The Bedford Anthology of
World Literature
The Twentieth Century, 1900–The Present

Book 6

The Bedford Anthology of
World Literature
The Twentieth Century, 1900–The Present

EDITED BY

Paul Davis
Gary Harrison
David M. Johnson
Patricia Clark Smith
John F. Crawford

THE UNIVERSITY OF NEW MEXICO

BEDFORD / ST. MARTIN'S   Boston ◆ New York

For Bedford/St. Martin's

Executive Editor: Alanya Harter
Developmental Editor: Genevieve Hamilton
Associate Developmental Editor: Joshua Levy
Senior Production Editor: Karen S. Baart
Production Editor: Stasia Zomkowski
Senior Production Supervisor: Nancy Myers
Marketing Manager: Jenna Bookin Barry
Editorial Assistant: Jeffrey Voccola
Production Assistants: Kerri Cardone, Tina Lai
Copyeditor: Melissa Cook
Map Coordinator: Tina Samaha
Text and Cover Design: Anna George
Cover Art: Cuban Portrait no. 10, 1996 (acrylic on canvas) by Marjorie Weiss (Contemporary Artist), Private Collection/Bridgeman Art Library
Composition: Stratford Publishing Services, Inc.
Printing and Binding: R. R. Donnelley & Sons Company

President: Joan E. Feinberg
Editorial Director: Denise B. Wydra
Editor in Chief: Karen S. Henry
Director of Marketing: Karen Melton
Director of Editing, Design, and Production: Marcia Cohen
Managing Editor: Elizabeth M. Schaaf

Library of Congress Control Number: 2002112262

1 0 9
k j i h

For information, write: Bedford/St. Martin's, 75 Arlington Street, Boston, MA 02116 (617-399-4000)

ISBN-10: 0–312–40266–X (paperback)
ISBN-13: 978–0–312–40266–2 (paperback)
ISBN: 0–312–41389–0 (hard cover)

Acknowledgments

Abé Kobo, "The Red Cocoon" and "The Stick," translated by Lane Dunlop, from *Late Chrysanthemum: 21 Stories from the Japanese* (San Francisco: North Point Press, 1986). Copyright © 1986 by Lane Dunlop. Reprinted with the permission of the translator.

Acknowledgments and copyrights are continued at the back of the book on pages 1437–42, which constitute an extension of the copyright page. It is a violation of the law to reproduce these selections by any means whatsoever without the written permission of the copyright holder.

PREFACE

◈ *The Bedford Anthology of World Literature* has a story behind it. In 1985, a group of us received a grant from the National Endowment for the Humanities. Our task: to develop and team teach a new kind of literature course—one that drew from the rich literary traditions of Asia, India, the Middle East, and the Americas as well as from the masterpieces of the Western world. We learned so much from that experience—from our students and from each other—that we applied those lessons to an anthology published in 1995, *Western Literature in a World Context*.

In that first edition of our anthology, our goal was to add works that truly represented *world* literature to the list of Western classics and to place great literary works in their historical and cultural contexts. We've kept that focus in the newly titled *Bedford Anthology*—but we've also drastically reshaped, redesigned, and reimagined it to make it the book you hold today. We talked to hundreds of instructors and students in an effort to identify and confirm what they considered challenging about the world literature course. The design and content of these pages represent our attempt to meet these challenges.

The study and teaching of world literature have changed significantly in the past twenty to thirty years. Formerly, most world literature courses consisted of masterpieces of Western literature, while the literary traditions of Asia, Africa, and Latin America were virtually ignored. The movement to broaden the canon to more accurately represent our world—and to better represent oral and marginalized traditions in the West—has greatly increased the number of texts taught in world literature courses today. Although the specifics remain controversial, nearly all teachers of literature are committed to the ongoing revaluation and expansion of the canon.

The last few decades have also seen instructors reconsidering the traditional methods of teaching world literature. In the past, most world literature courses were designed along formalistic or generic principles. But the expanded canon has complicated both of these approaches. There are no developed criteria for defining masterworks in such formerly ignored genres as letters and diaries or for unfamiliar forms from non-Western cultures, and we are frequently reminded that traditional approaches sometimes impose inappropriate Eurocentric perspectives on such works. As content and methodology for the course have been evolving, recent critical theory has reawakened interest in literature's historical and cultural contexts. All of these factors have both complicated and enriched the study of world literature. With this multivolume literature anthology, we don't claim to be presenting the definitive new canon of world literature or the last word on how to teach it. We have, however, tried to open new perspectives and possibilities for both students and teachers.

One anthology — six individual books. *The Bedford Anthology of World Literature* is now split into six separate books that correspond to the six time periods most commonly taught. These books are available in two packages: Books 1–3 and Books 4–6. Our motivation for changing the packaging is twofold and grows out of the extensive market research we did before shaping the development plan for the book. In our research, instructors from around the country confirmed that students just don't want to cart around a 2,500-page book — who would? Many also said that they focus on ancient literatures in the first semester of the course and on the twentieth

The Bedford Anthology of World Literature has been dynamically reimagined, redesigned, and restructured. We've added a second color, four hundred images, three hundred pronunciation guides, forty maps, six comparative time lines — and much more.

Portuguese Caravels Leaving to Explore the World, 1775 *The eighteenth century was a time of unprecedented global communication — political, social, economic, and literary. These painted blue tiles are found on the walls of the town of Paco de Arcos, near Lisbon, Portugal. (The Art Archive / Dagli Orti.)*

The Eighteenth Century

1650 - 1800

century in the second semester. In addition, many instructors teach an introduction to world literature that is tailored specifically to the needs of their students and their institution and thus want a text that can be adapted to *many* courses.

We believe that the extensive changes we've made to *The Bedford Anthology of World Literature* — breaking the anthology into six books rather than only two, creating a new two-color design, increasing the trim size, and adding maps, illustrations, numerous pedagogical features, an expanded instructor's manual, and a new companion Web site — will make the formidable task of teaching and taking a world literature course both manageable and pleasurable.

An expanded canon for the twenty-first century. In each of the six books of *The Bedford Anthology*, you'll find a superb collection of complete longer works, plays, prose, and poems — the best literature available in English or English translation. Five of the books are organized geographically and then by author in order of birth date. The exception to this rule is Book 6, which, reflecting our increasingly global identities, is organized by author without larger geographical groupings.

Aphra Behn's Oroonoko *is one of the texts we include in its entirety — highlighting important issues of race, gender, and slavery in the eighteenth century.*

❧ APHRA BEHN
1640–1689

Aphra Behn.
Engraving from
Histories and
Novels, 1696.
This is the earliest
surviving image
of Behn. (The
Huntington Library,
San Marino, CA)

Poet, playwright, and novelist Aphra Behn was one of the most prolific writers of her time. During a period in England when women were strongly discouraged from seeking literary recognition, she not only managed to earn a living as a professional writer but also directly engaged such traditionally "masculine" themes as political corruption, sexual politics, and social reform. In *Oroonoko* (1688), she openly addresses the complexities of rulership, sexual desire, and social injustice. Though her talent as a writer earned her much popularity and praise, the supposed presumptuousness and boldness of her work resulted in vicious attacks on her moral integrity. Associating her entrance into the public sphere of print and stage with prostitution, the satirist Robert Gould labeled her a vile "Punk[1] and Poetesse." Largely because of this stigma of indecency, publishers and scholars ignored Behn's work for years after her death. Only recently has she returned to center stage as a great literary talent, a major contributor to the development of the early English NOVEL, and a revolutionary figure in the tradition of women's writing in English.

Mystery, Travel, and Espionage. It is difficult to pin down the facts of Behn's early life. According to many sources, she was born near Canterbury to Bartholomew Johnson, a barber, and Elizabeth Denham. Her surprisingly advanced education and language skills (she was learned in Latin and French), might be attributed to a close association with the well-to-do family of Colonel Colepeper and to frequent exposure to Huguenot[2] and Dutch immigrants in Canterbury. Some recent scholarship, however, claims she was born in Kent and the daughter of John and Amy Amis or Amies. This would make her a possible relation, through her father, of Francis, Lord Willoughby of Parham, who at one time held a position for the British government in the West Indies. We know that in 1663 Behn traveled to the West Indies with her family after her father was named lieutenant-general of the colony of Surinam.[3] Though the stay in Surinam only lasted two months (her father died on the voyage), this experience influenced the writing of her most famous narrative work, *Oroonoko*.

The circumstances surrounding the adoption of Aphra Behn's last name are even more cloudy than those of her birth. Though there is no extant marriage record, scholars speculate that after the trip to Surinam, Behn wed a London merchant or seaman of Dutch or German descent. If

[1] punk: Prostitute.
[2] Huguenots: French Protestants who were members of the Reformed Church established in France by John Calvin circa 1555. Because of religious persecution, they fled to other countries in the sixteenth and seventeenth centuries.
[3] Surinam: A British sugar colony on the South American coast below Venezuela.

88

she married, she and her husband were together for only a short time before either he died or the two parted ways to live separate lives. More interesting is the suggestion that Behn imagined a spouse for herself so that she could gain the respectable title of widow. Several critics comment that, assuming Behn's maiden name was Johnson, taking the last name Behn creates an intriguing allusion to the famous seventeenth-century playwright Ben (Behn) Jonson.

The creation of a fictional husband may well seem like a bold act for a woman of the seventeenth century, but Behn was not one to shy away from taking chances or embarking on daring adventures. In 1666, for example, she served as a spy for Charles II (r. 1660–85) in the Anglo-Dutch War.[4] Recruited by secret agent Thomas Killigrew, she was charged with convincing one William Scot to be a double agent, reporting on expatriots, and providing information on Dutch military plans. Her foray into espionage was unsuccessful — what information she provided to the English crown was largely ignored, and she was never repaid for her expenses. Deep in debt and forced to borrow money for the cost of her return to England, it is likely that she spent some time in debtor's prison in 1688.

Writing Politics and the Politics of Writing. Aphra Behn lived through a period of monumental political unrest and social change. In 1642, two years after her birth, England became embroiled in a bloody civil war over religious authority, class privileges, and economic practices, among other issues. Charles I (r. 1625–49) was brought to trial and executed in 1649. Despite the promise of a new kind of governance, the ensuing rule of Oliver Cromwell[5] — under whom Britain was called the "Commonwealth," then the "Protectorate" — proved only that a citizen given the power to govern may be more ineffective and tyrannical than a monarch. The period known as the Restoration, beginning in 1660 with the restoration of Charles II as king of England, saw a newfound celebration of, and freedom in, the arts but did not provide long-term political stability. Charles's successor, James II (r. 1685–88), was quickly ousted and sent into exile, primarily because he was a professed Roman Catholic. In what is called the "Glorious Revolution" of 1688,[6] the Dutch Protestant William of Orange and his wife Mary came to power.

As shown by her service as a spy for Charles II, Behn was dedicated to the preservation of the monarchy and to the system of aristocratic rule. Much of her work is informed by this sociopolitical agenda. In texts

www For links to more information about Behn and a quiz on *Oroonoko*, see *World Literature Online* at bedfordstmartins .com/worldlit.

[4] Anglo-Dutch War: Battles between the British and the Dutch for control of the seas and trade routes (1652–84).
[5] Oliver Cromwell (1599–1658): A soldier, politician, and staunch Puritan who attacked the bishops of the Church of England and advocated widespread political and religious reform. He came to power as "Lord Protector" of England (1653–58) shortly after the execution of Charles I.
[6] Glorious Revolution: The birth of a son to the Catholic James II led prominent statesmen in England to invite Dutchman William of Orange and his wife, Mary, to assume the throne. William arrived in 1688, promising to protect the Protestant faith and the liberties of the English, and took the throne without opposition. James II, denounced by Parliament, fled to France.

We've tried to assemble a broad selection of the world's literatures. We've updated our selection of European texts; we have also included American writers who have had significant contact with world culture and who have influenced or defined who we are as Americans. And of course we have added many works from non-Western traditions, both frequently anthologized pieces and works unique to this anthology, including texts from Mesopotamia, Egypt, Israel, India, Persia, China, Japan, Arab countries of the Middle East, Africa, native America, Latin America, and the Caribbean.

Over thirty-five complete, longer works. These include Homer's *Odyssey* and *The Epic of Gilgamesh* in Book 1, Dante's *Inferno* and Kalidasa's *Shakuntala* in Book 2, Marlowe's *Doctor Faustus* and Shakespeare's *The Tempest* in Book 3, Bashō's *Narrow Road through the Backcountry* in Book 4, Dostoevsky's *Notes from Underground* in Book 5, and Achebe's *Things Fall Apart* in Book 6.

When a work is too long to be produced in its entirety, we've presented carefully edited selections from it; examples include the Rig Veda, *Ramayana, Mahabharata,* Qur'an, *The Song of Roland,* Ibn Hazm's *The Dove's Necklace, The Book of Margery Kempe,* Attar's *Conference of the Birds,* Cervantes's *Don Quixote,* Swift's *Gulliver's Travels,* Equiano's *Interesting Narrative,* Benjamin Franklin's *Autobiography,* Chikamatsu's *The Love Suicides at Amijima,* and Cao Xueqin's *The Story of the Stone.* In most cases the excerpts are not fragments but substantial selections wherein the structure and themes of the whole work are evident. The anthology also contains a generous selection of prose writing—short stories, letters, and essays.

Several hundred lyric poems. *The Bedford Anthology* includes the work of such fine poets as Sappho, Bhartrhari, Nezahualcoyotl, Petrarch, Kakinomoto Hitomaro, Rumi, Li Bai, Heine, Mirabai, Ramprasad, Baudelaire, Dickinson, Ghalib, Akhmatova, Neruda, Rich, and Walcott. Unique *In the Tradition* clusters collect poems that share a tradition or theme: poetry about love in Books 1, 2, and 3, Tang dynasty poetry in Book 2, Indian devotional poetry in Book 3, and poetry on war in Book 6.

∾ RAMPRASAD SEN
1718–1775

BAHK-tee

SHAHK-tee; KAH-lee
RAHM-pruh-sahd

The intensely religious village life of India produced not only storytellers—whose primary purpose was transmitting the stories of gods, goddesses, heroes, and heroines—but also poets who expressed ordinary people's spiritual longing for God. Emotional worship or surrender to God in Hinduism is called *bhakti,* a term that has its origins in the Upanishads. Bhakti became a religious movement in India during the religious reforms of the eighth, ninth, and tenth centuries. A particular version of bhakti was devoted to feminine divinity; in India there had been a long history of worshiping the greatgoddess **Shakti**[1]—also known as **Kali** and **Durga**—but a resurgence of her worship, led by the poet **Ramprasad** Sen, took place in Bengal[2] during the eighteenth century. Like medieval Christian poets devoted to the Virgin Mother, Bengal poets of this time favored the feminine dimension of God, which seemed to invite a personal relationship, an opportunity for conversation, and expressions of sadness and longing.

Ramprasad's poems, primarily songs to Kali, were extremely popular at the end of the eighteenth century when Bengal was in a time of darkness and despair. The region had been under Muslim rule for about five hundred years when the British defeated the Mughal army in the Battle of Plassey in 1757.[3] Robber barons controlled large parts of Bengal, and Kali was their patron deity. Regional kings promoted Kali worship by supporting court poets who composed and sang songs to the goddess. The songs became part of an extremely precarious village life. Bengal is a region of extremes, feast or famine, due to unpredictable rains. Some years bring little rain or droughts, while others have heavy rain and flooding. Occasionally there are years when just the right amount of rain falls at the appropriate times; these times are thought to be blessed by Kali.

Ramprasad's simple lyricism and familiar images touched a broad range of listeners; his songs appealed to scholars and peasants alike. His poetic skills influenced succeeding generations of Indian poets. Rabindranath Tagore,[4] the most famous Bengali writer of the late nineteenth cen-

www For links to more information about Ramprasad and a quiz on his poetry, see *World Literature Online* at bedfordstmartins.com/worldlit.

[1] **Shakti:** Shakti is the collective name for the consort of Shiva who has several names. **Shakti** is the feminine dynamic energy by which God creates, preserves, and dissolves the world. **Kali** is usually portrayed as terrifying: blue-black, three-eyed, and four-armed, with a necklace of human heads and a girdle of severed hands. **Durga,** "the unfathomable one," is one of the oldest versions of the Great Mother: fair complexioned and riding a lion, she releases humans from rebirth with her touch.

[2] **Bengal:** A region in the northeast Indian peninsula, now divided between India and Bangladesh.

[3] **Battle of Plassey:** Plassey is a village in West Bengal state where the British defeated the Bengal army in 1757, leading to Britain's control of northeast India.

[4] **Rabindranath Tagore** (1861–1941): A native of Bengal anxious to preserve the cultural richness of traditional village life while at the same time bridging the philosophical and literary gap between East and West. (See Book 5.)

612

Literature in context. In addition to individual authors presented in chronological order, *The Bedford Anthology* features two types of cross-cultural literary groupings. In the more than thirty **In the World** clusters, five to six in each book, writings around a single theme — such as the history of religions, science, love, human rights, women's rights, colonialism, the meeting of East and West, imperialism, and existentialism — and from different countries and cultural traditions are presented side by side, helping students understand that people of every culture have had their public gods, heroes, and revolutions, their private loves, lives, and losses. Titles include "Changing Gods: From Religion to Philosophy," in Book 1; "Muslim and Christian at War," in Book 2; "Humanism, Learning, and Education" in Book 3; "Love, Marriage, and the Education of Women," in Book 4; "Emancipation," in Book 5; and "Imagining Africa," in Book 6. The second type of grouping, **In the Tradition,** presents poetry on love in Books 1, 2, and 3 and literature on war and American multiculturalism in Book 6. These clusters gather together such widely disparate writers as Hammurabi, Heraclitus, Marcus Aurelius, Ibn Battuta, Marco Polo, Sei Shonagon, Galileo, Bartolomé de las Casas, Mary Wollstonecraft, Mary Astell, Shen Fu, Karl Marx, Elizabeth Cady Stanton, Swami Vivekananda, Aimé Césaire, and Bharati Mukherjee.

In the World clusters bring together texts from different literary traditions and help students make thematic connections and comparisons.

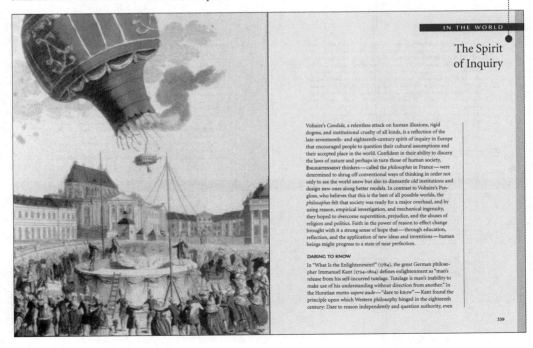

IN THE WORLD

The Spirit of Inquiry

Voltaire's *Candide*, a relentless attack on human illusions, rigid dogma, and institutional cruelty of all kinds, is a reflection of the late-seventeenth- and eighteenth-century spirit of inquiry in Europe that encouraged people to question their cultural assumptions and their accepted place in the world. Confident in their ability to discern the laws of nature and perhaps in turn those of human society, ENLIGHTENMENT thinkers — called the *philosophes* in France — were determined to shrug off conventional ways of thinking in order not only to see the world anew but also to dismantle old institutions and design new ones along better models. In contrast to Voltaire's Pangloss, who believes that this is the best of all possible worlds, the *philosophes* felt that society was ready for a major overhaul, and by using reason, empirical investigation, and mechanical ingenuity, they hoped to overcome superstition, prejudice, and the abuses of religion and politics. Faith in the power of reason to effect change brought with it a strong sense of hope that — through education, reflection, and the application of new ideas and inventions — human beings might progress to a state of near perfection.

DARING TO KNOW

In "What Is the Enlightenment?" (1784), the great German philosopher Immanuel Kant (1724–1804) defines enlightenment as "man's release from his self-incurred tutelage. Tutelage is man's inability to make use of his understanding without direction from another." In the Horatian motto *sapere aude* — "dare to know" — Kant found the principle upon which Western philosophy hinged in the eighteenth century: Dare to reason independently and question authority, even

339

Helping students and teachers navigate the wide world of literature. The hundreds of instructors we talked to before embarking on *The Bedford Anthology* shared with us their concerns about teaching an introduction to world literature course, no matter what their individual agendas were. One concern was the sheer difficulty for students of reading literature that not only spans the period from the beginning of recorded literatures to the present but also hails from vastly different cultures and historical moments. Another was the fact that no one instructor is an expert in *all* of world literature. We've put together *The Bedford Anthology of World Literature* with these factors in mind and hope that the help we offer both around and with the selected texts goes a long way toward bringing clarity to the abundance and variety of world writings.

Helping students understand the where and when of the literature in the anthology. Each book of *The Bedford Anthology* opens with an extended overview of its time period as well as with a **comparative time line** that lists what happened, where, and when in three overarching categories: history and politics; literature; and science, culture, and technology. An interactive version of each time line serves as the portal to the online support offered on our Book Companion Site. In addition,

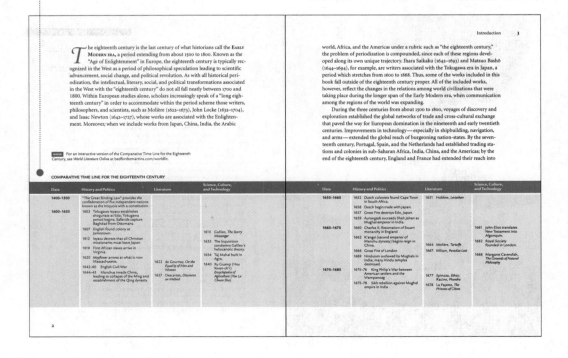

"Time and Place" boxes in the introductions to the different geographical groupings of writers further orient students in the era and culture connected with the literature they're reading by spotlighting something interesting and specific about a certain place and time.

    Maps included throughout the anthology show students where in the world various literatures came from. Besides the maps that open each geographical section and show countries in relation to the larger world at a given time in history, we've supplied maps that illustrate the shifting of national boundaries; industrial growth; the effects of conquest, conquerors, and colonialism; and the travels of Odysseus, Ibn Battuta, and Bashō.

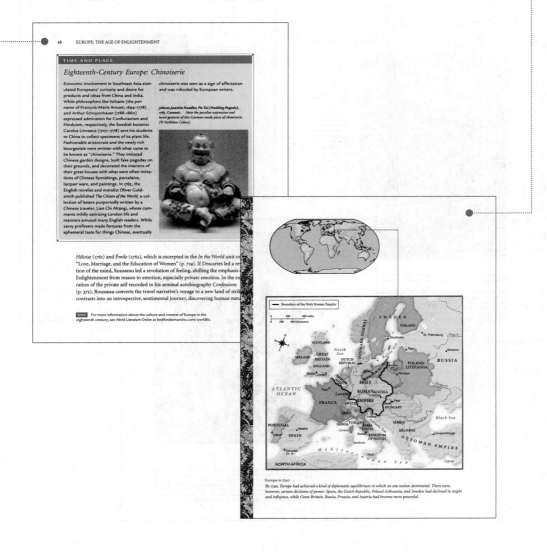

16   EUROPE: THE AGE OF ENLIGHTENMENT

TIME AND PLACE

Eighteenth-Century Europe: Chinoiserie

Economic involvement in Southeast Asia stimulated Europeans' curiosity and desire for products and ideas from China and India. While philosophers like Voltaire (the pen name of François-Marie Arouet; 1694–1778) and Arthur Schopenhauer (1788–1860) expressed admiration for Confucianism and Hinduism, respectively, the Swedish botanist Carolus Linnaeus (1707–1778) sent his students to China to collect specimens of its plant life. Fashionable aristocrats and the newly rich bourgeoisie were smitten with what came to be known as "chinoiserie." They imitated Chinese garden designs, built fake pagodas on their grounds, and decorated the interiors of their great houses with what were often imitations of Chinese furnishings, porcelains, lacquer ware, and paintings. In 1762, the English novelist and moralist Oliver Goldsmith published *The Citizen of the World*, a collection of letters purportedly written by a Chinese traveler, Lien Chi Altangi, whose comments mildly satirizing London life and manners amused many English readers. While savvy profiteers made fortunes from the ephemeral taste for things Chinese, eventually chinoiserie was seen as a sign of affectation and was ridiculed by European writers.

Johann Joachim Kandler, Pu-Tai (Nodding Pagoda), 1765. Ceramic. Note the peculiar expression and hand gestures of this German-made piece of chinoiserie. (© Kathleen Cohen)

Héloïse (1761) and *Émile* (1762), which is excerpted in the *In the World* unit on "Love, Marriage, and the Education of Women" (p. 719). If Descartes led a revolution of the mind, Rousseau led a revolution of feeling, shifting the emphasis of the Enlightenment from reason to emotion, especially private emotion. In the exploration of the private self recorded in his seminal autobiography *Confessions* (p. 372), Rousseau converts the travel narrative's voyage to a new land of striking contrasts into an introspective, sentimental journey, discovering human nature.

WWW   For more information about the culture and context of Europe in the eighteenth century, see *World Literature Online* at bedfordstmartins.com/worldlit.

Boundary of the Holy Roman Empire

Europe in 1740
By 1740, Europe had achieved a kind of diplomatic equilibrium in which no one nation dominated. There were, however, certain divisions of power: Spain, the Dutch Republic, Poland-Lithuania, and Sweden had declined in might and influence, while Great Britain, Russia, Prussia, and Austria had become more powerful.

The anthology's many illustrations—art, photographs, frontispieces, cartoons, and cultural artifacts—are meant to bring immediacy to literature that might otherwise feel spatially and temporally remote. A few examples are a photo of the Acropolis today juxtaposed with an artist's rendering of what it looked like newly built, a sketch of the first seven circles of Dante's hell, a scene from Hogarth's *Marriage à la Mode,* the ad Harriet Jacobs's owner ran for her capture and return, an editorial cartoon mocking Darwin's evolutionary theories, and a woodcut depicting Japanese boats setting out to greet Commodore Perry's warship in their harbor.

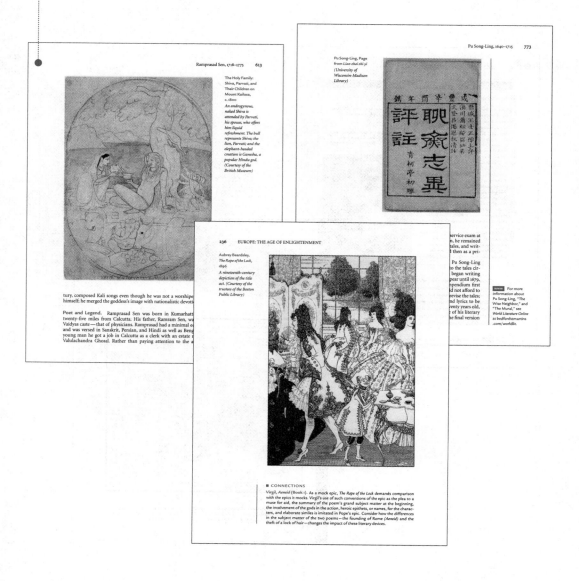

Practical and accessible editorial apparatus helps students understand what they read. Each author in the anthology is introduced by an informative and accessible literary and biographical discussion. The selections themselves are complemented with generous footnotes, marginal notes, cross-references, and critical quotations. Phonetic pronunciation guides are supplied in the margins of introductory material and before the selections for unfamiliar character and place names. Providing help with literary and historical vocabulary, bold-faced key terms throughout the text refer students to the comprehensive glossary at the end of each book.

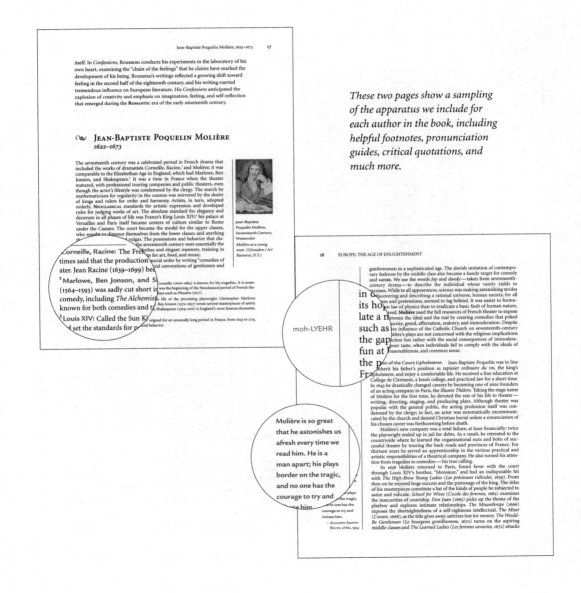

These two pages show a sampling of the apparatus we include for each author in the book, including helpful footnotes, pronunciation guides, critical quotations, and much more.

Jean-Baptiste Poquelin Molière, 1622–1673   17

itself. In *Confessions*, Rousseau conducts his experiments in the laboratory of his own heart, examining the "chain of the feelings" that he claims have marked the development of his being. Rousseau's writings reflected a growing shift toward feeling in the second half of the eighteenth century, and his writing exerted tremendous influence on European literature. His *Confessions* anticipated the explosion of creativity and emphasis on imagination, feeling, and self-reflection that emerged during the ROMANTIC era of the early nineteenth century.

JEAN-BAPTISTE POQUELIN MOLIÈRE
1622–1673

The seventeenth century was a celebrated period in French drama that included the works of Corneille, Racine,[1] and Molière; it was comparable to the Elizabethan Age in England, which had Marlowe, Ben Jonson, and Shakespeare.[2] It was a time in France when the theater matured, with professional touring companies and public theaters, even though the actor's lifestyle was condemned by the clergy. The search by mathematicians for regularity in the cosmos was mirrored by the desire of kings and rulers for order and harmony. Artists, in turn, adopted orderly, NEOCLASSICAL standards for artistic expression and developed rules for judging works of art. The absolute standard for elegance and decorum in all phases of life was France's King Louis XIV;[3] his palace at Versailles and Paris itself became centers of culture similar to Rome under the Caesars. The court became the model for the upper classes, who sought to distance themselves from the lower classes and anything vulgar. The possessions and behavior that dis[...]the seventeenth century were essentially the[...]for art, food, and music.

Jean-Baptiste Poquelin Molière, Seventeenth Century. Watercolor
Molière as a young man. (Giraudon / Art Resource, N.Y.)

Corneille, Racine: The Fre[...]times said that the production[...]ater. Jean Racine (1639–1699) be[...]

[2] Marlowe, Ben Jonson, and S[...] Corneille (1606–1684) is known for his tragedies. It is some-
(1564–1593) was sadly cut short i[...]was the beginning of the Neoclassical period of French the-
comedy, including *The Alchemi[...]plays such as *Phaedra* (1677).
known for both comedies and t[...]the life of the promising playwright Christopher Marlowe
                                        Ben Jonson (1572–1637) wrote several masterpieces of satiric
[3] Louis XIV: Called the Sun K[...]Shakespeare (1564–1616) is England's most famous dramatist,
[...]d set the standards for p[...]reigned for an unusually long period in France, from 1643 to 1715.
                                        social behavior.

moh-LYEHR

Molière is so great
that he astonishes us
afresh every time we
read him. He is a
man apart; his plays
border on the tragic,
and no one has the
courage to try and
[...]te him

— AUGUSTIN SAINTE-
BEUVE, critic, 1914

18   EUROPE: THE AGE OF ENLIGHTENMENT

gentlewomen in a sophisticated age. The slavish imitation of contemporary fashions by the middle class also became a handy target for comedy and SATIRE. We use the words *fop* and *dandy*—taken from seventeenth-century drama—to describe the individual whose vanity yields to excesses. While to all appearances, science was making astonishing strides in discovering and describing a rational universe, human society, for all its vices and pretensions, seemed to lag behind. It was easier to formulate a new law of physics than to eradicate a basic fault of human nature, such as greed. Molière used the full resources of French theater to expose the gap between the ideal and the real by creating comedies that poked fun at hypocrisy, greed, affectation, zealotry, and immoderation. Despite the pervasive influence of the Catholic Church on seventeenth-century French diction but rather on the social consequences of immoderate behavior and poor taste, when individuals fail to comply with the ideals of reasonableness, and common sense.

the pen of the Court Upholsterer.   Jean-Baptiste Poquelin was in line to inherit his father's position as *tapissier ordinaire du roi*, the king's upholsterer, and enjoy a comfortable life. He received a fine education at College de Clermont, a Jesuit college, and practiced law for a short term. In 1643 he drastically changed careers by becoming one of nine founders of an acting company in Paris, the *Illustre Théâtre*. Taking the stage name of Molière for the first time, he devoted the rest of his life to theater—writing, directing, staging, and producing plays. Although theater was popular with the general public, the acting profession itself was condemned by the clergy; in fact, an actor was automatically excommunicated by the church and denied Christian burial unless a renunciation of his chosen career was forthcoming before death.

Molière's new company was a total failure, at least financially; twice the playwright ended up in jail for debts. As a result, he retreated to the countryside where he learned the organizational nuts and bolts of successful theater by touring the back roads and provinces of France. For thirteen years he served an apprenticeship in the various practical and artistic responsibilities of a theatrical company. He also turned his attention from tragedies to comedies—his true calling.

In 1658 Molière returned to Paris, found favor with the court through Louis XIV's brother, "Monsieur," and had an indisputable hit with *The High-Brow Young Ladies* (*Les précieuses ridicules*, 1659). From then on he enjoyed huge success and the patronage of the king. The titles of his masterpieces constitute a list of the kinds of people he subjected to satire and ridicule. *School for Wives* (*L'école des femmes*, 1662) examines the insecurities of courtship. *Don Juan* (1665) picks up the theme of the playboy and explores intimate relationships. *The Misanthrope* (1666) exposes the shortsightedness of a self-righteous intellectual. *The Miser* (*L'avare*, 1668), as the title gives away, satirizes lust for money. *The Would-Be Gentleman* (*Le bourgeois gentilhomme*, 1670) turns on the aspiring middle classes and *The Learned Ladies* (*Les femmes savantes*, 1672) attacks

These terms cover the generic conventions of fiction, poetry, and drama; historical forms such as epic, epigram, and myth; and relevant historical periods such as the European Enlightenment or the Edo period in Japan.

Making connections among works from different times and places. At the end of each author introduction are two catalysts for further thought and discussion. **Questions** in the Connections apparatus tie together Western and world texts, both those within a single book and selections from other centuries, making the six books more of a unit and aiding in their interplay. **Further Research bibliographies**

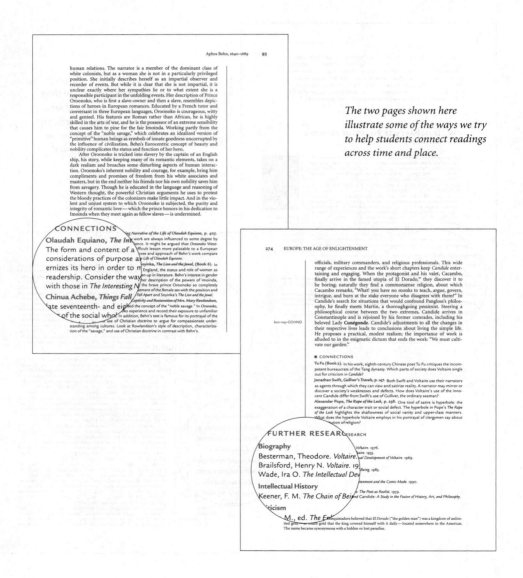

The two pages shown here illustrate some of the ways we try to help students connect readings across time and place.

provide sources for students who want to read more critical, biographical, or historical information about an author or a work.

Print and online ancillaries further support the anthology's material. Two instructor's manuals, *Resources for Teaching THE BEDFORD ANTHOLOGY OF WORLD LITERATURE*, accompany Books 1–3 and Books 4–6 (one for each package), providing additional information about the anthology's texts and the authors, suggestions for discussion and writing prompts in the classroom and beyond, and additional connections among texts in the six books.

We are especially enthusiastic about our integrated Book Companion Site, *World Literature Online*, which provides a wealth of content and information that only the interactive medium of the Web can offer. **Web links** throughout the anthology direct

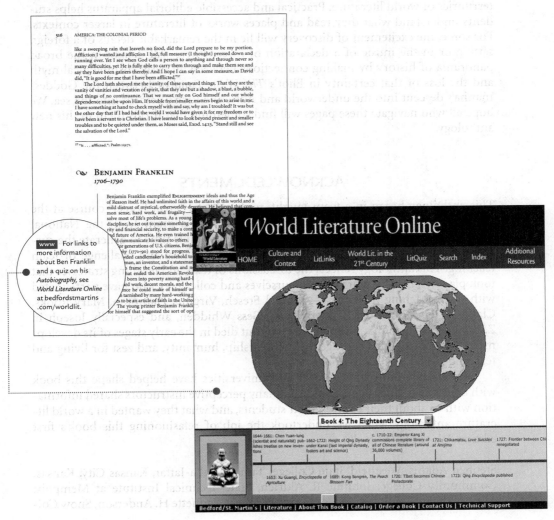

students to additional content on the Web site, where interactive illustrated time lines and maps serve as portals to more information about countries, texts, and authors. Culture and Context overviews offer additional historical background and annotated research links that students can follow to learn more on their own. Illustrated World Literature in the Twenty-First Century discussions trace the enduring presence in contemporary culture of the most frequently taught texts in world literature courses. Maps from the book are available online. Quizzes in LitQuiz offer an easy way for instructors to assess students' reading and comprehension. And LitLinks—annotated research links—provide a way for students to learn more about individual authors.

This wide variety of supplementary materials, as well as the broad spectrum of literary texts, offers teachers choices for navigating the familiar and the unfamiliar territories of world literature. Practical and accessible editorial apparatus helps students understand what they read and places works of literature in larger contexts. For some, the excitement of discovery will lie in the remarkable details of a foreign setting or in the music of a declaration of love. Others will delight in the broad panorama of history by making connections between an early cosmological myth and the loss of that certainty in Eliot's *The Waste Land* or between the Goddess Inanna's descent into the underworld and Adrienne Rich's descent into the sea. We hope all who navigate these pages will find something that thrills them in this new anthology.

ACKNOWLEDGMENTS

This anthology began in a team-taught, multicultural "great books" course at the University of New Mexico, initially developed with a grant from the National Endowment for the Humanities. The grant gave us ample time to generate the curriculum for the course, and it also supported the luxury and challenge of team teaching. This anthology reflects the discussions of texts and teaching strategies that took place over many years among ourselves and colleagues who have participated with us in teaching the course—Cheryl Fresch, Virginia Hampton, Mary Rooks, Claire Waters, Richard K. Waters, Mary Bess Whidden, and especially Joseph B. Zavadil, who began this anthology with us but died in the early stages of its development. Joe's spirit—his courage, wit, scholarship, humanity, and zest for living and teaching—endures in this book.

Reviewers from many colleges and universities have helped shape this book with their advice and suggestions. And many perceptive instructors shared information with us about their courses, their students, and what they wanted in a world literature anthology when we undertook the job of refashioning this book's first edition. We thank them all:

Stephen Adams, Westfield State College; Tamara Agha-Jaffar, Kansas City, Kansas, Community College; Johnnie R. Aldrich, State Technical Institute at Memphis; Allison Alison, Southeastern Community College; Jannette H. Anderson, Snow College; Kit Andrews, Western Oregon University; Joan Angelis, Woodbury University; Shirley Ariker, Empire State College; Sister Elena F. Arminio, College of Saint Elizabeth; Rose Lee Bancroft, Alice Lloyd College; John Bartle, Hamilton College; Amy M. Bawcom, University of Mary Hardin-Baylor; M. Susan Beck, University of Wisconsin-River Falls; Frank Beesley, Dalton State College; Peter Benson, Farleigh Dickinson University; Michael Bielmeier, Silver Lake College; Dale B. Billingsley, University of Louisville; Mark Bingham, Union University; Stephen Black, Dyersburg State Community College; Neil Blackadder, Knox College; Tyler Blake, MidAmerica Nazarene University; Gene Blanton, Jacksonville State University; James Boswell Jr., Harrisburg Area Community College; Lisa S. Bovelli, Itasca Community College; Lois Bragg, Gallaudet University; Kristin Ruth Brate, Arizona Western College; Marie Brenner, Bethel College; Linda Brown, Coastal Georgia Community College; Keith Callis, Crichton College; Charles P. Campbell, New Mexico Tech.; Zuoya Cao, Lincoln University; William Carpenter, College of ME Atlantic; May Charles, Wheeling Jesuit College; R. J. Clougherty, Tennessee Technical College; Helen Connell, Barry University; Lynn Conroy, Seton Hill College; Sue Coody, Weatherford College; Thomas A. Copeland, Youngstown State University; Peter Cortland, Quinnipiac College; R. Costomiris, Georgia Southern University; H. J. Coughlin, Eastern Connecticut State University; Marc D. Cyr, Georgia Southern University; Sarah Dangelantonio, Franklin Pierce College; James Davis, Troy State University; Barbara Dicey, Wallace College; Wilfred O. Dietrich, Blinn College; Michael Dinielli, Chaffey College; Matt Djos, Mesa State College; Marjorie Dobbin, Brewton-Parker College; Brian L. Dose, Martin Luther College; Dawn Duncan, Concordia College; Bernie Earley, Tompkins-Cortland Community College; Sarah M. Eichelman, Walters State Community College; Robert H. Ellison, East Texas Baptist University; Joshua D. Esty, Harvard University; Robert J. Ewald, University of Findlay; Shirley Felt, Southern California College; Lois Ferrer, CSU Dominguez Hills; Patricia Fite, University of the Incarnate Word; Sr. Agnes Fleck, St. Scholastica College; Robert Fliessner, Central State University; M. L. Flynn, South Dakota State University; Keith Foster, Arkansas State University; John C. Freeman, El Paso Community College; Doris Gardenshire, Trinity Valley Community College; Susan Gardner, University of North Carolina-Charlotte; Jerry D. Gibbens, Williams Baptist College; Susan Gilbert, Meredith College; Diana Glyer, Azusa Pacific University; Irene Gnarra, Kean University; R. C. Goetter, Glouster Community College; Nancy Goldfarb, Western Kentucky University; Martha Goodman, Central Virginia Community College; Lyman Grant, Austin Community College; Hazel Greenberg, San Jacinto College South; Janet Grose, Union University; Sharon Growney-Seals, Ouachita Technical College; Rachel Hadas, Rutgers University; Laura Hammons, East Central Community College; Carmen Hardin, University of Louisville; Darren Harris-Fain, Shawnee State University; Patricia B. Heaman, Wilkes University; Charles Heglan, University of South Florida; Dennis E. Hensley, Taylor University; Kathleen M. Herndon, Weber State University; Betty Higdon, Reedley College; David Hoegberg, Indiana University; Diane Long Hoeveler, Marquette University; Tyler Hoffman, Rutgers University; Lynn Hoggard, Midwestern State University; Greg Horn, Southwest VA Community College; Roger Horn, Charles County Community

College; Malinda Jay-Bartels, Gulf Coast Community College; Mell Johnson, Wallace State Community College; Kathryn Joyce, Santa Barbara City College; Steven Joyce, Ohio State University-Mansfield; Ronald A. T. Judy, University of Pittsburgh; Alan Kaufman, Bergen Community College; Tim Kelley, Northwest-Shoals Community College; Shoshanna Knapp, Virginia Technical College; Jim Knox, Roane State Community College; Mary Kraus, Bob Jones University; F. Kuzman, Bethel College; Kate Kysa, Anoka-Ramsey Community College; Linda L. Labin, Husson College; Barbara Laman, Dickinson State University; R. Scott Lamascus, GA-Southwestern State University; Sandi S. Landis, St. Johns River Community College; Ben Larson, York College; Craig Larson, Trinidad State Junior College; Linda M. Lawrence, Georgia Military College; Simon Lewis, C. of Charleston; Gary L. Litt, Moorhead State University; H. W. Lutrin, Borough of Manhattan Community College; Dennis Lynch, Elgin Community College; Donald H. Mager, Johnson C. Smith University; Barbara Manrique, California State University; W. E. Mason, Mid-Continent College; Judith Matsunobu, Atlantic Community College; Noel Mawer, Edward Waters College; Patrick McDarby, St. John's University; Judy B. McInnis, University of Delaware; Becky McLaughlin, University of Southern Alabama; Edward E. Mehok, Notre Dame College of Ohio; Patricia Menhart, Broward Community College; Arthur McA. Miller, New College of Florida; Mark James Morreale, Marist College; Toni Morris, University of Indianapolis; Philip Mosley, Penn State–Worthington; George Mower, Community College of Alleghany County; L. Carl Nadeau, University of St. Francis; Walter Nelson, Red Rocks Community College; Steven Neuwirth, Western Connecticut State University; Carol H. Oliver, St. Louis College of Pharmacy; Richard Orr, York Technical College; Geoffrey Orth, Longwood College; Ramenga M. Osotsi, James Madison University; Bonnie Pavlis, Riverside Community College; Craig Payne, Indian Hills College; Leialoha Perkins, University of Hawaii; Ralph Perrico, Mercyhurst College; Charles W. Pollard, Calvin College; Michael Popkin, Touro College; Victoria Poulakis, Northern Virginia Community College; Alan Powers, Bristol Community College; Andrew B. Preslar, Lamar University; Evan Radcliffe, Villanova University; Belle Randall, Cornish College of the Arts; Elaine Razzano, Lyndon State College; Lucia N. Robinson, Okaloosa-Walton Community College; John Rooks, Morris College; William T. Ross, University of South Florida; Andrew Rubenfeld, Stevens Institute of Technology; Elizabeth S. Ruleman, Tennessee Wesleyan College; Olena H. Saciuk, Inter-American University; Mary Lynn Saul, Worcester State College; MaryJane Schenck, University of Tampa; Kevin Schilbrack, Wesleyan College; Deborah Schlacks, University of Wisconsin; Michael Schroeder, Savannah State University; Helen Scott, Wilkes University; Asha Sen, University of Wisconsin; Mary Sheldon, Washburn University; Lisa Shoemaker, State Technical Community College; Jack Shreve, Allegany College of Maryland; Meg Simonton, Albertson College; Susan Sink, Joliet Junior College; Henry Sloss, Anne Arundel Community College; T. Sluberski, Concordia University; Betty Smith, The Criswell College; Jane Bouman Smith, Winthrop University; John Somerville, Hillsdale College; Claudia Stanger, Fullerton College; Patrick Sullivan, Manchester Community-Technical College; Joan S. Swartz, Baptist

Bible College of PA; Leah Swartz, Maryville University; Sister Renita Tadych, Silver Lake College; Janet Tarbuck, Kennebee Valley Technical College; Gina Teel, Southeast Arkansas College; Daniel Thurber, Concordia University; John Paul Vincent, Asbury College; Paul Vita, Morningside College; Tim Walsh, Otera Junior College; Julia Watson, Ohio State University; Patricia J. Webb, Maysville Community College; Lynne Weller, John Wood Community College; Roger West, Trident Technical College; Katherine Wikoff, Milwaukee School of Engineering; Evelyn M. Wilson, Tarrant County College; Carmen Wong, John Lyle Community College; Paul D. Wood, Paducah Community College; Fay Wright, North Idaho College; and finally, Pamela G. Xanthopoulos, Jackson State Community College.

We also want to thank a special group of reviewers who looked in depth at the manuscript for each book, offering us targeted advice about its strengths and weaknesses:

Cora Agatucci, Central Oregon Community College; Michael Austin, Shepherd College; Maryam Barrie, Washtenaw Community College; John Bartle, Hamilton College; Jeffry Berry, Adrian College; Lois Bragg, Gallaudet University; Ron Carter, Rappahannock Community College; Robin Clouser, Ursinus College; Eugene R. Cunnar, New Mexico State University; Karen Dahr, Ellsworth Community College; Kristine Daines, Arizona State University; Sarah Dangelantonio, Franklin Pierce College; Jim Doan, Nova SE University; Melora Giardetti, Simpson College; Audley Hall, North West Arkansas Community College; Dean Hall, Kansas State University; Wail Hassan, Illinois State University; Joris Heise, Sinclair Community College; Diane Long Hoeveler, Marquette University; Glenn Hopp, Howard Payne University; Mickey Jackson, Golden West College; Feroza Jussawalla, University of New Mexico; Linda Karch, Norwich University; David Karnos, Montana State University; William Laskowski, Jamestown College; Pat Lonchar, University of the Incarnate Word; Donald Mager, The Mott University; Judy B. McInnis, University of Delaware; Becky McLaughlin, University of South Alabama; Tony J. Morris, University of Indianapolis; Deborah Schlacks, University of Wisconsin; James Snowden, Cedarville University; David T. Stout, Luzerne County Community College; Arline Thorn, West Virginia State College; Ann Volin, University of Kansas; Mary Wack, Washington State University; Jayne A. Widmayer, Boise State University; and William Woods, Wichita State University.

No anthology of this size comes into being without critical and supportive friends and advisors. Our thanks go to the Department of English at the University of New Mexico (UNM); its chair, Scott Sanders, who encouraged and supported our work; and Margaret Shinn and the office staff, who provided administrative and technical assistance. Among our colleagues at UNM, we particularly want to thank Gail Baker, Helen Damico, Reed Dasenbrock, Patrick Gallacher, Feroza Jussawalla, Michelle LeBeau, Richard Melzer, Mary Power, Diana Robin, and Hugh Witemeyer. Several graduate students also helped with this project: Jana Giles contributed the final section on American multicultural literature; Mary Rooks wrote the sections on Aphra Behn and Wole Soyinka and served heroically as our assistant, record keeper, all-purpose editor, and consultant.

We have benefited from the knowledge and suggestions of those who have corrected our misunderstandings, illuminated topics and cultures with which we were unfamiliar, critiqued our work, and suggested ways to enrich the anthology: Paula Gunn Allen, Reynold Bean, Richard Bodner, Machiko Bomberger, Robert Dankoff, Kate Davis, Robert Hanning, Arthur Johnson, Dennis Jones, James Mischke, Harlan Nelson, Barrett Price, Clayton Rich, Julia Stein, Manjeet Tangri, William Witherup, Diane Wolkstein, and William Woods.

Resources for Teaching THE BEDFORD ANTHOLOGY OF WORLD LITERATURE was expertly developed, edited, and assembled by Mary Rooks, assisted by Julia Berrisford. Along with Mary, Shari Evans, Gabriel Gryffyn, and Rick Mott each wrote a section of the manual. The manual itself was a large and challenging endeavor; we are grateful to its authors for their enthusiasm and hard work.

A six-volume anthology is an undertaking that calls for a courageous, imaginative, and supportive publisher. Chuck Christensen, Joan Feinberg, Karen Henry, and Steve Scipione at Bedford/St. Martin's possess these qualities; we especially appreciate their confidence in our ability to carry out this task. Our editor, Alanya Harter, and her associate, Joshua Levy, have guided the project throughout, keeping us on track with a vision of the whole when we were discouraged and keeping the day-to-day work moving forward. In particular, they helped us to reconceptualize the anthology's format and content. Without their suggestions, unacknowledged contributions, and guidance, this anthology would not be what it is today. They were assisted by many others who undertook particular tasks: The brilliant design was conceived by Anna George; Genevieve Hamilton helped to manage the art program, and together with Julia Berrisford she managed the final stages of development. Martha Friedman served as photo researcher, and Tina Samaha was design consultant and map coordinator. Jeff Voccola acted as editorial assistant, taking on many tasks, including the onerous ones of pasting up and numbering the manuscript. Ben Fortson expertly and efficiently supplied the pronunciation guides. Harriet Wald tirelessly and imaginatively oversaw the content and production of the Web site, an enormous task; she was helped along the way by Coleen O'Hanley, Chad Crume, and Dave Batty. Jenna Bookin Barry enthusiastically developed and coordinated the marketing plan, especially challenging when six books publish over a span of six months.

We were blessed with a superb production team who took the book from manuscript to final pages. For Books 4 and 6, we owe special thanks to Senior Production Editor Karen Baart, whose dedication and eye for detail made the project better in every way. Stasia Zomkowski efficiently served as production editor for Books 3 and 5, Ara Salibian for Book 1, and Paula Carroll for Book 2; they were ably assisted by Courtney Jossart, Kerri Cardone, and Tina Lai. Melissa Cook's careful and thoughtful copyediting helped to give consistency and clarity to the different voices that contributed to the manuscript. Managing Editor Elizabeth Schaaf oversaw the whole process and Senior Production Supervisor Nancy Myers realized our final vision of design and content in beautifully bound and printed books.

Most of all, we thank our families, especially Mary Davis, Marlys Harrison, and Mona Johnson, for their advice, stamina, and patience during the past three years while this book has occupied so much of our time and theirs.

Paul Davis
Gary Harrison
David M. Johnson
Patricia Clark Smith
John F. Crawford

A NOTE ON TRANSLATION

Some translators of literary works into English tended to sacrifice form for literal meaning, while others subordinated literal meaning to the artistry of the original work. With the increasing number of translations of world literature available by a range of translators, it has become possible to select versions that are clear and accessible as well as literally and aesthetically faithful to the original. Thus our choice of Robert Fitzgerald's *Iliad* and *Odyssey,* Horace Gregory's poems by Catullus, Mary Barnard's poems by Sappho, Theodore Morrison's *Canterbury Tales,* Edward Seidensticker's *Tale of Genji,* and Willa and Edwin Muir's *The Metamorphosis,* among others.

There are those who question whether poetry can ever be adequately translated from one language and culture into another; our concern, however, is not with what might be lost in a translation but with what is gained. The best translations do not merely duplicate a work but re-create it in a new idiom. Coleman Barks's poems of Rumi, Stephen Mitchell's poems of Rilke, Miguel León-Portilla's translations of Nahuatl poetry, and David Hinton's poems of the Tang dynasty are in a way outstanding English poems in their own right. And William Kelly Simpson's love poems of ancient Egypt, Robert and Jean Hollander's *Inferno,* Richard Wilbur's *Tartuffe,* W. S. Merwin's poems of Ghalib, Judith Hemschemeyer's poems of Anna Akhmatova, and Robert Bly's poems of Pablo Neruda are examples of translations done by major poets whose renderings are now an important part of their own body of work.

Barbara Stoler Miller's translation of the Bhagavad Gita and Donald Keene's translation of Chikamatsu's *Love Suicides at Amijima* communicate the complexity of a literary work. Richard Bodner's contemporary translation of Bashō's *Narrow Road through the Backcountry,* especially commissioned, does justice to both the prose and the resonant haiku in that work. David Luke's excellent translation of *Death in Venice* pays tribute to Thomas Mann's original German and is at the same time very readable.

More is said about the translations in this book in the notes for individual works.

About the Editors

Paul Davis (Ph.D., University of Wisconsin), professor emeritus of English at the University of New Mexico, has been the recipient of several teaching awards and academic honors, including that of Master Teacher. He has taught courses since 1962 in composition, rhetoric, and nineteenth-century literature and has written and edited many scholarly books, including *The Penguin Dickens Companion* (1999), *Dickens A to Z* (1998), and *The Lives and Times of Ebeneezer Scrooge* (1990). He has also written numerous scholarly and popular articles on solar energy and Victorian book illustration.

Gary Harrison (Ph.D., Stanford University), professor and director of undergraduate studies at the University of New Mexico, has won numerous fellowships and awards for scholarship and teaching. He has taught courses in world literature, British Romanticism, and literary theory at the University of New Mexico since 1987. Harrison's publications include a critical study on William Wordsworth, *Wordsworth's Vagrant Muse: Poetry, Poverty and Power* (1994); and many articles on the literature and culture of the early nineteenth century.

David M. Johnson (Ph.D., University of Connecticut), professor emeritus of English at the University of New Mexico, has taught courses in world literature, mythology, the Bible as literature, philosophy and literature, and creative writing since 1965. He has written, edited, and contributed to numerous scholarly books and collections of poetry, including *Fire in the Fields* (1996) and *Lord of the Dawn: The Legend of Quetzalcoatl* (1987). He has also published scholarly articles, poetry, and translations of Nahuatl myths.

Patricia Clark Smith (Ph.D., Yale University), professor emerita of English at the University of New Mexico, has taught courses in world literature, creative writing, American literature, and Native American literature since 1971. Her many publications include a collection of poetry, *Changing Your Story* (1991); the biography *As Long as the Rivers Flow* (1996); and *On the Trail of Elder Brother* (2000).

John F. Crawford (Ph.D., Columbia University), associate professor of English at the University of New Mexico–Valencia, has taught medieval, world, and other literature courses since 1965 at a number of institutions, including California Institute of Technology, Herbert Lehmann College of CUNY, and, most recently, the University of New Mexico. The publisher of West End Press, Crawford has also edited *This Is About Vision: Interviews with Southwestern Writers* (1990) and written articles on multicultural women poets of the Southwest.

Pronunciation Key

This key applies to the pronunciation guides that appear in the margins and before most selections in *The Bedford Anthology of World Literature*. The syllable receiving the main stress is CAPITALIZED.

a	mat, alabaster, laugh	MAT, AL-uh-bas-tur, LAF
ah	mama, Americana, Congo	MAH-mah, uh-meh-rih-KAH-nuh, KAHNG-goh
ar	cartoon, Harvard	kar-TOON, HAR-vurd
aw	saw, raucous	SAW, RAW-kus
ay (or a)	may, Abraham, shake	MAY, AY-bruh-ham, SHAKE
b	bet	BET
ch	church, matchstick	CHURCH, MACH-stik
d	desk	DESK
e	Edward, melted	ED-wurd, MEL-tid
ee	meet, ream, petite	MEET, REEM, puh-TEET
eh	cherub, derriere	CHEH-rub, DEH-ree-ehr
f	final	FIGH-nul
g	got, giddy	GAHT, GIH-dee
h	happenstance	HAP-un-stans
i	mit, Ipswich, impression	MIT, IP-swich, im-PRESH-un
igh (or i)	eyesore, right, Anglophile	IGH-sore, RITE, ANG-gloh-file
ih	Philippines	FIH-luh-peenz
j	judgment	JUJ-mint
k	kitten	KIT-tun
l	light, allocate	LITE, AL-oh-kate
m	ramrod	RAM-rahd
n	ran	RAN
ng	rang, thinker	RANG, THING-ker
oh (or o)	open, owned, lonesome	OH-pun, OHND, LONE-sum
ong	wrong, bonkers	RONG, BONG-kurz
oo	moot, mute, super	MOOT, MYOOT, SOO-pur
ow	loud, dowager, how	LOWD, DOW-uh-jur, HOW
oy	boy, boil, oiler	BOY, BOYL, OY-lur
p	pet	PET
r	right, wretched	RITE, RECH-id
s	see, citizen	SEE, SIH-tuh-zun
sh	shingle	SHING-gul
t	test	TEST
th	thin	THIN
th	this, whether	*TH*IS, WEH-*th*ur
u	until, sumptuous, lovely	un-TIL, SUMP-choo-us, LUV-lee
uh	about, vacation, suddenly	uh-BOWT, vuh-KAY-shun, SUH-dun-lee
ur	fur, bird, term, beggar	FUR, BURD, TURM, BEG-ur
v	vacuum	VAK-yoo-um
w	western	WES-turn
y	yesterday	YES-tur-day
z	zero, loser	ZEE-roh, LOO-zur
zh	treasure	TREH-zhur

Where a name is given two pronunciations, usually the first is the most familiar pronunciation in English and the second is a more exact rendering of the native pronunciation.

In the pronunciations of French names, nasalized vowels are indicated by adding "ng" after the vowel.

Japanese words have no strong stress accent, so the syllables marked as stressed are so given only for the convenience of English speakers.

CONTENTS

IN THE TRADITION: The Literature of War, Conflict, and Resistance   *502*

IN THE WORLD: Crossing Cultures: The Example of India *1278*

The Bedford Anthology of
World Literature
The Twentieth Century, 1900–The Present

マクドナルド
ハンバーガ

エブリデー
ローブライス

Japanese McDonald's *Today — in part due to a new global economy, networks of communication, and cultural cross-pollination — world travelers of every origin can find something familiar away from home. For better or worse, there is probably a McDonald's in every major city around the world. This one is in Japan, a country with strong ties to the West today despite a policy of excluding all British and American influences for over 200 years (1640– 1853). (Travelsite / Neil Setchfield)*

The Twentieth Century

1900 –
The Present

The twentieth-century volume of this anthology opens with Joseph Conrad's *Heart of Darkness,* a work that can be seen as emblematic of the 1900s. Conrad, born Jósef Teodor Konrad Korzeniowski, left his native Poland when he was seventeen to work on a French ship. He later sailed on English ships and became a British citizen. Fluent in both French and English, he eventually settled in England and before he was forty published the first of his many novels in English, *Almayer's Folly* (1895), a story set in the Malay Peninsula in Southeast Asia. Most of his novels take place outside England—in Asia, Africa, eastern Europe, and Latin America. Today Conrad would probably be described as a "hybrid" writer, one whose life and work bring together more than one culture, among the first of many such twentieth-century writers who represent an emerging global perspective. Indeed, separating literatures into national categories, a habit of the nationalistic nineteenth century, makes less and less sense and

www For an interactive version of the Comparative Time Line for the Twentieth Century, see *World Literature Online* at bedfordstmartins.com/worldlit.

COMPARATIVE TIME LINE FOR THE TWENTIETH CENTURY

Date	History and Politics	Literature	Science, Culture, and Technology
1890–1900		1890 Williams, *An Open Letter to His Serene Majesty Leopold II*	1891 Kinescope movie camera invented by Thomas Edison.
	1895–1898 Spanish-American War		1896 Olympic Games revived in Athens.
	1899 Boxer Rebellion in China	1899 Kipling, "The White Man's Burden"	
	Boer War in South Africa		
1900–1910		1902 Conrad, *Heart of Darkness*	1900 Freud, *Interpretation of Dreams*
	1901 Cuba becomes protectorate of the United States.		1901 Marconi broadcasts radio signals.
	President McKinley assassinated.	Twain, *King Leopold's Soliloquy*	1903 Wright brothers make first powered flight.
	1904–1905 Russo-Japanese War won by Japan; Japan gains control of Korea.	1903 W. E. B. Du Bois, *The Souls of Black Folk*	1905 Einstein, theory of relativity
	1905 Norway separates from Sweden.	1905 Hossain, "Sultana's Dream"	
			Expressionist movement begun by group of German painters.
		1907 Kipling awarded Nobel Prize.	
		Synge, *Playboy of the Western World*	1907 Cubist exhibition in Paris
1910–1920	1910 Civil war in Mexico	1912 Mann, *Death in Venice*	1913 Armory Show introduces cubism and postimpressionism in United States.
	Japan annexes Korea.	1913 Lawrence, *Sons and Lovers*	
	1912 War in the Balkans	Proust, *Swann's Way*	
		Tagore awarded Nobel Prize.	Stravinsky, *The Rite of Spring*

becomes increasingly difficult with twentieth-century writings. Therefore, the geographical divisions used in earlier books of this anthology are not present here; the globalization of literature and culture that characterizes the modern period has blurred such separations.

FROM EUROPEAN DOMINANCE TO A GLOBAL CULTURE

The twentieth century began with Europe dominating the rest of the world. Controlling nearly four-fifths of the land surface of the earth, the West imagined itself as the force of peace and progress. A second wave of industrialization introduced electricity, chemicals, and oil; it especially transformed transportation and communications, making possible the automobile, the telephone, the radio, and the airplane. Science had achieved the status of a religion. Even nations like China that had previously resisted Westernization sought the benefits of science and industry.

By the time the century concluded, Europe had been displaced from its former centrality by an emerging global culture. Two world wars and numerous lesser

Date	History and Politics	Literature	Science, Culture, and Technology
1910–1920 (cont.)	1914–1918 World War I	1914 Death of Georg Trakl	1913 Ford pioneers the assembly line.
	1914 British protectorate in Egypt	Joyce, "The Dead"	
		1915 Death of August Stramm	1915 Einstein, general theory of relativity
	1916 Easter Rebellion of Irish nationalists against British rule.	Kafka, *The Metamorphosis*	Sanger indicted for *Family Limitation*
	Indian National Congress Party and All India Muslim League sign Lucknow Agreement calling for Indian independence.		Film: *Birth of a Nation*, Griffith
	1917 United States enters World War I		1916 Duchamp, beginnings of dada movement
	Russian Revolution	1918 Death of Wilfred Owen	
	1918 World War I armistice signed.	Death of Isaac Rosenberg	1918 Spengler, *Decline of the West*
	1919 Treaty of Versailles	Death of Guillaume Apollinaire	1919 First transatlantic flight
	British kill 400 Indian protesters at Amritsar.		Bauhaus founded by Gropius.
	Prohibition amendment ratified in U.S.	1921 Pirandello, *Six Characters in Search of an Author*	1921 Wittgenstein, *Tractatus Logico-Philosophicus*
1920–1930	1920 League of Nations established.	Hughes, "The Negro Speaks of Rivers"	
	Women's suffrage passed in United States.	1922 Eliot, *The Waste Land*	1922 Lord Carnarvon discovers the tomb of Tutankhamen.
	Irish independence	Rilke, *Sonnets to Orpheus*	
	Gandhi emerges as leader of Indian independence movement.		1923 Le Corbusier, *Towards a New Architecture*
	Sacco and Vanzetti arrested.		
	1921 First Indian parliament		

wars changed the maps and turned what had been virtually a European monologue into a conversation among many old and new nation-states throughout the world. The gas attacks of World War I, the scientific experimentation of the Nazis during the Holocaust, and the atomic bombs that ended World War II had undermined the belief that science brought only progress and prosperity. New sciences, such as psychology, anthropology, and sociology sought to understand the sources of irrationality, violence, and brutality. As they explored the human psyche, psychologists and anthropologists realized that savage impulses were not limited to "primitive" peoples. Eventually the simple dichotomy of "primitive" and "civilized" lost its validity.

In the colonial era that extended into the early twentieth century, industrialized nations exploited their colonies as sources of raw materials and as markets for manufactured goods. Although they claimed to be bringing European enlightenment to benighted parts of the globe, imperialists were really engaged in what Conrad's Marlow calls a "squeeze." They grabbed ivory, rubber, and oil but had little interest in the cultural productions of "savage" peoples. A cultural exchange began nevertheless. According to legend, some Japanese ceramics came to the West

Date	History and Politics	Literature	Science, Culture, and Technology
1920–1930 (cont.)	1922 League of Nations mandates establish European protectorates in the Middle East. Formation of the Soviet Union Irish Free State established.	1922 Tanizaki Junichiro, "Aguri" Lu Xun, "The True Story of Ah Q" McKay, *Harlem Shadows*	
		1923 Yeats awarded Nobel Prize.	1925 Scopes trial Film: *Battleship Potemkin*, Eisenstein Louis Armstrong makes first recording with his own band.
		1924 O'Casey, *Juno and the Paycock*	
	1925 Hindenberg elected president of Germany. Hitler, *Mein Kampf*, vol. 1.	1925 Cullen, "Heritage" Fitzgerald, *The Great Gatsby*	1927 Lindbergh's flight across the Atlantic
		1926 Hemingway, *The Sun Also Rises*	Film: *The Jazz Singer*; first talking picture
	1927 "Black Friday"; German economy collapses.	1927 Hesse, *Steppenwolf*	1928 Gershwin, *An American in Paris*
	1928 Stalin takes over leadership in Soviet Union. Kuomintang government established in China. Chiang Kai-shek becomes president of China.	1928 Sholokhov, *And Quiet Flows the Don* Yeats, *The Tower* 1929 Faulkner, *The Sound and the Fury* Woolf, *A Room of One's Own*	Ravel, *Bolero* Fleming discovers penicillin. Television demonstrated in Britain.
	1929 Stock market crash; beginning of Great Depression	Remarque, *All Quiet on the Western Front* Mann awarded Nobel Prize.	1929 St. Valentine's Day massacre O'Keeffe, *Black Flower and Blue Larkspur*

wrapped in the woodblock prints that inspired artists such as Vincent Van Gogh and James Whistler. African tribal art caught the attention of European modernist painters, especially Pablo Picasso. Hindu gurus from India and Zen masters from Japan promoted their spiritual disciplines in the West. In the first sixty-five years of the twentieth century, only two writers from outside Euro-American cultures had won the Nobel Prize for literature: Rabindranath Tagore of India in 1913 and Gabriela Mistral of Chile in 1945. In the past thirty-five years, however, ten writers from Africa, Asia, the Middle East, and Latin America have been awarded the prize. Like the world music movement that has put Ladysmith Black Mambazo on the American charts and made the Beatles big in Asia, the "world literature movement" begun in the middle of the last century has made literature global.

Nationalism in literature was replaced by cross-culturalism. Joseph Conrad, who migrated from Poland to France and then England at the beginning of the century to become an English novelist, would prove to be one of the first of the century's world citizens. His successors include Vladimir Nabokov and Aleksandr Solzhenitsyn, an émigré and an exile, respectively, who came from Russia to the United States; Derek Walcott, Claude McKay, Michelle Cliff, and V. S. Naipaul, who

Date	History and Politics	Literature	Science, Culture, and Technology
1930–1940	1930 Gandhi leads march against British salt monopoly.	1930 Musil, *The Man without Qualities*	1931 Dali, *Persistence of Memory*
	1931 Japan invades Manchuria.	1932 Neihardt, *Black Elk Speaks*	Empire State Building
	1932 F. D. Roosevelt elected U.S. president; New Deal begins.	Huxley, *Brave New World*	1932 Lindbergh kidnapping
	1933 Repeal of Prohibition	1933 Brecht, "When Evil-Doing Comes like Falling Rain"	Calder exhibits first mobiles in Paris.
	Hitler becomes German chancellor, granted dictatorial powers.	Stein, *The Autobiography of Alice B. Toklas*	Earhart first woman to fly solo across the Atlantic.
	1934 Dust Bowl in the Plains states	1934 Lorca, "Lament for Ignacio Sanchez Mejías"	
	1936 Abyssinian War ends; Italy annexes Ethiopia.		1936 Keynes, *General Theory of Employment, Interest and Money*
	Mussolini and Hitler proclaim Rome-Berlin Axis.	Pirandello awarded Nobel Prize.	Turing develops mathematical theory of computing.
	Edward VIII abdicates British throne.	1935 Neruda, *Residence on Earth*	1937 Picasso, *Guernica*
	Spanish civil war	1937 Rao, *Kanthapura*	Wright, Fallingwater house built in Pennsylvania.
	Chiang Kai-shek declares war on Japan.		1938 Carlson develops Xerography.
	1937 French suppress rebellion in Morocco.	1939 Césaire, *Notebook of a Return to the Native Land*	
	Japan invades China.	Steinbeck, *The Grapes of Wrath*	
	1938 Mexico nationalizes U.S. and British oil companies.		
	Germany mobilizes, occupies Sudetenland; Munich Conference		
	1939 World War II		

all migrated from the West Indies to the United States or Britain; Aimé Césaire from Martinique and Samuel Beckett from Ireland, who both went to Paris; and James Baldwin from the United States, who spent many years in Paris. Some of these migrants were driven into exile by political oppression, censorship, or poor economic conditions. *In the World:* Crossing Cultures draws upon writers from India, Pakistan, and the Indian diaspora to illustrate one aspect of this globalization of culture.

In addition to being globalized, literature also became diversified. Many formerly unheard voices joined the cultural conversation, especially women and members of ethnic and cultural minorities. New American literatures of ethnic subcultures, such as Chicano and Native American literature, developed themes of cultural pride and allegories of cultural history and mythology that recall the nationalistic literatures of Europe and America in the nineteenth century. They are part of a worldwide postcolonial movement through which many former colonies are constructing national identities. As industrialization has brought global culture to nearly every landscape on earth, an appreciation of the differences between cultures and individuals has also awakened.

Date	History and Politics	Literature	Science, Culture, and Technology
1940–1950	1940 Trotsky assassinated in Mexico.	1940 Wright, *Native Son*	1940 Lascaux caves discovered.
	1941 Japan attacks Pearl Harbor; United States enters war.	Koestler, *Darkness at Noon*	
	Italian forces expelled from East Africa.	1941 Brecht, *Mother Courage and Her Children*	
	1942 Battle of El Alamein drives Axis powers from North Africa.	1942 Camus, *The Stranger*	1942 Fermi splits the atom.
	1944 International Monetary Fund and World Bank established.	1943 Sartre, *The Flies*	1944 Wright, Johnson Administration and Research Building
	D day, June 6	1945 Senghor, *Shadow Songs*	
	1945 Germany surrenders; V-E Day, May 8		
	United States drops atomic bomb on Hiroshima and Nagasaki; Japan surrenders; VJ Day, August 14.		
	Arab League founded.		
	United Nations founded.		
	1946 Nuremberg Tribunal	1947 *The Diary of Anne Frank*	1947 Dead Sea Scrolls discovered.
	1947 Indian independence		
	U.N. develops plan for partitioning Palestine.	1948 Pound, *The Pisan Cantos*	1948 Bell Labs develops transistor.
	Truman Doctrine, offering support for countries opposing Communism	T. S. Eliot awarded Nobel Prize.	Pollock, *Composition No. 1*
	1948 Mohandas Gandhi assassinated.		

WORLD WAR I

The competition among European nations for control of disputed territories in eastern Europe and for sources of raw materials and new markets in Asia and Africa reached an impasse in the first decade of the twentieth century. When German expansionism threatened to engulf the rest of Europe, France, Russia, and Britain went to war to contain Germany and its allies, Austria and Italy. After the German strategy to defeat the French quickly and move on to other fronts failed, the war settled into a long and brutal siege in which millions of young men from all the European nations perished. Soldiers died hideous deaths in the massive trench warfare of World War I (1914–1918) — by gassing, shelling, and aerial bombardment — and more troops of more nationalities were slaughtered under grimmer conditions than in any previous war. The conflict ground to a stalemate in Western Europe in 1917. America belatedly entered the war in 1917, and the fresh American troops made enough of a difference that Germany surrendered by November 1918.

Although the war was fought with the expectation that it would produce lasting peace, it had just the opposite effect. The Treaty of Versailles (1919), which

Date	History and Politics		Literature		Science, Culture, and Technology	
1940–1950 (cont.)	1948	War in Palestine between Arabs and Jews; founding of Israel				
	1949	NATO established.				
		People's Republic of China proclaimed by Mao Zedong.				
		End of Greek civil war				
		Apartheid introduced in South Africa.				
1950–1960	1950	Korean War	1950	Abé Kobo, "The Red Cocoon"		
	1951	End of Allied occupation in Japan	1951	Salinger, *Catcher in the Rye*		
		Rosenbergs sentenced to death.				
	1952	First hydrogen bomb exploded by United States.	1952	Beckett, *Waiting for Godot*		
		Eisenhower elected president.				
		Mau Mau terror campaign against British in Kenya				
	1953	Yugoslav constitution; Tito elected president	1953	Kawabata Yasunari, "The Moon on the Water"	1953	Crick and Watson model structure of DNA.
		Stalin succeeded by Malenkov in USSR.				Skinner, *Science and Human Behavior*
		Shah Reza Pahlavi monarchy established in Iran.				Beauvoir, *The Second Sex*
		Laos gains independence from France.				

ended the war, reconfigured the map of Europe in ways that would soon antagonize both Germany and Russia, and it punished Germany with ruinous demands for reparations. In little more than a decade, the Germans, financially broken and restless for more *lebensraum* (living space), embraced an even more virulent nationalism—fascist National Socialism, or Nazism—and instigated a new war.

Although the protagonists in World War I were the major European powers, the war had reached far beyond the borders of Europe. By having chosen to side with Germany, the Ottoman empire, which had ruled the Middle East, southeastern Europe, and north Africa from its capital in Turkey since 1299, was brought to its final collapse. The resulting power vacuum allowed Turkish nationalists under the leadership of Mustapha Kemal Ataturk (1881–1938) to establish a secular republic. The new League of Nations placed other Ottoman lands in the Middle East under either French or British administration, a resolution that created many of the inequities and tensions in that region that still plague the world nearly a century later. The British and French roles in the Middle East differed from those that Britain and France had played in colonial Africa, for now they were administrators, not rulers. Nevertheless, the Europeans' interference in Middle Eastern

Date	History and Politics		Literature		Science, Culture, and Technology	
1950–1960 (cont.)	1954	Senator McCarthy censured by Senate.	1954	Amis, *Lucky Jim*		
		France surrenders to Vietminh; Vietnam divided at seventeenth parallel.				
		Southeast Asia Treaty Organization (SEATO) established.				
		National Liberation Front (FLN) established to fight for independence in Algeria.				
		Brown v. Board of Education desegregates public schools.				
	1955	Communist countries in Eastern Europe form Warsaw Pact.			1955	Montgomery bus boycott
		West Germany joins NATO.				
	1956	Suez crisis; Nasser nationalizes the Suez Canal.	1956	Ginsberg, *Howl*		
		Soviet invasion of Hungary		Osborne, *Look Back in Anger*		
		Islamic Republic of Pakistan declared.	1957	Baldwin, "Sonny's Blues"	1957	Launching of *Sputnik*, first space satellite
	1957	European Economic Community (EEC) established.		Pasternak, *Doctor Zhivago*		Bernstein, *West Side Story*
		Ghana, first sub-Saharan colony to win independence		Camus awarded Nobel Prize.		
	1958	Egypt and Syria form the United Arab Republic.	1958	Beckett, *Krapp's Last Tape*	1958	Beatnik movement
						Presley, "Heartbreak Hotel"

affairs was often resented and led to such confrontations as the Suez crisis between Egypt and Britain in 1956. In other parts of the world, European nations had recruited their colonial subjects to fight in the First World War. After the war, German colonies went to the victors: African colonies, for example, were divided among Britain, France, and Belgium; Japan was even able to seize some of the remote German possessions in the Pacific.

THE RUSSIAN REVOLUTION

Russia had entered World War I in 1914 ill prepared for battle. Russian industry was not capable of supplying the army that was under the personal charge of Tsar Nicholas II (1868–1918). Long-standing discontent with the autocratic tsar was intensified by his incompetence as a military commander and by the bungling of his generals. After two million Russian soldiers were killed in the first two years of the war and an economic crisis and food shortages wracked the homeland, Russia lost the will to continue fighting abroad. Nicholas was forced to abdicate early in 1917, and the country plunged into civil war. Loosely organized "White," or Menshevik, forces pursued a vague program of social democracy while "Red,"

Date	History and Politics	Literature	Science, Culture, and Technology
1950–1960 (cont.)	1959 Cuban revolution Chinese suppress rebellion in Tibet; Dalai Lama flees the country. Homelands established in South Africa.	1958 Achebe, *Things Fall Apart* 1959 Grass, *The Tin Drum* Soyinka, *The Lion and the Jewel* King, "My Trip to the Land of Gandhi"	
1960–1970	1960 Eichmann found guilty. Seventeen nations win independence from European powers. Sharpeville: 69 black demonstrators killed in South Africa. 1961 Bay of Pigs invasion Berlin Wall put up. 1962 Cuban missile crisis Algerian independence American combat troops sent to Vietnam. 1963 President Kennedy assassinated. 1964 China tests atomic bomb. 1965 Vietnam War escalates; United States begins bombing campaign. War between India and Pakistan 1966 Cultural Revolution in China	1961 Fanon, *The Wretched of the Earth* 1962 Borges, "The Garden of Forking Paths" 1963 Mahfouz, "Zaabalawi" Takenishi Hiroko, "The Rite" Akhmatova *Requiem* published in Germany. 1964 Sartre awarded Nobel Prize. 1965 Oe Kenzaburo, *Hiroshima Notes* 1966 al-Hakim, *The Fate of a Cockroach* Sachs awarded Nobel Prize.	1961 Gagarin first man in space. Beatles perform in Liverpool; Bob Dylan debuts in New York. 1962 Carson, *Silent Spring* 1963 Pop art 1965 Malcolm X shot. Op art

or Bolshevik, forces sought to institute a COMMUNIST government in what would later be known as the Russian or Communist Revolution. Under the leadership of Vladimir Ulianov Lenin (1870–1924), the Bolsheviks' Red Army won out by 1921, but the industrial and agricultural sectors of the Russian economy had been devastated. The first item on Lenin's postrevolution agenda was to rebuild Russia economically, a program that was cut short by his death in 1924. The subsequent struggle for power among the leaders of the politburo, the policy-making and executive arm of the Communist Party, led to the dictatorship of Josef Stalin (1879–1953), who consolidated his position by 1928 and ruled the nation for the next quarter century.

Many Western intellectuals saw the Great Depression that followed the stock market crash of 1929 as proof of Karl Marx's prediction of the collapse of capitalism. Although Karl Marx (1818–1883), the economist who developed communist theory, had asserted that communist revolutions would take place in the most advanced capitalist countries, Russia, the one existing communist state, had been the least industrialized of the European nations, and its brand of communism in fact emphasized dictatorship at the expense of the proletariat. In spite of its

Date	History and Politics	Literature	Science, Culture, and Technology
1960–1970 (cont.)	1967 Six-Day War between Israel and Arab nations		1967 Barnard performs first heart transplant.
	1968 Martin Luther King Jr. and Robert Kennedy assassinated.	1968 Kawabata Yasunari awarded Nobel Prize.	
	Prague Spring		Beatles, *Sgt. Pepper's Lonely Hearts Club Band*
	Student uprisings in France and West Germany		
	1969 Yasir Arafat elected chairman of the Palestine Liberation Organization (PLO).	1969 Beckett awarded Nobel Prize.	1969 Armstrong and Aldrin first men on the moon.
	Sectarian violence in Northern Ireland		
1970–1980		1970 Narayan, "A Horse and Two Goats"	
	1971 East Pakistan declares independence; Bangladesh founded.	1971 Neruda awarded Nobel Prize.	1971 Hoff invents computer chip.
	1972 President Nixon visits China.	1972 Márquez, "A Very Old Man with Enormous Wings"	
	1973 Arab states attack Israel and are defeated.	1973 Rich, *Diving into the Wreck*	
	OPEC cartel triples oil prices.	1974 Silko, "Lullaby"	
	U.S. troops leave Vietnam.	Kundera, "The Hitchhiking Game"	
	Britain, Ireland, and Denmark join EEC.	1975 Achebe, "An Image of Africa"	
	1974 Watergate scandal; Nixon resigns.		
	1975 War in Lebanon		

shortcomings, however, Russia was an alternative to the ruthless capitalist economies that seemed to produce wealth for the few and unemployment and misery for the many. The Great Depression did not bring any of the more advanced European countries to revolution, but it did encourage the growth of communist and socialist parties, on the left, and a reactionary nationalism, on the right, in the form of FASCISM. Fascists took power in Nazi Germany, the Italy of Benito Mussolini (1883–1945), the Spain of Francisco Franco (1892–1975), and the China of Chiang Kai-shek (1887–1975). Communism characterized itself as the movement that opposed fascism and transcended national interests to represent the international working class; in the eyes of many, it became the international alternative to nationalistic fascism.

As part of his international vision Lenin had encouraged the development of communist movements in many nonindustrial countries, particularly in colonial or formerly colonial countries in North Africa, the Middle East, and Asia. By allying themselves with the nationalistic and independence movements in those countries, communists appealed to people who resented colonial exploitation and wished to modernize without being Westernized. This strategy was most successful

Date	History and Politics		Literature		Science, Culture, and Technology	
1970–1980 (cont.)	1975	Franco dies; Juan Carlos becomes king of Spain.			1976	Haley, *Roots*
	1976	Deaths of Chinese leaders Mao Zedong and Zhou Enlai.				Wosniak and Jobs develop the personal computer.
		Soweto protests in South Africa	1977	Morrison, *Song of Solomon*		
	1977	President Sadat of Egypt visits Jerusalem.		Head, "The Deep River: A Story of Ancient Tribal Migration"		
	1979	Israel and Egypt sign peace treaty at Camp David.				
		Ayatollah Khomeini establishes Islamic republic in Iran.	1978	Desai, "The Farewell Party"	1978	Birth of first test-tube baby
		Soviet Union invades Afghanistan.				
		Saddam Hussein becomes president of Iraq.				
1980–1990	1980	Lech Walesa leads Solidarity strike in Gdańsk.	1980	Mnthali, "The Stranglehold of English Lit"		
	1980–1988	Iraq-Iran War	1981	Brooks, "To the Diaspora"	1981	AIDS first recognized as a disease.
	1981	President Sadat of Egypt assassinated.	1982	Márquez awarded Nobel Prize.	1982	Lin, Vietnam Veterans' Memorial
	1984	Indira Gandhi assassinated.	1984	Rifaat, "My World of the Unknown"		
	1985	Gorbachev becomes leader of USSR.	1986	Soyinka awarded Nobel Prize.		
	1986	Space shuttle *Challenger* explodes.	1987	Walcott, *The Arkansas Testament*		
		Chernobyl nuclear accident in the Ukraine				

in China, where the Communists joined forces with the nationalist revolution led by Sun Yat-sen (1866–1925) and his successor Chiang Kai-shek. When Chiang Kai-shek later tried to suppress the Communists, he inspired revolutionary opposition led by Mao Zedong (1893–1976) that eventually defeated the Nationalists and in 1949 established the People's Republic of China.

WORLD WAR II

Very soon after 1918 it became clear that the forces that had started the First World War were preparing for another confrontation. Competition among colonial powers, ultranationalism, the rise of dictators, and the stresses of a worldwide depression brought Europe and the rest of the world to the brink of explosion in the late 1930s. Two contradictory versions of Western civilization opposed each other. Fascists presented themselves as preservers or restorers of a pure European culture that would reverse the decline of the West. Their opponents saw Fascists as achieving order only by destroying the free democratic institutions that were the West's finest achievement. With the rise of fascism, many people were drawn to the Marxian conclusion that revolution was the inevitable result of the divide between

Date	History and Politics	Literature	Science, Culture, and Technology
1980–1990 (cont.)	1988 Soviet Union begins withdrawing troops from Afghanistan. 1989 End of Communist regimes in Eastern Europe Berlin Wall torn down. Tiananmen Square demonstrators shot.	1987 Chinweizu, *Decolonizing the African Mind* 1988 Rushdie, *The Satanic Verses* Mukherjee, "A Wife's Story" Mahfouz awarded Nobel Prize.	1988 Genome Project begun.
1990–2000	1990 East and West Germany are reunited. 1990–1991 Iraq invades Kuwait; Iraq defeated by U.S.-led coalition. 1990 Nelson Mandela released from prison. Mexico City becomes world's most populous city. 1991 Warsaw Pact dissolved. Gorbachev resigns as Soviet premier; USSR ceases to exist. 1992 Canada, Mexico, and United States form the North American Free Trade Association (NAFTA). Hindu extremists demolish Ayodhya mosque in India. Islamic rebels capture Kabul and overthrow Communist government.	1990 Fuentes, *The Prisoner of Las Lomas* Naipaul, "Our Universal Civilization" O'Brien, *The Things They Carried* Paz awarded Nobel Prize. 1991 Gordimer awarded Nobel Prize. 1992 Gao Xingjian, *Dialogue and Rebuttal* Walcott awarded Nobel Prize.	1990 *Hubble* space telescope placed in orbit.

capitalists and the working classes. Dismayed by the failure of capitalist governments to put a stop to Hitler, Mussolini, and Franco, people were drawn into affiliations with the communist parties and other leftist movements that formed a
diverse and committed Popular Front opposed to fascism. That opposition was
dramatically and tragically expressed in the Spanish civil war (1936–1939), in which
international brigades of idealistic leftists volunteered to fight beside the Spanish
Republicans in an unsuccessful effort to preserve the democratic second Spanish
Republic against the coalition of conservative and Fascist forces under General
Franco.

No one was prepared for the scope of World War II. The war reached beyond
Europe into China, Japan, and colonial possessions of the European powers in
Africa and Asia. Neither was anyone ready for the extent of the devastation, the
leveling of whole cities by aerial bombardment and the civilian genocide of the
Holocaust. The massive suffering, the torture, and the deaths of millions of Jews,
Gypsies, homosexuals, and others whom the Nazis deemed unfit to live was beyond
comprehension. These atrocities were carried out with a deliberate and scientific
efficiency that applied the principles of industrial organization and technological

Date	History and Politics		Literature		Science, Culture, and Technology	
1990–2000 (cont.)	1993	Czech and Slovak republics established as separate countries.	1993	Morrison awarded Nobel Prize.	1994	World Wide Web created.
	1994	Nelson Mandela becomes president of South Africa.	1994	Rushdie, "The Courter"		
		Palestinian Authority takes control of Gaza Strip.		Oe Kenzaburo awarded Nobel Prize.		
		Zapatista uprising in Mexico	1995	Paz, *In Light of India*		
	1995	Israeli prime minister Yitzhak Rabin assassinated.	1996	Szymborska awarded Nobel Prize.		
		Bosnian war				
		Uprising in Russian province of Chechnya				
		Terrorist bombing of federal building in Oklahoma City				
	1997	Hong Kong returned to China.	1997	Gordimer, "As Others See Us"	1997	Sheep cloned in Britain.
						Gehry, Guggenheim Museum in Bilbao, Spain
	1998	Arms inspectors driven from Iraq.				
	1999	War in Kosovo				
2000–2010			2000	Gao Xingjian awarded Nobel Prize.	2000	Human genome deciphered.
	2001	Terrorists destroy World Trade Center in New York City.			2002	Scientists confirm presence of water on Mars.

productivity to the business of mass murder. And the dropping of atomic bombs on Hiroshima and Nagasaki by the United States at the end of the war raised unsettling ethical and technological questions. Would atomic energy restore belief in science and progress or had it simply given humanity the power to create Armageddon?

In some ways, World War II fulfilled its stated mission: "to save the world for democracy." Not only were democratic governments established in the defeated countries — Germany, Italy, and Japan — but the war also forced democratic changes in the victorious nations as well, such as the decline of the class system in Britain and a move toward racial integration in the United States. The war also gave impetus to independence movements throughout the colonized world. Before World War II there was one independent country in Africa — Liberia; by the beginning of the twenty-first century, there were no remaining African colonies. World War II was the twentieth century's pivotal event. Its consequences and the issues it raised but did not settle, such as the realignment of the Middle East, are still shaping the world's experience today.

THE POSTWAR YEARS AND THE COLD WAR

Europe, Asia, parts of Africa, and the Middle East awoke from World War II as from a nightmare of devastation and suffering. Although some writers looked on the war as a prelude to the apocalypse, the biblical end of the world, others, especially in Europe and Japan, saw in the rubble an opportunity to rebuild a society now rid, they thought, of narrow nationalism, militarism, and expansionist designs. In the face of sometimes seemingly insurmountable obstacles and despite devastating setbacks, since World War II many nations took steps toward improving relations and understanding among the various countries and cultures of the world. The United Nations was founded in 1945 to mediate conflicts between member nations, to provide economic and technological assistance to countries in need, and to promote cooperation and cultural understanding. Fifty countries joined the four "sponsoring" nations — Britain, China, the Soviet Union, and the United States — to sign the original U.N. charter, and by 1960 another fifty had added their names to the document.

Despite the hope for world peace, the first decade after the war witnessed many regional conflicts, some of which, like the Greek civil war (1946–1949), the Chinese Communist revolution (1945–1949), and the Korean War (1950–1953), threatened to erupt into large-scale confrontations. Even as the peace agreements were being signed at Yalta in 1945, the frost of the cold war between the West and the Soviet Union was crystallizing. Treaties essentially had divided the world into Western and communist blocs, best symbolized perhaps by Germany, which was split into West and East. Both sides attempted to enlarge their spheres of influence, the West in the NATO alliance, the Soviet Union in the Warsaw Pact with its Eastern European satellite states. Both sides also sought to enlist the allegiance of countries in the Third World. Conflicts on the fringes, in Korea, for example, and Cuba, threatened to turn the cold war hot. When the Soviet Union announced in 1953 that it had developed a hydrogen bomb to match that of the United States, the standoff took on a more menacing aspect.

Europe and Japan lost most of their remaining colonies in Africa and Asia in the two decades following World War II. Often, as in the case of India and Pakistan, North and South Vietnam, Indonesia, and various African states, including South Africa, the collapse of colonialism introduced a turbulent period of civil, religious, and nationalist strife. The independence movements in these regions also marked a renewal of interest in traditional cultural practices, folklore, religion, and native languages. In Africa, for example, writers such as Jomo Kenyatta (1893–1978) and Ngugi Wa Thiong'o (b. 1938) of Kenya, Chinua Achebe (b. 1930) and Wole Soyinka (b. 1934) of Nigeria, and Alex La Guma (1925–1985) and Lewis Nkosi (b. 1936) of South Africa adapted traditional forms of oral storytelling to European narrative to celebrate African identity and articulate unique aspects of the African experience.

The colonial struggle in Indochina—Laos, Cambodia, and Vietnam—had far-reaching implications for the United States. Ho Chi Minh (1890–1969), who had lived in China, Moscow, and Paris, led the nationalist Vietminh against the French, who gave up their colonial holdings in Vietnam after a major defeat at Dien Bien Phu in 1954. Vietnam was then divided into two parts, North and South. The revolutionary nationalist leader Ho Chi Minh ruled the North while Diem Ngo Dinh (1901–1963), supported by the United States, was the official leader of the South. Diem's regime was unpopular, and a succession of coup attempts against him ultimately led to direct U.S. military intervention in 1964; America feared that a Communist takeover in South Vietnam would lead to further revolutions in the region. Arguably the United States's most unpopular war, the Vietnam War polarized public opinion throughout the country, especially after heavy U.S. losses during the Tet offensive of January 1968, which prompted massive antiwar demonstrations in both the United States and Europe. The antiwar and civil rights movements in the United States and the independence efforts around the world fomented a global struggle for basic human rights.

When the Berlin Wall came down in 1989, at least symbolically ending the cold war, some claimed that "the end of history" had been reached, for the separation of the world into three entities—the Free World, the Communist World, and the Third World—no longer stood. Every country had become a member of a single global community, a participant in an expanding free market connected to one network of communications. The arrogance of the assumption that the only significant differences in the world had been those between the capitalist West and the communist East was compounded in the notion that once those oppositions disappeared, the world had become homogenous. Some Asian observers of the world scene have described the almost continuous wars on their continent since World War II, wars that often involved Western interference, as World War III. In the wake of the cold war, many countries remained suspicious of modernization and Westernization, resisted the economic exploitation of the poor by rich nations, and viewed globalization as American subjugation of the rest of the world. History had not ended; it had merely been reconfigured.

MODERNISM

The first two decades of the twentieth century could be called the twilight of the ENLIGHTENMENT, the last time people held comforting beliefs in science and progress. The shock of the First World War shattered that faith and thrust the times into intellectual, cultural, and political crises. The following lines from "The Second Coming," written in 1920 by William Butler Yeats (1865–1939), one of Europe's most visionary poets, capture the spirit of the age that witnessed the Russian Revolution, the horrors of World War I, and the collapse of accepted truths in science, religion, and politics:

> Things fall apart, the center cannot hold;
> Mere anarchy is loosed upon the world,
> The blood-dimmed tide is loosed, and everywhere
> The ceremony of innocence is drowned;
> The best lack all conviction, while the worst
> Are full of passionate intensity.

Oswald Spengler (1880–1936) in *Decline of the West* (1918) asserted that the West had lived out its allotted cycle of glory, citing World War I as a point of no return in the downward spiral to final desolation. Since Europe had not suffered a widespread war for nearly a century, even the memories of earlier conflicts were distant. The young men who fought in the trenches had been nursed on comfortable pieties about God, country, and bravery, and had not even matured before they became the "lost generation," so called because so many had been wiped out on the battlefields or disillusioned by the destruction of the Great War. The wartime poets, many of whom died in combat, articulated the trauma in different ways. The traditionalism of the verse forms of Wilfred Owen (1893–1918) and Isaac Rosenberg (1890–1918) is undermined by the subject matter of trench warfare and gas attacks, while the expressionist imagery of Austrian poet Georg Trakl (1887–1914) turns the madness of war into surreal nightmare. The death and destruction wrought by the war seemed to confirm an assertion of German philosopher Friedrich Nietzsche (1844–1900), who in the preceding century had declared: "God is dead."

The Waste Land (1922) by T. S. Eliot (1888–1965), probably the classic description of modernist malaise, imagines modern urban society as a sterile, materialistic wasteland in which the search for meaning is filled with detours and dead ends. The poem pieces together realistic vignettes of banal urban life with fragments of great literary works from the past, shards of a broken and forgotten tradition. Communication between individuals is faulty or nonexistent, sexual relations mechanical and alienating. Although the end of the poem suggests potential sources of healing, *The Waste Land,* like much modernist writing from the first half of the twentieth century, is less concerned with a cure than with describing the societal sickness.

The chief diagnostician of the diseased modern psyche was Viennese physician Sigmund Freud (1856–1939), who described human beings in very different terms from those of the Enlightenment scientists. Instead of rational creatures who by seeking their own self-interests served the best interests of all, human beings, according to Freud, were driven by stifled desires and unconscious drives. Freud developed a scientific theory to explain the role of dreams, secret desires, personal history, and sexuality in defining the individual and to account for how modern urban society frustrates and forces suppression of those desires, causing neuroses. Freud developed psychoanalysis to enable individuals to overcome neuroses by becoming more aware of their suppressed inner life. Freud's ideas spurred an interest in consciousness, the role of sexuality in forming the individual, and the ways in which the perceiver affects his or her perceptions of the external world. Visual artists turned away from painting the exterior world to expressing on canvas their own interior visions. Sometimes this change in perspective produced pictures that distorted or transformed reality, as in the work of cubist painter Pablo Picasso (1881–1973). Other artists, known as abstract expressionists, or action painters, made no attempt to relate the images on their canvases to any exterior reality.

"Primitive" cultures, in which, Freud thought, natural impulses and instinctive drives were more openly expressed, became the focus of much scholarship. One of the early classics in the new fields of comparative religion and anthropology was *The Golden Bough* (1890) by Sir James Frazer (1854–1941). A broad survey of myth and ritual, this work was intended to defend the truth of Christianity against pagan religions, but it actually provided a rich symbolic tapestry for reevaluating the archetypal roots of Christianity and its resemblance to pagan religions. The similarities between "primitive" and modern cultures that Frazer brought to light appeared to argue against the myth of progress, especially when modern secularism was seen to be shallow and materialistic in comparison with the mythology of tribal or traditional societies. Bronislaw Malinowski (1884–1942), one of the first anthropologists to study native people in the field, challenged the nineteenth-century contention that myth represented prelogical or prescientific thinking and a rudimentary stage of civilization. By implication, Malinowski questioned any simplistic application of the idea of progress or lack of progress to native cultures.

Anthropologists and comparativists said that the truths and values of individual cultures and their religions were relative, a theory that came to be known as cultural relativism. They considered a particular religion or myth system merely a culture's language for addressing universal human needs, so that all surviving myths and mores from the hundreds of native cultures around the world are true in some sense. The primary issue was not universal truth but whether a particular mythology satisfied the social and psychological needs of those who embraced it. Ruth Benedict's (1887–1948) *Patterns of Culture* (1934) is a classic of the "new" relativism, in which anthropologists describe the behavior of a tribe but pass no value judgments on it. Investigators need to be ultrasensitive to their own cultural systems in order to minimize their cultural bias.

Some of the new social scientists found universal "deep structures" beneath the superficial differences among cultures. Carl Gustav Jung (1875–1961) believed that social codes governing religious, social, and cultural practices were not particular to certain cultures or historical periods but universal and timeless. In myth, literature, art, and religious symbolism, Jung found what he called "ARCHETYPES," or age-old symbols, such as the Quest, the Great Mother, and the Wise Man, that suggested that human beings in diverse times and cultures shared a common spiritual and psychic makeup. Moreover, although the outward or physical forms of religion changed or evolved, spiritual needs remained relatively constant for each new generation. Jung's explorations of world religions and his investigations of dreams, in stark contrast to the positivist philosophy of science that accepted only measurable observations of the physical world and turned its back on the soul, offered a path for spiritual rebirth.

The new focus on the perceiver and on consciousness prompted a growing uncertainty about the physical world and the nature of reality. After progressing in the nineteenth century to a place where they could explain nearly all material phenomena, the physical sciences were transformed by quantum physics and the theory of relativity in the twentieth century. The complex theories of such scientists as Max Planck (1858–1947), Albert Einstein (1879–1955), Niels Bohr (1885–1962), and Werner Heisenberg (1901–1976) constituted a paradigm shift that revised the Newtonian worldview in place since the seventeenth century. Einstein's theory of relativity modified the customary three-dimensional view of things, adding time as a necessary fourth dimension in any physical description of an object. In 1927, Werner Heisenberg's experiments with electrons led to his "uncertainty principle," which implied that scientists could not describe reality exactly because they could not simultaneously observe both the position and velocity of an electron. The work of these scientists paved the way for the discovery of a fascinating subatomic world that, to paraphrase Yeats's "The Second Coming," would eventually "vex the world to nightmare" with the nuclear bomb.

If such fundamental concepts as God, time, space, and matter were merely convenient and expedient "fictions," as the philosopher Hans Vaihinger concluded in 1911, what then of human values, language, literature, art, culture, the state, or the self? Philosophers known as logical positivists relegated questions of human ideals and metaphysics to the realm of emotions or the irrational and focused instead on language, recommending that abstract and imprecise terms such as *God, beauty,* and *truth* be exorcised from the lexicon. The Swiss linguist Ferdinand de Saussure (1857–1913) contended that languages were systems of arbitrary symbols that had identifiable connections within the system but no natural or necessary relationship to external reality. Languages were games and all we could ever really know were the rules of the games.

The general uncertainty about the nature of reality along with the alienation and fragmentation that followed the war produced feverish cultural activity as artists and writers sought new expressions for the unfamiliar world they confronted. AVANT-GARDE movements in art, music, and literature abounded, giving some credence to the insight of Mexican poet Octavio Paz (1914–1998) that "Modernity is a sort of creative self-destruction." Artists, musicians, and writers seemed to be trying to outpace the dizzying technological changes with artistic experimentation. In 1909 the Italian writer Filippo Marinetti (1876–1944) launched futurism, which strove to capture in the arts the aggressive and iconoclastic spirit of the new science and the rapidity of industrial and technological change. Other avant-garde schools, such as fauvism, expressionism, cubism, vorticism, and surrealism, challenged materialism, tepid conservatism, and the timid conformity of the bourgeoisie in social and cultural life.

Artists such as the French postimpressionist Paul Cézanne (1839–1906), the Russian Wassily Kandinsky (1866–1944), and Pablo Picasso took painting toward a complex, geometrical display of surfaces. In their creations, objects and figures were fragmented and distorted through multiple planes crisscrossing the canvas. American painter Jackson Pollock (1912–1956) went a step further, dripping paint on his canvases and making their subject the act of painting itself. In music, Viennese composer Arnold Schoenberg (1874–1951) and Russian composer Igor Stravinsky (1882–1971) challenged harmonic and melodic conventions by introducing atonality and polytonality. Atonality abandoned the concept of key;

polytonality allowed the composer to intermix keys at will. Both approaches resulted in a strange new music that replaced harmony with dissonance and discord. When Stravinsky's ballet *The Rite of Spring* opened in Paris in 1913, shocked patrons rioted. The distortion in these artists' works reflected the feel of early-twentieth-century Europe, which seemed to be spinning out of control.

Like the war that engendered it, MODERNISM began in Europe but its effects were global. As Western science and technology spread to many non-Western countries and as Western-educated artists and intellectuals carried modernism back to their native countries, experimentation in the arts and literature shaped movements in India, Japan, and many Latin American countries. Indian artists like Amrita Shergil (1913–1941) and Jamini Roy (1887–1972) melded Indian traditions with those of European modernism in their paintings. The fiction of Japanese novelist Tanizaki Junichiro (1886–1965) attempted to reconcile Western ideas, particularly those of Freud, with Japanese tradition. Even such anticolonial revolutionaries as Aimé Césaire (b. 1913) from Martinique and Léopold Senghor (1906–2001) from Senegal were profoundly influenced by European modernism.

MODERNIST LITERATURE

In "September 1913," Yeats lashes out at the Dublin middle classes whose obtuseness prevented a collection of impressionist paintings from being acquired by the city:

> What need you, being come to sense,
> But fumble in a greasy till
> And add the halfpence to the pence
> And prayer to shivering prayer, until
> You have dried the marrow from the bone?

Yeats's countryman James Joyce (1882–1941) also found fault with the Irish middle class in *Dubliners* (1914) and *A Portrait of the Artist as a Young Man* (1916) before shocking the sensibilities of the whole of Europe with the more experimental and sexually explicit *Ulysses* (1922). Italian playwright Luigi Pirandello (1867–1936) did away with the conventions of realistic theater in his experimental play *Six Characters in Search of an Author* (1921); at its premier performance in Rome, Pirandello had to be protected from offended audience members. The German novelist Franz Kafka (1883–1924) characterized modern life as a nightmare of bureaucratic anonymity that reduced his protagonists to paranoia. English novelist and poet D. H. Lawrence (1885–1930), putting into fiction the "vitalism" of French philosopher Henri Bergson (1859–1941), who celebrated an *élan vital* (vital spirit) against the deadening rationality of the logical positivists, featured sexually explicit themes and unabashedly sensual characters. Futurism, expressionism, and cubism found kindred spirits in writers such as Ezra Pound (1885–1972), Gottfried Benn (1886–1956), and Gertrude Stein (1874–1946), all of whom experimented with form, narrative structure, and language.

Twentieth-century novelists turned from social realism to psychological exploration, using first-person narration to tell stories that were more about their narrators than about the stories they told. In Japan, novelists such as Shimazaki Toson (1872–1943) developed a whole new genre known as the "I-Novel" (*shishosetsu*), autobiographical and confessional stories told in the first person. When modernists did employ a third-person voice, it was not that of the omniscient narrator of nineteenth-century fiction; this new point of view was limited to a single consciousness. Inheritors of nineteenth-century ROMANTICISM like Yeats and Russian poet Anna Akhmatova (1889–1966) used the first person even when writing about the momentous events of their time. Yeats writes of his personal involvement in the struggle for Irish independence and Akhmatova speaks directly of her suffering under Stalin's oppressive regime.

Many modernists attempted to mirror the era's changes in consciousness with nonlinear patterns of language. Gertrude Stein's work disrupted the reader's conventional expectations of narratives by exploding syntax, as in this "sentence" from "As a Wife Has a Cow":

> Has made, as it has made as it has made, has made has to be as a wife has a cow, a love story. Has made as to be as a wife has a cow a love story.

Imagist poets T. S. Eliot and Ezra Pound juxtaposed associated images in their work to convey a nondiscursive inner reality. Spanish poet Federico García Lorca (1898–1936) funneled folk and surrealist influences to picture the world of dreams in disconnected, evocative images. Joyce's *Finnegans Wake* (1939) carried experimentation with language to its logical conclusion, inventing words by assembling familiar sounds into strange and ambiguous new combinations.

The most important innovations in fiction were those of Joyce, Marcel Proust (1871–1922), and Virginia Woolf (1882–1941), who experimented with ways to represent consciousness in prose. In his monumental sequence of novels *Remembrance of Things Past* (*A la recherche du temps perdu*, 1913–1927), Proust explored the role of time and memory in shaping one's awareness of the world. Joyce and Woolf tried to replicate the "STREAM OF CONSCIOUSNESS"; in flowing, unpunctuated sentences that merged memory and present awareness and followed an associative logic, these writers evoked the inner life of their characters.

The modernists' experimentation with form, obscure personal symbolism, unfamiliar or invented language, and bleak subject matter alienated many readers. Often these writers were communicating with only a small cultural elite.

Modernists often made the artist himself the subject of a work, as in Joyce's *Portrait of the Artist as a Young Man* and Thomas Mann's (1875–1955) *Death in Venice* (1912). The artist appears in these works as an exiled, isolated, and alienated figure cut off from the common people.

POSTCOLONIALISM

The term POSTCOLONIALISM is sometimes used to describe the period following World War II; viewed from the point of view of colonized peoples, the struggle against colonialism is *the* important movement of the second half of the twentieth century. Although agitation to end colonial occupation had been organized in some countries, such as India, for example, as early as the late nineteenth century, it was not until after World War II that independence movements came to successful fruition. Led by Mohandas Gandhi (1869–1948), India gained independence in 1947. In the years that followed, independence movements and wars of liberation challenged colonialism throughout Asia and Africa. Although some colonial possessions remained intact at the end of the century — the Falkland Islands (Britain), the Canary Islands (Spain), New Caledonia (France), and Puerto Rico (United States) to name a few — the age of colonialism ended almost completely with the twentieth century.

The struggle to break the hold of colonial domination sometimes turned into civil war, as competing factions sought to control the destiny of a newly independent nation. In some cases, colonizers had created a single territory out of smaller tribal areas; when the colonial masters left, there was no longer an enforcer to hold disparate groups together and no natives prepared to take over the job of governing. In other places, governmental and social institutions had been well established and natives trained for leadership positions, but this native elite was often distrusted as being agents of the colonial culture that had been overthrown.

Educated and independent direction often came from writers, scholars, and intellectuals. Many writers, such as Nigerian poet Christopher Okibo (1932–1967) and Cape Verdean poet Amilcar Cabral (1924–1973), died while engaged in the struggle for independence. Frantz Fanon (1925–1961), a psychiatrist from Martinique who practiced in Algeria before joining the Algerian revolutionaries, wrote insightful social analyses of colonialism and passionate polemics against colonizers in *Black Skin, White Masks* (1952) and *The Wretched of the Earth* (1961). Writers who did not actively fight, like Indian novelist Raja Rao (b. 1909), who lived in an ashram and supported Gandhi's movement, wrote of the battle for independence. Writers and intellectuals who led independence movements or fought in revolutionary armies often took the lead in recovering or inventing an identity for their new nations after independence was gained. Aimé Césaire (b. 1913), a poet from

Martinique, attacked colonialism in his *Discourse on Colonialism* (1950) and fought for independence in the French Chamber of Deputies. Léopold Senghor (1906–2001), another poet, served as president of Senegal from 1960 to 1981. Postcolonial writers employed the tools of folklore, mythology, and realism inherited from the nineteenth-century European Romantics and REALISTS to construct that cultural history and identity for their homelands. Their Realist novels create what critic Frederic Jameson has called a "national allegory," stories that tell a myth of a nation through accounts of individual lives.

In the postcolonial context, however, the project of literary nation-building raises troubling questions. Can formerly colonized peoples retrieve their precolonial culture, or have they been forever changed by their engagement with the colonizers and cut off from the past by a hiatus often lasting several generations? Can the indigenous elements in a culture be distinguished from colonial accretions? Writers that had no precolonial written language worry that they can write only in the European languages learned in colonial schools, the "languages of the oppressors." By doing so, do they prolong the oppression and use a language ill-suited to express their culture's unique view of the world?

POSTCOLONIAL LITERATURE

In Joseph Conrad's (1857–1924) *Heart of Darkness* (1902), Conrad and his narrator, Marlow, are clearly appalled by the excesses of the colonizers, though neither is able to view the Congo through African eyes. *Heart of Darkness* is not so much about Africa as it is about Marlow and his demonic alter-ego, Kurtz, and the journey the novella chronicles is on one level a look into the divided psyche of the colonizers. Nigerian novelist Chinua Achebe (b. 1930) directly critiques Conrad's book in "An Image of Africa," and in his own novel *Things Fall Apart* (1958), he implicitly attacks the stereotypical objectification of Africans in *Heart of Darkness* by individualizing his own hero, Okonkwo, and describing the richness of his culture. In doing so, he challenges European racism while offering Africans an image of their cultural identity.

Such postcolonial cultural construction is a recent example of what European Romantics did in the nineteenth century, when they collected folklore and wrote novels to articulate an identity for the emerging nations of Europe, in what could be called the first wave of postcolonial literature. The writers of the Bengali Renaissance—Rabindranath Tagore (1861–1941) and others—based poems on Bengali folk songs and wrote fiction that explored the conflict between their Indian and British heritages. Writers of the Irish Renaissance, from the 1890s to the 1920s, active in the political struggle to free Ireland from British rule, wrote about their native culture. Yeats uses Irish mythology and history in his poems as a way of establishing a distinct cultural identity for the Irish and thus justify Ireland's independence from Britain. The Irish Renaissance, in turn, strongly influenced writers of the Harlem Renaissance of the 1920s and 1930s, who sought to establish a black culture with African roots and its own distinctive music, art, and literature. For the first generation of postcolonial African writers, such as Léopold Senghor of Senegal or Wole Soyinka (b. 1934) of Nigeria, the writers of the Harlem Renaissance — especially Claude McKay (1889–1948) and Langston Hughes (1902–1967) — were defining figures who had pioneered a black literature. This history is traced in some of the selections in *In the World:* Imagining Africa.

Several writers in *In the World:* Colonialism attack various aspects of colonial oppression: Frantz Fanon (1925–1961), the psychological infantilization of the black man; Césaire, the physical degradation of the colonized and their loss of personal pride and identity; Felix Mnthali (b. 1933), the cultural imperialism that denigrates native literary traditions. And in "The Deep River: A Story of Ancient Tribal Migration," South African Bessie Head (1937–1986) describes a whole culture that has lost its ties to the past and its identity.

To rebuild cultures undermined by colonialism, writers sometimes recovered, sometimes invented a history and mythology for their people. In poems like "The Lake Isle of Innisfree" and "Who Goes with Fergus?" Yeats creates an idealized Irish rural landscape and mythology that contrasts with the urban rationalism of Great Britain. Achebe places Okonkwo in a culture of stories and ritual practices that defines his difference from the Europeans and presages his confusion when caught between African and European influences. In recording Okonkwo's cultural heritage, Achebe confirms its reality and, by extension, its equality with European culture. A similar process of recording formerly oral cultures in writing occurs in Black Elk's (1863–1950) account of Lakota rituals and myths and Leslie Marmon Silko's (b. 1948) adaptations of traditional Pueblo Indian stories.

Nations that emerged from colonialism faced a dual challenge: to discover or create their own independent identity and to establish themselves amid a globalizing world. Increasingly, twentieth-century writers from all nations were becoming international citizens who melded their particular national identity with a global outlook. As writers moved from one nation to another, they became world citizens with what Salman Rushdie (b. 1947) calls "imaginary homelands," and their perspective changed from postcolonial to postmodernist.

POSTMODERNISM

In its simplest sense, the controversial term POSTMODERNISM refers to the period after the modernist period, roughly from World War II to the present. "Postcolonials" viewed the same period from the perspective of formerly colonized peoples. *Postmodern* describes the period from the perspective of the former colonizers. World War II, with its massive bombing of civilian populations, the genocidal destruction of the Holocaust, and the dropping of the atomic bomb magnified the horrors of the First World War and deepened postwar despair. T. S. Eliot had tried to piece together the fragments of Western culture after World War I; writers and artists after the Second World War, like the poets included in *In the Tradition: The Literature of War, Conflict, and Resistance*, wondered whether there were any fragments left. Takenishi Hiroko (b. 1929), in "The Rite," tells of a Hiroshima survivor who searches for a ceremony that will restore meaning to her life. The narration is broken into fragments from several periods of the survivor's life and does not pull the loose pieces together, suggesting that she will live out her life with a permanent sense of loss. Takenishi's search does not end, as Eliot's does, with hope. If the modernists were disillusioned and sought vainly for meaning, many postmodernists began with the assumption that there was no meaning to search for.

Postwar despair was formulated into a philosophy by the French EXISTENTIALISTS. Led by Jean-Paul Sartre (1905–1980), whose ideas were shaped by his experiences fighting in the French resistance movement during the war, the existentialists did not simply abandon the pieties of patriotism and honor. They called into question all the essential Truths of the Western tradition. Asserting that "existence precedes essence," they considered any attempt to find meaning beyond an individual's experience — in God, for example, in a national ideal, or in a concept of human nature — a form of "bad faith." One could not use Christianity or patriotism as justification for one's choices. Faced with radical isolation and the lack of any inherent meaning in the world, a condition the existentialists — especially Albert Camus (1913–1960) — referred to as "the absurd," the existential individual had to take total responsibility for his or her actions, for his or her existence. By doing so, individuals defined themselves. By rejecting the concept of essences, or established truths, existentialists established one of the tenets of postmodernism: that there are no essential truths.

The existentialists' rejection of established ideas was a prelude to the spurning of many institutions prompted by the antiwar and civil rights movements of the late 1960s. A worldwide quest for greater human rights challenged such institutions as the family, public schools, the university, police departments, and civil administrations. In May 1968, police moved in on rioting students at the Sorbonne, France's most prestigious university, setting off months of often violent protests. In what German-born philosopher Herbert Marcuse (1898–1979) called the "Great Refusal," students aimed to topple the elitist hierarchy of the university, to make the curriculum reflect more accurately the social and political realities of the time, and to provide greater access to education for minorities and the poor. A new generation of French intellectuals, including Jacques Lacan (1901–1981), Michel Foucault (1926–1984), Jean-François Lyotard (1924–1998), and Jacques Derrida (b. 1930), subverted such Establishment values as humanism and the priority of the individual; they repudiated the materialism and conservatism that, in their view, limited power and prestige to a privileged few. These writers continue to exert a significant influence among postmodern intellectuals, many of whom began their higher education during or just after the Vietnam era in the 1970s.

Postmodernists replaced essentialism (truths) with pluralism and seriousness with playfulness. Jean-François Lyotard reformulated the existential rejection of essences, calling it "incredulity toward metanarratives" (stories that explain an underlying truth). There is no one story, no eternal truth, no one set of laws that explains the world, Lyotard said. Rather, there are many narratives. Like other postmodern theorists, Lyotard could trace his intellectual ancestry back to Ferdinand de Saussure, whose linguistic theory described language not as a way of representing an external reality but as an arbitrary system of signs (words) that derive their meaning from the network of relationships within a language. Rejecting the high seriousness that characterizes discussions of the "big ideas" or the great books of the Western tradition, Lyotard employed the metaphor of "language games" to describe the way humanity's many stories relate to one another. Modernists often took art very seriously, but postmodernists indulge in artistic playfulness and parody. They mix genres, make paintings of soup cans, wrap buildings in massive curtains, record sounds in the street as a substitute for music. Unlike modernist architects who implemented the maxim that "form follows function" by attempting to reduce a building to its simplest functional components, postmodern architects mix styles, add unnecessary and playful decoration, and include stairways and doors that lead nowhere.

Postmodernists also "decenter" or "deconstruct" traditional notions. Jacques Derrida, whose work also builds on the linguistic theories of Saussure, calls essential ideas, or metanarratives, "centers." According to Derrida, centers are related to their opposites, the "others" that are "marginalized" in relation to them. For example, male marginalizes female, white marginalizes black, West marginalizes East, mind marginalizes body, speech marginalizes writing. Postmodernists "decenter" such pairs, opening up a free play between opposites and allowing the marginalized other, temporarily at least, to play a central role. Such decentering challenges established authority. "Man is no longer to be the measure of all things, the center of the universe," concludes Leonard Meyer, writing of "the end of the Renaissance" in 1963. Even the authority of the author is passé; for postmodernists, the formerly marginalized reader determines the meaning of a text.

Postmodernists also decentered traditional notions of character. For Jacques Lacan, the self is inevitably alienated since the "I" it uses to describe itself makes the self an object, an other. By decentering character, postmodernists also challenged traditional notions of plot, which depicts a character's growth through a causative series of actions.

Although manipulating the center and the margin can be seen as a kind of game, it also, of course, has serious political and social implications. By equating knowledge and power, philosopher Michel Foucault showed how some schools of thought become accepted and others rejected and how people construct a worldview and an understanding of themselves by adopting the terms of the dominant discourses around them. His analysis of prisons and mental institutions explores how those institutions are socially constructed and suggests ways in which different ideas about criminality or mental illness could change the world. Telling the world from the perspective of the repressed and marginalized has opened contemporary thought to many formerly ignored points of view—for example, those of women and of racial and cultural minorities.

Modernists assumed that some works of art were more serious and hence more valuable than others. Works of high culture—classical music or abstract expressionist painting, for example—were significant; popular songs or the illustrations of Norman Rockwell (1894–1978) were not. Postmodernists reject such hierarchical distinctions; there are simply many texts, many discourses, many pictures. Meaning is not inherent in the work, but is supplied by the reader, the listener, the viewer. In a culture where everything becomes a commodity and value is established in the marketplace, postmodernists make no distinction between fine and popular art, for all art is bought and sold. In the postmodern world, multiplicity rules. Distinctions between high and low, past and present, reality and illusion, serious and frivolous make little sense when everything is on the Internet. National borders are crossed with a keystroke. There are as many versions of reality as there are perspectives.

POSTMODERN LITERATURE

Modernism did not suddenly disappear after World War II. The aestheticism, experimentation, and engagement with interior reality that dominated literature in the first half of the twentieth century was continued in the work of later writers and incorporated into many postmodern works. The inventions in Argentinean writer Jorge Luis Borges's (1899–1986) labyrinthine short stories and in Abé Kobo's (1924–1993) "The Red Cocoon" are descended from the bizarre worlds in the stories of Franz Kafka. The aestheticism of Kawabata Yasunari's (1899–1972) "The Moon on the Water" recalls Virginia Woolf's short story "The Fascination of the Pool." Adrienne Rich's (b. 1929) psychological exploration in *Diving into the Wreck* (1973) builds on the work of earlier poets. But after World War II, modernism became international, comprising as many voices from the margins as from the white, male, European "center."

Existentialism's challenge to that center and to the relatively consistent story that it told is represented by several selections in this book. Sartre's play *The Flies* (1943) retells the story of Orestes in a way that challenges the patriarchal order represented by Zeus and Athena in Aeschylus's *Oresteia* and by the Nazis during World War II. Orestes takes full responsibility for the murders of Clytemnestra and Aegisthus; he does not justify his actions by appealing to any spiritual or temporal authority. Like Orestes, Daru, the hero of Albert Camus' story "The Guest," is "condemned to be free." Caught between the warring sides in the Algerian struggle for independence, he is misunderstood by both. In the dramas of the ABSURD, Samuel Beckett's (1906–1989) *Krapp's Last Tape* and Tawfiq al-Hakim's (1898–1987) *The Fate of a Cockroach*, the characters who take the absurdity of their situation for granted are considered insane.

Nearly all the postcolonial writers of the second half of the twentieth century similarly decentered the Western version of things by making formerly nameless natives into living persons. In his search for Zaabalawi, for example, Naguib Mahfouz's (b. 1911) narrator gives Cairo a history, a spiritual center, and a mystery independent of Western orientalism. R. K. Narayan (1906–2001), in "A Horse and Two Goats," makes a comedy of the misunderstandings between the Western traveler and the Indian villager, but he also demonstrates how a horse and two goats can be more valuable than a roadside statue. Postcolonial decentering combines with postmodern playfulness in *The Prisoner of Las Lomas*, by Mexican novelist Carlos Fuentes (b. 1928), and "The Courter," by Anglo-Indian Salman Rushdie (b. 1947). Both writers dramatize the relations between the margin and the center, using wordplay, puns, parody, allusions, serendipitous happenings, and bizarre surprises to facilitate the free play between them. In Fuentes's story, native peoples "imprison" a powerful businessman in his Mexico City mansion. Rushdie's adolescent hero is pulled between his Indian heritage and the lure of Western popular culture.

Language games become the subject as well as a technique in such stories as Borges's "The Garden of Forking Paths" and Milan Kundera's (b. 1929) "The Hitchhiking Game." Both challenge traditional ideas about character and plot by imagining worlds where everything is possible and where different aspects of characters emerge in alternating plots. In neither story is there a "metacharacter" — one who determines the possibilities of the story. As Borges's and Kundera's characters take on different personas, they change the characters around them and the course of the action.

Established categories for postmodern authors do not make much sense. Rushdie, for example, was born in India and educated in England; he worked in Pakistan, eventually claimed British citizenship, and now lives in New York. He has written novels reflecting each of these changing geographical identities, and he calls himself an "English writer" and a "translated man." He might be best described as a world writer. Fuentes's description of his situation holds true for many of his contemporaries. "I don't see myself as a nationalist writer at all," he commented. "I don't believe in nationalism in literature. Especially today, I think literature is an international event." Even when contemporary writers treat their native culture, they often do so with a broad audience in mind. Chinua Achebe, for example, was aware that he was writing about tribal culture in his native Nigeria for readers who would include many non-Nigerians. Indeed, in the essay "An Image of Africa," he implies that one important goal of his novel is to make Africans real to European and American readers by decentering their perspective on Africa. In similar ways, Leslie Marmon Silko, Alifa Rifaat (b. 1930), and Anita Desai (b. 1937) reestablish point of view by writing as women and former colonial subjects. Gao Xingjian (b. 1940) reimagines notions of life and death by presenting the second act of *Dialogue and Rebuttal* from the perspective of two characters who murdered each other at the end of Act One. Probably no writer has taken the notion of decentering further than Abé Kobo, who in "The Stick" writes from the point of view of a stick.

GLOBALIZING AMERICA

This anthology of twentieth-century world literature ends with selections by young American writers who do more than remind us that America is a multicultural society, a microcosm of the world. Sometimes called "hyphenated Americans" because of the ethnic groups they belong to and the countries they or their families emigrated from, these writers often revise our ideas about the United States and Americans. Many challenge, for example, the assumption that the United States is not an imperial power with colonial subjects, and they make clear how American culture, for both good and ill, reaches worldwide. They can help us to learn from the margins, as Europeans had to do in the last century, for we are connected worldwide. The voices from the margins, both within our own society and from remote parts of the world, can, as Nadine Gordimer illustrates, help us to see ourselves "as others see us." We don't need to be reminded, as we begin the twenty-first century, that it is much better to learn from the creators of stories and poems than from those who choose only to destroy.

JOSEPH CONRAD
B. POLAND, 1857–1924

Joseph Conrad's life and work cross cultural boundaries, making him representative of many writers of the twentieth century. Born a Pole in Russian-occupied Poland, Conrad went on to become a French merchant-seaman and then an English seaman and citizen. When he began writing he composed in English, his third language after Polish and French. Although he was a proud British citizen and a Polish nationalist, he was in a broad sense a European: a man whose political identity transcended any single national definition. Conrad's experience as a sailor in many parts of the world further broadened his identity, making him a kind of world citizen. Like most of his novels, *Heart of Darkness* (1902) is rooted in Conrad's own experience, but in this work his personal story is objectified to become the narrator Marlow's story, a story about storytelling itself and about the cultural experience of Europeans in Africa, a story that Thomas Mann[1] is reported to have said "prophetically inaugurated the twentieth century."

A Polish Nobleman Cased in British Tar. Conrad was born **Jósef Teodor Konrad Walecz Korzeniowski** in 1857 in **Berdyczew** in Russian-occupied Polish Ukraine. His father, Apollo, a writer and translator of French and English literature, was a Polish nationalist. His participation in revolutionary activities led to the family being exiled to the far north of Russia when Conrad was four. The physical hardships of the exile led to his mother's death when he was seven and to his father's death just a few years later. So Conrad, an imaginative and sensitive child, was raised from age eleven by an uncle, **Tadeusz Bobrowski**. Although he grew up far from the sea, the boy dreamed of a life as a sailor, and when he was sixteen he convinced his uncle to allow him to seek a seagoing career. He joined the French merchant service, became involved in gunrunning and an intense love affair, and attempted suicide. At twenty Conrad switched to the English merchant service, and for the next twenty years he worked his way up from seaman to mate and master. His voyages took him to many other parts of the world, including the East and West Indies, Asia, Africa, and South America. When he left the merchant service in 1894 he was fluent in three languages, a British citizen with multinational work experience, and a European with a knowledge of cultures throughout the world.

Novelist of the Sea. Conrad's second career—as an English novelist—began in 1895 with the publication of *Almayer's Folly* and lasted until his death in 1924. During that period Conrad wrote thirteen novels, two

---

[1] **Thomas Mann** (1875–1955): German novelist, essayist, and short-story writer. In symbolic stories like *Death in Venice* (1912; see p. 266), Mann treated the subject of the diseased condition of European civilization.

books of memoirs, and twenty-eight short stories. He established friendships with a large number of British and American writers of the time, including H. G. Wells, Rudyard Kipling, W. H. Hudson, John Galsworthy, Henry James, Stephen Crane, and Ford Madox Ford, with whom he collaborated on three books. Many of his novels and stories take place on ships isolated at sea, as do *Typhoon* (1902), *The Nigger of the "Narcissus"* (1898), and *The Secret Sharer* (1912). Others are set in exotic locations Conrad visited as a sailor: the Malay Peninsula in *An Outcast of the Islands* (1896) and *Lord Jim* (1900), a South Sea island in *Victory* (1915), and a South American mining town in *Nostromo* (1904). Conrad often studied the failure of Europeans to maintain their personal and cultural ideals in these exotic and alien places. His novels with European settings, such as *The Secret Agent* (1907), describing the activities of anarchist provocateurs in London, and *Under Western Eyes* (1911), about revolutionaries challenging Russian despotism, also treat failures of idealism. For this recurrent theme of lost or corrupted idealism, Conrad has been described as a deeply pessimistic writer. But in spite of their shortcomings his heroes are often engaging and sympathetic figures who have an idealistic belief in themselves and who follow a romantic desire for freedom. It may be that all Conrad's novels hearken back to his childhood experience as the son of a Polish nationalist who died for ideals that failed to become political realities because of the weaknesses of human beings and the complexities and imbalances of political relationships.

Although he is usually described as a novelist of the sea, Conrad used the sea and exotic settings symbolically to write about the human situation and the human spirit. In the preface to *Nigger of the "Narcissus,"* he said of its shipboard setting: "The problem . . . is not a problem of the sea, it is merely a problem that has arisen on board a ship where the conditions of complete isolation from all land entanglements make it stand out with particular force and colouring."

Conrad in Africa.

Heart of Darkness is based on Conrad's 1890 journey up the Congo River. Like his narrator, Marlow, Conrad was hired by a Belgian trading company to captain a steamship on the Congo, but when he arrived in Africa he found that the ship he was hired to pilot had sunk. Conrad was left to spend most of his time as a mate on another vessel, taking over as captain only briefly when the regular master was incapacitated. The journey upriver entailed bringing out the body of a trader, a man named Klein who had died at a trading post deep in the interior of Africa. In *Heart of Darkness,* Conrad spoke of his own experience in the Congo as a transforming one: "Before the Congo," he wrote, "I was just a mere animal." Shortly after returning from that trip, he gave up the sea and turned to storytelling as his profession. In retelling his African experiences in *Heart of Darkness,* Conrad transformed his personal history into myth.

Marlow's journey into the heart of Africa becomes a journey into the human spirit. Ostensibly it is an account of the truth about Kurtz, a man whose talents and achievements earned him regard as an "extraordinary" human being—a model of European enlightenment. But when Marlow

Portrait of Conrad
Joseph Conrad had a tenuous relationship with nationality; though he was born in Poland, he gained literary acclaim as a writer in English. (Hulton/Archive)

The point of my observations should be quite clear by now, namely that Conrad was a bloody racist.
– Chinua Achebe, 1975

TIME AND PLACE

Twentieth-Century America: Apocalypse Now

Apocalypse Now premiered at the Cannes Film Festival in 1979; director Francis Ford Coppola said of his now-legendary work: "My film is not about Vietnam. My film is Vietnam." Using Conrad's *Heart of Darkness* as inspiration, *Apocalypse Now* tells the tale of a journey upriver—the Mekong River rather than the Congo—in search of renegade Colonel Kurtz as well as some truths about the nature of the self and war.

Francis Ford Coppola, Apocalypse Now, 1979.   *In this film still, a small navy patrol boat reaches its destination, the wild jungle tribe led by the renegade colonel Kurtz. (The Kobal Collection / Zoetrope / USA)*

Apocalypse Now is one of many American movies about Vietnam; others include *The Green Berets* (1968), *The Deer Hunter* (1978), *Platoon* (1986), *Full Metal Jacket* (1987), and most recently, *We Were Soldiers* (2002). After the Vietnamese had defeated and expelled their French colonial rulers, the country plunged into civil war. The United States government, fearful of the spread of communism in southeast Asia, entered the civil war on the side of South Vietnam. President Lyndon Johnson escalated American involvement, calling for massive bombing raids and the commitment of thousands of troops, but American forces were unable to defeat the committed guerrilla fighters and were finally forced to retreat without victory in 1973. The conflict in Vietnam has played a huge role in the American imagination. It divided the nation, created a counterculture, and destroyed many lives. Several of the films about Vietnam—*Apocalypse Now* perhaps most spectacularly—dramatize the war's impact by showing characters caught in the middle of senseless slaughter as they ask themselves why they are fighting and who is in charge. These questions continue to trouble Americans to the present day.

arrives at Kurtz's camp, he discovers that in the depths of his being Kurtz is "a horror." Marlow also makes discoveries about himself and about his "kinship" with Kurtz.

Conrad and Marlow.   In many ways *Heart of Darkness* is as much about Marlow and storytelling as it is about Africa or Kurtz or ivory. As in much modern literature, the truth here is not in the tale but in the teller. The initial description of Marlow's method of storytelling, which opens the novel, is also a blueprint for Conrad's narrative technique: "The yarns of seamen have a direct simplicity, the whole meaning of which lies within the shell of a cracked nut. But Marlow was not typical . . . and to him the meaning of an episode was not inside like a kernel but outside, enveloping the tale which brought it out only as a glow brings out a haze, in the likeness of one of these misty halos that sometimes are made visible by the spectral illumination of moonshine." Although Marlow is never explicit about what he learns from his experiences, his psychological kinship with Kurtz, or why he lies to Kurtz's Intended, his account raises questions about how and why he was able to survive his journey and about the ways he differs from Kurtz and the other Europeans. Did he prevail through superior understanding or greater strength of will or moral character, or was it because he had a more repressed personality than the others? To what degree did he avoid complicity with Kurtz and the other colonizers? How much of what he tells us can we believe? What might he be trying to hide or repress that would make his account, at least to some extent, unreliable? What knowledge is he trying to pass on to those aboard the *Nellie*? There are hints but no definitive answers to these questions in the story.

Conrad and Colonialism.

Part of the "shell" that envelops Marlow's story is his critique of European colonialism. When Marlow compares Africa in the nineteenth century to England at the time of the Romans, he implies that his story is about colonialism and greed, about what he calls "the squeeze." Marlow's descriptions of the ivory trade and the European presence in Africa are solidly based on historical fact. In 1890, the Congo was in effect the personal domain of King Leopold II of Belgium, who promoted the commercial exploitation of the Congo's resources and the virtual enslavement of its native people. Historical accounts confirm that there is no exaggeration in the excesses described by Marlow. He is clearly appalled by what he finds in Africa: the mistreatment of natives, the venality and hypocrisy of the Europeans, the colossal corruption at the inner station. He also suggests that these shortcomings are not unique to colonizers in Africa, but rather are deep drives of the human character and will manifest themselves if allowed unrestrained expression. In Kurtz, Marlow sees a monstrous reflection of himself. He is, at least in part, horrified by what he sees.

Nigerian novelist **Chinua Achebe** has attacked this "European" story as an example of literary colonialism and European racism.[2] *Heart of Darkness* is not about Africa, Achebe argues, for Conrad's Africa has no reality and the natives no individuality, no names. For Conrad, Marlow, and Europeans, he says, Africa and Africans are "other" — objects against which the Europeans define their own individuality. As critical as they may be of the abuses of the ivory trade, they, too, are exploiting Africa to reconstruct a European civilization by contrasting it with both black and white savagery in Africa. Achebe delivered his attack in a 1975 speech, **"An Image of Africa,"** at the University of Massachusetts long after Conrad's

Heart of Darkness projects the image of Africa as "the other world," the antithesis of Europe and therefore of civilization, a place where a man's vaunted intelligence and refinement are finally mocked by triumphant bestiality.
– CHINUA ACHEBE, 1975

CHIN-wah
ah-CHAY-bay

p. 107

---

[2] Chinua Achebe (b. 1930): Nigerian novelist best known for *Things Fall Apart* (1958); see page 1023. Achebe's essay on *Heart of Darkness* appears in *In the World: Colonialism: Europe and Africa* on page 107.

death — testimony to the enduring currency of Conrad's story and to the centrality of the questions it raises.

A Story about European Culture. Marlow's experience is enlightening as well as horrifying. He has gained wisdom from his time in Africa, as his pose in the last scene as a meditating Buddha suggests. But he has acquired more than personal wisdom. Like epic heroes who journey to the underworld to gain the knowledge that will enable them to found nations, Marlow has traveled to Africa to recover what Europe — the "whited sepulchre" — has lost, repressed, or forgotten. In gaining that knowledge, Marlow's personal story becomes a cultural story, a modern epic about a deadened and wasted culture seeking to recover the vital heart of its humanity. His mission has been a dangerous and spiritually expensive one, and it is unclear how successful he was and whether what he gained was worth the horror.

■ CONNECTIONS

Chinua Achebe, "An Image of Africa," p. 107, *Things Fall Apart*, p. 1023; *In the World*: Colonialism, p. 97. In "An Image of Africa," Achebe accuses Conrad of being a "bloody racist" in *Heart of Darkness*. What aspects of Conrad's novel does Achebe consider racist? In what ways does *Things Fall Apart* correct the failings that Achebe finds in the novel? Do the materials in *In the World*: Colonialism offer any defense for Conrad?

Thomas Mann, *Death in Venice*, p. 266; T. S. Eliot, *The Waste Land*, p. 486; James Joyce, "The Dead," p. 372; W. B. Yeats, "The Second Coming," p. 193; *In the World*: Society and Its Discontents (Book 5). Many modern writers, continuing the critique developed by the nineteenth-century writers in *In the World*: Society and Its Discontents, considered European culture blighted, diseased, and lacking in vitality. Marlow, for example, describes Brussels as a "whited sepulchre," that lacks the heart-pounding life force of the Congo. Consider how this theme is handled in Mann's *Death in Venice*, T. S. Eliot's *The Waste Land*, and Joyce's "The Dead" as well as in *Heart of Darkness*. Do these writers share Yeats's vision in "The Second Coming" that a new age was about to be born?

Homer, *The Odyssey* (Book 1); Virgil, *The Aeneid* (Book 1); Dante, *The Inferno* (Book 2). One of the conventions of the epic is a journey to the underworld in which the hero learns from the dead truths not given to ordinary people. Odysseus, Aeneas, and Dante all make this harrowing trip. Compare Marlow's journey into Africa with those of the epic heroes. Are there any indications in *Heart of Darkness* that Marlow has gained extraordinary wisdom? What does he learn?

■ FURTHER RESEARCH

Biography
Baines, Jocelyn. *Joseph Conrad: A Critical Biography*. 1960.
Karl, Frederick. *Joseph Conrad: The Three Lives*. 1979.

Criticism
Adelman, Gary. *Heart of Darkness: Search for the Unconscious*. 1987.
Firchow, Peter Edgerly. *Envisioning Africa: Racism and Imperialism in Conrad's* Heart of Darkness. 2000.
Guerard, Albert. *Conrad the Novelist*. 1958.

Karl, Frederick. *A Reader's Guide to Joseph Conrad.* 1997.
Kimbrough, Robert, ed. Heart of Darkness: *An Authoritative Text, Backgrounds and Sources, Criticism.* 1988.
Lee, R. F. *Conrad's Colonialism.* 1969.
Murfin, Ross C., ed. *Joseph Conrad,* Heart of Darkness. *A Case Study in Contemporary Criticism.* 1989.
Page, Norman. *A Conrad Companion.* 1985.

www   For links to sites with more information about Conrad, a quiz on *Heart of Darkness,* and information about the culture and context of Europe in the twentieth century, see *World Literature Online* at bedfordstmartins .com/worldlit.

■ **PRONUNCIATION**

Chinua Achebe: CHIN-wah ah-CHAY-bay
Berdyczew: bare-DIH-chef
Tadeusz Bobrowski: tah-DAY-oosh boh-BRAWF-skee
Jósef Teodor Konrad Walecz Korzeniowski: YOO-zef tay-OH-dore KOHN-rahd VAH-wench koh-zheh-NYAWF-skee
Nostromo: nah-STROH-moh

∾ Heart of Darkness

1

The *Nellie,* a cruising yawl, swung to her anchor without a flutter of the sails, and was at rest. The flood had made, the wind was nearly calm, and being bound down the river, the only thing for it was to come to and wait for the turn of the tide.

The sea-reach of the Thames stretched before us like the beginning of an interminable waterway. In the offing[1] the sea and the sky were welded together without a joint, and in the luminous space the tanned sails of the barges drifting up with the tide seemed to stand still in red clusters of canvas sharply peaked, with gleams of varnished sprits. A haze rested on the low shores that ran out to sea in vanishing flatness. The air was dark above Gravesend, and farther back still seemed condensed into a mournful gloom, brooding motionless over the biggest, and the greatest, town on earth.

Heart of Darkness. Based on Conrad's personal experiences in the Congo in 1890, this novella was published as a serial in *Blackwood's Magazine* in 1899 and in 1902 was included in the collection *Youth and Two Other Tales.* Although at times the story reads like a nightmare version of Conrad's trip, the details of European exploitation it recounts are factually based. Beyond that, Conrad turns the facts of his actual experience into a myth of transformation. Marlow's journey into the interior of Africa becomes a descent into the darkness in himself and in humanity. The story contrasts Kurtz, who succumbs to his most elemental and savage impulses, with Marlow, who resists the powers of darkness and survives the ordeal. On his return to Europe, however, Marlow is unable or unwilling to reveal the truth of what he has seen, at least to Kurtz's Intended.

All notes are the editors'.

---

[1] **offing:** The horizon.

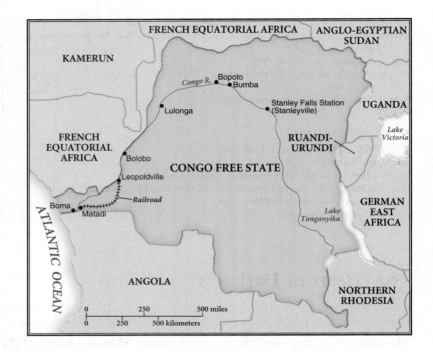

Congo Free State, 1890

The Congo of Conrad's time was, in fact, not a free state. A conference of European states in 1876 had assigned it to King Leopold II of Belgium as his personal property. Under Leopold's brutal rule, which lasted until his death in 1908, the people of the Congo were subjected to atrocities and forced labor. When Conrad journeyed through the Congo in 1890, many Congolese were virtual slaves under the harsh discipline of Leopold's officials.

The Director of Companies was our captain and our host. We four affectionately watched his back as he stood in the bows looking to seaward. On the whole river there was nothing that looked half so nautical. He resembled a pilot, which to a seaman is trustworthiness personified. It was difficult to realize his work was not out there in the luminous estuary, but behind him, within the brooding gloom.

Between us there was, as I have already said somewhere, the bond of the sea. Besides holding our hearts together through long periods of separation, it had the effect of making us tolerant of each other's yarns—and even convictions. The Lawyer—the best of old fellows—had, because of his many years and many virtues, the only cushion on deck, and was lying on the only rug. The Accountant had brought out already a box of dominoes, and was toying architecturally with the bones. Marlow sat cross-legged right aft, leaning against the mizzen-mast. He had sunken cheeks, a yellow complexion, a straight back, an ascetic aspect, and, with his arms dropped, the palms of hands outwards, resembled an idol. The director, satisfied the anchor had good hold, made his way aft and sat down amongst us. We exchanged a few words lazily. Afterwards there was silence on board the yacht. For some reason or other we did not begin that game of dominoes. We felt meditative, and fit for nothing but placid staring. The day was ending in a serenity of still and exquisite brilliance. The water shone pacifically; the sky, without a speck, was a benign immensity of unstained light; the very mist on the Essex marshes was like a gauzy and radiant fabric, hung from the wooded rises inland, and draping the low shores in diaphanous folds. Only the gloom to the west, brooding over the upper reaches, became more sombre every minute, as if angered by the approach of the sun.

And at last, in its curved and imperceptible fall, the sun sank low, and from glowing white changed to a dull red without rays and without heat, as if about to go out suddenly, stricken to death by the touch of that gloom brooding over a crowd of men.

Forthwith a change came over the waters, and the serenity became less brilliant but more profound. The old river in its broad reach rested unruffled at the decline of day, after ages of good service done to the race that peopled its banks, spread out in the tranquil dignity of a waterway leading to the uttermost ends of the earth. We looked at the venerable stream not in the vivid flush of a short day that comes and departs for ever, but in the august light of abiding memories. And indeed nothing is easier for a man who has, as the phrase goes, "followed the sea" with reverence and affection, than to evoke the great spirit of the past upon the lower reaches of the Thames. The tidal current runs to and fro in its unceasing service, crowded with memories of men and ships it had borne to the rest of home or to the battles of the sea. It had known and served all the men of whom the nation is proud, from Sir Francis Drake to Sir John Franklin,[2] knights all, titled and untitled—the great knights-errant of the sea. It had borne all the ships whose names are like jewels flashing in the night of time, from the *Golden Hind* returning with her round flanks full of treasure, to be visited by the Queen's Highness and thus pass out of the gigantic tale, to the *Erebus* and *Terror,* bound on other conquests—and that never returned. It had known the ships and the men. They had sailed from Deptford, from Greenwich, from Erith—the adventurers and the settlers; kings' ships and the ships of men on 'Change;[3] captains, admirals, the dark "interlopers" of the Eastern trade, and the commissioned "generals" of East India fleets. Hunters for gold or pursuers of fame, they all had gone out on that stream, bearing the sword, and often the torch, messengers of the might within the land, bearers of a spark from the sacred fire. What greatness had not floated on the ebb of that river into the mystery of an unknown earth! . . . The dreams of men, the seed of commonwealths, the germs of empires.

The sun set; the dusk fell on the stream, and lights began to appear along the shore. The Chapman lighthouse, a three-legged thing erect on a mud-flat, shone

---

[2]**Drake . . . Franklin:** Drake circumnavigated the globe from 1577 to 1580 on the *Golden Hind.* Franklin sought the Northwest Passage from 1845 to 1847 on the *Erebus* and the *Terror.*

[3]**'Change:** The Exchange, the British financial market.

strongly. Lights of ships moved in the fairway—a great stir of lights going up and going down. And farther west on the upper reaches the place of the monstrous town was still marked ominously on the sky, a brooding gloom in sunshine, a lurid glare under the stars.

"And this also," said Marlow suddenly, "has been one of the dark places of the earth."

He was the only man of us who still "followed the sea." The worst that could be said of him was that he did not represent his class. He was a seaman, but he was a wanderer, too, while most seamen lead, if one may so express it, a sedentary life. Their minds are of the stay-at-home order, and their home is always with them— the ship; and so is their country—the sea. One ship is very much like another, and the sea is always the same. In the immutability of their surroundings the foreign shores, the foreign faces, the changing immensity of life, glide past, veiled not by a sense of mystery but by a slightly disdainful ignorance; for there is nothing mysterious to a seaman unless it be the sea itself, which is the mistress of his existence and as inscrutable as Destiny. For the rest, after his hours of work, a casual stroll or a casual spree on shore suffices to unfold for him the secret of a whole continent, and generally he finds the secret not worth knowing. The yarns of seamen have a direct simplicity, the whole meaning of which lies within the shell of a cracked nut. But Marlow was not typical (if his propensity to spin yarns be excepted), and to him the meaning of an episode was not inside like a kernel but outside, enveloping the tale which brought it out only as a glow brings out a haze, in the likeness of one of these misty halos that sometimes are made visible by the spectral illumination of moonshine.

His remark did not seem at all surprising. It was just like Marlow. It was accepted in silence. No one took the trouble to grunt even; and presently he said, very slow—

"I was thinking of very old times, when the Romans first came here, nineteen hundred years ago—the other day. . . . Light came out of this river since—you say Knights? Yes; but it is like a running blaze on a plain, like a flash of lightning in the clouds. We live in the flicker—may it last as long as the old earth keeps rolling! But darkness was here yesterday. Imagine the feelings of a commander of a fine—what d'ye call 'em?—trireme in the Mediterranean, ordered suddenly to the north; run overland across the Gauls in a hurry; put in charge of one of these craft the legionaries—a wonderful lot of handy men they must have been, too—used to build, apparently by the hundred, in a month or two, if we may believe what we read. Imagine him here—the very end of the world, a sea the colour of lead, a sky the colour of smoke, a kind of ship about as rigid as a concertina—and going up this river with stores, or orders, or what you like. Sand-banks, marshes, forests, savages,—precious little to eat fit for a civilized man, nothing but Thames water to drink. No Falernian[4] wine here, no going ashore. Here and there a military camp lost in a wilderness, like a needle in a bundle of hay—cold, fog, tempests, disease, exile, and death,—death

---

[4] **Falernian:** A fine vintage wine.

skulking in the air, in the water, in the bush. They must have been dying like flies here. Oh, yes—he did it. Did it very well, too, no doubt, and without thinking much about it either, except afterwards to brag of what he had gone through in his time, perhaps. They were men enough to face the darkness. And perhaps he was cheered by keeping his eye on a chance of promotion to the fleet at Ravenna by and by, if he had good friends in Rome and survived the awful climate. Or think of a decent young citizen in a toga—perhaps too much dice, you know—coming out here in the train of some prefect, or tax-gatherer, or trader even, to mend his fortunes. Land in a swamp, march through the woods, and in some inland post feel the savagery, the utter savagery, had closed round him,—all that mysterious life of the wilderness that stirs in the forest, in the jungles, in the hearts of wild men. There's no initiation either into such mysteries. He has to live in the midst of the incomprehensible, which is also detestable. And it has a fascination, too, that goes to work upon him. The fascination of the abomination—you know, imagine the growing regrets, the longing to escape, the powerless disgust, the surrender, the hate."

He paused.

"Mind," he began again, lifting one arm from the elbow, the palm of the hand outwards, so that, with his legs folded before him, he had the pose of a Buddha preaching in European clothes and without a lotus-flower—"Mind, none of us would feel exactly like this. What saves us is efficiency—the devotion to efficiency. But these chaps were not much account, really. They were no colonists; their administration was merely a squeeze, and nothing more, I suspect. They were conquerors, and for that you want only brute force—nothing to boast of, when you have it, since your strength is just an accident arising from the weakness of others. They grabbed what they could get for the sake of what was to be got. It was just robbery with violence, aggravated murder on a great scale, and men going at it blind—as is very proper for those who tackle a darkness. The conquest of the earth, which mostly means the taking it away from those who have a different complexion or slightly flatter noses than ourselves, is not a pretty thing when you look into it too much. What redeems it is the idea only. An idea at the back of it; not a sentimental pretence but an idea; and an unselfish belief in the idea—something you can set up, and bow down before, and offer a sacrifice to. . . ."

He broke off. Flames glided in the river, small green flames, red flames, white flames, pursuing, overtaking, joining, crossing each other—then separating slowly or hastily. The traffic of the great city went on in the deepening night upon the sleepless river. We looked on, waiting patiently—there was nothing else to do till the end of the flood; but it was only after a long silence, when he said, in a hesitating voice, "I suppose you fellows remember I did once turn fresh-water sailor for a bit," that we knew we were fated, before the ebb began to run, to hear about one of Marlow's inconclusive experiences.

"I don't want to bother you much with what happened to me personally," he began, showing in this remark the weakness of many tellers of tales who seem so often unaware of what their audience would best like to hear; "yet to understand the effect of it on me you ought to know how I got out there, what I saw, how I went up that river to the place where I first met the poor chap. It was the farthest point of navigation and the culminating point of my experience. It seemed somehow to throw a kind of light on everything about me—and into my thoughts. It was sombre enough, too—and pitiful—not extraordinary in any way—not very clear either. No, not very clear. And yet it seemed to throw a kind of light.

"I had then, as you remember, just returned to London after a lot of Indian Ocean, Pacific, China Seas—a regular dose of the East—six years or so, and I was loafing about, hindering you fellows in your work and invading your homes, just as though I had got a heavenly mission to civilize you. It was very fine for a time, but after a bit I did get tired of resting. Then I began to look for a ship—I should think the hardest work on earth. But the ships wouldn't even look at me. And I got tired of that game, too.

"Now when I was a little chap I had a passion for maps. I would look for hours at South America, or Africa, or Australia, and lose myself in all the glories of exploration. At that time there were many blank spaces on the earth, and when I saw one that looked particularly inviting on a map (but they all look that) I would put my finger on it and say, When I grow up I will go there. The North Pole was one of these places, I remember. Well, I haven't been there yet, and shall not try now. The glamour's off. Other places were scattered about the Equator, and in every sort of latitude all over the two hemispheres. I have been in some of them, and . . . well, we won't talk about that. But there was one yet—the biggest, the most blank, so to speak— that I had a hankering after.

"True, by this time it was not a blank space any more. It had got filled since my boyhood with rivers and lakes and names. It had ceased to be a blank space of delightful mystery—a white patch for a boy to dream gloriously over. It had become a place of darkness. But there was in it one river especially, a mighty big river, that you could see on the map, resembling an immense snake uncoiled, with its head in the sea, its body at rest curving afar over a vast country, and its tail lost in the depths of the land. And as I looked at the map of it in a shop-window, it fascinated me as a snake would a bird—a silly little bird. Then I remembered there was a big concern, a Company for trade on that river. Dash it all! I thought to myself, they can't trade without using some kind of craft on that lot of fresh water—steamboats! Why shouldn't I try to get charge of one? I went on along Fleet Street, but could not shake off the idea. The snake had charmed me.

"You understand it was a Continental concern, that Trading society; but I have a lot of relations living on the Continent, because it's cheap and not so nasty as it looks, they say.

"I am sorry to own I began to worry them. This was already a fresh departure for me. I was not used to get things that way, you know. I always went my own road and on my own legs where I had a mind to go. I wouldn't have believed it of myself; but, then—you see—I felt somehow I must get there by hook or by crook. So I worried them. The men said 'My dear fellow,' and did nothing. Then—would you believe it?—I tried the women. I, Charlie Marlow, set the women to work—to get a job. Heavens! Well, you see, the notion drove me. I had an aunt, a dear enthusiastic soul. She wrote: 'It will be delightful. I am ready to do anything, anything for you. It is a glorious idea. I know the wife of a very high personage in the Administration, and also a man who has lots of influence with,' etc., etc. She was determined to make no end of fuss to get me appointed skipper of a river steamboat, if such was my fancy.

"I got my appointment — of course; and I got it very quick. It appears the Company had received news that one of their captains had been killed in a scuffle with the natives. This was my chance, and it made me the more anxious to go. It was only months and months afterwards, when I made the attempt to recover what was left of the body, that I heard the original quarrel arose from a misunderstanding about some hens. Yes, two black hens. Fresleven — that was the fellow's name, a Dane — thought himself wronged somehow in the bargain, so he went ashore and started to hammer the chief of the village with a stick. Oh, it didn't surprise me in the least to hear this, and at the same time to be told that Fresleven was the gentlest, quietest creature that ever walked on two legs. No doubt he was; but he had been a couple of years already out there engaged in the noble cause, you know, and he probably felt the need at last of asserting his self-respect in some way. Therefore he whacked the old nigger mercilessly, while a big crowd of his people watched him, thunderstruck, till some man — I was told the chief's son — in desperation at hearing the old chap yell, made a tentative jab with a spear at the white man — and of course it went quite easy between the shoulder-blades. Then the whole population cleared into the forest, expecting all kinds of calamities to happen, while, on the other hand, the steamer Fresleven commanded left also in a bad panic, in charge of the engineer, I believe. Afterwards nobody seemed to trouble much about Fresleven's remains, till I got out and stepped into his shoes. I couldn't let it rest, though; but when an opportunity offered at last to meet my predecessor, the grass growing through his ribs was tall enough to hide his bones. They were all there. The supernatural being had not been touched after he fell. And the village was deserted, the huts gaped black, rotting, all askew within the fallen enclosures. A calamity had come to it, sure enough. The people had vanished. Mad terror had scattered them, men, women, and children, through the bush, and they had never returned. What became of the hens I don't know either. I should think the cause of progress got them, anyhow. However, through this glorious affair I got my appointment, before I had fairly begun to hope for it.

"I flew around like mad to get ready, and before forty-eight hours I was crossing the Channel to show myself to my employers, and sign the contract. In a very few hours I arrived in a city[5] that always makes me think of a whited sepulchre.[6] Prejudice no doubt. I had no difficulty in finding the Company's offices. It was the biggest thing in the town, and everybody I met was full of it. They were going to run an over-sea empire, and make no end of coin by trade.

"A narrow and deserted street in deep shadow, high houses, innumerable windows with venetian blinds, a dead silence, grass sprouting between the stones, imposing carriage archways right and left, immense double doors standing ponderously ajar. I slipped through one of these cracks, went up a swept and ungarnished

---

[5] **a city:** The capital of Belgium. Between 1885 and 1908, when it became a Belgian colony, the Congo — now the Democratic Republic of the Congo — was owned by King Leopold II of Belgium.

[6] **whited sepulchre:** Jesus compared the hypocritical Pharisees to whited sepulchres, or tombs, which "outwardly appear beautiful, but inwardly are full of dead men's bones." See Matthew 23:27.

staircase, as arid as a desert, and opened the first door I came to. Two women, one fat and the other slim, sat on straw-bottomed chairs, knitting black wool. The slim one got up and walked straight at me — still knitting with down-cast eyes — and only just as I began to think of getting out of her way, as you would for a somnambulist, stood still, and looked up. Her dress was as plain as an umbrella-cover, and she turned round without a word and preceded me into a waiting-room. I gave my name, and looked about. Deal[7] table in the middle, plain chairs all round the walls, on one end a large shining map, marked with all the colours of a rainbow. There was a vast amount of red — good to see at any time, because one knows that some real work is done in there, a deuce of a lot of blue, a little green, smears of orange, and, on the East Coast, a purple patch, to show where the jolly pioneers of progress drink the jolly lager-beer. However, I wasn't going into any of these. I was going into the yellow. Dead in the centre. And the river was there — fascinating — deadly — like a snake. Ough! A door opened, a white-haired secretarial head, but wearing a compassionate expression, appeared, and a skinny forefinger beckoned me into the sanctuary. Its light was dim, and a heavy writing-desk squatted in the middle. From behind that structure came out an impression of pale plumpness in a frock-coat. The great man himself. He was five feet six, I should judge, and had his grip on the handle-end of ever so many millions. He shook hands, I fancy, murmured vaguely, was satisfied with my French. *Bon voyage.*

"In about forty-five seconds I found myself again in the waiting-room with the compassionate secretary, who, full of desolation and sympathy, made me sign some document. I believe I undertook amongst other things not to disclose any trade secrets. Well, I am not going to.

"I began to feel slightly uneasy. You know I am not used to such ceremonies, and there was something ominous in the atmosphere. It was just as though I had been let into some conspiracy — I don't know — something not quite right; and I was glad to get out. In the outer room the two women knitted black wool feverishly. People were arriving, and the younger one was walking back and forth introducing them. The old one sat on her chair. Her flat cloth slippers were propped up on a foot-warmer, and a cat reposed on her lap. She wore a starched white affair on her head, had a wart on one cheek, and silver-rimmed spectacles hung on the tip of her nose. She glanced at me above the glasses. The swift and indifferent placidity of that look troubled me. Two youths with foolish and cheery countenances were being piloted over, and she threw at them the same quick glance of unconcerned wisdom. She seemed to know all about them and about me, too. An eerie feeling came over me. She seemed uncanny and fateful. Often far away there I thought of these two, guarding the door of Darkness, knitting black wool as for a warm pall, one introducing, introducing continuously to the unknown, the other scrutinizing the cheery and foolish faces with unconcerned old eyes. *Ave!* Old knitter of black wool. *Morituri te salutant.*[8] Not many of those she looked at ever saw her again — not half, by a long way.

---

[7] **Deal:** Pine.

[8] *Ave . . . salutant:* "Hail! Those who are about to die salute you." This was the gladiators' salute to the Roman emperor in the Colosseum.

"There was yet a visit to the doctor. 'A simple formality,' assured me the secretary, with an air of taking an immense part in all my sorrows. Accordingly a young chap wearing his hat over the left eyebrow, some clerk I suppose,—there must have been clerks in the business, though the house was as still as a house in a city of the dead—came from somewhere upstairs, and led me forth. He was shabby and careless, with ink-stains on the sleeves of his jacket, and his cravat was large and billowy, under a chin shaped like the toe of an old boot. It was a little too early for the doctor, so I proposed a drink, and thereupon he developed a vein of joviality. As we sat over our vermuths he glorified the Company's business, and by and by I expressed casually my surprise at him not going out there. He became very cool and collected all at once. 'I am not such a fool as I look, quoth Plato to his disciples,' he said sententiously, emptied his glass with great resolution, and we rose.

"The old doctor felt my pulse, evidently thinking of something else the while. 'Good, good for there,' he mumbled, and then with a certain eagerness asked me whether I would let him measure my head. Rather surprised, I said Yes, when he produced a thing like calipers and got the dimensions back and front and every way, taking notes carefully. He was an unshaven little man in a threadbare coat like a gaberdine, with his feet in slippers, and I thought him a harmless fool. 'I always ask leave, in the interests of science, to measure the crania of those going out there,' he said. 'And when they come back, too?' I asked. 'Oh, I never see them,' he remarked; 'and, moreover, the changes take place inside, you know.' He smiled, as if at some quiet joke. 'So you are going out there. Famous. Interesting, too.' He gave me a searching glance, and made another note. 'Ever any madness in your family?' he asked, in a matter-of-fact tone. I felt very annoyed. 'Is that question in the interests of science, too?' 'It would be,' he said, without taking notice of my irritation, 'interesting for science to watch the mental changes of individuals, on the spot, but . . .' 'Are you an alienist?'[9] I interrupted. 'Every doctor should be—a little,' answered that original, imperturbably. 'I have a little theory which you Messieurs who go out there must help me to prove. This is my share in the advantages my country shall reap from the possession of such a magnificent dependency. The mere wealth I leave to others. Pardon my questions, but you are the first Englishman coming under my observation . . .' I hastened to assure him I was not in the least typical. 'If I were,' said I, 'I wouldn't be talking like this with you.' 'What you say is rather profound, and probably erroneous,' he said, with a laugh. 'Avoid irritation more than exposure to the sun. Adieu. How do you English say, eh? Good-bye. Ah! Good-bye. Adieu. In the tropics one must before everything keep calm.' . . . He lifted a warning forefinger. . . . '*Du calme, du calme. Adieu.*'

"One thing more remained to do—say good-bye to my excellent aunt. I found her triumphant. I had a cup of tea—the last decent cup of tea for many days—and in a room that most soothingly looked just as you would expect a lady's drawing-room to look, we had a long quiet chat by the fireside. In the course of these confidences it became quite plain to me I had been represented to the wife of the high

---

[9] **alienist:** A psychiatrist.

dignitary, and goodness knows to how many more people besides, as an exceptional and gifted creature—a piece of good fortune for the Company—a man you don't get hold of every day. Good heavens! and I was going to take charge of a two-penny-half-penny river-steamboat with a penny whistle attached! It appeared, however, I was also one of the Workers, with a capital—you know. Something like an emissary of light, something like a lower sort of apostle. There had been a lot of such rot let loose in print and talk just about that time, and the excellent woman, living right in the rush of all that humbug, got carried off her feet. She talked about 'weaning those ignorant millions from their horrid ways,' till, upon my word, she made me quite uncomfortable. I ventured to hint that the Company was run for profit.

"'You forget, dear Charlie, that the labourer is worthy of his hire,'[10] she said, brightly. It's queer how out of touch with truth women are. They live in a world of their own, and there has never been anything like it, and never can be. It is too beautiful altogether, and if they were to set it up it would go to pieces before the first sunset. Some confounded fact we men have been living contentedly with ever since the day of creation would start up and knock the whole thing over.

"After this I got embraced, told to wear flannel, be sure to write often, and so on—and I left. In the street—I don't know why—a queer feeling came to me that I was an impostor. Odd thing that I, who used to clear out for any part of the world at twenty-four hours' notice, with less thought than most men give to the crossing of a street, had a moment—I won't say of hesitation, but of startled pause, before this commonplace affair. The best way I can explain it to you is by saying that, for a second or two, I felt as though, instead of going to the centre of a continent, I were about to set off for the centre of the earth.

"I left in a French steamer, and she called in every blamed port they have out there, for, as far as I could see, the sole purpose of landing soldiers and custom-house officers. I watched the coast. Watching a coast as it slips by the ship is like thinking about an enigma. There it is before you—smiling, frowning, inviting, grand, mean, insipid, or savage, and always mute with an air of whispering, Come and find out. This one was almost featureless, as if still in the making, with an aspect of monotonous grimness. The edge of a colossal jungle, so dark-green as to be almost black, fringed with white surf, ran straight, like a ruled line, far, far away along a blue sea whose glitter was blurred by a creeping mist. The sun was fierce, the land seemed to glisten and drip with steam. Here and there grayish-whitish specks showed up clustered inside the white surf, with a flag flying above them perhaps. Settlements some centuries old, and still no bigger than pinheads on the untouched expanse of their background. We pounded along, stopped, landed soldiers; went on, landed custom-house clerks to levy toll in what looked like a God-forsaken wilderness, with a tin shed and a flag-pole lost in it; landed more soldiers—to take care of the custom-house clerks, presumably. Some, I heard, got drowned in the surf; but whether they did or not, nobody seemed particularly to care. They were just flung out there, and on we went. Every day the coast looked the same, as though we had

---

[10] **the labourer . . . his hire:** See Luke 10:7.

not moved; but we passed various places—trading places—with names like Gran' Bassam, Little Popo; names that seemed to belong to some sordid farce acted in front of a sinister back-cloth. The idleness of a passenger, my isolation amongst all these men with whom I had no point of contact, the oily and languid sea, the uniform sombreness of the coast, seemed to keep me away from the truth of things, within the toil of a mournful and senseless delusion. The voice of the surf heard now and then was a positive pleasure, like the speech of a brother. It was something natural, that had its reason, that had a meaning. Now and then a boat from the shore gave one a momentary contact with reality. It was paddled by black fellows. You could see from afar the white of their eyeballs glistening. They shouted, sang; their bodies streamed with perspiration; they had faces like grotesque masks—these chaps; but they had bone, muscle, a wild vitality, an intense energy of movement, that was as natural and true as the surf along their coast. They wanted no excuse for being there. They were a great comfort to look at. For a time I would feel I belonged still to a world of straightforward facts; but the feeling would not last long. Something would turn up to scare it away. Once, I remember, we came upon a man-of-war anchored off the coast. There wasn't even a shed there, and she was shelling the bush. It appears the French had one of their wars going on thereabouts. Her ensign dropped limp like a rag; the muzzles of the long six-inch guns stuck out all over the low hull; the greasy, slimy swell swung her up lazily and let her down, swaying her thin masts. In the empty immensity of earth, sky, and water, there she was, incomprehensible, firing into a continent. Pop, would go one of the six-inch guns; a small flame would dart and vanish, a little white smoke would disappear, a tiny projectile would give a feeble screech—and nothing happened. Nothing could happen. There was a touch of insanity in the proceeding, a sense of lugubrious drollery in the sight; and it was not dissipated by somebody on board assuring me earnestly there was a camp of natives—he called them enemies!—hidden out of sight somewhere.

"We gave her her letters (I heard the men in that lonely ship were dying of fever at the rate of three a day) and went on. We called at some more places with farcical names, where the merry dance of death and trade goes on in a still and earthy atmosphere as of an overheated catacomb; all along the formless coast bordered by dangerous surf, as if Nature herself had tried to ward off intruders; in and out of rivers, streams of death in life, whose banks were rotting into mud, whose waters, thickened into slime, invaded the contorted mangroves," that seemed to writhe at us in the extremity of an impotent despair. Nowhere did we stop long enough to get a particularized impression, but the general sense of vague and oppressive wonder grew upon me. It was like a weary pilgrimage amongst hints for nightmares.

"It was upward of thirty days before I saw the mouth of the big river. We anchored off the seat of the government. But my work would not begin till some two hundred miles farther on. So as soon as I could I made a start for a place thirty miles higher up.

"I had my passage on a little sea-going steamer. Her captain was a Swede, and

---

" **mangroves:** Tropical maritime trees.

knowing me for a seaman, invited me on the bridge. He was a young man, lean, fair, and morose, with lanky hair and a shuffling gait. As we left the miserable little wharf, he tossed his head contemptuously at the shore. 'Been living there?' he asked. I said, 'Yes.' 'Fine lot these government chaps—are they not?' he went on, speaking English with great precision and considerable bitterness. 'It is funny what some people will do for a few francs a month. I wonder what becomes of that kind when it goes up country?' I said to him I expected to see that soon. 'So-o-o!' he exclaimed. He shuffled athwart, keeping one eye ahead vigilantly. 'Don't be too sure,' he continued. 'The other day I took up a man who hanged himself on the road. He was a Swede, too.' 'Hanged himself! Why, in God's name?' I cried. He kept on looking out watchfully. 'Who knows? The sun too much for him, or the country perhaps.'

"At last we opened a reach. A rocky cliff appeared, mounds of turned-up earth by the shore, houses on a hill, others with iron roofs, amongst a waste of excavations, or hanging to the declivity. A continuous noise of the rapids above hovered over this scene of inhabited devastation. A lot of people, mostly black and naked, moved about like ants. A jetty projected into the river. A blinding sunlight drowned all this at times in a sudden recrudescence of glare. 'There's your Company's station,' said the Swede, pointing to three wooden barrack-like structures on the rocky slope. 'I will send your things up. Four boxes did you say? So. Farewell.'

"I came upon a boiler wallowing in the grass, then found a path leading up the hill. It turned aside for the boulders, and also for an undersized railway-truck lying there on its back with its wheels in the air. One was off. The thing looked as dead as the carcass of some animal. I came upon more pieces of decaying machinery, a stack of rusty rails. To the left a clump of trees made a shady spot, where dark things seemed to stir feebly. I blinked, the path was steep. A horn tooted to the right, and I saw the black people run. A heavy and dull detonation shook the ground, a puff of smoke came out of the cliff, and that was all. No change appeared on the face of the rock. They were building a railway. The cliff was not in the way or anything; but this objectless blasting was all the work going on.

"A slight clinking behind me made me turn my head. Six black men advanced in a file, toiling up the path. They walked erect and slow, balancing small baskets full of earth on their heads, and the clink kept time with their footsteps. Black rags were wound round their loins, and the short ends behind waggled to and fro like tails. I could see every rib, the joints of their limbs were like knots in a rope; each had an iron collar on his neck, and all were connected together with a chain whose bights[12] swung between them, rhythmically clinking. Another report from the cliff made me think suddenly of that ship of war I had seen firing into a continent. It was the same kind of ominous voice; but these men could by no stretch of imagination be called enemies. They were called criminals, and the outraged law, like the bursting shells, had come to them, an insoluble mystery from the sea. All their meagre breasts panted together, the violently dilated nostrils quivered, the eyes stared stonily up-hill. They passed me within six inches, without a glance, with that complete, death-

---

[12] **bights:** Slack sections.

like indifference of unhappy savages. Behind this raw matter one of the reclaimed, the product of the new forces at work, strolled despondently, carrying a rifle by its middle. He had a uniform jacket with one button off, and seeing a white man on the path, hoisted his weapon to his shoulder with alacrity. This was simple prudence, white men being so much alike at a distance that he could not tell who I might be. He was speedily reassured, and with a large, white, rascally grin, and a glance at his charge, seemed to take me into partnership in his exalted trust. After all, I also was a part of the great cause of these high and just proceedings.

"Instead of going up, I turned and descended to the left. My idea was to let that chain-gang get out of sight before I climbed the hill. You know I am not particularly tender; I've had to strike and to fend off. I've had to resist and to attack sometimes—that's only one way of resisting—without counting the exact cost, according to the demands of such sort of life as I had blundered into. I've seen the devil of violence, and the devil of greed, and the devil of hot desire; but, by all the stars! these were strong, lusty, red-eyed devils, that swayed and drove men—men, I tell you. But as I stood on this hillside, I foresaw that in the blinding sunshine of that land I would become acquainted with a flabby, pretending, weak-eyed devil of a rapacious and pitiless folly. How insidious he could be, too, I was only to find out several months later and a thousand miles farther. For a moment I stood appalled, as though by a warning. Finally I descended the hill, obliquely, towards the trees I had seen.

"I avoided a vast artificial hole somebody had been digging on the slope, the purpose of which I found it impossible to divine. It wasn't a quarry or a sandpit, anyhow. It was just a hole. It might have been connected with the philanthropic desire of giving the criminals something to do. I don't know. Then I nearly fell into a very narrow ravine, almost no more than a scar in the hillside. I discovered that a lot of imported drainage-pipes for the settlement had been tumbled in there. There wasn't one that was not broken. It was a wanton smash-up. At last I got under the trees. My purpose was to stroll into the shade for a moment; but no sooner within than it seemed to me I had stepped into the gloomy circle of some Inferno. The rapids were near, and an uninterrupted, uniform, headlong, rushing noise filled the mournful stillness of the grove, where not a breath stirred, not a leaf moved, with a mysterious sound—as though the tearing pace of the launched earth had suddenly become audible.

"Black shapes crouched, lay, sat between the trees leaning against the trunks, clinging to the earth, half coming out, half effaced within the dim light, in all the attitudes of pain, abandonment, and despair. Another mine on the cliff went off, followed by a slight shudder of the soil under my feet. The work was going on. The work! And this was the place where some of the helpers had withdrawn to die.

"They were dying slowly—it was very clear. They were not enemies, they were not criminals, they were nothing earthly now,—nothing but black shadows of disease and starvation, lying confusedly in the greenish gloom. Brought from all the recesses of the coast in all the legality of time contracts, lost in uncongenial surroundings, fed on unfamiliar food, they sickened, became inefficient, and were then allowed to crawl away and rest. These moribund shapes were free as air—and nearly as thin. I began to distinguish the gleam of the eyes under the trees. Then, glancing down, I saw a face near my hand. The black bones reclined at full length with one shoulder against the tree, and slowly the eyelids rose and the sunken eyes looked up at me, enormous and vacant, a kind of blind, white flicker in the depths of the orbs, which died out slowly. The man seemed young—almost a boy—but you know with them it's hard to tell. I found nothing else to do but to offer him one of my good Swede's ship's biscuits I had in my pocket. The fingers closed slowly on it and held—there was no other movement and no other glance. He had tied a bit of white worsted round his neck—Why? Where did he get it? Was it a badge—an ornament—a charm—a propitiatory act? Was there any idea at all connected with it? It looked startling round his black neck, this bit of white thread from beyond the seas.

"Near the same tree two more bundles of acute angles sat with their legs drawn up. One, with his chin propped on his knees, stared at nothing, in an intolerable and appalling manner: his brother phantom rested its forehead, as if overcome with a great weariness; and all about others were scattered in every pose of contorted collapse, as in some picture of a massacre or a pestilence. While I stood horror-struck, one of these creatures rose to his hands and knees, and went off on all-fours towards the river to drink. He lapped out of his hand, then sat up in the sunlight, crossing his shins in front of him, and after a time let his woolly head fall on his breastbone.

"I didn't want any more loitering in the shade, and I made haste towards the station. When near the buildings I met a white man, in such an unexpected elegance of get-up that in the first moment I took him for a sort of vision. I saw a high starched collar, white cuffs, a light alpaca jacket, snowy trousers, a clean necktie, and varnished boots. No hat. Hair parted, brushed, oiled, under a green-lined parasol held in a big white hand. He was amazing, and had a penholder behind his ear.

"I shook hands with this miracle, and I learned he was the Company's chief accountant, and that all the book-keeping was done at this station. He had come out for a moment, he said, 'to get a breath of fresh air.' The expression sounded wonderfully odd, with its suggestion of sedentary desk-life. I wouldn't have mentioned the fellow to you at all, only it was from his lips that I first heard the name of the man who is so indissolubly connected with the memories of that time. Moreover, I respected the fellow. Yes; I respected his collars, his vast cuffs, his brushed hair. His appearance was certainly that of a hairdresser's dummy; but in the great demoralization of the land he kept up his appearance. That's backbone. His starched collars and got-up shirt-fronts were achievements of character. He had been out nearly three years; and, later, I could not help asking him how he managed to sport such linen. He had just the faintest blush, and said modestly, 'I've been teaching one of the native women about the station. It was difficult. She had a distaste for the work.' Thus this man had verily accomplished something. And he was devoted to his books, which were in apple-pie order.

"Everything else in the station was in a muddle,—heads, things, buildings. Strings of dusty niggers with splay feet arrived and departed; a stream of manufactured goods, rubbishy cottons, beads, and brass-wire set into the depths of darkness, and in return came a precious trickle of ivory.

"I had to wait in the station for ten days—an eternity. I lived in a hut in the yard, but to be out of the chaos I would sometimes get into the accountant's office. It was built of horizontal planks, and so badly put together that, as he bent over his high desk, he was barred from neck to heels with narrow strips of sunlight. There was no need to open the big shutter to see. It was hot there, too; big flies buzzed fiendishly, and did not sting, but stabbed. I sat generally on the floor, while, of faultless appearance (and even slightly scented), perching on a high stool, he wrote, he wrote. Sometimes he stood up for exercise. When a truckle-bed with a sick man (some invalid agent from up-country) was put in there, he exhibited a gentle annoyance. 'The groans of this sick person,' he said, 'distract my attention. And without that it is extremely difficult to guard against clerical errors in this climate.'

"One day he remarked, without lifting his head, 'In the interior you will no doubt meet Mr. Kurtz.' On my asking who Mr. Kurtz was, he said he was a first-class agent; and seeing my disappointment at this information, he added slowly, laying down his pen, 'He is a very remarkable person.' Further questions elicited from him that Mr. Kurtz was at present in charge of a trading post, a very important one, in the true ivory-country, at 'the very bottom of there. Sends in as much ivory as all the others put together . . .' He began to write again. The sick man was too ill to groan. The flies buzzed in a great peace.

"Suddenly there was a growing murmur of voices and a great tramping of feet. A caravan had come in. A violent babble of uncouth sounds burst out on the other side of the planks. All the carriers were speaking together, and in the midst of the uproar the lamentable voice of the chief agent was heard 'giving it up' tearfully for the twentieth time that day. . . . He rose slowly. 'What a frightful row,' he said. He crossed the room gently to look at the sick man, and returning, said to me, 'He does not hear.' 'What! Dead?' I asked, startled. 'No, not yet,' he answered, with great composure. Then, alluding with a toss of the head to the tumult in the station-yard, 'When one has got to make correct entries, one comes to hate those savages—hate them to the death.' He remained thoughtful for a moment. 'When you see Mr. Kurtz,' he went on, 'tell him from me that everything here'—he glanced at the desk—'is very satisfactory. I don't like to write to him—with those messengers of ours you never know who may get hold of your letter—at that Central Station.' He stared at me for a moment with his mild, bulging eyes. 'Oh, he will go far, very far,' he began again. 'He will be somebody in the Administration before long. They, above—the Council in Europe, you know—mean him to be.'

"He turned to his work. The noise outside had ceased, and presently in going out I stopped at the door. In the steady buzz of flies the homeward-bound agent was lying flushed and insensible; the other, bent over his books, was making correct entries of perfectly correct transactions; and fifty feet below the doorstep I could see the still tree-tops of the grove of death.

"Next day I left that station at last, with a caravan of sixty men, for a two-hundred-mile tramp.

"No use telling you much about that. Paths, paths, everywhere; a stamped-in network of paths spreading over the empty land, through long grass, through burnt grass, through thickets, down and up chilly ravines, up and down stony hills ablaze with heat; and a solitude, a solitude, nobody, not a hut. The population had cleared out a long time ago. Well, if a lot of mysterious niggers armed with all kinds of fearful weapons suddenly took to travelling on the road between Deal and Gravesend, catching the yokels right and left to carry heavy loads for them, I fancy every farm and cottage thereabouts would get empty very soon. Only here the dwellings were gone, too. Still I passed through several abandoned villages. There's something pathetically childish in the ruins of grass walls. Day after day, with the stamp and shuffle of sixty pair of bare feet behind me, each pair under a 60-lb. load. Camp, cook, sleep, strike camp, march. Now and then a carrier dead in harness, at rest in the long grass near the path, with an empty water-gourd and his long staff lying by his side. A great silence around and above. Perhaps on some quiet night the tremor of far-off drums, sinking, swelling, a tremor vast, faint; a sound weird, appealing, suggestive, and wild—and perhaps with as profound a meaning as the sound of bells in a Christian country. Once a white man in an unbuttoned uniform, camping on the path with an armed escort of lank Zanzibaris, very hospitable and festive—not to say drunk. Was looking after the upkeep of the road he declared. Can't say I saw any road or any upkeep, unless the body of a middle-aged negro, with a bullet-hole in the forehead, upon which I absolutely stumbled three miles farther on, may be considered as a permanent improvement. I had a white companion, too, not a bad chap, but rather too fleshy and with the exasperating habit of fainting on the hot hillsides, miles away from the least bit of shade and water. Annoying, you know, to hold your own coat like a parasol over a man's head while he is coming-to. I couldn't help asking him once what he meant by coming there at all. 'To make money, of course. What do you think?' he said, scornfully. Then he got fever, and had to be carried in a hammock slung under a pole. As he weighed sixteen stone[13] I had no end of rows with the carriers. They jibbed,[14] ran away, sneaked off with their loads in the night—quite a mutiny. So, one evening, I made a speech in English with gestures, not one of which was lost to the sixty pairs of eyes before me, and the next morning I started the hammock off in front all right. An hour afterwards I came upon the whole concern wrecked in a bush—man, hammock, groans, blankets, horrors. The heavy pole had skinned his poor nose. He was very anxious for me to kill somebody, but there wasn't the shadow of a carrier near. I remembered the old doctor—'It would be interesting for science to watch the mental changes of individuals, on the spot.' I felt I was becoming scientifically interesting. However, all that is to no purpose. On the fifteenth day I came in sight of the big river again, and hobbled into the Central Station. It was on a back water surrounded by scrub and forest, with a pretty border of smelly mud on one side, and on the three others enclosed by a crazy fence of rushes. A neglected gap was all the gate it had, and the first glance at the place was enough to let you see the flabby devil was running that show. White men with long staves in their hands appeared languidly from amongst the buildings, strolling up to take a look at me, and then retired out of sight somewhere. One of them, a stout, excitable chap with black moustaches, informed me with great volubility and many disgressions, as soon as I told him who I was, that my

---

[13] **stone:** A British unit of weight equal to 14 pounds. Sixteen stone equals 224 pounds.
[14] **jibbed:** Balked.

steamer was at the bottom of the river. I was thunderstruck. What, how, why? Oh, it was 'all right.' The 'manager himself' was there. All quite correct. 'Everybody had behaved splendidly! splendidly!'—'you must,' he said in agitation, 'go and see the general manager at once. He is waiting!'

"I did not see the real significance of that wreck at once. I fancy I see it now, but I am not sure—not at all. Certainly the affair was too stupid—when I think of it—to be altogether natural. Still . . . But at the moment it presented itself simply as a confounded nuisance. The steamer was sunk. They had started two days before in a sudden hurry up the river with the manager on board, in charge of some volunteer skipper, and before they had been out three hours they tore the bottom out of her on stones, and she sank near the south bank. I asked myself what I was to do there, now my boat was lost. As a matter of fact, I had plenty to do in fishing my command out of the river. I had to set about it the very next day. That, and the repairs when I brought the pieces to the station, took some months.

"My first interview with the manager was curious. He did not ask me to sit down after my twenty-mile walk that morning. He was commonplace in complexion, in feature, in manners, and in voice. He was of middle size and of ordinary build. His eyes, of the usual blue, were perhaps remarkably cold, and he certainly could make his glance fall on one as trenchant and heavy as an axe. But even at these times the rest of his person seemed to disclaim the intention. Otherwise there was only an indefinable, faint expression of his lips, something stealthy—a smile—not a smile—I remember it, but I can't explain. It was unconscious, this smile was, though just after he had said something it got intensified for an instant. It came at the end of his speeches like a seal applied on the words to make the meaning of the commonest phrase appear absolutely inscrutable. He was a common trader, from his youth up employed in these parts—nothing more. He was obeyed, yet he inspired neither love nor fear, nor even respect. He inspired uneasiness. That was it! Uneasiness. Not a definite mistrust—just uneasiness—nothing more. You have no idea how effective such a . . . a . . . faculty can be. He had no genius for organizing, for initiative, or for order even. That was evident in such things as the deplorable state of the station. He had no learning, and no intelligence. His position had come to him—why? Perhaps because he was never ill . . . He had served three terms of three years out there . . . Because triumphant health in the general rout of constitutions is a kind of power in itself. When he went home on leave he rioted on a large scale—pompously. Jack[15] ashore—with a difference—in externals only. This one could gather from his casual talk. He originated nothing, he could keep the routine going—that's all. But he was great. He was great by this little thing that it was impossible to tell what could control such a man. He never gave that secret away. Perhaps there was nothing within him. Such a suspicion made one pause—for out there there were no external checks. Once when various tropical diseases had laid low almost every 'agent' in the station, he was heard to say, 'Men who come out here should have no entrails.' He sealed the utterance with that smile of his, as though it

---

[15] **Jack:** Jack Tar; a sailor.

had been a door opening into a darkness he had in his keeping. You fancied you had seen things—but the seal was on. When annoyed at meal-times by the constant quarrels of the white men about precedence, he ordered an immense round table to be made, for which a special house had to be built. This was the station's mess-room. Where he sat was the first place—the rest were nowhere. One felt this to be his unalterable conviction. He was neither civil nor uncivil. He was quiet. He allowed his 'boy'—an overfed young negro from the coast—to treat the white men, under his very eyes, with provoking insolence.

"He began to speak as soon as he saw me. I had been very long on the road. He could not wait. Had to start without me. The up-river stations had to be relieved. There had been so many delays already that he did not know who was dead and who was alive, and how they got on—and so on, and so on. He paid no attention to my explanations, and, playing with a stick of sealing-wax, repeated several times that the situation was 'very grave, very grave.' There were rumours that a very important station was in jeopardy, and its chief, Mr. Kurtz, was ill. Hoped it was not true. Mr. Kurtz was . . . I felt weary and irritable. Hang Kurtz, I thought. I interrupted him by saying I had heard of Mr. Kurtz on the coast. 'Ah! So they talk of him down there,' he murmured to himself. Then he began again, assuring me Mr. Kurtz was the best agent he had, an exceptional man, of the greatest importance to the Company; therefore I could understand his anxiety. He was, he said, 'very, very uneasy.' Certainly he fidgeted on his chair a good deal, exclaimed, 'Ah, Mr. Kurtz!' broke the stick of sealing-wax and seemed dumfounded by the accident. Next thing he wanted to know 'how long it would take to' . . . I interrupted him again. Being hungry, you know, and kept on my feet too, I was getting savage. 'How can I tell?' I said. 'I haven't even seen the wreck yet—some months, no doubt.' All this talk seemed to me so futile. 'Some months,' he said. 'Well, let us say three months before we can make a start. Yes. That ought to do the affair.' I flung out of his hut (he lived all alone in a clay hut with a sort of verandah) muttering to myself my opinion of him. He was a chattering idiot. Afterwards I took it back when it was borne in upon me startlingly with what extreme nicety he had estimated the time requisite for the 'affair.'

"I went to work the next day, turning, so to speak, my back on that station. In that way only it seemed to me I could keep my hold on the redeeming facts of life. Still, one must look about sometimes; and then I saw this station, these men strolling aimlessly about in the sunshine of the yard. I asked myself sometimes what it all meant. They wandered here and there with their absurd long staves in their hands, like a lot of faithless pilgrims bewitched inside a rotten fence. The word 'ivory' rang in the air, was whispered, was sighed. You would think they were praying to it. A taint of imbecile rapacity blew through it all, like a whiff from some corpse. By Jove! I've never seen anything so unreal in my life. And outside, the silent wilderness surrounding this cleared speck on the earth struck me as something great and invincible, like evil or truth, waiting patiently for the passing away of this fantastic invasion.

"Oh, these months! Well, never mind. Various things happened. One evening a grass shed full of calico, cotton prints, beads, and I don't know what else, burst into a blaze so suddenly that you would have thought the earth had opened to let an avenging fire consume all that trash. I was smoking my pipe quietly by my dismantled steamer, and saw them all cutting capers in the light, with their arms lifted high, when the stout man with moustaches came tearing down to the river, a tin pail in his hand, assured me that everybody was 'behaving splendidly, splendidly,' dipped about a quart of water and tore back again. I noticed there was a hole in the bottom of his pail.

"I strolled up. There was no hurry. You see the thing had gone off like a box of matches. It had been hopeless from the very first. The flame had leaped high, driven everybody back, lighted up everything—and collapsed. The shed was already a heap of embers glowing fiercely. A nigger was being beaten near by. They said he had caused the fire in some way; be that as it may, he was screeching most horribly. I saw him, later, for several days, sitting in a bit of shade looking very sick and trying to recover himself: afterwards he arose and went out—and the wilderness without a sound took him into its bosom again. As I approached the glow from the dark I found myself at the back of two men, talking. I heard the name of Kurtz pronounced, then the words, 'take advantage of this unfortunate accident.' One of the men was the manager. I wished him a good evening. 'Did you ever see anything like it—eh? it is incredible,' he said, and walked off. The other man remained. He was a first-class agent, young, gentlemanly, a bit reserved, with a forked little beard and a hooked nose. He was stand-offish with the other agents, and they on their side said he was the manager's spy upon them. As to me, I had hardly ever spoken to him before. We got into talk, and by and by we strolled away from the hissing ruins. Then he asked me to his room, which was in the main building of the station. He struck a match, and I perceived that this young aristocrat had not only a silver-mounted dressing-case but also a whole candle all to himself. Just at that time the manager was the only man supposed to have any right to candles. Native mats covered the clay walls; a collection of spears, assegais,[16] shields, knives was hung up in trophies. The business entrusted to this fellow was the making of bricks—so I had been informed; but there wasn't a fragment of a brick anywhere in the station, and he had been there more than a year—waiting. It seems he could not make bricks without something, I don't know what—straw maybe. Anyways, it could not be found there, and as it was not likely to be sent from Europe, it did not appear clear to me what he was waiting for. An act of special creation perhaps.[17] However, they were all waiting—all the sixteen or twenty pilgrims of them—for something; and upon my word it did not seem an uncongenial occupation, from the way they took it, though the only thing that ever came to them was disease—as far as I could see. They beguiled the time by backbiting and intriguing against each other in a foolish kind of way. There was an air of plotting about that station, but nothing came of it, of course. It was as unreal as everything else—as the philanthropic pretence of the whole concern, as their talk, as their government, as their show of work. The only real feeling was a desire to get appointed to a trading-post where ivory was to be had, so that they could earn percentages. They intrigued and slandered and hated each other only on that

---

[16] **assegais:** Javelins.

[17] **An act . . . perhaps:** Special creation was the belief, challenged by the evolutionists, that God created each species individually.

account,—but as to effectually lifting a little finger—oh, no. By heavens! there is
something after all in the world allowing one man to steal a horse while another
must not look at a halter. Steal a horse straight out. Very well. He has done it. Perhaps
he can ride. But there is a way of looking at a halter that would provoke the most
charitable of saints into a kick.

"I had no idea why he wanted to be sociable, but as we chatted in there it suddenly occurred to me the fellow was trying to get at something—in fact, pumping
me. He alluded constantly to Europe, to the people I was supposed to know there—
putting leading questions as to my acquaintances in the sepulchral city, and so on.
His little eyes glittered like mica discs—with curiosity—though he tried to keep up
a bit of superciliousness. At first I was astonished, but very soon I became awfully
curious to see what he would find out from me. I couldn't possibly imagine what I
had in me to make it worth his while. It was very pretty to see how he baffled himself,
for in truth my body was full only of chills, and my head had nothing in it but that
wretched steamboat business. It was evident he took me for a perfectly shameless
prevaricator. At last he got angry, and, to conceal a movement of furious annoyance,
he yawned. I rose. Then I noticed a small sketch in oils, on a panel, representing a
woman, draped and blindfolded, carrying a lighted torch. The background was
sombre—almost black. The movement of the woman was stately, and the effect of
the torch-light on the face was sinister.

"It arrested me, and he stood by civilly, holding an empty half-pint champagne
bottle (medical comforts) with the candle stuck in it. To my question he said Mr.
Kurtz had painted this—in this very station more than a year ago—while waiting
for means to go to his trading-post. 'Tell me, pray,' said I, 'who is this Mr. Kurtz?'

"'The chief of the Inner Station,' he answered in a short tone, looking away.
'Much obliged,' I said, laughing. 'And you are the brickmaker of the Central Station.
Everyone knows that.' He was silent for a while. 'He is a prodigy,' he said at last. 'He is
an emissary of pity, and science, and progress, and devil knows what else. We want,'
he began to declaim suddenly, 'for the guidance of the cause intrusted to us by
Europe, so to speak, higher intelligence, wide sympathies, a singleness of purpose.'
'Who says that?' I asked. 'Lots of them,' he replied. 'Some even write that; and so *he*
comes here, a special being, as you ought to know.' 'Why ought I to know?' I interrupted, really surprised. He paid no attention. 'Yes. To-day he is chief of the best station, next year he will be assistant-manager, two years more and . . . but I daresay
you know what he will be in two years' time. You are of the new gang—the gang of
virtue. The same people who sent him specially also recommended you. Oh, don't
say no. I've my own eyes to trust.' Light dawned upon me. My dear aunt's influential
acquaintances were producing an unexpected effect upon that young man. I nearly
burst into a laugh. 'Do you read the Company's confidential correspondence?' I
asked. He hadn't a word to say. It was great fun. 'When Mr. Kurtz,' I continued,
severely, 'is General Manager, you won't have the opportunity.'

"He blew the candle out suddenly, and we went outside. The moon had risen.
Black figures strolled about listlessly, pouring water on the glow, whence proceeded a
sound of hissing; steam ascended in the moonlight, the beaten nigger groaned
somewhere. 'What a row the brute makes!' said the indefatigable man with the

moustaches, appearing near us. 'Serve him right. Transgression—punishment—bang! Pitiless, pitiless. That's the only way. This will prevent all conflagrations for the future. I was just telling the manager . . .' He noticed my companion, and became crestfallen all at once. 'Not in bed yet,' he said, with a kind of servile heartiness; 'it's so natural. Ha! Danger—agitation.' He vanished. I went on to the river-side, and the other followed me. I heard a scathing murmur at my ear, 'Heap of muffs—go to.' The pilgrims could be seen in knots gesticulating, discussing. Several had still their staves in their hands. I verily believe they took these sticks to bed with them. Beyond the fence the forest stood up spectrally in the moonlight, and through the dim stir, through the faint sounds of that lamentable courtyard, the silence of the land went home to one's very heart—its mystery, its greatness, the amazing reality of its concealed life. The hurt nigger moaned feebly somewhere near by, and then fetched a deep sigh that made me mend my pace away from there. I felt a hand introducing itself under my arm. 'My dear sir,' said the fellow, 'I don't want to be misunderstood, and especially by you, who will see Mr. Kurtz long before I can have that pleasure. I wouldn't like him to get a false idea of my disposition. . . .'

"I let him run on, this papier-mâché Mephistopheles, and it seemed to me that if I tried I could poke my forefinger through him, and would find nothing inside but a little loose dirt, maybe. He, don't you see, had been planning to be assistant-manager by and by under the present man, and I could see that the coming of that Kurtz had upset them both not a little. He talked precipitately, and I did not try to stop him. I had my shoulders against the wreck of my steamer, hauled up on the slope like a carcass of some big river animal. The smell of mud, of primeval mud, by Jove! was in my nostrils, the high stillness of primeval forest was before my eyes; there were shiny patches on the black creek. The moon had spread over everything a thin layer of silver—over the rank grass, over the mud, upon the wall of matted vegetation standing higher than the wall of a temple, over the great river I could see through a sombre gap glittering, glittering, as it flowed broadly by without a murmur. All this was great, expectant, mute, while the man jabbered about himself. I wondered whether the stillness on the face of the immensity looking at us two were meant as an appeal or as a menace. What were we who had strayed in here? Could we handle that dumb thing, or would it handle us? I felt how big, how confoundedly big, was that thing that couldn't talk, and perhaps was deaf as well. What was in there? I could see a little ivory coming out from there, and I had heard Mr. Kurtz was in there. I had heard enough about it, too—God knows! Yet somehow it didn't bring any image with it—no more than if I had been told an angel or a fiend was in there. I believed it in the same way one of you might believe there are inhabitants in the planet Mars. I knew once a Scotch sailmaker who was certain, dead sure, there were people in Mars. If you asked him for some idea how they looked and behaved, he would get shy and mutter something about 'walking on all-fours.' If you as much as smiled, he would—though a man of sixty—offer to fight you. I would not have gone so far as to fight for Kurtz, but I went for him near enough to a lie. You know I hate, detest, and can't bear a lie, not because I am straighter than the rest of us, but simply because it appalls me. There is a taint of death, a flavour of mortality in lies—which is exactly what I hate and detest in the world—what I want to forget. It makes me miserable and sick, like biting something rotten would do. Temperament, I suppose. Well, I went near enough to it by letting the young fool there believe anything he liked to imagine as to my influence in Europe. I became in an instant as much of a pretence as the rest of the bewitched pilgrims. This simply because I had a notion it somehow would be of help to that Kurtz whom at the time I did not see—you understand. He was just a word for me. I did not see the man in the name any more than you do. Do you see him? Do you see the story? Do you see anything? It seems to me I am trying to tell you a dream—making a vain attempt, because no relation of a dream can convey the dream-sensation, that commingling of absurdity, surprise, and bewilderment in a tremor of struggling revolt, that notion of being captured by the incredible which is of the very essence of dreams. . . ."

He was silent for a while.

". . . No, it is impossible; it is impossible to convey the life-sensation of any given epoch of one's existence—that which makes its truth, its meaning—its subtle and penetrating essence. It is impossible. We live as we dream—alone. . . ."

He paused again as if reflecting, then added—

"Of course in this you fellows see more than I could then. You see me, whom you know. . . ."

It had become so pitch dark that we listeners could hardly see one another. For a long time already he, sitting apart, had been no more to us than a voice. There was not a word from anybody. The others might have been asleep, but I was awake. I listened, I listened on the watch for the sentence, for the word, that would give me the clue to the faint uneasiness inspired by this narrative that seemed to shape itself without human lips in the heavy night-air of the river.

". . . Yes—I let him run on," Marlow began again, "and think what he pleased about the powers that were behind me. I did! And there was nothing behind me! There was nothing but that wretched, old, mangled steamboat I was leaning against, while he talked fluently about 'the necessity for every man to get on.' 'And when one comes out here, you conceive, it is not to gaze at the moon.' Mr. Kurtz was a 'universal genius,' but even a genius would find it easier to work with 'adequate tools—intelligent men.' He did not make bricks—why, there was a physical impossibility in the way—as I was well aware; and if he did secretarial work for the manager, it was because 'no sensible man rejects wantonly the confidence of his superiors.' Did I see it? I saw it. What more did I want? What I really wanted was rivets, by heaven! Rivets. To get on with the work—to stop the hole. Rivets I wanted. There were cases of them down at the coast—cases—piled up—burst—split! You kicked a loose rivet at every second step in that station yard on the hillside. Rivets had rolled into the grove of death. You could fill your pockets with rivets for the trouble of stooping down—and there wasn't one rivet to be found where it was wanted. We had plates that would do, but nothing to fasten them with. And every week the messenger, a lone negro, letter-bag on shoulder and staff in hand, left our station for the coast. And several times a week a coast caravan came in with trade goods—ghastly glazed calico that made you shudder only to look at it, glass beads value about a penny a quart, confounded spotted cotton handkerchiefs. And no rivets. Three carriers could have brought all that was wanted to set that steamboat afloat.

"He was becoming confidential now, but I fancy my unresponsive attitude must have exasperated him at last, for he judged it necessary to inform me he feared neither God nor devil, let alone any mere man. I said I could see that very well, but what I wanted was a certain quantity of rivets — and rivets were what really Mr. Kurtz wanted, if he had only known it. Now letters went to the coast every week. . . . 'My dear sir,' he cried, 'I write from dictation.' I demanded rivets. There was a way — for an intelligent man. He changed his manner; became very cold, and suddenly began to talk about a hippopotamus; wondered whether sleeping on board the steamer (I stuck to my salvage night and day) I wasn't disturbed. There was an old hippo that had the bad habit of getting out on the bank and roaming at night over the station grounds. The pilgrims used to turn out in a body and empty every rifle they could lay hands on at him. Some even had sat up o' nights for him. All this energy was wasted, though. 'That animal has a charmed life,' he said; 'but you can say this only of brutes in this country. No man — you apprehend me? — no man here bears a charmed life.' He stood there for a moment in the moonlight with his delicate hooked nose set a little askew, and his mica eyes glittering without a wink, then, with a curt Good-night, he strode off. I could see he was disturbed and considerably puzzled, which made me feel more hopeful than I had been for days. It was a great comfort to turn from that chap to my influential friend, the battered, twisted, ruined, tin-pot steamboat. I clambered on board. She rang under my feet like an empty Huntley & Palmer biscuit-tin kicked along a gutter; she was nothing so solid in make, and rather less pretty in shape, but I had expended enough hard work on her to make me love her. No influential friend would have served me better. She had given me a chance to come out a bit — to find out what I could do. No, I don't like work. I had rather laze about and think of all the fine things that can be done. I don't like work — no man does — but I like what is in the work, — the chance to find yourself. Your own reality — for yourself, not for others — what no other man can ever know. They can only see the mere show, and never can tell what it really means.

"I was not surprised to see somebody sitting aft, on the deck, with his legs dangling over the mud. You see I rather chummed with the few mechanics there were in that station, whom the other pilgrims naturally despised — on account of their imperfect manners, I suppose. This was the foreman—a boiler-maker by trade—a good worker. He was a lank, bony, yellow-faced man, with big intense eyes. His aspect was worried, and his head was as bald as the palm of my hand; but his hair in falling seemed to have stuck to his chin, and had prospered in the new locality, for his beard hung down to his waist. He was a widower with six young children (he had left them in charge of a sister of his to come out there), and the passion of his life was pigeon-flying. He was an enthusiast and a connoisseur. He would rave about pigeons. After work hours he used sometimes to come over from his hut for a talk about his children and his pigeons; at work, when he had to crawl in the mud under the bottom of the steamboat, he would tie up that beard of his in a kind of white serviette[18] he brought for the purpose. It had loops to go over his ears. In the evening

---

[18] **serviette:** A napkin.

he could be seen squatted on the bank rinsing that wrapper in the creek with great care, then spreading it solemnly on a bush to dry.

"I slapped him on the back and shouted, 'We shall have rivets!' He scrambled to his feet exclaiming, 'No! Rivets!' as though he couldn't believe his ears. Then in a low voice, 'You . . . eh?' I don't know why we behaved like lunatics. I put my finger to the side of my nose and nodded mysteriously. 'Good for you!' he cried, snapped his fingers above his head, lifting one foot. I tried a jig. We capered on the iron deck. A frightful clatter came out of that hulk, and the virgin forest on the other bank of the creek sent it back in a thundering roll upon the sleeping station. It must have made some of the pilgrims sit up in their hovels. A dark figure obscured the lighted doorway of the manager's hut, vanished, then, a second or so after, the doorway itself vanished, too. We stopped, and the silence driven away by the stamping of our feet flowed back again from the recesses of the land. The great wall of vegetation, an exuberant and entangled mass of trunks, branches, leaves, boughs, festoons, motionless in the moonlight, was like a rioting invasion of soundless life, a rolling wave of plants, piled up, crested, ready to topple over the creek, to sweep every little man of us out of his little existence. And it moved not. A deadened burst of mighty splashes and snorts reached us from afar, as though an ichthyosaurus had been taking a bath of glitter in the great river. 'After all,' said the boiler-maker in a reasonable tone, 'why shouldn't we get the rivets?' Why not, indeed! I did not know of any reason why we shouldn't. 'They'll come in three weeks,' I said, confidently.

"But they didn't. Instead of rivets there came an invasion, an infliction, a visitation. It came in sections during the next three weeks, each section headed by a donkey carrying a white man in new clothes and tan shoes, bowing from that elevation right and left to the impressed pilgrims. A quarrelsome band of footsore sulky niggers trod on the heels of the donkey; a lot of tents, camp-stools, tin boxes, white cases, brown bales would be shot down in the courtyard, and the air of mystery would deepen a little over the muddle of the station. Five such instalments came, with their absurd air of disorderly flight with the loot of innumerable outfit shops and provision stores, that, one would think, they were lugging, after a raid, into the wilderness for equitable division. It was an inextricable mess of things decent in themselves but that human folly made look like the spoils of thieving.

"This devoted band called itself the Eldorado Exploring Expedition, and I believe they were sworn to secrecy. Their talk, however, was the talk of sordid buccaneers: it was reckless without hardihood, greedy without audacity, and cruel without courage; there was not an atom of foresight or of serious intention in the whole batch of them, and they did not seem aware these things are wanted for the work of the world. To tear treasure out of the bowels of the land was their desire, with no more moral purpose at the back of it than there is in burglars breaking into a safe. Who paid the expenses of the noble enterprise I don't know; but the uncle of our manager was leader of that lot.

"In exterior he resembled a butcher in a poor neighbourhood, and his eyes had a look of sleepy cunning. He carried his fat paunch with ostentation on his short legs, and during the time his gang infested the station spoke to no one but his nephew. You could see these two roaming about all day long with their heads close together in an everlasting confab.

"I had given up worrying myself about the rivets. One's capacity for that kind of folly is more limited than you would suppose. I said Hang!—and let things slide. I had plenty of time for meditation, and now and then I would give some thought to Kurtz. I wasn't very interested in him. No. Still, I was curious to see whether this man, who had come out equipped with moral ideas of some sort, would climb to the top after all and how he would set about his work when there.'"

2

"One evening as I was lying flat on the deck of my steamboat, I heard voices approaching—and there were the nephew and the uncle strolling along the bank. I laid my head on my arm again, and had nearly lost myself in a doze, when somebody said in my ear, as it were: 'I am as harmless as a little child, but I don't like to be dictated to. Am I the manager—or am I not? I was ordered to send him there. It's incredible.' . . . I became aware that the two were standing on the shore alongside the forepart of the steamboat, just below my head. I did not move; it did not occur to me to move: I was sleepy. 'It *is* unpleasant,' grunted the uncle. 'He has asked the Administration to be sent there,' said the other, 'with the idea of showing what he could do; and I was instructed accordingly. Look at the influence that man must have. Is it not frightful?' They both agreed it was frightful, then made several bizarre remarks: 'Make rain and fine weather—one man—the Council—by the nose'—bits of absurd sentences that got the better of my drowsiness, so that I had pretty near the whole of my wits about me when the uncle said, 'The climate may do away with this difficulty for you. Is he alone there?' 'Yes,' answered the manager; 'he sent his assistant down the river with a note to me in these terms: "Clear this poor devil out of the country, and don't bother sending more of that sort. I had rather be alone than have the kind of men you can dispose of with me." It was more than a year ago. Can you imagine such impudence!' 'Anything since then?' asked the other, hoarsely. 'Ivory,' jerked the nephew; 'lots of it—prime sort—lots—most annoying, from him.' 'And with that?' questioned the heavy rumble. 'Invoice,' was the reply fired out, so to speak. Then silence. They had been talking about Kurtz.

"I was broad awake by this time, but, lying perfectly at ease, remained still, having no inducement to change my position. 'How did that ivory come all this way?' growled the elder man, who seemed very vexed. The other explained that it had come with a fleet of canoes in charge of an English half-caste clerk Kurtz had with him; that Kurtz had apparently intended to return himself, the station being by that time bare of goods and stores, but after coming three hundred miles, had suddenly decided to go back, which he started to do alone in a small dugout with four paddlers, leaving the half-caste to continue down the river with the ivory. The two fellows there seemed astounded at anybody attempting such a thing. They were at a loss for an adequate motive. As to me, I seemed to see Kurtz for the first time. It was a distinct glimpse: the dugout, four paddling savages, and the lone white man turning his back suddenly on the headquarters, on relief, on thoughts of home—perhaps; setting his face towards the depths of the wilderness, towards his empty and desolate station. I did not know the motive. Perhaps he was just simply a fine fellow who stuck to his work for its own sake. His name, you understand, had not been pronounced once. He was 'that man.' The half-caste, who, as far as I could see, had conducted a difficult trip with great prudence and pluck, was invariably alluded to as 'that scoundrel.' The 'scoundrel' had reported that the 'man' had been very ill—had recovered imperfectly. . . . The two below me moved away then a few paces, and strolled back and forth at some little distance. I heard: 'Military post—doctor—two hundred miles—quite alone now—unavoidable delays—nine months—no news—strange rumours.' They approached again, just as the manager was saying, 'No one, as far as I know, unless a species of wandering trader—a pestilential fellow, snapping ivory from the natives.' Who was it they were talking about now? I gathered in snatches that this was some man supposed to be in Kurtz's district, and of whom the manager did not approve. 'We will not be free from unfair competition till one of these fellows is hanged for an example,' he said. 'Certainly,' grunted the other; 'get him hanged! Why not? Anything—anything can be done in this country. That's what I say; nobody here, you understand, *here*, can endanger your position. And why? You stand the climate—you outlast them all. The danger is in Europe; but there before I left I took care to——' They moved off and whispered, then their voices rose again. 'The extraordinary series of delays is not my fault. I did my best.' The fat man sighed. 'Very sad.' 'And the pestiferous absurdity of his talk,' continued the other; 'he bothered me enough when he was here. "Each station should be like a beacon on the road towards better things, a centre for trade of course, but also for humanizing, improving, instructing." Conceive you—that ass! And he wants to be manager! No, it's——' Here he got choked by excessive indignation, and I lifted my head the least bit. I was surprised to see how near they were—right under me. I could have spat upon their hats. They were looking on the ground, absorbed in thought. The manager was switching his leg with a slender twig: his sagacious relative lifted his head. 'You have been well since you came out this time?' he asked. The other gave a start. 'Who? I? Oh! Like a charm—like a charm. But the rest—oh, my goodness! All sick. They die so quick, too, that I haven't the time to send them out of the country—it's incredible!' 'H'm. Just so,' grunted the uncle. 'Ah! my boy, trust to this—I say, trust to this.' I saw him extend his short flipper of an arm for a gesture that took in the forest, the creek, the mud, the river,—seemed to beckon with a dishonouring flourish before the sunlit face of the land a treacherous appeal to the lurking death, to the hidden evil, to the profound darkness of its heart. It was so startling that I leaped to my feet and looked back at the edge of the forest, as though I had expected an answer of some sort to that black display of confidence. You know the foolish notions that come to one sometimes. The high stillness confronted these two figures with its ominous patience, waiting for the passing away of a fantastic invasion.

"They swore aloud together—out of sheer fright, I believe—then pretending not to know anything of my existence, turned back to the station. The sun was low; and leaning forward side by side, they seemed to be tugging painfully uphill their two ridiculous shadows of unequal length, that trailed behind them slowly over the tall grass without bending a single blade.

"In a few days the Eldorado Expedition went into the patient wilderness, that closed upon it as the sea closes over a diver. Long afterwards the news came that all the donkeys were dead. I know nothing as to the fate of the less valuable animals. They, no doubt, like the rest of us, found what they deserved. I did not inquire. I was then rather excited at the prospect of meeting Kurtz very soon. When I say very soon I mean it comparatively. It was just two months from the day we left the creek when we came to the bank below Kurtz's station.

"Going up that river was like travelling back to the earliest beginnings of the world, when vegetation rioted on the earth and the big trees were kings. An empty stream, a great silence, an impenetrable forest. The air was warm, thick, heavy, sluggish. There was no joy in the brilliance of sunshine. The long stretches of the waterway ran on, deserted, into the gloom of overshadowed distances. On silvery sandbanks hippos and alligators sunned themselves side by side. The broadening waters flowed through a mob of wooded islands; you lost your way on that river as you would in a desert, and butted all day long against shoals, trying to find the channel, till you thought yourself bewitched and cut off for ever from everything you had known once—somewhere—far away—in another existence perhaps. There were moments when one's past came back to one, as it will sometimes when you have not a moment to spare to yourself; but it came in the shape of an unrestful and noisy dream, remembered with wonder amongst the overwhelming realities of this strange world of plants, and water, and silence. And this stillness of life did not in the least resemble a peace. It was the stillness of an implacable force brooding over an inscrutable intention. It looked at you with a vengeful aspect. I got used to it afterwards; I did not see it any more; I had no time. I had to keep guessing at the channel; I had to discern, mostly by inspiration, the signs of hidden banks; I watched for sunken stones; I was learning to clap my teeth smartly before my heart flew out, when I shaved by a fluke some infernal sly old snag that would have ripped the life out of the tin-pot steamboat and drowned all the pilgrims; I had to keep a look-out for the signs of dead wood we could cut up in the night for next day's steaming. When you have to attend to things of that sort, to the mere incidents of the surface, the reality—the reality, I tell you—fades. The inner truth is hidden—luckily, luckily. But I felt it all the same; I felt often its mysterious stillness watching me at my monkey tricks, just as it watches you fellows performing on your respective tightropes for—what is it? half-a-crown a tumble——"

"Try to be civil, Marlow," growled a voice, and I knew there was at least one listener awake besides myself.

"I beg your pardon. I forgot the heartache which makes up the rest of the price. And indeed what does the price matter, if the trick be well done? You do your tricks very well. And I didn't do badly either, since I managed not to sink that steamboat on my first trip. It's a wonder to me yet. Imagine a blindfolded man set to drive a van over a bad road. I sweated and shivered over that business considerably, I can tell you. After all, for a seaman, to scrape the bottom of the thing that's supposed to float all the time under his care is the unpardonable sin. No one may know of it, but you never forget the thump—eh? A blow on the very heart. You remember it, you dream of it, you wake up at night and think of it—years after—and go hot and cold all over. I don't pretend to say that steamboat floated all the time. More than once she had to wade for a bit, with twenty cannibals splashing around and pushing. We had enlisted some of these chaps on the way for a crew. Fine fellows—cannibals—in their place. They were men one could work with, and I am grateful to them. And, after all, they did not eat each other before my face: they had brought along a provision of hippo-meat which went rotten, and made the mystery of the wilderness stink in my nostrils. Phoo! I can sniff it now. I had the manager on board and three or four pilgrims with their staves—all complete. Sometimes we came upon a station close by the bank, clinging to the skirts of the unknown, and the white men rushing out of a tumble-down hovel, with great gestures of joy and surprise and welcome, seemed very strange—had the appearance of being held there captive by a spell. The word ivory would ring in the air for a while—and on we went again into the silence, along empty reaches, round the still bends, between the high walls of our winding way, reverberating in hollow claps the ponderous beat of the stern-wheel. Trees, trees, millions of trees, massive, immense, running up high; and at their foot, hugging the bank against the stream, crept the little begrimed steamboat, like a sluggish beetle crawling on the floor of a lofty portico. It made you feel very small, very lost, and yet it was not altogether depressing, that feeling. After all, if you were small, the grimy beetle crawled on—which was just what you wanted it to do. Where the pilgrims imagined it crawled to I don't know. To some place where they expected to get something, I bet! For me it crawled towards Kurtz—exclusively; but when the steampipes started leaking we crawled very slow. The reaches opened before us and closed behind, as if the forest had stepped leisurely across the water to bar the way for our return. We penetrated deeper and deeper into the heart of darkness. It was very quiet there. At night sometimes the roll of drums behind the curtain of trees would run up the river and remain sustained faintly, as if hovering in the air high over our heads, till the first break of day. Whether it meant war, peace, or prayer we could not tell. The dawns were heralded by the descent of a chill stillness; the wood-cutters slept, their fires burned low; the snapping of a twig would make you start. We were wanderers on a prehistoric earth, on an earth that wore the aspect of an unknown planet. We could have fancied ourselves the first of men taking possession of an accursed inheritance, to be subdued at the cost of profound anguish and of excessive toil. But suddenly, as we struggled round a bend, there would be a glimpse of rush walls, of peaked grass-roofs, a burst of yells, a whirl of black limbs, a mass of hands clapping, of feet stamping, of bodies swaying, of eyes rolling, under the droop of heavy and motionless foliage. The steamer toiled along slowly on the edge of a black and incomprehensible frenzy. The prehistoric man was cursing us, praying to us, welcoming us—who could tell? We were cut off from the comprehension of our surroundings; we glided past like phantoms, wondering and secretly appalled, as sane men would be before an enthusiastic outbreak in a madhouse. We could not understand because we were too far and could not remember, because we were travelling in the night of first ages, of those ages that are gone, leaving hardly a sign—and no memories.

"The earth seemed unearthly. We are accustomed to look upon the shackled form of a conquered monster, but there—there you could look at a thing monstrous and free. It was unearthly, and the men were—— No, they were not inhuman. Well, you know, that was the worst of it—this suspicion of their not being inhuman. It would come slowly to one. They howled and leaped, and spun, and made horrid faces; but what thrilled you was just the thought of their humanity—like yours—the thought of your remote kinship with this wild and passionate uproar. Ugly. Yes, it was ugly enough; but if you were man enough you would admit to yourself that there was in you just the faintest trace of a response to the terrible frankness of that noise, a dim suspicion of there being a meaning in it which you—you so remote from the night of first ages—could comprehend. And why not? The mind of man is capable of any-thing—because everything is in it, all the past as well as all the future. What was there after all? Joy, fear, sorrow, devotion, valour, rage—who can tell?—but truth—truth stripped of its cloak of time. Let the fool gape and shudder—the man knows, and can look on without a wink. But he must at least be as much of a man as these on the shore. He must meet that truth with his own true stuff—with his own inborn strength. Principles won't do. Acquisitions, clothes, pretty rags—rags that would fly off at the first good shake. No; you want a deliberate belief. An appeal to me in this fiendish row—is there? Very well; I hear; I admit, but I have a voice, too, and for good or evil mine is the speech that cannot be silenced. Of course, a fool, what with sheer fright and fine sentiments, is always safe. Who's that grunting? You wonder I didn't go ashore for a howl and a dance? Well, no—I didn't. Fine sentiments, you say? Fine sen-timents, be hanged! I had no time. I had to mess about with white-lead and strips of woollen blanket helping to put bandages on those leaky steam-pipes—I tell you. I had to watch the steering, and circumvent those snags, and get the tin-pot along by hook or by crook. There was surface-truth enough in these things to save a wiser man. And between whiles I had to look after the savage who was fireman. He was an improved specimen; he could fire up a vertical boiler. He was there below me, and, upon my word, to look at him was as edifying as seeing a dog in a parody of breeches and a feather hat, walking on his hind-legs. A few months of training had done for that really fine chap. He squinted at the steam-gauge and at the water-gauge with an evident effort of intrepidity—and he had filed teeth, too, the poor devil, and the wool of his pate shaved into queer patterns, and three ornamental scars on each of his cheeks. He ought to have been clapping his hands and stamping his feet on the bank, instead of which he was hard at work, a thrall to strange witchcraft, full of improving knowledge. He was useful because he had been instructed; and what he knew was this—that should the water in that transparent thing disappear, the evil spirit inside the boiler would get angry through the greatness of his thirst, and take a terrible vengeance. So he sweated and fired up and watched the glass fearfully (with an impromptu charm, made of rags, tied to his arm, and a piece of polished bone, as big as a watch, stuck flat-ways through his lower lip), while the wooded banks slipped past us slowly, the short noise was left behind, the interminable miles of silence—and we crept on, towards Kurtz. But the snags were thick, the water was treacherous and shallow, the boiler seemed indeed to have a sulky devil in it, and thus neither that fire-man nor I had any time to peer into our creepy thoughts.

"Some fifty miles below the Inner Station we came upon a hut of reeds, an inclined and melancholy pole, with the unrecognizable tatters of what had been a flag of some sort flying from it, and a neatly stacked wood-pile. This was unexpected. We came to the bank, and on the stack of firewood found a flat piece of board with some faded pencil-writing on it. When deciphered it said: 'Wood for you. Hurry up. Approach cautiously.' There was a signature, but it was illegible—not Kurtz—a much longer word. 'Hurry up.' Where? Up the river? 'Approach cautiously.' We had not done so. But the warning could not have been meant for the place where it could be only found after approach. Something was wrong above. But what—and how much? That was the question. We commented adversely upon the imbecility of that telegraphic style. The bush around said nothing, and would not let us look very far, either. A torn curtain of red twill hung in the doorway of the hut, and flapped sadly in our faces. The dwelling was dismantled; but we could see a white man had lived there not very long ago. There remained a rude table—a plank on two posts; a heap of rubbish reposed in a dark corner, and by the door I picked up a book. It had lost its covers, and the pages had been thumbed into a state of extremely dirty softness; but the back had been lovingly stitched afresh with white cotton thread, which looked clean yet. It was an extraordinary find. Its title was, *An Inquiry into some Points of Seamanship,* by a man Towser, Towson—some such name—Master in his Majesty's Navy. The matter looked dreary reading enough, with illustrative diagrams and repulsive tables of figures, and the copy was sixty years old. I handled this amazing antiquity with the greatest possible tenderness, lest it should dissolve in my hands. Within, Towson or Towser was inquiring earnestly into the breaking strain of ships' chains and tackle, and other such matters. Not a very enthralling book; but at the first glance you could see there a singleness of intention, an honest concern for the right way of going to work, which made these humble pages, thought out so many years ago, luminous with another than a professional light. The simple old sailor, with his talk of chains and purchases,[19] made me forget the jungle and the pilgrims in a delicious sensation of having come upon something unmistakably real. Such a book being there was wonderful enough; but still more astounding were the notes pencilled in the margin, and plainly referring to the text. I couldn't believe my eyes! They were in cipher! Yes, it looked like cipher. Fancy a man lugging with him a book of that description into this nowhere and studying it—and making notes—in cipher at that! It was an extravagant mystery.

"I had been dimly aware for some time of a worrying noise, and when I lifted my eyes I saw the wood-pile was gone, and the manager, aided by all the pilgrims, was shouting at me from the river-side. I slipped the book into my pocket. I assure you to leave off reading was like tearing myself away from the shelter of an old and solid friendship.

"I started the lame engine ahead. 'It must be this miserable trader—this intruder,' exclaimed the manager, looking back malevolently at the place we had left. 'He must be English,' I said. 'It will not save him from getting into trouble if he is not

---

[19] **purchases:** Tackles or levers or similar mechanical devices.

careful,' muttered the manager darkly. I observed with assumed innocence that no man was safe from trouble in this world.

"The current was more rapid now, the steamer seemed at her last gasp, the stern-wheel flopped languidly, and I caught myself listening on tiptoe for the next beat of the boat, for in sober truth I expected the wretched thing to give up every moment. It was like watching the last flickers of a life. But still we crawled. Sometimes I would pick out a tree a little way ahead to measure our progress towards Kurtz by, but I lost it invariably before we got abreast. To keep the eyes so long on one thing was too much for human patience. The manager displayed a beautiful resignation. I fretted and fumed and took to arguing with myself whether or no I would talk openly with Kurtz; but before I could come to any conclusion it occurred to me that my speech or my silence, indeed any action of mine, would be a mere futility. What did it matter what any one knew or ignored? What did it matter who was manager? One gets sometimes such a flash of insight. The essentials of this affair lay deep under the surface, beyond my reach, and beyond my power of meddling.

"Towards the evening of the second day we judged ourselves about eight miles from Kurtz's station. I wanted to push on; but the manager looked grave, and told me the navigation up there was so dangerous that it would be advisable, the sun being very low already, to wait where we were till next morning. Moreover, he pointed out that if the warning to approach cautiously were to be followed, we must approach in daylight — not at dusk, or in the dark. This was sensible enough. Eight miles meant nearly three hours' steaming for us, and I could also see suspicious ripples at the upper end of the reach. Nevertheless, I was annoyed beyond expression at the delay, and most unreasonably, too, since one night more could not matter much after so many months. As we had plenty of wood, and caution was the word, I brought up in the middle of the stream. The reach was narrow, straight, with high sides like a railway cutting. The dusk came gliding into it long before the sun had set. The current ran smooth and swift, but a dumb immobility sat on the banks. The living trees, lashed together by the creepers and every living bush of the undergrowth, might have been changed into stone, even to the slenderest twig, to the lightest leaf. It was not sleep — it seemed unnatural, like a state of trance. Not the faintest sound of any kind could be heard. You looked on amazed, and began to suspect yourself of being deaf — then the night came suddenly, and struck you blind as well. About three in the morning some large fish leaped, and the loud splash made me jump as though a gun had been fired. When the sun rose there was a white fog, very warm and clammy, and more blinding than the night. It did not shift or drive; it was just there, standing all round you like something solid. At eight or nine, perhaps, it lifted as a shutter lifts. We had a glimpse of the towering multitude of trees, of the immense matted jungle, with the blazing little ball of the sun hanging over it — all perfectly still — and then the white shutter came down again, smoothly, as if sliding in greased grooves. I ordered the chain, which we had begun to heave in, to be paid out again. Before it stopped running with a muffled rattle, a cry, a very loud cry, as of infinite desolation, soared slowly in the opaque air. It ceased. A complaining clamour, modulated in savage discords, filled our ears. The sheer unexpectedness of it made my hair stir under my cap. I don't know how it struck the others: to me it seemed as though the mist itself had screamed, so suddenly, and apparently from all sides at once, did this tumultuous and mournful uproar arise. It culminated in a hurried outbreak of almost intolerably excessive shrieking, which stopped short, leaving us stiffened in a variety of silly attitudes, and obstinately listening to the nearly as appalling and excessive silence. 'Good God! What is the meaning——' stammered at my elbow one of the pilgrims,—a little fat man, with sandy hair and red whiskers, who wore side-spring boots, and pink pyjamas tucked into his socks. Two others remained open-mouthed a whole minute, then dashed into the little cabin, to rush out incontinently and stand darting scared glances, with Winchesters at 'ready' in their hands. What we could see was just the steamer we were on, her outlines blurred as though she had been on the point of dissolving, and a misty strip of water, perhaps two feet broad, around her—and that was all. The rest of the world was nowhere, as far as our eyes and ears were concerned. Just nowhere. Gone, disappeared; swept off without leaving a whisper or a shadow behind.

"I went forward, and ordered the chain to be hauled in short, so as to be ready to trip the anchor and move the steamboat at once if necessary. 'Will they attack?' whispered an awed voice. 'We will be all butchered in this fog,' murmured another. The faces twitched with the strain, the hands trembled slightly, the eyes forgot to wink. It was very curious to see the contrast of expressions of the white men and of the black fellows of our crew, who were as much strangers to that part of the river as we, though their homes were only eight hundred miles away. The whites, of course greatly discomposed, had besides a curious look of being painfully shocked by such an outrageous row. The others had an alert, naturally interested expression; but their faces were essentially quiet, even those of the one or two who grinned as they hauled at the chain. Several exchanged short, grunting phrases, which seemed to settle the matter to their satisfaction. Their headman, a young, broad-chested black, severely draped in dark-blue fringed cloths, with fierce nostrils and his hair all done up artfully in oily ringlets, stood near me. 'Aha!' I said, just for good fellowship's sake. 'Catch 'im,' he snapped, with a bloodshot widening of his eyes and a flash of sharp teeth—'catch 'im. Give 'im to us.' 'To you, eh?' I asked; 'what would you do with them?' 'Eat 'im!' he said, curtly, and, leaning his elbow on the rail, looked out into the fog in a dignified and profoundly pensive attitude. I would no doubt have been properly horrified, had it not occurred to me that he and his chaps must be very hungry: that they must have been growing increasingly hungry for at least this month past. They had been engaged for six months (I don't think a single one of them had any clear idea of time, as we at the end of countless ages have. They still belonged to the beginnings of time—had no inherited experience to teach them as it were), and of course, as long as there was a piece of paper written over in accordance with some farcical law or other made down the river, it didn't enter anybody's head to trouble how they would live. Certainly they had brought with them some rotten hippo-meat, which couldn't have lasted very long, anyway, even if the pilgrims hadn't, in the midst of a shocking hullabaloo, thrown a considerable quantity of it overboard. It looked like a high-handed proceeding; but it was really a case of legitimate self-defence. You can't breathe dead hippo waking, sleeping, and eating, and at the same time keep your precarious grip on existence. Besides that, they had given them every week three pieces of brass wire, each about nine inches long; and the theory was they were to buy their provisions with that currency in river-side villages. You can see how *that* worked. There were either no villages, or the people were hostile, or the director, who like the rest of us fed out of tins, with an occasional old he-goat thrown in, didn't want to stop the steamer for some more or less recondite reason. So, unless they swallowed the wire itself, or made loops of it to snare the fishes with, I don't see what good their extravagant salary could be to them. I must say it was paid with a regularity worthy of a large and honourable trading company. For the rest, the only thing to eat — though it didn't look eatable in the least — I saw in their possession was a few lumps of some stuff like half-cooked dough, of a dirty lavender colour, they kept wrapped in leaves, and now and then swallowed a piece of, but so small that it seemed done more for the looks of the thing than for any serious purpose of sustenance. Why in the name of all the gnawing devils of hunger they didn't go for us — they were thirty to five — and have a good tuck-in[20] for once, amazes me now when I think of it. They were big powerful men, with not much capacity to weigh the consequences, with courage, with strength, even yet, though their skins were no longer glossy and their muscles no longer hard. And I saw that something restraining, one of those human secrets that baffle probability, had come into play there. I looked at them with a swift quickening of interest — not because it occurred to me I might be eaten by them before very long, though I own to you that just then I perceived — in a new light, as it were — how unwholesome the pilgrims looked, and I hoped, yes I positively hoped, that my aspect was not so — what shall I say? — so — unappetizing: a touch of fantastic vanity which fitted well with the dream-sensation that pervaded all my days at that time. Perhaps I had a little fever, too. One can't live with one's finger everlastingly on one's pulse. I had often 'a little fever,' or a little touch of other things — the playful paw-strokes of the wilderness, the preliminary trifling before the more serious onslaught which came in due course. Yes; I looked at them as you would on any human being, with a curiosity of their impulses, motives, capacities, weaknesses, when brought to the test of an inexorable physical necessity. Restraint! What possible restraint? Was it superstition, disgust, patience, fear — or some kind of primitive honour? No fear can stand up to hunger, no patience can wear it out, disgust simply does not exist where hunger is; and as to superstition, beliefs, and what you may call principles, they are less than chaff in a breeze. Don't you know the devilry of lingering starvation, its exasperating torment, its black thoughts, its sombre and brooding ferocity? Well, I do. It takes a man all his inborn strength to fight hunger properly. It's really easier to face bereavement, dishonour, and the perdition of one's soul — than this kind of prolonged hunger. Sad, but true. And these chaps, too, had no earthly reason for any kind of scruple. Restraint! I would just as soon have expected restraint from a hyena prowling amongst the corpses of a battlefield. But there was the fact facing me — the fact dazzling, to be seen, like the foam on the depths of the sea, like a ripple on an unfathomable enigma, a mystery greater — when I thought of it — than the curious,

---

[20] **tuck-in:** A hearty meal.

inexplicable note of desperate grief in this savage clamour that had swept by us on the river-bank, behind the blind whiteness of the fog.

"Two pilgrims were quarrelling in hurried whispers as to which bank. 'Left.' 'No, no; how can you? Right, right, of course.' 'It is very serious,' said the manager's voice behind me; 'I would be desolated if anything should happen to Mr. Kurtz before we came up.' I looked at him, and had not the slightest doubt he was sincere. He was just the kind of man who would wish to preserve appearances. That was his restraint. But when he muttered something about going on at once, I did not even take the trouble to answer him. I knew, and he knew, that it was impossible. Were we to let go our hold of the bottom, we would be absolutely in the air — in space. We wouldn't be able to tell where we were going to — whether up or down stream, or across — till we fetched against one bank or the other, — and then we wouldn't know at first which it was. Of course I made no move. I had no mind for a smash-up. You couldn't imagine a more deadly place for a shipwreck. Whether drowned at once or not, we were sure to perish speedily in one way or another. 'I authorize you to take all the risks,' he said, after a short silence. 'I refuse to take any,' I said, shortly; which was just the answer he expected, though its tone might have surprised him. 'Well, I must defer to your judgment. You are captain,' he said, with marked civility. I turned my shoulder to him in sign of my appreciation, and looked into the fog. How long would it last? It was the most hopeless look-out. The approach to this Kurtz grubbing for ivory in the wretched bush was beset by as many dangers as though he had been an enchanted princess sleeping in a fabulous castle. 'Will they attack, do you think?' asked the manager, in a confidential tone.

"I did not think they would attack, for several obvious reasons. The thick fog was one. If they left the bank in their canoes they would get lost in it, as we would be if we attempted to move. Still, I had also judged the jungle of both banks quite impenetrable — and yet eyes were in it, eyes that had seen us. The river-side bushes were certainly very thick; but the undergrowth behind was evidently penetrable. However, during the short lift I had seen no canoes anywhere in the reach — certainly not abreast of the steamer. But what made the idea of attack inconceivable to me was the nature of the noise — of the cries we had heard. They had not the fierce character boding immediate hostile intention. Unexpected, wild, and violent as they had been, they had given me an irresistible impression of sorrow. The glimpse of the steamboat had for some reason filled those savages with unrestrained grief. The danger, if any, I expounded, was from our proximity to a great human passion let loose. Even extreme grief may ultimately vent itself in violence — but more generally takes the form of apathy. . . .

"You should have seen the pilgrims stare! They had no heart to grin, or even to revile me: but I believe they thought me gone mad — with fright, maybe. I delivered a regular lecture. My dear boys, it was no good bothering. Keep a look-out? Well, you may guess I watched the fog for the signs of lifting as a cat watches a mouse; but for anything else our eyes were of no more use to us than if we had been buried miles deep in a heap of cotton-wool. It felt like it, too — choking, warm, stifling. Besides, all I said, though it sounded extravagant, was absolutely true to fact. What we afterwards alluded to as an attack was really an attempt at repulse. The action was very far from being aggressive—it was not even defensive, in the usual sense: it was undertaken under the stress of desperation, and in its essence was purely protective.

"It developed itself, I should say, two hours after the fog lifted, and its commencement was at a spot, roughly speaking, about a mile and a half below Kurtz's station. We had just floundered and flopped round a bend, when I saw an islet, a mere grassy hummock of bright green, in the middle of the stream. It was the only thing of the kind; but as we opened the reach more, I perceived it was the head of a long sandbank, or rather of a chain of shallow patches stretching down the middle of the river. They were discoloured, just awash, and the whole lot was seen just under the water, exactly as a man's backbone is seen running down the middle of his back under the skin. Now, as far as I did see, I could go to the right or to the left of this. I didn't know either channel, of course. The banks looked pretty well alike, the depth appeared the same; but as I had been informed the station was on the west side, I naturally headed for the western passage.

"No sooner had we fairly entered it than I became aware it was much narrower than I had supposed. To the left of us there was the long uninterrupted shoal, and to the right a high, steep bank heavily overgrown with bushes. Above the bush the trees stood in serried ranks. The twigs overhung the current thickly, and from distance to distance a large limb of some tree projected rigidly over the stream. It was then well on in the afternoon, the face of the forest was gloomy, and a broad strip of shadow had already fallen on the water. In this shadow we steamed up—very slowly, as you may imagine. I sheered her well inshore—the water being deepest near the bank, as the sounding-pole informed me.

"One of my hungry and forbearing friends was sounding in the bows just below me. This steamboat was exactly like a decked scow. On the deck, there were two little teak-wood houses, with doors and windows. The boiler was in the fore-end, and the machinery right astern. Over the whole there was a light roof, supported on stanchions. The funnel projected through that roof, and in front of the funnel a small cabin built of light planks served for a pilot-house. It contained a couch, two camp-stools, a loaded Martini-Henry[21] leaning in one corner, a tiny table, and the steering-wheel. It had a wide door in front and a broad shutter at each side. All these were always thrown open, of course. I spent my days perched up there on the extreme fore-end of that roof, before the door. At night I slept, or tried to, on the couch. An athletic black belonging to some coast tribe, and educated by my poor predecessor, was the helmsman. He sported a pair of brass earrings, wore a blue cloth wrapper from the waist to the ankles, and thought all the world of himself. He was the most unstable kind of fool I had ever seen. He steered with no end of a swagger while you were by; but if he lost sight of you, he became instantly the prey of an abject funk, and would let that cripple of a steamboat get the upper hand of him in a minute.

"I was looking down at the sounding-pole, and feeling much annoyed to see at each try a little more of it stick out of that river, when I saw my poleman give up the business suddenly, and stretch himself flat on the deck, without even taking the

---

[21] **Martini-Henry:** A powerful rifle.

trouble to haul his pole in. He kept hold on it though, and it trailed in the water. At the same time the fireman, whom I could also see below me, sat down abruptly before his furnace and ducked his head. I was amazed. Then I had to look at the river mighty quick, because there was a snag in the fairway. Sticks, little sticks, were flying about—thick: they were whizzing before my nose, dropping below me, striking behind me against my pilot-house. All this time the river, the shore, the woods, were very quiet—perfectly quiet. I could only hear the heavy splashing thump of the stern-wheel and the patter of these things. We cleared the snag clumsily. Arrows, by Jove! We were being shot at! I stepped in quickly to close the shutter on the land-side. That fool-helmsman, his hands on the spokes, was lifting his knees high, stamping his feet, champing his mouth, like a reined-in horse. Confound him! And we were staggering within ten feet of the bank. I had to lean right out to swing the heavy shutter, and I saw a face amongst the leaves on the level with my own, looking at me very fierce and steady; and then suddenly, as though a veil had been removed from my eyes, I made out, deep in the tangled gloom, naked breasts, arms, legs, glaring eyes,—the bush was swarming with human limbs in movement, glistening, of bronze colour. The twigs shook, swayed, and rustled, the arrows flew out of them, and then the shutter came to. 'Steer her straight,' I said to the helmsman. He held his head rigid, face forward; but his eyes rolled, he kept on lifting and setting down his feet gently, his mouth foamed a little. 'Keep quiet!' I said in a fury. I might just as well have ordered a tree not to sway in the wind. I darted out. Below me there was a great scuffle of feet on the iron deck; confused exclamations; a voice screamed, 'Can you turn back?' I caught sight of a V-shaped ripple on the water ahead. What? Another snag! A fusillade burst out under my feet. The pilgrims had opened with their Win- chesters, and were simply squirting lead into that bush. A deuce of a lot of smoke came up and drove slowly forward. I swore at it. Now I couldn't see the ripple or the snag either. I stood in the doorway, peering, and the arrows came in swarms. They might have been poisoned, but they looked as though they wouldn't kill a cat. The bush began to howl. Our wood-cutters raised a warlike whoop; the report of a rifle just at my back deafened me. I glanced over my shoulder, and the pilot-house was yet full of noise and smoke when I made a dash at the wheel. The fool-nigger had dropped everything, to throw the shutter open and let off that Martini-Henry. He stood before the wide opening, glaring, and I yelled at him to come back, while I straightened the sudden twist out of that steamboat. There was no room to turn even if I had wanted to, the snag was somewhere very near ahead in that confounded smoke, there was no time to lose, so I just crowded her into the bank—right into the bank, where I knew the water was deep.

"We tore slowly along the overhanging bushes in a whirl of broken twigs and flying leaves. The fusillade below stopped short, as I had foreseen it would when the squirts got empty. I threw my head back to a glinting whizz that traversed the pilot-house, in at one shutter-hole and out at the other. Looking past that mad helmsman, who was shaking the empty rifle and yelling at the shore, I saw vague forms of men running bent double, leaping, gliding, distinct, incomplete, evanescent. Something big appeared in the air before the shutter, the rifle went overboard, and the man stepped back swiftly, looked at me over his shoulder in an extraordinary, profound, familiar manner, and fell upon my feet. The side of his head hit the wheel twice, and the end of what appeared a long cane clattered round and knocked over a little camp-stool. It looked as though after wrenching that thing from somebody ashore he had lost his balance in the effort. The thin smoke had blown away, we were clear of the snag, and looking ahead I could see that in another hundred yards or so I would be free to sheer off, away from the bank; but my feet felt so very warm and wet that I had to look down. The man had rolled on his back and stared straight up at me; both his hands clutched that cane. It was the shaft of a spear that, either thrown or lunged through the opening, had caught him in the side just below the ribs; the blade had gone in out of sight, after making a frightful gash; my shoes were full; a pool of blood lay very still, gleaming dark-red under the wheel; his eyes shone with an amazing lustre. The fusillade burst out again. He looked at me anxiously, gripping the spear like something precious, with an air of being afraid I would try to take it away from him. I had to make an effort to free my eyes from his gaze and attend to the steering. With one hand I felt above my head for the line of the steam whistle, and jerked out screech after screech hurriedly. The tumult of angry and warlike yells was checked instantly, and then from the depths of the woods went out such a tremulous and prolonged wail of mournful fear and utter despair as may be imagined to follow the flight of the last hope from the earth. There was a great commotion in the bush; the shower of arrows stopped, a few dropping shots rang out sharply—then silence, in which the languid beat of the stern-wheel came plainly to my ears. I put the helm hard a-starboard at the moment when the pilgrim in pink pyjamas, very hot and agitated, appeared in the doorway. 'The manager sends me——' he began in an official tone, and stopped short. 'Good God!' he said, glaring at the wounded man.

"We two whites stood over him, and his lustrous and inquiring glance enveloped us both. I declare it looked as though he would presently put to us some question in an understandable language; but he died without uttering a sound, without moving a limb, without twitching a muscle. Only in the very last moment, as though in response to some sign we could not see, to some whisper we could not hear, he frowned heavily, and that frown gave to his black death-mask an inconceivably sombre, brooding, and menacing expression. The lustre of inquiring glance faded swiftly into vacant glassiness. 'Can you steer?' I asked the agent eagerly. He looked very dubious; but I made a grab at his arm, and he understood at once I meant him to steer whether or no. To tell you the truth, I was morbidly anxious to change my shoes and socks. 'He is dead,' murmured the fellow, immensely impressed. 'No doubt about it,' said I, tugging like mad at the shoe-laces. 'And by the way, I suppose Mr. Kurtz is dead as well by this time.'

"For the moment that was the dominant thought. There was a sense of extreme disappointment, as though I had found out I had been striving after something altogether without a substance. I couldn't have been more disgusted if I had travelled all this way for the sole purpose of talking with Mr. Kurtz. Talking with . . . I flung one shoe overboard, and became aware that that was exactly what I had been looking forward to—a talk with Kurtz. I made the strange discovery that I had never imagined him as doing, you know, but as discoursing. I didn't say to myself, 'Now I will never see him,' or 'Now I will never shake him by the hand,' but, 'now I will never hear him.' The man presented himself as a voice. Not of course that I did not connect him with some sort of action. Hadn't I been told in all the tones of jealousy and admiration that he had collected, bartered, swindled, or stolen more ivory than all the other agents together? That was not the point. The point was in his being a gifted creature, and that of all his gifts the one that stood out preëminently, that carried with it a sense of real presence, was his ability to talk, his words — the gift of expression, the bewildering, the illuminating, the most exalted and the most contemptible, the pulsating stream of light, or the deceitful flow from the heart of an impenetrable darkness.

"The other shoe went flying unto the devil-god of that river. I thought, By Jove! it's all over. We are too late; he has vanished — the gift has vanished, by means of some spear, arrow, or club. I will never hear that chap speak after all, — and my sorrow had a startling extravagance of emotion, even such as I had noticed in the howling sorrow of these savages in the bush. I couldn't have felt more of lonely desolation somehow, had I been robbed of a belief or had missed my destiny in life. . . . Why do you sigh in this beastly way, somebody? Absurd? Well, absurd. Good Lord! mustn't a man ever —— Here, give me some tobacco." . . .

There was a pause of profound stillness, then a match flared, and Marlow's lean face appeared, worn, hollow, with downward folds and dropped eyelids, with an aspect of concentrated attention; and as he took vigorous draws at his pipe, it seemed to retreat and advance out of the night in the regular flicker of the tiny flame. The match went out.

"Absurd!" he cried. "This is the worst of trying to tell. . . . Here you all are, each moored with two good addresses, like a hulk with two anchors, a butcher round one corner, a policeman round another, excellent appetites, and temperature normal — you hear — normal from year's end to year's end. And you say, Absurd! Absurd be — exploded! Absurd! My dear boys, what can you expect from a man who out of sheer nervousness had just flung overboard a pair of new shoes! Now I think of it, it is amazing I did not shed tears. I am, upon the whole, proud of my fortitude. I was cut to the quick at the idea of having lost the inestimable privilege of listening to the gifted Kurtz. Of course I was wrong. The privilege was waiting for me. Oh, yes, I heard more than enough. And I was right, too. A voice. He was very little more than a voice. And I heard — him — it — this voice — other voices — all of them were so little more than voices — and the memory of that time itself lingers around me, impalpable, like a dying vibration of one immense jabber, silly, atrocious, sordid, savage, or simply mean, without any kind of sense. Voices, voices — even the girl herself — now ——"

He was silent for a long time.

"I laid the ghost of his gifts at last with a lie," he began, suddenly. "Girl! What? Did I mention a girl? Oh, she is out of it — completely. They — the women I mean — are out of it — should be out of it. We must help them to stay in that beautiful world of their own, lest ours gets worse. Oh, she had to be out of it. You should have heard the disinterred body of Mr. Kurtz saying, 'My Intended.' You would have perceived directly then how completely she was out of it. And the lofty frontal bone of

Mr. Kurtz! They say the hair goes on growing sometimes, but this—ah—specimen, was impressively bald. The wilderness had patted him on the head, and, behold, it was like a ball—an ivory ball; it had caressed him, and—lo!—he had withered; it had taken him, loved him, embraced him, got into his veins, consumed his flesh, and sealed his soul to its own by the inconceivable ceremonies of some devilish initiation. He was its spoiled and pampered favourite. Ivory? I should think so. Heaps of it, stacks of it. The old mud shanty was bursting with it. You would think there was not a single tusk left either above or below the ground in the whole country. 'Mostly fossil,' the manager had remarked, disparagingly. It was no more fossil than I am; but they call it fossil when it is dug up. It appears these niggers do bury the tusks sometimes—but evidently they couldn't bury this parcel deep enough to save the gifted Mr. Kurtz from his fate. We filled the steamboat with it, and had to pile a lot on the deck. Thus he could see and enjoy as long as he could see, because the appreciation of this favour had remained with him to the last. You should have heard him say, 'My ivory.' Oh, yes, I heard him. 'My Intended, my ivory, my station, my river, my——' everything belonged to him. It made me hold my breath in expectation of hearing the wilderness burst into a prodigious peal of laughter that would shake the fixed stars in their places. Everything belonged to him—but that was a trifle. The thing was to know what he belonged to, how many powers of darkness claimed him for their own. That was the reflection that made you creepy all over. It was impossible—it was not good for one either—trying to imagine. He had taken a high seat amongst the devils of the land—I mean literally. You can't understand. How could you?—with solid pavement under your feet, surrounded by kind neighbours ready to cheer you or to fall on you, stepping delicately between the butcher and the policeman, in the holy terror of scandal and gallows and lunatic asylums—how can you imagine what particular region of the first ages a man's untrammelled feet may take him into by the way of solitude—utter solitude without a policeman—by the way of silence—utter silence, where no warning voice of a kind neighbour can be heard whispering of public opinion? These little things make all the great difference. When they are gone you must fall back upon your own innate strength, upon your own capacity for faithfulness. Of course you may be too much of a fool to go wrong—too dull even to know you are being assaulted by the powers of darkness. I take it, no fool ever made a bargain for his soul with the devil: the fool is too much of a fool, or the devil too much of a devil—I don't know which. Or you may be such a thunderingly exalted creature as to be altogether deaf and blind to anything but heavenly sights and sounds. Then the earth for you is only a standing place—and whether to be like this is your loss or your gain I won't pretend to say. But most of us are neither one nor the other. The earth for us is a place to live in, where we must put up with sights, with sounds, with smells, too, by Jove!—breathe dead hippo, so to speak, and not be contaminated. And there, don't you see? your strength comes in, the faith in your ability for the digging of unostentatious holes to bury the stuff in—your power of devotion, not to yourself, but to an obscure, back-breaking business. And that's difficult enough. Mind, I am not trying to excuse or even explain—I am trying to account to myself for—for—Mr. Kurtz—for the shade of Mr. Kurtz. This initiated wraith from the back of Nowhere honoured me with its amazing confidence before it vanished altogether. This was because it could speak English to me. The original Kurtz had been educated partly in England, and—as he was good enough to say himself—his sympathies were in the right place. His mother was half-English, his father was half-French. All Europe contributed to the making of Kurtz; and by and by I learned that, most appropriately, the International Society for the Suppression of Savage Customs had intrusted him with the making of a report, for its future guidance. And he had written it, too. I've seen it. I've read it. It was eloquent, vibrating with eloquence, but too high-strung, I think. Seventeen pages of close writing he had found time for! But this must have been before his—let us say—nerves, went wrong, and caused him to preside at certain midnight dances ending with unspeakable rites, which—as far as I reluctantly gathered from what I heard at various times—were offered up to him—do you understand?—to Mr. Kurtz himself. But it was a beautiful piece of writing. The opening paragraph, however, in the light of later information, strikes me now as ominous. He began with the argument that we whites, from the point of development we had arrived at, 'must necessarily appear to them [savages] in the nature of supernatural beings—we approach them with the might as of a deity,' and so on, and so on. 'By the simple exercise of our will we can exert a power for good practically unbounded,' etc. etc. From that point he soared and took me with him. The peroration was magnificent, though difficult to remember, you know. It gave me the notion of an exotic Immensity ruled by an august Benevolence. It made me tingle with enthusiasm. This was the unbounded power of eloquence—of words—of burning noble words. There were no practical hints to interrupt the magic current of phrases, unless a kind of note at the foot of the last page, scrawled evidently much later, in an unsteady hand, may be regarded as the exposition of a method. It was very simple, and at the end of that moving appeal to every altruistic sentiment it blazed at you, luminous and terrifying, like a flash of lightning in a serene sky: 'Exterminate all the brutes!' The curious part was that he had apparently forgotten all about that valuable postscriptum, because, later on, when he in a sense came to himself, he repeatedly entreated me to take good care of 'my pamphlet' (he called it), as it was sure to have in the future a good influence upon his career. I had full information about all these things, and, besides, as it turned out, I was to have the care of his memory. I've done enough for it to give me the indisputable right to lay it, if I choose, for an everlasting rest in the dust-bin of progress, amongst all the sweepings and, figuratively speaking, all the dead cats of civilization. But then, you see, I can't choose. He won't be forgotten. Whatever he was, he was not common. He had the power to charm or frighten rudimentary souls into an aggravated witch-dance in his honour; he could also fill the small souls of the pilgrims with bitter misgivings: he had one devoted friend at least, and he had conquered one soul in the world that was neither rudimentary nor tainted with self-seeking. No; I can't forget him, though I am not prepared to affirm the fellow was exactly worth the life we lost in getting to him. I missed my late helmsman awfully,—I missed him even while his body was still lying in the pilot-house. Perhaps you will think it passing strange this regret for a savage who was no more account than a grain of sand in a black Sahara. Well, don't you see, he had done something, he had steered; for months I had him at my back—a help—an instrument. It was a kind of partnership. He steered for me—I had to look after him, I worried about his deficiencies, and thus a subtle bond had been created, of which I only became aware when it was suddenly broken. And the intimate profundity of that look he gave me when he received his hurt remains to this day in my memory—like a claim of distant kinship affirmed in a supreme moment.

"Poor fool! If he had only left that shutter alone. He had no restraint, no restraint—just like Kurtz—a tree swayed by the wind. As soon as I had put on a dry pair of slippers, I dragged him out, after first jerking the spear out of his side, which operation I confess I performed with my eyes shut tight. His heels leaped together over the little door-step; his shoulders were pressed to my breast; I hugged him from behind desperately. Oh! he was heavy, heavy; heavier than any man on earth, I should imagine. Then without more ado I tipped him overboard. The current snatched him as though he had been a wisp of grass, and I saw the body roll over twice before I lost sight of it for ever. All the pilgrims and the manager were then congregated on the awning-deck about the pilot-house, chattering at each other like a flock of excited magpies, and there was a scandalized murmur at my heartless promptitude. What they wanted to keep that body hanging about for I can't guess. Embalm it, maybe. But I had also heard another, and a very ominous, murmur on the deck below. My friends the wood-cutters were likewise scandalized, and with a better show of reason—though I admit that the reason itself was quite inadmissible. Oh, quite! I had made up my mind that if my late helmsman was to be eaten, the fishes alone should have him. He had been a very second-rate helmsman while alive, but now he was dead he might have become a first-class temptation, and possibly cause some startling trouble. Besides, I was anxious to take the wheel, the man in pink pyjamas showing himself a hopeless duffer at the business.

"This I did directly the simple funeral was over. We were going half-speed, keeping right in the middle of the stream, and I listened to the talk about me. They had given up Kurtz, they had given up the station; Kurtz was dead, and the station had been burnt—and so on—and so on. The red-haired pilgrim was beside himself with the thought that at least this poor Kurtz had been properly avenged. 'Say! We must have made a glorious slaughter of them in the bush. Eh? What do you think? Say?' He positively danced, the bloodthirsty little gingery[22] beggar. And he had nearly fainted when he saw the wounded man! I could not help saying, 'You made a glorious lot of smoke, anyhow.' I had seen, from the way the tops of the bushes rustled and flew, that almost all the shots had gone too high. You can't hit anything unless you take aim and fire from the shoulder; but these chaps fired from the hip with their eyes shut. The retreat, I maintained—and I was right—was caused by the screeching of the steam-whistle. Upon this they forgot Kurtz, and began to howl at me with indignant protests.

---

[22] **gingery:** Redheaded.

"The manager stood by the wheel murmuring confidentially about the necessity of getting well away down the river before dark at all events, when I saw in the distance a clearing on the river-side and the outlines of some sort of building. 'What's this?' I asked. He clapped his hands in wonder. 'The station!' he cried. I edged in at once, still going half-speed.

"Through my glasses I saw the slope of a hill interspersed with rare trees and perfectly free from undergrowth. A long decaying building on the summit was half buried in the high grass; the large holes in the peaked roof gaped black from afar; the jungle and the woods made a background. There was no enclosure or fence of any kind; but there had been one apparently, for near the house half-a-dozen slim posts remained in a row, roughly trimmed, and with their upper ends ornamented with round carved balls. The rails, or whatever there had been between, had disappeared. Of course the forest surrounded all that. The river-bank was clear, and on the water-side I saw a white man under a hat like a cart-wheel beckoning persistently with his whole arm. Examining the edge of the forest above and below, I was almost certain I could see movements—human forms gliding here and there. I steamed past prudently, then stopped the engines and let her drift down. The man on the shore began to shout, urging us to land. 'We have been attacked,' screamed the manager. 'I know—I know. It's all right,' yelled back the other, as cheerful as you please. 'Come along. It's all right. I am glad.'

"His aspect reminded me of something I had seen—something funny I had seen somewhere. As I manœuvred to get alongside, I was asking myself, 'What does this fellow look like?' Suddenly I got it. He looked like a harlequin. His clothes had been made of some stuff that was brown holland[23] probably, but it was covered with patches all over, with bright patches, blue, red, and yellow—patches on the back, patches on the front, patches on elbows, on knees; coloured binding around his jacket, scarlet edging at the bottom of his trousers; and the sunshine made him look extremely gay and wonderfully neat withal, because you could see how beautifully all this patching had been done. A beardless, boyish face, very fair, no features to speak of, nose peeling, little blue eyes, smiles and frowns chasing each other over that open countenance like sunshine and shadow on a wind-swept plain. 'Look out, captain!' he cried; 'there's a snag lodged in here last night.' What! Another snag? I confess I swore shamefully. I had nearly holed my cripple, to finish off that charming trip. The harlequin on the bank turned his little pug-nose up to me. 'You English?' he asked, all smiles. 'Are you?' I shouted from the wheel. The smiles vanished, and he shook his head as if sorry for my disappointment. Then he brightened up. 'Never mind!' he cried, encouragingly. 'Are we in time?' I asked. 'He is up there,' he replied, with a toss of the head up the hill, and becoming gloomy all of a sudden. His face was like the autumn sky, overcast one moment and bright the next.

"When the manager, escorted by the pilgrims, all of them armed to the teeth, had gone to the house this chap came on board. 'I say, I don't like this. These natives

---

[23] **holland:** Unbleached cotton or linen.

are in the bush,' I said. He assured me earnestly it was all right. 'They are simple people,' he added; 'well, I am glad you came. It took me all my time to keep them off.' 'But you said it was all right,' I cried. 'Oh, they meant no harm,' he said; and as I stared he corrected himself, 'Not exactly.' Then vivaciously, 'My faith, your pilot-house wants a clean-up!' In the next breath he advised me to keep enough steam on the boiler to blow the whistle in case of any trouble. 'One good screech will do more for you than all your rifles. They are simple people,' he repeated. He rattled away at such a rate he quite overwhelmed me. He seemed to be trying to make up for lots of silence, and actually hinted, laughing, that such was the case. 'Don't you talk with Mr. Kurtz?' I said. 'You don't talk with that man—you listen to him,' he exclaimed with severe exaltation. 'But now——' He waved his arm, and in the twinkling of an eye was in the uttermost depths of despondency. In a moment he came up again with a jump, possessed himself of both my hands, shook them continuously, while he gabbled: 'Brother sailor . . . honour . . . pleasure . . . delight . . . introduce myself . . . Russian . . . son of an arch-priest . . . Government of Tambov . . . What? Tobacco! English tobacco; the excellent English tobacco! Now, that's brotherly. Smoke? Where's a sailor that does not smoke?'

"The pipe soothed him, and gradually I made out he had run away from school, had gone to sea in a Russian ship; ran away again; served some time in English ships; was now reconciled with the arch-priest. He made a point of that. 'But when one is young one must see things, gather experience, ideas; enlarge the mind.' 'Here!' I interrupted. 'You can never tell! Here I met Mr. Kurtz,' he said, youthfully solemn and reproachful. I held my tongue after that. It appears he had persuaded a Dutch trading-house on the coast to fit him out with stores and goods, and had started for the interior with a light heart, and no more idea of what would happen to him than a baby. He had been wandering about that river for nearly two years alone, cut off from everybody and everything. 'I am not so young as I look. I am twenty-five,' he said. 'At first old Van Shuyten would tell me to go to the devil,' he narrated with keen enjoyment; 'but I stuck to him, and talked and talked, till at last he got afraid I would talk the hind-leg off his favourite dog, so he gave me some cheap things and a few guns, and told me he hoped he would never see my face again. Good old Dutchman, Van Shuyten. I've sent him one small lot of ivory a year ago, so that he can't call me a little thief when I get back. I hope he got it. And for the rest I don't care. I had some wood stacked for you. That was my old house. Did you see?'

"I gave him Towson's book. He made as though he would kiss me, but restrained himself. 'The only book I had left, and I thought I had lost it,' he said, looking at it ecstatically. 'So many accidents happen to a man going about alone, you know. Canoes get upset sometimes—and sometimes you've got to clear out so quick when the people get angry.' He thumbed the pages. 'You made notes in Russian?' I asked. He nodded. 'I thought they were written in cipher,' I said. He laughed, then became serious. 'I had lots of trouble to keep these people off,' he said. 'Did they want to kill you?' I asked. 'Oh, no!' he cried, and checked himself. 'Why did they attack us?' I pursued. He hesitated, then said shamefacedly, 'They don't want him to go.' 'Don't they?' I said, curiously. He nodded a nod full of mystery and wisdom. 'I tell you,' he cried, 'this man has enlarged my mind.' He opened his arms wide, staring at me with his little blue eyes that were perfectly round."

3

"I looked at him, lost in astonishment. There he was before me, in motley, as though he had absconded from a troupe of mimes, enthusiastic, fabulous. His very existence was improbable, inexplicable, and altogether bewildering. He was an insoluble problem. It was inconceivable how he had existed, how he had succeeded in getting so far, how he had managed to remain — why he did not instantly disappear. 'I went a little farther,' he said, 'then still a little farther — till I had gone so far that I don't know how I'll ever get back. Never mind. Plenty time. I can manage. You take Kurtz away quick — quick — I tell you.' The glamour of youth enveloped his particoloured rags, his destitution, his loneliness, the essential desolation of his futile wanderings. For months — for years — his life hadn't been worth a day's purchase; and there he was gallantly, thoughtlessly alive, to all appearance indestructible solely by the virtue of his few years and of his unreflecting audacity. I was seduced into something like admiration — like envy. Glamour urged him on, glamour kept him unscathed. He surely wanted nothing from the wilderness but space to breathe in and to push on through. His need was to exist, and to move onwards at the greatest possible risk, and with a maximum of privation. If the absolutely pure, uncalculating, unpractical spirit of adventure had ever ruled a human being, it ruled this be-patched youth. I almost envied him the possession of this modest and clear flame. It seemed to have consumed all thought of self so completely, that even while he was talking to you, you forgot that it was he — the man before your eyes — who had gone through these things. I did not envy him his devotion to Kurtz, though. He had not meditated over it. It came to him, and he accepted it with a sort of eager fatalism. I must say that to me it appeared about the most dangerous thing in every way he had come upon so far.

"They had come together unavoidably, like two ships becalmed near each other, and lay rubbing sides at last. I suppose Kurtz wanted an audience, because on a certain occasion, when encamped in the forest, they had talked all night, or more probably Kurtz had talked. 'We talked of everything,' he said, quite transported at the recollection. 'I forgot there was such a thing as sleep. The night did not seem to last an hour. Everything! Everything! . . . Of love too.' 'Ah, he talked to you of love!' I said, much amused. 'It isn't what you think,' he cried, almost passionately. 'It was in general. He made me see things — things.'

"He threw his arms up. We were on deck at the time, and the headman of my wood-cutters, lounging near by, turned upon him his heavy and glittering eyes. I looked around, and I don't know why, but I assure you that never, never before, did this land, this river, this jungle, the very arch of this blazing sky, appear to me so hopeless and so dark, so impenetrable to human thought, so pitiless to human weakness. 'And, ever since, you have been with him, of course?' I said.

"On the contrary. It appears their intercourse had been very much broken by various causes. He had, as he informed me proudly, managed to nurse Kurtz through two illnesses (he alluded to it as you would to some risky feat), but as a rule Kurtz wandered alone, far in the depths of the forest. 'Very often coming to this station, I had to wait days and days before he would turn up,' he said. 'Ah, it was worth waiting for!—sometimes.' 'What was he doing? exploring or what?' I asked. 'Oh, yes, of course'; he had discovered lots of villages, a lake, too—he did not know exactly in what direction; it was dangerous to inquire too much—but mostly his expeditions had been for ivory. 'But he had no goods to trade with by that time,' I objected. 'There's a good lot of cartridges left even yet,' he answered, looking away. 'To speak plainly, he raided the country,' I said. He nodded. 'Not alone, surely!' He muttered something about the villages round that lake. 'Kurtz got the tribe to follow him, did he?' I suggested. He fidgeted a little. 'They adored him,' he said. The tone of these words was so extraordinary that I looked at him searchingly. It was curious to see his mingled eagerness and reluctance to speak of Kurtz. The man filled his life, occupied his thoughts, swayed his emotions. 'What can you expect?' he burst out; 'he came to them with thunder and lightning, you know—and they had never seen anything like it—and very terrible. He could be very terrible. You can't judge Mr. Kurtz as you would an ordinary man. No, no, no! Now—just to give you an idea—I don't mind telling you, he wanted to shoot me, too, one day—but I don't judge him.' 'Shoot you!' I cried. 'What for?' 'Well, I had a small lot of ivory the chief of that village near my house gave me. You see I used to shoot game for them. Well, he wanted it, and wouldn't hear reason. He declared he would shoot me unless I gave him the ivory and then cleared out of the country, because he could do so, and had a fancy for it, and there was nothing on earth to prevent him killing whom he jolly well pleased. And it was true, too. I gave him the ivory. What did I care! But I didn't clear out. No, no. I couldn't leave him. I had to be careful, of course, till we got friendly again for a time. He had his second illness then. Afterwards I had to keep out of the way; but I didn't mind. He was living for the most part in those villages on the lake. When he came down to the river, sometimes he would take to me, and sometimes it was better for me to be careful. This man suffered too much. He hated all this, and somehow he couldn't get away. When I had a chance I begged him to try and leave while there was time; I offered to go back with him. And he would say yes, and then he would remain; go off on another ivory hunt; disappear for weeks; forget himself amongst these people—forget himself—you know.' 'Why! he's mad,' I said. He protested indignantly. Mr. Kurtz couldn't be mad. If I had heard him talk, only two days ago, I wouldn't dare hint at such a thing. . . . I had taken up my binoculars while we talked, and was looking at the shore, sweeping the limit of the forest at each side and at the back of the house. The consciousness of there being people in that bush, so silent, so quiet—as silent and quiet as the ruined house on the hill—made me uneasy. There was no sign on the face of nature of this amazing tale that was not so much told as suggested to me in desolate exclamations, completed by shrugs, in interrupted phrases, in hints ending in deep sighs. The woods were unmoved, like a mask—heavy, like the closed door of a prison—they looked with their air of hidden knowledge, of patient expectation, of unapproachable silence. The Russian was explaining to me that it was only lately that Mr. Kurtz had come down to the river, bringing along with him all the fighting men of that lake tribe. He had been absent for several months — getting himself adored, I suppose — and had come down unexpectedly, with the intention to all appearance of making a raid either across the river or down stream. Evidently the appetite for more ivory had got the better of the — what shall I say? — less material aspirations. However he had got much worse suddenly. 'I heard he was lying helpless, and so I came up — took my chance,' said the Russian. 'Oh, he is bad, very bad.' I directed my glass to the house. There were no signs of life, but there was the ruined roof, the long mud wall peeping above the grass, with three little square window-holes, no two of the same size; all this brought within reach of my hand, as it were. And then I made a brusque movement, and one of the remaining posts of that vanished fence leaped up in the field of my glass. You remember I told you I had been struck at the distance by certain attempts at ornamentation, rather remarkable in the ruinous aspect of the place. Now I had suddenly a nearer view, and its first result was to make me throw my head back as if before a blow. Then I went carefully from post to post with my glass, and I saw my mistake. These round knobs were not ornamental but symbolic; they were expressive and puzzling, striking and disturbing — food for thought and also for vultures if there had been any looking down from the sky; but at all events for such ants as were industrious enough to ascend the pole. They would have been even more impressive, those heads on the stakes, if their faces had not been turned to the house. Only one, the first I had made out, was facing my way. I was not so shocked as you may think. The start back I had given was really nothing but a movement of surprise. I had expected to see a knob of wood there, you know. I returned deliberately to the first I had seen — and there it was, black, dried, sunken, with closed eyelids, — a head that seemed to sleep at the top of that pole, and with the shrunken dry lips showing a narrow white line of the teeth, was smiling, too, smiling continuously at some endless and jocose dream of that eternal slumber.

"I am not disclosing any trade secrets. In fact, the manager said afterwards that Mr. Kurtz's methods had ruined the district. I have no opinion on that point, but I want you clearly to understand that there was nothing exactly profitable in these heads being there. They only showed that Mr. Kurtz lacked restraint in the gratification of his various lusts, that there was something wanting in him — some small matter which, when the pressing need arose, could not be found under his magnificent eloquence. Whether he knew of this deficiency himself I can't say. I think the knowledge came to him at last — only at the very last. But the wilderness had found him out early, and had taken on him a terrible vengeance for the fantastic invasion. I think it had whispered to him things about himself which he did not know, things of which he had no conception till he took counsel with this great solitude — and the whisper had proved irresistibly fascinating. It echoed loudly within him because he was hollow at the core. . . . I put down the glass, and the head that had appeared near enough to be spoken to seemed at once to have leaped away from me into inaccessible distance.

"The admirer of Mr. Kurtz was a bit crestfallen. In a hurried, indistinct voice he began to assure me he had not dared to take these — say, symbols — down. He was not afraid of the natives; they would not stir till Mr. Kurtz gave the word. His ascendancy was extraordinary. The camps of these people surrounded the place, and the

chiefs came every day to see him. They would crawl. . . . 'I don't want to know anything of the ceremonies used when approaching Mr. Kurtz,' I shouted. Curious, this
feeling that came over me that such details would be more intolerable than those
heads drying on the stakes under Mr. Kurtz's windows. After all, that was only a savage sight, while I seemed at one bound to have been transported into some lightless
region of subtle horrors, where pure, uncomplicated savagery was a positive relief,
being something that had a right to exist—obviously—in the sunshine. The young
man looked at me with surprise. I suppose it did not occur to him that Mr. Kurtz was
no idol of mine. He forgot I hadn't heard any of these splendid monologues on, what
was it? on love, justice, conduct of life—or what not. If it had come to crawling
before Mr. Kurtz, he crawled as much as the veriest savage of them all. I had no idea
of the conditions, he said: these heads were the heads of rebels. I shocked him excessively by laughing. Rebels! What would be the next definition I was to hear? There
had been enemies, criminals, workers—and these were rebels. Those rebellious
heads looked very subdued to me on their sticks. 'You don't know how such a life
tries a man like Kurtz,' cried Kurtz's last disciple. 'Well, and you?' I said. 'I! I! I am a
simple man. I have no great thoughts. I want nothing from anybody. How can you
compare me to . . . ?' His feelings were too much for speech, and suddenly he broke
down. 'I don't understand,' he groaned. 'I've been doing my best to keep him alive,
and that's enough. I had no hand in all this. I have no abilities. There hasn't been
a drop of medicine or a mouthful of invalid food for months here. He was shamefully abandoned. A man like this, with such ideas. Shamefully! Shamefully! I—I—
haven't slept for the last ten nights . . .'

"His voice lost itself in the calm of the evening. The long shadows of the forest
had slipped downhill while we talked, had gone far beyond the ruined hovel, beyond
the symbolic row of stakes. All this was in the gloom, while we down there were yet
in the sunshine, and the stretch of the river abreast of the clearing glittered in a still
and dazzling splendour, with a murky and overshadowed bend above and below.
Not a living soul was seen on the shore. The bushes did not rustle.

"Suddenly round the corner of the house a group of men appeared, as though
they had come up from the ground. They waded waist-deep in the grass, in a compact body, bearing an improvised stretcher in their midst. Instantly, in the emptiness
of the landscape, a cry arose whose shrillness pierced the still air like a sharp arrow
flying straight to the very heart of the land; and, as if by enchantment, streams of
human beings—of naked human beings—with spears in their hands, with bows,
with shields, with wild glances and savage movements, were poured into the clearing
by the dark-faced and pensive forest. The bushes shook, the grass swayed for a time,
and then everything stood still in attentive immobility.

"'Now, if he does not say the right thing to them we are all done for,' said the
Russian at my elbow. The knot of men with the stretcher had stopped, too, halfway
to the steamer, as if petrified. I saw the man on the stretcher sit up, lank and with an
uplifted arm, above the shoulders of the bearers. 'Let us hope that the man who can
talk so well of love in general will find some particular reason to spare us this time,'
I said. I resented bitterly the absurd danger of our situation, as if to be at the mercy
of that atrocious phantom had been a dishonouring necessity. I could not hear a

sound, but through my glasses I saw the thin arm extended commandingly, the lower jaw moving, the eyes of that apparition shining darkly far in its bony head that nodded with grotesque jerks. Kurtz—Kurtz—that means short in German—don't it? Well, the name was as true as everything else in his life—and death. He looked at least seven feet long. His covering had fallen off, and his body emerged from it pitiful and appalling as from a winding-sheet. I could see the cage of his ribs all astir, the bones of his arm waving. It was as though an animated image of death carved out of old ivory had been shaking its hand with menaces at a motionless crowd of men made of dark and glittering bronze. I saw him open his mouth wide—it gave him a weirdly voracious aspect, as though he had wanted to swallow all the air, all the earth, all the men before him. A deep voice reached me faintly. He must have been shouting. He fell back suddenly. The stretcher shook as the bearers staggered forward again, and almost at the same time I noticed that the crowd of savages was vanishing without any perceptible movement of retreat, as if the forest that had ejected these beings so suddenly had drawn them in again as the breath is drawn in a long aspiration.

"Some of the pilgrims behind the stretcher carried his arms—two shot-guns, a heavy rifle, and a light revolver-carbine—the thunderbolts of that pitiful Jupiter. The manager bent over him murmuring as he walked beside his head. They laid him down in one of the little cabins—just a room for a bedplace and a camp-stool or two, you know. We had brought his belated correspondence, and a lot of torn envelopes and open letters littered his bed. His hand roamed feebly amongst these papers. I was struck by the fire of his eyes and the composed languor of his expression. It was not so much the exhaustion of disease. He did not seem in pain. This shadow looked satiated and calm, as though for the moment it had had its fill of all the emotions.

"He rustled one of the letters, and looking straight in my face said, 'I am glad.' Somebody had been writing to him about me. These special recommendations were turning up again. The volume of tone he emitted without effort, almost without the trouble of moving his lips, amazed me. A voice! a voice! It was grave, profound, vibrating, while the man did not seem capable of a whisper. However, he had enough strength in him—factitious no doubt—to very nearly make an end of us, as you shall hear directly.

"The manager appeared silently in the doorway; I stepped out at once and he drew the curtain after me. The Russian, eyed curiously by the pilgrims, was staring at the shore. I followed the direction of his glance.

"Dark human shapes could be made out in the distance, flitting indistinctly against the gloomy border of the forest, and near the river two bronze figures, leaning on tall spears, stood in the sunlight under fantastic head-dresses of spotted skins, warlike and still in statuesque repose. And from right to left along the lighted shore moved a wild and gorgeous apparition of a woman.

"She walked with measured steps, draped in striped and fringed cloths, treading the earth proudly, with a slight jingle and flash of barbarous ornaments. She carried her head high; her hair was done in the shape of a helmet; she had brass leggings to the knee, brass wire gauntlets to the elbow, a crimson spot on her tawny cheek, innumerable necklaces of glass beads on her neck; bizarre things, charms, gifts of witch-men, that hung about her, glittered and trembled at every step. She must have had the value of several elephant tusks upon her. She was savage and superb, wild-eyed and magnificent; there was something ominous and stately in her deliberate progress. And in the hush that had fallen suddenly upon the whole sorrowful land, the immense wilderness, the colossal body of the fecund and mysterious life seemed to look at her, pensive, as though it had been looking at the image of its own tenebrous and passionate soul.

"She came abreast of the steamer, stood still, and faced us. Her long shadow fell to the water's edge. Her face had a tragic and fierce aspect of wild sorrow and of dumb pain mingled with the fear of some struggling, half-shaped resolve. She stood looking at us without a stir, and like the wilderness itself, with an air of brooding over an inscrutable purpose. A whole minute passed, and then she made a step forward. There was a low jingle, a glint of yellow metal, a sway of fringed draperies, and she stopped as if her heart had failed her. The young fellow by my side growled. The pilgrims murmured at my back. She looked at us all as if her life had depended upon the unswerving steadiness of her glance. Suddenly she opened her bared arms and threw them up rigid above her head, as though in an uncontrollable desire to touch the sky, and at the same time the swift shadows darted out on the earth, swept around on the river, gathering the steamer into a shadowy embrace. A formidable silence hung over the scene.

"She turned away slowly, walked on, following the bank, and passed into the bushes to the left. Once only her eyes gleamed back at us in the dusk of the thickets before she disappeared.

"'If she had offered to come aboard I really think I would have tried to shoot her,' said the man of patches, nervously. 'I have been risking my life every day for the last fortnight to keep her out of the house. She got in one day and kicked up a row about those miserable rags I picked up in the storeroom to mend my clothes with. I wasn't decent. At least it must have been that, for she talked like a fury to Kurtz for an hour, pointing at me now and then. I don't understand the dialect of this tribe. Luckily for me, I fancy Kurtz felt too ill that day to care, or there would have been mischief. I don't understand. . . . No—it's too much for me. Ah, well, it's all over now.'

"At this moment I heard Kurtz's deep voice behind the curtain: 'Save me!—save the ivory, you mean. Don't tell me. Save *me*! Why, I've had to save you. You are interrupting my plans now. Sick! Sick! Not so sick as you would like to believe. Never mind. I'll carry my ideas out yet—I will return. I'll show you what can be done. You with your little peddling notions—you are interfering with me. I will return. I. . . .'

"The manager came out. He did me the honour to take me under the arm and lead me aside. 'He is very low, very low,' he said. He considered it necessary to sigh, but neglected to be consistently sorrowful. 'We have done all we could for him—haven't we? But there is no disguising the fact, Mr. Kurtz has done more harm than good to the Company. He did not see the time was not ripe for vigorous action. Cautiously, cautiously—that's my principle. We must be cautious yet. The district is closed to us for a time. Deplorable! Upon the whole, the trade will suffer. I don't deny there is a remarkable quantity of ivory—mostly fossil. We must save it, at all events—but look how precarious the position is—and why? Because the method is unsound.' 'Do you,' said I, looking at the shore, 'call it "unsound method"?' 'Without doubt,' he exclaimed, hotly. 'Don't you?' . . . 'No method at all,' I murmured after a while. 'Exactly,' he exulted. 'I anticipated this. Shows a complete want of judgment. It is my duty to point it out in the proper quarter.' 'Oh,' said I, 'that fellow—what's his name?—the brickmaker, will make a readable report for you.' He appeared confounded for a moment. It seemed to me I had never breathed an atmosphere so vile, and I turned mentally to Kurtz for relief—positively for relief. 'Nevertheless I think Mr. Kurtz is a remarkable man,' I said with emphasis. He started, dropped on me a cold heavy glance, said very quietly, 'He *was*,' and turned his back on me. My hour of favour was over; I found myself lumped along with Kurtz as a partisan of methods for which the time was not ripe: I was unsound! Ah! but it was something to have at least a choice of nightmares.

"I had turned to the wilderness really, not to Mr. Kurtz, who, I was ready to admit, was as good as buried. And for a moment it seemed to me as if I also were buried in a vast grave full of unspeakable secrets. I felt an intolerable weight oppressing my breast, the smell of the damp earth, the unseen presence of victorious corruption, the darkness of an impenetrable night. . . . The Russian tapped me on the shoulder. I heard him mumbling and stammering something about 'brother seaman—couldn't conceal—knowledge of matters that would affect Mr. Kurtz's reputation.' I waited. For him evidently Mr. Kurtz was not in his grave; I suspect that for him Mr. Kurtz was one of the immortals. 'Well!' said I at last, 'speak out. As it happens, I am Mr. Kurtz's friend—in a way.'

"He stated with a good deal of formality that had we not been 'of the same profession,' he would have kept the matter to himself without regard to consequences. 'He suspected there was an active ill will towards him on the part of these white men that——' 'You are right,' I said, remembering a certain conversation I had overheard. 'The manager thinks you ought to be hanged.' He showed a concern at this intelligence which amused me at first. 'I had better get out of the way quietly,' he said, earnestly. 'I can do no more for Kurtz now, and they would soon find some excuse. What's to stop them? There's a military post three hundred miles from here.' 'Well, upon my word,' said I, 'perhaps you had better go if you have any friends amongst the savages near by.' 'Plenty,' he said. 'They are simple people—and I want nothing, you know.' He stood biting his lip, then: 'I don't want any harm to happen to these whites here, but of course I was thinking of Mr. Kurtz's reputation—but you are a brother seaman and——' 'All right,' said I, after a time. 'Mr. Kurtz's reputation is safe with me.' I did not know how truly I spoke.

"He informed me, lowering his voice, that it was Kurtz who had ordered the attack to be made on the steamer. 'He hated sometimes the idea of being taken away—and then again. . . . But I don't understand these matters. I am a simple man. He thought it would scare you away—that you would give it up, thinking him dead. I could not stop him. Oh, I had an awful time of it this last month.' 'Very well,' I said. 'He is all right now.' 'Ye-e-es,' he muttered, not very convinced apparently. 'Thanks,' said I; 'I shall keep my eyes open.' 'But quiet—eh?' he urged, anxiously. 'It would be awful for his reputation if anybody here——' I promised a complete discretion with great gravity. 'I have a canoe and three black fellows waiting not very far. I am off. Could you give me a few Martini-Henry cartridges?' I could, and did, with proper secrecy. He helped himself, with a wink at me, to a handful of my tobacco. 'Between sailors—you know—good English tobacco.' At the door of the pilot-house he turned round—'I say, haven't you a pair of shoes you could spare?' He raised one leg. 'Look.' The soles were tied with knotted strings sandal-wise under his bare feet. I rooted out an old pair, at which he looked with admiration before tucking it under his left arm. One of his pockets (bright red) was bulging with cartridges, from the other (dark blue) peeped 'Towson's Inquiry,' etc., etc. He seemed to think himself excellently well equipped for a renewed encounter with the wilderness. 'Ah! I'll never, never meet such a man again. You ought to have heard him recite poetry—his own, too, it was, he told me. Poetry!' He rolled his eyes at the recollection of these delights. 'Oh, he enlarged my mind!' 'Good-bye,' said I. He shook hands and vanished in the night. Sometimes I ask myself whether I had ever really seen him—whether it was possible to meet such a phenomenon! . . .

"When I woke up shortly after midnight his warning came to my mind with its hint of danger that seemed, in the starred darkness, real enough to make me get up for the purpose of having a look round. On the hill a big fire burned, illuminating fitfully a crooked corner of the station-house. One of the agents with a picket[24] of a few of our blacks, armed for the purpose, was keeping guard over the ivory; but deep within the forest, red gleams that wavered, that seemed to sink and rise from the ground amongst confused columnar shapes of intense blackness, showed the exact position of the camp where Mr. Kurtz's adorers were keeping their uneasy vigil. The monotonous beating of a big drum filled the air with muffled shocks and a lingering vibration. A steady droning sound of many men chanting each to himself some weird incantation came out from the black, flat wall of the woods as the humming of bees comes out of a hive, and had a strange narcotic effect upon my half-awake senses. I believe I dozed off leaning over the rail, till an abrupt burst of yells, an overwhelming outbreak of a pent-up and mysterious frenzy, woke me up in a bewildered wonder. It was cut short all at once, and the low droning went on with an effect of audible and soothing silence. I glanced casually into the little cabin. A light was burning within, but Mr. Kurtz was not there.

"I think I would have raised an outcry if I had believed my eyes. But I didn't believe them at first—the thing seemed so impossible. The fact is I was completely unnerved by a sheer blank fright, pure abstract terror, unconnected with any distinct shape of physical danger. What made this emotion so overpowering was—how shall I define it?—the moral shock I received, as if something altogether monstrous, intolerable to thought and odious to the soul, had been thrust upon me unexpectedly. This lasted of course the merest fraction of a second, and then the usual sense of commonplace, deadly danger, the possibility of a sudden onslaught and massacre, or something of the kind, which I saw impending, was positively welcome and composing. It pacified me, in fact, so much, that I did not raise an alarm.

---

[24] **picket:** A band of sentries.

"There was an agent buttoned up inside an ulster[25] and sleeping on a chair on deck within three feet of me. The yells had not awakened him; he snored very slightly; I left him to his slumbers and leaped ashore. I did not betray Mr. Kurtz—it was ordered I should never betray him—it was written I should be loyal to the nightmare of my choice. I was anxious to deal with this shadow by myself alone,— and to this day I don't know why I was so jealous of sharing with any one the peculiar blackness of that experience.

"As soon as I got on the bank I saw a trail—a broad trail through the grass. I remember the exultation with which I said to myself, 'He can't walk—he is crawling on all-fours—I've got him.' The grass was wet with dew. I strode rapidly with clenched fists. I fancy I had some vague notion of falling upon him and giving him a drubbing. I don't know. I had some imbecile thoughts. The knitting old woman with the cat obtruded herself upon my memory as a most improper person to be sitting at the other end of such an affair. I saw a row of pilgrims squirting lead in the air out of Winchesters held to the hip. I thought I would never get back to the steamer, and imagined myself living alone and unarmed in the woods to an advanced age. Such silly things—you know. And I remember I confounded the beat of the drum with the beating of my heart, and was pleased at its calm regularity.

"I kept to the track though—then stopped to listen. The night was very clear; a dark blue space, sparkling with dew and starlight, in which black things stood very still. I thought I could see a kind of motion ahead of me. I was strangely cocksure of everything that night. I actually left the track and ran in a wide semicircle (I verily believe chuckling to myself) so as to get in front of that stir, of that motion I had seen—if indeed I had seen anything. I was circumventing Kurtz as though it had been a boyish game.

"I came upon him, and, if he had not heard me coming, I would have fallen over him, too, but he got up in time. He rose, unsteady, long, pale, indistinct, like a vapour exhaled by the earth, and swayed slightly, misty and silent before me; while at my back the fires loomed between the trees, and the murmur of many voices issued from the forest. I had cut him off cleverly; but when actually confronting him I seemed to come to my senses, I saw the danger in its right proportion. It was by no means over yet. Suppose he began to shout? Though he could hardly stand, there was still plenty of vigour in his voice. 'Go away—hide yourself,' he said, in that profound tone. It was very awful. I glanced back. We were within thirty yards from the nearest fire. A black figure stood up, strode on long black legs, waving long black arms, across the glow. It had horns—antelope horns, I think—on its head. Some sorcerer, some witch-man, no doubt: it looked fiend-like enough. 'Do you know what you are doing?' I whispered. 'Perfectly,' he answered, raising his voice for that single word: it sounded to me far off and yet loud, like a hail through a speaking-trumpet. If he makes a row we are lost, I thought to myself. This clearly was not a case for fisticuffs, even apart from the very natural aversion I had to beat that Shadow—this wandering and tormented thing. 'You will be lost,' I said—'utterly

---

[25] **ulster**: A long overcoat.

lost.' One gets sometimes such a flash of inspiration, you know. I did say the right thing, though indeed he could not have been more irretrievably lost than he was at this very moment, when the foundations of our intimacy were being laid—to endure—to endure—even to the end—even beyond.

"'I had immense plans,' he muttered irresolutely. 'Yes,' said I; 'but if you try to shout I'll smash your head with——' There was not a stick or stone near. 'I will throttle you for good,' I corrected myself. 'I was on the threshold of great things,' he pleaded, in a voice of longing, with a wistfulness of tone that made my blood run cold. 'And now for this stupid scoundrel——' 'Your success in Europe is assured in any case,' I affirmed, steadily. I did not want to have the throttling of him, you under-stand—and indeed it would have been very little use for any practical purpose. I tried to break the spell—the heavy, mute spell of the wilderness—that seemed to draw him to its pitiless breast by the awakening of forgotten and brutal instincts, by the memory of gratified and monstrous passions. This alone, I was convinced, had driven him out to the edge of the forest, to the bush, towards the gleam of fires, the throb of drums, the drone of weird incantations; this alone had beguiled his unlaw-ful soul beyond the bounds of permitted aspirations. And, don't you see, the terror of the position was not in being knocked on the head—though I had a very lively sense of that danger, too—but in this, that I had to deal with a being to whom I could not appeal in the name of anything high or low. I had, even like the niggers, to invoke him—himself—his own exalted and incredible degradation. There was nothing either above or below him, and I knew it. He had kicked himself loose of the earth. Confound the man! he had kicked the very earth to pieces. He was alone, and I before him did not know whether I stood on the ground or floated in the air. I've been telling you what we said—repeating the phrases we pronounced—but what's the good? They were common everyday words—the familiar, vague sounds exchanged on every waking day of life. But what of that? They had behind them, to my mind, the terrific suggestiveness of words heard in dreams, of phrases spoken in nightmares. Soul! If anybody had ever struggled with a soul, I am the man. And I wasn't arguing with a lunatic either. Believe me or not, his intelligence was perfectly clear—concentrated, it is true, upon himself with horrible intensity, yet clear; and therein was my only chance—barring, of course, the killing him there and then, which wasn't so good, on account of unavoidable noise. But his soul was mad. Being alone in the wilderness, it had looked within itself, and, by heavens! I tell you, it had gone mad. I had—for my sins, I suppose—to go through the ordeal of looking into it myself. No eloquence could have been so withering to one's belief in mankind as his final burst of sincerity. He struggled with himself, too. I saw it—I heard it. I saw the inconceivable mystery of a soul that knew no restraint, no faith, and no fear, yet struggling blindly with itself. I kept my head pretty well; but when I had him at last stretched on the couch, I wiped my forehead, while my legs shook under me as though I had carried half a ton on my back down that hill. And yet I had only sup-ported him, his bony arm clasped round my neck—and he was not much heavier than a child.

"When next day we left at noon, the crowd, of whose presence behind the cur-tain of trees I had been acutely conscious all the time, flowed out of the woods again, filled the clearing, covered the slope with a mass of naked, breathing, quivering, bronze bodies. I steamed up a bit, then swung downstream, and two thousand eyes followed the evolutions of the splashing, thumping, fierce river-demon beating the water with its terrible tail and breathing black smoke into the air. In front of the first rank, along the river, three men, plastered with bright red earth from head to foot, strutted to and fro restlessly. When we came abreast again, they faced the river, stamped their feet, nodded their horned heads, swayed their scarlet bodies; they shook towards the fierce river-demon a bunch of black feathers, a mangy skin with a pendent tail — something that looked like a dried gourd; they shouted periodically together strings of amazing words that resembled no sounds of human language; and the deep murmurs of the crowd, interrupted suddenly, were like the responses of some satanic litany.

"We had carried Kurtz into the pilot-house: there was more air there. Lying on the couch, he stared through the open shutter. There was an eddy in the mass of human bodies, and the woman with helmeted head and tawny cheeks rushed out to the very brink of the stream. She put out her hands, shouted something, and all that wild mob took up the shout in a roaring chorus of articulated, rapid, breathless utterance.

" 'Do you understand this?' I asked.

"He kept on looking out past me with fiery, longing eyes, with a mingled expression of wistfulness and hate. He made no answer, but I saw a smile, a smile of indefinable meaning, appear on his colourless lips that a moment after twitched convulsively. 'Do I not?' he said slowly, gasping, as if the words had been torn out of him by a supernatural power.

"I pulled the string of the whistle, and I did this because I saw the pilgrims on deck getting out their rifles with an air of anticipating a jolly lark. At the sudden screech there was a movement of abject terror through that wedged mass of bodies. 'Don't! don't you frighten them away,' cried someone on deck disconsolately. I pulled the string time after time. They broke and ran, they leaped, they crouched, they swerved, they dodged the flying terror of the sound. The three red chaps had fallen flat, face down on the shore, as though they had been shot dead. Only the barbarous and superb woman did not so much as flinch, and stretched tragically her bare arms after us over the sombre and glittering river.

"And then that imbecile crowd down on the deck started their little fun, and I could see nothing more for smoke.

"The brown current ran swiftly out of the heart of darkness, bearing us down towards the sea with twice the speed of our upward progress; and Kurtz's life was running swiftly, too, ebbing, ebbing out of his heart into the sea of inexorable time. The manager was very placid, he had no vital anxieties now, he took us both in with a comprehensive and satisfied glance: the 'affair' had come off as well as could be wished. I saw the time approaching when I would be left alone of the party of 'unsound method.' The pilgrims looked upon me with disfavour. I was, so to speak, numbered with the dead. It is strange how I accepted this unforeseen partnership, this choice of nightmares forced upon me in the tenebrous land invaded by these mean and greedy phantoms.

"Kurtz discoursed. A voice! a voice! It rang deep to the very last. It survived his strength to hide in the magnificent folds of eloquence the barren darkness of his heart. Oh, he struggled! he struggled! The wastes of his weary brain were haunted by shadowy images now — images of wealth and fame revolving obsequiously round his unextinguishable gift of noble and lofty expression. My Intended, my station, my career, my ideas — these were the subjects for the occasional utterances of elevated sentiments. The shade of the original Kurtz frequented the bedside of the hollow sham, whose fate it was to be buried presently in the mould of primeval earth. But both the diabolic love and the unearthly hate of the mysteries it had penetrated fought for the possession of that soul satiated with primitive emotions, avid of lying fame, of sham distinction, of all the appearances of success and power.

"Sometimes he was contemptibly childish. He desired to have kings meet him at railway-stations on his return from some ghastly Nowhere, where he intended to accomplish great things. 'You show them you have in you something that is really profitable, and then there will be no limits to the recognition of your ability,' he would say. 'Of course you must take care of the motives — right motives — always.' The long reaches that were like one and the same reach, monotonous bends that were exactly alike, slipped past the steamer with their multitude of secular[26] trees looking patiently after this grimy fragment of another world, the forerunner of change, of conquest, of trade, of massacres, of blessings. I looked ahead — piloting. 'Close the shutter,' said Kurtz suddenly one day; 'I can't bear to look at this.' I did so. There was a silence. 'Oh, but I will wring your heart yet!' he cried at the invisible wilderness.

"We broke down — as I had expected — and had to lie up for repairs at the head of an island. This delay was the first thing that shook Kurtz's confidence. One morning he gave me a packet of papers and a photograph — the lot tied together with a shoe-string. 'Keep this for me,' he said. 'This noxious fool' (meaning the manager) 'is capable of prying into my boxes when I am not looking.' In the afternoon I saw him. He was lying on his back with closed eyes, and I withdrew quietly, but I heard him mutter, 'Live rightly, die, die . . .' I listened. There was nothing more. Was he rehearsing some speech in his sleep, or was it a fragment of a phrase from some newspaper article? He had been writing for the papers and meant to do so again, 'for the furthering of my ideas. It's a duty.'

"His was an impenetrable darkness. I looked at him as you peer down at a man who is lying at the bottom of a precipice where the sun never shines. But I had not much time to give him, because I was helping the engine-driver to take to pieces the leaky cylinders, to straighten a bent connecting-rod, and in other such matters. I lived in an infernal mess of rust, filings, nuts, bolts, spanners, hammers, ratchet-drills — things I abominate, because I don't get on with them. I tended the little forge we fortunately had aboard; I toiled wearily in a wretched scrap-heap — unless I had the shakes too bad to stand.

"One evening coming in with a candle I was startled to hear him say a little tremulously, 'I am lying here in the dark waiting for death.' The light was within a

---

[26] secular: Lasting from century to century.

foot of his eyes. I forced myself to murmur, 'Oh, nonsense!' and stood over him as if transfixed.

"Anything approaching the change that came over his features I have never seen before, and hope never to see again. Oh, I wasn't touched. I was fascinated. It was as though a veil had been rent. I saw on that ivory face the expression of sombre pride, of ruthless power, of craven terror—of an intense and hopeless despair. Did he live his life again in every detail of desire, temptation, and surrender during that supreme moment of complete knowledge? He cried in a whisper at some image, at some vision—he cried out twice, a cry that was no more than a breath—

"'The horror! The horror!'

"I blew the candle out and left the cabin. The pilgrims were dining in the mess-room, and I took my place opposite the manager, who lifted his eyes to give me a questioning glance, which I successfully ignored. He leaned back, serene, with that peculiar smile of his sealing the unexpressed depths of his meanness. A continuous shower of small flies streamed upon the lamp, upon the cloth, upon our hands and faces. Suddenly the manager's boy put his insolent black head in the doorway, and said in a tone of scathing contempt—

"'Mistah Kurtz—he dead.'

"All the pilgrims rushed out to see. I remained, and went on with my dinner. I believe I was considered brutally callous. However, I did not eat much. There was a lamp in there—light, don't you know—and outside it was so beastly, beastly dark. I went no more near the remarkable man who had pronounced a judgment upon the adventures of his soul on this earth. The voice was gone. What else had been there? But I am of course aware that next day the pilgrims buried something in a muddy hole.

"And then they very nearly buried me.

"However, as you see, I did not go to join Kurtz there and then. I did not. I remained to dream the nightmare out to the end, and to show my loyalty to Kurtz once more. Destiny. My destiny! Droll thing life is—that mysterious arrangement of merciless logic for a futile purpose. The most you can hope from it is some knowledge of yourself—that comes too late—a crop of unextinguishable regrets. I have wrestled with death. It is the most unexciting contest you can imagine. It takes place in an impalpable grayness, with nothing underfoot, with nothing around, without spectators, without clamour, without glory, without the great desire of victory, without the great fear of defeat, in a sickly atmosphere of tepid scepticism, without much belief in your own right, and still less in that of your adversary. If such is the form of ultimate wisdom, then life is a greater riddle than some of us think it to be. I was within a hair's breadth of the last opportunity for pronouncement, and I found with humiliation that probably I would have nothing to say. This is the reason why I affirm that Kurtz was a remarkable man. He had something to say. He said it. Since I had peeped over the edge myself, I understand better the meaning of his stare, that could not see the flame of the candle, but was wide enough to embrace the whole universe, piercing enough to penetrate all the hearts that beat in the darkness. He had summed up—he had judged. 'The horror!' He was a remarkable man. After all, this was the expression of some sort of belief; it had candour, it had conviction, it had a vibrating note of revolt in its whisper, it had the appalling face of a glimpsed truth—the strange commingling of desire and hate. And it is not my own extremity I remember best—a vision of grayness without form filled with physical pain, and a careless contempt for the evanescence of all things—even of this pain itself. No! It is his extremity that I seem to have lived through. True, he had made that last stride, he had stepped over the edge, while I had been permitted to draw back my hesitating foot. And perhaps in this is the whole difference; perhaps all the wisdom, and all truth, and all sincerity, are just compressed into that inappreciable moment of time in which we step over the threshold of the invisible. Perhaps! I like to think my summing-up would not have been a word of careless contempt. Better his cry— much better. It was an affirmation, a moral victory paid for by innumerable defeats, by abominable terrors, by abominable satisfactions. But it was a victory! That is why I have remained loyal to Kurtz to the last, and even beyond, when a long time after I heard once more, not his own voice, but the echo of his magnificent eloquence thrown to me from a soul as translucently pure as a cliff of crystal.

"No, they did not bury me, though there is a period of time which I remember mistily, with a shuddering wonder, like a passage through some inconceivable world that had no hope in it and no desire. I found myself back in the sepulchral city resenting the sight of people hurrying through the streets to filch a little money from each other, to devour their infamous cookery, to gulp their unwholesome beer, to dream their insignificant and silly dreams. They trespassed upon my thoughts. They were intruders whose knowledge of life was to me an irritating pretence, because I felt so sure they could not possibly know the things I knew. Their bearing, which was simply the bearing of commonplace individuals going about their business in the assurance of perfect safety, was offensive to me like the outrageous flauntings of folly in the face of a danger it is unable to comprehend. I had no particular desire to enlighten them, but I had some difficulty in restraining myself from laughing in their faces, so full of stupid importance. I daresay I was not very well at that time. I tottered about the streets—there were various affairs to settle—grinning bitterly at perfectly respectable persons. I admit my behaviour was inexcusable, but then my temperature was seldom normal in these days. My dear aunt's endeavours to 'nurse up my strength' seemed altogether beside the mark. It was not my strength that wanted nursing, it was my imagination that wanted soothing. I kept the bundle of papers given me by Kurtz, not knowing exactly what to do with it. His mother had died lately, watched over, as I was told, by his Intended. A clean-shaved man, with an official manner and wearing gold-rimmed spectacles, called on me one day and made inquiries, at first circuitous, afterwards suavely pressing, about what he was pleased to denominate certain 'documents.' I was not surprised, because I had had two rows with the manager on the subject out there. I had refused to give up the smallest scrap out of that package, and I took the same attitude with the spectacled man. He became darkly menacing at last, and with much heat argued that the Company had the right to every bit of information about its 'territories.' And said he, 'Mr. Kurtz's knowledge of unexplored regions must have been necessarily extensive and peculiar—owing to his great abilities and to the deplorable circumstances in which he had been placed: therefore——' I assured him Mr. Kurtz's knowledge, however extensive, did not bear upon the problems of commerce or administration. He invoked then the name of science. 'It would be an incalculable loss if,' etc., etc. I offered him the report on the 'Suppression of Savage Customs,' with the postscriptum torn off. He took it up eagerly, but ended by sniffing at it with an air of contempt. 'This is not what we had a right to expect,' he remarked. 'Expect nothing else,' I said. 'There are only private letters.' He withdrew upon some threat of legal proceedings, and I saw him no more; but another fellow, calling himself Kurtz's cousin, appeared two days later, and was anxious to hear all the details about his dear relative's last moments. Incidentally he gave me to understand that Kurtz had been essentially a great musician. 'There was the making of an immense success,' said the man, who was an organist, I believe, with lank gray hair flowing over a greasy coat-collar. I had no reason to doubt his statement; and to this day I am unable to say what was Kurtz's profession, whether he ever had any—which was the greatest of his talents. I had taken him for a painter who wrote for the papers, or else for a journalist who could paint—but even the cousin (who took snuff during the interview) could not tell me what he had been—exactly. He was a universal genius—on that point I agreed with the old chap, who thereupon blew his nose noisily into a large cotton handkerchief and withdrew in senile agitation, bearing off some family letters and memoranda without importance. Ultimately a journalist anxious to know something of the fate of his 'dear colleague' turned up. This visitor informed me Kurtz's proper sphere ought to have been politics 'on the popular side.' He had furry straight eyebrows, bristly hair cropped short, an eye-glass on a broad ribbon, and, becoming expansive, confessed his opinion that Kurtz really couldn't write a bit—'but heavens! how that man could talk. He electrified large meetings. He had faith—don't you see?—he had the faith. He could get himself to believe anything—anything. He would have been a splendid leader of an extreme party.' 'What party?' I asked. 'Any party,' answered the other. 'He was an—an—extremist.' Did I not think so? I assented. Did I know, he asked, with a sudden flash of curiosity, 'what it was that had induced him to go out there?' 'Yes,' said I, and forthwith handed him the famous Report for publication, if he thought fit. He glanced through it hurriedly, mumbling all the time, judged 'it would do,' and took himself off with this plunder.

"Thus I was left at last with a slim packet of letters and the girl's portrait. She struck me as beautiful—I mean she had a beautiful expression. I know that the sunlight can be made to lie, too, yet one felt that no manipulation of light and pose could have conveyed the delicate shade of truthfulness upon those features. She seemed ready to listen without mental reservation, without suspicion, without a thought for herself. I concluded I would go and give her back her portrait and those letters myself. Curiosity? Yes; and also some other feeling perhaps. All that had been Kurtz's had passed out of my hands: his soul, his body, his station, his plans, his ivory, his career. There remained only his memory and his Intended—and I wanted to give that up, too, to the past, in a way—to surrender personally all that remained of him with me to that oblivion which is the last word of our common fate. I don't defend myself. I had no clear perception of what it was I really wanted. Perhaps it was an impulse of unconscious loyalty, or the fulfilment of one of those ironic necessities that lurk in the facts of human existence. I don't know. I can't tell. But I went.

"I thought his memory was like the other memories of the dead that accumulate in every man's life—a vague impress on the brain of shadows that had fallen on it in their swift and final passage; but before the high and ponderous door, between the tall houses of a street as still and decorous as a well-kept alley in a cemetery, I had a vision of him on the stretcher, opening his mouth voraciously, as if to devour all the earth with all its mankind. He lived then before me; he lived as much as he had ever lived—a shadow insatiable of splendid appearances, of frightful realities; a shadow darker than the shadow of the night, and draped nobly in the folds of a gorgeous eloquence. The vision seemed to enter the house with me—the stretcher, the phantom-bearers, the wild crowd of obedient worshippers, the gloom of the forests, the glitter of the reach between the murky bends, the beat of the drum, regular and muffled like the beating of a heart—the heart of a conquering darkness. It was a moment of triumph for the wilderness, an invading and vengeful rush which, it seemed to me, I would have to keep back alone for the salvation of another soul. And the memory of what I had heard him say afar there, with the horned shapes stirring at my back, in the glow of fires, within the patient woods, those broken phrases came back to me, were heard again in their ominous and terrifying simplicity. I remembered his abject pleading, his abject threats, the colossal scale of his vile desires, the meanness, the torment, the tempestuous anguish of his soul. And later on I seemed to see his collected languid manner, when he said one day, 'This lot of ivory now is really mine. The Company did not pay for it. I collected it myself at a very great personal risk. I am afraid they will try to claim it as theirs though. H'm. It is a difficult case. What do you think I ought to do—resist? Eh? I want no more than justice.' . . . He wanted no more than justice—no more than justice. I rang the bell before a mahogany door on the first floor, and while I waited he seemed to stare at me out of the glassy panel—stare with that wide and immense stare embracing, condemning, loathing all the universe. I seemed to hear the whispered cry, 'The horror! The horror!'

"The dusk was falling. I had to wait in a lofty drawing-room with three long windows from floor to ceiling that were like three luminous and bedraped columns. The bent gilt legs and backs of the furniture shone in indistinct curves. The tall marble fireplace had a cold and monumental whiteness. A grand piano stood massively in a corner; with dark gleams on the flat surfaces like a sombre and polished sarcophagus. A high door opened—closed. I rose.

"She came forward, all in black, with a pale head, floating towards me in the dusk. She was in mourning. It was more than a year since his death, more than a year since the news came; she seemed as though she would remember and mourn for ever. She took both my hands in hers and murmured, 'I had heard you were coming.' I noticed she was not very young—I mean not girlish. She had a mature capacity for fidelity, for belief, for suffering. The room seemed to have grown darker, as if all the sad light of the cloudy evening had taken refuge on her forehead. This fair hair, this pale visage, this pure brow, seemed surrounded by an ashy halo from which the dark eyes looked out at me. Their glance was guileless, profound, confident, and trustful. She carried her sorrowful head as though she were proud of that sorrow, as though she would say, I—I alone know how to mourn for him as he deserves. But while we were still shaking hands, such a look of awful desolation came upon her face that I perceived she was one of those creatures that are not the playthings of Time. For her he had died only yesterday. And, by Jove! the impression was so powerful that for me, too, he seemed to have died only yesterday—nay, this very minute. I saw her and him in the same instant of time—his death and her sorrow—I saw her sorrow in the very moment of his death. Do you understand? I saw them together—I heard them together. She had said, with a deep catch of the breath, 'I have survived' while my strained ears seemed to hear distinctly, mingled with her tone of despairing regret, the summing up whisper of his eternal condemnation. I asked myself what I was doing there, with a sensation of panic in my heart as though I had blundered into a place of cruel and absurd mysteries not fit for a human being to behold. She motioned me to a chair. We sat down. I laid the packet gently on the little table, and she put her hand over it. . . . 'You knew him well,' she murmured, after a moment of mourning silence.

"'Intimacy grows quickly out there,' I said. 'I knew him as well as it is possible for one man to know another.'

"'And you admired him,' she said. 'It was impossible to know him and not to admire him. Was it?'

"'He was a remarkable man,' I said, unsteadily. Then before the appealing fixity of her gaze, that seemed to watch for more words on my lips, I went on, 'It was impossible not to——'

"'Love him,' she finished eagerly, silencing me into an appalled dumbness. 'How true! how true! But when you think that no one knew him so well as I! I had all his noble confidence. I knew him best.'

"'You knew him best,' I repeated. And perhaps she did. But with every word spoken the room was growing darker, and only her forehead, smooth and white, remained illumined by the unextinguishable light of belief and love.

"'You were his friend,' she went on. 'His friend,' she repeated, a little louder. 'You must have been, if he had given you this, and sent you to me. I feel I can speak to you—and oh! I must speak. I want you—you who have heard his last words—to know I have been worthy of him. . . . It is not pride. . . . Yes! I am proud to know I understood him better than any one on earth—he told me so himself. And since his mother died I have had no one—no one—to—to——'

"I listened. The darkness deepened. I was not even sure whether he had given me the right bundle. I rather suspect he wanted me to take care of another batch of his papers which, after his death, I saw the manager examining under the lamp. And the girl talked, easing her pain in the certitude of my sympathy; she talked as thirsty men drink. I had heard that her engagement with Kurtz had been disapproved by her people. He wasn't rich enough or something. And indeed I don't know whether he had not been a pauper all his life. He had given me some reason to infer that it was his impatience of comparative poverty that drove him out there.

"'. . . Who was not his friend who had heard him speak once?' she was saying. 'He drew men towards him by what was best in them.' She looked at me with intensity. 'It is the gift of the great,' she went on, and the sound of her low voice seemed to have the accompaniment of all the other sounds, full of mystery, desolation, and sorrow, I had ever heard — the ripple of the river, the soughing of the trees swayed by the wind, the murmurs of the crowds, the faint ring of incomprehensible words cried from afar, the whisper of a voice speaking from beyond the threshold of an eternal darkness. 'But you have heard him! You know!' she cried.

"'Yes, I know,' I said with something like despair in my heart, but bowing my head before the faith that was in her, before that great and saving illusion that shone with an unearthly glow in the darkness, in the triumphant darkness from which I could not have defended her — from which I could not even defend myself.

"'What a loss to me — to us!' — she corrected herself with beautiful generosity; then added in a murmur, 'To the world.' By the last gleams of twilight I could see the glitter of her eyes, full of tears — of tears that would not fall.

"'I have been very happy — very fortunate — very proud,' she went on. 'Too fortunate. Too happy for a little while. And now I am unhappy for — for life.'

"She stood up; her fair hair seemed to catch all the remaining light in a glimmer of gold. I rose, too.

"'And of all this,' she went on, mournfully, 'of all his promise, and of all his greatness, of his generous mind, of his noble heart, nothing remains — nothing but a memory. You and I ——'

"'We shall always remember him,' I said, hastily.

"'No!' she cried. 'It is impossible that all this should be lost — that such a life should be sacrificed to leave nothing — but sorrow. You know what vast plans he had. I knew of them, too — I could not perhaps understand — but others knew of them. Something must remain. His words, at least, have not died.'

"'His words will remain,' I said.

"'And his example,' she whispered to herself. 'Men looked up to him — his goodness shone in every act. His example ——'

"'True,' I said; 'his example, too. Yes, his example. I forgot that.'

"'But I do not. I cannot — I cannot believe — not yet. I cannot believe that I shall never see him again, that nobody will see him again, never, never, never.'

"She put out her arms as if after a retreating figure, stretching them back and with clasped pale hands across the fading and narrow sheen of the window. Never see him! I saw him clearly enough then. I shall see this eloquent phantom as long as I live, and I shall see her, too, a tragic and familiar Shade, resembling in this gesture another one, tragic also, and bedecked with powerless charms, stretching bare brown arms over the glitter of the infernal stream, the stream of darkness. She said suddenly very low, 'He died as he lived.'

"'His end,' said I, with dull anger stirring in me, 'was in every way worthy of his life.'

"'And I was not with him,' she murmured. My anger subsided before a feeling of infinite pity.

"'Everything that could be done ——' I mumbled.

"'Ah, but I believed in him more than any one on earth — more than his own mother, more than — himself. He needed me! Me! I would have treasured every sigh, every word, every sign, every glance.'

"I felt like a chill grip on my chest. 'Don't,' I said, in a muffled voice.

"'Forgive me. I—I—have mourned so long in silence—in silence. . . . You were with him—to the last? I think of his loneliness. Nobody near to understand him as I would have understood. Perhaps no one to hear. . . .'

"'To the very end,' I said, shakily. 'I heard his very last words. . . .' I stopped in a fright.

"'Repeat them,' she murmured in a heart-broken tone. 'I want—I want—something—something—to—to live with.'

"I was on the point of crying at her, 'Don't you hear them?' The dusk was repeating them in a persistent whisper all around us, in a whisper that seemed to swell menacingly like the first whisper of a rising wind. 'The horror! the horror!'

"'His last word—to live with,' she insisted. 'Don't you understand I loved him—I loved him—I loved him!'

"I pulled myself together and spoke slowly.

"'The last word he pronounced was—your name.'

"I heard a light sigh and then my heart stood still, stopped dead short by an exulting and terrible cry, by the cry of inconceivable triumph and of unspeakable pain. 'I knew it—I was sure!' . . . She knew. She was sure. I heard her weeping; she had hidden her face in her hands. It seemed to me that the house would collapse before I could escape, that the heavens would fall upon my head. But nothing happened. The heavens do not fall for such a trifle. Would they have fallen, I wonder, if I had rendered Kurtz that justice which was his due? Hadn't he said he wanted only justice? But I couldn't. I could not tell her. It would have been too dark—too dark altogether. . . ."

Marlow ceased, and sat apart, indistinct and silent, in the pose of a meditating Buddha. Nobody moved for a time. "We have lost the first of the ebb," said the Director, suddenly. I raised my head. The offing was barred by a black bank of clouds, and the tranquil waterway leading to the uttermost ends of the earth flowed sombre under an overcast sky—seemed to lead into the heart of an immense darkness.

Colonialism: Europe and Africa

Colonialism was one of the defining issues of the twentieth century, which began with most of Asia and Africa under the sway of European nations. In 1800, European powers controlled about 35 percent of the globe. The competition among them to gain additional colonies gathered momentum over the next hundred years until, by 1914, Europe—led by Britain, France, Holland, and Portugal—could claim approximately 85 percent of the earth's surface. European dominance of large areas of Asia, Africa, and Latin America continued until after World War II, when colonies worldwide fought to gain their independence and a new age of "decolonization" or "postcolonialism" was ushered in.

"THE WHITE MAN'S BURDEN"

The primary impetus behind the acquisition of colonies, called at the time "the great game," was, of course, economic. An increasing population in Europe and a lack of enough agricultural land fueled the colonial enterprise. By 1870, for example, England could no longer grow enough food to feed itself. Less developed countries and regions in Asia, Africa, and the Caribbean were exploited for cheap labor, raw materials used for manufactures in European factories, and land. On maps made by European cartographers, large areas of Asia and Africa appeared as "blank spaces," as Marlow says in *Heart of Darkness;* Europeans did not recognize the presence or the property rights of indigenous peoples, and these white spaces were colored in only when a European nation colonized an area. P. 35

Colonial conquest was justified in terms of the benefits it bestowed on the colonized. Along with economic development, the

L'AFRICA
È IL
CONTINENTE
DI DOMANI

LAVORO PER L'EUROPA
RESA DALL'ASSE

white man said he was bringing civilization and Christianity to unenlightened regions of the world. Furthermore, this was a mission, "the white man's burden," as it was referred to at the time, but as Rudyard Kipling claims in his poem of that title (1899), the job was often a thankless one. And there was always the danger of being engulfed like Kurtz in *Heart of Darkness* by the supposed darkness one had set out to enlighten.

p. 104

CONRAD AND ACHEBE

Conrad's *Heart of Darkness* and Chinua Achebe's **"An Image of Africa"** represent European colonialism and a postcolonial response to it, respectively. At the time it was written, *Heart of Darkness* (1899) was one of several literary attacks on the excesses of European colonialism in the Congo. Conrad recognizes that the colonizers are there only for "the squeeze," as he calls it, and that their promises to bring enlightenment and civilization to the "dark continent" hid their real intentions. But Achebe points out that neither Conrad nor his narrator, Marlow, question the assumption that European culture is superior to that in the jungle. Achebe's essay raises important literary as well as social and historical questions: Is it reasonable to expect a great work of literature to rise above the perspectives of its time and place? Can a literary work grounded in mistaken ideas still be great literature?

p. 107

COLONIALISM IN THE CONGO

The Free State of the Congo was one of the most cruel colonial enterprises of the late nineteenth century. In 1876 Leopold II of Belgium, a nation less than fifty years old with no overseas possessions, called a conference of the European powers to consider Africa and "to open to civilization the only part of our globe where Christianity has not penetrated and to pierce the darkness which envelops

The wealth of a common global culture will . . . be expressed in the particularities of our different languages and cultures very much like a universal garden of many-coloured flowers.
– Ngugi, "Creating Space . . ." in *Moving the Centre* 24

◀ **L'Africa É il Continente di Domani (Africa Is the Continent of Tomorrow). Poster, Late 1930s**
This piece of propaganda was created during Mussolini's Fascist regime in Italy. The Fascists, seeking to extend their reach by colonizing more of Africa (Italy had claimed Somalia in 1889), followed Great Britain, Germany, Portugal, Spain, and Belgium in acquiring parts of the continent. This poster was created to drum up public support for the campaign. (The Art Archive / Imperial War Museum)

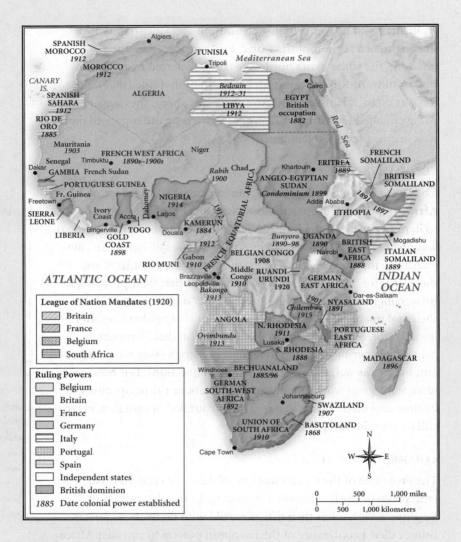

The Colonization of Africa, 1880–1939

From the late nineteenth century until the eve of World War II, most of Africa was divided up among seven European powers. The only independent states were Ethiopia and Liberia. After World War I, the newly formed League of Nations distributed Germany's African colonies to other countries, who were to govern them as "mandates," in preparation for eventual independence. Britain received German East Africa and Togo, South Africa was given German South-West Africa, while Kamerun (Cameroon) went to France and Ruandi-Urundi (Rwanda-Burundi) was assigned to Belgium.

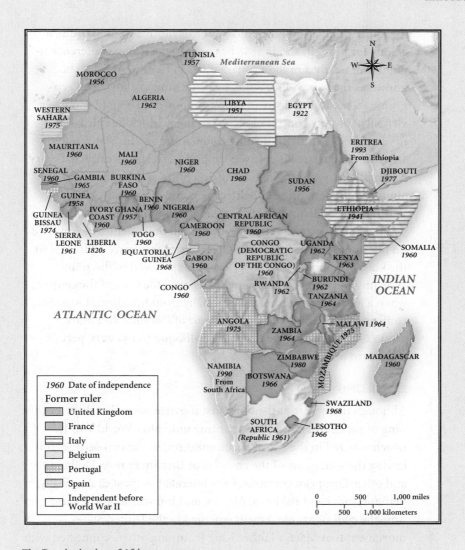

The Decolonization of Africa, 1951–2000

After World War II, African countries gained independence, sometimes peacefully and sometimes after armed struggle. The transition from European rule to self-governing nations was often followed by greater poverty, dictatorship, war, or famine in much of the continent. Striving for political, economic, and educational progress proved a difficult process.

Eng. Lit., my sister,
was more than a
cruel joke —
it was the heart
of alien conquest.
— FELIX MNTHALI

the entire population." Leopold's ulterior motive was to acquire a colony for himself, and in 1884 he convinced a Berlin conference to grant him nearly a million square miles in Central Africa to be known as the Congo Free State. By promising to allow open economic access and trade to all European powers, Leopold was given virtually absolute control over the territory, which he ruled—but never visited—until his death in 1908. Although his stated aims were humanitarian, his rule was despotic. His agents extracted ivory and rubber from the Congo using deception and violence and did almost nothing to bring enlightenment and civilization. George Washington Williams, an African American journalist and historian, was the first to expose Leopold's fraud and the cruelties he imposed p. 118 on the Congolese people in *An Open Letter,* a missive addressed to the king and published in 1890. Leopold managed to discredit Williams and cover up his own crimes until the turn of the century, when a journalistic onslaught, especially from Britain and America, confirmed Williams's allegations. *Heart of Darkness* and Mark p. 125 Twain's satiric essay *King Leopold's Soliloquy* (1905) were part of this storm of criticism.

DECOLONIZATION

Although there were anti-imperialist movements active at the beginning of the century, little change came until after World War II, which ushered in the age of decolonization. In the two decades following the war, many of the colonies of Britain, France, Holland, and other European countries were liberated—most dramatically, perhaps, India and Pakistan, Algeria, and Indonesia. At the same time the civil rights movement emerged in the United States, a movement that Martin Luther King Jr. among others connected with worldwide decolonization. By 1990 forty-nine new African nations had been formed. There were instances of peaceful resistance movements, like the nonviolent campaign led by Mohandas Gandhi in India, but more often independence was gained by bitter wars of liberation, as in Algeria.

The classic work on the psychology of colonialism is Frantz p. 129 Fanon's *The Wretched of the Earth* (1961). Fanon, a psychiatrist from the French colony of Martinique, left his medical post to join the struggle for Algerian independence. His experiences in the war contributed to his view that colonialism could be ended only by violence. Fanon's analysis of the polarities of colonizer and colonized is shared by his fellow Martinican Aimé Césaire, whose *Discourse on Colonialism* (1950) demonstrates "how colonization works to *decivilize* the colonizer, to *brutalize* him in the true sense of the word, to awaken him to buried instincts, to covetousness, violence, race hatred, and moral relativism." Kurtz enacts this drama, as does Prospero in Césaire's play, **A Tempest** (1969), a reworking of Shakespeare's *The Tempest*; Césaire's Prospero becomes a colonizing slave owner and Caliban his slave. In a selection from the final scene of the play included here, Césaire depicts the intractibility of the colonial situation that leaves Prospero and Caliban alone on an island locked in undying enmity. Nigerian writer Chinweizu (p. 142) uses characters from *The Tempest* to represent different positions in his analysis. He urges a generation of Calibans to challenge the Ariels and to re-Africanize the continent. Felix **Mnthali,** a poet from Malawi who now lives in Botswana, expresses his take on the role of English literature in Africa in his poem **"The Stranglehold of English Lit."** In **"Creating Space for a Hundred Flowers to Bloom,"** Kenyan writer **Ngugi Wa Thiong'o** takes a more positive view of the postcolonial situation. By rediscovering and affirming their native linguistic traditions, Africans can, Ngugi asserts, challenge the legacy of colonialism and enter the global culture on equal terms.

> When the native hears a speech about Western culture he pulls out his knife.
> – FRANTZ FANON, *The Wretched of the Earth*

p. 137

mun-THAH-lee

p. 148

p. 150

en-GOO-gee wah thee-ONG-oh

■ CONNECTIONS

In the World: Emancipation (Book 5); *In the World:* East and West (Book 5); "Imagining Africa," p. 853; *In the World:* Crossing Cultures, p. 1278. Colonialism is addressed by the abovementioned *In the World* sections in Books 5 and 6 of this anthology. How was the anticolonial struggle of the twentieth century brought about by the social and economic forces and by the ideal of freedom inherited from the European Enlightenment?

Chinua Achebe, *Things Fall Apart,* p. 1023; Léopold Senghor, "Prayer to the Masks," p. 886; Wole Soyinka, *The Lion and the Jewel,* p. 1146; Bessie Head, "Snapshots of a Wedding," p. 1213. Achebe's novel *Things Fall Apart* presents a Nigerian village disrupted by colonial intrusion. Senghor, the Senegalese writer who founded the Négritude movement along with Césaire, writes about being black in a white world in "Prayer to the Masks." Soyinka's play, *The Lion and the Jewel,* finds comedy in Nigerian natives like schoolmaster Lakunle, whose exaggerated respect for European culture makes him a fool. Head's "Snapshots of a Wedding" contrasts traditional village customs with urban—and Western—ways of doing things. How do these depictions of African life relate to one another? What elements of colonialism link them together?

William Butler Yeats, "Easter 1916," p. 190; Pablo Neruda, "The United Fruit Co.," p. 686. Although colonialism is usually associated with the "Third World," especially with Asia and Africa, it is also a theme in many of Yeats's poems. Poems like

> You know very well that I'm not interested in peace. I'm interested in being free! Free, you hear?
> – Caliban to Prospero, *A Tempest*

"Easter 1916" respond to the struggle of the Irish to free themselves from British rule. And Neruda's "The United Fruit Co." treats the exploitation of Central America by U.S. corporations. How do these colonized peoples' experiences differ from those in India and Africa? In what ways are their depictions of colonization similar?

■ **PRONUNCIATION**

Mnthali: mun-THAH-lee
Ngugi Wa Thiong'o: en-GOO-gee wah thee-ONG-oh

∾ RUDYARD KIPLING

B. INDIA, 1865–1936

Though many of Kipling's works, particularly his short stories and novels, demonstrate an understanding and appreciation of the Indian people and their culture, in other works, like the poem "The White Man's Burden" (1899), Kipling sounds like a jingoistic imperialist. The poem's unquestioned assumption of European superiority expresses the attitude that promoted colonialism in the first place and excused its excesses, an attitude nearly universal among nineteenth-century Europeans, even those critical of colonial enterprise.

∾ The White Man's Burden

Take up the White Man's burden —
    Send forth the best ye breed —
Go, bind your sons to exile
    To serve your captives' need;
To wait, in heavy harness,
    On fluttered folk and wild —
Your new-caught sullen peoples,
    Half devil and half child.

Take up the White Man's burden —
    In patience to abide,
To veil the threat of terror
    And check the show of pride;
By open speech and simple,
    An hundred times made plain,

10

The Rhodes Colossus. Drawing *Cecil Rhodes was prime minister of the Cape Colony, in what is now South Africa, from 1890 to 1897. Here pictured as a giant straddling and taking the measure of the continent of Africa, he dreamed of expanding the British empire "from the Cape to Cairo." (Hulton/Archive)*

To seek another's profit
    And work another's gain.

Take up the White Man's burden—
    The savage wars of peace—
Fill full the mouth of Famine,
    And bid the sickness cease;
And when your goal is nearest
    (The end for others sought)
Watch sloth and heathen folly
    Bring all your hope to nought.

Take up the White Man's burden—
    No iron rule of kings,
But toil of serf and sweeper—
    The tale of common things.
The ports ye shall not enter,
    The roads ye shall not tread,

Go, make them with your living
    And mark them with your dead.

Take up the White Man's burden,
    And reap his old reward—
The blame of those ye better
    The hate of those ye guard—
The cry of hosts ye humour
    (Ah, slowly?) toward the light:—
"Why brought ye us from bondage,
40   Our loved Egyptian night?"[1]

Take up the White Man's burden—
    Ye dare not stoop to less—
Nor call too loud on Freedom
    To cloak your weariness.
By all ye will or whisper,
    By all ye leave or do,
The silent sullen peoples
    Shall weigh your God and you.

Take up the White Man's burden!
50   Have done with childish days—
The lightly-proffered laurel,
    The easy ungrudged praise:
Comes now, to search your manhood
    Through all the thankless years,
Cold, edged with dear-bought wisdom,
    The judgment of your peers.

---

[1] **"Why . . . Egyptian night?":** When things got hard in the wilderness, the Israelites blamed Moses and Aaron for their troubles; see Exodus 16:23.

❧ CHINUA ACHEBE

B. NIGERIA, 1930

In the following transcript of a lecture delivered at the University of Massachusetts in February 1975, Nigerian novelist Chinua Achebe challenges the status of *Heart of Darkness* as one of the great books of Western literature. Conrad's novel, Achebe argues, does not treat its African characters as fully human. Achebe's own novel *Things Fall Apart* can be read as a response to Conrad's story. (For more on Chinua Achebe and the text of *Things Fall Apart,* see p. 1017.)

All notes are the editors' unless otherwise indicated.

❧ An Image of Africa

It was a fine autumn morning at the beginning of this academic year such as encouraged friendliness to passing strangers. Brisk youngsters were hurrying in all directions, many of them obviously freshmen in their first flush of enthusiasm. An older man, going the same way as I, turned and remarked to me how very young they came these days. I agreed. Then he asked me if I was a student too. I said no, I was a teacher. What did I teach? African literature. Now that was funny, he said, because he never had thought of Africa as having that kind of stuff, you know. By this time I was walking much faster. "Oh well," I heard him say finally, behind me, "I guess I have to take your course to find out."

A few weeks later I received two very touching letters from high-school children in Yonkers, New York, who — bless their teacher — had just read *Things Fall Apart.* One of them was particularly happy to learn about the customs and superstitions of an African tribe.

I propose to draw from these rather trivial encounters rather heavy conclusions which at first sight might seem somewhat out of proportion to them: But only at first sight.

The young fellow from Yonkers, perhaps partly on account of his age but I believe also for much deeper and more serious reasons, is obviously unaware that the life of his own tribesmen in Yonkers, New York, is full of odd customs and superstitions and, like everybody else in his culture, imagines that he needs a trip to Africa to encounter those things.

The other person being fully my own age could not be excused on the grounds of his years. Ignorance might be a more likely reason; but here again I believe that something more willful than a mere lack of information was at work. For did not that erudite British historian and Regius Professor at Oxford, Hugh Trevor Roper, pronounce a few years ago that African history did not exist?

If there is something in these utterances more than youthful experience, more than a lack of factual knowledge, what is it? Quite simply it is the desire — one might indeed say the need—in Western psychology to set up Africa as a foil to Europe, a place of negations at once remote and vaguely familiar in comparison with which Europe's own state of spiritual grace will be manifest.

This need is not new: which should relieve us of considerable responsibility and perhaps make us even willing to look at this phenomenon dispassionately. I have neither the desire nor, indeed, the competence to do so with the tools of the social and biological sciences. But, I can respond, as a novelist, to one famous book of European fiction, Joseph Conrad's *Heart of Darkness,* which better than any other work I know displays that Western desire and need which I have just spoken about. Of course, there are whole libraries of books devoted to the same purpose, but most of them are so obvious and so crude that few people worry about them today. Conrad, on the other hand, is undoubtedly one of the great stylists of modern fiction and a good storyteller into the bargain. His contribution therefore falls automatically into a different class—permanent literature—read and taught and constantly evaluated by serious academics. *Heart of Darkness* is indeed so secure today that a leading Conrad scholar has numbered it "among the half-dozen greatest short novels in the English language."[1] I will return to this critical opinion in due course because it may seriously modify my earlier suppositions about who may or may not be guilty in the things of which I will now speak.

Heart of Darkness projects the image of Africa as "the other world," the antithesis of Europe and therefore of civilization, a place where a man's vaunted intelligence and refinement are finally mocked by triumphant bestiality. The book opens on the River Thames, tranquil, resting peacefully "at the decline of day after ages of good service done to the race that peopled its banks." But the actual story takes place on the River Congo, the very antithesis of the Thames. The River Congo is quite decidedly not a River Emeritus. It has rendered no service and enjoys no old-age pension. We are told that "going up that river was like travelling back to the earliest beginning of the world."

Is Conrad saying then that these two rivers are very different, one good, the other bad? Yes, but that is not the real point. What actually worries Conrad is the lurking hint of kinship, of common ancestry. For the Thames, too, "has been one of the dark places of the earth." It conquered its darkness, of course, and is now at peace. But if it were to visit its primordial relative, the Congo, it would run the terrible risk of hearing grotesque, suggestive echoes of its own forgotten darkness, and of falling victim to an avenging recrudescence of the mindless frenzy of the first beginnings.

I am not going to waste your time with examples of Conrad's famed evocation of the African atmosphere. In the final consideration it amounts to no more than a steady, ponderous, fake-ritualistic repetition of two sentences, one about silence and the other about frenzy. An example of the former is "It was the stillness of an implacable force brooding over an inscrutable intention" and of the latter, "The

---

[1] "among . . . language": Albert J. Guerard, Introduction to *Heart of Darkness* (New York: New American Library, 1950), p. 9.

steamer toiled along slowly on the edge of a black and incomprehensible frenzy." Of course, there is a judicious change of adjective from time to time so that instead of "inscrutable," for example, you might have "unspeakable," etc., etc.

The eagle-eyed English critic, F. R. Leavis, drew attention nearly thirty years ago to Conrad's "adjectival insistence upon inexpressible and incomprehensible mystery." That insistence must not be dismissed lightly, as many Conrad critics have tended to do, as a mere stylistic flaw. For it raises serious questions of artistic good faith. When a writer, while pretending to record scenes, incidents and their impact, is in reality engaged in inducing hypnotic stupor in his readers through a bombardment of emotive words and other forms of trickery, much more has to be at stake than stylistic felicity. Generally, normal readers are well armed to detect and resist such underhand activity. But Conrad chose his subject well—one which was guaranteed not to put him in conflict with the psychological predisposition of his readers or raise the need for him to contend with their resistance. He chose the role of purveyor of comforting myths.

The most interesting and revealing passages in *Heart of Darkness* are, however, about people. I must quote a long passage from the middle of the story in which representatives of Europe in a steamer going down the Congo encounter the denizens of Africa:

> We were wanderers on a prehistoric earth, on an earth that wore the aspect of an unknown planet. We could have fancied ourselves the first of men taking possession of an accursed inheritance, to be subdued at the cost of profound anguish and of excessive toil. But suddenly, as we struggled round a bend, there would be a glimpse of rush walls, of peaked grass-roofs, a burst of yells, a whirl of black limbs, a mass of hands clapping, of feet stamping, of bodies swaying, of eyes rolling, under the droop of heavy and motionless foliage. The steamer toiled along slowly on the edge of a black and incomprehensible frenzy. The prehistoric man was cursing us, praying to us, welcoming us—who could tell? We were cut off from the comprehension of our surroundings; we glided past like phantoms, wondering and secretly appalled, as sane men would be before an enthusiastic outbreak in a madhouse. We could not remember because we were travelling in the night of first ages, of those ages that are gone, leaving hardly a sign—and no memories.
>
> The earth seemed unearthly. We are accustomed to look upon the shackled form of a conquered monster, but there—there you could look at a thing monstrous and free. It was unearthly, and the men were—No, they were not inhuman. Well, you know, that was the worst of it—this suspicion of their not being inhuman. It would come slowly to one. They howled and leaped, and spun, and made horrid faces; but what thrilled you was just the thought of your remote kinship with this wild and passionate uproar. Ugly. Yes, it was ugly enough; but if you were man enough you would admit to yourself that there was in you just the faintest trace of a response to the terrible frankness of that noise, a dim suspicion of there being a meaning in it which you—you so remote from the night of first ages—could comprehend.

Herein lies the meaning of *Heart of Darkness* and the fascination it holds over the Western mind: "What thrilled you was just the thought of their humanity—like yours. . . . Ugly."

Having shown us Africa in the mass, Conrad then zeros in on a specific example, giving us one of his rare descriptions of an African who is not just limbs or rolling eyes:

> And between whiles I had to look after the savage who was fireman. He was an improved specimen; he could fire up a vertical boiler. He was there below me, and, upon my word, to look at him was as edifying as seeing a dog in a parody of breeches and a feather hat, walking on his hind legs. A few months of training had done for that really fine chap. He squinted at the steam gauge and at the water gauge with an evident effort of intrepidity — and he had filed his teeth, too, the poor devil, and the wool of his pate shaved into queer patterns, and three ornamental scars on each of his cheeks. He ought to have been clapping his hands and stamping his feet on the bank, instead of which he was hard at work, a thrall to strange witchcraft, full of improving knowledge.

As everybody knows, Conrad is a romantic on the side. He might not exactly admire savages clapping their hands and stamping their feet but they have at least the merit of being in their place, unlike this dog in a parody of breeches. For Conrad, things (and persons) being in their place is of the utmost importance.

Towards the end of the story, Conrad lavishes great attention quite unexpectedly on an African woman who has obviously been some kind of mistress to Mr. Kurtz and now presides (if I may be permitted a little imitation of Conrad) like a formidable mystery over the inexorable imminence of his departure:

> She was savage and superb, wild-eyed and magnificent . . . She stood looking at us without a stir and like the wilderness itself, with an air of brooding over an inscrutable purpose.

This Amazon is drawn in considerable detail, albeit of a predictable nature, for two reasons. First, she is in her place and so can win Conrad's special brand of approval; and second, she fulfills a structural requirement of the story; she is a savage counterpart to the refined, European woman with whom the story will end:

> She came forward, all in black with a pale head, floating towards me in the dusk. She was in mourning. . . . She took both my hands in hers and murmured, "I had heard you were coming" . . . She had a mature capacity for fidelity, for belief, for suffering.

The difference in the attitude of the novelist to these two women is conveyed in too many direct and subtle ways to need elaboration. But perhaps the most significant difference is the one implied in the author's bestowal of human expression to the one and the withholding of it from the other. It is clearly not part of Conrad's purpose to confer language on the "rudimentary souls" of Africa. They only "exchanged short grunting phrases" even among themselves but mostly they were too busy with their frenzy. There are two occasions in the book, however, when Conrad departs somewhat from his practice and confers speech, even English speech, on the savages. The first occurs when cannibalism gets the better of them:

> "Catch 'im," he snapped, with a bloodshot widening of his eyes and a flash of sharp white teeth — "catch 'im. Give 'im to us." "To you, eh?" I asked; "what would you do with them?" "Eat 'im!" he said curtly . . .

The other occasion is the famous announcement:

> Mistah Kurtz—he dead.

At first sight, these instances might be mistaken for unexpected acts of generosity from Conrad. In reality, they constitute some of his best assaults. In the case of the cannibals, the incomprehensible grunts that had thus far served them for speech suddenly proved inadequate for Conrad's purpose of letting the European glimpse the unspeakable craving in their hearts. Weighing the necessity for consistency in the portrayal of the dumb brutes against the sensational advantages of securing their conviction by clear, unambiguous evidence issuing out of their own mouth, Conrad chose the latter. As for the announcement of Mr. Kurtz's death by the "insolent black head in the doorway," what better or more appropriate *finis* could be written to the horror story of that wayward child of civilization who willfully had given his soul to the powers of darkness and "taken a high seat amongst the devils of the land" than the proclamation of his physical death by the forces he had joined?

It might be contended, of course, that the attitude to the African in *Heart of Darkness* is not Conrad's but that of his fictional narrator, Marlow, and that far from endorsing it Conrad might indeed be holding it up to irony and criticism. Certainly, Conrad appears to go to considerable pains to set up layers of insulation between himself and the moral universe of his story. He has, for example, a narrator behind a narrator. The primary narrator is Marlow but his account is given to us through the filter of a second, shadowy person. But if Conrad's intention is to draw a *cordon sanitaire*[2] between himself and the moral and psychological malaise of his narrator, his care seems to me totally wasted because he neglects to hint however subtly or tentatively at an alternative frame of reference by which we may judge the actions and opinions of his characters. It would not have been beyond Conrad's power to make that provision if he had thought it necessary. Marlow seems to me to enjoy Conrad's complete confidence—a feeling reinforced by the close similarities between their careers.

Marlow comes through to us not only as a witness of truth, but one holding those advanced and humane views appropriate to the English liberal tradition which required all Englishmen of decency to be deeply shocked by atrocities in Bulgaria or the Congo of King Leopold of the Belgians or wherever. Thus Marlow is able to toss out such bleeding-heart sentiments as these:

> They were all dying slowly—it was very clear. They were not enemies, they were not criminals, they were nothing earthly now—nothing but black shadows of disease and starvation, lying confusedly in the greenish gloom. Brought from all the recesses of the coast in all the legality of time contracts, lost in uncongenial surroundings, fed on unfamiliar food, they sickened, became inefficient, and were then allowed to crawl away and rest.

The kind of liberalism espoused here by Marlow/Conrad touched all the best minds of the age in England, Europe, and America. It took different forms in the minds of

---

[2] *cordon sanitaire:* A buffer.

different people but almost always managed to sidestep the ultimate question of equality between white people and black people. That extraordinary missionary, Albert Schweitzer,[3] who sacrificed brilliant careers in music and theology in Europe for a life of service to Africans in much the same area as Conrad writes about, epitomizes the ambivalence. In a comment which I have often quoted but must quote one last time Schweitzer says: "The African is indeed my brother but my junior brother." And so he proceeded to build a hospital appropriate to the needs of junior brothers with standards of hygiene reminiscent of medical practice in the days before the germ theory of disease came into being. Naturally, he became a sensation in Europe and America. Pilgrims flocked, and I believe still flock even after he has passed on, to witness the prodigious miracle in Lamberene, on the edge of the primeval forest.

Conrad's liberalism would not take him quite as far as Schweitzer's, though. He would not use the word "brother" however qualified; the farthest he would go was "kinship." When Marlow's African helmsman falls down with a spear in his heart he gives his white master one final disquieting look.

> And the intimate profundity of that look he gave me when he received his hurt remains to this day in my memory—like a claim of distant kinship affirmed in a supreme moment.

It is important to note that Conrad, careful as ever with his words, is not talking so much about *distant kinship* as about someone *laying a claim* on it. The black man lays a claim on the white man which is well-nigh intolerable. It is the laying of this claim which frightens and at the same time fascinates Conrad, ". . . the thought of their humanity—like yours . . . Ugly."

The point of my observations should be quite clear by now, namely, that Conrad was a bloody racist. That this simple truth is glossed over in criticism of his work is due to the fact that white racism against Africa is such a normal way of thinking that its manifestations go completely undetected. Students of *Heart of Darkness* will often tell you that Conrad is concerned not so much with Africa as with the deterioration of one European mind caused by solitude and sickness. They will point out to you that Conrad is, if anything, less charitable to the Europeans in the story than he is to the natives. A Conrad student told me in Scotland last year that Africa is merely a setting for the disintegration of the mind of Mr. Kurtz.

Which is partly the point: Africa as setting and backdrop which eliminates the African as human factor. Africa as a metaphysical battlefield devoid of all recognizable humanity, into which the wandering European enters at his peril. Of course, there is a preposterous and perverse kind of arrogance in thus reducing Africa to the role of props for the breakup of one petty European mind. But that is not even the point. The real question is the dehumanization of Africa and Africans which this age-long attitude has fostered and continues to foster in the world. And the question

---

[3] **Albert Schweitzer** (1875–1965): Alsatian philosopher, theologian, musician, writer, physicist, and missionary; he gave his life to a medical mission and hospital at Lamberene, in Gabon, West Africa.

is whether a novel which celebrates this dehumanization, which depersonalizes a portion of the human race, can be called a great work of art. My answer is: No, it cannot. I would not call that man an artist, for example, who composes an eloquent instigation to one people to fall upon another and destroy them. No matter how striking his imagery or how beautifully his cadences fall, such a man is no more a great artist than another may be called a priest who reads the mass backwards or a physician who poisons his patients. All those men in Nazi Germany who lent their talent to the service of virulent racism whether in science, philosophy, or the arts have generally and rightly been condemned for their perversions. The time is long overdue for taking a hard look at the work of creative artists who apply their talents, alas often considerable as in the case of Conrad, to set people against people. This, I take it, is what Yevtushenko[4] is after when he tells us that a poet cannot be a slave trader at the same time, and gives the striking example of Arthur Rimbaud,[5] who was fortunately honest enough to give up any pretenses to poetry when he opted for slave trading. For poetry surely can only be on the side of man's deliverance and not his enslavement; for the brotherhood and unity of all mankind and against the doctrines of Hitler's master races or Conrad's "rudimentary souls."

Last year was the fiftieth anniversary of Conrad's death. He was born in 1857, the very year in which the first Anglican missionaries were arriving among my own people in Nigeria. It was certainly not his fault that he lived his life at a time when the reputation of the black man was at a particularly low level. But even after due allowances have been made for all the influences of contemporary prejudice on his sensibility, there remains still in Conrad's attitude a residue of antipathy to black people which his peculiar psychology alone can explain. His own account of his first encounter with a black man is very revealing:

> A certain enormous buck nigger encountered in Haiti fixed my conception of blind, furious, unreasoning rage, as manifested in the human animal to the end of my days. Of the nigger I used to dream for years afterwards.

Certainly, Conrad had a problem with niggers. His inordinate love of that word itself should be of interest to psychoanalysts. Sometimes his fixation on blackness is equally interesting as when he gives us this brief description:

> A black figure stood up, strode on long black legs, waving long black arms.

as though we might expect a black figure striding along on black legs to wave *white* arms! But so unrelenting is Conrad's obsession.

As a matter of interest Conrad gives us in *A Personal Record* what amounts to a companion piece to the buck nigger of Haiti. At the age of sixteen Conrad encountered

---

[4] **Yevtushenko:** Yevgeny Yevtushenko (b. 1933), Russian poet known in the West in particular for his poems criticizing Stalinism.

[5] **Arthur Rimbaud** (1854–1891): French symbolist poet who abandoned poetry for a life of adventure; among his later occupations were slave trading and gunrunning.

his first Englishman in Europe. He calls him "my unforgettable Englishman" and describes him in the following manner:

> [his] calves exposed to the public gaze . . . dazzled the beholder by the splendor of their marble-like condition and their rich tone of young ivory . . . The light of a headlong, exalted satisfaction with the world of men . . . illumined his face . . . and triumphant eyes. In passing he cast a glance of kindly curiosity and a friendly gleam of big, sound, shiny teeth . . . his white calves twinkled sturdily.

Irrational love and irrational hate jostling together in the heart of that tormented man. But whereas irrational love may at worst engender foolish acts of indiscretion, irrational hate can endanger the life of the community. Naturally, Conrad is a dream for psychoanalytic critics. Perhaps the most detailed study of him in this direction is by Bernard C. Meyer, M.D. In this lengthy book, Dr. Meyer follows every conceivable lead (and sometimes inconceivable ones) to explain Conrad. As an example, he gives us long disquisitions on the significance of hair and hair-cutting in Conrad. And yet not even one word is spared for his attitude to black people. Not even the discussion of Conrad's anti-Semitism was enough to spark off in Dr. Meyer's mind those other dark and explosive thoughts. Which only leads one to surmise that Western psychoanalysts must regard the kind of racism displayed by Conrad as absolutely normal despite the profoundly important work done by Frantz Fanon[6] in the psychiatric hospitals of French Algeria.

Whatever Conrad's problems were, you might say he is now safely dead. Quite true. Unfortunately, his heart of darkness plagues us still. Which is why an offensive and totally deplorable book can be described by a serious scholar as "among the half dozen greatest short novels in the English language," and why it is today perhaps the most commonly prescribed novel in the twentieth-century literature courses in our own English Department here. Indeed the time is long overdue for a hard look at things.

There are two probable grounds on which what I have said so far may be contested. The first is that it is no concern of fiction to please people about whom it is written. I will go along with that. But I am not talking about pleasing people. I am talking about a book which parades in the most vulgar fashion prejudices and insults from which a section of mankind has suffered untold agonies and atrocities in the past and continues to do so in many ways and many places today. I am talking about a story in which the very humanity of black people is called in question. It seems to me totally inconceivable that great art or even good art could possibly reside in such unwholesome surroundings.

Secondly, I may be challenged on the grounds of actuality. Conrad, after all, sailed down the Congo in 1890 when my own father was still a babe in arms, and recorded what he saw. How could I stand up in 1975, fifty years after his death and purport to contradict him? My answer is that as a sensible man I will not accept just any traveller's tales solely on the grounds that I have not made the journey myself. I

---

[6] **Frantz Fanon:** See the excerpt from *The Wretched of the Earth*, p. 129, for more on Fanon.

will not trust the evidence even of a man's very eyes when I suspect them to be as jaundiced as Conrad's. And we also happen to know that Conrad was, in the words of his biographer, Bernard C. Meyer, "notoriously inaccurate in the rendering of his own history."[7]

But more important by far is the abundant testimony about Conrad's savages which we could gather if we were so inclined from other sources and which might lead us to think that these people must have had other occupations besides merging into the evil forest or materializing out of it simply to plague Marlow and his dispirited band. For as it happened, soon after Conrad had written his book an event of far greater consequence was taking place in the art world of Europe. This is how Frank Willett, a British art historian, describes it:

> Gauguin had gone to Tahiti, the most extravagant individual act of turning to a non-European culture in the decades immediately before and after 1900, when European artists were avid for new artistic experiences, but it was only about 1904–5 that African art began to make its distinctive impact. One piece is still identifiable; it is a mask that had been given to Maurice Vlaminck in 1905. He records that Derain was "speechless" and "stunned" when he saw it, bought it from Vlaminck and in turn showed it to Picasso and Matisse, who were also greatly affected by it. Ambroise Vollard then borrowed it and had it cast in bronze . . . The revolution of twentieth century art was under way![8]

The mask in question was made by other savages living just north of Conrad's River Congo. They have a name, the Fang people, and are without a doubt among the world's greatest masters of the sculptured form. As you might have guessed, the event to which Frank Willett refers marked the beginning of cubism and the infusion of new life into European art that had run completely out of strength.

The point of all this is to suggest that Conrad's picture of the people of the Congo seems grossly inadequate even at the height of their subjection to the ravages of King Leopold's International Association for the Civilization of Central Africa. Travellers with closed minds can tell us little except about themselves. But even those not blinkered, like Conrad, with xenophobia, can be astonishingly blind.

Let me digress a little here. One of the greatest and most intrepid travellers of all time, Marco Polo, journeyed to the Far East from the Mediterranean in the thirteenth century and spent twenty years in the court of Kublai Khan in China. On his return to Venice he set down in his book entitled *Description of the World* his impressions of the peoples and places and customs he had seen. There are at least two extraordinary omissions in his account. He says nothing about the art of printing unknown as yet in Europe but in full flower in China. He either did not notice it at all or if he did, failed to see what use Europe could possibly have for it. Whatever reason, Europe had to wait another hundred years for Gutenberg. But even more spectacular was Marco Polo's omission of any reference to the Great Wall of China nearly

---

[7] **"notoriously . . . history"**: Meyer, p. 30.

[8] **Gaugin . . . under way**: Frank Willett, *African Art* (New York: Praeger, 1971), pp. 35–36.

four thousand miles long and already more than one thousand years old at the time of his visit. Again, he may not have seen it; but the Great Wall of China is the only structure built by man which is visible from the moon![9] Indeed, travellers can be blind.

As I said earlier, Conrad did not originate the image of Africa which we find in his book. It was and is the dominant image of Africa in the Western imagination and Conrad merely brought the peculiar gifts of his own mind to bear on it. For reasons which can certainly use close psychological inquiry, the West seems to suffer deep anxieties about the precariousness of its civilization and to have a need for constant reassurance by comparing itself to Africa. If Europe, advancing in civilization, could cast a backward glance periodically at Africa trapped in primordial barbarity, it could say with faith and feeling: There, but for the grace of God, go I. Africa is to Europe as the picture is to Dorian Gray[10] — a carrier onto whom the master unloads his physical and moral deformities so that he may go forward, erect and immaculate. Consequently, Africa is something to be avoided just as the picture has to be hidden away to safeguard the man's jeopardous integrity. Keep away from Africa, or else! Mr. Kurtz of *Heart of Darkness* should have heeded that warning and the prowling horror in his heart would have kept its place, chained to its lair. But he foolishly exposed himself to the wild irresistible allure of the jungle and lo! the darkness found him out.

In my original conception of this talk I had thought to conclude it nicely on an appropriately positive note in which I would suggest from my privileged position in African and Western culture some advantages the West might derive from Africa once it rid its mind of old prejudices and began to look at Africa not through a haze of distortions and cheap mystification but quite simply as a continent of people — not angels, but not rudimentary souls either — just people, often highly gifted people and often strikingly successful in their enterprise with life and society. But as I thought more about the stereotype image, about its grip and pervasiveness, about the willful tenacity with which the West holds it to its heart; when I thought of your television and the cinema and newspapers, about books read in schools and out of school, of churches preaching to empty pews about the need to send help to the heathen in Africa, I realized that no easy optimism was possible. And there is something totally wrong in offering bribes to the West in return for its good opinion of Africa. Ultimately, the abandonment of unwholesome thoughts must be its own and only reward. Although I have used the word *willful* a few times in this talk to characterize the West's view of Africa it may well be that what is happening at this stage is more akin to reflex action than calculated malice. Which does not make the situation more, but less, hopeful. Let me give you one last and really minor example of what I mean.

---

[9] About the omission of the Great Wall of China, I am indebted to *The Journey of Marco Polo* as recreated by artist Michael Foreman, published by *Pegasus Magazine*, 1974. [Achebe's note.]

[10] **Africa is . . . Dorian Gray:** In Oscar Wilde's novel *The Picture of Dorian Gray* (1891), a portrait of the hero bears all his marks of age and guilt while he himself remains young.

Last November the *Christian Science Monitor* carried an interesting article written by its education editor on the serious psychological and learning problems faced by little children who speak one language at home and then go to school where something else is spoken. It was a wide-ranging article taking in Spanish-speaking children in this country, the children of migrant Italian workers in Germany, the quadrilingual phenomenon in Malaysia, and so on. And all this while the article speaks unequivocally about *language.* But then out of the blue sky comes this:

> In London there is an enormous immigration of children who speak Indian or Nigerian dialects, or some other native language.[11]

I believe that the introduction of *dialects,* which is technically erroneous in the context, is almost a reflex action caused by an instinctive desire of the writer to downgrade the discussion to the level of Africa and India. And this is quite comparable to Conrad's withholding of language from his rudimentary souls. Language is too grand for these chaps; let's give them dialects. In all this business a lot of violence is inevitably done to words and their meaning. Look at the phrase "native language" in the above excerpt. Surely the only native language possible in London is Cockney English. But our writer obviously means something else—something Indians and Africans speak.

Perhaps a change will come. Perhaps this is the time when it can begin, when the high optimism engendered by the breathtaking achievements of Western science and industry is giving way to doubt and even confusion. There is just the possibility that Western man may begin to look seriously at the achievements of other people. I read in the papers the other day a suggestion that what America needs at this time is somehow to bring back the extended family. And I saw in my mind's eye future African Peace Corps Volunteers coming to help you set up the system.

Seriously, although the work which needs to be done may appear too daunting, I believe that it is not one day too soon to begin. And where better than at a University?

---

[11] In London . . . language: *Christian Science Monitor,* Nov. 15, 1974, p. 11.

GEORGE WASHINGTON WILLIAMS
B. UNITED STATES, 1849–1891

Lawyer, clergyman, journalist, and historian, George Washington Williams is best known for *History of the Negro Race in America from 1619 to 1880,* a work that prompted W. E. B. Du Bois to call him "the greatest historian of the race." After interviewing Leopold II in 1889, Williams described the king as "one of the noblest sovereigns in the world; an emperor whose highest ambition is to serve the cause of Christian civilization." However, his subsequent experience in the Congo would change his mind about the sovereign. He arranged to visit the colony in 1890 to gather material for a book and to evaluate the feasibility of sending skilled black American artisans there to help in the Congo's development. During his six months there, he became increasingly disenchanted with Leopold and his colony. Williams's *An Open Letter,* written from Stanley Falls, was the first published attack on Leopold's project. Williams makes nearly all the same points that would be raised in the journalistic onslaught several years later. *An Open Letter,* published as a pamphlet in Europe and America in 1890, prompted much controversy. Leopold sought to discredit Williams by revealing that the journalist had exaggerated or misrepresented some of his educational credentials and his achievements as a soldier in the Civil War. Although these revelations silenced the critics of the Congo Free State for several years, later investigators confirmed all that Williams had to say about the Congo.

A note on the spelling: Though an American, Williams uses British spellings here. At the time, it was common to use British phrases and spellings in order to appear cultured.

FROM

An Open Letter to His Serene Majesty Leopold II

Good and Great Friend,

I have the honour to submit for your Majesty's consideration some reflections respecting the Independant State of Congo, based upon a careful study and inspection of the country and character of the personal Government you have established upon the African Continent.

In order that you may know the truth, the whole truth, and nothing but the truth, I implore your most gracious permission to address you without restraint, and with the frankness of a man who feels that he has a duty to perform to *History, Humanity, Civilization* and to the *Supreme Being,* who is himself the "King of Kings." . . .

French and German Administrators Agreeing on New Franco-German Boundary Lines in Lobaye Marshes, Congo. *Le Petit journal*, 1913. Engraving

European administrators presumed to delineate borders where previously none had existed, creating African nations that did not reflect the tribal make-up of the land. (The Art Archive / Bibliothèque Municipale Dijon / Dagli Orti)

In your personal letter to the President of the Republic of the United States of America, bearing date of August 1st, 1885, you said that the possessions of the International Association of the Congo will hereafter form the Independent State of the Congo. "I have at the same time the honour to inform you and the Government of the Republic of the United States of America that, authorised by the Belgian Legislative Chambers to become the Chief of the new State, I have taken, in accord with the Association, the title of Sovereign of the Independent State of Congo." Thus you assumed the headship of the State of Congo, and at once organised a personal Government. You have named its officers, created its laws, furnished its finances, and every act of the Government has been clothed with the majesty of your authority.

On the 25th of February 1884, a gentleman, who has sustained an intimate relation to your Majesty for many years, and who then wrote as expressing your sentiments, addressed a letter to the United States in which the following language occurs:— "It may be safely asserted that no barbarous people have ever so readily adopted the fostering care of benevolent enterprise, as have the tribes of the Congo, and never was there a more honest and practical effort made to increase their knowledge and secure their welfare." The letter, from which the above is an excerpt, was written for the purpose of securing the friendly action of the Committee on Foreign Relations, which had under consideration a Senate Resolution in which the United States recognised the flag of the "Association Internationale du Congo" as the flag of a friendly Government. The letter was influential, because it was supposed to contain the truth respecting the natives, and the programme, not only of the Association, but of the new State, its legitimate successor, and of your Majesty.

When I arrived in the Congo, I naturally sought for the results of the brilliant programme: — *"fostering care," "benevolent enterprise,"* an *"honest and practical effort"* to increase the knowledge of the natives *"and secure their welfare."* I had never been able to conceive of Europeans, establishing a government in a tropical country, without building a hospital; and yet from the mouth of the Congo River to its headwaters, here at the seventh cataract, a distance of 1,448 miles, there is not a solitary hospital for Europeans, and only three sheds for sick Africans in the service of the State, not fit to be occupied by a horse. Sick sailors frequently die on board their vessels at Banana Point; and if it were not for the humanity of the Dutch Trading Company at that place — who have often opened their private hospital to the sick of other countries — many more might die. There is not a single chaplain in the employ of your Majesty's Government to console the sick or bury the dead. Your white men sicken and die in their quarters or on the caravan road, and seldom have Christian burial. With few exceptions, the surgeons of your Majesty's government have been gentlemen of professional ability, devoted to duty, but usually left with few medical stores and no quarters in which to treat their patients. The African soldiers and labourers of your Majesty's Government fare worse than the whites, because they have poorer quarters, quite as bad as those of the natives; and in the sheds, called hospitals, they languish upon a bed of bamboo poles without blankets, pillows or any food different from that served to them when well, rice and fish.

I was anxious to see to what extent the natives had *"adopted the fostering care"* of your Majesty's *"benevolent enterprise,"* and I was doomed to bitter disappointment. Instead of the natives of the Congo "adopting the fostering care" of your Majesty's Government, they everywhere complain that their land has been taken from them by force; that the Government is cruel and arbitrary, and declare that they neither love nor respect t[h]e Government and its flag. Your Majesty's Government has sequestered their land, burned their towns, stolen their property, enslaved their women and children, and committed other crimes too numerous to mention in detail. It is natural that they everywhere shrink from *"the fostering care"* your Majesty's Government so eagerly proffers them.

There has been, to my absolute knowledge, no *"honest and practical effort made to increase their knowledge and secure their welfare."* Your Majesty's Government has never spent one franc for educational purposes, nor institu[t]ed any practical system of industrialism. Indeed the most unpractical measures have been adopted *against* the natives in nearly every respect; and in the capital of your Majesty's Government at Boma there is not a native employed. The labour system is radically unpractical; the soldiers and labourers of your Majesty's Government are very largely imported from Zanzibar at a cost of £10 *per capita,* and from Sierre Leone, Liberia, Accra and Lagos at from £1 to £1/10. — *per capita.* These recruits are transported under circumstances more cruel than cattle in European countries. They eat their rice twice a day by the use of their fingers; they often thirst for water when the season is dry; they are exposed to the heat and rain, and sleep upon the damp and filthy decks of the vessels often so closely crowded as to lie in human ordure. And, of course, many die.

Upon the arrival of the survivors in the Congo they are set to work as labourers at one shilling a day; as soldiers they are promised sixteen shillings per month, in English money, but are usually paid off in cheap handkerchiefs and poisonous gin. The cruel and unjust treatment to which these people are subjected breaks the spirits of many of them, makes them distrust and despise your Majesty's Government. They are enemies, not patriots. . . .

From these general observations I wish now to pass to specific charges against your Majesty's Government.

FIRST.—Your Majesty's Government is deficient in the moral, military and financial strength, necessary to govern a territory of 1,508,000 square miles, 7,251 miles of navigation, and 31,694 square miles of lake surface. In the Lower Congo River there is but one post, in the cataract region one. From Leopoldville to N'Gombe, a distance of more than three hundred miles, there is not a single soldier or civilian. Not one out of every twenty State-officials know the language of the natives, although they are constantly issuing laws, difficult even for Europeans, and expect the natives to comprehend and obey them. Cruelties of the most astounding character are practised by the natives, such as burying slaves alive in the grave of a dead chief, cutting off the heads of captured warriors in native combats, and no effort is put forth by your Majesty's Government to prevent them. Between eight hundred and one thousand slaves are sold to be eaten by the natives of the Congo State annually; and slave raids, accomplished by the most cruel and murderous agencies, are carried on within the territorial limits of your Majesty's Government which is impotent. There are only 2,300 soldiers in the Congo.

SECOND.—Your Majesty's Government has established nearly fifty posts, consisting of from two to eight mercenary slave-soldiers from the East Coast. There is no white commissioned officer at these posts; they are in charge of the black Zanzibar soldiers, and the State expects them not only to sustain themselves, but to raid enough to feed the garrisons where the white men are stationed. These piratical, buccaneering posts compel the natives to furnish them with fish, goats, fowls, and vegetables at the mouths of their muskets; and whenever the natives refuse to feed these vampires, they report to the main station and white officers come with an expeditionary force and burn away the homes of the natives. These black soldiers, many of whom are slaves, exercise the power of life and death. They are ignorant and cruel, *because* they do not comprehend the natives; they are imposed upon them by the State. They make no report as to the number of robberies they commit, or the number of lives they take; they are only required to subsist upon the natives and thus relieve your Majesty's Government of the cost of feeding them. They are the greatest curse the country suffers now. . . .

FOURTH.—The Courts of your Majesty's Government are abortive, unjust, partial and delinquent. I have personally witnessed and examined their clumsy operations. The laws printed and circulated in Europe "for the protection of the blacks" in the Congo, are a dead letter and a fraud. I have heard an officer of the Belgian Army pleading the cause of a white man of low degree who had been guilty of beating and stabbing a black man, and urging race distinctions and prejudices as good and sufficient reasons why his client should be adjudged innocent. . . .

FIFTH. — Your Majesty's Government is excessively cruel to its prisoners, condemning them, for the slightest offences, to the chain gang, the like of which cannot be seen in any other Government in the civilised or uncivilised world. Often these ox-chains eat into the necks of the prisoners and produce sores about which the flies circle, aggravating the running wound; so the prisoner is constantly worried. These poor creatures are frequently beaten with a dried piece of hippopotamus skin, called a "chicote,"[1] and usually the blood flows at every stroke when well laid on. But the cruelties visited upon soldiers and workmen are not to be compared with the sufferings of the poor natives who, upon the slightest pretext, are thrust into the wretched prisons here in the Upper River. . . .

SIXTH. — Women are imported into your Majesty's Government for immoral purposes. They are introduced by two methods, viz., black men are dispatched to the Portuguese coast where they engage these women as mistresses of white men, who pay to the procurer a monthly sum. The other method is by capturing native women and condemning them to seven years' servitude for some imaginary crime against the State with which the villages of these women are charged. The State then hires these women out to the highest bidder, the officers having the first choice and then the men. Whenever children are born of such relations, the State maintains that the woman being its property the child belongs to it also. . . . There is only one post that I know of where there is not to be found children of the civil and military officers of your Majesty's Government abandoned to degradation; white men bringing their own flesh and blood under the lash of a most cruel master, the State of Congo.

SEVENTH. — Your Majesty's Government is engaged in trade and commerce, competing with the organised trade companies of Belgium, England, France, Portugal and Holland. It taxes all trading companies and exempts its own goods from export-duty, and makes many of its officers ivory-traders, with the promise of a liberal commission upon all they can buy or get for the State. State soldiers patrol many villages forbidding the natives to trade with any person but a State official, and when the natives refuse to accept the price of the State, their goods are seized by the Government that promised them "protection." When natives have persisted in trading with the trade-companies the State has punished their independence by burning the villages in the vicinity of the trading houses and driving the natives away. . . .

NINTH. — Your Majesty's Government has been, and is now, guilty of waging unjust and cruel wars against natives, with the hope of securing slaves and women, to minister to the behests of the officers of your Government. In such slave-hunting raids one village is armed by the State against the other, and the force thus secured is incorporated with the regular troops. I have no adequate terms with which to depict to your Majesty the brutal acts of your soldiers upon such raids as these. The soldiers who open the combat are usually the bloodthirsty cannibalistic Bangalas, who give

---

[1] chicote: A whip made of raw, sun-dried hippopotamus hide.

no quarter to the aged grandmother or nursing child at the breast of its mother. There are instances in which they have brought the heads of their victims to their white officers on the expeditionary steamers, and afterwards eaten the bodies of slain children. In one war two Belgian Army officers saw, from the deck of their steamer, a native in a canoe some distance away. He was not a combatant and was ignorant of the conflict in progress upon the shore, some distance away. The officers made a wager of £5 that they could hit the native with their rifles. Three shots were fired and the native fell dead, pierced through the head, and the trade canoe was transformed into a funeral barge and floated silently down the river.

In another war, waged without just cause, the Belgian Army officer in command of your Majesty's forces placed the men in two or three lines on the steamers and instructed them to commence firing when the whistles blew. The steamers approached the fated town, and, as was usual with them, the people came to the shore to look at the boats and sell different articles of food. There was a large crowd of men, women and children, laughing, talking and exposing their goods for sale. At once the shrill whistles of the steamers were heard, the soldiers levelled their guns and fired, and the people fell dead, and wounded, and groaning, and pleading for mercy. Many prisoners were made, and among them four comely looking young women. And now ensued a most revolting scene: your Majesty's officers quarreling over the selection of these women. The commander of this murderous expedition, with his garments stained with innocent blood, declared, that his rank entitled him to the first choice! Under the direction of this same officer the prisoners were reduced to servitude, and I saw them working upon the plantation of one of the stations of the State.

TENTH. — Your Majesty's Government is engaged in the slave-trade, wholesale and retail. It buys and sells and steals slaves. Your Majesty's Government gives £3 per head for able-bodied slaves for military service. Officers at the chief stations get the men and receive the money when they are transferred to the State; but there are some middle-men who only get from twenty to twenty-five francs per head. Three hundred and sixteen slaves were sent down the river recently, and others are to follow. These poor natives are sent hundreds of miles away from their villages, to serve among other natives whose language they do not know. When these men run away a reward of 1,000 N'taka is offered. Not long ago such a re-captured slave was given one hundred "chikote" each day until he died. Three hundred N'taka-brassrod is the price the State pays for a slave, when bought from a native. The labour force at the stations of your Majesty's Government in the Upper River is composed of slaves of all ages and both sexes. . . .

CONCLUSIONS

Against the deceit, fraud, robberies, arson, murder, slave-raiding, and general policy of cruelty of your Majesty's Government to the natives, stands their record of unexampled patience, long-suffering and forgiving spirit, which put the boasted civilisation and professed religion of your Majesty's Government to the blush. During thirteen years only one white man has lost his life by the hands of the natives, and only two white men have been killed in the Congo. Major Barttelot was shot by a Zanzibar soldier, and the captain of a Belgian trading-boat was the victim of his own rash and unjust treatment of a native chief.

All the crimes perpetrated in the Congo have been done in *your* name, and *you* must answer at the bar of Public Sentiment for the misgovernment of a people, whose lives and fortunes were entrusted to you by the august Conference of Berlin, 1884–1885. I now appeal to the Powers, which committed this infant State to your Majesty's charge, and to the great States which gave it international being; and whose majestic law you have scorned and trampled upon, to call and create an International Commission to investigate the charges herein preferred in the name of Humanity, Commerce, Constitutional Government and Christian Civilisation. . . .

I appeal to the Belgian people and to their Constitutional Government, so proud of its traditions, replete with the song and story of its champions of human liberty, and so jealous of its present position in the sisterhood of European States, — to cleanse itself from the imputation of the crimes with which your Majesty's personal State of Congo is polluted.

I appeal to Anti-Slavery Societies in all parts of Christendom, to Philanthropists, Christians, Statesmen, and to the great mass of people everywhere, to call upon the Governments of Europe, to hasten the close of the tragedy your Majesty's unlimited Monarchy is enacting in the Congo.

I appeal to our Heavenly Father, whose service is perfect love, in witness of the purity of my motives and the integrity of my aims; and to history and mankind I appeal for the demonstration and vindication of the truthfulness of the charges I have herein briefly outlined.

And all this upon the word of honour of a gentleman, I subscribe myself your Majesty's humble and obedient servant.

GEO. W. WILLIAMS.
Stanley Falls, Central Africa,
July 18th, 1890.

❧ Mark Twain (Samuel Clemens)
b. United States, 1835–1910

The great American humorist Mark Twain, known for his novels *Tom Sawyer* (1876) and *Huckleberry Finn* (1883), also wrote travel narratives, journalistic essays, and occasional satires. He was especially active in the anti-imperialist cause, announcing after the Spanish-American War, in which the United States acquired Puerto Rico, the Philippines, and Guam: "I am an anti-imperialist. I am opposed to having the eagle put its talons on any other land." In 1901 Twain became a vice-president of the Congo Reform Association, and the next year he composed *King Leopold's*

Soliloquy (1902). Written in the last decade of Twain's life, *Soliloquy* is an example of the kind of true "slanders" that his Leopold complains about. By casting his satire in the voice of the king, Twain exposes Leopold's duplicity, as he exults in the way he has tricked the Americans; his arrogance, as he asserts that a king should be above criticism; and his hypocrisy, as he spouts religious sentiments while shedding the blood of the Congolese.

FROM

❧ King Leopold's Soliloquy

[*Throws down pamphlets which he has been reading. Excitedly combs his flowing spread of whiskers with his fingers; pounds the table with his fists; lets off brisk volleys of unsanctified language at brief intervals, repentantly drooping his head, between volleys, and kissing the Louis XI crucifix hanging from his neck, accompanying the kisses with mumbled apologies; presently rises, flushed and perspiring, and walks the floor, gesticulating*]

—— ——!!—— ——!! If I had them by the throat! [*Hastily kisses the crucifix, and mumbles*] In these twenty years I have spent millions to keep the press of the two hemispheres quiet, and still these leaks keep on occurring. I have spent other millions on religion and art, and what do I get for it? Nothing. Not a compliment. These generosities are studiedly ignored, in print. In print I get nothing but slanders—and slanders again—and still slanders, and slanders on top of slanders! Grant them true, what of it? They are slanders all the same, when uttered against a king.

Miscreants—they are telling *everything!* Oh, everything: how I went pilgriming among the Powers in tears, with my mouth full of Bible and my pelt oozing piety at every pore, and implored them to place the vast and rich and populous Congo Free State in trust in my hands as their agent, so that I might root out slavery and stop the slave raids, and lift up those twenty-five millions of gentle and harmless blacks out of darkness into light, the light of our blessed Redeemer, the light that streams from his holy Word, the light that makes glorious our noble civilization—lift them up and dry their tears and fill their bruised hearts with joy and gratitude—lift them up and make them comprehend that they were no longer outcasts and forsaken, but our very brothers in Christ; how America and thirteen great European states wept in sympathy with me, and were persuaded; how their representatives met in convention in Berlin and made me Head Foreman and Superintendent of the Congo State, and drafted out my powers and limitations, carefully guarding the persons and liberties and properties of the natives against hurt and harm; forbidding whisky traffic and gun traffic; providing courts of justice; making commerce free and fetterless to the merchants and traders of all nations, and welcoming and safe-guarding all missionaries of all creeds and denominations. They have told how I planned and prepared my establishment and selected my horde of officials—"pals" and "pimps" of mine, "unspeakable Belgians" every one—and hoisted my flag, and "took in" a

President of the United States, and got him to be the first to recognize it and salute it. Oh, well, let them blackguard me if they like; it is a deep satisfaction to me to remember that I was a shade too smart for that nation that thinks itself so smart. Yes, I certainly did bunco a Yankee—as those people phrase it. Pirate flag? Let them call it so—perhaps it is. All the same, *they were the first to salute it.*

These meddlesome American missionaries! these frank British consuls! these blabbing Belgian-born traitor officials!—those tiresome parrots are always talking, always telling. They have told how for twenty years I have ruled the Congo State not as a trustee of the Powers, an agent, a subordinate, a foreman, but as a sovereign—sovereign over a fruitful domain four times as large as the German Empire—sovereign absolute, irresponsible, above all law; trampling the Berlin-made Congo charter under foot; barring out all foreign traders but myself; restricting commerce to myself, through concessionaires who are my creatures and confederates; seizing and holding the State as my personal property, the whole of its vast revenues as my private "swag"—mine, solely mine—claiming and holding its millions of people as my private property, my serfs, my slaves; their labor mine, with or without wage; the food they raise not their property but mine; the rubber, the ivory, and all the other riches of the land mine—mine solely—and gathered for me by the men, the women, and the little children under compulsion of lash and bullet, fire, starvation, mutilation, and the halter.

These pests!—it is as I say, they have kept back nothing! They have revealed these and yet other details which shame should have kept them silent about, since they were exposures of a king, a sacred personage and immune from reproach, by right of his selection and appointment to his great office by God himself; a king whose acts cannot be criticized without blasphemy, since God has observed them from the beginning and has manifested no dissatisfaction with them, nor shown disapproval of them, nor hampered nor interrupted them in any way. By this sign I recognize his approval of what I have done; his cordial and glad approval, I am sure I may say. Blest, crowned, beatified with this great reward, this golden reward, this unspeakably precious reward, why should I care for men's cursings and revilings of me? [*With a sudden outburst of feeling*] May they roast a million æons in— [*Catches his breath and effusively kisses the crucifix; sorrowfully murmurs, "I shall get myself damned yet, with these indiscretions of speech."*]

Yes, they go on telling everything, these chatterers! They tell how I levy incredibly burdensome taxes upon the natives—taxes which are a pure theft; taxes which they must satisfy by gathering rubber under hard and constantly harder conditions, and by raising and furnishing food supplies gratis—and it all comes out that, when they fall short of their tasks through hunger, sickness, despair, and ceaseless and exhausting labor without rest, and forsake their homes and flee to the woods to escape punishment, my black soldiers, drawn from unfriendly tribes, and instigated and directed by my Belgians, hunt them down and butcher them and burn their villages—reserving some of the girls. They tell it all: how I am wiping a nation of friendless creatures out of existence by every form of murder, for my private pocket's sake. But they never say, although they know it, that I have labored in the cause of religion at the same time and all the time, and have sent missionaries there (of a "convenient stripe," as they phrase it), to teach them the error of their ways and bring them to Him who is all mercy and love, and who is the sleepless guardian and friend of all who suffer. They tell only what is against me, they will not tell what is in my favor.

They tell how England required of me a Commission of Inquiry into Congo atrocities, and how, to quiet that meddling country, with its disagreeable Congo Reform Association, made up of earls and bishops and John Morleys and university grandees and other dudes, more interested in other people's business than in their own, I appointed it. Did it stop their mouths? No, they merely pointed out that it was a commission composed wholly of my "Congo butchers," "the very men whose acts were to be inquired into." They said it was equivalent to appointing a commission of wolves to inquire into depredations committed upon a sheepfold. *Nothing* can satisfy a cursed Englishman!

And are the fault-finders frank with my private character? They could not be more so if I were a plebeian, a peasant, a mechanic. They remind the world that from the earliest days my house has been chapel and brothel combined, and both industries working full time; that I practised cruelties upon my queen and my daughters, and supplemented them with daily shame and humiliations; that, when my queen lay in the happy refuge of her coffin, and a daughter implored me on her knees to let her look for the last time upon her mother's face, I refused; and that, three years ago, not being satisfied with the stolen spoils of a whole alien nation, I robbed my own child of her property and appeared by proxy in court, a spectacle to the civilized world, to defend the act and complete the crime. It is as I have said: They are unfair, unjust; they will resurrect and give new currency to such things as those, or to any other things that count against me, but they will not mention any act of mine that is in my favor. I have spent more money on art than any other monarch of my time, and they know it. Do they speak of it, do they tell about it? No, they do not. They prefer to work up what they call "ghastly statistics" into offensive kindergarten object lessons, whose purpose is to make sentimental people shudder, and prejudice them against me. They remark that "if the innocent blood shed in the Congo State by King Leopold were put in buckets and the buckets placed side by side, the line would stretch two thousand miles; if the skeletons of his ten millions of starved and butchered dead could rise up and march in single file, it would take them seven months and four days to pass a given point; if compacted together in a body, they would occupy more ground than St. Louis covers, World's Fair and all; if they should all clap their bony hands at once, the grisly crash would be heard at a distance of—" Damnation, it makes me tired! And they do similar miracles with the money I have distilled from that blood and put into my pocket. They pile it into Egyptian pyramids; they carpet Saharas with it; they spread it across the sky, and the shadow it casts makes twilight in the earth. And the tears I have caused, the hearts I have broken—oh, nothing can persuade them to let *them* alone!

❧ FRANTZ FANON
B. MARTINIQUE, 1925–1961

A psychiatrist from the French colonial island of Martinique in the Caribbean, Fanon is the leading theorist of the colonial mind. After leaving Martinique in 1943 to fight with the Free French in World War II, he studied medicine and psychiatry at Lyon and in 1953 became head of psychiatry at a hospital in Algeria. During the Algerian war for independence from France, Fanon sympathized with the rebels, resigning his post in 1956 to work with the independence movement. In *Black Skin, White Masks* (1952), Fanon analyzes how colonialism and racism make psychological health impossible for the black man. *The Wretched of the Earth,* published after Fanon's untimely death from leukemia in 1961, extends the argument of his earlier work to show how violent revolution is inevitable because of the colonial situation.

All notes are the editors' unless otherwise indicated.

FROM

 # The Wretched of the Earth

Translated by Constance Farrington

[DECOLONIZATION]

National liberation, national renaissance, the restoration of nationhood to the people, commonwealth: Whatever may be the headings used or the new formulas introduced, decolonization is always a violent phenomenon. At whatever level we study it — relationships between individuals, new names for sports clubs, the human admixture at cocktail parties, in the police, on the directing boards of national or private banks — decolonization is quite simply the replacing of a certain "species" of men by another "species" of men. Without any period of transition, there is a total, complete, and absolute substitution. It is true that we could equally well stress the rise of a new nation, the setting up of a new state, its diplomatic relations, and its economic and political trends. But we have precisely chosen to speak of that kind of *tabula rasa*[1] which characterizes at the outset all decolonization. Its unusual importance is that it constitutes, from the very first day, the minimum demands of the colonized. To tell the truth, the proof of success lies in a whole social structure being changed from the bottom up. The extraordinary importance of this change is that it is willed, called for, demanded. The need for this change exists in its crude state, impetuous and compelling, in the consciousness and in the lives of the men and women who are colonized. But the possibility of this change is equally experienced in the form of a terrifying future in the consciousness of another "species" of men and women: the colonizers.

Decolonization, which sets out to change the order of the world, is, obviously, a program of complete disorder. But it cannot come as a result of magical practices, nor of a natural shock, nor of a friendly understanding. Decolonization, as we know, is a historical process: That is to say that it cannot be understood, it cannot become intelligible nor clear to itself except in the exact measure that we can discern the movements which give it historical form and content. Decolonization is the meeting of two forces, opposed to each other by their very nature, which in fact owe their originality to that sort of substantification which results from and is nourished by the situation in the colonies. Their first encounter was marked by violence and their existence together — that is to say the exploitation of the native by the settler — was

---

[1] *tabula rasa:* Blank tablet.

carried on by dint of a great array of bayonets and cannons. The settler and the native are old acquaintances. In fact, the settler is right when he speaks of knowing "them" well. For it is the settler who has brought the native into existence and who perpetuates his existence. The settler owes the fact of his very existence, that is to say, his property, to the colonial system.

Decolonization never takes place unnoticed, for it influences individuals and modifies them fundamentally. It transforms spectators crushed with their inessentiality into privileged actors, with the grandiose glare of history's floodlights upon them. It brings a natural rhythm into existence, introduced by new men, and with it a new language and a new humanity. Decolonization is the veritable creation of new men. But this creation owes nothing of its legitimacy to any supernatural power; the "thing" which has been colonized becomes man during the same process by which it frees itself.

In decolonization, there is therefore the need of a complete calling in question of the colonial situation. If we wish to describe it precisely, we might find it in the well-known words: "The last shall be first and the first last." Decolonization is the putting into practice of this sentence. That is why, if we try to describe it, all decolonization is successful.

The naked truth of decolonization evokes for us the searing bullets and bloodstained knives which emanate from it. For if the last shall be first, this will only come to pass after a murderous and decisive struggle between the two protagonists. That affirmed intention to place the last at the head of things, and to make them climb at a pace (too quickly, some say) the well-known steps which characterize an organized society, can only triumph if we use all means to turn the scale, including, of course, that of violence.

You do not turn any society, however primitive it may be, upside down with such a program if you have not decided from the very beginning, that is to say from the actual formulation of that program, to overcome all the obstacles that you will come across in so doing. The native who decides to put the program into practice, and to become its moving force, is ready for violence at all times. From birth it is clear to him that this narrow world, strewn with prohibitions, can only be called in question by absolute violence.

The colonial world is a world divided into compartments. It is probably unnecessary to recall the existence of native quarters and European quarters, of schools for natives and schools for Europeans; in the same way we need not recall apartheid in South Africa. Yet, if we examine closely this system of compartments, we will at least be able to reveal the lines of force it implies. This approach to the colonial world, its ordering and its geographical layout will allow us to mark out the lines on which a decolonized society will be reorganized.

The colonial world is a world cut in two. The dividing line, the frontiers are shown by barracks and police stations. In the colonies it is the policeman and the soldier who are the official, instituted go-betweens, the spokesmen of the settler and his rule of oppression. In capitalist societies the educational system, whether lay or clerical, the structure of moral reflexes handed down from father to son, the exemplary honesty of workers who are given a medal after fifty years of good and loyal service, and the affection which springs from harmonious relations and good behavior—all these aesthetic expressions of respect for the established order serve to create around the exploited person an atmosphere of submission and of inhibition which lightens the task of policing considerably. In the capitalist countries a multitude of moral teachers, counselors, and "bewilderers" separate the exploited from those in power. In the colonial countries, on the contrary, the policeman and the soldier, by their immediate presence and their frequent and direct action maintain contact with the native and advise him by means of rifle butts and napalm not to budge. It is obvious here that the agents of government speak the language of pure force. The intermediary does not lighten the oppression, nor seek to hide the domination; he shows them up and puts them into practice with the clear conscience of an upholder of the peace; yet he is the bringer of violence into the home and into the mind of the native.

The zone where the natives live is not complementary to the zone inhabited by the settlers. The two zones are opposed, but not in the service of a higher unity. Obedient to the rules of pure Aristotelian logic, they both follow the principle of reciprocal exclusivity. No conciliation is possible, for of the two terms, one is superfluous. The settlers' town is a strongly built town, all made of stone and steel. It is a brightly lit town; the streets are covered with asphalt, and the garbage cans swallow all the leavings, unseen, unknown, and hardly thought about. The settler's feet are never visible, except perhaps in the sea; but there you're never close enough to see them. His feet are protected by strong shoes although the streets of his town are clean and even, with no holes or stones. The settler's town is a well-fed town, an easygoing town; its belly is always full of good things. The settlers' town is a town of white people, of foreigners.

The town belonging to the colonized people, or at least the native town, the Negro village, the medina, the reservation, is a place of ill fame, peopled by men of evil repute. They are born there, it matters little where or how; they die there, it matters not where, nor how. It is a world without spaciousness; men live there on top of each other, and their huts are built one on top of the other. The native town is a hungry town, starved of bread, of meat, of shoes, of coal, of light. The native town is a crouching village, a town on its knees, a town wallowing in the mire. It is a town of niggers and dirty Arabs. The look that the native turns on the settler's town is a look of lust, a look of envy; it expresses his dreams of possession—all manner of possession: to sit at the settler's table, to sleep in the settler's bed, with his wife if possible. The colonized man is an envious man. And this the settler knows very well; when their glances meet he ascertains bitterly, always on the defensive, "They want to take our place." It is true, for there is no native who does not dream at least once a day of setting himself up in the settler's place.

This world divided into compartments, this world cut in two is inhabited by two different species. The originality of the colonial context is that economic reality, inequality, and the immense difference of ways of life never come to mask the human realities. When you examine at close quarters the colonial context, it is evident that what parcels out the world is to begin with the fact of belonging to or not belonging to a given race, a given species. In the colonies the economic substructure is also a superstructure. The cause is the consequence; you are rich because you are white, you are white because you are rich. This is why Marxist analysis should always be slightly stretched every time we have to do with the colonial problem.

Everything up to and including the very nature of precapitalist society, so well explained by Marx, must here be thought out again. The serf is in essence different from the knight, but a reference to divine right is necessary to legitimize this statutory difference. In the colonies, the foreigner coming from another country imposed his rule by means of guns and machines. In defiance of his successful transplantation, in spite of his appropriation, the settler still remains a foreigner. It is neither the act of owning factories, nor estates, nor a bank balance which distinguishes the governing classes. The governing race is first and foremost those who come from elsewhere, those who are unlike the original inhabitants, "the others."

The violence which has ruled over the ordering of the colonial world, which has ceaselessly drummed the rhythm for the destruction of native social forms and broken up without reserve the systems of reference of the economy, the customs of dress and external life, that same violence will be claimed and taken over by the native at the moment when, deciding to embody history in his own person, he surges into the forbidden quarters. To wreck the colonial world is henceforward a mental picture of action which is very clear, very easy to understand and which may be assumed by each one of the individuals which constitute the colonized people. To break up the colonial world does not mean that after the frontiers have been abolished lines of communication will be set up between the two zones. The destruction of the colonial world is no more and no less than the abolition of one zone, its burial in the depths of the earth or its expulsion from the country.

The natives' challenge to the colonial world is not a rational confrontation of points of view. It is not a treatise on the universal, but the untidy affirmation of an original idea propounded as an absolute. The colonial world is a Manichean world. It is not enough for the settler to delimit physically, that is to say with the help of the army and the police force, the place of the native. As if to show the totalitarian character of colonial exploitation the settler paints the native as a sort of quintessence of evil.[2] Native society is not simply described as a society lacking in values. It is not enough for the colonist to affirm that those values have disappeared from, or still better never existed in, the colonial world. The native is declared insensible to ethics; he represents not only the absence of values, but also the negation of values. He is, let us dare to admit, the enemy of values, and in this sense he is the absolute evil. He is the corrosive element, destroying all that comes near him; he is the deforming element, disfiguring all that has to do with beauty or morality; he is the depository of maleficent powers, the unconscious and irretrievable instrument of blind forces. Monsieur Meyer could thus state seriously in the French National Assembly that the Republic must not be prostituted by allowing the Algerian people to become part of it. All values, in fact, are irrevocably poisoned and diseased as soon as they are allowed in contact with the colonized race. The customs of the colonized people,

---

[2] quintessence of evil: We have demonstrated the mechanism of this Manichean world in *Black Skin, White Masks* (New York: Grove Press, 1967). [Fanon's note.]

their traditions, their myths—above all, their myths—are the very sign of that poverty of spirit and of their constitutional depravity. That is why we must put the DDT which destroys parasites, the bearers of disease, on the same level as the Christian religion which wages war on embryonic heresies and instincts, and on evil as yet unborn. The recession of yellow fever and the advance of evangelization form part of the same balance sheet. But the triumphant *communiqués* from the missions are in fact a source of information concerning the implantation of foreign influences in the core of the colonized people. I speak of the Christian religion, and no one need be astonished. The Church in the colonies is the white people's Church, the foreigner's Church. She does not call the native to God's ways but to the ways of the white man, of the master, of the oppressor. And as we know, in this matter many are called but few chosen.

At times this Manicheism goes to its logical conclusion and dehumanizes the native, or to speak plainly, it turns him into an animal. In fact, the terms the settler uses when he mentions the native are zoological terms. He speaks of the yellow man's reptilian motions, of the stink of the native quarter, of breeding swarms, of foulness, of spawn, of gesticulations. When the settler seeks to describe the native fully in exact terms he constantly refers to the bestiary. The European rarely hits on a picturesque style; but the native, who knows what is in the mind of the settler, guesses at once what he is thinking of. Those hordes of vital statistics, those hysterical masses, those faces bereft of all humanity, those distended bodies which are like nothing on earth, that mob without beginning or end, those children who seem to belong to nobody, that laziness stretched out in the sun, that vegetative rhythm of life—all this forms part of the colonial vocabulary. General de Gaulle speaks of "the yellow multitudes" and François Mauriac[3] of the black, brown, and yellow masses which soon will be unleashed. The native knows all this, and laughs to himself every time he spots an allusion to the animal world in the other's words. For he knows that he is not an animal; and it is precisely at the moment he realizes his humanity that he begins to sharpen the weapons with which he will secure its victory.

As soon as the native begins to pull on his moorings, and to cause anxiety to the settler, he is handed over to well-meaning souls who in cultural congresses point out to him the specificity and wealth of Western values. But every time Western values are mentioned they produce in the native a sort of stiffening or muscular lockjaw. During the period of decolonization, the native's reason is appealed to. He is offered definite values, he is told frequently that decolonization need not mean regression, and that he must put his trust in qualities which are well tried, solid, and highly esteemed. But it so happens that when the native hears a speech about Western culture he pulls out his knife—or at least he makes sure it is within reach. The violence with which the supremacy of white values is affirmed and the aggressiveness which has permeated the victory of these values over the ways of life and of thought of the native mean that, in revenge, the native laughs in mockery when Western values are

---

[3] de Gaulle . . . Mauriac: Charles de Gaulle (1890–1970), French general and statesman; president of France from 1959 to 1969. François Mauriac (1885–1970), French novelist, critic, and essayist; recipient of the 1952 Nobel Prize in literature.

mentioned in front of him. In the colonial context the settler only ends his work of breaking in the native when the latter admits loudly and intelligibly the supremacy of the white man's values. In the period of decolonization, the colonized masses mock at these very values, insult them, and vomit them up. . . .

Colonialism is not satisfied merely with holding a people in its grip and emptying the native's brain of all form and content. By a kind of perverted logic, it turns to the past of the oppressed people, and distorts, disfigures, and destroys it. This work of devaluing precolonial history takes on a dialectical significance today.

When we consider the efforts made to carry out the cultural estrangement so characteristic of the colonial epoch, we realize that nothing has been left to chance and that the total result looked for by colonial domination was indeed to convince the natives that colonialism came to lighten their darkness. The effect consciously sought by colonialism was to drive into the natives' heads the idea that if the settlers were to leave, they would at once fall back into barbarism, degradation, and bestiality.

On the unconscious plane, colonialism therefore did not seek to be considered by the native as a gentle, loving mother who protects her child from a hostile environment, but rather as a mother who unceasingly restrains her fundamentally perverse offspring from managing to commit suicide and from giving free rein to its evil instincts. The colonial mother protects her child from itself, from its ego, and from its physiology, its biology, and its own unhappiness which is its very essence.

In such a situation the claims of the native intellectual are not a luxury but a necessity in any coherent program. The native intellectual who takes up arms to defend his nation's legitimacy and who wants to bring proofs to bear out that legitimacy, who is willing to strip himself naked to study the history of his body, is obliged to dissect the heart of his people.

Such an examination is not specifically national. The native intellectual who decides to give battle to colonial lies fights on the field of the whole continent. The past is given back its value. Culture, extracted from the past to be displayed in all its splendor, is not necessarily that of his own country. Colonialism, which has not bothered to put too fine a point on its efforts, has never ceased to maintain that the Negro is a savage; and for the colonist, the Negro was neither an Angolan nor a Nigerian, for he simply spoke of "the Negro." For colonialism, this vast continent was the haunt of savages, a country riddled with superstitions and fanaticism, destined for contempt, weighed down by the curse of God, a country of cannibals—in short, the Negro's country. Colonialism's condemnation is continental in its scope. The contention by colonialism that the darkest night of humanity lay over precolonial history concerns the whole of the African continent. The efforts of the native to rehabilitate himself and to escape from the claws of colonialism are logically inscribed from the same point of view as that of colonialism. The native intellectual who has gone far beyond the domains of Western culture and who has got it into his head to proclaim the existence of another culture never does so in the name of Angola or of Dahomey. The culture which is affirmed is African culture. The Negro, never so much a Negro as since he has been dominated by the whites, when he decides to prove that he has a culture and to behave like a cultured person, comes to realize that history points out a well-defined path to him: He must demonstrate that a Negro culture exists.

And it is only too true that those who are most responsible for this racialization of thought, or at least for the first movement toward that thought, are and remain those Europeans who have never ceased to set up white culture to fill the gap left by the absence of other cultures. Colonialism did not dream of wasting its time in denying the existence of one national culture after another. Therefore the reply of the colonized peoples will be straight away continental in its breadth. In Africa, the native literature of the last twenty years is not a national literature but a Negro literature. The concept of negritude, for example, was the emotional if not the logical antithesis of that insult which the white man flung at humanity. This rush of negritude against the white man's contempt showed itself in certain spheres to be the one idea capable of lifting interdictions and anathemas. Because the New Guinean or Kenyan intellectuals found themselves above all up against a general ostracism and delivered to the combined contempt of their overlords, their reaction was to sing praises in admiration of each other. The unconditional affirmation of African culture has succeeded the unconditional affirmation of European culture. On the whole, the poets of negritude oppose the idea of an old Europe to a young Africa, tiresome reasoning to lyricism, oppressive logic to high-stepping nature, and on one side stiffness, ceremony, etiquette, and scepticism, while on the other frankness, liveliness, liberty, and—why not?—luxuriance: but also irresponsibility.

The poets of negritude will not stop at the limits of the continent. From America, black voices will take up the hymn with fuller unison. The "black world" will see the light and Busia from Ghana, Birago Diop from Senegal, Hampaté Ba from the Soudan, and Saint-Clair Drake[4] from Chicago will not hesitate to assert the existence of common ties and a motive power that is identical.

---

[4] Busia . . . Drake: Black writers and intellectuals. Kofe A. Busia, Ghanaian scholar and writer, was prime minister of Ghana from 1969 to 1972; Birago Diop of Senegal was one of the earliest anticolonial African poets; Hampaté Ba was a Senegalese historian and author; Saint-Clair Drake was an anthropologist.

❧ AIMÉ CÉSAIRE
B. MARTINIQUE, 1913

Poet, playwright, and politician from the island of Martinique, Césaire brings a modernist perspective to bear on themes of decolonization, Western racism, and negritude, an affirmation of the independent validity of Negro culture. Educated in France in the 1930s, Césaire was influenced by the French modernists, particularly Andre Bréton and the surrealists. In Paris he also met Léopold Sédar Senghor from Senegal and Léon Gotran Damas from Guiana; together they founded the Négritude movement, which sought to counter European racism and establish

Native Soldiers
Surrendering to
French Commander
Nogues after Three
Months of Rebellion,
Ivory Coast.
Le Petit journal, 1910.
Engraving
*Formidable European
firepower and a
strong military
presence overwhelmed
the Africans who had
rebelled against the
colonialists. (The Art
Archive / Dagli Orti)*

positive meanings for blackness. After World War II, Césaire was elected
mayor of Fort-de-France, the capital of Martinique, and deputy to the
French Assembly, in which role he fought for anticolonialist causes until
he retired from politics in 1993. In *Discourse on Colonialism* (1950),
Césaire argues that fascism is simply colonialism turned on white Europeans, suggesting that the violence and racism in both colonialism and
fascism are inherent in Western culture. *A Tempest* (1969), Césaire's
reworking of Shakespeare's *The Tempest* (Book 3), casts Prospero as a
slave owner on the island where he has been exiled; he has enslaved the
native islanders, the mixed-race Ariel and the black Caliban. In the final
scene of the play presented here, Prospero, reconciled with his brother
Antonio, prepares to return to Europe to reclaim his throne as the duke of
Milan and to celebrate the marriage of his daughter, Miranda, to Ferdinand, son of Alonso and heir to the throne of Naples. Prospero plans to
set his slaves free before leaving, but in a confrontation with Caliban he
realizes he cannot do so; he remains on the island, an oppressor still.

꩜ A Tempest

Translated by Richard Miller

CAST

ALONSO	FERDINAND
ANTONIO	GONZALO
ARIEL	MIRANDA
CALIBAN	PROSPERO

ACT III

FROM *Scene 5*

Prospero's cave. MIRANDA *and* FERDINAND *are playing chess.*

MIRANDA: Sir, I think you're cheating.

FERDINAND: And what if I told you that I would not do so for twenty kingdoms?

MIRANDA: I would not believe a word of it, but I would forgive you. Now, be honest . . . you did cheat!

FERDINAND: I'm pleased that you were able to tell. (*Laughing*) That makes me less worried at the thought that soon you will be leaving your innocent flowery kingdom for my less-innocent world of men.

MIRANDA: Oh, you know that, hitched to your star, I would brave the demons of hell!

The Nobles enter.

ALONSO: My son! This marriage! The thrill of it has struck me dumb! The thrill and the joy!

GONZALO: A happy ending to a most opportune shipwreck!

ALONSO: A unique one, indeed, for it can legitimately be described as such.

GONZALO: Look at them! Isn't it wonderful! I've been too choked up to speak, or I would have already told these children all the joy my old heart feels at seeing them living love's young dream and cherishing each other so tenderly.

ALONSO: (*to* FERDINAND *and* MIRANDA) My children, give me your hands. May the Lord bless you.

GONZALO: Amen! Amen!

Enter PROSPERO.

PROSPERO: Thank you, Gentlemen, for having agreed to join in this little family party. Your presence has brought us comfort and joy. However, you must now think of getting some rest. Tomorrow morning, you will recover your vessels — they are undamaged — and your men, who I can guarantee are safe, hale and hearty. I shall return with you to Europe, and I can promise you — I should say: promise us — a rapid sail and propitious winds.

GONZALO: God be praised! We are delighted . . . delighted and overcome! What a happy, what a memorable day! With one voyage Antonio has found a brother, his brother has found a dukedom, his daughter has found a husband. Alonso has regained his son and gained a daughter. And what else? . . . Anyway, I am the only one whose emotion prevents him from knowing what he's saying . . .

PROSPERO: The proof of that, my fine Gonzalo, is that you are forgetting someone: Ariel, my loyal servant. *(Turning to* ARIEL*)* Yes, Ariel, today you will be free. Go, my sweet. I hope you will not be bored.

ARIEL: Bored! I fear that the days will seem all too short!
There, where the Cecropia gloves its impatient hands with silver,
Where the ferns free the stubborn black stumps
from their scored bodies with a green cry—
There where the intoxicating berry ripens the visit
of the wild ring-dove
through the throat of that musical bird
I shall let fall
one by one,
each more pleasing than the last
four notes so sweet that the last
will give rise to a yearning
in the heart of the most forgetful slaves
yearning for freedom!

PROSPERO: Come, come. All the same, you are not going to set my world on fire with your music, I trust!

ARIEL: *(with intoxication)*
Or on some stony plane
perched on an agave stalk
I shall be the thrush that launches
its mocking cry
to the benighted field-hand
"Dig, nigger! Dig, nigger!"
and the lightened agave will
straighten from my flight,
a solemn flag.

PROSPERO: That is a very unsettling agenda! Go! Scram! Before I change my mind! [. . .] Come here, Caliban. Have you got anything to say in your own defence? Take advantage of my good humor. I'm in a forgiving mood today.

CALIBAN: I'm not interested in defending myself. My only regret is that I've failed.

PROSPERO: What were you hoping for?

CALIBAN: To get back my island and regain my freedom.

PROSPERO: And what would you do all alone here on this island, haunted by the devil, tempest tossed?

CALIBAN: First of all, I'd get rid of you! I'd spit you out, all your works and pomps! Your "white" magic!

PROSPERO: That's a fairly negative program . . .

CALIBAN: You don't understand it . . . I say I'm going to spit you out, and that's very positive . . .

PROSPERO: Well, the world is really upside down . . . We've seen everything now: Caliban as a dialectician! However, in spite of everything I'm fond of you, Caliban. Come, let's make peace. We've lived together for ten years and worked side by side! Ten years count for something, after all! We've ended up by becoming compatriots!

CALIBAN: You know very well that I'm not interested in peace. I'm interested in being free! Free, you hear?

PROSPERO: It's odd . . . no matter what you do, you won't succeed in making me believe that I'm a tyrant!

CALIBAN: Understand what I say, Prospero:

For years I bowed my head
for years I took it, all of it—
your insults, your ingratitude . . .
and worst of all, more degrading than all the rest,
your condescension.
But now, it's over!
Over, do you hear?
Of course, at the moment
You're still stronger than I am.
But I don't give a damn for your power
or for your dogs or your police or your inventions!
And do you know why?
It's because I know I'll get you.
I'll impale you! And on a stake that you've sharpened yourself!
You'll have impaled yourself!
Prospero, you're a great magician:
you're an old hand at deception.
And you lied to me so much,
about the world, about myself,
that you ended up by imposing on me
an image of myself:
underdeveloped, in your words, undercompetent
that's how you made me see myself!
And I hate that image . . . and it's false!
But now I know you, you old cancer,
And I also know myself!
And I know that one day
my bare fist, just that,
will be enough to crush your world!
The old world is crumbling down!

Isn't it true? Just look!
It even bores you to death.
And by the way . . . you have a chance to get it over with:
You can pick up and leave.

You can go back to Europe.
But the hell you will!
I'm sure you won't leave.
You make me laugh with your "mission"!
Your "vocation"!
Your vocation is to hassle me.
And that's why you'll stay,
just like those guys who founded the colonies
and who now can't live anywhere else.
You're just an old addict, that's what you are!

PROSPERO: Poor Caliban! You know that you're headed towards your own ruin. You're sliding towards suicide! You know I will be the stronger, and stronger all the time. I pity you!

CALIBAN: And I hate you!

PROSPERO: Beware! My generosity has its limits.

CALIBAN: *(shouting)*

> *Shango marches with strength*
> *along his path, the sky!*
> *Shango is a fire-bearer,*
> *his steps shake the heavens*
> *and the earth*
> *Shango, Shango, ho!*

PROSPERO: I have uprooted the oak and raised the sea,
I have caused the mountain to tremble and have bared my chest to adversity.
With Jove I have traded thunderbolt for thunderbolt.
Better yet—from a brutish monster I have made man!
But ah! To have failed to find the path to man's heart . . .
if that be where man is.
(to CALIBAN)
Well, I hate you as well!
For it is you who have made me
doubt myself for the first time.
(to the Nobles)
. . . My friends, come near. We must say farewell . . . I shall not be going with you. My fate is here: I shall not run from it.

ANTONIO: What, Sire?

PROSPERO: Hear me well.
I am not in any ordinary sense a master,
as this savage thinks,
but rather the conductor of a boundless score:
this isle,
summoning voices, I alone,
and mingling them at my pleasure,
arranging out of confusion

one intelligible line.
Without me, who would be able to draw music from all that?
This isle is mute without me.
My duty, thus, is here,
and here I shall stay.

GONZALO: Oh day full rich in miracles!

PROSPERO: Do not be distressed. Antonio, be you the lieutenant of my goods and make use of them as procurator until that time when Ferdinand and Miranda may take effective possession of them, joining them with the Kingdom of Naples. Nothing of that which has been set for them must be postponed: Let their marriage be celebrated at Naples with all royal splendor. Honest Gonzalo, I place my trust in your word. You shall stand as father to our princess at this ceremony.

GONZALO: Count on me, Sire.

PROSPERO: Gentlemen, farewell.

They exit.

And now, Caliban, it's you and me!
What I have to tell you will be brief:
Ten times, a hundred times, I've tried to save you,
above all from yourself.
But you have always answered me with wrath
and venom,
like the opossum that pulls itself up by its own tail
the better to bite the hand that tears it from the darkness.
Well, my boy, I shall set aside my indulgent nature
and henceforth I will answer your violence
with violence!

Time passes, symbolized by the curtain's being lowered halfway and reraised. In semidarkness PROSPERO *appears, aged and weary. His gestures are jerky and automatic, his speech weak, toneless, trite.*

PROSPERO: Odd, but for some time now we seem to be overrun with opossums. They're everywhere. Peccarys, wild boar, all this unclean nature! But mainly opossums. Those eyes! The vile grins they have! It's as though the jungle was laying siege to the cave . . . But I shall stand firm . . . I shall not let my work perish! *(Shouting)* I shall protect civilization! *(He fires in all directions.)* They're done for! Now, this way I'll be able to have some peace and quiet for a while. But it's cold. Odd how the climate's changed. Cold on this island . . . Have to think about making a fire . . . Well, Caliban, old fellow, it's just us two now, here on the island . . . only you and me. You and me. You-me . . . me-you! What in the hell is he up to? *(Shouting)* Caliban!

In the distance, above the sound of the surf and the chirping of birds, we hear snatches of Caliban's song:

FREEDOM HI-DAY, FREEDOM HI-DAY!

❧ CHINWEIZU
B. NIGERIA, 1943

Scholar, poet, playwright, and critic Chinweizu was born and educated in Nigeria; he did graduate work in the United States, studying mathematics, philosophy, American studies, history, and economics. He is the author of several volumes of poetry and books on African history, literature, and culture. Of particular interest to students of literature are *Toward the Decolonisation of African Literature* (1980), written with Onwuchekwa Jemie and Ihechukwu Madubuike, and *Decolonising the African Mind* (1987), from which the following selection is taken. In it Chinweizu uses Ariel and Caliban from Shakespeare's *The Tempest* to characterize the two postcolonial factions in Africa.

A note on the spelling: Chinweizu's British spelling is reproduced here.

Young Black Woman in European Dress, 1900s. Wooden Figurine
This sculpture, made in Mali in West Africa, shows how European dominance usurped African dress style. (The Art Archive / Private Collection Paris / Dagli Orti)

❧ Decolonising the African Mind

FROM CALIBANS V. ARIELS

I

In *The Tempest,* Shakespeare's parable on colonialism, when Prospero, the ruler of the island, sailed back to his own country, he handed power over his colony to Ariel, his obedient native auxiliary, but not to Caliban who had fought against his rule. In each Third World country, the colonial administrator's mission, like Prospero's, was to conquer, pacify, and rule, and to extract as much wealth as possible for the West. The native auxiliaries of colonialism, the Ariels, were trained to assist this mission wholeheartedly.

The anticolonial nationalists—the Calibans of their world—aimed to expel the conquerors, revitalise the nation, and develop its resources for its people. With independence, the Ariels have had to adopt at least parts of the Calibans' programme in order to stay in power. But can minds conditioned for the first purpose accomplish the second without reeducation? Can Ariel carry out Caliban's mission, especially when it requires him to battle his mentor, Prospero?

There was once a stuntman who would stand his partner against a board and throw a knife at him, always missing him by a hair's breadth, until his partner's shape was outlined in knifepoints upon the board. One day the two quarrelled; the stuntman resolved to kill his partner during their next performance. But no matter how he tried, he could not hit him: He kept missing his partner's body by the habitual hair's breadth. His purpose had changed, but the habits of his eye and muscles had not.

Even if Ariel were to overcome his ingrained awe and turn on his creator, his conditioning would likewise conspire to defeat his new purpose.

For as long as Ariel leads in the Third World, Prospero's old world order—whether economic, cultural, political, or informational—will be safe. For the present Third World struggle to succeed, Caliban must press on with his old battle until he routs Prospero's agent, Ariel.

Ariel and Caliban symbolise two factions in the Third World; indeed two rival tendencies in each Third World mind. Ariel's rout would mean the eradication of the colonial mentality. The decolonisation of the mind required to accomplish this is a necessary step toward a new world order which will be more than a refurbished version of the old.

II

In decolonising the African mind, as distinct from the Third World mind, certain particulars of African history need to be taken into account. The most important is that, for the past thirteen centuries, Africa has been invaded, conquered, and colonised by Arabs and Europeans. Their cultural assimilation programmes, which continue till this day, have burdened Africa with Arabised and Europeanised Ariels.

Severed from his ancestral traditions and alienated from his natural African identity, the Arabised African strives to be even more Arab than his Arab master; and the Europeanised African strives to be even more European than his European master. Like Uthman Biri ibn Idris, a fourteenth century King of Borno, the Arabised African declares himself an Arab on the basis of his Arabised culture, or of a fictitious genealogy linking himself to some Arab ancestor, preferably to some alleged member of the Prophet Mohammed's tribe of the Quraish. The Europeanised African, like the late Kofi Busia, one-time Prime Minister of Ghana, declares himself a European because of his European education and culture. Fanon's famous phrase "Black Skin, White Mask" applies to both kinds of African Ariel. Both believe in the intrinsic superiority of the white invaders of Africa; each proselytises for the culture of his Prospero, is hostile to decolonisation, and is contemptuous of any re-Africanisation of African culture.

Believing that Arabs are Allah's chosen people, the Arabised African does not find it anomalous that there are so many "Arab Republics" on African soil. He is not moved to ask: How did they come into existence? What does their presence mean? Why are their numbers increasing? If anything, he views them as a matter for rejoicing. Obviously, he can't well resist Arab imperialism if he believes that Arabs are god's chosen mediators between man and god; or that Arabic, one of the major colonial languages in Africa, is the language of god himself. Any invitation to de-Arabise his culture would be viewed as sacrilegious; as an invitation to opt to spend eternity in hell.

The Europeanised African, for his part, is overwhelmed by the fantastic achievements of industrial civilisation. But having accepted the European propaganda that industrial civilisation is the genetic property of its European pioneers, he fails to distinguish industrial civilisation as a type from modern European civilisation as an instance of the type. His desire for the former is therefore perverted into a wish to assimilate himself into the latter. He overlooks the fact, which the Japanese and the Chinese have demonstrated, that industrial civilisation can be replicated by non-Europeans, and so cannot be regarded as somehow intrinsically European. And he is usually ignorant of the fact that Europeans were latecomers to scientific culture, and that their pioneering of the industrial revolution was based on the scientific heritage they borrowed from others—including the ancient Egyptian and Mesopotamian civilisations. Obviously, he can't resist European imperialism if he believes that Europeans are the sole owners of the paradise of industrial civilisation; or that European languages, which are colonial languages in Africa, are indispensable for participation in industrial civilisation. Any invitation to de-Europeanise his culture would be viewed as an invitation away from the industrial paradise and back to some pre-industrial hell.

Such veneration of alien cultures leaves the African Ariel susceptible to foreign domination. It makes him eager for approval and acclaim by Arab and European imperialists. He wants to write and read literature approved by these imperialists. He wants to contest in those sports that these imperialists organise and dominate. He wants to embark on the subservient economic development which these imperialists promote. He wants to accept the identity which these imperialists fashion for him. He is eager to abandon his ancestral religions for those concocted and dispensed by these imperialists. He wants to hear only the version of his history which these imperialists peddle. He is eager to join the "commonwealths" which these imperialists sponsor. If the African Ariel has his way, African countries would join or perpetually remain in the Arab commonwealth known as the Organisation of the Islamic Conference (OIC), the British Commonwealth, the French Community, and the COMECON[1] of the Russians. Yet these are only thinly disguised continuations today of the old Arab, British, French, and Russian empires.

The historic mission of present-day Africans is to effect a renaissance of African civilisation in an industrial mode so that Africa can henceforth defend itself against all invaders. In this connection, the African Ariel's commitment to alien religions has curious consequences for his defence of Africa. It was recently proclaimed that the Nigerian Army recognised only two religions: Christianity and Islam. This means that religions which were founded by Jews and Arabs, and which were imported into Nigeria, are the only ones recognized in the army of the leading nation of the Black World. Their shrines in Mecca, Rome, and Jerusalem are sacred to the Nigerian state, which helps fund pilgrimages to them; but shrines at Ife, Benin, Calabar, etc., which belong to religions founded by the ancestors of Nigerians, are given no place in the rites of the Nigerian state. Thus, if Nigeria ever went to war against invading Jews or Arabs (as might well happen, given Nigerian passions over the Arab-Israeli conflict), patriotic Nigerians would march out, praying to Jehovah of the Jews and Allah of the Arabs to help them vanquish these invaders. But what god would desert his chosen people and side with outsiders against them? A sorry fix Nigerians would then find themselves in for relying on the gods of others.

As that example shows, our historic mission demands a re-Africanisation of the African even in such matters as his religion. But at the core of its demands is a restoration of the African cultural personality in a version consistent with an industrial economy. Doing that requires that Africans exercise an independent cultural initiative. Decolonising the African mind, freeing it from alien control, is a necessary condition for such initiative.

The reason is simple. The colonised mind, like a well-conditioned slave, is incapable of initiative independent of its master. Initiative in pursuit of the slave's own interest would be tantamount to revolt. Given his conditioning, all his master need do to end his revolt is to speak in tones that trigger his deeply ingrained habit of obedience. Ending his habit of submission to his master's voice, destroying his master's authority over him, become necessary if that slave is to do things in his own interest. A renaissance of African civilisation in an industrial mode is not in the interest of Africa's Arab and European enemies. So long as they have any authority over what Africans do, they will assuredly use it to sabotage such a renaissance.

---

[1]COMECON: Acronym for the Council of Mutual Economic Assistance, an organization active from 1949 to 1991 that included the Soviet Union, Bulgaria, Czechoslovakia, Hungary, Poland, Romania, East Germany, Mongolia, Cuba, Vietnam, and Yugoslavia. [Editors' note.]

The central objective in decolonising the African mind is to overthrow the authority which alien traditions exercise over the African. This demands the dismantling of white supremacist beliefs, and the structures which uphold them, in every area of African life. It must be stressed, however, that decolonisation does not mean ignorance of foreign traditions; it simply means denial of their authority and withdrawal of allegiance from them. Foreign traditions are part of the harvest of human experience. One should certainly know about them, if only because one must know one's environment, and especially one's enemy. One should certainly use items from other traditions provided they are consistent with African cultural independence and serve African objectives; but one should neither ape nor revere them, let alone sacrifice the African interest to them.

The strategic importance of overthrowing the authority of alien traditions lies in this. A renaissance of African civilisation in an industrial mode implies a far-reaching renovation of African cultures. Renovation calls for selectivity guided by the new objectives. Like a plank, brick, or tile being used to renovate a house, every cultural item for use in renovating African civilisation has to be critically appraised to see if it meets the specifications demanded by the new objectives. Elements from African tradition, no less than elements from non-African traditions, have to be thus appraised. But such appraisal would be impaired, if not entirely prevented, if a tradition exercises an intimidating authority over Africans—as is now, alas, the case with the Arab and European traditions.

Overthrowing the authority of alien traditions will allow for the questioning of their contents, for selection of what is useful, for adapting to African conditions and needs whatever is selected as useful. It will prevent the unexamined importation of the harmful, as well as the unexamined importation of that for which equivalent, or even superior, African counterparts exist. If a foreign technique or principle (in law, medicine, politics, economics, architecture, etc.) has its analogue in the African tradition, there is no reason not to keep the African item, provided both are of equal benefit. And even if they are not, the foreign item would be selectable only if the African item cannot be adapted to do the job. Otherwise, we will clutter our culture with unnecessary borrowings.

It ought to be stressed that Europeanisation and Arabisation are, at best, superfluous to the creation of an industrial version of African civilisation. We need to remind ourselves that the Japanese and Chinese have not repudiated their civilisations, and did not abandon their identities when they set out to industrialise. The notion that industrialisation of a society demands Europeanisation of its culture (whether in the American, Russian, or other version) is a piece of imperialist propaganda. The cultures of the industrial societies differ profoundly from one another. What each has done is to take its pre-industrial culture and place it on an industrial foundation. In the process, each has had to extensively renovate its culture to install the scientific ethos, and to satisfy conditions necessary for industrialism. Africa's pre-industrial cultures can equally expect to be profoundly altered by the demands of an industrial foundation. Such changes should not be confused with Europeanisation, just because they were first manifested during the industrialisation of Europe.

If a case cannot even be made for Africa to Europeanise its culture; if Europeanisation is, at best, a pointless distortion; Arabisation would be pure retrogression, a flight into an archaic feudalism with an anti-industrial mentality. We must soberly ask ourselves: Has Arabic culture enabled the Arabs to achieve an industrial society? Have they been able to defeat the industrialised Israelis whom they outnumber some 75 to 1? If they have not, why would any sane African want to copy their impotent culture? Of course, the Arabs could claim to hold the keys to the Arab heaven. Africans should then emulate the moribund Arab culture if death, with entry into an Arab controlled hereafter, is their aim, rather than survival and prosperity in the here and now.

According to Fanon, with the withdrawal of the colonial masters, "the country finds itself in the hands of new managers; but the fact is that everything needs to be reformed and everything thought out anew."[2] The Ariels cannot see beyond merely managing their colonial inheritance; indeed, they see it as against their interest to do anything else. But the Calibans know, with Fanon, that the task is not to manage the colonial inheritance, but to reform everything, to think everything out anew. The task is to define our own objectives, set our own standards, and pick our own heroes from among those who outstandingly serve our own interests.

Clearly, those Ariels who are Arabising or Europeanising Africa must be defeated if Africa is to be free to concentrate on its historic tasks. A battle must be waged against them by the African Calibans, the inheritors of the movement for political decolonisation. The battle is against Ariels among our artists and critics who pine for Prospero's praise. It is against Ariels who parrot Prospero's version of our history. It is against economic and political Ariels who would keep us subservient to Prospero's economic and political systems. These are today's equivalents of the old slaving elites who destroyed Africa while hunting slaves for sale to Arabs and Europeans.

Decolonising the African mind may alternatively be seen as a battle between the Caliban and Ariel tendencies within each African, for bits of Ariel and Caliban exist within each of us. No African living in the twentieth century has escaped the taint of the colonial experience. None has freed himself from the colonial mentality in every department, or from the structures which maintain and reproduce that mentality. The decolonisation of the African mind must therefore be seen as a collective enterprise, as a communal exorcism through an intellectual bath in which we need one another's help to scrub those nooks of our minds which we cannot scour by ourselves.

---

[2] "the country . . . anew": Frantz Fanon, *The Wretched of the Earth*, Harmondsworth, Penguin, 1967, p. 79. [Chinweizu's note.]

FELIX MNTHALI
B. MALAWI, 1933

mun-THAH-lee | Felix **Mnthali,** Malawian poet, novelist, and scholar, was educated at Cambridge University, England. In Africa he has taught in the English departments at the University of Ibadan in Nigeria, Malawi University, and the University of Botswana. His published works include *When Sunset Comes to Saptiwa* (1980), a collection of poetry, and the novel *Yoranivyoto* (1998).

The Stranglehold of English Lit.

(for Molara Ogundipe-Leslie)

Those questions, sister,
those questions
                    stand
                    stab
                    jab
                    and gore
too close to the centre!

For if we had asked
why Jane Austen's people
10   carouse all day
and do no work

would Europe in Africa
have stood
the test of time?
and would she still maul
the flower of our youth
in the south?
Would she?

Your elegance of deceit,
20   Jane Austen,
lulled the sons and daughters
of the dispossessed
into a calf-love

with irony and satire
around imaginary people.

While history went on mocking
the victims of branding irons
and sugar-plantations
that made Jane Austen's people
30   wealthy beyond compare!

Eng. Lit., my sister,
was more than a cruel joke—
it was the heart
of alien conquest.

How could questions be asked
at Makerere and Ibadan,
Dakar and Ford Hare[1]—
with Jane Austen
at the centre?
40   How could they be answered?

---

[1] **Makerere . . . Ford Hare:** African universities: Makerere, in Uganda; Ibadan, in Nigeria; Dakar, in Senegal; and Ford Hare, in South Africa.

☙ NGUGI WA THIONG'O
B. KENYA, 1938

The novelist, playwright, and essayist **Ngugi Wa Thiong'o** from Kenya is one of East Africa's most important writers, whose works dealing with anticolonialism, class struggle, language, and national identity have exerted considerable influence throughout the world. Educated at Makerere College in Uganda and Leeds University in England, Ngugi has held academic positions at universities in Africa, Europe, and the United States, where he has taught at Yale, Smith, Amherst, and New York University. His first novel, *Weep Not, Child* (1964), a moving account of the Mau Mau rebellion, was written in English, under the name James Ngugi, as were other early novels dealing with cultural and class conflict in the wake of British colonialism in Kenya, such as *A Grain of Wheat* (1967) and *Petals of Blood* (1977). After 1977, Ngugi turned to his native Gikuyu tongue as a more appropriate medium for his plays and novels, which he aimed at the native Gikuyu audience. The 1977 play *Ngaahika Ndeenda* (*I Will Marry when I Please*), written in Gikuyu with the collaboration of

en-GOO-gee wah
thee-ONG-oh

Ngugi Wa Mirii, was so popular among the Gikuyu that the Kenyan government banned the play and detained Ngugi without trial out of fear that he was promoting political dissent. While in prison Ngugi wrote *Devil on the Cross* (1982), again in Gikuyu, and later translated it into English; his time in prison is the subject of *Detained: A Writer's Prison Diary* (1981). Further censorship from the government forced Ngugi to leave Kenya in 1982, and he has lived in exile ever since. He is currently professor of comparative literature at New York University.

As the author of critical works such as *Homecomings: Essays on African and Caribbean Literature, Culture and Politics* (1972), *Decolonizing the Mind: The Politics of Language in African Literature* (1986), and *Moving the Centre: The Struggle for Cultural Freedoms* (1993), from which the following selection is taken, Ngugi has emerged as perhaps the foremost advocate of preserving and indeed revitalizing native languages in the so-called postmodern era. He believes that "language as culture is the collective memory bank of a people's experience in history," and as such it empowers native language users, in his words, "to confront the world creatively." For his views Ngugi has been criticized as being nostalgic or for being a "nativist"; he responds, as he does in the following selection, that a common global culture can be achieved only when it is expressed "in the particularities of our different languages and cultures." His work to preserve the language and culture of native traditions does not point backward, he says, to reviving an antiquated tradition; rather, it revitalizes the present and contributes to the blending of cultures that he concedes is taking place already. Like Goethe, Ngugi contends that a world literature can flourish only when it acknowledges the linguistic and cultural particularities of the many traditions making up the global community.

All notes are the editors'.

FROM

 # Creating Space for a Hundred Flowers to Bloom
The Wealth of a Common Global Culture

Looking at the world today, one sees many countries, nations, peoples, customs, languages, and a multiplicity of apparently unsolvable conflicts and problems. But in reality the world is becoming one. Human beings who live in space circle the earth within only a few hours. They can hardly settle their eyes for long on any one country—even their own. On the earth itself, the ease of transportation has put every corner of the globe within general reach in a matter of hours, a far cry from the days of Phineas Fogg and his wager of going round the earth in eighty days.

Economic links are quite obvious. The leading financial institutions—banks, insurances, credit cards—operate in nearly all the capitals of the earth. Transnationals of all kinds link economic activities of several countries; some brands becoming almost national to many people so familiar a sight they have become in their daily lives. So a worker in Nairobi, Kenya, in an automobile warehouse can have the same employer as many others in North, Central, South American, and Asian cities. Messrs Coca-Cola and McDonalds, between themselves, are making the world in their own image. It is of course true that these processes are controlled by a handful of Western transnationals. IMF and the World Bank dictate the social and economic policies of many countries. But it does mean that many workers, many nations, even when they may not be consciously aware of it, are linked to the same controlling central forces. Their apparently individual struggles against any excesses of the central command are invisibly linked to others. Workers for instance could be struggling against the same employer even though they are located in the different capitals and nations of the earth. As for the distribution of power, a handful of Western nations still dominate various other nations. Hence the experiences of national liberation and even the internal social struggles of many nations might be shaped in a similar way by the fact of their being aimed against the practices of a common enemy.

Those global economic and political processes invariably give rise to cultural links. The evolution of the present global order over the last five hundred years has seen the world being dominated by a handful of languages; European languages of course and the cultures these have carried will have shaped the dominated in similar ways. The fax, the telex, the computer, while facilitating communications, also mean the instant spread of information and culture across national boundaries. Television images via satellites enable the whole world to experience the Palestinian uprising in the Middle East, the struggle for Amandla[1] in South Africa, the mass uprisings and calls for democratic accountability to the people in Eastern Europe, at about the same time. Mandela could speak to billions in the world from his platform at the Wembley stadium in London, the concert in his honour there becoming part of a global instant experience. His release from twenty-seven years in prison was watched by millions. Words like perestroika, glasnost, amandla, a luta continua,[2] people power, democracy, socialism have become part of a common vocabulary.

In terms of the structures of domination, subordination, and resistance, a common global experience is emerging. Gradually a vocabulary of concepts of domination and revolt become part of a shared intellectual tradition.

Literature, more than all the fleeting images brought about by the screen or newsprint, is one of the more enduring multinational cultural processes which have been building the basis of a shared common tradition. From the ancient and modern literatures names of characters like Rama, Sinbad, Ali Baba, Isis and Osiris,

---

[1] Amandla: From the Kwazulu phrase *amandla awethus,* meaning "power to the people."

[2] perestroika . . . continua: *Perestroika* and *glasnost* are terms associated with the opening of the Soviet Union under the leadership of Mikhail Gorbachev in the 1980s; *amandla* and *a luta continua* are freedom cries associated with the African liberation movements that followed World War II.

Abunuwasi, Anansi, Hercules, Odysseus, Achilles, Helen, Oedipus, Prometheus, Gargantua and Pantagruel, Faustus, Hamlet, Okonkwo,[3] to mention just a few; and writers like Aeschylus, Shakespeare, Pushkin, Dostoevsky, Tolstoy, Goethe, Schiller, Thomas Mann, Brecht, Richard Wright, Alice Walker, Faulkner, Melville, Lu Hsun, Kim Chi Ha, the Grimm brothers, Andersen, Chinua Achebe, Wole Soyinka, Alex la Guma, Sembene Ousmane,[4] have become part of a global inheritance.

Inevitably because of the position of domination of Europe *vis-à-vis* the rest of the globe over the last five hundred years, European literature has occupied a place of great prominence on the world stage. It has, unarguably, given rise to a great humanistic tradition. It has given us fantastic images of the world of struggle, of great upheavals, of change, of movement. When Shakespeare's King Lear breaks down under the storm occasioned by the fact of the old feudal order and conception of nature being challenged to the roots by the new bourgeois conception of nature and asks, who is that can tell me who I am, or the assassins in *Julius Caesar,* bathing themselves in the blood of the victim, and one of them wondering how many times their deeds would be duplicated in the world in times and states as yet unborn, could they not have been painting images of the twentieth century? When Adam and Eve are taken by the angel Gabriel on to a hill just before their expulsion from paradise in Milton's *Paradise Lost* and are shown visions of the world to be; they are actually being given a global vision of all the cities and civilisations of the world among which are the great African empires of Songhay and the twelfth-century city-states along the Kenyan coast such as Malindi and Mombasa.

The humanistic side of European literature reflects of course the democratic social struggles of the European peoples. But given the domination of the West over the rest of the world through such repressive historical moments as the slave trade and slavery, colonialism and currently neocolonialism, this literature tends to opt for silence or ambivalence or downright collaboration. Of course there are writers who show great sensitivity to the social evils perpetrated against other peoples: William Blake, Walt Whitman, Brecht, Sartre for instance. But taken as a whole this literature could not avoid being affected by the Eurocentric basis of its world view or global vision, and most of it, even when sympathetic, could not altogether escape from the racism inherent in Western enterprise in the rest of the world. . . .

Thus, if people were really to depend on European literature, even at its best, they would get a very distorted picture of the modern world, its evolution and its contemporary being. The twentieth century is a product of imperialist adventurism,

---

[3] Abunuwasi . . . Okonkwo: Abunuwasi and Anansi are trickster figures from East and West African legends, respectively; Okonkwo is the hero of Chinua Achebe's novel *Things Fall Apart* (1958).

[4] Lu Hsun . . . Ousmane: Lu Hsun (Lu Xun, 1881–1936), Chinese writer, see p. 331; Kim Chi Ha (b. 1941), a Korean poet imprisoned first in 1964 and sentenced to death in 1974 for his poems critical of the government of Park Chung Hee; before the sentence was carried out, it was commuted to life in prison in 1980, after Park was assassinated. Alex la Guma (1925–1985), South African writer and activist who was imprisoned and placed under house arrest on charges of treason, then forced into exile in 1966; his most famous novel is *In the Fog of the Season's End* (1972). Sembene Ousmane (b. 1923), Senegalese writer and film director, whose most well-known novel is *God's Bits of Wood* (*Les Bouts de bois de dieu,* 1960).

true, but also of resistance from the people of the Third World. This resistance is often reflected in the literature of the Third World and it is an integral part of the modern world, part of the forces which have been creating and are still creating the heritage of a common culture. They come from Asia. They come from South America. They come from Africa. And they come from the oppressed national sectors and social strata in North America, Australasia, and Europe. The Third World is all over the world. There is of course no absolute uniformity in this literature and within itself as a modern tradition, a twentieth-century tradition, it carries all sorts of tendencies. Let me concentrate on literature from the African continent.

There are, as you know, three traditions in the literature from Africa. First is that of the oral tradition or orature. It is the literature passed on from mouth to ear, generation to generation. It consists of songs, poems, drama, proverbs, riddles, sayings, and it is the richest and oldest of heritages. Furthermore, it is still very much alive and readily incorporates new elements. It can be extremely simple or very complex depending on the time, place, and the occasion. I can think of no better demonstration of this tradition than in the remarkable recording of the *Ozidi Saga* by J. P. Clark.[5] Here the epic of Ozidi and his grandmother Oreame is told over a period of seven nights. The section dealing with the education of the epic hero, Ozidi, by his very demanding grandmother, is a remarkable example of narrative in orature while the scene involving the empowerment of Ozidi illustrates even more remarkably the fusion of theatre, drama, poetry, magic, ritual, music, song, audience participation, the real and the marvellous in orature. Among the Agĩkũyũ of Kenya there used to be a Gĩkũyũ poetry festival, or shall I say, competition, which drew large crowds. The best poets of the various regions would meet in the arena, like in a battle, and compete with words and instant compositions. These poets had even developed a form of hierographics which they kept to themselves. This kind of festival was killed by the British for they did not want crowds of people meeting and practising things that they, in the colonial administration, could not understand. The importance of the oral tradition is that through its agency African languages in their most magical form have been kept alive. One of the highest developments of this was the *griot*[6] tradition in West Africa. Whole epics and histories of families and nations were banked in the memories of these keepers of the word.

The second tradition is that of Africans writing in European languages, particularly in those of the former colonisers. This is clearly a product of the fatal encounter between Africa and Europe in two ways. First is the question of language choice and this links it inevitably to the literatures carried by European languages. This literature is branded with the Europeanness of the word. A case of black skins in white linguistic masks? Secondly, it arose out of and was generally inspired by the great

---

[5] J. P. Clark: J. P. Clark-Bekederemo (b. 1935), Nigerian poet and playwright whose works include *A Reed in the Tide* (1965), *A Decade of Tongues* (1981), and *Mandela and Other Poems* (1988); Clark's research of the oral tradition of his Izon (Ijo) people in the delta of the former kingdom of Benin led to the publication of the *Ozidi Saga* (1977), the national epic of the Ijo.

[6] *griot:* West African bard or storyteller, whose performance of traditional epics and stories involves speech, song, and often dance.

anticolonial resistance of the African masses. Much of the literature was initially often a reaction to the conception of the universe in European literature in which the African was depicted as the negation of history. It had done a remarkable job in redrawing the images of the world as previously drawn by the literature of Europe. It has rescued the world defined by European languages from the total grip of Eurocentrism. But in another sense it continued and even aided in that Eurocentrism by its very choice of languages. In other words it does not really matter how much Caliban is able to curse in European languages. He can do very remarkable things with it as we can see in *The Tempest,* in that great poetic evocation of Caliban's love of the island and his total identification with its landscape. But in so far as he has not been forced to abandon his language, as happened in the case of the African diaspora, he is accepting Prospero's racist assumptions about the universe and contributing to Prospero's linguistic universe. He accepts that only by adopting the European tongue can he manage to express his humanity adequately. He has colluded in Prospero's uprooting of the African tongue à la Coetzee; the African peasant and worker in this literature reappears on the stage of world history speaking not his gabble but perfect English, French, or Portuguese, a remarkable case of literary surgery and transplant since in reality the masses of African people do continue speaking and using and creating in African languages. Note that the new Caliban comes to Prospero's linguistic high table with an offering, a linguistic bottle of wine so to speak. Thus, this tradition has tried to forge an identity by borrowing very heavily from African languages, that is from the rich harvest of orature as developed by African languages over the years. But note also that Caliban is not borrowing from Prospero to enrich his own gabble. On the contrary. He sees his role as that of borrowing from his own gabble to enlarge the possibilities of Prospero's languages. He gives nothing, absolutely nothing, back to his languages. This ultimately is the tragedy of the Europhone tradition which has come to wear the mask of African literature. It is now a case of black skins in white masks wearing black masks.

In the area of economics and geography, it is the raw materials of gold, diamonds, coffee, tea, which are taken from Africa and processed in Europe and then resold to Africa. In the area of culture, the raw material of African orature and histories developed by African languages are taken, repackaged through English or French or Portuguese and then resold back to Africa. In both cases one is not questioning the quality of the products for this is not really what is at issue.

The third tradition is that of Africans writing in African languages. In the precolonial era, this was a minority tradition among the nations in that not many of the African languages had been reduced to writing. But it has always been there and as Professor Abiola Irele has pointed out it is these languages which contain the classical era of African literature, a precolonial tradition. It is the one that owns the label, the title, the name, "African literature." It has been overshadowed by the more recent Europhone tradition. But African languages are coming back. The language debate has dominated every single literature conference to do with Africa over the last few years and it is going to continue to do so with even greater aggressive insistence as we face the twenty-first century. To the old voices of Cheikh Anita Diop and David Diop calling for reconnection with that tradition are newer voices from the oral tradition adding to the continental chorus of concern. The Somali poet of the oral tradition, Mohamed Ismail of Garce, has gone so far as to accuse the educated Africans of committing treason against their own languages:

> Oh my friends, the Somali language is very perplexed;
> It is all anxiety in its present condition;
> The value of its words and expressions are being gagged by its own people;
> Its very back and hips are broken, and it accuses its own speakers of neglect;
> It is weeping with deep sorrow;
> It is being orphaned and its value is vanishing.

A reconnection with the classic tradition of our languages to express the contemporary world will not be an easy, "walkover" kind of task. Writing in African languages has many difficulties and problems. Problems of literacy. Problems of publishing. Problems of the lack of a critical tradition. Problems of orthography. Problems of having very many languages in the same country. Problems of hostile governments with a colonised mentality. Abandonment by some of those who could have brought their genius—demonstrated by their excellent performance in foreign languages— to develop their own languages.

In short, literature in African languages suffers from a lack of a strong tradition, creative and critical. Writers in African languages are having to create several traditions simultaneously; publishing, critical vocabulary, orthography, and even words. But it has the advantage of being able to establish a natural give and take relationship to the rich heritage of orature. African writers in African languages are giving something back, however tiny, to the development of African languages.

That is why I still believe that despite the hue and cry about reductionism, nativism, backwardlookingness from the Europhonist opponents of this development, writing in African languages still holds the key for the positive development of new and vital traditions in African literature as we face the twenty-first century. Many more people are facing up to the creative necessity of writing in African languages and to do for African languages what Spenser, Shakespeare, and Milton did for English; what Cervantes did for Spanish; what Rabelais did for French; what Martin Luther, Goethe, and Schiller did for the German language; what Pushkin, Gogol, and Tolstoy did for Russian; what Elias Lonnrot of the Finnish classic, the *Kalevala,* did for Finnish; indeed what all writers in history have done for their languages. In short they are hearkening to the rescue call by the Somali poet quoted earlier.

African writers in African languages are engaged in the great adventure and drama of creating a new and great tradition. In this task they have at least two great reservoirs: the heritages of orature and of world literature and culture.

All great national literatures have rooted themselves in the culture and language of the peasantry. The Homeric *Iliad* and *Odyssey,* as was all Greek drama, were rooted in the legends and stories that everybody knew. The Russian writers of the nineteenth century, particularly Pushkin, rooted their work in the culture of the peasantry. The *Kalevala,* the founding text of modern Finnish literature and language, was rooted in the folklore of the peasantry. The oral tradition will then be the basis or the foundation of the new tradition in African literature.

African languages must not be afraid of also borrowing from the best in world culture. All the dynamic cultures of the world have borrowed from other cultures in a process of mutual fertilisation. In his very interesting essay on the relationships between languages and cultures *From the Prehistory of Novelistic Discourse,* Bakhtin[7] has this to say on the development of Latin:

> Latin literary language in all its generic diversity was created in the light of Greek literary language. Its national distinctiveness and the specific verbal thought process inherent in it were realised in creative literary consciousness in a way that would have been absolutely impossible under conditions of monoglossia. After all it is possible to objectivise one's own particular language, its internal form, the peculiarities of its world view, its special linguistic habitus only in the light of another language belonging to somebody else, which is almost as much "one's own" as one's own native language.

One could add the rhetorical question: and is it possible to conceive of the development of Greek literature and culture without Egyptian and other Mediterranean cultures? African languages, as we have seen, have contributed immensely to the development of European languages and extended their possibilities through the Europhone literary tradition of the modern African experience. Indeed the new *Oxford English Dictionary* has canonised quite a number of new words from Kiswahili and other African languages.

African languages will borrow from one another; they will borrow from their classical heritages; they will borrow from the world—from the Caribbean, from Afroamerica, from Latin America, from the Asian—and from the European worlds. In this, the new writing in African languages will do the opposite of the Europhone practice: Instead of being appropriated by the world, it will appropriate the world and one hopes on terms of equal exchange, at the very least, borrow on its own terms and needs.

The growth and the development of the new African literature in African languages will have vast implications for critical scholarship. Currently no expert on the so-called "African literature" need ever show even the slightest acquaintance with any African language. Can you imagine a professor of French literature and culture who does not know a single word of French? Unfortunately it is not just the case of non-African scholars. African scholars of African realities need never show any acquaintance with African languages, even with their mother tongues. An African-languages-based critical scholarship would have a very vital role to play in the further development of the new African literature. The Europhone would occupy its proper place; as an appendage of European literature or as a footnote in African literature.

---

[7] **Bakhtin:** Mikhail Mikhailovich Bakhtin (1895–1975), influential Russian critic and philosopher of language whose work focuses on the interrelationship between language, discourse, and society; his major works include *Problems of Dostoevski's Poetics (Problemy poetiki Dostoevskogo)*, first published in 1929, and *The Dialogic Imagination (Voprosi literatury i estetiki)*, a collection of important essays on discourse, epic, and the novel, first published between 1937 and 1941.

It is these revitalised African languages rooting themselves in the traditions of orature and of written African literature, inspired by the deepest aspirations of the African people for a meaningful social change, which will also be best placed to give and receive from the wealth of our common culture on an equal basis.

Similar cases can be made for the literature of Asia and South America over the last four hundred years. These literatures growing in the shadow of both great classical pasts and of European literatures, sometimes bitterly resisting their appeal, at other times borrowing from them, but absorbing the borrowed features to create their unique traditions, creating so to speak their own space in a world dominated by cultural imperialism from the West, all add to the literature and culture of resistance. They are an integral part of what makes up the twentieth century and the foundation of the literature and cultures of the twenty-first century. The languages and literatures of Asia, Africa, and South America, the literatures of peoples of non-European stock but who are now part of the economic, political, and cultural reality of the West, are all creating space for a hundred flowers to bloom on a global scale; and the organisation of cultural studies all over the world should reflect this multi-coloured reality of the human creative stream. The continued domination of the world by a handful of European languages and literatures can only make the world poorer not richer. The transition in African, Asian, South American, North American, and European letters is towards traditions that will freely give and take, on the basis of equality and mutual respect, from this vast heritage of human creativity.

The wealth of a common global culture will then be expressed in the particularities of our different languages and cultures very much like a universal garden of many-coloured flowers. The "flowerness" of the different flowers is expressed in their very diversity. But there is cross-fertilisation between them. And what is more, they all contain in themselves the seeds of a new tomorrow.

❧ BLACK ELK
b. UNITED STATES, 1863–1950

In 1932, Black Elk published *Black Elk Speaks*, an autobiographical account of the early life and teachings of a Sioux medicine man. In the 1960s, as groups like the Beatles and counterculture figures like Allen Ginsberg and Allen Watts were popularizing Indian gurus and Buddhism, people "re-discovered" *Black Elk Speaks* and its message about the sacredness of the natural world. Black Elk's spiritual vision promoted tolerance and respect for all peoples and their religions and brought Native American life into public view. His accounts of the life and religion of the Oglala Sioux in *Black Elk Speaks, When the Tree Flowered,* and *The Sacred Pipe* have been elevated, in the words of Vine Deloria Jr., noted Lakota author and lecturer, to the status of a "North American bible of all tribes." Furthermore, Black Elk's portrayal of life for the Oglala Lakota in the second half of the nineteenth century, the most important transitional period for American Indians west of the Mississippi, is an invaluable addition to the historical record. The American West has a special place in American mythology, and the Plains Indians played a heroic yet tragic role in that history.

The Westward Movement and Native Americans. The nineteenth century in the United States was a period of westward expansion across the Great Plains to the Rocky Mountains and beyond them to the abundance and beauty of the West Coast. The Lewis and Clark expedition of 1803 to 1806 drew attention to the frontier's immense natural resources and potential for white settlement. White voices like those of Ralph Waldo Emerson, Henry David Thoreau, John Muir, and John James Audubon[1] helped to create a myth of the West that decried the congested urbanization of the East Coast and celebrated the importance of wilderness and the preservation of the natural world. The migration of adventurers, pioneers, and settlers traveling in covered wagons was encouraged by a general belief in **MANIFEST DESTINY**,[2] which gave to the European immigrants what some believed to be a God-given right to exploit the New World's resources and run over any Native Americans who might be in their way. The discovery of gold in California at the end of the 1840s and the extension of the railroads across the Great Plains in the 1850s and 1860s spurred the drive westward.

---

[1] **Ralph Waldo Emerson . . . Audubon:** Emerson (1803–1882) was a poet and Transcendentalist philosopher who drew attention to the sacredness of nature. Author and naturalist Henry David Thoreau (1817–1862) wrote about the spirit of nature in *Walden* (1854) and believed that wilderness was important for urban America. John Muir (1838–1914) explored the American West and wrote about its value. John James Audubon (1785–1851), artist and writer, documented vanishing species of birds.

[2] **Manifest Destiny:** A nineteenth-century doctrine stating that the expansion of the United States into the West was part of God's plan for this country; used to justify acquisition of territory in the Southwest, Northwest, and the Caribbean, and political control of Latin America.

Black Elk and Elk in London, 1887

Black Elk (left) and Elk, an Oglala Lakota, toured for a time with Buffalo Bill's Wild West Show. This photograph shows Lakota men's grass dance costumes of the time, which included sheep and sleigh bells, otter fur waist and neck pieces, pheasant feather bustles, shell necklaces, and bone hairpieces with colored glass beads. (National Anthropological Archives)

Black Elk in
Manderson, South
Dakota, 1947
*Black Elk at the time
of the interviews for*
The Sacred Pipe.
*(National
Anthropological
Archives)*

www For links to
more information
about Black Elk,
quizzes on his work,
and more on the
culture and context
of America in the
twentieth century,
see *World Literature
Online* at
bedfordstmartins
.com/worldlit.

For Native Americans, the nineteenth century in the West resembled the 1700s in the Midwest, when attempts to preserve a traditional way of life became efforts to merely survive. In 1830 Andrew Jackson signed the Removal Act, which legislated the deportation of tribes east of the Mississippi River to the "Great American Desert." By 1840 the Great Plains was designated "Indian Territory," and native peoples were gradually exterminated or crowded onto reservations. There, in addition to crop failures and diseased livestock, Native Americans suffered from epidemics of measles, flu, whooping cough, and tuberculosis, and a great many died.

During the 1860s and 1870s, the Oglala Lakota tribe of the northern Great Plains came into increased contact with white settlers moving west, leading to skirmishes with the U.S. Army. The buffalo herds upon which all the Plains tribes depended for survival were being slaughtered by white hunters. From 1872 to 1874, about three million buffalo were killed for their hides; the meat was left to rot on the ground. Wiping out the buffalo became an unofficial program of the United States to starve the Native American people. By 1880 there were no buffalo on the southern plains; by 1885 buffalo had largely disappeared from the northern plains as well.

Native American Prophets and the Ghost Dance.   Native American prophets, or visionaries, attempted to organize tribes to preserve their traditional culture and actively resist white encroachment, though some predicted that like the buffalo their people were headed for complete annihilation. From the plight of the Plains Indians in the late 1800s emerged the Ghost Dance religion, a messianic, MILLENARIAN (anticipating a coming utopia) movement that promised the return of dead Native Americans and the restoration of abundant game animals. This message of hope spread rapidly through the Lakota, Arapaho, Cheyenne, and Kiowa tribes west of the Mississippi, which by the 1880s were poverty-stricken. West of the Rockies, the Paiute, Bannock, Shoshoni, Gosiute, and Ute tribes also began to perform the ritual dance. When two senior warriors, Red Cloud and Sitting Bull, became believers, anxiety spread through white frontier settlements; newspapers on the East Coast fed the fear of a significant Indian uprising. Following orders to eliminate the Ghost Dance, the U.S. Army killed Sitting Bull and eventually massacred several hundred Lakota men, women, and children at Wounded Knee on December 29, 1890, effectually ending resistance to white hegemony in the West.

Black Elk's Contact with the Spirit World.   Black Elk was born in 1863 into a family of Oglala Lakota medicine men. Their band, Big Road, lived a seminomadic life in the western portion of Lakota territory, west of the Black Hills in what is now Wyoming. When Black Elk was nine years old, he had a vision of the sacred spirit world that formed the basis of his later roles as healer, prophet, and advisor to his people. At age seventeen he told Black Road, a wise old medicine man, that he was afraid of the Thunder-beings, the leading powers from his childhood vision. Black Elk was told that he must reenact a portion of his vision in a horse dance ceremony and thereby claim medicine power from the spirit guides. As Black Elk performed several ceremonies and embarked on a vision quest, his reputation as a medicine man grew.

Black Elk and Buffalo Bill's Wild West Show.   Life on the Lakota's Pine Ridge Reservation became increasingly difficult as game animals disappeared. In an attempt to understand the white man's world, Black Elk joined Buffalo Bill's Wild West Show[3] in 1886, traveling first to New York

> Maybe it was the sheer space that seemed so fascinating to the whites. Or maybe it was the style of the Plains culture with its nomadism, its horse herds, hunters, warfare, and apparently aimless, leisurely movement over the land. Or maybe it was the immensely colorful costumes of these people who seemed to play at life with a sort of fierce artfulness. At bottom, maybe it was the sense that was to be gained over and again that the tribes loved this life, thought themselves the privileged and elect of all creation to be permitted the gusty, wide-skied joys of their world.
> – FREDERICK TURNER, critic, 1994

---

[3] Buffalo . . . Show: Buffalo Bill was the nickname of William Cody (1846–1917), a frontier scout who became famous for his Wild West Show, which romanticized the West and the conflict between the white man and the Native American.

City and then to England, where the show was performed at Queen Victoria's Golden Jubilee. Black Elk's Christian baptism—a condition of
employment for the touring company—prompted his search for the
spiritual basis of Christianity. He wondered whether the survival of his
subjugated people depended on their conversion to Christianity. Joining
a second Wild West Show, Black Elk traveled through Germany, France,
and Italy.

Wounded Knee.   Black Elk returned to Pine Ridge in 1889 and was
caught up in the intensity of the Ghost Dance religion. A shirt that incorporated the basic symbols of Black Elk's childhood vision was used by
Lakota Ghost Dancers. Rumors spread eastward that the Lakota Ghost
Dancers believed extermination of the whites was a precondition for the
restoration of a Native American paradise. The retaliation was the massacre at Wounded Knee at the end of 1890. Black Elk's Ghost Dance shirts
were not impervious to the bullets of white men's rifles. More than half of
the Great Sioux Reservation in southwest Dakota had been given over to
white settlers in 1889; what remained, mostly unproductive land, was
parceled into five reservations, and a period of economic desperation
began for their inhabitants.

Like many Native Americans, Black Elk was torn between his traditional culture and Christianity. Although he was personally denounced
for his practices by Jesuit priests, Black Elk continued his shamanic healing ceremonies, making use of medicinal plants. In 1904 a priest intervened in the case of a dying boy, grabbed Black Elk by the throat and
commanded, "Satan, get out!" Feeling beaten, Black Elk was baptized a
Roman Catholic on December 6 and given the name Nicholas; he ceased
performing Lakota religious ceremonies. Although he became a leader in
the Catholic community of Pine Ridge, South Dakota, it is not clear how
much of the Christian worldview Black Elk authentically adopted.

The Meeting between Black Elk and John G. Neihardt.   In 1930
Nebraskan poet John G. Neihardt went to Manderson, South Dakota,
to find someone who could tell him about the Ghost Dance for his
epic poem, *A Cycle of the West.* He found Black Elk. For his part, although
he spoke no English, Black Elk intuited that Neihardt could be trusted
with his knowledge of the spirit world and Lakota ceremonies. Through
Neihardt, Black Elk's vision would be immortalized. In May of 1931,
Neihardt returned to South Dakota to record Black Elk's teachings.
Black Elk told his story in Lakota; his son Ben translated the statements
into rather basic English. Neihardt rephrased the material into more
idiomatic English, and his daughter Enid wrote the proceedings down
in shorthand, later transcribing them with the help of a typewriter.
Neihardt then edited and reshaped the materials into *Black Elk Speaks:
Being the Life Story of a Holy Man of the Oglala Sioux.* The first edition,
published by William Morrow & Co. in 1932, listed the authorship "as told
to John G. Neihardt (Flaming Rainbow)." Neihardt changed this in the
University of Nebraska Press edition of 1961 to "as told through John G.
Neihardt. . . ."

Neihardt's own role in editing the materials led to a controversy in the 1970s; detractors claimed that *Black Elk Speaks* was really *John Neihardt Speaks,* and that Neihardt had falsely claimed to be transmitting authentic Native American teachings as actually communicated by Black Elk. That controversy was largely laid to rest when Raymond J. DeMallie edited and introduced the full transcription of Black Elk's words from the manuscripts preserved in the Neihardt Collection in the Western History Manuscripts Collection of the University of Missouri. DeMallie's conclusion in *The Sixth Grandfather: Black Elk's Teachings Given to John G. Neihardt* is that *Black Elk Speaks* is authentic but is shaped into a readable book by Neihardt's artistic skill. *The Sixth Grandfather,* with its extensive notes, photographs, and bibliography, makes it possible to probe the English translations of Black Elk's teachings, even though the original statements in Lakota died with him. Another set of Neihardt interviews in 1944 resulted in *When the Tree Flowered* (1951), published in the year after Black Elk's death, which includes additional material about Black Elk and another Oglala elder, Eagle Elk.

The Stages of Black Elk's Life and Teachings.   The first selection that follows, "The Gift of the Sacred Pipe," is a translation of Black Elk's account of the foundation myth of Lakota religion, which is to Lakota belief and ritual what Moses' reception of the Ten Commandments is to Judaism or Jesus' Last Supper is to Christianity. In the myth, the Lakota are visited by White Buffalo Calf Woman, a divine being who gives them an altar and a sacred pipe, which symbolically and ritually connects the people to their own world and to the spirit world.

"The Conclusion of Black Elk's Vision" tells of Black Elk's vision from the spirit world when he was a boy of nine years. In mythic terms, the vision provided Black Elk with a COSMOGONY, or a worldview, that revealed the essential relationships among the six directions—east, west, north, south, above, and below. Unlike some religions that locate spiritual power in a transcendent deity, Native Americans acknowledge spiritual power throughout the natural world as well as the cosmos. For Black Elk, the six directions were not points on a compass or indicators on a two-dimensional map, but grandfathers—that is, a network of beings who bind together the cycles of sun and moon, the heavens and the earth, seasons, colors, songs, plants, and animals. Behind all manifest forms is the Great Spirit, or *Wakan-Tanka.*[4] The six grandfathers, as embodiments of *Wakan-Tanka,* exemplify the connectedness and unity of all life, symbolized by the circle or sacred hoop. In the same vision, Black Elk learned how to use ceremony and sacred plants for healing.

"The Ghost Dance and Wounded Knee" (1889–91) is Black Elk's story of this powerful Native American millenarian movement and its demise at Wounded Knee. The use of a sacred tree symbolizing the center of the nation's hoop by the Ghost Dance religion convinced Black Elk that

I am fortunate in having met at least some of these men of the old days who possessed great human and spiritual qualities. But Black Elk had a special quality of power and kindliness and a sense of mission that was unique and which I am sure was recognized by all who had the opportunity to know him.

– JOSEPH EPES BROWN, preface to *The Sacred Pipe,* 1971

---

[4] *Wakan-Tanka:* The unmanifested spirit behind all of creation; comparable to the Christian God and the Hindu Nirguna-Brahman, or Ishvara.

there was a connection between his childhood vision and the messianic vision of the movement's founder, Wovoka. The apparent failure of Ghost Dance with the massacre at Wounded Knee was a tremendous disappointment to its followers. Black Elk was filled with feelings of personal failure, believing that somehow the suffering of his people was related to his inability to fully express and enact the vision he had been granted.

The most quoted passage from *Black Elk Speaks* is its conclusion, in which Black Elk expresses through Neihardt his devastation:

> When I look back now from this high hill of my old age, I can still see the butchered women and children lying heaped and scattered all along the crooked gulch. . . . And I can see that something else died there in the bloody mud, and was buried in the blizzard. A people's dream died there . . . And I, to whom so great a vision was given in my youth—you see me now a pitiful old man who has done nothing, for the nation's hoop is broken and scattered.

Black Elk's deep connection with John G. Neihardt, however, gave him hope that it was perhaps not too late, that his vision and its message would live on and eventually bring about the flowering of the "sacred tree" at the center of the world and harmony between whites and Native Americans. A portion of a conversation with the Neihardts, "Black Elk at Harney Peak," which ends this group of selections, shows Black Elk's humanity and hope for the future. His prayer was one that Neihardt continued to use as an emblem of brotherhood in his many lectures about Black Elk.

A Note on the Classification of Native Americans.   Accurate or proper names are a large part of any minority's bid for recognition, especially since it is common for a dominant culture to give minorities convenient, often derogatory, labels. The classification of Native Americans has been complicated by the large number of languages and dialects they use, even within the same region. Although there is ongoing disagreement among scholars, anthropologists and linguists frequently group the multitude of American Indian dialects into six major categories: Eskimo and Aleut, Algonquian, Athabascan, Uto-Aztecan, Chinookan, and Siouan or Hokan-Siouan or Dakota. Apparently the term *Sioux*, which means "adder" or "snake," was a French rendering of an insult used by Algonquian-speaking groups about non-Algonquian-speaking enemies. Nevertheless, *Sioux* is still used as a linguistic category by scholars and is also a common name for the famous warrior society of the Great Plains. It is now customary to distinguish seven Sioux tribes: Wahpekute, Mdewakanton, Wahpeton, Sisseton, Yankton, Yantonai, and Teton. The largest of these is the Teton Sioux, which is the western-most group and is also called Lakota. Among the Teton Sioux or Lakota are several bands, the largest of which is the Oglala. Other bands include Brule, Hunkpapa, Minneconjou, Itazipocho, Oohenonpa, and Sihasapa (Blackfoot). The term *Sioux* is also currently used interchangeably with *Lakota*; *Lakota* as the native word is usually considered to be preferable.

■ CONNECTIONS

Rabindranath Tagore, "The Hungry Stones" (Book 5). Disenchanted with Western materialism, twentieth-century Europeans and Americans searched for a spiritual identity by exploring the religions of India and the indigenous religious traditions of the Americas, from ancient Mexico to the Aleuts. Tagore used his writings to create a spiritual bridge between East and West. What evidence can be found in Black Elk's teachings of his awareness that his understanding could benefit both Native Americans and nonnatives?

Chinua Achebe, *Things Fall Apart*, p. 1023. There are a number of parallels between the colonial domination of Africa and the treatment of native peoples in the Americas by Europeans. Achebe focuses on the disintegration of Ibo society in Nigeria caused by the incursion of Europeans. As described by Black Elk, what are the signs that the culture of his Lakota people is threatened by the westward migration of Europeans?

Matsuo Bashō, *The Narrow Road through the Backcountry* (Book 4). Despite the differences between Eastern and Western cultures on the whole, there are often similarities among the individual spiritual teachers from both. In his poetry, Bashō conveys the spiritual power of certain shrines in Japan and how this power affected him. How does Black Elk relay the spiritual importance of the Black Hills? What is it about the place that moves him?

■ FURTHER RESEARCH

Historical Background
Brown, Dee. *Bury My Heart at Wounded Knee: An Indian History of the American West.* 1981.
Deloria, Vine Jr. *Custer Died for Your Sins: An Indian Manifesto.* 1970.
Densmore, Frances. *Teton Sioux Music.* 1918.
Standing Bear, Luther. *My People the Sioux.* 1933.
Utley, Robert M. *The Last Days of the Sioux Nation.* 1963.

Native American Religion
Gill, Sam D. *Native American Religions: An Introduction.* 1981.
Mooney, James. *The Ghost-Dance Religion and the Sioux Outbreak of 1890.* 1896.
Powers, William K. *Oglala Religion.* 1977.

Black Elk and John G. Neihardt
Aly, Lucile F. *John G. Neihardt: A Critical Biography.* 1977.
McCluskey, Sally. "*Black Elk Speaks:* And So Does John Neihardt." *Western American Literature* (winter 1972.)
Olson, Paul A. "*Black Elk Speaks* as Epic and Ritual Attempt to Reverse History." *Vision and Refuge: Essays on the Literature of the Great Plains.* Ed. Virginia Faulkner with Frederick C. Luebke. 1982.

∾ The Gift of the Sacred Pipe

Recorded and edited by Joseph Epes Brown

Early one morning, very many winters ago, two Lakota were out hunting with their bows and arrows, and as they were standing on a hill looking for game, they saw in the distance something coming towards them in a very strange and wonderful manner. When this mysterious thing came nearer to them, they saw that it was a very beautiful woman, dressed in white buckskin, and bearing a bundle on her back. Now this woman was so good to look at that one of the Lakota had bad intentions and told his friend of his desire, but this good man said that he must not have such thoughts, for surely this is a *wakan* woman.[1] The mysterious person was now very close to the men, and then putting down her bundle, she asked the one with bad intentions to come over to her. As the young man approached the mysterious woman, they were both covered by a great cloud, and soon when it lifted the sacred woman was standing there, and at her feet was the man with the bad thoughts who was now nothing but bones, and terrible snakes were eating him.[2]

"Behold what you see!" the strange woman said to the good man. "I am coming to your people and wish to talk with your chief *Hehlokecha Najin* [Standing Hollow Horn]. Return to him, and tell him to prepare a large tipi in which he should gather all his people, and make ready for my coming. I wish to tell you something of great importance!"

The young man then returned to the tipi of his chief, and told him all that had happened: that this *wakan* woman was coming to visit them and that they must all

---

The Gift of the Sacred Pipe. Joseph Epes Brown spent a very cold winter with Black Elk and his family in 1947, and with Benjamin Black Elk as a translator, recorded and edited the teachings in *The Sacred Pipe: Black Elk's Account of the Seven Rites of the Oglala Sioux* (1953). The first chapter, "The Gift of the Sacred Pipe," is Black Elk's account of the myth of the White Buffalo Calf Woman, a spirit being who brings the sacred pipe to the Lakota people and explains its role as a religious object and the center of ceremonial life. The parts of the pipe bring together basic elements of Lakota culture — earth, blood, buffalo, eagle, breath, smoke, fire. Together they provide an altar or mystical channel between mortal participant and the transcendent creator spirit, known by the Lakota as *Wakan-Tanka* — or Great Spirit.

All notes are adapted from Brown's.

---

[1] *wakan* **woman:** Throughout this work I shall translate the Lakota word *wakan* as "holy" or "sacred," rather than as "power" or "powerful" as used by some ethnologists. This latter term may be a true translation, yet is not really complete, for with the Sioux, and with all traditional peoples in general, the "power" (really the sacredness) of a being or a thing is in proportion to its nearness to its prototype.

[2] **man . . . eating him:** Black Elk emphasized that this should not only be taken as an event in time, but also as an eternal truth. "Any man," he said, "who is attached to the senses and to the things of this world, is one who lives in ignorance and is being consumed by the snakes which represent his own passions."

prepare. The chief, Standing Hollow Horn, then had several tipis taken down, and from them a great lodge[3] was made as the sacred woman had instructed. He sent out a crier to tell the people to put on their best buckskin clothes and to gather immediately in the lodge. The people were, of course, all very excited as they waited in the great lodge for the coming of the holy woman, and everybody was wondering where this mysterious woman came from and what it was that she wished to say.

Soon the young men who were watching for the coming of the *wakan* person announced that they saw something in the distance approaching them in a beautiful manner, and then suddenly she entered the lodge, walked around sun-wise,[4] and stood in front of Standing Hollow Horn.[5] She took from her back the bundle, and holding it with both hands in front of the chief, said: "Behold this and always love it! It is *lela wakan* [very sacred], and you must treat it as such. No impure man should ever be allowed to see it, for within this bundle there is a sacred pipe. With this you will, during the winters to come, send your voices to *Wakan-Tanka*, your Father and Grandfather."[6]

After the mysterious woman said this, she took from the bundle a pipe, and also a small round stone which she placed upon the ground. Holding the pipe up with its stem to the heavens, she said: "With this sacred pipe you will walk upon the Earth; for the Earth is your Grandmother and Mother,[7] and She is sacred. Every step that is taken upon Her should be as a prayer. The bowl of this pipe is of red stone; it is the Earth. Carved in the stone and facing the center is this buffalo calf[8] who represents all the four-leggeds who live upon your Mother. The stem of the pipe is of wood, and this represents all that grows upon the Earth. And these twelve feathers which hang

---

[3] **great lodge:** The Sioux ceremonial lodge is constructed with twenty-eight poles. One of these poles is the "key," holding up all the others, and this pole the holy men say represents *Wakan-Tanka*, who sustains the universe, which is represented by the lodge as a whole.

[4] **sun-wise:** The sun-wise or clockwise circumambulation is almost always used by the Sioux; occasionally, however, the counterclockwise movement is used in a dance or some occasion prior to or after a great catastrophe, for this movement is in imitation of the Thunder-beings who always act in an antinatural way and who come in a terrifying manner, often bringing destruction.

[5] **Standing Hollow Horn:** As leader of his people, he should be seated at the west, the place of honor; for in sitting at the west of a tipi, one faces the door, or east, from which comes the light, representing wisdom, and this illumination a leader must always possess if he is to guide his people in a sacred manner.

[6] **Father . . . Grandfather:** *Wakan-Tanka* as Grandfather is the Great Spirit independent of manifestation, unqualified, unlimited, identical to the Christian Godhead, or to the Hindu *Brahma-Nirguna*.

[7] **Grandmother . . . Mother:** As in the distinction made within *Wakan-Tanka* between Grandfather and Father, so the Earth is considered under two aspects, that of Mother and Grandmother. The former is the earth considered as the producer of all growing forms, in act; whereas Grandmother refers to the ground or substance of all growing things—potentiality.

[8] **buffalo calf:** The buffalo was to the Sioux the most important of all four-legged animals, for it supplied their food, their clothing, and even their houses, which were made from the tanned hides. Because the buffalo contained all these things within himself, and for many other reasons, he was a natural symbol of the universe, the totality of all manifested forms. Also the buffalo has four legs, and these represent the four ages which are an integral condition of creation.

here where the stem fits into the bowl are from *Wanbli Galeshka,* the Spotted Eagle,[9] and they represent the eagle and all the wingeds of the air. All these peoples, and all the things of the universe, are joined to you who smoke the pipe—all send their voices to *Wakan-Tanka,* the Great Spirit. When you pray with this pipe, you pray for and with everything."

The *wakan* woman then touched the foot of the pipe to the round stone which lay upon the ground, and said: "With this pipe you will be bound to all your relatives: your Grandfather and Father, your Grandmother and Mother. This round rock, which is made of the same red stone as the bowl of the pipe, your Father *Wakan-Tanka* has also given to you. It is the Earth, your Grandmother and Mother, and it is where you will live and increase. This Earth which He has given to you is red, and the two-leggeds who live upon the Earth are red; and the Great Spirit has also given to you a red day, and a red road.[10] All of this is sacred and so do not forget! Every dawn as it comes is a holy event, and every day is holy, for the light comes from your Father *Wakan-Tanka;* and also you must always remember that the two-leggeds and all the other peoples who stand upon this earth are sacred and should be treated as such.

"From this time on, the holy pipe will stand upon this red Earth, and the two-leggeds will take the pipe and will send their voices to *Wakan-Tanka.* These seven circles which you see on the stone have much meaning, for they represent the seven rites in which the pipe will be used. The first large circle represents the first rite which I shall give to you, and the other six circles represent the rites which will in time be revealed to you directly.[11] Standing Hollow Horn, be good to these gifts and to your people, for they are *wakan!* With this pipe the two-leggeds will increase, and there will come to them all that is good. From above *Wakan-Tanka* has given to you this sacred pipe, so that through it you may have knowledge. For this great gift you should always be grateful! But now before I leave I wish to give to you instructions for the first rite in which your people will use this pipe.

"It should be for you a sacred day when one of your people dies. You must then keep his soul[12] as I shall teach you, and through this you will gain much power; for if

---

[9] *Wanbli Galeshka,* the Spotted Eagle: Since He flies the highest of all created creatures and sees everything, the *Wanbli Galeshka* is regarded as *Wakan-Tanka* under certain aspects. He is a solar bird, His feathers being regarded as rays of the sun . . . .

[10] red road: That which runs north and south and is the good or straight way, for to the Sioux the north is purity and the south is the source of life. This "red road" is thus similar to the Christian "straight and narrow way"; it is the vertical of the cross, or the *ec-cirata el-mustaqim* of the Islamic tradition.

On the other hand, there is the "blue" or "black road" of the Sioux, which runs east and west and which is the path of error and destruction. He who travels on this path is, Black Elk has said, "one who is distracted, who is ruled by his senses, and who lives for himself rather than for his people."

[11] seven circles: According to Black Elk, two of these rites were known to the Sioux prior to the coming of the sacred Woman; these were the purification rites of the sweat lodge, and the *Hanblecheyapi* (crying for a vision); the ritual of the pipe was, however, now added to both of these.

[12] soul: In translating the Lakota word *wanagi,* I have used the term "soul" in preference to "spirit," which has been used by many ethnologists.

this soul is kept, it will increase in you your concern and love for your neighbor. So long as the person, in his soul, is kept with your people, through him you will be able to send your voice to *Wakan-Tanka*.[13]

"It should also be a sacred day when a soul is released and returns to its home, *Wakan-Tanka*, for on this day four women will be made holy, and they will in time bear children who will walk the path of life in a sacred manner, setting an example to your people. Behold Me, for it is I that they will take in their mouths, and it is through this that they will become *wakan*.

"He who keeps the soul of a person must be a good and pure man, and he should use the pipe so that all the people, with the soul, will together send their voices to *Wakan-Tanka*. The fruit of your Mother the Earth and the fruit of all that bears will be blessed in this manner, and your people will then walk the path of life in a sacred way. Do not forget that *Wakan-Tanka* has given you seven days in which to send your voices to Him. So long as you remember this you will live; the rest you will know from *Wakan-Tanka* directly."

The sacred woman then started to leave the lodge, but turning again to Standing Hollow Horn, she said: "Behold this pipe! Always remember how sacred it is, and treat it as such, for it will take you to the end. Remember, in me there are four ages.[14] I am leaving now, but I shall look back upon your people in every age, and at the end I shall return."

Moving around the lodge in a sun-wise manner, the mysterious woman left, but after walking a short distance she looked back towards the people and sat down. When she rose the people were amazed to see that she had become a young red and brown buffalo calf. Then this calf walked farther, lay down, and rolled, looking back at the people, and when she got up she was a white buffalo. Again the white buffalo walked farther and rolled on the ground, becoming now a black buffalo. This buffalo then walked farther away from the people, stopped, and after bowing to each of the four quarters of the universe, disappeared over the hill.

---

[13] "It is good," Black Elk has said, "to have a reminder of death before us, for it helps us to understand the impermanence of life on this earth, and this understanding may aid us in preparing for our own death. He who is well prepared is he who knows that he is nothing compared with *Wakan-Tanka*, who is everything; then he knows that world which is real."

[14] **four ages:** According to Siouan mythology, it is believed that at the beginning of the cycle a buffalo was placed at the west in order to hold back the waters. Every year this buffalo loses one hair, and every age he loses one leg. When all his hair and all four legs are gone, then the waters rush in once again, and the cycle comes to an end.

∿ The Conclusion of Black Elk's Vision

Recorded and edited by John Neihardt

Then a Voice said: "Behold this day, for it is yours to make. Now you shall stand upon the center of the earth to see, for there they are taking you." . . .

I looked ahead and saw the mountains there with rocks and forests on them, and from the mountains flashed all colors upward to the heavens. Then I was standing on the highest mountain of them all, and round about beneath me was the whole hoop of the world.[1] And while I stood there I saw more than I can tell and I understood more than I saw; for I was seeing in a sacred manner the shapes of all things in the spirit, and the shape of all shapes as they must live together like one being. And I saw that the sacred hoop of my people was one of many hoops that made one circle, wide as daylight and as starlight, and in the center grew one mighty flowering tree to shelter all the children of one mother and one father. And I saw that it was holy.

Then as I stood there, two men were coming from the east, head first like arrows flying, and between them rose the day-break star. They came and gave a herb to me and said: "With this on earth you shall undertake anything and do it." It was the day-break-star herb, the herb of understanding, and they told me to drop it on the earth. I saw it falling far, and when it struck the earth it rooted and grew and flowered, four blossoms on one stem, a blue, a white, a scarlet, and a yellow; and the rays from these streamed upward to the heavens so that all creatures saw it and in no place was there darkness.

The Conclusion of Black Elk's Vision.   In his boyhood vision, Black Elk is transported to the highest point of the Black Hills — Harney Peak — where he sees how the sacred hoop of his people is one of many such hoops that form one great circle of humankind. In the center is a mighty flowering tree that shelters all the people of the world, and it is holy. This is not simply a question of tolerating other belief systems; Black Elk sees the inner connection among them. Two messenger figures provide Black Elk with the "day-break-star" herb, which flowers into the colors of the four directions. Directions personified as "grandfathers" celebrate the completion of Black Elk's initiation by giving him appropriate gifts. The west gives him a cup of water, a bow, and arrows: the powers of divination, healing, and killing. The north, symbolized by white geese, gives him the power of cleansing. The east gives him a peace pipe, the channel that connects humans with spirit beings. And the south gives him a flowering stick, which represents the flowering tree at the center of the world and the source of life itself. Black Elk sees himself lying as if dead as he returns to ordinary reality.

A note on the edition: This selection is from *Black Elk Speaks.* All notes are the editors'.

---

[1]**Then . . . world:** The hoop represents the way that all life is connected. The "highest mountain" is Harney Peak, in the Black Hills.

Then the Voice said: "Your Six Grandfathers—now you shall go back to them."

I had not noticed how I was dressed until now, and I saw that I was painted red all over, and my joints were painted black,[2] with white stripes between the joints. My bay had lightning stripes all over him, and his mane was cloud. And when I breathed, my breath was lightning.

Now two men were leading me, head first like arrows slanting upward—the two that brought me from the earth. And as I followed on the bay, they turned into four flocks of geese that flew in circles, one above each quarter, sending forth a sacred voice as they flew: Br-r-r-p, br-r-r-p, br-r-r-p, br-r-r-p![3]

Then I saw ahead the rainbow flaming above the tepee of the Six Grandfathers, built and roofed with cloud and sewed with thongs of lightning; and underneath it were all the wings of the air and under them the animals and men. All these were rejoicing, and thunder was like happy laughter.

As I rode in through the rainbow door, there were cheering voices from all over the universe, and I saw the Six Grandfathers sitting in a row, with their arms held toward me and their hands, palms out; and behind them in the cloud were faces thronging, without number, of the people yet to be.

"He has triumphed!" cried the six together, making thunder. And as I passed before them there, each gave again the gift that he had given me before—the cup of water and the bow and arrows, the power to make live and to destroy; the white wing of cleansing and the healing herb; the sacred pipe; the flowering stick. And each one spoke in turn from west to south, explaining what he gave as he had done before, and as each one spoke he melted down into the earth and rose again; and as each did this, I felt nearer to the earth.

Then the oldest of them all said: "Grandson, all over the universe you have seen. Now you shall go back with power to the place from whence you came, and it shall happen yonder that hundreds shall be sacred, hundreds shall be flames! Behold!"

I looked below and saw my people there, and all were well and happy except one, and he was lying like the dead—and that one was myself.[4] Then the oldest Grandfather sang, and his song was like this:

There is someone lying on earth in a sacred manner.
There is someone—on earth he lies.
In a sacred manner I have made him to walk.

---

[2] **red . . . black:** Red, the color of blood and the east, is associated with birth and life; the color black is usually associated with the west and the setting sun, and therefore with death.

[3] **Br-r-r-p . . . br-r-r-p!:** By imitating the call of the geese, Black Elk could assume a goose's powers: that is, the power of flight and the cleansing powers associated with the north and with winter.

[4] **lying . . . myself:** In the shamanic tradition of Native Americans, initiates undergo a symbolic death, such as a serious illness, in order to receive the vision that will transform their lives. The death experience might involve a dismemberment and eventually a re-memberment.

Now the tepee, built and roofed with cloud, began to sway back and forth as in a wind, and the flaming rainbow door[5] was growing dimmer. I could hear voices of all kinds crying from outside: "Eagle Wing Stretches[6] is coming forth! Behold him!"

When I went through the door, the face of the day of earth was appearing with the day-break star upon its forehead; and the sun leaped up and looked upon me, and I was going forth alone.

And as I walked alone, I heard the sun singing as it arose, and it sang like this:

> With visible face I am appearing.
> In a sacred manner I appear.
> For the greening earth a pleasantness I make.
> The center of the nation's hoop I have made pleasant.
> With visible face, behold me!
> The four-leggeds and two-leggeds, I have made them to walk;
> The wings of the air, I have made them to fly.
> With visible face I appear.
> My day, I have made it holy.

When the singing stopped, I was feeling lost and very lonely. Then a Voice above me said: "Look back!" It was a spotted eagle that was hovering over me and spoke. I looked, and where the flaming rainbow tepee, built and roofed with cloud, had been, I saw only the tall rock mountain at the center of the world.

I was all alone on a broad plain now with my feet upon the earth, alone but for the spotted eagle guarding me. I could see my people's village far ahead, and I walked very fast, for I was homesick now. Then I saw my own tepee, and inside I saw my mother and my father bending over a sick boy that was myself. And as I entered the tepee, someone was saying: "The boy is coming to; you had better give him some water."

Then I was sitting up; and I was sad because my mother and my father didn't seem to know I had been so far away.

---

[5] **flaming rainbow door:** The rainbow in this vision, as in the story of the flood in the Hebrew Scriptures, symbolizes a sacred threshold between the heavens and the earth, a place for epiphanies and prophecies. A "flaming rainbow" signifies the outpouring of whatever meaning has been dispensed. Early in the interview process with Black Elk, the Neihardts were given ceremonial names. John Neihardt was "Flaming Rainbow" in anticipation of his future role in regard to Black Elk's teachings.

[6] **Eagle Wing Stretches:** The name given to Black Elk when he represents the six grandfathers on earth; it refers to the eagle in flight. Eagles, like angels, are feathered beings that mediate between the earth and the heavens.

FROM

◊ᐳ The Ghost Dance and Wounded Knee (1889–91)

THE MESSIAH'S DANCE

When I came back my people seemed to be in poverty. Before I went some of my people were looking well, but when I got back they all looked pitiful. There had been quite a famine. I returned in 1889.[1] While I was gone I had lost my power, but as soon as I returned I was called out to cure a sick person and just then my power returned.

At this time people were all talking about the land they had sold to Three Stars [General Crook] as a result of a treaty.[2] This fall I had another brother who went out on a show which went all over the world. He started out on this show.

This fall I heard that there were some men named Good Thunder, Brave Bear, and Yellow Breast who had gone and seen the Messiah.[3] It was toward the west right around Idaho somewhere. There was a sacred man there. These three men had gone to see this sacred man and they came back that following fall [1889] and reported that they had seen the Messiah and actually talked to him and that he had given them some sacred relics. They had had the meeting at the head of White Clay [Creek] and the people gathered together there to hear what these men had to say about it. I did not go over there, I just heard of it, that's all. These three men had

---

The Ghost Dance and Wounded Knee (1889–91). The description of Black Elk's participation in the Ghost Dance and his experiences at the 1890 massacre at Wounded Knee have contributed to Lakota history and provided an insider's view of the momentous events that mark the end of the traditional horse and buffalo culture of the Plains Indians. The Ghost Dance religion, the largest messianic movement among Native Americans in the nineteenth century, was largely crushed by the massacre at Wounded Knee. This massacre largely resulted from the fear, suspicion, and hatred of white America toward native peoples. Broken treaties and poverty-stricken reservations robbed Native America of direction and purpose.

Black Elk's descriptions of the Ghost Dance and the events at Wounded Knee are excerpted from Raymond J. DeMallie's edition, *The Sixth Grandfather,* which is a complete collection of Black Elk's accounts of his life given to John G. Neihardt. The footnotes are adapted from DeMallie's edition.

---

[1] Conditions had worsened significantly during the years Black Elk was away. The beef rations had been steadily decreased, and in 1889 they were again cut by more than half. There was famine at Pine Ridge, coupled with disease and drought. See Olson, *Red Cloud and the Sioux Problem,* pp. 320–21; Mooney, *The Ghost-Dance Religion,* pp. 826–42.

[2] **a treaty:** General George Crook headed the 1889 commission that secured the Indians' consent to the reduction and division of the Great Sioux Reservation.

[3] **the Messiah:** A Paiute Indian called Jack Wilson (Wovoka) who lived in Mason Valley, Nevada, forty miles northwest of the Walker Lake reservation. Sword also mentioned this first delegation to the Messiah in 1889; see Mooney, *The Ghost-Dance Religion,* pp. 767, 797.

brought some sacred red and white paint that the sacred man had given them. This paint was broken up into little pieces and distributed among the people.

These people told me that these men had actually seen the Messiah and that he had given them these things. They should put this paint on and have a ghost dance, and in doing this they would save themselves, that there is another world coming — a world just for the Indians, that in time the world would come and crush out all the whites. But if you want to get into this other world, you would have to have this paint on. It should be put all over the face and head,[4] and that this ghost dance would draw them to this other world and that the whites would have no power to get on so that it would crush them. In this other world there was plenty of meat — just like olden times — every dead person was alive again and all the buffalo that had been killed would be over there again roaming around. This world was to come like a cloud. This painting and ghost dance would make everyone get on the red road again. Everyone was eager to get back to the red road again.

This sacred man had presented two eagle feathers to Good Thunder, one of these three men. The sacred man had said to him: "Receive these eagle feathers and behold them, for my father will cause these two eagle feathers to bring your people back to him." This is all that was heard this whole winter. At first when I heard this I was bothered, because my vision was nearly like it and it looked as though my vision were really coming true and that if I helped, probably with my power that I had I could make the tree bloom and that I would get my people back into that sacred hoop again where they would prosper. This was in my mind but I still worked on as clerk in the store.[5] I wanted to see this man personally and find out and it was setting firmer in my mind every day.

It was now the spring of 1890. The winter of 1889–90 I heard that they wanted to find out more about that man. So Kicking Bear, Short Bull, Bear Comes Out, and [Mash the] Kettle and a party[6] started out to find out more about this sacred man and see him if possible. These fellows came home in the spring of 1890. I did not hear of the news that they had. But I heard that at the head of Cheyenne Creek, north of Pine Ridge, Kicking Bear had held the first ghost dance. From the rumors and gossips I heard that this Messiah was the son of the Great Spirit that had come out there. Then the next thing I heard was that they were dancing below Manderson on Wounded Knee.[7] I wanted to find out things, because it was setting strongly in my heart and something seemed to tell me to go and I resisted it for a while but then I could no longer resist, so I got on my horse and went to this ghost dance near Manderson and watched them dance.

---

[4] **face and head:** These instructions for performing the ceremonial dance were given by the Messiah Wovoka to the delegation from the Sioux reservation. The Ghost Dance religion was primarily spread by word of mouth.

[5] **the store:** Probably the store at Manderson.

[6] **Kicking Bear . . . a party:** These delegates represented the Pine Ridge, Rosebud, and Cheyenne River reservations. They were chosen at the autumn 1889 council mentioned above by Black Elk and were sent to learn more about the Messiah.

[7] Kicking Bear probably initiated the first ghost dance at Pine Ridge in August 1890; Good Thunder organized the dance on Wounded Knee Creek that Black Elk attended.

They had a sacred pole in the center. It was a circle in which they were dancing and I could clearly see that this was my sacred hoop and in the center they had an exact duplicate of my tree that never blooms and it came to my mind that perhaps with this power the tree would bloom and the people would get into the sacred hoop again. It seemed that I could recall all my vision in it. The more I thought about it, the stronger it got in my mind. Furthermore, the sacred articles that had been presented were scarlet relics and their faces were painted red. Furthermore, they had that pipe and the eagle feathers. It was all from my vision. So I sat there and felt sad. Then happiness overcame me all at once and it got ahold of me right there. I was to be intercessor for my people and yet I was not doing my duty. Perhaps it was this Messiah that had pointed me out and he might have set this to remind me to get to work again to bring my people back into the hoop and the old religion.

Again I recalled Harney Peak in the Black Hills [*the center of the earth*]. And I remembered my vision that the spirits had said to me: "Boy, take courage, they shall take you to the center of the earth." When they took me here, they said: "Behold all the universe, the good things of the earth. All this behold it, because they shall be your own." Then I saw people prospering all over. And I recalled my six grandfathers. They told me through their power I would be intercessor on earth for my people. They had told me that I should know everything so therefore I made up my mind to join them. What I went there first for was to find out what they had heard, but now I changed my mind and was going there to use my own power to bring the people together. The dance was [*all*] done that day, but the next day there was to be another dance, so I stayed all night for another one. . . .

BLACK ELK'S GHOST DANCE VISIONS

The next morning we danced again. As we started out to dance Kicking Bear offered a prayer saying: "Father, behold me, these people shall go forth today. They shall see their relatives that they may be happy over there day after day and there will be no end to that happiness." Then all the dancers around began to wail and cry. As we started to dance again some of the people would be laughing and some would be crying. Some of them would lie down for a vision and we just kept on dancing. I could see more of them staggering around panting and then they would fall down for visions. The people were crying for the old ways of living and [that] their religion would be with them again.[8]

It took quite a while for me to get in this condition. They sang all sorts of songs. Then I began to fear that my breath was coming up while we were dancing. The first feeling I had was that my legs seemed to be full of ants. We always danced with our eyes closed. Then we heard wailing of women and people were lying around all over as though they were having visions. It seemed as though I were swaying off the ground without touching it. This queer feeling came up [*farther*] and it was in my

---

[8] By this time all the traditional public rituals of the Lakota religion, including the sun dance, the soul-keeping ritual, and the give-aways (of material goods after a relative's death) were prohibited by the government.

heart now and I was panting. It was not a fear. It seemed that I would glide forward like a swing and swing back again. Of course it took me quite a while. I was panting hard and I must have fallen down, for they let me go.

All I saw was an eagle feather in front of my eyes at first. I felt as though I had fallen off a swing and gone out into the air. My arms were outstretched and right before me above I could see a spotted eagle dancing toward me with his wings fluttering and the shrill whistle he made. I could see a ridge right in front of me and I thought I was going to hit that ridge, but I went right over it. I did not move at all, I just looked ahead. After I reached the other side of the ridge I could see a beautiful land over there and people were camping there in circle[s] all over. I noticed that they had plenty, and I saw dried meat all over. I glided over the tipi. Then I went down feet first and lighted on the ground. As I was going down to the center of the hoop I could see a tree in full bloom with flowers on it. I could see two men coming toward me. They were dressed with ghost shirts like I was dressed. They came and said to me: "It is not yet time to see your Father, but we shall present to you something that you will carry home to your people and with this they shall come forth to see their loved ones." I could see fat horses all over and the wild animals ranging out over the country and hunters were returning with their meat. I was very happy to see that and I'm hungry for some of that meat right now. They told me to return at once and I was out in the air again and I glided the same as before back.

When I got right above the dance place, they were still dancing the ghost dance. I hoped to see that tree blooming [*but the day following it was not blooming*] and it was just seemingly faded. I went down to my body then and I could hear the voices. Then I got up from my vision. Whenever a man comes to, they ask you what you have seen. So most of the people came over there to see what I had dreamed. I told them the exact vision I had had. What I brought back was the memory of what they had shown me and I was to make an exact copy of it. This ghost shirt was to be used always in the ghost dances. So I started the ghost shirt.[9]

That evening we got together at Big Road's tipi; the chief dancers came. They decided there to use my ghost shirts. So the next day I made ghost shirts all day and they had to be painted by me. The first two shirts I made were made according to the Messiah vision. . . .

At this time there was quite a great famine among the people and some of them really believed in this Messiah business and were hoping that this land of promise would come soon so that they would be through with the poverty. Many of them wanted to know more about this. I told my vision through songs. As I sang one song, there were older men [*than I*] there to tell what they meant to the others. Before I told this everyone took out his pipe filled with kinnikinnick to make offer[ing]s to the sacred man that I had seen. Then I told my vision in song and I sang this song

---

[9] **ghost shirt:** A reservation schoolteacher, Mrs. Z. A. Parker, wrote an excellent description of a ghost dance she had witnessed on White Clay Creek in October 1890. She was told that the ghost shirts, which she understood that the Indians were wearing for the first time, had been seen in a vision by a woman, the wife of Return from Scout. It seems likely that several of the ghost dancers had had visions relating to sacred regalia for the ceremony.

three times. I sang a song the words of which were the same as the one the man on [beside] the tree had said, and the melody of it was that which I heard above the sixth village in my vision. [*I sang this song three times and*] the fourth time I sang it the people all began to cry, because the white man had taken our world from us and we were like prisoners of war.

I went to the sixth village in the vision because in the flaming rainbow of the first vision I had seen six grandfathers. The sixth one was myself. And this was to represent six grandfathers—the powers that the earth got from these six powers. I saw two men first in the vision and now I saw two men in the Messiah vision also. Here on earth I had six children; three have died. In my first vision I had seen twelve riders and again I saw twelve men in this vision. It represents the twelve moons in the year. This village might represent six generations from the first and perhaps in the sixth generation the tree will bloom as in my vision. . . .

THE WOUNDED KNEE MASSACRE

We moved camp to the Cheyenne River north of Pine Ridge. Most of the Oglalas were camping around Pine Ridge. I was out looking for horses and when I returned I learned that two policemen had come after me to be on their side as a scout.[10] Two days later I learned that the soldiers were marching toward Wounded Knee. This was in the Month of the Popping Trees—December. I heard that Big Foot was coming from a young man who had come there.[11] Rough Feather I heard was going to get Big Foot, who was coming from his camp near the mouth of Medicine Root Creek on White River. At that time there were some soldiers camping somewhere around there on the other side of the river. Rough Feather went over there in order to get Big Foot. He wanted them to come in a south-easterly direction, but they did not do it. They wanted to follow up Medicine Root. They followed it to the head and then scouts for the soldiers saw them here at the head of Medicine Root. The scouts represented this to the soldiers and from here it was represented to Pine Ridge. On this same evening the soldiers went toward where Big Foot was camped at the head of Medicine Root. Big Foot's camp came to the creek of Porcupine Butte where the soldiers met them and they nearly had a fight here. The soldiers brought Big Foot back to Wounded Knee.[12] That evening the soldiers gathered around where they had camped. The soldiers had them well guarded all night.

It was December 29, 1890, the next morning. They carried Big Foot over to the officers, for he was sick. They told the rest of Big Foot's people to bring their guns

---

[10] Although Black Elk himself apparently never joined the Indian scouts, another Oglala with the same name— probably Black Elk's brother—did enlist as a scout. A photograph of this man, in uniform, is in the Nebraska State Historical Society, in Lincoln.

[11] Big Foot and his band of some three hundred Minneconjous had fled from the Cheyenne River Reservation on December 23. They were alarmed by the news of Sitting Bull's death on Standing Rock Reservation, December 15, and feared the soldiers on their own reservation.

[12] Big Foot surrendered to Major Samuel M. Whitside on December 28, and together the Indians and soldiers camped for the night on Wounded Knee Creek, twenty miles northeast of Pine Ridge agency.

over there. Everyone stacked their guns and even their knives up in the office [at the officers' headquarters]. The soldiers were searching all the tipis for weapons. There were two men near Big Foot's tipi who wore blankets made out of white sheets, with just their eyes showing. Some of them had probably hidden their knives. The officer who was taking the guns from them went up to these men and pulled their white blankets apart and one of them had his gun concealed inside the sheet. He proceeded to the other one and opened it and just as he was going to get his gun, this man shot him. This man's name was Yellow Bird. This fellow did not want to give up his gun, and did not intend to shoot the white man at all — the gun just went off. Of course the soldiers were all around there already with their [wagon] guns on the hill north, across the flat east, and across the creek. The Indian scouts were behind the soldiers on the south. Yellow Bird and the white officer were wrestling with this gun and they had rolled down together on the ground and were wrestling with it. Dog Chief was right there where they took the guns and was standing right by these men while wrestling. This man was a friend of mine and he saw the whole thing.

Big Foot was the first Indian that was killed by an officer before the [wagon] guns began [to shoot]. They had carried Big Foot over to where the guns were being given up and immediately after the shot of Yellow Bird the officer shot Big Foot. Yellow Bird went into a tipi nearby and killed lots of them probably before he died. The Indians all ran to the stacks of guns and got their guns during a lull while the soldiers were loading again. A soldier ran up to tear the tipi away to get at Yellow Bird, but the latter shot at them as they came up and killed them. They fired at the tipi and the soldiers' guns set it afire and he died in there.

The night before this I was over in the camp at Pine Ridge and I couldn't sleep. When I saw the soldiers going out it seemed that I knew there would be trouble. I was walking around all night until daylight. After my meal early that morning I got my horse and while I was out I heard shooting over to the east — I heard wagon guns going off.[13] This was a little distance from the camp and when I heard this gun I felt it right in my body, so I went out and drove the horses back to the camp for I knew there was trouble. Just as I got back with the horses there was a man who returned from Pine Ridge and had come back because he had heard this. He said: "Hey, hey son, the people that are coming are fired upon, I know it."

I took my buckskin and saddled up. I had no gun. The only thing I had was the sacred red stick. I put on my sacred shirt. This was a shirt I had made to be worn by no one but myself, which had a spotted eagle outstretched on the back of it, a star on the left shoulder, the rainbow diagonally across the breast from the left shoulder downward toward the hip. I made another rainbow around the neck, like a necklace with a star at the bottom. At the shoulder, elbows, and wrists were eagle feathers. And over the whole shirt I had red streaks of lightning. This was a bullet-proof shirt. I painted my face red. I had another eagle feather thrust through my hair at the top of my head. . . .

---

[13] **guns going off:** The troops had four Hotchkiss machine guns, which they used against the Lakotas at Wounded Knee.

We went back to Pine Ridge just after dark. It was about fifteen miles by the old road. When the soldiers gathered on the hill they began to go back on that ridge over there. After the soldiers did their dirty work over there they began to march up Wounded Knee. The soldiers wanted to fight yet, but we did not care so much about charging at them. I wanted to see the place where Big Foot and his people got killed and as I followed down the draw I could see men and women lying dead all along there. Soldiers and Indians afterwards were here and there. [*Then as I got nearer there were more of them lying there.*] Right at the beginning of the draw there were many Indians and there were more soldiers further down.

This was a good day—the sun was shining. In the evening it began to snow. It was a very bad snow. The day was cold even though it was sunny. That night the snow covered us and we all died from the cold. As I went down toward the village, I could see children dying all over—it was just a sight. I did not get as far as Big Foot's body though. Somehow I did not feel sorry about these women and children. There was a time that I did not use my first vision, but I used the power of the vision about the Messiah. I was not sorry, I was not feeling bad about it, but I thought there will be a day. I was not sorry about the women and children because I was figuring on dying and then I would join them somewhere. I just thought I would probably die before this thing was over and I just figured that there would be a day when I could either take revenge or die.

∾ Black Elk at Harney Peak

The more I talk about these things the more I think of old times, and it makes me feel sad, but I hope that we can make the tree bloom for your children and for mine. We know each other now, and from now on we will be like relatives; and we have been that so far, but we will think of that deeply and set that remembrance down deep in our hearts—not just thinly, but deeply in our hearts it should be marked. From here we can see the Black Hills and the high peak to which I was taken to see the whole world and [the spirits] showed me the good things; and when I think of that it was hopeless it seems before I saw you, but here you came. Somehow the spirits have made you come to revive the tree that never bloomed. We see here the strange lands of the world [the badlands], and on this side you see the greenness of the world [the plains] and down there the wideness of the world [the prairies], the colors of the earth. And you will set them in your mind. This is my land. Someday

---

Black Elk at Harney Peak. In this final piece, Black Elk refers to himself as the sixth grandfather, that is, the representative of or channel for the spirit world on earth. Black Elk and his son Benjamin, and Neihardt and his daughters, Enid and Hilda, embody the reconciliation of two peoples and two worlds, the possibility for the blooming of the "flowering stick." It should be noted, however, that despite repeated petitions from the Lakota people, no portion of the Black Hills, which the Lakota were forced to relinquish in 1876, has been returned to them.

we'll be here again; thus I will do a little prayer before we go home, and you will have that down in your heart that you will make a success out of this. So we shall name that butte Remembrance Butte. You will remember the six grandfathers, and the sixth one [*is myself and perhaps I am the sixth one*] that stands before you, and I am speaking of the truth that really happens. And furthermore, that Remembrance Butte will always be remembered because this is the land that I have assigned to my children. This was the land that was my favorite, and in this land my children will prosper; and with this proposition I hope you will have success in it. Perhaps some day we will be here again, and whenever we see this butte we will always think of what it means.

The six grandfathers set upon this world many things, all of which should be happy. Every little thing is sent for something, and in that thing there should be happiness and making each other happy. With the tender grasses showing their tender faces to each other, thus we should do, and this was the wish of the six grandfathers.

As Black Elk began his prayer, he had his son Ben stand at his right hand to represent his generations on into the future; Neihardt with Enid and Hilda stood on Black Elk's left, representing their generations. Then he prayed:

Hey-a-a-hey! (four times)
Grandfather, the Great Spirit, behold us on earth,
      the two-leggeds. The flowering stick
      that you have given to me has not bloomed,
      and my people are in despair.
To where the sun goes down to the six grandfathers where
      you have placed them, thus guarding the whole universe
      and the guidance of all beings.
And to the center of the earth you have set a sacred stick
      that should bloom, but it failed.
But nevertheless, grandfathers, behold it and guide us; you
      have beheld us. I myself, Black Elk, and my nephew,
      Mr. Neihardt. Thus the tree may bloom.
Oh hear me, grandfathers, and help us, that our generation
      in the future will live and walk the good road with the
      flowering stick to success.
Also, the pipe of peace we will offer it as we walk the good
      road to success.
Hear me, and hear our plea.

❧ WILLIAM BUTLER YEATS
B. IRELAND, 1865–1939

Spanning the dizzying changes in aesthetics and politics between 1890 and 1939, the work of William Butler Yeats epitomizes the contradictory impulses of early modernist society and culture—its recognition of a world consumed by violent conflict, emptied of value and tradition, and yet struggling to find some idea, some system, some myth to hold itself together. As Yeats wrote in a prophetic poem, "Things fall apart; the centre cannot hold; / . . . and everywhere / The ceremony of innocence is drowned." As a leading figure of the **IRISH LITERARY RENAISSANCE**,[1] a poet, statesman, critic, and visionary, Yeats strove in his research of the occult, in his revitalization of Irish myth and legend, and in his poetry to bring meaning and purpose to his contemporaries. Often considered to be the greatest poet writing in English in the early modernist period, Yeats spoke not only to Ireland and to his generation, but, as Chinua Achebe's *Things Fall Apart* attests, to people of all countries and to the generation of writers that followed him.

William Butler Yeats, 1908. Photograph
Yeats as a young man. (Hulton / Archive)

Sligo and Dublin.   William Butler Yeats was born in Sandymount, a suburb of Dublin, Ireland, on June 13, 1865. Through his father, the lawyer-turned-painter John Butler Yeats, William was linked to a line of clergymen; and through his mother, Susan Pollexfen, to a line of seafarers who captured the imagination of the young boy. When William was three years old, he accompanied his family to London where his father took up the study of painting. William attended the Godolphin School and cultivated a strong sense of nostalgia for Ireland. Fortunately, his family on both sides had connections to county Sligo, on the west coast of Ireland, where the young boy visited his grandfather in the shadow of his revered Ben Bulben, the chief peak of the Sligo Mountains. Here, on summer vacations and holidays in later years, Yeats would ramble in the country-side and listen to tales about fairies and Irish folk heroes. In 1880, the family returned to Ireland, eventually taking a house overlooking Howth harbor just north of Dublin. Yeats's father, who had maintained a caring but stern supervision over his son's education, placed William in Erasmus High School where he began writing poetry. After leaving high school, Yeats attended art school at the Metropolitan School of Art where his father taught. There he met George Russell (1867–1935), or A. E., an artist, poet, and mystic in whom the young Yeats found a kindred spirit.

www   For links to more information about Yeats, a quiz on his poetry, and information about his twenty-first-century relevance, see *World Literature Online* at bedfordstmartins .com/worldlit.

---

[1] **Irish Literary Renaissance:** A movement in the 1890s among Irish writers aimed at revitalizing Irish literature and renewing interest in and revaluating Irish myth, legend, folklore, history, and literature. The literary renaissance was part of a broader cultural interest in things Irish in the late 1890s, which included promoting the Irish language, the restoration of Irish sports, and the founding of the National Literary Society and the Irish National Theatre.

The Making of a Poet. Another significant meeting came in 1885, when Yeats met the Irish Fenian[2] leader John O'Leary (1830–1907), whom Yeats later described as the embodiment of "Romantic Ireland." Through O'Leary, Yeats associated with some of the soon-to-be leaders of the Irish nationalist movement. In the next year, Yeats gave up his studies in art and returned to London, where he devoted his energies to writing and joined in quasi-philosophical and occult discussions with Madame Blavatsky (1831–1891) and her Theosophical Society.[3] These two often contradictory elements of Yeats's character, the political and the spiritual, lent to his life and poetry their characteristic tension and ambiguity. Both his life and work were marked by a struggle to attain a pure vision of art out of an exacting confrontation with the cold imperfections of human life. Those imperfections were compounded by the political strife of early twentieth-century Ireland and by the advent of World War I.

Yeats's embrace of Theosophy inspired a mind already well stocked in the legends and folklore of Ireland. In 1889, with the help of O'Leary, the young poet published his first book, *The Wanderings of Oisin and Other Poems*. This collection of early lyrics and ballads accompanying the long title poem, an allegorical story of a journey into the land of the fairies based on Irish legend, shows an influence of the PRE-RAPHAELITES[4] in its sensuous imagery and dreamy medievalism and an influence of Theosophy in its Indian subjects.

During the next few years Yeats edited several collections of Irish folktales, fairy tales, and ballads, and even collaborated with F. J. Ellis on an edition of the works of the Romantic poet William Blake (1757–1827), whose myth-making and visionary spirituality Yeats found congenial to his literary sensibility. In the early 1890s, Yeats also helped to found the Rhymers' Club, the National Literary Society in Dublin, and the London-Irish Literary Society. In this same period he wrote *The Countess Cathleen* (1892), a play inspired by Maud Gonne, with whom Yeats had fallen in love two years earlier. An uncompromising Irish nationalist determined to free Ireland from English rule, Gonne did not return the love Yeats so passionately offered her. Although Yeats accompanied her on some of her many travels between Dublin, London, and Paris to support the Irish cause, she would not consent to marry him when he asked for her hand in 1891. This was only the first of many refusals from Gonne that would haunt the poet's life and work to the very end.

---

[2] **Fenian:** The Fenian Society was a secret organization of Irish nationalists founded in 1858 that promoted Irish independence from England by means of violent revolution; it was named after the Fenians, professional soldiers who served Irish kings in third-century Ireland.

[3] **Theosophical Society:** Founded in London in 1875 by Helena Petrovna Blavatsky to promote the reconciliation of Eastern religious doctrines with Western mysticism.

[4] **Pre-Raphaelites:** A group of artists and writers, including John Everett Millais (1829–1896), Dante Gabriel Rossetti (1828–1882), and William Holman Hunt (1827–1910), who rebelled against convention in poetry and painting by means of a strict adherence to details of nature; they aimed to capture what they perceived as the truth, simplicity, and clarity of medieval painting—its pure colors, spiritual or mystical ambience, and sensuousness.

The Irish Poet.   In 1892 a second publication, *The Countess Cathleen and Various Legends and Lyrics,* was published, and a few of Yeats's lyrics appeared in *The Yellow Book,* a notorious periodical associated with Aubrey Beardsley (1872–1898), Max Beerbohm (1872–1956), and Ernest Dowson (1867–1900), key figures of the aesthete movement in FIN-DE-SIÈCLE London, which held that the pursuit of beauty was the sole purpose of art. Yeats's London circle also included the poets and critics Lionel Johnson (1867–1902), George Moore (1852–1933), and Arthur Symons (1865–1945), who shared Yeats's interest in Blake and the FRENCH SYMBOL-ISTS.[5] The year 1893 saw the publication of *The Rose,* a collection of poems on Irish themes that includes "The Lake Isle of Innisfree" and "Who Goes with Fergus?" In 1896, Yeats met Lady Augusta Gregory (1852–1932), a writer, Irish patriot, and wealthy patron of Irish literature, and the following year he spent the first of many summers at her country house at Coole Park, Galway, in the west of Ireland. Here Yeats, Lady Gregory, and playwrights Edward Martyn and J. M. Synge (1871–1909) planned the Irish National Theatre, which they founded in 1899. That year marks the beginning of the Irish Literary Renaissance; it was also the year that *The Wind Among the Reeds* was published, a collection that brought Yeats's synthesis of Irish legend, private reverie, and esoteric symbolism to perfection.

As a founder of the Irish National Theatre, which found a home in the Abbey Theatre, Dublin, in 1904, Yeats had to deal with its practical problems, not the least of which was protecting it from the narrow-minded provincialism, petty morality, and rank hypocrisy of the Irish middle classes. Bitter and out of patience with protests over the production of J. M. Synge's *The Playboy of the Western World* (1907) and with the Dublin Corporation's refusal to provide a gallery for the collection of French paintings offered it by Sir Hugh Lane, Yeats roundly condemned the shopkeeper mentality of Dubliners in "September 1913" and other poems published in *Responsibilities* (1914), which first appeared in 1913 as *Poems Written in Discouragement.* Up to that time, Yeats had published two important collections of poems, *In the Seven Woods* (1904) and *The Green Helmet and Other Poems* (1910), and he had produced some of his plays, including *Cathleen ni Houlihan* (1902) and *On Baile's Strand* (1904), which opened the Abbey Theatre. The American poet Ezra Pound (1885–1972), whom Yeats met in 1909, encouraged the Irishman to study Japanese *Nō* plays,[6] and in the year of one of Ireland's greatest political crises, 1916, Yeats produced *At the Hawk's Well,* a play for masked dancers based on his study of Japanese theater.

---

[5] **French Symbolists:** Symbolism generally refers to a movement among poets in France anticipated in the work of Charles Baudelaire (1821–1867) and Arthur Rimbaud (1854–1891) but practiced as a self-conscious movement by Stéphane Mallarmé (1842–1898), Paul Verlaine (1844–1896), and Jules Laforgue (1860–1887). The Symbolists sought to effect the fluidity and evocative harmony of music in their work—to capture tones, fragrances, sensations, and intuitions rather than concrete images or rational ideas.

[6] **Japanese *Nō* plays:** The highly elaborate and ritualistic classical theater of Japan known for its minimalist approach to plot, scenery, and stage effects and the stately performance and Zen-like mastery of its actors; *Nō* means "talent" or "accomplishment."

The Abbey Theatre, Dublin, c. 1930

The Abbey Theatre, cofounded and directed by Yeats and Lady Gregory, was home to the Irish National Theatre, which helped further the cause of Irish independence and cultural revival through its productions of nationalistic and political plays, some of which were written by Yeats himself. (Hulton/Archive)

In 1916, Yeats's attention was caught by the "terrible beauty" of the Easter Rebellion in Dublin. Because he had spent much of his time since 1907 in England, the rising of the Irish nationalists who seized the Dublin post office in a bold but failed attempt to throw off English rule took Yeats by surprise. His qualified praise in "Easter 1916" for the leaders of the Easter Rebellion, many of whom were executed, marked a sort of reconciliation with Ireland, to which he returned. Yeats married Georgie Hyde-Lees (but not before he'd proposed to Iseult Gonne, Maud's daughter), took up residence at Ballylee, in Galway, and eventually became a senator of the newly established Irish Free State in 1922. Through the medium of Hyde-Lees, who professed to have psychic powers, Yeats wrote *A Vision* (1925), a prophetic work that sets out the esoteric system of symbols and the complex theory of cyclical history that informs his greatest collections of poetry, *The Tower* (1928) and *The Winding Stair* (1933).

After contracting a lung disease, Yeats retired from the senate in 1928 and in the following year left Ballylee to travel in Italy and southern France. The nearly seventy-year-old poet continued writing poetry and plays and in his last years produced a stunning series of poems that cut to the brute realities of life, old age, and the body, what Yeats called his return to the "foul rag-and-bone shop of the heart." Yeats died in 1939 in the south of France, "in the dead of winter," to quote from W. H. Auden's (1907–1973) poetic tribute to Yeats, but his "gift survived it all."

Twentieth-Century Ireland: Irish Independence

On April 24, 1916, while England was engaged in war on the continent of Europe, Irish nationalists staged the Easter Rising in an attempt to overthrow British rule. The fighting was chaotic and fierce, but short-lived. When it subsided five days after it began, 450 were dead, more than 2,500 injured, and many parts of Dublin destroyed. In May the British executed fifteen of the rebels after a series of public court-martials. The rebellion was memorialized by the great Irish literary figures of the day who, like William Butler Yeats (1865–1939), a committed nationalist and one-time member of the Irish Republican Brother-hood, shared the fighters' patriotic sentiment. (See "Easter 1916," p. 190, for Yeats's poetic memorial to the uprising.) Yeats wrote of Patrick Henry Pearse (1879–1916), the leader who was also a poet and an educator who championed education for Irish children in Gaelic. Pearse had become the first president of the newly declared 1916 Irish republic before the British executed him in May for his part in the rebellion. James Connolly (1868–1916), the leader of the Irish Citizen Army, which had participated in the rebellion, also lost his life.

Michael Collins (1890–1922), imprisoned for his actions in the Rising, went on to reorganize the Irish Republican Army (IRA) and launch full-scale guerrilla war against British government forces in Ireland, which resulted in 1921 in a treaty partitioning Ireland into Ulster (Northern Ireland) and the Irish Republic in the south. Collins was killed in an ambush in the civil war in 1922. Writers such as Yeats, Sean O'Casey, Samuel Beckett, Brendan Behan, James Joyce, and George Bernard Shaw were inspired by, if sometimes critical of, those who fought for Irish independence.

Derailment of Train by Guerrillas, Belfast, 1923. A violent struggle between the Irish and the British arose from the Irish independence movement, which often employed guerrilla tactics, as in this Belfast scene where Irish guerrillas derail a train. Many Irish writers, like Yeats, were conflicted by the physical-force wing of Irish nationalism. (The Art Archive / Dagli Orti)

That gift was great and varied, and in following the course of Yeats's poetry from the Pre-Raphaelite dreaminess of *The Wanderings of Oisin,* to the spare colloquialism and symbolic density of *The Tower* and *The Winding Stair,* to the tightly wrought, concrete realism of *Last Poems,* one can track some of the important transformations of early-twentieth-century poetry. Yeats's distinctive signature, however—the deeply felt tension between his spiritual, aesthetic ideals and his unflinching grasp of the contradictions and disturbing complexities of mortal life—insistently qualifies any attempt to see Yeats's work as merely representative of a given movement. With its mellifluous tone and natural simplicity, "The Lake Isle of Innisfree" captures some of the Pre-Raphaelite qualities of Yeats's poetry of the 1890s. "Who Goes with Fergus?", from the same collection, combines those same qualities with the Irish legend of a hero who turned away from life's dreary business to devote his life to poetry and to "brood / Upon love's bitter mystery." This poem typifies the otherworldliness of Yeats's early work, before he made the radical turn in the late 1890s to face the world head-on and to become the poet-legislator of Ireland and its culture.

In "September 1913" Yeats criticizes the cultural and political indolence of the middle classes and in "Easter 1916" cautiously praises their awakening in the "terrible beauty" of the Easter Rebellion. The language of these poems is precise and colloquial, aimed at a broader audience. Moreover, the poems of this period, without abandoning the symbolism of the earlier period, more immediately engage the concerns of the present and more directly confront the harsh truths of everyday reality.

The Poetry of Vision.   Yeats's verse of the twenties and thirties is partly contingent on the symbolic system of *A Vision* (1925), which Yeats received in part from his wife's automatic writing and in part from a complex synthesis of his studies of esoteric and occult thinkers ranging from Greek philosopher Empedocles (c. 495–c. 435 B.C.E.) to William Blake. This complex system involves a web of correspondences, derived from twenty-eight phases of the moon, between cosmic, national, and personal history. Most important for the poems included here, *A Vision* describes history as the movement of two intersecting cones or spinning "gyres." These gyres, which symbolize the opposites of subjectivity and objectivity, beauty and truth, and value and fact, expand and contract at regular intervals of two thousand years. Thus, every two thousand years a new system of values gains ascendancy. An avatar—Helen of Troy, Christ, the unnameable "beast" of "The Second Coming"—marks the beginning of each new age. Yeats saw the beginning of the twentieth century as the beginning of an objective cycle, which would mean a period hostile to art, spiritual vision, and individuality. This system underlies the symbolism of poems such as "Leda and the Swan" and "The Second Coming," both of which inaugurate ages of brutality and objective values before and after the subjective age of Christ, which reached its height in the flourishing of art and humanism in the Renaissance. Yeats's celebration of a world of pure art in "Sailing to Byzantium" pays tribute to the Byzantine period when, according to Yeats's view, art appeared to transcend the fleshly frailties of human experience. For Yeats, in early Byzantium "the painter, the mosaic worker, the worker in gold and silver, the illuminator of sacred books, were almost impersonal, almost perhaps without the consciousness of individual design, absorbed in their subject-matter and that the vision of a whole people."

Stubborn Mortality.   Yeats was never able to reconcile his passionate search for a systematic pattern behind human events with his insistence that we "Cast a cold eye / On life, on death." The poetry of his late period embodies a struggle between the quiet permanence of art and the mortality of life, the joy of spiritual desire and the grief of human love. "The Circus Animals' Desertion," for example, demonstrates Yeats's characteristic questioning of the projects of men and women, including his own — his refusal to accept simple explanations to describe human motives, and his consummate skill in abstracting emblems and themes from his passionate engagement with life, complete with its wicked and mad old men and women, its "mound of refuse or the sweepings of the street."

■ CONNECTIONS

Chinua Achebe, *Things Fall Apart,* p. 1023. Yeats's "A Second Coming" symbolizes the upheaval in Western culture that Yeats, like T. S. Eliot, saw taking place after World War I. Achebe's novel takes its title from Yeats's "A Second Coming," suggesting that a similar disintegration of culture and values was taking place in Africa. What parallels are there between Yeats's view of this cultural dissolution, as an Irish writer, and Achebe's as an African writer? What does each writer see as falling apart in his world?

William Blake, Poems (Book 5). Yeats admired the work of the visionary British Romantic poet, William Blake, particularly visionary works like *The Marriage of Heaven and Hell.* Blake's poems anticipate Yeats's interest in mysticism and esoteric philosophy as well as Yeats's mythmaking. How does Yeats's use of Celtic folklore lead to a different kind of mythmaking than that which we find in Blake?

Rabindranath Tagore, "Broken Ties" (Book 5). Yeats promoted Rabindranath Tagore's writings for Western audiences. Both writers were interested in questions of national identity, folklore, and spirituality. On the basis of the poems you have read by these authors, what do you think would have particularly interested Yeats in Tagore's "Broken Ties"?

■ FURTHER RESEARCH

Editions
Albright, Daniel, ed. *W. B. Yeats: The Poems.* 1990.
Allt, Peter, and Russell K. Alspach, eds. *The Variorum Edition of the Poems of W. B. Yeats.* 1957.
Finneran, Richard J., ed. *Yeats, The Poems: A New Edition.* 1983.

Biography
Brown, Terence. *The Life of W. B. Yeats: A Critical Biography.* 1999.
Ellman, Richard. *Yeats: The Man and the Masks.* Revised ed. 1978.
Jeffares, Norman A. *W. B. Yeats: A New Biography.* 1988.

Criticism
Bloom, Harold, ed. *William Butler Yeats.* 1986.
Cullingford, Elizabeth. *Gender and History in Yeats's Love Poetry.* 1993.
Ellman, Richard. *The Identity of Yeats.* 1964.

Finneran, Richard J., ed. *Critical Essays on W. B. Yeats.* 1986.
Fleming, Deborah, ed. *Learning the Trade: Essays on W. B. Yeats and Contemporary Poetry.* 1993.
Jeffares, Norman A. *A New Commentary on the Collected Poems of W. B. Yeats.* 1983.
Malins, Edward. *A Preface to Yeats.* 1977.
O'Donnell, William H. *The Poetry of William Butler Yeats: An Introduction.* 1986.
Rosenthal, M. L. *Running to Paradise: Yeats's Poetic Art.* 1994.

Spoken Word
"William Butler Yeats." Caedmon Records.

☙ The Lake Isle of Innisfree[1]

I will arise and go now, and go to Innisfree,
And a small cabin build there, of clay and wattles made:
Nine bean-rows will I have there, a hive for the honeybee,
And live alone in the bee-loud glade.

And I shall have some peace there, for peace comes dropping slow,
Dropping from the veils of the morning to where the cricket sings;
There midnight's all a glimmer, and noon a purple glow,
And evening full of the linnet's wings.

I will arise and go now, for always night and day
I hear lake water lapping with low sounds by the shore;
While I stand on the roadway, or on the pavements grey,
I hear it in the deep heart's core.

10

"The Lake Isle of Innisfree." First appearing in *National Observer* on December 13, 1890, this poem was republished in Yeats's 1893 collection *The Rose*. It is one of the first poems that marked Yeats's singularity as an artist, especially his mastery of sound and symbol. In the autobiographical essay *The Trembling of the Veil* (1922), Yeats describes the moment of inspiration for the poem. Walking through London's Fleet Street, feeling homesick, he "heard a little tinkle of water and saw a fountain in a shop-window which balanced a little ball upon its jet. . . ." The sound of the trickling fountain reminded him of lake water at Innisfree, an island in Lough Gill, county Sligo, where Yeats spent time as a child. He describes this poem as his "first lyric with anything in its rhythm of my own music."

---

[1] **Innisfree:** An island in Lough Gill, county Sligo, in northwestern Ireland.

❧ Who Goes with Fergus?[1]

Who will go drive with Fergus now,
And pierce the deep wood's woven shade,
And dance upon the level shore?
Young man, lift up your russet brow,
And lift your tender eyelids, maid,
And brood on hopes and fear no more.

And no more turn aside and brood
Upon love's bitter mystery;
For Fergus rules the brazen cars,
10   And rules the shadows of the wood,
And the white breast of the dim sea
And all dishevelled wandering stars.

"Who Goes with Fergus?" This lyric first appeared as part of Yeats's play, *The Countess Cathleen*, published in *The Countess Cathleen and Various Legends and Lyrics* (1892). The next year Yeats included the verse in *The Rose* (1893), a collection of poems reflecting his studies in Irish folklore, songs, and legends as well as his deep interest in esoteric philosophy and mysticism, including Theosophy, cabala, and Rosicrucianism. Fergus MacRoy, the "Fergus" to whom the poem refers, was a king of Ulster and one of the heroes in a series of legends known as the Red Branch or Ulster cycle. After losing his crown to rival king Conchubar, Fergus spent the remainder of his life living peacefully in the woods. For Yeats, who believed that Fergus was the poet of the cycle, Fergus came to signify the poet-legislator, a person occupying the transitional space between the world of imagination and dreams and the world of politics. As the somewhat ambiguous tone of the poem suggests, Yeats could never completely privilege one of these worlds over the other.

---

[1] **Fergus:** A legendary Irish hero; king of the Red Branch Kings who gave up his power to follow the less worldly pursuits of poetry and philosophy.

Easter 1916[1]

I have met them at close of day
Coming with vivid faces
From counter or desk among grey
Eighteenth-century houses.
I have passed with a nod of the head
Or polite meaningless words,
Or have lingered awhile and said
Polite meaningless words,
And thought before I had done
Of a mocking tale or a gibe
To please a companion
Around the fire at the club,
Being certain that they and I
But lived where motley is worn:
All changed, changed utterly:
A terrible beauty is born.

That woman's[2] days were spent
In ignorant good-will,

"Easter 1916." This poem was first published in a privately printed, limited edition of only twenty-five copies entitled *Easter, 1916,* and later in *New Statesman,* on October 23, 1920; it was again published in the collection *Michael Robartes and the Dancer* in 1921. Composed in September 1916, when Yeats was staying with Maud Gonne MacBride, the poem records Yeats's deeply felt response to the failed Easter Rising in Dublin, which began on Easter Monday, April 24, 1916. During the rebellion, members of the Irish Volunteers, the Irish Republican Brotherhood, and the Irish Citizen Army occupied several important buildings, including the General Post Office in Dublin, and read a Proclamation of the Provisional Government, declaring independent nationhood for Ireland. The rebellion was effectively quashed by the British five days later; fifteen of its leaders were executed. Troubled by the event and "despondent about the future," Yeats wrote to Lady Gregory that he was "trying to write a poem on the men executed — 'terrible beauty has been born again.'" Often seen as a eulogy to the martyred revolutionaries, "Easter 1916" begins with the speaker recollecting his casual encounters with them and his criticism of their single-minded devotion to their cause and ends with the sudden and powerful awareness that their sacrifice, although a tragic excess, has perhaps been necessary to galvanize the Irish spirit. The poem does not, however, unequivocally celebrate the rebellion and the changes it wrought — to Ireland, to the poet, and to the revolutionaries themselves.

---

[1] Easter 1916: The Easter Rebellion to which the poem refers actually began on the Monday after Easter 1916. A group of Irish nationalists seized the Dublin post office in a failed attempt to throw off the yoke of British rule. After a week-long fight, the rebels surrendered and were imprisoned; fifteen of the leaders, some of whom Yeats knew personally, were executed by firing squad.

[2] That woman: Constance Gore-Booth, an Irish nationalist from county Sligo.

Her nights in argument
20   Until her voice grew shrill.
What voice more sweet than hers
When, young and beautiful,
She rode to harriers?[3]
This man[4] had kept a school
And rode our wingèd horse;
This other[5] his helper and friend
Was coming into his force;
He might have won fame in the end,
So sensitive his nature seemed,
30   So daring and sweet his thought.
This other man[6] I had dreamed
A drunken, vainglorious lout.
He had done most bitter wrong
To some who are near my heart,
Yet I number him in the song;
He, too, has resigned his part
In the casual comedy;
He, too, has been changed in his turn,
Transformed utterly:
40   A terrible beauty is born.

Hearts with one purpose alone
Through summer and winter seem
Enchanted to a stone
To trouble the living stream.
The horse that comes from the road,
The rider, the birds that range
From cloud to tumbling cloud,
Minute by minute they change;
A shadow of cloud on the stream
50   Changes minute by minute;
A horse-hoof slides on the brim,
And a horse plashes within it;
The long-legged moor-hens dive,
And hens to moor-cocks call;

---

[3] harriers: Dogs resembling small foxhounds used in packs for hunting rabbits.

[4] This man: Patrick Pearse, a schoolmaster and Gaelic poet; the winged horse is Pegasus, horse of the Muses.

[5] This other: Thomas MacDonagh, a poet and playwright.

[6] This other man: Major John MacBride, who had married then separated from Maud Gonne, Yeats's lifelong love.

Minute by minute they live:
The stone's in the midst of all.

Too long a sacrifice
Can make a stone of the heart.
O when may it suffice?
60   That is Heaven's part, our part
To murmur name upon name,
As a mother names her child
When sleep at last has come
On limbs that had run wild.
What is it but nightfall?
No, no, not night but death;
Was it needless death after all?
For England may keep faith
For all that is done and said.
70   We know their dream; enough
To know they dreamed and are dead;
And what if excess of love
Bewildered them till they died?
I write it out in a verse—
MacDonagh and MacBride
And Connolly[7] and Pearse
Now and in time to be,
Wherever green is worn,
Are changed, changed utterly:
80   A terrible beauty is born.

---

[7] **Connolly:** James Connolly, the chief leader of the Easter Rebellion.

∽ The Second Coming

Turning and turning in the widening gyre[1]
The falcon cannot hear the falconer;
Things fall apart; the centre cannot hold;
Mere anarchy is loosed upon the world,
The blood-dimmed tide is loosed, and everywhere
The ceremony of innocence is drowned;
The best lack all conviction, while the worst
Are full of passionate intensity.

Surely some revelation is at hand;
10   Surely the Second Coming is at hand.
The Second Coming! Hardly are those words out
When a vast image out of *Spiritus Mundi*[2]
Troubles my sight: somewhere in sands of the desert
A shape with lion body and the head of a man,
A gaze blank and pitiless as the sun,
Is moving its slow thighs, while all about it
Reel shadows of the indignant desert birds.
The darkness drops again; but now I know
That twenty centuries of stony sleep
20   Were vexed to nightmare by a rocking cradle,
And what rough beast, its hour come round at last,
Slouches towards Bethlehem to be born?

"The Second Coming." First appearing in *The Dial* in November 1920, this poem was published the following year in Yeats's collection *Michael Robartes and the Dancer*. Based on the cosmological system detailed in Yeats's *A Vision* as well as on the Revelation of St. John the Divine, "The Second Coming" predicts the birth of a new and terrible god whose arrival would usher in an age of calculated brutality and objective indifference to human feeling and human rights. Although Yeats denied that he ever foresaw "the growing murderousness of the world," this poem's prophecy of the rise of ruthless regimes is eerily parallel with what came later—Hitler, Stalin, the massive destruction of human life in World War II, and more. But Yeats had plenty on which to base his dark vision: namely, the machinelike devastation of World War I and the political violence and repression at home and abroad. His apparent prescience, however, as well as the apocalyptic theme and tone of "The Second Coming" and its terse phrasing and precise imagery make it one of Yeats's most memorable works.

---

[1] **the widening gyre:** The gyre refers to Yeats's theory of historical cycles developed in *A Vision*. Yeats imagines history as a dynamic set of interlocking cone-shaped spirals. At the end of each two-thousand-year cycle, a new spirit governs human consciousness and the affairs of the world. This poem, which envisions an age dominated by indifference and authoritarianism, ironically announces itself as the second coming, which refers to the second coming of Christ and the end of the world.

[2] *Spiritus Mundi:* Spirit of the World; in Yeats's scheme a sort of collective consciousness or "Great Memory" that links the human race by a shared set of archetypes and symbols.

∾ Sailing to Byzantium

1

That is no country for old men. The young
In one another's arms, birds in the trees
—Those dying generations—at their song,
The salmon-falls, the mackerel-crowded seas,
Fish, flesh, or fowl, commend all summer long
Whatever is begotten, born, and dies.
Caught in that sensual music all neglect
Monuments of unageing intellect.

2

An aged man is but a paltry thing,
10   A tattered coat upon a stick, unless
Soul clap its hands and sing, and louder sing
For every tatter in its mortal dress,
Nor is there singing school but studying
Monuments of its own magnificence;
And therefore I have sailed the seas and come
To the holy city of Byzantium.

3

O sages standing in God's holy fire
As in the gold mosaic of a wall,

"Sailing to Byzantium." This work was first published in *October Blast* in 1927 and collected in *The Tower* in 1928. The poems of this period show Yeats, now in his sixties, confronting the problems of age, including his own mortality, as well as engaging in a wide range of topical issues, such as the War of Independence (1919–1921), the partitioning of Ireland, and the Irish Civil War (1922–1923). Critics have noted a certain bitterness in the poems of this collection stemming at least in part from Yeats's continued ambivalence about his ability to shape his own destiny and that of Ireland. He described "Sailing to Byzantium" as a poem about the journey of the poet's soul toward a city of spiritual and aesthetic bliss. In *A Vision* Yeats idealized Byzantium—today's Istanbul—as a holy city, a site of spiritual fullness and artistic creativity, a place where he could find "in some little wine-shop some philosophical worker in mosaic who could answer all my questions, the supernatural descending nearer to him than to Plotinus, . . ." Ireland—"that country"—was no place for old men, but Byzantium, with its promise of immortality through an art that transcended personal interests, offered fulfillment and sanctuary from a world gone stale or sterile. Indeed, Yeats's Byzantium is a stark contrast to Eliot's "Unreal City" in *The Waste Land* (p. 486).

Come from the holy fire, perne in a gyre,[1]
20   And be the singing-masters of my soul.
Consume my heart away; sick with desire
And fastened to a dying animal
It knows not what it is; and gather me
Into the artifice of eternity.

4

Once out of nature I shall never take
My bodily form from any natural thing,
But such a form as Grecian goldsmiths make
Of hammered gold and gold enamelling
To keep a drowsy Emperor awake;
30   Or set upon a golden bough to sing
To lords and ladies of Byzantium
Of what is past, or passing, or to come.

---

[1] **perne in a gyre:** To spin in a cone-shaped spiral; see "The Second Coming," note 1.

❧ Leda and the Swan

A sudden blow: the great wings beating still
Above the staggering girl, her thighs caressed
By the dark webs, her nape caught in his bill,
He holds her helpless breast upon his breast.

How can those terrified vague fingers push
The feathered glory from her loosening thighs?

"Leda and the Swan." One of the poems from *The Tower* (1928), this work was first published in *The Dial* (June 1924), then in a limited edition entitled *The Cat and the Moon and Certain Poems* (July 1924). In "Leda and the Swan" Yeats returns to the apocalyptic view of "The Second Coming." As he explained to Lady Gregory, "Leda and the Swan" began with the idea "that the reign of democracy is over for the present, and in reaction there will be violent government from above, as now in Russia, and is beginning here." The political subtext of the poem, however, is overshadowed, if you will, by the dynamic and shocking rape of Leda. For Yeats, this particular violent intervention of a supernatural force into the mortal world began one of the cosmic cycles of history, giving rise to the Trojan War and the foundation of Greek civilization and culture. In the sonnet's final two lines, Yeats, who was a reader of the German philosopher Friedrich Nietzsche (1844–1900), raises a question fundamental to twentieth-century philosophy — Do the cataclysmic events of history bring us knowledge or power, and what is the relation of knowledge and power to the making of history? The Catholic Church attacked Yeats and labeled his poem the "Stinking Sonnet"; its explicit, emotionally restrained treatment of rape still disturbs some readers today.

And how can body, laid in that white rush,
But feel the strange heart beating where it lies?

A shudder in the loins engenders there
10   The broken wall, the burning roof and tower
And Agamemnon[1] dead.
                        Being so caught up,
So mastered by the brute blood of the air,
Did she put on his knowledge with his power
Before the indifferent beak could let her drop?

---

[1] **Agamemnon:** King of Mycenae and leader of the Greek forces against Troy; because he sacrificed his daughter Iphigenia to gain favorable winds to reach Troy, Agamemnon was murdered by his wife, Clytemnestra, on his return home from the war.

∞ Among School Children

1

I walk through the long schoolroom questioning;
A kind old nun in a white hood replies;
The children learn to cipher and to sing,
To study reading-books and history,
To cut and sew, be neat in everything
In the best modern way—the children's eyes

"Among School Children." A poem from *The Tower* (1928), this work first appeared in August 1927 in *The Dial* and in *London Mercury*. Occasioned in part by Yeats's visit to St. Otteran's School, in Waterford, it blends a general reflection on the potential bankruptcy of early dreams and promises with a personal meditation on Yeats's own unmet hopes, particularly his unrequited love for Maud Gonne. In some ways a modernist version of Wordsworth's "Ode: Intimations of Immortality," Yeats looks back from what Wordsworth calls the "years that bring the philosophic mind" on the stages of his and Maud Gonne's history, whose images fade in and out of the mind's eye. The poem weighs the burden of physical aging and mortality against the vitality of sexual generation and the hopes of youth. In the final stanzas, Yeats suggests that the images people project for themselves and for their children potentially set them up for disappointment or lead to life-sapping projects that deprive one of the fullness or immediacy of a life lived truly in the moment. Rather than project images or set one's sights upon some plan, it is better to fuse the image with the lived experience so that dancer and the dance merge as one indistinct being.

In momentary wonder stare upon
A sixty-year-old smiling public man.[1]

2

I dream of a Ledaean body,[2] bent
Above a sinking fire, a tale that she
Told of a harsh reproof, or trivial event
That changed some childish day to tragedy—
Told, and it seemed that our two natures blent
Into a sphere from youthful sympathy,
Or else, to alter Plato's parable,
Into the yolk and white of the one shell.[3]

3

And thinking of that fit of grief or rage
I look upon one child or t'other there
And wonder if she stood so at that age—
For even daughters of the swan can share
Something of every paddler's heritage—
And had that colour upon cheek or hair,
And thereupon my heart is driven wild:
She stands before me as a living child.

4

Her present image floats into the mind—
Did Quattrocento finger[4] fashion it
Hollow of cheek as though it drank the wind
And took a mess of shadows for its meat?
And I though never of Ledaean kind
Had pretty plumage once—enough of that,
Better to smile on all that smile, and show
There is a comfortable kind of old scarecrow.

---

[1] **public man:** In 1922, Yeats was elected senator of the Irish Free State.

[2] **Ledaean body:** As beautiful as Leda, mother of Helen of Troy (see "Leda and the Swan," note 1).

[3] **Plato's . . . shell:** Plato's *Symposium* explains that true lovers are the two halves of a once complete being; when torn asunder by the gods, the two halves continually seek reunion with each other.

[4] **Quattrocento finger:** The hand of a fifteenth-century Italian painter or artist, such as Masaccio (1401–1428), Leonardo da Vinci (1452–1519), or Sandro Botticelli (1444–1510).

5

What youthful mother, a shape upon her lap
Honey of generation had betrayed,
And that must sleep, shriek, struggle to escape
As recollection or the drug decide,
Would think her son, did she but see that shape
With sixty or more winters on its head,
A compensation for the pang of his birth,
40   Or the uncertainty of his setting forth?

6

Plato thought nature but a spume that plays
Upon a ghostly paradigm of things;
Solider Aristotle played the taws
Upon the bottom of a king of kings;
World-famous golden-thighed Pythagoras[5]
Fingered upon a fiddle-stick or strings
What a star sang and careless Muses heard:
Old clothes upon old sticks to scare a bird.

7

Both nuns and mothers worship images,
50   But those the candles light are not as those
That animate a mother's reveries,
But keep a marble or a bronze repose.
And yet they too break hearts—O Presences
That passion, piety or affection knows,
And that all heavenly glory symbolise—
O self-born mockers of man's enterprise;

8

Labour is blossoming or dancing where
The body is not bruised to pleasure soul,
Nor beauty born out of its own despair,
60   Nor blear-eyed wisdom out of midnight oil.

---

[5] **Plato . . . Pythagoras:** Plato (427–347 B.C.E.) believed that things in nature were mere shadows of a perfect ideal form beyond the reach of ordinary sensibility; Aristotle (384–322 B.C.E.), who studied the natural world more closely than Plato, was Alexander the Great's tutor and so perhaps "played the taws," that is, spanked his young pupil; Pythagoras (582–507 B.C.E.) studied mathematics and music and was said to have a golden thigh-bone.

O chestnut-tree, great-rooted blossomer,
Are you the leaf, the blossom or the bole?
O body swayed to music, O brightening glance,
How can we know the dancer from the dance?

∾ The Circus Animals' Desertion

1

I sought a theme and sought for it in vain,
I sought it daily for six weeks or so.
Maybe at last, being but a broken man,
I must be satisfied with my heart, although
Winter and summer till old age began
My circus animals were all on show,
Those stilted boys, that burnished chariot,
Lion and woman and the Lord knows what.[1]

2

What can I but enumerate old themes?
First that sea-rider Oisin[2] led by the nose
Through three enchanted islands, allegorical dreams,
Vain gaiety, vain battle, vain repose,
Themes of the embittered heart, or so it seems,
That might adorn old songs or courtly shows;

10

"The Circus Animals' Desertion." This work was published in both *The Atlantic Monthly* and *London Mercury* in 1939 and was collected in the volume *Last Poems and Two Plays* in 1939, after Yeats's death. Many poems in that collection deal specifically with mortality and death, with reactions ranging from outrage and fear to acceptance and resignation. In "The Circus Animals' Desertion," Yeats summarizes his life's work, looking back over its changing themes as they pass before him in a kind of pageant. Most important, Yeats acknowledges that his work, however much it may devolve from political realities and esoteric philosophies, at base is motivated by the vital energies of the heart and body, which, in the end, is where one returns — to the "foul rag-and-bone shop of the heart." No matter that the images in his poetry "Grew in pure mind," the generative power of that poetry was rooted in robust desire and profound engagement with life in all of its facets.

---

[1]**My circus . . . what:** The Irish heroes of Yeats's early work and images from his plays; the "lion and woman" alludes to the Sphinx in his poem "The Double Vision of Michael Robartes."

[2]**Oisin:** A legendary Irish hero and poet who appears in Yeats's first book *The Wanderings of Oisin and Other Poems* (1889).

But what cared I that set him on to ride,
I, starved for the bosom of his faery bride?

And then a counter-truth filled out its play,
The Countess Cathleen[3] was the name I gave it;
She, pity-crazed, had given her soul away,
20   But masterful Heaven had intervened to save it.
I thought my dear must her own soul destroy,
So did fanaticism and hate enslave it,
And this brought forth a dream and soon enough
This dream itself had all my thought and love.

And when the Fool and Blind Man stole the bread
Cuchulain[4] fought the ungovernable sea;
Heart-mysteries there, and yet when all is said
It was the dream itself enchanted me:
Character isolated by a deed
30   To engross the present and dominate memory.
Players and painted stage took all my love,
And not those things that they were emblems of.

3

Those masterful images because complete
Grew in pure mind, but out of what began?
A mound of refuse or the sweepings of a street,
Old kettles, old bottles, and a broken can,
Old iron, old bones, old rags, that raving slut
Who keeps the till. Now that my ladder's gone,
I must lie down where all the ladders start,
40   In the foul rag-and-bone shop of the heart.

---

[3] *The Countess Cathleen:* Yeats's play (1892) in which an Irish countess who sells her soul to the devil to buy food for the peasants is rescued from damnation by a forgiving Heaven.
[4] **Cuchulain:** From Yeats's *On Baile's Strand* (1904); Cuchulain is a legendary Irish hero.

∿ LUIGI PIRANDELLO
B. *ITALY, 1867–1936*

Italian dramatist, poet, novelist, and writer of short stories, Luigi Pirandello transformed drama from the Realist plays of the nineteenth century into the self-conscious, reflexive theater of modernism. Pirandello
more than any other pioneered modernist stage conventions and themes,
exploring the psychological and philosophical connections between
illusion and reality in a venue that made no pretense of being other than
a theater. His works introduce the EXISTENTIALIST interest in consciousness that would concern such later writers as Camus and Sartre, and his
plays lead thematically to the absurdist dramas of Beckett, Pinter, and
Stoppard.[1]

Sicilian Roots.   Pirandello was born in 1867 in Sicily in the village of
Girgenti (now Arguento), where his father was a well-to-do proprietor
of a sulfur mine. Although his father expected him to enter the family
business, Pirandello showed an early aptitude for learning and went from
the University of Palermo in Sicily to the University of Rome and ultimately to Bonn where he earned a doctorate in philology in 1891. The
subject of his doctoral thesis, written in German, was the dialect of his
home village, a dialect he would imaginatively re-create in many of his
novels, stories, and plays.

An arranged marriage to Antonietta Portulano, the daughter of a
wealthy sulfur merchant, in 1894 made Pirandello financially independent, enabling him to go to Rome and embark on a writer's life. There he
published several volumes of poetry, translations, and short stories.
When a landslide destroyed the sulfur mine that supported him in 1904,
he started to earn a living as a professor at a women's college in Rome. He
taught there until 1922, when his success as a playwright enabled him
to give up his teaching income. The failure of the sulfur mine had pre-
cipitated Antonietta's mental illness, a paranoia that erupted in jealous
suspicion of Pirandello and necessitated her hospitalization. Her illness
shadowed Pirandello's life until he committed her to an institution in
1919, where she was confined until her death in 1959. Her condition also
spurred his interest in psychology, madness, and the difficulties of knowing and understanding oneself and others, all recurring themes in his
writings.

Portrait of Luigi
Pirandello, 1928.
Painting
*Pirandello is shown
here looking dark and
foreboding, suggesting
an air of seriousness.
(Courtesy of the
Biblioteca e Raccolta
Teatrale del Burcado,
S.I.A.E.)*

www   For more
information about
Pirandello and a quiz
on *Six Characters in
Search of an Author,*
and for more on the
culture and context
of Europe in the
twentieth century,
see *World Literature
Online* at
bedfordstmartins
.com/worldlit.

---

[1] **Beckett . . . Stoppard:** Three modern dramatists who are among the most notable practitioners of the theater of the absurd. Samuel Beckett (1906–1989), Irish novelist, poet, and dramatist whose works include *Waiting for Godot* (1952); Harold Pinter (b. 1930), English dramatist, screenwriter, poet, and actor; author of *The
Caretaker* (1960), *The Homecoming* (1965), and many other plays. Tom Stoppard (b. 1937), English playwright
and screenwriter; author of *Rosencrantz and Guildenstern Are Dead* (1967) and many other plays.

Pirandello's Early Writings.   Although he began his literary career by publishing three volumes of poems, Pirandello wrote mostly fiction early on. From 1890 to 1930, he published several novels and a dozen volumes of short stories. As a writer of short fiction, he is the Maupassant[2] of Italy. The early stories were realistic in the VERISIMO manner of Giovanni Verga,[3] often describing the customs and dialects of his native Sicily. Later stories became increasingly philosophical and psychological, developing themes that he would explore more fully in his novels and plays. In the best known of his novels, *The Late Mattia Pascal* (1904), Pirandello moves away from the conventions of nineteenth-century Realism to explore bizarre and fantastic situations. The plot of the novel, unbelievable from a realistic point of view, becomes a symbolic rendering of the inner life of its characters. A series of chance occurrences enable the hero to assume a new identity, initiating themes — the instability of identity and the multiple personalities that make up the individual — that Pirandello would explore in many of his plays, the works for which he is most remembered.

Playwrighting.   It was World War I that gave impetus to Pirandello's career in drama. "It was the war that revealed the theatre to me," he wrote, "mine is a theatre of war: The passions were unchained, and I made my living creatures suffer those passions on stage." During the war, when his two sons were prisoners of war, and afterwards, as his wife's illness worsened, Pirandello wrote plays at the rate of two or more a year. Their titles often suggest their Pirandellian themes: *Right You Are, If You Think You Are* (1917), for example, or *The Game of Role Playing* (1918).

He earned worldwide recognition with *Six Characters in Search of an Author* (1921) and *Henry IV* (1922). These plays most fully develop the philosophical and psychological themes that Pirandello is known for. At the premiere performance of *Six Characters* in Rome, the audience booed, yelled "madhouse," and mobbed the author afterwards to the point that he had to be rescued by the police. The production in Milan later that year, however, was enthusiastically received. And the production in Paris by the Pitoëff Company in 1923 established Pirandello as a major dramatist of international importance.

Fascism.   In 1925, with the aid of Mussolini, Pirandello founded his own art theater in Rome. Partly out of gratitude for Mussolini's support, perhaps, he joined the Fascist party, asserting "I am a Fascist because I am an Italian"; his continued support for Mussolini has puzzled many commentators. Pirandello saw in Mussolini a leader who confronted the ambiguity, uncertainty, and suffering in the modern situation. "Mussolini is one of the few people," he told an interviewer, "who know that

---

[2] Maupassant: Guy de Maupassant (1850–1893), French Realist; considered the father of the Realist short story, he influenced the work of writers worldwide in constructing and writing short fiction.

[3] *verisimo* . . . **Verga**: Giovanni Verga (1840–1922), Sicilian novelist whose realistic works, influenced by the writings of French Realists Flaubert and Zola, define the Realist school in Italy, known as *verisimo*. Several of Verga's novels, including *Cavalleriarusticane* (1880), were translated into English by D. H. Lawrence.

reality exists in man's power to create it, and that one creates it only through the activity of the mind." His plays express similar themes, though perhaps more tentatively than in this bold assertion. Even though his commitment was to his art, not to politics, and his belief in Mussolini would eventually diminish with time, he remained enough of a believer in him and his cause to donate his Nobel medal to be melted down to support the Italian invasion of Abyssinia.

Pirandello spent much of the last fifteen years of his life attending productions of his work throughout Europe and the Americas. He saw some of his work made into film, and in 1934 he was awarded the Nobel Prize in literature. At his death in 1936, he had written more than forty plays.

From Realism to Modernism.   Although he began his career as a REALIST, by the time of his great plays Pirandello had adopted the techniques and themes of modernism. His plays trade the devices of the realistic theater for theatrical illusion. They explore psychological themes like madness, the instability of identity, and the multiple personalities that make up individuals, and such philosophical issues as the relativity of truth to the perceiver and the relationship between art and life, illusion and reality. In *Henry IV* (*Enrico IV,* 1922), for example, a young man going to a masquerade ball as Holy Roman Emperor Henry IV falls from his horse, forgets who he really is, and believes he is the emperor. His wealthy family indulges his illusion, giving him a castle and servants. When he recovers his memory a dozen years later, he chooses to maintain the illusion, creating a situation in which reality and illusion, sanity and madness become nearly impossible to disentangle.

Six Characters, **a Play about the Theater.**   *Six Characters in Search of an Author* breaks from the conventions of Realist drama to explore similar themes. Abandoning the "fiction" that the audience is looking into an illusion of the real world from which the fourth wall has been removed, Pirandello's play is about the theater itself and the nature of theatrical illusion. There is no assumption of an invisible wall between the audience and the stage: Characters enter through the audience and make no pretense of being anywhere other than on a stage.

By implication, Pirandello's approach is a criticism of the attempt of Realist theater to create an illusion of reality. The six characters who interrupt a rehearsal of another of Pirandello's plays extend this critique. The characters are seeking to have their story performed; the playwright has imagined them but has not given them a script. Their melodramatic story is raw material not yet shaped by art. This soap opera, involving incest, infidelity, prostitution, poverty, and suicide, exaggerates the subjects treated by social-problem playwrights like Ibsen.[4] The characters

> Each of us thinks of himself as *one,* but that, well, it's not true, each of us is many, oh so many, sir, according to the possibilities of being that are in us. We are one thing for this person, another for that! Already *two* utterly different things! And with it all, the illusion of being always one thing for all men, and always this one thing in every single action. It's not true! Not true!
>
> – PIRANDELLO, *Six Characters in Search of an Author*

> It was the war that revealed the theatre to me, mine is a theatre of war: The passions were unchained, and I made my living creatures suffer those passions on stage.
>
> – PIRANDELLO

---

[4] **Ibsen:** Henrik Ibsen (1828–1906), Norwegian playwright whose social-problem plays often included such melodramatic material as suicide *(Hedda Gabler),* syphilis *(Ghosts),* and abandonment of husband and children *(A Doll's House).*

become **"ABSURD"**[5] because they are incapable of changing themselves and their story is improbable. The Father defends their reality by asserting that "life is full of infinite absurdities which . . . do not need to appear probable, because they're true." When the actors re-create the characters' story, it becomes conventional, and the characters do not recognize themselves in the performance.

Ironically, the living actors change the characters, turning their immutable truth into uncertain and changing reality. Thus the play distinguishes reality from "truth," because in life, people's identities are not fixed. "Each of us thinks of himself as *one,*" the Father remarks, "but that, well, it's not true, each of us is many, oh so many, sir, according to the possibilities of being that are in us. We are one thing for this person, another for that! Already *two* utterly different things! And with it all, the illusion of being always one thing for all men, and always this one thing in every single action. It's not true! Not true!" Truth is relative to the situation and to the limited understanding that words allow. "How can we understand each other, sir" the Father asks the Director, "if, in the words I speak, I put the sense and value of things as they are inside me, whereas the man who hears them inevitably receives them in the sense and with the value they have for him, the sense and value of the world inside him?"

Pirandello does not answer the questions he raises about reality and illusion, the nature of communication, and the relativity of truth. Nor does he — abandoning another theatrical convention — resolve the tension between his play and the play within his play. Instead, he leaves the audience disturbed and thinking, wondering what they have just seen is all about.

■ CONNECTIONS

Henrik Ibsen, *Hedda Gabler* (Book 5). The "characters" in *Six Characters in Search of an Author* constitute a dysfunctional family, reminiscent of the families in Ibsen's social-problem plays. By exaggerating their melodramatic story, Pirandello is able to critique the notion of Realism in theater, especially as it was practiced by Ibsen and his contemporaries. In what ways is Hedda Gabler's story melodramatic? How does Ibsen make it believable? What theatrical techniques does Pirandello use to highlight the extreme elements in the characters' story?

Samuel Beckett, *Krapp's Last Tape*, p. 774; Tawfiq al-Hakim, *The Fate of a Cockroach*, p. 590. In much modern literature, language calls attention to itself rather than to what it is talking about. This "reflexivity" makes the art of the work one of the work's subjects. Reflexive works are thus often about difficulties in communication, for words are often inadequate to convey what the characters are trying to express. Consider the language in *Six Characters in Search of an Author,* al-Hakim's *The Fate of a Cockroach,* and Beckett's *Krapp's Last Tape.* How does language call attention to itself? What is the significance of language to the theme of each play?

William Shakespeare, *The Tempest* (Book 3). Modern theater is sometimes characterized as theater that does not seek to create an illusion of reality but instead pre-

---

[5] "absurd": Pirandello uses the term in a manner similar to the existentialists and the dramatists of the absurd, that is, to describe a situation in which human beings find no inherent meaning, truth, or value. See Camus, p. 756, and In the World: Existentialism, p. 746.

sents itself as theatrical illusion. Pirandello does this by using the theater itself as the stage and making his play about play-making. Such theatricality, however, is not solely modern. In *The Tempest,* Shakespeare's final play, Shakespeare uses Prospero as an alter-ego who bids his creator's farewell to the stage. How would you distinguish between the theatricality of *Six Characters* and that of *The Tempest*? Can you think of any other plays where the theater and dramatic illusion become the subject of the drama?

■ **FURTHER RESEARCH**

Biography
Bassnett-McGuire, Susan. *Pirandello.* 1984.

Criticism
Bassanese, Fiora A. *Understanding Luigi Pirandello.* 1997.
Bentley, Eric. *The Pirandello Commentaries.* 1986.
Cambon, Glauco, ed. *Pirandello: A Collection of Critical Essays.* 1967.
Esslin, Martin. *The Theatre of the Absurd.* 1961.
Oliver, Roger W. *Dreams of Passion: The Theater of Luigi Pirandello.* 1979.
Starkie, Walter. *Luigi Pirandello, 1867–1936.* 1965.

 # Six Characters in Search of an Author

Translated by Eric Bentley

CHARACTERS OF THE PLAY-IN-THE-MAKING

THE FATHER	THE BOY, *14*
THE MOTHER	THE LITTLE GIRL, *4*
THE SON, *aged 22*	*(these two last do not speak)*
THE STEPDAUGHTER, *18*	*Then, called into being:* MADAM PACE

Six Characters in Search of an Author. One of a trilogy of plays, along with *Each in His Own Way* (1924) and *Tonight We Improvise* (1930), *Six Characters in Search of an Author* is a play about the theater itself. At its first production in Rome in 1921, the play so violated the expectations of the audience that Pirandello had to be rescued from an angry crowd after the performance. Pirandello's offensive innovations—revealing the stage machinery to the audience and making the apparatus of the production visible, questioning the nature and reality of theatrical illusion—would soon become common in modern drama.

   Six Characters is also a play about the creative process. Characters imagined by the playwright but given no script are at various stages of completeness. The two most realized figures, the Father and the Stepdaughter, center the story. The less-defined characters, the Son and younger children, for example, have only marginal roles to play. Their incompleteness reflects the point in the creative process at which their author released them into the world. Without a script to act out, these characters are forever fixed, immutably true to their original conception. When they are given expression in a performance by a theater company, however, they lose some of their "truth," suggesting the inevitable gap between an artist's conception and its realization in a work of art.

   All notes are the editors' unless otherwise indicated.

ACTORS IN THE COMPANY

THE DIRECTOR (DIRETTORE-CAPOCOMICO)	STAGE MANAGER
LEADING LADY	PROMPTER
LEADING MAN	PROPERTY MAN
SECOND ACTRESS	TECHNICIAN
INGENUE	DIRECTOR'S SECRETARY
JUVENILE LEAD	STAGE DOOR MAN
OTHER ACTORS AND ACTRESSES	STAGE CREW

THE PLACE: *The stage of a playhouse.*

The play has neither acts nor scenes. The performance should be interrupted twice: first—without any lowering of the curtain—when the Director and the chief among the Characters retire to put the scenario together and the Actors leave the stage; second when the Technician lets the curtain down by mistake.

When the audience arrives in the theater, the curtain is raised; and the stage, as normally in the daytime, is without wings or scenery and almost completely dark and empty. From the beginning we are to receive the impression of an unrehearsed performance.

Two stairways, left and right respectively, connect the stage with the auditorium.

On stage the dome of the prompter's box has been placed on one side of the box itself. On the other side, at the front of the stage, a small table and an armchair with its back to the audience, for the DIRETTORE-CAPOCOMICO [DIRECTOR].

Two other small tables of different sizes with several chairs around them have also been placed at the front of the stage, ready as needed for the rehearsal. Other chairs here and there, left and right, for the actors, and at the back, a piano, on one side and almost hidden.

As soon as the houselights dim, the TECHNICIAN *is seen entering at the door on stage. He is wearing a blue shirt, and a tool bag hangs from his belt. From a corner at the back he takes several stagebraces, then arranges them on the floor downstage, and kneels down to hammer some nails in. At the sound of the hammering, the* STAGE MANAGER *comes running from the door that leads to the dressing rooms.*

STAGE MANAGER: Oh! What are you doing?

TECHNICIAN: What am I doing? Hammering.

STAGE MANAGER: At this hour? [*He looks at the clock*] It's ten-thirty already. The Director will be here any moment. For the rehearsal.

TECHNICIAN: I gotta have time to work, too, see.

STAGE MANAGER: You will have. But not now.

TECHNICIAN: When?

STAGE MANAGER: Not during rehearsal hours. Now move along, take all this stuff away, and let me set the stage for the second act of, um, *The Game of Role Playing.*

[*Muttering, grumbling, the* TECHNICIAN *picks up the stage-braces and goes away. Meanwhile, from the door on stage, the* ACTORS OF THE COMPANY *start coming in, both men and women, one at a time at first, then in twos, at random, nine or ten of them, the number one would expect as the cast in rehearsals of Pirandello's play,* The Game of Role Playing, *which is the order of the day. They enter, greet the* STAGE MANAGER *and each other, all saying good-morning to all. Several go to their dressing rooms. Others, among them the* PROMPTER, *who has a copy of the script rolled up under his arm, stay on stage, waiting for the* DIRECTOR *to begin the rehearsal. Meanwhile, either seated in conversational groups, or standing, they exchange a few words among themselves. One lights a cigarette, one complains about the part he has been assigned, one reads aloud to his companions items of news from a theater journal. It would be well if both the Actresses and the Actors wore rather gay and brightly colored clothes and if this first improvised scene* [scena a soggetto] *combined vivacity with naturalness. At a certain point, one of the actors can sit down at the piano and strike up a dance tune. The younger actors and actresses start dancing.*]

STAGE MANAGER [*clapping his hands to call them to order*]: All right, that's enough of that. The Director's here.

[*The noise and the dancing stop at once. The Actors turn and look toward the auditorium from the door of which the* DIRECTOR *is now seen coming. A bowler hat on his head, a walking stick under his arm, and a big cigar in his mouth, he walks down the aisle and, greeted by the Actors, goes on stage by one of the two stairways. The* SECRETARY *hands him his mail: several newspapers and a script in a wrapper.*]

DIRECTOR: Letters?

SECRETARY: None. That's all the mail there is.

DIRECTOR [*handing him the script*]: Take this to my room. [*Then, looking around and addressing himself to the* STAGE MANAGER] We can't see each other in here. Want to give us a little light?

STAGE MANAGER: OK.

[*He goes to give the order, and shortly afterward, the whole left side of the stage where the Actors are is lit by a vivid white light. Meanwhile, the* PROMPTER *has taken up his position in his box. He uses a small lamp and has the script open in front of him.*]

DIRECTOR [*clapping his hands*]: Very well, let's start. [*To the* STAGE MANAGER] Someone missing?

STAGE MANAGER: The Leading Lady.

DIRECTOR: As usual! [*He looks at the clock*] We're ten minutes late already. Fine her for that, would you, please? Then she'll learn to be on time.

[*He has not completed his rebuke when the voice of the* LEADING LADY *is heard from the back of the auditorium.*]

LEADING LADY: No, no, for Heaven's sake! I'm here! I'm here! [*She is dressed all in white with a big, impudent hat on her head and a cute little dog in her arms. She runs down the aisle and climbs one of the sets of stairs in great haste.*]

DIRECTOR: You've sworn an oath always to keep people waiting.

LEADING LADY: You must excuse me. Just couldn't find a taxi. But you haven't even begun, I see. And I'm not on right away. [*Then, calling the* STAGE MANAGER *by name, and handing the little dog over to him*] Would you please shut him in my dressing room?

DIRECTOR [*grumbling*]: And the little dog to boot! As if there weren't enough dogs around here. [*He claps his hands again and turns to the* PROMPTER.] Now then, the second act of *The Game of Role Playing*. [*As he sits down in his armchair*] Quiet, gentlemen. Who's on stage?

[*The Actresses and Actors clear the front of the stage and go and sit on one side, except for the three who will start the rehearsal and the* LEADING LADY *who, disregarding the* DIRECTOR'*s request, sits herself down at one of the two small tables.*]

DIRECTOR [*to the* LEADING LADY]: You're in this scene, are you?

LEADING LADY: Me? No, no.

DIRECTOR [*irritated*]: Then how about getting up, for Heaven's sake?

[*The* LEADING LADY *rises and goes and sits beside the other Actors who have already gone to one side.*]

DIRECTOR [*to the* PROMPTER]: Start, start.

PROMPTER [*reading from the script*]: "In the house of Leone Gala. A strange room, combined study and dining room."

DIRECTOR [*turning to the* STAGE MANAGER]: We'll use the red room.

STAGE MANAGER [*making a note on a piece of paper*]: Red room. Very good.

PROMPTER [*continuing to read from the script*]: "The table is set and the desk has books and papers on it. Shelves with books on them, and cupboards with lavish tableware. Door in the rear through which one goes to Leone's bedroom. Side door on the left through which one goes to the kitchen. The main entrance is on the right."

DIRECTOR [*rising and pointing*]: All right, now listen carefully. That's the main door. This is the way to the kitchen. [*Addressing himself to the Actor playing the part of Socrates*] You will come on and go out on this side. [*To the* STAGE MANAGER] The compass at the back. And curtains. [*He sits down again.*]

STAGE MANAGER [*making a note*]: Very good.

PROMPTER [*reading as before*]: "Scene One. Leone Gala, Guido Venanzi, Filippo called Socrates." [*To the* DIRECTOR] Am I supposed to read the stage directions, too?

DIRECTOR: Yes, yes, yes! I've told you that a hundred times!

PROMPTER [*reading as before*]: "At the rise of the curtain, Leone Gala, wearing a chef's hat and apron, is intent on beating an egg in a saucepan with a wooden spoon. Filippo, also dressed as a cook, is beating another egg. Guido Venanzi, seated, is listening."

LEADING ACTOR [*to the* DIRECTOR]: Excuse me, but do I really have to wear a chef's hat?

DIRECTOR [*annoyed by this observation*]: I should say so! It's in the script. [*And he points at it.*]

LEADING ACTOR: But it's ridiculous, if I may say so.

DIRECTOR [*leaping to his feet, furious*]: "Ridiculous, ridiculous!" What do you want me to do? We never get a good play from France any more, so we're reduced to producing plays by Pirandello, a fine man and all that, but neither the actors, the critics, nor the audience are ever happy with his plays, and if you ask me, he does it all on purpose. [*The Actors laugh. And now he rises and coming over to the* LEADING ACTOR *shouts:*] A cook's hat, yes, my dear man! And you beat eggs. And you think you have nothing more on your hands than the beating of eggs? Guess again. You symbolize the shell of those eggs. [*The Actors resume their laughing, and start making ironical comments among themselves.*] Silence! And pay attention while I explain. [*Again addressing himself to the* LEADING ACTOR] Yes, the shell: that is to say, the empty *form* of reason without the *content* of instinct, which is blind. You are reason, and your wife is instinct in the game of role playing. You play the part assigned you, and you're your own puppet—of your own free will. Understand?

LEADING ACTOR [*extending his arms, palms upward*]: Me? No.

DIRECTOR [*returning to his place*]: Nor do I. Let's go on. Wait and see what I do with the ending. [*In a confidential tone*] I suggest you face three-quarters front. Otherwise, what with the abstruseness of the dialogue, and an audience that can't hear you, good-bye play! [*Again clapping*] Now, again, order! Let's go.

PROMPTER: Excuse me, sir, may I put the top back on the prompter's box? There's rather a draft.

DIRECTOR: Yes, yes, do that.

[*The* STAGE DOOR MAN *has entered the auditorium in the meanwhile, his braided cap on his head. Proceeding down the aisle, he goes up on stage to announce to the* DIRECTOR *the arrival of the Six Characters, who have also entered the auditorium, and have started following him at a certain distance, a little lost and perplexed, looking around them.*

Whoever is going to try and translate this play into scenic terms must take all possible measures not to let these Six Characters get confused with the Actors of the Company. Placing both groups correctly, in accordance with the stage directions, once the Six are on stage, will certainly help, as will lighting the two groups in contrasting colors. But the most suitable and effective means to be suggested here is the use of special masks for the Characters: masks specially made of material which doesn't go limp when sweaty and yet masks which are not too heavy for the Actors wearing them, cut out and worked over so they leave eyes, nostrils, and mouth free. This will also bring out the inner significance of the play. The Characters in fact should not be presented as ghosts but as created realities, unchanging constructs of the imagination, and therefore more solidly real than the Actors with their fluid naturalness. The masks will help to give the impression of figures constructed by art, each one unchangeably fixed in the expression of its own fundamental sentiment, thus:

remorse *in the case of the* FATHER; revenge *in the case of the* STEPDAUGHTER; disdain *in the case of the* SON; grief *in the case of the* MOTHER, *who should have wax tears fixed in the rings under her eyes and on her cheeks, as with the sculpted and painted images of the* mater dolorosa *in church. Their clothes should be of special material and design, without extravagance, with rigid, full folds like a statue, in short not suggesting a material you might buy at any store in town, cut out and tailored at any dressmaker's.*

The FATHER *is a man of about fifty, hair thin at the temples, but not bald, thick mustache coiled round a still youthful mouth that is often open in an uncertain, pointless smile. Pale, most notably on his broad forehead: blue eyes, oval, very clear and piercing; dark jacket and light trousers: at times gentle and smooth, at times he has hard, harsh outbursts.*

The MOTHER *seems scared and crushed by an intolerable weight of shame and self-abasement. Wearing a thick black crepe widow's veil, she is modestly dressed in black, and when she lifts the veil, the face does not show signs of suffering, and yet seems made of wax. Her eyes are always on the ground.*

The STEPDAUGHTER, *eighteen, is impudent, almost insolent. Very beautiful, and also in mourning, but mourning of a showy elegance. She shows contempt for the timid, afflicted, almost humiliated manner of her little brother, rather a mess of a* BOY, *fourteen, also dressed in black, but a lively tenderness for her little sister, a* LITTLE GIRL *of around four, dressed in white with black silk sash round her waist.*

The SON, *twenty-two, tall, almost rigid with contained disdain for the* FATHER *and supercilious indifference toward the* MOTHER, *wears a mauve topcoat and a long green scarf wound round his neck.*]

STAGE DOOR MAN [*beret in hand*]: Excuse me, your honor.

DIRECTOR [*rudely jumping on him*]: What is it now?

STAGE DOOR MAN [*timidly*]: There are some people here asking for you.

[*The* DIRECTOR *and the Actors turn in astonishment to look down into the auditorium.*]

DIRECTOR [*furious again*]: But I'm rehearsing here! And you know perfectly well no one can come in during rehearsal! [*Turning again toward the house*] Who are these people? What do they want?

THE FATHER [*stepping forward, followed by the others, to one of the two little stairways to the stage*]: We're here in search of an author.

DIRECTOR [*half angry, half astounded*]: An author? What author?

FATHER: Any author, sir.

DIRECTOR: There's no author here at all. It's not a new play we're rehearsing.

STEPDAUGHTER [*very vivaciously as she rushes up the stairs*]: Then so much the better, sir! *We* can be your new play!

ONE OF THE ACTORS [*among the racy comments and laughs of the others*]: Did you hear that?

FATHER [*following the* STEPDAUGHTER *onstage*]: Certainly, but if the author's not here . . . [*to the* DIRECTOR] Unless *you'd* like to be the author?

[*The* MOTHER, *holding the* LITTLE GIRL *by the hand, and the* BOY *climb the first steps of the stairway and remain there waiting. The* SON *stays morosely below.*]

DIRECTOR: Is this your idea of a joke?

FATHER: Heavens, no! Oh, sir, on the contrary: we bring you a painful drama.

STEPDAUGHTER: We can make your fortune for you.

DIRECTOR: Do me a favor, and leave. We have no time to waste on madmen.

FATHER [*wounded, smoothly*]: Oh, sir, you surely know that life is full of infinite absurdities which, brazenly enough, do not need to appear probable, because they're true.

DIRECTOR: What in God's name are you saying?

FATHER: I'm saying it can actually be considered madness, sir, to force oneself to do the opposite: that is, to give probability to things so they will seem true. But permit me to observe that, if this is madness, it is also the *raison d'être* of your profession.

[*The Actors become agitated and indignant.*]

DIRECTOR [*rising and looking him over*]: It is, is it? It seems to you an affair for madmen, our profession?

FATHER: Well, to make something seem true which is not true . . . without any need, sir: just for fun . . . Isn't it your job to give life on stage to creatures of fantasy?

DIRECTOR [*immediately, making himself spokesman for the growing indignation of his Actors*]: Let me tell you something, my good sir. The actor's profession is a very noble one. If, as things go nowadays, our new playwrights give us nothing but stupid plays, with puppets in them instead of men, it is our boast, I'd have you know, to have given life—on these very boards—to immortal works of art.

[*Satisfied, the Actors approve and applaud their* DIRECTOR.]

FATHER [*interrupting and bearing down hard*]: Exactly! That's just it. You have created living beings—*more* alive than those that breathe and wear clothes! Less real, perhaps; but more true! We agree completely!

[*The Actors look at each other, astounded.*]

DIRECTOR: What? You were saying just now . . .

FATHER: No, no, don't misunderstand me. You shouted that you hadn't time to waste on madmen. So I wanted to tell you that no one knows better than you that Nature employs the human imagination to carry her work of creation on to a higher plane!

DIRECTOR: All right, all right. But what are you getting at, exactly?

FATHER: Nothing, sir. I only wanted to show that one may be born to this life in many modes, in many forms: as tree, as rock, water or butterfly . . . or woman. And that . . . characters are born too.

DIRECTOR [*his amazement ironically feigned*]: And you—with these companions of yours—were born a character?

FATHER: Right, sir. And alive, as you see.

[*The* DIRECTOR *and the Actors burst out laughing as at a joke.*]

FATHER [*wounded*]: I'm sorry to hear you laugh, because, I repeat, we carry a painful drama within us, as you all might deduce from the sight of that lady there, veiled in black.

[*As he says this, he gives his hand to the* MOTHER *to help her up the last steps and, still holding her by the hand, he leads her with a certain tragic solemnity to the other side of the stage, which is suddenly bathed in fantastic light. The* LITTLE GIRL *and the* BOY *follow the* MOTHER; *then the* SON, *who stands on one side at the back; then the* STEPDAUGHTER *who also detaches herself from the others—downstage and leaning against the proscenium arch. At first astonished at this development, then overcome with admiration, the Actors now burst into applause as at a show performed for their benefit.*]

DIRECTOR [*bowled over at first, then indignant*]: Oh, stop this! Silence please! [*Then, turning to the Characters*] And you, leave! Get out of here! [*To the* STAGE MANAGER] For God's sake, get them out!

STAGE MANAGER [*stepping forward but then stopping, as if held back by a strange dismay*]: Go! Go!

FATHER [*to the* DIRECTOR]: No, look, we, um—

DIRECTOR [*shouting*]: I tell you we've got to work!

LEADING MAN: It's not right to fool around like this . . .

FATHER [*resolute, stepping forward*]: I'm amazed at your incredulity! You're accustomed to seeing the created characters of an author spring to life, aren't you, right here on this stage, the one confronting the other? Perhaps the trouble is there's no script *there* [*pointing to the* PROMPTER's *box*] with us in it?

STEPDAUGHTER [*going right up to the* DIRECTOR, *smiling, coquettish*]: Believe me, we really are six characters, sir. Very interesting ones at that. But lost. Adrift.

FATHER [*brushing her aside*]: Very well: lost, adrift. [*Going right on*] In the sense, that is, that the author who created us, made us live, did not wish, or simply and materially was not able, to place us in the world of art. And that was a real crime, sir, because whoever has the luck to be born a living character can also laugh at death. He will never die! The man will die, the writer, the instrument of creation; the creature will never die! And to have eternal life it doesn't even take extraordinary gifts, nor the performance of miracles. Who was Sancho Panza?[1] Who was Don Abbondio?[2] But they live forever because, as live germs, they have the luck to find a fertile matrix, an imagination which knew how to raise and nourish them, make them live through all eternity!

DIRECTOR: That's all well and good. But what do you people want here?

FATHER: We want to live, sir.

DIRECTOR [*ironically*]: Through all eternity?

FATHER: No, sir. But for a moment at least. In you.

AN ACTOR: Well, well, well!

LEADING LADY: They want to live in us.

JUVENILE LEAD [*pointing to the* STEPDAUGHTER]: Well, I've no objection, so long as I get that one.

FATHER: Now look, look. The play is still in the making. [*To the* DIRECTOR] But if you wish, and your actors wish, we can make it right away. Acting in concert.

LEADING MAN [*annoyed*]: Concert? We don't put on concerts! We do plays, dramas, comedies!

FATHER: Very good. That's why we came.

DIRECTOR: Well, where's the script?

FATHER: Inside us, sir. [*The Actors laugh.*] The drama is inside us. It *is* us. And we're impatient to perform it. According to the dictates of the passion within us.

STEPDAUGHTER [*scornful, with treacherous grace, deliberate impudence*]: My passion—if you only knew, sir! My passion—for him! [*She points to the* FATHER *and makes as if to embrace him but then breaks into a strident laugh.*]

FATHER [*an angry interjection*]: You keep out of this now. And please don't laugh that way!

STEPDAUGHTER: No? Then, ladies and gentlemen, permit me. A two months' orphan, I shall dance and sing for you all. Watch how! [*She mischievously starts to sing "Beware of Chu Chin Chow"*[3] *by Dave Stamper, reduced to fox trot or slow one-step by Francis Salabert: the first verse, accompanied by a step or two of dancing. While*

---

[1] **Sancho Panza:** Don Quixote's unforgettable servant and companion in Cervantes's *Don Quixote* (1605, 1615), who counters the knight's idealism with realism and common sense.

[2] **Don Abbondio:** A humble priest in Manzoni's *The Betrothed*. [Translator's note.]

[3] **"Beware of Chu Chin Chow":** A song from the Ziegfeld Follies, 1917.

she sings and dances, the Actors, especially the young ones, as if drawn by some strange fascination, move toward her and half raise their hands as if to take hold of her. She runs away and when the Actors burst into applause she just stands there, remote, abstracted, while the DIRECTOR *protests.*]

ACTORS AND ACTRESSES [*laughing and clapping*]: Brava! Fine! Splendid!

DIRECTOR [*annoyed*]: Silence! What do you think this is, a night spot? [*Taking the* FATHER *a step or two to one side, with a certain amount of consternation*] Tell me something. Is she crazy?

FATHER: Crazy? Of course not. It's much worse than that.

STEPDAUGHTER [*running over at once to the* DIRECTOR]: Worse! Worse! Not crazy but worse! Just listen: I'll play it for you right now, this drama, and at a certain point you'll see me—when this dear little thing—[*She takes the* LITTLE GIRL *who is beside the* MOTHER *by the hand and leads her to the* DIRECTOR.]—isn't she darling? [*Takes her in her arms and kisses her.*] Sweetie! Sweetie! [*Puts her down again and adds with almost involuntary emotion.*] Well, when God suddenly takes this little sweetheart away from her poor mother, and that idiot there—[*thrusting the* BOY *forward, rudely seizing him by a sleeve*] does the stupidest of things, like the nitwit that he is, [*with a shove she drives him back toward the* MOTHER] then you will see me take to my heels. Yes, ladies and gentlemen, take to my heels! I can hardly wait for that moment. For after what happened between him and me—[*She points to the* FATHER *with a horrible wink.*] something very intimate, you understand—I can't stay in such company any longer, witnessing the anguish of our mother on account of that fool there—[*She points to the* SON.] Just look at him, look at him!—how indifferent, how frozen, because he is the legitimate son, that's what he is, full of contempt for me, for him [*the* BOY], and for that little creature [*the* LITTLE GIRL], because we three are bastards, d'you see? bastards. [*Goes to the* MOTHER *and embraces her.*] And this poor mother, the common mother of us all, he—well, he doesn't want to acknowledge her as *his* mother too, and he looks down on her, that's what he does, looks on her as only the mother of us three bastards, the wretch! [*She says this rapidly in a state of extreme excitement. Her voice swells to the word: "bastards!" and descends again to the final "wretch," almost spitting it out.*]

MOTHER [*to the* DIRECTOR, *with infinite anguish*]: In the name of these two small children, sir, I implore you . . . [*She grows faint and sways.*] Oh, heavens . . .

FATHER [*rushing over to support her with almost all the Actors who are astonished and scared*]: Please! Please, a chair, a chair for this poor widow!

ACTORS [*rushing over*]: —Is it true then?—She's *really* fainting?

DIRECTOR: A chair!

[*One of the Actors proffers a chair. The others stand around, ready to help. The* MOTHER, *seated, tries to stop the* FATHER *from lifting the veil that hides her face.*]

FATHER [*to the* DIRECTOR]: Look at her, look at her . . .

MOTHER: Heavens, no, stop it!

FATHER: Let them see you. [*He lifts her veil.*]

MOTHER [*rising and covering her face with her hands, desperate*]: Oh, sir, please stop this man from carrying out his plan. It's horrible for me!

DIRECTOR [*surprised, stunned*]: I don't know where we're at! What's this all about? [*To the* FATHER] Is this your wife?

FATHER [*at once*]: Yes, sir, my wife.

DIRECTOR: Then how is she a widow, if you're alive?

[*The Actors relieve their astonishment in a loud burst of laughter.*]

FATHER [*wounded, with bitter resentment*]: Don't laugh! Don't laugh like that! Please! Just that is her drama, sir. She had another man. Another man who should be here!

MOTHER [*with a shout*]: No! No!

STEPDAUGHTER: He had the good luck to die. Two months ago, as I told you. We're still in mourning, as you see.

FATHER: But he's absent, you see, not just because he's dead. He's absent—take a look at her, sir, and you will understand at once!—Her drama wasn't in the love of two men for whom she was incapable of feeling anything—except maybe a little gratitude [not to me, but to him]—She is not a woman, she is a mother!—And her drama—a powerful one, very powerful—is in fact all in those four children which she bore to her two men.

MOTHER: *My* men? Have you the gall to say I wanted two men? It was him, sir. He forced the other man on me. Compelled—yes, compelled—me to go off with him!

STEPDAUGHTER [*cutting in, roused*]: It's not true!

MOTHER [*astounded*]: How d'you mean, not true?

STEPDAUGHTER: It's not true! It's not true!

MOTHER: And what can you know about it?

STEPDAUGHTER: It's not true. [*To the* DIRECTOR] Don't believe it. Know why she says it? For his sake. [*Pointing to the* SON] His indifference tortures her, destroys her. She wants him to believe that, if she abandoned him when he was two, it was because he [*the* FATHER] compelled her to.

MOTHER [*with violence*]: He did compel me, he did compel me, as God is my witness! [*To the* DIRECTOR] Ask him if that isn't true. [*Her husband*] Make him tell him. [*The* SON] She couldn't know anything about it.

STEPDAUGHTER: With my father, while he lived, I know you were always happy and content. Deny it if you can.

MOTHER: I don't deny it, I don't . . .

STEPDAUGHTER: He loved you, he cared for you! [*To the* BOY, *with rage*] Isn't that so? Say it! Why don't you speak, you dope?

MOTHER: Leave the poor boy alone. Why d'you want to make me out ungrateful, daughter? I have no wish to offend your father! I told him [*the* FATHER] I didn't abandon my son and my home for my own pleasure. It wasn't my fault.

FATHER: That's true, sir. It was mine.

[*Pause*]

LEADING MAN [*to his companions*]: What a show!

LEADING LADY: And *they* put it on—for us.

JUVENILE LEAD: Quite a change!

DIRECTOR [*who is now beginning to get very interested*]: Let's listen to this, let's listen! [*And saying this, he goes down one of the stairways into the auditorium, and stands in front of the stage, as if to receive a spectator's impression of the show.*]

SON [*without moving from his position, cold, quiet, ironic*]: Oh yes, you can now listen to the philosophy lecture. He will tell you about the Demon of Experiment.

FATHER: You are a cynical idiot, as I've told you a hundred times. [*To the* DIRECTOR, *now in the auditorium*] He mocks me, sir, on account of that phrase I found to excuse myself with.

SON [*contemptuously*]: Phrases!

FATHER: Phrases! Phrases! As if they were not a comfort to everyone: in the face of some unexplained fact, in the face of an evil that eats into us, to find a word that says nothing but at least quiets us down!

STEPDAUGHTER: Quiets our guilt feelings too. That above all.

FATHER: Our guilt feelings? Not so. I have never quieted my guilt feelings with words alone.

STEPDAUGHTER: It took a little money as well, didn't it, it took a little dough! The hundred lire he was going to pay me, ladies and gentlemen!

[*Movement of horror among the Actors.*]

SON [*with contempt toward the* STEPDAUGHTER]: That's filthy.

STEPDAUGHTER: Filthy? The dough was there. In a small pale blue envelope on the mahogany table in the room behind the shop. Madam Pace's [*she pronounces it "Pah-chay"*] shop. One of those Madams who lure us poor girls from good families into their *ateliers* under the pretext of selling *Robes et Manteaux.*[4]

SON: And with those hundred lire he was going to pay she has bought the right to tyrannize over us all. Only it so happens—I'd have you know—that he never actually incurred the debt.

STEPDAUGHTER: Oh, oh, but we were really going to it, I assure you! [*She bursts out laughing.*]

MOTHER [*rising in protest*]: Shame, daughter! Shame!

STEPDAUGHTER [*quickly*]: Shame? It's my revenge! I am frantic, sir, frantic to live it, live that scene! The room . . . here's the shopwindow with the coats in it; there's the bed-sofa; the mirror; a screen; and in front of the window the little mahogany table with the hundred lire in the pale blue envelope. I can see it. I could take it. But you men should turn away now: I'm almost naked. I don't blush any more. It's he that blushes now. [*Points to the* FATHER.] But I assure you he was very pale, very pale, at that moment. [*To the* DIRECTOR] You must believe me, sir.

DIRECTOR: You lost me some time ago.

FATHER: Of course! Getting it thrown at you like that! Restore a little order, sir, and let *me* speak. And never mind this ferocious girl. She's trying to heap opprobrium on me by withholding the relevant explanations!

STEPDAUGHTER: This is no place for long-winded narratives!

---

[4] *ateliers . . . Robes et Manteaux:* Workshops; supposedly to sell dresses and coats.

FATHER: I said—explanations.

STEPDAUGHTER: Oh, certainly. Those that suit your turn.

[*At this point, the* DIRECTOR *returns to the stage to restore order.*]

FATHER: But that's the whole root of the evil. Words. Each of us has, inside him, a world of things—to everyone, his world of things. And how can we understand each other, sir, if, in the words I speak, I put the sense and value of things as they are inside me, whereas the man who hears them inevitably receives them in the sense and with the value they have for him, the sense and value of the world inside him? We think we understand each other but we never do. Consider: the compassion, all the compassion I feel for this woman [*the* MOTHER] has been received by her as the most ferocious of cruelties!

MOTHER: You ran me out of the house.

FATHER: Hear that? Ran her out. It *seemed to her* that I ran her out.

MOTHER: You can talk; I can't . . . But, look, sir, after he married me . . . and who knows why he did? I was poor, of humble birth . . .

FATHER: And that's why. I married you for your . . . humility. I loved you for it, believing . . . [*He breaks off, seeing her gestured denials; seeing the impossibility of making himself understood by her, he opens his arms wide in a gesture of despair, and turns to the* DIRECTOR] See that? She says No. It's scarifying, isn't it, sir, scarifying, this deafness of hers, this mental deafness! She has a heart, oh yes, where her children are concerned! But she's deaf, deaf in the brain, deaf, sir, to the point of desperation!

STEPDAUGHTER [*to the* DIRECTOR]: All right, but now make him tell you what his intelligence has ever done for us.

FATHER: If we could only foresee all the evil that can result from the good we believe we're doing!

[*At this point, the* LEADING LADY, *who has been on hot coals seeing the* LEADING MAN *flirt with the* STEPDAUGHTER, *steps forward and asks of the* DIRECTOR:]

LEADING LADY: Excuse me, is the rehearsal continuing?

DIRECTOR: Yes, of course! But let me listen a moment.

JUVENILE LEAD: This is something quite new.

INGENUE: Very interesting!

LEADING LADY: If that sort of thing interests you. [*And she darts a look at the* LEADING MAN.]

DIRECTOR [*to the* FATHER]: But you must give us *clear* explanations. [*He goes and sits down.*]

FATHER: Right. Yes. Listen. There was a man working for me. A poor man. As my secretary. Very devoted to me. Understood *her* [*the* MOTHER] very well. There was mutual understanding between them. Nothing wrong in it. They thought no harm at all. Nothing off-color about it. No, no, he knew his place, as she did. They didn't do anything wrong. Didn't even think it.

STEPDAUGHTER: So he thought it *for* them. And did it.

FATHER: It's not true! I wanted to do them some good. And myself too, oh yes, I admit. I'd got to this point, sir: I couldn't say a word to either of them but they would exchange a significant look. The one would consult the eyes of the other, asking how what I had said should be taken, if they didn't want to put me in a rage. That sufficed, you will understand, to keep me continually in a rage, in a state of unbearable exasperation.

DIRECTOR: Excuse me, why didn't you fire him, this secretary?

FATHER: Good question! That's what I did do, sir. But then I had to see that poor woman remain in my house, a lost soul. Like an animal without a master that one takes pity on and carries home.

MOTHER: No, no, it's—

FATHER [*at once, turning to her to get it in first*]: Your son? Right?

MOTHER: He'd already snatched my son from me.

FATHER: But not from cruelty. Just so he'd grow up strong and healthy. In touch with the soil.

STEPDAUGHTER [*pointing at the latter, ironic*]: And just look at him!

FATHER [*at once*]: Uh? Is it also my fault if he then grew up this way? I sent him to a wet nurse, sir, in the country, a peasant woman. I didn't find her [*the* MOTHER] strong enough, despite her humble origin. I'd married her for similar reasons, as I said. All nonsense maybe, but there we are. I always had these confounded aspirations toward a certain solidity, toward what is morally sound. [*Here the* STEPDAUGHTER *bursts out laughing.*] Make her stop that! It's unbearable!

DIRECTOR: Stop it. I can't hear, for Heaven's sake!

[*Suddenly, again, as the* DIRECTOR *rebukes her, she is withdrawn and remote, her laughter cut off in the middle. The* DIRECTOR *goes down again from the stage to get an impression of the scene.*]

FATHER: I couldn't bear to be with that woman any more. [*Points to the* MOTHER] Not so much, believe me, because she irritated me, and even made me feel physically ill, as because of the pain—a veritable anguish—that I felt on her account.

MOTHER: And he sent me away!

FATHER: Well provided for. And to that man. Yes, sir. So she could be free of me.

MOTHER: And so *he* could be free.

FATHER: That, too. I admit it. And much evil resulted. But I intended good. And more for her than for me, I swear it! [*He folds his arms across his chest. Then, suddenly, turning to the* MOTHER] I never lost sight of you, never lost sight of you till, from one day to the next, unbeknown to me, he carried you off to another town. He noticed I was interested in her, you see, but that was silly, because my interest was absolutely pure, absolutely without ulterior motive. The interest I took in her new family, as it grew up, had an unbelievable tenderness to it. Even she should bear witness to that! [*He points to the* STEPDAUGHTER.]

STEPDAUGHTER: Oh, very much so! I was a little sweetie. Pigtails over my shoulders. Panties coming down a little bit below my skirt. A little sweetie. He would see me coming out of school, at the gate. He would come and see me as I grew up . . .

FATHER: This is outrageous. You're betraying me!

STEPDAUGHTER: I'm not! What do you mean?

FATHER: Outrageous. Outrageous. [*Immediately, still excited, he continues in a tone of explanation, to the* DIRECTOR.] My house, sir, when she had left it, at once seemed empty. [*Points to the* MOTHER] She was an incubus. But she filled my house for me. Left alone, I wandered through these rooms like a fly without a head. This fellow here [*the* SON] was raised away from home. Somehow, when he got back, he didn't seem mine any more. Without a mother between me and him, he grew up on his own, apart, without any relationship to me, emotional or intellectual. And then — strange, sir, but true — first I grew curious, then I was gradually attracted toward *her* family, which I had brought into being. The thought of *this* family began to fill the void around me. I had to — really had to — believe she was at peace, absorbed in the simplest cares of life, lucky to be away and far removed from the complicated torments of my spirit. And to have proof of this, I would go and see that little girl at the school gate.

STEPDAUGHTER: Correct! He followed me home, smiled at me and, when I was home, waved to me, like this! I would open my eyes wide and look at him suspiciously. I didn't know who it was. I told mother. And she guessed right away it was him. [*The* MOTHER *nods.*] At first she didn't want to send me back to school for several days. When I did go, I saw him again at the gate — the clown! — with a brown paper bag in his hand. He came up to me, caressed me, and took from the bag a lovely big Florentine straw hat with a ring of little May roses round it — for me!

DIRECTOR: You're making too long a story of this.

SON [*contemptuously*]: Story is right! Fiction! Literature!

FATHER: Literature? This is life, sir. Passion!

DIRECTOR: Maybe! But not actable!

FATHER: I agree. This is all preliminary. I wouldn't *want* you to act it. As you see, in fact, she [*the* STEPDAUGHTER] is no longer that little girl with pigtails —

STEPDAUGHTER: — and the panties showing below her skirt!

FATHER: The drama comes now, sir. Novel, complex —

STEPDAUGHTER [*gloomy, fierce, steps forward*]: — What my father's death meant for us was —

FATHER [*Not giving her time to continue*]: — poverty, sir. They returned, unbeknownst to me. She's so thickheaded. [*Pointing to the* MOTHER] It's true she can hardly write herself, but she could have had her daughter write, or her son, telling me they were in need!

MOTHER: But, sir, how could I have guessed he felt the way he did?

FATHER: Which is just where you always went wrong. You could never guess how I felt about anything!

MOTHER: After so many years of separation, with all that had happened . . .

FATHER: And is it my fault if that fellow carried you off as he did? [*Turning to the* DIRECTOR] From one day to the next, as I say. He'd found some job someplace. I couldn't even trace them. Necessarily, then, my interest dwindled, with the years. The drama breaks out, sir, unforeseen and violent, at their return. When I, alas, was impelled by the misery of my still living flesh . . . Oh, and what misery

that is for a man who is alone, who has not wanted to form debasing relationships, not yet old enough to do without a woman, and no longer young enough
to go and look for one without shame! Misery? It's horror, horror, because no
woman can give him love any more.—Knowing this, one should go without!
Well, sir, on the outside, when other people are watching, each man is clothed in
dignity: but, on the inside, he knows what unconfessable things are going on
within him. One gives way, gives way to temptation, to rise again, right afterward, of course, in a great hurry to put our dignity together again, complete,
solid, a stone on a grave that hides and buries from our eyes every sign of our
shame and even the very memory of it! It's like that with everybody. Only the
courage to say it is lacking—to say certain things.

STEPDAUGHTER: The courage to do them, though—everybody's got that.

FATHER: Everybody. But in secret. That's why it takes more courage to say them. A
man only has to say them and it's all over: he's labeled a cynic. But, sir, he isn't!
He's just like everybody else. Better! He's better because he's not afraid to reveal,
by the light of intelligence, the red stain of shame, there, in the human beast,
which closes its eyes to it. Woman—yes, woman—what is she like, actually?
She looks at us, inviting, tantalizing. You take hold of her. She's no sooner in
your arms than she shuts her eyes. It is the sign of her submission. The sign with
which she tells the man: Blind yourself for I am blind.

STEPDAUGHTER: How about when she no longer keeps them shut? When she no
longer feels the need to hide the red stain of shame from herself by closing her
eyes, and instead, her eyes dry now and impassive, sees the shame of the man,
who has blinded himself even without love? They make me vomit, all those
intellectual elaborations, this philosophy that begins by revealing the beast and
then goes on to excuse it and save its soul . . . I can't bear to hear about it!
Because when a man feels obliged to *reduce* life this way, reduce it all to "the
beast," throwing overboard every vestige of the truly human, every aspiration
after chastity, all feelings of purity, of the ideal, of duties, of modesty, of shame,
then nothing is more contemptible, more nauseating than his wretched guilt
feelings! Crocodile tears!

DIRECTOR: Let's get to the facts, to the facts! This is just discussion.

FATHER: Very well. But a fact is like a sack. When it's empty, it won't stand up. To
make it stand up you must first pour into it the reasons and feelings by which it
exists. I couldn't know that—when that man died and they returned here in
poverty—she went out to work as a dressmaker to support the children, nor
that the person she went to work for was that . . . that Madam Pace!

STEPDAUGHTER: A high-class dressmaker, if you'd all like to know! To all appearances, she serves fine ladies, but then she arranges things so that the fine ladies
serve *her* . . . without prejudice to ladies not so fine!

MOTHER: Believe me, sir, I never had the slightest suspicion that that old witch hired
me because she had her eye on my daughter . . .

STEPDAUGHTER: Poor mama! Do you know, sir, what the woman did when I brought
her my mother's work? She would point out to me the material she'd ruined by
giving it to my mother to sew. And she deducted for that, she deducted. And so,

you understand, *I* paid, while that poor creature thought she was making sacrifices for me and those two by sewing, even at night, Madam Pace's material!

[*Indignant movements and exclamations from the Actors.*]

DIRECTOR [*without pause*]: And there, one day, you met—

STEPDAUGHTER [*pointing to the* FATHER]: —him, him, yes sir! An old client! Now there's a scene for you to put on! Superb!

FATHER: Interrupted by her—the mother—

STEPDAUGHTER [*without pause, treacherously*]: —almost in time!—

FATHER [*shouting*]: No, no, *in* time! Because, luckily, I recognized the girl in time. And I took them all back, sir, into my home. Now try to visualize my situation and hers, the one confronting the other—she as you see her now, myself unable to look her in the face any more.

STEPDAUGHTER: It's too absurd! But—afterward—was it possible for me to be a modest little miss, virtuous and well-bred, in accordance with those confounded aspirations toward a certain solidity, toward what is morally sound?

FATHER: And therein lies the drama, sir, as far as I'm concerned: in my awareness that each of us thinks of himself as *one* but that, well, it's not true, each of us is many, oh so many, sir, according to the possibilities of being that are in us. We are one thing for this person, another for that! Already *two* utterly different things! And with it all, the illusion of being always one thing for all men, and always this one thing in every single action. It's not true! Not true! We realize as much when, by some unfortunate chance, in one or another of our acts, we find ourselves suspended, hooked. We see, I mean, that we are not wholly in that act, and that therefore it would be abominably unjust to judge us by that act alone, to hold us suspended, hooked, in the pillory, our whole life long, as if our life were summed up in that act! Now do you understand this girl's treachery? She surprised me in a place, in an act, in which she should never have had to know me—I couldn't be that way for her. And she wants to give me a reality such as I could never have expected I would have to assume for her, the reality of a fleeting moment, a shameful one, in my life! This, sir, this is what I feel most strongly. And you will see that the drama will derive tremendous value from this. But now add the situation of the others! His . . . [*He points to the* SON.]

SON [*shrugging contemptuously*]: Leave me out of this! It's none of my business.

FATHER: What? None of your business?

SON: None. And I *want* to be left out. I wasn't made to be one of you, and you know it.

STEPDAUGHTER: We're common, aren't we?—And he's so refined.—But from time to time I give him a hard, contemptuous look, and he looks down at the ground. You may have noticed that, sir. He looks down at the ground. For he knows the wrong he's done me.

SON [*hardly looking at her*]: Me?

STEPDAUGHTER: You! You! I'm on the streets because of you! [*A movement of horror from the Actors*] Did you or did you not, by your attitude, deny us—I won't say the intimacy of home but even the hospitality which puts guests at their ease? We were the intruders, coming to invade the kingdom of your legitimacy! I'd like to have you see, sir, certain little scenes between just him and me! He says I tyrannized over them all. But it was entirely because of his attitude that I started to exploit the situation he calls filthy, a situation which had brought me into his home with my mother, who is also *his* mother, *as its mistress!*

SON [*coming slowly forward*]: They can't lose, sir, three against one, an easy game. But figure to yourself a son, sitting quietly at home, who one fine day sees a young woman arrive, an impudent type with her nose in the air, asking for his father, with whom she has heaven knows what business; and then he sees her return, in the same style, accompanied by that little girl over there; and finally he sees her treat his father — who can say why? — in a very ambiguous and cool manner, demanding money, in a tone that takes for granted that he *has* to give it, has to, is obligated —

FATHER: — but I *am* obligated: it's for your mother!

SON: How would I know? When, sir, [*to the* DIRECTOR] have I ever seen her? When have I ever heard her spoken of? One day I see her arrive with her, [*the* STEP-DAUGHTER] with that boy, with that little girl. They say to me: "It's your mother too, know that?" I manage to figure out from her carryings-on [*pointing at the* STEPDAUGHTER] why they arrived in our home from one day to the next . . . What I'm feeling and experiencing I can't put into words, and wouldn't want to. I wouldn't want to confess it, even to myself. It cannot therefore result in any action on my part. You can see that. Believe me, sir, I'm a character that, dramatically speaking, remains unrealized. I'm out of place in their company. So please leave me out of it all!

FATHER: What? But it's just because you're so —

SON [*in violent exasperation*]: — I'm so what? How would *you* know? When did you ever care about me?

FATHER: *Touché! Touché!* But isn't even that a dramatic situation? This withdrawn-ness of yours, so cruel to me, and to your mother who, on her return home is seeing you almost for the first time, a grown man she doesn't recognize, though she knows you're her son . . . [*Pointing out the* MOTHER *to the* DIRECTOR] Just look at her, she's crying.

STEPDAUGHTER [*angrily, stamping her foot*]: Like the fool she is!

FATHER [*pointing her out to the* DIRECTOR]: And she can't abide him, you know. [*Again referring to the* SON] — He says it's none of his business. The truth is he's almost the pivot of the action. Look at that little boy, clinging to his mother all the time, scared, humiliated . . . It's all because of *him*. [*the* SON] Perhaps the most painful situation of all is that little boy's: he feels alien, more than all the others, and the poor little thing is so mortified, so anguished at being taken into our home — out of charity, as it were . . . [*Confidentially*] He's just like his father: humble, doesn't say anything . . .

DIRECTOR: He won't fit anyway. You've no idea what a nuisance children are on stage.

FATHER: But he wouldn't be a nuisance for long. Nor would the little girl, no, she's the first to go . . .

DIRECTOR: Very good, yes! The whole thing interests me very much indeed. I have a hunch, a definite hunch, that there's material here for a fine play!

STEPDAUGHTER [*trying to inject herself*]: With a character like me in it!

FATHER [*pushing her to one side in his anxiety to know what the* DIRECTOR *will decide*]: You be quiet!

DIRECTOR [*going right on, ignoring the interruption*]: Yes, it's new stuff . . .

FATHER: Very new!

DIRECTOR: You had some gall, though, to come and throw it at me this way . . .

FATHER: Well, you see, sir, born as we are to the stage . . .

DIRECTOR: You're amateurs, are you?

FATHER: No. I say: "born to the stage" because . . .

DIRECTOR: Oh, come on, you must have done some acting!

FATHER: No, no, sir, only as every man acts the part assigned to him—by himself or others—in this life. In me you see passion itself, which—in almost all people, as it rises—invariably becomes a bit theatrical . . .

DIRECTOR: Well, never mind! Never mind about that!—You see, my dear sir, without the author . . . I could direct you to an author . . .

FATHER: No, no, look: You be the author!

DIRECTOR: Me? What are you talking about?

FATHER: Yes, you. You. Why not?

DIRECTOR: Because I've never been an author, that's why not!

FATHER: Couldn't you be one now, hm? There's nothing to it. Everyone's doing it. And your job is made all the easier by the fact that you have us—here—alive—right in front of your nose!

DIRECTOR: It wouldn't be enough.

FATHER: Not enough? Seeing us live our own drama . . .

DIRECTOR: I know, but you always need someone to write it!

FATHER: No. Just someone to take it down, maybe, since you have us here—in action—scene by scene. It'll be enough if we piece together a rough sketch for you, then you can rehearse it.

DIRECTOR [*tempted, goes up on stage again*]: Well, I'm almost, almost tempted . . . Just for kicks . . . We could actually rehearse . . .

FATHER: Of course you could! What scenes you'll see emerge! I can list them for you right away.

DIRECTOR: I'm tempted . . . I'm tempted . . . Let's give it a try . . . Come to my office. [*Turns to the Actors*] Take a break, will you? But don't go away. We'll be back in fifteen or twenty minutes. [*To the* FATHER] Let's see what we can do . . . Maybe we can get something very extraordinary out of all this . . .

FATHER: We certainly can. Wouldn't it be better to take *them* along? [*He points to the Characters.*]

DIRECTOR: Yes, let them all come. [*Starts going off, then comes back to address the Actors*] Now don't forget. Everyone on time. Fifteen minutes.

[DIRECTOR *and Six Characters cross the stage and disappear. The Actors stay there and look at one another in amazement.*]

LEADING MAN: Is he serious? What's he going to do?

JUVENILE: This is outright insanity.

A THIRD ACTOR: We have to improvise a drama right off the bat?

JUVENILE LEAD: That's right. Like Commedia dell'Arte.[5]

LEADING LADY: Well, if he thinks *I'm* going to lend myself to that sort of thing . . .

INGENUE: Count me out.

A FOURTH ACTOR [*alluding to the Characters*]: I'd like to know who those people are.

THE THIRD ACTOR: Who would they be? Madmen or crooks!

JUVENILE LEAD: And he's going to pay attention to them?

INGENUE: Carried away by vanity! Wants to be an author now . . .

LEADING MAN: It's out of this world. If this is what the theater is coming to, my friends . . .

A FIFTH ACTOR: I think it's rather fun.

THE THIRD ACTOR: Well! We shall see. We shall see. [*And chatting thus among themselves, the Actors leave the stage, some using the little door at the back, others returning to their dressing rooms.*]

The curtain remains raised. The performance is interrupted by a twenty-minute intermission.

Bells ring. The performance is resumed.

   From dressing rooms, from the door, and also from the house, the Actors, the STAGE MANAGER, *the* TECHNICIAN, *the* PROMPTER, *the* PROPERTY MAN *return to the stage; at the same time the* DIRECTOR *and the Six Characters emerge from the office.*

   As soon as the house lights are out, the stage lighting is as before.

DIRECTOR: Let's go, everybody! Is everyone here? Quiet! We're beginning. [*Calls the* TECHNICIAN *by name.*]

TECHNICIAN: Here!

DIRECTOR: Set the stage for the parlor scene. Two wings and a backdrop with a door in it will do, quickly please!

[*The* TECHNICIAN *at once runs to do the job, and does it while the* DIRECTOR *works things out with the* STAGE MANAGER, *the* PROPERTY MAN, *the* PROMPTER, *and the Actors. This indication of a set consists of two wings, a drop with a door in it, all in pink and gold stripes.*]

DIRECTOR [*to the* PROPERTY MAN]: See if we have some sort of bed-sofa in the prop room.

PROPERTY MAN: Yes, sir, there's the green one.

STEPDAUGHTER: No, no, not green! It was yellow, flowered, plush, and very big. Extremely comfortable.

PROPERTY MAN: Well, we have nothing like that.

DIRECTOR: But it doesn't matter. Bring the one you have.

STEPDAUGHTER: Doesn't matter? Madam Pace's famous chaise longue!

DIRECTOR: This is just for rehearsal. Please don't meddle! [*To the* STAGE MANAGER] See if we have a display case — long and rather narrow.

STEPDAUGHTER: The table, the little mahogany table for the pale blue envelope!

STAGE MANAGER [*to the* DIRECTOR]: There's the small one. Gilded.

---

[5] **Commedia dell'Arte:** Improvised Italian street drama dating from the Middle Ages that featured certain stock figures, such as Harlequin.

DIRECTOR: All right. Get that one.

FATHER: A large mirror.

STEPDAUGHTER: And the screen. A screen, please, or what'll I do?

STAGE MANAGER: Yes, ma'am, we have lots of screens, don't worry.

DIRECTOR [*to the* STEPDAUGHTER]: A few coat hangers?

STEPDAUGHTER: A great many, yes.

DIRECTOR [*to the* STAGE MANAGER]: See how many we've got, and have them brought on.

STAGE MANAGER: Right, sir, I'll see to it.

[*The* STAGE MANAGER *also hurries to do his job and while the* DIRECTOR *goes on talking with the* PROMPTER *and then with the Characters and the Actors, has the furniture carried on by stagehands and arranges it as he thinks fit.*]

DIRECTOR [*to the* PROMPTER]: Meanwhile you can get into position. Look: This is the outline of the scenes, act by act. [*He gives him several sheets of paper.*] You'll have to be a bit of a virtuoso today.

PROMPTER: Shorthand?

DIRECTOR [*Pleasantly surprised*]: Oh, good! You know shorthand?

PROMPTER: I may not know prompting, but shorthand . . . [*Turning to a stagehand*] Get me some paper from my room — quite a lot — all you can find!

[*The stagehand runs off and returns a little later with a wad of paper which he gives to the* PROMPTER.]

DIRECTOR [*Going right on, to the* PROMPTER]: Follow the scenes line by line as we play them, and try to pin down the speeches, at least the most important ones. [*Then, turning to the Actors*] Clear the stage please, everyone! Yes, come over to this side and pay close attention. [*He indicates the left.*]

LEADING LADY: Excuse me but —

DIRECTOR [*forestalling*]: There'll be no improvising, don't fret.

LEADING MAN: Then what are we to do?

DIRECTOR: Nothing. For now, just stop, look, and listen. Afterward you'll be given written parts. Right now we'll rehearse. As best we can. With them doing the rehearsing for us. [*He points to the Characters.*]

FATHER [*amid all the confusion on stage, as if he'd fallen from the clouds*]: We're rehearsing? How d'you mean?

DIRECTOR: Yes, for them. You rehearse for them. [*Indicates the Actors.*]

FATHER: But if we are the characters . . .

DIRECTOR: All right, you're characters, but, my dear sir, characters don't perform here, actors perform here. The characters are there, in the script [*He points to the* PROMPTER's *box.*] — when there *is* a script!

FATHER: Exactly! Since there isn't, and you gentlemen have the luck to have them right here, alive in front of you, those characters . . .

DIRECTOR: Oh, great! Want to do it all yourselves? Appear before the public, do the acting yourselves?

FATHER: Of course. Just as we are.

DIRECTOR [*Ironically*]: I'll bet you'd put on a splendid show!

LEADING MAN: Then what's the use of staying?

DIRECTOR [*without irony, to the Characters*]: Don't run away with the idea that you can act! That's laughable . . . [*And in fact the Actors laugh.*] Hear that? They're laughing. [*Coming back to the point*] I was forgetting. I must cast the show. It's quite easy. It casts itself. [*To the* SECOND ACTRESS] You, ma'am, will play the Mother. [*To the* FATHER] You'll have to find her a name.

FATHER: Amalia, sir.

DIRECTOR: But that's this lady's real name. We wouldn't want to call her by her real name!

FATHER: Why not? If that is her name . . . But of course, if it's to be this lady . . . [*He indicates the* SECOND ACTRESS *with a vague gesture.*] To me she [*The* MOTHER] is Amalia. But suit yourself . . . [*He is getting more and more confused.*] I don't know what to tell you . . . I'm beginning to . . . oh, I don't know . . . to find my own words ringing false, they sound different somehow.

DIRECTOR: Don't bother about that, just don't bother about it. We can always find the right sound. As for the name, if you say Amalia, Amalia it shall be; or we'll find another. For now, we'll designate the characters thus: [*To the* JUVENILE LEAD] You're the Son. [*To the* LEADING LADY] You, ma'am, are of course the Stepdaughter.

STEPDAUGHTER [*excitedly*]: What, what? That one there is me? [*She bursts out laughing.*]

DIRECTOR [*mad*]: What is there to laugh at?

LEADING LADY [*aroused*]: No one has ever dared laugh at me! I insist on respect—or I quit!

STEPDAUGHTER: But, excuse me, I'm not laughing at you.

DIRECTOR [*to the* STEPDAUGHTER]: You should consider yourself honored to be played by . . .

LEADING LADY [*without pause, contemptuously*]: —"That one there!"

STEPDAUGHTER: But I wasn't speaking of you, believe me. I was speaking of me. I don't see me in you, that's all. I don't know why . . . I guess you're just not like me!

FATHER: That's it, exactly, my dear sir! What is *expressed* in us . . .

DIRECTOR: Expression, expression! You think that's your business? Not at all!

FATHER: Well, but what *we* express . . .

DIRECTOR: But you don't. You don't express. You provide us with raw material. The actors give it body and face, voice and gesture. They've given expression to much loftier material, let me tell you. Yours is on such a small scale that, if it stands up on stage at all, the credit, believe me, should all go to my actors.

FATHER: I don't dare contradict you, sir, but it's terribly painful for us who are as you see us—with these bodies, these faces—

DIRECTOR [*cutting in, out of patience*]: —that's where make-up comes in, my dear sir, for whatever concerns the face, the remedy is make-up!

FATHER: Yes. But the voice, gesture—

DIRECTOR: Oh, for Heaven's sake! You can't exist here! Here the actor acts you, and that's that!

FATHER: I understand, sir. But now perhaps I begin to guess also why our author who saw us, alive as we are, did not want to put us on stage. I don't want to offend your actors. God forbid! But I feel that seeing myself acted . . . I don't know by whom . . .

LEADING MAN [*rising with dignity and coming over, followed by the gay young Actresses who laugh*]: By me, if you've no objection.

FATHER [*humble, smooth*]: I'm very honored, sir. [*He bows.*] But however much art and willpower the gentleman puts into absorbing me into himself . . . [*He is bewildered now.*]

LEADING MAN: Finish. Finish.

[*The Actresses laugh.*]

FATHER: Well, the performance he will give, even forcing himself with make-up to resemble me, well, with that figure [*all the Actors laugh*] he can hardly play me as I am. I shall rather be — even apart from the face — what he interprets me to be, as he feels I am — if he feels I am anything — and not as I feel myself inside myself. And it seems to me that whoever is called upon to judge us should take this into account.

DIRECTOR: So now you're thinking of what the critics will say? And I was still listening! Let the critics say what they want. We will concentrate on putting on your play! [*He walks away a little, and looks around.*] Come on, come on. Is the set ready? [*To the Actors and the Characters*] Don't clutter up the stage, I want to be able to see! [*He goes down from the stage.*] Let's not lose any more time! [*To the* STEPDAUGHTER] Does the set seem pretty good to you?

STEPDAUGHTER: Oh! But I can't recognize it!

DIRECTOR: Oh my God, don't tell me we should reconstruct Madam Pace's back room for you! [*To the* FATHER] Didn't you say a parlor with flowered wallpaper?

FATHER: Yes, sir. White.

DIRECTOR: It's not white. Stripes. But it doesn't matter. As for furniture we're in pretty good shape. That little table — bring it forward a bit! [*Stagehands do this. To the* PROPERTY MAN] Meanwhile you get an envelope, possibly a light blue one, and give it to the gentleman. [*indicating the* FATHER]

PROPERTY MAN: A letter envelope?

DIRECTOR AND FATHER: Yes, a letter envelope.

PROPERTY MAN: I'll be right back. [*He exits.*]

DIRECTOR: Come on, come on. It's the young lady's scene first. [*The* LEADING LADY *comes forward.*] No, no, wait. I said the young lady. [*Indicating the* STEPDAUGHTER] You will just watch —

STEPDAUGHTER [*adding, without pause*]: — watch me live it!

LEADING LADY [*resenting this*]: I'll know how to live it too, don't worry, once I put myself in the role!

DIRECTOR [*raising his hands to his head*]: Please! No more chatter! Now, scene one. The Young Lady with Madam Pace. Oh, and how about this Madam Pace? [*Bewildered, looking around him, he climbs back on stage.*]

FATHER: She isn't with us, sir.

DIRECTOR: Then what do we do?

FATHER: But she's alive. She's alive too.

DIRECTOR: Fine. But where?

FATHER: I'll tell you. [*Turning to the Actresses*] If you ladies will do me the favor of giving me your hats for a moment.

THE ACTRESSES [*surprised a little, laughing a little, in chorus*]: —What?—Our hats?—What does he say?—Why?—Oh, dear!

DIRECTOR: What are you going to do with the ladies' hats?

[*The Actors laugh.*]

FATHER: Oh, nothing. Just put them on these coathooks for a minute. And would some of you be so kind as to take your coats off too?

ACTORS [*as before*]: Their coats too?—And then?—He's nuts!

AN ACTRESS OR TWO [*as above*]: —But why?—Just the coats?

FATHER: Just so they can be hung there for a moment. Do me this favor. Will you?

ACTRESSES [*taking their hats off, and one or two of them their coats, too, continuing to laugh, and going to hang the hats here and there on the coathooks*]: —Well, why not?—There!—This is getting to be really funny!—Are we to put them on display?

FATHER: Exactly! That's just right, ma'am: on display!

DIRECTOR: May one inquire *why* you are doing this?

FATHER: Yes, sir. If we set the stage better, who knows but she may come to us, drawn by the objects of her trade . . . [*Inviting them to look toward the entrance at the back*] Look! Look!

[*The entrance at the back opens, and* MADAM PACE *walks a few paces downstage, a hag of enormous fatness with a pompous wig of carrot-colored wool and a fiery red rose on one side of it, à l'espagnole,*[6] *heavily made up, dressed with gauche elegance in garish red silk, a feathered fan in one hand and the other hand raised to hold a lighted cigarette between two fingers. At the sight of this apparition, the* DIRECTOR *and the Actors at once dash off the stage with a yell of terror, rushing down the stairs and making as if to flee up the aisle. The* STEPDAUGHTER, *on the other hand, runs to* MADAM PACE—*deferentially, as to her boss.*]

STEPDAUGHTER [*running to her*]: Here she is, here she is!

FATHER [*beaming*]: It's she! What did I tell you? Here she is!

DIRECTOR [*overcoming his first astonishment, and incensed now*]: What tricks are these?

[*The next four speeches are more or less simultaneous.*]

LEADING MAN: What goes on around here?

JUVENILE LEAD: Where on earth did she come from?

INGENUE: They must have been holding her in reserve.

LEADING LADY: Hocus pocus! Hocus pocus!

FATHER [*dominating these protests*]: Excuse me, though! Why, actually, would you want to destroy this prodigy in the name of vulgar truth, this miracle of a reality that is born of the stage itself—called into being by the stage, drawn here by the

---

[6] à l'espagnole: In a Spanish fashion.

stage, and shaped by the stage—and which has more right to live on the stage than you have because it is much truer? Which of you actresses will later re-create Madam Pace? This lady *is* Madam Pace. You must admit that the actress who re-creates her will be less true than this lady—who is Madam Pace. Look: My daughter recognized her, and went right over to her. Stand and watch the scene!

[*Hesitantly, the* DIRECTOR *and the Actors climb back on stage. But the scene between the* STEP-DAUGHTER *and* MADAM PACE *has begun during the protest of the Actors and the* FATHER's *answer: sotto voce, very quietly, in short naturally—as would never be possible on a stage. When, called to order by the* FATHER, *the Actors turn again to watch, they hear* MADAM PACE, *who has just placed her hand under the* STEPDAUGHTER's *chin in order to raise her head, talk unintelligibly. After trying to hear for a moment, they just give up.*]

DIRECTOR: Well?

LEADING MAN: What's she saying?

LEADING LADY: One can't hear a thing.

JUVENILE LEAD: Louder!

STEPDAUGHTER [*leaving* MADAM PACE, *who smiles a priceless smile, and walking down toward the Actors*]: Louder, huh? How d'you mean: louder? These aren't things that can be said louder. *I* was able to say them loudly—to shame him [*indicating the* FATHER]—that was my revenge. For Madam, it's different, my friends: It would mean—jail.

DIRECTOR: Oh my God! It's like that, is it? But, my dear young lady, in the theater one must be heard. And even we couldn't hear you, right here on the stage. How about an audience out front? There's a scene to be done. And anyway you *can* speak loudly—it's just between yourselves, we won't be standing here listening like now. Pretend you're alone. In a room. The back room of the shop. No one can hear you. [*The* STEPDAUGHTER *charmingly and with a mischievous smile tells him No with a repeated movement of the finger.*] Why not?

STEPDAUGHTER [*sotto voce, mysteriously*]: There's someone who'll hear if she [MADAM PACE] speaks loudly.

DIRECTOR [*in consternation*]: Is someone else going to pop up now?

[*The Actors make as if to quit the stage again.*]

FATHER: No, no, sir. She means me. I'm to be there—behind the door—waiting. And Madam knows. So if you'll excuse me. I must be ready for my entrance. [*He starts to move.*]

DIRECTOR [*stopping him*]: No, wait. We must respect the exigencies of the theater. Before you get ready—

STEPDAUGHTER [*interrupting him*]: Let's get on with it! I tell you I'm dying with desire to live it, to live that scene! If he's ready, I'm more than ready!

DIRECTOR [*shouting*]: But first we have to get that scene out of you and her! [*Indicating* MADAM PACE] Do you follow me?

STEPDAUGHTER: Oh dear, oh dear, she was telling me things you already know—that my mother's work had been badly done once again, the material is ruined, and I'm going to have to bear with her if I want her to go on helping us in our misery.

MADAM PACE [*coming forward with a great air of importance*]: Si, si, senor, porque yo no want profit. No advantage, no.[7]

DIRECTOR [*almost scared*]: What, what? She talks like *that?!*

[*All the Actors loudly burst out laughing.*]

STEPDAUGHTER [*also laughing*]: Yes, sir, she talks like that—halfway between Spanish and English—very funny, isn't it?

MADAM PACE: Now that is not good manners, no, that you laugh at me! Yo hablo[8] the English as good I can, senor!

DIRECTOR: And it *is* good! Yes! Do talk that way, ma'am! It's a surefire effect! There couldn't be anything better to, um, soften the crudity of the situation! Do talk that way! It's fine!

STEPDAUGHTER: Fine! Of course! To have certain propositions put to you in a lingo like that. Surefire, isn't it? Because, sir, it seems almost a joke. When I hear there's "an old senor" who wants to "have good time conmigo,"[9] I start to laugh—don't I, Madam Pace?

MADAM PACE: Old, viejo, no. Viejito—leetle beet old, si, darling? Better like that: If he no give you fun, he bring you prudencia.[10]

MOTHER [*jumping up, to the stupefaction and consternation of all the Actors, who had been taking no notice of her, and who now respond to her shouts with a start and, smiling, try to restrain her, because she has grabbed* MADAM PACE*'s wig and thrown it on the floor*]: Witch! Witch! Murderess! My daughter!

STEPDAUGHTER [*running over to restrain her* MOTHER]: No, no, mama, no, please!

FATHER [*running over too at the same time*]: Calm down, calm down! Sit here.

MOTHER: Then send that woman away!

STEPDAUGHTER [*to the* DIRECTOR, *who also has run over*]: It's not possible, not possible that my mother should be here!

FATHER [*also to the* DIRECTOR]: They can't be together. That's why, you see, the woman wasn't with us when we came. Their being together would spoil it, you understand.

DIRECTOR: It doesn't matter, doesn't matter at all. This is just a preliminary sketch. Everything helps. However confusing the elements, I'll piece them together somehow. [*Turning to the* MOTHER *and sitting her down again in her place*] Come along, come along, ma'am, calm down: Sit down again.

STEPDAUGHTER [*who meanwhile has moved center stage again. Turning to* MADAM PACE]: All right, let's go!

MADAM PACE: Ah, no! No thank you! Yo aqui no do nada[11] with your mother present.

STEPDAUGHTER: Oh, come on! Bring in that old senor who wants to have good time conmigo! [*Turning imperiously to all the others*] Yes, we've got to have it, this scene!—Come on, let's go! [*To* MADAM PACE] You may leave.

MADAM PACE: Ah si, I go, I go, go seguramente[12] . . . [*She makes her exit furiously,*

---

[7] **porque . . . no:** Because I don't want any profit.   [8] **Yo hablo:** I speak.   [9] **conmigo:** With me.   [10] **viejo:** Old; **Viejito:** A little old; **prudencia:** Discretion.   [11] **Yo aqui no do nada:** I will do nothing here.   [12] **seguramente:** Certainly.

putting her wig back on, and looking haughtily at the Actors who applaud mockingly.]

STEPDAUGHTER [*to the* FATHER]: And you can make your entrance. No need to go out and come in again. Come here. Pretend, you're already in. Right. Now I'm here with bowed head, modest, huh? Let's go! Speak up! With a different voice, the voice of someone just in off the street: "Hello, miss."

DIRECTOR [*by this time out front again*]: Now look: Are you directing this, or am I? [*To the* FATHER *who looks undecided and perplexed.*] Do it, yes. Go to the back. Don't leave the stage, though. And then come forward.

[*The* FATHER *does it, almost dismayed. Very pale; but already clothed in the reality of his created life, he smiles as he approaches from the back, as if still alien to the drama which will break upon him. The Actors now pay attention to the scene which is beginning.*]

DIRECTOR [*softly, in haste, to the* PROMPTER *in the box*]: And you, be ready now, ready to write!

THE SCENE

FATHER [*coming forward, with a different voice*]: Hello, miss.

STEPDAUGHTER [*with bowed head and contained disgust*]: Hello.

FATHER [*scrutinizing her under her hat which almost hides her face and noting that she is very young, exclaims, almost to himself, a little out of complaisance and a little out of fear of compromising himself in a risky adventure*]: Oh . . . — Well, I was thinking, it wouldn't be the first time, hm? The first time you came here.

STEPDAUGHTER [*as above*]: No, sir.

FATHER: You've been here other times? [*And when the* STEPDAUGHTER *nods*] More than one? [*He waits a moment for her to answer, then again scrutinizes her under her hat; smiles; then says*] Well then, hm . . . it shouldn't any longer be so . . . May I take this hat off for you?

STEPDAUGHTER [*without pause, to forestall him, not now containing her disgust*]: No, sir, I will take it off! [*And she does so in haste, convulsed.*]

[*The* MOTHER, *watching the scene with the* SON *and with the two others, smaller and more her own, who are close to her all the time, forming a group at the opposite side of the stage from the Actors, is on tenterhooks as she follows the words and actions of* FATHER *and* STEPDAUGHTER *with varied expression: grief, disdain, anxiety, horror, now hiding her face, now emitting a moan.*]

MOTHER: Oh God! My God!

FATHER [*is momentarily turned to stone by the moaning; then he reassumes the previous tone*]: Now give it to me: I'll hang it up for you. [*He takes the hat from her hands.*] But I could wish for a little hat worthier of such a dear, lovely little head! Would you like to help me choose one? From the many Madam has? — You wouldn't?

INGENUE [*interrupting*]: Oh now, come on, those are *our* hats!

DIRECTOR [*without pause, very angry*]: Silence, for Heaven's sake, don't try to be funny!—This is the stage. [*Turning back to the* STEPDAUGHTER] Would you begin again, please?

STEPDAUGHTER [*beginning again*]: No, thank you, sir.

FATHER: Oh, come on now, don't say no. Accept one from me. To please me . . . There are some lovely ones you know. And we would make Madam happy. Why else does she put them on display?

STEPDAUGHTER: No, no, sir, look: I wouldn't even be able to wear it.

FATHER: You mean because of what the family would think when they saw you come home with a new hat on? Think nothing of it. Know how to handle that? What to tell them at home?

STEPDAUGHTER [*breaking out, at the end of her rope*]: But that's not why, sir. I couldn't wear it because I'm . . . as you see me. You might surely have noticed! [*Points to her black attire.*]

FATHER: In mourning, yes. Excuse me. It's true: I do see it. I beg your pardon. I'm absolutely mortified, believe me.

STEPDAUGHTER [*forcing herself and plucking up courage to conquer her contempt and nausea*]: Enough! Enough! It's for me to thank you, it is not for you to be mortified or afflicted. Please pay no more attention to what I said. Even for me, you understand . . . [*She forces herself to smile and adds*] I need to forget I am dressed like this.

DIRECTOR [*interrupting, addressing himself to the* PROMPTER *in his box, and going up on stage again*]: Wait! Wait! Don't write. Leave that last sentence out, leave it out! [*Turning to the* FATHER *and* STEPDAUGHTER] It's going very well indeed. [*Then to the* FATHER *alone*] This is where you go into the part we prepared. [*To the Actors*] Enchanting, that little hat scene, don't you agree?

STEPDAUGHTER: Oh, but the best is just coming. Why aren't we continuing?

DIRECTOR: Patience one moment. [*Again addressing himself to the Actors*] Needs rather delicate handling, of course . . .

LEADING MAN: —With a certain *ease*—

LEADING LADY: Obviously. But there's nothing to it. [*To the* LEADING MAN] We can rehearse it at once, can't we?

LEADING MAN: As far as I'm . . . Very well, I'll go out and make my entrance. [*And he does go out by the back door, ready to re-enter.*]

DIRECTOR [*to the* LEADING LADY]: And so, look, your scene with that Madam Pace is over. I'll write it up later. You are standing . . . Hey, where are you going?

LEADING LADY: Wait. I'm putting my hat back on . . . [*She does so, taking the hat from the hook.*]

DIRECTOR: Oh yes, good. —Now, you're standing here with your head bowed.

STEPDAUGHTER [*amused*]: But she's not wearing black!

LEADING LADY: I *shall* wear black! And I'll carry it better than you!

DIRECTOR [*to the* STEPDAUGHTER]: Keep quiet, please! Just watch. You can learn something. [*Claps his hands*] Get going, get going! The entrance! [*And he goes back out front to get an impression of the stage.*]

[*The door at the back opens, and the* LEADING MAN *comes forward, with the relaxed, waggish manner of an elderly Don Juan. From the first speeches, the performance of the scene by the Actors is quite a different thing, without, however, having any element of parody in it—rather, it seems corrected, set to rights. Naturally, the* STEPDAUGHTER *and the* FATHER, *being quite unable to recognize themselves in this* LEADING LADY *and* LEADING MAN *but hearing them speak their own words express in various ways, now with gestures, now with smiles, now with open protests, their surprise, their wonderment, their suffering, etc., as will be seen forthwith. The* PROMPTER's *voice is clearly heard from the box.*[13]

LEADING MAN: Hello, miss.

FATHER [*without pause, unable to contain himself*]: No, no!

[*The* STEPDAUGHTER, *seeing how the* LEADING MAN *makes his entrance, has burst out laughing.*]

DIRECTOR [*coming from the proscenium, furious*]: Silence here! And stop that laughing at once! We can't go ahead till it stops.

STEPDAUGHTER [*coming from the proscenium*]: How can I help it? This lady [*the* LEADING LADY] just stands there. If she's supposed to be me, let me tell you that if anyone said hello to me in that manner and that tone of voice, I'd burst out laughing just as I actually did!

FATHER [*coming forward a little too*]: That's right . . . the manner, the tone . . .

DIRECTOR: Manner! Tone! Stand to one side now, and let me see the rehearsal.

LEADING MAN [*coming forward*]: If I'm to play an old man entering a house of ill—

DIRECTOR: Oh, pay no attention, please. Just begin again. It was going fine. [*Waiting for the Actors to resume*] Now then . . .

LEADING MAN: Hello, miss.

LEADING LADY: Hello.

LEADING MAN [*recreating the* FATHER's *gesture of scrutinizing her under her hat, but then expressing very distinctly first the complaisance and then the fear*]: Oh . . . Well . . . I was thinking it wouldn't be the first time, I hope . . .

FATHER [*unable to help correcting him*]: Not "I hope." "Would it?" "Would it?"

DIRECTOR: He says: "would it?" A question.

LEADING MAN [*pointing to the* PROMPTER]: I heard: "I hope."

DIRECTOR: Same thing! "Would it." Or: "I hope." Continue, continue. — Now, maybe a bit less affected . . . Look, I'll do it for you. Watch me . . . [*Returns to the stage, then repeats the bit since the entrance*] — Hello, miss.

LEADING LADY: Hello.

DIRECTOR: Oh, well . . . I was thinking . . . [*Turning to the* LEADING MAN *to have him note how he has looked at the* LEADING LADY *under her hat*] Surprise . . . fear and complaisance. [*Then, going on, and turning to the* LEADING LADY] It wouldn't be the first time, would it? The first time you came here. [*Again turning to the* LEADING MAN *with an inquiring look*] Clear? [*To the* LEADING LADY] Then you say: No, sir. [*Back to the* LEADING MAN] How shall I put it? Plasticity! [*Goes back out front.*]

LEADING LADY: No, sir.

---

[13] **the box:** In Italian rehearsals, traditionally, the prompter reads all the lines a few seconds ahead of the actors until the latter have completely memorized their roles, if indeed they ever do. [Translator's note.]

LEADING MAN: You came here other times? More than one?

DIRECTOR: No, no, wait. [*Indicating the* LEADING LADY] First let her nod. "You came here other times?"

[*The* LEADING LADY *raises her head a little, closes her eyes painfully as if in disgust, then nods twice at the word "Down" from the* DIRECTOR.]

STEPDAUGHTER [*involuntarily*]: Oh, my God! [*And she at once puts her hand on her mouth to keep the laughter in.*]

DIRECTOR [*turning round*]: What is it?

STEPDAUGHTER [*without pause*]: Nothing, nothing.

DIRECTOR [*to the* LEADING MAN]: That's your cue. Go straight on.

LEADING MAN: More than one? Well then, hm . . . it shouldn't any longer be so . . . May I take this little hat off for you?

[*The* LEADING MAN *says this last speech in such a tone and accompanies it with such a gesture that the* STEPDAUGHTER, *her hands on her mouth, much as she wants to hold herself in, cannot contain her laughter, which comes bursting out through her fingers irresistibly and very loud.*]

LEADING LADY [*returning to her place, enraged*]: Now look, I'm not going to be made a clown of by that person!

LEADING MAN: Nor am I. Let's stop.

DIRECTOR [*to the* STEPDAUGHTER, *roaring*]: Stop it! Stop it!

STEPDAUGHTER: Yes, yes. Forgive me, forgive me . . .

DIRECTOR: You have no manners! You're presumptuous! So there!

FATHER [*seeking to intervene*]: That's true, yes, that's true, sir, but forgive . . .

DIRECTOR [*on stage again*]: Forgive nothing! It's disgusting!

FATHER: Yes, sir. But believe me, it has such a strange effect—

DIRECTOR: Strange? Strange? What's strange about it?

FATHER: I admire your actors, sir, I really admire them, this gentleman [LEADING MAN] and that lady [LEADING LADY] but assuredly . . . well, they're not us . . .

DIRECTOR: So what? How *could* they be you, if they're the actors?

FATHER: Exactly, the actors! And they play our parts well, both of them. But of course, to us, they seem something else—that tries to be the same but simply isn't!

DIRECTOR: How d'you mean: isn't? What is it then?

FATHER: Something that . . . becomes theirs. And stops being ours.

DIRECTOR: Necessarily! I explained that to you!

FATHER: Yes. I understand, I do under—

DIRECTOR: Then that will be enough! [*Turning to the Actors.*] We'll be rehearsing by ourselves as we usually do. Rehearsing with authors present has always been hell, in my experience. There's no satisfying them. [*Turning to the* FATHER *and the* STEPDAUGHTER] Come along then. Let's resume. And let's hope you find it possible not to laugh this time.

STEPDAUGHTER: Oh, no, I won't be laughing this time around. My big moment comes up now. Don't worry!

DIRECTOR: Very well, when she says: "Please pay no more attention to what I said . . . Even for me—you understand . . ." [*Turning to the* FATHER] You'll have to cut right in with: "I understand, oh yes, I understand . . ." and ask her right away—

STEPDAUGHTER [*interrupting*]: Oh? Ask me what?

DIRECTOR: —why she is in mourning.

STEPDAUGHTER: No, no, look: When I told him I needed to forget I was dressed like this, do you know what his answer was? "Oh, good! Then let's take that little dress right off, shall we?"

DIRECTOR: Great! Terrific! It'll knock 'em right out of their seats!

STEPDAUGHTER: But it's the truth.

DIRECTOR: Truth, is it? Well, well, well. This is the theater! Our motto is: truth up to a certain point!

STEPDAUGHTER: Then what would you propose?

DIRECTOR: You'll see. You'll see it. Just leave me alone.

STEPDAUGHTER: Certainly not. From my nausea—from all the reasons one more cruel than another why I am what I am, why I am "that one there"—you'd like to cook up some romantic, sentimental concoction, wouldn't you? He asks me why I'm in mourning, and I tell him, through my tears, that Papa died two months ago! No, my dear sir! He has to say what he did say: "Then let's take that little dress right off, shall we?" And I, with my two-months mourning in my heart, went back there—you see? behind that screen—and—my fingers quivering with shame, with loathing—I took off my dress, took off my corset . . .

DIRECTOR [*running his hands through his hair*]: Good God, what are you saying?

STEPDAUGHTER [*shouting frantically*]: The truth, sir, the truth!

DIRECTOR: Well, yes, of course, that must be the truth . . . and I quite understand your horror, young lady. Would you try to understand that all that is impossible *on the stage*?

STEPDAUGHTER: Impossible? Then, thanks very much, I'm leaving.

DIRECTOR: No, no, look . . .

STEPDAUGHTER: I'm leaving, I'm leaving! You went in that room, you two, didn't you, and figured out "what is possible on the stage"? Thanks very much. I see it all. He wants to skip to the point where he can act out his [*exaggerating*] spiritual travail! But I want to play *my* drama. Mine!

DIRECTOR [*annoyed, and shrugging haughtily*]: Oh well, *your* drama. This is not just your drama, if I may say so. How about the drama of the others? His drama [*the* FATHER], hers [*the* MOTHER]? We can't let one character hog the limelight, just taking the whole stage over, and overshadowing all the others! Everything must be placed within the frame of one harmonious picture! We must perform only what is performable! I know as well as you do that each of us has a whole life of his own inside him and would like to bring it all out. But the difficult thing is this: to bring out only as much as is needed—in relation to the others—and in this to *imply* all the rest, *suggest* what remains inside! Oh, it would be nice if every character could come down to the footlights and tell the audience just what is brewing inside him—in a fine monologue or, if you will, a lecture! [*Good-natured, conciliatory*] Miss, you will have to *contain yourself*. And it will be in your interest. It could make a bad impression—let me warn you—this tearing fury, this desperate disgust—since, if I may say so, you confessed having been with others at Madam Pace's—before him—more than once!

STEPDAUGHTER [*lowering her head, pausing to recollect, a deeper note in her voice*]: It's true. But to me the others are also *him,* all of them equally!

DIRECTOR [*not getting it*]: The others? How d'you mean?

STEPDAUGHTER: People "go wrong." And wrong follows on the heels of wrong. Who is responsible, if not whoever it was who first brought them down? Isn't that always the case? And for me that is him. Even before I was born. Look at him, and see if it isn't so.

DIRECTOR: Very good. And if he has so much to feel guilty about, can't you appreciate how it must weigh him down? So let's at least permit him to act it out.

STEPDAUGHTER: And how, may I ask, how could he act out all that "noble" guilt, all those so "moral" torments, if you propose to spare him the horror of one day finding in his arms—after having bade her take off the black clothes that marked her recent loss—a woman now, and already gone wrong—that little girl, sir, that little girl whom he used to go watch coming out of school?

[*She says these last words in a voice trembling with emotion. The* MOTHER, *hearing her say this, overcome with uncontrollable anguish, which comes out first in suffocated moans and subsequently bursts out in bitter weeping. The emotion takes hold of everyone. Long pause.*]

STEPDAUGHTER [*as soon as the* MOTHER *gives signs of calming down, somber, determined*]: We're just among ourselves now. Still unknown to the public. Tomorrow you will make of us the show you have in mind. You will put it together in your way. But would you like to really see—our drama? Have it explode—the real thing?

DIRECTOR: Of course. Nothing I'd like better. And I'll use as much of it as I possibly can!

STEPDAUGHTER: Very well. Have this Mother here go out.

MOTHER [*ceasing to weep, with a loud cry*]: No, no! Don't allow this, don't allow it!

DIRECTOR: I only want to take a look, ma'am.

MOTHER: I can't, I just can't!

DIRECTOR: But if it's already happened? Excuse me but I just don't get it.

MOTHER: No, no, it's happening now. It's always happening. My torment is not a pretense! I am alive and present—always, in every moment of my torment—it keeps renewing itself, it too is alive and always present. But those two little ones over there—have you heard them speak? They cannot speak, sir, not any more! They still keep clinging to me—to keep my torment alive and present. For themselves they don't exist, don't exist any longer. And she [*the* STEPDAUGHTER], she just fled, ran away from me, she's lost, lost . . . If I see her before me now, it's for the same reason: to renew the torment, keep it always alive and present forever—the torment I've suffered on her account too—forever!

FATHER [*solemn*]: The eternal moment, sir, as I told you. She [*the* STEPDAUGHTER] is here to catch me, fix me, hold me there in the pillory, hanging there forever, hooked, in that single fleeting shameful moment of my life! She cannot give it up. And, actually, sir, *you* cannot spare me.

DIRECTOR: But I didn't say I wouldn't use that. On the contrary, it will be the nucleus of the whole first act. To the point where she [*the* MOTHER] surprises you.

FATHER: Yes, exactly. Because that is the sentence passed upon me: all our passion which has to culminate in her [*the* MOTHER's] final cry!

STEPDAUGHTER: It still rings in my ears. It's driven me out of my mind, that cry!—You can present me as you wish, sir, it doesn't matter. Even dressed. As long as at least my arms—just my arms—are bare. Because it was like this. [*She goes to the* FATHER *and rests her head on his chest.*] I was standing like this with my head on his chest and my arms round his neck like this. Then I saw something throbbing right here on my arm. A vein. Then, as if it was just this living vein that disgusted me, I jammed my eyes shut, like this, d'you see? and buried my head on his chest. [*Turning to the* MOTHER] Scream, scream, mama! [*Buries her head on the* FATHER's *chest and with her shoulders raised as if to avoid hearing the scream she adds in a voice stifled with torment.*] Scream as you screamed then!

MOTHER [*rushing forward to part them*]: No! My daughter! My daughter! [*Having pulled her from him*] Brute! Brute! It's my daughter, don't you see—my daughter!

DIRECTOR [*the outburst having sent him reeling to the footlights, while the Actors show dismay*]: Fine! Splendid! And now: curtain, curtain!

FATHER [*running to him, convulsed*]: Right! Yes! Because that, sir, is how it actually was!

DIRECTOR [*in admiration and conviction*]: Yes, yes, of course! Curtain! Curtain!

[*Hearing this repeated cry of the* DIRECTOR, *the* TECHNICIAN *lets down the curtain, trapping the* DIRECTOR *and the* FATHER *between curtain and footlights.*]

DIRECTOR [*looking up, with raised arms*]: What an idiot! I say Curtain, meaning that's how the act should end, and they let down the actual curtain! [*He lifts a corner of the curtain so he can get back on stage. To the* FATHER] Yes, yes, fine, splendid! Absolutely surefire! Has to end that way. I can vouch for the first act. [*Goes behind the curtain with the* FATHER.]

[*When the curtain rises we see that the stagehands have struck that first "indication of a set," and have put on stage in its stead a small garden fountain. On one side of the stage, the Actors are sitting in a row, and on the other are the Characters. The* DIRECTOR *is standing in the middle of the stage, in the act of meditating with one hand, fist clenched, on his mouth.*]

DIRECTOR [*shrugging after a short pause*]: Yes, well then, let's get to the second act. Just leave it to me as we agreed beforehand and everything will be all right.

STEPDAUGHTER: Our entrance into his house [*the* FATHER] in spite of him. [*the* SON]

DIRECTOR [*losing patience*]: Very well. But leave it all to me, I say.

STEPDAUGHTER: In spite of him. Just let that be clear.

MOTHER [*shaking her head from her corner*]: For all the good that's come out of it . . .

STEPDAUGHTER [*turning quickly on her*]: It doesn't matter. The more damage to us, the more guilt feelings for him.

DIRECTOR [*still out of patience*]: I understand, I understand. All this will be taken into account, especially at the beginning. Rest assured.

MOTHER [*supplicatingly*]: Do make them understand, I beg you, sir, for my conscience sake, for I tried in every possible way—

STEPDAUGHTER [*continuing her* MOTHER's *speech, contemptuously*]: To placate me, to advise me not to give him trouble. [*To the* DIRECTOR] Do what she wants, do it because it's true. I enjoy the whole thing very much because, look: The more she plays the suppliant and tries to gain entrance into his heart, the more he holds himself aloof: he's an absentee! How I relish this!

DIRECTOR: We want to get going—on the second act, don't we?

STEPDAUGHTER: I won't say another word. But to play it all in the garden, as you want to, won't be possible.

DIRECTOR: Why won't it be possible?

STEPDAUGHTER: Because he [*the* SON] stays shut up in his room, on his own. Then again we need the house for the part about this poor bewildered little boy, as I told you.

DIRECTOR: Quite right. But on the other hand, we can't change the scenery in view of the audience three or four times in one act, nor can we stick up signs—

LEADING MAN: They used to at one time . . .

DIRECTOR: Yes, when the audiences were about as mature as that little girl.

LEADING LADY: They got the illusion more easily.

FATHER [*suddenly, rising*]: The illusion, please don't say illusion! Don't use that word! It's especially cruel to us.

DIRECTOR [*astonished*]: And why, if I may ask?

FATHER: Oh yes, cruel, cruel! You should understand that.

DIRECTOR: What word would you have us use anyway? The illusion of creating here for our spectators—

LEADING MAN: —By our performance—

DIRECTOR: —the illusion of a reality.

FATHER: I understand, sir, but perhaps you do not understand us. Because, you see, for you and for your actors all this—quite rightly—is a game—

LEADING LADY [*indignantly interrupting*]: Game! We are not children, sir. We act in earnest.

FATHER: I don't deny it. I just mean the game of your art which, as this gentleman rightly says, must provide a perfect illusion of reality.

DIRECTOR: Yes, exactly.

FATHER: But consider this. We [*he quickly indicates himself and the other five Characters*], we have no reality outside this illusion.

DIRECTOR [*astonished, looking at his Actors who remain bewildered and lost*]: And that means?

FATHER [*after observing them briefly, with a pale smile*]: Just that, ladies and gentlemen. How should we have any other reality? What for you is an illusion, to be created, is for us our unique reality. [*Short pause. He takes several short steps toward the* DIRECTOR, *and adds*] But not for us alone, of course. Think a moment. [*He looks into his eyes.*] Can you tell me who you are? [*And he stands there pointing his first finger at him.*]

DIRECTOR [*Upset, with a half-smile*]: How do you mean, who I am? I am I.

FATHER: And if I told you that wasn't true because you are me?

DIRECTOR: I would reply that you are out of your mind. [*The Actors laugh.*]

FATHER: You are right to laugh: because this is a game. [*To the* DIRECTOR] And you can object that it's only in a game that that gentleman there [LEADING MAN], who is himself, must be me, who am *myself*. I've caught you in a trap, do you see that?

[*Actors start laughing again.*]

DIRECTOR [*Annoyed*]: You said all this before. Why repeat it?

FATHER: I won't—I didn't intend to say that. I'm inviting you to emerge from this game. [*He looks at the* LEADING LADY *as if to forestall what she might say.*] This game of art which you are accustomed to play here with your actors. Let me again ask quite seriously: Who are you?

DIRECTOR [*turning to the Actors, amazed and at the same time irritated*]: The gall of this fellow! Calls himself a character and comes here to ask me who I am!

FATHER [*dignified, but not haughty*]: A character, sir, can always ask a man who he is. Because a character really has his own life, marked with his own characteristics, by virtue of which he is always someone. Whereas, a man—I'm not speaking of you now—a man can be no one.

DIRECTOR: Oh sure. But you are asking me! And I am the manager, understand?

FATHER [*quite softly with mellifluous modesty*]: Only in order to know, sir, if you as you now are see yourself . . . for example, at a distance in time. Do you see the man you once were, with all the illusions you had then, with everything, inside you and outside, as it seemed then—as it was then for you!—Well sir, thinking back to those illusions which you don't have any more, to all those things which no longer seem to be what at one time they were for you, don't you feel, not just the boards of this stage, but the very earth beneath slipping away from you? For will not all that you feel yourself to be now, your whole reality of today, as it is now, inevitably seem an illusion tomorrow?

DIRECTOR [*who has not followed exactly, but has been staggered by the plausibilities of the argument*]: Well, well, what do you want to prove?

FATHER: Oh nothing sir. I just wanted to make you see that if *we* [*pointing again at himself and the other Characters*] have no reality outside of illusion, it would be well if you should distrust your reality because, though you breathe it and touch it today, it is destined like that of yesterday to stand revealed to you tomorrow as illusion.

DIRECTOR [*deciding to mock him*]: Oh splendid! And you'll be telling me next that you and this play that you have come to perform for me are truer and more real than I am.

FATHER [*quite seriously*]: There can be no doubt of that, sir.

DIRECTOR: Really?

FATHER: I thought you had understood that from the start.

DIRECTOR: More real than me?

FATHER: If your reality can change overnight . . .

DIRECTOR: Of course it can, it changes all the time, like everyone else's.

FATHER [*with a cry*]: But ours does not, sir. You see, that is the difference. It does not change, it cannot ever change or be otherwise because it is already fixed, it is what is, just that, forever—a terrible thing, sir!—an immutable reality. You should shudder to come near us.

DIRECTOR [*suddenly struck by a new idea, he steps in front of the* FATHER]: I should like to know, however, when anyone ever saw a character get out of his part and set about expounding and explicating it, delivering lectures on it. Can you tell me? I have never seen anything like that.

FATHER: You have never seen it, sir, because authors generally hide the travail of their creations. When characters are alive and turn up, living, before their author, all that author does is follow the words and gestures which they propose to him. He has to want them to be as they themselves want to be. Woe betide him if he doesn't! When a character is born, he at once acquires such an independence, even of his own author, that the whole world can imagine him in innumerable situations other than those the author thought to place him in. At times he acquires a meaning that the author never dreamt of giving him.

DIRECTOR: Certainly, I know that.

FATHER: Then why all this astonishment at us? Imagine what a misfortune it is for a character such as I described to you—given life in the imagination of an author who then wished to deny him life—and tell me frankly: Isn't such a character, given life and left without life, isn't he right to set about doing just what we are doing now as we stand here before you, after having done just the same—for a very long time, believe me—before *him,* trying to persuade him, trying to push him . . . I would appear before him sometimes, sometimes she [*looks at* STEP-DAUGHTER] would go to him, sometimes that poor mother . . .

STEPDAUGHTER [*coming forward as if in a trance*]: It's true. I too went there, sir, to tempt him, many times, in the melancholy of that study of his, at the twilight hour, when he would sit stretched out in his armchair, unable to make up his mind to switch the light on, and letting the evening shadows invade the room, knowing that these shadows were alive with us and that we were coming to tempt him . . . [*As if she saw herself still in that study and felt only annoyance at the presence of all of these Actors*] Oh, if only you would all go away! Leave us alone! My mother there with her son—I with this little girl—the boy there always alone—then I with him [*the* FATHER]—then I by myself, I by myself . . . in those shadows. [*Suddenly she jumps up as if she wished to take hold of herself in the vision she has of herself lighting up the shadows and alive.*] Ah my life! What scenes, what scenes we went there to propose to him: I, I tempted him more than the others.

FATHER: Right, but perhaps that was the trouble: You insisted too much. You thought you could seduce him.

STEPDAUGHTER: Nonsense. He wanted me that way. [*She comes up to the* DIRECTOR *to tell him as in confidence.*] If you ask me, sir, it was because he was so depressed, or because he despised the theater the public knows and wants . . .

DIRECTOR: Let's continue. Let's continue, for Heaven's sake. Enough theories, I'd like some facts. Give me some facts.

STEPDAUGHTER: It seems to me that we have already given you more facts than you can handle—with our entry into his [*the* FATHER's] house! You said you couldn't change the scene every five minutes or start hanging signs.

DIRECTOR: Nor can we, of course not, we have to combine the scenes and group them in one simultaneous close-knit action. Not your idea at all. You'd like to see your brother come home from school and wander through the house like a ghost, hiding behind the doors, and brooding on a plan which — how did you put it — ?

STEPDAUGHTER: — shrivels him up, sir, completely shrivels him up, sir.

DIRECTOR: "Shrivels!" What a word! All right then: His growth was stunted except for his eyes. Is that what you said?

STEPDAUGHTER: Yes, sir. Just look at him. [*She points him out next to the* MOTHER.]

DIRECTOR: Good girl. And then at the same time you want this little girl to be playing in the garden, dead to the world. Now, the boy in the house, the girl in the garden, is that possible?

STEPDAUGHTER: Happy in the sunshine! Yes, that is my only reward, her pleasure, her joy in that garden! After the misery, the squalor of a horrible room where we slept, all four of us, she with me: Just think, of the horror of my contaminated body next to hers! She held me tight, oh so tight with her loving innocent little arms! In the garden she would run and take my hand as soon as she saw me. She did not see the big flowers, she ran around looking for the teeny ones and wanted to show them to me, oh the joy of it!

[*Saying this and tortured by the memory she breaks into prolonged desperate sobbing, dropping her head onto her arms which are spread out on the work table. Everyone is overcome by her emotion. The* DIRECTOR *goes to her almost paternally and says to comfort her*]

DIRECTOR: We'll do the garden. We'll do the garden, don't worry, and you'll be very happy about it. We'll bring all the scenes together in the garden. [*Calling a stagehand by name*] Hey, drop me a couple of trees, will you, two small cypress trees, here in front of the fountain.

[*Two small cypress trees are seen descending from the flies. A* STAGEHAND *runs on to secure them with nails and a couple of braces.*]

DIRECTOR [*to the* STEPDAUGHTER]: Something to go on with anyway. Gives us an idea. [*Again calling the* STAGEHAND *by name*] Hey, give me a bit of sky.

STAGEHAND [*From above*]: What?

DIRECTOR: Bit of sky, a backcloth, to go behind that fountain. [*A white backdrop is seen descending from the flies.*] Not white, I said sky. It doesn't matter, leave it, I'll take care of it. [*Shouting*] Hey, Electrician, put these lights out. Let's have a bit of atmosphere, lunar atmosphere, blue background, and give me a blue spot on that backcloth. That's right. That's enough. [*At his command a mysterious lunar scene is created which induces the Actors to talk and move as they would on an evening in the garden beneath the moon.*] [*To* STEPDAUGHTER] You see? And now instead of hiding behind doors in the house the boy could move around here in the garden and hide behind trees. But it will be difficult, you know, to find a little girl to play the scene where she shows you the flowers. [*Turning to the* BOY] Come down this way a bit. Let's see how this can be worked out. [*And when the* BOY *doesn't move*] Come on, come on. [*Then dragging him forward he tries to make him hold his head up but it falls down again every time.*] Oh dear, another problem, this boy . . . What *is* it? . . . My God, he'll have to say something . . . [*He goes up to him, puts a hand on his shoulder and leads him behind one of the tree drops.*] Come on. Come on. Let me see. You can hide a bit here . . . Like this . . . You can stick your head out a bit to look . . . [*He goes to one side to see the effect. The* BOY *has scarcely run through the actions when the Actors are deeply affected; and they remain quite overwhelmed.*] Ah! Fine! Splendid! [*He turns again to the* STEPDAUGHTER.] If the little girl surprises him looking out and runs over to him, don't you think she might drag a few words out of him too?

STEPDAUGHTER [*jumping to her feet*]: Don't expect him to speak while *he's* here. [*She points to the* SON.] You have to send *him* away first.

SON [*going resolutely toward one of the two stairways*]: Suits me. Glad to go. Nothing I want more.

DIRECTOR [*immediately calling him*]: No. Where are you going? Wait.

[*The* MOTHER *rises, deeply moved, in anguish at the thought that he is really going. She instinctively raises her arms as if to halt him, yet without moving away from her position.*]

SON [*arriving at the footlights, where the* DIRECTOR *stops him*]: I have absolutely nothing to do here. So let me go please. Just let me go.

DIRECTOR: How do you mean, you have nothing to do?

STEPDAUGHTER [*placidly, with irony*]: Don't hold him! He won't go.

FATHER: He has to play the terrible scene in the garden with his mother.

SON [*unhesitating, resolute, proud*]: I play nothing. I said so from the start. [*To the* DIRECTOR] Let me go.

STEPDAUGHTER [*running to the* DIRECTOR *to get him to lower his arms so that he is no longer holding the* SON *back*]: Let him go. [*Then turning to the* SON *as soon as the* DIRECTOR *has let him go*] Very well, go. [*The* SON *is all set to move toward the stairs but, as if held by some occult power, he cannot go down the steps. While the Actors are both astounded and deeply troubled, he moves slowly across the footlights straight to the other stairway. But having arrived there he remains poised for the descent but unable to descend. The* STEPDAUGHTER, *who has followed him with her eyes in an attitude of defiance, bursts out laughing.*] He can't, you see. He can't. He has to stay here, has to. Bound by a chain, indissolubly. But if I who do take flight, sir, when that happens which has to happen, and precisely because of the hatred I feel for him, precisely so as not to see him again — very well, if *I* am still here and can bear the sight of him and his company — you can imagine whether *he* can go away. He who really must, must remain here with that fine father of his and that mother there who no longer has any other children. [*Turning again to the* MOTHER] Come on, Mother, come on. [*Turning again to the* DIRECTOR *and pointing to the* MOTHER] Look, she got up to hold him back. [*To the* MOTHER, *as if exerting a magical power over her*] Come. Come . . . [*Then to the* DIRECTOR] You can imagine how little she wants to display her love in front of your actors. But so great is her desire to get at him that — look, you see — she is even prepared to live her scene.

[*In fact the* MOTHER *has approached and no sooner has the* STEPDAUGHTER *spoken her last words than she spreads her arms to signify consent.*]

SON [*without pause*]: But *I* am not, *I* am not. If I can not go I will stay here, but I repeat: I will play nothing.

FATHER [*to the* DIRECTOR, *enraged*]: You can force him, sir.

SON: No one can force me.

FATHER: I will force you.

STEPDAUGHTER: Wait, wait. First the little girl must be at the fountain. [*She runs to take the* LITTLE GIRL, *drops on her knees in front of her, takes her little face in her hands.*] My poor little darling, you look bewildered with those lovely big eyes of yours. Who knows where you think you are? We are on a stage my dear. What is a stage? It is a place where you play at being serious, a place for play-acting, where we will now play-act. But seriously! For real! You too . . . [*She embraces her, presses her to her bosom and rocks her a little.*] Oh, little darling, little darling, what an ugly play you will enact! What a horrible thing has been planned for you, the garden, the fountain . . . All pretense, of course, that's the trouble, my sweet, everything is make-believe here, but perhaps for you, my child, a make-believe fountain is nicer than a real one for playing in, hmm? It will be a game for the others, but not for you, alas, because you are real, my darling, and are actually playing in a fountain that is real, beautiful, big, green with many bamboo plants reflected in it and giving it shade. Many, many ducklings can swim in it, breaking the shade to bits. You want to take hold of one of these ducklings . . . [*With a shout that fills everyone with dismay*] No! No, my Rosetta! Your mother is not looking after you because of that beast of a son. A thousand devils are loose in my head . . . and he . . . [*She leaves the* LITTLE GIRL *and turns with her usual hostility to the* BOY.] And what are you doing here, always looking like a beggar child? It will be your fault too if this little girl drowns—with all your standing around like that. As if I hadn't paid for everybody when I got you all into this house. [*Grabbing one of his arms to force him to take a hand out of his pocket*] What have you got there? What are you hiding? Let's see this hand. [*Tears his hand out of his pocket, and to the horror of everyone discovers that it holds a small revolver. She looks at it for a moment as if satisfied and then says*] Ah! Where did you get that and how? [*And as the* BOY *in his confusion, with his eyes staring and vacant all the time, does not answer her*] Idiot, if I were you I wouldn't have killed myself, I would have killed one of those two—or both of them—the father and the son! [*She hides him behind the small cypress tree from which he had been looking out, and she takes the* LITTLE GIRL *and hides her in the fountain, having her lie down in it in such a way as to be quite hidden. Finally, the* STEPDAUGHTER *goes down on her knees with her face in her hands, which are resting on the rim of the fountain.*]

DIRECTOR: Splendid! [*Turning to the* SON] And at the same time . . .

SON [*with contempt*]: And at the same time, nothing. It is not true, sir. There was never any scene between me and her. [*He points to the* MOTHER.] Let her tell you herself how it was.

[*Meanwhile the* SECOND ACTRESS *and the* JUVENILE LEAD *have detached themselves from the group of Actors. The former has started to observe the* MOTHER, *who is opposite her, very closely. And the other has started to observe the* SON. *Both are planning how they will re-create the roles.*]

MOTHER: Yes, it is true, sir. I had gone to his room.

SON: My room, did you hear that? Not the garden.

DIRECTOR: That is of no importance. We have to rearrange the action, I told you that.

SON [*noticing that the* JUVENILE LEAD *is observing him*]: What do *you* want?

JUVENILE LEAD: Nothing. I am observing you.

SON [*turning to the other side where the* SECOND ACTRESS *is*]: Ah, and here we have you to re-create the role, eh? [*He points to the* MOTHER.]

DIRECTOR: Exactly, exactly. You should be grateful, it seems to me, for the attention they are giving you.

SON: Oh yes, thank you. But you still haven't understood that you cannot do this drama. We are not inside you, not in the least, and your actors are looking at us from the outside. Do you think it's possible for us to live before a mirror which, not content to freeze us in the fixed image it provides of our expression, also throws back at us an unrecognizable grimace purporting to be ourselves?

FATHER: That is true. That is true. You must see that.

DIRECTOR [*to the* JUVENILE LEAD *and the* SECOND ACTRESS]: Very well, get away from here.

SON: No good. I won't cooperate.

DIRECTOR: Just be quiet a minute and let me hear your mother. [*To the* MOTHER] Well? You went into his room?

MOTHER: Yes sir, into his room. I was at the end of my tether. I wanted to pour out all of the anguish which was oppressing me. But as soon as he saw me come in—

SON: —There was no scene. I went away. I went away so there would be no scene. Because I have never made scenes, never, understand?

MOTHER: That's true. That's how it was. Yes.

DIRECTOR: But now there's got to be a scene between you and him. It is indispensable.

MOTHER: As for me, sir, I am ready. If only you could find some way to have me speak to him for one moment, to have me say what is in my heart.

FATHER [*going right up to the* SON, *very violent*]: You will do it! For your mother! For your mother!

SON [*more decisively than ever*]: I will do nothing!

FATHER [*grabbing him by the chest and shaking him*]: By God, you will obey! Can't you hear how she is talking to you? Aren't you her son?

SON [*grabbing his* FATHER]: No! No! Once and for all let's have done with it!

[*General agitation. The* MOTHER, *terrified, tries to get between them to separate them.*]

MOTHER [*as before*]: Please, please!

FATHER [*without letting go of the* SON]: You must obey, you must obey!

SON [*wrestling with his* FATHER *and in the end throwing him to the ground beside the little stairway, to the horror of everyone*]: What's this frenzy that's taken hold of you? To show your shame and ours to everyone? Have you no restraint? I won't cooperate, I won't cooperate! And that is how I interpret the wishes of the man who did not choose to put us on stage.

DIRECTOR: But you came here.

SON [*pointing to his* FATHER]: He came here—not me!

DIRECTOR: But aren't you here too?

SON: It was he who wanted to come, dragging the rest of us with him, and then getting together with you to plot not only what really happened, but also—as if that did not suffice—*what did not happen.*

DIRECTOR: Then tell me. Tell me what did happen. Just tell me. You came out of your room without saying a thing?

SON [*after a moment of hesitation*]: Without saying a thing. In order not to make a scene.

DIRECTOR [*driving him on*]: Very well, and then, what did you do then?

SON [*while everyone looks on in anguished attention, he moves a few steps on the front part of the stage*]: Nothing . . . crossing the garden . . . [*He stops, gloomy, withdrawn.*]

DIRECTOR [*always driving him on to speak, impressed by his reticence*]: Very well, crossing the garden?

SON [*desperate, hiding his face with one arm*]: Why do you want to make me say it, sir? It is horrible.

[*The* MOTHER *trembles all over, and stifles groans, looking toward the fountain.*]

DIRECTOR [*softly, noticing this look of hers, turning to the* SON, *with growing apprehension*]: The little girl?

SON [*looking out into the auditorium*]: Over there—in the fountain . . .

FATHER [*on the ground, pointing compassionately toward the* MOTHER]: And she followed him, sir.

DIRECTOR [*to the* SON, *anxiously*]: And then you . . .

SON [*slowly, looking straight ahead all the time*]: I ran out. I started to fish her out . . . but all of a sudden I stopped. Behind those trees I saw something that froze me: the boy, the boy was standing there, quite still. There was madness in the eyes. He was looking at his drowned sister in the fountain. [*The* STEPDAUGHTER, *who has been bent over the fountain, hiding the* LITTLE GIRL, *is sobbing desperately, like an echo from the bottom. Pause*] I started to approach and then . . .

[*From behind the trees where the* BOY *has been hiding, a revolver shot rings out.*]

MOTHER [*running up with a tormented shout, accompanied by the* SON *and all the Actors in a general tumult*]: Son! My son! [*And then amid the hubbub and the disconnected shouts of the others*] Help! Help!

DIRECTOR [*amid the shouting, trying to clear a space while the* BOY *is lifted by his head and feet and carried away behind the backcloth*]: Is he wounded, is he wounded, really?

[*Everyone except the* DIRECTOR *and the* FATHER, *who has remained on the ground beside the steps, has disappeared behind the backcloth which has served for a sky, where they can still be heard for a while whispering anxiously. Then from one side and the other of this curtain, the Actors come back on stage.*]

LEADING LADY [*re-entering from the right, very much upset*]: He's dead! Poor boy! He's dead! What a terrible thing!

LEADING MAN [*re-entering from the left, laughing*]: How do you mean, dead? Fiction, fiction, one doesn't believe such things.

OTHER ACTORS [*on the right*]: Fiction? Reality! Reality! He is dead!

OTHER ACTORS [*on the left*]: No! Fiction! Fiction!

FATHER [*rising, and crying out to them*]: Fiction indeed! Reality, reality, gentlemen, reality! [*Desperate, he too disappears at the back.*]

DIRECTOR [*at the end of his rope*]: Fiction! Reality! To hell with all of you! Lights, lights, lights! [*At a single stroke the whole stage and auditorium is flooded with very bright light. The* DIRECTOR *breathes again, as if freed from an incubus, and they all look each other in the eyes, bewildered and lost.*] Things like this don't happen to me, they've made me lose a whole day. [*He looks at his watch.*] Go, you can all go. What could we do now anyway? It is too late to pick up the rehearsal where we left off. See you this evening. [*As soon as the Actors have gone he talks to the* ELECTRICIAN *by name.*] Hey, Electrician, lights out. [*He has hardly said the words when the theater is plunged for a moment into complete darkness.*] Hey, for God's sake, leave me at least one light! I like to see where I am going!

[*Immediately, from behind the backcloth, as if the wrong switch had been pulled, a green light comes on which projects the silhouettes, clear-cut and large, of the Characters, minus the* BOY *and the* LITTLE GIRL. *Seeing the silhouettes, the* DIRECTOR, *terrified, rushes from the stage. At the same time the light behind the backcloth goes out and the stage is again lit in nocturnal blue as before.*

Slowly, from the right side of the curtain, the SON *comes forward first, followed by the* MOTHER *with her arms stretched out toward him; then from the left side, the* FATHER. *They stop in the middle of the stage and stay there as if in a trance. Last of all from the right, the* STEPDAUGHTER *comes out and runs toward the two stairways. She stops on the first step, to look for a moment at the other three, and then breaks into a harsh laugh before throwing herself down the steps; she runs down the aisle between the rows of seats; she stops one more time and again laughs, looking at the three who are still on stage; she disappears from the auditorium, and from the lobby her laughter is still heard. Shortly thereafter the curtain falls.*]

✎ RAINER MARIA RILKE
B. PRAGUE, 1875–1926

Rainer Maria Rilke lived a life full of contradictions. A native speaker of German, he was a spiritual citizen of France and the rest of the European continent during most of his adult life. Though hyperconscious of his role as a poet and solitary figure, he was also a sensual, neurotically dependent man involved in a lifelong relationship with a powerful and famous woman. Rilke spent his life in a kind of self-imposed exile, wandering through Russia, France, Italy, and Germany making observations, visiting museums, libraries, parks, gardens, and bookstores, and writing — poems, notebooks, and letters. In the broadest terms, his was a religious quest in search of a wholeness that would counter the fragmentation and sadness of the modern world.

www   For links to more information about Rilke and a quiz on his poetry and for more on the culture and context of Europe in the twentieth century, see *World Literature Online* at bedfordstmartins .com/worldlit.

Rilke reacted to the ugliness and materialism of modern society by deliberately withdrawing from the world, and in the tradition of the nineteenth-century SYMBOLISTS focused on the reality of art, which could reconcile and harmonize disparate elements. Like many other artists of the World War I period, Rilke turned inward for refuge. He was attacked by the generation to follow for his lack of concern for society in general; but in fact he had tremendous sympathy for the downtrodden. He gloried in the mysteries of childhood, the magic of animals, and the feelings of women. Out of the rich tapestry of his quasi-mystical personality and the visual imagery in his work emerged the most important German poet since Goethe.[1]

Passionate Relations.   Rilke was born in Prague of Austrian parents in 1875. His father, Josef, although briefly the commander of the citadel at Brescia during the Franco-Austrian War in 1859, served most of his life as a minor railroad official. His mother, Sophie or "Phia," a writer whose privately printed book of aphorisms shows feminist leanings, appears to have dominated Rilke's early life both emotionally and artistically. Rilke was also pressured by an uncle who pushed him toward military school. His mother had wanted a daughter and thus named her son Maria and dressed him in girl's clothing until he was six. Rilke's dependence on his mother was matched by his fury at her influence on his life; his remarks about her in later years are scathing:

> When I must see this lost, unreal, entirely unrelated woman, who cannot grow old, then I feel that I tried to get away from her even as a child and am deeply afraid that after years and years of running and walking I am still not far enough from her, that I still have somewhere in me inner movements which are the other half of her withered gestures, broken pieces of memory which she carries in her; I am horrified then at her distracted piety, her obstinate faith, all the disfigured and distorted things she clings to, herself empty as a dress, ghostlike and terrible. And that I am yet her child; that some hardly recognizable wallpaper door in this faded wall, which belongs nowhere, was my entrance into the world (if indeed such an entrance can lead to the world).

The major influence on Rilke's life after his mother was Lou Andreas-Salomé, daughter of a Russian general whom Rilke met in Munich while he was establishing a reputation as a writer. He was twenty-two, Andreas-Salomé thirty-six. She had already had romantic and intellectual relationships with a number of famous men, including Nietzsche and his friend, the philosopher Paul Ree. She then married a lecturer on the Orient at the University of Berlin, Friedrich Carl Andreas. Rilke fell in love with her, besieging her with flowers and poems, and became her lover in the summer of 1897. She encouraged his journey to Italy in 1898 and

---

[1] **Goethe:** Johann Wolfgang von Goethe (1749–1832), a German novelist and intellectual who wrote *The Sorrows of Young Werther* (1774) and *Faust* (1808, 1832). See Book 5.

introduced him to Russian culture in 1899, inviting him on a tour along with her husband. Their sexual relationship appeared to liberate Rilke — the substance of his poetry changed, taking on a celebratory quality — and she candidly remarked of it at a later time:

> If I belonged to you for some years it was because you represented absolute reality for me for the first time, body and person indistinguishably one and the same, an unquestionable element of life itself.

Rilke destroyed many poems to Andreas-Salomé, but some remain in his volume *The Book of Hours*. One reads:

> Put out my eyes, and I can see you,
> wall up my ears, and I shall hear,
> and without limbs, I will draw near,
> and without mouth I call your name.
> Break off my arms, I shall embrace you
> with all my heart, as with a hand;
> throw my heart shut, my brain will face you,
> and if you fan my brain to flame,
> my blood shall carry and encase you.

Philosophy and Art.   As Andreas-Salomé soon recognized, Rilke was a depressive personality, returning obsessively to feelings of spiritual alienation. Though not a systematic philosopher, he had studied the works of Kierkegaard[2] and Nietzsche,[3] especially concerning humanity's distance from God and isolation in the universe. These concerns, coupled with his temporary separation from Andreas-Salomé and other friends after his unhappy marriage to Clara Westhoff in 1901, led to his semi-autobiographical novel *The Notebooks of Malte Laurids Brigge* and the poems that would make up *The Book of Hours* and *New Poems, First and Second Series* in the years immediately after. The dominant note of loneliness in these writings, which is often made into a virtue, may be seen in the early poem "Autumn Day" from *The Book of Pictures*, published in 1902.

Some of Rilke's most famous poems were written in the two collections of *New Poems*, published in 1907 and 1908. These show the benefit of his studies in art, particularly his Italian tour in 1898 and his association with the French sculptor Auguste Rodin[4] (1840–1917) after 1900.

---

[2] **Kierkegaard:** Søren Kierkegaard (1813–1855), a Danish philosopher and religious writer who emphasized self-examination and the subjectivity of truth. His works include *The Concluding Unscientific Postscript* (1846) and *Either/Or* (1843). See Book 5.

[3] **Nietzsche:** Friedrich Wilhelm Nietzsche (1844–1900), German philosopher known for his attack on the "slave morality" of Judaeo-Christian culture and his celebration of the "superman"; his works include *Thus Spake Zarathustra* (1883–1891) and *Beyond Good and Evil* (1886).

[4] **Auguste Rodin** (1840–1917): French sculptor associated with realistic figures: his best-known works are *The Thinker* in bronze and *The Kiss* in marble.

C. F. MacIntyre, a
mid-twentieth-
century critic and
translator, described
Rilke in the period
from 1900 to 1908,
"as a man who
during a certain
period of his life rode
the twin fillies of the
wing'd horse, sculp-
ture and painting,
keeping a firm foot
on each, and singing
as he went, his beau-
tifully formed and
colored sonnets, or
polishing and paint-
ing small concert and
salon pieces, sonatas
in miniature."

In poems like "The Panther" and "Archaic Torso of Apollo," Rilke uses detailed observations to evoke the living quality of his subjects. Art takes on an active role, promoting the only useful kind of activity possible in the world, that of transformation.

Duino Castle and the Elegies.   In his busiest period, between 1900 and 1910, Rilke began appealing to wealthy and influential patrons, often clever and talented women. In 1911, he stayed with Princess Marie von Thurn und Taxis-Hohenlohe at Duino Castle in Italy, where he conceived his greatest work, *Duino Elegies.* He wrote two elegies there, leaving his sanctuary for a series of travels abroad, and completed a third elegy in Paris in 1913. He left Paris for Munich in July 1914, where he wrote a fourth elegy late in the year, just before being drafted as a private in the Austrian army at age forty. He was transferred to the Austrian War Ministry and left the army the following year. At that point his writing underwent a long period of paralysis. Rilke did not complete the rest of the cycle of *Duino Elegies* until February 1922, when in a small castle in Switzerland named the Château de Muzot, leased and later purchased for him by friends, he wrote the last six elegies as well as most of *Sonnets to Orpheus* in a single week. Rilke died from complications from a previously undetected form of leukemia in 1926, a few years after completing *Elegies* and *Sonnets.*

The Early Lyrics.   As Rilke matured as a writer his poems became quite complex and allusive, but his early lyrics are accessible, highly fashioned pieces of art. C. F. MacIntyre describes the Rilke of the period from 1900 to 1908 "as a man who during a certain period of his life rode the twin fillies of the wing'd horse, sculpture and painting, keeping a firm foot on each, and singing as he went, his beautifully formed and colored sonnets, or polishing and painting small concert and salon pieces, sonatas in miniature." In 1900 Rilke lived in Worpswede, a colony of painters, and had opportunity to observe visual artists at work. In 1902 he met Rodin, became his secretary, and wrote a book about him. Rodin's craft is reflected in Rilke's poems about statues, animals, people, and architecture.

Although quite different from Keats's "Ode to Autumn," Rilke's "Autumn Day" is certainly within the Romantic tradition of linking the autumnal season to a state of mind or feelings. The last stanza connects autumn to a stage of life and concludes that patterns have largely been set for old age. The most noteworthy quality about "The Panther," one of the first poems in the new collection, is its focus on the creature's gaze as it crosses back and forth behind the bars of its cage. Here Rilke makes visual perspective the center of his poem's content. In a 1914 letter to Rudolf Kassner, an Austrian writer, Rilke describes what he calls "in-seeing": "I love in-seeing. Can you imagine with me how glorious it is to in-see a dog, for example . . . by *in-see* I don't mean to look *through* . . . what I mean is to let yourself precisely into the dog's center, the point from which it begins to be a dog, the place in it where God, as it were, would have sat down for a moment when the dog was finished, in order to watch it during its first embarrassments and inspirations and to nod that it was good, that nothing was lacking, that it couldn't have been better made." "The Panther," a poem about a caged animal, is also about the poet living in a caged world. The meaning of the last stanza is ambiguous; what, after all, is the effect of the moment of consciousness that lifts the panther's pupils?

"Archaic Torso of Apollo" begins with a sudden recognition that the sculpture, even in its incomplete state, is filled with a life force. Rilke dramatizes his studies of classical art by making the rippling chest and curved loins of Apollo stand for sexual energy. At one extreme is the animal nature of this energy; at another, it becomes a transcendent and perfect star that reflects the inadequacies of the reader. Then comes the urgent mandate: "You must change your life."

The mythic story of Leda and the swan, the basis for Rilke's poem "Leda," was a favorite story in ancient Greece and has been used by a number of artists and poets since. In Rilke's "Leda," as well as in W. B. Yeats's **"Leda and the Swan,"** the interest lies in the confrontation between the two realms, the godhead and the mortal, and in what takes place when these two meet. p. 195

The last lyric presented here, "The Buddha in the Glory," also was inspired by a statue and is the climactic, final poem in *New Poems, Second Part.* While most of the other poems in that collection were grounded in the world of people and objects, the Buddha becomes the self-contained seed of the transcendent, spiritual realm.

Duino Elegies. In *The Notebooks of Malte Laurids Brigge,* Rilke comments on his early work and the sources of creativity: "Alas, those verses one writes in youth aren't much. One should wait and gather sweetness and light all his life . . . and then maybe at the end he might write ten good lines. For poetry isn't, as people imagine, merely feelings (these come soon enough); it is experiences. To write one line, a man ought to see many cities, people, and things; he must learn to know animals and the way of birds in the air, and how little flowers open in the morning . . . one must have memories of many nights of love, no two alike . . . and the screams of women in childbed . . . one must have sat by the dying, one must have sat by the dead in a room with open windows."

The conclusion of a poem from 1914 called "Turning-point" ("Wendung") suggests a new direction for a maturing Rilke:

Work of the eyes is done, now
go and do heart-work
on all the images imprisoned creatures within you; for you
overpowered them: but even now you don't know them.
Learn, inner man, to look on your inner woman,
the one attained from a thousand
natures, the merely attained but
not yet beloved form.

Walking along the Adriatic seashore at Duino Castle, reputedly once a place of refuge for the Florentine exile Dante,[5] Rilke seemed to hear the first line of the first elegy rise directly from the boiling sea: "Who, if I cried out, would hear me among the angels' hierarchies?" After sketching the terrifying remoteness of the angels and the theme of transcendence presented as an object both of admiration and terror, Rilke considers the artist's lonely life of creation here on earth. He turns to the condition of the unfulfilled, both those unfulfilled in passion and those who have died young. To answer the question in the second stanza, "Ah, whom can we ever turn to in our need?" Rilke eventually looks inward; the real power, he seems to say, comes from that which is stored up inside us. This is the power of art; he contrasts it with the natural passions, which are expended by normal living.

Sonnets to Orpheus.   The unworldliness of art, its home among the isolated, the unfulfilled, and the early dead—themes of the first elegy—are transformed in Rilke's last major work, *Sonnets to Orpheus,* in which he commemorates the early death at age eighteen of a talented dancer, Vera Ouckama Knoop, the daughter of a friend. Rilke chose the title because, as he tells the grieving mother, Orpheus, the "singing god," speaks through him. In these poems he turns lament into praise, just as in *Elegies* he transforms the fear of the angels into a song that rivals angelic music. Put another way, the abstraction of *Elegies* is given shape in *Sonnets,* where grief is transformed into rejoicing and the angel of transcendence is turned into the spirit of Orpheus and eventually into Eurydice, the "inner woman" of the poem "Turning."

In many respects Rilke's work was a working out of an interior monologue unconnected with the destruction that lay about him at the end of World War I. Like his fellow writer from Prague Franz Kafka,[6] Rilke was a citizen of no country; a practitioner of art, he employed a rich personal symbolism in order to create an aesthetic image of the world. Incapable of sustaining a human relationship, his real strength lay in his refusal to allow the daily claims of life to overwhelm him. With William Butler Yeats, Marcel Proust, James Joyce,[7] and a few others, he was one of the artistic geniuses of modernism; after him would come a generation of more practical men and women hoping to portray the world realistically and at the same time make it nearer to their liking.

---

[5] **Dante** (1265–1321): One of the greatest Italian poets, he wrote *The Divine Comedy,* the journey of a pilgrim through hell, purgatory, and heaven.

[6] **Franz Kafka** (1883–1924): Known for his nightmarish writings about modern life, including *The Metamorphosis* (1915) and *The Penal Colony* (1919). See p. 423.

[7] **William Butler Yeats . . . Joyce:** Yeats (1865–1939), an Irish poet; see p. 181. Marcel Proust (1871–1922), a French novelist known for his sixteen-volume *Remembrance of Things Past.* James Joyce (1882–1941), an Irish novelist; see p. 366.

■ CONNECTIONS

W. B. Yeats, "Sailing to Byzantium," p. 194. Poets have long contrasted the eternal existence of works of art with the passing, sensual frailty of mortal existence. Yeats's "Sailing to Byzantium" presents that city as a symbol of artistic brilliance and achievement, "Monuments of unageing intellect." What is Rilke doing differently in "Archaic Torso of Apollo" by transforming a statue into a living presence that can transform lives?

Adrienne Rich, "I Dream I'm the Death of Orpheus," p. 995. Orpheus, with his capacity for turning suffering into art and his ability to descend into the Underworld, has been a popular model for artists and writers in the West. Adrienne Rich provides a new twist to this tradition by adopting the point of view of Eurydice and pointing toward women's emancipation struggle. How does Rilke use the Orpheus myth in his sonnets?

John Keats, "To Autumn" (Book 5). The influence of nineteenth-century Romanticism on twentieth-century European poets can often be seen in their attitudes toward nature and their use of images drawn from nature. Keats's "Ode to Autumn" recognizes the inevitable changes of the seasons and celebrates the numerous meanings of harvest. How does the ripeness of fruit in Rilke point beyond harvest to the solitude of someone who is in the "autumn" of his or her life?

■ FURTHER RESEARCH

English Editions
Herder-Norton, M. D. *Sonnets to Orpheus.* 1942.
Kinnell, Galway, and Hannah Leibmann. *The Essential Rilke.* 1999.
Leishman, J. B., and Stephen Spender. *The Duino Elegies.* 1939.
MacIntyre, C. F. *Selected Poems.* 1962.
Mitchell, Stephen. *The Selected Poetry of Rainer Maria Rilke.* 1989.
Snow, Edward. *Uncollected Poems of Rainer Maria Rilke.* 1997.

Historical Background
Bernstein, Michael André. *Five Portraits: Modernity and the Imagination in Twentieth-Century German Writing.* 2000.

Biography
Hendry, J. F. *The Sacred Threshold: A Life of Rainer Maria Rilke.* 1983.
Leppmann, Wolfgang. *Rilke: A Life.* 1984.

Criticism
Heep, Hartmut. *A Different Poem: Rainer Maria Rilke's American Translators: Randall Jarrell, Robert Lowell, and Robert Bly.* 1996.
Peters, H. F. *Rainer Maria Rilke: Masks and the Man.* 1977.
Sword, Helen. *Engendering Inspiration: Visionary Strategies in Rilke, Lawrence, and H. D.* 1995.

ᘒ Autumn Day

Translated by C. F. MacIntyre

Lord, it is time. The summer was too long.
Lay now thy shadow over the sundials,
and on the meadows let the winds blow strong.

Bid the last fruit to ripen on the vine;
allow them still two friendly southern days
to bring them to perfection and to force
the final sweetness in the heavy wine.

Who has no house now will not build him one.
Who is alone now will be long alone,
will waken, read, and write long letters
and through the barren pathways up and down
restlessly wander when dead leaves are blown.

10

Early Lyrics. The "Archaic Torso of Apollo" was probably inspired by the fifth-century B.C.E. *Torso of a Youth from Miletus,* one of three torsos of Apollo in the Archaic Room of the Louvre Museum in Paris.

The story of Leda is very popular among Western artists and writers, as is any encounter between the gods and mortals. According to Greek myth, Zeus took the form of a swan in order to seduce Leda, who then became the mother of quadruplets: Pollux and Helen, by Zeus, and Castor and Clytemnestra, by Tyndareus, her mortal husband.

"The Buddha in the Glory" was published as the last poem of *New Poems.* In a letter to Clara Rilke in 1905, he describes a Buddha below his window: "Soon after supper I retire, and am in my little house by 8:30 at the latest. Then I have in front of me the vast blossoming starry night, and below, in front of the window, the gravel walk goes up a little hill on which, in fanatic taciturnity, a statue of the Buddha rests, distributing, with silent discretion, the unutterable self-consciousness of his gesture beneath all the skies of the day and night. C'est le centre du monde [He is the center of the world], I say to Rodin."

A note on the translation: The two translators of these lyrics, C. F. MacIntyre and Stephen Mitchell, do an excellent job of rendering the complexities of Rilke's German into English. All notes are the editors'.

༄ The Panther

Translated by Stephen Mitchell

In the Jardin des Plantes, Paris

His vision, from the constantly passing bars,
has grown so weary that it cannot hold
anything else. It seems to him there are
a thousand bars; and behind the bars, no world.

As he paces in cramped circles, over and over,
the movement of his powerful soft strides
is like a ritual dance around a center
in which a mighty will stands paralyzed.

10   Only at times, the curtain of the pupils
lifts, quietly——. An image enters in,
rushes down through the tensed, arrested muscles,
plunges into the heart and is gone.

༄ Archaic Torso of Apollo

Translated by Stephen Mitchell

We cannot know his legendary head
with eyes like ripening fruit. And yet his torso
is still suffused with brilliance from inside,
like a lamp, in which his gaze, now turned to low,

gleams in all its power. Otherwise
the curved breast could not dazzle you so, nor could
a smile run through the placid hips and thighs
to that dark center where procreation flared.[1]

---

[1] **procreation flared:** This particular phrase raises a problem for the translator. Rilke uses the German *Zeugung*, which literally means "procreation" or "breeding." The question is whether the word "procreation" carries the bright, flaming sexuality envisioned by Rilke. C. F. MacIntyre's translation reads "where the genitals burned."

Otherwise this stone would seem defaced
10   beneath the translucent cascade of the shoulders
and would not glisten like a wild beast's fur:

would not; from all the borders of itself,
burst like a star: for here there is no place
that does not see you. You must change your life.

Leda

Translated by C. F. MacIntyre

When the god in his need advanced toward
the swan, its beauty left him nigh dismayed;
but, though perplexed, he vanished in the bird.
Already his deft trickery betrayed

it to the deed before he had yet proved
the untried creature's feelings. But *she* knew
already who was in the swan and moved
the outcome of the one thing she must do.

Struggling and confused, she knew not whither
10   to hide from him, nor how she could withstand . . .
his neck slipped through her ever-weakening hands,

and in the belov'd he let his godhead leap.
Then he first felt delight in all his feathers
and verily became swan in her lap.

The Buddha in the Glory

Translated by C. F. MacIntyre

Center of centers, of all seeds the germ,
O almond self-enclosed[1] and growing sweeter,
from here clear to the starry swarms
your fruit's flesh grows. I greet you.

---

[1] **almond self-enclosed:** An almond-shaped aureole (called the *vesica piscis* in Latin) is used in early Christian art to surround the figure of Jesus or Mary; in Italian this shape is called a *mandorla* and indicates divinity as well as a threshold between worlds.

Lo, you feel how nothing more depends
on you; into infinity your shell
waxes; there the strong sap works and fills you.
And from beyond a gloriole descends

10

to help, for high above your head your suns,
full and fulgurating, turn.
And yet, already in you is begun
something which longer than the suns shall burn.

ᚙ Duino Elegies

Translated by Stephen Mitchell

THE FIRST ELEGY

Who, if I cried out, would hear me among the angels'[1]
hierarchies? and even if one of them pressed me
suddenly against his heart: I would be consumed
in that overwhelming existence. For beauty is nothing
but the beginning of terror, which we still are just able to endure,
and we are so awed because it serenely disdains
to annihilate us. Every angel is terrifying.
      And so I hold myself back and swallow the call-note
of my dark sobbing. Ah, whom can we ever turn to

10 in our need? Not angels, not humans,

The First Elegy. *Duino Elegies (Duinester Elegien)* was written over the years 1912 to 1923, the year it was published. The individual elegies reflect the feelings of desolation of the World War I period. The sections of the elegies that are abstract and philosophical tend to be difficult to understand, as Rilke wrestles with the idealistic claims of art versus the transiency and volatility of life. In our selection, Rilke deals with the ultimate claims of the infinite and transcendent while acknowledging the human longing for the immanent, or that which is sensual and tangible. In a letter to his Polish translator, Witold Hulewicz, Rilke deals with the themes of his elegies, one of which involves the visible and the invisible: "It is our task to imprint this temporary, perishable earth into ourselves so deeply, so painfully and passionately, that its essence can rise again, 'invisibly,' inside us. We are the bees of the invisible. We wildly collect the honey of the visible, to store it in the great golden hive of the invisible."

---

[1] **angels:** Rilke is not referring to Christian angels; he explains in a letter to Witold Hulewicz: "The angel of the Elegies is that creature in whom the transformation of the visible into the invisible, which we are accomplishing, already appears in its completion . . . ; that being who guarantees the recognition of a higher level of reality in the invisible. — Therefore 'terrifying' for us, because we, its lovers and transformers, still cling to the visible."

and already the knowing animals are aware
that we are not really at home in
our interpreted world.[2] Perhaps there remains for us
some tree on a hillside, which every day we can take
into our vision; there remains for us yesterday's street
and the loyalty of a habit so much at ease
when it stayed with us that it moved in and never left.
      Oh and night: there is night, when a wind full of infinite space
gnaws at our faces. Whom would it not remain for — that longed-after,

20 mildly disillusioning presence, which the solitary heart
so painfully meets. Is it any less difficult for lovers?
But they keep on using each other to hide their own fate.
      Don't you know *yet*? Fling the emptiness out of your arms
into the spaces we breathe; perhaps the birds
will feel the expanded air with more passionate flying.

Yes — the springtimes needed you. Often a star
was waiting for you to notice it. A wave rolled toward you
out of the distant past, or as you walked
under an open window, a violin

30 yielded itself to your hearing. All this was mission.
But could you accomplish it? Weren't you always
distracted by expectation, as if every event
announced a beloved? (Where can you find a place
to keep her, with all the huge strange thoughts inside you
going and coming and often staying all night.)
But when you feel longing, sing of women in love;
for their famous passion is still not immortal. Sing
of women abandoned and desolate (you envy them, almost)
who could love so much more purely than those who were gratified.

40 Begin again and again the never-attainable praising;
remember: the hero lives on; even his downfall was
merely a pretext for achieving his final birth.
But Nature, spent and exhausted, takes lovers back
into herself, as if there were not enough strength
to create them a second time. Have you imagined
Gaspara Stampa[3] intensely enough so that any girl
deserted by her beloved might be inspired
by that fierce example of soaring, objectless love
and might say to herself, "Perhaps I can be like her"?

---

[2] **our interpreted world**: Unlike animals, human beings interpret reality and are therefore separate from it.

[3] **Gaspara Stampa** (1523–1554): Italian noblewoman who wrote some two hundred sonnets about how she was abandoned by Count Collalto.

50 Shouldn't this most ancient of sufferings finally grow
more fruitful for us? Isn't it time that we lovingly
freed ourselves from the beloved and, quivering, endured:
as the arrow endures the bowstring's tension, so that
gathered in the snap of release it can be more than
itself. For there is no place where we can remain.

Voices. Voices. Listen, my heart, as only
saints have listened: until the gigantic call lifted them
off the ground; yet they kept on, impossibly,
kneeling and didn't notice at all:
60 so complete was their listening. Not that you could endure
God's voice — far from it. But listen to the voice of the wind
and the ceaseless message that forms itself out of silence.
It is murmuring toward you now from those who died young.[4]
Didn't their fate, whenever you stepped into a church
in Naples or Rome, quietly come to address you?
Or high up, some eulogy entrusted you with a mission,
as, last year, on the plaque in Santa Maria Formosa.[5]
What they want of me is that I gently remove the appearance
of injustice about their death — which at times
70 slightly hinders their souls from proceeding onward.
Of course, it is strange to inhabit the earth no longer,
to give up customs one barely had time to learn,
not to see roses and other promising Things
in terms of a human future; no longer to be
what one was in infinitely anxious hands; to leave
even one's own first name behind, forgetting it
as easily as a child abandons a broken toy.
Strange to no longer desire one's desires. Strange
to see meanings that clung together once, floating away
80 in every direction. And being dead is hard work
and full of retrieval before one can gradually feel
a trace of eternity. — Though the living are wrong to believe
in the too-sharp distinctions which they themselves have created.
Angels (they say) don't know whether it is the living
they are moving among, or the dead. The eternal torrent

---

[4] **those who died young:** In Padua, Rilke visited the tombstones of young men who had died as students at the university.

[5] **plaque . . . Formosa:** Santa Maria Formosa was a church in Venice that Rilke visited in 1911; in it a plaque carried the words of Willem Hellemans, who died in 1593: (in translation) "I lived for others while life lasted; now, after death, / I have not perished, but in cold marble I live for myself. . . ."

whirls all ages along in it, through both realms
forever, and their voices are drowned out in its thunderous roar.

In the end, those who were carried off early no longer need us:
they are weaned from earth's sorrows and joys, as gently as children
90   outgrow the soft breasts of their mothers. But we, who do need
such great mysteries, we for whom grief is so often
the source of our spirit's growth—: could we exist without *them*?
Is the legend meaningless that tells how, in the lament for Linus,[6]
the daring first notes of song pierced through the barren numbness;
and then in the startled space which a youth as lovely as a god
had suddenly left forever, the Void felt for the first time
that harmony which now enraptures and comforts and helps us.

---

[6]**lament for Linus:** Linus was a legendary poet-musician first mentioned by Homer in *The Iliad* (XVIII.569–72); there are different versions of his death, but it is thought that the lament was sung in the autumn for harvested crops or dying vegetation.

∿ Sonnets to Orpheus

Translated by Stephen Mitchell

I, 1

A tree ascended there. Oh pure transcendence!
Oh Orpheus sings! Oh tall tree in the ear!
And all things hushed. Yet even in that silence
a new beginning, beckoning, change appeared.

Creatures of stillness crowded from the bright
unbound forest, out of their lairs and nests;

Sonnets to Orpheus. First published as *Die Sonette an Orpheus* in 1923, fifty-nine of the elegies in this collection were written in less than a month after the completion of *Duino Elegies*. After wandering from city to city in the wake of World War I, Rilke settled in the solitude of the Château de Muzot, a small house in the Valais region of Switzerland in the winter of 1922. A friend had left a pen and an ink drawing of Orpheus playing for an audience of birds and animals tacked to the wall opposite Rilke's desk when she left Muzot in 1921. Rilke read the story of Orpheus and Eurydice in a French prose version of Ovid's *Metamorphoses* and learned how even rocks and trees gathered to hear Orpheus's enchanted singing. Early in the sonnets presented here, Rilke announces the importance of listening to Orpheus, who is worthy of attention because he has journeyed to the underworld to retrieve his dead wife, Eurydice.

and it was not from any dullness, not
from fear, that they were so quiet in themselves,

but from simply listening. Bellow, roar, shriek
seemed small inside their hearts. And where there had been
just a makeshift hut to receive the music,

a shelter nailed up out of their darkest longing,
with an entryway that shuddered in the wind—
you built a temple deep inside their hearing.

I, 2

And it was almost a girl[1] who, stepping from
this single harmony of song and lyre,
appeared to me through her diaphanous form
and made herself a bed inside my ear.

And slept in me. Her sleep was everything:
the awesome trees, the distances I had felt
so deeply that I could touch them, meadows in spring:
all wonders that had ever seized my heart.

She slept the world. Singing god, how was that first
sleep so perfect that she had no desire
ever to wake? See: she arose and slept.

Where is her death now? Ah, will you discover
this theme before your song consumes itself?—
Where is she vanishing? . . . A girl, almost . . . .

I, 3

A god can do it. But will you tell me how
a man can penetrate through the lyre's strings?
Our mind is split. And at the shadowed crossing
of heart-roads, there is no temple for Apollo.[2]

Song, as you have taught it, is not desire,
not wooing any grace that can be achieved;

---

[1] **almost a girl:** See the lines from Rilke's poem "Turning-point" (p. 249): "Learn, inner man, to look on your inner woman. . . ." The creative spirit within is feminine.

[2] **no temple for Apollo:** The sanctuaries that stood at the crossroads in ancient Greece were dedicated to gods of the underworld like Hecate, not to a god of light like Apollo.

song is reality. Simple, for a god.
But when can *we* be real? When does he pour

the earth, the stars, into us? Young man,
10 it is not your loving, even if your mouth
was forced wide open by your own voice — learn

to forget that passionate music. It will end.
True singing is a different breath, about
nothing. A gust inside the god. A wind.

I, 5

Erect no gravestone to his memory; just
let the rose blossom each year for his sake.
For it *is* Orpheus. Wherever he has passed
through this or that. We do not need to look

for other names. When there is poetry,
it is Orpheus singing.[3] He lightly comes and goes.
Isn't it enough if sometimes he can stay
with us a few days longer than a rose?

Though he himself is afraid to disappear,
10 he *has* to vanish: don't you understand?
The moment his word steps out beyond our life here,

he moves where you will never find his trace.
The lyre's strings do not constrict his hands.
And it is in overstepping that he obeys.

---

[3] **When . . . singing:** In a letter to Nanny Wunderly-Volkart in 1920, Rilke wrote: "Ultimately there is only *one* poet, that infinite one who makes himself felt, here and there through the ages, in a mind that can surrender to him."

❧ THOMAS MANN
B. GERMANY, 1875–1955

Thomas Mann was one of the monumental figures of his time, an author whose cultural awareness, understanding of history, psychological depth, and command of the novel as a literary form made him a worthy successor to his nineteenth-century predecessors, Gustave Flaubert, Fyodor Dostoyevsky, and Leo Tolstoy.[1] He was regarded as the modern inheritor of the German literary tradition, which included Johann Wolfgang von Goethe and Friedrich Schiller.[2] Mann, who was richly endowed with the German cultural heritage of the nineteenth century, especially the philosophical works of Arthur Schopenhauer and Friedrich Nietzsche and the Romantic music of Richard Wagner,[3] was thrust, as fate would have it, into the special horror of twentieth-century Europe. After an early inclination toward German nationalism, Mann opposed the upstart Nazi Party in the 1920s and departed the country in 1933 following the rise to power of Adolf Hitler. He fled to the United States in 1938, returned to visit a divided Germany after the war, and resettled in Switzerland in 1952.

Portrait of Thomas Mann, 1935
Thomas Mann in middle age. (Hulton / Archive)

Added to the outward disruptions of politics and war were Mann's own personal conflicts stemming from his early family life; both worlds come into play in his work. His novels often treat the complexities of reconciling an individual's artistic temperament with the changing faces and needs of society and choosing between personal passions and social duty. Like other writers of his time, Mann questions whether the legacy of European culture can heal the ruptures brought about by social change and world war, whether the internal split between intellect and sensuality can be reconciled.

Family Life. Thomas Mann was born in 1875, the second son of Thomas Johann Heinrich Mann, in Lubeck, Germany. The elder Mann was a renowned German burgher, or middle-class citizen, of his day, president of a granary and shipping business and later consul to the Netherlands

---

[1] **Flaubert . . . Tolstoy:** Three great European novelists of the nineteenth century. Gustave Flaubert (1821–1880) created the character of Emma Bovary in *Madame Bovary* (1856); Fyodor Dostoevsky (1821–1881) penned the two Russian masterpieces *Crime and Punishment* (1866) and *The Brothers Karamazov* (1880); and Leo Tolstoy (1828–1910) wrote the epic novel *War and Peace* (1869) and the Romantic novel *Anna Karenina* (1877).

[2] **Goethe . . . Schiller:** Towering figures of German literature in the late eighteenth and early nineteenth centuries. Johann Wolfgang von Goethe (1749–1832) and Friedrich Schiller (1759–1805) were both members of the Romantic Sturm und Drang (storm and stress) movement in the 1770s; in the last decade of Schiller's life, the two collaborated on several literary projects.

[3] **Schopenhauer . . . Wagner:** Arthur Schopenhauer (1788–1860) influenced German thought with his major work, *The World as Will and Representation* (1819). He argued for the centrality of the human will in artistic creation and intellectual understanding. Friedrich Nietzsche's (1844–1900) brilliant distinction between Apollonian and Dionysian art is developed in *The Birth of Tragedy* (1789). Richard Wagner (1813–1883) composed operas based in large part on medieval German sagas; the drama and patriotism of his "Ring Series" influenced Mann.

and a senator in the German parliament. The family business collapsed, however, shortly after his death and sumptuous funeral. His widow, Julia da Silva Bruhns, a dark-haired woman from Rio de Janeiro whose mother had been a Portuguese Creole, was a passionate, strict, opinionated woman who embraced young Thomas as her favorite of her five children; he in turn adored her piano performances of Chopin. Thomas and his youngest brother, Heinrich, were rivals almost from the beginning; Heinrich would later become a well-known novelist in his own right. One of Thomas's sisters, Lula, had been said by her father to be a victim of her own passionate nature; eventually, both she and her sister, Carla, committed suicide.

After the father's death in 1891, the Manns moved to Munich. Thomas did not finish college but like many Germans during that time of national unification and a search for national identity, he read widely in European works from England, Scandinavia, and Russia; Tolstoy was his favorite novelist. While on vacation in 1897 in Rome, he began to write a story about a bourgeois Lubeck family that resembled his own. Originally titled *Decline* (*Verfall*), the manuscript grew to epic length and was published in 1900 as *Buddenbrooks*. This work, which began as an autobiography, ended up as a story of society at large: middle-class values versus artistic rebellion, the stolid, Teutonic North versus the passionate, Mediterranean South, and bourgeois decline versus the moral corruption of the artist. In the novel, the death due to typhoid of Hanno, the last of the Buddenbrooks, symbolizes the decay of family life. *Buddenbrooks* caught on several years after its publication and sold tens of thousands of copies. Mann could later say without exaggeration that it "was the German novel's breakthrough into world literature."

Marriage and Onset of the War. Mann would treat the same themes more richly in the novellas and short stories he published after the turn of the century. The first of these, the novella *Tonio Kröger* (1903), created a memorable character. The shy, aristocratic, and ineffectual Tonio came to represent the artist as a young man. Mann himself commented later: "When I wrote in *Tonio Kröger* that quite a number of people go astray because there is absolutely no right way for them, I didn't think that would be the most revealing thing I could say about myself." Shortly after the success of that work, Mann met Katia Pringsheim, the daughter of a professor of mathematics at the University of Munich. The Pringsheims, Jews who had converted to Christianity, were a wealthy and established Munich family. Though Mann spurned the attractions of wealth, he found much to outweigh his reservations in Katia; he wrote to her: "Only happiness can cure me!" The marriage lasted fifty years and produced six children.

Left to his own inclinations, Mann probably would have continued to explore the contrast between the stuffy middle class and artistic decadence. Although his novella *Death in Venice* (*Der Tod in Venedig*, 1912) projects this conflict into the future with the story of an aging German writer vacationing in southern Europe, whose passion for a young boy has tragic consequences, Mann would have no time to develop the theme

www For links to more information about Mann and a quiz on *Death in Venice* and for more on the culture and context of Europe in the twentieth century, see *World Literature Online* at bedfordstmartins .com/worldlit.

further. Germany's disastrous defeat in World War I led to his nationalist tract, *Reflections of an Unpolitical Man* (1918), which defended the Romantic, irrational, Wagnerian side of the German psyche. And after witnessing the rise of Hitler in the 1920s, Mann took a stand for democracy. The historical and moral upheaval of the times led to the publication of Mann's second major novel, *The Magic Mountain* (*Der Zauberberg*), in 1924. In this story an impressionable young German, Hans Castorp, visits his cousin in a tuberculosis sanatorium where he converses with other inmates on the state of the world. The novel presents a long debate between an Italian humanist, Settembrini, and a fanatical totalitarian figure, Herr Naphta. After seven years Castorp returns to Germany cautiously supporting the cause of humanism only to be pressed into service in World War I. The influence and popularity of this classic BILDUNGS-ROMAN — a novel of psychological development — was largely responsible for Thomas Mann being awarded a Nobel Prize in 1929. In 1930 he delivered an address in Berlin, "An Appeal to Reason," calling for resistance to the Nazi Party. He left the country when Hitler seized power in 1933 and was stripped of his German citizenship by the Nazis a year later.

Life in Exile.   In exile, first in America and later in Europe, after World War II, Mann continued to write novels about the big picture. The most ambitious were a cycle of four entitled *Joseph and His Brothers* (1933–45), which suggest through their treatment of biblical legend the fate of a modern-day exile such as Mann himself. *Doctor Faustus* (1947) is an allegory of the descent of Germany into the evil of Nazi barbarism. In all of these works as well as in *The Magic Mountain,* Mann relies deeply on his humanistic education, applying world myths, Bible stories, and the legend of Faust[4] to contemporary events.

As Mann reached middle age, he used his art to explore and resolve conflicts from his personal life. Work claimed more and more of his energies. Though the suicides of his two sisters and his son, Klaus, his own battle with lung cancer in 1945, his staunch defense of the political victims of the McCarthy era in America, and the death of his brother Heinrich in 1950 all contributed to his personal pain and torment in later life, he rebounded time and again to pursue new projects. "I would not lack ideas," he told an old friend, "even if I reached 120." His recent biographer suggests that he was one of the last great writers to seriously claim that art had saved his life. Lucid to the end, he died at the age of eighty in a hospital in Zurich, Switzerland, in 1955.

Death in Venice.   Much in *Death in Venice* is based on actual events. In 1911 Mann, then thirty-six, his wife, Katia, and his brother Heinrich traveled to the Lido, the fabled island resort near Venice, where according to Mann "a series of curious circumstances and impressions combined with

> . . . the conflict between passion and puritanism . . . seems also to underlie [Mann's] continuing interest in the . . . erotic visitation, the emotional invasion that changes a whole existence.
>
> – DAVID DUKE, Norton Critical Edition, *Death in Venice*, 1994

---

[4] **legend of Faust:** In a bargain with the devil, Faust sold his soul for knowledge and exotic experience. Faust was the hero of medieval legends and was dramatized by the English playwright Christopher Marlowe (1564–1593) in *Doctor Faustus* (1589) and by Goethe (1749–1832) in *Faust.* See Books 3 and 5.

my subconscious search for something new to give birth to a productive idea, which then developed into the story *Death in Venice.*" In Mann's *A Sketch of My Life,* he lists the events from 1911 that were transferred to the novel: "Nothing is invented: the wanderer at the Northern Cemetery in Munich, the gloomy ship from Pola, the foppish old man, the suspect gondolier, Tadzio and his family, the departure prevented by a muddle with the luggage, the cholera, the honest clerk at the travel agency, the sinister singer. . . ." The seed for the character of Aschenbach, pictured in the novel as an eminent German man of letters with a fatal weakness, came from the life of Germany's most distinguished man of letters, Johann Wolfgang von Goethe, who at the age of seventy-four fell in love with a seventeen-year-old, Ulrike von Levetzow, while vacationing in Marienbad. Goethe actually initiated a proposal of marriage before coming to his senses.

Mann paid close attention to his portrait of Aschenbach, a living link to the Greek and Latin classical tradition, a man who has renounced youthful rebellion and adopted his rightful place as an upholder of cultural tradition. He is, however, also a man of great weakness: He is lonely and vulnerable, he has not made his peace with the temptations of the world, and he harbors still buried emotions that easily betray him.

In his notebooks, it is clear that Mann researched every aspect of the tale, from the origins of cholera in India to the Greek classics that increasingly intrude on Aschenbach's mind as he becomes more and more obsessed with a beautiful boy. Katia's memoirs, published after Mann's death, describe the real-life situation that lay behind the central incident of the story, the appearance of a handsome Polish boy at their Venetian resort. She says of her husband: "He immediately had a weakness for this youth, he liked him inordinately, and he always watched him on the beach with his friends. He did not follow him through all of Venice, but the youth did fascinate him. . . ." The challenge for Mann the artist became the psychological portrayal of a writer who is awakened from an orderly but emotionally barren existence by sensuous beauty.

Crucial in the novella is the role of the classics: At various points in the story they correspond to stages of Aschenbach's inner turmoil. First comes the uncorrupted world of heroes, natural beauty, and epic actions of *The Odyssey.*[5] Then, as Aschenbach tries to rationalize his feelings for the boy, comes the intellectual world of Plato,[6] especially as seen in *The Symposium,* in which intellectual or spiritual love between males is declared to be a higher form of love than a man's love for his wife. Plato's doctrine of eros — sexual love or desire — suggests that sensuous beauty has the potential to revive in the soul a memory of ideal beauty so that sexual love can be transformed into a higher intellectual or spiritual rela-

---

[5] *The Odyssey:* Homer's epic (c. 700 B.C.E.) about Odysseus's journey home from the Trojan War.

[6] Plato: One of the great philosophers of ancient Greece, Plato (429–347 B.C.E.) founded the Academy; Aristotle (384–322 B.C.E.), another influential Greek philosopher, was one of his pupils. Plato's thought is colored by his belief in the existence of ideals, like Beauty and Goodness, which transcend the real world of sensuous experience.

tionship. But for Mann, sexuality, once unleashed, can as easily lead to lust and the destructive consequences of instinct as to the refined ideals of the imagination and art.

As Aschenbach enters his decline, reference is made to the dangerous world of sexual excess found in *The Bacchae,* the play by Euripedes[7] about the Dionysian love cults of ancient Greece. Mann also refers in the novella to the distinction philosopher Friedrich Nietzsche makes between two views of art and life: the Apollonian (orderly, restrained, sculptured) and the Dionysian (free, expressive, chaotic, excessive), both part of ancient Greek culture. In a letter to Carl Maria Weber in 1920, Mann states that the ideal would be the equilibrium of sensuality and morality, a balance "between the Dionysian spirit of lyric poetry as it individualistically and irresponsibly pours itself out, and the Apolline spirit of epic narrative with its objective commitment and its moral responsibilities to society." Mann does not choose this balance for his protagonist.

Finally, Aschenbach's sensual homosexual yearnings cannot be allowed into his experience and are repudiated. The doctrine of eros represented by the boy, Tadzio, brings death rather than a new life in which the intellectual, the artistic, and the instinctual could have been reconciled and harmonized. Tadzio turns from Eros into the messenger, Hermes,[8] who will bear the once-esteemed professor to the land of the dead. Starting in Munich and increasing as Aschenbach draws near his final destination, figures of death seem to stalk him. Aschenbach's decline is reflected in his use of cosmetics and in his admission to his family of his interest in Tadzio. The ultimate moral failure involves sins of omission: Aschenbach does not warn the Polish family about the cholera epidemic and doesn't heed the advice to depart Venice before it is too late.

This was the German novel's breakthrough into world literature.

– THOMAS MANN, of his novel *Buddenbrooks*

■ CONNECTIONS

T. S. Eliot, "The Love Song of J. Alfred Prufrock," p. 482. For some writers, the corrupting influences of modern urban life are best depicted in the microcosm of love and sexuality. In both "The Love Song of J. Alfred Prufrock" and *The Waste Land,* Eliot portrays a spiritual sickness that has infected the intimate relationships of men and women. How does Mann present the unfortunate consequences of Aschenbach's eroticism?

James Baldwin, "Sonny's Blues," p. 830. In "Sonny's Blues," Baldwin uses jazz as musical motif to reveal the personalities of two brothers. How does Mann develop the motif, or theme, of the traveler in *Death in Venice*? How is the figure of Hermes from Greek mythology particularly appropriate for Aschenbach's journey into death?

Leo Tolstoy, *The Death of Ivan Ilych* (Book 5). A favorite subject of European writers and intellectuals at the turn of the twentieth century was the individual trapped by

---

[7] **Euripides** (485–406 B.C.E.): Greek playwright of more than ninety plays that criticized contemporary society and challenged the military values carried over from the Trojan War and the wisdom of the Olympian religion. His plays include *Medea* (c. 413 B.C.E.), *Trojan Women* (415 B.C.E.), and *The Bacchae* (405 B.C.E.).

[8] **Hermes:** Pictured with winged sandals and the staff of a herald, Hermes is the messenger god of the ancient Greeks; he also conducted the souls of the dead to Hades.

his or her social class and/or vocation who was somehow blind to the deeper meanings of the self. Tolstoy's Ivan Ilych was caught up in bureaucratic values and impervious to the emotional needs of his family. How does Aschenbach's role as a writer and intellectual hinder his discovery of his emotional needs and desires?

■ **FURTHER RESEARCH**

Editions
Koelb, Clayton, ed. and trans. *Death in Venice: A New Translation, Backgrounds and Contexts, Criticism.* 1994.
Luke, David, trans. *Death in Venice and Other Stories.* 1988.

Biographies
Feuerlicht, Ignace. *Thomas Mann.* 1969.
Heilbut, Anthony. *Thomas Mann: Eros and Literature.* 1995.
Winston, Richard. *Thomas Mann: The Making of an Artist, 1875–1911.* 1981.

Criticism
Berlin, Jeffrey B. *Approaches to Teaching Mann's "Death in Venice" and Other Short Fiction.* 1992.
Bloom, Harold, ed. *Thomas Mann.* 1986.
Ezergailis, Inta M., ed. *Critical Essays on Thomas Mann.* 1988.
Hatfield, Henry, ed. *Thomas Mann: A Collection of Critical Essays.* 1964.
Reed, Terence J. *Thomas Mann: The Uses of Tradition.* 1974.

∾ Death in Venice

Translated by David Luke

1

On a spring afternoon in 19——, the year in which for months on end so grave a threat seemed to hang over the peace of Europe,[1] Gustav Aschenbach, or von[2] Aschenbach as he had been officially known since his fiftieth birthday, had set out from his apartment on the Prinzregentenstrasse[3] in Munich to take a walk of some length by himself. The morning's writing had overstimulated him: his work had now reached a difficult and dangerous point which demanded the utmost care and circumspection, the most insistent and precise effort of will, and the productive

---

Death in Venice. Originally published in German as *Der Tod in Venedig* in 1912, this work and nearly all Thomas Mann's original writings in German—twenty-four volumes in all—were translated into English by Helen T. Lowe-Porter between 1924 and 1951, with another volume added in 1960. This astonishing production by a single translator—who held exclusive rights for the time period involved—did not come without controversy. While Mann is not an easy writer to

---

[1] **On . . . Europe:** A number of diplomatic crises occurred in 1911 that eventually led to the outbreak of World War I, in 1914.   [2] **von:** Indicates a noble rank, which had been bestowed on Aschenbach on his fiftieth birthday.
[3] **Prinzregentenstrasse:** A street in Munich.

mechanism in his mind—that *motus animi continuus* which according to Cicero[4] is the essence of eloquence—had so pursued its reverberating rhythm that he had been unable to halt it even after lunch, and had missed the refreshing daily siesta which was now so necessary to him as he became increasingly subject to fatigue. And so, soon after taking tea, he had left the house hoping that fresh air and movement would set him to rights and enable him to spend a profitable evening.

It was the beginning of May, and after a succession of cold, wet weeks a premature high summer had set in. The Englischer Garten, although still only in its first delicate leaf, had been as sultry as in August, and at its city end full of traffic and pedestrians. Having made his way to the Aumeister along less and less frequented paths, Aschenbach had briefly surveyed the lively scene at the popular open-air restaurant, around which a few cabs and private carriages were standing; then, as the sun sank, he had started homeward across the open meadow beyond the park, and since he was now tired and a storm seemed to be brewing over Föhring,[5] he had stopped by the Northern Cemetery to wait for the tram that would take him straight back to the city.

As it happened, there was not a soul to be seen at or near the tram-stop. Not one vehicle passed along the Föhringer Chaussee or the paved Ungererstrasse on which solitary gleaming tramrails pointed toward Schwabing;[6] nothing stirred behind the fencing of the stonemasons' yards, where crosses and memorial tablets and monuments, ready for sale, composed a second and untenanted burial ground; across the street, the mortuary chapel with its Byzantine styling stood silent in the glow of the westering day. Its facade, adorned with Greek crosses and brightly painted

translate clearly and faithfully at every turn, it has been shown that Lowe-Porter took some liberties with Mann's texts. In 1988, when the work was no longer copyrighted, David Luke translated seven of Mann's stories; Luke's translation of *Death in Venice* is the one presented here.

The literary style of *Death in Venice* invites considerable discussion. Mann is one of the most difficult German stylists in modern times—his long, entangled sentences that end with the main verb, following German syntax, have plagued even native speakers of German, and the writing in *Death in Venice* in particular is especially complex, suggesting the voice of Gustav von Aschenbach himself: learned, pedantic, not quite of this world. (Mann admitted to "an element of parody" in his character's overblown and sometimes pompous musings.) Moreover, Mann borrows a stylistic feature from the operatic dramas of Richard Wagner: LEITMOTIFS. These are repetitions within a work of themes, brief passages, or even single words designed to intensify sensations in the reader's mind. Aschenbach fantasizes about a tiger in a jungle, for example, while still in Munich. Later in Venice, when he becomes aware of the plague and its source in India, the tiger reappears in his thoughts. This demonic foreshadowing confirms the reader's original premonition that something dangerous is going to happen. Within a seemingly leisurely account of the vacation of Gustav von Aschenbach in Venice, Mann builds a story of winding and subterranean passageways, secrets, and decadence much like the city of Venice itself in the summer heat and humidity. Alert readers will notice leitmotifs developing throughout the story.

All notes are the editors' unless otherwise indicated.

[4] **Cicero:** Marcus Tullius Cicero (106–43 B.C.E.), a Roman orator; *motus animi continuus* means "the continuous motion of the spirit." [5] **Föhring:** A district of Munich. [6] **Schwabing:** A district of Munich.

hieratic motifs, is also inscribed with symmetrically arranged texts in gilt lettering, selected scriptural passages about the life to come, such as: "They shall go in unto the dwelling-place of the Lord," or "May light perpetual shine upon them." The waiting Aschenbach had already been engaged for some minutes in the solemn pastime of deciphering the words and letting his mind wander in contemplation of the mystic meaning that suffused them, when he noticed something that brought him back to reality: in the portico of the chapel, above the two apocalyptic beasts that guard the steps leading up to it, a man was standing, a man whose slightly unusual appearance gave his thoughts an altogether different turn.

It was not entirely clear whether he had emerged through the bronze doors from inside the chapel or had suddenly appeared and mounted the steps from outside. Aschenbach, without unduly pondering the question, inclined to the former hypothesis. The man was moderately tall, thin, beardless, and remarkably snub-nosed; he belonged to the red-haired type and had its characteristic milky, freckled complexion. He was quite evidently not of Bavarian origin; at all events he wore a straw hat with a broad straight brim which gave him an exotic air, as of someone who had come from distant parts. It is true that he also had the typical Bavarian rucksack strapped to his shoulders and wore a yellowish belted outfit of what looked like frieze,[7] as well as carrying a gray rain-cape over his left forearm which was propped against his waist, and in his right hand an iron-pointed walking stick which he had thrust slantwise into the ground, crossing his feet and leaning his hip against its handle. His head was held high, so that the Adam's apple stood out stark and bare on his lean neck where it rose from the open shirt; and there were two pronounced vertical furrows, rather strangely ill-matched to his turned-up nose, between the colorless red-lashed eyes with which he peered sharply into the distance. There was thus—and perhaps the raised point of vantage on which he stood contributed to this impression—an air of imperious survey, something bold or even wild about his posture; for whether it was because he was dazzled into a grimace by the setting sun or by reason of some permanent facial deformity, the fact was that his lips seemed to be too short and were completely retracted from his teeth, so that the latter showed white and long between them, bared to the gums.

Aschenbach's half-absentminded, half-inquisitive scrutiny of the stranger had no doubt been a little less than polite, for he suddenly became aware that his gaze was being returned: the man was in fact staring at him so aggressively, so straight in the eye, with so evident an intention to make an issue of the matter and out-stare him, that Aschenbach turned away in disagreeable embarrassment and began to stroll along the fence, casually resolving to take no further notice of the fellow. A minute later he had put him out of his mind. But whether his imagination had been stirred by the stranger's itinerant appearance, or whether some other physical or psychological influence was at work, he now became conscious, to his complete surprise, of an extraordinary expansion of his inner self, a kind of roving restlessness, a youthful craving for far-off places, a feeling so new or at least so long

---

[7] **frieze:** Wool cloth with an uncut nap on one side.

unaccustomed and forgotten that he stood as if rooted, with his hands clasped behind his back and his eyes to the ground, trying to ascertain the nature and purport of his emotion.

It was simply a desire to travel; but it had presented itself as nothing less than a seizure, with intensely passionate and indeed hallucinatory force, turning his craving into vision. His imagination, still not at rest from the morning's hours of work, shaped for itself a paradigm of all the wonders and terrors of the manifold earth, of all that it was now suddenly striving to envisage: he saw it, saw a landscape, a tropical swampland under a cloud-swollen sky, moist and lush and monstrous, a kind of primeval wilderness of islands, morasses and muddy alluvial channels; far and wide around him he saw hairy palm-trunks thrusting upward from rank jungles of fern, from among thick fleshy plants in exuberant flower; saw strangely misshapen trees with roots that arched through the air before sinking into the ground or into stagnant shadowy-green glassy waters where milk-white blossoms floated as big as plates, and among them exotic birds with grotesque beaks stood hunched in the shallows, their heads tilted motionlessly sideways; saw between the knotted stems of the bamboo thicket the glinting eyes of a crouching tiger; and his heart throbbed with terror and mysterious longing. Then the vision faded; and with a shake of his head Aschenbach resumed his perambulation along the fencing of the gravestone yards.

His attitude to foreign travel, at least since he had had the means at his disposal to enjoy its advantages as often as he pleased, had always been that it was nothing more than a necessary health precaution, to be taken from time to time however disinclined to it one might be. Too preoccupied with the tasks imposed upon him by his own sensibility and by the collective European psyche, too heavily burdened with the compulsion to produce, too shy of distraction to have learned how to take leisure and pleasure in the colorful external world, he had been perfectly well satisfied to have no more detailed a view of the earth's surface than anyone can acquire without stirring far from home, and he had never even been tempted to venture outside Europe. This had been more especially the case since his life had begun its gradual decline and his artist's fear of not finishing his task—the apprehension that his time might run out before he had given the whole of himself by doing what he had it in him to do—was no longer something he could simply dismiss as an idle fancy; and during this time his outward existence had been almost entirely divided between the beautiful city which had become his home and the rustic mountain retreat he had set up for himself and where he passed his rainy summers.

And sure enough, the sudden and belated impulse that had just overwhelmed him very soon came under the moderating and corrective influence of common sense and of the self-discipline he had practiced since his youth. It had been his intention that the book to which his life was at present dedicated should be advanced to a certain point before he moved to the country, and the idea of a jaunt in the wide world that would take him away from his work for months now seemed too casual, too upsetting to his plans to be considered seriously. Nevertheless, he knew the reason for the unexpected temptation only too well. This longing for the distant and the new, this craving for liberation, relaxation, and forgetfulness—it had been, he was bound to admit, an urge to escape, to run away from his writing, away from the humdrum scene of his cold, inflexible, passionate duty. True, it was a duty he loved, and by now he had almost even learned to love the enervating daily struggle between his proud, tenacious, tried and tested will and that growing weariness which no one must be allowed to suspect nor his finished work betray by any telltale sign of debility or lassitude. Nevertheless, it would be sensible, he decided, not to span the bow too far and willfully stifle a desire that had erupted in him with such vivid force. He thought of his work, thought of the passage at which he had again, today as yesterday, been forced to interrupt it—that stubborn problem which neither patient care could solve nor a decisive *coup de main*[8] dispel. He reconsidered it, tried to break or dissolve the inhibition, and, with a shudder of repugnance, abandoned the attempt. It was not a case of very unusual difficulty, he was simply paralyzed by a scruple of distaste, manifesting itself as a perfectionistic fastidiousness which nothing could satisfy. Perfectionism, of course, was something which even as a young man he had come to see as the innermost essence of talent, and for its sake he had curbed and cooled his feelings; for he knew that feeling is apt to be content with high-spirited approximations and with work that falls short of supreme excellence. Could it be that the enslaved emotion was now avenging itself by deserting him, by refusing from now on to bear up his art on its wings, by taking with it all his joy in words, all his appetite for the beauty of form? Not that he was writing badly: it was at least the advantage of his years to be master of his trade, a mastery of which at any moment he could feel calmly confident. But even as it brought him national honor he took no pleasure in it himself, and it seemed to him that his work lacked that element of sparkling and joyful improvisation, that quality which surpasses any intellectual substance in its power to delight the receptive world. He dreaded spending the summer in the country, alone in that little house with the maid who prepared his meals and the servant who brought them to him; dreaded the familiar profile of the mountain summits and mountain walls which would once again surround his slow discontented toil. So what did he need? An interlude, some impromptu living, some *dolce far niente*,[9] the invigoration of a distant climate, to make his summer bearable and fruitful. Very well then—he would travel. Not all that far, not quite to where the tigers were. A night in the wagon-lit and a siesta of three or four weeks at some popular holiday resort in the charming south . . .

Such were his thoughts as the tram clattered toward him along the Ungererstrasse, and as he stepped into it he decided to devote that evening to the study of maps and timetables. On the platform it occurred to him to look round and see what had become of the man in the straw hat, his companion for the duration of this not inconsequential wait at a tram stop. But the man's whereabouts remained a mystery, for he was no longer standing where he had stood, nor was he to be seen anywhere else at the stop or in the tramcar itself.

---

[8] *coup de main:* French for "bold stroke."   [9] *dolce far niente:* Italian for "sweet doing nothing" or "pleasant idleness."

2

The author of the lucid and massive prose-epic about the life of Frederic of Prussia;[10] the patient artist who with long toil had woven the great tapestry of the novel called *Maya,*[11] so rich in characters, gathering so many human destinies together under the shadow of one idea; the creator of that powerful tale entitled *A Study in Abjection,* which earned the gratitude of a whole younger generation by pointing to the possibility of moral resolution even for those who have plumbed the depths of knowledge; the author (lastly but not least in this summary enumeration of his maturer works) of that passionate treatise *Intellect and Art* which in its ordering energy and antithetical eloquence has led serious critics to place it immediately alongside Schiller's disquisition *On Naive and Reflective Literature:*[12] in a word, Gustav Aschenbach, was born in L. . . , an important city in the province of Silesia, as the son of a highly-placed legal official. His ancestors had been military officers, judges, government administrators; men who had spent their disciplined, decently austere life in the service of the king and the state. A more inward spirituality had shown itself in one of them who had been a preacher; a strain of livelier, more sensuous blood had entered the family in the previous generation with the writer's mother, the daughter of a director of music from Bohemia. Certain exotic racial characteristics in his external appearance had come to him from her. It was from this marriage between hard-working, sober conscientiousness and darker, more fiery impulses that an artist, and indeed this particular kind of artist, had come into being.

With his whole nature intent from the start upon fame, he had displayed not exactly precocity, but a certain decisiveness and personal trenchancy in his style of utterance, which at an early age made him ripe for a life in the public eye and well suited to it. He had made a name for himself when he had scarcely left school. Ten years later he had learned to perform, at his writing desk, the social and administrative duties entailed by his reputation; he had learned to write letters which, however brief they had to be (for many claims beset the successful man who enjoys the confidence of the public), would always contain something kindly and pointed. By the age of forty he was obliged, wearied though he might be by the toils and vicissitudes of his real work, to deal with a daily correspondence that bore postage-stamps from every part of the globe.

His talent, equally remote from the commonplace and from the eccentric, had a native capacity both to inspire confidence in the general public and to win admiration and encouragement from the discriminating connoisseur. Ever since his boyhood the duty to achieve—and to achieve exceptional things—had been imposed on him from all sides, and thus he had never known youth's idleness, its carefree negligent ways. When in his thirty-fifth year he fell ill in Vienna, a subtle observer remarked of him on a social occasion: "You see, Aschenbach has always only lived

---

[10] **Frederic of Prussia:** Frederick the Great, king of Prussia from 1740 to 1786. [11] *Maya:* In Hindu thought, the illusionary nature of the phenomenal world, behind which exists the "real." [12] *On Naive . . . Literature:* An important essay by Friedrich Schiller (1759–1805).

like *this*"—and the speaker closed the fingers of his left hand tightly into a fist—
"and never like *this*"—and he let his open hand hang comfortably down along the
back of the chair. It was a correct observation; and the morally courageous aspect of
the matter was that Aschenbach's native constitution was by no means robust, and
that the constant harnessing of his energies was something to which he had been
called, but not really born.

As a young boy, medical advice and care had made school attendance impossible and obliged him to have his education at home. He had grown up by himself,
without companions, and had nevertheless had to recognize in good time that he
belonged to a breed not seldom talented, yet seldom endowed with the physical basis
which talent needs if it is to fulfill itself—a breed that usually gives of its best in
youth, and in which the creative gift rarely survives into mature years. But he would
"stay the course"—it was his favorite motto, he saw his historical novel about Frederic the Great as nothing if not the apotheosis of this, the king's word of command,
"durchhalten!"[13] which to Aschenbach epitomized a manly ethos of suffering action.
And he dearly longed to grow old, for it had always been his view that an artist's gift
can only be called truly great and wide-ranging, or indeed truly admirable, if it has
been fortunate enough to bear characteristic fruit at all the stages of human life.

They were not broad, the shoulders on which he thus carried the tasks laid
upon him by his talent; and since his aims were high, he stood in great need of discipline—and discipline, after all, was fortunately his inborn heritage on his father's
side. At the age of forty or fifty, and indeed during those younger years in which
other men live prodigally and dilettantishly, happily procrastinating the execution of
great plans, Aschenbach would begin his day early by dashing cold water over his
chest and back, and then, with two tall wax candles in silver candlesticks placed at
the head of his manuscript, he would offer up to art, for two or three ardently conscientious morning hours, the strength he had gathered during sleep. It was a par-
donable error, indeed it was one that betokened as nothing else could the triumph of
his moral will, that uninformed critics should mistake the great world of *Maya,* or
the massive epic unfolding of Frederic's life, for the product of solid strength and
long stamina, whereas in fact they had been built up to their impressive size from
layer upon layer of daily opuscula, from a hundred or a thousand separate inspirations; and if they were indeed so excellent, wholly and in every detail, it was only
because their creator, showing that same constancy of will and tenacity of purpose
as had once conquered his native Silesia,[14] had held out for years under the pressure
of one and the same work, and had devoted to actual composition only his best and
worthiest hours.

For a significant intellectual product to make a broad and deep immediate appeal, there must be a hidden affinity, indeed a congruence, between the personal destiny of the author and the wider destiny of his generation. The public does not know
why it grants the accolade of fame to a work of art. Being in no sense connoisseurs,

---

[13] *durchhalten!:* German for "Hold out!"   [14] Silesia: Frederick the Great conquered Silesia, a region of central
Europe, from Austria.

readers imagine they perceive a hundred good qualities in it which justify their admiration; but the real reason for their applause is something imponderable, a sense of sympathy. Hidden away among Aschenbach's writings was a passage directly asserting that nearly all the great things that exist owe their existence to a defiant despite: it is despite grief and anguish, despite poverty, loneliness, bodily weakness, vice, and passion and a thousand inhibitions, that they have come into being at all. But this was more than an observation, it was an experience, it was positively the formula of his life and his fame, the key to his work; is it surprising then that it was also the moral formula, the outward gesture, of his work's most characteristic figures?

The new hero-type favored by Aschenbach, and recurring in his books in a multiplicity of individual variants, had already been remarked upon at an early stage by a shrewd commentator, who had described his conception as that of "an intellectual and boyish manly virtue, that of a youth who clenches his teeth in proud shame and stands calmly on as the swords and spears pass through his body." That was well put, perceptive and precisely true, for all its seemingly rather too passive emphasis. For composure under the blows of fate, grace in the midst of torment—this is not only endurance: it is an active achievement, a positive triumph, and the figure of Saint Sebastian[15] is the most perfect symbol if not of art in general, then certainly of the kind of art here in question. What did one see if one looked in any depth into the world of this writer's fiction? Elegant self-control concealing from the world's eyes until the very last moment a state of inner disintegration and biological decay; sallow ugliness, sensuously marred and worsted, which nevertheless is able to fan its smouldering concupiscence to a pure flame, and even to exalt itself to mastery in the realm of beauty; pallid impotence, which from the glowing depths of the spirit draws strength to cast down a whole proud people at the foot of the Cross and set its own foot upon them as well; gracious poise and composure in the empty austere service of form; the false, dangerous life of the born deceiver, his ambition and his art which lead so soon to exhaustion—to contemplate all these destinies, and many others like them, was to doubt if there is any other heroism at all but the heroism of weakness. In any case, what other heroism could be more in keeping with the times? Gustav Aschenbach was the writer who spoke for all those who work on the brink of exhaustion, who labor and are heavy-laden, who are worn out already but still stand upright, all those moralists of achievement who are slight of stature and scanty of resources, but who yet, by some ecstasy of the will and by wise husbandry, manage at least for a time to force their work into a semblance of greatness. There are many such, they are the heroes of our age. And they all recognized themselves in his work, they found that it confirmed them and raised them on high and celebrated them; they were grateful for this, and they spread his name far and wide.

He had been young and raw with the times: ill advised by fashion, he had publicly stumbled, blundered, made himself look foolish, offended in speech and writing against tact and balanced civility. But he had achieved dignity, that goal toward

---

[15] **Saint Sebastian:** Third-century Christian martyr whose sufferings were the subject of Renaissance paintings.

which, as he declared, every great talent is innately driven and spurred; indeed it can be said that the conscious and defiant purpose of his entire development had been, leaving all the inhibitions of skepticism and irony behind him, an ascent to dignity.

Lively, clear-outlined, intellectually undemanding presentation is the delight of the great mass of the middle-class public, but passionate radical youth is interested only in problems: and Aschenbach had been as problematic and as radical as any young man ever was. He had been in thrall to intellect, had exhausted the soil by excessive analysis and ground up the seed corn of growth; he had uncovered what is better kept hidden, made talent seem suspect, betrayed the truth about art—indeed, even as the sculptural vividness of his descriptions was giving pleasure to his more naive devotees and lifting their minds and hearts, he, this same youthful artist, had fascinated twenty-year-olds with his breathtaking cynicisms about the questionable nature of art and of the artist himself.

But it seems that there is nothing to which a noble and active mind more quickly becomes inured than that pungent and bitter stimulus, the acquisition of knowledge; and it is very sure that even the most gloomily conscientious and radical sophistication of youth is shallow by comparison with Aschenbach's profound decision as a mature master to repudiate knowledge as such, to reject it, to step over it with head held high—in the recognition that knowledge can paralyze the will, paralyze and discourage action and emotion and even passion, and rob all these of their dignity. How else is the famous short story *A Study in Abjection* to be understood but as an outbreak of disgust against an age indecently undermined by psychology and represented by the figure of that spiritless, witless semiscoundrel who cheats his way into a destiny of sorts when, motivated by his own ineptitude and depravity and ethical whimsicality, he drives his wife into the arms of a callow youth—convinced that his intellectual depths entitle him to behave with contemptible baseness? The forthright words of condemnation which here weighed vileness in the balance and found it wanting—they proclaimed their writer's renunciation of all moral skepticism, of every kind of sympathy with the abyss; they declared his repudiation of the laxity of that compassionate principle which holds that to understand all is to forgive all. And the development that was here being anticipated, indeed already taking place, was that "miracle of reborn naiveté" to which, in a dialogue written a little later, the author himself had referred with a certain mysterious emphasis. How strange these associations! Was it an intellectual consequence of this "rebirth," of this new dignity and rigor, that, at about the same time, his sense of beauty was observed to undergo an almost excessive resurgence, that his style took on the noble purity, simplicity, and symmetry that were to set upon all his subsequent works that so evident and evidently intentional stamp of the classical master? And yet: moral resoluteness at the far side of knowledge, achieved in despite of all corrosive and inhibiting insight—does this not in its turn signify a simplification, a morally simplistic view of the world and of human psychology, and thus also a resurgence of energies that are evil, forbidden, morally impossible? And is form not two-faced? Is it not at one and the same time moral and immoral—moral as the product and expression of discipline, but immoral and even antimoral inasmuch as it houses within itself an innate moral indifference, and indeed essentially strives for nothing less than to bend morality under its proud and absolute scepter?

Be that as it may! A development is a destiny; and one that is accompanied by the admiration and mass confidence of a wide public must inevitably differ in its course from one that takes place far from the limelight and from the commitments of fame. Only the eternal intellectual vagrant is bored and prompted to mockery when a great talent grows out of its libertinistic chrysalis stage, becomes an expressive representative of the dignity of mind, takes on the courtly bearing of that solitude which has been full of hard, uncounseled, self-reliant sufferings and struggles, and has achieved power and honor among men. And what a game it is too, how much defiance there is in it and how much satisfaction, this self-formation of a talent! As time passed, Gustav Aschenbach's presentations took on something of an official air, of an educator's stance; his style in later years came to eschew direct audacities, new and subtle nuances, it developed toward the exemplary and definitive, the fastidiously conventional, the conservative and formal and even formulaic; and as tradition has it of Louis XIV,[16] so Aschenbach as he grew older banned from his utterance every unrefined word. It was at this time that the education authority adopted selected pages from his works for inclusion in the prescribed school readers. And when a German ruler who had just come to the throne granted personal nobilitation to the author of *Frederic of Prussia* on his fiftieth birthday, he sensed the inner appropriateness of this honor and did not decline it.

After a few restless years of experimental living in different places, he soon chose Munich as his permanent home and lived there in the kind of upper-bourgeois status which is occasionally the lot of certain intellectuals. The marriage which he had contracted while still young with the daughter of an academic family had been ended by his wife's death after a short period of happiness. She had left him a daughter, now already married. He had never had a son.

Gustav von Aschenbach was of rather less than average height, dark and clean-shaven. His head seemed a little too large in proportion to his almost delicate stature. His brushed-back hair, thinning at the top, very thick and distinctly gray over the temples, framed a high, deeply lined, scarred-looking forehead. The bow of a pair of gold spectacles with rimless lenses cut into the base of his strong, nobly curved nose. His mouth was large, often relaxed, often suddenly narrow and tense; the cheeks were lean and furrowed, the well-formed chin slightly cleft. Grave visitations of fate seemed to have passed over this head, which usually inclined to one side with an air of suffering. And yet it was art that had here performed that fashioning of the physiognomy which is usually the work of a life full of action and stress. The flashing exchanges of the dialogue between Voltaire and the king on the subject of war had been born behind that brow; these eyes that looked so wearily and deeply through their glasses had seen the bloody inferno of the Seven Years' War[17] sick bays.

---

[16] **Louis XIV:** King of France from 1638 to 1715; the "Sun King."　[17] **Seven Years' War:** War lasting from 1756 to 1763 between Prussia and an alliance of Austria, France, Russia, Sweden, Saxony, and Spain. Frederick the Great invited Voltaire (1694–1778), the prominent French philosopher, novelist, and satirist, to reside at his court.

Even in a personal sense, after all, art is an intensified life. By art one is more deeply satisfied and more rapidly used up. It engraves on the countenance of its servant the traces of imaginary and intellectual adventures, and even if he has outwardly existed in cloistral tranquillity, it leads in the long term to overfastidiousness, overrefinement, nervous fatigue, and overstimulation, such as can seldom result from a life full of the most extravagant passions and pleasures.

3

Mundane and literary business of various kinds delayed Aschenbach's eagerly awaited departure until about a fortnight after that walk in Munich. Finally he gave instructions that his country house was to be made ready for occupation in four weeks' time, and then, one day between the middle and end of May, he took the night train to Trieste, where he stayed only twenty-four hours, embarking on the following morning for Pola.[18]

What he sought was something strange and random, but in a place easily reached, and accordingly he took up his abode on an Adriatic island which had been highly spoken of for some years: a little way off the Istrian coast, with colorful ragged inhabitants speaking a wild unintelligible dialect, and picturesque fragmented cliffs overlooking the open sea. But rain and sultry air, a self-enclosed provincial Austrian hotel clientele, the lack of that restful intimate contact with the sea which can only be had on a gentle, sandy coast, filled him with vexation and with a feeling that he had not yet come to his journey's end. He was haunted by an inner impulse that still had no clear direction; he studied shipping timetables, looked up one place after another—and suddenly his surprising yet at the same time self-evident destination stared him in the face. If one wanted to travel overnight to somewhere incomparable, to a fantastic mutation of normal reality, where did one go? Why, the answer was obvious. What was he doing here? He had gone completely astray. *That* was where he had wanted to travel. He at once gave notice of departure from his present, mischosen stopping place. Ten days after his arrival on the island, in the early morning mist, a rapid motor launch carried him and his luggage back over the water to the naval base, and here he landed only to re-embark immediately, crossing the gangway onto the damp deck of a ship that was waiting under steam to leave for Venice.

It was an ancient Italian boat, out of date and dingy and black with soot. Aschenbach was no sooner aboard than a grubby hunchbacked seaman, grinning obsequiously, conducted him to an artificially lit cavelike cabin in the ship's interior. Here, behind a table, with his cap askew and a cigarette end in the corner of his mouth, sat a goat-bearded man with the air of an old-fashioned circus director and a slick caricatured business manner, taking passengers' particulars and issuing their tickets. "To Venice!" he exclaimed, echoing Aschenbach's request, and extending his arm he pushed his pen into some coagulated leftover ink in a tilted inkstand. "One first class to Venice. Certainly, sir!" He scribbled elaborately, shook some blue sand

---

[18] **Pola:** Now called Pula, on the Adriatic Sea, about thirty miles south of Trieste, another seaport.

from a box over the writing and ran it off into an earthenware dish, then folded the paper with his yellow bony fingers and wrote on it again. "A very happily chosen destination!" he chattered as he did so. "Ah, Venice! A splendid city! A city irresistibly attractive to the man of culture, by its history no less than by its present charms!" There was something hypnotic and distracting about the smooth facility of his movements and the glib empty talk with which he accompanied them, almost as if he were anxious that the traveler might have second thoughts about his decision to go to Venice. He hastily took Aschenbach's money and with the dexterity of a croupier dropped the change on the stained tablecloth. *"Buon divertimento, signore,"*[9] he said, bowing histrionically. "It is an honor to serve you . . . Next, please, gentlemen!" he exclaimed with a wave of the arm, as if he were doing a lively trade, although in fact there was no one else there to be dealt with. Aschenbach returned on deck.

Resting one elbow on the handrail, he watched the idle crowd hanging about the quayside to see the ship's departure, and watched the passengers who had come aboard. Those with second-class tickets were squatting, men and women together, on the forward deck, using boxes and bundles as seats. The company on the upper deck consisted of a group of young men, probably shop or office workers from Pola, a high-spirited party about to set off on an excursion to Italy. They were making a considerable exhibition of themselves and their enterprise, chattering, laughing, fatuously enjoying their own gesticulations, leaning overboard and shouting glibly derisive ribaldries at their friends on the harbor-side street, who were hurrying about their business with briefcases under their arms and waved their sticks peevishly at the holiday-makers. One of the party, who wore a light yellow summer suit of extravagant cut, a scarlet necktie and a rakishly tilted Panama hat, was the most conspicuous of them all in his shrill hilarity. But as soon as Aschenbach took a slightly closer look at him, he realized with a kind of horror that the man's youth was false. He was old, there was no mistaking it. There were wrinkles round his eyes and mouth. His cheeks' faint carmine was rouge, the brown hair under his straw hat with its colored ribbon was a wig, his neck was flaccid and scrawny, his small stuck-on moustache and the little imperial on his chin were dyed, his yellowish full complement of teeth, displayed when he laughed, were a cheap artificial set, and his hands, with signet rings on both index fingers, were those of an old man. With a spasm of distaste Aschenbach watched him as he kept company with his young friends. Did they not know, did they not notice that he was old, that he had no right to be wearing foppish and garish clothes like theirs, no right to be acting as if he were one of them? They seemed to be tolerating his presence among them as something habitual and to be taken for granted, they treated him as an equal, reciprocated without embarrassment when he teasingly poked them in the ribs. How was this possible? Aschenbach put his hand over his forehead and closed his eyes, which were hot from too little sleep. He had a feeling that something not quite usual was beginning to happen, that the world was undergoing a dreamlike alienation, becoming increasingly deranged and bizarre, and that perhaps this process might be arrested if he

---

[9] *"Buon . . . signore":* Italian for "Have a good vacation, sir."

were to cover his face for a little and then take a fresh look at things. But at that moment he had the sensation of being afloat, and starting up in irrational alarm, he noticed that the dark heavy hulk of the steamer was slowly parting company with the stone quayside. Inch by inch, as the engine pounded and reversed, the width of the dirty glinting water between the hull and the quay increased, and after clumsy maneuverings the ship turned its bows toward the open sea. Aschenbach crossed to the starboard side, where the hunchback had set up a deck chair for him and a steward in a grease-stained frock coat offered his services.

The sky was gray, the wind damp. The port and the islands had been left behind, and soon all land was lost to view in the misty panorama. Flecks of sodden soot drifted down on the washed deck, which never seemed to get dry. After only an hour an awning was set up, as it was beginning to rain.

Wrapped in his overcoat, a book lying on his lap, the traveler rested, scarcely noticing the hours as they passed him by. It had stopped raining; the canvas shelter was removed. The horizon was complete. Under the turbid dome of the sky the desolate sea surrounded him in an enormous circle. But in empty, unarticulated space our mind loses its sense of time as well, and we enter the twilight of the immeasurable. As Aschenbach lay there, strange and shadowy figures, the foppish old man, the goat-bearded purser from the ship's interior, passed with uncertain gestures and confused dream-words through his mind, and he fell asleep.

At midday he was requested to come below for luncheon in the long, narrow dining saloon, which ended in the doors to the sleeping berths; here he ate at the head of the long table, at the other end of which the group of apprentices, with the old man among them, had been quaffing since ten o'clock with the good-humored ship's captain. The meal was wretched and he finished it quickly. He needed to be back in the open air, to look at the sky: perhaps it would clear over Venice.

It had never occurred to him that this would not happen, for the city had always received him in its full glory. But the sky and the sea remained dull and leaden, from time to time misty rain fell, and he resigned himself to arriving by water in a different Venice, one he had never encountered on the landward approach. He stood by the foremast, gazing into the distance, waiting for the sight of land. He recalled that poet[20] of plangent inspiration who long ago had seen the cupolas and bell-towers of his dream rise before him out of these same waters; inwardly he recited a few lines of the measured music that had been made from that reverence and joy and sadness, and effortlessly moved by a passion already shaped into language, he questioned his grave and weary heart, wondering whether some new inspiration and distraction, some late adventure of the emotions, might yet be in store for him on his leisured journey.

And now, on his right, the flat coastline rose above the horizon, the sea came alive with fishing vessels, the island resort appeared: the steamer left it on its port side, glided at half speed through the narrow channel named after it, entered the lagoon, and presently, near some shabby miscellaneous buildings, came to a complete halt, as this was where the launch carrying the public health inspector must be awaited.

---

[20] **that poet:** August Graf von Platen (1796–1855), author of *Sonnets on Venice* (1825).

An hour passed before it appeared. One had arrived and yet not arrived; there was no hurry, and yet one was impelled by impatience. The young men from Pola had come on deck, no doubt also patriotically attracted by the military sound of bugle calls across the water from the direction of the Public Gardens; and elated by the Asti[21] they had drunk, they began cheering the *bersaglieri*[22] as they drilled there in the park. But the dandified old man, thanks to his spurious fraternization with the young, was now in a condition repugnant to behold. His old head could not carry the wine as his sturdy youthful companions had done, and he was lamentably drunk. Eyes glazed, a cigarette between his trembling fingers, he stood swaying, tilted to and fro by inebriation and barely keeping his balance. Since he would have fallen at his first step he did not dare move from the spot, and was nevertheless full of wretched exuberance, clutching at everyone who approached him, babbling, winking, sniggering, lifting his ringed and wrinkled forefinger as he uttered some bantering inanity, and licking the corners of his mouth with the tip of his tongue in a repellently suggestive way. Aschenbach watched him with frowning disapproval, and once more a sense of numbness came over him, a feeling that the world was somehow, slightly yet uncontrollably, sliding into some kind of bizarre and grotesque derangement. It was a feeling on which, to be sure, he was unable to brood further in present circumstances, for at this moment the thudding motion of the engine began again, and the ship, having stopped short so close to its destination, resumed its passage along the San Marco Canal.[23]

Thus it was that he saw it once more, that most astonishing of all landing places, that dazzling composition of fantastic architecture which the Republic presented to the admiring gaze of approaching seafarers: the unburdened splendor of the Ducal Palace, the Bridge of Sighs, the lion and the saint on their two columns at the water's edge, the magnificently projecting side wing of the fabulous basilica, the vista beyond it of the gate tower and the Giants' Clock; and as he contemplated it all he reflected that to arrive in Venice by land, at the station, was like entering a palace by a back door: that only as he was now doing, only by ship, over the high sea, should one come to this most extraordinary of cities.

The engine stopped, gondolas pressed alongside, the gangway was let down, customs officers came on board and perfunctorily discharged their duties; disembarkation could begin. Aschenbach indicated that he would like a gondola to take him and his luggage to the stopping place of the small steamboats that ply between the city and the Lido,[24] since he intended to stay in a hotel by the sea. His wishes were approved, his orders shouted down to water level, where the gondoliers were quarreling in Venetian dialect. He was still prevented from leaving the ship, held up by his trunk which at that moment was being laboriously dragged and maneuvered down the ladderlike gangway; and thus, for a full minute or two, he could not avoid the importunate attentions of the dreadful old man, who on some obscure drunken

---

[21] **Asti:** A sparkling, white Italian wine. [22] *bersaglieri:* Elite Italian soldiers. [23] **San Marco Canal:** One of the central canals of Venice, which is a collection of 118 islands interlaced by a series of canals and bridges. [24] **Lido:** A famous resort near Venice.

impulse felt obliged to do this stranger the parting honors. "We wish the signore a most enjoyable stay!" he bleated, bowing and scraping. "We hope the signore will not forget us! *Au revoir, excusez and bon jour,*[25] your Excellency!" He drooled, he screwed up his eyes, licked the corners of his mouth, and the dyed imperial on his senile underlip reared itself upward. "Our compliments," he driveled, touching his lips with two fingers, "our compliments to your sweetheart, to your most charming, beautiful sweetheart . . ." And suddenly the upper set of his false teeth dropped half out of his jaw. Aschenbach was able to escape. "Your sweetheart, your pretty sweetheart!" he heard from behind his back, in gurgling, cavernous, encumbered tones, as he clung to the rope railing and descended the gangway.

Can there be anyone who has not had to overcome a fleeting sense of dread, a secret shudder of uneasiness, on stepping for the first time or after a long interval of years into a Venetian gondola? How strange a vehicle it is, coming down unchanged from times of old romance, and so characteristically black, the way no other thing is black except a coffin—a vehicle evoking lawless adventures in the plashing stillness of night, and still more strongly evoking death itself, the bier, the dark obsequies, the last silent journey! And has it been observed that the seat of such a boat, that armchair with its coffin-black lacquer and dull black upholstery, is the softest, the most voluptuous, most enervating seat in the world? Aschenbach became aware of this when he had settled down at the gondolier's feet, sitting opposite his luggage, which was neatly assembled at the prow. The oarsmen were still quarreling; raucously, unintelligibly, with threatening gestures. But in the peculiar silence of this city of water their voices seemed to be softly absorbed, to become bodiless, dissipated above the sea. It was sultry here in the harbor. As the warm breath of the sirocco[26] touched him, as he leaned back on cushions over the yielding element, the traveler closed his eyes in the enjoyment of this lassitude as sweet as it was unaccustomed. It will be a short ride, he thought; if only it could last forever! In a gently swaying motion he felt himself gliding away from the crowd and the confusion of voices.

How still it was growing all round him! There was nothing to be heard except the plashing of the oar, the dull slap of the wave against the boat's prow where it rose up steep and black and armed at its tip like a halberd, and a third sound also: that of a voice speaking and murmuring—it was the gondolier, whispering and muttering to himself between his teeth, in intermittent grunts pressed out of him by the labor of his arms. Aschenbach looked up and noticed with some consternation that the lagoon was widening round him and that his gondola was heading out to sea. It was thus evident that he must not relax too completely, but give some attention to the proper execution of his instructions.

"Well! To the *vaporetto*[27] stop!" he said, half turning round. The muttering ceased, but no answer came.

---

[25] *Au revoir . . . jour:* French for "good-bye," "excuse me," and "good day."

[26] *sirocco:* A hot wind blowing from the Sahara that picks up moisture over the Mediterranean.

[27] *vaporetto:* A "little steamboat" used for public transportation.

"I said to the *vaporetto* stop!" he repeated, turning round completely and look-ing up into the face of the gondolier, who was standing behind him on his raised deck, towering between him and the pale sky. He was a man of displeasing, indeed brutal appearance, wearing blue seaman's clothes, with a yellow scarf round his waist and a shapeless, already fraying straw hat tilted rakishly on his head. To judge by the cast of his face and the blond curling moustache under his snub nose, he was quite evidently not of Italian origin. Although rather slightly built, so that one would not have thought him particularly well suited to his job, he plied his oar with great energy, putting his whole body into every stroke. Occasionally the effort made him retract his lips and bare his white teeth. With his reddish eyebrows knitted, he stared right over his passenger's head as he answered peremptorily, almost insolently:

"You are going to the Lido."

Aschenbach replied:

"Of course. But I only engaged this gondola to row me across to San Marco. I wish to take the *vaporetto*."

"You cannot take the *vaporetto*, signore."

"And why not?"

"Because the *vaporetto* does not carry luggage."

That was correct, as Aschenbach now remembered. He was silent. But the man's abrupt, presumptuous manner, so uncharacteristic of the way foreigners were usu-ally treated in this country, struck him as unacceptable. He said:

"That is my business. I may wish to deposit my luggage. Will you kindly turn round."

There was silence. The oar plashed, the dull slap of the water against the bow continued, and the talking and muttering began again: the gondolier was talking to himself between his teeth.

What was to be done? Alone on the sea with this strangely contumacious, un-cannily resolute fellow, the traveler could see no way of compelling him to obey his instructions. And in any case, how luxurious a rest he might have here if he simply accepted the situation! Had he not wished the trip were longer, wished it to last for-ever? It was wisest to let things take their course, and above all it was very agreeable to do so. A magic spell of indolence seemed to emanate from his seat, from this low black-upholstered armchair, so softly rocked by the oarstrokes of the high-handed gondolier behind him. The thought that he had perhaps fallen into the hands of a criminal floated dreamily across Aschenbach's mind—powerless to stir him to any active plan of self-defence. There was the more annoying possibility that the whole thing was simply a device for extorting money from him. A kind of pride or sense of duty, a recollection, so to speak, that there are precautions to be taken against such things, impelled him to make one further effort. He asked:

"What is your charge for the trip?"

And looking straight over his head, the gondolier answered:

"You will pay, signore."

The prescribed retort to this was clear enough. Aschenbach answered mechanically:

"I shall pay nothing, absolutely nothing, if you take me where I do not want to go."

"The signore wants to go to the Lido."

"But not with you."

"I can row you well."

True enough, thought Aschenbach, relaxing. True enough, you will row me well. Even if you are after my cash and dispatch me to the house of Hades[28] with a blow of your oar from behind, you will have rowed me well.

But nothing of the sort happened. He was even provided with company: a boat full of piratical musicians, men and women singing to the guitar or mandolin, importunately traveling hard alongside the gondola and for the foreigner's benefit filling the silence of the waters with mercenary song. Aschenbach threw some money into the outheld hat, whereupon they fell silent and moved off. And the gondolier's muttering became audible again, as in fits and starts he continued his self-colloquy.

And so in due course one arrived, bobbing about in the wake of a *vaporetto* bound for the city. Two police officers, with their hands on their backs, were pacing up and down the embankment and looking out over the lagoon. Aschenbach stepped from the gondola onto the gangway, assisted by the old man with a boat hook who turns up for this purpose at every landing stage in Venice; and having run out of small change, he walked across to the hotel opposite the pier, intending to change money and pay off the oarsman with some suitable gratuity. He was served at the hall desk, and returned to the landing stage to find his luggage loaded onto a trolley on the embankment: the gondola and the gondolier had vanished.

"He cleared off," said the old man with the boat hook. "A bad man, a man without a licence, signore. He is the only gondolier who has no licence. The others telephoned across to us. He saw the police waiting for him. So he cleared off."

Aschenbach shrugged his shoulders.

"The signore has had a free trip," said the old man, holding out his hat. Aschenbach threw coins into it. He directed that his luggage should be taken to the Hotel des Bains,[29] and followed the trolley along the avenue, that white-blossoming avenue, bordered on either side by taverns and bazaars and guesthouses, which runs straight across the island to the beach.

He entered the spacious hotel from the garden terrace at the back, passing through the main hall and the vestibule to the reception office. As his arrival had been notified in advance, he was received with obsequious obligingness. A manager, a soft-spoken, flatteringly courteous little man with a black moustache and a frock coat of French cut, accompanied him in the lift to the second floor and showed him to his room, an agreeable apartment with cherry-wood furniture, strongly scented flowers put out to greet him, and a view through tall windows to the open sea. He went and stood by one of them when the manager had withdrawn, and as his luggage was brought in behind him and installed in the room, he gazed out over the beach, uncrowded at this time of the afternoon, and over the sunless sea

---

[28] **Hades:** The mythical underworld in Greek mythology, ruled by the god Hades; the dead were rowed across the river Styx by the boatman Charon.   [29] **Hotel des Bains:** French for "bathing hotel"; a seaside resort.

which was at high tide, its long low waves beating with a quiet regular rhythm on the shore.

The observations and encounters of a devotee of solitude and silence are at once less distinct and more penetrating than those of the sociable man; his thoughts are weightier, stranger, and never without a tinge of sadness. Images and perceptions which might otherwise be easily dispelled by a glance, a laugh, an exchange of comments, concern him unduly, they sink into mute depths, take on significance, become experiences, adventures, emotions. The fruit of solitude is originality, something daringly and disconcertingly beautiful, the poetic creation. But the fruit of solitude can also be the perverse, the disproportionate, the absurd, and the forbidden. And thus the phenomena of his journey to this place, the horrible old made-up man with his maudlin babble about a sweetheart, the illicit gondolier who had been done out of his money, were still weighing on the traveler's mind. Without in any way being rationally inexplicable, without even really offering food for thought, they were nevertheless, as it seemed to him, essentially strange, and indeed it was no doubt this very paradox that made them disturbing. In the meantime he saluted the sea with his gaze and rejoiced in the knowledge that Venice was now so near and accessible. Finally he turned round, bathed his face, gave the room maid certain instructions for the enhancement of his comfort, and then had himself conveyed by the green-uniformed Swiss lift attendant to the ground floor.

He took tea on the front terrace, then went down to the esplanade and walked some way along it in the direction of the Hotel Excelsior. When he returned, it was already nearly time to be changing for dinner. He did so in his usual leisurely and precise manner, for it was his custom to work when performing his toilet; despite this, he arrived a little early in the hall, where he found a considerable number of the hotel guests assembled, unacquainted with each other and affecting a studied mutual indifference, yet all united in expectancy by the prospect of their evening meal. He picked up a newspaper from the table, settled down in a leather armchair and took stock of the company, which differed very agreeably from what he had encountered at his previous hotel.

A large horizon opened up before him, tolerantly embracing many elements. Discreetly muted, the sounds of the major world languages mingled. Evening dress, that internationally accepted uniform of civilization, imparted a decent outward semblance of unity to the wide variations of mankind here represented. One saw the dry elongated visages of Americans, many-membered Russian families, English ladies, German children with French nurses. The Slav component seemed to predominate. In his immediate vicinity he could hear Polish being spoken.

It was a group of adolescent and barely adult young people, sitting round a cane table under the supervision of a governess or companion: three young girls, of fifteen to seventeen as it seemed, and a long-haired boy of about fourteen. With astonishment Aschenbach noticed that the boy was entirely beautiful. His countenance, pale and gracefully reserved, was surrounded by ringlets of honey-colored hair, and with its straight nose, its enchanting mouth, its expression of sweet and divine gravity, it recalled Greek sculpture of the noblest period; yet despite the purest formal perfection, it had such unique personal charm that he who now contemplated it felt he had never beheld, in nature or in art, anything so consummately successful. What also struck him was an obvious contrast of educational principles in the way the boy and his sisters were dressed and generally treated. The system adopted for the three girls, the eldest of whom could be considered to be grown-up, was austere and chaste to the point of disfigurement. They all wore exactly the same slate-colored half-length dresses, sober and of a deliberately unbecoming cut, with white turnover collars as the only relieving feature, and any charm of figure they might have had was suppressed and negated from the outset by this cloistral uniform. Their hair, smoothed and stuck back firmly to their heads, gave their faces a nunlike emptiness and expressionlessness. A mother was clearly in charge here; and it had not even occurred to her to apply to the boy the same pedagogic strictness as she thought proper for the girls. In his life, softness and tenderness were evidently the rule. No one had ever dared to cut short his beautiful hair; like that of the *Boy Extracting a Thorn*[30] it fell in curls over his forehead, over his ears, and still lower over his neck. The English sailor's suit, with its full sleeves tapering down to fit the fine wrists of his still childlike yet slender hands, and with its lanyards and bows and embroideries, enhanced his delicate shape with an air of richness and indulgence. He was sitting, in semiprofile to Aschenbach's gaze, with one foot in its patent leather shoe advanced in front of the other, with one elbow propped on the arm of his basket chair, with his cheek nestling against the closed hand, in a posture of relaxed dignity, without a trace of the almost servile stiffness to which his sisters seemed to have accustomed themselves. Was he in poor health? For his complexion was white as ivory against the dark gold of the surrounding curls. Or was he simply a pampered favorite child, borne up by the partiality of a capricious love? Aschenbach was inclined to think so. Inborn in almost every artistic nature is a luxuriant, treacherous bias in favor of the injustice that creates beauty, a tendency to sympathize with aristocratic preference and pay it homage.

A waiter circulated and announced in English that dinner was served. Gradually the company disappeared through the glass door into the dining room. Latecomers passed, coming from the vestibule or the lifts. The service of dinner had already begun, but the young Poles were still waiting round their cane table, and Aschenbach, comfortably ensconced in his deep armchair, and additionally having the spectacle of beauty before his eyes, waited with them.

The governess, a corpulent and rather unladylike, red-faced little woman, finally gave the signal for them to rise. With arched brows she pushed back her chair and bowed as a tall lady, dressed in silvery gray and very richly adorned with pearls, entered the hall. This lady's attitude was cool and poised, her lightly powdered coiffure and the style of her dress both had that simplicity which is the governing principle of taste in circles where piety is regarded as one of the aristocratic values. In Germany she might have been the wife of a high official. The only thing that did give her appearance a fantastic and luxurious touch was her jewelry, which was indeed beyond price, consisting of earrings as well as a very long three-stranded necklace of gently shimmering pearls as big as cherries.

---

[30] *Boy . . . Thorn:* First-century B.C.E. Greek statue of a boy admired for his beauty.

The brother and sisters had quickly risen to their feet. They bowed over their mother's hand to kiss it, while she, with a restrained smile on her well-maintained but slightly weary and angular face, looked over their heads and addressed a few words in French to the governess. Then she walked toward the glass door. Her children followed her: the girls in order of age, after them the governess, finally the boy. For some reason or other he turned round before crossing the threshold, and as there was now no one else in the hall, his strangely twilight-gray eyes met those of Aschenbach, who with his paper in his lap, lost in contemplation, had been watching the group leave.

What he had seen had certainly not been remarkable in any particular. One does not go in to table before one's mother, they had waited for her, greeted her respectfully, and observed normal polite precedence in entering the dining room. But this had all been carried out with such explicitness, with such a strongly accented air of discipline, obligation, and self-respect, that Aschenbach felt strangely moved. He lingered for another few moments, then he too crossed into the dining room and had himself shown to his table—which, as he noticed with a brief stirring of regret, was at some distance from that of the Polish family.

Tired and yet intellectually stimulated, he beguiled the long and tedious meal with abstract and indeed transcendental reflections. He meditated on the mysterious combination into which the canonical and the individual must enter for human beauty to come into being, proceeded from this point to general problems of form and art, and concluded in the end that his thoughts and findings resembled certain seemingly happy inspirations that come to us in dreams, only to be recognized by the sober senses as completely shallow and worthless. After dinner he lingered for a while, smoking and sitting and walking about, in the evening fragrance of the hotel garden, then retired early and passed the night in sleep which was sound and long, though dream images enlivened it from time to time.

Next day the weather did not seem to be improving. The wind was from landward. Under a pallid overcast sky the sea lay sluggishly still and shrunken-looking, with the horizon in prosaic proximity and the tide so far out that several rows of long sandbars lay exposed. When Aschenbach opened his window, he thought he could smell the stagnant air of the lagoon.

Vexation overcame him. The thought of leaving occurred to him then and there. Once before, years ago, after fine spring weeks, this same weather had come on him here like a visitation, and so adversely affected his health that his departure from Venice had been like a precipitate escape. Were not the same symptoms now presenting themselves again, that unpleasant feverish sensation, the pressure in the temples, the heaviness in the eyelids? To move elsewhere yet again would be tiresome; but if the wind did not change, then there was no question of his staying here. As a precaution he did not unpack completely. At nine he breakfasted in the buffet between the hall and the main restaurant which was used for serving breakfast.

The kind of ceremonious silence prevailed here which a large hotel always aims to achieve. The serving waiters moved about noiselessly. A clink of crockery, a half-whispered word, were the only sounds audible. In one corner, obliquely opposite the door and two tables away from his own, Aschenbach noticed the Polish girls with their governess. Perched very upright, their ash-blond hair newly brushed and with reddened eyes, in stiff blue linen dresses with little white turnover collars and cuffs, they sat there passing each other a jar of preserves. They had almost finished their breakfast. The boy was missing.

Aschenbach smiled. Well, my little Phaeacian![31] he thought. You seem, unlike these young ladies, to enjoy the privilege of sleeping your fill. And with his spirits suddenly rising, he recited to himself the line: "Varied garments to wear, warm baths and restful reposing."

He breakfasted unhurriedly, received some forwarded mail from the porter who came into the breakfast room with his braided cap in hand, and opened a few letters as he smoked a cigarette. Thus it happened that he was still present to witness the entry of the lie-abed they were waiting for across the room.

He came through the glass door and walked in the silence obliquely across the room to his sisters' table. His walk was extraordinarily graceful, in the carriage of his upper body, the motion of his knees, the placing of his white-shod foot; it was very light, both delicate and proud, and made still more beautiful by the childlike modesty with which he twice, turning his head toward the room, raised and lowered his eyes as he passed. With a smile and a murmured word in his soft liquescent language, he took his seat; and now especially, as his profile was exactly turned to the watching Aschenbach, the latter was again amazed, indeed startled, by the truly god-like beauty of this human creature. Today the boy was wearing a light casual suit of blue and white striped linen material with a red silk breast-knot, closing at the neck in a simple white stand-up collar. But on this collar — which did not even match the rest of the suit very elegantly — there, like a flower in bloom, his head was gracefully resting. It was the head of Eros,[32] with the creamy luster of Parian marble,[33] the brows fine-drawn and serious, the temples and ear darkly and softly covered by the neat right-angled growth of the curling hair.

Good, good! thought Aschenbach, with that cool professional approval in which artists confronted by a masterpiece sometimes cloak their ecstasy, their rapture. And mentally he added: Truly, if the sea and the shore did not await me, I should stay here as long as you do! But as it was, he went, went through the hall accompanied by the courteous attentions of the hotel staff, went down over the great terrace and straight along the wooden passageway to the enclosed beach reserved for hotel guests. Down there, a barefooted old man with linen trousers, sailor's jacket, and straw hat functioned as bathing attendant: Aschenbach had himself conducted by him to his reserved beach cabin, had his table and chair set up on the sandy wooden platform in front of it, and made himself comfortable in the deck chair which he had drawn further out toward the sea onto the wax-yellow sand.

---

[31] **Phaeacian:** The Phaeacians were a contented, peaceful, island people who showed hospitality to Odysseus in Homer's *Odyssey* (Book VIII).

[32] **Eros:** The Greek god of love. In early Greek mythology, Eros was born out of Chaos and is thought to be the creative, binding force in all relationships. In later mythology, he is the son of Aphrodite; his role is reduced to sensuous desire, and he is portrayed as a beautiful boy with wings — the same as the Roman god Cupid.

[33] **Parian marble:** White marble from the Greek island of Paros.

The scene on the beach, the spectacle of civilization taking its carefree sensuous ease at the brink of the element, entertained and delighted him as much as ever. Already the gray shallow sea was alive with children wading, with swimmers, with assorted figures lying on the sandbars, their crossed arms under their heads. Others were rowing little keelless boats painted red and blue, and capsizing with shrieks of laughter. In front of the long row of *capanne*,[34] with their platforms like little verandahs to sit on, there was animated play and leisurely sprawling repose, there was visiting and chattering, there was punctilious morning elegance as well as unabashed nakedness contentedly enjoying the liberal local conventions. Further out, on the moist firm sand, persons in white bathing robes, in loose-fitting colorful shirtwear wandered to and fro. On the right, a complicated sand castle built by children was bedecked by flags in all the national colors. Vendors of mussels, cakes, and fruit knelt to display their wares. On the left, in front of one of the huts in the row that was set at right angles to the others and to the sea, forming a boundary to the beach at this end, a Russian family was encamped: men with beards and big teeth, overripe indolent women, a Baltic spinster sitting at an easel and with exclamations of despair painting the sea, two good-natured hideous children, an old nanny in a headcloth who behaved in the caressingly deferential manner of the born serf. There they all were, gratefully enjoying their lives, tirelessly shouting the names of their disobediently romping children, mustering a few Italian words to joke at length with the amusing old man who sold them sweets, kissing each other on the cheeks and caring not a jot whether anyone was watching their scene of human solidarity.

Well, I shall stay, thought Aschenbach. What better place could I find? And with his hands folded in his lap, he let his eyes wander in the wide expanse of the sea, let his gaze glide away, dissolve and die in the monotonous haze of this desolate emptiness. There were profound reasons for his attachment to the sea: he loved it because as a hard-working artist he needed rest, needed to escape from the demanding complexity of phenomena and lie hidden on the bosom of the simple and tremendous; because of a forbidden longing deep within him that ran quite contrary to his life's task and was for that very reason seductive, a longing for the unarticulated and immeasurable, for eternity, for nothingness. To rest in the arms of perfection is the desire of any man intent upon creating excellence; and is not nothingness a form of perfection? But now, as he mused idly on such profound matters, the horizontal line of the sea's shore was suddenly intersected by a human figure, and when he had retrieved his gaze from limitless immensity and concentrated it again, he beheld the beautiful boy, coming from the left and walking past him across the sand. He walked barefoot, ready for wading, his slender legs naked to above the knees; his pace was leisured, but as light and proud as if he had long been used to going about without shoes. As he walked he looked round at the projecting row of huts: but scarcely had he noticed the Russian family, as it sat there in contented concord and going about its natural business, than a storm of angry contempt gathered over his face. He frowned darkly, his lips pouted, a bitter grimace pulled them to one side and

---

[34] *capanne:* Beach cabins.

distorted his cheek; his brows were contracted in so deep a scowl that his eyes seemed to have sunk right in under their pressure, glaring forth a black message of hatred. He looked down, looked back again menacingly, then made with one shoulder an emphatic gesture of rejection as he turned his back and left his enemies behind him.

A kind of delicacy or alarm, something like respect and embarrassment, moved Aschenbach to turn away as if he had seen nothing; for no serious person who witnesses a moment of passion by chance will wish to make any use, even privately, of what he has observed. But he was at one and the same time entertained and moved, that is to say he was filled with happiness. Such childish fanaticism, directed against so harmless a piece of good-natured living—it gave a human dimension to mute divinity, it made a statuesque masterpiece of nature, which had hitherto merely delighted the eyes, seem worthy of a profounder appreciation as well; and it placed the figure of this adolescent, remarkable already by his beauty, in a context which enabled one to take him seriously beyond his years.

With his head still averted, Aschenbach listened to the boy's voice, his high, not very strong voice, as he called out greetings to his playmates working at the sand castle, announcing his arrival when he was still some way from them. They answered, repeatedly shouting his name or a diminutive of his name, and Aschenbach listened for this with a certain curiosity, unable to pick up anything more precise than two melodious syllables that sounded something like "Adgio" or still oftener "Adgiu," called out with a long *u* at the end. The sound pleased him, he found its euphony befitting to its object, repeated it quietly to himself and turned again with satisfaction to his letters and papers.

With his traveling writing-case on his knees, he took out his fountain pen and began to deal with this and that item of correspondence. But after no more than a quarter of an hour he felt that it was a great pity to turn his mind away like this from the present situation, this most enjoyable of all situations known to him, and to miss the experience of it for the sake of an insignificant activity. He threw his writing materials aside, he returned to the sea; and before long, his attention attracted by the youthful voices of the sand castle builders, he turned his head comfortably to the right against the back of his chair, to investigate once more the whereabouts and doings of the excellent Adgio.

His first glance found him; the red breast-knot was unmistakable. He and some others were busy laying an old plank as a bridge across the damp moat of the sand castle, and he was supervising this work, calling out instructions and motioning with his head. With him were about ten companions, both boys and girls, of his age and some of them younger, all chattering together in tongues, in Polish, in French, and even in Balkan idioms. But it was his name that was most often heard. It was obvious that he was sought after, wooed, admired. One boy in particular, a Pole like him, a sturdy young fellow whom they called something like "Jashu," with glossy black hair and wearing a linen belted suit, seemed to be his particular vassal and friend. When the work on the sand castle ended for the time being, they walked along the beach with their arms round each other, and the boy they called "Jashu" kissed his beautiful companion.

Aschenbach was tempted to shake his finger at him. "But I counsel you, Critobulus," he thought with a smile, "to go traveling for a year! You will need that much time at least before you are cured."[35] And he then breakfasted on some large, fully ripe strawberries which he bought from a vendor. It had grown very warm, although the sun was unable to break through the sky's layer of cloud. Even as one's senses enjoyed the tremendous and dizzying spectacle of the sea's stillness, lassitude paralyzed the mind. To the mature and serious Aschenbach it seemed an appropriate, fully satisfying task and occupation for him to guess or otherwise ascertain what name this could be that sounded approximately like "Adgio." And with the help of a few Polish recollections he established that what was meant must be "Tadzio," the abbreviation of "Tadeusz" and changing in the vocative to "Tadziu."

Tadzio was bathing. Aschenbach, who had lost sight of him, identified his head and his flailing arm far out to sea; for the water was evidently still shallow a long way out. But already he seemed to be giving cause for alarm, already women's voices were calling out to him from the bathing huts, again shrieking this name which ruled the beach almost like a rallying-cry, and which with its soft consonants, its long-drawn-out *u*-sound at the end, had both a sweetness and a wildness about it: "Tadziu! Tadziu!" He returned, he came running, beating the resisting water to foam with his feet, his head thrown back, running through the waves. And to behold this living figure, lovely and austere in its early masculinity, with dripping locks and beautiful as a young god, approaching out of the depths of the sky and the sea, rising and escaping from the elements—this sight filled the mind with mythical images, it was like a poet's tale from a primitive age, a tale of the origins of form and of the birth of the gods. Aschenbach listened with closed eyes to this song as it began its music deep within him, and once again he reflected that it was good to be here and that here he would stay.

Later on, Tadzio lay in the sand resting from his bathe, wrapped in his white bathing robe which he had drawn through under his right shoulder, and cradling his head on his naked arm; and even when Aschenbach was not watching him but reading a few pages in his book, he almost never forgot that the boy was lying there, and that he need only turn his head slightly to the right to have the admired vision again in view. It almost seemed to him that he was sitting here for the purpose of protecting the half-sleeping boy—busy with doings of his own and yet nevertheless constantly keeping watch over this noble human creature there on his right, only a little way from him. And his heart was filled and moved by a paternal fondness, the tender concern by which he who sacrifices himself to beget beauty in the spirit is drawn to him who possesses beauty.

After midday he left the beach, returned to the hotel and took the lift up to his room. Here he spent some time in front of the looking glass studying his gray hair, his weary sharp-featured face. At that moment he thought of his fame, reflected that many people recognized him on the streets and would gaze at him respectfully,

---

[35] **"But I counsel . . . cured"**: This is the advice that Socrates gave to Critobulus, who had kissed Alcibiades' handsome son (Xenophon, *Memorabilia*, Bk. 1, ch. 3).

saluting the unerring and graceful power of his language—he recalled all the external successes he could think of that his talent had brought him, even calling to mind his elevation to the nobility. Then he went down to the restaurant and took lunch at his table. When he had finished and was entering the lift again, a group of young people who had also just been lunching crowded after him into the hovering cubicle, and Tadzio came with them. He stood quite near Aschenbach, so near that for the first time the latter was not seeing him as a distant image, but perceiving and taking precise cognizance of the details of his humanity. The boy was addressed by someone, and as he replied, with an indescribably charming smile, he was already leaving the lift again as it reached the first floor, stepping out backward with downcast eyes. The beautiful are modest, thought Aschenbach, and began to reflect very intensively on why this should be so. Nevertheless, he had noticed that Tadzio's teeth were not as attractive as they might have been: rather jagged and pale, lacking the luster of health and having that peculiar brittle transparency that is sometimes found in cases of anemia. "He's very delicate, he's sickly," thought Aschenbach, "he'll probably not live to grow old." And he made no attempt to explain to himself a certain feeling of satisfaction or relief that accompanied this thought.

He spent two hours in his room, and in mid-afternoon took the *vaporetto* across the stale-smelling lagoon to Venice. He got out at San Marco, took tea on the Piazza,[36] and then, in accordance with the daily program he had adopted for his stay here, set off on a walk through the streets. But it was this walk that brought about a complete change in his mood and intentions.

An unpleasant sultriness pervaded the narrow streets; the air was so thick that the exhalations from houses and shops and hot food stalls, the reek of oil, the smell of perfume, and many other odors hung about in clouds instead of dispersing. Cigarette smoke lingered and was slow to dissipate. The throng of people in the alleyways annoyed him as he walked instead of giving him pleasure. The further he went, the more overwhelmingly he was afflicted by that appalling condition sometimes caused by a combination of the sea air with the sirocco, a condition of simultaneous excitement and exhaustion. He began to sweat disagreeably. His eyes faltered, his chest felt constricted, he was feverish, the blood throbbed in his head. He fled from the crowded commercial thoroughfares, over bridges, into the poor quarters. There he was besieged by beggars, and the sickening stench from the canals made it difficult to breathe. In a silent square, one of those places in the depths of Venice that seem to have been forgotten and put under a spell, he rested on the edge of a fountain, wiped the sweat from his forehead, and realized that he would have to leave.

For the second time, and this time definitively, it had become evident that this city, in this state of the weather, was extremely injurious to him. To stay on willfully would be contrary to good sense, the prospect of a change in the wind seemed quite uncertain. He must make up his mind at once. To return straight home was out of the question. Neither his summer nor his winter quarters were ready to receive him. But this was not the only place with the sea and a beach, and elsewhere they were to

---

[36] **Piazza:** A large, central plaza in front of Saint Mark's Church.

be had without the harmful additional ingredient of this lagoon with its mephitic vapors. He remembered a little coastal resort not far from Trieste which had been recommended to him. Why not go there? And he must do so without delay, if it was to be worthwhile changing to a different place yet again. He declared himself resolved and rose to his feet. At the next gondola stop he took a boat and had himself conveyed back to San Marco through the murky labyrinth of canals, under delicate marble balconies flanked with carved lions, round the slimy stone corners of buildings, past the mournful facades of *palazzi*[37] on which boards bearing the names of commercial enterprises were mirrored in water where refuse bobbed up and down. He had some trouble getting to his destination, as the gondolier was in league with lace factories and glassworks and tried to land him at every place where he might view the wares and make a purchase; and whenever this bizarre journey through Venice might have cast its spell on him, he was effectively and irksomely disenchanted by the cutpurse mercantile spirit of the sunken queen of the Adriatic.[38]

Back in the hotel, before he had even dined, he notified the office that unforeseen circumstances obliged him to leave on the following morning. Regret was expressed, his bill was settled. He took dinner and spent the warm evening reading newspapers in a rocking chair on the back terrace. Before going to bed he packed completely for departure.

He slept fitfully, troubled by his impending further journey. When he opened his windows in the morning, the sky was still overcast, but the air seemed fresher, and—he began even now to regret his decision. Had he not given notice too impulsively, had it not been a mistake, an action prompted by a mere temporary indisposition? If only he had deferred it for a little, if only, without giving up so soon, he had taken a chance on acclimatizing himself to Venice or waiting for the wind to change, then he would now have before him not the hurry and flurry of a journey, but a morning on the beach like that of the previous day. Too late. What he had wanted yesterday he must go on wanting now. He got dressed and took the lift down to breakfast at eight o'clock.

When he entered the breakfast room it was still empty of guests. A few came in as he was sitting waiting for what he had ordered. As he sipped his tea he saw the Polish girls arrive with their companion: strict and matutinal, with reddened eyes, they proceeded to their table in the window corner. Shortly after this the porter approached with cap in hand and reminded him that it was time to leave. The motor coach was standing ready to take him and other passengers to the Hotel Excelsior, from which point the motor launch would convey the ladies and gentlemen through the company's private canal and across to the station. Time is pressing, signore.—In Aschenbach's opinion time was doing nothing of the sort. There was more than an hour till his train left. He found it extremely annoying that hotels should make a practice of getting their departing clients off the premises unnecessarily early, and

---

[37] *palazzi:* "Palaces" built during the Renaissance that were turned into commercial buildings.

[38] **queen of the Adriatic:** Venice had reached the height of its wealth and power in the fifteenth century and was known as "Queen of the Seas."

indicated to the porter that he wished to have his breakfast in peace. The man hesitantly withdrew, only to reappear five minutes later. It was impossible, he said, for the automobile to wait any longer. Aschenbach retorted angrily that in that case it should leave, and take his trunk with it. He himself would take the public steamboat when it was time, and would they kindly leave it to him to deal with the problem of his own departure. The hotel servant bowed. Aschenbach, glad to have fended off these tiresome admonitions, finished his breakfast unhurriedly, and even got the waiter to hand him a newspaper. It was indeed getting very late by the time he rose. It so happened that at that same moment Tadzio entered through the glass door.

As he walked to his family's table his path crossed that of the departing guest. Meeting this gray-haired gentleman with the lofty brow, he modestly lowered his eyes, only to raise them again at once in his enchanting way, in a soft and full glance; and then he had passed. Good-bye, Tadzio! thought Aschenbach. How short our meeting was. And he added, actually shaping the thought with his lips and uttering it aloud to himself, as he normally never did: "May God bless you!"—He then went through the routine of departure, distributed gratuities, received the parting courtesies of the soft-spoken little manager in the French frock coat, and left the hotel on foot as he had come, walking along the white-blossoming avenue with the hotel servant behind him carrying his hand luggage, straight across the island to the *vaporetto* landing stage. He reached it, he took his seat on board—and what followed was a voyage of sorrow, a grievous passage that plumbed all the depths of regret.

It was the familiar trip across the lagoon, past San Marco, up the Grand Canal. Aschenbach sat on the semicircular bench in the bows, one arm on the railing, shading his eyes with his hand. The Public Gardens fell away astern, the Piazzetta revealed itself once more in its princely elegance and was left behind, then came the great flight of the *palazzi,* with the splendid marble arch of the Rialto appearing as the waterway turned. The traveler contemplated it all, and his heart was rent with sorrow. The atmosphere of the city, this slightly moldy smell of sea and swamp from which he had been so anxious to escape—he breathed it in now in deep, tenderly painful drafts. Was it possible that he had not known, had not considered how deeply his feelings were involved in all these things? What had been a mere qualm of compunction this morning, a slight stirring of doubt as to the wisdom of his behavior, now became grief, became real suffering, an anguish of the soul, so bitter that several times it brought tears to his eyes, and which as he told himself he could not possibly have foreseen. What he found so hard to bear, what was indeed at times quite unendurable, was evidently the thought that he would never see Venice again, that this was a parting forever. For since it had become clear for a second time that this city made him ill, since he had been forced a second time to leave it precipitately, he must of course from now on regard it as an impossible and forbidden place to which he was not suited, and which it would be senseless to attempt to revisit. Indeed, he felt that if he left now, shame and pride must prevent him from ever setting eyes again on this beloved city which had twice physically defeated him; and this contention between his soul's desire and his physical capacities suddenly seemed to the aging Aschenbach so grave and important, the bodily inadequacy so shameful, so necessary to overcome at all costs, that he could not understand the facile resignation with which he had decided yesterday, without any serious struggle, to tolerate that inadequacy and to acknowledge it.

In the meantime the *vaporetto* was approaching the station, and Aschenbach's distress and sense of helplessness increased to the point of distraction. In his torment he felt it to be impossible to leave and no less impossible to turn back. He entered the station torn by this acute inner conflict. It was very late, he had not a moment to lose if he was to catch his train. He both wanted to catch it and wanted to miss it. But time was pressing, lashing him on; he hurried to get his ticket, looking round in the crowded concourse for the hotel company's employee who would be on duty here. The man appeared and informed him that his large trunk had been sent off as registered baggage. Sent off already? Certainly—to Como.[39] To Como? And from hasty comings and goings, from angry questions and embarrassed replies, it came to light that the trunk, before even leaving the luggage room in the Hotel Excelsior, had been put with some quite different baggage and dispatched to a totally incorrect address.

Aschenbach had some difficulty preserving the facial expression that would be the only comprehensible one in these circumstances. A wild joy, an unbelievable feeling of hilarity, shook him almost convulsively from the depths of his heart. The hotel employee rushed to see if it was still possible to stop the trunk, and needless to say returned without having had any success. Aschenbach accordingly declared that he was not prepared to travel without his luggage, that he had decided to go back and wait at the Hotel des Bains for the missing article to turn up again. Was the company's motor launch still at the station? The man assured him that it was waiting immediately outside. With Italian eloquence he prevailed upon the official at the ticket office to take back Aschenbach's already purchased ticket. He swore that telegrams would be sent, that nothing would be left undone and no effort spared to get the trunk back in no time at all—and thus it most strangely came about that the traveler, twenty minutes after arriving at the station, found himself back on the Grand Canal and on his way back to the Lido.

How unbelievably strange an experience it was, how shaming, how like a dream in its bizarre comedy: to be returning, by a quirk of fate, to places from which one has just taken leave forever with the deepest sorrow—to be sent back and to be seeing them again within the hour! With spray tossing before its bows, deftly and entertainingly tacking to and fro between gondolas and *vaporetti,* the rapid little boat darted toward its destination, while its only passenger sat concealing under a mask of resigned annoyance the anxiously exuberant excitement of a truant schoolboy. From time to time he still inwardly shook with laughter at this mishap, telling himself that even a man born under a lucky star could not have had a more welcome piece of ill luck. There would be explanations to be given, surprised faces to be

---

[39] **Como:** A lake and resort area in northwest Italy.

confronted—and then, as he told himself, everything would be well again, a disaster would have been averted, a grievous mistake corrected, and everything he thought he had turned his back on for good would lie open again for him to enjoy, would be his for as long as he liked . . . And what was more, did the rapid movement of the motor launch deceive him, or was there really now, to crown all else, a breeze blowing from the sea?

The bow waves dashed against the concrete walls of the narrow canal that cuts across the island to the Hotel Excelsior. There a motor omnibus was waiting for the returning guest and conveyed him along the road above the rippling sea straight to the Hotel des Bains. The little manager with the moustache and the fancily-cut frock coat came down the flight of steps to welcome him.

In softly flattering tones he expressed regret for the incident, described it as highly embarrassing for himself and for the company, but emphatically endorsed Aschenbach's decision to wait here for his luggage. His room, to be sure, had been relet, but another, no less comfortable, was immediately at his disposal. *"Pas de chance, monsieur!"*[40] said the Swiss lift-attendant as they glided up. And thus the fugitive was once more installed in a room situated and furnished almost exactly like the first.

Exhausted and numbed by the confusion of this strange morning, he had no sooner distributed the contents of his hand luggage about the room than he collapsed into a reclining chair at the open window. The sea had turned pale green, the air seemed clearer and purer, the beach with its bathing cabins and boats more colorful, although the sky was still gray. Aschenbach gazed out, his hands folded in his lap, pleased to be here again but shaking his head with displeasure at his irresolution, his ignorance of his own wishes. Thus he sat for about an hour, resting and idly daydreaming. At midday he caught sight of Tadzio in his striped linen suit with the red breast-knot, coming from the sea, through the beach barrier and along the boarded walks back to the hotel. From up here at his window Aschenbach recognized him at once, before he had even looked at him properly, and some such thought came to him as: Why, Tadzio, there you are again too! But at the same instant he felt that casual greeting die on his lips, stricken dumb by the truth in his heart—he felt the rapturous kindling of his blood, the joy and the anguish of his soul, and realized that it was because of Tadzio that it had been so hard for him to leave.

He sat quite still, quite unseen at his high vantage point, and began to search his feelings. His features were alert, his eyebrows rose, an attentive, intelligently inquisitive smile parted his lips. Then he raised his head, and with his arms hanging limply down along the back of his chair, described with both of them a slowly rotating and lifting motion, the palms of his hands turning forward, as if to sketch an opening and outspreading of the arms. It was a gesture that gladly bade welcome, a gesture of calm acceptance.

---

[40] *"Pas . . . monsieur!"*: French for "No luck, sir!"

4

Now day after day the god with the burning cheeks[41] soared naked, driving his four fire-breathing steeds through the spaces of heaven, and now, too, his yellow-gold locks fluttered wide in the outstorming east wind. Silk-white radiance gleamed on the slow-swelling deep's vast waters. The sand glowed. Under the silvery quivering blue of the ether, rust-colored awnings were spread out in front of the beach cabins, and one spent the morning hours on the sharply defined patch of shade they provided. But exquisite, too, was the evening, when the plants in the park gave off a balmy fragrance, and the stars on high moved through their dance, and the softly audible murmur of the night-surrounded sea worked its magic on the soul. Such an evening carried with it the delightful promise of a new sunlit day of leisure easily ordered, and adorned with countless close-knit possibilities of charming chance encounter.

The guest whom so convenient a mishap had detained here was very far from seeing the recovery of his property as a reason for yet another departure. For a couple of days he had had to put up with some privations and appear in the main dining room in his traveling clothes. Then, when finally the errant load was once more set down in his room, he unpacked completely and filled the cupboards and drawers with his possessions, resolving for the present to set no time limit on his stay; he was glad now to be able to pass his hours on the beach in a tussore[42] suit and to present himself again in seemly evening attire at the dinner table.

The lulling rhythm of this existence had already cast its spell on him; he had been quickly enchanted by the indulgent softness and splendor of this way of life. What a place this was indeed, combining the charms of a cultivated seaside resort in the south with the familiar ever-ready proximity of the strange and wonderful city! Aschenbach did not enjoy enjoying himself. Whenever and wherever he had to stop work, have a breathing space, take things easily, he would soon find himself driven by restlessness and dissatisfaction—and this had been so in his youth above all— back to his lofty travail, to his stern and sacred daily routine. Only this place bewitched him, relaxed his will, gave him happiness. Often in the forenoon, under the awning of his hut, gazing dreamily at the blue of the southern sea, or on a mild night perhaps, reclining under a star-strewn sky on the cushions of a gondola that carried him back to the Lido from the Piazza where he had long lingered—and as the bright lights, the melting sounds of the serenade dropped away behind him— often he recalled his country house in the mountains, the scene of his summer labors, where the low clouds would drift through his garden, violent evening thunderstorms would put out all the lights, and the ravens he fed would take refuge in the tops of the pine trees. Then indeed he would feel he had been snatched away now to the Elysian land,[43] to the ends of the earth, where lightest of living is granted to

---

[41] **the god . . . cheeks:** Helios, Greek god of the sun.   [42] **tussore:** A coarse silk.   [43] **Elysian land:** In Greek mythology, some fortunate mortals spend their afterlife in the bliss of the Elysian Fields, or Islands of the Blest, rather than in Hades.

mortals, where no snow is nor winter, no storms and no rain downstreaming, but where Oceanus[44] ever causes a gentle cooling breeze to ascend, and the days flow past in blessed idleness, with no labor or strife, for to the sun alone and its feasts they are all given over.

Aschenbach saw much of the boy Tadzio, he saw him almost constantly; in a confined environment, with a common daily program, it was natural for the beautiful creature to be near him all day, with only brief interruptions. He saw him and met him everywhere: in the ground-floor rooms of the hotel, on their cooling journeys by water to the city and back, in the sumptuous Piazza itself, and often elsewhere from time to time, in alleys and byways, when chance had played a part. But it was during the mornings on the beach above all, and with the happiest regularity, that he could devote hours at a time to the contemplation and study of this exquisite phenomenon. Indeed, it was precisely this ordered routine of happiness, this equal daily repetition of favorable circumstances, that so filled him with contentment and zest for life, that made this place so precious to him, that allowed one sunlit day to follow another in such obligingly endless succession.

He rose early, as he would normally have done under the insistent compulsion of work, and was down at the beach before most of the other guests, when the sun's heat was still gentle and the sea lay dazzling white in its morning dreams. He greeted the barrier attendant affably, exchanged familiar greetings also with the barefooted, white-bearded old man who had prepared his place for him, spread the brown awning and shifted the cabin furniture out to the platform where Aschenbach would settle down. Three hours or four were then his, hours in which the sun would rise to its zenith and to terrible power, hours in which the sea would turn a deeper and deeper blue, hours in which he would be able to watch Tadzio.

He saw him coming, walking along from the left by the water's edge, saw him from behind as he emerged between the cabins, or indeed would sometimes look up and discover, gladdened and startled, that he had missed his arrival and that the boy was already there, already in the blue and white bathing costume which now on the beach was his sole attire. There he would be, already busy with his customary activities in the sun and the sand—this charmingly trivial, idle yet ever-active life that was both play and repose, a life of sauntering, wading, digging, snatching, lying about, and swimming, under the watchful eyes and at the constant call of the women on their platform, who with their high-pitched voices would cry out his name: "Tadziu! Tadziu!" and to whom he would come running with eager gesticulation, to tell them what he had experienced, to show them what he had found, what he had caught: jellyfish, little seahorses, and mussels, and crabs that go sideways. Aschenbach understood not a word of what he said, and commonplace though it might be, it was liquid melody in his ears. Thus the foreign sound of the boy's speech exalted it to music, the sun in its triumph shed lavish brightness all over him, and the sublime perspective of the sea was the constant contrasting background against which he appeared.

---

[44] **Oceanus:** In Greek mythology, the Titan who rules over a river encircling the world.

Soon the contemplative beholder knew every line and pose of that noble, so freely displayed body, he saluted again with joy each already familiar perfection, and there was no end to his wonder, to the delicate delight of his senses. The boy would be summoned to greet a guest who was making a polite call on the ladies in their cabin; he would run up, still wet perhaps from the sea, throw back his curls, and as he held out his hand, poised on one leg with the other on tiptoe, he had an enchanting way of turning and twisting his body, gracefully expectant, charmingly shamefaced, seeking to please because good breeding required him to do so. Or he would be lying full-length, his bathing robe wrapped round his chest, his finely chiseled arm propped on the sand, his hand cupping his chin; the boy addressed as "Jashu" would squat beside him caressing him, and nothing could be more bewitching than the way the favored Tadzio, smiling with his eyes and lips, would look up at this lesser and servile mortal. Or he would be standing at the edge of the sea, alone, some way from his family, quite near Aschenbach, standing upright with his hands clasped behind his neck, slowly rocking to and fro on the balls of his feet and dreamily gazing into the blue distance, while little waves ran up and bathed his toes. His honey-colored hair nestled in ringlets at his temples and at the back of his neck, the sun gleamed in the down on his upper spine, the subtle outlining of his ribs and the symmetry of his breast stood out through the scanty covering of his torso, his armpits were still as smooth as those of a statue, the hollows of his knees glistened and their bluish veins made his body seem composed of some more translucent material. What discipline, what precision of thought was expressed in that outstretched, youthfully perfect physique! And yet the austere pure will that had here been darkly active, that had succeeded in bringing this divine sculptured shape to light—was it not well known and familiar to Aschenbach as an artist? Was it not also active in him, in the sober passion that filled him as he set free from the marble mass of language that slender form which he had beheld in the spirit,[45] and which he was presenting to mankind as a model and mirror of intellectual beauty?

A model and mirror! His eyes embraced that noble figure at the blue water's edge, and in rising ecstasy he felt he was gazing on Beauty itself, on Form as a thought of God, on the one and pure perfection which dwells in the spirit and of which a human image and likeness had here been lightly and graciously set up for him to worship. Such was his emotional intoxication; and the aging artist welcomed it unhesitatingly, even greedily. His mind was in labor, its store of culture was in ferment, his memory threw up thoughts from ancient tradition which he had been taught as a boy, but which had never yet come alive in his own fire. Had he not read that the sun turns our attention from spiritual things to the things of the senses?[46] He had read that it so numbs and bewitches our intelligence and memory that the soul, in its joy, quite forgets its proper state and clings with astonished admiration to that most beautiful of all the things the sun shines upon: yes, that only with the help

---

[45] **set free . . . spirit:** Michelangelo (1475–1564), Italian painter and sculptor who believed that he released the figure encased in a block of marble by his carving.

[46] **the sun turns . . . senses:** A reference to Plutarch (46–120 C.E.) and his *Dialogue on Love.*

of a bodily form is the soul then still able to exalt itself to a higher vision. That Cupid, indeed, does as mathematicians do, when they show dull-witted children tangible images of the pure Forms: so too the love god, in order to make spiritual things visible, loves to use the shapes and colors of young men, turning them into instruments of Recollection by adorning them with all the reflected splendor of Beauty, so that the sight of them will truly set us on fire with pain and hope.

Such were the thoughts the god inspired in his enthusiast, such were the emotions of which he grew capable. And a delightful vision came to him, spun from the sea's murmur and the glittering sunlight. It was the old plane tree not far from the walls of Athens—that place of sacred shade, fragrant with chaste-tree blossoms, adorned with sacred statues and pious gifts in honor of the nymphs and of Acheloüs.[47] The stream trickled crystal clear over smooth pebbles at the foot of the great spreading tree; the crickets made their music. But on the grass, which sloped down gently so that one could hold up one's head as one lay, there reclined two men, sheltered here from the heat of the noonday: one elderly and one young, one ugly and one beautiful, the wise beside the desirable. And Socrates, wooing him with witty compliments and jests, was instructing Phaedrus on desire and virtue. He spoke to him of the burning tremor of fear which the lover will suffer when his eye perceives a likeness of eternal Beauty; spoke to him of the lusts of the profane and base who cannot turn their eyes to Beauty when they behold its image and are not capable of reverence; spoke of the sacred terror that visits the noble soul when a god-like countenance, a perfect body appears to him—of how he trembles then and is beside himself and hardly dares look at the possessor of beauty, and reveres him and would even sacrifice to him as to a graven image, if he did not fear to seem foolish in the eyes of men. For Beauty, dear Phaedrus, only Beauty is at one and the same time divinely desirable and visible: it is, mark well, the only form of the spiritual that we can receive with our senses and endure with our senses. For what would become of us if other divine things, if Reason and Virtue and Truth were to appear to us sensuously? Should we not perish in a conflagration of love, as once upon a time Semele[48] did before Zeus? Thus Beauty is the lover's path to the spirit—only the path, only a means, little Phaedrus . . . And then he uttered the subtlest thing of all, that sly wooer: he who loves, he said, is more divine than the beloved, because the god is in the former, but not in the latter—this, the tenderest perhaps and the most mocking thought ever formulated, a thought alive with all the mischievousness and most secret voluptuousness of the heart.

The writer's joy is the thought that can become emotion, the emotion that can wholly become a thought. At that time the solitary Aschenbach took possession and control of just such a pulsating thought, just such a precise emotion: namely, that Nature trembles with rapture when the spirit bows in homage before Beauty. He

---

[47] **Acheloüs:** A river god in ancient Athens. The passage describes Plato's Academy, which was located in a grove of plane trees. A number of Plato's dialogues are devoted to the teachings of Socrates (469–399 B.C.E.).

[48] **Semele:** The mortal mother of Dionysus, whose father is Zeus. She was consumed in flames when she insisted on viewing Zeus in his divine form.

suddenly desired to write. Eros indeed, we are told, loves idleness and is born only for the idle. But at this point of Aschenbach's crisis and visitation his excitement was driving him to produce. The occasion was almost a matter of indifference. An inquiry, an invitation to express a personal opinion on a certain important cultural problem, a burning question of taste, had been circulated to the intellectual world and had been forwarded to him on his travels. The theme was familiar to him, it was close to his experience; the desire to illuminate it in his own words was suddenly irresistible. And what he craved, indeed, was to work on it in Tadzio's presence, to take the boy's physique for a model as he wrote, to let his style follow the lineaments of this body which he saw as divine, and to carry its beauty on high into the spiritual world, as the eagle once carried the Trojan shepherd boy[49] up into the ether. Never had he felt the joy of the word more sweetly, never had he known so clearly that Eros dwells in language, as during those perilously precious hours in which, seated at his rough table under the awning, in full view of his idol and with the music of his voice in his ears, he used Tadzio's beauty as a model for his brief essay—that page and a half of exquisite prose which with its limpid nobility and vibrant controlled passion was soon to win the admiration of many. It is as well that the world knows only a fine piece of work and not also its origins, the conditions under which it came into being; for knowledge of the sources of an artist's inspiration would often confuse readers and shock them, and the excellence of the writing would be of no avail. How strange those hours were! How strangely exhausting that labor! How mysterious this act of intercourse and begetting between a mind and a body! When Aschenbach put away his work and left the beach, he felt worn out, even broken, and his conscience seemed to be reproaching him as if after some kind of debauch.

On the following morning, just as he was leaving the hotel, he noticed from the steps that Tadzio, already on his way to the sea—and alone—was just approaching the beach barrier. The wish to use this opportunity, the mere thought of doing so, and thereby lightly, lightheartedly, making the acquaintance of one who had unknowingly so exalted and moved him: the thought of speaking to him, of enjoying his answer and his glance—all this seemed natural, it was the irresistibly obvious thing to do. The beautiful boy was walking in a leisurely fashion, he could be overtaken, and Aschenbach quickened his pace. He reached him on the boarded way behind the bathing cabins, he was just about to lay his hand on his head or his shoulder, and some phrase or other, some friendly words in French were on the tip of his tongue—when he felt his heart, perhaps partly because he had been walking fast, hammering wildly inside him, felt so breathless that he would only have been able to speak in a strangled and trembling voice. He hesitated, struggled to control himself, then was suddenly afraid that he had already been walking too long close behind the beautiful boy, afraid that Tadzio would notice this, that he would turn and look at him questioningly; he made one more attempt, failed, gave up, and hurried past with his head bowed.

---

[49] **as the eagle . . . shepherd boy:** In the form of an eagle, Zeus kidnapped the Trojan shepherd Ganymede, who became the cupbearer for the Olympian gods.

Too late! he thought at that moment. Too late! But was it too late? This step he had failed to take would very possibly have been all to the good, it might have had a lightening and gladdening effect, led perhaps to a wholesome disenchantment. But the fact now seemed to be that the aging lover no longer wished to be disenchanted, that the intoxication was too precious to him. Who shall unravel the mystery of an artist's nature and character! Who shall explain the profound instinctual fusion of discipline and dissoluteness on which it rests! For not to be able to desire wholesome disenchantment is to be dissolute. Aschenbach was no longer disposed to self-criticism; taste, the intellectual mold of his years, self-respect, maturity, and late simplicity all disinclined him to analyze his motives and decide whether what had prevented him from carrying out his intention had been a prompting of conscience or a disreputable weakness. He was confused, he was afraid that someone, even if only the bathing attendant, might have witnessed his haste and his defeat; he was very much afraid of exposure to ridicule. For the rest, he could not help inwardly smiling at his comic-sacred terror. "Crestfallen," he thought, "spirits dashed, like a frightened cock hanging its wings in a fight! Truly this is the god who at the sight of the desired beauty so breaks our courage and dashes our pride so utterly to the ground . . ."[50] He toyed with the theme, gave rein to his enthusiasm, plunged into emotions he was too proud to fear.

He was no longer keeping any tally of the leisure time he had allowed himself; the thought of returning home did not even occur to him. He had arranged for ample funds to be made available to him here. His one anxiety was that the Polish family might leave; but he had surreptitiously learned, by a casual question to the hotel barber, that these guests had begun their stay here only very shortly before he had arrived himself. The sun was browning his face and hands, the stimulating salty breeze heightened his capacity for feeling, and whereas formerly, when sleep or food or contact with nature had given him any refreshment, he would always have expended it completely on his writing, he now, with high-hearted prodigality, allowed all the daily revitalization he was receiving from the sun and leisure and sea air to burn itself up in intoxicating emotion.

He slept fleetingly; the days of precious monotony were punctuated by brief, happily restless nights. To be sure, he would retire early, for at nine o'clock, when Tadzio had disappeared from the scene, he judged his day to be over. But at the first glint of dawn a pang of tenderness would startle him awake, his heart would remember its adventure, he could bear his pillows no longer, he would get up, and lightly wrapped against the early morning chill he would sit down at the open window to wait for the sunrise. His soul, still fresh with the solemnity of sleep, was filled with awe by this wonderful event. The sky, the earth, and the sea still wore the glassy paleness of ghostly twilight; a dying star still floated in the void. But a murmur came, a winged message from dwelling places no mortal may approach, that Eos[51] was rising from her husband's side; and now it appeared, that first sweet blush at the furthest

---

[50] **"Crestfallen . . . to the ground":** Quoted from Plutarch's *Dialogue on Love.*

[51] **Eos:** The Greek goddess of dawn who loved the young men Cleitus, Cephalus, and the hunter Orion.

horizon of the sky and sea, which heralds the sensuous disclosure of creation. The goddess approached, that ravisher of youth, who carried off Cleitus and Cephalus and defied the envy of all the Olympians to enjoy the love of the beautiful Orion. A scattering of roses began, there at the edge of the world, an ineffably lovely shining and blossoming: childlike clouds, transfigured and transparent with light, hovered like serving *amoretti*[52] in the vermilion and violet haze; crimson light fell across the waves, which seemed to be washing it landward; golden spears darted from below into the heights of heaven, the gleam became a conflagration, noiselessly and with overwhelming divine power the glow and the fire and the blazing flames reared upward, and the sacred steeds of the goddess's brother Helios, tucking their hooves, leapt above the earth's round surface. With the splendor of the god irradiating him, the lone watcher sat; he closed his eyes and let the glory kiss his eyelids. Feelings he had had long ago, early and precious dolors of the heart, which had died out in his life's austere service and were now, so strangely transformed, returning to him — he recognized them with a confused and astonished smile. He meditated, he dreamed, slowly a name shaped itself on his lips, and still smiling, with upturned face, his hands folded in his lap, he fell asleep in his chair once more.

With such fiery ceremony the day began, but the rest of it, too, was strangely exalted and mythically transformed. Where did it come from, what was its origin, this sudden breeze that played so gently and speakingly around his temples and ears, like some higher insufflation? Innumerable white fleecy clouds covered the sky, like the grazing flocks of the gods. A stronger wind rose, and the horses of Poseidon[53] reared and ran; his bulls too, the bulls of the blue-haired sea god, roared and charged with lowered horns. But among the rocks and stones of the more distant beach the waves danced like leaping goats. A sacred, deranged world, full of Panic[54] life, enclosed the enchanted watcher, and his heart dreamed tender tales. Sometimes, as the sun was sinking behind Venice, he would sit on a bench in the hotel park to watch Tadzio, dressed in white with a colorful sash, at play on the rolled gravel tennis court; and in his mind's eye he was watching Hyacinthus, doomed to perish because two gods loved him.[55] He could even feel Zephyr's grievous envy of his rival, who had forgotten his oracle and his bow and his zither to be forever playing with the beautiful youth; he saw the discus, steered by cruel jealousy, strike the lovely head; he himself, turning pale too, caught the broken body in his arms, and the flower that sprang from that sweet blood bore the inscription of his undying lament.

Nothing is stranger, more delicate, than the relationship between people who know each other only by sight — who encounter and observe each other daily, even hourly, and yet are compelled by the constraint of convention or by their own temperament to keep up the pretense of being indifferent strangers, neither greeting nor

---

[52] *amoretti:* Cupids.   [53] **Poseidon:** Greek god of the sea.   [54] **Panic:** Pan, the goat-god associated with nature and sexuality, is responsible for panic.   [55] **Hyacinthus . . . loved him:** In Greek mythology, Zephyr (god of the west wind) and Apollo (the sun god; also the god of archery and music) competed for the love of Hyacinthus, who was accidentally killed in a discus game. The hyacinth flower, marked with the syllables of lament, *ai ai* ("Alas, alas"), arose from his blood.

speaking to each other. Between them is uneasiness and overstimulated curiosity, the nervous excitement of an unsatisfied, unnaturally suppressed need to know and to communicate; and above all, too, a kind of strained respect. For man loves and respects his fellow man for as long as he is not yet in a position to evaluate him, and desire is born of defective knowledge.

It was inevitable that some kind of relationship and acquaintance should develop between Aschenbach and the young Tadzio, and with a surge of joy the older man became aware that his interest and attention were not wholly unreciprocated. Why, for example, when the beautiful creature appeared in the morning on the beach, did he now never use the boarded walk behind the bathing cabins, but always take the front way through the sand, passing Aschenbach's abode and often passing unnecessarily close to him, almost touching his table or his chair, as he sauntered toward the cabin where his family sat? Was this the attraction, the fascination exercised by a superior feeling on its tender and thoughtless object? Aschenbach waited daily for Tadzio to make his appearance and sometimes pretended to be busy when he did so, letting the boy pass him seemingly unnoticed. But sometimes, too, he would look up, and their eyes would meet. They would both be deeply serious when this happened. In the cultured and dignified countenance of the older man, nothing betrayed an inner emotion; but in Tadzio's eyes there was an inquiry, a thoughtful questioning, his walk became hesitant, he looked at the ground, looked sweetly up again, and when he had passed, something in his bearing seemed to suggest that only good breeding restrained him from turning to look back.

But once, one evening, it was different. The Poles and their governess had been absent from dinner in the main restaurant — Aschenbach had noticed this with concern. After dinner, very uneasy about where they might be, he was walking in evening dress and a straw hat in front of the hotel, at the foot of the terrace, when suddenly he saw the nunlike sisters appearing with their companion, in the light of the arc lamps, and four paces behind them was Tadzio. Obviously they had come from the *vaporetto* pier, having for some reason dined in the city. The crossing had been chilly perhaps; Tadzio was wearing a dark blue reefer jacket with gold buttons and a naval cap to match. The sun and sea air never burned his skin, it was marble-pale as always; but today he seemed paler than usual, either because of the cool weather or in the blanching moonlight of the lamps. His symmetrical eyebrows stood out more sharply, his eyes seemed much darker. He was more beautiful than words can express, and Aschenbach felt, as so often already, the painful awareness that language can only praise sensuous beauty, but not reproduce it.

He had not been prepared for the beloved encounter, it came unexpectedly, he had not had time to put on an expression of calm and dignity. Joy no doubt, surprise, admiration, were openly displayed on his face when his eyes met those of the returning absentee — and in that instant it happened that Tadzio smiled: smiled at him, speakingly, familiarly, enchantingly, and quite unabashed, with his lips parting slowly as the smile was formed. It was the smile of Narcissus[56] as he bows his head

---

[56] **Narcissus:** A beautiful but vain Greek youth who was condemned by the gods to fall in love with his own reflection.

over the mirroring water, that profound, fascinated, protracted smile with which he reaches out his arms toward the reflection of his own beauty—a very slightly contorted smile, contorted by the hopelessness of his attempt to kiss the sweet lips of his shadow; a smile that was provocative, curious, and imperceptibly troubled, bewitched and bewitching.

He who had received this smile carried it quickly away with him like a fateful gift. He was so deeply shaken that he was forced to flee the lighted terrace and the front garden and hurry into the darkness of the park at the rear. Words struggled from his lips, strangely indignant and tender reproaches: "You mustn't smile like that! One mustn't, do you hear, mustn't smile like that at anyone!" He sank down on one of the seats, deliriously breathing the nocturnal fragrance of the flowers and trees. And leaning back, his arms hanging down, overwhelmed, trembling, shuddering all over, he whispered the standing formula of the heart's desire—impossible here, absurd, depraved, ludicrous, and sacred nevertheless, still worthy of honor even here: "I love you!"

5

During the fourth week of his stay at the Lido Gustav von Aschenbach began to notice certain uncanny developments in the outside world. In the first place it struck him that as the height of the season approached, the number of guests at his hotel was diminishing rather than increasing, and in particular that the German language seemed to be dying away into silence all round him, so that in the end only foreign sounds fell on his ear at table and on the beach. Then one day the hotel barber, whom he visited frequently now, let slip in conversation a remark that aroused his suspicions. The man had mentioned a German family who had just left after only a brief stay, and in his chattering, flattering manner he added: "But you are staying on, signore; you are not afraid of the sickness." Aschenbach looked at him. "The sickness?" he repeated. The fellow stopped his talk, pretended to be busy, had not heard the question. And when it was put to him again more sharply, he declared that he knew nothing and tried with embarrassed loquacity to change the subject.

That was at midday. In the afternoon with the sea dead calm and the sun burning, Aschenbach crossed to Venice, for he was now driven by a mad compulsion to follow the Polish boy and his sisters, having seen them set off toward the pier with their companion. He did not find his idol at San Marco. But at tea, sitting at his round wrought-iron table on the shady side of the Piazza, he suddenly scented in the air a peculiar aroma, one which it now seemed to him he had been noticing for days without really being conscious of it—a sweetish, medicinal smell that suggested squalor and wounds and suspect cleanliness. He scrutinized it, pondered and identified it, finished his tea and left the Piazza at the far end opposite the basilica. In the narrow streets the smell was stronger. At corners, printed notices had been pasted up in which the civic authorities, with fatherly concern, gave warning to the local population that since certain ailments of the gastric system were normal in this weather, they should refrain from eating oysters and mussels and indeed from using water from the canals. The euphemistic character of the announcement was obvious. Groups of people were standing about silently on bridges or in squares, and the stranger stood among them, brooding and scenting the truth.

He found a shopkeeper leaning against his vaulted doorway, surrounded by coral necklaces and trinkets made of imitation amethyst, and asked him about the unpleasant smell. The man looked him over with heavy eyes, and hastily gathered his wits. "A precautionary measure, signore," he answered, gesticulating. "The police have laid down regulations, and quite right too, it must be said. This weather is oppressive, the sirocco is not very wholesome. In short, the signore will understand—an exaggerated precaution no doubt . . ." Aschenbach thanked him and walked on. Even on the *vaporetto* taking him back to the Lido he now noticed the smell of the bactericide.

Back at the hotel, he went at once to the table in the hall where the newspapers were kept, and carried out some research. In the foreign papers he found nothing. Those in his own language mentioned rumors, quoted contradictory statistics, reported official denials and questioned their veracity. This explained the withdrawal of the German and Austrian clientele. Visitors of other nationalities evidently knew nothing, suspected nothing, still had no apprehensions. "They want it kept quiet!" thought Aschenbach in some agitation, throwing the newspapers back on the table. "They're hushing this up!" But at the same time his heart filled with elation at the thought of the adventure in which the outside world was about to be involved. For to passion, as to crime, the assured everyday order and stability of things is not opportune, and any weakening of the civil structure, any chaos and disaster afflicting the world, must be welcome to it, as offering a vague hope of turning such circumstances to its advantage. Thus Aschenbach felt an obscure sense of satisfaction at what was going on in the dirty alleyways of Venice, cloaked in official secrecy— this guilty secret of the city, which merged with his own innermost secret and which it was also so much in his own interests to protect. For in his enamored state his one anxiety was that Tadzio might leave, and he realized with a kind of horror that he would not be able to go on living if that were to happen.

Lately he had not been content to owe the sight and proximity of the beautiful boy merely to daily routine and chance: he had begun pursuing him, following him obtrusively. On Sunday, for example, the Poles never appeared on the beach; he rightly guessed that they were attending mass in San Marco, and hastened to the church himself. There, stepping from the fiery heat of the Piazza into the golden twilight of the sanctuary, he would find him whom he had missed, bowed over a prie-dieu[57] and performing his devotions. Then he would stand in the background, on the cracked mosaic floor, amid a throng of people kneeling, murmuring, and crossing themselves, and the massive magnificence of the oriental temple would weigh sumptuously on his senses. At the front, the ornately vested priest walked to and fro, doing his business and chanting. Incense billowed up, clouding the feeble flames of the altar candles, and with its heavy, sweet sacrificial odor another seemed to mingle: the smell of the sick city. But through the vaporous dimness and the flickering lights

---

[57] **prie-dieu:** French for "pray-god"; a kneeling bench for prayers.

Aschenbach saw the boy, up there at the front, turn his head and seek him with his eyes until he found him.

Then, when the great doors were opened and the crowd streamed out into the shining Piazza swarming with pigeons, the beguiled lover would hide in the ante-basilica, he would lurk and lie in wait. He would see the Poles leave the church, see the brother and sisters take ceremonious leave of their mother, who would then set off home, turning toward the Piazzetta; he would observe the boy, the cloistral sisters, and the governess turn right and walk through the clock tower gateway into the Merceria,[58] and after letting them get a little way ahead he would follow them — follow them furtively on their walk through Venice. He had to stop when they lingered, had to take refuge in hot food stalls and courtyards to let them pass when they turned round; he would lose them, search for them frantically and exhaustingly, rushing over bridges and along filthy culs-de-sac, and would then have to endure minutes of mortal embarrassment when he suddenly saw them coming toward him in a narrow passageway where no escape was possible. And yet one cannot say that he suffered. His head and his heart were drunk, and his steps followed the dictates of that dark god[59] whose pleasure it is to trample man's reason and dignity underfoot.

Presently, somewhere or other, Tadzio and his family would take a gondola, and while they were getting into it Aschenbach, hiding behind a fountain or the projecting part of a building, would wait till they were a little way from the shore and then do the same. Speaking hurriedly and in an undertone, he would instruct the oarsman, promising him a large tip, to follow that gondola ahead of them that was just turning the corner, to follow it at a discreet distance; and a shiver would run down his spine when the fellow, with the roguish compliance of a pander, would answer him in the same tone, assuring him that he was at his service, entirely at his service.

Thus he glided and swayed gently along, reclining on soft black cushions, shadowing that other black, beaked craft, chained to its pursuit by his infatuation. Sometimes he would lose sight of it and become distressed and anxious, but his steersman, who seemed to be well practiced in commissions of this kind, would always know some cunning maneuver, some side-canal or short cut that would again bring Aschenbach in sight of what he craved. The air was stagnant and malodorous, the sun burned oppressively through the haze that had turned the sky to the color of slate. Water lapped against wood and stone. The gondolier's call, half warning and half greeting, was answered from a distance out of the silent labyrinth, in accordance with some strange convention. Out of little overhead gardens umbelliferous blossoms spilled over and hung down the crumbling masonry, white and purple and almond scented. Moorish windows were mirrored in the murky water. The marble steps of a church dipped below the surface; a beggar squatted on them, protesting his misery, holding out his hat and showing the whites of his eyes as if he were blind; an antiques dealer beckoned to them with crawling obsequiousness as they passed his den, inviting them to stop and be swindled. This was Venice, the flattering and suspect beauty — this city, half fairy tale and half tourist trap, in whose

---

[58] **the Merceria:** A shopping district.   [59] **that dark god:** Dionysus, the god of wine, intoxication, and ecstasy.

insalubrious air the arts once rankly and voluptuously blossomed, where composers have been inspired to lulling tones of somniferous eroticism. Gripped by his adventure, the traveler felt his eyes drinking in this sumptuousness, his ears wooed by these melodies; he remembered, too, that the city was stricken with sickness and concealing it for reasons of cupidity, and he peered around still more wildly in search of the gondola that hovered ahead.

So it was that in his state of distraction he could no longer think of anything or want anything except this ceaseless pursuit of the object that so inflamed him: nothing but to follow him, to dream of him when he was not there, and after the fashion of lovers to address tender words to his mere shadow. Solitariness, the foreign environment, and the joy of an intoxication of feeling that had come to him so late and affected him so profoundly—all this encouraged and persuaded him to indulge himself in the most astonishing ways: as when it had happened that late one evening, returning from Venice and reaching the first floor of the hotel, he had paused outside the boy's bedroom door, leaning his head against the doorframe in a complete drunken ecstasy, and had for a long time been unable to move from the spot, at the risk of being surprised and discovered in this insane situation.

Nevertheless, there were moments at which he paused and half came to his senses. Where is this leading me! he would reflect in consternation at such moments. Where was it leading him! Like any man whose natural merits move him to take an aristocratic interest in his origins, Aschenbach habitually let the achievements and successes of his life remind him of his ancestors, for in imagination he could then feel sure of their approval, of their satisfaction, of the respect they could not have withheld. And he thought of them even here and now, entangled as he was in so impermissible an experience, involved in such exotic extravagances of feeling; he thought, with a sad smile, of their dignified austerity, their decent manliness of character. What would they say? But for that matter, what would they have said about his entire life, a life that had deviated from theirs to the point of degeneracy, this life of his in the compulsive service of art, this life about which he himself, adopting the civic values of his forefathers, had once let fall such mocking observations—and which nevertheless had essentially been so much like theirs! He too had served, he too had been a soldier and a warrior, like many of them: for art was a war, an exhausting struggle, it was hard these days to remain fit for it for long. A life of self-conquest and of defiant resolve, an astringent, steadfast, and frugal life which he had turned into the symbol of that heroism for delicate constitutions, that heroism so much in keeping with the times—surely he might call this manly, might call it courageous? And it seemed to him that the kind of love that had taken possession of him did, in a certain way, suit and befit such a life. Had it not been highly honored by the most valiant of peoples, indeed had he not read that in their cities it had flourished by inspiring valorous deeds? Numerous warrior-heroes of olden times had willingly borne its yoke, for there was no kind of abasement that could be reckoned as such if the god had imposed it; and actions that would have been castigated as signs of cowardice had their motives been different, such as falling to the ground in supplication, desperate pleas, and slavish demeanor—these were accounted no disgrace to a lover, but rather won him still greater praise.

Such were the thoughts with which love beguiled him, and thus he sought to sustain himself, to preserve his dignity. But at the same time he kept turning his attention, inquisitively and persistently, to the disreputable events that were evolving in the depths of Venice, to that adventure of the outside world which darkly mingled with the adventure of his heart, and which nourished his passion with vague and lawless hopes. Obstinately determined to obtain new and reliable information about the status and progress of the malady, he would sit in the city's coffee houses searching through the German newspapers, which several days ago had disappeared from the reading table in the hotel foyer. They carried assertions and retractions by turns. The number of cases, the number of deaths, was said to be twenty, or forty, or a hundred and more, such reports being immediately followed by statements flatly denying the outbreak of an epidemic, or at least reducing it to a few quite isolated cases brought in from outside the city. Scattered here and there were warning admonitions, or protests against the dangerous policy being pursued by the Italian authorities. There was no certainty to be had.

The solitary traveler was nevertheless conscious of having a special claim to participation in this secret, and although excluded from it, he took a perverse pleasure in putting embarrassing questions to those in possession of the facts, and thus, since they were pledged to silence, forcing them to lie to him directly. One day, at luncheon in the main dining room, he interrogated the hotel manager in this fashion, the soft-footed little man in the French frock coat who was moving around among the tables supervising the meal and greeting the clients, and who also stopped at Aschenbach's table for a few words of conversation. Why, in fact, asked his guest in a casual and nonchalant way, why on earth had they begun recently to disinfect Venice? — "It is merely a police measure, sir," answered the trickster, "taken in good time, as a safeguard against various disagreeable public health problems that might otherwise arise from this sultry and exceptionally warm weather—a precautionary measure which it is their duty to take." — "Very praiseworthy of the police," replied Aschenbach; and after exchanging a few meteorological observations with him the manager took his leave.

On the very same day, in the evening after dinner, it happened that a small group of street singers from the city gave a performance in the front garden of the hotel. They stood by one of the iron arc lamp standards, two men and two women, their faces glinting white in the glare, looking up at the great terrace where the hotel guests sat over their coffee and cooling drinks, resigned to watching this exhibition of folk culture. The hotel staff, the lift boys, waiters, office employees, had come out to listen in the hall doorways. The Russian family, eager to savor every pleasure, had had cane chairs put out for them down in the garden in order to be nearer the performers and were contentedly sitting there in a semicircle. Behind her master and mistress, in a turbanlike headcloth, stood their aged serf.

The beggar virtuosi were playing a mandolin, a guitar, a harmonica, and a squeaking fiddle. Instrumental developments alternated with vocal numbers, as when the younger of the women, shrill and squawky of voice, joined the tenor with his sweet falsetto notes in an ardent love duet. But the real talent and leader of the ensemble was quite evidently the other man, the one who had the guitar and was a kind of buffo-baritone[60] character, with hardly any voice but with a mimic gift and remarkable comic verve. Often he would detach himself from the rest of the group and come forward, playing his large instrument and gesticulating, toward the terrace, where his pranks were rewarded with encouraging laughter. The Russians in their parterre seats took special delight in all this southern vivacity, and their plaudits and admiring shouts led him on to ever further and bolder extravagances.

Aschenbach sat by the balustrade, cooling his lips from time to time with the mixture of pomegranate juice and soda water that sparkled ruby-red in the glass before him. His nervous system greedily drank in the jangling tones, for passion paralyzes discrimination and responds in all seriousness to stimuli which the sober senses would either treat with humorous tolerance or impatiently reject. The antics of the mountebank had distorted his features into a rictus-like smile which he was already finding painful. He sat on with a casual air, but inwardly he was utterly engrossed; for six paces from him Tadzio was leaning against the stone parapet.

There he stood, in the white belted suit he occasionally put on for dinner, in a posture of innate and inevitable grace, his left forearm on the parapet, his feet crossed, his right hand on the supporting hip; and he was looking down at the entertainers with an expression that was scarcely a smile, merely one of remote curiosity, a polite observation of the spectacle. Sometimes he straightened himself, stretching his chest, and with an elegant movement of both arms drew his white tunic down through his leather belt. But sometimes, too, and the older man noticed it with a mind-dizzying sense of triumph as well as with terror, he would turn his head hesitantly and cautiously, or even quickly and suddenly as if to gain the advantage of surprise, and look over his left shoulder to where his lover was sitting. Their eyes did not meet, for an ignominious apprehension was forcing the stricken man to keep his looks anxiously in check. Behind them on the terrace sat the women who watched over Tadzio, and at the point things had now reached, the enamored Aschenbach had reason to fear that he had attracted attention and aroused suspicion. Indeed, he had several times, on the beach, in the hotel foyer, and on the Piazza San Marco, been frozen with alarm to notice that Tadzio was being called away if he was near him, that they were taking care to keep them apart—and although his pride writhed in torments it had never known under the appalling insult that this implied, he could not in conscience deny its justice.

In the meantime the guitarist had begun a solo to his own accompaniment, a song in many stanzas which was then a popular hit all over Italy, and which he managed to perform in a graphic and dramatic manner, with the rest of his troupe joining regularly in the refrain. He was a lean fellow, thin and cadaverous in the face as well, standing there on the gravel detached from his companions, with a shabby felt hat on the back of his head and a quiff of his red hair bulging out under the brim, in a posture of insolent bravado; strumming and thrumming on his instrument, he tossed his pleasantries up to the terrace in a vivid *parlando*,[61] enacting it all so strenuously that the veins swelled on his forehead. He was quite evidently not of Venetian

---

[60] **buffo-baritone:** Comic baritone.   [61] *parlando:* A musical term meaning in a speaking or declamatory manner.

origin, but rather of the Neapolitan comic type, half pimp, half actor, brutal and bold-faced, dangerous and entertaining. The actual words of his song were merely foolish, but in his presentation, with his grimaces and bodily movements, his way of winking suggestively and lasciviously licking the corner of his mouth, it had something indecent and vaguely offensive about it. Though otherwise dressed in urban fashion he wore a sports shirt, out of the soft collar of which his skinny neck projected, displaying a remarkably large and naked Adam's apple. His pallid snub-nosed face, the features of which gave little clue to his age, seemed to be lined with contortions and vice, and the grinning of his mobile mouth was rather strangely ill-matched to the two deep furrows that stood defiantly, imperiously, almost savagely, between his reddish brows. But what really fixed the solitary Aschenbach's deep attention on him was his observation that this suspect figure seemed to be carrying his own suspect atmosphere about with him as well. For every time the refrain was repeated the singer would perform, with much grimacing and wagging of his hand as if in greeting, a grotesque march round the scene, which brought him immediately below where Aschenbach sat; and every time this happened a stench of carbolic[62] from his clothes or his body drifted up to the terrace.

Having completed his ballad he began to collect money. He started with the Russians, who were seen to give generously, and then came up the steps. Saucy as his performance had been, up here he was humility itself. Bowing and scraping, he crept from table to table, and a sly obsequious grin bared his prominent teeth, although the two furrows still stood threateningly between his red eyebrows. The spectacle of this alien being gathering in his livelihood was viewed with curiosity and not a little distaste; one threw coins with the tips of one's fingers into the hat, which one took care not to touch. Removal of the physical distance between the entertainer and decent folk always causes, however great one's pleasure has been, a certain embarrassment. He sensed this, and sought to make amends by cringing. He approached Aschenbach, and with him came the smell, which no one else in the company appeared to have noticed.

"Listen to me!" said the solitary traveler in an undertone and almost mechanically. "Venice is being disinfected. Why?" — The comedian answered hoarsely: "Because of the police! It's the regulations, signore, when it's so hot and when there's sirocco. The sirocco is oppressive. It is not good for the health . . ." He spoke in a tone of surprise that such a question could be asked, and demonstrated with his outspread hand how oppressive the sirocco was. — "So there is no sickness in Venice?" asked Aschenbach very softly and between his teeth. — The clown's muscular features collapsed into a grimace of comic helplessness. "A sickness? But what sickness? Is the sirocco a sickness? Is our police a sickness perhaps? The signore is having his little joke! A sickness! Certainly not, signore! A preventive measure, you must understand, a police precaution against the effects of the oppressive weather . . ." He gesticulated. "Very well," said Aschenbach briefly, still without raising his voice, and quickly dropped an unduly large coin into the fellow's hat. Then he motioned him

---

[62] **carbolic:** Carbolic acid used for a disinfectant.

with his eyes to clear off. The man obeyed, grinning and bowing low. But he had not even reached the steps when two hotel servants bore down on him, and with their faces close to his subjected him to a whispered cross-examination. He shrugged, gave assurances, swore that he had been discreet; it was obvious. Released, he returned to the garden, and after a brief consultation with his colleagues under the arc lamp he came forward once more, to express his thanks in a parting number.

It was a song that Aschenbach could not remember ever having heard before; a bold hit in an unintelligible dialect, and having a laughing refrain in which the rest of the band regularly and loudly joined. At this point both the words and the instrumental accompaniment stopped, and nothing remained except a burst of laughter, to some extent rhythmically ordered but treated with a high degree of naturalism, the soloist in particular showing great talent in his lifelike rendering of it. With artistic distance restored between himself and the spectators, he had recovered all his impudence, and the simulated laughter which he shamelessly directed at the terrace was a laughter of mockery. Even before the end of the articulated part of each stanza he would pretend to be struggling with an irresistible impulse of hilarity. He would sob, his voice would waver, he would press his hand against his mouth and hunch his shoulders, till at the proper moment the laughter would burst out of him, exploding in a wild howl, with such authenticity that it was infectious and communicated itself to the audience, so that a wave of objectless and merely self-propagating merriment swept over the terrace as well. And precisely this seemed to redouble the singer's exuberance. He bent his knees, slapped his thighs, held his sides, he nearly burst with what was now no longer laughing but shrieking; he pointed his finger up at the guests, as if that laughing company above him were itself the most comical thing in the world, and in the end they were all laughing, everyone in the garden and on the verandah, the waiters and the lift boys and the house servants in the doorways.

Aschenbach reclined in his chair no longer, he was sitting bolt upright as if trying to fend off an attack or flee from it. But the laughter, the hospital smell drifting toward him, and the nearness of the beautiful boy, all mingled for him into an immobilizing nightmare, an unbreakable and inescapable spell that held his mind and senses captive. In the general commotion and distraction he ventured to steal a glance at Tadzio, and as he did so he became aware that the boy, returning his glance, had remained no less serious than himself, just as if he were regulating his attitude and expression by those of the older man, and as if the general mood had no power over him while Aschenbach kept aloof from it. There was something so disarming and overwhelmingly moving about this childlike submissiveness, so rich in meaning, that the gray-haired lover could only with difficulty restrain himself from burying his face in his hands. He had also had the impression that the way Tadzio from time to time drew himself up with an intake of breath was like a kind of sighing, as if from a constriction of the chest. "He's sickly, he'll probably not live long," he thought again, with that sober objectivity into which the drunken ecstasy of desire sometimes strangely escapes; and his heart was filled at one and the same time with pure concern on the boy's behalf and with a certain wild satisfaction.

In the meantime the troupe of Venetians had finished their performance and were leaving. Applause accompanied them, and their leader took care to embellish even his exit with comical pranks. His bowing and scraping and hand-kissing amused the company, and so he redoubled them. When his companions were already outside, he put on yet another act of running backward and painfully colliding with a lamppost, then hobbling to the gate apparently doubled up in agony. When he got there however, he suddenly discarded the mask of comic underdog, uncoiled like a spring to his full height, insolently stuck out his tongue at the hotel guests on the terrace, and slipped away into the darkness. The company was dispersing; Tadzio had left the balustrade some time ago. But the solitary Aschenbach, to the annoyance of the waiters, sat on and on at his little table over his unfinished pomegranate drink. The night was advancing, time was ebbing away. In his parents' house, many years ago, there had been an hourglass—he suddenly saw that fragile symbolic little instrument as clearly as if it were standing before him. Silently, subtly, the rust-red sand trickled through the narrow glass aperture, dwindling away out of the upper vessel, in which a little whirling vortex had formed.

On the very next day, in the afternoon, Aschenbach took a further step in his persistent probing of the outside world, and this time his success was complete. What he did was to enter the British travel agency just off the Piazza San Marco, and after changing some money at the cash desk, he put on the look of a suspicious foreigner and addressed his embarrassing question to the clerk who had served him. The clerk was a tweed-clad Englishman, still young, with his hair parted in the middle, his eyes close set, and having that sober, honest demeanor which makes so unusual and striking an impression amid the glib knaveries of the south. "No cause for concern, sir," he began. "An administrative measure, nothing serious. They often issue directives of this kind, as a precaution against the unhealthy effects of the heat and the sirocco . . ." But raising his blue eyes he met those of the stranger, which were looking wearily and rather sadly at his lips, with an expression of slight contempt. At this the Englishman colored. "That is," he continued in an undertone and with some feeling, "the official explanation, which the authorities here see fit to stick to. I can tell you that there is rather more to it than that." And then, in his straightforward comfortable language, he told Aschenbach the truth.

For several years now, Asiatic cholera had been showing an increased tendency to spread and migrate. Originating in the sultry morasses of the Ganges delta,[63] rising with the mephitic exhalations of that wilderness of rank useless luxuriance, that primitive island jungle shunned by man, where tigers crouch in the bamboo thickets, the pestilence had raged with unusual and prolonged virulence all over northern India; it had struck eastward into China, westward into Afghanistan and Persia, and following the main caravan routes, it had borne its terrors to Astrakhan and even to Moscow. But while Europe trembled with apprehension that from there the specter might advance and arrive by land, it had been brought by Syrian traders over the sea; it had appeared almost simultaneously in several Mediterranean ports, raising its head in Toulon and Malaga, showing its face repeatedly in Palermo and Naples, and taking a seemingly permanent hold all over Calabria and Apulia.[64] The northern half

---

[63] **Ganges delta:** In India.   [64] **Astrakhan . . . Apulia:** Seaports in Russia, France, Spain, and Sicily, respectively; the last two are districts in southern Italy.

of the peninsula had still been spared. But in the middle of May this year, in Venice, the dreadful comma-bacilli had been found on one and the same day in the emaciated and blackened corpses of a ship's hand and of a woman who sold greengroceries. The two cases were hushed up. But a week later there were ten, there were twenty and then thirty, and they occurred in different quarters of the city. A man from a small provincial town in Austria who had been taking a few days' holiday in Venice died with unmistakable symptoms after returning home, and that was why the first rumors of a Venetian outbreak had appeared in German newspapers. The city authorities replied with a statement that the public health situation in Venice had never been better, and at the same time adopted the most necessary preventive measures. But the taint had probably now passed into foodstuffs, into vegetables or meat or milk; for despite every denial and concealment, the mortal sickness went on eating its way through the narrow little streets, and with the premature summer heat warming the water in the canals, conditions for the spread of infection were particularly favorable. It even seemed as if the pestilence had undergone a renewal of its energy, as if the tenacity and fertility of its pathogens had redoubled. Cases of recovery were rare; eighty percent of the victims died, and they died in a horrible manner, for the sickness presented itself in an extremely acute form and was frequently of the so-called "dry" type, which is the most dangerous of all. In this condition the body could not even evacuate the massive fluid lost from the blood-vessels. Within a few hours the patient would become dehydrated, his blood would thicken like pitch and he would suffocate with convulsions and hoarse cries. He was lucky if, as sometimes happened, the disease took the form of a slight malaise followed by a deep coma from which one never, or scarcely at all, regained consciousness. By the beginning of June the isolation wards in the Ospedale Civile[65] were quietly filling, the two orphanages were running out of accommodation, and there was a gruesomely brisk traffic between the quayside of the Fondamente Nuove[66] and the cemetery island of San Michele. But fear of general detriment to the city, concern for the recently opened art exhibition in the Public Gardens, consideration of the appalling losses which panic and disrepute would inflict on the hotels, on the shops, on the whole nexus of the tourist trade, proved stronger in Venice than respect for the truth and for international agreements; it was for this reason that the city authorities obstinately adhered to their policy of concealment and denial. The city's chief medical officer, a man of high repute, had resigned from his post in indignation and had been quietly replaced by a more pliable personality. This had become public knowledge; and such corruption in high places, combined with the prevailing insecurity, the state of crisis into which the city had been plunged by the death that walked its streets, led at the lower social levels to a certain breakdown of moral standards, to an activation of the dark and antisocial forces, which manifested itself in intemperance, shameless license, and growing criminality. Drunkenness in the evenings became noticeably more frequent; thieves and ruffians, it was said, were making the streets unsafe at night; there were repeated robberies and even murders, for it had already twice come

---

[65] **Ospedale Civile:** City Hospital.   [66] **Fondamente Nuove:** New Piers.

to light that persons alleged to have died of the plague had in fact been poisoned by their own relatives; and commercial vice now took on obtrusive and extravagant forms which had hitherto been unknown in this area and indigenous only to southern Italy or oriental countries.

The Englishman's narrative conveyed the substance of all this to Aschenbach. "You would be well advised, sir," he concluded, "to leave today rather than tomorrow. The imposition of quarantine can be expected any day now." — "Thank you," said Aschenbach, and left the office.

The Piazza was sunless and sultry. Unsuspecting foreigners were sitting at the cafés, or standing in front of the church with pigeons completely enveloping them, watching the birds swarm and beat their wings and push each other out of the way as they snatched with their beaks at the hollow hands offering them grains of maize. Feverish with excitement, triumphant in his possession of the truth, yet with a taste of disgust on his tongue and a fantastic horror in his heart, the solitary traveler paced up and down the flagstones of the magnificent precinct. He was considering a decent action which would cleanse his conscience. Tonight, after dinner, he might approach the lady in the pearls and address her with words which he now mentally rehearsed: "Madam, allow me as a complete stranger to do you a service, to warn you of something which is being concealed from you for reasons of self-interest. Leave here at once with Tadzio and your daughters! Venice is plague-stricken." He might then lay his hand in farewell on the head of a mocking deity's instrument, turn away, and flee from this quagmire. But at the same time he sensed an infinite distance between himself and any serious resolve to take such a step. It would lead him back to where he had been, give him back to himself again; but to one who is beside himself, no prospect is so distasteful as that of self-recovery. He remembered a white building adorned with inscriptions that glinted in the evening light, suffused with mystic meaning in which his mind had wandered; remembered then that strange itinerant figure who had wakened in him, in his middle age, a young man's longing to rove to far-off and strange places; and the thought of returning home, of level-headedness and sobriety, of toil and mastery, filled him with such repugnance that his face twisted into an expression of physical nausea. "They want it kept quiet!" he whispered vehemently. And: "I shall say nothing!" The consciousness of his complicity in the secret, of his share in the guilt, intoxicated him as small quantities of wine intoxicate a weary brain. The image of the stricken and disordered city, hovering wildly before his mind's eye, inflamed him with hopes that were beyond comprehension, beyond reason and full of monstrous sweetness. What, compared with such expectations, was that tender happiness of which he had briefly dreamed a few moments ago? What could art and virtue mean to him now, when he might reap the advantages of chaos? He said nothing, and stayed on.

That night he had a terrible dream, if dream is the right word for a bodily and mental experience which did indeed overtake him during deepest sleep, in complete independence of his will and with complete sensuous vividness, but with no perception of himself as present and moving about in any space external to the events themselves; rather, the scene of the events was his own soul, and they irrupted into it from outside, violently defeating his resistance — a profound, intellectual resistance—as they passed through him, and leaving his whole being, the culture of a lifetime, devastated and destroyed.

It began with fear, fear and joy and a horrified curiosity about what was to come. It was night, and his senses were alert; for from far off a hubbub was approaching, an uproar, a compendium of noise, a clangor and blare and dull thundering, yells of exultation and a particular howl with a long-drawn-out *u* at the end—all of it permeated and dominated by a terrible sweet sound of flute music: by deep-warbling, infamously persistent, shamelessly clinging tones that bewitched the innermost heart. Yet he was aware of a word, an obscure word, but one that gave a name to what was coming: *"the stranger-god!"*[67] There was a glow of smoky fire: in it he could see a mountain landscape, like the mountains round his summer home. And in fragmented light, from wooded heights, between tree trunks and mossy boulders, it came tumbling and whirling down: a human and animal swarm, a raging rout, flooding the slope with bodies, with flames, with tumult and frenzied dancing. Women, stumbling on the hide garments that fell too far about them from the waist, held up tambourines and moaned as they shook them above their thrown-back heads; they swung blazing torches, scattering the sparks, and brandished naked daggers; they carried snakes with flickering tongues which they had seized in the middle of the body, or they bore up their own breasts in both hands, shrieking as they did so. Men with horns over their brows, hairy-skinned and girdled with pelts, bowed their necks and threw up their arms and thighs, clanging brazen cymbals and beating a furious tattoo on drums, while smooth-skinned boys prodded goats with leafy staves, clinging to their horns and yelling with delight as the leaping beasts dragged them along. And the god's enthusiasts howled out the cry with the soft consonants and long-drawn-out final *u*, sweet and wild both at once, like no cry that was ever heard: here it was raised, belled out into the air as by rutting stags, and there they threw it back with many voices, in ribald triumph, urging each other on with it to dancing and tossing of limbs, and never did it cease. But the deep, enticing flute music mingled irresistibly with everything. Was it not also enticing him, the dreamer who experienced all this while struggling not to, enticing him with shameless insistence to the feast and frenzy of the uttermost surrender? Great was his loathing, great his fear, honorable his effort of will to defend to the last what was his and protect it against the Stranger, against the enemy of the composed and dignified intellect. But the noise, the howling grew louder, with the echoing cliffs reiterating it: it increased beyond measure, swelled up to an enrapturing madness. Odors besieged the mind, the pungent reek of the goats, the scent of panting bodies and an exhalation as of staling waters, with another smell, too, that was familiar: that of wounds and wandering disease. His heart throbbed to the drumbeats, his brain whirled, a fury seized him, a blindness, a dizzying lust, and his soul craved to join the round-dance of the god. The obscene symbol,[68] wooden and gigantic, was uncovered and

---

[67] *"the stranger-god!"*: Dionysus, a god whose cult originated in Thrace and Phrygia—north and east of the Greek peninsula. The dream is about the orgiastic rites associated with the worship of Dionysus.

[68] **The obscene symbol**: The phallus.

raised on high: and still more unbridled grew the howling of the rallying-cry. With foaming mouths they raged, they roused each other with lewd gestures and licentious hands, laughing and moaning they thrust the prods into each other's flesh and licked the blood from each other's limbs. But the dreamer now was with them and in them, he belonged to the Stranger-God. Yes, they were himself as they flung themselves, tearing and slaying, on the animals and devoured steaming gobbets of flesh, they were himself as an orgy of limitless coupling, in homage to the god, began on the trampled, mossy ground. And his very soul savored the lascivious delirium of annihilation.

Out of this dream the stricken man woke unnerved, shattered and powerlessly enslaved to the daemon-god. He no longer feared the observant eyes of other people; whether he was exposing himself to their suspicions he no longer cared. In any case they were running away, leaving Venice; many of the bathing cabins were empty now, there were great gaps in the clientele at dinner, and in the city one scarcely saw any foreigners. The truth seemed to have leaked out, and however tightly the interested parties closed ranks, panic could no longer be stemmed. But the lady in the pearls stayed on with her family, either because the rumors were not reaching her or because she was too proud and fearless to heed them. Tadzio stayed on; and to Aschenbach, in his beleaguered state, it sometimes seemed that all these unwanted people all round him might flee from the place or die, that every living being might disappear and leave him alone on this island with the beautiful boy—indeed, as he sat every morning by the sea with his gaze resting heavily, recklessly, incessantly on the object of his desire, or as he continued his undignified pursuit of him in the evenings along streets in which the disgusting mortal malady wound its underground way, then indeed monstrous things seemed full of promise to him, and the moral law no longer valid.

Like any other lover, he desired to please and bitterly dreaded that he might fail to do so. He added brightening and rejuvenating touches to his clothes, he wore jewelery and used scent, he devoted long sessions to his toilet several times a day, arriving at table elaborately attired and full of excited expectation. As he beheld the sweet youthful creature who had so entranced him he felt disgust at his own aging body, the sight of his gray hair and sharp features filled him with a sense of shame and hopelessness. He felt a compulsive need to refresh and restore himself physically; he paid frequent visits to the hotel barber.

Cloaked in a hairdressing gown, leaning back in the chair as the chatterer's hands tended him, he stared in dismay at his reflection in the looking glass.

"Gray," he remarked with a wry grimace.

"A little," the man replied. "And the reason? A slight neglect, a slight lack of interest in outward appearances, very understandable in persons of distinction, but not altogether to be commended, especially as one would expect those very persons to be free from prejudice about such matters as the natural and the artificial. If certain people who profess moral disapproval of cosmetics were to be logical enough to extend such rigorous principles to their teeth, the result would be rather disgusting. After all, we are only as old as we feel in our minds and hearts, and sometimes gray hair is actually further from the truth than the despised corrective would be. In your case, signore, one has a right to the natural color of one's hair. Will you permit me simply to give your color back to you?"

"How so?" asked Aschenbach.

Whereupon the eloquent tempter washed his client's hair in two kinds of water, one clear and one dark; and his hair was as black as when he had been young. Then he folded it into soft waves with the curling tongs, stepped back and surveyed his handiwork.

"Now the only other thing," he said, "would be just to freshen up the signore's complexion a little."

And like a craftsman unable to finish, unable to satisfy himself, he passed busily and indefatigably from one procedure to another. Aschenbach, reclining comfortably, incapable of resistance, filled rather with exciting hopes by what was happening, gazed at the glass and saw his eyebrows arched more clearly and evenly, the shape of his eyes lengthened, their brightness enhanced by a slight underlining of the lids; saw below them a delicate carmine come to life as it was softly applied to skin that had been brown and leathery; saw his lips that had just been so pallid now burgeoning cherry-red; saw the furrows on his cheeks, round his mouth, the wrinkles by his eyes, all vanishing under face cream and an aura of youth—with beating heart he saw himself as a young man in his earliest bloom. The cosmetician finally declared himself satisfied, with the groveling politeness usual in such people, by profusely thanking the client he had served. "An insignificant adjustment, signore," he said as he gave a final helping hand to Aschenbach's outward appearance. "Now the signore can fall in love as soon as he pleases." And the spellbound lover departed, confused and timorous but happy as in a dream. His necktie was scarlet, his broad-brimmed straw hat encircled with a many-colored ribbon.

A warm gale had blown up; it rained little and lightly, but the air was humid and thick and filled with smells of decay. The ear was beset with fluttering, flapping, and whistling noises, and to the fevered devotee, sweating under his makeup, it seemed that a vile race of wind demons was disporting itself in the sky, malignant sea birds that churn up and gnaw and befoul a condemned man's food.[69] For the sultry weather was taking away his appetite, and he could not put aside the thought that what he ate might be tainted with infection.

One afternoon, dogging Tadzio's footsteps, Aschenbach had plunged into the confused network of streets in the depths of the sick city. Quite losing his bearings in this labyrinth of alleys, narrow waterways, bridges, and little squares that all looked so much like each other, not sure now even of the points of the compass, he was intent above all on not losing sight of the vision he so passionately pursued. Ignominious caution forced him to flatten himself against walls and hide behind the backs of people walking in front of him; and for a long time he was not conscious of the weariness, the exhaustion that emotion and constant tension had inflicted on his body and mind. Tadzio walked behind his family; he usually gave precedence in narrow passages to his attendant and his nunlike sisters, and as he strolled along by

---

[69] birds . . . food: "*Harpies:* horribly gaunt. They quickly flew in, falling upon all the food with insatiable gluttony, fed, unable to become satiated, and *defiled* what they left behind with their ordure." [Mann's note.]

himself he sometimes turned his head and glanced over his shoulder with his strange twilight-gray eyes, to ascertain that his lover was still following him. He saw him, and did not give him away. Drunk with excitement as he realized this, lured onward by those eyes, helpless in the leading strings of his mad desire, the infatuated Aschenbach stole upon the trail of his unseemly hope—only to find it vanish from his sight in the end. The Poles had crossed a little humpbacked bridge; the height of the arch hid them from their pursuer, and when in his turn he reached the top of it, they were no longer to be seen. He looked frantically for them in three directions, straight ahead and to left and right along the narrow, dirty canal-side, but in vain. Unnerved and weakened, he was compelled to abandon his search.

His head was burning, his body was covered with sticky sweat, his neck quivered, a no longer endurable thirst tormented him; he looked round for something, no matter what, that would instantly relieve it. At a little greengrocer's shop he bought some fruit, some overripe soft strawberries, and ate some of them as he walked. A little square, one that seemed to have been abandoned, to have been put under a spell, opened up in front of him: he recognized it, he had been here, it was where he had made that vain decision weeks ago to leave Venice. On the steps of the well in its center he sank down and leaned his head against the stone rim. The place was silent, grass grew between the cobblestones, garbage was lying about. Among the dilapidated houses of uneven height all round him there was one that looked like a *palazzo*, with Gothic windows that now had nothing behind them, and little lion balconies. On the ground floor of another there was a chemist's shop. From time to time warm gusts of wind blew the stench of carbolic across to him.

There he sat, the master, the artist who had achieved dignity, the author of *A Study in Abjection*, he who in such paradigmatically pure form had repudiated intellectual vagrancy and the murky depths, who had proclaimed his renunciation of all sympathy with the abyss, who had weighed vileness in the balance and found it wanting; he who had risen so high, who had set his face against his own sophistication, grown out of all his irony, and taken on the commitments of one whom the public trusted; he, whose fame was official, whose name had been ennobled, and on whose style young boys were taught to model their own—there he sat, with his eyelids closed, with only an occasional mocking and rueful sideways glance from under them which he hid again at once; and his drooping, cosmetically brightened lips shaped the occasional word of the discourse his brain was delivering, his half-asleep brain with its tissue of strange dream-logic.

"For Beauty, Phaedrus, mark well! only Beauty is at one and the same time divine and visible, and so it is indeed the sensuous lover's path, little Phaedrus, it is the artist's path to the spirit.[70] But do you believe, dear boy, that the man whose path to the spiritual passes through the senses can ever achieve wisdom and true manly dignity? Or do you think rather (I leave it to you to decide) that this is a path of dangerous charm, very much an errant and sinful path which must of necessity lead us astray? For I must tell you that we artists cannot tread the path of Beauty without

---

[70] **"For Beauty, . . . spirit"**: In his delirious fantasy, Aschenbach assumes the role of Socrates in Plato's *Phaedrus* and applies Platonic ideas to his own situation.

Eros keeping company with us and appointing himself as our guide; yes, though we may be heroes in our fashion and disciplined warriors, yet we are like women, for it is passion that exalts us, and the longing of our soul must remain the longing of a lover—that is our joy and our shame. Do you see now perhaps why we writers can be neither wise nor dignified? That we necessarily go astray, necessarily remain dissolute emotional adventurers? The magisterial poise of our style is a lie and a farce, our fame and social position are an absurdity, the public's faith in us is altogether ridiculous, the use of art to educate the nation and its youth is a reprehensible undertaking which should be forbidden by law. For how can one be fit to be an educator when one has been born with an incorrigible and natural tendency toward the abyss? We try to achieve dignity by repudiating that abyss, but whichever way we turn we are subject to its allurement. We renounce, let us say, the corrosive process of knowledge—for knowledge, Phaedrus, has neither dignity nor rigor: it is all insight and understanding and tolerance, uncontrolled and formless; it sympathizes with the abyss, it *is* the abyss. And so we reject it resolutely, and henceforth our pursuit is of Beauty alone, of Beauty which is simplicity, which is grandeur and a new kind of rigor and a second naiveté, of Beauty which is Form. But form and naiveté, Phaedrus, lead to intoxication and lust; they may lead a noble mind into terrible criminal emotions, which his own fine rigor condemns as infamous; they lead, they too lead, to the abyss. I tell you, that is where they lead us writers; for we are not capable of self-exaltation, we are merely capable of self-debauchery. And now I shall go, Phaedrus, and you shall stay here; and leave this place only when you no longer see me."

A few days later Gustav von Aschenbach, who had been feeling unwell, left the Hotel des Bains at a later morning hour than usual. He was being attacked by waves of dizziness, only half physical, and with them went an increasing sense of dread, a feeling of hopelessness and pointlessness, though he could not decide whether this referred to the external world or to his personal existence. In the foyer he saw a large quantity of luggage standing ready for dispatch, asked one of the doormen which guests were leaving, and was given in reply the aristocratic Polish name which he had inwardly been expecting to hear. As he received the information there was no change in his ravaged features, only that slight lift of the head with which one casually notes something one did not need to know. He merely added the question: "When?" and was told: "After lunch." He nodded and went down to the sea.

It was a bleak spectacle there. Tremors gusted outward across the water between the beach and the first long sandbar, wrinkling its wide flat surface. An autumnal, out-of-season air seemed to hang over the once so colorful and populous resort, now almost deserted, with litter left lying about on the sand. An apparently abandoned camera stood on its tripod at the edge of the sea, and the black cloth over it fluttered and flapped in the freshening breeze.

Tadzio, with the three or four playmates he still had, was walking about on the right in front of his family's bathing cabin; and reclining in his deck chair with a rug over his knees, about midway between the sea and the row of cabins, Aschenbach once more sat watching him. The boys' play was unsupervised, as the women were probably busy with travel preparations; it seemed to be unruly and degenerating into roughness. The sturdy boy he had noticed before, the one in the belted suit with glossy black hair who was addressed as "Jashu," had been angered and blinded by some sand thrown into his face: he forced Tadzio to a wrestling match, which soon ended in the downfall of the less muscular beauty. But as if in this hour of leave-taking the submissiveness of the lesser partner had been transformed into cruel brutality, as if he were now bent on revenge for his long servitude, the victor did not release his defeated friend even then, but knelt on his back and pressed his face into the sand so hard and so long that Tadzio, breathless from the fight in any case, seemed to be on the point of suffocation. His attempts to shake off the weight of his tormentor were convulsive; they stopped altogether for moments on end and became a mere repeated twitching. Appalled, Aschenbach was about to spring to the rescue when the bully finally released his victim. Tadzio, very pale, sat up and went on sitting motionless for some minutes, propped on one arm, his hair tousled and his eyes darkening. Then he stood right up and walked slowly away. His friends called to him, laughingly at first, then anxiously and pleadingly; he took no notice. The dark-haired boy, who had no doubt been seized at once by remorse at having gone so far, ran after him and tried to make up the quarrel. A jerk of Tadzio's shoulder rejected him. Tadzio walked on at an angle down to the water. He was barefooted and wearing his striped linen costume with the red bow.

At the edge of the sea he lingered, head bowed, drawing figures in the wet sand with the point of one foot, then walked into the shallow high water, which at its deepest point did not even wet his knees; he waded through it, advancing easily, and reached the sandbar. There he stood for a moment looking out into the distance and then, moving left, began slowly to pace the length of this narrow strip of unsubmerged land. Divided from the shore by a width of water, divided from his companions by proud caprice, he walked, a quite isolated and unrelated apparition, walked with floating hair out there in the sea, in the wind, in front of the nebulous vastness. Once more he stopped to survey the scene. And suddenly, as if prompted by a memory, by an impulse, he turned at the waist, one hand on his hip, with an enchanting twist of the body, and looked back over his shoulder at the beach. There the watcher sat, as he had sat once before when those twilight-gray eyes, looking back at him then from that other threshold, had for the first time met his. Resting his head on the back of his chair, he had slowly turned it to follow the movements of the walking figure in the distance; now he lifted it toward this last look; then it sank down on his breast, so that his eyes stared up from below, while his face wore the inert, deep-sunken expression of profound slumber. But to him it was as if the pale and lovely soul-summoner[71] out there were smiling to him, beckoning to him; as if he loosed his hand from his hip and pointed outward, hovering ahead and onward, into an immensity rich with unutterable expectation. And as so often, he set out to follow him.

Minutes passed, after he had collapsed sideways in his chair, before anyone hurried to his assistance. He was carried to his room. And later that same day the world was respectfully shocked to receive the news of his death.

---

[71] **soul-summoner:** The Greek god Hermes leads souls to the Underworld; his official title is *Psychopompos,* "Escort of Souls."

ᚙ ROKEYA SAKHAWAT HOSSAIN
B. INDIA, 1880–1932

Western women writing in the late nineteenth and early twentieth centuries often focused on characters and situations that illustrated the psychological and social toll of a patriarchal society. The young widow in Emilia Pardo Bazán's "The Revolver" is driven into paralytic passivity by the threat of her husband's gun. The new mother in Charlotte Perkins Gilman's "The Yellow Wallpaper" is driven mad by imagining a woman trapped inside the wallpaper, which has been read as an extreme expression of the limitations that Western women experience under patriarchy. Most of these women would wish for Virginia Woolf's "room of one's own,"[1] space in which to assert their independence from male control. In many non-Western societies, however, physical separation and confinement of women in rooms of their own are the very media of oppression. The PURDAH system in India, practiced in somewhat different ways by Muslims and Hindus, mandates that women be kept in their own section of the house, one that can be visited only by other women or by a narrowly restricted circle of male relatives. In public, women are hidden from view by curtains, robes, and veils. For Begum **Rokeya Sakhawat Hossain**, one of the foremost feminist writers of early-twentieth-century India, challenging this system became a lifelong crusade.

roh-KAY-yuh
sah-kah-WAHT
hoh-SINE

Although Hossain herself wore a traditional robe throughout her life, she objected to the physical constraints, the denial of opportunity, and the psychological impact purdah had on women, who colluded with their own confinement. In *The Secluded Ones* (1928), a collection of true stories about the effects of the system, Hossain tells of a woman whose house caught on fire. When the woman attempted to escape, Hossain writes, "she found the courtyard full of strangers fighting the fire. She would not come out in front of them. So she went back to her bedroom . . . and hid under the bed. She burned to death but did not come out." Such were the debilitating results of the purdah system that Hossain set out to change.

A Secret Education.   Hossain was born in 1880 into a prominent and well-to-do Muslim family in the village of Pairaband in northern Bengal, in what is now Bangladesh. Her brothers were educated at home and later at a school in Calcutta, but the girls were not given any systematic education. Rokeya was encouraged to learn only enough Arabic to read the Qur'an (Koran) and enough Urdu to read some primers on feminine conduct. Luckily, her older brother, Ibrahim Saber, believed in education for women and at night secretly taught his sisters English and Bangla (Bengali), languages their parents had forbidden because they were spoken by non-Muslims. Ibrahim Saber was also instrumental in persuading

---

[1] **"room . . . own":** Asked to speak on the topic of "Women and Fiction," English novelist Virginia Woolf (1882–1941; see p. 402) asserted, "a woman must have money and a room of her own if she is to write fiction." Her essay, *A Room of One's Own,* was published in 1929.

the family to marry Rokeya to Syed Sakhawat Hossain, a liberal district magistrate educated in Calcutta and London who was committed to the cause of women's education. Rokeya expressed her gratitude to her brother in the dedication of her novel *Padmaraga* (1924): "You have moulded me from childhood . . . your love is sweeter than honey which after all has a bitter after-taste; [your love] is pure and divine like Kausar."[2]

Promoting Women's Education.   The newly married couple moved to Rangpur where Sakhawat was stationed; there he encouraged Rokeya to associate with other educated women, Hindus and Christians as well as Muslims. He also encouraged her to write. "If my dear husband had not been so supportive," Hossain commented later, "I might never have written or published anything." After eleven years of marriage—when Hossain was twenty-seven—her husband died, leaving her sufficient money to live on as well as a substantial sum designated to be spent on women's education. Hossain used the money to start a girl's school in Bhagalpur in 1909, moving the school a year later to Calcutta, where it is still operating as the Sakhawat Memorial Girl's School. She designed the school as a model of the women's educational programs she advocated and promoted through the Anjuman-e-Khawatin-e-Islam, the Muslim Women's Association, an activist group she founded in 1916.

Hossain in fact devoted her life to women's education, which she saw as essential to female liberation. Most of her writings are directed to bringing about the social changes in the culture of northern India that she saw as essential for achieving a measure of equality for Muslims and for liberating Muslim women. She advocated a curriculum for women that included the sciences; practical training in horticulture, personal hygiene, health care, and nutrition; and painting and the other fine arts. Education must lead to freedom from male domination, she asserted, so it needed to develop potential vocational skills in women. By the time of her death in 1932, Hossain was recognized as a national leader in the cause of Muslim rights and women's education. The day of her death, December 9, is celebrated in Bangladesh as Rokeya Day.

Hossain's Literary Work.   Hossain wrote most of her literary works in Bangla (Bengali), the vernacular language of her region of northern India. Since she was writing to raise the consciousness of her compatriots, especially Muslim women, she wrote in the language most familiar to them. Of her Bangla writings, only parts of *The Secluded Ones* have been translated into English. She also wrote many articles, essays, and speeches as well as a novel, *Padmaraga* (*Ruby,* 1924), in Bangla. Her collected works, entitled *Racanavali,* were published in Bangla in 1973.

"Sultana's Dream."   Unlike most of Hossain's work, "Sultana's Dream" (1905) was written in English and initially published in an English magazine, *The Indian Ladies' Magazine.* Hossain wrote the story while her

> If our liberation from male domination depends on our ability to earn independently, then we should begin. We should be lawyers, magistrates, judges, clerks. . . . The sort of labour we put in our households can bring us wages if we use it outside.
>
> – ROKEYA SAKHAWAT HOSSAIN

www   For links to more information about Hossain, a quiz on "Sultana's Dream," and for information on the culture and context of India in the twentieth century, see *World Literature Online* at bedfordstmartins .com/worldlit.

---

[2] **Kausar:** A stream of nectar in Paradise, mentioned in the Qur'an.

That women may possess faculties and talents equivalent to or greater than men — that they are capable of developing themselves to a stage where they may attain complete mastery over nature without any help from men and create a new world of perfect beauty, great wealth, and goodness — this is what "Sultana's Dream" depicts.

– ABDUL HUSSAIN, critic, 1921

husband was away on a business trip to pass the time and to demonstrate to him her proficiency in English. When he returned, she showed him the story and, she recalled, "he read the whole thing without even bothering to sit down. 'A terrible revenge!' he said when he was finished." Clearly the story's utopian fantasy was an angry indictment of purdah and the oppression of women in Bengal. The "revenge" was Hossain's satiric reversal of gender roles, which placed men in seclusion and belittled their desires. Another aspect of Hossain's vision of an ideal society, one devoted to horticulture and life-enhancing sciences rather than warfare, was apparently less immediately striking. Like Jonathan Swift (1667–1745),[3] to whose *Gulliver's Travels* "Sultana's Dream" has often been compared, Hossain was accused of misanthropy and sexism, but ultimately these attitudes did not deter the positive impact her story had on its Indian readers.

■ CONNECTIONS

Virginia Woolf, *A Room of One's Own*, p. 408. Although Hossain does not focus specifically on the situation of women writers, as Woolf does in *A Room of One's Own*, she is interested in how things might be different if women had their own space. What things do the two writers see as distinctively feminine? Where do their visions of a woman's world significantly differ?

Francis Bacon, *The New Atlantis* (Book 3); Jonathan Swift, *Gulliver's Travels* (Book 4); Aristophanes, *Lysistrata* (Book 1). "Sultana's Dream" is written within a tradition of utopian literature that satirizes existing social arrangements by imagining alternative societies. Compare Ladyland with Bacon's New Atlantis and Swift's Houyhnhnmland. What existing social institutions do the authors criticize and how do their alternative societies correct social ills? What would Swift and Bacon think of Ladyland? Can Aristophanes' *Lysistrata* be considered a work of utopian literature? Does it envision a feminine society similar to Ladyland?

***In the World*: Love, Marriage, and the Education of Women (Book 4).** Education has been a centerpiece of feminist proposals for social reform in the last several centuries. Consider Hossain's educational ideas in relation to those in *In the World*: Love, Marriage, and the Education of Women. Is Hossain's curriculum similar to what Western feminists would propose? In what way do her views seem most determined by her cultural situation?

■ FURTHER RESEARCH

Hossain, Rokeya Sakhawat. *"Sultana's Dream" and Selections from* The Secluded Ones, Roushan Jahan, trans. and ed. 1988.

■ PRONUNCIATION

Koh-i-Noor: KOH-ee-noor
Padmaraga: pud-muh-RAH-guh
Rokeya Sakhawat Hossain: roh-KAY-yuh sah-kah-WAHT hoh-SINE
Zenana: zay-NAH-nah

---

[3] **Jonathan Swift:** Swift's fantasy travel narrative *Gulliver's Travels* (1726) satirized human foibles and suggested that horses were wiser and more rational than humans. (See Book 4.)

∾ Sultana's Dream

One evening I was lounging in an easy chair in my bedroom and thinking lazily of the condition of Indian womanhood. I am not sure whether I dozed off or not. But, as far as I remember, I was wide awake. I saw the moonlit sky sparkling with thousands of diamondlike stars, very distinctly.

All of a sudden a lady stood before me; how she came in, I do not know. I took her for my friend, Sister Sara.

"Good morning," said Sister Sara. I smiled inwardly as I knew it was not morning, but starry night. However, I replied to her, saying, "How do you do?"

"I am all right, thank you. Will you please come out and have a look at our garden?"

I looked again at the moon through the open window, and thought there was no harm in going out at that time. The menservants outside were fast asleep just then, and I could have a pleasant walk with Sister Sara.

I used to have my walks with Sister Sara, when we were at Darjeeling.[1] Many a time did we walk hand in hand and talk lightheartedly in the botanical gardens there. I fancied Sister Sara had probably come to take me to some such garden, and I readily accepted her offer and went out with her.

When walking I found to my surprise that it was a fine morning. The town was fully awake and the streets alive with bustling crowds. I was feeling very shy, thinking I was walking in the street in broad daylight, but there was not a single man visible.

Some of the passersby made jokes at me. Though I could not understand their language, yet I felt sure they were joking. I asked my friend, "What do they say?"

"The women say you look very mannish."

"Mannish?" said I. "What do they mean by that?"

"They mean that you are shy and timid like men."

"Sultana's Dream." Published in 1905 in *Indian Ladies' Magazine,* an English periodical produced in Madras, this story has been described by Roushan Jahan as "one of the earliest 'self-consciously feminist' utopian stories written in English by a woman." Characterizing Hossain as "the first and foremost feminist of Bengali Muslim society," Jahan goes on to observe: "One hesitates to use a term that is not content-free and *feminist* does mean different things to different people, yet it is the term that automatically occurs to many who read Rokeya's work now." By reversing the gender roles of Bengali Muslim society so that women take charge of public affairs while men are sequestered in their houses, Hossain satirizes the system of purdah that confined and controlled women in Indian society. She also speculates about the ways in which a feminine society would differ from a masculine one, especially in environmental and educational practices and in the marriage laws. Jahan describes her edition of "Sultana's Dream" as one that "retains the style of Rokeya's early-twentieth-century, Bangla-influenced English." Jahan normalized capitalization, spelling, and punctuation to contemporary U.S. standards.

All notes are the editors' unless otherwise indicated.

---

[1] **Darjeeling:** A resort city in northwest Bengal in the foothills of the Himalayas.

"Shy and timid like men?" It was really a joke. I became very nervous when I found that my companion was not Sister Sara, but a stranger. Oh, what a fool had I been to mistake this lady for my dear old friend Sister Sara.

She felt my fingers tremble in her hand, as we were walking hand in hand.

"What is the matter, dear, dear?" she said affectionately.

"I feel somewhat awkward," I said, in a rather apologizing tone, "as being a purdahnishin woman[2] I am not accustomed to walking about unveiled."

"You need not be afraid of coming across a man here. This is Ladyland, free from sin and harm. Virtue herself reigns here."

By and by I was enjoying the scenery. Really it was very grand. I mistook a patch of green grass for a velvet cushion. Feeling as if I were walking on a soft carpet, I looked down and found the path covered with moss and flowers.

"How nice it is," said I.

"Do you like it?" asked Sister Sara. (I continued calling her "Sister Sara," and she kept calling me by my name.)

"Yes, very much; but I do not like to tread on the tender and sweet flowers."

"Never mind, dear Sultana. Your treading will not harm them; they are street flowers."

"The whole place looks like a garden," said I admiringly. "You have arranged every plant so skillfully."

"Your Calcutta could become a nicer garden than this, if only your countrymen wanted to make it so."

"They would think it useless to give so much attention to horticulture, while they have so many other things to do."

"They could not find a better excuse," said she with [a] smile. I became very curious to know where the men were. I met more than a hundred women while walking there, but not a single man.

"Where are the men?" I asked her.

"In their proper places, where they ought to be."

"Pray let me know what you mean by 'their proper places.'"

"Oh, I see my mistake, you cannot know our customs, as you were never here before. We shut our men indoors."

"Just as we are kept in the zenana?"[3]

"Exactly so."

"How funny." I burst into a laugh. Sister Sara laughed too.

"But, dear Sultana, how unfair it is to shut in the harmless women and let loose the men."

"Why? It is not safe for us to come out of the zenana, as we are naturally weak."

"Yes, it is not safe so long as there are men about the streets, nor is it so when a wild animal enters a marketplace."

"Of course not."

---

[2] **purdahnishin woman:** A woman who practices purdah.

[3] **zenana:** Women's living quarters, separate from the public rooms of the house.

"Suppose some lunatics escape from the asylum and begin to do all sorts of mischief to men, horses, and other creatures: In that case what will your countrymen do?"

"They will try to capture them and put them back into their asylum."

"Thank you! And you do not think it wise to keep sane people inside an asylum and let loose the insane?"

"Of course not!" said I, laughing lightly.

"As a matter of fact, in your country this very thing is done! Men, who do or at least are capable of doing no end of mischief, are let loose and the innocent women shut up in the zenana! How can you trust those untrained men out of doors?"

"We have no hand or voice in the management of our social affairs. In India man is lord and master. He has taken to himself all powers and privileges and shut up the women in the zenana."

"Why do you allow yourselves to be shut up?"

"Because it cannot be helped as they are stronger than women."

"A lion is stronger than a man, but it does not enable him to dominate the human race. You have neglected the duty you owe to yourselves, and you have lost your natural rights by shutting your eyes to your own interests."

"But my dear Sister Sara, if we do everything by ourselves, what will the men do then?"

"They should not do anything, excuse me; they are fit for nothing. Only catch them and put them into the zenana."

"But would it be very easy to catch and put them inside the four walls?" said I. "And even if this were done, would all their business—political and commercial—also go with them into the zenana?"

Sister Sara made no reply. She only smiled sweetly. Perhaps she thought it was useless to argue with one who was no better than a frog in a well.

By this time we reached Sister Sara's house. It was situated in a beautiful heart-shaped garden. It was a bungalow with a corrugated iron roof. It was cooler and nicer than any of our rich buildings. I cannot describe how neat and nicely furnished and how tastefully decorated it was.

We sat side by side. She brought out of the parlor a piece of embroidery work and began putting on a fresh design.

"Do you know knitting and needlework?"

"Yes: We have nothing else to do in our zenana."

"But we do not trust our zenana members with embroidery!" she said laughing, "as a man has not patience enough to pass thread through a needlehole even!"

"Have you done all this work yourself?" I asked her, pointing to the various pieces of embroidered teapoy[4] cloths.

"Yes."

"How can you find time to do all these? You have to do the office work as well? Have you not?"

"Yes. I do not stick to the laboratory all day long. I finish my work in two hours."

---

[4] **teapoy:** A small, three-legged table used for serving tea.

"In two hours! How do you manage? In our land the officers, magistrates, for instance, work seven hours daily."

"I have seen some of them doing their work. Do you think they work all the seven hours?"

"Certainly they do!"

"No, dear Sultana, they do not. They dawdle away their time in smoking. Some smoke two or three choroots during the office time. They talk much about their work, but do little. Suppose one choroot takes half an hour to burn off, and a man smokes twelve choroots daily; then, you see, he wastes six hours every day in sheer smoking."

We talked on various subjects; and I learned that they were not subject to any kind of epidemic disease, nor did they suffer from mosquito bites as we do. I was very much astonished to hear that in Ladyland no one died in youth except by rare accident.

"Will you care to see our kitchen?" she asked me.

"With pleasure," said I, and we went to see it. Of course the men had been asked to clear off when I was going there. The kitchen was situated in a beautiful vegetable garden. Every creeper, every tomato plant, was itself an ornament. I found no smoke, nor any chimney either in the kitchen — it was clean and bright; the windows were decorated with flower garlands. There was no sign of coal or fire.

"How do you cook?" I asked.

"With solar heat," she said, at the same time showing me the pipe, through which passed the concentrated sunlight and heat. And she cooked something then and there to show me the process.

"How did you manage to gather and store up the sun heat?" I asked her in amazement.

"Let me tell you a little of our past history, then. Thirty years ago, when our present Queen was thirteen years old, she inherited the throne. She was Queen in name only, the Prime Minister really ruling the country.

"Our good Queen liked science very much. She circulated an order that all the women in her country should be educated. Accordingly a number of girls' schools were founded and supported by the Government. Education was spread far and wide among women. And early marriage also was stopped. No woman was to be allowed to marry before she was twenty-one. I must tell you that, before this change, we had been kept in strict purdah."

"How the tables are turned," I interposed with a laugh.

"But the seclusion is the same," she said. "In a few years we had separate universities, where no men were admitted.

"In the capital, where our Queen lives, there are two universities. One of these invented a wonderful balloon, to which they attached a number of pipes. By means of this captive balloon, which they managed to keep afloat above the cloudland, they could draw as much water from the atmosphere as they pleased. As the water was incessantly being drawn by the university people, no cloud gathered and the ingenious Lady Principal stopped rain and storms thereby."

"Really! Now I understand why there is no mud here!" said I. But I could not understand how it was possible to accumulate water in the pipes. She explained to me how it was done; but I was unable to understand her, as my scientific knowledge was very limited. However, she went on:

"When the other university came to know of this, they became exceedingly jealous and tried to do something more extraordinary still. They invented an instrument by which they could collect as much sun heat as they wanted. And they kept the heat stored up to be distributed among others as required.

"While the women were engaged in scientific researches, the men of this country were busy increasing their military power. When they came to know that the female universities were able to draw water from the atmosphere and collect heat from the sun, they only laughed at the members of the universities and called the whole thing 'a sentimental nightmare!'"

· "Your achievements are very wonderful indeed! But tell me how you managed to put the men of your country into the zenana. Did you entrap them first?"

"No."

"It is not likely that they would surrender their free and open air life of their own accord and confine themselves within the four walls of the zenana! They must have been overpowered."

"Yes, they have been!"

"By whom?—by some lady warriors, I suppose?"

"No, not by arms."

"Yes, it cannot be so. Men's arms are stronger than women's. Then?"

"By brain."

"Even their brains are bigger and heavier than women's. Are they not?"

"Yes, but what of that? An elephant also has got a bigger and heavier brain than a man has. Yet man can enchain elephants and employ them, according to his own wishes."

"Well said, but tell me, please, how it all actually happened. I am dying to know it!"

"Women's brains are somewhat quicker than men's. Ten years ago, when the military officers called our scientific discoveries 'a sentimental nightmare,' some of the young ladies wanted to say something in reply to those remarks. But both the Lady Principals restrained them and said they should reply not by word but by deed, if ever they got the opportunity. And they had not long to wait for that opportunity."

"How marvelous!" I heartily clapped my hands.

"And now the proud gentlemen are dreaming sentimental dreams themselves.

"Soon afterward certain persons came from a neighboring country and took shelter in ours. They were in trouble, having committed some political offense. The King, who cared more for power than for good government, asked our kindhearted Queen to hand them over to his officers. She refused, as it was against her principle to turn out refugees. For this refusal the king declared war against our country.

"Our military officers sprang to their feet at once and marched out to meet the enemy.

"The enemy, however, was too strong for them. Our soldiers fought bravely, no doubt. But in spite of all their bravery the foreign army advanced step by step to invade our country.

"Nearly all the men had gone out to fight; even a boy of sixteen was not left home. Most of our warriors were killed, the rest driven back, and the enemy came within twenty-five miles of the capital.

"A meeting of a number of wise ladies was held at the Queen's palace to advise [as] to what should be done to save the land.

"Some proposed to fight like soldiers; others objected and said that women were not trained to fight with swords and guns, nor were they accustomed to fighting with any weapons. A third party regretfully remarked that they were hopelessly weak of body.

"'If you cannot save your country for lack of physical strength,' said the Queen, 'try to do so by brain power.'

"There was a dead silence for a few minutes. Her Royal Highness said again, 'I must commit suicide if the land and my honor are lost.'

"Then the Lady Principal of the second university (who had collected sun heat), who had been silently thinking during the consultation, remarked that they were all but lost; and there was little hope left for them. There was, however, one plan [that] she would like to try, and this would be her first and last effort; if she failed in this, there would be nothing left but to commit suicide. All present solemnly vowed that they would never allow themselves to be enslaved, no matter what happened.

"The Queen thanked them heartily, and asked the Lady Principal to try her plan.

"The Lady Principal rose again and said, 'Before we go out the men must enter the zenanas. I make this prayer for the sake of purdah.' 'Yes, of course,' replied Her Royal Highness.

"On the following day the Queen called upon all men to retire into zenanas for the sake of honor and liberty.

"Wounded and tired as they were, they took that order rather for a boon! They bowed low and entered the zenanas without uttering a single word of protest. They were sure that there was no hope for this country at all.

"Then the Lady Principal with her two thousand students marched to the battle-field, and arriving there directed all the rays of the concentrated sunlight and heat toward the enemy.

"The heat and light were too much for them to bear. They all ran away panic-stricken, not knowing in their bewilderment how to counteract that scorching heat. When they fled away leaving their guns and other ammunitions of war, they were burned down by means of the same sun heat.

"Since then no one has tried to invade our country any more."

"And since then, your countrymen never tried to come out of the zenana?"

"Yes, they wanted to be free. Some of the Police Commissioners and District Magistrates sent word to the Queen to the effect that the Military Officers certainly deserved to be imprisoned for their failure; but they [had] never neglected their duty and therefore they should not be punished, and they prayed to be restored to their respective offices.

"Her Royal Highness sent them a circular letter, intimating to them that if their services should ever be needed they would be sent for, and that in the meanwhile they should remain where they were.

"Now that they are accustomed to the purdah system and have ceased to grumble at their seclusion, we call the system *mardana*[5] instead of zenana."

"But how do you manage," I asked Sister Sara, "to do without the police or magistrates in case of theft or murder?"

"Since the mardana system has been established, there has been no more crime or sin; therefore we do not require a policeman to find out a culprit, nor do we want a magistrate to try a criminal case."

"That is very good, indeed. I suppose if there were any dishonest person, you could very easily chastise her. As you gained a decisive victory without shedding a single drop of blood, you could drive off crime and criminals too without much difficulty!"

"Now, dear Sultana, will you sit here or come to my parlor?" she asked me.

"Your kitchen is not inferior to a queen's boudoir!" I replied with a pleasant smile, "but we must leave it now; for the gentlemen may be cursing me for keeping them away from their duties in the kitchen so long." We both laughed heartily.

"How my friends at home will be amused and amazed, when I go back and tell them that in the far-off Ladyland, ladies rule over the country and control all social matters, while gentlemen are kept in the mardanas to mind babies, to cook, and to do all sorts of domestic work; and that cooking is so easy a thing that it is simply a pleasure to cook!"

"Yes, tell them about all that you see here."

"Please let me know how you carry on land cultivation and how you plow the land and do other hard manual work."

"Our fields are tilled by means of electricity, which supplies motive power for other hard work as well, and we employ it for our aerial conveyances too. We have no railroad nor any paved streets here."

"Therefore neither street nor railway accidents occur here," said I. "Do not you ever suffer from want of rainwater?" I asked.

"Never since the 'water balloon' has been set up. You see; the big balloon and pipes attached thereto. By their aid we can draw as much rainwater as we require. Nor do we ever suffer from flood or thunderstorms. We are all very busy making nature yield as much as she can. We do not find time to quarrel with one another as we never sit idle. Our noble Queen is exceedingly fond of botany; it is her ambition to convert the whole country into one grand garden."

"The idea is excellent. What is your chief food?"

"Fruits."

"How do you keep your country cool in hot weather? We regard the rainfall in summer as a blessing from heaven."

"When the heat becomes unbearable, we sprinkle the ground with plentiful showers drawn from the artificial fountains. And in cold weather we keep our rooms warm with sun heat."

She showed me her bathroom, the roof of which was removable. She could

---

[5] *mardana:* Men's quarters where guests are received; the public rooms in the house.

enjoy a shower [or] bath whenever she liked, by simply removing the roof (which was like the lid of a box) and turning on the tap of the shower pipe.

"You are a lucky people!" ejaculated I. "You know no want. What is your religion, may I ask?"

"Our religion is based on Love and Truth. It is our religious duty to love one another and to be absolutely truthful. If any person lies, she or he is . . ."

"Punished with death?"

"No, not with death. We do not take pleasure in killing a creature of God— especially a human being. The liar is asked to leave this land for good and never to come to it again."

"Is an offender never forgiven?"

"Yes, if that person repents sincerely."

"Are you not allowed to see any man, except your own relations?"

"No one except sacred relations."

"Our circle of sacred relations is very limited, even first cousins are not sacred."

"But ours is very large; a distant cousin is as sacred as a brother."

"That is very good. I see Purity itself reigns over your land. I should like to see the good Queen, who is so sagacious and farsighted and who has made all these rules."

"All right," said Sister Sara.

Then she screwed a couple of seats onto a square piece of plank. To this plank she attached two smooth and well-polished balls. When I asked her what the balls were for, she said they were hydrogen balls and they were used to overcome the force of gravity. The balls were of different capacities, to be used according to the different weights desired to be overcome. She then fastened to the air-car two winglike blades, which, she said, were worked by electricity. After we were comfortably seated she touched a knob and the blades began to whirl, moving faster and faster every moment. At first we were raised to the height of about six or seven feet and then off we flew. And before I could realize that we had commenced moving, we reached the garden of the Queen.

My friend lowered the air-car by reversing the action of the machine, and when the car touched the ground the machine was stopped and we got out.

I had seen from the air-car the Queen walking on a garden path with her little daughter (who was four years old) and her maids of honor.

"Halloo! you here!" cried the Queen, addressing Sister Sara. I was introduced to Her Royal Highness and was received by her cordially without any ceremony.

I was very much delighted to make her acquaintance. In [the] course of the conversation I had with her, the Queen told me that she had no objection to permitting her subjects to trade with other countries. "But," she continued, "no trade was possible with countries where the women were kept in the zenanas and so unable to come and trade with us. Men, we find, are rather of lower morals and so we do not like dealing with them. We do not covet other people's land, we do not fight for a piece of diamond though it may be a thousandfold brighter than the Koh-i-Noor,[6]

---

[6] **Koh-i-Noor:** Meaning "mountain of light," this is the name of a large and exceptionally brilliant diamond in the possession of the Mughal rulers of India, currently part of the British crown jewels; a symbol of great wealth. [Jahan's note.]

nor do we grudge a ruler his Peacock Throne.[7] We dive deep into the ocean of knowledge and try to find out the precious gems [that] Nature has kept in store for us. We enjoy Nature's gifts as much as we can."

After taking leave of the Queen, I visited the famous universities, and was shown over some of their factories, laboratories, and observatories.

After visiting the above places of interest, we got again into the air-car, but as soon as it began moving I somehow slipped down and the fall startled me out of my dream. And on opening my eyes, I found myself in my own bedroom still lounging in the easy chair!

---

[7] **Peacock Throne:** A famous jewel-encrusted throne built for the Mughal emperor Shah Jahan, who was responsible for the Taj Mahal. The throne was carried away from Delhi by the Persian invader Nadir Shah. Its current location is the cause of much speculation. Many think that one of the thrones displayed in the Istanbul Museum is the Peacock Throne. It is a longstanding Indian symbol of royal power and splendor. [Jahan's note.]

℘ LU XUN
B. CHINA, 1881–1936

Lu Xun, the pen name of Zhou Shuren, was born into comfortable circumstances and expected to become an educated member of the professional classes. He first challenged those expectations when he turned his back on a career in the civil service and left China to study medicine in Japan. Once trained as a surgeon, however, he realized that what he wished to cure most was the backward condition of the Chinese people, not merely their bodily illnesses. "The most important thing," he wrote, "was to change their spirit, and since at that time I felt that literature was the best means to that end, I decided to promote a literary movement." Creating a new school of writing called CRITICAL REALISM[1] that examined social tendencies through the actions of realistic characters, Lu Xun's writing was marked by a tough-mindedness that exposed those within China who prevented social progress. Lu Xun was a fierce opponent of the conventional Chinese morality that was handed down to each new generation through the doctrines of CONFUCIANISM, which stresses obedience, reverence for the past, and constricting rules of acceptable behavior. Confucianism, he said, had "cannibalized" China. Although he died

loo-SHWEN

> My themes were usually the unfortunates of this abnormal society. My aim was to expose the disease and draw attention to it so that it might be cured.
>
> – LU XUN

---

[1] **critical realism:** The idea of critical realism became increasingly connected to Lu Xun's notion of revolution. In an address to the League of Left-Wing Writers (1930), a group he had helped to form, Lu Xun stated: "Revolution is a bitter thing, mixed with filth and blood, not as lovely or perfect as poets think. Of course there is destruction in a revolution, but construction is even more necessary to it; and while destruction is straightforward, construction is troublesome."

before **Mao Zedong** and the Chinese Communist Party[2] seized control of the country after World War II, Lu Xun was recognized by the Communist leader as the spiritual father of the Chinese Revolution.

Portrait of Lu Xun, c. 1900

The writer Lu Xun was revered by Mao Zedong and the Communists. (© Bettmann / CORBIS)

A Revolutionary Life.   While a medical student in Japan, Lu Xun came across a photograph from the Russo-Japanese War of 1904–05. The picture showed a Chinese prisoner about to be beheaded by the Japanese surrounded by a group of Chinese who appeared indifferent to the fate of their countryman. Lu Xun decided to challenge the apathy of the Chinese by returning home and creating a movement to win the youth of China to the cause of social change, starting the literary journal *New Youth* and working as a teacher. His first short story, "Diary of a Madman" (1918), is a scathing attack on what Lu Xun saw as a cannibalistic society that was devouring itself. Considered the first work of modern Chinese literature, it was written in vernacular and colloquial Chinese rather than in the usual literary language. The "madman" who narrates the story is obsessed by the growing paranoia that he lives in a society of cannibals. "In ancient times," he writes in an early entry in his diary, "as I recollect, people often ate human beings, but I am rather hazy about it. I tried to look this up but my history book has no chronology, and scrawled over each page are the words 'virtue' and 'morality.' Since I could not sleep anyway, I read hard half the night, until I began to see words between the lines, the whole book being filled with two words — 'Eat People.'" As his "dementia" grows, the madman realizes that cannibalism is not just a thing of the past. The disease has been passed down from father to son for four thousand years. By the end of the diary, he sees only one glimmer of hope: "Perhaps there are still children who have not eaten men? Save the children." This hope was also Lu Xun's revolutionary program for China and the aim of his literary work.

From 1920 to 1926 Lu Xun worked in the anti-imperialist movement in Beijing (Peking), and in 1927 he moved to Canton, then a seat of revolutionary activity. After the coup d'état of **Chiang Kai-shek** and his **Kuomintang** army[3] later that year, Lu Xun retreated to Shanghai, where he lived his last ten years fighting the Japanese imperialists on the one hand and Chiang Kai-shek's rightist government on the other. He organized the League of Left-Wing Writers and wrote more than six hundred essays under many pen names while dodging political repression. Though encouraged by the successes of the Chinese Communists, he never joined the Communist Party. He died of tuberculosis in Shanghai in 1936.

---

[2] **Mao . . . Party:** Mao Zedong (1893–1976) was a founding member of the Chinese Communist Party (1921). After breaking with the Kuomintang nationalists in 1927, Mao Zedong consolidated his authority against both the invading Japanese and the Kuomintang and ousted the Chinese nationalists in 1949.

[3] **Chiang . . . army:** Chiang Kai-shek (1887–1975) originally supported the separatist Chinese government of Sun Yat-sen in 1918, occupied the capital of Beijing in 1928, then lost ground to the Communist Party and was finally forced to withdraw with his army to the island of Taiwan in 1949.

Political Fiction.   Lu Xun wrote many political essays, commentaries, literary sketches, and reminiscences, but his literary reputation is based on the twenty-six short stories that were published between 1918 and 1935 and gathered in three collections: *Call to Arms* (1922), *Wandering* (1925), and *Old Tales Retold* (1935). The recurrent theme in nearly all of the stories is the oppressive hold of the past on the present. Influenced by the work of European Realists, especially Nikolai Gogol and Maxim Gorky,[4] Lu Xun described his subject as "the unfortunates of this abnormal society. My aim was to expose the disease and draw attention to it so that it might be cured." In "The New Year's Sacrifice," for example, he shows how the feudal family system in China "murders" a woman who is treated as property and sold into two wretched marriages and who finally dies as an outcast beggar on New Year's day. The story's irony and bleak satire are characteristic of Lu Xun's work. In "Regret for the Past," he writes of two lovers who defy social rules by living together and rejecting established gender roles. The social rejection and financial hardship they suffer as a result of their defiance, however, destroys their love, drives them apart, and presages their deaths. Lu Xun's stories always lead to the conclusion that so destructive a culture has to be changed.

"The True Story of Ah Q."   Lu Xun's fictional masterpiece, "The True Story of Ah Q," was written in 1921. In this cautionary tale, set in 1911, an old farmhand who has suffered bullying and persecution all his life and dreamed of deliverance at the hands of revolutionaries is charged with committing an act of common thievery and executed in the town square at the moment of liberation. The story is typically complex. It exposes the folly of the laborer himself, who cringes before authority and lives in a fantasy world, and the weakness of the old order in the subplot of the rich man who is robbed of his possessions. It also reveals the hypocrisy of the young "revolutionaries" who execute Ah Q to give the appearance of maintaining law and order. The opposing forces in prerevolutionary China are all here: a hapless individual out of touch with society; the old order, helpless to defend itself; and the new order about to be born — callow, superficial, as yet unable to do the right thing. "Ah Q" does not have a happy ending: It is a look at false notions of social revolution, and its irony and satire leave no group untouched.

Lu Xun was wont to use irony and satire to scrutinize the social conventions of China's past and the revolutionary excesses of his day, making it difficult for readers to identify the author's point of view in his work, hidden as it is behind the mask of the SATIRIST.[5] At the beginning of "The True Story of Ah Q," Lu Xun seems to be making fun of the narrator's obsessive attempt to find the proper literary name for the story and his

> Regarded as a national hero and canonized by the Chinese Communist Party, Lu Xun has been revered as the intellectual source of the Chinese Revolution who prepared the ideological ground for Mao Zedong.
>
> – DANIEL S. BURT, critic, 2001

> Lu Xun was the major leader in the Chinese cultural revolution. He was not only a great writer but a great thinker and a great revolutionist. . . . Lu Xun breached and stormed the enemy citadel; on the cultural front he was the bravest and most correct, the firmest, the most loyal, and the most ardent national hero, a hero without parallel in our history.
>
> – MAO ZEDONG

---

[4] **Gogol . . . Gorky:** The Russian writers Nikolai Gogol (1809–1852), author of "The Overcoat" (1842) and *Dead Souls* (1842), and Maxim Gorky (1868–1936), author of *The Lower Depths* (1902) and *Mother* (1907).

[5] **mask of the satirist:** Satirists often write through the personae of narrators, like Gulliver in Swift's *Gulliver's Travels,* who obscure the author's point of view from the reader.

www For links to more information about Lu Xun, a quiz on "The True Story of Ah Q," and more on the culture and content of twentieth-century China, see *World Literature Online* at bedfordstmartins .com/worldlit.

pedantic references to seemingly meaningless episodes in Chinese history. Indeed, for the first half of the story, the narrator's straight-faced depiction of the adventures of Ah Q makes comedy of the "hero," who is for the most part a fool. In the second half of the story, however, the tone becomes less comic as the serious consequences of Ah Q's foolishness are revealed. The society's power to devour turns comedy into pathos. Unaware of the real forces that may doom him whatever his actions, Ah Q has no idea what is about to happen to him, and his flights of equivocation, self-deception, and bravado only hasten his fate.

■ CONNECTIONS

Franz Kafka, *The Metamorphosis*, p. 428; Chinua Achebe, *Things Fall Apart*, p. 1023; Anton Chekhov, *The Cherry Orchard* (Book 5). Like Kafka's Gregor Samsa, the aristocrats in Chekhov's *The Cherry Orchard*, and Achebe's Okonkwo, Ah Q is a victim of historical forces largely beyond his comprehension. Identify the historical changes that undo the characters in each of these works. What is the outcome of the characters' failure to understand their situations? Is it tragic? Comic? Pathetic?

Jonathan Swift, *Gulliver's Travels* (Book 4); Voltaire, *Candide* (Book 4). Like Swift's Gulliver and Voltaire's Candide, Ah Q is naive and gullible. His naiveté highlights the cruelty of the social forces that oppress and eventually kill him. The positive social vision that Swift and Voltaire hold in opposition to the societies they satirize is more visible, implicitly at least, than that of Lu Xun. What alternative does each satirist offer to the social ills he attacks? How is it suggested in each work?

Sophocles, *Oedipus Rex* (Book 1). Ah Q is an example of the type of protagonist sometimes called an "anti-hero." Although his story broadly follows a tragic plot that ends with his execution, he is not noble and has no largeness of spirit. Compare Ah Q with a tragic hero like Oedipus. What about Ah Q's story might be considered tragic? Is its overall effect cathartic?

■ FURTHER RESEARCH

Translations
Yang, Xianyi, and Gladys Yang, trans. *The Complete Stories of Lu Xun*. 1981.

Criticism
Lee, Leo Ou-fan. *Voices from the Iron House: A Study of Lu Xun*. 1987.
Lyell, William A. *Lu Hsun's Vision of Reality*. 1976.

■ PRONUNCIATION

Ah Gui: ah-GWAY
Bao Si: bow-SUH
Chen Duxiu: chun-doo-SHYOO
Chiang Kai-shek: jahng-kigh-SHEK
Chong Zhen: chohng-JUN
Da Ji: dah-JEE
Diao Chan: dyow-CHAHN
Dong Zhuo: dohng-JWOH
Fu Xi: foo-SHEE
Kuomintang: gwoh-min-DAHNG, kwoh-min-TAHNG
Lu Xun: loo-SHWEN
Mao Zedong: mow-dzuh-DOHNG

Qian: chee-EN
Qing: CHING
Shaoxing: show-SHING
Tianshui: tyen-SHWAY
Xuan De, Xuan Tong: shwen-DUH, shwen-TOHNG
Weizhuang: way-JWAHNG
Zhang: JAHNG
Zhao, Zhao Baiyan, Zhao Sichen: JOW, jow-bah-YAN, jow-suh-CHUN
Zhou: JOH
Zi You Dang: dzuh-yoh-DAHNG
Zou: DZOH
Zuo Zhuan: dzwoh-JWEN

The True Story of Ah Q

Translated by Xianyi Yang and Gladys Yang

CHAPTER 1

Introduction

For several years now I have been meaning to write the true story of Ah Q. But while wanting to write I was in some trepidation too, which goes to show that I am not one of those who achieve glory by writing; for an immortal pen has always been required to record the deeds of an immortal man, the man becoming known to posterity through the writing and the writing known to posterity through the man—until finally it is not clear who is making whom known. But in the end, as though possessed by some fiend, I always came back to the idea of writing the story of Ah Q.

And yet no sooner had I taken up my pen than I became conscious of tremendous difficulties in writing this far-from-immortal work. The first was the question of what to call it. Confucius said, "If the name is not correct, the words will not ring

---

"The True Story of Ah Q." Written in 1921 and collected in the volume *Call to Arms* (1922), this story takes place a decade earlier, in 1911, at the time of the revolution in China that overthrew the Manchu dynasty and installed a republic under Sun Yat-sen. The story can be taken as a parable about the diseased condition of China at the beginning of the twentieth century. Ah Q, representing China, is incapable of understanding his situation or taking any responsibility for it. On the contrary, he interprets every defeat as a victory and is convinced of his superiority relative to everyone else. Finally, his delusions entangle him in a revolution and lead to his destruction. Lu Xun's harsh satire, intended to motivate his readers to want to change China, combines an ironic narration that mocks rule-bound Confucianism with a "hero" who values nothing except his own narrow and immediate self-interest in a black comedy that ends up with the protagonist's execution. No characters in the story offer hope for a better society. The rich are interested only in maintaining their privileged position, the revolutionaries are out to prove they are in control and can ensure law and order, and Ah Q never awakens.

A note on the translation: The translation is by Xianyi and Gladys Yang, who have translated many of Lu Xun's stories. All notes are the editors'.

true"; and this axiom should be most scrupulously observed. There are many types of biography: official biographies, autobiographies, unauthorized biographies, legends, supplementary biographies, family histories, sketches . . . but unfortunately none of these suited my purpose. "Official biography"? This account will obviously not be included with those of many eminent people in some authentic history. "Autobiography"? But I am obviously not Ah Q. If I were to call this an "unauthorized biography," then where is his "authenticated biography"? The use of "legend" is impossible because Ah Q was no legendary figure. "Supplementary biography"? But no president has ever ordered the National Historical Institute to write a "standard life" of Ah Q. It is true that although there are no "lives of gamblers" in authentic English history, the well-known author Conan Doyle nevertheless wrote *Rodney Stone*;[1] but while this is permissible for a well-known author it is not permissible for such as I. Then there is "family history"; but I do not know whether I belong to the same family as Ah Q or not, nor have his children or grandchildren ever entrusted me with such a task. If I were to use "sketch," it might be objected that Ah Q has no "complete account." In short, this is really a "life," but since I write in vulgar vein using the language of hucksters and pedlars, I dare not presume to give it so high-sounding a title. So I will take as my title the last two words of a stock phrase of the novelists, who are not reckoned among the Three Cults and Nine Schools.[2] "Enough of this digression, and back to the *true story*"; and if this is reminiscent of the *True Story of Calligraphy*[3] of the ancients, it cannot be helped.

The second difficulty confronting me was that a biography of this type should start off something like this: "So-and-so, whose other name was so-and-so, was a native of such-and-such a place"; but I don't really know what Ah Q's surname was. Once, he seemed to be named Zhao, but the next day there was some confusion about the matter again. This was after Mr. Zhao's son had passed the county examination and, to the sound of gongs, his success was announced in the village. Ah Q, who had just drunk two bowls of yellow wine, began to prance about declaring that this reflected credit on him too, since he belonged to the same clan as Mr. Zhao and by an exact reckoning was three generations senior to the successful candidate. At the time several bystanders even began to stand slightly in awe of Ah Q. But the next day the bailiff summoned him to Mr. Zhao's house. When the old gentleman set eyes on him his face turned crimson with fury and he roared:

"Ah Q, you miserable wretch! Did you say I belonged to the same clan as you?"

Ah Q made no reply.

The more he looked at him the angrier Mr. Zhao became. Advancing menacingly a few steps he said, "How dare you talk such nonsense! How could I have such a relative as you? Is your surname Zhao?"

---

[1] **Doyle . . . *Stone*:** Sir Arthur Conan Doyle (1859–1930), popular British novelist best known for the Sherlock Holmes stories. *Rodney Stone* (1896) is a historical novel about the sporting (and gambling) life during the Regency period in early-nineteenth-century England.

[2] **Three Cults and Nine Schools:** The Three Cults were Confucianism, Buddhism, and Daoism (Taoism); the Nine Schools comprised the Confucian, Daoist, Legalist, and Mohist schools and five others.

[3] *True Story of Calligraphy:* A book by Feng Wu of the Qing dynasty (1644–1911).

Ah Q made no reply and was planning a retreat, when Mr. Zhao darted forward and gave him a slap on the face.

"How could *you* be named Zhao? Are you worthy of the name Zhao?"

Ah Q made no attempt to defend his right to the name Zhao but rubbing his left cheek went out with the bailiff from whom, once outside, he had to listen to another torrent of abuse. He then by way of atonement paid him two hundred cash. All who heard this said Ah Q was a great fool to ask for a beating like that. Even if his surname *were* Zhao—which wasn't likely—he should have known better than to boast like that when there was a Mr. Zhao living in the village. After this no further mention was made of Ah Q's ancestry, thus I still have no idea what his surname really was.

The third difficulty I encountered in writing this work was that I don't know how Ah Q's personal name should be written either. During his lifetime everybody called him Ah Gui, but after his death not a soul mentioned Ah Gui again; for he was obviously not one of those whose name is "preserved on bamboo tablets and silk."[4] If there is any question of preserving his name, this essay must be the first attempt at doing so. Hence I am confronted with this difficulty at the outset. I have given the question careful thought. Ah Gui—would that be the "Gui" meaning fragrant osmanthus[5] or the "Gui" meaning nobility? If his other name had been Moon Pavilion, or if he had celebrated his birthday in the month of the Moon Festival, then it would certainly be the "Gui" for fragrant osmanthus. But since he had no other name—or if he had, no one knew it—and since he never sent out invitations on his birthday to secure complimentary verses, it would be arbitrary to write Ah Gui (fragrant osmanthus). Again, if he had had an elder or younger brother called Ah Fu (prosperity), then he would certainly be called Ah Gui (nobility). But he was all on his own; thus there is no justification for writing Ah Gui (nobility). All the other, unusual characters with the sound *gui* are even less suitable. I once put this question to Mr. Zhao's son, the successful county candidate, but even such a learned man as he was baffled by it. According to him, however, the reason why this name could not be traced was that Chen Duxiu[6] had brought out the magazine *New Youth* advocating the use of the Western alphabet, hence the national culture was going to the dogs. As a last resort, I asked someone from my district to go and look up the legal documents recording Ah Q's case, but after eight months he sent me a letter saying that there was no name anything like Ah Gui in those records. Although uncertain whether this was the truth or whether my friend had simply done nothing, after failing to trace the name this way I could think of no other means of finding it. Since I am afraid the new system of phonetics has not yet come into common use, there is nothing for it but to use the Western alphabet, writing the name according to the English spelling as Ah Gui and abbreviating it to Ah Q. This approximates to blindly

---

[4] "preserved on . . . silk": Preserved in ancient texts, before the invention of paper.

[5] fragrant osmanthus: The fragrant osmanthus blooms in the month of the Moon Festival; in Chinese folklore, the shadow on the moon is an osmanthus tree.

[6] Chen Duxiu (1880–1942): Editor of *New Youth* and an advocate of the modernization of Chinese culture.

following *New Youth,* and I am thoroughly ashamed of myself; but since even such a learned man as Mr. Zhao's son could not solve my problem, what else can I do?

My fourth difficulty was with Ah Q's place of origin. If his surname were Zhao, then according to the old custom which still prevails of classifying people by their district, one might look up the commentary in *The Hundred Surnames*[7] and find "Native of Tianshui in Gansu." But unfortunately this surname is open to question, with the result that Ah Q's place of origin must also remain uncertain. Although he lived for the most part in Weizhuang, he often stayed in other places, so that it would be wrong to call him a native of Weizhuang. It would, in fact, amount to a distortion of history.

The only thing that consoles me is the fact that the character "Ah" is absolutely correct. This is definitely not the result of false analogy, and is well able to stand the test of scholarly criticism. As for the other problems, it is not for such unlearned people as myself to solve them, and I can only hope that disciples of Dr. Hu Shi, who has such "a passion for history and research," may be able in future to throw new light on them. I am afraid, however, that by that time my "True Story of Ah Q" will have long since passed into oblivion.

The foregoing may be considered as an introduction.

Chapter 2

A Brief Account of Ah Q's Victories

In addition to the uncertainty regarding Ah Q's surname, personal name, and place of origin, there is even some uncertainty regarding his "background." This is because the people of Weizhuang only made use of his services or treated him as a laughing-stock, without ever paying the slightest attention to his "background." Ah Q himself remained silent on this subject, except that when quarreling with someone he might glare at him and say, "We used to be much better off than you! Who do you think you are?"

Ah Q had no family but lived in the Tutelary God's Temple at Weizhuang. He had no regular work either, being simply an odd-job man for others: When there was wheat to be cut he would cut it, when there was rice to be hulled he would hull it, when there was a boat to be punted he would punt it. If the work lasted for any length of time he might stay in the house of his temporary employer, but as soon as it was finished he would leave. Thus whenever people had work to be done they would remember Ah Q, but what they remembered was his service and not his "background." By the time the job was done even Ah Q himself was forgotten, to say nothing of his "background." Once indeed an old man remarked, "What a worker Ah Q is!" Ah Q, bare-backed scrawny sluggard, was standing before him at the time, and others could not tell whether the remark was serious or derisive, but Ah Q was overjoyed.

Ah Q, again, had a very high opinion of himself. He looked down on all the inhabitants of Weizhuang, thinking even the two young "scholars" not worth a smile, though most young scholars were likely to pass the official examinations. Mr.

---

[7] *The Hundred Surnames:* A school reading primer.

Zhao and Mr. Qian were held in great respect by the villagers, for in addition to being rich they were both the fathers of young scholars. Ah Q alone showed them no exceptional deference, thinking to himself, "My sons may be much greater."

Moreover, after Ah Q had been to town several times he naturally became even more conceited, although at the same time he had the greatest contempt for towns-people. For instance, a bench made of a wooden plank three feet by three inches the Weizhuang villagers called a "long bench." Ah Q called it a "long bench" too; but the townspeople called it a "straight bench," and he thought, "This is wrong. Ridicu-lous!" Again, when they fried large-headed fish in oil the Weizhuang villagers all added shallots sliced half an inch thick, whereas the townspeople added finely shred-ded shallots, and he thought, "This is wrong too. Ridiculous!" But the Weizhuang villagers were really ignorant rustics who had never seen fish fried in town.

Ah Q who "used to be much better off," who was a man of the world and a "worker," would have been almost the perfect man had it not been for a few unfortu-nate physical blemishes. The most annoying were some patches on his scalp where at some uncertain date shiny ringworm scars had appeared. Although these were on his own head, apparently Ah Q did not consider them as altogether honourable, for he refrained from using the word "ringworm" or any words that sounded anything like it. Later he improved on this, making "bright" and "light" forbidden words, while later still even "lamp" and "candle" were taboo. Whenever this taboo was disre-garded, whether intentionally or not, Ah Q would fly into a rage, his ringworm scars turning scarlet. He would look over the offender, and if it were someone weak in repartee he would curse him, while if it were a poor fighter he would hit him. Yet, curiously enough, it was usually Ah Q who was worsted in these encounters, until finally he adopted new tactics, contenting himself in general with a furious glare.

It so happened, however, that after Ah Q had taken to using this furious glare, the idlers in Weizhuang grew even more fond of making jokes at his expense. As soon as they saw him they would pretend to give a start and say:

"Look! It's lighting up."

Ah Q rising to the bait as usual would glare in fury.

"So there is a paraffin lamp here," they would continue, unafraid.

Ah Q could do nothing but rack his brains for some retort. "You don't even deserve. . . ." At this juncture it seemed as if the bald patches on his scalp were noble and honourable, not just ordinary ringworm scars. However, as we said above, Ah Q was a man of the world: He knew at once that he had nearly broken the "taboo" and refrained from saying any more.

If the idlers were still not satisfied but continued to pester him, they would in the end come to blows. Then only after Ah Q had to all appearances been defeated, had his brownish queue pulled and his head bumped against the wall four or five times, would the idlers walk away, satisfied at having won. And Ah Q would stand there for a second thinking to himself, "It's as if I were beaten by my son. What the world is coming to nowadays! . . ." Thereupon he too would walk away, satisfied at having won.

Whatever Ah Q thought he was sure to tell people later; thus almost all who made fun of Ah Q knew that he had this means of winning a psychological victory.

So after this anyone who pulled or twisted his brown queue would forestall him by saying, "Ah Q, this is not a son beating his father, it is a man beating a beast. Let's hear you say it: A man beating a beast!"

Then Ah Q, clutching at the root of his queue, his head on one side, would say, "Beating an insect—how about that? I am an insect—now will you let me go?"

But although he was an insect the idlers would not let him go until they had knocked his head five or six times against something nearby, according to their custom, after which they would walk away satisfied that they had won, confident that this time Ah Q was done for. In less than ten seconds, however, Ah Q would walk away also satisfied that he had won, thinking that he was the "Number One self-belittler," and that after subtracting "self-belittler" what remained was "Number One." Was not the highest successful candidate in the official examination also "Number One"? "And who do you think *you* are?"

After employing such cunning devices to get even with his enemies, Ah Q would make his way cheerfully to the tavern to drink a few bowls of wine, joke with the others again, quarrel with them again, come off victorious again, and return cheerfully to the Tutelary God's Temple, there to fall asleep as soon as his head touched the pillow. If he had money he would gamble. A group of men would squat on the ground, Ah Q sandwiched in their midst, his face streaming with sweat; and his voice would shout the loudest: "Four hundred on the Green Dragon!"

"Hey—open there!"

The stake-holder, his face streaming with sweat too, would open the box and chant: "Heavenly Gate!—Nothing for the Corner! . . . No stakes on Popularity Passage! Pass over Ah Q's coppers!"

"The Passage—one hundred—one hundred and fifty."

To the tune of this chanting, Ah Q's money would gradually vanish into the pockets of other sweating players. Finally he would be forced to squeeze his way out of the crowd and watch from the back, taking a vicarious interest in the game until it broke up, when he would return reluctantly to the Tutelary God's Temple. The next day he would go to work with swollen eyes.

However, the truth of the proverb "Misfortune may prove a blessing in disguise" was shown when Ah Q was unfortunate enough to win and almost suffered defeat in the end.

This was the evening of the Festival of the Gods in Weizhuang. According to custom there was an opera; and close to the stage, also according to custom, were numerous gambling tables. The drums and gongs of the opera sounded miles away to Ah Q who had ears only for the stake-holder's chant. He staked successfully again and again, his coppers turning into silver coins, his silver coins into dollars, and his dollars mounting up. In his excitement he cried out, "Two dollars on Heavenly Gate!"

He never knew who started the fight, nor for what reason. Curses, blows, and footsteps formed a confused medley of sound in his head, and by the time he clambered to his feet the gambling tables had vanished and so had the gamblers. Several parts of his body seemed to be aching as if he had been kicked and knocked about, while a number of people were looking at him in astonishment. Feeling as if something were amiss he walked back to the Tutelary God's Temple, and by the time he had calmed down again he realized that his pile of dollars had gone. Since most of the people who ran gambling tables at the Festival were not natives of Weizhuang, where could he look for the culprits?

So white and glittering a pile of silver! All of it his . . . but now it had disappeared. Even to consider this tantamount to being robbed by his son did not comfort him. To consider himself as an insect did not comfort him either. This time he really tasted something of the bitterness of defeat.

But presently he changed defeat into victory. Raising his right hand he slapped his own face hard, twice, so that it tingled with pain. After this slapping his heart felt lighter, for it seemed as if the one who had given the slap was himself, the one slapped some other self, and soon it was just as if he had beaten someone else — in spite of the fact that his face was still tingling. He lay down satisfied that he had gained the victory.

Soon he was asleep.

Chapter 3

A Further Account of Ah Q's Victories

Although Ah Q was always gaining victories, it was only after he was favoured with a slap in the face by Mr. Zhao that he became famous.

After paying the bailiff two hundred cash he lay down angrily. Then he said to himself, "What is the world coming to nowadays, with sons beating their fathers!" And then the thought of the prestige of Mr. Zhao, who was now his son, gradually raised his spirits. He scrambled up and made his way to the tavern singing *The Young Widow at Her Husband's Grave*.[8] At that time he did feel that Mr. Zhao was a cut above most people.

After this incident, strange to relate, it was true that everybody seemed to pay him unusual respect. He probably attributed this to the fact that he was Mr. Zhao's father, but actually such was not the case. In Weizhuang, as a rule, if the seventh child hit the eighth child or Li So-and-so hit Zhang So-and-so, it was not taken seriously. A beating had to be connected with some important personage like Mr. Zhao before the villagers thought it worth talking about. But once they thought it worth talking about, since the beater was famous the one beaten enjoyed some of his reflected fame. As for the fault being Ah Q's, that was naturally taken for granted, the reason being that Mr. Zhao could do no wrong. But if Ah Q were wrong, why did everybody seem to treat him with unusual respect? This is difficult to explain. We may put forward the hypothesis that it was because Ah Q had said he belonged to the same family as Mr. Zhao; thus, although he had been beaten, people were still afraid there might be some truth in his assertion and therefore thought it safer to treat him more respectfully. Or, alternatively, it may have been like the case of the sacrificial beef in the Confucian temple: Although the beef was in the same category as the pork and

---

[8] *The Young Widow at Her Husband's Grave:* A popular opera in Shaoxing.

mutton, being of animal origin just as they were, later Confucians did not dare touch it since the sage had enjoyed it.

After this Ah Q prospered for several years.

One spring, when he was walking along in a state of happy intoxication, he saw Whiskers Wang sitting stripped to the waist in the sunlight at the foot of a wall, catching lice; and at this sight his own body began to itch. Since Whiskers Wang was scabby and bewhiskered, everybody called him "Ringworm Whiskers Wang." Although Ah Q omitted the word "Ringworm," he had the greatest contempt for the man. To Ah Q, while scabs were nothing to take exception to, such hairy cheeks were really too outlandish and could excite nothing but scorn. So Ah Q sat down by his side. Had it been any other idler, Ah Q would never have dared sit down so casually; but what had he to fear by the side of Whiskers Wang? In fact, his willingness to sit down was doing the fellow an honour.

Ah Q took off his tattered lined jacket and turned it inside out; but either because he had washed it recently or because he was too clumsy, a long search yielded only three or four lice. He saw that Whiskers Wang, on the other hand, was catching first one and then another in swift succession, cracking them between his teeth with a popping sound.

Ah Q felt first disappointed, then resentful: The despicable Whiskers Wang had so many, he himself so few—what a great loss of face! He longed to find one or two big ones, but there were none, and when at last he managed to catch a middle-sized one, stuffed it fiercely between his thick lips and bit hard, the resultant pop was again inferior to the noise made by Whiskers Wang.

All Ah Q's ringworm patches turned scarlet. He flung his jacket on the ground, spat, and swore, "Hairy worm!"

"Mangy dog, who are you calling names?" Whiskers Wang looked up contemptuously.

Although the relative respect accorded him in recent years had increased Ah Q's pride, he was still rather timid when confronted by those loafers accustomed to fighting. But today he was feeling exceptionally pugnacious. How dare a hairy-cheeked creature like this insult him?

"If the cap fits wear it," he retorted, standing up and putting his hands on his hips.

"Are your bones itching?" demanded Whiskers Wang, standing up too and draping his jacket over his shoulders.

Thinking that the fellow meant to run away, Ah Q lunged forward to punch him. But before his fist reached the target, his opponent seized him and gave him a tug which sent him staggering. Then Whiskers Wang seized his queue and started dragging him towards the wall to knock his head in the time-honoured manner.

"'A gentleman uses his tongue but not his hands!'" protested Ah Q, his head on one side.

Apparently Whiskers Wang was no gentleman, for without paying the slightest attention to what Ah Q said he knocked his head against the wall five times in succession, then with a great push shoved him two yards away, after which he walked off in triumph.

As far as Ah Q could remember, this was the first humiliation of his life, because he had always scoffed at Whiskers Wang on account of his ugly bewhiskered cheeks, but had never been scoffed at, much less beaten by him. And now, contrary to all expectations, Whiskers Wang had beaten him. Could it really be true, as they said in the marketplace: "The Emperor has abolished the official examinations, so that scholars who have passed them are no longer in demand"? This must have undermined the Zhao family's prestige. Was this why people were treating him contemptuously too?

Ah Q stood there irresolutely.

From the distance approached another of Ah Q's enemies. This was Mr. Qian's eldest son whom Ah Q thoroughly despised. After studying in a foreign-style school in the city, it seemed he had gone to Japan. When he came home half a year later his legs were straight[9] and his queue had disappeared. His mother wept bitterly a dozen times, and his wife tried three times to jump into the well. Later his mother told everyone, "His queue was cut off by some scoundrel when he was drunk. By rights he ought to be a big official, but now he'll have to wait till it's grown again." Ah Q, however, did not believe this, and insisted on calling him a "Bogus Foreign Devil" or "Traitor in Foreign Pay." At sight of him he would start cursing under his breath.

What Ah Q despised and detested most in him was his false queue. When it came to having a false queue, a man could scarcely be considered human; and the fact that his wife had not attempted to jump into the well a fourth time showed that she was not a good woman either.

Now this "Bogus Foreign Devil" was approaching.

"Baldhead! Ass. . . ." In the past Ah Q had just cursed under his breath, inaudibly; but today, because he was in a rage and itching for revenge, the words slipped out involuntarily.

Unfortunately this Baldhead was carrying a shiny brown cane which looked to Ah Q like the "staff carried by a mourner." With great strides he bore down on Ah Q who, guessing at once that a beating was in the offing, hastily flexed his muscles and hunched his shoulders in anticipation. Sure enough, *Thwack!* something struck him on the head.

"I meant him!" explained Ah Q, pointing to a nearby child.

Thwack! Thwack! Thwack!

As far as Ah Q could remember, this was the second humiliation of his life. Fortunately after the thwacking stopped it seemed to him that the matter was closed, and he even felt somewhat relieved. Moreover, the precious "ability to forget" handed down by his ancestors stood him in good stead. He walked slowly away and by the time he approached the tavern door he was quite cheerful again.

Just then, however, a little nun from the Convent of Quiet Self-Improvement came walking towards him. The sight of a nun always made Ah Q swear; how much more so, then, after these humiliations? When he recalled what had happened, his anger flared up again.

---

[9] **his legs were straight:** Foreigners were thought to walk stiffly, with straight legs.

"I couldn't think what made my luck so bad today—so it's meeting you that did it!" he fumed to himself.

Going towards her he spat noisily. "Ugh! . . . Pah!"

The little nun paid not the least attention but walked on with lowered head. Ah Q stepped up to her and shot out a hand to rub her newly shaved scalp, then with a guffaw cried, "Baldhead! Go back quick, your monk's waiting for you. . . ."

"Who are you pawing? . . ." demanded the nun, flushing all over her face as she quickened her pace.

The men in the tavern roared with laughter. This appreciation of his feat added to Ah Q's elation.

"If the monk paws you, why can't I?" He pinched her cheek.

Again the men in the tavern roared with laughter. More bucked than ever, and eager to please his admirers, Ah Q pinched her hard again before letting her go.

This encounter had made him forget Whiskers Wang and the Bogus Foreign Devil, as if all the day's bad luck had been avenged. And strange to relate, even more completely relaxed than after the thwacking, he felt as light as if he were walking on air.

"Ah Q, may you die sonless!" wailed the little nun already some distance away.

Ah Q roared with delighted laughter.

The men in the tavern joined in, with only a shade less gusto in their laughter.

Chapter 4

The Tragedy of Love

There are said to be some victors who take no pleasure in a victory unless their opponents are as fierce as tigers or eagles: In the case of foes as timid as sheep or chickens they find their triumph empty. There are other victors who, having carried all before them, with the enemy slain or surrendered, utterly cowed, realize that now no foe, no rival, no friend is left—none but themselves, supreme, lonely, lost, and forlorn. Then they find their triumph a tragedy. But not so our hero: He was always exultant. This may be a proof of the moral supremacy of China over the rest of the world.

Look at Ah Q, elated as if he were walking on air!

This victory was not without strange consequences, though. For after walking on air for quite a time he floated into the Tutelary God's Temple, where he would normally have started snoring as soon as he lay down. This evening, however, he found it very hard to close his eyes, being struck by something odd about his thumb and first finger, which seemed to be smoother than usual. It is impossible to say whether something soft and smooth on the little nun's face had stuck to his fingers, or whether his fingers had been rubbed smooth against her cheek.

"Ah Q, may you die sonless!"

These words sounded again in Ah Q's ears, and he thought, "Quite right, I should take a wife; for if a man dies sonless he has no one to sacrifice a bowl of rice to his spirit. . . . I ought to have a wife." As the saying goes, "There are three forms of unfilial conduct, of which the worst is to have no descendants,"[10] and it is one of the tragedies of life that "spirits without descendants go hungry."[11] Thus his view was absolutely in accordance with the teachings of the saints and sages, and it is indeed a pity that later he should have run amok.

"Woman, woman! . . ." he thought.

". . . The monk paws. . . . Woman, woman! . . . Woman!" he thought again.

We shall never know when Ah Q finally fell asleep that evening. After this, however, he probably always found his fingers rather soft and smooth, and always remained a little lightheaded. "Woman . . ." he kept thinking.

From this we can see that woman is a menace to mankind.

The majority of Chinese men could become saints and sages, were it not for the unfortunate fact that they are ruined by women. The Shang Dynasty was destroyed by Da Ji, the Zhou Dynasty was undermined by Bao Si; as for the Qin Dynasty, although there is no historical evidence to that effect, if we assume that it fell on account of some woman we shall probably not be far wrong. And it is a fact that Dong Zhuo's death was caused by Diao Chan.[12]

Ah Q, too, was a man of strict morals to begin with. Although we do not know whether he was guided by some good teacher, he had always shown himself most scrupulous in observing "strict segregation of the sexes," and was righteous enough to denounce such heretics as the little nun and the Bogus Foreign Devil. His view was, "All nuns must carry on in secret with monks. If a woman walks alone on the street, she must want to seduce bad men. When a man and a woman talk together, it must be to arrange to meet." In order to correct such people, he would glare furiously, pass loud, cutting remarks, or, if the place were deserted, throw a small stone from behind.

Who could tell that close on thirty, when a man should "stand firm,"[13] he would lose his head like this over a little nun? Such lightheadedness, according to the classical canons, is most reprehensible; thus women certainly are hateful creatures. For if the little nun's face had not been soft and smooth, Ah Q would not have been bewitched by her; nor would this have happened if the little nun's face had been covered by a cloth. Five or six years before, when watching an open-air opera, he had pinched the leg of a woman in the audience; but because it was separated from him by the cloth of her trousers he had not had this lightheaded feeling afterwards. The little nun had not covered her face, however, and this is another proof of the odiousness of the heretic.

"Woman . . ." thought Ah Q.

---

[10] **"There are . . . descendants"**: Quotation from Mencius (372–289 B.C.E.), a Confucian philosopher.

[11] **"spirits . . . hungry"**: Quotation from the classic text *Zuo Zhuan*, a historical chronicle from the seventh century B.C.E.

[12] **Da Ji . . . Diao Chan**: Concubines supposedly responsible for the downfalls of dynasties. Dong Zhuo was a powerful figure at the end of the Han dynasty.

[13] **"stand firm"**: Confucius said that at the age of thirty he "stood firm." The phrase is used proverbially to indicate that a man is thirty years old.

He kept a close watch on those women who he believed must "want to seduce men," but they did not smile at him. He listened very carefully to those women who talked to him, but not one of them mentioned anything relevant to a secret rendezvous. Ah! This was simply another example of the odiousness of women: They all assumed a false modesty.

One day when Ah Q was grinding rice in Mr. Zhao's house, he sat down in the kitchen after supper to smoke a pipe. If it had been anyone else's house, he could have gone home after supper, but they dined early in the Zhao family. Although it was the rule that you must not light a lamp but go to bed after eating, there were occasional exceptions to the rule. Before Mr. Zhao's son passed the county examination he was allowed to light a lamp to study the examination essays, and when Ah Q went to do odd jobs he was allowed to light a lamp to grind rice. Because of this latter exception to the rule, Ah Q still sat in the kitchen smoking before going on with his work.

When Amah Wu, the only maidservant in the Zhao household, had finished washing the dishes, she sat down on the long bench too and started chatting to Ah Q:

"Our mistress hasn't eaten anything for two days, because the master wants to get a concubine. . . ."

"Woman . . . Amah Wu . . . this little widow," thought Ah Q.

"Our young mistress is going to have a baby in the eighth moon. . . ."

"Woman . . ." thought Ah Q.

He put down his pipe and stood up.

"Our young mistress—" Amah Wu chattered on.

"Sleep with me!" Ah Q suddenly rushed forward and threw himself at her feet.

There was a moment of absolute silence.

"*Aiya!*" Dumbfounded for an instant, Amah Wu suddenly began to tremble, then rushed out shrieking and could soon be heard sobbing.

Ah Q kneeling opposite the wall was dumbfounded too. He grasped the empty bench with both hands and stood up slowly, dimly aware that something was wrong. In fact, by this time he was in rather a nervous state himself. In a flurry, he stuck his pipe into his belt and decided to go back to grind rice. But—*Bang!*—a heavy blow landed on his head, and he spun round to see the successful county candidate standing before him brandishing a big bamboo pole.

"How dare you . . . you. . . ."

The big bamboo pole came down across Ah Q's shoulders. When he put up both hands to protect his head, the blow landed on his knuckles, causing him considerable pain. As he escaped through the kitchen door it seemed as if his back also received a blow.

"Turtle's egg!" shouted the successful candidate, cursing him in Mandarin from behind.

Ah Q fled to the hulling-floor where he stood alone, his knuckles still aching and still remembering that "Turtle's egg!" because it was an expression never used by the Weizhuang villagers but only by the rich who had seen something of official life.

This made it the more alarming, the more impressive. By now, however, all thought of "Woman . . ." had flown. After this cursing and beating it seemed as if something were done with, and quite lightheartedly he began to grind rice again. Soon this made him hot, and he stopped to take off his shirt.

While taking off his shirt he heard an uproar outside, and since Ah Q was all for excitement he went out in search of the sound. Step by step he traced it into Mr. Zhao's inner courtyard. Although it was dusk he could see many people there: all the Zhao family including the mistress who had not eaten for two days. In addition, their neighbour Mrs. Zou was there, as well as their relatives Zhao Baiyan and Zhao Sichen.

The young mistress was leading Amah Wu out of the servants' quarters, saying as she did so:

"Come outside . . . don't stay brooding in your own room."

"Everybody knows you are a good woman," put in Mrs. Zou from the side. "You mustn't think of committing suicide."

Amah Wu merely wailed, muttering something inaudible.

"This is interesting," thought Ah Q. "What mischief can this little widow be up to?" Wanting to find out, he was approaching Zhao Sichen when suddenly he caught sight of Mr. Zhao's eldest son rushing towards him with, what was worse, the big bamboo pole in his hand. The sight of this big bamboo pole reminded him that he had been beaten by it, and he realized that apparently he was connected in some way with all this excitement. He turned and ran, hoping to escape to the hulling-floor, not foreseeing that the bamboo pole would cut off his retreat. When it did, he turned and ran in the other direction, leaving without further ado by the back gate. Soon he was back in the Tutelary God's Temple.

After Ah Q had been sitting down for a time, he broke out in goose-flesh and felt cold, because although it was spring the nights were still chilly and not suited to bare backs. He remembered that he had left his shirt in the Zhaos' house but was afraid that if he went to fetch it he might get another taste of the successful candidate's bamboo pole.

Then the bailiff came in.

"Curse you, Ah Q!" said the bailiff. "So you can't even keep your hands off the Zhao family servants, you rebel! You've made me lose my sleep, damn it! . . ."

Under this torrent of abuse Ah Q naturally had nothing to say. Finally, since it was nighttime, he had to pay the bailiff double: four hundred cash. Because he happened to have no ready money by him, he gave his felt hat as security, and agreed to the following five terms:

1.   The next morning Ah Q must take a pair of red candles, weighing one pound each, and a bundle of incense sticks to the Zhao family to atone for his misdeeds.

2.   Ah Q must pay for the Taoist priests whom the Zhao family had called to exorcize evil spirits.

3.   Ah Q must never again set foot in the Zhao household.

4. If anything unfortunate should happen to Amah Wu, Ah Q must be held responsible.

5. Ah Q must not go back for his wages or shirt.

Ah Q naturally agreed to everything, but unfortunately he had no ready money. Luckily it was already spring, so it was possible to do without his padded quilt which he pawned for two thousand cash to comply with the terms stipulated. After kow-towing with bare back he still had a few cash left, but instead of using these to redeem his felt hat from the bailiff, he spent them all on drink.

Actually, the Zhao family burned neither the incense nor the candles, because these could be used when the mistress worshipped Buddha and were put aside for that purpose. Most of the ragged shirt was made into diapers for the baby which was born to the young mistress in the eighth moon, while the tattered remainder was used by Amah Wu to make shoe soles.

Chapter 5

The Problem of Making a Living

After Ah Q had kowtowed and complied with the Zhao family's terms, he went back as usual to the Tutelary God's Temple. The sun had gone down, and he began to feel that something was wrong. Careful thought led him to the conclusion that this was probably because his back was bare. Remembering that he still had a ragged lined jacket, he put it on and lay down, and when he opened his eyes again the sun was already shining on the top of the west wall. He sat up, saying, "Curse it!"

After getting up he loafed about the streets as usual, until he began to feel that something else was wrong, though this was not to be compared to the physical dis-comfort of a bare back. Apparently, from that day onwards all the women in Weizhuang fought shy of Ah Q: Whenever they saw him coming they took refuge indoors. In fact, even Mrs. Zou who was nearing fifty retreated in confusion with the rest, calling her eleven-year-old daughter to go inside. This struck Ah Q as very strange. "The bitches!" he thought. "All of a sudden they're behaving like young ladies. . . ."

A good many days later, however, he felt even more forcibly that something was wrong. First, the tavern refused him credit; secondly, the old man in charge of the Tutelary God's Temple made some uncalled-for remarks, as if he wanted Ah Q to leave; and thirdly, for many days — how many exactly he could not remember — not a soul had come to hire him. To be refused credit in the tavern he could put up with; if the old man kept urging him to leave, he could just ignore his complaints; but when no one came to hire him he had to go hungry, and this was really a "cursed" state to be in.

When Ah Q could stand it no longer he went to his former employers' homes to find out what was the matter — it was only Mr. Zhao's threshold that he was not allowed to cross. But he met with a strange reception. The one to appear was always a man looking thoroughly annoyed who waved him away as if he were a beggar, saying:

"There's nothing for you, get out!"

Ah Q found it more and more extraordinary. "These people always needed help in the past," he thought. "They can't suddenly have nothing to be done. This looks fishy." After making careful inquiries he found out that when they had any odd jobs they all called in Young D. Now this Young D was a thin and weakly pauper, even lower in Ah Q's eyes than Whiskers Wang. Who could have thought that this low fellow would steal his living from him? So this time Ah Q's indignation was greater than usual, and going on his way, fuming, he suddenly raised his arm and sang:

"Steel mace in hand I shall trounce you. . . ."[14]

A few days later he did indeed meet Young D in front of Mr. Qian's house. "When two foes meet, there is no mistaking each other." As Ah Q advanced upon him, Young D stood his ground.

"Beast!" spluttered Ah Q, glaring.

"I'm an insect—will that do?" rejoined Young D.

Such modesty only enraged Ah Q even more, but since he had no steel mace in his hand all he could do was rush forward to grab at Young D's queue. Young D, protecting his own queue with one hand, grabbed at Ah Q's with the other, whereupon Ah Q also used his free hand to protect his own queue. In the past Ah Q had never considered Young D worth taking seriously, but owing to his recent privations he was now as thin and weak as his opponent, so that they presented a spectacle of evenly matched antagonists, four hands clutching at two heads, both men bending at the waist, casting a blue, rainbow-shaped shadow on the Qian family's white wall for over half an hour.

"All right! All right!" exclaimed some of the onlookers, probably by way of mediation.

"Good, good!" exclaimed others, but whether to mediate, applaud the fighters, or spur them on to further efforts, is not certain.

The two combatants turned deaf ears to them all, however. If Ah Q advanced three paces, Young D would recoil three paces, and there they would stand. If Young D advanced three paces, Ah Q would recoil three paces, and there they would stand again. After about half an hour—Weizhuang had few clocks, so it is difficult to tell the time; it may have been twenty minutes—when steam was rising from their heads and sweat pouring down their cheeks, Ah Q let fall his hands, and in the same second Young D's hands fell too. They straightened up simultaneously and stepped back simultaneously, pushing their way out through the crowd.

"Just you wait, curse you!" called Ah Q over his shoulder.

"Curse you! Just you wait . . ." echoed Young D, also over his shoulder.

This epic struggle had apparently ended in neither victory nor defeat, and it is not known whether the spectators were satisfied or not, for none of them expressed any opinion. But still not a soul came to hire Ah Q for odd jobs.

One warm day, when a balmy breeze seemed to give some foretaste of summer, Ah Q actually felt cold; but he could put up with this—his greatest worry was an

---

[14] *"Steel mace . . .":* From *The Battle of the Dragon and the Tiger,* a popular opera in Shaoxing.

empty stomach. His cotton quilt, felt hat, and shirt had long since disappeared, and after that he had sold his padded jacket. Now nothing was left but his trousers, and these of course he could not take off. He had a ragged lined jacket, it is true; but this was certainly worthless, unless he gave it away to be made into shoe soles. He had long been dreaming of finding some money on the road, but hitherto he had not come across any; he had also been hoping he might suddenly discover some money in his tumble-down room, and had frantically ransacked it, but the room was quite, quite empty. Then he made up his mind to go out in search of food.

As he walked along the road "in search of food" he saw the familiar tavern and the familiar steamed bread, but he passed them by without pausing for a second, without even hankering after them. It was not these he was looking for, although what exactly he was looking for he did not know himself.

Since Weizhuang was not a big place, he soon left it behind. Most of the country outside the village consisted of paddy fields, green as far as the eye could see with the tender shoots of young rice, dotted here and there with round black, moving objects — peasants cultivating their fields. But blind to the delights of country life, Ah Q simply went on his way, for he knew instinctively that this was far removed from his "search for food." Finally, however, he came to the walls of the Convent of Quiet Self-Improvement.

The convent too was surrounded by paddy fields, its white walls standing out sharply in the fresh green, and inside the low earthen wall at the back was a vegetable garden. Ah Q hesitated for a time, looking around him. Since there was no one in sight he scrambled on to the low wall, holding on to some milkwort. The mud wall started crumbling, and Ah Q shook with fear; however, by clutching at the branch of a mulberry tree he managed to jump over it. Within was a wild profusion of vegetation, but no sign of yellow wine, steamed bread, or anything edible. A clump of bamboos by the west wall had put forth many young shoots, but unfortunately these were not cooked. There was also rape which had long since gone to seed, mustard already about to flower, and some tough old cabbages.

Resentful as a scholar who has failed the examinations, Ah Q walked slowly towards the gate of the garden. Suddenly, however, he gave a start of joy, for what did he see there but a patch of turnips! He knelt down and had just begun pulling when a round head appeared from behind the gate, only to be promptly withdrawn. This was no other than the little nun. Now though Ah Q had always had the greatest contempt for such people as little nuns, there are times when "Discretion is the better part of valour." He hastily pulled up four turnips, tore off the leaves, and stuffed them under his jacket. By this time an old nun had already come out.

"May Buddha preserve us, Ah Q! How dare you climb into our garden to steal turnips! . . . Mercy on us, what a wicked thing to do! *Aiya*, Buddha preserve us!"

"When did I ever climb into your garden and steal turnips?" retorted Ah Q as he started off, keeping his eyes on her.

"Now — aren't you?" The old nun pointed at the bulge in his jacket.

"Are these yours? Will they come when you call? You. . . ."

Leaving his sentence unfinished, Ah Q took to his heels as fast as he could, followed by a huge fat black dog. Originally this dog had been at the front gate, and how it reached the back garden was a mystery. With a snarl the black dog gave chase and was just about to bite Ah Q's leg when most opportunely a turnip fell from his jacket, and the dog, taken by surprise, stopped for a second. During this time Ah Q scrambled up the mulberry tree, scaled the mud wall, and fell, turnips and all, outside the convent. He left the black dog still barking by the mulberry tree, and the old nun saying her prayers.

Fearing that the nun would let the black dog out again, Ah Q gathered together his turnips and ran, picking up a few small stones as he went. But the black dog did not reappear. Ah Q threw away the stones and walked on, eating as he went, thinking to himself, "There is nothing to be had here: Better go to town. . . ."

By the time the third turnip was finished he had made up his mind to go to town.

Chapter 6

From Resurgence to Decline

Weizhuang did not see Ah Q again till just after the Moon Festival that year. Everybody was surprised to hear of his return, and this made them think back and wonder where he had been all that time. In the past Ah Q had usually taken great pleasure in announcing his few visits to town; but since he had not done so this time, his going had passed unnoticed. He may have told the old man in charge of the Tutelary God's Temple, but according to the custom of Weizhuang only a trip to town by Mr. Zhao, Mr. Qian, or the successful county candidate counted as important. Even the Bogus Foreign Devil's going was not talked about, much less Ah Q's. This would explain why the old man had not spread the news for him, with the result that the villagers remained in the dark.

Ah Q's return this time was very different from before, and in fact quite enough to occasion astonishment. The day was growing dark when he showed up, bleary-eyed, at the tavern door, walked up to the counter, and tossed down on it a handful of silver and coppers produced from his belt. "Cash!" he announced. "Bring the wine!" He was wearing a new lined jacket and at his waist hung a large purse, the great weight of which caused his belt to sag in a sharp curve.

It was the custom in Weizhuang that anyone in any way unusual should be treated with respect rather than disregarded, and now, although they knew quite well that this was Ah Q, still he was very different from the Ah Q of the ragged coat. The ancients say, "A scholar who has been away three days must be looked at with new eyes." So the waiter, tavern keeper, customers, and passersby all quite naturally expressed a kind of suspicion mingled with respect. The tavern keeper started off by nodding, following this up with the words:

"So you're back, Ah Q!"

"Yes, I'm back."

"Made a pretty packet, eh? . . . Where. . . ?"

"I've been in town."

By the next day this piece of news had spread through Weizhuang. And since everybody wanted to hear the success story of this Ah Q of the ready money and the new lined jacket, in the tavern, teahouse, and under the temple eaves, the villagers gradually ferreted out the news. The result was that they began to treat Ah Q with a new deference.

According to Ah Q, he had been a servant in the house of a successful provincial candidate. This part of the story filled all who heard it with awe. This successful provincial candidate was named Bai, but because he was the only successful provincial candidate in the whole town there was no need to use his surname: Whenever anyone spoke of the successful provincial candidate, it meant him. And this was so not only in Weizhuang, for almost everyone within a radius of a hundred li imagined his name to be Mr. Successful Provincial Candidate. To have worked in the household of such a man naturally called for respect; but according to Ah Q's further statements, he was unwilling to go on working there because this successful candidate was really too much of a "turtle's egg." This part of the story made all who heard it sigh, but with a sense of pleasure, because it showed that Ah Q was unworthy to work in the household of such a man, yet not to work there was a pity.

According to Ah Q, his return was also due to his dissatisfaction with the townspeople because they called a long bench a straight bench, used shredded shallots to fry fish, and—a defect he had recently discovered—the women did not sway in a very satisfactory manner as they walked. However, the town had its good points too; for instance, in Weizhuang everyone played with thirty-two bamboo counters and only the Bogus Foreign Devil could play mahjong, but in town even the street urchins excelled at mahjong. You had only to place the Bogus Foreign Devil in the hands of these young rascals in their teens for him straightway to become like "a small devil before the King of Hell." This part of the story made all who heard it blush.

"Have you seen an execution?" asked Ah Q. "Ah, that's a fine sight. . . . When they execute the revolutionaries. . . . Ah, that's a fine sight, a fine sight. . . ." He shook his head, sending his spittle flying onto the face of Zhao Sichen who was standing opposite him. This part of the story made all who heard it tremble. Then with a glance around, he suddenly raised his right hand and dropped it on the neck of Whiskers Wang who, craning forward, was listening with rapt attention.

"Off with his head!" shouted Ah Q.

Whiskers Wang gave a start, and jerked back his head as fast as lightning or a spark struck from a flint, while the bystanders shivered with pleasurable apprehension. After this, Whiskers Wang went about in a daze for many days and dared not go near Ah Q, nor did the others.

Although we cannot say that in the eyes of the inhabitants of Weizhuang Ah Q's status at this time was superior to that of Mr. Zhao, we can at least affirm without any danger of inaccuracy that it was approximately equivalent.

Not long after, Ah Q's fame suddenly spread into the women's apartments of Weizhuang too. Although the only two families of any pretensions in Weizhuang were those of Qian and Zhao, and nine-tenths of the rest were poor, still women's apartments are women's apartments, and the way Ah Q's fame spread into them was quite miraculous. When the womenfolk met they would say to each other, "Mrs. Zou bought a blue silk skirt from Ah Q. Although it was old, it only cost ninety cents.

And Zhao Baiyan's mother (this has yet to be verified, because some say it was Zhao Sichen's mother) bought a child's costume of crimson foreign calico which was nearly new for only three hundred cash, less eight per cent discount."

Then those who had no silk skirt or needed foreign calico were most anxious to see Ah Q in order to buy from him. Far from avoiding him now, they sometimes followed him when he passed, calling to him to stop.

"Ah Q, have you any more silk skirts?" they would ask. "No? We want foreign calico too. Do you have any?"

This news later spread from the poor households to the rich ones, because Mrs. Zou was so pleased with her silk skirt that she took it to Mrs. Zhao for her approval, and Mrs. Zhao told Mr. Zhao, speaking very highly of it.

Mr. Zhao discussed the matter that evening at dinner with his son the successful county candidate, suggesting that there was certainly something strange about Ah Q and that they should be more careful about their doors and windows. They did not know, though, what if anything Ah Q had left—he might still have something good. Since Mrs. Zhao happened to want a good cheap fur jacket, after a family council it was decided to ask Mrs. Zou to find Ah Q for them at once. For this a third exception was made to the rule, special permission being given that evening for a lamp to be lit.

A considerable amount of oil had been burned, but still there was no sign of Ah Q. The whole Zhao household was yawning with impatience, some of them resenting Ah Q's casualness, others blaming Mrs. Zou for not making a greater effort. Mrs. Zhao was afraid that Ah Q dared not come because of the terms agreed upon that spring, but Mr. Zhao did not think this anything to worry about because, as he said, "This time *I* sent for him." Sure enough, Mr. Zhao proved himself a man of insight, for Ah Q finally arrived with Mrs. Zou.

"He keeps saying he has nothing left," panted Mrs. Zou as she came in. "When I told him to come and tell you so himself he kept talking back. I told him. . . ."

"Sir!" cried Ah Q with an attempt at a smile, coming to a halt under the eaves.

"I hear you did well for yourself in town, Ah Q," said Mr. Zhao, going up to him and looking him over carefully. "Very good. Now . . . they say you have some old things. . . . Bring them all here for us to look at. This is simply because I happen to want. . . ."

"I told Mrs. Zou—there's nothing left."

"Nothing left?" Mr. Zhao could not help sounding disappointed. "How could they go so quickly?"

"They belonged to a friend, and there wasn't much to begin with. People bought some. . . ."

"There must be something left."

"Only a door curtain."

"Then bring the door curtain for us to see," said Mrs. Zhao hurriedly.

"Well, tomorrow will do," said Mr. Zhao without much enthusiasm. "When you have anything in future, Ah Q, you must bring it to us first. . . ."

"We certainly won't pay less than other people!" said the successful county candidate. His wife shot a hasty glance at Ah Q to see his reaction.

"I need a fur jacket," said Mrs. Zhao.

Although Ah Q agreed, he slouched out so carelessly that they did not know whether he had taken their instructions to heart or not. This so disappointed, annoyed, and worried Mr. Zhao that he even stopped yawning. The successful candidate was also far from satisfied with Ah Q's attitude. "People should be on their guard against such a turtle's egg," he said. "It might be best to order the bailiff to forbid him to live in Weizhuang."

Mr. Zhao did not agree, saying that then Ah Q might bear a grudge, and that in a business like this it was probably a case of "the eagle does not prey on its own nest": His own village need not worry so long as they were a little more watchful at night. The successful candidate, much impressed by this parental instruction, immediately withdrew his proposal for banishing Ah Q but cautioned Mrs. Zou on no account to repeat what had been said.

The next day, however, when Mrs. Zou took her blue skirt to be dyed black she repeated these insinuations about Ah Q, although not actually mentioning what the successful candidate had said about driving him away. Even so, it was most damaging to Ah Q. In the first place, the bailiff appeared at his door and took away the door curtain. Although Ah Q protested that Mrs. Zhao wanted to see it, the bailiff would not give it back and even demanded monthly hush money. In the second place, the villagers' respect for Ah Q suddenly changed. Although they still dared not take liberties, they avoided him as much as possible. While this differed from their previous fear of his "Off with his head!" it closely resembled the attitude of the ancients to spirits: They kept a respectful distance.

Some idlers who wanted to get to the bottom of the business went to question Ah Q carefully. And with no attempt at concealment Ah Q told them proudly of his experiences. They learned that he had merely been a petty thief, not only unable to climb walls but even unable to go through openings: He simply stood outside an opening to receive the stolen goods.

One night he had just received a package and his chief had gone in again, when he heard a great uproar inside and took to his heels as fast as he could. He fled from the town that same night, back to Weizhuang; and after this he dared not return to do any more thieving. This story, however, was even more damaging to Ah Q, since the villagers had been keeping a respectful distance because they did not want to incur his enmity; for who could have guessed that he was only a thief who dared not steal again? Now they knew he was really too low to inspire fear.

CHAPTER 7

The Revolution

On the fourteenth day of the ninth moon of the third year in the reign of Emperor Xuan Tong[15]—the day on which Ah Q sold his purse to Zhao Baiyan—at midnight, after the fourth stroke of the third watch, a large boat with a big black awning

---

[15] **On the fourteenth . . . Tong:** November 4, 1911, the day revolutionaries freed Shaoxing from the rule of the Manchu dynasty.

arrived at the Zhao family's landing place. This boat floated up in the darkness while the villagers were sound asleep, so that they knew nothing about it; but it left again about dawn, when quite a number of people saw it. Investigation revealed that this boat actually belonged to the successful provincial candidate!

This incident caused great uneasiness in Weizhuang, and before midday the hearts of all the villagers were beating faster. The Zhao family kept very quiet about the errand of the boat, but according to gossip in the teahouse and tavern, the revolutionaries were going to enter the town and the successful provincial candidate had come to the country to take refuge. Mrs. Zou alone thought otherwise, maintaining that the successful candidate merely wanted to deposit a few battered cases in Weizhuang, but that Mr. Zhao had sent them back. Actually the successful provincial candidate and the successful county candidate in the Zhao family were not on good terms, so that it was scarcely logical to expect them to prove friends in adversity; moreover, since Mrs. Zou was a neighbour of the Zhao family and had a better idea of what was going on, she ought to have known.

Then a rumour spread to the effect that although the scholar had not come in person, he had sent a long letter tracing some distant relationship with the Zhao family; and since Mr. Zhao after thinking it over had decided it could after all do him no harm to keep the cases, they were now stowed under his wife's bed. As for the revolutionaries, some people said they had entered the town that night in white helmets and white armour—in mourning for Emperor Chong Zhen.[16]

Ah Q had long since known of revolutionaries and this year with his own eyes had seen revolutionaries decapitated. But since it had occurred to him that the revolutionaries were rebels and that a rebellion would make things difficult for him, he had always detested and kept away from them. Who could have guessed that they could strike such fear into a successful provincial candidate renowned for a hundred li around? In consequence, Ah Q could not help feeling rather fascinated, the terror of all the villagers only adding to his delight.

"Revolution is not a bad thing," thought Ah Q. "Finish off the whole lot of them . . . curse them! . . . I'd like to go over to the revolutionaries myself."

Ah Q had been hard up recently, which no doubt made him rather dissatisfied; moreover he had drunk two bowls of wine at noon on an empty stomach. Consequently he became drunk very quickly; and as he walked along thinking to himself, he seemed again to be treading on air. Suddenly, in some curious way, he felt as if he were a revolutionary and all the people in Weizhuang were his captives. Unable to contain himself for joy, he shouted at the top of his voice:

"Rebellion! Rebellion!"

All the villagers stared at him in consternation. Ah Q had never seen such pitiful looks before; they refreshed him as much as a drink of iced water in summer. So he walked on even more happily, shouting:

"Fine! . . . I shall take what I want! I shall like whom I please!

---

[16] **Emperor Chong Zhen:** An ironic reference to an emperor who committed suicide when revolutionaries approached the city gates of Beijing in 1644.

"Tra la tra la!
Alas, in my cups I have slain my sworn brother Zheng,
Alas, ya-ya-ya . . .
Tra la, tra la, tum ti tum tum!
Steel mace in hand I shall trounce you."

Mr. Zhao and his son were standing at their gate with two relatives discussing the revolution. Ah Q did not see them as he passed with his head thrown back, singing, *"Tra la la, tum ti tum!"*

"Q, old fellow!" called Mr. Zhao timidly in a low voice.

"Tra la," sang Ah Q, unable to imagine that his name could be linked with those words "old fellow." Sure that he had heard wrongly and was in no way concerned, he simply went on singing, *"Tra la la, tum ti tum!"*

"Q, old fellow!"

"Alas, in my cups. . . ."

"Ah Q!" The successful candidate had no choice but to name him outright.

Only then did Ah Q come to a stop. "Well?" he asked with his head on one side.

"Q, old fellow . . . now. . . ." But Mr. Zhao was at a loss for words again. "Are you well off now?"

"Well off? Of course. I get what I want. . . ."

"Ah Q, old man, poor friends of yours like us are of no consequence . . ." faltered Zhao Baiyan, as if sounding out the revolutionaries' attitude.

"Poor friends? You're richer anyway than I am." With this Ah Q walked away.

This left them in speechless dismay. Back home that evening Mr. Zhao and his son discussed the question until it was time to light the lamps. And Zhao Baiyan once home took the purse from his waist and gave it to his wife to hide for him at the bottom of a chest.

For a while Ah Q walked upon air, but by the time he reached the Tutelary God's Temple he had come down to earth again. That evening the old man in charge of the temple was also unexpectedly friendly and offered him tea. Then Ah Q asked him for two flat cakes, and after eating these demanded a four-ounce candle that had been lighted once and a candlestick. He lit the candle and lay down alone in his little room feeling inexpressibly refreshed and happy, while the candlelight leaped and flickered as if this were the Lantern Festival and his imagination soared with it.

"Revolt? It would be fine. . . . A troop of revolutionaries would come, all in white helmets and white armour, with swords, steel maces, bombs, foreign guns, sharp-pointed double-edged knives, and spears with hooks. When they passed this temple they would call out, 'Ah Q! Come along with us!' And then I would go with them. . . .

"Then the fun would start. All the villagers, the whole lousy lot, would kneel down and plead, 'Ah Q, spare us!' But who would listen to them! The first to die would be Young D and Mr. Zhao, then the successful county candidate and the Bogus Foreign Devil. . . . But perhaps I would spare a few. I would once have spared Whiskers Wang, but now I don't even want him. . . .

"Things . . . I would go straight in and open the cases: silver ingots, foreign coins, foreign calico jackets. . . . First I would move the Ningbo bed of the successful county candidate's wife to the temple, as well as the Qian family tables and chairs—or else just use the Zhao family's. I wouldn't lift a finger myself, but order Young D to move the things for me, and to look smart about it if he didn't want his face slapped. . . .

"Zhao Sichen's younger sister is very ugly. In a few years Mrs. Zou's daughter might be worth considering. The Bogus Foreign Devil's wife is willing to sleep with a man without a queue, hah! She can't be a good woman! The successful county candidate's wife has scars on her eyelids. . . . I haven't seen Amah Wu for a long time and don't know where she is—what a pity her feet are so big."

Before Ah Q had reached a satisfactory conclusion, there was a sound of snoring. The four-ounce candle had burned down only half an inch, and its flickering red light lit up his open mouth.

"Ho, ho!" shouted Ah Q suddenly, raising his head and looking wildly around. But at sight of the four-ounce candle, he lay back and fell asleep again.

The next morning he got up very late, and when he went out into the street everything was the same as usual. He was still hungry, but though he racked his brains he did not seem able to think of anything. All of a sudden, however, an idea struck him and he walked slowly off until, either by design or accident, he reached the Convent of Quiet Self-Improvement.

The convent was as peaceful as it had been that spring, with its white wall and shining black gate. After a moment's reflection he knocked at the gate, whereupon a dog on the other side started barking. He hastily picked up some broken bricks, then went back again to knock more heavily, knocking until the black gate was pitted with pock-marks. At last he heard someone coming to open up.

Clutching a brick, Ah Q straddled there prepared to do battle with the black dog. The convent gate opened a crack, but no black dog rushed out. When he looked in all he could see was the old nun.

"What are you here for again?" she asked with a start.

"There's a revolution . . . didn't you know?" said Ah Q vaguely.

"Revolution, revolution . . . we've already had one." The old nun's eyes were red. "What more do you want to do to us?"

"What?" demanded Ah Q, dumbfounded.

"Didn't you know? The revolutionaries have already been here!"

"Who?" demanded Ah Q, still more dumbfounded.

"The successful county candidate and the Foreign Devil."

This completely took the wind out of Ah Q's sails. When the old nun saw there was no fight left in him she promptly shut the gate, so that when Ah Q pushed it again he could not budge it, and when he knocked again there was no answer.

It had happened that morning. The successful county candidate in the Zhao family was quick to learn the news. As soon as he heard that the revolutionaries had entered the town that night, he wound his queue up on his head and went out first thing to call on the Bogus Foreign Devil in the Qian family, with whom he had never been on very good terms. Because this was a time for all to work for reforms, they had a most satisfactory talk and on the spot became comrades who saw eye to eye and pledged themselves to make revolution.

After racking their brains for some time, they remembered that in the Convent of Quiet Self-Improvement there was an imperial tablet inscribed "Long live the Emperor" which ought to be done away with immediately. Thereupon they lost no time in going to the convent to carry out their revolutionary activities. Because the old nun tried to stop them and passed a few remarks, they considered her as the Qing government and gave her quite a few knocks on the head with a stick and with their knuckles. The nun, pulling herself together after they had gone, made an inspection. Naturally the imperial tablet had been smashed into fragments on the ground and the valuable Xuan De censer[17] before the shrine of Guanyin, the goddess of mercy, had also disappeared.

Ah Q only learned this later. He deeply regretted having been asleep at the time, and resented the fact that they had not come to call him. Then he said to himself, "Maybe they still don't know I have joined the revolutionaries."

Chapter 8

Barred from the Revolution

The people of Weizhuang felt easier in their minds with each passing day. From the news brought they knew that although the revolutionaries had entered the town their coming had not made a great deal of difference. The magistrate was still the highest official, it was only his title that had changed; and the successful provincial candidate also had some post—the Weizhuang villagers could not remember these names clearly—some kind of official post; while the head of the military was still the same old captain. The only cause for alarm was that, the day after their arrival, some bad revolutionaries made trouble by cutting off people's queues. It was said that the boatman Seven-pounder from the next village had fallen into their clutches, and that he no longer looked presentable. Still, the danger of this was not great, because the Weizhuang villagers seldom went to town to begin with, and those who had been considering a trip there at once changed their minds in order to avoid this risk. Ah Q had been thinking of going to town to look up his old friends, but as soon as he heard the news he gave up the idea.

It would be wrong, however, to say that there were no reforms in Weizhuang. During the next few days the number of people who coiled their queues on their heads gradually increased and, as has already been said, the first to do so was naturally the successful county candidate; the next were Zhao Sichen and Zhao Baiyan, and after them Ah Q. If it had been summer it would not have been considered strange if everybody had coiled their queues on their heads or tied them in knots; but this was late autumn, so that this autumn observance of a summer practice on the part of those who coiled their queues could be considered nothing short of a heroic decision, and as far as Weizhuang was concerned it could not be said to have had no connection with the reforms.

---

[17] **Xuan De censer:** Bronze censer, or covered incense burner, made during the Xuan De period of the Ming dynasty (1426–35).

When Zhao Sichen approached with the nape of his neck bare, people who saw him remarked, "Ah! Here comes a revolutionary!"

When Ah Q heard this he was greatly impressed. Although he had long since heard how the successful county candidate had coiled his queue on his head, it had never occurred to him to do the same. Only now when he saw that Zhao Sichen had followed suit was he struck with the idea of doing the same himself. He made up his mind to copy them. He used a bamboo chopstick to twist his queue up on his head, and after some hesitation eventually summoned up the courage to go out.

As he walked along the street people looked at him, but without any comment. Ah Q, disgruntled at first, soon waxed indignant. Recently he had been losing his temper very easily. As a matter of fact he was no worse off than before the revolution, people treated him politely, and the shops no longer demanded payment in cash, yet Ah Q still felt dissatisfied. A revolution, he thought, should mean more than this. When he saw Young D, his anger boiled over.

Young D had also coiled his queue up on his head and, what was more, had actually used a bamboo chopstick to do so too. Ah Q had never imagined that Young D would also have the courage to do this; he certainly could not tolerate such a thing! Who was Young D anyway? He was greatly tempted to seize him then and there, break his bamboo chopstick, let down his queue and slap his face several times into the bargain to punish him for forgetting his place and for his presumption in becoming a revolutionary. But in the end he let him off, simply fixing him with a furious glare, spitting, and exclaiming, "Pah!"

These last few days the only one to go to town was the Bogus Foreign Devil. The successful county candidate in the Zhao family had thought of using the deposited cases as a pretext to call on the successful provincial candidate, but the danger that he might have his queue cut off had made him defer his visit. He had written an extremely formal letter, and asked the Bogus Foreign Devil to take it to town; he had also asked the latter to introduce him to the Freedom Party. When the Bogus Foreign Devil came back he collected four dollars from the successful county candidate, after which the latter wore a silver peach on his chest. All the Weizhuang villagers were overawed, and said that this was the badge of the Persimmon Oil Party, equivalent to the rank of a Han Lin.[18] As a result, Mr. Zhao's prestige suddenly increased, far more so in fact than when his son first passed the official examination; consequently he started looking down on everyone else and when he saw Ah Q tended to ignore him a little.

Ah Q, disgruntled at finding himself cold-shouldered all the time, realized as soon as he heard of this silver peach why he was left out in the cold. Simply to say that you had gone over was not enough to make anyone a revolutionary; nor was it enough merely to wind your queue up on your head; the most important thing was to get into touch with the revolutionary party. In all his life he had known only two revolutionaries, one of whom had already lost his head in town, leaving only the

---

[18] **Persimmon . . . Han Lin:** A satirical remark. The villagers misunderstand the characters for "freedom" (zi you dang) to mean "persimmon oil" (shi you dang). Han Lin was a ranking official in the Qing dynasty.

Bogus Foreign Devil. His only course was to go at once to talk things over with the Bogus Foreign Devil.

The front gate of the Qian house happened to be open, and Ah Q crept timidly in. Once inside he gave a start, for there was the Bogus Foreign Devil standing in the middle of the courtyard dressed entirely in black, no doubt in foreign dress, and also wearing a silver peach. In his hand he held the stick with which Ah Q was already acquainted to his cost, while the foot-long queue which he had grown again had been combed out to hang loosely over his shoulders, giving him a resemblance to the immortal Liu Hai.[19] Standing respectfully before him were Zhao Baiyan and three others, all of them listening with the utmost deference to what the Bogus Foreign Devil was saying.

Ah Q tiptoed inside and stood behind Zhao Baiyan, eager to pronounce some greeting, but not knowing what to say. Obviously he could not call the man "Bogus Foreign Devil," and neither "Foreigner" nor "Revolutionary" seemed quite the thing. Perhaps the best form of address would be "Mr. Foreigner."

But Mr. Foreigner had not seen him, because with eyes upraised he was holding forth with great gusto:

"I am so impetuous that when we met I kept urging, 'Old Hong, let's get down to business!' But he always answered 'Nein!'—that's a foreign word which you wouldn't understand. Otherwise we should have succeeded long ago. This just goes to show how cautious he is. Time and again he asked me to go to Hubei, but I've not yet agreed. Who wants to work in a small district town? . . ."

"Er—well—" Ah Q waited for him to pause, then screwed up his courage to speak. But for some reason or other he still did not call him Mr. Foreigner.

The four men who had been listening gave a start and turned to stare at Ah Q. Mr. Foreigner too caught sight of him for the first time.

"What is it?"

"I. . . ."

"Clear out!"

"I want to join. . . ."

"Get out!" Mr. Foreigner raised the "mourner's stick."

Thereupon Zhao Baiyan and the others shouted, "Mr. Qian tells you to get out, don't you hear!"

Ah Q put up his hands to protect his head, and without knowing what he was doing fled through the gate; but this time Mr. Foreigner did not give chase. After running more than sixty steps Ah Q slowed down, and now his heart filled with dismay, because if Mr. Foreigner would not allow him to be a revolutionary, there was no other way open to him. In future he could never hope to have men in white helmets and white armour come to call him. All his ambitions, aims, hope, and future had been blasted at one fell swoop. The fact that gossips might spread the news and make him a laughingstock for the likes of Young D and Whiskers Wang was only a secondary consideration.

---

[19] Liu Hai: A folk character with long, flowing hair.

Never before had he felt so flat. Even coiling his queue on his head now struck him as pointless and ridiculous. As a form of revenge he was very tempted to let his queue down at once, but he did not do so. He wandered about till evening, when after drinking two bowls of wine on credit he began to feel in better spirits, and in his mind's eye saw fragmentary visions of white helmets and white armour once more.

One day he loafed about until late at night. Only when the tavern was about to close did he start to stroll back to the Tutelary God's Temple.

Crash-bang!

He suddenly heard an unusual sound, which could not have been firecrackers. Ah Q, always fond of excitement and of poking his nose into other people's business, headed straight for the noise in the darkness. He thought he heard footsteps ahead, and was listening carefully when a man fled past from the opposite direction. Ah Q instantly wheeled round to follow him. When that man turned, Ah Q turned too, and when having turned a corner that man stopped, Ah Q followed suit. He saw that there was no one after them and that the man was Young D.

"What's up?" demanded Ah Q resentfully.

"The Zhao . . . Zhao family has been robbed," panted Young D.

Ah Q's heart went pit-a-pat. After saying this, Young D went off. But Ah Q kept on running by fits and starts. However, having been in the business himself made him unusually bold. Rounding the corner of a lane, he listened carefully and thought he heard shouting; while by straining his eyes he thought he could see a troop of men in white helmets and white armour carrying off cases, carrying off furniture, even carrying off the Ningbo bed of the successful county candidate's wife. He could not, however, see them very clearly. He wanted to go nearer, but his feet were rooted to the ground.

There was no moon that night, and Weizhuang was very still in the pitch darkness, as quiet as in the peaceful days of Emperor Fu Xi.[20] Ah Q stood there until his patience ran out, yet there seemed no end to the business, distant figures kept moving to and fro, carrying off cases, carrying off furniture, carrying off the Ningbo bed of the successful county candidate's wife . . . carrying until he could hardly believe his own eyes. But he decided not to go any closer, and went back to the temple.

It was even darker in the Tutelary God's Temple. When he had closed the big gate he groped his way into his room, and only after he had been lying down for some time did he calm down sufficiently to begin thinking how this affected him. The men in white helmets and white armour had evidently arrived, but they had not come to call him; they had taken away fine things, but there was no share for him — this was all the fault of the Bogus Foreign Devil, who had barred him from the rebellion. Otherwise how could he have failed to have a share this time?

The more Ah Q thought of it the angrier he grew, until he was in a towering rage. "So no rebellion for me, only for you, eh?" he fumed, nodding furiously. "Curse you, you Bogus Foreign Devil — all right, be a rebel! That's a crime for which you get

---

[20] **Emperor Fu Xi:** Legendary Chinese monarch.

your head chopped off. I'll turn informer, then see you dragged off to town to have your head cut off—your whole family executed. . . . To hell with you!"

CHAPTER 9

The Grand Finale

After the Zhao family was robbed most of the people in Weizhuang felt pleased yet fearful, and Ah Q was no exception. But four days later Ah Q was suddenly dragged into town in the middle of the night. It happened to be a dark night. A squad of soldiers, a squad of militia, a squad of police, and five secret servicemen made their way quietly to Weizhuang and, after posting a machine-gun opposite the entrance, under cover of darkness surrounded the Tutelary God's Temple. But Ah Q did not bolt for it. For a long time nothing stirred till the captain, losing patience, offered a reward of twenty thousand cash. Only then did two militiamen summon up courage to jump over the wall and enter. With their cooperation, the others rushed in and dragged Ah Q out. But not until he had been carried out of the temple to somewhere near the machine-gun did he begin to wake up to what was happening.

It was already midday by the time they reached town, and Ah Q found himself carried to a dilapidated yamen[21] where, after taking five or six turnings, he was pushed into a small room. No sooner had he stumbled inside than the door, in the form of a wooden grille, was slammed on his heels. The rest of the cell consisted of three blank walls, and when he looked carefully he saw two other men in a corner.

Although Ah Q was feeling rather uneasy, he was by no means depressed, because the room where he slept in the Tutelary God's Temple was in no way superior to this. The two other men also seemed to be villagers. They gradually fell into conversation with him, and one of them told him that the successful provincial candidate wanted to dun him for the rent owed by his grandfather; the other did not know why he was there. When they questioned Ah Q he answered quite frankly, "Because I wanted to revolt."

That afternoon he was dragged out through the grille and taken to a big hall, at the far end of which sat an old man with a cleanly shaven head. Ah Q took him for a monk at first, but when he saw soldiers standing guard and a dozen men in long coats on both sides, some with their heads clean shaven like this old man and some with a foot or so of hair hanging over their shoulders like the Bogus Foreign Devil, all glaring furiously at him with grim faces, he knew that this man must be someone important. At once his knee-joints relaxed of their own accord, and he sank to his knees.

"Stand up to speak! Don't kneel!" shouted all the men in the long coats.

Although Ah Q understood, he felt quite incapable of standing up. He had involuntarily started squatting, improving on this finally to kneel down.

"Slave!" exclaimed the long-coated men contemptuously. They did not insist on his getting up, however.

---

[21]**yamen:** The office of a magistrate or government official.

"Tell the truth and you will receive a lighter sentence," said the old man with the shaven head in a low but clear voice, fixing his eyes on Ah Q. "We know everything already. When you have confessed, we will let you go."

"Confess!" repeated the long-coated men loudly.

"The fact is I wanted . . . to join . . ." muttered Ah Q disjointedly after a moment's confused thinking.

"In that case, why didn't you?" asked the old man gently.

"The Bogus Foreign Devil wouldn't let me."

"Nonsense. It's too late to talk now. Where are your accomplices?"

"What? . . ."

"The gang who robbed the Zhao family that night."

"They didn't come to call me. They moved the things away themselves." Mention of this made Ah Q indignant.

"Where are they now? When you have told me I will let you go," repeated the old man even more gently.

"I don't know. . . . They didn't come to call me. . . ."

Then, at a sign from the old man, Ah Q was dragged back through the grille. The following morning he was dragged out once more.

Everything was unchanged in the big hall. The old man with the clean-shaven head was still sitting there, and Ah Q knelt down again as before.

"Have you anything else to say?" asked the old man gently.

Ah Q thought, and decided there was nothing to say, so he answered, "Nothing."

Then a man in a long coat brought a sheet of paper and held a brush in front of Ah Q, which he wanted to thrust into his hand. Ah Q was now nearly frightened out of his wits, because this was the first time in his life that his hand had ever come into contact with a writing brush. He was just wondering how to hold it when the man pointed out a place on the paper and told him to sign his name.

"I—I—can't write," said Ah Q, shamefaced, nervously holding the brush.

"In that case, to make it easy for you, draw a circle!"

Ah Q tried to draw a circle, but the hand with which he grasped the brush trembled, so the man spread the paper on the ground for him. Ah Q bent down and, as painstakingly as if his life depended on it, drew a circle. Afraid people would laugh at him, he determined to make the circle round; however, not only was that wretched brush very heavy, but it would not do his bidding. Instead it wobbled from side to side; and just as the line was about to close it swerved out again, making a shape like a melon seed.

While Ah Q was still feeling mortified by his failure to draw a circle, the man took back the paper and brush without any comment. A number of people then dragged him back for the third time through the grille.

By now he felt not too upset. He supposed that in this world it was the fate of everybody at some time to be dragged in and out of prison and to have to draw circles on paper; it was only his circle not being round that he felt a blot on his escutcheon. Presently, however, he regained composure by thinking, "Only idiots can make perfect circles." And with this thought he fell asleep.

That night, however, the successful provincial candidate was unable to sleep, because he had quarrelled with the captain. The successful provincial candidate had insisted that the main thing was to recover the stolen goods, while the captain said the main thing was to make a public example. Recently the captain had come to treat the successful provincial candidate quite disdainfully. So banging his fist on the table he said, "Punish one to awe one hundred! See now, I have been a member of the revolutionary party for less than twenty days, but there have been a dozen cases of robbery, none of them yet solved; think how badly that reflects on me. Now this one has been solved, you come and haggle. It won't do. This is my affair."

The successful provincial candidate, most put out, insisted that if the stolen goods were not recovered he would resign immediately from his post as assistant civil administrator.

"As you please," said the captain.

In consequence the successful provincial candidate did not sleep that night; but happily he did not hand in his resignation the next day after all.

The third time that Ah Q was dragged out of the grille-door was the morning following the night on which the successful provincial candidate had been unable to sleep. When he reached the hall, the old man with the clean-shaven head was sitting there as usual. And Ah Q knelt down as usual.

Very gently the old man questioned him, "Have you anything more to say?"

Ah Q thought, and decided there was nothing to say, so he answered, "Nothing."

A number of men in long coats and short jackets put on him a white vest of foreign cloth with some black characters on it. Ah Q felt most disconcerted, because this was very like mourning dress and to wear mourning was unlucky. At the same time his hands were bound behind his back, and he was dragged out of the yamen.

Ah Q was lifted onto an uncovered cart, and several men in short jackets sat down beside him. The cart started off at once. In front were a number of soldiers and militiamen shouldering foreign rifles, and on both sides were crowds of gaping spectators, while what was behind Ah Q could not see. Suddenly it occurred to him—"Can I be going to have my head cut off?" Panic seized him and everything turned dark before his eyes, while there was a humming in his ears as if he had fainted. But he did not really faint. Although he felt frightened some of the time, the rest of the time he was quite calm. It seemed to him that in this world probably it was the fate of everybody at some time to have his head cut off.

He still recognized the road and felt rather surprised: Why were they not going to the execution ground? He did not know that he was being paraded round the streets as a public example. But if he had known, it would have been the same: He would only have thought that in this world probably it was the fate of everybody at some time to be made a public example of.

Then he realized that they were making a detour to the execution ground, so after all he must be going to have his head cut off. He looked round him regretfully at the people swarming after him like ants, and unexpectedly in the crowd by the roadside he caught sight of Amah Wu. So that was why he had not seen her for so long: She was working in town.

Ah Q suddenly became ashamed of his lack of spirit, because he had not sung any lines from an opera. His thoughts revolved like a whirlwind: *The Young Widow at*

Her Husband's Grave was not heroic enough. The passage "Alas, in my cups" in *The Battle of the Dragon and the Tiger* was too feeble. "Steel mace in hand I shall trounce you" was still the best. But when he wanted to raise his hands, he remembered that they were bound together; so he did not sing "Steel mace in hand" either.

"In twenty years I shall be another. . . ."[22] In his agitation Ah Q uttered half a saying which he had picked up for himself but never used before. "Good!!!" The roar of the crowd sounded like the growl of a wolf.

The cart moved steadily forward. During the shouting Ah Q's eyes turned in search of Amah Wu, but she did not seem to have seen him for she was looking intently at the foreign rifles carried by the soldiers.

So Ah Q took another look at the shouting crowd.

At that instant his thoughts revolved again like a whirlwind. Four years before, at the foot of the mountain, he had met a hungry wolf which had followed him at a set distance, wanting to eat him. He had nearly died of fright, but luckily he happened to have a knife in his hand which gave him the courage to get back to Weizhuang. He had never forgotten that wolf's eyes, fierce yet cowardly, gleaming like two will-o'-the-wisps, as if boring into him from a distance. Now he saw eyes more terrible even than the wolf's: dull yet penetrating eyes that having devoured his words still seemed eager to devour something beyond his flesh and blood. And these eyes kept following him at a set distance.

These eyes seemed to have merged into one, biting into his soul.

"Help, help!"

But Ah Q never uttered these words. All had turned black before his eyes, there was a buzzing in his ears, and he felt as if his whole body were being scattered like so much light dust.

As for the aftereffects of the robbery, the most affected was the successful provincial candidate, because the stolen goods were never recovered. All his family lamented bitterly. Next came the Zhao household; for when the successful county candidate went into town to report the robbery, not only did he have his queue cut off by bad revolutionaries, but he had to pay a reward of twenty thousand cash into the bargain; so all the Zhao family lamented bitterly too. From that day forward they gradually assumed the air of the survivors of a fallen dynasty.

As for any discussion of the event, no question was raised in Weizhuang. Naturally all agreed that Ah Q had been a bad man, the proof being that he had been shot; for if he had not been bad, how could he have been shot? But the consensus of opinion in town was unfavourable. Most people were dissatisfied, because a shooting was not such a fine spectacle as a decapitation; and what a ridiculous culprit he had been too, to pass through so many streets without singing a single line from an opera. They had followed him for nothing.

---

[22] **"In twenty . . .":** Popular saying used by prisoners before their execution; it indicates a belief in the transmigration of the soul after death.

JAMES JOYCE
B. *IRELAND, 1882–1941*

Portrait of James Joyce, age 22
Joyce left Ireland for Europe in 1902. Frustrated by the provinciality and "paralysis" he depicts in Dubliners, *he would return to Ireland only for brief periods of time.* (Hulton / Archive)

With the publication in Paris of his greatest work of fiction, *Ulysses* (1922; 1936 in England), James Joyce inaugurated a revolution in the writing of the novel. Boldly innovative in language, style, and structure, *Ulysses,* along with T. S. Eliot's *The Waste Land,* quickly became a landmark of European **MODERNISM**[1] and brought charges of obscurity and obscenity against its author. Joyce's genius in depicting the interior workings of the mind as it encounters the myriad, often fragmented, details of everyday life became a model for many novelists; Joyce is one of the original architects of the **STREAM-OF-CONSCIOUSNESS**[2] technique in fiction. From his early works, *Dubliners* (1914) and *A Portrait of the Artist as a Young Man* (1914–15), to his radical experiment, *Finnegans Wake* (1939), Joyce showed that he was a master of language, pushing the boundaries of linguistic possibility and upending conventional grammar and sentence structure. His experiments with novelistic form and with language exerted a profound influence on twentieth-century literature, not just in Ireland where he was born or in Europe, but throughout the world.

A Failing Household. James Joyce's father, John Joyce, was a charming, spendthrift alcoholic with passionate political sympathies for freeing Ireland from British rule. The elder Joyce especially championed Charles Stuart Parnell (1846–1891), the brilliant Protestant Irish nationalist leader. Joyce's mother, May, a woman with musical gifts and a forbearing disposition, had ten children over a twelve-year period. James Augustine Joyce, born on February 2, 1882, was the first. Although John Joyce managed family properties and had been given a political appointment in the office of the Rates Collector in Dublin, he handily brought his family down from moderate prosperity into wracking poverty by the time he was in his forties; between Joyce's birth in 1882 and the day he left Ireland for good at the age of twenty-two, his father had moved the family twenty times, from one shabby house to another. Joyce deplored his father's reckless waste but admired his fine tenor voice, his flair for mimicry, his flashing wit, and his lively way with a story.

Joyce's parents nicknamed him "Sunny Jim" for his intelligence and beaming good nature. Like many eldest children of unstable households,

---

[1] **modernism:** Refers to the spirit of innovation and experimentation, the break with nineteenth-century aesthetic and literary conventions, and the exploration of psychological states of mind, alienation, and social rupture that characterized the era between the two world wars.

[2] **stream of consciousness:** First coined by the American philosopher and psychologist William James to denote the often disjointed, sometimes incoherent, flow of ideas, sensations, thoughts, and images running through the conscious mind at any given moment, "stream of consciousness" generally refers to psychological Realism through the depiction of the raw, unedited contents of a character's mind as they present themselves in the character's consciousness.

he was precociously able to control his temper and to care for himself and his brothers and sisters, leading them and the neighboring children in games and adventures. Joyce's brother Stanislaus vividly recalled being cast in a backyard production as Adam to his sister Margaret Alice's Eve, while Joyce starred as the hissing, wriggling serpent. The only problem James seemed to manifest in his boyhood was his poor eyesight, which was to trouble him throughout his life.

From Catholicism to Art.   Despite financial woes, John Joyce saw to it that his eldest received an excellent Jesuit education; long after Joyce had rejected Roman Catholicism, he praised the Jesuits for teaching him "to arrange things in such a way that they become easy to survey and judge." The early chapters of *A Portrait of the Artist as a Young Man* (1916) suggest the rigorous atmosphere of that education. A brilliant student who easily won prizes and scholarships, Joyce took from his Jesuit teachers not only their vaunted skill in logic and debate but also a deep appreciation of symbolism and of the sheer power of language. When he was about seventeen, however, convinced that his Jesuit teachers were repressive and narrow, Joyce left the church resolved to replace his faith with a commitment to becoming a writer. At University College in Dublin, where he solidified his conception of himself as an artist, he lost interest in the rigid academic work expected of him and tried his hand at poetry, short stories, and criticism of contemporary literature. Unlike other Irish writers such as Yeats and Synge, Joyce was not drawn to the revival of Gaelic writing and Irish themes in vogue at the time. Instead, he avidly read and praised Continental writers such as Ibsen, whom he thought of as more universal and "impersonal" than Irish artists.

Exile and Marriage.   In 1900, when *The Fortnightly Review* published a review essay Joyce wrote on the drama of Norwegian playwright Henrik Ibsen (1826–1906), the great man himself sent a message to Joyce thanking him. This heady event was transformative to an eighteen-year-old aspiring writer. As biographer Richard Ellmann puts it, "Before Ibsen's letter Joyce was an Irishman; after it, he was a European." Joyce threw himself into the study of languages and literature envisioning a life beyond Ireland. After 1902 he went to live on the Continent, returning to Ireland only for brief periods. Close to starvation, he eked out a living in Paris by teaching English while he worked on his "Epiphanies," short notebook entries that recorded overheard conversations or sights glimpsed in passing that seemed to embody flashes of insight into the human condition. He returned to Dublin in April 1903 to be at his mother's deathbed. When May Joyce died in August after a drawn-out struggle with cancer, Joyce stayed on in Dublin and taught, but by the following year he was back on the Continent, disgusted by the political corruption and smug provincialism of his homeland. On this trip he brought the beautiful Nora Barnacle, an uneducated, perceptive, earthy young woman from Galway in the west of Ireland, an isolated region Joyce identified with life lived simply and passionately, as opposed to the artificiality and hypocrisy he found in Dublin.

www   For links to more information about James Joyce, a quiz on "The Dead," and more on the culture and context of twentieth-century Europe, see *World Literature Online* at bedfordstmartins .com/worldlit.

Dubliners and *A Portrait of the Artist.*   Though Joyce and Barnacle did

not marry until 1931, they were a devoted couple from the beginning. In 1904, they moved to Trieste, then part of Austria, where Joyce taught English in the Berlitz school and began work on *Dubliners* (1914), a collection of short stories that sought to capture the city of Dublin and its people, and on the autobiographical novel *A Portrait of the Artist as a Young Man* (1916). In *Dubliners,* Joyce shepherds realistic and detailed renderings of everyday life into moments of deep insight, moments he called "epiphanies." In a texture of rich detail, Joyce portrays what he sees as the parochial and narrow-minded habits of the Irish middle classes. *A Portrait of the Artist as a Young Man* recounts the story of Stephen Dedalus, a character modeled on Joyce himself before 1902, at a time when he was torn between powerful sexual urges and religious guilt, conflicted between a call to religion and a devotion to art. As Stephen struggles with his desires, he develops a theory of art and the artist, whom he believes must finally go into exile, as did Joyce, in order to embrace the cosmopolitan world of art. Although similar in narrative design to the Realist and Naturalist novels popular at the time, *Dubliners* and *A Portrait* anticipate the symbolic density and linguistic experimentation of Joyce's later works, *Ulysses* (1922) and *Finnegans Wake* (1939), for which Joyce is especially known.

Ulysses.   Structured in episodes that roughly follow those of Homer's

Odyssey, Ulysses tracks the intricate thoughts and ordinary experiences over a twenty-four-hour period of the advertising man Leopold Bloom and the teacher Stephen Dedalus, whom Joyce had introduced in *Portrait.* Unlike Homer's Odysseus, Leopold Bloom is the most common of men,

Liffey Tram, Dublin,
c. 1900
*The center of Dublin
as Joyce knew it.*
(Hulton / Archive)

but his anxieties and apparent aimlessness are representative of the alienation, boredom, and futility that characterized the European psyche in the early twentieth century. Disrupting conventions of syntax and narrative structure, Joyce sought to capture the uncensored flow of thoughts as they spilled over into consciousness. This "interior monologue" would come to typify the "stream-of-consciousness" style of fiction wherein a writer attempts to imitate or create the free association and amplification of ideas in a person's mind. Joyce's frank, realistic descriptions of the full range of human experience — from sex to defecation — led to strong criticism from a prudish public. Though first published in 1922, *Ulysses* was not available to American readers until 1933, when a landmark U.S. District Court decision overruled the Post Office's charge that the book was obscene.

Finnegans Wake.   Joyce spent more than fifteen years working on *Finnegans Wake* (1939), a work that challenged all previous ideas about the nature of fiction. The novel constitutes a sprawling epic dream of a representative Irishman, an imagined vision that seeks to embrace all human history. In it, Joyce energetically disassembles syntax, grammatical structure, and narrative order; puns wildly in a multitude of languages; borrows freely from the vocabularies of music halls, sports, and advertising; takes ideas from contemporary sciences, medieval histories, and colloquial bar conversations; and superimposes the Homeric, Celtic, and Teutonic myth-cycles on the lives of his urban Irish characters, thereby revealing the extraordinary dimensions of even the most ordinary lives. Joyce considered *Finnegans Wake* his masterpiece, but its complex structure, inventiveness, and intricate play with diction and syntax have made it less accessible to readers than his other writings.

Flight and Death.   The latter years of Joyce's life were troubled by his failing eyesight and by his daughter Lucia's schizophrenia; Joyce had great difficulty accepting the gravity of his daughter's illness and refused for many years to institutionalize her, thus ensuring a chaotic home life. In December 1940, after the German occupation of France, the Joyces fled their home in Paris with their grandson and crossed the border into Switzerland with what belongings they could carry, wheeling the little boy's treasured bicycle before them. Joyce died suddenly in Zurich a few weeks later of a perforated ulcer.

Dubliners.   Of *Dubliners,* the collection in which "The Dead" appears, Joyce said,

> My intention was to write a chapter of the moral history of my country and I chose Dublin for the scene because that city seemed to me the center of paralysis. I have tried to present it to the indifferent public under four of its aspects: childhood, adolescence, maturity, and public life.

In this collection, three or four stories apiece center on one of these phases of life. A child feels helpless anger when he learns the bazaar about

All of the stories in *Dubliners* are studies in paralysis or frustration, and the total epiphany is of the nature of modern city life — the submission to routines and the fear of breaking them; the emancipation that is sought, but is not sought hard enough; the big noble attitudes that are punctured by the weakness of the flesh.

– ANTHONY BURGESS, novelist, 1965

which he has spun romantic fantasies is nothing but a tawdry commercial venture; a young woman, bound by a promise made to her dead mother, lacks the courage to board the ship where her lover waits to take her to a new life abroad; men in their middle years who have not fulfilled their dreams of adventure now feel trapped in their marriages and numbing clerical jobs and take out their alcoholic bitterness on their families; the ineffectual complacency of a group of small-time political hacks sitting in a darkened room on an election day is thrown into relief when one of them reads aloud an impassioned ode to the fallen Irish nationalist leader Parnell. Seemingly everyday events bloom with quiet import, as the stories reveal subtle parallels and symbolic interconnections. For example, abandoned houses, darkened rooms, blind alleys, and shadowy passageways and staircases appear throughout the stories, accumulating meaning as symbols of moral blindness, spiritual emptiness, and emotional repression.

"The Dead." Of the fifteen stories in *Dubliners*, "The Dead" was written last and placed at the end of the collection, gathering together the imagery and the import of all the other stories. It is also the most tender of the *Dubliners* stories; while Joyce was quite capable of savaging the complacent pieties of bourgeois Irish people, he told his brother Stanislaus that he wanted to honor one native trait he felt he could honestly praise, namely, Irish hospitality. In this quiet and beautifully textured story, the Misses Morkan, two elderly music teachers, give their annual banquet and musicale for their relations, friends, and pupils. Their nephew, Gabriel Conroy, through whose consciousness the story is largely filtered, is a critical if polite observer of the evening's events. As he prepares himself to give his after-dinner speech on Irish warmth, he coldly notes the superficiality and social hypocrisy going on all around him. Gabriel is a mildly pompous intellectual who feels superior to most of the other guests. Indeed, many of the people at his aunts' party are in one way or another "paralyzed"—frozen into fixed opinions, smug in their moral certainties, or shackled by inhibitions, alcoholism, or old age.

As the evening passes and the snow deepens outside, it becomes clear that for the guests gathered together in a temporary refuge of warmth and light, memories of the past are more vivid than their present lives. Old-time tenors, long-ago parties, and dead friends and relatives are evoked with much laughter and wistfulness and regret, and the middle-aged Gabriel finds himself restlessly wishing to assert his own present sexuality and vitality. He longs to be outside walking briskly through the snow and then conceives an intense desire to make love to his wife, Gretta. But Gretta's own secret memories of the dead have been stirred, and Gabriel's epiphany comes when he discovers the wife to whom he hoped to make love grieves afresh for a passionate working-class boy she once knew, a boy who died for love of her. In the breathtaking final image of the snow "falling faintly through the universe," obliterating all individual detail, Joyce's story expands into a vision of the mortality that unites everyone, the living and the dead alike.

■ CONNECTIONS

William Butler Yeats, "Easter 1916," p. 190. *Dubliners* depicts the middle classes of Dublin, with which Joyce, like Gabriel in "The Dead," had an ambivalent relationship. Similarly, "Easter 1916" reflects Yeats's changing attitudes toward what he first sees as the complacent and passionless Irish middle class. What is the image of Ireland that emerges from these works? On what grounds do Yeats and Joyce base their criticism of Ireland or the middle classes? Do they sympathize or identify with them at all?

Anita Desai, "The Farewell Party," p. 1196. At a party in the home of the Misses Morkan, Joyce brings together diverse perspectives on Anglo-Irish relations, Irish history, and Irish politics and culture. Similarly, in "The Farewell Party," Desai assembles at a party several characters of diverse opinion on Euro-Indian relations whose seemingly banal conversation reveals a great deal about themselves and the postcolonial world they inhabit. How do these stories use the *topoi,* or literary themes, of a party and dialogue to present the complexities of their characters and of intercultural and colonial relations? Are there other similarities in these stories?

In the World: **Colonialism, p. 97.** In Miss Ivors, who nettles Gabriel with questions about politics and national identity, Joyce's "The Dead" broaches the question of Irish nationalism. Ivors accuses Gabriel of being a West Briton — an Irish person with stronger affiliations to England and the Continent than to Ireland — and goads him by flaunting her preference for the language and culture of Ireland. Drawing on some of the works in *In the World:* Colonialism, consider Joyce's presentation of Irish nationalism in this story. What does his position on Anglo-Irish relations seem to be?

■ FURTHER RESEARCH

Biography
Beja, Morris. *James Joyce: A Literary Life.* 1992.
Ellmann, Richard. *James Joyce.* 2nd ed. 1982.

Criticism
Attridge, Derek. *The Cambridge Companion to James Joyce.* 1990.
————. *Joyce Effects: Transforming Language, History, and Theory.* 2000.
Cheng, Vincent John, and Timothy Peter Martin. *Joyce in Context.* 1992.
MacCabe, Colin, ed. *James Joyce: New Perspectives.* 1982.
Reynolds, Mary T., ed. *James Joyce: A Collection of Critical Essays.* 1993.

Culture and History
Attridge, Derek, and Marjorie Elizabeth Howes, eds. *Semicolonial Joyce.* 2000.
Bidwell, Brice, and Linda Heffer. *The Joycean Way: A Topographic Guide to* Dubliners
    and A Portrait of the Artist as a Young Man. 1982.
Pierce, David. *James Joyce's Ireland.* 1992.

∾ The Dead

Lily, the caretaker's daughter, was literally run off her feet. Hardly had she brought one gentleman into the little pantry behind the office on the ground floor and helped him off with his overcoat than the wheezy hall-door bell clanged again and she had to scamper along the bare hallway to let in another guest. It was well for her she had not to attend to the ladies also. But Miss Kate and Miss Julia had thought of that and had converted the bathroom upstairs into a ladies' dressing-room. Miss Kate and Miss Julia were there, gossiping and laughing and fussing, walking after each other to the head of the stairs, peering down over the banisters and calling down to Lily to ask her who had come.

It was always a great affair, the Misses Morkan's annual dance. Everybody who knew them came to it, members of the family, old friends of the family, the members of Julia's choir, any of Kate's pupils that were grown up enough, and even some of Mary Jane's pupils too. Never once had it fallen flat. For years and years it had gone off in splendid style as long as anyone could remember; ever since Kate and Julia, after the death of their brother Pat, had left the house in Stoney Batter and taken Mary Jane, their only niece, to live with them in the dark gaunt house on Usher's Island, the upper part of which they had rented from Mr. Fulham, the cornfactor[1] on the ground floor. That was a good thirty years ago if it was a day. Mary Jane, who was then a little girl in short clothes, was now the main prop of the household for she

---

"**The Dead.**" Perhaps Joyce's masterpiece in the genre of the short story, this is the last of fifteen stories in *Dubliners,* Joyce's collection of intimate portraits of the ordinary lives of the men and women, largely from the middle classes, of his native city. Joyce had completed all of the stories except "The Dead" by 1905, submitting the manuscript to publishers who rejected it on grounds of obscenity because of its candid treatment of sexuality and its explicit language. When Joyce added "The Dead," he placed it at the end of the collection as a kind of afterword. He thought it would temper his somewhat harsh treatment of Dublin, a place he associated with stifling provincialism, in the rest of the work. As he told his brother Stanislaus, "The Dead" added to his sketch of Dublin its "ingenuous insularity" and "hospitality," which was missing from the previous stories. As with *A Portrait of the Artist as a Young Man,* "The Dead" derives in part from Joyce's own life. His wife, Nora, who was from Galway, serves as the model for Gretta, just as the cosmopolitan Gabriel Conroy is fashioned after Joyce. Nora did have a passionate friend, Michael Bodkin, who died just a year before she met Joyce. Like Michael Furey in the story, Bodkin took ill after standing in the rain under an apple tree to sing goodbye to Nora, who was leaving for Dublin. These biographical details and connections are transformed within the work, whose interest lies not so much in its parallels with Joyce's life but in its symbolic depiction of a conflicted intellectual struggling to transcend the numbing routines and superficial banter of middle-class life even as he demonstrates his affinities with them. In the concluding symbol of "The Dead," snow falling on Ireland, Joyce evokes a unity and interconnectedness that aim to reconcile the conflicts of the story as well as those of the collection as a whole.

---

[1] **cornfactor:** Mr. Fulham is an agent who buys and sells grain according to the market price.

had the organ in Haddington Road.[2] She had been through the Academy and gave a pupils' concert every year in the upper room of the Antient Concert Rooms. Many of her pupils belonged to better-class families on the Kingstown and Dalkey line. Old as they were, her aunts also did their share. Julia, though she was quite grey, was still the leading soprano in Adam and Eve's,[3] and Kate, being too feeble to go about much, gave music lessons to beginners on the old square piano in the back room. Lily, the caretaker's daughter, did housemaid's work for them. Though their life was modest they believed in eating well; the best of everything: diamond-bone sirloins, three-shilling tea, and the best bottled stout. But Lily seldom made a mistake in the orders so that she got on well with her three mistresses. They were fussy, that was all. But the only thing they would not stand was back answers.

Of course they had good reason to be fussy on such a night. And then it was long after ten o'clock and yet there was no sign of Gabriel and his wife. Besides they were dreadfully afraid that Freddy Malins might turn up screwed.[4] They would not wish for worlds that any of Mary Jane's pupils should see him under the influence; and when he was like that it was sometimes very hard to manage him. Freddy Malins always came late but they wondered what could be keeping Gabriel: and that was what brought them every two minutes to the banisters to ask Lily had Gabriel or Freddy come.

— O, Mr. Conroy, said Lily to Gabriel when she opened the door for him, Miss Kate and Miss Julia thought you were never coming. Good-night, Mrs. Conroy.

— I'll engage they did, said Gabriel, but they forget that my wife here takes three mortal hours to dress herself.

He stood on the mat, scraping the snow from his goloshes, while Lily led his wife to the foot of the stairs and called out:

— Miss Kate, here's Mrs. Conroy.

Kate and Julia came toddling down the dark stairs at once. Both of them kissed Gabriel's wife, said she must be perished alive and asked was Gabriel with her.

— Here I am as right as the mail, Aunt Kate! Go on up. I'll follow, called out Gabriel from the dark.

He continued scraping his feet vigorously while the three women went upstairs, laughing, to the ladies' dressing-room. A light fringe of snow lay like a cape on the shoulders of his overcoat and like toecaps on the toes of his goloshes; and, as the buttons of his overcoat slipped with a squeaking noise through the snow-stiffened frieze,[5] a cold fragrant air from out-of-doors escaped from crevices and folds.

— Is it snowing again, Mr. Conroy? asked Lily.

She had preceded him into the pantry to help him off with his overcoat. Gabriel smiled at the three syllables she had given his surname and glanced at her. She was a

---

[2] **had the organ . . . Road:** Mary Jane plays the organ for services held at Saint Mary's Church in the well-to-do southeastern quarter of Dublin. Saint Mary's was noted in Joyce's time for its fine music.

[3] **Adam and Eve's:** A Franciscan church located on a Dublin quay and named for a nearby tavern.

[4] **screwed:** Drunk.

[5] **frieze:** A coarse woolen fabric.

slim, growing girl, pale in complexion and with hay-coloured hair. The gas in the pantry made her look still paler. Gabriel had known her when she was a child and used to sit on the lowest step nursing a rag doll.

—Yes, Lily, he answered, and I think we're in for a night of it.

He looked up at the pantry ceiling, which was shaking with the stamping and shuffling of feet on the floor above, listened for a moment to the piano and then glanced at the girl, who was folding his overcoat carefully at the end of a shelf.

—Tell me, Lily, he said in a friendly tone, do you still go to school?

—O no, sir, she answered. I'm done schooling this year and more.

—O, then, said Gabriel gaily, I suppose we'll be going to your wedding one of these fine days with your young man, eh?

The girl glanced back at him over her shoulder and said with great bitterness:

—The men that is now is only all palaver and what they can get out of you.

Gabriel coloured as if he felt he had made a mistake and, without looking at her, kicked off his goloshes and flicked actively with his muffler at his patent-leather shoes.

He was a stout tallish young man. The high colour of his cheeks pushed upwards even to his forehead where it scattered itself in a few formless patches of pale red; and on his hairless face there scintillated restlessly the polished lenses and the bright gilt rims of the glasses which screened his delicate and restless eyes. His glossy black hair was parted in the middle and brushed in a long curve behind his ears where it curled slightly beneath the groove left by his hat.

When he had flicked lustre into his shoes he stood up and pulled his waistcoat down more tightly on his plump body. Then he took a coin rapidly from his pocket.

—O Lily, he said, thrusting it into her hands, it's Christmas-time, isn't it? Just . . . here's a little. . . .

He walked rapidly towards the door.

—O no, sir! cried the girl, following him. Really, sir, I wouldn't take it.

—Christmas-time! Christmas-time! said Gabriel, almost trotting to the stairs and waving his hand to her in deprecation.

The girl, seeing that he had gained the stairs, called out after him:

—Well, thank you, sir.

He waited outside the drawing-room door until the waltz should finish, listening to the skirts that swept against it and to the shuffling of feet. He was still discomposed by the girl's bitter and sudden retort. It had cast a gloom over him which he tried to dispel by arranging his cuffs and the bows of his tie. Then he took from his waistcoat pocket a little paper and glanced at the headings he had made for his speech. He was undecided about the lines from Robert Browning for he feared they would be above the heads of his hearers. Some quotation that they could recognise from Shakespeare or from the Melodies[6] would be better. The indelicate clacking of the men's heels and the shuffling of their soles reminded him that their grade of

---

[6] the Melodies: Thomas Moore's *Irish Melodies* (1807–1834) was a popular collection of verses set to traditional Irish airs.

culture differed from his. He would only make himself ridiculous by quoting poetry to them which they could not understand. They would think that he was airing his superior education. He would fail with them just as he had failed with the girl in the pantry. He had taken up a wrong tone. His whole speech was a mistake from first to last, an utter failure.

Just then his aunts and his wife came out of the ladies' dressing-room. His aunts were two small plainly dressed old women. Aunt Julia was an inch or so taller. Her hair, drawn low over the tops of her ears, was grey; and grey also, with darker shadows, was her large flaccid face. Though she was stout in build and stood erect her slow eyes and parted lips gave her the appearance of a woman who did not know where she was or where she was going. Aunt Kate was more vivacious. Her face, healthier than her sister's, was all puckers and creases, like a shrivelled red apple, and her hair, braided in the same old-fashioned way, had not lost its ripe nut colour.

They both kissed Gabriel frankly. He was their favourite nephew, the son of their dead elder sister, Ellen, who had married T. J. Conroy of the Port and Docks.

— Gretta tells me you're not going to take a cab back to Monkstown to-night, Gabriel, said Aunt Kate.

— No, said Gabriel, turning to his wife, we had quite enough of that last year, hadn't we? Don't you remember, Aunt Kate, what a cold Gretta got out of it? Cab windows rattling all the way, and the east wind blowing in after we passed Merrion. Very jolly it was. Gretta caught a dreadful cold.

Aunt Kate frowned severely and nodded her head at every word.

— Quite right, Gabriel, quite right, she said. You can't be too careful.

— But as for Gretta there, said Gabriel, she'd walk home in the snow if she were let.

Mrs. Conroy laughed.

— Don't mind him, Aunt Kate, she said. He's really an awful bother, what with green shades for Tom's eyes at night and making him do the dumb-bells, and forcing Eva to eat the stirabout.[7] The poor child! And she simply hates the sight of it! . . . O, but you'll never guess what he makes me wear now!

She broke out into a peal of laughter and glanced at her husband, whose admiring and happy eyes had been wandering from her dress to her face and hair. The two aunts laughed heartily too, for Gabriel's solicitude was a standing joke with them.

— Goloshes! said Mrs. Conroy. That's the latest. Whenever it's wet underfoot I must put on my goloshes. To-night even he wanted me to put them on, but I wouldn't. The next thing he'll buy me will be a diving suit.

Gabriel laughed nervously and patted his tie reassuringly while Aunt Kate nearly doubled herself, so heartily did she enjoy the joke. The smile soon faded from Aunt Julia's face and her mirthless eyes were directed towards her nephew's face. After a pause she asked:

— And what are goloshes, Gabriel?

---

[7] **stirabout:** Porridge.

—Goloshes, Julia! exclaimed her sister. Goodness me, don't you know what goloshes are? You wear them over your . . . over your boots, Gretta, isn't it?

—Yes, said Mrs. Conroy. Guttapercha[8] things. We both have a pair now. Gabriel says everyone wears them on the continent.

—O, on the continent, murmured Aunt Julia, nodding her head slowly.

Gabriel knitted his brows and said, as if he were slightly angered:

—It's nothing very wonderful but Gretta thinks it very funny because she says the word reminds her of Christy Minstrels.[9]

—But tell me, Gabriel, said Aunt Kate, with brisk tact. Of course, you've seen about the room. Gretta was saying . . .

—O, the room is all right, replied Gabriel. I've taken one in the Gresham.

—To be sure, said Aunt Kate, by far the best thing to do. And the children, Gretta, you're not anxious about them?

—O, for one night, said Mrs. Conroy. Besides, Bessie will look after them.

—To be sure, said Aunt Kate again. What a comfort it is to have a girl like that, one you can depend on! There's that Lily, I'm sure I don't know what has come over her lately. She's not the girl she was at all.

Gabriel was about to ask his aunt some questions on this point but she broke off suddenly to gaze after her sister who had wandered down the stairs and was craning her neck over the banisters.

—Now, I ask you, she said, almost testily, where is Julia going? Julia! Julia! Where are you going?

Julia, who had gone halfway down one flight, came back and announced blandly:

—Here's Freddy.

At the same moment a clapping of hands and a final flourish of the pianist told that the waltz had ended. The drawing-room door was opened from within and some couples came out. Aunt Kate drew Gabriel aside hurriedly and whispered into his ear:

—Slip down, Gabriel, like a good fellow and see if he's all right, and don't let him up if he's screwed. I'm sure he's screwed. I'm sure he is.

Gabriel went to the stairs and listened over the banisters. He could hear two persons talking in the pantry. Then he recognised Freddy Malins' laugh. He went down the stairs noisily.

—It's such a relief, said Aunt Kate to Mrs. Conroy, that Gabriel is here. I always feel easier in my mind when he's here. . . . Julia, there's Miss Daly and Miss Power will take some refreshment. Thanks for your beautiful waltz, Miss Daly. It made lovely time.

A tall wizen-faced man, with a stiff grizzled moustache and swarthy skin, who was passing out with his partner said:

—And may we have some refreshment, too, Miss Morkan?

---

[8] **Guttapercha:** A tough, waterproof, rubberlike material.

[9] **Christy Minstrels:** A famous troupe of American blackface entertainers who danced, sang, and bantered in exaggerated African American dialect.

—Julia, said Aunt Kate summarily, and here's Mr. Browne and Miss Furlong. Take them in, Julia, with Miss Daly and Miss Power.

—I'm the man for the ladies, said Mr. Browne, pursing his lips until his moustache bristled and smiling in all his wrinkles. You know, Miss Morkan, the reason they are so fond of me is—

He did not finish his sentence, but, seeing that Aunt Kate was out of earshot, at once led the three young ladies into the back room. The middle of the room was occupied by two square tables and placed end to end, and on these Aunt Julia and the caretaker were straightening and smoothing a large cloth. On the sideboard were arrayed dishes and plates, and glasses and bundles of knives and forks and spoons. The top of the closed square piano served also as a sideboard for viands and sweets. At a smaller sideboard in one corner two young men were standing, drinking hop-bitters.

Mr. Browne led his charges thither and invited them all, in jest, to some ladies' punch, hot, strong and sweet. As they said they never took anything strong he opened three bottles of lemonade for them. Then he asked one of the young men to move aside, and, taking hold of the decanter, filled out for himself a goodly measure of whisky. The young men eyed him respectfully while he took a trial sip.

—God help me, he said, smiling, it's the doctor's orders.

His wizened face broke into a broader smile, and the three young ladies laughed in musical echo to his pleasantry, swaying their bodies to and fro, with nervous jerks of their shoulders. The boldest said:

—O, now, Mr. Browne, I'm sure the doctor never ordered anything of the kind.

Mr. Browne took another sip of his whisky and said, with sidling mimicry:

—Well, you see, I'm like the famous Mrs. Cassidy, who is reported to have said: *Now, Mary Grimes, if I don't take it, make me take it, for I feel I want it.*

His hot face had leaned forward a little too confidentially and he had assumed a very low Dublin accent so that the young ladies, with one instinct, received his speech in silence. Miss Furlong, who was one of Mary Jane's pupils, asked Miss Daly what was the name of the pretty waltz she had played; and Mr. Browne, seeing that he was ignored, turned promptly to the two young men who were more appreciative.

A red-faced young woman, dressed in pansy, came into the room, excitedly clapping her hands and crying:

—Quadrilles! Quadrilles![10]

Close on her heels came Aunt Kate, crying:

—Two gentlemen and three ladies, Mary Jane!

—O, here's Mr. Bergin and Mr. Kerrigan, said Mary Jane. Mr. Kerrigan, will you take Miss Power? Miss Furlong, may I get you a partner, Mr. Bergin. O, that'll just do now.

—Three ladies, Mary Jane, said Aunt Kate.

The two young gentlemen asked the ladies if they might have the pleasure, and Mary Jane turned to Miss Daly.

---

[10] **Quadrilles:** A complex sort of square dance requiring sets of four couples apiece.

—O, Miss Daly, you're really awfully good, after playing for the last two dances, but really we're so short of ladies to-night.

—I don't mind in the least, Miss Morkan.

—But I've a nice partner for you, Mr. Bartell D'Arcy, the tenor. I'll get him to sing later on. All Dublin is raving about him.

—Lovely voice, lovely voice! said Aunt Kate.

As the piano had twice begun the prelude to the first figure Mary Jane led her recruits quickly from the room. They had hardly gone when Aunt Julia wandered slowly into the room, looking behind her at something.

—What is the matter, Julia? asked Aunt Kate anxiously. Who is it?

Julia, who was carrying in a column of table-napkins, turned to her sister and said, simply, as if the question had surprised her:

—It's only Freddy, Kate, and Gabriel with him.

In fact right behind her Gabriel could be seen piloting Freddy Malins across the landing. The latter, a young man of about forty, was of Gabriel's size and build, with very round shoulders. His face was fleshy and pallid, touched with colour only at the thick hanging lobes of his ears and at the wide wings of his nose. He had coarse features, a blunt nose, a convex and receding brow, tumid and protruded lips. His heavy-lidded eyes and the disorder of his scanty hair made him look sleepy. He was laughing heartily in a high key at a story which he had been telling Gabriel on the stairs and at the same time rubbing the knuckles of his left fist backwards and forwards into his left eye.

—Good-evening, Freddy, said Aunt Julia.

Freddy Malins bade the Misses Morkan good-evening in what seemed an off-hand fashion by reason of the habitual catch in his voice and then, seeing that Mr. Browne was grinning at him from the sideboard, crossed the room on rather shaky legs and began to repeat in an undertone the story he had just told to Gabriel.

—He's not so bad, is he? said Aunt Kate to Gabriel.

Gabriel's brows were dark but he raised them quickly and answered:

—O no, hardly noticeable.

—Now, isn't he a terrible fellow! she said. And his poor mother made him take the pledge on New Year's Eve. But come on, Gabriel, into the drawing-room.

Before leaving the room with Gabriel she signalled to Mr. Browne by frowning and shaking her forefinger in warning to and fro. Mr. Browne nodded in answer and, when she had gone, said to Freddy Malins:

—Now, then, Teddy, I'm going to fill you out a good glass of lemonade just to buck you up.

Freddy Malins, who was nearing the climax of his story, waved the offer aside impatiently but Mr. Browne, having first called Freddy Malins' attention to a disarray in his dress, filled out and handed him a full glass of lemonade. Freddy Malins' left hand accepted the glass mechanically, his right hand being engaged in the mechanical readjustment of his dress. Mr. Browne, whose face was once more wrinkling with mirth, poured out for himself a glass of whisky while Freddy Malins exploded, before he had well reached the climax of his story, in a kink of high-pitched bronchitic laughter and, setting down his untasted and overflowing glass, began to rub the knuckles of his left fist backwards and forwards into his left eye, repeating words of his last phrase as well as his fit of laughter would allow him.

Gabriel could not listen while Mary Jane was playing her Academy piece,[11] full of runs and difficult passages, to the hushed drawing-room. He liked music but the piece she was playing had no melody for him and he doubted whether it had any melody for the other listeners, though they had begged Mary Jane to play something. Four young men, who had come from the refreshment-room to stand in the doorway at the sound of the piano, had gone away quietly in couples after a few minutes. The only persons who seemed to follow the music were Mary Jane herself, her hands racing along the keyboard or lifted from it at the pauses like those of a priestess in momentary imprecation, and Aunt Kate standing at her elbow to turn the page.

Gabriel's eyes, irritated by the floor, which glittered with beeswax under the heavy chandelier, wandered to the wall above the piano. A picture of the balcony scene in *Romeo and Juliet* hung there and beside it was a picture of the two murdered princes in the Tower[12] which Aunt Julia had worked in red, blue, and brown wools when she was a girl. Probably in the school they had gone to as girls that kind of work had been taught, for one year his mother had worked for him as a birthday present a waistcoat of purple tabinet,[13] with little foxes' heads upon it, lined with brown satin and having round mulberry buttons. It was strange that his mother had had no musical talent though Aunt Kate used to call her the brains carrier of the Morkan family. Both she and Julia had always seemed a little proud of their serious and matronly sister. Her photograph stood before the pierglass. She held an open book on her knees and was pointing out something in it to Constantine who, dressed in a man-o'-war suit, lay at her feet. It was she who had chosen the names for her sons for she was very sensible of the dignity of family life. Thanks to her, Constantine was now senior curate in Balbriggan and, thanks to her, Gabriel himself had taken his degree in the Royal University. A shadow passed over his face as he remembered her sullen opposition to his marriage. Some slighting phrases she had used still rankled in his memory; she had once spoken of Gretta as being country cute[14] and that was not true of Gretta at all. It was Gretta who had nursed her during all her last long illness in their house at Monkstown.

He knew that Mary Jane must be near the end of her piece for she was playing again the opening melody with runs of scales after every bar and while he waited for the end the resentment died down in his heart. The piece ended with a trill of octaves in the treble and a final deep octave in the bass. Great applause greeted Mary Jane as, blushing and rolling up her music nervously, she escaped from the room.

---

[11] **Academy piece:** A piece of music noted for its technical difficulty that showcases the skills of the musician.

[12] **two . . . Tower:** The two little sons of Edward IV who were rumored to have been imprisoned and murdered in the Tower of London by their usurping uncle, the future Richard III, in 1483.

[13] **tabinet:** A material similar to poplin.

[14] **country cute:** Sly, calculating; from the expression "country cute and city clever."

The most vigorous clapping came from the four young men in the doorway who had gone away to the refreshment-room at the beginning of the piece but had come back when the piano had stopped.

Lancers[15] were arranged. Gabriel found himself partnered with Miss Ivors. She was a frank-mannered talkative young lady, with a freckled face and prominent brown eyes. She did not wear a low-cut bodice and the large brooch which was fixed in the front of her collar bore on it an Irish device.

When they had taken their places she said abruptly:

—I have a crow to pluck with you.

—With me? said Gabriel.

She nodded her head gravely.

—What is it? asked Gabriel, smiling at her solemn manner.

—Who is G.C.? answered Miss Ivors, turning her eyes upon him.

Gabriel coloured and was about to knit his brows, as if he did not understand, when she said bluntly:

—O, innocent Amy! I have found out that you write for *The Daily Express*. Now, aren't you ashamed of yourself?

—Why should I be ashamed of myself? asked Gabriel, blinking his eyes and trying to smile.

—Well, I'm ashamed of you, said Miss Ivors frankly. To say you'd write for a rag like that. I didn't think you were a West Briton.[16]

A look of perplexity appeared on Gabriel's face. It was true that he wrote a literary column every Wednesday in *The Daily Express,* for which he was paid fifteen shillings. But that did not make him a West Briton surely. The books he received for review were almost more welcome than the paltry cheque. He loved to feel the covers and turn over the pages of newly printed books. Nearly every day when his teaching in the college was ended he used to wander down the quays to the second-hand booksellers, to Hickey's on Bachelor's Walk, to Webb's or Massey's on Aston's Quay, or to O'Clohissey's in the by-street. He did not know how to meet her charge. He wanted to say that literature was above politics. But they were friends of many years' standing and their careers had been parallel, first at the University and then as teachers: he could not risk a grandiose phrase with her. He continued blinking his eyes and trying to smile and murmured lamely that he saw nothing political in writing reviews of books.

When their turn to cross[17] had come he was still perplexed and inattentive. Miss Ivors promptly took his hand in a warm grasp and said in a soft friendly tone:

—Of course, I was only joking. Come, we cross now.

When they were together again she spoke of the University question and Gabriel felt more at ease. A friend of hers had shown her his review of Browning's poems. That was how she had found out the secret: but she liked the review immensely. Then she said suddenly:

---

[15] **Lancers:** A kind of quadrille.

[16] **West Briton:** An Irish person whose main loyalty is to Great Britain.

[17] **cross:** One of the steps in a lancer quadrille.

—O, Mr. Conroy, will you come for an excursion to the Aran Isles this summer? We're going to stay there a whole month. It will be splendid out in the Atlantic. You ought to come. Mr. Clancy is coming, and Mr. Kilkelly and Kathleen Kearney. It would be splendid for Gretta too if she'd come. She's from Connacht, isn't she?

—Her people are, said Gabriel shortly.

—But you will come, won't you? said Miss Ivors, laying her warm hand eagerly on his arm.

—The fact is, said Gabriel, I have already arranged to go—

—Go where? asked Miss Ivors.

—Well, you know, every year I go for a cycling tour with some fellows and so—

—But where? asked Miss Ivors.

—Well, we usually go to France or Belgium or perhaps Germany, said Gabriel awkwardly.

—And why do you go to France and Belgium, said Miss Ivors, instead of visiting your own land?

—Well, said Gabriel, it's partly to keep in touch with the languages and partly for a change.

—And haven't you your own language to keep in touch with—Irish? asked Miss Ivors.

—Well, said Gabriel, if it comes to that, you know, Irish is not my language.

Their neighbours had turned to listen to the cross-examination. Gabriel glanced right and left nervously and tried to keep his good humour under the ordeal which was making a blush invade his forehead.

—And haven't you your own land to visit, continued Miss Ivors, that you know nothing of, your own people, and your own country?

—O, to tell you the truth, retorted Gabriel suddenly, I'm sick of my own country, sick of it!

—Why? asked Miss Ivors.

Gabriel did not answer for his retort had heated him.

—Why? repeated Miss Ivors.

They had to go visiting together[18] and, as he had not answered her, Miss Ivors said warmly:

—Of course, you've no answer.

Gabriel tried to cover his agitation by taking part in the dance with great energy. He avoided her eyes for he had seen a sour expression on her face. But when they met in the long chain he was surprised to feel his hand firmly pressed. She looked at him from under her brows for a moment quizzically until he smiled. Then, just as the chain was about to start again, she stood on tiptoe and whispered into his ear:

—West Briton!

When the lancers were over Gabriel went away to a remote corner of the room where Freddy Malins' mother was sitting. She was a stout feeble old woman with white hair. Her voice had a catch in it like her son's and she stuttered slightly. She had

---

[18] **to go visiting together:** Visiting and making the long chain are two other steps in the dance.

been told that Freddy had come and that he was nearly all right. Gabriel asked her whether she had had a good crossing. She lived with her married daughter in Glasgow and came to Dublin on a visit once a year. She answered placidly that she had had a beautiful crossing and that the captain had been most attentive to her. She spoke also of the beautiful house her daughter kept in Glasgow, and of all the nice friends they had there. While her tongue rambled on Gabriel tried to banish from his mind all memory of the unpleasant incident with Miss Ivors. Of course the girl or woman, or whatever she was, was an enthusiast but there was a time for all things. Perhaps he ought not to have answered her like that. But she had no right to call him a West Briton before people, even in joke. She had tried to make him ridiculous before people, heckling him and staring at him with her rabbit's eyes.

He saw his wife making her way towards him through the waltzing couples. When she reached him she said into his ear:

—Gabriel, Aunt Kate wants to know won't you carve the goose as usual. Miss Daly will carve the ham and I'll do the pudding.

—All right, said Gabriel.

—She's sending in the younger ones first as soon as this waltz is over so that we'll have the tables to ourselves.

—Were you dancing? asked Gabriel.

—Of course I was. Didn't you see me? What words had you with Molly Ivors?

—No words. Why? Did she say so?

—Something like that. I'm trying to get that Mr. D'Arcy to sing. He's full of conceit, I think.

—There were no words, said Gabriel moodily, only she wanted me to go for a trip to the west of Ireland and I said I wouldn't.

His wife clasped her hands excitedly and gave a little jump.

—O, do go, Gabriel, she cried. I'd love to see Galway again.

—You can go if you like, said Gabriel coldly.

She looked at him for a moment, then turned to Mrs. Malins and said:

—There's a nice husband for you, Mrs. Malins.

While she was threading her way back across the room Mrs. Malins, without adverting to the interruption, went on to tell Gabriel what beautiful places there were in Scotland and beautiful scenery. Her son-in-law brought them every year to the lakes and they used to go fishing. Her son-in-law was a splendid fisher. One day he caught a fish, a beautiful big big fish, and the man in the hotel boiled it for their dinner.

Gabriel hardly heard what she said. Now that supper was coming near he began to think again about his speech and about the quotation. When he saw Freddy Malins coming across the room to visit his mother Gabriel left the chair free for him and retired into the embrasure of the window. The room had already cleared and from the back room came the clatter of plates and knives. Those who still remained in the drawing-room seemed tired of dancing and were conversing quietly in little groups. Gabriel's warm trembling fingers tapped the cold pane of the window. How cool it must be outside! How pleasant it would be to walk out alone, first along by the river and then through the park! The snow would be lying on the branches of the trees and forming a bright cap on the top of the Wellington Monument. How much more pleasant it would be there than at the supper-table!

He ran over the headings of his speech: Irish hospitality, sad memories, the Three Graces, Paris, the quotation from Browning. He repeated to himself a phrase he had written in his review: *One feels that one is listening to a thought-tormented music.* Miss Ivors had praised the review. Was she sincere? Had she really any life of her own behind all her propagandism? There had never been any ill-feeling between them until that night. It unnerved him to think that she would be at the supper-table, looking up at him while he spoke with her critical quizzing eyes. Perhaps she would not be sorry to see him fail in his speech. An idea came into his mind and gave him courage. He would say, alluding to Aunt Kate and Aunt Julia: *Ladies and Gentlemen, the generation which is now on the wane among us may have had its faults but for my part I think it had certain qualities of hospitality, of humour, of humanity, which the new and very serious and hypereducated generation that is growing up around us seems to me to lack.* Very good: that was one for Miss Ivors. What did he care that his aunts were only two ignorant old women?

A murmur in the room attracted his attention. Mr. Browne was advancing from the door, gallantly escorting Aunt Julia, who leaned upon his arm, smiling and hanging her head. An irregular musketry of applause escorted her also as far as the piano and then, as Mary Jane seated herself on the stool, and Aunt Julia, no longer smiling, half turned so as to pitch her voice fairly into the room, gradually ceased. Gabriel recognised the prelude. It was that of an old song of Aunt Julia's — *Arrayed for the Bridal.*[19] Her voice, strong and clear in tone, attacked with great spirit the runs which embellish the air and though she sang very rapidly she did not miss even the smallest of the grace notes. To follow the voice, without looking at the singer's face, was to feel and share the excitement of swift and secure flight. Gabriel applauded loudly with all the others at the close of the song and loud applause was borne in from the invisible supper-table. It sounded so genuine that a little colour struggled into Aunt Julia's face as she bent to replace in the music-stand the old leather-bound songbook that had her initials on the cover. Freddy Malins, who had listened with his head perched sideways to hear her better, was still applauding when everyone else had ceased and talking animatedly to his mother who nodded her head gravely and slowly in acquiescence. At last, when he could clap no more, he stood up suddenly and hurried across the room to Aunt Julia whose hand he seized and held in both his hands, shaking it when words failed him or the catch in his voice proved too much for him.

—I was just telling my mother, he said, I never heard you sing so well, never. No, I never heard your voice so good as it is tonight. Now! Would you believe that now? That's the truth. Upon my word and honour that's the truth. I never heard your voice sound so fresh and so . . . so clear and fresh, never.

---

[19] *Arrayed for the Bridal:* An arrangement by George Linley of a popular aria from Bellini's opera *I Puritani di Scozia* (1835) about a dewy young bride breathlessly awaiting her groom; it is an inappropriate selection for the elderly Julia to perform.

Aunt Julia smiled broadly and murmured something about compliments as she released her hand from his grasp. Mr. Browne extended his open hand towards her and said to those who were near him in the manner of a showman introducing a prodigy to an audience:

—Miss Julia Morkan, my latest discovery!

He was laughing very heartily at this himself when Freddy Malins turned to him and said:

—Well, Browne, if you're serious you might make a worse discovery. All I can say is I never heard her sing half so well as long as I am coming here. And that's the honest truth.

—Neither did I, said Mr. Browne. I think her voice has greatly improved.

Aunt Julia shrugged her shoulders and said with meek pride:

—Thirty years ago I hadn't a bad voice as voices go.

—I often told Julia, said Aunt Kate emphatically, that she was simply thrown away in that choir. But she never would be said by me.

She turned as if to appeal to the good sense of the others against a refractory child while Aunt Julia gazed in front of her, a vague smile of reminiscence playing on her face.

—No, continued Aunt Kate, she wouldn't be said or led by anyone, slaving there in that choir night and day, night and day. Six o'clock on Christmas morning! And all for what?

—Well, isn't it for the honour of God, Aunt Kate? asked Mary Jane, twisting round on the piano-stool and smiling.

Aunt Kate turned fiercely on her niece and said:

—I know all about the honour of God, Mary Jane, but I think it's not at all honourable for the pope to turn out the women out of the choirs that have slaved there all their lives and put little whipper-snappers of boys over their heads. I suppose it is for the good of the Church if the pope does it. But it's not just, Mary Jane, and it's not right.

She had worked herself into a passion and would have continued in defence of her sister for it was a sore subject with her but Mary Jane, seeing that all the dancers had come back, intervened pacifically:

—Now, Aunt Kate, you're giving scandal to Mr. Browne who is of the other persuasion.

Aunt Kate turned to Mr. Browne, who was grinning at this allusion to his religion, and said hastily:

—O, I don't question the pope's being right. I'm only a stupid old woman and I wouldn't presume to do such a thing. But there's such a thing as common everyday politeness and gratitude. And if I were in Julia's place I'd tell that Father Healy straight up to his face . . .

—And besides, Aunt Kate, said Mary Jane, we really are all hungry and when we are hungry we are all very quarrelsome.

—And when we are thirsty we are also quarrelsome, added Mr. Browne.

—So that we had better go to supper, said Mary Jane, and finish the discussion afterwards.

On the landing outside the drawing-room Gabriel found his wife and Mary Jane trying to persuade Miss Ivors to stay for supper. But Miss Ivors, who had put on her hat and was buttoning her cloak, would not stay. She did not feel in the least hungry and she had already overstayed her time.

—But only for ten minutes, Molly, said Mrs. Conroy. That won't delay you.

—To take a pick itself,[20] said Mary Jane, after all your dancing.

—I really couldn't, said Miss Ivors.

—I am afraid you didn't enjoy yourself at all, said Mary Jane hopelessly.

—Ever so much, I assure you, said Miss Ivors, but you really must let me run off now.

—But how can you get home? asked Mrs. Conroy.

—O, it's only two steps up the quay.

Gabriel hesitated a moment and said:

—If you will allow me, Miss Ivors, I'll see you home if you really are obliged to go.

But Miss Ivors broke away from them.

—I won't hear of it, she cried. For goodness sake go in to your suppers and don't mind me. I'm quite well able to take care of myself.

—Well, you're the comical girl, Molly, said Mrs. Conroy frankly.

—*Beannacht libh,*[21] cried Miss Ivors, with a laugh, as she ran down the staircase.

Mary Jane gazed after her, a moody puzzled expression on her face, while Mrs. Conroy leaned over the banisters to listen for the hall-door. Gabriel asked himself was he the cause of her abrupt departure. But she did not seem to be in ill humour: she had gone away laughing. He stared blankly down the staircase.

At that moment Aunt Kate came toddling out of the supper-room, almost wringing her hands in despair.

—Where is Gabriel? she cried. Where on earth is Gabriel? There's everyone waiting in there, stage to let, and nobody to carve the goose!

—Here I am, Aunt Kate! cried Gabriel, with sudden animation, ready to carve a flock of geese, if necessary.

A fat brown goose lay at one end of the table and at the other end, on a bed of creased paper strewn with sprigs of parsley, lay a great ham, stripped of its outer skin and peppered over with crust crumbs, a meat paper frill round its shin and beside this was a round of spiced beef. Between these two rival ends ran parallel lines of side-dishes: two little minsters of jelly, red and yellow; a shallow dish full of blocks of blancmange and red jam, a large green leaf-shaped dish with a stalk-shaped handle, on which lay bunches of purple raisins and peeled almonds, a companion dish on which lay a solid rectangle of Smyrna figs, a dish of custard topped with grated nutmeg, a small bowl full of chocolates and sweets wrapped in gold and silver papers and a glass vase in which stood some tall celery stalks. In the centre of the table there stood, as sentries to a fruit-stand which upheld a pyramid of oranges

---

[20] **To take . . . itself:** To have a small bite to eat.

[21] *Beannacht libh:* "Blessing to ye"; a Gaelic good-night.

and American apples, two squat old-fashioned decanters of cut glass, one containing port and the other dark sherry. On the closed square piano a pudding in a huge yellow dish lay in waiting and behind it were three squads of bottles of stout and ale and minerals, drawn up according to the colours of their uniforms, the first two black, with brown and red labels, the third and smallest squad white, with transverse green sashes.

Gabriel took his seat boldly at the head of the table and, having looked to the edge of the carver, plunged his fork firmly into the goose. He felt quite at ease now for he was an expert carver and liked nothing better than to find himself at the head of a well-laden table.

— Miss Furlong, what shall I send you? he asked. A wing or a slice of the breast?

— Just a small slice of the breast.

— Miss Higgins, what for you?

— O, anything at all, Mr. Conroy.

While Gabriel and Miss Daly exchanged plates of goose and plates of ham and spiced beef Lily went from guest to guest with a dish of hot floury potatoes wrapped in a white napkin. This was Mary Jane's idea and she had also suggested apple sauce for the goose but Aunt Kate had said that plain roast goose without apple sauce had always been good enough for her and she hoped she might never eat worse. Mary Jane waited on her pupils and saw that they got the best slices and Aunt Kate and Aunt Julia opened and carried across from the piano bottles of stout and ale for the gentlemen and bottles of minerals for the ladies. There was a great deal of confusion and laughter and noise, the noise of orders and counter-orders, of knives and forks, of corks and glass-stoppers. Gabriel began to carve second helpings as soon as he had finished the first round without serving himself. Everyone protested loudly so that he compromised by taking a long draught of stout for he had found the carving hot work. Mary Jane settled down quietly to her supper but Aunt Kate and Aunt Julia were still toddling round the table, walking on each other's heels, getting in each other's way and giving each other unheeded orders. Mr. Browne begged of them to sit down and eat their suppers and so did Gabriel but they said there was time enough so that, at last, Freddy Malins stood up and, capturing Aunt Kate, plumped her down on her chair amid general laughter.

When everyone had been well served Gabriel said, smiling:

— Now, if anyone wants a little more of what vulgar people call stuffing let him or her speak.

A chorus of voices invited him to begin his own supper and Lily came forward with three potatoes which she had reserved for him.

— Very well, said Gabriel amiably, as he took another preparatory draught, kindly forget my existence, ladies and gentlemen, for a few minutes.

He set to his supper and took no part in the conversation with which the table covered Lily's removal of the plates. The subject of talk was the opera company which was then at the Theatre Royal. Mr. Bartell D'Arcy, the tenor, a dark-complexioned young man with a smart moustache, praised very highly the leading contralto of the company but Miss Furlong thought she had a rather vulgar style of production.

Freddy Malins said there was a negro chieftain singing in the second part of the Gaiety pantomime[22] who had one of the finest tenor voices he had ever heard.

—Have you heard him? he asked Mr. Bartell D'Arcy across the table.

—No, answered Mr. Bartell D'Arcy carelessly.

—Because, Freddy Malins explained, now I'd be curious to hear your opinion of him. I think he has a grand voice.

—It takes Teddy to find out the really good things, said Mr. Browne familiarly to the table.

—And why couldn't he have a voice too? asked Freddy Malins sharply. Is it because he's only a black?

Nobody answered this question and Mary Jane led the table back to the legitimate opera. One of her pupils had given her a pass for *Mignon.* Of course it was very fine, she said, but it made her think of poor Georgina Burns.[23] Mr. Browne could go back farther still, to the old Italian companies that used to come to Dublin—Tietjens, Ilma de Murzka, Campanini, the great Trebelli, Giuglini, Ravelli, Aramburo.[24] Those were the days, he said, when there was something like singing to be heard in Dublin. He told too of how the top gallery of the old Royal used to be packed night after night, of how one night an Italian tenor had sung five encores to *Let Me Like a Soldier Fall,*[25] introducing a high C every time, and of how the gallery boys would sometimes in their enthusiasm unyoke the horses from the carriage of some great *prima donna* and pull her themselves through the streets to her hotel. Why did they never play the grand old operas now, he asked, *Dinorah, Lucrezia Borgia?*[26] Because they could not get the voices to sing them: that was why.

—O, well, said Mr. Bartell D'Arcy, I presume there are as good singers today as there were then.

—Where are they? asked Mr. Browne defiantly.

—In London, Paris, Milan, said Mr. Bartell D'Arcy warmly. I suppose Caruso,[27] for example, is quite as good, if not better than any of the men you have mentioned.

—Maybe so, said Mr. Browne. But I may tell you I doubt it strongly.

—O, I'd give anything to hear Caruso sing, said Mary Jane.

—For me, said Aunt Kate, who had been picking a bone, there was only one tenor. To please me, I mean. But I suppose none of you ever heard of him.

---

[22] **Gaiety pantomime:** The Gaiety theater featured popular dramas, musicals, and comic revues, entertainment considerably less elegant than what the rest of the guests have been discussing.

[23] *Mignon . . .* **Burns:** *Mignon* is an 1866 opera by Ambroise Thomas; Georgina Burns was a famous soprano in the 1880s.

[24] **Tietjens . . . Aramburo:** The names of celebrated nineteenth-century opera singers.

[25] *Let Me . . . Fall:* Aria from William Vincent Wallace's 1845 opera *Maritana,* a melodramatic vow to die bravely and honorably.

[26] *Dinorah . . . Borgia: Dinorah* is an 1859 Giacomo Meyerbeer opera; *Lucrezia Borgia* (1833) was composed by Gaetano Donizetti.

[27] **Caruso:** Enrico Caruso (1873–1921), the great tenor who was just coming into his fame in 1904, the time in which the story is set.

—Who was he, Miss Morkan? asked Mr. Bartell D'Arcy politely.

—His name, said Aunt Kate, was Parkinson.[28] I heard him when he was in his prime and I think he had then the purest tenor voice that was ever put into a man's throat.

—Strange, said Mr. Bartell D'Arcy. I never even heard of him.

—Yes, yes, Miss Morkan is right, said Mr. Browne. I remember hearing of old Parkinson but he's too far back for me.

—A beautiful pure sweet mellow English tenor, said Aunt Kate with enthusiasm.

Gabriel having finished, the huge pudding was transferred to the table. The clatter of forks and spoons began again. Gabriel's wife served out spoonfuls of the pudding and passed the plates down the table. Midway down they were held up by Mary Jane, who replenished them with raspberry or orange jelly or with blancmange and jam. The pudding was of Aunt Julia's making and she received praises for it from all quarters. She herself said that it was not quite brown enough.

—Well, I hope, Miss Morkan, said Mr. Browne, that I'm brown enough for you because, you know, I'm all brown.

All the gentlemen, except Gabriel, ate some of the pudding out of compliment to Aunt Julia. As Gabriel never ate sweets the celery had been left for him. Freddy Malins also took a stalk of celery and ate it with his pudding. He had been told that celery was a capital thing for the blood and he was just then under the doctor's care. Mrs. Malins, who had been silent all through the supper, said that her son was going down to Mount Melleray[29] in a week or so. The table then spoke of Mount Melleray, how bracing the air was down there, how hospitable the monks were and how they never asked for a penny-piece from their guests.

—And do you mean to say, asked Mr. Browne incredulously, that a chap can go down there and put up there as if it were a hotel and live on the fat of the land and then come away without paying a farthing?

—O, most people give some donation to the monastery when they leave, said Mary Jane.

—I wish we had an institution like that in our Church, said Mr. Browne candidly.

He was astonished to hear that the monks never spoke, got up at two in the morning, and slept in their coffins. He asked what they did it for.

—That's the rule of the order, said Aunt Kate firmly.

—Yes, but why? asked Mr. Browne.

Aunt Kate repeated that it was the rule, that was all. Mr. Browne still seemed not to understand. Freddy Malins explained to him, as best he could, that the monks were trying to make up for the sins committed by all the sinners in the outside world. The explanation was not very clear for Mr. Browne grinned and said:

—I like that idea very much but wouldn't a comfortable spring bed do them as well as a coffin?

—The coffin, said Mary Jane, is to remind them of their last end.

---

[28] **Parkinson:** A tenor named Parkinson sang with the Carl Rosa Opera Company in the late nineteenth century.

[29] **Mount Melleray:** A Trappist monastery in the south of Ireland; although all politely avoid saying so, the alcoholic Freddy is going there to dry out.

As the subject had grown lugubrious it was buried in a silence of the table during which Mrs. Malins could be heard saying to her neighbour in an indistinct undertone:

—They are very good men, the monks, very pious men.

The raisins and almonds and figs and apples and oranges and chocolates and sweets were now passed about the table and Aunt Julia invited all the guests to have either port or sherry. At first Mr. Bartell D'Arcy refused to take either but one of his neighbours nudged him and whispered something to him upon which he allowed his glass to be filled. Gradually as the last glasses were being filled the conversation ceased. A pause followed, broken only by the noise of the wine and by unsettlings of chairs. The Misses Morkan, all three, looked down at the tablecloth. Someone coughed once or twice and then a few gentlemen patted the table gently as a signal for silence. The silence came and Gabriel pushed back his chair and stood up.

The patting at once grew louder in encouragement and then ceased altogether. Gabriel leaned his ten trembling fingers on the tablecloth and smiled nervously at the company. Meeting a row of upturned faces he raised his eyes to the chandelier. The piano was playing a waltz tune and he could hear the skirts sweeping against the drawing-room door. People, perhaps, were standing in the snow on the quay outside, gazing up at the lighted windows and listening to the waltz music. The air was pure there. In the distance lay the park where the trees were weighted with snow. The Wellington Monument wore a gleaming cap of snow that flashed westward over the white field of Fifteen Acres.

He began:

—Ladies and Gentlemen.

—It has fallen to my lot this evening, as in years past, to perform a very pleasing task but a task for which I am afraid my poor powers as a speaker are all too inadequate.

—No, no! said Mr. Browne.

—But, however that may be, I can only ask you tonight to take the will for the deed and to lend me your attention for a few moments while I endeavour to express to you in words what my feelings are on this occasion.

—Ladies and Gentlemen. It is not the first time that we have gathered together under this hospitable roof, around this hospitable board. It is not the first time that we have been the recipients—or perhaps, I had better say, the victims—of the hospitality of certain good ladies.

He made a circle in the air with his arm and paused. Everyone laughed or smiled at Aunt Kate and Aunt Julia and Mary Jane who all turned crimson with pleasure. Gabriel went on more boldly:

—I feel more strongly with every recurring year that our country has no tradition which does it so much honour and which it should guard so jealously as that of its hospitality. It is a tradition that is unique as far as my experience goes (and I have visited not a few places abroad) among the modern nations. Some would say, perhaps, that with us it is rather a failing than anything to be boasted of. But granted even that, it is, to my mind, a princely failing, and one that I trust will long be cultivated among us. Of one thing, at least, I am sure. As long as this one roof shelters the good ladies aforesaid—and I wish from my heart it may do so for many and many a long year to come—the tradition of genuine warm-hearted courteous Irish hospitality, which our forefathers have handed down to us and which we in turn must hand down to our descendants, is still alive among us.

A hearty murmur of assent ran round the table. It shot through Gabriel's mind that Miss Ivors was not there and that she had gone away discourteously: and he said with confidence in himself:

—Ladies and Gentlemen.

—A new generation is growing up in our midst, a generation actuated by new ideas and new principles. It is serious and enthusiastic for these new ideas and its enthusiasm, even when it is misdirected, is, I believe, in the main sincere. But we are living in a sceptical and, if I may use the phrase, a thought-tormented age: and sometimes I fear that this new generation, educated or hypereducated as it is, will lack those qualities of humanity, of hospitality, of kindly humour which belonged to an older day. Listening tonight to the names of all those great singers of the past it seemed to me, I must confess, that we were living in a less spacious age. Those days might, without exaggeration, be called spacious days: and if they are gone beyond recall let us hope, at least, that in gatherings such as this we shall still speak of them with pride and affection, still cherish in our hearts the memory of those dead and gone great ones whose fame the world will not willingly let die.

—Hear, hear! said Mr. Browne loudly.

—But yet, continued Gabriel, his voice falling into a softer inflection, there are always in gatherings such as this sadder thoughts that will recur to our minds: thoughts of the past, of youth, of changes, of absent faces that we miss here tonight. Our path through life is strewn with many such sad memories: and were we to brood upon them always we could not find the heart to go on bravely with our work among the living. We have all of us living duties and living affections which claim, and rightly claim, our strenuous endeavours.

—Therefore, I will not linger on the past. I will not let any gloomy moralising intrude upon us here tonight. Here we are gathered together for a brief moment from the bustle and rush of our everyday routine. We are met here as friends, in the spirit of good-fellowship, as colleagues, also to a certain extent, in the true spirit of *camaraderie,* and as the guests of—what shall I call them?—the Three Graces of the Dublin musical world.

The table burst into applause and laughter at this sally. Aunt Julia vainly asked each of her neighbours in turn to tell her what Gabriel had said.

—He says we are the Three Graces, Aunt Julia, said Mary Jane.

Aunt Julia did not understand but she looked up, smiling, at Gabriel, who continued in the same vein:

—Ladies and Gentlemen.

—I will not attempt to play tonight the part that Paris[30] played on another occasion. I will not attempt to choose between them. The task would be an invidious one

---

[30] **Paris:** In Greek myth, Paris was the Trojan shepherd prince compelled to choose the most beautiful from among Hera, Athena, and Aphrodite. When he chose Aphrodite, she awarded him the already-married Helen as his bride, precipitating the Trojan War.

and one beyond my poor powers. For when I view them in turn, whether it be our chief hostess herself, whose good heart, whose too good heart, has become a byword with all who know her, or her sister, who seems to be gifted with perennial youth and whose singing must have been a surprise and a revelation to us all to-night, or, last but not least, when I consider our youngest hostess, talented, cheerful, hard-working, and the best of nieces, I confess, Ladies and Gentlemen, that I do not know to which of them I should award the prize.

Gabriel glanced down at his aunts and, seeing the large smile on Aunt Julia's face and the tears which had risen to Aunt Kate's eyes, hastened to his close. He raised his glass of port gallantly, while every member of the company fingered a glass expectantly, and said loudly:

—Let us toast them all three together. Let us drink to their health, wealth, long life, happiness, and prosperity and may they long continue to hold the proud and self-won position which they hold in their profession and the position of honour and affection which they hold in our hearts.

All the guests stood up, glass in hand, and, turning towards the three seated ladies, sang in unison, with Mr. Browne as leader:

For they are jolly gay fellows,
For they are jolly gay fellows,
For they are jolly gay fellows,
Which nobody can deny.

Aunt Kate was making frank use of her handkerchief and even Aunt Julia seemed moved. Freddy Malins beat time with his pudding-fork and the singers turned towards one another, as if in melodious conference, while they sang, with emphasis:

Unless he tells a lie,
Unless he tells a lie.

Then, turning once more towards their hostesses, they sang:

For they are jolly gay fellows,
For they are jolly gay fellows,
For they are jolly gay fellows,
Which nobody can deny.

The acclamation which followed was taken up beyond the door of the supper-room by many of the other guests and renewed time after time, Freddy Malins acting as officer with his fork on high.

The piercing morning air came into the hall where they were standing so that Aunt Kate said:

—Close the door, somebody. Mrs. Malins will get her death of cold.

—Browne is out there, Aunt Kate, said Mary Jane.

—Browne is everywhere, said Aunt Kate, lowering her voice.

Mary Jane laughed at her tone.

—Really, she said archly, he is very attentive.

—He has been laid on here like the gas, said Aunt Kate in the same tone, all during the Christmas.

She laughed herself this time good-humouredly and then added quickly:

—But tell him to come in, Mary Jane, and close the door. I hope to goodness he didn't hear me.

At that moment the hall-door was opened and Mr. Browne came in from the doorstep, laughing as if his heart would break. He was dressed in a long green overcoat with mock astrakhan cuffs and collar and wore on his head an oval fur cap. He pointed down the snow-covered quay from where the sound of shrill prolonged whistling was borne in.

—Teddy will have all the cabs in Dublin out, he said.

Gabriel advanced from the little pantry behind the office, struggling into his overcoat and, looking round the hall, said:

—Gretta not down yet?

—She's getting on her things, Gabriel, said Aunt Kate.

—Who's playing up there? asked Gabriel.

—Nobody. They're all gone.

—O no, Aunt Kate, said Mary Jane. Bartell D'Arcy and Miss O'Callaghan aren't gone yet.

—Someone is strumming at the piano, anyhow, said Gabriel.

Mary Jane glanced at Gabriel and Mr. Browne and said with a shiver:

—It makes me feel cold to look at you two gentlemen muffled up like that. I wouldn't like to face your journey home at this hour.

—I'd like nothing better this minute, said Mr. Browne stoutly, than a rattling fine walk in the country or a fast drive with a good spanking goer between the shafts.[31]

—We used to have a very good horse and trap at home, said Aunt Julia sadly.

—The never-to-be-forgotten Johnny, said Mary Jane, laughing.

Aunt Kate and Gabriel laughed too.

—Why, what was wonderful about Johnny? asked Mr. Browne.

—The late lamented Patrick Morkan, our grandfather, that is, explained Gabriel, commonly known in his later years as the old gentleman, was a glue-boiler.

—O, now, Gabriel, said Aunt Kate, laughing, he had a starch mill.

—Well, glue or starch, said Gabriel, the old gentleman had a horse by the name of Johnny. And Johnny used to work in the old gentleman's mill, walking round and round in order to drive the mill. That was all very well; but now comes the tragic part about Johnny. One fine day the old gentleman thought he'd like to drive out with the quality to a military review in the park.

—The Lord have mercy on his soul, said Aunt Kate compassionately.

—Amen, said Gabriel. So the old gentleman, as I said, harnessed Johnny and put on his very best tall hat and his very best stock collar and drove out in grand style from his ancestral mansion somewhere near Back Lane, I think.

---

[31]**fast drive . . . shafts:** A fast carriage drive with a spirited horse.

Everyone laughed, even Mrs. Malins, at Gabriel's manner and Aunt Kate said:

—O now, Gabriel, he didn't live in Back Lane, really. Only the mill was there.

—Out from the mansion of his forefathers, continued Gabriel, he drove with Johnny. And everything went on beautifully until Johnny came in sight of King Billy's statue: and whether he fell in love with the horse King Billy sits on or whether he thought he was back again in the mill, anyhow he began to walk round the statue.

Gabriel paced in a circle round the hall in his goloshes amid the laughter of the others.

—Round and round he went, said Gabriel, and the old gentleman, who was a very pompous old gentleman, was highly indignant. *Go on, sir! What do you mean, sir? Johnny! Johnny! Most extraordinary conduct! Can't understand the horse!*

The peals of laughter which followed Gabriel's imitation of the incident were interrupted by a resounding knock at the hall-door. Mary Jane ran to open it and let in Freddy Malins. Freddy Malins, with his hat well back on his head and his shoulders humped with cold, was puffing and steaming after his exertions.

—I could only get one cab, he said.

—O, we'll find another along the quay, said Gabriel.

—Yes, said Aunt Kate. Better not keep Mrs. Malins standing in the draught.

Mrs. Malins was helped down the front steps by her son and Mr. Browne and, after many manœuvres, hoisted into the cab. Freddy Malins clambered in after her and spent a long time settling her on the seat, Mr. Browne helping him with advice. At last she was settled comfortably and Freddy Malins invited Mr. Browne into the cab. There was a good deal of confused talk, and then Mr. Browne got into the cab. The cabman settled his rug over his knees, and bent down for the address. The confusion grew greater and the cabman was directed differently by Freddy Malins and Mr. Browne, each of whom had his head out through a window of the cab. The difficulty was to know where to drop Mr. Browne along the route and Aunt Kate, Aunt Julia, and Mary Jane helped the discussion from the doorstep with cross-directions and contradictions and abundance of laughter. As for Freddy Malins he was speechless with laughter. He popped his head in and out of the window every moment, to the great danger of his hat, and told his mother how the discussion was progressing till at last Mr. Browne shouted to the bewildered cabman above the din of everybody's laughter:

—Do you know Trinity College?

—Yes, sir, said the cabman.

—Well, drive bang up against Trinity College gates, said Mr. Browne, and then we'll tell you where to go. You understand now?

—Yes, sir, said the cabman.

—Make like a bird for Trinity College.

—Right, sir, cried the cabman.

The horse was whipped up and the cab rattled off along the quay amid a chorus of laughter and adieus.

Gabriel had not gone to the door with the others. He was in a dark part of the hall gazing up the staircase. A woman was standing near the top of the first flight, in the shadow also. He could not see her face but he could see the terracotta and salmonpink panels of her skirt which the shadow made appear black and white. It was his wife. She was leaning on the banisters, listening to something. Gabriel was surprised at her stillness and strained his ear to listen also. But he could hear little save the noise of laughter and dispute on the front steps, a few chords struck on the piano and a few notes of a man's voice singing.

He stood still in the gloom of the hall, trying to catch the air that the voice was singing and gazing up at his wife. There was grace and mystery in her attitude as if she were a symbol of something. He asked himself what is a woman standing on the stairs in the shadow, listening to distant music, a symbol of. If he were a painter he would paint her in that attitude. Her blue felt hat would show off the bronze of her hair against the darkness and the dark panels of her skirt would show off the light ones. *Distant Music* he would call the picture if he were a painter.

The hall-door was closed; and Aunt Kate, Aunt Julia, and Mary Jane came down the hall, still laughing.

—Well, isn't Freddy terrible? said Mary Jane. He's really terrible.

Gabriel said nothing but pointed up the stairs towards where his wife was standing. Now that the hall-door was closed the voice and the piano could be heard more clearly. Gabriel held up his hand for them to be silent. The song seemed to be in the old Irish tonality and the singer seemed uncertain both of his words and of his voice. The voice, made plaintive by distance and by the singer's hoarseness, faintly illuminated the cadence of the air with words expressing grief:

> O, the rain falls on my heavy locks
> And the dew wets my skin,
> My babe lies cold . . .

—O, exclaimed Mary Jane. It's Bartell D'Arcy singing and he wouldn't sing all the night. O, I'll get him to sing a song before he goes.

—O do, Mary Jane, said Aunt Kate.

Mary Jane brushed past the others and ran to the staircase but before she reached it the singing stopped and the piano was closed abruptly.

—O, what a pity! she cried. Is he coming down, Gretta?

Gabriel heard his wife answer yes and saw her come down towards them. A few steps behind her were Mr. Bartell D'Arcy and Miss O'Callaghan.

—O, Mr. D'Arcy, cried Mary Jane, it's downright mean of you to break off like that when we were all in raptures listening to you.

—I have been at him all the evening, said Miss O'Callaghan, and Mrs. Conroy too and he told us he had a dreadful cold and couldn't sing.

—O, Mr. D'Arcy, said Aunt Kate, now that was a great fib to tell.

—Can't you see that I'm as hoarse as a crow? said Mr. D'Arcy roughly.

He went into the pantry hastily and put on his overcoat. The others, taken aback by his rude speech, could find nothing to say. Aunt Kate wrinkled her brows and made signs to the others to drop the subject. Mr. D'Arcy stood swathing his neck carefully and frowning.

—It's the weather, said Aunt Julia, after a pause.

—Yes, everybody has colds, said Aunt Kate readily, everybody.

—They say, said Mary Jane, we haven't had snow like it for thirty years; and I read this morning in the newspapers that the snow is general all over Ireland.

—I love the look of snow, said Aunt Julia sadly.

—So do I, said Miss O'Callaghan. I think Christmas is never really Christmas unless we have the snow on the ground.

—But poor Mr. D'Arcy doesn't like the snow, said Aunt Kate, smiling.

Mr. D'Arcy came from the pantry, fully swathed and buttoned, and in a repentant tone told them the history of the cold. Everyone gave him advice and said it was a great pity and urged him to be very careful of his throat in the night air. Gabriel watched his wife who did not join in the conversation. She was standing right under the dusty fanlight and the flame of the gas lit up the rich bronze of her hair which he had seen her drying at the fire a few days before. She was in the same attitude and seemed unaware of the talk about her. At last she turned towards them and Gabriel saw that there was colour on her cheeks and that her eyes were shining. A sudden tide of joy went leaping out of his heart.

—Mr. D'Arcy, she said, what is the name of that song you were singing?

—It's called *The Lass of Aughrim*,[32] said Mr. D'Arcy, but I couldn't remember it properly. Why? Do you know it?

—*The Lass of Aughrim,* she repeated. I couldn't think of the name.

—It's a very nice air, said Mary Jane. I'm sorry you were not in voice tonight.

—Now, Mary Jane, said Aunt Kate, don't annoy Mr. D'Arcy. I won't have him annoyed.

Seeing that all were ready to start she shepherded them to the door where good-night was said:

—Well, good-night, Aunt Kate, and thanks for the pleasant evening.

—Good-night, Gabriel. Good-night, Gretta!

—Good-night, Aunt Kate, and thanks ever so much. Good-night, Aunt Julia.

—O, good-night, Gretta, I didn't see you.

—Good-night, Mr. D'Arcy. Good-night, Miss O'Callaghan.

—Good-night, Miss Morkan.

—Good-night, again.

—Good-night, all. Safe home.

—Good-night. Good-night.

The morning was still dark. A dull yellow light brooded over the houses and the river; and the sky seemed to be descending. It was slushy underfoot; and only streaks and patches of snow lay on the roofs, on the parapets of the quay and on the area railings. The lamps were still burning redly in the murky air and, across the river, the palace of the Four Courts stood out menacingly against the heavy sky.

She was walking on before him with Mr. Bartell D'Arcy, her shoes in a brown parcel tucked under one arm and her hands holding her skirt up from the slush. She had no longer any grace of attitude but Gabriel's eyes were still bright with

---

[32] *The Lass of Aughrim*: Child Ballad number 76, also called "Lord Gregory," in which a peasant girl stands outside a castle and pleads with her noble lover to acknowledge her and their child.

happiness. The blood went bounding along his veins; and the thoughts went rioting through his brain, proud, joyful, tender, valorous.

She was walking on before him so lightly and so erect that he longed to run after her noiselessly, catch her by the shoulders and say something foolish and affection-ate into her ear. She seemed to him so frail that he longed to defend her against something and then to be alone with her. Moments of their secret life together burst like stars upon his memory. A heliotrope envelope was lying beside his breakfast-cup and he was caressing it with his hand. Birds were twittering in the ivy and the sunny web of the curtain was shimmering along the floor: he could not eat for happiness. They were standing on the crowded platform and he was placing a ticket inside the warm palm of her glove. He was standing with her in the cold, looking in through a grated window at a man making bottles in a roaring furnace. It was very cold. Her face, fragrant in the cold air, was quite close to his; and suddenly she called out to the man at the furnace.

—Is the fire hot, sir?

But the man could not hear her with the noise of the furnace. It was just as well. He might have answered rudely.

A wave of yet more tender joy escaped from his heart and went coursing in warm flood along his arteries. Like the tender fires of stars moments of their life together, that no one knew of or would ever know of, broke upon and illumined his memory. He longed to recall to her those moments, to make her forget the years of their dull existence together and remember only their moments of ecstasy. For the years, he felt, had not quenched his soul or hers. Their children, his writing, her household cares had not quenched all their souls' tender fire. In one letter that he had written to her then he had said: *Why is it that words like these seem to me so dull and cold? Is it because there is no word tender enough to be your name?*

Like distant music these words that he had written years before were borne towards him from the past. He longed to be alone with her. When the others had gone away, when he and she were in their room in the hotel, then they would be alone together. He would call her softly:

—Gretta!

Perhaps she would not hear at once: she would be undressing. Then something in his voice would strike her. She would turn and look at him. . . .

At the corner of Winetavern Street they met a cab. He was glad of its rattling noise as it saved him from conversation. She was looking out of the window and seemed tired. The others spoke only a few words, pointing out some building or street. The horse galloped along wearily under the murky morning sky, dragging his old rattling box after his heels, and Gabriel was again in a cab with her, galloping to catch the boat, galloping to their honeymoon.

As the cab drove across O'Connell Bridge Miss O'Callaghan said:

—They say you never cross O'Connell Bridge without seeing a white horse.

—I see a white man this time, said Gabriel.

—Where? asked Mr. Bartell D'Arcy.

Gabriel pointed to the statue, on which lay patches of snow. Then he nodded familiarly to it and waved his hand.

—Good-night, Dan, he said gaily.[33]

When the cab drew up before the hotel Gabriel jumped out and, in spite of Mr. Bartell D'Arcy's protest, paid the driver. He gave the man a shilling over his fare. The man saluted and said:

—A prosperous New Year to you, sir.

—The same to you, said Gabriel cordially.

She leaned for a moment on his arm in getting out of the cab and while standing at the curbstone, bidding the others good-night. She leaned lightly on his arm, as lightly as when she had danced with him a few hours before. He had felt proud and happy then, happy that she was his, proud of her grace and wifely carriage. But now, after the kindling again of so many memories, the first touch of her body, musical and strange and perfumed, sent through him a keen pang of lust. Under cover of her silence he pressed her arm closely to his side; and, as they stood at the hotel door, he felt that they had escaped from their lives and duties, escaped from home and friends and run away together with wild and radiant hearts to a new adventure.

An old man was dozing in a great hooded chair in the hall. He lit a candle in the office and went before them to the stairs. They followed him in silence, their feet falling in soft thuds on the thickly carpeted stairs. She mounted the stairs behind the porter, her head bowed in the ascent, her frail shoulders curved as with a burden, her skirt girt tightly about her. He could have flung his arms about her hips and held her still for his arms were trembling with desire to seize her and only the stress of his nails against the palms of his hands held the wild impulse of his body in check. The porter halted on the stairs to settle his guttering candle. They halted too on the steps below him. In the silence Gabriel could hear the falling of the molten wax into the tray and the thumping of his own heart against his ribs.

The porter led them along a corridor and opened a door. Then he set his unstable candle down on a toilet-table and asked at what hour they were to be called in the morning.

—Eight, said Gabriel.

The porter pointed to the tap of the electric-light and began a muttered apology but Gabriel cut him short.

—We don't want any light. We have light enough from the street. And I say, he added, pointing to the candle, you might remove that handsome article, like a good man.

The porter took up his candle again, but slowly for he was surprised by such a novel idea. Then he mumbled good-night and went out. Gabriel shot the lock to.

A ghostly light from the street lamp lay in a long shaft from one window to the door. Gabriel threw his overcoat and hat on a couch and crossed the room towards the window. He looked down into the street in order that his emotion might calm a little. Then he turned and leaned against a chest of drawers with his back to the light. She had taken off her hat and cloak and was standing before a large swinging

---

[33] **Good-night . . . gaily:** Gabriel salutes the snow-covered statue of Daniel O'Connell (1775–1847), poet and Irish nationalist.

mirror, unhooking her waist. Gabriel paused for a few moments, watching her, and then said:

—Gretta!

She turned away from the mirror slowly and walked along the shaft of light towards him. Her face looked so serious and weary that the words would not pass Gabriel's lips. No, it was not the moment yet.

—You look tired, he said.

—I am a little, she answered.

—You don't feel ill or weak?

—No, tired: that's all.

She went on to the window and stood there, looking out. Gabriel waited again and then, fearing that diffidence was about to conquer him, he said abruptly:

—By the way, Gretta!

—What is it?

—You know that poor fellow Malins? he said quickly.

—Yes. What about him?

—Well, poor fellow, he's a decent sort of chap after all, continued Gabriel in a false voice. He gave me back that sovereign I lent him and I didn't expect it really. It's a pity he wouldn't keep away from that Browne, because he's not a bad fellow at heart.

He was trembling now with annoyance. Why did she seem so abstracted? He did not know how he could begin. Was she annoyed, too, about something? If she would only turn to him or come to him of her own accord! To take her as she was would be brutal. No, he must see some ardour in her eyes first. He longed to be master of her strange mood.

—When did you lend him the pound? she asked, after a pause.

Gabriel strove to restrain himself from breaking out into brutal language about the sottish Malins and his pound. He longed to cry to her from his soul, to crush her body against his, to overmaster her. But he said:

—O, at Christmas, when he opened that little Christmas-card shop in Henry Street.

He was in such a fever of rage and desire that he did not hear her come from the window. She stood before him for an instant, looking at him strangely. Then, suddenly raising herself on tiptoe and resting her hands lightly on his shoulders, she kissed him.

—You are a very generous person, Gabriel, she said.

Gabriel, trembling with delight at her sudden kiss and at the quaintness of her phrase, put his hands on her hair and began smoothing it back, scarcely touching it with his fingers. The washing had made it fine and brilliant. His heart was brimming over with happiness. Just when he was wishing for it she had come to him of her own accord. Perhaps her thoughts had been running with his. Perhaps she had felt the impetuous desire that was in him and then the yielding mood had come upon her. Now that she had fallen to him so easily he wondered why he had been so diffident.

He stood, holding her head between his hands. Then, slipping one arm swiftly about her body and drawing her towards him, he said softly:

—Gretta dear, what are you thinking about?

She did not answer nor yield wholly to his arm. He said again, softly:

—Tell me what it is, Gretta. I think I know what is the matter. Do I know?

She did not answer at once. Then she said in an outburst of tears:

—O, I am thinking about that song, *The Lass of Aughrim.*

She broke loose from him and ran to the bed and, throwing her arms across the bed-rail, hid her face. Gabriel stood stock-still for a moment in astonishment and then followed her. As he passed in the way of the cheval-glass he caught sight of himself in full length, his broad, well-filled shirt-front, the face whose expression always puzzled him when he saw it in a mirror, and his glimmering gilt-rimmed eyeglasses. He halted a few paces from her and said:

—What about the song? Why does that make you cry?

She raised her head from her arms and dried her eyes with the back of her hand like a child. A kinder note than he had intended went into his voice.

—Why, Gretta? he asked.

—I am thinking about a person long ago who used to sing that song.

—And who was the person long ago? asked Gabriel, smiling.

—It was a person I used to know in Galway when I was living with my grandmother, she said.

The smile passed away from Gabriel's face. A dull anger began to gather again at the back of his mind and the dull fires of his lust began to glow angrily in his veins.

—Someone you were in love with? he asked ironically.

—It was a young boy I used to know, she answered, named Michael Furey. He used to sing that song, *The Lass of Aughrim.* He was very delicate.

Gabriel was silent. He did not wish her to think that he was interested in this delicate boy.

—I can see him so plainly, she said after a moment. Such eyes as he had: big dark eyes! And such an expression in them—an expression!

—O, then, you were in love with him? said Gabriel.

—I used to go out walking with him, she said, when I was in Galway.

A thought flew across Gabriel's mind.

—Perhaps that was why you wanted to go to Galway with that Ivors girl? he said coldly.

She looked at him and asked in surprise:

—What for?

Her eyes made Gabriel feel awkward. He shrugged his shoulders and said:

—How do I know? To see him perhaps.

She looked away from him along the shaft of light towards the window in silence.

—He is dead, she said at length. He died when he was only seventeen. Isn't it a terrible thing to die so young as that?

—What was he? asked Gabriel, still ironically.

—He was in the gasworks, she said.

Gabriel felt humiliated by the failure of his irony and by the evocation of this figure from the dead, a boy in the gasworks. While he had been full of memories of their secret life together, full of tenderness and joy and desire, she had been comparing him in her mind with another. A shameful consciousness of his own person assailed him. He saw himself as a ludicrous figure, acting as a pennyboy[34] for his aunts, a nervous well-meaning sentimentalist, orating to vulgarians and idealising his own clownish lusts, the pitiable fatuous fellow he had caught a glimpse of in the mirror. Instinctively he turned his back more to the light lest she might see the shame that burned upon his forehead.

He tried to keep up his tone of cold interrogation but his voice when he spoke was humble and indifferent.

—I suppose you were in love with this Michael Furey, Gretta, he said.

—I was great with him at that time, she said.

Her voice was veiled and sad. Gabriel, feeling now how vain it would be to try to lead her whither he had purposed, caressed one of her hands and said, also sadly:

—And what did he die of so young, Gretta? Consumption, was it?

—I think he died for me, she answered.

A vague terror seized Gabriel at this answer as if, at that hour when he had hoped to triumph, some impalpable and vindictive being was coming against him, gathering forces against him in its vague world. But he shook himself free of it with an effort of reason and continued to caress her hand. He did not question her again for he felt that she would tell him of herself. Her hand was warm and moist: it did not respond to his touch but he continued to caress it just as he had caressed her first letter to him that spring morning.

—It was in the winter, she said, about the beginning of the winter when I was going to leave my grandmother's and come up here to the convent. And he was ill at the time in his lodgings in Galway and wouldn't be let out and his people in Oughterard were written to. He was in decline, they said, or something like that. I never knew rightly.

She paused for a moment and sighed.

—Poor fellow, she said. He was very fond of me and he was such a gentle boy. We used to go out together, walking, you know, Gabriel, like the way they do in the country. He was going to study singing only for his health. He had a very good voice, poor Michael Furey.

—Well; and then? asked Gabriel.

—And then when it came to the time for me to leave Galway and come up to the convent he was much worse and I wouldn't be let see him so I wrote a letter saying I was going up to Dublin and would be back in the summer and hoping he would be better then.

She paused for a moment to get her voice under control and then went on:

—Then the night before I left I was in my grandmother's house in Nuns' Island, packing up, and I heard gravel thrown up against the window. The window was so wet I couldn't see so I ran downstairs as I was and slipped out the back into the garden and there was the poor fellow at the end of the garden, shivering.

—And did you not tell him to go back? asked Gabriel.

---

[34] **pennyboy:** An errand boy, or a cheap entertainer who would sing or dance for spare change.

—I implored him to go home at once and told him he would get his death in the rain. But he said he did not want to live. I can see his eyes as well as well! He was standing at the end of the wall where there was a tree.

—And did he go home? asked Gabriel.

—Yes, he went home. And when I was only a week in the convent he died and he was buried in Oughterard where his people came from. O, the day I heard that, that he was dead!

She stopped, choking with sobs, and, overcome by emotion, flung herself face downward on the bed, sobbing in the quilt. Gabriel held her hand for a moment longer, irresolutely, and then, shy of intruding on her grief, let it fall gently and walked quietly to the window.

She was fast asleep.

Gabriel, leaning on his elbow, looked for a few moments unresentfully on her tangled hair and half-open mouth, listening to her deep-drawn breath. So she had had that romance in her life: a man had died for her sake. It hardly pained him now to think how poor a part he, her husband, had played in her life. He watched her while she slept as though he and she had never lived together as man and wife. His curious eyes rested long upon her face and on her hair: and, as he thought of what she must have been then, in that time of her first girlish beauty, a strange friendly pity for her entered his soul. He did not like to say even to himself that her face was no longer beautiful but he knew that it was no longer the face for which Michael Furey had braved death.

Perhaps she had not told him all the story. His eyes moved to the chair over which she had thrown some of her clothes. A petticoat string dangled to the floor. One boot stood upright, its limp upper fallen down: the fellow of it lay upon its side. He wondered at his riot of emotions of an hour before. From what had it proceeded? From his aunt's supper, from his own foolish speech, from the wine and dancing, the merry-making when saying good-night in the hall, the pleasure of the walk along the river in the snow. Poor Aunt Julia! She, too, would soon be a shade with the shade of Patrick Morkan and his horse. He had caught that haggard look upon her face for a moment when she was singing *Arrayed for the Bridal.* Soon, perhaps, he would be sitting in that same drawing-room, dressed in black, his silk hat on his knees. The blinds would be drawn down and Aunt Kate would be sitting beside him, crying and blowing her nose and telling him how Julia had died. He would cast about his mind for some words that might console her, and would find only lame and useless ones. Yes, yes: that would happen very soon.

The air of the room chilled his shoulders. He stretched himself cautiously along under the sheets and lay down beside his wife. One by one they were all becoming shades. Better pass boldly into that other world, in the full glory of some passion, than fade and wither dismally with age. He thought of how she who lay beside him had locked in her heart for so many years that image of her lover's eyes when he had told her that he did not wish to live.

Generous tears filled Gabriel's eyes. He had never felt like that himself towards any woman but he knew that such a feeling must be love. The tears gathered more thickly in his eyes and in the partial darkness he imagined he saw the form of a young man standing under a dripping tree. Other forms were near. His soul had approached that region where dwell the vast hosts of the dead. He was conscious of, but could not apprehend, their wayward and flickering existence. His own identity was fading out into a grey impalpable world: the solid world itself which these dead had one time reared and lived in was dissolving and dwindling.

A few light taps upon the pane made him turn to the window. It had begun to snow again. He watched sleepily the flakes, silver and dark, falling obliquely against the lamplight. The time had come for him to set out on his journey westward. Yes, the newspapers were right: snow was general all over Ireland. It was falling on every part of the dark central plain, on the treeless hills, falling softly upon the Bog of Allen and, farther westward, softly falling into the dark mutinous Shannon waves. It was falling, too, upon every part of the lonely churchyard on the hill where Michael Furey lay buried. It lay thickly drifted on the crooked crosses and headstones, on the spears of the little gate, on the barren thorns. His soul swooned slowly as he heard the snow falling faintly through the universe and faintly falling, like the descent of their last end, upon all the living and the dead.

✍ VIRGINIA WOOLF
B. ENGLAND, 1882–1941

Virginia Woolf, 1929
Woolf at age forty-seven. (Hulton / Archive)

Virginia Woolf's novels break away from early-twentieth-century literary conventions to reflect women's thought patterns, viewpoints, and sense of time. Although in her private life Woolf avoided Freudian analysis,[1] in her fiction she advanced the MODERNIST narrative techniques of STREAM OF CONSCIOUSNESS and SYMBOLISM that drew heavily on Freud's theories, and she and her husband, Leonard Woolf, made Freud's works widely available in English translation through their Hogarth Press. Though wary like many of her female contemporaries of being labeled a "feminist," Woolf wrote two volumes of pioneering feminist essays exploring women's creativity and the factors that might inhibit it.

Virginia Woolf is too often remembered not for her accomplishments but for the intermittent mental illness that ultimately led to her suicide during the dark days of early World War II. Woolf was much more than her illness and her death: a woman with a genius for friendship; in her own, soft-spoken manner, a feminist; a devoted wife and partner; and above all, a brilliant, innovative writer who was by turns playful, philosophical, lyrical, analytical, sensuous, affectionate, perceptive, and fiercely life-affirming.

---

[1]**Freudian analysis:** Sigmund Freud (1856–1939) is the father of psychoanalysis.

A Stimulating Childhood.   Adeline Virginia Stephen was born in London on January 25, 1882, the third child and second daughter of Leslie and Julia Princep Stephen. Woolf and her older sister, Vanessa, were close companions all their lives, and Virginia adored her older brother, Thoby. A younger brother, Adrian, was born in 1883. Both parents had been previously married and widowed, and Woolf had half siblings on both sides of the family. The children of her mother's first marriage—Stella, George, and Gerald Duckworth—were to figure importantly in Woolf's early life.

Woolf's father was the epitome of the eminent VICTORIAN.[2] Not wealthy but sufficiently well-off, he was a literary man—a critic, scholar, magazine editor, and biographer. Woolf's mother, Julia Stephen, was celebrated for her lively charm and her perfect profile, and Virginia was the uneasy heir of her mother's beauty. The Duckworth and Stephen children grew up in the heady intellectual atmosphere of a household that regularly entertained such luminaries of late Victorian culture as the writers Alfred, Lord Tennyson; Henry James; and George Meredith;[3] the painters Holman Hunt and Edward Burne-Jones; and the actress Ellen Terry.[4] Woolf's great-aunt on her mother's side was the pioneering photographer Julia Cameron.

There were pleasures and injuries in this upbringing, especially during the summers spent in the family's country house on the Cornwall coast, and, overall, Woolf described her early family experience as "tangled and matted with emotion." The most sinister element was the sexual abuse she and Vanessa suffered at the hands of their two Duckworth half brothers in childhood and adolescence. As an adult Woolf wrote of the abuse, but like many victims she seems never to have connected the past abuse with her problems in adulthood, namely her sexual frigidity and her mental illness. Instead, she concluded that she was born naturally deficient in sensuality and mental health.

Like most girls of their social class, Woolf and her sister were tutored at home by their mother and a series of governesses. Formal education was reserved for boys, but Leslie Stephen was wise enough to discern his daughter Virginia's gifts. When she asked to learn ancient Greek, he was happy to hire a tutor. He allowed her to read any book in his library and enjoyed discussing literature with her. Her mother imparted a different sort of influence, imbued as she was with the Victorian ideal that women fulfilled their highest natures by serving others cheerfully. When grown, Woolf would characterize that ideal as "The Angel in the House" and identify it as the dangerous spirit that keeps women from expressing themselves, making them intent on pleasing men rather than being true to their own natures and talents.

www For links to more information about Woolf, a quiz on *A Room of One's Own,* and information about the culture and context of twentieth-century Europe, see *World Literature Online* at bedfordstmartins .com/worldlit.

---

[2] **Victorian:** In English history, "Victorian" refers to the age of Queen Victoria (r. 1837–1901) and the values of respectability, conservatism, and prudery.

[3] **Tennyson . . . Meredith:** Alfred, Lord Tennyson (1809–1892) was poet laureate of England. Henry James (1843–1916) was an American novelist. George Meredith (1828–1909) was an English novelist and poet.

[4] **Hunt . . . Terry:** Holman Hunt (1827–1910) was an English painter. Edward Burne-Jones (1833–1898) was an English painter and designer. Ellen Terry (1848–1928) was a renowned English actress.

Death and Depression.   More traumatic events marred Woolf's adolescence, beginning with the sudden death of her mother when Virginia was thirteen. Her much-beloved half sister, Stella Duckworth, became the maternal figure for her stepfamily, but a scant two years later, while honeymooning with her new husband, she too died, of a sudden acute infection. Virginia's father grew more and more depressed and withdrawn, and Virginia and Vanessa had to run the household until his death in 1904. Although Virginia's grief for him was enough to precipitate a second breakdown — the first occurred after her mother's death — his death eventually freed her. She began teaching at a night school for working-class people, joined the suffrage movement, and wrote book reviews.

By 1905, Thoby, Vanessa, Virginia, and Adrian Stephen had moved together into a flat in the Bloomsbury section of London and began keeping lively company with Thoby's friends, a household arrangement that lasted until Thoby's death of typhoid fever the following year. Many of the brilliant men who came to the Stephen children's home were members of a society at Cambridge called the Apostles. Most were on their way to becoming the intellectual lights of their generation. Many were bisexual or gay, and their uninhibited discussions often centered on sexuality as well as art and politics. Eventually their circle, called "Bloomsbury" by social historians, included historian Lytton Strachey; economic theorist John Maynard Keynes; novelist E. M. Forster; art critic Roger Fry; artist and art critic Clive Bell,[5] whom Vanessa would marry in 1907; and civil administrator Leonard Woolf, later a policy developer for the Labour party who became Virginia's husband in 1912.

Creating a Space for Writing.   For Virginia Stephen, Leonard Woolf proved the wisest choice she could have made. Always held as something of an outsider because he was Jewish, Leonard provided for Virginia a slight distancing from the intense, intellectual involvements of Bloomsbury. For the rest of his life, his real occupation would be to care tenderly for his wife, nursing her through her terrifying bouts of illness, arranging her life, protecting and supporting her, and keeping her as well and productive as possible. Leonard Woolf's presence enabled his wife to write; it was only after their marriage that she managed to complete her first novel, *The Voyage Out* (1915), which she had begun in 1907. With *Jacob's Room* (1922), Woolf began to experiment with subject and narrative form. In her next novel, *Mrs. Dalloway* (1925), Woolf centered on a single day in the lives of a London society woman and a shell-shocked veteran of World War I.

---

[5] **Strachey . . . Bell:** Bloomsbury began as a social group, but through its members' writings developed into a cultural force that broke free from Victorian restrictions. Lytton Strachey (1880–1932) wrote biographies. John Maynard Keynes (1883–1946) became known for Keynesian economics, which involves government control of interest and tax rates. E. M. Forster (1879–1970) wrote very important novels about the English middle class, including *A Passage to India* (1924). Roger Fry (1866–1934) was an art critic who championed Cézanne and other French painters. Clive Bell (1881–1964) was an art critic whose books include *Landmarks in Nineteenth-Century Painting* (1927).

Until she was forty-four and had written *To the Lighthouse* (1927), whose main character, Mrs. Ramsey, is based on her mother, Woolf was literally haunted by the apparition and voice of Julia Stephen. The ebullient tour de force, *Orlando* (1928), was inspired by Woolf's delight in her adventurous cross-dressing friend, Vita Sackville-West. *Orlando*'s protagonist begins as a male adolescent in Elizabethan England, undergoes a mysterious sex change around the time of the Restoration, and while still in her thirties and a woman, ends up as a successful female writer in contemporary London. In 1928, Woolf delivered the lectures on women and creativity at Newnham College, Cambridge, that would become *A Room of One's Own* (1929), excerpts of which are presented here. With her next book, *The Waves* (1931), Woolf's work began to grow less exuberant, reflecting her difficulty in the last decade of her life of maintaining the mental health necessary to write.

One offshoot of Woolf's long quest for health was the establishment of Hogarth Press, originally conceived as a project that would engage Virginia in simple therapeutic tasks such as typesetting and bookbinding. The press, however, became a commercial and artistic success, publishing authors such as Katherine Mansfield[6] and T. S. Eliot[7] as well as the Woolfs' own work. Leonard Woolf's greatest literary achievement would prove to be the sensitive, detailed memoirs and diaries in which he chronicled his and Virginia's years together. Despite at least one significant affair between Virginia and another woman—the flamboyant Sackville-West—the Woolfs remained a devoted couple from the time of their marriage until Virginia's death twenty-nine years later. Together she and Leonard wrote and ran Hogarth Press when she was well; and together they contrived to get her through the major breakdowns that came regularly with the completion of each book.

Virginia's Suicide.   In March 1941, anguished by the death of a favorite nephew in the Spanish civil war and by the Nazi bombings that destroyed both her and Leonard's London house and the building that housed Hogarth Press, Virginia feared that she was about to undergo a permanent breakdown that would leave her a burden to her husband. On March 28, she weighted her pockets with heavy stones and waded into the River Ouse below their country house in Sussex. After her body was recovered, Leonard buried Virginia's ashes beneath one of the great elms there and chose for her epitaph a sentence from *The Waves* (1931): "Against you I will fling myself, unvanquished and unyielding, O Death!"

New Directions for the Novel.   Both *The Voyage Out* and Woolf's second novel, *Night and Day* (1919), are relatively conventional novels about young women not unlike herself exploring questions of marriage and art. *Jacob's Room*, which is about a young man who resembles Virginia's

Something, she meant, is immune from change, and shines out (she glanced at the window with its ripple of reflected lights) in the face of the flowing, the fleeting, the spectral, like a ruby; so that again tonight she had the feeling she had had once today, already, of peace, of rest. Of such moments, she thought, the thing is made that endures.

– VIRGINIA WOOLF, *To the Lighthouse*, 1927

---

[6] **Katherine Mansfield** (1888–1923): A short-story writer born in New Zealand.

[7] **T. S. Eliot** (1888–1965): An American-born poet who moved to England; he gave expression to the destruction of World War I with his startling poem *The Waste Land* (1922). See page 473.

Life is not a series of gig lamps symmetrically arranged; but a luminous halo, a semitransparent envelope surrounding us from the beginning of consciousness to the end. Is it not the task of the novelist to convey this varying, this unknown and uncircumscribed spirit, whatever aberration or complexity it may display, with as little mixture of the alien and external as possible?

– VIRGINIA WOOLF, 1925

brother, Thoby, represents a stylistic departure; it does not present the major incidents in the protagonist's life either chronologically or directly—we learn of Jacob's death only by way of his mother's cleaning out his room and wondering how to dispose of his personal effects. The main theme seems to be the impossibility of truly knowing the inner workings of Jacob or any other person. *Mrs. Dalloway* furthers the experimentation with the stream-of-consciousness technique. Woolf moves the narrative point of view back and forth between Mrs. Dalloway and the person who is in some sense her alter ego, one a sane and the other an insane character, gradually revealing the deep similarities between them, although they never meet. In the lyrical, semiautobiographical *To the Lighthouse* (1927), the novel that was to exorcise her mother's presence, Woolf explores the theme of women's roles while continuing to advance the stream-of-consciousness narrative technique by using an impressionistic sense of time rather than the hours of a day.

Thought by many to be her masterpiece, *The Waves* is Woolf's most experimental novel, with six different characters' stream-of-consciousness monologues all meditating on the death of a friend they hold in common, a character again modeled on Thoby. *The Years* (1937) brought Woolf her first wide popularity, setting forth the history of an upper-class English family, from the late Victorian age to the present. As political events in Europe darkened, she wrote *I Take Three Guineas* (1938), a brilliant feminist and pacifist work in which she explores the connections between FASCISM and the patriarchy in which she had been raised. Not surprisingly, the book received many negative reviews as a tract for what E. M. Forster called "extreme feminism." *Between the Acts* (1941), the book Woolf finished drafting just before her death, is a complex narrative: Neighboring families in the country anticipate and then attend a village pageant. The work considers issues of time, history, loss, and the question of what endures despite and beyond them.

A Room of One's Own.   In the following chapter from *A Room of One's Own* (1929), Woolf's imagining of the fate of the fictional Judith Shakespeare begins after the narrator returns home frustrated after a visit to the British Museum library, where she has been unable to find any text to help her understand why women have not achieved equality with men. She is desperate to account for the disparity, but none of the books helps. Glancing through her own copy of Trevelyan's *History of England,* the narrator sees that women are all but excised from history, save for the most cursory and condescending references, and she understands that she will need to fashion for herself a model of what life might have been like for an Elizabethan woman with Shakespeare's gifts. The sensuous detail with which Woolf fleshes out this sadly predictable story and the beautifully controlled tone in which she tells it are essayist and feminist Virginia Woolf at her best.

"Three Pictures" and "The Fascination of the Pool."   The second piece that follows, "Three Pictures," was published in *The Death of the Moth* (1942) after Woolf's death. In it Woolf imaginatively discusses three pictures, creating a thin line between essay and fiction. By using the metaphor of pictures and how "we must needs be pictures to each other," Woolf illustrates the layers of reality that lie beneath surface impressions, the difference between appearance and reality, and how difficult it is to penetrate beneath the "picture" and really know another person and his or her situation.

In "The Fascination of the Pool," Woolf uses the metaphor of a pool to explore the meanderings of memory, the ways that thoughts become layered in the mind and shift from one story to another; as Woolf says, beneath the surface of the water "went on some profound under-water life like the brooding, the ruminating of a mind." The mind contains bits of experiences that in their disembodied state float freely through the "water" of consciousness. When these pieces join together, individuals emerge with their kernels of history and intersecting stories. In the third paragraph, time itself becomes layered with meaning. We long to get to the bottom of the pool, to finally understand all the voices, and at times it seems as if we actually approach this possibility, only to have the moment slip away.

■ CONNECTIONS

Kawabata Yasunari, "The Moon on the Water," p. 659. Modern writers use such metaphors as mirrors, pools of water, panes of glass, and ice on a lake for the different layers of reality and for the contrast between appearance and reality. In "The Moon on the Water" a mirror illustrates the tangential relationships of the story's characters. How does Woolf employ pictures in "Three Pictures" to raise questions about the nature and truthfulness of human perception?

Adrienne Rich, "Diving into the Wreck," p. 996. A number of women writers in the twentieth century promoted the cause of women's liberation and political equality through their writings. Both Rich and Woolf are considered feminists, but their ideas about women's liberation differ, reflecting their respective generations and countries. According to Woolf in the excerpt from *A Room of One's Own,* what does a woman need in order to realize her potential as a human being? How does Rich develop the journey of self-discovery in her poem "Diving into the Wreck"?

Charlotte Perkins Gilman, "The Yellow Wallpaper" (Book 5). An artist can symbolize the limitations of psychological space through constricted physical space. Perkins Gilman brilliantly uses a wall and wallpaper to circumscribe the mental realm of her narrator. What are the several meanings of "room" in the excerpt from Woolf's *A Room of One's Own?*

■ FURTHER RESEARCH

Biography
Bell, Quentin. *Virginia Woolf.* 1972.
Reid, Panthea. *Art and Affection: A Life of Virginia Woolf.* 1996.
Rose, Phyllis. *Woman of Letters: A Life of Virginia Woolf.* 1978.

Bibliography
Dick, Susan. *The Complete Shorter Fiction of Virginia Woolf.* 1989.
Kirkpatrick, B. J. *A Bibliography of Virginia Woolf.* 1997.

History and Culture

Bell, Quentin. *Bloomsbury.* 1968.

Laurence, Patricia Ondek. *The Reading of Silence: Virginia Woolf in the English Tradition.*
1991.

Todd, Pamela. *Bloomsbury at Home.* 1999.

Criticism

Clements, Patricia, and Isobel Grundy, eds. *Virginia Woolf: New Critical Essays.* 1983.

Homans, Margaret, ed. *Virginia Woolf: A Collection of Critical Essays.* 1993.

Nalbantian, Suzanne. *Aesthetic Autobiography: From Life to Art in Marcel Proust, James
Joyce, Virginia Woolf, and Anaïs Nin.* 1994.

❧ A Room of One's Own

CHAPTER 3 [SHAKESPEARE'S SISTER][1]

It was disappointing not to have brought back in the evening some important statement, some authentic fact. Women are poorer than men because—this or that. Perhaps now it would be better to give up seeking for the truth, and receiving on one's
head an avalanche of opinion hot as lava, discoloured as dish-water. It would be better to draw the curtains; to shut out distractions; to light the lamp; to narrow the
enquiry and to ask the historian, who records not opinions but facts, to describe
under what conditions women lived, not throughout the ages, but in England, say in
the time of Elizabeth.

For it is a perennial puzzle why no woman wrote a word of that extraordinary
literature when every other man, it seemed, was capable of song or sonnet. What
were the conditions in which women lived, I asked myself; for fiction, imaginative
work that is, is not dropped like a pebble upon the ground, as science may be; fiction
is like a spider's web, attached ever so lightly perhaps, but still attached to life at all
four corners. Often the attachment is scarcely perceptible; Shakespeare's plays, for
instance, seem to hang there complete by themselves. But when the web is pulled

---

A Room of One's Own. Published in 1929, this work as a whole is concerned with the second-class
role of women in modern society. From its title has come the now-popular idea that a woman
writer needs "a room of her own" to pursue her calling. In the chapter reprinted here, Woolf
returns frustrated from the British Museum library, wondering about the absence of women in
literate culture. In her copy of Trevelyan's *History of England,* she discovers that women have been
largely excluded from history. Woolf must then create a suitable context for her fictional Judith
Shakespeare.

All notes are the editors' unless otherwise indicated.

---

[1]Woolf has just returned from the library of the British Museum, where she has had no success in finding
books that might help her understand why women seem to have achieved so much less than men throughout
history.

askew, hooked up at the edge, torn in the middle, one remembers that these webs are not spun in mid-air by incorporeal creatures, but are the work of suffering human beings, and are attached to grossly material things, like health and money and the houses we live in.

I went, therefore, to the shelf where the histories stand and took down one of the latest, Professor Trevelyan's *History of England*.[2] Once more I looked up Women, found "position of," and turned to the pages indicated. "Wife-beating," I read, "was a recognised right of man, and was practised without shame by high as well as low. . . . Similarly," the historian goes on, "the daughter who refused to marry the gentleman of her parents' choice was liable to be locked up, beaten and flung about the room, without any shock being inflicted on public opinion. Marriage was not an affair of personal affection, but of family avarice, particularly in the 'chivalrous' upper classes. . . . Betrothal often took place while one or both of the parties was in the cradle, and marriage when they were scarcely out of the nurses' charge." That was about 1470, soon after Chaucer's time. The next reference to the position of women is some two hundred years later, in the time of the Stuarts. "It was still the exception for women of the upper and middle class to choose their own husbands, and when the husband had been assigned, he was lord and master, so far at least as law and custom could make him. Yet even so," Professor Trevelyan concludes, "neither Shakespeare's women nor those of authentic seventeenth-century memoirs, like the Verneys and the Hutchinsons,[3] seem wanting in personality and character." Certainly, if we consider it, Cleopatra must have had a way with her; Lady Macbeth, one would suppose, had a will of her own; Rosalind, one might conclude, was an attractive girl.[4] Professor Trevelyan is speaking no more than the truth when he remarks that Shakespeare's women do not seem wanting in personality and character. Not being a historian, one might go even further and say that women have burnt like beacons in all the works of all the poets from the beginning of time — Clytemnestra, Antigone, Cleopatra, Lady Macbeth, Phèdre, Cressida, Rosalind, Desdemona, the Duchess of Malfi, among the dramatists; then among the prose writers: Millamant, Clarissa, Becky Sharp, Anna Karenina, Emma Bovary, Madame de Guermantes[5] — the names flock to mind, nor do they recall women "lacking in personality and character." Indeed, if woman had no existence save in the fiction written by men, one would imagine her a person of the utmost importance; very various; heroic and mean; splendid and sordid; infinitely beautiful and hideous in the extreme; as great

---

[2] *History of England:* G. M. Trevelyan's *History of England* (1926) was, in Woolf's day, the most popular short history of the nation.

[3] Verneys . . . Hutchinsons: Authors of family memoirs of seventeenth-century England.

[4] Cleopatra . . . girl: Shakespeare's heroines from the plays *Antony and Cleopatra, Macbeth,* and *As You Like It,* respectively. Woolf is using the irony of understatement here.

[5] Clytemnestra . . . Guermantes: All are famous women characters from drama and fiction. In order, they are from Aeschylus's *Agamemnon;* Sophocles' *Antigone;* Shakespeare's *Antony and Cleopatra* and *Macbeth;* Racine's *Phèdre;* Shakespeare's *Troilus and Cressida, As You Like It,* and *Othello;* Webster's *The Duchess of Malfi;* Congreve's *The Way of the World;* Richardson's *Clarissa;* Thackeray's *Vanity Fair;* Tolstoy's *Anna Karenina;* Flaubert's *Madame Bovary;* and Proust's *Remembrance of Things Past.*

as a man, some think even greater.[6] But this is woman in fiction. In fact, as Professor Trevelyan points out, she was locked up, beaten and flung about the room.

A very queer, composite being thus emerges. Imaginatively she is of the highest importance; practically she is completely insignificant. She pervades poetry from cover to cover; she is all but absent from history. She dominates the lives of kings and conquerors in fiction; in fact she was the slave of any boy whose parents forced a ring upon her finger. Some of the most inspired words, some of the most profound thoughts in literature fall from her lips; in real life she could hardly read, could scarcely spell, and was the property of her husband.

It was certainly an odd monster that one made up by reading the historians first and the poets afterwards—a worm winged like an eagle; the spirit of life and beauty in a kitchen chopping up suet. But these monsters, however amusing to the imagination, have no existence in fact. What one must do to bring her to life was to think poetically and prosaically at one and the same moment, thus keeping in touch with fact—that she is Mrs. Martin, aged thirty-six, dressed in blue, wearing a black hat and brown shoes; but not losing sight of fiction either—that she is a vessel in which all sorts of spirits and forces are coursing and flashing perpetually. The moment, however, that one tries this method with the Elizabethan woman, one branch of illumination fails; one is held up by the scarcity of facts. One knows nothing detailed, nothing perfectly true and substantial about her. History scarcely mentions her. And I turned to Professor Trevelyan again to see what history meant to him. I found by looking at his chapter headings that it meant—

"The Manor Court and the Methods of Open-field Agriculture . . . The Cistercians and Sheep-farming . . . The Crusades . . . The University . . . The House of Commons . . . The Hundred Years' War . . . The Wars of the Roses . . . The Renaissance Scholars . . . The Dissolution of the Monasteries . . . Agrarian and Religious Strife . . . The Origin of English Sea-power . . . The Armada . . ." and so on. Occasionally an individual woman is mentioned, an Elizabeth, or a Mary; a queen or a great lady. But by no possible means could middle-class women with nothing but brains and character at their command have taken part in any one of the great movements which, brought together, constitute the historian's view of the past. Nor shall we find her in any collection of anecdotes. Aubrey[7] hardly mentions her. She

---

[6] **a person of . . . even greater:** "It remains a strange and almost inexplicable fact that in Athena's city, where women were kept in almost Oriental suppression as odalisques or drudges, the stage should yet have produced figures like Clytemnestra and Cassandra, Atossa and Antigone, Phèdre and Medea, and all the other heroines who dominate play after play of the 'misogynist' Euripides. But the paradox of this world where in real life a respectable woman could hardly show her face alone in the street, and yet on the stage woman equals or surpasses man, has never been satisfactorily explained. In modern tragedy the same predominance exists. At all events, a very cursory survey of Shakespeare's work (similarly with Webster, though not with Marlowe or Jonson) suffices to reveal how this dominance, this initiative of women, persists from Rosalind to Lady Macbeth. So too in Racine; six of his tragedies bear their heroines' names; and what male characters of his shall we set against Hermione and Andromaque, Bérénice and Roxane, Phèdre and Athalie? So again with Ibsen; what men shall we match with Solveig and Nora, Hedda and Hilda Wangel and Rebecca West?"—F. L. Lucas, *Tragedy,* pp. 114–15. [Woolf's note.]

[7] **Aubrey:** John Aubrey (1626–1697) was a British diarist.

never writes her own life and scarcely keeps a diary; there are only a handful of her letters in existence. She left no plays or poems by which we can judge her. What one wants, I thought — and why does not some brilliant student at Newnham or Girton[8] supply it? — is a mass of information; at what age did she marry; how many children had she as a rule; what was her house like; had she a room to herself; did she do the cooking; would she be likely to have a servant? All these facts lie somewhere, presumably, in parish registers and account books; the life of the average Elizabethan woman must be scattered about somewhere, could one collect it and make a book of it. It would be ambitious beyond my daring, I thought, looking about the shelves for books that were not there, to suggest to the students of those famous colleges that they should rewrite history, though I own that it often seems a little queer as it is, unreal, lopsided; but why should they not add a supplement to history? calling it, of course, by some inconspicuous name so that women might figure there without impropriety? For one often catches a glimpse of them in the lives of the great, whisking away into the background, concealing, I sometimes think, a wink, a laugh, perhaps a tear. And, after all, we have lives enough of Jane Austen; it scarcely seems necessary to consider again the influence of the tragedies of Joanna Baillie upon the poetry of Edgar Allan Poe;[9] as for myself, I should not mind if the homes and haunts of Mary Russell Mitford[10] were closed to the public for a century at least. But what I find deplorable, I continued, looking about the bookshelves again, is that nothing is known about women before the eighteenth century. I have no model in my mind to turn about this way and that. Here am I asking why women did not write poetry in the Elizabethan age, and I am not sure how they were educated; whether they were taught to write; whether they had sitting-rooms to themselves; how many women had children before they were twenty-one; what, in short, they did from eight in the morning till eight at night. They had no money evidently; according to Professor Trevelyan they were married whether they liked it or not before they were out of the nursery, at fifteen or sixteen very likely. It would have been extremely odd, even upon this showing, had one of them suddenly written the plays of Shakespeare, I concluded, and I thought of that old gentleman, who is dead now, but was a bishop, I think, who declared that it was impossible for any woman, past, present, or to come, to have the genius of Shakespeare. He wrote to the papers about it. He also told a lady who applied to him for information that cats do not as a matter of fact go to heaven, though they have, he added, souls of a sort. How much thinking those old gentlemen used to save one! How the borders of ignorance shrank back at their approach! Cats do not go to heaven. Women cannot write the plays of Shakespeare.

Be that as it may, I could not help thinking, as I looked at the works of Shakespeare on the shelf, that the bishop was right at least in this; it would have been impossible, completely and entirely, for any woman to have written the plays of

---

[8] **Newnham or Girton:** Women's colleges of Cambridge University.

[9] **Baillie . . . Poe:** Baillie was an English dramatist (1762–1851); Edgar Allan Poe (1809–1849) was an American poet and fiction writer.

[10] **Mitford:** Mary Russell Mitford (1787–1855) wrote accounts of life in the English countryside.

Shakespeare in the age of Shakespeare. Let me imagine, since facts are so hard to come by, what would have happened had Shakespeare had a wonderfully gifted sister, called Judith, let us say. Shakespeare himself went, very probably—his mother was an heiress—to the grammar school, where he may have learnt Latin—Ovid, Virgil, and Horace[11]—and the elements of grammar and logic. He was, it is well known, a wild boy who poached rabbits, perhaps shot a deer, and had, rather sooner than he should have done, to marry a woman in the neighbourhood, who bore him a child rather quicker than was right. That escapade sent him to seek his fortune in London. He had, it seemed, a taste for the theatre; he began by holding horses at the stage door. Very soon he got work in the theatre, became a successful actor, and lived at the hub of the universe, meeting everybody, knowing everybody, practising his art on the boards, exercising his wits in the streets, and even getting access to the palace of the queen. Meanwhile his extraordinarily gifted sister, let us suppose, remained at home. She was as adventurous, as imaginative, as agog to see the world as he was. But she was not sent to school. She had no chance of learning grammar and logic, let alone of reading Horace and Virgil. She picked up a book now and then, one of her brother's perhaps, and read a few pages. But then her parents came in and told her to mend the stockings or mind the stew and not moon about with books and papers. They would have spoken sharply but kindly, for they were substantial people who knew the conditions of life for a woman and loved their daughter—indeed, more likely than not she was the apple of her father's eye. Perhaps she scribbled some pages up in an apple loft on the sly, but was careful to hide them or set fire to them. Soon, however, before she was out of her teens, she was to be betrothed to the son of a neighbouring wool-stapler.[12] She cried out that marriage was hateful to her, and for that she was severely beaten by her father. Then he ceased to scold her. He begged her instead not to hurt him, not to shame him in this matter of her marriage. He would give her a chain of beads or a fine petticoat, he said; and there were tears in his eyes. How could she disobey him? How could she break his heart? The force of her own gift alone drove her to it. She made up a small parcel of her belongings, let herself down by a rope one summer's night and took the road to London. She was not seventeen. The birds that sang in the hedge were not more musical than she was. She had the quickest fancy, a gift like her brother's, for the tune of words. Like him, she had a taste for the theatre. She stood at the stage door; she wanted to act, she said. Men laughed in her face. The manager—a fat, loose-lipped man—guffawed. He bellowed something about poodles dancing and women acting—no woman, he said, could possibly be an actress. He hinted—you can imagine what. She could get no training in her craft. Could she even seek her dinner in a tavern or roam the streets at midnight? Yet her genius was for fiction and lusted to feed abundantly upon the lives of men and women and the study of their ways. At last—for she was very young, oddly like Shakespeare the poet in her face, with the same grey eyes and rounded brows—at last Nick Greene the actor-manager took pity on her; she found

---

[11] **Ovid . . . Horace:** Great Roman poets of the Augustan Age, standard fare for any schoolboy learning Latin.

[12] **wool-stapler:** Wool-dealer.

herself with child by that gentleman and so—who shall measure the heat and violence of the poet's heart when caught and tangled in a woman's body?—killed herself one winter's night and lies buried at some crossroads where the omnibuses now stop outside the Elephant and Castle.[13]

That, more or less, is how the story would run, I think, if a woman in Shakespeare's day had had Shakespeare's genius. But for my part, I agree with the deceased bishop, if such he was—it is unthinkable that any woman in Shakespeare's day should have had Shakespeare's genius. For genius like Shakespeare's is not born among labouring, uneducated, servile people. It was not born in England among the Saxons and the Britons. It is not born today among the working classes. How, then, could it have been born among women whose work began, according to Professor Trevelyan, almost before they were out of the nursery, who were forced to it by their parents and held to it by all the power of law and custom? Yet genius of a sort must have existed among women as it must have existed among the working classes. Now and again an Emily Brontë or a Robert Burns[14] blazes out and proves its presence. But certainly it never got itself on to paper. When, however, one reads of a witch being ducked, of a woman possessed by devils, of a wise woman selling herbs, or even of a very remarkable man who had a mother, then I think we are on the track of a lost novelist, a suppressed poet, of some mute and inglorious Jane Austen, some Emily Brontë who dashed her brains out on the moor or mopped and mowed about the highways crazed with the torture that her gift had put her to. Indeed, I would venture to guess that Anon, who wrote so many poems without signing them, was often a woman. It was a woman Edward Fitzgerald,[15] I think, suggested who made the ballads and the folk-songs, crooning them to her children, beguiling her spinning with them, or the length of the winter's night.

This may be true or it may be false—who can say?—but what is true in it, so it seemed to me, reviewing the story of Shakespeare's sister as I had made it, is that any woman born with a great gift in the sixteenth century would certainly have gone crazed, shot herself, or ended her days in some lonely cottage outside the village, half witch, half wizard, feared and mocked at. For it needs little skill in psychology to be sure that a highly gifted girl who had tried to use her gift for poetry would have been so thwarted and hindered by other people, so tortured and pulled asunder by her own contrary instincts, that she must have lost her health and sanity to a certainty. No girl could have walked to London and stood at a stage door and forced her way into the presence of actor-managers without doing herself a violence and suffering an anguish which may have been irrational—for chastity may be a fetish invented by certain societies for unknown reasons—but were none the less inevitable. Chastity had then, it has even now, a religious importance in a woman's life, and has

---

[13] **Elephant and Castle:** A pub. As a suicide, Judith could not be buried in consecrated ground. Burial at a crossroads was thought to keep the restless spirits of suicides safely in their graves.

[14] **Brontë . . . Burns:** The Scots poet Robert Burns (1759–1796) came from the working class; the novelist Emily Brontë (1818–1848) had been raised as the sheltered and isolated daughter of a country curate.

[15] **Edward Fitzgerald** (1809–1883): A popular poet and translator.

so wrapped itself round with nerves and instincts that to cut it free and bring it to the light of day demands courage of the rarest. To have lived a free life in London in the sixteenth century would have meant for a woman who was poet and playwright a nervous stress and dilemma which might well have killed her. Had she survived, whatever she had written would have been twisted and deformed, issuing from a strained and morbid imagination. And undoubtedly, I thought, looking at the shelf where there are no plays by women, her work would have gone unsigned. That refuge she would have sought certainly. It was the relic of the sense of chastity that dictated anonymity to women even so late as the nineteenth century. Currer Bell, George Eliot, George Sand,[16] all the victims of inner strife as their writings prove, sought ineffectively to veil themselves by using the name of a man. Thus they did homage to the convention, which if not implanted by the other sex was liberally encouraged by them (the chief glory of a woman is not to be talked of, said Pericles,[17] himself a much-talked-of man), that publicity in women is detestable. Anonymity runs in their blood. The desire to be veiled still possesses them. They are not even now as concerned about the health of their fame as men are, and, speaking generally, will pass a tombstone or a signpost without feeling an irresistible desire to cut their names on it, as Alf, Bert, or Chas. must do in obedience to their instinct, which murmurs if it sees a fine woman go by, or even a dog, Ce chien est à moi.[18] And, of course, it may not be a dog, I thought, remembering Parliament Square, the Sièges Allée[19] and other avenues; it may be a piece of land or a man with curly black hair. It is one of the great advantages of being a woman that one can pass even a very fine negress without wishing to make an Englishwoman of her.

That woman, then, who was born with a gift of poetry in the sixteenth century, was an unhappy woman, a woman at strife against herself. All the conditions of her life, all her own instincts, were hostile to the state of mind which is needed to set free whatever is in the brain. But what is the state of mind that is most propitious to the act of creation, I asked. Can one come by any notion of the state that furthers and makes possible that strange activity? Here I opened the volume containing the Tragedies of Shakespeare. What was Shakespeare's state of mind, for instance, when he wrote *Lear* and *Antony and Cleopatra*? It was certainly the state of mind most favourable to poetry that there has ever existed. But Shakespeare himself said nothing about it. We only know casually and by chance that he "never blotted a line."[20] Nothing indeed was ever said by the artist himself about his state of mind until the eighteenth century perhaps. Rousseau perhaps began it. At any rate, by the nineteenth century self-consciousness had developed so far that it was the habit for men

---

[16] **Currer Bell . . . Sand:** The male pen names of the writers Charlotte Brontë, Marian Evans, and Aurore Dupin.

[17] **Pericles** (c. 500–429 B.C.E.): A powerful Athenian statesman.

[18] **Ce chien . . . moi:** "That dog is mine" (French).

[19] **Parliament . . . Allée:** The seats of power of England and France; Woolf sees the root of colonialism in the male desire to possess.

[20] **"never . . . line":** Ben Jonson claimed this in *Timber, or Discoveries* (1691).

of letters to describe their minds in confessions and autobiographies. Their lives also were written, and their letters were printed after their deaths. Thus, though we do not know what Shakespeare went through when he wrote *Lear,* we do know what Carlyle went through when he wrote the *French Revolution;* what Flaubert went through when he wrote *Madame Bovary;* what Keats[21] was going through when he tried to write poetry against the coming of death and the indifference of the world.

And one gathers from this enormous modern literature of confession and self-analysis that to write a work of genius is almost always a feat of prodigious difficulty. Everything is against the likelihood that it will come from the writer's mind whole and entire. Generally material circumstances are against it. Dogs will bark; people will interrupt; money must be made; health will break down. Further, accentuating all these difficulties and making them harder to bear is the world's notorious indifference. It does not ask people to write poems and novels and histories; it does not need them. It does not care whether Flaubert finds the right word or whether Carlyle scrupulously verifies this or that fact. Naturally, it will not pay for what it does not want. And so the writer, Keats, Flaubert, Carlyle, suffers, especially in the creative years of youth, every form of distraction and discouragement. A curse, a cry of agony, rises from those books of analysis and confession. "Mighty poets in their misery dead"[22] — that is the burden of their song. If anything comes through in spite of all this, it is a miracle, and probably no book is born entire and uncrippled as it was conceived.

But for women, I thought, looking at the empty shelves, these difficulties were infinitely more formidable. In the first place, to have a room of her own, let alone a quiet room or a sound-proof room, was out of the question, unless her parents were exceptionally rich or very noble, even up to the beginning of the nineteenth century. Since her pin money, which depended on the good will of her father, was only enough to keep her clothed, she was debarred from such alleviations as came even to Keats or Tennyson or Carlyle, all poor men, from a walking tour, a little journey to France, from the separate lodging which, even if it were miserable enough, sheltered them from the claims and tyrannies of their families. Such material difficulties were formidable; but much worse were the immaterial. The indifference of the world which Keats and Flaubert and other men of genius have found so hard to bear was in her case not indifference but hostility. The world did not say to her as it said to them, Write if you choose; it makes no difference to me. The world said with a guffaw, Write? What's the good of your writing? Here the psychologists of Newnham and Girton might come to our help, I thought, looking again at the blank spaces on the shelves. For surely it is time that the effect of discouragement upon the mind of the artist should be measured, as I have seen a dairy company measure the effect of ordinary milk and Grade A milk upon the body of the rat. They set two rats in cages side

---

[21] **Carlyle . . . Keats:** All these authors encountered adversity. The first draft of Thomas Carlyle's *The French Revolution* (1837) was accidentally burned; Gustave Flaubert was charged with obscenity for writing *Madame Bovary* (1857); Keats wrote his great odes knowing he was soon to die of tuberculosis.

[22] **"Mighty . . . dead":** A line from William Wordsworth's poem "Resolution and Independence."

by side, and of the two one was furtive, timid, and small, and the other was glossy, bold, and big. Now what food do we feed women as artists upon? I asked, remembering, I suppose, that dinner of prunes and custard.[23] To answer that question I had only to open the evening paper and to read that Lord Birkenhead[24] is of opinion — but really I am not going to trouble to copy out Lord Birkenhead's opinion upon the writing of women. What Dean Inge[25] says I will leave in peace. The Harley Street[26] specialist may be allowed to rouse the echoes of Harley Street with his vociferations without raising a hair on my head. I will quote, however, Mr. Oscar Browning,[27] because Mr. Oscar Browning was a great figure in Cambridge at one time, and used to examine the students at Girton and Newnham. Mr. Oscar Browning was wont to declare "that the impression left on his mind, after looking over any set of examination papers, was that, irrespective of the marks he might give, the best woman was intellectually the inferior of the worst man." After saying that Mr. Browning went back to his rooms — and it is this sequel that endears him and makes him a human figure of some bulk and majesty — he went back to his rooms and found a stableboy lying on the sofa — "a mere skeleton, his cheeks were cavernous and sallow, his teeth were black, and he did not appear to have the full use of his limbs. . . . 'That's Arthur' [said Mr. Browning]. 'He's a dear boy really and most high-minded.'" The two pictures always seem to me to complete each other. And happily in this age of biography the two pictures often do complete each other, so that we are able to interpret the opinions of great men not only by what they say, but by what they do.

But though this is possible now, such opinions coming from the lips of important people must have been formidable enough even fifty years ago. Let us suppose that a father from the highest motives did not wish his daughter to leave home and become writer, painter, or scholar. "See what Mr. Oscar Browning says," he would say; and there was not only Mr. Oscar Browning; there was the *Saturday Review;* there was Mr. Greg[28] — the "essentials of a woman's being," said Mr. Greg emphatically, "are that *they are supported by, and they minister to, men*" — there was an enormous body of masculine opinion to the effect that nothing could be expected of women intellectually. Even if her father did not read out loud these opinions, any girl could read them for herself; and the reading, even in the nineteenth century, must have lowered her vitality, and told profoundly upon her work. There would always have been that assertion — you cannot do this, you are incapable of doing that — to protest against, to overcome. Probably for a novelist this germ is no longer of much effect; for there have been women novelists of merit. But for painters it must still have some sting in it; and for musicians, I imagine, is even now active and poisonous in the extreme. The

---

[23] dinner . . . custard: Earlier, Woolf describes eating such a meal at a women's college while male students dine heartily.

[24] Lord Birkenhead: The Earl of Birkenhead, lord chancellor of England from 1919 to 1922, reportedly said women's achievements amounted to nothing.

[25] Dean Inge: William Ralph Inge, dean of St. Paul's Cathedral, 1911–1934.

[26] Harley Street: Location of fashionable London doctors' offices.

[27] Oscar Browning (1837–1923): Lecturer in history at Cambridge.

[28] Mr. Greg: W. W. Greg (1875–1959), editor, librarian, and reviewer.

woman composer stands where the actress stood in the time of Shakespeare. Nick Greene, I thought, remembering the story I had made about Shakespeare's sister, said that a woman acting put him in mind of a dog dancing. Johnson repeated the phrase two hundred years later of women preaching. And here, I said, opening a book about music, we have the very words used again in this year of grace, 1928, of women who try to write music. "Of Mlle. Germaine Tailleferre one can only repeat Dr. Johnson's dictum concerning a woman preacher, transposed into terms of music. 'Sir, a woman's composing is like a dog's walking on his hind legs. It is not done well, but you are surprised to find it done at all.'"[29] So accurately does history repeat itself.

Thus, I concluded, shutting Mr. Oscar Browning's life and pushing away the rest, it is fairly evident that even in the nineteenth century a woman was not encouraged to be an artist. On the contrary, she was snubbed, slapped, lectured, and exhorted. Her mind must have been strained and her vitality lowered by the need of opposing this, of disproving that. For here again we come within range of that very interesting and obscure masculine complex which has had so much influence upon the woman's movement; that deep-seated desire, not so much that *she* shall be inferior as that *he* shall be superior, which plants him wherever one looks, not only in front of the arts, but barring the way to politics too, even when the risk to himself seems infinitesimal and the suppliant humble and devoted. Even Lady Bessborough, I remembered, with all her passion for politics, must humbly bow herself and write to Lord Granville Leveson-Gower: ". . . notwithstanding all my violence in politics and talking so much on that subject, I perfectly agree with you that no woman has any business to meddle with that or any other serious business, farther than giving her opinion (if she is ask'd)."[30] And so she goes on to spend her enthusiasm where it meets with no obstacle whatsoever upon that immensely important subject, Lord Granville's maiden speech in the House of Commons. The spectacle is certainly a strange one, I thought. The history of men's opposition to women's emancipation is more interesting perhaps than the story of that emancipation itself. An amusing book might be made of it if some young student at Girton or Newnham would collect examples and deduce a theory — but she would need thick gloves on her hands, and bars to protect her of solid gold.

But what is amusing now, I recollected, shutting Lady Bessborough, had to be taken in desperate earnest once. Opinions that one now pastes in a book labelled cock-a-doodle-dum and keeps for reading to select audiences on summer nights once drew tears, I can assure you. Among your grandmothers and great-grandmothers there were many that wept their eyes out. Florence Nightingale shrieked aloud in her agony.[31] Moreover, it is all very well for you, who have got yourselves to college and enjoy sitting-rooms — or is it only bed-sitting-rooms? — of your own to say that

---

[29] "Of Mlle. . . . at all'": *A Survey of Contemporary Music* [1924], Cecil Gray, p. 246. [Woolf's note.] Germaine Tailleferre (1892–1983) was a French composer, a disciple of Erik Satie.

[30] ". . . notwithstanding . . . ask'd)": Henrietta Spencer's correspondence with Lord Granville, Foreign Secretary under William Gladstone, was well known.

[31] Florence . . . agony: See *Cassandra*, by Florence Nightingale, printed in *The Cause*, by R. Strachey. [Woolf's note.] Ray Strachey's 1928 book was a history of British feminism with an appendix by Nightingale.

genius should disregard such opinions; that genius should be above caring what is said of it. Unfortunately, it is precisely the men or women of genius who mind most what is said of them. Remember Keats. Remember the words he had cut on his tombstone.[32] Think of Tennyson; think—but I need hardly multiply instances of the undeniable, if very unfortunate, fact that it is the nature of the artist to mind excessively what is said about him. Literature is strewn with the wreckage of men who have minded beyond reason the opinions of others.

And this susceptibility of theirs is doubly unfortunate, I thought, returning again to my original enquiry into what state of mind is most propitious for creative work, because the mind of an artist, in order to achieve the prodigious effort of freeing whole and entire the work that is in him, must be incandescent, like Shakespeare's mind, I conjectured, looking at the book which lay open at *Antony and Cleopatra*. There must be no obstacle in it, no foreign matter unconsumed.

For though we say that we know nothing about Shakespeare's state of mind, even as we say that, we are saying something about Shakespeare's state of mind. The reason perhaps why we know so little of Shakespeare—compared with Donne or Ben Jonson or Milton—is that his grudges and spites and antipathies are hidden from us. We are not held up by some "revelation" which reminds us of the writer. All desire to protest, to preach, to proclaim an injury, to pay off a score, to make the world the witness of some hardship or grievance was fired out of him and consumed. Therefore his poetry flows from him free and unimpeded. If ever a human being got his work expressed completely, it was Shakespeare. If ever a mind was incandescent, unimpeded, I thought, turning again to the bookcase, it was Shakespeare's mind.

---

[32] **words . . . tombstone:** "Here lies one whose name was writ in water."

෴ Three Pictures

THE FIRST PICTURE

It is impossible that one should not see pictures; because if my father was a blacksmith and yours was a peer of the realm, we must needs be pictures to each other. We cannot possibly break out of the frame of the picture by speaking natural words. You see me leaning against the door of the smithy with a horseshoe in my hand and you think as you go by: "How picturesque!" I, seeing you sitting so much at your ease in

---

"Three Pictures." Although not published until 1942 in *The Death of the Moth*, Leonard Woolf indicated that this essay was written in 1929. The third picture comes from "A graveyard scene" in Woolf's diary for September 1927. Pictures here are a metaphor of people's first impressions of one another. The fact that one elaborates on these pictures and fills in a history for them creates misunderstandings in relationships. "Three Pictures" becomes a lesson in projection versus reality and looks at the human yearning to create meaning from sense impressions and the black holes of ignorance.

the car, almost as if you were going to bow to the populace, think what a picture of old luxurious aristocratic England! We both are quite wrong in our judgments no doubt, but that is inevitable.

So now at the turn of the road I saw one of these pictures. It might have been called "The Sailor's Homecoming" or some such title. A fine young sailor carrying a bundle; a girl with her hand on his arm; neighbours gathering round; a cottage garden ablaze with flowers; as one passed one read at the bottom of that picture that the sailor was back from China, and there was a fine spread waiting for him in the parlor; and he had a present for his young wife in his bundle; and she was soon going to bear him their first child. Everything was right and good and as it should be, one felt about that picture. There was something wholesome and satisfactory in the sight of such happiness; life seemed sweeter and more enviable than before.

So thinking I passed them, filling in the picture as fully, as completely as I could, noticing the colour of her dress, of his eyes, seeing the sandy cat slinking round the cottage door.

For some time the picture floated in my eyes, making most things appear much brighter, warmer, and simpler than usual; and making some things appear foolish; and some things wrong and some things right, and more full of meaning than before. At odd moments during that day and the next the picture returned to one's mind, and one thought with envy, but with kindness, of the happy sailor and his wife; one wondered what they were doing, what they were saying now. The imagination supplied other pictures springing from that first one, a picture of the sailor cutting firewood, drawing water; and they talked about China; and the girl set his present on the chimneypiece where everyone who came could see it; and she sewed at her baby clothes, and all the doors and windows were open into the garden so that the birds were flittering and the bees humming, and Rogers — that was his name — could not say how much to his liking all this was after the China seas. As he smoked his pipe, with his foot in the garden.

THE SECOND PICTURE

In the middle of the night a loud cry rang through the village. Then there was a sound of something scuffling; and then dead silence. All that could be seen out of the window was the branch of lilac tree hanging motionless and ponderous across the road. It was a hot still night. There was no moon. The cry made everything seem ominous. Who had cried? Why had she cried? It was a woman's voice, made by some extremity of feeling almost sexless, almost expressionless. It was as if human nature had cried out against some iniquity, some inexpressible horror. There was dead silence. The stars shone perfectly steadily. The fields lay still. The trees were motionless. Yet all seemed guilty, convicted, ominous. One felt that something ought to be done. Some light ought to appear tossing, moving agitatedly. Someone ought to come running down the road. There should be lights in the cottage windows. And then perhaps another cry, but less sexless, less wordless, comforted, appeased. But no light came. No feet were heard. There was no second cry. The first had been swallowed up, and there was dead silence.

One lay in the dark listening intently. It had been merely a voice. There was nothing to connect it with. No picture of any sort came to interpret it, to make it intelligible to the mind. But as the dark arose at last all one saw was an obscure human form, almost without shape, raising a gigantic arm in vain against some overwhelming iniquity.

THE THIRD PICTURE

The fine weather remained unbroken. Had it not been for that single cry in the night one would have felt that the earth had put into harbour; that life had ceased to drive before the wind; that it had reached some quiet cove and there lay anchored, hardly moving, on the quiet waters. But the sound persisted. Wherever one went, it might be for a long walk up into the hills, something seemed to turn uneasily beneath the surface, making the peace, the stability all round one seem a little unreal. There were the sheep clustered on the side of the hill; the valley broke in long tapering waves like the fall of smooth waters. One came on solitary farmhouses. The puppy rolled in the yard. The butterflies gambolled over the gorse. All was as quiet, as safe [as] could be. Yet, one kept thinking, a cry had rent it; all this beauty had been an accomplice that night; had consented to remain calm, to be still beautiful; at any moment it might be sundered again. This goodness, this safety were only on the surface.

And then to cheer oneself out of this apprehensive mood one turned to the picture of the sailor's homecoming. One saw it all over again producing various little details — the blue colour of her dress, the shadow that fell from the yellow flowering tree — that one had not used before. So they had stood at the cottage door, he with his bundle on his back, she just lightly touching his sleeve with her hand. And a sandy cat had slunk round the door. Thus gradually going over the picture in every detail, one persuaded oneself by degrees that it was far more likely that this calm and content and goodwill lay beneath the surface than anything treacherous, sinister. The sheep grazing, the waves of the valley, the farmhouse, the puppy, the dancing butterflies were in fact like that all through. And so one turned back home, with one's mind fixed on the sailor and his wife, making up picture after picture of them so that one picture after another of happiness and satisfaction might be laid over that unrest, that hideous cry, until it was crushed and silenced by their pressure out of existence.

Here at last was the village, and the churchyard through which one must pass; and the usual thought came, as one entered it, of the peacefulness of the place, with its shady yews, its rubbed tombstones, its nameless graves. Death is cheerful here, one felt. Indeed, look at that picture! A man was digging a grave, and children were picnicking at the side of it while he worked. As the shovels of yellow earth were thrown up, the children were sprawling about eating bread and jam and drinking milk out of large mugs. The gravedigger's wife, a fat fair woman, had propped herself against a tombstone and spread her apron on the grass by the open grave to serve as a tea-table. Some lumps of clay had fallen among the tea things. Who was going to be buried, I asked. Had old Mr Dodson died at last? "Oh! no. It's for young Rogers, the sailor," the woman answered, staring at me. "He died two nights ago, of some foreign fever. Didn't you hear his wife? She rushed into the road and cried out . . . Here, Tommy, you're all covered with earth!"

What a picture it made!

ᕐ The Fascination of the Pool

It may have been very deep—certainly one could not see to the bottom of it. Round the edge was so thick a fringe of rushes that their reflections made a darkness like the darkness of very deep water. However in the middle was something white. The big farm a mile off was to be sold and some zealous person, or it may have been a joke on the part of a boy, had stuck one of the posters advertising the sale, with farm horses, agricultural implements, and young heifers, on a tree stump by the side of the pool. The centre of the water reflected the white placard and when the wind blew the centre of the pool seemed to flow and ripple like a piece of washing. One could trace the big red letters in which Romford Mill was printed in the water. A tinge of red was in the green that rippled from bank to bank.

But if one sat down among the rushes and watched the pool—pools have some curious fascination, one knows not what—the red and black letters and the white paper seemed to lie very thinly on the surface, while beneath went on some profound underwater life like the brooding, the ruminating of a mind. Many, many people must have come there alone, from time to time, from age to age, dropping their thoughts into the water, asking it some question, as one did oneself this summer evening. Perhaps that was the reason of its fascination—that it held in its waters all kinds of fancies, complaints, confidences, not printed or spoken aloud, but in a liquid state, floating one on top of another, almost disembodied. A fish would swim through them, be cut in two by the blade of a reed; or the moon would annihilate them with its great white plate. The charm of the pool was that thoughts had been left there by people who had gone away and without their bodies their thoughts wandered in and out freely, friendly and communicative, in the common pool.

"The Fascination of the Pool." This piece comes from a typescript with holograph revisions, dated May 29, 1929. Leonard Woolf relates that when Virginia had an idea for a short story she would quickly sketch out the theme and then put the notes in a desk drawer; the sketch might or might not be retrieved later for revision. In fact, the only book of short stories that appeared in Virginia Woolf's lifetime was *Monday or Tuesday* (1921). "The Fascination of the Pool" lay in manuscript form until it was collected in *The Complete Shorter Fiction of Virginia Woolf* (1985). In this work, Woolf notices how pools hold people's imagination and identifies them as repositories of reflection and memory. She also associates the depths of the pool with consciousness and the disconnected pieces of history.

All footnotes come from the Susan Dick edition of the work.

Among all these liquid thoughts some seemed to stick together and to form recognisable people—just for a moment. And one saw a whiskered red face formed in the pool leaning low over it, drinking it. I came here in 1851 after the heat of the Great Exhibition.[1] I saw the Queen open it. And the voice chuckled liquidly, easily, as if he had thrown off his elastic side boots and put his top hat on the edge of the pool. Lord, how hot it was! and now all gone, all crumbled, of course, the thoughts seemed to say, swaying among the reeds. But I was a lover, another thought began, sliding over the other silently and orderly as fish not impeding each other. A girl; we used to come down from the farm (the placard of its sale was reflected on the top of the water) that summer, 1662. The soldiers never saw us from the road. It was very hot. We lay here. She was lying hidden in the rushes with her lover, laughing into the pool and slipping into it, thoughts of eternal love, of fiery kisses and despair. And I was very happy, said another thought glancing briskly over the girl's despair (for she had drowned herself). I used to fish here. We never caught the giant carp but we saw him once—the day Nelson fought at Trafalgar.[2] We saw him under the willow—my word! what a great brute he was! They say he was never caught. Alas, alas sighed a voice, slipping over the boy's voice. So sad a voice must come from the very bottom of the pool. It raised itself under the others as a spoon lifts all the things in a bowl of water. This was the voice we all wished to listen to. All the voices slipped gently away to the side of the pool to listen to the voice[3] which so sad it seemed—it must surely know the reason of all this. For they all wished to know.

One drew closer to the pool and parted the reeds so that one could see deeper, through the reflections, through the faces, through the voices to the bottom. But there under the man who had been to the Exhibition; and the girl who had drowned herself and the boy who had seen the fish; and the voice which cried alas alas! yet there was always something else. There was always another face, another voice. One thought came and covered another. For though there are moments when a spoon seems about to lift all of us, and our thoughts and longings and questions and confessions and disillusions into the light of day, somehow the spoon always slips beneath and we flow back again over the edge into the pool. And once more the whole of its centre is covered over with the reflection of the placard which advertises the sale of Romford Mill Farm. That perhaps is why one loves to sit and look into pools.

---

[1] **the Great Exhibition:** Held in the Crystal Palace in Hyde Park and opened by Queen Victoria on May 1, 1851.

[2] **Nelson . . . Trafalgar:** Lord Nelson was killed while defeating Napoleon's fleet in a battle off Cape Trafalgar on October 21, 1805.

[3] **the voice:** VW has cancelled "of the great seer" here.

✌ FRANZ KAFKA
B. PRAGUE, 1883–1924

The writings of Franz Kafka courageously explore the fears and frustrations of life in the modern age, how it feels to be manipulated by large institutions and betrayed by family and friends. The Industrial Revolution of the nineteenth century had undoubtedly produced immense wealth and a new middle class, but the centers of power in the expanding cities were large bureaucracies in which individuals were lost and dehumanized. Much of Kafka's writing deals with the intimidation of the individual by governments and courts of law. Kafka also wrote of faceless, heartless, modern corporations in which individuals become nonentities caught up in legalistic, administrative maneuvers. Often these governmental or corporate systems are too complex and elusive for people to understand and, finally, survive.

Kafka did not officially belong to the French school of SURREALISM,[1] but his blend of precise detail, ordinary reality, and nightmare is surreal in nature. Making use of Freud's revelations about the subconscious, Kafka accepts the dominance of dream realities and portrays the everyday as something that can turn in an instant into a nightmare in which lives are distorted. Kafka's work embodies a disturbing loss of faith in the fundamental institutions of Western civilization—universities, churches, courts, and governments—and implicitly argues that if God still exists in the post–World War I era—and many doubted He did—then He has retreated into the vast recesses of the cosmos, out of touch and out of hearing. Given the absence of both rational control in the world and a model of the universe that included God, Kafka was brilliantly prophetic about the rise of TOTALITARIANISM in the twentieth century and the horrifying effect that Fascist and Communist regimes would have on millions—as well as about the alienating influence of international corporations. It is no wonder that at this seemingly hopeless time European intellectuals turned to some variety of EXISTENTIALISM.

An Early Conflict: Work and Writing. Franz Kafka was born in Prague (then part of the Austro-Hungarian empire) in 1883 to Julie Lowy, a kindly woman from a family of rabbis, and Hermann Kafka, a self-made man who had worked his way from village butcher to city entrepreneur. The aggressive and domineering Hermann pressured his son into becoming a businessman; Franz was well-educated, earning a doctor of law degree from German University in Prague. Despite an early passion for writing, he took a job in the semigovernmental Workers' Accident

Franz Kafka, c. 1910
Kafka at around the age of twenty-seven. (Hulton / Archive)

www For links to more information about Kafka, a quiz on *The Metamorphosis,* and for information on the twenty-first-century relevance of Kafka, see *World Literature Online* at bedfordstmartins .com/worldlit.

---

[1] French . . . surrealism: Founded by André Breton (1896–1966), who believed that Freud's discoveries about the world of dreams should be incorporated into literature. Breton defined *surrealism* as the attempt to blend ordinary reality with dream realities in order to better reflect the movements and profundities of modern consciousness.

Insurance Institute, where he had ample opportunity to observe the laborious machinations of a bureaucracy in the Austro-Hungarian empire.

Kafka felt caught between his continued passion for writing and his desire to do well in his career, as he remarks in this journal entry:

> Now these two vocations (writing and working in an office) cannot be compatible and have a fortunate outcome in common. The smallest success in the one field becomes a great disaster in the other . . . At the office I fulfill my obligations outwardly, but not my inner ones, and every unfulfilled inner obligation turns into a misfortune which does not find its way out of me.

Somehow he managed to succeed at both endeavors, becoming a respected executive handling claims and litigation as well as a successful writer.

An Overwhelming Father.   Exacerbating the pain he felt in his relationship with his father, Kafka lived at home for most of his life. In the essay, "A Letter to My Father," he writes of his feelings of inferiority and humiliation, feelings that not surprisingly pervade the consciousness of his fictional characters:

> I was, after all, depressed even by your mere physical presence. I remember for instance how often we undressed together in the same bathing-hut. There was I, skinny, weakly, slight, you strong, tall, broad. Even inside the hut I felt myself a miserable specimen, and what's more not only in your eyes but in the eyes of the whole world, for you were for me the measure of all things.

Kafka was twice engaged to Felice Bauer but didn't marry, and the failure of this relationship became an additional burden. Although his stories were praised by his friends, he was insecure about his writing and resisted publishing his work; only a few of his short stories and two novellas, *The Metamorphosis* (*Die Verwandlung,* 1915) and *The Penal Colony* (*Die Strafkolonie,* 1919) were published during his lifetime.

Tuberculosis.   In 1917 Kafka was found to have tuberculosis, and he eventually suffered from tuberculosis of the larynx, a particularly hateful illness for someone who spent his life struggling to communicate. After living in various sanatoriums in Prague, Kafka moved to Berlin in 1922, where his relationship with Dora Dymant brought him some happiness before he died on June 3, 1924. Before dying he asked his friend and executor, Max Brod, to burn his unpublished papers, which included three unfinished novels. Brod disregarded his friend's request and published a number of short stories and sketches as well as the incomplete novels *The Trial* (*Der Prozess,* 1925), *The Castle* (*Das Schloss,* 1926), and *Amerika* (1927), all of which deal with the effects of totalitarianism on individuals.

Cracking the Frozen Sea Within.   Kafka wrote, "The books we need are the kind that act upon us like a nightmare, that make us suffer like the death of someone we love more than ourselves . . . a book should serve as

I was, after all, depressed even by your mere physical presence. I remember for instance how often we undressed together in the same bathing-hut. There was I, skinny, weakly, slight, you strong, tall, broad. Even inside the hut I felt myself a miserable specimen, and what's more not only in your eyes but in the eyes of the whole world, for you were for me the measure of all things.

– KAFKA to his father, 1919

Twentieth-Century Europe: Sigmund Freud

The man who challenged the nineteenth-century view of the rational man and set the psychological agenda for the twentieth century was Sigmund Freud (1856–1937): *The Interpretation of Dreams* (published in 1899 but dated 1900) found and unlatched the door to the psyche and the unconscious. Freud's hypothesis concerning the repressed contents of the unconscious seemed to confirm everyone's worst fear, namely that darkness was capable of overwhelming and controlling the daytime world of ordinary reality.

Born of Jewish parents on May 6, 1856, in a small town in Moravia — a region today in the Czech Republic — Freud spent most of his life in Vienna, Austria. Given the importance Freud later placed on childhood, it is ironic that very little is known about his own. After studying medicine with a specialty in neurology, he went to Paris in 1885 to investigate hysteria. A Viennese physician, Josef Breuer, told Freud about curing the symptoms of hysteria by "getting the patient to recollect in hypnosis the circumstances of their origin and to express the emotions accompanying them." Together they published a book on the "cathartic method," *Studies in Hysteria* (*Studien über Hysterie*, 1895), which was the starting point of psychoanalysis. When Freud later discovered that hypnosis was not a satisfactory tool for treating hysteria, he developed free association and dream analysis as ways of exploring the unconscious. He proposed that neuroses could be healed when traumatic experiences from childhood that had been repressed or denied are re-experienced as an adult through recounting one's personal history. Freud did not discover the inner world of the psyche, nor was he the first to proclaim the importance of dreams or the power of sexuality, but in writings such as *The History of the Psychoanalytic Movement* (1914) and *Three Contributions to the Theory of Sex* (1905) he made

Portrait of Sigmund Freud. *The father of psychoanalysis, Freud made contributions to psychology and culture that still resonate today. (The Art Archive / Museum der Stadt Wien / Dagli Orti [A])*

the unconscious, dreams, and sex central to the twentieth century's understanding of human nature. The journey into the self, into the hidden and repressed corridors and closets of childhood, has become a paradigm of the modern spiritual journey.

Freud's work validated the importance of storytelling by maintaining that the painful effects of childhood trauma can be alleviated when an individual learns how to tell his or her story. As Freud discovered a symbolic language for interpreting the discontinuous realities of dreams, he influenced modern fiction writers, whose stream-of-consciousness and surrealistic narratives challenged the conventional, chronological narrative forms inherited from the nineteenth century.

The books we need are the kind that act upon us like a nightmare, that make us suffer like the death of someone we love more than ourselves . . . a book should serve as the ax for the frozen sea within us.

– KAFKA

the ax for the frozen sea within us"—and he proceeded to write such books. Kafka typically takes the point of view of a victim, someone who is confused about a particular system of power, the people in control, and how to gain access. In *The Trial,* the accused actually has an opportunity to speak to his accusers, but he knows neither the nature of his crime nor why he has been found guilty. In *The Castle,* contact with decision makers is not possible. There might be a telephone line into the interior of a power structure, but it is uncertain who might pick up the phone on the other end and what transaction might take place. Social power, like God, has receded into anonymity, not unlike the contemporary frustration of trying to reach an actual person at a phone company, but instead having to deal with recorded messages and an automated system.

Kafka is a master of the short sketch that ends with a twist; he actually revived the biblical form of the PARABLE[2] for a modern audience. A short parable called "Before the Law," an ALLEGORY[3] of modern life, encapsulates Kafka's persistent themes. A man approaches the gateway of the Law, but a gatekeeper prevents him from entering. Finally, after years in front of the gate and endless discussions with the gatekeeper, the man asks one final question before dying: "Everyone strives to reach the Law, so how does it happen that for all these many years no one but myself has ever begged for admittance?" The gatekeeper answers, "No one else could ever be admitted here, since this gate was made only for you. I am now going to shut it." For Kafka, this gateway stands for all the institutional, doctrinal, and religious barriers that individuals confront over a lifetime.

Metamorphosis into an Insect.   The demeaning, dehumanizing distance in *The Metamorphosis* is found within the home and the family, where parents and adult children live together without caring for one another, where people talk without communicating. *The Metamorphosis* is typical of a number of Kafka's works in that it places an everyday, ordinary world side by side with extraordinary phenomena. The story begins with Gregor Samsa's discovery that in his physical form he has been turned into an insect. Gregor's condition corresponds to the psychological state of an individual who awakens to the full dimensions of being trapped in a sense of helplessness and alienation in his or her everyday life. Gregor's family, to whom he has dedicated his working life, is unsympathetic to his plight. Even though the unfortunate, pitiable change in him is completely out of his control, his parents and, eventually, even his sister feel he has let them down. One of the most dehumanizing scenes in the story occurs when Mr. Samsa reasserts his authority as the head of the household and drives his son back into his room, throwing fruit at him. One of the apples that lodges in Gregor's back rots and festers until Gregor dies without understanding what has happened to him. Gregor's

---

[2] **parable:** A short narrative designed to present a lesson about life; parables were popular during biblical times.

[3] **allegory:** An allegory explains a concept or theory by turning the parts of the theory into characters in a narration.

misfortune ironically forces his family out of their passive dependence; as they detach themselves from his suffering, they appear to take charge of their own lives and make plans for the future.

The heartless bureaucracy was not unknown to the nineteenth century; after all, Tolstoy's Ivan Ilych[4] became a cog in Russia's legal system. But Franz Kafka's haunting version of the modern world, which makes the line between the ruling elite and the rest of society impossibly vague and suffocating, has been immensely influential in the twentieth century. Although Kafka's writings had very little impact during his lifetime, audiences after World War II have found his portrayal of modern bureaucratic alienation and the paralyzing insecurities that individuals suffer in their private lives both prescient and profound. He continues to strike a deep chord in Western consciousness.

■ CONNECTIONS

T. S. Eliot, "The Love Song of J. Alfred Prufrock," p. 482. The modern city that emerged in the twentieth century engendered an entirely different lifestyle than any that had been previously known. Franz Kafka was particularly in tune with the effect modern bureaucracy had on human beings, how individuals are lost in office labyrinths and paperwork. Eliot's Prufrock seems incapable of making significant choices for his life in "The Love Song of J. Alfred Prufrock." How does Kafka's Gregor Samsa become an almost passive cog in the machinery of his company—an "insect"—before his metamorphosis?

Jean-Paul Sartre, The Flies, p. 697. Some writers use crisis to shock the reader into recognition of a serious problem confronting modern society. Sartre's works underscore the necessity for modern individuals to take charge of their lives. How does Kafka convince readers that the transformation of Gregor Samsa is a consequence of modern life to which anyone might be subject?

Anton Chekhov, The Cherry Orchard (Book 5). The breakdown of the family was one consequence of the shift of population from farms and small towns to the modern city at the turn of the twentieth century. In The Cherry Orchard, Chekhov pays particular attention to the lack of real communication between family members and how this affects their actions. What are the reactions of Gregor's family to his change? Does Gregor's suffering provide an explanation for the improved situation of his family after his death?

■ FURTHER RESEARCH

Biography
Brod, Max. Franz Kafka: A Biography. 1960.
Hayman, Ronald. Kafka: A Biography. 1982.
Pawel, Ernest. The Nightmare of Reason, A Life of Franz Kafka. 1984.

Criticism
Bloom, Harold, ed. Franz Kafka's The Metamorphosis. 1988.
Fickert, Kurt. End of a Mission: Kafka's Search for Truth in His Last Stories. 1993.
Gray, Ronald, ed. Kafka: A Collection of Critical Essays. 1962.

Metamorphosis . . . certainly represents the horrible imagery of an ethic of lucidity. But it is also the product of that incalculable amazement man feels at being conscious of the beast he becomes effortlessly. In this fundamental ambiguity lies Kafka's secret. These perpetual oscillations between the natural and the extraordinary, the individual and the universal, the tragic and the everyday, the absurd and the logical, are found throughout his work. . . .

– ALBERT CAMUS, 1955

---

[4] **Ivan Ilych:** Tolstoy's *The Death of Ivan Ilych* deals with a man who spends his life working to attain a middle-class, comfortable existence and ends up depressed and alone on his deathbed. (See Book 5.)

✑ The Metamorphosis

Translated by Willa and Edwin Muir

1

As Gregor Samsa awoke one morning from uneasy dreams he found himself transformed in his bed into a gigantic insect. He was lying on his hard, as it were armorplated, back and when he lifted his head a little he could see his domelike brown belly divided into stiff arched segments on top of which the bed quilt could hardly keep in position and was about to slide off completely. His numerous legs, which were pitifully thin compared to the rest of his bulk, waved helplessly before his eyes.

What has happened to me? he thought. It was no dream. His room, a regular human bedroom, only rather too small, lay quiet between the four familiar walls. Above the table on which a collection of cloth samples was unpacked and spread out—Samsa was a commercial traveler—hung the picture which he had recently cut out of an illustrated magazine and put into a pretty gilt frame. It showed a lady, with a fur cap on and a fur stole, sitting upright and holding out to the spectator a huge fur muff into which the whole of her forearm had vanished!

Gregor's eyes turned next to the window, and the overcast sky—one could hear raindrops beating on the window gutter—made him quite melancholy. What about sleeping a little longer and forgetting all this nonsense, he thought, but it could not be done, for he was accustomed to sleep on his right side and in his present condition he could not turn himself over. However violently he forced himself toward his right side he always rolled onto his back again. He tried it at least a hundred times, shutting his eyes to keep from seeing his struggling legs, and only desisted when he began to feel in his side a faint dull ache he had never experienced before.

Oh God, he thought, what an exhausting job I've picked on! Traveling about day in, day out. It's much more irritating work than doing the actual business in the

---

The Metamorphosis. First published in 1915 as *Die Verwandlung,* the English translation by Willa and Edwin Muir didn't appear until 1948 in *The Penal Colony: Stories and Short Pieces,* indicating that interest in Kafka in the English-speaking world really began after World War II, when Kafka's prophetic voice was noticed.

The Metamorphosis begins with a scene told in shockingly simple fashion that haunts the reader, who like Gregor must search for a framework to accommodate the strange events that unfold with a sense of inevitability: "As Gregor Samsa awoke one morning from uneasy dreams he found himself transformed in his bed into a gigantic insect." Although the line between reality and unreality, between nightmare and sanity, fluctuates in Kafka's writings, he intends for Gregor's misfortune to be taken literally—at least initially. Fate has dealt Gregor Samsa an incredible blow. What could have prepared him for this? Kafka proceeds to fill in the background for Gregor's condition and to detail its effects on Gregor's family, whose concern for him deteriorates as the story progresses. The story ends with a number of questions unresolved, such as whether the Samsa family learned anything at all from Gregor's life and death or whether it is in the nature of the middle class to simply bumble onward.

office, and on top of that there's the trouble of constant traveling, of worrying about train connections, the bed and irregular meals, casual acquaintances that are always new and never become intimate friends. The devil take it all! He felt a slight itching up on his belly; slowly pushed himself on his back nearer to the top of the bed so that he could lift his head more easily; identified the itching place which was surrounded by many small white spots the nature of which he could not understand and made to touch it with a leg, but drew the leg back immediately, for the contact made a cold shiver run through him.

He slid down again into his former position. This getting up early, he thought, makes one quite stupid. A man needs his sleep. Other commercials live like harem women. For instance, when I come back to the hotel of a morning to write up the orders I've got, these others are only sitting down to the breakfast. Let me just try that with my chief; I'd be sacked on the spot. Anyhow, that might be quite a good thing for me, who can tell? If I didn't have to hold my hand because of my parents I'd have given notice long ago, I'd have gone to the chief and told him exactly what I think of him. That would knock him endways from his desk! It's a queer way of doing, too, this sitting on high at a desk and talking down to employees, especially when they have to come quite near because the chief is hard of hearing. Well, there's still hope; once I've saved enough money to pay back my parents' debts to him — that should take another five or six years — I'll do it without fail. I'll cut myself completely loose then. For the moment, though, I'd better get up, since my train goes at five.

He looked at the alarm clock ticking on the chest. Heavenly Father! he thought. It was half-past six o'clock and the hands were quietly moving on, it was even past the half-hour, it was getting on toward a quarter to seven. Had the alarm clock not gone off? From the bed one could see that it had been properly set for four o'clock; of course it must have gone off. Yes, but was it possible to sleep quietly through that ear-splitting noise? Well, he had not slept quietly, yet apparently all the more soundly for that. But what was he to do now? The next train went at seven o'clock; to catch that he would need to hurry like mad and his samples weren't even packed up, and he himself wasn't feeling particularly fresh and active. And even if he did catch the train he wouldn't avoid a row with the chief, since the firm's porter would have been waiting for the five o'clock train and would have long since reported his failure to turn up. The porter was a creature of the chief's, spineless and stupid. Well, supposing he were to say he was sick? But that would be most unpleasant and would look suspicious, since during his five years' employment he had not been ill once. The chief himself would be sure to come with the sick-insurance doctor, would reproach his parents with their son's laziness, and would cut all excuses short by referring to the insurance doctor, who of course regarded all mankind as perfectly healthy malingerers. And would he be so far wrong on this occasion? Gregor really felt quite well, apart from a drowsiness that was utterly superfluous after such a long sleep, and he was even unusually hungry.

As all this was running through his mind at top speed without his being able to decide to leave his bed — the alarm clock had just struck a quarter to seven — there came a cautious tap at the door behind the head of his bed. "Gregor," said a voice — it was his mother's — "it's a quarter to seven. Hadn't you a train to catch?" That gentle voice! Gregor had a shock as he heard his own voice answering hers, unmistakably his own voice, it was true, but with a persistent horrible twittering squeak behind it like an undertone, which left the words in their clear shape only for the first moment and then rose up reverberating around them to destroy their sense, so that one could not be sure one had heard them rightly. Gregor wanted to answer at length and explain everything, but in the circumstances he confined himself to saying: "Yes, yes, thank you, Mother, I'm getting up now." The wooden door between them must have kept the change in his voice from being noticeable outside, for his mother contented herself with this statement and shuffled away. Yet this brief exchange of words had made the other members of the family aware that Gregor was still in the house, as they had not expected, and at one of the side doors his father was already knocking, gently, yet with his fist. "Gregor, Gregor," he called, "What's the matter with you?" And after a little while he called again in a deeper voice: "Gregor! Gregor!" At the other side door his sister was saying in a low, plaintive tone: "Gregor? Aren't you well? Are you needing anything?" He answered them both at once: "I'm just ready," and did his best to make his voice sound as normal as possible by enunciating the words very clearly and leaving long pauses between them. So his father went back to his breakfast, but his sister whispered: "Gregor, open the door, do." However, he was not thinking of opening the door, and felt thankful for the prudent habit he had acquired in traveling of locking all doors during the night, even at home.

His immediate intention was to get up quietly without being disturbed, to put on his clothes and above all eat his breakfast, and only then consider what else was to be done, since in bed, he was well aware, his meditations would come to no sensible conclusion. He remembered that often enough in bed he had felt small aches and pains, probably caused by awkward postures, which had proved purely imaginary once he got up, and he looked forward eagerly to seeing this morning's delusions gradually fall away. That the change in his voice was nothing but the precursor of a severe chill, a standing ailment of commercial travelers, he had not the least possible doubt.

To get rid of the quilt was quite easy; he had only to inflate himself a little and it fell off by itself. But the next move was difficult, especially because he was so uncommonly broad. He would have needed arms and hands to hoist himself up; instead he had only the numerous little legs which never stopped waving in all directions and which he could not control in the least. When he tried to bend one of them it was the first to stretch itself straight; and did he succeed at last in making it do what he wanted, all the other legs meanwhile waved the more wildly in a high degree of unpleasant agitation. "But what's the use of lying idle in bed," said Gregor to himself.

He thought that he might get out of bed with the lower part of his body first, but this lower part, which he had not yet seen and of which he could form no clear conception, proved too difficult to move; it shifted so slowly; and when finally, almost wild with annoyance, he gathered his forces together and thrust out recklessly, he had miscalculated the direction and bumped heavily against the lower end of the bed, and the stinging pain he felt informed him that precisely this lower part of his body was at the moment probably the most sensitive.

So he tried to get the top part of himself out first, and cautiously moved his head toward the edge of the bed. That proved easy enough, and despite its breadth and mass the bulk of his body at last slowly followed the movement of his head. Still, when he finally got his head free over the edge of the bed he felt too scared to go on advancing, for after all if he let himself fall in this way it would take a miracle to keep his head from being injured. And at all costs he must not lose consciousness now, precisely now; he would rather stay in bed.

But when after a repetition of the same efforts he lay in his former position again, sighing, and watched his little legs struggling against each other more wildly than ever, if that were possible, and saw no way of bringing any order into this arbitrary confusion, he told himself again that it was impossible to stay in bed and that the most sensible course was to risk everything for the smallest hope of getting away from it. At the same time he did not forget to remind himself occasionally that cool reflection, the coolest possible, was much better than desperate resolves. In such moments he focused his eyes as sharply as possible on the window, but, unfortunately, the prospect of the morning fog, which muffled even the other side of the narrow street, brought him little encouragement and comfort. "Seven o'clock already," he said to himself when the alarm clock chimed again, "seven o'clock already and still such a thick fog." And for a little while he lay quiet, breathing lightly, as if perhaps expecting such complete repose to restore all things to their real and normal condition.

But then he said to himself: "Before it strikes a quarter past seven I must be quite out of this bed, without fail. Anyhow, by that time someone will have come from the office to ask for me, since it opens before seven." And he set himself to rocking his whole body at once in a regular rhythm, with the idea of swinging it out of the bed. If he tipped himself out in that way he could keep his head from injury by lifting it at an acute angle when he fell. His back seemed to be hard and was not likely to suffer from a fall on the carpet. His biggest worry was the loud crash he would not be able to help making, which would probably cause anxiety, if not terror, behind all the doors. Still, he must take the risk.

When he was already half out of the bed—the new method was more a game than an effort, for he needed only to hitch himself across by rocking to and fro—it struck him how simple it would be if he could get help. Two strong people—he thought of his father and the servant girl—would be amply sufficient; they would only have to thrust their arms under his convex back, lever him out of the bed, bend down with their burden, and then be patient enough to let him turn himself right over onto the floor, where it was to be hoped his legs would then find their proper function. Well, ignoring the fact that the doors were all locked, ought he really to call for help? In spite of his misery he could not suppress a smile at the very idea of it.

He had got so far that he could barely keep his equilibrium when he rocked himself strongly, and he would have to nerve himself very soon for the final decision since in five minutes' time it would be quarter past seven—when the front doorbell rang. "That's someone from the office," he said to himself, and grew almost rigid, while his little legs only jigged about all the faster. For a moment everything stayed quiet. "They're not going to open the door," said Gregor to himself, catching at some kind of irrational hope. But then of course the servant girl went as usual to the door with her heavy tread and opened it. Gregor needed only to hear the first good morning of the visitor to know immediately who it was—the chief clerk himself. What a fate, to be condemned to work for a firm where the smallest omission at once gave rise to the gravest suspicion! Were all employees in a body nothing but scoundrels, was there not among them one single loyal devoted man who, had he wasted only an hour or so of the firm's time in a morning, was so tormented by conscience as to be driven out of his mind and actually incapable of leaving his bed? Wouldn't it really have been sufficient to send an apprentice to inquire—if any inquiry were necessary at all—did the chief clerk himself have to come and thus indicate to the entire family, an innocent family, that this suspicious circumstance could be investigated by no one less versed in affairs than himself? And more through the agitation caused by these reflections than through any act of will Gregor swung himself out of bed with all his strength. There was a loud thump, but it was not really a crash. His fall was broken to some extent by the carpet, his back, too, was less stiff than he thought, and so there was merely a dull thud, not so very startling. Only he had not lifted his head carefully enough and had hit it; he turned it and rubbed it on the carpet in pain and irritation.

"That was something falling down in there," said the chief clerk in the next room to the left. Gregor tried to suppose to himself that something like what had happened to him today might someday happen to the chief clerk; one really could not deny that it was possible. But as if in brusque reply to this supposition the chief clerk took a couple of firm steps in the next-door room and his patent leather boots creaked. From the right-hand room his sister was whispering to inform him of the situation: "Gregor, the chief clerk's here." "I know," muttered Gregor to himself; but he didn't dare to make his voice loud enough for his sister to hear it.

"Gregor," said his father now from the left-hand room, "the chief clerk has come and wants to know why you didn't catch the early train. We don't know what to say to him. Besides, he wants to talk to you in person. So open the door, please. He will be good enough to excuse the untidiness of your room." "Good morning, Mr. Samsa," the chief clerk was calling amiably meanwhile. "He's not well," said his mother to the visitor, while his father was still speaking through the door, "he's not well, sir, believe me. What else would make him miss a train! The boy thinks about nothing but his work. It makes me almost cross the way he never goes out in the evenings; he's been here the last eight days and has stayed at home every single evening. He just sits there quietly at the table reading a newspaper or looking through railway timetables. The only amusement he gets is doing fretwork. For instance, he spent two or three evenings cutting out a little picture frame; you would be surprised to see how pretty it is; it's hanging in his room; you'll see it in a minute when Gregor opens the door. I must say I'm glad you've come, sir; we should never have got him to unlock the door by ourselves; he's so obstinate; and I'm sure he's unwell, though he wouldn't have it to be so this morning." "I'm just coming," said Gregor slowly and carefully, not moving an inch for fear of losing one word of the conversation. "I can't think of any other explanation, madame," said the chief clerk, "I hope it's nothing serious. Although on the other hand I must say that we men of business—fortunately or unfortunately—very often simply have to ignore any slight indisposition, since business must be attended to." "Well, can the chief clerk come in now?" asked Gregor's father impatiently, again knocking on the door. "No," said Gregor. In the left-hand room a painful silence followed this refusal, in the right-hand room his sister began to sob.

Why didn't his sister join the others? She was probably newly out of bed and hadn't even begun to put on her clothes yet. Well, why was she crying? Because he wouldn't get up and let the chief clerk in, because he was in danger of losing his job, and because the chief would begin dunning his parents again for the old debts? Surely these were things one didn't need to worry about for the present. Gregor was still at home and not in the least thinking of deserting the family. At the moment, true, he was lying on the carpet and no one who knew the condition he was in could seriously expect him to admit the chief clerk. But for such a small discourtesy, which could plausibly be explained away somehow later on, Gregor could hardly be dismissed on the spot. And it seemed to Gregor that it would be much more sensible to leave him in peace for the present than to trouble him with tears and entreaties. Still, of course, their uncertainty bewildered them all and excused their behavior.

"Mr. Samsa," the chief clerk called now in a louder voice, "what's the matter with you? Here you are, barricading yourself in your room, giving only 'yes' and 'no' for answers, causing your parents a lot of unnecessary trouble and neglecting—I mention this only in passing—neglecting your business duties in an incredible fashion. I am speaking here in the name of your parents and of your chief, and I beg you quite seriously to give me an immediate and precise explanation. You amaze me, you amaze me. I thought you were a quiet, dependable person, and now all at once you seem bent on making a disgraceful exhibition of yourself. The chief did hint to me early this morning a possible explanation for your disappearance—with reference to the cash payments that were entrusted to you recently—but I almost pledged my solemn word of honor that this could not be so. But now that I see how incredibly obstinate you are, I no longer have the slightest desire to take your part at all. And your position in the firm is not so unassailable. I came with the intention of telling you all this in private, but since you are wasting my time so needlessly I don't see why your parents shouldn't hear it too. For some time past your work has been most unsatisfactory; this is not the season of the year for a business boom, of course, we admit that, but a season of the year for doing no business at all, that does not exist, Mr. Samsa, must not exist."

"But, sir," cried Gregor, beside himself and in his agitation forgetting everything else, "I'm just going to open the door this very minute. A slight illness, an attack of giddiness, has kept me from getting up. I'm still lying in bed. But I feel all right again. I'm getting out of bed now. Just give me a moment or two longer! I'm not quite so well as I thought. But I'm all right, really. How a thing like that can suddenly strike one down! Only last night I was quite well, my parents can tell you, or rather I did have a slight presentiment. I must have showed some sign of it. Why didn't I report it at the office! But one always thinks that an indisposition can be got over without staying in the house. Oh sir, do spare my parents! All that you're reproaching me with now has no foundation; no one has ever said a word to me about it. Perhaps you haven't looked at the last orders I sent in. Anyhow, I can still catch the eight o'clock train, I'm much the better for my few hours' rest. Don't let me detain you here, sir; I'll be attending to business very soon, and do be good enough to tell the chief so and to make my excuses to him!"

And while all this was tumbling out pell-mell and Gregor hardly knew what he was saying, he had reached the chest quite easily, perhaps because of the practice he had had in bed, and was now trying to lever himself upright by means of it. He meant actually to open the door, actually to show himself and speak to the chief clerk; he was eager to find out what the others, after all their insistence, would say at the sight of him. If they were horrified then the responsibility was no longer his and he could stay quiet. But if they took it calmly, then he had no reason either to be upset, and could really get to the station for the eight o'clock train if he hurried. At first he slipped down a few times from the polished surface of the chest, but at length with a last heave he stood upright; he paid no more attention to the pains in the lower part of his body, however they smarted. Then he let himself fall against the back of a nearby chair, and clung with his little legs to the edges of it. That brought him into control of himself again and he stopped speaking, for now he could listen to what the chief clerk was saying.

"Did you understand a word of it?" the chief clerk was asking; "surely he can't be trying to make fools of us?" "Oh dear," cried his mother, in tears, "perhaps he's terribly ill and we're tormenting him. Grete! Grete!" she called out then. "Yes Mother?" called his sister from the other side. They were calling to each other across Gregor's room. "You must go this minute for the doctor. Gregor is ill. Go for the doctor, quick. Did you hear how he was speaking?" "That was no human voice," said the chief clerk in a voice noticeably low beside the shrillness of the mother's. "Anna! Anna!" his father was calling through the hall to the kitchen, clapping his hands, "get a locksmith at once!" And the two girls were already running through the hall with a swish of skirts—how could his sister have got dressed so quickly?—and were tearing the front door open. There was no sound of its closing again; they had evidently left it open, as one does in houses where some great misfortune has happened.

But Gregor was now much calmer. The words he uttered were no longer understandable, apparently, although they seemed clear enough to him, even clearer than before, perhaps because his ear had grown accustomed to the sound of them. Yet at any rate people now believed that something was wrong with him, and were ready to help him. The positive certainty with which these first measures had been taken comforted him. He felt himself drawn once more into the human circle and hoped for great and remarkable results from both the doctor and the locksmith, without really distinguishing precisely between them. To make his voice as clear as possible for the decisive conversation that was now imminent he coughed a little, as quietly as he could, of course, since this noise too might not sound like a human cough for all he was able to judge. In the next room meanwhile there was complete silence. Perhaps his parents were sitting at the table with the chief clerk, whispering, perhaps they were all leaning against the door and listening.

Slowly Gregor pushed the chair toward the door, then let go of it, caught hold of the door for support—the soles at the end of his little legs were somewhat sticky—

and rested against it for a moment after his efforts. Then he set himself to turning the key in the lock with his mouth. It seemed, unhappily, that he hadn't really any teeth—what could he grip the key with?—but on the other hand his jaws were certainly very strong; with their help he did manage to set the key in motion, heedless of the fact that he was undoubtedly damaging them somewhere, since a brown fluid issued from his mouth, flowed over the key, and dripped on the floor. "Just listen to that," said the chief clerk next door; "he's turning the key." That was a great encouragement to Gregor; but they should all have shouted encouragement to him, his father and mother too: "Go on, Gregor," they should have called out, "keep going, hold on to that key!" And in the belief that they were all following his efforts intently, he clenched his jaws recklessly on the key with all the force at his command. As the turning of the key progressed he circled around the lock, holding on now only with his mouth, pushing on the key, as required, or pulling it down again with all the weight of his body. The louder click of the finally yielding lock literally quickened Gregor. With a deep breath of relief he said to himself: "So I didn't need the locksmith," and laid his head on the handle to open the door wide.

Since he had to pull the door toward him, he was still invisible when it was really wide open. He had to edge himself slowly around the near half of the double door, and to do it very carefully if he was not to fall plump upon his back just on the threshold. He was still carrying out this difficult maneuver, with no time to observe anything else, when he heard the chief clerk utter a loud "Oh!"—it sounded like a gust of wind—and now he could see the man, standing as he was nearest to the door, clapping one hand before his open mouth and slowly backing away as if driven by some invisible steady pressure. His mother—in spite of the chief clerk's being there her hair was still undone and sticking up in all directions—first clasped her hands and looked at his father, then took two steps toward Gregor and fell on the floor among her outspread skirts, her face quite hidden on her breast. His father knotted his fist with a fierce expression on his face as if he meant to knock Gregor back into his room, then looked uncertainly around the living room, covered his eyes with his hands, and wept till his great chest heaved.

Gregor did not go now into the living room, but leaned against the inside of the firmly shut wing of the door, so that only half his body was visible and his head above it bending sideways to look at the others. The light had meanwhile strengthened; on the other side of the street one could see clearly a section of the endlessly long, dark gray building opposite—it was a hospital—abruptly punctuated by its row of regular windows; the rain was still falling, but only in large singly discernible and literally singly splashing drops. The breakfast dishes were set out on the table lavishly, for breakfast was the most important meal of the day to Gregor's father, who lingered it out for hours over various newspapers. Right opposite Gregor on the wall hung a photograph of himself in military service, as a lieutenant, hand on sword, a carefree smile on his face, inviting one to respect his uniform and military bearing. The door leading to the hall was open, and one could see that the front door stood open too, showing the landing beyond and the beginning of the stairs going down.

"Well," said Gregor, knowing perfectly that he was the only one who had retained any composure, "I'll put my clothes on at once, pack up my samples, and start off. Will you only let me go? You see, sir, I'm not obstinate, and I'm willing to work; traveling is a hard life, but I couldn't live without it. Where are you going, sir? To the office? Yes? Will you give a true account of all this? One can be temporarily incapacitated, but that's just the moment for remembering former services and bearing in mind that later on, when the incapacity has been got over, one will certainly work with all the more industry and concentration. I'm loyally bound to serve the chief, you know that very well. Besides, I have to provide for my parents and my sister. I'm in great difficulties, but I'll get out of them again. Don't make things any worse for me than they are. Stand up for me in the firm. Travelers are not popular there, I know. People think they earn sacks of money and just have a good time. A prejudice there's no particular reason for revising. But you, sir, have a more comprehensive view of affairs than the rest of the staff, yes, let me tell you in confidence, a more comprehensive view than the chief himself, who, being the owner, lets his judgment easily be swayed against one of his employees. And you know very well that the traveler, who is never seen in the office almost the whole year around, can so easily fall a victim to gossip and ill luck and unfounded complaints, which he mostly knows nothing about, except when he comes back exhausted from his rounds, and only then suffers in person from their evil consequences, which he can no longer trace back to the original causes. Sir, sir, don't go away without a word to me to show that you think me in the right at least to some extent!"

But at Gregor's very first words the chief clerk had already backed away and only stared at him with parted lips over one twitching shoulder. And while Gregor was speaking he did not stand still one moment but stole away toward the door, without taking his eyes off Gregor, yet only an inch at a time, as if obeying some secret injunction to leave the room. He was already at the hall, and the suddenness with which he took his last step out of the living room would have made one believe he had burned the sole of his foot. Once in the hall he stretched his right arm before him toward the staircase, as if some supernatural power were waiting there to deliver him.

Gregor perceived that the chief clerk must on no account be allowed to go away in this frame of mind if his position in the firm were not to be endangered to the utmost. His parents did not understand this so well; they had convinced themselves in the course of years that Gregor was settled for life in this firm, and besides they were so preoccupied with their immediate troubles that all foresight had forsaken them. Yet Gregor had this foresight. The chief clerk must be detained, soothed, persuaded, and finally won over; the whole future of Gregor and his family depended on it! If only his sister had been there! She was intelligent; she had begun to cry while Gregor was still lying quietly on his back. And no doubt the chief clerk, so partial to ladies, would have been guided by her; she would have shut the door of the flat and in the hall talked him out of his horror. But she was not there, and Gregor would have to handle the situation himself. And without remembering that he was still unaware what powers of movement he possessed, without even remembering that his words in all possibility, indeed in all likelihood, would again be unintelligible, he let go the wing of the door, pushed himself through the opening, started to walk toward the chief clerk, who was already ridiculously clinging with both hands to the railing on the landing; but immediately, as he was feeling for a support, he fell down with a little cry upon all his numerous legs. Hardly was he down when he experienced for the first time this morning a sense of physical comfort; his legs had firm ground under them; they were completely obedient, as he noted with joy; they even strove to carry him forward in whatever direction he chose; and he was inclined to believe that a final relief from all his sufferings was at hand. But in the same moment as he found himself on the floor, rocking with suppressed eagerness to move, not far from his mother, indeed just in front of her, she, who had seemed so completely crushed, sprang all at once to her feet, her arms and fingers outspread, cried: "Help, for God's sake, help!" bent her head down as if to see Gregor better, yet on the contrary kept backing senselessly away; had quite forgotten that the laden table stood behind her; sat upon it hastily, as if in absence of mind, when she bumped into it; and seemed altogether unaware that the big coffeepot beside her was upset and pouring coffee in a flood over the carpet.

"Mother, Mother," said Gregor in a low voice, and looked up at her. The chief clerk, for the moment, had quite slipped from his mind; instead, he could not resist snapping his jaws together at the sight of the streaming coffee. That made his mother scream again, she fled from the table and fell into the arms of his father, who hastened to catch her. But Gregor had now no time to spare for his parents; the chief clerk was already on the stairs; with his chin on the banisters he was taking one last backward look. Gregor made a spring, to be as sure as possible of overtaking him; the chief clerk must have divined his intention, for he leaped down several steps and vanished; he was still yelling "Ugh!" and it echoed through the whole staircase.

Unfortunately, the flight of the chief clerk seemed completely to upset Gregor's father, who had remained relatively calm until now, for instead of running after the man himself, or at least not hindering Gregor in his pursuit, he seized in his right hand the walking stick that the chief clerk had left behind on a chair, together with a hat and greatcoat, snatched in his left hand a large newspaper from the table, and began stamping his feet and flourishing the stick and the newspaper to drive Gregor back into his room. No entreaty of Gregor's availed, indeed no entreaty was even understood, however humbly he bent his head his father only stamped on the floor the more loudly. Behind his father his mother had torn open a window, despite the cold weather, and was leaning far out of it with her face in her hands. A strong draught set in from the street to the staircase, the window curtains blew in, the newspapers on the table fluttered, stray pages whisked over the floor. Pitilessly Gregor's father drove him back, hissing and crying "Shoo!" like a savage. But Gregor was quite unpracticed in walking backwards, it really was a slow business. If he only had a chance to turn around he could get back to his room at once, but he was afraid of exasperating his father by the slowness of such a rotation and at any moment the stick in his father's hand might hit him a fatal blow on the back or on the head. In the end, however, nothing else was left for him to do since to his horror he observed that in moving backwards he could not even control the direction he took; and so, keeping an anxious eye on his father all the time over his shoulder, he began to turn around as quickly as he could, which was in reality very slowly. Perhaps his father noted his good intentions, for he did not interfere except every now and then to help him in the maneuver from a distance with the point of the stick. If only he would have stopped making that unbearable hissing noise! It made Gregor quite lose his head. He had turned almost completely around when the hissing noise so distracted him that he even turned a little the wrong way again. But when at last his head was fortunately right in front of the doorway, it appeared that his body was too broad simply to get through the opening. His father, of course, in his present mood was far from thinking of such a thing as opening the other half of the door, to let Gregor have enough space. He had merely the fixed idea of driving Gregor back into his room as quickly as possible. He would never have suffered Gregor to make the circumstantial preparations for standing up on end and perhaps slipping his way through the door. Maybe he was now making more noise than ever to urge Gregor forward, as if no obstacle impeded him; to Gregor, anyhow, the noise in his rear sounded no longer like the voice of one single father; this was really no joke, and Gregor thrust himself—come what might—into the doorway. One side of his body rose up, he was tilted at an angle in the doorway, his flank was quite bruised, horrid blotches stained the white door, soon he was stuck fast and, left to himself, could not have moved at all, his legs on one side fluttered trembling in the air, those on the other were crushed painfully to the floor—when from behind his father gave him a strong push which was literally a deliverance and he flew far into the room, bleeding freely. The door was slammed behind him with the stick, and then at last there was silence.

2

Not until it was twilight did Gregor awake out of a deep sleep, more like a swoon than a sleep. He would certainly have waked up of his own accord not much later, for he felt himself sufficiently rested and well slept, but it seemed to him as if a fleeting step and a cautious shutting of the door leading into the hall had aroused him. The electric lights in the street cast a pale sheen here and there on the ceiling and the upper surfaces of the furniture, but down below, where he lay, it was dark. Slowly, awkwardly trying out his feelers, which he now first learned to appreciate, he pushed his way to the door to see what had been happening there. His left side felt like one single long, unpleasantly tense scar, and he had actually to limp on his two rows of legs. One little leg, moreover, had been severely damaged in the course of that morning's events—it was almost a miracle that only one had been damaged—and trailed uselessly behind him.

He had reached the door before he discovered what had really drawn him to it: the smell of food. For there stood a basin filled with fresh milk in which floated little sops of white bread. He could almost have laughed with joy, since he was now still hungrier than in the morning, and he dipped his head almost over the eyes straight into the milk. But soon in disappointment he withdrew it again; not only did he find it difficult to feed because of his tender left side—and he could only feed with the palpitating collaboration of his whole body—he did not like the milk either, although milk had been his favorite drink and that was certainly why his sister had set it there for him, indeed it was almost with repulsion that he turned away from the basin and crawled back to the middle of the room.

He could see through the crack of the door that the gas was turned on in the living room, but while usually at this time his father made a habit of reading the afternoon newspaper in a loud voice to his mother and occasionally to his sister as well, not a sound was now to be heard. Well, perhaps his father had recently given up this habit of reading aloud, which his sister had mentioned so often in conversation and in her letters. But there was the same silence all around, although the flat was certainly not empty of occupants. "What a quiet life our family has been leading," said Gregor to himself, and as he sat there motionless staring into the darkness he felt great pride in the fact that he had been able to provide such a life for his parents and sister in such a fine flat. But what if all the quiet, the comfort, the contentment were now to end in horror? To keep himself from being lost in such thoughts Gregor took refuge in movement and crawled up and down the room.

Once during the long evening one of the side doors was opened a little and quickly shut again, later the other side door too; someone had apparently wanted to come in and then thought better of it. Gregor now stationed himself immediately before the living-room door, determined to persuade any hesitating visitor to come in or at least to discover who it might be; but the door was not opened again and he waited in vain. In the early morning, when the doors were locked, they had all wanted to come in, now that he had opened one door and the other had apparently been opened during the day, no one came in and even the keys were on the other side of the doors.

It was late at night before the gas went out in the living room, and Gregor could easily tell that his parents and his sister had all stayed awake until then, for he could clearly hear the three of them stealing away on tiptoe. No one was likely to visit him, not until the morning, that was certain; so he had plenty of time to meditate at his leisure on how he was to arrange his life afresh. But the lofty, empty room in which he had to lie flat on the floor filled him with an apprehension he could not account for, since it had been his very own room for the past five years — and with a half-unconscious action, not without a slight feeling of shame, he scuttled under the sofa, where he felt comfortable at once, although his back was a little cramped and he could not lift his head up, and his only regret was that his body was too broad to get the whole of it under the sofa.

He stayed there all night, spending the time partly in a light slumber, from which his hunger kept waking him up with a start, and partly in worrying and sketching vague hopes, which all led to the same conclusion, that he must lie low for the present and, by exercising patience and the utmost consideration, help the family to bear the inconvenience he was bound to cause them in his present condition.

Very early in the morning, it was still almost night, Gregor had the chance to test the strength of his new resolutions, for his sister, nearly fully dressed, opened the door from the hall and peered in. She did not see him at once, yet when she caught sight of him under the sofa — well, he had to be somewhere, he couldn't have flown away, could he? — she was so startled that without being able to help it she slammed the door shut again. But as if regretting her behavior she opened the door again immediately and came in on tiptoe, as if she were visiting an invalid or even a stranger. Gregor had pushed his head forward to the very edge of the sofa and watched her. Would she notice that he had left the milk standing, and not for lack of hunger, and would she bring in some other kind of food more to his taste? If she did not do it of her own accord, he would rather starve than draw her attention to the fact, although he felt a wild impulse to dart out from under the sofa, throw himself at her feet, and beg her for something to eat. But his sister at once noticed, with surprise, that the basin was still full, except for a little milk that had been spilled all around it, she lifted it immediately, not with her bare hands, true, but with a cloth and carried it away. Gregor was wildly curious to know what she would bring instead, and made various speculations about it. Yet what she actually did next, in the goodness of her heart, he could never have guessed at. To find out what he liked she brought him a whole selection of food, all set out on an old newspaper. There were old, half-decayed vegetables, bones from last night's supper covered with a white sauce that had thickened; some raisins and almonds; a piece of cheese that Gregor would have called uneatable two days ago; a dry roll of bread, a buttered roll, and a roll both buttered and salted. Besides all that, she set down again the same basin, into which she had poured some water, and which was apparently to be reserved for his exclusive use. And with fine tact, knowing that Gregor would not eat in her presence, she withdrew quickly and even turned the key, to let him understand that he could take his ease as much as he liked. Gregor's legs all whizzed toward the food. His wounds must have healed completely, moreover, for he felt no disability, which amazed him and made him reflect how more than a month ago he had cut one finger a little with a knife and had still suffered pain from the wound only the day before yesterday. Am I less sensitive now? he thought, and sucked greedily at the cheese, which above all the other edibles attracted him at once and strongly. One after another and with tears of satisfaction in his eyes he quickly devoured the cheese, the vegetables, and the sauce; the fresh food, on the other hand, had no charms for him, he could not even stand the smell of it and actually dragged away to some little distance the things he could eat. He had long finished his meal and was only lying lazily on the same spot when his sister turned the key slowly as a sign for him to retreat. That roused him at once, although he was nearly asleep, and he hurried under the sofa again. But it took considerable self-control for him to stay under the sofa, even for the short time his sister was in the room, since the large meal had swollen his body somewhat and he was so cramped he could hardly breathe. Slight attacks of breathlessness afflicted him and his eyes were starting a little out of his head as he watched his unsuspecting sister sweeping together with a broom not only the remains of what he had eaten but even the things he had not touched, as if these were now of no use to anyone, and hastily shoveling it all into a bucket, which she covered with a wooden lid and carried away. Hardly had she turned her back when Gregor came from under the sofa and stretched and puffed himself out.

In this manner Gregor was fed, once in the early morning while his parents and the servant girl were still asleep, and a second time after they had all had their midday dinner, for then his parents took a short nap and the servant girl could be sent out on some errand or other by his sister. Not that they would have wanted him to starve, of course, but perhaps they could not have borne to know more about his feeding than from hearsay, perhaps too his sister wanted to spare them such little anxieties wherever possible, since they had quite enough to bear as it was.

Under what pretext the doctor and the locksmith had been got rid of on that first morning Gregor could not discover, for since what he said was not understood by the others it never struck any of them, not even his sister, that he could understand what they said, and so whenever his sister came into his room he had to content himself with hearing her utter only a sigh now and then and an occasional appeal to the saints. Later on, when she had got a little used to the situation—of course she could never get completely used to it—she sometimes threw out a remark which was kindly meant or could be so interpreted. "Well, he liked his dinner today," she would say when Gregor had made a good clearance of his food; and when he had not eaten, which gradually happened more and more often, she would say almost sadly: "Everything's been left standing again."

But although Gregor could get no news directly, he overheard a lot from the neighboring rooms, and as soon as voices were audible, he would run to the door of the room concerned and press his whole body against it. In the first few days especially there was no conversation that did not refer to him somehow, even if only indirectly. For two whole days there were family consultations at every mealtime about what should be done; but also between meals the same subject was discussed, for there were always at least two members of the family at home, since no one wanted to be alone in the flat and to leave it quite empty was unthinkable. And on the very first of these days the household cook—it was not quite clear what and how much she knew of the situation—went down on her knees to his mother and begged leave to go, and when she departed, a quarter of an hour later, gave thanks for her dismissal with tears in her eyes as if for the greatest benefit that could have been conferred on her, and without any prompting swore a solemn oath that she would never say a single word to anyone about what had happened.

Now Gregor's sister had to cook too, helping her mother; true, the cooking did not amount to much, for they ate scarcely anything. Gregor was always hearing one of the family vainly urging another to eat and getting no answer but: "Thanks, I've had all I want," or something similar. Perhaps they drank nothing either. Time and again his sister kept asking his father if he wouldn't like some beer and offered kindly to go and fetch it herself, and when he made no answer suggested that she could ask the concierge to fetch it, so that he need feel no sense of obligation, but then a round "No" came from his father and no more was said about it.

In the course of that very first day Gregor's father explained the family's financial position and prospects to both his mother and his sister. Now and then he rose from the table to get some voucher or memorandum out of the small safe he had rescued from the collapse of his business five years earlier. One could hear him opening the complicated lock and rustling papers out and shutting it again. This statement made by his father was the first cheerful information Gregor had heard since his imprisonment. He had been of the opinion that nothing at all was left over from his father's business, at least his father had never said anything to the contrary, and of course he had not asked him directly. At that time Gregor's sole desire was to do his utmost to help the family to forget as soon as possible the catastrophe that had overwhelmed the business and thrown them all into a state of complete despair. And so he had set to work with unusual ardor and almost overnight had become a commercial traveler instead of a little clerk, with of course much greater chances of earning money, and his success was immediately translated into good round coin which he could lay on the table for his amazed and happy family. These had been fine times, and they had never recurred, at least not with the same sense of glory, although later on Gregor had earned so much money that he was able to meet the expenses of the whole household and did so. They had simply got used to it, both the family and Gregor; the money was gratefully accepted and gladly given, but there was no special uprush of warm feeling. With his sister alone had he remained intimate, and it was a secret plan of his that she, who loved music, unlike himself, and could play movingly on the violin, should be sent next year to study at the Conservatorium, despite the great expense that would entail, which must be made up in some other way. During his brief visits home the Conservatorium was often mentioned in the talks he had with his sister, but always merely as a beautiful dream which could never come true, and his parents discouraged even these innocent references to it; yet Gregor had made up his mind firmly about it and meant to announce the fact with due solemnity on Christmas Day.

Such were the thoughts, completely futile in his present condition, that went through his head as he stood clinging upright to the door and listening. Sometimes out of sheer weariness he had to give up listening and let his head fall negligently against the door, but he always had to pull himself together again at once, for even the slight sound his head made was audible next door and brought all conversation to a stop. "What can he be doing now?" his father would say after a while, obviously turning toward the door, and only then would the interrupted conversation gradually be set going again.

Gregor was now informed as amply as he could wish—for his father tended to repeat himself in his explanations, partly because it was a long time since he had handled such matters and partly because his mother could not always grasp things at once—that a certain amount of investments, a very small amount it was true, had survived the wreck of their fortunes and had even increased a little because the dividends had not been touched meanwhile. And besides that, the money Gregor brought home every month—he had kept only a few dollars for himself—had never been quite used up and now amounted to a small capital sum. Behind the door Gregor nodded his head eagerly, rejoiced at this evidence of unexpected thrift and foresight. True, he could really have paid off some more of his father's debts to the chief with this extra money, and so brought much nearer the day on which he could quit his job, but doubtless it was better the way his father had arranged it.

Yet this capital was by no means sufficient to let the family live on the interest of it; for one year, perhaps, or at the most two, they could live on the principal, that was all. It was simply a sum that ought not to be touched and should be kept for a rainy day; money for living expenses would have to be earned. Now his father was still hale enough but an old man, and he had done no work for the past five years and could not be expected to do much; during these five years, the first years of leisure in his laborious though unsuccessful life, he had grown rather fat and become sluggish. And Gregor's old mother, how was she to earn a living with her asthma, which troubled her even when she walked through the flat and kept her lying on a sofa every other day panting for breath beside an open window? And was his sister to earn her bread, she who was still a child of seventeen and whose life hitherto had been so pleasant, consisting as it did in dressing herself nicely, sleeping long, helping in the housekeeping, going out to a few modest entertainments, and above all playing the violin? At first whenever the need for earning money was mentioned Gregor let go his hold on the door and threw himself down on the cool leather sofa beside it, he felt so hot with shame and grief.

Often he just lay there the long nights through without sleeping at all, scrabbling for hours on the leather. Or he nerved himself to the great effort of pushing an armchair to the window, then crawled up over the window sill and, braced against the chair, leaned against the windowpanes, obviously in some recollection of the sense of freedom that looking out of a window always used to give him. For in reality day by day things that were even a little way off were growing dimmer to his sight; the hospital across the street, which he used to execrate for being all too often before his eyes, was now quite beyond his range of vision, and if he had not known that he lived in Charlotte Street, a quiet street but still a city street, he might have believed that his window gave on a desert waste where gray sky and gray land blended indistinguishably into each other. His quick-witted sister only needed to observe twice that the armchair stood by the window; after that whenever she had tidied the room she always pushed the chair back to the same place at the window and even left the inner casements open.

If he could have spoken to her and thanked her for all she had to do for him, he could have borne her ministrations better; as it was, they oppressed him. She certainly tried to make as light as possible of whatever was disagreeable in her task, and as time went on she succeeded, of course, more and more, but time brought more enlightenment to Gregor too. The very way she came in distressed him. Hardly was she in the room when she rushed to the window, without even taking time to shut the door, careful as she was usually to shield the sight of Gregor's room from the others, and as if she were almost suffocating tore the casements open with hasty fingers, standing then in the open draught for a while even in the bitterest cold and drawing deep breaths. This noisy scurry of hers upset Gregor twice a day; he would crouch trembling under the sofa all the time, knowing quite well that she would certainly have spared him such a disturbance had she found it at all possible to stay in his presence without opening the window.

On one occasion, about a month after Gregor's metamorphosis, when there was surely no reason for her to be still startled at his appearance, she came a little earlier than usual and found him gazing out of the window, quite motionless, and thus well placed to look like a bogey. Gregor would not have been surprised had she not come in at all, for she could not immediately open the window while he was there, but not only did she retreat, she jumped back as if in alarm and banged the door shut; a stranger might well have thought that he had been lying in wait for her there meaning to bite her. Of course he hid himself under the sofa at once, but he had to wait until midday before she came again, and she seemed more ill at ease than usual. This made him realize how repulsive the sight of him still was to her, and that it was bound to go on being repulsive, and what an effort it must cost her not to run away even from the sight of the small portion of his body that stuck out from under the sofa. In order to spare her that, therefore, one day he carried a sheet on his back to the sofa—it cost him four hours' labor—and arranged it there in such a way as to hide him completely, so that even if she were to bend down she could not see him. Had she considered the sheet unnecessary, she would certainly have stripped it off the sofa again, for it was clear enough that this curtaining and confining of himself was not likely to conduce to Gregor's comfort, but she left it where it was, and Gregor even fancied that he caught a thankful glance from her eye when he lifted the sheet carefully a very little with his head to see how she was taking the new arrangement.

For the first fortnight his parents could not bring themselves to the point of entering his room, and he often heard them expressing their appreciation of his sister's activities, whereas formerly they had frequently scolded her for being as they thought a somewhat useless daughter. But now, both of them often waited outside the door, his father and his mother, while his sister tidied his room, and as soon as she came out she had to tell them exactly how things were in the room, what Gregor had eaten, how he had conducted himself this time, and whether there was not perhaps some slight improvement in his condition. His mother, moreover, began relatively soon to want to visit him, but his father and sister dissuaded her at first with arguments which Gregor listened to very attentively and altogether approved. Later, however, she had to be held back by main force, and when she cried out: "Do let me in to Gregor, he is my unfortunate son! Can't you understand that I must go to him?" Gregor thought that it might be well to have her come in, not every day, of course, but perhaps once a week; she understood things, after all, much better than his sister, who was only a child despite the efforts she was making and had perhaps taken on so difficult a task merely out of childish thoughtlessness.

Gregor's desire to see his mother was soon fulfilled. During the daytime he did not want to show himself at the window, out of consideration for his parents, but he could not crawl very far around the few square yards of floor space he had, nor could he bear lying quietly at rest all during the night, while he was fast losing any interest he had ever taken in food, so that for mere recreation he had formed the habit of crawling crisscross over the walls and ceiling. He especially enjoyed hanging suspended from the ceiling; it was much better than lying on the floor; one could breathe more freely; one's body swung and rocked lightly; and in the almost blissful absorption induced by this suspension it could happen to his own surprise that he let go and fell plump on the floor. Yet he now had his body much better under control than formerly, and even such a big fall did him no harm. His sister at once remarked the new distraction Gregor had found for himself—he left traces behind him of the sticky stuff on his soles wherever he crawled—and she got the idea in her head of giving him as wide a field as possible to crawl in and of removing the pieces of furniture that hindered him, above all the chest of drawers and the writing desk. But that was more than she could manage all by herself; she did not dare ask her father to help her; and as for the servant girl, a young creature of sixteen who had had the courage to stay on after the cook's departure, she could not be asked to help, for she had begged as a special favor that she might keep the kitchen door locked and open it only on a definite summons; so there was nothing left but to apply to her mother at an hour when her father was out. And the old lady did come, with exclamations of joyful eagerness, which, however, died away at the door of Gregor's room. Gregor's sister, of course, went in first, to see that everything was in order before letting his mother enter. In great haste Gregor pulled the sheet lower and tucked it more in folds so that it really looked as if it had been thrown accidentally over the sofa. And this time he did not peer out from under it; he renounced the pleasure of seeing his mother on this occasion and was only glad that she had come at all. "Come in, he's out of sight," said his sister, obviously leading her mother in by the hand. Gregor could now hear the two women struggling to shift the heavy old chest from its place, and his sister claiming the greater part of the labor for herself, without listening to the admonitions of her mother, who feared she might overstrain herself. It took a long time. After at least a quarter of an hour's tugging his mother objected that the chest had better be left where it was, for in the first place it was too heavy and could never be got out before his father came home, and standing in the middle of the room like that it would only hamper Gregor's movements, while in the second place it was not at all certain that removing the furniture would be doing a service to Gregor. She was inclined to think to the contrary; the sight of the naked walls made her own heart heavy, and why shouldn't Gregor have the same feeling, considering that he had been used to his furniture for so long and might feel forlorn without it. "And doesn't it look," she concluded in a low voice—in fact she had been almost whispering all the time as if to avoid letting Gregor, whose exact whereabouts she did not know, hear even the tones of her voice, for she was convinced that he could not understand her words—"doesn't it look as if we were showing him, by taking away his furniture, that we have given up hope of his ever getting better and are just leaving him coldly to himself? I think it would be best to keep his room exactly as it has always been, so that when he comes back to us he will find everything unchanged and be able all the more easily to forget what has happened in between."

On hearing these words from his mother Gregor realized that the lack of all direct human speech for the past two months together with the monotony of family life must have confused his mind, otherwise he could not account for the fact that he had quite earnestly looked forward to having his room emptied of furnishing. Did he really want his warm room, so comfortably fitted with old family furniture, to be turned into a naked den in which he would certainly be able to crawl unhampered in all directions but at the price of shedding simultaneously all recollection of his human background? He had indeed been so near the brink of forgetfulness that only the voice of his mother, which he had not heard for so long, had drawn him back from it. Nothing should be taken out of his room; everything must stay as it was; he could not dispense with the good influence of the furniture on his state of mind; and even if the furniture did hamper him in his senseless crawling around and around, that was no drawback but a great advantage.

Unfortunately his sister was of the contrary opinion; she had grown accustomed, and not without reason, to consider herself an expert in Gregor's affairs as against her parents, and so her mother's advice was now enough to make her determined on the removal not only of the chest and the writing desk, which had been her first intention, but of all the furniture except the indispensable sofa. This determination was not, of course, merely the outcome of childish recalcitrance and of the self-confidence she had recently developed so unexpectedly and at such cost; she had in fact perceived that Gregor needed a lot of space to crawl about in, while on the other hand he never used the furniture at all, so far as could be seen. Another factor might also have been the enthusiastic temperament of an adolescent girl, which seeks to indulge itself on every opportunity and which now tempted Grete to exaggerate the horror of her brother's circumstances in order that she might do all the more for him. In a room where Gregor lorded it all alone over empty walls no one save herself was likely ever to set foot.

And so she was not to be moved from her resolve by her mother, who seemed moreover to be ill at ease in Gregor's room and therefore unsure of herself, was soon reduced to silence, and helped her daughter as best she could to push the chest outside. Now, Gregor could do without the chest, if need be, but the writing desk he must retain. As soon as the two women had got the chest out of his room, groaning as they pushed it, Gregor stuck his head out from under the sofa to see how he might intervene as kindly and cautiously as possible. But as bad luck would have it, his mother was the first to return, leaving Grete clasping the chest in the room next door where she was trying to shift it all by herself, without of course moving it from the spot. His mother however was not accustomed to the sight of him, it might sicken her and so in alarm Gregor backed quickly to the other end of the sofa, yet could not prevent the sheet from swaying a little in front. That was enough to put her on the alert. She paused, stood still for a moment, and then went back to Grete.

Although Gregor kept reassuring himself that nothing out of the way was happening, but only a few bits of furniture were being changed around, he soon had to admit that all this trotting to and fro of the two women, their little ejaculations, and the scraping of furniture along the floor affected him like a vast disturbance coming from all sides at once, and however much he tucked in his head and legs and cowered to the very floor he was bound to confess that he would not be able to stand it for long. They were clearing his room out, taking away everything he loved; the chest in which he kept his fret saw and other tools was already dragged off; they were now loosening the writing desk which had almost sunk into the floor, the desk at which he had done all his homework when he was at the commercial academy, at the grammar school before that, and, yes, even at the primary school—he had no more time to waste in weighing the good intentions of the two women, whose existence he had by now almost forgotten, for they were so exhausted that they were laboring in silence and nothing could be heard but the heavy scuffling of their feet.

And so he rushed out—the women were just leaning against the writing desk in the next room to give themselves a breather—and four times changed his direction, since he really did not know what to rescue first, then on the wall opposite, which was already otherwise cleared, he was struck by the picture of the lady muffled in so much fur and quickly crawled up to it and pressed himself to the glass, which was a good surface to hold on to and comforted his hot belly. This picture at least, which was entirely hidden beneath him, was going to be removed by nobody. He turned his head toward the door of the living room so as to observe the women when they came back.

They had not allowed themselves much of a rest and were already coming; Grete had twined her arm around her mother and was almost supporting her. "Well, what shall we take now?" said Grete, looking around. Her eyes met Gregor's from the wall. She kept her composure, presumably because of her mother, bent her head down to her mother, to keep her from looking up, and said, although in a fluttering, unpremeditated voice: "Come, hadn't we better go back to the living room for a moment?" Her intentions were clear enough to Gregor, she wanted to bestow her mother in safety and then chase him down from the wall. Well, just let her try it! He clung to his picture and would not give it up. He would rather fly in Grete's face.

But Grete's words had succeeded in disquieting her mother, who took a step to one side, caught sight of the huge brown mass on the flowered wallpaper, and before she was really conscious that what she saw was Gregor, screamed in a loud, hoarse voice: "Oh God, oh God!" fell with outspread arms over the sofa as if giving up, and did not move. "Gregor!" cried his sister, shaking her fist and glaring at him. This was the first time she had directly addressed him since his metamorphosis. She ran into the next room for some aromatic essence with which to rouse her mother from her fainting fit. Gregor wanted to help too—there was still time to rescue the picture— but he was stuck fast to the glass and had to tear himself loose; he then ran after his sister into the next room as if he could advise her, as he used to do; but then had to stand helplessly behind her; she meanwhile searched among various small bottles and when she turned around started in alarm at the sight of him; one bottle fell on the floor and broke; a splinter of glass cut Gregor's face and some kind of corrosive medicine splashed him; without pausing a moment longer Grete gathered up all the bottles she could carry and ran to her mother with them; she banged the door shut with her foot. Gregor was now cut off from his mother, who was perhaps nearly dying because of him; he dared not open the door for fear of frightening away his sister, who had to stay with her mother; there was nothing he could do but wait; and harassed by self-reproach and worry he began now to crawl to and fro, over everything, walls, furniture, and ceiling, and finally in his despair, when the whole room seemed to be reeling around him, fell down onto the middle of the big table.

A little while elapsed, Gregor was still lying there feebly and all around was quiet, perhaps that was a good omen. Then the doorbell rang. The servant girl was of course locked in her kitchen, and Grete would have to open the door. It was his father. "What's been happening?" were his first words; Grete's face must have told him everything. Grete answered in a muffled voice, apparently hiding her head on his breast: "Mother has been fainting, but she's better now. Gregor's broken loose." "Just what I expected," said his father, "just what I've been telling you, but you women would never listen." It was clear to Gregor that his father had taken the worst interpretation of Grete's all too brief statement and was assuming that Gregor had been guilty of some violent act. Therefore Gregor must now try to propitiate his father, since he had neither time nor means for an explanation. And so he fled to the door of his own room and crouched against it, to let his father see as soon as he came in from the hall that his son had the good intention of getting back into his room immediately and that it was not necessary to drive him there, but that if only the door were opened he would disappear at once.

Yet his father was not in the mood to perceive such fine distinctions. "Ah!" he cried as soon as he appeared, in a tone that sounded at once angry and exultant. Gregor drew his head back from the door and lifted it to look at his father. Truly, this was not the father he had imagined to himself; admittedly he had been too absorbed of late in his new recreation of crawling over the ceiling to take the same interest as before in what was happening elsewhere in the flat, and he ought really to be prepared for some changes. And yet, and yet, could that be his father? The man who used to lie wearily sunk in bed whenever Gregor set out on a business journey; who welcomed him back of an evening lying in a long chair in a dressing gown; who could not really rise to his feet but only lifted his arms in greeting, and on the rare occasions when he did go out with his family, on one or two Sundays a year and on highest holidays, walked between Gregor and his mother, who were slow walkers anyhow, even more slowly than they did, muffled in his old greatcoat, shuffling laboriously forward with the help of his crook-handled stick which he set down most cautiously at every step and, whenever he wanted to say anything, nearly always came to a full stop and gathered his escort around him? Now he was standing there in fine shape; dressed in a smart blue uniform with gold buttons, such as bank messengers wear; his strong double chin bulged over the stiff high collar of his jacket; from under his bushy eyebrows his black eyes darted fresh and penetrating glances; his onetime tangled white hair had been combed flat on either side of a shining and carefully exact parting. He pitched his cap, which bore a gold monogram, probably the badge of some bank, in a wide sweep across the whole room onto a sofa and with the tail-ends of his jacket thrown back, his hands in his trouser pockets, advanced with a grim visage toward Gregor. Likely enough he did not himself know what he meant to do; at any rate he lifted his feet uncommonly high, and Gregor was dumbfounded at the enormous size of his shoe soles. But Gregor could not risk standing up to him, aware as he had been from the very first day of his new life that his father believed only the severest measures suitable for dealing with him. And so he ran before his father, stopping when he stopped and scuttling forward again when his father made any kind of move. In this way they circled the room several times without anything decisive happening, indeed the whole operation did not even look like a pursuit because it was carried out so slowly. And so Gregor did not leave the floor, for he feared that his father might take as a piece of peculiar wickedness any excursion of his over the walls or the ceiling. All the same, he could not stay this course much longer, for while his father took one step he had to carry out a whole series of movements. He was already beginning to feel breathless, just as in his former life his lungs had not been very dependable. As he was staggering along, trying to concentrate his energy on running, hardly keeping his eyes open; in his dazed state never even thinking of any other escape than simply going forward; and having almost forgotten that the walls were free to him, which in this room were well provided with finely carved pieces of furniture full of knobs and crevices—suddenly something lightly flung landed close behind him and rolled before him. It was an apple; a second apple followed immediately; Gregor came to a stop in alarm; there was no point in running on, for his father was determined to bombard him. He had filled his pockets with fruit from the dish on the sideboard and was now shying apple after apple, without taking particularly good aim for the moment. The small red apples rolled about the floor as if magnetized and cannoned into each other. An apple thrown without much force grazed Gregor's back and glanced off harmlessly. But another following immediately landed right on his back and sank in; Gregor wanted to drag himself forward, as if this startling, incredible pain could be left behind him; but he felt as if nailed to the spot and flattened himself out in a complete derangement of all his senses. With his last conscious look he saw the door of his room being torn open and his mother rushing out ahead of his screaming sister, in her underbodice, for her daughter had loosened her clothing to let her breathe more freely and recover from her swoon, he saw his mother rushing toward his father, leaving one after another behind her on the floor her loosened petticoats, stumbling over her petticoats straight to his father and embracing him, in complete union with him— but here Gregor's sight began to fail—with her hands clasped around his father's neck as she begged for her son's life.

3

The serious injury done to Gregor, which disabled him for more than a month—the apple went on sticking in his body as a visible reminder, since no one ventured to remove it—seemed to have made even his father recollect that Gregor was a member of the family, despite his present unfortunate and repulsive shape, and ought not to be treated as an enemy, that, on the contrary, family duty required the suppression of disgust and the exercise of patience, nothing but patience.

And although his injury had impaired, probably forever, his powers of movement, and for the time being it took him long, long minutes to creep across his room like an old invalid—there was no question now of crawling up the wall—yet in his own opinion he was sufficiently compensated for this worsening of his condition by the fact that toward evening the living-room door, which he used to watch intently for an hour or two beforehand, was always thrown open, so that lying in the darkness of his room, invisible to the family, he could see them all at the lamp-lit table and listen to their talk, by general consent as it were, very different from his earlier eavesdropping.

True, their intercourse lacked the lively character of former times, which he had always called to mind with a certain wistfulness in the small hotel bedrooms where he had been wont to throw himself down, tired out, on damp bedding. They were now mostly very silent. Soon after supper his father would fall asleep in his armchair; his mother and sister would admonish each other to be silent; his mother, bending low over the lamp, stitched at fine sewing for an underwear firm; his sister, who had taken a job as a salesgirl, was learning shorthand and French in the evenings on the chance of bettering herself. Sometimes his father woke up, and as if quite unaware that he had been sleeping said to his mother: "What a lot of sewing you're doing today!" and at once fell asleep again, while the two women exchanged a tired smile.

With a kind of mulishness his father persisted in keeping his uniform on even in the house; his dressing gown hung uselessly on its peg and he slept fully dressed where he sat, as if he were ready for service at any moment and even here only at the beck and call of his superior. As a result, his uniform, which was not brand-new to start with, began to look dirty, despite all the loving care of the mother and sister to keep it clean, and Gregor often spent whole evenings gazing at the many greasy spots on the garment, gleaming with gold buttons always in a high state of polish, in which the old man sat sleeping in extreme discomfort and yet quite peacefully.

As soon as the clock struck ten his mother tried to rouse his father with gentle words and to persuade him after that to get into bed, for sitting there he could not have a proper sleep and that was what he needed most, since he had to go on duty at six. But with the mulishness that had obsessed him since he became a bank messenger he always insisted on staying longer at the table, although he regularly fell asleep again and in the end only with the greatest trouble could be got out of his armchair and into his bed. However insistently Gregor's mother and sister kept urging him with gentle reminders, he would go on slowly shaking his head for a quarter of an hour, keeping his eyes shut, and refuse to get to his feet. The mother plucked at his sleeve, whispering endearments in his ear, the sister left her lessons to come to her mother's help, but Gregor's father was not to be caught. He would only sink down deeper in his chair. Not until the two women hoisted him up by the armpits did he open his eyes and look at them both, one after the other, usually with the remark: "This is a life. This is the peace and quiet of my old age." And leaning on the two of them he would heave himself up, with difficulty, as if he were a great burden to himself, suffer them to lead him as far as the door and then wave them off and go on alone, while the mother abandoned her needlework and the sister her pen in order to run after him and help him farther.

Who could find time, in this overworked and tired-out family, to bother about Gregor more than was absolutely needful? The household was reduced more and more; the servant girl was turned off; a gigantic bony charwoman with white hair flying around her head came in morning and evening to do the rough work; everything else was done by Gregor's mother, as well as great piles of sewing. Even various family ornaments, which his mother and sister used to wear with pride at parties and celebrations, had to be sold, as Gregor discovered of an evening from hearing them all discuss the prices obtained. But what they lamented most was the fact that they could not leave the flat which was much too big for their present circumstances, because they could not think of any way to shift Gregor. Yet Gregor saw well enough that consideration for him was not the main difficulty preventing the removal, for they could have easily shifted him in some suitable box with a few air holes in it; what really kept them from moving into another flat was rather their own complete hopelessness and the belief that they had been singled out for a misfortune such as had never happened to any of their relations or acquaintances. They fulfilled to the uttermost all that the world demands of poor people, the father fetched breakfast for the small clerks in the bank, the mother devoted her energy to making underwear for strangers, the sister trotted to and fro behind the counter at the behest of customers, but more than this they had not the strength to do. And the wound in Gregor's back began to nag at him afresh when his mother and sister, after getting his father into bed, came back again, left their work lying, drew close to each other, and sat cheek by cheek; when his mother, pointing toward his room, said: "Shut that door now, Grete," and he was left again in darkness, while next door the women mingled their tears or perhaps sat dry-eyed staring at the table.

Gregor hardly slept at all by night or by day. He was often haunted by the idea that next time the door opened he would take the family's affairs in hand again just as he used to do; once more, after this long interval, there appeared in his thoughts the figures of the chief and the chief clerk, the commercial travelers and the apprentices, the porter who was so dull-witted, two or three friends in other firms, a chambermaid in one of the rural hotels, a sweet and fleeting memory, a cashier in a milliner's shop, whom he had wooed earnestly but too slowly — they all appeared, together with strangers or people he had quite forgotten, but instead of helping him and his family they were one and all unapproachable and he was glad when they vanished. At other times he would not be in the mood to bother about his family, he was only filled with rage at the way they were neglecting him, and although he had no clear idea of what he might care to eat he would make plans for getting into the larder to take the food that was after all his due, even if he were not hungry. His sister no longer took thought to bring him what might especially please him, but in the morning and at noon before she went to business hurriedly pushed into his room with her foot any food that was available, and in the evening cleared it out again with one sweep of the broom, heedless of whether it had been merely tasted, or — as most frequently happened — left untouched. The cleaning of his room, which she now did always in the evenings, could not have been more hastily done. Streaks of dirt stretched along the walls, here and there lay balls of dust and filth. At first Gregor used to station himself in some particularly filthy corner when his sister arrived, in order to reproach her with it, so to speak. But he could have sat there for weeks without getting her to make any improvement; she could see the dirt as well as he did, but she had simply made up her mind to leave it alone. And yet, with a touchiness that was new to her, which seemed anyhow to have infected the whole family, she jealously guarded her claim to be the sole caretaker of Gregor's room. His mother once subjected his room to a thorough cleaning, which was achieved only by means of several buckets of water — all this dampness of course upset Gregor too and he lay widespread, sulky, and motionless on the sofa — but she was well punished for it. Hardly had his sister noticed the changed aspect of his room that evening than she rushed in high dudgeon into the living room and, despite the imploringly raised hands of her mother, burst into a storm of weeping, while her parents — her father had of course been startled out of his chair — looked on at first in helpless amazement; then they too began to go into action; the father reproached the mother on his right for not having left the cleaning of Gregor's room to his sister; shrieked at the sister on his left that never again was she to be allowed to clean Gregor's room; while the mother tried to pull the father into his bedroom, since he was beyond himself with agitation; the sister, shaken with sobs, then beat upon the table with her small fists; and Gregor hissed loudly with rage because not one of them thought of shutting the door to spare him such a spectacle and so much noise.

Still, even if the sister, exhausted by her daily work, had grown tired of looking after Gregor as she did formerly, there was no need for his mother's intervention or for Gregor's being neglected at all. The charwoman was there. This old widow, whose strong bony frame had enabled her to survive the worst a long life could offer, by no means recoiled from Gregor. Without being in the least curious she had once by chance opened the door of his room and at the sight of Gregor, who, taken by surprise, began to rush to and fro although no one was chasing him, merely stood there with her arms folded. From that time she never failed to open his door a little for a moment, morning and evening, to have a look at him. At first she even used to call him to her, with words which apparently she took to be friendly, such as: "Come along, then, you old dung beetle!" or "Look at the old dung beetle, then!" To such allocutions Gregor made no answer, but stayed motionless where he was, as if the door had never been opened. Instead of being allowed to disturb him so senselessly whenever the whim took her, she should rather have been ordered to clean out his room daily, that charwoman! Once, early in the morning—heavy rain was lashing on the windowpanes, perhaps a sign that spring was on the way—Gregor was so exasperated when she began addressing him again that he ran at her, as if to attack her, although slowly and feebly enough. But the charwoman instead of showing fright merely lifted high a chair that happened to be beside the door, and as she stood there with her mouth wide open it was clear that she meant to shut it only when she brought the chair down on Gregor's back. "So you're not coming any nearer?" she asked, as Gregor turned away again, and quietly put the chair back into the corner.

Gregor was now eating hardly anything. Only when he happened to pass the food laid out for him did he take a bit of something in his mouth as a pastime, kept it there for an hour at a time, and usually spat it out again. At first he thought it was chagrin over the state of his room that prevented him from eating, yet he soon got used to the various changes in his room. It had become a habit in the family to push into his room things there was no room for elsewhere, and there were plenty of these now, since one of the rooms had been let to three lodgers. These serious gentlemen—all three of them with full beards, as Gregor once observed through a crack in the door—had a passion for order, not only in their own room but, since they were now members of the household, in all its arrangements, especially in the kitchen. Superfluous, not to say dirty, objects they could not bear. Besides, they had brought with them most of the furnishings they needed. For this reason many things could be dispensed with that it was no use trying to sell but that should not be thrown away either. All of them found their way into Gregor's room. The ash can likewise and the kitchen garbage can. Anything that was not needed for the moment was simply flung into Gregor's room by the charwoman, who did everything in a hurry; fortunately Gregor usually saw only the object, whatever it was, and the hand that held it. Perhaps she intended to take the things away again as time and opportunity offered, or to collect them until she could throw them all out in a heap, but in fact they just lay wherever she happened to throw them, except when Gregor pushed his way through the junk heap and shifted it somewhat, at first out of necessity, because he had not room enough to crawl, but later with increasing enjoyment, although after such excursions, being sad and weary to death, he would lie motionless for hours. And since the lodgers often ate their supper at home in the common living room, the living-room door stayed shut many an evening, yet Gregor reconciled himself quite easily to the shutting of the door, for often enough on evenings when it was opened he had disregarded it entirely and lain in the darkest corner of his room, quite unnoticed by the family. But on one occasion the charwoman left the door open a little and it stayed ajar even when the lodgers came in for supper and the lamp was lit. They set themselves at the top end of the table where formerly Gregor and his father and mother had eaten their meals, unfolded their napkins, and took knife and fork in hand. At once his mother appeared in the other doorway with a dish of meat and close behind her his sister with a dish of potatoes piled high. The food steamed with a thick vapor. The lodgers bent over the food set before them as if to scrutinize it before eating, in fact the man in the middle, who seemed to pass for an authority with the other two, cut a piece of meat as it lay on the dish, obviously to discover if it were tender or should be sent back to the kitchen. He showed satisfaction, and Gregor's mother and sister, who had been watching anxiously, breathed freely and began to smile.

The family itself took its meals in the kitchen. Nonetheless, Gregor's father came into the living room before going into the kitchen and with one prolonged bow, cap in hand, made a round of the table. The lodgers all stood up and murmured something in their beards. When they were alone again they ate their food in almost complete silence. It seemed remarkable to Gregor that among the various noises coming from the table he could always distinguish the sound of their masticating teeth, as if this were a sign to Gregor that one needed teeth in order to eat, and that with toothless jaws even of the finest make one could do nothing. "I'm hungry enough," said Gregor sadly to himself, "but not for that kind of food. How these lodgers are stuffing themselves, and here am I dying of starvation!"

On that very evening—during the whole of his time there Gregor could not remember ever having heard the violin—the sound of violin-playing came from the kitchen. The lodgers had already finished their supper, the one in the middle had brought out a newspaper and given the other two a page apiece, and now they were leaning back at ease reading and smoking. When the violin began to play they pricked up their ears, got to their feet, and went on tiptoe to the hall door where they stood huddled together. Their movements must have been heard in the kitchen, for Gregor's father called out: "Is the violin-playing disturbing you, gentlemen? It can be stopped at once." "On the contrary," said the middle lodger, "could not Fräulein Samsa come and play in this room, beside us, where it is much more convenient and comfortable?" "Oh certainly," cried Gregor's father, as if he were the violin-player. The lodgers came back into the living room and waited. Presently Gregor's father arrived with the music stand, his mother carrying the music and his sister with the violin. His sister quietly made everything ready to start playing; his parents, who had never let rooms before and so had an exaggerated idea of the courtesy due to lodgers, did not venture to sit down on their own chairs; his father leaned against the door, the right hand thrust between two buttons of his livery coat, which was formally buttoned up; but his mother was offered a chair by one of the lodgers and, since she left the chair just where he had happened to put it, sat down in a corner to one side.

Gregor's sister began to play; the father and mother, from either side, intently watched the movements of her hands. Gregor, attracted by the playing, ventured to move forward a little until his head was actually inside the living room. He felt hardly any surprise at his growing lack of consideration for the others; there had been a time when he prided himself on being considerate. And yet just on this occasion he had more reason than ever to hide himself, since, owing to the amount of dust that lay thick in his room and rose into the air at the slightest movement, he too was covered with dust; fluff and hair and remnants of food trailed with him, caught on his back and along his sides; his indifference to everything was much too great for him to turn on his back and scrape himself clean on the carpet, as once he had done several times a day. And in spite of his condition, no shame deterred him from advancing a little over the spotless floor of the living room.

To be sure, no one was aware of him. The family was entirely absorbed in the violin-playing; the lodgers, however, who first of all had stationed themselves, hands in pockets, much too close behind the music stand so that they could all have read the music, which must have bothered his sister, had soon retreated to the window, half whispering with downbent heads, and stayed there while his father turned an anxious eye on them. Indeed, they were making it more than obvious that they had been disappointed in their expectation of hearing good or enjoyable violin-playing, that they had had more than enough of the performance and only out of courtesy suffered a continued disturbance of their peace. From the way they all kept blowing the smoke of their cigars high in the air through nose and mouth one could divine their irritation. And yet Gregor's sister was playing so beautifully. Her face leaned sideways, intently and sadly her eyes followed the notes of music. Gregor crawled a little farther forward and lowered his head to the ground so that it might be possible for his eyes to meet hers. Was he an animal, that music had such an effect upon him? He felt as if the way were opening before him to the unknown nourishment he craved. He was determined to push forward till he reached his sister, to pull at her skirt and so let her know that she was to come into his room with her violin, for no one here appreciated her playing as he would appreciate it. He would never let her out of his room, at least, not so long as he lived; his frightful appearance would become, for the first time, useful to him; he would watch all the doors of his room at once and spit at intruders; but his sister should need no constraint, she should stay with him of her own free will; she should sit beside him on the sofa, bend down her ear to him, and hear him confide that he had had the firm intention of sending her to the Conservatorium, and that, but for his mishap, last Christmas—surely Christmas was long past?—he would have announced it to everybody without allowing a single objection. After this confession his sister would be so touched that she would burst into tears, and Gregor would then raise himself to her shoulder and kiss her on the neck, which, now that she went to business, she kept free of any ribbon or collar.

"Mr. Samsa!" cried the middle lodger to Gregor's father, and pointed, without wasting any more words, at Gregor, now working himself slowly forward. The violin fell silent, the middle lodger first smiled to his friends with a shake of the head and then looked at Gregor again. Instead of driving Gregor out, his father seemed to think it more needful to begin by soothing down the lodgers, although they were not at all agitated and apparently found Gregor more entertaining than the violin-playing. He hurried toward them and, spreading out his arms, tried to urge them back into their own room and at the same time to block their view of Gregor. They now began to be really a little angry, one could not tell whether because of the old man's behavior or because it had just dawned on them that all unwittingly they had such a neighbor as Gregor next door. They demanded explanations of his father, they waved their arms like him, tugged uneasily at their beards, and only with reluctance backed toward their room. Meanwhile Gregor's sister, who stood there as if lost when her playing was so abruptly broken off, came to life again, pulled herself together all at once after standing for a while holding violin and bow in nervelessly hanging hands and staring at her music, pushed her violin into the lap of her mother, who was still sitting in her chair fighting asthmatically for breath, and ran into the lodgers' room to which they were now being shepherded by her father rather more quickly than before. One could see the pillows and blankets on the beds flying under her accustomed fingers and being laid in order. Before the lodgers had actually reached their room she had finished making the beds and slipped out.

The old man seemed once more to be so possessed by his mulish self-assertiveness that he was forgetting all the respect he should show to his lodgers. He kept driving them on and driving them on until in the very door of the bedroom the middle lodger stamped his foot loudly on the floor and so brought him to a halt. "I beg to announce," said the lodger, lifting one hand and looking also at Gregor's mother and sister, "that because of the disgusting conditions prevailing in this household and family"—here he spat on the floor with emphatic brevity—"I give you notice on the spot. Naturally I won't pay you a penny for the days I have lived here, on the contrary I shall consider bringing an action for damages against you, based on claims—believe me—that will be easily susceptible of proof." He ceased and stared straight in front of him, as if he expected something. In fact his two friends at once rushed into the breach with these words: "And we too give notice on the spot." On that he seized the door handle and shut the door with a slam.

Gregor's father, groping with his hands, staggered forward and fell into his chair; it looked as if he were stretching himself there for his ordinary evening nap, but the marked jerkings of his head, which were as if uncontrollable, showed that he was far from asleep. Gregor had simply stayed quietly all the time on the spot where the lodgers had espied him. Disappointment at the failure of his plan, perhaps also the weakness arising from extreme hunger, made it impossible for him to move. He feared, with a fair degree of certainty, that at any moment the general tension would discharge itself in a combined attack upon him, and he lay waiting. He did not react even to the noise made by the violin as it fell off his mother's lap from under her trembling fingers and gave out a resonant note.

"My dear parents," said his sister, slapping her hand on the table by way of introduction, "things can't go on like this. Perhaps you don't realize that, but I do. I won't utter my brother's name in the presence of this creature, and so all I say is: we must try to get rid of it. We've tried to look after it and to put up with it as far as is humanly possible, and I don't think anyone could reproach us in the slightest."

"She is more than right," said Gregor's father to himself. His mother, who was still choking for lack of breath, began to cough hollowly into her hand with a wild look in her eyes.

His sister rushed over to her and held her forehead. His father's thoughts seemed to have lost their vagueness at Grete's words, he sat more upright, fingering his service cap that lay among the plates still lying on the table from the lodgers' supper, and from time to time looked at the still form of Gregor.

"We must try to get rid of it," his sister now said explicitly to her father, since her mother was coughing too much to hear a word, "it will be the death of both of you, I can see that coming. When one has to work as hard as we do, all of us, one can't stand this continual torment at home on top of it. At least I can't stand it any longer." And she burst into such a passion of sobbing that her tears dropped on her mother's face, where she wiped them off mechanically.

"My dear," said the old man sympathetically, and with evident understanding, "but what can we do?"

Gregor's sister merely shrugged her shoulders to indicate the feeling of helplessness that had now overmastered her during her weeping fit, in contrast to her former confidence.

"If he could understand us," said her father, half questioningly; Grete, still sobbing, vehemently waved a hand to show how unthinkable that was.

"If he could understand us," repeated the old man, shutting his eyes to consider his daughter's conviction that understanding was impossible, "then perhaps we might come to some agreement with him. But as it is——"

"He must go," cried Gregor's sister, "that's the only solution, Father. You must just try to get rid of the idea that this is Gregor. The fact that we've believed it for so long is the root of all our trouble. But how can it be Gregor? If this were Gregor, he would have realized long ago that human beings can't live with such a creature, and he'd have gone away on his own accord. Then we wouldn't have any brother, but we'd be able to go on living and keep his memory in honor. As it is, this creature persecutes us, drives away our lodgers, obviously wants the whole apartment to himself, and would have us all sleep in the gutter. Just look, Father," she shrieked all at once, "he's at it again!" And in an access of panic that was quite incomprehensible to Gregor she even quitted her mother, literally thrusting the chair from her as if she would rather sacrifice her mother than stay so near to Gregor, and rushed behind her father, who also rose up, being simply upset by her agitation, and half spread his arms out as if to protect her.

Yet Gregor had not the slightest intention of frightening anyone, far less his sister. He had only begun to turn around in order to crawl back to his room, but it was certainly a startling operation to watch, since because of his disabled condition he could not execute the difficult turning movements except by lifting his head and then bracing it against the floor over and over again. He paused and looked around. His good intentions seemed to have been recognized; the alarm had only been momentary. Now they were all watching him in melancholy silence. His mother lay in her chair, her legs stiffly outstretched and pressed together, her eyes almost closing for sheer weariness; his father and his sister were sitting beside each other, his sister's arm around the old man's neck.

Perhaps I can go on turning around now, thought Gregor, and began his labors again. He could not stop himself from panting with the effort, and had to pause now and then to take breath. Nor did anyone harass him, he was left entirely to himself. When he had completed the turn-around he began at once to crawl straight back. He was amazed at the distance separating him from his room and could not understand how in his weak state he had managed to accomplish the same journey so recently, almost without remarking it. Intent on crawling as fast as possible, he barely noticed that not a single word, not an ejaculation from his family, interfered with his progress. Only when he was already in the doorway did he turn his head around, not completely, for his neck muscles were getting stiff, but enough to see that nothing had changed behind him except that his sister had risen to her feet. His last glance fell on his mother, who was not quite overcome by sleep.

Hardly was he well inside his room when the door was hastily pushed shut, bolted, and locked. The sudden noise in his rear startled him so much that his little legs gave beneath him. It was his sister who had shown such haste. She had been standing ready waiting and had made a light spring forward, Gregor had not even heard her coming, and she cried "At last!" to her parents as she turned the key in the lock.

"And what now?" said Gregor to himself, looking around in the darkness. Soon he made the discovery that he was now unable to stir a limb. This did not surprise him, rather it seemed unnatural that he should ever actually have been able to move on these feeble little legs. Otherwise he felt relatively comfortable. True, his whole body was aching, but it seemed that the pain was gradually growing less and would finally pass away. The rotting apple in his back and the inflamed area around it, all covered with soft dust, already hardly troubled him. He thought of his family with tenderness and love. The decision that he must disappear was one that he held to even more strongly than his sister, if that were possible. In this state of vacant and peaceful meditation he remained until the tower clock struck three in the morning. The first broadening of light in the world outside the window entered his consciousness once more. Then his head sank to the floor of its own accord and from his nostrils came the last faint flicker of his breath.

When the charwoman arrived early in the morning—what between her strength and her impatience she slammed all the doors so loudly, never mind how often she had been begged not to do so, that no one in the whole apartment could enjoy any quiet sleep after her arrival—she noticed nothing unusual as she took her customary peep into Gregor's room. She thought he was lying motionless on purpose, pretending to be in the sulks; she credited him with every kind of intelligence. Since she happened to have the long-handled broom in her hand she tried to tickle him up with it from the doorway. When that too produced no reaction she felt provoked and poked at him a little harder, and only when she had pushed him along the floor without meeting any resistance was her attention aroused. It did not take her long to establish the truth of the matter, and her eyes widened, she let out a whistle, yet did not waste much time over it but tore open the door of the Samsas' bedroom and yelled into the darkness at the top of her voice: "Just look at this, it's dead; it's lying here dead and done for!"

Mr. and Mrs. Samsa started up in their double bed and before they realized the nature of the charwoman's announcement had some difficulty in overcoming the shock of it. But then they got out of bed quickly, one on either side, Mr. Samsa throwing a blanket over his shoulders, Mrs. Samsa in nothing but her nightgown; in this array they entered Gregor's room. Meanwhile the door of the living room opened, too, where Grete had been sleeping since the advent of the lodgers; she was completely dressed as if she had not been to bed, which seemed to be confirmed also by the paleness of her face. "Dead?" said Mrs. Samsa, looking questioningly at the charwoman, although she could have investigated for herself, and the fact was obvious enough without investigation. "I should say so," said the charwoman, proving her words by pushing Gregor's corpse a long way to one side with her broomstick. Mrs. Samsa made a movement as if to stop her, but checked it. "Well," said Mr. Samsa, "now thanks be to God." He crossed himself, and the three women followed his example. Grete, whose eyes never left the corpse, said: "Just see how thin he was. It's such a long time since he's eaten anything. The food came out again just as it went in." Indeed, Gregor's body was completely flat and dry, as could only now be seen when it was no longer supported by the legs and nothing prevented one from looking closely at it.

"Come in beside us, Grete, for a little while," said Mrs. Samsa with a tremulous smile, and Grete, not without looking back at the corpse, followed her parents into their bedroom. The charwoman shut the door and opened the window wide. Although it was so early in the morning a certain softness was perceptible in the fresh air. After all, it was already the end of March.

The three lodgers emerged from their room and were surprised to see no breakfast; they had been forgotten. "Where's our breakfast?" said the middle lodger peevishly to the charwoman. But she put her finger to her lips and hastily, without a word, indicated by gestures that they should go into Gregor's room. They did so and stood, their hands in the pockets of their somewhat shabby coats, around Gregor's corpse in the room where it was now fully light.

At that the door of the Samsas' bedroom opened and Mr. Samsa appeared in his uniform, his wife on one arm, his daughter on the other. They all looked a little as if they had been crying; from time to time Grete hid her face on her father's arm.

"Leave my house at once!" said Mr. Samsa, and pointed to the door without disengaging himself from the women. "What do you mean by that?" said the middle lodger, taken somewhat aback, with a feeble smile. The two others put their hands behind them and kept rubbing them together, as if in gleeful expectation of a fine set-to in which they were bound to come off the winners. "I mean just what I say," answered Mr. Samsa, and advanced in a straight line with his two companions toward the lodger. He stood his ground at first quietly, looking at the floor as if his thoughts were taking a new pattern in his head. "Then let us go, by all means," he said, and looked up at Mr. Samsa as if in a sudden access of humility he were expecting some renewed sanction for this decision. Mr. Samsa merely nodded briefly once or twice with meaning eyes. Upon that the lodger really did go with long strides into the hall, his two friends had been listening and had quite stopped rubbing their hands for some moments and now went scuttling after him as if afraid that Mr. Samsa might get into the hall before them and cut them off from their leader. In the hall they all three took their hats from the rack, their sticks from the umbrella stand, bowed in silence, and quitted the apartment. With a suspiciousness that proved quite unfounded Mr. Samsa and the two women followed them out to the landing; leaning over the banister they watched the three figures slowly but surely going down the long stairs, vanishing from sight at a certain turn of the staircase on every floor and coming into view again after a moment or so; the more they dwindled, the more the Samsa family's interest in them dwindled, and when a butcher's boy met them and passed them on the stairs coming up proudly with a tray on his head, Mr. Samsa and the two women soon left the landing and as if a burden had been lifted from them went back into their apartment.

They decided to spend this day in resting and going for a stroll; they had not only deserved such a respite from work, but absolutely needed it. And so they sat down at the table and wrote three notes of excuse, Mr. Samsa to his board of management, Mrs. Samsa to her employer, and Grete to the head of her firm. While they were writing, the charwoman came in to say that she was going now, since her morning's work was finished. At first they only nodded without looking up, but as she kept hovering there they eyed her irritably. "Well?" said Mr. Samsa. The charwoman stood grinning in the doorway as if she had good news to impart to the family but meant not to say a word unless properly questioned. The small ostrich feather standing upright on her hat, which had annoyed Mr. Samsa ever since she was engaged, was waving gaily in all directions. "Well, what is it then?" asked Mrs. Samsa, who obtained more respect from the charwoman than the others. "Oh," said the charwoman, giggling so amiably that she could not at once continue, "just this, you don't need to bother about how to get rid of the thing next door. It's been seen to already." Mrs. Samsa and Grete bent over their letters again, as if preoccupied; Mr. Samsa, who perceived that she was eager to begin describing it all in detail, stopped her with a decisive hand. But since she was not allowed to tell her story, she remembered the great hurry she was in, obviously deeply huffed: "Bye, everybody," she said, whirling off violently, and departed with a frightful slamming of doors.

"She'll be given notice tonight," said Mr. Samsa, but neither from his wife nor his daughter did he get any answer, for the charwoman seemed to have shattered again the composure they had barely achieved. They rose, went to the window and stayed there, clasping each other tight. Mr. Samsa turned in his chair to look at them and quietly observed them for a little. Then he called out: "Come along, now, do. Let bygones be bygones. And you might have some consideration for me." The two of them complied at once, hastened to him, caressed him, and quickly finished their letters.

Then they all three left the apartment together, which was more than they had done for months, and went by tram into the open country outside the town. The tram, in which they were the only passengers, was filled with warm sunshine. Leaning comfortably back in their seats they canvassed their prospects for the future, and it appeared on closer inspection that these were not at all bad, for the jobs they had got, which so far they had never really discussed with each other, were all three admirable and likely to lead to better things later on. The greatest immediate improvement in their condition would of course arise from moving to another house; they wanted to take a smaller and cheaper but also better situated and more easily run apartment than the one they had, which Gregor had selected. While they were thus conversing, it struck both Mr. and Mrs. Samsa, almost at the same moment, as they became aware of their daughter's increasing vivacity, that in spite of all the sorrow of recent times, which had made her cheeks pale, she had bloomed into a pretty girl with a good figure. They grew quieter and half unconsciously exchanged glances of complete agreement, having come to the conclusion that it would soon be time to find a good husband for her. And it was like a confirmation of their new dreams and excellent intentions that at the end of their journey their daughter sprang to her feet first and stretched her young body.

‿ TANIZAKI JUNICHIRO
B. JAPAN, 1886–1965

tah-nee-ZAH-kee
joo-nee-CHEE-roh

Tanizaki Junichiro is one of modern Japan's most prolific and acclaimed writers, rivaling in popularity and reputation Nobel Prize–winning writer Kawabata Yasunari (1899–1972) (p. 659), a contemporary of his, and the younger Japanese novelist Mishima Yukio (1925–1970). Beginning his writing career in 1909 with the publication of a one-act play, Tanizaki achieved notoriety a year later with "The Tattooer," the story of a tattoo artist obsessed with a desire to cover the entire body of a beautiful young woman with his work. This piece anticipates the exoticism, decadence, sexual tension, fascination with the past, and quest for the beautiful that recur throughout Tanizaki's writings. His work exercised a profound influence on Japanese writing in the twentieth century and in 1949 earned him the Imperial Culture Prize, the highest official sanction for a writer's work given in Japan, and in 1964 an honorary membership in the American Academy and Institute of Arts and Letters.

www For links to more information about Tanizaki, a quiz on "Aguri," and for information on the culture and context of Japan in the twentieth century, see *World Literature Online* at bedfordstmartins .com/worldlit.

Early Influences.   Tanizaki Junichiro was born in 1886 in Tokyo and raised in the old merchant quarter. During Tanizaki's childhood, his father struggled to keep up the once-prosperous family's social position, attempting several business enterprises and intermittently relying on Tanizaki's maternal grandfather's printing business for support. With his mother, a woman recognized for her beauty and accustomed to the finer things in life, Tanizaki attended **Kabuki** theater,[1] where he developed the keen sensitivity and love for music, spectacle, and drama that characterize his work. A frequenter of nearby book shops, Tanizaki cultivated his interest in heroic tales of the samurai, even as his mother nurtured his appreciation for handmade paper and fine fabrics. Perhaps fittingly, his fiction features characters who despite their mastery of creating appearances do not measure up to their nobler ambitions.

Because of financial difficulties, in 1910 Tanizaki left the Tokyo Imperial University, where he had been studying Japanese literature. At the time, Tanizaki was fascinated with the West, and his early work shows the influence of Western writers, including the French poet Charles Baudelaire (1821–1867), the American fiction writer Edgar Allan Poe (1809–1849), and the Irish satirist Oscar Wilde (1854–1900), whose *The Picture of Dorian Gray* Tanizaki translated into Japanese. Setting up household in Yokohama, a cosmopolitan port city south of Tokyo, Tanizaki sought out European ideas and influences and even built a Western-style house in the foreign enclave of the city. There he continued his writing and produced several screenplays for the developing Japanese movie industry.

Kyoto Culture.   After the great earthquake of 1923 that devastated parts of Tokyo and Yokohama, Tanizaki moved to Ashihi in the Kyoto-Osaka region. In this more traditional region of Japan, Tanizaki shrugged off his Euro-American ways and began seriously to explore the history and culture of his homeland. In the novel *A Fool's Love* (*Chijin no Ai*, 1924), written just after his move to Ashihi, Tanizaki self-consciously parodied and criticized his and his generation's infatuation with the West, particularly with American culture. As in Nigerian playwright Wole Soyinka's **The Lion and the Jewel** (1963), as a result of mimicking Western ways, the protagonist in *A Fool's Love* is shown to be a hollow man, emptied of identity and caught up in a self-destructive attraction to a simplified version of the West. The novel also continues Tanizaki's exploration of the destructiveness of sexuality.

The move to Ashihi marked a turning point for Tanizaki, and in his later fiction, such as *Some Prefer Nettles* (*Tade Kuu Mushi*, 1928–29), the Kyoto region would be identified with traditional Japanese culture while Tokyo and its environs would symbolize Japan under the influence of the West. To further his reorientation to his country's indigenous traditions and history, Tanizaki for several years undertook the overwhelming task of translating the classic Japanese novel *The Tale of Genji* (see Book 2) into modern Japanese, making the text accessible to his contemporaries. Moreover, many of his novels and short stories, such as "A Blind Man's Tale" and "A Portrait of Shunkin," turn on themes drawn from Japanese history and are remarkable for their display of historical scholarship as well as their creativity. The latter story takes place during the Japanese

Tanizaki's reputation has at times been controversial, owing to his preoccupation with the bizarre and with sexual aberration. He never forgot the novelist's duty to entertain, but his work is a serious exploration of a psyche tormented by a dual vision of woman as both devil and nurturer, and forced also to choose between the reticence of Japanese culture and the hard brashness of the West.

– Phillip Tudor Harries, literary critic, 1993

p. 1146

---

[1]**Kabuki theater:** A form of popular Japanese drama using only male actors that is aimed primarily at the middle classes; Kabuki developed in the sixteenth and seventeenth centuries parallel to *joruri*, or puppet theater, which often shares the same plots and stories and even the same plays.

civil war of the sixteenth century that culminated in the rise of Tokugawa Ieyasu, the first shogun of the newly united Japan after whom the TOKU-GAWA, or EDO, era (1603–1867) is named.[2] Following the events in the life of a servant named Yaichi, Tanizaki re-creates the chaotic atmosphere of war and the shifting alliances that characterized sixteenth-century Japan. Like Mori Ogai before him (see Book 5) and Kawabata Yasunari, Tanizaki increasingly was drawn in his work to the historical past, which became for each of these writers a sanctuary for the values of order and beauty.

In one of the great essays of twentieth-century literature, "In Praise of Shadows" ("In'ei Raisan," 1933), Tanizaki describes his project as a recuperation of the "world of shadows"—that is, the cultivated traditions of the past—that were giving way to the desire to emulate the West:

> No matter what complaints we may have, Japan has chosen to fol-low the West, and there is nothing for her to do but move bravely ahead and leave us old ones behind. But we must be resigned to the fact that as long as our skin is the color it is the loss we have suffered cannot be remedied. I have written all this because I have thought that there might still be somewhere, possibly in literature or the arts, where something could be saved. I would call back at least for literature this world of shadows we are losing. In the mansion called literature I would have the eaves deep and the walls dark, I would push back into the shadows the things that come forward too clearly, I would strip away the useless decoration. I do not ask that this be done everywhere, but perhaps we may be allowed at least one mansion where we can turn off the electric lights and see what it is like without them.

In this brilliant essay, the dark contours of *Nō* drama, the shadowed interiors of Japanese houses, the soft light of the candle lantern—all things that evoke the subtle tones of Japanese culture—are contrasted with the bewildering glare of the electric lamp that illuminates in the West everything from the commode to the low ceilings of the Western-style Miyaho Hotel in Kyoto. Thus, the shadow world is that of the receding traditions of old Japan, while the overly illuminated spaces of contemporary Japan are those abandoned to Westernization.

Ties to Tradition.   In 1930, in what would be only halfway through his long career, a "Complete Works" of Tanizaki appeared. But the writer had just begun his prolific exploration of numerous genres—short stories, novels, plays, screenplays, poetry, essays, and criticism—that today fill twenty-eight volumes. Twice married and divorced, in 1935 Tanizaki

---

[2] **Tokugawa era** (1603–1867): Period of Japanese history named after Tokugawa Ieyasu (1542–1616), who was named *shogun* in 1603; also known as the Edo era, named after the capital (now Tokyo). The early Tokugawa period was one of international isolation, political stability, and nation building when the middle classes rose to power and influence; it was a period of great literary and cultural growth, particularly among popular art forms—such as Kabuki and *joruri* (puppet) theater, the popular novel, and colored woodblock art—produced for the flourishing middle-class audiences. The era ended in 1867 when a group of resentful samurai restored imperial rule under the teenage emperor Meiji (r. 1867–1912) and opened Japan to Western trade and cultural exchange.

wed Mrs. Nezu Matsuko, the recently widowed daughter of a rich merchant from **Osaka**. With Matsuko, the now-famous writer found a lifelong companion, whose sense of custom and traditional values further strengthened his own. During World War II, Tanizaki wrote *The Makioka Sisters* (*Sasameyuki*, 1943–48), a novel of manners that was at first banned in Japan as an impediment to the war effort. At the end of the war, however, he received the prestigious Imperial Culture Prize in part for his novel, which traces the history of four sisters living in Osaka and clinging to outmoded ways as they attempt to find a husband for the second sister, Yukiko. The work marked a way of life that was passing quickly out of existence in the war years.

OH-sah-kah

Postwar Novels.   Tanizaki's postwar novels return to the realm of the senses, to the shadowy side of fantasy and sadomasochism that he had first broached in "The Tattooer." *The Key* (*Kagi,* 1956) and *Diary of a Mad Old Man* (*Futen Rojin Nikki,* 1961–62), his last completed novel, are both written in the form of a diary and record the sexual escapades of an aging professor and his wife, and those of a seventy-year-old man. In both novels, as in **"Aguri,"** Western commodities and fashions heighten eroticism. Also as in "Aguri," the world of appearances is confused with fact, and imagined fictions influence life. Picking up the themes of his youthful writing, Tanizaki rounds out his oeuvre with an ironic celebration of the power of imagination and desire to construct the beautiful, however idiosyncratic or perverse it may appear to others. His explorations of sexuality place him in the company of Western writers such as D. H. Lawrence and Milan Kundera, whose **"The Hitchhiking Game"** similarly engages in playing games as a way to explore the psychological dimensions of its characters and their relationships. After completing the *Diary of a Mad Old Man,* Tanizaki continued to write but did not complete another novel before his death in Yugawara, south of Tokyo, on July 30, 1965.

ah-GOO-ree

p. 1005

■ CONNECTIONS

Emilia Pardo Bazán, "The Revolver" (Book 5); Milan Kundera, "The Hitchhiking Game," p. 1005. Tanizaki's "Aguri" presents a couple whose game playing upsets the tenuous balance of an already strained relationship. Similarly, Kundera's story recounts the erotically charged adventure of a couple involved in a game that leads them into confusion and then to some serious self-reflection about the meaning and nature of their relationship as well as their own identities. Pardo Bazán's story depicts from a feminist perspective the consequences of game playing as a means of controlling a partner. Taken together, what do these stories suggest about the stability and formation of identity in the modern world? How do they negotiate or define the boundary between art and life?

T. S. Eliot, *The Waste Land,* p. 486. As in "Aguri," Tanizaki's fiction often concerns itself with the erosion of traditional Japanese values in the modern world, often figured by a superficial and misguided fascination with Western fashion, movies, architecture, and the like. Eliot's *The Waste Land* similarly presents a picture of London uprooted from its traditional moorings. In what ways do Eliot and Tanizaki share the same concerns about the loss of meaning or value in the modern world?

> . . . it is likely that if any one writer of the period will stand the test of time and be accepted as a figure of world stature, it will be Tanizaki.
>
> – DONALD KEENE, critic and literary historian, 1984

Thomas Mann, *Death in Venice,* **p. 266.** Writers in the early twentieth century were interested in such psychological conditions as neurosis, narcissism, schizophrenia, obsession, and compulsion. Tanizaki's early fiction often deals with sexual obsession, and "Aguri" explores what might be called the erotic economy of the beautiful: that is, the difference between love and desire, between the beautiful object and the fetish. Similarly, in *Death in Venice,* Gustave Aschenbach's attraction to Tadzio blurs the distinction between erotic desire and aesthetic appreciation, and the novella explores the psychology of obsession as Aschenbach both recoils from and is consumed by his desire. Compare Okada and Aschenbach in terms of their narcissism, or egocentricity, and obsessive behavior. What is each author's purpose in creating such characters?

■ **FURTHER RESEARCH**

Chambers, Anthony Hood. *The Secret Window: Ideal Worlds in Tanizaki's Fiction.* 1994.
Ito, Ken. *Visions of Desire: Tanizaki's Fictional Worlds.* 1991.
Keene, Donald. *Dawn to the West: Japanese Literature of the Modern Era.* 1984.
Petersen, Gwen Boardman. *The Moon in the Water: Understanding Tanizaki, Kawabata, and Mishima.* 1979.
Van Gessel, C. *Three Modern Novelists: Soseki, Tanizaki, Kawabata.* 1993.

■ **PRONUNCIATION**

Aguri: ah-GOO-ree
Okada: oh-KAH-dah
Osaka: OH-sah-kah, oh-SAH-kah
Tanizaki Junichiro: tah-nee-ZAH-kee joo-nee-CHEE-roh

 # Aguri

Translated by Howard Hibbert

"Getting a bit thinner, aren't you? Is anything wrong? You're not looking well these days. . . ."

That was what his friend T. had said in passing when they happened to meet him along the Ginza a little while ago. It reminded Okada that he had spent last night with Aguri too, and he felt more fatigued than ever. Of course T. could scarcely have been teasing him about *that*—his relations with Aguri were too well known, there was nothing unusual about being seen strolling on the Ginza in downtown Tokyo with her. But to Okada, with his taut-stretched nerves and his vanity, T.'s

---

"Aguri." First published in 1922, this work is the story of both Okada, a man in his thirties suffering from poor health due in part to overindulgence—"sexual and otherwise"—and the title character, Aguri, a woman half his age. Compelled by sexual desire, Okada lives out his fantasy of seeing Aguri dressed in Western clothes. Aguri becomes a symbol, in turn, of the Japanese desire for Euro-American culture, in this case a near-fatal attraction.

remark was disturbing. Everyone he met said he was "getting thinner"—he had worried about it himself for over a year. In the last six months you could almost see the change from one day to the next, as his fine rich flesh slowly melted away. He'd got into the habit of furtively examining his body in the mirror whenever he took a bath, to see how emaciated it was becoming, but by now he was afraid to look. In the past (until a year or two ago, at least) people said he had a feminine sort of figure. He had rather prided himself on it. "The way I'm built makes you think of a woman, doesn't it?" he used to say archly to his friends at the bathhouse. "Don't get any funny ideas!" But now . . .

It was from the waist down that his body had seemed most feminine. He remembered often standing before a mirror entranced by his own reflection, running his hand lovingly over his plump white buttocks, as well rounded as a young girl's. His thighs and calves were almost *too* bulging, but it had delighted him to see how fat they looked—the legs of a chophouse waitress—alongside Aguri's slim ones. She was only fourteen then, and her legs were as slender and straight as those of any Western girl: Stretched out beside his in the bath, they looked more beautiful than ever, which pleased him as much as it did Aguri. She was a tomboy, and used to push him over on his back and sit on him, or walk over him, or trample on his thighs as if she were flattening a lump of dough. . . . But now what miserable skinny legs he had! His knees and ankles had been nicely dimpled, but for some time now the bones had stuck out pathetically, you could see them moving under the skin. The exposed blood vessels looked like earthworms. His buttocks were flattening out too: When he sat on something hard it felt as if a pair of boards had been clapped together. Yet it was only lately that his ribs began to show: One by one they had come into sharp relief, from the bottom up, till now you could see the whole skeleton of his chest so distinctly that it made a somewhat grim anatomy lesson. He was such a heavy eater that his little round belly had seemed safe enough, but even *that* was gradually shriveling—at this rate, you'd soon be able to make out his inner organs! Next to his legs, he had prided himself on his smooth "feminine" arms; at the slightest excuse he rolled up his sleeves to show them off. Women admired and envied them, and he used to joke with his girl friends about it. Now, even to the fondest eye, they didn't look at all feminine—or masculine either for that matter. They weren't so much human arms as two sticks of wood. Two pencils hanging down beside his body. All the little hollows between one bone and the next were deepening, the flesh dwindling away. How much longer can I go on losing weight like this? he asked himself. It's amazing that I can still get around at all, when I'm so horribly emaciated! He felt grateful to be alive, but also a little terrified. . . .

These thoughts were so unnerving that Okada had a sudden attack of giddiness. There was a heavy, numbing sensation in the back of his head; he felt as if his knees were shaking and his legs buckling under him, as if he were being knocked over backward. No doubt the state of his nerves had something to do with it, but he knew very well that it came from long overindulgence, sexual and otherwise—as did his diabetes, which caused some of his symptoms. There was no use feeling sorry now, but he *did* regret having to pay for it so soon, and pay, moreover, by the deterioration of his good looks, his proudest possession. I'm still in my thirties, he thought. I don't see why my health has to fail so badly. . . . He wanted to cry and stamp his feet in rage.

"Wait a minute—look at that ring! An aquamarine, isn't it? I wonder how it would look on me."

Aguri had stopped short and tugged at his sleeve; she was peering into a Ginza show window. As she spoke she waved the back of her hand under Okada's nose, flexing and extending her fingers. Her long slender fingers—so soft they seemed made only for pleasure—gleamed in the bright May afternoon sunlight with an especially seductive charm. Once in Nanking he had looked at a singsong girl's fingers resting gracefully on the table like the petals of some exquisite hothouse flower, and thought there could be no more delicate beauty than a Chinese woman's hands. But Aguri's hands were only a little larger, only a little more like those of an ordinary human being. If the singsong girl's hands were hothouse flowers, hers were fresh young wildflowers: The fact that they were not so artificial only made them more appealing. How pretty a bouquet of flowers with petals like these would be. . . .

"What do you think? Would it look nice?" She poised her fingertips on the railing in front of the window, pressed them back in the half-moon curve of a dancer's gesture, and stared at them as if she had lost all interest in the ring.

Okada mumbled something in reply but forgot it immediately. He was staring at her hands too, at the beautiful hands he knew so well. . . . Several years had passed since he began playing with those delicious morsels of flesh: squeezing them in his palms like clay, putting them inside his clothes like a pocket warmer, or in his mouth, under his arm, under his chin. But while he was steadily aging, her mysterious hands looked younger every year. When Aguri was only fourteen they seemed yellow and dry, with tiny wrinkles, but now at seventeen the skin was white and smooth, and yet even on the coldest day so sleek you'd think the oil would cloud the gold band of her ring. Childish little hands, as tender as a baby's and as voluptuous as a whore's—how fresh and youthful they were, always restlessly seeking pleasure! . . . But why had his health failed like this? Just to look at her hands made him think of all they had provoked him to, all that went on in those secret rooms where they met; and his head ached from the potent stimulus. . . . As he kept his eyes fixed on them, he began to think of the rest of her body. Here in broad daylight on the crowded Ginza he saw her naked shoulders . . . her breasts . . . her belly . . . buttocks . . . legs . . . one by one all the parts of her body came floating up before his eyes with frightening clarity in queer, undulating shapes. And he felt crushed under the solid weight of her hundred and fifteen or twenty pounds. . . . For a moment Okada thought he was going to faint—his head was reeling, he seemed on the verge of falling. . . . Idiot! Suddenly he drove away his fantasies, steadied his tottering legs. . . .

"Well, are we going shopping?"

"All right."

They began walking toward Shimbashi Station. . . . Now they were off to Yokohama.

Today Aguri must be happy, he thought, I'll be buying her a whole new outfit. You'll find the right things for yourself in the foreign shops of Yokohama, he had told her; in Arthur Bond's and Lane Crawford, and that Indian jeweler, and the Chinese dressmaker. . . . You're the exotic type of beauty; Japanese kimonos cost more than they're worth, and they're not becoming to you. Notice the Western and the Chinese ladies: They know how to set off their faces and figures to advantage, and without spending too much money at it. You ought to do the same from now on. . . . And so Aguri had been looking forward to today. As she walks along, breathing a little heavily in the early-summer heat, her white skin damp with sweat under the heavy flannel kimono that hampers her long, youthful limbs, she imagines herself shedding these "unbecoming" clothes, fixing jewels on her ears, hanging a necklace around her throat, slipping into a near-transparent blouse of rustling silk or cambric, swaying elegantly on tiptoes in fragile high-heeled shoes. . . . She sees herself looking like the Western ladies who pass them on the street. Whenever one of them comes long Aguri studies her from head to toe, following her with her eyes and badgering him with questions about how he likes that hat, or that necklace, or whatever.

But Okada shared her preoccupation. All the smart young foreign ladies made him think of an Aguri transfigured by Western clothes. . . . I'd like to buy that for you, he thought; and this too. . . . Yet why couldn't he be a little more cheerful? Later on they would play their enchanting game together. It was a clear day with a refreshing breeze, a fine May afternoon for any kind of outing . . . for dressing her up in airy new garments, grooming her like a beloved pet, and then taking her on the train in search of a delightful hiding place. Somewhere with a balcony overlooking the blue sea, or a room at a hot-spring resort where the young leaves of the forest glisten beyond glass doors, or else a gloomy, out-of-the-way hotel in the foreign quarter. And there the game would begin, the enchanting game that he was always dreaming of, that gave him his only reason for living. . . . Then she would stretch herself out like a leopard. A leopard in necklace and earrings. A leopard brought up as a house pet, knowing exactly how to please its master, but one whose occasional flashes of ferocity made its master cringe. Frisking, scratching, striking, pouncing on him — finally ripping and tearing him to shreds, and trying to suck the marrow out of his bones. . . . A deadly game! The mere thought of it had an ecstatic lure for him. He found himself trembling with excitement. Once again his head was swimming, he thought he was going to faint. . . . He wondered if he might be dying, now at last, aged thirty-four, collapsing here in the street. . . .

"Oh, are you dead? How tiresome!" Aguri glances absent-mindedly at the corpse lying at her feet. The two-o'clock sun beats down on it, casting dark shadows in the hollows of its sunken cheeks. . . . If he *had* to die he might have waited half a day longer, till we finished our shopping. . . . Aguri clicks her tongue in annoyance. I don't want to get mixed up in this if I can help it, she thinks, but I suppose I can't just leave him here. And there are hundreds of yen in his pocket. That money was *mine* — he might at least have willed it to me before he died. The poor fool was so crazy about me he couldn't possibly resent it if I take the money and buy anything I please, or flirt with any man I please. He knew I was fickle — he even seemed to enjoy it, sometimes. . . . As she makes excuses to herself Aguri extracts the money from his pocket. If he tries to haunt me I won't be afraid of *him* — he'll listen to me whether he's alive or dead. I'll have my way. . . .

"Look, Mr. Ghost! I bought this wonderful ring with your money. I bought this beautiful lace-trimmed skirt. And see!" (She pulls up her skirt to show her legs.) "See these legs you're so fond of, these gorgeous legs? I bought a pair of white silk stockings, and pink garters too—all with your money! Don't you think I have good taste? Don't you think I look angelic? Although you're dead I'm wearing the right clothes for me, just the way you wanted, and I'm having a marvelous time! I'm so happy, really happy! You must be happy too, for having given me all this. Your dreams have come true in me, now that I'm so beautiful, so full of life! Well, Mr. Ghost, my poor love-struck Mr. Ghost who can't rest in peace—how about a smile?"

Then I'll hug that cold corpse as hard as I can, hug it till his bones crack, and he screams: "Stop! I can't bear any more!" If he doesn't give in, I'll find a way to seduce him. I'll love him till his withered skin is torn to shreds, till his last drop of blood is squeezed out, till his dry bones fall apart. Then even a ghost ought to feel satisfied. . . .

"What's the matter? Is something on your mind?"

"Uh-h . . ." Okada began mumbling under his breath.

They looked as if they were having a pleasant walk together—it ought to have been extremely pleasant—and yet he couldn't share her gaiety. One sad thought after another welled up, and he felt exhausted even before they began their game. It's only nerves, he had told himself; nothing serious, I'll get over it as soon as I go outside. That was how he had talked himself into coming, but he'd been wrong. It wasn't nerves alone: His arms and legs were so tired they were ready to drop off, and his joints creaked as he walked. Sometimes being tired was a mild, rather enjoyable sensation, but when it got this bad it might be a dangerous symptom. At this very moment, all unknown to him, wasn't his system being invaded by some grave disease? Wasn't he staggering along letting the disease take its own course till it overwhelmed him? Better to collapse right away than be so ghastly tired! He'd like to sink down into a soft bed. Maybe his health had demanded it long ago. Any doctor would be alarmed and say: "Why in heaven's name are you out walking in *your* condition? You belong in bed—it's no wonder you're dizzy!"

The thought left Okada feeling more exhausted than ever; walking became an even greater effort. On the Ginza sidewalk—that dry, stony surface he so much enjoyed striding over when he was well—every step sent a shock of pain vibrating up from his heel to the top of his head. First of all, his feet were cramped by these tan box-calf shoes that compressed them in a narrow mold. Western clothes were intended for healthy, robust men: To anyone in a weakened condition they were quite insupportable. Around the waist, over the shoulders, under the arms, around the neck—every part of the body was pressed and squeezed by clasps and buttons and rubber and leather, layer over layer, as if you were strapped to a cross. And of course you had to put on stockings before the shoes, stretching them carefully up on your legs by garters. Then you put on a shirt, and then trousers, cinching them in with a buckle at the back till they cut into your waist and hanging them from your shoulders with suspenders. Your neck was choked in a close-fitting collar, over which you fastened a nooselike necktie, and stuck a pin in it. If a man is well filled out, the tighter you squeeze him, the more vigorous and bursting with vitality he seems; but a man who is only skin and bones can't stand that. The thought that he was wearing such appalling garments made Okada gasp for breath, made his arms and legs even wearier. It was only because these Western clothes held him together that he was able to keep on walking at all — but to think of stiffening a limp, helpless body, shackling it hand and foot, and driving it ahead with shouts of "Keep going! Don't you dare collapse!" It was enough to make a man want to cry. . . .

Suddenly Okada imagined his self-control giving way, imagined himself breaking down and sobbing. . . . This sprucely dressed middle-aged gentleman who was strolling along the Ginza until a moment ago, apparently out to enjoy the fine weather with the young lady at his side, a gentleman who looks as if he might be the young lady's uncle — all at once screws up his face into a dreadful shape and begins to bawl like a child! He stops there in the street and pesters her to carry him. "*Please, Aguri! I can't go another step! Carry me piggyback!*"

"What's wrong with you?" says Aguri sharply, glaring at him like a stern auntie. "Stop acting like that! Everybody's looking at you!" . . . Probably she doesn't notice that he has gone mad: It's not unusual for her to see him in tears. This is the first time it's happened on the street, but when they're alone together he always cries like this. . . . How silly of him! she must be thinking. There's nothing for him to cry about in public — if he wants to cry I'll let him cry his heart out later! "Shh! Be quiet! You're embarrassing me!"

But Okada won't stop crying. At last he begins to kick and struggle, tearing off his necktie and collar and throwing them down. And then, dog-tired, panting for breath, he falls flat on the pavement. "I can't walk any more. . . . I'm sick . . . ," he mutters, half delirious. "Get me out of these clothes and put me in something soft! Make a bed for me here, I don't care if it *is* in the street!"

Aguri is at her wit's end, so embarrassed her face is as red as fire. There is no escape — a huge crowd of people has swarmed around them under the blazing sun. A policeman turns up. . . . He questions Aguri in front of everyone. ("Who do you suppose she is?" people begin whispering to one another. "Some rich man's daughter?" "No, I don't think so." "An actress?") "What's the matter there?" the policeman asks Okada, not unkindly. He regards him as a lunatic. "How about getting up now, instead of sleeping in a place like this?"

"I won't! I won't! I'm sick, I tell you! How can I ever get up?" Still sobbing weakly, Okada shakes his head. . . .

He could see the spectacle vividly before his eyes. He felt as if he were actually sobbing. . . .

"Papa . . ." A faint voice is calling — a sweet little voice, not Aguri's. It is the voice of a chubby four-year-old girl in a printed muslin kimono, who beckons to him with her tiny hand. Behind her stands a woman whose hair is done up in a chignon; she looks like the child's mother. . . . "Teruko! Teruko! Here I am! . . . Ah, Osaki! Are you there too?" And then he sees his own mother, who died several years ago. She is gesturing eagerly and trying hard to tell him something, but she is too far away, a veil of mist hangs between them. . . . Yet he realizes that tears of loneliness and sorrow are streaming down her cheeks. . . .

I'm going to stop thinking sad thoughts like that, Okada told himself; thoughts about Mother, about Osaki and the child, about death. . . . Why did they weigh so heavily on him? No doubt because of his poor health. Two or three years ago when he was well they wouldn't have seemed so overpowering, but now they combined with physical exhaustion to thicken and clog all his veins. And when he was sexually excited the clogging became more and more oppressive. . . . As he walked along in the bright May sunshine he felt himself isolated from the world around him: His sight was dimmed, his hearing faded, his mind turned darkly, obstinately in upon itself.

"If you have enough money left," Aguri was saying, "how about buying me a wrist watch?" They had just come to Shimbashi Station; perhaps she thought of it when she saw the big clock.

"They have good watches in Shanghai. I should have bought you one when I was there."

For a moment Okada's fancies flew off to China. . . . At Soochow, aboard a beautiful pleasure boat, being poled along a serene canal toward the soaring Tiger Hill Pagoda . . . Inside the boat two young lovers sit blissfully side by side like turtle-doves. . . . He and Aguri transformed into a Chinese gentleman and a singsong girl. . . .

Was he in love with Aguri? If anyone asked, of course he would answer "Yes." But at the thought of Aguri his mind became a pitch-dark room hung with black velvet curtains—a room like a conjurer's stage set—in the center of which stood the marble statue of a nude woman. Was that really Aguri? Surely the Aguri he loved was the living, breathing counterpart of that marble figure. This girl walking beside him now through the foreign shopping quarter of Yokohama—he could see the lines of her body through the loose flannel clothing that enveloped it, could picture to himself the statue of the "woman" under her kimono. He recalled each elegant trace of the chisel. Today he would adorn the statue with jewels and silks. He would strip off that shapeless, unbecoming kimono, reveal that naked "woman" for an instant, and then dress her in Western clothes: He would accentuate every curve and hollow, give her body a brilliant surface and lively flowing lines; he would fashion swelling contours, make her wrists, ankles, neck, all strikingly slender and graceful. Really, shopping to enhance the beauty of the woman you love ought to be like a dream come true.

A dream . . . There was indeed something dreamlike about walking along this quiet, almost deserted street lined with massive Western-style buildings, looking into show windows here and there. It wasn't garish, like the Ginza; even in daytime a hush lay over it. Could anyone be alive in these silent buildings, with their thick gray walls where the window glass glittered like fish eyes, reflecting the blue sky? It seemed more like a museum gallery than a street. And the merchandise displayed behind the glass on both sides was bright and colorful, with the fascinating, mysterious luster of a garden at the bottom of the sea.

A curio-shop sign in English caught his eye: ALL KINDS OF JAPANESE FINE ARTS: PAINTINGS, PORCELAINS, BRONZE STATUES. . . . And one that must have been for a Chinese tailor: MAN CHANG DRESS MAKER FOR LADIES AND GENTLEMEN. . . . And also: JAMES BERGMAN JEWELLERY . . . RINGS, EARRINGS, NECKLACES. . . . E & B CO. FOREIGN DRY GOODS AND GROCERIES . . . LADY'S UNDERWEARS . . . DRAPERIES, TAP-ESTRIES, EMBROIDERIES. . . . Somehow the very ring of these words in his ear had the heavy, solemn beauty of the sound of a piano. . . . Only an hour by streetcar from Tokyo, yet you felt as if you had arrived at some far-off place. And you hesitated to go inside these shops when you saw how lifeless they looked, their doors firmly shut. In these show windows—perhaps because they were meant for foreigners—goods were set out on display in a cold, formal arrangement well behind the glass, quite unlike the ingratiating clutter of the windows along the Ginza. There seemed to be no clerks or shop-boys at work; all kinds of luxuries were on display, but these dimly lit rooms were as gloomy as a Buddhist shrine. . . . Still, that made the goods within seem all the more curiously enticing.

Okada and Aguri went up and down the street several times: past a shoeshop, a milliner's shop, a jeweler, a furrier, a textile merchant. . . . If he handed over a little of his money, any of the things in these shops would cling fast to her white skin, coil around her lithe, graceful arms and legs, become a part of her. . . . European women's clothes weren't "things to wear"—they were a second layer of skin. They weren't merely wrapped over and around the body but dyed into its very surface like a kind of tattooed decoration. When he looked again, all the goods in the show windows seemed to be so many layers of Aguri's skin, flecked with color, with drops of blood. She ought to choose what she likes and make it part of herself. If you buy jade earrings, he wanted to tell her, think of yourself with beautiful green pendants growing from your earlobes. If you put on that squirrel coat, the one in the furrier's window, think of yourself as an animal with a velvety sleek coat of hair. If you buy the celadon-colored stockings hanging over there, the moment you pull them on, your legs will have a silken skin, warmed by your own coursing blood. If you slip into patent-leather shoes, the soft flesh of your heels will turn into glittering lacquer. My darling Aguri! All these were molded to the statue of woman which is you: blue, purple, crimson skins—all were formed to your body. It's *you* they are selling there, your outer skin is waiting to come to life. Why, when you have such superb things of your own, do you wrap yourself up in clothes like that baggy, shapeless kimono?

"Yes, sir. For the young lady? . . . Just what does she have in mind?"

A Japanese clerk had emerged out of the dark back room of the shop and was eying Aguri suspiciously. They had gone into a modest little dress shop because it seemed least forbidding: Not a very attractive one, to be sure, but there were glass-covered cases along both sides of the narrow room, and the cases were full of dresses. Blouses and skirts—women's breasts and hips—dangled overhead. There were low glass cases in the middle of the room, too, displaying petticoats, chemises, hosiery, corsets, and all manner of little lacy things. Nothing but cool, slippery, soft fabrics, literally softer than a woman's skin: delicately crinkled silk crepe, glossy white silk, fine satin. When Aguri realized that she would soon be clothed in these fabrics, like a mannequin, she seemed ashamed at being eyed by the clerk and shrank back shyly, losing all her usual vivaciousness. But her eyes were sparkling as if to say: "I want this, and that, and that. . . ."

"I don't really know what I'd like. . . ." She seemed puzzled and embarrassed. "What do *you* think?" she whispered to Okada, hiding behind him to avoid the clerk's gaze.

"Let me see now," the clerk spoke up briskly. "I imagine any of these would look good on you." He spread out a white linen-like dress for her inspection. "How about this one? Just hold it up to yourself and look at it — you'll find a mirror over there."

Aguri went before the mirror and tucked the white garment under her chin, letting it hang down loosely. Eyes upturned, she stared at it with the glum look of a fretful child.

"How do you like it?" Okada asked.

"Mmm. Not bad."

"It doesn't seem to be linen, though. What's the material?"

"That's cotton voile, sir. It's a fresh, crisp kind of fabric, very pleasant to the touch."

"And the price?"

"Let's see. . . . Now this one . . ." The clerk turned toward the back room and called in a startlingly loud voice: "Say, how much is this cotton voile — forty-five yen?"

"It'll have to be altered," Okada said. "Can you do it today?"

"Today? Are you sailing tomorrow?"

"No, but we *are* rather in a hurry."

"Hey, how about it?" The clerk turned and shouted toward the back room again. "He says he wants it today — can you manage it? See if you can, will you?" Though a little rough-spoken, he seemed kind and good-natured. "We'll start right now, but it'll take at least two hours."

"That will be fine. We still need to buy shoes and a hat and the rest, and she'll want to change into the new things here. But what is she supposed to wear underneath? It's the first time she's ever had Western clothes."

"Don't worry, we have all those too — here's what you start with." He slipped a silk brassière out of a glass case. "Then you put this on over it, and then step into this and this, below. They come in a different style too, but there's no opening, so you have to take it off if you want to go to the toilet. That's why Westerners hold their water as long as they can. Now, this kind is more convenient: It has a button here, you see? Just unbutton it and you'll have no trouble! . . . The chemise is eight yen, the petticoat is about six yen — they're cheap compared with kimonos, but see what beautiful white silk they're made of! Please step over here and I'll take your measurements."

Through the flannel cloth the dimensions of the hidden form were measured; around her legs, under her arms, the leather tape was wound to investigate the bulk and shape of her body.

"How much is this woman worth?" Was that what the clerk was calculating? It seemed to Okada that he was having a price set on Aguri, that he was putting her on sale in a slave market.

About six o'clock that evening they came back to the dress shop with their other purchases: shoes, a hat, a pearl necklace, a pair of amethyst earrings. . . .

"Well, come in! Did you find some nice things?" The clerk greeted them in a breezy, familiar tone. "It's all ready! The fitting room is over here — just go in and change your clothes!"

Okada followed Aguri behind the screen, gently holding over one arm the soft, snowy garments. They came to a full-length mirror, and Aguri, still looking glum, slowly began to undo her sash. . . .

The statue of woman in Okada's mind stood naked before him. The fine silk snagged on his fingers as he helped apply it to her skin, going round and round the white figure, tying ribbons, fastening buttons and hooks. . . . Suddenly Aguri's face lit up with a radiant smile. Okada felt his head begin to swim. . . .

∾ T. S. ELIOT
b. UNITED STATES, 1888–1965

T. S. Eliot, 1948
Eliot in his office at the Institute for Advanced Study. (Hulton / Archive)

T. S. Eliot's poem *The Waste Land,* the most notable twentieth-century poem in English, appeared in the November 1922 issue of the literary magazine *The Dial. The Waste Land* depicts the modern world as a devastated place whose land has lost its regenerative capacity, whose cities are sites of pollution and despair, and whose human relationships are empty and sterile, without moral or spiritual value. More than any other single work, it also reflects the disillusionment of American intellectuals, some of them European expatriates, with Western society at the end of World War I. Nonlinear in structure, fragmented in organization, and obscure in its references, the poem seemed destined for a limited audience; but after being augmented by notes by the author and supported by interpretive reviews and essays, it went on to establish itself as a monument of its age.

It is now common to identify the postwar period in Europe and America as the "wasteland," the spiritual and intellectual condition that promoted the spread of EXISTENTIALISM in the 1930s, '40s, and '50s. In 1948, twenty-six years after the poem's publication, Eliot was awarded the Nobel Prize in literature, and as Elizabeth Drew recounts, a symposium held to pay tribute to his influence "contained contributions from forty-seven writers from more than a dozen different countries, and hailed the poet-critic-dramatist as perhaps the most powerful literary influence in the civilized world of today." Eliot was like an entire literary movement in himself: a poet, an enormously popular lecturer on both sides of the Atlantic, a leading critic, a publisher of an influential literary magazine, and a director of a prominent publishing house in London.

Eliot came to symbolize the traditional and the conservative in religion, politics, and literature, but his poems are marvelously innovative and experimental. He was heavily influenced by the FRENCH SYMBOLISTS,[1]

---

[1] French Symbolists: Nineteenth-century French Symbolists Charles Baudelaire (1821–1867), Stéphane Mallarmé (1842–1898), and Paul Verlaine (1844–1896) made use of symbols as a means of evoking the inner world of consciousness.

www   For links to
more information
about Eliot, quizzes
on his poetry, and for
information on
Eliot's twenty-first-
century relevance,
see *World Literature
Online* at
bedfordstmartins
.com/worldlit.

who had broken with traditional subject matter and polite, poetic language. He was attracted to STREAM-OF-CONSCIOUSNESS writing, which
could pull together experiences and images from disparate periods and
locales. Above all, he was well read and in favor of drawing from the
broad reaches of European and world literature. He once described the
challenge for the twentieth-century writer: "Our civilization comprehends great variety and complexity, and this variety and complexity,
playing upon a refined sensibility, must produce various and complex
results. The poet must become more and more comprehensive, more
allusive, more indirect, in order to force, to dislocate if necessary, language into meaning."

Eliot and *The Waste Land* had their detractors, especially among
American poets. It was believed that the poem turned the attention of
American writers away from the tradition of Walt Whitman[2]—optimistic,
democratic, and nationalistic—to a more pessimistic, elitist, and cosmopolitan aesthetic that virtually silenced homegrown literature for a
decade and made the recovery of a native literature difficult even in the
Depression years of the 1930s, when new struggles produced new literary
impulses. American poet William Carlos Williams[3] commented in retrospect that *The Waste Land* "wiped out our world as if an atomic bomb
had been dropped on it."

From St. Louis to Harvard.   Thomas Stearns Eliot was born September 26, 1888, in St. Louis, Missouri, the youngest son of seven children.
His family, which was highly intellectual and literary, had come from
Massachusetts and maintained strong connections to New England.
Eliot's grandfather William Greenleaf Eliot, a graduate of Harvard Divin-
ity School, moved to St. Louis in 1834 where he founded the first Unitar-
ian church; he also founded Washington University in 1859. Eliot's mother,
Charlotte Champe Stearns, was a writer of biographies and religious
verse. Eliot spent his summers in New England, eventually attending
Milton Academy in Massachusetts, and in 1906 he entered Harvard University and came under the influence of Irving Babbit, the classical, anti-
Romantic author of *Rousseau and Romanticism*. Three years later he began
graduate work in philosophy, again at Harvard. He completed a master's
degree in one year and went to Paris to study at the Sorbonne; he then
returned to Harvard and began a doctoral dissertation on F. H. Bradley.[4]
Around this time he wrote "The Love Song of J. Alfred Prufrock," a poem
that captures the frustration and disillusionment of the age.

---

[2] Walt Whitman (1819–1892): America's poet of democracy; he used images and rhythms available to ordinary
people.

[3] William Carlos Williams (1883–1963): Developed a poetic idiom close to ordinary speech; much of his poetry
deals with common experience.

[4] F. H. Bradley (1846–1924): English philosopher who emphasized the private nature of individual experience
in *Appearance and Reality* (1893); influenced Eliot's private imagery.

Critical Years of Transition.   The years 1914 and 1915 figure prominently in Eliot's life as a writer. World War I broke out while he was studying in Germany on a traveling fellowship from Harvard, pushing him to England where he settled down and lived for the rest of his life. He did not return to Harvard to finish his doctorate, and he turned from philosophy to poetry. In 1915 he married Vivien Haigh-Wood and in London met Ezra Pound, a transplanted American poet from the Midwest who loved to shepherd new talent into the public eye. Pound persuaded Harriet Monroe, the editor of the Chicago-based *Poetry,* to publish "The Love Song of J. Alfred Prufrock" (June 1915) and introduced Eliot to the director of Egoist Press, Harriet Weaver. Weaver published Eliot's first book of poems, *Prufrock and Other Observations,* in 1917, the same year the poet took a job as a clerk in a bank, Lloyd's of London. Eliot became a forerunner of the "Lost Generation," the international set of American writers who declared their disaffection with European politics and society after the slaughter of so many young soldiers in World War I. The attitude of these writers is best summarized in lines written by Eliot's closest collaborator, Pound, in 1920:

> There died a myriad,
> And of the best, among them,
> For an old bitch gone in the teeth,
> For a botched civilization . . .
>
> For two gross of broken statues,
> For a few thousand battered books.

The Waste Land.   Clearly Eliot was in crisis in 1921 and 1922 when he wrote *The Waste Land,* as his security and happiness were being challenged on several fronts. For some time he had struggled to overcome the puritanical element in his family history; poems such as "Prufrock" treated the theme of sexual repression, whereas other early poems were surprisingly bawdy and crude, often self-consciously primitive in their depiction of characters and situations. His wife, Vivien, who was mentally unstable, was suffering from bouts of neuralgia and insomnia. Meanwhile, Eliot's family had withdrawn their financial support, thinking that Eliot was wasting his life in literature; then his father died in 1919. When Eliot had a breakdown, a neurologist suggested he take a leave from his work at the bank, and Eliot found psychiatric help in Lausanne, Switzerland, in the winter of 1921, the time of the writing of *The Waste Land.* Again Pound came to his aid: He collected money for Eliot's support and helped edit the poem in manuscript, seeing it through to publication in 1922. A number of letters written by Eliot during the creation of *The Waste Land* corroborate his vulnerable and sometimes desperate emotional and financial circumstances. One close friend, the American critic Edmund Wilson, called the poem "nothing more or less than a most distressingly moving account of Eliot's own agonized state of mind," and Eliot himself said of the poem in 1947 that he had written it "simply to relieve" his feelings. Nevertheless the work elevated Eliot into

Our civilization comprehends great variety and complexity, and this variety and complexity, playing upon a refined sensibility, must produce various and complex results. The poet must become more and more comprehensive, more allusive, more indirect, in order to force, to dislocate if necessary, language into meaning.

– T. S. ELIOT, 1921

the top tier of modern poetry; no one in the twentieth century had painted such an inclusive portrait of the world as it was after World War I while making use of the diverse conventions of Western literature.

Christianity and Conservatism.   In 1922, Eliot resigned from the edito-rial board of *The Dial* and started a heavily influential cultural magazine, *The Criterion,* the critical focus of which was a conservative assessment of the relationship between culture and society. From this point on, Eliot's life and work turned toward literary and religious orthodoxy and politi-cal conservatism. He became a British subject in 1927, and in the same year he took communion in the Anglican Church. He committed his first wife to a mental institution and was able to overcome his own emotional distress. In 1930, he published *Ash Wednesday,* a poem of religious con-version, and later in the decade wrote the first section of a long Christian poem, *Four Quartets,* which he completed in 1943. When Eliot turned to writing drama, most of it too held a religious message. Two of his major plays, the early historical drama *Murder in the Cathedral* (1935) and the later contemporary work *The Cocktail Party* (1949), both concern Chris-tian martyrdom, an unusual topic for the twentieth century. In later life Eliot worked as a senior editor for Faber and Faber, a leading British pub-lisher, rarely traveling to the United States. He eventually remarried — happily this time — and died peacefully in 1965.

Prufrock and Alienation.   Written when Eliot was twenty-three years old, "The Love Song of J. Alfred Prufrock" was Eliot's first mature poem with an unsettling message. The title itself ironically links romance with the stodgy name "J. Alfred Prufrock." The epigraph from Dante's *In-ferno* suggests that Prufrock himself, who lives in a kind of "inferno," or hell, can speak frankly about his life without fear of infamy. The shock, however, begins with the opening image of this DRAMATIC MONOLOGUE,[5] which compares the evening to an etherized patient, and then mentions tawdry "one-night cheap hotels." The narrator in this poem is speaking in a completely original way, which continues, after an interjection about women who "come and go / Talking of Michelangelo," with a description of the night that makes the atmosphere into an animal whose "muzzle" and "tongue" make contact with the city streets. And yet, as its title sug-gests, this poem is about love, a theme of many of Eliot's poems and a central motif of *The Waste Land.*

The poem's questions about time, personal appearance, and courage lead into accounts of failed encounters with the opposite sex. The re-peated questioning — "So how should I presume?"; "How should I begin . . . ?"; "Would it have been worth it?" — indicate Prufrock's divided consciousness. He then identifies with "lonely men in shirt-sleeves, lean-ing out of windows. . . ." At social events, the conversation is superficial;

---

[5] **dramatic monologue:** A poetic form made popular by the English poet Robert Browning (1812–1889) in the nineteenth century, in which a fictional character speaking to a silent audience reveals as much about himself as he does about his particular situation in life.

real communication is nonexistent. Eventually, it becomes clear that Prufrock is not simply inept in social situations filled with empty forms who perhaps lack real humanity in the first place; Prufrock is afraid of life itself. The poem ends with superficial questions: "Shall I part my hair behind? Do I dare to eat a peach?"

This early poem exhibits what would become Eliot's stylistic trademarks: disconnected lines, ironic side comments, colloquialisms mixed with fragments of past masters, like Shakespeare, and animal or fish imagery. Prufrock's world, if not as radical as Kafka's, in which a man can awaken one morning as a pitiable beetle, is nevertheless modern, decadent, despairing, sad.

The Complexities of *The Waste Land*.   Two characteristics of *The Waste Land* are immediately challenging. The first is its composition: It moves from one image to another and from situation to situation without any explanation or transition. David Daiches explains: "Eliot's real novelty — and the cause of much bewilderment when his poems first appeared — was his deliberate elimination of all merely connective and transitional passages, his building up of the total pattern of meaning through the immediate juxtaposition of images. . . ." In fact, it was American poet Ezra Pound who in editing the poem cut away much of that connective tissue, making the work both startling and hard to follow. The second challenge of *The Waste Land* are the many literary excerpts quoted in their original languages: Greek and Latin classics, medieval Romance, Elizabethan drama, German opera, French Symbolist poetry, and religious writings, from Christian to Buddhist sources to the Indian Upanishads.[6]

Eliot introduced his notes for the publication of *The Waste Land* in book form with a comment about his influences:

> Not only the title, but the plan and a good deal of the incidental symbolism of the poem were suggested by Miss Jessie L. Weston's book on the Grail legend: *From Ritual to Romance* (Cambridge). . . . To another work of anthropology I am indebted in general, one which has influenced our generation profoundly; I mean *The Golden Bough;* I have used especially the two volumes *Adonis, Attis, Osiris.* Anyone who is acquainted with these works will immediately recognize in the poem certain references to vegetation ceremonies.

The Grail Legend.   In the European Middle Ages a Christian myth developed around the Grail, which according to legend was the cup or platter used by Jesus at the Last Supper and then used by Joseph of Arimathea to collect Jesus' blood at the Crucifixion. The Grail became the possession of a series of Grail kings in an uncertain location. In the stories that were told of it, a brave knight from King Arthur's court — usually Perceval — endures a perilous journey in order to find the Grail, which is hidden away in the castle of the sexually wounded Fisher King. By asking the

---

[6]**Upanishads:** A series of writings containing the ancient wisdom of India; written between c. the ninth and the first centuries B.C.E.

right questions, the knight can heal the king and reinvigorate the land. Jessie Weston in her book connects the Grail stories to older fertility rituals involved with the annual plant cycle of birth, death, and rebirth. Elizabeth Drew explains:

> Miss Weston found the Grail legends to be Christianized versions, via the "mystery" religions,[7] of the ancient fertility cults. She believed the knight's "quest" to be a version of older initiation rites into religious mysteries concerned with the union of the physical with the source of spiritual being. These faiths, she thinks, were spread into western Europe by Syrian merchants and later transformed into the stories of the Grail.

James George Frazer's *The Golden Bough* (1890) is a brilliant work of comparative mythology about early fertility myths and rituals in the ancient Near East and Mediterranean region, with a focus on the dying-and-rising god-hero-king whose life and sacrificial death were annually reenacted in imitation of the seasonal cycle of plants. Eliot translates the Grail quest into the modern search for meaning.

The underlying theme of *The Waste Land* concerns time: The present time can be appreciated and understood only in the context of the past. Only within the context and continuity of past wisdom can a pattern be found that will comprehend the fragmentation of modern society. The death images of rock, dust, bones, and polluted water are paradoxically also the potential of new life. The blind Tiresias, who becomes an amalgam of modern men in the poem, needs a new vision, a new set of eyes by which he can be healed and the modern city transformed.

Eliot's tendency to combine emotional, historical, mythical, and literary references is complicated enough; the footnotes he provided in later editions of the work attest to the obscurity of some of his sources and the compression of his ideas and images.

The Sections of the Poem.   The work begins with April, usually the month of new growth but here "the cruellest month" because it stirs "memory and desire." The speakers in the first section shift rapidly: Marie, a member of the aristocracy who has memories of an alpine childhood but now goes "south in the winter"; an unidentified speaker who paints a ghastly scene of a junk-filled, lifeless desert; a "hyacinth girl" who was perhaps raped in a garden; an aged fortune-teller, a fugitive, telling a guarded fortune; and the speaker of the poem, contemplating fog-ridden, dirty modern London when he meets a stranger who has a sinister, doom-filled message for him. "Memory and desire" here conjure nothing positive; modern life is seen to be bleak, dangerous, and unfulfilling.

---

[7] **"mystery" religions:** Mystery cults were very popular in ancient Greece and Rome for at least one thousand years, beginning c. 1000 B.C.E. The details of their inner workings were kept secret, but all shared a rigorous rite of initiation, a concern about death, and a hope for immortality centered on a deity who had personal knowledge of the afterlife. The most popular Greek versions were the Orphic and Eleusinian mysteries. The mysteries of Isis and Mithra were favored in the Roman world.

The second section begins in an exotic setting with artistic panels on the walls depicting metamorphosis. The woman who cries out "Speak . . . Think" is apparently modeled on Eliot's first wife. The grim, dry voice of the narrator is not enclosed in quotation marks; it is apparently the poet speaking in his own dramatic voice. The scene changes with the words "When Lil's husband got demobbed," introducing a conversation in a London pub. The voices saying HURRY UP PLEASE ITS TIME and singing "Good Night, Ladies" are meant to signify more than the voice of the tavern keeper or the drunken song of the departing company; the narrator's voice creeps in, too—a voice of despair.

The third section begins with a description of the modern-day Thames River in London. The rubbish along the bank includes "other testimony of summer nights," possibly the contraceptives of that time. A mixture of images recalls the Fisher King of the Grail legend, two lower-class Londoners, the rape of Philomela from an earlier section, a homosexual proposition from a decadent Greek businessman, and a long scene narrated by Tiresias, the prophet fated by the gods to be both man and woman. He witnesses an empty and cheap modern sexual encounter, followed by contrasting scenes of London in her glory in the time of Elizabeth and the filthy Thames River district known to the poet. In both times, it seems, there were scenes of defilement, and Tiresias has witnessed them all. The section ends with St. Augustine's description of arriving as a young man in the city of Carthage (c. 370), a site of worldly lust and fornication.

The fourth section, very short, describes the death of a Phoenician sailor; these early sailors connected the port cities of the classical world through the watery medium of the Mediterranean. The sailor's death is apparently symbolic; all "commerce"—all significant exchange—may be similarly dead in modern Europe.

The fifth section connects some of the themes of the first four. It begins in a reddish desert area with "torchlight red on sweaty faces." In this surreal landscape, where there is "no water but only rock," there is a mysterious "third who walks . . . beside you." In this poem, so full of intrusions and mysteries, this could be one or many of the other figures already encountered; in the same way, the city of London, which is now depicted as "falling down" in the taunting music of the nursery rhyme, could be many other capitals as well. Finally, after these speculations comes the rain, and with it a Hindu formula for achieving a blessed state: *Datta, Dayadhvam, Damyata*—Give, Sympathize, Control. The closest the poet comes to assembling the materials of the poem, not to mention his life or the life of Europe, is the line "Shall I at least set my lands in order?" This is certainly not an answer to the problems of the age, but it could be a beginning. The final invocation, *"Shantih shantih shantih,"* again a Hindu formula, is a call for abiding peace.

Like the knight Perceval in search of the answer to the riddle of the Holy Grail, the poet, locating himself somewhere in the chorus of voices in *The Waste Land,* is a quester. The decay of Europe, especially the moral decay, which Eliot depicts in terms of psychological and sexual depravity, is what necessitates his search for meaning. The promise in the poem

Eliot wants to suggest in the rhythms of his verse the movement of thought in a living mind, and thus to communicate the exact pattern of his meaning not so much by logical structure as by emotional suggestion.
– F. O. MATTHIESSEN, 1947

seems to rest in the undifferentiated religious figures and symbols in the fifth section. Eliot seems to be saying that if the West is to be restored, it will be through the symbolic operations of the world's great myths and religions. His faith seems to want to rest not in people but in the individual consciousness and in symbolic processes, especially those of renewal. Whether his intellectualized vision is appealing or seems artificial and contrived may depend on the reader's tolerance for a form of poetry that is for many far removed from daily life.

Reactions to *The Waste Land*.   *The Waste Land*'s first generation of critics were kept busy trying to explain the poem to a somewhat baffled literary audience. Edmund Wilson led the way in a long essay in *The Dial* in December 1922, illuminating a number of references based on his reading of Eliot's own notes, which were soon being published with the poem. Critic Kathleen Raine, however, not only understood the work but thought *it* had understood everything:

> For my generation T. S. Eliot's early poetry, more than the work of any other poet, has enabled us to know our world imaginatively. All those who have lived in the Waste Land of London, can, I suppose, remember the particular occasion on which, reading T. S. Eliot's poems for the first time, an experience of the contemporary world that had been nameless and formless, suddenly received its apotheosis.

And American critic Malcolm Cowley feels he and other young writers understood the poem well but that it didn't speak for them:

> The idea was a simple one. Beneath the rich symbolism of *The Waste Land,* the wide learning expressed in seven languages, the actions conducted on three planes, the musical episodes, the geometrical structure—beneath and by means of all this, we felt the poet was saying that the present is inferior to the past. The past was dignified; the present is barren of emotion. The past was a landscape nourished by living fountains; now the fountains of spiritual grace are dry. . . . It happened that we were excited by the adventure of living in the present. The famous "postwar mood of aristocratic disillusionment" was a mood we had never really shared. It happened that Eliot's subjective truth was not our own.

E. E. Cummings, an American poet, asked why Eliot could not write his own lines instead of borrowing from dead poets. And modern American novelist Ernest Hemingway wrote in *Transatlantic Review:* "If I knew that by grinding Mr. Eliot into a fine dry powder and sprinkling that powder over Mr. Conrad's grave Mr. Conrad would shortly appear, looking very annoyed at the forced return, and commence writing, I would leave for London early tomorrow with a sausage grinder."

■ **CONNECTIONS**

Joseph Conrad, *Heart of Darkness,* **p. 35.** Writers at the turn of the century were particularly interested in the psychological effects of the modernizing world: how, for example, cities affected interpersonal relationships. *Heart of Darkness* explores the influence of colonialism on an individual's ability to relate to others. How does Eliot depict relationships in *The Waste Land*?

Franz Kafka, *The Metamorphosis*, p. 428. Modern writers face the challenge of portraying the fragmentation or disintegration of consciousness in the medium of the written word, which by its nature depends on coherent, linear patterns to communicate meaning. Kafka uses the metaphor of a man's metamorphosis into an insect to dramatize the effect of modern bureaucracy on the human consciousness. How does Eliot show the disconnectedness of the modern psyche in *The Waste Land*?

Rabindranath Tagore, "Broken Ties" (Book 5). Although the Enlightenment placed great faith in reason to solve human problems, some writers in the nineteenth century questioned the implications of rationalism for the emotional and spiritual life of individuals. Tagore suggests in "Broken Ties" that while philosophers such as John Stuart Mill can use reason to raise legitimate questions about religion and society, a simplistic use of logic can lead individuals astray. How does Prufrock's questioning in "The Love Song of J. Alfred Prufrock" affect his ability to make healthy choices?

■ **FURTHER RESEARCH**

Biography
Ackroyd, Peter. *T. S. Eliot: A Life.* 1984.
Bush, Ronald. *T. S. Eliot: A Study in Character and Style.* 1984.
Childs, Donald J. *T. S. Eliot: Mystic, Son and Lover.* 1997.

Criticism
Albright, Daniel. *Quantum Poetics.* 1997.
Bush, Ronald, ed. *T. S. Eliot: The Modernist in History.* 1991.
Cattaui, Georges. *T. S. Eliot.* 1966.
Julius, Anthony. *T. S. Eliot: Anti-Semitism and Literary Form.* 1995.
Knoll, Robert E., ed. *Storm over* The Waste Land. 1964.
Moody, David A., ed. *The Cambridge Companion to T. S. Eliot.* 1994.
Palmer, Marja. *Men and Women in T. S. Eliot's Early Poetry.* 1996.
Smith, Grover. *The Waste Land.* 1983.

∾ The Love Song of J. Alfred Prufrock

S'io credesse che mia risposta fosse
A persona che mai tornasse al mondo,
Questa fiamma staria senza piu scosse.
Ma perciocche giammai di questo fondo
Non torno vivo alcun, s'i'odo il vero,
Senza tema d'infamia ti rispondo.[1]

Let us go then, you and I,
When the evening is spread out against the sky
Like a patient etherized upon a table;
Let us go, through certain half-deserted streets,
The muttering retreats
Of restless nights in one-night cheap hotels
And sawdust restaurants with oyster shells:
Streets that follow like a tedious argument
Of insidious intent
10 To lead you to an overwhelming question . . .
Oh, do not ask, "What is it?"
Let us go and make our visit.

In the room the women come and go
Talking of Michelangelo.[2]

The yellow fog that rubs its back upon the windowpanes,
The yellow smoke that rubs its muzzle on the windowpanes
Licked its tongue into the corners of the evening,
Lingered upon the pools that stand in drains,
Let fall upon its back the soot that falls from chimneys,

"The Love Song of J. Alfred Prufrock." This poem, a masterful portrait of the spirit of ennui, of weariness and boredom, first appeared in the Chicago literary magazine *Poetry* in June 1915 and was included in Eliot's first book of poems, *Prufrock and Other Observations,* published in 1917. Prufrock appears to embody the debilitating self-consciousness of the modern middle class and its inability to create meaningful human relationships. Trapped within social manners and unable to get beyond decorousness, Prufrock is separated from passion and sexuality.

All notes are the editors'.

---

[1] *S'io credesse . . . rispondo:* The epigraph is from Dante's *Inferno* (27.61–66); Guido da Montefeltro, whose punishment for fraud is being wrapped in a flame, agrees to identify himself: "If I thought that I was speaking to someone who would ever return to the world, this flame would shake no more, but since no one has ever returned alive from this place, if what I hear is true, I answer you without fear of infamy." Thus, the implication is that Prufrock, the narrator in Eliot's poem, can speak honestly.

[2] **In the room . . . Michelangelo:** It appears that Prufrock is going to this room to visit a woman friend; women speak of Michelangelo (1475–1564), the famous Italian painter and sculptor.

20 Slipped by the terrace, made a sudden leap,
And seeing that it was a soft October night,
Curled once about the house, and fell asleep.

     And indeed there will be time
For the yellow smoke that slides along the street,
Rubbing its back upon the windowpanes;
There will be time, there will be time
To prepare a face to meet the faces that you meet;
There will be time to murder and create,
And time for all the works and days of hands[3]
30 That lift and drop a question on your plate;
Time for you and time for me,
And time yet for a hundred indecisions,
And for a hundred visions and revisions,
Before the taking of a toast and tea.

     In the room the women come and go
Talking of Michelangelo.

     And indeed there will be time
To wonder, "Do I dare?" and, "Do I dare?"
Time to turn back and descend the stair,
40 With a bald spot in the middle of my hair—
(They will say: "How his hair is growing thin!")
My morning coat, my collar mounting firmly to the chin,
My necktie rich and modest, but asserted by a simple pin—
(They will say: "But how his arms and legs are thin!")
Do I dare
Disturb the universe?
In a minute there is time
For decisions and revisions which a minute will reverse.

     For I have known them all already, known them all—
50 Have known the evenings, mornings, afternoons,
I have measured out my life with coffee spoons;
I know the voices dying with a dying fall
Beneath the music from a farther room.
     So how should I presume?

     And I have known the eyes already, known them all—
The eyes that fix you in a formulated phrase,

---

[3] **works . . . hands:** The ancient Greek poet Hesiod (eighth century B.C.E.) wrote a long poem, *Works and Days*, about farm work; Eliot is contrasting meaningful work to empty social gestures.

And when I am formulated, sprawling on a pin,
When I am pinned and wriggling on the wall,
Then how should I begin
60   To spit out all the butt-ends of my days and ways?
  And how should I presume?

  And I have known the arms already, known them all —
Arms that are braceleted and white and bare
(But in the lamplight, downed with light brown hair!)
Is it perfume from a dress
That makes me so digress?
Arms that lie along a table, or wrap about a shawl.
  And should I then presume?
  And how should I begin?

70   Shall I say, I have gone at dusk through narrow streets
And watched the smoke that rises from the pipes
Of lonely men in shirt-sleeves, leaning out of windows? . . .

  I should have been a pair of ragged claws
Scuttling across the floors of silent seas.

  And the afternoon, the evening, sleeps so peacefully!
Smoothed by long fingers,
Asleep . . . tired . . . or it malingers,
Stretched on the floor, here beside you and me.
Should I, after tea and cakes and ices,
80   Have the strength to force the moment to its crisis?
But though I have wept and fasted, wept and prayed,
Though I have seen my head (grown slightly bald) brought in upon a platter,[4]
I am no prophet — and here's no great matter;
I have seen the moment of my greatness flicker,
And I have seen the eternal Footman hold my coat, and snicker,
And in short, I was afraid.

  And would it have been worth it, after all,
After the cups, the marmalade, the tea,
Among the porcelain, among some talk of you and me,
90   Would it have been worth while,

---

[4] **Though I . . . platter:** John the Baptist was beheaded by King Herod; his head was brought to Queen Herodias on a silver platter (Matthew 14:3–11).

To have bitten off the matter with a smile,
To have squeezed the universe into a ball
To roll it toward some overwhelming question,
To say: "I am Lazarus,[5] come from the dead,
Come back to tell you all, I shall tell you all"—
If one, settling a pillow by her head,
    Should say: "That is not what I meant at all.
    That is not it, at all."

    And would it have been worth it, after all,
100 Would it have been worth while,
After the sunsets and the dooryards and the sprinkled streets,
After the novels, after the teacups, after the skirts that trail along the floor—
And this, and so much more?—
It is impossible to say just what I mean!
But as if a magic lantern threw the nerves in patterns on a screen:
Would it have been worth while
If one, settling a pillow or throwing off a shawl,
And turning toward the window, should say:
    "That is not it at all,
110   That is not what I meant, at all."

    No! I am not Prince Hamlet,[6] nor was meant to be;
Am an attendant lord, one that will do
To swell a progress,[7] start a scene or two,
Advise the prince; no doubt, an easy tool,
Deferential, glad to be of use,
Politic, cautious, and meticulous;
Full of high sentence,° but a bit obtuse;   opinions
At times, indeed, almost ridiculous—
Almost, at times, the Fool.

120   I grow old . . . I grow old . . .
I shall wear the bottoms of my trousers rolled.

    Shall I part my hair behind? Do I dare to eat a peach?
I shall wear white flannel trousers, and walk upon the beach.
I have heard the mermaids singing, each to each.

---

[5] **Lazarus:** Raised from the dead by Jesus (John 11:1–44).

[6] **Prince Hamlet:** Shakespeare's Hamlet (c. 1602) is known for his indecision.

[7] **progress:** A journey made by members of the royal court.

I do not think that they will sing to me.

I have seen them riding seaward on the waves
Combing the white hair of the waves blown back
When the wind blows the water white and black.

We have lingered in the chambers of the sea
By sea-girls wreathed with seaweed red and brown
130   Till human voices wake us, and we drown.

∾ The Waste Land[1]

"Nam Sibyllam quidem Cumis ego ipse oculis meis vidi in ampulla pendere, et cum illi pueri dicerent: Σίβυλλα τί θέλεις; respondebat illa: ἀποθανεῖν θέλω."[2]

For Ezra Pound
il miglior fabbro.[3]

I. The Burial of the Dead[4]

April is the cruellest month, breeding
Lilacs out of the dead land, mixing
Memory and desire, stirring
Dull roots with spring rain.

The Waste Land. This work first appeared in England in the first issue of *Criterion* (October 1922), and in America in *The Dial* (November 1922). Eliot's original poem, before it was edited and drastically reduced by Ezra Pound, and unpublished drafts of the poem were made available to scholars in 1968 from the manuscript collections of John Quinn, a New York patron of the arts. A facsimile edition of the poem with original drafts was edited by Valerie Eliot, his second wife, and published in 1971.

The Waste Land is difficult to grasp because it jumps around a lot and because of its numerous allusions to other literary works; the reader may not be familiar with the work cited or its

---

[1] Eliot added some notes for the publication of *The Waste Land* in book form by Boni and Liveright, New York, December 1922. These are identified by (E). We have omitted or departed from these notes as has seemed fitting, while adding additional notes for clarification.

[2] "For I saw with my own eyes the Sibyl from Cumae hanging in a bottle, and when the boys asked her, 'Sibyl, what do you want?' she would reply, 'I want to die.'"—Petronius, *Satyricon,* 48. According to legend, the prophetess had been granted a long life but not perpetual youth, and so she was hideously shriveled with age. Compare Madame Sosostris and Tiresias, fortune-tellers later to appear in *The Waste Land*.

[3] *il miglior fabbro:* "The better maker [poet]." Eliot compliments his friend Ezra Pound, who edited the poem into its final form during the period of Eliot's hospitalization. The Italian original is Dante's praise of the poet Arnaut Daniel, from the *Purgatorio,* 26, 117.

[4] **The Burial of the Dead:** Title of the funeral service in *The Book of Common Prayer*.

Winter kept us warm, covering
Earth in forgetful snow, feeding
A little life with dried tubers.
Summer surprised us, coming over the Starnbergersee
With a shower of rain; we stopped in the colonnade,
10 And went on in sunlight, into the Hofgarten,
And drank coffee, and talked for an hour.
Bin gar keine Russin, stamm' aus Litauen, echt deutsch.[5]
And when we were children, staying at the archduke's,
My cousin's, he took me out on a sled,
And I was frightened. He said, Marie,
Marie, hold on tight. And down we went.
In the mountains, there you feel free.
I read, much of the night, and go south in the winter.

What are the roots that clutch, what branches grow
20 Out of this stony rubbish? Son of man,[6]
You cannot say, or guess, for you know only
A heap of broken images, where the sun beats,
And the dead tree gives no shelter, the cricket no relief,[7]
And the dry stone no sound of water. Only
There is shadow under this red rock,
(Come in under the shadow of this red rock),
And I will show you something different from either
Your shadow at morning striding behind you
Or your shadow at evening rising to meet you;
30 I will show you fear in a handful of dust.[8]
      Frisch weht der Wind
      Der Heimat zu

---

language and is not sure how it contributes to the meaning of the poem. The best way to read *The Waste Land*—at least the first time—is to *disregard* the footnotes, to simply struggle through, paying attention in particular to whatever feelings are called up by the reading. Such feelings as bewilderment, frustration, anger, inadequacy, curiosity, and excitement could be interpreted as reactions to the modern world. Eliot's implicit message has to do with both the assault to comprehension and meaning that World War I among other things constituted and the search for a new way of seeing that will recover meaning.

All footnotes are the editors' unless identified with "(E)" for Eliot.

---

[5] Bin . . . deutsch: "I'm not Russian at all; I come from Lithuania, pure German." The remark is ironical; little is "pure" in the poem. The scene is from the vicinity of Munich, in south Germany.

[6] Son of man: God's address to the prophet Ezekiel (Ezekiel 2:1).

[7] the cricket no relief: Compare Ecclesiastes 12:5.

[8] handful of dust: Compare "Ashes to ashes, dust to dust" in the funeral service.

Mein Irisch Kind,
Wo weilest du?[9]
"You gave me hyacinths first a year ago;
"They called me the hyacinth girl."
—Yet when we came back, late, from the Hyacinth garden,
Your arms full, and your hair wet, I could not
Speak, and my eyes failed, I was neither
40 Living nor dead, and I knew nothing,
Looking into the heart of light, the silence.
Oed' und leer das Meer.[10]

Madame Sosostris,[11] famous clairvoyante,
Had a bad cold, nevertheless
Is known to be the wisest woman in Europe,
With a wicked pack of cards.[12] Here, said she,
Is your card, the drowned Phoenician Sailor,
(Those are pearls that were his eyes.[13] Look!)
Here is Belladonna,[14] the Lady of the Rocks,
50 The lady of situations.
Here is the man with three staves, and here the Wheel,[15]
And here is the one-eyed merchant, and this card,
Which is blank, is something he carries on his back,
Which I am forbidden to see. I do not find
The Hanged Man.[16] Fear death by water.
I see crowds of people, walking round in a ring.
Thank you. If you see dear Mrs. Equitone,

---

[9] *Frisch . . . du?:* The lyric in German is from Wagner's opera version of *Tristan and Isolde:* "Fresh blows the wind / toward the homeland. / My Irish girl / where do you abide?"

[10] *Oed' . . . Meer:* From *Tristan and Isolde:* "Waste and empty the sea." The dying Tristan looks out to sea and finds no sign of Isolde's ship.

[11] Madame Sosostris: A fortune-teller; her name is close to that of the Egyptian pharaoh Seostris.

[12] wicked . . . cards: Tarot cards, thought to have originated in ancient Egypt for the purposes of divination.

[13] Those . . . eyes: Shakespeare, *The Tempest*, I, ii, 399–402. Consolation of Ariel to Ferdinand over his father, who is feared drowned:

> Those are pearls that were his eyes;
> Nothing of him that doth fade,
> But doth suffer a sea-change
> Into something rich and strange.

[14] Belladonna: Italian for "lovely lady," but also a poison.

[15] the man . . . the Wheel: Eliot says that he associates, "quite arbitrarily," the "man with three staves" with the Fisher King, who appears later. The Wheel could be the wheel of fortune.

[16] Hanged Man: Eliot himself confesses that he has "departed to suit my own convenience" from the symbolism of the Tarot pack (E).

Tell her I bring the horoscope myself:
One must be so careful these days.

60   Unreal City,
Under the brown fog of a winter dawn,[17]
A crowd flowed over London Bridge, so many,
I had not thought death had undone so many.[18]
Sighs, short and infrequent, were exhaled,
And each man fixed his eyes before his feet.
Flowed up the hill and down King William Street,
To where Saint Mary Woolnoth kept the hours
With a dead sound on the final stroke of nine.[19]
There I saw one I knew, and stopped him, crying: "Stetson!
70 "You who were with me in the ships at Mylae![20]
"That corpse you planted last year in your garden,
"Has it begun to sprout? Will it bloom this year?
"Or has the sudden frost disturbed its bed?
"Oh keep the Dog far hence, that's friend to men,
"Or with his nails he'll dig it up again![21]
"You! hypocrite lecteur! — mon semblable, — mon frère!"[22]

II. A Game of Chess[23]

The Chair she sat in, like a burnished throne,[24]
Glowed on the marble, where the glass
Held up by standards wrought with fruited vines

---

[17] **Unreal . . . dawn:** Echoes Baudelaire's "Swarming city, city full of dreams, / where the specter in broad daylight accosts the passerby," from *The Flowers of Evil.*

[18] **I . . . many:** Dante's comment in the *Inferno,* seeing the citizens of Hell: "Such a long procession / of people, I had not thought / death had undone so many" (*Inferno,* 3, 55–57).

[19] **Sighs . . . nine:** Eliot supplies commonplace scenes from London: St. Mary Woolnoth, a church in the business district, and the dead sound in the tower clock, "a phenomenon which I have often noticed" (E).

[20] **"Stetson . . . Mylae!":** Stetson is the name of the average businessman, perhaps connected to the American hat manufacturer; Mylae is the site of a victorious Roman sea battle against Carthage in 260 B.C.E., a pointless war fought over commercial interests and thereby comparable to World War I.

[21] **"Oh keep . . . up again!":** Compare the nearly identical passage in John Webster, *The White Devil* (1612), V, iv, 97–98, where the dog is called "foe to man."

[22] **"You! . . . frère!":** Baudelaire, preface to *Flowers of Evil;* French for "Hypocrite reader! My double, my brother!"

[23] **A Game of Chess:** Eliot appears to be recalling two plays by Thomas Middleton: for the title, *A Game of Chess* (1624), and for the plot, *Women Beware Women* (1657), in which a woman is seduced while her mother-in-law is engrossed in a chess game.

[24] **The Chair . . . throne:** Note the description of Cleopatra in Shakespeare, *Antony and Cleopatra,* II, ii, 190: "The barge she sat in, like a burnished throne. . . ."

80 From which a golden Cupidon peeped out
    (Another hid his eyes behind his wing)
    Doubled the flames of sevenbranched candelabra
    Reflecting light upon the table as
    The glitter of her jewels rose to meet it,
    From satin cases poured in rich profusion;
    In vials of ivory and coloured glass
    Unstoppered, lurked her strange synthetic perfumes,
    Unguent, powdered, or liquid—troubled, confused
    And drowned the sense in odours; stirred by the air
90 That freshened from the window, these ascended
    In fattening the prolonged candle-flames,
    Flung their smoke into the laquearia,[25]
    Stirring the pattern on the coffered ceiling.
    Huge sea-wood fed with copper
    Burned green and orange, framed by the coloured stone,
    In which sad light a carvèd dolphin swam.
    Above the antique mantel was displayed
    As though a window gave upon the sylvan scene[26]
    The change of Philomel, by the barbarous king
100 So rudely forced;[27] yet there the nightingale
    Filled all the desert with inviolable voice
    And still she cried, and still the world pursues,
    "Jug Jug" to dirty ears.
    And other withered stumps of time
    Were told upon the walls; staring forms
    Leaned out, leaning, hushing the room enclosed.
    Footsteps shuffled on the stair.
    Under the firelight, under the brush, her hair
    Spread out in fiery points
110 Glowed into words, then would be savagely still.

        "My nerves are bad to-night. Yes, bad. Stay with me.
    "Speak to me. Why do you never speak. Speak.
        "What are you thinking of? What thinking? What?
    "I never know what you are thinking. Think."[28]

---

[25] laquearia: A panelled ceiling; Eliot here refers to a banquet scene in Virgil's *Aeneid* prepared by Dido for Aeneas: "Lighted lamps hung from the coffered ceiling / Rich with gold leaf, and torches with high flames / Prevailed over the night." (Robert Fizgerald, trans.)

[26] sylvan scene: Eliot notes Milton's use of "Sylvan scene" in a description of Eden in *Paradise Lost*, 4, 140.

[27] The change . . . forced: "Ovid, *Metamorphoses*, VI, Philomela" (E). Philomela is raped by her brother-in-law, who cuts out her tongue; the gods, taking pity on her, transform her into a nightingale.

[28] "My nerves . . . Think": Commonly thought to reflect Eliot's own marital experience with his first wife, Vivien.

I think we are in rats' alley
Where the dead men lost their bones.

    "What is that noise?"
                 The wind under the door.
"What is that noise now? What is the wind doing?"
120   Nothing again nothing.
                           "Do
"You know nothing? Do you see nothing? Do you remember
"Nothing?"
    I remember
Those are pearls that were his eyes.
"Are you alive, or not? Is there nothing in your head?"
                               But

O O O O that Shakespeherian Rag—
It's so elegant
130 So intelligent[29]
"What shall I do now? What shall I do?"
"I shall rush out as I am, and walk the street
"With my hair down, so. What shall we do to-morrow?
"What shall we ever do?"
                 The hot water at ten.
And if it rains, a closed car at four.
And we shall play a game of chess,
Pressing lidless eyes and waiting for a knock upon the door.

    When Lil's husband got demobbed,[30] I said—
140 I didn't mince my words, I said to her myself,
HURRY UP PLEASE ITS TIME[31]
Now Albert's coming back, make yourself a bit smart.
He'll want to know what you done with that money he gave you
To get yourself some teeth. He did, I was there.
You have them all out, Lil, and get a nice set,
He said, I swear, I can't bear to look at you.
And no more can't I, I said, and think of poor Albert,
He's been in the army four years, he wants a good time,
And if you don't give it him, there's others will, I said.
150 Oh is there, she said. Something o' that, I said.
Then I'll know who to thank, she said, and give me a straight look.

---

[29] O . . . intelligent: Adapted from "The Shakespearean Rag," a popular dance song (1912).

[30] demobbed: Demobilized from military service.

[31] HURRY . . . TIME: Announcement of closing time in a London pub.

HURRY UP PLEASE ITS TIME
If you don't like it you can get on with it, I said.
Others can pick and choose if you can't.
But if Albert makes off, it won't be for lack of telling.
You ought to be ashamed, I said, to look so antique.
(And her only thirty-one.)
I can't help it, she said, pulling a long face,
It's them pills I took, to bring it off, she said.
160 (She's had five already, and nearly died of young George.)
The chemist[32] said it would be all right, but I've never been the same.
You are a proper fool, I said.
Well, if Albert won't leave you alone, there it is, I said,
What you get married for if you don't want children?
HURRY UP PLEASE ITS TIME
Well, that Sunday Albert was home, they had a hot gammon,[33]
And they asked me in to dinner, to get the beauty of it hot—
HURRY UP PLEASE ITS TIME
HURRY UP PLEASE ITS TIME
170 Goonight Bill. Goonight Lou. Goonight May. Goonight.
Ta ta. Goonight. Goonight.
Good night, ladies, good night, sweet ladies, good night, good night.[34]

III. THE FIRE SERMON[35]

The river's tent is broken: the last fingers of leaf
Clutch and sink into the wet bank. The wind
Crosses the brown land, unheard. The nymphs are departed.
Sweet Thames, run softly, till I end my song.[36]
The river bears no empty bottles, sandwich papers,
Silk handkerchiefs, cardboard boxes, cigarette ends
Or other testimony of summer nights. The nymphs are departed.
180 And their friends, the loitering heirs of city directors;
Departed, have left no addresses.
By the waters of Leman I sat down and wept . . .[37]
Sweet Thames, run softly till I end my song,
Sweet Thames, run softly, for I speak not loud or long.

---

[32] chemist: Druggist. [33] gammon: Ham.

[34] Good . . . night: Ophelia's mad song from Shakespeare, *Hamlet*, IV, v, 69–70.

[35] The Fire Sermon: A sermon by Buddha against the fires of the senses, against the flames of passion and desire.

[36] my song: From "Prothalamion," a marriage song by Edmund Spenser (1596).

[37] By . . . wept . . .: Compare Psalm 137:1: "By the rivers of Babylon, there we sat down, yea, we wept, when we remembered Zion." Leman is the French name of Lake Geneva in Switzerland, where Eliot was hospitalized while completing *The Waste Land*. The word also means "lover" in early English.

But at my back in a cold blast I hear
The rattle of the bones, and chuckle spread from ear to ear.[38]
A rat crept softly through the vegetation
Dragging its slimy belly on the bank
While I was fishing in the dull canal
190 On a winter evening round behind the gashouse
Musing upon the king my brother's wreck
And on the king my father's death before him.[39]
White bodies naked on the low damp ground
And bones cast in a little low dry garret,
Rattled by the rat's foot only, year to year.
But at my back from time to time I hear
The sound of horns and motors, which shall bring
Sweeney to Mrs. Porter in the spring.
O the moon shone bright on Mrs. Porter
200 And on her daughter
They wash their feet in soda water[40]
Et O ces voix d'enfants, chantant dans la coupole![41]

     Twit twit twit
Jug jug jug jug jug jug
So rudely forc'd.
Tereu[42]

     Unreal City
Under the brown fog of a winter noon
Mr. Eugenides, the Smyrna merchant
210 Unshaven, with a pocket full of currants
C.i.f. London: documents at sight,

---

[38] But at . . . ear: Compare "But at my back I always hear / Time's wingèd chariot hurrying near," Andrew Marvell, "To His Coy Mistress," 21–22. (E)

[39] Musing . . . before him: Recalls Ferdinand's presumed loss of his father in Shakespeare, *The Tempest*, I, ii, 389–91 (E):

        . . . Sitting on a bank,
    Weeping against the king my father's wreck,
    This music crept by me on the waters.

This reference also recalls the story of the Fisher King from anthropological sources.

[40] O the moon . . . soda water: Eliot says, "I do not know the origin of the ballad from which these lines are taken: It was reported to me from Sydney, Australia" (E). The ballad was a soldier's song from World War I; in the song Mrs. Porter and her daughter are prostitutes, and the soda water is a douche, not a foot wash. In other contexts, however, washing the feet is a ritual of purification.

[41] Et . . . coupole!: "And Oh, those voices of children, singing in the cupola!" The final line of Paul Verlaine's sonnet "Parsifal."

[42] Twit . . . Tereu: Recalls the rape of Philomela and the song of the nightingale, II, 98–103.

Asked me in demotic French
To luncheon at the Cannon Street Hotel
Followed by a weekend at the Metropole.[43]

At the violet hour, when the eyes and back
Turn upward from the desk, when the human engine waits
Like a taxi throbbing waiting,
I Tiresias, though blind, throbbing between two lives,
Old man with wrinkled female breasts,[44] can see
220   At the violet hour, the evening hour that strives
Homeward, and brings the sailor home from sea,
The typist home at teatime, clears her breakfast, lights
Her stove, and lays out food in tins.
Out of the window perilously spread
Her drying combinations touched by the sun's last rays,
On the divan are piled (at night her bed)
Stockings, slippers, camisoles, and stays.
I Tiresias, old man with wrinkled dugs
Perceived the scene, and foretold the rest—
230   I too awaited the expected guest.
He, the young man carbuncular,[45] arrives,
A small house agent's clerk, with one bold stare,
One of the low on whom assurance sits
As a silk hat on a Bradford[46] millionaire.
The time is now propitious, as he guesses,
The meal is ended, she is bored and tired,
Endeavours to engage her in caresses
Which still are unreproved, if undesired.
Flushed and decided, he assaults at once;
240   Exploring hands encounter no defence;
His vanity requires no response,
And makes a welcome of indifference.

---

[43] **Mr. Eugenides . . . Metropole:** A Greek merchant from a Turkish port city with a pocketful of currants shipped duty-free to London invites the narrator in vulgar French to lunch in a businessman's hotel in London followed by an illicit weekend in an expensive tourist hotel in Brighton.

[44] **I . . . breasts:** The speaker is Tiresias, who because of spells cast by the gods has been both a man and a woman. When asked who has the greater sexual pleasure, he answers that a woman does; in anger, the goddess Juno strikes him blind, but her husband Jupiter gives him the gift of prophecy (Ovid, *Metamorphoses*, 3, 320–38). "Tiresias, although a mere spectator and not indeed a 'character,' is yet the most important personage in the poem, uniting all the rest" (E).

[45] **carbuncular:** Suffering from acne.

[46] **Bradford:** A town in the north of England where fortunes were made off profiteering during World War I.

(And I Tiresias have foresuffered all
Enacted on this same divan or bed;
I who have sat by Thebes below the wall
And walked among the lowest of the dead.)
Bestows one final patronising kiss,
And gropes his way, finding the stairs unlit . . .
    She turns and looks a moment in the glass,
250 Hardly aware of her departed lover;
Her brain allows one half-formed thought to pass:
"Well now that's done: and I'm glad it's over."
When lovely woman stoops to folly[47] and
Paces about her room again, alone,
She smoothes her hair with automatic hand,
And puts a record on the gramophone.

    "This music crept by me upon the waters"
And along the Strand, up Queen Victoria Street.
O City city, I can sometimes hear
260 Beside a public bar in Lower Thames Street,
The pleasant whining of a mandoline
And a clatter and a chatter from within
Where fishmen lounge at noon: where the walls
Of Magnus Martyr[48] hold
Inexplicable splendour of Ionian white and gold.

       The river sweats
       Oil and tar
       The barges drift
       With the turning tide
270   Red sails
       Wide
       To leeward, swing on the heavy spar.
       The barges wash
       Drifting logs
       Down Greenwich reach

---

[47] When . . . folly: First line of a song by Olivia in *The Vicar of Wakefield*, a novel by Oliver Goldsmith (1766):
    When lovely woman stoops to folly
    And finds too late that men betray
    What harm can soothe her melancholy,
    What art can wash the guilt away?
[48] Magnus Martyr: London church with a beautiful interior praised by Eliot in his notes; built by Sir Christopher Wren at the end of the seventeenth century.

Past the Isle of Dogs.
             Weialala leia
             Wallala leialala[49]

           Elizabeth and Leicester
280 Beating oars[50]
The stern was formed
A gilded shell
Red and gold
The brisk swell
Rippled both shores
Southwest wind
Carried down stream
The peal of bells
White towers
290   Weialala leia
             Wallala leialala

       "Trams and dusty trees.
Highbury bore me. Richmond and Kew
Undid me. By Richmond I raised my knees
Supine on the floor of a narrow canoe."

       "My feet are at Moorgate, and my heart
Under my feet. After the event
He wept. He promised 'a new start.'
I made no comment. What should I resent?"

300   "On Margate Sands.
I can connect
Nothing with nothing.
The broken fingernails of dirty hands.
My people humble people who expect
Nothing."
             la la

---

[49] Weialala . . . leialala: "The Song of the (three) Thames-daughters begins here" (E). These creations of the poet's, parodies of Wagner's Rhine Maidens from the opera *Twilight of the Gods,* sing their refrain in lines 277–78 and 290–91 and speak separately in lines 292–306, each identifying a place along the Thames where she was debauched.

[50] Elizabeth . . . oars: The story of the dalliance of Queen Elizabeth and Robert Dudley, Earl of Leicester, while cruising in a barge down the Thames. Eliot took the story from James A. Froude's biography *Elizabeth,* vol. I, ch. 4.

> To Carthage then I came[51]
> Burning burning burning burning[52]
> O Lord Thou pluckest me out
> O Lord Thou pluckest[53]
>
> burning

IV. DEATH BY WATER[54]

Phlebas the Phoenician, a fortnight dead,
Forgot the cry of gulls, and the deep sea swell
And the profit and loss.
                              A current under sea
Picked his bones in whispers. As he rose and fell
He passed the stages of his age and youth
Entering the whirlpool.
                              Gentile or Jew
O you who turn the wheel and look to windward,
Consider Phlebas, who was once handsome and tall as you.

V. WHAT THE THUNDER SAID[55]

After the torchlight red on sweaty faces
After the frosty silence in the gardens
After the agony in stony places
The shouting and the crying
Prison and palace and reverberation
Of thunder of spring over distant mountains
He who was living is now dead[56]

---

[51] To Carthage . . . came: St. Augustine, *The Confessions*, III, 1.

[52] Burning . . . burning: Refrain from Buddha's "Fire Sermon," which argues against the fires of passion (E).

[53] O Lord . . . pluckest: "From St. Augustine's *Confessions* again. The collocation of these two representatives of Eastern and Western asceticism, as the culmination of this part of the poem, is not an accident" (E).

[54] Death by Water: Phlebas is a poetic creation, perhaps an ancestor of Mr. Eugenides, who in drowning is purified by being stripped of his worldly attributes. The reader is left to decide whether Phlebas's death is a sacrificial act leading to rebirth or a pointless waste.

[55] What the Thunder Said: Eliot comments: "In the first part of Part V three themes are employed: the journey to Emmaus, the approach to the Chapel Perilous . . . and the present decay of eastern Europe" (E). The opening lines of the section refer to the story of the betrayal and Crucifixion of Christ.

[56] Of thunder of spring . . . dead: The Passion of Christ in the Garden of Gethsemane is merged here with the vegetation cycle.

We who were living are now dying
330   With a little patience

Here is no water but only rock
Rock and no water and the sandy road
The road winding above among the mountains
Which are mountains of rock without water
If there were water we should stop and drink
Amongst the rock one cannot stop or think
Sweat is dry and feet are in the sand
If there were only water amongst the rock
Dead mountain mouth of carious[57] teeth that cannot spit
340   Here one can neither stand nor lie nor sit
There is not even silence in the mountains
But dry sterile thunder without rain
There is not even solitude in the mountains
But red sullen faces sneer and snarl
From doors of mudcracked houses
                                    If there were water

And no rock
If there were rock
And also water
350   And water
A spring
A pool among the rock
If there were the sound of water only
Not the cicada
And dry grass singing
But sound of water over a rock
Where the hermit-thrush sings in the pine trees
Drip drop drip drop drop drop drop
But there is no water

360   Who is the third who walks always beside you?[58]
When I count, there are only you and I together
But when I look ahead up the white road
There is always another one walking beside you
Gliding wrapt in a brown mantle, hooded

---

[57] carious: From carrion: decaying (flesh).

[58] the third . . . beside you?: Eliot refers to an Antarctic expedition in which a party of explorers "had the constant delusion that there was *one more member* than could actually be counted" (E). Also, in the story of the journey to Emmaus (Luke 24:13–34), a third person appears to join the two disciples: Jesus.

I do not know whether a man or a woman[59]
—But who is that on the other side of you?

What is that sound high in the air[60]
Murmur of maternal lamentation
Who are those hooded hordes swarming
370 Over endless plains, stumbling in cracked earth
Ringed by the flat horizon only
What is the city over the mountains
Cracks and reforms and bursts in the violet air
Falling towers
Jerusalem Athens Alexandria
Vienna London
Unreal

A woman drew her long black hair out tight
And fiddled whisper music on those strings
380 And bats with baby faces in the violet light
Whistled, and beat their wings
And crawled head downward down a blackened wall
And upside down in air were towers
Tolling reminiscent bells, that kept the hours
And voices singing out of empty cisterns and exhausted wells.

In this decayed hole among the mountains
In the faint moonlight, the grass is singing
Over the tumbled graves, about the chapel
There is the empty chapel, only the wind's home.[61]
390 It has no windows, and the door swings,
Dry bones can harm no one.
Only a cock stood on the rooftree
Co co rico co co rico[62]
In a flash of lightning. Then a damp gust
Bringing rain

---

[59] **a man or a woman:** May refer to the prophet Tiresias.

[60] **that sound . . . air:** Eliot cites a comment by Hermann Hesse that "already half of Europe . . . is on the way to chaos, going drunk in holy madness along the edge of the abyss, and sings, sings drunkenly and hymnlike as Dmitri Karamazov sang." (Hesse, *Look into Chaos* [*Blick ins Chaos*], 1920.)

[61] **the chapel . . . home:** The Chapel Perilous of the Grail legend, cited in Jessie Weston's *From Ritual to Romance.*

[62] **Co co . . . rico:** The cock's crow suggests the breaking of a spell.

Ganga[63] was sunken, and the limp leaves
Waited for rain, while the black clouds
Gathered far distant, over Himavant.[64]
The jungle crouched, humped in silence.
400 Then spoke the thunder
D A
Datta:[65] what have we given?
My friend, blood shaking my heart
The awful daring of a moment's surrender
Which an age of prudence can never retract
By this, and this only, we have existed
Which is not to be found in our obituaries
Or in memories draped by the beneficent spider[66]
Or under seals broken by the lean solicitor
410 In our empty rooms
D A
Dayadhvam: I have heard the key
Turn in the door once and turn once only[67]
We think of the key, each in his prison
Thinking of the key, each confirms a prison
Only at nightfall, aethereal rumours
Revive for a moment a broken Coriolanus[68]
D A
Damyata: The boat responded
420 Gaily, to the hand expert with sail and oar
The sea was calm, your heart would have responded
Gaily, when invited, beating obedient
To controlling hands

                    I sat upon the shore
Fishing,[69] with the arid plain behind me

---

[63] Ganga: The Ganges River in India.

[64] Himavant: The Himalaya Mountains.

[65] *Datta . . . Damyata:* The words *datta* (give), l. 402; *dayadhvam* (sympathize), l. 412; and *damyata* (control), l. 419. According to the Brihadaranyaka Upanishads (c. 900–800 B.C.E.), the thunder god Prajapati commands that humans practice charity, sympathy, and self-control as a spiritual exercise. Apparently Eliot saw this as a redemptive or cleansing activity.

[66] memories . . . spider: Compare Webster, *The White Devil*, V, vi: "They'll remarry / . . . ere the spider / Make a thin curtain for your epitaphs."

[67] I have . . . once only: Compare Dante, *The Inferno*, 33, 46–47: "And I heard them below locking the door / Of the horrible tower," from Count Ugolino's story of being locked in a tower to starve, along with his children.

[68] Coriolanus: That is, a tyrant, possibly a betrayer.

[69] Fishing: The Fisher King of the Grail legend, in whose voice the poem ends.

Shall I at last set my lands in order?[70]
London Bridge is falling down falling down falling down
Poi s'ascose nel foco che gli affina[71]
Quando fiam uti chelidon—O swallow swallow[72]
430 *Le Prince d'Aquitaine à la tour abolie*[73]
These fragments I have shored against my ruins
Why then Ile fit you. Hieronymo's mad againe.[74]
Datta. Dayadhvam. Damyata.
       Shantih   shantih   shantih[75]

---

[70] set . . . order?: Isaiah 38:1, "Set thine house in order, for thou shalt die and not live."

[71] *Poi . . . affina*: The *Purgatorio*, 26, 48, "Then he hid himself in the purifying fire." The poet Arnaut Daniel leaves Dante, imploring him to remember his suffering.

[72] O . . . swallow: "When will I be like the swallow?" Eliot cites "The Vigil of Venus," a late Latin poem in which Philomela is turned into a swallow, and also the story of Philomela in parts II and III of *The Waste Land*.

[73] *Le Prince . . . abolie:* "The prince of Aquitaine at the ruined tower," from a sonnet by the symbolist poet Gerard de Nerval, "El Desdichado" (1854). The disinherited prince is expressing "the black sun of melancholy."

[74] Ile fit . . . againe: See Thomas Kyd, *The Spanish Tragedy* (1594). Hieronymo "fits" (serves) his enemies by writing a play for them that exposes their crimes, then revenging himself upon them.

[75] shantih: Repeated as here, a formal ending to an Upanishad. "The Peace which passeth understanding" is our equivalent to this word (E).

The Literature of War, Conflict, and Resistance

The twentieth century will be remembered as one of the bloodiest in the history of mankind. Among other disasters, two great "world" wars swept through Europe and parts of Asia and Africa and drew the United States into the fighting, ultimately threatening European influence around the globe. The First World War is said to have killed off an entire generation of European men and the Second World War, in some ways a continuation of the first, decimated civilian populations with aerial bombing and culminated in the nuclear destruction of two Japanese cities, Hiroshima and Nagasaki, at the hands of the United States. Moreover, the century was rife with civil war, revolution, wars against colonial domination, and ethnic and religious conflicts. From the bloody revolutions in Mexico (1910–1920) and Russia (1918–1920) to the fighting between Hindu India and Muslim Pakistan and between Israel and Palestine, the century was marked with violent confrontation.

The works presented in this section attempt to come to terms with the horrors of war and its meaning for humanity. The section comprises selections from the two world wars; poems of the Holocaust, the most horrific of the "ethnic cleansing" operations of the century; a story from the American war in Vietnam (1964–1973); poems from the ongoing struggle between the Israelis and the Palestinians; and, finally, poems by a Chinese dissident living in exile from his native land. Many other works in this anthology could be placed in this section: T. S. Eliot's *The Waste Land,* for example, García Lorca's **"Lament for Ignacio Sanchez Mejías,"** the poems of Anna Akhmatova, Fuentes's *The Prisoner of Las Lomas,* and Takenishi Hiroko's **"The Rite,"** to name a few. That so much writing of

p. 486
p. 579
p. 938
p. 971

Mercedes Vallejo, Free Drawing, 1938
Mercedes Vallejo was just fourteen when he was wounded during the Spanish civil war. He drew this recollection of the capture of Teruel while he was being treated in the hospital. (Mandeveille Special Collections, UC San Diego)

the twentieth century is about war is one testimony to the pervasiveness of the era's conflict and violence.

THE WORLD WARS

World War I (1914–18) was fought on two fronts: the eastern front, where scores of casualties were exacted from the Balkan states and from Russia, and the western front, where bitter trench warfare led to the slaughter of millions of soldiers from France, England, Germany, Italy, the United States, and other countries. Civilian populations also came under attack from artillery bombardment and armies of occupation.

The Second World War (1939–45) originated in Germany and was brought about in part by the harsh surrender terms imposed on that country at the end of the First World War and in part by the racist and expansionist ambitions of German leader Adolf Hitler. Tens of millions of lives in Russia, Germany, and throughout Europe

"The blood-dimmed tide is loosed, and everywhere /
The ceremony of innocence is drowned" — With these words, Yeats, in 1921, announced the dominant theme of the twentieth century's consciousness and much of its serious literature.

— DANIEL STERN,
New York Times

Europe in 1914

In the summer of 1914, most of Europe was divided into two camps: the Triple Alliance of Germany, Austria-Hungary, and Italy and the Triple Entente—Great Britain, France, and Russia. This division was intensified by the nationalist aspirations of ethnic groups within the European empires, especially in the Balkans. There Serbian nationalists were inflamed by Austria's annexation in 1908 of Bosnia-Herzegovina, which they coveted as part of a "greater Serbia." On June 28, 1914, Archduke Francis Ferdinand, the heir to the Austro-Hungarian throne, was assassinated in the Bosnian capital Sarajevo by a Serbian. This event triggered military mobilizations by the rival alliances, plunging Europe into World War I.

were lost. At the same time, Japan, allied with Germany, conquered China, the rest of Southeast Asia, and Burma. The United States and its allies fought Japan on the islands and at sea, in the Pacific. Aerial bombing, as in the First World War, accounted for enormous civilian casualties, this time throughout Europe, the British Isles, and Japan.

Scene during the Siege of
Teruel, Spain. April 1, 1938
*The Spanish civil war (1936–39)
was a battle between the leftist
Republicans and Francisco
Franco's Fascists. Franco, who
was backed by Hitler and
Mussolini, ultimately won,
ruling until his death in 1975.
(Library of Congress, LC-USZ62
112445)*

Perhaps the most horrifying aspect of this war was the attempt by
Nazi Germany to bring about the "Final Solution of the Jewish
Question"—the planned extermination of an entire people. Some
seven million Jews were murdered, most of them in Nazi concentration camps, during the course of the war.

THE LOST GENERATION

The two world wars marked a turning point in the consciousness of
Western Europe. At issue was the concept of Western civilization by
which Europe had justified its political and economic domination of
non-Western peoples.

The American émigré poet Ezra Pound, commenting on the
decimation of Europe as the First World War raged on, spoke of the
decline of the West:

> There died a myriad,
> And of the best, among them,
> For an old bitch gone in the teeth,
> For a botched civilization. . . .

The sense of loss and dissolution that followed the First World
War eventually grew beyond that of a generation or even Western
civilization as a whole. As T. S. Eliot asked between the wars, "After
such knowledge, what forgiveness?" And after the terror of the

Second World War, language itself seemed to falter. The ability of authors to represent the common concerns of humanity was called into question, as confidence in political and moral authority declined in the West. Some writers turned from modernity to embrace one of the world religions. Others sought relief in rebuilding their languages and cultures from the fragments of the devastated societies of Europe and the Far East.

THEMES AND PERSPECTIVES

The First World War saw the rise of the machine, an increased use of artillery, and the failed strategy of trench warfare, in addition to the utter dehumanization of the soldiers who were injured and killed by these "advances" in the art of war. The idealism of those sent to fight, many of them college trained and well read in the classics, was shattered along the nearly stationary western front that ran from Belgium to Switzerland, where their comrades didn't simply fall to the ground and die but were sent flying through the air or were exploded where they stood. Poets such as the well-born Austrian **Georg Trakl** and the moralistic young Englishmen Wilfred Owen and Isaac Rosenberg either returned broken from their injuries or they died in battle; all their honesty in reporting what they experienced could not save them or those who followed them.

GAY-org TRAH-kuhl

British Soldiers with Gas Masks
This image from World War I illustrates one of the terrors of the new warfare. (© Hulton-Deutsch Collection / CORBIS)

In the period "between the two wars," as a French phrase puts it, writers warned in vain of what was still to come, trying to rouse an already battered humanity to confront evil where it first appeared. German novelist **Erich Maria Remarque** recalled the horror of trench warfare in ***All Quiet on the Western Front*** (1929), and Bertolt Brecht, a German socialist poet and playwright, warned his countrymen of the coming of "the house painter," his contemptuous term for the future dictator Adolf Hitler. Those and other premonitions went unheeded or were heard too late.

EH-rik muh-REE-uh
ruh-MARK

p. 520

WAR ACROSS THE WORLD

The formerly mostly exclusive role of the writer changed somewhat in the Second World War. Although some were soldiers who still wrote of battles, World War II spared precious few of its experience; often it was the ordinary citizen who wrote of the destruction of cities or of being in hiding or of surviving the Holocaust. Those closest to the suffering remembered it in later years in their poems, sometimes living only long enough to finish the work of recording

Franciszek Jazwieki, Portrait of an Unknown Prisoner, 1942–43. Pencil and Crayon on Cardboard
Jazwieki, a prisoner in Auschwitz, the horrendous concentration camp in Poland, completed over one hundred portraits of his fellow prisoners between 1942 and 1945. Note the prisoner number visible in this portrait. (Courtesy of the Auschwitz-Birkenau State Museum)

Holocaust Survivors at Buchenwald
This photograph was taken at the Buchenwald concentration camp upon its liberation by U.S. troops. The Nobel Prize–winning author Elie Wiesel can be seen on the right of the center bunk. (© Bettmann / CORBIS)

the horror of Nazi extermination. Nellie Sachs, a survivor of both world wars, struggled to write down her memories of the death camps of World War II. Paul Celan, whose parents died in the death camps, finished writing of his experiences at the hands of the Nazis only to commit suicide when his work was done. With terrible irony the war had democratized suffering and death, bringing it home to the people of more than half the world.

People lost a fundamental trust in the outcome of human action. The enormity of the Holocaust and the nightmarish destruction wrought by nuclear weapons dwarfed the human perspective even further. The poetry that was written at this time struggled to recover its grounding in language. **Tamura Ryuichi**, a leading poet of Japan and a foe of Japanese militarism, borrowed the idea from T. S. Eliot that the modern world was a wasteland consisting of fragments among the ruins. For Polish Nobelist **Wislawa Szymborska**, the postwar world was one in which terrorists blew up pubs on a Saturday evening and in which the scale of things had become inverted. Russian poet Andrei **Voznesensky**, celebrating the victory of the Soviet Union over the German invaders, becomes a latter-day Goya, the Spanish artist whose etchings "Disasters of War" shocked sensibilities in the early nineteenth century.

tah-MOO-rah
ree-oo-EE-chee

vis-WAH-vah
shim-BORE-skah

VUZ-nih-SYEN-skee

VIETNAM

For Americans the world wars were triumphs. The United States entered the First World War late enough to escape much of the devastation that decimated the armies of Europe; the victories of the Second World War, though attained through great sacrifice, had brought down the evil Nazi regime and saved at least some of the world for democracy. The Vietnam War, however, brought home to Americans the disillusionment experienced by Europeans in the earlier conflicts. An undeclared war without clear objectives, the fighting in Vietnam divided the United States and ended with retreat rather than victory. Tim O'Brien, a veteran of the war and the American writer who has proved most able to express the mixed feelings prompted by it, describes the reaction of an American recruit to having killed for the first time in the short story **"The Man I Killed."** p. 535 Like the moving passage from Remarque's *All Quiet on the Western Front,* in which a German soldier recognizes his common humanity with the Frenchman he has slain, O'Brien's soldier imagines the life of the young Vietnamese man whose corpse lay before him.

American Troops Wading across River, Ben Khe, South Vietnam, 1965
American troops in Vietnam were fighting in terrain previously unknown to them. In addition to challenging topographical elements and weather conditions, Americans were fighting an enemy they couldn't actually see most of the time and for reasons that became increasingly unclear. (© Bettmann / CORBIS)

PALESTINE AND ISRAEL

In the wake of the Holocaust, Western powers took the lead in responding to demands for a Jewish state. A United Nations commission in 1948, which overruled the objections of the Palestinians and neighboring Arab states, divided Palestine into two parts, a Jewish region and a Palestinian one. The turmoil that has ensued led to the first of several wars between the new state of Israel and its Arab neighbors. A war in 1948 left Palestine with even less land than the partition had proposed and left many Palestinians refugees living in crowded camps in surrounding countries or in exile elsewhere in the world. Several wars between Israel and Middle Eastern Arab countries have erupted since, each ending in Palestinian defeat and deepened resentment.

fah-DWAH too-KAHN

p. 540

For dispossessed Palestinians, loss of their land is a great hardship, as is seen in the poems of **Fadwa Tuqan**. In **"Song of Becoming"** Tuqan writes of schoolboys who once played games and flew kites in the wind but who grew up and became angry and, finally, gave their lives to martyrdom. Mahmoud Darwish, a Palestinian of a later generation than Tuqan, may be one of those boys. His response to the situation is resistance rather than despair. In his eyes, the land is sodden with the blood of forty-nine villagers slain by Israeli troops, and he issues the warning, "Beware of my anger," after he

Israeli Soldiers by the Dome of the Rock, 1967
Israeli soldiers celebrate the capture of Old Jerusalem from the Jordanians in the Six Day War. They cheer in front of the Dome of the Rock, a mosque sacred to all Muslims. (© Bettmann / CORBIS)

catalogs the humiliations inflicted on the colonized Palestinians as they pass through Israeli checkpoints. **Yehuda Amichai,** Israel's most prominent poet, also writes about schoolchildren. Acknowledging the human toll on both sides of the warfare, Amichai laments kindergartners who will grow up in a world without pity.

yeh-HOO-duh
ah-mee-CHIGH

TIANANMEN SQUARE

In 1989, when the People's Army crushed the student movement that was demonstrating for democratic reforms in Tiananmen Square, in Beijing, hundreds of students were killed and many more imprisoned or driven into exile. On the banners carried by protesters in the square were passages from the poetry of **Bei Dao**, a leading writer in the democracy movement who had earlier gone into exile in the West. In poems like **"The Answer," "Declaration,"** and **"An End or a Beginning,"** Bei Dao gives expression to the hopes and later the disillusionment of those in the People's Republic of China who sought democratic reform.

bay DOW

pp. 548–49

■ CONNECTIONS

T. S. Eliot, *The Waste Land,* p. 486; Anna Akhmatova, Poems, p. 558; Federico García Lorca, "Lament for Ignacio Sanchez Mejías," p. 579; Pablo Neruda, Poems, p. 677; Samuel Beckett, *Krapp's Last Tape,* p. 774; Takenishi Hiroko, "The Rite," p. 971. The authors in this section should be read alongside other major figures in contemporary literature. These include T. S. Eliot, author of *The Waste Land*; Akhmatova, the Russian poet who chronicled the repression of the Stalin era in the Soviet Union; Lorca, who was murdered at the beginning of the Spanish civil war; Neruda, the Communist poet from Chile; Irish-French playwright Beckett, who fought as a French partisan in World War II; and Takenishi, who lived through the Hiroshima bombing. What do these major thinkers have in common with those who are included in this section? Does the fact that they are "writers" necessarily separate them from the "real" issues of war?

Samuel Beckett, *Krapp's Last Tape,* p. 774; Gabriel García Márquez, "A Very Old Man with Enormous Wings," p. 928; Milan Kundera, "The Hitchhiking Game," p. 1005; Salman Rushdie, "The Courter," p. 1261; Leslie Marmon Silko, "Lullaby," p. 1333. The twentieth century saw the decline of confidence in "the master narrative," the idea that one *can tell* a story that reflects the values of "civilized society"; an increasing lack of faith in such storytelling can be seen in the works of many writers of the latter half of the 1900s, including Beckett, García Márquez, Kundera, Rushdie, and Silko. How do the works cited here reflect this loss of confidence?

■ FURTHER RESEARCH

Anthologies
Eberhart, Richard, and Selden Rodman, eds. *War and the Poet.* 1945.
Forché, Carolyn, ed. *Against Forgetting: Twentieth-Century Poetry of Witness.* 1993.
Silkin, Jon, ed. *The Penguin Book of First World War Poetry.* 1981.
Stallworthy, Jon. *The Oxford Book of War Poetry.* 1984.

Criticism and Comment

Cohen, J. M. *Poets of This Age: 1908–1965.* 1966.

Fussell, Paul. *The Great War and Modern Memory.* 1975.

Hamburger, Michael. *The Truth of Poetry.* 1982.

■ PRONUNCIATION

Yehuda Amichai: yeh-HOO-duh ah-mee-CHIGH
Bei Dao: bay DOW
Erich Maria Remarque: EH-rik muh-REE-uh ruh-MARK
Wislawa Szymborska: vis-WAH-vah shim-BORE-skah
Tamura Ryuichi: tah-MOO-rah ree-oo-EE-chee
Georg Trakl: GAY-org TRAH-kuhl
Fadwa Tuqan: fah-DWAH too-KAHN
Voznesensky: vuz-nih-SYEN-skee

GEORG TRAKL
B. AUSTRIA, 1887–1914

After achieving early recognition as a poet, Georg Trakl received a personal stipend from the philosopher Ludwig Wittgenstein in July 1914 to enable him to continue writing. Instead, he enlisted in the army as a pharmacist on the eastern front. Following a defeat in Grodek, Poland, with ninety wounded men in his care and no medicine to give them, Trakl attempted suicide and was transferred to a mental hospital in Krakow, where his second suicide attempt succeeded. His poetry, highly personal and reflecting an early life of privilege, gained in intensity as he became absorbed in the war. His personification of the night and the moon in "Eastern Front" and the blood in the field in "Grodek" are examples of his powerful symbolism. As an EXPRESSIONIST, Trakl sought to objectify inner experience rather than to describe the world outside the self. He was mourned as the greatest German expressionist poet lost in the war.

Eastern Front

Translated by Christopher Middleton

The wrath of the people is dark,
Like the wild organ notes of winter storm,
The battle's crimson wave, a naked
Forest of stars.

With ravaged brows, with silver arms
To dying soldiers night comes beckoning.
In the shade of the autumn ash
Ghosts of the fallen are sighing.

Thorny wilderness girdles the town about.
10   From bloody doorsteps the moon
Chases terrified women.
Wild wolves have poured through the gates.

Grodek[1]

Translated by Michael Hamburger

At nightfall the autumn woods cry out
With deadly weapons and the golden plains,
The deep blue lakes, above which more darkly
Rolls the sun; the night embraces
Dying warriors, the wild lament
Of their broken mouths.
But quietly there in the pastureland
Red clouds in which an angry god resides,
The shed blood gathers, lunar coolness.
10   All the roads lead to blackest carrion.
Under golden twigs of the night and stars
The sister's shade now sways through the silent copse
To greet the ghosts of the heroes, the bleeding heads;
And softly the dark flutes of autumn sound in the reeds.
O prouder grief! You brazen altars,
Today a great pain feeds the hot flame of the spirit,
The grandsons yet unborn.

---

[1]Grodek: A town in Galicia, Poland, where Trakl served as a chemist with the Austrian army. After a battle there, he was placed in charge of a large number of serious casualties whose sufferings he could not relieve; he tried to shoot himself but was prevented from doing so. "Grodek" is the last poem Trakl wrote: Soon after its composition, the poet was sent to Kracow and placed under observation as a mental patient. He died in a military hospital in that city from a self-induced overdose of drugs. [Translator's note.]

WILFRED OWEN
B. ENGLAND, 1893–1918

The British poet Wilfred Owen is generally regarded, like the German Georg Trakl, as the great national poet of his generation; Owen's life, too, was tragically cut short on the battlefield. He saw World War I from a soldier's point of view and related it in matter-of-fact, public language to his countrymen. He rejected the idealism of upper-class British schoolboys who had studied war from Latin authors. Thus he calls the prescription of Horace, "Dulce et decorum est pro patria mori," the "old Lie."

All notes are the editors'.

Dulce et Decorum Est[1]

Bent double, like old beggars under sacks,
Knock-kneed, coughing like hags, we cursed through sludge,
Till on the haunting flares we turned our backs
And towards our distant rest began to trudge.
Men marched asleep. Many had lost their boots
But limped on, blood-shod. All went lame; all blind;
Drunk with fatigue; deaf even to the hoots
Of tired, outstripped Five-Nines[2] that dropped behind.

Gas! Gas![3] Quick, boys! —An ecstasy of fumbling,
10   Fitting the clumsy helmets just in time;
But someone still was yelling out and stumbling,
And flound'ring like a man in fire or lime . . .
Dim, through the misty panes[4] and thick green light,
As under a green sea, I saw him drowning.

In all my dreams, before my helpless sight,
He plunges at me, guttering, choking, drowning.

If in some smothering dreams you too could pace
Behind the wagon that we flung him in,

---

[1] Dulce et Decorum Est: The beginning of a line from Horace, which in full means "Sweet and fitting it is to die for your country."

[2] Five-Nines: 5.9 inch–caliber shells.

[3] Gas! Gas!: Poison gas, usually mustard gas, was commonly used in trench warfare in World War I.

[4] the misty panes: The cloudy eye lenses on the gas mask.

And watch the white eyes writhing in his face,
20 His hanging face, like a devil's sick of sin;
If you could hear, at every jolt, the blood
Come gargling from the froth-corrupted lungs,
Obscene as cancer, bitter as the cud
Of vile, incurable sores on innocent tongues,—
My friend, you would not tell with such high zest
To children ardent for some desperate glory,
The old Lie: Dulce et decorum est
Pro patria mori.

Anthem for Doomed Youth

What passing-bells for these who die as cattle?
—Only the monstrous anger of the guns.
Only the stuttering rifles' rapid rattle
Can patter out their hasty orisons.°   prayers
No mockeries now for them; no prayers nor bells;
Nor any voice of mourning save the choirs,—
The shrill, demented choirs of wailing shells;
And bugles calling for them from sad shires.

What candles may be held to speed them all?
10 Not in the hands of boys but in their eyes
Shall shine the holy glimmers of goodbyes.
The pallor of girls' brows shall be their pall;
Their flowers the tenderness of patient minds,
And each slow dusk a drawing-down of blinds.

Strange Meeting

It seemed that out of battle I escaped
Down some profound dull tunnel, long since scooped
Through granites which titanic wars had groined.

Yet also there encumbered sleepers groaned,
Too fast in thought or death to be bestirred.
Then, as I probed them, one sprang up, and stared
With piteous recognition in fixed eyes,
Lifting distressful hands, as if to bless.
And by his smile, I knew that sullen hall,—

10   By his dead smile I knew we stood in Hell.
With a thousand pains that vision's face was grained;
Yet no blood reached there from the upper ground,
And no guns thumped, or down the flues made moan.
"Strange friend," I said, "here is no cause to mourn."
"None," said that other, "save the undone years,
The hopelessness. Whatever hope is yours,
Was my life also; I went hunting wild
After the wildest beauty in the world,
Which lies not calm in eyes, or braided hair,
20   But mocks the steady running of the hour,
And if it grieves, grieves richlier than here.
For by my glee might many men have laughed,
And of my weeping something had been left,
Which must die now. I mean the truth untold,
The pity of war, the pity war distilled.
Now men will go content with what we spoiled,
Or, discontent, boil bloody, and be spilled.
They will be swift with swiftness of the tigress.
None will break ranks, though nations trek from progress.
30   Courage was mine, and I had mystery,
Wisdom was mine, and I had mastery:
To miss the march of this retreating world
Into vain citadels that are not walled.
Then, when much blood had clogged their chariot-wheels,
I would go up and wash them from sweet wells,
Even with truths that lie too deep for taint.
I would have poured my spirit without stint
But not through wounds; not on the cess° of war.   fortunes
Foreheads of men have bled where no wounds were.

40   "I am the enemy you killed, my friend.
I knew you in this dark: for so you frowned
Yesterday through me as you jabbed and killed.
I parried; but my hands were loath and cold.
Let us sleep now. . . ."

❧ ISAAC ROSENBERG
B. ENGLAND, 1890–1918

Isaac Rosenberg was aware of the risk he was taking by serving at the front. In 1916 he wrote: "I am determined that this war, with all its powers for devastation, shall not master my poeting; that is, if I am lucky enough to come through all right. I will not leave a corner of my consciousness covered up, but saturate myself with the strange and extraordinary new conditions of this life, and it will all refine itself into poetry later on." Perhaps the most realistic British poet of the war, Rosenberg also wrote of what he witnessed with passion. "Returning, We Hear the Larks" and "Dead Man's Dump" reveal specific human truths through powerful images.

All notes are the editors'.

❧ Returning, We Hear the Larks

Sombre the night is.
And though we have our lives, we know
What sinister threat lurks there.

Dragging these anguished limbs we only know
This poison-blasted track opens on our camp—
On a little safe sleep.

But hark! joy—joy—strange joy.
Lo! heights of night ringing with unseen larks.
Music showering on our upturned list'ning faces.

10 Death could drop from the dark
As easily as song—
But song only dropped,
Like a blind man's dreams on the sand
By dangerous tides,
Like a girl's dark hair for she dreams no ruin lies there,
Or her kisses where a serpent hides.

Dead Man's Dump

The plunging limbers[1] over the shattered track
Racketed with their rusty freight,
Stuck out like many crowns of thorns,
And the rusty stakes like sceptres old
To stay the flood of brutish men
Upon our brothers dear.

The wheels lurched over sprawled dead
But pained them not, though their bones crunched,
Their shut mouths made no moan.
They lie there huddled, friend and foeman,
Man born of man, and born of woman,
And shells go crying over them
From night till night and now.

Earth has waited for them,
All the time of their growth
Fretting for their decay:
Now she has them at last!
In the strength of their strength
Suspended — stopped and held.

What fierce imaginings their dark souls lit?
Earth! have they gone into you!
Somewhere they must have gone,
And flung on your hard back
Is their soul's sack
Emptied of God-ancestralled essences.
Who hurled them out? Who hurled?

None saw their spirits' shadow shake the grass,
Or stood aside for the half used life to pass
Out of those doomed nostrils and the doomed mouth,
When the swift iron burning bee
Drained the wild honey of their youth.

What of us who, flung on the shrieking pyre,
Walk, our usual thoughts untouched,
Our lucky limbs as on ichor[2] fed,

---

[1] limbers: Two-wheeled vehicles for transporting guns.
[2] ichor: An ethereal fluid taking the place of blood in the veins of Greek gods.

Immortal seeming ever?
Perhaps when the flames beat loud on us,
A fear may choke in our veins
And the startled blood may stop.

The air is loud with death,
40   The dark air spurts with fire,
The explosions ceaseless are.
Timelessly now, some minutes past,
These dead strode time with vigorous life,
Till the shrapnel called "An end!"
But not to all. In bleeding pangs
Some borne on stretchers dreamed of home,
Dear things, war-blotted from their hearts.

Maniac Earth! howling and flying, your bowel
Seared by the jagged fire, the iron love,
50   The impetuous storm of savage love.
Dark Earth! dark Heavens! swinging in chemic smoke,
What dead are born when you kiss each soundless soul
With lightning and thunder from your mined heart,
Which man's self dug, and his blind fingers loosed?

A man's brains splattered on
A stretcher-bearer's face;
His shook shoulders slipped their load,
But when they bent to look again
The drowning soul was sunk too deep
60   For human tenderness.

They left this dead with the older dead,
Stretched at the cross roads.

Burnt black by strange decay
Their sinister faces lie,
The lid over each eye,
The grass and coloured clay
More motion have than they,
Joined to the great sunk silences.

Here is one not long dead;
70   His dark hearing caught our far wheels,
And the choked soul stretched weak hands
To reach the living word the far wheels said,
The blood-dazed intelligence beating for light,

Crying through the suspense of the far torturing wheels
Swift for the end to break
Or the wheels to break,
Cried as the tide of the world broke over his sight.

Will they come? Will they ever come?
Even as the mixed hoofs of the mules,
80 The quivering-bellied mules,
And the rushing wheels all mixed
With his tortured upturned sight.
So we crashed round the bend,
We heard his weak scream,
We heard his very last sound,
And our wheels grazed his dead face.

❧ ERICH MARIA REMARQUE
B. GERMANY, 1898–1970

German novelist Erich Maria Remarque wrote *All Quiet on the Western Front* (*Im Westen nichts Neues*) in 1929. The work was immediately praised throughout Europe and America and made into a film the following year. In the passage reprinted here, a German soldier kills a French soldier, a printer named Gérard Duval who had the bad luck of falling into the same trench. The German conducts a "conversation" with Duval after he has died of his wounds, even promising in his guilt to write the Frenchman's wife and become a printer himself. Remarque's stark, realistic portrayal of trench warfare had a profound effect on the public — only four years before Hitler's rise to power in Germany. The translation by the Australian writer Arthur Wheen done in 1929, the year of the novel's publication in German, contributed to making *All Quiet on the Western Front* a worldwide best-seller.

FROM

❧ All Quiet on the Western Front

Translated by Arthur Wheen

Already it has become somewhat lighter. Steps hasten over me. The first. Gone. Again, another. The rattle of machine-guns becomes an unbroken chain. Just as I am about to turn round a little, something heavy stumbles, and with a crash a body falls over me into the shell-hole, slips down, and lies across me—

I do not think at all, I make no decision—I strike madly home, and feel only how the body suddenly convulses, then becomes limp, and collapses. When I recover myself, my hand is sticky and wet.

The man gurgles. It sounds to me as though he bellows, every gasping breath is like a cry, a thunder—but it is only my heart pounding. I want to stop his mouth, stuff it with earth, stab him again, he must be quiet, he is betraying me; now at last I regain control of myself, but have suddenly become so feeble that I cannot any more lift my hand against him.

So I crawl away to the farthest corner and stay there, my eyes glued on him, my hand grasping the knife—ready, if he stirs, to spring at him again. But he won't do so any more, I can hear that already in his gurgling.

I can see him indistinctly. I have but one desire, to get away. If it is not soon it will be too light; it will be difficult enough now. Then as I try to raise up my head I see it is impossible already. The machine-gun fire so sweeps the ground that I would be shot through and through before I could make one jump.

I test it once with my helmet, which I take off and hold up to find out the level of the shots. The next moment it is knocked out of my hand by a bullet. The fire is sweeping very low over the ground. I am not far enough from the enemy line to escape being picked off by one of the snipers if I attempt to get away.

The light increases. Burning I wait for our attack. My hands are white at the knuckles, I clench them so tightly in my longing for the fire to cease so that my comrades may come.

Minute after minute trickles away. I dare not look again at the dark figure in the shell-hole. With an effort I look past it and wait, wait. The bullets hiss, they make a steel net, never ceasing, never ceasing.

Then I notice my bloody hand and suddenly feel nauseated. I take some earth and rub the skin with it, now my hand is muddy and the blood cannot be seen any more.

The fire does not diminish. It is equally heavy from both sides. Our fellows have probably given me up for lost long ago.

It is early morning, clear and grey. The gurgling continues, I stop my ears, but soon take my fingers away again, because then I cannot hear the other sound.

The figure opposite me moves. I shrink together and involuntarily look at it. Then my eyes remain glued to it. A man with a small pointed beard lies there, his head is fallen to one side, one arm is half-bent, his head rests helplessly upon it. The other hand lies on his chest, it is bloody.

He is dead, I say to myself, he must be dead, he doesn't feel anything any more; it is only the body that is gurgling there. Then the head tries to raise itself, for a moment the groaning becomes louder, his forehead sinks back upon his arm. The man is not dead, he is dying, but he is not dead. I drag myself toward him, hesitate, support myself on my hands, creep a bit farther, wait, again a terrible journey of three yards, a long, a terrible journey. At last I am beside him.

Then he opens his eyes. He must have heard me and gazes at me with a look of utter terror. The body lies still, but in the eyes there is such an extraordinary expression of flight that for a moment I think they have power enough to carry the body off with them. Hundreds of miles away with one bound. The body is still, perfectly still, without sound, the gurgle has ceased, but the eyes cry out, yell, all the life is gathered together in them for one tremendous effort to flee, gathered together there in a dreadful terror of death, of me.

My legs give way and I drop on my elbows. "No, no," I whisper.

The eyes follow me. I am powerless to move so long as they are there.

Then his hand slips slowly from his breast, only a little bit, it sinks just a few inches, but this movement breaks the power of the eyes. I bend forward, shake my head and whisper: "No, no, no." I raise one hand, I must show him that I want to help him, I stroke his forehead.

The eyes shrink back as the hand comes, then they lose their stare, the eyelids droop lower, the tension is past. I open his collar and place his head more comfortably upright.

His mouth stands half open, it tries to form words. The lips are dry. My water bottle is not there. I have not brought it with me. But there is water in the mud, down at the bottom of the crater. I climb down, take out my handkerchief, spread it out, push it under, and scoop up the yellow water that strains through into the hollow of my hand.

He gulps it down. I fetch some more. Then I unbutton his tunic in order to bandage him if it is possible. In any case I must do it, so that if the fellows over there capture me they will see that I wanted to help him, and so will not shoot me. He tries to resist, but his hand is too feeble. The shirt is stuck and will not come away, it is buttoned at the back. So there is nothing for it but to cut it off.

I look for the knife and find it again. But when I begin to cut the shirt the eyes open once more and the cry is in them again and the demented expression, so that I must close them, press them shut and whisper: "I want to help you, Comrade, *camerade, camerade, camerade——*" eagerly repeating the word, to make him understand.

There are three stabs. My field dressing covers them, the blood runs out under it, I press it tighter; there; he groans.

That is all I can do. Now we must wait, wait.

These hours. . . . The gurgling starts again—but how slowly a man dies! For this I know—he cannot be saved. Indeed, I have tried to tell myself that he will be, but at noon this pretence breaks down and melts before his groans. If only I had not lost my revolver crawling about, I would shoot him. Stab him I cannot.

By noon I am groping on the outer limits of reason. Hunger devours me, I could almost weep for something to eat, I cannot struggle against it. Again and again I fetch water for the dying man and drink some myself.

This is the first man I have killed with my hands, whom I can see close at hand, whose death is my doing. Kat and Kropp and Müller have experienced it already, when they have hit someone; it happens to many, in hand-to-hand fighting especially—

But every gasp lays my heart bare. This dying man has time with him, he has an invisible dagger with which he stabs me: Time and my thoughts.

I would give much if he would but stay alive. It is hard to lie here and to have to see and hear him.

In the afternoon, about three, he is dead.

I breathe freely again. But only for a short time. Soon the silence is more unbearable than the groans. I wish the gurgling were there again, gasping, hoarse, now whistling softly, and again hoarse and loud.

It is mad, what I do. But I must do something. I prop the dead man up again so that he lies comfortably although he feels nothing any more. I close his eyes. They are brown, his hair is black and a bit curly at the sides.

The mouth is full and soft beneath his moustache; the nose is slightly arched, the skin brownish; it is now not so pale as it was before, when he was still alive. For a moment the face seems almost healthy;—then it collapses suddenly into the strange face of the dead that I have so often seen, strange faces, all alike.

No doubt his wife still thinks of him; she does not know what has happened. He looks as if he would often have written to her;—she will still be getting mail from him—Tomorrow, in a week's time—perhaps even a stray letter a month hence. She will read it, and in it he will be speaking to her.

My state is getting worse, I can no longer control my thoughts. What would his wife look like? Like the little brunette on the other side of the canal? Does she belong to me now? Perhaps by this act she becomes mine. I wish Kantorek were sitting here beside me. If my mother could see me—The dead man might have had thirty more years of life if only I had impressed the way back to our trench more sharply on my memory. If only he had run two yards farther to the left, he might now be sitting in the trench over there and writing a fresh letter to his wife.

But I will get no further that way; for that is the fate of all of us: if Kemmerich's legs had been six inches to the right; if Haie Westhus had bent his back three inches further forward—

The silence spreads. I talk and must talk. So I speak to him and say to him: "Comrade, I did not want to kill you. If you jumped in here again, I would not do it, if you would be sensible too. But you were only an idea to me before, an abstraction that lived in my mind and called forth its appropriate response. It was that abstraction I stabbed. But now, for the first time, I see you are a man like me. I thought of your hand-grenades, of your bayonet, of your rifle; now I see your wife and your face and our fellowship. Forgive me, comrade. We always see it too late. Why do they never tell us that you are just poor devils like us, that your mothers are just as anxious as ours, and that we have the same fear of death, and the same dying and the same agony—Forgive me, comrade; how could you be my enemy? If we threw away these rifles and this uniform you could be my brother just like Kat and Albert. Take twenty years of my life, comrade, and stand up—take more, for I do not know what I can even attempt to do with it now."

It is quiet, the front is still except for the crackle of rifle-fire. The bullets rain over, they are not fired haphazard, but shrewdly aimed from all sides. I cannot get out.

"I will write to your wife," I say hastily to the dead man, "I will write to her, she must hear it from me, I will tell her everything I have told you, she shall not suffer, I will help her, and your parents too, and your child—"

His tunic is half open. The pocketbook is easy to find. But I hesitate to open it. In it is the book with his name. So long as I do not know his name perhaps I may still forget him, time will obliterate it, this picture. But his name, it is a nail that will be hammered into me and never come out again. It has the power to recall this for ever, it will always come back and stand before me.

Irresolutely I take the wallet in my hand. It slips out of my hand and falls open. Some pictures and letters drop out. I gather them up and want to put them back again, but the strain I am under, the uncertainty, the hunger, the danger, these hours with the dead man have confused me, I want to hasten the relief, to intensify and to end the torture, as one strikes an unendurably painful hand against the trunk of a tree, regardless of everything.

There are portraits of a woman and a little girl, small amateur photographs taken against an ivy-clad wall. Along with them are letters. I take them out and try to read them. Most of it I do not understand, it is so hard to decipher and I know scarcely any French. But each word I translate pierces me like a shot in the chest;—like a stab in the chest.

My brain is taxed beyond endurance. But I realize this much, that I will never dare to write to these people as I intended. Impossible. I look at the portraits once more; they are clearly not rich people. I might send them money anonymously if I earn anything later on. I seize upon that, it is at least something to hold on to. This dead man is bound up with my life, therefore I must do everything, promise everything, in order to save myself; I swear blindly that I mean to live only for his sake and his family, with wet lips I try to placate him—and deep down in me lies the hope that I may buy myself off in this way and perhaps even yet get out of this; it is a little stratagem: If only I am allowed to escape, then I will see to it. So I open the book and read slowly:—Gérard Duval, compositor.

With the dead man's pencil I write the address on an envelope, then swiftly thrust everything back into his tunic.

I have killed the printer, Gérard Duval. I must be a printer, I think confusedly, be a printer, printer—

BERTOLT BRECHT
B. GERMANY, 1898–1956

German expressionist Bertolt Brecht created a theater of political agitation. A voice on the German left before the rise of Nazism, Brecht
went into exile in 1933 under threat of death, fleeing to northern Europe
and then to the United States, where he endured further persecution at
the hands of the House Un-American Activities Committee after World
War II. He returned to East Berlin in 1949 and was honored as the major
Communist playwright of Eastern Europe. "When Evil-Doing Comes
like Falling Rain" was written to call the attention of the German people
to the atrocities committed by the Nazis as they rose to power in the
1930s.

When Evil-Doing Comes like Falling Rain

Translated by John Willett

Like one who brings an important letter to the counter after office hours: the
     counter is already closed.
Like one who seeks to warn the city of an impending flood, but speaks another
     language. They do not understand him.
Like a beggar who knocks for the fifth time at a door where he has four times been
     given something: the fifth time he is hungry.
Like one whose blood flows from a wound and who awaits the doctor: his blood
     goes on flowing.
So do we come forward and report that evil has been done us.

The first time it was reported that our friends were being butchered there was a cry
     of horror. Then a hundred were butchered. But when a thousand were
     butchered and there was no end to the butchery, a blanket of silence spread.
When evil-doing comes like falling rain, nobody calls out "stop!"

When crimes begin to pile up they become invisible. When sufferings become
     unendurable the cries are no longer heard. The cries, too, fall like rain in
     summer.

NELLIE SACHS
B. GERMANY, 1891–1970

Nellie Sachs, a German Jew, survived Nazi persecution and emigrated to Sweden in the late 1930s. Her first book of poems had been published before the Nazi takeover; she spent her later life as a translator while writing about the Holocaust and won the Nobel Prize in literature in 1966. "O the Chimneys" remembers the ovens in the extermination camps.

O the Chimneys

Translated by Michael Roloff

And though after my skin worms destroy this body, yet in my flesh shall I see God.
— JOB 19:26

O the chimneys
On the ingeniously devised habitations of death
When Israel's body drifted as smoke
Through the air —
Was welcomed by a star, a chimney sweep,
A star that turned black
Or was it a ray of sun?

O the chimneys!
Freedomway for Jeremiah and Job's dust —
Who devised you and laid stone upon stone
The road for refugees of smoke?

O the habitations of death,
Invitingly appointed
For the host who used to be a guest —
O you fingers
Laying the threshold
Like a knife between life and death —

O you chimneys,
O you fingers
And Israel's body as smoke through the air!

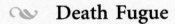

PAUL CELAN

B. ROMANIA, 1920–1970

Paul Celan was born Paul Antschel in Romania in 1920, the son of German-speaking Jews. After medical studies in France, he returned to Romania in 1939 where he taught Romance languages. In 1940, when political control of the area passed from the Russians to the Nazis and the Romanian Fascists, Celan's mother and father were arrested and placed in a Nazi concentration camp where they both died; Paul himself was freed from a forced labor camp in 1944. After 1948, Celan lived in Paris until he drowned himself in the Seine when he was fifty. He wrote his poetry—most of it about the trauma he, his countrymen, and other Jews had experienced in World War II—in a broken, nearly hysterical language reminiscent of the work of German expressionist poet August Stramm. Celan was chief among those who raised the question of whether German could again be a literary language after the war. "Death Fugue," with its repetition of unrelated lines and phrases, is a haunting evocation of the state of postwar European society. Translator John Felstiner calls the haunting image that opens the poem, the "Black milk of daybreak," the best-known lines in Celan's poetry since they evoke the bleakness of the Holocaust turning light to darkness. In his version of the poem, Felstiner enhances the traumatic repetitions by leaving some of them, especially at the end, in the original German, suggesting that one can never forget so painful a past.

All notes are the editors'.

Death Fugue

Translated by John Felstiner

Black milk of daybreak we drink it at evening
we drink it at midday and morning we drink it at night
we drink and we drink
we shovel a grave in the air there you won't lie too cramped
A man lives in the house he plays with his vipers he writes
he writes when it grows dark to Deutschland° your golden hair Marguerite[1]   Germany
he writes it and steps out of doors and the stars are all sparkling
        he whistles his hounds to come close

---

[1]golden hair Marguerite: Allusions to the heroine of Goethe's *Faust* and Heinrich Heine's golden-haired Lorelei, two familiar symbols of the feminine in classic German literature.

he whistles his Jews into rows has them shovel a grave in the ground
10 he orders us strike up and play for the dance

Black milk of daybreak we drink you at night
we drink you at morning and midday we drink you at evening
we drink and we drink
A man lives in the house he plays with his vipers he writes
he writes when it grows dark to Deutschland your golden hair Marguerite
your ashen hair Shulamith[2] we shovel a grave in the air
                                   there you won't lie too cramped
He shouts jab this earth deeper you lot there you others sing up and play
he grabs for the rod in his belt he swings it his eyes are blue
20 jab your spades deeper you lot there you others play on for the dancing

Black milk of daybreak we drink you at night
we drink you at midday and morning we drink you at evening
we drink and we drink
a man lives in the house your goldenes Haar Marguerite
your aschenes Haar Shulamith he plays with his vipers
He shouts play death more sweetly Death is a master from Deutschland
he shouts scrape your strings darker you'll rise then in smoke to the sky
you'll have a grave then in the clouds there you won't lie too cramped

Black milk of daybreak we drink you at night
30 we drink you at midday Death is a master aus Deutschland
we drink you at evening and morning we drink and we drink
this Death is ein Meister aus Deutschland his eye it is blue
he shoots you with shot made of lead shoots you level and true
a man lives in the house your goldenes Haar Margarete
he looses his hounds on us grants us a grave in the air
he plays with his vipers and daydreams
                                   der Tod ist ein Meister aus Deutschland
dein goldenes Haar Margarete
dein aschenes Haar Shulamith

---

[2] **ashen hair Shulamith:** The "black and comely" princess in the Song of Songs in the Hebrew Scriptures, often seen as a symbol of the Jewish people.

TAMURA RYUICHI

B. JAPAN, 1923–1998

Tamura Ryuichi was first exposed to English and American literary culture while attending high school in Tokyo, just before the outbreak of World War II. He attempted to avoid the draft by entering university but was conscripted in 1943. When he returned to Tokyo, a city devastated by aerial bombing, he found work as an editor and helped establish a literary group named "The Waste Land" after the poem by T. S. Eliot. Tamura's war experience informs part of a highly ambitious body of work that has won him world recognition. "October Poem" reflects on the Japanese defeat and surrender; "A Vertical Coffin" addresses, much in the spirit of Eliot and Ezra Pound, civilization as a whole.

The translations by Samuel Grolmes and Tsumura Yumiko are from their volume of Tamura's work in English, the most comprehensive selection of his work in any language other than Japanese.

October Poem

Translated by Samuel Grolmes and Tsumura Yumiko

Crisis is my nature
There is a fierce hurricane of feelings
under my smooth skin   There is
a fresh corpse thrown up
on the desolate shore of October

     October is my Empire
     My delicate hands control things to be lost
     My small eyes watch things that are to disappear
     My soft ears listen to the silence of people who are to die

10 Fear is my nature
The Time that murders everything
flows in my rich blood   There is
a new hunger trembling
in the cold sky of October

     October is my Empire
     My dead armies occupy all cities where rain falls
     My dead patrol planes circle in the sky above the lost souls
     My dead mobs sign their names for the people who are going to die

A Vertical Coffin

Translated by Samuel Grolmes and Tsumura Yumiko

I

Do not touch my corpse with your hands
Your hands
cannot touch "death"
As for my corpse
mix it in the crowd
let the rain fall on it

> We do not have hands
> We do not have hands that should touch death

I know the windows of the city
10 I know the windows where there is no one
No matter what city I go to
you have never been inside the room
Marriage and work
passion and sleep   and even death too
are chased out of your rooms
and become unemployed like you are

> We do not have a profession
> We do not have a profession that should touch death

I know the rain in the city
20 I know that crowd of umbrellas
No matter what city I go to
you have never been under the roof
Value and belief
revolution and hope   and even life
were kicked out from under your roof
and became unemployed like you are

> We do not have a profession
> We do not have a profession that should touch life

II

Do not let my corpse sleep on the ground
30 Your death
cannot rest on the ground

As for my corpse
put it in a vertical coffin
and let it stand up

     There is no grave on the earth for us
     There is no grave on the earth to put our corpses in
I know death on the earth
I know the meaning of death on the earth
No matter what country I go to
40 your death has never been put into a grave
The young girls' corpses go floating down the river
The blood of a small bird that was shot to death   and man voices that were
     slaughtered
have been chased out of your earth
and will become an exile like you are

     There is no country on the earth for us
     There is no country on the earth worth our deaths

I know the value of this earth
I know the lost value of the earth
No matter what country I go to
50 your life has never been fulfilled with great things
The wheat that was mowed as far as into the future
the trapped beasts   also little sisters
are chased out of your lives
become exiles like you are

     There is no country on the earth for us
     There is no country on the earth worth our lives

III

Do not burn my corpse in the fire
Your deaths
cannot be burned with fire
60 As for my corpse
hang it inside civilization
Let it rot

     We do not have fire
     We do not have a fire which should burn a corpse

I know your civilization
I know your civilization that has neither love nor death

No matter which house I go to
you have never been with a family
A father's single tear
70   the painful joy of a mother delivering a baby   and even the matter of heart
was chased out of your houses
became sick people like you are

    We do not have love
    We have nothing but the love of a sick person

I know your hospital rooms
I know your dreams that continue from bed to bed
No matter what hospital room I go to
you have never been really asleep
Drooping hands from the bed
80   eyes that were opened by great things   also thirsty hearts
are chased out of your hospital rooms
become sick people like you are

    We do not have poison
    We do not have a poison to heal us

WISLAWA SZYMBORSKA
B. POLAND, 1923

Wislawa Szymborska, a self-described private person, has spent her whole life in western Poland, where she was born, attended school, and has worked for nearly thirty years as a columnist and poetry editor for the literary magazine *Zycie Literacia*. In spite of her differences with the Communist regime in Poland and her disillusionment with its aims, she was able to publish sixteen volumes of poetry and several volumes of essays during the Communist era. Accepting the Nobel Prize in 1996, she remarked, "inspiration is not the exclusive privilege of poets or artists generally. There is, has been, and will always be a certain group of people whom inspiration visits. It's made up of all who've consciously chosen their calling and do their job with love and imagination." The humility in this statement is also apparent in Szymborska's poems, which treat big events with modest matter-of-factness and quiet irony.

The Terrorist, He Watches

Translated by Robert A. Maguire and Magnus Jan Krynski

The bomb will go off in the bar at one twenty p.m.
Now it's only one sixteen p.m.
Some will still have time to get in,
some to get out.

The terrorist has already crossed to the other side of the street.
The distance protects him from any danger,
and what a sight for sore eyes:

A woman in a yellow jacket, she goes in.
A man in dark glasses, he comes out.
10   Guys in jeans, they are talking.
One seventeen and four seconds.
That shorter guy's really got it made, and gets on a scooter,
and that taller one, he goes in.

One seventeen and forty seconds.
That girl there, she's got a green ribbon in her hair.
Too bad that bus just cut her off.
One eighteen p.m.
The girl's not there any more.
Was she dumb enough to go in, or wasn't she?
20   That we'll see when they carry them out.

One nineteen p.m.
No one seems to be going in.
Instead a fat baldy's coming out.
Like he's looking for something in his pockets and
at one nineteen and fifty seconds
he goes back for those lousy gloves of his.

It's one twenty p.m.
The time, how it drags.
Should be any moment now.
30   Not yet.
Yes, this is it.
The bomb, it goes off.

ANDREI VOZNESENSKY
B. RUSSIA, 1933

Andrei Voznesensky was first published in the Soviet *Literaturnaya Gazeta* in 1958, during the "thaw" in the cold war that lasted until 1961 under Premier Nikita Khrushchev. Voznesensky's trips to the United States with poet Yevgeni Yevtushenko and their friendship with American poets Lawrence Ferlinghetti and Allen Gisberg helped renew cultural relations between the two countries. Voznesensky disclaimed politics as a motivating force in his work, advocating a "pure poetry" that looks "deep into the human mind, right inside the brain" and arguing that "our poetry's future lies in association, metaphors reflecting the interdependence of phenomena, their mutual transformation." Ironically, his best-known poem is patriotic. "I Am Goya" celebrates the Russian victory over the Nazis in the German invasion of the Soviet Union in August 1944 and recalls Spanish painter Francisco de Goya (1746–1828), whose images of slaughter and resistance dignified the situation of the peasantry in the Napoleonic Wars at the beginning of the nineteenth century.

A note on the translation: Voznesensky's most famous poem, "I Am Goya," is translated here by American poet Stanley Kunitz, who translated the works of several of Russia's most important modern poets.

I Am Goya

Translated by Stanley Kunitz

I am Goya[1]
of the bare field, by the enemy's beak gouged
till the craters of my eyes gape
I am grief

I am the tongue
of war, the embers of cities
on the snows of the year 1941
I am hunger

I am the gullet
10   of a woman hanged whose body like a bell

---

[1] Goya: Francisco de Goya (1746–1828), Spanish artist whose etchings late in life of the horrors of war have endured in the collective European memory. [Editors' note.]

tolled over a blank square
I am Goya

O grapes of wrath!
I have hurled westward
                    the ashes of the uninvited guest!
and hammered stars into the unforgetting sky — like nails
I am Goya

❧ TIM O'BRIEN
B. UNITED STATES, 1946

Born and raised in rural Minnesota, Tim O'Brien was drafted into the infantry in 1968 after graduating from Macalester College. Opposed to the Vietnam War, he served for two years as a foot soldier in Vietnam and was awarded the Purple Heart. After leaving the military he did graduate work at Harvard School of Government, worked as a reporter at the *Washington Post,* and has written numerous books, several of which are based on his experience in Vietnam, including the novel *Going After Cacciato* (1978), the memoir *If I Die in a Combat Zone, Box Me Up and Ship Me Home* (1973), and the volume of short stories *The Things They Carried* (1990). "The Man I Killed" comes from that collection of stories and describes an incident similar to the one in the passage from Remarque's **All Quiet on the Western Front,** also included in this section.

p. 520

❧ The Man I Killed

His jaw was in his throat, his upper lip and teeth were gone, his one eye was shut, his other eye was a star-shaped hole, his eyebrows were thin and arched like a woman's, his nose was undamaged, there was a slight tear at the lobe of one ear, his clean black hair was swept upward into a cowlick at the rear of the skull, his forehead was lightly freckled, his fingernails were clean, the skin at his left cheek was peeled back in three ragged strips, his right cheek was smooth and hairless, there was a butterfly on his chin, his neck was open to the spinal cord and the blood there was thick and shiny and it was this wound that had killed him. He lay face-up in the center of the trail, a slim, dead, almost dainty young man. He had bony legs, a narrow waist, long shapely fingers. His chest was sunken and poorly muscled — a scholar, maybe. His wrists were the wrists of a child. He wore a black shirt, black pajama pants, a gray

ammunition belt, a gold ring on the third finger of his right hand. His rubber sandals had been blown off. One lay beside him, the other a few meters up the trail. He
had been born, maybe, in 1946 in the village of My Khe near the central coastline of
Quang Ngai Province, where his parents farmed, and where his family had lived for
several centuries, and where, during the time of the French, his father and two
uncles and many neighbors had joined in the struggle for independence. He was not
a Communist. He was a citizen and a soldier. In the village of My Khe, as in all of
Quang Ngai, patriotic resistance had the force of tradition, which was partly the
force of legend, and from his earliest boyhood the man I killed would have listened
to stories about the heroic Trung sisters and Tran Hung Dao's famous rout of the
Mongols and Le Loi's final victory against the Chinese at Tot Dong. He would have
been taught that to defend the land was a man's highest duty and highest privilege.
He had accepted this. It was never open to question. Secretly, though, it also frightened him. He was not a fighter. His health was poor, his body small and frail. He
liked books. He wanted someday to be a teacher of mathematics. At night, lying on
his mat, he could not picture himself doing the brave things his father had done, or
his uncles, or the heroes of the stories. He hoped in his heart that he would never be
tested. He hoped the Americans would go away. Soon, he hoped. He kept hoping and
hoping, always, even when he was asleep.

"Oh, man, you fuckin' trashed the fucker," Azar said. "You scrambled his sorry
self, look at that, you *did*, you laid him out like Shredded fuckin' Wheat."

"Go away," Kiowa said.

"I'm just saying the truth. Like oatmeal."

"Go," Kiowa said.

"Okay, then, I take it back," Azar said. He started to move away, then stopped
and said, "Rice Krispies, you know? On the dead test, this particular individual gets
A-plus."

Smiling at this, he shrugged and walked up the trail toward the village behind
the trees.

Kiowa kneeled down.

"Just forget that crud," he said. He opened up his canteen and held it out for a
while and then sighed and pulled it away. "No sweat, man. What else could you do?"

Later, Kiowa said, "I'm serious. Nothing *anybody* could do. Come on, stop
staring."

The trail junction was shaded by a row of trees and tall brush. The slim young
man lay with his legs in the shade. His jaw was in his throat. His one eye was shut and
the other was a star-shaped hole.

Kiowa glanced at the body.

"All right, let me ask a question," he said. "You want to trade places with him?
Turn it all upside down — you *want* that? I mean, be honest."

The star-shaped hole was red and yellow. The yellow part seemed to be getting
wider, spreading out at the center of the star. The upper lip and gum and teeth were
gone. The man's head was cocked at a wrong angle, as if loose at the neck, and the
neck was wet with blood.

"Think it over," Kiowa said.

Then later he said, "Tim, it's a *war*. The guy wasn't Heidi—he had a weapon, right? It's a tough thing, for sure, but you got to cut out that staring."

Then he said, "Maybe you better lie down a minute."

Then after a long empty time he said, "Take it slow. Just go wherever the spirit takes you."

The butterfly was making its way along the young man's forehead, which was spotted with small dark freckles. The nose was undamaged. The skin on the right cheek was smooth and fine-grained and hairless. Frail-looking, delicately boned, the young man would not have wanted to be a soldier and in his heart would have feared performing badly in battle. Even as a boy growing up in the village of My Khe, he had often worried about this. He imagined covering his head and lying in a deep hole and closing his eyes and not moving until the war was over. He had no stomach for violence. He loved mathematics. His eyebrows were thin and arched like a woman's, and at school the boys sometimes teased him about how pretty he was, the arched eyebrows and long shapely fingers, and on the playground they mimicked a woman's walk and made fun of his smooth skin and his love for mathematics. The young man could not make himself fight them. He often wanted to, but he was afraid, and this increased his shame. If he could not fight little boys, he thought, how could he ever become a soldier and fight the Americans with their airplanes and helicopters and bombs? It did not seem possible. In the presence of his father and uncles, he pretended to look forward to doing his patriotic duty, which was also a privilege, but at night he prayed with his mother that the war might end soon. Beyond anything else, he was afraid of disgracing himself, and therefore his family and village. But all he could do, he thought, was wait and pray and try not to grow up too fast.

"Listen to me," Kiowa said. "You feel terrible, I know that."

Then he said, "Okay, maybe I *don't* know."

Along the trail there were small blue flowers shaped like bells. The young man's head was wrenched sideways, not quite facing the flowers, and even in the shade a single blade of sunlight sparkled against the buckle of his ammunition belt. The left cheek was peeled back in three ragged strips. The wounds at his neck had not yet clotted, which made him seem animate even in death, the blood still spreading out across his shirt.

Kiowa shook his head.

There was some silence before he said, "Stop *staring*."

The young man's fingernails were clean. There was a slight tear at the lobe of one ear, a sprinkling of blood on the forearm. He wore a gold ring on the third finger of his right hand. His chest was sunken and poorly muscled—a scholar, maybe. His life was now a constellation of possibilities. So, yes, maybe a scholar. And for years, despite his family's poverty, the man I killed would have been determined to continue his education in mathematics. The means for this were arranged, perhaps, through the village liberation cadres, and in 1964 the young man began attending classes at the university in Saigon, where he avoided politics and paid attention to the problems of calculus. He devoted himself to his studies. He spent his nights alone, wrote romantic poems in his journal, took pleasure in the grace and beauty of differential equations. The war, he knew, would finally take him, but for the time being he would not let himself think about it. He had stopped praying; instead, now, he waited. And as he waited, in his final year at the university, he fell in love with a classmate, a girl of seventeen, who one day told him that his wrists were like the wrists of a child, so small and delicate, and who admired his narrow waist and the cowlick that rose up like a bird's tail at the back of his head. She liked his quiet manner; she laughed at his freckles and bony legs. One evening, perhaps, they exchanged gold rings.

Now one eye was a star.

"You okay?" Kiowa said.

The body lay almost entirely in shade. There were gnats at the mouth, little flecks of pollen drifting above the nose. The butterfly was gone. The bleeding had stopped except for the neck wounds.

Kiowa picked up the rubber sandals, clapping off the dirt, then bent down to search the body. He found a pouch of rice, a comb, a fingernail clipper, a few soiled piasters, a snapshot of a young woman standing in front of a parked motorcycle. Kiowa placed these items in his rucksack along with the gray ammunition belt and rubber sandals.

Then he squatted down.

"I'll tell you the straight truth," he said. "The guy was dead the second he stepped on the trail. Understand me? We all had him zeroed. A good kill—weapon, ammunition, everything." Tiny beads of sweat glistened at Kiowa's forehead. His eyes moved from the sky to the dead man's body to the knuckles of his own hands. "So listen, you best pull your shit together. Can't just sit here all day."

Later he said, "Understand?"

Then he said, "Five minutes, Tim. Five more minutes and we're moving out."

The one eye did a funny twinkling trick, red to yellow. His head was wrenched sideways, as if loose at the neck, and the dead young man seemed to be staring at some distant object beyond the bell-shaped flowers along the trail. The blood at the neck had gone to a deep purplish black. Clean fingernails, clean hair—he had been a soldier for only a single day. After his years at the university, the man I killed returned with his new wife to the village of My Khe, where he enlisted as a common rifleman with the 48th Vietcong Battalion. He knew he would die quickly. He knew he would see a flash of light. He knew he would fall dead and wake up in the stories of his village and people.

Kiowa covered the body with a poncho.

"Hey, you're looking better," he said. "No doubt about it. All you needed was time—some mental R&R."

Then he said, "Man, I'm sorry."

Then later he said, "Why not talk about it?"

Then he said, "Come on, man, talk."

He was a slim, dead, almost dainty young man of about twenty. He lay with one leg bent beneath him, his jaw in his throat, his face neither expressive nor inexpressive. One eye was shut. The other was a star-shaped hole.

"Talk," Kiowa said.

∾ FADWA TUQAN
B. PALESTINE, 1917

One of Palestine's most important poets, Fadwa Tuqan was born in the West Bank town of Nablus in 1917. Raised in a conservative, middle-class Islamic household, she describes in her early poetry what it was like growing up under strict rules that limited her freedom of expression and movement. Nonetheless, in part due to the assistance of her brother, the celebrated poet Ibrahim Tuqan (1905–1941), Fadwa read widely in Islamic literature and moved to Jerusalem in 1939, a city that she describes as having lifted the veil separating the two sexes. After her brother's death, she returned to Nablus, which has remained her primary place of residence throughout her life. Her early *divan,* or collections of poetry, including *I Found It* (1957), were celebrated for their candid portrayal of a woman's love and feelings. After the Israeli occupation of the West Bank and Gaza that followed the Six-Day War of 1967, Fadwa turned to more political themes in her writing, calling for justice for the Palestinians and recognition of Palestine as a nation. Her poetic works include *In Front of the Closed Door* (1967), *Horsemen of the Night* (1969), *Alone on the Summit of the World* (1973), and *Daily Nightmares* (1988). Her important autobiography, *Mountainous Journey* (1985), describes her life up to the 1967 war.

∾ Enough for Me

Translated by Olive Kenny

Enough for me to die on her earth
be buried in her
to melt and vanish into her soil
then sprout forth as a flower
played with by a child from my country.
Enough for me to remain
in my country's embrace
to be in her close as a handful of dust
a sprig of grass
a flower.

Song of Becoming

Translated by Naomi Shihab Nye

They're only boys
who used to frolic and play
releasing in the western wind
their blue red green kites
the colour of the rainbow
jumping, whistling, exchanging spontaneous jokes
and laughter
fencing with branches, assuming the roles
of great heroes in history.

10   They've grown suddenly now
grown more than the years of a lifetime
grown, merged with a secret word of love
carried its letters like a Bible, or a Quran
read in whispers

They've grown more than the years of a lifetime
become the trees plunging deep into the earth
and soaring high towards the sun
They're now the voice that rejects
they're the dialectics of destruction and building anew
20   the anger burning on the fringes of a blocked horizon
invading classroom, streets, city quarters
centering on the squares
and facing sullen tanks with a stream of stones.

With plain rejection they now shake the gallows of the dawn
assailing the night and its deluge
They've grown, grown more than the years of a lifetime
become the worshipped and the worshipper
When their torn limbs merged with the stuff of our earth,
they became a legend
30   They grew, and became the bridge
they grew, grew and became
larger than all poetry.

YEHUDA AMICHAI
B. GERMANY, 1924–2000

Israel's most renowned contemporary poet, Yehuda Amichai was born in
Würzburg in 1924. Seeking refuge from the Nazis, his family emigrated
to what was at the time Palestine and took up residence in Jerusalem,
where Yehuda attended school and studied Hebrew. During World War II
Amichai served in the British army, and in the war of independence and
the wars of 1956 and 1973 he was a commando in the Israeli army.
Between the wars Amichai enrolled at Hebrew University, where he studied Hebrew literature and wrote poetry. His first book of poems, *Now and
in Other Days,* appeared in 1955. After graduating, Amichai worked as a
teacher in secondary schools and continued to write verse. With his second volume, *Two Hopes Away* (1958), he fully realized the poetic power
of the colloquial language of the emerging state of Israel—a modernized form of Hebrew—and received international recognition. In the
1970s and '80s, Amichai held visiting professorships at several American
higher-learning institutions, including University of California, Berkeley,
and New York University. When Shimon Peres, Yitzhak Rabin, and Yasir
Arafat shared the Nobel Peace Prize in 1994, Amichai's poems were read
at the ceremony. By his death in September 2000, Amichai had published
two novels, several short stories, and eleven collections of poetry. His
memories of war drive the imagery and themes of many of his poems,
and his firsthand experience of brutal killings inspired the longing for
peace that permeates his work.

Sort of an Apocalypse

Translated by Chana Bloch and Stephen Mitchell

The man under his fig tree telephoned the man under his vine:
"Tonight they definitely might come. Assign
positions, armor-plate the leaves, secure the tree,
tell the dead to report home immediately."

The white lamb leaned over, said to the wolf:
"Humans are bleating and my heart aches with grief.
I'm afraid they'll get to gunpoint, to bayonets in the dust.
At our next meeting this matter will be discussed."

All the nations (united) will flow to Jerusalem
to see if the Torah has gone out. And then,

10

inasmuch as it's spring, they'll come down
and pick flowers from all around.

And they'll beat swords into plowshares and plowshares into swords,
and so on and so on, and back and forth.

Perhaps from being beaten thinner and thinner,
the iron of hatred will vanish, forever.

God Has Pity on Kindergarten Children

Translated by Assia Gutmann

God has pity on children in kindergartens,
He pities school children — less.
But adults he pities not at all.

He abandons them,
Sometimes they have to crawl on all fours
In the roasting sand
To reach the dressing station,
And they are streaming with blood.

But perhaps
10   He will have pity on those who love truly
And take care of them
And shade them,
Like a tree over the sleeper on the public bench.

Perhaps even we will spend on them
Our last pennies of kindness
Inherited from mother,

So that their own happiness will protect us
Now and on other days.

❧ Mahmoud Darwish

B. Palestine, 1941

The foremost Palestinian poet of the conflict between Israel and Palestine, Mahmoud Darwish was about seven years old in 1948 when the Israelis occupied his native village of Al-Birwah, near Akka (Acre). For a year his family took refuge in Lebanon, after which they returned to Galilee and Mahmoud began writing poetry as an elementary-school student. He published his first volume of poems, *Birds without Wings,* in 1960 and followed with three more collections by 1967. In 1969 he was awarded the Lotus Prize at the Fourth Afro-Asian Writers Conference.

As his reputation as a writer grew, Darwish became increasingly active in the pro-Arab branch of the Israeli Communist Party, *Rakah,* and served for a while as editor of its newspaper, *Al-Ittihad (Unity),* published biweekly in Haifa. While working as a journalist and editor, Darwish was continually under surveillance by the Israelis and several times was placed under house arrest. In 1971 he announced his exile from Israel and settled for a year in Cairo, where he contributed to the newspaper *al-Ahram.* In the next year he published *I Love You, I Love You Not* and moved to Beirut, where he lived for the next ten years, writing poetry, directing the Palestinian Center for Research, and editing *Shu'un Falastiniyya (Palestinian Affairs* magazine). Later Darwish moved to Damascus, Syria, working again as an editor and journalist. He eventually became president of the Union of Arab Poets, and he served as a member of the Executive Committee of the Palestine Liberation Organization until 1993. After residing for some time in Paris and serving as editor of the Palestinian literary review, *Al-Karmel,* in 1996 Darwish returned for the first time to Israel and was greeted by crowds of celebrating Palestinians. After that visit he said, "As long as my soul is alive no one can smother my feeling of nostalgia to a country which I still consider as Palestine."

As a poet living outside of his homeland, Darwish communicates an exile's powerful sense of loss and desire for his land in his work. He also celebrates the human dignity of the Palestinians and dramatically describes the fear and suffering of his people. He has published more than thirty books of poetry and prose; two of his most recent books are *Memory for Forgetfulness: August, Beirut, 1982* (1995) and *Bed of a Stranger* (1998). The poem "Identity Card," one of the most celebrated of all his poems among Palestinians, stems from an incident when an Israeli censor changed the word "Palestine" in one of his poems to "Eretz Israel," or land of Israel.

All notes are the editors'.

∽ Identity Card

Translated by Denys Johnson-Davies

Put it on record.
    I am an Arab
And the number of my card is fifty thousand
I have eight children
And the ninth is due after summer.
What's there to be angry about?

Put it on record.
    I am an Arab
Working with comrades of toil in a quarry.
I have eight children
For them I wrest the loaf of bread,
The clothes and exercise books
From the rocks
And beg for no alms at your door,
    Lower not myself at your doorstep.
    What's there to be angry about?

Put it on record.
    I am an Arab.
I am a name without a title,[1]
Patient in a country where everything
Lives in a whirlpool of anger.
    My roots
    Took hold before the birth of time
    Before the burgeoning of the ages,
    Before cypress and olive trees,
    Before the proliferation of weeds.
My father is from the family of the plough
    Not from highborn nobles.
And my grandfather was a peasant
    Without line or genealogy.
My house is a watchman's hut
    Made of sticks and reeds.

---

[1] **without a title:** Arabs often use titles, such as "Bey" or "Pasha"; to lack a title is an indication of his lack of official acknowledgment of his identity.

Does my status satisfy you?
    I am a name without a surname.

Put it on record.
    I am an Arab.
Colour of hair: jet black.
Colour of eyes: brown.
My distinguishing features:

40   On my head the *'iqal* cords over a *keffiyeh*[2]
    Scratching him who touches it.
My address:
    I'm from a village, remote, forgotten,
    Its streets without name
    And all its men in the fields and quarry.

    What's there to be angry about?

Put it on record.
    I am an Arab.
You stole my forefathers' vineyards

50   And land I used to till,
    I and all my children,
    And you left us and all my grandchildren
    Nothing but these rocks.
    Will your government be taking them too
    As is being said?

    So!
    Put it on record at the top of page one:
    I don't hate people,
    I trespass on no one's property.

60 And yet, if I were to become hungry
    I shall eat the flesh of my usurper.
    Beware, beware of my hunger
    And of my anger!

---

[2] *'iqal . . . keffiyeh:* A *keffiyeh* is a head scarf worn by Arab men, which is held in place by a black cord known as an *'iqal.*

Victim Number 18[1]

Translated by Denys Johnson-Davies

Once the olive grove was green.
It was, and the sky
A grove of blue. It was, my love.
What changed it that evening?

At the bend in the track they stopped the lorry of workers.
So calm they were.
They turned us round towards the east. So calm they were.

Once my heart was a blue bird, O nest of my beloved.
The handkerchiefs I had of yours were all white. They were, my love.
What stained them that evening?
I do not understand at all, my love.

At the bend in the track they stopped the lorry of workers.
So calm they were.
They turned us round towards the east. So calm they were.

From me you'll have everything,
Yours the shade and yours the light,
A wedding-ring and all you want,
And an orchard of trees, of olive and fig.
And as on every night I'll come to you.
In the dream I'll enter by the window and throw you jasmine.
Blame me not if I'm a little late:
They stopped me.

---

[1] Victim Number 18: This title refers to the massacre at Kafr Qassem in 1956, in which Israeli troops killed forty-nine unarmed villagers, an incident leading to the 1956 war.

༄ BEI DAO
B. CHINA, 1949

Bei Dao, which literally means North Island, is the pen name of Zhao Zhenkai, one of China's most important and widely acclaimed contemporary poets, now living in exile in the United States. Born in Beijing in 1949, Bei Dao was educated at the prestigious Fourth Middle School. In 1966, as a young member of the Red Guard, he took part in the Cultural Revolution, a movement that from 1966 to 1976 sent thousands of city dwellers into exile in the country as part of an effort to unify the nation by making urban intellectuals, writers, and academics share the life and work of peasants. After three years, his hopes for a meaningful transformation of culture disappointed, he turned to construction work and began writing poetry. He participated in the demonstrations at Tiananmen Square in 1976, protesting the policies of Chairman Mao Zedong and the so-called "Gang of Four." His most famous poem, "The Answer," which was read at the demonstrations, established his as an important voice of the democratic movement in China.

After the death of Mao Zedong that same year, party restrictions on literary and cultural production were loosened, and in 1979 Bei Dao started a groundbreaking literary magazine, *Jintian* (*Today*). Already known as a writer of subversive verse that expressed the hopes of those looking for democratic reforms from the new leader, Deng Xiaoping, Bei Dao became the leader of the Misty school of poets, so named for its experiments with form and syntax and often obscure and surrealistic imagery. The difficult works of Misty poets challenged both official party ideology and the outworn, orthodox conventions of Socialist Realism.

Bei Dao's work has helped to create a new poetic idiom for contemporary Chinese poets, and he has also been a leader in transforming contemporary Chinese literature by experimenting with and publishing new narrative and poetic forms. *Today* was banned in 1980, and as the promise of Deng Xiaoping's government dimmed and Bei Dao faced official censure for his work, his poetry began to reflect the bitter disappointment of his generation.

In the mid-1980s Bei Dao left China to travel through the United States and Europe. He returned to China in 1988 and in the following year helped to launch a petition for the release of Wei Jingsheng and others imprisoned for taking part in the democracy movement. This drive eventually exploded in the massacre at Tiananmen Square on June 4, 1989. This time Bei Dao was in Europe during the demonstration, but the student protesters had printed lines of his poetry on their banners. Remaining in exile, Bei Dao has spent the last several years teaching in Europe and the United States, holding positions at the University of Michigan and Beloit College in Wisconsin, among others.

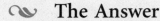 # The Answer

Translated by Bonnie S. McDougall

Debasement is the password of the base.
Nobility the epitaph of the noble.
See how the gilded sky is covered
With the drifting twisted shadows of the dead.

The Ice Age is over now,
Why is there ice everywhere?
The Cape of Good Hope has been discovered,
Why do a thousand sails contest the Dead Sea?

I came into this world
Bringing only paper, rope, a shadow,
To proclaim before the judgment
The voice that has been judged:

Let me tell you, world,
I — do — not — believe!
If a thousand challengers lie beneath your feet,
Count me as number one thousand and one.

I don't believe the sky is blue;
I don't believe in thunder's echoes;
I don't believe that dreams are false;
I don't believe that death has no revenge.

If the sea is destined to breach the dikes
Let all the brackish water pour into my heart;
If the land is destined to rise
Let humanity choose a peak for existence again.

A new conjunction and glimmering stars
Adorn the unobstructed sky now:
They are the pictographs from five thousand years.
They are the watchful eyes of future generations.

Declaration

for Yu Luoke[1]

Translated by Bonnie S. McDougall

Perhaps the final hour is come
I have left no testament
Only a pen, for my mother
I am no hero
In an age without heroes
I just want to be a man

The still horizon
Divides the ranks of the living and the dead
I can only choose the sky
10   I will not kneel on the ground
Allowing the executioners to look tall
The better to obstruct the wind of freedom

From star-like bullet holes shall flow
A blood-red dawn

---

[1] *for Yu Luoke:* The first draft of this poem was written in 1975. Some good friends of mine fought side by side with Yu Luoke, and two of them were thrown into prison where they languished for three years. This poem records our tragic and indignant protest in that tragic and indignant period. [Author's note.]

An End or a Beginning

for Yu Luoke

Translated by Bonnie S. McDougall

Here I stand
Replacing another, who has been murdered
So that each time the sun rises
A heavy shadow, like a road
Shall run across the land

A sorrowing mist
Covers the uneven patchwork of roofs
Between one house and another

Chimneys spout ashy crowds
10   Warmth effuses from gleaming trees
Lingering on the wretched cigarette stubs
Low black clouds arise
From every tired hand

In the name of the sun
Darkness plunders openly
Silence is still the story of the East
People on age-old frescoes
Silently live forever
Silently die and are gone

20   Ah, my beloved land
Why don't you sing any more
Can it be true that even the ropes of the Yellow River towmen
Like sundered lute-strings
Reverberate no more
True that time, this dark mirror
Has also turned its back on you forever
Leaving only stars and drifting clouds behind

I look for you
In every dream
30   Every foggy night or morning
I look for spring and apple trees
Every wisp of breeze stirred up by honey bees
I look for the seashore's ebb and flow
The seagulls formed from sunlight on the waves
I look for the stories built into the wall
Your forgotten name and mine

If fresh blood could make you fertile
The ripened fruit
On tomorrow's branches
40   Would bear my colour

I must admit
That I trembled
In the death-white chilly light
Who wants to be a meteorite
Or a martyr's ice-cold statue
Watching the unextinguished fire of youth
Pass into another's hand
Even if doves alight on its shoulder

It can't feel their bodies' warmth and breath
50 They preen their wings
And quickly fly away

I am a man
I need love
I long to pass each tranquil dusk
Under my love's eyes
Waiting in the cradle's rocking
For the child's first cry
On the grass and fallen leaves
On every sincere gaze
60 I write poems of life
This universal longing
Has now become the whole cost of being a man

I have lied many times
In my life
But I have always honestly kept to
The promise I made as a child
So that the world which cannot tolerate
A child's heart
Has still not forgiven me

70 Here I stand
Replacing another, who has been murdered
I have no other choice
And where I fall
Another will stand
A wind rests on my shoulders
Stars glimmer in the wind

Perhaps one day
The sun will become a withered wreath
To hang before
80 The growing forest of gravestones
Of each unsubmitting fighter
Black crows the night's tatters
Flock thick around

✆ ANNA AKHMATOVA
B. RUSSIA, 1889–1966

ahk-MAH-tuh-vuh

Increasingly recognized as one of the greatest poets of the twentieth century, Anna **Akhmatova** was one of the leading figures in a group of Russian poets known as the ACMEISTS that included her first husband, Nikolai Gumilev (1886–1921) and Osip Mandelstam (1891–1938). They rejected what they saw as the mystifications of SYMBOLISM in favor of a poetry of linguistic clarity and precision. While other writers were killed during Stalin's regime, Akhmatova survived the postrevolutionary repression; her work is a testament to the generation of Russians whose lives span the period from just before the Russian Revolution to the post-Stalinist fifties and sixties. Tracing her work from the early love lyrics that began to appear in 1907 to the elegiac national poems of the 1920s to the 1960s, the reader of Akhmatova is caught up in the tragic sweep of Russian and Soviet history as told through the powerful voice of an artist who chose to stay behind and bear witness for her country and its people.

From Tsarskoe Selo to Paris. Anna Akhmatova was born Anya Gorenko on June 23, 1889, in Odessa, Russia; she was the daughter of Inna Stogova and Andrei Gorenko, a well-to-do officer in the Russian merchant marine. Much of her childhood was spent in **Tsarskoe Selo** (now Pushkin), near St. Petersburg, to which she pays fond tribute in her poetry. The family spent many summers at Streletskiy Bay on the Black Sea coast, where the young Akhmatova fell in love with the sea. Early in life she read the French Symbolists and her beloved Alexander Pushkin,[1] and soon showed signs of being a poet herself. Her father, oddly, despised the idea of having a poet in the family, so much so that, when she was seventeen, Anya took the Tatar name of her great-grandmother, Anna Akhmatova, to avoid bringing disgrace to the Gorenko name. Her youthful happiness was disrupted by two major shocks: the defeat of the Russian fleet by the Japanese in 1905 and, in the same year, the attempted suicide of the poet Nikolai Gumilev (1886–1921), whom she had met two years before and whose desperation stemmed from her refusal to return his ardent love. Shortly after beginning the study of law at Kiev College for Women in 1907, Akhmatova returned to St. Petersburg to study literature. In April 1910, she married Gumilev and visited Paris, met the Italian painter Modigliani (1884–1920), and absorbed the excitement of turn-of-the-century Paris, where Braque, Picasso, and Stravinsky,[2] among others,

TSAR-sku-yuh
syih-LOH

www For links to more information about Akhmatova, a quiz on her poems, and for more information about the culture and context of Russia in the twentieth century, see *World Literature Online* at bedfordstmartins .com/worldlit.

---

[1] **Alexander Pushkin** (1799–1837): The greatest of all Russian Romantic writers, whose works include the satiric masterpiece *Eugene Onegin* (1823–1830) and the "little plays," such as "The Bronze Horseman." (See Book 5.)

[2] **Braque . . . Stravinsky:** Georges Braque (1882–1963) and Pablo Picasso (1881–1973), French and Spanish artists whose experiments with form and structure transformed art in the early twentieth century; Picasso is the founder of cubism. Igor Stravinsky (1882–1971), Russian American composer whose experiments with dissonance, irregular rhythm, and tonality transformed early-twentieth-century music. All three, among the elite of avant-garde artists, worked for some time in Paris, where Akhmatova met them.

Nathan Altman, *Portrait of Anna Akhmatova*, 1914
Akhmatova's striking physical appearance led many artists and photographers to produce her portrait. (Scala / Art Resource, NY)

were breaking upon the cultural scene. The couple returned after three months in Paris to settle in Tsarskoe Selo.

Lyrical Love Poems.   Akhmatova's first collection of poetry, *Evening* (*Vecher*), appeared in 1912, and poems of hers had appeared earlier, in Gumilev's journal, *Sirius*. By now Gumilev had founded The Poets' Guild, the name that the Acmeists chose for themselves, and the journal *Apollon*, which carried the Acmeist manifestos repudiating the doctrines of Symbolism, particularly as embodied in the Russian poet Vyacheslav

A poet is someone to
whom it is impossible
to give anything and
from whom it is
impossible to take
anything away.

— ANNA AKHMATOVA

Ivanov (1866–1949), the most dazzling figure of The Tower, a literary
salon in St. Petersburg.

Evening consists primarily of love poems, many written while
Gumilev traveled in Africa and Akhmatova was alone. These elegiac love
poems are notable for their precision and brevity—their ability to imply
a tragic story in a few elegant lines. Lyrical but again elegiac love poems
fill her second and third collections—*Rosary* (*Chyotkti*, 1914), which
enjoyed a wide and enthusiastic reception, and *White Flock* (*Belaya staya*,
1917). In these poems, Akhmatova often displaces onto the speakers her
own loneliness and grief over her growing alienation from Gumilev, the
suicide of the poet Vsevolod Knyazev (1891–1913), and other incidents
that immediately affected her life; yet a whisper of hope in the poems
turns what would be despair into Keatsian[3] melancholy.

Postrevolutionary Persecution.   After the revolution, Akhmatova and
Gumilev divorced, and in 1918 she married—as it turned out, again
unhappily—Vladimir Shileiko (1891–1930), an ORIENTALIST and a minor
poet. Despite what she calls the "suicidal anguish" of Russia during these
years, she refused to abandon her country, although it would soon betray
her when the censors of the 1920s suspected her very private and apoliti-
cal poetry to be counterrevolutionary. In 1921, the year her friend and fellow poet Aleksander Blok (1880–1921) died, Gumilev was executed for
taking part in an anti-Bolshevik conspiracy; in the next year Akhmatova
published *Anno Domini MCMXXI*, composed in part of poems published in *Plantain* (*Podorozhnik*, 1921). *Anno Domini* often strikes a foreboding tone as Akhmatova attests to the devastation of the civil war and
the deterioration of politics and human rights after the revolution. Many
of its poems are more personal, recording her protest against Shileiko,
who didn't want her to write and reportedly burned some of her poems,
and whom she quickly divorced.

From 1922 to 1940 the government effectively banned Akhmatova's
poetry. During these years she wrote little verse, turning to literary criticism and publishing studies of Pushkin in the mid 1930s. In May 1934,
Akhmatova witnessed the arrest of Osip Mandelstam in Moscow; in the
next year Akhmatova's third husband, N. N. Punin (1888–1953) and her
only child, Lev Gumilev (1912–1992), were arrested in the first wave of
purges following the assassination of Josef Stalin's deputy, Sergei Kirov.
Akhmatova petitioned Stalin successfully to have her husband and son
released, but both were arrested again in 1949. Punin died in a Siberian
prison camp in 1953; Akhmatova's son did not leave prison again until
1956. *Requiem* (*Rekviem*), included here, offers poetic testimony to these
arrests and to her wretched experiences during those years.

---

[3] **Keatsian:** Referring to the lyrical poetry of English Romantic poet John Keats (1795–1821), who often elides
beauty and melancholy, pleasure and sadness in his work. (See Book 5.)

In 1940 Akhmatova published a collection of some old and some new poems, *From Six Books* (*Iz Shesti Knig*), but Soviet censors withdrew it from circulation after only six months. In the following year she was evacuated from Leningrad to Tashkent, where she remained until 1944. Stalin's culture minister, Zhdanov, attacked her work again in the following year and ousted her from the Writers' Union. Meanwhile, she worked on what some critics see as her masterpiece, the cryptic and autobiographical *Poem Without a Hero* (*Poema Bez Geroya*), begun in 1940 and finished in 1962. A poem of epic proportion and power like Pushkin's *Eugene Onegin*, *Poem Without a Hero* contains the allusive density and symbolic compression of T. S. Eliot's **The Waste Land**. Its story, set in St. Petersburg just before World War I, alludes to the death of a soldier-poet and is dotted with fragments of memories of the Silver Age days — of her friends, musicians, poets, and dancers as they witness, and sometimes fall with, the death of that great city.

p. 486

Public Recognition.   With the death of Stalin in 1953, Akhmatova was restored to her rightful place as a publicly honored poet. In her last years she was again able to publish her work with a minimal degree of censorship, and she was elected to the presidium of the Writer's Union. In addition to writing poetry, she also wrote translations (as she had from the 1930s); composed various memoirs, including one of the painter Modigliani; and enjoyed the company of various friends and admirers, including the young poets Anatoly Naiman and Joseph Brodsky (1940–1996), whom she encouraged. *Poems 1909–1960* (*Stikotvoreniya 1909–1960*) appeared in 1961 and *The Flight of Time* (*Beg vremeni*) in 1965; because of censorship, neither *Requiem* nor *Poem Without a Hero* was published in Russian, leading her to comment, "The contemporary reader does not know my poems, either the new ones or the old ones." A pirated edition of *Requiem* did appear from a West German press in 1963, and its haunting record of the harrowing experiences of Stalinism won Akhmatova international fame. In 1964 she went to Italy to receive the Taormina Prize for Poetry and in the next year to Oxford, England, to accept an honorary Doctor of Letters degree. On March 5, 1966, Anna Akhmatova died in a nursing home near Moscow, leaving behind a poetic monument to the history and spirit of the country and the people she loved.

A Poetry of Loss.   Profound but detached grief, loss, and sometimes guilt pervade Akhmatova's work. Her verse achieves a kind of classical poise that prevents her meditations on private experience, love, and loss from becoming sentimental or effusive. Indeed, her work fuses private with collective experience in a lyrical verse that is always precise and controlled, often ironic, and sometimes, as in *Poem Without a Hero,* surrealistic. Like that of T. S. Eliot and other modernist poets, Akhmatova's language, colloquial and precise, appears deceptively simple. From fragments of experience that appear directly in the work, she creates an elegiac poetry that resonates with the personal and national tragedies of her time.

Akhmatova's poetry ranks with the best of world poetry: Her works concluded the classical period of nineteenth-century Russian literature and served as a foundation and one of the main components of the new art. Her life gave to her contemporaries a model of dignity, loyalty, courage, and strength which people can discover within themselves during times of hardship. Her existence proved that a fragile, lonely person — who could have led a life burdened by vulnerability and helplessness — can achieve heroic stature.

— ANATOLY NAIMAN,
critic, 1992

vah-ROH-nyish

"Voronezh" and "To the Memory of M. B." **"Voronezh,"** published without its last four lines in 1940, is dedicated to Osip Mandelstam, who was exiled to this city south of Moscow from 1934 to 1937. Through historical allusions to Peter the Great, who built a flotilla at Voronezh that stands on a tributary to the river Don, and to the battle of Kulikovo in 1380, which marked a Russian victory over the Mongols, Akhmatova contrasts the present disgrace of Mandelstam's exile with two triumphant moments in the city's past. The result is a poignant critique of the disintegration of the nation under Stalin, as well as a tribute to Mandelstam. The final four lines invoke the melancholy and uncertainty of the mid 1930s and attribute to the Muse the responsibility of wakefulness during times of trouble and disgrace. "To the Memory of M. B.," dedicated to Mikhail Bulgakov (1891–1940), an important Russian novelist, pays tribute to her friend and to the stoic power of those who braced themselves against opposition and threat to continue their work. The poem can also be seen as a memorial and a testimony to Akhmatova's own strength as a writer and witness of the nation's tragedy as it played out in the lives of her friends.

Requiem. *Requiem* is a cycle of poems reflecting on Stalin's Great Terror, in particular the imprisonment of Akhmatova's son at Leningrad. The poem vividly portrays the women who waited in lines outside of prisons to hear some news of relatives and friends rounded up during the Terror. The outer frame of the poem—the dedication, prologue, and epilogues—speaks directly to the common experience of Russians. The individual sections within that frame focus particularly on Akhmatova's own experiences: the arrests of her third husband, Nikolai Punin, and her son, Lev Gumilev, and the execution of her first husband, Nikolai Gumilev. As in "Voronezh," Akhmatova broadens the historical perspective of these incidents by alluding to the historical past. The poem becomes increasingly grim, invoking apocalyptic imagery, as she tries to come to terms with the possibility that her son, like her husband, may well be executed. In the final epilogue, Akhmatova describes herself as a sort of Niobe, transformed into a weeping statue outside the Leningrad prison, a monument to the suffering that she and others like her withstood during the purges. Working on the poem in the midst of the Terror between 1935 and 1940, Akhmatova committed parts of it to memory as she composed, fearing reprisals against her or her son. Although an ever-widening circle of friends knew of parts of the poem by word of mouth, *Requiem* was not published in the Soviet Union until 1987.

■ CONNECTIONS

T. S. Eliot, *The Waste Land,* p. 486. Both Eliot's *The Waste Land* and Akhmatova's *Requiem* may be considered modernist epics that evoke a world evacuated of meaning and value but that also attempt to recuperate what has been lost and contain in themselves the strong convictions of their authors. How do these poems convey value and hope out of the profound despair and tragedy to which they bear witness?

Federico García Lorca, "Lament for Ignacio Sanchez Mejías," p. 579. Akhmatova's *Requiem,* as its title suggests, takes the form of an elegy, a meditative poem commemorating and reflecting on the death of a person or some other loss. Often, as in the case of *Requiem,* a person's death is also a symbol of other kinds of diminutions—of values, of order, of tradition, of hope. Lorca's elegy laments the loss of something larger in Spanish culture through the death of bullfighter Ignacio Sanchez Mejías. How do the deaths mourned and commemorated in these poems occasion reflection on larger issues? (Pablo Neruda's "Alberto Rojas Jimenez Comes Flying" [p. 680] may also be considered in this context.)

Takenishi Hiroko, "The Rite," p. 971. Akhmatova's *Requiem* was composed during Stalin's pogroms, a time of political and personal trauma and crisis for the Russian people. Takenishi Hiroko's "The Rite" is a postwar meditation on the loss and grief surrounding the survivors of the U.S. bombing of Hiroshima. It is an implicit critique of the bombing and of Japan's treatment of its survivors and their children. What image of the twentieth century emerges from these two works? What if any possibility for hope or renewal do they hold out to the reader?

■ FURTHER RESEARCH

Biography
Haight, Amanda. *Anna Akhmatova: A Poetic Pilgrimage.* 1976.
Reeder, Roberta. *Anna Akhmatova: Poet and Prophet.* 1995.

Criticism
Amert, Susan. *In a Shattered Mirror: The Later Poetry of Anna Akhmatova.* 1992.
Hingley, Ronald. *Nightingale Fever: Russian Poets in Revolution.* 1981.
Leiter, Sharon. *Akhmatova's Petersburg.* 1983.

■ PRONUNCIATION

Akhmatova: ahk-MAH-tuh-vuh
Tsarskoe Selo: TSAR-sku-yuh syih-LOH
Voronezh: vah-ROH-nyish
Yenisey: YEN-ih-say
Yezhov: yih-ZHAWF

∾ Voronezh

Translated by Judith Hemschemeyer

O. M.

And the whole town is encased in ice,
Trees, walls, snow, as if under glass.
Timidly, I walk on crystals,
Gaily painted sleds skid.
And over the Peter of Voronezh[1] — crows,
Poplar trees, and the dome, light green,
Faded, dulled, in sunny haze,
And the battle of Kulikovo[2] blows from the slopes
Of the mighty, victorious land.
And the poplars, like cups clashed together,
Roar over us, stronger and stronger,
As if our joy were toasted by
A thousand guests at a wedding feast.
But in the room of the poet in disgrace,
Fear and the Muse keep watch by turns.
And the night comes on
That knows no dawn.

10

"Voronezh." After Stalin came to power in 1924, Akhmatova was increasingly subject to censorship. Thus, after the publication of *Anno Domini* in 1922, Akhmatova did not prepare another volume of poems until 1940. That collection, which is known as *Reed*, and which contained "Voronezh," was never published as a book, but poems from the collection appeared in several books, including *From Six Books* (1940), *Poems 1909–1960* (1961), and *The Flight of Time* (1965). "Voronezh" was dedicated to the Russian poet Osip Mandelstam (1891–1938), who was arrested for writing an anti-Stalinist poem and exiled to the city of the poem's title in 1936. Alluding to two important Russian achievements at Voronezh—Peter the Great's construction of a flotilla, or navy, and the battle of Kulikovo in 1380—the poem contrasts Mandelstam's exile with these triumphant moments in the city's past, powerfully criticizing the disintegration of the nation under Stalin and paying tribute to Mandelstam at the same time.

A note on the translation: The translations of "Voronezh" and the two poems following are by Judith Hemschemeyer, published by Zephyr Press, 1992. The notes are the editors'.

---

[1] **the Peter of Voronezh:** A statue of Peter the Great, who had built a flotilla in Voronezh, which is on a tributary of the river Don.

[2] **Kulikovo:** In 1380, the Russians led by Dmitry Donskoy defeated the Mongols in this field near Voronezh.

To the Memory of M. B.

Translated by Judith Hemschemeyer

I give you this instead of roses on your grave,
Instead of the burning of incense;
You lived so sparely and, to the end, maintained
That magnificent disdain.
You drank wine, you joked like nobody else
And suffocated between those stifling walls,
And you yourself let in the terrible guest
And stayed with her alone.
And you are no more, and nothing is heard anywhere
About your noble and sorrowful life.
Only my voice, like a flute, sounds
At your silent funeral service.
Oh, who dared believe that I, half mad,
I, the mourner of perished days,
I, smoldering over a low flame,
Having lost everything and forgotten everyone—
I would have to commemorate the one who, full of strength,
And will, and brilliant schemes,
Talked to me just yesterday it seems,
Concealing the trembling of mortal pain.

"To the Memory of M. B." This poem, dedicated to the novelist Mikhail Bulgakov, does not appear in any of the collections published in Akhmatova's lifetime. It pays tribute to the poet's close friend and to the power of those writers who in the face of censorship and the threat of imprisonment continued their work. The poem can also be seen as an incidental tribute to Akhmatova's own strength as a writer, one who bore witness to the nation's tragedy as it played out in the lives of her family and friends.

ॐ Requiem

Translated by Judith Hemschemeyer

No, not under the vault of alien skies,[1]
And not under the shelter of alien wings—
I was with my people then,
There, where my people, unfortunately, were.

Instead of a Preface

In the terrible years of the Yezhov terror,[2] I spent seventeen months in the prison lines of Leningrad.[3] Once, someone "recognized" me. Then a woman with bluish lips standing behind me, who, of course, had never heard me called by name before, woke up from the stupor to which everyone had succumbed and whispered in my ear (everyone spoke in whispers there):

"Can you describe this?"

And I answered: "Yes, I can."

Then something that looked like a smile passed over what had once been her face.

Dedication

Mountains bow down to this grief,
Mighty rivers cease to flow,

Requiem. This cycle of poems is a powerful memorial to the grave suffering of the Russian people during Josef Stalin's Great Terror of the late 1930s. A modern epic comparable to T. S. Eliot's *The Waste Land,* the poem is a series of short, lyric and narrative verses written in a variety of forms that record Akhmatova's stages of grieving for the loss of her husband and son framed by a Dedication, Prologue, and two Epilogues. Invoking classical and religious myth, *Requiem* transcends the personal and serves as a testimony of all who lost family members to exile, imprisonment, or execution during Stalin's regime, which lasted from the late 1920s until his death in 1953. In Part 10, Crucifixion, a grieving mother, who stands for all the women waiting in line for a glimpse of their loved ones through the prison windows, identifies with Mary witnessing the death of Jesus. Similarly Epilogue II alludes to the myth of Niobe, who turned into a weeping statue on Mount Sipylus after her children are slain by Apollo and Artemis. Through these figures, the poem becomes trans-historical, pointing to the tragedy that is human history.

---

[1] **vault . . . skies:** An allusion to Alexander Pushkin's "Message to Siberia."

[2] **Yezhov terror:** Nikolai Yezhov (1895–1939) was chief of Stalin's secret police from 1936 to 1938, during the Purge, or Terror.

[3] **I spent . . . Leningrad:** Akhmatova's son, Lev Gumilev, had been imprisoned in Leningrad.

But the prison gates hold firm,
And behind them are the "prisoners' burrows"
And mortal woe.
20   For someone a fresh breeze blows,
For someone the sunset luxuriates—
We wouldn't know, we are those who everywhere
Hear only the rasp of the hateful key
And the soldiers' heavy tread.
We rose as if for an early service,
Trudged through the savaged capital
And met there, more lifeless than the dead;
The sun is lower and the Neva[4] mistier,
But hope keeps singing from afar.
30   The verdict . . . And her tears gush forth,
Already she is cut off from the rest,
As if they painfully wrenched life from her heart,
As if they brutally knocked her flat,
But she goes on . . . Staggering . . . Alone . . .
Where now are my chance friends
Of those two diabolical years?
What do they imagine is in Siberia's storms,
What appears to them dimly in the circle of the moon?
I am sending my farewell greeting to them.

PROLOGUE

40   That was when the ones who smiled
Were the dead, glad to be at rest.
And like a useless appendage, Leningrad
Swung from its prisons.
And when, senseless from torment,
Regiments of convicts marched,
And the short songs of farewell
Were sung by locomotive whistles.
The stars of death stood above us
And innocent Russia writhed
50   Under bloody boots
And under the tires of the Black Marias.[5]

---

[4] Neva: The river that flows through Leningrad.
[5] Black Marias: Cars used to conduct convicts to prison.

1

They led you[6] away at dawn,
I followed you, like a mourner,
In the dark front room the children were crying,
By the icon shelf the candle was dying.
On your lips was the icon's chill.
The deathly sweat on your brow . . . Unforgettable! —
I will be like the wives of the Streltsy,[7]
Howling under the Kremlin towers.

2

60 Quietly flows the quiet Don,[8]
Yellow moon slips into a home.

He slips in with cap askew,
He sees a shadow, yellow moon.

This woman is ill,
This woman is alone,

Husband in the grave,[9] son in prison,
Say a prayer for me.

3

No, it is not I, it is somebody else who is suffering.
I would not have been able to bear what happened,
70 Let them shroud it in black,
And let them carry off the lanterns . . .
                                        Night.

4

You should have been shown, you mocker,
Minion of all your friends,

---

[6] you: Nikolai Punin, Akhmatova's third husband, who was arrested in 1935.

[7] the Streltsy: An elite troop who mutinied against Peter the Great in 1698; their wives pleaded in vain under the "Kremlin towers" as nearly 2,500 of the men were executed.

[8] Don: One of the major rivers of Russia; it flows south into the Sea of Azov.

[9] Husband . . . grave: Her first husband, Nikolai Gumilev, who was executed in 1921.

Gay little sinner of Tsarskoe Selo,
What would happen in your life—
How three-hundredth in line, with a parcel,
You would stand by the Kresty prison,[10]
Your fiery tears
Burning through the New Year's ice.
Over there the prison poplar bends,
And there's no sound—and over there how many
Innocent lives are ending now . . .

5

For seventeen months I've been crying out,
Calling you home.
I flung myself at the hangman's feet,
You are my son and my horror.
Everything is confused forever,
And it's not clear to me
Who is a beast now, who is a man,
And how long before the execution.
And there are only dusty flowers,
And the chinking of the censer, and tracks
From somewhere to nowhere.
And staring me straight in the eyes,
And threatening impending death,
Is an enormous star.[11]

6

The light weeks will take flight,
I won't comprehend what happened.
Just as the white nights[12]
Stared at you, dear son, in prison,
So they are staring again,
With the burning eyes of a hawk,
Talking about your lofty cross,
And about death.

---

[10] **Kresty prison:** The Leningrad prison where her son was held.

[11] **Who is a beast . . . star:** The apocalyptic imagery here derives in part from Revelation 8:10–12 and 9:7–11.

[12] **white nights:** Leningrad is far enough north that in the summer it never becomes completely dark.

7. THE SENTENCE[13]

And the stone word fell
On my still-living breast.
Never mind, I was ready.
I will manage somehow.

110   Today I have so much to do:
I must kill memory once and for all,
I must turn my soul to stone,
I must learn to live again—

Unless . . . Summer's ardent rustling
Is like a festival outside my window.
For a long time I've foreseen this
Brilliant day, deserted house.

8. TO DEATH

You will come in any case—so why not now?
I am waiting for you—I can't stand much more.
120   I've put out the light and opened the door
For you, so simple and miraculous.
So come in any form you please,
Burst in as a gas shell
Or, like a gangster, steal in with a length of pipe,
Or poison me with typhus fumes.
Or be that fairy tale you've dreamed up.
So sickeningly familiar to everyone—
In which I glimpse the top of a pale blue cap
And the house attendant white with fear.
130   Now it doesn't matter anymore. The Yenisey[14] swirls,
The North Star shines.
And the final horror dims
The blue luster of beloved eyes.

9

Now madness half shadows
My soul with its wing,

---

[13] The Sentence: This section is dated on the day of her son's sentencing to labor camp, June 22, 1939.

[14] The Yenisey: A river in Siberia, along which were located many concentration camps.

And makes it drunk with fiery wine
And beckons toward the black ravine.

And I've finally realized
That I must give in,
140   Overhearing myself
Raving as if it were somebody else.

And it does not allow me to take
Anything of mine with me
(No matter how I plead with it,
No matter how I supplicate):

Not the terrible eyes of my son —
Suffering turned to stone,
Not the day of the terror,
Not the hour I met with him in prison,

150   Not the sweet coolness of his hands,
Not the trembling shadow of the lindens,
Not the far-off, fragile sound —
Of the final words of consolation.

10. CRUCIFIXION

*"Do not weep for Me, Mother,
I am in the grave."*[15]

1

A choir of angels sang the praises of that momentous hour,
And the heavens dissolved in fire.
To his Father He said: "Why hast Thou forsaken me!"[16]
And to his Mother: "Oh, do not weep for Me . . ."

2

Mary Magdalene beat her breast and sobbed,
The beloved disciple turned to stone,
160   But where the silent Mother stood, there
No one glanced and no one would have dared.

---

[15] *"Do not . . . grave":* A refrain from a Russian Orthodox prayer sung during the Easter or Holy Week service.
[16] *"Why . . . me!":* Jesus' last words according to Matthew 27:46.

EPILOGUE I

I learned how faces fall,
How terror darts from under eyelids,
How suffering traces lines
Of stiff cuneiform on cheeks,
How locks of ashen-blonde or black
Turn silver suddenly,
Smiles fade on submissive lips
And fear trembles in a dry laugh.

170   And I pray not for myself alone,
But for all those who stood there with me
In cruel cold, and in July's heat,
At that blind, red wall.

EPILOGUE II

Once more the day of remembrance[17] draws near.
I see, I hear, I feel you:

The one they almost had to drag at the end,
And the one who tramps her native land no more,

And the one who, tossing her beautiful head,
Said: "Coming here's like coming home."

180   I'd like to name them all by name,
But the list has been confiscated and is nowhere to be found.

I have woven a wide mantle for them
From their meager, overheard words.

I will remember them always and everywhere,
I will never forget them no matter what comes.

And if they gag my exhausted mouth
Through which a hundred million scream,

Then may the people remember me
On the eve of my remembrance day.

---

[17] **day of remembrance:** Literally translated, this line refers to Remembrance Day, a memorial service of the Russian Orthodox Church held one year after a person's death.

190   And if ever in this country
           They decide to erect a monument to me,

           I consent to that honor
           Under these conditions — that it stand

           Neither by the sea, where I was born:
           My last tie with the sea is broken,

           Nor in the tsar's garden near the cherished pine stump,[18]
           Where an inconsolable shade looks for me,

           But here, where I stood for three hundred hours,
           And where they never unbolted the doors for me

200   This, lest in blissful death
           I forget the rumbling of the Black Marias,

           Forget how that detested door slammed shut
           And an old woman howled like a wounded animal.

           And may the melting snow stream like tears
           From my motionless lids of bronze,[19]

           And a prison dove coo in the distance,
           And the ships of the Neva sail calmly on.

---

[18] Nor . . . pine stump: Alluding to her childhood, when she had taken walks around Tsarkoe Selo, the site of some of her fondest memories, including those of her first husband.

[19] motionless lids of bronze: The children of Niobe, the daughter of Tantalus, were slain by Artemis and Apollo after Niobe had offended their mother, Leto. Niobe turned into a weeping statue that has become a classic symbol of maternal grief.

FEDERICO GARCÍA LORCA
B. SPAIN, 1898–1936

www For links to more information about Lorca, a quiz on his poetry, and for more information about the culture and context of Europe in the twentieth century, see *World Literature Online* at bedfordstmartins .com/worldlit.

At dawn on August 19, 1936, a month after the beginning of the Spanish civil war, the internationally celebrated poet Federico García Lorca was shot by a firing squad near an ancient Moorish spring outside the city of Granada and buried in an unmarked grave. He was thirty-eight years old. The month before, he had told his friend Damaso Alonso, "I will never be political. I am a revolutionary because there are no true poets who are not revolutionaries. But political I will never, never be!" But Lorca, who also made a habit of saying "I am on the side of the poor," whose homosexuality was apparent in several of his most accessible works, and who had publicly stated that the fall of Moorish Granada in 1492 was a "disastrous event," was evidently political enough to merit assassination in the eyes of the "black squads"—Fascist gunmen who roamed the major cities of Spain in those terrible days. After his martyrdom, Lorca became the world's poet and playwright. Today his works survive in all the languages of Europe.

Lorca's early reputation rested on collections of lyrics—especially *Gypsy Ballads*—that were heavily influenced by his roots in Andalusia and possessed a primal, almost mythic, energy associated with gypsies and flamenco. His residence in New York City in 1929 and 1930 led to a more surrealistic stage in his poetry; in *Poet in New York,* the city, on the edge of the Great Depression, becomes a symbol of the blackness and inhumanity that threaten Spain and has been seen as a premonition of Lorca's own death. In the second half of his brief writing career Lorca emerged as one of the great Spanish dramatists, perhaps the greatest since the Golden Age of Spanish drama in the sixteenth and seventeenth centuries, when Lope de Vega (1562–1635) and Pedro Calderón de la Barca (1600–1681) lived. In highly poetic language and imaginative settings, Lorca's plays deal with the dark, earthy forces of sexuality, fertility, and the moon. His technical experimentation has been compared to that of Pirandello and Brecht[1] (see pp. 201 and 525). His fiery, emotional, often surrealistic writing—poetry and drama alike—is unique in tone and impact, and brings together a variety of materials ranging from Spanish nursery rhymes and children's songs to the "deep songs" of the Andalusian provinces, folk songs, and ballads of Moorish and Gypsy influence. Though dark-complexioned, Lorca claimed no Moorish or Gypsy blood. His sympathy for these peoples (as well as for the *indios* of the Americas and the *negros* of Harlem), however, is a marked component of his work.

---

[1] **Pirandello and Brecht:** Luigi Pirandello (1867–1936), an Italian playwright, uses a play within a play in order to challenge the line between art and reality in his most famous drama, *Six Characters in Search of an Author* (1921). Bertolt Brecht (1898–1956), a German playwright known for *The Threepenny Opera* (1928) and *Mother Courage* (1939), employs unusual stage effects and lighting to comment on society's problems.

The Young Writer. The first child of a well-to-do family, Lorca was born in 1898 in the rural town of Fuente Vaqueros in the province of Granada; his family moved to the city in 1909. Educated in private schools, Federico showed an affinity for music, but his father, a practical man who distrusted the arts, insisted that he study law. (A revealing anecdote has his father telling the family servant, "Give him an omelette of chrysanthemums! of violets! of twilight!" when the teenage Lorca came in late to dinner because he had been gazing too long at the twilight.) Although Lorca was indifferent toward his studies at the University of Madrid, he did immerse himself in the classical writers of Spain, including Cervantes, Lope de Vega, Calderón de la Barca, Tirso de Molina, and Góngora.[2] He traveled to central Spain in 1916 and 1917, where he studied folk music and storytelling. His first book, *Impressions and Landscapes* (*Impressiones y Paiajes*, 1918), financed by his father once he was convinced of its artistic merit, is a record of these early explorations.

Fortunate to have both artistic connections and family support—whatever his father's misgivings—Lorca was able to join the Students' Residence in Madrid, a renowned center for young artists, scholars, and writers, in 1919. He lived there for nine years, gaining celebrity as a musician and poet. Frequenting the center were older poets such as Juan Ramón Jiménez and Antonio Machado,[3] and Lorca's contemporaries Rafael Alberti and Jorge Guillen[4]—altogether two generations of the world's greatest Spanish-language poets. Other resident artists included filmmaker Luis Buñuel[5] and painter Salvador Dalí.[6] Dalí was important to Lorca in two respects: He helped introduce the young poet to the doctrines of SURREALISM, a leading art movement of the twenties, and for years he was the object of Lorca's romantic passion. The relationship lasted from 1922 to 1928, when Lorca left the Residence.

By 1922, Lorca had organized folk festivals of "deep song," the passionate lyrics of the province of Andalusia. His own volume of poetic imitations of this music was published in 1931. Meanwhile, still at the Residence, Lorca had published small editions of his poetry, organized puppet shows based on folk stories, written and directed a play (a critical disaster in its single stage appearance), presented an exhibit of his drawings, and participated in a 1927 literary conference organized by the highly cultivated bullfighter Ignacio Sanchez Mejías, whom Lorca was to eulogize seven years later in his most famous poem.

> ... there has been no more beautiful mind than Lorca's.
> – STARK YOUNG, critic, 1948

[2] **Cervantes ... Góngora:** Cervantes (1547–1616) wrote the brilliant novel *Don Quixote;* Lope de Vega (1562–1635), Calderón de la Barca (1600–1681), and Tirso de Molina (1580–1648) were playwrights; Góngora (1561–1627) was a poet.

[3] **Jiménez ... Machado:** Juan Ramón Jiménez (1881–1958) is known for poems in *Diary of a Newly Married Poet* and *Platero and I.* Antonio Machado (1875–1939) draws on the Andalusian landscape in *New Songs.*

[4] **Alberti ... Guillen:** Rafael Alberti (1902–1999) shows his surrealistic bent in *Concerning the Angels.* Josef Guillen (1893–1984) wrote *Cantico,* a collection of poems.

[5] **Luis Buñuel** (1900–1983): Filmmaker who collaborated with Salvador Dalí (see note 6) in surreal, poetic films and also made films of social criticism such as *Los olvidados* (1949).

[6] **Salvador Dalí** (1904–1989): Dalí became a surrealist painter in the 1920s; his painting *The Persistence of Memory* (1931) is an otherworldly landscape filled with limp watches.

If it was not given to [Lorca] to explore the full scope of tragic art, as it was given to Shakespeare and the Greeks to do, he remains at least the chief lyric dramatist of the first half of the century.

– JOHN GASSNER,
critic, 1967

Lorca's first real collections of poetry, *Book of Poems* (*Libro de Poemas*, 1921) and *Songs* (*Canciones*, 1921–1924), showed his promise as a young writer, but *Gypsy Ballads* (*Romancero Gitano*, 1928) brought him fame throughout his country. The later volume shows Lorca's attraction to colorful landscapes, the earthy sensuality of rural life, and the theme of death, exemplified in the poem "The Faithless Wife."

Maturity and Early Death.   In 1928, the year *Gypsy Ballads* was published, Lorca was to undergo the deepest emotional crisis of his life, probably attributable to his inner conflicts over his homosexuality and the merciless exposure occasioned by his sudden fame. He accepted the offer of a former professor, Fernando de los Ríos, to visit New York City in June 1929. Although he studied at Columbia University through the fall semester, he learned very little English, and the poetry he wrote is replete with images of cultural and emotional alienation. Most of the volume *Poet in New York* (*Poeta en Nueva York*) was written during this stay in New York; it was published posthumously in 1940. Its poems, many of which challenge the reader's imagination with their unique and surreal images, are filled with pictures and sounds of the desolation Lorca discovered through his numerous walks in the city at this difficult time in America. He was particularly troubled by the plight of the blacks in Harlem—a short distance from Columbia University. In the poem "Ode to Walt Whitman"—included here—Lorca laments what he sees as the corruption of the healthy sexuality envisioned by Whitman.

Lorca returned to Spain at the time of the establishment of the Second Republic, celebrating with his countrymen the fragile victory of a broadly based democratic movement (1931–36). He initiated an arts project called "The Hut," literally a house on wheels that transported classical theater to small towns and villages. Traveling with the company, Lorca edited classical drama to conform to ordinary people's tastes and thus developed a strong rapport with the popular audience. This experience prepared him to write his own drama. Lorca's earlier plays, like *The Shoemaker's Marvelous Wife* (*La zapatera prodigosa*), were influenced by the folk elements of puppet theater and the tradition of sixteenth-century Italian *commedia dell'arte*. (*Commedia* was a type of comedy that used stock characters like the silly old man, the clever servant, and the lover to weave a play around an elaborate, absurd plot.) Lorca became renowned, however, primarily for three later plays dealing with elemental passions that challenge the limitations of social mores and result in death. His first great tragedy, *Blood Wedding* (*Bodas de sangre*), originally performed in 1933, is about a fatal attraction between a married man and a woman who run away on the day of her wedding. *Blood Wedding* is called a poetic drama, which in this play means realistic drama with lyrical interludes. Although based on a newspaper story of a bride who ran off with her lover on the night of her wedding, Lorca elevates the journalistic account to tragedy by surrounding the actions of the characters with the larger forces of fate. Since the end of the drama is known or at least suspected by the first act, the real focus of the play is the characters and what drives them, as if the play were a primitive wedding ritual involving primal emotions. Themes of love and death and marriage and funerals pervade Lorca's poetry as well as his plays. The Spanish title, *Bodas de sangre* (*Blood Weddings*), is plural; several "weddings" take place during the play.

Yerma, performed in 1934, is about a woman who yearns for motherhood, but her husband is sterile. The traveling performances of "The Hut" ceased production in the face of growing political tension in April 1936. Lorca finished his last great play about women in the spring of 1936, just before the beginning of the Spanish civil war and Lorca's death that summer. *The House of Bernarda Alba* (*La casa de Bernarda Alba*) is about a mother whose tyranny over her daughters leads to a tragic suicide. It was not performed until 1945.

"Lament for Ignacio Sanchez Mejías."   Lorca's last great poetic work, "Llanto por Ignácio Sánchez Mejías" (1935), was inspired by the death of his friend, the bullfighter Ignacio Sanchez Mejías, in August 1934, following the former champion's return to the ring after a seven-year absence. The poem, organized in four movements, is recognized as a classic of Spanish literature. Preceding Lorca's execution by less than two years, the "Lament" is often regarded as Lorca's anticipation of his own death.

The poem uses a variety of forms and themes. The repeated phrase "five in the afternoon" in the work's first section draws on the repetition of the *cante jondo,* or "deep song," to create a haunting chorus of sadness and a sense of inevitability. This chorus is a good example of the difficulty of translating Lorca. The first two lines of "Lament" are quite simple and yet difficult to duplicate in English:

> *A las cinco de la tarde.*
> *Eran las cinco en punto de la tarde.*

> At five in the afternoon.
> It was exactly five in the afternoon.

The first line in Spanish is made up of two anapests—two unstressed syllables followed by a stressed syllable. The second line immediately interrupts that pattern by beginning with a stressed syllable, thereby urgently qualifying the time frame for the reader. The second line of the translation, dissimilarly, begins with three unstressed syllables, which diminishes the insistence on the exact time. *En punto* means "exactly," but with an extra precision and sharpness, since *punto* also carries the sense of "dot, point, sharp, precision"—a distant echo of the sharp point of a bull's horn or a matador's sword.

The poem's second section, "The Spilled Blood," surrounds the bullfighter's death with tactile images of a bleeding body. In the last two sections of "Lament," "The Laid Out Body" and "Absent Soul," Lorca explores the consequences and injustice of Mejías's death. The Catholic consolation of heaven does not appease the profound sorrow of his passing. In fact, Lorca thinks the beautiful, remarkable man will soon be forgotten, "like all the dead of the Earth, / like all the dead who are forgotten / in a heap of lifeless dogs." Of course, quite the reverse is true—Lorca's "Lament" immortalizes Ignacio Sanchez Mejías along with its creator.

It should not be overlooked that, from the first childlike and ingratiating lyrics of his youth, there is a bitter root *(raíz amarga)*. At its most revealing level, we find in Lorca a spirit obsessed with primitive passion, with earthy emotion and, above all, with a vision of death — his great and all-embracing theme.

– ÁNGEL DEL RÍO, *Poet in New York,* 1955

■ CONNECTIONS

Aeschylus, *The Oresteia* (Book 1); Sophocles, *Oedipus Rex* (Book 1). Greek tragedies like *The Oresteia* and *Oedipus Rex* are known for their spare style, the intensity of their plots, and their ritualistic elements. The events that befall Oedipus, for example, have implications for the entire community, and his story has become a model for the psychological struggle between fathers and sons. Which elements in Lorca's poetry reflect the ritualistic and stylistic character of Greek tragedies? How does his poetry demonstrate the spare, ritualistic qualities found in Aeschylus and Sophocles?

Anna Akhmatova, *Requiem*, p. 560. Lorca's "Lament for Ignacio Sanchez Mejías" is an elegy, a meditative poem commemorating the death of a person or lamenting some other kind of loss. Often in elegies the death of a person stands for other kinds of loss — loss of values, of order, of tradition, of hope, and the like. Akhmatova's *Requiem*, while expressing the poet's grief for the loss of her husband and son, also points to the death of something greater in Russian culture and history. How do the deaths these poems mourn and commemorate occasion reflection on larger issues? (Pablo Neruda's "Alberto Rojas Jimenez Comes Flying" [p. 680] may also be considered in this context.)

Abé Kobo, "The Stick," p. 920; Pablo Neruda, "Sexual Water" and "Alberto Rojas Jimenez Comes Flying," pp. 678 and 680; Aimé Césaire, "Notebook of a Return to the Native Land, p. 888. Abé, Neruda, and Césaire were influenced by surrealism, a movement in art and literature that attempted to capture the immediacy of the unconscious in its bizarre and grotesque images and in its defiance of logical patterns. What elements of surrealism do you find in Lorca's poetry, and how do they compare with the surreal elements in Abé, Neruda, and Césaire?

■ FURTHER RESEARCH

Biography
Gibson, Ian. *Federico García Lorca: A Life.* 1989.
Londre, Felicia Hardinson. *Federico García Lorca.* 1984.
MacCurdy, G. Grant. *Federico García Lorca: Life, Work, and Criticism.* 1986.

Criticism
Adams, Mildred. *García Lorca: Playwright and Poet.* 1984.
Anderson, Andrew. *Lorca's Late Poetry.* 1990.
Morris, C. Brian. *Son of Andalusia: The Lyrical Landscapes of Federico García Lorca.* 1997.
Pollin, Alice, and Philip H. Smith. *Concordance to the Plays and Poems of Federico García Lorca.* 1975.
Predmore, Richard L. *Lorca's New York Poetry.* 1980.
Stainton, Leslie. *Lorca: A Dream of Life.* 1999.

‿ The Faithless Wife

Translated by Stephen Spender and J. L. Gili

So I took her to the river
believing she was a maiden,
but she already had a husband.
It was on Saint James's night[1]
and almost as if I was obliged to.
The lanterns went out
and the crickets lighted up.
In the farthest street corners
I touched her sleeping breasts,
10   and they opened to me suddenly
like spikes of hyacinth.
The starch of her petticoat
sounded in my ears
like a piece of silk
rent by ten knives.
Without silver light on their foliage
the trees had grown larger
and a horizon of dogs
barked very far from the river.

20   Past the blackberries,
the reeds and the hawthorn,
underneath her cluster of hair
I made a hollow in the earth.
I took off my tie.
She took off her dress.

"The Faithless Wife." This poem was included in *The Gypsy Ballads* (*Romancero gitano,* 1928), the collection that brought Lorca national fame and was his most popular book. It contains eighteen ballads that draw their themes from Lorca's home province of Andalusia and a mixture of eroticism and violence. The Gypsies in the poems represent at once a kind of primitive energy and freedom while being subjugated to oppression. "The Faithless Wife" was so popular that people would recite it to Lorca when they met him. The power of the poem depends on suggestion, what is left unsaid and only hinted at. The links between sexuality, horsemanship, and the river contribute to an image of the Gypsy, who in the last stanza, follows certain conventions associated with seduction.

All notes are the editors'.

---

[1] **Saint James's night:** According to tradition, James was one of the original twelve disciples; in Spain he is called Santiago. His shrine is at Compostela, Spain, and his feast day is July 25.

I my belt with the revolver.
She her four bodices.
Nor nard[2] nor mother-o'-pearl
have skin so fine,
30   nor does glass with silver
shine with such brilliance.
Her thighs slipped away from me
like startled fish,
half full of fire,
half full of cold.
That night I ran
on the best of roads
mounted on a nacre° mare   mother-of-pearl
without bridle or stirrups.
40   As a man, I won't repeat
the things she said to me.
The light of understanding
has made me most discreet.
Smeared with sand and kisses
I took her away from the river.
The swords of the lilies
battled with the air.

I behaved like what I am.
Like a proper gypsy.
50   I gave her a large sewing basket,
of straw-coloured satin,
and I did not fall in love
for although she had a husband
she told me she was a maiden
when I took her to the river.

---

[2] **nard:** Short for spikenard, a plant of the valerian family that yields a fragrant ointment.

∾ Ode to Walt Whitman[1]

Translated by Stephen Spender and J. L. Gili

Along the East River and the Bronx
the boys were singing showing their waists,
with the wheel, the oil, the leather and the hammer.
Ninety thousand miners extracted silver from rocks
and children drew stairs and perspectives.

But none would sleep,
none wanted to be a river,
none loved the great leaves,
none, the blue tongue of the beach.

10   Along the East River and the Queensborough
the boys were fighting with Industry,
and the Jews were selling to the faun of the river
the rose of the Circumcision,[2]
and the sky rushed through bridges and roofs
herds of bison pushed by the wind.

But none would pause,
none wanted to be a cloud,

"Ode to Walt Whitman." This poem is included in the collection *Poet in New York (Poeta en Nueva York)*, which was largely written during Lorca's stay in New York, 1929 to 1930. The "Ode" appeared separately in Mexico in 1933, in a limited edition. The entire collection was published posthumously by Editorial Séneca (Ediciones Arbol) in Mexico City, 1940. Lorca probably read Whitman in Spanish translations by León Felipe, whom Lorca met in New York. Undoubtedly they talked about Whitman's immense democratic vision as well as the characteristics of Whitman's poetry that Lorca uses in his ode: long lines, repetitions, catalogs, and a prophetic tone.

Lorca found New York to be very depressing, a symbol of modern decay. He draws from the tradition of surrealism with its uses of dream imagery to suggest the nightmare of the metropolis. In the last line of the second stanza, Lorca stretches the imagination with "the blue tongue of the beach," and yet there are a number of associations between "blue tongue" and "beach," including lapping, protruding, lifeless, and polluted. In a broader sense Lorca links the ugliness and destruction of the city with what he sees as the sick and predatory lives of New York's effeminate homosexuals. He contrasts them with the healthy sexuality—both heterosexual and homosexual—symbolized by Walt Whitman.

All notes are the editors'.

---

[1] For a discussion of Walt Whitman and his poetry, see Book 5.

[2] **Circumcision:** The Spanish version does not capitalize *circuncisión,* which is used as a sign of the covenant between Yahweh, the God of Israel, and Jewish men.

none searched for the ferns
nor the yellow wheel of the tambourine.

20 When the moon rises,
the pulleys will turn to disturb the sky:
a boundary of needles will fence in the memory
and the coffins will carry away those who do not work.

New York of slime,
New York of wires and death:
What angel do you carry hidden in your cheek?
What perfect voice will tell the truths of the wheat?
Who, the terrible dream of your stained anemones?

Not for one moment, beautiful aged Walt Whitman,
30 have I failed to see your beard full of butterflies,
nor your shoulders of corduroy worn out by the moon,
nor your thighs of virginal Apollo,
nor your voice like a pillar of ashes:
ancient and beautiful as the mist,
you moaned like a bird
with the sex transfixed by a needle,
enemy of the satyr,
enemy of the vine,
and lover of bodies under the rough cloth.
40 Not for one moment; virile beauty,
who in mountains of coal, posters and railways,
dreamed of being a river and sleeping like a river
with that comrade who would place in your breast
the small pain of an ignorant leopard.

Not for one moment, Adam of blood, male,
lone man in the sea, beautiful aged Walt Whitman,
because through the terraces,
clustered around the bars,
pouring out of sewers in bunches,
50 trembling between the legs of chauffeurs
or revolving on the platforms of absinthe,
the pansies,[3] Walt Whitman, dreamed of you.

This one also! This one! And they fall
on your chaste and luminous beard,

---

[3] **pansies:** Lorca uses the Spanish *maricas,* which is the feminine version of *maricón,* both of which are negative names for effeminate gay men—in the same category as "pansy," "fairy," and "sissy." Interestingly, Lorca uses the masculine article with a feminine noun: *los maricas.*

Northern blonds, Negroes of the sands,
multitudes of shrieks and gestures,
like cats or like snakes,
the pansies, Walt Whitman, the pansies,
muddy with tears, flesh for the whip,
60   boot or bite of subduers.

This one also! This one! Tainted fingers
appear on the shore of your dreams
when the friend eats your apple
with a faint taste of petrol
and the sun sings along the navels
of boys that play under bridges.

But you did not search for the scratched eyes,
or the very dark swamp where children are submerged,
or the frozen saliva,
70   or the wounded curves resembling toad's bellies
which the pansies carry in cars and terraces
while the moon strikes at them along the corners of fear.

You searched for a nude who was like a river.
Bull and dream that would join the wheel with the seaweed,
father of your agony, camellia of your death,
and would moan in the flames of your hidden Equator.

Because it is just that man does not search for his delight
in the jungle of blood of the following morning.
The sky has shores where to avoid life,
80   and certain bodies must not repeat themselves in the dawn.

Agony, agony, dream, ferment and dream.
This is the world, my friend, agony, agony.
The corpses decompose under the clock of the cities.
War passes weeping with a million grey rats,
the rich give to their mistresses
small illuminated moribunds,
and Life is not noble, nor good, nor sacred.

Man can, if he wishes, lead his desire
through vein of coral or celestial nude:
90   tomorrow love will be rocks, and Time
a breeze which comes sleeping through the branches.

That is why I do not raise my voice, aged Walt Whitman,
against the little boy who writes

a girl's name on his pillow,
nor the boy who dresses himself in the bride's trousseau
in the darkness of the wardrobe,
nor the solitary men in clubs
who drink the water of prostitution with nausea,
nor the men with a green stare
100   who love man and burn their lips in silence.
But against you, yes, pansies of the cities,
of tumescent flesh and unclean mind,
mud of drains, harpies, unsleeping enemies
of Love which distributes crowns of joy.

Against you always, you who give boys
drops of soiled death with bitter poison.
Against you always,
Fairies of North America,
Pájaros of Havana,
110   *Jotos* of Mexico,
Sarasas of Cadiz,
Apios of Seville,
Cancos of Madrid,
Floras of Alicante,
Adelaidas of Portugal.[4]

Pansies of the world, murderers of doves!
Women's slaves, bitches of their boudoirs,
opened with the fever of fans in public squares
or ambushed in frigid landscapes of hemlock.

120   Let there be no quarter! Death
flows from your eyes
and clusters grey flowers on the shores.
Let there be no quarter! Take heed!
Let the perplexed, the pure,
the classicists, the noted, the supplicants,
close the gates of the Bacchanalia.

And you, beautiful Walt Whitman, sleep on the Hudson's banks,
with your beard toward the Pole and your hands open.
Bland clay or snow, your tongue is calling for
130   comrades that keep watch on your gazelle without a body.

---

[4] *Pájaros, jotos, sarasas, apios, cancos, floras, adelaidas:* Colloquial versions of *maricas*, but with different connotations. For example, *pájaros* means "birds" and *floras* means "flowers." See note 3.

Sleep; nothing remains.
A dance of walls agitates the meadows
and America drowns itself in machines and lament.
I want the strong air of the most profound night
to remove flowers and words from the arch where you sleep,
and a black boy to announce to the gold-minded whites
the arrival of the reign of the ear of corn.

Lament for Ignacio Sanchez Mejías

Translated by Stephen Spender and J. L. Gili

1. Cogida[1] and Death

At five in the afternoon.[2]
It was exactly five in the afternoon.
A boy brought the white sheet
at five in the afternoon.
A frail of lime[3] ready prepared
at five in the afternoon.
The rest was death, and death alone
at five in the afternoon.

10 The wind carried away the cottonwool
at five in the afternoon.

"Lament for Ignacio Sanchez Mejías." "Llanto por Ignacio Sanchez Mejías" was published in Madrid in 1935. The grand sweep of the poem's imagery coupled with the restraint and dignity of the verse make this work one of Lorca's greatest achievements. Ignacio Sanchez Mejías (1891–1934), a cultivated, handsome son of a doctor, was an avant-garde playwright and a patron of the arts as well as a bullfighter. He competed as a matador between 1920 and 1922 and again between 1924 and 1927. He came out of his second retirement in 1934 and agreed to fight one additional time, stepping in for his injured rival, Domingo Ortega. On August 11 he was fatally gored by the bull Granadino and died two days later from a gangrene infection after a twelve-hour ambulance ride to Madrid. Lorca was a good friend of the bullfighter. This poem, with its repetition of the time of day, joins in the Spanish tradition of speaking of the deceased as having had an *emplazamiento,* an "appointment with death" or a "summons by Death to an appointment."

A note on the translation: The translation is by Stephen Spender and J. L. Gili; the notes are the editors'.

---

[1] **Cogida:** Goring by a bull; also means "harvesting."
[2] **At five . . . afternoon:** The body of Sanchez Mejías, removed from a mortuary in Madrid at five in the afternoon on August 14, 1934, was carried through the streets, then transported by train to Seville for burial.
[3] **frail of lime:** A basket of lime used to disinfect a dead body.

And the oxide scattered crystal and nickel[4]
at five in the afternoon.
Now the dove and the leopard[5] wrestle
at five in the afternoon.
And a thigh with a desolate horn
at five in the afternoon.
The bass-string struck up
at five in the afternoon.
Arsenic bells and smoke
at five in the afternoon.
Groups of silence in the corners
at five in the afternoon.
And the bull alone with a high heart!
At five in the afternoon.
When the sweat of snow was coming
at five in the afternoon,
when the bull ring was covered in iodine
at five in the afternoon,
death laid eggs in the wound
at five in the afternoon.
At five in the afternoon.
Exactly at five o'clock in the afternoon.

A coffin on wheels is his bed
at five in the afternoon.
Bones and flutes resound in his ears
at five in the afternoon.
Now the bull was bellowing through his forehead
at five in the afternoon.
The room was iridescent with agony
at five in the afternoon.
In the distance the gangrene now comes
at five in the afternoon.

Horn of the lily through green groins
at five in the afternoon.
The wounds were burning like suns
at five in the afternoon,

---

[4] **cottonwool . . . nickel:** Cottonwool suggests cotton surgical dressing; oxide (rust) suggests the color of blood; crystal suggests the doctors' glass beakers; nickel suggests medical instruments. This stanza rather surrealistically describes the actual goring and attempts at treatment.

[5] **dove . . . leopard:** Symbols of peace and violence, respectively. The inscription on the cover of the printed edition of the poem reads "a dove . . . gathered him up."

and the crowd was breaking the windows[6]
at five in the afternoon.
At five in the afternoon.
Ah, that fatal five in the afternoon!
It was five by all the clocks!
It was five in the shade of the afternoon!

2. The Spilled Blood

I will not see it!

Tell the moon to come[7]
for I do not want to see the blood
of Ignacio on the sand.

I will not see it!

The moon wide open.
Horse of still clouds,
and the grey bull ring of dreams
with willows in the barreras.
I will not see it!

Let my memory kindle!
Warn the jasmines
of such minute whiteness!

I will not see it!

The cow of the ancient world
passed her sad tongue
over a snout of blood
spilled on the sand,
and the bulls of Guisando,[8]
partly death and partly stone,
bellowed like two centuries
sated with treading the earth.
No.

---

[6] **the crowd . . . windows:** Suggests a crowd of followers clamoring to see Sanchez Mejías on his deathbed. No such incident is known to have occurred.

[7] **Tell . . . come:** According to tradition, the moon comes to suck up the blood of the world before turning red in a lunar eclipse.

[8] **bulls of Guisando:** Weathered, ancient stone statuary depicting bulls, in Madrid.

I do not want to see it!
I will not see it!

Ignacio goes up the tiers[9]
with all his death on his shoulders.
80   He sought for the dawn
but the dawn was no more.
He seeks for his confident profile
and the dream bewilders him.
He sought for his beautiful body
and encountered his opened blood.
I will not see it!
I do not want to hear it spurt
each time with less strength:
that spurt that illuminates
90   the tiers of seats, and spills
over the corduroy and the leather
of a thirsty multitude.
Who shouts that I should come near!
Do not ask me to see it!

His eyes did not close
when he saw the horns near,
but the terrible mothers[10]
lifted their heads.
And across the ranches,
100   an air of secret voices rose,
shouting to celestial bulls,
herdsmen of pale mist.
There was no prince in Seville
who could compare with him,
nor sword like his sword
nor heart so true.
Like a river of lions
was his marvellous strength,
and like a marble torso
110   his firm drawn moderation.
The air of Andalusian Rome°   Seville
gilded his head
where his smile was a spikenard[11]

---

[9] **Ignacio . . . tiers:** Lorca imagines a scene in which the bullfighter goes up the tiers of the arena.

[10] **terrible mothers:** Lorca envisioned these awesome presences as the Three Fates who announce the hour of death.

[11] **spikenard:** A white flower common to Andalusia; suggests his teeth.

of wit and intelligence.
What a great torero in the ring!
What a good peasant in the sierra!
How gentle with the sheaves!
How hard with the spurs!
How tender with the dew!
120   How dazzling in the fiesta!
How tremendous with the final
banderillas of darkness!¹²

But now he sleeps without end.
Now the moss and the grass
open with sure fingers
the flower of his skull.
And now his blood comes out singing;
singing along marshes and meadows,
sliding on frozen horns,
130   faltering soulless in the mist,
stumbling over a thousand hoofs
like a long, dark, sad tongue,
to form a pool of agony
close to the starry Guadalquivir.¹³
Oh, white wall of Spain!
Oh, black bull of sorrow!
Oh, hard blood of Ignacio!
Oh, nightingale of his veins!
No.
140   I will not see it!
No chalice can contain it,
no swallows can drink it,
no frost of light can cool it,
nor song nor deluge of white lilies,
no glass can cover it with silver.
No.
I will not see it!

3. The Laid Out Body

Stone is a forehead where dreams grieve
without curving waters and frozen cypresses.

---

¹² *banderillas* of darkness: Colorful, barbed darts stuck into the shoulders of the bull to aggravate him.
¹³ **Guadalquivir**: River in Andalusia associated with the bullfighter's blood.

150   Stone is a shoulder on which to bear Time
with trees formed of tears and ribbons and planets.

I have seen grey showers move towards the waves
raising their tender riddled arms,
to avoid being caught by the lying stone
which loosens their limbs without soaking the blood.

For stone gathers seed and clouds,
skeleton larks and wolves of penumbra:[14]
but yields not sounds nor crystals nor fire,
only bull rings and bull rings and more bull rings without walls.

160   Now, Ignacio the well born lies on the stone.
All is finished. What is happening? Contemplate his face:
death has covered him with pale sulphur
and has placed on him the head of a dark minotaur.[15]

All is finished. The rain penetrates his mouth.
The air, as if mad, leaves his sunken chest,
and Love, soaked through with tears of snow,
warms itself on the peak of the herd.

What are they saying? A stenching silence settles down.
We are here with a body laid out which fades away,
170   with a pure shape which had nightingales
and we see it being filled with depthless holes.

Who creases the shroud? What he says is not true![16]
Nobody sings here, nobody weeps in the corner,
nobody pricks the spurs, nor terrifies the serpent.
Here I want nothing else but the round eyes
to see this body without a chance of rest.

Here I want to see those men of hard voice.
Those that break horses and dominate rivers;
those men of sonorous skeleton who sing
180   with a mouth full of sun and flint.

Here I want to see them. Before the stone.
Before this body with broken reins.

---

[14] **penumbra:** A shadowy, borderline area.

[15] **minotaur:** The bullfighter is compared to a mythical sacrificial creature, half bull and half man.

[16] **not true!:** Lorca does not want to be distracted from the reality of the dead body by conventional pieties.

I want to know from them the way out
for this captain strapped down by death.

I want them to show me a lament like a river
which will have sweet mists and deep shores,
to take the body of Ignacio where it loses itself
without hearing the double panting of the bulls.

190   Loses itself in the round bull ring of the moon
which feigns in its youth a sad quiet bull:
loses itself in the night without song of fishes
and in the white thicket of frozen smoke.

I don't want them to cover his face with handkerchiefs
that he may get used to the death he carries.
Go, Ignacio; feel not the hot bellowing.
Sleep, fly, rest: even the sea dies!

4. Absent Soul

The bull does not know you, nor the fig tree,
nor the horses, nor the ants in your own house.
The child and the afternoon do not know you
200   because you have died for ever.

The back of the stone does not know you,
nor the black satin in which you crumble.
Your silent memory does not know you
because you have died for ever.

The autumn will come[17] with small white snails,
misty grapes and with clustered hills,
but no one will look into your eyes
because you have died for ever.

Because you have died for ever,
210   like all the dead of the Earth,
like all the dead who are forgotten
in a heap of lifeless dogs.

Nobody knows you. No. But I sing of you.
For posterity I sing of your profile and grace.
Of the signal maturity of your understanding.

---

[17] **The autumn will come:** Autumn is the season following Sanchez Mejías's death.

Of your appetite for death and the taste of its mouth.
Of the sadness of your once valiant gaiety.

It will be a long time, if ever, before there is born
an Andalusian so true, so rich in adventure.
220   I sing of his elegance with words that groan,
and I remember a sad breeze through the olive trees.

∾ TAWFIQ AL-HAKIM
B. EGYPT, 1898–1987

tah-FEEK
ahl-hah-KEEM

One of the leading figures in the modernist movement among Arabic writers of the twentieth century, **Tawfiq al-Hakim** has worked in nearly every literary genre, writing plays, novels, short stories, essays, biographies, and nonfiction. He is best known as a dramatist, and with little exaggeration, he can be said to have created Arabic drama. In more than seventy plays in nearly every dramatic genre, al-Hakim pioneered a type of literature previously unknown in Arabic.

Creating Modern Arabic Literature.   Classical Arabic literature had its golden age in the ninth, tenth, and eleventh centuries and then went into a decline. It had virtually disappeared by the seventeenth and eighteenth centuries, when the powerful Ottoman empire displaced Arabic with Turkish as the language of government and commerce in much of the Islamic world. Arabic remained the language of religion, somewhat like Latin in the liturgies of the Roman Catholic Church. As Islamic nations emerged from Ottoman rule in the nineteenth century, writers sought to revive Arabic literature. After centuries of disuse, literary Arabic was an ancient language quite unlike the spoken Arabic of the time; and the colloquial language, because it had not been used for writing, lacked the refinement and versatility needed for literary purposes. Classical Arabic literature, devoted almost exclusively to poetry and poetic forms, also couldn't provide models for modern literary genres, especially the drama and the novel. Writers who sought to revive and modernize Arabic literature needed to discover or create a language that would be both literary and accessible to the modern reader. They also needed to adapt modern literary forms to Islamic culture. Tawfiq al-Hakim did both for Arabic drama; Naguib Mahfouz (b. 1911; p. 797), al-Hakim's younger Egyptian contemporary, would perform a similar service for the novel.

His name was virtually synonymous with serious Arabic drama during the 1930s and 1940s; and the best of his plays are unquestionably masterpieces, the potential appeal of which goes far beyond the Arab world.

– PAUL STARKEY, critic

A Day Job in Public Service.   Born in Alexandria in 1898 into a middle-class family that directed him toward a career in law, Tawfiq al-Hakim preferred the arts to the courts. When he was sent to Paris to complete a doctorate in law in the 1920s, he spent his time going to the theater, reading French literature, and trying his hand at writing musical comedies. He returned to Cairo in 1928 without a degree but with the intention to become a writer.

To support himself al-Hakim took a job in government service. His first position, for the Ministry of Legal Affairs, was as a prosecutor in a village in the Nile delta, an experience he drew on for his novel *Maze of Justice* (1937). He went on to work for the Ministry of Education and the Ministry of Social Affairs. He left government service in 1943 to work as a journalist and to have more time for writing but returned in 1951 to become director of the National Library. In 1959 he was sent to Paris as the permanent Egyptian delegate to UNESCO, an agency of the United Nations that promotes international collaboration on culture, education, and science.

His Literary Career.   In spite of working full-time, al-Hakim was a prolific author, writing some seventy plays, five novels, numerous articles and short stories, and several biographies and autobiographies as well as books on political and intellectual topics. His plays range from religious pageantry to adaptations of classical stories, social-problem plays, and absurdist theater. *Muhammad, the Prophet* (1936) presents the main events in Muhammad's life as a spectacular pageant. Al-Hakim drew on classical Arabic sources for *Isis* (1955), a play based on ancient Egyptian myth, and *Shahrazad* (1934), a sequel to the central story in *The Arabian Nights*. His handling of the story of Shahrazad's marriage, however, owed as much to the SYMBOLIST techniques of Belgian dramatist Maurice Maeterlinck (1862–1949) as it did to *The Thousand and One Nights*. When adapting such Western stories as *Pygmalian* (1942) and *King Oedipus* (1949), al-Hakim similarly attempted to combine occidental and Egyptian perspectives. In his *Oedipus,* for example, Tiresias is cast as the villain who causes the suffering of Oedipus; according to al-Hakim, a Muslim audience would not accept the idea that the gods would inflict such pain on the heroic king. Al-Hakim also tackled contemporary themes, as in the social-problem play *Boss Kudrez's Building* (1948), an attack on war profiteering. After a stay in Paris in 1959 and 1960, many of al-Hakim's plays, like *The Fate of a Cockroach* (*Masir Sarsar,* 1966), were influenced by the THEATER OF THE ABSURD.[1]

Although many of al-Hakim's plays were published, not many were produced. During the early years of his career, especially, there were few theaters and few experienced actors in Egypt. He would, through the

www   For links to more information about Tawfiq al-Hakim, a quiz on *The Fate of a Cockroach,* and for more information about the culture and context of the Middle East in the twentieth century, see *World Literature Online* at bedfordstmartins .com/worldlit.

The most prominent playwright in the Arab theatre. . . . "The Father of Modern Arabic Theatre."

– ELSAID BADAWI, "Arab Theatre and Language," 1999

---

[1] **theater of the absurd:** A movement in European drama after World War II that grew out of prewar expressionism and surrealism; it described the human situation, in the words of playwright Eugene Ionesco, thus: "Cut off from his religious, metaphysical, and transcendental roots, man is lost; all his actions become senseless, absurd, useless." This worldview is presented most forcefully in Albert Camus' essay "The Myth of Sisyphus" (p. 757). The major playwrights of the movement include the Irish-French dramatist Samuel Beckett (1906–1989; p. 770), author of *Waiting for Godot* (1952), and Italian dramatist Eugene Ionesco (1909–1994), who wrote *The Bald Soprano* (1950) and *Rhinoceros* (1960).

power of his work, encourage the development of Egyptian theater, and his invention of a language somewhere between classical literary Arabic and the Arabic of the streets would be a suitable vehicle for a literary Arabic drama. Since his plays were often read rather than seen, al-Hakim gained a reputation as a "playwright of ideas," and he characterized his role as a writer in such terms: "The core of my philosophy is not to make the reader adopt my opinion without thinking and speculating, rather to stimulate the average reader's ability to weigh matters, while reaching his own opinion." His plays typically pose philosophical questions, about the morality of power, the relationship between the artist and his work, the choice between law or force as a way of dealing with social problems, and whether the end justifies the means.

An Absurd Drama of Ideas.   *The Fate of a Cockroach* is a wonderfully comic example of the theater of the absurd. From the beginning, when the curtain opens to a world of cockroaches who measure their importance by the length of their whiskers and live in fear of the organized power of the ants, al-Hakim is able to satirize human absurdities in the pretensions and foibles of the insects. The satiric technique here is not unlike that in *Gulliver's Travels* (1726; see Book 4), in which English satirist Jonathan Swift (1667–1745) attacks the pettiness of human beings through the pretensions of the miniature people of Lilliput. Al-Hakim's manipulation of scale turns the bathroom that the cockroaches occupy into a kingdom, the bathtub into a lake. The mysterious powers that swat them with towels from above and make their existence precarious are so far beyond their comprehension that they view them as gods and undefined mysteries. Along the way, al-Hakim is able to satirize academics, politicians, and priests and to make comedy out of the battle between the sexes. At the same time his magnification of the cockroaches into characters with human desires and quirks makes them self-aware, and hence sympathetic, figures.

This sympathy is important in the last two acts when the world of the bathroom is newly seen from a human point of view. As Adil, Samia, and the Doctor watch the struggles of the cockroach in the bathtub, the audience remembers the King of the first act. The drama of his fruitless attempts to climb the side of the tub, like the unending frustration of Camus' Sisyphus as he rolls his rock up the hill, is magnified because "its hero is conscious"—the cockroach being the absurd hero of the play. Like Gregor Samsa in Kafka's ***The Metamorphosis,*** a human consciousness inside a beetle's body, the cockroach must face the meaninglessness of his existence. The humans in al-Hakim's play may identify with the cockroach and wonder if he will give up, but in the end they are indifferent and do not come to his aid or mourn his demise.

p. 428

■ CONNECTIONS

Franz Kafka, *The Metamorphosis*, p. 428. Consider the literary significance of cockroaches. Kafka's Gregor Samsa, the human-turned-cockroach of *The Metamorphosis*, has become one of the most widely recognized characters in twentieth-century literature. (Samsa is also referred to as a beetle.) What qualities of cockroaches lead

Kafka and al-Hakim to use them? How do *The Metamorphosis* and *The Fate of a Cockroach* draw on the revulsion many people connect with these insects? Are there ways in which they are admirable in both works? How would you describe their symbolic role in the two texts?

Jonathan Swift, *Gulliver's Travels* (Book 4). The dual perspectives in *The Fate of a Cockroach* are a satiric device similar to the changing perspectives that Swift uses in *Gulliver's Travels* when he places Gulliver first in a land of Lilliputians who are only six inches tall and then in a land of giants. How do the perspective of the cockroaches and that of the humans differ in al-Hakim's play? Could Adil be considered a Gulliver who gains perspective on things by observing the fate of the cockroach, or does he, like Gulliver, end up insane? Is al-Hakim's satiric intent similar to Swift's?

Albert Camus, "The Myth of Sisyphus," p. 757. *The Fate of a Cockroach* can be seen as a work inspired by the myth of Sisyphus, for the cockroach king's efforts to climb the bathtub and frustrations in falling are almost identical to the punishment of the eternally frustrated Sisyphus. For his part, Camus uses the myth to develop his concept of "the absurd." Is al-Hakim also exploring the absurd? What do the attitudes of the various human characters toward the cockroach contribute to al-Hakim's exploration of the human condition?

■ FURTHER RESEARCH

Criticism

Hutchins, William, ed. *Critical Perspectives on Tawfiq al-Hakim.* 1998.
Long, Richard. *Tawfiq al-Hakim, Playwright of Egypt.* 1979.
Starkey, Paul. *From the Ivory Tower: A Critical Analysis of Tawfiq al-Hakim.* 1988.

Translations

Hutchins, W. M., trans. *Plays, Prefaces and Postscripts of Tawfiq al-Hakim.* 1981, 1983.
Johnson-Davies, Denys, trans. *The Fate of a Cockroach and Other Plays.* 1973.
———. *The Tree Climber.* 1966.

■ PRONUNCIATION

Tawfiq al-Hakim: tah-FEEK ahl-hah-KEEM

❧ The Fate of a Cockroach

Translated by Denys Johnson-Davies

CHARACTERS

Cockroaches
KING
QUEEN
MINISTER
SAVANT
PRIEST
A SUBJECT COCKROACH

Procession of Ants

Mortals
SAMIA, *a housewife*
ADIL, *her husband*
COOK
DOCTOR

ACT ONE—THE COCKROACH AS KING

The scene is a spacious courtyard—as viewed of course by the cockroaches. In actual fact the courtyard is nothing more than the bathroom floor in an ordinary flat. In the front part of this courtyard stands an immense wall, which is nothing but the outer wall of the bath. The time is night, though from the point of view of the cockroaches it is daytime—our bright daylight being so blinding to them that it causes them either to disappear or go to sleep. At the beginning of the play, night has not completely fallen, which is to say that the cockroaches' day is about to begin. The King is standing in sprightly fashion next to a hole in the wall, perhaps the doorway to his palace, and is calling to the Queen who is asleep inside the palace.

KING: Come along—wake up! It's time for work.

QUEEN *(from inside)*: The darkness of evening has not yet appeared.

KING: Any moment now it will.

QUEEN: Has the blinding light of day completely disappeared?

KING: Any moment now it will.

QUEEN: Until it disappears completely and night has completely come, let me be and don't bother me.

KING: What laziness! What laziness!

QUEEN *(making her appearance)*: I wasn't sleeping. You must remember that I have my toilet and make-up to do.

KING: Make-up and toilet! If all wives were like you, then God help all husbands!

QUEEN *(aroused to anger)*: I'm a queen! Don't forget I'm the Queen!

The Fate of a Cockroach. First published in 1966 as *Masir Sarsar* and performed in 1969, this play appeared in English translation in 1973. Now it is frequently performed in theaters in Europe and the United States as well as in the Middle East. The play combines the traditional battle of the sexes with a Swiftian shift in perspective to produce a satiric comedy of the absurd. Along the way al-Hakim makes fun of the pretensions of politicians, academics, clergymen, and psychiatrists while implying the more serious absurdist concept that all human endeavor takes place in an alien universe that holds no ultimate meaning.

KING: And I'm the King!

QUEEN: I'm exactly the same as you—there's no difference between us at all.

KING: There is a difference.

QUEEN: And what, prithee, might this difference be?

KING: My whiskers.

QUEEN: Just as you have whiskers, so have I.

KING: Yes, but my whiskers are longer than yours.

QUEEN: That is a trifling difference.

KING: So it seems to you.

QUEEN: To you rather. It is your sickly imagination that always makes it appear to you that there is a difference between us.

KING: The difference exists—it can be clearly seen by anyone with eyes to see. If you don't believe me, ask the Minister, the Priest, the Savant, and all those worthy gentlemen connected with the court . . .

QUEEN (*sarcastically*): The court!

KING: Please—no sarcasm! I have an ever-growing feeling that you're always trying to belittle my true worth.

QUEEN: Your worth?

KING: Yes, and my authority. You are always trying to diminish my authority.

QUEEN (*even more sarcastically*): Your authority? Your authority over whom? Not over me at any rate—you are in no way better than me. You don't provide me with food or drink. Have you ever fed me? I feed myself, just as you feed yourself. Do you deny it?

KING: In the whole cockroach kingdom there is no one who feeds another. Every cockroach strives for his own daily bread.

QUEEN: Then I am free to do as I like?

KING: And who ever said you weren't?

QUEEN: Let me be then. It is I who will decide when I shall work and when be lazy, when to sleep and when to get up.

KING: Of course you are free to do as you like but, in your capacity as Queen, you must set a good example.

QUEEN: A good example to whom?

KING: To the subjects, naturally.

QUEEN: The subjects? And where might they be? In my whole life I've never seen anyone around you but those three: the Minister, the Priest, and the learned Savant.

KING: They are enough, they are the élite, the cream . . .

QUEEN: But if you are the King you should be surrounded by the people.

KING: Have you forgotten the characteristics of our species? We are not like those small creatures called "ants," who gather together in their thousands on the slightest pretext.

QUEEN: Don't remind me of ants! A king like you claiming you have worth and authority and you don't know how to solve the ant problem!

KING: The ant problem! Ah . . . um . . .

QUEEN: Ah . . . um . . . is that all you can say?

KING: What reminded you of ants?

QUEEN: Their being a continual threat to us. A queen like me, in my position and with my beauty, elegance, and pomp, can't take a step without trembling for fear that I might slip and fall on my back—and woe to me should I fall on my back, for I would quickly become a prey to the armies of ants.

KING: Be careful, therefore, that you do not fall on your back!

QUEEN: Is that the only solution you have?

KING: Do you want, from one day to the next, a solution to a problem that is as old as time?

QUEEN: Then shut up and don't boast about the length of your whiskers!

KING: Please! Don't talk to the King in such a tone!

QUEEN: King! I would just like to ask *who* made you a king.

KING: I made myself a king.

QUEEN: And what devious means and measures brought you to the throne and placed you on the seat of kingship?

KING *(indignantly)*: Means and measures? Pardon me for saying so, but you're stupid!

QUEEN: I confess I'm stupid about this . . .

KING: What means and what measures, Madam? The question's a lot simpler than that. One morning I woke up and looked at my face in the mirror—or rather in a pool of water near the drain. You yourself know this drain well—it's the one at which we first met. Do you remember?

QUEEN: Of course I remember, but what's the connection between the drain, your face, and the throne?

KING: Have a little patience and you'll find out. I told you that I looked at my face in the mirror—something that you naturally do every day, perhaps every hour, in order to assure yourself of the beauty of your face.

QUEEN: At present we're talking about *your* face. Speak and don't get away from the subject.

KING *(rather put out by now)*: As I told you, I looked at my face in the mirror—this was of course by chance . . . that is to say by sheer accident . . . meaning that it was not intentional, I swear to you.

QUEEN: That's neither here nor there. You looked at your face in the drain—what did you discover?

KING: I discovered something that surprised me and aroused in me . . .

QUEEN: A feeling of dejection.

KING: Not at all—of admiration.

QUEEN: Admiration of what?

KING: Of the length of my whiskers. I was really delighted at the length of my whiskers. I immediately rose up and challenged all the cockroaches to compare their whiskers with mine, and that if it was apparent that mine were the longest then I should become king over them all.

QUEEN: And they accepted the challenge?

KING: No, they conceded it to me there and then, saying that they had no time for whisker-measuring.

QUEEN: And so you automatically became His Majesty!

KING: Just so.

QUEEN: And did they tell you what your privileges were to be?

KING: No.

QUEEN: And did they tell you what their duties towards you were?

KING: No. They merely said that as I was pleased with the title and rank, I could do as I pleased. So long as this cost them nothing and they were not required to feed me, then they had no objection to my calling myself what I liked. And so they left me, each in his own way in search of his daily bread.

QUEEN: Then how was it that I became Queen?

KING: By commonsense logic. As I was King and you were the female I loved and lived with, so you were of necessity Queen.

QUEEN: And your Minister? How did he become a minister?

KING: His talents nominated him for the office of Minister, just as mine did for the throne.

QUEEN: We know about your talents—the length of your whiskers. But what are your Minister's talents?

KING: His consummate concern with proposing disconcerting problems and producing unpleasant news.

QUEEN: And the Priest, what are his talents?

KING: The completely incomprehensible things he says.

QUEEN: And the learned Savant?

KING: The strange information he has about things that have no existence other than in his own head.

QUEEN: And what induced you to put up with these people?

KING: Necessity. I found no one but them wanting to be close to me. They are in need of someone to whom they can pour out their absurdities, whereas I am in need of close companions who will call me "Your Majesty."

QUEEN: All of which was brought upon you by your long whiskers.

KING: And am I responsible? I was born with them like this.

QUEEN: Maybe there was someone with longer whiskers than you and yet he never thought of declaring himself a king.

KING: Very likely, yet it was I who thought . . .

QUEEN: A stupid idea in any case.

KING (*indignantly*): And who are you to say? You understand nothing!

QUEEN: I understand more than you.

KING: You're a garrulous and conceited cockroach!

QUEEN: And you're a . . .

KING: Hush! The Minister's coming.

QUEEN: Then have some self-respect in front of him and treat me with respect.

KING: To hear is to obey, Your Majesty.

QUEEN: That's better! Husbands like you are submissive only to a woman who maintains her rights.

The Minister makes his appearance, wailing.

MINISTER: My Lord King! Help, my Lord King!

KING: What is it?

MINISTER: A calamity! A great calamity, my Lord!

KING: Goodness gracious! *(aside)* I told you his hobby was to bring unpleasant news. *(loudly)* Yes? Tell us, delight our ears!

MINISTER: My son, Your Majesty — my one and only son.

KING: What's wrong with him?

MINISTER: He has been taken in the prime of youth — has died in the spring of life — he has been killed! Killed!

KING: Killed? How? Who killed him?

MINISTER: The ants.

KING: The ants again?

QUEEN: There, you see? The ants. The ants.

MINISTER: Yes, Your Majesty, the ants — none but the ants.

KING: Ah, those ants! Tell us what happened.

MINISTER: What always happens.

KING: Be more explicit.

MINISTER: My son was walking along the wall, just going for a stroll for amusement's sake, like anyone else at his age — a perfectly innocent stroll of course, for you well know what a well-behaved person he is. He's exceedingly serious, with no inclinations towards flirtations or foolhardy ventures, all those kinds of nonsensical pastimes . . .

KING *(impatiently)*: That's neither here nor there — what happened?

MINISTER: His foot slipped and he fell to the ground. Of course he fell on his back and was unable to turn on to his front and get to his feet. And then the ants spotted him. They brought along their troops and armies, surrounded him, smothered him, and carried him off to their towns and villages.

QUEEN: What a terrible thing! Truly a catastrophe!

MINISTER: A great catastrophe, Your Majesty — a national catastrophe!

KING: I share your feelings of sadness for the deceased. Don't, though, ask that I announce public mourning.

MINISTER: I have not asked for an announcement of mourning, Your Majesty.

KING: That's extremely intelligent of you.

MINISTER: I am merely announcing that it is a catastrophe for the whole of our species.

KING: The whole of our species? The death of your son?

MINISTER: I mean rather the ants' aggression against us all in this manner.

QUEEN *(to the Minister)*: He understands what you mean perfectly well. He merely pretends not to. He turns the matter into a personal one so that he need not bother himself about the decisive solution which everyone awaits from him.

KING: What are you saying? Are you trying to accuse me of neglecting the duties of my position?

QUEEN: I am not accusing you, I am merely drawing your attention to the necessity for finding a solution to the problem of the ants.

KING: And is the problem of the ants a new one? Speak, Minister?

MINISTER: No, Your Majesty.

KING: Then you know that it is not new, that it is old as Time itself.

MINISTER: Certainly, Your Majesty.

KING: We grew up, our fathers, our grandfathers, and our grandfathers' grandfathers grew up, with the problem of the ants there.

MINISTER: Truly, Your Majesty.

KING: Seeing that you know all that, why do you today assign me the task of solving it? Why should it be my bad luck that I, out of all those fathers and grandfathers who came before me, should alone be asked to find the solution?

QUEEN: Because before you came along there had been no one who was so delighted with the length of his whiskers that he demanded to be made king!

KING: Shut up, you . . .

QUEEN: Mind what you say!

KING (*between his teeth*): Your . . . Your Majesty!

QUEEN: Yes, that's the polite way in which you should address me.

KING: And with all politeness I would like to ask you how you know that before me there was no cockroach who wanted to be king?

QUEEN: Because such ideas only occur to someone like you.

KING: Like me?

QUEEN: Yes, because you're my husband and I know you well.

KING: Kindly note that we are not alone now, also that I am now fulfilling my official functions.

QUEEN: Go ahead and fulfil your official functions!

KING: Speak, Minister.

MINISTER: Before you, Your Majesty, we lived in an age of primitive barbarism. We had neither a king nor a minister, then you came along, with your sense of organization and sound thinking, and ascended the throne.

KING: Then I have a sense of organization and sound thinking?

MINISTER: Without doubt, Your Majesty.

KING: Tell Her Majesty that!

QUEEN (*sarcastically*): Her Majesty is primarily concerned with the practical results. I want to see the fruit of this thinking and organization. Come on, produce a solution to the problem of the ants!

KING (*impatiently*): Come along, Minister — suggest something!

MINISTER: As you think best, Your Majesty.

KING: Yes, but it's up to you first to put forward an opinion, even if it's a stupid one. I'll then look into it.

MINISTER: Put forward an opinion?

KING: Yes, any opinion. Speak — quickly. It's one of the duties of your position to put forward an opinion — and for me to make fun of it.

QUEEN: Perhaps his opinion will be sound.

KING: I don't think so — I know his opinions.

QUEEN: Why, then, did you appoint him Minister?

KING: I didn't appoint him. I told you so a thousand times — I never appointed anyone. It's he who appointed himself. I accepted because he had no rival.

MINISTER: I volunteered to act without a salary.

KING: Talk seriously, Minister, and don't waste the State's time.

MINISTER: I've found it! Your Majesty, I think we could overcome the ants with the same weapon they use.

KING: And what's their weapon?

MINISTER: Armies. They attack us with huge armies. Now if we were able to mobilize ourselves and assemble in great numbers we'd find it easy to attack them, to scatter and to crush them under our great feet.

KING: A stupid idea.

QUEEN: Why do you make fun of it before you have discussed it?

KING: It's clearly unacceptable and absurd.

QUEEN: First of all, encourage him to speak and then talk things over with him.

KING (turning to Minister; peevishly): I have encouraged you and here I am talking things over with you. Speak. Tell me how many there will be in the army of cockroaches you want to mobilize?

MINISTER: Let's say twenty. Twenty cockroaches assembled together could trample underfoot and destroy a long column of ants — nay, a whole village, a whole township.

KING: Of that there is no doubt, but has it ever happened in the whole of our long history that twenty cockroaches have gathered together in one column?

MINISTER: It has not, but we can try . . .

KING: How can we try? We are quite different from ants. The ants know the discipline of forming themselves into columns, but we cockroaches don't know discipline.

MINISTER: Perhaps by learning and training . . .

KING: And who will teach and train us.

MINISTER: We can look around for someone who will undertake it.

KING: Marvellous! So we end up with looking around for a teacher and a trainer! Tell me, then, if we find the teacher and the trainer, after how many generations will the species of cockroaches be taught and trained to walk in columns?

MINISTER: Such information, Your Majesty, does not fall within my province. I have merely given my opinion as to the plan of action. It is for others to talk about the details.

KING: Who are those others? For example?

MINISTER: Our learned Savant for example. He is the man to be asked about such information.

QUEEN: He is right. These are things about which the learned Savant can talk.

KING: And where is the learned Savant?

MINISTER: We'll ask him to come immediately, Your Majesty.

KING: Ask for him and let him come — we are waiting.

Hardly has the Minister made a move than the learned Savant makes his appearance, panting.

MINISTER (to the Savant): My dear chap, we were just about to inquire about you. His Majesty wants you on an important matter.

SAVANT: Good.

MINISTER: His Majesty will tell you . . .

KING: No, you tell him.

MINISTER: Shall I put the whole matter to him?

KING: Yes—quickly.

MINISTER: The matter in question is the problem of the ants.

SAVANT: What about the problem of the ants?

MINISTER: We want to find a decisive solution to it.

SAVANT: And what have I to do with this? This is a political problem. It is for you to solve—you in your capacity as Minister and His Majesty in his capacity as King.

MINISTER (*now baffled*): A political problem?

SAVANT: In any case, it's an old problem. It does not fall within the province of science or scientists.

KING: But the Minister has turned it into a scientific problem, because he wants the cockroaches to be taught to walk in columns.

SAVANT: That can never happen.

MINISTER: But it must do, because we can't go on like this for ever, having the ants attacking us and not being able to drive them off.

QUEEN: The Minister is right, we must think seriously about this danger.

SAVANT: What exactly is required of me?

QUEEN: To assist with your knowledge. All hope now lies with science.

SAVANT: Define exactly what is required. What is required of me precisely? In science things must be precisely defined.

QUEEN: Define things for him, Minister.

MINISTER: You know that the ants attack us with their armies. If we also were able to mobilize an army of twenty, or even ten, cockroaches with which to attack them, we would be able to destroy their towns and villages.

SAVANT: Then mobilize ten cockroaches!

MINISTER: And who will do so?

SAVANT: You and His Majesty the King—that's your job.

KING: Our job!

SAVANT: Naturally. If the King can't order ten cockroaches to assemble together, then what authority has the King got?

KING (*haughtily*): It seems that you're living in a daze, learned Savant!

MINISTER: The problem is how to gather these cockroaches together.

KING: Tell him! Tell him!

QUEEN: Inform us, Savant, has it ever happened that you have seen ten cockroaches gathered together in one spot?

SAVANT: Yes, I once saw—a very long time ago, in the early days of my youth—several cockroaches gathered together at night in the kitchen round a piece of tomato.

QUEEN: Tomato?

SAVANT: Yes.

KING: An extraordinary idea—this matter of a tomato!

MINISTER: We begin from here.

QUEEN: And you say that science cannot solve the problem?

SAVANT: What has science to do with this? That was no more than a general observation.

KING: This is the modesty of a true Savant. The idea is, however, useful. If we were able to get a piece of tomato, then a number of cockroaches would gather together round it.

SAVANT: The real problem is how to get hold of a piece of tomato.

KING: How is it, therefore, that we do sometimes get hold of a piece?

SAVANT: By sheer chance.

QUEEN: And when does sheer chance occur?

SAVANT: That is something one cannot predict.

KING: You have therefore arrived at solving one problem by presenting us with another.

QUEEN: Suggest for us something other than tomatoes.

SAVANT: Any other sort of food puts us in the same position, for though we can find food we are unable to make a particular sort of food available.

QUEEN: Can't we get cockroaches together without food?

SAVANT: Neither cockroaches nor anything else.

MINISTER: That's true. The armies of the ant species themselves assemble only round food, to carry off food, or to store food.

KING: Our sole method of getting cockroaches together is food?

SAVANT: That's right—from the theoretical point of view.

QUEEN: What do you mean?

SAVANT: I mean, Your Majesty, from the practical point of view it's all neither here nor there, because the cockroaches assembling round the food won't make a bit of difference—they'll just eat and fill their stomachs, then each will take himself off.

KING: That's true. It has happened before. Remember how after I was installed as King a number of cockroaches happened to assemble round a piece of sugar we found—it was sheer good luck—and I seized the opportunity of this gathering to deliver the speech from the throne. I rose to my feet to speak, with them having eaten their fill, and hardly had I uttered two words than I found each one of them waving his whiskers and going off on his own. They left me shouting into thin air!

MINISTER: That's just our trouble!

QUEEN: Is there no cure for this, O Savant?

SAVANT: It is something ingrained.

QUEEN: There must be a reason.

SAVANT: I have thought about this a lot and have hit upon a reason. The fact is that a strong link has been observed between the assembling of cockroaches in one place and the occurrence of catastrophes of a certain sort.

MINISTER: You mean the moving mountains?

SAVANT: Exactly—and the annihilating, choking rain.

KING: That's true. I have heard news of just such calamities.

SAVANT: This has today become confirmed from a scientific point of view. If a number of cockroaches gather together in one place, and there is bright, dazzling light, mountains that have neither pinnacles nor peaks move and trample upon our troop, utterly squashing them. At other times there teems down a choking rain that destroys every one of us.

QUEEN: And what is the reason for this, O Savant?

SAVANT: Natural phenomena.

KING: And why do these natural phenomena only occur when several cockroaches are assembled?

SAVANT: Science has not yet arrived at an explanation.

KING: And what is the true nature of these moving mountains and this annihilating, choking rain?

QUEEN: These moving mountains and this choking rain, are they intended to destroy us?

SAVANT: These are all questions which cannot be answered scientifically.

QUEEN: Then why do these catastrophes only occur when we are assembled together?

SAVANT: I do not know, Your Majesty. All that science can do is to record these phenomena, to link up the connection between them and deduce a scientific law.

KING: You mean to say therefore that our fear of such calamities has made our species from time immemorial afraid of assembling together?

SAVANT: Exactly, it is from here that this characteristic has arisen—the fact that each one of us goes off on his own in a different direction: an instinctive defence mechanism.

MINISTER: But the ants do exactly the opposite to us.

SAVANT: The ants, because of their tiny size, can do what they like, but we larger creatures are in a special position.

MINISTER: But by their coming together they overcome us.

SAVANT: Yes—regretfully.

MINISTER: And the solution? We want a solution, O Savant.

KING: The Minister's son was torn to pieces by troops of ants who carried him off to their villages.

SAVANT: My sincere condolences, Minister.

MINISTER: Thank you, but this is not all we expect of you.

KING: That's right—we want of you something more useful than merely condoling with the Minister.

QUEEN: We want a definite remedy.

SAVANT: Give me time in which to examine the matter. With me everything must be done on a proper basis, with one step following another. First we must start by knowing ourselves, by discovering what is round about us in this vast cosmos. Do you know for example what is to be found behind this shiny wall underneath which we stand? *(He points at the outer wall of the bath.)*

KING: What is there behind it?

SAVANT: I have climbed to the top of it many times and have seen the strangest of things.

ALL: What did you see?

SAVANT: I saw a vast chasm—probably a large lake, though the strange thing is that it is sometimes without water, at others full of water.

ALL: And why is that?

SAVANT: I do not yet know, but after having observed this phenomenon, I was able to observe a constant factor, namely that this lake was full of water in the glare of light, but was empty of water in the darkness.

KING: And what is the relationship between light and the water?

SAVANT: There is some sort of relationship but I do not yet know the reason for it. Nevertheless we have been able to deduce a constant law in the form of a true scientific equation, namely that light equals water and darkness equals dryness.

KING: At such a moment, therefore . . .

SAVANT: At such a moment the lake is dry and it has a very beautiful appearance. Its sides are smooth and snow-white—as though strewn with jasmine flowers.

QUEEN: I wish I could see them.

SAVANT: With great pleasure. If Your Majesty would permit me, I shall lead you to the top of the wall, and then you can look down at the deep chasm—a marvellous sight.

KING: I too would like to see it.

SAVANT: I am at your disposal—let's all go.

MINISTER: Wait—the Priest is coming.

The Priest makes his appearance.

KING: Come and join us, O venerable Priest!

PRIEST: That's exactly what I'd like to do, for I have just passed by a most sad sight.

KING: A sad sight?

PRIEST: Yes, a procession of ants carrying a cockroach. The cockroach, it seems, was dead and motionless. An ant at the head was dragging him by his whiskers, while at the rear a group of them were pushing him. There was nothing I could do but ask the gods to have mercy on him.

QUEEN: Do you not know who it was?

PRIEST: No.

QUEEN: That was the Minister's son.

PRIEST *(turning to the Minister)*: Your son?

MINISTER *(lowering his head in sorrow)*: Yes.

PRIEST: May the gods grant you comfort! I shall say a prayer for you.

MINISTER: Thank you!

KING: We were just now discussing what we should do about these catastrophes, for the time has come to search for a remedy. Have you any suggestion, O Priest?

PRIEST: I have only one suggestion.

KING: Don't you dare say to offer up sacrifices!

PRIEST: There is nothing else.

MINISTER: Do you see, Majesty? We have now entered into another difficulty—the search for sacrifices. We may find them and we may not. Also, who will go looking for them and bring them back? I personally am not prepared to do so—my psychological state does not permit me.

SAVANT: I certainly am not prepared to do so, because I naturally do not believe in such methods.

PRIEST: Apostasy is rife in this kingdom!

QUEEN: Do not say such a thing, O Priest! You know well that I am a firm believer.

KING: Yes, we are believers, but the question of these sacrifices has become tiresome—and a trifle old-fashioned. In the past we have offered some of the sacrifices you demanded but they gave no result.

PRIEST: The result is not in my hands—I offer the sacrifices and the gods are free to accept or refuse them.

SAVANT: Your gods always refuse the sacrifices—only the ants accept them.

MINISTER: Truly. We noticed that with the piece of sugar you demanded as a sacrifice—it was the ants who ate it.

KING: Listen, O Priest—ask the gods to help us without it costing us anything.

PRIEST: Do you want them to serve you for free?

MINISTER: And why not? Does not our King undertake his official duties for free?

QUEEN: And I myself—the Queen—no one has given me anything, not even my dear husband. I strive for my daily bread like him, without any difference at all.

SAVANT: Nor I of course—no one has laid down any salary or wage for me.

MINISTER: Nor I too. I am the Minister of the kingdom and all my official functions are performed for no wage.

KING: Then why do you demand wages for your gods?

PRIEST: I will not *demand* anything.

KING: On the contrary, you must demand of them that they help us, but on the condition that such help is free and for nothing—god-sent!

PRIEST: I can't put conditions on the gods.

SAVANT: Do they stipulate the fee to you, or do you volunteer it?

PRIEST: There is no stipulation or volunteering, but anyone who asks something of someone should aim to tempt him.

SAVANT: So it's a question of tempting . . .

PRIEST: Describe it how you will, but I cannot make a request of the gods while I am empty-handed.

SAVANT: And do you think the gods are concerned with what you have in your hands?

PRIEST: What kind of question is that?

SAVANT: Have the gods ever listened to you?

PRIEST: Naturally.

SAVANT: When was that?

PRIEST: Once, I was lying ill in a corner when I saw the armies of ants approaching. I was certain that I was done for. I called upon the gods with a prayer that came from the depths of my heart. Suddenly I saw that something looking like a large dark cloud full of water had descended from the skies and swooped down upon the armies of ants and swept them quite away, clearing them off the face of the earth.

QUEEN: How extraordinary!

SAVANT: The scientific composition of this cloud is well known: It consists of a network of many threads from a large piece of moistened sacking.

KING: Neither the cloud's origin nor yet its scientific composition is of interest. What is important is who sent it down and wiped away the ants with it.

PRIEST: Speak to him, O King, and ask him who sent it down from the sky and with it destroyed the armies of the ants. Who? Who?

SAVANT: This is not a question that science can answer. However, I very much doubt the existence of any connection between this priest's prayer and the descent of this cloud.

PRIEST: How is it then that the cloud descended only after my prayer?

SAVANT: Pure coincidence.

PRIEST: What blasphemy! What apostasy!

QUEEN: I am against blasphemy and apostasy, and you, my husband who are King, must be like me in this.

KING: Of course I am like you in this. Listen, O reverend Priest, I believe, must believe, that your prayer was beneficial. In any event, seeing that your prayer was efficacious and successful the once, it will clearly be so again. I would therefore ask you to pray and pray long.

MINISTER: Particularly as cost-free prayer without sacrifice has been successful.

QUEEN: Because, as he said, it issued forth from the depths of his heart.

PRIEST (irritably): Yes, all right—I shall pray.

QUEEN (shouting): Look! Look!

A procession of ants carrying a cockroach makes its appearance.

THE ANTS (chanting):

> *Here is your great feast.*
> *We carry it together, together,*
> *To our towns, our villages:*
> *A great and splendid cockroach—*
> *Provision for the winter long.*
> *With it our storerooms we shall fill.*
> *None of us will hunger know,*
> *Because we all lend a hand,*
> *We're members of a single body.*
> *There is amongst us no one sad,*
> *There is amongst us none who's lonesome,*
> *There is amongst us none who says*
> *"I am not concerned with others."*

The ants move towards the wall with their heavy load, while the cockroaches continue to watch them in glum silence and stupefaction.

KING: It grieves us, O Minister, to see your son borne off in this manner.

PRIEST: May the gods have mercy upon him! May the gods have mercy upon him!

KING: It's certainly a most dignified funeral!

SAVANT: So it seems, although logic dictates that it should be otherwise, for in relation to the ants it means food, that is to say a universal blessing, and the carrying of blessings and food should be accompanied by manifestations of joy, acclamations and singing.

KING: But we hear nothing—groups walking in utter silence.

SAVANT: That is so. We hear no sound from them because they are such tiny creatures. Who knows, though—perhaps they are making thunderous sounds?

KING: Perhaps they have a language?

SAVANT: Perhaps they were singing?

KING: Naturally—for them—this was a most suitable occasion for joy and singing.

QUEEN: I implore you! I implore you! Do not stir up the grief of a sorrowing father
with such talk! Let us either do something for him or keep quiet.

KING: Forgive me, Minister, this was merely general talk about the ants, but—as the
Queen says—something must be done, and this has occupied us since our
meeting up today.

QUEEN: This meeting which up till now has achieved nothing useful.

KING: My dear! My dear! Your Majesty! We are still at the stage of conferring and
exchanging points of view.

QUEEN: What conferring and what points of view? There are the ants in front of you!
They are carrying off the Minister's son to make a good, wholesome meal of
him. Is it so difficult for you, being as you are four hulking males, to attack and
crush them, and to rescue the Minister's son from their hands?

KING: Are we four? Where's the fourth?

QUEEN: You of course.

KING: Ah, quite right. But I . . . leave me out of it. I am the King and the King rules
and does not fight.

PRIEST: Leave me also out of it. I am the Priest and the Priest prays and does not
fight.

SAVANT: And I too, naturally. You must leave me out of it, for I am the Savant and the
Savant makes research but does not brawl.

QUEEN: Then I shall go—I, the Queen—yet I shall not say I am the Queen, but
merely a female. Stand, you males, and watch with folded arms while females go
to war.

KING: And the Minister? Is he not a male like us? Why is he standing by silently when
the matter concerns him?

MINISTER: I do not want to put you in such predicaments because of my son.

QUEEN: As we have said, the matter is no longer merely that of your son.

MINISTER: I am grateful, Your Majesty, but . . .

QUEEN: The question is too important to be purely a personal one—they all know
that, these most excellent leaders of the Kingdom. However, they don't want to
know so they pretend not to, because they are without resolution, without
willpower.

KING: My dear Majesty . . .

QUEEN: Shut up, you effete weakling! Leave the matter in my hands!

KING: Do you want me to give up the throne in your favour?

QUEEN: No, my dear sir. This throne of yours does not interest me, does not tempt
me. All I want is for you to let me act.

KING: Don't be so headstrong, my dear. You can do nothing. You want to attack, to
make war, and to fight like the ants, but this cannot happen.

QUEEN: And why not?

KING: Ask the eminent Savant — he has the answer.

QUEEN: Speak, O eminent Savant!

KING: Speak and tell her why the ants know methods of warfare and we don't. Tell her, explain to her!

SAVANT: First, the ants have a Minister of War.

QUEEN: A Minister of War?

SAVANT: Naturally. A minister who devotes all his attention to the business of organizing armies. Is it reasonable that all these vast troops should march with such discipline and order in serried ranks without somebody responsible behind them, somebody specialized in organizing them?

QUEEN: The question's a simple one — why don't we too have a specialized Minister of War?

SAVANT: That is a political matter, and I don't understand politics. Ask His Majesty about that.

QUEEN: Please be so good as to reply, Your Majesty!

KING: What's the question?

QUEEN: Why do you not appoint a specialized Minister of War?

KING: A specialized Minister of War? Is that in my hands? Where is he? Let me find him and I'll appoint him immediately. We had quite enough trouble finding one Minister, our friend here. He was good enough to accept being a general minister to look after everything without understanding anything.

MINISTER: If I do not enjoy your confidence, then I am ready to proffer my resignation.

KING: Your resignation? Do you hear? Now here's our one and only minister threatening to resign!

QUEEN: No, honourable Minister. You enjoy the confidence of everyone. Don't listen to what the King says — he sometimes lets his tongue run away with him.

MINISTER: My thanks to Your Majesty!

KING: Your most gracious Majesty!

QUEEN: Then, O venerable Savant, the whole difference is that the ants have a specialized Minister of War?

SAVANT: That is not all they have.

QUEEN: What do they have as well?

SAVANT: A brilliant Minister of Supply.

QUEEN: A Minister of Supply?

SAVANT: A brilliant one — the operation of storing food in warehouses on that enormous scale must have some remarkable economic planning behind it.

KING: We have no need for any supply or any Minister of Supply because we don't have a food crisis and have no need to plan or store.

SAVANT: Certainly, our economy runs by sheer good luck — and we boast about it!

QUEEN: Boast about it?

KING: Certainly, my dear. Certainly we have many things to boast about which should not be sneezed at.

SAVANT: In confirmation of His Majesty's opinion I would say that we have a characteristic not found among the ants, namely birth control. The ants let their numbers increase so enormously that they are driven into a food and storage crisis, and the need for food leads to war.

KING: We are certainly in no need of food, of the storage of food, or of war.

SAVANT: And so we are superior creatures.

KING: Without doubt. We attack no living creature; we harm no one. We do not know greed or the desire to acquire and store things away.

QUEEN: Are there no creatures superior to us?

SAVANT: No, we are the most superior creatures on the face of the earth.

QUEEN: That's right, and yet we suffer because of those other, inferior creatures.

SAVANT: Inferiority is always a cause of trouble, but we must be patient. We cannot bring those creatures who are lower than us up to the same standard of civilization as ourselves. To each his own nature, his own environment, and his own circumstances. The ant, for instance, is concerned solely with food. As for us, we are more concerned with knowledge.

QUEEN: Knowledge?

SAVANT: Certainly. These long whiskers we have we do not use only to touch food. Very often we touch with them things which are not eaten, merely in order to seek out their nature, to discover their reality. Do you not, Your Majesty, often do just that?

QUEEN: Certainly. Certainly. I am very interested in touching strange substances with my whiskers, not merely from my desire for food but from sheer curiosity.

SAVANT: Yes, from curiosity, a love of knowledge, a desire to know.

KING: And yet you say, my dear Queen, that we are weak-willed. We are the sturdiest of creatures on earth, is that not so, O venerable Savant?

SAVANT: Most certainly, Majesty.

KING: Are the ants stronger than us? Impossible! They do not know us; all they know is how to eat us. But they do not know who we are. Do the ants know us?

SAVANT: Of course not.

KING: Have they got the slightest idea of the true facts about us, about our nature? Do they realize that we are thinking creatures?

SAVANT: The only knowledge they have about us is that we are food for them.

KING: And so, in relation to ourselves, they are inferior creatures.

QUEEN: Which doesn't prevent them eating us. We must find some way of protecting ourselves from being harmed by them.

KING: The only way is for us not to fall on our backs.

QUEEN: This, then, in your view is the whole solution?

KING: In the view of us all.

QUEEN: We have in short ended up where we began, that is to say at nought, nought, nought! Our meeting, our discussions, our investigations have all led us to nought, nought, nought!

SAVANT: In research there is no such thing as nought. Every investigation is useful. When we touch things with our whiskers we derive profit even though we do not exactly understand the true nature of those things. Which reminds me, a few moments ago I was saying that I had just come from making a very important discovery but no one appeared ready to listen.

KING: Ah, yes, it seems to me that I did hear you say so. And what is the discovery? Speak—I am a ready listener.

SAVANT: This lake . . .

KING: What lake? Ah yes, of course—we were talking about a lake and you wanted to take the Queen and me there so that we might see it.

SAVANT: And we were in fact on the point of going except that the Priest came along.

KING: Yes, that is true. Let us go then. Come, let's go now. That is at least more worthwhile than talking about fairy tales and fanciful projects! After you, my dear Majesty!

QUEEN: I shall not go with you. I shall stay here and the Minister will stay with me. He is naturally in no psychological state for sightseeing.

KING: As you both wish. And you, O illustrious Priest, will you come with us?

PRIEST: Such reconnoitrings have nothing to do with me.

KING: Then let us away, O Savant!

The King and the Savant go off. The Queen, the Minister, and the Priest remain.

QUEEN: I am very sad about your loss. However, I am also sad and distressed about the shameful attitude of my husband.

MINISTER: Do not blame your husband, Your Majesty. Your husband, the King, is capable of doing nothing.

QUEEN: He is at least capable of being serious and of making up his mind; of being up to the situation.

MINISTER: The situation is difficult.

QUEEN: Certainly, and it needs a strong character to face up to it, but I am sorry to say that my husband is of a weak character. Have you not remarked this?

MINISTER: We rely on you, Your Majesty.

QUEEN: Were it not that I am at his side, what would he do? Deep down inside he feels this. I am a stronger personality than he, but he's always trying to fool himself, to make himself out as superior.

MINISTER: We all have our particular natures and characteristics. He is nevertheless good-hearted.

QUEEN: I don't deny that. He is a truly good person but . . .

PRIEST: But going around with that atheist of a Savant and listening to his nonsense bodes no good.

MINISTER: He also listens a lot to you, O venerable Priest!

PRIEST: And likewise he listens to you, O high-minded Minister!

MINISTER: He listens to everyone and to everything. It is only fair of us to say that he is a man with an open mind.

QUEEN: You defend him despite everything because without him you'd be without a job.

MINISTER: I, Your Majesty?

QUEEN: Yes, you. You in particular. The Priest has things to occupy him, so does the Savant, but you the Minister would have no work to do without the King.

MINISTER: And you, Your Majesty? You are the Queen and the Queen . . .

QUEEN: Understood—she too hasn't got a job without the King! I know that.

MINISTER: Sorry, I . . .

QUEEN: Don't apologize! My position is like yours. I know that. The difference, however, is that I'm female and he's always wanting to remind me that he's male — and that he's got longer whiskers than me!

A cockroach appears; he is singing.

COCKROACH *(singing):*

> O night, O lovely night
> During which our eyes we close
> On things both dear and dread.
> O night, O lovely night.
> With one eye we go to sleep,
> With the other we impatiently await
> The breaking of the lucent dawn.
> O night, O lovely night.

QUEEN: Who's that singing?

MINISTER *(looking):* He is a subject cockroach.

QUEEN: One of our subjects? Singing while we're thinking, thinking from early morning about his problem! Bring him here.

MINISTER *(calling to him):* Hey you, come here!

COCKROACH *(approaching):* Yes.

MINISTER: Who are you?

COCKROACH: Someone who sings and strives after his daily bread.

MINISTER: You are singing when we are thinking for you?

COCKROACH: And who asked you to think for me? I think for myself.

MINISTER: I'm the Minister.

COCKROACH *(sarcastically):* It's an honour I'm sure.

MINISTER: We are thinking about an important problem that threatens your life — the problem of the ants. You've come along at the right time. We'd like you and others to cooperate with us. What do you think?

COCKROACH: I think you should let me be.

He turns his back on him and departs singing:

> O night, O lovely night
> During which our eyes we close.

MINISTER *(to the Queen):* It's no good!

QUEEN: It really isn't!

The Savant looks down from on top of the outer wall of the bath.

SAVANT *(calling out from on top of the wall):* Help! Help!

QUEEN: What's happened?

SAVANT: The King.

QUEEN *(anxiously):* What's happened to the King?

SAVANT: His foot slipped — he fell into the lake!

QUEEN: Fallen into the lake? How terrible!

MINISTER: Is the King dead?

SAVANT: Not yet. The lake's dry, it's got no water in it. Its walls are slippery and he's at the foot of them trying to get out.

QUEEN: Then let's go and help him to get out. Help him! Save him! For Heaven's sake, save my husband!

SAVANT (*shouting*): Stay where you are! There is no way of saving him — you can't get down to him.

QUEEN: We must do something for him. Let's all go.

SAVANT: Do not move! The walls along the edge of the lake are slippery and your feet too may slip and you'll fall in.

QUEEN: My husband must be saved! Save my husband! I beseech you — save him!

MINISTER: Yes, the King must be saved!

SAVANT: No one can do so. He is in the very depths of the chasm. The walls are slippery. One's feet will slip on the smooth walls. Only he can save himself, only by his own efforts — or a miracle from the skies!

PRIEST: A miracle from the skies! Now *you* speak of a miracle from the skies!

MINISTER: This is your chance, O Priest!

QUEEN: Yes, I implore you, O Priest, to do something about my husband. I implore you!

PRIEST: Has not this Savant said that there is no one in the Heavens to hear us?

SAVANT: Don't seize the opportunity to be coy! Anyone who is able to do something now should do so.

QUEEN: Yes. Do something, O Priest — please!

MINISTER: It's your duty, O Priest — save the King!

PRIEST: There is nothing for me to do but pray.

MINISTER: Then we ask you to pray.

PRIEST: All of us must pray. Even this Savant must pray with us, but he will not accept to do so.

QUEEN: He will, he will accept for our sake, for the sake of my husband.

SAVANT: I shall accept to do so so that I may invalidate his argument. If there really is someone up there who hears our voices, understands our language, and pays attention to our entreaties, that's fine. If not, we have lost nothing.

MINISTER: So he has accepted.

PRIEST: A most grudging acceptance.

SAVANT: I told you he'd get coy and start making excuses.

MINISTER: Please, O Priest, be obliging.

QUEEN: Be sure that our hearts are all with you at this moment.

PRIEST: Not all of you.

MINISTER: Pay no heed to him. Pretend he's not here. Won't our three voices suffice?

SAVANT: I said I would join my voice to yours — what more do you want of me?

PRIEST: I don't want your voice to be with ours — it's enough to have one doubting voice to spoil the rest.

SAVANT: And what's my voice to you? Is it being addressed to you or to the Heavens? Leave it to the Heavens to listen or not, whether you yourself accept or not.

MINISTER: That is reasonable.

QUEEN: Truly. Leave the matter to the Heavens, oh venerable Priest, and don't bother yourself about it. Who knows? Maybe, unbeknownst to us, it will be acceptable.

PRIEST: So be it!

QUEEN: Then let us all pray.

PRIEST: Pray! Lift up your hands with me! Oh gods!

ALL *(lifting up their hands and calling out)*: Oh gods! Oh gods!

CURTAIN

ACT TWO — THE COCKROACH'S STRUGGLE

A bedroom with a bed, a wardrobe, and a small table on which rests an alarm clock. A large table stands between two chairs: On it are papers and books. The room has a small door leading to the bathroom, which contains a bath and a basin with a mirror above it, also a shelf on which are toothbrushes and tubes of toothpaste. From the bedroom another door opens onto the rest of the flat. The room is rather dark; day is beginning to dawn, light seeping through the room. As it gets lighter, Adil suddenly sits up and then gets out of bed; he performs various vigorous gymnastic movements. His wife Samia wakes up and half rises in the bed. She puts on a small bedside light.

SAMIA *(turning to her husband)*: You're up, Adil?

ADIL: Of course.

SAMIA: Has the alarm gone off?

ADIL: Of course not — as usual I got up by myself.

SAMIA: What an odd alarm! Didn't we set it for six before going to bed?

ADIL: We did — as we do every night. However, it waits till I get up by myself and then rings. *(The alarm clock goes off.)*

SAMIA: There — it's ringing.

ADIL: It does it on purpose, I assure you.

SAMIA: No harm done so long as you're . . .

ADIL: As I'm ringing in its stead?

SAMIA: And that you wake up on time.

ADIL: For you that's all that matters.

He moves towards the bathroom.

SAMIA: Where are you going?

ADIL: To the bathroom of course.

SAMIA *(jumping out of bed)*: Off with you — I'm first.

ADIL: Yes, as usual. I get up before you and it's you who get to the bathroom before me.

SAMIA: That's only right.

ADIL: How is it right? As I wake up before you I should have the bathroom first. From today onwards I'm sticking to my rights.

SAMIA: You say that every day — it's a record I've heard only too often.

ADIL: Because it's my right! It's my right, I say!

SAMIA: Off with you! Don't waste time! I'm going in before you because my work demands . . .

ADIL: Your work! I suppose I'm out of work? If you're a company employee, I happen to be also employed by the same company, and if you're in a hurry so am I. Besides, I've got to shave which you haven't.

SAMIA: I've got something more important than having to shave.

ADIL: And what might that be?

SAMIA: To do my make-up, my dear man. You don't have to make up.

ADIL: And what do you have to make up when you're going off to work in an oils, paints, and chemicals factory?

SAMIA: What a fatuous question!

ADIL: Give me an answer.

SAMIA: Listen! Don't waste any more time. Please get away from the bathroom and let me in.

ADIL: No, you don't! Today I'll not weaken — I'll stick to my rights. I'll not give in today.

SAMIA: You're rebelling?

ADIL: Yes.

SAMIA: You say "yes"?

ADIL: Yes.

SAMIA: And you repeat it?

ADIL: Yes.

SAMIA: I warn you. This is a warning.

ADIL: What are you going to do?

SAMIA: Get out of my way — at once!

ADIL: Only over my dead body!

SAMIA: Is that so? All right, then!

She pushes him roughly. He almost falls, but catches hold of the bed.

ADIL: Good God! Have you gone crazy, Samia? Why are you shoving me about like this?

SAMIA: It's you who wants to use force. Everything can be settled nice and quietly. 'Bye!

She enters the bathroom. He hurries after her. She locks the bathroom door in his face.
He raps on it.

ADIL: Open it! Open it! This is no way to behave! It's not a question of force. You seize your rights by force — I mean my rights. It's my right. You seize my right by sheer force. Open up! Open up!

SAMIA (*inside the bathroom — she is doing her hair in front of the mirror and humming to herself*): Please shut up. Don't annoy me by knocking like that!

ADIL: By what right do you go in before me?

SAMIA: I came in and there's an end to it.

ADIL: But it's a matter of principle.

SAMIA: A matter of what?

ADIL: Of principle—of principles. Don't you know what principles are?

SAMIA: I haven't yet read the morning papers.

ADIL: What *are* you talking about?

SAMIA: I'm telling you to occupy yourself usefully until I've finished having my bath.

ADIL: Occupy myself?

SAMIA: Yes, with anything, because I want quiet—quiet.

ADIL: Quiet? You tell me to be quiet?

SAMIA: Listen, Adil, turn on the radio.

ADIL: Turn on what?

SAMIA *(turning on the basin tap)*: Turn the tap on.

ADIL: The tap? You want me to turn the tap on for you as well? But the tap's where you are.

SAMIA: I told you to turn on the radio.

ADIL: The radio?

SAMIA: Yes, the radio.

ADIL: You said the tap.

SAMIA: The tap? Would I be so crazy as to say such a thing? I told you to turn on the radio! The radio! Can you hear me properly?

ADIL: I'm sorry, it's my fault. It's always my fault.

SAMIA *(moistening the toothbrush and taking up the tube of toothpaste)*: What horrible toothpaste! One of your lordship's purchases!

ADIL *(going towards the radio standing on the table)*: Why am I so weak with you? But—but is it really weakness? No, it's impossible—it's merely that I spoil you. I spoil you because you're a woman, a weak woman, the weaker sex.

He turns on the radio and the voice of the announcer bursts forth.

ANNOUNCER: And here is the summary of the news: The black nationals rose up in revolt following the occupation by the white colonialists by force of . . .

ADIL *(lowering the volume)*: They rose up in revolt!

SAMIA: I told you to turn on the radio.

ADIL: It's on.

SAMIA: But I can't hear any singing or music.

ADIL: It's the news. The news! Am I also responsible for the radio programmes?

SAMIA: Turn to another station, man.

ADIL: As you say.

He turns to another station and a song is heard:

> "The attainment of desires is not by hoping;
> Things of this world are gained by striving."

SAMIA *(humming the song to herself in the bathroom)*: "Things of this world are gained . . ."

ADIL: Happy?

SAMIA: Of course—it's a beautiful song.

ADIL: Things of this world are gained by striving! *(He lowers the volume.)*

ADIL *(forcefully)*: Look here, Samia! Open up! Open up! I want to say something important to you!

SAMIA: I haven't had my bath yet.

ADIL: I want to know, I want a quick explanation: Who am I?

SAMIA: What are you saying?

ADIL: I'm asking you who I am.

SAMIA: What a question! You're Adil of course.

ADIL: Adil who?

SAMIA: Adil my husband.

ADIL: Is that all?

SAMIA: What do you mean? Do you want your surname, job, and date of birth? It's all written down for you on your identity card.

ADIL: I know. I wasn't asking about that. I was asking about my true identity. Do you know what my true identity is?

SAMIA: No, you tell me.

ADIL: I'm the world!

SAMIA: The world?

ADIL: Yes, the world that is gained by striving. You take everything I have and I take nothing of yours. You get hold of the whole of my salary and I can't touch a millieme of yours. All the payments, expenses, bills, instalments, all come out of *my* pocket: *your* dressmaker—*your* hairdresser—the instalments on *your* car—*your* petrol—*your* 'fridge—*your* washing machine—*your* Butagas . . .

SAMIA: My Butagas? Talking about the Butagas, listen, Adil—don't forget to get in touch with them to send a fresh bottle.

ADIL: And it's I who always has to get in touch!

SAMIA: I've got work to do as you know.

ADIL: And I've got no work? Your job's *work* and mine's play?

SAMIA: Won't you stop tyrannizing me with your chatter!

ADIL: And now it's I who tyrannize you!

SAMIA: Please—I've got a headache. I want to have my bath in peace—in peace, do you hear? I've told you a thousand times to occupy yourself with something, man. Read the morning paper, take a needle and thread and sew the buttons on your shirt, get the breakfast ready . . .

ADIL: Shall I get your breakfast?

SAMIA: Yes, instead of talking a lot of rubbish.

ADIL *(sitting on his bed and placing his head in the palms of his hands)*: Ah . . .

SAMIA: Why are you so quiet? *(Adil remains gloomily immersed in silence.)* Adil! *(Adil does not reply. He gets up and walks about the room.)* Why are you so quiet, Adil? What are you doing out there? *(Adil does not reply but stands himself in front of her framed photo standing on the table by the bed.)* Why don't you reply, Adil? Are you in the room?

ADIL: Yes, in the room.

SAMIA: What are you doing now?

ADIL: I'm looking at your picture.

He is in fact looking at the picture—but with fury; he makes a gesture of wanting to strangle her.

SAMIA: Are you looking at my picture?

ADIL: Yes—with longing.

SAMIA: Is this the time for it? I told you to do something useful.

ADIL: Such as?

SAMIA: Go to the kitchen and put on the milk to heat until the cook comes. By the way, did you turn on the Butagas? I'll be lighting the water heater in a while—are you listening?

ADIL: I'm listening.

SAMIA: Hurry up and do it, please.

ADIL: Certainly. This is unnatural. It must be that I'm not a normal person. *(He knocks at the bathroom door.)*

SAMIA *(cleaning her teeth and rinsing her mouth)*: What do you want?

ADIL *(shouting)*: I'm not a normal person! Can you hear? Not normal!

SAMIA: Not normal? Who's not normal?

ADIL: I'm not—I'm not normal.

SAMIA: Are you ill?

ADIL: I shall carry out your orders: the Butagas—the heater—the bath—the heater—the bath—the Butagas—the heater—the bath—the bath—the bath—

SAMIA: Hurry up, Adil!

ADIL: Right away. *(He goes to the telephone on the table, lifts the receiver and dials a number.)* Hullo. Hullo. Raafat? Good morning, Raafat. Listen. Listen. No, no, I'm not upset. Do you think I sound upset? No, no, not at all. I . . . I'm only . . . tell me: Are you awake? Ah, of course you're awake seeing that you're talking to me. No, no . . . I meant . . . have you had your bath? Oh yes . . . good. No, I haven't done anything yet. I got up early. That's the root of the problem. Tell me, talking about baths . . . yes, baths . . . has your wife . . . no, sorry . . . it's a stupid question. No, no, nothing. I only wanted to talk to you, merely to . . . merely to . . . nothing. Yes. Yes. Nothing at all. No, no . . . don't be alarmed. I'm only . . . actually, I feel that I'm . . . yes, I'm not completely all right. No, it's not all that bad. Of course I'll go out. Yes, we'll meet at the factory as usual. Samia . . . she's in the bath. In the bath, old man . . . in the bath. I'll give her your regards. No, no, don't worry yourself. I'm fine . . . fine, Raafat. 'Bye. 'Bye.

During the telephone conversation Samia has been trying in vain to put on the water heater.
At last, as Adil puts down the receiver, she opens the door.

SAMIA: Your lordship was chatting on the telephone while I thought you'd gone to the kitchen to put on the Butagas.

ADIL: A hurried conversation.

SAMIA: With someone at the company?

ADIL: With a lady.

SAMIA: A lady?

ADIL: Yes, a lady . . . a friend.

SAMIA: Do I know her?

ADIL: No, she's a new friend — a most pleasant person.

SAMIA: Married?

ADIL: Of course not.

SAMIA: Someone who works in the company?

ADIL: No, someone far away from that atmosphere. Just a lady, a beautiful lady, a refined lady, amenable and unassuming.

SAMIA: Adil, this is no time for these glorious imaginings.

ADIL: Imaginings?

SAMIA: Of course, imaginings. After five years of marriage, don't you think I know what you are?

ADIL: And what am I?

SAMIA: Don't go on asking me that question every moment. Will you please note that I haven't yet had my bath, that I haven't done my hair, in fact haven't done a thing up until now except to talk nonsense with my respected husband. I haven't even lit the heater because you've refused to be serious and have just sat around chatting on the phone.

ADIL: God Almighty!

SAMIA *(motioning to him to go to the kitchen)*: Do you mind?

ADIL *(making his way meekly to the kitchen)*: Why trouble to say "do you mind"? You know I'll comply with the order.

SAMIA: Of course I know that. *(She examines her hair in the mirror.)*

ADIL *(from offstage, in the kitchen)*: Of course. I'm now in the kitchen turning on the Butagas for you.

SAMIA: Thank you. *(She goes to the heater in the bathroom and lights it as she hums to herself.)*

ADIL *(from offstage)*: And the bottle of milk by the door — I'm taking it in and putting it on to heat. Any other orders?

Samia continues humming to herself.

ADIL *(entering, wiping his hands and singing)*: The attainment of desires is not by hoping.

SAMIA *(going towards the bathroom door)*: Adil, pass me the towel, will you?

ADIL *(passes her the towel)*: The towel.

SAMIA: And the bathrobe too.

ADIL *(presenting her with the bathrobe)*: And the bathrobe. You've got the soap and sponge?

SAMIA: The bottle of eau-de-Cologne please.

ADIL *(passing her the bottle)*: And the eau-de-Cologne.

SAMIA: And the tin of powder.

Adil passes her the powder.

SAMIA: And now get out!

ADIL: I'm out!

Samia closes the door of the bathroom and walks forward, humming to herself, towards the bath. She no sooner looks inside it than she lets out a scream.

ADIL (*sitting with lowered head and then rising up in alarm at her scream*): What's wrong?

SAMIA (*opening the door of the bathroom and screaming*): Adil! Adil! Come quickly and look!

ADIL (*going towards the bathroom*): What is it? What's happened?

SAMIA (*pointing to the inside of the bath*): Look!

ADIL (*looks into the bath*): It's a cockroach.

SAMIA: Of course it's a cockroach, but how did it get in here?

ADIL: In the same way any cockroach gets into a house.

SAMIA: I mean here, into the tub, into the bath.

ADIL: Perhaps it fell from the ceiling.

SAMIA: The bath must be cleaned at once, but first it must be killed.

ADIL: Killed?

SAMIA: At once. You've got the insecticide in the kitchen.

ADIL: It's I who's going to be entrusted with killing it?

SAMIA: Of course.

ADIL: Of course, but look! It's going to come out by itself.

SAMIA: It would be better if it came out by itself because killing it in the bath will make a mess.

ADIL: Yes, it would be preferable if it were to come out nice and quietly so that it doesn't dirty the bath for you.

SAMIA: And when it comes out you can deal with it far away.

ADIL: Yes, far away from you.

SAMIA (*looking into the bath*): It doesn't look as if it will be able to.

ADIL (*looking closely*): It's trying.

SAMIA: It's slipping.

ADIL: The walls of the bath are slippery.

SAMIA: Yes, no sooner does it start climbing than it slips and falls.

ADIL: But it goes on trying.

SAMIA: And goes on again and again.

ADIL: With the same procedure.

SAMIA (*continuing to look*): Yes. Yes.

ADIL: Look, Samia. With all its strength it's climbing up the slippery wall.

SAMIA: And there it is slipping back again. There—it's fallen all the way back.

ADIL: And it's starting off to repeat the attempt.

SAMIA: Up it goes, up it goes. It's slipped! It's slipped! It's fallen!

ADIL: Don't you notice something, Samia?

SAMIA: What?

ADIL: That it's always at the same place.

SAMIA: Approximately a third of the way to the top of the bath.

ADIL: Yes, then it falls.

SAMIA: So it's unable to climb more than that.

ADIL: Because the walls of the bath are less steep near the bottom, which makes climbing easier. After that, though, it's straight up.

SAMIA: That's not the reason. Cockroaches can easily climb up a perpendicular wall, also along a ceiling. The reason is because it's slippery—no wall or ceiling is as slippery as this.

ADIL: How then can a cockroach climb up a wall of porcelain tiles, which is as slippery as this bathtub?

SAMIA: And who told you that cockroaches can climb up a porcelain tile wall?

ADIL: Can't they?

SAMIA: Have you ever seen it?

ADIL: I rather imagined I had.

SAMIA: Imagined you had? So your lordship is imagining things!

ADIL: And you—have you seen it?

SAMIA: No, and so long as I have not seen a cockroach climbing up a wall of porcelain tiles I am unable to say that it could happen.

ADIL: Sounds logic.

SAMIA: Aren't you pleased with my logic?

ADIL: Did I say I wasn't? I was wondering, merely wondering. Is it impossible that something one hasn't seen with one's own eyes can happen?

SAMIA: Whoever said such a thing?

ADIL: I imagined you said something like that.

SAMIA: You imagined! Once again you're imagining things. Please don't imagine!

ADIL: As you say. I shall not imagine any more. As you wish me to be so positivistic, allow me to look in the dictionary.

SAMIA: Look for what?

ADIL: For the habits of cockroaches. Just a moment.

He hurries to the shelf of books by the bed and brings back a dictionary.

SAMIA: Hurry up, please.

ADIL *(turning over the pages)*: Right away. Co . . . cock . . . cockroach, also known as black-beetle.

SAMIA: Black-beetle?

ADIL: Yes, black-beetle.

SAMIA: I prefer the word cockroach.

ADIL: I too.

SAMIA: What else does the dictionary say?

ADIL: The cockroach or black-beetle is a harmful insect that infests cloth, food, and paper. It is often found in lavatories and has long hairy horns or whiskers. It spoils more food than it actually requires as nourishment. It can live for about a year.

SAMIA: A year? It lives for a year?

ADIL: If it's not done away with and is left to enjoy its life.

SAMIA: Spoiling our food and clothes!

ADIL *(closing the dictionary)*: That's all it says in the dictionary.

SAMIA: And now?

ADIL: And now what?

SAMIA: Are we going to go on like this looking at the cockroach?

ADIL: It's an enjoyable spectacle—don't you find it so?

SAMIA: What about the work we've got to do?

ADIL: Quite right — work.

SAMIA: We've got to put an end to it.

ADIL: And how do we put an end to it? This is something which is not in our hands.

SAMIA: In whose hands, then?

ADIL (*pointing to the cockroach*): In *its* hands. It's still climbing.

SAMIA: And also still falling.

ADIL: Yes, it climbs, then it rolls over, then it falls. Note the procedure: climbs, then slips, then rolls over, then falls to the bottom of the bathtub.

SAMIA: It climbs, then slips, then rolls over, then falls to the bottom of the bathtub.

ADIL: Exactly. Then it starts off again, without resting, without respite. It climbs . . .

SAMIA: Then it slips . . .

ADIL: Then it rolls over . . .

SAMIA: Then it falls . . .

ADIL: Then it climbs . . .

SAMIA: Listen, Adil — and then what?

ADIL: It hasn't had its final word.

SAMIA: I think that's plenty.

ADIL: Are you saying that to me?

SAMIA: Please, if you've got time to waste I haven't.

ADIL: Good God, and is that my fault?

SAMIA: Am I going to have my bath or aren't I?

ADIL: Go ahead! Have I stopped you?

SAMIA: And the cockroach?

ADIL: I am responsible only for myself.

SAMIA: Which means that you intend to leave it like this inside the bath?

ADIL: I think it's better to leave it as it is so that it can solve its problem by itself.

SAMIA: Are you joking, Adil? Is this a time for joking?

ADIL: On the contrary, I'm being extremely serious. Do you not see that it's still trying to save itself, so let's leave it to try.

SAMIA: Until when?

ADIL: We cannot — either you or I — decide when. That depends on its willpower — and up until now it has shown no intention of discontinuing its attempts. Look! So far it is showing no sign of being tired.

SAMIA: But I'm tired.

ADIL: Unfortunately.

SAMIA: And you? Aren't you tired?

ADIL: Of course, the same as you, but there's nothing to be done about it.

SAMIA: In short, I'm not having my bath today, or dressing, or going off to my job — all because of a cockroach which has fallen into the bathtub and my solicitous husband who stands watching it and talking drivel.

ADIL: Thank you!

SAMIA: As one cannot depend upon you, I suppose I must act.

ADIL: What are you going to do?

SAMIA: Get the insecticide and look after things myself.

ADIL: You're going to destroy the cockroach?

SAMIA: Right away.

ADIL: Then go off and bring the insecticide.

SAMIA: I'll do just that.

Samia hurries off to the kitchen and Adil quickly locks the bathroom door from the inside. Samia, noting what has happened, turns back and raps at the locked door. Adil, inside the bathroom, moves towards the bath, humming to himself.

SAMIA: What have you done, Adil? Open it!

Adil does not reply to her: He is looking at the cockroach in the bath.

SAMIA: Have you done it, Adil?

ADIL *(pointing at the cockroach)*: Up you go . . . up . . . up. Another step. Go on . . . go on . . .

SAMIA *(rapping at the door)*: Adil, open it!

ADIL *(to the cockroach)*: Stick to it! Stick to it! Struggle for your life!

SAMIA *(knocking vigorously)*: I told you to open up, Adil. Open it! Can't you hear me?

ADIL *(to the cockroach)*: They want to kill you with insecticide. Don't be afraid—I'll not open the door. Stick to it! Stick to it!

SAMIA *(rapping at the door)*: Open the door, Adil! Open up, I tell you!

ADIL *(to the cockroach)*: What a shame! You slipped, you rolled over and fell down as you do each time.

SAMIA *(rapping at the door)*: Can't you hear all this knocking?

ADIL *(to the cockroach)*: You want to have another go. Once again you're starting to climb. Why don't you rest a while? Rest for a moment, brother! Give yourself a breather? But what's the point? *(shouting)* There's no point!

SAMIA: No point? You say there's no point?

ADIL: Not to you!

SAMIA: So you've uttered at last! Are you going to open up eventually or not?

ADIL: No.

SAMIA: Are you saying no?

ADIL: Yes.

SAMIA: Are you saying no or yes?

ADIL: No and yes.

SAMIA: Speak intelligibly. Are you going to open up or not?

ADIL: I'll open up and I'll not open up.

SAMIA: Don't annoy me—define your attitude!

ADIL: You define yours!

SAMIA: Mine's clear—very clear.

ADIL: In relation to whom?

SAMIA: To you of course.

ADIL: I'm not asking about your attitude in relation to myself, I'm asking about your attitude in relation to it.

SAMIA: What's it?

ADIL: The cockroach.

SAMIA: No, you've really gone mad! *(The telephone rings. She hurries off to it and lifts up the receiver.)* Hullo. Who is it speaking? Ah, good morning, Mr. Raafat. No, we're not dressed yet, nor had breakfast, nor done a thing all morning — neither he nor I. He spoke to you? Ah, it was he who rang you. I have, in fact, noticed something strange about him: unnatural, sick. Yes, he's in the bathroom. No, he's locked himself in. A cockroach, my dear sir. Yes, an ordinary cockroach. No. No. It's a long story. Yes, when we meet. No, I don't think he's intending to go to work. I myself am late. Quite definitely something's happened to him. No, don't you worry. The company doctor? And what can the company doctor do? I'm most grateful, Mr. Raafat. Where's Yusriyya? Good morning, Yusriyya. Your husband noticed and told you? No, don't you worry, Yusriyya. I'm very grateful to both you and Mr. Raafat. Thank you. Thank you. *(She puts down the receiver.)*

The cook enters; she is carrying the saucepan of milk.

COOK: Who put the milk on the fire and left it? The milk's all boiled over on to the floor and the saucepan's quite empty.

SAMIA *(pointing to the bathroom)*: It's his lordship.

COOK: And what's he been interfering in the kitchen for?

SAMIA: And why are *you* late today?

COOK: Transport.

SAMIA: Jam packed, not even a place to stand, isn't that so?

COOK: Exactly.

SAMIA: I know your excuse, know it in advance!

COOK: Shall I prepare the breakfast?

SAMIA: Breakfast? You'd better wait till we see where it's all going to end. *(She points at the bathroom.)*

COOK *(looking towards the bathroom)*: It's him?

SAMIA: Yes, inside — he's locked himself in.

COOK: Why? I hope nothing's wrong.

SAMIA: The cockroach.

COOK: Cockroach?

SAMIA: Look here, Umm Attiya, did you clean the bath well yesterday?

COOK: Of course, Ma'am — with carbolic acid.

SAMIA: Impossible.

COOK: The bottle's along by the kitchen.

SAMIA: You're sure?

COOK: I swear to you.

SAMIA: Then where's this wretched cockroach come from?

COOK: From the skylight, from the stairs, from the pipes, from out of the cracks in the walls — however much you clean a house it's bound to have cockroaches and ants.

All this time Adil has been in the bathroom engrossed in watching the cockroach. He makes gestures to it as he follows it climbing up and falling down; by sighs and miming he expresses all his emotions and concern.

SAMIA *(suddenly shouting)*: Oh, and where's it all going to end? My poor nerves! My poor nerves!

COOK: Shall I bring you a cup of tea?

SAMIA: No, you go about your work and let me be for the moment.

COOK: The insecticide's along by the kitchen, Ma'am. I'll bring it and . . .

SAMIA: I know the insecticide's in the kitchen but the trouble is . . . Off you go and let me alone, Umm Attiya—I know what I'm about.

COOK: As you say, Ma'am. *(She goes out.)*

SAMIA *(going towards the bathroom and rapping at the door)*: Listen, Adil, I want to have a few words with you. Are you listening?

ADIL *(without moving or interrupting his watching of the cockroach)*: I'm listening.

SAMIA: I think things have gone on quite long enough.

ADIL *(automatically echoing her words)*: Long enough.

SAMIA: And there's a limit to one's patience.

ADIL: One's patience.

SAMIA: And my nerves are in ribbons.

ADIL: In ribbons.

SAMIA: And you're behaving ridiculously.

ADIL: Ridiculously.

SAMIA *(shouting)*: This is unbearable! Won't you answer me? Answer anything! Answer! Answer! Answer!

ADIL: Answer! Answer! Answer!

SAMIA *(leaving the bathroom door in despair)*: It's hopeless! There's no longer any point in speaking to that creature. He just repeats my words like a parrot. We've now got a cockroach and a parrot in the bathroom!

COOK *(entering)*: Today you're both later than usual, Ma'am.

SAMIA: Of course.

COOK: Today's a holiday?

SAMIA: It's not a holiday or anything of the sort—it's a working day as usual.

COOK: All right but . . .

SAMIA: But what? His lordship's locked himself up in the bathroom and doesn't want to open it, nor does he want to answer me. I've given up knocking and trying to talk to him. I've come to the end of my tether with him . . . there's no way of making contact with him.

COOK: Seeing that he's bolted himself in . . .

SAMIA: There's only one way.

COOK: Let's try it.

SAMIA: Do you know what it is?

COOK: No.

SAMIA: Break down the door.

COOK: Break down the bathroom door?

SAMIA: Yes.

COOK: And who's going to do that?

SAMIA: Can't you?

COOK: Me?

SAMIA: Certainly, you'd not be able to.

COOK: It's a solid door and would need a carpenter . . .

SAMIA: Go and fetch a carpenter.

COOK: There's no carpenter nearby in the district.

SAMIA: What's to be done?

COOK: Leave it in the hands of the Almighty. We'll let him be for a while until he gets fed up and opens up of his own accord.

SAMIA: He won't get fed up. So long as that wretched thing's got a breath of life in it.

COOK: But he'll have to come out so as to go to work.

SAMIA: He'll forget work or pretend to. I know him—sometimes he forgets himself. Many times he's unable to get any control over himself or over his time.

COOK: And your own work, Ma'am?

SAMIA: That's the trouble. I can't go without him because they'll ask me about him. What shall I say to them? Shall I say that he hasn't turned up to work because he's engrossed in watching a cockroach in the bath?

COOK: Say that he's tired, indisposed.

SAMIA: They'll immediately send round the company doctor.

COOK: Let him come and good luck to him!

SAMIA: And if he examines him and finds he's not indisposed at all?

COOK: That's true.

SAMIA: He's always getting me into such embarrassing situations. If I weren't always alongside him to rescue him and guide him he'd get into any number of scrapes.

COOK: May the Almighty keep you and give you strength!

SAMIA: He always yields to me, he never disobeys me.

COOK: That's evident.

SAMIA: What's happened to him then this morning? I said to him: Open up! Open up! but he seemed stone-deaf.

COOK: All his life he's paid attention to what you have to say.

SAMIA: Except for today. I don't know what's happened to him.

COOK: Somebody's put the evil eye on him.

SAMIA: And where will be the end of it?

COOK: Be patient, Ma'am. Patience is a virtue.

SAMIA: My patience has run out, it's finished, it's had it!

COOK (*looking in the direction of the bathroom*): But you mean to say that all he's doing is just watching a cockroach?

SAMIA: You don't believe it?

COOK: Honestly, Ma'am, if it weren't that I believe every word you say I'd not make head or tail of it.

SAMIA: Of course—this wouldn't happen with a normal man.

COOK: Shall I speak to him, Ma'am?

SAMIA: You?

COOK: I'll have a go.

SAMIA: Go on!

The cook knocks on the bathroom door. Adil, motionless, is still watching what is going on in the bathtub.

COOK (*she knocks again, then again and again, and finally shouts out*): I'm Umm Attiya.

ADIL (*raising his head*): Umm Attiya? What do you want?

COOK: To wash the bathroom floor.

ADIL: It's forbidden.

COOK: Forbidden?

ADIL: Today it's forbidden.

COOK: I'll bring a new piece of soap for the bath.

ADIL: There's soap here.

COOK: A clean towel?

ADIL: There is one. There's everything.

COOK: Don't you need anything?

ADIL: All I need is for you to take yourself off and shut up.

COOK: Just as you say.

The cook returns despondently to Samia.

SAMIA: I told you it was no good.

COOK: You're quite right.

SAMIA: So what's to be done? One's got to do something, one's simply got to.

COOK: Calm down, Ma'am, and leave things to the Almighty!

SAMIA: One can't just shut up about it — one can't!

She walks nervously about the room, while the cook watches her and sighs. There is a ring at the door.

COOK: It's the front door!

SAMIA: Who could it be?

COOK: I'll go and see. (*She goes out.*)

SAMIA (*standing up and listening, then calling out*): Who is it, Umm Attiya?

COOK (*entering in a state of flurry*): It's the doctor, Ma'am!

SAMIA: Doctor? What doctor?

COOK: He said he was the company doctor. I put him in the lounge.

SAMIA: The company doctor? Ah, no doubt Raafat sent him, thinking that the situation demanded it. And now what's to be done? This is just what I feared. (*She moves towards the bathroom door and knocks.*) Adil! Open up, Adil — there's something very important.

ADIL (*his gaze directed at the inside of the bath*): I know — very important.

SAMIA: The situation's critical.

ADIL: No doubt about it. (*He points to the cockroach in the bath.*) Its situation is indeed critical, and you know its situation is critical.

SAMIA: Whose situation? I'm talking about your situation.

ADIL: That also is only too well known.

SAMIA: Open up, Adil. Open up so I can explain the situation to you.

ADIL: The situation's clear and requires no explaining.

SAMIA: You're wrong, something new's occurred: the doctor's come.

ADIL: Doctor? You've brought a doctor? — to do away with this poor thing? An entomologist of course?

SAMIA: Entomologist? What are you talking about? The doctor's come about you. Open up — the doctor's here for you.

ADIL: For me? An entomologist?

SAMIA: What entomologist, Adil? The company doctor; the company doctor's come to examine you.

ADIL *(jumping to his feet)*: What's that you're saying?

SAMIA: Open up and I'll explain to you.

ADIL *(realizing what she's up to)*: Open up? Not likely! I've heard that one before!

SAMIA: I'm not fooling, Adil, and I'm not playing a trick. I'm talking seriously: The company doctor has arrived and is in the lounge. It seems Raafat sent him thinking you were ill.

ADIL: Me ill?

SAMIA: So Raafat understood, and the doctor's actually come.

ADIL: If he's actually come, why don't I hear his voice?

SAMIA: He's in the lounge. I told you he was in the lounge — and please don't make him wait any longer!

ADIL: In short, you want me to open up?

SAMIA: Of course, in order to be able to deal with the question of the doctor.

ADIL: Cut this story of the doctor out!

SAMIA: Don't you believe he's here?

ADIL: If he's really come for me, let him speak to me himself.

SAMIA: You want him to come in here?

ADIL: Isn't that the normal thing?

SAMIA: All right. *(She calls out.)* Umm Attiya — ask the doctor to come in here.

COOK: Certainly, Ma'am.

Samia hurriedly arranges her hair and clothes preparatory to meeting the doctor.

COOK *(at the door)*: Please, in here, Doctor.

SAMIA *(meeting him)*: Please come in, Doctor.

DOCTOR *(enters carrying a small bag)*: Good morning.

SAMIA: Good morning. It seems we've put you out for no . . .

DOCTOR: Not at all. I was already dressed and was about to leave when Mr. Raafat contacted me by telephone. I came along immediately — my house is just nearby.

SAMIA: We are extremely grateful but . . .

DOCTOR: And how does Mr. Adil feel?

SAMIA: The fact is he's . . .

DOCTOR: In any event everything will become clear when I've examined him. Where is he, might I ask?

SAMIA: He's . . . he's . . . he's here in the bathroom. I'll call him.

DOCTOR: Let him take his bath in peace.

SAMIA: He's not taking a bath. He's . . . just a moment. *(She knocks at the bathroom door.)* Adil! Open up, Adil — the doctor's waiting.

ADIL: Where is he?

SAMIA: Here in the room. Answer him, Doctor!

DOCTOR: Mr. Adil!

ADIL: Good God! It's true!

DOCTOR *(to Samia)*: What's he saying?

SAMIA *(to Adil)*: You believe me? Now open up!

ADIL *(opening the door of the bathroom and standing by it)*: Doctor? Truly I'm most embarrassed . . .

DOCTOR: How are you now, Mr. Adil?

ADIL: I? I'm fine.

DOCTOR: Fine?

ADIL: Naturally.

SAMIA: But he felt slightly unwell early this morning.

ADIL: I?

SAMIA: Of course you. Since early this morning you haven't been feeling right.

ADIL: And you know the reason why?

SAMIA: Whatever the reason, the doctor's come and there's an end to it. In any case you're late for work and there's no harm in the doctor giving you a day off, isn't that so, Doctor?

DOCTOR: Before prescribing anything I must make an examination. Please lie down on the bed, Mr. Adil.

ADIL: But I . . .

SAMIA: Listen to what the doctor has to say, Adil, and let him examine you.

ADIL: Examine? And say it appears . . .

SAMIA: Anyway, you're run down.

ADIL: But that's not sufficient reason . . .

SAMIA: It's enough for now.

ADIL: I prefer him to know the real reason.

SAMIA: The real reason?

ADIL: Yes, come along, Doctor.

DOCTOR: Where to?

ADIL *(drawing him towards the bathroom)*: In here.

SAMIA: You're mad, Adil! *(She draws the doctor away from the bathroom.)* Please, Doctor, come away.

ADIL: Leave him alone, Samia. Let me tell him of the real reason. *(Pulls the doctor towards him.)* Come along, Doctor.

SAMIA: Don't listen to him, Doctor. *(Pulls the doctor towards her.)* Come along.

DOCTOR *(at a loss, being pulled in opposite directions by the two of them)*: Please! Please!

SAMIA: Let the doctor go, Adil. It's not right.

ADIL: You let him go!

SAMIA: Allow him to examine you—that's what he's come for.

ADIL: No, I'll tell him the real reason.

SAMIA: But that won't . . . won't . . .

ADIL: It must be done.

SAMIA: You don't realize what you're doing. Come here, Doctor, please. *(She pulls him.)*

ADIL: But the doctor is interested to know what it is I want to show him. I'm sure of that. Please, Doctor, listen to what I have to say. Come along! *(He pulls at the doctor.)*

DOCTOR: Excuse me! Excuse me! *(He tries to release himself from the two of them.)*

SAMIA: I'm sorry, Doctor, but my husband Adil doesn't appreciate . . .

ADIL: Doesn't appreciate what? In what way don't I appreciate? I know exactly what I'm doing. My mind's quite made up.

SAMIA: I've warned you, Adil, I've warned you.

ADIL: I'll take the responsibility.

SAMIA: All right, you're free to do as you please.

DOCTOR *(bewildered)*: What's it all about? Please—tell me.

ADIL *(drawing him into the bathroom)*: Come along with me, Doctor, and I'll explain things to you.

DOCTOR *(in astonishment)*: Where to?

ADIL *(standing in front of the bath)*: Here, look! What do you see inside the bathtub?

DOCTOR *(looking)*: Nothing. There's no water in it.

ADIL: Of course there's no water in it, but isn't there something else?

DOCTOR: No, nothing—it's empty.

ADIL: Yet even so, there is something there.

DOCTOR: Something? Such as?

ADIL: Do you find it absolutely sparkling white?

DOCTOR: Yes, absolutely.

ADIL: But you can't say that it's absolutely clean.

DOCTOR: Who am I to criticize your cleanliness?

ADIL: Thank you for your kind words but the obvious truth of the matter is that there is something dirty in the bath.

SAMIA: So you've admitted it's dirty and must be done away with?

ADIL: Dirty's something and doing away with it is something else.

DOCTOR *(looks at them both uncomprehendingly)*: If you'll allow me . . .

ADIL: Look down here into the bath, Doctor, and you'll understand.

The doctor looks down with great attention.

ADIL: Do you not see something moving?

DOCTOR *(without interest)*: A cockroach.

ADIL: A cockroach? Well done!

DOCTOR: And so?

ADIL: This cockroach is the very core and essence.

DOCTOR: Very core and essence?

ADIL: Look at it well, Doctor. What do you notice about it?

DOCTOR: From what point of view?

ADIL: From the point of view of its behaviour.

DOCTOR: Its behaviour?

SAMIA: Keep quiet, Adil—let me explain to the doctor.

ADIL: No, please, Samia—let me do the speaking.

SAMIA: And why should I not speak? At least I won't tell it wrong.

ADIL: And I'll tell it wrong?

SAMIA: Don't complicate things for me. Let me do the talking, because I'm better than you at explaining things.

ADIL: Of course, but it's only I who . . .

SAMIA: Today you're opposing me all along the line in a quite unreasonable way.

ADIL: It's not opposition. I didn't mean . . . it's just . . .

SAMIA: Just what? Listen, Doctor . . .

ADIL: A moment, Samia, please! Let me speak first because I've got my own point of view.

SAMIA: And I too have a point of view.

ADIL: Of course. Of course—and your point of view is respected, very respected. But allow me a minute, one single minute and no more.

SAMIA: No, not even half a minute.

ADIL: Please, Samia.

SAMIA: Out of the question.

ADIL: Samia!

DOCTOR: Friends, there's no reason for all this disagreement. Explain to me first of all exactly what the problem's all about.

SAMIA: The problem, Doctor . . .

ADIL: For which of us did the Doctor come? Was it not for me? Tell me, Doctor, for whom did you come here?

DOCTOR: For you.

ADIL: For me, then it is I who shall explain to you . . .

DOCTOR: You or the lady—the important thing is for me to know what it's about.

SAMIA: Do you hear, Adil: You or I, and as I'm the woman I have priority.

ADIL: Heavens! Even in this, even in my own illness?

SAMIA: You've now admitted you're ill.

ADIL: In the doctor's view. Of course he has come because there's an ill person in the house, and the ill person is supposed to be me, but the fact, Doctor, is . . .

SAMIA: The fact is that he's . . .

ADIL: The fact is that I'm . . .

SAMIA (violently): Whatever next, Adil? Please, don't force me to . . .

ADIL: It's my fault, my fault as usual, because it's always my fault.

DOCTOR: The important thing, friends, is: What's it all about?

SAMIA: I'm sorry, Doctor—we're taking up too much of your time.

DOCTOR: No, not at all, only I'd like to understand . . .

SAMIA: You'll understand, Doctor, you'll understand—if he'd just shut up for a moment I'd be able to explain to you.

ADIL: Just the opposite.

SAMIA: What's just the opposite?

ADIL: If I keep silent he'll not understand what it's about.

SAMIA: Meaning that I'm incapable of making him understand, or do you mean I'm a liar and will falsify the facts?

ADIL: God forbid! Would I ever insinuate such a thing!

DOCTOR: Allow me, so as to put an end to all disagreement, just let me find out what it's about by myself. Please, Mr. Adil, please lie down on the bed so that I can examine you and then I'll know the truth for myself.

ADIL: No, Doctor—the truth's not to be found on the bed but in the bath.

DOCTOR: In the bath?

ADIL: Yes, in this bath—this cockroach.

DOCTOR: Permit me, please excuse me, but I . . . I don't understand anything at all.

SAMIA: It's not his fault—of course he can't understand.

ADIL: I'll explain the matter in a few words—listen, Doctor, look carefully at this cockroach and tell me what it's doing now?

DOCTOR *(looking into the bath)*: What's it doing? It's doing nothing.

ADIL: Look carefully, Doctor.

DOCTOR: What are you getting at exactly?

SAMIA: What Adil is getting at is that . . .

ADIL: No, no, let the doctor discover it for himself.

DOCTOR *(looking intently into the bath)*: Discover?

ADIL: Don't you see, for example, that the cockroach is trying to do something?

DOCTOR: Of course, it's trying to get out of the bath.

ADIL: Marvellous! Marvellous! We've got there.

DOCTOR *(looking at him)*: Where have we got?

ADIL: To the heart of the whole matter.

DOCTOR *(nodding his head)*: Understood. Understood. It's all quite clear now.

ADIL: You understand what I'm driving at, Doctor? This is the point of departure and I shall explain my attitude to you.

DOCTOR: No, no, there's no need to explain—I've understood. *(He goes out of the bathroom and whispers to Samia)* Might I have a word with you?

SAMIA *(following him)*: Of course, Doctor, go ahead.

DOCTOR *(whispering)*: He's really overdoing it. How many hours does he work at the factory?

SAMIA: The usual hours, but there's something else to it.

DOCTOR: Does he do other work?

SAMIA: He is preparing a thesis for his doctorate, but this condition of his . . .

DOCTOR: Understood, understood. He's certainly in need of rest. I'll write down for him all that's necessary. Would you allow me, Mr. Adil?

ADIL *(coming out of the bathroom)*: What, Doctor?

DOCTOR: Nothing—it's just that having visited you at home in my capacity of company doctor, I must examine you, if only for the purpose of establishing that I've been here.

ADIL: But I'm not ill.

DOCTOR: I know that, but I am required to put in a report and the report must show that an examination has been made.

ADIL: You came in an official capacity?

DOCTOR: Of course.

ADIL: Ah, in that case I must help you. However, what are you going to write in your report seeing that I'm not ill?

DOCTOR: Leave things to me. First of all, would you just lie down here on the bed.

ADIL: I've put on weight these last years.

DOCTOR: That's obvious—you're getting flabby before your time.

SAMIA: He's grown himself a real paunch!

ADIL: From fatty food — Umm Attiya's cooking!

DOCTOR: Maybe also from lack of exercise.

ADIL: I've got no time for exercise.

DOCTOR: You overdo things at work.

ADIL: I have to.

DOCTOR (*examining his chest and back with the stethoscope*): Take a deep breath. Enough, enough. Do you smoke?

ADIL: A little.

DOCTOR: Drink a lot of coffee?

ADIL: A couple of cups a day.

DOCTOR: Alcohol? Drugs?

ADIL: No, no. Never, never.

DOCTOR: You naturally sometimes stay up late at night.

ADIL: Sometimes, when my work requires me to, but in any case it's never later than midnight.

DOCTOR: Do you sleep well?

ADIL: Like a log.

DOCTOR: Do you have unpleasant dreams?

ADIL: Neither pleasant nor unpleasant, I don't dream at all.

DOCTOR: Perhaps you dream and don't remember your dreams.

ADIL: Maybe.

DOCTOR: You don't suffer from anything unusual?

ADIL: No, not at all.

DOCTOR: Thank you.

The doctor sets about writing out his prescription to one side of the room.

SAMIA (*approaching the doctor*): I hope everything's all right, Doctor?

DOCTOR: Fine, everything's just fine — he's in splendid health, thanks be to God. There's not a thing wrong with him. I'll write him out a prescription for some tranquillizers and give him three days' sick leave.

SAMIA: Three days?

DOCTOR: Too little?

SAMIA: No, it's a lot, too much.

ADIL (*jumping to his feet*): What's too much?

SAMIA: The doctor wants to give you three days' sick leave.

ADIL: Three days?

SAMIA: One day's plenty, Doctor.

ADIL: Of course one day, and there wasn't even any reason to have today off if it hadn't been that you came, Doctor — so as to justify your coming here.

DOCTOR: As you say — one day, my dear sir.

ADIL: Thank you, Doctor.

DOCTOR: On condition that you stay in bed.

ADIL: Stay in bed?

DOCTOR: It's necessary.

ADIL: And what's the necessity?

DOCTOR: For complete rest and relaxation.

ADIL: And if I find complete rest and relaxation somewhere else?

DOCTOR: Where?

ADIL: In the bathroom, for example?

SAMIA: Do you hear, Doctor? He'll be spending the day in the bathroom.

DOCTOR: There's no harm in his taking a warm bath, it'll help him to relax.

SAMIA: He'll not be taking a bath at all, neither warm nor cold.

DOCTOR: What, then, will he do in the bathroom?

SAMIA: Ask him.

ADIL: I shall watch the cockroach. What's wrong with that?

SAMIA: You've heard with your very own ears, haven't you, Doctor?

DOCTOR: The cockroach? Again?

ADIL: Come along to the bath with me and I'll explain things to you.

DOCTOR (*looking at his watch*): Another time, it's getting late and I've got some urgent work to do.

ADIL: My explanation will take no more than a minute.

DOCTOR: I promise to visit you again shortly when, God willing, your nerves will have calmed down.

ADIL: My nerves are perfectly calm. I would have liked you to stay for a while so that . . .

DOCTOR: I'll come back. I'll come back.

ADIL: When?

DOCTOR: In the afternoon. In the afternoon.

ADIL: When you return in the afternoon everything will have changed.

DOCTOR: What will have changed?

ADIL: The cockroach will—will have been destroyed. Do you think my wife will leave things as they are?

SAMIA: Of course not. You can't stop me from using the bath the whole day—it's unreasonable.

ADIL (*to the doctor*): Do you hear?

SAMIA: Judge, Doctor! Don't I have to go off to my work at the factory? Hasn't his lordship already made me late enough?

ADIL: Doctor, it's not I who've made her late. Her being late has another reason. Ask her about it!

SAMIA: What's the other reason?

ADIL: Your insistence on taking a bath today.

SAMIA: Ask him, Doctor, what the reason was for my not taking a bath today.

ADIL: I'll tell you the reason, Doctor: The reason is that she wants to destroy this cockroach.

SAMIA: There you are, Doctor!

DOCTOR: The fact is that the question . . .

ADIL: I'm certain, Doctor, you'll come down on the side of truth, for the question is clear.

SAMIA: Of course it's clear, but don't try to influence the doctor. He understands everything.

ADIL: I'm not trying to influence the doctor. It's you who from the very beginning were trying to influence him, but he understands perfectly my purpose.

SAMIA: Your purpose?

ADIL: Of course.

SAMIA: Tell us, Doctor: Have you really understood anything of him?

ADIL: And have you understood anything of her, Doctor?

SAMIA: Answer, Doctor!

ADIL: Yes, answer!

DOCTOR (*at a loss between the two of them*): The truth of the matter is I . . . is I . . .

ADIL: Listen, Doctor; the essence of the matter can be put into a few words: Put yourself in the same position.

DOCTOR: Your position?

ADIL: The position of the cockroach.

DOCTOR (*hurriedly taking up his bag*): No—please excuse me.

He rushes out with Samia and Adil in his wake calling out to him.

SAMIA: Wait, Doctor!

ADIL: Just a moment, Doctor!

CURTAIN

ACT THREE—THE FATE OF THE COCKROACH

The same scene less than a minute later. Samia and Adil are returning to the room after the doctor's hasty departure.

ADIL: Why did the doctor leave like that?

SAMIA: Ask yourself.

ADIL: Ask myself? Why? Did I do anything wrong?

SAMIA: You? From the moment you woke up this morning you haven't stopped doing things wrong.

ADIL: Good Heavens!

SAMIA: We woke up in the morning in fine shape, got ourselves ready to go out to work, and then your lordship causes us all this unnecessary delay.

ADIL: It's I who've caused it?

SAMIA: Your cockroach!

ADIL: And was it I who placed it in the bath?

SAMIA: What it amounts to is that you've got the day off—official sick leave. As for me, I've got to go off to my work. It's true I'm late but I'll make the best of it and give as an excuse your being ill and the company doctor coming to the house.

The doctor reappears.

DOCTOR: Please excuse me! I went off in a most impolite manner.

ADIL: No, don't mention it, Doctor.

DOCTOR: I was afraid I'd be late for my other work. On thinking it over, though, I feel that my prime duty lies here. I have therefore returned quickly to ask that I might continue my examination of the case.

SAMIA: Thank you, Doctor.

DOCTOR: I'd like to have a word in private with your wife—would you allow me, Mr. Adil?

ADIL: Of course. Of course. I'll go into the bathroom.

DOCTOR: Take your time!

Adil goes into the bathroom and locks the door on himself. He goes back to watching the bath with interest. He makes signs and gestures as he follows the cockroach's movements, like someone following a game of chess.

SAMIA: Is anything wrong, Doctor?

DOCTOR: I want to ask you about certain things.

SAMIA: Go ahead!

DOCTOR: My questions will perhaps be a trifle embarrassing in that they may touch upon some personal aspects, but my duty as a practising doctor demands that I do so. May I put my questions?

SAMIA: Of course, Doctor, go ahead!

DOCTOR: What's your opinion about your husband's personality?

SAMIA: In what respect?

DOCTOR: In respect of strength and weakness.

SAMIA: In relation to whom?

DOCTOR: In relation to yourself of course.

SAMIA: I . . . I believe his personality to be weaker than mine.

DOCTOR: Does he know it?

SAMIA: Certainly.

DOCTOR: He has told you so openly?

SAMIA: No, but he believes it deep inside him.

DOCTOR: How do you know?

SAMIA: He is always stating that I boss him and make him obey my orders and tyrannize him.

DOCTOR: Tyrannize him?

SAMIA: That's what he says.

DOCTOR: Then he believes or imagines that you are tyrannizing him?

SAMIA: Yes.

DOCTOR: My diagnosis is appropriate.

SAMIA: What diagnosis?

DOCTOR: This question of the cockroach.

SAMIA: And what's the connection?

DOCTOR: You want to do away with the cockroach and he wants to save it from your hands.

SAMIA: You mean, Doctor . . .

DOCTOR: Yes, in his inner consciousness he has identified himself with the cockroach, and this is the secret of his concern and affection for it.

SAMIA: Extraordinary! D'you think so, Doctor?

DOCTOR: There can be no other reason.

SAMIA: But . . .

DOCTOR: This is a very obvious example from modern psychology. I am not a specialist in psychiatry, but I have made a private study of it as a hobby and I am indeed lucky to have come across this case today.

SAMIA: Are you certain it's a psychological state?

DOCTOR: A typical case.

SAMIA: Can it be treated?

DOCTOR: The treatment is easy, extremely easy.

SAMIA: Whatever you order me to do I shall carry out immediately.

DOCTOR: The treatment requires no more than your persuading your husband that there is no similarity between him and the cockroach.

SAMIA: And how shall I persuade him?

DOCTOR: That's the problem.

SAMIA: A way must be found.

DOCTOR: First of all you must on your side show affection for the cockroach.

SAMIA: Show affection for the cockroach?

DOCTOR: That's essential, because any hurt done by you to the cockroach would, in your husband's view, be a hurt done to him personally.

SAMIA: But this is madness.

DOCTOR: Naturally—it's a pathological condition.

SAMIA: But he's perfectly sane. Up until this morning he could not have been more balanced in all his behaviour, performing his company work perfectly well.

DOCTOR: He is in fact extremely well balanced and will always be able to perform his company work in the best possible manner, of that I'm sure.

SAMIA: Then he's a normal person.

DOCTOR: Normal in all things except one—that of the cockroach.

SAMIA: That's right, no sooner is the cockroach mentioned than . . .

DOCTOR: Than he begins to speak and act strangely.

SAMIA: That is so.

DOCTOR: Yet even so there's no cause for worry. With a little wisdom and patience, kindness and adjustment, we shall quickly be able to sort things out for the best.

SAMIA: You may be confident, Doctor, that I shall employ both wisdom and patience and shall be kind and compliant with him in everything he wants.

DOCTOR: That is all that is now required, so let's begin trying.

SAMIA: Yes, we shall try.

DOCTOR: First of all, we must go along and participate in what he's doing.

SAMIA (she goes with the doctor behind her and gently knocks on the bathroom door): Adil!

ADIL (getting to his feet and opening the door to them): Have you finished your little private talk?

SAMIA: Yes, the doctor was advising me . . .

DOCTOR: To put you on a special diet. I'd like you to be a little slimmer.

ADIL: Slimmer? Me?

DOCTOR: Why not? Do you want to let your body get flabby?

ADIL: Has my wife complained about my physique?

DOCTOR: No, I'm talking medically—an increase in weight leads to lethargy, and you are in need of energy.

ADIL: I'm exceedingly energetic, extremely energetic, which can be seen from the fact that I wake up in the morning before the alarm goes off. Ask Samia.

SAMIA: Quite correct.

DOCTOR: Then you admit your husband possesses this quality.

SAMIA: No doubt about it—he's exceedingly energetic.

DOCTOR: Do you hear that, Mr. Adil? Your wife is being very complimentary about you.

ADIL: She can't deny I'm energetic, though of course I'm not as energetic as this cockroach.

DOCTOR: The cockroach? Ah, yes, of course.

ADIL: Look, Doctor. Look, Samia. It's still struggling—with the same perseverance. I tried to catch it out slacking or giving up, but never . . . never . . . never.

SAMIA *(looking into the bathtub with feigned interest)*: It's certainly courageous.

ADIL: And what courage!

SAMIA: I've begun to love it.

ADIL *(looking at her)*: Love it?

SAMIA: Yes, doesn't its courage deserve love?

ADIL: You wanted to destroy it with insecticide.

SAMIA: I was stupid.

ADIL: Thanks be to God!

SAMIA: Look at its whiskers—they're beautiful!

ADIL: Whose whiskers?

SAMIA: The cockroach's of course.

ADIL: Its whiskers are beautiful?

SAMIA: Don't you think so?

ADIL: You making fun of me?

SAMIA: Of you? No, no—I swear to you, Adil. Please don't be angry. I swear to you I'm not making fun of you. I'm being absolutely serious now. I'm sincere in what I say, and when I say that its whiskers please me, be sure that I really mean it.

ADIL: And since when did you discover its whiskers were so beautiful?

SAMIA: Since . . . since a moment ago when I looked carefully at it.

ADIL: I myself have been looking carefully at it from early morning and can't find anything beautiful about it.

SAMIA: You're being modest.

ADIL: Modest? Me? What's the connection?

SAMIA: Oh none, none at all.

DOCTOR: Certainly there's no connection whatsoever.

SAMIA: Of course, Adil, be sure there's no connection.

ADIL *(looking at the two of them)*: What's all this confusion about?

SAMIA: Nothing at all, Adil—everything's quite in order. All that's happened is that the doctor and I have come to understand your point of view completely.

DOCTOR: Certainly. Certainly.

ADIL *(doubting them)*: And what is my point of view?

SAMIA: It's — it's that this cockroach . . .

DOCTOR: Should not come to any harm.

SAMIA: Yes. Yes.

ADIL: Do you know why?

SAMIA: We know all right.

ADIL: No, Samia, I'm certain you don't really know. I shall explain it to you and the
doctor.

SAMIA: No, there's no need, Adil, no need at all. We know and appreciate the position. God willing, everything will return to normal with a little wisdom and
patience.

ADIL: Yes, a little patience. All that's wanted is a little patience, because things may go
on for a while. In any case, it's both interesting and exciting. I don't get bored
watching, and so long as this cockroach goes on putting up such a struggle to get
out of its impasse, it is not right that we should destroy it.

SAMIA: Who said we were going to destroy it? On the contrary, Adil, I'll look after it
with every care. I'll sacrifice myself for it.

ADIL: Sacrifice yourself for it? Please, Samia — there's no need to make fun.

SAMIA: Absolutely not, Adil. What can I do to convince you that I'm definitely not
making fun?

ADIL: When all's said and done, the struggle this cockroach is putting up stirs within
me a feeling of respect.

SAMIA: And who said we had less respect for it than you? We are at one with you,
Adil — absolutely at one. Maybe we have even more respect and appreciation for
it than you, isn't that so, Doctor?

DOCTOR: Of course. Of course.

ADIL: More than me? No, I don't think so.

SAMIA: And why not?

ADIL: Because I've been watching it since early morning, following its every movement. It amazes me the amount of strength that's stored up in it — quite remarkable strength.

SAMIA: I'm in agreement with you about that, Adil, and I really do find that it has an
extraordinarily strong personality.

ADIL: Strong personality?

SAMIA: Don't you think so?

ADIL: I think it's an exaggeration to say it's got a personality.

SAMIA: Honestly, Adil, it's got a strong personality — you must believe that.

ADIL: Listen, Samia — don't get characteristics mixed up. The fact that a cockroach
has such strength and determination is both acceptable and reasonable, but to
say it's got a personality is going too far.

SAMIA: I insist it has got a personality. Maybe even its personality is stronger than
mine — wouldn't you agree with me there, Doctor?

DOCTOR: Very likely.

ADIL: What's very likely, Doctor? That this cockroach's personality is stronger than Samia's?

DOCTOR: Don't, Mr. Adil, overestimate the personality of your lady wife — with all due deference to her.

ADIL: I'm not overestimating but — but to compare my wife with a cockroach!

SAMIA: But I'm in agreement, Adil.

ADIL: It's not a question of whether you're in agreement or not in agreement — we're talking about the comparison itself.

SAMIA: And why should we reject the comparison, seeing that the cockroach commands respect? It does me honour.

ADIL: Are we back again at making fun?

SAMIA: Not at all, I swear to you, Adil. I'm absolutely serious — just ask the doctor.

ADIL: Listen, Samia, when words lose their normal dimensions, then everything loses its seriousness. I've begun to feel that you're in league with the doctor to ridicule my ideas.

DOCTOR: God forbid, Mr. Adil!

SAMIA: No, Adil, please don't make such an accusation against the doctor. He is the last person to wish to harm your self-respect. He hasn't interrupted his other work and devoted all his time to us in order to make fun of you and your ideas.

DOCTOR: On the contrary, the . . . the fact of the matter is that I . . .

SAMIA: Don't say anything, Doctor — it's obvious what your feelings are.

ADIL: I'm sorry — I no doubt misunderstood.

SAMIA: Be sure, Adil, that we are of the same opinion as you. There is now no disagreement between us. The cockroach is as much an object of affection to us as to you.

ADIL: Affection?

SAMIA: Yes, and in deference to it and to you I have decided not to have a bath today in order to prove to you I won't attempt to harm it.

ADIL: Thank you.

SAMIA: Doesn't that please you?

ADIL: Of course it pleases me.

SAMIA: Everything that pleases you, Adil, everything that makes you happy, I shall at once put into effect for you.

ADIL: What's all this tenderness about?

SAMIA: I regret all my hasty actions.

ADIL: What hasty actions?

SAMIA: I haven't always been nice to you.

ADIL: That is your right as a woman and a wife, but it is my duty as a man and a husband to endure.

SAMIA: No, from now on you shall not endure, I shall not make you endure.

ADIL: What's happened now? What's come over the universe?

DOCTOR: Your wife is one of the best of wives, Mr. Adil, and is blindly obedient to you.

ADIL: Since when?

SAMIA: Since today.

ADIL: And why today?

SAMIA: Because it . . . because I . . .

DOCTOR: Because she naturally doesn't want to see you being ill.

ADIL: But I'm not ill.

DOCTOR: Of course. Of course you're not ill at all.

SAMIA: What the doctor means is you're . . .

DOCTOR: Certainly. What I mean is that it's clear you're not ill. That was established by examining you, be sure of that. However, the whole object is to remove the *idea* of illness, not illness itself. Just the fact of seeing a doctor in the house, a doctor who has come because of you, has made your wife feel towards you a certain . . .

SAMIA: Yes. Yes. As soon as I saw you would need sick leave . . .

ADIL: I don't need sick leave. It's the doctor who made me take it at the time he made out his report. As for me, I'm in no need of any leave.

DOCTOR: That's quite so.

SAMIA: In any case, Adil, I was unfair to you.

ADIL: Sometimes.

SAMIA: I admit it.

ADIL: Then you won't go to the bathroom before me?

SAMIA: No, never—I've turned over a new leaf, I promise.

ADIL: You won't tell me to get breakfast?

SAMIA: No, I promise. I promise.

ADIL: You won't impose your will and orders on me?

SAMIA: No, I promise. I promise.

ADIL: And what's the secret of this sudden transformation?

SAMIA: I didn't realize that this behaviour of mine towards you would have such results.

ADIL: What results?

DOCTOR: She means . . . she means your being angry.

ADIL: But I haven't been angry. I used sometimes to feel annoyance at your behaviour. I was only too often annoyed with you, but I've never been angry with you.

DOCTOR: You used to repress it.

ADIL: Repress it?

DOCTOR: Repress it deep within yourself. It's this repression that leads to . . . that leads to . . .

ADIL: Leads to what?

DOCTOR: Leads to . . . to temperamental upsets.

ADIL: Certainly I feel upset, but only for a while.

SAMIA: But maybe you keep some feeling lurking deep inside you.

ADIL: Because of you? No, not at all.

SAMIA: I almost believed this morning you hated me.

ADIL: Hated you?

SAMIA: Yes, because of the insecticide.

ADIL: Do you call that hate? A mere feeling of slight annoyance at your wish to destroy this cockroach.

SAMIA: I didn't recognize its importance.

ADIL: And do you now honestly recognize its importance?

SAMIA: Of course.

ADIL: I doubt it.

SAMIA: And why do you doubt it?

ADIL: Because you don't watch it with sufficient attention. Look! For example, it has now begun to stand for long periods on the bottom of the bath. What's the meaning of that?

SAMIA *(looking with attention)*: It means that . . .

ADIL: That it's beginning to take rests.

SAMIA: Yes.

ADIL: After that continuous effort it must be in need of rest periods during which it lies prostrate, as you see, quietly moving its whiskers before carrying on anew with its climbing.

DOCTOR *(looking with attention)*: It's actually begun moving slowly so as to start climbing again.

SAMIA: That's right—it's started to climb.

ADIL: Note carefully the spot at which it begins to slip.

SAMIA: Yes, yes—the same spot. There it goes—it's slipped!

DOCTOR: And fallen once more to its place at the bottom.

ADIL: Look, it's getting up from its fall and is beginning to climb again.

SAMIA: And it will slip down again. There it is—it's slipped down! The poor thing! It's been doing exactly the same thing since early morning.

ADIL: And maybe since last night, because when we got up we found it already in the bath. It must therefore have fallen into it from the ceiling during the night.

SAMIA: I have a question, Adil? May I?

ADIL: Of course, Samia—ask it.

SAMIA: Have you not thought of rescuing it from its predicament?

ADIL: Rescuing it?

SAMIA: Yes, why don't you rescue it?

ADIL: It's rescuing itself.

SAMIA: How can it rescue itself? It will never be able to. All the time its attempts are in vain because the bath is empty and slippery; there's nothing for it to climb up but the slippery sides on which it loses its foothold.

ADIL: That's up to it.

SAMIA: At least help it. Give it a little help, Adil. For example, let the end of the towel hang over inside the bath, or bring a piece of string and dangle it over the side— or anything that'll help it to get out.

ADIL: And why should we do that?

SAMIA: To get it out, to get it out alive. Don't you want it to be saved?

ADIL: Who said I wanted it to be saved?

SAMIA: How odd! You don't want it to be saved? Then you want its death?

ADIL: I don't want its death either.

SAMIA: Then what do you want for it?

ADIL: I don't want anything for it. It is no concern of mine.

SAMIA: Of course not. Of course not. It's absolutely no concern of yours. You have no connection with it, no connection at all. You are something and it is something else. We know that only too well, isn't that so, Doctor?

DOCTOR: Without doubt.

SAMIA: Be sure, Adil, that we're *completely* convinced that you have no connection with this cockroach. We wish you to know this well and to believe it.

ADIL: And don't I know this?

SAMIA: The important thing is that you should believe it deep inside you.

ADIL: Believe what?

SAMIA: Believe that there is no relationship and not the slightest similarity between you and it.

ADIL: Similarity between me and it? Whatever next, Samia? Have things come to this pass? You talk of a similarity between me and the cockroach?

SAMIA: On the contrary, it makes me happy to know there's no similarity.

ADIL: Then such a similarity does exist in your view?

SAMIA: Not in mine, Adil.

ADIL: Then in whose?

SAMIA: In your own view?

ADIL: Mine! In my view I resemble the cockroach?

SAMIA: Then you no longer think this is so?

ADIL: Think what? That I resemble the cockroach? In what way do I resemble it? Please let me know. You've really gone too far; this is too much, Samia, much too much. Me resemble a cockroach? Me? In what way? From what point of view? Whiskers? If it's from the point of view of whiskers, I am clean-shaven, as you can see. From the point of view of features? Of lineaments of face? Speak! Speak! Speak!

SAMIA: Please, Doctor, you speak!

DOCTOR (*to Samia*): Be so good as to allow us a moment in private.

SAMIA: I'll go and prepare you a cup of coffee, Doctor. (*She goes out, leaving the doctor and Adil on their own.*)

DOCTOR: Listen, Mr. Adil—you should, first of all, know that your wife is wholly loyal to you and does not at all intend to hurt your feelings.

ADIL: After what I've heard?

DOCTOR: Believe me, she respects you, appreciates you, and has a very high regard for you, despite your belief that your personality is weaker than hers.

ADIL: My personality weaker than hers! Who said so?

DOCTOR: No one at all—a mere supposition, a mere possibility that this was your inner belief.

ADIL: Such a supposition or possibility never occurred to me.

DOCTOR: Maybe, for example, her demands, or what might have been understood as orders, were . . .

ADIL: Certainly she is a person of many demands and orders, even arbitrary actions and a desire to be the boss.

DOCTOR: You admit this point?

ADIL: For sure.

DOCTOR: Then you find that she has a desire to be the boss?

ADIL: Of course, like most wives, and especially those who, like her, have graduated with their husbands from the same college and are employed in the same line of work.

DOCTOR: Equality, then, between the two of you is total in everything?

ADIL: In everything.

DOCTOR: And yet she wants to have the advantage, to be the boss, to dominate.

ADIL: That is exactly my wife's attitude.

DOCTOR: And you let her be the boss and dominate.

ADIL: Yes, and do you know why?

DOCTOR: Because she . . .

ADIL: No, please wait! Don't be too hasty and conclude from that that she has a stronger personality than me — those are merely her pretensions.

DOCTOR: Her pretensions?

ADIL: Tell me frankly, Doctor, was it not she who said something of that sort to you?

DOCTOR: I believe . . .

ADIL: Yes, I know this of her: Deep within her she believes I have a weaker personality than her.

DOCTOR: And is that not true?

ADIL: Of course it's not at all true. She's free to believe whatever she likes about herself. If her conceit portrays things to her in that light, then let her imagine as she will.

DOCTOR: But this does not obviate the fact that you obey her and carry out all her orders.

ADIL: It's a desire on my part to please her, because she's a woman, a weak woman, taken up with her youth, her advancement, her talent. I don't like to shake her belief in her own strength and superiority. I would regard that as meanness, meanness on my part as a strong man. I hold that real manliness demands that she be made to feel her strength and her importance and to raise her morale.

DOCTOR: Raise her morale? Extraordinary! The problem's reversed.

ADIL: What problem?

DOCTOR: Another question, Mr. Adil: the problem of the cockroach?

ADIL: What about the cockroach?

DOCTOR: It's your interest in it?

ADIL: And what's the secret of your interest in my interest?

DOCTOR: None at all, it's just . . .

ADIL: Listen here, Doctor — the whole thing's becoming clear to me. I've now understood. I've understood its beauty and its whiskers and its personality and the similarity. What you were getting at, therefore, was that I . . .

DOCTOR: Frankly, Mr. Adil, sir, yes.

ADIL: Yes?

DOCTOR: Our whole object was merely to assist and to . . .

ADIL: Participate — to assist and participate with my wife in such talk.

DOCTOR: No, Mr. Adil, this is a well-known theory.

ADIL: Theory? What theory?

DOCTOR: To tell you the truth I've not specialized in psychiatry, I've only studied it purely as a hobby, and so . . .

ADIL: Quite understood. And so you came to believe that I belonged to the cockroach species.

DOCTOR: No, it's not quite like that. In any case I've now changed my opinion.

ADIL: Thank God! You now see that I'm a human being!

DOCTOR: You must excuse me, Mr. Adil, but all the surrounding circumstances drew one in that direction.

ADIL: Please, Doctor, explain to me in detail what got into your mind, according to your psychiatry.

DOCTOR: No, there's no point now. I'm sorry.

ADIL: And my wife Samia knew of this opinion of yours?

DOCTOR: Yes.

ADIL: And she it was who helped you to see me as a cockroach?

DOCTOR: No, Mr. Adil, no. It's not like that. It's not, I assure you, quite like that. I assure you.

ADIL: Listen, Doctor, I want to tell you in all frankness that any similarity between me and the cockroach is mere . . .

DOCTOR: My apologies. My apologies, Mr. Adil. Our intentions were well meant, I swear they were.

ADIL: Allow me to complete what I had to say: If you believed that I resembled a cockroach, then you were mistaken.

DOCTOR: Of course—and how! I admit I made a wrong analysis, that I'm mistaken, a hundred percent mistaken.

ADIL: Yes, a grave mistake, because I am unable to attain the magnificent level reached by cockroaches.

DOCTOR: What are you saying? The magnificent level?

ADIL: Yes.

DOCTOR: Are you being serious?

ADIL: Wholly serious—and I'm prepared to repeat what I said.

DOCTOR: Then you admire this cockroach?

ADIL: And I appreciate it.

DOCTOR: And you appreciate it?

ADIL: And I respect it.

DOCTOR: And you respect it?

ADIL: And I understand it well.

DOCTOR (*scrutinizing him closely*): Understood. Understood. And you take after it and imagine yourself . . .

ADIL: In its place?

DOCTOR: Yes, like it.

ADIL: Yes, I imagine that.

DOCTOR: Then you, you . . .

ADIL: I what?

DOCTOR: I don't know any longer. You've bewildered me, Mr. Adil.

ADIL: Please, Doctor, that's quite enough. Once again you're applying your psychiatry to me. It's a lot simpler than all that. I shall explain it to you clearly if you'll allow me.

DOCTOR: Please go ahead.

ADIL: First of all, imagine you're a cockroach.

DOCTOR: Me?

ADIL: Or that the cockroach is you.

DOCTOR: Mr. Adil . . .

ADIL: Please don't look at me like that. I understand exactly the meaning of your glances. You are still doubting. You are really at a loss about me, but I assure you once again that it's altogether different from what you have in mind.

DOCTOR: Then your employment of these words is in the nature of a pleasantry or . . .

ADIL: Take it in any meaning you like. The important thing is for you to leave out, as far as I'm concerned, this psychiatric business and be natural with me.

DOCTOR: Be natural?

ADIL: Yes, are you being natural now?

DOCTOR: By God, I'm . . . to tell the truth . . .

ADIL: You're not sure?

DOCTOR: I no longer know anything.

ADIL: I'll tell you what to do: Just let yourself go, forget you're a doctor and let's examine the matter with the utmost simplicity. Are you ready to do this?

DOCTOR: Yes.

ADIL: Great! What was I asking you?

DOCTOR: You asked me about . . .

ADIL: Yes, I remember. I asked you to imagine that you . . .

DOCTOR: That I was a cockroach.

ADIL: Or that the cockroach was you.

DOCTOR: Indeed. Indeed.

ADIL: And now to the second step.

DOCTOR: But wait, in my situation I can't . . .

ADIL: Can't what?

DOCTOR: I can't be a cockroach.

ADIL: Why not.

DOCTOR: Because I've never been married.

ADIL: What's that got to do with it?

DOCTOR: It seems that I . . . that I expressed myself badly.

ADIL: No, you merely misunderstood me. I did not ask you to be a family cockroach, in the psychological sense. No, I meant the actual cockroach in front of you there in the bath.

DOCTOR (*pointing at the cockroach in the bath*): That?

ADIL: Yes, that hero.

DOCTOR: Hero?

ADIL: Indeed a hero. Imagine yourself in a deep well with walls of smooth marble and that you found it impossible to get out despite having made exhausting efforts to do so, what would you do?

DOCTOR: I'd give up of course.

ADIL: But it hasn't given up.

DOCTOR: By no means — I see it repeating its attempts dozens of times.

ADIL: Even hundreds. Since early morning I've been occupied in counting up the number of times.

DOCTOR: Is that what you were engaged in since morning?

ADIL: Yes, I wanted to know when its struggle would come to an end.

DOCTOR (*looking into the bath with real interest*): As of now it looks as if it won't give up yet.

ADIL: Indeed. We're tired from watching but it's not tired from trying.

DOCTOR (*continuing to watch it*): What hope has it of escaping?

ADIL: No hope of course.

DOCTOR: Unless you were to intervene and save it.

ADIL: And I shall not intervene.

DOCTOR: Why not, seeing that you admire it?

ADIL: I must leave it to its fate.

DOCTOR: Were it able to scream, and it screamed to you for help, would you not take pity on it?

ADIL: Perhaps, but it's mute and doesn't scream.

DOCTOR: Who are you to say that?

ADIL: What are you saying?

DOCTOR: I am saying that who are we to say it is not screaming now and asking for help — just that the oscillations of its voice are not picked up by the human ear.

ADIL: Very possibly.

DOCTOR: Imagine that it is now screaming and beseeching, and you don't hear and don't understand its language.

ADIL: It also doesn't hear me and see me.

DOCTOR: Yes, every contact between the two of you is severed.

ADIL: Not completely severed, as is borne out by the fact that I am interested in it.

DOCTOR: You are interested in its struggle for life.

ADIL: This, then, is its voice, its pleading, its language which I can hear and under-stand.

DOCTOR: Certainly, it explains our being so interested in its struggle.

ADIL: Is that not what has kept me in front of the bath since early morning?

DOCTOR (*looking into the bath*): It is in reality an entertaining spectacle.

ADIL (*also looking*): Isn't it.

DOCTOR: Truly, though, I'm surprised at your refraining to help it a little, even by way of remuneration for the spectacle.

ADIL: It really deserves it.

DOCTOR: We're in this together — let's get it out of its plight!

ADIL: Get it out alive?

DOCTOR: Of course.

ADIL: And will Samia accept that?

DOCTOR: She's got a kind heart.

ADIL: I personally prefer not to introduce sentiment into a situation like this, otherwise our position is going to appear truly ridiculous.

Samia appears in the doorway carrying the coffee.

DOCTOR: Quite the contrary, the position now is no longer ridiculous at all. It's become understood and acceptable, and I myself have begun to find the subject worth following.

SAMIA *(offering him the coffee)*: Coffee, Doctor.

DOCTOR *(without raising his eyes from the bath)*: Thanks, I'll have it in a moment.

SAMIA: It seems that the cockroach is also occupying you, Doctor?

DOCTOR *(continuing his viewing)*: Certainly it's begun to interest me.

SAMIA: No doubt the disease is catching!

ADIL *(turning to her)*: What disease?

SAMIA: The doctor understands what I mean.

DOCTOR *(rousing himself)*: Come along, let's drink the coffee first.

They all go into the bedroom. The doctor sits down in a chair and Samia puts the tray of coffee on a small table beside him.

SAMIA: Have you finished your examination, Doctor?

ADIL: Whose examination? My examination?

SAMIA: No, Adil, I'm just having a word with the doctor.

DOCTOR: I think it's best now to talk openly, for there's no reason or necessity for hiding anything. Mr. Adil is in perfect health and vigour, and can put on his clothes and go out as of now if he wants.

SAMIA: And the sick leave, Doctor?

DOCTOR: That's another question. However, Madam, your husband is in the right about everything and I completely endorse his behaviour, there being nothing at all untoward about it.

SAMIA: And the cockroach?

DOCTOR: What about the cockroach? I myself hope that I could become like the cockroach.

SAMIA *(winking at the doctor)*: Ah, understood. I understand, Doctor.

DOCTOR: No, honestly, I'm speaking seriously.

SAMIA: Speaking seriously?

ADIL: Of course, Samia, it's serious. The doctor has explained everything to me, has been absolutely open with me. In any case, may God be indulgent towards you!

SAMIA: Is that right, Doctor?

DOCTOR: The fact is that we had understood the situation wrongly and took up an erroneous attitude.

SAMIA: Meaning that Adil . . .

DOCTOR: Absolutely, a hundred percent.

SAMIA: Thanks be to God. Thanks be to God. I was extremely worried about you, Adil.

ADIL: You thought there was some sort of kinship between me and the cockroach!

SAMIA: You shouldn't blame me, Adil; your great love for it . . .

DOCTOR: On the contrary, it appears it wasn't love or anything of the sort, because if he'd loved it he'd have had pity on it and saved it. Our whole hope now lies in your compassion.

SAMIA: My compassion?

DOCTOR: Yes — and I personally would ask you, I would intercede with you . . .

SAMIA: Intercede for whom, Doctor?

DOCTOR: For the cockroach.

SAMIA (*shouting*): Doctor! Doctor! Adil, what's happened to the doctor?

DOCTOR: Don't be upset. Don't be upset. I'm fine and well.

SAMIA: Fine and well — like my husband!

ADIL: Yes, like me of course.

SAMIA: What a disaster — you and the doctor! There's only Umm Attiya and I left. It'll be our turn next. No, it can't be — I'm going out at once. Umm Attiya! Umm Attiya!

ADIL: What's happened, Samia? Have you gone mad?

SAMIA: Is it I who've gone mad?

DOCTOR: Calm down, Madam, and allow us to explain things to you.

COOK (*appearing*): You called, Ma'am?

SAMIA: Yes, I'm going out. Prepare my bath.

COOK: Certainly, Ma'am.

She quickly enters the bathroom and turns on the bath tap.

ADIL (*not conscious of what is happening in the bathroom, he walks towards his wife*): Calm down, Samia. Calm down a little and allow us to explain things to you.

DOCTOR: Your nerves are upset, Madam, without proper reason — if you'd only allow us to say a word.

SAMIA: No, there's no point, Doctor.

ADIL: Don't you want to come to an understanding?

SAMIA: It's enough the understanding between you and the doctor — you're both in league against me.

DOCTOR: Not against you, Madam. Would it be reasonable? It's only that I've become convinced by Mr. Adil's point of view; I've understood the true meaning of his purpose and behaviour.

SAMIA: And so you've become like him.

ADIL: Like me? You mean like a cockroach.

DOCTOR: That's an honour for me.

SAMIA: You see, it really is catching!

The cook in the bathroom, having turned on the tap and filled the bath, stretches out her hand and removes the cockroach, dead, with the tip of her fingers, throwing it into a corner of the bathroom.

COOK: I've run the bath, Ma'am!

ADIL (*realizing what has happened*): She's filled the bath! (*He hurries into the bathroom and gives a shout after looking into the bath.*) Come along here, Doctor — what we feared has happened.

DOCTOR (*following him*): What's happened?

ADIL: The cockroach is dead.

DOCTOR: Dead?

ADIL: It was no doubt drowned. But where is it? Umm Attiya, where's the cockroach that was here in the bath?

COOK (*pointing to the corner of the bathroom*): I threw it down there, for the time being. (*She goes out.*)

ADIL: What a pity!

DOCTOR: Yes, it certainly is a pity.

SAMIA: Shall I get you a professional mourner? Shall we bring some music and you can walk in its funeral procession?

ADIL: That's quite enough sarcasm, thank you!

DOCTOR: Let the matter rest, Mr. Adil. What's happened has happened. In any case you wanted to leave it to its fate, and this is its fate.

ADIL: Yes, it had to end—somehow. Let us cast a last look at its corpse.

DOCTOR: Where's its corpse?

SAMIA: Its corpse? Even you, Doctor!

Adil and the doctor look round for the cockroach in the corner of the bathroom.

ADIL: Look. Look, Doctor, at these ants. Where have they come from?

DOCTOR (*looks*): Yes, a horde of ants is carrying it off.

SAMIA: Ants?

ADIL: Yes, ants carrying off the corpse of the cockroach. Come, Samia, look! It's a really extraordinary sight—a crowd of ants carrying off the cockroach and taking it up the wall. Look, Doctor, they're taking it towards one of those cracks.

DOCTOR (*continuing to look*): It's obviously their house, or their village, or their warehouse in which they'll store this booty.

ADIL: Take note of that ant in the front. Do you see it?

DOCTOR: Yes, it's dragging the cockroach by its whiskers.

ADIL: As though it were a ship's tow rope.

DOCTOR: And this group of ants in the rear, they're pushing it from the back. Do you see?

ADIL: The work's distributed amongst them with extraordinary discipline.

DOCTOR: And the most extraordinary thing is that they're going up at speed, despite their heavy load.

ADIL: There's only a short distance left between them and the crack or warehouse. But look, Doctor, it seems as if the opening is too small for the size of the cockroach. How can it be got in?

DOCTOR: Don't be afraid, it'll get in—nothing is too difficult for the genius of ants.

SAMIA (*looking at them from the door*): Having finished with the heroism of cockroaches we've now started on the genius of ants!

ADIL (*continuing to watch*): I doubt if it's possible to get the cockroach into that small crack.

DOCTOR (*also watching*): We'll soon see.

The telephone rings.

SAMIA *(hurrying to the phone)*: Telephone, Adil! Perhaps it's for you.

ADIL *(turns and joins her)*: For me?

SAMIA *(taking up the receiver)*: Hullo. Who did you say? The doctor? Yes, he's here. Just a moment. *(She calls out.)* It's for you, Doctor.

DOCTOR *(hurrying over and taking up the receiver)*: Hullo. The company. Yes, I'm the doctor. How do you do? Where's this case? Street . . . number . . . Wait while I write it down. *(Takes out a small notebook and writes.)* What did you say the number was? Thank you. The case I'm on at present? Oh, I've finished with that now. Quite satisfactory. No, not at all serious. Merely indisposed. I'll tell him. Thanks. *(He puts down the receiver.)*

ADIL: They're asking about me at the company?

DOCTOR: Naturally.

SAMIA: They thought it was a serious case.

DOCTOR *(to Adil)*: They express their hopes for your recovery.

ADIL: Recovery?

SAMIA: And I too join my voice to theirs.

ADIL: Yes? Yes?

In the meantime the cook has slipped into the bathroom carrying a bucket of water and a rag and has begun cleaning it and removing the ants from off the wall. The others, occupied in their conversation, have not noticed.

DOCTOR *(looking at his watch)*: I must leave you—there's another case waiting for me.

SAMIA: Another case?

DOCTOR: In a far-away street. I mustn't be late. Goodbye.

ADIL: Wait, Doctor. Are you going off just like that without taking a look at the ants?

SAMIA: Do you want to hold the doctor up for the ants as well?

DOCTOR: It would in fact interest me, let's go and have a look.

ADIL: Off we go, perhaps the ants will have succeeded in getting the cockroach into that crack.

SAMIA *(looking at them in wonder)*: By God, it's amazing!

As Adil and the doctor reach the bathroom the cook leaves it with her bucket.

COOK *(to Samia)*: I've cleaned the bathroom, Ma'am.

Samia is busy taking her clothes out of the wardrobe.

ADIL *(in the bathroom)*: What a disaster it would be if Umm Attiya's done it.

COOK *(without understanding)*: Done it?

ADIL *(shouting as he stands in front of the wall)*: What a pity! What a pity!

DOCTOR *(standing behind him and looking at the wall)*: She's done it!

ADIL: She's done it. Look—she's removed the ants, the cockroach, and the lot. She's cleared the wall of everything.

DOCTOR *(coming out of the bathroom)*: Bad luck!

ADIL *(to the cook as he comes out)*: Why, Umm Attiya? Why?

COOK: What have I done?

ADIL: Nothing, nothing at all—just carry on with your work, God damn you!

The cook goes out in bewilderment. The doctor takes up his bag.

DOCTOR: I trust you'll spend your day resting and return to work tomorrow feeling a lot better, God willing.

ADIL: And what's keeping me till tomorrow? I'll get dressed now and go to work immediately.

DOCTOR: No, please, you're supposed to be on leave today.

ADIL: And what can I do now with this leave? Can't you cancel it?

DOCTOR: How can I cancel it? The company knows I'm here and that I've come to see you. What shall I say to them? Shall I say that he's . . .

SAMIA: That he's been sitting and watching a cockroach!

DOCTOR: Don't complicate things, Mr. Adil—a day's sick leave and that's that and the problem's solved.

SAMIA *(taking up her clothes)*: I'm going into the bathroom. If you'll excuse me. I think it's no longer forbidden to go into the bathroom!

ADIL: Lucky you!

SAMIA: Advise him, Doctor, to spend his day off doing something useful.

ADIL: And what, in your view, is doing something useful?

DOCTOR: Anyway, Mr. Adil knows how to spend his time usefully and enjoyably.

SAMIA: I can bet he'll be spending the day sitting down writing memoirs about the fate of the cockroach!

DOCTOR: And where's the cockroach now? No sign is left of it, not even one of its whiskers.

ADIL: The important thing was its struggle for life.

DOCTOR: Yes, and that is what will remain fixed in my memory. Goodbye, everyone.

SAMIA: We're most grateful, Doctor. We're sorry for having kept you with us all this time without proper reason.

DOCTOR: Not at all. Not at all.

SAMIA: I hope that the case to which you are going is a little more serious!

DOCTOR: You may be sure that I didn't waste my time uselessly with yourselves. Goodbye. *(He leaves hurriedly.)*

SAMIA *(as she enters the bathroom)*: Listen, Adil, you've got the day off today. You should know that I want you to spend this day usefully. D'you hear? There are my clothes and dresses all crumpled up in the wardrobe—get down to sorting them out and hang them up at your leisure one by one so that when I come back from work I'll find everything nicely sorted out and organized. Understood?

Adil remains silent, his head lowered.

SAMIA: D'you hear what I say?

ADIL: I do.

SAMIA: And let's not find a single dress creased or crumpled. Understood?

ADIL *(shouting)*: Understooooood!

SAMIA: I'm warning you. *(She goes into the bathroom and locks herself in.)*

ADIL *(shouting)*: Umm Attiya, bring the bucket and rag and wipe me out of existence!

CURTAIN

❧ JORGE LUIS BORGES
B. ARGENTINA, 1899–1986

Jorge Luis Borges

Although popular in Argentina, Borges's work did not find an international audience until later in the writer's life, and then he was showered with praise. (Charles H. Phillips / Timepix)

HOR-hay loo-EES
BOR-hays

Jorge Luis Borges created his own version of the short story in which he expresses the modern dissolution of conventional reality by blurring the traditional line between fiction and historical scholarship. In the aftermath of World War I, many writers felt that traditional, understandable models of reality were shattered and that reality was at best fragmented. As a native of Argentina, Borges set the stage for other experimental Latin American writers to follow, like Gabriel García Márquez, Julio Cortázar, and Carlos Fuentes,[1] by exploring the psychological boundaries between interior and exterior reality, playing with multiple identities, and intersecting different times and places.

Borges has been compared to Kafka, whom he translated. Indeed, both were devoted to the exploration of consciousness, but while Kafka's stories deal with the dreamlike landscapes of the emotions, Borges's are very intellectual, drawing from the storehouse of world literature. Borges draws on esoteric literature and the wisdom traditions of world cultures to create subtle connections and unusual synchronicity in his stories. An international writer, Borges moves easily from one language to another in his work, just as his characters cross national boundaries with ease, pursuing their livelihoods abroad. Nowhere, of course, does Borges provide a magic key that unlocks a comprehensive, previously hidden plan for the cosmos, but like the ancient Gnostics,[2] he tantalizes us with the possibility that such a key exists, and that reality—for the artist at least—is an act of the imagination.

Crossing Cultures. Born on August 24, 1899, in Buenos Aires, Argentina, **Jorge Luis Borges** was raised in a home where languages and books were important. Jorge's mother, Lenore Acevedo Suarez, was a translator, and his father, Jorge Guillermos Borges, was a teacher, lawyer, and writer. Since his paternal grandmother was English and lived with the family, Borges grew up speaking both English and Spanish. When asked about the central event of his childhood, he answered, "I should say my father's library." In that library filled with English as well as Spanish books, the young Borges read a large number of classics. His father expected him to be a writer, and he was not disappointed. Borges began early, writing his

---

[1] **Márquez . . . Fuentes:** Gabriel García Márquez (b. 1928) is the Colombian author of *One Hundred Years of Solitude,* among other works. Julio Cortázar (1914–1984), a writer from Argentina, gained notoriety for his experimental novel *Hopscotch* in 1965. Carlos Fuentes's (b. 1928) many novels deal with Mexico's history and its social struggles; he is Mexico's most famous living writer. See Márquez and Fuentes on pages 924 and 933.

[2] **Gnostics:** Members of an ancient sect in the Middle East whose adherents believed that hidden knowledge held the key to the universe. Throughout history there have been Gnostics who have formed secret societies with secret scriptures and who have believed they understood the workings of the cosmos.

first story at age seven and publishing a Spanish translation of Oscar Wilde's[3] "The Happy Prince" in a Buenos Aires newspaper at age nine.

In 1914 World War I broke out and the Borges family, then traveling in Europe, was stranded in Geneva, Switzerland, where Borges completed secondary school at the Collège de Genève. He became proficient in Latin and French in school and taught himself German and German philosophy at home. In Spain, after the war, Borges became acquainted with a group of young writers called the ULTRAISTS[4] who rejected middle-class materialism and sought refuge in the artifice of poetry, in exotic images and metaphor. Returning to Buenos Aires in 1921, Borges became very active in the literary scene of that city, where from 1920 to 1930 he published four books of essays and three books of poetry. He founded three literary magazines and contributed to numerous others, including *Sur* (*South*), the most famous literary review of South America, and published three collections of unusual short stories: *The Garden of Forking Paths* (*El jardín de los senderos que se bifurcan*) in 1941, *Fictions* (*Ficciones*) in 1944, and *El Aleph* (1949).

Borges worked in a library in Buenos Aires from 1938 to 1946, but his opposition to the dictatorship of Juan Perón, who came to power in 1946, led to his dismissal from the job. The Perónistas offered him work as a chicken inspector in the city market, but he found a teaching job instead. After the fall of Perón in 1955, Borges was made director of the National Library, a position emblematic of his love for literature and vast learning. Unfortunately, his eyesight gradually failed in the mid 1950s; concerning his appointment and his eyesight, he said, "I speak of God's splendid irony in granting me at once 800,000 books and darkness." He was forced to dictate his writing. In 1961 he won the International Publishers' Prize, which he shared with Samuel Beckett.[5] He published a final collection of stories in 1970, *Doctor Brodie's Report* (*El informe de Brodie*). Besides traveling to various parts of the world, he spent his final years lecturing and teaching in universities, including the University of Texas and Michigan State. For most of Borges's life his mother lived with him, but late in life he married twice. His first marriage was to Elsa Astela Millán in 1967, the second to his longtime secretary, María Kodama, in 1986, shortly before he died of liver cancer in Geneva, Switzerland, where he is buried.

The Many Facets of Borges's Mind.   Early on Borges was interested in writing poetry and essays. From 1936 to 1939 he wrote a weekly column for the newspaper *El Hogar* in which he covered a broad range of literatures and was interested in connecting Argentinean literature to the traditions of Europe and America. His first real fame, however, came with

www   For links to more information about Borges and a quiz on "The Garden of Forking Paths," information about Borges's relevance in the twenty-first century, and information about the culture and context of South America in the twentieth century, see *World Literature Online* at bedfordstmartins .com/worldlit.

---

[3] **Oscar Wilde** (1854–1900): Irish writer who published various kinds of literature, from plays to fairy tales.

[4] **Ultraists:** Members of the literary movement in Spain after World War I that advocated the use of image and metaphor to create a poetry divorced from ordinary reality and politics.

[5] **Samuel Beckett** (1906–1989): Irish novelist, poet, and dramatist whose experimental works make use of stream-of-consciousness techniques. See page 770.

Philosophy, comparative philologies, archaeology, everything has been evolving, progressing, breaking new ground. But we know little as ever about why we are born again each morning. Despite the comings and goings of the collective unconscious, we know equally little about the meanings of our very symbols. Borges restates, in a few allegorical pages, the circular, ceremonial direction of our curious, groping, thrilling, and atrocious ignorance.

– ANTHONY KERRIGAN, critic, 1962

the publication of short stories in the collections *Ficciones* and *El Aleph.* Borges was influenced by the **IDEALISTIC**[6] belief that reality is essentially a network of ideas rather than a collection of material sensations; thus many of the stories in these collections read like essays, with frequent references to books, authors, and translations—some real, some imaginary. The short stories take their themes from mythology, ancient religions, Gnosticism, Jewish mysticism,[7] and various esoteric authors. Often a story's plot involves a puzzle and a search for an answer that is intricately intertwined with obscure details and that has an unexpected twist—a kind of mind game. In "Death and the Compass," for example, the detective Erik Lönnrot discovers the identity of a murderer by using the lore surrounding the Tetragrammaton,[8] the mystical name of God, but becomes trapped in the labyrinth of his own knowledge. In Borges's writings, the library is a symbol of the world's knowledge; somewhere there is an answer, but it is buried under thousands, if not millions, of layers.

"The Garden of Forking Paths."   Borges's detective story "The Garden of Forking Paths" was originally published in a collection of the same name in 1941 and eventually republished in *Labyrinths* (1962), an appropriate title for Borges's writings, since he is a master at creating tantalizing mazes that can be navigated only by picking up on the nearly invisible thread of clues Borges weaves into his narration. One dimension of the story consists of Yu Tsun's communicating the location of a British bombing target to his chief in Berlin, but another aspect entirely is the labyrinth discovered in a text by Yu Tsun's ancestor called *The Garden of Forking Paths,* which in its very structure models a universe comprising multiple planes of time in which individuals play several diverse roles. Even though the detective story is resolved in the final paragraph, Borges leaves the reader with the unmistakable impression that he or she is part of a larger network of relationships that transcend everyday understanding.

At times Borges's concerns with multiple planes of consciousness and esoteric learning are a game wherein he plays with the frontiers of the mind; at other times he seems to be reaching for a **SYNCRETISTIC** mythology—one that would blend ancient wisdom with modern psychology. He challenges a modern society that has lost contact with the meaningful symbols of its own traditions and lacks the vision for unifying whatever cultural fragments remain. After his extensive meanderings through

---

[6] **Idealistic:** Philosophical idealism in its various kinds held that objects of perception were in reality mental constructs and not the material objects themselves.

[7] **Jewish mysticism:** Like all forms of mysticism, Jewish mysticism focuses on learning and practices that lead to unity with the creator. Its teachings are called the Cabala or Kabala. Cabala dates from the beginnings of Judaism but gained a significant following in the eleventh century in Spain. It strives to discover hidden meanings in every letter, number, and word of the Hebrew Scriptures. The two primary texts are *Sefer Yezirah* (*Book of Creation,* c. third century) and *Zohar* (*Book of Brightness,* second and thirteenth centuries).

[8] **Tetragrammaton:** The four letters in the Hebrew alphabet said to make up god's unspeakable name, YHWH; this name and its uses are believed to contain special powers.

archaeology, philology, philosophy, comparative religion, and world literature, Borges offers this final epigraph from the German mystic Angelus Silesius (seventeenth century), which concludes *Other Inquisitions 1937–1952*, a collection of essays.

> *Freund, es ist auch genug. Im Fall du mehr willst lesen,*
> *So geh und werde selbst die Schrift und selbst das Wesen.*

> Friend, this is enough. If finally you want to read more,
> Go and be yourself the letter and yourself the spirit.

■ CONNECTIONS

Carlos Fuentes, "The Prisoner of Las Lomas," p. 938. Twentieth-century writers in the Third-World countries of Latin America were often torn between the attractions of international culture and the values of the indigenous populace of their countries of origin. Fuentes makes consistent use of Mexican history and culture to provide a context for his stories. How does Borges employ multiple nationalities to create an international world for his stories?

Alifa Rifaat, "My World of the Unknown," p. 1130. To suggest the complexity of human consciousness, modern writers layer their stories with dream-realities and fantasies. Rifaat skillfully creates what may be either a supernatural or a private psychological dimension in "My World of the Unknown." How does Borges manipulate apparently historical matters in order to ultimately create a larger sense of the role of fate or destiny?

Machado de Assis, "Adam and Eve" (Book 5). The popularity of scientific thinking in the nineteenth and twentieth century opened up the possibility of questioning the Bible and providing new interpretations or versions of its stories. Machado de Assis's story is an alternative version of the Adam and Eve story in Genesis. How does Borges suggest a new version of reality using materials from different cultures and ages?

■ FURTHER RESEARCH

Biography
McMurray, George R. *Jorge Luis Borges.* 1980.
Monegal, Emir Rodriquez. *Jorge Luis Borges.* 1978.

Criticism
Alazraki, Jaime, ed. *Critical Essays on Jorge Luis Borges.* 1987.
Dunham, Lowell, and Ivar Ivask, eds. *The Cardinal Points of Borges.* 1971.
Fishburn, Evelyn, and Psiche Hughes. *A Dictionary of Borges.* 1990.
Isbister, Rob, and Peter Standish. *A Concordance to the Works of Jorge Luis Borges, 1899–1986.* 1992.

■ PRONUNCIATION

Jorge Luis Borges: HOR-hay loo-EES BOR-hays

When one thinks of Borges, one thinks more of a literature than of a writer. Borges's stories and poems are aimed at the universe, unlike the writer with clearly defined scopes and goals. . . . Throughout his vast oeuvre, one keeps discovering the man of refined intellect, the philosopher, the "writer for writers" as he was considered some twenty years ago. . . ."

– MAURICIO BETANCOURT, 2001

❧   The Garden of Forking Paths

Translated by Donald A. Yates

On page 22 of Liddell Hart's *History of World War I* you will read that an attack against the Serre-Montauban line by thirteen British divisions (supported by 1,400 artillery pieces), planned for the 24th of July, 1916, had to be postponed until the morning of the 29th. The torrential rains, Captain Liddell Hart comments, caused this delay, an insignificant one, to be sure.

The following statement, dictated, reread, and signed by Dr. Yu Tsun, former professor of English at the *Hochschule*[1] at Tsingtao, throws an unsuspected light over the whole affair. The first two pages of the document are missing.

". . . and I hung up the receiver. Immediately afterwards, I recognized the voice that had answered in German. It was that of Captain Richard Madden. Madden's presence in Viktor Runeberg's apartment meant the end of our anxieties and—but this seemed, *or should have seemed,* very secondary to me—also the end of our lives. It meant that Runeberg had been arrested or murdered.[2] Before the sun set on that day, I would encounter the same fate. Madden was implacable. Or rather, he was obliged to be so. An Irishman at the service of England, a man accused of laxity and perhaps of treason, how could he fail to seize and be thankful for such a miraculous opportunity: the discovery, capture, maybe even the death of two agents of the German Reich? I went up to my room; absurdly I locked the door and threw myself on my back on the narrow iron cot. Through the window I saw the familiar roofs and the cloud-shaded six o'clock sun. It seemed incredible to me that that day without

---

"The Garden of Forking Paths."   Originally published as "El jardín de senderos que se bifurcan" in a collection of the same name in 1941, this story was later included in *Ficciones* (1945, 1956).

With mention of a book of history, data, and dates, this story begins seemingly rooted in a reality as substantial as an automobile or a brick house, but as soon as the second paragraph, the historical account is qualified by a newly discovered document by Dr. Yu Tsun, a scholar who taught English at a German university in China. From this point onward, ordinary reality begins to slip away into a series of fragments and innuendos. As is typical of Borges, two of the main characters in this story are foreigners seeking to prove their loyalties to a particular cause; the third character is, like Borges himself, a sinologist, or specialist in the study of Chinese language, culture, and history. Part of the enjoyment of this work is rereading it one or more times to pick up on the clues Borges has planted in the text that tie its loose ends together.

A note on the translation: The following translation by Donald A. Yates was published in *Michigan Alumnus Quarterly Review* (Spring 1958) and eventually republished in *Labyrinths: Selected Stories and Other Writings* (1962). All notes are the editors' unless otherwise indicated.

---

[1] **Hochschule:** University (German).

[2] **Runeberg . . . murdered:** A hypothesis both hateful and odd. The Prussian spy Hans Rabener, alias Viktor Runeberg, attacked with drawn automatic the bearer of the warrant for his arrest, Captain Richard Madden. The latter, in self-defense, inflicted the wound which brought about Runeberg's death. (Editor's note.) [Borges provided this "Editor's note" as part of the story.]

premonitions or symbols should be the one of my inexorable death. In spite of my dead father, in spite of having been a child in a symmetrical garden of Hai Feng, was I—now—going to die? Then I reflected that everything happens to a man precisely, precisely *now*. Centuries of centuries and only in the present do things happen; countless men in the air, on the face of the earth and the sea, and all that really is happening is happening to me . . . The almost intolerable recollection of Madden's horse-like face banished these wanderings. In the midst of my hatred and terror (it means nothing to me now to speak of terror, now that I have mocked Richard Madden, now that my throat yearns for the noose) it occurred to me that that tumultuous and doubtless happy warrior did not suspect that I possessed the Secret. The name of the exact location of the new British artillery park on the River Ancre. A bird streaked across the gray sky and blindly I translated it into an airplane and that airplane into many (against the French sky) annihilating the artillery station with vertical bombs. If only my mouth, before a bullet shattered it, could cry out that secret name so it could be heard in Germany . . . My human voice was very weak. How might I make it carry to the ear of the Chief? To the ear of that sick and hateful man who knew nothing of Runeberg and me save that we were in Staffordshire and who was waiting in vain for our report in his arid office in Berlin, endlessly examining newspapers . . . I said out loud: *I must flee*. I sat up noiselessly, in a useless perfection of silence, as if Madden were already lying in wait for me. Something—perhaps the mere vain ostentation of proving my resources were nil—made me look through my pockets. I found what I knew I would find. The American watch, the nickel chain and the square coin, the key ring with the incriminating useless keys to Runeberg's apartment, the notebook, a letter which I resolved to destroy immediately (and which I did not destroy), a crown, two shillings and a few pence, the red and blue pencil, the handkerchief, the revolver with one bullet. Absurdly, I took it in my hand and weighed it in order to inspire courage within myself. Vaguely I thought that a pistol report can be heard at a great distance. In ten minutes my plan was perfected. The telephone book listed the name of the only person capable of transmitting the message; he lived in a suburb of Fenton, less than a half hour's train ride away.

I am a cowardly man. I say it now, now that I have carried to its end a plan whose perilous nature no one can deny. I know its execution was terrible. I didn't do it for Germany, no. I care nothing for a barbarous country which imposed upon me the abjection of being a spy. Besides, I know of a man from England—a modest man—who for me is no less great than Goethe.[3] I talked with him for scarcely an hour, but during that hour he was Goethe . . . I did it because I sensed that the Chief somehow feared people of my race—for the innumerable ancestors who merge within me. I wanted to prove to him that a yellow man could save his armies. Besides, I had to flee from Captain Madden. His hands and his voice could call at my door at any moment. I dressed silently, bade farewell to myself in the mirror, went downstairs, scrutinized the peaceful street and went out. The station was not far from my home, but I judged it wise to take a cab. I argued that in this way I ran less risk of being

---

[3] **Goethe:** Johann Wolfgang von Goethe (1749–1832), a German writer.

recognized; the fact is that in the deserted street I felt myself visible and vulnerable, infinitely so. I remember that I told the cab driver to stop a short distance before the main entrance. I got out with voluntary, almost painful slowness; I was going to the village of Ashgrove but I bought a ticket for a more distant station. The train left within a very few minutes, at eight-fifty. I hurried; the next one would leave at nine-thirty. There was hardly a soul on the platform. I went through the coaches; I remember a few farmers, a woman dressed in mourning, a young boy who was reading with fervor the *Annals* of Tacitus,[4] a wounded and happy soldier. The coaches jerked forward at last. A man whom I recognized ran in vain to the end of the platform. It was Captain Richard Madden. Shattered, trembling, I shrank into the far corner of the seat, away from the dreaded window.

From this broken state I passed into an almost abject felicity. I told myself that the duel had already begun and that I had won the first encounter by frustrating, even if for forty minutes, even if by a stroke of fate, the attack of my adversary. I argued that this slightest of victories foreshadowed a total victory. I argued (no less fallaciously) that my cowardly felicity proved that I was a man capable of carrying out the adventure successfully. From this weakness I took strength that did not abandon me. I foresee that man will resign himself each day to more atrocious undertakings; soon there will be no one but warriors and brigands; I give them this counsel: *The author of an atrocious undertaking ought to imagine that he has already accomplished it, ought to impose upon himself a future as irrevocable as the past.* Thus I proceeded as my eyes of a man already dead registered the elapsing of that day, which was perhaps the last, and the diffusion of the night. The train ran gently along, amid ash trees. It stopped, almost in the middle of the fields. No one announced the name of the station. "Ashgrove?" I asked a few lads on the platform. "Ashgrove," they replied. I got off.

A lamp enlightened the platform but the faces of the boys were in shadow. One questioned me, "Are you going to Dr. Stephen Albert's house?" Without waiting for my answer, another said, "The house is a long way from here, but you won't get lost if you take this road to the left and at every crossroads turn again to your left." I tossed them a coin (my last), descended a few stone steps and started down the solitary road. It went downhill, slowly. It was of elemental earth; overhead the branches were tangled; the low, full moon seemed to accompany me.

For an instant, I thought that Richard Madden in some way had penetrated my desperate plan. Very quickly, I understood that that was impossible. The instructions to turn always to the left reminded me that such was the common procedure for discovering the central point of certain labyrinths. I have some understanding of labyrinths: Not for nothing am I the great grandson of that Ts'ui Pên who was governor of Yunnan and who renounced worldly power in order to write a novel that might be even more populous than the *Hung Lu Meng*[5] and to construct a labyrinth

---

[4]**Tacitus:** Roman historian (55–117 C.E.).

[5]*Hung Lu Meng: The Dream of the Red Chamber,* also called *The Story of the Stone* (1791), a long, very famous Chinese novel. (See Book 4.)

in which all men would become lost. Thirteen years he dedicated to these heterogeneous tasks, but the hand of a stranger murdered him—and his novel was incoherent and no one found the labyrinth. Beneath English trees I meditated on that lost maze: I imagined it inviolate and perfect at the secret crest of a mountain; I imagined it erased by rice fields or beneath the water; I imagined it infinite, no longer composed of octagonal kiosks and returning paths, but of rivers and provinces and kingdoms . . . I thought of a labyrinth of labyrinths, of one sinuous spreading labyrinth that would encompass the past and the future and in some way involve the stars. Absorbed in these illusory images, I forgot my destiny of one pursued. I felt myself to be, for an unknown period of time, an abstract perceiver of the world. The vague, living countryside, the moon, the remains of the day worked on me, as well as the slope of the road which eliminated any possibility of weariness. The afternoon was intimate, infinite. The road descended and forked among the now confused meadows. A high-pitched, almost syllabic music approached and receded in the shifting of the wind, dimmed by leaves and distance. I thought that a man can be an enemy of other men, of the moments of other men, but not of a country: not of fireflies, words, gardens, streams of water, sunsets. Thus I arrived before a tall, rusty gate. Between the iron bars I made out a poplar grove and a pavilion. I understood suddenly two things, the first trivial, the second almost unbelievable: The music came from the pavilion, and the music was Chinese. For precisely that reason I had openly accepted it without paying it any heed. I do not remember whether there was a bell or whether I knocked with my hand. The sparkling of the music continued.

From the rear of the house within a lantern approached: a lantern that the trees sometimes striped and sometimes eclipsed, a paper lantern that had the form of a drum and the color of the moon. A tall man bore it. I didn't see his face, for the light blinded me. He opened the door and said slowly, in my own language: "I see that the pious Hsi P'êng persists in correcting my solitude. You no doubt wish to see the garden?"

I recognized the name of one of our consuls and I replied, disconcerted, "The garden?"

"The garden of forking paths."

Something stirred in my memory and I uttered with incomprehensible certainty, "The garden of my ancestor Ts'ui Pên."

"Your ancestor? Your illustrious ancestor? Come in."

The damp path zigzagged like those of my childhood. We came to a library of Eastern and Western books. I recognized bound in yellow silk several volumes of the Lost Encyclopedia, edited by the Third Emperor of the Luminous Dynasty[6] but never printed. The record on the phonograph revolved next to a bronze phoenix. I also recall a *famille rose*[7] vase and another, many centuries older, of that shade of blue which our craftsmen copied from the potters of Persia . . .

---

[6] **Third . . . Dynasty:** The Yung-lo emperor of the Ming dynasty who commissioned an extensive encyclopedia in the fifteenth century.

[7] *famille rose:* Pink family (French), referring to Chinese enamelware.

Stephen Albert observed me with a smile. He was, as I have said, very tall, sharp-featured, with gray eyes and a gray beard. He told me that he had been a missionary in Tientsin "before aspiring to become a Sinologist."

We sat down—I on a long, low divan, he with his back to the window and a tall circular clock. I calculated that my pursuer, Richard Madden, could not arrive for at least an hour. My irrevocable determination could wait.

"An astounding fate, that of Ts'ui Pên," Stephen Albert said. "Governor of his native province, learned in astronomy, in astrology, and in the tireless interpretation of the canonical books, chess player, famous poet and calligrapher—he abandoned all this in order to compose a book and a maze. He renounced the pleasures of both tyranny and justice, of his populous couch, of his banquets and even of erudition—all to close himself up for thirteen years in the Pavilion of the Limpid Solitude. When he died, his heirs found nothing save chaotic manuscripts. His family, as you may be aware, wished to condemn them to the fire; but his executor—a Taoist or Buddhist monk—insisted on their publication."

"We descendants of Ts'ui Pên," I replied, "continue to curse that monk. Their publication was senseless. The book is an indeterminate heap of contradictory drafts. I examined it once: In the third chapter the hero dies, in the fourth he is alive. As for the other undertaking of Ts'ui Pên, his labyrinth . . ."

"Here is Ts'ui Pên's labyrinth," he said, indicating a tall lacquered desk.

"An ivory labyrinth!" I exclaimed. "A minimum labyrinth."

"A labyrinth of symbols," he corrected. "An invisible labyrinth of time. To me, a barbarous Englishman, has been entrusted the revelation of this diaphanous mystery. After more than a hundred years, the details are irretrievable; but it is not hard to conjecture what happened. Ts'ui Pên must have said once: *I am withdrawing to write a book.* And another time: *I am withdrawing to construct a labyrinth.* Everyone imagined two works; to no one did it occur that the book and the maze were one and the same thing. The Pavilion of the Limpid Solitude stood in the center of a garden that was perhaps intricate; that circumstance could have suggested to the heirs a physical labyrinth. Ts'ui Pên died; no one in the vast territories that were his came upon the labyrinth; the confusion of the novel suggested to me that *it* was the maze. Two circumstances gave me the correct solution of the problem. One: the curious legend that Ts'ui Pên had planned to create a labyrinth which would be strictly infinite. The other: a fragment of a letter I discovered."

Albert rose. He turned his back on me for a moment; he opened a drawer of the black and gold desk. He faced me and in his hands he held a sheet of paper that had once been crimson, but was now pink and tenuous and cross-sectioned. The fame of Ts'ui Pên as a calligrapher had been justly won. I read, uncomprehendingly and with fervor, these words written with a minute brush by a man of my blood: *I leave to the various futures (not to all) my garden of forking paths.* Wordlessly, I returned the sheet. Albert continued:

"Before unearthing this letter, I had questioned myself about the ways in which a book can be infinite. I could think of nothing other than a cyclic volume, a circular one. A book whose last page was identical with the first, a book which had the possibility of continuing indefinitely. I remembered too that night which is at the middle of the Thousand and One Nights when Scheherezade (through a magical oversight of the copyist) begins to relate word for word the story of the Thousand and One Nights, establishing the risk of coming once again to the night when she must repeat it, and thus on to infinity. I imagined as well a Platonic, hereditary work, transmitted from father to son, in which each new individual adds a chapter or corrects with pious care the pages of his elders. These conjectures diverted me; but none seemed to correspond, not even remotely, to the contradictory chapters of Ts'ui Pên. In the midst of this perplexity, I received from Oxford the manuscript you have examined. I lingered, naturally, on the sentence: *I leave to the various futures (not to all) my garden of forking paths.* Almost instantly, I understood: 'the garden of forking paths' was the chaotic novel; the phrase 'the various futures (not to all)' suggested to me the forking in time, not in space. A broad rereading of the work confirmed the theory. In all fictional works, each time a man is confronted with several alternatives, he chooses one and eliminates the others; in the fiction of Ts'ui Pên, he chooses—simultaneously—all of them. *He creates,* in this way, diverse futures, diverse times which themselves also proliferate and fork. Here, then, is the explanation of the novel's contradictions. Fang, let us say, has a secret; a stranger calls at his door; Fang resolves to kill him. Naturally, there are several possible outcomes: Fang can kill the intruder, the intruder can kill Fang, they both can escape, they both can die, and so forth. In the work of Ts'ui Pên, all possible outcomes occur; each one is the point of departure for other forkings. Sometimes, the paths of this labyrinth converge: For example, you arrive at this house, but in one of the possible pasts you are my enemy, in another, my friend. If you will resign yourself to my incurable pronunciation, we shall read a few pages."

His face, within the vivid circle of the lamplight, was unquestionably that of an old man, but with something unalterable about it, even immortal. He read with slow precision two versions of the same epic chapter. In the first, an army marches to a battle across a lonely mountain; the horror of the rocks and shadows makes the men undervalue their lives and they gain an easy victory. In the second, the same army traverses a palace where a great festival is taking place; the resplendent battle seems to them a continuation of the celebration and they win the victory. I listened with proper veneration to these ancient narratives, perhaps less admirable in themselves than the fact that they had been created by my blood and were being restored to me by a man of a remote empire, in the course of a desperate adventure, on a Western isle. I remember the last words, repeated in each version like a secret commandment: *Thus fought the heroes, tranquil their admirable hearts, violent their swords, resigned to kill and to die.*

From that moment on, I felt about me and within my dark body an invisible, intangible swarming. Not the swarming of the divergent, parallel, and finally coalescent armies, but a more inaccessible, more intimate agitation that they in some manner prefigured. Stephen Albert continued:

"I don't believe that your illustrious ancestor played idly with these variations. I don't consider it credible that he would sacrifice thirteen years to the infinite execution of a rhetorical experiment. In your country, the novel is a subsidiary form of literature; in Ts'ui Pên's time it was a despicable form. Ts'ui Pên was a brilliant novelist, but he was also a man of letters who doubtless did not consider himself a mere novelist. The testimony of his contemporaries proclaims—and his life fully confirms—his metaphysical and mystical interests. Philosophic controversy usurps a good part of the novel. I know that of all problems, none disturbed him so greatly nor worked upon him so much as the abysmal problem of time. Now then, the latter is the only problem that does not figure in the pages of the *Garden*. He does not even use the word that signifies *time*. How do you explain this voluntary omission?"

I proposed several solutions—all unsatisfactory. We discussed them. Finally, Stephen Albert said to me:

"In a riddle whose answer is chess, what is the only prohibited word?"

I thought a moment and replied, "The word *chess*."

"Precisely," said Albert. "*The Garden of Forking Paths* is an enormous riddle, or parable, whose theme is time; this recondite cause prohibits its mention. To omit a word always, to resort to inept metaphors and obvious periphrases, is perhaps the most emphatic way of stressing it. That is the tortuous method preferred, in each of the meanderings of his indefatigable novel, by the oblique Ts'ui Pên. I have compared hundreds of manuscripts, I have corrected the errors that the negligence of the copyists has introduced, I have guessed the plan of this chaos, I have reestablished—I believe I have reestablished—the primordial organization, I have translated the entire work: It is clear to me that not once does he employ the word 'time.' The explanation is obvious: *The Garden of Forking Paths* is an incomplete, but not false, image of the universe as Ts'ui Pên conceived it. In contrast to Newton and Schopenhauer,[8] your ancestor did not believe in a uniform, absolute time. He believed in an infinite series of times, in a growing, dizzying net of divergent, convergent, and parallel times. This network of times which approached one another, forked, broke off, or were unaware of one another for centuries, embraces *all* possibilities of time. We do not exist in the majority of these times; in some you exist, and not I; in others I, and not you; in others, both of us. In the present one, which a favorable fate has granted me, you have arrived at my house; in another, while crossing the garden, you found me dead; in still another, I utter these same words, but I am a mistake, a ghost."

"In every one," I pronounced, not without a tremble to my voice, "I am grateful to you and revere you for your re-creation of the garden of Ts'ui Pên."

"Not in all," he murmured with a smile. "Time forks perpetually toward innumerable futures. In one of them I am your enemy."

Once again I felt the swarming sensation of which I have spoken. It seemed to me that the humid garden that surrounded the house was infinitely saturated with invisible persons. Those persons were Albert and I, secret, busy, and multiform in other dimensions of time. I raised my eyes and the tenuous nightmare dissolved. In the yellow and black garden there was only one man; but this man was as strong as a statue . . . this man was approaching along the path and he was Captain Richard Madden.

---

[8] **Newton and Schopenhauer:** Isaac Newton (1642–1727), an English mathematician; Arthur Schopenhauer (1788–1860), a German philosopher.

"The future already exists," I replied, "but I am your friend. Could I see the letter again?"

Albert rose. Standing tall, he opened the drawer of the tall desk; for the moment his back was to me. I had readied the revolver. I fired with extreme caution. Albert fell uncomplainingly, immediately. I swear his death was instantaneous—a lightning stroke.

The rest is unreal, insignificant. Madden broke in, arrested me. I have been condemned to the gallows. I have won out abominably; I have communicated to Berlin the secret name of the city they must attack. They bombed it yesterday; I read it in the same papers that offered to England the mystery of the learned Sinologist Stephen Albert who was murdered by a stranger, one Yu Tsun. The Chief had deciphered this mystery. He knew my problem was to indicate (through the uproar of the war) the city called Albert, and that I had found no other means to do so than to kill a man of that name. He does not know (no one can know) my innumerable contrition and weariness.

～ KAWABATA YASUNARI
B. JAPAN, 1899–1972

One of Japan's most highly praised yet also most difficult modern writers, Kawabata Yasunari has found an enthusiastic audience in the West as well as in Japan. In 1968 he was the first Japanese writer to win the Nobel Prize in literature. In addition to short stories, novels, and literature for children, Kawabata has written major critical works on the novel and numerous essays and reviews. In his fiction Kawabata is a master of subtle imagery, writing in a hauntingly lyrical and delicate prose that lends itself readily to the short story or novella and for which he has been highly praised. The poetic density of his writing is sustained in his novels, such as *Snow Country* and *The Master of Go,* for which he is primarily known in the West.

Kawabata Yasunari
The Japanese writer and Nobel prize–winner in Stockholm, Sweden, in the late 1960s. (© Bettmann / CORBIS)

A Lonely Child.   Kawabata Yasunari was born in Osaka on June 11, 1899, the son of a physician who died when Kawabata was only two years old, the first of a series of untimely deaths that left the boy without a family by age fourteen. *Diary of a Sixteen-Year-Old,* published in 1925 but recounting twelve days in May 1914, describes his experience attending the slow and painful death of his demanding grandfather, with whom he had lived since his grandmother died nine years before. He had lost his mother when he was three and his sister when he was nine. The loneliness and longing of many of his stories are no doubt linked to these traumatic events; of his childhood, Kawabata wrote,

> Perhaps it is because I was an orphan with nowhere I could call home that I have never lost my taste for melancholic wanderings. I am always dreaming, though I never manage to forget myself in any dream. I am awake even as I dream but I cover this up with my taste for back-streets.

Despite having to take care of his grandfather, Kawabata completed school in Osaka, then went on to Tokyo for the equivalent of high school and enrolled in Tokyo Imperial University. Already steeped in the Japanese classics, Kawabata studied Japanese literature; he published his first story, heavily influenced by European MODERNISM, in 1921 and became a leading figure in the literary avant-garde while serving on the staff of the journal *Bungei Shunju.* In 1927, the year after his graduation, Kawabata published his first novel, the partly autobiographical *The Izu Dancer* (*Izu no Odoriko*). At the time of publishing this story about a young student who falls in love with a fourteen-year-old daughter of traveling entertainers, Kawabata had already attracted the attention of the literary world with his short stories; but this novel—a novella—was his first popular success and clinched his literary reputation. With another novelist, Riichi Yokomitsu, Kawabata later founded *The Literary Age,* a magazine associated with the NEO-SENSUALIST movement,[1] or *Shin-kankaku-ha,* an avant-garde group that preferred aesthetic values and emotional delicacy in literature to the scientific REALISM and NATURALISM that had dominated the Japanese literary scene in the 1920s. Groundbreaking in their use of free association and STREAM OF CONSCIOUSNESS, Kawabata's early novels offer in theme and technique an intriguing blend of traditional Japanese fiction and European modernism, filtered through the transforming art of a self-conscious and delicate craftsman. Unlike such cosmopolitan artists as fellow writer Mishima Yukio and filmmaker Kurosawa Akira (1925–1970), Kawabata soon minimized the Western elements of his work, but one senses even in his later fiction the influence of his neo-Sensualist days and his early experiments in stream-of-consciousness technique, SURREALISM, CUBISM, and DADAISM. His most modernist work is the unfinished *Crystal Fantasies* (*Suisho Genso,* 1931), written during a short period of fascination with James Joyce's *Ulysses,* which he read first in Japanese and then in English.

Spirit of Sorrow.   Throughout the thirties Kawabata published short stories, bringing out a collection titled *Of Birds and Beasts* (*Kinjū*) in 1933 and a partly completed novel, *Snow Country* (*Yukiguni*), in 1937 (com-

---

[1] **neo-Sensualist movement:** Also known as the New Sensibilities or New Perceptionist school; founded by Kawabata and other avant-garde writers, including Riichi Yokomitsu (1898–1947), and headquartered at the University of Tokyo in the 1920s. In 1924 the group founded a magazine called *The Literary Age.* Influenced by European writers as well as by Japanese poetic traditions and *Nō* drama, the neo-Sensualists sought to break with the confessional style of Realist and Naturalist writers and aimed for a more purely aesthetic, nonlinear style of fiction writing.

pleted in 1947). *Snow Country,* his most famous novel, like *The Izu Dancer,* conveys a sadness and loneliness tinged with a lyrical eroticism that characterizes Kawabata's work as a whole. Negotiating the boundaries of EROS and THANATOS, love and death, the motif of refined melancholy goes back to such Japanese classics as *The Tale of Genji* (see Book 2), which Kawabata read during the war. After Japan's defeat, Kawabata wrote, "Since Japan has surrendered the only thing left for me to do is to return to the traditional sorrow of spirit of the Japanese people." That sorrow of spirit is the *mono-no-aware,* a delicate sense of the fleetingness of life and love. *Snow Country* tells the story of Shimamura, a wealthy man from Tokyo, and Komako, an aging geisha; its episodic structure, its scenes of delicate encounter, and its mood are reminiscent of the structure and sensibility of *Genji.*

In his postwar novel *Thousand Cranes* (*Sembazuru,* 1949), Kawabata writes about his beloved tea ceremony (he was a collector of items used in the ancient tea ceremonies), which, despite his stated intentions, becomes an elaborate metaphor for the pursuit of beauty in life. Two other postwar novels, *The Master of Go* (*Meijin,* 1954) and *The Lake* (*Mizuumi,* 1954), also concern the pursuit of beauty. In the latter, that pursuit takes on a somewhat bizarre form in the character of a retired teacher who compulsively and surreptitiously spies on beautiful women. This kind of eroticism, bordering on the perverse, appears again in *House of the Sleeping Beauties* (*Nemureru bijo,* 1961), in which the protagonist, Eguchi, an old man, spends the night in a secret establishment that caters to his need to sleep with beautiful young girls, who are drugged for the purpose. His friend and fellow novelist Mishima called this story an "esoteric masterpiece," a story that "is dominated not by openness and clarity but by a strangling tightness." The reader of this story, Mishima writes, "knows with the greatest immediacy the terror of lust urged on by the approach of death." Rather than a tale of sexual perversion, however, Kawabata's story is an evocation of a tragic sense of the gap between the elderly man's proximity to death, his decrepitude and ugliness, and the vitality and beauty of the young women. One critic has suggested that Kawabata is a master at "dredging . . . the sexual depths" of human experience and that the lyrical quality of his work, along with its emphasis on the larger issues of life's transience and melancholy, rescues the novels from any misguided charges of prurience or pornography. Indeed, in these works Kawabata captures the essence of the "FLOATING WORLD," the realm of the senses that ground us in life and fill us with regret at its temporality. Another work of the 1950s, *The Sound of the Mountain* (*Yama no Oto,* 1954), which some have called Kawabata's greatest achievement, also focuses on an elderly man's tragic awareness of his mortality. In associating beauty with melancholy, Kawabata is reminiscent of the English poet John Keats (1795–1821); the hauntingly lyrical quality of Kawabata's short stories and novels, their eroticism and their obscurity, invite other comparisons to European ROMANTICISM.

International Acclaim.   From the 1920s through the 1960s he published some 140 short short stories, or "stories that fit in the palm of the hand"

www For links to more information about Kawabata, quizzes on his work, and for information about the culture and context of Japan in the twentieth century, see *World Literature Online* at bedfordstmartins .com/worldlit.

(*tanagokor no shosetsu*), short fiction, critical essays, and autobiographical works. Many of these were collected in edited editions, but relatively few have been translated into English. Among Kawabata's later works translated into English are *Beauty and Sadness* (*Utsukushisa to kanashimi to,* 1965); his Nobel Prize acceptance speech, *Japan the Beautiful and Myself* (*Utsukushii Nihon no watakushi,* 1969); and *The Existence and Discovery of Beauty* (*Bi no sonzai to hakken,* 1969).

In 1948 Kawabata became president of the Japanese P.E.N. club and was highly regarded and rewarded for his work. In 1937 he had won the *Bungei Konwa Kai* prize, and in 1952 he won the *Geijutsuin-sho* literary prize and an award from the Japanese Academy of Arts. In 1961 he won the *Bunka Kunsho* (Cultural Decoration), Japan's most distinguished award, for *The Old Capital* (*Koto,* 1961), and in that same year *House of the Sleeping Beauties* won the Mainichi Cultural Prize. In the sixties Kawabata traveled through Europe and the United States, receiving the Nobel Prize in literature in 1968. In 1971 he made a rare move by actively entering into politics as a supporter of a conservative candidate for governor of Tokyo. For unknown reasons, he committed suicide in his studio in April 1972, two years after the suicide of his friend Mishima, over whose funeral ceremonies Kawabata had presided.

"The Moon on the Water."   Through its theme of hopeless longing, its subtle evocation of the beautiful amidst the most melancholic conditions, and its lyrical language and poetic imagery, this story ("Suigetsu," 1953) captures the essence of Kawabata. The love that can never be grasped, that seems to fly on the wing, like Kyōko's love for her dying husband, is shown here to be more powerful and pure than that which she can bestow on her second husband. Moreover, Kawabata shows the inseparability of love from melancholy, youth from age, and desire from death, as the first husband who longs to watch his beautiful wife in the garden must see his own ghastly face in the mirror he uses to watch her. Moreover, there is a tragic loneliness and detachment to voyeuristically taking in the world through a mirror—the object of desire being a mere reflection, or simulacrum, of the palpable world Kyōko experiences. Yet even Kyōko recognizes "the richness of the world in the mirror," which becomes a focal point of her conversation with her husband and seems nearly to displace her world as a primary reality. Like a work of art, the world in the mirror takes on a life of its own, a life that is somehow purer, more beautiful, than the actual world it reflects. Kawabata has created, Mishima says of "The Moon on the Water," a "decadent literature which has a perfect formal beauty and which has a fragrance reminiscent of the rotting smell of overripe fruit." For beauty, and even life, finds its most intense expression at the moment it begins to give way to decrepitude and death. In Kawabata's fiction the dying man or woman has the greatest appreciation of beauty, here represented by the purity of the intangible world in the mirror and by the dying man's longing as mediated through the moon's image in the pool reflected in his mirror. It is that reflection of a reflection that Kyōko keeps in her heart after her husband's death.

"Snow."   From the beginning of his career, Kawabata wrote what he called "palm-of-the-hand stories," short short stories such as "Snow." Haiku-like in their impressionistic brevity, they show Kawabata's mastery of creating characters and atmosphere in spare and precise but powerfully suggestive prose. Like a miniature, "Snow" is a synthesis of many important themes in Kawabata's fiction — the need for solitude, the pursuit of beauty, the escape into imagination or imaginative works, and hope. "Snow" also is a good example of Kawabata's sensitive depiction of the natural world, whether real or, in the case of the billowy "peony snowflakes" falling on the mountain lake in the story, imagined.

■ CONNECTIONS

Kate Chopin, "The Story of an Hour" (Book 5). Kawabata was influenced by the modernist conception of stream of consciousness, by surrealism, and by Buddhism. Linking their characters' moods to their settings, "The Moon on the Water" and "Snow" offer striking psychological profiles of their protagonists. Chopin's "The Story of an Hour" similarly presents depth of feeling with great economy, using setting to reflect the main character's inner world. How do Chopin's and Kawabata's techniques reveal interiority through external description?

James Joyce, "The Dead," p. 372. Critics have praised Kawabata's ability to capture states of mind and to create mood by means of scrupulous detail and poetic imagery; critics praise the same skills in Joyce. In *The Dead,* especially in the closing paragraphs, Joyce infuses snow with symbolic value in a passage that culminates in a vision of transcendent interconnectedness linking past and present. In Kawabata's short short story, the snow also accrues symbolic weight and is affiliated with past experiences that relieve the work-weary Sankichi. Despite their different cultures, both writers seem to find similar resonances in snow. In what ways are Sankichi and Gabriel similar? How does each character make use of the snow psychologically?

■ FURTHER RESEARCH

Criticism

Keene, Donald. *Dawn to the West.* 1984.

Miyoshi, Masao. *Accomplices of Silence: The Modern Japanese Novel.* 1974.

Petersen, Gwen Boardman. *The Moon in the Water: Understanding Tanizaki, Kawabata, and Mishima.* 1979.

Pollack, David. *Reading against Culture: Ideology and Narrative in the Japanese Novel.* 1992.

Rimer, J. Thomas. *Modern Japanese Fiction and Its Traditions: An Introduction.* 1978.

❧ The Moon on the Water

Translated by George Saitō

It occurred to Kyōko one day to let her husband, in bed upstairs, see her vegetable garden by reflecting it in her hand mirror. To one who had been so long confined, this opened a new life. The hand mirror was part of a set in Kyōko's trousseau. The mirror stand was not very big. It was made of mulberry wood, as was the frame of the mirror itself. It was the hand mirror that still reminded her of the bashfulness of her early married years when, as she was looking into it at the reflection of her back hair in the stand mirror, her sleeve would slip and expose her elbow.

When she came from the bath, her husband seemed to enjoy reflecting the nape of her neck from all angles in the hand mirror. Taking the mirror from her, he would say: "How clumsy you are! Here, let me hold it." Maybe he found something new in the mirror. It was not that Kyōko was clumsy, but that she became nervous at being looked at from behind.

Not enough time had passed for the color of the mulberry-wood frame to change. It lay in a drawer. War came, followed by flight from the city and her husband's becoming seriously ill; by the time it first occurred to Kyōko to have her husband see the garden through the mirror, its surface had become cloudy and the rim had been smeared with face powder and dirt. Since it still reflected well enough, Kyōko did not worry about this cloudiness—indeed she scarcely noticed it. Her husband, however, would not let the mirror go from his bedside and polished it and its frame in his idleness with the peculiar nervousness of an invalid. Kyōko sometimes imagined that tuberculosis germs had found their way into the imperceptible cracks in the frame. After she had combed her husband's hair with a little camellia oil, he sometimes ran the palm of his hand through his hair and then rubbed the mirror. The wood of the mirror stand remained dull, but that of the mirror grew lustrous.

When Kyōko married again, she took the same mirror stand with her. The hand mirror, however, had been buried in the coffin of her dead husband. A hand mirror with a carved design had now taken its place. She never told her second husband about this.

"The Moon on the Water." This story, published in 1953, captures the essence of Kawabata in its theme of longing, its sensuous evocation of pathos and beauty, and its lyrical syntax and imagery. Fleeting love, like that of Kyōko for her dying husband, is more powerful and pure than the love she can bestow on her second husband, suggesting that beauty finds its most intense and pure expression at the moment it begins to slip out of reach. In Kawabata's fiction, as in this story, the dying man or woman has perhaps the greatest appreciation of beauty, here represented by an intangible reflection in a mirror and by a dying man's longing as mediated through the moon's image in a pool, itself reflected in the mirror. That reflection of a reflection remains in Kyōko's heart after her husband's death. By way of poetic imagery and subtle evocation, this story succeeds in expressing the state of mind of both its characters, much like the approach seen in the modernist fiction of European writers James Joyce and Virginia Woolf.

All notes are the editors'.

According to custom, the hands of her dead husband had been clasped and his fingers crossed, so that it was impossible to make them hold the hand mirror after he had been put into the coffin. She laid the mirror on his chest.

"Your chest hurt you so. Even this must be heavy."

Kyōko moved the mirror down to his stomach. Because she thought of the important role that the mirror had played in their marital life, Kyōko had first laid it on his chest. She wanted to keep this little act as much as possible from the eyes even of her husband's family. She had piled white chrysanthemums on the mirror. No one had noticed it. When the ashes were being gathered after the cremation, people noticed the glass which had been melted into a shapeless mass, partly sooty and partly yellowish. Someone said: "It's glass. What is it, I wonder?" She had in fact placed a still smaller mirror on the hand mirror. It was the sort of mirror usually carried in a toilet case, a long, narrow, double-faced mirror. Kyōko had dreamed of using it on her honeymoon trip. The war had made it impossible for them to go on a honeymoon. During her husband's lifetime she never was able to use it on a trip.

With her second husband, however, she went on a honeymoon. Since her leather toilet case was now very musty, she bought a new one—with a mirror in it too.

On the very first day of their trip, her husband touched Kyōko and said: "You are like a little girl. Poor thing!" His tone was not in the least sarcastic. Rather it suggested unexpected joy. Possibly it was good for him that Kyōko was like a little girl. At this remark, Kyōko was assailed by an intense sorrow. Her eyes filled with tears and she shrank away. He might have taken that to be girlish too.

Kyōko did not know whether she had wept for her own sake or for the sake of her dead husband. Nor was it possible to know. The moment this idea came to her, she felt very sorry for her second husband and thought she had to be coquettish.

"Am I so different?" No sooner had she spoken than she felt very awkward, and shyness came over her.

He looked satisfied and said: "You never had a child . . ."

His remark pierced her heart. Before a male force other than her former husband Kyōko felt humiliated. She was being made sport of.

"But it was like looking after a child all the time."

This was all she said by way of protest. It was as if her first husband, who had died after a long illness, had been a child inside her. But if he was to die in any case, what good had her continence done?

"I've only seen Mori from the train window." Her second husband drew her to him as he mentioned the name of her home town. "From its name,[1] it sounds like a pretty town in the woods. How long did you live there?"

"Until I graduated from high school. Then I was drafted to work in a munitions factory in Sanjō."

"Is Sanjō near, then? I've heard a great deal about Sanjō beauties. I see why you're so beautiful."

"No, I'm not." Kyōko brought her hand to her throat.

---

[1] **its name:** *Mori* means "grove."

"Your hands are beautiful, and I thought your body should be beautiful too."

"Oh no."

Finding her hands in the way, Kyōko quietly drew them back.

"I'm sure I'd have married you even if you had had a child. I could have adopted the child and looked after it. A girl would have been better," he whispered in Kyōko's ear. Maybe it was because he had a boy, but his remark seemed odd even as an expression of love. Possibly he had planned the long, ten-day honeymoon so that she would not have to face the stepson quite so soon.

Her husband had a toilet case for traveling, made of what seemed to be good leather. Kyōko's did not compare with it. His was large and strong, but it was not new. Maybe because he often traveled or because he took good care of it, the case had a mellow luster. Kyōko thought of the old case, never used, which she had left to mildew. Only its small mirror had been used by her first husband, and she had sent it with him in death.

The small glass had melted into the hand mirror, so that no one except Kyōko could tell that they had been separate before. Since Kyōko had not said that the curious mass had been mirrors, her relatives had no way of knowing.

Kyōko felt as if the numerous worlds reflected in the two mirrors had vanished in the fire. She felt the same kind of loss when her husband's body was reduced to ashes. It had been with the hand mirror that came with the mirror stand that Kyōko first reflected the vegetable garden. Her husband always kept that mirror beside his pillow. Even the hand mirror seemed to be too heavy for the invalid, and Kyōko, worried about his arms and shoulders, gave him a lighter and smaller one.

It was not only Kyōko's vegetable garden that her husband had observed through the two mirrors. He had seen the sky, clouds, snow, distant mountains, and nearby woods. He had seen the moon. He had seen wildflowers, and birds of passage had made their way through the mirror. Men walked down the road in the mirror and children played in the garden.

Kyōko was amazed at the richness of the world in the mirror. A mirror which had until then been regarded only as a toilet article, a hand mirror which had served only to show the back of one's neck, had created for the invalid a new life. Kyōko used to sit beside his bed and talk about the world in the mirror. They looked into it together. In the course of time it became impossible for Kyōko to distinguish between the world that she saw directly and the world in the mirror. Two separate worlds came to exist. A new world was created in the mirror and it came to seem like the real world.

"The sky shines silver in the mirror," Kyōko said. Looking up through the window, she added: "When the sky itself is grayish." The sky in the mirror lacked the leaden and heavy quality of the actual sky. It was shining.

"Is it because you are always polishing the mirror?"

Though he was lying down, her husband could see the sky by turning his head.

"Yes, it's a dull gray. But the color of the sky is not necessarily the same to dogs' eyes and sparrows' eyes as it is to human eyes. You can't tell which eyes see the real color."

"What we see in the mirror — is that what the mirror eye sees?"

Kyōko wanted to call it the eye of their love. The trees in the mirror were a fresher green than real trees, and the lilies a purer white.

"This is the print of your thumb, Kyōko. Your right thumb."

He pointed to the edge of the mirror. Kyōko was somehow startled. She breathed on the mirror and erased the fingerprint.

"That's all right, Kyōko. Your fingerprint stayed on the mirror when you first showed me the vegetable garden."

"I didn't notice it."

"You may not have noticed it. Thanks to this mirror, I've memorized the prints of your thumbs and index fingers. Only an invalid could memorize his wife's fingerprints."

Her husband had done almost nothing but lie in bed since their marriage. He had not gone to war. Toward the end of the war he had been drafted, but he fell ill after several days of labor at an airfield and came home at the end of the war. Since he was unable to walk, Kyōko went with his elder brother to meet him. After her husband had been drafted, she stayed with her parents. They had left the city to avoid the bombings. Their household goods had long since been sent away. As the house where their married life began had been burned down, they had rented a room in the home of a friend of Kyōko's. From there her husband commuted to his office. A month in their honeymoon house and two months at the house of a friend—that was all the time Kyōko spent with her husband before he fell ill.

It was then decided that her husband should rent a small house in the mountains and convalesce there. Other families had been in the house, also fugitives from the city, but they had gone back to Tokyo after the war ended, and Kyōko took over their vegetable garden. It was only some six yards square, a clearing in the weeds. They could easily have bought vegetables, but Kyōko worked in the garden. She became interested in vegetables grown by her own hand. It was not that she wanted to stay away from her sick husband, but such things as sewing and knitting made her gloomy. Even though she thought of him always, she had brighter hopes when she was out in the garden. There she could indulge her love for her husband. As for reading, it was all she could do to read aloud at his bedside. Then Kyōko thought that by working in the garden she might regain that part of herself which it seemed she was losing in the fatigue of the long nursing.

It was in the middle of September that they moved to the mountains. The summer visitors had almost all gone and a long spell of early autumn rains came, chilly and damp.

One afternoon the sun came out to the clear song of a bird. When she went into the garden, she found the green vegetables shining. She was enraptured by the rosy clouds on the mountain tops. Startled by her husband's voice calling her, she hurried upstairs, her hands covered with mud, and found him breathing painfully.

"I called and called. Couldn't you hear me?"

"I'm sorry. I couldn't."

"Stop working in the garden. I'd be dead in no time if I had to keep calling you like that. In the first place, I can't see where you are and what you're doing."

"I was in the garden. But I'll stop."

He was calmer.

"Did you hear the lark?"

That was all he had wanted to tell her. The lark sang in the nearby woods again. The woods were clear against the evening glow. Thus Kyōko learned to know the song of the lark.

"A bell will help you, won't it? How about having something you can throw until I get a bell for you?"

"Shall I throw a cup from here? That would be fun."

It was settled that Kyōko might continue her gardening; but it was after spring had come to end the long, harsh mountain winter that Kyōko thought of showing him the garden in the mirror.

The single mirror gave him inexhaustible joy, as if a lost world of fresh green had come back. It was impossible for him to see the worms she picked from the vegetables. She had to come upstairs to show him. "I can see the earthworms from here, though," he used to say as he watched her digging in the earth.

When the sun was shining into the house, Kyōko sometimes noticed a light and, looking up, discovered that her husband was reflecting the sun in the mirror. He insisted that Kyōko remake the dark-blue kimono he had used during his student days into pantaloons for herself. He seemed to enjoy the sight of Kyōko in the mirror as she worked in the garden, wearing the dark blue with its white splashes.

Kyōko worked in the garden half-conscious and half-unconscious of the fact that she was being seen. Her heart warmed to see how different her feelings were now from the very early days of her marriage. Then she had blushed even at showing her elbow when she held the smaller glass behind her head. It was, however, only when she remarried that she started making up as she pleased, released from the long years of nursing and the mourning that had followed. She saw that she was becoming remarkably beautiful. It now seemed that her husband had really meant it when he said that her body was beautiful.

Kyōko was no longer ashamed of her reflection in the mirror—after she had had a bath, for instance. She had discovered her own beauty. But she had not lost that unique feeling that her former husband had planted in her toward the beauty in the mirror. She did not doubt the beauty she was in the mirror. Quite the reverse: She could not doubt the reality of that other world. But between her skin as she saw it and her skin as reflected in the mirror she could not find the difference that she had found between that leaden sky and the silver sky in the mirror. It may not have been only the difference in distance. Maybe the longing of her first husband confined to his bed had acted upon her. But then, there was now no way of knowing how beautiful she had looked to him in the mirror as she worked in the garden. Even before his death, Kyōko herself had not been able to tell.

Kyōko thought of, indeed longed for, the image of herself working in the garden, seen through the mirror in her husband's hand, and for the white of the lilies, the crowd of village children playing in the field, and the morning sun rising above the far-off snowy mountains—for that separate world she had shared with him. For the sake of her present husband, Kyōko suppressed this feeling, which seemed about to become an almost physical yearning, and tried to take it for something like a distant view of the celestial world.

One morning in May, Kyōko heard the singing of wild birds over the radio. It was a broadcast from a mountain near the heights where she had stayed with her first husband until his death. As had become her custom, after seeing her present husband off to work, Kyōko took the hand mirror from the drawer of the stand and reflected the clear sky. Then she gazed at her face in the mirror. She was astonished by a new discovery. She could not see her own face unless she reflected it in the mirror. One could not see one's own face. One felt one's own face, wondering if the face in the mirror was one's actual face. Kyōko was lost in thought for some time. Why had God created man's face so that he might not see it himself?

"Suppose you could see your own face, would you lose your mind? Would you become incapable of acting?"

Most probably man had evolved in such a way that he could not see his own face. Maybe dragonflies and praying mantises could see their own faces.

But then perhaps one's own face was for others to see. Did it not resemble love? As she was putting the hand mirror back in the drawer, Kyōko could not even now help noticing the odd combination of carved design and mulberry. Since the former mirror had burned with her first husband, the mirror stand might well be compared to a widow. But the hand mirror had had its advantages and disadvantages. Her husband was constantly seeing his face in it. Perhaps it was more like seeing death itself. If his death was a psychological suicide by means of a mirror, then Kyōko was the psychological murderer. Kyōko had once thought of the disadvantages of the mirror, and tried to take it from him. But he would not let her.

"Do you intend to have me see nothing? As long as I live, I want to keep loving something I can see," her husband said. He would have sacrificed his life to keep the world in the mirror. After heavy rains they would gaze at the moon through the mirror, the reflection of the moon from the pool in the garden. A moon which could hardly be called even the reflection of a reflection still lingered in Kyōko's heart.

∾ Snow

Translated by Lane Dunlop and J. Martin Holman

For the past four or five years, Noda Sankichi had secluded himself at a Tokyo high-rise hotel from the evening of New Year's Day until the morning of the third. Although the hotel had an imposing name, Sankichi's name for it was the Dream Hotel.

"Snow." One of Kawabata's many very short "palm-of-the-hand" stories, this piece condenses Kawabata's characteristic exploration of themes such as solitude, beauty, the imagination, and hope. It also presents a fine example of Kawabata's sensitivity to nature and his subtle evocation of atmosphere and mood.

A note on the translation: The translation is by Lane Dunlop and J. Martin Holman, published in North Point Press, 1988.

"Father has gone to the Dream Hotel," his son or his daughter would say to New Year's visitors who came to the house. The visitors would take it as a joke meant to conceal Sankichi's whereabouts.

"That's a nice place. He must be having a good New Year's there." Some of them even said this.

However, not even Sankichi's family knew that Sankichi actually did have dreams at the Dream Hotel.

The room at the hotel was the same every year. It was the Snow Room. Again, only Sankichi knew that he always called whatever room it was the Snow Room.

When he'd arrive at the hotel, Sankichi would draw the curtains of the room, immediately get into bed, and close his eyes. For two or three hours, he would lie there quietly. It was true that he was seeking rest from the irritation and fatigue of a busy, agitated year, but, even when the fretful tiredness had gone away, a deeper weariness welled up and spread out within him. Understanding this, Sankichi waited for his weariness to reach its fullest extent. When he had been pulled down to the bottom of the weariness, his head gone numb with it, then the dream would begin to rise toward the surface.

In the darkness behind his eyelids, tiny millet-sized grains of light would begin to dance and flow. The grains were of a pale, golden, transparent hue. As their gold chilled to a faint whiteness, they turned into snowflakes, all flowing in the same direction and at the same slow speed. They were powdery flakes, falling in the distance.

"This New Year's, too, the snow has come."

With this thought, the snow would belong to Sankichi. It was falling in Sankichi's heart.

In the darkness of his closed eyes, the snow came nearer. Falling thick and fast, it changed into peony snowflakes. The big, petal-like snowflakes fell more slowly than the powdery snowflakes. Sankichi was enfolded in the silent, peaceful blizzard.

It was all right to open his eyes now.

When Sankichi opened his eyes, the wall of the room had become a snowscape. What he'd seen behind his eyelids was merely the snow falling; what he saw on the wall was the landscape in which the snow had fallen.

In a large field in which stood only five or six bare-branched trees, peony snowflakes were falling. As the snow drifted higher, neither earth nor grass was visible. There were no houses, no sign of a human being. It was a lonely scene, and yet Sankichi, in his electrically heated bed, did not feel the coldness of the snowy field. But the snowy landscape was all there was. Sankichi himself was not there.

"Where shall I go? Whom shall I call?" Although the thought came to him, it was not his own. It was the voice of the snow.

The snowy plain, in which nothing moved but falling snow, presently, of its own accord, flowed away, shifting to the scenery of a mountain gorge. On the far side, the mountain towered up. A stream wound along its base. Although the narrow stream seemed choked with snow, it was flowing without a ripple. A mass of snow that had fallen in from the bank was floating along. Halted by a boulder that jutted out into the current, it melted into the water.

The boulder was a huge mass of amethyst quartz.

At the top of the quartz boulder, Sankichi's father appeared. His father was holding the three- or four-year-old Sankichi in his arms.

"Father, it's dangerous—standing on that sort of sharp, jagged rock. The soles of your feet must hurt." From the bed, the fifty-four-year-old Sankichi spoke to his father in the snowy landscape.

The crown of the boulder was a cluster of pointed quartz crystals that looked as if they could pierce his father's feet. At Sankichi's words, his father shifted his weight for a better footing. As he did so, the snow atop the boulder crumbled and fell into the stream. Perhaps frightened by that, Sankichi's father held him tighter.

"It's strange that this narrow little stream isn't buried under so much snow," his father said.

There was snow on his father's head and shoulders and on his arms, which held Sankichi.

The snow scene on the wall was shifting, moving upstream. A lake came into view. It was a small lake, in the depths of the mountains, but, as the source of such a narrow little stream, it seemed too large. The white peony snowflakes, the farther away they were, took on a tinge of gray. Heavy clouds hovered in the distance. The mountains on the far shore were indistinct.

Sankichi gazed for a while at the steadily falling peony snowflakes as they melted into the lake's surface. On the mountains of the far shore, something was moving. It was coming nearer through the gray sky. It was a flock of birds. They had great snow-colored wings. As if the snow itself had become their wings, even when they flew past Sankichi's eyes, there was no sound of wingbeats. Were their wings extended in silent, slow waves? Was the falling snow bearing up the birds?

When he tried to count the birds, there were seven, there were eleven . . . He lost count. But Sankichi felt it as a pleasure rather than as a puzzlement.

"What birds are those? What are those wings?"

"We're not birds. Don't you see who's riding on the wings?" A voice answered from one of the snowbirds.

"Ah, I see," Sankichi said.

Riding on the birds through the falling snow, all the women who had loved Sankichi had come to him. Which of them had spoken first?

In his dream, Sankichi could freely call up those who had loved him in the past.

From the evening of New Year's Day to the morning of the third, in the Snow Room of the Dream Hotel, drawing the curtains, having his meals brought to the room, never leaving his bed, Sankichi communed with those souls.

❧ PABLO NERUDA

B. CHILE, 1904–1973

www For links to more information about Neruda, a quiz on his poems, and for information about the culture and context of South America in the twentieth century, see *World Literature Online* at bedfordstmartins .com/worldlit.

Not only is Pablo Neruda one of the greatest poets to have written in Spanish, he is also one of the finest poets of the twentieth century to have written in any language. Like William Blake, Walt Whitman, and William Butler Yeats,[1] Neruda created poems in which history, politics, and personal experience coalesce into language. Neruda's unabashed devotion to his native Chile is reminiscent of Walt Whitman's passionate love for the people and places of the United States. Neruda's poems are intimately tied to the soil and sea of Chile, and, like Whitman, he delighted in the common things around him, objects of simple grace like spoons, salt, and socks. He also incorporated history into his poems, especially the conquest and exploitation of Latin America by Europe and the United States. His large body of work helped bring to the people of Chile and all of Latin America a sense of pride and an identity separate from that of their conquerors.

Although he won a number of international peace awards and literary prizes, including the Nobel Prize in literature in 1971, Neruda did not become widely known or popular in the United States in his lifetime; his bold mixture of leftist politics and poetry alienated American critics and publishers. In his later years, without relinquishing his Chilean roots, Neruda searched for bonds that would reach across national boundaries and draw men and women together in a joint human enterprise.

Exposure to World Culture.   Pablo Neruda was born Ricardo Eliezer Neftali Reyes y Basoalto on July 12, 1904, in the southern Chilean town of Parral. His father, Jose del Carmen Reyes, was a railroad worker. His mother, Rosa de Basoalto, died when Pablo was three or four years old; his father's second wife, Trinidad Candia, was described by Neruda as "the tutelary angel of my childhood." They moved south of Parral to the small town of Temuco, where Pablo spent his childhood in a lush environment of dense forest, sultry rains, and pungent odors—the sensorium of experience at the center of Neruda's poems. As a child he announced, "I'm going out to hunt poems," and he was enormously successful: From childhood on he seemed to see his life in terms of language, of fitting words to the occasion. To that end Neruda was blessed with a mentor early on, the poet Gabriela Mistral,[2] a headmistress in Temuco.

---

[1] **Blake . . . Yeats:** William Blake (1757–1827), English prophetic poet who wove together contemporary politics and mythic visions. See Book 5. Walt Whitman (1819–1892), American poet and spokesman for democracy who celebrated variety in people, places, and occupations; the first edition of *Leaves of Grass* was published in 1855. See Book 5. William Butler Yeats (1865–1939), Irish poet who contributed to Ireland's search for an identity separate from England's by introducing politics into his poems. See page 181.

[2] **Gabriela Mistral** (1889–1957): Received the Nobel Prize in literature in 1945, the first Latin American writer to be so honored. Mistral was a teacher, consul, poet, and essayist famous for her writings on women's issues and social justice.

Mistral took Neruda under her wing and exposed him to European literature. In 1920 at the age of sixteen, he published poems and articles under his new name, Pablo Neruda, after a nineteenth-century Czech writer, Jan Neruda. He adopted the pseudonym out of fear of ridicule from his family. Mistral recommended him for a scholarship when he was seventeen to study French literature at the Instituto Pedagogica in Santiago, the cultural and political capital of Chile. Leading a bohemian lifestyle in the capital city, Neruda read poets like the FRENCH SYMBOLISTS Rimbaud and Baudelaire.[3] Between 1923 and 1926 he wrote five books of poetry, but it was the second, *Twenty Love Poems and a Song of Despair* (*Veinte poemas de amor y una cancion desesperada,* 1924), that brought him praise and national recognition at the age of twenty.

Like other Latin American countries, Chile rewards its writers with diplomatic posts, and for more than fifteen years Neruda was a Chilean consul in various countries. At the young age of twenty-three he was sent to Southeast Asia; he lived in Rangoon, Colombo, Singapore, and Batavia between 1927 and 1932, bearing witness to a troubled period when countries were struggling for their independence from Europe. Neruda's poems of this time, which show the influence of SURREALISM, were collected in *Residence on Earth* (*Residencia en la tierra*). In 1933 he returned to Chile and was then assigned to Buenos Aires, then to Madrid, where *Residence on Earth,* Parts I and II, were published in 1935 to much acclaim and the admiration of Spanish poets. When the SPANISH CIVIL WAR[4] broke out in 1936 and Neruda's friend the brilliant poet Federico García Lorca (p. 568) was executed by the Civil Guard, Neruda, whose poems had become angry and sad, became outspokenly anti-Fascist. In an interview he spoke of those years: "The most intense memories . . . are those of my life in Spain — that great brotherhood of poets. It was terrible to see that republic of friends destroyed by the civil war. My friends were scattered: Some were exterminated right there — like García Lorca and Miguel Hernández;[5] others went into exile."

Into Politics.   Neruda was recalled from Madrid by the Chilean government in 1937, then reassigned to Spain and France to aid Republican Spanish refugees. Then from 1939 to 1943 he acted as Chilean consul to Mexico before returning to Santiago, where he became a member of the central committee of the Chilean Communist Party and was elected to the senate. In a series of letters beginning in 1947, Neruda accused Chile's president, Gonzalez Videla, of betraying Chile in dealings with the United States. When he lost his case against Videla before Chile's Supreme Court and Communism was declared illegal by Chile's Congress, Neruda was

---

[3] **Rimbaud and Baudelaire:** Arthur Rimbaud (1854–1891) and Charles Baudelaire (1821–1867), French Symbolist poets who used associative language to explore antisocial themes and the dark side of consciousness.

[4] **Spanish civil war** (1936–1939): Pitted Republican forces against a Fascist army supported by the German Nazis and led by Francisco Franco, who became the dictator of Spain from 1939 to 1975.

[5] **Miguel Hernández** (1910–1942): Spanish poet whose work dealt with social injustice.

On the one hand is the soil of the continent itself, before names were devised for it, with its natural riches, its fertility, and its prototypal people augmented in the course of time by men of all races who felt . . . a flame of freedom and charity in their hearts, from fray Bartolomé de las Casas or Alonso de Ercilla, to San Martín, Lincoln, and Martí to the striker jailed in Iquique or an *ejidatario* from Sonora: all Americans. On the other hand, there are rapacious and covetous men, from Columbus to Cortés, to Rosas and García Moreno, to a Somoza or a Trujillo and the masters of Anaconda Copper and United Fruit.

– LUIS MONGUIÓ, 1961, on the theme of *General Song*

forced into exile; he traveled to Mexico, France, Italy, the Soviet Union, and China.

Chile had been unique in Latin America in that it democratically elected presidents, a tradition that ended with the military dictatorship of Pinochet in 1974. But even within its democracies, there had been an ongoing power struggle in Chile in the modern period between the conservative upper classes and the working classes—not unlike other Latin American countries, in which the distribution of wealth was radically disproportionate. Chilean labor unions had clamored for recognition and peasants had demanded land reform. Neruda's evident sympathies with the downtrodden began to appear in his poetry.

A major collection of Neruda's poems, *General Song* (*Canto general*, 1950)—340 poems grouped into fifteen sections—caught the world's attention with its depiction of Latin American history, geography, and the politics of its dictators. Neruda raised the hackles of U.S. government officials with his depiction of the exploitation of Latin American people and resources by huge corporations like the United Fruit Company. The poet himself celebrated the people of the United States even while he criticized U.S. corporations and politicos; a few years earlier he had paid tribute to American writers, the American frontier, and Abraham Lincoln in "Let the Rail Splitter Awake" (1948), expressing the belief that the United States shared in the destiny of all the Americas.

World Fame.   Neruda was translated and honored all over the world, especially in socialist countries, in the 1950s and '60s. Settling into his famous house, Isla Negra, on the Pacific coast in Chile, Neruda carried on a love affair with the Chilean people while cultivating a fellowship with a wide circle of poets both at home and abroad. His poetic voice mellowed and his attitude toward life was celebratory in more than a dozen new collections, including *The Stones of Chile* (*Las piedras de Chile*, 1969), *Isla Negra: A Notebook* (*Memorial de Isla Negra*, 1964), and *World's End* (*Fin de mundo*, 1969).

Neruda was appointed the Chilean ambassador to France when Salvador Allende was elected president of Chile in 1970, the first duly elected socialist in the Americas, and Chile declared a national holiday when the poet was awarded the Nobel Prize in 1971. Neruda returned to Chile in 1973 in poor health and died in a Santiago clinic on September 23, heartbroken by the military coup that had led to the assassination of Allende just days before, on September 11, and led to the brutally repressive dictatorship of General Augusto Pinochet. Neruda's *Memoirs* (*Confiso que he vivido: Memorias*) was published in 1974; an English translation appeared in 1977. Nine additional volumes of his poetry were published posthumously.

A Sampling of Poems.   Despite his active commitment to politics, Neruda's poetic output was enormous; a 1962 edition of his poems, set in small print, ran to 1,832 pages. The genius of his poetry lies in its earthy imagery, in his use of all the senses to create a strong and vigorous language. Neruda was instrumental in helping to free Latin American writers from artificial restraints and cerebral quaintness. The poems on the following pages are a sampling from the different periods of his long writing career. The first three, "Ode with a Lament," "Sexual Water," and "Alberto Rojas Jimenez Comes Flying," are from *Residence on Earth*, which presents Neruda's version of the post–World War I "wasteland," a disheveled world unhinged from destiny and purpose. There is an underlying sadness in these poems even as Neruda looks to surreal images in the hope of discovering a deeper pattern of connections through dreamlike associations. "Ode with a Lament" immediately links a conventional image with the startling phrase, "O pressure of doves." A dazzling combination of traditional poetic images juxtaposed with exotic metaphors follow as the poem develops the themes of death, sorrow, and broken things.

"Sexual Water" is an extended treatment of sexual energy or libido. Like Walt Whitman, Neruda was devoted to the world of real objects and he loved to make lists and to shade them with potential danger. An ongoing theme of these poems seems to be that if there is any way to reassemble the world, it must begin with the physical world and not with some abstract, metaphysical system.

"Alberto Rojas Jimenez Comes Flying," one of Neruda's most popular poems, is both an exuberantly energetic evocation of a dead man's spirit and a critique of modern life. The extended litany of grief in this poem ties death to the physical memories of the close friendship between Neruda and Jimenez. "Ode of the Sun to the People's Army," published in *Spain in the Heart* (*Espana en el corazon*, 1937), is part of a series of hymns to the Spanish people. A bold and spirited voice rallies the Republican forces in the Spanish civil war in "Ode," an oral poem, meant to be sung or chanted; in fact, it was first printed and distributed by soldiers on the battlefront. Intellectuals and artists of Spanish America were deeply affected by the Spanish civil war, a struggle for human dignity and freedom against the spread of Fascism in Europe.

General Song (1950), the large collection of Neruda's poems, represents a change in the poet's writing style and purpose. His earlier surreal poems, which were keyed to the natural world, had developed a personal, even private lexicon of meaning. In *General Song*, Neruda connects with the history of the Americas, with the intent to communicate the ongoing struggle for its heart and soul. "Hymn and Return," collected in Part VII of *General Song*, points to the new direction of the whole volume: Neruda's love affair with Chile will spread throughout the Americas. In a visionary sequence of poems early in *General Song*, *The Heights of Macchu Picchu*, inspired by a pilgrimage to the ancient Inca stronghold in the Peruvian Andes, the poet arrives at Macchu Picchu and connects with an ancient civilization. It is as if he finds a source of hope in the airy vastness of the Andean stronghold. The succeeding sections deal with the greed, power, wealth, suffering, and hope in the social and political struggles of the colonial history of the Americas. The prosaic language of "The United Fruit Co." borders on simple propaganda in poetic form. Its declarative statements are direct indictments of various dictators—listed by name—and ruthless corporations that exploited various

Now let us use the good word "Americanism." Neruda constantly reminds us of Whitman, much more for his deep breath and that ease of the American man, who knows neither hindrances nor obstacles, than for his verse of huge proportions. His Americanism is present in his works in the form of a vigorous freedom, in a blessed audacity, and in a bitter fertility.

– GABRIELA MISTRAL

Latin American countries for cheap labor and natural resources. The concluding stanza about the suffering of Indians is similar to a number of other Latin American works that convey the evils of European colonialism through the plight of the Indian in the Americas.

In *Elementary Odes* (*Odas elementales*, 1954 and 1956) Neruda uses a simple voice as a means of reaching Latin American working classes and produces a charming series of poems about simple objects like socks, tomatoes, and lemons. "Poet's Obligation," published in *Full Powers* (*Plenos poderes*, 1962), echoes Walt Whitman's empathy for other and diverse human beings and his desire to give voice to the silent. The poet, according to Neruda, has an obligation to free those people who live in prisons — whether they be prison cells, factories, or offices.

■ CONNECTIONS

William Butler Yeats, "Easter 1916" and "The Second Coming," pp. 190, 193. Some modern poets incorporate political events into their poems as a means of speaking to the larger social issues of the day. In "Easter 1916" Yeats portrays the role of the English in Irish affairs in a conflict that is ongoing today. How does Neruda use political leaders in "The United Fruit Co." to address larger issues of colonialism in Latin America?

Gabriel García Márquez, "A Very Old Man with Enormous Wings," p. 928. A number of Latin American writers create a sense of spiritual depth in their writings through surrealism. García Márquez, associated with "magical realism," bends conventional reality to engage the reader in extraordinary dimensions of consciousness. How do the exotic metaphors in "Ode with a Lament" and "Sexual Water" stretch the imagination of readers and facilitate new interpretations of the poems' themes?

Walt Whitman, *Song of Myself* (Book 5). Several American writers have attempted to create a uniquely American poetry. Whitman celebrated the whole range of American lifestyles in homegrown images and an American idiom. How does Neruda, in poems like "Hymn and Return" and *The Heights of Macchu Picchu,* discover and employ materials indigenous to Chile to evoke the connectedness of various countries of the Americas?

■ FURTHER RESEARCH

Biography
Teitelboim, Volodia. *Neruda: An Intimate Biography.* 1991.

Editions
Neruda, Pablo. *Neruda's Garden: An Anthology of Odes.* Maria Jacketti, trans. 1995.
————. *Odes to Common Things.* Ken Krabbenhoft, trans. 1994.

History and Culture
Rodman, Selden. "Pablo Neruda's Chile." In *South America of the Poets.* 1970.

Criticism
Costa, Rene de. *The Poetry of Pablo Neruda.* 1979.
Duran, Manuel, and Margery Safir. *Earth Tones: The Poetry of Pablo Neruda.* 1981.
Riess, Frank. *The World and the Stone: Language and Imagery in Neruda's* Canto General. 1972.
Santi, Enrico Mario. *Pablo Neruda, The Poetics of Prophecy.* 1982.

∾ Ode with a Lament

Translated by H. R. Hays

O girl among the roses, O pressure of doves,
O citadel of fishes and rosebushes,
Your soul is a bottle full of dry salt
And your skin is a bell full of grapes.

Unfortunately I have nothing to give you except fingernails
Or eyelashes, or melted pianos,
Or dreams which pour from my heart in torrents,
Dusty dreams that race like black riders,
Dreams full of speed and affliction.

10   I can only love you with kisses and poppies,
With garlands wet by the rain,
Gazing at yellow dogs and horses red as ashes.

I can only love you with waves behind me,
Between wandering gusts of sulphur and pensive waters,
Swimming toward cemeteries that flow in certain rivers
With wet pasturage growing above sad tombs of plaster,
Swimming through submerged hearts
And pale catalogues of unburied children.
There is much death, many funereal events
20   In my forsaken passions and desolate kisses,
There is a water that falls on my head,
While my hair grows,
A water like time, a black torrential water,
With a nocturnal voice, with a cry
Of a bird in the rain, like an interminable
Shadow of a wet wing sheltering my bones,
While I dress myself, while

"Ode with a Lament." The translation by H. R. Hays of "Oda con un lamento," which first appeared in Spanish in *Residentia en la tierra* in 1935, was published in *12 Spanish American Poets: An Anthology* in 1943. The poem seems to be addressed to a young woman and draws on the conventions associated with a poet's devotion to a woman and the gifts that a poet might offer his beloved. Although "roses" and "doves" are often linked with love, Neruda indicates that he is exploring new territory when the speaker says, "Your soul is a bottle of dry salt / And your skin is a bell full of grapes." Are those compliments? The poem unfolds in more nontraditional, often startling poetic images, many of which have to do with death. Salvador Dalí and the surrealists are invoked with the "melted pianos" in line six.

Interminably I look at myself in mirrors and windows,
I hear someone calling me, calling me with sobs,
30 With a sad voice rotted by time.
You are on foot, on the earth, full
Of fangs and lightings.
You generate kisses and you kill ants.
You weep with health, with onions, with bees,
With burning alphabet.
You are like a blue and green sword
And you ripple when touched like a river.

Come to my soul dressed in white, like a branch
Of bleeding roses and cups of ashes,
40 Come with an apple and a horse,
Because there is a dark room there and a broken candelabra,
Some twisted chairs that wait for winter,
And a dead dove with a number.

❧ Sexual Water

Translated by H. R. Hays

Running in single drops,
In drops like teeth,
In thick drops of marmalade and blood,
Running in drops,
The water falls,
Like a sword of drops
Like a rending river of glass,
It falls biting,
Striking the axis of symmetry, hitting on the
10 Ribs of the soul,
Breaking castoff things, soaking the darkness.

It is only a gust, damper than tears,
A liquid, a sweat, a nameless oil,
A sharp movement,

"Sexual Water." This H. R. Hays translation was published in *12 Spanish American Poets: An Anthology* in 1943, eight years after "Agua sexual" first appeared in *Residentia en la tierra.* "Sexual Water" is a long list of objects and situations associated with sexuality. It becomes a kind of test for the reader to discover the links.

Creating itself, thickening itself,
The water falls,
In slow drops,
Toward the sea, toward its dry ocean,
Toward its wave without water.

20 I see a long summer and a death rattle coming out of a granary,
Cellars, cicadas,
Towns, stimuli,
Habitations, girl children
Sleeping with hands on their hearts,
Dreaming with pirates, with fire,
I see ships,
I see trees of spinal cord
Bristling like furious cats,
I see blood, daggers, and women's stockings,
30 I see men's hair,
I see beds, I see corridors where a virgin screams,
I see blankets and organs and hotels.

I see stealthy dreams,
I accept the preceding days,
And also origins and also memories,
Like an eyelid dreadfully raised by force
I am watching.

And then there is this sound:
A red noise of bones,
40 An adhering of flesh,
And legs yellow as grain stalks joining together.
I am listening among explosions of kisses,
I am listening, shaken among breathing and sobs.

I am watching, hearing
With half my soul on sea and half my soul on land,
And with both halves of my soul I look at the world.

And though I close my eyes and cover my heart
Completely,
I see a deaf water falling
50 In deaf drops.

It is like a hurricane of gelatin,
Like a cataract of sperm and medusas.
I see a muddy rainbow flowing.
I see its waters passing through my bones.

❧ Alberto Rojas Jimenez Comes Flying[1]

Translated by H. R. Hays

Between fearful feathers, between the nights,
Between the magnolias, between telegrams,
Between the south wind and the sea wind of the west,
     You come flying.

Below tombs, below ashes,
Below frozen snails,
Below the deepest terrestrial waters,
     You come flying.

10   Lower still, among submerged girl-children
And blind plants and wounded fishes,
Lower still, once more among clouds,
     You come flying.

Farther than the blood, farther than the bones,
Farther than bread, farther than wine,
Farther than fire,
     You come flying.

Farther than vinegar and death,
Among putrefactions and violets,
With your celestial voice and your moist shoes,
20   You come flying.

Above deputations and drugstores
And wheels and lawyers and ocean liners
And red teeth, recently extracted,
     You come flying.

Above cities with submerged roof tops,
In which large women unplait their hair

"Alberto Rojas Jimenez Comes Flying." This translation of "Alberto Rojas Jimenez viene volando," also by H. R. Hays and also published in *12 Spanish American Poets: An Anthology* in 1943, first appeared in *Residentia en la tierra* in 1935. "Alberto Rojas Jimenez Comes Flying" collects images into four-line stanzas. The poem's extended litany of grief ranges over numerous memories and associations with death as a way of paying tribute to Jimenez's untimely death and his lingering memory.

---

[1] **Alberto Rojas Jimenez:** A poet and friend of Neruda who died by drowning. [Editors' note.]

With broad hands and lost combs,
        You come flying.

Close to a cellar where the wine matures,
30   With tepid, muddy hands, in silence,
        With slow hands, red and wooden,
        You come flying.

Among vanished aviators,
Beside canals and shadows,
Beside buried white lilies,
        You come flying.

Among bottles with a bitter color,
Among rings of anise seed and misfortune,
Raising your hands and weeping,
40   You come flying.

Over dentists and congregations,
Over cinemas, ears, and tunnels,
In a new suit, with extinguished eyes,
        You come flying.

Over your unwalled cemetery
Where the sailors go astray,
While the rain of your death falls,
        You come flying.

While the rain of your fingers falls,
50   While the rain of your bones falls,
While your marrow and your laughter fall,
        You come flying.

Over the stones into which you are melting,
Flowing, down winter, down time,
While your heart descends in a shower of drops,
        You come flying.

You are not there, circled with cement
And the black hearts of notaries
And the maddened bones of riders:
60   You come flying.

O poppy of the sea, O my kinsman,
O guitar player dressed in bees,

It is not true there is all this shadow in your hair:
>   You come flying.

It is not true that all this shadow pursues you,
It is not true there are all these dead swallows,
All this obscure region of lamentation:
>   You come flying.

The black wind of Valparaiso[2]
70 Spreads its wings of smoke and foam
To sweep the sky where you pass:
>   You come flying.

There are steamers and the cold of a dead sea
And whistles and months and an odor
Of a rainy morning and filthy fishes:
>   You come flying.

There is rum, and you and I, and my soul that I weep in,
And no one and nothing, except for a staircase
With broken steps and an umbrella:
80 >   You come flying.

There is the sea. I descend at night and I hear you
Come flying below the deserted sea,
Below the sea that lives in me, in obscurity:
>   You come flying.

I hear your wings and your slow flight
And the water of the dead strikes me
Like blind moist doves:
>   You come flying.

You come flying, alone, solitary,
90 Alone among corpses, forever alone,
You come flying without a shadow, nameless,
Without sugar, without a mouth, without rosebushes,
>   You come flying.

---

[2] **Valparaiso:** A seaport in central Chile. [Editors' note.]

～ Ode of the Sun to the People's Army

Translated by H. R. Hays

Arms of the people! This way! Menace and siege
Still are wasting the earth, mixing it with death,
With the sharpness of goads! Salud, salud,
The mothers of the world cry salud to you,
The schools cry salud, the old carpenters,
Army of the People, they cry salud with ears of grain,
With milk, with potatoes, with the lemon and the laurel,
All that is of the earth and the mouth
Of man.

10   All, like a necklace
Of hands, like a
Palpitating girdle, like the obstinacy of lightning,
All prepares for you, all converges toward you!
            Day of steel,
Fortified blueness!
            Forward, brothers,
Forward through the plowed fields,
Forward through the dry and sleepless night, threadbare and delirious,
Forward among grapevines, treading the cold color of the rocks,

20 Salud, salud, press on! Sharper than the voice of winter,
More sensitive than the eyelid, more certain than the point of thunder,
Punctual as the swift diamond, now in warfare,
Warriors like steel gray water of the midlands,
Like the flower and the wine, like the spiral heart of the earth,
Like the roots of all the leaves, of all the fragrant merchandise of the earth.
Salud, soldiers, salud, red plow furrows,
Salud, sturdy clover, salud, ranks of the people
In the light of the lightning, salud, salud, salud,
Forward, forward, forward, forward,

30 Over the mines, over the cemeteries, against the abominable
Appetite of death, against the spiny
Terror of traitors,

"Ode of the Sun to the People's Army." "Oda solar al erjercito del pueblo" was published in
Spain in the Heart (*España en la corazon,* 1937) and translated by H. R. Hays in *12 Spanish American
Poets: An Anthology* (1943). The Spanish civil war was extremely important for Latin America, associated as it was with Spanish colonialism and the struggle of fledgling democracies against dictatorships throughout the Americas. Spain became a test case for the fight against Fascism in
Europe, during which Neruda's poem was actually circulated among soldiers at the front. As a
public propaganda piece, "Ode" is best read aloud.

People, capable people, heart and rifles,
Heart and rifles, forward.
Photographers, miners, railworkers, brothers
Of the coal mine and stone quarry, kinsmen
Of the hammer, the forest, joyful shooting festival, forward,
Guerrillas, majors, sergeants, political commissars,
Aviators of the people, night fighters,
40 Sea fighters, forward!
Against you
There is nothing but a human chain gang, a pit full
Of rotten fish; forward!
There is nothing but dying corpses,
Swamps of terrible bloody pus,
There are no enemies: forward, Spain,
Forward, bells of the people,
Forward, regions of apple orchards,
Forward, banners of grain,
50 Forward, capital letters of fire,
For in the struggle on the waves, in the fields,
In the mountains, in the twilight loaded with acrid perfume,
You are giving birth to permanence, a thread
Of difficult strength.
       In the meanwhile,
Root and garland arise from silence
To await the ore of victory:
Each tool, each red wheel,
Each saw handle, the plume of each plow,
60 Each product of soil, each tremor of blood
Seeks to follow your footsteps, Army of the People:
Your organized light reaches the poor,
The forgotten men, your definite star
Nails its hoarse rays in death
And enacts the new eyes of hope.

Hymn and Return

Translated by Robert Bly

Country, my country, I turn my blood in your direction.
But I am begging you the way a child begs its mother,
with tears:
               take this blind guitar
and these lost features.
I left to find sons for you over the earth,
I left to comfort those fallen with your name made of snow,
I left to build a house with your pure timber,
I left to carry your star to the wounded heroes.

10   Now I want to fall asleep in your substance.
Give me your clear night of piercing strings,
your night like a ship, your altitude covered with stars.

My country: I want to change my shadow.
My country: I want to have another rose.
I want to put my arm around your narrow waist
and sit down on your stones whitened by the sea
and hold the wheat back and look deep into it.
I am going to pick the thin flower of nitrate,[1]
I am going to feel the icy wool of the field,
20   and staring at your famous and lonesome sea-foam
I'll weave with them a wreath on the shore for your beauty.

Country, my country,
entirely surrounded by aggressive water
and fighting snow,
the eagle and the sulphur come together in you,

"Hymn and Return." "Hymno y regreso" appeared in Part VII of *Canto general (General Song)* in 1950 but is dated 1939, the year of the defeat of the Spanish Republican army and Neruda's decision to return to Chile. The poem marks a change in Neruda's writing; earlier poems had often been private affairs, but those in *Canto general*, as the title suggests, were meant to embrace all the peoples of the Americas as well as the poet's countrymen. This translation by Robert Bly was published in *Neruda and Vallejo: Selected Poems* in 1971.

---

[1] **nitrate:** Nitrates are an important part of the economy in Chile; they can be very dangerous to the workmen who mine them. [Editors' note.]

and a drop of pure human light
burns in your antarctic hand of ermine and sapphire,
lighting up the hostile sky.

My country, take care of your light! Hold up
30   your stiff straw of hope
into the blind and frightening air.
All of this difficult light has fallen on your isolated land,
this future of the race,
that makes you defend a mysterious flower
alone, in the hugeness of an America that lies asleep.

✑ The United Fruit Co.

Translated by Robert Bly

When the trumpet sounded, it was
all prepared on the earth,
and Jehovah parceled out the earth
to Coca-Cola, Inc., Anaconda,
Ford Motors, and other entities:
The Fruit Company, Inc.
reserved for itself the most succulent,
the central coast of my own land,
the delicate waist of America.
10   It rechristened its territories
as the "Banana Republics"
and over the sleeping dead,
over the restless heroes
who brought about the greatness,
the liberty and the flags,
it established the comic opera:
abolished the independencies,

"The United Fruit Co." Translated by Robert Bly in *Neruda and Vallejo: Selected Poems* (1971), "La United Fruit Co." was first published in *Canto general* in 1950. The poem is grouped with others in *Canto general* devoted to men who thwarted progress toward democracy in Central and South America through dictatorships or collaboration with the economic colonialism of the United States. The language of "The United Fruit Co." is so direct it borders on prose. The company of the work's title stands for the many corporations that have exploited various Latin American countries for labor and natural resources. The poem's last stanza points to the oppression of indigenous workers at the bottom of the social ladder, the worst example of colonial exploitation.

presented crowns of Caesar,
unsheathed envy, attracted
20   the dictatorship of the flies,
Trujillo flies, Tacho flies,
Carias flies, Martinez flies,
Ubico flies,¹ damp flies
of modest blood and marmalade,
drunken flies who zoom
over the ordinary graves,
circus flies, wise flies
well trained in tyranny.

Among the bloodthirsty flies
30   the Fruit Company lands its ships,
taking off the coffee and the fruit;
the treasure of our submerged
territories flows as though
on plates into the ships.

Meanwhile Indians are falling
into the sugared chasms
of the harbors, wrapped
for burial in the mist of the dawn:
a body rolls, a thing
40   that has no name, a fallen cipher,
a cluster of dead fruit
thrown down on the dump.

---

¹**Trujillo flies . . . Ubico flies:** Dictators in Central America: Rafael Leonidas Trujillo Molina in the Dominican Republic, 1930–38 and 1942–52; Maximiliano Hernández Martínez in El Salvador 1931–44; Tiburcio Carías Andino in Honduras, 1933–49; Jorge Ubico in Guatemala, 1931–44. [Editors' note.]

∾ The Heights of Macchu Picchu

Translated by Jack Schmitt

VI

And so I scaled the ladder of the earth
amid the atrocious maze of lost jungles
up to you, Macchu Picchu.
High citadel of terraced stones,
at long last the dwelling of him whom the earth
did not conceal in its slumbering vestments.
In you, as in two parallel lines,
the cradle of lightning and man
was rocked in a wind of thorns.

10   Mother of stone, sea spray of the condors.

Towering reef of the human dawn.

Spade lost in the primal sand.

This was the dwelling, this is the site:
here the full kernels of corn rose
and fell again like red hailstones.

Here the golden fiber emerged from the vicuña[1]
to clothe love, tombs, mothers,
the king, prayers, warriors.

Here man's feet rested at night
20   beside the eagle's feet, in the high gory

The Heights of Macchu Picchu. Part II of *Canto general* is called *Alturas de Macchu Picchu*, a sequence of twelve poems inspired by a visit to Macchu Picchu, the sky city built by the Incas. Section VI, presented here, was translated by Jack Schmitt and published in *Canto general* in 1991. In sections III through V, Neruda dwells on the suffering and death that attends the history of common people and is almost overcome by the sadness of his reflections. But as he arrives in Macchu Picchu in VI and connects with an ancient civilization, his spirits rise. The moment when he realizes that the ruins were once the habitat and thoroughfares of human beings is luminous; the stones come alive along with the air.

All notes are the editors'.

---

[1] **vicuña:** An animal that was found wild in the Andes; it is related to the llama and well known for its soft, shaggy wool.

retreats, and at dawn
they trod the rarefied mist with feet of thunder
and touched lands and stones
until they recognized them in the night or in death.

I behold vestments and hands,
the vestige of water in the sonorous void,
the wall tempered by the touch of a face
that beheld with my eyes the earthen lamps,
that oiled with my hands the vanished
30   wood: because everything—clothing, skin, vessels,
words, wine, bread—
is gone, fallen to earth.

And the air flowed with orange-blossom
fingers over all the sleeping:
a thousand years of air, months, weeks of air,
of blue wind, of iron cordillera,[2]
like gentle hurricanes of footsteps
polishing the solitary precinct of stone.

---

[2] **cordillera:** A mountain range.

ᘯ Ode to Salt

Translated by Robert Bly

I saw the salt
in this shaker
in the salt flats.
I know
you
will never believe me,
but
it sings,
the salt sings, the hide

"Ode to Salt." Pablo Neruda was popular with all classes of people throughout Latin America. In *Elemental Odes* (*Odas elementales,* 1954 and 1956), he wrote about everyday objects, like salt and tomatoes, in a simple voice as a means of reaching the working classes. In "Ode to Salt," the poet connects salt with various places and crystals so that by the end of the poem there is much that "the tiniest / wave of the shaker / brings home to us." This translation by Robert Bly was published in *Neruda and Vallejo: Selected Poems* (1971).

10 of the salt plains,
 it sings
 through a mouth smothered
 by earth.
 I shuddered in those deep
 solitudes
 when I heard
 the voice
 of
 the salt
20 in the desert.
 Near Antofagasta°   a city in northern Chile
 the entire
 salt plain
 speaks:
 it is a
 broken
 voice,
 a song full
 of grief.
30 Then in its own mines
 rock salt, a mountain
 of buried light,
 a cathedral through which light passes,
 crystal of the sea, abandoned
 by the waves.

 And then on every table
 on this earth,
 salt,
 your nimble
40 body
 pouring out
 the vigorous light
 over
 our foods.
 Preserver
 of the stores
 of the ancient ships,
 you were
 an explorer
50 in the ocean,
 substance
 going first
 over the unknown, barely open

routes of the sea-foam.
Dust of the sea, the tongue
receives a kiss
of the night sea from you:
taste recognizes
the ocean in each salted morsel,
60   and therefore the smallest,
the tiniest
wave of the shaker
brings home to us
not only your domestic whiteness
but the inward flavor of the infinite.

❧ Poet's Obligation

Translated by Alastair Reid

To whoever is not listening to the sea
this Friday morning, to whoever is cooped up
in house or office, factory or woman
or street or mine or harsh prison cell:
to him I come, and, without speaking or looking,
I arrive and open the door of his prison,
and a vibration starts up, vague and insistent,
a great fragment of thunder sets in motion
the rumble of the planet and the foam,
10   the raucous rivers of the ocean flood,
the star vibrates swiftly in its corona,
and the sea is beating, dying and continuing.

So, drawn on by my destiny,
I ceaselessly must listen to and keep
the sea's lamenting in my awareness,
I must feel the crash of the hard water
and gather it up in a perpetual cup
so that, wherever those in prison may be,
wherever they suffer the autumn's castigation,

"Poet's Obligation." "Deber del poeta" was published in *Full Powers (Plenos poderes)* in 1962 and translated by Alastair Reid as "Poet's Obligation" in *Neruda: Selected Poems* in 1970. Here Neruda sees the role of the poet in terms of two central images: The poet as oracle is compared to the "sea," and as such is able to pass through barriers and into the various "prisons" that enclose people, entrapments of everyday life. Poetry and the poet become vehicles of freedom.

20   I may be there with an errant wave,
      I may move, passing through windows,
      and hearing me, eyes will glance upward
      saying "How can I reach the sea?"
      And I shall broadcast, saying nothing,
      the starry echoes of the wave,
      a breaking up of foam and of quicksand,
      a rustling of salt withdrawing,
      the grey cry of sea-birds on the coast.

      So, through me, freedom and the sea
30   will make their answer to the shuttered heart.

❧ JEAN-PAUL SARTRE
B. FRANCE, 1905–1980

zhawng-POLE SART

Philosopher, playwright, journalist, literary theorist, novelist, and political and social critic, **Jean-Paul Sartre** is perhaps the foremost French writer and intellectual of the twentieth century. His name is virtually synonymous with EXISTENTIALISM, the dominant European philosophical school in the years following World War II. Sartre's choice to present his philosophical ideas in the form of novels and plays makes him a literary figure in the tradition of Plato, Voltaire, and Rousseau.[1] Like Plato's dialogues and Voltaire's *Candide* (see Book 4), many of Sartre's works transcend their philosophic intent and are compelling works of literature in their own right. Their influence on writers and thinkers throughout the world has been profound.

www   For links to more information about Sartre, a quiz on *The Flies,* and for information about the culture and context of Europe in the twentieth century, see *World Literature Online* at bedfordstmartins .com/worldlit.

A Childhood with Books.   Born in Paris in 1905, Sartre had a lonely childhood. After his father died when Sartre was very young, his mother returned to her family so the boy was raised in the home of his maternal grandfather, Carl Schweitzer, a professor of German at the Sorbonne and the uncle of missionary Albert Schweitzer (1875–1965). Small, cross-eyed, and rejected by other children, Sartre retreated into the world of

---

[1] **Plato . . . Rousseau:** Three philosophers who expressed their ideas through literary works. Plato (427–347 B.C.E.), Greek philosopher who used the Socratic dialogue—conversations between Socrates, who mainly posed questions, and others—to express his philosophy (see Book 1); Voltaire (1694–1778), French satirist, playwright, and essayist best known for *Candide* (1759) (see Book 4); Jean-Jacques Rousseau (1712–1778), French philosopher and political and educational theorist who often presented his philosophical concepts in novels, such as *Émile* (1762) and *Julie, or the New Heloise* (1761) (see Book 4).

Jean-Paul Sartre with Simone de Beauvoir, January 1, 1959
Sartre and Beauvoir, the early feminist writer, were lifelong companions who wrote and lived together, although they never married. (© Pierre George / Corbis-Sygma)

books and spent much of his time in solitary reading in his grandfather's library, a room he called his "temple." In his autobiography, *The Words* (*Les Mots*, 1963), he describes how words served as a refuge from the world that had not accepted him and became a means to construct another world of his own imagination.

Nausea. Sartre attended college at the École Normale Supérieure, where he earned his doctorate in philosophy in 1929. While a student he met philosopher and feminist theorist Simone de Beauvoir (1908–1986), forming a lifelong relationship with her that never became the "bourgeois marriage" that both of them intellectually rejected. In the years before the war, he taught in secondary schools in Le Havre, Lyon, and Paris, and published a novel, *Nausea* (*La Nausée*, 1938). A controversial and iconoclastic work, this novelistic diary presents Roquentin's revulsion as he confronts the physical world, other people, and his own body. His "nausea"—the realization that things have no meaning in themselves, that the world is "absurd"—makes him an outsider, for he refuses to accept the conventional explanations of meaning that others use to avoid the unsettling sickness. Eventually, he comes to believe that the world can only have the meaning that he chooses to give it. That belief became a cornerstone of Sartre's existential philosophy. "Existence precedes essence," Sartre asserted, meaning that the world has no inherent meaning and human beings have no predetermined identity. Life is absurd, and "man is condemned to be free."

Men are not created but create themselves through their choices.

– JEAN-PAUL SARTRE, "Forgers of Myths," 1946

The Crucible of World War II.   It was the Second World War that crystallized Sartre's philosophy and focused his literary work. Drafted in 1939 and taken prisoner in 1940, Sartre was released (or he escaped) a year later. Reentering a society occupied by the German army and "ruled" by the French collaborationist government under Marshal Philippe Pétain, he realized that he had three choices: collaboration, quiet self-preservation, or resistance. For Sartre, the first two were not really choices at all: To collaborate or to ignore the occupation was to surrender one's freedom. His philosophical emphasis on freedom, the core concept in existentialism, emerged from his wartime experiences. In 1943 he published his massive philosophical treatise *Being and Nothingness* (*L'Être et le néant*) and produced *The Flies* (*Les Mouches*) on the Parisian stage. The play was an act of resistance dressed in the guise of the classical story of Orestes as a way of getting it past the German censors. In both these works Sartre asserts the freedom of consciousness from determination by the material world so long as the individual takes responsibility to choose this freedom. Without so choosing one lives in "bad faith," directed by forces outside the self, be they political and religious tyrants or conventional, unexamined ideas.

Later Work.   During the final years of the war and afterwards, Sartre continued to publish both philosophic and literary works. *No Exit* (*Huis clos*), his most well-known play, appeared in 1944. Set in hell, it presents the eternal torment of three individuals who lived their lives in bad faith. This play was followed by several more; a series of novels under the general title *Roads to Freedom* (*Les Chemins de la liberté*, 1945–1950); and many other works of philosophy, literary criticism, biography, psychology, and political polemics. Sartre's autobiography *The Words* tells the story of his life up to 1963, when the book was published, and Simone de Beauvoir's memoirs tell some of the rest. His prolific writings, his position as editor of the important intellectual journal *Les Temps modernes,* and his controversial and outspoken views made Sartre a very visible figure in France during his lifetime. He was working on the fourth volume of a biography of Gustave Flaubert when he died in 1980. His funeral, like Victor Hugo's a century earlier, was a national event. It was attended by some twenty-five thousand mourners.

The Flies.   *The Flies* is a drama that presents the same action as *The Libation Bearers,* the second of three plays in Aeschylus's *Oresteia.*[2] After the murder of Agamemnon by Clytemnestra, the subject of the first play,

---

[2] **Aeschylus's *Oresteia*** (458 B.C.E.): Three plays that tell the story of Orestes as a means of depicting the transformation of ancient Greece from a primitive matriarchy that settled scores through blood revenge to a patriarchal society based on courts and law. The first play in the trilogy, *Agamemnon,* is about Clytemnestra's murder of Agamemnon upon his return from the Trojan War, vengeance for his sacrifice of their daughter Iphegenia. In the second play, *The Libation Bearers (Choephori),* Orestes murders Clytemnestra and her consort, Ægisthus, to avenge his father's death. And in *The Eumenides,* the third play, Orestes defends his action before Athene and the Athenian court. The drama ends with Athene's absolving Orestes of his crime.

Orestes, Agamemnon's son, returns to Argos and to the palace of the Atreides, now ruled by Clytemnestra and the usurper Ægisthus. After revealing himself to his sister Electra, Orestes avenges his father's death by killing both Ægisthus and Clytemnestra. At the end of the play, pursued by the Furies, he leaves Argos to go to Athens where, in the third play of the trilogy, *The Eumenides,* Orestes and the Furies plead their cases to Athene. Athene exonerates Orestes and reconciles the Furies to a new role as patronesses of the city of Athens.

In *The Flies,* Sartre reinterprets this material. In the Greek classic, Orestes' murders of Ægistheus and Clytemnestra are the final acts in a familial sequence of blood justice. When Orestes is pardoned by Athene and the court in Athens, a new order of rational and deliberative justice is established. Sartre's Orestes, by contrast, is not so much seeking to redress his father's murder as he is asserting his own freedom and liberating the citizens of Argos from their "bad faith" and systematic remorse. He must overthrow the political and religious tyrants Ægistheus and Zeus, with their "passion for order," and replace them with a new era of freedom. Sartre compared his play with Aeschylus's in the following terms: "My intention was to consider the tragedy of freedom as contrasted with the tragedy of fate. In other words, what my play is about can be summed up as the question, 'How does a man behave toward an act committed by him, for which he takes the full consequences and full responsibility upon himself, even if he is otherwise horrified by his act?'" In *Oresteia,* the characters are agents of the gods, carrying out a pre-established pattern of divine retribution and expiating the crimes of the past. Sartre's Orestes must free himself from the past and from Zeus by discovering and choosing his own freedom.

Sartre's protagonist is a distinctly modern hero. He is not defined by family or destiny. Exiled from Argos as a child, he is a man without a country. Even his "multicultural" education, as the tutor who accompanies him on his wanderings reminds him, has freed him from prior definition. "Did I not, from the very first," the tutor asks him, "set you a-reading all the books there are, so as to make clear to you the infinite diversity of men's opinions? And did I not remind you, time and again, how variable are human creeds and customs? . . . [Y]our mind is free from prejudice and superstition; you have no family ties, no religion, and no calling; you are free to turn your hand to anything. But you know better than to commit yourself—and there lies your strength." These negative virtues of "the man without qualities" are not sufficient to give Orestes an identity or a direction for his life. The tutor's notion of freedom describes only an absence. To be truly free, Orestes must choose his life and take committed action. His decision to murder Ægistheus and Clytemnestra fulfills those conditions.

Though it got past the German censors in 1943, *The Flies* was recognized by its French audience as an attack on the Pétain government—located at Vichy about two hundred miles south of Paris—and its cowardly collaboration with the Germans. The official line of the Vichy regime was that the suffering of the war was a just punishment for the frivolousness and godlessness of the prewar years. In its attempt to

> **Man is condemned to be free.**
>
> – Jean-Paul Sartre

restore a "moral order," the Vichy government was supported by the Catholic Church. In Sartre's play, Ægistheus (the occupying Nazis), Clytemnestra (the Vichy collaborators), and Zeus (the church) form an alliance to oppress the people of Argos (the French population) and engage them in unending rituals of remorse. "By writing my play," Sartre said, "I was trying by my own unaided effort, feeble though it might be, to do what I could to root out this sickness of repentance, this complacence in repentance and shame. What was needed at the time was to revive the French people, to restore their courage." At that time, to discourage resistance to the occupation and to keep the French people in line, the Nazis had a policy of killing randomly selected French citizens in response to attacks from the Underground. Sartre pointed out that "anyone who committed an attack . . . had to know that, unless he gave himself up, fellow Frenchmen would be shot at random. So he was liable to a second form of repentance: He had to resist the temptation to give himself up. This is how the allegory in my play is to be understood." In Sartre's view it is not only Orestes' acts that are important but also the fact that he takes responsibility for them. He has no remorse.

The end of *The Flies* is significantly different from the conclusion of *The Libation Bearers*. In the former, Orestes is now positively free, for he has acted, has taken responsibility for his acts, and has no remorse. He is a savior to the city, but he will not be their ruler, for that would continue their enslavement and their dependence on rule from outside themselves. By his act, they too are condemned to be free. For Sartre, living in a world where God had died and where the dissolution of external authority had left human beings in "dread," "anguish," and "absurdity" was not reason for despair. The necessity of choice made his existentialism, in the end, an optimistic philosophy.

■ **CONNECTIONS**

In the World: **Existentialism, p. 746.** As a play intended to embody philosophical ideas, *The Flies* presents some of the concepts developed in *In the World:* Existentialism. What ideas developed by the writers there are also developed in Sartre's play? Is the play convincing as a drama, or is it merely a vehicle for ideas?

Aeschylus, *The Oresteia* **(Book 1).** For *The Flies*, Sartre draws from the same myth found in Aeschylus's *Oresteia*, the story of Orestes' retribution for the murder of his father, Agamemnon. Consider the character of Orestes in the two plays. In what ways is Sartre's hero different from the Orestes in Aeschylus? Would Sartre accept Aeschylus's worldview? Would Aeschylus agree with Sartre's interpretation of the Greek myth?

Fyodor Dostoevsky, "The Grand Inquisitor" (Book 5). Like Sartre's Orestes, Dostoevsky's Jesus in "The Grand Inquisitor" calls on human beings to choose freedom. Is Dostoevsky's concept of freedom similar to Sartre's? Is the point of view of the Grand Inquisitor represented by any of the characters in Sartre's play?

■ **FURTHER RESEARCH**

Background on Existentialism
La Capra, Dominick. *A Preface to Sartre.* 1978.
Sartre, Jean-Paul. *Existentialism.* 1947.

Criticism

Contat, Michel, and Michel Rybalka, eds. *Sartre on Theater*. 1976.
Howells, Christina, ed. *Sartre*. 1995.
Howells, Christina. *Sartre: The Necessity of Freedom*. 1988.
McBride, William L., ed. *Existentialist Literature and Aesthetics*. 1997.
Thody, Philip. *Jean-Paul Sartre: A Literary and Political Study*. 1960.
Wilcocks, Robert, ed. *Critical Essays on Jean-Paul Sartre*. 1988.
Woods, Philip R. *Understanding Jean-Paul Sartre*. 1990.

■ **PRONUNCIATION**

Jean-Paul Sartre: zhawng-POLE SART

 **The Flies**

Translated by Stuart Gilbert

CHARACTERS IN THE PLAY

ZEUS	THE HIGH PRIEST
ORESTES	A YOUNG WOMAN
ELECTRA	AN OLD WOMAN
ÆGISTHEUS	AN IDIOT BOY
CLYTEMNESTRA	FIRST SOLDIER
THE TUTOR	SECOND SOLDIER
FIRST FURY	MEN AND WOMEN, *townsfolk of Argos*
SECOND FURY	FURIES, SERVANTS, PALACE GUARDS
THIRD FURY	

ACT I

A public square in Argos, dominated by a statue of ZEUS, *god of flies and death. The image has white eyes and blood-smeared cheeks.*

A procession of OLD WOMEN *in black, carrying urns, advances; they make libations to the statue. An* IDIOT BOY *is squatting in the background.* ORESTES *enters, accompanied by* THE TUTOR.

The Flies. First staged in Paris in 1943, this drama is an allegorical play that presents the Greek myth of Orestes as a parallel to the situation of France in World War II. Sartre adopted the Greek subject matter to get the play—which made a case for the French resistance—past the Nazi censors. "The Flies" of the title are his transformation of the Furies in the old myth. The Furies tormented the people of Argos, prompting rituals of guilt and remorse so that they accepted the usurper Ægistheus as the French accepted the Vichy government that collaborated with the Nazis. Although intensely topical at the time of its initial production, *The Flies* also has a lasting philosophical message. Sartre calls on individuals to live authentically by choosing their lives, taking responsibility for their choices, and refusing to be the tool of others who would seek to control them.

A note on the translation: The translation presented here is by Stuart Gilbert. Gilbert has translated many works of French literature, especially those of the existentialists.

ORESTES: Listen, my good women.

[*The* OLD WOMEN *swing round, emitting little squeals.*]

THE TUTOR: Would you kindly tell us—[*The* OLD WOMEN *spit on the ground and move back a pace.*] Steady, good ladies, steady. I only want a piece of simple information. We are travelers and we have lost our way. [*Dropping their urns, the* WOMEN *take to their heels.*] Stupid old hags! You'd think I had intentions on their virtue! [*Ironically*] Ah, young master, truly this has been a pleasant journey. And how well inspired you were to come to this city of Argos, when there are hundreds of towns in Greece and Italy where the drink is good, the inns are hospitable, and the streets full of friendly, smiling people! But these uncouth hillmen—one would suppose they'd never seen a foreigner before. A hundred times and more I've had to ask our way, and never once did I get a straight answer. And then the grilling heat! This Argos is a nightmare city. Squeals of terror everywhere, people who panic the moment they set eyes on you, and scurry to cover, like black beetles, down the glaring streets. Pfoo! I can't think how you bear it—this emptiness, the shimmering air, that fierce sun overhead. What's deadlier than the sun?

ORESTES: I was born here.

THE TUTOR: So the story goes. But, if I were you, I wouldn't brag about it.

ORESTES: I was born here—and yet I have to ask my way, like any stranger. Knock at that door.

THE TUTOR: What do you expect? That someone will open it? Only look at those houses and tell me how they strike you. You will observe there's not a window anywhere. They open on closed courtyards, I suppose, and turn their backsides to the street. [ORESTES *makes a fretful gesture.*] Very good, sir. I'll knock—but nothing will come of it.

[*He knocks. Nothing happens. He knocks again, and the door opens a cautious inch.*]

A VOICE: What do you want?

THE TUTOR: Just a word of information. Can you tell me where—? [*The door is slammed in his face.*] Oh, the devil take you! Well, my lord Orestes, is that enough, or must I try elsewhere? If you wish, I'll knock at every door.

ORESTES: No, that's enough.

THE TUTOR: Well, I never! There's someone here. [*He goes up to the* IDIOT BOY.] Excuse me, sir . . .

THE IDIOT: Hoo! Hoo! Hoo!

THE TUTOR [*bowing again*]: My noble lord . . .

THE IDIOT: Hoo!

THE TUTOR: Will Your Highness deign to show us where Ægistheus lives?

THE IDIOT: Hoo!

THE TUTOR: Ægistheus, King of Argos.

THE IDIOT: Hoo! Hoo! Hoo!

[ZEUS *passes by, back stage.*]

THE TUTOR: We're out of luck. The only one who doesn't run away is a half-wit. [ZEUS *retraces his steps.*] Ah, that's odd! He's followed us here.

ORESTES: Who?

THE TUTOR: That bearded fellow.

ORESTES: You're dreaming.

THE TUTOR: I tell you, I saw him go by.

ORESTES: You must be mistaken.

THE TUTOR: Impossible. Never in my life have I seen such a beard—or, rather, only one: the bronze beard on the chin of Zeus Ahenobarbos at Palermo. Look, there he is again. What can he want of us?

ORESTES: He is only a traveler like ourselves.

THE TUTOR: Only that? We met him on the road to Delphi. And when we took the boat at Itea, there he was, fanning that great beard in the bows. At Nauplia we couldn't move a step without having him at our heels, and now—here he is again! Do you think that chance explains it? [*He brushes the flies off his face.*] These flies in Argos are much more sociable than its townsfolk. Just look at them! [*Points to the* IDIOT BOY.] There must be a round dozen pumping away at each of his eyes, and yet he's smiling quite contentedly; probably he likes having his eyes sucked. That's not surprising; look at that yellow muck oozing out of them. [*He flaps his hands at the flies.*] Move on, my little friends. Hah! They're on you now. Allow me! [*He drives them away.*] Well, this should please you—you who are always complaining of being a stranger in your native land. These charming insects, anyhow, are making you welcome; one would think they know who you are. [*He whisks them away.*] Now leave us in peace, you buzzers. We know you like us, but we've had enough of you. . . . Where can they come from? They're as big as bumble-bees and noisy as a swarm of locusts.

[*Meanwhile* ZEUS *has approached them.*]

ZEUS: They are only bluebottles, a trifle larger than usual. Fifteen years ago a mighty stench of carrion drew them to this city, and since then they've been getting fatter and fatter. Give them another fifteen years, and they'll be as big as toads.

[*A short silence.*]

THE TUTOR: Pray, whom have I the honor of addressing?

ZEUS: Demetrios is my name, and I hail from Athens.

ORESTES: Did I not see you on the boat, a fortnight ago?

ZEUS: Yes, and I saw you, too.

[*Hideous shrieks come from the palace.*]

THE TUTOR: Listen to that! I don't know if you will agree with me, young master, but I think we'd do better to leave this place.

ORESTES: Keep quiet!

ZEUS: You have nothing to fear. It's what they call Dead Men's Day today. Those cries announce the beginning of the ceremony.

ORESTES: You seem well posted on the local customs.

ZEUS: Yes, I often visit Argos. As it so happened, I was here on the great day of Agamemnon's homecoming, when the Greek fleet, flushed with victory, anchored in the Nauplia roads. From the top of the rampart one saw the bay dappled with their white sails. [*He drives the flies away.*] There were no flies then. Argos was only a small country town, basking in the sun, yawning the years away. Like everyone else I went up to the sentry-path to see the royal procession, and I watched it for many an hour wending across the plain. At sundown on the second day Queen Clytemnestra came to the ramparts, and with her was Ægistheus, the present King. The people of Argos saw their faces dyed red by the sunset, and they saw them leaning over the battlements, gazing for a long while seawards. And the people thought: "There's evil brewing." But they kept silence. Ægistheus, you should know, was the Queen's lover. A hard, brutal man, and even in those days he had the cast of melancholy. . . . But you're looking pale, young sir.

ORESTES: It's the long journey I have made, and this accursed heat. But pray go on; you interest me.

ZEUS: Agamemnon was a worthy man, you know, but he made one great mistake. He put a ban on public executions. That was a pity. A good hanging now and then—that entertains folk in the provinces and robs death of its glamour. . . . So the people here held their tongues; they looked forward to seeing, for once, a violent death. They still kept silent when they saw their King entering by the city gates. And when Clytemnestra stretched forth her graceful arms, fragrant and white as lilies, they still said nothing. Yet at that moment a word, a single word, might have sufficed. But no one said it; each was gloating in imagination over the picture of a huge corpse with a shattered face.

ORESTES: And you, too, said nothing?

ZEUS: Does that rouse your indignation? Well, my young friend, I like you all the better for it; it proves your heart's in the right place. No, I admit I, too, held my peace. I'm a stranger here, and it was no concern of mine. And next day when it started, when the folks of Argos heard their King screaming his life out in the palace, they still kept silence, but they rolled their eyes in a sort of ecstasy, and the whole town was like a woman in heat.

ORESTES: So now the murderer is on the throne. For fifteen years he has enjoyed the fruits of crime. And I thought the gods were just!

ZEUS: Steady, my friend! Don't blame the gods too hastily. Must they always punish? Wouldn't it be better to use such breaches of the law to point a moral?

ORESTES: And is that what they did?

ZEUS: They sent the flies.

THE TUTOR: The flies? How do the flies come in?

ZEUS: They are a symbol. But if you want to know what the gods did, look around you. See that old creature over there, creeping away like a beetle on her little black feet, and hugging the walls. Well, she's a good specimen of the squat black vermin that teem in every cranny of this town. Now watch me catch our specimen, it's well worth inspection. Here it is. A loathsome object, you'll agree. . . . Hah! You're blinking now. Still, you're an Argive and you should be used to the white-hot rapiers of the sun. . . . Watch her wriggling, like a hooked fish! . . . Now, old lady, let's hear your tale of woe. I see you're in black from head to foot. In mourning for a whole regiment of sons, is that it? Tell us, and I'll release you—perhaps. For whom are you in mourning?

OLD WOMAN: Sir, I am not in mourning. Everyone wears black at Argos.

ZEUS: Everyone wears black? Ah, I see. You're in mourning for your murdered King.

OLD WOMAN: Whisht! For God's sake, don't talk of that.

ZEUS: Yes, you're quite old enough to have heard those huge cries that echoed and re-echoed for a whole morning in the city streets. What did you do about it?

OLD WOMAN: My good man was in the fields, at work. What could I do, a woman alone? I bolted my door.

ZEUS: Yes, but you left your window not quite closed, so as to hear the better, and, while you peeped behind the curtains and held your breath, you felt a little tingling itch between your loins, and didn't you enjoy it!

OLD WOMAN: Oh, please stop, sir!

ZEUS: And when you went to bed that night, you had a grand time with your man. A real gala night.

OLD WOMAN: A what? . . . No, my lord, that was a dreadful, dreadful night.

ZEUS: A real gala, I tell you, and you've never been able to blot out its memory.

OLD WOMAN: Mercy on us! Are you—are you one of the Dead?

ZEUS: I dead? You're crazy, woman. . . . Anyhow, don't trouble your head who I am; you'd do better to think of yourself, and try to earn forgiveness by repenting of your sins.

OLD WOMAN: Oh, sir, I do repent, most heartily I repent. If you only knew how I repent, and my daughter too, and my son-in-law offers up a heifer every year, and my little grandson has been brought up in a spirit of repentance. He's a pretty lad, with flaxen hair, and he always behaves as good as gold. Though he's only seven, he never plays or laughs, for thinking of his original sin.

ZEUS: Good, you old bitch, that's as it should be—and be sure you die in a nice bitchy odor of repentance. It's your one hope of salvation. [*The* OLD WOMAN *runs away.*] Unless I'm much mistaken, my masters, we have there the real thing, the good old piety of yore, rooted in terror.

ORESTES: What man are you?

ZEUS: Who cares what I am? We were talking of the gods. Well now, should they have struck Ægistheus down?

ORESTES: They should. . . . They should. . . . Oh, how would I know what they should have done? What do I care, anyhow? I'm a stranger here. . . . Does Ægistheus feel contrition?

ZEUS: Ægistheus? I'd be much surprised. But what matter? A whole city's repenting on his account. And it's measured by the bushel, is repentance. [*Eerie screams in the palace.*] Listen! Lest they forget the screams of the late King in his last agony, they keep this festival of death each year when the day of the King's murder comes round. A herdsman from the hills—he's chosen for his lung-power—is set to bellow in the Great Hall of the palace. [ORESTES *makes a gesture of disgust.*] Bah! That's nothing. I wonder what you'll say presently, when they let the Dead loose. Fifteen years ago, to a day, Agamemnon was murdered. And what a change has come over the light-hearted folk of Argos since that day; how near and dear to me they are at present!

ORESTES: Dear to you?

ZEUS: Pay no heed, young man. That was a slip of the tongue. Near and dear to the gods, I meant.

ORESTES: You surprise me. Then those blood-smeared walls, these swarms of flies, this reek of shambles and the stifling heat, these empty streets and yonder god with his gashed face, and all those creeping, half-human creatures beating their breasts in darkened rooms, and those shrieks, those hideous, blood-curdling shrieks—can it be that Zeus and his Olympians delight in these?

ZEUS: Young man, do not sit in judgment on the gods. They have their secrets—and their sorrows.

[*A short silence.*]

ORESTES: Am I right in thinking Agamemnon had a daughter? A daughter named Electra?

ZEUS: Yes. She lives there, in the palace—that building yonder.

ORESTES: So that's the palace? . . . And what does Electra think of—all this?

ZEUS: Oh, she's a mere child. There was a son, too, named Orestes. But he's dead, it seems.

ORESTES: Dead? Well, really . . .

THE TUTOR: Of course he's dead, young master. I thought you knew it. Don't you remember what they told us at Nauplia—about Ægistheus's having him murdered, soon after Agamemnon's death?

ZEUS: Still, some say he's alive. The story goes that the men ordered to kill the child had pity on him and left him in the forest. Some rich Athenians found him there and took him home. For my part, I'd rather he were dead.

ORESTES: Pray, why?

ZEUS: Suppose that one day he appeared in this city, and—

ORESTES: Continue, please.

ZEUS: As you wish. . . . Well, I'd say this to him. "My lad—," I'd say, "My lad," as he's your age or thereabouts—if he's alive, of course. By the way, young lord, may I know your name?

ORESTES: Philebus is my name, and I hail from Corinth. I am traveling to improve my mind, and this old slave accompanying me used to be my tutor.

ZEUS: Thank you. Well, I'd say something like this. "My lad, get you gone! What business have you here? Do you wish to enforce your rights? Yes, you're brave and strong and spirited. I can see you as a captain in an army of good fighters. You have better things to do than reigning over a dead-and-alive city, a carrion city plagued by flies. These people are great sinners but, as you see, they're working out their atonement. Let them be, young fellow, let them be; respect their sorrowful endeavor, and begone on tiptoe. You cannot share in their repentance, since you did not share their crime. Your brazen innocence makes a gulf between you and them. So if you have any care for them, be off! Be off, or you will work their doom. If you hinder them on their way, if even for a moment you turn their thoughts from their remorse, all their sins will harden on them—like cold fat. They have guilty consciences, they're afraid—and fear and guilty consciences have a good savor in the nostrils of the gods. Yes, the gods take pleasure in such poor souls. Would you oust them from the favor of the gods? What, moreover, could you give them in exchange? Good digestions, the gray monotony of provincial life, and the boredom—ah, the soul-destroying boredom—of long days of mild content. Go your way, my lad, go your way. The repose of cities and men's souls hangs on a thread; tamper with it and you bring disaster. [*Looking him in the eyes*] A disaster which will recoil on you.

ORESTES: Yes? So that is what you'd say? Well, if I were that young man, I'd answer—[*They eye each other truculently.* THE TUTOR *coughs.*] No, I don't know how I'd answer you. Perhaps you're right, and anyhow it's no concern of mine.

ZEUS: Good. I only hope Orestes would show as much sense. . . . Well, peace be with you, my friend; I must go about my business.

ORESTES: Peace be with you.

ZEUS: By the way, if those flies bother you, here's a way of getting rid of them. You see that swarm buzzing round your head? Right. Now watch! I flick my wrist—so—and wave my arm once, and then I say: Abraxas, galla, galla, tsay, tsay. See! They're falling down and starting to crawl on the ground like caterpillars.

ORESTES: By Jove!

ZEUS: Oh, that's nothing. Just a parlor trick. I'm a fly-charmer in my leisure hours. Good day to you. We shall meet again.

[*Exit* ZEUS.]

THE TUTOR: Take care. That man knows who you are.

ORESTES: "Man," you say. But *is* he a man?

THE TUTOR: What else should he be? You grieve me, my young master. Have all my lessons, all my precepts, the smiling skepticism I taught you, been wasted on your ears? "Is he a man?" you ask. There's nothing else but men—what more would you have? And that bearded fellow is a man, sure enough; probably one of Ægistheus's spies.

ORESTES: A truce to your philosophy! It's done me too much harm already.

THE TUTOR: Harm? Do you call it doing harm to people when one emancipates their minds? Ah, how you've changed! Once I read you like an open book. . . . But at least you might tell me your plans. Why bring me to this city, and what's your purpose here?

ORESTES: Did I say I had a purpose? But that's enough. Be silent now. [*He takes some steps towards the palace.*] This is *my* palace. My father's birthplace. And it's there a whore and her paramour foully butchered him. I, too, was born there. I was nearly three when that usurper's bravoes carried me away. Most likely we went out by that door. One of them held me in his arms, I had my eyes wide open, and no doubt I was crying. And yet I have no memories, none whatever. I am looking at a huge, gloomy building, solemn and pretentious in the worst provincial taste. I am looking at it, but I *see* it for the first time.

THE TUTOR: No memories, master? What ingratitude, considering that I gave ten years of my life to stocking you with them! And what of all the journeys we have made together, all the towns we visited? And the course in archæology I composed specially for you? No memories, indeed! Palaces, shrines, and temples—with so many of them is your memory peopled that you could write a guidebook of all Greece.

ORESTES: Palaces—that's so. Palaces, statues, pillars—stones, stones, stones! Why, with all those stones in my head, am I not heavier? While you are about it, why not remind me of the three hundred and eighty-seven steps of the temple at Ephesus? I climbed them, one by one, and I remember each. The seventeenth, if my memory serves me, was badly broken. And yet—! Why, an old, mangy dog, warming himself at the hearth, and struggling to his feet with a little whimper to welcome his master home—why, that dog has more memories than I! At least he recognizes his master. *His* master. But what can I call mine?

THE TUTOR: And what of your culture, Lord Orestes? What of that? All that wise lore I culled for you with loving care, like a bouquet, matching the fruits of my knowledge with the finest flowers of my experience? Did I not, from the very first, set you a-reading all the books there are, so as to make clear to you the infinite diversity of men's opinions? And did I not remind you, time and again, how variable are human creeds and customs? So, along with youth, good looks, and wealth, you have the wisdom of far riper years; your mind is free from prejudice and superstition; you have no family ties, no religion, and no calling; you are free to turn your hand to anything. But you know better than to commit yourself—and there lies your strength. So, in a word, you stand head and shoulders above the ruck and, what's more, you could hold a chair of philosophy or architecture in a great university. And yet you cavil at your lot!

ORESTES: No, I do not cavil. What should I cavil at? You've left me free as the strands torn by the wind from spiders' webs that one sees floating ten feet above the ground. I'm light as gossamer and walk on air. I know I'm favored, I appreciate my lot at its full value. [*A pause.*] Some men are born bespoken; a certain path has been assigned them, and at its end there is something they *must* do, a deed allotted. So on and on they trudge, wounding their bare feet on the flints. I suppose that strikes *you* as vulgar—the joy of going somewhere definite. And there are others, men of few words, who bear deep down in their hearts a load of dark imaginings; men whose whole life was changed because one day in childhood, at the age of five or seven—Right; I grant you these are no great men. When I was seven, I know I had no home, no roots. I let sounds and scents, the patter of rain on housetops, the golden play of sunbeams, slip past my body and fall round me—and I knew these were for others, I could never make them *my* memories. For memories are luxuries reserved for people who own houses, cattle, fields, and servants. Whereas I—! I'm free as air, thank God. My mind's my own, gloriously aloof. [*He goes nearer to the palace.*] I might have lived there. I'd not have read any of your books; perhaps I'd not have learned to read. It's rare for a Greek prince to know how to read. But I'd have come in and gone out by that door ten thousand times. As a child I'd have played with its leaves, and when I pushed at them with all my little might, they'd have creaked without yielding, and I'd have taken the measure of my weakness. Later on, I'd have pushed them open furtively by night and gone out after girls. And some years later, when I came of age, the slaves would have flung the doors wide open and I'd have crossed the threshold on horseback. My old wooden door! I'd have been able to find your keyhole with my eyes shut. And that notch there—I might have made it showing off, the first day they let me hold a spear. [*He steps back.*]

Let's see. That's the Dorian style, isn't it? And what do you make of that gold inlay? I saw the like at Dodona; a pretty piece of craftsmanship. And now I'm going to say something that will rejoice you. This is not *my* palace, nor *my* door. And there's nothing to detain us here.

THE TUTOR: Ah, that's talking sense. For what would you have gained by living in Argos? By now your spirit would be broken, you'd be wallowing in repentance.

ORESTES: Still, it would be *my* repentance. And this furnace heat singeing my hair would be *mine*. Mine, too, the buzz of all these flies. At this moment I'd be lying naked in some dark room at the back of the palace, and watching a ribbon of red light lengthen across the floor. I'd be waiting for sundown; waiting for the cool dusk of an Argos evening to rise like perfume from the parched earth; an Argos evening like many a thousand others, familiar yet ever new, another evening that should be *mine*. . . . Well, well, my worthy pedagogue, let's be off. We've no business to be luxuriating in others' heat.

THE TUTOR: Ah, my young lord, how you've eased my mind! During these last few months—to be exact, ever since I revealed to you the secret of your birth—I could see you changing day by day, and it gave me many a sleepless night. I was afraid—

ORESTES: Of what?

THE TUTOR: No, it will anger you.

ORESTES: Speak.

THE TUTOR: Be it so. Well, though from one's earliest years one has been trained to skeptic irony, one can't help having foolish fancies now and then. And I wondered if you weren't hatching some wild scheme to oust Ægistheus and take his place.

ORESTES [*thoughtfully*]: To oust Ægistheus. Ah—[*A pause.*] No, my good slave, you need not fear; the time for that is past. True, nothing could please me better than to grip that sanctimonious ruffian by the beard and drag him from my father's throne. But what purpose would it serve? These folk are no concern of mine. I have not seen one of their children come into the world, nor been present at their daughters' weddings; I don't share their remorse, I don't even know a single one of them by name. That bearded fellow was right; a king should share his subjects' memories. So we'll let them be, and begone on tiptoe. . . . But, mind you, if there were something I could do, something to give me the freedom of the city; if, even by a crime, I could acquire their memories, their hopes and fears, and fill with these the void within me, yes, even if I had to kill my own mother—

THE TUTOR: Hush! For heaven's sake, hush!

ORESTES: Yes, these are idle dreams. Let's be off. Now go and see if we can get some horses here, and we'll move on to Sparta, where I have good friends.

[ELECTRA *comes forward, carrying a large ashcan. She goes up to the statue of* ZEUS, *without seeing them.*]

ELECTRA: Yes, you old swine, scowl away at me with your goggle eyes and your fat face all smeared with raspberry juice—scowl away, but you won't scare me, not you! They've been to worship you, haven't they?—those pious matrons in black dresses. They've been padding around you in their big creaky shoes. And you were pleased, old bugaboo, it warmed your silly wooden heart. You like them old, of course; the nearer they're to corpses, the more you love them. They've poured their choicest wines out at your feet, because it's your festival today, and the stale smell from their petticoats tickled your nostrils. [*She rubs herself against him.*] Now smell me for a change, smell the perfume of a fresh, clean body. But, of course, I'm young, I'm alive—and you loathe youth and life. I, too, am bringing you offerings, while all the others are at prayers. Here they are: ashes from the hearth, peelings, scraps of offal crawling with maggots, a chunk of bread too filthy even for our pigs. But your darling flies will love it, won't they, Zeus? A good feast day to you, old idol, and let's hope it is your last. I'm not strong enough to pull you down. All I can do is to spit at you. But some day he will come, the man I'm waiting for, carrying a long, keen sword. He'll look you up and down and chuckle, with his hands on his hips, like this, and his head thrown back. Then he'll draw his sword and chop you in two, from top to bottom—like this! So the two halves of Zeus will fall apart, one to the left, one to the right, and everyone will see he's made of common wood. Just a lump of cheap white deal, the terrible God of Death! And all that frightfulness, the blood on his face, his dark green eyes, and all the rest—they'll see it was only a coat of paint. *You,* anyhow, you know you're white inside, white as a child's body, and you know, too, that a sword can rip you limb from limb, and you won't even bleed. Just a log of deal—anyhow it will serve to light our fires next winter. [*She notices* ORESTES.] Oh!

ORESTES: Don't be alarmed.

ELECTRA: I'm not alarmed. Not a bit. Who are you?

ORESTES: A stranger.

ELECTRA: Then you are welcome. All that's foreign to this town is dear to me. Your name?

ORESTES: Philebus. I've come from Corinth.

ELECTRA: Ah? From Corinth. My name's Electra.

ORESTES: Electra—[*To* THE TUTOR] Leave us.

[*Exit* THE TUTOR.]

ELECTRA: Why are you looking at me like that?

ORESTES: You're very beautiful. Not at all like the people in these parts.

ELECTRA: I beautiful? Can you really mean it? As beautiful as the Corinthian girls?

ORESTES: Yes.

ELECTRA: Well, here they never tell me that I'm beautiful. Perhaps they don't want me to know it. Anyhow, what use would beauty be to me? I'm only a servant.

ORESTES: What! You a servant?

ELECTRA: The least of the servants in the palace. I wash the King's and the Queen's underlinen. And how dirty it is, all covered with spots and stains! Yes, I have to wash everything they wear next to their skin, the shifts they wrap their rotting bodies in, the nightdresses Clytemnestra has on when the King shares her bed. I shut my eyes and scrub with all my might. I have to wash up, too. You don't believe me? See my hands, all chapped and rough. Why are you looking at them in that funny way? Do they, by any chance, look like the hands of a princess?

ORESTES: Poor little hands. No, they don't look like a princess's hands. . . . But tell me more. What else do they make you do?

ELECTRA: Every morning I've to empty the ashcan. I drag it out of the palace, and then — well, you saw what I do with the refuse. That big fellow in wood is Zeus, God of Death and Flies. The other day, when the High Priest came here to make his usual bows and scrapings, he found himself treading on cabbage stumps and rotten turnips and mussel shells. He looked startled, I can tell you! I say! You won't tell on me, will you?

ORESTES: No.

ELECTRA: Really I don't care if you do. They can't make things much worse for me than they are already. I'm used to being beaten. Perhaps they'd shut me up in one of the rooms in the tower. That wouldn't be so bad; at least I wouldn't have to see their faces. Just imagine what I get by way of thanks at bedtime, when my day's work is done. I go up to a tall, stout lady with dyed hair, with thick lips and very white hands, a queen's hands, that smell of honey. Then she puts her hands on my shoulders and dabs my forehead with her lips and says: "Good night, Electra. Good night." Every evening. Every evening I have to feel that woman slobbering on my face. Ugh! Like a piece of raw meat on my forehead. But I hold myself up, I've never fallen yet. She's my mother, you know. If I was up in the tower, she wouldn't kiss me anymore.

ORESTES: Have you never thought of running away?

ELECTRA: I haven't the courage; I daren't face the country roads at night all by myself.

ORESTES: Is there no one, no girlfriend of yours, who'd go with you?

ELECTRA: No, I'm quite alone. Ask any of the people here, and they'll tell you I'm a pest, a public nuisance. I've no friends.

ORESTES: Not even an old nurse, who saw you into the world and has kept a little affection for you?

ELECTRA: Not even an old nurse. Mother will tell you; I freeze even the kindest hearts — that's how I am.

ORESTES: Do you propose to spend your life here?

ELECTRA [*excitedly*]: My life? Oh no, no! Of course not! Listen. I'm waiting for — for something.

ORESTES: Something, or someone?

ELECTRA: That's my secret. Now it's your turn to speak. You're good-looking, too. Will you be here long?

ORESTES: Well, I'd thought of leaving today. But, as it is —

ELECTRA: Yes?

ORESTES: As it is, I'm not so sure.

ELECTRA: Is Corinth a pretty place?

ORESTES: Very pretty.

ELECTRA: Do you like it? Are you proud of Corinth?

ORESTES: Yes.

ELECTRA: How strange that sounds! I can't imagine myself being proud of my home town. Tell me what it feels like.

ORESTES: Well—No, I don't know. I can't explain.

ELECTRA: You can't? I wonder why. [*A short silence.*] What's Corinth like? Are there shady streets and squares? Places where one can stroll in the cool of the evening?

ORESTES: Yes.

ELECTRA: And everyone comes out of doors? People go for walks together?

ORESTES: Almost everyone is out and about at sundown.

ELECTRA: Boys and girls together?

ORESTES: Oh yes, one often sees them going for walks together.

ELECTRA: And they always find something to say to each other? They like each other's company, and one hears them laughing in the streets quite late at night?

ORESTES: Yes.

ELECTRA: I suppose you think I'm very childish. But it's so hard for me to picture a life like that—going for walks, laughing and singing in the streets. Everybody here is sick with fear. Everyone except me. And I—

ORESTES: Yes? And you?

ELECTRA: Oh, I—I'm sick with—hatred. And what do they do all day, the girls at Corinth?

ORESTES: Well, they spend quite a while making themselves pretty; then they sing or play on lutes. Then they call on their friends, and at night they go to dances.

ELECTRA: But don't they have any worries?

ORESTES: Only quite little ones.

ELECTRA: Yes? Now listen well, please. Don't the people at Corinth feel remorse?

ORESTES: Sometimes. Not very often.

ELECTRA: So they do what they like and, afterwards, don't give another thought to it?

ORESTES: That's their way.

ELECTRA: How strange! [*A short silence.*] Please tell me something else; I want to know it because of—of someone I'm expecting. Suppose one of the young fellows you've been telling about, who walk and laugh with girls in the evenings— suppose one of these young men came home after a long journey and found his father murdered, and his mother living with the murderer, and his sister treated like a slave—what would he do, that young man from Corinth? Would he just take it for granted and slink out of his father's house and look for consolation with his girl friends? Or would he draw his sword and hurl himself at the assassin, and slash his brains out? . . . Why are you silent?

ORESTES: I was wondering—

ELECTRA: What? You can't say what he'd do?

CLYTEMNESTRA [*offstage, calling*]: Electra!

ELECTRA: Hush!

ORESTES: What is it?

ELECTRA: That was my mother, Queen Clytemnestra. [CLYTEMNESTRA *enters.*] What's this, Philebus? Are you afraid of her?

ORESTES [*to himself*]: So that's the face I tried to picture, night after night, until I came to see it, really *see* it, drawn and haggard under the rosy mask of paint. But I hadn't counted on those dead eyes.

CLYTEMNESTRA: Electra, hear the King's order. You are to make ready for the ceremony. You must wear your black dress and your jewels. . . . Well, what does this behavior mean? Why are you pressing your elbows to your hips and staring at the ground? Oh, I know your tricks, my girl, but they don't deceive me any longer. Just now I was watching at the window and I saw a very different Electra, a girl with flashing eyes, bold gestures. . . . Why don't you answer?

ELECTRA: Do you really think a scullery maid would add to the splendor of your festival?

CLYTEMNESTRA: No playacting. You are a princess, Electra, and the townsfolk expect to see you, as in former years.

ELECTRA: A princess—yes, the princess of a day. Once a year, when this day comes round, you remember who I am; because, of course, the people want an edifying glimpse of our family life. A strange princess, indeed, who herds pigs and washes up. Tell me, will Ægistheus put his arm round my neck as he did last time? Will he smile tenderly on me, while he mumbles horrible threats in my ear?

CLYTEMNESTRA: If you would have him otherwise, it rests with you.

ELECTRA: Yes—if I let myself be tainted by your remorse; if I beg the gods' forgiveness for a crime I never committed. Yes—if I kiss your royal husband's hand and call him father. Ugh! The mere thought makes me sick. There's dry blood under his nails.

CLYTEMNESTRA: Do as you will. I have long ceased giving you orders in my name. It is the King's command I bring you.

ELECTRA: And why should I obey him? Ægistheus is your husband, Mother, your dearly beloved husband—not mine.

CLYTEMNESTRA: That is all I have to say, Electra. Only too well I see you are determined to bring ruin on yourself, and on us all. Yet who am I to counsel you, I who ruined my whole life in a single morning? You hate me, my child, but what disturbs me more is your likeness to me, as I was once. I used to have those clean-cut features, that fever in the blood, those smoldering eyes—and nothing good came of them.

ELECTRA: No! Don't say I'm like you! Tell me, Philebus—you can see us side by side—am I really like her?

ORESTES: How can I tell? Her face is like a pleasant garden that hail and storms have ravaged. And upon yours I see a threat of storm; one day passion will sear it to the bone.

ELECTRA: A threat of storm? Good! So far I welcome the likeness. May your words come true!

CLYTEMNESTRA: And you, young man, who stare so boldly at us, who are you and why have you come here? Let me look at you more closely.

ELECTRA [*quickly*]: He's a Corinthian, of the name of Philebus. A traveler.

CLYTEMNESTRA: Philebus? Ah!

ELECTRA: You seemed to fear another name.

CLYTEMNESTRA: To fear? If the doom I brought on my life has taught me anything, it is that I have nothing left to fear. . . . Welcome to Argos, stranger. Yes, come nearer. How young you seem! What's your age?

ORESTES: Eighteen.

CLYTEMNESTRA: Are your parents alive?

ORESTES: My father's dead.

CLYTEMNESTRA: And your mother? Is she about my age? Ah, you don't answer. I suppose she looks much younger; she still laughs and sings when you are with her. Do you love her? Answer me, please. Why did you leave her?

ORESTES: I am on my way to Sparta, to enlist in the army.

CLYTEMNESTRA: Most travelers give our city a wide berth. Some go twenty leagues out of their way to avoid it. Were you not warned? The people of the Plain have put us in quarantine; they see our repentance as a sort of pestilence and are afraid of being infected.

ORESTES: I know.

CLYTEMNESTRA: Did they tell you that we bear the burden of an inexpiable crime, committed fifteen years ago?

ORESTES: Yes, they told me that.

CLYTEMNESTRA: And that Queen Clytemnestra bears the heaviest load of guilt — that men shudder at her name?

ORESTES: That, too, I heard.

CLYTEMNESTRA: And yet you've come here! Stranger, I am Queen Clytemnestra.

ELECTRA: Don't pity her, Philebus. The Queen is indulging in our national pastime, the game of public confession. Here everyone cries his sins on the housetops. On holidays you'll often see a worthy shopkeeper dragging himself along on his knees, covering his hair with dust, and screaming out that he's a murderer, a libertine, a liar, and all the rest of it. But the folk of Argos are getting a little tired of these amusements; everyone knows his neighbor's sins by heart. The Queen's, especially, have lost interest; they're official — our basic crimes, in fact. So you can imagine her delight when she finds someone like you, somebody raw and young, who doesn't even know her name, to hear her tale of guilt. A marvelous opportunity! It's as if she were confessing for the first time.

CLYTEMNESTRA: Be silent. Anyone has the right to spit in my face, to call me murderess and whore. But no one has the right to speak ill of my remorse.

ELECTRA: Note her words, Philebus. That's a rule of the game. People will beg you to condemn them, but you must be sure to judge them only on the sins they own to; their other evil deeds are no one's business, and they wouldn't thank you for detecting them.

CLYTEMNESTRA: Fifteen years ago men said I was the loveliest woman in Greece. Look at me now and judge my sufferings. Let me be frank, young stranger; it is not the death of that old lecher that I regret. When I saw his blood tingeing the water in the bath, I sang and danced for joy. And even now, after fifteen years, whenever I recall it, I have a thrill of pleasure. But — but I had a son; he would be your age now. When Ægistheus handed him over to his bravoes, I —

ELECTRA: You had a daughter too, my mother, if I'm not mistaken. And you've made of her a scullion. But that crime, it seems, sits lightly on your conscience.

CLYTEMNESTRA: You are young, Electra. It is easy for young people, who have not yet had a chance of sinning, to condemn. But wait, my girl; one day you, too, will be trailing after you an inexpiable crime. At every step you will think that you are leaving it behind, but it will remain as heavy as before. Whenever you look back you will see it there, just at arm's length, glowing darkly like a black crystal. And you will have forgotten what it really is, and murmur to yourself: "It wasn't I, it could not have been I, who did that." Yet, though you disown it time and time again, always it will be there, a dead weight holding you back. And then at last you will realize that you staked your life on a single throw of the dice, and nothing remains for you but to drag your crime after you until you die. For that is the law, just or unjust, of repentance. Ah, then we'll see a change come over your young pride.

ELECTRA: My young pride? So it's your lost youth you are regretting, still more than your crime. It's my youth you detest, even more than my innocence.

CLYTEMNESTRA: What I detest in you, Electra, is—myself. Not your youth—far from it!—but my own.

ELECTRA: And I—it's you, it's *you* I hate.

CLYTEMNESTRA: For shame, Electra! Here we are, scolding each other like two women of the same age in love with the same man! And yet I am your mother. . . . I do not know who you are, young man, nor what brings you here, but your presence bodes no good. Electra hates me—that, of course, I always knew. But for fifteen years we have kept the peace; only our eyes betrayed our feelings. And now you have come, you have spoken, and here we are showing our teeth and snapping at each other like two curs in the street. An ancient law of Argos compels us to give you hospitality, but, I make no secret of it, I had rather you were gone. As for you, my child, too faithful copy of myself, 'tis true I have no love for you. But I had rather cut off my right hand than do you harm. Only too well you know it, and you trade on my weakness. But I advise you not to rear your anxious little head against Ægistheus; he has a short way with vipers. Mark my words, do his bidding—or you will rue it.

ELECTRA: Tell the King that I shall not attend the rite. Do you know what they do, Philebus? Above the town there's a great cavern; none of our young men, not even the bravest, has ever found its end. People say that it leads down to hell, and the High Priest has had the entrance blocked with a great stone. Well—would you believe it?—each year when this anniversary comes round, the townspeople gather outside the cavern, soldiers roll away the stone, and our dead, so they say, come up from hell and roam the city. Places are laid for them at every table, chairs and beds made ready, and the people in the house huddle in corners to make room for them during the night watches. For the dead are everywhere, the whole town's at their mercy. You can imagine how our townsfolk plead with them. "My poor dead darling, I didn't mean to wrong you. Please be kind." Tomorrow, at cockcrow, they'll return underground, the stone will be rolled back, and that will be the end of it until this day next year.

Well, I refuse to take part in this mummery. Those dead folk are *their* dead, not mine.

CLYTEMNESTRA: If you will not obey his summons willingly, the King will have you brought to him by force.

ELECTRA: By force? . . . I see. Very well, then. My good kind mother, will you please tell the King that I shall certainly obey. I shall attend the rite, and if the townsfolk wish to see me, they won't be disappointed. . . . Philebus, will you do something for me? Please don't go at once, but stay here for the ceremony. Perhaps some parts of it may entertain you. Now I'll go and make myself ready.

[*Exit* ELECTRA.]

CLYTEMNESTRA [*to* ORESTES]: Leave this place. I feel that you are going to bring disaster on us. You have no cause to wish us ill; we have done nothing to you. So go, I beg you. By all you hold most sacred, for your mother's sake, I beg you, go.

[*Exit* CLYTEMNESTRA.]

ORESTES [*thoughtfully*]: For my mother's sake.

[ZEUS *enters and comes up to him.*]

ZEUS: Your attendant tells me you wish to leave. He has been looking for horses all over Argos, but can find none. Well, I can procure for you two sturdy mares and riding gear at a very low figure.

ORESTES: I've changed my mind. I am not leaving Argos.

ZEUS [*meditatively*]: Ah, so you're not leaving, after all. [*A short pause. Then, in a quicker tempo*] In that case I shall stay with you and be your host. I know an excellent inn in the lower town where we can lodge together. You won't regret my company, I can assure you. But first—Abraxas, galla, galla, tsay, tsay—let me rid you of those flies. A man of my age can often be very helpful to lads like you. I'm old enough to be your father; you must tell me all about yourself and your troubles. So come, young man, don't try to shake me off. Meetings like this are often of more use than one would think. Consider the case of Telemachus— you know whom I mean, King Ulysses' son. One fine day he met an old worthy of the name of Mentor, who joined forces with him. Now I wonder if you know who that old fellow Mentor really was. . . .

[*He escorts* ORESTES *off the stage, holding him in conversation, while the curtain falls.*]

ACT II

Scene 1

A mountain terrace, with a cavern on the right. Its entrance is blocked by a large black boulder. On the left is a flight of steps leading up to a temple. A crowd of men and women have gathered for the ceremony.

A WOMAN [*kneeling before her little son, as she straightens the kerchief round his neck*]: There! That's the third time I've had to straighten it for you. [*She dusts his clothes.*] That's better. Now try to behave properly, and mind you start crying when you're told.

THE CHILD: Is that where they come from?

THE WOMAN: Yes.

THE CHILD: I'm frightened.

THE WOMAN: And so you should be, darling. Terribly frightened. That's how one grows up into a decent, god-fearing man.

A MAN: They'll have good weather today.

ANOTHER MAN: Just as well. It seems they still like sunlight, shadows though they are. Last year, when it rained, they were fierce, weren't they?

FIRST MAN: Ay, that's the word. Fierce.

SECOND MAN: A shocking time we had!

THIRD MAN: Once they've gone back to their cave and left us to ourselves, I'll climb up here again and look at that there stone, and I'll say to myself: "Now we've a year's peace before us."

FOURTH MAN: Well, I'm not like you, I ain't consoled that easily. From tomorrow I'll start wondering how they'll be next year. Every year they're getting nastier and nastier, and—

SECOND MAN: Hold your tongue, you fool! Suppose one of them has crept out through a crevice and is prowling round us now, eavesdropping, like. There's some of the Dead come out ahead of time, so I've heard tell.

[*They eye each other nervously.*]

A YOUNG WOMAN: If only it would start! What are they up to, those palace folk? They're never in a hurry, and it's all this waiting gets one down, what with the blazing sun and only that big black stone to look at. Just think! They're all there, crowded up behind the stone, gloating over the cruel things they're going to do to us.

AN OLD WOMAN: That's enough, my girl. . . . We all know she's no better than she should be; that's why she's so scared of her ghost. Her husband died last spring, and for ten years she'd been fooling the poor man.

YOUNG WOMAN: I don't deny it. Sure enough, I fooled him to the top of his bent; but I always liked him and I led him a pleasant life, that he can't deny. He never knew a thing about the other men, and when he died, you should have seen the way he looked at me, so tenderly, like a grateful dog. Of course, he knows everything now, and it's bitter pain for him, poor fellow, and all his love has turned to hate. Presently I'll feel him coiling round me, like a wisp of smoke, and he'll cling to me more closely than any living man has ever clung. I'll bring him home with me, wound round my neck like a tippet. I've a tasty little meal all ready, with the cakes and honey that he always liked. But it's all no use, I know. He'll never forgive me, and tonight—oh, how I dread it!—he will share my bed.

A MAN: Ay, she's right. What's Ægistheus doing? We can't bear this suspense much longer. It ain't fair to keep us waiting like this.

ANOTHER MAN: Sorry for yourself, are you? But do you think Ægistheus is less afraid than we? Tell me, how'd you like to be in his shoes, and have Agamemnon gibbering at you for twenty-four hours?

YOUNG WOMAN: Oh, this horrible, horrible suspense! Do you know, I have a feeling that all of you are drifting miles and miles away, leaving me alone. The stone is not yet rolled aside, but each of us is shut up with his dead, and lonely as a raindrop.

[ZEUS *enters, followed by* ORESTES *and* THE TUTOR.]

ZEUS: This way, young man; you'll have a better view.

ORESTES: So here we have them, the citizens of Argos, King Agamemnon's loyal subjects!

THE TUTOR: What an ugly lot! Observe, young master, their sallow cheeks and sunken eyes. These folk are perishing of fear. What better example could we have of the effects of superstition? Just look at them! And if you need another proof of the soundness of my teaching, look on me and my rosy cheeks.

ZEUS: Much good they do you, your pink cheeks. For all your roses, my good man, you're no more than a sack of dung, like all those others, in the eyes of Zeus. Yes, though you may not guess it, you stink to heaven. These folk, at least, are wise in their generation; they know how bad they smell.

A MAN [*climbing onto the temple steps, harangues the crowd*]: Do they want to drive us mad? Let's raise our voices all together and summon Ægistheus. Make him understand we will not suffer any more delay.

THE CROWD: Ægistheus! King Ægistheus! Have pity on us!

A WOMAN: Pity, yes, pity, you cry. And will none have pity on me? He'll come with his slit throat, the man I loathed so bitterly, and clammy, unseen arms will maul me in the darkness, all through the night.

ORESTES: But this is madness! Why doesn't someone tell these wretched people—?

ZEUS: What's this, young man? Why this ado over a woman who's lost her nerve? Wait and see; there's worse to come.

A MAN [*falling on his knees*]: I stink! Oh, how I stink! I am a mass of rottenness. See how the flies are teeming round me, like carrion crows. . . . That's right, my harpies, sting and gouge and scavenge me; bore through my flesh to my black heart. I have sinned a thousand times, I am a sink of ordure, and I reek to heaven.

ZEUS: O worthy man!

SOME MAN [*helping him to his feet*]: That's enough. You shall talk about it later, when *they* are out.

[*Gasping, rolling his eyes, the man stares at them.*]

THE CROWD: Ægistheus! Ægistheus! For mercy's sake, give the order to begin. We can bear no more.

[ÆGISTHEUS *comes onto the temple steps, followed by* CLYTEMNESTRA, THE HIGH PRIEST, *and* BODYGUARDS.]

ÆGISTHEUS: Dogs! How dare you bewail your lot? Have you forgotten your disgrace? Then, by Zeus, I shall refresh your memories. [*He turns to* CLYTEMNESTRA.] We must start without her, it seems. But let her beware! My punishment will be condign.

CLYTEMNESTRA: She promised to attend. No doubt she is making ready, lingering in front of her mirror.

ÆGISTHEUS [*to* THE SOLDIERS]: Go seek Electra in the palace and bring her here by force, if need be. [SOLDIERS *file out. He addresses* THE CROWD.] Take your usual places. The men on my right, women and children on my left. Good.

[*A short silence.* ÆGISTHEUS *is waiting.*]

HIGH PRIEST: Sire, these people are at breaking point.

ÆGISTHEUS: I know. But I am waiting for—

[THE SOLDIERS *return.*]

A SOLDIER: Your Majesty, we have searched for the princess everywhere. But there is no one in the palace.

ÆGISTHEUS: So be it. We shall deal with her tomorrow. [*To* THE HIGH PRIEST] Begin.

HIGH PRIEST: Roll away the stone.

THE CROWD: Ah!

[THE SOLDIERS *roll away the stone.* THE HIGH PRIEST *goes to the entrance of the cavern.*]

HIGH PRIEST: You, the forgotten and forsaken, all you whose hopes were dupes, who creep along the ground darkling like smoke wraiths and have nothing left you but your great shame—you, the dead, arise; this is your day of days. Come up, pour forth like a thick cloud of fumes of brimstone driven by the wind; rise from the bowels of the earth, ye who have died a hundred deaths, ye whom every heartbeat in our breasts strikes dead again. In the name of anger unappeased and unappeasable, and the lust of vengeance, I summon you to wreak your hatred on the living. Come forth and scatter like a dark miasma in our streets, weave between the mother and her child, the lover and his beloved; make us regret that we, too, are not dead. Arise, spectres, harpies, ghouls, and goblins of our night. Soldiers arise, who died blaspheming; arise, downtrodden victims, children of disgrace; arise, all ye who died of hunger, whose last sigh was a curse. See, the living are here to greet you, fodder for your wrath. Arise and have at them like a great rushing wind, and gnaw them to the bone. Arise! Arise! Arise!

[*A tom-tom sounds, and* THE PRIEST *dances at the entrance of the cavern, slowly at first, then quickening his gyrations until he falls to the ground exhausted.*]

ÆGISTHEUS: They are coming forth.

THE CROWD: Heaven help us!

ORESTES: I can bear this no longer. I must go—

ZEUS: Look at me, young man. In the eyes. Good; you understand. Now, keep quiet.

ORESTES: Who—who are you?

ZEUS: You shall know soon.

[ÆGISTHEUS *comes slowly down the temple steps.*]

ÆGISTHEUS: They are there. All of them. [*A short silence.*] There he is, Aricië, the husband you used so ill. There he is, beside you, kissing you tenderly, clasping you in his dead arms. How he loves you! And ah, how he hates you! . . . There she is, Nicias, your mother, who died of your neglect. . . . And you there, Segestes, you bloodsucker—they are all round you, the wretched men who borrowed of you; those who starved to death, and those who hanged themselves because of you.

In your debt they died, but today they are your creditors. And you, fathers and mothers, loving parents, lower your eyes humbly. They are there, your dead children, stretching their frail arms towards you, and all the happiness you denied them, all the tortures you inflicted, weigh like lead on their sad, childish, unforgiving hearts.

THE CROWD: Have mercy!

ÆGISTHEUS: Mercy? You ask for mercy! Do you not know the dead have no mercy? Their grievances are time-proof, adamant; rancor without end. Do you hope, Nicias, to atone by deeds of kindness for the wrong you did your mother? But what act of kindness can ever reach her now? Her soul is like a sultry, windless noon, in which nothing stirs, nothing changes, nothing lives. Only a fierce unmoving sun beats down on bare rocks forever. The dead have ceased to be—think what that implies in all its ruthlessness—yes, they are no more, and in their eternal keeping your crimes have no reprieve.

THE CROWD: Mercy!

ÆGISTHEUS: Well you may cry mercy! Play your parts, you wretched mummers, for today you have a full house to watch you. Millions of staring, hopeless eyes are brooding darkly on your faces and your gestures. They can see us, read our hearts, and we are naked in the presence of the dead. Ah, that makes you squirm; it burns and sears you, that stern, calm gaze unchanging as the gaze of eyes remembered.

THE CROWD: Mercy!

THE MEN: Forgive us for living while you are dead.

THE WOMEN: Have mercy! Tokens of you are ever with us, we see your faces everywhere we turn. We wear mourning unceasingly, and weep for you from dawn till dusk, from dusk till dawn. But somehow, try as we may, your memory dwindles and slips through our fingers; daily it grows dimmer and we know ourselves the guiltier. Yes, you are leaving us, ebbing away like lifeblood from a wound. And yet, know you well—if this can mollify your bitter hatred—that you, our dear departed, have laid waste our lives.

THE MEN: Forgive us for living while you are dead.

THE CHILDREN: Please forgive us. We didn't want to be born, we're ashamed of growing up. What wrong can we have done you? It's not our fault if we're alive. And only just alive; see how small we are, how pale and puny. We never laugh or sing, we glide about like ghosts. And we're so frightened of you, so terribly afraid. Have mercy on us.

THE MEN: Forgive us for living while you are dead.

ÆGISTHEUS: Hold your peace! If you voice your sorrow thus, what will be left for me, your King, to say? For my ordeal has begun; the earth is quaking, and the light failing, and the greatest of the dead is coming forth—he whom I slew with my own hand, King Agamemnon.

ORESTES [*drawing his sword*]: I forbid you to drag my father's name into this mummery.

ZEUS [*clutching his arms*]: Stop, young fellow! Stop that!

ÆGISTHEUS [*looking round*]: Who dares to—?

[ELECTRA, *wearing a white dress, comes onto the temple steps.* ÆGISTHEUS *sees her.*]
　　Electra!

THE CROWD: Electra!

ÆGISTHEUS: What is the meaning of this, Electra? Why are you in white?

ELECTRA: It's my prettiest dress. The city holds high festival today, and I thought I'd look my best.

HIGH PRIEST: Would you insult our dead? This day is *their* day, and well you know it. You should be in mourning.

ELECTRA: Why? I'm not afraid of *my* dead, and yours mean nothing to me.

ÆGISTHEUS: That is so; your dead are not our dead. . . . Remember the breed she comes of, the breed of Atreus, who treacherously cut his nephews' throats. What are you, Electra, but the last survivor of an accursed race? Ay, that whorish dress becomes you. I suffered your presence in the palace out of pity, but now I know I erred; the old foul blood of the house of Atreus flows in your veins. And if I did not see to it, you would taint us all. But bide awhile, my girl, and you will learn how I can punish. Your eyes will be red with weeping for many a day.

THE CROWD: Sacrilege! Sacrilege! Away with her!

ÆGISTHEUS: Hear, miserable girl, the murmurs of these good folk you have outraged. Were I not here to curb their anger, they would tear you in pieces.

THE CROWD: Away with her, the impious wretch!

ELECTRA: Is it impious to be gay? Why can't these good folk of yours be gay? What prevents them?

ÆGISTHEUS: She is laughing, the wanton — and her dead father is standing there with blood on his face.

ELECTRA: How dare you talk of Agamemnon? How can you be so sure he doesn't visit me by night and tell me all his secrets? Ah, if you knew the love and longing that hoarse, dead voice breathes in my ears! Yes, I'm laughing — laughing for the first time in my life; for the first time I'm happy. And can you be so sure my new-won happiness doesn't rejoice my father's heart? More likely, if he's here and sees his daughter in her white dress — his daughter of whom you've made a wretched drudge — if he sees her holding her head high, keeping her pride intact, more likely the last thing he dreams of is to blame me. No, his eyes are sparkling in the havoc of his face, he's twisting his blood-stained lips in the shadow of a smile.

THE YOUNG WOMAN: Can it be true, what she says?

VOICES: No, no. She's talking nonsense. She's gone mad. Electra, go, for pity's sake, or your sins will be visited on us.

ELECTRA: But what is it you're so frightened of? I can see all round you and there's nothing but your own shadows. Now listen to what I've just been told, something you may not know. In Greece there are cities where men live happily. White, contented cities, basking like lizards in the sun. At this very moment, under this same sky, children are playing in the streets of Corinth. And their mothers aren't asking forgiveness for having brought them into the world. No, they're smiling tenderly at them, they're proud of their motherhood. Mothers of Argos, can't you understand? Does it mean nothing to you, the pride of a mother who looks at her son and thinks: "It's I who bore him, brought him up"?

ÆGISTHEUS: That's enough. Keep silent, or I'll thrust your words down your throat.

VOICES: Yes, yes. Make her stop. She's talked enough.

OTHER VOICES: No, let her speak. It's Agamemnon speaking through her.

ELECTRA: The sun is shining. Everywhere down in the plains men are looking up and saying: "It's a fine day," and they're happy. Are you so set on making yourselves wretched that you've forgotten the simple joy of the peasant who says as he walks across his fields: "It's a fine day"? No, there you stand hanging your heads, moping and mumbling, more dead than alive. You're too terrified to lift a finger, afraid of jolting your precious ghosts if you make any movement. That would be dreadful, wouldn't it, if your hand suddenly went through a patch of clammy mist, and it was your grandmother's ghost! Now look at me. I'm spreading out my arms freely, and I'm stretching like someone just roused from sleep. I have my place in the sunlight, my full place and to spare. And does the sky fall on my head? Now I'm dancing, see, I'm dancing, and all I feel is the wind's breath fanning my cheeks. Where are the dead? Do you think they're dancing with me, in step?

HIGH PRIEST: People of Argos, I tell you that this woman is a profaner of all we hold most holy. Woe to her and to all of you who listen to her words!

ELECTRA: Oh, my beloved dead—Iphigeneia, my elder sister, and Agamemnon, my father and my only King—hear my prayer. If I am an evildoer, if I offend your sorrowing shades, make some sign that I may know. But if, my dear ones, you approve, let no leaf stir, no blade of grass be moved, and no sound break in on my sacred dance. For I am dancing for joy, for peace among men; I dance for happiness and life. My dead ones, I invoke your silence that these people around me may know your hearts are with me.

[*She dances.*]

VOICES IN THE CROWD: Look how she's dancing, light as a flame. Look how her dress is rippling, like a banner in the wind. And the dead—the dead do nothing.

THE YOUNG WOMAN: And see her look of ecstasy—oh, no, no, that's not the face of a wicked woman. Well, Ægistheus, what have you to say? Why are you silent?

ÆGISTHEUS: I waste no words on her. Does one argue with malignant vermin? No, one stamps them out. My kindness to her in the past was a mistake, but a mistake that can be remedied. Have no fear, I shall make short work of her and end her accursed race.

VOICES IN THE CROWD: Answer us, King Ægistheus. Threats are no answer.

THE YOUNG WOMAN: She's dancing, smiling, oh, so happily and the dead seem to protect her. Oh fortunate, too fortunate Electra! Look, I, too, am holding out my arms, baring my neck to the sunlight.

A VOICE IN THE CROWD: The dead hold their peace. Ægistheus, you have lied.

ORESTES: Dear Electra!

ZEUS: This is too much. I'll shut that foolish wench's tongue. [*Stretches out his right arm.*] Poseidon, carabou, carabou, roola. [*The big stone which blocked the entrance to the cavern rumbles across the stage and crashes against the temple steps.* ELECTRA *stops dancing.*]

THE CROWD: Ah! . . . Mercy on us!

[*A long silence.*]

HIGH PRIEST: Froward and fickle race, now you have seen how the dead avenge themselves. Mark how the flies are beating down on you, in thick, swirling clouds. You have hearkened to the tempter's voice, and a curse has fallen on the city.

THE CROWD: It is not our fault, we are innocent. That woman came and tempted us, with her lying tongue. To the river with her! Drown the witch.

AN OLD WOMAN [*pointing to* THE YOUNG WOMAN]: That young huzzy there was lapping up her words like milk. Strip her naked and lash her till she squeals. [THE WOMEN *seize* THE YOUNG WOMAN, *while* THE MEN *surge up the temple steps, towards* ELECTRA.]

ÆGISTHEUS [*straightening up*]: Silence, dogs! Back to your places! Vengeance is mine, not yours. [*A short silence.*] Well, you have seen what comes of disobeying me. Henceforth you will know better than to misdoubt your ruler. Disperse to your homes, the dead will keep you company and be your guests until tomorrow's dawn. Make place for them at your tables, at your hearths, and in your beds. And see that your good behavior blots out the memory of what has happened here. As for me—grieved though I am by your mistrust, I forgive you. But you, Electra—

ELECTRA: Yes? What of it? I failed to bring it off this time. Next time I'll do better.

ÆGISTHEUS: There shall be no next time. The custom of the city forbids my punishing you on the day the dead are with us. This you knew, and you took advantage of it. But you are no longer one of us; I cast you out forever. You shall go hence barefooted, with nothing in your hands, wearing that shameless dress. And I hereby order any man who sees you within our gates after the sun has risen to strike you down and rid the city of its bane.

[*He goes out, followed by* THE SOLDIERS. THE CROWD *file past* ELECTRA, *shaking their fists at her.*]

ZEUS [*to* ORESTES]: Well, young master, were you duly edified? For, unless I'm much mistaken, the tale has a moral. The wicked have been punished and the good rewarded. [*He points to* ELECTRA.] As for that woman—

ORESTES [*sharply*]: Mind what you say. That woman is my sister. Now go; I want to talk to her.

ZEUS [*observes him for a moment, then shrugs his shoulders*]: Very good.

[*Exit* ZEUS *followed by* THE TUTOR.]

ORESTES: Electra!

ELECTRA [*still standing on the temple steps, she raises her eyes and gazes at him*]: Ah, you're still there, Philebus?

ORESTES: You're in danger, Electra. You mustn't stay a moment longer in this city.

ELECTRA: In danger? Yes, that's true. You saw how I failed to bring it off. It was a bit your fault, you know—but I'm not angry with you.

ORESTES: My fault? How?

ELECTRA: You deceived me. [*She comes down the steps towards him.*] Let me look at your eyes. Yes, it was your eyes that made a fool of me.

ORESTES: There's no time to lose. Listen, Electra! We'll escape together. Someone's getting a horse for me and you can ride pillion.

ELECTRA: No.

ORESTES: What? You won't come away with me?

ELECTRA: I refuse to run away.

ORESTES: I'll take you with me to Corinth.

ELECTRA [*laughing*]: Corinth? Exactly! I know you mean well, but you're fooling me again. What could a girl like me do in Corinth? I've got to keep a level head, you know. Only yesterday my desires were so simple, so modest. When I waited at table, with meek, downcast eyes, I used to watch the two of them—the handsome old woman with the dead face, and the fat, pale King with the slack mouth and that absurd beard like a regiment of spiders running round his chin. And then I'd dream of what I'd see one day—a wisp of steam, like one's breath on a cold morning, rising from their split bellies. That was the only thing I lived for, Philebus, I assure you. I don't know what you're after, but this I know: that I mustn't believe you. Your eyes are too bold for my liking. . . . Do you know what I used to tell myself before I met you? That a wise person can want nothing better from life than to pay back the wrong that has been done to him.

ORESTES: If you come with me, Electra, you'll see there are many, many other things to ask of life—without one's ceasing to be wise.

ELECTRA: No, I won't listen anymore, you've done me quite enough harm already. You came here with your kind, girlish face and your eager eyes—and you made me forget my hatred. I unlocked my hands and I let my one and only treasure slip through them. You lured me into thinking one could cure the people here by words. Well, you saw what happened. They nurse their disease; they've got to like their sores so much that they scratch them with their dirty nails to keep them festering. Words are no use for such as they. An evil thing is conquered only by another evil thing, and only violence can save them. So good-by, Philebus, and leave me to my bad dreams.

ORESTES: They'll kill you.

ELECTRA: We have a sanctuary here, Apollo's shrine. Often criminals take shelter there, and so long as they are in the temple, no one can touch a hair of their heads. That's where I'll go.

ORESTES: But why refuse my help?

ELECTRA: It's not for you to help me. Someone else will come, to set me free. [*A short silence.*] My brother isn't dead; I know that. And I'm waiting for his coming.

ORESTES: Suppose he doesn't come?

ELECTRA: He *will* come; he's bound to come. He is of our stock, you see; he has crime and tragedy in his blood, as I have—the bad blood of the house of Atreus. I picture him as a big, strong man, a born fighter, with bloodshot eyes like our father's, always smoldering with rage. He, too, is doomed; tangled up in his destiny, like a horse whose belly is ripped open and his legs are caught up in his guts. And now at every step he tears his bowels out. Yes, one day he will come, this city draws him. Nothing can hinder his coming, for it is here he can do the greatest harm, and suffer the greatest harm. I often seem to see him coming, with lowered head, sullen with pain, muttering angry words. He scares me; every night I see him in my dreams, and I wake screaming with terror. But I'm waiting for him and I love him. I must stay here to direct his rage—for I, any-how, keep a clear head—to point to the guilty and say: "Those are they, Orestes. Strike!"

ORESTES: And suppose he isn't like that at all?

ELECTRA: How can he be otherwise? Don't forget he's the son of Agamemnon and Clytemnestra.

ORESTES: But mightn't he be weary of all that tale of wickedness and bloodshed; if, for instance, he'd been brought up in a happy, peaceful city?

ELECTRA: Then I'd spit in his face, and I'd say: "Go away, you cur; go and keep com-pany where you belong, with women. But you're reckoning without your doom, poor fool. You're a grandson of Atreus, and you can't escape the heritage of blood. You prefer shame to crime; so be it. But Fate will come and hunt you down in your bed; you'll have the shame to start with, and then you will commit the crime, however much you shirk it."

ORESTES: Electra, I am Orestes.

ELECTRA [*with a cry*]: Oh! . . . You liar!

ORESTES: By the shades of my father, Agamemnon, I swear I am Orestes. [*A short silence.*] Well? Why don't you carry out your threat and spit in my face?

ELECTRA: How could I? [*She gazes at him earnestly.*] So those shining eyes, that noble forehead, are—my brother's! Orestes. . . . Oh, I'd rather you had stayed Phile-bus, and my brother was dead. [*Shyly*] Was it true, what you said about your having lived at Corinth?

ORESTES: No. I was brought up by some well-to-do Athenians.

ELECTRA: How young you look! Have you ever been in battle? Has that sword you carry ever tasted blood?

ORESTES: Never.

ELECTRA: It's strange. I felt less lonely when I didn't know you. I was waiting for the Orestes of my dream; always thinking of his strength and of my weakness. And now you're there before me; Orestes, the real Orestes, was you all the time. I look at you and I see we're just a boy and a girl, two young orphans. But, you know, I love you. More than I'd have loved the other Orestes.

ORESTES: Then, if you love me, come away. We'll leave this place together.

ELECTRA: Leave Argos? No. It's here the doom of the Atrides must be played out, and I am of the house of Atreus. I ask nothing of you. I've nothing more to ask of Philebus. But here I stay.

[ZEUS *enters, back stage, and takes cover to listen to them.*]

ORESTES: Electra, I'm Orestes, your brother. I, too, am of the house of Atreus, and my place is at your side.

ELECTRA: No. You're not my brother; you're a stranger. Orestes is dead, and so much the better for him. From now on I'll do homage to his shade, along with my father's and my sister's. You, Philebus, claim to be of our house. So be it! But can you truly say that you are one of *us*? Was *your* childhood darkened by the shadow of a murder? No, more likely you were a quiet little boy with happy, trustful eyes, the pride of your adoptive father. Naturally you could trust people—they always had a smile for you—just as you could trust the solid friendly things around you: tables, beds, and stairs. And because you were rich, and always nicely dressed, and had lots of toys, you must have often thought the world was quite a nice world to live in, like a big warm bath in which one can splash and loll contentedly. My childhood was quite different. When I was six I was a drudge, and I mistrusted everything and everyone. [*A short pause.*] So go away, my noble-souled brother. I have no use for noble souls; what I need is an accomplice.

ORESTES: How could I leave you alone; above all, now that you've lost even your last hope? . . . What do you propose to do here?

ELECTRA: That's my business. Good-by, Philebus.

ORESTES: So you're driving me away? [*He takes some steps, then halts and faces her.*] Is it my fault if I'm not the fierce young swashbuckler you expected? Him you'd have taken by the hand at once and said: "Strike!" Of me you asked nothing. But, good heavens, why should I be outcast by my own sister—when I've not even been put to the test?

ELECTRA: No, Philebus, I could never lay such a load upon a heart like yours; a heart that has no hatred in it.

ORESTES: You are right. No hatred; but no love, either. You, Electra, I might have loved. And yet—I wonder. Love or hatred calls for self-surrender. He cuts a fine figure, the warm-blooded, prosperous man, solidly entrenched in his well-being, who one fine day surrenders all to love—or to hatred; himself, his house, his land, his memories. But who am I, and what have I to surrender? I'm a mere shadow of a man; of all the ghosts haunting this town today, none is ghostlier than I. The only loves I've known were phantom loves, rare and vacillating as will-o'-the-wisps. The solid passions of the living were never mine. Never! [*A short silence.*] But, oh, the shame of it. Here I am, back in the town where I was born, and my own sister disavows me. And now—where shall I go? What city must I haunt?

ELECTRA: Isn't there some pretty girl waiting for you—somewhere in the world?

ORESTES: Nobody is waiting for me anywhere. I wander from city to city, a stranger to all others and to myself, and the cities close again behind me like the waters of a pool. If I leave Argos, what trace of my coming will remain, except the cruel disappointment of your hope?

ELECTRA: You told me about happy towns—

ORESTES: What do I care for happiness? I want my share of memories, my native soil, my place among the men of Argos. [*A short silence.*] Electra, I shall not leave Argos.

ELECTRA: Please, please, Philebus, go away. If you have any love for me, go. It hurts me to think what may come to you here—nothing but evil, that I know—and your innocence would ruin all my plans.

ORESTES: I shall not go.

ELECTRA: How can you think I'd let you stay beside me—you with your stubborn uprightness—to pass silent judgment on my acts? Oh, why are you so obstinate? Nobody wants you here.

ORESTES: It's my one chance, and you, Electra—surely you won't refuse it to me? Try to understand. I want to be a man who belongs to some place, a man among comrades. Only consider. Even the slave bent beneath his load, dropping with fatigue and staring dully at the ground a foot in front of him—why, even that poor slave can say he's in *his* town, as a tree is in a forest, or a leaf upon the tree. Argos is all around him, warm, compact, and comforting. Yes, Electra, I'd gladly be that slave and enjoy that feeling of drawing the city round me like a blanket and curling myself up in it. No, I shall not go.

ELECTRA: Even if you stayed a hundred years among us, you'd still be a stranger here, and lonelier than if you were tramping the highroads of Greece. The townspeople would be watching you all the time from the corner of an eye, and they'd lower their voices when you came near.

ORESTES: Is it really so hard to win a place among you? My sword can serve the city, and I have gold to help the needy.

ELECTRA: We are not short of captains, or of charitable souls.

ORESTES: In that case—[*He takes some steps away from her, with lowered eyes.* ZEUS *comes forward and gazes at him, rubbing his hands.* ORESTES *raises his eyes heavenwards.*] Ah, if only I knew which path to take! O Zeus, our Lord and King of Heaven, not often have I called on you for help, and you have shown me little favor; yet this you know: that I have always tried to act aright. But now I am weary and my mind is dark; I can no longer distinguish right from wrong. I need a guide to point my way. Tell me, Zeus, is it truly your will that a king's son, hounded from this city, should meekly school himself to banishment and slink away from his ancestral home like a whipped cur? I cannot think it. And yet—and yet you have forbidden the shedding of blood. . . . What have I said? Who spoke of bloodshed? . . . O Zeus, I beseech you, if meek acceptance, the bowed head and lowly heart are what you would have of me, make plain your will by some sign; for no longer can I see my path.

ZEUS [*aside*]: Ah, that's where I can help, my young friend. Abraxas, abraxas, tsou, tsou.

[*Light flashes out round the stone.*]

ELECTRA [*laughing*]: Splendid! It's raining miracles today! See what comes of being a pious young man and asking counsel of the gods. [*She is convulsed with laughter and can hardly get the words out.*] Oh, noble youth, Philebus, darling of the gods! "Show me a sign," you asked. "Show me a sign." Well, now you've had your sign—a blaze of light round that precious, sacred stone of theirs. So off you go to Corinth! Off you go!

ORESTES [*staring at the stone*]: So that is the Right Thing. To live at peace—always at perfect peace. I see. Always to say "Excuse me," and "Thank you." That's what's wanted, eh? [*He stares at the stone in silence for some moments.*] The Right Thing. *Their* Right Thing. [*Another silence.*] Electra!

ELECTRA: Hurry up and go. Don't disappoint your fatherly old friend, who has bent down from Olympus to enlighten you. [*She stops abruptly, a look of wonder on her face.*] But—but what's come over you?

ORESTES [*slowly, in a tone he has not used till now*]: There is another way.

ELECTRA [*apprehensively*]: No, Philebus, don't be stubborn. You asked the gods for orders; now you have them.

ORESTES: Orders? What do you mean? Ah yes, the light round that big stone. But it's not for me, that light; from now on I'll take no one's orders, neither man's nor god's.

ELECTRA: You're speaking in riddles.

ORESTES: What a change has come on everything, and, oh, how far away you seem! Until now I felt something warm and living round me, like a friendly presence. That something has just died. What emptiness! What endless emptiness, as far as eye can reach! [*He takes some steps away from her.*] Night is coming on. The air is getting chilly, isn't it? But what was it—what was it that died just now?

ELECTRA: Philebus—

ORESTES: I say there is another path—*my* path. Can't you see it? It starts here and leads down to the city. I must go down—do you understand?—I must go down into the depths, among you. For you are living, all of you, at the bottom of a pit. [*He goes up to* ELECTRA.] You are *my* sister, Electra, and that city is *my* city. *My* sister. [*He takes her arm.*]

ELECTRA: Don't touch me. You're hurting me, frightening me—and I'm *not* yours.

ORESTES: I know. Not yet. I'm still too—too light. I must take a burden on my shoulders, a load of guilt so heavy as to drag me down, right down into the abyss of Argos.

ELECTRA: But what—what do you mean to do?

ORESTES: Wait. Give me time to say farewell to all the lightness, the aery lightness that was mine. Let me say good-by to my youth. There are evenings at Corinth and at Athens, golden evenings full of songs and scents and laughter; these I shall never know again. And mornings, too, radiant with promise. Good-by to them all, good-by. . . . Come, Electra, look at our city. There it lies, rose-red in the sun, buzzing with men and flies, drowsing its doom away in the languor of a summer afternoon. It fends me off with its high walls, red roofs, locked doors. And yet it's mine for the taking; I've felt that since this morning. You, too, Electra, are mine for the taking—and I'll take you, too. I'll turn into an ax and hew those walls asunder, I'll rip open the bellies of those stolid houses and there will steam up from the gashes a stench of rotting food and incense. I'll be an iron wedge driven into the city, like a wedge rammed into the heart of an oak tree.

ELECTRA: Oh, how you've changed! Your eyes have lost their glow; they're dull and smoldering. I'm sorry for that, Philebus; you were so gentle. But now you're talking like the Orestes of my dreams.

ORESTES: Listen! All these people quaking with fear in their dark rooms, with their dear departed round them—supposing I take over all their crimes. Supposing I set out to win the name of "guilt-stealer," and heap on myself all their remorse; that of the woman unfaithful to her husband, of the tradesman who let his mother die, of the usurer who bled his victims white? Surely once I am plagued with all those pangs of conscience, innumerable as the flies of Argos—surely then I shall have earned the freedom of your city. Shall I not be as much at home within your red walls as the red-aproned butcher in his shop, among the carcasses of flayed sheep and cattle?

ELECTRA: So you wish to atone for us?

ORESTES: To atone? No. I said I'd house your penitence, but I did *not* say what I'd do with all those cackling fowls; maybe I'll wring their necks.

ELECTRA: And how can you take over our sense of guilt?

ORESTES: Why, all of you ask nothing better than to be rid of it. Only the King and Queen force you to nurse it in your foolish hearts.

ELECTRA: The King and Queen—Oh, Philebus!

ORESTES: The gods bear witness that I had no wish to shed their blood.

[*A long silence.*]

ELECTRA: You're too young, too weak.

ORESTES: Are you going to draw back—*now*? Hide me somewhere in the palace, and lead me tonight to the royal bedchamber—and then you'll see if I am too weak!

ELECTRA: Orestes!

ORESTES: Ah! For the first time you've called me Orestes.

ELECTRA: Yes. I know you now. You are indeed Orestes. I didn't recognize you at first, I'd expected somebody quite different. But this throbbing in my blood, this sour taste on my lips—I've had them in my dreams, and I know what they mean. So at last you have come, Orestes, and your resolve is sure. And here I am beside you—just as in my dreams—on the brink of an act beyond all remedy. And I'm frightened; that, too, was in my dreams. How long I've waited for this moment, dreading and hoping for it! From now on, all the moments will link up, like the cogs in a machine, and we shall never rest again until they both are lying on their backs, with faces like crushed mulberries. In a pool of blood. To think it's you who are going to shed it, you with those gentle eyes! I'm sorry now, sorry that never again I'll see that gentleness, never again see Philebus. Orestes, you are my elder brother, and head of our house; fold me in your arms, protect me. Much suffering, many perils lie ahead of both of us.

[ORESTES *takes her in his arms.* ZEUS *leaves his hiding place and creeps out on tiptoe.*]

CURTAIN

Scene 2

The throne room in the palace. An awe-inspiring, blood-smeared image of ZEUS *occupies a prominent position. The sun is setting.*

[ELECTRA *enters, then beckons to* ORESTES *to follow her.*]

ORESTES: Someone's coming.

[*He begins to draw his sword.*]

ELECTRA: It's the sentries on their rounds. Follow me. I know where to hide.

[*Two* SOLDIERS *enter.*]

FIRST SOLDIER: I can't think what's come over the flies this evening. They're all crazy-like.

SECOND SOLDIER: They smell the dead; that's why they're in such a state. Why, I daren't open my mouth to yawn for fear they all come teeming down my throat and start a round dance in my gullet. [ELECTRA *peeps from her hiding place, then quickly withdraws her head.*] Hear that? Something creaked yonder.

FIRST SOLDIER: Oh, it's only Agamemnon, sitting down on his throne.

SECOND SOLDIER: And the seat creaked when he planted his fat bottom on it? No, it couldn't be that; a dead man's light as air.

FIRST SOLDIER: That goes for common folk like you and me. But a king, he's different. Mind you, Agamemnon always did himself proud at table. Why, he weighed two hundred pounds or more if he weighed one. It would be surprising if there wasn't some pounds left of all that flesh.

SECOND SOLDIER: So — so you think he's here, do you?

FIRST SOLDIER: Where else should he be? If I was a dead king and I had twenty-four hours' leave each year, you may be sure I'd spend them squatting on my throne, just to remind me of the high old times I had when I was His Almighty Majesty. And I'd stay put; I wouldn't run round pestering folk in their houses.

SECOND SOLDIER: Ah, wouldn't you? You say that because you're alive. But if you were dead, you'd be just as nasty as the others. [FIRST SOLDIER *smacks his face.*] Hey! What are you up to?

FIRST SOLDIER: I'm doing you a good turn. Look, I've killed seven of 'em, all at a go.

SECOND SOLDIER: Seven what? Seven dead 'uns?

FIRST SOLDIER: O' course not. *Flies.* Look, my hand's all bloody. [*He wipes it on his pants.*] Ugh, the filthy brutes!

SECOND SOLDIER: Pity you can't swat the lot of them while you're about it. The dead men, now — they don't do nothing, they know how to behave. If the flies were all killed off, we'd have some peace.

FIRST SOLDIER: Peace, you say? No, if I thought there were ghost-flies here as well, that'd be the last straw.

SECOND SOLDIER: Why?

FIRST SOLDIER: Don't you see? They die by millions every day, the little buzzers. Well, if all the flies that have died since last summer were set loose in the town, there'd be three hundred and sixty-five dead flies for every one that's here. The air'd be laced with flies, we'd breathe flies, eat flies, sweat flies; they'd be rolling down our throats in clusters and bunging up our lungs. . . . I wonder, now — maybe that's why there's such a funny smell in this room.

SECOND SOLDIER: No, no, it ain't that. They say our dead men have foul breaths, you know. And this room's not so big as it looks — a thousand square feet or so, I should say. Two or three dead men would be enough to foul the air.

FIRST SOLDIER: That's so. Fussing and fuming like they do.

SECOND SOLDIER: I tell you there's something amiss here. I heard a floorboard creak over there.

[*They go behind the throne to investigate.* ORESTES *and* ELECTRA *slip out on the left and tiptoe past the steps of the throne, returning to their hiding place just as the* SOLDIERS *emerge on the left.*]

FIRST SOLDIER: You see, there ain't nobody. It's only that old sod Agamemnon. Like as not, he's sitting on them cushions, straight as a poker. I shouldn't be surprised if he's watching you and me for want of anything else to do.

SECOND SOLDIER: Ay, and we'd better have a good look round, I ain't easy in my mind. These flies are something wicked, but it can't be helped.

FIRST SOLDIER: I wish I was back in the barracks. At least the dead folk there are old chums come back to visit us, just ordinary folk like us. But when I think that His Late Lamented Majesty is there, like as not counting the buttons missing on my tunic, well it makes me dithery, like when the general's doing an inspection.

[*Enter* ÆGISTHEUS *and* CLYTEMNESTRA, *followed by* SERVANTS *carrying lamps.*]

ÆGISTHEUS: Go, all of you.

[*Exeunt* SOLDIERS *and* SERVANTS.]

CLYTEMNESTRA: What is troubling you tonight?

ÆGISTHEUS: You saw what happened? Had I not played upon their fear, they'd have shaken off their remorse in the twinkling of an eye.

CLYTEMNESTRA: Is that all? Then be reassured. You will always find a way to freeze their courage when the need arises.

ÆGISTHEUS: I know. Oh, I'm only too skillful in the art of false pretense. [*A short silence.*] I am sorry I had to rebuke Electra.

CLYTEMNESTRA: Why? Because she is my daughter? It pleased you to so do, and all you do has my approval.

ÆGISTHEUS: Woman, it is not on your account that I regret it.

CLYTEMNESTRA: Then—why? You used not to have much love for Electra.

ÆGISTHEUS: I am tired. So tired. For fifteen years I have been upholding the remorse of a whole city, and my arms are aching with the strain. For fifteen years I have been dressing a part, playing the scaremonger, and the black of my robes has seeped through to my soul.

CLYTEMNESTRA: But, sire, I, too—

ÆGISTHEUS: I know, woman, I know. You are going to tell me of your remorse. I wish I shared it. It fills out the void of your life. I have no remorse—and no man in Argos is sadder than I.

CLYTEMNESTRA: My sweet lord—

[*She goes up to him affectionately.*]

ÆGISTHEUS: Keep off, you whore! Are you not ashamed—under his eyes?

CLYTEMNESTRA: Under his eyes? Who can see us here?

ÆGISTHEUS: Why, the King. The dead came forth this morning.

CLYTEMNESTRA: Sire, I beg you—the dead are underground and will not trouble us for many a long day. Have you forgotten it was you yourself who invented that fable to impress your people?

ÆGISTHEUS: That's so. Well, it only shows how tired I am, how sick at heart. Now leave me to my thoughts. [*Exit* CLYTEMNESTRA.] Have you in me, Lord Zeus, the king you wished for Argos? I come and go among my people, I speak in trumpet tones, I parade the terror of my frown, and all who see me cringe in an agony of repentance. But I—what am I but an empty shell? Some creature has devoured me unawares, gnawed out my inner self. And now, looking within, I see I am more dead than Agamemnon. Did I say I was sad? I lied. Neither sad nor gay is the desert—a boundless waste of sand under a burning waste of sky. Not sad, nor gay, but—sinister. Ah, I'd give my kingdom to be able to shed a tear.

[ZEUS *enters.*]

ZEUS: That's right. Complain away! You're only a king, like every other king.

ÆGISTHEUS: Who are you? What are you doing here?

ZEUS: So you don't recognize me?

ÆGISTHEUS: Be gone, stranger, or I shall have you thrown out by my guards.

ZEUS: You don't recognize me? Still, you have seen me often enough in dreams. It's true I looked more awe inspiring. [*Flashes of lightning, a peal of thunder.* ZEUS *assumes an awe-inspiring air.*] And now you do know me?

ÆGISTHEUS: Zeus!

ZEUS: Good! [*Affable again, he goes up to the statue.*] So that's meant to be me? It's thus the Argives picture me at their prayers? Well, well, it isn't often that a god can study his likeness, face to face. [*A short silence.*] How hideous I am! They cannot like me much.

ÆGISTHEUS: They fear you.

ZEUS: Excellent! I've no use for love. Do you, Ægistheus, love me?

ÆGISTHEUS: What do you want of me? Have I not paid heavily enough?

ZEUS: Never enough.

ÆGISTHEUS: But it's killing me, the task I have undertaken.

ZEUS: Come now! Don't exaggerate! Your health is none too bad; you're fat. Mind, I'm not reproaching you. It's good, royal fat, yellow as tallow—just as it should be. You're built to live another twenty years.

ÆGISTHEUS: Another twenty years!

ZEUS: Would you rather die?

ÆGISTHEUS: Yes.

ZEUS: So, if anyone came here now, with a drawn sword, would you bare your breasts to him?

ÆGISTHEUS: I—I cannot say.

ZEUS: Now mark my words. If you let yourself be slaughtered like a dumb ox, your doom will be exemplary. You shall be King in hell for all eternity. That's what I came here to tell you.

ÆGISTHEUS: Is someone planning to kill me?

ZEUS: So it seems.

ÆGISTHEUS: Electra?

ZEUS: Not only Electra.

ÆGISTHEUS: Who?

ZEUS: Orestes.

ÆGISTHEUS: Oh! . . . Well, that's in the natural order of things, no doubt. What can I do against it?

ZEUS [*mimicking his tone*]: What can I do? [*Imperiously*] Bid your men arrest a young stranger going under the name of Philebus. Have him and Electra thrown into a dungeon—and if you leave them there to rot, I'll think no worse of you. Well, what are you waiting for? Call your men.

ÆGISTHEUS: No.

ZEUS: Be good enough to tell me why that no.

ÆGISTHEUS: I am tired.

ZEUS: Don't stare at the ground. Raise your big, bloodshot eyes and look at me. That's better. Yes, you're majestically stupid, like a horse; a kingly fool. But yours is not the stubbornness that vexes me; rather, it will add a spice to your surrender. For I know you will obey me in the end.

ÆGISTHEUS: I tell you I refuse to fall in with your plans. I have done so far too often.

ZEUS: That's right. Show your mettle! Resist! Resist! Ah, how I cherish souls like yours! Your eyes flash, you clench your fists, you fling refusal in the teeth of Zeus. None the less, my little rebel, my restive little horse, no sooner had I warned you than your heart said yes. Of course you'll obey. Do you think I leave Olympus without good reason? I wished to warn you of this crime because it is my will to avert it.

ÆGISTHEUS: To warn me! How strange!

ZEUS: Why "strange"? Surely it's natural enough. Your life's in danger and I want to save it.

ÆGISTHEUS: Who asked you to save it? What about Agamemnon? Did you warn *him*? And yet *he* wished to live.

ZEUS: O miserable man, what base ingratitude! You are dearer to me than Agamemnon, and when I prove this, you complain!

ÆGISTHEUS: Dearer than Agamemnon? I? No, it's Orestes whom you cherish. You allowed me to work my doom, you let me rush in, ax in hand, to King Agamemnon's bath—and no doubt you watched from high Olympus, licking your lips at the thought of another damned soul to gloat over. But today you are protecting young Orestes against himself; and I, whom you egged on to kill his father—you have chosen me to restrain the young man's hand. I was a poor creature, just qualified for murder; but for Orestes, it seems, you have higher destinies in view.

ZEUS: What strange jealousy is this! But have no fear; I love him no more than I love you. I love nobody.

ÆGISTHEUS: Then see what you have made of me, unjust god that you are. And tell me this. If today you hinder the crime Orestes has in mind, why did you permit mine of fifteen years ago?

ZEUS: All crimes do not displease me equally. And now, Ægistheus, I shall speak to you frankly, as one king to another. The first crime was mine: I committed it when I made man mortal. Once I had done that, what was left for you, poor human murderers, to do? To kill your victims? But they already had the seed of death in them; all you could do was to hasten its fruition by a year or two. Do you know what would have befallen Agamemnon if you had not killed him?

Three months later he'd have died of apoplexy in a pretty slave-girl's arms. But your crime served my ends.

ÆGISTHEUS: What ends? For fifteen years I have been atoning for it—and you say it served your ends!

ZEUS: Exactly. It's because you are atoning for it that it served my ends. I like crimes that *pay*. I like yours because it was a clumsy, boorish murder, a crime that did not know itself, a crime in the antique mode, more like a cataclysm than an act of man. Not for one moment did you defy me. You struck in a frenzy of fear and rage. And then, when your frenzy had died down, you looked back on the deed with loathing and disowned it. Yet what a profit I have made on it! For one dead man, twenty thousand living men wallowing in repentance. Yes, it was a good bargain I struck that day.

ÆGISTHEUS: I see what lies behind your words. Orestes will have no remorse.

ZEUS: Not a trace of it. At this moment he is thinking out his plan, coolly, methodically, cheerfully. What good to me is a carefree murder, a shameless, sedate crime, that lies light as thistledown on the murderer's conscience? No, I won't allow it. Ah, how I loathe the crimes of this new generation; thankless and sterile as the wind! Yes, that nice-minded young man will kill you as he'd kill a chicken; he'll go away with red hands and a clean heart. In your place I should feel humiliated. So—call your men!

ÆGISTHEUS: Again I tell you, I will *not*. The crime that is being hatched displeases you enough for me to welcome it.

ZEUS: Ægistheus, you are a king, and it's to your sense of kingship I appeal, for you enjoy wielding the scepter.

ÆGISTHEUS: Continue.

ZEUS: You may hate me, but we are akin; I made you in my image. A king is a god on earth, glorious and terrifying as a god.

ÆGISTHEUS: You terrifying?

ZEUS: Look at me. [*A long silence.*] I told you you were made in my image. Each keeps order; you in Argos, I in heaven and on earth—and you and I harbor the same dark secret in our hearts.

ÆGISTHEUS: I have no secret.

ZEUS: You have. The same as mine. The bane of gods and kings. The bitterness of knowing men are free. Yes, Ægistheus, they are free. But your subjects do not know it, and you do.

ÆGISTHEUS: Why, yes. If they knew it, they'd send my palace up in flames. For fifteen years I've been playing a part to mask their power from them.

ZEUS: So you see we are alike.

ÆGISTHEUS: Alike? A god likening himself to me—what freak of irony is this? Since I came to the throne, all I said, all my acts, have been aimed at building up an image of myself. I wish each of my subjects to keep that image in the foreground of his mind, and to feel, even when alone, that my eyes are on him, severely judging his most private thoughts. But I have been trapped in my own net. I have come to see myself only as they see me. I peer into the dark pit of their souls, and there, deep down, I see the image that I have built up. I shudder, but I cannot take my eyes off it. Almighty Zeus, who am I? Am I anything more than the dread that others have of me?

ZEUS: And I—who do you think *I* am? [*Points to the statue.*] I, too, have my image, and do you suppose it doesn't fill me with confusion? For a hundred thousand years I have been dancing a slow, dark ritual dance before men's eyes. Their eyes are so intent on me that they forget to look into themselves. If I forgot myself for a single moment, if I let their eyes turn away—

ÆGISTHEUS: Yes?

ZEUS: Enough. That is *my* business. Ægistheus, I know that you are weary of it all; but why complain? You'll die one day—but I shall not. So long as there are men on earth, I am doomed to go on dancing before them.

ÆGISTHEUS: Alas! But who has doomed us?

ZEUS: No one but ourselves. For we have the same passion. You, Ægistheus, have, like me, a passion for order.

ÆGISTHEUS: For order? That is so. It was for the sake of order that I wooed Clytemnestra, for order that I killed my King; I wished that order should prevail, and that it should prevail through me. I have lived without love, without hope, even without lust. But I have kept order. Yes, I have kept good order in my kingdom. That has been my ruling passion; a godlike passion, but how terrible!

ZEUS: We could have no other, you and I; I am God, and you were born to be a king.

ÆGISTHEUS: Ay, more's the pity!

ZEUS: Ægistheus, my creature and my mortal brother, in the name of this good order that we serve, both you and I, I ask you—nay, I command you—to lay hands on Orestes and his sister.

ÆGISTHEUS: Are they so dangerous?

ZEUS: Orestes knows that he is free.

ÆGISTHEUS [*eagerly*]: He knows he's free? Then, to lay hands on him, to put him in irons, is not enough. A free man in a city acts like a plague spot. He will infect my whole kingdom and bring my work to nothing. Almighty Zeus, why stay your hand? Why not fell him with a thunderbolt?

ZEUS [*slowly*]: Fell him with a thunderbolt? [*A pause. Then, in a muffled voice*] Ægistheus, the gods have another secret.

ÆGISTHEUS: Yes?

ZEUS: Once freedom lights its beacon in a man's heart, the gods are powerless against him. It's a matter between man and man, and it is for other men, and for them only, to let him go his gait, or to throttle him.

ÆGISTHEUS [*observing him closely*]: To throttle him? Be it so. Well, I shall do your will, no doubt. But say no more, and stay here no longer—I could not bear it. [*As* ZEUS *departs,* ELECTRA *leaps forward and rushes to the door.* ORESTES *comes forward.*]

ELECTRA: Strike him down! Don't give him time to call for help. I'll bar the door.

ÆGISTHEUS: So you, young man, are Orestes?

ORESTES: Defend yourself.

ÆGISTHEUS: I shall not defend myself. It's too late for me to call for help, and I am glad it is too late. No, I shall not resist. I *wish* you to kill me.

ORESTES: Good. Little I care how it is done. . . . So I am to be a murderer.

[ORESTES *strikes him with his sword.*]

ÆGISTHEUS [*tottering*]: Ah! You struck well, Orestes. [*He clings to* ORESTES.] Let me look at you. Is it true you feel no remorse?

ORESTES: Remorse? Why should I feel remorse? I am only doing what is right.

ÆGISTHEUS: What is right is the will of God. You were hidden here and you heard the words of Zeus.

ORESTES: What do I care for Zeus? Justice is a matter between men, and I need no god to teach me it. It's right to stamp you out, like the foul brute you are, and to free the people of Argos from your evil influence. It is right to restore to them their sense of human dignity.

ÆGISTHEUS [*groaning*]: Pain! What agony!

ELECTRA: Look! Look! He's swaying; his face has gone quite gray. What an ugly sight's a dying man!

ORESTES: Keep silent! Let him carry with him to the grave no other memory than the memory of our joy.

ÆGISTHEUS: My curse on you both!

ORESTES: Won't you have done with dying?

[*He strikes again.* ÆGISTHEUS *falls.*]

ÆGISTHEUS: Beware of the flies, Orestes, beware of the flies. All is not over.

[*Dies.*]

ORESTES [*giving the body a kick*]: For him, anyhow, all is over. Now lead me to the Queen's room.

ELECTRA: Orestes!

ORESTES: What?

ELECTRA: She—she can do us no more harm.

ORESTES: What of it? What has come over you? This is not how you spoke a little while ago.

ELECTRA: Orestes! You, too, have changed. I hardly recognize you.

ORESTES: Very well. I'll go alone.

[*Exit.*]

ELECTRA [*to herself*]: Will she scream? [*Silence. She is listening.*] He's walking down the passage. When he opens the fourth door—Oh, I wanted this to happen. And I—I want it now, I *must* want it. [*She looks at* ÆGISTHEUS.] That one—yes, he's dead. So this is what I wanted. I didn't realize how it would be. [*She comes closer to the body.*] A hundred times I've seen him, in my dreams, lying just where he is now, with a sword through his heart. His eyes were closed, he seemed asleep. How I hated him, what joy I got from hating him! But he doesn't seem asleep; his eyes are open, staring up at me. He is dead, and my hatred is dead, too. And I'm standing here, waiting, waiting. That woman is still alive, she's in her bedroom, and presently she'll be screaming. Screaming like an animal in pain. No, I can't bear those eyes any longer. [*Kneeling, she lays a mantle over the King's face.*] What was it, then, I wanted? What? [*A short silence.*

CLYTEMNESTRA *screams.*] He's struck her. She was our mother—and he's struck her. [*She rises to her feet.*] It's done; my enemies are dead. For years and years I've reveled in the thought of this, and, now it's happened, my heart is like a lump of ice. Was I lying to myself all those years? No, that's not true, it can't be true. I'm not a coward. Only a moment ago I wanted it, and I haven't changed. I'm glad, glad, to see that swine lying at my feet. [*She jerks the mantle off the dead King's face.*] Those dead-fish eyes goggling up at nothing—why should they trouble me? That's how I wanted to see them, dead and staring, and I'm glad, glad— [CLYTEMNESTRA'*s screams are weakening.*] Let her scream! Make her scream, Orestes. I want her to suffer. [*The screams cease.*] Oh joy, joy! I'm weeping for joy; my enemies are dead, my father is avenged. [ORESTES *returns, his sword dripping blood.* ELECTRA *runs to him and flings herself into his arms.*]

ELECTRA: Orestes! . . . Oh! . . .

ORESTES: You're frightened. Why?

ELECTRA: I'm not frightened. I'm drunk. Drunk with joy. What did she say? Did she beg for mercy long?

ORESTES: Electra. I shall not repent of what I have done, but I think fit not to speak of it. There are some memories one does not share. It is enough for you to know she's dead.

ELECTRA: Did she die cursing us? That's all I want you to tell me. Did she curse us?

ORESTES: Yes. She died cursing us.

ELECTRA: Take me in your arms, beloved, and press me to your breast. How dark the night is! I never knew such darkness; those torches have no effect on it. . . . Do you love me?

ORESTES: It is not night; a new day is dawning. We are free, Electra. I feel as if I'd brought you into life and I, too, had just been born. Yes, I love you, and you belong to me. Only yesterday I was empty-handed, and today I have *you.* Ours is a double tie of blood; we two come of the same race and we two have shed blood.

ELECTRA: Let go your sword. Give me that hand, your strong right hand. [*She clasps and kisses it.*] Your fingers are short and square, made to grasp and hold. Dear hand! It's whiter than mine. But how heavy it became to strike down our father's murderers! Wait! [*She takes a torch and holds it near* ORESTES.] I must light up your face; it's getting so dark that I can hardly see you. And I *must* see you; when I stop seeing, I'm afraid of you. I daren't take my eyes off you. I must tell myself again and again that I love you. But—how strange you look!

ORESTES: I am free, Electra. Freedom has crashed down on me like a thunderbolt.

ELECTRA: Free? But I—I don't feel free. And you—can you undo what has been done? Something has happened and we are no longer free to blot it out. Can you prevent our being the murderers of our mother—for all time?

ORESTES: Do you think I'd wish to prevent it? I have done *my* deed, Electra, and that deed was good. I shall bear it on my shoulders as a carrier at a ferry carries the traveler to the farther bank. And when I have brought it to the farther bank I shall take stock of it. The heavier it is to carry, the better pleased I shall be; for that burden is my freedom. Only yesterday I walked the earth haphazard; thousands of roads I tramped that brought me nowhere, for they were other men's roads. Yes, I tried them all; the haulers' tracks along the riverside, the mule-paths in the mountains, and the broad, flagged highways of the charioteers. But none of these was mine. Today I have one path only, and heaven knows where it leads. But it is *my* path. . . . What is it, Electra?

ELECTRA: I can't see you any more. Those torches give no light. I hear your voice, but it hurts me, it cuts like a knife. Will it always be as dark as this — always, even in the daytime? . . . Oh, Orestes! There they are!

ORESTES: Who?

ELECTRA: There they are! Where have they come from? They're hanging from the ceiling like clusters of black grapes; the walls are alive with them; they're swirling down across the torchlight and it's their shadows that are hiding your face from me.

ORESTES: The flies —

ELECTRA: Listen! The sound of their wings is like a roaring furnace. They're all round us, Orestes, watching, biding their time. Presently they'll swoop down on us and I shall feel thousands of tiny clammy feet crawling over me. Oh, look! They're growing bigger, bigger; now they're as big as bees. We'll never escape them, they'll follow us everywhere in a dense cloud. Oh God, now I can see their eyes, millions of beady eyes all staring at us!

ORESTES: What do the flies matter to us?

ELECTRA: They're the Furies, Orestes, the goddesses of remorse.

VOICE [*from behind the door*]: Open! Open! . . . If you don't, we'll smash the door in.

[*Heavy thuds. They are battering at the door.*]

ORESTES: Clytemnestra's cries must have brought them here. Come! Lead me to Apollo's shrine. We will spend the night there, sheltered from men and flies. And tomorrow I shall speak to my people.

CURTAIN

Act III

The temple of Apollo. Twilight. A statue of Apollo in the center of the stage. ELECTRA *and* ORESTES *are sleeping at the foot of the statue, their arms clasped round its legs. The* FURIES *ring them round; they sleep standing, like cranes.*

At the back is a huge bronze door.

FIRST FURY [*stretching herself*]: Aaaah! I slept the night out standing, stiff with rage, and my sleep was glorious with angry dreams. Ah, how lovely is the flower of anger, the red flower in my heart! [*She circles round* ORESTES *and* ELECTRA.] Still sleeping. How white and soft they are! I'll roll on their breasts and bellies, like a torrent over stones. And I shall polish hour by hour their tender flesh; rub it, scour it, wear it to the bone. [*She comes a few steps forward.*] Oh clear, bright dawn of hate! A superb awakening. They're sleeping, sweating, a smell of fever rises from them. But I am awake; cool and hard and gemlike. My soul is adamant — and I feel my sanctity.

ELECTRA [*sighing in her sleep*]: No! No!

FIRST FURY: She's sighing. Wait, my pretty one, wait till you feel our teeth. Soon you'll be screaming with the agony of our caresses. I'll woo you like a man, for you're my bride, and you shall feel my love crushing your life out. You, Electra, are more beautiful than I; but you'll see how my kisses age you. Within six months I'll have you raddled like an old hag; but I stay young forever. [*She bends over* ORESTES *and* ELECTRA.] Ah, this lovely human carrion, what a tasty meal we have in store! As I gaze down at them and breathe their breath, I choke with rage. Nothing is sweeter, nothing, than to feel a dawn of hatred spreading like quickfire in one's veins; teeth and talons ready for their task. Hatred is flooding through me, welling up in my breasts like milk. Awake, sisters, awake! The day has come.

SECOND FURY: I dreamt I was biting them.

FIRST FURY: Be patient. Today they are protected by a god, but soon hunger and thirst will drive them out of sanctuary. And then you shall bite them to your heart's content.

THIRD FURY: Aaah! How I want to claw them!

FIRST FURY: Your turn will come. In a little while your iron talons will be ribboning the flesh of those young criminals with angry red. Come closer, sisters, come and look at them.

A FURY: How young they are!

ANOTHER FURY: And how beautiful!

FIRST FURY: Yes, we are favored. Only too often criminals are old and ugly. Too seldom do we have the joy, the exquisite delight, of ruining what's beautiful.

THE FURIES: Heiah! Heiahah!

THIRD FURY: Orestes is almost a child. I shall mother him, oh so tenderly, with my hatred; I shall take his pale head on my knees and stroke his hair.

FIRST FURY: And then?

THIRD FURY: Then, when he least expects it, I shall dig these two fingers into his eyes.

[*All laugh.*]

FIRST FURY: See, they're stretching, sighing, on the brink of waking. And now, my sisters, flies my sisters, let's sing the sinners from their sleep.

THE FURIES [*together*]: Bzz. Bzz. Bzz. Bzz.
    We shall settle on your rotten hearts like flies on butter;
    Rotten hearts, juicy, luscious hearts.
    Like bees, we'll suck the pus and matter from your hearts,
    And we'll turn it into honey, rich, green honey.
    What love could ravish us as hatred does?
    Bzz. Bzz. Bzz. Bzz.
    We shall be the staring eyes of the houses,
    The growls of the kenneled mastiff baring his fangs as you go by,
    A drone of wings pulsing in high air,
    Sounds of the forest,
    Whistlings, whinings, creakings, hissings, howlings.

We shall be the darkness,
The clotted darkness of your souls.
Bzz. Bzz. Bzz. Bzz.
Heiah, heiah, heiahah!
Bzz. Bzz. Bzz. Bzz.
We are the flies, the suckers of pus,
We shall have open house with you,
We shall gather our food from your mouths,
And our light from the depths of your eyes.
All your life we will be with you,
Until we make you over to the worms.

[*They dance.*]

ELECTRA [*still half asleep*]: Was someone speaking? Who—who are you?

THE FURIES: Bzz. Bzz. Bzz.

ELECTRA: Ah, yes. There you are. Well? Have we really killed them?

ORESTES [*waking*]: Electra!

ELECTRA: You, who are you? Ah, yes. Orestes. Go away.

ORESTES: But—what's wrong, Electra?

ELECTRA: You frighten me. I had a dream. I saw our mother lying on her back. Blood was pouring from her, gushing under the doors. A dream. . . . Feel my hands. They're icy. No, don't. Don't touch me. Did she really bleed much?

ORESTES: Don't!

ELECTRA [*waking up completely*]: Let me look at you. You killed them. It was you, you who killed them. You are here beside me, you have just waked up, there's nothing written on your face, no brand. . . . And yet you killed them.

ORESTES: Why, yes. I killed them. [*A short silence.*] You, too, make me afraid. Yesterday you were so beautiful. And now you look as if some wild beast had clawed your face.

ELECTRA: No beast. Your crime. It's tearing off my cheeks and eyelids; I feel as if my eyes and teeth were naked. . . . But what are those creatures?

ORESTES: Take no notice of them. They can do you no harm.

FIRST FURY: No harm? Let her dare to come among us and you'll see if we can do no harm!

ORESTES: Keep quiet. Back to your kennel, bitches. [*The* FURIES *growl.*] Is it possible that the girl who only yesterday was dancing in a white dress on the temple steps—is it possible you were that girl?

ELECTRA: I've grown old. In a single night.

ORESTES: You have not lost your beauty, but—Where, now, have I seen dead eyes like those? Electra—you are like *her.* Like Clytemnestra. What use, then, was it killing her? When I see my crime in those eyes, it revolts me.

FIRST FURY: That is because *you* revolt *her.*

ORESTES: Is that true, Electra? Do I revolt you?

ELECTRA: Oh, let me be!

FIRST FURY: Well? Can you still have any doubt? How should she not hate you? She lived in peace, dreaming her dreams; and then you came, bringing murder and impiety upon her. So now she has to share your guilt and hug that pedestal, the only scrap of earth remaining to her.

ORESTES: Do not listen.

FIRST FURY: Away! Away! Make him go, Electra; don't let him touch you! He's a butcher. He reeks of fresh, warm blood. He used the poor old woman very foully, you know; he killed her piecemeal.

ELECTRA: Oh no! That's a lie, surely?

FIRST FURY: You can believe me; I was there all the time, buzzing in the air around them.

ELECTRA: So he struck her several times?

FIRST FURY: Ten times at least. And each time the sword squelched in the wound. She tried to shield her face and belly with her hands, and he carved her hands to ribbons.

ELECTRA: So it wasn't a quick death. Did she suffer much?

ORESTES: Put your fingers in your ears, do not look at them, and, above all, ask no questions. If you question them, you're lost.

FIRST FURY: Yes, she suffered—horribly.

ELECTRA [*covering her face with her hands*]: Oh!

ORESTES: She wants to part us, she is building up a wall of solitude around you. But beware; once you are alone, alone and helpless, they will fling themselves upon you. Electra, we planned this crime together and we should bear its brunt together.

ELECTRA: You dare to say I planned it with you?

ORESTES: Can you deny it?

ELECTRA: Of course I deny it. Wait! Well, perhaps—in a way. . . . Oh, I don't know. I dreamt the crime, but you carried it out, you murdered your own mother.

THE FURIES [*shrieking and laughing*]: Murderer! Murderer! Butcher!

ORESTES: Electra, behind that door is the outside world. A world of dawn. Out there the sun is rising, lighting up the roads. Soon we shall leave this place, we shall walk those sunlit roads, and these hags of darkness will lose their power. The sunbeams will cut through them like swords.

ELECTRA: The sun—

FIRST FURY: You will never see the sun again, Electra. We shall mass between you and the sun like a swarm of locusts; you will carry darkness round your head wherever you go.

ELECTRA: Oh, let me be! Stop torturing me!

ORESTES: It's your weakness gives them their strength. Mark how they dare not speak to me. A nameless horror has descended on you, keeping us apart. And yet why should this be? What have you lived through that I have not shared? Do you imagine that my mother's cries will ever cease ringing in my ears? Or that my eyes will ever cease to see her great sad eyes, lakes of lambent darkness in the pallor of her face? And the anguish that consumes you—do you think it will ever cease ravaging my heart? But what matter? I am free. Beyond anguish, beyond remorse. Free. And at one with myself. No, you must not loathe yourself, Electra. Give me your hand. I shall never forsake you.

ELECTRA: Let go of my hand! Those hell-hounds frighten me, but you frighten me more.

FIRST FURY: You see! You see! . . . That's quite true, little doll; you're less afraid of us than of that man. Because you need us, Electra. You are our child, our little girl. You need our nails to score your skin, our teeth to bite your breast, and all our savage love to save you from your hatred of yourself. Only the suffering of your body can take your mind off your suffering soul. So come and let us hurt you. You have only those two steps to come down, and we will take you in our arms. And when our kisses sear your tender flesh, you'll forget all in the cleansing fires of pain.

THE FURIES: Come down to us! Come down!

[*Slowly they dance round her, weaving their spell.* ELECTRA *rises to her feet.*]

ORESTES [*gripping her arm*]: No, no, for pity's sake. Don't go to them. Once they get you, all is lost.

ELECTRA [*freeing herself violently*]: Let go! Oh, how I hate you!

[*She goes down the steps, and the* FURIES *fling themselves on her.*]
    Help!

[ZEUS *enters.*]

ZEUS: Kennel up!

FIRST FURY: The master!

[*The* FURIES *slink off reluctantly, leaving* ELECTRA *lying on the ground.*]

ZEUS: Poor children. [*He goes up to* ELECTRA.] So to this you've come, unhappy pair? My heart is torn between anger and compassion. Get up, Electra. So long as I am here, my Furies will not hurt you. [*He helps her to rise and gazes at her face.*] Ah, what a cruel change! In a night, a single night, all the wild-rose bloom has left your cheeks. In one night your body has gone to ruin, lungs, gall, and liver all burnt out. The pride of headstrong youth—see what it has brought you to, poor child.

ORESTES: Stop talking in that tone, fellow. It is unbecoming for the king of the gods.

ZEUS: And you, my lad, drop that haughty tone. It's unbecoming for a criminal atoning for his crime.

ORESTES: I am no criminal, and you have no power to make me atone for an act I don't regard as a crime.

ZEUS: So you may think, but wait awhile. I shall cure you of that error before long.

ORESTES: Torture me to your heart's content; I regret nothing.

ZEUS: Not even the doom you have brought upon your sister?

ORESTES: Not even that.

ZEUS: Do you hear, Electra? And this man professed to love you!

ORESTES: She is dearer to me than life. But her suffering comes from within, and only she can rid herself of it. For she is free.

ZEUS: And you? You, too, are free, no doubt?

ORESTES: Yes, and well you know it.

ZEUS: A pity you can't see yourself as you are now, you fool, for all your boasting! What a heroic figure you cut there, cowering between the legs of a protecting god, with a pack of hungry vixen keeping guard on you! If you *can* brag of freedom, why not praise the freedom of a prisoner languishing in fetters, or a slave nailed to the cross?

ORESTES: Certainly. Why not?

ZEUS: Take care. You play the braggart now because Apollo is protecting you. But Apollo is my most obedient servant. I have but to lift a finger and he will abandon you.

ORESTES: Then do so. Lift a finger, lift your whole hand while you are about it.

ZEUS: No, that is not my way. Haven't I told you that I take no pleasure in punishment? I have come to save you both.

ELECTRA: To save us? No, it is too cruel to make sport of us. You are the lord of vengeance and of death, but, god though you are, you have no right to delude your victims with false hopes.

ZEUS: Within a quarter of an hour you can be outside that door.

ELECTRA: Safe and sound?

ZEUS: You have my word for it.

ELECTRA: And what do you want from me in return?

ZEUS: Nothing, my child. Nothing.

ELECTRA: Nothing? Did I hear right? Then you are a kind god, a lovable god.

ZEUS: Or next to nothing. A mere trifle. What you can give most easily—a little penitence.

ORESTES: Take care, Electra. That trifle will weigh like a millstone on your soul.

ZEUS [*to* ELECTRA]: Don't listen to him. Answer me, instead. Why hesitate to disavow that crime? It was committed by someone else; one could hardly say even that you were his accomplice.

ORESTES: Electra! Are you going to go back on fifteen years of hope and hatred?

ZEUS: What has she to go back on? Never did she really wish that impious deed to be accomplished.

ELECTRA: If only that were true!

ZEUS: Come now! Surely you can trust my word. Do I not read in men's hearts?

ELECTRA [*incredulously*]: And you read in mine that I never really desired that crime? Though for fifteen years I dreamt of murder and revenge?

ZEUS: Bah! I know you nursed bloodthirsty dreams—but there was a sort of innocence about them. They made you forget your servitude, they healed your wounded pride. But you never really thought of making them come true. Well, am I mistaken?

ELECTRA: Ah, Zeus, dear Zeus, how I long to think you are not mistaken!

ZEUS: You're a little girl, Electra. A mere child. Most little girls dream of becoming the richest or the loveliest woman on earth. But you were haunted by the cruel destiny of your race, you dreamt of becoming the saddest, most criminal of women. You never willed to do evil; you willed your own misfortune. At an age when most children are playing hopscotch or with their dolls, you, poor child, who had no friends or toys, you toyed with dreams of murder, because that's a game to play alone.

ELECTRA: Yes, yes! I'm beginning to understand.

ORESTES: Listen, Electra! It's *now* you are bringing guilt upon you. For who except yourself can know what you really wanted? Will you let another decide that for you? Why distort a past that can no longer stand up for itself? And why disown the firebrand that you were, that glorious young goddess, vivid with hatred, that I loved so much? Can't you see this cruel god is fooling you?

ZEUS: No, Electra. I'm not fooling you. And now hear what I offer. If you repudiate your crime, I'll see that you two occupy the throne of Argos.

ORESTES: Taking the places of our victims?

ZEUS: How else?

ORESTES: And I shall put on the royal robe, still warm from the dead King's wearing?

ZEUS: That or another. What can it matter?

ORESTES: Nothing of course—provided that it's black.

ZEUS: Are you not in mourning?

ORESTES: Yes, I was forgetting; in mourning for my mother. And my subjects—must I have them, too, wear black?

ZEUS: They wear it already.

ORESTES: True. We can give them time to wear out their old clothes. . . . Well, Electra, have you understood? If you shed some tears, you'll be given Clytemnestra's shifts and petticoats—those dirty, stinking ones you had to wash for fifteen years. And the part she played is yours for the asking. Now that you have come to look so much like her, you will play the part superbly; everyone will take you for your mother. But I—I fear I am more squeamish—I refuse to wear the breeches of the clown I killed.

ZEUS: You talk big, my boy. You butchered a defenseless man and an old woman who begged for mercy. But, to hear you speak, one would think you'd bravely fought, one against a crowd, and were the savior of your city.

ORESTES: Perhaps I was.

ZEUS: You a savior! Do you know what's afoot behind that door? All the good folk of Argos are waiting there. Waiting to greet you with stones and pikes and pitchforks. Oh, they are very grateful to their savior! . . . You are lonely as a leper.

ORESTES: Yes.

ZEUS: So you take pride in being an outcast, do you? But the solitude you're doomed to, most cowardly of murderers, is the solitude of scorn and loathing.

ORESTES: The most cowardly of murderers is he who feels remorse.

ZEUS: Orestes, I created you, and I created all things. Now see! [*The walls of the temple draw apart, revealing the firmament, spangled with wheeling stars.* ZEUS *is standing in the background. His voice becomes huge—amplified by loudspeakers—but his form is shadowy.*] See those planets wheeling on their appointed ways, never swerving, never clashing. It was I who ordained their courses, according to the law of justice. Hear the music of the spheres, that vast, mineral hymn of praise, sounding and resounding to the limits of the firmament. [*Sounds of music.*] It is my work that living things increase and multiply, each according to his kind. I have ordained that man shall always beget man, and dog give birth to dog. It is my work that the tides with their innumerable tongues creep up to lap the sand and draw back at the appointed hour. I make the plants grow, and my breath fans round the earth the yellow clouds of pollen. You are not in your own home, intruder; you are a foreign body in the world, like a splinter in flesh, or a poacher in his lordship's forest. For the world is good; I made it according to my will, and I am Goodness. But you, Orestes, you have done evil, the very rocks and stones cry out against you. The Good is everywhere, it is the coolness of the wellspring, the pith of the reed, the grain of flint, the weight of stone. Yes, you will find it even in the heart of fire and light; even your own body plays you false, for it abides perforce by my law. Good is everywhere, in you and about you; sweeping through you like a scythe, crushing you like a mountain. Like an ocean it buoys you up and rocks you to and fro, and it enabled the success of your evil plan, for it was in the brightness of the torches, the temper of your blade, the strength of your right arm. And that of which you are so vain, the Evil that you think is your creation, what is it but a reflection in a mocking mirror, a phantom thing that would have no being but for Goodness. No, Orestes, return to your saner self; the universe refutes you, you are a mite in the scheme of things. Return to Nature, Nature's thankless son. Know your sin, abhor it, and tear it from you as one tears out a rotten, noisome tooth. Or else—beware lest the very seas shrink back at your approach, springs dry up when you pass by, stones and rocks roll from your path, and the earth crumbles under your feet.

ORESTES: Let it crumble! Let the rocks revile me, and flowers wilt at my coming. Your whole universe is not enough to prove me wrong. You are the king of gods, king of stones and stars, king of the waves of the sea. But you are not the king of man.

[*The walls draw together.* ZEUS *comes into view, tired and dejected, and he now speaks in his normal voice.*]

ZEUS: Impudent spawn! So I am not your king? Who, then, made you?

ORESTES: You. But you blundered; you should not have made me free.

ZEUS: I gave you freedom so that you might serve me.

ORESTES: Perhaps. But now it has turned against its giver. And neither you nor I can undo what has been done.

ZEUS: Ah, at last! So this is your excuse?

ORESTES: I am not excusing myself.

ZEUS: No? Let me tell you it sounds much like an excuse, this freedom whose slave you claim to be.

ORESTES: Neither slave nor master. I *am* my freedom. No sooner had you created me than I ceased to be yours.

ELECTRA: Oh, Orestes! By all you hold most holy, by our father's memory, I beg you do not add blasphemy to your crime!

ZEUS: Mark her words, young man. And hope no more to win her back by arguments like these. Such language is somewhat new to her ears—and somewhat shocking.

ORESTES: To my ears, too. And to my lungs, which breathe the words, and to my tongue, which shapes them. In fact, I can hardly understand myself. Only yesterday you were still a veil on my eyes, a clot of wax in my ears; yesterday, indeed, I had an excuse. *You* were my excuse for being alive, for you had put me in the world to fulfill your purpose, and the world was an old pander prating to me about your goodness, day in, day out. And then you forsook me.

ZEUS: *I* forsook you? How?

ORESTES: Yesterday, when I was with Electra, I felt at one with Nature, this Nature of your making. It sang the praises of Good—*your* Good—in siren tones, and lavished intimations. To lull me into gentleness, the fierce light mellowed and grew tender as a lover's eyes. And, to teach me the forgiveness of offenses, the sky grew bland as a pardoner's face. Obedient to your will, my youth rose up before me and pleaded with me like a girl who fears her lover will forsake her. That was the last time, the last, I saw my youth. Suddenly, out of the blue, freedom crashed down on me and swept me off my feet. Nature sprang back, my youth went with the wind, and I knew myself alone, utterly alone in the midst of this well-meaning little universe of yours. I was like a man who's lost his shadow. And there was nothing left in heaven, no right or wrong, nor anyone to give me orders.

ZEUS: What of it? Do you want me to admire a scabby sheep that has to be kept apart; or the leper mewed in a lazar-house? Remember, Orestes, you once were of my flock, you fed in my pastures among my sheep. Your vaunted freedom isolates you from the fold; it means exile.

ORESTES: Yes, exile.

ZEUS: But the disease can't be deeply rooted yet; it began only yesterday. Come back to the fold. Think of your loneliness; even your sister is forsaking you. Your eyes are big with anguish, your face is pale and drawn. The disease you're suffering from is inhuman, foreign to my nature, foreign to yourself. Come back. I am forgetfulness, I am peace.

ORESTES: Foreign to myself—I know it. Outside nature, against nature, without excuse, beyond remedy, except what remedy I find within myself. But I shall not return under your law; I am doomed to have no other law but mine. Nor shall I come back to nature, the nature you found good; in it are a thousand beaten paths all leading up to you—but I must blaze my trail. For I, Zeus, am a man, and every man must find out his own way. Nature abhors man, and you too, god of gods, abhor mankind.

ZEUS: That is true; men like you I hold in abhorrence.

ORESTES: Take care; those words were a confession of your weakness. As for me, I do not hate you. What have I to do with you, or you with me? We shall glide past each other, like ships in a river, without touching. You are God and I am free; each of us is alone, and our anguish is akin. How can you know I did not try to feel remorse in the long night that has gone by? And to sleep? But no longer can I feel remorse, and I can sleep no more.

[*A short silence.*]

ZEUS: What do you propose to do?

ORESTES: The folk of Argos are my folk. I must open their eyes.

ZEUS: Poor people! Your gift to them will be a sad one; of loneliness and shame. You will tear from their eyes the veils I had laid on them, and they will see their lives as they are, foul and futile, a barren boon.

ORESTES: Why, since it is their lot, should I deny them the despair I have in me?

ZEUS: What will they make of it?

ORESTES: What they choose. They're free; and human life begins on the far side of despair.

[*A short silence.*]

ZEUS: Well, Orestes, all this was foreknown. In the fullness of time a man was to come, to announce my decline. And you're that man, it seems. But seeing you yesterday—you with your girlish face—who'd have believed it?

ORESTES: Could I myself have believed it? . . . The words I speak are too big for my mouth, they tear it; the load of destiny I bear is too heavy for my youth and has shattered it.

ZEUS: I have little love for you, yet I am sorry for you.

ORESTES: And I, too, am sorry for *you.*

ZEUS: Good-by, Orestes. [*He takes some steps forward.*] As for you, Electra, bear this in mind. My reign is not yet over—far from it!—and I shall not give up the struggle. So choose if you are with me or against me. Farewell.

ORESTES: Farewell. [ZEUS *goes out.* ELECTRA *slowly rises to her feet.*] Where are you going?

ELECTRA: Leave me alone. I'm done with you.

ORESTES: I have known you only for a day, and must I lose you now forever?

ELECTRA: Would to God that I had never known you!

ORESTES: Electra! My sister, dear Electra! My only love, the one joy of my life, do not leave me. Stay with me.

ELECTRA: Thief! I had so little, so very little to call mine; only a few weak dreams, a morsel of peace. And now you've taken my all; you've robbed a pauper of her mite! You were my brother, the head of our house, and it was your duty to protect me. But no, you needs must drag me into carnage; I am red as a flayed ox, these loathsome flies are swarming after me, and my heart is buzzing like an angry hive.

ORESTES: Yes, my beloved, it's true, I have taken all from you, and I have nothing to offer in return; nothing but my crime. But think how vast a gift that is! Believe me, it weighs on my heart like lead. We were too light, Electra; now our feet sink into the soil, like chariot wheels in turf. So come with me; we will tread heavily on our way, bowed beneath our precious load. You shall give me your hand, and we will go—

ELECTRA: Where?

ORESTES: I don't know. Towards ourselves. Beyond the rivers and mountains are an Orestes and an Electra waiting for us, and we must make our patient way towards them.

ELECTRA: I won't hear any more from you. All you have to offer me is misery and squalor. [*She rushes out into the center of the stage. The* FURIES *slowly close in on her.*] Help! Zeus, king of gods and men, my king, take me in your arms, carry me from this place, and shelter me. I will obey your law, I will be your creature and your slave, I will embrace your knees. Save me from the flies, from my brother, from myself! Do not leave me lonely and I will give up my whole life to atonement. I repent, Zeus. I bitterly repent.

[*She runs off the stage. The* FURIES *make as if to follow her, but the* FIRST FURY *holds them back.*]

FIRST FURY: Let her be, sisters. She is not for us. But that man is ours, and ours, I think, for many a day. His little soul is stubborn. He will suffer for two.

[*Buzzing, the* FURIES *approach* ORESTES.]

ORESTES: I am alone, alone.

FIRST FURY: No, no, my sweet little murderer, I'm staying with you, and you'll see what merry games I'll think up to entertain you.

ORESTES: Alone until I die. And after that—?

FIRST FURY: Take heart, sisters, he is weakening. See how his eyes dilate. Soon his nerves will be throbbing like harp strings, in exquisite arpeggios of terror.

SECOND FURY: And hunger will drive him from his sanctuary before long. Before nightfall we shall know how his blood tastes.

ORESTES: Poor Electra!

[THE TUTOR *enters.*]

THE TUTOR: Master! Young master! Where are you? It's so dark one can't see a thing. I'm bringing you some food. The townspeople have surrounded the temple; there's no hope of escape by daylight. We shall have to try our chance when night comes. Meanwhile, eat this food to keep your strength up. [*The* FURIES *bar his way.*] Hey! Who are these? More of those primitive myths! Ah, how I regret that pleasant land of Attica, where reason's always right.

ORESTES: Do not try to approach me, or they will tear you in pieces.

THE TUTOR: Gently now, my lovelies. See what I've brought you, some nice meat and fruit. Here you are! Let's hope it will calm you down.

ORESTES: So the people of Argos have gathered outside the temple, have they?

THE TUTOR: Indeed they have, and I can't say which are the fiercer, the thirstier for your blood: these charming young creatures here, or your worthy subjects.

ORESTES: Good. [*A short silence.*] Open that door.

THE TUTOR: Have you lost your wits? They're waiting behind it, and they're armed.

ORESTES: Do as I told you.

THE TUTOR: For once permit me, sir, to disobey your orders. I tell you, they will stone you. It's madness.

ORESTES: Old man, I am your master, and I order you to unbar that door.

[THE TUTOR *opens one leaf of the double doors a few inches.*]

THE TUTOR: Oh dear! Oh dear!

ORESTES: Open both leaves.

[THE TUTOR *half opens both leaves of the door and takes cover behind one of them.* THE CROWD *surges forward, thrusting the doors wide open; then stops, bewildered, on the threshold. The stage is flooded with bright light. Shouts rise from* THE CROWD: "Away with him!" "Kill him!" "Stone him!" "Tear him in pieces!"]*

ORESTES [*who has not heard them*]: The sun!

THE CROWD: Murderer! Butcher! Blasphemer! We'll tear you limb from limb. We'll pour molten lead into your veins.

A WOMAN: I'll pluck out your eyes.

A MAN: I'll eat your gizzard!

ORESTES [*drawing himself up to his full height*]: So here you are, my true and loyal subjects? I am Orestes, your King, son of Agamemnon, and this is my coronation day. [*Exclamations of amazement, mutterings among* THE CROWD.] Ah, you are lowering your tone? [*Complete silence.*] I know; you fear me. Fifteen years ago to the day, another murderer showed himself to you, his arms red to the elbows, gloved in blood. But him you did not fear; you read in his eyes that he was of your kind, he had not the courage of his crimes. A crime that its doer disowns becomes ownerless—no man's crime; that's how you see it, isn't it? More like an accident than a crime?

So you welcomed the criminal as your King, and that crime without an owner started prowling round the city, whimpering like a dog that has lost its master. You see me, men of Argos, you understand that my crime is wholly mine; I claim it as my own, for all to know; it is my glory, my life's work, and you can neither punish me nor pity me. That is why I fill you with fear.

And yet, my people, I love you, and it was for your sake that I killed. For your sake. I had come to claim my kingdom, and you would have none of me because I was not of your kind. Now I am of your kind, my subjects; there is a bond of blood between us, and I have earned my kingship over you.

As for your sins and your remorse, your night-fears, and the crime Ægistheus committed—all are mine, I take them all upon me. Fear your dead no longer; they are *my* dead. And, see, your faithful flies have left you and come to me. But have no fear, people of Argos. I shall not sit on my victim's throne or take the scepter in my blood-stained hands. A god offered it to me, and I said no. I wish to be a king without a kingdom, without subjects.

Farewell, my people. Try to reshape your lives. All here is new, all must begin anew. And for me, too, a new life is beginning. A strange life. . . .

Listen now to this tale. One summer there was a plague of rats in Scyros. It was like a foul disease; they soiled and nibbled everything, and the people of the city were at their wits' end. But one day a flute player came to the city. He took his stand in the marketplace. Like this. [ORESTES *rises to his feet.*] He began playing on his flute and all the rats came out and crowded round him. Then he started off, taking long strides—like this. [*He comes down from the pedestal.*] And he called to the people of Scyros: "Make way!" [THE CROWD *makes way for him.*] And all the rats raised their heads and hesitated—as the flies are doing. Look! Look at the flies! Then all of a sudden they followed in his train. And the flute player, with his rats, vanished forever. Thus.

[*He strides out into the light. Shrieking, the* FURIES *fling themselves after him.*]

CURTAIN

Existentialism

zhawng-POLE SART

p. 697

At the time of his death in 1980, **Jean-Paul Sartre**—philosopher, playwright, novelist, and passionate defender of justice—had become one of the most famous European intellectuals of the twentieth century. Associated with a loose collection of ideas and writers called EXISTENTIALISM, Sartre used his plays and novels to dramatize his ideas about the nature of personal freedom and the necessity to make a commitment to a social cause. At the beginning of Sartre's play *The Flies*, Orestes' tutor describes Orestes as the modern, secular man who has been liberated by a good university education: ". . . your mind is free from prejudice and superstition; you have no family ties, no religion, and no calling; you are free to turn your hand to anything." The cornerstone of Sartre's philosophy of individual freedom is described by the scholar and translator Walter Kaufmann: "All man's alibis are unacceptable: No gods are responsible for his condition; no original sin; no heredity and no environment; no race, no caste, no father and no mother; no wrong-headed education, no governess, no teacher; not even an impulse or a disposition, a complex or childhood trauma. Man is free. . . ." Having recognized that his freedom has isolated him from human relationships, Orestes experiences the great paradox of adolescence: Once you have freed yourself through rebellion against family, society, and tradition, you yearn to belong again to a community. The rest of *The Flies* involves Orestes' search for a cause and the courage to consciously commit to it.

Existentialism had its roots in the nineteenth-century idea that individuals live in an unpredictable, unreasonable world that no existing religion or philosophy adequately explains. A fundamental

Alberto Giacometti,
Diego, **1953. Oil on**
canvas. 39½ × 31¾
inches
*This painting of
Giacometti's brother
conveys an existential
loneliness much like
that found in the
work of Camus and
Sartre. (Solomon R.
Guggenheim
Museum, New York.
55.1436 © 2003 Artists
Rights Society [ARS],
New York/ADAGP,
Paris. Photograph by
Robert E. Mates. ©
The Solomon R.
Guggenheim
Foundation, New
York)*

shift of consciousness took place in the second half of the nineteenth century and continued into the twentieth. The liberal progressive thinkers of the nineteenth century believed that science, technology, education, democracy, Christianity, and the INDUSTRIAL REVOLUTION would together create an increasingly humane, free, and prosperous world. But their belief that the cosmos supported their dreams of a rational society was seriously challenged by forerunners of existentialism such as Danish theologian Søren Kierkegaard (1813–1855) and Russian novelist Fyodor Dostoevsky (1821–1881). Kierkegaard, a dedicated Christian, attacked rational explanations of God and the institutional church and focused on the desperate, despairing alone-ness of each individual, one's yearning for contact with God, the subjective nature of faith, and the need to make choices. He asked that his tombstone be inscribed: "That Individual." The voice of Dostoevsky's protagonist in *Notes from Underground* (1864) also protests against any rational system that attempts to limit the indi-vidual. Dostoevsky's novels are preoccupied with self-consciousness and the uncertainty of the world as well as with the difficulty of acting coherently, of integrating one's ideas, beliefs, and acts. The world, in fact, does not provide meaning for the individual.

The **ENLIGHTENMENT** worldview was fundamentally eroded when people lost faith in any transcendent powers shaping and con-trolling the destiny of the earth, whether that power was called God or Reason or Destiny. The term **AGNOSTIC**, meaning someone who holds that the human mind cannot know of the existence of God or of anything beyond material phenomena, was first used by English biology professor Thomas Huxley in 1869. In 1883 the German philosopher Friedrich Nietzsche announced that "God is dead," adding, "We have killed him—you and I." Although Kierkegaard was a Christian and Nietzsche an **ATHEIST**, both attacked what they saw as the complacency and dishonesty of the Christianity of their day. Whether God never existed, no longer exists, or has become so distant that his purposes are ambiguous and communication is uncertain, the implications of humanity's sense of aloneness were manifold, setting the stage for both the radical freedom and the debilitating anxiety that existentialism articulates.

By the end of the nineteenth century, advancements in the fields of physics and biology were such that it appeared as though scien-tific laws and mathematics would largely replace religious explana-tions for the functioning of the universe and the processes of nature. But while science challenged traditional religions, it did not replace them; there was little human consolation in quantum mechanics or in one of Einstein's theories. In 1904 psychologist Sigmund Freud contributed to the shift of religious truth to the inner world of the psyche by stating that religion "is nothing but psychology projected to the outer world." At about this time, knowledge was divided into two types, a classification that largely continues to the present day: Science in its many guises provides information about the *external reality* of nature and the universe, while religion and myth, along with art and poetry, shed light on *interior reality*—the psyche, soul, or spirit.

The idea that human beings were essentially alone in the universe, living without God on the planet Earth, brought feelings of profound despair and alienation to the educated classes of Europe and America. Industrial cities were filled with slums. Intellectuals referred to the new middle class as the masses and not the enlightened. Finally, the senseless destruction of the two world wars seemed ample confirmation that God did not control the world, that there was no single religion or philosophy that provided an explanation and consolation for the wasted lives and institutional decay in the West. The inescapable conclusion seemed to be that individual human beings were solely and totally responsible for their lives: for making choices and creating meaning or purpose. Images of meaninglessness and brokenness permeated most of Western artistic

Jean Dubuffet, *Parois d'Oreines*, c. 1955. Reed pen and ink *Expressing alienation and isolation, Dubuffet's works shocked the art world. (Victoria & Albert Museum, London / Art Resource, NY. © 2003 Artists Rights Society [ARS], New York / ADAGP, Paris)*

All man's alibis are unacceptable: No gods are responsible for his condition; no original sin; no heredity and no environment; no race, no caste, no father and no mother; no wrong-headed education, no governess, no teacher; not even an impulse or a disposition, a complex or childhood trauma. Man is free. . . .
– WALTER KAUFMANN, scholar and translator

p. 752

p. 757

culture in the first half of the twentieth century: in art, through movements such as EXPRESSIONISM and SURREALISM; and in literature, in the work of such writers as Kafka (p. 423), Rilke (p. 245), and Eliot (p. 473). Existential freedom exists in the lonely, absurd world of the twentieth century in which the labels associated with political, educational, and religious institutions are called into question.

Karl Jaspers (1883–1969), considered religious, was a leader of German existentialism. He coined the phrase "existence philosophy" in *Existenzphilosophie* (1938), a work that celebrates personal choice in the context of total freedom. Jaspers, in turn, influenced other Christian existentialists like writer and playwright Gabriel Marcel (1889–1973) and theologian, teacher, and writer Paul Tillich (1886–1965). For existentialists, religion is, in Kierkegaard's phrase, a "leap of faith." The term *existentialism,* however, is most strongly associated with the French school of philosophy whose most famous exponents are Jean-Paul Sartre (p. 692) and Albert Camus (p. 756).

Sartre's experiences as a soldier fighting Hitler in World War II provided a foundation for the discussion of the stark realities of life and death in his writings. In his work Sartre was indebted to German philosopher Martin Heidegger (1889–1976), who explored the nature of subjectivity, the truths associated with one's being, and the awareness of being "abandoned" in this world. The excerpt from Sartre's **"Existentialism Is a Humanism"** explores the consequences of living in a world without God's direction or plan. Sartre explains his dictum "Existence precedes essence" by saying that humans create who they are through their choices. Existentialists must then answer the fundamental moral question: Without the rewards and punishments for human behavior described by religion, what is the basis for doing good rather than evil? For, as Dostoevsky states, "If God didn't exist, everything would be possible." In **"The Myth of Sisyphus,"** Camus becomes a myth-maker, proposing a means of achieving dignity in a world without ultimate purpose or meaning. The ultimate hero for Camus is the person who faces the emptiness and silence of the universe honestly and courageously—without excuses, without whining, and without retreating into superstition and fantasy.

When Sartre died in 1980, the political and social controversies that surrounded him and his partner, the important feminist writer Simone de Beauvoir, died with him. What is striking is that no philosophy or theology has arisen since then that has influenced the general consciousness or caught the public's eye quite like Sartre and his peers did. The beliefs surrounding existentialism have permeated the post–World War II world, East and West. **Frantz Fanon**'s *Black Skin, White Masks* (1952) presents Fanon's own experience of alienation, racism, and colonization in France and Algeria. Fanon turns European existentialism on its head by analyzing the crippling effects of past colonialism on blacks and describes how he seeks an existential freedom from labels and neurosis. The devastation of World War II shaped the attitudes of Japan's young writers and intellectuals as they coped with disillusionment, despair, anger, and rebellion. *Hiroshima Notes,* by **Oe Kenzaburo**, contains conversations with A-bomb survivors. Having lived through the dropping of the atomic bomb, these individuals were confronted with the ultimate existential question: In a broken, meaningless world, why go on? The excerpt included from the third chapter, **"The Moralists of Hiroshima,"** presents portraits of individuals who, having survived the abyss of suffering and death, achieve heroism through their affirmations of life.

FRAHNTS fah-NONG
p. 761

OH-eh
ken-zah-BOO-roh

p. 766

The challenges of existentialism live on. Most contemporary writers and artists address the notion that individuals must create meaning for themselves in an uncertain world, a world for which no existing system provides a coherent, universally accepted explanation. On the contrary, at the beginning of the twenty-first century, the world is teeming with conflicting, even dangerously opposing, worldviews and philosophies.

■ CONNECTIONS

Jean-Paul Sartre, *The Flies* **(p. 697); Albert Camus, "The Guest" (p. 816).** Existentialist writers commonly place their protagonists in situations calling for courageous, and even dangerous, choices. How do Sartre and Camus create the context for choice in their respective works?

Franz Kafka, *The Metamorphosis,* **p. 428.** Alienation does not necessarily lead to a recognition of personal freedom and the decision to take decisive action. How does Kafka, in *The Metamorphosis,* show the shadow side of alienation in the passivity of his characters?

James Baldwin, "Sonny's Blues," p. 830. In Baldwin's short story, a middle-class black man learns about his authentic voice through his jazz-playing brother. How does his experience relate to existentialism as it is discussed here?

■ PRONUNCIATION

Frantz Fanon: FRAHNTS fah-NONG
Oe Kenzaburo: OH-eh ken-zah-BOO-roh
Jean-Paul Sartre: zhawng-POLE SART

Jean-Paul Sartre

B. France, 1905–1980

In addition to being a major spokesman for French existentialism as a philosopher, Sartre wrote plays, novels, and essays. A central message of his writings is that we humans must courageously face the fact that we are alone in the cosmos, that there is no overall divine plan that can give us direction or comfort. Individuals must therefore consciously make choices for themselves that are consistent with choices that would benefit other human beings. The tenet "existence precedes essence" means that there is no preexistent plan for a human life prior to birth; existence comes first, and, out of one's succeeding choices, essence is created.

A note on the translation: "Existentialism Is a Humanism" is Walter Kaufmann's translation of "L'Existentialisme est un humanisme," a famous lecture given by Sartre in 1946. All notes are the editors'.

FROM

Existentialism Is a Humanism

Translated by Walter Kaufmann

Most of those who are making use of this word would be highly confused if required to explain its meaning. For since it has become fashionable, people cheerfully declare that this musician or that painter is "existentialist." A columnist in *Clartés* signs himself "The Existentialist," and, indeed, the word is now so loosely applied to so many things that it no longer means anything at all. It would appear that, for the lack of any novel doctrine such as that of surrealism, all those who are eager to join in the latest scandal or movement now seize upon this philosophy in which, however, they can find nothing to their purpose. For in truth this is of all teachings the least scandalous and the most austere: It is intended strictly for technicians and philosophers. All the same, it can easily be defined.

The question is only complicated because there are two kinds of existentialists. There are, on the one hand, the Christians, amongst whom I shall name Jaspers and Gabriel Marcel,[1] both professed Catholics; and on the other the existential atheists, amongst whom we must place Heidegger[2] as well as the French existentialists and myself. What they have in common is simply the fact that they believe that *existence*

---

[1] **Jaspers . . . Marcel:** Karl Jaspers (1883–1969), German philosopher who was not in fact a professed Catholic; Gabriel Marcel (1889–1973), French philosopher and Christian existentialist who converted to Roman Catholicism in 1929.

[2] **Heidegger:** Martin Heidegger (1889–1976), important German philosopher who did not consider himself an existentialist; nevertheless his writings on existence, time, and death influenced Jean-Paul Sartre and others.

comes before *essence*—or, if you will, that we must begin from the subjective. What exactly do we mean by that?

If one considers an article of manufacture—as, for example, a book or a paper-knife—one sees that it has been made by an artisan who had a conception of it; and he has paid attention, equally, to the conception of a paper-knife and to the pre-existent technique of production which is a part of that conception and is, at bottom, a formula. Thus the paper-knife is at the same time an article producible in a certain manner and one which, on the other hand, serves a definite purpose, for one cannot suppose that a man would produce a paper-knife without knowing what it was for. Let us say, then, of the paper-knife that its essence—that is to say the sum of the formulae and the qualities which made its production and its definition possible—precedes its existence. The presence of such-and-such a paper-knife or book is thus determined before my eyes. Here, then, we are viewing the world from a technical standpoint, and we can say that production precedes existence.

When we think of God as the creator, we are thinking of him, most of the time, as a supernal artisan. Whatever doctrine we may be considering, whether it be a doctrine like that of Descartes, or of Leibnitz[3] himself, we always imply that the will follows, more or less, from the understanding or at least accompanies it, so that when God creates he knows precisely what he is creating. Thus, the conception of man in the mind of God is comparable to that of the paper-knife in the mind of the artisan: God makes man according to a procedure and a conception, exactly as the artisan manufactures a paper-knife, following a definition and a formula. Thus each individual man is the realization of a certain conception which dwells in the divine understanding. In the philosophic atheism of the eighteenth century, the notion of God is suppressed, but not, for all that, the idea that essence is prior to existence; something of that idea we still find everywhere, in Diderot, in Voltaire, and even in Kant.[4] Man possesses a human nature; that "human nature," which is the conception of human being, is found in every man; which means that each man is a particular example of a universal conception, the conception of Man. In Kant, this universality goes so far that the wild man of the woods, man in the state of nature, and the bourgeois are all contained in the same definition and have the same fundamental qualities. Here again, the essence of man precedes that historic existence which we confront in experience.

Atheistic existentialism, of which I am a representative, declares with greater consistency that if God does not exist there is at least one being whose existence comes before its essence, a being which exists before it can be defined by any conception of it. That being is man or, as Heidegger has it, the human reality. What do we

---

[3] **Descartes . . . Leibnitz:** René Descartes (1596–1650), French mathematician and philosopher who believed in a profound distinction between mental and material realities. Gottfreid Wilhelm Leibniz (1646–1716), German mathematician and philosopher. See Book 4.

[4] **Diderot . . . Kant:** Denis Diderot (1713–1784), French encyclopedist, philosopher, and writer. See Book 4. François-Marie Arouet de Voltaire (1694–1778), great eighteenth-century French philosopher and author of several satirical works, including *Candide* (1759); see Book 4. Immanuel Kant (1724–1804), German philosopher who believed that reason could be used to ascertain truth.

mean by saying that existence precedes essence? We mean that man first of all exists, encounters himself, surges up in the world—and defines himself afterwards. If man as the existentialist sees him is not definable, it is because to begin with he is nothing. He will not be anything until later, and then he will be what he makes of himself. Thus, there is no human nature, because there is no God to have a conception of it. Man simply is. Not that he is simply what he conceives himself to be, but he is what he wills, and as he conceives himself after already existing—as he wills to be after that leap towards existence. Man is nothing else but that which he makes of himself. That is the first principle of existentialism. And this is what people call its "subjectivity," using the word as a reproach against us. But what do we mean to say by this, but that man is of a greater dignity than a stone or a table? For we mean to say that man primarily exists—that man is, before all else, something which propels itself towards a future and is aware that it is doing so. Man is, indeed, a project which possesses a subjective life, instead of being a kind of moss, or a fungus or a cauliflower. Before that projection of the self nothing exists; not even in the heaven of intelligence: Man will only attain existence when he is what he purposes to be. Not, however, what he may wish to be. For what we usually understand by wishing or willing is a conscious decision taken—much more often than not—after we have made ourselves what we are. I may wish to join a party, to write a book, or to marry—but in such a case what is usually called my will is probably a manifestation of a prior and more spontaneous decision. If, however, it is true that existence is prior to essence, man is responsible for what he is. Thus, the first effect of existentialism is that it puts every man in possession of himself as he is, and places the entire responsibility for his existence squarely upon his own shoulders. And, when we say that man is responsible for himself, we do not mean that he is responsible only for his own individuality, but that he is responsible for all men.

The word "subjectivism" is to be understood in two senses, and our adversaries play upon only one of them. Subjectivism means, on the one hand, the freedom of the individual subject and, on the other, that man cannot pass beyond human subjectivity. It is the latter which is the deeper meaning of existentialism. When we say that man chooses himself, we do mean that every one of us must choose himself; but by that we also mean that in choosing for himself he chooses for all men. For in effect, of all the actions a man may take in order to create himself as he wills to be, there is not one which is not creative, at the same time, of an image of man such as he believes he ought to be. To choose between this or that is at the same time to affirm the value of that which is chosen; for we are unable ever to choose the worse. What we choose is always the better; and nothing can be better for us unless it is better for all. If, moreover, existence precedes essence and we will to exist at the same time as we fashion our image, that image is valid for all and for the entire epoch in which we find ourselves. Our responsibility is thus much greater than we had supposed, for it concerns mankind as a whole. If I am a worker, for instance, I may choose to join a Christian rather than a Communist trade union. And if, by that membership, I choose to signify that resignation is, after all, the attitude that best becomes a man, that man's kingdom is not upon this earth, I do not commit myself alone to that view. Resignation is my will for everyone, and my action is, in consequence, a commitment on behalf of all mankind. Or if, to take a more personal case, I decide to marry and to have children, even though this decision proceeds simply from my situation, from my passion or my desire, I am thereby committing not only myself, but humanity as a whole, to the practice of monogamy. I am thus responsible for myself and for all men, and I am creating a certain image of man as I would have him to be. In fashioning myself I fashion man. . . .

Towards 1880, when the French professors endeavored to formulate a secular morality, they said something like this:—God is a useless and costly hypothesis, so we will do without it. However, if we are to have morality, a society, and a law-abiding world, it is essential that certain values should be taken seriously; they must have an *a priori* existence ascribed to them. It must be considered obligatory *a priori* to be honest, not to lie, not to beat one's wife, to bring up children and so forth; so we are going to do a little work on this subject, which will enable us to show that these values exist all the same, inscribed in an intelligible heaven although, of course, there is no God. In other words—and this is, I believe, the purport of all that we in France call radicalism—nothing will be changed if God does not exist; we shall rediscover the same norms of honesty, progress, and humanity, and we shall have disposed of God as an out-of-date hypothesis which will die away quietly of itself. The existentialist, on the contrary, finds it extremely embarrassing that God does not exist, for there disappears with Him all possibility of finding values in an intelligible heaven. There can no longer be any good *a priori,* since there is no infinite and perfect consciousness to think it. It is nowhere written that "the good" exists, that one must be honest or must not lie, since we are now upon the plane where there are only men. Dostoevsky[5] once wrote "If God did not exist, everything would be permitted"; and that, for existentialism, is the starting point. Everything is indeed permitted if God does not exist, and man is in consequence forlorn, for he cannot find anything to depend upon either within or outside himself. He discovers forthwith, that he is without excuse. For if indeed existence precedes essence, one will never be able to explain one's action by reference to a given and specific human nature; in other words, there is no determinism—man is free, man *is* freedom. Nor, on the other hand, if God does not exist, are we provided with any values or commands that could legitimize our behavior. Thus we have neither behind us, nor before us in a luminous realm of values, any means of justification or excuse. We are left alone, without excuse. That is what I mean when I say that man is condemned to be free. Condemned, because he did not create himself, yet is nevertheless at liberty, and from the moment that he is thrown into this world he is responsible for everything he does.

---

[5] **Dostoevsky:** Fyodor Dostoevsky (1821–1881), Russian novelist who penned *Crime and Punishment* (1866) and *The Brothers Karamazov* (1880).

❧ ALBERT CAMUS
B. ALGERIA, 1913–1960

cah-MOO

"The Myth of Sisyphus" is a short section of a book called *The Myth of Sisyphus and Other Essays,* in which **Camus** writes about the consequences of living in a world where there are apparently no universal rules, no boundaries validated by transcendent rewards and punishments. Camus uses the word *absurd* to describe the gap between what humans yearn for and actual reality: We yearn for clarity, for example, but see that the world science has created is incomprehensible. We would like to belong to the world, to feel at home on the earth, and yet, with all our learning, we feel estranged. The unbelievably beautiful cosmos that

Jean Dubuffet, *Je Vous Écoute,* **1956. Reed pen and ink**

The title of this piece translates to "I hear you." (Visual Arts Library / Art Resource, NY. © 2003 Artists Rights Society [ARS], New York / ADAGP, Paris)

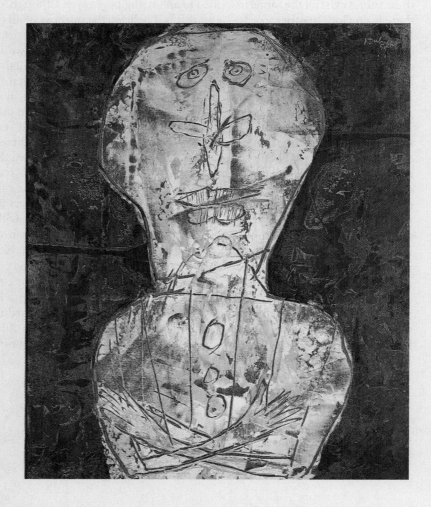

stretches beyond our vision in the night sky remains cool and indifferent; nothing in nature reaches out to us, nothing takes us in its arms. In this kind of world Camus creates a hero who attends to the business of pushing a rock up a hill without any hope of ultimate redemption. Sisyphus's heroism in the underworld is exhibited by his courageous attentiveness to his eternal task. There is no god to pat Sisyphus on the back and tell him that his struggle was worth it, that it all fit into an eternal plan.

A note on the translation: The translation is by Justin O'Brien and the notes are the editors'.

The Myth of Sisyphus

Translated by Justin O'Brien

The gods had condemned Sisyphus[1] to ceaselessly rolling a rock to the top of a mountain, whence the stone would fall back of its own weight. They had thought with some reason that there is no more dreadful punishment than futile and hopeless labor.

If one believes Homer, Sisyphus was the wisest and most prudent of mortals. According to another tradition, however, he was disposed to practice the profession of highwayman. I see no contradiction in this. Opinions differ as to the reasons why he became the futile laborer of the underworld. To begin with, he is accused of a certain levity in regard to the gods. He stole their secrets. Ægina, the daughter of Æsopus, was carried off by Jupiter. The father was shocked by that disappearance and complained to Sisyphus. He, who knew of the abduction, offered to tell about it on condition that Æsopus would give water to the citadel of Corinth. To the celestial thunderbolts he preferred the benediction of water. He was punished for this in the underworld. Homer tells us also that Sisyphus had put Death in chains. Pluto could not endure the sight of his deserted, silent empire. He dispatched the god of war, who liberated Death from the hands of her conqueror.

It is said also that Sisyphus, being near to death, rashly wanted to test his wife's love. He ordered her to cast his unburied body into the middle of the public square. Sisyphus woke up in the underworld. And there, annoyed by an obedience so contrary to human love, he obtained from Pluto permission to return to earth in order to chastise his wife. But when he had seen again the face of this world, enjoyed water and sun, warm stones and the sea, he no longer wanted to go back to the infernal darkness. Recalls, signs of anger, warnings were of no avail. Many years more he

---

[1] **Sisyphus:** In order to spite his brother Salmoneus, Sisyphus seduced Salmoneus's daughter Tyro and had two children with her; she killed them when she learned the reason for his love. Sisyphus then committed an impious act for which he was condemned to Hades where for eternity he had to push an enormous boulder to the top of a hill. Near the top, the stone was fated to roll down again.

lived facing the curve of the gulf, the sparkling sea, and the smiles of earth. A decree of the gods was necessary. Mercury came and seized the impudent man by the collar and, snatching him from his joys, led him forcibly back to the underworld, where his rock was ready for him.

You have already grasped that Sisyphus is the absurd hero. He *is,* as much through his passions as through his torture. His scorn of the gods, his hatred of death, and his passion for life won him that unspeakable penalty in which the whole being is exerted toward accomplishing nothing. This is the price that must be paid for the passions of this earth. Nothing is told us about Sisyphus in the underworld. Myths are made for the imagination to breathe life into them. As for this myth, one sees merely the whole effort of a body straining to raise the huge stone, to roll it and push it up a slope a hundred times over; one sees the face screwed up, the cheek tight against the stone, the shoulder bracing the clay-covered mass, the foot wedging it, the fresh start with arms outstretched, the wholly human security of two earth-clotted hands. At the very end of his long effort measured by skyless space and time without depth, the purpose is achieved. Then Sisyphus watches the stone rush down in a few moments toward that lower world whence he will have to push it up again toward the summit. He goes back down to the plain.

It is during that return, that pause, that Sisyphus interests me. A face that toils so close to stones is already stone itself! I see that man going back down with a heavy yet measured step toward the torment of which he will never know the end. That hour like a breathing-space which returns as surely as his suffering, that is the hour of consciousness. At each of those moments when he leaves the heights and gradually sinks toward the lairs of the gods, he is superior to his fate. He is stronger than his rock.

If this myth is tragic, that is because its hero is conscious. Where would his torture be, indeed, if at every step the hope of succeeding upheld him? The workman of today works every day in his life at the same tasks, and this fate is no less absurd. But it is tragic only at the rare moments when it becomes conscious. Sisyphus, proletarian of the gods, powerless and rebellious, knows the whole extent of his wretched condition: It is what he thinks of during his descent. The lucidity that was to constitute his torture at the same time crowns his victory. There is no fate that cannot be surmounted by scorn.

If the descent is thus sometimes performed in sorrow, it can also take place in joy. This word is not too much. Again I fancy Sisyphus returning toward his rock, and the sorrow was in the beginning. When the images of earth cling too tightly to memory, when the call of happiness becomes too insistent, it happens that melancholy rises in man's heart: This is the rock's victory, this is the rock itself. The boundless grief is too heavy to bear. These are our nights of Gethsemane. But crushing truths perish from being acknowledged. Thus, Œdipus at the outset obeys fate without knowing it. But from the moment he knows, his tragedy begins. Yet at the same moment, blind and desperate, he realizes that the only bond linking him to the world is the cool hand of a girl. Then a tremendous remark rings out: "Despite so many ordeals, my advanced age and the nobility of my soul make me conclude that all is well." Sophocles' Œdipus, like Dostoevsky's Kirilov,[2] thus gives the recipe for the absurd victory. Ancient wisdom confirms modern heroism.

One does not discover the absurd without being tempted to write a manual of happiness. "What! by such narrow ways—?" There is but one world, however. Happiness and the absurd are two sons of the same earth. They are inseparable. It would be a mistake to say that happiness necessarily springs from the absurd discovery. It happens as well that the feeling of the absurd springs from happiness. "I conclude that all is well," says Œdipus, and that remark is sacred. It echoes in the wild and limited universe of man. It teaches that all is not, has not been, exhausted. It drives out of this world a god who had come into it with dissatisfaction and a preference for futile sufferings. It makes of fate a human matter, which must be settled among men.

All Sisyphus's silent joy is contained therein. His fate belongs to him. His rock is his thing. Likewise, the absurd man, when he contemplates his torment, silences all the idols. In the universe suddenly restored to its silence, the myriad wondering little voices of the earth rise up. Unconscious, secret calls, invitations from all the faces, they are the necessary reverse and price of victory. There is no sun without shadow, and it is essential to know the night. The absurd man says yes and his effort will henceforth be unceasing. If there is a personal fate, there is no higher destiny, or at least there is but one which he concludes is inevitable and despicable. For the rest, he knows himself to be the master of his days. At that subtle moment when man glances backward over his life, Sisyphus returning toward his rock, in that slight pivoting he contemplates that series of unrelated actions which becomes his fate, created by him, combined under his memory's eye and soon sealed by his death. Thus, convinced of the wholly human origin of all that is human, a blind man eager to see who knows that the night has no end, he is still on the go. The rock is still rolling.

I leave Sisyphus at the foot of the mountain! One always finds one's burden again. But Sisyphus teaches the higher fidelity that negates the gods and raises rocks. He too concludes that all is well. This universe henceforth without a master seems to him neither sterile nor futile. Each atom of that stone, each mineral flake of that night-filled mountain, in itself forms a world. The struggle itself toward the heights is enough to fill a man's heart. One must imagine Sisyphus happy.

---

[2] **Kirilov:** A character in Dostoevsky's novel *The Possessed* who believed that men would become gods by overcoming their fear of death.

FRANTZ FANON
B. MARTINIQUE, 1925–1961

Frantz Fanon was born in 1925 on the island of Martinique in the Caribbean where he received his early education. In 1943 he went to France to join the resistance and fight with the Free French against the Germans in World War II. After the war he received a scholarship to study medicine and psychiatry in Lyon. Before leaving France, he published *Black Skin, White Masks* in 1952, an analysis of the profound and long-lasting psychological effects of white colonization and racism on blacks. In 1953, Fanon took a position in the Blida-Joinville Hospital in Algeria as head of psychiatry. When the Algerian civil war broke out (1954), he was shocked by stories of French torturers; in 1956 he resigned from his official position with the French government and joined the Algerian rebels, the Algerian National Liberation Front, or FLN. In his letter of resignation, Fanon wrote: "If psychiatry is the medical technique that aims to enable man no longer to be a stranger to his environment, I owe it myself to affirm that the Arab, permanently an alien in his own country, lives in a state of absolute depersonalization. . . . The events in Algeria are the logical consequence of an abortive attempt to decerebralize a people."

Fleeing to Tunisia, Fanon attended to patients and wrote articles openly supporting the FLN for publications like Jean-Paul Sartre's *Les Temps modernes* and the FLN newspaper *el Moudjahid*. While serving as ambassador to Ghana for the Provisional Algerian Government, Fanon developed leukemia and, refusing to rest, finished his provocative indictment of colonialism, *The Wretched of the Earth*, which Sartre published in 1961, the year of Fanon's death. Frantz Fanon died in Bethesda, Maryland, where he had sought medical aid for his cancer at the National Institutes of Health. His body was buried by the Algerian National Army of Liberation in Algeria.

The author's first task in *Black Skin, White Masks,* originally titled "An Essay for the Disalienation of Blacks," was to describe the process of alienation. Born into a culture that spoke French and then schooled in French history and culture, the young Fanon thought of himself as a Frenchman until he encountered racism in France. Racism made him doubt both his identity as a Frenchman and his manhood as a black individual. To speak French was to adopt the values of French culture, which identified blacks as evil and inferior. In an attempt to transcend this characterization, the black man wears a white mask; he focuses on the idealized values of equality and tolerance in white culture while nevertheless experiencing racism. The black man becomes split between his consciousness and his skin, and thus alienated from himself.

Fanon proposes a program for "disalienation." Essentially, it means a profound change of consciousness whereby a man lets go of those labels from the past that have conditioned his behavior—he drops his secondary identity as a black man or a white man—in order to live as a human being in the present. The goal is not to get involved in the past and argue about the appropriateness of racist categories but to free one's self from labels and make choices as an individual. In this way, Fanon appropriates existential concepts for blacks.

A note on the translation: The translation is by Charles Lam Markmann; all notes are the editors'.

ꙮ Black Skin, White Masks

Translated by Charles Lam Markmann

FROM BY WAY OF CONCLUSION

The problem considered here is one of time. Those Negroes and white men will be disalienated who refuse to let themselves be sealed away in the materialized Tower of the Past. For many other Negroes, in other ways, disalienation will come into being through their refusal to accept the present as definitive.

I am a man, and what I have to recapture is the whole past of the world. I am not responsible solely for the revolt in Santo Domingo.[1]

Every time a man has contributed to the victory of the dignity of the spirit, every time a man has said no to an attempt to subjugate his fellows, I have felt solidarity with his act.

In no way should I derive my basic purpose from the past of the peoples of color.

In no way should I dedicate myself to the revival of an unjustly unrecognized Negro civilization. I will not make myself the man of any past. I do not want to exalt the past at the expense of my present and of my future.

It is not because the Indo-Chinese has discovered a culture of his own that he is in revolt. It is because "quite simply" it was, in more than one way, becoming impossible for him to breathe. When one remembers the stories with which, in 1938, old regular sergeants described the land of piastres and rickshaws, of cut-rate boys and women, one understands only too well the rage with which the men of the Viet-Minh go into battle.

An acquaintance with whom I served during the Second World War recently returned from Indo-China. He has enlightened me on many things. For instance, the serenity with which young Vietnamese of sixteen or seventeen faced firing squads. "On one occasion," he told me, "we had to shoot from a kneeling position: The soldiers' hands were shaking in the presence of those young 'fanatics.'" Summing up, he added: "The war that you and I were in was only a game compared to what is going on out there."

---

[1] **Santo Domingo:** The inhabitants of Santo Domingo—what is today the Dominican Republic, in the Caribbean—rebelled against French rule in 1808 and 1809.

Seen from Europe, these things are beyond understanding. There are those who talk of a so-called Asiatic attitude toward death. But these basement philosophers cannot convince anyone. This Asiatic serenity, not so long ago, was a quality to be seen in the "bandits" of Vercors and the "terrorists" of the Resistance.

The Vietnamese who die before the firing squads are not hoping that their sacrifice will bring about the reappearance of a past. It is for the sake of the present and of the future that they are willing to die.

If the question of practical solidarity with a given past ever arose for me, it did so only to the extent to which I was committed to myself and to my neighbor to fight for all my life and with all my strength so that never again would a people on the earth be subjugated. It was not the black world that laid down my course of conduct. My black skin is not the wrapping of specific values. It is a long time since the starry sky that took away Kant's breath revealed the last of its secrets to us. And the moral law is not certain of itself.

As a man, I undertake to face the possibility of annihilation in order that two or three truths may cast their eternal brilliance over the world.

Sartre has shown that, in the line of an unauthentic position,[2] the past "takes" in quantity, and, when solidly constructed, *informs* the individual. He is the past in a changed value. But, too, I can recapture my past, validate it, or condemn it through my successive choices.

The black man wants to be like the white man. For the black man there is only one destiny. And it is white. Long ago the black man admitted the unarguable superiority of the white man, and all his efforts are aimed at achieving a white existence.

Have I no other purpose on earth, then, but to avenge the Negro of the seventeenth century?[3]

In this world, which is already trying to disappear, do I have to pose the problem of black truth?

Do I have to be limited to the justification of a facial conformation?

I as a man of color do not have the right to seek to know in what respect my race is superior or inferior to another race.

I as a man of color do not have the right to hope that in the white man there will be a crystallization of guilt toward the past of my race.

I as a man of color do not have the right to seek ways of stamping down the pride of my former master.

I have neither the right nor the duty to claim reparation for the domestication of my ancestors.

There is no Negro mission; there is no white burden.

I find myself suddenly in a world in which things do evil; a world in which I am summoned into battle; a world in which it is always a question of annihilation or triumph.

---

[2] **unauthentic position:** Authenticity results from an individual making conscious choices for himself rather than having others make choices for him.

[3] **Negro . . . century?:** The Negro who was enslaved and oppressed by slavery.

I find myself—I, a man—in a world where words wrap themselves in silence; in a world where the other endlessly hardens himself.

No, I do not have the right to go and cry out my hatred at the white man. I do not have the duty to murmur my gratitude to the white man.

My life is caught in the lasso of existence. My freedom turns me back on myself. No, I do not have the right to be a Negro.

I do not have the duty to be this or that. . . .

If the white man challenges my humanity, I will impose my whole weight as a man on his life and show him that I am not that "sho' good eatin'" that he persists in imagining.

I find myself suddenly in the world and I recognize that I have one right alone: that of demanding human behavior from the other.

One duty alone: that of not renouncing my freedom through my choices.

I have no wish to be the victim of the *Fraud* of a black world.

My life should not be devoted to drawing up the balance sheet of Negro values.

There is no white world, there is no white ethic, any more than there is a white intelligence.

There are in every part of the world men who search.

I am not a prisoner of history. I should not seek there for the meaning of my destiny.

I should constantly remind myself that the real *leap* consists in introducing invention into existence.

In the world through which I travel, I am endlessly creating myself.

I am a part of Being to the degree that I go beyond it.

And, through a private problem, we see the outline of the problem of Action. Placed in this world, in a situation, "embarked," as Pascal would have it, am I going to gather weapons?

Am I going to ask the contemporary white man to answer for the slave ships of the seventeenth century?

Am I going to try by every possible means to cause Guilt to be born in minds?

Moral anguish in the face of the massiveness of the Past? I am a Negro, and tons of chains, storms of blows, rivers of expectoration flow down my shoulders.

But I do not have the right to allow myself to bog down. I do not have the right to allow the slightest fragment to remain in my existence. I do not have the right to allow myself to be mired in what the past has determined.

I am not the slave of the Slavery that dehumanized my ancestors.

To many colored intellectuals European culture has a quality of exteriority. What is more, in human relationships, the Negro may feel himself a stranger to the Western world. Not wanting to live the part of a poor relative, of an adopted son, of a bastard child, shall he feverishly seek to discover a Negro civilization?

Let us be clearly understood. I am convinced that it would be of the greatest interest to be able to have contact with a Negro literature or architecture of the third century before Christ. I should be very happy to know that a correspondence had flourished between some Negro philosopher and Plato. But I can absolutely not see how this fact would change anything in the lives of the eight-year-old children who labor in the cane fields of Martinique or Guadeloupe.

No attempt must be made to encase man, for it is his destiny to be set free.

The body of history does not determine a single one of my actions.

I am my own foundation.

And it is by going beyond the historical, instrumental hypothesis that I will initiate the cycle of my freedom.

The disaster of the man of color lies in the fact that he was enslaved.

The disaster and the inhumanity of the white man lie in the fact that somewhere he has killed man.

And even today they subsist, to organize this dehumanization rationally. But I as a man of color, to the extent that it becomes possible for me to exist absolutely, do not have the right to lock myself into a world of retroactive reparations.

I, the man of color, want only this:

That the tool never possess the man. That the enslavement of man by man cease forever. That is, of one by another. That it be possible for me to discover and to love man, wherever he may be.

The Negro is not. Any more than the white man.

Both must turn their backs on the inhuman voices which were those of their respective ancestors in order that authentic communication be possible. Before it can adopt a positive voice, freedom requires an effort at disalienation. At the beginning of his life a man is always clotted, he is drowned in contingency. The tragedy of the man is that he was once a child.

It is through the effort to recapture the self and to scrutinize the self, it is through the lasting tension of their freedom that men will be able to create the ideal conditions of existence for a human world.

Superiority? Inferiority?

Why not the quite simple attempt to touch the other, to feel the other, to explain the other to myself?

Was my freedom not given to me then in order to build the world of the *You*?

At the conclusion of this study, I want the world to recognize, with me, the open door of every consciousness.

My final prayer:

O my body, make of me always a man who questions!

OE KENZABURO

B. JAPAN, 1935

Oe Kenzaburo was born in 1935 on Shikoku, probably the most isolated of Japan's four main islands, into a family of wealthy landowners. He was raised in the strong, antinationalistic village culture of his region until World War II brought the death of his father, the loss of family property, and sweeping changes to all of Japan. After Japan's defeat in 1945, democratic ideas from the West began to replace the hierarchical emperor system. In 1953, Oe left his village and moved to Tokyo, and in 1954 he enrolled in Tokyo University to study French literature, which influenced the writing that he began in 1957. His story "The Catch" won the Akutagawa Award. His early works, including his first novel, *Nip the Buds, Shoot the Kids* (1958; trans. 1995), deal with the uprooting of village life in Japan after the war and its effects on young people. He gained the reputation of being the most promising writer since Mishima Yukio, who also wrote about the social turbulence that followed the war in novels like *The Temple of the Golden Pavilion* (1959). After graduating from Tokyo University in 1959 Oe became a full-time writer. His works of this period increasingly focus on the effects of the U.S. occupation of Japan and the struggles of young intellectuals.

Oe's first son, Hikari, was born mentally handicapped due to a brain deformity. Learning how to live with this tragedy is the subject of *A Personal Matter* (1964; trans. 1968), his best-known and possibly his finest novel. After a visit to Hiroshima, Oe made an extraordinary connection between his son and the survivors of the atomic bombings in Hiroshima and Nagasaki; he wrote a long essay on the issues of survival and the challenge of living amidst pain and destruction in *Hiroshima Notes* (1965). His interest in the history and culture of Okinawa resulted in *The Silent Cry* (1967), which examines the tension between villages and modern life. After that work, Oe's writings centered around two major subjects. One was the challenges of life with his son and the search for his own father in *Teach Us to Outgrow Our Madness* (1969) and *My Deluged Soul* (1973); Hikari's transition to young manhood is dealt with in *Rouse Up, O Young Men of the New Age* (1983), Oe's culminating confessional work on raising his handicapped son who has, in actuality, become an accomplished composer. The other was the reconciliation of the myths and culture of traditional village life with the modern age of technology, as begun in *The Silent Cry*. He draws on cultural anthropology for *Letters to My Sweet Bygone Years* (1987) and *Wonders of the Forest* (1986). Oe's output includes more than twenty novels, several short story collections, and the extended essay *Hiroshima Notes*. He writes that his ultimate goal is "to contribute to the healing and reconciliation of all peoples." He received the Nobel Prize in literature in 1994.

In the summer of 1963, Oe was asked to go to Hiroshima and write a report on an international rally to abolish nuclear weapons. He began a series of interviews with survivors of the atomic bombing of that city,

Michael Schwartz, *Oe Kenzaburo*, 1995 *The 1994 winner of the Nobel Prize in literature, Oe Kenzaburo.* (© *Michael Schwartz/The Image Works*)

p. 757

including a number of doctors. Their memories and reflections formed the basis for what Oe calls a nonreligious conversion that influenced his life and writing from then on. Since the survivors themselves believe their sufferings are ultimately due to Japan's modern expansionism and its wars in Asia, which led to the bombings, Oe repeatedly asks whether Japan has learned the lessons of its defeat in 1945. And like Camus in **The Myth of Sisyphus**, Oe asks the ultimate question in the face of an absurd world: Why not commit suicide? Why should the survivors go on living? In the following excerpt from Chapter 3 of *Hiroshima Notes*— "The Moralists of Hiroshima"— Oe highlights the wisdom of an old woman and then turns to the incredible courage of young mothers. As he says, ". . . I regain courage when I encounter the thoroughly and fundamentally human sense of morality in the Hiroshima people 'who do not kill themselves in spite of their misery.'"

All footnotes are the author's.

Hiroshima Notes

Translated by David L. Swain and Toshi Yonezawa

FROM THE MORALISTS OF HIROSHIMA

September 1964

In talking with A-bomb victims in various hospitals, in their homes, and on the streets of Hiroshima, and hearing what they have been through and how they feel about things now, I have come to realize that they, one and all, possess unique powers of observation and expression concerning what it means to be human. I have noticed that they understand in very concrete ways such words as courage, hope, sincerity, and even "miserable death." The way they use these terms makes them what in Japanese has traditionally been called "interpreters of human nature," and what today would translate as "moralists." The reason they became moralists is that they experienced the cruelest days in human history and have endured nineteen years since. Whenever I think of the moralists of Hiroshima, I recall first an old woman who is one of the leading members of the Hiroshima Mothers' Group which publishes the splendid small magazine *The Rivers of Hiroshima*. She is a woman who speaks her mind boldly, and how attractive her vivid, incisive expression is— especially when describing the life and opinions of a certain local conservative politician who managed to rise to prominence during and after the Second World War. . . .

On the other hand, the old woman's husband, a doctor, was purged for having been a town assembly leader during the war. The old doctor lamented, "My reputation is ruined." He was afflicted with neurosis and, in his disappointment, took to buying all sorts of new medicines and trying them all. For several days following the atomic bombing, the aged doctor had been one of the doctors who worked devotedly to help the people of Hiroshima. As he, too, had been exposed to the atomic bomb, it was not unnatural that he should obtain and himself use sizeable quantities of each new medicine that came out as soon as he heard of it. But he indulged this interest to excess; and, according to his old wife, he died because his internal organs were eroded by the poisons produced by the reaction of all the new medicinal substances in his stomach. The old woman was also an A-bomb victim but had enjoyed good health, so she firmly refused to take any of the new medicines. Instead, she took a traditional herbal medicine, which cost her five thousand yen each month; and she criticized her husband for his indulgence. Herbal medicines are not used by the hospitals in Hiroshima for the treatment of A-bomb diseases; consequently, she could not depend upon the national assistance for medical expenses available to certified A-bomb victims. The old doctor and his old wife had both been healthy before the atomic bombing; that they both grew remarkably weaker after the bombing indicates clearly that they suffered various symptoms due to exposure to the atomic bomb, regardless of the fact that one had an obsession for new medicines and the other a preference for traditional herbals.

The truth is, though, that A-bomb victims cannot obtain certification for government medical assistance unless they have one or more of certain specific symptoms designated by the Ministry of Health and Welfare. How often I have had A-bomb victims tell me confidentially that they had no illness before the bombing and no definite symptoms of A-bomb disease afterward, yet they are certainly not in good health. Thus, for the A-bomb victims, there are two conflicting factors involved: On the one hand, almost any symptom may be related to the massive and multiple impact of heat, blast, and radiation, including long-term aftereffects— conditions which the human race, including the medical profession, never before experienced and has yet to comprehend fully; and, on the other hand, they cannot qualify for government protection unless their complaints fall within the rather narrow range of specified symptoms, many of which are fatal.

Now, this old woman has no connection whatsoever with any authoritarian belief or value system. She is a stubborn, independent-minded person who bases her judgments on what she sees with her own eyes and hears with her own ears. She has no use for dogmatic or conventional ideas; she has seen too many people struggle to overcome difficulties which established ideas and norms could not have solved anyway. It is people like this woman whom I call the moralists of Hiroshima. According to her, people who drowned their cares in liquor immediately after exposure to the atomic bomb did not suffer radiation illness, for the radioactivity turned to froth and oozed out of their skin.[1] Hot-bath therapy and moxa cauterization[2] of infected skin areas have been tried, with good effect, by some people. These traditional therapies cannot be simply rejected out of hand. The point is that Dr. Shigeto and others of the A-bomb Hospital staff have recorded everything done in the treatment of

---

[1] This explanation may have been a layperson's guess; but at least one medical specialist reported that drinking alcohol gave rapid relief from radiation symptoms.

[2] **moxa cauterization:** In moxa therapy, powdered moxa is burned on the skin's surface at one of the invisible sensitive points, traditionally 365 in number, which are also the loci of acupuncture therapy.

A-bomb diseases because they were coping with unprecedented conditions; they were pioneering in virgin territory. Thus the old woman continued to speak eloquently. But when she came to reporting on fellow bomb victims with whom the Hiroshima Mothers' Group is always in contact, a certain sadness crept into her forceful expression.

A young mother, who is a friend of the old woman's daughter, gave birth to a stillborn, deformed child. The young mother was an A-bomb victim who had suffered burns and consequent keloid scars; she had prepared herself for misfortune, but wanted to have a look at her baby. When the doctor refused to permit it, she asked her husband to look at it. He went to see the baby, only to find that it had already been disposed of. I am told that the young mother lamented, "If only I could see my baby, I would have courage." I was astonished by the word "courage" in her otherwise grief-stricken and hopeless statement. The word belongs among those which have been given a new depth of meaning by the existentialists. The hospital policy of not showing deformed stillborn babies to their mothers is certainly humane. Limits need to be maintained on what we are allowed to see so that we will remain human. But if a mother wants to see her dead deformed child so as to regain her own courage, she is attempting to live at the minimum limit under which a human being can remain human. This may be interpreted as a valiant expression of humanism beyond popular humanism—a new humanism sprouting from the misery of Hiroshima. Who is not moved by the spirit of this young mother, for whom even a deformed stillborn baby would be a sign to which she could cling in order to regain her courage?

Another young mother was obsessed with anxiety throughout her pregnancy at the thought of bearing a deformed child—so much so that her fear disturbed the physical functions necessary to delivery. As a result, when her time came, her labor pains came and went, off and on, for many hours. She finally had a normal baby, but her own body never fully recovered from that time on.

Although many young mothers suffer neurosis, the fact that they reject abortion and choose to go ahead and bear children shows the bravery of these young A-bomb victims. The overall picture, however, is not always so encouraging. Not a few couples among the A-bomb victims have divorced because they could not have children; and some young wives, compelled by those around them to appear brave, must struggle secretly with neuroses.

There are, of course, even sadder stories. One girl, for example, happened to see her hospital chart, on which was written "myeloid leukemia," and then hanged herself. Whenever I hear such stories, I feel we are fortunate that ours is not a Christian country. I feel an almost complete relief that a dogmatic Christian sense of guilt did not prevent the girl from taking her own life. None of us survivors can morally blame her. We have only the freedom to remember the existence of "people who do not kill themselves in spite of their misery." My personal feeling about myself is that I, as a Japanese, might be the kind of person who, if attacked by cancer, would hang himself without any sense of guilt or fear of hell. At least, I doubt that I am qualified to prevent others from committing suicide. I am, as it were, too corroded by a sort of spiritless mold. Being such a person, I regain courage when I encounter the thoroughly and fundamentally human sense of morality in the Hiroshima people "who do not kill themselves in spite of their misery."

The political scandal in the newspapers this third week of September as I write this section opens with a sensational account of Khrushchev's statement that the Russians now possess "a fearful weapon capable of exterminating mankind." Several days later this was revised as "fearful new-style weapons," using the plural form. However wide the gap between the two expressions may be, I cannot rid myself of the impression that these awesome weapons reign over our age like raving-mad gods. In this nuclear age, should not the morality of "people who do not kill themselves in spite of their misery" apply universally to us all? Certainly we share naturally the morality of people in Hiroshima who were unavoidably degraded and, yet, did not commit suicide.

SAMUEL BECKETT
B. IRELAND, 1906–1989

Samuel Beckett

Beckett in middle age.
(© Topham / The
Image Works)

Samuel Beckett, Irish-born playwright, novelist, story writer, poet, and translator, emigrated to Paris where he created a substantial body of work in which many memorable characters search for meaning in a confusing and enigmatic world. In his mature work Beckett is guided by a sense of comedy that nevertheless rarely dilutes his bleak view of life. While he is comparable to a variety of literary figures—including his mentor, the Irish word wizard James Joyce (p. 366)—his spiritual kinship extends to an even more diverse lot, including Italian playwright Luigi Pirandello (p. 201), Dutch artist Bram van Velde,[1] and comedic film actors such as Buster Keaton.[2]

Like many writers of his time, Beckett contributed to the broad literary and artistic movement that today is called MODERNISM. Influenced by the psychoanalytic theories of Sigmund Freud (p. 425; 1856–1939), which sought the cure to neurosis in the individual's buried past, and by Carl Jung (1875–1961), who found in world myths and symbols evidence of a collective unconscious, modernist writers and artists endeavored to express the hidden inner life of the individual. A member of the French Underground during the Nazi occupation of France in the Second World War, Beckett emerged from the experience as one of the most profound voices of the European generation that sought to understand the human predicament—"L'ABSURD," as the French called it. Although he shared the interests of many of his peers, Beckett, characteristically, worked alone. While Jean-Paul Sartre (p. 692), Albert Camus (p. 756), and other French writers created a literary movement based on *l'absurd,* Beckett wrote largely without recognition in the Paris that they, too, inhabited.

Beckett's play *Waiting for Godot* (1952) will probably number among the great works of literature of all time. His early writings in English, influenced by Joyce, and his adept translations of poetry and fiction from several European languages quickly established his reputation as a master stylist. But he separated himself from such prose masters as Joyce later in his career, making his own mark with dramatic dialogues written with poetic brevity. Time and again Beckett's characters drive home a point, often painfully, by saying the unsayable in simple language. Beckett so strove after simplicity that he switched from writing in English to writing

---

[1] Bram van Velde (1895–1981): A close friend of Beckett's and the principal subject of an article he wrote on the state of painting in modern Europe. Beckett frequently appears to be describing his own position when writing of van Velde: He speaks of modern art being "in mourning for the object" and of the artist's "fidelity to failure," so that, being "obliged to act, he makes an expressive act, even if only of itself, of its impossibility, of its obligation."

[2] Buster Keaton (1895–1966): One of the early generation of film comedians that included Charlie Chaplin and Harold Lloyd. Beckett was a great admirer of the art of slapstick comedy and was pleased when Buster Keaton was engaged to play in *Film,* Beckett's only work for the cinema, a short film produced in 1964.

in French because, he said, he was less tempted by the subtleties of his adopted tongue.

Early Life. Samuel Beckett was born on the outskirts of Dublin on April 13, 1906. Driven to apply himself while still very young by a domineering Protestant mother who recognized his extraordinary intellectual abilities, he was later educated at Trinity College, Dublin, receiving his bachelor's degree in 1928. Although he joined the Trinity College faculty, he resigned his post at the end of 1931, disappointing friends and supporters. Beckett lived miserably for a time in London, traveled in Germany, and finally settled in Paris in 1936. He wrote his two earliest novels, *Murphy* (1938) and *Watt* (written between 1942 and 1944), in English but was already writing in French at the start of World War II.

Although Beckett, a habitual loner except for infrequent forays into society, would probably have preferred to shun the world and devote himself solely to his writing, the times would not allow it. Despite his professed desire to remain neutral in politics, Beckett joined the French resistance against the German occupation in 1941, following the German invasion of France and the fall of Paris in 1940. At first, the resistance did little more than remind the French people that the war against Germany was ongoing outside France. But soon Beckett's apartment in Paris became a "drop" for microfilm photographs destined for Britain of German installations. Matters heated up in 1942, when some of Beckett's friends were arrested, and many Parisians, primarily Jews, were either shot or sent to concentration camps. Beckett moved south to Roussillon, then a free city but later occupied by the Germans as they, too, moved south. Beckett stayed a step ahead of the German Gestapo, or secret police, until the war ended. He was awarded the croix de guerre, the French medal for bravery, in 1945.

The Siege in the Room. Restored to Paris in 1946, Beckett began to conduct what he called "the siege in the room." Biographer Anthony Cronin describes this as "a reduction to bare necessities, being driven back on oneself, being stripped of all resources save the ultimate ones of desperation and self-reliance." Writing in French, Beckett produced many of his major works in these years: the two novels *Molloy* (1951) and *Malone Dies* (1951), *Waiting for Godot* (1952), and the novel *The Unnameable* (1953). He followed these with a number of other plays and short pieces originally intended for radio, including *Krapp's Last Tape* (1958).

By now Beckett lived in some degree of comfort. His reputation had been established and his small circle of friends proved impressively loyal. Even so, he suffered from a number of minor illnesses: cysts, rashes, insomnia, dizzy spells, stomach pains, bad teeth, panic attacks, and hypochondria. He had been the victim of a stabbing on a Paris street in 1938, possibly the result of an argument with a pimp, which resulted in lung damage that lasted for the rest of his life. But as he approached old age his complaints lessened. The grimness of his work did not. He referred to *Texts for Nothing*, thirteen short pieces written after *The Unnameable*, as "nothing more than the grisly afterbirth" of that novel.

www For links to more information about Beckett and a quiz on *Krapp's Last Tape*, and for information about the culture and context of Europe in the twentieth century, see *World Literature Online* at bedfordstmartins.com/worldlit.

In 1969, largely as a result of the success of *Waiting for Godot*, Beckett was awarded the Nobel Prize in literature. The citation for the prize remarked that it was for "a body of work that, in new forms of fiction and the theatre, has transmuted the destitution of modern man into his exaltation." Beckett himself remained somewhat aloof from the award, commenting that he was "lacking in Nobel fiber" and worrying aloud whether he would even try to write again after all the commotion. He asked his publisher, Jerome Lindon, to accept the award in his place. In fact, though he lived twenty years longer, he wrote little new work after receiving the honor, devoting himself instead to the staging of his existing dramas. He died in December 1989.

The Beckett Man.   All Beckett's works present in one form or another what one of his biographers has called the "Beckett man"—a seriocomic character who rejects the central Western European beliefs in the life of reason, progress, and liberal optimism. Typically unemployed and without ambition in the ordinary sense, the Beckett man reels from his memory of education, society's attempt to instill in him such traditional values as honor, dignity, and courage. His experience of love is limited, though he dimly recalls the influence of his mother when he was a child. He regards physical distress, including paralysis, as ordinary and even vaguely pleasurable. The only virtue he appears to possess is a capacity to endure. Beckett's characters become increasingly enfeebled, even paralyzed, in later works until in *The Unnameable* the main character is reduced to a creature who hangs in a bottle and has only the power of reflection.

After the war, Beckett began to question the stance of his earlier characters like Murphy and Watt who had cleverly tried to deny or demolish their relationship to what they called "the big world." Perhaps moved by his participation in and knowledge of the real dangers of the French resistance, Beckett detected a certain arrogance in his early work. Instead of infusing new characters with his own learning and cleverness, he left them alone in the world, which they saw as an ominous and unknowable place. The more vulnerable Beckett made them to outside forces, the more their stature tended to grow in the eyes of the audience. Of the novel *Molloy* (written between 1947 and 1949), Beckett said, "I conceived *Molloy* and what followed the day I realized my own stupidity."

Waiting for Godot.   *Waiting for Godot* (written between 1947 and 1949, and published in French in 1952) followed *Molloy*. In *Godot*, the characters Vladimir and Estragon assemble to meet a mysterious character named Godot. Both complain of small maladies, both occasionally rise to the expectation that Godot will arrive, but both ultimately give up again. The theme of the play is repeated throughout in one way or another: "Nothing to be done." The actors, as a critic has noted, are imprisoned by their own dialogue, which always comes back to the same place. Not that nothing ever happens; someone comes, but it is not Godot. It is Pozzo, whom Estragon and Vladimir first mistakenly identify as Godot only to disavow their hasty error. Eventually, Pozzo leaves for the fair, where he has determined to sell his slave, Lucky. But in the second act of the play, Pozzo and Lucky return through the same door through which they had left. Both are enfeebled: Pozzo is blind and Lucky is unable to speak. At the end of each of the two acts there appears a boy who announces that Godot will not come today, "but surely tomorrow." But Godot does not arrive the next day either. Vladimir summarizes the action of the play in a speech during the second act:

> Tomorrow, when I wake, or think I do, what shall I say of today? That with Estragon my friend, at this place, until the fall of night, I waited for Godot? That Pozzo passed, with his carrier, and that he spoke to us? Probably. But in all that what truth will there be?

Waiting for Godot is a work that has been interpreted as operating on many levels: as slapstick comedy; as a play about the death of God (*God-ot* could be heard as a pun in English); as an EXISTENTIALIST drama in which man is left alone to act in the world but can find no basis for action; as a play about time and its destruction of possibility. But no matter how one sees it, in the end the theatergoer is caught up in the spare beauty of the play's dialogue, the amount of interest it creates in the midst of apparent hopelessness, the surprising degree to which one identifies with the characters, however weak they are. A play about despair, *Waiting for Godot* maintains an atmosphere of faint, unreasonable hope that carries both the audience and the actors, however reluctantly, through to the drama's conclusion.

Krapp's Last Tape.   Beckett saw his writings of the late 1940s as the height of his creativity, disparaging subsequent works for their lack of development. In 1956 he commented, "For some authors writing gets easier the more they write. For me it gets more and more difficult. For me the area of possibilities gets smaller and smaller." Beckett made an effort to escape this narrowing field of possibilities in a radio play called *All that Fall,* broadcast in 1956. The piece recounts memories of Beckett's youth in the Irish landscape, a theme more accessible to the listening audience than was his other work at the time. But while *All that Fall* was scripted in a public voice, *Krapp's Last Tape* (1958), Beckett's next major play, returned fiercely to inner reflection. Beckett, who had not so much as seen a tape recorder when he wrote this play, imagined a reclusive, ineffectual drunkard on his sixty-ninth birthday listening to tapes he had recorded on his twenty-eighth and thirty-ninth birthdays. (To account for the earlier use of the tape recorder, invented only around 1950, the play is set on "a late evening in the future.") The unsettling bleakness of the play emerges from the conflicts and disharmonies between the three persons that constitute Krapp at twenty-eight, thirty-nine, and sixty-nine.

Throughout Beckett's work we can find evidence of his conviction that everything is hopeless, meaningless, purposeless, and, above all, agonizing to endure.

– GEORGE WELLWARTH, critic, 1964

■ CONNECTIONS

Luigi Pirandello, *Six Characters in Search of an Author,* p. 205. The groundbreaking modernist play *Six Characters in Search of an Author* established the convention of actors speaking to one another outside of a fabricated plot, with their feelings in full view of the audience. How is Beckett's use of this modernist convention similar to that in Pirandello's play?

Fyodor Dostoevsky, *Notes from Underground* (Book 5). Dostoevsky's *Notes from Underground* is often considered one of the seminal texts of existentialism for its treatment of alienation, isolation, and suffering as well as the ideal of freedom. Beckett's use of the confessional voice and an isolated, alienated figure in *Krapp's Last Tape* recalls Dostoevsky's story. Can Krapp be seen as an "underground man"? How is he similar to and different from Dostoevsky's monologuist? Would you consider *Krapp's Last Tape* an existentialist play?

Tawfiq al-Hakim, *The Fate of a Cockroach*, p. 590; Albert Camus, "The Myth of Sisyphus," p. 757. *Krapp's Last Tape* and al-Hakim's *The Fate of a Cockroach* are both examples of what critic Martin Esslin called the "theatre of the absurd." In what sense is the human situation presented in each of these plays "absurd"? Does Albert Camus' essay "The Myth of Sisyphus" suggest some meanings of *absurd*? What dramatic techniques do Beckett's and al-Hakim's plays share?

■ FURTHER RESEARCH

Biographies
Bair, Deidre. *Samuel Beckett: A Biography*. 1978.
Cronin, Anthony. *Samuel Beckett: The Last Modernist*. 1999.

Criticism
Esslin, Martin, ed. *Samuel Beckett: A Collection of Critical Essays*. 1965.
Fletcher, John, and John Spurling. *Beckett the Playwright*. 1985.
Harvey, Lawrence. *Samuel Beckett: Poet and Critic*. 1970.
Kenner, Hugh. *Samuel Beckett: A Critical Study*. 1965.
———, ed. *A Reader's Guide to Samuel Beckett*. 1973.
Mercier, Vivien. *Beckett/Beckett*. 1977.

∽ Krapp's Last Tape

A late evening in the future.

Krapp's den.

Front center a small table, the two drawers of which open towards audience.

Sitting at the table, facing front, i.e., across from the drawers, a wearish[1] old man: Krapp.

Krapp's Last Tape. This play was first performed at the Royal Court Theatre in London on October 28, 1958. The single figure onstage is an old man who, on his sixty-ninth birthday, is listening to tape recordings he made on earlier birthdays at ages twenty-eight and thirty-nine. The young Krapp mostly recalls his efforts to make love to a girl; the middle-aged Krapp, at the height of his creative powers, stresses the moment of breakthrough when he finally acquires self-understanding

---

[1] **wearish:** Lean, wizened.

Rusty black narrow trousers too short for him. Rusty black sleeveless waistcoat, four capacious pockets. Heavy silver watch and chain. Grimy white shirt open at neck, no collar. Surprising pair of dirty white boots, size ten at least, very narrow and pointed.

White face. Purple nose. Disordered grey hair. Unshaven.

Very nearsighted (but unspectacled). Hard of hearing.

Cracked voice. Distinctive intonation.

Laborious walk.

On the table a tape recorder with microphone and a number of cardboard boxes containing reels of recorded tapes.

Table and immediately adjacent area in strong white light. Rest of stage in darkness.

Krapp remains a moment motionless, heaves a great sigh, looks at his watch, fumbles in his pockets, takes out an envelope, puts it back, fumbles, takes out a small bunch of keys, raises it to his eyes, chooses a key, gets up and moves to front of table. He stoops, unlocks first drawer, peers into it, feels about inside it, takes out a reel of tape, peers at it, puts it back, locks drawer, unlocks second drawer, peers into it, feels about inside it, takes out a large banana, peers at it, locks drawer, puts keys back in his pocket. He turns, advances to edge of stage, halts, strokes banana, peels it, drops skin at his feet, puts end of banana in his mouth and remains motionless, staring vacuously before him. Finally he bites off the end, turns aside and begins pacing to and fro at edge of stage, in the light, i.e. not more than four or five paces either way, meditatively eating banana. He treads on skin, slips, nearly falls, recovers himself, stoops and peers at skin and finally pushes it, still stooping, with his foot over the edge of stage into pit. He resumes his pacing, finishes banana, returns to table, sits down, remains a moment motionless, heaves a great sigh, takes keys from his pockets, raises them to his eyes, chooses key, gets up and moves to front of table, unlocks second drawer, takes out a second large banana, peers at it, locks drawer, puts back keys in his pocket, turns, advances to edge of stage, halts, strokes banana, peels it, tosses skin into pit, puts end of banana in his mouth and remains motionless, staring vacuously before him. Finally he has an idea, puts banana in his waistcoat pocket, the end emerging, and goes with all the speed he can muster backstage into darkness. Ten seconds. Loud pop of cork. Fifteen seconds. He comes back into light carrying an old ledger and sits down at table. He lays ledger on table, wipes his mouth, wipes his hands on the front of his waistcoat, brings them smartly together and rubs them.

---

as an artist; the older Krapp, barely concealing his longing for the past, envies both versions of his younger self while finding fault with their presumption and foolishness. His love life virtually ended and his creative life thwarted, Krapp sees the promise and error of his life from the perspective of his darkened room. But his engagement with the past is severely limited: It comes down to his purely negative control of the tape recorder. He can stop, reverse, or fast-forward the tapes, but he cannot change the words or the history that they partially reveal. This play's commentary on man's helplessness to change the past reflects Beckett's mature view that although the artist never loses his vision, he also can never completely satisfy it.

A note on the text: Beckett wrote the play in English and subsequently translated it into French. All notes are the editors'.

KRAPP *(briskly)*: Ah! *(He bends over ledger, turns the pages, finds the entry he wants, reads.)* Box . . . thrree . . . spool . . . five. *(He raises his head and stares front. With relish.)* Spool! *(Pause.)* Spooool! *(Happy smile. Pause. He bends over table, starts peering and poking at the boxes.)* Box . . . thrree . . . thrree . . . four . . . two . . . *(with surprise)* nine! good God! . . . seven . . . ah! the little rascal! *(He takes up box, peers at it.)* Box thrree. *(He lays it on table, opens it, and peers at spools inside.)* Spool . . . *(he peers at ledger)* . . . five . . . *(he peers at spools)* . . . five . . . five . . . ah! the little scoundrel! *(He takes out a spool, peers at it.)* Spool five. *(He lays it on table, closes box three, puts it back with the others, takes up the spool.)* Box thrree, spool five. *(He bends over the machine, looks up. With relish.)* Spooool! *(Happy smile. He bends, loads spool on machine, rubs his hands.)* Ah! *(He peers at ledger, reads entry at foot of page.)* Mother at rest at last . . . Hm . . . The black ball . . . *(He raises his head, stares blankly front. Puzzled.)* Black ball? . . . *(He peers again at ledger, reads.)* The dark nurse . . . *(He raises his head, broods, peers again at ledger, reads.)* Slight improvement in bowel condition . . . Hm . . . Memorable . . . what? *(He peers closer.)* Equinox, memorable equinox. *(He raises his head, stares blankly front. Puzzled.)* Memorable equinox? . . . *(Pause. He shrugs his shoulders, peers again at ledger, reads.)* Farewell to— *(he turns the page)*—love.

He raises his head, broods, bends over machine, switches on and assumes listening posture, i.e. leaning forward, elbows on table, hand cupping ear towards machine, face front.

TAPE *(strong voice, rather pompous, clearly Krapp's at a much earlier time)*: Thirty-nine today, sound as a— *(Settling himself more comfortably he knocks one of the boxes off the table, curses, switches off, sweeps boxes and ledger violently to the ground, winds tape back to beginning, switches on, resumes posture.)* Thirty-nine today, sound as a bell, apart from my old weakness, and intellectually I have now every reason to suspect at the . . . *(hesitates)* . . . crest of the wave—or thereabouts. Celebrated the awful occasion, as in recent years, quietly at the Winehouse. Not a soul. Sat before the fire with closed eyes, separating the grain from the husks. Jotted down a few notes, on the back of an envelope. Good to be back in my den, in my old rags. Have just eaten I regret to say three bananas and only with difficulty refrained from a fourth. Fatal things for a man with my condition. *(Vehemently.)* Cut 'em out! *(Pause.)* The new light above my table is a great improvement. With all this darkness round me I feel less alone. *(Pause.)* In a way. *(Pause.)* I love to get up and move about in it, then back here to . . . *(hesitates)* . . . me. *(Pause.)* Krapp.

Pause.

The grain, now what I wonder do I mean by that, I mean . . . *(hesitates)* . . . I suppose I mean those things worth having when all the dust has—when all *my* dust has settled. I close my eyes and try and imagine them.

Pause. Krapp closes his eyes briefly.

Extraordinary silence this evening, I strain my ears and do not hear a sound. Old Miss McGlome always sings at this hour. But not tonight. Songs of her girlhood, she says. Hard to think of her as a girl. Wonderful woman though.

Connaught,[2] I fancy. *(Pause.)* Shall I sing when I am her age, if I ever am? No. *(Pause.)* Did I sing as a boy? No. *(Pause.)* Did I ever sing? No.

Pause.

Just been listening to an old year, passages at random. I did not check in the book, but it must be at least ten or twelve years ago. At that time I think I was still living on and off with Bianca in Kedar Street. Well out of that, Jesus yes! Hopeless business. *(Pause.)* Not much about her, apart from a tribute to her eyes. Very warm. I suddenly saw them again. *(Pause.)* Incomparable! *(Pause.)* Ah well . . . *(Pause.)* These old P.M.s[3] are gruesome, but I often find them — *(Krapp switches off, broods, switches on)* — a help before embarking on a new . . . *(hesitates)* . . . retrospect. Hard to believe I was ever that young whelp. The voice! Jesus! And the aspirations! *(Brief laugh in which Krapp joins.)* And the resolutions! *(Brief laugh in which Krapp joins.)* To drink less, in particular. *(Brief laugh of Krapp alone.)* Statistics. Seventeen hundred hours, out of the preceding eight thousand odd, consumed on licensed premises[4] alone. More than 20%, say 40% of his waking life. *(Pause.)* Plans for a less . . . *(hesitates)* . . . engrossing sexual life. Last illness of his father. Flagging pursuit of happiness. Unattainable laxation. Sneers at what he calls his youth and thanks to God that it's over. *(Pause.)* False ring there. *(Pause.)* Shadows of the opus . . . magnum.[5] Closing with a — *(brief laugh)* — yelp to Providence. *(Prolonged laugh in which Krapp joins.)* What remains of all that misery? A girl in a shabby green coat, on a railway-station platform? No?

Pause.
When I look —

Krapp switches off, broods, looks at his watch, gets up, goes backstage into darkness. Ten seconds. Pop of cork. Ten seconds. Second cork. Ten seconds. Third cork. Ten seconds. Brief burst of quavering song.

KRAPP *(sings)*:   Now the day is over,
                Night is drawing nigh-igh,
                Shadows —

Fit of coughing. He comes back into light, sits down, wipes his mouth, switches on, resumes his listening posture.

TAPE: — back on the year that is gone, with what I hope is perhaps a glint of the old eye to come, there is of course the house on the canal where mother lay a-dying, in the late autumn, after her long viduity *(Krapp gives a start)*, and the — *(Krapp switches off, winds back tape a little, bends his ear closer to machine, switches on)* — a-dying, after her long viduity, and the —

Krapp switches off, raises his head, stares blankly before him. His lips move in the syllables of "viduity." No sound. He gets up, goes backstage into darkness, comes back with an enormous dictionary, lays it on table, sits down, and looks up the word.

---

[2] **Connaught:** Northwestern county of Ireland.   [3] **P.M.s:** Postmortems.   [4] **licensed premises:** A pub or liquor store.   [5] **opus magnum:** *Magnum opus,* Latin for "great work."

KRAPP *(reading from dictionary)*: State—or condition of being—or remaining—a widow—or widower. *(Looks up. Puzzled.)* Being—or remaining? . . . *(Pause. He peers again at dictionary. Reading.)* "Deep weeds of viduity" . . . Also of an animal, especially a bird . . . the vidua or weaver-bird . . . Black plumage of male . . . *(He looks up. With relish.)* The vidua-bird!

Pause. He closes dictionary, switches on, resumes listening posture.

TAPE: —bench by the weir[6] from where I could see her window. There I sat, in the biting wind, wishing she were gone. *(Pause.)* Hardly a soul, just a few regulars, nursemaids, infants, old men, dogs. I got to know them quite well—oh by appearance of course I mean! One dark young beauty I recollect particularly, all white and starch, incomparable bosom, with a big black hooded perambulator, most funereal thing. Whenever I looked in her direction she had her eyes on me. And yet when I was bold enough to speak to her—not having been introduced—she threatened to call a policeman. As if I had designs on her virtue! *(Laugh. Pause.)* The face she had! The eyes! Like . . . *(hesitates)* . . . chrysolite![7] *(Pause.)* Ah well . . . *(Pause.)* I was there when—*(Krapp switches off, broods, switches on again)*—the blind went down, one of those dirty brown roller affairs, throwing a ball for a little white dog, as chance would have it. I happened to look up and there it was. All over and done with, at last. I sat on for a few moments with the ball in my hand and the dog yelping and pawing at me. *(Pause.)* Moments. Her moments, my moments. *(Pause.)* The dog's moments. *(Pause.)* In the end I held it out to him and he took it in his mouth, gently, gently. A small, old, black, hard, solid rubber ball. *(Pause.)* I shall feel it, in my hand, until my dying day. *(Pause.)* I might have kept it. *(Pause.)* But I gave it to the dog.

Pause.
Ah well . . .

Pause.
Spiritually a year of profound gloom and indigence until that memorable night in March, at the end of the jetty, in the howling wind, never to be forgotten, when suddenly I saw the whole thing. The vision, at last. This I fancy is what I have chiefly to record this evening, against the day when my work will be done and perhaps no place left in my memory, warm or cold, for the miracle that . . . *(hesitates)* . . . for the fire that set it alight. What I suddenly saw then was this, that the belief I had been going on all my life, namely—*(Krapp switches off impatiently, winds tape forward, switches on again)*—great granite rocks the foam flying up in the light of the lighthouse and the wind-gauge spinning like a propellor, clear to me at last that the dark I have always struggled to keep under is in reality my most—*(Krapp curses, switches off, winds tape forward, switches on again)*—unshatterable association until my dissolution of storm and night with the light of the understanding and the fire—*(Krapp curses louder, switches*

---

[6] **weir**: Millpond.   [7] **chrysolite**: A pale green semiprecious stone.

off, winds tape forward, switches on again) — my face in her breasts and my hand on her. We lay there without moving. But under us all moved, and moved us, gently, up and down, and from side to side.

Pause.

Past midnight. Never knew such silence. The earth might be uninhabited.

Pause.

Here I end—

Krapp switches off, winds tape back, switches on again.

—upper lake, with the punt, bathed off the bank, then pushed out into the stream and drifted. She lay stretched out on the floorboards with her hands under her head and her eyes closed. Sun blazing down, bit of a breeze, water nice and lively. I noticed a scratch on her thigh and asked her how she came by it. Picking gooseberries, she said. I said again I thought it was hopeless and no good going on, and she agreed, without opening her eyes. *(Pause.)* I asked her to look at me and after a few moments— *(pause)*—after a few moments she did, but the eyes just slits, because of the glare. I bent over her to get them in the shadow and they opened. *(Pause. Low.)* Let me in. *(Pause.)* We drifted in among the flags and stuck. The way they went down, sighing, before the stem! *(Pause.)* I lay down across her with my face in her breasts and my hand on her. We lay there without moving. But under us all moved, and moved us, gently, up and down, and from side to side.

Pause.

Past midnight. Never knew—

Krapp switches off, broods. Finally he fumbles in his pockets, encounters the banana, takes it out, peers at it, puts it back, fumbles, brings out the envelope, fumbles, puts back envelope, looks at his watch, gets up, and goes backstage into darkness. Ten seconds. Sound of bottle against glass, then brief siphon. Ten seconds. Bottle against glass alone. Ten seconds. He comes back a little unsteadily into light, goes to front of table, takes out keys, raises them to his eyes, chooses key, unlocks first drawer, peers into it, feels about inside, takes out reel, peers at it, locks drawer, puts keys back in his pocket, goes and sits down, takes reel off machine, lays it on dictionary, loads virgin reel on machine, takes envelope from his pocket, consults back of it, lays it on table, switches on, clears his throat, and begins to record.

KRAPP: Just been listening to that stupid bastard I took myself for thirty years ago, hard to believe I was ever as bad as that. Thank God that's all done with anyway. *(Pause.)* The eyes she had! *(Broods, realizes he is recording silence, switches off, broods. Finally.)* Everything there, everything, all the— *(Realizes this is not being recorded, switches on.)* Everything there, everything on this old muckball, all the light and dark and famine and feasting of . . . *(hesitates)* . . . the ages! *(In a shout.)* Yes! *(Pause.)* Let that go! Jesus! Take his mind off his homework! Jesus! *(Pause. Weary.)* Ah well, maybe he was right. *(Pause.)* Maybe he was right. *(Broods. Realizes. Switches off. Consults envelope.)* Pah! *(Crumples it and throws it away. Broods. Switches on.)* Nothing to say, not a squeak. What's a year now? The sour cud and the iron stool. *(Pause.)* Revelled in the word spool. *(With relish.)*

Spooool! Happiest moment of the past half million. *(Pause.)* Seventeen copies sold, of which eleven at trade price to free circulating libraries beyond the seas. Getting known. *(Pause.)* One pound six and something, eight I have little doubt. *(Pause.)* Crawled out once or twice, before the summer was cold. Sat shivering in the park, drowned in dreams and burning to be gone. Not a soul. *(Pause.)* Last fancies. *(Vehemently.)* Keep 'em under! *(Pause.)* Scalded the eyes out of me reading *Effie*[8] again, a page a day, with tears again. Effie . . . *(Pause.)* Could have been happy with her, up there on the Baltic, and the pines, and the dunes. *(Pause.)* Could I? *(Pause.)* And she? *(Pause.)* Pah! *(Pause.)* Fanny came in a couple of times. Bony old ghost of a whore. Couldn't do much, but I suppose better than a kick in the crutch. The last time wasn't so bad. How do you manage it, she said, at your age? I told her I'd been saving up for her all my life. *(Pause.)* Went to Vespers once, like when I was in short trousers. *(Pause. Sings.)*

> Now the day is over,
> Night is drawing nigh-igh,
> Shadows— *(coughing, then almost inaudible)* —of the evening
> Steal across the sky.

(Gasping.) Went to sleep and fell off the pew. *(Pause.)* Sometimes wondered in the night if a last effort mightn't— *(Pause.)* Ah finish your booze now and get to your bed. Go on with this drivel in the morning. Or leave it at that. *(Pause.)* Leave it at that. *(Pause.)* Lie propped up in the dark—and wander. Be again in the dingle[9] on a Christmas Eve, gathering holly, the red-berried. *(Pause.)* Be again on Croghan on a Sunday morning, in the haze, with the bitch, stop and listen to the bells. *(Pause.)* And so on. *(Pause.)* Be again, be again. *(Pause.)* All that old misery. *(Pause.)* Once wasn't enough for you. *(Pause.)* Lie down across her.

Long pause. He suddenly bends over machine, switches off, wrenches off tape, throws it away, puts on the other, winds it forward to the passage he wants, switches on, listens staring front.

TAPE: —gooseberries, she said. I said again I thought it was hopeless and no good going on, and she agreed, without opening her eyes. *(Pause.)* I asked her to look at me and after a few moments— *(pause)* —after a few moments she did, but the eyes just slits, because of the glare. I bent over her to get them in the shadow and they opened. *(Pause. Low.)* Let me in. *(Pause.)* We drifted in among the flags and stuck. The way they went down, sighing, before the stem! *(Pause.)* I lay down across her with my face in her breasts and my hand on her. We lay there without moving. But under us all moved, and moved us, gently, up and down, and from side to side.

Pause. Krapp's lips move. No sound.
Past midnight. Never knew such silence. The earth might be uninhabited.

Pause.

---

[8] *Effie*: *Effi Briest* (1895), a novel by Theodor Fontane.   [9] **dingle**: Wooded hollow.

Here I end this reel. Box—*(pause)*—three, spool—*(pause)*—five. *(Pause.)* Perhaps my best years are gone. When there was a chance of happiness. But I wouldn't want them back. Not with the fire in me now. No, I wouldn't want them back.

Krapp motionless staring before him. The tape runs on in silence.

CURTAIN

❧ R. K. NARAYAN
B. INDIA, 1906–2001

Many of R. K. Narayan's novels and stories describe the people and the life in the mythical Indian town of Malgudi, a place much like Madras and Mysore, the cities in southern India where Narayan spent nearly all his life. The rich and varied gallery of characters in Narayan's work gives Malgudi the density and presence of a real place—of India itself. Narayan has remarked that "the material available to the story writer in India is limitless. Within a broad climate of inherited culture there are endless variations. . . . Under such conditions the writer has only to look out of the window to pick up a character (and thereby a story)." The many memorable characters that populate Narayan's novels and stories have led critics to compare Malgudi to William Faulkner's Yoknapatawpha County and Gabriel García Márquez's Macondo, places imagined and made real by the power of literature.[1]

R. K. Narayan
The author rarely left his home area in southern India.
(© DPA / The Image Works)
ruh-see-POO-rum
krish-nuh-SWAH-mee
nuh-RIGH-yun

The Creator of Malgudi.   Born in 1906 into a Brahman family, **Rasipuram Krishnaswami Narayan** spent his early childhood in the house of his maternal grandmother in Madras. While he was there, he attended a Lutheran mission school where he was disliked by the teachers and students as one of the few non-Christians. When he reached high-school age, he rejoined his parents in Mysore and attended the school where his father was headmaster. He was not a particularly dedicated student; when he finished school in 1924, he failed the university entrance exam in English and had to delay his university studies for a year. He spent his free time reading books of all sorts, but mainly fiction by such novelists as

---

[1] **Faulkner . . . Márquez:** William Faulkner (1897–1962), American novelist; in works like *The Sound and the Fury* (1929) and *Intruder in the Dust* (1948), Faulkner created a whole history and sociology for his home area of northeastern Mississippi—and implicitly the American South—depicting the dissolution of its values and social traditions. In *One Hundred Years of Solitude* (1967), Gabriel García Márquez (b. 1928; see p. 924) similarly creates a history and sociology for Macondo, based on the village in northern Colombia where he grew up.

Dickens, Conan Doyle, Sir Walter Scott, Tagore, and H. G. Wells.[2] Gradu-ated from Maharaja's College (now the University of Mysore) in 1930, he briefly tried secondary-school teaching before taking up writing, the pro-fession he pursued for the rest of his life.

Narayan wrote about the life and the people he observed around him in Mysore, the town he fictionalized as Malgudi. His work as the Mysore correspondent for a Madras newspaper sent him out daily in search of stories and established the discipline of daily writing that accounts for his prolific output. Beginning in 1935 when *Swami and Friends,* his first novel, was published, Narayan produced more than fifteen novels, twelve volumes of short stories and essays, and an autobiography as well as retellings of *The Ramayana* (1972) and *The Mahabharata* (1978), and numerous articles and stories in his lifetime. The best known of his nov-els are *The Bachelor of Arts* (1937), *Mr. Sampath* (1949), *The Financial Expert* (1952), *Waiting for the Mahatma: A Novel* (1955), *The Guide* (1958), *The Vendor of Sweets* (1967), and *A Tiger for Malgudi* (1983).

A Tradition of Storytelling.   Unlike many Indian writers who in the last century either left or spent much of their lives outside of India, R. K. Narayan was content to remain at home. He traveled abroad only rarely, remaining in the region of India where he had grown up. In many ways he was a traditional village storyteller, a figure he celebrates in the short story "Under the Banyan Tree" (1985). Narayan did not experiment with the form of the novel or that of the short story; he aimed to tell a good tale and record the lives of the people he knew. Discussing the differences between America and India in an essay in *In the World:* Crossing Cultures (see p. 1278), Narayan contrasts the pragmatic American temperament with the Indian way: "From childhood," he writes, "an Indian is brought up on the notion that austerity and a contented life is good, and also a certain otherworldliness is inculcated through the tales a grandmother narrates, the discourses at the temple hall, and through moral books." Narayan sought to give expression to the values of his upbringing in his fiction.

Narayan's Themes.   Narayan's novels document the transition of a society from an agrarian village culture to middle-class urban life. His works tend to center on middle-class people — schoolteachers, financial managers, and merchants — in the mythical town of Malgudi. These self-conscious characters seek to grow and establish an identity distinct from

The material avail-able to the story writer in India is limitless. Within a broad climate of inherited culture there are endless variations. . . . Under such circum-stances the writer has only to look out of the window to pick up a character (and thereby a story).

– R. K. NARAYAN

---

[2] **Dickens . . . Wells:** Writers of the nineteenth and early twentieth century, many of whom influenced Indian letters. Charles Dickens (1812–1870), English novelist, is best known for *David Copperfield* (1850) and *Great Expectations* (1861). Sir Arthur Conan Doyle (1859–1930), English novelist and short-story writer, composed the Sherlock Holmes stories. Scottish novelist Sir Walter Scott (1771–1832) wrote a history of Scotland and its emer-gence as a nation in novels like *Waverley* (1814) and *Rob Roy* (1818). Scott also wrote historical romances about the Middle Ages. Rabindranath Tagore (1861–1941) was a Bengali poet, novelist, and playwright who inspired almost all later Indian writers of the twentieth century; see Book 5. H. G. Wells (1866–1946), English novelist, science-fiction writer, and popular historian, wrote *Tono-Bungay* (1909) and *The Time Machine* (1895).

TIME AND PLACE

Twentieth-Century India: Caste and Gender in an Indian Village

Its major cities such as Bombay and Calcutta notwithstanding, India is still a village culture, and many Indians, like Muni in "A Horse and Two Goats," follow traditional ways of life little affected by modern technology. Many rural Indians are poor and illiterate, deprivations magnified for many village women who also suffer the constraints traditional Indian culture places on their gender. Novelist and short-story writer Mahasweta Devi (b. 1926) has devoted her life to alleviating the sufferings of such women, by both her writing and her social work among the indigenous villagers in Bengal. Her short story "Rudali" (1980) tells of a widow of the untouchable caste left to fend for herself after her husband, children, and grandchildren either die or leave the village. Exploited by landowners and priests, the widow subsists by grinding grain into flour, never sure where her next meal will come from. Her lot improves when she and another widow challenge the mores of traditional village life by living together and starting a business as *rudali*, or professional mourners, sometimes employing the local prostitutes. The story, made into a controversial play in 1992 by Usha Gangali and into a film nominated for the foreign film Oscar in 1994, celebrates the power of women to take

Low Caste Indian Family.   *India's rigid caste system dictates that those born into a lower caste must endure a life of hardship. (© Bettmann / CORBIS)*

charge of their lives and through mutual support to overturn the centuries-old restrictions of caste and gender.

family and community. The resulting tension between individuality and tradition forms a recurrent theme in the novels. In Malgudi, as in the works of Rabindranath Tagore, education and a middle-class way of life bring a degree of Westernization, raising questions about cultural identity and the relationship between the traditional and the modern. Although Narayan is not a political novelist, Malgudi inevitably embodies the key social and political issues of India—its urbanization and its colonial heritage.

[Narayan's stories are] comedies of sadness . . . lighted with the glint of mockery of both self and others.

– WILLIAM R. WALSH, critic, 1971

Even though many of Narayan's characters speak the vernacular languages of India — like the villager Muni in "A Horse and Two Goats" (1970), who speaks Tamil and does not understand English — Narayan himself writes in English. Commenting on this choice, he said, "English has been with us [Indians] for over a century and a half. I am particularly fond of the language. I was never aware that I was using a different, a foreign, language when I wrote in English, because it came very easily." Indeed, the ease and natural rhythms of Narayan's prose demonstrate the author's comfort with English; however, the invasiveness of British colonialism on the subcontinent is perhaps evidenced by that very comfort level.

"A Horse and Two Goats."   Narayan's short stories are often less "modern" than his novels. Tales such as "A Horse and Two Goats" describe traditional village life and retain the character of stories that are told rather than written. The story of Muni the goatherd is a comic folktale about the misunderstandings that arise when a traditional culture meets the modern world. Its humor is similar to that in *The Gods Must Be Crazy,* a film about a Kalahari Bushman's contact with Western culture. Narayan's story does not condescend to the villager or make him out to be a simpleton. Its sympathetic portrayal of Muni and his situation allows the reader to both laugh at his absurd negotiations and celebrate his good fortune.

■ **CONNECTIONS**

Joseph Conrad, *Heart of Darkness,* **p. 35; Chinua Achebe,** *Things Fall Apart,* **p. 1023, and "An Image of Africa," p. 107; Wole Soyinka,** *The Lion and the Jewel,* **p. 1146; Carlos Fuentes,** *The Prisoner of Las Lomas,* **p. 938.** Like Conrad's *Heart of Darkness,* Achebe's *Things Fall Apart,* Soyinka's *The Lion and the Jewel,* and Fuentes's *The Prisoner of Las Lomas,* "A Horse and Two Goats" is a story about cross-cultural misunderstanding. Achebe, in his essay "An Image of Africa," argues that point of view in such stories is a critical factor. What is the point of view in each of the works listed above? Does it reveal the assumptions made on both sides of the misunderstanding addressed by these texts? What are the issues in each?

In the World: **Crossing Cultures, p. 1278.** "A Horse and Two Goats" is an implicit commentary on some of the issues in *In the World:* Crossing Cultures, which includes several Indian writers, among them Narayan, who comment on Indian culture and globalism. How does Narayan's point of view differ from that of many of the Indian writers in that section? How does "A Horse and Two Goats" articulate the point of view that Narayan develops in "My America"?

In the World: **Travel Narratives (Book 4);** *In the World:* **Discovery and Confrontation (Book 3); Jonathan Swift,** *Gulliver's Travels* **(Book 4); William Shakespeare,** *The Tempest* **(Book 3); Montaigne, "Of Cannibals" (Book 3).** "A Horse and Two Goats" might be considered an unusual travel narrative, one told by a nontraveler. Ponder how this shift in perspective makes this story different from usual travel narratives, such as those in *In the World* sections on travel in Books 3 and 4 of this anthology. How might Gulliver's voyage to the land of the Houyhnhnms have been different had it been told from the Houyhnhnms' point of view? How successful is Shakespeare in understanding Caliban? How well does Montaigne understand cannibals?

■ **FURTHER RESEARCH**

Autobiography
Narayan, R. K. *My Days: A Memoir.* 1974.

Criticism
Hariprasanna, A. *The World of Malgudi.* 1994.
Ram, Susan, and N. Ram. *R. K. Narayan: Early Years 1906–1945.* 1996.
Sharan, N. N. *Critical Study of the Novels of R. K. Narayan.* 1993.
Walsh, William. *R. K. Narayan.* 1971.

■ **PRONUNCIATION**
Avvaiyar: uh-VIGH-yar
Bhagwan: BAH-gwahn
dhall: DAHL
dhobi: DOH-bee
dhoti: DOH-tee
lakh: LAHK
Lakshmi: LUK-shmee
Rasipuram Krishnaswami Narayan: ruh-see-POO-rum krish-nuh-SWAH-mee
    nuh-RIGH-yun
swarga: SWAR-guh

> India's most distinguished literary career of recent times.
>
> – SHASHI THAROOR,
> 1994

> Narayan is a master, in control of his subtle effects. He is very funny: His use of irony is superb, and there is much going on in the tiny world he describes.
>
> – HANIF KUREISHI,
> writer, 1990

❦ A Horse and Two Goats

Of the seven hundred thousand villages dotting the map of India, in which the majority of India's five hundred million live, flourish, and die, Kritam was probably the tiniest, indicated on the district survey map by a microscopic dot, the map being meant more for the revenue official out to collect tax than for the guidance of the motorist, who in any case could not hope to reach it since it sprawled far from the highway at the end of a rough track furrowed up by the iron-hooped wheels of bullock carts. But its size did not prevent its giving itself the grandiose name Kritam, which meant in Tamil "coronet" or "crown" on the brow of this subcontinent. The village consisted of less than thirty houses, only one of them built with brick and cement. Painted a brilliant yellow and blue all over with gorgeous carvings of gods and gargoyles on its balustrade, it was known as the Big House. The other houses, distributed in four streets, were generally of bamboo thatch, straw, mud, and other

---

"A Horse and Two Goats." This piece of short fiction serves as the title story for the R. K. Narayan collection that appeared in 1970. Although not set in Malgudi, the city that serves as the setting for nearly all his longer works of fiction, this story develops themes that are central to all Narayan's work. In the confrontation of the Indian villager and the American businessman, Narayan makes comedy of the differences between the culture of traditional rural India and that of the industrialized urban world. Within the comedy, he questions whether there are values inherent in village life, ponders the differences in scale of the traditional agrarian world and the industrialized world, and challenges the notion of what is valued by each culture.

All notes are the editors'.

unspecified material. Muni's was the last house in the fourth street, beyond which stretched the fields. In his prosperous days Muni had owned a flock of forty sheep and goats and sallied forth every morning driving the flock to the highway a couple of miles away. There he would sit on the pedestal of a clay statue of a horse while his cattle grazed around. He carried a crook at the end of a bamboo pole and snapped foliage from the avenue trees to feed his flock; he also gathered faggots and dry sticks, bundled them, and carried them home for fuel at sunset.

His wife lit the domestic fire at dawn, boiled water in a mud pot, threw into it a handful of millet flour, added salt, and gave him his first nourishment for the day. When he started out, she would put in his hand a packed lunch, once again the same millet cooked into a little ball, which he could swallow with a raw onion at midday. She was old, but he was older and needed all the attention she could give him in order to be kept alive.

His fortunes had declined gradually, unnoticed. From a flock of forty which he drove into a pen at night, his stock had now come down to two goats, which were not worth the rent of a half rupee a month the Big House charged for the use of the pen in their back yard. And so the two goats were tethered to the trunk of a drumstick tree which grew in front of his hut and from which occasionally Muni could shake down drumsticks. This morning he got six. He carried them in with a sense of triumph. Although no one could say precisely who owned the tree, it was his because he lived in its shadow.

She said, "If you were content with the drumstick leaves alone, I could boil and salt some for you."

"Oh, I am tired of eating those leaves. I have a craving to chew the drumstick out of sauce, I tell you."

"You have only four teeth in your jaw, but your craving is for big things. All right, get the stuff for the sauce, and I will prepare it for you. After all, next year you may not be alive to ask for anything. But first get me all the stuff, including a measure of rice or millet, and I will satisfy your unholy craving. Our store is empty today. Dhall,[1] chili, curry leaves, mustard, coriander, gingelley[2] oil, and one large potato. Go out and get all this." He repeated the list after her in order not to miss any item and walked off to the shop in third street.

He sat on an upturned packing case below the platform of the shop. The shopman paid no attention to him. Muni kept clearing his throat, coughing, and sneezing until the shopman could not stand it any more and demanded, "What ails you? You will fly off that seat into the gutter if you sneeze so hard, young man." Muni laughed inordinately, in order to please the shopman, at being called "young man." The shopman softened and said, "You have enough of the imp inside to keep a second wife busy, but for the fact the old lady is still alive." Muni laughed appropriately again at this joke. It completely won the shopman over; he liked his sense of humour to be appreciated. Muni engaged his attention in local gossip for a few minutes, which

---

[1] **dhall:** A grain like lentils or split peas.

[2] **gingelley:** An Indian plant whose seeds are pressed into a cooking oil.

always ended with a reference to the postman's wife who had eloped to the city some months before.

The shopman felt most pleased to hear the worst of the postman, who had cheated him. Being an itinerant postman, he returned home to Kritam only once in ten days and every time managed to slip away again without passing the shop in the third street. By thus humouring the shopman, Muni could always ask for one or two items of food, promising repayment later. Some days the shopman was in a good mood and gave in, and sometimes he would lose his temper suddenly and bark at Muni for daring to ask for credit. This was such a day, and Muni could not progress beyond two items listed as essential components. The shopman was also displaying a remarkable memory for old facts and figures and took out an oblong ledger to support his observations. Muni felt impelled to rise and flee. But his self-respect kept him in his seat and made him listen to the worst things about himself. The shopman concluded, "If you could find five rupees and a quarter, you will have paid off an ancient debt and then could apply for admission to swarga.[3] How much have you got now?"

"I will pay you everything on the first of the next month."

"As always, and whom do you expect to rob by then?"

Muni felt caught and mumbled, "My daughter has sent word that she will be sending me money."

"Have you a daughter?" sneered the shopman. "And she is sending you money! For what purpose, may I know?"

"Birthday, fiftieth birthday," said Muni quietly.

"Birthday! How old are you?"

Muni repeated weakly, not being sure of it himself, "Fifty." He always calculated his age from the time of the great famine when he stood as high as the parapet around the village well, but who could calculate such things accurately nowadays with so many famines occurring? The shopman felt encouraged when other customers stood around to watch and comment. Muni thought helplessly, "My poverty is exposed to everybody. But what can I do?"

"More likely you are seventy," said the shopman. "You also forget that you mentioned a birthday five weeks ago when you wanted castor oil for your holy bath."

"Bath! Who can dream of a bath when you have to scratch the tank-bed for a bowl of water? We would all be parched and dead but for the Big House, where they let us take a pot of water from their well." After saying this Muni unobtrusively rose and moved off.

He told his wife, "That scoundrel would not give me anything. So go out and sell the drumsticks for what they are worth."

He flung himself down in a corner to recoup from the fatigue of his visit to the shop. His wife said, "You are getting no sauce today, nor anything else. I can't find anything to give you to eat. Fast till the evening, it'll do you good. Take the goats and be gone now," she cried and added, "Don't come back before the sun is down." He

---

[3] **swarga:** Heaven.

knew that if he obeyed her she would somehow conjure up some food for him in the evening. Only he must be careful not to argue and irritate her. Her temper was undependable in the morning but improved by evening time. She was sure to go out and work—grind corn in the Big House, sweep or scrub somewhere, and earn enough to buy foodstuff and keep a dinner ready for him in the evening.

Unleashing the goats from the drumstick tree, Muni started out, driving them ahead and uttering weird cries from time to time in order to urge them on. He passed through the village with his head bowed in thought. He did not want to look at anyone or be accosted. A couple of cronies lounging in the temple corridor hailed him, but he ignored their call. They had known him in the days of affluence when he lorded over a flock of fleecy sheep, not the miserable gawky goats that he had today. Of course he also used to have a few goats for those who fancied them, but real wealth lay in sheep; they bred fast and people came and bought the fleece in the shearing season; and then that famous butcher from the town came over on the weekly market days bringing him betel leaves, tobacco, and often enough some *bhang*,[4] which they smoked in a hut in the coconut grove, undisturbed by wives and well-wishers. After a smoke one felt light and elated and inclined to forgive everyone including that brother-in-law of his who had once tried to set fire to his home. But all this seemed like the memories of a previous birth. Some pestilence afflicted his cattle (he could of course guess who had laid his animals under a curse), and even the friendly butcher would not touch one at half the price . . . and now here he was left with the two scraggy creatures. He wished someone would rid him of their company too. The shopman had said that he was seventy. At seventy, one only waited to be summoned by God. When he was dead what would his wife do? They had lived in each other's company since they were children. He was told on their day of wedding that he was ten years old and she was eight. During the wedding ceremony they had had to recite their respective ages and names. He had thrashed her only a few times in their career, and later she had the upper hand. Progeny, none. Perhaps a large progeny would have brought him the blessing of the gods. Fertility brought merit. People with fourteen sons were always so prosperous and at peace with the world and themselves. He recollected the thrill he had felt when he mentioned a daughter to that shopman; although it was not believed, what if he did not have a daughter?— his cousin in the next village had many daughters, and any one of them was as good as his; he was fond of them all and would buy them sweets if he could afford it. Still, everyone in the village whispered behind their backs that Muni and his wife were a barren couple. He avoided looking at anyone; they all professed to be so high up, and everyone else in the village had more money than he. "I am the poorest fellow in our caste and no wonder that they spurn me, but I won't look at them either," and so he passed on with his eyes downcast along the edge of the street, and people left him also very much alone, commenting only to the extent, "Ah, there he goes with his two goats; if he slits their throats, he may have more peace of mind." "What has he to worry about anyway? They live on nothing and have none to worry about." Thus

---

[4] *bhang:* A narcotic made from hemp.

people commented when he passed through the village. Only on the outskirts did he lift his head and look up. He urged and bullied the goats until they meandered along to the foot of the horse statue on the edge of the village. He sat on its pedestal for the rest of the day. The advantage of this was that he could watch the highway and see the lorries[5] and buses pass through to the hills, and it gave him a sense of belonging to a larger world. The pedestal of the statue was broad enough for him to move around as the sun travelled up and westward; or he could also crouch under the belly of the horse, for shade.

The horse was nearly life-size, moulded out of clay, baked, burnt, and brightly coloured, and reared its head proudly, prancing its forelegs in the air and flourishing its tail in a loop; beside the horse stood a warrior with scythe-like mustachios, bulging eyes, and aquiline nose. The old image-makers believed in indicating a man of strength by bulging out his eyes and sharpening his moustache tips, and also decorated the man's chest with beads which looked today like blobs of mud through the ravages of sun and wind and rain (when it came), but Muni would insist that he had known the beads to sparkle like the nine gems at one time in his life. The horse itself was said to have been as white as a dhobi-washed[6] sheet, and had had on its back a cover of pure brocade of red and black lace, matching the multicoloured sash around the waist of the warrior. But none in the village remembered the splendour as no one noticed its existence. Even Muni, who spent all his waking hours at its foot, never bothered to look up. It was untouched even by the young vandals of the village who gashed tree trunks with knives and tried to topple off milestones and inscribed lewd designs on all walls. This statue had been closer to the population of the village at one time, when this spot bordered the village; but when the highway was laid through (or perhaps when the tank and wells dried up completely here) the village moved a couple of miles inland.

Muni sat at the foot of the statue, watching his two goats graze in the arid soil among the cactus and lantana bushes. He looked at the sun; it had tilted westward no doubt, but it was not the time yet to go back home; if he went too early his wife would have no food for him. Also he must give her time to cool off her temper and feel sympathetic, and then she would scrounge and manage to get some food. He watched the mountain road for a time signal. When the green bus appeared around the bend he could leave, and his wife would feel pleased that he had let the goats feed long enough.

He noticed now a new sort of vehicle coming down at full speed. It looked like both a motor car and a bus. He used to be intrigued by the novelty of such spectacles, but of late work was going on at the source of the river on the mountain and an assortment of people and traffic went past him, and he took it all casually and described to his wife, later in the day, everything he saw. Today, while he observed the yellow vehicle coming down, he was wondering how to describe it later to his wife when it sputtered and stopped in front of him. A red-faced foreigner, who had been

---

[5] **lorries:** Trucks.

[6] **dhobi-washed:** Clothes washed by the riverside by a native washerwoman.

driving it, got down and went round it, stooping, looking, and poking under the vehicle; then he straightened himself up, looked at the dashboard, stared in Muni's direction, and approached him. "Excuse me, is there a gas station nearby, or do I have to wait until another car comes—" He suddenly looked up at the clay horse and cried, "Marvellous," without completing his sentence. Muni felt he should get up and run away, and cursed his age. He could not readily put his limbs into action; some years ago he could outrun a cheetah, as happened once when he went to the forest to cut fuel and it was then that two of his sheep were mauled—a sign that bad times were coming. Though he tried, he could not easily extricate himself from his seat, and then there was also the problem of the goats. He could not leave them behind.

The red-faced man wore khaki clothes—evidently a policeman or a soldier. Muni said to himself, "He will chase or shoot if I start running. Some dogs chase only those who run—oh, Shiva protect me. I don't know why this man should be after me." Meanwhile the foreigner cried, "Marvellous!" again, nodding his head. He paced around the statue with his eyes fixed on it. Muni sat frozen for a while, and then suddenly fidgeted and tried to edge away. Now the other man suddenly pressed his palms together in a salute, smiled, and said, "Namaste![7] How do you do?"

At which Muni spoke the only English expressions he had learnt, "Yes, no." Having exhausted his English vocabulary, he started in Tamil: "My name is Muni. These two goats are mine, and no one can gainsay it—though our village is full of slanderers these days who will not hesitate to say that what belongs to a man doesn't belong to him." He rolled his eyes and shuddered at the thought of evil-minded men and women peopling his village.

The foreigner faithfully looked in the direction indicated by Muni's fingers, gazed for a while at the two goats and the rocks, and with a puzzled expression took out his silver cigarette case and lit a cigarette. Suddenly remembering the courtesies of the season, he asked, "Do you smoke?" Muni answered, "Yes, no." Whereupon the red-faced man took a cigarette and gave it to Muni, who received it with surprise, having had no offer of a smoke from anyone for years now. Those days when he smoked bhang were gone with his sheep and the large-hearted butcher. Nowadays he was not able to find even matches, let alone bhang. (His wife went across and borrowed a fire at dawn from a neighbour.) He had always wanted to smoke a cigarette; only once did the shopman give him one on credit, and he remembered how good it had tasted. The other flicked the lighter open and offered a light to Muni. Muni felt so confused about how to act that he blew on it and put it out. The other, puzzled but undaunted, flourished his lighter, presented it again, and lit Muni's cigarette. Muni drew a deep puff and started coughing; it was racking, no doubt, but extremely pleasant. When his cough subsided he wiped his eyes and took stock of the situation, understanding that the other man was not an Inquisitor of any kind. Yet, in order to make sure, he remained wary. No need to run away from a man who gave him such a potent smoke. His head was reeling from the effect of one of those

---

[7] **Namaste!:** A word of greeting.

strong American cigarettes made with roasted tobacco. The man said, "I come from New York," took out a wallet from his hip pocket, and presented his card.

Muni shrank away from the card. Perhaps he was trying to present a warrant and arrest him. Beware of khaki, one part of his mind warned. Take all the cigarettes or bhang or whatever is offered, but don't get caught. Beware of khaki. He wished he weren't seventy as the shopman had said. At seventy one didn't run, but surrendered to whatever came. He could only ward off trouble by talk. So he went on, all in the chaste Tamil for which Kritam was famous. (Even the worst detractors could not deny that the famous poetess Avvaiyar was born in this area, although no one could say whether it was in Kritam or Kuppam, the adjoining village.) Out of this heritage the Tamil language gushed through Muni in an unimpeded flow. He said, "Before God, sir, Bhagwan,[8] who sees everything, I tell you, sir, that we know nothing of the case. If the murder was committed, whoever did it will not escape. Bhagwan is all-seeing. Don't ask me about it. I know nothing." A body had been found mutilated and thrown under a tamarind tree at the border between Kritam and Kuppam a few weeks before, giving rise to much gossip and speculation. Muni added an explanation. "Anything is possible there. People over there will stop at nothing." The foreigner nodded his head and listened courteously though he understood nothing.

"I am sure you know when this horse was made," said the red man and smiled ingratiatingly.

Muni reacted to the relaxed atmosphere by smiling himself, and pleaded, "Please go away, sir, I know nothing. I promise we will hold him for you if we see any bad character around, and we will bury him up to his neck in a coconut pit if he tries to escape; but our village has always had a clean record. Must definitely be the other village."

Now the red man implored, "Please, please, I will speak slowly, please try to understand me. Can't you understand even a simple word of English? Everyone in this country seems to know English. I have gotten along with English everywhere in this country, but you don't speak it. Have you any religious or spiritual scruples against English speech?"

Muni made some indistinct sounds in his throat and shook his head. Encouraged, the other went on to explain at length, uttering each syllable with care and deliberation. Presently he sidled over and took a seat beside the old man, explaining, "You see, last August, we probably had the hottest summer in history, and I was working in shirt-sleeves in my office on the fortieth floor of the Empire State Building. We had a power failure one day, you know, and there I was stuck for four hours, no elevator, no air conditioning. All the way in the train I kept thinking, and the minute I reached home in Connecticut, I told my wife Ruth, 'We will visit India this winter, it's time to look at other civilizations.' Next day she called the travel agent first thing and told him to fix it, and so here I am. Ruth came with me but is staying back at Srinagar,[9] and I am the one doing the rounds and joining her later."

---

[8] **Bhagwan:** Master.

[9] **Srinagar:** Capital of Kashmir; a popular vacation spot.

Muni looked reflective at the end of this long oration and said, rather feebly, "Yes, no," as a concession to the other's language, and went on in Tamil, "When I was this high" — he indicated a foot high — "I had heard my uncle say . . ."

No one can tell what he was planning to say, as the other interrupted him at this stage to ask, "Boy, what is the secret of your teeth? How old are you?"

The old man forgot what he had started to say and remarked, "Sometimes we too lose our cattle. Jackals or cheetahs may sometimes carry them off, but sometimes it is just theft from over in the next village, and then we will know who has done it. Our priest at the temple can see in the camphor flame the face of the thief, and when he is caught . . ." He gestured with his hands a perfect mincing of meat.

The American watched his hands intently and said, "I know what you mean. Chop something? Maybe I am holding you up and you want to chop wood? Where is your axe? Hand it to me and show me what to chop. I do enjoy it, you know, just a hobby. We get a lot of driftwood along the backwater near my house, and on Sundays I do nothing but chop wood for the fireplace. I really feel different when I watch the fire in the fireplace, although it may take all the sections of the Sunday *New York Times* to get a fire started." And he smiled at this reference.

Muni felt totally confused but decided the best thing would be to make an attempt to get away from this place. He tried to edge out, saying, "Must go home," and turned to go. The other seized his shoulder and said desperately, "Is there no one, absolutely no one here, to translate for me?" He looked up and down the road, which was deserted in this hot afternoon; a sudden gust of wind churned up the dust and dead leaves on the roadside into a ghostly column and propelled it towards the mountain road. The stranger almost pinioned Muni's back to the statue and asked, "Isn't this statue yours? Why don't you sell it to me?"

The old man now understood the reference to the horse, thought for a second, and said in his own language, "I was an urchin this high when I heard my grandfather explain this horse and warrior, and my grandfather himself was this high when he heard his grandfather, whose grandfather . . ."

The other man interrupted him. "I don't want to seem to have stopped here for nothing. I will offer you a good price for this," he said, indicating the horse. He had concluded without the least doubt that Muni owned this mud horse. Perhaps he guessed by the way he sat on its pedestal, like other souvenir sellers in this country presiding over their wares.

Muni followed the man's eyes and pointing fingers and dimly understood the subject matter and, feeling relieved that the theme of the mutilated body had been abandoned at least for the time being, said again, enthusiastically, "I was this high when my grandfather told me about this horse and the warrior, and my grandfather was this high when he himself . . ." and he was getting into a deeper bog of reminiscence each time he tried to indicate the antiquity of the statue.

The Tamil that Muni spoke was stimulating even as pure sound, and the foreigner listened with fascination. "I wish I had my tape-recorder here," he said, assuming the pleasantest expression. "Your language sounds wonderful. I get a kick out of every word you utter, here" — he indicated his ears — "but you don't have to waste your breath in sales talk. I appreciate the article. You don't have to explain its points."

"I never went to a school, in those days only Brahmin[10] went to schools, but we had to go out and work in the fields morning till night, from sowing to harvest time . . . and when Pongal[11] came and we had cut the harvest, my father allowed me to go out and play with others at the tank, and so I don't know the Parangi language you speak, even little fellows in your country probably speak the Parangi language, but here only learned men and officers know it. We had a postman in our village who could speak to you boldly in your language, but his wife ran away with someone and he does not speak to anyone at all nowadays. Who would if a wife did what she did? Women must be watched; otherwise they will sell themselves and the home." And he laughed at his own quip.

The foreigner laughed heartily, took out another cigarette, and offered it to Muni, who now smoked with ease, deciding to stay on if the fellow was going to be so good as to keep up his cigarette supply. The American now stood up on the pedestal in the attitude of a demonstrative lecturer and said, running his finger along some of the carved decorations around the horse's neck, speaking slowly and uttering his words syllable by syllable, "I could give a sales talk for this better than anyone else. . . . This is a marvellous combination of yellow and indigo, though faded now. . . . How do you people of this country achieve these flaming colours?"

Muni, now assured that the subject was still the horse and not the dead body, said, "This is our guardian, it means death to our adversaries. At the end of Kali Yuga,[12] this world and all other worlds will be destroyed, and the Redeemer will come in the shape of a horse called 'Kalki'; this horse will come to life and gallop and trample down all bad men." As he spoke of bad men the figures of his shopman and his brother-in-law assumed concrete forms in his mind, and he revelled for a moment in the predicament of the fellow under the horse's hoof: served him right for trying to set fire to his home. . . .

While he was brooding on this pleasant vision, the foreigner utilized the pause to say, "I assure you that this will have the best home in the U.S.A. I'll push away the bookcase, you know I love books and am a member of five book clubs, and the choice and bonus volumes mount up to a pile really in our living room, as high as this horse itself. But they'll have to go. Ruth may disapprove, but I will convince her. The T.V. may have to be shifted too. We can't have everything in the living room. Ruth will probably say what about when we have a party? I'm going to keep him right in the middle of the room. I don't see how that can interfere with the party—we'll stand around him and have our drinks."

Muni continued his description of the end of the world. "Our pundit[13] discoursed at the temple once how the oceans are going to close over the earth in a huge wave and swallow us—this horse will grow bigger than the biggest wave and carry on its back only the good people and kick into the floods the evil ones—plenty of

---

[10] **Brahmin:** Members of the highest or priestly Hindu caste.

[11] **Pongal:** A festival that is observed in early January.

[12] **Kali Yuga:** One of the cycles of time in Hindu mythology; a destructive period.

[13] **pundit:** A Brahmin scholar.

them about—" he said reflectively. "Do you know when it is going to happen?" he asked.

The foreigner now understood by the tone of the other that a question was being asked and said, "How am I transporting it? I can push the seat back and make room in the rear. That van can take in an elephant"—waving precisely at the back of the seat.

Muni was still hovering on visions of avatars and said again, "I never missed our pundit's discourses at the temple in those days during every bright half of the month, although he'd go on all night, and he told us that Vishnu[14] is the highest god. Whenever evil men trouble us, he comes down to save us. He has come many times. The first time he incarnated as a great fish, and lifted the scriptures on his back when the floods and sea waves . . ."

"I am not a millionaire, but a modest businessman. My trade is coffee."

Amidst all this wilderness of obscure sound Muni caught the word "coffee" and said, "If you want to drink 'kapi,' drive further up, in the next town, they have Friday market, and there they open 'kapi-otels'—so I learn from passers-by. Don't think I wander about. I go nowhere and look for nothing." His thoughts went back to the avatars. "The first avatar was in the shape of a little fish in a bowl of water, but every hour it grew bigger and bigger and became in the end a huge whale which the seas could not contain, and on the back of the whale the holy books were supported, saved and carried." Once he had launched on the first avatar, it was inevitable that he should go on to the next, a wild boar on whose tusk the earth was lifted when a vicious conqueror of the earth carried it off and hid it at the bottom of the sea. After describing this avatar Muni concluded, "God will always save us whenever we are troubled by evil beings. When we were young we staged at full moon the story of the avatars. That's how I know the stories; we played them all night until the sun rose, and sometimes the European collector would come to watch, bringing his own chair. I had a good voice and so they always taught me songs and gave me the women's roles. I was always Goddess Lakshmi,[15] and they dressed me in a brocade sari, loaned from the Big House . . ."

The foreigner said, "I repeat I am not a millionaire. Ours is a modest business; after all, we can't afford to buy more than sixty minutes of T.V. time in a month, which works out to two minutes a day, that's all, although in the course of time we'll maybe sponsor a one-hour show regularly if our sales graph continues to go up . . ."

Muni was intoxicated by the memory of his theatrical days and was about to explain how he had painted his face and worn a wig and diamond earrings when the visitor, feeling that he had spent too much time already, said, "Tell me, will you accept a hundred rupees or not for the horse? I'd love to take the whiskered soldier also but no space for him this year. I'll have to cancel my air ticket and take a boat home, I suppose. Ruth can go by air if she likes, but I will go with the horse and keep him in my cabin all the way if necessary." And he smiled at the picture of himself

---

[14] **Vishnu:** One of the chief Hindu gods.

[15] **Lakshmi:** Goddess of wealth and good fortune; symbol of all domestic virtues.

voyaging across the seas hugging this horse. He added, "I will have to pad it with straw so that it doesn't break . . ."

"When we played *Ramayana,* they dressed me as Sita,"[16] added Muni. "A teacher came and taught us the songs for the drama and we gave him fifty rupees. He incarnated himself as Rama, and He alone could destroy Ravana, the demon with ten heads who shook all the worlds; do you know the story of *Ramayana?*"

"I have my station wagon as you see. I can push the seat back and take the horse in if you will just lend me a hand with it."

"Do you know *Mahabharata?*[17] Krishna was the eighth avatar of Vishnu, incarnated to help the Five Brothers regain their kingdom. When Krishna was a baby he danced on the thousand-hooded giant serpent and trampled it to death; and then he suckled the breasts of the demoness and left them flat as a disc though when she came to him her bosoms were large, like mounds of earth on the banks of a dug up canal." He indicated two mounds with his hands. The stranger was completely mystified by the gesture. For the first time he said, "I really wonder what you are saying because your answer is crucial. We have come to the point when we should be ready to talk business."

"When the tenth avatar comes, do you know where you and I will be?" asked the old man.

"Lend me a hand and I can lift off the horse from its pedestal after picking out the cement at the joints. We can do anything if we have a basis of understanding."

At this stage the mutual mystification was complete, and there was no need even to carry on a guessing game at the meaning of words. The old man chattered away in a spirit of balancing off the credits and debits of conversational exchange, and said in order to be on the credit side, "Oh, honourable one, I hope God has blessed you with numerous progeny. I say this because you seem to be a good man, willing to stay beside an old man and talk to him, while all day I have none to talk to except when somebody stops by to ask for a piece of tobacco. But I seldom have it, tobacco is not what it used to be at one time, and I have given up chewing. I cannot afford it nowadays." Noting the other's interest in his speech, Muni felt encouraged to ask, "How many children have you?" with appropriate gestures with his hands. Realizing that a question was being asked, the red man replied, "I said a hundred," which encouraged Muni to go into details. "How many of your children are boys and how many girls? Where are they? Is your daughter married? Is it difficult to find a son-in-law in your country also?"

In answer to these questions the red man dashed his hand into his pocket and brought forth his wallet in order to take immediate advantage of the bearish trend in the market. He flourished a hundred-rupee currency note and said, "Well, this is what I meant."

---

[16] **Sita:** The wife of Rama, hero of the *Ramayana,* an Indian epic. At one point in the story Sita is abducted by Ravana, a demon king.

[17] *Mahabharata:* An Indian epic. In the most famous section of the poem, reprinted separately as the Bhagavad Gita, Krishna gives spiritual counsel to the hero of the epic, Arjuna.

The old man now realized that some financial element was entering their talk. He peered closely at the currency note, the like of which he had never seen in his life; he knew the five and ten by their colours although always in other people's hands, while his own earning at any time was in coppers and nickels. What was this man flourishing the note for? Perhaps asking for change. He laughed to himself at the notion of anyone coming to him for changing a thousand- or ten-thousand-rupee note. He said with a grin, "Ask our village headman, who is also a moneylender; he can change even a lakh[18] of rupees in gold sovereigns if you prefer it that way; he thinks nobody knows, but dig the floor of his puja[19] room and your head will reel at the sight of the hoard. The man disguises himself in rags just to mislead the public. Talk to the headman yourself because he goes mad at the sight of me. Someone took away his pumpkins with the creeper and he, for some reason, thinks it was me and my goats . . . that's why I never let my goats be seen anywhere near the farms." His eyes travelled to his goats nosing about, attempting to wrest nutrition from minute greenery peeping out of rock and dry earth.

The foreigner followed his look and decided that it would be a sound policy to show an interest in the old man's pets. He went up casually to them and stroked their backs with every show of courteous attention. Now the truth dawned on the old man. His dream of a lifetime was about to be realized. He understood that the red man was actually making an offer for the goats. He had reared them up in the hope of selling them some day and, with the capital, opening a small shop on this very spot. Sitting here, watching towards the hills, he had often dreamt how he would put up a thatched roof here, spread a gunny sack out on the ground, and display on it fried nuts, coloured sweets, and green coconut for the thirsty and famished wayfarers on the highway, which was sometimes very busy. The animals were not prize ones for a cattle show, but he had spent his occasional savings to provide them some fancy diet now and then, and they did not look too bad. While he was reflecting thus, the red man shook his hand and left on his palm one hundred rupees in tens now, suddenly realizing that this was what the old man was asking. "It is all for you or you may share it if you have a partner."

The old man pointed at the station wagon and asked, "Are you carrying them off in that?"

"Yes, of course," said the other, understanding the transportation part of it.

The old man said, "This will be their first ride in a motor car. Carry them off after I get out of sight, otherwise they will never follow you, but only me even if I am travelling on the path to Yama Loka."[20] He laughed at his own joke, brought his palms together in a salute, turned round and went off, and was soon out of sight beyond a clump of thicket.

The red man looked at the goats grazing peacefully. Perched on the pedestal of the horse, as the westerly sun touched off the ancient faded colours of the statue with a fresh splendour, he ruminated, "He must be gone to fetch some help, I suppose!" and settled down to wait. When a truck came downhill, he stopped it and got the

---

[18] **lakh:** One hundred thousand; a large number.   [19] **puja:** A rite or ceremony.   [20] **Yama Loka:** The underworld.

help of a couple of men to detach the horse from its pedestal and place it in his station wagon. He gave them five rupees each, and for a further payment they siphoned off gas from the truck, and helped him to start his engine.

Muni hurried homeward with the cash securely tucked away at his waist in his dhoti.[21] He shut the street door and stole up softly to his wife as she squatted before the lit oven wondering if by a miracle food would drop from the sky. Muni displayed his fortune for the day. She snatched the notes from him, counted them by the glow of the fire, and cried, "One hundred rupees! How did you come by it? Have you been stealing?"

"I have sold our goats to a red-faced man. He was absolutely crazy to have them, gave me all this money and carried them off in his motor car!"

Hardly had these words left his lips when they heard bleating outside. She opened the door and saw the two goats at her door. "Here they are!" she said. "What's the meaning of all this?"

He muttered a great curse and seized one of the goats by its ears and shouted, "Where is that man? Don't you know you are his? Why did you come back?" The goat only wriggled in his grip. He asked the same question of the other too. The goat shook itself off. His wife glared at him and declared, "If you have thieved, the police will come tonight and break your bones. Don't involve me. I will go away to my parents. . . ."

---

[21]**dhoti:** Loincloth.

❧ NAGUIB MAHFOUZ
B. EGYPT, 1911

When Naguib Mahfouz received the Nobel Prize in 1988, he was the first Arabic writer to be so recognized. Although he was Egypt's premier novelist and deserving of such a distinction for his work, the prize was widely regarded in the Arab world as recognition for Arabic literature generally. Mahfouz and fellow Egyptian writer Tawfiq al-Hakim had been pioneers in creating modern Arabic literature, al-Hakim largely in drama, Mahfouz in fiction. Both writers had managed to create, indeed invent, a new Arabic literary idiom, one that was free of the formality and remoteness of classical literary Arabic but that also had a refinement and a versatility that contemporary colloquial Arabic lacked. The prize was seen as an acknowledgment of both men's achievement in remaking the language and establishing a literature comparable to those of Europe, America, and Asia.

Naguib Mahfouz
Mahfouz was the first Egyptian to win the Nobel Prize in literature.
(© Topham / The Image Works)

Creating a Modern Arabic Literature.   After its golden age in the ninth, tenth, and eleventh centuries, Arabic literature went into decline. When

www For links to more information about Mahfouz and a quiz on "Zaabalawi," and for information about the culture and context of the Middle East in the twentieth century, see *World Literature Online* at bedfordstmartins .com/worldlit.

nuh-GEEB mah-FOOZ

the Ottoman empire established Turkish as the language of commerce and government in the early modern period, Arabic literature virtually disappeared. As the Ottomans lost power in the nineteenth and early twentieth centuries, however, Arabic was revived, but the hiatus in its use as a literary language meant that there were no models for such modern literary forms as the novel. Traditional Arabic literature was almost exclusively poetry. Those who hoped to revive Arabic literature and make it modern had to discover or create a literary and accessible language and adapt modern literary forms to the Islamic culture.

A Career in Government Service. Born in 1911 in the Gamaliya district of Cairo, the seventh child in a middle-class family of modest means, **Naguib Mahfouz** spent his earliest years in the crowded districts of the old city. He attended government schools and graduated with a degree in philosophy from the University of Cairo in 1934. After graduation he decided to become a professional writer and worked for a few years as a journalist before entering the Egyptian civil service in 1939, where he worked for the next thirty-two years. There he adapted novels for the movies and television before going on to become the director of the national Cinema Organization, the governmental agency that manages the film industry in Egypt. He retired from the civil service in 1971.

A Literary Career. Mahfouz's first book, *The Whisper of Madness,* a collection of short stories, appeared in 1938. He continued to write during his years with the civil service and in his retirement, producing more than forty novels and fourteen volumes of short stories. His writing career can be divided into four periods. From 1939 to 1944, Mahfouz set out to write a series of historical novels modeled after the novels of Sir Walter Scott,[1] tracing the history of Egypt from ancient times to Mahfouz's day. He completed only three of the thirty books he planned to write, all on ancient Egypt, and in them indirectly critiqued contemporary Egypt. *The Struggle for Thebes* (1944), for example, was interpreted as an allegory, or a symbolic representation, of the British occupation and the presence in Egypt of a ruling aristocracy of foreigners. Many of Mahfouz's novels are a fictional representation of the history and contemporary situation of Egypt, articulating the author's view that the novelist serves as an "informer that engages in re-creating a collective memory and thus produces and offers knowledge of a given society and an alternative articulation of that society's history."

The novelist serves as an "informer that engages in re-creating a collective memory and thus produces and offers knowledge of a given society and an alternative articulation of that society's history.

– NAGUIB MAHFOUZ

Social Realism. With *A New Cairo* (1945), Mahfouz entered a second stage of his writing career, during which he produced the SOCIAL-REALIST novels about contemporary Egypt for which he is widely known. *The*

---

[1] **novels . . . Scott:** The Waverley novels of Sir Walter Scott (1771–1832), which dealt with Scottish history in the seventeenth and eighteenth centuries, were written as an allegory of Scotland's emergence into nationhood and national identity. The novels were an important literary statement for many nineteenth- and twentieth-century authors, especially in nations that were just developing their own identities.

Cairo, c. 1912
This street scene shows the great Mohammed-el-Worde mosque in the background.
(Library of Congress, LC USZ62 099022)

Cairo Trilogy, made up of *Palace Walk, Palace of Desire,* and *Sugar Street,* written in the early fifties but not published until 1956 and 1957, trace three generations of a Cairo family from 1918 to 1944. In the tumultuous period between the two world wars, Egypt went through continuous political and social upheaval, much of it involving the place of Britain in Egyptian affairs and the growing movement for Egyptian independence. The repeated attempts to get rid of the British army, to expel foreigners who controlled the Egyptian government and economy, and to replace a corrupt monarchy with a constitutional government boiled over into revolution in 1919 and again in the 1950s. Meanwhile a rapidly growing population exacerbated the social inequities and poverty that plagued the nation. Mahfouz's realistic novels about the suffering and struggles of the middle and lower classes chronicle the human consequences of the

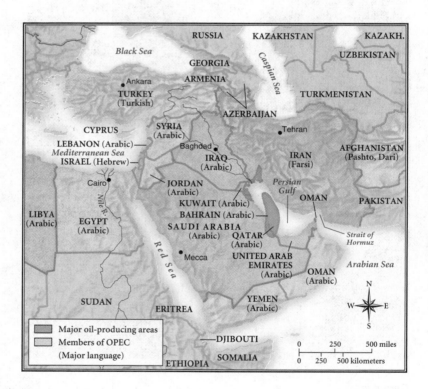

The Middle East, 2000

The twentieth century saw the end of colonial interests in the Middle East, but as in Africa, the postcolonial states were the product not of historical national identities but of borders drawn up by the colonial powers. Inevitably, problems arose. The discovery of oil, however, brought unprecedented wealth to the region and endowed it with a strategic importance for the United States and the Soviet Union, who struggled during the cold war to maintain influence with oil-rich states such as Saudi Arabia and Iraq.

government's and the foreign powers' neglect of the people of Egypt. Edward Fox describes politics in Mahfouz's books as "simply another of the evils that afflict humankind, a force whose harm one may be lucky enough to avoid." Mahfouz may have temporarily suspended this persistent cynicism in the early fifties, in hopes that Gamal Abdel Nasser[2] would bring positive political change. He had completed the *Cairo* trilogy before Nasser came to power in 1952 but delayed its publication until 1956, when he lost hope that Nasser would make a difference in the lives of the people. Mahfouz's novels of the sixties openly criticize the Nasser regime.

Existential Modernism and Arabic Traditions.   After the publication of the trilogy, Mahfouz's work changed again. The transitional novel, published in 1959 and translated as *Children of Gebelawi* and *Children of the Alley,* is a history of mankind in which God, Adam, Moses, Jesus, and Muhammad appear as figures in a modern family saga that is also an allegory of mankind's religious history. Unable to secure a publisher in Egypt, Mahfouz published the book in Lebanon. It was subsequently attacked for taking license with sacred history and was banned in nearly every Islamic country, even though its theme could be said to be how greed for material things takes humanity away from God. Mahfouz further developed this theme in his EXISTENTIALIST and MODERNIST novels of the 1960s, works such as *The Thief and the Dogs* (1961) that probe the inner workings of an individual's mind, making use of STREAM-OF-CONSCIOUSNESS and SURREALIST techniques. In the fourth stage of his career, beginning in about the mid seventies, Mahfouz turned from European modernism to the traditions of Arabic literature, drawing on *Arabian Nights* and other Arabic classics and folklore for novels like *Arabian Nights and Days* (1982) and *The Journey of Ibn Fattouma* (1983).

"Zaabalawi."   Written in the early 1960s, Mahfouz's story "Zaabalawi" raises many of the same concerns as the controversial *Children of the Alley.* Like that novel, the story is concerned with the secularization of Egyptian life and the loss of religious traditions. The narrator's search for **Zaabalawi** is a quest for his own spiritual roots, for the truths hidden in the memories of old men living in the older parts of Cairo and for an understanding that transcends the rational and scientific explanations of things.

■ CONNECTIONS

Joseph Conrad, *Heart of Darkness*, p. 35. Like Conrad's *Heart of Darkness,* "Zaabalawi" is a quest story. In both works, the narrators are looking for something

> Through works rich in nuance — now clear-sightedly realistic, now evocatively ambiguous — [Mahfouz] has formed an Arabic narrative art that applies to all mankind.
>
> – SWEDISH ACADEMY
>   FOR THE NOBEL
>   AWARDS, 1988

zah-bah-LAH-wee

---

[2] **Gamal Abdel Nasser** (1918–1970): Egyptian military officer who led the army coup that deposed the corrupt king Farouk in 1952. Nasser was named the first president of the republic of Egypt in 1956. Although he sought to modernize Egypt and improve the lives of the poor through measures such as land reform, his changes, in Mahfouz's view, simply brought more suffering.

missing in their lives, something that has personal as well as larger social and cultural significance. What are these characters searching for? How clearly does each know what he seeks, and what does each find by the end of his quest?

Søren Kierkegaard, "The Sickness unto Death" (Book 5), Franz Kafka, *The Metamorphosis*, p. 428. Kierkegaard characterizes modern life as diseased and modern man's mission as seeking a cure. In a similar vein Kafka dramatizes modern man's condition or "illness" through the transformation of Gregor Samsa into an insect in *The Metamorphosis*. Is the disease "for which no one possesses a remedy" in Mahfouz's story similar to that defined by Kierkegaard and made into a parable by Kafka? What are its symptoms? Do you think it can be cured? Would you describe "Zaabalawi" as an "existential" story?

Wu Ch'eng-en, *Monkey* (Book 3). Like Tripitaka, the monk who brings the Buddhist scriptures back to China from India, the narrator of "Zaabalawi" sets out to recover or discover spiritual knowledge. Both characters must pass a series of tests before they can succeed. Think about the tests that each undergoes. Do they have symbolic import? Are the two pilgrims similar in character? Is each ultimately successful in achieving the goal of his mission?

■ FURTHER RESEARCH

Background
Allen, Roger M. A. *The Arabic Novel: An Historical and Critical Introduction.* 1982.

Criticism
El-Enany, Rasheed, ed. *Naguib Mahfouz: The Pursuit of Meaning.* 1993.
Gordon, Hayim. *Naguib Mahfouz's Egypt.* 1990.
Le Gassick, Trevor, ed. *Perspectives on Naguib Mahfouz.* 1991.
Mikhail, Mona. *Studies in the Short Fiction of Mahfouz and Idris.* 1992.
Somekh, Sasson. "'Zaabalawi'—Author, Theme, and Technique," *Journal of Arabic Literature,* I (1970), 24–35.

■ PRONUNCIATION

Hassanein: hah-sah-NANE
Naguib Mahfouz: nuh-GEEB mah-FOOZ
Qamar: kah-MAR
Tabakshiyya: tah-bahk-SHEE-yah
Umm al-Ghulam: OOM ahl-goo-LAHM
Wanas al-Damanhouri: wah-NAHS ahl-dah-mahn-HOO-ree
Zaabalawi: zah-bah-LAH-wee

∾　Zaabalawi

Translated by Denys Johnson-Davies

Finally I became convinced that I had to find Sheikh[1] Zaabalawi.
The first time I had heard of his name had been in a song:

Oh what's become of the world, Zaabalawi?
They've turned it upside down and taken away its taste.

It had been a popular song in my childhood, and one day it had occurred to me
to demand of my father, in the way children have of asking endless questions:
"Who is Zaabalawi?"
He had looked at me hesitantly as though doubting my ability to understand the
answer. However, he had replied, "May his blessing descend upon you, he's a true

---

"Zaabalawi." Included in a collection of short stories first published in 1963, this work comes
from the same period in Mahfouz's career as the controversial novel *Children of the Alley*. The story
takes place in the old neighborhoods of Cairo where Mahfouz grew up and that provide the settings for many of his novels. The narrator remembers hearing in his childhood of Zaabalawi, an
elusive figure who could work miracles of healing. His search for Zaabalawi takes him from the
modern offices of a lawyer to the old city and to figures from the past. In meetings with a calligrapher, a composer, and, finally, an old drunkard, the narrator gradually surrenders more and more
control of his quest until he succumbs to a drunken sleep. While he is sleeping, Zaabalawi
appears—only to disappear again before the narrator awakens. At the end of the story the narrator still seeks to meet Zaabalawi.

The simple folktale structure of "Zaabalawi" is made complex by several crucial ambiguities.
The nature of the narrator's illness is unclear, for it is described simply as an illness "for which no
one possesses a remedy." Exactly who Zaabalawi is or was is also left vague. Most of those who have
known him knew him only in the past, while others only know of him or of others who know him.
Even after he appears at the end of the story, questions remain about his reality and his whereabouts. Indeed, the final ambiguity in the story is whether Zaabalawi appeared at all, for the narrator has only Wanas's report, a dream of paradise, and some drops of water on his forehead as signs
of Zaabalawi's visit, and even after his evening at the Negma Bar he still seeks to know that Zaabalawi is not "a mere myth."

The narrator's quest can be read as a spiritual one, a search for certainty and assurance in the
face of despair. It can also be viewed as a search for something from the past that has been lost,
something from the narrator's childhood or from his father's generation. The allegory also suggests that the story is about the creative process, the discoveries an artist, composer, or writer
makes when he or she relaxes and gives up the search only to have the thing sought after appear of
its own accord.

A note on the translation: This translation from the Arabic captures the folktale qualities of
Mahfouz's story; translator Denys Johnson-Davies was challenged by the process of translating
into English a grammatically and structurally very different language. All notes are the editors'.

---

[1] **Sheikh:** Title of respect, especially for older, important men.

saint of God, a remover of worries and troubles. Were it not for him I would have died miserably—"

In the years that followed, I heard my father many a time sing the praises of this good saint and speak of the miracles he performed. The days passed and brought with them many illnesses, for each one of which I was able, without too much trouble and at a cost I could afford, to find a cure, until I became afflicted with that illness for which no one possesses a remedy. When I had tried everything in vain and was overcome by despair, I remembered by chance what I had heard in my childhood: Why, I asked myself, should I not seek out Sheikh Zaabalawi? I recollected my father saying that he had made his acquaintance in Khan Gaafar[2] at the house of Sheikh Qamar, one of those sheikhs who practiced law in the religious courts, and so I took myself off to his house. Wishing to make sure that he was still living there, I made inquiries of a vendor of beans whom I found in the lower part of the house.

"Sheikh Qamar!" he said, looking at me in amazement. "He left the quarter ages ago. They say he's now living in Garden City and has his office in al-Azhar Square."[3]

I looked up the office address in the telephone book and immediately set off to the Chamber of Commerce Building, where it was located. On asking to see Sheikh Qamar, I was ushered into a room just as a beautiful woman with a most intoxicating perfume was leaving it. The man received me with a smile and motioned me toward a fine leather-upholstered chair. Despite the thick soles of my shoes, my feet were conscious of the lushness of the costly carpet. The man wore a lounge suit and was smoking a cigar; his manner of sitting was that of someone well satisfied both with himself and with his worldly possessions. The look of warm welcome he gave me left no doubt in my mind that he thought me a prospective client, and I felt acutely embarrassed at encroaching upon his valuable time.

"Welcome!" he said, prompting me to speak.

"I am the son of your old friend Sheikh Ali al-Tatawi," I answered so as to put an end to my equivocal position.

A certain languor was apparent in the glance he cast at me; the languor was not total in that he had not as yet lost all hope in me.

"God rest his soul," he said. "He was a fine man."

The very pain that had driven me to go there now prevailed upon me to stay.

"He told me," I continued, "of a devout saint named Zaabalawi whom he met at Your Honor's. I am in need of him, sir, if he be still in the land of the living."

The languor became firmly entrenched in his eyes, and it would have come as no surprise if he had shown the door to both me and my father's memory.

"That," he said in the tone of one who has made up his mind to terminate the conversation, "was a very long time ago and I scarcely recall him now."

Rising to my feet so as to put his mind at rest regarding my intention of going, I asked, "Was he really a saint?"

"We used to regard him as a man of miracles."

---

[2] **Khan Gaafar:** A shopping district in Cairo.

[3] **al-Azhar Square:** A section of Cairo near a famous mosque and the university.

"And where could I find him today?" I asked, making another move toward the door.

"To the best of my knowledge he was living in the Birgawi Residence in al-Azhar," and he applied himself to some papers on his desk with a resolute movement that indicated he would not open his mouth again. I bowed my head in thanks, apologized several times for disturbing him, and left the office, my head so buzzing with embarrassment that I was oblivious to all sounds around me.

I went to the Birgawi Residence, which was situated in a thickly populated quarter. I found that time had so eaten at the building that nothing was left of it save an antiquated façade and a courtyard that, despite being supposedly in the charge of a caretaker, was being used as a rubbish dump. A small, insignificant fellow, a mere prologue to a man, was using the covered entrance as a place for the sale of old books on theology and mysticism.

When I asked him about Zaabalawi, he peered at me through narrow, inflamed eyes and said in amazement, "Zaabalawi! Good heavens, what a time ago that was! Certainly he used to live in this house when it was habitable. Many were the times he would sit with me talking of bygone days, and I would be blessed by his holy presence. Where, though, is Zaabalawi today?"

He shrugged his shoulders sorrowfully and soon left me, to attend to an approaching customer. I proceeded to make inquiries of many shopkeepers in the district. While I found that a large number of them had never even heard of Zaabalawi, some, though recalling nostalgically the pleasant times they had spent with him, were ignorant of his present whereabouts, while others openly made fun of him, labeled him a charlatan, and advised me to put myself in the hands of a doctor—as though I had not already done so. I therefore had no alternative but to return disconsolately home.

With the passing of days like motes in the air, my pains grew so severe that I was sure I would not be able to hold out much longer. Once again I fell to wondering about Zaabalawi and clutching at the hope his venerable name stirred within me. Then it occurred to me to seek the help of the local sheikh of the district; in fact, I was surprised I had not thought of this to begin with. His office was in the nature of a small shop, except that it contained a desk and a telephone, and I found him sitting at his desk, wearing a jacket over his striped galabeya.[4] As he did not interrupt his conversation with a man sitting beside him, I stood waiting till the man had gone. The sheikh then looked up at me coldly. I told myself that I should win him over by the usual methods, and it was not long before I had him cheerfully inviting me to sit down.

"I'm in need of Sheikh Zaabalawi," I answered his inquiry as to the purpose of my visit.

He gazed at me with the same astonishment as that shown by those I had previously encountered.

"At least," he said, giving me a smile that revealed his gold teeth, "he is still alive.

---

[4] **galabeya:** Traditional Arab robe.

The devil of it is, though, he has no fixed abode. You might well bump into him as you go out of here, on the other hand you might spend days and months in fruitless searching."

"Even you can't find him!"

"Even I! He's a baffling man, but I thank the Lord that he's still alive!"

He gazed at me intently, and murmured, "It seems your condition is serious."

"Very."

"May God come to your aid! But why don't you go about it systematically?" He spread out a sheet of paper on the desk and drew on it with unexpected speed and skill until he had made a full plan of the district, showing all the various quarters, lanes, alleyways, and squares. He looked at it admiringly and said, "These are dwelling-houses, here is the Quarter of the Perfumers, here the Quarter of the Coppersmiths, the Mouski,[5] the police and fire stations. The drawing is your best guide. Look carefully in the cafés, the places where the dervishes perform their rites, the mosques and prayer-rooms, and the Green Gate,[6] for he may well be concealed among the beggars and be indistinguishable from them. Actually, I myself haven't seen him for years, having been somewhat preoccupied with the cares of the world, and was only brought back by your inquiry to those most exquisite times of my youth."

I gazed at the map in bewilderment. The telephone rang, and he took up the receiver.

"Take it," he told me, generously. "We're at your service."

Folding up the map, I left and wandered off through the quarter, from square to street to alleyway, making inquiries of everyone I felt was familiar with the place. At last the owner of a small establishment for ironing clothes told me, "Go to the calligrapher Hassanein in Umm al-Ghulam — they were friends."

I went to Umm al-Ghulam,[7] where I found old Hassanein working in a deep, narrow shop full of signboards and jars of color. A strange smell, a mixture of glue and perfume, permeated its every corner. Old Hassanein was squatting on a sheepskin rug in front of a board propped against the wall; in the middle of it he had inscribed the word "Allah"[8] in silver lettering. He was engrossed in embellishing the letters with prodigious care. I stood behind him, fearful of disturbing him or breaking the inspiration that flowed to his masterly hand. When my concern at not interrupting him had lasted some time, he suddenly inquired with unaffected gentleness, "Yes?"

Realizing that he was aware of my presence, I introduced myself. "I've been told that Sheikh Zaabalawi is your friend; I'm looking for him," I said.

His hand came to a stop. He scrutinized me in astonishment. "Zaabalawi! God be praised!" he said with a sigh.

"He *is* a friend of yours, isn't he?" I asked eagerly.

---

[5] the Mouski: A central market bazaar.   [6] the Green Gate: Medieval gate in Cairo.   [7] Umm al-Ghulam: Street in Cairo.   [8] "Allah": "God" in Arabic.

"He was, once upon a time. A real man of mystery: He'd visit you so often that people would imagine he was your nearest and dearest, then would disappear as though he'd never existed. Yet saints are not to be blamed."

The spark of hope went out with the suddenness of a lamp snuffed by a power-cut.

"He was so constantly with me," said the man, "that I felt him to be a part of everything I drew. But where is he today?"

"Perhaps he is still alive?"

"He's alive, without a doubt. . . . He had impeccable taste, and it was due to him that I made my most beautiful drawings."

"God knows," I said, in a voice almost stifled by the dead ashes of hope, "how dire my need for him is, and no one knows better than you of the ailments in respect of which he is sought."

"Yes, yes. May God restore you to health. He is, in truth, as is said of him, a man, and more. . . ."

Smiling broadly, he added, "And his face possesses an unforgettable beauty. But where is he?"

Reluctantly I rose to my feet, shook hands, and left. I continued wandering eastward and westward through the quarter, inquiring about Zaabalawi from everyone who, by reason of age or experience, I felt might be likely to help me. Eventually I was informed by a vendor of lupine[9] that he had met him a short while ago at the house of Sheikh Gad, the well-known composer. I went to the musician's house in Tabakshiyya,[10] where I found him in a room tastefully furnished in the old style, its walls redolent with history. He was seated on a divan, his famous lute beside him, concealing within itself the most beautiful melodies of our age, while somewhere from within the house came the sound of pestle and mortar and the clamor of children. I immediately greeted him and introduced myself, and was put at my ease by the unaffected way in which he received me. He did not ask, either in words or gesture, what had brought me, and I did not feel that he even harbored any such curiosity. Amazed at his understanding and kindness, which boded well, I said, "O Sheikh Gad, I am an admirer of yours, having long been enchanted by the renderings of your songs."

"Thank you," he said with a smile.

"Please excuse my disturbing you," I continued timidly, "but I was told that Zaabalawi was your friend, and I am in urgent need of him."

"Zaabalawi!" he said, frowning in concentration. "You need him? God be with you, for who knows, O Zaabalawi, where you are."

"Doesn't he visit you?" I asked eagerly.

"He visited me some time ago. He might well come right now; on the other hand I mightn't see him till death!"

I gave an audible sigh and asked, "What made him like that?"

---

[9] lupine: Beans.   [10] Tabakshiyya: District in Cairo named for the straw trays that are made and sold there.

The musician took up his lute. "Such are saints or they would not be saints," he said, laughing.

"Do those who need him suffer as I do?"

"Such suffering is part of the cure!"

He took up the plectrum and began plucking soft strains from the strings. Lost in thought, I followed his movements. Then, as though addressing myself, I said, "So my visit has been in vain."

He smiled, laying his cheek against the side of the lute. "God forgive you," he said, "for saying such a thing of a visit that has caused me to know you and you me!"

I was much embarrassed and said apologetically, "Please forgive me; my feelings of defeat made me forget my manners."

"Do not give in to defeat. This extraordinary man brings fatigue to all who seek him. It was easy enough with him in the old days when his place of abode was known. Today, though, the world has changed, and after having enjoyed a position attained only by potentates, he is now pursued by the police on a charge of false pretenses. It is therefore no longer an easy matter to reach him, but have patience and be sure that you will do so."

He raised his head from the lute and skillfully fingered the opening bars of a melody. Then he sang:

> I make lavish mention, even though I blame myself, of those I love,
> For the stories of the beloved are my wine.[11]

With a heart that was weary and listless, I followed the beauty of the melody and the singing.

"I composed the music to this poem in a single night," he told me when he had finished. "I remember that it was the eve of the Lesser Bairam.[12] Zaabalawi was my guest for the whole of that night, and the poem was of his choosing. He would sit for a while just where you are, then would get up and play with my children as though he were one of them. Whenever I was overcome by weariness or my inspiration failed me, he would punch me playfully in the chest and joke with me, and I would bubble over with melodies, and thus I continued working till I finished the most beautiful piece I have ever composed."

"Does he know anything about music?"

"He is the epitome of things musical. He has an extremely beautiful speaking voice, and you have only to hear him to want to burst into song and to be inspired to creativity. . . ."

"How was it that he cured those diseases before which men are powerless?"

"That is his secret. Maybe you will learn it when you meet him."

But when would that meeting occur? We relapsed into silence, and the hubbub of children once more filled the room.

---

[11] **"I make . . . wine":** Lines from a poem by the medieval mystic Ibn al-Farid.

[12] **Lesser Bairam:** Holiday celebrated at the end of the month of Ramadan.

Again the sheikh began to sing. He went on repeating the words "and I have a memory of her" in different and beautiful variations until the very walls danced in ecstasy. I expressed my wholehearted admiration, and he gave me a smile of thanks. I then got up and asked permission to leave, and he accompanied me to the front door. As I shook him by the hand, he said, "I hear that nowadays he frequents the house of Hagg Wanas al-Damanhouri. Do you know him?"

I shook my head, though a modicum of renewed hope crept into my heart.

"He is a man of private means," the sheikh told me, "who from time to time visits Cairo, putting up at some hotel or other. Every evening, though, he spends at the Negma Bar in Alfi Street."

I waited for nightfall and went to the Negma Bar. I asked a waiter about Hagg Wanas, and he pointed to a corner that was semisecluded because of its position behind a large pillar with mirrors on all four sides. There I saw a man seated alone at a table with two bottles in front of him, one empty, the other two-thirds empty. There were no snacks or food to be seen, and I was sure that I was in the presence of a hardened drinker. He was wearing a loosely flowing silk galabeya and a carefully wound turban; his legs were stretched out toward the base of the pillar, and as he gazed into the mirror in rapt contentment, the sides of his face, rounded and handsome despite the fact that he was approaching old age, were flushed with wine. I approached quietly till I stood but a few feet away from him. He did not turn toward me or give any indication that he was aware of my presence.

"Good evening, Mr. Wanas," I greeted him cordially.

He turned toward me abruptly, as though my voice had roused him from slumber, and glared at me in disapproval. I was about to explain what had brought me to him when he interrupted in an almost imperative tone of voice that was none the less not devoid of an extraordinary gentleness. "First, please sit down, and, second, please get drunk!"

I opened my mouth to make my excuses but, stopping up his ears with his fingers, he said, "Not a word till you do what I say."

I realized I was in the presence of a capricious drunkard and told myself that I should at least humor him a bit. "Would you permit me to ask one question?" I said with a smile, sitting down.

Without removing his hands from his ears he indicated the bottle. "When engaged in a drinking bout like this, I do not allow any conversation between myself and another unless, like me, he is drunk, otherwise all propriety is lost and mutual comprehension is rendered impossible."

I made a sign indicating that I did not drink.

"That's your lookout," he said offhandedly. "And that's my condition!"

He filled me a glass, which I meekly took and drank. No sooner had the wine settled in my stomach than it seemed to ignite. I waited patiently till I had grown used to its ferocity, and said, "It's very strong, and I think the time has come for me to ask you about—"

Once again, however, he put his fingers in his ears. "I shan't listen to you until you're drunk!"

He filled up my glass for the second time. I glanced at it in trepidation; then, overcoming my inherent objection, I drank it down at a gulp. No sooner had the wine come to rest inside me than I lost all willpower. With the third glass, I lost my memory, and with the fourth the future vanished. The world turned round about me and I forgot why I had gone there. The man leaned toward me attentively, but I saw him—saw everything—as a mere meaningless series of colored planes. I don't know how long it was before my head sank down onto the arm of the chair and I plunged into deep sleep. During it, I had a beautiful dream the like of which I had never experienced. I dreamed that I was in an immense garden surrounded on all sides by luxuriant trees, and the sky was nothing but stars seen between the entwined branches, all enfolded in an atmosphere like that of sunset or a sky overcast with cloud. I was lying on a small hummock of jasmine petals, more of which fell upon me like rain, while the lucent spray of a fountain unceasingly sprinkled the crown of my head and my temples. I was in a state of deep contentedness, of ecstatic serenity. An orchestra of warbling and cooing played in my ear. There was an extraordinary sense of harmony between me and my inner self, and between the two of us and the world, everything being in its rightful place, without discord or distortion. In the whole world there was no single reason for speech or movement, for the universe moved in a rapture of ecstasy. This lasted but a short while. When I opened my eyes, consciousness struck at me like a policeman's fist and I saw Wanas al-Damanhouri regarding me with concern. Only a few drowsy customers were left in the bar.

"You have slept deeply," said my companion. "You were obviously hungry for sleep."

I rested my heavy head in the palms of my hands. When I took them away in astonishment and looked down at them, I found that they glistened with drops of water.

"My head's wet," I protested.

"Yes, my friend tried to rouse you," he answered quietly.

"Somebody saw me in this state?"

"Don't worry, he is a good man. Have you not heard of Sheikh Zaabalawi?"

"Zaabalawi!" I exclaimed, jumping to my feet.

"Yes," he answered in surprise. "What's wrong?"

"Where is he?"

"I don't know where he is now. He was here and then he left."

I was about to run off in pursuit but found I was more exhausted than I had imagined. Collapsed over the table, I cried out in despair, "My sole reason for coming to you was to meet him! Help me to catch up with him or send someone after him."

The man called a vendor of prawns and asked him to seek out the sheikh and bring him back. Then he turned to me. "I didn't realize you were afflicted. I'm very sorry. . . ."

"You wouldn't let me speak," I said irritably.

"What a pity! He was sitting on this chair beside you the whole time. He was playing with a string of jasmine petals he had around his neck, a gift from one of his admirers, then, taking pity on you, he began to sprinkle some water on your head to bring you around."

"Does he meet you here every night?" I asked, my eyes not leaving the doorway through which the vendor of prawns had left.

"He was with me tonight, last night, and the night before that, but before that I hadn't seen him for a month."

"Perhaps he will come tomorrow," I answered with a sigh.

"Perhaps."

"I am willing to give him any money he wants."

Wanas answered sympathetically, "The strange thing is that he is not open to such temptations, yet he will cure you if you meet him."

"Without charge?"

"Merely on sensing that you love him."

The vendor of prawns returned, having failed in his mission.

I recovered some of my energy and left the bar, albeit unsteadily. At every street corner I called out "Zaabalawi!" in the vague hope that I would be rewarded with an answering shout. The street boys turned contemptuous eyes on me till I sought refuge in the first available taxi.

The following evening I stayed up with Wanas al-Damanhouri till dawn, but the sheikh did not put in an appearance. Wanas informed me that he would be going away to the country and would not be returning to Cairo until he had sold the cotton crop.

I must wait, I told myself; I must train myself to be patient. Let me content myself with having made certain of the existence of Zaabalawi, and even of his affection for me, which encourages me to think that he will be prepared to cure me if a meeting takes place between us.

Sometimes, however, the long delay wearied me. I would become beset by despair and would try to persuade myself to dismiss him from my mind completely. How many weary people in this life know him not or regard him as a mere myth! Why, then, should I torture myself about him in this way?

No sooner, however, did my pains force themselves upon me than I would again begin to think about him, asking myself when I would be fortunate enough to meet him. The fact that I ceased to have any news of Wanas and was told he had gone to live abroad did not deflect me from my purpose; the truth of the matter was that I had become fully convinced that I had to find Zaabalawi.

Yes, I have to find Zaabalawi.

ALBERT CAMUS
B. ALGERIA, 1913–1960

Albert Camus, c. 1945
*Algerian-born
Camus, photographed
here at about age
thirty-two, died in a
car accident in 1960
at the age of forty-
seven. (Hulton/
Archive)*

ahl-BARE kah-MOO

Albert Camus is usually associated with EXISTENTIALISM, the popular philosophical and literary movement of the mid twentieth century exemplified in the writings of Jean-Paul Sartre. In a secular world that seemed to run according to natural law rather than God's will and that resonated with Kafka's nightmares and T. S. Eliot's "wasteland," existentialism focused on the freedom that humans must exercise when making choices, when deciding who they are and how they will act. In Camus' early writings, such as *The Stranger* (1942) and *The Myth of Sisyphus and Other Essays* (1942), the author depicts a world that offers no purpose and little meaning to its inhabitants. Camus, calling this secular reality ABSURD, was quickly identified as the philosopher of the absurd, the outsider, and the gentle hedonist.

The two great wars of the first half of the twentieth century, with their massive destruction of human life and social ideals, left many wondering whether there was anything or anyone in which to believe. Camus looked at the postwar era with courage, honesty, and sensitivity. He became the quintessential rebel, starting a peoples' theater, joining and then rejecting the Communist Party, writing social polemics for newspapers, fighting in the French Underground against the Nazis, and refusing to side with either the French or the Algerians in the Algerian struggle for independence in the 1950s. He denounced tyranny, terrorism, and FASCISM, whether they occurred on the extreme right or the extreme left. And he searched for the basis of meaning and social commitment in a world disillusioned with traditional beliefs, movements, and institutions.

Since his death in 1960, Camus' popularity has periodically waxed and waned, but his writings have consistently encouraged a serious discussion of social issues and invited readers to commit themselves to bettering the human condition.

Beginning Life in Poverty. **Albert Camus** was born on November 7, 1913, in Mondovi, Algeria, in what was then French North Africa. His father, a transplanted Frenchman, was an illiterate farmer who was killed at the first Battle of Marne in World War I. His mother, who was originally from Spain, moved her family—Albert and his brother, uncle, and grandmother—to a two-room apartment in Belcourt, a working-class suburb of Algiers, where she worked as a charwoman. Raised by his maternal grandmother who used a whip to discipline him, Camus was permanently affected by the silence in his relationship with his illiterate, deaf mother who rarely spoke.

Ordinarily, he would have worked after completing elementary school, but a teacher, Louis Germain, to whom Camus would later dedicate his Nobel Prize speech, recognized his intellectual gifts and arranged for a scholarship to the lycée in the European section of Algiers (now Lycée Albert Camus). As a scholarship student from a poor, working-class neighborhood, the young Camus met with the prejudice and arrogance of his schoolmates, sons of wealth and privilege whose first allegiance was to Europe rather than to North Africa. These experiences influenced the youthful writings of Camus in 1932 when he took the side of the oppressed, seeking to give voice to the sufferings of those who like his mother were largely silent. His sympathy for the plight of the working class guided his moral and political struggles for the rest of his life. Winning honors both as a young scholar of philosophy and as a passionate goalie for the soccer team at the University of Algiers, Camus' world collapsed at age seventeen when he was diagnosed with tuberculosis; a year's convalescence was prescribed. Undoubtedly, his brush with death and subsequent unreliable health had a profound effect on the young man.

Left-Wing Politics.   Camus married Simone Hie in 1933. Influenced by the liberal writings of such French writers as **André Gide** and **André Malraux**[1] and the apparent sympathy Communists showed toward the plight of the Arabs, Camus joined the Algerian Communist Party in 1934 and founded The Labor Theater (*Le Théâtre du Travail*). While working at various jobs, Camus directed, wrote, and adapted plays for this peoples' theater, which performed on the docks in Algiers. Camus broke with the Communist Party in 1937 because of its growing hostility toward the Arab cause. His first collection of essays, *The Wrong and the Right Side* (*L'Envers et l'endroit,* 1937) reveals his passionate attachment to the people and landscapes of North Africa. As an **AGNOSTIC**, he characterizes the twin poles of his secular religion in these essays as Yes and No: a passionate Yes to "life with its face of tears and sun, life in the salt sea and on warm stones," but a resounding No to injustice and oppression. In "Return to Tipasa" he writes, "Yes, there is beauty and there are the humiliated. Whatever may be the difficulties of the undertaking, I should like never to be unfaithful either to one or to the others." In 1938 he joined the staff of a left-wing newspaper, *Alger-Républicain,* for which he wrote book reviews and a series of articles critical of the government's treatment of the Kabyles, a mountain people south of Algiers. He was eventually forced out of Algeria because of his politics. Living in Paris, he worked for *Paris-Soir* and continued to write.

Pursuing the Absurd.   It was at this time that Camus devised an ambitious plan that reflected his extraordinary gifts as a writer and thinker: He would write a philosophical essay, a novel, and a play around one particular theme and if possible publish all three works together. For his first theme he chose the absurd. *The Myth of Sisyphus* (*Le Mythe de Sisyphe,* 1942), a collection of essays, explains how absurdity arises from one's longing for clear answers about the nature of reality in an

www   For links to more information about Camus and a quiz on "The Guest," and for information about the culture and context of Algeria in the twentieth century, see *World Literature Online* at bedfordstmartins .com/worldlit.

ahn-DRAY ZHEED;
ahn-DRAY mahl-ROH

p. 757

---

[1] **Gide . . . Malraux:** André Gide (1869–1951) wrote poems, plays, and novels that focused on the importance of self-examination and the life of the senses. André Malraux (1901–1976), like Camus, was a French intellectual who combined writing with political action; his most famous novel, *Man's Fate* (1934), is about the Shanghai uprising and the Communist encroachment in China.

irrational, incomprehensible world—absurdity exists in the gulf between human need and the "unreasonable silence of the world." *The Stranger* (*L'Étranger*, 1942), Camus' most famous—and disturbing—novel, presents an absurd hero, **Meursault**, who refuses to adopt the social and religious conventions of his day and is therefore a stranger to his society. The play *Caligula* (1945) takes the idea of liberty to destructive extremes and completes the triumvirate on the absurd.

World War II interfered with Camus' plans for developing a second theme. He joined the French resistance movement in 1942, and in 1943, after another attack of tuberculosis, became a publisher's reader and a member of the administrative staff at Gallimard, a position he held until he died. The next year he became editor of the underground newspaper *Combat,* writing editorials and articles. In most of his writing of this period, and as a consequence of his associations with French existentialism and Jean-Paul Sartre, Camus examines the grounds for moral responsibility in a world in which God and religious institutions no longer provide a comprehensive vision and an imperative for ethical action. In a secular world, what connects us to the plight of our neighbors and thrusts us into the social arena? Several of Camus' plays depict life in a world in which restraints have been lifted and anything is possible: *The Misunderstanding* (*Le Malentendu*, 1944), *The State of Siege* (*L'État de siège*, 1948), and *The Just Assassins* (*Les Justes*, 1948).

Revolution and Morality.   In 1947 Camus published *The Plague* (*La Peste*), a novel that sets up a situation in which he can test his ideas: He gradually reveals the ethical motivations and psychological needs of the book's characters in a North African city besieged and isolated by the plague. *The Rebel* (*L'Homme révolté*, 1951), written as a complement to *The Plague,* discusses the nature of revolution and the relation of means and ends in political movements. Camus asks if the sacrifices demanded by the new secular prophets like Marx and Lenin[2] will lead ultimately to better societies. These works were attacked by Sartre and others. In 1952, Camus broke with Sartre over a fundamental issue: The latter accepted the evils of Stalinism[3] as a means to an end—a more humane society. Camus refused to exchange present sufferings for abstract promises of a better future, regardless of whether those promises were made by a socialist philosopher or a religious prophet.

Camus's final novel, *The Fall* (*La Chute*, 1956), is a strange, ironic monologue about personal responsibility and the darkness surrounding human motivation. His last volume of short stories, *Exile and the Kingdom* (*L'Exil et le royaume*, 1957), captures the poignant loneliness of being caught between two cultures: of being born in North Africa and yet

> . . . there is a *passion* of the absurd. The absurd man will not commit suicide; he wants to live, without relinquishing any of his certainty, without a future, without hope, without illusion, and without resignation either. He stares at death with passionate attention and this fascination liberates him. He experiences the "divine irresponsibility" of the condemned man.
>
> – JEAN-PAUL SARTRE, 1955

---

[2] **Marx and Lenin:** Karl Marx (1818–1883) was a social philosopher and founder of modern socialism. Nikolai Lenin (1870–1924) led the Communist Revolution of 1917 in Russia.

[3] **Stalinism:** A form of Marxism associated with Josef Stalin (1879–1953), the Communist dictator of the Soviet Union from 1922 to 1953. Stalin harshly repressed all dissent and upheld the absolute central authority of his government. Millions died under his brutal orchestration of the USSR's industrialization.

feeling like a colonial and an exile, all the while searching for a home, a "kingdom." This colonial dilemma was repeated for Europeans throughout Africa, India, and Southeast Asia, but for Camus it represented a universal condition: To have been born anywhere with full consciousness was to be an exile, estranged in one's own country or kingdom.

Albert Camus received the Nobel Prize in literature in 1957, one of the youngest persons to be awarded that honor. Tragically, he died in a car crash en route to Paris on January 4, 1960 — a rather absurd conclusion to a tremendously productive and worthwhile life.

"The Guest."   The Algerian struggle for independence from France in the 1950s amply illustrated the complexity of revolutionary situations. Recognizing the deep loyalties that both the Algerian-born French and Arab Algerians had toward their homeland, Camus risked the criticism of leftists and sought a reconciliation between the French government and the Algerian rebels, the FLN. This struggle, which polarized attitudes and forced an unwanted partisanship on both the Algerian Arabs and the Algerian French, serves as the volatile setting for Camus' "The Guest," taken from his collection *Exile and the Kingdom*. In this story, colonialism has reached into the Algerian backcountry, but Camus creates a situation in which the ideal of individual freedom takes precedence over political ideology and local politics. Even though French domination is symbolized in the local schoolteacher Daru, who distributes food to his drought-stricken region and teaches French geography to his pupils, the remote desert setting of the story provides an open arena for individual choices — Daru is free to act.

Real class differences are first introduced by showing Balducci, the gendarme, riding on his horse while the Arab prisoner, with hands bound, is walking. When Daru is given custody of the prisoner, he seeks ways to give the Arab his freedom. Through small signs of decency, Daru affirms the prisoner's common humanity and at the same time preserves his own set of values. Although there is little real, verbal communication between them, Daru acknowledges the minimal bond of their shared meals and lodgings. Daru resents both the legal system that interposed itself in the Arab's family quarrel and the subjugated Arab who failed to avoid capture. Even when presented with his freedom, the Arab ironically is incapable of escaping. Furthermore, Daru returns to the schoolhouse to find that his efforts on behalf of the Arab are totally misunderstood by other Arabs. Like Camus himself, Daru feels the loneliness of one who is neither an exile nor at home in the kingdom, a situation reflected in the collection title *Exile and the Kingdom*.

■ CONNECTIONS

In the World: **Existentialism, p. 746;** *In the World:* **Emancipation (Book 5); Dostoevsky, "The Grand Inquisitor" (Book 5).** The concept of freedom is central to existentialism. Consider Daru's feelings about holding the Arab captive and the prisoner's refusal to run away when Daru releases him. What is Camus saying about freedom? Is his point the same as that made by Sartre or by Dostoevsky in "The Grand Inquisitor"?

Some time ago I summed up *The Stranger* by a statement which I recognize is highly paradoxical: "In our society, any man who does not weep at the funeral of his mother risks being sentenced to death." I only wished to say that the hero of the book was sentenced because he did not play the game . . . he refuses to lie. To lie is not only to say what is not. It is also, it is above all, to say more than what is, and, in matters of the human heart, to say more than what one feels. This is what we do, all of us, every day, to simplify life. . . . One would not be greatly mistaken in reading in *The Stranger* the account of a man who, without any heroic posturing, consents to die for the truth.

— ALBERT CAMUS, preface to the 1955 edition of *L'Étranger*

Jean-Paul Sartre, *The Flies*, p. 697. One of the most important social and artistic movements of the twentieth century was existentialism. Sartre, one of the founders of French existentialism, created characters in *The Flies* who are brought to a recognition of responsibility for their choices. Camus, also considered an existentialist, created a character who is an outsider in society; does Daru in any way fit the existential label?

Voltaire, *Candide* (Book 4). Writers of satire often speak through an innocent protagonist to create the illusion of an unbiased observer or participant. The innocence of Voltaire's Candide allows the author to comment on the irrationalities of social institutions like religion. How does Camus use Daru as a means of social criticism?

■ FURTHER RESEARCH

Biography
Bronner, St. E. *Albert Camus, the Thinker, the Artist, the Man.* 1996.
Lottman, Herbert. *Albert Camus: A Biography.* 1980.

History and Culture
Brée, Germaine. *Albert Camus.* 1961.
McBride, Joseph. *Albert Camus, Philosopher and Litterateur.* 1992.

Criticism
Bosman, Catherine S. *Albert Camus.* 2001.
Brée, Germaine. *Camus: A Collection of Critical Essays.* 1961.
Douglas, Kenneth, ed. *Yale French Studies: Albert Camus.* 1960.
Eastman, Jennifer. *Albert Camus: The Mythic and the Real.* 2001.
Ellison, David R. *Understanding Albert Camus.* 1990.
Rizzuto, Anthony. *Camus: Love and Sexuality.* 1998.
Thody, Philip. *Albert Camus: A Study of His Work.* 1957.

■ PRONUNCIATION

Albert Camus: ahl-BARE kah-MOO
André Gide: ahn-DRAY ZHEED
André Malraux: ahn-DRAY mahl-ROH
Meursault: mur-SOH

↬ The Guest

Translated by Justin O'Brien

The schoolmaster was watching the two men climb toward him. One was on horseback, the other on foot. They had not yet tackled the abrupt rise leading to the schoolhouse built on the hillside. They were toiling onward, making slow progress in the snow, among the stones, on the vast expanse of the high, deserted plateau. From time to time the horse stumbled. Without hearing anything yet, he could see the

---

"The Guest." For Camus, life in an absurd world meant making choices without the assurance of universally accepted guidelines or principles. In fact, the complex secular world often presents individuals with conflicting sets of values and conflicting ethical codes. The question then becomes "How do I live a socially committed life in a culture where I feel so alienated that I am

breath issuing from the horse's nostrils. One of the men, at least, knew the region. They were following the trail although it had disappeared days ago under a layer of dirty white snow. The schoolmaster calculated that it would take them half an hour to get onto the hill. It was cold; he went back into the school to get a sweater.

He crossed the empty, frigid classroom. On the blackboard the four rivers of France,[1] drawn with four different colored chalks, had been flowing toward their estuaries for the past three days. Snow had suddenly fallen in mid-October after eight months of drought without the transition of rain, and the twenty pupils, more or less, who lived in the villages scattered over the plateau had stopped coming. With fair weather they would return. Daru now heated only the single room that was his lodging, adjoining the classroom and giving also onto the plateau to the east. Like the class windows, his window looked to the south too. On that side the school was a few kilometers from the point where the plateau began to slope toward the south. In clear weather could be seen the purple mass of the mountain range where the gap opened onto the desert.

Somewhat warmed, Daru returned to the window from which he had first seen the two men. They were no longer visible. Hence they must have tackled the rise. The sky was not so dark, for the snow had stopped falling during the night. The morning had opened with a dirty light which had scarcely become brighter as the ceiling of clouds lifted. At two in the afternoon it seemed as if the day were merely beginning. But still this was better than those three days when the thick snow was falling amidst unbroken darkness with little gusts of wind that rattled the double door of the classroom. Then Daru had spent long hours in his room, leaving it only to go to the shed and feed the chickens or get some coal. Fortunately the delivery truck from Tadjid, the nearest village to the north, had brought his supplies two days before the blizzard. It would return in forty-eight hours.

Besides, he had enough to resist a siege, for the little room was cluttered with bags of wheat that the administration left as a stock to distribute to those of his pupils whose families had suffered from the drought. Actually they had all been victims because they were all poor. Every day Daru would distribute a ration to the children. They had missed it, he knew, during these bad days. Possibly one of the fathers or big brothers would come this afternoon and he could supply them with grain. It was just a matter of carrying them over to the next harvest. Now shiploads of wheat were arriving from France and the worst was over. But it would be hard to forget that

tempted to withdraw into a private world?" In "The Guest," Daru appears to be living quite contentedly "in exile," a distant, out-of-the-way place where moral issues are simplified. Then his privacy is shattered when he experiences a conflict between his European background and the indigenous Arab culture. Since there are no guarantees that Daru's attempt to do the right thing will be met with success or recognition, he is faced with a classic existential situation in which the individual has only his inner resources to guide him in making a decision.

The translation is by Justin O'Brien; the notes are the editors'.

[1]**four rivers of France:** The Seine, Loire, Rhône, and Gironde rivers; French geography is being taught rather than Algerian.

poverty, that army of ragged ghosts wandering in the sunlight, the plateaus burned to a cinder month after month, the earth shriveled up little by little, literally scorched, every stone bursting into dust under one's foot. The sheep had died then by thousands and even a few men, here and there, sometimes without anyone's knowing.

In contrast with such poverty, he who lived almost like a monk in his remote schoolhouse, nonetheless satisfied with the little he had and with the rough life, had felt like a lord with his whitewashed walls, his narrow couch, his unpainted shelves, his well, and his weekly provision of water and food. And suddenly this snow, without warning, without the foretaste of rain. This is the way the region was, cruel to live in, even without men—who didn't help matters either. But Daru had been born here. Everywhere else, he felt exiled.

He stepped out onto the terrace in front of the schoolhouse. The two men were now halfway up the slope. He recognized the horseman as Balducci, the old gendarme he had known for a long time. Balducci was holding on the end of a rope an Arab who was walking behind him with hands bound and head lowered. The gendarme waved a greeting to which Daru did not reply, lost as he was in contemplation of the Arab dressed in a faded blue jellaba,[2] his feet in sandals but covered with socks of heavy raw wool, his head surmounted by a narrow, short *chèche*.[3] They were approaching. Balducci was holding back his horse in order not to hurt the Arab, and the group was advancing slowly.

Within earshot, Balducci shouted: "One hour to do the three kilometers from El Ameur!" Daru did not answer. Short and square in his thick sweater, he watched them climb. Not once had the Arab raised his head. "Hello," said Daru when they got up onto the terrace. "Come in and warm up." Balducci painfully got down from his horse without letting go the rope. From under his bristling mustache he smiled at the schoolmaster. His little dark eyes, deep-set under a tanned forehead, and his mouth surrounded with wrinkles made him look attentive and studious. Daru took the bridle, led the horse to the shed, and came back to the two men, who were now waiting for him in the school. He led them into his room. "I am going to heat up the classroom," he said. "We'll be more comfortable there." When he entered the room again, Balducci was on the couch. He had undone the rope tying him to the Arab, who had squatted near the stove. His hands still bound, the *chèche* pushed back on his head, he was looking toward the window. At first Daru noticed only his huge lips, fat, smooth, almost Negroid; yet his nose was straight, his eyes were dark and full of fever. The *chèche* revealed an obstinate forehead and, under the weathered skin now rather discolored by the cold, the whole face had a restless and rebellious look that struck Daru when the Arab, turning his face toward him, looked him straight in the eyes. "Go into the other room," said the schoolmaster, "and I'll make you some mint tea." "Thanks," Balducci said. "What a chore! How I long for retirement." And addressing his prisoner in Arabic: "Come on, you." The Arab got up and, slowly, holding his bound wrists in front of him, went into the classroom.

---

[2] **jellaba:** "Djellaba": a long, loose robe worn by men and women in some Arab countries.

[3] *chèche:* A head scarf or turban.

With the tea, Daru brought a chair. But Balducci was already enthroned on the nearest pupil's desk and the Arab had squatted against the teacher's platform facing the stove, which stood between the desk and the window. When he held out the glass of tea to the prisoner, Daru hesitated at the sight of his bound hands. "He might perhaps be untied." "Sure," said Balducci. "That was for the trip." He started to get to his feet. But Daru, setting the glass on the floor, had knelt beside the Arab. Without saying anything, the Arab watched him with his feverish eyes. Once his hands were free, he rubbed his swollen wrists against each other, took the glass of tea, and sucked up the burning liquid in swift little sips.

"Good," said Daru. "And where are you headed?"

Balducci withdrew his mustache from the tea. "Here, son."

"Odd pupils! And you're spending the night?"

"No. I'm going back to El Ameur. And you will deliver this fellow to Tinguit. He is expected at police headquarters."

Balducci was looking at Daru with a friendly little smile.

"What's this story?" asked the schoolmaster. "Are you pulling my leg?"

"No, son. Those are the orders."

"The orders? I'm not . . ." Daru hesitated, not wanting to hurt the old Corsican. "I mean, that's not my job."

"What! What's the meaning of that? In wartime people do all kinds of jobs."

"Then I'll wait for the declaration of war!"

Balducci nodded.

"O.K. But the orders exist and they concern you too. Things are brewing, it appears. There is talk of a forthcoming revolt. We are mobilized, in a way."

Daru still had his obstinate look.

"Listen, son," Balducci said. "I like you and you must understand. There's only a dozen of us at El Ameur to patrol throughout the whole territory of a small department[4] and I must get back in a hurry. I was told to hand this guy over to you and return without delay. He couldn't be kept there. His village was beginning to stir; they wanted to take him back. You must take him to Tinguit tomorrow before the day is over. Twenty kilometers shouldn't faze a husky fellow like you. After that, all will be over. You'll come back to your pupils and your comfortable life."

Behind the wall the horse could be heard snorting and pawing the earth. Daru was looking out the window. Decidedly, the weather was clearing and the light was increasing over the snowy plateau. When all the snow was melted, the sun would take over again and once more would burn the fields of stone. For days, still, the unchanging sky would shed its dry light on the solitary expanse where nothing had any connection with man.

"After all," he said, turning around toward Balducci, "what did he do?" And, before the gendarme had opened his mouth, he asked: "Does he speak French?"

"No, not a word. We had been looking for him for a month, but they were hiding him. He killed his cousin."

---

[4] **department:** A territorial unit.

"Is he against us?"

"I don't think so. But you can never be sure."

"Why did he kill?"

"A family squabble, I think. One owed the other grain, it seems. It's not at all clear. In short, he killed his cousin with a billhook. You know, like a sheep, *kreezk!*"

Balducci made the gesture of drawing a blade across his throat and the Arab, his attention attracted, watched him with a sort of anxiety. Daru felt a sudden wrath against the man, against all men with their rotten spite, their tireless hates, their blood lust.

But the kettle was singing on the stove. He served Balducci more tea, hesitated, then served the Arab again, who, a second time, drank avidly. His raised arms made the jellaba fall open and the schoolmaster saw his thin, muscular chest.

"Thanks, kid," Balducci said. "And now, I'm off."

He got up and went toward the Arab, taking a small rope from his pocket.

"What are you doing?" Daru asked dryly.

Balducci, disconcerted, showed him the rope.

"Don't bother."

The old gendarme hesitated. "It's up to you. Of course, you are armed?"

"I have my shotgun."

"Where?"

"In the trunk."

"You ought to have it near your bed."

"Why? I have nothing to fear."

"You're crazy, son. If there's an uprising, no one is safe, we're all in the same boat."

"I'll defend myself. I'll have time to see them coming."

Balducci began to laugh, then suddenly the mustache covered the white teeth.

"You'll have time? O.K. That's just what I was saying. You have always been a little cracked. That's why I like you, my son was like that."

At the same time he took out his revolver and put it on the desk.

"Keep it; I don't need two weapons from here to El Ameur."

The revolver shone against the black paint of the table. When the gendarme turned toward him, the schoolmaster caught the smell of leather and horseflesh.

"Listen, Balducci," Daru said suddenly, "every bit of this disgusts me, and first of all your fellow here. But I won't hand him over. Fight, yes, if I have to. But not that."

The old gendarme stood in front of him and looked at him severely.

"You're being a fool," he said slowly. "I don't like it either. You don't get used to putting a rope on a man even after years of it, and you're even ashamed — yes, ashamed. But you can't let them have their way."

"I won't hand him over," Daru said again.

"It's an order, son, and I repeat it."

"That's right. Repeat to them what I've said to you: I won't hand him over."

Balducci made a visible effort to reflect. He looked at the Arab and at Daru. At last he decided.

"No, I won't tell them anything. If you want to drop us, go ahead; I'll not denounce you. I have an order to deliver the prisoner and I'm doing so. And now you'll just sign this paper for me."

"There's no need. I'll not deny that you left him with me."

"Don't be mean with me. I know you'll tell the truth. You're from hereabouts and you are a man. But you must sign, that's the rule."

Daru opened his drawer, took out a little square bottle of purple ink, the red wooden penholder with the "sergeant-major" pen he used for making models of penmanship, and signed. The gendarme carefully folded the paper and put it into his wallet. Then he moved toward the door.

"I'll see you off," Daru said.

"No," said Balducci. "There's no use being polite. You insulted me."

He looked at the Arab, motionless in the same spot, sniffed peevishly, and turned away toward the door. "Good-by, son," he said. The door shut behind him. Balducci appeared suddenly outside the window and then disappeared. His footsteps were muffled by the snow. The horse stirred on the other side of the wall and several chickens fluttered in fright. A moment later Balducci reappeared outside the window leading the horse by the bridle. He walked toward the little rise without turning around and disappeared from sight with the horse following him. A big stone could be heard bouncing down. Daru walked back toward the prisoner, who, without stirring, never took his eyes off him. "Wait," the schoolmaster said in Arabic and went toward the bedroom. As he was going through the door, he had a second thought, went to the desk, took the revolver, and stuck it in his pocket. Then, without looking back, he went into his room.

For some time he lay on his couch watching the sky gradually close over, listening to the silence. It was this silence that had seemed painful to him during the first days here, after the war. He had requested a post in the little town at the base of the foothills separating the upper plateaus from the desert. There, rocky walls, green and black to the north, pink and lavender to the south, marked the frontier of eternal summer. He had been named to a post farther north, on the plateau itself. In the beginning, the solitude and the silence had been hard for him on these wastelands peopled only by stones. Occasionally, furrows suggested cultivation, but they had been dug to uncover a certain kind of stone good for building. The only plowing here was to harvest rocks. Elsewhere a thin layer of soil accumulated in the hollows would be scraped out to enrich paltry village gardens. This is the way it was: Bare rock covered three quarters of the region. Towns sprang up, flourished, then disappeared; men came by, loved one another or fought bitterly, then died. No one in this desert, neither he nor his guest, mattered. And yet, outside this desert neither of them, Daru knew, could have really lived.

When he got up, no noise came from the classroom. He was amazed at the unmixed joy he derived from the mere thought that the Arab might have fled and that he would be alone with no decision to make. But the prisoner was there. He had merely stretched out between the stove and the desk. With eyes open, he was staring at the ceiling. In that position, his thick lips were particularly noticeable, giving him a pouting look. "Come," said Daru. The Arab got up and followed him. In the bedroom, the schoolmaster pointed to a chair near the table under the window. The Arab sat down without taking his eyes off Daru.

"Are you hungry?"

"Yes," the prisoner said.

Daru set the table for two. He took flour and oil, shaped a cake in a frying-pan, and lighted the little stove that functioned on bottled gas. While the cake was cooking, he went out to the shed to get cheese, eggs, dates, and condensed milk. When the cake was done he set it on the window sill to cool, heated some condensed milk diluted with water, and beat up the eggs into an omelette. In one of his motions he knocked against the revolver stuck in his right pocket. He set the bowl down, went into the classroom, and put the revolver in his desk drawer. When he came back to the room, night was falling. He put on the light and served the Arab. "Eat," he said. The Arab took a piece of the cake, lifted it eagerly to his mouth, and stopped short.

"And you?" he asked.

"After you. I'll eat too."

The thick lips opened slightly. The Arab hesitated, then bit into the cake determinedly.

The meal over, the Arab looked at the schoolmaster. "Are you the judge?"

"No, I'm simply keeping you until tomorrow."

"Why do you eat with me?"

"I'm hungry."

The Arab fell silent. Daru got up and went out. He brought back a folding bed from the shed, set it up between the table and the stove, perpendicular to his own bed. From a large suitcase which, upright in a corner, served as a shelf for papers, he took two blankets and arranged them on the camp bed. Then he stopped, felt useless, and sat down on his bed. There was nothing more to do or to get ready. He had to look at this man. He looked at him, therefore, trying to imagine his face bursting with rage. He couldn't do so. He could see nothing but the dark yet shining eyes and the animal mouth.

"Why did you kill him?" he asked in a voice whose hostile tone surprised him.

The Arab looked away.

"He ran away. I ran after him."

He raised his eyes to Daru again and they were full of a sort of woeful interrogation. "Now what will they do to me?"

"Are you afraid?"

He stiffened, turning his eyes away.

"Are you sorry?"

The Arab stared at him openmouthed. Obviously he did not understand. Daru's annoyance was growing. At the same time he felt awkward and self-conscious with his big body wedged between the two beds.

"Lie down there," he said impatiently. "That's your bed."

The Arab didn't move. He called to Daru:

"Tell me!"

The schoolmaster looked at him.

"Is the gendarme coming back tomorrow?"

"I don't know."

"Are you coming with us?"

"I don't know. Why?"

The prisoner got up and stretched out on top of the blankets, his feet toward the window. The light from the electric bulb shone straight into his eyes and he closed them at once.

"Why?" Daru repeated, standing beside the bed.

The Arab opened his eyes under the blinding light and looked at him, trying not to blink.

"Come with us," he said.

In the middle of the night, Daru was still not asleep. He had gone to bed after undressing completely; he generally slept naked. But when he suddenly realized that he had nothing on, he hesitated. He felt vulnerable and the temptation came to him to put his clothes back on. Then he shrugged his shoulders; after all, he wasn't a child and, if need be, he could break his adversary in two. From his bed he could observe him, lying on his back, still motionless with his eyes closed under the harsh light. When Daru turned out the light, the darkness seemed to coagulate all of a sudden. Little by little, the night came back to life in the window where the starless sky was stirring gently. The schoolmaster soon made out the body lying at his feet. The Arab still did not move, but his eyes seemed open. A faint wind was prowling around the schoolhouse. Perhaps it would drive away the clouds and the sun would reappear.

During the night the wind increased. The hens fluttered a little and then were silent. The Arab turned over on his side with his back to Daru, who thought he heard him moan. Then he listened for his guest's breathing, become heavier and more regular. He listened to that breath so close to him and mused without being able to go to sleep. In this room where he had been sleeping alone for a year, this presence bothered him. But it bothered him also by imposing on him a sort of brotherhood he knew well but refused to accept in the present circumstances. Men who share the same rooms, soldiers or prisoners, develop a strange alliance as if, having cast off their armor with their clothing, they fraternized every evening, over and above their differences, in the ancient community of dream and fatigue. But Daru shook himself; he didn't like such musings, and it was essential to sleep.

A little later, however, when the Arab stirred slightly, the schoolmaster was still not asleep. When the prisoner made a second move, he stiffened, on the alert. The Arab was lifting himself slowly on his arms with almost the motion of a sleepwalker. Seated upright in bed, he waited motionless without turning his head toward Daru, as if he were listening attentively. Daru did not stir; it had just occurred to him that the revolver was still in the drawer of his desk. It was better to act at once. Yet he continued to observe the prisoner, who, with the same slithery motion, put his feet on the ground, waited again, then began to stand up slowly. Daru was about to call out to him when the Arab began to walk, in a quite natural but extraordinarily silent way. He was heading toward the door at the end of the room that opened into the shed. He lifted the latch with precaution and went out, pushing the door behind him but without shutting it. Daru had not stirred. "He is running away," he merely thought. "Good riddance!" Yet he listened attentively. The hens were not fluttering; the guest must be on the plateau. A faint sound of water reached him, and he didn't know what it was until the Arab again stood framed in the doorway, closed the door carefully, and came back to bed without a sound. Then Daru turned his back on him and fell asleep. Still later he seemed, from the depths of his sleep, to hear furtive steps around the schoolhouse. "I'm dreaming! I'm dreaming!" he repeated to himself. And he went on sleeping.

When he awoke, the sky was clear; the loose window let in a cold, pure air. The Arab was asleep, hunched up under the blankets now, his mouth open, utterly relaxed. But when Daru shook him, he started dreadfully, staring at Daru with wild eyes as if he had never seen him and such a frightened expression that the schoolmaster stepped back. "Don't be afraid. It's me. You must eat." The Arab nodded his head and said yes. Calm had returned to his face, but his expression was vacant and listless.

The coffee was ready. They drank it seated together on the folding bed as they munched their pieces of the cake. Then Daru led the Arab under the shed and showed him the faucet where he washed. He went back into the room, folded the blankets and the bed, made his own bed, and put the room in order. Then he went through the classroom and out onto the terrace. The sun was already rising in the blue sky; a soft, bright light was bathing the deserted plateau. On the ridge the snow was melting in spots. The stones were about to reappear. Crouched on the edge of the plateau, the schoolmaster looked at the deserted expanse. He thought of Balducci. He had hurt him, for he had sent him off in a way as if he didn't want to be associated with him. He could still hear the gendarme's farewell and, without knowing why, he felt strangely empty and vulnerable. At that moment, from the other side of the schoolhouse, the prisoner coughed. Daru listened to him almost despite himself and then, furious, threw a pebble that whistled through the air before sinking into the snow. That man's stupid crime revolted him, but to hand him over was contrary to honor. Merely thinking of it made him smart with humiliation. And he cursed at one and the same time his own people who had sent him this Arab and the Arab too who had dared to kill and not managed to get away. Daru got up, walked in a circle on the terrace, waited motionless, then went back into the schoolhouse.

The Arab, leaning over the cement floor of the shed, was washing his teeth with two fingers. Daru looked at him and said: "Come." He went back into the room ahead of the prisoner. He slipped a hunting-jacket on over his sweater and put on walking-shoes. Standing, he waited until the Arab had put on his *chèche* and sandals. They went into the classroom and the schoolmaster pointed to the exit, saying: "Go ahead." The fellow didn't budge. "I'm coming," said Daru. The Arab went out. Daru went back into the room and made a package of pieces of rusk, dates, and sugar. In the classroom, before going out, he hesitated a second in front of his desk, then crossed the threshold and locked the door. "That's the way," he said. He started toward the east, followed by the prisoner. But, a short distance from the schoolhouse, he thought he heard a slight sound behind them. He retraced his steps and examined the surroundings of the house, there was no one there. The Arab watched him without seeming to understand. "Come on," said Daru.

They walked for an hour and rested beside a sharp peak of limestone. The snow was melting faster and faster and the sun was drinking up the puddles at once, rapidly cleaning the plateau, which gradually dried and vibrated like the air itself. When they resumed walking, the ground rang under their feet. From time to time a bird rent the space in front of them with a joyful cry. Daru breathed in deeply the fresh morning light. He felt a sort of rapture before the vast familiar expanse, now almost entirely yellow under its dome of blue sky. They walked an hour more, descending toward the south. They reached a level height made up of crumbly rocks. From there on, the plateau sloped down, eastward, toward a low plain where there were a few spindly trees and, to the south, toward outcroppings of rock that gave the landscape a chaotic look.

Daru surveyed the two directions. There was nothing but the sky on the horizon. Not a man could be seen. He turned toward the Arab, who was looking at him blankly. Daru held out the package to him. "Take it," he said. "There are dates, bread, and sugar. You can hold out for two days. Here are a thousand francs too." The Arab took the package and the money but kept his full hands at chest level as if he didn't know what to do with what was being given him. "Now look," the schoolmaster said as he pointed in the direction of the east, "there's the way to Tinguit. You have a two-hour walk. At Tinguit you'll find the administration and the police. They are expecting you." The Arab looked toward the east, still holding the package and the money against his chest. Daru took his elbow and turned him rather roughly toward the south. At the foot of the height on which they stood could be seen a faint path. "That's the trail across the plateau. In a day's walk from here you'll find pasturelands and the first nomads. They'll take you in and shelter you according to their law." The Arab had now turned toward Daru and a sort of panic was visible in his expression. "Listen," he said. Daru shook his head: "No, be quiet. Now I'm leaving you." He turned his back on him, took two long steps in the direction of the school, looked hesitantly at the motionless Arab, and started off again. For a few minutes he heard nothing but his own step resounding on the cold ground and did not turn his head. A moment later, however, he turned around. The Arab was still there on the edge of the hill, his arms hanging now, and he was looking at the schoolmaster. Daru felt something rise in his throat. But he swore with impatience, waved vaguely, and started off again. He had already gone some distance when he again stopped and looked. There was no longer anyone on the hill.

Daru hesitated. The sun was now rather high in the sky and was beginning to beat down on his head. The schoolmaster retraced his steps, at first somewhat uncertainly, then with decision. When he reached the little hill, he was bathed in sweat. He climbed it as fast as he could and stopped, out of breath, at the top. The rock-fields to the south stood out sharply against the blue sky, but on the plain to the east a steamy heat was already rising. And in that slight haze, Daru, with heavy heart, made out the Arab walking slowly on the road to prison.

A little later, standing before the window of the classroom, the schoolmaster was watching the clear light bathing the whole surface of the plateau, but he hardly saw it. Behind him on the blackboard, among the winding French rivers, sprawled the clumsily chalked-up words he had just read: "You handed over our brother. You will pay for this." Daru looked at the sky, the plateau, and, beyond, the invisible lands stretching all the way to the sea. In this vast landscape he had loved so much, he was alone.

JAMES BALDWIN
B. UNITED STATES, 1924–1987

James Baldwin

Baldwin's stepfather was a preacher, a vocation that influenced Baldwin's style as a writer and a speaker.
(Steve Shapiro / Stockphoto.com)

I grew up with music, . . . much more than with any other language. In a way the music I grew up with saved my life.

– JAMES BALDWIN

Writers have always gravitated to the city. In cities they could immerse themselves in intellectual life, meet fellow writers and artists, and seek out publishers and patrons. In the twentieth century the migration from country to city also often involved the crossing of national borders, as writers sought out such artistic enclaves as New York's Greenwich Village, the Bloomsbury section of London, or the Left Bank of the Seine, in Paris. They went to the city to shed the provincialism and isolation of small towns; they went abroad to escape persecution at home or to distance themselves from the familiar and thus gain a new perspective on the world they had left behind. Refugees like Bertolt Brecht and Alexander Solzhenitsyn[1] sought the political freedom to write and publish their work. The "Lost Generation"[2] of American writers—including Ernest Hemingway and F. Scott Fitzgerald—fled to Paris between the two world wars, seeking excitement as well as liberation from the puritanical restraints in America. In the postcolonial years after World War II, many writers from former British colonies migrated to London; writers from former French colonies, like Léopold Senghor and Aimé Césaire, went to Paris. James Baldwin, who came of age after World War II, spent much of his adult life in Europe and the Middle East, where distance gave him perspective on the racial and sexual attitudes in America; nearly all of his novels and essays written abroad are about his homeland, its character and psyche.

From Harlem to Paris.   Baldwin was born to Emma Jones, an unmarried domestic worker in Harlem, in 1924. Three years later Jones married David Baldwin, a factory hand and lay preacher whose Pentecostal God embodied the anger and bitterness he felt toward white society. When David's only son from a previous marriage left the household in 1932, James, the eldest of the nine remaining children, was left to bear the brunt of his stepfather's rancor. James escaped the poverty and bitterness of his home life through reading, and he credited in particular one of his teachers, Orilla Miller, for showing him a way out of his domestic despair. He said it was "certainly because of her, who arrived in my terrifying life so soon, that I never really managed to hate white people." At

---

[1] **Brecht . . . Solzhenitsyn:** Bertolt Brecht (1898–1956), German poet, playwright, and screenwriter who escaped Nazi persecution by fleeing to northern Europe and then to the United States; see page 525. Alexander Solzhenitsyn (b. 1918), Russian novelist; author of *One Day in the Life of Ivan Denisovich* (1962) and other novels. He escaped Soviet persecution by spending several years in exile in Vermont.

[2] **"Lost Generation":** The name coined by Gertrude Stein (1874–1946) for a group of American writers who came of age after World War I and formed an American artists' colony in Paris. The early work of Ernest Hemingway (1899–1961), especially *The Sun Also Rises* (1926), is regarded as emblematic of these artists' situation and attitude.

age fourteen, Baldwin converted to the Pentecostal faith of his stepfather and, perhaps trying to please him, took up preaching for the four years until his graduation from high school in 1942. A young man with eight younger siblings and no job, James then concluded that religion offered no solution to the problems of the poor in Harlem. In 1943, following the death of his stepfather, Baldwin began a fictionalized account of his family that would eventually become *Go Tell It on the Mountain* (1953).

Baldwin left Harlem to seek out the artistic community of Greenwich Village, especially the novelist Richard Wright,[3] who became a kind of mentor to the young writer. When Wright moved to Paris in 1947, Baldwin followed in 1948, but the relationship between the two soon soured when Baldwin published the essay "Everybody's Protest Novel" (1949), which used Wright's *Native Son* (1940) to illustrate the limitations and excesses of ideological fiction. Baldwin didn't return to America until 1957. In the intervening years he moved frequently from one country to another, buying time and space in which to write extensively on two themes: race relations in the United States and the situation of the black homosexual. In the early sixties Baldwin lived intermittently in the Middle East, where he could purchase obscurity more easily than in Paris or New York, and made visits to the United States to lend support to the civil rights movement. In 1963 he met with Attorney General Robert Kennedy and prominent civil rights supporters, marched on Washington, D.C., with Dr. Martin Luther King Jr., and joined the voter-registration campaign in Selma, Alabama. Fearing the climate of violence he felt everywhere he went, he withdrew from Selma in October of that year, a month before the assassination of President John F. Kennedy. Frequent return trips to the States and repeated demonstrations of solidarity with the civil rights movement notwithstanding, Baldwin spent increasingly more time in Europe and the Middle East later in the decade. In the 1970s and 1980s, as the quality and freshness of his writing slowly diminished, Baldwin kept his home in Paris and on the French Riviera. After suffering two heart attacks, he died of cancer in 1987.

Baldwin's Literary Career.   In his first novel, *Go Tell It on the Mountain*, Baldwin told the story of his stern and bitter stepfather, a story he also documented two years later in the nonfiction work *Notes of a Native Son* (1955). His second novel, *Giovanni's Room* (1956), drew on his experience as an alienated bisexual and nearly cost him his audience. He treated the same theme more cautiously in a later novel, *Another Country* (1962). Although he later published several less successful novels — *Tell Me How Long the Train's Been Gone* (1968), *If Beale Street Could Talk* (1974), and *Just above My Head* (1979) — it was as an essayist that he made his mark. In the essays collected in *Notes of a Native Son, Nobody Knows My Name* (1961), and *The Fire Next Time* (1963), Baldwin, writing in the voices of

www   For links to more information about Baldwin and a quiz on "Sonny's Blues," and for information about the culture and context of America in the twentieth century, see *World Literature Online* at bedfordstmartins.com/worldlit.

Jimmy's voice, as much as Dr. King's or Malcolm X's, helped shepherd and guide us toward black liberation.

– AMIRI BARAKA, writer, 1987

---

[3] **Richard Wright** (1908–1960): Mississippi-born African American novelist who wrote Social-Realist novels on the oppression of blacks in America such as *Native Son* (1940) and the autobiographical *Black Boy* (1945). After settling in France in 1947, Wright was significantly influenced by the French existentialists.

prophet, moralist, and preacher, addressed the issues of his time to appeal to the conscience of the nation.

For Baldwin, racial and sexual issues were connected. America, he asserted, did not have a Negro problem but a white problem. "Whatever white people do not know about Negroes," Baldwin writes in *The Fire Next Time*, "reveals, precisely and inexorably, what they do not know about themselves." Unable to accept themselves or the truth about American history, those who ground their identity in being white project their inadequacies and repressed fears onto an alien other. Those others, black or homosexual, have a role to play, Baldwin argues, in healing the denial and repression of the white community: "We, with love, shall force our brothers to see themselves as they are, to cease fleeing from reality and begin to change it. . . . We cannot be free until they are free." His message, delivered in a didactic style derived from his training as an Evangelical preacher, was in keeping with the message of Dr. King.

Baldwin and Controversy.   Baldwin made enemies through both his words and his actions. He alienated Wright when he rejected Wright's *Native Son* character, the murderer and rapist Bigger Thomas, as a dangerous black wish fulfillment. His open homosexuality and his choice to live abroad angered Black Panther Eldridge Cleaver, author of *Soul on Ice* (1968), who asserted that Baldwin had "the most grueling, agonizing total hatred of blacks, particularly of himself." Baldwin refused to focus on racism and ignore sexual issues as Cleaver and some other black militants wanted him to. In the mid 1960s, as the schism deepened between moderates in the civil rights movement and militants such as Cleaver, Baldwin reached an anguished decision to distance himself from U.S. racial politics. He questioned how a writer could be most effective as a political instrument. What, he asked, is the most effective strategy for political engagement—words or actions? And he wondered if he could keep his necessary concentration as a writer if he was physically engaged in the struggle. Baldwin decided to avoid physical confrontation in order to concentrate on writing. This was not necessarily a mark of cowardice. It was Baldwin, for instance, who wrote in 1971 in support of Professor Angela Davis, about to stand trial on capital charges in California:

> We must fight for your life as though it were our own—which it is—and render impassable with our bodies the corridor to the gas chamber. For, if they take you in the morning, they will be coming for us that night.

"Sonny's Blues."   Although Baldwin is primarily regarded as an essayist and novelist, his short stories, frequently anthologized, also have tremendous appeal. "Sonny's Blues" (1957) is typical of Baldwin's work in that it approaches a commonplace subject from a complex perspective. The story begins with the arrest of Sonny, a young black musician, for possession of narcotics, followed by his release from jail to rejoin his peers. Sonny's story is told by his older brother, who has resisted Sonny's social and artistic world, opting instead for the relative security of a teaching position. A series of brief dramatic scenes show a friend of Sonny's as he confronts the brother about Sonny's chances for rehabilitation and his need for love; Sonny himself, just out of prison and unsure of his next move; and the older brother's tangled memories of his evasions of Sonny and his resistance to connections with Sonny's world. In the story's final scene, the brother accepts Sonny's invitation to see him perform with his friends in a downtown club. Returning to the piano after a year in prison, Sonny triumphs; the drink his brother has sent over to him shines like a halo on the piano top above his head.

Baldwin treats Sonny's fragile victory with understanding and skill; he is equally interested in the older brother, who must come to terms with the distance he has put between himself and Sonny. Thus Baldwin tells a double tale, part linear and exterior (Sonny's fate), part circular and interior (the hidden fate of the older brother). In his doubleness, his introspection, and his sense of our inability to fully comprehend or control our fate, Baldwin acknowledges his debt to Freud and the French EXISTENTIALISTS. In his realistic portrayal of life in Harlem and his use of the blues and jazz in the story's subject and structure, Baldwin draws on his African American heritage. Like Algerian-born French existentialist Albert Camus (p. 812), who reflects on the ambiguity of his double French and Algerian heritage, Baldwin is poised between two worlds: "European" white America and black America.

■ CONNECTIONS

W. E. B. Du Bois, *The Souls of Black Folk:* **"The Sorrow Songs," p. 865; African American Folk Songs (Book 5); James Joyce, "The Dead," p. 372; Anita Desai, "The Farewell Party," p. 1196.** The blues featured in Baldwin's story expresses the suffering of two brothers as well as the black experience in general in much the same way that the sorrow songs tell of the hardships of the slaves. Think about the role of music in Baldwin's story, both thematic and structural. Could the story itself be considered blues? Music also has important roles in Joyce's "The Dead" and Desai's "The Farewell Party." Are those roles similar to the part that jazz and the blues play in "Sonny's Blues"?

Naguib Mahfouz, "Zaabalawi," p. 803. Like the main character in Mahfouz's "Zaabalawi," the narrator of "Sonny's Blues" is searching for healing, recovery from the grief of his daughter's death and from the guilt he feels at having failed to carry out his promise to his mother regarding Sonny. Is his "condition" like that of the narrator in "Zaabalawi," who suffers from "a disease for which no one possesses a remedy"? Is he healed by the end of the story? Compare the ending of "Sonny's Blues" with that of "Zaabalawi."

Sophocles, *Antigone* **(Book 1); Goethe,** *Faust* **(Book 5).** Baldwin's worldview, grounded in a recognition and acceptance of suffering, is shared by many writers. Consider the role of suffering in Sophocles' *Antigone* and Goethe's *Faust* in relation to Baldwin's story. To what extent does the protagonist in each of these works bring suffering on herself or himself? Can the reasons for the suffering in any of these works be explained or justified or is it simply an inevitable part of the nature of things? Is "Sonny's Blues" a tragedy?

The name James Baldwin had been around the house for as long as I could remember, and it meant almost as much as that of Martin Luther King. . . . Baldwin gave expression to the longings of blacks in exalted prose. He was embraced, in the tradition of Negro Firstism, even by those who never sat down with a book, as *our* preeminent literary spokesman, whether he liked it or not.

– DARRYL PINCKNEY, critic, 1988

We, with love, shall force our brothers to see themselves as they are, to cease fleeing from reality and begin to change it. . . . We cannot be free until they are free.

– JAMES BALDWIN

■ **FURTHER RESEARCH**

Biography
Campbell, James. *Talking at the Gates: A Life of James Baldwin.* 1991.
Leeming, David. *James Baldwin: A Biography.* 1994.
Weatherby, William J. *James Baldwin: Artist on Fire: A Portrait.* 1990.

Criticism
Auger, Philip. *Native Sons in No Man's Land: Rewriting Afro-American Manhood in the Novels of Baldwin, Walker, Wideman, and Gaines.* 2000.
Balfour, Lawrie. *The Evidence of Things not Said: James Baldwin and the Promise of American Democracy.* 2001.
Eckman, Fern M. *The Furious Passage of James Baldwin.* 1966.
Kinnamon, Kenneth, ed. *James Baldwin: A Collection of Critical Essays.* 1974.
Pratt, L. H. *James Baldwin.* 1978.
Standley, Fred, and Nancy Burt, eds. *Critical Essays on James Baldwin.* 1988.

❧ Sonny's Blues

I read about it in the paper, in the subway, on my way to work. I read it, and I couldn't believe it, and I read it again. Then perhaps I just stared at it, at the newsprint spelling out his name, spelling out the story. I stared at it in the swinging lights of the subway car, and in the faces and bodies of the people, and in my own face, trapped in the darkness which roared outside.

It was not to be believed and I kept telling myself that, as I walked from the subway station to the high school. And at the same time I couldn't doubt it. I was scared, scared for Sonny. He became real to me again. A great block of ice got settled in my

---

"Sonny's Blues." Written in 1957 and collected in the volume *Going to Meet the Man* (1965), this short story invokes the traditions of oral storytelling as well as the blues to heal the rift between two brothers. Sonny, a jazz musician and heroin user who has just been released from prison, returns to the home of his older brother, the narrator of the story, a math teacher who rejects Sonny's music and way of life. The reunion of the two brothers prompts the recollection of family stories — like the death of their father's brother who was run over by a car full of drunken white men — and occasions a review of the divergent directions their lives have taken. The musical motif that runs through and shapes the story turns the story itself into a kind of musical performance, one that goes back and forth between scenes of the two boys' lives and culminates in the final scene at the club. Baldwin said of his own life: "I grew up with music, . . . much more than with any other language. In a way the music I grew up with saved my life." The same might be said for the two brothers in the story. By the time of Sonny's performance in the final scene, the narrator has come to understand that the suffering in Sonny's music is expressive not only of the pain of Sonny's own life but also of that of their family and all the people of Harlem. The music enables him to come to terms with his grief for his daughter. Opened to the suffering in their lives, the two brothers can understand and love each other. Music, a language beyond words, brings together stories of the past and creates community — literally a brotherhood — between them.

All notes are the editors'.

belly and kept melting there slowly all day long, while I taught my classes algebra. It was a special kind of ice. It kept melting, sending trickles of ice water all up and down my veins, but it never got less. Sometimes it hardened and seemed to expand until I felt my guts were going to come spilling out or that I was going to choke or scream. This would always be at a moment when I was remembering some specific thing Sonny had once said or done.

When he was about as old as the boys in my classes his face had been bright and open, there was a lot of copper in it; and he'd had wonderfully direct brown eyes, and great gentleness and privacy. I wondered what he looked like now. He had been picked up, the evening before, in a raid on an apartment downtown, for peddling and using heroin.

I couldn't believe it: but what I mean by that is that I couldn't find any room for it anywhere inside me. I had kept it outside me for a long time. I hadn't wanted to know. I had had suspicions, but I didn't name them, I kept putting them away. I told myself that Sonny was wild, but he wasn't crazy. And he'd always been a good boy, he hadn't ever turned hard or evil or disrespectful, the way kids can, so quick, so quick, especially in Harlem. I didn't want to believe that I'd ever see my brother going down, coming to nothing, all that light in his face gone out, in the condition I'd already seen so many others. Yet it had happened and here I was, talking about algebra to a lot of boys who might, every one of them for all I knew, be popping off needles every time they went to the head. Maybe it did more for them than algebra could.

I was sure that the first time Sonny had ever had horse, he couldn't have been much older than these boys were now. These boys, now, were living as we'd been living then, they were growing up with a rush and their heads bumped abruptly against the low ceiling of their actual possibilities. They were filled with rage. All they really knew were two darknesses, the darkness of their lives, which was now closing in on them, and the darkness of the movies, which had blinded them to that other darkness, and in which they now, vindictively, dreamed, at once more together than they were at any other time, and more alone.

When the last bell rang, the last class ended, I let out my breath. It seemed I'd been holding it for all that time. My clothes were wet—I may have looked as though I'd been sitting in a steam bath, all dressed up, all afternoon. I sat alone in the classroom a long time. I listened to the boys outside, downstairs, shouting and cursing and laughing. Their laughter struck me for perhaps the first time. It was not the joyous laughter which—God knows why—one associates with children. It was mocking and insular, its intent was to denigrate. It was disenchanted, and in this, also, lay the authority of their curses. Perhaps I was listening to them because I was thinking about my brother and in them I heard my brother. And myself.

One boy was whistling a tune, at once very complicated and very simple, it seemed to be pouring out of him as though he were a bird, and it sounded very cool and moving through all that harsh, bright air, only just holding its own through all those other sounds.

I stood up and walked over to the window and looked down into the courtyard. It was the beginning of the spring and the sap was rising in the boys. A teacher passed through them every now and again, quickly, as though he or she couldn't wait to get out of that courtyard, to get those boys out of their sight and off their minds. I started collecting my stuff. I thought I'd better get home and talk to Isabel.

The courtyard was almost deserted by the time I got downstairs. I saw this boy standing in the shadow of a doorway, looking just like Sonny. I almost called his name. Then I saw that it wasn't Sonny, but somebody we used to know, a boy from around our block. He'd been Sonny's friend. He'd never been mine, having been too young for me, and, anyway, I'd never liked him. And now, even though he was a grown-up man, he still hung around that block, still spent hours on the street corners, was always high and raggy. I used to run into him from time to time and he'd often work around to asking me for a quarter or fifty cents. He always had some real good excuse, too, and I always gave it to him, I don't know why.

But now, abruptly, I hated him. I couldn't stand the way he looked at me, partly like a dog, partly like a cunning child. I wanted to ask him what the hell he was doing in the school courtyard.

He sort of shuffled over to me, and he said, "I see you got the papers. So you already know about it."

"You mean about Sonny? Yes, I already know about it. How come they didn't get you?"

He grinned. It made him repulsive and it also brought to mind what he'd looked like as a kid. "I wasn't there. I stay away from them people."

"Good for you." I offered him a cigarette and I watched him through the smoke. "You come all the way down here just to tell me about Sonny?"

"That's right." He was sort of shaking his head and his eyes looked strange, as though they were about to cross. The bright sun deadened his damp dark brown skin and it made his eyes look yellow and showed up the dirt in his kinked hair. He smelled funky. I moved a little away from him and I said, "Well, thanks. But I already know about it and I got to get home."

"I'll walk you a little ways," he said. We started walking. There were a couple of kids still loitering in the courtyard and one of them said goodnight to me and looked strangely at the boy beside me.

"What're you going to do?" he asked me. "I mean, about Sonny?"

"Look. I haven't seen Sonny for over a year, I'm not sure I'm going to do anything. Anyway, what the hell *can* I do?"

"That's right," he said quickly, "ain't nothing you can do. Can't much help old Sonny no more, I guess."

It was what I was thinking and so it seemed to me he had no right to say it.

"I'm surprised at Sonny, though," he went on — he had a funny way of talking, he looked straight ahead as though he were talking to himself — "I thought Sonny was a smart boy, I thought he was too smart to get hung."

"I guess he thought so too," I said sharply, "and that's how he got hung. And how about you? You're pretty goddamn smart, I bet."

Then he looked directly at me, just for a minute. "I ain't smart," he said. "If I was smart, I'd have reached for a pistol a long time ago."

"Look. Don't tell *me* your sad story, if it was up to me, I'd give you one." Then I felt guilty—guilty, probably, for never having supposed that the poor bastard *had* a story of his own, much less a sad one, and I asked, quickly, "What's going to happen to him now?"

He didn't answer this. He was off by himself some place. "Funny thing," he said, and from his tone we might have been discussing the quickest way to get to Brooklyn, "when I saw the papers this morning, the first thing I asked myself was if I had anything to do with it. I felt sort of responsible."

I began to listen more carefully. The subway station was on the corner, just before us, and I stopped. He stopped, too. We were in front of a bar and he ducked slightly, peering in, but whoever he was looking for didn't seem to be there. The juke box was blasting away with something black and bouncy and I half watched the barmaid as she danced her way from the juke box to her place behind the bar. And I watched her face as she laughingly responded to something someone said to her, still keeping time to the music. When she smiled one saw the little girl, one sensed the doomed, still-struggling woman beneath the battered face of the semi-whore.

"I never *give* Sonny nothing," the boy said finally, "but a long time ago I come to school high and Sonny asked me how it felt." He paused, I couldn't bear to watch him, I watched the barmaid, and I listened to the music which seemed to be causing the pavement to shake. "I told him it felt great." The music stopped, the barmaid paused and watched the juke box until the music began again. "It did."

All this was carrying me some place I didn't want to go. I certainly didn't want to know how it felt. It filled everything, the people, the houses, the music, the dark, quicksilver barmaid, with menace; and this menace was their reality.

"What's going to happen to him now?" I asked again.

"They'll send him away some place and they'll try to cure him." He shook his head. "Maybe he'll even think he's kicked the habit. Then they'll let him loose"—he gestured, throwing his cigarette into the gutter. "That's all."

"What do you mean, that's *all*?"

But I knew what he meant.

"I *mean*, that's *all*." He turned his head and looked at me, pulling down the corners of his mouth. "Don't you know what I mean?" he asked, softly.

"How the hell *would* I know what you mean?" I almost whispered it, I don't know why.

"That's right," he said to the air, "how would *he* know what I mean?" He turned toward me again, patient and calm, and yet I somehow felt him shaking, shaking as though he were going to fall apart. I felt that ice in my guts again, the dread I'd felt all afternoon; and again I watched the barmaid, moving about the bar, washing glasses, and singing. "Listen. They'll let him out and then it'll just start all over again. That's what I mean."

"You mean—they'll let him out. And then he'll just start working his way back in again. You mean he'll never kick the habit. Is that what you mean?"

"That's right," he said, cheerfully. "*You* see what I mean."

"Tell me," I said at last, "why does he want to die? He must want to die, he's killing himself, why does he want to die?"

He looked at me in surprise. He licked his lips. "He don't want to die. He wants to live. Don't nobody want to die, ever."

Then I wanted to ask him—too many things. He could not have answered, or if he had, I could not have borne the answers. I started walking. "Well, I guess it's none of my business."

"It's going to be rough on old Sonny," he said. We reached the subway station. "This is your station?" he asked. I nodded. I took one step down. "Damn!" he said, suddenly. I looked up at him. He grinned again. "Damn it if I didn't leave all my money home. You ain't got a dollar on you, have you? Just for a couple of days, is all."

All at once something inside gave and threatened to come pouring out of me. I didn't hate him any more. I felt that in another moment I'd start crying like a child.

"Sure," I said. "Don't sweat." I looked in my wallet and didn't have a dollar, I only had a five. "Here," I said. "That hold you?"

He didn't look at it—he didn't want to look at it. A terrible, closed look came over his face, as though he were keeping the number on the bill a secret from him and me. "Thanks," he said, and now he was dying to see me go. "Don't worry about Sonny. Maybe I'll write him or something."

"Sure," I said. "You do that. So long."

"Be seeing you," he said. I went on down the steps.

And I didn't write Sonny or send him anything for a long time. When I finally did, it was just after my little girl died, he wrote me back a letter which made me feel like a bastard.

Here's what he said:

Dear brother,

You don't know how much I needed to hear from you. I wanted to write you many a time but I dug how much I must have hurt you and so I didn't write. But now I feel like a man who's been trying to climb up out of some deep, real deep and funky hole and just saw the sun up there, outside. I got to get outside.

I can't tell you much about how I got here. I mean I don't know how to tell you. I guess I was afraid of something or I was trying to escape from something and you know I have never been very strong in the head (smile). I'm glad Mama and Daddy are dead and can't see what's happened to their son and I swear if I'd known what I was doing I would never have hurt you so, you and a lot of other fine people who were nice to me and who believed in me.

I don't want you to think it had anything to do with me being a musician. It's more than that. Or maybe less than that. I can't get anything straight in my head down here and I try not to think about what's going to happen to me when I get out-side again. Sometime I think I'm going to flip and *never* get outside and sometime I think I'll come straight back. I tell you one thing, though, I'd rather blow my brains out than go through this again. But that's what they all say, so they tell me. If I tell you when I'm coming to New York and if you could meet me, I sure would appreciate it. Give my love to Isabel and the kids and I was sure sorry to hear about little Gracie. I wish I could be like Mama and say the Lord's will be done, but I don't know it seems to me that trouble is the one thing that never does get stopped and I don't know what good it does to blame it on the Lord. But maybe it does some good if you believe it.

Your brother,
Sonny

Then I kept in constant touch with him and I sent him whatever I could and I went to meet him when he came back to New York. When I saw him many things I thought I had forgotten came flooding back to me. This was because I had begun, finally, to wonder about Sonny, about the life that Sonny lived inside. This life, whatever it was, had made him older and thinner and it had deepened the distant stillness in which he had always moved. He looked very unlike my baby brother. Yet, when he smiled, when we shook hands, the baby brother I'd never known looked out from the depths of his private life, like an animal waiting to be coaxed into the light.

"How you been keeping?" he asked me.

"All right. And you?"

"Just fine." He was smiling all over his face. "It's good to see you again."

"It's good to see you."

The seven years' difference in our ages lay between us like a chasm: I wondered if these years would ever operate between us as a bridge. I was remembering, and it made it hard to catch my breath, that I had been there when he was born; and I had heard the first words he had ever spoken. When he started to walk, he walked from our mother straight to me. I caught him just before he fell when he took the first steps he ever took in this world.

"How's Isabel?"

"Just fine. She's dying to see you."

"And the boys?"

"They're fine, too. They're anxious to see their uncle."

"Oh, come on. You know they don't remember me."

"Are you kidding? Of course they remember you."

He grinned again. We got into a taxi. We had a lot to say to each other, far too much to know how to begin.

As the taxi began to move, I asked, "You still want to go to India?"

He laughed. "You still remember that. Hell, no. This place is Indian enough for me."

"It used to belong to them," I said.

And he laughed again. "They damn sure knew what they were doing when they got rid of it."

Years ago, when he was around fourteen, he'd been all hipped on the idea of going to India. He read books about people sitting on rocks, naked, in all kinds of weather, but mostly bad, naturally, and walking barefoot through hot coals and arriving at wisdom. I used to say that it sounded to me as though they were getting away from wisdom as fast as they could. I think he sort of looked down on me for that.

"Do you mind," he asked, "if we have the driver drive alongside the park? On the west side—I haven't seen the city in so long."

"Of course not," I said. I was afraid that I might sound as though I were humoring him, but I hoped he wouldn't take it that way.

So we drove along, between the green of the park and the stony, lifeless elegance of hotels and apartment buildings, toward the vivid, killing streets of our childhood. These streets hadn't changed, though housing projects jutted up out of them now like rocks in the middle of a boiling sea. Most of the houses in which we had grown up had vanished, as had the stores from which we had stolen, the basements in which we had first tried sex, the rooftops from which we had hurled tin cans and bricks. But houses exactly like the houses of our past yet dominated the landscape, boys exactly like the boys we once had been found themselves smothering in these houses, came down into the streets for light and air and found themselves encircled by disaster. Some escaped the trap, most didn't. Those who got out always left something of themselves behind, as some animals amputate a leg and leave it in the trap. It might be said, perhaps, that I had escaped, after all, I was a school teacher; or that Sonny had, he hadn't lived in Harlem for years. Yet, as the cab moved uptown through streets which seemed, with a rush, to darken with dark people, and as I covertly studied Sonny's face, it came to me that what we both were seeking through our separate cab windows was that part of ourselves which had been left behind. It's always at the hour of trouble and confrontation that the missing member aches.

We hit 110th Street and started rolling up Lenox Avenue. And I'd known this avenue all my life, but it seemed to me again, as it had seemed on the day I'd first heard about Sonny's trouble, filled with a hidden menace which was its very breath of life.

"We almost there," said Sonny.

"Almost." We were both too nervous to say anything more.

We live in a housing project. It hasn't been up long. A few days after it was up it seemed uninhabitably new, now, of course, it's already rundown. It looks like a parody of the good, clean, faceless life—God knows the people who live in it do their best to make it a parody. The beat-looking grass lying around isn't enough to make their lives green, the hedges will never hold out the streets, and they know it. The big windows fool no one, they aren't big enough to make space out of no space. They don't bother with the windows, they watch the TV screen instead. The playground is most popular with the children who don't play at jacks, or skip rope, or roller skate, or swing, and they can be found in it after dark. We moved in partly because it's not too far from where I teach, and partly for the kids; but it's really just like the houses in which Sonny and I grew up. The same things happen, they'll have the same things to remember. The moment Sonny and I started into the house I had the feeling that I was simply bringing him back into the danger he had almost died trying to escape.

Sonny has never been talkative. So I don't know why I was sure he'd be dying to talk to me when supper was over the first night. Everything went fine, the oldest boy remembered him, and the youngest boy liked him, and Sonny had remembered to bring something for each of them; and Isabel, who is really much nicer than I am, more open and giving, had gone to a lot of trouble about dinner and was genuinely glad to see him. And she's always been able to tease Sonny in a way that I haven't. It was nice to see her face so vivid again and to hear her laugh and watch her make Sonny laugh. She wasn't, or, anyway, she didn't seem to be, at all uneasy or embarrassed. She chatted as though there were no subject which had to be avoided and she got Sonny past his first, faint stiffness. And thank God she was there, for I was filled with that icy dread again. Everything I did seemed awkward to me, and everything I said sounded freighted with hidden meaning. I was trying to remember everything I'd heard about dope addiction and I couldn't help watching Sonny for signs. I wasn't doing it out of malice. I was trying to find out something about my brother. I was dying to hear him tell me he was safe.

"Safe!" my father grunted, whenever Mama suggested trying to move to a neighborhood which might be safer for children. "Safe, hell! Ain't no place safe for kids, nor nobody."

He always went on like this, but he wasn't, ever, really as bad as he sounded, not even on weekends, when he got drunk. As a matter of fact, he was always on the lookout for "something a little better," but he died before he found it. He died suddenly, during a drunken weekend in the middle of the war, when Sonny was fifteen. He and Sonny hadn't ever got on too well. And this was partly because Sonny was the apple of his father's eye. It was because he loved Sonny so much and was frightened for him, that he was always fighting with him. It doesn't do any good to fight with Sonny. Sonny just moves back, inside himself, where he can't be reached. But the principal reason that they never hit it off is that they were so much alike. Daddy was big and rough and loud-talking, just the opposite of Sonny, but they both had—that same privacy.

Mama tried to tell me something about this, just after Daddy died. I was home on leave from the army.

This was the last time I ever saw my mother alive. Just the same, this picture gets all mixed up in my mind with pictures I had of her when she was younger. The way I always see her is the way she used to be on a Sunday afternoon, say, when the old folks were talking after the big Sunday dinner. I always see her wearing pale blue. She'd be sitting on the sofa. And my father would be sitting in the easy chair, not far from her. And the living room would be full of church folks and relatives. There they sit, in chairs all around the living room, and the night is creeping up outside, but nobody knows it yet. You can see the darkness growing against the windowpanes and you hear the street noises every now and again, or maybe the jangling beat of a tambourine from one of the churches close by, but it's real quiet in the room. For a moment nobody's talking, but every face looks darkening, like the sky outside. And my mother rocks a little from the waist, and my father's eyes are closed. Everyone is looking at something a child can't see. For a minute they've forgotten the children. Maybe a kid is lying on the rug, half asleep. Maybe somebody's got a kid in his lap and is absent-mindedly stroking the kid's head. Maybe there's a kid, quiet and big-eyed, curled up in a big chair in the corner. The silence, the darkness coming, and the darkness in the faces frightens the child obscurely. He hopes that the hand which strokes his forehead will never stop—will never die. He hopes that there will never come a time when the old folks won't be sitting around the living room, talking about where they've come from, and what they've seen, and what's happened to them and their kinfolk.

But something deep and watchful in the child knows that this is bound to end, is already ending. In a moment someone will get up and turn on the light. Then the old folks will remember the children and they won't talk any more that day. And when light fills the room, the child is filled with darkness. He knows that every time this happens he's moved just a little closer to that darkness outside. The darkness outside is what the old folks have been talking about. It's what they've come from. It's what they endure. The child knows that they won't talk any more because if he knows too much about what's happened to *them,* he'll know too much too soon, about what's going to happen to *him.*

The last time I talked to my mother, I remember I was restless. I wanted to get out and see Isabel. We weren't married then and we had a lot to straighten out between us.

There Mama sat, in black, by the window. She was humming an old church song, *Lord, you brought me from a long ways off.* Sonny was out somewhere. Mama kept watching the streets.

"I don't know," she said, "if I'll ever see you again, after you go off from here. But I hope you'll remember the things I tried to teach you."

"Don't talk like that," I said, and smiled. "You'll be here a long time yet."

She smiled, too, but she said nothing. She was quiet for a long time. And I said, "Mama, don't you worry about nothing. I'll be writing all the time, and you be getting the checks. . . ."

"I want to talk to you about your brother," she said, suddenly. "If anything happens to me he ain't going to have nobody to look out for him."

"Mama," I said, "ain't nothing going to happen to you *or* Sonny. Sonny's all right. He's a good boy and he's got good sense."

"It ain't a question of his being a good boy," Mama said, "nor of his having good sense. It ain't only the bad ones, nor yet the dumb ones that gets sucked under." She stopped, looking at me. "Your Daddy once had a brother," she said, and she smiled in a way that made me feel she was in pain. "You didn't never know that, did you?"

"No," I said, "I never knew that," and I watched her face.

"Oh, yes," she said, "your Daddy had a brother." She looked out of the window again. "I know you never saw your Daddy cry. But *I* did—many a time, through all these years."

I asked her, "What happened to his brother? How come nobody's ever talked about him?"

This was the first time I ever saw my mother look old.

"His brother got killed," she said, "when he was just a little younger than you are now. I knew him. He was a fine boy. He was maybe a little full of the devil, but he didn't mean nobody no harm."

Then she stopped and the room was silent, exactly as it had sometimes been on those Sunday afternoons. Mama kept looking out into the streets.

"He used to have a job in the mill," she said, "and, like all young folks, he just liked to perform on Saturday nights. Saturday nights, him and your father would drift around to different places, go to dances and things like that, or just sit around with people they knew, and your father's brother would sing, he had a fine voice, and play along with himself on his guitar. Well, this particular Saturday night, him and your father was coming home from some place, and they were both a little drunk and there was a moon that night, it was bright like day. Your father's brother was feeling kind of good, and he was whistling to himself, and he had his guitar slung over his shoulder. They was coming down a hill and beneath them was a road that turned off from the highway. Well, your father's brother, being always kind of frisky, decided to run down this hill, and he did, with that guitar banging and clanging behind him, and he ran across the road, and he was making water behind a tree. And your father was sort of amused at him and he was still coming down the hill, kind of slow. Then he heard a car motor and that same minute his brother stepped from behind the tree, into the road, in the moonlight. And he started to cross the road. And your father started to run down the hill, he says he don't know why. This car was full of white men. They was all drunk, and when they seen your father's brother they let out a great whoop and holler and they aimed the car straight at him. They was having fun, they just wanted to scare him, the way they do sometimes, you know. But they was drunk. And I guess the boy, being drunk, too, and scared, kind of lost his head. By the time he jumped it was too late. Your father says he heard his brother scream when the car rolled over him, and he heard the wood of that guitar when it give, and he heard them strings go flying, and he heard them white men shouting, and the car kept on a-going and it ain't stopped till this day. And, time your father got down the hill, his brother weren't nothing but blood and pulp."

Tears were gleaming on my mother's face. There wasn't anything I could say.

"He never mentioned it," she said, "because I never let him mention it before you children. Your Daddy was like a crazy man that night and for many a night thereafter. He says he never in his life seen anything as dark as that road after the lights of that car had gone away. Weren't nothing, weren't nobody on that road, just your Daddy and his brother and that busted guitar. Oh, yes. Your Daddy never did really get right again. Till the day he died he weren't sure but that every white man he saw was the man that killed his brother."

She stopped and took out her handkerchief and dried her eyes and looked at me.

"I ain't telling you all this," she said, "to make you scared or bitter or to make you hate nobody. I'm telling you this because you got a brother. And the world ain't changed."

I guess I didn't want to believe this. I guess she saw this in my face. She turned away from me, toward the window again, searching those streets.

"But I praise my Redeemer," she said at last, "that He called your Daddy home before me. I ain't saying it to throw no flowers at myself, but, I declare, it keeps me from feeling too cast down to know I helped your father get safely through this world. Your father always acted like he was the roughest, strongest man on earth. And everybody took him to be like that. But if he hadn't had *me* there—to see his tears!"

She was crying again. Still, I couldn't move. I said, "Lord, Lord, Mama, I didn't know it was like that."

"Oh, honey," she said, "there's a lot that you don't know. But you are going to find it out." She stood up from the window and came over to me. "You got to hold on to your brother," she said, "and don't let him fall, no matter what it looks like is happening to him and no matter how evil you gets with him. You going to be evil with him many a time. But don't you forget what I told you, you hear?"

"I won't forget," I said. "Don't you worry, I won't forget. I won't let nothing happen to Sonny."

My mother smiled as though she were amused at something she saw in my face. Then, "You may not be able to stop nothing from happening. But you got to let him know you's *there.*"

Two days later I was married, and then I was gone. And I had a lot of things on my mind and I pretty well forgot my promise to Mama until I got shipped home on a special furlough for her funeral.

And, after the funeral, with just Sonny and me alone in the empty kitchen, I tried to find out something about him.

"What do you want to do?" I asked him.

"I'm going to be a musician," he said.

For he had graduated, in the time I had been away, from dancing to the juke box to finding out who was playing what, and what they were doing with it, and he had bought himself a set of drums.

"You mean, you want to be a drummer?" I somehow had the feeling that being a drummer might be all right for other people but not for my brother Sonny.

"I don't think," he said, looking at me very gravely, "that I'll ever be a good drummer. But I think I can play a piano."

I frowned. I'd never played the role of the older brother quite so seriously before, had scarcely ever, in fact, *asked* Sonny a damn thing. I sensed myself in the presence of something I didn't really know how to handle, didn't understand. So I made my frown a little deeper as I asked: "What kind of musician do you want to be?"

He grinned. "How many kinds do you think there are?"

"Be *serious,*" I said.

He laughed, throwing his head back, and then looked at me. "I *am* serious."

"Well, then, for Christ's sake, stop kidding around and answer a serious question. I mean, do you want to be a concert pianist, you want to play classical music and all that, or—or what?" Long before I finished he was laughing again. "For Christ's *sake,* Sonny!"

He sobered, but with difficulty. "I'm sorry. But you sound so—*scared!*" and he was off again.

"Well, you may think it's funny now, baby, but it's not going to be so funny when you have to make your living at it, let me tell you *that.*" I was furious because I knew he was laughing at me and I didn't know why.

"No," he said, very sober now, and afraid, perhaps, that he'd hurt me, "I don't want to be a classical pianist. That isn't what interests me. I mean"—he paused, looking hard at me, as though his eyes would help me to understand, and then gestured helplessly, as though perhaps his hand would help—"I mean, I'll have a lot of studying to do, and I'll have to study *everything*, but, I mean, I want to play *with*—jazz musicians." He stopped. "I want to play jazz," he said.

Well, the word had never before sounded as heavy, as real, as it sounded that afternoon in Sonny's mouth. I just looked at him and I was probably frowning a real frown by this time. I simply couldn't see why on earth he'd want to spend his time hanging around nightclubs, clowning around on bandstands, while people pushed each other around a dance floor. It seemed—beneath him, somehow. I had never thought about it before, had never been forced to, but I suppose I had always put jazz musicians in a class with what Daddy called "good-time people."

"Are you *serious*?"

"Hell, *yes*, I'm serious."

He looked more helpless than ever, and annoyed, and deeply hurt.

I suggested, helpfully: "You mean—like Louis Armstrong?"

His face closed as though I'd struck him. "No. I'm not talking about none of that old-time, down home crap."

"Well, look, Sonny, I'm sorry, don't get mad. I just don't altogether get it, that's all. Name somebody—you know, a jazz musician you admire."

"Bird."

"Who?"

"Bird! Charlie Parker! Don't they teach you nothing in the goddamn army?"

I lit a cigarette. I was surprised and then a little amused to discover that I was trembling. "I've been out of touch," I said. "You'll have to be patient with me. Now. Who's this Parker character?"

"He's just one of the greatest jazz musicians alive," said Sonny, sullenly, his hands in his pockets, his back to me. "Maybe *the* greatest," he added, bitterly, "that's probably why *you* never heard of him."

"All right," I said, "I'm ignorant. I'm sorry. I'll go out and buy all the cat's records right away, all right?"

"It don't," said Sonny, with dignity, "make any difference to me. I don't care what you listen to. Don't do me no favors."

I was beginning to realize that I'd never seen him so upset before. With another part of my mind I was thinking that this would probably turn out to be one of those things kids go through and that I shouldn't make it seem important by pushing it too hard. Still, I didn't think it would do any harm to ask: "Doesn't all this take a lot of time? Can you make a living at it?"

He turned back to me and half leaned, half sat, on the kitchen table. "Everything takes time," he said, "and—well, yes, sure, I can make a living at it. But what I don't seem to be able to make you understand is that it's the only thing I want to do."

"Well, Sonny," I said, gently, "you know people can't always do exactly what they *want* to do—"

"*No*, I don't know that," said Sonny, surprising me. "I think people *ought* to do what they want to do, what else are they alive for?"

"You getting to be a big boy," I said desperately, "it's time you started thinking about your future."

"I'm thinking about my future," said Sonny, grimly. "I think about it all the time."

I gave up. I decided, if he didn't change his mind, that we could always talk about it later. "In the meantime," I said, "you got to finish school." We had already decided that he'd have to move in with Isabel and her folks. I knew this wasn't the ideal arrangement because Isabel's folks are inclined to be dicty[1] and they hadn't especially wanted Isabel to marry me. But I didn't know what else to do. "And we have to get you fixed up at Isabel's."

There was a long silence. He moved from the kitchen table to the window. "That's a terrible idea. You know it yourself."

"Do you have a *better* idea?"

He just walked up and down the kitchen for a minute. He was as tall as I was. He had started to shave. I suddenly had the feeling that I didn't know him at all.

He stopped at the kitchen table and picked up my cigarettes. Looking at me with a kind of mocking, amused defiance, he put one between his lips. "You mind?"

"You smoking already?"

He lit the cigarette and nodded, watching me through the smoke. "I just wanted to see if I'd have the courage to smoke in front of you." He grinned and blew a great cloud of smoke to the ceiling. "It was easy." He looked at my face. "Come on, now. I bet you was smoking at my age, tell the truth."

I didn't say anything but the truth was on my face, and he laughed. But now there was something very strained in his laugh. "Sure. And I bet that ain't all you was doing."

He was frightening me a little. "Cut the crap," I said. "We already decided that you was going to go and live at Isabel's. Now what's got into you all of a sudden?"

"*You* decided it," he pointed out. "*I* didn't decide nothing." He stopped in front of me, leaning against the stove, arms loosely folded. "Look, brother. I don't want to stay in Harlem no more, I really don't." He was very earnest. He looked at me, then over toward the kitchen window. There was something in his eyes I'd never seen before, some thoughtfulness, some worry all his own. He rubbed the muscle of one arm. "It's time I was getting out of here."

"Where do you want to *go*, Sonny?"

"I want to join the army. Or the navy, I don't care. If I say I'm old enough, they'll believe me."

Then I got mad. It was because I was so scared. "You must be crazy. You god-damn fool, what the hell do you want to go and join the *army* for?"

"I just told you. To get out of Harlem."

"Sonny, you haven't even finished *school*. And if you really want to be a musician, how do you expect to study if you're in the *army*?"

He looked at me, trapped, and in anguish. "There's ways. I might be able to work out some kind of deal. Anyway, I'll have the G.I. Bill when I come out."

"*If* you come out." We stared at each other. "Sonny, please. Be reasonable. I know the setup is far from perfect. But we got to do the best we can."

"I ain't learning nothing in school," he said. "Even when I go." He turned away

---

[1] **dicty:** Snobbish or bossy.

from me and opened the window and threw his cigarette out into the narrow alley. I watched his back. "At least, I ain't learning nothing you'd want me to learn." He slammed the window so hard I thought the glass would fly out, and turned back to me. "And I'm sick of the stink of these garbage cans!"

"Sonny," I said, "I know how you feel. But if you don't finish school now, you're going to be sorry later that you didn't." I grabbed him by the shoulders. "And you only got another year. It ain't so bad. And I'll come back and I swear I'll help you do *whatever* you want to do. Just try to put up with it till I come back. Will you please do that? For me?"

He didn't answer and he wouldn't look at me.

"Sonny. You hear me?"

He pulled away. "I hear you. But you never hear anything *I* say."

I didn't know what to say to that. He looked out of the window and then back at me. "OK," he said, and sighed. "I'll try."

Then I said, trying to cheer him up a little, "They got a piano at Isabel's. You can practice on it."

And as a matter of fact, it did cheer him up for a minute. "That's right," he said to himself. "I forgot that." His face relaxed a little. But the worry, the thoughtfulness, played on it still, the way shadows play on a face which is staring into the fire.

But I thought I'd never hear the end of that piano. At first, Isabel would write me, saying how nice it was that Sonny was so serious about his music and how, as soon as he came in from school, or wherever he had been when he was supposed to be at school, he went straight to that piano and stayed there until suppertime. And, after supper, he went back to that piano and stayed there until everybody went to bed. He was at the piano all day Saturday and all day Sunday. Then he bought a record player and started playing records. He'd play one record over and over again, all day long sometimes, and he'd improvise along with it on the piano. Or he'd play one section of the record, one chord, one change, one progression, then he'd do it on the piano. Then back to the record. Then back to the piano.

Well, I really don't know how they stood it. Isabel finally confessed that it wasn't like living with a person at all, it was like living with sound. And the sound didn't make any sense to her, didn't make any sense to any of them—naturally. They began, in a way, to be afflicted by this presence that was living in their home. It was as though Sonny were some sort of god, or monster. He moved in an atmosphere which wasn't like theirs at all. They fed him and he ate, he washed himself, he walked in and out of their door; he certainly wasn't nasty or unpleasant or rude, Sonny isn't any of those things; but it was as though he were all wrapped up in some cloud, some fire, some vision all his own; and there wasn't any way to reach him.

At the same time, he wasn't really a man yet, he was still a child, and they had to watch out for him in all kinds of ways. They certainly couldn't throw him out. Neither did they dare to make a great scene about that piano because even they dimly sensed, as I sensed, from so many thousands of miles away, that Sonny was at that piano playing for his life.

But he hadn't been going to school. One day a letter came from the school board and Isabel's mother got it—there had, apparently, been other letters but Sonny had torn them up. This day, when Sonny came in, Isabel's mother showed him the letter and asked where he'd been spending his time. And she finally got it out of him that he'd been down in Greenwich Village, with musicians and other characters, in a white girl's apartment. And this scared her and she started to scream at him and what came up, once she began—though she denies it to this day—was what sacrifices they were making to give Sonny a decent home and how little he appreciated it.

Sonny didn't play the piano that day. By evening, Isabel's mother had calmed down but then there was the old man to deal with, and Isabel herself. Isabel says she did her best to be calm but she broke down and started crying. She says she just watched Sonny's face. She could tell, by watching him, what was happening with him. And what was happening was that they penetrated his cloud, they had reached him. Even if their fingers had been a thousand times more gentle than human fingers ever are, he could hardly help feeling that they had stripped him naked and were spitting on that nakedness. For he also had to see that his presence, that music, which was life or death to him, had been torture for them and that they had endured it, not at all for his sake, but only for mine. And Sonny couldn't take that. He can take it a little better today than he could then but he's still not very good at it and, frankly, I don't know anybody who is.

The silence of the next few days must have been louder than the sound of all the music ever played since time began. One morning, before she went to work, Isabel was in his room for something and she suddenly realized that all of his records were gone. And she knew for certain that he was gone. And he was. He went as far as the navy would carry him. He finally sent me a postcard from some place in Greece and that was the first I knew that Sonny was still alive. I didn't see him any more until we were both back in New York and the war had long been over.

He was a man by then, of course, but I wasn't willing to see it. He came by the house from time to time, but we fought almost every time we met. I didn't like the way he carried himself, loose and dreamlike all the time, and I didn't like his friends, and his music seemed to be merely an excuse for the life he led. It sounded just that weird and disordered.

Then we had a fight, a pretty awful fight, and I didn't see him for months. By and by I looked him up, where he was living, in a furnished room in the Village, and I tried to make it up. But there were lots of other people in the room and Sonny just lay on his bed, and he wouldn't come downstairs with me, and he treated these other people as though they were his family and I weren't. So I got mad and then he got mad, and then I told him that he might just as well be dead as live the way he was living. Then he stood up and he told me not to worry about him any more in life, that he *was* dead as far as I was concerned. Then he pushed me to the door and the other people looked on as though nothing were happening, and he slammed the door behind me. I stood in the hallway, staring at the door. I heard somebody laugh in the room and then the tears came to my eyes. I started down the steps, whistling to keep from crying, I kept whistling to myself, *You going to need me, baby, one of these cold, rainy days.*

I read about Sonny's trouble in the spring. Little Grace died in the fall. She was a beautiful little girl. But she only lived a little over two years. She died of polio and she suffered. She had a slight fever for a couple of days, but it didn't seem like anything and we just kept her in bed. And we would certainly have called the doctor, but the fever dropped, she seemed to be all right. So we thought it had just been a cold. Then, one day, she was up, playing, Isabel was in the kitchen fixing lunch for the two boys when they'd come in from school, and she heard Grace fall down in the living room. When you have a lot of children you don't always start running when one of them falls, unless they start screaming or something. And, this time, Grace was quiet. Yet, Isabel says that when she heard that *thump* and then that silence, something happened in her to make her afraid. And she ran to the living room and there was little Grace on the floor, all twisted up, and the reason she hadn't screamed was that she couldn't get her breath. And when she did scream, it was the worst sound, Isabel says, that she'd ever heard in all her life, and she still hears it sometimes in her dreams. Isabel will sometimes wake me up with a low, moaning, strangled sound and I have to be quick to awaken her and hold her to me and where Isabel is weeping against me seems a mortal wound.

I think I may have written Sonny the very day that little Grace was buried. I was sitting in the living room in the dark, by myself, and I suddenly thought of Sonny. My trouble made his real.

One Saturday afternoon, when Sonny had been living with us, or, anyway, been in our house, for nearly two weeks, I found myself wandering aimlessly about the living room, drinking from a can of beer, and trying to work up the courage to search Sonny's room. He was out, he was usually out whenever I was home, and Isabel had taken the children to see their grandparents. Suddenly I was standing still in front of the living room window, watching Seventh Avenue. The idea of searching Sonny's room made me still. I scarcely dared to admit to myself what I'd be searching for. I didn't know what I'd do if I found it. Or if I didn't.

On the sidewalk across from me, near the entrance to a barbecue joint, some people were holding an old-fashioned revival meeting. The barbecue cook, wearing a dirty white apron, his conked hair[2] reddish and metallic in the pale sun, and a cigarette between his lips, stood in the doorway, watching them. Kids and older people paused in their errands and stood there, along with some older men and a couple of very tough-looking women who watched everything that happened on the avenue, as though they owned it, or were maybe owned by it. Well, they were watching this, too. The revival was being carried on by three sisters in black, and a brother. All they had were their voices and their Bibles and a tambourine. The brother was testifying and while he testified two of the sisters stood together, seeming to say, amen, and the

---

[2] **conked hair:** Hair that has been straightened and coated heavily with grease.

third sister walked around with the tambourine outstretched and a couple of people dropped coins into it. Then the brother's testimony ended and the sister who had been taking up the collection dumped the coins into her palm and transferred them to the pocket of her long black robe. Then she raised both hands, striking the tambourine against the air, and then against one hand, and she started to sing. And the two other sisters and the brother joined in.

It was strange, suddenly, to watch, though I had been seeing these street meetings all my life. So, of course, had everybody else down there. Yet, they paused and watched and listened and I stood still at the window. "*Tis the old ship of Zion,*" they sang, and the sister with the tambourine kept a steady, jangling beat, "*it has rescued many a thousand!*" Not a soul under the sound of their voices was hearing this song for the first time, not one of them had been rescued. Nor had they seen much in the way of rescue work being done around them. Neither did they especially believe in the holiness of the three sisters and the brother, they knew too much about them, knew where they lived, and how. The woman with the tambourine, whose voice dominated the air, whose face was bright with joy, was divided by very little from the woman who stood watching her, a cigarette between her heavy, chapped lips, her hair a cuckoo's nest, her face scarred and swollen from many beatings, and her black eyes glittering like coal. Perhaps they both knew this, which was why, when, as rarely, they addressed each other, they addressed each other as Sister. As the singing filled the air the watching, listening faces underwent a change, the eyes focusing on something within; the music seemed to soothe a poison out of them; and time seemed, nearly, to fall away from the sullen, belligerent, battered faces, as though they were fleeing back to their first condition, while dreaming of their last. The barbecue cook half shook his head and smiled, and dropped his cigarette and disappeared into his joint. A man fumbled in his pockets for change and stood holding it in his hand impatiently, as though he had just remembered a pressing appointment further up the avenue. He looked furious. Then I saw Sonny, standing on the edge of the crowd. He was carrying a wide, flat notebook with a green cover, and it made him look, from where I was standing, almost like a schoolboy. The coppery sun brought out the copper in his skin, he was very faintly smiling, standing very still. Then the singing stopped, the tambourine turned into a collection plate again. The furious man dropped in his coins and vanished, so did a couple of the women, and Sonny dropped some change in the plate, looking directly at the woman with a little smile. He started across the avenue, toward the house. He has a slow, loping walk, something like the way Harlem hipsters walk, only he's imposed on this his own half-beat. I had never really noticed it before.

I stayed at the window, both relieved and apprehensive. As Sonny disappeared from my sight, they began singing again. And they were still singing when his key turned in the lock.

"Hey," he said.

"Hey, yourself. You want some beer?"

"No. Well, maybe." But he came up to the window and stood beside me, looking out. "What a warm voice," he said.

They were singing *If I could only hear my mother pray again!*

"Yes," I said, "and she can sure beat that tambourine."

"But what a terrible song," he said, and laughed. He dropped his notebook on the sofa and disappeared into the kitchen. "Where's Isabel and the kids?"

"I think they went to see their grandparents. You hungry?"

"No." He came back into the living room with his can of beer. "You want to come some place with me tonight?"

I sensed, I don't know how, that I couldn't possibly say no. "Sure. Where?"

He sat down on the sofa and picked up his notebook and started leafing through it. "I'm going to sit in with some fellows in a joint in the Village."

"You mean, you're going to play, tonight?"

"That's right." He took a swallow of his beer and moved back to the window. He gave me a sidelong look. "If you can stand it."

"I'll try," I said.

He smiled to himself and we both watched as the meeting across the way broke up. The three sisters and the brother, heads bowed, were singing *God be with you till we meet again.* The faces around them were very quiet. Then the song ended. The small crowd dispersed. We watched the three women and the lone man walk slowly up the avenue.

"When she was singing before," said Sonny, abruptly, "her voice reminded me for a minute of what heroin feels like sometimes—when it's in your veins. It makes you feel sort of warm and cool at the same time. And distant. And—and sure." He sipped his beer, very deliberately not looking at me. I watched his face. "It makes you feel—in control. Sometimes you've got to have that feeling."

"Do you?" I sat down slowly in the easy chair.

"Sometimes." He went to the sofa and picked up his notebook again. "Some people do."

"In order," I asked, "to play?" And my voice was very ugly, full of contempt and anger.

"Well"—he looked at me with great, troubled eyes, as though, in fact, he hoped his eyes would tell me things he could never otherwise say—"they *think* so. And *if* they think so—!"

"And what do *you* think?" I asked.

He sat on the sofa and put his can of beer on the floor. "I don't know," he said, and I couldn't be sure if he were answering my question or pursuing his thoughts. His face didn't tell me. "It's not so much to *play.* It's to *stand* it, to be able to make it at all. On any level." He frowned and smiled: "In order to keep from shaking to pieces."

"But these friends of yours," I said, "they seem to shake themselves to pieces pretty goddamn fast."

"Maybe." He played with the notebook. And something told me that I should curb my tongue, that Sonny was doing his best to talk, that I should listen. "But of course you only know the ones that've gone to pieces. Some don't—or at least they haven't *yet* and that's just about all *any* of us can say." He paused. "And then there are some who just live, really, in hell, and they know it and they see what's happening and they go right on. I don't know." He sighed, dropped the notebook, folded his arms. "Some guys, you can tell from the way they play, they on something *all* the time. And you can see that, well, it makes something real for them. But of course," he picked up his beer from the floor and sipped it and put the can down again, "they *want* to, too, you've got to see that. Even some of them that say they don't—*some,* not all."

"And what about you?" I asked—I couldn't help it. "What about you? Do *you* want to?"

He stood up and walked to the window and remained silent for a long time. Then he sighed. "Me," he said. Then: "While I was downstairs before, on my way here, listening to that woman sing, it struck me all of a sudden how much suffering she must have had to go through—to sing like that. It's *repulsive* to think you have to suffer that much."

I said: "But there's no way not to suffer—is there, Sonny?"

"I believe not," he said and smiled, "but that's never stopped anyone from trying." He looked at me. "Has it?" I realized, with this mocking look, that there stood between us, forever, beyond the power of time or forgiveness, the fact that I had held silence—so long!—when he had needed human speech to help him. He turned back to the window. "No, there's no way not to suffer. But you try all kinds of ways to keep from drowning in it, to keep on top of it, and to make it seem—well, like *you.* Like you did something, all right, and now you're suffering for it. You know?" I said nothing. "Well you know," he said, impatiently, "why *do* people suffer? Maybe it's better to do something to give it a reason, *any* reason."

"But we just agreed," I said, "that there's no way not to suffer. Isn't it better, then, just to—take it?"

"But nobody just takes it," Sonny cried, "that's what I'm telling you! *Everybody* tries not to. You're just hung up on the *way* some people try—it's not *your* way!"

The hair on my face began to itch, my face felt wet. "That's not true," I said, "that's not true. I don't give a damn what other people do, I don't even care how they suffer. I just care how *you* suffer." And he looked at me. "Please believe me," I said, "I don't want to see you—die—trying not to suffer."

"I won't," he said, flatly, "die trying not to suffer. At least, not any faster than anybody else."

"But there's no need," I said, trying to laugh, "is there? in killing yourself."

I wanted to say more, but I couldn't. I wanted to talk about will power and how life could be—well, beautiful. I wanted to say that it was all within; but was it? or, rather, wasn't that exactly the trouble? And I wanted to promise that I would never fail him again. But it would all have sounded—empty words and lies.

So I made the promise to myself and prayed that I would keep it.

"It's terrible sometimes, inside," he said, "that's what's the trouble. You walk these streets, black and funky and cold, and there's not really a living ass to talk to, and there's nothing shaking, and there's no way of getting it out—that storm inside. You can't talk it and you can't make love with it, and when you finally try to get with it and play it, you realize *nobody's* listening. So *you've* got to listen. You got to find a way to listen."

And then he walked away from the window and sat on the sofa again, as though all the wind had suddenly been knocked out of him. "Sometimes you'll do *anything* to play, even cut your mother's throat." He laughed and looked at me. "Or your brother's." Then he sobered. "Or your own." Then: "Don't worry. I'm all right now and I think I'll *be* all right. But I can't forget—where I've been. I don't mean just the physical place I've been, I mean where I've *been*. And *what* I've been."

"What have you been, Sonny?" I asked.

He smiled—but sat sideways on the sofa, his elbow resting on the back, his fingers playing with his mouth and chin, not looking at me. "I've been something I didn't recognize, didn't know I could be. Didn't know anybody could be." He stopped, looking inward, looking helplessly young, looking old. "I'm not talking about it now because I feel *guilty* or anything like that—maybe it would be better if I did, I don't know. Anyway, I can't really talk about it. Not to you, not to anybody," and now he turned and faced me. "Sometimes, you know, and it was actually when I was most *out* of the world, I felt that I was in it, that I was *with* it, really, and I could play or I didn't really have to *play,* it just came out of me, it was there. And I don't know how I played, thinking about it now, but I know I did awful things, those times, sometimes, to people. Or it wasn't that I *did* anything to them—it was that they weren't real." He picked up the beer can; it was empty; he rolled it between his palms: "And other times—well, I needed a fix, I needed to find a place to lean, I needed to clear a space to *listen*—and I couldn't find it, and I—went crazy, I did terrible things to *me,* I was terrible *for* me." He began pressing the beer can between his hands, I watched the metal begin to give. It glittered, as he played with it, like a knife, and I was afraid he would cut himself, but I said nothing. "Oh well. I can never tell you. I was all by myself at the bottom of something, stinking and sweating and crying and shaking, and I smelled it, you know? *my* stink, and I thought I'd die if I couldn't get away from it and yet, all the same, I knew that everything I was doing was just locking me in with it. And I didn't know," he paused, still flattening the beer can, "I didn't know, I still *don't* know, something kept telling me that maybe it was good to smell your own stink, but I didn't think that *that* was what I'd been trying to do—and—who can stand it?" and he abruptly dropped the ruined beer can, looking at me with a small, still smile, and then rose, walking to the window as though it were the lodestone rock. I watched his face, he watched the avenue, "I couldn't tell you when Mama died—but the reason I wanted to leave Harlem so bad was to get away from drugs. And then, when I ran away, that's what I was running from—really. When I came back, nothing had changed, *I* hadn't changed, I was just—older." And he stopped, drumming with his fingers on the windowpane. The sun had vanished, soon darkness would fall. I watched his face. "It can come again," he said, almost as though speaking to himself. Then he turned to me. "It can come again," he repeated. "I just want you to know that."

"All right," I said, at last. "So it can come again. All right."

He smiled, but the smile was sorrowful. "I had to try to tell you," he said.

"Yes," I said. "I understand that."

"You're my brother," he said, looking straight at me, and not smiling at all.

"Yes," I repeated, "yes. I understand that."

He turned back to the window, looking out. "All that hatred down there," he said, "all that hatred and misery and love. It's a wonder it doesn't blow the avenue apart."

We went to the only nightclub on a short, dark street, downtown. We squeezed through the narrow, chattering, jam-packed bar to the entrance of the big room, where the bandstand was. And we stood there for a moment, for the lights were very dim in this room and we couldn't see. Then, "Hello, boy," said a voice and an enormous black man, much older than Sonny or myself, erupted out of all that atmospheric lighting and put an arm around Sonny's shoulder. "I been sitting right here," he said, "waiting for you."

He had a big voice, too, and heads in the darkness turned toward us.

Sonny grinned and pulled a little away, and said, "Creole, this is my brother. I told you about him."

Creole shook my hand. "I'm glad to meet you, son," he said, and it was clear that he was glad to meet me *there,* for Sonny's sake. And he smiled, "You got a real musician in *your* family," and he took his arm from Sonny's shoulder and slapped him, lightly, affectionately, with the back of his hand.

"Well. Now I've heard it all," said a voice behind us. This was another musician, and a friend of Sonny's, a coal-black, cheerful-looking man, built close to the ground. He immediately began confiding to me, at the top of his lungs, the most terrible things about Sonny, his teeth gleaming like a lighthouse and his laugh coming up out of him like the beginning of an earthquake. And it turned out that everyone at the bar knew Sonny, or almost everyone; some were musicians, working there, or nearby, or not working, some were simply hangers-on, and some were there to hear Sonny play. I was introduced to all of them and they were all very polite to me. Yet, it was clear that, for them, I was only Sonny's brother. Here, I was in Sonny's world. Or, rather: his kingdom. Here, it was not even a question that his veins bore royal blood.

They were going to play soon and Creole installed me, by myself, at a table in a dark corner. Then I watched them, Creole, and the little black man, and Sonny, and the others, while they horsed around, standing just below the bandstand. The light from the bandstand spilled just a little short of them and, watching them laughing and gesturing and moving about, I had the feeling that they, nevertheless, were being most careful not to step into that circle of light too suddenly: that if they moved into the light too suddenly, without thinking, they would perish in flame. Then, while I watched, one of them, the small, black man, moved into the light and crossed the bandstand and started fooling around with his drums. Then—being funny and being, also, extremely ceremonious—Creole took Sonny by the arm and led him to the piano. A woman's voice called Sonny's name and a few hands started clapping. And Sonny, also being funny and being ceremonious, and so touched, I think, that he could have cried, but neither hiding it nor showing it, riding it like a man, grinned, and put both hands to his heart and bowed from the waist.

Creole then went to the bass fiddle and a lean, very bright-skinned brown man jumped up on the bandstand and picked up his horn. So there they were, and the atmosphere on the bandstand and in the room began to change and tighten. Someone stepped up to the microphone and announced them. Then there were all kinds of murmurs. Some people at the bar shushed others. The waitress ran around, frantically getting in the last orders, guys and chicks got closer to each other, and the lights on the bandstand, on the quartet, turned to a kind of indigo. Then they all looked different there. Creole looked about him for the last time, as though he were making certain that all his chickens were in the coop, and then he—jumped and struck the fiddle. And there they were.

All I know about music is that not many people ever really hear it. And even then, on the rare occasions when something opens within, and the music enters, what we mainly hear, or hear corroborated, are personal, private, vanishing evocations. But the man who creates the music is hearing something else, is dealing with the roar rising from the void and imposing order on it as it hits the air. What is evoked in him, then, is of another order, more terrible because it has no words, and triumphant, too, for that same reason. And his triumph, when he triumphs, is ours. I just watched Sonny's face. His face was troubled, he was working hard, but he wasn't with it. And I had the feeling that, in a way, everyone on the bandstand was waiting for him, both waiting for him and pushing him along. But as I began to watch Creole, I realized that it was Creole who held them all back. He had them on a short rein. Up there, keeping the beat with his whole body, wailing on the fiddle, with his eyes half closed, he was listening to everything, but he was listening to Sonny. He was having a dialogue with Sonny. He wanted Sonny to leave the shoreline and strike out for the deep water. He was Sonny's witness that deep water and drowning were not the same thing—he had been there, and he knew. And he wanted Sonny to know. He was waiting for Sonny to do the things on the keys which would let Creole know that Sonny was in the water.

And, while Creole listened, Sonny moved, deep within, exactly like someone in torment. I had never before thought of how awful the relationship must be between the musician and his instrument. He has to fill it, this instrument, with the breath of life, his own. He has to make it do what he wants it to do. And a piano is just a piano. It's made out of so much wood and wires and little hammers and big ones, and ivory. While there's only so much you can do with it, the only way to find this out is to try; to try and make it do everything.

And Sonny hadn't been near a piano for over a year. And he wasn't on much better terms with his life, not the life that stretched before him now. He and the piano stammered, started one way, got scared, stopped; started another way, panicked, marked time, started again; then seemed to have found a direction, panicked again, got stuck. And the face I saw on Sonny I'd never seen before. Everything had been burned out of it, and, at the same time, things usually hidden were being burned in, by the fire and fury of the battle which was occurring in him up there.

Yet, watching Creole's face as they neared the end of the first set, I had the feeling that something had happened, something I hadn't heard. Then they finished, there was scattered applause, and then, without an instant's warning, Creole started into something else, it was almost sardonic, it was *Am I Blue*. And, as though he commanded, Sonny began to play. Something began to happen. And Creole let out the reins. The dry, low, black man said something awful on the drums, Creole answered, and the drums talked back. Then the horn insisted, sweet and high, slightly detached perhaps, and Creole listened, commenting now and then, dry, and driving, beautiful and calm and old. Then they all came together again, and Sonny was part of the family again. I could tell this from his face. He seemed to have found, right there beneath his fingers, a damn brand-new piano. It seemed that he couldn't get over it. Then, for awhile, just being happy with Sonny, they seemed to be agreeing with him that brand-new pianos certainly were a gas.

Then Creole stepped forward to remind them that what they were playing was the blues. He hit something in all of them, he hit something in me, myself, and the music tightened and deepened, apprehension began to beat the air. Creole began to tell us what the blues were all about. They were not about anything very new. He and his boys up there were keeping it new, at the risk of ruin, destruction, madness, and death, in order to find new ways to make us listen. For, while the tale of how we suffer, and how we are delighted, and how we may triumph is never new, it always must be heard. There isn't any other tale to tell, it's the only light we've got in all this darkness.

And this tale, according to that face, that body, those strong hands on those strings, has another aspect in every country, and a new depth in every generation. Listen, Creole seemed to be saying, listen. Now these are Sonny's blues. He made the little black man on the drums know it, and the bright, brown man on the horn. Creole wasn't trying any longer to get Sonny in the water. He was wishing him Godspeed. Then he stepped back, very slowly, filling the air with the immense suggestion that Sonny speak for himself.

Then they all gathered around Sonny and Sonny played. Every now and again one of them seemed to say, amen. Sonny's fingers filled the air with life, his life. But that life contained so many others. And Sonny went all the way back, he really began with the spare, flat statement of the opening phrase of the song. Then he began to make it his. It was very beautiful because it wasn't hurried and it was no longer a lament. I seemed to hear with what burning he had made it his, with what burning we had yet to make it ours, how we could cease lamenting. Freedom lurked around us and I understood, at last, that he could help us to be free if we would listen, that he would never be free until we did. Yet, there was no battle in his face now. I heard what he had gone through, and would continue to go through until he came to rest in earth. He had made it his: that long line, of which we knew only Mama and Daddy. And he was giving it back, as everything must be given back, so that, passing through death, it can live forever. I saw my mother's face again, and felt, for the first time, how the stones of the road she had walked on must have bruised her feet. I saw the moonlit road where my father's brother died. And it brought something else back to me, and carried me past it, I saw my little girl again and felt Isabel's tears again, and I felt my own tears begin to rise. And I was yet aware that this was only a moment, that the world waited outside, as hungry as a tiger, and that trouble stretched above us, longer than the sky.

Then it was over. Creole and Sonny let out their breath, both soaking wet, and grinning. There was a lot of applause and some of it was real. In the dark, the girl came by and I asked her to take drinks to the bandstand. There was a long pause, while they talked up there in the indigo light and after awhile I saw the girl put a Scotch and milk on top of the piano for Sonny. He didn't seem to notice it, but just before they started playing again, he sipped from it and looked toward me, and nodded. Then he put it back on top of the piano. For me, then, as they began to play again, it glowed and shook above my brother's head like the very cup of trembling.

Imagining Africa

Book 6 begins with Joseph Conrad's **Heart of Darkness**, a story about Africa written at the turn of the century that depicts Africa from a white European perspective. Even though Conrad's novel may offer a more sympathetic treatment of Africa than that found in the Tarzan stories of Edgar Rice Burroughs (1875–1950), written at about the same time, *Heart of Darkness* is nonetheless, as Chinua Achebe demonstrates in **"An Image of Africa,"** a distorted, one-sided view, an imperial perspective that constructs Africa as a savage continent in need of civilizing and Christianizing. It is black to Europe's white; dark instead of light. It is violent, wild, Other. Africa, identified by modern anthropologists as the site of *Homo sapiens'* first emergence, was not thought of at the turn of the century as a homeland. The West traced its origins to Greece and Rome, not to Cairo and Timbuktu. Many colonized blacks and those of the DIASPORA living in Europe and America absorbed this Eurocentric point of view, and as they denigrated Africa, they denied their heritage and themselves. **W. E. B. Du Bois** describes this phenomenon in **The Souls of Black Folk** as the African American "double-consciousness," a state in which the African is in conflict with the American. Along with many other black writers of the twentieth century, Du Bois sought to heal this racial self-alienation by changing the Western image of Africa, challenging the colonial oppression that supported it, and celebrating a positive account of African heritage.

p. 35

p. 107

doo-BOYZ

p. 861

PAN-AFRICANISM

By affirming his own African heritage and encouraging other blacks to do the same, Du Bois allied himself with a movement later called

Aaron Douglas, *Into Bondage*, 1936. Oil on canvas *Douglas, an artist of the Harlem Renaissance, painted murals on public buildings and founded the art department at Fisk University in Nashville, Tennessee. (In the Collection of The Corcoran Gallery of Art, Museum Purchase and partial gift from Thurlow Evans Tibbs Jr., The Evans Tibbs Collection)*

One ever feels his two-ness, — an American, a Negro; two souls, two thoughts, two unreconciled strivings; two warring ideals in one dark body, whose dogged strength alone keeps it from being torn asunder.

— W. E. B. Du Bois

Pan-Africanism that was based on the idea that blacks everywhere shared a common heritage and a common destiny. Historians trace the roots of the movement back to the late eighteenth century, when Sierra Leone was established in 1787 as a refuge in west Africa for freed and runaway slaves. American abolitionists facilitated the founding of a similar state, Liberia, in the 1820s. By the mid nineteenth century some historians had begun to develop a perspective on Africa that highlighted the greatness in the African past, including the achievements of the ancient Egyptians. Yet even apologists for "the dark continent," such as Liberian author Edward Blyden (1832–1912), considered late-nineteenth-century Africa to be in a "state of barbarism." Blyden accepted a Western progressivist view of Africa and seems to echo Conrad's Marlow when he asserts: "There is not a single mental or moral deficiency now existing among Africans, . . . to which we cannot find a parallel in the past history of Europe." Blyden and his contemporaries thought that blacks who returned to Africa would bring with them the civilizing influences of the West and that these would help to transform the continent.

Du Bois, who coined the term *Pan-Negroism* to characterize his ideas, was part of a philosophical tradition that can be traced to the

Romantic nationalism of German philosopher Johann Gottfried
Herder (1744–1803). Herder, who influenced European nationalism
in such countries as Italy and Germany, described world history as
the development of groups of people bound together by language,
culture, mythology, and traditions. Du Bois sought to reconnect
blacks in the diaspora with their African heritage. He saw African
Americans as the "advance guard of the Negro people," for they had
the education and the experience of the modern world that would
enable them to lead the movement, which Du Bois considered part
of the international struggle for social justice. He organized a Pan-
African Congress in Paris in 1919 to coincide with the Versailles
peace conference that ended World War I, hoping to convince world
leaders that the Wilsonian principle of self-determination should be
applied to Africans as well as Europeans, giving Africans the power
to decide their future.

Du Bois saw the Pan-African movement as part of the larger
fight against European colonialism; his contemporary at the beginning of the century, Marcus Garvey (1887–1940), a Jamaican who
had emigrated to New York City, emphasized another dimension of
the movement — the desire of American blacks to return to the
African homeland. Known as the "Black Moses," Garvey preached
"Back to Africa" and "Africa for the Africans," leading thousands in a
march through the streets of Harlem. Few of his followers actually
returned to Africa, however, and Garvey's crusade fell apart in the
mid twenties when he was imprisoned for mail fraud.

Du Bois, however, maintained the Pan-African dream throughout his long life. He convened several Pan-African congresses in the
period between the wars, finally passing the mantle of leadership to
a younger generation, in particular to **Kwame Nkrumah** (1909–1972)
of Ghana at the fifth Pan-African Congress held in Manchester,
England, in 1945. Just after World War II, when colonies throughout
Africa were seeking independence, Nkrumah, who would become
the first prime minister of the newly independent nation of Ghana
in 1957, was the first African to lead the Pan-African movement. He
envisioned a United States of Africa, which would unite the continent and welcome back Africans from the diaspora. Although his
dream soon gave way to the more powerful forces of tribalism and
nationalism in Africa, it had in a small way a symbolic realization
when in 1961 Du Bois emigrated to Ghana.

KWAH-may
en-KROO-mah

THE HARLEM RENAISSANCE

Although Garvey's movement failed to populate Africa with black Americans, its energy, broad appeal, and positive view of Africa contributed to a cultural awakening in the States that in the arts became known as the Harlem Renaissance. Led by writers, artists, and musicians, many from the Caribbean and the American South, this movement that began in the 1920s was characterized by an affirmation of blackness, a celebration of African culture and traditions, and a search for an African heritage. Like the Romantic nationalists of nineteenth-century Europe, the writers of the Harlem Renaissance collected their people's folklore and celebrated their own culture. Du Bois wrote about the sorrow songs—the songs of the slaves—in *The Souls of Black Folk,* and James Weldon Johnson put together what is now the standard collection of Negro spirituals, songs that in p. 873 his poem **"O Black and Unknown Bards"** Johnson traces to Africa. Claude McKay, a Jamaican emigrant to Harlem, turned conventional connotations of "black" and "white" on their heads and celebrated p. 876 blackness in such poems as **"Harlem Shadows"** and **"Outcast."** p. 880 Countee Cullen's **"Heritage"** and Langston Hughes's **"The Negro** p. 878 **Speaks of Rivers"** imagine a romantic Africa. Inspired in part by the writers of the **IRISH RENAISSANCE,**[1] these poets implicitly compared their situation to that of the Irish, and like the mythic Ireland celebrated by Yeats and his fellow Irish poets, similarly looked to the past, to a time before slavery and the ravages of colonial oppression. Although none of the Harlem writers of the twenties and thirties except Du Bois actually emigrated to Africa, they made it into an "imaginary homeland" as well as a destination for the many artists, writers, and civil rights activists who traveled to Africa or settled there in the later years of the century.

NÉGRITUDE

In the influential novel *Banjo* (1929), Claude McKay's hero advises a skeptical black student to read the writers of the Irish Renaissance: "If you were sincere in your feelings about racial advancement," he

For I was born, far from my native clime, / Under the white man's menace, out of time.

– CLAUDE McKAY, "Outcast"

---

[1]Irish Renaissance: Also called the Celtic Renaissance, this movement of the late-nineteenth and early-twentieth centuries was marked by a rebirth of Irish literature that drew on Irish mythology and history and promoted the cause of Irish independence. Some of its major writers were William Butler Yeats (1865–1939; see p. 181), John Millington Synge (1871–1909), and Sean O'Casey (1880–1964).

says, "you would turn for example to whites of a different type. You would study the Irish cultural and social movement." The Irish writers had turned to Celtic mythology and Irish history as sources of ethnic identity and used their writing to promote Irish independence from British colonialism. The Harlem artists were also devoted to the cause of liberation. When blacks from the French colonies looked for writers to emulate, they discovered the Parisian avant-garde, particularly the SURREALISTS, and the writers of the Harlem Renaissance, most notably Claude McKay. The founders of the NÉGRITUDE movement in Paris in the early thirties, three students from French colonies in Africa and the Caribbean—**Léopold Sédar Senghor** (p. 884) from Senegal, **Aimé Césaire** (p. 887) from Martinique, and Léon Damas from French Guiana—set out with aims similar to those of the Harlem group. Senghor characterized McKay as their spiritual mentor, "the true inventor of Négritude," he wrote. "I speak not of the word, but of the values of Négritude. . . . Far from seeing in one's blackness an inferiority, one accepts it, one lays claim to it with pride, one cultivates it, lovingly." Senghor expressed this acceptance in poems like **"Black Woman,"** which metaphorically celebrates Africa, and **"Prayer to the Masks,"** an evocation of Senghor's African heritage. In *Notebook of a Return to the Native Land*, one of the most important works of French SURREALISM, Césaire returns to Martinique to confront its poverty, suffering, and history of slavery; by the end of the poem, in the sections presented below, he has come to accept his homeland in all its pain and suffering.

Describing Négritude poetry as "in our time, the only great revolutionary poetry," French existentialist philosopher Jean-Paul Sartre (1905–1980), in the influential essay "Black Orpheus," catalogs the themes of the poems as "exile, slavery, the Africa-Europe couple and the great . . . division of the world into black and white." He describes the map of the world imagined by the Négritude poets as composed of three circles whose centers overlap:

> . . . in the foreground—forming the first of three concentric circles—extends the land of exile, colorless Europe; then comes the dazzling circle of the Islands and of childhood; . . . the last circle is Africa, burnt, oily like a snake's skin, flickering like a flame, between being and nothingness, more *real* than the "eternal boulevards with cops" but absent, beyond attainment, disintegrating Europe with its black but invisible rays: Africa, an *imaginary* continent.

lay-oh-POHLD
say-DAR sawng-GORE;
eh-MAY seh-ZAR

p. 885
p. 886
p. 888

What would you
expect to find, when
the muzzle that has
silenced the voices
of black men is
removed? That they
would thunder your
praise? . . . For the
white man has
enjoyed for three
thousand years the
privilege of seeing
without being seen. It
was a seeing pure
and uncomplicated;
the light of his eyes
drew all things from
their primeval dark-
ness. . . . Today
these black men have
fixed their gaze upon
us and our gaze is
thrown back in our
eyes. . . . black
torches, in their turn,
light the world.

– JEAN-PAUL SARTRE

OH-kot puh-buh-TEK

Sartre saw self-conscious absorption in blackness as a stage in a dialectical process—a process of change involving a thing and its opposite—that would eventually bring about a society that transcends racial categories. Although Senghor described Négritude as an evolutionary dynamic, his categories seem fixed. He characterizes, for example, the African personality type as emotional, intuitive, physical, and creative, and the European as rational, mechanical, and mental. "Emotion is black," he asserted, "as Reason is Hellenic." For such delineations he has been criticized as an "essentialist," one who adopts the categories of nineteenth-century European racism while rejecting their valuation. Césaire, who coined the term *Négritude,* seems to have the more evolutionary notion: "My Négritude has a ground," he wrote. "It is a fact that there is a black culture: It is historical, there is nothing biological about it." By recognizing Négritude as part of a historical process and not an essential category, Césaire can choose to change history; in the existential moment of his return to Martinique, he can choose to transform suffering into celebration.

POSTCOLONIAL AFRICA

As African nations achieved political independence after World War II, there was great ambivalence regarding how much of the colonial past had to be given up in order to reach a collective psychic independence. Many Africans hoped to retain the benefits of Western culture while others argued that all traces of European influence had to be eradicated. For writers, that could mean rejecting the language in which they were educated and the language in which they wrote. Ugandan poet **Okot p'Bitek** (p. 893) captures this postcolonial predicament in two narrative poems, one written in the voice of a woman who wishes to be simply African and the other in the voice of her husband who is captivated by Western ways. The domestic argument between husband and wife becomes emblematic of the debate throughout Africa.

Many Africans have found fault with the Pan-African and Négritude movements. Since both were led by blacks in the diaspora, they appeared to some as a black imperialism that would simply replace white imperialism and continue to direct the course of Africa from outside the continent. Furthermore, in the postwar struggles for independence, many former colonies in Africa were more concerned with their national identity than with their "pan-African" connections to other nations. Négritude was criticized for its unrealistic romanticism, its failure to acknowledge the inequities and injustices within many African societies.

During the second half of the twentieth century, many African American writers made pilgrimages to decolonized Africa and continued to celebrate the dream of return, albeit with a more realistic view of the continent's difficulties. James Baldwin was prompted to skepticism, however (see p. 899). Already a resident of North Africa for some time, he attended the Conference of Black Writers held in Paris in 1956 at which Senghor called for black authors worldwide to celebrate their common culture. Baldwin asked what, beyond suffering, all blacks had in common and doubted that the African elements in his own heritage were more important than the American ones. Although some African American writers — Alice Walker, for example, in *The Color Purple* (1982) — continued to see a return to Africa as a utopian project, others recognized its difficulties and believed the real journey called for looking within. Gwendolyn Brooks (p. 902), after visiting Africa, acknowledged that the "Afrika" she sought was herself and that the continent she visited had much "work . . . to be done." In **Song of Solomon,** Toni Morrison's hero, on a quest to recover his identity, also discovers the Africa within him. Morrison transforms the motif of return into myth as her hero learns that his identity is caught up in the legend of his great-grandfather Solomon, a slave said to have flown back to Africa.

Many postcolonial African writers challenge the Romanticism of their peers both within Africa and in the diaspora. Chinweizu (p. 907) and his fellow Nigerian colleagues, for example, call for a more realistic assessment of the challenges facing Africans as they struggle for genuine independence and national identity. The desire to romanticize Africa's past and present distorts the image of Africa and misdirects efforts toward social change. Nadine Gordimer (p. 910), a white South African, believes that much, in fact, has already been achieved on the continent and suggests that African Americans must search for their identity in America, not Africa.

Since our past has been vilified by imperialism, and since an imperialist education has tried to equip us with all manner of absurd views and reactions to our past, we need to reclaim and rehabilitate our genuine past, to repossess our true and entire history in order to acquire a secure launching pad into our future.

— CHINWEIZU ET AL.

p. 904

■ CONNECTIONS

**Joseph Conrad, *Heart of Darkness*, p. 35; Chinua Achebe, "An Image of Africa,"
p. 107.** *Heart of Darkness* and Achebe's response to it, "An Image of Africa," are both
concerned with the central issue of this *In the World* section: the image of Africa in
Western, African, and African American eyes. How does Conrad's European analysis differ from Achebe's?

***In the World:* Colonialism, p. 97; *In the World:* Emancipation (Book 5).** How are the
anticolonial and independence themes that appear in much of the material in this
section related to similar themes in the *In the World* sections on colonialism and
emancipation?

James Baldwin, "Sonny's Blues," p. 830. "Sonny's Blues" is a story about African
American identity. What Sonny and his brother find they have in common could be
characterized as "African," "American," or "African American." In which category
or categories would you place their shared heritage?

■ PRONUNCIATION

Aimé Césaire: eh-MAY seh-ZAR
W. E. B. Du Bois: doo-BOYZ
Kwame Nkrumah: KWAH-may en-KROO-mah
Okot p'Bitek: OH-kot puh-buh-TEK
Léopold Sédar Senghor: lay-oh-POHLD say-DAR sawng-GORE

∾ W. E. B. DU BOIS
B. UNITED STATES, 1868–1963

W. E. B. Du Bois

*(Photographs and
Prints Division,
Schomburg Center for
Research in Black
Culture, The New
York Pulic Library,
Astor, Lenox, and
Tilden Foundations)*

William Edward Burghardt Du Bois was born in Great Barrington, Massachusetts, where he was brought up to love liberty and democracy and
was not subjected to racial discrimination. In 1885 he traveled to Fisk
University, a black college in Nashville, where he encountered a world
sharply divided between black and white. Returning to New England for
graduate studies at Harvard University, he majored in philosophy and
history and wrote a celebrated dissertation, "The Suppression of the Slave
Trade in the United States of America," in 1896. He became, in the words
of African American studies professor Cornel West, the greatest "American intellectual of African descent . . . produced in this country." Du Bois
taught at several universities, including Wilberforce and the University of
Pennsylvania, and he served for many years as the Director of Publicity
and Research for the National Association for the Advancement of Colored People (NAACP), an organization he helped to found. Among his
many important books are *The Philadelphia Negro* (1899), *The Souls of
Black Folk* (1903), *John Brown* (1909), *Black Reconstruction* (1935), and
Dusk of Dawn: An Essay Toward an Autobiography of a Race Concept
(1940). In 1961 he moved to Ghana and became a citizen two years later,
the year he died.

In the following first selection from *The Souls of Black Folk,* Du Bois analyzes the African American's "double-consciousness"—the apparently irreconcilable duality of being both American and black in which many African Americans are compelled to live. The second selection, the chapter entitled "The Sorrow Songs," discusses the artistry of slave songs and the historical situation that inspired them.

All notes are the editors'.

❧ The Souls of Black Folk

FROM CHAPTER 1

OF OUR SPIRITUAL STRIVINGS

After the Egyptian and Indian, the Greek and Roman, the Teuton and Mongolian, the Negro is a sort of seventh son, born with a veil, and gifted with second-sight in this American world,—a world which yields him no true self-consciousness, but only lets him see himself through the revelation of the other world. It is a peculiar sensation, this double-consciousness, this sense of always looking at one's self through the eyes of others, of measuring one's soul by the tape of a world that looks on in amused contempt and pity. One ever feels his two-ness,—an American, a Negro; two souls, two thoughts, two unreconciled strivings; two warring ideals in one dark body, whose dogged strength alone keeps it from being torn asunder.

The history of the American Negro is the history of this strife,—this longing to attain self-conscious manhood, to merge his double self into a better and truer self. In this merging he wishes neither of the older selves to be lost. He would not Africanize America, for America has too much to teach the world and Africa. He would not bleach his Negro soul in a flood of white Americanism, for he knows that Negro blood has a message for the world. He simply wishes to make it possible for a man to be both a Negro and an American, without being cursed and spit upon by his fellows, without having the doors of Opportunity closed roughly in his face.

This, then, is the end of his striving: to be a co-worker in the kingdom of culture, to escape both death and isolation, to husband and use his best powers and his latent genius. These powers of body and mind have in the past been strangely wasted, dispersed, or forgotten. The shadow of a mighty Negro past flits through the tale of Ethiopia the Shadowy and of Egypt the Sphinx. Throughout history, the powers of single black men flash here and there like falling stars, and die sometimes before the world has rightly gauged their brightness. Here in America, in the few days since Emancipation, the black man's turning hither and thither in hesitant and doubtful striving has often made his very strength to lose effectiveness, to seem like absence of power, like weakness. And yet it is not weakness,—it is the contradiction of double aims. The double-aimed struggle of the black artisan—on the one hand to escape white contempt for a nation of mere hewers of wood and drawers of water, and on the other hand to plough and nail and dig for a poverty-stricken horde— could only result in making him a poor craftsman, for he had but half a heart in either cause. By the poverty and ignorance of his people, the Negro minister or doctor was tempted toward quackery and demagogy; and by the criticism of the other world, toward ideals that made him ashamed of his lowly tasks. The would-be black *savant* was confronted by the paradox that the knowledge his people needed was a twice-told tale to his white neighbors, while the knowledge which would teach the white world was Greek to his own flesh and blood. The innate love of harmony and beauty that set the ruder souls of his people a-dancing and a-singing raised but confusion and doubt in the soul of the black artist; for the beauty revealed to him was the soul-beauty of a race which his larger audience despised, and he could not articulate the message of another people. This waste of double aims, this seeking to satisfy two unreconciled ideals, has wrought sad havoc with the courage and faith and deeds of ten thousand thousand people,—has sent them often wooing false gods and invoking false means of salvation, and at times has even seemed about to make them ashamed of themselves. . . .

The first decade was merely a prolongation of the vain search for freedom, the boon that seemed ever barely to elude their grasp,—like a tantalizing will-o'-the-wisp, maddening and misleading the headless host. The holocaust of war, the terrors of the Ku-Klux Klan, the lies of carpet-baggers, the disorganization of industry, and the contradictory advice of friends and foes, left the bewildered serf with no new watchword beyond the old cry for freedom. As the time flew, however, he began to grasp a new idea. The ideal of liberty demanded for its attainment powerful means, and these the Fifteenth Amendment gave him. The ballot, which before he had looked upon as a visible sign of freedom, he now regarded as the chief means of gaining and perfecting the liberty with which war had partially endowed him. And why not? Had not votes made war and emancipated millions? Had not votes enfranchised the freedmen? Was anything impossible to a power that had done all this? A million black men started with renewed zeal to vote themselves into the kingdom. So the decade flew away, the revolution of 1876 came, and left the half-free serf weary, wondering, but still inspired. Slowly but steadily, in the following years, a new vision began gradually to replace the dream of political power,—a powerful movement, the rise of another ideal to guide the unguided, another pillar of fire by night after a clouded day. It was the ideal of "book-learning"; the curiosity, born of compulsory ignorance, to know and test the power of the cabalistic letters of the white man, the longing to know. Here at last seemed to have been discovered the mountain path to Canaan; longer than the highway of Emancipation and law, steep and rugged, but straight, leading to heights high enough to overlook life.

Up the new path the advance guard toiled, slowly, heavily, doggedly; only those who have watched and guided the faltering feet, the misty minds, the dull understandings, of the dark pupils of these schools know how faithfully, how piteously, this people strove to learn. It was weary work. The cold statistician wrote down the inches of progress here and there, noted also where here and there a foot had slipped or some one had fallen. To the tired climbers, the horizon was ever dark, the mists were often cold, the Canaan was always dim and far away. If, however, the vistas disclosed as yet no goal, no resting-place, little but flattery and criticism, the journey at least gave leisure for reflection and self-examination; it changed the child of Emancipation to the youth with dawning self-consciousness, self-realization, self-respect.

In those sombre forests of his striving his own soul rose before him, and he saw himself,—darkly as through a veil; and yet he saw in himself some faint revelation of his power, of his mission. He began to have a dim feeling that, to attain his place in the world, he must be himself, and not another. For the first time he sought to analyze the burden he bore upon his back, that dead-weight of social degradation partially masked behind a half-named Negro problem. He felt his poverty; without a cent, without a home, without land, tools, or savings, he had entered into competition with rich, landed, skilled neighbors. To be a poor man is hard, but to be a poor race in a land of dollars is the very bottom of hardships. He felt the weight of his ignorance,—not simply of letters, but of life, of business, of the humanities; the accumulated sloth and shirking and awkwardness of decades and centuries shackled his hands and feet. Nor was his burden all poverty and ignorance. The red stain of bastardy, which two centuries of systematic legal defilement of Negro women had stamped upon his race, meant not only the loss of ancient African chastity, but also the hereditary weight of a mass of corruption from white adulterers, threatening almost the obliteration of the Negro home.

A people thus handicapped ought not to be asked to race with the world, but rather allowed to give all its time and thought to its own social problems. But alas! while sociologists gleefully count his bastards and his prostitutes, the very soul of the toiling, sweating black man is darkened by the shadow of a vast despair. Men call the shadow prejudice, and learnedly explain it as the natural defence of culture against barbarism, learning against ignorance, purity against crime, the "higher" against the "lower" races. To which the Negro cries Amen! and swears that to so much of this strange prejudice as is founded on just homage to civilization, culture, righteousness, and progress, he humbly bows and meekly does obeisance. But before that nameless prejudice that leaps beyond all this he stands helpless, dismayed, and wellnigh speechless; before that personal disrespect and mockery, the ridicule and systematic humiliation, the distortion of fact and wanton license of fancy, the cynical ignoring of the better and the boisterous welcoming of the worse, the all-pervading desire to inculcate disdain for everything black, from Toussaint[1] to the devil,— before this there rises a sickening despair that would disarm and discourage any nation save that black host to whom "discouragement" is an unwritten word.

But the facing of so vast a prejudice could not but bring the inevitable selfquestioning, self-disparagement, and lowering of ideals which ever accompany repression and breed in an atmosphere of contempt and hate. Whisperings and portents came borne upon the four winds: Lo! we are diseased and dying, cried the dark hosts; we cannot write, our voting is vain; what need of education, since we must always cook and serve? And the Nation echoed and enforced this self-criticism, saying: Be content to be servants, and nothing more; what need of higher culture for half-men? Away with the black man's ballot, by force or fraud,—and behold the suicide of a race! Nevertheless, out of the evil came something of good,—the more

---

[1]**Toussaint:** Toussaint Louverture (1743?–1803), a freed slave who became a general and liberator of Haiti in the 1790s. Arrested by the French in 1802, he died in prison only to become a symbol of freedom and the struggle for independence.

careful adjustment of education to real life, the clearer perception of the Negroes' social responsibilities, and the sobering realization of the meaning of progress.

So dawned the time of *Sturm und Drang:*[2] storm and stress today rocks our little boat on the mad waters of the world-sea; there is within and without the sound of conflict, the burning of body and rending of soul; inspiration strives with doubt, and faith with vain questionings. The bright ideals of the past, — physical freedom, political power, the training of brains and the training of hands, — all these in turn have waxed and waned, until even the last grows dim and overcast. Are they all wrong, — all false? No, not that, but each alone was over-simple and incomplete, — the dreams of a credulous race-childhood, or the fond imaginings of the other world which does not know and does not want to know our power. To be really true, all these ideals must be melted and welded into one. The training of the schools we need today more than ever, — the training of deft hands, quick eyes and ears, and above all the broader, deeper, higher culture of gifted minds and pure hearts. The power of the ballot we need in sheer self-defence, — else what shall save us from a second slavery? Freedom, too, the long-sought, we still seek, — the freedom of life and limb, the freedom to work and think, the freedom to love and aspire. Work, culture, liberty, — all these we need, not singly but together, not successively but together, each growing and aiding each, and all striving toward that vaster ideal that swims before the Negro people, the ideal of human brotherhood, gained through the unifying ideal of Race; the ideal of fostering and developing the traits and talents of the Negro, not in opposition to or contempt for other races, but rather in large conformity to the greater ideals of the American Republic, in order that some day on American soil two world-races may give each to each those characteristics both so sadly lack. We the darker ones come even now not altogether empty-handed: There are today no truer exponents of the pure human spirit of the Declaration of Independence than the American Negroes; there is no true American music but the wild sweet melodies of the Negro slave; the American fairy tales and folk-lore are Indian and African; and, all in all, we black men seem the sole oasis of simple faith and reverence in a dusty desert of dollars and smartness. Will America be poorer if she replace her brutal dyspeptic blundering with lighthearted but determined Negro humility? or her coarse and cruel wit with loving jovial good-humor? or her vulgar music with the soul of the Sorrow Songs?

Merely a concrete test of the underlying principles of the great republic is the Negro Problem, and the spiritual striving of the freedmen's sons is the travail of souls whose burden is almost beyond the measure of their strength, but who bear it in the name of an historic race, in the name of this the land of their fathers' fathers, and in the name of human opportunity.

And now what I have briefly sketched in large outline let me on coming pages tell again in many ways, with loving emphasis and deeper detail, that men may listen to the striving in the souls of black folk.

---

[2] *Sturm und Drang:* Storm and stress; refers to a period of intense literary activity in the late eighteenth century associated with idealism and the revolt against stale convention. The movement, named after a play about the American Revolution, is associated with Goethe, Rousseau, and Schiller.

CHAPTER 14

The Sorrow Songs

I walk through the churchyard
*   To lay this body down;*
I know moon-rise, I know star-rise;
I walk in the moonlight, I walk in the starlight;
I'll lie in the grave and stretch out my arms,
I'll go to judgment in the evening of the day,
And my soul and thy soul shall meet that day,
*   When I lay this body down.*
                                                    — Negro Song

They that walked in darkness sang songs in the olden days—Sorrow Songs—for they were weary at heart. And so before each thought that I have written in this book I have set a phrase, a haunting echo of these weird old songs in which the soul of the black slave spoke to men. Ever since I was a child these songs have stirred me strangely. They came out of the South unknown to me, one by one, and yet at once I knew them as of me and of mine. Then in after years when I came to Nashville I saw the great temple builded of these songs towering over the pale city. To me Jubilee Hall seemed ever made of the songs themselves, and its bricks were red with the blood and dust of toil. Out of them rose for me morning, noon, and night, bursts of wonderful melody, full of the voices of my brothers and sisters, full of the voices of the past.

Little of beauty has America given the world save the rude grandeur God himself stamped on her bosom; the human spirit in this new world has expressed itself in vigor and ingenuity rather than in beauty. And so by fateful chance the Negro folk-song—the rhythmic cry of the slave—stands today not simply as the sole American music, but as the most beautiful expression of human experience born this side the seas. It has been neglected, it has been, and is, half despised, and above all it has been persistently mistaken and misunderstood; but notwithstanding, it still remains as the singular spiritual heritage of the nation and the greatest gift of the Negro people.

Away back in the thirties the melody of these slave songs stirred the nation, but the songs were soon half forgotten. Some, like "Near the lake where drooped the willow," passed into current airs and their source was forgotten; others were caricatured on the "minstrel" stage and their memory died away. Then in war-time came the singular Port Royal experiment after the capture of Hilton Head, and perhaps for the first time the North met the Southern slave face to face and heart to heart with no third witness. The Sea Islands of the Carolinas, where they met, were filled with a black folk of primitive type, touched and moulded less by the world about them than any others outside the Black Belt. Their appearance was uncouth, their language funny, but their hearts were human and their singing stirred men with a mighty power. Thomas Wentworth Higginson hastened to tell of these songs, and Miss McKim and others urged upon the world their rare beauty. But the world listened only half credulously until the Fisk Jubilee Singers sang the slave songs so deeply into the world's heart that it can never wholly forget them again.

There was once a blacksmith's son born at Cadiz, New York, who in the changes of time taught school in Ohio and helped defend Cincinnati from Kirby Smith. Then he fought at Chancellorsville and Gettysburg and finally served in the Freedman's Bureau at Nashville. Here he formed a Sunday-school class of black children in 1866, and sang with them and taught them to sing. And then they taught him to sing, and when once the glory of the Jubilee songs passed into the soul of George L. White, he knew his life-work was to let those Negroes sing to the world as they had sung to him. So in 1871 the pilgrimage of the Fisk Jubilee Singers began. North to Cincinnati they rode,—four half-clothed black boys and five girl-women,—led by a man with a cause and a purpose. They stopped at Wilberforce, the oldest of Negro schools, where a black bishop blessed them. Then they went, fighting cold and starvation, shut out of hotels, and cheerfully sneered at, ever northward; and ever the magic of their song kept thrilling hearts, until a burst of applause in the Congregational Council at Oberlin revealed them to the world. They came to New York and Henry Ward Beecher dared to welcome them, even though the metropolitan dailies sneered at his "Nigger Minstrels." So their songs conquered till they sang across the land and across the sea, before Queen and Kaiser, in Scotland and Ireland, Holland and Switzerland. Seven years they sang, and brought back a hundred and fifty thousand dollars to found Fisk University.

Since their day they have been imitated—sometimes well, by the singers of Hampton and Atlanta, sometimes ill, by straggling quartettes. Caricature has sought again to spoil the quaint beauty of the music, and has filled the air with many debased melodies which vulgar ears scarce know from the real. But the true Negro folk-song still lives in the hearts of those who have heard them truly sung and in the hearts of the Negro people.

What are these songs, and what do they mean? I know little of music and can say nothing in technical phrase, but I know something of men, and knowing them, I know that these songs are the articulate message of the slave to the world. They tell us in these eager days that life was joyous to the black slave, careless and happy. I can easily believe this of some, of many. But not all the past South, though it rose from the dead, can gainsay the heart-touching witness of these songs. They are the music of an unhappy people, of the children of disappointment; they tell of death and suffering and unvoiced longing toward a truer world, of misty wanderings and hidden ways.

The songs are indeed the siftings of centuries; the music is far more ancient than the words, and in it we can trace here and there signs of development. My grandfather's grandmother was seized by an evil Dutch trader two centuries ago; and coming to the valleys of the Hudson and Housatonic, black, little, and lithe, she shivered and shrank in the harsh north winds, looked longingly at the hills, and often crooned a heathen melody to the child between her knees, thus:

Do ba - na co - ba, ge - ne   me, ge - ne me !

Do ba - na co - ba, ge - ne   me, ge - ne me !

Ben d' nu – li, nu – li, nu – li, nu – li, ben d'   le.

The child sang it to his children and they to their children's children, and so two hundred years it has travelled down to us and we sing it to our children, knowing as little as our fathers what its words may mean, but knowing well the meaning of its music.

This was primitive African music; it may be seen in larger form in the strange chant which heralds "The Coming of John":

> *"You may bury me in the East,*
> *You may bury me in the West,*
> *But I'll hear the trumpet sound in that morning,"*

—the voice of exile.

Ten master songs, more or less, one may pluck from this forest of melody—songs of undoubted Negro origin and wide popular currency, and songs peculiarly characteristic of the slave. One of these I have just mentioned. Another whose strains begin this book is "Nobody knows the trouble I've seen." When, struck with a sudden poverty, the United States refused to fulfil its promises of land to the freedmen, a brigadier-general went down to the Sea Islands to carry the news. An old woman on the outskirts of the throng began singing this song; all the mass joined with her, swaying. And the soldier wept.

The third song is the cradle-song of death which all men know,—"Swing low, sweet chariot,"—whose bars begin the life story of "Alexander Crummell." Then there is the song of many waters, "Roll, Jordan, roll," a mighty chorus with minor cadences. There were many songs of the fugitive like that which opens "The Wings of Atalanta," and the more familiar "Been a-listening." The seventh is the song of the End and the Beginning—"My Lord, what a mourning! when the stars begin to fall"; a strain of this is placed before "The Dawn of Freedom." The song of groping—"My way's cloudy"—

begins "The Meaning of Progress"; the ninth is the song of this chapter—"Wrestlin' Jacob, the day is a-breaking,"—a pæan of hopeful strife. The last master song is the song of songs—"Steal away,"—sprung from "The Faith of the Fathers."

There are many others of the Negro folk-songs as striking and characteristic as these, as, for instance, the three strains in the third, eighth, and ninth chapters; and others I am sure could easily make a selection on more scientific principles. There are, too, songs that seem to me a step removed from the more primitive types: There is the maze-like medley, "Bright sparkles," one phrase of which heads "The Black Belt"; the Easter carol, "Dust, dust and ashes"; the dirge, "My mother's took her flight and gone home"; and that burst of melody hovering over "The Passing of the First-Born"—"I hope my mother will be there in that beautiful world on high."

These represent a third step in the development of the slave song, of which "You may bury me in the East" is the first, and songs like "March on" and "Steal away" are the second. The first is African music, the second Afro-American, while the third is a blending of Negro music with the music heard in the foster land. The result is still distinctively Negro and the method of blending original, but the elements are both Negro and Caucasian. One might go further and find a fourth step in this develop-ment, where the songs of white America have been distinctively influenced by the slave songs or have incorporated whole phrases of Negro melody, as "Swanee River" and "Old Black Joe." Side by side, too, with the growth has gone the debasements and imitations—the Negro "minstrel" songs, many of the "gospel" hymns, and some of the contemporary "coon" songs,—a mass of music in which the novice may easily lose himself and never find the real Negro melodies.

In these songs, I have said, the slave spoke to the world. Such a message is natu-rally veiled and half articulate. Words and music have lost each other and new and cant phrases of a dimly understood theology have displaced the older sentiment. Once in a while we catch a strange word of an unknown tongue, as the "Mighty Myo," which figures as a river of death; more often slight words or mere doggerel are joined to music of singular sweetness. Purely secular songs are few in number, partly because many of them were turned into hymns by a change of words, partly because the frolics were seldom heard by the stranger, and the music less often caught. Of nearly all the songs, however, the music is distinctly sorrowful. The ten master songs I have mentioned tell in word and music of trouble and exile, of strife and hiding; they grope toward some unseen power and sigh for rest in the End.

The words that are left to us are not without interest, and, cleared of evident dross, they conceal much of real poetry and meaning beneath conventional theology and unmeaning rhapsody. Like all primitive folk, the slave stood near to Nature's heart. Life was a "rough and rolling sea" like the brown Atlantic of the Sea Islands; the "Wilderness" was the home of God, and the "lonesome valley" led to the way of life. "Winter'll soon be over," was the picture of life and death to a tropical imagina-tion. The sudden wild thunder-storms of the South awed and impressed the Negroes,—at times the rumbling seemed to them "mournful," at times imperious:

> *"My Lord calls me,*
> *He calls me by the thunder,*
> *The trumpet sounds it in my soul."*

The monotonous toil and exposure is painted in many words. One sees the ploughmen in the hot, moist furrow, singing:

"Dere's no rain to wet you,
Dere's no sun to burn you,
Oh, push along, believer,
I want to go home."

The bowed and bent old man cries, with thrice-repeated wail:

"O Lord, keep me from sinking down,"

and he rebukes the devil of doubt who can whisper:

"Jesus is dead and God's gone away."

Yet the soul-hunger is there, the restlessness of the savage, the wail of the wanderer, and the plaint is put in one little phrase:

Over the inner thoughts of the slaves and their relations one with another the shadow of fear ever hung, so that we get but glimpses here and there, and also with them, eloquent omissions and silences. Mother and child are sung, but seldom father; fugitive and weary wanderer call for pity and affection, but there is little of wooing and wedding; the rocks and the mountains are well known, but home is unknown. Strange blending of love and helplessness sings through the refrain:

"Yonder's my ole mudder,
Been waggin' at de hill so long;
'Bout time she cross over,
Git home bime-by."

Elsewhere comes the cry of the "motherless" and the "Farewell, farewell, my only child."

Love-songs are scarce and fall into two categories—the frivolous and light, and the sad. Of deep successful love there is ominous silence, and in one of the oldest of these songs there is a depth of history and meaning:

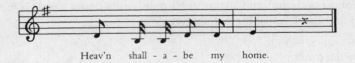

Heav'n   shall - a - be   my   home.

A black woman said of the song, "It can't be sung without a full heart and a troubled sperrit." The same voice sings here that sings in the German folk-song:

"Jetz Geh i' an's brunele, trink' aber net."

Of death the Negro showed little fear, but talked of it familiarly and even fondly as simply a crossing of the waters, perhaps—who knows?—back to his ancient forests again. Later days transfigured his fatalism, and amid the dust and dirt the toiler sang:

"Dust, dust and ashes, fly over my grave,
But the Lord shall bear my spirit home."

The things evidently borrowed from the surrounding world undergo character-istic change when they enter the mouth of the slave. Especially is this true of Bible phrases. "Weep, O captive daughter of Zion," is quaintly turned into "Zion, weep-a-low," and the wheels of Ezekiel are turned every way in the mystic dreaming of the slave, till he says:

"There's a little wheel a-turnin' in-a-my heart."

As in olden time, the words of these hymns were improvised by some leading minstrel of the religious band. The circumstances of the gathering, however, the rhythm of the songs, and the limitations of allowable thought, confined the poetry for the most part to single or double lines, and they seldom were expanded to quat-rains or longer tales, although there are some few examples of sustained efforts, chiefly paraphrases of the Bible. Three short series of verses have always attracted me,—the one that heads this chapter, of one line of which Thomas Wentworth Hig-ginson has fittingly said, "Never, it seems to me, since man first lived and suffered was his infinite longing for peace uttered more plaintively." The second and third are descriptions of the Last Judgment,—the one a late improvisation, with some traces of outside influence:

"Oh, the stars in the elements are falling,
And the moon drips away into blood,
And the ransomed of the Lord are returning unto God,
Blessed be the name of the Lord."

And the other earlier and homelier picture from the low coast lands:

"Michael, haul the boat ashore,
Then you'll hear the horn they blow,
Then you'll hear the trumpet sound,
Trumpet sound the world around,
Trumpet sound for rich and poor,

Trumpet sound the Jubilee,
Trumpet sound for you and me."

Through all the sorrow of the Sorrow Songs there breathes a hope—a faith in the ultimate justice of things. The minor cadences of despair change often to triumph and calm confidence. Sometimes it is faith in life, sometimes a faith in death, sometimes assurance of boundless justice in some fair world beyond. But whichever it is, the meaning is always clear: that sometime, somewhere, men will judge men by their souls and not by their skins. Is such a hope justified? Do the Sorrow Songs sing true?

The silently growing assumption of this age is that the probation of races is past, and that the backward races of today are of proven inefficiency and not worth the saving. Such an assumption is the arrogance of peoples irreverent toward Time and ignorant of the deeds of men. A thousand years ago such an assumption, easily possible, would have made it difficult for the Teuton to prove his right to life. Two thousand years ago such dogmatism, readily welcome, would have scouted the idea of blond races ever leading civilization. So woefully unorganized is sociological knowledge that the meaning of progress, the meaning of "swift" and "slow" in human doing, and the limits of human perfectability, are veiled, unanswered sphinxes on the shores of science. Why should Æschylus have sung two thousand years before Shakespeare was born? Why has civilization flourished in Europe, and flickered, flamed, and died in Africa? So long as the world stands meekly dumb before such questions, shall this nation proclaim its ignorance and unhallowed prejudices by denying freedom of opportunity to those who brought the Sorrow Songs to the Seats of the Mighty?

Your country? How came it yours? Before the Pilgrims landed we were here. Here we have brought our three gifts and mingled them with yours: a gift of story and song—soft, stirring melody in an ill-harmonized and unmelodious land; the gift of sweat and brawn to beat back the wilderness, conquer the soil, and lay the foundations of this vast economic empire two hundred years earlier than your weak hands could have done it; the third, a gift of the Spirit. Around us the history of the land has centred for thrice a hundred years; out of the nation's heart we have called all that was best to throttle and subdue all that was worst; fire and blood, prayer and sacrifice, have billowed over this people, and they have found peace only in the altars of the God of Right. Nor has our gift of the Spirit been merely passive. Actively we have woven ourselves with the very warp and woof of this nation,—we fought their battles, shared their sorrow, mingled our blood with theirs, and generation after generation have pleaded with a headstrong, careless people to despise not Justice, Mercy, and Truth, lest the nation be smitten with a curse. Our song, our toil, our cheer, and warning have been given to this nation in blood-brotherhood. Are not these gifts worth the giving? Is not this work and striving? Would America have been America without her Negro people?

Even so is the hope that sang in the songs of my fathers well sung. If somewhere in this whirl and chaos of things there dwells Eternal Good, pitiful yet masterful, then anon in His good time America shall rend the Veil and the prisoned shall go free. Free, free as the sunshine trickling down the morning into these high windows of mine, free as yonder fresh young voices welling up to me from the caverns of brick and mortar below—swelling with song, instinct with life, tremulous treble and darkening bass. My children, my little children, are singing to the sunshine, and thus they sing:

Let us cheer the wea - ry trav - el - ler,

Cheer the wea - ry trav - el - ler, Let us

cheer the wea - ry trav - el - ler A -

- long the heav - en - ly way.

And the traveller girds himself, and sets his face toward the Morning, and goes his way.

JAMES WELDON JOHNSON
B. UNITED STATES, 1871–1938

Born in Jacksonville, Florida, into a supportive middle-class environment, James Weldon Johnson was educated at Atlanta University, Columbia University, and the Boston Conservatory of Music. He undertook and excelled in a variety of jobs — teacher, school principal, lawyer, journalist, official of the National Association for the Advancement of Colored People, lobbyist, and diplomat. A talented writer, Johnson produced the novel *Autobiography of an Ex-Colored Man* in 1912 and three collections of poetry in his lifetime. He is best known perhaps for his poem "Lift Every Voice and Sing" (1900), later called "the Black National Anthem." In "O Black and Unknown Bards" (1930) Johnson invokes the ancestral African poets whose genius was passed down to the anonymous poets who composed the slave songs of America.

All notes are the editors'.

O Black and Unknown Bards

O black and unknown bards of long ago,
How came your lips to touch the sacred fire?
How, in your darkness, did you come to know
The power and beauty of the minstrel's lyre?
Who first from midst his bonds lifted his eyes?
Who first from out the still watch, lone and long,
Feeling the ancient faith of prophets rise
Within his dark-kept soul, burst into song?

Heart of what slave poured out such melody
10   As "Steal away to Jesus"?[1] On its strains
His spirit must have nightly floated free,
Though still about his hands he felt his chains.
Who heard great "Jordan roll"? Whose starward eye
Saw chariot "swing low"? And who was he
That breathed that comforting, melodic sigh,
"Nobody knows de trouble I see"?

What merely living clod, what captive thing,
Could up toward God through all its darkness grope,

---

[1] **"Steal away to Jesus"**: The titles in this stanza and in stanza four are of various Negro spirituals.

20   And find within its deadened heart to sing
These songs of sorrow, love and faith, and hope?
How did it catch that subtle undertone,
That note in music heard not with the ears?
How sound the elusive reed so seldom blown,
Which stirs the soul or melts the heart to tears.

Not that great German master[2] in his dream
Of harmonies that thundered amongst the stars
At the creation, ever heard a theme
Nobler than "Go down, Moses." Mark its bars
How like a mighty trumpet-call they stir
30   The blood. Such are the notes that men have sung
Going to valorous deeds; such tones there were
That helped make history when Time was young.

There is a wide, wide wonder in it all,
That from degraded rest and servile toil
The fiery spirit of the seer should call
These simple children of the sun and soil.
O black slave singers, gone, forgot, unfamed,
You—you alone, of all the long, long line
Of those who've sung untaught, unknown, unnamed,
40   Have stretched out upward, seeking the divine.

You sang not deeds of heroes or of kings;
No chant of bloody war, no exulting pean
Of arms-won triumphs; but your humble strings
You touched in chord with music empyrean.
You sang far better than you knew; the songs
That for your listeners' hungry hearts sufficed
Still live,—but more than this to you belongs:
You sang a race from wood and stone to Christ.

---

[2] German master: Probably German composer Ludwig van Beethoven (1770–1827).

CLAUDE McKAY
b. Jamaica, 1889–1948

Claude McKay began writing poems in Caribbean dialect while still a child. Recognized by the Jamaican Institute of Arts and Sciences for two volumes of poetry he published in 1912, McKay was awarded a scholarship to study in the United States. After two years of studying agriculture at Tuskegee Institute and Kansas State University, McKay went to New York, where he became a writer and editor for radical journals. His most important collection of poems, *Harlem Shadows* (1922), was published at the beginning of the Harlem Renaissance. His short and very intense lyric poetry is technically conservative, following English literary forms, but politically radical: McKay was the most militant writer of the Harlem Renaissance.

McKay left New York in 1923, living abroad in France, Britain, and North Africa, where he published several novels including *Home to Harlem* (1928) and *Banjo* (1929). In identifying McKay as the spiritual founder of the Négritude movement, Léopold Senghor said,

> Claude McKay can rightfully be considered the true inventor of Négritude. I speak not of the word, but of the values of Négritude. . . . Far from seeing in one's blackness an inferiority, one accepts it, one lays claim to it with pride, one cultivates it lovingly.

McKay's novel *Banjo* was particularly influential for the Négritude writers, who responded to its frank and affirmative treatment of blackness.

James L. Allen,
Claude McKay
McKay wrote novels
and short stories as
well as poetry.
*(Photographs and
Print Division,
Schomburg Center for
Research in Black
Culture, The New
York Public Library,
Astor, Lenox, and
Tilden Foundations)*

To the White Fiends

Think you I am not fiend and savage too?
Think you I could not arm me with a gun
And shoot down ten of you for every one
Of my black brothers murdered, burnt by you?
Be not deceived, for every deed you do
I could match — out-match: am I not Afric's son,
Black of that black land where black deeds are done?
But the Almighty from the darkness drew
My soul and said: Even thou shalt be a light
Awhile to burn on the benighted earth,
Thy dusky face I set among the white
For thee to prove thyself of higher worth;
Before the world is swallowed up in night,
To show thy little lamp: go forth, go forth!

10

Harlem Shadows

I hear the halting footsteps of a lass
    In Negro Harlem when the night lets fall
Its veil. I see the shapes of girls who pass
    To bend and barter at desire's call.
Ah, little dark girls who in slippered feet
Go prowling through the night from street to street!

Through the long night until the silver break
    Of day the little gray feet know no rest;
Through the lone night until the last snow-flake
10   Has dropped from heaven upon the earth's white breast,
The dusky, half-clad girls of tired feet
Are trudging, thinly shod, from street to street.

Ah, stern harsh world, that in the wretched way
    Of poverty, dishonor and disgrace,
Has pushed the timid little feet of clay,
    The sacred brown feet of my fallen race!
Ah, heart of me, the weary, weary feet
In Harlem wandering from street to street.

Outcast

For the dim regions whence my fathers came
My spirit, bondaged by the body, longs.
Words felt, but never heard, my lips would frame;
My soul would sing forgotten jungle songs.
I would go back to darkness and to peace,
But the great western world holds me in fee,
And I may never hope for full release
While to its alien gods I bend my knee.
Something in me is lost, forever lost,
10 Some vital thing has gone out of my heart,
And I must walk the way of life a ghost
Among the sons of earth, a thing apart.

For I was born, far from my native clime,
Under the white man's menace, out of time.

❧ LANGSTON HUGHES
B. *UNITED STATES, 1902–1967*

Langston Hughes was born and raised in the Midwest, influenced by such writers as Paul Lawrence Dunbar and Carl Sandburg. After attending Columbia University briefly in 1922, he left school and worked his way across the Atlantic to Europe and Africa on a freighter. His first book of poems, *The Weary Blues* (1925), reveals his fascination with jazz and the blues as well as the spirituals of his youth. Besides twelve volumes of poetry, Hughes wrote novels, plays, essays, and historical works. He is perhaps best known for his short stories, many of which are included in a late collection, *I Wonder as I Wander* (1956). Known for his generosity and his support of many younger writers, Hughes defended the right of young black authors "to express our dark-skinned selves without fear or shame." An early star of the Harlem Renaissance, Hughes dedicated "The Negro Speaks of Rivers" to W. E. B. Du Bois. In that poem Hughes traces his heritage by associating the Mississippi, the river near his childhood home in St. Louis, with rivers in Africa and the Middle East.

William H. Johnson, *Jitterbugs,* 1940–45. Oil on plywood *Johnson, a painter during the Harlem Renaissance, was known for his renderings of black New York nightlife. Jazz figured greatly in his work, as it did in the poetry of his friend Langston Hughes. (Smithsonian American Art Museum, Washington, DC/ Art Resource, NY)*

877

The Negro Speaks of Rivers

I've known rivers:
I've known rivers ancient as the world and older than the flow of human
    blood in human veins.

My soul has grown deep like the rivers.

I bathed in the Euphrates when dawns were young.
I built my hut near the Congo and it lulled me to sleep.
I looked upon the Nile[1] and raised the pyramids above it.

I heard the singing of the Mississippi when Abe Lincoln went down to New
    Orleans, and I've seen its muddy bosom turn all golden in the sunset.

I've known rivers:
Ancient, dusky rivers.

My soul has grown deep like the rivers.

---

[1] **Euphrates . . . Nile:** The Euphrates River flows through the ancient kingdom of Babylon, from present-day Turkey through Syria and Iraq; the Congo flows through the Republic of Congo in central Africa into the Atlantic Ocean; the Nile runs through Egypt into the Mediterranean Sea. [Editors' note.]

The Weary Blues

Droning a drowsy syncopated tune,
Rocking back and forth to a mellow croon,
    I heard a Negro play.
Down on Lenox Avenue the other night
By the pale dull pallor of an old gas light
    He did a lazy sway . . .
    He did a lazy sway . . .
To the tune o' those Weary Blues.
With his ebony hands on each ivory key
He made that poor piano moan with melody.
    O Blues!
Swaying to and fro on his rickety stool
He played that sad raggy tune like a musical fool.
    Sweet Blues!
Coming from a black man's soul.
    O Blues!
In a deep song voice with a melancholy tone

I heard that Negro sing, that old piano moan —
    "Ain't got nobody in all this world,
20   Ain't got nobody but ma self.
    I's gwine to quit ma frownin'
    And put ma troubles on the shelf."
Thump, thump, thump, went his foot on the floor.
He played a few chords then he sang some more —
    "I got the Weary Blues
    And I can't be satisfied.
    Got the Weary Blues
    And can't be satisfied —
    I ain't happy no mo'
30   And I wish that I had died."
And far into the night he crooned that tune.
    The stars went out and so did the moon.
    The singer stopped playing and went to bed
    While the Weary Blues echoed through his head.
    He slept like a rock or a man that's dead.

Jazzonia

Oh, silver tree!
Oh, shining rivers of the soul!

In a Harlem cabaret
Six long-headed jazzers play.
A dancing girl whose eyes are bold
Lifts high a dress of silken gold.

Oh, singing tree!
Oh, shining rivers of the soul!

Were Eve's eyes
10 In the first garden
Just a bit too bold?
Was Cleopatra gorgeous
In a gown of gold?

Oh, shining tree!
Oh, silver rivers of the soul!

In a whirling cabaret
Six long-headed jazzers play.

Yet do I marvel at this curious thing: / To make a poet black, and bid him sing!

— COUNTEE CULLEN

Countee Cullen, the adopted son of a Methodist minister living in New York, earned a B.A. at New York University and an M.A. at Harvard before returning to teach school in New York City. As with many writers of the Harlem Renaissance, Cullen's first collection of poems, reflecting the energies of the group, was his strongest. After *Color* was published in 1925, Cullen served as the editor of the important black magazine *Opportunity*, and his poems appeared in many periodicals. Like the work of Claude McKay, Cullen's verse is formally traditional but at the same time intense and political. The last line of "Yet Do I Marvel" was a watchword among the early writers of the Harlem Renaissance.

All notes are the editors'.

∾ Heritage

For Harold Jackman

What is Africa to me:
Copper sun or scarlet sea,
Jungle star or jungle track,
Strong bronzed men, or regal black
Women from whose loins I sprang
When the birds of Eden sang?
One three centuries removed
From the scenes his fathers loved,
Spicy grove, cinnamon tree,
What is Africa to me?

So I lie, who all day long
Want no sound except the song
Sung by wild barbaric birds
Goading massive jungle herds,
Juggernauts of flesh that pass
Trampling tall defiant grass
Where young forest lovers lie,
Plighting troth beneath the sky.
So I lie, who always hear,
Though I cram against my ear
Both my thumbs, and keep them there,
Great drums throbbing through the air.
So I lie, whose fount of pride,

Dear distress, and joy allied.
Is my somber flesh and skin,
With the dark blood dammed within
Like great pulsing tides of wine
That, I fear, must burst the fine
Channels of the chafing net
30   Where they surge and foam and fret.
Africa? A book one thumbs
Listlessly, till slumber comes.
Unremembered are her bats
Circling through the night, her cats
Crouching in the river reeds,
Stalking gentle flesh that feeds
By the river brink; no more
Does the bugle-throated roar
Cry that monarch claws have leapt
40   From the scabbards where they slept.
Silver snakes that once a year
Doff the lovely coats you wear,
Seek no covert in your fear
Lest a mortal eye should see;
What's your nakedness to me?
Here no leprous flowers rear
Fierce corollas in the air;
Here no bodies sleek and wet,
Dripping mingled rain and sweat,
50   Tread the savage measures of
Jungle boys and girls in love.
What is last year's snow to me,
Last year's anything? The tree
Budding yearly must forget
How its past arose or set—
Bough and blossom, flower, fruit,
Even what shy bird with mute
Wonder at her travail there,
Meekly labored in its hair.
60   *One three centuries removed*
From the scenes his fathers loved,
Spicy grove, cinnamon tree,
What is Africa to me?

So I lie, who find no peace
Night or day, no slight release
From the unremittant beat
Made by cruel padded feet

Walking through my body's street.
Up and down they go, and back,
70   Treading out a jungle track.
So I lie, who never quite
Safely sleep from rain at night—
I can never rest at all
When the rain begins to fall;
Like a soul gone mad with pain
I must match its weird refrain;
Ever must I twist and squirm,
Writhing like a baited worm,
While its primal measures drip
80   Through my body, crying, "Strip!
Doff this new exuberance.
Come and dance the Lover's Dance!"
In an old remembered way
Rain works on me night and day.

Quaint, outlandish heathen gods
Black men fashion out of rods,
Clay, and brittle bits of stone,
In a likeness like their own,
My conversion came high-priced;
90   I belong to Jesus Christ,
Preacher of humility,
Heathen gods are naught to me.

Father, Son, and Holy Ghost,
So I make an idle boast;
Jesus of the twice-turned cheek,
Lamb of God, although I speak
With my mouth thus, in my heart
Do I play a double part.
Ever at Thy glowing altar
100   Must my heart grow sick and falter,
Wishing He I served were black,
Thinking then it would not lack
Precedent of pain to guide it,
Let who would or might deride it;
Surely then this flesh would know
Yours had borne a kindred woe.
Lord, I fashion dark gods, too,
Daring even to give You
Dark despairing features where,

110 Crowned with dark rebellious hair,
Patience wavers just so much as
Mortal grief compels, while touches
Quick and hot, of anger, rise
To smitten cheek and weary eyes.
Lord, forgive me if my need
Sometimes shapes a human creed.
All day long and all night through,
One thing only must I do:
Quench my pride and cool my blood,
120 *Lest I perish in the flood,*
Lest a hidden ember set
Timber that I thought was wet
Burning like the dryest flax,
Melting like the merest wax,
Lest the grave restore its dead.
Not yet has my heart or head
In the least way realized
They and I are civilized.

∾ Yet Do I Marvel

I doubt not God is good, well-meaning, kind,
And did He stoop to quibble could tell why
The little buried mole continues blind,
Why flesh that mirrors Him must some day die,
Make plain the reason tortured Tantalus[1]
Is baited by the fickle fruit, declare
If merely brute caprice dooms Sisyphus[2]
To struggle up a never-ending stair.
Inscrutable His ways are, and immune
10 To catechism by a mind too strewn
With petty cares to slightly understand
What awful brain compels his awful hand.
Yet do I marvel at this curious thing:
To make a poet black, and bid him sing!

---

[1] Tantalus: In Greek mythology, Tantalus is a king who stole food from the gods and divulged divine secrets. He was punished in Hades by being offered food and drink that is always just beyond his reach.

[2] Sisyphus: In Greek mythology, Sisyphus is a king who did not show proper respect for the gods. He was punished in Hades by having to roll a heavy stone up a hill only to have it roll down again as he reaches the top. (See p. 757.)

LÉOPOLD SÉDAR SENGHOR

B. SENEGAL, 1906–2001

Léopold Sédar Senghor, the son of a wealthy Catholic merchant, was born in 1906 in Joal, a predominantly Muslim port town in Senegal. As a child, Senghor received a traditional African education as well as a formal introduction to European culture. Eventually, he completed his education, first at the Lycée Louis le Grand and later at the Sorbonne. In Paris Senghor joined with other French-speaking African and Caribbean writers, including Aimé Césaire (b. 1913) from Martinique, to lay the foundations of what would become known as the Négritude movement. Together Senghor, Césaire, and Léon Damas founded *Black Student* (*L'Éudiant noir*), a journal exploring questions of race and celebrating African culture. After obtaining the equivalent of a master's degree from the Sorbonne in 1932 with a thesis on Baudelaire, Senghor went on to become the first African to receive the prestigious *agrégation,* a fellowship for advanced study in France, for which he had to become a French citizen.

Senghor's teaching career was interrupted by World War II; he fought on the northern front and was captured by the Germans in 1940. While in the prison camps, Senghor wrote many of the poems that would later appear in *Shadow Songs* (*Chants d'ombre,* 1945) and *Black Hosts* (*Hosties noires,* 1948). Released in 1942, Senghor returned to teaching and in 1944 became the Professor of African Languages at the École Nationale de la France d'Outre Mer (National School of the Overseas French Territories). After the war Senghor entered a new phase of his career, publishing *Chants d'ombre* and being elected to the French Constituent Assembly as a deputy for Senegal.

Starting in his student years, Senghor wrote for and organized the then-burgeoning Négritude movement. In addition to founding the short-lived journal *L'Étudiant noir,* Senghor helped to found two other journals, *The Human Condition* (*Condition humaine*) and *African Presence* (*Présence Africaine*). Throughout his career, Senghor's writings celebrated Africa's cultural heritage and attempted to promote a new view of African culture and society.

In 1948, the year he published his second collection of poetry, *Hosties noires,* Senghor also published *Anthology of the New Black and Madagascan Poetry* (*Anthologie de la nouvelle poésie nègre et malgache*) with a preface by Jean-Paul Sartre. Sartre's introduction to the groundbreaking work that brought together works of French-speaking black writers articulated for the first time the constituent features of Négritude and its historical and cultural importance. *Songs for Naett* (*Chants pour Naëtt*), Senghor's third volume of poetry, appeared in 1949; his next book of poems, *Ethiopiques,* would not appear until 1960, as he devoted much time and energy to politics. In the forties and fifties, Senghor founded several political parties and sat on various political committees. Representing the interests of Senegal in particular and French Africa in general, Senghor attempted to reshape the relationship between France and its colonies into one of an equal balance of power. After Senegal finally won its independence in 1960, Senghor was elected president of that nation, holding the position until 1981 when he retired.

In the selection that follows, Senghor's definition of Négritude comes from his essay "Pierre Teilhard de Chardin et la Politique Africaine" ("Pierre Teilhard de Chardin and African Politics"), published in 1962.

All notes are the editors'.

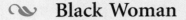 Négritude

Translated by John Reed and Clive Wake

It is time to define this word which so lends itself to polemical and to contradictory interpretations. Quite simply, *négritude* is the *sum total of the values of the civilization of the African world.* It is not racialism, it is culture. It is the embracing and domination of a situation in order to apprehend the cosmos by the process of coming to terms with it. Because it is a symbiosis of particular determinisms . . . geographical and ethnic . . . *négritude* is rooted in these and takes from them the color of its original style. But historically, it does this in order to transcend these, as life transcends the matter from which it arises. This Teilhardian[1] concept of *négritude* was not however at the outset, in the years from 1928 to 1935, to be our own. *Négritude* as we had then begun to conceive and define it was a weapon of defense and attack and inspiration rather than an instrument of construction. Of its values we held on only to those which were opposed to the values of Europe, to the reason which is discursive, logical, instrumental, chrematistic. *Négritude* then was intuitive reason, reason which is embrace and not reason which is eye. More precisely, it was *the communal warmth, the image-symbol and the cosmic rhythm which instead of dividing and sterilizing, unified and made fertile.*

---

[1] Teilhardian: Refers to Pierre Teilhard de Chardin (1881–1955), Jesuit philosopher and scientist who promulgated an evolutionary theory of the development of the collective spiritual consciousness of mankind and of the earth itself.

Black Woman

Translated by Melvin Dixon

Naked woman, black woman
Dressed in your color[1] that is life, in your form that is beauty!
I grew up in your shadow. The softness of your hands
Shielded my eyes, and now at the height of Summer and Noon,

---

[1] your color: Both the green of the African landscape and the black of the woman's skin.

From the crest of a charred hilltop I discover you, Promised Land[2]
And your beauty strikes my heart like an eagle's lightning flash.

Naked woman, dark woman
Ripe fruit with firm flesh, dark raptures of black wine,
Mouth that gives music to my mouth
10   Savanna of clear horizons, savanna quivering to the fervent caress
Of the the East Wind,[3] sculptured tom-tom, stretched drumskin
Moaning under the hands of the conqueror
Your deep contralto voice is the spiritual song of the Beloved.

Naked woman, dark woman
Oil no breeze can ripple, oil soothing the thighs
Of athletes and the thighs of the princes of Mali[4]
Gazelle with celestial limbs, pearls are stars
Upon the night of your skin. Delight of the mind's riddles,
The reflections of red gold from your shimmering skin
20   In the shade of your hair, my despair
Lightens in the close suns of your eyes.

Naked woman, black woman
I sing your passing beauty and fix it for all Eternity
before jealous Fate reduces you to ashes to nourish the roots of life.

---

[2] **Promised Land:** An allusion to the land promised to the exiled Israelites in the Book of Exodus.

[3] **East Wind:** The Hamattan, a wind that blows across Senegal between November and April from the Sahara Desert to the northeast.

[4] **Mali:** African nation east of Senegal that has roots in the ancient African kingdom of Mali.

❧ Prayer to the Masks

Translated by Melvin Dixon

Masks![1] O Masks!
Black mask, red mask, you white-and-black masks
Masks of the four cardinal points where the Spirit blows
I greet you in silence!
And you, not the least of all, Ancestor with the lion head.[2]
You keep this place safe from women's laughter
And any wry, profane smiles

---

[1] **Masks!:** African ancestral masks, kept in a sacred place and believed to contain the spirits of ancestors who provide protection for the living.

[2] **Ancestor with the lion head:** The lion is the totem animal, the symbolic emblem, of the Senghor family.

You exude the immortal air where I inhale
The breath of my Fathers.
10 Masks with faces without masks, stripped of every dimple
And every wrinkle
You created this portrait, my face leaning
On an altar of blank paper
And in your image, listen to me!
The Africa of empires is dying—it is the agony
Of a sorrowful princess
And Europe, too, tied to us at the navel.
Fix your steady eyes on your oppressed children
Who give their lives like the poor man his last garment.
20 Let us answer "present" at the rebirth of the World
As white flour cannot rise without the leaven.
Who else will teach rhythm to the world
Deadened by machines and cannons?
Who will sound the shout of joy at daybreak to wake orphans and the dead?
Tell me, who will bring back the memory of life
To the man of gutted hopes?
They call us men of cotton, coffee, and oil
They call us men of death.
But we are men of dance, whose feet get stronger
30 As we pound upon firm ground.

∾ AIMÉ CÉSAIRE
B. MARTINIQUE, 1913

Poet, playwright, and politician from the island of Martinique in the French Caribbean, Césaire brings a MODERNIST perspective to bear on the themes of decolonization, Western racism, and negritude. Educated in France in the 1930s, Césaire was influenced by the French modernists, particularly André Breton and the SURREALISTS. In Paris he also met Léopold Sédar Senghor from Senegal and Léon Gotran Damas from Guiana; together they founded the NÉGRITUDE movement, which sought to counter European racism with positive meanings for blackness. After World War II Césaire was elected mayor of Fort-de-France, the capital of Martinique, and deputy to the French Assembly, in which role he fought for anticolonialist causes until he retired from politics in 1993. Césaire's long poem *Notebook of a Return to the Native Land* (*Cahier d'un retour au pays natal*, 1939; English translation, 1947) became the manifesto and masterwork of the Négritude movement. It is also one of the most important works of French surrealism. The selection presented here is taken from the

I say right on! The old negritude / progressively cadavers itself / the horizon breaks, recoils and expands / and through the shredding of clouds the flashing of a sign / the slave ship cracks everywhere . . .

— AIMÉ CÉSAIRE,
*Notebook of a Return
to the Native Land*

end of the poem where Césaire accepts and celebrates his race, his heritage, and his identity. Earlier in the poem, he has cataloged the poverty and misery of his native land, the cruelty and brutality of slavery, and the debased sense of self that he and his countrymen have adopted.

An excerpt from Césaire's reworking of Shakespeare's *The Tempest* appears in *In the World:* Colonialism (see p. 137).

All notes are the editors' unless otherwise marked.

FROM

 # Notebook of a Return to the Native Land

Translated by Clayton Eshleman and Annette Smith

And my special geography too; the world map made for my own use, not tinted with the arbitrary colors of scholars, but with the geometry of my spilled blood, I accept both the determination of my biology, not a prisoner to a facial angle, to a type of hair, to a well-flattened nose, to a clearly Melanian coloring, and negritude, no longer a cephalic index, or plasma, or soma, but measured by the compass of
suffering
and the Negro every day more base, more cowardly, more sterile, less profound, more spilled out of himself, more separated from himself, more wily with himself, less immediate to himself,

I accept, I accept it all

and far from the palatial sea that foams beneath the suppurating syzygy[1] of blisters, miraculously lying in the despair of my arms the body of my country, its bones shocked and, in its veins, the blood hesitating like a drop of vegetal milk at the injured point of the bulb . . .

Suddenly now strength and life assail me like a bull and the water of life overwhelms the papilla[2] of the morne, now all the veins and veinlets are bustling with new blood and the enormous breathing lung of cyclones and the fire hoarded in volcanoes and the gigantic seismic pulse which now beats the measure of a living body in my firm conflagration.

And we are standing now, my country and I, hair in the wind, my hand puny in its enormous fist and now the strength is not in us but above us, in a voice that drills the night and the hearing like the penetrance of an apocalyptic wasp.[3] And the voice

---

[1] suppurating syzygy: The festering tides.

[2] papilla: Nipple.

[3] apocalyptic wasp: Like the plagues suffered by the Israelites in Egypt. See Exodus, Ch. 5–11.

proclaims that for centuries Europe has force-fed us with lies and bloated us with pestilence,
for it is not true that the work of man is done
that we have no business being on earth
that we parasite the world
that it is enough for us to heel to the world
where the work has only begun
and man still must overcome all the interdictions wedged in the recesses of his fervor and no race has a monopoly on beauty, on intelligence, on strength

and there is room for everyone at the convocation of conquest and we know now that the sun turns around our earth lighting the parcel designated by our will alone and that every star falls from sky to earth at our omnipotent command.

I now see the meaning of this trial by the sword: my country is the "lance of night" of my Bambara[4] ancestors. It shrivels and its point desperately retreats toward the haft when it is sprinkled with chicken blood and it says that its nature requires the blood of man, his fat, his liver, his heart, not chicken blood.

And I seek for my country not date hearts, but men's hearts which, in order to enter the silver cities through the great trapezoidal gate, beat with warrior blood, and as my eyes sweep my kilometers of paternal earth I number its sores almost joyfully and I pile one on top of the other like rare species, and my total is ever lengthened by unexpected mintings of baseness.

And there are those who will never get over not being made in the likeness of God but of the devil, those who believe that being a nigger is like being a second-class clerk; waiting for a better deal and upward mobility; those who beat the drum of compromise in front of themselves, those who live in their own dungeon pit; those who drape themselves in proud pseudomorphosis;[5] those who say to Europe: "You see, I *can* bow and scrape, like you I pay my respects, in short, I am no different from you; pay no attention to my black skin: the sun did it."

And there is the nigger pimp, the nigger askari,[6] and all the zebras shaking themselves in various ways to get rid of their stripes in a dew of fresh milk. And in the midst of all that I say right on! my grandfather dies, I say right on! the old negritude progressively cadavers itself.

No question about it: he was a good nigger. The Whites say he was a good nigger, a really good nigger, massa's good ole darky. I say right on!

He was a good nigger, indeed,
poverty had wounded his chest and back and they had stuffed into his poor brain

---

[4] **Bambara:** An ethnic group in Mali. The ritual referred to is one in which human blood is sprinkled on spears to make them effective.

[5] **pseudomorphosis:** A false personality.

[6] **askari:** The Swahili term in East Africa for African colonial soldiers.

that a fatality impossible to trap weighed on him; that he had no control over his own fate; that an evil Lord had for all eternity inscribed Thou Shall Not in his pelvic constitution; that he must be a good nigger; must sincerely believe in his worthlessness, without any perverse curiosity to check out the fatidic hieroglyphs.

He was a very good nigger

and it never occurred to him that he could hoe, burrow, cut anything, anything else really than insipid cane

He was a very good nigger.

And they threw stones at him, bits of scrap iron, broken bottles, but neither these stones, nor this scrap iron, nor these bottles . . . O peaceful years of God on this terraqueous clod!

and the whip argued with the bombilation[7] of the flies over the sugary dew of our sores.

I say right on! The old negritude
progressively cadavers itself
the horizon breaks, recoils and expands
and through the shredding of clouds the flashing of a sign
the slave ship cracks everywhere . . . Its belly convulses and resounds . . . The
ghastly tapeworm of its cargo gnaws the fetid guts of the strange suckling of the sea!

And neither the joy of sails filled like a pocket stuffed with doubloons, nor the tricks
played on the dangerous stupidity of the frigates of order[8] prevent it from hearing
the threat of its intestinal rumblings

In vain to ignore them the captain hangs the biggest loudmouth nigger from the
main yard or throws him into the sea, or feeds him to his mastiffs

Reeking of fried onions the nigger scum rediscovers the bitter taste of freedom in its
spilled blood

And the nigger scum is on its feet

the seated nigger scum
unexpectedly standing
standing in the hold

---

[7] bombilation: Swarming.

[8] frigates of order: Ships sent out from England to enforce Britain's abolition of slavery.

standing in the cabins
standing on deck
standing in the wind
standing under the sun
standing in the blood
    standing
        and
            free
standing and no longer a poor madwoman in her maritime freedom and
destitution gyrating in perfect drift[9]
and there she is:
most unexpectedly standing
standing in the rigging
standing at the tiller
standing at the compass
standing at the map
standing under the stars
    standing
        and
            free
and the lustral[10] ship fearlessly advances on the crumbling water.

And now our ignominious plops are rotting away!
by the clanking noon sea
by the burgeoning midnight sun
listen sparrow hawk who holds the keys to the orient
by the disarmed day
by the stony spurt of the rain

listen dogfish that watches over the occident

listen white dog of the north, black serpent of the south that cinches the sky girdle
There still remains one sea to cross
oh still one sea to cross
that I may invent my lungs
that the prince may hold his tongue
that the queen may lay me
still one old man to murder
one madman to deliver
that my soul may shine bark shine

---

[9] **drift:** An allusion to the Ship of Fools on which the insane were put out to sea and set adrift. Here the slave ship is adrift after the slaves have taken it over.

[10] **lustral:** Purifying. By revolting the slaves are purified.

bark bark bark
and the owl[11] my beautiful inquisitive angel may hoot.
The master of laughter?
The master of ominous silence?
The master of hope and despair?
The master of laziness? Master of the dance?
    It is I!
and for this reason, Lord,
the frail-necked men
receive and perceive deadly triangular calm[12]

Rally to my side my dances
you bad nigger dances
the carcan-cracker dance[13]
the prison-break dance
the it-is-beautiful-good-and-legitimate-to-be-a-nigger-dance
Rally to my side my dances and let the sun bounce on the racket of my hands

but no the unequal sun is not enough for me
coil, wind, around my new growth
light on my cadenced fingers
to you I surrender my conscience and its fleshy rhythm
to you I surrender the fire in which my weakness smolders
to you I surrender the "chain-gang"
to you the swamps
to you the nontourist of the triangular circuit
devour wind
to you I surrender my abrupt words
devour and encoil yourself
and self-encoiling embrace me with a more ample shudder
embrace me unto furious us
embrace, embrace US
but after having drawn from us blood
drawn by our own blood!
embrace, my purity mingles only with yours
so then embrace
like a field of even filagos[14]
at dusk

---

[11] the owl: Césaire's guardian angel.

[12] triangular calm: Césaire associates the triangular slave trade—operating between Europe, Africa, and America—with the Christian Holy Trinity, traditionally represented by a triangle.

[13] carcan-cracker dance: The carcan was an iron collar fixed around the necks of slaves, and this dance was a dance of freedom.

[14] filagos: Casuarina trees.

our multicolored purities
and bind, bind me without remorse
bind me with your vast arms to the luminous clay
bind my black vibration to the very navel of the world
bind, bind me, bitter brotherhood
then, strangling me with your lasso of stars
rise,
Dove[15]
rise
rise
rise
I follow you who are imprinted on my ancestral white cornea.
rise sky licker
and the great black hole where a moon ago I wanted to drown it is there I will now
fish the malevolent tongue of the night in its motionless veerition![16]

---

[15] Dove: The Christian symbol of the Pentecost.

[16] veerition: Coined from the Latin verb *verri*, meaning "to sweep," "to scrape a surface," and ultimately "to scan." (Translators' note.)

❧ OKOT P'BITEK
B. *UGANDA, 1931–1982*

Ugandan poet and novelist Okot p'Bitek combined soccer playing with writing as a young man. When he went to England with the Ugandan national team in 1958, he stayed there for several years, earning degrees in education from Bristol University, in law from the University of Wales, and in anthropology from Oxford. Returning to Africa, he taught at Makerere University in Uganda and Nairobi University in Kenya. His most famous works, from which the selections here are taken, are two long poems written in the traditional song style of Acholi, Okot p'Bitek's native town. *Song of Lawino* (1969) is a woman's extended lament about her college-educated husband, who has abandoned her for Western ways and a Westernized woman. In *Song of Ocol* (1970), the woman's husband responds, decrying the backwardness of his wife and praising European customs and values. This argument between husband and wife articulates the debate over the same issues taking place throughout Africa.

A note on the translation: These poems, written in Okot p'Bitek's native language of Acholi, have been translated into English by the author. All notes are the editors'.

FROM

Song of Lawino

MY HUSBAND'S TONGUE IS BITTER

Husband, now you despise me
Now you treat me with spite
And say I have inherited the stupidity of my aunt;
Son of the Chief,
Now you compare me
With the rubbish in the rubbish pit,
You say you no longer want me
Because I am like the things left behind
In the deserted homestead.
10   You insult me
You laugh at me
You say I do not know the letter A
Because I have not been to school
And I have not been baptized
You compare me with a little dog,
A puppy.

My friend, age-mate of my brother,
Take care,
Take care of your tongue,
20   Be careful what your lips say.

First take a deep look, brother,
You are now a man
You are not a dead fruit!
To behave like a child does not befit you!

Listen Ocol, you are the son of a Chief,
Leave foolish behavior to little children,
It is not right that you should be laughed at in a song!
Songs about you should be songs of praise!

Stop despising people
30   As if you were a little foolish man,
Stop treating me like a saltless ash[1]

---

[1] **saltless ash:** The ash remaining after salt has been removed from it.

Become barren of insults and stupidity;
Who has ever uprooted the Pumpkin?

My clansmen, I cry
Listen to my voice:
The insults of my man
Are painful beyond bearing.

My husband abuses me together with my parents;
He says terrible things about my mother
40 And I am so ashamed!

He abuses me in English
And he is so arrogant.

He says I am rubbish,
He no longer wants me!
In cruel jokes, he laughs at me,
He says I am primitive
Because I cannot play the guitar,
He says my eyes are dead
And I cannot read,
50 He says my ears are blocked
And cannot hear a single foreign word,
That I cannot count the coins.
He says I am like sheep,
The fool,

Ocol treats me
As if I am no longer a person,
He says I am silly
Like the *ojuu* insects that sit on the beer pot
My husband treats me roughly.
60 The insults!
Words cut more painfully than sticks!
He says my mother is a witch,
That my clansmen are fools
Because they eat rats,
He says we are all Kaffirs.[2]
We do not know the ways of God,
We sit in deep darkness

---

[2] **Kaffirs:** Arabic for "nonbelievers."

And do not know the Gospel,
He says my mother hides her charms
70   In her necklace
And that we are all sorcerers.

My husband's tongue
Is bitter like the roots of the *lyonno* lily,
It is hot like the penis of the bee,
Like the sting of the *kalang*![3]
Ocol's tongue is fierce like the arrow of the scorpion,
Deadly like the spear of the buffalo-hornet.
It is ferocious
Like the poison of a barren woman
80   And corrosive like the juice of the gourd.

My husband pours scorn
On Black People,
He behaves like a hen
That eats its own eggs
A hen that should be imprisoned under a basket.

His eyes grow large
Deep black eyes
Ocol's eyes resemble those of the Nile Perch!
90   He becomes fierce
Like a lioness with cubs,
He begins to behave like a mad hyena.

He says Black People are primitive
And their ways are utterly harmful,
Their dances are mortal sins
They are ignorant, poor, and diseased!

Ocol says he is a modern man,
A progressive and civilized man,
He says he has read extensively and widely
100   And he can no longer live with a thing like me
Who cannot distinguish between good and bad,

He says I am just a village woman,
I am of the old type,
And no longer attractive.

---

[3] *kalang:* A large African fruit bat.

He says I am blocking his progress,
My head, he says,
Is as big as that of an elephant
But it is only bones,
There is no brain in it,
He says I am only wasting his time.

FROM

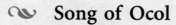 Song of Ocol

WHAT IS AFRICA TO ME?

What is Africa
To me?

Blackness,
Deep, deep fathomless
Darkness;

Africa,
Idle giant
Basking in the sun,
Sleeping, snoring,
Twitching in dreams;

10

Diseased with a chronic illness,
Choking with black ignorance,
Chained to the rock
Of poverty,
And yet laughing,
Always laughing and dancing,
The chains on his legs
Jangling;

Displaying his white teeth
In bright pink gum,
Loose white teeth
That cannot bite,
Joking, giggling, dancing . . .

20

Stuck in the stagnant mud
Of superstitions,
Frightened by the spirits
Of the bush, the stream,

The rock,
Scared of corpses . . .

30 He hears eerie noises
From the lakeside
And from the mountain top,
Sees snakes
In the whirlwind
And at both ends
Of the rainbow;

The caves house his gods
Or he carries them
On his head
40 Or on his shoulder
As he roams the wilderness,
Led by his cattle,
Or following the spoor
Of the elephant
That he has speared
But could not kill;

Child,
Lover of toys,
Look at his toy weapons,
50 His utensils, his hut . . .
Toy garden, toy chickens,
Toy cattle,
Toy children . . .

Timid,
Unadventurous,
Scared of the unbeaten track,
Unweaned,
Clinging to mother's milkless breasts
Clinging to brother,
60 To uncle, to clan,
To tribe

To blackness,

To Africa,

Africa
This rich granary

Of taboos, customs,
Traditions . . .

Mother, mother,
Why,
70   Why was I born
Black?

∾ JAMES BALDWIN
B. UNITED STATES, 1924–1987

As one of the most important black writers of the civil rights era of the
1960s, James Baldwin commented on nearly all of the racial controversies
of his time. In 1956 he was asked to report on the first Conference of Black
Writers held in Paris, a meeting that sought to articulate a unified voice
for black writers worldwide. In the section of his essay included here,
Baldwin ponders whether there is a common black culture shared by
Africans, African Americans, and blacks from around the world. Unlike
Senghor and the spokesmen for the Négritude movement, Baldwin is
skeptical that such a culture exists.

   All notes are the editors'.

**Children in the Silent
Protest Parade, 1917**
*A silent march, part
of which is captured
in this photograph,
was held on July 28,
1917, in Harlem to
protest a massacre in
East St. Louis and
lynchings in Waco,
Texas. (Manuscripts,
Archives & Rare
Books Division,
Schomburg Center
for Research in Black
Culture, The New
York Public Library,
Astor, Lenox, and
Tilden Foundations)*

FROM

∾ Nobody Knows My Name

[Is There a Single Black Culture?]

The evening debate rang perpetual changes on two questions. These questions—each of which splintered, each time it was asked, into a thousand more—were, first: What *is* a culture? This is a difficult question under the most serene circumstances—under which circumstances, incidentally, it mostly fails to present itself. (This implies, perhaps, one of the possible definitions of a culture, at least at a certain stage of its development.) In the context of the conference, it was a question which was helplessly at the mercy of another one. And the second question was this: Is it possible to describe as a culture what may simply be, after all, a history of oppression? That is, is this history and these present facts, which involve so many millions of people who are divided from each other by so many miles of the globe, which operates, and has operated, under such very different conditions, to such different effects, and which has produced so many different subhistories, problems, traditions, possibilities, aspirations, assumptions, languages, hybrids—is this history enough to have made of the earth's black populations anything that can legitimately be described as a culture? For what, beyond the fact that all black men at one time or another left Africa, or have remained there, do they really have in common?

And yet, it became clear as the debate wore on, that there *was* something which all black men held in common, something which cut across opposing points of view, and placed in the same context their widely dissimilar experience. What they held in common was their precarious, their unutterably painful relation to the white world. What they held in common was the necessity to remake the world in their own image, to impose this image on the world, and no longer be controlled by the vision of the world, and of themselves, held by other people. What, in sum, black men held in common was their ache to come into the world as men. And this ache united people who might otherwise have been divided as to what a man should be.

Yet, whether or not this could properly be described as a *cultural* reality remained another question. Haiti's Jacques Alexis[1] made the rather desperate observation that a cultural survey must have *something* to survey; but then seemed confounded, as, indeed, we all were, by the dimensions of the particular cultural survey in progress. It was necessary, for example, before one could relate the culture of Haiti to that of Africa, to know what the Haitian culture was. Within Haiti there were a great many cultures. Frenchmen, Negroes, and Indians had bequeathed it quite dissimilar ways of life; Catholics, voodooists, and animists cut across class and color lines. Alexis described as "pockets" of culture those related and yet quite specific and dissimilar ways of life to be found within the borders of any country in the world and wished to know by what alchemy these opposing ways of life became a

---

[1]Jacques Alexis (1922–1961): Haitian novelist and political activist driven into exile by the dictatorial Duvalier regime. His best-known novel is *General Sun, My Brother* (*Compère général soleil*, 1955).

national culture. And he wished to know, too, what relation national culture bore to national independence—was it possible, really, to speak of a national culture when speaking of nations which were not free?

Senghor remarked, apropos of this question, that one of the great difficulties posed by this problem of cultures within cultures, particularly within the borders of Africa herself, was the difficulty of establishing and maintaining contact with the people if one's language had been formed in Europe. And he went on, somewhat later, to make the point that the heritage of the American Negro was an African heritage. He used, as proof of this, a poem of Richard Wright's[2] which was, he said, involved with African tensions and symbols, even though Wright himself had not been aware of this. He suggested that the study of African sources might prove extremely illuminating for American Negroes. For, he suggested, in the same way that white classics exist—classic here taken to mean an enduring revelation and statement of a specific, peculiar, cultural sensibility—black classics must also exist. This raised in my mind the question of whether or not white classics *did* exist, and, with this question, I began to see the implications of Senghor's claim.

For, if white classics existed, in distinction, that is, to merely French or English classics, these could only be the classics produced by Greece and Rome. If *Black Boy,* said Senghor, were to be analyzed, it would undoubtedly reveal the African heritage to which it owed its existence; in the same way, I supposed, that Dickens's *A Tale of Two Cities,* would, upon analysis, reveal its debt to Aeschylus. It did not seem very important.

And yet, I realized, the question had simply never come up in relation to European literature. It was not, now, the European necessity to go rummaging in the past, and through all the countries of the world, bitterly staking out claims to its cultural possessions.

Yet *Black Boy* owed its existence to a great many other factors, by no means so tenuous or so problematical; in so handsomely presenting Wright with his African heritage, Senghor rather seemed to be taking away his identity. *Black Boy* is the study of the growing up of a Negro boy in the Deep South, and is one of the major American autobiographies. I had never thought of it, as Senghor clearly did, as one of the major *African* autobiographies, only one more document, in fact, like one more book in the Bible, speaking of the African's long persecution and exile.

Senghor chose to overlook several gaps in his argument, not the least of which was the fact that Wright had not been in a position, as Europeans had been, to remain in contact with his hypothetical African heritage. The Greco-Roman tradition had, after all, been *written down;* it was by this means that it had kept itself alive. Granted that there was something African in *Black Boy,* as there was undoubtedly something African in all American Negroes, the great question of what this was, and how it had survived, remained wide open. Moreover, *Black Boy* had been written in the English language which Americans had inherited from England, that is, if you

---

[2] Richard Wright (1908–1960): African American novelist, playwright, and poet who wrote the autobiographical *Black Boy* (1945) and the novel *Native Son* (1940). He was a mentor to Baldwin at the beginning of Baldwin's career, though they later had a falling-out.

like, from Greece and Rome; its form, psychology, moral attitude, preoccupations, in short, its cultural validity, were all due to forces which had nothing to do with Africa. Or was it simply that we had been rendered unable to recognize Africa in it? — for, it seemed that, in Senghor's vast re-creation of the world, the footfall of the African would prove to have covered more territory than the footfall of the Roman.

❧ GWENDOLYN BROOKS
B. UNITED STATES, 1917–2000

> You did not know the Black continent / that had to be reached / was you.
> — GWENDOLYN BROOKS, "To the Diaspora"

Gwendolyn Brooks was born in Kansas but is identified with Chicago, the city where she grew up and whose Negro ghetto, Bronzeville, is the subject of many of her poems. She began writing early and was a regular contributor to the black Chicago newspaper *The Defender* by the time she was sixteen. Brooks was inspired by the work of Langston Hughes, whom she met at church and who became a friend and mentor. Her work mixes the language of black preachers with street talk and draws on the rhythms of jazz and the blues to describe the everyday life of blacks. Many of her finest early poems are verbal portraits of the inhabitants of "Bronzeville." After attending the Second Black Writers' Conference at Fisk University in 1967, Brooks adopted a more activist voice and, addressing her poems to a black audience, wrote about the issues raised by the civil rights movement and the Black Nationalists. She traveled to Africa in 1971 and 1974. Among her many books of poetry are *A Street in Bronzeville* (1945), *Bronzeville Boys and Girls* (1956), and *Blacks* (1987).

❧ To the Diaspora[1]

you did not know you were Afrika

When you set out for Afrika
you did not know you were going.
Because
you did not know you were Afrika.
You did not know the Black continent

---

[1]Diaspora: A dispersion of people from their native land; here, specifically, Africans living outside of Africa. [Editors' note.]

that had to be reached
was you.

I could not have told you then that some sun
would come,
10 somewhere over the road,
would come evoking the diamonds
of you, the Black continent—
somewhere over the road.
You would not have believed my mouth.

When I told you, meeting you somewhere close
to the heat and youth of the road,
liking my loyalty, liking belief,
you smiled and you thanked me but very little believed me.

Here is some sun. Some.
20 Now off into the places rough to reach.
Though dry, though drowsy, all unwillingly a-wobble,
into the dissonant and dangerous crescendo.
Your work, that was done, to be done to be done to be done.

❧ Toni Morrison
b. United States, 1931

Born into a black working-class family in Lorain, Ohio, Toni Morrison early learned the joys of storytelling—her parents told stories to their four children and encouraged the children to tell stories in return. An avid reader as a child, Morrison later earned degrees in English and classics at Howard University and Cornell, began a career as a university professor, and then worked for twenty-five years as an editor for Random House. Since 1989 she has held the Goheen Chair in the Humanities at Princeton University. Morrison received the Nobel Prize in literature in 1993.

Morrison's first novel, *The Bluest Eye* (1970), has since been followed by six more, evocative and mythic stories of the black experience in America. Among them are *Beloved* (1987), a harrowing latter-day slave narrative in which a mother kills her infant daughter rather than allow her to be taken into slavery, and *Song of Solomon* (1977), from which the selection presented here is taken. The central figure in the novel,

Macon (Milkman) Dead, a young man from a well-to-do black family in Michigan, goes to Virginia in search of gold, not fully realizing that his quest is really for his roots. In Virginia he meets an older woman, Susan Byrd, who holds the clues to his heritage. On Milkman's first visit, Byrd is constrained by the presence of her friend Grace Long and misrepresents or omits important parts of the story that she tells to Milkman. On Milkman's second visit, excerpted here, Grace is absent and Byrd tells Milkman the story of Solomon, a slave celebrated in a children's rhyme and in a legend of his flight back to Africa. As he listens to Byrd's story, Milkman realizes that Solomon was his great-grandfather and that Byrd is his second cousin. The legend that discloses these connections, a mythic version of the return-to-Africa motif, enables Milkman to "fly" to a knowledge of his identity.

FROM

❧ Song of Solomon

[FLYING TO AFRICA]

Perhaps it was because the sun had hit the rim of the horizon, but Susan Byrd's house looked different. The cedar tree was a silvery gray and its bark crinkled all the way up. It looked to Milkman like the leg of an ancient elephant. And now he noticed that the ropes that held the swing were frayed and the picket fence that had looked so bright and perky before was really flaked, peeling, even leaning to the left. The blue steps leading to the porch were faded into a watery gray. In fact the whole house looked seedy.

He lifted his hand to knock on the door and noticed the doorbell. He rang it and Susan Byrd opened the door.

"Hello again," he said.

"Well," she said, "you're as good as your word."

"I'd like to talk to you some more, if you don't mind. About Sing. May I come in?"

"Of course." She stood back from the door and the odor of another batch of gingerbread wafted out. Again they sat in the living room—he in the gray wing-back chair, she on the sofa this time. Miss Long was nowhere in sight.

"I know you don't know who Sing married or if she married, but I was wondering—"

"Of course I know who she married. That is if they *did* marry. She married Jake, that black boy her mother took care of."

Milkman felt dizzy. Everybody kept changing right in front of him. "But yesterday you said nobody heard from her after she left."

"Nobody did. But they knew who she left with!"

"Jake?"

"Jake. Black Jake. Black as coal."

"Where—where did they live? Boston?"

"I don't know where they ended up. North, I guess. We never heard."

"I thought you said she went to a private school in Boston."

She dismissed the whole notion with a wave of her hand. "I just said that in front of *her*, Grace. She talks so much, you know. Carries tales all over the county. It's true she was supposed to go to some school, but she didn't. She left on that double-team wagon with that black boy, Jake. A whole lot of slaves got together. Jake was driving. Can you imagine it? Riding off with a wagonload of slaves?"

"What was Jake's last name? Can you tell me?"

She shrugged. "I don't think he had one. He was one of those flying African children. They must all be dead a long time now."

"Flying African children?"

"Um hm, one of Solomon's children. Or Shalimar. Papa said Heddy always called him Shalimar."

"And Heddy was . . ."

"My grandmother. Sing's mother and Papa's too. An Indian woman. She was the one who took care of Jake when his father left them all. She found him and took him home and raised him. She didn't have any boy children then. My father, Crowell, came later." She leaned forward and whispered, "She didn't have a husband, Heddy. I didn't want to go into all of that with Grace. You can imagine what she'd do with that information. You're a stranger, so it doesn't matter. But Grace . . ." Susan Byrd looked pleadingly at the ceiling. "This Jake was a baby she found, and he and Sing grew up together, and I guess rather than be packed off to some Quaker school, she ran away with him. You know colored people and Indians mixed a lot, but sometimes, well, some Indians didn't like it—the marrying, I mean. But neither one of them knew their own father, Jake nor Sing. And my own father didn't know his. Heddy never said. I don't know to this day if he was white, red, or—well—*what*. Sing's name was Singing Bird. And my father's name was Crow at first. Later he changed it to Crowell Byrd. After he took off his buckskin." She smiled.

"Why did you call Solomon a flying African?"

"Oh, that's just some old folks' lie they tell around here. Some of those Africans they brought over here as slaves could fly. A lot of them flew back to Africa. The one around here who did was this same Solomon, or Shalimar—I never knew which was right. He had a slew of children, all over the place. You may have noticed that everybody around here claims kin to him. Must be over forty families spread in these hills calling themselves Solomon something or other. I guess he must have been hot stuff." She laughed. "But anyway, hot stuff or not, he disappeared and left everybody. Wife, everybody, including some twenty-one children. And they say they all saw him go. The wife saw him and the children saw him. They were all working in the fields. They used to try to grow cotton here. Can you imagine? In these hills? But cotton was king then. Everybody grew it until the land went bad. It was cotton even when I was a girl. Well, back to this Jake boy. He was supposed to be one of Solomon's original twenty-one—all boys and all of them with the same mother. Jake was the baby. The baby and the wife were right next to him when he flew off."

"When you say 'flew off' you mean he ran away, don't you? Escaped?"

"No, I mean flew. Oh, it's just foolishness, you know, but according to the story he wasn't running away. He was flying. He flew. You know, like a bird. Just stood up in the fields one day, ran up some hill, spun around a couple of times, and was lifted up in the air. Went right on back to wherever it was he came from. There's a big double-headed rock over the valley named for him. It like to killed the woman, the wife. I guess you could say 'wife.' Anyway she's supposed to have screamed out loud for days. And there's a ravine near here they call Ryna's Gulch, and sometimes you can hear this funny sound by it that the wind makes. People say it's the wife, Solomon's wife, crying. Her name was Ryna. They say she screamed and screamed, lost her mind completely. You don't hear about women like that anymore, but there used to be more—the kind of woman who couldn't live without a particular man. And when the man left, they lost their minds, or died or something. Love, I guess. But I always thought it was trying to take care of children by themselves, you know what I mean?"

She talked on and on while Milkman sat back and listened to gossip, stories, legends, speculations. His mind was ahead of hers, behind hers, with hers, and bit by bit, with what she said, what he knew, and what he guessed, he put it all together.

Sing had said she was going to a Quaker school, but she joined Jake on his wagonful of ex-slaves heading for Boston or somewhere. They must have dropped their passengers all along the way. And then Jake, at the reins, took a wrong turn, because he couldn't read, and they ended up in Pennsylvania.

"But there's a children's game they play around here. And in the game they sing, 'Jake the *only* son of Solomon.' *Only.*" He looked at her, hoping she wouldn't mind the interruption.

"Well, they're wrong. He wasn't the only son. There were twenty others. But he was the only one Solomon tried to take with him. Maybe that's what it means. He lifted him up, but dropped him near the porch of the big house. That's where Heddy found him. She used to come over there and help with the soapmaking and the candlemaking. She wasn't a slave, but she worked over at the big house certain times of year. She was melting tallow when she looked up and saw this man holding a baby and flying toward the ridge. He brushed too close to a tree and the baby slipped out of his arms and fell through the branches to the ground. He was unconscious, but the trees saved him from dying. Heddy ran over and picked him up. She didn't have any male children, like I said, just a little bitty girl, and this one just dropped out of the sky almost in her lap. She never named him anything different; she was afraid to do that. She found out the baby was Ryna's, but Ryna was out of her mind. Heddy lived a good ways off from the place Solomon and them others worked on. She tried to keep the girl away from that place too. And you can imagine how she felt when both of them ran off. Just my father was left."

"Did Jake have to register at the Freedmen's Bureau before he left the state?"

"Everybody did. Everybody who had been slaves, that is. Whether they left the state or not. But we were never slaves, so—"

"You told me that. Weren't any of Jake's brothers registering too?"

"I couldn't say. Those must have been some times, back then. Some bad times. It's a wonder anybody knows who anybody is."

"You've helped me a lot, Miss Byrd. I'm grateful." He thought then about asking her if she had a photo album. He wanted to see Sing, Crowell, even Heddy. But he decided against it. She might start asking him questions, and he didn't want to trouble her with a new-found relative who was as black as Jake.

"Now, that's not the woman you're looking for, is it? Pilate?"

"No," he said. "Couldn't be." He made motions of departure and then remembered his watch.

"By the way, did I leave my watch here? I'd like it back."

"Watch?"

"Yes. Your friend wanted to see it. Miss Long. I handed it to her but I forgot—" Milkman stopped. Susan Byrd was laughing out loud.

"Well, you can say goodbye to it, Mr. Macon. Grace will go to dinner all over the county telling people about the watch you gave her."

"What?"

"Well, you know. She doesn't mean any real harm, but it's a quiet place. We don't have many visitors, especially young men who wear gold watches and have northern accents. I'll get it back for you."

CHINWEIZU
B. NIGERIA, 1943

ONWUCHEKWA JEMIE

IHECHUKWU MADUBUIKE

In their sometimes controversial book, *Toward the Decolonization of African Literature: African Fiction and Poetry and Their Critics* (1980), Nigerian scholars and critics Chinweizu, Onwuchekwa Jemie, and Ihechukwu Madubuike articulate an African perspective on Africa and its literature. Since earlier writing on these topics was done by Western critics and blacks in the diaspora, these three native authors set out to challenge the existing scholarship, in which they saw both white imperialism and black romanticism. In the excerpt that follows, they call for "critical realism" in the treatment of Africa and its literature.

All notes are the editors'.

∽ The African Writer and the African Past

In contemporary African literature and criticism there have been three dominant attitudes towards the African past: shamefaced rejection; romantic embrace;
and realistic appraisal. Those who reject the African past and would have as little to
do with it as possible are those who, shamed by imperialist propaganda and misrep-
resentation, would wish to forget it entirely and to hurry off into a euromodernist
African future. Prominent among them are those champions of tigritude, those
African neo-Tarzanists who dismiss African literature that deals with the African
past as a "literature of self-worship," a literature of narcissism. Against this school of
thought headed by Wole Soyinka,[1] it must be emphasized that since our past has
been vilified by imperialism, and since an imperialist education has tried to equip us
with all manner of absurd views and reactions to our past, we do need to reclaim and
rehabilitate our genuine past, to repossess our true and entire history in order to
acquire a secure launching pad into our future. Thus, a concern with our past will
never be out of place.

Those African writers and critics who understand the need for us to repossess
and rehabilitate our past have approached it with either romanticism or critical realism. In our view, there are excellent grounds for avoiding a romanticization of our
past and for according it a critical and realistic appraisal. Most important is the fact
that we cannot afford to build on misinformation, and romanticism has a tendency
to put misleading glosses upon whatever it gazes upon. In this regard, the romanticism of the negritude school is notorious. But before proceeding to examine this, we
should first disentangle three important aspects of negritude and state our attitudes
to them.

First, there is its African nationalist consciousness which revolts against European cultural imperialism. As we argued earlier, an active African nationalist consciousness is indispensable to the task of African liberation. For its stand and
contributions in this department, African nationalism is indebted to negritude. To
its champions we offer our salute!

The second important aspect of negritude is its concern with recapturing for
modern literature the technical repertory of traditional African orature. This again
is a crucial project in cultural retrieval. Without it, the task of ensuring continuity
between traditional and modern African culture would be practically impossible.
For its pioneering efforts in this department, African nationalism is again indebted
to negritude. To its champions, we also offer our salute!

The third important aspect of negritude is the image of traditional Africa which
it has held up to view. This is highly questionable. In reaction to colonial insults the

---

[1] **Wole Soyinka** (b. 1934; see p. 1141): Nigerian playwright and novelist. In "Myth, Literature, and the African
World" (1976), Soyinka attacks the Négritude writers, stating that "the tiger does not stalk about crying his
tigritude."

negritude poets generally salve their wounds with extravagant nostalgia for a vaguely conceived past. But ought we to persist in this disservice to our past, and even to our present? Was our past one uninterrupted orgy of sensuality? One boring canvas of idyllic goodness, fraternity, and harmony? Were our ancestors a parade of plaster saints who never, among themselves, struck a blow, or hurt a fly, and who suffered all psychic and physical pain gladly and cheerfully, or never suffered at all?

No doubt, at its inception, even this romanticism filled a historic need. It was an understandably extreme reaction, offering blanket praise in retort to Europe's blanket condemnation of Africa. But that mythical portrait of traditional Africa can prove to be a new prison. In the task of decolonization we cannot afford an uncritical glorification of the past. We may brandish our memories of empires of ages ago as shields against Western disparagement, but we also know that before colonialism came there was slavery. Who hunted the slaves? And who sold them for guns, trinkets, and gin? And the African attitudes and roles which made that slave trade possible, are they not part of that nostalgic past? Are those attitudes not still with us, poisoning our present? How much of this illusion of purity and sanctity can survive the events of the past two decades? After all, "When a nigger kicks a nigger / Where is the negritude?" (Madubuike). Even though other parts of the blame belong elsewhere, we cannot deny our own share of the responsibility.

As regards the arts, romanticism of the negritude kind, because it venerates what it considers a gold past, could discourage our use of exemplars from that past as points of contemporary departure. By encouraging the minting of facsimiles, it could imprison the contemporary imagination in a bygone era. As has happened in the plastic arts, especially in the lamentable case of airport art, the romantic minting of facsimiles from a golden past could saddle us with anachronistic imagery, and prevent the evolution of new literary forms out of the old, resulting in a fossilization of forms and a literary stasis.

In contrast, critical realism, because it does not spread a gloss of sanctity on the past, does not extol every aspect of it. It is content to praise what it sees as praiseworthy, and to dispraise what it sees as not praiseworthy. It thereby treats our past like any other valid era of culture. This enables us to see welcome as well as objectionable similarities between our present and our past, and such discrimination and selectivity enables us to adopt desirable features from the arts of our past as we endeavor to anchor our modern culture in our tradition. Because critical realism prevents us from treating exemplars as sacrosanct, it allows for the evolution of new forms through adaptations from the old. When, as in Okigbo's "Path of Thunder,"[2] contemporary events and objects are put into the traditional image matrix and described with traditional terms of rhetoric, the effect is refreshing. We thereby obtain a modernism that has emerged from a clearly African poetic tradition.

Other examples in which aspects of our modern literature have been successfully

---

[2] **"Path of Thunder"** (1965): Written by Nigerian novelist Christopher Okigbo (1932–1967), who died fighting for Biafra's independence from Nigeria.

grafted onto traditional trunks include the following: Tutuola's *Palm-Wine Drinkard,*[3] *My Life in the Bush of Ghosts,* and other novels, which are embedded in the Yoruba mythic imagination; Achebe's *Things Fall Apart*[4] and *Arrow of God* which capture, in English, Igbo speech patterns, proverbs, and idiom; and Okot p'Bitek's[5] *Song of Lawino, Song of Ocol, Song of a Prisoner,* and *Song of Malaya,* each of which uses authentic African imagery and Acholi rhetorical devices to examine an aspect of the contemporary African condition.

---

[3] *Palm-Wine Drinkard* (1952): Authored by Nigerian novelist Amos Tutuola (1920–1997), this work draws on Yoruba mythology.

[4] *Things Fall Apart* (1958; see p. 1023): Nigerian novelist Chinua Achebe (b. 1930) penned this work as well as *Arrow of God* (1964); both are novels about the impact of colonialism on tribal societies in Nigeria.

[5] **Okot p'Bitek** (1931–1982): Ugandan novelist and poet who wrote a series of poems in the style of traditional Acholi song: *Song of Lawino* (1969; see p. 894), *Song of Ocol* (1969; see p. 897), *Song of a Prisoner* (1971), and *Song of Malaya* (1971).

❧ NADINE GORDIMER
B. SOUTH AFRICA, 1923

Described by Irish poet Seamus Heaney as one of the "guerrillas of the imagination," South African novelist and short-story writer Nadine Gordimer has devoted her long writing career to exploring the racial divide in her native land and in writing across the color line. Born into a middle-class white family in the suburbs of Johannesburg, Gordimer published her first story when she was still a teenager. In the fourteen novels and more than two hundred short stories she as written since, Gordimer provides an inside view of the transformation of South Africa during the last half century. An ardent opponent of APARTHEID, South Africa's official system of racial segregation, Gordimer joined the African National Congress (ANC) while it was still illegal to do so, and many of her works are written from the point of view of South African blacks. She considers the proudest day of her life to be not the one on which she received the Nobel Prize, in 1991, but the day in 1986 when she testified at a trial to save the lives of twenty-two ANC members accused of treason. Her many novels include *A Guest of Honor* (1970), *Burger's Daughter* (1979), and *My Son's Story* (1990). In "As Others See Us" (1997), Gordimer compares race relations in postapartheid South Africa with those in the United States, offering an African point of view on America and suggesting that Americans may not see themselves clearly and that what they imagine about Africa may not be the whole truth.

∾ As Others See Us

There is nothing more presumptuous than a foreigner telling other people what is wrong with their country. I know how I react when pundits who are not South African make flip judgments of our problems on the basis of the slim experience of visits to our country. This does not mean that a reasoned, critical look is not useful; just that the onlooker understands not most, but only half of the game. So it is right that I provide my modest credentials for an opinion on race relations in the U.S.A. in contrast to race relations in my own country—relations I have been part of since birth.

I have visited America once a year or more since the 1950s, usually only for several weeks but twice for several months, spent in New York and Cambridge, with forays to the Midwest, the West Coast, and the South. I began in the McCarthy era and have gathered my impressions through the eras of Martin Luther King Jr., Stokely Carmichael, Andy Young, Louis Farrakhan, and your roster of presidents up to the present incumbent. In my early visits as a young writer I mixed in an easy fashion with a good number of my peers, black men and women whose interests in the arts and in Africa coincided with mine. I remember parties in Queens, welcoming visits to homey apartments, jazz evenings in Harlem not as a gaping tourist but as an individual sharing the leisure diversion of newfound friends themselves. These were not people with big names; all of us were starting out.

As time went by, on subsequent visits to the U.S., I found I was meeting fewer and fewer black Americans. Those that I did meet—and much enjoyed—were Du Bois's Talented Tenth: Harry Belafonte, Charlayne Hunter-Gault, Jamaica Kincaid, Randall Robinson, Toni Morrison, Henry Louis Gates, and Cornel West, for example.

While housed in an apartment adjacent to a student residence at Harvard, in 1995, when I gave the Charles Eliot Norton Lectures, almost the only black Americans I met were through the efforts of Skip Gates. The Talented Tenth again. At the homes of my white American friends, people to whom colour truly means nothing, I now find I meet blacks from Africa, but rarely a black American. Whites from Africa who came from active antiracist backgrounds, and now live in the States, have no black men and women among their friends. Why? A paradox, since back home in South Africa they mixed in tough friendship with blacks, and were totally accepted by them, under conditions that made this difficult, to say the least. The reason seems to be that black Americans do not want to mix with whites, however much compatibility is beckoning to be recognized. The old, old answer I think not only survives but seems to have grown in bitterness, for reasons (of economics and opportunity?) Americans know best: When you have been so long rejected, your collective consciousness tells you that the open door, open arms, have come too late. You assert your self-respect only by saying "no." No no no: I read that playwright August Wilson wants black theatre for *blacks only*—black writers, actors, audiences. If even the doors of the arts are slammed shut, how shall people find their common humanity?

And how to live together, in the end, without it? This theatre is Greek tragedy where wars and violence become the only means of communication, the curse of gods on humans.

Why does self-respect, identity, rest on this ancient and terrible tragedy of white rejection of black?

One has to look at race relations in South Africa for an explanation of the U.S.A.'s realities. Over three hundred and fifty years of oppression and racist exploitation unequalled in place or time, black South Africans nevertheless have had their own earth under their feet. Despite neglect in official education, their languages have remained intact as mother tongues. Their names are their own ancestral names. Nothing—neither cruel apartheid denigration nor liberal paternalism—has destroyed their identity. *They know who they are.* In relations with whites, now that everyone is equal before the law, they do not have to say "no" in order to assert pride of identity and self-respect. It is for the average white to discover, earn, and affirm a valid identity in a society with a black majority. There are those whites to whom this is anathema, but surprising numbers who followed the white flock in racism before are making the adjustment. What matter that the process begins as pragmatism. Groups of extremists who cannot adjust will die out with the present middle-aged generation, I believe. And as for those whites who threw in their lot with the black struggle—they are recognized as brothers and sisters and are active in all areas of reconstruction: They are long accustomed to contributing under the direction of blacks.

Unemployment, inequalities in employment opportunities are a heritage of the hopelessly inadequate, segregated education of blacks under apartheid. There is frustration, over this, among blacks, but at the same time black empowerment is a reality moving both at government level (in the civil service and police, more slowly than one would wish, but there are valid reasons in the problems of transition) and the new black private sector. There, black empowerment is moving boldly into the white enclaves round the stock market. If the black entrepreneurs are in some way a home-grown product out of black poverty, like the "Tough Love Crowd"[1] of successful black American capitalists, the neoconservatists who advocate unsparing self-criticism as the way to empower blacks, the resemblance ends there. Black South Africans "climbing the corporate ladder," because of their records of active participation in the liberation struggle, including political detention and imprisonment in many cases, can rightfully maintain their brotherhood with the masses, and defy any questioning of their motives in empowering their people through infiltration of capitalist enterprises within a state where capitalist exploitation was allied with racism. While some say they are betraying the revolution, others see these moves as a necessary phase of struggle: First came the political kingdom, now comes the economic one, to be fought, inevitably, on white economic supremacy's home ground.

---

[1] **"Tough Love Crowd"**: Ronald Suresh Roberts, *Clarence Thomas: Tough Love Crowd; Counterfeit Heroes and Unhappy Truths* (New York University Press, 1995). [Author's note.]

Lack of capital inhibits these entrepreneurs; they have to borrow finance from whites, but are alert to the way the balance must be precariously held, the frontier of black ownership must be pushed hard and continuously against shareholdings that still entrench white economic power.

In the South African theatre, a cross-pollination of European experimental dramatic structures and African resources of mime, living experiences, shared body-language with whites produces a theatre that is nonracial not only in mixed casting that reflects the tensions and truth of our mixed society, but also in that "black" plays and "white" plays are recognized as opportunities opening to each the experience of the other. And all are welcome in the audience.

It is unfortunate to have to say it: History is against you, in the U.S.A. Alas, Martin Luther King is dead and you have no Nelson Mandela. White Americans cannot give back to blacks a stolen and lost identity; black Americans are reluctant to accept that it cannot be found in an avatar of apartheid in reverse. They are Americans, and whether whites like it or not, and whether blacks like it or not, a common destiny has to be worked out. This is not simple, in South Africa either, but in my observation and participation we are doing rather better than the U.S.A., despite our staggering problems of poverty, unemployment, and vast number of the homeless, a legacy from the apartheid regime.

As Wislawa Szymborska, the Polish Nobel laureate poet, writes: "We know how to divide ourselves. But to put ourselves together?"

✢ ABÉ KOBO

B. JAPAN, 1924–1993

AH-bay KOH-boh

Abé Kobo, best known outside of Japan for the novel *The Woman in the Dunes* (1962), is one of Japan's most acclaimed writers. Abé, heavily influenced by Western writers such as the novelist Franz Kafka (1883–1924) and the EXISTENTIALISTS Jean-Paul Sartre (1905–1980) and Albert Camus (1913–1960), has been compared to those writers as well as to the avant-garde writers Samuel Beckett (1906–1989), Eugène Ionesco (1909–1994), and the novelist Gabriel García Márquez (b. 1928). Dealing with themes of alienation and displacement like many of his European, African, and Latin American peers, Abé views human existence in the modern world of mass production and consumption as a condition of absurdity. His plays, short stories, and novels feature characters who are forced to accept or endure the sometimes nightmarish and always bizarre situations in which they find themselves: a man forced to dig himself out of the sand every day, a man turned into a stick, a man whose leg unravels and forms a cocoon around him. While Abé's settings and characters are Japanese, the circumstances they face and the struggle they undertake to find meaning and to discover identity extend beyond national boundaries and speak to readers everywhere.

Early Life. Abé Kimifusa, who later changed his name to **Abé Kobo,** was born in Tokyo in 1924. Abé's father, a medical doctor, moved his family to the Japanese colonial state of Manchuria (then called Manchukuo), where he practiced medicine and taught at the Imperial Medical College. Abé grew up in Mukden (now Shanyeng), Manchuria, where he showed a great deal of intellectual curiosity, collecting insects, studying mathematics, and reading European philosophy and literature, including the works of Edgar Allan Poe (1809–1849) and Kafka, whose fantastic stories stirred Abé's imagination. In 1941 Abé, like many sons of colonial administrators, returned to Tokyo to study at the Sejo Koko School, a private high school; after graduation he studied medicine at Tokyo University, taking his degree in 1948. Abé reported that the degree was granted only under the condition that he never actually practice medicine, and he never did. Instead, he chose a literary career.

Return to Tokyo. Before completing his medical studies and after being excused from military service because of a respiratory illness, Abé returned to Manchuria just before the end of the war to attend his father, who was dying of cholera. In Manchuria, conditions had grown quite desperate. Overrun with refugees competing for scarce resources and plagued with armed bands of robbers, the colonized state presented a spectacle of despair and suffering that haunted Abé and would inspire his fiction. Abé believed that as one of the colonizers he was complicitous in the suffering he saw and later recalled: "Living on the side of the rulers had an abstract evil. The sensitive individual still feels guilt, remorse, shame." After his father's death, Abé took up writing in earnest, returning first to Hokkaido, his father's hometown, and then to Tokyo, where he married **Yamada Matiko**, known as Abé Machi, an accomplished artist who collaborated with Abé throughout his career, designing stage sets as well as Abé's books.

yeh-MAH-dah
mah-TEE-koh

Critique of Modern Life.   Abé's novella *The Crime of S. Karuma,* published in *The Wall,* won the Akutagawa Prize in 1951, the first of many awards Abé would receive for his fiction and drama. About this time he joined the literary group called "Night Association"; among his influences was **Hanada Kiyoteru**, a MARXIST who was once editor of *New Japanese Literature* and who founded the Organization of the Documentary Arts. Like many Japanese intellectuals after the Second World War, Abé embraced Marxism, and he actively supported the unionization of workers. Some of his early plays invoke Marxist themes, in particular the alienation of human beings in industrialized society. Both Hanada and Abé sought in their work to reconcile SURREALIST literary and psychoanalytic ideas with a Marxist analysis of society. Eventually, however, perhaps in part because their sensibility was more anarchist than communist and their aesthetics more AVANT-GARDE than REALIST, both were expelled from the Communist Party in 1962. For the next thirty years Abé continued his critique of what he saw as the devaluation of life in a rapidly industrializing nation and world. While directing his own theater company in Tokyo and writing several plays each year for his troupe, Abé also wrote the novels and short stories that have won international acclaim and been widely translated. In his later years the author moved to the Hakone Mountains, in Shizuoka Prefecture, southwest of Tokyo, where he continued writing. He died on January 22, 1993.

hah-NAH-dah
kee-yoh-TEH-roo

Experiments in Fiction.   Abé's first published novel, *The Road Sign at the End of the Road* (1948), is the story of a self-exiled man dying of tuberculosis and drug addiction while held hostage in Manchuria by a robber. The work broaches the themes of alienation and displacement that characterize Abé's later fiction, such as *The Wall* (1951), *The Beasts Go Homeward* (1957), and *Inter Ice Age 4* (1959), which moved Abé's writing into the genre of science fiction. While these same themes circulate throughout much of postwar Japanese literature, Abé's surreal, avant-garde style marks a significant departure from the more realistic narratives written by many of his contemporaries, such as **Mishima Yukio** (1925–1970) and **Oe Kenzaburo** (b. 1935).[1] *Inter Ice Age 4* concerns a scientist, involved in a web of intrigue after the death of one of his subjects, who peers into the

MEE-shee-mah
YOO-kee-oh
OH-eh
ken-zah-BOO-roh

---

[1]Mishima . . . Oe: Mishima Yukio was a novelist, essayist, and playwright whose works include *The Sailor Who Fell from Grace with the Sea, The Decay of the Angel,* and *Confessions of a Mask;* Oe Kenzaburo, who won the Nobel Prize in literature in 1994, is the author of several novels and short stories, including *A Personal Matter, The Silent Cry,* and *Teach Us to Outgrow Our Madness.* (See p. 765.)

future by means of a machine he has invented and foresees a "water world" where humans must have gills in order to live. *The Woman in the Dunes* (1962), perhaps the most widely known of Abé's works, won the Yomiuri Prize for literature and brought Abé's work worldwide recognition in 1963 when it was made into a film directed by Teshigahara Hiroshi that won the Special Jury Award at the Cannes Film Festival the next year. The novel recounts the story of a schoolteacher and amateur entomologist, Jumpei Niki, who is taken prisoner in a remote village while on vacation collecting insects for his hobby. Jumpei takes refuge with a young widow who lives in a house continuously buried by collapsing sand dunes. Accepting his Sisyphean task of survival under these conditions, Jumpei helps the woman in her never-ending struggle to survive by shoveling sand. When he finally has the chance to escape, he chooses in an act of existential good faith to stay.

The Strength of the Mask.   Later Abé novels include *The Face of Another* (1964), which, like Mary Shelley's *Frankenstein,* questions the relationship of identity and physical appearance through the trials of its protagonist, a scientist who reconstructs his face according to his wife's ideal of beauty after it is disfigured in a laboratory accident; *The Ruined Map* (1967), a detective story in which the pursuer begins to lose his sense of self as he imagines the motives of the man he seeks; and *The Box Man* (1973), in which a man takes up living in a carefully fashioned cardboard box from which he safely observes the world of others. While Abé's protagonists often begin in desperation, they usually learn to accept the bizarre accidents that befall them and move beyond acceptance to positive determination. As Abé has said of *The Box Man,* for example, "Being no one means at the same time that one can be anyone." In addition to these novels, Abé wrote and directed many plays, including *The Ghost Is Here* (1958), *Friends* (1967), and *The Green Stocking* (1974); he also wrote scripts for radio, television, and film. His plays and scripts reflect with characteristic satire and irony the fragility of identity and the helplessness of the individual before social and economic forces. In *Friends,* for example, which won the Tanizaki Junichiro award, eight people occupy a man's apartment and take over his life, eventually imprisoning him in a cage for disobedience and then murdering him. All the while they claim they are acting upon the principles of goodwill and brotherly love. Abé's last novel, *Kangaroo Notebook,* was published in 1996, three years after his death.

Throughout his work, as the stories included here demonstrate, Abé transformed into surreal and sometimes nightmarish metaphors the alienation and absurdity he found in the modern industrializing world of postwar Japan. With "The Red Cocoon" (1950), Abé began a series of stories about metamorphoses that includes *The Wall* and "The Stick" (1955). Comparable to Kafka's **The Metamorphosis,** though written in a more self-consciously surrealistic style, these stories have as their themes the precariousness of identity and the devaluation of individuality in a

p. 428

postwar world that has witnessed genocide, massive civilian casualties in war, and the use of devastating weapons, including the atomic bomb.

■ **CONNECTIONS**

Franz Kafka, *The Metamorphosis*, p. 428. One of the persistent themes in twentieth-century literature is alienation. Both Abé Kobo and Franz Kafka, whose work influenced Abé, symbolize alienation as a metamorphosis from human into nonhuman form in "The Stick" and *The Metamorphosis,* respectively. Yet both authors wrote within unique cultural and historical contexts. How does their use of the theme of transformation evoke those distinctive contexts? How does the mood or tone in these stories affect the way the reader thinks about alienation?

Samuel Beckett, *Krapp's Last Tape*, p. 774. Some critics see Abé Kobo's dramas as a Japanese version of the theater of the absurd, of which Beckett's play is a key example. How do Abé's short stories draw upon the techniques or devices of the theater of the absurd? What do his stories share with Beckett's play thematically, stylistically, and philosophically?

Albert Camus, "The Myth of Sisyphus," p. 757. Like the work of his contemporary Oe Kenzaburo, Abé Kobo's writing often takes on what appears to be an existentialist quality. In Abé's stories, individuals sometimes engage in a heroic struggle to make meaning out of the ordinary events of everyday life. What do you see as the similarities between the circumstances in Abé's and Camus' work, and what do you think is the philosophical significance of those works?

■ **FURTHER RESEARCH**

Biography
Serafin, Steven R., ed. *Encyclopedia of World Literature in the 20th Century.* Vol 1. 1999.

Criticism
Kimball, Arthur G. *Crisis in Identity and Contemporary Japanese Novels.* 1973.
Rimer, J. Thomas. *Modern Japanese Fiction and Its Traditions.* 1978.
Shields, Nancy K. *Fake Fish: The Theater of Kobo Abé.* 1966.
Tsuruta, Kinya, and Thomas E. Swann, eds. *Approaches to the Modern Japanese Novel.* 1976.
Yamanouchi, Hisaaki. *The Search for Authenticity in Modern Japanese Literature.* 1978.

■ **PRONUNCIATION**

Abé Kobo: AH-bay KOH-boh
Hanada Kiyoteru: hah-NAH-dah kee-yoh-TEH-roo
Mishima Yukio: MEE-shee-mah YOO-kee-oh
Yamada Matiko: yeh-MAH-dah mah-TEE-koh

✺ The Red Cocoon

Translated by Lane Dunlop

The sun is starting to set. It's the time when people hurry home to their roosts, but I don't have a roost to go back to. I go on walking slowly down the narrow cleft between the houses. Although there are so many houses lined up along the streets, why is there not one house which is mine? I think, repeating the same question for the hundredth time.

When I take a piss against a telephone pole, sometimes there's a scrap of rope hanging down, and I want to hang myself. The rope, looking at my neck out of the corner of its eye, says: "Let's rest, brother." And I want to rest, too. But I can't rest. I'm not the rope's brother, and besides, I still can't understand why I don't have a house.

Every day, night comes. When night comes, you have to rest. Houses are to rest in. If that's so, it's not that I don't have a house, is it?

Suddenly, I get an idea. Maybe I've been making a serious mistake in my thinking. Maybe it's not that I don't have a house, but that I've forgotten it. That's right, it could be. For example, I stop in front of this house I happen to be passing. Might not this be my house? Of course, compared to other houses, it has no special feature that particularly breathes out that possibility, but one could say the same of any house. That cannot be a proof canceling the fact that this may be my house. I'm feeling brave. OK, let's knock on the door.

I'm in luck. The smiling face of a woman looks out of a half-opened window. She seems kind. The wind of hope blows through the neighborhood of my heart. My

---

"The Red Cocoon" and "The Stick." Like Kafka's *The Metamorphosis,* in which an unsuspecting Gregor Samsa awakens to find himself transformed into a giant insect, Abé's "The Red Cocoon" (1950) and "The Stick" (1955) symbolize the absurdity of modern life through the metamorphosis of the human body. Abé's unnamed protagonists find themselves transformed into a caterpillar and a stick, respectively, and as is Gregor, they are forced to come to terms with their new mode of existence; unlike Gregor's, however, their new bodies are not inherently disgusting or revolting. Trapped in their transfiguration, Abé's characters do not despair but rather seem reconciled to their predicaments, either out of a positive choice to endure or out of a lack of alternatives. Part of Abé's genius as a writer is in presenting these absurd situations from the point of view of characters who seem to take their metamorphoses for granted. Through them, Abé metaphorically depicts human beings subjected to social and economic powers beyond their control. In "The Red Cocoon," the narrator's transformation suggests that the only thing we can really possess is our own identity; paradoxically, it also implies that withdrawal into the self — into the isolation of the cocoon — essentially effaces the "I," whose essence is perhaps grounded in contingency and communication with others. In "The Stick," the character's transformation reflects the apparent insignificance of most individual lives. Human beings in the modern — or postmodern — world tend to be overlooked, affecting only a small group of others beyond their families. The story's cries of "Daddy, Daddy," seem to give utterance to people's often frustrated search for a connection with others.

heart becomes a flag that spreads out flat and flutters in the wind. I smile, too. Like a real gentleman, I say:

"Excuse me, but this isn't my house by any chance?"

The woman's face abruptly hardens. "What? Who are you?"

About to explain, all of a sudden I can't. I don't know what I should explain. How can I make her understand that it's not a question now of who I am? Getting a little desperate, I say:

"Well, if you think this isn't my house, will you please prove it to me?"

"My god . . ." The woman's face is frightened. That gets me angry.

"If you have no proof, it's all right for me to think it's mine."

"But this is my house."

"What does that matter? Just because you say it's yours doesn't mean it's not mine. That's so."

Instead of answering, the woman turns her face into a wall and shuts the window. That's the true form of a woman's smiling face. It's always this transformation that gives away the incomprehensible logic by which, because something belongs to someone, it does not belong to me.

But, why . . . why does everything belong to someone else and not to me? Even if it isn't mine, can't there be just one thing that doesn't belong to anyone?

Sometimes, I have delusions. That the concrete pipes on construction sites or in storage yards are my house. But they're already on the way to belonging to somebody. Because they become someone else's, they disappear without any reference to my wishes or interest in them. Or they turn into something that is clearly not my house.

Well then, how about park benches? They'd be fine, of course. If they were really my house, and if only he didn't come and chase me off them with his stick . . . Certainly they belong to everybody, not to anybody. But he says:

"Hey, you, get up. This bench belongs to everybody. It doesn't belong to anybody, least of all you. Come on, start moving. If you don't like it, you can spend the night in the basement lockup at the precinct house. If you stop anyplace else, no matter where, you'll be breaking the law."

The Wandering Jew—is that who I am?

The sun is setting. I keep walking.

A house . . . houses that don't disappear, turn into something else, that stand on the ground and don't move. Between them, the cleft that keeps changing, that doesn't have any one face that stays the same . . . the street. On rainy days, it's like a paint-loaded brush, on snowy days it becomes just the width of the tire ruts, on windy days it flows like a conveyor belt. I keep walking. I can't understand why I don't have a house, and so I can't even hang myself.

Hey, who's holding me around the ankle? If it's the rope for hanging, don't get so excited, don't be in such a hurry. But that's not what it is. It's a sticky silk thread. When I grab it and pull it, the end's in a split between the upper and sole of my shoe. It keeps getting longer and longer, slippery-like. This is weird. My curiosity makes me keep pulling it in. Then something even weirder happens. I'm slowly leaning over. I can't stand up at a right angle to the ground. Has the earth's axis tilted or the gravitational force changed direction?

A thud. My shoe drops off and hits the ground. I see what's happening. The earth's axis hasn't tilted, one of my legs has gotten shorter. As I pull at the thread, my leg rapidly gets shorter and shorter. Like the elbow of a frayed jacket unraveling, my leg's unwinding. The thread, like the fiber of a snake gourd, is my disintegrating leg.

I can't take one more step. I don't know what to do. I keep on standing. In my hand that doesn't know what to do either, my leg that has turned into a silk thread starts to move by itself. It crawls out smoothly. The tip, without any help from my hand, unwinds itself and like a snake starts wrapping itself around me. When my left leg's all unwound, the thread switches as natural as you please to my right leg. In a little while, the thread has wrapped my whole body in a bag. Even then, it doesn't stop but unwinds me from the hips to the chest, from the chest to the shoulders, and as it unwinds it strengthens the bag from inside. In the end, I'm gone.

Afterward, there remained a big empty cocoon.

Ah, now at last I can rest. The evening sun dyes the cocoon red. This, at least, is my house for sure, which nobody can keep me out of. The only trouble is now that I have a house, there's no "I" to return to it.

Inside the cocoon, time stopped. Outside, it was dark, but inside the cocoon it was always evening. Illumined from within, it glowed red with the colors of sunset. This outstanding peculiarity was bound to catch his sharp policeman's eye. He spotted me, the cocoon, lying between the rails of the crossing. At first he was angry, but soon changing his mind about this unusual find, he put me into his pocket. After tumbling around in there for a while, I was transferred to his son's toy box.

❧ The Stick

Translated by Lane Dunlop

It was a muggy Sunday in June . . .

On the crowded roof of the department store across from the station, supervising my two kids, I looked down at the avenue swollen with cars and people after the rain.

Spotting an opening, just vacated, between the ventilator and the stairs, I quickly wedged myself into it. I lifted each of the children in turn so they could see over the railing. They soon got tired of this, but now I was interested. It was nothing unusual, I thought. Actually, there were more adults clinging to the rail than children. Most of the children, quickly getting bored, started badgering their parents to go home. The adults, though, scolding them as if they'd interrupted their work, dreamily nestled their chins on their forearms on the railing again.

Of course, it may have been a slightly guilty pleasure. Even so, it wasn't anything to particularly call into question. I was simply in an absentminded mood. Or at least

I was not thinking of anything that later on I would have to try to remember. Only—perhaps it was the humid air—I grew curiously irritable and lost my temper with the kids.

The oldest, as if he were angry at me, was yelling "Daddy!" Without thinking, as if to escape his voice, I leaned way out over the railing. It was just a momentary impulse, nothing dangerous. But all of a sudden my body was floating in air. The voice yelling "Daddy!" still in my ears, I started falling.

I don't know if it was while falling that it happened, or if it happened, and then I fell, but when I came to, still falling, I'd turned into a stick. Not thick, not slender—I was a straight, handy stick about three feet long. The voice yelled "Daddy!" again. An opening appeared in the quickly moving crowd on the pavement below. Aiming at it, turning end over end, I fell faster and faster. Bouncing off the pavement with a sharp, dry sound, I hit a tree and lodged in a crack in the gutter between the sidewalk and the trolley tracks. Along the railing above, the pale little faces of my children were neatly lined up side by side.

The passersby glared angrily up at the roof. The doorman standing guard at the entrance, saying he would really get those brats for this, sprinted up the stairs. Excitedly, people shook their fists and made threats. Because of that, I stayed where I was in the gutter unnoticed by anyone for a while.

Finally a student noticed me. He was with two companions. One was a student like himself, dressed in the same uniform, and the other seemed to be their teacher. The two students, in stature, expression, and way of wearing their hats, were as alike as twins. The teacher, with a white mustache and powerful spectacles, was a very serene, tall gentleman.

Pulling me free, the first student said in a somehow regretful tone:

"Even this kind of thing, when it's no longer any use, has to perish."

"Let me have it," the teacher said with a smile. Receiving me from the student, he shook me two or three times, then said: "It's lighter than I thought. But nobody wants it for anything. Such as it is, though, it's a good object of study for you two. Perhaps just the thing for your first practical exercise. Let's think a little, shall we, of what can be learned from this stick."

Using me as a walking stick, the old gentleman started walking. The two students followed behind. Avoiding the crowd, they came out into the square in front of the station and looked around for a bench. The benches all being taken, though, they sat down side by side on the edge of the grass. Holding me up in both hands, the teacher narrowed his eyes as he scrutinized me against the light. Just then, I noticed a strange thing. Apparently noticing it at the same moment, the students said almost in unison: "Teacher, your mustache . . ." It seemed to be a false mustache. The left end had come unstuck and was flapping in the breeze. The teacher, calmly nodding agreement, pressed the mustache back in place with a saliva-moistened fingertip. As if nothing had happened, he turned to the students on either side of him and spoke.

"Now, what sort of things can you infer from this stick? Try analyzing it, judging it, and deciding on its punishment."

First, the student on the right took me and looked at me from various angles. "The first thing one notices is that this stick has an upper and a lower part." Sliding me through his hand closed in a tube, he continued: "The upper part is fairly ingrained with grime. The lower part is rather worn and abraded. This means, I take it, that this stick was not merely thrown away by the roadside but was used by people for some specific purpose. However, this stick was subjected to pretty hard use. There are nicks and scratches all over it. Furthermore, doesn't the fact that it was used for a long time without being thrown away mean that this stick, during its lifetime, was a simple, honest tool?"

"What you say is correct. But it's a little too sentimental," the teacher said, a smile in his voice.

Whereupon, whether it was to refute those words or not, the student on the left said, in a tone almost harsh:

"I think that this stick was probably completely useless. It's much *too* simple, isn't it? It's degrading for a human being to use a mere stick as a tool. Even a monkey can use a stick."

"But, to state the reverse," the student on the right rejoined, "cannot one say that the stick is the origin of all tools? What's more, without being especially altered, its uses are many. It can guide the blind man and train the dog. As a lever, it can move heavy objects, and it can thrash an adversary."

"The stick guides the blind man? I am unable to agree with that opinion. It's not the case that the blind man is guided by the stick. I believe that, using the stick, he guides himself."

"Well, isn't that to say that this was an honest stick?"

"Perhaps so. However, if Teacher is able to thrash me with this stick, I am also able to thrash Teacher with it."

Finally the teacher burst out laughing. "It's a real pleasure listening to you two argue. You're as alike as a pair of melons. However, you are simply saying the same thing in different ways. To summarize your statements, this man was a stick. That, for the necessity of referring to this man, is an adequate answer . . . In brief, this stick was a stick."

"But . . ." the student on the right said, a lingering regret in his voice. "To say that it was able to be a stick, don't we have to recognize its special characteristics? I have seen all sorts of human beings in our specimen room, but I've never once seen a stick. This kind of simple honesty is unusual, after all . . ."

"No, no. Just because it's not in our specimen room doesn't mean it's unusual," the teacher replied. "On the contrary, it's all too commonplace. In short, it's absolutely banal, and therefore we do not recognize any necessity to deliberately pick it up and examine it."

The students, simultaneously, as if they'd agreed on it, raised their faces and looked at the crowd around them. The teacher smiled. "No, it's not the case that all these people are sticks. When I say that being a stick is excessively ordinary, I speak in the qualitative rather than the quantitative sense. It's the same thing as mathematicians not saying much about the properties of a triangle. Because there are no new discoveries to be made from it." Pausing, he added: "By the way, what punishment do you two intend to hand down?"

"Do we have to inflict a punishment even on this stick?" the student on the right asked, as if in a quandary.

"What do you think?" The teacher turned to the student on the left.

"Of course we must punish it. To punish the dead is our raison d'être. We exist, therefore we must punish."

"Well, then, what is the appropriate punishment?"

The two students each thought hard for a while. The teacher, taking me, idly began drawing something in the dirt. It was a diagram without any abstract meaning. It soon sprouted arms and legs and became the figure of a monster. Then he began erasing the picture. When he'd finished, he stood up and, gazing into the distance, he muttered:

"Even you two must have thought long enough by now. The answer is so difficult because it's too simple. Surely you remember it from one of my lectures . . . Those who are judged by not being judged . . ."

"I remember," both students said at once. "It's enough for courts on earth to judge a certain percentage of the population. But we, until there are immortal human beings, have to judge them all. Compared to the number of people, however, we are extremely few. If we had to judge all the dead in the same way, we would probably work ourselves to death. Fortunately, there exists this convenient category of people whom we judge by not judging . . ."

"This stick is a representative example of that category." Smiling, the teacher let go of me. I fell down, and started to roll away. Stopping me with the tip of his shoe, the teacher said: "Therefore, the best punishment is to leave it behind like this. Most likely someone will pick it up and, just as during its lifetime, use it as a stick in various ways."

One of the students, as if it had just occurred to him, said: "What would this stick have thought if it could have heard us?"

The teacher looked at the student as if pitying him, but said nothing. Then, urging the two, he started walking. The students, seemingly worried about me, turned around and looked back at me several times. Soon, however, they were swallowed up by the crowd and disappeared. Somebody stepped on me. I was pressed halfway into the rain-softened dirt.

"Daddy, Daddy, Daddy . . ." I heard voices calling. They sounded like my children, and they didn't sound like my children. It would not be strange if, among the thousands of children in this crowd, there were many others who had to call out their father's name.

GABRIEL GARCÍA MÁRQUEZ

B. COLOMBIA, 1927

Ben Martin, *Gabriel García Márquez*, 1984 *García Márquez in his home library in Colombia. (Ben Martin / Timepix)*

GAH-bree-el
gar-SEE-ah MAR-kes

www For links to more information about García Márquez and a quiz on "A Very Old Man with Enormous Wings," and for information on the culture and context of South America in the twentieth century, see *World Literature Online* at bedfordstmartins .com/worldlit.

At one point in *One Hundred Years of Solitude,* Gabriel García Márquez's best-known novel, the characters succumb to a case of collective amnesia. To combat this contagion, the villagers label everything in town: "Thus they went on living in a reality that was slipping away, momentarily captured by words, but which would escape irremediably when they forgot the values of the written letters." This episode and the narrator's comment on it are emblematic of García Márquez's work as a whole. The fictional village of Macondo, where García Márquez sets many of his novels and stories, is based on the obscure village of Aracataca in northeastern Colombia where the author spent his early childhood. Although he left the village when he was eight, he guaranteed its literary survival by naming it "Macondo" in his work and making it one of modern literature's mythic places of the imagination along with William Faulkner's Yoknapatawpha County and R. K. Narayan's Malgudi.[1]

A Tradition of Storytelling.   Raised by his maternal grandparents in Aracataca, a village they helped to found, **Gabriel García Márquez** listened to tales of his grandfather's military exploits in the civil war and of the massacre of the striking workers on the local banana plantations in 1928, the year after Gabriel was born, when the workers resisted exploitation by the United Fruit Company. The young García Márquez especially listened to his grandmother's stories of ghosts, haunted houses, omens, and the lives and superstitions of the local people. Looking back years later, García Márquez would remark: "I feel that all my writing has been about the experiences of the time I spent with my grandparents."

Gabriel was sent to a boarding school in Barranquilla after his grandfather died. Eight years old, he was nicknamed "the old man" by his schoolmates, who thought him bookish and too serious; he eventually developed a rapport with them by writing stories, drawing cartoons, and reading aloud in the dormitory. In time his classmates came to regard him as a writer. He went on to study law and journalism at the Universities of Bogotá and Cartagena and then worked as a journalist in Bogotá, Havana, New York, Barcelona, and Mexico City. Though he has lived and worked internationally, his writings almost always go back to Macondo, whose history and mythology distill his experience and embody his view of the human condition.

---

[1]**Faulkner . . . Narayan's Malgudi:** William Faulkner (1897–1962), American novelist who in works like *The Sound and the Fury* (1929) and *Intruder in the Dust* (1948) created a history and sociology for his home area of northeastern Mississippi—and implicitly the American South—describing the dissolution of its values and social traditions. R. K. Narayan (1906–2001), Indian novelist who wrote about Malgudi, an imagined city in southern India, in many of his novels and stories, including *The Financial Expert* (1952) and *The Guide* (1958); see page 781.

A Career in Journalism.   Although García Márquez began publishing stories in the late forties, literary work remained a sideline for many years. After his first book of fiction appeared in 1955 to little notice, he continued to support himself by working as a journalist, earning a measure of notoriety for a series of reports that revealed the incompetence of the Colombian navy. To escape the government's retribution for those reports, he took an assignment as a foreign correspondent in Europe and eventually settled in Paris, intending to devote himself full-time to writing stories. In the early sixties he published several volumes: the novels *No One Writes to the Colonel* (1961) and *The Evil Hour* (1962), and a collection of stories, *Big Mama's Funeral* (1962). While those works enjoyed some critical recognition, their sales did not produce enough money to enable García Márquez to give up journalism; he continued to work off and on as a journalist and screenwriter. Much of his journalism was devoted to politics, such as his opposition to the Pinochet dictatorship in Chile and his support of the Cuban revolution. He used some of the money he received with the Nobel Prize in literature in 1982 to fund his antifascist magazine, *Alternativa*. His position with *Prensa Latina*, the Cuban news agency, as well as his friendship with Fidel Castro led the U.S. government to deny him a visa for many years.

The Impact of Modernism.   García Márquez was inspired to write fiction by reading the MODERNIST writers of the early twentieth century, especially Hemingway, Faulkner, Kafka, and Borges.[2] From Hemingway he learned an objective, bare-bones, Realist style; Faulkner's use of local myths and legends to construct an imaginary world recalled for the Colombian his grandmother's stories and inspired the village of Macondo; the work of Kafka and Borges suggested ways to meld dreams and nightmares with everyday reality. Reading Kafka's *The Metamorphosis* (Borges's Spanish translation) was a watershed for García Márquez: "I thought to myself that I didn't know anyone was allowed to write things like that. If I had known, I would have started writing much earlier." But the most important influence on the author's writing, it turned out, was his grandmother. García Márquez recounts an incident that occurred in the mid sixties as he was driving from Mexico City to Acapulco. Suddenly he had the beginning of his next novel—*One Hundred Years of Solitude* (*Cien años de soledad*, 1967), over which he had been fruitlessly struggling for a long time—so clearly in mind that he could have dictated it verbatim. He had remembered his grandmother's way of telling stories:

> The tone that I eventually used in *One Hundred Years of Solitude* was based on the way my grandmother used to tell stories. She told

The tone that I eventually used in *One Hundred Years of Solitude* was based on the way my grandmother used to tell stories. She told things that sounded supernatural and fantastic, but she told them with complete naturalness. . . . What was most important was the expression she had on her face. She did not change her expression at all when telling her stories and everyone was surprised. In previous attempts to write, I tried to tell the story without believing in it. I discovered that what I had to do was believe in them myself and write them with the same expression with which my grandmother told them: with a brick face.

– GABRIEL GARCÍA MÁRQUEZ

[2] **Hemingway . . . Borges:** Ernest Hemingway (1899–1961), American novelist and short-story writer noted for his blunt, terse, and starkly objective style in novels like *For Whom the Bell Tolls* (1940) and stories like "The Killers." Franz Kafka (1883–1924), German novelist and short-story writer; García Márquez was profoundly influenced by reading *The Metamorphosis*. "A Very Old Man with Enormous Wings" has many similarities to Kafka's "The Hunger Artist," a story about a carnival performer who makes not eating an attraction and ultimately starves himself to death. Jorge Luis Borges (1899–1986), Argentine writer especially noted for his enigmatic and fantastic short stories; see page 648.

things that sounded supernatural and fantastic, but she told them with complete naturalness. . . . What was most important was the expression she had on her face. She did not change her expression at all when telling her stories and everyone was surprised. In previous attempts to write, I tried to tell the story without believing in it. I discovered that what I had to do was believe in them myself and write them with the same expression with which my grandmother told them: with a brick face.

After the revelation on the Acapulco highway, García Márquez spent the next eighteen months writing night and day.

Magical Realism. *One Hundred Years of Solitude,* the saga of the founding of Macondo and its rise and fall over a century, combines realistic detail with folk legends and myths; hyperbolic, archetypal characters; and fantastic, dreamlike events. It chronicles seven generations of the

family of the founder, José Arcadio **Buendía**. The town and its history become an imaginative microcosm of the Latin American experience and, indeed, the human experience, for its mythic dimensions reach from the Garden of Eden to the Flood to the Apocalypse. Its mixture of realism, myth, and the miraculous has been called "**MAGICAL REALISM**,"[3] the dominant mode adopted by the writers of *el boom* (the boom), a movement in Latin American literature during the 1960s and 1970s, in the

works of García Márquez, Carlos Fuentes of Mexico, Mario Vargas **Llosa** of Peru, Julio Cortázar of Argentina, and others. These writers combine the realistic details of everyday life with extraordinary, even miraculous events.

The success of *One Hundred Years of Solitude* freed García Márquez from the necessity of having to hold another job, and with it began a period of rich productivity in the writer's creative life. *The Incredible and Sad Tale of Innocent Eréndira and Her Heartless Grandmother,* García Márquez's third collection of short stories, appeared in 1972. *The Autumn of the Patriarch (El otoño del patriarca),* a novel about a South American dictator, an all-powerful madman who, somewhere between the ages of 107 and 232, still rules his nation in lonely solitude, followed in 1975. *Chronicle of a Death Foretold* (1981) is a fictional version of an actual murder case; *Love in the Time of Cholera (El amor en los tiempos del cólera,* 1985) tells the story of a lifelong love affair. And *The General in His Labyrinth* (1989) is a historical novel recounting the last days of the Latin American liberator Simón Bolívar.

---

[3] **magical realism:** Fiction in which a Realist technique is used to narrate stories that combine mundane and miraculous events, everyday realities and the supernatural. The term is most often used to describe the work of the Latin American writers of *el boom:* García Márquez; Carlos Fuentes (b. 1928; see p. 933), Mexican novelist and author of such works as *Christopher Unborn* (1989); Mario Vargas Llosa (b. 1936), Peruvian novelist and journalist, and author of *The Time of the Hero* (1963), *Conversation in the Cathedral* (1969), and other works; and Julio Cortázar (1914–1984), Argentine author best known for the novel *Hopscotch* (1963) and the short story "Blow-Up," which was made into a successful film. Critics have also applied the term to other modern writers, especially Kafka (see p. 423), Thomas Mann (see p. 261), and Borges.

"A Very Old Man with Enormous Wings." García Márquez stresses the realism in his work; "my work as a whole," he has written, "is founded on a geographical and historical reality." The description of the fallen angel in "A Very Old Man with Enormous Wings" (1972) illustrates this fundamental realism. Bald and dirty, with missing teeth, ragged clothes, and an unbearable smell, the stranger who appears in the courtyard of **Pelayo** and **Elisenda**'s house is first of all "an old man." The priest concludes that "seen close up he was much too human." Even the wings that mark him as an angel are bedraggled and "strewn with parasites." His presence in the village may be magical, but it is also absurd, and the reactions of the villagers quickly transform the unfamiliar creature into something familiar. Father Gonzaga is convinced that the old man is an impostor and writes to the Pope for confirmation of his suspicions; the villagers treat the angel as a sideshow spectacle, one that is outdone when the spider woman comes to town. The story she tells of her suffering provides a conventional explanation for her situation, unlike the "haughty" silence of the angel. In the end, when the angel miraculously flies away, Elisenda is relieved that the "annoyance" is gone from her life. The angel may be magical, but the various responses of the villagers—from indifference to exploitation—deflate his significance and lead readers to wonder about the place of magic in the modern world.

pay-LAH-yoh;
eh-lee-SEN-dah

■ CONNECTIONS

Franz Kafka, *The Metamorphosis*, p. 428. Like García Márquez, Kafka begins his story with a miraculous event—Gregor's transformation into a bug—and then realistically explores its consequences. The angel and the cockroach provoke reactions from others. What do the angel and the cockroach symbolize? Do people's reactions to them satirize similar human failings?

Carlos Fuentes, *The Prisoner of Las Lomas*, p. 938; Jorge Luis Borges, "The Garden of Forking Paths," p. 652; Pablo Neruda, poems, p. 677; Abé Kobo, "The Red Cocoon" and "The Stick," pp. 918 and 920. Several modern works in this anthology adopt the magical realist technique of mixing the uncanny, bizarre, or supernatural with the realistic and the mundane: Fuentes's *The Prisoner of Las Lomas*, Borges's "The Garden of Forking Paths," Abé Kobo's "The Red Cocoon" and "The Stick," and Neruda's poems could all be considered, in a broad sense, "magical realism." What is fantastic in each work? How does each author make the fantastic believable? Is the same point being made in each work through magical realism?

Samuel Taylor Coleridge, "The Rime of the Ancient Mariner" (Book 5). The Romantics in the early nineteenth century were fascinated with supernatural and uncanny events, often using the conventions of the folktale to give credence to an extraordinary story. In the story told by Coleridge's Ancient Mariner, the albatross has similarities to García Márquez's angel. Both, for example, have a religious dimension. What does each symbolize? Are Pelayo and Elisenda likely to become compulsive storytellers like the mariner, waylaying people to listen to their tale?

■ FURTHER RESEARCH

Criticism
Bell, Michael. *Gabriel García Márquez: Solitude and Solidarity.* 1993.
McMurray, George R., ed. *Critical Essays on Gabriel García Márquez.* 1987.

McNerney, Kathleen. *Understanding Gabriel García Márquez.* 1989.

Oberhelman, Harley D. *Gabriel García Márquez: A Study of the Short Fiction.* 1991.

Shaw, Bradley A., and Nora Vera-Goodwin, eds. *Critical Perspectives on Gabriel García Márquez.* 1986.

Vergara, Isabel Rodríguez. *Haunting Demons: Critical Essays on the Works of Gabriel García Márquez.* 1998.

Williams, Raymond. *Gabriel García Márquez.* 1984.

■ PRONUNCIATION

Buendía: bwayn-*THEE*-ah

Cartagena: kar-tah-HAY-nah

Elisenda: eh-lee-SEN-dah

Gabriel García Márquez: GAH-bree-el gar-SEE-ah MAR-kes

Llosa: YOH-sah

Pelayo: pay-LAH-yoh

Yoknapatawpha: yahk-nuh-puh-TAW-puh

∾ A Very Old Man with Enormous Wings

Translated by Gregory Rabassa

On the third day of rain they had killed so many crabs inside the house that Pelayo had to cross his drenched courtyard and throw them into the sea, because the newborn child had a temperature all night and they thought it was due to the stench. The world had been sad since Tuesday. Sea and sky were a single ash-gray thing and the sands of the beach, which on March nights glimmered like powdered light, had become a stew of mud and rotten shellfish. The light was so weak at noon that when Pelayo was coming back to the house after throwing away the crabs, it was hard for him to see what it was that was moving and groaning in the rear of the courtyard. He had to go very close to see that it was an old man, a very old man, lying face down in the mud, who, in spite of his tremendous efforts, couldn't get up, impeded by his enormous wings.

Frightened by that nightmare, Pelayo ran to get Elisenda, his wife, who was putting compresses on the sick child, and he took her to the rear of the courtyard. They both looked at the fallen body with mute stupor. He was dressed like a ragpicker.

"A Very Old Man with Enormous Wings." This short story, written shortly after *One Hundred Years of Solitude* and included in a collection of García Márquez's stories in 1972, recounts in deadpan, realistic narration a series of bizarre and miraculous events—a voice characteristic of the author's magical realism. The angel of the story's title does not have the appearance of a supernatural being but rather that of an unkempt and disheveled old man. As each of the villagers seeks to "explain" the angel and deny or ignore his supernatural nature, García Márquez reveals their superstition and self-interest and satirizes institutions such as the church. The ending may surprise readers as it does the villagers; it also raises questions about the presence of the miraculous in the midst of the mundane.

There were only a few faded hairs left on his bald skull and very few teeth in his mouth, and his pitiful condition of a drenched great-grandfather had taken away any sense of grandeur he might have had. His huge buzzard wings, dirty and half-plucked, were forever entangled in the mud. They looked at him so long and so closely that Pelayo and Elisenda very soon overcame their surprise and in the end found him familiar. Then they dared speak to him, and he answered in an incomprehensible dialect with a strong sailor's voice. That was how they skipped over the inconvenience of the wings and quite intelligently concluded that he was a lonely castaway from some foreign ship wrecked by the storm. And yet, they called in a neighbor woman who knew everything about life and death to see him, and all she needed was one look to show them their mistake.

"He's an angel," she told them. "He must have been coming for the child, but the poor fellow is so old that the rain knocked him down."

On the following day everyone knew that a flesh-and-blood angel was held captive in Pelayo's house. Against the judgment of the wise neighbor woman, for whom angels in those times were the fugitive survivors of a celestial conspiracy, they did not have the heart to club him to death. Pelayo watched over him all afternoon from the kitchen, armed with his bailiff's club, and before going to bed he dragged him out of the mud and locked him up with the hens in the wire chicken coop. In the middle of the night, when the rain stopped, Pelayo and Elisenda were still killing crabs. A short time afterward the child woke up without a fever and with a desire to eat. Then they felt magnanimous and decided to put the angel on a raft with fresh water and provisions for three days and leave him to his fate on the high seas. But when they went out into the courtyard with the first light of dawn, they found the whole neighborhood in front of the chicken coop having fun with the angel, without the slightest reverence, tossing him things to eat through the openings in the wire as if he weren't a supernatural creature but a circus animal.

Father Gonzaga arrived before seven o'clock, alarmed at the strange news. By that time onlookers less frivolous than those at dawn had already arrived and they were making all kinds of conjectures concerning the captive's future. The simplest among them thought that he should be named mayor of the world. Others of sterner mind felt that he should be promoted to the rank of five-star general in order to win all wars. Some visionaries hoped that he could be put to stud in order to implant on earth a race of winged wise men who could take charge of the universe. But Father Gonzaga, before becoming a priest, had been a robust woodcutter. Standing by the wire, he reviewed his catechism in an instant and asked them to open the door so that he could take a close look at that pitiful man who looked more like a huge decrepit hen among the fascinated chickens. He was lying in a corner drying his open wings in the sunlight among the fruit peels and breakfast leftovers that the early risers had thrown him. Alien to the impertinences of the world, he only lifted his antiquarian eyes and murmured something in his dialect when Father Gonzaga went into the chicken coop and said good morning to him in Latin. The parish priest had his first suspicion of an impostor when he saw that he did not understand the language of God or know how to greet His ministers. Then he noticed that seen close up he was much too human: He had an unbearable smell of the outdoors, the back

side of his wings was strewn with parasites and his main feathers had been mistreated by terrestrial winds, and nothing about him measured up to the proud dignity of angels. Then he came out of the chicken coop and in a brief sermon warned
the curious against the risks of being ingenuous. He reminded them that the devil
had the bad habit of making use of carnival tricks in order to confuse the unwary. He
argued that if wings were not the essential element in determining the difference
between a hawk and an airplane, they were even less so in the recognition of angels.
Nevertheless, he promised to write a letter to his bishop so that the latter would write
to his primate so that the latter would write to the Supreme Pontiff in order to get
the final verdict from the highest courts.

His prudence fell on sterile hearts. The news of the captive angel spread with
such rapidity that after a few hours the courtyard had the bustle of a marketplace
and they had to call in troops with fixed bayonets to disperse the mob that was about
to knock the house down. Elisenda, her spine all twisted from sweeping up so much
marketplace trash, then got the idea of fencing in the yard and charging five cents
admission to see the angel.

The curious came from far away. A traveling carnival arrived with a flying acro-
bat who buzzed over the crowd several times, but no one paid any attention to him
because his wings were not those of an angel but, rather, those of a sidereal bat. The
most unfortunate invalids on earth came in search of health: a poor woman who
since childhood had been counting her heartbeats and had run out of numbers; a
Portuguese man who couldn't sleep because the noise of the stars disturbed him; a
sleepwalker who got up at night to undo the things he had done while awake; and
many others with less serious ailments. In the midst of that shipwreck disorder that
made the earth tremble, Pelayo and Elisenda were happy with fatigue, for in less than
a week they had crammed their rooms with money and the line of pilgrims waiting
their turn to enter still reached beyond the horizon.

The angel was the only one who took no part in his own act. He spent his time
trying to get comfortable in his borrowed nest, befuddled by the hellish heat of the
oil lamps and sacramental candles that had been placed along the wire. At first they
tried to make him eat some mothballs, which, according to the wisdom of the wise
neighbor woman, were the food prescribed for angels. But he turned them down,
just as he turned down the papal lunches that the penitents brought him, and they
never found out whether it was because he was an angel or because he was an old
man that in the end he ate nothing but eggplant mush. His only supernatural virtue
seemed to be patience. Especially during the first days, when the hens pecked at him,
searching for the stellar parasites that proliferated in his wings, and the cripples
pulled out feathers to touch their defective parts with, and even the most merciful
threw stones at him, trying to get him to rise so they could see him standing. The
only time they succeeded in arousing him was when they burned his side with an
iron for branding steers, for he had been motionless for so many hours that they
thought he was dead. He awoke with a start, ranting in his hermetic language and
with tears in his eyes, and he flapped his wings a couple of times, which brought on a
whirlwind of chicken dung and lunar dust and a gale of panic that did not seem to
be of this world. Although many thought that his reaction had been one not of rage

but of pain, from then on they were careful not to annoy him, because the majority understood that his passivity was not that of a hero taking his ease but that of a cataclysm in repose.

Father Gonzaga held back the crowd's frivolity with formulas of maidservant inspiration while awaiting the arrival of a final judgment on the nature of the captive. But the mail from Rome showed no sense of urgency. They spent their time finding out if the prisoner had a navel, if his dialect had any connection with Aramaic, how many times he could fit on the head of a pin, or whether he wasn't just a Norwegian with wings. Those meager letters might have come and gone until the end of time if a providential event had not put an end to the priest's tribulations.

It so happened that during those days, among so many other carnival attractions, there arrived in town the traveling show of the woman who had been changed into a spider for having disobeyed her parents. The admission to see her was not only less than the admission to see the angel, but people were permitted to ask her all manner of questions about her absurd state and to examine her up and down so that no one would ever doubt the truth of her horror. She was a frightful tarantula the size of a ram and with the head of a sad maiden. What was most heartrending, however, was not her outlandish shape but the sincere affliction with which she recounted the details of her misfortune. While still practically a child she had sneaked out of her parents' house to go to a dance, and while she was coming back through the woods after having danced all night without permission, a fearful thunderclap rent the sky in two and through the crack came the lightning bolt of brimstone that changed her into a spider. Her only nourishment came from the meatballs that charitable souls chose to toss into her mouth. A spectacle like that, full of so much human truth and with such a fearful lesson, was bound to defeat without even trying that of a haughty angel who scarcely deigned to look at mortals. Besides, the few miracles attributed to the angel showed a certain mental disorder, like the blind man who didn't recover his sight but grew three new teeth, or the paralytic who didn't get to walk but almost won the lottery, and the leper whose sores sprouted sunflowers. Those consolation miracles, which were more like mocking fun, had already ruined the angel's reputation when the woman who had been changed into a spider finally crushed him completely. That was how Father Gonzaga was cured forever of his insomnia and Pelayo's courtyard went back to being as empty as during the time it had rained for three days and crabs walked through the bedrooms.

The owners of the house had no reason to lament. With the money they saved they built a two-story mansion with balconies and gardens and high netting so that crabs wouldn't get in during the winter, and with iron bars on the windows so that angels wouldn't get in. Pelayo also set up a rabbit warren close to town and gave up his job as bailiff for good, and Elisenda bought some satin pumps with high heels and many dresses of iridescent silk, the kind worn on Sunday by the most desirable women in those times. The chicken coop was the only thing that didn't receive any attention. If they washed it down with creolin and burned tears of myrrh inside it every so often, it was not in homage to the angel but to drive away the dungheap stench that still hung everywhere like a ghost and was turning the new house into an old one. At first, when the child learned to walk, they were careful that he not get too close to the chicken coop. But then they began to lose their fears and got used to the smell, and before the child got his second teeth he'd gone inside the chicken coop to play, where the wires were falling apart. The angel was no less standoffish with him than with other mortals, but he tolerated the most ingenious infamies with the patience of a dog who had no illusions. They both came down with chicken pox at the same time. The doctor who took care of the child couldn't resist the temptation to listen to the angel's heart, and he found so much whistling in the heart and so many sounds in his kidneys that it seemed impossible for him to be alive. What surprised him most, however, was the logic of his wings. They seemed so natural on that completely human organism that he couldn't understand why other men didn't have them too.

When the child began school it had been some time since the sun and rain had caused the collapse of the chicken coop. The angel went dragging himself about here and there like a stray dying man. They would drive him out of the bedroom with a broom and a moment later find him in the kitchen. He seemed to be in so many places at the same time that they grew to think that he'd been duplicated, that he was reproducing himself all through the house, and the exasperated and unhinged Elisenda shouted that it was awful living in that hell full of angels. He could scarcely eat and his antiquarian eyes had also become so foggy that he went about bumping into posts. All he had left were the bare cannulae of his last feathers. Pelayo threw a blanket over him and extended him the charity of letting him sleep in the shed, and only then did they notice that he had a temperature at night, and was delirious with the tongue twisters of an old Norwegian. That was one of the few times they became alarmed, for they thought he was going to die and not even the wise neighbor woman had been able to tell them what to do with dead angels.

And yet he not only survived his worst winter, but seemed improved with the first sunny days. He remained motionless for several days in the farthest corner of the courtyard, where no one would see him, and at the beginning of December some large, stiff feathers began to grow on his wings, the feathers of a scarecrow, which looked more like another misfortune of decrepitude. But he must have known the reason for those changes, for he was quite careful that no one should notice them, that no one should hear the sea chanteys that he sometimes sang under the stars. One morning Elisenda was cutting some bunches of onions for lunch when a wind that seemed to come from the high seas blew into the kitchen. Then she went to the window and caught the angel in his first attempts at flight. They were so clumsy that his fingernails opened a furrow in the vegetable patch and he was on the point of knocking the shed down with the ungainly flapping that slipped on the light and couldn't get a grip on the air. But he did manage to gain altitude. Elisenda let out a sigh of relief, for herself and for him, when she saw him pass over the last houses, holding himself up in some way with the risky flapping of a senile vulture. She kept watching him even when she was through cutting the onions and she kept on watching until it was no longer possible for her to see him, because then he was no longer an annoyance in her life but an imaginary dot on the horizon of the sea.

CARLOS FUENTES
B. PANAMA, 1928

For many in the United States, Mexicans are, as one commentator has described them, "distant neighbors." Americans know more about European culture than they do about that of the nation next door. The work of Carlos Fuentes, Mexico's foremost contemporary novelist, is a good introduction to contemporary Mexico, as he writes about Mexican history and culture in nearly all of his books. He is also a very cosmopolitan writer, involved with Europe, the United States, and the traditions of Western culture generally. His interest in relations between industrial nations and developing nations and his experiments with narrative point of view and MAGICAL REALISM place his work in the mainstream of contemporary world literature. He is the first Mexican novelist to have had one of his works — *The Old Gringo* (1985) — on the *New York Times* bestseller list.

A Citizen of the World.   Fuentes has been an internationalist from birth. The son of a career diplomat, he was born in Panama and spent most of his childhood outside Mexico—in the United States, Latin America, and Europe. He learned English at age four in Washington, D.C., and he attended schools in the United States, Brazil, Chile, and Mexico. He has suggested that this childhood dislocation helped to ignite his literary career: "I had to imagine Mexico before I ever lived in Mexico," he remarked in a 1988 interview, "so when I went to live in Mexico, the first thing I had to do was to contrast my imagination of the country to the reality of the country, which is the kind of tension from which literature is born." After studying law at the University of Mexico and at the Institute of Advanced International Studies in Geneva, Switzerland, Fuentes became a diplomat himself, serving as a cultural officer and on other diplomatic missions and as Mexico's ambassador to France in the 1970s. Even though his support for the Marxist revolution in Cuba led to disputes with the U. S. State Department and he has been barred on occasion from entering the United States, he has spent a great deal of time in this country, teaching at many American universities, including Columbia, Harvard, George Mason, and the Universities of California, Oklahoma, and Pennsylvania. He has also taught at the University of Paris; Cambridge University, in England; and the University of Concepción, in Chile.

The Early Novels.   Carlos Fuentes began his writing career in the late forties. In 1958 he published his first novel, *Where the Air Is Clear* (*La región mas transparente*), the story of an old revolutionary, Federico Robles, who has become a financial tycoon preoccupied with making money. Robles symbolizes a Mexico that has lost direction, betrayed its revolution, and adopted the empty values of materialistic capitalism. In the course of the novel, Robles's financial empire falls, and he leaves the city to return to the country and reestablish contact with some mythic

Bob Daemmrich, *Carlos Fuentes,* 1999
This photograph of Fuentes was taken while the author was attending the Latin American Studies symposium at Southwestern University. (© Bob Daemmrich / The Image Works)

KAR-lohs FWEN-tays

www   For links to more information about Fuentes and a quiz on *The Prisoner of Las Lomas,* and for information about the culture and context of Mexico in the twentieth century, see *World Literature Online* at bedfordstmartins .com/worldlit.

sources of Mexican culture. *The Death of Artemio Cruz* (*La muerte de Artemio Cruz,* 1962) further developed these cultural themes. Like Robles, Cruz is a businessman who has betrayed the revolution of 1910–1920, in which he fought as a young man. Although he came from peasant origins, he used the revolution as a way of acquiring personal wealth and power. He lied and married his way into a wealthy family, made opportunistic political alliances, and abandoned the ideal of land reform for which the revolution was fought so that he could inhabit the mansions of the prerevolutionary landowners. He has increased his wealth by becoming a Mexican front man for large American corporations. An old man on his deathbed at the time of the narration, he tells of his life in several voices representing the fragmentation of his character and of Mexican culture. The story of his life thus becomes an account of the history of Mexico in the twentieth century.

Mexico and Its History.   Nearly all of Fuentes's novels take up the themes of these early works: the class domination and polarization of Mexican culture; its lost contact with its own mythic and historic roots through materialism and "Americanization"; the financial corruption of modern, urban life; and the betrayal of Mexico's revolutionary ideals, especially the failure to carry out land reform. These social themes have made Mexican history important elements in Fuentes's work. Many of the characters and situations in his novels are defined in historical terms. Eruptions from the Aztec past, for example, intrude on the contemporary scene. The bloody revolution of 1910–1920 is a particularly defining event in Fuentes's work. Fought at the same time as the **BOLSHEVIK** Revolution in Russia, the Mexican Revolution sought to limit the power of the Catholic Church, overthrow the large landowners, and, by redistributing the land among the *campesinos* (peasants), create a more equitable distribution of the national wealth. Although the single-party government that took power in the revolution and ruled for the rest of the twentieth century paid lip service to revolutionary ideals, it failed to carry out a program of land reform. For Fuentes this betrayal is the defining fact about modern Mexico.

What strikes the reader first in Fuentes's work may be his erudition and intellectual rigour, but what remains in the mind is his sympathy, his concern to commemorate the countless lives sacrificed in pain and obscurity so that we might live.

– MICHAEL KERRIGAN,
Times Literary Supplement, 1994

Fuentes has said that "the theme of the country, the culture, and the society in which I work . . . has been [my] most powerful external impulse." The divisions between primitive and modern, past and present, revolutionary idealism and continuing corruption, the rural countryside and the sprawl of the world's largest city, and a mythic past and a materialistic present become the defining contradictions in his work. Fuentes's Mexico City, a microcosm of Mexican culture that centers most of his novels, is reminiscent of Dickens's London, Balzac's Paris, and the urban wasteland of T. S. Eliot's vision of the modern world.[1] Banal, anonymous,

---

[1] **Fuentes's Mexico City . . . world:** The Romantic Realists of the nineteenth century—Honoré de Balzac (1799–1850) and Charles Dickens (1812–1870), for example—were noted for creating mythic versions of the cities they wrote about. T. S. Eliot's 1922 poem *The Waste Land* (see p. 486), similarly creates a mythic version of modern London that symbolically represents the spiritually empty post–World War I modern cities.

Twentieth-Century Mexico: The Mexican Revolution

The Mexican Revolution (1910–1920) was the first great social revolution of the twentieth century and one of the bloodiest conflicts in the history of North America. Contemporary Mexico cannot be understood without refer-

Defiende las Conquistas, c. 1910–1920.   This advertisement, featuring the Mexican revolutionary Emiliano Zapata, translates, "Defend the Conquests for which We Gave Our Lives." (The Art Archive)

ence to it. Mexican dictator Porfirio Díaz (1830–1915) steered Mexico into the twentieth century with the slogan "Order and progress," but by the end of his rule landowners had amassed inordinate power while the poor had slipped deep into poverty and deprivation. During the second decade of the twentieth century, a series of revolutionary leaders — among them Francisco I. Madero, Victoriano Huerta, Venustiano Carranza, Francisco Villa, and Emiliano Zapata — fought to control the country and institute liberal reforms. The revolution was not a clear-cut struggle between oppression and liberty but a succession of shifting allegiances among a wide-ranging assortment of leaders in which attempts to create stability were ineffective and overly complicated. During this period some industries, railroads and mining, for example, were nationalized; some common lands were restored to indigenous peoples; and modest reforms were made in labor laws, agricultural policy, and education. Church and state were separated and anticlericalism was institutionalized, as was the Party of the Revolution (P.R.I.), which ruled Mexican government for the rest of the twentieth century. Although some argue that the revolution continued for another twenty years in varying degrees, the 1910s, the most turbulent decade of violent civil war, cost an estimated one and a half to two million lives.

> The theme of the country, the culture, and the society in which I work . . . has been [my] most powerful external impulse.
>
> – CARLOS FUENTES

ah-YEN-day

and spiritually empty, the product of technology and greed, Mexico City is part of an international network and is cut off from its own history and traditions. Fuentes has also acknowledged kinship with William Faulkner as a "novelist of defeat," for in Faulkner's Yoknapatawpha County Fuentes finds a fragmented and declining rural culture similar to Mexico's. This suppressed peasant culture and the sacred traditions of the Aztec past show up in the present in recollections of Aztec myth or in mysterious events that cannot be explained in the more logical or scientific terms of the city. These touches of "magical realism" give a surreal edge to Fuentes's vision and ally him with the most important movement in Latin American literature in the last thirty years. Like other magical realists — such writers as Alejo Carpentier, Isabel **Allende**,[2] and Gabriel García Márquez — Fuentes juxtaposes the everyday and the miraculous as a way of revealing the discontinuities and contradictions of modern life. Besides *Artemio Cruz,* the novels by which Fuentes is known in the United States are *Terra Nostra* (1975), an exploration of Mexico's Spanish heritage; *The Old Gringo* (*El gringo viejo,* 1985) a novel about the disappearance of American writer Ambrose Bierce in Mexico in 1913, during the revolution; and *Christopher Unborn* (*Cristobal nonato,* 1989), a satiric commentary on Columbus and his impact on the Western Hemisphere. Fuentes has also written many short stories, collected in *The Masked Days* (*Los días enmascarados,* 1954), *Songs of the Blind* (*Candar de ciegos,* 1964), *Constancia and Other Stories for Virgins* (*Constancia y otros novelas para vírgenes,* 1989), and *Distant Relations, a Novel in Nine Stories* (*La frontera de cristal: una novela en nueve cuentos,* 1995).

> I had to imagine Mexico before I ever lived in Mexico, so when I went to live in Mexico, the first thing I had to do was to contrast my imagination of the country to the reality of the country, which is the kind of tension from which literature is born.
>
> – CARLOS FUENTES, in a 1988 interview

■ **CONNECTIONS**

Joseph Conrad, *Heart of Darkness,* **p. 35;** *In the World:* **Colonialism, p. 97.** The issues of colonialism raised by Conrad's *Heart of Darkness* and *In the World:* Colonialism are implicit in the uneasy relationship between Fuentes's lawyer-narrator, an inheritor of the culture of the Europeans who settled Mexico, and the country peasants who come to occupy the courtyard of his house and "imprison" him. Like Kurtz, Nicolás is a captive of the people he has conquered. Does he share Kurtz's initial idealism or his ultimate recognition of "the horror"? What does he learn?

Milan Kundera, "The Hitchhiking Game," p. 1005. *The Prisoner of Las Lomas* and Kundera's "The Hitchhiking Game" contain similar contemporary versions of the Don Juan myth, narrated in both cases by the Don Juan figure in the story. What role does sexual conquest play in the lives of these characters? What does the Don Juan motif contribute thematically to these stories? Can these stories be interpreted as commentary on patriarchal cultures?

Anton Chekhov, *The Cherry Orchard* **(Book 5); Rabindranath Tagore, "The Hungry Stones" (Book 5).** The house in *The Prisoner of Las Lomas* represents Mexican culture and history; it "owns" Nicolás as much as he owns it. It is similar to the palace

---

[2] **Carpentier . . . Allende:** Alejo Carpentier (1904–1980), Cuban novelist and musicologist influenced by French surrealism and the author of *The Kingdom of this World* (1949) and other works; Isabel Allende (b. 1942), Chilean novelist and short-story writer who has penned *House of the Spirits* (1982), *Daughter of Fortune* (1999), and other works.

haunted by its Indian past in Tagore's "The Hungry Stones" and to the estate in Chekhov's *The Cherry Orchard,* which represents the Russian past. Consider the qualities of these domiciles and what they add to the picture of the past of their three cultures. How do they function symbolically in the outcomes of these three works?

■ **FURTHER RESEARCH**

Background
Paz, Octavio. *The Labyrinth of Solitude: Life and Thought in Mexico.* 1961.

Criticism
Brody, Robert, and Charles Rossmann. *Carlos Fuentes, a Critical View.* 1982.
Delden, Maarten van. *Carlos Fuentes, Mexico and Modernity.* 1998.
Durán, Gloria. *The Archetypes of Carlos Fuentes: From Witch to Androgyne.* 1980.
Faris, Wendy B. *Carlos Fuentes.* 1983.
Guzmán, Daniel de. *Carlos Fuentes.* 1972.
Helmuth, Chalene. *The Postmodern Fuentes.* 1997.
Williams, Raymond. *The Writings of Carlos Fuentes.* 1996.

■ **PRONUNCIATION**

Allende: ah-YEN-day
Calle de Córdoba: KAH-yay *thay* KORE-*thoh*-vah
Camino Real: kah-MEE-noh ray-AHL
Chapultepec: chuh-PUL-tuh-peck, chah-pool-teh-PECK
Cinco de Mayo: SEENG-koh *thay* MAH-yoh
Escobedo: ays-koh-VAY-*thoh*
Eulalia: yoo-LAY-lee-uh
Carlos Fuentes: KAR-lohs FWEN-tays
Guanajuanto: gwah-nah-WAHN-toh
Ixtapa-Zihuatenejo: ees-TAH-pah thee-wah-tah-NAY-hoh
Michoacán: mee-choh-ah-KAHN
Morelos: moh-RAY-lohs
Oaxaca: wah-HAH-kah
Potosí: poh-toh-SEE
Prisciliano Nieves: pree-see-LYAH-noh NYAY-vays
Querétaro: kay-RAY-tah-roh
Quezada: kay-THAH-*thah*, kay-*THAH*-dah
Sarita Palazuelos: sah-REE-tah pah-lah-THWAY-lohs
Solomillo: soh-loh-MEE-yoh
Tehuacán: tay-wah-KAHN
Virreyes: vee-RAY-yes

The first active and conscious agent of the internationalization of the Spanish American novel.

– JOSE DONOSO, 1977

∾ The Prisoner of Las Lomas

Translated by Thomas Christensen

[*To Valerio Adami, for a Sicilian story*]

1

As incredible as this story is, I might as well begin at the beginning and continue straight on to the end. Easy to say. The minute I get set to begin, I realize I begin with an enigma. It follows that difficulties ensue. Oh, fuck! It can't be helped: the story begins with a mystery; my hope, I swear, is that by the end you'll understand everything. That you will understand me. You'll see: I leave out nothing. But the truth is that when I entered the sickroom of Brigadier General Prisciliano Nieves on February 23, 1960, in the British hospital then located in the Avenida Mariano Escobedo (present site of the Camino Real Hotel, to orient my younger listeners), I myself had to believe in the enigma, or what I was planning would not succeed. I want to be understood. The mystery was true. (The truth was the mystery.) But if I was not myself convinced of it, I would not convince the old and astute Brigadier Nieves, not even on his sickbed.

He was, as I said, a general. You know that already. I was a young lawyer who had

---

The Prisoner of Las Lomas. Written in 1987 and included in the volume *Constancia and Other Stories for Virgins* (*Constancia y otros novelas para vírgenes*, 1989; English translation, 1990), this work displays many of Fuentes's characteristic themes. Like *Artemio Cruz, Prisoner* is a first-person narrative. Although Nicolás Sarmiento's personal history does not reach back to the revolution, his personal story does, for he has linked his life with that of General Prisciliano Nieves, a legendary hero of the war. Sarmiento, a cynical opportunist, uses his serendipitous knowledge of the truth about Nieves's role in the war to blackmail the general and establish himself as his heir. His hard-headed realism, urbanity, and lack of sentimentality make him a successful blackmailer, businessman, and Don Juan. But these same traits also make him incapable of understanding the appeal of the legend about General Nieves and of recognizing the emotional bonds that link the Mexican people into "family." His education in the mysteries of emotion and cultural solidarity begins when he departs from his rule of emotional detachment and becomes involved with Lala, a mysterious woman with ties to rural Mexico. Her murder implicates him and forces him to recognize his servants as individuals with names. Ironically, he discovers his alter ego Dimas Palmero, the servant charged with murdering Lala. They both become prisoners—Palmero in the jail where he is held without trial, and Sarmiento in his mansion in Las Lomas de Chapultepec, where he is surrounded by a host of nameless peasants, Lala's kin, who take control of his life. Both the peasant and the *patrón* are entangled in the tragedy, as they are in the truth and legends of Mexican history and culture. By the end of the story, faced with its power to control his destiny, Sarmiento has learned just how limited his knowledge of Mexican history is.

A note on the translation: The translation is by Thomas Christensen, who has translated the works of many Latin American writers, including Alejo Carpentier, Julio Cortázar, and Laura Esquivel. The notes are the editors'.

recently received my degree—news for you and for me. I knew everything about him. He, nothing about me. So when I found the door to his private room in the hospital ajar and pushed it open, he didn't recognize me, but neither did he draw back. Lax as security is in Mexican hospitals, there was no reason for the brigadier to be alarmed. I saw him lying there in one of those beds that are like the throne of death, a white throne, as if cleanliness were the compensation that dying offers us. His name *Nieves* means *snow,* but lying in all that bleached linen he was like a fly in milk. The brigadier was very dark, his head was shaved, his mouth a long, sourish crack, his eyes masked by two thick, livid veils. But why describe him, when he was so soon gone? You can look up his photo in the Casasola Archives.

Who knows why he was dying? I went by his house and they said to me:

—The general's bad.

—It's just he's so old.

I scarcely noticed them. The one who spoke first seemed a cook, the second a young girl servant. I made out a sort of majordomo inside the house, and there was a gardener tending the roses outside. You see: only of the gardener was I able to say definitely, that man is a gardener. The others were just one thing or another. They didn't exist for me.

But the brigadier did. Propped up in his hospital bed, surrounded by a parapet of cushions, he looked at me as he must have looked at his troops the day he single-handedly saved the honor of his regiment, of the Northeast Corps, almost of the very Revolution, and maybe even of the country itself—why not?—in the encounter of La Zapotera, when the wild Colonel Andrés Solomillo, who confused extermination with justice, occupied the Santa Eulalia sugar mill and lined both masters and workers against its wall to face the firing squad, saying the servants were as bad as those they served.

—The one who holds the cow is as bad as the one who slaughters it.

So said Solomillo, helping himself to the possessions of the Escalona family, masters of the hacienda: quickly grabbing all the gold coins he'd found in the library, behind the complete works of Auguste Comte, he proposed to Prisciliano: —Take these, my captain, so that for once those who are as hungry as you and I may be invited to the banquet of life.

Prisciliano Nieves—the legend goes—not only refused the gold his superior offered him but, when it came time for the execution, he placed himself between the firing squad and the condemned and said to Colonel Andrés Solomillo: —The soldiers of the Revolution are neither murderers nor thieves. These poor people are guilty of nothing. Separate the poor from the rich, please.

What happened then—so the story goes—was this: the colonel, furious, told Prisciliano that if he didn't shut up he would be the second feature in the morning's firing; Prisciliano shouted to the troops not to kill other poor people; the squad hesitated; Solomillo gave the order to fire at Prisciliano; Prisciliano gave the order to fire at the colonel; and in the end the squad obeyed Prisciliano:

—Mexican soldiers do not murder the people, because they are the people, said Prisciliano beside the body of Solomillo, and the soldiers cheered him and felt satisfied.

This phrase, associated ever since with the fame, the life, and the virtues of the instantly Colonel and soon-to-be Brigadier General Don Prisciliano Nieves, surely would be engraved on the base of his monument: THE HERO OF SANTA EULALIA.

And now here I come, forty-five years later, to put a damper on the final glory of General Prisciliano Nieves.

—General Nieves, listen carefully. I know the truth of what happened that morning in Santa Eulalia.

The maraca that sounded in the throat of my brigadier Prisciliano Nieves was not his death rattle, not yet. In the dim light of the hospital, my middle-class lawyer's young breath smelling of Sen-Sen mixed with Don Prisciliano's ancient respiration, a drumroll scented of chloroform and *chile chipotle.*[1] No, my general, don't die without signing here. For your honor, my general: worry no more about your honor, and rest in peace.

2

My house in Las Lomas de Chapultepec has one outstanding virtue: it shows the advantages of immortality. I don't know how people felt about it when it was constructed, when the forties were dawning. The Second World War brought Mexico a lot of money. We exported raw materials at high prices and the farmworkers entered the churches on their knees, praying for the war to go on. Cotton, hemp, vegetables, strategic minerals; it all went out in every direction. I don't know how many cows had to die in Sonora for this great house to be erected in Las Lomas, or how many black-market deals lay behind its stone and mortar. You have seen such houses along the Paseo de la Reforma and the Boulevard de los Virreyes and in the Polanco neighborhood: they are architectural follies of pseudo-colonial inspiration, resembling the interior of the Alameda movie house, which in turn mimics the Plateresque of Taxco with its cupolas, towers, and portals. Not to mention that movie house's artificial ceiling, dappled with hundred-watt stars and adorned with scudding little clouds. My house in Boulevard de los Virreyes stopped short of that.

Surely the Churrigueresque[2] delirium of the house I have lived in for more than twenty years was an object of derision. I imagine two or three caricatures by Abel Quezada[3] making fun of the cathedral-like portal, the wrought-iron balconies, the nightmare ornamentation of decorations, reliefs, curves, angels, madonnas, cornucopias, fluted plaster columns, and stained-glass windows. Inside, things don't get any better, believe me. *Inside* reproduces *outside*: once again, in a hall that rises two stories, we encounter the blue-tile stairs, the iron railing and balconies overlooking the hall from the bedrooms, the iron candelabra with its artificial candles dripping fake wax of petrified plastic, the floor of Talavera tile, the uncomfortable wood-and-leather furniture, straight and stiff as if for receiving a sentence from the Holy Inquisition. What a production . . . !

---

[1] *chile chipotle:* A hot chile sauce.   [2] **Churrigueresque:** An elaborate and extravagantly decorated style of Spanish baroque architecture.   [3] **Abel Quezada:** A Mexican painter and cartoonist.

But the extraordinary thing, as I was saying, is that this white elephant, this symbol of vulgar pretension and the new money of the entrepreneurs who made a profit off the war, has been converted, with time, into a relic of a better era. Today, when things are fast going downhill, we fondly recall a time when things were looking up. Better vulgar and satisfied than miserable but refined. You don't need me to tell you that. Bathed in the glow of nostalgia, unique and remote in a new world of skyscrapers, glass, and concrete, my grotesque quasimodel home (my Quasimodo[4] abode, my friends, ha ha! it might be hunchbacked, but it's mine, all mine!) has now become a museum piece. It's enough to say that first the neighbors and then the authorities came to me, imploring:

—Never, sir, sell your house or let it be demolished. There aren't many examples left of the Neocolonial architecture of the forties. Don't even think of sacrificing it to the crane or (heaven protect us!) (we would never imagine such a thing of you!) to vile pecuniary interests.

I had a strange friend once, named Federico Silva, whom his friends called the Mandarin and who lived in another kind of house, an elegant villa dating from the adolescent decade of the century (1915? 1920?), squeezed and dwarfed by the looming skyscrapers lining the Calle de Córdoba. He wouldn't let it go on principle: he would not cave in to the modernization of the city. Obviously, nostalgia makes demands on me. But if I don't let go of my house, it's not because of my neighbors' pleas, or because I have an inflated sense of its value as an architectural curiosity, or anything like that. I remain in my house because I have lived like a king in it for twenty-five years: from the time I was twenty-five until I turned fifty, what do you think of that? An entire life!

Nicolás Sarmiento, be honest with those who are good enough to hear you out, pipes up the little inner voice of my Jiminy Cricket. Tell them the truth. You don't leave this house for the simple reason that it belonged to Brigadier General Prisciliano Nieves.

3

An entire life: I was about to tell you that when I took over this meringue of a house I was a miserable little lawyer, only the day before a clerk in an insignificant law office on the Avenida Cinco de Mayo. My world, on my word of honor, went no farther than the Celaya candy store; I would look through the windows of my office and imagine being rewarded with mountains of toffees, rock candy, candy kisses, and *morelianas.* Maybe the world was a great candied orange, I said to my beloved fiancée, Miss Buenaventura del Rey, from one of the best families of the Narvarte district. Bah, if I had stayed with her I would have been turned into a candied orange, a lemon drop. No: the world was the sugared orange, I would take one bite and then, with disdain and the air of a conquistador, I would throw it over my shoulder. Give me a hug, sweetheart!

---

[4] **Quasimodo:** The hunchback of Notre Dame in Victor Hugo's novel.

Buenaventura, on the other hand, wanted to eat the orange down to the last seed, because who knows if tomorrow will bring another. When I walked into the house in Las Lomas for the first time, I knew that there was no room in it for Miss Buenaventura del Rey. Shall I confess something to you? My sainted fiancée seemed to me less fine, less interesting than the servants that my general had in his service. Adieu, Buenaventura, and give your papa my warmest thanks for having given away to me, without even realizing it, the secret of Prisciliano Nieves. But goodbye also, worthy cook, lovely girl servant, stupid waiter, and stooped gardener of the Hero of Santa Eulalia. Let no one remain here who served or knew Prisciliano Nieves when he was alive. Let them all be gone!

The women tied their bundles and went proudly off. The waiter, on the other hand, half argued and half whined that it wasn't his fault the general died, that nobody ever thought of them, what would become of them now, would they die of hunger, or would they have to steal? I would like to have been more generous with them. I couldn't afford it; no doubt, I was not the first heir that couldn't use the battalion of servants installed in the house he inherited. The gardener returned now and again to look at his roses from a distance. I asked myself if it wouldn't be a good idea to have him come back and take care of them. But I didn't succumb: I subscribed to the motto *Nothing from the past!* From that moment, I started a new life: new girlfriend, new servants, new house. Nobody who might know anything about the battle of La Zapotera, the hacienda of Santa Eulalia, or the life of Brigadier Prisciliano Nieves. Poor little Buenaventura; she shed a lot of tears and even made a fool of herself calling me up and getting the brush-off from my servants. The poor thing never found out that our engagement was the source of my fortune; her father, an old army accountant, cross-eyed from constantly making an ass of himself, had been in Santa Eulalia and knew the truth, but for him it was just a funny story, it had no importance, it was a bit of table talk; he didn't act on the precious information he possessed, whereas I did, and at that moment I realized that information is the source of power, but the crucial thing is to know how to use it or, if the situation demands, not use it: silence, too, can be power.

New life, new house, new girlfriend, new servants. Now I'm reborn: Nicolás Sarmiento, at your service.

I was reborn, yes, gentlemen: an entire life. Who knew better than anyone that there was a device called the telephone with which a very foxy lawyer could communicate better than anyone with the world, that great sugared orange? You are listening to him now. Who knew better than anyone that there is a seamless power called information? Who knows knows—so the saying goes. But I amended it: who knows can do, who can do knows—power is knowledge. Who subscribed to every gringo review available on technology, sports, fashion, communications, interior decoration, architecture, domestic appliances, shows, whatever you need and desire? Who? Why, you're listening to him, he's talking to you: the lawyer Nicolás Sarmiento, who joined information to telephone: as soon as I found out about a product that was unknown in Mexico, I would use the telephone and in a flash obtain the license to exploit it here.

All by telephone: patents for Dishwasher A and Microcomputer B, for telephone answering machines and electromagnetic recorders, rights to Parisian *prêt-à-porter*[5] and jogging shoes, licenses for drills and marine platforms, for photocopiers and vitamins, for betablockers for cardiacs and small aircraft for magnates: what didn't I patent for Mexico and Central America in those twenty-five years, sirs, finding the financial dimension for every service, tying my Mexican sub-licenses in with the fortunes of the manufacturing company in Wall Street, the Bourse, and the City? And all, I tell you, without stirring from the house of my Brigadier Prisciliano Nieves, who to do his business had, as they say, to shunt cattle all around the ranch. Whereas, with telephone raised, I almost singlehandedly brought Mexico into the modern era. Without anybody realizing. In the place of honor in my library were the telephone directories of Manhattan, Los Angeles, Houston . . . St. Louis, Missouri: home of the McDonnell Douglas airplane factory and Ralston cereals; Topeka, Kansas: home of Wishwashy detergent; and Dearborn, Michigan, of the auto factory in the birthplace of Henry Ford; not to mention nacho manufacturing in Amarillo, Texas, and the high-tech conglomerates on Route 128 in Massachusetts.

The directory, my friends, the phone book, the area code followed by seven numbers: an invisible operation, and, if not quite silent, at least as modulated as a murmur of love. Listen well: in my office at Las Lomas I have a console of some fifty-seven direct telephone lines. Everything I need is at my fingertips: notaries, patent experts, and sympathetic bureaucrats.

In view of what has happened, I'm speaking to you, as they say, with all my cards on the table and nothing up my sleeve. But you still don't have to believe me. I'm a bit more refined than in those long-ago days of my visit to the British hospital and my abandonment of Miss Buenaventura del Rey. I'm half chameleon, you can't tell me from any middle-class Mexican who has become polished by taking advantage of trips, conversations, lectures, films, and good music available to . . . well, get rich, everyone has a chance, there's a field marshal's baton in every knapsack. I read Emil Ludwig[6] in a pocket edition and learned that Napoleon has been the universal super-model of ascent by merit, in Europe and in the so-called Third World. The gringos, so dull in their references, speak of self-made men like Horatio Alger and Henry Ford. We, of Napoleon or nothing: Come, my Josephine, here is your very own Corsican, St. Helena is far away, the pyramids are watching us, even if they are in Teotihuacán,[7] and from here to Waterloo is a country mile. We're half Napoleon, half Don Juan, we can't help it, and I tell you, my terror of falling back to where I'd come from was as great as my ambition: you see, I hold nothing back. But the women, the women I desired, the anti-Buenaventuras, I desired them as they desired me, refined, cosmopolitan, sure, it cost me a little something, but self-confident, at times imperious, I made them understand (and it was true) that there was no commitment between us: grand passion today, fading memory tomorrow . . . That was another story, although they soon learned to count on my discretion and they forgave my

---

[5] *prêt-à-porter:* Ready-to-wear.   [6] **Emil Ludwig** (1881–1948): Author of *Napoleon* (1924).   [7] **Teotihuacán:** The ancient city of Mexico, located about thirty miles northeast of the present Mexico City, the site of Aztec ceremonial pyramids.

failings. Women and servants. From my colonial watchtower of Las Lomas, armed with telephones that passed through all the styles, country black, Hollywood white, October crisis red, bright green Technicolor, golden Barbie Doll, detached speaker, hand-dialed, to telephones like the one I am using at present, pure you-talk-to-me-when-I-press-the-button, to my little black Giorgio Armani number with TV screen, which I use only for my conquests.

Women: in the sixties there were still some foreign castaways from the forties, a little weather-beaten now but eager to acquire a young lover and a large house where they could throw parties and dazzle the Aztecs; it was through them that I burst on the scene and went on to charm the second wave of women, that is, girls who wanted to marry a young lawyer on the way up who had already had as lover the Princess of Salm-Salm or the heiress of the Fresno, California, cardboard-recycling factory. Such is this business of love. I used those young girls to tell the world I was on the make. I seduced all I could, the rest went running to confide to their coreligionists that the spirits that flowed here were strong but fleeting: Nicolás Sarmiento isn't going to lead you to the altar, dearie. I made myself interesting, because the sixties demanded it. I tried to seduce the two Elenas, mother and daughter, though without success. They still kept their particular domestic arrangements. But after them came a generation of desperate Mexican women who believed that to be interesting was to be melancholy, miserable, and a reader of Proust. As soon as they satisfied me they would try to commit suicide in my bathroom, with such frequency that I turned, in reaction, to the working class. Secretaries, manicurists, shop clerks who wanted to hook a husband the same as the Mexican princesses, but whom I sidetracked with sweet talk, educating them, teaching them how to walk, dress themselves, and use a finger bowl after eating shrimp (things the women of my first generation had taught me). They coaxed me into educating them, instead of being educated, as I had been by the three preceding generations. So where was my golden mean? The fifth generation left me at a loss. Now they wanted neither to teach me nor to learn from me, only to vie and divide. Sure of themselves, they acted like men and told me that was what it meant to be women. Can that be true? But the philosophy of the good Don Juan is simply this: check out the chicks and chalk them up. And although, when I talk about it, this all sounds quite orderly, the truth is that in my bed, ladies and gentlemen listeners, a great chaos reigned, because there was always an Austro-Hungarian of generation number one who had left a prescription in the medicine cabinet ten years before and returned to reclaim it (in the hope of fanning old flames) and who, seated under said cabinet in a compromising position, would find a potential Galatea[8] throwing up an unknown (to her) kir and, in the bathtub, smothered in soapsuds scented of German woods, a potential Maria Vetsera from the Faculty of Letters and, knocking at the front door, an ex-girlfriend, now married and with five children, with a mind to show me all of them, lined up like marimba keys, simply to make me see what I had lost! I won't even mention the girls (most

---

[8] **Galatea:** The statue brought to life by Aphrodite in response to the plea of the sculptor, Pygmalion, who had fallen in love with his creation.

amusing!) who, during the eighties, began to appear at my house unexpectedly, on pogo sticks, leaping fences behind the Churrigueresque mansions of Virreyes, hopping here and there, from house to house, demonstrating thereby that:

— Private property is okay, pal, but only if it's shared!

They passed like wisps in the breeze, on their pogo sticks, so nubile, ah, as I, turning fifty, saw them bound by as if in a dream, all of them under twenty, assuming the right to enter all the houses, rich or poor, and to talk, to talk, nothing else, with everyone, saying: Get with it, get with what's happening, now!

If you're still listening to me, you might conclude that my destiny was to end up with a woman who would combine the qualities (and the defects, there's no way around it!) of the five generations of ladies I had seduced. You see: the essence of Don Juan is to move, to travel, to scoff at boundaries, whether between countries, gardens, balconies, or beds. For Don Juan there are no doors, or, rather, there is always an unforeseen door for his escape. Now my merry bands of girls on pogo sticks were the Doña Juanitas (damned if they don't smell of pot!) and I, as you know by now, tied to the phone, doing everything by phone, meetings, business deals, love affairs . . .

And servants. I needed them, and very good ones, to throw my famous parties, to receive equally a woman in intimate and attentive circumstances and a crowd of five hundred guests for an epochal bash — the frosting on my house of meringue! But eventually they went out of style, those offensive shows of extravagance, as the richest politicians in Mexico called them, and although I never made a public display of crying over the poverty of my countrymen, at least I always tried to give them honest work. Honest but temporary: What I never could stand was a servant staying with me too long. He would gain power from my past. He would remember the previous women. He couldn't help making comparisons. He would treat the new ones the way he treated the old ones, as if he were trying to serve me well and perform satisfactorily, when the sly fellow would know perfectly well that he was performing poorly and making me look bad: Here's your hot-water bottle, madam, the way you like it. Listen, dog, who are you confusing me with? The diuretic morning grapefruit for the pudgy lady who prefers cheese and tortillas. The confusion becomes an allusion, and no Mexican woman was ever born who can't see, smell, and catch those subtle little innuendos. (Except one from Chiapas who was so out of it that I had to clap like crazy to wake her up when she fell asleep in the middle of the action, and then the cunt would pop up and start doing her regional dance. It must be something in the genes. Send them all back to Guatemala!)

Besides denying them the power that cumulative memory gave them over me, I refused to retain my servants, to keep them from intriguing with each other. A servant who stayed more than two years would end up conspiring with other servants against me. The first year, they idolize me and compete with each other; the second, they hate the one they see as my favorite; the third, they join together to throw me out on my ear. All right, then! Here no one passes more than two Christmases in a row. Before the Wise Men make their third trip through the desert on their camels, let the Star of Bethlehem be put out: my butcher and baker and candlestick maker, hey diddle diddle, out on your asses! Cook, upstairs maid, boy, gardener, and a chauffeur who only runs errands because, tied to my telephones and computers, I hardly ever leave my colonial house. That's all I need.

Since I inherited the house, I've kept an exact list of lovers and servants. The first is already rather long, though not like Don Juan's; besides, it's pretty personalized. The servants' list, on the other hand, I try to do seriously, with statistics. Into the computer I put their birthplace, previous occupation. In that way, I have on hand a most interesting sort of sociological profile, since the regions that provide me servants have come down, over the years, to Querétaro, Puebla, the state of Mexico, and Morelos.[9] Next, within each of these, come the cities (Toluca wins by a long shot), the towns, the villages, the old haciendas. Thanks to the relative speed with which I change servants, I think I'll end up covering every square inch of those four federal states. It will be highly entertaining to see what sorts of coincidences, exceptions, and convergences, among them and in relation to my own life, the detailed memories of my computers will provide. How many instances will there be of servants coming from Zacatlán de las Manzanas, state of Puebla? Or, how many members of the same family will end up in my service? How many will know each other and will gossip about me and my house? The possible combinations of their employment and my accounting are obvious: both are infinite, but the calculation of probabilities is, by definition, finite—repetition is not dispersion but, finally, unity. We all end up looking at ourselves in the mirror of the world and seeing our own foolish faces and nothing more.

The world comes to me and the proof is that here you are, listening to me and hanging on my wise and statistical words. Ahem, as they say in the funnies, and also: How fickle is fate, and how often it manages to give a kick in the pants to the best-laid plans!

The present revolving odalisque[10] was, in a certain sense, my ideal lover. We met by telephone. Tell me if there could be a more perfect *class action,* as we Mexican legal types say; or *serendipity* (what a word!), as the gringo yuppies, who keep on looking for it, say; or *birds of a feather flocking together,* as the prole Indian types around here whom we call *nacos* say. (*Naco* hero on a train: Nacozari. Jealous *naco* in an inn: Nacothello. Corsican *naco* imprisoned on a remote island: Nacoleon. Anarchist *nacos* executed in the electric chair: Naco and Vanzetti.)

—Nacolás Sarmiento.

So she addressed me, mocking me, my last conquest, my latest love, my last girlfriend, how could she fail to conquer me if she entered my game list in this way? Nacolás Sarmiento, she called me, putting me down and tickling me at the same time; her name was Lala and she possessed characteristics of each of the generations that preceded her. She was polyglot like my first round of women (although I suspect that Lala didn't learn languages in an ancestral castle surrounded by governesses, but by the Berlitz method here in the Avenida Chapultepec, or serving meals to the gringo tourists in Ixtapa–Zihuatanejo). Her melancholy was the genuine

---

[9] **Querétaro . . . Morelos:** The states that include Mexico City and the surrounding countryside.

[10] **odalisque:** A concubine or harem girl.

article, not put in her skull by a decadent prof of philosophy and letters; she didn't know Proust, not even by the book covers—her melancholy was more in the style of the mariachi singer José Alfredo Jimenez:

> *And if they want to know about my past,*
> *I'll have to tell them another lie,*
> *I'll tell them I came from a different world . . .*

I mean that she was pretty mysterious, too good to be true, and when she sang that hold-me-tight, I'd rush to bury myself in her arms and whisper sweet nothings in my tenderest manner . . . Ah, Lala, how I adored you, love, how I adored your tight little ass, my sweet, your savage howling and biting each time I entered your divine zoology, my love, so wild and so refined, so submissive and so mad at the same time, so full of unforgettable details: Lala, you who left me flowers drawn with shaving cream on the bathroom mirror; you who filled champagne bottles with soil; you who highlighted in yellow your favorite names in my telephone books; you who always slept face-down, with your hair disheveled and your mouth half-open, solitary and defenseless, with your hands pressed against your tummy; you who never cut your toenails in my presence, who brushed your teeth with baking soda or ground tortilla, Lala, is it true that I surprised you praying one night, kneeling, and you laughed nervously and showed me a sore knee as excuse, and I said, Let Daddy kiss it and make it better? Lala, you existed only for me, in my bed, in my house, I never saw you outside my vast Churrigueresque prison, but you never felt yourself a prisoner, isn't that so? I never wanted to know about you; as I've said: in all this, the truth is the mystery. Light streaks ran through your hair; you drank carbonated *Tehuacán* before sleeping; you paid the price for a ravenous appetite; you knew how to walk barefoot.

But let's take things in order: of the fourth generation, Lala had a certain lack of breeding that I was going to refine—and to which she submitted willingly, which was the part of her makeup she got from the fifth generation of young little Mexicans, sure of themselves, open to education, experience, professional responsibility. Women, ladies and gentlemen, are like computers: they have passed from the simplest operations, such as adding, subtracting, carrying sums and totaling columns of figures, successively, to the simultaneous operations of the fifth generation: instead of turning each tortilla in turn, we'll turn them all at once. I know this because I've brought to Mexico all the innovations of computation, from the first to the fourth, and now I wait for the fifth and know that the country that discovers it is going to dominate the twenty-first century, which is now approaching, as the old song says, in the murk of night, like an unknown soul, through streets ever winding this way and that, passing like an old-time lover, cloaked in a trailing cape . . . and then the surprise: Who'd known all along? Why, who else but Nicolás Sarmiento, the same son of a bitch who subscribes to the gringo magazines and does business by phone and has a new squeeze, dark and silky, called Lala, a true guava of a girl, in his house in Las Lomas.

Who lacked a past. And yet it didn't matter that I learned nothing, I sensed that part of my conquest of Lala consisted in not asking her anything, that what was new about these new Mexicans was that they had no past, or if they had one it was from another time, another incarnation. If that was the case, it only increased Lala's mysterious spell. If her origins were unknown, her present was not: soft, small, burning in all her recesses, dark, always half open and mistress of a pair of eyes that never closed because they never opened; the deliberation of her movements restraining an impetuousness that she and I shared; it was the fear that once exhausted it would not return. No, Lala, always slow, long nights, endless hope, patient flesh, and the soul, my love, always quicker than the body: closer to decadence and death, Lala.

Now I must reveal a fact to you. I don't know if it's ridiculous or painful. Maybe it's simply what I've just said: a fact. I need to have servants because physically I'm a complete idiot. In business I'm a genius, as I've established. But I can't manage practical things. Cooking, for example: zilch. Even for a couple of eggs, I have to get someone to fix them for me. I don't know how to drive; I need a chauffeur. I don't know how to tie my tie or untie my shoes. The result: nothing but these monkey ties with clips that stick in your shirt collars; nothing but slip-ons, never shoes with laces. To women, this all seems sort of endearing and they become maternal with me. They see me so useless in this, such a shark in everything else; they're moved, and they love me that much more. It's true.

But nobody but Lala has known how to kneel before me, with such tenderness, with such devotion, just as if praying, and what's more, with such efficiency: what more perfect way to tie a shoe, leaving the loop expansive as a butterfly ready to fly, yet bound like a link yoked to its twin; and the shoe itself, secure, exact, comfortable, neither too tight nor too loose, a shoe kind to my body, neither constricting nor loose. Lala was perfection, I tell you: *purr-fec-tion.* Neither more nor less. And I say so myself, I who classify my servants by provinces on my computer, but my girls by neighborhoods.

What else should I tell you before I tell you what happened? You suspect already, or maybe not. I had a vasectomy when I was about thirty to avoid having children and so no one can show up in these parts with a brat in her arms, weeping: "Your baby, Nicolás! Aren't you going to acknowledge it? Bastard!" I arranged everything by telephone; it was my business weapon, and although I traveled from time to time, each time I stayed shut up longer in Las Lomas de Chapultepec afterwards. The women came to me and I used my parties to take new ones. I replaced my servants so they wouldn't get the idea that here in Don Nico we've found our gold mine. I never cared, as other Mexican politicians and magnates do, to employ procurers for my women. I make my conquests by myself. As long as I always have someone around to drive my car, cook my beans, and tie my shoes.

All this came to a head one night in July 1982, when the economic crisis was upon us and I was getting nervous, pondering the significance of a declaration of national bankruptcy, the interplanetary travels of Silva Herzog,[11] the debt, Paul

---

[11]**Silva Herzog:** Mexican finance minister in 1982 at the time of a major devaluation of the Mexican peso; Paul Volcker was chairman of the U.S. Federal Reserve Board.

Volcker, and my patents and licenses business, in the middle of all this turmoil. Better to throw a big party to forget the crisis, and I ordered a bar and buffet by the pool. The waiter was new, I didn't know his name; my relationship with Lala had lasted two months now and the lady was growing on me, I was liking her more and more, she made me, I confess, hot and bothered, if the truth be told. She arrived late, when I was already mingling with a hundred revelers, calling on my waiters and the guests alike to sample the Taittinger; who knew when we would see it again, much less taste it!

Lala appeared, and her Saint Laurent strapless gown, of black silk, with a red wrap, would likewise not be seen again *pour longtemps*[12]—believe me, who had arranged for her to wear it. How she glowed, my beautiful love, how all eyes followed her, each and every one, you hear me? to the edge of the pool, where the waiter offered her a glass of champagne; she stood for a long time looking at the *naco* dressed in a white cotton jacket, black pants shiny from so much use by previous boys in my service, bow tie—it was impossible to tell him from the others who had had the same position, the same clothes, the same manner. Manner? The servant lifted his head, she emptied the glass into his face, he dropped the tray in the pool, grabbed Lala's arm violently, she drew away, said something, he answered, everyone watched, I moved forward calmly, took her arm (I saw where his fingers had pressed my lady's soft skin), I told him (I didn't know his name) to go inside, we would talk later. I noticed he seemed confused, a wild uncertainty in his black eyes, his dark jaw quivering. He arranged his glossy hair, parted in the middle, and walked away with his shoulders slumped. I thought he was going to fall into the pool. It's nothing, I told the guests, and everything seemed fine, ladies and gentlemen who are listening to me. I laughed: Remember, the pretexts for parties like this are going fast. Everyone laughed with me and I said nothing to Lala. But she went up to bed and waited for me there. She was asleep when the party ended and I got in. I stepped on a champagne glass as I entered the room. I left it on the floor; and in bed, Lala was sleeping in her elegant Saint Laurent dress. I took off her shoes. I studied her. We were tired. I slept. The next day, I got up around six, with that faint sense of absence that takes shape as we wake—and *she* wasn't there. The tracks of her bare feet, on the other hand, were. Bloody tracks; Lala had cut her feet because of my carelessness in not cleaning up the broken glass. I went out the rococo balcony to the pool. There she was, floating face-down, dressed, barefoot, her feet cut, as if she had gone all night without huaraches, walking on thorns, surrounded by a sea of blood. When I turned her over, there was a gaping wound in her belly; the dagger had been withdrawn. They took my servant Dimas Palmero to the Reclusorio Norte, where he was held, awaiting the slow march of Mexican justice, accused of murder. And I was given the same sentence, though in the Churrigueresque palace of Las Lomas de Chapultepec, once the residence of Brigadier General Prisciliano Nieves, who died one morning in 1960 in the old British hospital on the Avenida Mariano Escobedo.

---

[12] *pour longtemps:* For a long time.

4

The morning of the tragedy, I had only four servants in the big colonial house of Las Lomas, apart from the said Dimas Palmero: a cook, a maid, a chauffeur, and a gardener. I confess that I can barely recall their features or their names. That is perhaps because, as I work in my house, I have rendered them invisible. If I went out every day to an office, I would notice them, by contrast, on my return. But they stayed out of sight so as not to disturb me. I don't know their names, or what they are like. My secretary, Sarita Palazuelos, dealt with them; I was busy with my work in the house, I'm not married, the servants are invisible. They don't exist, as they say.

I think I'm alone in my house. I hear a voice, I ask:

— Who's there?

— Nobody, sir, answers the maid's little voice.

They prefer to be invisible. But there must be someone.

— Take this gift, girl.

— Oh, sir, you shouldn't. I'm nobody to get presents from you, oh, no!

— Happy birthday, I insist.

— Oh, but you shouldn't be thinking of me, sir.

They return to being invisible.

— Oh! Excuse me!

— Please excuse my boldness, sir.

— I won't bother you for even a moment, sir. I'm just going to dust the furniture.

Now one of them had a name: Dimas Palmero.

I couldn't bear to see him. Hate kept me from sleeping; I hugged the pillow that held the scent, each day fainter, of Lala my love, and I cried in despair. Then, to torture myself, I racked my mind with her memory and imagined the worst: Lala with that boy; Lala in the arms of Dimas Palmero; Lala with a past. Then I realized that I couldn't recall the face of the young murderer. Young: I said that and began to remember. I began to draw him out from the original anonymity with which I regarded him that fatal night. Uniformed as a waiter, white cotton jacket, shiny pants, bow tie, identical to all, same as none. I began to wonder how Lala might have regarded him. Young, I said; was he handsome as well? But, besides being young and handsome, was he interesting? and was he interesting because he held some secret? I induced and deduced like mad those first days of my solitude, and from his secret I passed to his interest, from his interest to his youth, and from there to his good looks. Dimas Palmero, in my strange fiftyish pseudo-widowhood, was the Lucifer who warned me: For the first time in your life, you have lost a woman, cuckold Nicolás, not because you left her, or chased her out, not even because *she* left you, but because I took her away from you and I took her forever. Dimas had to be handsome, and he had to have a secret. No other way a cheap *naco* could have defeated me. It couldn't be. It would have to take a youth who was handsome, at least, and who held a secret, to defeat me.

I had to see him. One night it became an obsession: to see Dimas Palmero, speak with him, convince myself that at least I deserved my grief and my defeat.

They had been bringing me trays of food. I barely touched them. I never saw who brought the tray three times a day, or who took it away. Miss Palazuelos sent a note that she was waiting for my instructions, but what instructions could I give, drowned as I was in melancholy? I told her to take a vacation while I got over my broken heart. I noticed the eyes of the boy who took the message. I didn't know him. Surely Miss Palazuelos had substituted a new boy for Dimas Palmero. But I was obsessed: I saw in this new servant a double, almost, of the incarcerated Dimas. How I wanted to confront my rival!

I was obsessed, and my obsession was to go to the Reclusorio and speak with Dimas, to see him face to face. For the first time in ten days, I showered, I shaved, I put on a decent suit, and I left my bedroom, I went down the stairs of gargoyled ironwork to the colonial hall surrounded by little balconies, with a glazed-tile fountain in the corner, burbling water. I reached the front door and tried, with a natural gesture, to open it. It was locked. Such security! The help had turned cautious, indeed, after the crime. Skittish and, as I've said, invisible. Where were the damned bastards? How did I call them? What did I call them?? Boy, girl! Ah, my good woman, my good man! . . . Fuck it!

Nobody answered. I looked out the stained-glass windows of the hall, parting the curtains. They were there in the gardens. Settled in. Sprawled over the grass, trampling it, smoking cigarettes and crushing the butts in the rose mulch; squatting, pulling from their food bags steaming pigs' feet in green mole[13] and steaming sweet and hot tamales, strewing the ground with the burnt maize leaves; the women coquettishly clipping my roses, sticking them in their shiny black hair, while the kids pricked their hands on the thorns and the piglets crackled over the flame . . . I ran to one of the side windows: they were playing marbles and ball-and-cup, they had set some suspicious, leaking casks by the side of the garage. I ran to the right wing of the mansion: a man was urinating in the narrow, shady part of the garden, a man in a lacquered straw hat was pissing against the wall between my house and . . .

I was surrounded.

A smell of purslane came from the kitchen. I entered. I had never seen the new cook, a fat woman, square as a die, with jet-black hair and a face aged by skepticism.

—I am Lupe, the new cook—she told me—and this is Don Zacarías, the new chauffeur.

Said chauffeur did not even rise from the table where he was eating purslane tacos. I looked at him with astonishment. He was the image of the ex-president Don Adolfo Ruiz Cortines,[14] who in turn was identified, in popular wit, with the actor Boris Karloff: bushy eyebrows, deep eyes, huge bags under the eyes, wrinkles deeper than the Grand Canyon, high forehead, high cheekbones, compressed skull, graying hair brushed to the back.

—Pleased, I said, like a perfect idiot.

I returned to the bedroom and, almost instinctively, I decided to put on some of the few shoes with laces that I have. I looked at myself there, seated on the unmade bed, by the pillow that held her scent, with my shoelaces untied and hanging loose like inert but hungry earthworms. I pulled the bell cord by the headboard, to see who would answer my call.

---

[13] **green mole:** A chile sauce.   [14] **Cortines:** President of Mexico from 1952 to 1959.

A few minutes passed. Then knuckles rapped.

He entered, the young man who resembled (according to my fancy) the incarcerated Dimas Palmero. I decided, nonetheless, to tell them apart, to separate them, not to allow any confusion. The murderer was locked away. This was someone else.

—What is your name?

—Marco Aurelio.

You'll notice he didn't say "At your service, sir," or "What may I do for you, *patrón.*" Nor did he look at me sideways, eyes hooded, head lowered.

—Tie my shoes.

He looked at me a moment.

—Right now, I said. He continued to look at me, and then knelt before me. He tied the laces.

—Tell the chauffeur I'm going out after eating. And tell the cook to come up so I can plan some menus. And another thing, Marco Aurelio . . .

Now back on his feet, he looked at me fixedly.

—Clear all the intruders out of my garden. If they're not gone within half an hour, I'll call the police. You may go, Marco Aurelio. That's all, you hear?

I dressed, ostentatiously and ostensibly, to go out, I who had gone out so seldom. I decided to try for the first time—almost—a beige gabardine double-breasted suit, blue shirt, stupid yellow clip tie, and, sticking out of my breast pocket, a Liberty[15] handkerchief an Englishwoman had given me.

Real sharp, real shark: I spoke my name and, stomping loudly, I went downstairs. But there it was the same story. Locked door, people surrounding the house. A full-fledged party, and a piñata in the garage. The children squealing happily. A child making a hubbub, trapped in a strange metal crib, all barred in up to the top, like a furnace grate.

—Marco Aurelio!

I sat down in the hall of stained-glass windows. Marco Aurelio solicitously undid my shoes, and, solicitously, offered me my most comfortable slippers. Would I like my pipe? Did I want a brandy? I would lack nothing. The chauffeur would go out and get me any videotape I wanted: new pictures or old, sports, sex, music . . . The family has told me to tell you not to worry. You know, Don Nico, in this country (he was saying as he knelt before me, taking off my shoes, this horrendous *naco*) we survive the worst calamities because we take care of each other, you'll see, I was in Los Angeles as an illegal and the American families there are scattered all around, they live far apart from each other, parents without children, the old ones abandoned, the young ones looking to break away, but here it's just the opposite, Don Nico, how can you have forgotten that? you're so solitary, God help you, not us—if you don't have a job, the family will feed you, it will put a roof over your head, if the cops are after you, or you want to escape the army, the family will hide you, send you back from Las Lomas to Morelos and from there to Los Angeles and back into circulation: the family knows how to move by night, the family is almost always invisible,

---

[15] **Liberty:** A London department store noted for its fine printed fabrics.

but what the fuck, Don Nico, it can make its presence felt, how it can make its presence felt! You'll see. So you're going to call the police if we don't go? Then I assure you that the police will not find us here when they arrive, although they will find you, quite stiff, floating in the pool, just like Eduardita, whom God has taken onto . . . But listen, Don Nico, there's no need to look like you've seen a ghost, our message is real simple: you'll lead your usual life, phone all you like, manage your business, throw parties, receive your pals and their dolls, and we'll take care of you, the only thing is, you'll never leave this place as long as our brother Dimas is in the pen: the day that Dimas leaves jail, you leave your house, Don Nico, not a minute before, not a minute later, unless you don't play straight with us, and then you'll leave here first—but they'll carry you out, that much I swear.

He pressed together his thumb and index finger and kissed them noisily as I buried myself in the pillow of Eduardita—my Lala!

5

So began my new life, and the first thing that will strike you, my listeners, is the same thought that occurred to me, in my own house in Las Lomas: Well, really my life hasn't changed; indeed, now I'm more protected than ever; they let me throw my parties, manage my business affairs by telephone, receive the girls who console me for the death of Lala (my cup runneth over: I'm a tragic lover, howboutthat!), and to the cops who showed up to ask why all these people have surrounded my house, packed in the garden, frying quesadillas[16] by the rosebushes, urinating in the garage, they explained: Because this gentleman is very generous, every day he brings us the leftovers from his parties—*every day!* I confirmed this personally to the police, but they looked at me with a mournful smirk (Mexican officials are expert at looking at you with a sardonic grimace) and I understood: So be it. From then on, I would have to pay them their weekly bribe. I recorded it in my expense books, and I had to fire Miss Palazuelos, so that she wouldn't suspect anything. She herself hadn't an inkling why she was fired. I was famous for what I've mentioned: nobody lasted very long with me, not secretary or chauffeur or lover. I'm my own boss, and that's the end of it! You will note that this whole fantastic situation was simply an echo of my normal situation, so there was no reason for anyone to be alarmed: neither the exterior world that kept on doing business with me nor the interior world (I, my servants, my lovers, the same as ever . . .).

The difference, of course, is that this fantastic situation (masquerading as my usual situation) contained one element of abnormality that was both profound and intolerable: it was not the work of my own free will.

There was that one little thing; this situation did not respond to my whim; I responded to it. And it was up to me to end it; if Dimas Palmero went free, I would be freed as well.

But how was I going to arrange for said Dimas to get off? Although I was the one

---

[16] **quesadillas:** Tortillas with melted cheese.

who called the police to have him arrested, he was now charged with murder by the District Attorney's office.

I decided to put on shoes with laces; it was a pretext for asking the valet Marco Aurelio to come up to help me, chat with me, inform me: Were all those people in the garden really the family of the jailed Dimas Palmero? Yes, answered Marco Aurelio, a fine, very extended Mexican family, we all help each other out, as they say. And what else? I insisted, and he laughed at that: We're all Catholic, never the pill, never a condom, the children that God sends . . . Where were they from? From the state of Morelos, all *campesinos,*[17] workers in the cane fields; no, the fields were not abandoned, didn't they tell you, Don Nico? this is hardly the full contingent, ha ha, this is no more than a delegation, we're good in Morelos at organizing delegations and sending them to the capital to demand justice, surely you remember General Emiliano Zapata;[18] well, now you can see that we've learned something. Now we don't ask for justice. Now we make justice. But I am innocent, I said to Marco Aurelio kneeling before me, I lost Lala, I am . . . He lifted his face, black and yellow as the flag of an invisible, hostile nation: — Dimas Palmero is our brother.

Beyond that, I couldn't make him budge. These people are tight-lipped. Our brother: did he mean it literally, or by solidarity? (Stubborn sons of that fucking Zapata!) A lawyer knows that everything in the world (words, the law, love . . .) can be interpreted in the *strict* sense or in the *loose* sense. Was the brotherhood of Marco Aurelio, my extraordinary servant, and Dimas, my incarcerated servant, of blood, or was it figurative? Narrow, or broad? I would have to know to understand my situation. Marco Aurelio, I said one day, even if I withdraw the charges against your brother, as you call him (poker-faced, bilious silence), the prosecutor will try him because too many people witnessed the scene by the pool between Lala and your brother, it doesn't depend on me, they will proceed ex officio, understand? it's not a question of avenging Lala's death . . .

— Our sister . . . But not a whore, no way.

He was kneeling in front of me, tying my shoelaces, and on hearing him say this, I gave him a kick in the face. I assure you it wasn't intentional; it was a brutal reflex responding to a brutal assertion. I gave him a brutal kick in the jaw, I knocked him good, he fell on his back, and I followed my blind instinct, left reason aside (left it sound asleep), and ran down the stairs to the hall just as an unfamiliar maid was sweeping the entrance, and the open door invited me to go out into the morning of Las Lomas, the air sharp with pollution, the distant whoosh of a balloon and the flight of the red, blue, yellow spheres, liberated, far from the empty barranca[19] that surrounded us, its high eucalyptuses with their peeling bark fighting the smell of shit from the bluff's recesses: globes of colors greeted me as I went out and breathed poison and rubbed my eyes.

My garden was the site of a pilgrimage. The scent of fried food mixed with the odor of shit and eucalyptus: smoke from cookstoves, squeals of children, the strum-

---

[17] *campesinos:* Fieldworkers, peasants.   [18] **General Emiliano Zapata** (1879–1919): Revolutionary who led an army of peasants during the Mexican Revolution in a fight for land reform.   [19] **barranca:** A steep slope or escarpment.

ming of guitars, click of marbles, two policemen flirting with the girls in braids and aprons on the other side of the gargoyled grillwork of my mansion, an old, toothless, graying man in patched pants and huaraches, his lacquered straw hat in his hand and an invitation—he came over to me: Please try something, sir, there are good tacos, sir. I looked at the policemen, who didn't look at me but laughed wickedly with the country girls and I thought the stupid cunts were practically pregnant already, who said they weren't whores, giving birth in the open fields to the bastard kids of these bastard cops, their children adding to the family of, of, of this old patriarch who offered me tacos instead of protecting the two girls being seduced by this pair of sinister uniformed bandits, smiling, indifferent to my presence on the steps of my house. Was he going to protect them the way he protected Lala? I got up. I studied him, trying to understand.

What could I do? I thanked him and sat down with him in my own garden and a woman offered us hot tortillas in a willow basket. The old man asked me to take the first bite and I repeated the atavistic gesture of taking the moistened bread of the gods out from under the damp colored napkin, as if the earth itself had opened up to offer me the Proustian madeleine[20] of the Mexican: the warm tortilla. (You who are listening to me will remember that I had plied a whole generation of young readers with Marcel Proust, and he who reads Proust, said a staunch nationalistic friend of mine, Proustitutes himself!) Awful! The truth is that, sitting there with the old patriarch eating hot salted tortillas, I felt so transported, so back in my mama's arms again or something like that, that I was already telling myself, forget it, let's have the tortillas, let's have those casks of *pulque*[21] that I saw going into the garage the other day; they brought us brimming glasses of thick liquor, tasting of pineapple, and Marco Aurelio must have had a pretty good knock, because there wasn't a trace of him to be seen. I sat with my legs crossed on my own lawn, the old man feeding me, I questioning him: How long are you going to be here? Don't worry, we don't have to return to Morelos, this could go on for years, do you realize that, señor? He looked at me with his ageless face, the old goat, and told me that they were taking turns, hadn't I caught on? They came and went, they were never the same twice, every day some went home and others arrived, because it's a question of making a sacrifice for Dimas Palmero and for Eduardita, poor child, too, hadn't I realized? Did I think it was always the same folk outside here? He laughed a little, tapping his gummy mouth: the truth was that I had never really noticed them, to me they had, indeed, all appeared the same . . .

But each one is different, the old man said quickly, with a dark seriousness that filled me with fear, each one comes into the world to aid his people, and although most die in infancy, those who have the good fortune to grow, those, señor, are a treasure for an old man like me, they are going to inherit the earth, they are going to go to work there in the North with the gringos, they are going to come to the capital to serve you; and they won't send money to the old folks, you can't argue with that,

---

[20] **madeleine:** French novelist Marcel Proust (1871–1922) in *Remembrance of Things Past* describes a boyhood experience of eating a small French cake, a madeleine, that becomes a defining sensory memory in his life.
[21] *pulque:* A fermented drink made from agave.

señor (he resumed his usual cordiality), if the old folks don't know who each of their children are, their names, what they do, what they look like, if we depend on them to keep from dying of hunger when we grow old? Just one condition, he said, pausing:

— Poor, señor, but proud.

He looked over my shoulder, waved. I followed his look. Marco Aurelio in his white shirt and his black pants was rubbing his chin, resting against the door of the house. I got up, thanked the old man, brushed the dirt from my rear, and walked toward Marco Aurelio. I knew that, from then on, it would be nothing but loafers for me.

6

That night I had a terrifying dream that those people would stay here forever, renewing themselves again and again, generation after generation, without concern for any one individual destiny, least of all that of a little half-elegant lawyer: the canny dandy of Las Lomas de Chapultepec. They could hold out until I died. But I still couldn't understand how my death would avenge that of Dimas Palmero, who languished in preventive custody, waiting for the Mexican judicial tortoise to summon him to justice. Listen close. I said tortoise, not torture. That could take years, didn't I know it. If they observed the law limiting the amount of time a man can be detained before being tried, Mexico would stop being what it always has been: a reign of influence, whim, and injustice. So I tell you, and you, like it or not, you have to listen. If I'm the prisoner of Las Lomas, you're the prisoners of my telephones — you listen to me.

Don't imagine I haven't thought of all the ways I could make this my link to the outside, my Ariadne's thread,[22] my vox humana. I have a videotape I often watch, given the circumstances: poor Barbara Stanwyck lying paralyzed in bed,[23] listening to the footsteps of the murderer climbing the stairs to kill her and take control of her millions (will it be her husband? suspense!), and she is trying to call the police and the telephone is out of order, a voice answering, sorry, wrong number . . . What a thriller! — *La voix humaine*, a French girlfriend told me . . . But this was not a Universal picture, only a modest Huaraches Films production, or some such totally asshole thing. All right, I know that I speak to you to take my mind off things for a while; don't think, however, that I have ever stopped plotting my escape. It would be so easy, I tell myself, to go on strike, stop using my phones to make money, neglect my bank accounts, stop talking to you, to my public auditors, my stockbrokers . . . My immediate conclusion: these people wouldn't give a fuck about my poverty. They are not here to take my cash. If I didn't feed them, they would feed me. I suspect that this Morelos operation functions as efficiently as a Japanese assembly line. If I became poor, they would come to my assistance!

You are free as I was once, and you will understand when I say that, come what may, one doesn't easily resign oneself to giving up one's liberty just like that. Very

---

[22] **Ariadne's thread:** In Greek mythology Ariadne gave Theseus the thread that he could follow to find his way out of the Minotaur's labyrinth.   [23] **a videotape . . . in bed:** The film is *Sorry, Wrong Number* (1948).

well: They have sworn to kill me if I denounce them. But what if I managed to escape, hide, set the authorities on them from afar? Don't try it, Don Nico, said my recovered jailer, Marco Aurelio, we are many, we will find you; he laughed: there are branches of the family in Los Angeles, in Texas, in Chicago, even in Paris and London, where rich Mexican señoras take their Agripinas, their Rudecindas, and their Dalmacias to work abroad . . . It wouldn't surprise me to see some guy in a big sombrero get off a jumbo jet at Charles de Gaulle Airport and chop me to bits in the middle of Paris, laughing wickedly, brandishing the machete that dangles eternally from him like a spare penis. How I hated Marco Aurelio! How dare one of these cheap *nacos* talk so familiarly about General de Gaulle! That's instant communications for you!

They knew my intentions. I took advantage of one of my parties to put on the overcoat and hat of a friend, without his noticing, and while everyone was drinking the last bottle of Taittinger (the pretext for the party) and eating exquisite canapés prepared by the block-shaped fat woman of the kitchen, Doña Lupe (a genius, that woman!), with the hat pulled down over my ears and my lapels turned up, I slipped through the door, which was open that night (and every night: you must realize that my jailers no longer imagined that I would escape, what for? if my life was the same as ever!—me inside with my parties and my telephones; they outside, invisible: as always!). As I say, they no longer locked the door. But I disguised myself and slipped through the door because I didn't want to accept a sentence of confinement imposed by others. I did so without caring about success or failure. The door, freedom, the street, the jumbo to Paris, even if I was met there by Rudecinda, the cousin of Marco Aurelio, rolling pin in hand . . .

—You forgot to tie your shoes, Don Nico, said Marco Aurelio, holding high a tray heaped with canapés, looking at my feet, and blocking the way to the front door.

I laughed, sighed, took off the overcoat and the hat, returned to my guests.

I tried it several times, I wouldn't give up, to keep my self-respect. But one time I couldn't get beyond the garden, because the children, instinctively, surrounded me, forming a circle, and sang a play song to me. Another time, escaping at night by the balcony, I was hanging by my fingernails when I heard a group at my feet serenading me: it was my birthday and I had forgotten! Many happy returns, Don Nico, these are the years of your life that . . . ! I was in despair: fifty springtimes in these circumstances! In desperation I resorted to Montecristo's strategy:[24] I feigned death, lying very stiff in my bed; not to give up, as I say, to touch all the bases. Marco Aurelio poured a bucket of cold water on me and I cried out, and he just stood there, saying: Don Nico, when you die on me, I'll be the first to let you know, you can be sure. Will you cry for me, Marco Aurelio, you bastard? I was incensed! I thought first of poisoning my immediate jailers, the valet Marco Aurelio, the cubic cook, the Karloff car man; but not only did I suspect that others would rush in to replace them, I also feared (inconsistent of me!) that while the lawsuit against the miserable Dimas

---

[24] **Montecristo's strategy:** In Alexandre Dumas's novel *The Count of Monte Cristo* (1844), the hero escapes from prison by pretending to be dead.

Palmero dragged on indefinitely, an action against me for poisoning my servants would be thunderous, scandalous, trumpeted in the press: Heartless Millionaire Poisons Faithful Servants! From time to time, a few fat morsels must be cast to the (nearly starved) sharks of justice . . . Besides, when I entered the kitchen, Doña Lupe was so kind to me: Do sit down, Don Nico, do you know what I'm fixing today? Can you smell it? Don't you like your cheese and squash? Or would you rather have what we're fixing ourselves, *chilaquilitos*[25] in green sauce? This made my mouth water and made life seem bearable. The chauffeur and the boy sat down to eat with Doña Lupe and me, they told me stories, they were quite amusing, they made me remember, remember her . . .

So why didn't I explain my situation to the girls who passed through my parties and my bed? What would they think of such a thing? Can you imagine the ridicule, the incredulity? So just leave when you want to, Nicolás, who's going to stop you? But they'll kill me, baby. Then I'm going to save you, I'm going to inform the police. Then they'll kill you along with me, my love. Or would you rather live on the run, afraid for your life? Of course I never told them a thing, nor did they suspect anything. I was famous as a recluse. And they came to console me for the death of Lala. Into my arms, goddesses, for life is short, but the night is long.

7

I saw her. I tell you I saw her yesterday, in the garden.

8

I called a friend of mine, an influential man in the District Attorney's office: What do you know about the case of my servant, Dimas Palmero? My friend stopped laughing and said: Whatever you want, Nicolás, is how we'll handle it. You understand: if you like, we'll keep him locked up without a trial until Judgment Day; if you prefer, we'll move up the court date and try him tomorrow; if what you want is to see him free, that can be arranged, and, look, Nicolás, why play dumb, there are people who disappear, who just simply disappear. Whatever you like, I repeat.

Whatever I liked. I was on the point of saying no, this Dimas or Dimass or Dimwit or whatever he's called isn't the real problem, I'm the prisoner, listen, call my lawyer, have the house surrounded, make a big fuss, kill these bastards . . .

I thanked my friend for his offer and hung up without indicating a preference. What for? I buried my head in my pillow. There is nothing left of Lala, not even the aroma. I racked my brains thinking: What should I do? What solution have I overlooked? What possibilities have I left in the inkwell? I had an inspiration; I decided to speed things up. I went down to the kitchen. It was the hour when Marco Aurelio, Doña Lupe, and the chauffeur with the face of the former president ate. The smell of pork in purslane came up the rococo stairway, stronger than the scent, ever fainter, of Lala — Eduardita, as they called her. I went down berating myself furiously: What

---

[25] **chilaquilitos:** A snack of eggs, chiles, and tortillas.

was I thinking? Why this terrible helplessness? Why did I think only of myself, not of her, who was the victim, after all? I deserved what had happened to me; I was the prisoner of Las Lomas even before all this happened, I was imprisoned by my own habits, my comfortable life, my easy business deals, my even easier loves. But also—I said when my bare feet touched the cold tile of the living room—I was bound by a sort of devotion and respect for my lovers: I didn't ask questions, I didn't check out their stories: —I have no past, Nico, my life commenced the moment we met, and I might whistle a tune as my only comment, but that was all.

The three were sitting comfortably eating their lunch.

—May I? I inquired cordially.

Doña Lupe got up to prepare something for me. The two men didn't budge, although Marco Aurelio waved for me to sit down. The presidential double merely looked at me, without blinking, from the imperturbable depths of his baggy eyes.

—Thank you. I came down just to ask a question. It occurred to me that what is important to you is not to keep me imprisoned here but to free Dimas. That's right, isn't it?

The cook served me an aromatic dish of pork with purslane, and I began to eat, looking at them. I had said the same thing that they had always said to me: You leave here the day our brother Dimas Palmero gets out of jail. Why now these little looks exchanged between them, this air of uncertainty, if I had only repeated what we all knew: the unwritten rule of our covenant? Give me statutory law; down with *common law,* which is subject to all sorts of interpretations and depends too much on the ethics and good sense of the people. But these peasants from Morelos must be, like me, inheritors of Roman law, where all that counts is what is written, not what is done or not done, even if it violates the letter of the law. The law, sirs, is august, and supersedes all exceptions. These people's lands always had depended on a statute, a royal decree; and now I felt that my life also was going to depend on a written contract. I looked at the looks of my jailers as they looked at each other.

—Tell me if you are willing to put this in writing: The day that Dimas Palmero gets out of the pen, Nicolás Sarmiento goes free from Las Lomas. Agreed?

I began to lose confidence; they didn't answer; they looked at each other, suspicious, tight-lipped, let me tell you, the faces of all three marked with a feline wariness; but hadn't I merely asked them to confirm in writing what they had always said! Why this unforeseen suspicion all of a sudden?

—We've been thinking, Don Nico, said Marco Aurelio finally, and we have reached the conclusion that you could quickly arrange for our brother Dimas Palmero to be freed; then we let you go; but you could still play us a trick and have the law spread its net over Dimas again. —And over us, too, said the cook, not even sighing.

—That game has been played on us plenty, said the pale, baggy-eyed chauffeur gloomily, arranging his hair with his five-fingered comb.

—Come on, come on, the cook emphatically exhorted the electric stove, atavistically airing it with her hands and lips, as if it were a charcoal brazier. The old idiot!

—So what we're willing to write down, Don Nico, is that you'll be freed when you confess to the murder of Eduardita, so that our brother cannot be judged for a crime committed by another.

I won't give them the pleasure of spitting out the pork (anyway, it's quite tasty), or of spilling my glass of fermented pineapple juice, which, quite complacently, the cook has just set in front of my nose. I'm going to give them a lesson in cool, even though my head is spinning like a carousel.

— That was not our original agreement. We've been shut up together here more than three months. Our accord is now binding, as they say.

— Nobody ever respected any agreement with us, the cook quickly replied, waving her hands furiously, as though they were straw fans, in front of the electric burner.

— Nobody, said the chauffeur sepulchrally. All they do is send us to hell.

And I was going to pay for all the centuries of injustice toward the people of Morelos? I didn't know whether to laugh or cry. The simple truth was, I didn't know what to say. I was too busy taking in my new situation. I pushed my plate aside and left the kitchen without saying a word. I climbed the stairs with the sensation that my body was a sick friend I was following with great difficulty. I sat down in the bathroom and there I remained, sleeping. But even my dreams betrayed me. I dreamed that they were right. Damn! They were right.

9

And it is you who wake me, with a furious ringing, a buzz of alarm, calling me on the phone, questioning me urgently, sympathizing with me: Why don't I ask them about her? About whom? I say, playing the fool. About Lala, la Eduarda, la Eduardita, as they called her, la Lala, la . . . Why? She's the key to the whole business! You're completely in the dark: what was behind that scene between Lala and Dimas by the pool? Who was Lala? Have all these people besieged you because of her, or him, or both of them? Why not find out? Fool!

Both of them. I laughed, fell back to sleep, sitting on the toilet in the bathroom, with my pajama bottoms rolled down around my ankles, in a stupor: both of them, you said, without realizing that I can't bear to imagine, much less to pursue the thought, of her with another — she with another, that thought I cannot bear, and you laugh at me, I hear your laughter on the telephone line, you say goodbye, you accuse me, you ask when I got so delicate and sentimental? You, Nicolás Sarmiento, who have had dozens of women just as dozens of women have had you, both you and they members of a city and a society that abandoned all that colonial-catholiccantabrian hypocrisy a few generations ago and cheerfully dedicated themselves to fucking anyone, you who know perfectly well that your dames come to you from others and go from you to others, just as they know that you weren't a monk before you knew them, nor will you become one after leaving them: you, Nicolás Sarmiento, the Don Juan of venture capital, are going to tell us now that you can't bear the thought of your Lala in the arms of Dimas Palmero? Why? It turns your stomach to think that she slept with a servant? Could it be that your horror is more social than sexual? Tell us! Wake up!

I tell you I saw her in the garden.

I got up slowly from the bathroom, I pulled up my pajamas, I didn't have to tie them, they closed with a snap, thank God, I'm hopeless for daily life, I'm only good at making money and making love; does that justify a life?

I look at the garden from the window of my bedroom.

Tell me if you don't see her, standing, with her long braids, a knee slightly bent, looking toward the barranca, surprised to be caught between the city and nature, unable to tell where one begins and the other ends, or which imitates the other: the barranca doesn't smell of the mountains, it smells of the buried city and the city no longer smells of city but of infirm nature: she longs for the country, looking toward the barranca, now Doña Lupe goes out for air, approaches the girl, puts a hand on her shoulder, and says: Don't be sad, you mustn't, you're in the city now and the city can be ugly and hard, but so can the country, the country is at least as violent as the city, I could tell you stories, Eduarda . . .

I'll say it straight out. There is only one redeeming thing in my life and that is the respect I've shown my women. You can condemn me as egotistical, or frivolous, or condescending, or manipulating, or unable to tie my shoes. The one thing you can't accuse me of is sticking my nose where it doesn't belong. I think that's all that has saved me. I think that's why women have loved me: I don't ask for explanations, I don't check out their pasts. No one can check the past of anyone in a society as fluid as ours. Where are you from? What do you do? Who were your mama and papa? Each of our questions can be a wound that doesn't heal. A wound that keeps us from loving or being loved. Everything betrays us: the body sends us one signal and an expression reveals another, words turn against themselves, the mind cons us, death deceives death . . . Beware!

10

I saw Lala that afternoon in the garden, when she was nobody, when she was someone else, when she looked dreamily over a barranca, when she was still a virgin. I saw her and realized that she had a past and that I loved her. These, then, were her people. This, then, was all that remained of her, her family, her people, her land, her nostalgia. Dimas Palmero, was he her lover or her brother, either one longing for revenge? Marco Aurelio, was he really the brother of Dimas or, perhaps, of Eduardita? What was her relationship to the cook Doña Lupe, the baggy-eyed chauffeur, the shabby old patriarch?

I dressed. I went down to the living room. I went out to the garden. There was no longer any reason to bar my way. We all knew the rules, the contract. One day we would sit down to write it out and formalize it. I walked among the running children, took a piece of jerky without asking permission, a plump red-cheeked woman smiled at me, I waved cordially to the old man, the old man looked up and caught my eye, he put out his hand for me to help him up, he looked at me with an incredible intensity, as if only he could see that second body of mine, my sleepy companion struggling behind me through life.

I helped the old man up and he took my arm with a grip as firm as his gaze, and said: "I will grow old but never die. You understand." He led me to the edge of the property. The girl was still standing there, and Doña Lupe put her arms around her, enveloping her shoulders in her huge embrace. We went over to her, and Marco Aurelio, too, half whistling, half smoking. We were a curious quintet, that night in Las Lomas de Chapultepec, far from their land, Morelos, the country, the cane fields, the rice fields, the blue sculpted mountains cut off at the top, secret, where it is said the immortal guerrilla Zapata still rides his white horse . . .

I approached them. Or, rather, the old patriarch who had also decided to be immortal came to me, and the old man almost forced me to join them, to embrace them. I looked at the pretty girl, dark, ripe as those sweet oranges, oranges with an exciting navel and juices slowly evaporating in the sun. I took her dark arm and thought of Lala. Only this girl didn't smell of perfume, she smelled of soap. These, then, were her people, I repeated. This, then, was all that remained of her, of her feline grace, her fantastic capacity for learning conventions and mimicking fashions, speaking languages, being independent, loving herself and loving me, letting go her beautiful body with its rhythmic hips, shaking her small sweet breasts, looking at me orgasmically, as if a tropical river suddenly flowed through her eyes at the moment she desired me, oh my adored Lala, only this remains of you: your rebel land, your peasant forebears and fellows, your province as a genetic pool, bloody as the pool where you died, Lala, your land as an immense liquid pool of cheap arms for cutting cane and tending the moist rows of rice, your land as the ever-flowing fountain of workers for industry and servants for Las Lomas residences and secretary-typists for ministries and clerks in department stores and salesgirls in markets and garbage collectors and chorus girls in the Margo Theater and starlets in the national cinema and assembly-line workers in the border factories and counter help in Texas Taco Huts and servants in mansions like mine in Beverly Hills and young housewives in Chicago and young lawyers like me in Detroit and young journalists in New York: all swept in a dark flow from Morelos, Oaxaca, Guanajuanto, Michoacán, and Potosí, all tossed about the world in currents of revolution, war, liberation, the glory of some, the poverty of others, the audacity of a few, the contempt of many . . . liberty and crime.

Lala, after all, had a past. But I had not imagined it.

11

It wasn't necessary to formalize our agreement. It all started long ago, when the father of my sainted fiancée, Buenaventura del Rey, gave me the key to blackmail General Prisciliano Nieves in his hospital bed and force him to bequeath me his large house in Las Lomas in exchange for his honor as hero of Santa Eulalia. Like me, you have probably asked yourselves: Why didn't Buenaventura's father use that same information? And you know the answer as well as I. In our modern world, things come only to those who know how to use information. That's the recipe for power now, and those who let information slip through their fingers will fail miserably. On one side, weak-knees like the papa of Buenaventura del Rey. On the other side, sharks like Nicolás Sarmiento your servant. And in between, these poor, decent people who don't have any information, who have only memory, a memory that brings them suffering.

Sometimes, audaciously, I cast pebbles into that genetic pool, just to study the ripples. Santa Eulalia? La Zapotera? General Nieves, whose old house in Las Lomas we all inhabit, they unaware and me well informed, naturally? What did they know?

In my computer were entered the names and birthplaces of this sea of people who served me, most from the state of Morelos, which is, after all, the size of Switzerland. What information did Dimas Palmero possess?

(*So you come from La Zapotera in Morelos. Yes, Don Nico. Then you know the hacienda of Santa Eulalia? Of course, Don Nico, but to call it a hacienda . . . you know, there's only a burnt-out shell. It's what they called a sugar mill. Ah yes, you probably played in it as a child, Dimas. That's right, señor. And you heard stories about it? Yes, of course. The wall where the Escalona family was lined up in front of a firing squad must still be there? Yes, my grandfather was one of those who was going to be shot. But your grandfather was not a landowner. No, but the colonel said he was going to wipe out both the owners and those who served them. And then what happened? Then another commander said no, Mexican soldiers don't murder the people, because they are the people. And then, Dimas? Then they say that the first officer gave the order to fire on the masters and the servants, but the second officer gave a counterorder. Then the soldiers shot the first officer, and then the Escalona family. They didn't fire at the servants. And then? Then they say the soldiers and the servants embraced and cheered, señor. But you don't remember the names of those officers, Dimas? No, even the old ones no longer remember. But if you like I can try to find out, Don Nico. Thank you, Dimas. At your service, sir.*)

12

Yes, I imagine that Dimas Palmero had some information, who knows—but I'm sure that his relatives, crammed into my garden, kept the memory alive.

I approached them. Or, rather, I approached the old patriarch and he practically forced me to join them, to greet the others. I looked at the pretty, dark girl. I touched her dark arm. I thought of Lala. Doña Lupe had her arm around the girl. The bluish-haired grandfather, that old man as wrinkled as an old piece of silk, supported by the solid body of the cook, playing with the braids of the red-cheeked girl, all looking together toward the barranca of Las Lomas de Chapultepec: I was anxious to find out if they had a collective memory, however faint, of their own land, the same land about which I had information exclusively for my advantage; I asked them if someone had told them the names, did the old men remember the names? Nieves? Does that name mean anything to you—Nieves? Solomillo? Do you remember these old names? I asked, smiling, in an offhand manner, to see if the laws of probability projected by my computer would hold: the officers, the death of the Escalona family, Santa Eulalia, the Zapotera . . . One of those you mention said he was going to free us from servitude, the old man said very evenly, but when the other one put all of us, masters and servants, in front of a wall, Prisciliano, yes, Prisciliano, now I remember, said, "Mexican soldiers don't murder the people, because they are the people," and the other officer gave the order to fire, Prisciliano gave the counterorder, and the soldiers fired first at Prisciliano, then at the landowners, and finally at the second officer.

—Solomillo? Andrés Solomillo.

—No, Papa, you're getting mixed up. First they shot the landowners, then the revolutionary leaders began to shoot each other.

—Anyway, they all died, said the old survivor with something like resigned sadness.

—Oh, it was a long time ago, Papa.

—And you, what happened to you?

—The soldiers shouted hurray and threw their caps in the air, we tossed our sombreros in the air too, we all embraced, and I swear, sir, no one who was present that morning in Santa Eulalia will ever forget that famous line, "The soldiers are the people . . ." Well, the important thing, really, was that we'd gotten rid of the landowners first and the generals after.

He paused a moment, looking at the barranca, and said: *And it didn't do us a bit of good.*

The old man shrugged, his memory was beginning to fail him, surely; besides, they told so many different stories about what happened at Santa Eulalia, you could just about believe them all; it was the only way not to lie, and the old man laughed.

—But in the midst of so much death, there's no way to know who survived and who didn't.

—No, Papa, if you don't remember, who is going to?

—You are, said the old man. That is why I tell you. That is how it has always been. The children remember for you.

—Does Dimas know this story? I ventured to ask, immediately biting my tongue for my audacity, my haste, my . . . The old man showed no reaction.

—It all happened a long time ago. I was a child then and the soldier just told us: You're free, there's no more hacienda, or landowners, or bosses, nothing but freedom, our chains were removed, *patrón,* we were free as air. And now see how we end up, serving still, or in jail.

—Long live our chains! Marco Aurelio gave a laugh, a cross between sorrow and cynicism, as he passed by, hoisting a Dos Equis,[26] and I watched him, thinking of Eduarda as a child, how she must have struggled to reach my arms, and I thought of Dimas Palmero in prison and of how he would stay there, with his memory, not realizing that memory was information, Dimas in his cell knowing the same story as everyone, conforming to the memory of the world and not the memory of his people—Prisciliano Nieves was the hero of Santa Eulalia—while the old man knew what Dimas forgot, didn't know, or rejected: Prisciliano Nieves had died in Santa Eulalia; but neither of them knew how to convert his memory into information, and my life depended on their doing nothing, on their memory, accurate or not, remaining frozen forever, an imprisoned memory, you understand, my accomplices? Memory their prisoner, information my prisoner, and both of us here, not moving from the house, both of us immobile, both prisoners, and everyone happy, so I immediately said to Marco Aurelio: Listen, when you visit your brother, tell him he'll lack for nothing, you hear me? Tell him that they'll take good care of him, I promise, he can get married, have conjugal visits, you know: I've heard it said in the house that he likes this red-cheeked girl with the bare arms, well, he can marry her, she's

---

[26] **Dos Equis:** A brand of beer.

not going to run off with one of these bandits, you've seen what they're like, Marco Aurelio, but tell Dimas not to worry, he can count on me, I'll pay for the wedding and give the girl a dowry, tell him I'm taking him, and all of you, into my care, you will all be well cared for, I'll see to it that you'll never lack for anything, neither you here nor Dimas in the pen, he won't have to work, or you either, I'll look after the family, resigned to the fact that the real criminal will never be found: Who killed Eduarda? We'll never know, I swear, when a girl like that comes to the city and becomes independent, neither you nor I, nobody, is guilty of anything . . .

That was my decision. I preferred to remain with them and leave Dimas in jail rather than declare myself guilty or pin the crime on someone else. They understood. I thought of Dimas Palmero locked up and also of the day I presented myself to Brigadier Prisciliano Nieves in his hospital room.

—Sign here, my general. I promise to take care of your servants and your honor. You can rest in peace. Your reputation is in my hands. I wouldn't want it to be lost, believe me. I will be as silent as the grave; I will be your heir.

The dying Brigadier Prisciliano Nieves looked at me with enormous brazenness. I knew then that his possessions no longer mattered to him, that he wouldn't bat an eyelash.

—Do you have any heirs, other than your servants, I asked, and the old man surely had not expected that question, which I put to him as I took a hand mirror from the table next to the bed and held it in front of the sick face of the general, in this way registering his surprise.

Who knows what the false Prisciliano saw there.

—No, I have no one.

Well informed, I already knew that. The old man ceased to look at his death's face and looked instead at mine, young, alert, perhaps resembling his own anonymous youthful look.

—My general, you are not you. Sign here, please, and die in peace.

To each his own memory. To each his own information. The world believed that Prisciliano Nieves killed Andrés Solomillo at Santa Eulalia. The old patriarch installed in my house knew that they had all killed each other. My first sweetheart Buenaventura del Rey's papa, paymaster of the constitutionalist army, knew that as well. Between the two memories lay my twenty-five years of prosperity. But Dimas Palmero, in jail, believed like everyone else that Prisciliano Nieves was the hero of Santa Eulalia, its survivor and its enforcer of justice. His information *was* the world's. The old men, by contrast, *held* the world's information, which isn't the same. Prisciliano Nieves died, along with Andrés Solomillo, at Santa Eulalia, when the former said that the soldiers, being the people, would not kill the people, and the latter proved the contrary right there, and barely had Prisciliano fallen when Solomillo, too, was cut down by the troops. Who usurped the legend of Prisciliano Nieves? What had been that man's name? Who profited from the slaughter of the leaders? No doubt, someone just as anonymous as those who had invaded my garden and surrounded my house. That was the man I visited one morning in the hospital and blackmailed. I converted memory to information. Buenaventura's papa and the ragged old man residing in my garden retained memory but lacked information. Only I had both, but as yet I could do nothing with them except to ensure that everything would go on the same as always, that nothing would be questioned, that it would never occur to Dimas Palmero to translate the memory of his clan into information, that neither the information nor the memory would ever do anyone any good anymore, except for me. But the price of that deadlock was that I would remain forever in my house in Las Lomas, Dimas Palmero in jail, and his family in my garden.

In the final analysis, was it I who won, he who lost? That I leave for you to decide. Over my telephone lines, you have heard all I've said. I've been completely honest with you. I've put all my cards on the table. If there are loose ends in my story, you can gather them up and tie them in a bow yourselves. My memory and my information are now yours. You have the right to criticize, to finish the story, to reverse the tapestry and change the weave, to point out the lapses of logic, to imagine you have resolved all the mysteries that I, the narrator crushed under the press of reality, have let escape through the net of my telephones, which is the net of my words.

And still I'll bet you won't know what to do with what you know. Didn't I say so from the beginning? My story is hard to believe.

Now I no longer had to take risks and struggle. Now I had my place in the world, my house, my servants, and my secrets. I no longer had the guts to go see Dimas Palmero in prison and ask him what he knew about Prisciliano Nieves or what he knew about Lala: Why did you kill her? On your own? Because the old man ordered you to? For the honor of the family? Or for your own?

—Lala, I sighed, my Lala . . .

Then through the gardens of Virreyes came the girls on pogo sticks, hopping like nubile kangaroos, wearing sweatshirts with the names of Yankee universities on them and acid-washed jeans with Walkmans hooked between blue jean and belt and the fantastic look of Martians, radio operators, telephone operators, aviators all rolled into one, with their black earphones over their ears, hopping on their springy pogo sticks over the hedges that separate the properties of Las Lomas—spectacular, Olympic leaps—waving to me, inviting me to follow them, to find myself through others, to join the party, to take a chance with them: Let's all crash the parties, they say, that's more fun, hopping by like hares, like fairies, like Amazons, like Furies, making private property moot, seizing their right to happiness, community, entertainment, and God knows what . . . Free, they would never make any demands on me, ask for marriage, dig into my affairs, discover my secrets, the way the alert Lala did . . . Oh, Lala, why were you so ambitious?

I wave to them from a distance, surrounded by servants, goodbye, goodbye, I toss them kisses and they smile at me, free, carefree, dazzling, dazzled, inviting me to follow them, to abandon my prison, and I wave and would like to tell them no, I am not the prisoner of Las Lomas, no, they are my prisoners, an entire people . . .

I enter the house and disconnect my bank of telephones. The fifty-seven lines on which you're listening to me. I have nothing else to tell you. Soon there will be no one to repeat these fictions, and they will all be true. I thank you for listening.

❧ TAKENISHI HIROKO

B. JAPAN, 1929

In *Children of the A-Bomb* (1959), Osado Arata records the testimony of a boy who was a fourth-grader in Hiroshima, Japan, on August 6, 1945, when the crew of the B-29 bomber *Enola Gay* dropped the atomic weapon innocuously named Little Boy on that city. He remembers the refugee camp in some field in the Hiroshima suburbs, the stench of rotting flesh and bodies being cremated, the clouds of flies and mosquitoes, and his mother dying there of wounds and radiation sickness after almost two weeks of agony. He concludes his flat list of horrors by saying, "Too much sorrow makes me like a stranger to myself, and yet despite my grief I cannot cry." By the 1950s and 1960s, Japanese writers who had been children and adolescents in the year of the Hiroshima and Nagasaki bombings began to tell the story of their sorrow to help them to recognize themselves. Takenishi Hiroko's "The Rite" is one of the most powerful of these semiautobiographical retellings.

A Hiroshima Survivor.   Takenishi Hiroko was born in April 1929 into an upper-middle-class family in Hiroshima. In "The Rite," Takenishi's narrator, Aki, recalls in fleeting snatches some of the sorts of early pleasures Takenishi herself had grown up with in a childhood fairly insulated from the consciousness of war: She tends the carp pond in her parents' pleasant suburban garden, scaring off the marauding night heron and eavesdropping while her elders speak over a late dinner; she visits the great stone feudal castle with its white pagoda tower, the monument that until 1945 defined the skyline of the city built on the delta islands of the Honshu River, the monument after which the city was named: *Hiro-shima-jo,* "Broad-island-castle."

Takenishi was a sixteen-year-old schoolgirl when the United States dropped on Hiroshima the first nuclear bomb to be used against an enemy population, thereby instantly erasing most of the world Takenishi had known. As "The Rite" implies, an especially large number of young women in Hiroshima were killed instantly on that day; eight thousand of them, including Takenishi, were called out of their regular classes to special civilian defense duty, ordered to raze houses in the central part of the city to create firebreaks against the ordinary incendiary bomb attack the military feared was in the offing. Osado, the oral historian of Hiroshima, quotes one of those women, a student at a junior college, describing the first minutes after the blast:

> The vicinity was in pitch darkness; from the depths of the gloom, bright red flames rise crackling, and spread moment by moment. The faces of my friends who just before were working energetically are now burned and blistered, their clothes torn to rags; to what shall I liken their trembling appearance as they stagger about? Our teacher is holding her students close to her like a mother hen protecting her chicks, and like baby chicks paralyzed with terror, the students were thrusting their heads under her arms. . . .

www For links to more information about Takenishi and a quiz on "The Rite," and for information about the culture and context of Japan in the twentieth century, see *World Literature Online* at bedfordstmartins .com/worldlit.

Too much sorrow makes me like a stranger to myself, and yet despite my grief I cannot cry.

– *Children of the A-Bomb*

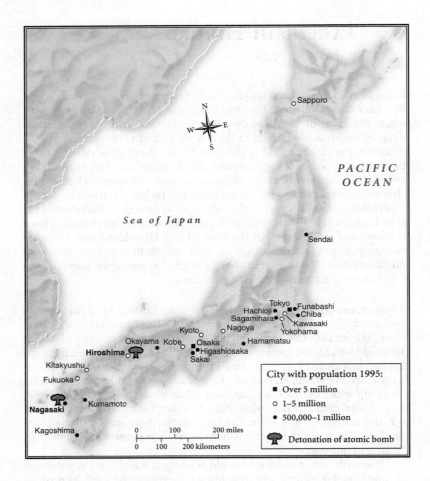

Nuclear Bombs Dropped on Japan, August 1945

The destruction caused by the bombs dropped on Hiroshima and Nagasaki was unprecedented and total: Hundreds of thousands of people were killed in a moment, many vaporized by the blast; cities were razed; survivors were traumatized and, in most cases, made ill.

Deaths directly resulting from the Hiroshima bombing numbered at least one hundred forty thousand at the end of 1945; by 1950, some sixty thousand more people had died from long-term effects of the blast. It is difficult to assess the even further-reaching outcomes, such as rises in the rates of birth defects and cancers for Hiroshima survivors, their children, and their grandchildren. Like Takenishi's narrator, Aki, many who did not suffer illnesses resulting from radiation were riddled with survivor guilt, including those who still live today.

Twentieth-Century Japan: Hiroshima

On the Monday morning of August 6, 1945, an American B-29 bomber called *Enola Gay* dropped an atomic bomb on the Japanese city of Hiroshima. In "The Rite," Takenishi Hiroko describes the terror of that day and its long-term effects from the point of view of a Japanese schoolgirl. It was the first time the A-bomb had been used in warfare. Three days later, the United States dropped a second bomb, nicknamed "Fat Man," on the Japanese city of Nagasaki. One week later, on August 14, 1945, Japan announced its surrender, and the Second World War was over. The day the atomic bomb dropped on Hiroshima remains one of the most horrifying of the twentieth century, both because of its immediate effec-

tiveness and because of the scope of its impact. The atomic bomb that killed an estimated two hundred thousand people in the city of Hiroshima marks the beginning of the epoch of nuclear warfare. President Harry S. Truman's decision to drop the bomb showed his faith in the new science that had created the weapon, but it also promised to change the way war would be waged in the future. The bombing of Hiroshima was particularly horrific because the A-bomb did not discriminate between military and civilian targets. In his speech to the American people about what the U.S. government had just done, Truman called Hiroshima a "military base" and urged the Japanese to leave industrialized cities, saying those cities would be next. Hiroshima was not a military base; it was a city teeming with life; the near total destruction the A-bomb wreaked on Hiroshima changed it forever and made unthinkable the prospect of future atomic wars.

Aftermath of Hiroshima. *The scene of devastation in Hiroshima after August 6, 1945. Takenishi Hiroko was sixteen when the bomb was dropped on the city she had lived in all her life. (The Art Archive)*

The great anger, the deep hate, come after the event. The thing that parted me from Junko, that kept Kiyoko from me although she wanted to see me again, that made me cower all night in a hollow in the ground — if I could catch the real nature of that thing and fling the fullness of my anger and hate at it, I would not be in torment to this day, well over ten years after, tied to this fierce anger that still finds no proper outlet.

– TAKENISHI HIROKO, "The Rite"

Takenishi's Writing Career.   Takenishi survived to graduate from Waseda University, where she majored in Japanese literature. After obtaining her degree, she worked for two major Japanese publishing houses until 1962, when she began to concentrate on writing and publishing both her own fiction and critical essays on classical Japanese literature. In 1964 a collection of those essays, *Two Ways Between the Ancient and Contemporary Times,* won a prestigious literary award, the Tomara Tashiki Prize. In 1978, Takenishi was awarded the Women's Literature Prize for "The Orchestra Festival" *(Kai Gen Sai),* a story that also deals with the bomb. Her critical work *A Theory on the Tales of Genji* (1975) is considered a definitive study of that classic work. Her fictional work *Barracks* won the Kawabata Yasunari Prize in 1980.

"The Rite."   This stunning work appeared in 1963, as the world approached the twentieth anniversary of Hiroshima and Nagasaki. The story's fragmented structure and its flashbacks that seem to meld into one another befit Aki's inner life. The narrator is still in shock from the blast, even though on the surface she goes calmly about her daily routine of arranging remodeling jobs for a construction company, going out on dates, and seeing friends. Her deepest experience, her repressed inner life, is hinged on the moment of the blast, a moment readers do not see until the near end of the story.

The reader never learns about the fate of Aki's own family or even very much about Aki's own experience of the bomb, but as she goes about her daily routine among the living, more than a decade after the blast, she looks about her at the bereaved mothers who have gone mad, at the surviving sisters who kill themselves out of guilt. She visits the hospital bed of her friend Setsuko, who vows she will soon be well even as she lies dying of metastasized cancer. And she goes to the house of her friend Tomiko who has summoned Aki on business, vaguely wishing to "remodel" her house, to make it "what we want"; her husband, she assures Aki, desires that, too, though he never shows up. Aki realizes that Tomiko, who keeps two miscarried fetuses in jars on her Buddhist altar, is almost certainly heading for a third miscarriage, but Tomiko insists that this time "everything is going to be all right." Everyone denies there is something wrong; almost no one speaks of the bomb, of the dead, of the dying, of his or her own past and present pain, or of fears for the future. When Aki verges on speaking about her memories and fears to her lover, he says, "If you really loved me, you would be able to put that sort of thing right out of your mind!" She knows then that she must break off with him.

As the story ends, Aki seems less spiritually depleted, more conscious of her own needs and the sources of her terror, tentatively planning to return to Hiroshima to see what might still be there for her and resolved "to live without wiping out the memory of that day."

■ CONNECTIONS

Joseph Conrad, *Heart of Darkness,* **p. 35.** "The Rite," like *Heart of Darkness,* is narrated several years after the traumatic event that prompts its telling, and in the narrative both Aki and Marlow are seeking an understanding of their experience and its significance in their lives. What signs are there in the lives of the two narrators that their experiences were traumatic? What indicates that the stories are emotionally difficult for the characters to remember?

James Joyce, "The Dead," p. 372; Tanizaki Junichiro, "Aguri," p. 464; Franz Kafka, *The Metamorphosis*, p. 428. The fragmented scenes, stream-of-consciousness narration, and disjointed temporal sequences and dreams in "The Rite" are features of modernist narrative technique found in the work of several writers in this anthology, especially that of Joyce, Tanizaki, and Kafka. Identify other modernist stories that share these features. Do the same elements have the same impact in each of the stories?

T. S. Eliot, *The Waste Land*, p. 486. Eliot's wasteland is often interpreted as a symbolic representation of the spiritual devastation wrought by World War I. Hiroshima was literally a wasteland after the atomic bomb was dropped there, and Takenishi uses images of the physical "warscape" to suggest the psychological and spiritual impact of the bombing. Does Takenishi find the kind of cultural devastation in postwar Japan that Eliot sees in post–World War I Europe?

■ **FURTHER RESEARCH**

Background
Oe Kenzaburo. *Hiroshima Notes*. 1965.
Osado Arata. *Children of the A-Bomb*. 1982.
Rhodes, Richard. *The Making of the Atomic Bomb*. 1986.

∾ The Rite

Translated by Eileen Kato

To the riverside house with the tin roof on which several bunches of red chili peppers had been set out to dry they brought at evening an injured man, stretched out on a wooden shutter. By the entrance to the small dirt-floored front area stood two pickling tubs with big stone weights on the lids, casting long shadows in the westerly sun. The hill that pressed in on the house from behind was fully exposed to the late sunlight, so that even the texture of its soil showed clearly. Holding the shutter front and rear were two sturdy young men with towels around their necks and

---

"The Rite." Published in 1963, eighteen years after the bombing of Hiroshima, this story indicates one of its important themes in its title: the search for a ritual that will express the grief and heal the traumas caused by the attack. Aki, the protagonist, is obsessed with death and the rites of death, hunting for the proper feelings to have in the wake of death and suffering. Of all her childhood memories, Aki keeps returning to three that predate the bomb—the death of a poor man who lived behind her parents' house, whose family could afford no burial save to haul his body away in a cart; the crying of an unseen woman at the bottom of her parents' garden, which stirred the young Aki deeply; and the beautiful lantern festivals in honor of ancestor spirits. In the present, when she chooses a magazine at a newsstand, she is drawn strongly to one with a picture of an ancient Egyptian funerary jar on the cover. The ancient peoples of the world gave much thought to how to grieve, how to mourn, how to lay their dead to rest. But no rite has been

split-toed tabi sneakers[1] on their feet. The doorway was so narrow there was no way they could get in. They appeared to be talking about it and trying to figure out what to do. The injured man's head was thickly bandaged and from under the thin quilt that covered his body, his gaitered legs stuck out, also shod with tabi sneakers. The goings-on beyond the river were so unusual that Aki couldn't tear herself away from the lattice window. Her school satchel, flap open, lay there unheeded by her side.

A middle-aged woman emerged from the front room. It was the woman who washed rice and rinsed clothes every day at the river. Crying in a shrill voice, she clutched at the injured man, and then throwing her arms in the air and screaming something at the top of her voice, she ran to the next house some distance away. Between there and the next house was a rough log cabin that looked like some sort of storage shed. At the foot of the hill the only inhabited buildings were the woman's house and the house next door that she had run to. Both were roofed with tin, and judging by their size, other than the dirt-floored front area, there couldn't be more than one room worth calling a room.

Soon the woman hurried back from the next house, bringing an old woman with her. The door panel had been removed and now, the makeshift stretcher slid easily inside. The injured man must be the husband who came home drunk late every night, thought Aki. The woman who ran to the neighboring house must be the wife, and the one she brought back with her must be the mother of one of them. The two young men leaned over the injured man and peered into his face. Three small children had climbed on top of the quilt and seemed to be patting and stroking the injured man. When one of the children slithered off the quilt and wandered away, the other two did the same, and then all three left the house.

Already dusk was closing in. The three children each started picking up pebbles, and then together, facing the stream, they began seeing who could throw the farthest.

That night, mingling with the river noises, there came to Aki's ears a low sound of crying. But it grew steadily louder and there was no sign that it would ever stop. And as Aki opened the shutters a little to try to see what was happening beyond the river, the thought struck her that now, under that naked electric light over there, a man's death was drawing near. Was it through his own carelessness he got hurt, she wondered, or had he been attacked by someone? And those people left behind, how would they be able to live now?

Aki remembered when that house was built. One day a man and a woman and three children came to the riverside with a pushcart full of lumber and sheets of tin. They chose a site at the foot of the hill and drove stakes into the ground. First of all,

---

performed—and perhaps no rite will suffice—to lay to rest the dead of Hiroshima, many of whom disappeared at the moment of the blast, charred, reduced to smears of ash, vaporized. The adult Aki longs for a whole litany of girlfriends—Junko, Kiyoko, Kazue, Emiko, Ikuko, Yayoi—whom she secretly imagines may still be living, for their deaths have left no trace.

All notes are the editors'.

---

[1] **tabi sneakers:** Tabis are soft-soled shoes that separate the big toe from the rest of the toes.

they built the little log cabin. Then they built one house with a tin roof. All day long the man swung his hammer and wielded his saw; the children romped and raced around; the wife washed vegetables in the river. Then, when the second house was finished, the old woman appeared from somewhere and took up her abode there. It was shortly after this that the man started going out every day, dressed in a workman's happi coat,[2] his legs in gaiters and tabi sneakers on his feet, and then, more and more often, he could be heard late at night, singing off key in a loud voice. The man had a slurred pronunciation that jarred the ear, but this was not simply because he was drunk. The woman's speech too, and even the way the children talked, were quite different from Aki's own manner of speaking.

The day after the injured man was brought home and the day following that, the dried red peppers were left where they were on the roof. The hearse that Aki thought must surely come to that house in the end did not come after all. All she saw was a canvas covered pushcart, escorted by the two women and the three children and several brawny looking men, going slowly along the road by the river.

From the far off days of her childhood, long before Aki had ever experienced such things as the sickness or death of her own flesh and blood, that was a funeral that stayed like a weight on her mind.

There's lightning flashing!

Aki wakes up with the feeling she has just come out of a queer disturbing dream. She seems to have woken up in the middle of her own scream. With her mind on this, Aki gropes for the switch of the bedside lamp. Finds it. Presses it. There is the familiar ceiling of her four-and-a-half-mat rented room. It is just after two in the morning. In the dusty vase, the fresh summer flowers she had put there only yesterday are already wilted and drooping. By her bed a weekly magazine, a cigarette case, a lighter, an ashtray.

From time to time the wind rustles the branches of the trees and bushes. Aki turns over and lies face down, lights a cigarette, inhales.

Pictured on the cover of the weekly that Aki had bought yesterday at the subway station entrance was the lid of a jar. When she left the construction company where she worked, she walked along the pavement that her heels always caught in, to the shop run by a German near the subway station. Often on Saturday afternoons Aki would come to this shop for a late lunch of tea and pie. She had done so yesterday. And then, to buy a weekly, she had gone to the station newsstand at the side of the ticket window. While she was looking for one with an interesting cover, her hand, as though it were the natural thing to do, reached for the one with that lid.

Except for the magazine's title, the whole cover was taken up by the face of a young Egyptian nobleman, drawn big against a vermillion background. When Aki learned that this was the lid of an urn used in ancient Egypt as a container for the viscera of corpses to be mummified, a strange thrill ran through a corner of her

---

[2] **happi coat:** A loose-fitting cloth jacket that fastens with ties in the front.

heart. It was as if she alone in the midst of a multitude was experiencing a secret joy, but this joy was overshadowed by a heavy, helpless gloom. "There's someone watching me!" Suddenly Aki had this uneasy feeling and looked up, shifting her gaze in the direction of the ticket gate.

A young man approaching and a woman, turning her back on him without a word, and going out to the sidewalk. A man in a sudden outburst of anger at a woman who appeared to have come late for their date. A group of girl students, each hand in hand with a friend, their free hands separately hailing a taxi. A plump middle-aged woman approaching with rapid mincing steps. Every face looking totally intent on some immediate, intimate aim. Relieved, Aki lifted up the handbag on her arm and went through the ticket gate onto the platform. She sat down on an empty bench, and then resumed her examination of the urn lid.

The nobleman had a wig and his eyes were of obsidian and quartzite. According to the explanation, a glass image of the sacred serpent had originally been attached to the forehead. His loved ones left behind would have assembled before him to mourn this dead man. Some would have prayed, some would have waved incense censers, some would have made funeral offerings of great price. The lid of the alabaster urn would then have been removed and his internal organs gently placed within. What memories would have stirred then in those people as lid met jar again?

There without a doubt was a fitting way to start out on death's journey, with the dead well tended and watched over by the living. Thinking of that man who had left behind a part of his own flesh, and his people who had taken it into their keeping, in what was surely a most dignified and solemn ceremony, it seemed to Aki that there indeed was a secure and reassuring way to die.

It was three days now since she had gone to the suburb where Tomiko lived in front of the station, carrying Tomiko's postcard asking for help in her handbag.

Tomiko's house had a little shop in it that sold the latest books and magazines, along with cigarettes. Whenever a train stopped at the station, a couple of customers would drop in at the shop. Although it was a hot sticky evening, Tomiko was there minding the shop, dressed in a maternity smock that was a little on the long side. The moment she caught sight of Aki, she let out a sudden cry of joy and grabbed her by the arms. It had been four or five years since they had last met. Watching Tomiko's friendly, darting eyes, Aki thought, "She's just the same as ever!"

"I want to have the shop remodeled. I've been telling my husband all along that when it came time for that, I'd call on your place."

The husband in question did not put in an appearance. For Aki, it was not that Tomiko's request was in any way unusual, but willy-nilly she had to bear in mind the likely reaction of her section chief, who much preferred new jobs to remodeling. Anyway, Aki got most of the necessary data for the estimate from her friend and briskly wrote it down. There was nothing further she needed to be told. At this point Tomiko said, "My husband is still on his rounds. Anyway, that's what we want. Please do the best you can for us!" Aki said she needed about a week.

"Sure! That's fine!"

Then Tomiko bowed formally from the waist and that was the end of the business talk.

A boy's voice was saying the conventional "Excuse me for eating first! That was a good meal!" The boy had come out from under the door curtain of a side door that seemed to communicate with the kitchen, and now with lowered head, was standing facing Tomiko.

Who does that remind me of! thought Aki.

The moment of confusion, then the self-conscious look on the boy's face! That was the face that Noboru had often shown her when he was late for a date. With his nervous temperament, he was such a stickler for punctuality that whenever he was late, Aki used to wonder uneasily if she herself hadn't made a mistake. "I got caught by the prof." — that's all he would say as he sat down, so boyishly that sometimes Aki found it hard to believe that Noboru was older than she. If Aki asked Noboru a question about the university research laboratory where he worked, he would answer in great detail, but he never took the initiative in talking about himself or his work. Whenever Aki came late, Noboru would immediately start telling her about what he had been reading while waiting, and before she could even apologize for being late she would be drawn into Noboru's conversation, and as often as not they would soon be deep in talk about something else altogether.

"Why don't you eat supper here with me before you go!" Invited thus by Tomiko, Aki walked under the door curtain. More than ten years had gone by since they had graduated together from the same girls' school. Aki had never once met Tomiko's husband. But seeing Tomiko so little changed, and judging too from the fact that at this hour he was still out on his rounds, leaving the estimate for the remodeling and all that up to his wife, Aki decided he must be a hard worker and a nice fellow but a timid, ineffectual sort of man.

Every time a train pulled in or out of the station, a minor tremor shook the room, but by the time they were drinking their after-dinner cup of tea, she didn't mind it so much.

"How are you? Any change since I saw you last?" Being suddenly questioned like this by Tomiko made Aki start. "Me?" she rejoined quizzically. "Oh, nothing in particular!" she said with a laugh, and then fell silent. Ever since she had first noticed Tomiko's smock, she had been thinking she must sooner or later broach the subject as casually as she could and ask about Tomiko's condition. Now's the time, she thought.

"Let's forget about me! What about you? When is it?" she asked in a low voice. Now, for a moment, it was Tomiko's turn to be taken aback, or so it appeared to Aki.

"If all goes according to schedule — January. No matter what, this time everything is going to be all right. My husband says so too."

The light had gone out of Tomiko's face. Her eyes had a fixed look about them. Aki searched for words to say, but no word she came up with seemed to be the right one; anything she said would only make matters worse!

"Look there!"

As she spoke, Tomiko pointed to a corner of the living room. When Aki had first been shown into the room, she had seen a corner heaped with flowers and just thought, There's the Buddha altar! But until they were now called to her attention, she had stupidly failed to notice the two small jars, standing low there side by side and all but buried under the flowers. The fetuses that had miscarried, as if this were determined by the waxing and the waning of the moon, and then the mourning rites that had to be gone through, as though it were all a matter of course. Tomiko talked about these things in a low voice, as if she were talking about someone else. She continued staring fixedly at the edge of the table while her fingertips groped for the chopsticks.

"But never mind! This time, you'll see! I'll have my baby properly!" And as she said this, Tomiko's eyes grew warm and smiling again.

But to Aki, it seemed as if she had suddenly been thrown into the middle of a thicket of prickly cactus, and no matter where she turned or how she looked about, she could see nothing like a path leading out of it. The overlapping fleshy leaves were slowly but deliberately swelling, getting fatter and fatter. The way they stretched upward, they seemed to be showing her how much they could grow. She felt a chill, as though convulsions had seized her body here and there; only her cheeks were burning.

On the way back from Tomiko's house, where a field of corn lay along the station railing, Aki vomited twice. She crouched there, steadying herself by holding on to several corn stalks bunched together, her back arched in misery like some stray cat that might have wandered that way. She had a vision of all those miscarried babies, clustered like so many grapes, gushing out over and over there before her eyes, feebly-thrusting tiny hands and feet, rubbing up against each other, and after wriggling for a while, coming to rest quietly at last, in a white jar no bigger than a saké pourer.

Suddenly now, the end of her nightmare of a while ago comes back to Aki.

I seemed to be in a big room. Or maybe it wasn't that big after all. Pitch blackness all around, except for one single disc of light. I did not know what I was doing there, but as I stood there perfectly still, I thought, it's cold! Then that round brightness, which was the shining surface of some thick, dark solution, began to congeal with the cold and gave off a gleam that reminded me of blood. The surface of the liquid wavered. At first the gleam undulated gently. Then gradually the undulation changed into a great swell, and the liquid surface began to spread slowly. The liquid, fed from some unknown source, was surely increasing in volume, or so it appeared to me. In the interval between one swell and the next, some terribly soft-looking pinkish thing would rise up out of the top of the liquid and then sink back again, only to reappear from another part and sink back once more. Now the thick fluid was whirling and overflowing all around. I was going to be sucked into the maelstrom of that viscous gleam! Thinking only of how to escape from my rapidly mounting terror, I screamed "Quick!" as if urging someone to do something.

And then before I knew it, in a corner of the darkness, a pale face appeared, shining like a light. It did not immediately come close to me. I was at the limit of my endurance, but the rate of approach of that pale face was excruciatingly slow. I wanted to beckon to it, but my hand seemed to be pulled down by a great weight and I could not move it. When finally the face came close enough to see, I gave a start —

"Noboru!"

I do not know how many seconds later, how many hours later it was, but in the instant when his tenderness tried to reach out to me, I shivered all over and pushed him away.

Aki takes a resolute puff of her cigarette, then stubs it out in the ashtray. She switches off the bedside lamp. In the room below there is not a sound.

At this hour, when the cactuses and sago palms lift up their clustering limbs to the night sky, underneath the leaves the sleeping breath of animals will be wafted forth. The earth is white. The little spring is surely shining silver. Lazy but stubborn, that crowd of oh so very animal-like plants! A beating of the wings of unseen birds. A wild beast suddenly will rise from sleep and come crashing through the thicket and then violently shake itself, its eyes shining gold in the cool air of night.

Or again . . . in the heart of the city the buildings have at last recovered the coldness of the stone, while at the foundry, flames enwrap the furnace. The blistering cries of things that leave the womb and the gossamer-weak whimpers from the beds in the old people's home must melt and run together somewhere in the sky at night. Good fellowship and shame and boastfulness, the groans of the oppressed and long deep sighs like the receding tide; perhaps these also come together somewhere, whirling, whirling round and round. In the shade of all sorts of things are little sprouting lives making a secret gamble. But however secret the bet, however poor the chance, the thing that once begins to breathe alive will go on living in the dark night of the womb, deep in the amniotic sea, until the moon is full; untouched by doubt or hesitation, as if saying that the destiny laid down for it is simply this, to live.

Soon now, there will be a death that I must face. Aki is thinking of Setsuko, who must be asleep at this hour in her room at the university hospital. The day cannot be far off when all the malignancies spreading here and there through Setsuko's body, accompanied by unbearable pain, will plunge her senses into disorder. "The end has come," her doctor will say. With downcast eyes the nurse will cover her with a white starched sheet brought in from the laundry room, and they will gently carry her down to the morgue in the basement.

Just a week ago, I bought the eau de Cologne that Setsuko always uses and went and knocked lightly on the door of her sickroom. The woman attendant said "Please" as she showed me into the room, and went out looking happy to get away for a while. Setsuko's eyes were like two beads of glass that might have been set temporarily in the bone sockets. Her meager flesh hung around her bones as if it were some sort of thick wrapping paper covering her temporarily. What I saw that day deep inside her were the thin burned-up bones; what I heard was the brittle crumbling of their white calcinated remains.

Setsuko's hospitalization had been decided on just half a year after her marriage.

Then Setsuko's husband was appointed to a foreign post very shortly after. According to her, just like the diplomat her husband now accompanied, he himself was destined in the future to become a distinguished diplomat. From a café terrace that had a view of the Sphynx, from a brick-built city with rain-washed pavements, from the shores of a lake with a range of snow-clad mountains behind, he frequently sent her picture postcards. As soon as she recovered from this illness, he would come back and fetch her. "When that is done, next thing I will invite you to come and visit us. How many days can you get off from work?" And it seemed that Setsuko was making these plans in all seriousness.

Yes, but soon now Setsuko will be enveloped in rites of great solemnity. Summoned back from his foreign post, her husband will be reunited with his young wife in that dark room in the basement. His colleagues, Setsuko's friends, and the relatives on both sides will gather around Setsuko, now a corpse, and then soon they will hurry away again about their business. The husband will probably sit by Setsuko's side for a night. There will be the casket, the cremation, the solemn chanting of the sutras, the funeral flowers, the requiem music, the incense. Then he will take his wife in his arms, or all that's left of her—the calcinated bones and ashes—and he will leave, with all the other mourners following. In the deserted place of mourning there will be no sign of life until the garbageman appears, his hand towel round his head. He will come from the doorway and approach the altar and begin to clear away the funeral flower-wreaths.

There are caskets in hearses that glide gently forward, followed by the long chain of the funeral procession, and there are coffins dragged along on screeching pushcarts, tied down roughly with a common rope. There are people who gouge out the viscera of their dead and then wait upon the mountains for the birds, and there are people who scale precipices, their dead stuffed into leather bags upon their backs. There are secluded tombs away at the far end of well-kept avenues of approach flanked with statues of lions and of camels and of elephants, while by the shores of northern seas, are graves marked only by the native rocks forever lashed by stormy waves.

There are all kinds of rites to go with death.

In the royal palace there are rites that well befit the palaces of kings. Under roofs of tin are other rites more suited for a tin-roofed house. Sunlight, the stars, the trees, the honey in the flower, love . . . even lives that were snuffed out before they could know any of these things have their own special rites.

Aki has never seen Junko's dead body.

That big tilled field at twilight under great columns of cloud . . . that had become the backdrop for Aki's last memory of Junko in that place. With the orange-colored book she had taken from Aki's bookshelf under her arm, she had stopped in front of the farm-tool shed at the entrance to the field and said, "See you tomorrow." "'Bye! Say hello to your big sister for me, won't you!" Aki rejoined, to which Junko retorted, "And what about my big brother?" and then she stuck out her tongue. Their two laughing voices died away in the squeals of a child chasing dragonflies.

The little girl with the bucktoothed smile and hair in long plaits down her back never changed or grew an inch in Aki's mind from that time on. Even now, when the smell of hay comes to her, Aki will sometimes start. The pile of hay by the toolshed in that big tilled field was always hollowed by the weight of the two of them. On top of the hay Junko would go on and on talking about people she had never met as if they were acquaintances of long years' standing; even people who had been dead and buried for decades or even centuries, she would talk about in the same familiar way. And that is why, whenever she had to go off somewhere in connection with her work, if the wind happened to carry a whiff of new-mown hay through the window of the suburban train, Aki would find herself thinking that her relations with Junko, severed so many years before, were about to be resumed. With an upward glance she would scrutinize all the faces in the car she was riding in. But she never had any recollection of having seen a single one of those faces before. And yet, surely there was a smell of hay! Or was she just imagining things? And so, deciding she had been mistaken and trying to think of something else, she would lower her eyes again.

Aki has never seen Kiyoko's dead body.

Kiyoko had left Aki's house late that night. And that was the end of that. In the calm of the evening, the incessant croaking of the frogs intensified the impression of sultriness. After dinner, the two of them started on some beading work in Aki's room. They took turns going out on the veranda every time they heard a splash to chase away the night heron that stalked the carp in the garden pond. Then, while they were huddled together looking at some gold dust fallen from a large moth, Kiyoko promised to come to Aki's house again in two or three days' time. But that promise has yet to be kept. If Kiyoko were to walk into this room in a moment or two and stand there right in front of her, Aki would find nothing particularly strange or startling about that. It would merely be like a piece of movie film that had broken and was now patched together, restoring them to each other. "What happened? What have you been up to?" First of all they would look each other in the eye to make sure it was really the two of them, and then no doubt they'd grab and poke each other to make doubly sure, and everything would be all right again. Yes, thinks Aki, I am still waiting for Kiyoko!

Aki has never seen Kazue's dead body.

Nor Emiko's dead body.

No, nor Ikuko's.

Nor has she ever come across anyone else who witnessed their end or verified the deaths of Junko or Kiyoko or Kazue or Yayoi.

After that summer there were lots of people who for reasons of their own preferred to keep silent. Something must have happened to her friends to make them feel they didn't want Aki to see them. One of these days, surely, she'd meet Junko. Maybe she'll run into someone who has news of Kazue! And with these thoughts, Aki just went on waiting.

Sometimes the thought strikes Aki, maybe Junko is living right here in this same town without knowing that I am here too! Maybe she too is looking for me! Only, I am not in any of the places where she has looked. And she is not in any of the places where I have searched. Have we not perhaps gone on and on missing each other like that? Maybe in the train we have stood close together any number of times, back to back, and then got off and gone our separate ways. Maybe we have even sat in the same row at the theater, and then, unaware of each other's presence, left by different exits, one to the right, the other to the left. Maybe she was standing at the back of that elevator whose doors closed just as I was about to get on.

A year or so after that time, one day I ran into Yayoi's mother quite by chance, and she smiled and laughed at me, and not only at me but at all the people going by, and didn't seem the least bit embarrassed that she was in her bare feet. A few years later, the bloated corpse of Ikuko's younger sister was recovered from below the wharf where the logs are left to season in the water. The evening papers carried her picture and gave the cause of death as extreme nervous exhaustion. Tatsuo, who was to marry into Kazue's family in two or three years, because Kazue was missing, moved away and no longer lived in that place. An old established merchant family like that, and now, unless Kazue some day reappears, their line is doomed to die out.

In the devastated schoolground a mound of black earth had been raised and on top of it was just one plain wooden marker. Buried beneath in unglazed urns, indiscriminately gathered up with all those other deaths, must I recognize the deaths of Junko and Kiyoko and Kazue as well? Even so, if the dead, as they say, are never truly dead and will not rest in peace until the appropriate rites of mourning are performed for them, then the deaths of Junko and of Kiyoko and Kazue are not yet, so to speak, fully accomplished.

Now it is just three o'clock in the morning.

Aki gets up and opens the west window. She adjusts the collar of her robe and sits in the window, surveying the garden below. All the other lights in the building seem to be out, but the garden lamp casts a round of glimmering brightness on the ground. At the center of this circle of light is a small potting shovel that someone threw aside. A tricycle sits astride the line of the circumference.

Still from time to time the lightning streaks in its erratic course across the night sky. After its light goes out, the trees and houses seem to plunge into an even deeper blackness.

Spreading beyond the edge of the garden is a vegetable field. If you cross that you come to the riverbeach. Since we've had no rain for some time, the water level will have dropped. Maybe you can even see the pebbles in the riverbed. Where the weir has dammed the water up, will the river fish be sleeping soundly?

Last evening, for the first time in days, there was a beautiful sunset. Intending to go to the public bath, she began to put her toilet things together. Then with her washbasin under her arm, Aki leaned out of the window.

"Hands up!"

The block of apartments had a bend in the middle like a hook: From the downstairs apartment diagonally opposite, two little boys, brothers, barefoot and dressed only in swimming trunks, came dashing out together. Then, as if they had planned it in advance, they suddenly darted apart, one to the right, the other to the left, and from behind the trunks of the garden's few trees they started shooting at each other. Bang, Baanng! Bang, Baanng!

The young mother began scolding from inside the apartment. "What's happened to your shoes? And your caps?"

After a little bout of gunning, the boys raced into the house again, still making shooting noises. As they ran in, they met a girl in a yellow dress coming out. She emptied the water out of a bucket with a boat floating in it and collected the sneakers they had trampled and knocked every which way, and as she went around tidying everything up, she turned and shouted to the inside of the house, "Uncle will be home early today, won't he, Auntie?"

Because it is Saturday, of course. Soon now, "Uncle" will be honking the horn of his Publica and the boys will go dashing out, yelling, "Papa's home!" And the two will start tugging at the coattails of their father who will be carrying a box of pastries for dessert and rattling his car keys as he comes. They will grab at the keys. Aki can see it all as if it were already happening before her eyes. The window pane of the apartment the boys ran into now has six palms spread against it like so many pressed flowers.

All of a sudden everything went quiet. The stillness was so deep it made you wonder that even a block of apartments like this one could experience such an hour. Aki looked slowly about the place. A watering can abandoned in the sandbox; a plastic pool, blobs of sand on the bottom looking like a map; a path of dried plaster; under the eaves a lizard that seemed as if it had been pasted on; a clothes line already gone slack; trees bent low as if their own weight had been too much for them to bear; a bucket only half full, left behind in the common laundry area; the rubbish dump with papers sticking out of it; an improvised garage that looked more like a box for toys . . . the sound of the cicadas, penetrating as a brush stroke on paper, had now died away.

Aki put the washbasin she had been holding on the table and then, leaning against the window frame, inhaled her cigarette. She blew the first puff of smoke straight at the middle of the sky. Just then, the western sky was one great blaze of splendor.

Yes, straight over there, at the far edge of the vegetable field that stretches out beyond the block of apartments, yesterday's setting sun went right down the chimney of that brick house. It was majestic, solemn. Moment by moment the colors changed; it was like watching scenery in a series of hurriedly shifted slides. A quiet peaceful Saturday. It was indeed a fitting end to a fine summer's day.

But at the close of that other summer's day, the bright evening glow was not caused simply by the setting sun. The blue first faded from the eastern sky and gradually it sank into black ink, but though the darkness grew and deepened, the evening glow was not the least bit dimmed. On the contrary, as the other side of the sky darkened, it burned all the more brightly, and seemed to be spreading and spreading. Aki crouched low in a hollow in a field with people she had never seen before that day, and stared steadily up at that night sky.

The morning, the great flash, the big bang, the squall of wind, the fire . . . all these I can remember very clearly, but what happened to me next? That was a blank in her memory that Aki was not able to fill in.

When she recovered her senses she found herself running in the direction of the sea, borne along in a rush of total strangers. Shirts in shreds, scorched trousers, blood-soaked blouses, yukatas with a sleeve missing, seared and blistered skin, an old man just sitting there watching the people rush by before his eyes, a woman with a child in each arm, a barefoot university student, someone screaming, "The fire is coming!" When she looked back at the town it was engulfed in black smoke. As for what was happening inside it, at the time Aki had no idea, and even to think of it was too horrifying.

Why did she have this thing with her? Aki was crouching in the hollow she had managed to struggle to, an empty bucket in front of her. The eyes of the people gathered there were abnormally bright and their voices strangely high-pitched. Whenever there was a moment's lull in the noise and confusion, the low roar of the sea could be heard. As evening wore on, the crowd of grotesque figures in the hollow continued to grow.

It was already the hour of the afterglow, but the sky was blazing with the excess of heat from the earth, and all through the night it continued to burn a fiery red, until at last, in the brightness slowly spreading from the east, it lost its incandescent glow. Up to daybreak, ominous noises like an avalanche shook the hollow several times. When the wind shifted, it carried a reek of burning fat. Now and then, a frog croaked somewhere.

Aki longed for the morning. With morning everything would be better. If she could just make it through this night, things would be all right. That was the feeling that sustained her.

Ah, but that morning, so breathlessly awaited it had hurt, what did it have to show to Aki? Things that for so long she had seen with her own eyes and touched with her own hands, and whose existence she had never even thought to doubt, taking their being there so much for granted, she now could find no more, except in some far corner of her memory, deep in her consciousness. With her lips slightly parted, Aki stood transfixed with horror. Broken stumps of old trees were still smouldering. Molten metal ran along the pavement. A great geyser gushed out where the lid of the water main had exploded. All around as far as eye could see, nothing but ruin and rubble, and strewn on top of all, as if left behind there by mistake, strange objects of some whitish chalky substance. The far-off hills, in some strange way, seemed to be closing in upon the town.

It is not an act of Heaven.

It is not an act of Earth.

No! It can't be that!

But at the time, Aki had not an inkling of the real nature of this thing that set her knees knocking together in sheer terror.

And Aki, standing petrified there, now became aware of an eery stillness that seemed to be about to envelop her body. Presently it wrapped her round with a gentleness she had never known or felt before. Perhaps I am going to be shut in for all eternity somewhere at the bottom of the earth, she thought. It was not long before she felt herself being sucked down into a black abyss. Innumerable little yellow arrows flew before her eyes, bewildering her, and she felt herself falling, falling down into a blank that had cut off the light. There was no longer anything left of the great gentleness. Aki was now being manipulated by something hard and resistant. Something was over; she could not but think that. Rather than question the existence of the thing that now sought to gain control of her, she merely felt the pity of it all.

Suddenly, something white jumped out of the rubbish dump and streaked across the garden in a straight line, making for the vegetable field beyond. A cat, most likely. As if suddenly remembering to do so, the wind now shook the branches of the trees.

It was not quite true for Aki to say that she had never experienced before that summer's day the feeling of being all at once enveloped in an eery stillness and then falling, falling down into the blank that cut the light off. Why? Because although dim and far away, she now suddenly remembered a night long ago, when she had felt herself slip all at once into a black abyss, a night she now was dredging up from the immeasurable depths of her subconscious.

"Good night! Now go to sleep!" the nurse said, moving away from Aki's side. After looking at the thermometer hung on a post, she left the room. Aki stretched herself under the quilt. She was full of that feeling of well-being that comes when a high temperature returns to normal. Tonight too, no doubt, there will be lots of guests. Father and mother, but especially mother, will be tired out attending to them. The maid too will be busily bustling about. From the main house on the other side of the patio came the clatter of a late dinner. In the moonlight, the dwarfed pine lifted its twisted trunk, and the white sand spread around it in the pot gleamed silvery white.

When all the shutters were put up in the main house, she felt how isolated was the little detached room where she now slept.

How much time had passed she did not know, but after a while Aki thought she heard voices outside the earthen wall. They stopped for a while and then went on again in low tones. They were voices she did not remember ever having heard before. They were certainly not the voices of the gatekeeper and his wife. Because a stream from the hill had been diverted through their garden, sometimes people coming down the hill strayed in by mistake. Maybe the voices of a while ago belonged to some people like that. But no matter how much time went by, there was no change in the location of the voices. After a while, they began to grow gradually louder. There was a man's voice, low but somehow angry. At long intervals the thin voice of a woman mingled with it. The hard-to-catch voice of the man grew louder and rougher. The woman's voice presently changed to a low convulsive sobbing. Then there was a dull thump, as though part of one body had struck a terrible blow at a part of the other body. Aki instinctively hid her head under the quilt. She had heard what she was not supposed to hear, hadn't she? A ringing started deep within her ears. She had a strange feeling of being shot at with countless yellow arrows, all coming straight at her.

Why was she upsetting herself over that unknown woman who was undoubtedly cowering on the other side of the garden wall? Aki, still only a child, did not know, but in some obscure hurt way she felt a sense of identity with the woman beyond the wall. Are all women doomed to weep like that when they grow up? Even women whose tears I have never once seen; for example, that nurse so attentive and good with sick people and apparently trusted by the doctor, or the teacher of my elementary school class who stands on her platform every day looking as if she never gave a thought to anything but the government textbooks: Do women like that too, late in the night, go someplace we don't know and cry their hearts out there in floods of tears? Aki felt that she was falling, falling down into a black abyss, and then discovered that she herself was crying.

The day of her visit to Tomiko, just as they were settling down with the table between them, Tomiko had looked Aki in the eye and asked, "When did you last go back home?"

The place where Tomiko was born and which she calls her home she seems to think is naturally "home" for Aki too. But when Tomiko questioned her like that, Aki found she could not answer right away. As she looked at Tomiko, it seemed that already the words were breaking into fragments in her head, GO—BA—CK—HO—ME.

Since we two had not seen each other for four or five years, it was not inappropriate for Tomiko to start talking about that place, thought Aki. It's not just Tomiko. Lots of other people, either by way of greeting or because they really want to know how things are now in that place, ask me the same question. They probably don't mean anything by it. But that place where Tomiko and I were born and raised and from which the fire drove us out—is that a proper place for me to go back to, just like that, as Tomiko says, without the slightest hesitation? What exactly in that place would I be going home to? If there is something there that's fitting to return to, I want it to be a something that endures unchanged and transcends time. Something of which it may be said, now *that* at least is certain. People should return to something that, no matter what may happen, will endure and still be seen as the true root and source of what they are.

When the night of the Bon Lantern Festival came around, Tomiko and I would often go down to the pier together. On several occasions we got on the same boat. "Mr. Boatman, please row out that way; no! further out into the offing," and the two of us side by side at the gunwale would watch the other boats pass by. "Ah! that one was the Masudaya's boat, and the one coming from over there is surely the Sasaya's boat!" And chattering away like that, we would stay on until quite late, blown by the night winds. Scattered over the waters, then brushing against each other again, those lanterns for the departed souls were as vivid in Aki's mind as something she might have seen just now on the riverbeach beyond the vegetable field.

Does Tomiko still remember? The thin little bones, the pale pink insides of the nearly transparent fish in their shoals? The wharf bridge darkening the water below? The five-colored pinwheels stuck between the cotton candy stall and the white mice cages, and that resonance of expectancy along the shrine path at the time of the clan god's festival? The window full of the Milky Way, and when you opened it that smell of oil from the armory that nearly knocked you out? The castle tower,[3] the parade ground, the napes of the young men's necks, the henhouse, the greenhouse, the shipyard, the schoolhouse, the warehouse, the heat shimmer, the carrying chest, the armor case . . . ?

The old men, gathered under the ornamental light that looked like a sea anemone, would soon be deep in talk. Hiding behind her back, I would slip in with the maid who went to serve them their black tea. The first of them to spot me would beckon with his hand and say, "Aki, there's a good little girl, come over here to grandpa!"

The wallpaper was pretty well faded but you could still clearly make out the picture pattern. The Pyramids towered in the distance. A woman was washing a jar in the stream. The animals seemed to be asleep in the shade of the trees while a man sat nearby. The old men talked on and on as if they were never going to stop. "Salt-broiling is the only thing for *ayu* trout, eh!" "What's happened to all the women?" "Now the difference between the treeleaf butterfly of the Ryūkyūs and the treeleaf butterfly of Taiwan is this. . . ."

That time when, in the bright sunshine, I gazed on the vast multitude of dead in all the chaos of that ruined ground, laid waste and desolate by someone or by something yet unknown, with my knees knocking together out of control, the thing I kept telling myself was this: It is only a temporary phenomenon! I kept on pursuing the original appearance of that place as it had been before, and as I was sure it would be again. Maybe tomorrow I will see Junko! Maybe I'll come across someone who knows how Kiyoko is! When I was trying to sleep out under the starry sky with such thoughts in my mind, the awareness that began to seep through the depths of my consciousness, the thing I took to thinking as if it were most natural was this: Junko and Kiyoko, sometime, somewhere, will surely appear before me once again!

At that time, what on earth did I consider the original appearance of that place? Was it the limpid flowing stream, so clear that you could see the pebbles in the riverbed? Was it the trees along the roads with their load of soft green buds? Was it the tilled field where the earth was neither hard nor black nor dry when turned over? Was it the harmony that prevailed among all these? Or was it the dawn city when the fish peddlers went by? The sound of rackets batting the ball back and forth until near twilight on the schoolyard tennis court? The white walled castle? But all these, alas, are things doomed to change, now no longer fit to bear the weight of changelessness! I felt I had been witness on that morning to a temporary phenomenon that later, sometime, must be overcome and gone beyond. But perhaps I was wrong. The term temporary phenomenon should not have referred only to the scene of devastation; it should have covered, too, the great flash, the big bang, the squall of wind, and it should perhaps also have included that place that dawned and darkened to the low

---

[3] **castle tower:** The feudal castle of Hiroshima, built in 1859, had a white pagoda-like tower five stories high. Destroyed in the 1945 blast, the castle was restored in 1958.

roar of the sea. It struck me then that something certainly had ended there. I was perhaps one of the witnesses to the end of a particular phenomenon.

But that thought too may have been wrong. Its present condition, its broad paved streets, its tall buildings, its airport, its foreign cars, its stadium, its cinemas, its bars . . . all those things are enough to make one doubt the reality of what once happened in that place. From now on, too, new schools will be put up. More and more trees will line the city's streets. There will be more and more roller coasters in more amusement parks. But there are times, nevertheless, when I am struck with the dread premonition that suddenly one day all those tall buildings will come tumbling down. I have visions of the pavements splitting open, of the foreign cars abandoned in the streets and turned to lumps of burnt-down metal. They will be like these other things in the world of my memory, that in a twinkling were all changed and lost. And this is true not only of that place as it is now. All these familiar things about me every day, this table, this bookshelf, this mirror, this clock, these people boxed into their several compartments, and—standing here and holding all of that—this block of apartments, the street lights, the suspension bridge, the superhighway, the lockers in the drafting room, the bones of kindly gentle people. It seems to me I hear the sound of all these things crumbling down. And I myself am nothing more than another of these things doomed to crumble! Aki thinks of her own self, her body blown to bits, reduced to chalky handfuls left exposed to every wind. But, just like life, is not death, too, simply one of the many faces of existence?

Even if it has only a tin roof I don't mind! I want to sleep somewhere that isn't out on the bare ground!

I don't mind if it isn't in a glass! I want some clean water that you're not afraid to drink!

Even a piece so small it fits into the hollow of my hand, I don't mind! I want to see myself in something you could call a mirror!

Even if it's that mean, nasty Taeko, I don't mind! I want to talk to someone that is not a grown-up stranger wrapped in bandages!

But several nights were to pass in the hollow before even a single one of these simple wishes of Aki's would come true.

The great anger, the deep hate, come after the event. The thing that parted me from Junko, that kept Kiyoko from me although she wanted to see me again, that made me cower all night in a hollow in the ground—if I could catch the real nature of that thing and fling the fullness of my anger and hate at it, I would not be in torment to this day, well over ten years after, tied to this fierce anger that still finds no proper outlet. I would not be tortured by this nameless hate that yet finds no clear object. This is what Aki thinks.

Sometimes Aki, on her way to the office in the morning, would suddenly think she had found it, would see that object clearly. At the midday break, opening the window of the drafting room and looking up at a cloudless sky, there were times she felt she saw it float up quite clearly, with no further need for doubt. I must not let this out of my sight! Now, how can I get my anger and indignation across to this, their object? Aki would begin to lay her plan with meticulous care. But as she pursued that object, its contours would grow vague, and then some other object more or less linked with it would intrude. The new object was always inevitably linked with the old. One after another new objects would appear and then grow vague and blurred. And a further trouble: Aki began to suspect uneasily that the hazy something that had lost its clear outlines might be her own self.

I am ashamed to say I still cannot see where I had best direct my hate and anger, but . . . and Aki went on thinking. The rite that should have been performed and never was, and my unassuaged thirst for it, I must recognize as the beginning of a questioning of "being" that I must now develop. Wherein lies the realness of things? Can you say that a thing that's really there and that you can be sure of is one your eyes can see, your hands can touch, your skin can feel? The things in your consciousness, that you can neither see nor touch, are they less truly there?

But what degree of realness is there in things your eyes can see, your hands can touch, or your skin can feel? Setsuko's husband was not by her side in that sickroom. But when Setsuko looked up at the map of the world pasted on the wall beside her bed and thought about her husband in his foreign post, was he not truly there within her mind? Surely then he was a more weighty presence in her consciousness than when he was beside her, touching her, and she would waken with a sense that he was slipping far away from her like a draft of wind. And can the senses grasp reality as well as she could with her consciousness, once she could cease to treat as an unreal thing the presence in it?

"What do you think of it? Those people starting out simultaneously from the far ends of the Silk Road[4] to meet in the middle?"

Noboru put this question to Aki as they were having dinner in a restaurant that overlooked the nighttime sea. With a vivacity unusual for him, his eyes slightly clouded from the little whiskey he had drunk, he kept on talking to Aki of one thing after another. He seemed to have a compulsion to talk. He even felt impelled to speak to the waiter who came to clear the table, saying such things as "The butter sauce with the fish-meunière is very good here" or "This coffee must be a blend of at least three varieties of beans." There were not many customers. The air conditioning in the room was too cold for Aki in her short-sleeved blouse.

After dinner, Aki walked along the shore road with Noboru. As they walked, Aki, comforted by Noboru, had her spirits restored but saw it all as too late. I want to go on walking for a long, long time, she thought. But that same evening, when Noboru had reduced to nothing the distance that separated them, Aki found herself caught up in the eery stillness. Feeling as if someone else had suddenly come up behind and

---

[4] **the Silk Road:** The Great Silk Road was the ancient trade route linking China to the Mediterranean; Noboru seems to be speaking of a commemorative celebration of the road.

laid a hand on her shoulder to pull her back, she shuddered. She said, "Any moment now, I am going to fall into that black abyss!" And then Noboru, anguish showing in his face, muttered in a low voice, "I know; but you must forget all about that kind of thing. If you really loved me, you would be able to put that sort of thing right out of your mind!"

What Aki, in the grip of that eery stillness, foresaw in dire premonition was Noboru, blind still himself to all the signs, Noboru hideously changed beyond all recognition, as Aki herself must change! In the taxi on the way back, the two of them hardly opened their mouths. Noboru looked out the window. In his rear view mirror, the driver kept darting quizzical glances at the back seat.

Aki lit a fresh cigarette.

After that I didn't meet him for quite a while, not until the winter. On that bookshelf there will be several books lent to me by Noboru. "If you want to study the houses of Granada, this one is good. If you are more interested in Madrid, this one here is best." It seems to her she can hear his voice.

I still had his books and I should have returned them to him when I saw him for the last time in the winter, yet I failed to do so! There is something wrong with me. . . .

Rejected, Noboru's slightly twisted face drew slowly back. Aki had felt the reproach in his eyes as she turned her cheek away. Gently she loosened his arm. The utter wretchedness of letting go of warmth and tenderness went right through her. Her voice was very low and small when she said, "I'm sorry," and it was swallowed up immediately in the dark sea before her eyes. The risen tide was beating steadily against the breakwater. The invisible thread that had drawn Noboru and herself together had now snapped, thought Aki, while another Aki whispered to her, "But it is you yourself, isn't it, who let go of the thread! It is you yourself, isn't it, who refuse to see him any more! You're a fool, that's what you are! Maybe so, but. . . ."

It was snowing.

Far out a ship's siren wailed.

Aki, who had lowered her gaze to the water's surface, now raised it gradually and then turned her whole face up. The snow was not coming from any very high place, but rather seemed to be gushing quietly out and falling softly down from somewhere quite near.

Noboru must think I didn't really love him. But I don't have the strength to go on explaining about that dread awareness that suddenly took hold of me.

Aki bit her lip. The snow was falling cold on her cheeks. Only the backs of her eyes were scalding hot. She could feel his gaze on her from behind, so piercing that it hurt, as she said "Let's go!" Taking the lead, she set off walking ahead of him. Naturally, he must have been terribly hurt and have taken this to mean that his love was not returned. Children hooded against the cold were running about the deck of one of the boats at anchor in the canal. On the deck of another, a number of young sailors were warming themselves around a fire they had made in an oil drum. They spotted Noboru and Aki and their individual spontaneous whistles came together in a chorus. That was the end of the year before last.

It is a little after four in the morning.

That small light beyond the vegetable garden—is it from the brick house? Or maybe it's some nearer light. The trees and houses are still plunged in darkness. Aki automatically smooths her front hair with the palm of her left hand. Her eyes pick out a tree. When I think of Noboru, quite often I remember at the same time that night so long ago when I broke down and cried for an unknown woman. Of all past nights, why do I have to pick out that one? Or is it perhaps that I am trying to relive it in the unconscious? All that is very vague. The two things seem to be totally unconnected, yet in some obscure way you can also see that they are profoundly linked. But that summer when I witnessed in that place the sudden loss of all I thought was mine and the omission of the rite that should have been performed, something that lay dormant until then suddenly colored me, and its dye deepened rapidly. I think I can say that. Now, on the contrary, that thing is trying to gain control of me, and I am questioning anew the meaning of existence. What we call dying, what we call living, things that are or that are not—what exactly are all these things? No doubt I'll go on groping, questioning, bearing the burden of this anger that I cannot vent, and this hate that still finds no clear object. I want to live without wiping out the memory of that day! My ancestors were slaves in Egypt . . . like the people of Israel, who at the Feast of the Passover, yearning to break free from bondage, woke from sleep and resumed reading their dark records. At that time, their thoughts probably ran like this—Someone who can just casually wipe out the memory of his own history will not be fit, as history unfolds, to play the role of a great hero.

That place of mine that was so beautiful—if it was truly mine, then that same place when hideously changed by someone or some force unknown to me was surely also mine. To the question of which is really the true place, I cannot answer now with any confidence. If one speaks in terms of a phenomenon, then both were that. If asked which was reality, I am inclined to say that both were also that. But surely what I called unchanging, the abiding source one can always go home to, must be something richer far than either, rejecting neither of them but transcending both. It must be something solidly sustained by an imperturbable order, although it may reveal itself under the varying aspects of separate phenomena. Yes, I shall no doubt go to that place again, but I will not be going home. What makes me think so is that host of things lost to my sight, no more reliable than fluff or down, and the uncertainty of all the things I see before me every day. To my regret, that imperturbable order is now known to me only within the world of wishful intimations. But I must know if it really exists. If I could know it, even in a flash of intuition, then perhaps I would no longer be the prey of this eery stillness that takes hold of me. I would be freed then from my terror of being sucked into that void that blocks out the light and of falling down, down, down into that black abyss. I want to know.

Slowly, softly now, a whiteness starts to spread, beneath a sky that seems to be melting quietly away, and the shapes of trees and houses at last stand out. A thick mist will be creeping along the river, brushing the wings of the still sleeping crane flies on the dewy grasses of the riverbeach. Any moment now, the alarm bell at the grade crossing will start ringing. Soon the garden swing will be encircled by the joyous shrieks of children. A man still in his night clothes will cut through the squeals of delight with a yell of "Breakfast!" A woman will come out to fetch them, and the children, with a hand in each of hers, will disappear again inside the door. A deliveryman will appear beyond the shrubbery. A bill collector, taking advantage of the holiday with everyone at home, will be approaching from beyond the rubbish heap. In the makeshift garage, the engine of the Publica will soon be starting up. "'Bye! See you later! Have a nice holiday!"

Soon the night will be over. Let me get some sleep! And Aki draws the window curtain shut.

✿ ADRIENNE RICH
B. UNITED STATES, 1929

www For links to more information about Rich and a quiz on her poetry, and for information about the culture and context of America in the twentieth century, see *World Literature Online* at bedfordstmartins .com/worldlit.

With about twenty volumes of poetry and several volumes of essays and notebooks, Adrienne Rich has exerted a tremendous influence on modern American letters. Her importance extends beyond the world of literature into cultural history and contemporary social change. When the poets Sylvia Plath and Anne Sexton,[1] Rich's brilliant contemporaries, took their own lives in their early middle years, they involuntarily lent credence to the belief that women writers must suffer and probably die in the effort to accommodate their gender and their art. In contrast, for almost five decades Rich has been continuously looked to by readers not only for the excellence of her work in and of itself but also because the woman and her work together have come to be seen as talismans for hope and courage, for what Rich herself has called "the will to change."

Her first book of poetry, *A Change of World,* appeared in 1951, when the poet was only twenty-two. In the years since, Rich has steadily published books of poetry, feminist literary criticism, autobiographical essays, and social commentary, all of which reflect the widening and changing concerns of American women since the 1950s. To read through her work

---

[1]**Plath . . . Sexton:** Sylvia Plath (1932–1963), the author of the posthumously published *Ariel* (1968), was an accomplished poet in her middle years when she killed herself. Anne Sexton (1928–1974), the author of *The Death Notebooks* (1974), suffered from depression for many years before taking her life. Both Plath and Sexton are known as "confessional" poets, since their poems appear to be very personal in content.

chronologically is to witness a fluid, uncompromisingly honest approach to the pain and beauty inherent in growth and survival.

Early Expectations.   In her autobiographical essay "Split at the Root: An Essay on Jewish Identity" (1982), Rich writes of some of her life from childhood through college. Born on May 16, 1929, into an upper-middle-class family in Baltimore, she was inculcated with ideas about the behavior proper to Southern women by her Christian mother, who had set aside her own gifts in musical composition and performance to attend to her husband and two daughters. Rich's father was the descendant of Jewish immigrants from Austria-Hungary and the Middle East who had raised their son to assimilate into the world of white, Southern, gentile professionals. He was accepted into the fold at Johns Hopkins Hospital, in Baltimore, despite being the only Jewish physician on staff. As Rich says in another autobiographical essay, "When We Dead Awaken: Writing As Re-Vision" (1971), her father, intent upon achievement, was the appreciative and demanding audience for whom she first wrote, although "the obverse side of this, of course, was that I tried for a long time to please him, or rather, not to displease him."

Adrienne Rich,
c. 1950s
This undated publicity photograph was circulated after Rich won a $1,500 grant in literature from the National Institute of Arts and Letters. (© Bettmann/CORBIS)

At Radcliffe in the late forties and early fifties, she had the common experience of reading male poets taught by male professors and, naturally, modeled her early work on the **FORMALIST**,[2] measured, and somewhat cerebral poems of writers such as Frost, Auden, MacNeice, and Stevens,[3] then in vogue. In a preface to Rich's first collection, *A Change of World* (1951), which won the Yale Younger Poets Prize, Auden himself praised Rich for what seems to be in retrospect the rather subservient virtues of mildness and obedience; her poems, he said, "speak quietly but do not mumble, respect their elders, but are not cowed by them."

Imbued with the assumption of most people of her generation that marriage and a family were the normal way for a woman to proceed toward a fulfilling life, in 1953 Rich married Alfred Conrad, a Harvard faculty member in economics, and gave birth to three sons, David, Paul, and Jacob, in a period of six years. In 1955, the year of her eldest son's birth, Rich brought out her second volume of poems, *The Diamond Cutters,* another volume of technically accomplished and graceful formalist poems. It would be eight years before her next book appeared. Although in the intervening years Rich received many grants and awards, that time in her life was mostly shaped by the incessant tasks of housekeeping and mothering, a growing frustration at not having enough uninterrupted time to work, and a terrifying sense of "being pulled along on a current which called itself my destiny, but in which I seemed to be losing touch with whoever I had been." Motherhood, as Rich has observed, can be a

---

[2] formalist: Formalism in modern poetry refers to the use of conventional meters and stanza forms, as opposed to the varying line lengths and irregular sound patterns, usually unrhymed, of "free verse."

[3] Frost . . . Stevens: The American poets Robert Frost (1874–1963), W. H. Auden (1907–1973), and Wallace Stevens (1879–1955), and the British Louis MacNeice (1907–1963), wrote formalist poems with complex, compactly expressed ideas; their poems tend to challenge the mind rather than stimulate the emotions.

great radicalizer. In her 1976 book *Of Woman Born: Motherhood as Experience and Institution,* she looks back on her life as a daughter and as a mother to examine the paradoxes and dilemmas attendant upon those years in women's lives, the tension between conventional roles and artistry.

Finding Her Voice.   *Snapshots of a Daughter-in-Law,* the title poem of which took Rich more than two years to write, came out in 1963. It was a breakthrough in that the line and meter of the poems had become looser than in her earlier work, even as Rich more directly addressed issues such as women's anger and the separations and quarrels between the sexes and generations. Still, the poems keep a relatively safe distance from their subjects; the poet rarely speaks in her own voice as herself.

Like many in academic communities in the late fifties, Rich was drawn to civil rights issues; throughout the sixties and early seventies, she became increasingly involved in protesting the U.S. presence in Indochina. Rich's family moved to New York City in 1966 after her husband accepted a post at City College. Rich, too, began to teach there, in the SEEK and Open Admissions programs, which made a college education accessible to disadvantaged and nontraditional students and often proved to be as radicalizing and transformative for the participating teachers as they were for the students. Her collections of poems from those years— *Necessities of Life* (1966), *Leaflets* (1969), and *The Will to Change* (1971)— reveal in both their subject matter and experimentation the poet's increasingly strong political commitments. Rich was finding her own voice and ways of integrating social issues and poetry. *Leaflets,* for example, includes a series of poems written in the ancient Arabic form of the *GHAZAL;*[4] Rich uses that strongly imagistic tradition to address in colloquial language the Vietnam War, the racial politics of inner-city life, and her experience as a teacher.

Social Activist and Writer.   In the sixties and early seventies, Rich found that questions raised about one kind of injustice or oppression inevitably led her to question other areas of her life, and political transformation led to personal change, none of it easily undertaken. In 1970, Rich left Alfred Conrad, who took his own life later that same year. By 1976, Rich and Michelle Cliff, the Jamaican-born poet and essayist, had become partners in life and enterprise. For several years they coedited *Sinister Wisdom,* a lesbian feminist journal that was especially focused on the work of women of color. Rather than writing confessional poetry, a tendency among a number of women poets, Rich took on the role of observer and commentator, providing a voice for those who previously had been speechless or silenced.

For more than twenty years, Rich has taught in numerous colleges

---

[4] *ghazal: Ghazals* are defined in Islamic literature as lyric poems; they are made up of five couplets that are linked by theme or association.

and universities, including Swarthmore, Columbia, Brandeis, Rutgers, and Stanford. In addition to giving lectures and workshops across the country, she has been active in movements for women's reproductive rights, gay and lesbian rights, and the New Jewish Agenda. In essays such as "It Is the Lesbian in Us" (1976) and "Compulsory Heterosexuality and Lesbian Existence" (1980), reprinted in *Blood, Bread, and Poetry* (1986), she has become an articulator of lesbian consciousness and a major theorist of the politics of sexuality and the effects of patriarchy on both men and women. When *Diving into the Wreck* won the 1974 National Book Award, Rich declined to accept the honor as an individual. Together with her sister nominees, Alice Walker and Audre Lorde, she drafted a statement accepting the prize on behalf of all women. Her awards since then have included a MacArthur Fellowship, the Ruth Lilly Poetry Prize, the Academy of American Poets' Wallace Stevens Award for outstanding mastery of the art of poetry (1997), and the Lifetime Achievement Award (1999) from the Lannan Foundation.

Unlike many poets whose productivity diminishes with age, Rich continues to write and publish; collections from the 1980s and 1990s include *The Fact of a Doorframe: Poems Selected and New* (1984); *Time's Power: Poems 1985–1988* (1989); *An Atlas of the Difficult World: Poems 1988–1991* (1992); *Dark Fields of the Republic: Poems 1991–1995* (1995); *Midnight Salvage: Poems 1995–1998* (1999). At present, Rich makes her home in California.

A Sampling of Poems.   "Aunt Jennifer's Tigers," one of the selections that follow, is a poem from Rich's first collection that articulates the split between female creativity and the feminine wish to please a man. The poem illustrates Rich's early involvement with formalism. The poem "I Dream I'm the Death of Orpheus" (1971), draws on the Greek myth of Orpheus, the consummate poet who failed in an attempt to lead his beloved Eurydice out of the realm of the dead, all because he broke the rules and gazed longingly at her face before they had emerged from the underworld; he was later killed by Maenads on a mountain. Rich's poem is written from the point of view of a liberated Eurydice who has assumed her feminine powers. The title poem from *Diving into the Wreck* (1973) centers on the themes of risk and loss, of courageous acts of discovery and recovery. The poem, itself multilayered, suggests through images and symbols that the richness and adventure of getting to know one's self parallels a descent into the sea.

Twenty-One Love Poems (1976) is a collection of SONNETS[5] featuring images from everyday life in the city, moments of estrangement and tenderness that sound the chords of love. Against the backdrop of a raucous city, the four poems from the collection presented here capture the softness, the shelter provided by a deep relationship.

> Adrienne Rich's poems, volume after volume, have been the makings of one of the authentic, unpredictable, urgent, essential voices of our time. All of her life she has been in love with the hope of telling the utter truth, and her command of language from the first has been startlingly powerful.
> – W. S. MERWIN, poet

---

[5] sonnets: Common in the fifteenth and sixteenth centuries in England, sonnets are tightly structured, fourteen-line poems with elaborate rhyme schemes.

■ CONNECTIONS

Langston Hughes, "The Negro Speaks of Rivers," p. 878. The search for an authentic voice or language to express personal experience is particularly vexing for minorities like blacks, Native Americans, and women, who feel they are using the language of the oppressor, whether that oppressor be white society or men. With dialect and a careful choice of images, Hughes was able to create a "black voice" in his poetry and thereby honor "black experience." How does Rich deal with language of feminism and lesbianism in poems like "I Dream I'm the Death of Orpheus" and the selections from *Twenty-One Love Poems*?

T. S. Eliot, *The Waste Land*, p. 486. A number of poets disillusioned with traditional, institutional belief systems such as Christianity and democracy have sought a "new myth" or paradigm for modern society. Eliot is primarily occupied with displaying the fragmentation of modern society in *The Waste Land*, but the last section of that poem presents some possibilities for healing. What does Rich propose in "Diving into the Wreck" as a substitute for "the book of myths / in which / our names do not appear"?

Andrew Marvell, "To His Coy Mistress" (Book 3). Love poems in the carpe diem, or "seize the day," tradition urge lovers to make the most of their time because death will soon overtake them. Marvell's "To His Coy Mistress" is one of the most famous instances from the European Renaissance of using "time's winged chariot" as an argument for lovemaking. What attitudes about time and love does Rich present in sonnet III: "Since we're not young, weeks have to do time"?

■ FURTHER RESEARCH

Criticism

Cooper, J. R. *Reading Adrienne Rich: Reviews and Revisions 1951–1981.* 1984.
Gelpi, Barbara Charlesworth, and Albert Gelpi, eds. *Adrienne Rich's Poetry and Prose: Poems, Prose, Reviews and Criticism.* 1993.
Keyes, C. *The Aesthetics of Power: The Poetry of Adrienne Rich.* 1986.
Ratcliffe, Krista. *Anglo-American Feminist Challenges to the Rhetorical Traditions: Virginia Woolf, Mary Daly, Adrienne Rich.* 1996.
Sielke, Sabine. *Fashioning the Female Subject: The Intertextual Networking of Dickinson, Moore, and Rich.* 1997.
Templeton, Alice. *The Dream and the Dialogue: Adrienne Rich's Feminist Poetics.* 1994.

Aunt Jennifer's Tigers

Aunt Jennifer's tigers prance across a screen,
Bright topaz denizens of a world of green.
They do not fear the men beneath the tree;
They pace in sleek chivalric certainty.

"Aunt Jennifer's Tigers." Rich herself has observed that, while this poem, published in *A Change of World* (1951), articulates the tension between female creativity and the feminine wish to please a man, at the time of its writing she scarcely realized it might be about herself: "It was important that Aunt Jennifer was a person as distinct from myself as possible—distanced by the formalism of the poem, by its objective, observant tone—even by putting the woman in a different generation." The final stanza of the poem affirms the lasting quality of art.

Aunt Jennifer's fingers fluttering through her wool
Find even the ivory needle hard to pull.
The massive weight of Uncle's wedding band
Sits heavily upon Aunt Jennifer's hand.

When Aunt is dead, her terrified hands will lie
10   Still ringed with ordeals she was mastered by.
The tigers in the panel that she made
Will go on prancing, proud and unafraid.

❧ I Dream I'm the Death of Orpheus[1]

I am walking rapidly through striations of light and dark thrown under an
    arcade.

I am a woman in the prime of life, with certain powers
and those powers severely limited
by authorities whose faces I rarely see.
I am a woman in the prime of life
driving her dead poet in a black Rolls-Royce
through a landscape of twilight and thorns.
A woman with a certain mission
which if obeyed to the letter will leave her intact.
10   A woman with the nerves of a panther
a woman with contacts among Hell's Angels[2]
a woman feeling the fullness of her powers
at the precise moment when she must not use them

"I Dream I'm the Death of Orpheus." This poem was first published in *The Will to Change*
(1971). Although Rich uses the Orpheus of Greek mythology to evoke the image of an artist, she
draws more specifically on Jean Cocteau's 1950 film *Orphée*. In the film, the figure of Death is a
woman, accompanied by motorcyclists in black leather jackets, who comes for Orpheus. Rich
projects the strength of this woman onto a powerful poet who has been repressed by the male
Romantic tradition that has idolized women. She is angry, and she is fighting for her own existence
as an individual and an artist.

    All notes are the editors'.

---

[1] **Orpheus:** In Greek mythology, Orpheus was the greatest musician of his time. When his wife, Eurydice, dies
from a snakebite, Orpheus convinces the powers of the Underworld to release her. They agree on one condition: On the journey to the upper world, Orpheus must not look back at her. He cannot resist a glance, however, whereupon she disappears immediately back into Hades.

[2] **Hell's Angels:** A motorcycle club started in California that symbolizes freedom and independence to its
admirers.

a woman sworn to lucidity
who sees through the mayhem, the smoky fires
of these underground streets
her dead poet learning to walk backward against the wind
on the wrong side of the mirror

∽ Diving into the Wreck

First having read the book of myths,
and loaded the camera,
and checked the edge of the knife-blade,
I put on
the body-armor of black rubber
the absurd flippers
the grave and awkward mask.
I am having to do this
not like Cousteau[1] with his
10   assiduous team
aboard the sun-flooded schooner
but here alone.

There is a ladder.
The ladder is always there
hanging innocently
close to the side of the schooner.
We know what it is for,
we who have used it.
Otherwise
20   it's a piece of maritime floss
some sundry equipment.

I go down.
Rung after rung and still

"Diving into the Wreck." The title poem of the award-winning collection *Diving into the Wreck* (1973) is about the richness and adventure of the pursuit of self-knowledge, which is akin to a descent into the sea. The downward journey moves the speaker toward wholeness, dredging up from terrible experience that which is worth keeping: "something more permanent / than fish or weed . . . / the wreck and not the story of the wreck / the thing itself and not the myth." The underworld treasure ultimately becomes a discovery of self.

---

[1]**Cousteau:** Jacques-Yves Cousteau (1910–1997), well-known French oceanographer who explored marine life while aboard the *Calypso*. [Editors' note.]

the oxygen immerses me
the blue light
the clear atoms
of our human air.
I go down.
My flippers cripple me,

30   I crawl like an insect down the ladder
and there is no one
to tell me when the ocean
will begin.

First the air is blue and then
it is bluer and then green and then
black I am blacking out and yet
my mask is powerful
it pumps my blood with power
the sea is another story

40   the sea is not a question of power
I have to learn alone
to turn my body without force
in the deep element.

And now: it is easy to forget
what I came for
among so many who have always
lived here
swaying their crenellated fans
between the reefs

50   and besides
you breathe differently down here.

I came to explore the wreck.
The words are purposes.
The words are maps.
I came to see the damage that was done
and the treasures that prevail.
I stroke the beam of my lamp
slowly along the flank
of something more permanent

60   than fish or weed

the thing I came for:
the wreck and not the story of the wreck
the thing itself and not the myth
the drowned face always staring

toward the sun
the evidence of damage
worn by salt and sway into this threadbare beauty
the ribs of the disaster
curving their assertion
70   among the tentative haunters.

This is the place.
And I am here, the mermaid whose dark hair
streams black, the merman in his armored body
We circle silently
about the wreck
we dive into the hold.
I am she: I am he

whose drowned face sleeps with open eyes
whose breasts still bear the stress
80   whose silver, copper, vermeil cargo lies
obscurely inside barrels
half-wedged and left to rot
we are the half-destroyed instruments
that once held to a course
the water-eaten log
the fouled compass

We are, I am, you are
by cowardice or courage
the one who find our way
90   back to this scene
carrying a knife, a camera
a book of myths
in which
our names do not appear.

❧ Twenty-One Love Poems

I: WHEREVER IN THIS CITY, SCREENS FLICKER

Wherever in this city, screens flicker
with pornography, with science-fiction vampires,
victimized hirelings bending to the lash,
we also have to walk . . . if simply as we walk
through the rainsoaked garbage, the tabloid cruelties
of our own neighborhoods.
We need to grasp our lives inseparable
from those rancid dreams, that blurt of metal, those disgraces,
and the red begonia perilously flashing
from a tenement sill six stories high,   10
or the long-legged young girls playing ball
in the junior highschool playground.
No one has imagined us. We want to live like trees,
sycamores blazing through the sulfuric air,
dappled with scars, still exuberantly budding,
our animal passion rooted in the city.

III: SINCE WE'RE NOT YOUNG, WEEKS HAVE TO DO TIME

Since we're not young, weeks have to do time
for years of missing each other. Yet only this odd warp
in time tells me we're not young.
Did I ever walk the morning streets at twenty,
my limbs streaming with a purer joy?
did I lean from any window over the city
listening for the future
as I listen here with nerves tuned for your ring?
And you, you move toward me with the same tempo.
Your eyes are everlasting, the green spark   10
of the blue-eyed grass of early summer,

Twenty-One Love Poems. In this collection, first published separately as a small volume in 1976 and then incorporated into *The Dream of a Common Language* (1978), Rich takes the Elizabethan sonnet sequence—the epitome of what she has called "all those poems about women written by men" in the sixteenth century in England—and uses it as a means to explore the sexual and spiritual dimensions of a woman's love for another woman. These sonnets celebrate a love relationship that becomes an oasis from the cold, often violent, dramas of the big city. Moments of tenderness become a refuge and salvation.

the green-blue wild cress washed by the spring.
At twenty, yes: we thought we'd live forever.
At forty-five, I want to know even our limits.
I touch you knowing we weren't born tomorrow,
and somehow, each of us will help the other live,
and somewhere, each of us must help the other die.

IV: I COME HOME FROM YOU THROUGH THE EARLY LIGHT OF SPRING

I come home from you through the early light of spring
flashing off ordinary walls, the Pez Dorado,
the Discount Wares, the shoe-store. . . . I'm lugging my sack
of groceries, I dash for the elevator
where a man, taut, elderly, carefully composed
lets the door almost close on me.—*For god's sake hold it!*
I croak at him.—*Hysterical,*—he breathes my way.
I let myself into the kitchen, unload my bundles,
make coffee, open the window, put on Nina Simone
singing *Here comes the sun.* . . . I open the mail,
drinking delicious coffee, delicious music,
my body still both light and heavy with you. The mail
lets fall a Xerox of something written by a man
aged 27, a hostage, tortured in prison:
My genitals have been the object of such a sadistic display
they keep me constantly awake with the pain . . .
Do whatever you can to survive.
You know, I think that men love wars . . .
And my incurable anger, my unmendable wounds
break open further with tears, I am crying helplessly,
and they still control the world, and you are not in my arms.

VI: YOUR SMALL HANDS, PRECISELY EQUAL TO MY OWN—

Your small hands, precisely equal to my own—
only the thumb is larger, longer—in these hands
I could trust the world, or in many hands like these,
handling power-tools or steering-wheel
or touching a human face. . . . Such hands could turn
the unborn child rightways in the birth canal
or pilot the exploratory rescue-ship
through icebergs, or piece together
the fine, needle-like sherds of a great krater-cup
bearing on its sides

figures of ecstatic women striding
to the sibyl's den or the Eleusinian cave —[1]
such hands might carry out an unavoidable violence
with such restraint, with such a grasp
of the range and limits of violence
that violence ever after would be obsolete.

---

[1] **sibyl's . . . cave:** Ancient Greek art portrays the processionals of the Eleusinian mysteries, which centered on the goddess Demeter and her daughter Persephone. The "Eleusinian cave" is the original sanctuary of Demeter and the archetypal entrance to the Underworld. The "sibyl's den" is the place where the oracle prophesies. [Editors' note.]

❧ MILAN KUNDERA
B. CZECHOSLOVAKIA, 1929

With a mixture of philosophy, autobiography, and fiction, Milan Kundera continues to reinvent and reinvigorate the modern novel. Although he does not dwell on the totalitarian legacy of Eastern Europe under the USSR, the relationships of his characters, their betrayals and fantasies, are usually shaped by political events. Kundera is not easily placed within a specific literary tradition. Unlike French activist writers like André Malraux, Jean-Paul Sartre, and Albert Camus, who promoted leftist political agendas in their work, Kundera probes the essential question of finding meaning and purpose in the modern, technological, and bureaucratic world, thus transcending political boundaries and platforms. The political oppression that hangs like a backdrop in Kundera's fiction can as easily erupt into comedy and farce as it can crystalize into tragedy.

Life under Communism.   Milan Kundera was born April 1, 1929, in Brno, Czechoslovakia. Following the example of his father, the well-known pianist Ludvik Kundera, Milan initially studied music as well as film and literature at Charles University in Prague and worked as a laborer and jazz musician. As a student he joined the **COMMUNIST** Party, as did many other young intellectuals,[1] but due to an untimely remark, he was debarred at about the time of the Communist takeover of Prague in 1947. After graduation in 1952 he became a lecturer in world literature at the Film Academy. In 1956 he enrolled in the Academy of Music and

www   For links to more information about Kundera and a quiz on "The Hitchhiking Game," and for information about the culture and context of Europe in the twentieth century, see *World Literature Online* at bedfordstmartins.com/worldlit.

---

[1] **Communist . . . intellectuals:** The Communist Party was attractive to young intellectuals since it ostensibly took the side of the working class against the moneyed, ruling upper classes and promised a program of social reform.

Dramatic Arts in Prague, where, after two years, he became an assistant professor from 1957 to 1969. He was admitted back into the Communist Party in 1956.

Kundera's first three publications were books of poetry: *Man: A Broad Garden* (*Clovek zahrada sira*, 1953), *The Last May* (*Posledni maf*, 1955), and *Monologues* (*Monology*, 1957). His play *The Owners of the Keys* (*Majitele klicu*) was first produced in Prague in April 1962 at the National Theatre and won the Klement Lukes Prize in 1963. Kundera then began writing fiction and published three volumes of short stories under the collective title *Laughable Loves* (*Mesne lasky;* 1963, 1965, 1968). A turning point in his career occurred with the publication of his first novel in 1967, *The Joke (Zert),* which explores the role of humor in a totalitarian regime, with reference to Stalinism. Along with other writers, Kundera was an outspoken advocate of opening up Czechoslovakia's socialism to criticism and liberal reform. Steps, in fact, were taken in that direction, and for a brief period Czechoslovakians enjoyed the cultural freedom of what became known as the Prague Spring of 1968, while dreaming of independence from the Soviet Union. When *The Joke* was finally published after resistance from state censorship, it quickly went through three voluminous printings and made Kundera into a major literary voice in Eastern Europe. Then, within four months, the political situation reversed: The reform movement was snuffed out when troops from the USSR, Poland, and East Germany invaded Czechoslovakia on August 21, 1968. In 1970, after Kundera lost his teaching job and left the party, his books were removed from bookstores and libraries, and he was forbidden to publish in his country.

The Move to France.   Two of Kundera's novels, consequently, were first published abroad; the French version of *Life Is Elsewhere, La Vie est ailleurs,* appeared in 1973 and received the Prix Medicis for the best foreign novel published in France in that year. *The Farewell Waltz* (*Valcik na rozloucenou,* translated earlier as *The Farewell Party*) was published in French in 1976 and then in Italian, receiving the Premio Mondello for the best novel published in Italy in that same year. Both works combine eroticism with political satire. In 1975 Kundera was allowed to leave Czechoslovakia to accept a teaching position in comparative literature at the University of Rennes, in France. After the publication in 1979 of *The Book of Laughter and Forgetting* (*La Livre de rire et de l'oubli,* 1980), which combines autobiography, history, and fiction, the Czech government revoked Kundera's citizenship. In 1981 the author became a French citizen and returned to the theater with *Jacques and His Master (Jacques et son maitre: Hommage a Denis Diderot),* a play based on a work by Diderot.[2] His prose work *The Art of the Novel* (*L' Art du roman*), a seven-part essay written in French, was first published in 1986. Three novels have been published

---

[2] **Diderot:** Denis Diderot (1713–1784), encyclopedist and philosopher known for his interest in travel and native peoples. See Book 4.

recently: a French translation of *Slowness* in 1995; *Identity,* in Icelandic, in 1997; *Ignorance (La Ignorancia)* in Spanish in 2000.

Kundera currently lives in Paris with his wife, Vera Hrabankova, and is on the editorial board of the prestigious Paris publishing house of Gallimard. Since 1985 Kundera has granted only written interviews, feeling that he had been incorrectly quoted in the past. *Testaments Betrayed* (*Testaments trahis,* 1993) is a nonfiction work of nine parts that addresses the ways in which Kundera feels he has been harmed by translators and interpreters. Kundera has become one of the leading intellectuals of Europe, but the fame he has inherited does not sit easily on his shoulders. In a *Village Voice* interview he said, "When I was a little boy in short pants I dreamed about a miraculous ointment that would make me invisible. Then I became an adult, began to write, and wanted to be successful. Now I'm successful and would like to have the ointment that would make me invisible."

Themes and Influences.   *The Unbearable Lightness of Being* (1984), translated from the original Czech manuscript, *Nesnesitelna lehkost byti,* is probably Kundera's most well-known novel in the West; it was also made into a popular movie starring Daniel Day-Lewis and Lena Olin. In an essay on the art of the novel, Kundera describes the modern situation of his characters:

> . . . I thought of the fate of Descartes' famous formulation: man as "master and proprietor of nature." Having brought off miracles in science and technology, this "master and proprietor" is suddenly realizing that he owns nothing and is master neither of nature (it is vanishing, little by little, from the planet), nor of History (it has escaped him), nor of himself (he is led by the irrational forces of his soul). But if God is gone and man is no longer master, then who is master? The planet is moving through the void without any master. There it is, the unbearable lightness of being.

Kundera acknowledges the influence of writers like Laurence Sterne[3] from England, Denis Diderot from France, and Hermann Broch[4] from Germany; but from Kundera's own Prague came the brilliant, disturbing artistry of Franz Kafka (see p. 423). Kundera explains the influence of Kafka's critique of the modern world:

> There are tendencies in modern history that produce the *Kafkan* in the broad social dimension: the progressive concentration of power, tending to deify itself; the bureaucratization of social activity that turns all institutions into *boundless labyrinths;* and the resulting depersonalization of the individual.

> Sex, in Kundera, is a means of rebelling against authority. Often, it's the only means.
>
> – J. HOBERMAN, critic, 1983

---

[3] **Laurence Sterne** (1713–1768): English novelist who authored *Tristram Shandy* (1767), which features eccentricities, digressions, and incoherences.

[4] **Hermann Broch** (1886–1951): Austrian novelist who critiqued modern life and is known for his stream-of-consciousness novel *The Death of Virgil* (1945).

Sexual Politics and "The Hitchhiking Game." A central theme in Kundera's writings, as in Kafka's, is the dispensing and manipulation of power. Publicly, power is a question of politics and institutions; privately, the machinations of power involve sex and love. In a world of perceived shrinking possibilities, sex might be the ultimate rebellion against authority or the only available arena for adventure and heroism. In *The Unbearable Lightness of Being,* two sets of lovers play out the endless varieties of betrayal and fulfillment. In the more recent novel *Immortality* (1990), love is again the central theme, explored in seven parts — a common structural pattern in Kundera's novels — by a writer named Kundera who becomes preoccupied with a fascinating woman who is part imaginary, part real. In the marvelously subtle and intricate short story "The Hitchhiking Game," a young couple on vacation begin a game in which they play uncharacteristic roles. Although politics is not an essential ingredient in this story, the young couple live most of the year in a regimented society that restricts their freedom to be who they really are or wish to be. The hitchhiking game provides them with the opportunity to explore new social and sexual roles and to test previously untapped dimensions of their personalities. As might be expected, the role-playing begins to dominate the relationship, and the man and woman's identities become confused. In this way Kundera dramatizes the role of games in modern relationships and how limited self-awareness and partial communication create obstacles to intimacy.

■ CONNECTIONS

Kawabata Yasunari, "The Moon on the Water," p. 664. One area of cultural differences between Japan and Europe is sexual mores. Kawabata treats the love relationship in his story with utmost delicacy and nuance. How would you characterize Kundera's treatment of the sexual game in "The Hitchhiking Game"? What parts of this game are as hidden and disguised in the European story as in the Japanese?

Chinua Achebe, *Things Fall Apart,* p. 1023. The health of a culture is partially measured by how cultural mores do or do not assist the individual in coping with crises. *Things Fall Apart* raises the question of whether Ibo society is equipped to deal with the threatening influence of British law and religion. How does Kundera measure the health of Czech culture?

Henrik Ibsen, *Hedda Gabler* (Book 5). In order to examine and criticize gender roles in the nineteenth century, writers had to portray the middle-class society from which the female rebel had to emerge. Ibsen outraged the conventional society of his time, creating strong female characters in the midst of a stultifying culture. How does Kundera develop the gender roles of his characters in his story? Have women achieved some kind of equality in "The Hitchhiking Game"?

■ FURTHER RESEARCH

Biography
Porter, Robert. *Milan Kundera: A Voice from Central Europe.* 1981.

History and Culture
French, A. *Czech Writers and Politics, 1945–1969.* 1982.
Zeman, Z. A. B. *Prague Spring.* 1969.

Criticism
Aji, Aron, ed. *Milan Kundera and the Art of Fiction.* 1992.
Misurella, Fred. *Understanding Milan Kundera: Public Events, Private Affairs.* 1993.
Nemcova Banerjee, Maria. *Terminal Paradox: The Novels of Milan Kundera.* 1990.
O'Brien, John. *Milan Kundera and Feminism: Dangerous Intersections.* 1995.
Roth, Philip. Introduction to *Laughable Loves.* 1975.
———. *Reading Myself and Others.* 1975.

∾ The Hitchhiking Game

Translated by Suzanne Rappaport

1

The needle on the gas gauge suddenly dipped toward empty and the young driver of the sports car declared that it was maddening how much gas the car ate up. "See that we don't run out of gas again," protested the girl (about twenty-two), and reminded the driver of several places where this had already happened to them. The young man replied that he wasn't worried, because whatever he went through with her had the charm of adventure for him. The girl objected; whenever they had run out of gas on the highway it had, she said, always been an adventure only for her. The young man had hidden and she had had to make ill use of her charms by thumbing a ride and letting herself be driven to the nearest gas station, then thumbing a ride back with a can of gas. The young man asked the girl whether the drivers who had given her a ride had been unpleasant, since she spoke as if her task had been a hardship. She replied (with awkward flirtatiousness) that sometimes they had been *very* pleasant but that it hadn't done her any good as she had been burdened with the can and had had to leave them before she could get anything going. "Pig," said the young man. The girl protested that she wasn't a pig, but that he really was. God knows how many girls stopped him on the highway, when he was driving the car alone! Still driving, the young man put his arm around the girl's shoulders and kissed her gently on the forehead. He knew that she loved him and that she was jealous. Jealousy isn't a pleasant quality, but if it isn't overdone (and if it's combined with modesty), apart from its inconvenience there's even something touching about it. At least that's what the young man thought. Because he was only twenty-eight, it seemed to him that he was old and knew everything that a man could know about women. In the girl

---

"**The Hitchhiking Game.**" Included in the short-story collection *Laughable Loves* (*Smesne lasky*) and translated by Suzanne Rappaport in 1974, this story recounts a game played by a young man and woman that stretches the psychological makeup of both but does not ultimately enhance intimacy. In fact, something appears to be lost; at the beginning of the story, the young man sees something special in the young woman, irrespective of "the law of universal transience, which made even his girl's shyness a precious thing to him." At the end of the story the woman poignantly attempts to reclaim this identity by asserting, "I am me, I am me, I am me. . . ." Their game could be seen as a mirror of society's games.

sitting beside him he valued precisely what, until now, he had met with least in women: purity.

The needle was already on empty, when to the right the young man caught sight of a sign, announcing that the station was a quarter of a mile ahead. The girl hardly had time to say how relieved she was before the young man was signaling left and driving into a space in front of the pumps. However, he had to stop a little way off, because beside the pumps was a huge gasoline truck with a large metal tank and a bulky hose, which was refilling the pumps. "We'll have to wait," said the young man to the girl and got out of the car. "How long will it take?" he shouted to the man in overalls. "Only a moment," replied the attendant, and the young man said: "I've heard that one before." He wanted to go back and sit in the car, but he saw that the girl had gotten out the other side. "I'll take a little walk in the meantime," she said. "Where to?" the young man asked on purpose, wanting to see the girl's embarrassment. He had known her for a year now but she would still get shy in front of him. He enjoyed her moments of shyness, partly because they distinguished her from the women he'd met before, partly because he was aware of the law of universal transience, which made even his girl's shyness a precious thing to him.

2

The girl really didn't like it when during the trip (the young man would drive for several hours without stopping) she had to ask him to stop for a moment somewhere near a clump of trees. She always got angry when, with feigned surprise, he asked her why he should stop. She knew that her shyness was ridiculous and old-fashioned. Many times at work she had noticed that they laughed at her on account of it and deliberately provoked her. She always got shy in advance at the thought of how she was going to get shy. She often longed to feel free and easy about her body, the way most of the women around her did. She had even invented a special course in self-persuasion: She would repeat to herself that at birth every human being received one out of the millions of available bodies, as one would receive an allotted room out of the millions of rooms in an enormous hotel. Consequently, the body was fortuitous and impersonal, it was only a ready-made, borrowed thing. She would repeat this to herself in different ways, but she could never manage to feel it. This mind-body dualism was alien to her. She was too much one with her body; that is why she always felt such anxiety about it.

She experienced this same anxiety even in her relations with the young man, whom she had known for a year and with whom she was happy, perhaps because he never separated her body from her soul and she could live with him *wholly*. In this unity there was happiness, but right behind the happiness lurked suspicion, and the girl was full of that. For instance, it often occurred to her that the other women (those who weren't anxious) were more attractive and more seductive and that the young man, who did not conceal the fact that he knew this kind of woman well, would someday leave her for a woman like that. (True, the young man declared that he'd had enough of them to last his whole life, but she knew that he was still much younger than he thought.) She wanted him to be completely hers and she to be completely his, but it often seemed to her that the more she tried to give him everything, the more she denied him something: the very thing that a light and superficial love or a flirtation gives to a person. It worried her that she was not able to combine seriousness with lightheartedness.

But now she wasn't worrying and any such thoughts were far from her mind. She felt good. It was the first day of their vacation (of their two-week vacation, about which she had been dreaming for a whole year), the sky was blue (the whole year she had been worrying about whether the sky would really be blue), and he was beside her. At his, "Where to?" she blushed, and left the car without a word. She walked around the gas station, which was situated beside the highway in total isolation, surrounded by fields. About a hundred yards away (in the direction in which they were traveling), a wood began. She set off for it, vanished behind a little bush, and gave herself up to her good mood. (In solitude it was possible for her to get the greatest enjoyment from the presence of the man she loved. If his presence had been continuous, it would have kept on disappearing. Only when alone was she able to *hold on* to it.)

When she came out of the wood onto the highway, the gas station was visible. The large gasoline truck was already pulling out and the sports car moved forward toward the red turret of the pump. The girl walked on along the highway and only at times looked back to see if the sports car was coming. At last she caught sight of it. She stopped and began to wave at it like a hitchhiker waving at a stranger's car. The sports car slowed down and stopped close to the girl. The young man leaned toward the window, rolled it down, smiled, and asked, "Where are you headed, miss?" "Are you going to Bystritsa?" asked the girl, smiling flirtatiously at him. "Yes, please get in," said the young man, opening the door. The girl got in and the car took off.

3

The young man was always glad when his girlfriend was gay. This didn't happen too often; she had a quite tiresome job in an unpleasant environment, many hours of overtime without compensatory leisure and, at home, a sick mother. So she often felt tired. She didn't have either particularly good nerves or self-confidence and easily fell into a state of anxiety and fear. For this reason he welcomed every manifestation of her gaiety with the tender solicitude of a foster parent. He smiled at her and said: "I'm lucky today. I've been driving for five years, but I've never given a ride to such a pretty hitchhiker."

The girl was grateful to the young man for every bit of flattery; she wanted to linger for a moment in its warmth and so she said, "You're very good at lying."

"Do I look like a liar?"

"You look like you enjoy lying to women," said the girl, and into her words there crept unawares a touch of the old anxiety, because she really did believe that her young man enjoyed lying to women.

The girl's jealousy often irritated the young man, but this time he could easily overlook it for, after all, her words didn't apply to him but to the unknown driver. And so he just casually inquired, "Does it bother you?"

"If I were going with you, then it would bother me," said the girl and her words contained a subtle, instructive message for the young man; but the end of her sentence applied only to the unknown driver, "but I don't know you, so it doesn't bother me."

"Things about her own man always bother a woman more than things about a stranger" (this was now the young man's subtle, instructive message to the girl), "so seeing that we are strangers, we could get on well together."

The girl purposely didn't want to understand the implied meaning of his message, and so she now addressed the unknown driver exclusively:

"What does it matter, since we'll part company in a little while?"

"Why?" asked the young man.

"Well, I'm getting out at Bystritsa."

"And what if I get out with you?"

At these words the girl looked up at him and found that he looked exactly as she imagined him in her most agonizing hours of jealousy. She was alarmed at how he was flattering her and flirting with her (an unknown hitchhiker), and *how becoming it was to him*. Therefore she responded with defiant provocativeness, "What would *you* do with me, I wonder?"

"I wouldn't have to think too hard about what to do with such a beautiful woman," said the young man gallantly and at this moment he was once again speaking far more to his own girl than to the figure of the hitchhiker.

But this flattering sentence made the girl feel as if she had caught him at something, as if she had wheedled a confession out of him with a fraudulent trick. She felt toward him a brief flash of intense hatred and said, "Aren't you rather too sure of yourself?"

The young man looked at the girl. Her defiant face appeared to him to be completely convulsed. He felt sorry for her and longed for her usual, familiar expression (which he used to call childish and simple). He leaned toward her, put his arm around her shoulders, and softly spoke the name with which he usually addressed her and with which he now wanted to stop the game.

But the girl released herself and said: "You're going a bit too fast!"

At this rebuff the young man said: "Excuse me, miss," and looked silently in front of him at the highway.

4

The girl's pitiful jealousy, however, left her as quickly as it had come over her. After all, she was sensible and knew perfectly well that all this was merely a game. Now it even struck her as a little ridiculous that she had repulsed her man out of jealous rage. It wouldn't be pleasant for her if he found out why she had done it. Fortunately women have the miraculous ability to change the meaning of their actions after the event. Using this ability, she decided that she had repulsed him not out of anger but so that she could go on with the game, which, with its whimsicality, so well suited the first day of their vacation.

So again she was the hitchhiker, who had just repulsed the overenterprising driver, but only so as to slow down his conquest and make it more exciting. She half turned toward the young man and said caressingly:

"I didn't mean to offend you, mister!"

"Excuse me, I won't touch you again," said the young man.

He was furious with the girl for not listening to him and refusing to be herself when that was what he wanted. And since the girl insisted on continuing in her role, he transferred his anger to the unknown hitchhiker whom she was portraying. And all at once he discovered the character of his own part: He stopped making the gallant remarks with which he had wanted to flatter his girl in a roundabout way, and began to play the tough guy who treats women to the coarser aspects of his masculinity: willfulness, sarcasm, self-assurance.

This role was a complete contradiction of the young man's habitually solicitous approach to the girl. True, before he had met her, he had in fact behaved roughly rather than gently toward women. But he had never resembled a heartless tough guy, because he had never demonstrated either a particularly strong will or ruthlessness. However, if he did not resemble such a man, nonetheless he had *longed* to at one time. Of course it was a quite naive desire, but there it was. Childish desires withstand all the snares of the adult mind and often survive into ripe old age. And this childish desire quickly took advantage of the opportunity to embody itself in the proffered role.

The young man's sarcastic reserve suited the girl very well—it freed her from herself. For she herself was, above all, the epitome of jealousy. The moment she stopped seeing the gallantly seductive young man beside her and saw only his inaccessible face, her jealousy subsided. The girl could forget herself and give herself up to her role.

Her role? What was her role? It was a role out of trashy literature. The hitchhiker stopped the car not to get a ride, but to seduce the man who was driving the car. She was an artful seductress, cleverly knowing how to use her charms. The girl slipped into this silly, romantic part with an ease that astonished her and held her spellbound.

5

There was nothing the young man missed in his life more than lightheartedness. The main road of his life was drawn with implacable precision. His job didn't use up merely eight hours a day, it also infiltrated the remaining time with the compulsory boredom of meetings and home study, and, by means of the attentiveness of his countless male and female colleagues, it infiltrated the wretchedly little time he had left for his private life as well. This private life never remained secret and sometimes even became the subject of gossip and public discussion. Even two weeks' vacation didn't give him a feeling of liberation and adventure; the gray shadow of precise planning lay even here. The scarcity of summer accommodations in our country compelled him to book a room in the Tatras six months in advance, and since for that he needed a recommendation from his office, its omnipresent brain thus did not cease knowing about him even for an instant.

He had become reconciled to all this, yet all the same from time to time the terrible thought of the straight road would overcome him — a road along which he was being pursued, where he was visible to everyone, and from which he could not turn aside. At this moment that thought returned to him. Through an odd and brief conjunction of ideas the figurative road became identified with the real highway along which he was driving — and this led him suddenly to do a crazy thing.

"Where did you say you wanted to go?" he asked the girl.

"To Banska Bystritsa," she replied.

"And what are you going to do there?"

"I have a date there."

"Who with?"

"With a certain gentleman."

The car was just coming to a large crossroads. The driver slowed down so he could read the road signs, then turned off to the right.

"What will happen if you don't arrive for that date?"

"It would be your fault and you would have to take care of me."

"You obviously didn't notice that I turned off in the direction of Nove Zamky."

"Is that true? You've gone crazy!"

"Don't be afraid. I'll take care of you," said the young man.

So they drove and chatted thus — the driver and the hitchhiker who did not know each other.

The game all at once went into a higher gear. The sports car was moving away not only from the imaginary goal of Banska Bystritsa, but also from the real goal, toward which it had been heading in the morning: the Tatras and the room that had been booked. Fiction was suddenly making an assault upon real life. The young man was moving away from himself and from the implacable straight road, from which he had never strayed until now.

"But you said you were going to the Low Tatras!" The girl was surprised.

"I am going, miss, wherever I feel like going. I'm a free man and I do what I want and what it pleases me to do."

6

When they drove into Nove Zamky it was already getting dark.

The young man had never been here before and it took him a while to orient himself. Several times he stopped the car and asked the passersby directions to the hotel. Several streets had been dug up, so that the drive to the hotel, even though it was quite close by (as all those who had been asked asserted), necessitated so many detours and roundabout routes that it was almost a quarter of an hour before they finally stopped in front of it. The hotel looked unprepossessing, but it was the only one in town and the young man didn't feel like driving on. So he said to the girl, "Wait here," and got out of the car.

Out of the car he was, of course, himself again. And it was upsetting for him to find himself in the evening somewhere completely different from his intended destination—the more so because no one had forced him to do it and as a matter of fact he hadn't even really wanted to. He blamed himself for this piece of folly, but then became reconciled to it. The room in the Tatras could wait until tomorrow and it wouldn't do any harm if they celebrated the first day of their vacation with something unexpected.

He walked through the restaurant—smoky, noisy, and crowded—and asked for the reception desk. They sent him to the back of the lobby near the staircase, where behind a glass panel a superannuated blonde was sitting beneath a board full of keys. With difficulty, he obtained the key to the only room left.

The girl, when she found herself alone, also threw off her role. She didn't feel ill-humored, though, at finding herself in an unexpected town. She was so devoted to the young man that she never had doubts about anything he did, and confidently entrusted every moment of her life to him. On the other hand the idea once again popped into her mind that perhaps—just as she was now doing—other women had waited for her man in his car, those women whom he met on business trips. But surprisingly enough this idea didn't upset her at all now. In fact, she smiled at the thought of how nice it was that today she was this other woman, this irresponsible, indecent other woman, one of those women of whom she was so jealous. It seemed to her that she was cutting them all out, that she had learned how to use their weapons; how to give the young man what until now she had not known how to give him: lightheartedness, shamelessness, and dissoluteness. A curious feeling of satisfaction filled her, because she alone had the ability to be all women and in this way she alone could completely captivate her lover and hold his interest.

The young man opened the car door and led the girl into the restaurant. Amid the din, the dirt, and the smoke he found a single, unoccupied table in a corner.

7

"So how are you going to take care of me now?" asked the girl provocatively.

"What would you like for an aperitif?"

The girl wasn't too fond of alcohol, still she drank a little wine and liked vermouth fairly well. Now, however, she purposely said: "Vodka."

"Fine," said the young man. "I hope you won't get drunk on me."

"And if I do?" said the girl.

The young man did not reply but called over a waiter and ordered two vodkas and two steak dinners. In a moment the waiter brought a tray with two small glasses and placed it in front of them.

The man raised his glass, "To you!"

"Can't you think of a wittier toast?"

Something was beginning to irritate him about the girl's game. Now sitting face to face with her, he realized that it wasn't just the *words* which were turning her into a stranger, but that her *whole persona* had changed, the movements of her body and her facial expression, and that she unpalatably and faithfully resembled that type of woman whom he knew so well and for whom he felt some aversion.

And so (holding his glass in his raised hand), he corrected his toast: "O.K., then I won't drink to you, but to your kind, in which are combined so successfully the better qualities of the animal and the worse aspects of the human being."

"By 'kind' do you mean all women?" asked the girl.

"No, I mean only those who are like you."

"Anyway it doesn't seem very witty to me to compare a woman with an animal."

"O.K.," the young man was still holding his glass aloft, "then I won't drink to your kind, but to your soul. Agreed? To your soul, which lights up when it descends from your head into your belly, and which goes out when it rises back up to your head."

The girl raised her glass. "O.K., to my soul, which descends into my belly."

"I'll correct myself once more," said the young man. "To your belly, into which your soul descends."

"To my belly," said the girl, and her belly (now that they had named it specifically), as it were, responded to the call; she felt every inch of it.

Then the waiter brought their steaks and the young man ordered them another vodka and some soda water (this time they drank to the girl's breasts), and the conversation continued in this peculiar, frivolous tone. It irritated the young man more and more how *well able* the girl was to become the lascivious miss. If she was able to do it so well, he thought, it meant that she really *was* like that. After all, no alien soul had entered into her from somewhere in space. What she was acting now was she herself; perhaps it was that part of her being which had formerly been locked up and which the pretext of the game had let out of its cage. Perhaps the girl supposed that by means of the game she was *disowning* herself, but wasn't it the other way around? Wasn't she becoming herself only through the game? Wasn't she freeing herself through the game? No, opposite him was not sitting a strange woman in his girl's body; it was his girl, herself, no one else. He looked at her and felt growing aversion toward her.

However, it was not only aversion. The more the girl withdrew from him *psychically,* the more he longed for her *physically*. The alien quality of her soul drew attention to her body, yes, as a matter of fact it turned her body into a body for *him* as if until now it had existed for the young man hidden within clouds of compassion, tenderness, concern, love, and emotion, as if it had been lost in these clouds (yes, as if this body had been lost!). It seemed to the young man that today he was seeing his girl's body for the first time.

After her third vodka and soda the girl got up and said flirtatiously, "Excuse me."

The young man said, "May I ask you where you are going, miss?"

"To piss, if you'll permit me," said the girl and walked off between the tables back toward the plush screen.

8

She was pleased with the way she had astounded the young man with this word, which—in spite of all its innocence—he had never heard from her. Nothing seemed to her truer to the character of the woman she was playing than this flirtatious emphasis placed on the word in question. Yes, she was pleased, she was in the best of moods. The game captivated her. It allowed her to feel what she had not felt till now: a *feeling* of *happy-go-lucky irresponsibility.*

She, who was always uneasy in advance about her every next step, suddenly felt completely relaxed. The alien life in which she had become involved was a life without shame, without biographical specifications, without past or future, without obligations. It was a life that was extraordinarily free. The girl, as a hitchhiker, could do anything, *everything was permitted her.* She could say, do, and feel whatever she liked.

She walked through the room and was aware that people were watching her from all the tables. It was a new sensation, one she didn't recognize: *indecent joy caused by her body.* Until now she had never been able to get rid of the fourteen-year-old girl within herself who was ashamed of her breasts and had the disagreeable feeling that she was indecent, because they stuck out from her body and were visible. Even though she was proud of being pretty and having a good figure, this feeling of pride was always immediately curtailed by shame. She rightly suspected that feminine beauty functioned above all as sexual provocation and she found this distasteful. She longed for her body to relate only to the man she loved. When men stared at her breasts in the street it seemed to her that they were invading a piece of her most secret privacy which should belong only to herself and her lover. But now she was the hitchhiker, the woman without a destiny. In this role she was relieved of the tender bonds of her love and began to be intensely aware of her body. And her body became more aroused the more alien the eyes watching it.

She was walking past the last table when an intoxicated man, wanting to show off his worldliness, addressed her in French: *"Combien, mademoiselle?"*

The girl understood. She thrust out her breasts and fully experienced every movement of her hips, then disappeared behind the screen.

9

It was a curious game. This curiousness was evidenced, for example, in the fact that the young man, even though he himself was playing the unknown driver remarkably well, did not for a moment stop seeing his girl in the hitchhiker. And it was precisely this that was tormenting. He saw his girl seducing a strange man, and had the bitter privilege of being present, of seeing at close quarters how she looked and of hearing what she said when she was cheating on him (when she had cheated on him, when she would cheat on him). He had the paradoxical honor of being himself the pretext for her unfaithfulness.

This was all the worse because he worshipped rather than loved her. It had always seemed to him that her inward nature was *real* only within the bounds of fidelity and purity, and that beyond these bounds it simply didn't exist. Beyond these bounds she would cease to be herself, as water ceases to be water beyond the boiling point. When he now saw her crossing this horrifying boundary with nonchalant elegance, he was filled with anger.

The girl came back from the rest room and complained: "A guy over there asked me: *Combien, mademoiselle?*"

"You shouldn't be surprised," said the young man, "after all, you look like a whore."

"Do you know that it doesn't bother me in the least?"

"Then you should go with the gentleman!"

"But I have you."

"You can go with him after me. Go and work out something with him."

"I don't find him attractive."

"But in principle you have nothing against it, having several men in one night."

"Why not, if they're good-looking."

"Do you prefer them one after the other or at the same time?"

"Either way," said the girl.

The conversation was proceeding to still greater extremes of rudeness; it shocked the girl slightly but she couldn't protest. Even in a game there lurks a lack of freedom; even a game is a trap for the players. If this had not been a game and they had really been two strangers, the hitchhiker could long ago have taken offense and left. But there's no escape from a game. A team cannot flee from the playing field before the end of the match, chess pieces cannot desert the chessboard: The boundaries of the playing field are fixed. The girl knew that she had to accept whatever form the game might take, just because it was a game. She knew that the more extreme the game became, the more it would be a game and the more obediently she would have to play it. And it was futile to evoke good sense and warn her dazed soul that she must keep her distance from the game and not take it seriously. Just because it was only a game her soul was not afraid, did not oppose the game, and narcotically sank deeper into it.

The young man called the waiter and paid. Then he got up and said to the girl, "We're going."

"Where to?" The girl feigned surprise.

"Don't ask, just come on," said the young man.

"What sort of way is that to talk to me?"

"The way I talk to whores," said the young man.

10

They went up the badly lit staircase. On the landing below the second floor a group of intoxicated men was standing near the rest room. The young man caught hold of the girl from behind so that he was holding her breast with his hand. The men by the rest room saw this and began to call out. The girl wanted to break away, but the young man yelled at her: "Keep still!" The men greeted this with general ribaldry and addressed several dirty remarks to the girl. The young man and the girl reached the second floor. He opened the door of their room and switched on the light.

It was a narrow room with two beds, a small table, a chair, and a washbasin. The young man locked the door and turned to the girl. She was standing facing him in a defiant pose with insolent sensuality in her eyes. He looked at her and tried to discover behind her lascivious expression the familiar features which he loved tenderly. It was as if he were looking at two images through the same lens, at two images superimposed one upon the other with the one showing through the other. These two images showing through each other were telling him that *everything* was in the girl, that her soul was terrifyingly amorphous, that it held faithfulness and unfaithfulness, treachery and innocence, flirtatiousness and chastity. This disorderly jumble seemed disgusting to him, like the variety to be found in a pile of garbage. Both images continued to show through each other and the young man understood that the girl differed only on the surface from other women, but deep down was the same as they: full of all possible thoughts, feelings, and vices, which justified all his secret misgivings and fits of jealousy. The impression that certain outlines delineated her as an individual was only a delusion to which the other person, the one who was looking, was subject — namely himself. It seemed to him that the girl he loved was a creation of his desire, his thoughts, and his faith and that the *real* girl now standing in front of him was hopelessly alien, hopelessly *ambiguous*. He hated her.

"What are you waiting for? Strip," he said.

The girl flirtatiously bent her head and said, "Is it necessary?"

The tone in which she said this seemed to him very familiar; it seemed to him that once long ago some other woman had said this to him, only he no longer knew which one. He longed to humiliate her. Not the hitchhiker, but his own girl. The game merged with life. The game of humiliating the hitchhiker became only a pretext for humiliating his girl. The young man had forgotten that he was playing a game. He simply hated the woman standing in front of him. He stared at her and took a fifty-crown bill from his wallet. He offered it to the girl. "Is that enough?"

The girl took the fifty crowns and said: "You don't think I'm worth much."

The young man said: "You aren't worth more."

The girl nestled up against the young man. "You can't get around me like that! You must try a different approach, you must work a little!"

She put her arms around him and moved her mouth toward his. He put his fingers on her mouth and gently pushed her away. He said: "I only kiss women I love."

"And you don't love me?"

"No."

"Whom do you love?"

"What's that got to do with you? Strip!"

11

She had never undressed like this before. The shyness, the feeling of inner panic, the dizziness, all that she had always felt when undressing in front of the young man (and she couldn't hide in the darkness), all this was gone. She was standing in front of him self-confident, insolent, bathed in light, and astonished at where she had all of a sudden discovered the gestures, heretofore unknown to her, of a slow, provocative striptease. She took in his glances, slipping off each piece of clothing with a caressing movement and enjoying each individual stage of this exposure.

But then suddenly she was standing in front of him completely naked and at this moment it flashed through her head that now the whole game would end, that, since she had stripped off her clothes, she had also stripped away her dissimulation, and that being naked meant that she was now herself and the young man ought to come up to her now and make a gesture with which he would wipe out everything and after which would follow only their most intimate lovemaking. So she stood naked in front of the young man and at this moment stopped playing the game. She felt embarrassed and on her face appeared the smile, which really belonged to her — a shy and confused smile.

But the young man didn't come to her and didn't end the game. He didn't notice the familiar smile. He saw before him only the beautiful, alien body of his own girl, whom he hated. Hatred cleansed his sensuality of any sentimental coating. She wanted to come to him, but he said: "Stay where you are, I want to have a good look at you." Now he longed only to treat her as a whore. But the young man had never had a whore and the ideas he had about them came from literature and hearsay. So he turned to these ideas and the first thing he recalled was the image of a woman in black underwear (and black stockings) dancing on the shiny top of a piano. In the little hotel room there was no piano, there was only a small table covered with a linen cloth leaning against the wall. He ordered the girl to climb up on it. The girl made a pleading gesture, but the young man said, "You've been paid."

When she saw the look of unshakable obsession in the young man's eyes, she tried to go on with the game, even though she no longer could and no longer knew how. With tears in her eyes she climbed onto the table. The top was scarcely three feet square and one leg was a little bit shorter than the others so that standing on it the girl felt unsteady.

But the young man was pleased with the naked figure, now towering above him, and the girl's shy insecurity merely inflamed his imperiousness. He wanted to see her body in all positions and from all sides, as he imagined other men had seen it and would see it. He was vulgar and lascivious. He used words that she had never heard from him in her life. She wanted to refuse, she wanted to be released from the game. She called him by his first name, but he immediately yelled at her that she had no right to address him so intimately. And so eventually in confusion and on the verge of tears, she obeyed, she bent forward and squatted according to the young man's wishes, saluted, and then wiggled her hips as she did the Twist for him. During a slightly more violent movement, when the cloth slipped beneath her feet and she nearly fell, the young man caught her and dragged her to the bed.

He had intercourse with her. She was glad that at least now finally the unfortunate game would end and they would again be the two people they had been before and would love each other. She wanted to press her mouth against his. But the young man pushed her head away and repeated that he only kissed women he loved. She burst into loud sobs. But she wasn't even allowed to cry, because the young man's furious passion gradually won over her body, which then silenced the complaint of her soul. On the bed there were soon two bodies in perfect harmony, two sensual bodies, alien to each other. This was exactly what the girl had most dreaded all her life and had scrupulously avoided till now: love-making without emotion or love. She knew that she had crossed the forbidden boundary, but she proceeded across it without objections and as a full participant — only somewhere, far off in a corner of her consciousness, did she feel horror at the thought that she had never known such pleasure, never so much pleasure as at this moment—beyond that boundary.

12

Then it was all over. The young man got up off the girl and, reaching out for the long cord hanging over the bed, switched off the light. He didn't want to see the girl's face. He knew that the game was over, but didn't feel like returning to their customary relationship. He feared this return. He lay beside the girl in the dark in such a way that their bodies would not touch.

After a moment he heard her sobbing quietly. The girl's hand diffidently, childishly touched his. It touched, withdrew, then touched again, and then a pleading, sobbing voice broke the silence, calling him by his name and saying, "I am me, I am me. . . ."

The young man was silent, he didn't move, and he was aware of the sad emptiness of the girl's assertion, in which the unknown was defined in terms of the same unknown quantity.

And the girl soon passed from sobbing to loud crying and went on endlessly repeating this pitiful tautology: "I am me, I am me, I am me. . . ."

The young man began to call compassion to his aid (he had to call it from afar, because it was nowhere near at hand), so as to be able to calm the girl. There were still thirteen days' vacation before them.

❧ CHINUA ACHEBE
B. NIGERIA, 1930

A novelist, poet, short-story writer, writer of children's literature, essayist, editor, and teacher, **Chinua Achebe** is one of the most influential West African writers of the twentieth century. Achebe has also worked as a producer, writer, and director for radio, including a stint with the Voice of Nigeria, of which he was director from 1961 to 1966. In an explicitly political vein, he served on diplomatic missions for Biafra during the Nigerian civil war and was deputy president of the People's Redemption Party in 1983. With subtlety and complexity, Achebe's novels portray from an insider's point of view traditional African society and culture, especially as it clashes with the forces of colonialism and the vestiges of its ghost in postcolonial Nigeria. Like fellow African writers Wole Soyinka (b. 1934) from Nigeria and **Ngugi Wa Thiong'o** (b. 1938) from Kenya, Achebe has articulated in his work a sustaining moral vision for African consciousness and identity, engaging directly the difficult problems Africa faces in

CHIN-wah
ah-CHAY-bay

en-GOO-gee wah
thee-ONG-oh

Chinua Achebe, 1988
The Nigerian author in his home in Amherst, Massachusetts. (Hulton / Archive)

EE-boh

www For links to more information about Chinua Achebe and a quiz on *Things Fall Apart,* and for information about Achebe's twenty-first-century relevance and the culture and context of Africa in the twentieth century, see *World Literature Online* at bedfordstmartins .com/worldlit.

the postcolonial era and recovering a sense of the African spirit as it emerges from traditional folktales, stories, and customs. Though Achebe writes in English, his novels capture the rich imagery and rhythms of his native country's proverbs and tales.

English and Ibo Education. Chinua Achebe was born November 16, 1930, in Ogidi, Nigeria, the fifth child of Isaiah Okafor Achebe and Janet Iloegbunam, Ibo missionary teachers who raised him in a Christian household. Although he received his education in English at the British missionary schools in Ogidi, he developed an attachment to traditional Ibo stories through his mother and sister. In his teens he studied at the Government College in Umuahia and then attended University College in Ibadan from 1948 to 1953, receiving a bachelor's degree. He had entered college on a scholarship to study medicine, but after his first year he switched to the liberal arts, including English literature. His reading in European, especially British, literature brought home to Achebe the often condescending and false image of Africa presented by European writers such as Joyce Cary (1888–1957) and Joseph Conrad. Achebe began writing his first novel, *Things Fall Apart* (1958), as a direct repudiation of the image of Nigeria presented in Cary's *Mister Johnson* (1939).

Civil War and Independence. Upon graduation from the university at Ibadan, Achebe worked as a producer and director for the Nigerian Broadcasting Service until civil war erupted in 1967. Nigeria had gained its independence from Britain in 1960, the year before Achebe's marriage to Christie Chinwe Okoli. In the vacuum created by the withdrawal of British colonial authority, three tribal groups — the **Ibo**, Hausa-Fulani, and Yoruba — competed against one another for power. The civil war, which lasted until 1970, did little to resolve those rivalries, and since the time of the war Nigeria has been ruled by a succession of dictators, some posing as supporters of democracy. During the war, Biafra, a state of Ibo speakers in eastern Nigeria, seceded from the rest of the country. Achebe supported the Biafran independence movement, working for the Biafran Ministry of Information. That experience served him well, especially in *A Man of the People* (1966) and *Anthills of the Savannah* (1987), in which he focuses on the corruption, power-mongering, and hope for democratic freedoms that characterize Nigerian politics even today. A collection of poetry, *Christmas in Biafra,* winner of the Commonwealth Poetry Prize, and a collection of short stories, *Girls at War,* were written during the civil war.

International Acclaim. In the early 1970s Achebe accepted visiting professorships at the University of Massachusetts, Amherst, where he again taught from 1987 to 1988, and the University of Connecticut at Storrs. During this time he taught literature and founded and edited *Okike,* a journal of African literature and criticism. In addition, he founded the Heinemann African Writers Series, which has established African literature written in English as a major force in contemporary world literature. In 1976 Achebe returned to Nigeria as a teacher and senior research fellow at the University of Nigeria, Nsukka. He has continued to be involved in Nigerian political life, primarily as a commentator, and in 1983 he published *The Trouble with Nigeria,* a nonfiction critique of the political corruption of his country.

Representing Africa.   Achebe describes himself as a "political writer" whose work is "concerned with universal human communication across racial and cultural boundaries as a means of fostering respect for all people." He set out to correct the distorted representation of Africa that European writers had delivered to European audiences and to show the adverse impact that colonization had had upon indigenous cultures. His first three novels, which make up a kind of trilogy, directly accomplish those objectives. *Things Fall Apart* (1958), chosen here to represent Achebe, shows Nigeria at the advent of British colonization. It takes place in the Ibo villages of **Umuofia** in the late 1880s, a time when English missionaries and administrators first began to appear. The Europeans were interested in the Niger delta region for its palm oil, and in 1879 Englishman George Goldie formed the United Africa Company to drive out the French, who had conquered most of western Africa in the previous decade. Eventually becoming the Royal Niger Company and granted a royal charter, Goldie's company established a monopoly in the region by about 1884. By 1893, Nigeria was declared a British colony, and cocoa, timber, rubber, coconuts, and palm oil began to flow out of the country on British ships. The novel focuses on the psychological and cultural consequences of that history as it affects the leader Okonkwo, who struggles to preserve his and his people's integrity and sovereignty in the face of the changes in law and religion that the colonizers have brought.

oo-MWOH-fee-ah

No Longer at Ease.   Achebe's next two novels, *No Longer at Ease* (1960) and *Arrow of God* (1964), continue the story of Umuofia in the two generations after Okonkwo's. Although *Arrow of God* is the third novel in the series, it tells the story of the second generation in Umuofia in the 1920s. Ezeulu, a spiritual leader, also must grapple with the gap between European and African ways. Another flawed hero, Ezeulu plans to use his son to spy on Western schools. The scheme fails when the son, Oduche, is converted and turns against his father and his father's god. Ezeulu manages to get arrested, is imprisoned by the British, and finally embitters his own people by carrying out a heavy penalty on them; the entire village turns against him. *No Longer at Ease* takes readers into the 1950s, when a grandson of Okonkwo, the English-educated Obi Okonkwo, fails to integrate Ibo tradition with European ideals. The would-be hero represents the educated elite, whose aspirations have more often than not failed to materialize in Nigeria. Obi returns to his country a kind of stranger, turns against his people, and falls into the political corruption he'd hoped to eradicate.

Anthills of the Savannah.   Achebe's next three novels focus primarily on political corruption in the post-1960 period—after Nigerian independence. *A Man of the People* (1966) condemns the abuse of power and

The Igbo have always lived in a world of continual struggle, motion, and change—a feature conspicuous in the tautness, overreach, and torsion of their art; it is like a tightrope walk, a hairbreadth brush with the boundaries of anarchy.

– CHINUA ACHEBE

corruption, as does *Anthills of the Savannah* (1988). The latter novel, one of the most highly acclaimed of Achebe's works, follows a set of friends— Ikem, Sam, and Chris—whose friendship falls apart as Sam, who has become a military dictator of the imaginary West African country of Kangan, loses the support and confidence of Ikem, an editor, and Chris, the Minister of Information. To preserve his power, Sam resorts to propaganda, repression, and finally, the extermination of opponents and critics. As in the case of *A Man of the People*, which seemed to anticipate much of the corruption of the 1970s, *Anthills of the Savannah* appears to have prophesied the duplicity and arbitrary wielding of power of the present regime in Nigeria. *Anthills* ends with cautious optimism, noting the important role of women in the movement for reform. With his latest novel pointing to the uncertain future, Achebe's work so far constitutes a history, in fiction, of colonialism and independence in Nigeria from the nineteenth century to the present.

Things Fall Apart. *Things Fall Apart,* one of the first and finest novels of postindependence African literature in English, launched Achebe on the project of tracing Nigeria's history in his fiction. The title comes from William Butler Yeats's **"The Second Coming,"** a visionary poem announcing the birth of a "rough beast . . . slouching toward Bethlehem." That beast here appears to be the erosion of Ibo society, portrayed in unsurpassed detail, sensitivity, and understanding, after its devastating encounter with European colonialism. Set in roughly the same period as Conrad's **Heart of Darkness** (1902), the novel presents the early encounter with European missionaries from the African—specifically, the Ibo—point of view. Some of the incidents of this encounter, such as the raid on Abame mentioned in Chapter 15, are based on actual historical incidents—in this case, a British attack on the town of Ahiara, which took place in 1905, to avenge the killing of a missionary. Achebe's critique of British colonialism, however, comes less through the documentation of such incidents and more through the celebration of Ibo culture. To counteract the portrayal of the African as a shadowy figure in novels such as Joyce Cary's *Mister Johnson* (1939) and Conrad's *Heart of Darkness,* Achebe in this novel and others honors, without resorting to sentimentality, the humanity and dignity of the African people. In *Things Fall Apart,* Achebe presents that humanity in part through the character of the village leader, Okonkwo, whose actions involve him in almost every aspect of the complex culture and religious life of the Ibo in Umuofia.

Okonkwo is a complex and tragic hero who is as noble and flawed as an Achilles or a Creon.[1] While Okonkwo embodies many of the virtues of his society—courage, industry, and material success—he also demonstrates a dangerous stubbornness and self-satisfaction. His killing of **Ikemefuna** and his rejection of his son Nwoye are presented unsympathetically; indeed, like Creon's in *Antigone,* Okonkwo's rigidity and

p. 193

p. 35

ee-kay-may-FOO-nah

---

[1] **Creon:** The king of Thebes; represented in Sophocles' (496–406 B.C.E.) play *Antigone* as a man who refuses to bend the rules of the state.

heavy-handedness eventually lead to his downfall. As in later novels, and like his compatriot writer Wole Soyinka, Achebe, in *Things Fall Apart,* recognizes the need for the preservation of tradition but also affirms a cautious and controlled acceptance of those European ideas and practices that can enhance African culture and make it stronger.

Ibo Proverbs and Lore. One of the features of *Things Fall Apart,* carried even further in *Arrow of God,* is the presence of Ibo proverbs found throughout the story. In these proverbs can be seen some of the values of Ibo culture, which include, as critic Emmanuel Ngara points out, "bravery, hard work, material wealth . . . eloquence and dignity," values rarely associated with Africa in the eyes of some Western readers. Moreover, the proverbs are aligned with important, often contradictory, motifs and themes in the novel. One of the key proverbs from *Things Fall Apart,* "when a man says yes his *chi* says yes also," points to Okonkwo's pride in the self-determination that led to his success and that won him the praise of his people. When he accidentally kills Ezeudu's son, he begins to face the hard reality that even a self-made man like himself is subject to forces beyond his control. Now barred forever from becoming one of the lords of the clan, Okonkwo had worked hard to take control of his life, saying yes to his *chi,* and yet his *chi,* or personal god, denied him his ultimate desire. Other proverbs note the need for those who have been blessed to be humble, and for the great to accept greatness in others; the tale of the greedy tortoise in Chapter 11 also cautions against greed and excessive pride. Okonkwo's contempt for those who have been less successful than he is the first sign of the trouble to come.

"An Image of Africa." The English missionaries and administration officials exacerbate the misfortunes visited upon Okonkwo. The white missionary at Mbanta articulates the uninformed prejudice against native religion and culture, which the novel has just elaborated in fine detail. Achebe introduces the missionary comically; the villagers mock his interpreter's use of their language as he mistakes the word meaning "my buttocks" for "myself." Many of the Mbanta men are astounded at the missionaries' pronouncements that their gods are dead and have no power; they laugh with incredulity at a missionary's claims that his is the only living and powerful god. In **"An Image of Africa,"** delivered as a Chancellor's Lecture at the University of Massachusetts, Amherst, on February 18, 1975, Achebe spoke of an aim that could well describe the achievement of this novel: "to look at Africa not through a haze of distortions and cheap mystification but quite simply as a continent of people—not angels, but not rudimentary souls either—just people, often highly gifted people and often strikingly successful in their enterprise with life and society." *Things Fall Apart* ends tragically, with Okonkwo humiliated by the beating he received in the white man's jail and with his deep disappointment that the men of Umuofia would not stand up, as he had, to the encroachment of the English. Okonkwo's death is symbolic, in many ways, of the death of Ibo society itself; the novel questions whether that death was necessary and gives its African

[Achebe's characters] have a vital relationship with the social and economic landscape. We can see, and feel, how his characters, their worldview, their very aspirations, have been shaped by a particular environment in a particular historical place. They live in history . . . because they are the makers of history.

– NGUGI WA
THIONG'O, novelist
and critic, 1972

p. 107

readers reason to believe in the importance of preserving what is best in their traditions.

■ CONNECTIONS

Olaudah Equiano, *The Interesting Narrative of the Life of Olaudah Equiano* **(Book 4).** Achebe's novels, including *Things Fall Apart*, draw heavily on folklore and the ways of the Ibo. In "The African Writer and the English Language," Achebe describes Equiano as an African writer who appropriated the "master's discourse" to produce a powerful text that challenged the slanderous image of Africa presented by those perpetuating the slave trade. Compare the depiction of the Ibo in the first chapter of Equiano's narrative with that in Achebe's novel. What is the "image of Africa" in these texts?

Joseph Conrad, *Heart of Darkness,* **p. 35.** Ever since Achebe wrote the essay "The Image of Africa" (see *In the World:* Colonialism, p. 107), which sharply renounces Conrad's depiction of Africa in *Heart of Darkness,* Conrad's novel — as well as Joyce Cary's *Mister Johnson* — has served to point up the differences between representations of Africa and Africans by non-African writers and those by African writers. Compare Conrad's "image of Africa" with Achebe's. How does Achebe's novel engage in a dialogue with Conrad's?

William Butler Yeats, "The Second Coming," p. 193. Achebe deliberately borrowed a phrase from Yeats's poem "The Second Coming" for the title of his novel. "The Second Coming" points to a new cosmic order following some kind of powerful upheaval. Why would Achebe allude to Yeats's apocalyptic vision in naming his novel? What catastrophic transformation does the novel explicitly point to? What catastrophic form of renewal might it imply?

■ FURTHER RESEARCH

Gikandi, Simon. *Reading Chinua Achebe: Language and Ideology in Fiction.* 1991.
Innes, C. L. *Chinua Achebe.* 1990.
Innes, C. L. and Bernth Lindfors, eds. *Critical Perspectives on Chinua Achebe.* 1978.
Killam, G. D. *The Writings of Chinua Achebe.* 1977.
Turkington, Kate. *Chinua Achebe:* Things Fall Apart. 1977.
Wren, Robert M. *Achebe's World: The Historical and Cultural Context of the Novels of Chinua Achebe.* 1980.

■ PRONUNCIATION

Chinua Achebe: CHIN-wah ah-CHAY-bay
Chielo: chee-AY-loh
egwugwu: ay-GWOO-gwoo
Erulu: ay-ROO-loo
Ezeani: ay-zay-AH-nee
Ezeugo: ay-zay-OO-goh
Ibo: EE-boh
Idemili: ee-DAY-mee-lee
Ikemefuna: ee-kay-may-FOO-nah
Mbari: em-BAH-ree
Ndulue: en-doo-loo-AY
Ngugi Wa Thiong'o: en-GOO-gee wah thee-ONG-oh
Nwakibie: nwah-kee-BEE-ay
Nwayieke: nwah-yee-AY-kay
Umuofia: oo-MWOH-fee-ah

✺ Things Fall Apart

PART I

1

Okonkwo was well known throughout the nine villages and even beyond. His fame rested on solid personal achievements. As a young man of eighteen he had brought honor to his village by throwing Amalinze the Cat. Amalinze was the great wrestler who for seven years was unbeaten, from Umuofia to Mbaino. He was called the Cat because his back would never touch the earth. It was this man that Okonkwo threw in a fight which the old men agreed was one of the fiercest since the founder of their town engaged a spirit of the wild for seven days and seven nights.

The drums beat and the flutes sang and the spectators held their breath. Amalinze was a wily craftsman, but Okonkwo was as slippery as a fish in water. Every nerve and every muscle stood out on their arms, on their backs and their thighs, and one almost heard them stretching to breaking point. In the end Okonkwo threw the Cat.

That was many years ago, twenty years or more, and during this time Okonkwo's fame had grown like a bush-fire in the harmattan. He was tall and huge, and his bushy eyebrows and wide nose gave him a very severe look. He breathed heavily, and it was said that, when he slept, his wives and children in their houses could hear him breathe. When he walked, his heels hardly touched the ground and he seemed to walk on springs, as if he was going to pounce on somebody. And he did pounce on people quite often. He had a slight stammer and whenever he was angry and could not get his words out quickly enough, he would use his fists. He had no patience with unsuccessful men. He had had no patience with his father.

Things Fall Apart. Achebe's first novel, published in 1958, was written as a direct response to the image of Africa presented in Joyce Cary's *Mister Johnson,* a novel depicting a shallow, comic African who is totally obedient and devoted to his white master. Achebe wanted his novel to "teach my readers that their past—with all its imperfections—was not one long night of savagery from which the first Europeans acting on God's behalf delivered them." The title of the work comes from William Butler Yeats's "The Second Coming," a poem that evokes a catastrophic upheaval of order, one that Achebe links with the arrival of Europeans in Umuofia, the homeland of the novel's protagonist, Okonkwo. Through Okonkwo's heroic struggle against the disturbances introduced by the colonizers, *Things Fall Apart* records the psychological and cultural struggles of an entire nation in the throes of crisis and change. Moreover, true to his stated aim, Achebe brilliantly depicts the social complexity and cultural diversity of Ibo society before the arrival of the Europeans. In the figure of Okonkwo, Achebe presents a complex and tragic hero as noble and flawed as an Achilles or a Hamlet; upholding the military values of the former, Okonkwo displays the conflicted psyche of the latter. In the end, like those tragic heroes, Okonkwo suffers separation and ultimately death, despite—or perhaps because of—his efforts to maintain his dignity and to preserve the integrity of his community.

All notes are the editors'.

Unoka, for that was his father's name, had died ten years ago. In his day he was lazy and improvident and was quite incapable of thinking about tomorrow. If any money came his way, and it seldom did, he immediately bought gourds of palm-wine, called round his neighbors and made merry. He always said that whenever he saw a dead man's mouth he saw the folly of not eating what one had in one's lifetime. Unoka was, of course, a debtor, and he owed every neighbor some money, from a few cowries[1] to quite substantial amounts.

He was tall but very thin and had a slight stoop. He wore a haggard and mournful look except when he was drinking or playing on his flute. He was very good on his flute, and his happiest moments were the two or three moons after the harvest when the village musicians brought down their instruments, hung above the fireplace. Unoka would play with them, his face beaming with blessedness and peace. Sometimes another village would ask Unoka's band and their dancing *egwugwu*[2] to come and stay with them and teach them their tunes. They would go to such hosts for as long as three or four markets,[3] making music and feasting. Unoka loved the good fare and the good fellowship, and he loved this season of the year, when the rains had stopped and the sun rose every morning with dazzling beauty. And it was not too hot either, because the cold and dry harmattan wind was blowing down from the north. Some years the harmattan was very severe and a dense haze hung on the atmosphere. Old men and children would then sit round log fires, warming their bodies. Unoka loved it all, and he loved the first kites that returned with the dry season, and the children who sang songs of welcome to them. He would remember his own childhood, how he had often wandered around looking for a kite sailing leisurely against the blue sky. As soon as he found one he would sing with his whole being, welcoming it back from its long, long journey, and asking it if it had brought home any lengths of cloth.

That was years ago, when he was young. Unoka, the grown-up, was a failure. He was poor and his wife and children had barely enough to eat. People laughed at him because he was a loafer, and they swore never to lend him any more money because he never paid back. But Unoka was such a man that he always succeeded in borrowing more, and piling up his debts.

One day a neighbor called Okoye came in to see him. He was reclining on a mud bed in his hut playing on the flute. He immediately rose and shook hands with Okoye, who then unrolled the goatskin which he carried under his arm, and sat down. Unoka went into an inner room and soon returned with a small wooden disc containing a kola nut, some alligator pepper, and a lump of white chalk.[4]

---

[1] **cowries:** A sixty-pound bag of cowries—mollusk shells used as currency—was worth about one pound sterling.

[2] *egwugwu:* Dancers who masquerade as spirits of the village ancestors.

[3] **three or four markets:** One-and-a-half to two weeks; the Ibo week has four days—Eke, the market day; Afo, a half-working day; and Oye and Nkwo, full working days.

[4] **kola . . . chalk:** All items used in hospitality ceremonies. Kola nuts, like coffee, contain caffeine and so offer a mild stimulant; alligator pepper is a black pepper reserved especially for kola; and the chalk is used for visitors to draw their personal mark.

"I have kola," he announced when he sat down, and passed the disc over to his guest.

"Thank you. He who brings kola brings life. But I think you ought to break it," replied Okoye, passing back the disc.

"No, it is for you, I think," and they argued like this for a few moments before Unoka accepted the honor of breaking the kola. Okoye, meanwhile, took the lump of chalk, drew some lines on the floor, and then painted his big toe.

As he broke the kola, Unoka prayed to their ancestors for life and health, and for protection against their enemies. When they had eaten they talked about many things: about the heavy rains which were drowning the yams, about the next ancestral feast and about the impending war with the village of Mbaino. Unoka was never happy when it came to wars. He was in fact a coward and could not bear the sight of blood. And so he changed the subject and talked about music, and his face beamed. He could hear in his mind's ear the blood-stirring and intricate rhythms of the *ekwe* and the *udu* and the *ogene*,[5] and he could hear his own flute weaving in and out of them, decorating them with a colorful and plaintive tune. The total effect was gay and brisk, but if one picked out the flute as it went up and down and then broke up into short snatches, one saw that there was sorrow and grief there.

Okoye was also a musician. He played on the *ogene*. But he was not a failure like Unoka. He had a large barn full of yams and he had three wives. And now he was going to take the Idemili[6] title, the third highest in the land. It was a very expensive ceremony and he was gathering all his resources together. That was in fact the reason why he had come to see Unoka. He cleared his throat and began:

"Thank you for the kola. You may have heard of the title I intend to take shortly."

Having spoken plainly so far, Okoye said the next half a dozen sentences in proverbs. Among the Ibo the art of conversation is regarded very highly, and proverbs are the palm-oil with which words are eaten. Okoye was a great talker and he spoke for a long time, skirting round the subject and then hitting it finally. In short, he was asking Unoka to return the two hundred cowries he had borrowed from him more than two years before. As soon as Unoka understood what his friend was driving at, he burst out laughing. He laughed loud and long and his voice rang out clear as the *ogene*, and tears stood in his eyes. His visitor was amazed, and sat speechless. At the end, Unoka was able to give an answer between fresh outbursts of mirth.

"Look at that wall," he said, pointing at the far wall of his hut, which was rubbed with red earth so that it shone. "Look at those lines of chalk"; and Okoye saw groups of short perpendicular lines drawn in chalk. There were five groups, and the smallest group had ten lines. Unoka had a sense of the dramatic and so he allowed a pause, in which he took a pinch of snuff and sneezed noisily, and then he continued: "Each group there represents a debt to someone, and each stroke is one hundred cowries. You see, I owe that man a thousand cowries. But he has not come to wake me up in

---

[5] *ekwe . . . ogene:* A wooden drum, clay drum, and iron gong, respectively.

[6] **Idemili:** A river god, associated with the sacred python.

the morning for it. I shall pay you, but not today. Our elders say that the sun will shine on those who stand before it shines on those who kneel under them. I shall pay my big debts first." And he took another pinch of snuff, as if that was paying the big debts first. Okoye rolled his goatskin and departed.

When Unoka died he had taken no title at all and he was heavily in debt. Any wonder then that his son Okonkwo was ashamed of him? Fortunately, among these people a man was judged according to his worth and not according to the worth of his father. Okonkwo was clearly cut out for great things. He was still young but he had won fame as the greatest wrestler in the nine villages. He was a wealthy farmer and had two barns full of yams, and had just married his third wife. To crown it all he had taken two titles and had shown incredible prowess in two inter-tribal wars. And so although Okonkwo was still young, he was already one of the greatest men of his time. Age was respected among his people, but achievement was revered. As the elders said, if a child washed his hands he could eat with kings. Okonkwo had clearly washed his hands and so he ate with kings and elders. And that was how he came to look after the doomed lad who was sacrificed to the village of Umuofia by their neighbors to avoid war and bloodshed. The ill-fated lad was called Ikemefuna.

2

Okonkwo had just blown out the palm-oil lamp and stretched himself on his bamboo bed when he heard the *ogene* of the town crier piercing the still night air. *Gome, gome, gome, gome,* boomed the hollow metal. Then the crier gave his message, and at the end of it beat his instrument again. And this was the message. Every man of Umuofia was asked to gather at the market place tomorrow morning. Okonkwo wondered what was amiss, for he knew certainly that something was amiss. He had discerned a clear overtone of tragedy in the crier's voice, and even now he could still hear it as it grew dimmer and dimmer in the distance.

The night was very quiet. It was always quiet except on moonlight nights. Darkness held a vague terror for these people, even the bravest among them. Children were warned not to whistle at night for fear of evil spirits. Dangerous animals became even more sinister and uncanny in the dark. A snake was never called by its name at night, because it would hear. It was called a string. And so on this particular night as the crier's voice was gradually swallowed up in the distance, silence returned to the world, a vibrant silence made more intense by the universal trill of a million million forest insects.

On a moonlight night it would be different. The happy voices of children playing in open fields would then be heard. And perhaps those not so young would be playing in pairs in less open places, and old men and women would remember their youth. As the Ibo say: "When the moon is shining the cripple becomes hungry for a walk."

But this particular night was dark and silent. And in all the nine villages of Umuofia a town crier with his *ogene* asked every man to be present tomorrow morning. Okonkwo on his bamboo bed tried to figure out the nature of the emergency—war with a neighboring clan? That seemed the most likely reason, and he was not afraid of war. He was a man of action, a man of war. Unlike his father he could stand the look of blood. In Umuofia's latest war he was the first to bring home a human head. That was his fifth head; and he was not an old man yet. On great occasions such as the funeral of a village celebrity he drank his palm-wine from his first human head.

In the morning the market place was full. There must have been about ten thousand men there, all talking in low voices. At last Ogbuefi Ezeugo stood up in the midst of them and bellowed four times, *"Umuofia kwenu,"*[7] and on each occasion he faced a different direction and seemed to push the air with a clenched fist. And ten thousand men answered *"Yaa!"* each time. Then there was perfect silence. Ogbuefi Ezeugo was a powerful orator and was always chosen to speak on such occasions. He moved his hand over his white head and stroked his white beard. He then adjusted his cloth, which was passed under his right armpit and tied above his left shoulder.

"Umuofia kwenu," he bellowed a fifth time, and the crowd yelled in answer. And then suddenly like one possessed he shot out his left hand and pointed in the direction of Mbaino, and said through gleaming white teeth firmly clenched: "Those sons of wild animals have dared to murder a daughter of Umuofia." He threw his head down and gnashed his teeth, and allowed a murmur of suppressed anger to sweep the crowd. When he began again, the anger on his face was gone and in its place a sort of smile hovered, more terrible and more sinister than the anger. And in a clear unemotional voice he told Umuofia how their daughter had gone to market at Mbaino and had been killed. That woman, said Ezeugo, was the wife of Ogbuefi Udo, and he pointed to a man who sat near him with a bowed head. The crowd then shouted with anger and thirst for blood.

Many others spoke, and at the end it was decided to follow the normal course of action. An ultimatum was immediately dispatched to Mbaino asking them to choose between war on the one hand, and on the other the offer of a young man and a virgin as compensation.

Umuofia was feared by all its neighbors. It was powerful in war and in magic, and its priests and medicine men were feared in all the surrounding country. Its most potent war-medicine was as old as the clan itself. Nobody knew how old. But on one point there was general agreement—the active principle in that medicine had been an old woman with one leg. In fact, the medicine itself was called *agadi-nwayi*, or old woman. It had its shrine in the centre of Umuofia, in a cleared spot. And if anybody was so foolhardy as to pass by the shrine after dusk he was sure to see the old woman hopping about.

And so the neighboring clans who naturally knew of these things feared Umuofia, and would not go to war against it without first trying a peaceful settlement. And in fairness to Umuofia it should be recorded that it never went to war unless its case was clear and just and was accepted as such by its Oracle—the Oracle of the Hills and the Caves. And there were indeed occasions when the Oracle had

---

[7] *"Umuofia kwenu"*: "Umuofia united."

forbidden Umuofia to wage a war. If the clan had disobeyed the Oracle they would surely have been beaten, because their dreaded *agadi-nwayi* would never fight what the Ibo call a *fight of blame*.

But the war that now threatened was a just war. Even the enemy clan knew that. And so when Okonkwo of Umuofia arrived at Mbaino as the proud and imperious emissary of war, he was treated with great honor and respect, and two days later he returned home with a lad of fifteen and a young virgin. The lad's name was Ikemefuna, whose sad story is still told in Umuofia unto this day.

The elders, or *ndichie,* met to hear a report of Okonkwo's mission. At the end they decided, as everybody knew they would, that the girl should go to Ogbuefi Udo to replace his murdered wife. As for the boy, he belonged to the clan as a whole, and there was no hurry to decide his fate. Okonkwo was, therefore, asked on behalf of the clan to look after him in the interim. And so for three years Ikemefuna lived in Okonkwo's household.

Okonkwo ruled his household with a heavy hand. His wives, especially the youngest, lived in perpetual fear of his fiery temper, and so did his little children. Perhaps down in his heart Okonkwo was not a cruel man. But his whole life was dominated by fear, the fear of failure and of weakness. It was deeper and more intimate than the fear of evil and capricious gods and of magic, the fear of the forest, and of the forces of nature, malevolent, red in tooth and claw. Okonkwo's fear was greater than these. It was not external but lay deep within himself. It was the fear of himself, lest he should be found to resemble his father. Even as a little boy he had resented his father's failure and weakness, and even now he still remembered how he had suffered when a playmate had told him that his father was *agbala*. That was how Okonkwo first came to know that *agbala* was not only another name for a woman, it could also mean a man who had taken no title. And so Okonkwo was ruled by one passion—to hate everything that his father Unoka had loved. One of those things was gentleness and another was idleness.

During the planting season Okonkwo worked daily on his farms from cockcrow until the chickens went to roost. He was a very strong man and rarely felt fatigue. But his wives and young children were not as strong, and so they suffered. But they dared not complain openly. Okonkwo's first son, Nwoye, was then twelve years old but was already causing his father great anxiety for his incipient laziness. At any rate, that was how it looked to his father, and he sought to correct him by constant nagging and beating. And so Nwoye was developing into a sad-faced youth.

Okonkwo's prosperity was visible in his household. He had a large compound enclosed by a thick wall of red earth. His own hut, or *obi,* stood immediately behind the only gate in the red walls. Each of his three wives had her own hut, which together formed a half moon behind the *obi.* The barn was built against one end of the red walls, and long stacks of yam stood out prosperously in it. At the opposite end of the compound was a shed for the goats, and each wife built a small attachment to her hut for the hens. Near the barn was a small house, the "medicine house" or shrine where Okonkwo kept the wooden symbols of his personal god and of his ancestral spirits. He worshipped them with sacrifices of kola nut, food, and palm-wine, and offered prayers to them on behalf of himself, his three wives and eight children. So when the daughter of Umuofia was killed in Mbaino, Ikemefuna came into Okonkwo's household. When Okonkwo brought him home that day he called his most senior wife and handed him over to her.

"He belongs to the clan," he told her. "So look after him."

"Is he staying long with us?" she asked.

"Do what you are told, woman," Okonkwo thundered, and stammered. "When did you become one of the *ndichie* of Umuofia?"

And so Nwoye's mother took Ikemefuna to her hut and asked no more questions.

As for the boy himself, he was terribly afraid. He could not understand what was happening to him or what he had done. How could he know that his father had taken a hand in killing a daughter of Umuofia? All he knew was that a few men had arrived at their house, conversing with his father in low tones, and at the end he had been taken out and handed over to a stranger. His mother had wept bitterly, but he had been too surprised to weep. And so the stranger had brought him, and a girl, a long, long way from home, through lonely forest paths. He did not know who the girl was, and he never saw her again.

3

Okonkwo did not have the start in life which many young men usually had. He did not inherit a barn from his father. There was no barn to inherit. The story was told in Umuofia, of how his father, Unoka, had gone to consult the Oracle of the Hills and the Caves to find out why he always had a miserable harvest.

The Oracle was called Agbala, and people came from far and near to consult it. They came when misfortune dogged their steps or when they had a dispute with their neighbors. They came to discover what the future held for them or to consult the spirits of their departed fathers.

The way into the shrine was a round hole at the side of a hill, just a little bigger than the round opening into a henhouse. Worshippers and those who came to seek knowledge from the god crawled on their belly through the hole and found themselves in a dark, endless space in the presence of Agbala. No one had ever beheld Agbala, except his priestess. But no one who had ever crawled into his awful shrine had come out without the fear of his power. His priestess stood by the sacred fire which she built in the heart of the cave and proclaimed the will of the god. The fire did not burn with a flame. The glowing logs only served to light up vaguely the dark figure of the priestess.

Sometimes a man came to consult the spirit of his dead father or relative. It was said that when such a spirit appeared, the man saw it vaguely in the darkness, but never heard its voice. Some people even said that they had heard the spirits flying and flapping their wings against the roof of the cave.

Many years ago when Okonkwo was still a boy his father, Unoka, had gone to consult Agbala. The priestess in those days was a woman called Chika. She was full of the power of her god, and she was greatly feared. Unoka stood before her and began his story.

"Every year," he said sadly, "before I put any crop in the earth, I sacrifice a cock to Ani, the owner of all land. It is the law of our fathers. I also kill a cock at the shrine of Ifejioku, the god of yams. I clear the bush and set fire to it when it is dry. I sow the yams when the first rain has fallen, and stake them when the young tendrils appear. I weed—"

"Hold your peace!" screamed the priestess, her voice terrible as it echoed through the dark void. "You have offended neither the gods nor your fathers. And when a man is at peace with his gods and his ancestors, his harvest will be good or bad according to the strength of his arm. You, Unoka, are known in all the clan for the weakness of your machete and your hoe. When your neighbors go out with their ax to cut down virgin forests, you sow your yams on exhausted farms that take no labor to clear. They cross seven rivers to make their farms; you stay at home and offer sacrifices to a reluctant soil. Go home and work like a man."

Unoka was an ill-fated man. He had a bad *chi*[8] or personal god, and evil fortune followed him to the grave, or rather to his death, for he had no grave. He died of the swelling which was an abomination to the earth goddess. When a man was afflicted with swelling in the stomach and the limbs he was not allowed to die in the house. He was carried to the Evil Forest and left there to die. There was the story of a very stubborn man who staggered back to his house and had to be carried again to the forest and tied to a tree. The sickness was an abomination to the earth, and so the victim could not be buried in her bowels. He died and rotted away above the earth, and was not given the first or the second burial. Such was Unoka's fate. When they carried him away, he took with him his flute.

With a father like Unoka, Okonkwo did not have the start in life which many young men had. He neither inherited a barn nor a title, nor even a young wife. But in spite of these disadvantages, he had begun even in his father's lifetime to lay the foundations of a prosperous future. It was slow and painful. But he threw himself into it like one possessed. And indeed he was possessed by the fear of his father's contemptible life and shameful death.

There was a wealthy man in Okonkwo's village who had three huge barns, nine wives and thirty children. His name was Nwakibie and he had taken the highest but one title which a man could take in the clan. It was for this man that Okonkwo worked to earn his first seed yams.

He took a pot of palm-wine and a cock to Nwakibie. Two elderly neighbors were sent for, and Nwakibie's two grown-up sons were also present in his *obi*. He presented a kola nut and an alligator pepper, which were passed round for all to see and then returned to him. He broke the nut saying: "We shall all live. We pray for life, children, a good harvest, and happiness. You will have what is good for you and I will have what is good for me. Let the kite perch and let the eagle perch too. If one says no to the other, let his wing break."

---

[8] *chi:* Literally, one's personal god; the *chi* may be thought of as the spiritual double of the person existing in the world, which acts as a guide to the fulfillment of one's destiny. To act against the *chi* is to act against one's own best interests, as Okonkwo will do later when he kills Ikemefuna.

After the kola nut had been eaten Okonkwo brought his palm-wine from the corner of the hut where it had been placed and stood it in the center of the group. He addressed Nwakibie, calling him "Our father."

"*Nna ayi*,"[9] he said. "I have brought you this little kola. As our people say, a man who pays respect to the great paves the way for his own greatness. I have come to pay you my respects and also to ask a favor. But let us drink the wine first."

Everybody thanked Okonkwo and the neighbors brought out their drinking horns from the goatskin bags they carried. Nwakibie brought down his own horn, which was fastened to the rafters. The younger of his sons, who was also the youngest man in the group, moved to the center, raised the pot on his left knee and began to pour out the wine. The first cup went to Okonkwo, who must taste his wine before anyone else. Then the group drank, beginning with the eldest man. When everyone had drunk two or three horns, Nwakibie sent for his wives. Some of them were not at home and only four came in.

"Is Anasi not in?" he asked them. They said she was coming. Anasi was the first wife and the others could not drink before her, and so they stood waiting.

Anasi was a middle-aged woman, tall and strongly built. There was authority in her bearing and she looked every inch the ruler of the womenfolk in a large and prosperous family. She wore the anklet of her husband's titles, which the first wife alone could wear.

She walked up to her husband and accepted the horn from him. She then went down on one knee, drank a little, and handed back the horn. She rose, called him by his name and went back to her hut. The other wives drank in the same way, in their proper order, and went away.

The men then continued their drinking and talking. Ogbuefi Idigo was talking about the palm-wine tapper, Obiako, who suddenly gave up his trade.

"There must be something behind it," he said, wiping the foam of wine from his mustache with the back of his left hand. "There must be a reason for it. A toad does not run in the daytime for nothing."

"Some people say the Oracle warned him that he would fall off a palm tree and kill himself," said Akukalia.

"Obiako has always been a strange one," said Nwakibie. "I have heard that many years ago, when his father had not been dead very long, he had gone to consult the Oracle. The Oracle said to him, 'Your dead father wants you to sacrifice a goat to him.' Do you know what he told the Oracle? He said, 'Ask my dead father if he ever had a fowl when he was alive.'" Everybody laughed heartily except Okonkwo, who laughed uneasily because, as the saying goes, an old woman is always uneasy when dry bones are mentioned in a proverb. Okonkwo remembered his own father.

At last the young man who was pouring out the wine held up half a horn of the thick, white dregs and said, "What we are eating is finished." "We have seen it," the others replied. "Who will drink the dregs?" he asked. "Whoever has a job in hand," said Idigo, looking at Nwakibie's elder son Igwelo with a malicious twinkle in his eye.

---

[9] "*Nna ayi*": "Our father."

Everybody agreed that Igwelo should drink the dregs. He accepted the half-full horn from his brother and drank it. As Idigo had said, Igwelo had a job in hand because he had married his first wife a month or two before. The thick dregs of palm-wine were supposed to be good for men who were going in to their wives.

After the wine had been drunk Okonkwo laid his difficulties before Nwakibie.

"I have come to you for help," he said. "Perhaps you can already guess what it is. I have cleared a farm but have no yams to sow. I know what it is to ask a man to trust another with his yams, especially these days when young men are afraid of hard work. I am not afraid of work. The lizard that jumped from the high iroko tree to the ground said he would praise himself if no one else did. I began to fend for myself at an age when most people still suck at their mothers' breasts. If you give me some yam seeds I shall not fail you."

Nwakibie cleared his throat. "It pleases me to see a young man like you these days when our youth has gone so soft. Many young men have come to me to ask for yams but I have refused because I knew they would just dump them in the earth and leave them to be choked by weeds. When I say no to them they think I am hard hearted. But it is not so. Eneke the bird says that since men have learned to shoot without missing, he has learned to fly without perching. I have learned to be stingy with my yams. But I can trust you. I know it as I look at you. As our fathers said, you can tell a ripe corn by its look. I shall give you twice four hundred yams. Go ahead and prepare your farm."

Okonkwo thanked him again and again and went home feeling happy. He knew that Nwakibie would not refuse him, but he had not expected he would be so generous. He had not hoped to get more than four hundred seeds. He would now have to make a bigger farm. He hoped to get another four hundred yams from one of his father's friends at Isiuzo.

Share-cropping was a very slow way of building up a barn of one's own. After all the toil one only got a third of the harvest. But for a young man whose father had no yams, there was no other way. And what made it worse in Okonkwo's case was that he had to support his mother and two sisters from his meagre harvest. And supporting his mother also meant supporting his father. She could not be expected to cook and eat while her husband starved. And so at a very early age when he was striving desperately to build a barn through share-cropping Okonkwo was also fending for his father's house. It was like pouring grains of corn into a bag full of holes. His mother and sisters worked hard enough, but they grew women's crops, like coco-yams, beans, and cassava. Yam, the king of crops, was a man's crop.

The year that Okonkwo took eight hundred seed-yams from Nwakibie was the worst year in living memory. Nothing happened at its proper time; it was either too early or too late. It seemed as if the world had gone mad. The first rains were late, and, when they came, lasted only a brief moment. The blazing sun returned, more fierce than it had ever been known, and scorched all the green that had appeared with the rains. The earth burned like hot coals and roasted all the yams that had been sown. Like all good farmers, Okonkwo had begun to sow with the first rains. He had sown four hundred seeds when the rains dried up and the heat returned. He watched the sky all day for signs of rain clouds and lay awake all night. In the morn-ing he went back to his farm and saw the withering tendrils. He had tried to protect them from the smoldering earth by making rings of thick sisal leaves around them. But by the end of the day the sisal rings were burned dry and gray. He changed them every day, and prayed that the rain might fall in the night. But the drought contin-ued for eight market weeks and the yams were killed.

Some farmers had not planted their yams yet. They were the lazy easy-going ones who always put off clearing their farms as long as they could. This year they were the wise ones. They sympathized with their neighbors with much shaking of the head, but inwardly they were happy for what they took to be their own foresight.

Okonkwo planted what was left of his seed-yams when the rains finally returned. He had one consolation. The yams he had sown before the drought were his own, the harvest of the previous year. He still had the eight hundred from Nwak-ibie and the four hundred from his father's friend. So he would make a fresh start.

But the year had gone mad. Rain fell as it had never fallen before. For days and nights together it poured down in violent torrents, and washed away the yam heaps. Trees were uprooted and deep gorges appeared everywhere. Then the rain became less violent. But it went from day to day without a pause. The spell of sunshine which always came in the middle of the wet season did not appear. The yams put on luxuri-ant green leaves, but every farmer knew that without sunshine the tubers would not grow.

That year the harvest was sad, like a funeral, and many farmers wept as they dug up the miserable and rotting yams. One man tied his cloth to a tree branch and hanged himself.

Okonkwo remembered that tragic year with a cold shiver throughout the rest of his life. It always surprised him when he thought of it later that he did not sink under the load of despair. He knew that he was a fierce fighter, but that year had been enough to break the heart of a lion.

"Since I survived that year," he always said, "I shall survive anything." He put it down to his inflexible will.

His father, Unoka, who was then an ailing man, had said to him during that terrible harvest month: "Do not despair. I know you will not despair. You have a manly and a proud heart. A proud heart can survive a general failure because such a failure does not prick its pride. It is more difficult and more bitter when a man fails *alone.*"

Unoka was like that in his last days. His love of talk had grown with age and sick-ness. It tried Okonkwo's patience beyond words.

4

"Looking at a king's mouth," said an old man, "one would think he never sucked at his mother's breast." He was talking about Okonkwo, who had risen so suddenly from great poverty and misfortune to be one of the lords of the clan. The old man bore no ill will towards Okonkwo. Indeed he respected him for his industry and suc-cess. But he was struck, as most people were, by Okonkwo's brusqueness in dealing with less successful men. Only a week ago a man had contradicted him at a kindred meeting which they held to discuss the next ancestral feast. Without looking at the man Okonkwo had said: "This meeting is for men." The man who had contradicted him had no titles. That was why he had called him a woman. Okonkwo knew how to kill a man's spirit.

Everybody at the kindred meeting took sides with Osugo when Okonkwo called him a woman. The oldest man present said sternly that those whose palm-kernels were cracked for them by a benevolent spirit should not forget to be humble. Okonkwo said he was sorry for what he had said, and the meeting continued.

But it was really not true that Okonkwo's palm-kernels had been cracked for him by a benevolent spirit. He had cracked them himself. Anyone who knew his grim struggle against poverty and misfortune could not say he had been lucky. If ever a man deserved his success, that man was Okonkwo. At an early age he had achieved fame as the greatest wrestler in all the land. That was not luck. At the most one could say that his *chi* or personal god was good. But the Ibo people have a proverb that when a man says yes his *chi* says yes also. Okonkwo said yes very strongly; so his *chi* agreed. And not only his *chi* but his clan too, because it judged a man by the work of his hands. That was why Okonkwo had been chosen by the nine villages to carry a message of war to their enemies unless they agreed to give up a young man and a virgin to atone for the murder of Udo's wife. And such was the deep fear that their enemies had for Umuofia that they treated Okonkwo like a king and brought him a virgin who was given to Udo as wife, and the lad Ikemefuna.

The elders of the clan had decided that Ikemefuna should be in Okonkwo's care for a while. But no one thought it would be as long as three years. They seemed to forget all about him as soon as they had taken the decision.

At first Ikemefuna was very much afraid. Once or twice he tried to run away, but he did not know where to begin. He thought of his mother and his three-year-old sister and wept bitterly. Nwoye's mother was very kind to him and treated him as one of her own children. But all he said was: "When shall I go home?" When Okonkwo heard that he would not eat any food he came into the hut with a big stick in his hand and stood over him while he swallowed his yams, trembling. A few moments later he went behind the hut and began to vomit painfully. Nwoye's mother went to him and placed her hands on his chest and on his back. He was ill for three market weeks, and when he recovered he seemed to have overcome his great fear and sadness.

He was by nature a very lively boy and he gradually became popular in Okonkwo's household, especially with the children. Okonkwo's son, Nwoye, who was two years younger, became quite inseparable from him because he seemed to know everything. He could fashion out flutes from bamboo stems and even from the elephant grass. He knew the names of all the birds and could set clever traps for the little bush rodents. And he knew which trees made the strongest bows.

Even Okonkwo himself became very fond of the boy—inwardly of course. Okonkwo never showed any emotion openly, unless it be the emotion of anger. To show affection was a sign of weakness; the only thing worth demonstrating was strength. He therefore treated Ikemefuna as he treated everybody else—with a heavy hand. But there was no doubt that he liked the boy. Sometimes when he went to big village meetings or communal ancestral feasts he allowed Ikemefuna to accompany him, like a son, carrying his stool and his goatskin bag. And, indeed, Ikemefuna called him father.

Ikemefuna came to Umuofia at the end of the carefree season between harvest and planting. In fact he recovered from his illness only a few days before the Week of Peace began. And that was also the year Okonkwo broke the peace, and was punished, as was the custom, by Ezeani, the priest of the earth goddess.

Okonkwo was provoked to justifiable anger by his youngest wife, who went to plait her hair at her friend's house and did not return early enough to cook the afternoon meal. Okonkwo did not know at first that she was not at home. After waiting in vain for her dish he went to her hut to see what she was doing. There was nobody in the hut and the fireplace was cold.

"Where is Ojiugo?" he asked his second wife, who came out of her hut to draw water from a gigantic pot in the shade of a small tree in the middle of the compound.

"She has gone to plait her hair."

Okonkwo bit his lips as anger welled up within him.

"Where are her children? Did she take them?" he asked with unusual coolness and restraint.

"They are here," answered his first wife, Nwoye's mother. Okonkwo bent down and looked into her hut. Ojiugo's children were eating with the children of his first wife.

"Did she ask you to feed them before she went?"

"Yes," lied Nwoye's mother, trying to minimize Ojiugo's thoughtlessness.

Okonkwo knew she was not speaking the truth. He walked back to his *obi* to await Ojiugo's return. And when she returned he beat her very heavily. In his anger he had forgotten that it was the Week of Peace. His first two wives ran out in great alarm pleading with him that it was the sacred week. But Okonkwo was not the man to stop beating somebody half-way through, not even for fear of a goddess.

Okonkwo's neighbors heard his wife crying and sent their voices over the compound walls to ask what was the matter. Some of them came over to see for themselves. It was unheard of to beat somebody during the sacred week.

Before it was dusk Ezeani, who was the priest of the earth goddess, Ani, called on Okonkwo in his *obi*. Okonkwo brought out kola nut and placed it before the priest.

"Take away your kola nut. I shall not eat in the house of a man who has no respect for our gods and ancestors."

Okonkwo tried to explain to him what his wife had done, but Ezeani seemed to pay no attention. He held a short staff in his hand which he brought down on the floor to emphasize his points.

"Listen to me," he said when Okonkwo had spoken. "You are not a stranger in Umuofia. You know as well as I do that our forefathers ordained that before we plant any crops in the earth we should observe a week in which a man does not say a harsh word to his neighbor. We live in peace with our fellows to honor our great goddess of the earth without whose blessing our crops will not grow. You have committed a great evil." He brought down his staff heavily on the floor. "Your wife was at fault, but even if you came into your *obi* and found her lover on top of her, you would still have committed a great evil to beat her." His staff came down again. "The evil you have done can ruin the whole clan. The earth goddess whom you have insulted may refuse to give us her increase, and we shall all perish." His tone now changed from anger to command. "You will bring to the shrine of Ani tomorrow one she-goat, one hen, a length of cloth, and a hundred cowries." He rose and left the hut.

Okonkwo did as the priest said. He also took with him a pot of palm-wine. Inwardly, he was repentant. But he was not the man to go about telling his neighbors that he was in error. And so people said he had no respect for the gods of the clan. His enemies said his good fortune had gone to his head. They called him the little bird *nza* who so far forgot himself after a heavy meal that he challenged his *chi*.

No work was done during the Week of Peace. People called on their neighbors and drank palm-wine. This year they talked of nothing else but the *nso-ani*[10] which Okonkwo had committed. It was the first time for many years that a man had broken the sacred peace. Even the oldest men could only remember one or two other occasions somewhere in the dim past.

Ogbuefi Ezeudu, who was the oldest man in the village, was telling two other men who came to visit him that the punishment for breaking the Peace of Ani had become very mild in their clan.

"It has not always been so," he said. "My father told me that he had been told that in the past a man who broke the peace was dragged on the ground through the village until he died. But after a while this custom was stopped because it spoiled the peace which it was meant to preserve."

"Somebody told me yesterday," said one of the younger men, "that in some clans it is an abomination for a man to die during the Week of Peace."

"It is indeed true," said Ogbuefi Ezeudu. "They have that custom in Obodoani. If a man dies at this time he is not buried but cast into the Evil Forest. It is a bad custom which these people observe because they lack understanding. They throw away large numbers of men and women without burial. And what is the result? Their clan is full of the evil spirits of these unburied dead, hungry to do harm to the living."

After the Week of Peace every man and his family began to clear the bush to make new farms. The cut bush was left to dry and fire was then set to it. As the smoke rose into the sky kites appeared from different directions and hovered over the burning field in silent valediction. The rainy season was approaching when they would go away until the dry season returned.

Okonkwo spent the next few days preparing his seed-yams. He looked at each yam carefully to see whether it was good for sowing. Sometimes he decided that a yam was too big to be sown as one seed and he split it deftly along its length with his sharp knife. His eldest son, Nwoye, and Ikemefuna helped him by fetching the yams in long baskets from the barn and in counting the prepared seeds in groups of four

---

[10] *nso-ani:* "Earth's taboo," a serious offense against the earth goddess Ani.

hundred. Sometimes Okonkwo gave them a few yams each to prepare. But he always found fault with their effort, and he said so with much threatening.

"Do you think you are cutting up yams for cooking?" he asked Nwoye. "If you split another yam of this size, I shall break your jaw. You think you are still a child. I began to own a farm at your age. And you," he said to Ikemefuna, "do you not grow yams where you come from?"

Inwardly Okonkwo knew that the boys were still too young to understand fully the difficult art of preparing seed-yams. But he thought that one could not begin too early. Yam stood for manliness, and he who could feed his family on yams from one harvest to another was a very great man indeed. Okonkwo wanted his son to be a great farmer and a great man. He would stamp out the disquieting signs of laziness which he thought he already saw in him.

"I will not have a son who cannot hold up his head in the gathering of the clan. I would sooner strangle him with my own hands. And if you stand staring at me like that," he swore, "Amadiora[11] will break your head for you!"

Some days later, when the land had been moistened by two or three heavy rains, Okonkwo and his family went to the farm with baskets of seed-yams, their hoes and machetes, and the planting began. They made single mounds of earth in straight lines all over the field and sowed the yams in them.

Yam, the king of crops, was a very exacting king. For three or four moons it demanded hard work and constant attention from cock-crow till the chickens went back to roost. The young tendrils were protected from earth-heat with rings of sisal leaves. As the rains became heavier the women planted maize, melons, and beans between the yam mounds. The yams were then staked, first with little sticks and later with tall and big tree branches. The women weeded the farm three times at definite periods in the life of the yams, neither early nor late.

And now the rains had really come, so heavy and persistent that even the village rain-maker no longer claimed to be able to intervene. He could not stop the rain now, just as he would not attempt to start it in the heart of the dry season, without serious danger to his own health. The personal dynamism required to counter the forces of these extremes of weather would be far too great for the human frame.

And so nature was not interfered with in the middle of the rainy season. Sometimes it poured down in such thick sheets of water that earth and sky seemed merged in one gray wetness. It was then uncertain whether the low rumbling of Amadiora's thunder came from above or below. At such times, in each of the countless thatched huts of Umuofia, children sat around their mother's cooking fire telling stories, or with their father in his *obi* warming themselves from a log fire, roasting and eating maize. It was a brief resting period between the exacting and arduous planting season and the equally exacting but light-hearted month of harvests.

Ikemefuna had begun to feel like a member of Okonkwo's family. He still thought about his mother and his three-year-old sister, and he had moments of sadness and

---

[11]**Amadiora:** The god of thunder and lightning.

depression. But he and Nwoye had become so deeply attached to each other that such moments became less frequent and less poignant. Ikemefuna had an endless stock of folk tales. Even those which Nwoye knew already were told with a new freshness and the local flavor of a different clan. Nwoye remembered this period very vividly till the end of his life. He even remembered how he had laughed when Ikemefuna told him that the proper name for a corn cob with only a few scattered grains was *eze-agadi-nwayi,* or the teeth of an old woman. Nwoye's mind had gone immediately to Nwayieke, who lived near the udala tree. She had about three teeth and was always smoking her pipe.

Gradually the rains became lighter and less frequent, and earth and sky once again became separate. The rain fell in thin, slanting showers through sunshine and quiet breeze. Children no longer stayed indoors but ran about singing:

> *"The rain is falling, the sun is shining,*
> *Alone Nnadi is cooking and eating."*

Nwoye always wondered who Nnadi was and why he should live all by himself, cooking and eating. In the end he decided that Nnadi must live in that land of Ikemefuna's favorite story where the ant holds his court in splendor and the sands dance forever.

5

The Feast of the New Yam was approaching and Umuofia was in a festival mood. It was an occasion for giving thanks to Ani, the earth goddess and the source of all fertility. Ani played a greater part in the life of the people than any other deity. She was the ultimate judge of morality and conduct. And what was more, she was in close communion with the departed fathers of the clan whose bodies had been committed to earth.

The Feast of the New Yam was held every year before the harvest began, to honor the earth goddess and the ancestral spirits of the clan. New yams could not be eaten until some had first been offered to these powers. Men and women, young and old, looked forward to the New Yam Festival because it began the season of plenty—the new year. On the last night before the festival, yams of the old year were all disposed of by those who still had them. The new year must begin with tasty, fresh yams and not the shriveled and fibrous crop of the previous year. All cooking pots, calabashes, and wooden bowls were thoroughly washed, especially the wooden mortar in which yam was pounded. Yam foo-foo and vegetable soup was the chief food in the celebration. So much of it was cooked that, no matter how heavily the family ate or how many friends and relatives they invited from neighboring villages, there was always a large quantity of food left over at the end of the day. The story was always told of a wealthy man who set before his guests a mound of foo-foo so high that those who sat on one side could not see what was happening on the other, and it was not until late in the evening that one of them saw for the first time his in-law who had arrived during the course of the meal and had fallen to on the opposite side. It was only then that they exchanged greetings and shook hands over what was left of the food.

The New Yam Festival was thus an occasion for joy throughout Umuofia. And every man whose arm was strong, as the Ibo people say, was expected to invite large numbers of guests from far and wide. Okonkwo always asked his wives' relations, and since he now had three wives his guests would make a fairly big crowd.

But somehow Okonkwo could never become as enthusiastic over feasts as most people. He was a good eater and he could drink one or two fairly big gourds of palm-wine. But he was always uncomfortable sitting around for days waiting for a feast or getting over it. He would be very much happier working on his farm.

The festival was now only three days away. Okonkwo's wives had scrubbed the walls and the huts with red earth until they reflected light. They had then drawn patterns on them in white, yellow, and dark green. They then set about painting themselves with cam wood and drawing beautiful black patterns on their stomachs and on their backs. The children were also decorated, especially their hair, which was shaved in beautiful patterns. The three women talked excitedly about the relations who had been invited, and the children reveled in the thought of being spoiled by these visitors from the motherland. Ikemefuna was equally excited. The New Yam Festival seemed to him to be a much bigger event here than in his own village, a place which was already becoming remote and vague in his imagination.

And then the storm burst. Okonkwo, who had been walking about aimlessly in his compound in suppressed anger, suddenly found an outlet.

"Who killed this banana tree?" he asked.

A hush fell on the compound immediately.

"Who killed this tree? Or are you all deaf and dumb?"

As a matter of fact the tree was very much alive. Okonkwo's second wife had merely cut a few leaves off it to wrap some food, and she said so. Without further argument Okonkwo gave her a sound beating and left her and her only daughter weeping. Neither of the other wives dared to interfere beyond an occasional and tentative, "It is enough, Okonkwo," pleaded from a reasonable distance.

His anger thus satisfied, Okonkwo decided to go out hunting. He had an old rusty gun made by a clever blacksmith who had come to live in Umuofia long ago. But although Okonkwo was a great man whose prowess was universally acknowledged, he was not a hunter. In fact he had not killed a rat with his gun. And so when he called Ikemefuna to fetch his gun, the wife who had just been beaten murmured something about guns that never shot. Unfortunately for her, Okonkwo heard it and ran madly into his room for the loaded gun, ran out again and aimed at her as she clambered over the dwarf wall of the barn. He pressed the trigger and there was a loud report accompanied by the wail of his wives and children. He threw down the gun and jumped into the barn, and there lay the woman, very much shaken and frightened but quite unhurt. He heaved a heavy sigh and went away with the gun.

In spite of this incident the New Yam Festival was celebrated with great joy in Okonkwo's household. Early that morning as he offered a sacrifice of new yam and palm-oil to his ancestors he asked them to protect him, his children, and their mothers in the new year.

As the day wore on his in-laws arrived from three surrounding villages, and each party brought with them a huge pot of palm-wine. And there was eating and drinking till night, when Okonkwo's in-laws began to leave for their homes.

The second day of the new year was the day of the great wrestling match between Okonkwo's village and their neighbors. It was difficult to say which the people enjoyed more—the feasting and fellowship of the first day or the wrestling contest of the second. But there was one woman who had no doubt whatever in her mind. She was Okonkwo's second wife, Ekwefi, whom he nearly shot. There was no festival in all the seasons of the year which gave her as much pleasure as the wrestling match. Many years ago when she was the village beauty Okonkwo had won her heart by throwing the Cat in the greatest contest within living memory. She did not marry him then because he was too poor to pay her bride-price. But a few years later she ran away from her husband and came to live with Okonkwo. All this happened many years ago. Now Ekwefi was a woman of forty-five who had suffered a great deal in her time. But her love of wrestling contests was still as strong as it was thirty years ago.

It was not yet noon on the second day of the New Yam Festival. Ekwefi and her only daughter, Ezinma, sat near the fireplace waiting for the water in the pot to boil. The fowl Ekwefi had just killed was in the wooden mortar. The water began to boil, and in one deft movement she lifted the pot from the fire and poured the boiling water over the fowl. She put back the empty pot on the circular pad in the corner, and looked at her palms, which were black with soot. Ezinma was always surprised that her mother could lift a pot from the fire with her bare hands.

"Ekwefi," she said, "is it true that when people are grown up, fire does not burn them?" Ezinma, unlike most children, called her mother by her name.

"Yes," replied Ekwefi, too busy to argue. Her daughter was only ten years old but she was wiser than her years.

"But Nwoye's mother dropped her pot of hot soup the other day and it broke on the floor."

Ekwefi turned the hen over in the mortar and began to pluck the feathers.

"Ekwefi," said Ezinma, who had joined in plucking the feathers, "my eyelid is twitching."

"It means you are going to cry," said her mother.

"No," Ezinma said, "it is this eyelid, the top one."

"That means you will see something."

"What will I see?" she asked.

"How can I know?" Ekwefi wanted her to work it out herself.

"Oho," said Ezinma at last. "I know what it is—the wrestling match."

At last the hen was plucked clean. Ekwefi tried to pull out the horny beak but it was too hard. She turned round on her low stool and put the beak in the fire for a few moments. She pulled again and it came off.

"Ekwefi!" a voice called from one of the other huts. It was Nwoye's mother, Okonkwo's first wife.

"Is that me?" Ekwefi called back. That was the way people answered calls from outside. They never answered yes for fear it might be an evil spirit calling.

"Will you give Ezinma some fire to bring to me?" Her own children and Ikemefuna had gone to the stream.

Ekwefi put a few live coals into a piece of broken pot and Ezinma carried it across the clean swept compound to Nwoye's mother.

"Thank you, Nma," she said. She was peeling new yams, and in a basket beside her were green vegetables and beans.

"Let me make the fire for you," Ezinma offered.

"Thank you, Ezigbo," she said. She often called her Ezigbo, which means "the good one."

Ezinma went outside and brought some sticks from a huge bundle of firewood. She broke them into little pieces across the sole of her foot and began to build a fire, blowing it with her breath.

"You will blow your eyes out," said Nwoye's mother, looking up from the yams she was peeling. "Use the fan." She stood up and pulled out the fan which was fastened into one of the rafters. As soon as she got up, the troublesome nanny-goat, which had been dutifully eating yam peelings, dug her teeth into the real thing, scooped out two mouthfuls and fled from the hut to chew the cud in the goats' shed. Nwoye's mother swore at her and settled down again to her peeling. Ezinma's fire was now sending up thick clouds of smoke. She went on fanning it until it burst into flames. Nwoye's mother thanked her and she went back to her mother's hut.

Just then the distant beating of drums began to reach them. It came from the direction of the *ilo*, the village playground. Every village had its own *ilo* which was as old as the village itself and where all the great ceremonies and dances took place. The drums beat the unmistakable wrestling dance—quick, light, and gay, and it came floating on the wind.

Okonkwo cleared his throat and moved his feet to the beat of the drums. It filled him with fire as it had always done from his youth. He trembled with the desire to conquer and subdue. It was like the desire for woman.

"We shall be late for the wrestling," said Ezinma to her mother.

"They will not begin until the sun goes down."

"But they are beating the drums."

"Yes. The drums begin at noon but the wrestling waits until the sun begins to sink. Go and see if your father has brought out yams for the afternoon."

"He has. Nwoye's mother is already cooking."

"Go and bring our own, then. We must cook quickly or we shall be late for the wrestling."

Ezinma ran in the direction of the barn and brought back two yams from the dwarf wall.

Ekwefi peeled the yams quickly. The troublesome nanny-goat sniffed about, eating the peelings. She cut the yams into small pieces and began to prepare a pottage, using some of the chicken.

At that moment they heard someone crying just outside their compound. It was very much like Obiageli, Nwoye's sister.

"Is that not Obiageli weeping?" Ekwefi called across the yard to Nwoye's mother.

"Yes," she replied. "She must have broken her water-pot."

The weeping was now quite close and soon the children filed in, carrying on their heads various sizes of pots suitable to their years. Ikemefuna came first with the biggest pot, closely followed by Nwoye and his two younger brothers. Obiageli brought up the rear, her face streaming with tears. In her hand was the cloth pad on which the pot should have rested on her head.

"What happened?" her mother asked, and Obiageli told her mournful story. Her mother consoled her and promised to buy her another pot.

Nwoye's younger brothers were about to tell their mother the true story of the accident when Ikemefuna looked at them sternly and they held their peace. The fact was that Obiageli had been making *inyanga*[12] with her pot. She had balanced it on her head, folded her arms in front of her, and began to sway her waist like a grown-up young lady. When the pot fell down and broke she burst out laughing. She only began to weep when they got near the iroko tree outside their compound.

The drums were still beating, persistent and unchanging. Their sound was no longer a separate thing from the living village. It was like the pulsation of its heart. It throbbed in the air, in the sunshine, and even in the trees, and filled the village with excitement.

Ekwefi ladled her husband's share of the pottage into a bowl and covered it. Ezinma took it to him in his *obi*.

Okonkwo was sitting on a goatskin already eating his first wife's meal. Obiageli, who had brought it from her mother's hut, sat on the floor waiting for him to finish. Ezinma placed her mother's dish before him and sat with Obiageli.

"Sit like a woman!" Okonkwo shouted at her. Ezinma brought her two legs together and stretched them in front of her.

"Father, will you go to see the wrestling?" Ezinma asked after a suitable interval.

"Yes," he answered. "Will you go?"

"Yes." And after a pause she said: "Can I bring your chair for you?"

"No, that is a boy's job." Okonkwo was specially fond of Ezinma. She looked very much like her mother, who was once the village beauty. But his fondness only showed on very rare occasions.

"Obiageli broke her pot today," Ezinma said.

"Yes, she has told me about it," Okonkwo said between mouthfuls.

"Father," said Obiageli, "people should not talk when they are eating or pepper may go down the wrong way."

"That is very true. Do you hear that, Ezinma? You are older than Obiageli but she has more sense."

He uncovered his second wife's dish and began to eat from it. Obiageli took the first dish and returned to her mother's hut. And then Nkechi came in, bringing the third dish. Nkechi was the daughter of Okonkwo's third wife.

In the distance the drums continued to beat.

6

The whole village turned out on the *ilo*, men, women, and children. They stood round in a huge circle leaving the center of the playground free. The elders and grandees of the village sat on their own stools brought there by their young sons or slaves. Okonkwo was among them. All others stood except those who came early

---

[12] *inyanga:* Bragging or showing off.

enough to secure places on the few stands which had been built by placing smooth logs on forked pillars.

The wrestlers were not there yet and the drummers held the field. They too sat just in front of the huge circle of spectators, facing the elders. Behind them was the big and ancient silk-cotton tree which was sacred. Spirits of good children lived in that tree waiting to be born. On ordinary days young women who desired children came to sit under its shade.

There were seven drums and they were arranged according to their sizes in a long wooden basket. Three men beat them with sticks, working feverishly from one drum to another. They were possessed by the spirit of the drums.

The young men who kept order on these occasions dashed about, consulting among themselves and with the leaders of the two wrestling teams, who were still outside the circle, behind the crowd. Once in a while two young men carrying palm fronds ran round the circle and kept the crowd back by beating the ground in front of them or, if they were stubborn, their legs and feet.

At last the two teams danced into the circle and the crowd roared and clapped. The drums rose to a frenzy. The people surged forward. The young men who kept order flew around, waving their palm fronds. Old men nodded to the beat of the drums and remembered the days when they wrestled to its intoxicating rhythm.

The contest began with boys of fifteen or sixteen. There were only three such boys in each team. They were not the real wrestlers; they merely set the scene. Within a short time the first two bouts were over. But the third created a big sensation even among the elders who did not usually show their excitement so openly. It was as quick as the other two, perhaps even quicker. But very few people had ever seen that kind of wrestling before. As soon as the two boys closed in, one of them did something which no one could describe because it had been as quick as a flash. And the other boy was flat on his back. The crowd roared and clapped and for a while drowned the frenzied drums. Okonkwo sprang to his feet and quickly sat down again. Three young men from the victorious boy's team ran forward, carried him shoulder high, and danced through the cheering crowd. Everybody soon knew who the boy was. His name was Maduka, the son of Obierika.

The drummers stopped for a brief rest before the real matches. Their bodies shone with sweat, and they took up fans and began to fan themselves. They also drank water from small pots and ate kola nuts. They became ordinary human beings again, talking and laughing among themselves and with others who stood near them. The air, which had been stretched taut with excitement, relaxed again. It was as if water had been poured on the tightened skin of a drum. Many people looked around, perhaps for the first time, and saw those who stood or sat next to them.

"I did not know it was you," Ekwefi said to the woman who had stood shoulder to shoulder with her since the beginning of the matches.

"I do not blame you," said the woman. "I have never seen such a large crowd of people. Is it true that Okonkwo nearly killed you with his gun?"

"It is true indeed, my dear friend. I cannot yet find a mouth with which to tell the story."

"Your *chi* is very much awake, my friend. And how is my daughter, Ezinma?"

"She has been very well for some time now. Perhaps she has come to stay."

"I think she has. How old is she now?"

"She is about ten years old."

"I think she will stay. They usually stay if they do not die before the age of six."

"I pray she stays," said Ekwefi with a heavy sigh.

The woman with whom she talked was called Chielo. She was the priestess of Agbala, the Oracle of the Hills and the Caves. In ordinary life Chielo was a widow with two children. She was very friendly with Ekwefi and they shared a common shed in the market. She was particularly fond of Ekwefi's only daughter, Ezinma, whom she called "my daughter." Quite often she bought beancakes and gave Ekwefi some to take home to Ezinma. Anyone seeing Chielo in ordinary life would hardly believe she was the same person who prophesied when the spirit of Agbala was upon her.

The drummers took up their sticks and the air shivered and grew tense like a tightened bow.

The two teams were ranged facing each other across the clear space. A young man from one team danced across the center to the other side and pointed at whomever he wanted to fight. They danced back to the center together and then closed in.

There were twelve men on each side and the challenge went from one side to the other. Two judges walked around the wrestlers and when they thought they were equally matched, stopped them. Five matches ended in this way. But the really exciting moments were when a man was thrown. The huge voice of the crowd then rose to the sky and in every direction. It was even heard in the surrounding villages.

The last match was between the leaders of the teams. They were among the best wrestlers in all the nine villages. The crowd wondered who would throw the other this year. Some said Okafo was the better man; others said he was not the equal of Ikezue. Last year neither of them had thrown the other even though the judges had allowed the contest to go on longer than was the custom. They had the same style and one saw the other's plans beforehand. It might happen again this year.

Dusk was already approaching when their contest began. The drums went mad and the crowds also. They surged forward as the two young men danced into the circle. The palm fronds were helpless in keeping them back.

Ikezue held out his right hand. Okafo seized it, and they closed in. It was a fierce contest. Ikezue strove to dig in his right heel behind Okafo so as to pitch him backwards in the clever *ege* style. But the one knew what the other was thinking. The crowd had surrounded and swallowed up the drummers, whose frantic rhythm was no longer a mere disembodied sound but the very heartbeat of the people.

The wrestlers were now almost still in each other's grip. The muscles on their arms and their thighs and on their backs stood out and twitched. It looked like an equal match. The two judges were already moving forward to separate them when Ikezue, now desperate, went down quickly on one knee in an attempt to fling his man backwards over his head. It was a sad miscalculation. Quick as the lightning of Amadiora, Okafo raised his right leg and swung it over his rival's head. The crowd burst into a thunderous roar. Okafo was swept off his feet by his supporters and carried home shoulder high. They sang his praise and the young women clapped their hands:

> *"Who will wrestle for our village?*
>   *Okafo will wrestle for our village.*
> *Has he thrown a hundred men?*
>   *He has thrown four hundred men.*
> *Has he thrown a hundred Cats?*
>   *He has thrown four hundred Cats.*
> *Then send him word to fight for us."*

7

For three years Ikemefuna lived in Okonkwo's household and the elders of Umuofia seemed to have forgotten about him. He grew rapidly like a yam tendril in the rainy season, and was full of the sap of life. He had become wholly absorbed into his new family. He was like an elder brother to Nwoye, and from the very first seemed to have kindled a new fire in the younger boy. He made him feel grown-up; and they no longer spent the evenings in mother's hut while she cooked, but now sat with Okonkwo in his *obi,* or watched him as he tapped his palm tree for the evening wine. Nothing pleased Nwoye now more than to be sent for by his mother or another of his father's wives to do one of those difficult and masculine tasks in the home, like splitting wood, or pounding food. On receiving such a message through a younger brother or sister, Nwoye would feign annoyance and grumble aloud about women and their troubles.

Okonkwo was inwardly pleased at his son's development, and he knew it was due to Ikemefuna. He wanted Nwoye to grow into a tough young man capable of ruling his father's household when he was dead and gone to join the ancestors. He wanted him to be a prosperous man, having enough in his barn to feed the ancestors with regular sacrifices. And so he was always happy when he heard him grumbling about women. That showed that in time he would be able to control his womenfolk. No matter how prosperous a man was, if he was unable to rule his women and his children (and especially his women) he was not really a man. He was like the man in the song who had ten and one wives and not enough soup for his foo-foo.

So Okonkwo encouraged the boys to sit with him in his *obi,* and he told them stories of the land—masculine stories of violence and bloodshed. Nwoye knew that it was right to be masculine and to be violent, but somehow he still preferred the stories that his mother used to tell, and which she no doubt still told to her younger children—stories of the tortoise and his wily ways, and of the bird *eneke-nti-oba*[13] who challenged the whole world to a wrestling contest and was finally thrown by the cat. He remembered the story she often told of the quarrel between Earth and Sky long ago, and how Sky withheld rain for seven years, until crops withered and the dead could not be buried because the hoes broke on the stony Earth. At last Vulture

---

[13] *eneke-nti-oba:* "Swallow with the ear of a crocodile," a kind of bird that appears in many fables and proverbs.

was sent to plead with Sky, and to soften his heart with a song of the suffering of the sons of men. Whenever Nwoye's mother sang this song he felt carried away to the distant scene in the sky where Vulture, Earth's emissary, sang for mercy. At last Sky was moved to pity, and he gave to Vulture rain wrapped in leaves of coco-yam. But as he flew home his long talon pierced the leaves and the rain fell as it had never fallen before. And so heavily did it rain on Vulture that he did not return to deliver his message but flew to a distant land, from where he had espied a fire. And when he got there he found it was a man making a sacrifice. He warmed himself in the fire and ate the entrails.

That was the kind of story that Nwoye loved. But he now knew that they were for foolish women and children, and he knew that his father wanted him to be a man. And so he feigned that he no longer cared for women's stories. And when he did this he saw that his father was pleased, and no longer rebuked him or beat him. So Nwoye and Ikemefuna would listen to Okonkwo's stories about tribal wars, or how, years ago, he had stalked his victim, overpowered him, and obtained his first human head. And as he told them of the past they sat in darkness or the dim glow of logs, waiting for the women to finish their cooking. When they finished, each brought her bowl of foo-foo and bowl of soup to her husband. An oil lamp was lit and Okonkwo tasted from each bowl, and then passed two shares to Nwoye and Ikemefuna.

In this way the moons and the seasons passed. And then the locusts came. It had not happened for many a long year. The elders said locusts came once in a generation, reappeared every year for seven years, and then disappeared for another lifetime. They went back to their caves in a distant land, where they were guarded by a race of stunted men. And then after another lifetime these men opened the caves again and the locusts came to Umuofia.

They came in the cold harmattan season after the harvests had been gathered, and ate up all the wild grass in the fields.

Okonkwo and the two boys were working on the red outer walls of the compound. This was one of the lighter tasks of the after-harvest season. A new cover of thick palm branches and palm leaves was set on the walls to protect them from the next rainy season. Okonkwo worked on the outside of the wall and the boys worked from within. There were little holes from one side to the other in the upper levels of the wall, and through these Okonkwo passed the rope, or *tie-tie,* to the boys and they passed it round the wooden stays and then back to him; and in this way the cover was strengthened on the wall.

The women had gone to the bush to collect firewood, and the little children to visit their playmates in the neighboring compounds. The harmattan was in the air and seemed to distill a hazy feeling of sleep on the world. Okonkwo and the boys worked in complete silence, which was only broken when a new palm frond was lifted on to the wall or when a busy hen moved dry leaves about in her ceaseless search for food.

And then quite suddenly a shadow fell on the world, and the sun seemed hidden behind a thick cloud. Okonkwo looked up from his work and wondered if it was going to rain at such an unlikely time of the year. But almost immediately a shout of joy broke out in all directions, and Umuofia, which had dozed in the noon-day haze, broke into life and activity.

"Locusts are descending," was joyfully chanted everywhere, and men, women, and children left their work or their play and ran into the open to see the unfamiliar sight. The locusts had not come for many, many years, and only the old people had seen them before.

At first, a fairly small swarm came. They were the harbingers sent to survey the land. And then appeared on the horizon a slowly moving mass like a boundless sheet of black cloud drifting towards Umuofia. Soon it covered half the sky, and the solid mass was now broken by tiny eyes of light like shining star dust. It was a tremendous sight, full of power and beauty.

Everyone was now about, talking excitedly and praying that the locusts should camp in Umuofia for the night. For although locusts had not visited Umuofia for many years, everybody knew by instinct that they were very good to eat. And at last the locusts did descend. They settled on every tree and on every blade of grass; they settled on the roofs and covered the bare ground. Mighty tree branches broke away under them, and the whole country became the brown-earth color of the vast, hungry swarm.

Many people went out with baskets trying to catch them, but the elders counseled patience till nightfall. And they were right. The locusts settled in the bushes for the night and their wings became wet with dew. Then all Umuofia turned out in spite of the cold harmattan, and everyone filled his bags and pots with locusts. The next morning they were roasted in clay pots and then spread in the sun until they became dry and brittle. And for many days this rare food was eaten with solid palm-oil.

Okonkwo sat in his *obi* crunching happily with Ikemefuna and Nwoye, and drinking palm-wine copiously, when Ogbuefi Ezeudu came in. Ezeudu was the oldest man in this quarter of Umuofia. He had been a great and fearless warrior in his time, and was now accorded great respect in all the clan. He refused to join in the meal, and asked Okonkwo to have a word with him outside. And so they walked out together, the old man supporting himself with his stick. When they were out of earshot, he said to Okonkwo:

"That boy calls you father. Do not bear a hand in his death." Okonkwo was surprised, and was about to say something when the old man continued:

"Yes, Umuofia has decided to kill him. The Oracle of the Hills and the Caves has pronounced it. They will take him outside Umuofia as is the custom, and kill him there. But I want you to have nothing to do with it. He calls you his father."

The next day a group of elders from all the nine villages of Umuofia came to Okonkwo's house early in the morning, and before they began to speak in low tones Nwoye and Ikemefuna were sent out. They did not stay very long, but when they went away Okonkwo sat still for a very long time supporting his chin in his palms. Later in the day he called Ikemefuna and told him that he was to be taken home the next day. Nwoye overheard it and burst into tears, whereupon his father beat him heavily. As for Ikemefuna, he was at a loss. His own home had gradually become very faint and distant. He still missed his mother and his sister and would be very glad to see them. But somehow he knew he was not going to see them. He remembered once when men had talked in low tones with his father; and it seemed now as if it was happening all over again.

Later, Nwoye went to his mother's hut and told her that Ikemefuna was going home. She immediately dropped her pestle with which she was grinding pepper, folded her arms across her breast and sighed, "Poor child."

The next day, the men returned with a pot of wine. They were all fully dressed as if they were going to a big clan meeting or to pay a visit to a neighboring village. They passed their cloths under the right armpit, and hung their goatskin bags and sheathed machetes over their left shoulders. Okonkwo got ready quickly and the party set out with Ikemefuna carrying the pot of wine. A deathly silence descended on Okonkwo's compound. Even the very little children seemed to know. Throughout that day Nwoye sat in his mother's hut and tears stood in his eyes.

At the beginning of their journey the men of Umuofia talked and laughed about the locusts, about their women, and about some effeminate men who had refused to come with them. But as they drew near to the outskirts of Umuofia silence fell upon them too.

The sun rose slowly to the center of the sky, and the dry, sandy footway began to throw up the heat that lay buried in it. Some birds chirruped in the forests around. The men trod dry leaves on the sand. All else was silent. Then from the distance came the faint beating of the *ekwe*. It rose and faded with the wind—a peaceful dance from a distant clan.

"It is an *ozo*[14] dance," the men said among themselves. But no one was sure where it was coming from. Some said Ezimili, others Abame or Aninta. They argued for a short while and fell into silence again, and the elusive dance rose and fell with the wind. Somewhere a man was taking one of the titles of his clan, with music and dancing and a great feast.

The footway had now become a narrow line in the heart of the forest. The short trees and sparse undergrowth which surrounded the men's village began to give way to giant trees and climbers which perhaps had stood from the beginning of things, untouched by the ax and the bush-fire. The sun breaking through their leaves and branches threw a pattern of light and shade on the sandy footway.

Ikemefuna heard a whisper close behind him and turned round sharply. The man who had whispered now called out aloud, urging the others to hurry up.

"We still have a long way to go," he said. Then he and another man went before Ikemefuna and set a faster pace.

Thus the men of Umuofia pursued their way, armed with sheathed machetes, and Ikemefuna, carrying a pot of palm-wine on his head, walked in their midst. Although he had felt uneasy at first, he was not afraid now. Okonkwo walked behind him. He could hardly imagine that Okonkwo was not his real father. He had never been fond of his real father, and at the end of three years he had become very distant indeed. But his mother and his three-year-old sister . . . of course she would not be

---

[14] *ozo:* One of the four titles or ranks in the Ibo society; they are Ozo, Idemili, Omalo, and Erulu.

three now, but six. Would he recognize her now? She must have grown quite big. How his mother would weep for joy, and thank Okonkwo for having looked after him so well and for bringing him back. She would want to hear everything that had happened to him in all these years. Could he remember them all? He would tell her about Nwoye and his mother, and about the locusts. . . . Then quite suddenly a thought came upon him. His mother might be dead. He tried in vain to force the thought out of his mind. Then he tried to settle the matter the way he used to settle such matters when he was a little boy. He still remembered the song:

> *Eze elina, elina!*
> > *Sala*
>
> *Eze ilikwa ya*
> *Ikwaba akwa oligholi*
> *Ebe Danda nechi eze*
> *Ebe Uzuzu nete egwu*
> > *Sala*[15]

He sang it in his mind, and walked to its beat. If the song ended on his right foot, his mother was alive. If it ended on his left, she was dead. No, not dead, but ill. It ended on the right. She was alive and well. He sang the song again, and it ended on the left. But the second time did not count. The first voice gets to Chukwu, or God's house. That was a favorite saying of children. Ikemefuna felt like a child once more. It must be the thought of going home to his mother.

One of the men behind him cleared his throat. Ikemefuna looked back, and the man growled at him to go on and not stand looking back. The way he said it sent cold fear down Ikemefuna's back. His hands trembled vaguely on the black pot he carried. Why had Okonkwo withdrawn to the rear? Ikemefuna felt his legs melting under him. And he was afraid to look back.

As the man who had cleared his throat drew up and raised his machete, Okonkwo looked away. He heard the blow. The pot fell and broke in the sand. He heard Ikemefuna cry, "My father, they have killed me!" as he ran towards him. Dazed with fear, Okonkwo drew his machete and cut him down. He was afraid of being thought weak.

As soon as his father walked in, that night, Nwoye knew that Ikemefuna had been killed, and something seemed to give way inside him, like the snapping of a tightened bow. He did not cry. He just hung limp. He had had the same kind of feeling not long ago, during the last harvest season. Every child loved the harvest season. Those who were big enough to carry even a few yams in a tiny basket went with grownups to the farm. And if they could not help in digging up the yams, they could gather firewood together for roasting the ones that would be eaten there on the farm. This roasted yam soaked in red palm-oil and eaten in the open farm was

---

[15] *Eze elina, . . . Sala:* "King don't eat, don't eat! / Sala / King if you eat it / You will weep for the abomination / Where Danda installs a king / Where Uzuzu dances / Sala." *Danda* means "ant"; *Uzuzu,* "sand"; and *Sala,* which has no meaning, is a refrain.

sweeter than any meal at home. It was after such a day at the farm during the last harvest that Nwoye had felt for the first time a snapping inside him like the one he now felt. They were returning home with baskets of yams from a distant farm across the stream when they heard the voice of an infant crying in the thick forest. A sudden hush had fallen on the women, who had been talking, and they had quickened their steps. Nwoye had heard that twins were put in earthenware pots and thrown away in the forest, but he had never yet come across them. A vague chill had descended on him and his head had seemed to swell, like a solitary walker at night who passes an evil spirit on the way. Then something had given way inside him. It descended on him again, this feeling, when his father walked in, that night after killing Ikemefuna.

8

Okonkwo did not taste any food for two days after the death of Ikemefuna. He drank palm-wine from morning till night, and his eyes were red and fierce like the eyes of a rat when it was caught by the tail and dashed against the floor. He called his son, Nwoye, to sit with him in his *obi*. But the boy was afraid of him and slipped out of the hut as soon as he noticed him dozing.

He did not sleep at night. He tried not to think about Ikemefuna, but the more he tried the more he thought about him. Once he got up from bed and walked about his compound. But he was so weak that his legs could hardly carry him. He felt like a drunken giant walking with the limbs of a mosquito. Now and then a cold shiver descended on his head and spread down his body.

On the third day he asked his second wife, Ekwefi, to roast plantains for him. She prepared it the way he liked—with slices of oil-bean and fish.

"You have not eaten for two days," said his daughter Ezinma when she brought the food to him. "So you must finish this." She sat down and stretched her legs in front of her. Okonkwo ate the food absent-mindedly. "She should have been a boy," he thought as he looked at his ten-year-old daughter. He passed her a piece of fish.

"Go and bring me some cold water," he said. Ezinma rushed out of the hut, chewing the fish, and soon returned with a bowl of cool water from the earthen pot in her mother's hut.

Okonkwo took the bowl from her and gulped the water down. He ate a few more pieces of plantain and pushed the dish aside.

"Bring me my bag," he asked, and Ezinma brought his goatskin bag from the far end of the hut. He searched in it for his snuff-bottle. It was a deep bag and took almost the whole length of his arm. It contained other things apart from his snuff-bottle. There was a drinking horn in it, and also a drinking gourd, and they knocked against each other as he searched. When he brought out the snuff-bottle he tapped it a few times against his kneecap before taking out some snuff on the palm of his left hand. Then he remembered that he had not taken out his snuff-spoon. He searched his bag again and brought out a small, flat, ivory spoon, with which he carried the brown snuff to his nostrils.

Ezinma took the dish in one hand and the empty water bowl in the other and went back to her mother's hut. "She should have been a boy," Okonkwo said to himself again. His mind went back to Ikemefuna and he shivered. If only he could find some work to do he would be able to forget. But it was the season of rest between the harvest and the next planting season. The only work that men did at this time was covering the walls of their compound with new palm fronds. And Okonkwo had already done that. He had finished it on the very day the locusts came, when he had worked on one side of the wall and Ikemefuna and Nwoye on the other.

"When did you become a shivering old woman," Okonkwo asked himself, "you, who are known in all the nine villages for your valor in war? How can a man who has killed five men in battle fall to pieces because he has added a boy to their number? Okonkwo, you have become a woman indeed."

He sprang to his feet, hung his goatskin bag on his shoulder and went to visit his friend, Obierika.

Obierika was sitting outside under the shade of an orange tree making thatches from leaves of the raffia-palm. He exchanged greetings with Okonkwo and led the way into his *obi*.

"I was coming over to see you as soon as I finished that thatch," he said, rubbing off the grains of sand that clung to his thighs.

"Is it well?" Okonkwo asked.

"Yes," replied Obierika. "My daughter's suitor is coming today and I hope we will clinch the matter of the bride-price. I want you to be there."

Just then Obierika's son, Maduka, came into the *obi* from outside, greeted Okonkwo and turned towards the compound.

"Come and shake hands with me," Okonkwo said to the lad. "Your wrestling the other day gave me much happiness." The boy smiled, shook hands with Okonkwo and went into the compound.

"He will do great things," Okonkwo said. "If I had a son like him I should be happy. I am worried about Nwoye. A bowl of pounded yams can throw him in a wrestling match. His two younger brothers are more promising. But I can tell you, Obierika, that my children do not resemble me. Where are the young suckers that will grow when the old banana tree dies? If Ezinma had been a boy I would have been happier. She has the right spirit."

"You worry yourself for nothing," said Obierika. "The children are still very young."

"Nwoye is old enough to impregnate a woman. At his age I was already fending for myself. No, my friend, he is not too young. A chick that will grow into a cock can be spotted the very day it hatches. I have done my best to make Nwoye grow into a man, but there is too much of his mother in him."

"Too much of his grandfather," Obierika thought, but he did not say it. The same thought also came to Okonkwo's mind. But he had long learned how to lay that ghost. Whenever the thought of his father's weakness and failure troubled him he expelled it by thinking about his own strength and success. And so he did now. His mind went to his latest show of manliness.

"I cannot understand why you refused to come with us to kill that boy," he asked Obierika.

"Because I did not want to," Obierika replied sharply. "I had something better to do."

"You sound as if you question the authority and the decision of the Oracle, who said he should die."

"I do not. Why should I? But the Oracle did not ask me to carry out its decision."

"But someone had to do it. If we were all afraid of blood, it would not be done. And what do you think the Oracle would do then?"

"You know very well, Okonkwo, that I am not afraid of blood; and if anyone tells you that I am, he is telling a lie. And let me tell you one thing, my friend. If I were you I would have stayed at home. What you have done will not please the Earth. It is the kind of action for which the goddess wipes out whole families."

"The Earth cannot punish me for obeying her messenger," Okonkwo said. "A child's fingers are not scalded by a piece of hot yam which its mother puts into its palm."

"That is true," Obierika agreed. "But if the Oracle said that my son should be killed I would neither dispute it nor be the one to do it."

They would have gone on arguing had Ofoedu not come in just then. It was clear from his twinkling eyes that he had important news. But it would be impolite to rush him. Obierika offered him a lobe of the kola nut he had broken with Okonkwo. Ofoedu ate slowly and talked about the locusts. When he finished his kola nut he said:

"The things that happen these days are very strange."

"What has happened?" asked Okonkwo.

"Do you know Ogbuefi Ndulue?" Ofoedu asked.

"Ogbuefi Ndulue of Ire village," Okonkwo and Obierika said together.

"He died this morning," said Ofoedu.

"That is not strange. He was the oldest man in Ire," said Obierika.

"You are right," Ofoedu agreed. "But you ought to ask why the drum has not beaten to tell Umuofia of his death."

"Why?" asked Obierika and Okonkwo together.

"That is the strange part of it. You know his first wife who walks with a stick?"

"Yes. She is called Ozoemena."

"That is so," said Ofoedu. "Ozoemena was, as you know, too old to attend Ndulue during his illness. His younger wives did that. When he died this morning, one of these women went to Ozoemena's hut and told her. She rose from her mat, took her stick and walked over to the *obi*. She knelt on her knees and hands at the threshold and called her husband, who was laid on a mat. 'Ogbuefi Ndulue,' she called, three times, and went back to her hut. When the youngest wife went to call her again to be present at the washing of the body, she found her lying on the mat, dead."

"That is very strange, indeed," said Okonkwo. "They will put off Ndulue's funeral until his wife has been buried."[16]

---

[16] "That is . . . buried": A wife who died soon after her husband might be blamed for his death, therefore the concern here.

"That is why the drum has not been beaten to tell Umuofia."

"It was always said that Ndulue and Ozoemena had one mind," said Obierika. "I remember when I was a young boy there was a song about them. He could not do anything without telling her."

"I did not know that," said Okonkwo. "I thought he was a strong man in his youth."

"He was indeed," said Ofoedu.

Okonkwo shook his head doubtfully.

"He led Umuofia to war in those days," said Obierika.

Okonkwo was beginning to feel like his old self again. All that he required was something to occupy his mind. If he had killed Ikemefuna during the busy planting season or harvesting it would not have been so bad; his mind would have been centered on his work. Okonkwo was not a man of thought but of action. But in absence of work, talking was the next best.

Soon after Ofoedu left, Okonkwo took up his goatskin bag to go.

"I must go home to tap my palm trees for the afternoon," he said.

"Who taps your tall trees for you?" asked Obierika.

"Umezulike," replied Okonkwo.

"Sometimes I wish I had not taken the *ozo* title," said Obierika. "It wounds my heart to see these young men killing palm trees in the name of tapping."

"It is so indeed," Okonkwo agreed. "But the law of the land must be obeyed."

"I don't know how we got that law," said Obierika. "In many other clans a man of title is not forbidden to climb the palm tree. Here we say he cannot climb the tall tree but he can tap the short ones standing on the ground. It is like Dimaragana, who would not lend his knife for cutting up dog-meat because the dog was taboo to him, but offered to use his teeth."

"I think it is good that our clan holds the *ozo* title in high esteem," said Okonkwo. "In those other clans you speak of, *ozo* is so low that every beggar takes it."

"I was only speaking in jest," said Obierika. "In Abame and Aninta the title is worth less than two cowries. Every man wears the thread of title on his ankle, and does not lose it even if he steals."

"They have indeed soiled the name of *ozo*," said Okonkwo as he rose to go.

"It will not be very long now before my in-laws come," said Obierika.

"I shall return very soon," said Okonkwo, looking at the position of the sun.

There were seven men in Obierika's hut when Okonkwo returned. The suitor was a young man of about twenty-five, and with him were his father and uncle. On Obierika's side were his two elder brothers and Maduka, his sixteen-year-old son.

"Ask Akueke's mother to send us some kola nuts," said Obierika to his son. Maduka vanished into the compound like lightning. The conversation at once centered on him, and everybody agreed that he was as sharp as a razor.

"I sometimes think he is too sharp," said Obierika, somewhat indulgently. "He hardly ever walks. He is always in a hurry. If you are sending him on an errand he flies away before he has heard half of the message."

"You were very much like that yourself," said his eldest brother. "As our people say, 'When mother-cow is chewing grass its young ones watch its mouth.' Maduka has been watching your mouth."

As he was speaking the boy returned, followed by Akueke, his half-sister, carrying a wooden dish with three kola nuts and alligator pepper. She gave the dish to her father's eldest brother and then shook hands, very shyly, with her suitor and his relatives. She was about sixteen and just ripe for marriage. Her suitor and his relatives surveyed her young body with expert eyes as if to assure themselves that she was beautiful and ripe.

She wore a coiffure which was done up into a crest in the middle of the head. Cam wood was rubbed lightly into her skin, and all over her body were black patterns drawn with *uli*.[7] She wore a black necklace which hung down in three coils just above her full, succulent breasts. On her arms were red and yellow bangles, and on her waist four or five rows of *jigida*, or waist beads.

When she had shaken hands, or rather held out her hand to be shaken, she returned to her mother's hut to help with the cooking.

"Remove your *jigida* first," her mother warned as she moved near the fireplace to bring the pestle resting against the wall. "Every day I tell you that *jigida* and fire are not friends. But you will never hear. You grew your ears for decoration, not for hearing. One of these days your *jigida* will catch fire on your waist, and then you will know."

Akueke moved to the other end of the hut and began to remove the waist-beads. It had to be done slowly and carefully, taking each string separately, else it would break and the thousand tiny rings would have to be strung together again. She rubbed each string downwards with her palms until it passed the buttocks and slipped down to the floor around her feet.

The men in the *obi* had already begun to drink the palm-wine which Akueke's suitor had brought. It was a very good wine and powerful, for in spite of the palm fruit hung across the mouth of the pot to restrain the lively liquor, white foam rose and spilled over.

"That wine is the work of a good tapper," said Okonkwo.

The young suitor, whose name was Ibe, smiled broadly and said to his father: "Do you hear that?" He then said to the others: "He will never admit that I am a good tapper."

"He tapped three of my best palm trees to death," said his father, Ukegbu.

"That was about five years ago," said Ibe, who had begun to pour out the wine, "before I learned how to tap." He filled the first horn and gave to his father. Then he poured out for the others. Okonkwo brought out his big horn from the goatskin bag, blew into it to remove any dust that might be there, and gave it to Ibe to fill.

As the men drank, they talked about everything except the thing for which they had gathered. It was only after the pot had been emptied that the suitor's father cleared his voice and announced the object of their visit.

---

[7] *uli*: A black dye used to decorate the body.

Obierika then presented to him a small bundle of short broomsticks. Ukegbu counted them.

"They are thirty?" he asked.

Obierika nodded in agreement.

"We are at last getting somewhere," Ukegbu said, and then turning to his brother and his son he said: "Let us go out and whisper together." The three rose and went outside. When they returned Ukegbu handed the bundle of sticks back to Obierika. He counted them; instead of thirty there were now only fifteen. He passed them over to his eldest brother, Machi, who also counted them and said:

"We had not thought to go below thirty. But as the dog said, 'If I fall down for you and you fall down for me, it is play.' Marriage should be a play and not a fight; so we are falling down again." He then added ten sticks to the fifteen and gave the bundle to Ukegbu.

In this way Akueke's bride-price was finally settled at twenty bags of cowries. It was already dusk when the two parties came to this agreement.

"Go and tell Akueke's mother that we have finished," Obierika said to his son, Maduka. Almost immediately the women came in with a big bowl of foo-foo. Obierika's second wife followed with a pot of soup, and Maduka brought in a pot of palm-wine.

As the men ate and drank palm-wine they talked about the customs of their neighbors.

"It was only this morning," said Obierika, "that Okonkwo and I were talking about Abame and Aninta, where titled men climb trees and pound foo-foo for their wives."

"All their customs are upside-down. They do not decide bride-price as we do, with sticks. They haggle and bargain as if they were buying a goat or a cow in the market."

"That is very bad," said Obierika's eldest brother. "But what is good in one place is bad in another place. In Umunso they do not bargain at all, not even with broomsticks. The suitor just goes on bringing bags of cowries until his in-laws tell him to stop. It is a bad custom because it always leads to a quarrel."

"The world is large," said Okonkwo. "I have even heard that in some tribes a man's children belong to his wife and her family."

"That cannot be," said Machi. "You might as well say that the woman lies on top of the man when they are making the children."

"It is like the story of white men who, they say, are white like this piece of chalk," said Obierika. He held up a piece of chalk, which every man kept in his *obi* and with which his guests drew lines on the floor before they ate kola nuts. "And these white men, they say, have no toes."

"And have you never seen them?" asked Machi.

"Have you?" asked Obierika.

"One of them passes here frequently," said Machi. "His name is Amadi."

Those who knew Amadi laughed. He was a leper, and the polite name for leprosy was "the white skin."

9

For the first time in three nights, Okonkwo slept. He woke up once in the middle of the night and his mind went back to the past three days without making him feel uneasy. He began to wonder why he had felt uneasy at all. It was like a man wondering in broad daylight why a dream had appeared so terrible to him at night. He stretched himself and scratched his thigh where a mosquito had bitten him as he slept. Another one was wailing near his right ear. He slapped the ear and hoped he had killed it. Why do they always go for one's ears? When he was a child his mother had told him a story about it. But it was as silly as all women's stories. Mosquito, she had said, had asked Ear to marry him, whereupon Ear fell on the floor in uncontrollable laughter. "How much longer do you think you will live?" she asked. "You are already a skeleton." Mosquito went away humiliated, and any time he passed her way he told Ear that he was still alive.

Okonkwo turned on his side and went back to sleep. He was roused in the morning by someone banging on his door.

"Who is that?" he growled. He knew it must be Ekwefi. Of his three wives Ekwefi was the only one who would have the audacity to bang on his door.

"Ezinma is dying," came her voice, and all the tragedy and sorrow of her life were packed in those words.

Okonkwo sprang from his bed, pushed back the bolt on his door and ran into Ekwefi's hut.

Ezinma lay shivering on a mat beside a huge fire that her mother had kept burning all night.

"It is *iba*,"[18] said Okonkwo as he took his machete and went into the bush to collect the leaves and grasses and barks of trees that went into making the medicine for *iba*.

Ekwefi knelt beside the sick child, occasionally feeling with her palm the wet, burning forehead.

Ezinma was an only child and the center of her mother's world. Very often it was Ezinma who decided what food her mother should prepare. Ekwefi even gave her such delicacies as eggs, which children were rarely allowed to eat because such food tempted them to steal. One day as Ezinma was eating an egg Okonkwo had come in unexpectedly from his hut. He was greatly shocked and swore to beat Ekwefi if she dared to give the child eggs again. But it was impossible to refuse Ezinma anything. After her father's rebuke she developed an even keener appetite for eggs. And she enjoyed above all the secrecy in which she now ate them. Her mother always took her into their bedroom and shut the door.

Ezinma did not call her mother *Nne* like all children. She called her by her name, Ekwefi, as her father and other grown-up people did. The relationship between them was not only that of mother and child. There was something in it like the companionship of equals, which was strengthened by such little conspiracies as eating eggs in the bedroom.

---

[18] *iba*: Fever.

Ekwefi had suffered a good deal in her life. She had borne ten children and nine of them had died in infancy, usually before the age of three. As she buried one child after another her sorrow gave way to despair and then to grim resignation. The birth of her children, which should be a woman's crowning glory, became for Ekwefi mere physical agony devoid of promise. The naming ceremony after seven market weeks became an empty ritual. Her deepening despair found expression in the names she gave her children. One of them was a pathetic cry, Onwumbiko — "Death, I implore you." But Death took no notice; Onwumbiko died in his fifteenth month. The next child was a girl, Ozoemena — "May it not happen again." She died in her eleventh month, and two others after her. Ekwefi then became defiant and called her next child Onwuma — "Death may please himself." And he did.

After the death of Ekwefi's second child, Okonkwo had gone to a medicine man, who was also a diviner of the Afa Oracle, to inquire what was amiss. This man told him that the child was an *ogbanje*,[19] one of those wicked children who, when they died, entered their mothers' wombs to be born again.

"When your wife becomes pregnant again," he said, "let her not sleep in her hut. Let her go and stay with her people. In that way she will elude her wicked tormentor and break its evil cycle of birth and death."

Ekwefi did as she was asked. As soon as she became pregnant she went to live with her old mother in another village. It was there that her third child was born and circumcised on the eighth day. She did not return to Okonkwo's compound until three days before the naming ceremony. The child was called Onwumbiko.

Onwumbiko was not given proper burial when he died. Okonkwo had called in another medicine man who was famous in the clan for his great knowledge about *ogbanje* children. His name was Okagbue Uyanwa. Okagbue was a very striking figure, tall, with a full beard and a bald head. He was light in complexion and his eyes were red and fiery. He always gnashed his teeth as he listened to those who came to consult him. He asked Okonkwo a few questions about the dead child. All the neighbors and relations who had come to mourn gathered round them.

"On what market-day was it born?" he asked.

"*Oye*," replied Okonkwo.

"And it died this morning?"

Okonkwo said yes, and only then realized for the first time that the child had died on the same market-day as it had been born. The neighbors and relations also saw the coincidence and said among themselves that it was very significant.

"Where do you sleep with your wife, in your *obi* or in her own hut?" asked the medicine man.

"In her hut."

"In future call her into your *obi*."

The medicine man then ordered that there should be no mourning for the dead child. He brought out a sharp razor from the goatskin bag slung from his left

---

[19] child . . . *ogbanje*: The *ogbanje* is locked into a pattern of early death and cyclic rebirth unless its *iyi-uwa,* a stone that links it to the spirit world, is found and destroyed so that the child can live.

shoulder and began to mutilate the child. Then he took it away to bury in the Evil Forest, holding it by the ankle and dragging it on the ground behind him. After such treatment it would think twice before coming again, unless it was one of the stubborn ones who returned, carrying the stamp of their mutilation—a missing finger or perhaps a dark line where the medicine man's razor had cut them.

By the time Onwumbiko died Ekwefi had become a very bitter woman. Her husband's first wife had already had three sons, all strong and healthy. When she had borne her third son in succession, Okonkwo had gathered a goat for her, as was the custom. Ekwefi had nothing but good wishes for her. But she had grown so bitter about her own *chi* that she could not rejoice with others over their good fortune. And so, on the day that Nwoye's mother celebrated the birth of her three sons with feasting and music, Ekwefi was the only person in the happy company who went about with a cloud on her brow. Her husband's wife took this for malevolence, as husbands' wives were wont to. How could she know that Ekwefi's bitterness did not flow outwards to others but inwards into her own soul; that she did not blame others for their good fortune but her own evil *chi* who denied her any?

At last Ezinma was born, and although ailing she seemed determined to live. At first Ekwefi accepted her, as she had accepted others—with listless resignation. But when she lived on to her fourth, fifth, and sixth years, love returned once more to her mother, and, with love, anxiety. She determined to nurse her child to health, and she put all her being into it. She was rewarded by occasional spells of health during which Ezinma bubbled with energy like fresh palm-wine. At such times she seemed beyond danger. But all of a sudden she would go down again. Everybody knew she was an *ogbanje*. These sudden bouts of sickness and health were typical of her kind. But she had lived so long that perhaps she had decided to stay. Some of them did become tired of their evil rounds of birth and death, or took pity on their mothers, and stayed. Ekwefi believed deep inside her that Ezinma had come to stay. She believed because it was that faith alone that gave her own life any kind of meaning. And this faith had been strengthened when a year or so ago a medicine man had dug up Ezinma's *iyi-uwa*. Everyone knew then that she would live because her bond with the world of *ogbanje* had been broken. Ekwefi was reassured. But such was her anxiety for her daughter that she could not rid herself completely of her fear. And although she believed that the *iyi-uwa* which had been dug up was genuine, she could not ignore the fact that some really evil children sometimes misled people into digging up a specious one.

But Ezinma's *iyi-uwa* had looked real enough. It was a smooth pebble wrapped in a dirty rag. The man who dug it up was the same Okagbue who was famous in all the clan for his knowledge in these matters. Ezinma had not wanted to cooperate with him at first. But that was only to be expected. No *ogbanje* would yield her secrets easily, and most of them never did because they died too young—before they could be asked questions.

"Where did you bury your *iyi-uwa*?" Okagbue had asked Ezinma. She was nine then and was just recovering from a serious illness.

"What is *iyi-uwa*?" she asked in return.

"You know what it is. You buried it in the ground somewhere so that you can die and return again to torment your mother."

Ezinma looked at her mother, whose eyes, sad and pleading, were fixed on her.

"Answer the question at once," roared Okonkwo, who stood beside her. All the family were there and some of the neighbors too.

"Leave her to me," the medicine man told Okonkwo in a cool, confident voice. He turned again to Ezinma. "Where did you bury your *iyi-uwa*?"

"Where they bury children," she replied, and the quiet spectators murmured to themselves.

"Come along then and show me the spot," said the medicine man.

The crowd set out with Ezinma leading the way and Okagbue following closely behind her. Okonkwo came next and Ekwefi followed him. When she came to the main road, Ezinma turned left as if she was going to the stream.

"But you said it was where they bury children?" asked the medicine man.

"No," said Ezinma, whose feeling of importance was manifest in her sprightly walk. She sometimes broke into a run and stopped again suddenly. The crowd followed her silently. Women and children returning from the stream with pots of water on their heads wondered what was happening until they saw Okagbue and guessed that it must be something to do with *ogbanje*. And they all knew Ekwefi and her daughter very well.

When she got to the big udala tree Ezinma turned left into the bush, and the crowd followed her. Because of her size she made her way through trees and creepers more quickly than her followers. The bush was alive with the tread of feet on dry leaves and sticks and the moving aside of tree branches. Ezinma went deeper and deeper and the crowd went with her. Then she suddenly turned round and began to walk back to the road. Everybody stood to let her pass and then filed after her.

"If you bring us all this way for nothing I shall beat sense into you," Okonkwo threatened.

"I have told you to let her alone. I know how to deal with them," said Okagbue.

Ezinma led the way back to the road, looked left and right and turned right. And so they arrived home again.

"Where did you bury your *iyi-uwa*?" asked Okagbue when Ezinma finally stopped outside her father's *obi*. Okagbue's voice was unchanged. It was quiet and confident.

"It is near that orange tree," Ezinma said.

"And why did you not say so, you wicked daughter of Akalogoli?" Okonkwo swore furiously. The medicine man ignored him.

"Come and show me the exact spot," he said quietly to Ezinma.

"It is here," she said when they got to the tree.

"Point at the spot with your finger," said Okagbue.

"It is here," said Ezinma touching the ground with her finger. Okonkwo stood by, rumbling like thunder in the rainy season.

"Bring me a hoe," said Okagbue.

When Ekwefi brought the hoe, he had already put aside his goatskin bag and his big cloth and was in his underwear, a long and thin strip of cloth wound round the waist like a belt and then passed between the legs to be fastened to the belt behind. He immediately set to work digging a pit where Ezinma had indicated. The neighbors sat around watching the pit becoming deeper and deeper. The dark top soil soon gave way to the bright red earth with which women scrubbed the floors and walls of huts. Okagbue worked tirelessly and in silence, his back shining with perspiration. Okonkwo stood by the pit. He asked Okagbue to come up and rest while he took a hand. But Okagbue said he was not tired yet.

Ekwefi went into her hut to cook yams. Her husband had brought out more yams than usual because the medicine man had to be fed. Ezinma went with her and helped in preparing the vegetables.

"There is too much green vegetable," she said.

"Don't you see the pot is full of yams?" Ekwefi asked. "And you know how leaves become smaller after cooking."

"Yes," said Ezinma, "that was why the snake-lizard killed his mother."

"Very true," said Ekwefi.

"He gave his mother seven baskets of vegetables to cook and in the end there were only three. And so he killed her," said Ezinma.

"That is not the end of the story."

"Oho," said Ezinma. "I remember now. He brought another seven baskets and cooked them himself. And there were again only three. So he killed himself too."

Outside the *obi* Okagbue and Okonkwo were digging the pit to find where Ezinma had buried her *iyi-uwa*. Neighbors sat around, watching. The pit was now so deep that they no longer saw the digger. They only saw the red earth he threw up mounting higher and higher. Okonkwo's son, Nwoye, stood near the edge of the pit because he wanted to take in all that happened.

Okagbue had again taken over the digging from Okonkwo. He worked, as usual, in silence. The neighbors and Okonkwo's wives were now talking. The children had lost interest and were playing.

Suddenly Okagbue sprang to the surface with the agility of a leopard.

"It is very near now," he said. "I have felt it."

There was immediate excitement and those who were sitting jumped to their feet.

"Call your wife and child," he said to Okonkwo. But Ekwefi and Ezinma had heard the noise and run out to see what it was.

Okagbue went back into the pit, which was now surrounded by spectators. After a few more hoe-fuls of earth he struck the *iyi-uwa*. He raised it carefully with the hoe and threw it to the surface. Some women ran away in fear when it was thrown. But they soon returned and everyone was gazing at the rag from a reasonable distance. Okagbue emerged and without saying a word or even looking at the spectators he went to his goatskin bag, took out two leaves and began to chew them. When he had swallowed them, he took up the rag with his left hand and began to untie it. And then the smooth, shiny pebble fell out. He picked it up.

"Is this yours?" he asked Ezinma.

"Yes," she replied. All the women shouted with joy because Ekwefi's troubles were at last ended.

All this had happened more than a year ago and Ezinma had not been ill since. And then suddenly she had begun to shiver in the night. Ekwefi brought her to the fireplace, spread her mat on the floor and built a fire. But she had got worse and worse. As she knelt by her, feeling with her palm the wet, burning forehead, she prayed a thousand times. Although her husband's wives were saying that it was nothing more than *iba,* she did not hear them.

Okonkwo returned from the bush carrying on his left shoulder a large bundle of grasses and leaves, roots and barks of medicinal trees and shrubs. He went into Ekwefi's hut, put down his load and sat down.

"Get me a pot," he said, "and leave the child alone."

Ekwefi went to bring the pot and Okonkwo selected the best from his bundle, in their due proportions, and cut them up. He put them in the pot and Ekwefi poured in some water.

"Is that enough?" she asked when she had poured in about half of the water in the bowl.

"A little more . . . I said *a little.* Are you deaf?" Okonkwo roared at her.

She set the pot on the fire and Okonkwo took up his machete to return to his *obi.*

"You must watch the pot carefully," he said as he went, "and don't allow it to boil over. If it does its power will be gone." He went away to his hut and Ekwefi began to tend the medicine pot almost as if it was itself a sick child. Her eyes went constantly from Ezinma to the boiling pot and back to Ezinma.

Okonkwo returned when he felt the medicine had cooked long enough. He looked it over and said it was done.

"Bring me a low stool for Ezinma," he said, "and a thick mat."

He took down the pot from the fire and placed it in front of the stool. He then roused Ezinma and placed her on the stool, astride the steaming pot. The thick mat was thrown over both. Ezinma struggled to escape from the choking and overpowering steam, but she was held down. She started to cry.

When the mat was at last removed she was drenched in perspiration. Ekwefi mopped her with a piece of cloth and she lay down on a dry mat and was soon asleep.

10

Large crowds began to gather on the village *ilo* as soon as the edge had worn off the sun's heat and it was no longer painful on the body. Most communal ceremonies took place at that time of the day, so that even when it was said that a ceremony would begin "after the midday meal" everyone understood that it would begin a long time later, when the sun's heat had softened.

It was clear from the way the crowd stood or sat that the ceremony was for men. There were many women, but they looked on from the fringe like outsiders. The titled men and elders sat on their stools waiting for the trials to begin. In front of them was a row of stools on which nobody sat. There were nine of them. Two little groups of people stood at a respectable distance beyond the stools. They faced the elders. There were three men in one group and three men and one woman in the other. The woman was Mgbafo and the three men with her were her brothers. In the other group were her husband, Uzowulu, and his relatives. Mgbafo and her brothers were as still as statues into whose faces the artist has molded defiance. Uzowulu and his relative, on the other hand, were whispering together. It looked like whispering, but they were really talking at the top of their voices. Everybody in the crowd was talking. It was like the market. From a distance the noise was a deep rumble carried by the wind.

An iron gong sounded, setting up a wave of expectation in the crowd. Everyone looked in the direction of the *egwugwu* house. *Gome, gome, gome, gome* went the gong, and a powerful flute blew a high-pitched blast. Then came the voices of the *egwugwu*, guttural and awesome. The wave struck the women and children and there was a backward stampede. But it was momentary. They were already far enough where they stood and there was room for running away if any of the *egwugwu* should go towards them.

The drum sounded again and the flute blew. The *egwugwu* house was now a pandemonium of quavering voices: *Aru oyim de de de dei!*[20] filled the air as the spirits of the ancestors, just emerged from the earth, greeted themselves in their esoteric language. The *egwugwu* house into which they emerged faced the forest, away from the crowd, who saw only its back with the many-colored patterns and drawings done by specially chosen women at regular intervals. These women never saw the inside of the hut. No woman ever did. They scrubbed and painted the outside walls under the supervision of men. If they imagined what was inside, they kept their imagination to themselves. No woman ever asked questions about the most powerful and the most secret cult in the clan.

Aru oyim de de de dei! flew around the dark, closed hut like tongues of fire. The ancestral spirits of the clan were abroad. The metal gong beat continuously now and the flute, shrill and powerful, floated on the chaos.

And then the *egwugwu* appeared. The women and children sent up a great shout and took to their heels. It was instinctive. A woman fled as soon as an *egwugwu* came in sight. And when, as on that day, nine of the greatest masked spirits in the clan came out together it was a terrifying spectacle. Even Mgbafo took to her heels and had to be restrained by her brothers.

Each of the nine *egwugwu* represented a village of the clan. Their leader was called Evil Forest. Smoke poured out of his head.

The nine villages of Umuofia had grown out of the nine sons of the first father of the clan. Evil Forest represented the village of Umueru, or the children of Eru, who was the eldest of the nine sons.

"*Umuofia kwenu!*" shouted the leading *egwugwu*, pushing the air with his raffia arms. The elders of the clan replied, "*Yaa!*"

"*Umuofia kwenu!*"

"*Yaa!*"

"*Umuofia kwenu!*"

"*Yaa!*"

Evil Forest then thrust the pointed end of his rattling staff into the earth. And it began to shake and rattle, like something agitating with a metallic life. He took the

---

[20] *Aru . . . dei!:* "Body of my friend, greetings."

first of the empty stools and the eight other *egwugwu* began to sit in order of seniority after him.

Okonkwo's wives, and perhaps other women as well, might have noticed that the second *egwugwu* had the springy walk of Okonkwo. And they might also have noticed that Okonkwo was not among the titled men and elders who sat behind the row of *egwugwu*. But if they thought these things they kept them within themselves. The *egwugwu* with the springy walk was one of the dead fathers of the clan. He looked terrible with the smoked raffia body, a huge wooden face painted white except for the round hollow eyes and the charred teeth that were as big as a man's fingers. On his head were two powerful horns.

When all the *egwugwu* had sat down and the sound of the many tiny bells and rattles on their bodies had subsided, Evil Forest addressed the two groups of people facing them.

"Uzowulu's body, I salute you," he said. Spirits always addressed humans as "bodies." Uzowulu bent down and touched the earth with his right hand as a sign of submission.

"Our father, my hand has touched the ground," he said.

"Uzowulu's body, do you know me?" asked the spirit.

"How can I know you, father? You are beyond our knowledge."

Evil Forest then turned to the other group and addressed the eldest of the three brothers.

"The body of Odukwe, I greet you," he said, and Odukwe bent down and touched the earth. The hearing then began.

Uzowulu stepped forward and presented his case.

"That woman standing there is my wife, Mgbafo. I married her with my money and my yams. I do not owe my in-laws anything. I owe them no yams. I owe them no coco-yams. One morning three of them came to my house, beat me up, and took my wife and children away. This happened in the rainy season. I have waited in vain for my wife to return. At last I went to my in-laws and said to them, 'You have taken back your sister. I did not send her away. You yourselves took her. The law of the clan is that you should return her bride-price.' But my wife's brothers said they had nothing to tell me. So I have brought the matter to the fathers of the clan. My case is finished. I salute you."

"Your words are good," said the leader of the *egwugwu*. "Let us hear Odukwe. His words may also be good."

Odukwe was short and thickset. He stepped forward, saluted the spirits, and began his story.

"My in-law has told you that we went to his house, beat him up, and took our sister and her children away. All that is true. He told you that he came to take back her bride-price and we refused to give it him. That also is true. My in-law, Uzowulu, is a beast. My sister lived with him for nine years. During those years no single day passed in the sky without his beating the woman. We have tried to settle their quarrels time without number and on each occasion Uzowulu was guilty—"

"It is a lie!" Uzowulu shouted.

"Two years ago," continued Odukwe, "when she was pregnant, he beat her until she miscarried."

"It is a lie. She miscarried after she had gone to sleep with her lover."

"Uzowulu's body, I salute you," said Evil Forest, silencing him. "What kind of lover sleeps with a pregnant woman?" There was a loud murmur of approbation from the crowd. Odukwe continued:

"Last year when my sister was recovering from an illness, he beat her again so that if the neighbors had not gone in to save her she would have been killed. We heard of it, and did as you have been told. The law of Umuofia is that if a woman runs away from her husband her bride-price is returned. But in this case she ran away to save her life. Her two children belong to Uzowulu. We do not dispute it, but they are too young to leave their mother. If, in the other hand, Uzowulu should recover from his madness and come in the proper way to beg his wife to return she will do so on the understanding that if he ever beats her again we shall cut off his genitals for him."

The crowd roared with laughter. Evil Forest rose to his feet and order was immediately restored. A steady cloud of smoke rose from his head. He sat down again and called two witnesses. They were both Uzowulu's neighbors, and they agreed about the beating. Evil Forest then stood up, pulled out his staff and thrust it into the earth again. He ran a few steps in the direction of the women; they all fled in terror, only to return to their places almost immediately. The nine *egwugwu* then went away to consult together in their house. They were silent for a long time. Then the metal gong sounded and the flute was blown. The *egwugwu* had emerged once again from their underground home. They saluted one another and then reappeared on the *ilo*.

"*Umuofia kwenu!*" roared Evil Forest, facing the elders and grandees of the clan.

"*Yaa!*" replied the thunderous crowd; then silence descended from the sky and swallowed the noise.

Evil Forest began to speak and all the while he spoke everyone was silent. The eight other *egwugwu* were as still as statues.

"We have heard both sides of the case," said Evil Forest. "Our duty is not to blame this man or to praise that, but to settle the dispute." He turned to Uzowulu's group and allowed a short pause.

"Uzowulu's body, I salute you," he said.

"Our father, my hand has touched the ground," replied Uzowulu, touching the earth.

"Uzowulu's body, do you know me?"

"How can I know you, father? You are beyond our knowledge," Uzowulu replied.

"I am Evil Forest. I kill a man on the day that his life is sweetest to him."

"That is true," replied Uzowulu.

"Go to your in-laws with a pot of wine and beg your wife to return to you. It is not bravery when a man fights with a woman." He turned to Odukwe, and allowed a brief pause.

"Odukwe's body, I greet you," he said.

"My hand is on the ground," replied Odukwe.

"Do you know me?"

"No man can know you," replied Odukwe.

"I am Evil Forest, I am Dry-meat-that-fills-the-mouth, I am Fire-that-burns-without-faggots. If your in-law brings wine to you, let your sister go with him. I salute you." He pulled his staff from the hard earth and thrust it back.

"*Umuofia kwenu!*" he roared, and the crowd answered.

"I don't know why such a trifle should come before the *egwugwu*," said one elder to another.

"Don't you know what kind of man Uzowulu is? He will not listen to any other decision," replied the other.

As they spoke two other groups of people had replaced the first before the *egwugwu*, and a great land case began.

11

The night was impenetrably dark. The moon had been rising later and later every night until now it was seen only at dawn. And whenever the moon forsook evening and rose at cock-crow the nights were as black as charcoal.

Ezinma and her mother sat on a mat on the floor after their supper of yam foo-foo and bitter-leaf soup. A palm-oil lamp gave out yellowish light. Without it, it would have been impossible to eat; one could not have known where one's mouth was in the darkness of that night. There was an oil lamp in all the four huts on Okonkwo's compound, and each hut seen from the others looked like a soft eye of yellow half-light set in the solid massiveness of night.

The world was silent except for the shrill cry of insects, which was part of the night, and the sound of wooden mortar and pestle as Nwayieke pounded her foo-foo. Nwayieke lived four compounds away, and she was notorious for her late cooking. Every woman in the neighborhood knew the sound of Nwayieke's mortar and pestle. It was also part of the night.

Okonkwo had eaten from his wives' dishes and was now reclining with his back against the wall. He searched his bag and brought out his snuff-bottle. He turned it on to his left palm, but nothing came out. He hit the bottle against his knee to shake up the tobacco. That was always the trouble with Okeke's snuff. It very quickly went damp, and there was too much saltpeter in it. Okonkwo had not bought snuff from him for a long time. Idigo was the man who knew how to grind good snuff. But he had recently fallen ill.

Low voices, broken now and again by singing, reached Okonkwo from his wives' huts as each woman and her children told folk stories. Ekwefi and her daughter, Ezinma, sat on a mat on the floor. It was Ekwefi's turn to tell a story.

"Once upon a time," she began, "all the birds were invited to a feast in the sky. They were very happy and began to prepare themselves for the great day. They painted their bodies with red cam wood and drew beautiful patterns on them with *uli*.

"Tortoise saw all these preparations and soon discovered what it all meant. Nothing that happened in the world of the animals ever escaped his notice; he was full of cunning. As soon as he heard of the great feast in the sky his throat began to itch at the very thought. There was a famine in those days and Tortoise had not eaten a good meal for two moons. His body rattled like a piece of dry stick in his empty shell. So he began to plan how he would go to the sky."

"But he had no wings," said Ezinma.

"Be patient," replied her mother. "That is the story. Tortoise had no wings, but he went to the birds and asked to be allowed to go with them.

" 'We know you too well,' said the birds when they had heard him. 'You are full of cunning and you are ungrateful. If we allow you to come with us you will soon begin your mischief.'

" 'You do not know me,' said Tortoise. 'I am a changed man. I have learned that a man who makes trouble for others is also making it for himself.'

"Tortoise had a sweet tongue, and within a short time all the birds agreed that he was a changed man, and they each gave him a feather, with which he made two wings.

"At last the great day came and Tortoise was the first to arrive at the meeting place. When all the birds had gathered together, they set off in a body. Tortoise was very happy and voluble as he flew among the birds, and he was soon chosen as the man to speak for the party because he was a great orator.

" 'There is one important thing which we must not forget,' he said as they flew on their way. 'When people are invited to a great feast like this, they take new names for the occasion. Our hosts in the sky will expect us to honor this age-old custom.'

"None of the birds had heard of this custom but they knew that Tortoise, in spite of his failings in other directions, was a widely traveled man who knew the customs of different peoples. And so they each took a new name. When they had all taken, Tortoise also took one. He was to be called *All of you.*

"At last the party arrived in the sky and their hosts were very happy to see them. Tortoise stood up in his many-colored plumage and thanked them for their invitation. His speech was so eloquent that all the birds were glad they had brought him, and nodded their heads in approval of all he said. Their hosts took him as the king of the birds, especially as he looked somewhat different from the others.

"After kola nuts had been presented and eaten, the people of the sky set before their guests the most delectable dishes Tortoise had ever seen or dreamed of. The soup was brought out hot from the fire and in the very pot in which it had been cooked. It was full of meat and fish. Tortoise began to sniff aloud. There was pounded yam and also yam pottage cooked with palm-oil and fresh fish. There were also pots of palm-wine. When everything had been set before the guests, one of the people of the sky came forward and tasted a little from each pot. He then invited the birds to eat. But Tortoise jumped to his feet and asked: 'For whom have you prepared this feast?'

" 'For all of you,' replied the man.

"Tortoise turned to the birds and said: 'You remember that my name is *All of you.* The custom here is to serve the spokesman first and the others later. They will serve you when I have eaten.'

"He began to eat and the birds grumbled angrily. The people of the sky thought it must be their custom to leave all the food for their king. And so Tortoise ate the best part of the food and then drank two pots of palm-wine, so that he was full of food and drink and his body filled out in his shell.

"The birds gathered round to eat what was left and to peck at the bones he had thrown all about the floor. Some of them were too angry to eat. They chose to fly home on an empty stomach. But before they left each took back the feather he had lent to Tortoise. And there he stood in his hard shell full of food and wine but without any wings to fly home. He asked the birds to take a message for his wife, but they all refused. In the end Parrot, who had felt more angry than the others, suddenly changed his mind and agreed to take the message.

"'Tell my wife,' said Tortoise, 'to bring out all the soft things in my house and cover the compound with them so that I can jump down from the sky without very great danger.'

"Parrot promised to deliver the message, and then flew away. But when he reached Tortoise's house he told his wife to bring out all the hard things in the house. And so she brought out her husband's hoes, machetes, spears, guns, and even his cannon. Tortoise looked down from the sky and saw his wife bringing things out, but it was too far to see what they were. When all seemed ready he let himself go. He fell and fell and fell until he began to fear that he would never stop falling. And then like the sound of his cannon he crashed on the compound."

"Did he die?" asked Ezinma.

"No," replied Ekwefi. "His shell broke into pieces. But there was a great medicine man in the neighborhood. Tortoise's wife sent for him and he gathered all the bits of shell and stuck them together. That is why Tortoise's shell is not smooth."

"There is no song in the story," Ezinma pointed out.

"No," said Ekwefi. "I shall think of another one with a song. But it is your turn now."

"Once upon a time," Ezinma began, "Tortoise and Cat went to wrestle against Yams — no, that is not the beginning. Once upon a time there was a great famine in the land of animals. Everybody was lean except Cat, who was fat and whose body shone as if oil was rubbed on it . . ."

She broke off because at that very moment a loud and high-pitched voice broke the outer silence of the night. It was Chielo, the priestess of Agbala, prophesying. There was nothing new in that. Once in a while Chielo was possessed by the spirit of her god and she began to prophesy. But tonight she was addressing her prophecy and greetings to Okonkwo, and so everyone in his family listened. The folk stories stopped.

"*Agbala do-o-o-o! Agbala ekeneo-o-o-o-o,*" came the voice like a sharp knife cutting through the night. "*Okonkwo! Agbala ekene gio-o-o-o! Agbala cholu ifu ada ya Ezinmao-o-o-o!*" [21]

At the mention of Ezinma's name Ekwefi jerked her head sharply like an animal that had sniffed death in the air. Her heart jumped painfully within her.

---

[21] "*Agbala do-o-o-o! . . . Ezinmao-o-o-o!*": "Agbala wants something! Agbala greets," . . . "Okonkwo! Agbala greets you! Agbala wants to see his daughter Ezinma!"

The priestess had now reached Okonkwo's compound and was talking with him outside his hut. She was saying again and again that Agbala wanted to see his daughter, Ezinma. Okonkwo pleaded with her to come back in the morning because Ezinma was now asleep. But Chielo ignored what he was trying to say and went on shouting that Agbala wanted to see his daughter. Her voice was as clear as metal, and Okonkwo's women and children heard from their huts all that she said. Okonkwo was still pleading that the girl had been ill of late and was asleep. Ekwefi quickly took her to their bedroom and placed her on their high bamboo bed.

The priestess screamed. "Beware, Okonkwo!" she warned. "Beware of exchanging words with Agbala. Does a man speak when a god speaks? Beware!"

She walked through Okonkwo's hut into the circular compound and went straight toward Ekwefi's hut. Okonkwo came after her.

"Ekwefi," she called, "Agbala greets you. Where is my daughter, Ezinma? Agbala wants to see her."

Ekwefi came out from her hut carrying her oil lamp in her left hand. There was a light wind blowing, so she cupped her right hand to shelter the flame. Nwoye's mother, also carrying an oil lamp, emerged from her hut. The children stood in the darkness outside their hut watching the strange event. Okonkwo's youngest wife also came out and joined the others.

"Where does Agbala want to see her?" Ekwefi asked.

"Where else but in his house in the hills and the caves?" replied the priestess.

"I will come with you, too," Ekwefi said firmly.

"*Tufia-a!*"[22] the priestess cursed, her voice cracking like the angry bark of thunder in the dry season. "How dare you, woman, to go before the mighty Agbala of your own accord? Beware, woman, lest he strike you in his anger. Bring me my daughter."

Ekwefi went into her hut and came out again with Ezinma.

"Come, my daughter," said the priestess. "I shall carry you on my back. A baby on its mother's back does not know that the way is long."

Ezinma began to cry. She was used to Chielo calling her "my daughter." But it was a different Chielo she now saw in the yellow half-light.

"Don't cry, my daughter," said the priestess, "lest Agbala be angry with you."

"Don't cry," said Ekwefi, "she will bring you back very soon. I shall give you some fish to eat." She went into the hut again and brought down the smoke-black basket in which she kept her dried fish and other ingredients for cooking soup. She broke a piece in two and gave it to Ezinma, who clung to her.

"Don't be afraid," said Ekwefi, stroking her head, which was shaved in places, leaving a regular pattern of hair. They went outside again. The priestess bent down on one knee and Ezinma climbed on her back, her left palm closed on her fish and her eyes gleaming with tears.

"*Agbala do-o-o-o! Agbala ekeneo-o-o-o!* . . ." Chielo began once again to chant greetings to her god. She turned round sharply and walked through Okonkwo's hut,

---

[22] *"Tufia-a!":* An oath; literally, "spitting out."

bending very low at the eaves. Ezinma was crying loudly now, calling on her mother. The two voices disappeared into the thick darkness.

A strange and sudden weakness descended on Ekwefi as she stood gazing in the direction of the voices like a hen whose only chick has been carried away by a kite. Ezinma's voice soon faded away and only Chielo was heard moving farther and farther into the distance.

"Why do you stand there as though she had been kidnapped?" asked Okonkwo as he went back to his hut.

"She will bring her back soon," Nwoye's mother said.

But Ekwefi did not hear these consolations. She stood for a while, and then, all of a sudden, made up her mind. She hurried through Okonkwo's hut and went outside. "Where are you going?" he asked.

"I am following Chielo," she replied and disappeared in the darkness. Okonkwo cleared his throat, and brought out his snuff-bottle from the goatskin bag by his side.

The priestess's voice was already growing faint in the distance. Ekwefi hurried to the main footpath and turned left in the direction of the voice. Her eyes were useless to her in the darkness. But she picked her way easily on the sandy footpath hedged on either side by branches and damp leaves. She began to run, holding her breasts with her hands to stop them flapping noisily against her body. She hit her left foot against an outcropped root, and terror seized her. It was an ill omen. She ran faster. But Chielo's voice was still a long way away. Had she been running too? How could she go so fast with Ezinma on her back? Although the night was cool, Ekwefi was beginning to feel hot from her running. She continually ran into the luxuriant weeds and creepers that walled in the path. Once she tripped up and fell. Only then did she realize, with a start, that Chielo had stopped her chanting. Her heart beat violently and she stood still. Then Chielo's renewed outburst came from only a few paces ahead. But Ekwefi could not see her. She shut her eyes for a while and opened them again in an effort to see. But it was useless. She could not see beyond her nose.

There were no stars in the sky because there was a rain-cloud. Fireflies went about with their tiny green lamps, which only made the darkness more profound. Between Chielo's outbursts the night was alive with the shrill tremor of forest insects woven into the darkness.

"*Agbala do-o-o-o!* . . . *Agbala ekeneo-o-o-o!* . . ." Ekwefi trudged behind, neither getting too near nor keeping too far back. She thought they must be going towards the sacred cave. Now that she walked slowly she had time to think. What would she do when they got to the cave? She would not dare to enter. She would wait at the mouth, all alone in that fearful place. She thought of all the terrors of the night. She remembered that night, long ago, when she had seen *Ogbu-agali-odu*, one of those evil essences loosed upon the world by the potent "medicines" which the tribe had made in the distant past against its enemies but had now forgotten how to control. Ekwefi had been returning from the stream with her mother on a dark night like this when they saw its glow as it flew in their direction. They had thrown down their water-pots and lain by the roadside expecting the sinister light to descend on them and kill them. That was the only time Ekwefi ever saw *Ogbu-agali-odu*. But although it had happened so long ago, her blood still ran cold whenever she remembered that night.

The priestess's voice came at longer intervals now, but its vigor was undiminished. The air was cool and damp with dew. Ezinma sneezed. Ekwefi muttered, "Life to you." At the same time the priestess also said, "Life to you, my daughter." Ezinma's voice from the darkness warmed her mother's heart. She trudged slowly along.

And then the priestess screamed. "Somebody is walking behind me!" she said. "Whether you are spirit or man, may Agbala shave your head with a blunt razor! May he twist your neck until you see your heels!"

Ekwefi stood rooted to the spot. One mind said to her: "Woman, go home before Agbala does you harm." But she could not. She stood until Chielo had increased the distance between them and she began to follow again. She had already walked so long that she began to feel a slight numbness in the limbs and in the head. Then it occurred to her that they could not have been heading for the cave. They must have by-passed it long ago; they must be going towards Umuachi, the farthest village in the clan. Chielo's voice now came after long intervals.

It seemed to Ekwefi that the night had become a little lighter. The cloud had lifted and a few stars were out. The moon must be preparing to rise, its sullenness over. When the moon rose late in the night, people said it was refusing food, as a sullen husband refuses his wife's food when they have quarrelled.

"Agbala do-o-o-o! Umuachi! Agbala ekene unuo-o-o!" It was just as Ekwefi had thought. The priestess was now saluting the village of Umuachi. It was unbelievable, the distance they had covered. As they emerged into the open village from the narrow forest track the darkness was softened and it became possible to see the vague shape of trees. Ekwefi screwed her eyes up in an effort to see her daughter and the priestess, but whenever she thought she saw their shape it immediately dissolved like a melting lump of darkness. She walked numbly along.

Chielo's voice was now rising continuously, as when she first set out. Ekwefi had a feeling of spacious openness, and she guessed they must be on the village *ilo,* or playground. And she realized too with something like a jerk that Chielo was no longer moving forward. She was, in fact, returning. Ekwefi quickly moved away from her line of retreat. Chielo passed by, and they began to go back the way they had come.

It was a long and weary journey and Ekwefi felt like a sleepwalker most of the way. The moon was definitely rising, and although it had not yet appeared on the sky its light had already melted down the darkness. Ekwefi could now discern the figure of the priestess and her burden. She slowed down her pace so as to increase the distance between them. She was afraid of what might happen if Chielo suddenly turned round and saw her.

She had prayed for the moon to rise. But now she found the half-light of the incipient moon more terrifying than darkness. The world was now peopled with vague, fantastic figures that dissolved under her steady gaze and then formed again in new shapes. At one stage Ekwefi was so afraid that she nearly called out to Chielo for companionship and human sympathy. What she had seen was the shape of a man climbing a palm tree, his head pointing to the earth and his legs skywards. But at that very moment Chielo's voice rose again in her possessed chanting, and Ekwefi recoiled, because there was no humanity there. It was not the same Chielo who sat with her in the market and sometimes bought beancakes for Ezinma, whom she called her daughter. It was a different woman—the priestess of Agbala, the Oracle of the Hills and Caves. Ekwefi trudged along between two fears. The sound of her benumbed steps seemed to come from some other person walking behind her. Her arms were folded across her bare breasts. Dew fell heavily and the air was cold. She could no longer think, not even about the terrors of night. She just jogged along in a half-sleep, only waking to full life when Chielo sang.

At last they took a turning and began to head for the caves. From then on, Chielo never ceased in her chanting. She greeted her god in a multitude of names—the owner of the future, the messenger of earth, the god who cut a man down when his life was sweetest to him. Ekwefi was also awakened and her benumbed fears revived.

The moon was now up and she could see Chielo and Ezinma clearly. How a woman could carry a child of that size so easily and for so long was a miracle. But Ekwefi was not thinking about that. Chielo was not a woman that night.

"Agbala do-o-o-o! Agbala ekeneo-o-o-o! Chi negbu madu ubosi ndu ya nato ya uto daluo-o-o!" [23]

Ekwefi could already see the hills looming in the moonlight. They formed a circular ring with a break at one point through which the foot-track led to the center of the circle.

As soon as the priestess stepped into this ring of hills her voice was not only doubled in strength but was thrown back on all sides. It was indeed the shrine of a great god. Ekwefi picked her way carefully and quietly. She was already beginning to doubt the wisdom of her coming. Nothing would happen to Ezinma, she thought. And if anything happened to her could she stop it? She would not dare to enter the underground caves. Her coming was quite useless, she thought.

As these things went through her mind she did not realize how close they were to the cave mouth. And so when the priestess with Ezinma on her back disappeared through a hole hardly big enough to pass a hen, Ekwefi broke into a run as though to stop them. As she stood gazing at the circular darkness which had swallowed them, tears gushed from her eyes, and she swore within her that if she heard Ezinma cry she would rush into the cave to defend her against all the gods in the world. She would die with her.

Having sworn that oath, she sat down on a stony ledge and waited. Her fear had vanished. She could hear the priestess's voice, all its metal taken out of it by the vast emptiness of the cave. She buried her face in her lap and waited.

She did not know how long she waited. It must have been a very long time. Her back was turned on the footpath that led out of the hills. She must have heard a noise behind her and turned round sharply. A man stood there with a machete in his hand. Ekwefi uttered a scream and sprang to her feet.

---

[23] *"Agbala . . . daluo-o-o!"*: "Agbala wants something! Agbala greets. . . . *Chi* who kills a man on the day his life is so pleasant he gives thanks!"

"Don't be foolish," said Okonkwo's voice. "I thought you were going into the shrine with Chielo," he mocked.

Ekwefi did not answer. Tears of gratitude filled her eyes. She knew her daughter was safe.

"Go home and sleep," said Okonkwo. "I shall wait here."

"I shall wait too. It is almost dawn. The first cock has crowed."

As they stood there together, Ekwefi's mind went back to the days when they were young. She had married Anene because Okonkwo was too poor then to marry. Two years after her marriage to Anene she could bear it no longer and she ran away to Okonkwo. It had been early in the morning. The moon was shining. She was going to the stream to fetch water. Okonkwo's house was on the way to the stream. She went in and knocked at his door and he came out. Even in those days he was not a man of many words. He just carried her into his bed and in the darkness began to feel around her waist for the loose end of her cloth.

12

On the following morning the entire neighborhood wore a festive air because Okonkwo's friend, Obierika, was celebrating his daughter's *uri*. It was the day on which her suitor (having already paid the greater part of her bride-price) would bring palm-wine not only to her parents and immediate relatives but to the wide and extensive group of kinsmen called *umunna*. Everybody had been invited— men, women, and children. But it was really a woman's ceremony and the central figures were the bride and her mother.

As soon as day broke, breakfast was hastily eaten and women and children began to gather at Obierika's compound to help the bride's mother in her difficult but happy task of cooking for a whole village.

Okonkwo's family was astir like any other family in the neighborhood. Nwoye's mother and Okonkwo's youngest wife were ready to set out for Obierika's compound with all their children. Nwoye's mother carried a basket of coco-yams, a cake of salt, and smoked fish which she would present to Obierika's wife. Okonkwo's youngest wife, Ojiugo, also had a basket of plantains and coco-yams and a small pot of palm-oil. Their children carried pots of water.

Ekwefi was tired and sleepy from the exhausting experiences of the previous night. It was not very long since they had returned. The priestess, with Ezinma sleeping on her back, had crawled out of the shrine on her belly like a snake. She had not as much as looked at Okonkwo and Ekwefi or shown any surprise at finding them at the mouth of the cave. She looked straight ahead of her and walked back to the village. Okonkwo and his wife followed at a respectful distance. They thought the priestess might be going to her house, but she went to Okonkwo's compound, passed through his *obi* and into Ekwefi's hut and walked into her bedroom. She placed Ezinma carefully on the bed and went away without saying a word to anybody.

Ezinma was still sleeping when everyone else was astir, and Ekwefi asked Nwoye's mother and Ojiugo to explain to Obierika's wife that she would be late. She had got ready her basket of coco-yams and fish, but she must wait for Ezinma to wake.

"You need some sleep yourself," said Nwoye's mother. "You look very tired."

As they spoke Ezinma emerged from the hut, rubbing her eyes and stretching her spare frame. She saw the other children with their water-pots and remembered that they were going to fetch water for Obierika's wife. She went back to the hut and brought her pot.

"Have you slept enough?" asked her mother.

"Yes," she replied. "Let us go."

"Not before you have had your breakfast," said Ekwefi. And she went into her hut to warm the vegetable soup she had cooked last night.

"We shall be going," said Nwoye's mother. "I will tell Obierika's wife that you are coming later." And so they all went to help Obierika's wife—Nwoye's mother with her four children and Ojiugo with her two.

As they trooped through Okonkwo's *obi* he asked: "Who will prepare my afternoon meal?"

"I shall return to do it," said Ojiugo.

Okonkwo was also feeling tired, and sleepy, for although nobody else knew it, he had not slept at all last night. He had felt very anxious but did not show it. When Ekwefi had followed the priestess, he had allowed what he regarded as a reasonable and manly interval to pass and then gone with his machete to the shrine, where he thought they must be. It was only when he had got there that it had occurred to him that the priestess might have chosen to go round the villages first. Okonkwo had returned home and sat waiting. When he thought he had waited long enough he again returned to the shrine. But the Hills and the Caves were as silent as death. It was only on his fourth trip that he had found Ekwefi, and by then he had become gravely worried.

Obierika's compound was as busy as an anthill. Temporary cooking tripods were erected on every available space by bringing together three blocks of sun-dried earth and making a fire in their midst. Cooking pots went up and down the tripods, and foo-foo was pounded in a hundred wooden mortars. Some of the women cooked the yams and the cassava, and others prepared vegetable soup. Young men pounded the foo-foo or split firewood. The children made endless trips to the stream.

Three young men helped Obierika to slaughter the two goats with which the soup was made. They were very fat goats, but the fattest of all was tethered to a peg near the wall of the compound. It was as big as a small cow. Obierika had sent one of his relatives all the way to Umuike to buy that goat. It was the one he would present alive to his in-laws.

"The market of Umuike is a wonderful place," said the young man who had been sent by Obierika to buy the giant goat. "There are so many people on it that if you threw up a grain of sand it would not find a way to fall to earth again."

"It is the result of a great medicine," said Obierika. "The people of Umuike wanted their market to grow and swallow up the markets of their neighbors. So they made a powerful medicine. Every market day, before the first cock-crow, this medicine stands on the market ground in the shape of an old woman with a fan. With this magic fan she beckons to the market all the neighboring clans. She beckons in front of her and behind her, to her right and to her left."

"And so everybody comes," said another man, "honest men and thieves. They can steal your cloth from off your waist in that market."

"Yes," said Obierika. "I warned Nwankwo to keep a sharp eye and a sharp ear. There was once a man who went to sell a goat. He led it on a thick rope which he tied round his wrist. But as he walked through the market he realized that people were pointing at him as they do to a madman. He could not understand it until he looked back and saw that what he led at the end of the tether was not a goat but a heavy log of wood."

"Do you think a thief can do that kind of thing single-handed?" asked Nwankwo.

"No," said Obierika. "They use medicine."

When they had cut the goats' throats and collected the blood in a bowl, they held them over an open fire to burn off the hair, and the smell of burning hair blended with the smell of cooking. Then they washed them and cut them up for the women who prepared the soup.

All this anthill activity was going smoothly when a sudden interruption came. It was a cry in the distance: *Oji odu achu ijiji-o-o! (The one that uses its tail to drive flies away!)* Every woman immediately abandoned whatever she was doing and rushed out in the direction of the cry.

"We cannot all rush out like that, leaving what we are cooking to burn in the fire," shouted Chielo, the priestess. "Three or four of us should stay behind."

"It is true," said another woman. "We will allow three or four women to stay behind."

Five women stayed behind to look after the cooking-pots, and all the rest rushed away to see the cow that had been let loose. When they saw it they drove it back to its owner, who at once paid the heavy fine which the village imposed on anyone whose cow was let loose on his neighbors' crops. When the women had exacted the penalty they checked among themselves to see if any woman had failed to come out when the cry had been raised.

"Where is Mgbogo?" asked one of them.

"She is ill in bed," said Mgbogo's next-door neighbor. "She has *iba.*"

"The only other person is Udenkwo," said another woman, "and her child is not twenty-eight days yet."

Those women whom Obierika's wife had not asked to help her with the cooking returned to their homes, and the rest went back, in a body, to Obierika's compound.

"Whose cow was it?" asked the women who had been allowed to stay behind.

"It was my husband's," said Ezelagbo. "One of the young children had opened the gate of the cow-shed."

Early in the afternoon the first two pots of palm-wine arrived from Obierika's in-laws. They were duly presented to the women, who drank a cup or two each, to help them in their cooking. Some of it also went to the bride and her attendant maidens, who were putting the last delicate touches of razor to her coiffure and cam wood on her smooth skin.

When the heat of the sun began to soften, Obierika's son, Maduka, took a long broom and swept the ground in front of his father's *obi.* And as if they had been waiting for that, Obierika's relatives and friends began to arrive, every man with his goatskin bag hung on one shoulder and a rolled goatskin mat under his arm. Some of them were accompanied by their sons bearing carved wooden stools. Okonkwo was one of them. They sat in a half-circle and began to talk of many things. It would not be long before the suitors came.

Okonkwo brought out his snuff-bottle and offered it to Ogbuefi Ezenwa, who sat next to him. Ezenwa took it, tapped it on his kneecap, rubbed his left palm on his body to dry it before tipping a little snuff into it. His actions were deliberate, and he spoke as he performed them:

"I hope our in-laws will bring many pots of wine. Although they come from a village that is known for being closefisted, they ought to know that Akueke is the bride for a king."

"They dare not bring fewer than thirty pots," said Okonkwo. "I shall tell them my mind if they do."

At that moment Obierika's son, Maduka, led out the giant goat from the inner compound, for his father's relatives to see. They all admired it and said that that was the way things should be done. The goat was then led back to the inner compound.

Very soon after, the in-laws began to arrive. Young men and boys in single file, each carrying a pot of wine, came first. Obierika's relatives counted the pots as they came. Twenty, twenty-five. There was a long break, and the hosts looked at each other as if to say, "I told you." Then more pots came. Thirty, thirty-five, forty, forty-five. The hosts nodded in approval and seemed to say, "Now they are behaving like men." Altogether there were fifty pots of wine. After the pot-bearers came Ibe, the suitor, and the elders of his family. They sat in a half-moon, thus completing a circle with their hosts. The pots of wine stood in their midst. Then the bride, her mother, and a half a dozen other women and girls emerged from the inner compound, and went round the circle shaking hands with all. The bride's mother led the way, followed by the bride and the other women. The married women wore their best cloths and the girls wore red and black waist-beads and anklets of brass.

When the women retired, Obierika presented kola nuts to his in-laws. His eldest brother broke the first one. "Life to all of us," he said as he broke it. "And let there be friendship between your family and ours."

The crowd answered: "*Ee-e-e!*"

"We are giving you our daughter today. She will be a good wife to you. She will bear you nine sons like the mother of our town."

"*Ee-e-e!*"

The oldest man in the camp of the visitors replied: "It will be good for you and it will be good for us."

"*Ee-e-e!*"

"This is not the first time my people have come to marry your daughter. My mother was one of you."

"*Ee-e-e!*"

"And this will not be the last, because you understand us and we understand you. You are a great family."

"*Ee-e-e!*"

"Prosperous men and great warriors." He looked in the direction of Okonkwo. "Your daughter will bear us sons like you."

"*Ee-e-e!*"

The kola was eaten and the drinking of palm-wine began. Groups of four or five men sat round with a pot in their midst. As the evening wore on, food was presented to the guests. There were huge bowls of foo-foo and steaming pots of soup. There were also pots of yam pottage. It was a great feast.

As night fell, burning torches were set on wooden tripods and the young men raised a song. The elders sat in a big circle and the singers went round singing each man's praise as they came before him. They had something to say for every man. Some were great farmers, some were orators who spoke for the clan; Okonkwo was the greatest wrestler and warrior alive. When they had gone round the circle they settled down in the center, and girls came from the inner compound to dance. At first the bride was not among them. But when she finally appeared holding a cock in her right hand, a loud cheer rose from the crowd. All the other dancers made way for her. She presented the cock to the musicians and began to dance. Her brass anklets rattled as she danced and her body gleamed with cam wood in the soft yellow light. The musicians with their wood, clay, and metal instruments went from song to song. And they were all gay. They sang the latest song in the village:

> "*If I hold her hand*
>> *She says, 'Don't touch!'*
> *If I hold her foot*
>> *She says, 'Don't touch!'*
> *But when I hold her waist-beads*
>> *She pretends not to know.*"

The night was already far spent when the guests rose to go, taking their bride home to spend seven market weeks with her suitor's family. They sang songs as they went, and on their way they paid short courtesy visits to prominent men like Okonkwo, before they finally left for their village. Okonkwo made a present of two cocks to them.

13

Go-di-di-go-go-di-go. Di-go-go-di-go. It was the *ekwe* talking to the clan. One of the things every man learned was the language of the hollowed-out wooden instrument. Diim! Diim! Diim! boomed the cannon at intervals.

The first cock had not crowed, and Umuofia was still swallowed up in sleep and silence when the *ekwe* began to talk, and the cannon shattered the silence. Men stirred on their bamboo beds and listened anxiously. Somebody was dead. The cannon seemed to rend the sky. Di-go-go-di-go-di-di-go-go floated in the message-laden night air. The faint and distant wailing of women settled like a sediment of sorrow on the earth. Now and again a full-chested lamentation rose above the wailing whenever a man came into the place of death. He raised his voice once or twice in manly sorrow and then sat down with the other men listening to the endless wailing of the women and the esoteric language of the *ekwe*. Now and again the cannon boomed. The wailing of the women would not be heard beyond the village, but the *ekwe* carried the news to all the nine villages and even beyond. It began by naming the clan: *Umuofia obodo dike*, "the land of the brave." *Umuofia obodo dike! Umuofia obodo dike!* It said this over and over again, and as it dwelt on it, anxiety mounted in every heart that heaved on a bamboo bed that night. Then it went nearer and named the village: *"Iguedo of the yellow grinding-stone!"* It was Okonkwo's village. Again and again Iguedo was called and men waited breathlessly in all the nine villages. At last the man was named and people sighed "E-u-u, Ezeudu is dead." A cold shiver ran down Okonkwo's back as he remembered the last time the old man had visited him. "That boy calls you father," he had said. "Bear no hand in his death."

Ezeudu was a great man, and so all the clan was at his funeral. The ancient drums of death beat, guns and cannon were fired, and men dashed about in frenzy, cutting down every tree or animal they saw, jumping over walls and dancing on the roof. It was a warrior's funeral, and from morning till night warriors came and went in their age groups. They all wore smoked raffia skirts and their bodies were painted with chalk and charcoal. Now and again an ancestral spirit or *egwugwu* appeared from the underworld, speaking in a tremulous, unearthly voice and completely covered in raffia. Some of them were very violent, and there had been a mad rush for shelter earlier in the day when one appeared with a sharp machete and was only prevented from doing serious harm by two men who restrained him with the help of a strong rope tied round his waist. Sometimes he turned round and chased those men, and they ran for their lives. But they always returned to the long rope he trailed behind. He sang, in a terrifying voice, that Ekwensu, or Evil Spirit, had entered his eye.

But the most dreaded of all was yet to come. He was always alone and was shaped like a coffin. A sickly odor hung in the air wherever he went, and flies went with him. Even the greatest medicine men took shelter when he was near. Many years ago another *egwugwu* had dared to stand his ground before him and had been transfixed to the spot for two days. This one had only one hand and it carried a basket full of water.

But some of the *egwugwu* were quite harmless. One of them was so old and infirm that he leaned heavily on a stick. He walked unsteadily to the place where the corpse was laid, gazed at it a while, and went away again — to the underworld.

The land of the living was not far removed from the domain of the ancestors. There was coming and going between them, especially at festivals and also when an old man died, because an old man was very close to the ancestors. A man's life from birth to death was a series of transition rites which brought him nearer and nearer to his ancestors.

Ezeudu had been the oldest man in his village, and at his death there were only three men in the whole clan who were older, and four or five others in his own age group. Whenever one of these ancient men appeared in the crowd to dance unsteadily the funeral steps of the tribe, younger men gave way and the tumult subsided.

It was a great funeral, such as befitted a noble warrior. As the evening drew near, the shouting and the firing of guns, the beating of drums, and the brandishing and clanging of machetes increased.

Ezeudu had taken three titles in his life. It was a rare achievement. There were only four titles in the clan, and only one or two men in any generation ever achieved the fourth and highest. When they did, they became the lords of the land. Because he had taken titles, Ezeudu was to be buried after dark with only a glowing brand to light the sacred ceremony.

But before this quiet and final rite, the tumult increased tenfold. Drums beat violently and men leaped up and down in frenzy. Guns were fired on all sides and sparks flew out as machetes clanged together in warriors' salutes. The air was full of dust and the smell of gunpowder. It was then that the one-handed spirit came, carrying a basket full of water. People made way for him on all sides and the noise subsided. Even the smell of gunpowder was swallowed in the sickly smell that now filled the air. He danced a few steps to the funeral drums and then went to see the corpse.

"Ezeudu!" he called in his guttural voice. "If you had been poor in your last life I would have asked you to be rich when you come again. But you were rich. If you had been a coward, I would have asked you to bring courage. But you were a fearless warrior. If you had died young, I would have asked you to get life. But you lived long. So I shall ask you to come again the way you came before. If your death was the death of nature, go in peace. But if a man caused it, do not allow him a moment's rest." He danced a few more steps and went away.

The drums and the dancing began again and reached fever-heat. Darkness was around the corner, and the burial was near. Guns fired the last salute and the cannon rent the sky. And then from the center of the delirious fury came a cry of agony and shouts of horror. It was as if a spell had been cast. All was silent. In the center of the crowd a boy lay in a pool of blood. It was the dead man's sixteen-year-old son, who with his brothers and half-brothers had been dancing the traditional farewell to their father. Okonkwo's gun had exploded and a piece of iron had pierced the boy's heart.

The confusion that followed was without parallel in the tradition of Umuofia. Violent deaths were frequent, but nothing like this had ever happened.

The only course open to Okonkwo was to flee from the clan. It was a crime against the earth goddess to kill a clansman, and a man who committed it must flee from the land. The crime was of two kinds, male and female. Okonkwo had committed the female, because it had been inadvertent. He could return to the clan after seven years.

That night he collected his most valuable belongings into head-loads. His wives wept bitterly and their children wept with them without knowing why. Obierika and half a dozen other friends came to help and to console him. They each made nine or ten trips carrying Okonkwo's yams to store in Obierika's barn. And before the cock crowed Okonkwo and his family were fleeing to his motherland. It was a little village called Mbanta, just beyond the borders of Mbaino.

As soon as the day broke, a large crowd of men from Ezeudu's quarter stormed Okonkwo's compound, dressed in garbs of war. They set fire to his houses, demolished his red walls, killed his animals, and destroyed his barn. It was the justice of the earth goddess, and they were merely her messengers. They had no hatred in their hearts against Okonkwo. His greatest friend, Obierika, was among them. They were merely cleansing the land which Okonkwo had polluted with the blood of a clansman.

Obierika was a man who thought about things. When the will of the goddess had been done, he sat down in his *obi* and mourned his friend's calamity. Why should a man suffer so grievously for an offense he had committed inadvertently? But although he thought for a long time he found no answer. He was merely led into greater complexities. He remembered his wife's twin children, whom he had thrown away. What crime had they committed? The Earth had decreed that they were an offense on the land and must be destroyed. And if the clan did not exact punishment for an offense against the great goddess, her wrath was loosed on all the land and not just on the offender. As the elders said, if one finger brought oil it soiled the others.

Part II

14

Okonkwo was well received by his mother's kinsmen in Mbanta. The old man who received him was his mother's younger brother, who was now the eldest surviving member of that family. His name was Uchendu, and it was he who had received Okonkwo's mother twenty and ten years before when she had been brought home from Umuofia to be buried with her people. Okonkwo was only a boy then and Uchendu still remembered him crying the traditional farewell: "Mother, mother, mother is going."

That was many years ago. Today Okonkwo was not bringing his mother home to be buried with her people. He was taking his family of three wives and their children to seek refuge in his motherland. As soon as Uchendu saw him with his sad and weary company he guessed what had happened, and asked no questions. It was not until the following day that Okonkwo told him the full story. The old man listened silently to the end and then said with some relief: "It is a female *ochu*."[24] And he arranged the requisite rites and sacrifices.

Okonkwo was given a plot of ground on which to build his compound, and two or three pieces of land on which to farm during the coming planting season. With the help of his mother's kinsmen he built himself an *obi* and three huts for his wives. He then installed his personal god and the symbols of his departed fathers. Each of Uchendu's five sons contributed three hundred seed-yams to enable their cousin to plant a farm, for as soon as the first rain came farming would begin.

At last the rain came. It was sudden and tremendous. For two or three moons the sun had been gathering strength till it seemed to breathe a breath of fire on the

---

[24] *ochu:* Manslaughter; because the killing was unintentional, it is a "female" crime.

earth. All the grass had long been scorched brown, and the sands felt like live coals to the feet. Evergreen trees wore a dusty coat of brown. The birds were silenced in the forests, and the world lay panting under the live, vibrating heat. And then came the clap of thunder. It was an angry, metallic, and thirsty clap, unlike the deep and liquid rumbling of the rainy season. A mighty wind arose and filled the air with dust. Palm trees swayed as the wind combed their leaves into flying crests like strange and fantastic coiffure.

When the rain finally came, it was in large, solid drops of frozen water which the people called "the nuts of the water of heaven." They were hard and painful on the body as they fell, yet young people ran about happily picking up the cold nuts and throwing them into their mouths to melt.

The earth quickly came to life and the birds in the forests fluttered around and chirped merrily. A vague scent of life and green vegetation was diffused in the air. As the rain began to fall more soberly and in smaller liquid drops, children sought for shelter, and all were happy, refreshed, and thankful.

Okonkwo and his family worked very hard to plant a new farm. But it was like beginning life anew without the vigor and enthusiasm of youth, like learning to become left-handed in old age. Work no longer had for him the pleasure it used to have, and when there was no work to do he sat in a silent half-sleep.

His life had been ruled by a great passion — to become one of the lords of the clan. That had been his life-spring. And he had all but achieved it. Then everything had been broken. He had been cast out of his clan like a fish onto a dry, sandy beach, panting. Clearly his personal god or *chi* was not made for great things. A man could not rise beyond the destiny of his *chi*. The saying of the elders was not true — that if a man said yea his *chi* also affirmed. Here was a man whose *chi* said nay despite his own affirmation.

The old man, Uchendu, saw clearly that Okonkwo had yielded to despair and he was greatly troubled. He would speak to him after the *isa-ifi*[25] ceremony.

The youngest of Uchendu's five sons, Amikwu, was marrying a new wife. The bride-price had been paid and all but the last ceremony had been performed. Amikwu and his people had taken palm-wine to the bride's kinsmen about two moons before Okonkwo's arrival in Mbanta. And so it was time for the final ceremony of confession.

The daughters of the family were all there, some of them having come a long way from their homes in distant villages. Uchendu's eldest daughter had come from Obodo, nearly half a day's journey away. The daughters of Uchendu's brothers were also there. It was a full gathering of *umuada*,[26] in the same way as they would meet if a death occurred in the family. There were twenty-two of them.

They sat in a big circle on the ground and the bride sat in the center with a hen in her right hand. Uchendu sat by her, holding the ancestral staff of the family. All

---

[25] *isa-ifi:* A ceremony held to determine the fidelity of a wife who has been separated from her husband for a long period of time.

[26] *umuada:* A celebration of the female members of a clan upon their return home.

the other men stood outside the circle, watching. Their wives watched also. It was evening and the sun was setting.

Uchendu's eldest daughter, Njide, asked the questions.

"Remember that if you do not answer truthfully you will suffer or even die at childbirth," she began. "How many men have lain with you since my brother first expressed the desire to marry you?"

"None," she answered simply.

"Answer truthfully," urged the other women.

"None?" asked Njide.

"None," she answered.

"Swear on this staff of my fathers," said Uchendu.

"I swear," said the bride.

Uchendu took the hen from her, slit its throat with a sharp knife, and allowed some of the blood to fall on his ancestral staff.

From that day Amikwu took the young bride to his hut and she became his wife. The daughters of the family did not return to their homes immediately but spent two or three days with their kinsmen.

On the second day Uchendu called together his sons and daughters and his nephew, Okonkwo. The men brought their goatskin mats, with which they sat on the floor, and the women sat on a sisal mat spread on a raised bank of earth. Uchendu pulled gently at his gray beard and gnashed his teeth. Then he began to speak, quietly and deliberately, picking his words with great care:

"It is Okonkwo that I primarily wish to speak to," he began. "But I want all of you to note what I am going to say. I am an old man and you are all children. I know more about the world than any of you. If there is any one among you who thinks he knows more let him speak up." He paused, but no one spoke.

"Why is Okonkwo with us today? This is not his clan. We are only his mother's kinsmen. He does not belong here. He is an exile, condemned for seven years to live in a strange land. And so he is bowed with grief. But there is just one question I would like to ask him. Can you tell me, Okonkwo, why it is that one of the commonest names we give our children is Nneka, or 'Mother is Supreme'? We all know that a man is the head of the family and his wives do his bidding. A child belongs to its father and his family and not to its mother and her family. A man belongs to his fatherland and not to his motherland. And yet we say Nneka—'Mother is Supreme.' Why is that?"

There was silence. "I want Okonkwo to answer me," said Uchendu.

"I do not know the answer," Okonkwo replied.

"You do not know the answer? So you see that you are a child. You have many wives and many children—more children than I have. You are a great man in your clan. But you are still a child, *my* child. Listen to me and I shall tell you. But there is one more question I shall ask you. Why is it that when a woman dies she is taken home to be buried with her own kinsmen? She is not buried with her husband's kinsmen. Why is that? Your mother was brought home to me and buried with my people. Why was that?"

Okonkwo shook his head.

"He does not know that either," said Uchendu, "and yet he is full of sorrow because he has come to live in his motherland for a few years." He laughed a mirthless laughter, and turned to his sons and daughters. "What about you? Can you answer my question?"

They all shook their heads.

"Then listen to me," he said and cleared his throat. "It's true that a child belongs to its father. But when a father beats his child, it seeks sympathy in its mother's hut. A man belongs to his fatherland when things are good and life is sweet. But when there is sorrow and bitterness he finds refuge in his motherland. Your mother is there to protect you. She is buried there. And that is why we say that mother is supreme. Is it right that you, Okonkwo, should bring to your mother a heavy face and refuse to be comforted? Be careful or you may displease the dead. Your duty is to comfort your wives and children and take them back to your fatherland after seven years. But if you allow sorrow to weigh you down and kill you, they will all die in exile." He paused for a long while. "These are now your kinsmen." He waved at his sons and daughters. "You think you are the greatest sufferer in the world? Do you know that men are sometimes banished for life? Do you know that men sometimes lose all their yams and even their children? I had six wives once. I have none now except that young girl who knows not her right from her left. Do you know how many children I have buried—children I begot in my youth and strength? Twenty-two. I did not hang myself, and I am still alive. If you think you are the greatest sufferer in the world ask my daughter, Akueni, how many twins she has borne and thrown away. Have you not heard the song they sing when a woman dies?

> "'*For whom is it well, for whom is it well?*
> *There is no one for whom it is well.*'

"I have no more to say to you."

15

It was in the second year of Okonkwo's exile that his friend, Obierika, came to visit him. He brought with him two young men, each of them carrying a heavy bag on his head. Okonkwo helped them put down their loads. It was clear that the bags were full of cowries.

Okonkwo was very happy to receive his friend. His wives and children were very happy too, and so were his cousins and their wives when he sent for them and told them who his guest was.

"You must take him to salute our father," said one of the cousins.

"Yes," replied Okonkwo. "We are going directly." But before they went he whispered something to his first wife. She nodded, and soon the children were chasing one of their cocks.

Uchendu had been told by one of his grandchildren that three strangers had come to Okonkwo's house. He was therefore waiting to receive them. He held out his hands to them when they came into his *obi,* and after they had shaken hands he asked Okonkwo who they were.

"This is Obierika, my great friend. I have already spoken to you about him."

"Yes," said the old man, turning to Obierika. "My son has told me about you, and I am happy you have come to see us. I knew your father, Iweka. He was a great man. He had many friends here and came to see them quite often. Those were good days when a man had friends in distant clans. Your generation does not know that. You stay at home, afraid of your next-door neighbor. Even a man's motherland is strange to him nowadays." He looked at Okonkwo. "I am an old man and I like to talk. That is all I am good for now." He got up painfully, went into an inner room, and came back with a kola nut.

"Who are the young men with you?" he asked as he sat down again on his goat-skin. Okonkwo told him.

"Ah," he said. "Welcome, my sons." He presented the kola nut to them, and when they had seen it and thanked him, he broke it and they ate.

"Go into that room," he said to Okonkwo, pointing with his finger. "You will find a pot of wine there."

Okonkwo brought the wine and they began to drink. It was a day old, and very strong.

"Yes," said Uchendu after a long silence. "People traveled more in those days. There is not a single clan in these parts that I do not know very well. Aninta, Umuazu, Ikeocha, Elumelu, Abame—I know them all."

"Have you heard," asked Obierika, "that Abame is no more?"

"How is that?" asked Uchendu and Okonkwo together.

"Abame has been wiped out," said Obierika. "It is a strange and terrible story. If I had not seen the few survivors with my own eyes and heard their story with my own ears, I would not have believed. Was it not on an Eke day that they fled into Umuofia?" he asked his two companions, and they nodded their heads.

"Three moons ago," said Obierika, "on an Eke market day a little band of fugitives came into our town. Most of them were sons of our land whose mothers had been buried with us. But there were some too who came because they had friends in our town, and others who could think of nowhere else open to escape. And so they fled into Umuofia with a woeful story." He drank his palm-wine, and Okonkwo filled his horn again. He continued:

"During the last planting season a white man had appeared in their clan."

"An albino," suggested Okonkwo.

"He was not an albino. He was quite different." He sipped his wine. "And he was riding an iron horse. The first people who saw him ran away, but he stood beckoning to them. In the end the fearless ones went near and even touched him. The elders consulted their Oracle and it told them that the strange man would break their clan and spread destruction among them." Obierika again drank a little of his wine. "And so they killed the white man and tied his iron horse to their sacred tree because it looked as if it would run away to call the man's friends. I forgot to tell you another thing which the Oracle said. It said that other white men were on their way. They were locusts, it said, and that first man was their harbinger sent to explore the terrain. And so they killed him."

"What did the white man say before they killed him?" asked Uchendu.

"He said nothing," answered one of Obierika's companions.

"He said something, only they did not understand him," said Obierika. "He seemed to speak through his nose."

"One of the men told me," said Obierika's other companion, "that he repeated over and over again a word that resembled Mbaino. Perhaps he had been going to Mbaino and had lost his way."

"Anyway," resumed Obierika, "they killed him and tied up his iron horse. This was before the planting season began. For a long time nothing happened. The rains had come and yams had been sown. The iron horse was still tied to the sacred silk-cotton tree. And then one morning three white men led by a band of ordinary men like us came to the clan. They saw the iron horse and went away again. Most of the men and women of Abame had gone to their farms. Only a few of them saw these white men and their followers. For many market weeks nothing else happened. They have a big market in Abame on every other Afo day and, as you know, the whole clan gathers there. That was the day it happened. The three white men and a very large number of other men surrounded the market. They must have used a powerful medicine to make themselves invisible until the market was full. And they began to shoot. Everybody was killed, except the old and the sick who were at home and a handful of men and women whose *chi* were wide awake and brought them out of that market." He paused.

"Their clan is now completely empty. Even the sacred fish in their mysterious lake have fled and the lake has turned the color of blood. A great evil has come upon their land as the Oracle had warned."

There was a long silence. Uchendu ground his teeth together audibly. Then he burst out:

"Never kill a man who says nothing. Those men of Abame were fools. What did they know about the man?" He ground his teeth again and told a story to illustrate his point. "Mother Kite once sent her daughter to bring food. She went, and brought back a duckling. 'You have done very well,' said Mother Kite to her daughter, 'but tell me, what did the mother of this duckling say when you swooped and carried its child away?' 'It said nothing,' replied the young kite. 'It just walked away.' 'You must return the duckling,' said Mother Kite. 'There is something ominous behind the silence.' And so Daughter Kite returned the duckling and took a chick instead. 'What did the mother of this chick do?' asked the old kite. 'It cried and raved and cursed me,' said the young kite. 'Then we can eat the chick,' said her mother. 'There is nothing to fear from someone who shouts.' Those men of Abame were fools."

"They were fools," said Okonkwo after a pause. "They had been warned that danger was ahead. They should have armed themselves with their guns and their machetes even when they went to market."

"They have paid for their foolishness," said Obierika. "But I am greatly afraid. We have heard stories about white men who made the powerful guns and the strong drinks and took slaves away across the seas, but no one thought the stories were true."

"There is no story that is not true," said Uchendu. "The world has no end, and what is good among one people is an abomination with others. We have albinos among us. Do you not think that they came to our clan by mistake, that they have strayed from their way to a land where everybody is like them?"

Okonkwo's first wife soon finished her cooking and set before their guests a big meal of pounded yams and bitter-leaf soup. Okonkwo's son, Nwoye, brought in a pot of sweet wine tapped from the raffia palm.

"You are a big man now," Obierika said to Nwoye. "Your friend Anene asked me to greet you."

"Is he well?" asked Nwoye.

"We are all well," said Obierika.

Ezinma brought them a bowl of water with which to wash their hands. After that they began to eat and to drink the wine.

"When did you set out from home?" asked Okonkwo.

"We had meant to set out from my house before cock-crow," said Obierika. "But Nweke did not appear until it was quite light. Never make an early morning appointment with a man who has just married a new wife." They all laughed.

"Has Nweke married a wife?" asked Okonkwo.

"He has married Okadigbo's second daughter," said Obierika.

"That is very good," said Okonkwo. "I do not blame you for not hearing the cock crow."

When they had eaten, Obierika pointed at the two heavy bags.

"That is the money from your yams," he said. "I sold the big ones as soon as you left. Later on I sold some of the seed-yams and gave out others to sharecroppers. I shall do that every year until you return. But I thought you would need the money now and so I brought it. Who knows what may happen tomorrow? Perhaps green men will come to our clan and shoot us."

"God will not permit it," said Okonkwo. "I do not know how to thank you."

"I can tell you," said Obierika. "Kill one of your sons for me."

"That will not be enough," said Okonkwo.

"Then kill yourself," said Obierika.

"Forgive me," said Okonkwo, smiling. "I shall not talk about thanking you any more."

16

When nearly two years later Obierika paid another visit to his friend in exile the circumstances were less happy. The missionaries had come to Umuofia. They had built their church there, won a handful of converts, and were already sending evangelists to the surrounding towns and villages. That was a source of great sorrow to the leaders of the clan; but many of them believed that the strange faith and the white man's god would not last. None of his converts was a man whose word was heeded in the assembly of the people. None of them was a man of title. They were mostly the kind of people that were called *efulefu*, worthless, empty men. The imagery of an *efulefu* in the language of the clan was a man who sold his machete and wore the sheath to battle. Chielo, the priestess of Agbala, called the converts the excrement of the clan, and the new faith was a mad dog that had come to eat it up.

What moved Obierika to visit Okonkwo was the sudden appearance of the latter's son, Nwoye, among the missionaries in Umuofia.

"What are you doing here?" Obierika had asked when after many difficulties the missionaries had allowed him to speak to the boy.

"I am one of them," replied Nwoye.

"How is your father?" Obierika asked, not knowing what else to say.

"I don't know. He is not my father," said Nwoye, unhappily.

And so Obierika went to Mbanta to see his friend. And he found that Okonkwo did not wish to speak about Nwoye. It was only from Nwoye's mother that he heard scraps of the story.

The arrival of the missionaries had caused a considerable stir in the village of Mbanta. There were six of them and one was a white man. Every man and woman came out to see the white man. Stories about these strange men had grown since one of them had been killed in Abame and his iron horse tied to the sacred silk-cotton tree. And so everybody came to see the white man. It was the time of the year when everybody was at home. The harvest was over.

When they had all gathered, the white man began to speak to them. He spoke through an interpreter who was an Ibo man, though his dialect was different and harsh to the ears of Mbanta. Many people laughed at his dialect and the way he used words strangely. Instead of saying "myself" he always said "my buttocks." But he was a man of commanding presence and the clansmen listened to him. He said he was one of them, as they could see from his color and his language. The other four black men were also their brothers, although one of them did not speak Ibo. The white man was also their brother because they were all sons of God. And he told them about this new God, the Creator of all the world and all the men and women. He told them that they worshipped false gods, gods of wood and stone. A deep murmur went through the crowd when he said this. He told them that the true God lived on high and that all men when they died went before Him for judgment. Evil men and all the heathen who in their blindness bowed to wood and stone were thrown into a fire that burned like palm-oil. But good men who worshipped the true God lived forever in His happy kingdom. "We have been sent by this great God to ask you to leave your wicked ways and false gods and turn to Him so that you may be saved when you die," he said.

"Your buttocks understand our language," said someone light-heartedly and the crowd laughed.

"What did he say?" the white man asked his interpreter. But before he could answer, another man asked a question: "Where is the white man's horse?" he asked. The Ibo evangelists consulted among themselves and decided that the man probably meant bicycle. They told the white man and he smiled benevolently.

"Tell them," he said, "that I shall bring many iron horses when we have settled down among them. Some of them will even ride the iron horse themselves." This was interpreted to them but very few of them heard. They were talking excitedly among themselves because the white man had said he was going to live among them. They had not thought about that.

At this point an old man said he had a question. "Which is this god of yours," he asked, "the goddess of the earth, the god of the sky, Amadiora or the thunderbolt, or what?"

The interpreter spoke to the white man and he immediately gave his answer. "All the gods you have named are not gods at all. They are gods of deceit who tell you to kill your fellows and destroy innocent children. There is only one true God and He has the earth, the sky, you and me and all of us."

"If we leave our gods and follow your god," asked another man, "who will protect us from the anger of our neglected gods and ancestors?"

"Your gods are not alive and cannot do you any harm," replied the white man. "They are pieces of wood and stone."

When this was interpreted to the men of Mbanta they broke into derisive laughter. These men must be mad, they said to themselves. How else could they say that Ani and Amadiora were harmless? And Idemili and Ogwugwu too? And some of them began to go away.

Then the missionaries burst into song. It was one of those gay and rollicking tunes of evangelism which had the power of plucking at silent and dusty chords in the heart of an Ibo man. The interpreter explained each verse to the audience, some of whom now stood enthralled. It was a story of brothers who lived in darkness and in fear, ignorant of the love of God. It told of one sheep out on the hills, away from the gates of God and from the tender shepherd's care.

After the singing the interpreter spoke about the Son of God whose name was Jesu Kristi. Okonkwo, who only stayed in the hope that it might come to chasing the men out of the village or whipping them, now said:

"You told us with your own mouth that there was only one god. Now you talk about his son. He must have a wife, then." The crowd agreed.

"I did not say He had a wife," said the interpreter, somewhat lamely.

"Your buttocks said he had a son," said the joker. "So he must have a wife and all of them must have buttocks."

The missionary ignored him and went on to talk about the Holy Trinity. At the end of it Okonkwo was fully convinced that the man was mad. He shrugged his shoulders and went away to tap his afternoon palm-wine.

But there was a young lad who had been captivated. His name was Nwoye, Okonkwo's first son. It was not the mad logic of the Trinity that captivated him. He did not understand it. It was the poetry of the new religion, something felt in the marrow. The hymn about brothers who sat in darkness and in fear seemed to answer a vague and persistent question that haunted his young soul—the question of the twins crying in the bush and the question of Ikemefuna who was killed. He felt a relief within as the hymn poured into his parched soul. The words of the hymn were like the drops of frozen rain melting on the dry palate of the panting earth. Nwoye's callow mind was greatly puzzled.

17

The missionaries spent their first four or five nights in the marketplace, and went into the village in the morning to preach the gospel. They asked who the king of the village was, but the villagers told them that there was no king. "We have men of high title and the chief priests and the elders," they said.

It was not very easy getting the men of high title and the elders together after the excitement of the first day. But the missionaries persevered, and in the end they were received by the rulers of Mbanta. They asked for a plot of land to build their church.

Every clan and village had its "evil forest." In it were buried all those who died of the really evil diseases, like leprosy and smallpox. It was also the dumping ground for the potent fetishes of great medicine men when they died. An "evil forest" was, therefore, alive with sinister forces and powers of darkness. It was such a forest that the rulers of Mbanta gave to the missionaries. They did not really want them in their clan, and so they made them that offer which nobody in his right senses would accept.

"They want a piece of land to build their shrine," said Uchendu to his peers when they consulted among themselves. "We shall give them a piece of land." He paused, and there was a murmur of surprise and disagreement. "Let us give them a portion of the Evil Forest. They boast about victory over death. Let us give them a real battlefield in which to show their victory." They laughed and agreed, and sent for the missionaries, whom they had asked to leave them for a while so that they might "whisper together." They offered them as much of the Evil Forest as they cared to take. And to their greatest amazement the missionaries thanked them and burst into song.

"They do not understand," said some of the elders. "But they will understand when they go to their plot of land tomorrow morning." And they dispersed.

The next morning the crazy men actually began to clear a part of the forest and to build their house. The inhabitants of Mbanta expected them all to be dead within four days. The first day passed and the second and third and fourth, and none of them died. Everyone was puzzled. And then it became known that the white man's fetish had unbelievable power. It was said that he wore glasses on his eyes so that he could see and talk to evil spirits. Not long after, he won his first three converts.

Although Nwoye had been attracted to the new faith from the very first day, he kept it secret. He dared not go too near the missionaries for fear of his father. But whenever they came to preach in the open marketplace or the village playground, Nwoye was there. And he was already beginning to know some of the simple stories they told.

"We have now built a church," said Mr. Kiaga, the interpreter, who was now in charge of the infant congregation. The white man had gone back to Umuofia, where he built his headquarters and from where he paid regular visits to Mr. Kiaga's congregation at Mbanta.

"We have now built a church," said Mr. Kiaga, "and we want you all to come in every seventh day to worship the true God."

On the following Sunday, Nwoye passed and re-passed the little red-earth and thatch building without summoning enough courage to enter. He heard the voice of singing and although it came from a handful of men it was loud and confident. Their church stood on a circular clearing that looked like the open mouth of the Evil Forest. Was it waiting to snap its teeth together? After passing and re-passing by the church, Nwoye returned home.

It was well known among the people of Mbanta that their gods and ancestors were sometimes long-suffering and would deliberately allow a man to go on defying them. But even in such cases they set their limit at seven market weeks or twenty-eight days. Beyond that limit no man was suffered to go. And so excitement mounted in the village as the seventh week approached since the impudent missionaries built their church in the Evil Forest. The villagers were so certain about the doom that awaited these men that one or two converts thought it wise to suspend their allegiance to the new faith.

At last the day came by which all the missionaries should have died. But they were still alive, building a new red-earth and thatch house for their teacher, Mr. Kiaga. That week they won a handful more converts. And for the first time they had a woman. Her name was Nneka, the wife of Amadi, who was a prosperous farmer. She was very heavy with child.

Nneka had had four previous pregnancies and childbirths. But each time she had borne twins, and they had been immediately thrown away. Her husband and his family were already becoming highly critical of such a woman and were not unduly perturbed when they found she had fled to join the Christians. It was a good riddance.

One morning Okonkwo's cousin, Amikwu, was passing by the church on his way from the neighboring village, when he saw Nwoye among the Christians. He was greatly surprised, and when he got home he went straight to Okonkwo's hut and told him what he had seen. The women began to talk excitedly, but Okonkwo sat unmoved.

It was late afternoon before Nwoye returned. He went into the *obi* and saluted his father, but he did not answer. Nwoye turned round to walk into the inner compound when his father, suddenly overcome with fury, sprang to his feet and gripped him by the neck.

"Where have you been?" he stammered.

Nwoye struggled to free himself from the choking grip.

"Answer me," roared Okonkwo, "before I kill you!" He seized a heavy stick that lay on the dwarf wall and hit him two or three savage blows.

"Answer me!" he roared again. Nwoye stood looking at him and did not say a word. The women were screaming outside, afraid to go in.

"Leave that boy at once!" said a voice in the outer compound. It was Okonkwo's uncle, Uchendu. "Are you mad?"

Okonkwo did not answer. But he left hold of Nwoye, who walked away and never returned.

He went back to the church and told Mr. Kiaga that he had decided to go to Umuofia where the white missionary had set up a school to teach young Christians to read and write.

Mr. Kiaga's joy was very great. "Blessed is he who forsakes his father and his mother for my sake," he intoned. "Those that hear my words are my father and my mother."

Nwoye did not fully understand. But he was happy to leave his father. He would return later to his mother and his brothers and sisters and convert them to the new faith.

As Okonkwo sat in his hut that night, gazing into a log fire, he thought over the matter. A sudden fury rose within him and he felt a strong desire to take up his machete, go to the church, and wipe out the entire vile and miscreant gang. But on further thought he told himself that Nwoye was not worth fighting for. Why, he cried in his heart, should he, Okonkwo, of all people, be cursed with such a son? He saw clearly in it the finger of his personal god or *chi*. For how else could he explain his great misfortune and exile and now his despicable son's behavior? Now that he had time to think of it, his son's crime stood out in its stark enormity. To abandon the gods of one's father and go about with a lot of effeminate men clucking like old hens was the very depth of abomination. Suppose when he died all his male children decided to follow Nwoye's steps and abandon their ancestors? Okonkwo felt a cold shudder run through him at the terrible prospects, like the prospect of annihilation. He saw himself and his fathers crowding round their ancestral shrine waiting in vain for worship and sacrifice and finding nothing but ashes of bygone days, and his children the while praying to the white man's god. If such a thing were ever to happen, he, Okonkwo, would wipe them off the face of the earth.

Okonkwo was popularly called the "Roaring Flame." As he looked into the log fire he recalled the name. He was a flaming fire. How then could he have begotten a son like Nwoye, degenerate and effeminate? Perhaps he was not his son. No! he could not be. His wife had played him false. He would teach her! But Nwoye resembled his grandfather, Unoka, who was Okonkwo's father. He pushed the thought out of his mind. He, Okonkwo, was called a flaming fire. How could he have begotten a woman for a son? At Nwoye's age Okonkwo had already become famous throughout Umuofia for his wrestling and his fearlessness.

He sighed heavily, and as if in sympathy the smoldering log also sighed. And immediately Okonkwo's eyes were opened and he saw the whole matter clearly. Living fire begets cold, impotent ash. He sighed again, deeply.

18

The young church in Mbanta had a few crises early in its life. At first the clan had assumed that it would not survive. But it had gone on living and gradually becoming stronger. The clan was worried, but not overmuch. If a gang of *efulefu* decided to live in the Evil Forest it was their own affair. When one came to think of it, the Evil Forest was a fit home for such undesirable people. It was true they were rescuing twins from the bush, but they never brought them into the village. As far as the villagers were concerned, the twins still remained where they had been thrown away. Surely the earth goddess would not visit the sins of the missionaries on the innocent villagers?

But on one occasion the missionaries had tried to overstep the bounds. Three converts had gone into the village and boasted openly that all the gods were dead and impotent and that they were prepared to defy them by burning all their shrines.

"Go and burn your mothers' genitals," said one of the priests. The men were seized and beaten until they streamed with blood. After that nothing happened for a long time between the church and the clan.

But stories were already gaining ground that the white man had not only brought a religion but also a government. It was said that they had built a place of judgment in Umuofia to protect the followers of their religion. It was even said that they had hanged one man who killed a missionary.

Although such stories were now often told they looked like fairy-tales in Mbanta and did not as yet affect the relationship between the new church and the clan. There was no question of killing a missionary here, for Mr. Kiaga, despite his madness, was quite harmless. As for his converts, no one could kill them without having to flee from the clan, for in spite of their worthlessness they still belonged to the clan. And so nobody gave serious thought to the stories about the white man's government or the consequences of killing the Christians. If they became more troublesome than they already were they would simply be driven out of the clan.

And the little church was at that moment too deeply absorbed in its own troubles to annoy the clan. It all began over the question of admitting outcasts.

These outcasts, or *osu,* seeing that the new religion welcomed twins and such abominations, thought that it was possible that they would also be received. And so one Sunday two of them went into the church. There was an immediate stir; but so great was the work the new religion had done among the converts that they did not immediately leave the church when the outcasts came in. Those who found themselves nearest to them merely moved to another seat. It was a miracle. But it only lasted till the end of the service. The whole church raised a protest and was about to drive these people out, when Mr. Kiaga stopped them and began to explain.

"Before God," he said, "there is no slave or free. We are all children of God and we must receive these our brothers."

"You do not understand," said one of the converts. "What will the heathen say of us when they hear that we receive *osu* into our midst? They will laugh."

"Let them laugh," said Mr. Kiaga. "God will laugh at them on the judgment day. Why do the nations rage and the peoples imagine a vain thing? He that sitteth in the heavens shall laugh. The Lord shall have them in derision."

"You do not understand," the convert maintained. "You are our teacher, and you can teach us the things of the new faith. But this is a matter which we know." And he told him what an *osu* was.

He was a person dedicated to a god, a thing set apart—a taboo forever, and his children after him. He could neither marry nor be married by the free-born. He was in fact an outcast, living in a special area of the village, close to the Great Shrine. Wherever he went he carried with him the mark of his forbidden caste—long, tangled, and dirty hair. A razor was taboo to him. An *osu* could not attend an assembly of the free-born, and they, in turn, could not shelter under his roof. He could not take any of the four titles of the clan, and when he died he was buried by his kind in the Evil Forest. How could such a man be a follower of Christ?

"He needs Christ more than you and I," said Mr. Kiaga.

"Then I shall go back to the clan," said the convert. And he went. Mr. Kiaga stood firm, and it was his firmness that saved the young church. The wavering converts drew inspiration and confidence from his unshakable faith. He ordered the outcasts to shave off their long, tangled hair. At first they were afraid they might die.

"Unless you shave off the mark of your heathen belief I will not admit you into the church," said Mr. Kiaga. "You fear that you will die. Why should that be? How are you different from other men who shave their hair? The same God created you and them. But they have cast you out like lepers. It is against the will of God, who has promised everlasting life to all who believe in His holy name. The heathen say you will die if you do this or that, and you are afraid. They also said I would die if I built my church on this ground. Am I dead? They said I would die if I took care of twins. I am still alive. The heathen speak nothing but falsehood. Only the word of our God is true."

The two outcasts shaved off their hair, and soon they were the strongest adherents of the new faith. And what was more, nearly all the *osu* in Mbanta followed their example. It was in fact one of them who in his zeal brought the church into serious conflict with the clan a year later by killing the sacred python, the emanation of the god of water.

The royal python was the most revered animal in Mbanta and all the surrounding clans. It was addressed as "Our Father," and was allowed to go wherever it chose, even into people's beds. It ate rats in the house and sometimes swallowed hens' eggs. If a clansman killed a royal python accidentally, he made sacrifices of atonement and performed an expensive burial ceremony such as was done for a great man. No punishment was prescribed for a man who killed the python knowingly. Nobody thought that such a thing could ever happen.

Perhaps it never did happen. That was the way the clan at first looked at it. No one had actually seen the man do it. The story had arisen among the Christians themselves.

But, all the same, the rulers and elders of Mbanta assembled to decide on their action. Many of them spoke at great length and in fury. The spirit of wars was upon them. Okonkwo, who had begun to play a part in the affairs of his motherland, said that until the abominable gang was chased out of the village with whips there would be no peace.

But there were many others who saw the situation differently, and it was their counsel that prevailed in the end.

"It is not our custom to fight for our gods," said one of them. "Let us not presume to do so now. If a man kills the sacred python in the secrecy of his hut, the matter lies between him and the god. We did not see it. If we put ourselves between the god and his victim we may receive blows intended for the offender. When a man blasphemes, what do we do? Do we go and stop his mouth? No. We put our fingers into our ears to stop us hearing. That is a wise action."

"Let us not reason like cowards," said Okonkwo. "If a man comes into my hut and defecates on the floor, what do I do? Do I shut my eyes? No! I take a stick and break his head. That is what a man does. These people are daily pouring filth over us, and Okeke says we should pretend not to see." Okonkwo made a sound full of disgust. This was a womanly clan, he thought. Such a thing could never happen in his fatherland, Umuofia.

"Okonkwo has spoken the truth," said another man. "We should do something. But let us ostracize these men. We would then not be held accountable for their abominations."

Everybody in the assembly spoke, and in the end it was decided to ostracize the Christians. Okonkwo ground his teeth in disgust.

That night a bell-man went through the length and breadth of Mbanta proclaiming that the adherents of the new faith were thenceforth excluded from the life and privileges of the clan.

The Christians had grown in number and were now a small community of men, women, and children, self-assured and confident. Mr. Brown, the white missionary, paid regular visits to them. "When I think that it is only eighteen months since the Seed was first sown among you," he said, "I marvel at what the Lord hath wrought."

It was Wednesday in Holy Week and Mr. Kiaga had asked the women to bring red earth and white chalk and water to scrub the church for Easter; and the women had formed themselves into three groups for this purpose. They set out early that morning, some of them with their water-pots to the stream, another group with hoes and baskets to the village red-earth pit, and the others to the chalk quarry.

Mr. Kiaga was praying in the church when he heard the women talking excitedly. He rounded off his prayer and went to see what it was all about. The women had come to the church with empty water-pots. They said that some young men had chased them away from the stream with whips. Soon after, the women who had gone for red earth returned with empty baskets. Some of them had been heavily whipped. The chalk women also returned to tell a similar story.

"What does it all mean?" asked Mr. Kiaga, who was greatly perplexed.

"The village has outlawed us," said one of the women. "The bell-man announced it last night. But it is not our custom to debar anyone from the stream or the quarry."

Another woman said, "They want to ruin us. They will not allow us into the markets. They have said so."

Mr. Kiaga was going to send into the village for his men-converts when he saw them coming on their own. Of course they had all heard the bell-man, but they had never in all their lives heard of women being debarred from the stream.

"Come along," they said to the women. "We will go with you to meet those cowards." Some of them had big sticks and some even machetes.

But Mr. Kiaga restrained them. He wanted first to know why they had been outlawed.

"They say that Okoli killed the sacred python," said one man.

"It is false," said another. "Okoli told me himself that it was false."

Okoli was not there to answer. He had fallen ill on the previous night. Before the day was over he was dead. His death showed that the gods were still able to fight their own battles. The clan saw no reason then for molesting the Christians.

19

The last big rains of the year were falling. It was the time for treading red earth with which to build walls. It was not done earlier because the rains were too heavy and would have washed away the heap of trodden earth; and it could not be done later because harvesting would soon set in, and after that the dry season.

It was going to be Okonkwo's last harvest in Mbanta. The seven wasted and weary years were at last dragging to a close. Although he had prospered in his motherland Okonkwo knew that he would have prospered even more in Umuofia, in the land of his fathers where men were bold and warlike. In these seven years he would have climbed to the utmost heights. And so he regretted every day of his exile. His mother's kinsmen had been very kind to him, and he was grateful. But that did not alter the facts. He had called the first child born to him in exile Nneka — "Mother is Supreme" — out of politeness to his mother's kinsmen. But two years later when a son was born he called him Nwofia — "Begotten in the Wilderness."

As soon as he entered his last year in exile Okonkwo sent money to Obierika to build him two huts in his old compound where he and his family would live until he built more huts and the outside wall of his compound. He could not ask another man to build his own *obi* for him, nor the walls of his compound. Those things a man built for himself or inherited from his father.

As the last heavy rains of the year began to fall, Obierika sent word that the two huts had been built and Okonkwo began to prepare for his return, after the rains. He would have liked to return earlier and build his compound that year before the rains stopped, but in doing so he would have taken something from the full penalty of seven years. And that could not be. So he waited impatiently for the dry season to come.

It came slowly. The rain became lighter and lighter until it fell in slanting showers. Sometimes the sun shone through the rain and a light breeze blew. It was a gay and airy kind of rain. The rainbow began to appear, and sometimes two rainbows, like a mother and her daughter, the one young and beautiful, and the other an old and faint shadow. The rainbow was called the python of the sky.

Okonkwo called his three wives and told them to get things together for a great feast. "I must thank my mother's kinsmen before I go," he said.

Ekwefi still had some cassava left on her farm from the previous year. Neither of the other wives had. It was not that they had been lazy, but that they had many children to feed. It was therefore understood that Ekwefi would provide cassava for the feast. Nwoye's mother and Ojiugo would provide the other things like smoked fish, palm-oil, and pepper for the soup. Okonkwo would take care of meat and yams.

Ekwefi rose early on the following morning and went to her farm with her daughter, Ezinma, and Ojiugo's daughter, Obiageli, to harvest cassava tubers. Each of them carried a long cane basket, a machete for cutting down the soft cassava stem, and a little hoe for digging out the tuber. Fortunately, a light rain had fallen during the night and the soil would not be very hard.

"It will not take us long to harvest as much as we like," said Ekwefi.

"But the leaves will be wet," said Ezinma. Her basket was balanced on her head, and her arms folded across her breasts. She felt cold. "I dislike cold water dropping on my back. We should have waited for the sun to rise and dry the leaves."

Obiageli called her "Salt" because she said that she disliked water. "Are you afraid you may dissolve?"

The harvesting was easy, as Ekwefi had said. Ezinma shook every tree violently with a long stick before she bent down to cut the stem and dig out the tuber. Sometimes it was not necessary to dig. They just pulled the stump, and earth rose, roots snapped below, and the tuber was pulled out.

When they had harvested a sizable heap they carried it down in two trips to the stream, where every woman had a shallow well for fermenting her cassava.

"It should be ready in four days or even three," said Obiageli. "They are young tubers."

"They are not all that young," said Ekwefi. "I planted the farm nearly two years ago. It is a poor soil and that is why the tubers are so small."

Okonkwo never did things by halves. When his wife Ekwefi protested that two goats were sufficient for the feast he told her that it was not her affair.

"I am calling a feast because I have the wherewithal. I cannot live on the bank of a river and wash my hands with spittle. My mother's people have been good to me and I must show my gratitude."

And so three goats were slaughtered and a number of fowls. It was like a wedding feast. There was foo-foo and yam pottage, egusi soup and bitter-leaf soup and pots and pots of palm-wine.

All the *umunna*[27] were invited to the feast, all the descendants of Okolo, who had lived about two hundred years before. The oldest member of this extensive family was Okonkwo's uncle, Uchendu. The kola nut was given him to break, and he prayed to the ancestors. He asked them for health and children. "We do not ask for wealth because he that has health and children will also have wealth. We do not pray to have more money but to have more kinsmen. We are better than animals because we have kinsmen. An animal rubs its itching flank against a tree, a man asks his kinsman to scratch him." He prayed especially for Okonkwo and his family. He then broke the kola nut and threw one of the lobes on the ground for the ancestors.

As the broken kola nuts were passed round, Okonkwo's wives and children and those who came to help them with the cooking began to bring out the food. His sons brought out the pots of palm-wine. There was so much food and drink that many kinsmen whistled in surprise. When all was laid out, Okonkwo rose to speak.

"I beg you to accept this little kola," he said. "It is not to pay you back for all you did for me in these seven years. A child cannot pay for its mother's milk. I have only called you together because it is good for kinsmen to meet."

Yam pottage was served first because it was lighter than foo-foo and because yam always came first. Then the foo-foo was served. Some kinsmen ate it with egusi

---

[27] *umunna:* The male members of the clan.

soup and others with bitter-leaf soup. The meat was then shared so that every member of the *umunna* had a portion. Every man rose in order of years and took a share. Even the few kinsmen who had not been able to come had their shares taken out for them in due term.

As the palm-wine was drunk one of the oldest members of the *umunna* rose to thank Okonkwo:

"If I say that we did not expect such a big feast I will be suggesting that we did not know how open-handed our son, Okonkwo, is. We all know him, and we expected a big feast. But it turned out to be even bigger than we expected. Thank you. May all you took out return again tenfold. It is good in these days when the younger generation consider themselves wiser than their sires to see a man doing things in the grand, old way. A man who calls his kinsmen to a feast does not do so to save them from starving. They all have food in their own homes. When we gather together in the moonlit village ground it is not because of the moon. Every man can see it in his own compound. We come together because it is good for kinsmen to do so. You may ask why I am saying all this. I say it because I fear for the younger generation, for you people." He waved his arm where most of the young men sat. "As for me, I have only a short while to live, and so have Uchendu and Unachukwu and Emefo. But I fear for you young people because you do not understand how strong is the bond of kinship. You do not know what it is to speak with one voice. And what is the result? An abominable religion has settled among you. A man can now leave his father and his brothers. He can curse the gods of his fathers and his ancestors, like a hunter's dog that suddenly goes mad and turns on his master. I fear for you; I fear for the clan." He turned again to Okonkwo and said, "Thank you for calling us together."

PART III

20

Seven years was a long time to be away from one's clan. A man's place was not always there, waiting for him. As soon as he left, someone else rose and filled it. The clan was like a lizard; if it lost its tail it soon grew another.

Okonkwo knew these things. He knew that he had lost his place among the nine masked spirits who administered justice in the clan. He had lost the chance to lead his warlike clan against the new religion, which, he was told, had gained ground. He had lost the years in which he might have taken the highest titles in the clan. But some of these losses were not irreparable. He was determined that his return should be marked by his people. He would return with a flourish, and regain the seven wasted years.

Even in his first year in exile he had begun to plan for his return. The first thing he would do would be to rebuild his compound on a more magnificent scale. He would build a bigger barn than he had had before and he would build huts for two new wives. Then he would show his wealth by initiating his sons into the *ozo* society. Only the really great men in the clan were able to do this. Okonkwo saw clearly the high esteem in which he would be held, and he saw himself taking the highest title in the land.

As the years of exile passed one by one it seemed to him that his *chi* might now be making amends for the past disaster. His yams grew abundantly, not only in his motherland but also in Umuofia, where his friend gave them out year by year to sharecroppers.

Then the tragedy of his first son had occurred. At first it appeared as if it might prove too great for his spirit. But it was a resilient spirit, and in the end Okonkwo overcame his sorrow. He had five other sons and he would bring them up in the way of the clan.

He sent for the five sons and they came and sat in his *obi*. The youngest of them was four years old.

"You have all seen the great abomination of your brother. Now he is no longer my son or your brother. I will only have a son who is a man, who will hold his head up among my people. If any one of you prefers to be a woman, let him follow Nwoye now while I am alive so that I can curse him. If you turn against me when I am dead I will visit you and break your neck."

Okonkwo was very lucky in his daughters. He never stopped regretting that Ezinma was a girl. Of all his children she alone understood his every mood. A bond of sympathy had grown between them as the years had passed.

Ezinma grew up in her father's exile and became one of the most beautiful girls in Mbanta. She was called Crystal of Beauty, as her mother had been called in her youth. The young ailing girl who had caused her mother so much heartache had been transformed, almost overnight, into a healthy, buoyant maiden. She had, it was true, her moments of depression when she would snap at everybody like an angry dog. These moods descended on her suddenly and for no apparent reason. But they were very rare and short-lived. As long as they lasted, she could bear no other person but her father.

Many young men and prosperous middle-aged men of Mbanta came to marry her. But she refused them all, because her father had called her one evening and said to her: "There are many good and prosperous people here, but I shall be happy if you marry in Umuofia when we return home."

That was all he had said. But Ezinma had seen clearly all the thought and hidden meaning behind the few words. And she had agreed.

"Your half-sister, Obiageli, will not understand me," Okonkwo said. "But you can explain to her."

Although they were almost the same age, Ezinma wielded a strong influence over her half-sister. She explained to her why they should not marry yet, and she agreed also. And so the two of them refused every offer of marriage in Mbanta.

"I wish she were a boy," Okonkwo thought within himself. She understood things so perfectly. Who else among his children could have read his thoughts so well? With two beautiful grown-up daughters his return to Umuofia would attract considerable attention. His future sons-in-law would be men of authority in the clan. The poor and unknown would not dare to come forth.

Umuofia had indeed changed during the seven years Okonkwo had been in exile. The church had come and led many astray. Not only the low-born and the outcast but sometimes a worthy man had joined it. Such a man was Ogbuefi Ugonna, who had taken two titles, and who like a madman had cut the anklet of his titles and cast it away to join the Christians. The white missionary was very proud of him and he was one of the first men in Umuofia to receive the sacrament of Holy Communion, or Holy Feast as it was called in Ibo. Ogbuefi Ugonna had thought of the Feast in terms of eating and drinking, only more holy than the village variety. He had therefore put his drinking-horn into his goatskin bag for the occasion.

But apart from the church, the white men had also brought a government. They had built a court where the District Commissioner judged cases in ignorance. He had court messengers who brought men to him for trial. Many of these messengers came from Umuru on the bank of the Great River, where the white men first came many years before and where they had built the center of their religion and trade and government. These court messengers were greatly hated in Umuofia because they were foreigners and also arrogant and high-handed. They were called *kotma*, and because of their ash-colored shorts they earned the additional name of Ashy-Buttocks. They guarded the prison, which was full of men who had offended against the white man's law. Some of these prisoners had thrown away their twins and some had molested the Christians. They were beaten in the prison by the *kotma* and made to work every morning clearing the government compound and fetching wood for the white Commissioner and the court messengers. Some of these prisoners were men of title who should be above such mean occupation. They were grieved by the indignity and mourned for their neglected farms. As they cut grass in the morning the younger men sang in time with the strokes of their machetes:

> Kotma *of the ash buttocks,*
> > *He is fit to be a slave.*
> *The white man has no sense,*
> > *He is fit to be a slave.*

The court messengers did not like to be called Ashy-Buttocks, and they beat the men. But the song spread in Umuofia.

Okonkwo's head was bowed in sadness as Obierika told him these things.

"Perhaps I have been away too long," Okonkwo said, almost to himself. "But I cannot understand these things you tell me. What is it that has happened to our people? Why have they lost the power to fight?"

"Have you not heard how the white man wiped out Abame?" asked Obierika.

"I have heard," said Okonkwo. "But I have also heard that Abame people were weak and foolish. Why did they not fight back? Had they no guns and machetes? We would be cowards to compare ourselves with the men of Abame. Their fathers had never dared to stand before our ancestors. We must fight these men and drive them from the land."

"It is already too late," said Obierika sadly. "Our own men and our sons have joined the ranks of the stranger. They have joined his religion and they help to uphold his government. If we should try to drive out the white men in Umuofia we should find it easy. There are only two of them. But what of our own people who are following their way and have been given power? They would go to Umuru and bring the soldiers, and we would be like Abame." He paused for a long time and then said: "I told you on my last visit to Mbanta how they hanged Aneto."

"What has happened to that piece of land in dispute?" asked Okonkwo.

"The white man's court has decided that it should belong to Nnama's family, who had given much money to the white man's messengers and interpreter."

"Does the white man understand our custom about land?"

"How can he when he does not even speak our tongue? But he says that our customs are bad; and our own brothers who have taken up his religion also say that our customs are bad. How do you think we can fight when our own brothers have turned against us? The white man is very clever. He came quietly and peaceably with his religion. We were amused at his foolishness and allowed him to stay. Now he has won our brothers, and our clan can no longer act like one. He has put a knife on the things that held us together and we have fallen apart."

"How did they get hold of Aneto to hang him?" asked Okonkwo.

"When he killed Oduche in the fight over the land, he fled to Aninta to escape the wrath of the earth. This was about eight days after the fight, because Oduche had not died immediately from his wounds. It was on the seventh day that he died. But everybody knew that he was going to die and Aneto got his belongings together in readiness to flee. But the Christians had told the white man about the accident, and he sent his *kotma* to catch Aneto. He was imprisoned with all the leaders of his family. In the end Oduche died and Aneto was taken to Umuru and hanged. The other people were released, but even now they have not found the mouth with which to tell of their suffering."

The two men sat in silence for a long while afterwards.

21

There were many men and women in Umuofia who did not feel as strongly as Okonkwo about the new dispensation. The white man had indeed brought a lunatic religion, but he had also built a trading store and for the first time palm-oil and kernel became things of great price, and much money flowed into Umuofia.

And even in the matter of religion there was a growing feeling that there might be something in it after all, something vaguely akin to method in the overwhelming madness.

This growing feeling was due to Mr. Brown, the white missionary, who was very firm in restraining his flock from provoking the wrath of the clan. One member in particular was very difficult to restrain. His name was Enoch and his father was the priest of the snake cult. The story went around that Enoch had killed and eaten the sacred python, and that his father had cursed him.

Mr. Brown preached against such excess of zeal. Everything was possible, he told his energetic flock, but everything was not expedient. And so Mr. Brown came to be respected even by the clan, because he trod softly on its faith. He made friends with some of the great men of the clan and on one of his frequent visits to the neighboring villages he had been presented with a carved elephant tusk, which was a sign of dignity and rank. One of the great men in that village was called Akunna and he had given one of his sons to be taught the white man's knowledge in Mr. Brown's school.

Whenever Mr. Brown went to that village he spent long hours with Akunna in his *obi* talking through an interpreter about religion. Neither of them succeeded in converting the other but they learned more about their different beliefs.

"You say that there is one supreme God who made heaven and earth," said Akunna on one of Mr. Brown's visits. "We also believe in Him and call Him Chukwu. He made all the world and the other gods."

"There are no other gods," said Mr. Brown. "Chukwu is the only God and all others are false. You carve a piece of wood—like that one" (he pointed at the rafters from which Akunna's carved *Ikenga*[28] hung), "and you call it a god. But it is still a piece of wood."

"Yes," said Akunna. "It is indeed a piece of wood. The tree from which it came was made by Chukwu, as indeed all minor gods were. But He made them for His messengers so that we could approach Him through them. It is like yourself. You are the head of your church."

"No," protested Mr. Brown. "The head of my church is God Himself."

"I know," said Akunna, "but there must be a head in this world among men. Somebody like yourself must be the head here."

"The head of my church in that sense is in England."

"That is exactly what I am saying. The head of your church is in your country. He has sent you here as his messenger. And you have also appointed your own messengers and servants. Or let me take another example, the District Commissioner. He is sent by your king."

"They have a queen," said the interpreter on his own account.

"Your queen sends her messenger, the District Commissioner. He finds that he cannot do the work alone and so he appoints *kotma* to help him. It is the same with God, or Chukwu. He appoints the smaller gods to help Him because His work is too great for one person."

"You should not think of Him as a person," said Mr. Brown. "It is because you do so that you imagine He must need helpers. And the worst thing about it is that you give all the worship to the false gods you have created."

"That is not so. We make sacrifices to the little gods, but when they fail and there is no one else to turn to we go to Chukwu. It is right to do so. We approach a great man through his servants. But when his servants fail to help us, then we go to the last source of hope. We appear to pay greater attention to the little gods but that is not so. We worry them more because we are afraid to worry their Master. Our fathers knew that Chukwu was the Overlord and that is why many of them gave their children the name Chukwuka—'Chukwu is Supreme.'"

"You said one interesting thing," said Mr. Brown. "You are afraid of Chukwu. In my religion Chukwu is a loving Father and need not be feared by those who do His will."

---

[28] *Ikenga:* A carved figure symbolizing a man's strength, made from wood and the horns of a ram.

"But we must fear Him when we are not doing His will," said Akunna. "And who is to tell His will? It is too great to be known."

In this way Mr. Brown learned a good deal about the religion of the clan and he came to the conclusion that a frontal attack on it would not succeed. And so he built a school and a little hospital in Umuofia. He went from family to family begging people to send their children to his school. But at first they only sent their slaves or sometimes their lazy children. Mr. Brown begged and argued and prophesied. He said that the leaders of the land in the future would be men and women who had learned to read and write. If Umuofia failed to send her children to the school, strangers would come from other places to rule them. They could already see that happening in the Native Court, where the D.C. was surrounded by strangers who spoke his tongue. Most of these strangers came from the distant town of Umuru on the bank of the Great River where the white man first went.

In the end Mr. Brown's arguments began to have an effect. More people came to learn in his school, and he encouraged them with gifts of singlets and towels. They were not all young, these people who came to learn. Some of them were thirty years old or more. They worked on their farms in the morning and went to school in the afternoon. And it was not long before the people began to say that the white man's medicine was quick in working. Mr. Brown's school produced quick results. A few months in it were enough to make one a court messenger or even a court clerk. Those who stayed longer became teachers; and from Umuofia laborers went forth into the Lord's vineyard. New churches were established in the surrounding villages and a few schools with them. From the very beginning religion and education went hand in hand.

Mr. Brown's mission grew from strength to strength, and because of its link with the new administration it earned a new social prestige. But Mr. Brown himself was breaking down in health. At first he ignored the warning signs. But in the end he had to leave his flock, sad and broken.

It was in the first rainy season after Okonkwo's return to Umuofia that Mr. Brown left for home. As soon as he had learned of Okonkwo's return five months earlier, the missionary had immediately paid him a visit. He had just sent Okonkwo's son, Nwoye, who was now called Isaac, to the new training college for teachers in Umuru. And he had hoped that Okonkwo would be happy to hear of it. But Okonkwo had driven him away with the threat that if he came into his compound again, he would be carried out of it.

Okonkwo's return to his native land was not as memorable as he had wished. It was true his two beautiful daughters aroused great interest among suitors and marriage negotiations were soon in progress, but, beyond that, Umuofia did not appear to have taken any special notice of the warrior's return. The clan had undergone such profound change during his exile that it was barely recognizable. The new religion and government and the trading stores were very much in the people's eyes and minds. There were still many who saw these new institutions as evil, but even they talked and thought about little else, and certainly not about Okonkwo's return.

And it was the wrong year too. If Okonkwo had immediately initiated his two sons into the *ozo* society as he had planned he would have caused a stir. But the initiation rite was performed once in three years in Umuofia, and he had to wait for nearly two years for the next round of ceremonies.

Okonkwo was deeply grieved. And it was not just a personal grief. He mourned for the clan, which he saw breaking up and falling apart, and he mourned for the warlike men of Umuofia, who had so unaccountably become soft like women.

22

Mr. Brown's successor was the Reverend James Smith, and he was a different kind of man. He condemned openly Mr. Brown's policy of compromise and accommodation. He saw things as black and white. And black was evil. He saw the world as a battlefield in which the children of light were locked in mortal conflict with the sons of darkness. He spoke in his sermons about sheep and goats and about wheat and tares. He believed in slaying the prophets of Baal.

Mr. Smith was greatly distressed by the ignorance which many of his flock showed even in such things as the Trinity and the Sacraments. It only showed that they were seeds sown on a rocky soil. Mr. Brown had thought of nothing but numbers. He should have known that the kingdom of God did not depend on large crowds. Our Lord Himself stressed the importance of fewness. Narrow is the way and few the number. To fill the Lord's holy temple with an idolatrous crowd clamoring for signs was a folly of everlasting consequence. Our Lord used the whip only once in His life — to drive the crowd away from His church.

Within a few weeks of his arrival in Umuofia Mr. Smith suspended a young woman from the church for pouring new wine into old bottles. This woman had allowed her heathen husband to mutilate her dead child. The child had been declared an *ogbanje,* plaguing its mother by dying and entering her womb to be born again. Four times this child had run its evil round. And so it was mutilated to discourage it from returning.

Mr. Smith was filled with wrath when he heard of this. He disbelieved the story which even some of the most faithful confirmed, the story of really evil children who were not deterred by mutilation, but came back with all the scars. He replied that such stories were spread in the world by the Devil to lead men astray. Those who believed such stories were unworthy of the Lord's table.

There was a saying in Umuofia that as a man danced so the drums were beaten for him. Mr. Smith danced a furious step and so the drums went mad. The overzealous converts who had smarted under Mr. Brown's restraining hand now flourished in full favor. One of them was Enoch, the son of the snake-priest who was believed to have killed and eaten the sacred python. Enoch's devotion to the new faith had seemed so much greater than Mr. Brown's that the villagers called him the outsider who wept louder than the bereaved.

Enoch was short and slight of build, and always seemed in great haste. His feet were short and broad, and when he stood or walked his heels came together and his feet opened outwards as if they had quarreled and meant to go in different directions. Such was the excessive energy bottled up in Enoch's small body that it was always erupting in quarrels and fights. On Sundays he always imagined that the sermon was preached for the benefit of his enemies. And if he happened to sit near one of them he would occasionally turn to give him a meaningful look, as if to say, "I told you so." It was Enoch who touched off the great conflict between church and clan in Umuofia which had been gathering since Mr. Brown left.

It happened during the annual ceremony which was held in honor of the earth deity. At such times the ancestors of the clan who had been committed to Mother Earth at their death emerged again as *egwugwu* through tiny ant-holes.

One of the greatest crimes a man could commit was to unmask an *egwugwu* in public, or to say or do anything which might reduce its immortal prestige in the eyes of the uninitiated. And this was what Enoch did.

The annual worship of the earth goddess fell on a Sunday, and the masked spirits were abroad. The Christian women who had been to church could not therefore go home. Some of their men had gone out to beg the *egwugwu* to retire for a short while for the women to pass. They agreed and were already retiring, when Enoch boasted aloud that they would not dare to touch a Christian. Whereupon they all came back and one of them gave Enoch a good stroke of the cane, which was always carried. Enoch fell on him and tore off his mask. The other *egwugwu* immediately surrounded their desecrated companion, to shield him from the profane gaze of women and children, and led him away. Enoch had killed an ancestral spirit, and Umuofia was thrown into confusion.

That night the Mother of the Spirits walked the length and breadth of the clan, weeping for her murdered son. It was a terrible night. Not even the oldest man in Umuofia had ever heard such a strange and fearful sound, and it was never to be heard again. It seemed as if the very soul of the tribe wept for a great evil that was coming—its own death.

On the next day all the masked *egwugwu* of Umuofia assembled in the marketplace. They came from all the quarters of the clan and even from the neighboring villages. The dreaded Otakagu came from Imo, and Ekwensu, dangling a white cock, arrived from Uli. It was a terrible gathering. The eerie voices of countless spirits, the bells that clattered behind some of them, and the clash of machetes as they ran forwards and backwards and saluted one another, sent tremors of fear into every heart. For the first time in living memory the sacred bull-roarer was heard in broad daylight.

From the marketplace the furious band made for Enoch's compound. Some of the elders of the clan went with them, wearing heavy protections of charms and amulets. These were men whose arms were strong in *ogwu*, or medicine. As for the ordinary men and women, they listened from the safety of their huts.

The leaders of the Christians had met together at Mr. Smith's parsonage on the previous night. As they deliberated they could hear the Mother of Spirits wailing for her son. The chilling sound affected Mr. Smith, and for the first time he seemed to be afraid.

"What are they planning to do?" he asked. No one knew, because such a thing had never happened before. Mr. Smith would have sent for the District Commissioner and his court messengers, but they had gone on tour on the previous day.

"One thing is clear," said Mr. Smith. "We cannot offer physical resistance to them. Our strength lies in the Lord." They knelt down together and prayed to God for delivery.

"O Lord, save Thy people," cried Mr. Smith.

"And bless Thine inheritance," replied the men.

They decided that Enoch should be hidden in the parsonage for a day or two. Enoch himself was greatly disappointed when he heard this, for he had hoped that a holy war was imminent; and there were a few other Christians who thought like him. But wisdom prevailed in the camp of the faithful and many lives were thus saved.

The band of *egwugwu* moved like a furious whirlwind to Enoch's compound and with machete and fire reduced it to a desolate heap. And from there they made for the church, intoxicated with destruction.

Mr. Smith was in his church when he heard the masked spirits coming. He walked quietly to the door which commanded the approach to the church compound, and stood there. But when the first three or four *egwugwu* appeared on the church compound he nearly bolted. He overcame this impulse and instead of running away he went down the two steps that led up to the church and walked towards the approaching spirits.

They surged forward, and a long stretch of the bamboo fence with which the church compound was surrounded gave way before them. Discordant bells clanged, machetes clashed and the air was full of dust and weird sounds. Mr. Smith heard a sound of footsteps behind him. He turned round and saw Okeke, his interpreter. Okeke had not been on the best of terms with his master since he had strongly condemned Enoch's behavior at the meeting of the leaders of the church during the night. Okeke had gone as far as to say that Enoch should not be hidden in the parsonage, because he would only draw the wrath of the clan on the pastor. Mr. Smith had rebuked him in very strong language, and had not sought his advice that morning. But now, as he came up and stood by him confronting the angry spirits, Mr. Smith looked at him and smiled. It was a wan smile, but there was deep gratitude there.

For a brief moment the onrush of the *egwugwu* was checked by the unexpected composure of the two men. But it was only a momentary check, like the tense silence between blasts of thunder. The second onrush was greater than the first. It swallowed up the two men. Then an unmistakable voice rose above the tumult and there was immediate silence. Space was made around the two men, and Ajofia began to speak.

Ajofia was the leading *egwugwu* of Umuofia. He was the head and spokesman of the nine ancestors who administered justice in the clan. His voice was unmistakable and so he was able to bring immediate peace to the agitated spirits. He then addressed Mr. Smith, and as he spoke clouds of smoke rose from his head.

"The body of the white man, I salute you," he said, using the language in which immortals spoke to men.

"The body of the white man, do you know me?" he asked.

Mr. Smith looked at his interpreter, but Okeke, who was a native of distant Umuru, was also at a loss.

Ajofia laughed in his guttural voice. It was like the laugh of rusty metal. "They are strangers," he said, "and they are ignorant. But let that pass." He turned round to his comrades and saluted them, calling them the fathers of Umuofia. He dug his rattling spear into the ground and it shook with metallic life. Then he turned once more to the missionary and his interpreter.

"Tell the white man that we will not do him any harm," he said to the interpreter. "Tell him to go back to his house and leave us alone. We liked his brother who was with us before. He was foolish, but we liked him, and for his sake we shall not harm his brother. But this shrine which he built must be destroyed. We shall no longer allow it in our midst. It has bred untold abominations and we have come to put an end to it." He turned to his comrades. "Fathers of Umuofia, I salute you"; and they replied with one guttural voice. He turned again to the missionary. "You can stay with us if you like our ways. You can worship your own god. It is good that a man should worship the gods and the spirits of his fathers. Go back to your house so that you may not be hurt. Our anger is great but we have held it down so that we can talk to you."

Mr. Smith said to his interpreter: "Tell them to go away from here. This is the house of God and I will not live to see it desecrated."

Okeke interpreted wisely to the spirits and leaders of Umuofia: "The white man says he is happy you have come to him with your grievances, like friends. He will be happy if you leave the matter in his hands."

"We cannot leave the matter in his hands because he does not understand our customs, just as we do not understand his. We say he is foolish because he does not know our ways, and perhaps he says we are foolish because we do not know his. Let him go away."

Mr. Smith stood his ground. But he could not save his church. When the *egwugwu* went away the red-earth church which Mr. Brown had built was a pile of earth and ashes. And for the moment the spirit of the clan was pacified.

23

For the first time in many years Okonkwo had a feeling that was akin to happiness. The times which had altered so unaccountably during his exile seemed to be coming round again. The clan which had turned false on him appeared to be making amends.

He had spoken violently to his clansmen when they had met in the marketplace to decide on their action. And they had listened to him with respect. It was like the good old days again, when a warrior was a warrior. Although they had not agreed to kill the missionary or drive away the Christians, they had agreed to do something substantial. And they had done it. Okonkwo was almost happy again.

For two days after the destruction of the church, nothing happened. Every man in Umuofia went about armed with a gun or a machete. They would not be caught unawares, like the men of Abame.

Then the District Commissioner returned from his tour. Mr. Smith went immediately to him and they had a long discussion. The men of Umuofia did not take any notice of this, and if they did, they thought it was not important. The missionary often went to see his brother white man. There was nothing strange in that.

Three days later the District Commissioner sent his sweet-tongued messenger to the leaders of Umuofia asking them to meet him in his headquarters. That also was not strange. He often asked them to hold such palavers, as he called them. Okonkwo was among the six leaders he invited.

Okonkwo warned the others to be fully armed. "An Umuofia man does not refuse a call," he said. "He may refuse to do what he is asked; he does not refuse to be asked. But the times have changed, and we must be fully prepared."

And so the six men went to see the District Commissioner, armed with their machetes. They did not carry guns, for that would be unseemly. They were led into the courthouse where the District Commissioner sat. He received them politely. They unslung their goatskin bags and their sheathed machetes, put them on the floor, and sat down.

"I have asked you to come," began the Commissioner, "because of what happened during my absence. I have been told a few things but I cannot believe them until I have heard your own side. Let us talk about it like friends and find a way of ensuring that it does not happen again."

Ogbuefi Ekwueme rose to his feet and began to tell the story.

"Wait a minute," said the Commissioner. "I want to bring in my men so that they too can hear your grievances and take warning. Many of them come from distant places and although they speak your tongue they are ignorant of your customs. James! Go and bring in the men." His interpreter left the courtroom and soon returned with twelve men. They sat together with the men of Umuofia, and Ogbuefi Ekwueme began to tell the story of how Enoch murdered an *egwugwu*.

It happened so quickly that the six men did not see it coming. There was only a brief scuffle, too brief even to allow the drawing of a sheathed machete. The six men were handcuffed and led into the guardroom.

"We shall not do you any harm," said the District Commissioner to them later, "if only you agree to cooperate with us. We have brought a peaceful administration to you and your people so that you may be happy. If any man ill-treats you we shall come to your rescue. But we will not allow you to ill-treat others. We have a court of law where we judge cases and administer justice just as it is done in my own country under a great queen. I have brought you here because you joined together to molest others, to burn people's houses and their place of worship. That must not happen in the dominion of our queen, the most powerful ruler in the world. I have decided that you will pay a fine of two hundred bags of cowries. You will be released as soon as you agree to this and undertake to collect that fine from your people. What do you say to that?"

The six men remained sullen and silent and the Commissioner left them for a while. He told the court messengers, when he left the guardroom, to treat the men with respect because they were the leaders of Umuofia. They said, "Yes, sir," and saluted.

As soon as the District Commissioner left, the head messenger, who was also the prisoners' barber, took down his razor and shaved off all the hair on the men's heads. They were still handcuffed, and they just sat and moped.

"Who is the chief among you?" the court messengers asked in jest. "We see that every pauper wears the anklet of title in Umuofia. Does it cost as much as ten cowries?"

The six men ate nothing throughout that day and the next. They were not even given any water to drink, and they could not go out to urinate or go into the bush when they were pressed. At night the messengers came in to taunt them and to knock their shaven heads together.

Even when the men were left alone they found no words to speak to one another. It was only on the third day, when they could no longer bear the hunger and the insults, that they began to talk about giving in.

"We should have killed the white man if you had listened to me," Okonkwo snarled.

"We could have been in Umuru now waiting to be hanged," someone said to him.

"Who wants to kill the white man?" asked a messenger who had just rushed in. Nobody spoke.

"You are not satisfied with your crime, but you must kill the white man on top of it." He carried a strong stick, and he hit each man a few blows on the head and back. Okonkwo was choked with hate.

As soon as the six men were locked up, court messengers went into Umuofia to tell the people that their leaders would not be released unless they paid a fine of two hundred and fifty bags of cowries.

"Unless you pay the fine immediately," said their head-man, "we will take your leaders to Umuru before the big white man, and hang them."

This story spread quickly through the villages, and was added to as it went. Some said that the men had already been taken to Umuru and would be hanged on the following day. Some said that their families would also be hanged. Others said that soldiers were already on their way to shoot the people of Umuofia as they had done in Abame.

It was the time of the full moon. But that night the voice of children was not heard. The village *ilo* where they always gathered for a moon-play was empty. The women of Iguedo did not meet in their secret enclosure to learn a new dance to be displayed later to the village. Young men who were always abroad in the moonlight kept their huts that night. Their manly voices were not heard on the village paths as they went to visit their friends and lovers. Umuofia was like a startled animal with ears erect, sniffing the silent, ominous air and not knowing which way to run.

The silence was broken by the village crier beating his sonorous *ogene*. He called every man in Umuofia, from the Akakanma age group upwards, to a meeting in the marketplace after the morning meal. He went from one end of the village to the other and walked all its breadth. He did not leave out any of the main footpaths.

Okonkwo's compound was like a deserted homestead. It was as if cold water had been poured on it. His family was all there, but everyone spoke in whispers. His daughter Ezinma had broken her twenty-eight day visit to the family of her future husband, and returned home when she heard that her father had been imprisoned, and was going to be hanged. As soon as she got home she went to Obierika to ask what the men of Umuofia were going to do about it. But Obierika had not been home since morning. His wives thought he had gone to a secret meeting. Ezinma was satisfied that something was being done.

On the morning after the village crier's appeal the men of Umuofia met in the marketplace and decided to collect without delay two hundred and fifty bags of cowries to appease the white man. They did not know that fifty bags would go to the court messengers, who had increased the fine for that purpose.

24

Okonkwo and his fellow prisoners were set free as soon as the fine was paid. The District Commissioner spoke to them again about the great queen, and about peace and good government. But the men did not listen. They just sat and looked at him and at his interpreter. In the end they were given back their bags and sheathed machetes and told to go home. They rose and left the courthouse. They neither spoke to anyone nor among themselves.

The courthouse, like the church, was built a little way outside the village. The footpath that linked them was a very busy one because it also led to the stream, beyond the court. It was open and sandy. Footpaths were open and sandy in the dry season. But when the rains came the bush grew thick on either side and closed in on the path. It was now dry season.

As they made their way to the village the six men met women and children going to the stream with their water-pots. But the men wore such heavy and fearsome looks that the women and children did not say "*nno*" or "welcome" to them, but edged out of the way to let them pass. In the village little groups of men joined them until they became a sizable company. They walked silently. As each of the six men got to his compound, he turned in, taking some of the crowd with him. The village was astir in a silent, suppressed way.

Ezinma had prepared some food for her father as soon as news spread that the six men would be released. She took it to him in his *obi*. He ate absent-mindedly. He had no appetite; he only ate to please her. His male relations and friends had gathered in his *obi*, and Obierika was urging him to eat. Nobody else spoke, but they noticed the long stripes on Okonkwo's back where the warder's whip had cut into his flesh.

The village crier was abroad again in the night. He beat his iron gong and announced that another meeting would be held in the morning. Everyone knew that Umuofia was at last going to speak its mind about the things that were happening.

Okonkwo slept very little that night. The bitterness in his heart was now mixed with a kind of childlike excitement. Before he had gone to bed he had brought down his war dress, which he had not touched since his return from exile. He had shaken out his smoked raffia skirt and examined his tall feather head-gear and his shield. They were all satisfactory, he had thought.

As he lay on his bamboo bed he thought about the treatment he had received in the white man's court, and he swore vengeance. If Umuofia decided on war, all would be well. But if they chose to be cowards he would go out and avenge himself. He thought about wars in the past. The noblest, he thought, was the war against Isike.

In those days Okudo was still alive. Okudo sang a war song in a way that no other man could. He was not a fighter, but his voice turned every man into a lion.

"Worthy men are no more," Okonkwo sighed as he remembered those days. "Isike will never forget how we slaughtered them in that war. We killed twelve of their men and they killed only two of ours. Before the end of the fourth market week they were suing for peace. Those were days when men were men."

As he thought of these things he heard the sound of the iron gong in the distance. He listened carefully, and could just hear the crier's voice. But it was very faint. He turned on his bed and his back hurt him. He ground his teeth. The crier was drawing nearer and nearer until he passed by Okonkwo's compound.

"The greatest obstacle in Umuofia," Okonkwo thought bitterly, "is that coward, Egonwanne. His sweet tongue can change fire into cold ash. When he speaks he moves our men to impotence. If they had ignored his womanish wisdom five years ago, we would not have come to this." He ground his teeth. "Tomorrow he will tell them that our fathers never fought a 'war of blame.' If they listen to him I shall leave them and plan my own revenge."

The crier's voice had once more become faint, and the distance had taken the harsh edge off his iron gong. Okonkwo turned from one side to the other and derived a kind of pleasure from the pain his back gave him. "Let Egonwanne talk about a 'war of blame' tomorrow and I shall show him my back and head." He ground his teeth.

The marketplace began to fill as soon as the sun rose. Obierika was waiting in his *obi* when Okonkwo came along and called him. He hung his goatskin bag and his sheathed machete on his shoulder and went out to join him. Obierika's hut was close to the road and he saw every man who passed to the marketplace. He had exchanged greetings with many who had already passed that morning.

When Okonkwo and Obierika got to the meeting place there were already so many people that if one threw up a grain of sand it would not find its way to the earth again. And many more people were coming from every quarter of the nine villages. It warmed Okonkwo's heart to see such strength of numbers. But he was looking for one man in particular, the man whose tongue he dreaded and despised so much.

"Can you see him?" he asked Obierika.

"Who?"

"Egonwanne," he said, his eyes roving from one corner of the huge marketplace to the other. Most of the men sat on wooden stools they had brought with them.

"No," said Obierika, casting his eyes over the crowd. "Yes, there he is, under the silk-cotton tree. Are you afraid he would convince us not to fight?"

"Afraid? I do not care what he does to *you*. I despise him and those who listen to him. I shall fight alone if I choose."

They spoke at the top of their voices because everybody was talking, and it was like the sound of a great market.

"I shall wait till he has spoken," Okonkwo thought. "Then I shall speak."

"But how do you know he will speak against war?" Obierika asked after a while.

"Because I know he is a coward," said Okonkwo. Obierika did not hear the rest of what he said because at that moment somebody touched his shoulder from behind and he turned round to shake hands and exchange greetings with five or six friends. Okonkwo did not turn round even though he knew the voices. He was in no mood to exchange greetings. But one of the men touched him and asked about the people of his compound.

"They are well," he replied without interest.

The first man to speak to Umuofia that morning was Okika, one of the six who had been imprisoned. Okika was a great man and an orator. But he did not have the booming voice which a first speaker must use to establish silence in the assembly of the clan. Onyeka had such a voice; and so he was asked to salute Umuofia before Okika began to speak.

"*Umuofia kwenu!*" he bellowed, raising his left arm and pushing the air with his open hand.

"*Yaa!*" roared Umuofia.

"*Umuofia kwenu!*" he bellowed again, and again and again, facing a new direction each time. And the crowd answered, "*Yaa!*"

There was immediate silence as though cold water had been poured on a roaring flame.

Okika sprang to his feet and also saluted his clansmen four times. Then he began to speak:

"You all know why we are here, when we ought to be building our barns or mending our huts, when we should be putting our compounds in order. My father used to say to me: 'Whenever you see a toad jumping in broad daylight, then know that something is after its life.' When I saw you all pouring into this meeting from all the quarters of our clan so early in the morning, I knew that something was after our life." He paused for a brief moment and then began again:

"All our gods are weeping. Idemili is weeping, Ogwugwu is weeping, Agbala is weeping, and all the others. Our dead fathers are weeping because of the shameful sacrilege they are suffering and the abomination we have all seen with our eyes." He stopped again to steady his trembling voice.

"This is a great gathering. No clan can boast of greater numbers or greater valor. But are we all here? I ask you: Are all the sons of Umuofia with us here?" A deep murmur swept through the crowd.

"They are not," he said. "They have broken the clan and gone their several ways. We who are here this morning have remained true to our fathers, but our brothers have deserted us and joined a stranger to soil their fatherland. If we fight the stranger we shall hit our brothers and perhaps shed the blood of a clansman. But we must do it. Our fathers never dreamed of such a thing, they never killed their brothers. But a white man never came to them. So we must do what our fathers would never have done. Eneke the bird was asked why he was always on the wing and he replied: 'Men have learned to shoot without missing their mark and I have learned to fly without perching on a twig.' We must root out this evil. And if our brothers take the side of evil we must root them out too. And we must do it *now*. We must bail this water now that it is only ankle deep. . . ."

At this point there was a sudden stir in the crowd and every eye was turned in one direction. There was a sharp bend in the road that led from the marketplace to the white man's court, and to the stream beyond it. And so no one had seen the approach of the five court messengers until they had come round the bend, a few paces from the edge of the crowd. Okonkwo was sitting at the edge.

He sprang to his feet as soon as he saw who it was. He confronted the head messenger, trembling with hate, unable to utter a word. The man was fearless and stood his ground, his four men lined up behind him.

In that brief moment the world seemed to stand still, waiting. There was utter silence. The men of Umuofia were merged into the mute backcloth of trees and giant creepers, waiting.

The spell was broken by the head messenger. "Let me pass!" he ordered.

"What do you want here?"

"The white man whose power you know too well has ordered this meeting to stop."

In a flash Okonkwo drew his machete. The messenger crouched to avoid the blow. It was useless. Okonkwo's machete descended twice and the man's head lay beside his uniformed body.

The waiting backcloth jumped into tumultuous life and the meeting was stopped. Okonkwo stood looking at the dead man. He knew that Umuofia would not go to war. He knew because they had let the other messengers escape. They had broken into tumult instead of action. He discerned fright in that tumult. He heard voices asking: "Why did he do it?"

He wiped his machete on the sand and went away.

25

When the District Commissioner arrived at Okonkwo's compound at the head of an armed band of soldiers and court messengers he found a small crowd of men sitting wearily in the *obi*. He commanded them to come outside, and they obeyed without a murmur.

"Which among you is called Okonkwo?" he asked through his interpreter.

"He is not here," replied Obierika.

"Where is he?"

"He is not here!"

The Commissioner became angry and red in the face. He warned the men that unless they produced Okonkwo forthwith he would lock them all up. The men murmured among themselves, and Obierika spoke again.

"We can take you where he is, and perhaps your men will help us."

The Commissioner did not understand what Obierika meant when he said, "Perhaps your men will help us." One of the most infuriating habits of these people was their love of superfluous words, he thought.

Obierika with five or six others led the way. The Commissioner and his men followed, their firearms held at the ready. He had warned Obierika that if he and his men played any monkey tricks they would be shot. And so they went.

There was a small bush behind Okonkwo's compound. The only opening into this bush from the compound was a little round hole in the red-earth wall through which fowls went in and out in their endless search for food. The hole would not let a man through. It was to this bush that Obierika led the Commissioner and his men. They skirted round the compound, keeping close to the wall. The only sound they made was with their feet as they crushed dry leaves.

Then they came to the tree from which Okonkwo's body was dangling, and they stopped dead.

"Perhaps your men can help us bring him down and bury him," said Obierika. "We have sent for strangers from another village to do it for us, but they may be a long time coming."

The District Commissioner changed instantaneously. The resolute administrator in him gave way to the student of primitive customs.

"Why can't you take him down yourselves?" he asked.

"It is against our custom," said one of the men. "It is an abomination for a man to take his own life. It is an offense against the Earth, and a man who commits it will not be buried by his clansmen. His body is evil, and only strangers may touch it. That is why we ask your people to bring him down, because you are strangers."

"Will you bury him like any other man?" asked the Commissioner.

"We cannot bury him. Only strangers can. We shall pay your men to do it. When he has been buried we will then do our duty by him. We shall make sacrifices to cleanse the desecrated land."

Obierika, who had been gazing steadily at his friend's dangling body, turned suddenly to the District Commissioner and said ferociously: "That man was one of the greatest men in Umuofia. You drove him to kill himself; and now he will be buried like a dog. . . ." He could not say any more. His voice trembled and choked his words.

"Shut up!" shouted one of the messengers, quite unnecessarily.

"Take down the body," the Commissioner ordered his chief messenger, "and bring it and all these people to the court."

"Yes, sah," the messenger said, saluting.

The Commissioner went away, taking three or four of the soldiers with him. In the many years in which he had toiled to bring civilization to different parts of Africa he had learned a number of things. One of them was that a District Commissioner must never attend to such undignified details as cutting a hanged man from the tree. Such attention would give the natives a poor opinion of him. In the book which he planned to write he would stress that point. As he walked back to the court he thought about that book. Every day brought him some new material. The story of this man who had killed a messenger and hanged himself would make interesting reading. One could almost write a whole chapter on him. Perhaps not a whole chapter but a reasonable paragraph, at any rate. There was so much else to include, and one must be firm in cutting out details. He had already chosen the title of the book, after much thought: *The Pacification of the Primitive Tribes of the Lower Niger.*

⟡ DEREK WALCOTT
B. ST. LUCIA, 1930

Growing up on the Caribbean island of St. Lucia, Derek Walcott was exposed at an early age to a wide range of peoples and customs whose roots extended to Africa, Asia, and Europe. The history of the region also included indigenous peoples who had been largely exterminated by Spanish explorers in the sixteenth century. Walcott's substantial body of work—poetry and plays—addresses the social and political realities of a diverse and turbulent history. Like other West Indian writers and artists, Walcott is interested in the search for identity within such a cultural collage.

After the decimation of the original West Indians through slavery and disease, some five million Africans were brought in to work as slaves on the islands' plantations in the seventeenth and eighteenth centuries. After the abolition of slavery in the nineteenth century, East Indian, Chinese, Portuguese, and Irish immigrants were recruited to work the fields of sugar cane. An early pattern of an elite white ruling class dominating a peasant working class comprising various ethnic groups prevailed into the twentieth century. Thus, the most basic question of identity concerning the West Indies has to do with the name of these islands and their residents. The current name, "West Indies," perpetuates the misnomer coined by Columbus in 1492 when he called the native peoples of the Americas "Indians" and used "West" to distinguish them from the "East Indians" of India. The terms *Greater* and *Lesser Antilles* have also been used for the region, but *Antilles* was the name of a legendary island located between Europe and Japan on medieval maps; after Columbus's "discovery," the Spanish called the islands *Antillas*. Residents of the West Indies have a complicated relationship not only with their personal identity but with that of their land as well.

Walcott's writings are a personal odyssey, a search for a mosaic that would harmonize the diversity of his native region, a vision complicated by the multiplicity of languages spoken there—English, Spanish, French, and Dutch—not to mention a variety of CREOLE dialects and island PATOIS (a regional form of a language). Walcott, himself a combination of different ethnic groups, sympathizes with the various social classes and mores on the islands. His writings appeal to many who see themselves as ethnic and cultural *MESTIZOS*[1]—peoples of mixed origins. The experience of native peoples under European colonizers is one of the fundamental stories of the Americas and of central importance to such modern writers as Pablo Neruda of Chile, Carlos Fuentes of Mexico, and Leslie Marmon Silko of the southwestern United States.

Rune Hellestad,
***Derek Walcott,* 1992**
The Nobel Prize–winning poet and playwright. (© Rune Hellestad / CORBIS)

www For links to more information about Derek Walcott and a quiz on his poetry, and for information about the culture and context of the Caribbean in the twentieth century, see *World Literature Online* at bedfordstmartins .com/worldlit.

---

[1] ***mestizos:*** *Mestizo,* a Spanish word meaning "mixed," was first used in Latin American countries to refer to children of a mixed couple, a Spanish or a Portuguese with an indigenous person; with the intermarrying of various immigrant groups since, *mestizo* has come to have a broader application.

Walcott's Mixed Heritage.   Derek Walcott was born of racially mixed
parentage on January 23, 1930, in Castries, the capital of St. Lucia. His
mother was white and his father black, an official and artist who died
shortly after Derek's birth. His mother then became headmistress at a
Methodist elementary school. Derek, who was Protestant and middle
class in a largely black, Roman Catholic, working-class society, experienced the tension between contrasting cultures at an early age. Moreover,
his first language was English in a society that spoke French creole.[2]

Early in his secondary education at St. Mary's College, in Castries,
Walcott discovered his calling as a poet, his responsibility to protect his
island's heritage, and his sympathy for the poor. His first two volumes of
poetry, *25 Poems* (1948) and *Epitaph for the Young* (1949), are about his
childhood on St. Lucia. In 1950, along with Maurice Mason, Walcott
founded the St. Lucian Arts Guild, where he produced *Henri Christophe*
(1950), a historical play about the Haitian revolution. Derek's twin
brother, Roddy, ran this influential theater when Derek left to attend the
University of the West Indies in Kingston, Jamaica, on a scholarship. After
receiving a B.A., Walcott taught school in Kingston, later working as a
feature writer for *The Sunday Guardian,* out of Port-of-Spain, Trinidad.

**Education in the United States and the Search for Roots in the West
Indies.**   A Rockefeller Fellowship in theater brought Walcott to New York
University in 1957. The civil rights movement in the United States during
the late 1950s and the 1960s opened Walcott's eyes to the complexities of
race issues. Returning to Port-of-Spain in 1959, Walcott founded Trinidad
Theatre Workshop (known originally as Little Carib Theatre Workshop),
which occupied him for close to two decades, until 1976. In his first important collection of poems, *In a Green Night: Poems 1948–1962* (1962), work
that extended his reputation beyond the Caribbean, Walcott explored his
heritage as a West Indian. During this time he also wrote one of his most
impressive plays, *Dream on Monkey Mountain* (1967), in which the dreams
of the hero, Makak, give voice to the history of colonial oppression and a
peoples' ties to Africa. *The Castaway* (1969) uses the figure of Robinson
Crusoe to embody the solitary search for identity. *Another Life* (1973) is a
series of autobiographical poems that invoke the spirit of the ancient
Greek traveler Odysseus and the meaning of the search for home.

In his next two collections of poetry, *Sea Grapes* (1976) and *Star
Apple Kingdom* (1977), Walcott wrote about the role of the poet as well as
the legacy of slavery, "the MIDDLE PASSAGE," and colonial domination.
The plays *Ti-Jean and His Brothers* (1958) and *Pantomime* (1978) also deal
with the consequences and the legacy of slavery. *The Joker of Seville* (1974)
retells Tirso de Molina's sixteenth-century story of Don Juan in a West
Indian setting. *O Babylon!* was published with *The Joker* and involves a
RASTAFARIAN[3] cult in Jamaica.

---

[2] **French creole:** A blend of French and the language originally spoken on the islands.

[3] **Rastafarian:** Having to do with a religious cult in Jamaica that regards the late Haile Selassie of Ethiopia as
the messiah; reggae music and the late Bob Marley are associated with Rastafarianism.

In 1979, Walcott was named an honorary member of the American Academy of Arts and Letters. His travels between the United States and the Caribbean stimulated the poems in *The Fortunate Traveler* (1981), in which he recognizes the stark contrast of the powerful, wealthy United States with the impoverished Caribbean. Walcott's *Collected Poems* was published in 1986. In *Omeros* (1990), an epic poem loosely related to Homer's epics and to Dante's *Divine Comedy*,[4] Walcott weaves together many of the themes of his previous writing while celebrating the rich folk traditions of African descendants in the West Indies. In 1991, he was awarded the Nobel Prize in literature.

Selected Poems.   The poems selected here touch on themes central to Walcott's writings. Like a number of writers sympathetic to the impact of colonization on indigenous peoples, Walcott was carried by his work into the very culture that symbolizes domination and oppression — that of white America. The poem "A Latin Primer" deals with the influence of Walcott's education on the process of his becoming a poet, the tension between the educational opportunities provided by the privileged elite and the richness of the folk traditions preserved by the oppressed majority. "White Magic" further explores the cultural conflict between white secularism and the folk traditions of the islands. The United States provides Walcott with the opportunity to publish and work at universities, but his involvement with its culture has the potential to estrange him from the Caribbean culture of his childhood. His poetry, in fact, voices the yearning of an outsider for the rich textures of island life. In the two poems that follow, Walcott writes tightly, compactly, employing end rhyme with a light touch.

"The Light of the World" reveals the anatomy of estrangement through the symbol of a beautiful island woman. Though a looser rhythm prevails here, the poem's images are characteristically dense and thoughtful. In "For Pablo Neruda," Walcott pays tribute to a fellow American poet — a Chilean — whose broad sympathies embraced the ethnic and historical extremes of North and South America. Walcott's poetic style has affinities with Neruda's: Both make use of rich, complex metaphors as a means of yoking the disparate suffering caused by European conquest and the potential contradictions of living in a multicultural society.

> The Caribbean has remained a green place, even if, as Derek Walcott has written, "the golden apples of this sun are shot with acid." Between the nightmare of the slave barracoons [barracks], and the vision of Adamic islands, have emerged the imagined worlds. . . .
>
> – LOUIS JAMES, critic, 1999

■ CONNECTIONS

James Baldwin, "Sonny's Blues," p. 830. The situation of blacks in the United States is similar to that of blacks in the Caribbean: Though their roots are in Africa, they have both nevertheless created a rich culture of their own in America and the islands. In "Sonny's Blues," black music affords the story's characters an opportunity

---

[4] **Homer's . . . *Comedy*:** Homer (eighth century B.C.E.) wrote the *Iliad* and the *Odyssey;* Dante (1265–1321) wrote the *Divine Comedy,* a trilogy about a spiritual pilgrimage to the underworld and then to purgatory and heaven.

to discover pieces of their ethnicity. How does "A Latin Primer" describe Walcott's search for a culture consistent with the basic ingredients of his childhood?

T. S. Eliot, *The Waste Land,* p. 486. A number of modern writers, willing to risk obscurity, believe that their language and form should reflect the density and complexities of life in the modern world. Eliot's adherence to this idea is reflected in the difficulty of finding meaning in *The Waste Land.* What might be the justification for the complex images in Walcott's "White Magic" and "The Light of the World"?

William Wordsworth, "Lines Composed a Few Miles Above Tintern Abbey" (Book 5). The Romantic poets of England and the Continent were fond of using images from nature to suggest states of mind. Wordsworth masterfully integrates emotions, nature, and periods of time in "Lines Composed a Few Miles Above Tintern Abbey." How does Walcott portray the rich, layered culture of Caribbean life through the sea, plant life, food, and smell?

■ **FURTHER RESEARCH**

Historical and Cultural Background

Brathwaite, Kamau. *Roots.* 1993.
Hulme, Peter, and Neil L. Whitehead, eds. *Wild Majesty: Encounters with Caribs from Columbus to the Present Day.* 1992.
James, Louis. *Caribbean Literature in English.* 1999.

Critical Works on Derek Walcott

Erada, Rei. *Derek Walcott's Poetry: American Mimicry.* 1992.
Goldstraw, Irma. *Derek Walcott: An Annotated Bibliography of His Writings, 1944–1984.* 1984.
Hamner, Robert D. *Derek Walcott.* 1994.
Hamner, Robert D., ed. *Critical Perspectives on Derek Walcott.* 1993.
King, Bruce L. *The Theatre of Derek Walcott.* 1996.

A Latin Primer

(In Memoriam: H. D. Boxill)

I had nothing against which
to notch the growth of my work
but the horizon, no language
but the shallows in my long walk

home, so I shook all the help
my young right hand could use

"**A Latin Primer.**" This poem was first published in *The Arkansas Testament* (1987), a collection of poems about St. Lucia. The title poem is about a visit to Arkansas where Walcott was made painfully aware of the color of his skin. "A Latin Primer" describes the poet's struggle to find a language suitable for his direct personal experiences. His formal education and teaching role seem to have alienated him until a frigate bird provides a poetic breakthrough.

All notes are the editors'.

from the sand-crusted kelp
of distant literatures.

The frigate bird[1] my phoenix,[2]
10 I was high on iodine,
one drop from the sun's murex
stained the foam's fabric wine;

ploughing white fields of surf
with a boy's shins, I kept
staggering as the shelf
of sand under me slipped,

then found my deepest wish
in the swaying words of the sea,
and the skeletal fish
20 of that boy is ribbed in me;

but I saw how the bronze
dusk of imperial palms
curled their fronds into questions
over Latin exams.

I hated signs of scansion.
Those strokes across the line
drizzled on the horizon
and darkened discipline.

They were like Mathematics
30 that made delight Design,
arranging the thrown sticks
of stars to sine and cosine.[3]

Raging, I'd skip a pebble
across the sea's page; it still
scanned its own syllable:
trochee, anapest, dactyl.[4]

---

[1] **frigate bird:** A large, tropical seabird with V-shaped wings and tail; the *Fregata magnificens.*

[2] **phoenix:** A mythical bird from ancient Egypt; said to renew itself by rising out of its own ashes, it symbolizes immortality.

[3] **sine and cosine:** Technical terms in trigonometry.

[4] **trochee . . . dactyl:** Common patterns of accented and unaccented syllables of words in a line of verse.

Miles,[5] foot soldier. *Fossa,*
a trench or a grave. My hand
hefts a last sand bomb to toss
40   at slowly fading sand.

I failed Matriculation
in Maths; passed it; after that,
I taught Love's basic Latin:
Amo, amas, amat.[6]

In tweed jacket and tie
a master at my college
I watched the old words dry
like seaweed on the page.

I'd muse from the roofed harbour
50   back to my desk, the boys'
heads plunged in paper
softly as porpoises.

The discipline I preached
made me a hypocrite;
their lithe black bodies, beached,
would die in dialect;

I spun the globe's meridian,
showed its sealed hemispheres,
but where were those brows heading
60   when neither world was theirs?

Silence clogged my ears
with cotton, a cloud's noise;
I climbed white tiered arenas
trying to find my voice,

and I remember: it was on a
Saturday near noon, at Vigie,[7]

---

[5] *Miles:* Latin for "soldier"; also refers to Nelson Appleton Miles (1839–1925), a U.S. soldier who worked his way up from foot soldier to general. After the Civil War, Miles led troops against Native Americans in the West and fought in the Caribbean during the Spanish-American War (1895–1898).

[6] *Amo, amas, amat:* The first conjugation of the Latin *amare,* "to love."

[7] **Vigie:** The Vigie peninsula forms the northern side of the Castries Harbor of St. Lucia, an island in the Caribbean.

that my heart, rounding the corner
of Half-Moon Battery,[8]

70   stopped to watch the foundry
of midday cast in bronze
the trunk of a gommier tree
on a sea without seasons,

while ochre Rat Island
was nibbling the sea's lace,
that a frigate bird came sailing
through a tree's net, to raise

its emblem in the cirrus,
named with the common sense
of fishermen: sea scissors,
80   *Fregata magnificens,*

ciseau-la-mer,[9] the patois[10]
for its cloud-cutting course;
and that native metaphor
made by the strokes of oars,

with one wing beat for scansion,
that slowly levelling V
made one with my horizon
as it sailed steadily

beyond the sheep-nibbled columns
90   of fallen marble trees,
or the roofless pillars once
sacred to Hercules.[11]

---

[8] Half-Moon Battery: Remnant of a fortification from the three hundred years of fighting between England and France over ownership of St. Lucia.

[9] *ciseau-la-mer:* French for "sea scissors," or "scissors of the sea."

[10] patois: A local dialect that is a variation of an area's standard language.

[11] Hercules: Roman name of the Greek hero and god Heracles; the ancient Pillars of Hercules flanked the Strait of Gibraltar between Gibraltar, in Europe, and Mt. Acha, in Africa.

∾ White Magic

(For Leo St. Helene)

The *gens-gagée*[1] kicks off her wrinkled skin.
Clap her soul in a jar! The half-man wolf
can trot with bending elbows, rise, and grin
in lockjawed lycanthropia.[2] Censers dissolve
the ground fog with its whistling, wandering souls,
the unbaptized, unfinished, and uncursed
by holy fiat. The island's griots[3] love
our mushroom elves, the devil's parasols
who creep like grubs from a trunk's rotten holes,
10   their mouths a sewn seam, their clubfeet reversed.
Exorcism cannot anachronize
those signs we hear past midnight in a wood
where a pale woman like a blind owl flies
to her forked branch, with scarlet moons for eyes
bubbling with doubt. You heard a silver splash?
It's nothing. If it slid from mossed rocks
dismiss it as a tired crab, a fish,
unless our water-mother with dank locks
is sliding under this page below your pen,
20   only a simple people think they happen.
Dryads and hamadryads[4] were engrained
in the wood's bark, in papyrus, and this paper;
but when our dry leaves crackle to the deer-
footed, hobbling hunter, Papa Bois,[5]

"White Magic." Also first published in *The Arkansas Testament* (1987), this poem delves into the spirit world of island culture and contrasts folk belief with the secular views of the white world. In an almost defensive posture, the poem concludes: "Our myths are ignorance, theirs are literature."
    All notes are the editors'.

---

[1] *gens-gagée:* Island patois for "spirit being."

[2] **lycanthropia:** From the Greek *lykoi* (wolf) and *anthropos* (man); lycanthropy is the belief that one has become a wolf.

[3] **griots:** Members of a hereditary caste among the peoples of western Africa whose function is to keep an oral history of the tribe or village and to tell the stories, songs, and poems of the people.

[4] **Dryads and hamadryads:** Deities or nymphs of the woods; hamadryads are spirits of particular trees.

[5] **Papa Bois:** Refers to a notorious pirate, Jambe de Bois (French for "wooden leg"), who had a hideout on Pigeon Island, off the west coast of St. Lucia.

he's just Pan's[6] clone, one more translated satyr.
The crone who steps from her jute sugar sack
(though you line moonlit lintels with white flour),
the *beau l'homme*[7] creeping towards you, front to back,
the ferny footed, faceless, mouse-eared elves,
30   these fables of the backward and the poor
marbled by moonlight, will grow white and richer.
Our myths are ignorance, theirs are literature.

---

[6] **Pan:** Greek god of pastures, flocks, and shepherds; symbolic of the sexual energy of nature, which took the form of a goatlike creature, the satyr. This figure was "translated" by medieval Christians into Satan.
[7] *beau l'homme:* French for "handsome man."

∾   The Light of the World

Kaya now, got to have kaya now,
Got to have kaya now,
For the rain is falling.
                    – BOB MARLEY[1]

Marley was rocking on the transport's stereo
and the beauty was humming the choruses quietly.
I could see where the lights on the planes of her cheek
streaked and defined them; if this were a portrait
you'd leave the highlights for last, these lights
silkened her black skin; I'd have put in an earring,
something simple, in good gold, for contrast, but she
wore no jewelry. I imagined a powerful and sweet
odour coming from her, as from a still panther,
10   and the head was nothing else but heraldic.
When she looked at me, then away from me politely
because any staring at strangers is impolite,

"The Light of the World." This poem, also first published in *The Arkansas Testament* (1987), begins with the description of a beautiful woman from the islands, which in turn evokes memories from childhood: the sadness of drunk women, the smells of the Market, the images of family. Walcott struggles with the feeling that by living away from the islands he has abandoned an already abandoned people.

All notes are the editors'.

---

[1] **Bob Marley** (1945–1981): Jamaican-born reggae singer committed to nonviolence and the Rastafarian religion.

it was like a statue, like a black Delacroix's[2]
Liberty Leading the People, the gently bulging
whites of her eyes, the carved ebony mouth,
the heft of the torso solid, and a woman's,
but gradually even that was going in the dusk,
except the line of her profile, and the highlit cheek,
and I thought, O Beauty, you are the light of the world!

20   It was not the only time I would think of that phrase
in the sixteen-seater transport that hummed between
Gros-Islet[3] and the Market, with its grit of charcoal
and the litter of vegetables after Saturday's sales,
and the roaring rum shops, outside whose bright doors
you saw drunk women on pavements, the saddest of all things,
winding up their week, winding down their week.
The Market, as it closed on this Saturday night,
remembered a childhood of wandering gas lanterns
hung on poles at street corners, and the old roar
30   of vendors and traffic, when the lamplighter climbed,
hooked the lantern on its pole and moved on to another,
and the children turned their faces to its moth, their
eyes white as their nighties; the Market
itself was closed in its involved darkness
and the shadows quarrelled for bread in the shops,
or quarrelled for the formal custom of quarrelling
in the electric rum shops. I remember the shadows.

The van was slowly filling in the darkening depot.
I sat in the front seat, I had no need for time.
40   I looked at two girls, one in a yellow bodice
and yellow shorts, with a flower in her hair,
and lusted in peace, the other less interesting.
That evening I had walked the streets of the town
where I was born and grew up, thinking of my mother
with her white hair tinted by the dyeing dusk,
and the tilting box houses that seemed perverse
in their cramp; I had peered into parlours
with half-closed jalousies, at the dim furniture,

---

[2] **Delacroix:** Eugène Delacroix (1798–1863), French Romantic painter whose visit to Morocco in 1832 inspired
an interest in "exotic" subjects.

[3] **Gros-Islet:** Fishing village on the northwest coast of St. Lucia known for its weekly carnivals.

Morris chairs,[4] a centre table with wax flowers,
and the lithograph of *Christ of the Sacred Heart*,[5]
vendors still selling to the empty streets—
sweets, nuts, sodden chocolates, nut cakes, mints.

An old woman with a straw hat over her headkerchief
hobbled towards us with a basket; somewhere,
some distance off, was a heavier basket
that she couldn't carry. She was in a panic.
She said to the driver: *"Pas quittez moi à terre,"*
which is, in her patois: "Don't leave me stranded,"
which is, in her history and that of her people:
"Don't leave me on earth," or, by a shift of stress:
"Don't leave me the earth" [for an inheritance];
"Pas quittez moi à terre, Heavenly transport,
Don't leave me on earth, I've had enough of it."
The bus filled in the dark with heavy shadows
that would not be left on earth; no, that would be left
on the earth, and would have to make out.
Abandonment was something they had grown used to.

And I had abandoned them, I knew that there
sitting in the transport, in the sea-quiet dusk,
with men hunched in canoes, and the orange lights
from the Vigie[6] headland, black boats on the water;
I, who could never solidify my shadow
to be one of their shadows, had left them their earth,
their white rum quarrels, and their coal bags,
their hatred of corporals, of all authority.
I was deeply in love with the woman by the window.
I wanted to be going home with her this evening.
I wanted her to have the key to our small house
by the beach at Gros-Islet; I wanted her to change
into a smooth white nightie that would pour like water
over the black rocks of her breasts, to lie

[4] **Morris chairs:** Large armchairs with adjustable backs and removable cushions, named after the English artist and poet William Morris (1834–1896).

[5] ***Christ of the Sacred Heart:*** Image depicting the exposed heart of Jesus encircled by either flames or thorns. Partly because of St. Margaret Mary Alacoque's visions in the seventeenth century, the Roman Catholic Church approved the "enthronement" of this image in the home, symbolizing the sovereignty of Christ over the family.

[6] **Vigie:** See note 7 for "A Latin Primer."

simply beside her by the ring of a brass lamp
with a kerosene wick, and tell her in silence
that her hair was like a hill forest at night,
that a trickle of rivers was in her armpits,
that I would buy her Benin[7] if she wanted it,
and never leave her on earth. But the others, too.

Because I felt a great love that could bring me to tears,
and a pity that prickled my eyes like a nettle,
90   I was afraid I might suddenly start sobbing
on the public transport with the Marley going,
and a small boy peering over the shoulders
of the driver and me at the lights coming,
at the rush of the road in the country darkness,
with lamps in the houses on the small hills,
and thickets of stars; I had abandoned them,
I had left them on earth, I left them to sing
Marley's songs of a sadness as real as the smell
of rain on dry earth, or the smell of damp sand,
100   and the bus felt warm with their neighbourliness,
their consideration, and the polite partings

in the light of its headlamps. In the blare,
in the thud-sobbing music, the claiming scent
that came from their bodies. I wanted the transport
to continue forever, for no one to descend
and say a good night in the beams of the lamps
and take the crooked path up to the lit door,
guided by fireflies; I wanted her beauty
to come into the warmth of considerate wood,
110   to the relieved rattling of enamel plates
in the kitchen, and the tree in the yard,
but I came to my stop. Outside the Halcyon Hotel.
The lounge would be full of transients like myself.
Then I would walk with the surf up the beach.
I got off the van without saying good night.
Good night would be full of inexpressible love.
They went on in their transport, they left me on earth.

Then, a few yards ahead, the van stopped. A man
shouted my name from the transport window.
120   I walked up towards him. He held out something.

---

[7] **Benin**: West African nation on the Gulf of Guinea; also a city in southern Nigeria known for its art.

A pack of cigarettes had dropped from my pocket.
He gave it to me. I turned, hiding my tears.
There was nothing they wanted, nothing I could give them
but this thing I have called "The Light of the World."

For Pablo Neruda[1]

I am not walking on sand,
but I feel I am walking on sand,
this poem is accompanying me on sand.
Fungus lacing the rock,
on the ribs, mould. Moss
feathering the mute roar
of the staved-in throat
of the wreck, the crab gripping.

Why this loop of correspondences,
10   as your voice grows hoarser
than the chafed Pacific? Your voice
falling soundless as snow on
the petrified Andes, the snow
like feathers from the tilting
rudderless condors,[2]
emissary in a black suit, who
walks among eagles, hand, whose
five-knuckled peninsula
bars the heartbreaking ocean?

20   Hear the ambassador of velvet
open the felt-hinged door,

"**For Pablo Neruda.**"   This tribute to the great Chilean poet Pablo Neruda, who, like Walcott and others, created a connection between indigenous peoples and European settlers in his work, was first published in *Sea Grapes* (1976). In "The Heights of Macchu Picchu," especially, Neruda celebrated the grandeur of Inca civilization.

All notes are the editors'.

---

[1] **Pablo Neruda** (1904–1973): Chilean poet who wrote about the effects of colonialism on the Americas; a number of his poems depict the oppression of the Indians. (See p. 672.)

[2] **condors:** In a famous line in *The Heights of Macchu Picchu,* a collection of poems about the ancient Inca city of the title located high in the Andes, Neruda mentions condors, a bird with a wingspread of twelve feet common to the Andes.

the black flag flaps toothless
over Isla Negra.[3] You said
when others like me despaired:
climb the moss-throated stairs
to the crest of Macchu Picchu,[4]
break your teeth like a pick on
the obdurate, mottled terraces,
wear the wind, soaked with rain
30   like a cloak, above absences,

and for us, in the New World,
our older world, you became
a benign, rigorous uncle,
and through you we fanned open
to others, to the sand-rasped
mutter of César Vallejo,[5] to
the radiant, self-circling
sunstone of Octavio,[6] men
who, unlike the Saxons,[7] I am tempted
40   to call by their Christian names;

we were all netted to one rock
by vines of iron, our livers
picked by corbeaux and condors
in the New World, in a new word,
brotherhood, word which arrests
the crests of the snowblowing ocean
in its flash to a sea of sierras,
the round fish mouths of our children,
the word *cantan*.[8] All this
50   you have done for me. Gracias.

---

[3] **Isla Negra:** Pablo Neruda had a house in Isla Negra, on the Pacific coast in Chile. When he was in residence there, he flew a flag.

[4] **Macchu Picchu:** See note 2.

[5] **César Vallejo** (1892–1938): Peruvian poet particularly interested in social change.

[6] **Octavio:** Octavio Paz (1914–1998), a Nobel Prize–winner from Mexico who often wrote about the Mexican search for identity in its Indian past; Paz's long poem "Sunstone" is a critique of Mexican apathy. *Sunstone* can also refer to gold.

[7] **Saxons:** Originally, a Germanic tribe, some of whom conquered England in the fifth and sixth centuries; the term *Anglo-Saxon* usually refers to England and the English.

[8] *cantan:* Spanish for "You (plural) sing" or "They sing."

⮺ ALIFA RIFAAT
B. EGYPT, 1930

Contrary to the stereotype of submissive, veiled, and voiceless victims of a male-dominated society, Arab women have been amassing a considerable body of work in Arabic literature. Some of this writing takes a vigorous feminist stand on issues of women's rights and women's sexuality. One of the first feminist writers in Arabic literature was the poet Aisha al-Taymuriyya (1840–1902), a member of the Turkish aristocracy in Egypt. Between 1892 and 1920 several journals focusing on and produced by women came out of Egypt and circulated throughout the Arabic world. In 1995, at the first Arab Women Book Fair, held in Cairo, more than 150 women writers participated from throughout the Arab world and more than 1,500 titles were on display by publishers. Among the principal Arabic feminists writing today are Hanan al-Shaykh (b. Lebanon, 1945); Ghada al-Samman (b. Syria, 1942); Fadia Faqir (b. Jordan, 1956); Alia Mamdouh (b. Iraq, 1944); Liana Badr (b. Palestine, 1952); and Nawal el-Saadawi (b. 1931) and **Alifa Rifaat** from Egypt. Through translations, al-Shaykh, el-Saadawi, and Rifaat in particular have received widespread attention and acclaim throughout the East and West, and the reception of their work has generated interest in and controversy over the role of women in the Arab world as well as the politics of literary reception in a global culture. The award-winning Rifaat has been recognized abroad and in Egypt as a gifted stylist and a controversial pioneer in writing about social conditions and sexual politics concerning Egyptian women.

Education and Marriage.   Fatma Abdulla Rifaat was born on June 5, 1930, in Cairo, into the family of a well-to-do architect, Abdulla, and his wife, Zakia. Raised in the countryside where her family owned property, Fatma was a precocious child who demonstrated early her gift for writing. At the age of nine, she wrote a short story describing "despair in our village," for which she was punished. After receiving her primary school diploma, Rifaat attended the British Institute in Cairo from 1946 to 1949. Though she wanted to enroll in the College of Fine Arts at Cairo and go on to the university, her father, who believed that arts and literature would interfere with her duties as a wife and mother, refused her wishes and forced her to marry. Of that situation, Rifaat explains: "All decisions in our family are made by the menfolk; we are proud of our Arab origin and hold on to certain Arab customs, among which is the belief that the marriage of girls and their education remains the business of the man. The men taught us to be ladies in society and mistresses of the home only. As for the arts and literature, they were a waste of time and even forbidden." After an eight-month unconsummated marriage with a mining engineer, in July 1952 Fatma married a cousin with the same surname, Hussein Rifaat, a police officer with whom she had a daughter and two sons. Because Hussein's work took him to several posts at a number of

www   For links to more information about Alifa Rifaat and a quiz on "My World of the Unknown," and for information about the culture and context of the Middle East in the twentieth century, see *World Literature Online* at bedfordstmartins .com/worldlit.

AH-lee-fah ree-FAHT

towns and villages, Rifaat, like the wife in "My World of the Unknown," had the opportunity to observe Egyptian life in all its diversity.

Reclaiming the Writer.   Having experimented with oil painting and music, Rifaat returned to writing short stories, "a thing," she explains, "that clashed with my marriage." When her first story was published in 1955, her husband "created a storm," even though she had published her work under a pseudonym, Alifa Rifaat. She nevertheless continued to publish until 1960, when her husband demanded that she stop writing altogether. For more than a decade Rifaat complied, during which time she avidly studied literature and read on Sufism, science, astronomy, and history. In about 1973, after she had suffered a long bout of illness, her husband conceded that she might resume her writing. During that time of reclaiming her voice, Rifaat wrote "My World of the Unknown," a story that immediately garnered her both praise and blame for its treatment of the protagonist's sexuality. Beginning in 1974, Rifaat published many short stories in the literary journal *al-Thaqafa al-usbu'iya,* followed by the collection of short stories *Eve Returns with Adam to Paradise* (1975) and the novel *The Jewel of Pharo* (1978). After her husband's death in 1979 Rifaat met the British translator Denys Johnson-Davies, who, Rifaat explains, encouraged her to abandon some of the Romantic elements of her early work and to use colloquial language for dialogue. Several collections of her stories were published in the early 1980s, including *Who Can This Man Be?* (1981), *The Prayer of Love* (1983), *A House in the Land of the Dead* (1984), and *Love Conspired on Me* (1985). In 1983, *Distant View of a Minaret,* a collection of stories selected and translated by Denys Johnson-Davies, among them "My World of the Unknown," was published in English before appearing in Arabic two years later. In 1984 Rifaat won the Excellence Award from the Modern Literature Assembly. She has contributed nearly one hundred short stories to Arabic and English magazines, and her work has been produced for British, Egyptian, and German radio and television. Her novel *Girls of Baurdin* was published in 1995.

Awakening.   Unlike some of her contemporaries, such as el-Saadawi and al-Shaykh, Rifaat draws primarily on Arab tradition in her fiction. A devout Muslim well read in the Islamic holy book, the QUR'AN (KORAN), and in the collected laws and traditions of Islam, the HADITH, she seeks to reconcile Islamic teachings, which she believes have been misinterpreted with regard to women, with current practices. However, as recently as 1999, *Distant View of a Minaret* was pulled from the shelves of the bookstore at the American University in Cairo for offending public morality and injuring good taste. Critics oppose Rifaat's frank exploration of female sexuality. "Most of my stories," Rifaat has observed, "revolve around a woman's right to a fully effective and complete sexual life in marriage; that and the sexual and emotional problems encountered by women in marriages are the most important themes of my stories." Her own marriage was initially unfulfilling because she had been told nothing about the act of making love. She adds, however, that Western models of sexual education and sexual liberation are inappropriate for Arab peoples,

sexual education and sexual liberation are inappropriate for Arab peoples, who have a strong commitment to Muslim religion and Arabic culture. "Our society," she explains, "does not allow us to experience sex freely as Western women may. We have our traditions and our religion in which we believe." In this story, Rifaat indeed does not express Western notions of libido but accounts for the narrator's sexual awakening by way of Islamic myth and Arabic folk belief.

"My World of the Unknown."   In Rifaat's "My World of the Unknown," the known world the narrator inhabits is that of middle-class, somewhat Westernized Egyptian women whose menfolk are thoroughly absorbed in the gray workaday world of urban bureaucracy and whose children are off at school, leaving them to occupy their days with supervising households. Though she says little about her life prior to the action of the story, it is apparent that the narrator's wifely existence has left her feeling dry and depleted in body and soul. When her preoccupied husband is transferred to a post in the countryside, her subconscious stirs and directs her toward the mysterious house where the deeper needs of her imagination, her sexuality, and her spirit may be met. In the house on the canal, she feels alive and open to the natural world, and her whole being is refreshed and quickened when she enters into a magical love affair with a beautiful female snake. The snake is apparently a **djinn**— one of a host of corporeal beings Allah created from smokeless fire who are said to live in a parallel universe to ours. Arab folklore abounds with tales of comings and goings between these worlds, and such encounters may be for good or for ill, since the djinn, like human beings, may be evil or helpful. In any case, to glimpse their world of the unknown alters a human being forever; such an experience seems to have driven Aneesa, the house's previous occupant, into madness, and by the end of the story, when the husband clumsily destroys his wife's idyll by killing one of the snake's own kind, the narrator may be mad as well, for her whole life is focused on the slim hope that she will be reunited with her snake lover. Like the supernatural world, human sexuality is at once a territory of great beauty and joy and, equally, of great risk. By daring to explore her own desires and by reaching out sexually and spiritually toward a very different—and female—being, the narrator invites danger and sorrow, but to have drawn back from the adventure would have meant continuing to live out a mechanical, meaningless existence.

■ **CONNECTIONS**

Charlotte Perkins Gilman, "The Yellow Wallpaper" (Book 5). "My World of the Unknown" presents women's space and women's desire in a context in which women experience only limited power and freedom. Their desire for more seems to be reflected in an encounter with a mysterious Other who offers some form of liberation or alternative to oppressive conventions. How are the conditions in these two stories similar? In what ways are these stories culturally or historically specific?

Franz Kafka, *The Metamorphosis*, p. 428; Abé Kobo, "The Stick," p. 920. Rifaat's "My World of the Unknown" invokes the genre known as the "fantastic," or fantasy,

Alifa Rifaat's revolt falls far short of suggesting that there be any change in the traditional role of women in Muslim society, and the last place she would look for inspiration for any change would be the Christian West.

  – DENYS JOHNSON-DAVIES, translator

JIN

works in which events and characters appear that would not manifest in real life. Such stories invite readers to "suspend our disbelief," to paraphrase the poet Samuel Taylor Coleridge, and treat the impossible as plausible. In Rifaat's story, the narrator's encounter with the snake is presented as if it were actually taking place. Similarly, in Kafka's *The Metamorphosis* and Abé's "The Stick," Gregor's transformation into an insect and the narrator's becoming a stick, respectively, are described as real events. By means of the fantastic — one branch of which is science fiction — authors often are able to criticize the real world, its social conventions or politics and its follies. How do these writers use fantasy to deal with very serious subjects?

■ **FURTHER RESEARCH**

Ahmed, Leila. "Arab Culture and Writing Women's Bodies." *Feminist Issues* 12 (2): 41–55.

al-Ali, Nadje Sadig. *Gender Writing/Writing Gender: The Representation of Women in a Selection of Modern Egyptian Literature.* 1994.

Elkhadem, Saad. "The Representation of Women in Early Egyptian Fiction: A Survey." *The International Fiction Review* 23 (1996): 76–90.

Olive, Barbara A. "Writing Women's Bodies: A Study of Alifa Rifaat's Short Fiction." *The International Fiction Review* 23 (1996): 44–50.

Salti, Ramzi. "Feminism and Religion in Alifa Rifaat's Short Stories." *The International Fiction Review* 18.2 (1991): 108–12.

■ **PRONUNCIATION**

djinn: JIN
Alifa Rifaat: AH-lee-fah ree-FAHT
souk: SOOK

✎ My World of the Unknown

Translated by Denys Johnson-Davies

There are many mysteries in life, unseen powers in the universe, worlds other than our own, hidden links and radiations that draw creatures together and whose effect is interacting. They may merge or be incompatible, and perhaps the day will come when science will find a method for connecting up these worlds in the same way as it has made it possible to voyage to other planets. Who knows?

Yet one of these other worlds I have explored; I have lived in it and been linked with its creatures through the bond of love. I used to pass with amazing speed

---

"My World of the Unknown." The first English translation of this story was published in 1983 in the collection *Distant View of a Minaret and Other Stories* translated by Denys Johnson-Davies. The same collection was published two years later in Arabic under the title, as translated into English, *The Long Night of Winter and Other Stories.* Based in part on her experiences with her husband, whose travels to various posts acquainted Rifaat with rural Egypt, "My World of the Unknown" was the first story to attract wide attention to the writer's fiction. Although Rifaat has

between this tangible world of ours and another invisible earth, mixing in the two worlds on one and the same day, as though living it twice over.

When entering into the world of my love, and being summoned and yielding to its call, no one around me would be aware of what was happening to me. All that occurred was that I would be overcome by something resembling a state of languor and would go off into a semi-sleep. Nothing about me would change except that I would become very silent and withdrawn, though I am normally a person who is talkative and eager to go out into the world of people. I would yearn to be on my own, would long for the moment of surrender as I prepared myself for answering the call.

Love had its beginning when an order came through for my husband to be transferred to a quiet country town and, being too busy with his work, delegated to me the task of going to this town to choose suitable accommodation prior to his taking up the new appointment. He cabled one of his subordinates named Kamil and asked him to meet me at the station and to assist me.

I took the early morning train. The images of a dream I had had that night came to me as I looked out at the vast fields and gauged the distances between the towns through which the train passed and reckoned how far it was between the new town in which we were fated to live and beloved Cairo.

The images of the dream kept reappearing to me, forcing themselves upon my mind: images of a small white house surrounded by a garden with bushes bearing yellow flowers, a house lying on the edge of a broad canal in which were swans and tall sailing boats. I kept on wondering at my dream and trying to analyse it. Perhaps it was some secret wish I had had, or maybe the echo of some image that my unconscious had stored up and was chewing over.

As the train arrived at its destination, I awoke from my thoughts. I found Kamil awaiting me. We set out in his car, passing through the local *souk.*[1] I gazed at the mounds of fruit with delight, chatting away happily with Kamil. When we emerged from the *souk* we found ourselves on the bank of the Mansoura canal, a canal on which swans swam and sailing boats moved to and fro. I kept staring at them with uneasy longing. Kamil directed the driver to the residential buildings the governorate had put up for housing government employees. While gazing at the opposite bank a large boat with a great fluttering sail glided past. Behind it could be seen a white house that had a garden with trees with yellow flowers and that lay on its own amidst vast fields. I shouted out in confusion, overcome by the feeling that I had been here before.

---

said that death is one of the main subjects of her writing, women's sexuality—particularly the right of married women to enjoy a full and rewarding sex life—has been equally her focus. In many ways the suppression of sexual desire in a woman's life symbolizes the blocking of other desires whose expression might lead to happiness, joy, and fulfillment.

All notes are the editors'.

---

[1] *souk:* An outdoor market or bazaar.

"Go to that house," I called to the driver. Kamil leapt up, objecting vehemently: "No, no,—no one lives in that house. The best thing is to go to the employees' buildings."

I shouted insistently, like someone hypnotized: "I must have a look at that house." "All right," he said. "You won't like it, though—it's old and needs repairing." Giving in to my wish, he ordered the driver to make his way there.

At the garden door we found a young woman, spare and of fair complexion. A fat child with ragged clothes encircled her neck with his burly legs. In a strange silence, she stood as though nailed to the ground, barring the door with her hands and looking at us with doltish enquiry.

I took a sweet from my bag and handed it to the boy. He snatched it eagerly, tightening his grip on her neck with his podgy, mud-bespattered feet so that her face became flushed from his high-spirited embrace. A half-smile showed on her tightly closed lips. Taking courage, I addressed her in a friendly tone: "I'd like to see over this house." She braced her hands resolutely against the door. "No," she said quite simply. I turned helplessly to Kamil, who went up to her and pushed her violently in the chest so that she staggered back. "Don't you realize," he shouted at her, "that this is the director's wife? Off with you!"

Lowering her head so that the child all but slipped from her, she walked off dejectedly to the canal bank where she lay down on the ground, put the child on her lap, and rested her head in her hands in silent submission.

Moved by pity, I remonstrated: "There's no reason to be so rough, Mr. Kamil. Who is the woman?" "Some mad woman," he said with a shrug of his shoulders, "who's a stranger to the town. Out of kindness the owner of this house put her in charge of it until someone should come along to live in it."

With increased interest I said: "Will he be asking a high rent for it?" "Not at all," he said with an enigmatic smile. "He'd welcome anyone taking it over. There are no restrictions and the rent is modest—no more than four pounds."

I was beside myself with joy. Who in these days can find somewhere to live for such an amount? I rushed through the door into the house with Kamil behind me and went over the rooms: five spacious rooms with wooden floors, with a pleasant hall, modern lavatory, and a beautifully roomy kitchen with a large verandah over-looking vast pistachio-green fields of generously watered rice. A breeze, limpid and cool, blew, playing with the tips of the crop and making the delicate leaves move in continuous dancing waves.

I went back to the first room with its spacious balcony overlooking the road and revealing the other bank of the canal where, along its strand, extended the houses of the town. Kamil pointed out to me a building facing the house on the other side. "That's where we work," he said, "and behind it is where the children's schools are."

"Thanks be to God," I said joyfully. "It means that everything is within easy reach of this house—and the *souk*'s nearby too." "Yes," he said, "and the fishermen will knock at your door to show you the fresh fish they've caught in their nets. But

the house needs painting and re-doing, also there are all sorts of rumours about it —
the people around here believe in djinn[2] and spirits."

"This house is going to be my home," I said with determination. "Its low rent
will make up for whatever we may have to spend on re-doing it. You'll see what this
house will look like when I get the garden arranged. As for the story about djinn and
spirits, just leave them to us — we're more spirited than them."

We laughed at my joke as we left the house. On my way to the station we agreed
about the repairs that needed doing to the house. Directly I reached Cairo I cabled
my husband to send the furniture from the town we had been living in, specifying a
suitable date to fit in with the completion of the repairs and the house being ready
for occupation.

On the date fixed I once again set off and found that all my wishes had been carried out and that the house was pleasantly spruce with its rooms painted a cheerful
orange tinge, the floors well polished and the garden tidied up and made into small
flowerbeds.

I took possession of the keys and Kamil went off to attend to his business, having put a chair on the front balcony for me to sit on while I awaited the arrival of the
furniture van. I stretched out contentedly in the chair and gazed at the two banks
with their towering trees like two rows of guards between which passed the boats
with their lofty sails, while around them glided a male swan heading a flotilla of
females. Halfway across the canal he turned and flirted with them, one after the
other, like a sultan amidst his harem.

Relaxed, I closed my eyes. I projected myself into the future and pictured to
myself the enjoyment I would have in this house after it had been put in order
and the garden fixed up. I awoke to the touch of clammy fingers shaking me by the
shoulders.

I started and found myself staring at the fair-complexioned woman with her
child squatting on her shoulders as she stood erect in front of me staring at me in
silence. "What do you want?" I said to her sharply. "How did you get in?" "I got in
with this," she said simply, revealing a key between her fingers.

I snatched the key from her hand as I loudly rebuked her: "Give it here. We have
rented the house and you have no right to come into it like this." "I have a lot of other
keys," she answered briefly. "And what," I said to her, "do you want of this house?" "I
want to stay on in it and for you to go," she said. I laughed in amazement at her
words as I asked myself: Is she really mad? Finally I said impatiently: "Listen here,
I'm not leaving here and you're not entering this house unless I wish it. My husband
is coming with the children, and the furniture is on the way. He'll be arriving in a

---

[2] djinn: The djinn are intelligent corporeal beings created by Allah out of smokeless fire. They inhabit a sort of
parallel universe to ours, although Arabic folklore recounts comings and goings between the two worlds. They
may appear to human beings in the guise of an animal or in human form; the narrator's lover in this story
does both. One whole sura of the Qur'an (Koran) is devoted to the djinn. The English word *genie* is derived
from *djinn*.

little while and we'll be living here for such period of time as my husband is required to work in this town."

She looked at me in a daze. For a long time she was silent, then she said: "All right, your husband will stay with me and you can go." Despite my utter astonishment I felt pity for her. "I'll allow you to stay on with us for the little boy's sake," I said to her gently, "until you find yourself another place. If you'd like to help me with the housework I'll pay you what you ask."

Shaking her head, she said with strange emphasis: "I'm not a servant. I'm Aneesa." "You're not staying here," I said to her coldly, rising to my feet. Collecting all my courage and emulating Kamil's determination when he rebuked her, I began pushing her in the chest as I caught hold of the young boy's hand. "Get out of here and don't come near this house," I shouted at her. "Let me have all the keys. I'll not let go of your child till you've given them all to me."

With a set face that did not flicker she put her hand to her bosom and took out a ring on which were several keys, which she dropped into my hand. I released my grip on the young boy. Supporting him on her shoulders, she started to leave. Regretting my harshness, I took out several piastres from my bag and placed them in the boy's hand. With the same silence and stiffness she wrested the piastres from the boy's hand and gave them back to me. Then she went straight out. Bolting the door this time, I sat down, tense and upset, to wait.

My husband arrived, then the furniture, and for several days I occupied myself with putting the house in order. My husband was busy with his work and the children occupied themselves with making new friends and I completely forgot about Aneesa, that is until my husband returned one night wringing his hands with fury: "This woman Aneesa, can you imagine that since we came to live in this house she's been hanging around it every night. Tonight she was so crazy she blocked my way and suggested I should send you off so that she might live with me. The woman's gone completely off her head about this house and I'm afraid she might do something to the children or assault you."

Joking with him and masking the jealousy that raged within me, I said: "And what is there for you to get angry about? She's a fair and attractive enough woman—a blessing brought to your very doorstep!" With a sneer he took up the telephone, muttering: "May God look after her!"

He contacted the police and asked them to come and take her away. When I heard the sound of the police van coming I ran to the window and saw them taking her off. The poor woman did not resist, did not object, but submitted with a gentle sadness that as usual with her aroused one's pity. Yet, when she saw me standing in tears and watching her, she turned to me and, pointing to the wall of the house, called out: "I'll leave her to you." "Who?" I shouted. "Who, Aneesa?" Once again pointing at the bottom of the house, she said: "Her."

The van took her off and I spent a sleepless night. No sooner did day come than I hurried to the garden to examine my plants and to walk round the house and carefully inspect its walls. All I found were some cracks, the house being old, and I laughed at the frivolous thought that came to me: Could, for example, there be jewels buried here, as told in fairy tales?

Who could "she" be? What was the secret of this house? Who was Aneesa and was she really mad? Where were she and her son living? So great did my concern for Aneesa become that I began pressing my husband with questions until he brought me news of her. The police had learnt that she was the wife of a well-to-do teacher living in a nearby town. One night he had caught her in an act of infidelity, and in fear she had fled with her son and had settled here, no one knowing why she had betaken herself to this particular house. However, the owner of the house had been good enough to allow her to put up in it until someone should come to live in it, while some kind person had intervened on her behalf to have her name included among those receiving monthly allowances from the Ministry of Social Affairs. There were many rumours that cast doubt upon her conduct: People passing by her house at night would hear her conversing with unknown persons. Her madness took the form of a predilection for silence and isolation from people during the daytime as she wandered about in a dream world. After the police had persuaded them to take her in to safeguard the good repute of her family, she was returned to her relatives.

The days passed and the story of Aneesa was lost in oblivion. Winter came and with it heavy downpours of rain. The vegetation in my garden flourished though the castor-oil plants withered and their yellow flowers fell. I came to find pleasure in sitting out on the kitchen balcony looking at my flowers and vegetables and enjoying the belts of sunbeams that lay between the clouds and lavished my balcony with warmth and light.

One sunny morning my attention was drawn to the limb of a nearby tree whose branches curved up gracefully despite its having dried up and its dark bark being cracked. My gaze was attracted by something twisting and turning along the tip of a branch: Bands of yellow and others of red, intermingled with bands of black, were creeping forward. It was a long, smooth tube, at its end a small striped head with two bright, wary eyes.

The snake curled round on itself in spiral rings, then tautened its body and moved forward. The sight gripped me; I felt terror turning my blood cold and freezing my limbs.

My senses were numbed, my soul intoxicated with a strange elation at the exciting beauty of the snake. I was rooted to the spot, wavering between two thoughts that contended in my mind at one and the same time: Should I snatch up some implement from the kitchen and kill the snake, or should I enjoy the rare moment of beauty that had been afforded me?

As though the snake had read what was passing through my mind, it raised its head, tilting it to right and left in thrilling coquetry. Then, by means of two tiny fangs like pearls, and a golden tongue like a twig of *arak* wood, it smiled at me and fastened its eyes on mine in one fleeting, commanding glance. The thought of killing left me. I felt a current, a radiation from its eyes that penetrated to my heart ordering me to stay where I was. A warning against continuing to sit out there in front of it surged inside me, but my attraction to it paralysed my limbs and I did not move. I kept on watching it, utterly entranced and captivated. Like a bashful virgin being lavished with compliments, it tried to conceal its pride in its beauty, and, having made certain of captivating its lover, the snake coyly twisted round and gently, gracefully glided away until swallowed up by a crack in the wall. Could the snake be the "she" that Aneesa had referred to on the day of her departure?

At last I rose from my place, overwhelmed by the feeling that I was on the brink of a new world, a new destiny, or rather, if you wish, the threshold of a new love. I threw myself onto the bed in a dreamlike state, unaware of the passage of time. No sooner, though, did I hear my husband's voice and the children with their clatter as they returned at noon than I regained my sense of being a human being, wary and frightened about itself, determined about the existence and continuance of its species. Without intending to I called out: "A snake—there's a snake in the house."

My husband took up the telephone and some men came and searched the house. I pointed out to them the crack into which the snake had disappeared, though racked with a feeling of remorse at being guilty of betrayal. For here I was denouncing the beloved, inviting people against it after it had felt safe with me.

The men found no trace of the snake. They burned some wormwood and fumigated the hole but without result. Then my husband summoned Sheikh Farid, Sheikh of the Rifa'iyya[3] order in the town, who went on chanting verses from the Qur'an as he tapped the ground with his stick. He then asked to speak to me alone and said:

"Madam, the sovereign of the house has sought you out and what you saw is no snake, rather it is one of the monarchs of the earth—may God make your words pleasant to them—who has appeared to you in the form of a snake. Here in this house there are many holes of snakes, but they are of the non-poisonous kind. They inhabit houses and go and come as they please. What you saw, though, is something else."

"I don't believe a word of it," I said, stupefied. "This is nonsense. I know that the djinn are creatures that actually exist, but they are not in touch with our world, there is no contact between them and the world of humans."

With an enigmatic smile he said: "My child, the Prophet[4] went out to them and read the Qur'an to them in their country. Some of them are virtuous and some of them are Muslims, and how do you know there is no contact between us and them? Let your prayer be 'O Lord, increase me in knowledge' and do not be nervous. Your purity of spirit, your translucence of soul have opened to you doors that will take you to other worlds known only to their Creator. Do not be afraid. Even if you should find her one night sleeping in your bed, do not be alarmed but talk to her with all politeness and friendliness."

"That's enough of all that, Sheikh Farid. Thank you," I said, alarmed, and he left us.

We went on discussing the matter. "Let's be practical," suggested my husband, "and stop all the cracks at the bottom of the outside walls and put wire-mesh over the windows, also paint wormwood all round the garden fence."

---

[3] **Sheikh of the Rifa'iyya:** The sheikh is the local head of a conservative Islamic order.

[4] **the Prophet:** Muhammad (c. 570–632 C.E.), the founder of Islam.

We set about putting into effect what we had agreed. I, though, no longer dared to go out onto the balconies. I neglected my garden and stopped wandering about in it. Generally I would spend my free time in bed. I changed to being someone who liked to sit around lazily and was disinclined to mix with people; those diversions and recreations that previously used to tempt me no longer gave me any pleasure. All I wanted was to stretch myself out and drowse. In bewilderment I asked myself: Could it be that I was in love? But how could I love a snake? Or could she really be one of the daughters of the monarchs of the djinn? I would awake from my musings to find that I had been wandering in my thoughts and recalling to mind how magnificent she was. And what is the secret of her beauty? I would ask myself. Was it that I was fascinated by her multi-coloured, supple body? Or was it that I had been dazzled by that intelligent, commanding way she had of looking at me? Or could it be the sleek way she had of gliding along, so excitingly dangerous, that had captivated me?

Excitingly dangerous! No doubt it was this excitement that had stirred my feelings and awakened my love, for did they not make films to excite and frighten? There was no doubt but that the secret of my passion for her, my preoccupation with her, was due to the excitement that had aroused, through intense fear, desire within myself; an excitement that was sufficiently strong to drive the blood hotly through my veins whenever the memory of her came to me, thrusting the blood in bursts that made my heart beat wildly, my limbs limp. And so, throwing myself down in a pleasurable state of torpor, my craving for her would be awakened and I would wish for her coil-like touch, her graceful gliding motion.

And yet I fell to wondering how union could come about, how craving be quenched, the delights of the body be realized, between a woman and a snake. And did she, I wondered, love me and want me as I loved her? An idea would obtrude itself upon me sometimes: Did Cleopatra, the very legend of love, have sexual intercourse with her serpent after having given up sleeping with men, having wearied of amorous adventures with them so that her sated instincts were no longer moved other than by the excitement of fear, her senses no longer aroused other than by bites from a snake? And the last of her lovers had been a viper that had destroyed her.

I came to live in a state of continuous torment, for a strange feeling of longing scorched my body and rent my senses, while my circumstances obliged me to carry out the duties and responsibilities that had been placed on me as the wife of a man who occupied an important position in the small town, he and his family being objects of attention and his house a Kaaba[5] for those seeking favours; also as a mother who must look after her children and concern herself with every detail of their lives so as to exercise control over them; there was also the house and its chores, this house that was inhabited by the mysterious lover who lived in a world other than mine. How, I wondered, was union between us to be achieved? Was wishing for this love a sin or was there nothing to reproach myself about?

---

[5] **Kaaba:** Metaphorically, the house is a pilgrimage site; the Kaaba is the small cubical building within the Great Mosque at Mecca that houses the Black Stone, the holiest relic in Islam. Muslims worldwide face toward the Kaaba when they pray.

And as my self-questioning increased so did my yearning, my curiosity, my desire. Was the snake from the world of reptiles or from the djinn? When would the meeting be? Was she, I wondered, aware of me and would she return out of pity for my consuming passion?

One stormy morning with the rain pouring down so hard that I could hear the drops rattling on the window pane, I lit the stove and lay down in bed between the covers seeking refuge from an agonizing trembling that racked my yearning body which, ablaze with unquenchable desire, called out for relief.

I heard a faint rustling sound coming from the corner of the wall right beside my bed. I looked down and kept my eyes fixed on one of the holes in the wall, which I found was slowly, very slowly, expanding. Closing my eyes, my heart raced with joy and my body throbbed with mounting desire as there dawned in me the hope of an encounter. I lay back in submission to what was to be. No longer did I care whether love was coming from the world of reptiles or from that of the djinn, sovereigns of the world. Even were this love to mean my destruction, my desire for it was greater.

I heard a hissing noise that drew nearer, then it changed to a gentle whispering in my ear, calling to me: "I am love, O enchantress. I showed you my home in your sleep; I called you to my kingdom when your soul was dozing on the horizon of dreams, so come, my sweet beloved, come and let us explore the depths of the azure sea of pleasure. There, in the chamber of coral, amidst cool, shady rocks where reigns deep, restful silence lies our bed, lined with soft, bright green damask, inlaid with pearls newly wrenched from their shells. Come, let me sleep with you as I have slept with beautiful women and have given them bliss. Come, let me prise out your pearl from its shell that I may polish it and bring forth its splendour. Come to where no one will find us, where no one will see us, for the eyes of swimming creatures are innocent and will not heed what we do nor understand what we say. Down there lies repose, lies a cure for all your yearnings and ills. Come, without fear or dread, for no creature will reach us in our hidden world, and only the eye of God alone will see us; He alone will know what we are about and He will watch over us."

I began to be intoxicated by the soft musical whisperings. I felt her cool and soft and smooth, her coldness producing a painful convulsion in my body and hurting me to the point of terror. I felt her as she slipped between the covers, then her two tiny fangs, like two pearls, began to caress my body; arriving at my thighs, the golden tongue, like an *arak* twig, inserted its pronged tip between them and began sipping and exhaling; sipping the poisons of my desire and exhaling the nectar of my ecstasy, till my whole body tingled and started to shake in sharp, painful, rapturous spasms—and all the while the tenderest of words were whispered to me as I confided to her all my longings.

At last the cool touch withdrew, leaving me exhausted. I went into a deep slumber to awake at noon full of energy, all of me a joyful burgeoning to life. Curiosity and a desire to know who it was seized me again. I looked at the corner of the wall and found that the hole was wide open. Once again I was overcome by fear. I pointed out the crack to my husband, unable to utter, although terror had once again awakened in me passionate desire. My husband filled up the crack with cement and went to sleep.

Morning came and everyone went out. I finished my housework and began roaming around the rooms in boredom, battling against the desire to surrender myself to sleep. I sat in the hallway and suddenly she appeared before me, gentle as an angel, white as day, softly undulating and flexing herself, calling to me in her bewitching whisper: "Bride of mine, I called you and brought you to my home. I have wedded you, so there is no sin in our love, nothing to reproach yourself about. I am the guardian of the house, and I hold sway over the snakes and vipers that inhabit it, so come and I shall show you where they live. Have no fear so long as we are together. You and I are in accord. Bring a container with water and I shall place my fingers over your hand and we shall recite together some verses from the Qur'an, then we shall sprinkle it in the places from which they emerge and shall thus close the doors on them, and it shall be a pact between us that your hands will not do harm to them."

"Then you are one of the monarchs of the djinn?" I asked eagerly. "Why do you not bring me treasures and riches as we hear about in fables when a human takes as sister her companion among the djinn?"

She laughed at my words, shaking her golden hair that was like dazzling threads of light. She whispered to me, coquettishly: "How greedy is mankind! Are not the pleasures of the body enough? Were I to come to you with wealth we would both die consumed by fire."

"No, no," I called out in alarm. "God forbid that I should ask for unlawful wealth. I merely asked it of you as a test, that it might be positive proof that I am not imagining things and living in dreams."

She said: "And do intelligent humans have to have something tangible as evidence? By God, do you not believe in His ability to create worlds and living beings? Do you not know that you have an existence in worlds other than that of matter and the transitory? Fine, since you ask for proof, come close to me and my caresses will put vitality back into your limbs. You will retain your youth. I shall give you abiding youth and the delights of love—and they are more precious than wealth in the world of man. How many fortunes have women spent in quest of them? As for me I shall feed from the poisons of your desire, the exhalations of your burning passion, for that is my nourishment and through it I live."

"I thought that your union with me was for love, not for nourishment and the perpetuation of youth and vigour," I said in amazement.

"And is sex anything but food for the body and an interaction in union and love?" she said. "Is it not this that makes human beings happy and is the secret of feeling joy and elation?"

She stretched out her radiant hand to my body, passing over it like the sun's rays and discharging into it warmth and a sensation of languor.

"I am ill," I said. "I am ill. I am ill," I kept on repeating. When he heard me my husband brought the doctor, who said: "High blood pressure, heart trouble, nervous depression." Having prescribed various medicaments he left. The stupidity of doctors! My doctor did not know that he was describing the symptoms of love, did not even know it was from love I was suffering. Yet I knew my illness and the secret of my cure. I showed my husband the enlarged hole in the wall and once again he stopped it up. We then carried the bed to another corner.

After some days had passed I found another hole alongside my bed. My beloved came and whispered to me: "Why are you so coy and flee from me, my bride? Is it fear of your being rebuffed or is it from aversion? Are you not happy with our being together? Why do you want for us to be apart?"

"I am in agony," I whispered back. "Your love is so intense and the desire to enjoy you so consuming. I am frightened I shall feel that I am tumbling down into a bottomless pit and being destroyed."

"My beloved," she said. "I shall only appear to you in beauty's most immaculate form."

"But it is natural for you to be a man," I said in a precipitate outburst, "seeing that you are so determined to have a love affair with me."

"Perfect beauty is to be found only in woman," she said, "so yield to me and I shall let you taste undreamed of happiness; I shall guide you to worlds possessed of such beauty as you have never imagined."

She stretched out her fingers to caress me, while her delicate mouth sucked in the poisons of my desire and exhaled the nectar of my ecstasy, carrying me off into a trance of delicious happiness.

After that we began the most pleasurable of love affairs, wandering together in worlds and living on horizons of dazzling beauty, a world fashioned of jewels, a world whose every moment was radiant with light and formed a thousand shapes, a thousand colours.

As for the opening in the wall, I no longer took any notice. I no longer complained of feeling ill, in fact there burned within me abounding vitality. Sometimes I would bring a handful of wormwood and, by way of jest, would stop up the crack, just as the beloved teases her lover and closes the window in his face that, ablaze with desire for her, he may hasten to the door. After that I would sit for a long time and enjoy watching the wormwood powder being scattered in spiral rings by unseen puffs of wind. Then I would throw myself down on the bed and wait.

For months I immersed myself in my world, no longer calculating time or counting the days, until one morning my husband went out on the balcony lying behind our favoured wall alongside the bed. After a while I heard him utter a cry of alarm. We all hurried out to find him holding a stick, with a black, ugly snake almost two metres long, lying at his feet.

I cried out with a sorrow whose claws clutched at my heart so that it began to beat wildly. With crazed fury I shouted at my husband: "Why have you broken the pact and killed it? What harm has it done?" How cruel is man! He lets no creature live in peace.

I spent the night sorrowful and apprehensive. My lover came to me and embraced me more passionately than ever. I whispered to her imploringly: "Be kind, beloved. Are you angry with me or sad because of me?"

"It is farewell," she said. "You have broken the pact and have betrayed one of my subjects, so you must both depart from this house, for only love lives in it."

In the morning I packed up so that we might move to one of the employees' buildings, leaving the house in which I had learnt of love and enjoyed incomparable pleasures.

I still live in memory and in hope. I crave for the house and miss my secret love. Who knows, perhaps one day my beloved will call me. Who really knows?

⌘ WOLE SOYINKA
B. NIGERIA, 1934

One of Africa's most influential and prolific modern authors, Wole Soyinka is a persistent and outspoken human rights advocate whose campaigns against violence, exploitation, and political corruption have generated both controversy and critical acclaim. The eclectic nature of Soyinka's vision as well as his writing allows him to explore the intellectual, political, and literary heritage of a wide array of cultures and belief systems. Credited with professionalizing the English-language theater in Nigeria and revitalizing interest in Yoruban culture, Soyinka speaks to both a local and a world audience in his literary battle for freedom and justice. On his ability to unite art and activism and cross cultural boundaries, he once commented: "I have one abiding religion, human liberty." Though he celebrates the traditions and rituals of his cultural heritage, he also recognizes the necessity of negotiating the challenges of a modern, industrialized world. His writing, which draws heavily on indigenous values, beliefs, and artistic conventions, also reflects the influence of Western myths, archetypes, and literary techniques. "Soyinka seems fated to bridge elements in our world which are poles apart," one critic observed.

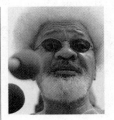

Wole Soyinka, 2002
Soyinka was photographed here speaking at the burial rites for slain Nigerian justice minister Bola Ige. (© Reuters NewMedia Inc. / CORBIS)

Colonial Christianity and Yoruban Tradition.   Born Akinwande Oluwole Soyinka in 1934 in Nigeria, then under British rule, Soyinka was raised in an English-speaking environment. His mother, whom he nicknamed the "Wild Christian," was a teacher, performer, trader, and activist. His father was headmaster of an Anglican primary school, which Soyinka attended, in the town of Aké. As a center for European activities in western Nigeria, Aké suffered the erosion of its traditional Nigerian values and customs under wave upon wave of Western influence. Soyinka's witness to this process is contained in the autobiographical *Aké: The Years of Childhood* (1981), in which is found a child's exploration of the conflict between and occasional blending of European Christianity and traditional Yoruban culture.

The Yoruba, a group of peoples in southwestern Nigeria bound by a shared language and culture, have diverse religious beliefs connected by common underlying threads. In Yoruban religion, humans are surrounded by gods and spirits with whom interaction is inevitable: Trees and rivers, for example, might be inhabited and made sacred by ancestral spirits. These spirit ancestors are worshiped in annual festivals and masquerade processions through the *egungun,* masked figures who become possessed by a particular spirit and are able to speak with special wisdom. The *egungun opidan,* a kind of traveling theater that staged MASQUE-like[1] productions in open spaces—such as the one that took place across from

www   For links to more information about Wole Soyinka and a quiz on *The Lion and the Jewel,* and for information about the culture and context of Africa in the twentieth century, see *World Literature Online* at bedfordstmartins.com/worldlit.

---

[1]**masque:** Developed in the Renaissance, a masque is a highly stylized and structured performance that usually focuses on a mythological or allegorical plot, combining drama, music, song, and dance in an elaborate display.

Soyinka's mother's shop in the local market—exposed the young man to important figures and themes of Yoruban belief and to native conventions of drama such as drumming, stylized and patterned dances, and the use of representative as well as recognizable characters. Soyinka's visits to the relatively isolated town of Isara, where his grandfather lived and where many traditional festivals were still celebrated, certainly contributed to his later work. Here might have begun, for example, his view of the ritualized experience of the divine as an essentially therapeutic and creative communal activity. In contrast to his own home environment, which was dominated by Christian doctrine (his mother insisted on this), Nigeria's indigenous cultural heritage must have seemed rich with color, mystery, and pageantry.

Education, Imprisonment, Exile.   During the time of their control of Nigeria, the English appointed warrant chiefs to supplant village leaders and rule over native communities. These warrant chiefs were accused of unjustified seizure of property, undermining the value of the bride-price,[2] and other gross abuses. In 1929 a group of women, among them Soyinka's mother, became concerned that a head count being carried out by the British might lead to a tax on women. Through songs and dance, their traditional means of protest, the women launched a campaign against the exploitative colonial government that would last for years.

Given his early exposure to political controversy and protest, it is not surprising that Soyinka became deeply devoted to the struggle for Nigerian political independence and cultural autonomy. The pursuit of knowledge led him to Government College in Nigeria in 1952 and later to the University of Leeds in England. He studied at Leeds under the famous Shakespearean scholar G. Wilson Knight, then worked as an actor, script reader, and director at the Royal Court Theatre in London. Awarded a Rockefeller Research Grant to study West African drama, Soyinka returned home to the University of Ibadan in 1960, the year that Nigeria declared independence from Great Britain. During that year he assembled his own acting company, The 1960 Masks, began to write radio plays denouncing the abuse of power in government, and wrote and produced *A Dance of the Forests,* a play critical of the widespread corruption and dishonesty of native politicians. Its release timed to coincide with Nigeria's celebration of independence, the play was received with hostility by both the newly installed leaders for its attack on corruption and the traditionalists for its blending of Yoruban folk heritage with European dramatic techniques. In the years immediately following his return to Africa, Soyinka worked to establish a strong Nigerian theater. He headed theater troupes at various universities, co-founded the Drama Association of Nigeria in 1964, and produced such plays as *Kongi's Harvest* (1965), *The Trials of Brother Jero* (1966), and *The Strong Breed* (1967). After working as a lecturer in the English department at the University of Ife (1962–63) and

---

[2] **bride-price:** The money or goods that a man brings to a woman's family when he marries her.

then at the University of Lagos (1965–67), he became head of the department of theater arts at the University of Ibadan in 1967.

An outspoken activist for human rights, Soyinka was imprisoned twice during the early years of Nigerian independence, first for three months in 1965, under the specious accusation that he had broadcast false election results, then for more than two years (1967–69) for allegedly conspiring to aid the Biafran independence movement.[3] During the latter period of imprisonment, most of which Soyinka spent in solitary confinement, the author wrote on cigarette packages, in the blank spaces of books he secretly acquired, even on toilet paper to keep his mind active and focused. These notes contributed to *The Man Died: The Prison Notes of Wole Soyinka* (1972), in which Soyinka asserts that "books and all forms of writing have always been objects of terror to all those who seek to suppress the truth."

After his release, Soyinka taught and lectured at universities in Nigeria and in other parts of the world, including at Cambridge, Harvard, Yale, and Cornell Universities. Twice exiled from his homeland, voluntarily in 1975 and by force in 1994, he was eventually charged with treason by the regime of dictator General Sani Abacha. In spite of the threat of physical harm, he continued to use the written and spoken word to pursue his campaign for individual rights and his hopes for a reborn Nigeria. He won the Nobel Prize in literature in 1986.

Progress and the Human Condition.   Though known foremost as a dramatist, Soyinka has written poetry, novels, and criticism renowned for their experimentation, originality, and richness. In collections like *Indanre and Other Poems* (1967) and *Poems from Prison* (1969), Soyinka explores the human condition in both a domestic and global context through a combination of biblical and classical references with the imagery of African landscapes and Yoruban spiritual beliefs. Ogun, the Yoruban god of war, ruler of the road, and master metallurgist, appears in much of Soyinka's poetry (as well as in his other work) as a symbol of the forces of creation and destruction so influential in human destiny. Soyinka's frequent use of archetypes, such as the isolated individual searching for his true path in life, often universalizes a local experience. His first novel, *The Interpreters* (1965), is about a group of young Nigerian intellectuals searching for meaning and purpose in a world in which traditional codes of conduct have been challenged by modern attitudes and technology. Soyinka explores the role of tradition and cultural history and the influence of Western intellectual and artistic worldviews as applied to literature in the essay collections *Myth, Literature and the African World* (1976) and *Art, Dialogue and Outrage* (1988). Soyinka's literary eclecticism — his frequent blending of potentially contradictory images, themes, and artistic techniques and forms — reflects

Soyinka seems fated to bridge elements in our world which are poles apart.

– UNKNOWN CRITIC

---

[3] **Biafran independence movement:** The Ibo people of several regions in Nigeria seceded from the national government in May 1967 to create an independent state. Their efforts were defeated by Nigerian forces in 1970.

his philosophy of social change wherein a community selectively integrates new or external influences with its own customs and traditions to create a new and authentic cultural identity.

Soyinka's plays often dramatize moments or periods of social crisis. *Kongi's Harvest* (1966), for example, presents the social and political aftermath of a confrontation between a newly installed dictator, Kongi, and the hereditary monarch he has deposed. Both leaders are satirized in the play, but the brunt of the attack is on "Kongism," an unjust rulership unsanctioned by the people. In a program note to the 1969 performance of the play, Soyinka called attention to the universality of the play's theme, noting "there are a thousand and more forms of Kongism — from the crude and blasphemous to the subtle and sanctimonious." *The Strong Breed* (1967) depicts a village in need of a ritual sacrifice in order to expiate an undefined evil. The Christ-figure Eman, an outsider in a community distrustful of strangers, is the only character in the play whose compassion for others transcends social boundaries; he is hanged on a sacred tree at the end of the play. *Madmen and Specialists* (1970), notably lacking in specific references to time and place, depicts a society overpowered by the "out there" force of violent authoritarian rule. Cut off from the creative and regenerative power of the earth, the past, and the communal festival, the play's characters lose their humanity and degenerate into monsters. As is typical of Soyinka's drama, both plays are rich in symbolism and ritual, draw on archetypal figures, and experiment with fluidity of place and character. Steeped in Yoruban culture and values, *Death and the King's Horseman* (1975) tells the story of Elesin, the king's horseman, who after the death of the king is required to commit ritual suicide in order to preserve peace and progress in the land. His destiny is thwarted when he is arrested by a British colonial officer. Elesin's son, Olunde, takes his own life in order to wash away the curse.

The Lion and the Jewel.   The encounter of European theatrical conventions and techniques with the masquerade and pageantry of Yoruban heritage in Soyinka's early play *The Lion and the Jewel* (1963) underscores the meeting of Western innovation, capitalism, and Christian doctrine with the world of tradition, chieftains, and paganism in the story of the drama. Motorcycles, photo layouts, unions, and stamp machines clash and blend with the sacred "odan" tree, wood spirits, and fertility rites. The forces of progress and conservatism, however, are not entirely oppositional in the text. Instead, Soyinka depicts a community in the process of change, struggling to selectively incorporate various aspects of modern life while preserving its own heritage.

Many of the themes that dominate Soyinka's writing — political corruption, the creative and destructive power of the god Ogun, the centrality of ritual and festival to communal health and growth — are introduced in this play. However, in contrast to much of his later work, which some consider obscure, mostly due to its elevated language, *The Lion and the Jewel* is relatively lighthearted and accessible. Lakunle's speech, for example, though cluttered with quotations from Romantic fiction and Christian liturgy, is more humorous and misguided than learned. While some critics say the dialogue in the play is overextended, physical action, particularly dance-drama, interrupts it periodically and shifts the emphasis from speech to performance. The "plays within the play," *The Mime of the White Surveyor,* for example, function in a variety of ways — including providing historical background, facilitating a communal interpretation of events, and adding dimension to the characters. Stylized dance, song, drumming, and mime introduce the powerful forces of gesture and rhythm into Soyinka's dramatic world.

■ CONNECTIONS

Aristophanes, *Lysistrata* (Book 1). *Lysistrata* uses sexual comedy to make a political point about the folly of war as well as to highlight the difference between domestic and martial, or military, values. Soyinka also employs sexual comedy as a way of talking about gender, class, and colonial politics. How does Soyinka present the chief's alleged impotence as a subject for comedy? How does this comedy generate questions about social, political, and gender issues? Is *The Lion and the Jewel* a comedy, do you think, or a tragedy?

Chinua Achebe, *Things Fall Apart,* p. 1023. Twentieth-century African fiction often deals with contact between Africa and Europe. Achebe's *Things Fall Apart* and Soyinka's *The Lion and the Jewel* both depict the way in which European colonial intervention exacerbates the psychological and social difficulties already faced by African people. Compare Achebe's protagonist, Okonkwo, with Soyinka's Chief Baroka. In what ways do these men represent African identity? How are their conflicts interwoven with those of their people?

Anita Desai, "The Farewell Party," p. 1196. Colonial and postcolonial literature often dramatize the shaping of personal identity through the cultural and national affiliations that are possible in a colonial context. "The Farewell Party" depicts a community in which European and Indian ideologies combine and collide; Soyinka's *The Lion and the Jewel* is set in a community that comprises European and African ideologies. How do these texts treat the "company men and women" — to use Desai's phrase — who deny their native origins and accept European culture and values?

■ FURTHER RESEARCH

Biography
Jones, Eldred. *Wole Soyinka.* 1973.

Criticism
Gibbs, James. *Critical Perspectives on Wole Soyinka.* 1980.
Jones, Eldred. *The Writing of Wole Soyinka.* 1988.
Maduakor, Obi. *Wole Soyinka: An Introduction to His Writing.* 1986.
Wright, D. *Wole Soyinka: Life Work and Criticism.* 1996.

ᴗ The Lion and the Jewel

CHARACTERS

SIDI, *the village belle*
LAKUNLE, *school teacher*
BAROKA, *the "Bale" of Ilujinle*
SADIKU, *his head wife*
THE FAVOURITE
VILLAGE GIRLS

A WRESTLER
A SURVEYOR
SCHOOLBOYS
ATTENDANTS ON THE "BALE"
MUSICIANS, DANCERS, MUMMERS,
PRISONERS, TRADERS, THE VILLAGE

MORNING

A clearing on the edge of the market, dominated by an immense odan tree. It is the village centre. The wall of the bush school flanks the stage on the right, and a rude window opens on to the stage from the wall. There is a chant of the "Arithmetic Times" issuing from this window. It begins a short while before the action begins. Sidi enters from left, carrying a small pail of water on her head. She is a slim girl with plaited hair. A true village belle. She balances the pail on her head with accustomed ease. Around her is wrapped the familiar broad cloth which is folded just above her breasts, leaving the shoulders bare.

Almost as soon as she appears on the stage, the schoolmaster's face also appears at the window. (The chanting continues— "Three times two are six," "Three times three are nine," etc.) The teacher Lakunle, disappears. He is replaced by two of his pupils, aged roughly eleven, who make a buzzing noise at Sidi, repeatedly clapping their hands across the mouth. Lakunle now reappears below the window and makes for Sidi, stopping only to give the boys admonitory whacks on the head before they can duck. They vanish with a howl and he shuts the window on them. The chanting dies away. The schoolmaster is nearly twenty-three. He is dressed in an old-style English suit, threadbare but not ragged, clean but not ironed, obviously a size or two too small. His tie is done in a very small knot, disappearing beneath a shiny black waistcoat. He wears twenty-three-inch-bottom trousers, and blanco-white tennis shoes.

The Lion and the Jewel. Written while Wole Soyinka was in England, this play was produced in Ibadan, Nigeria, in 1959 and at the Royal Court Theatre in London in 1966. One of his most popular plays, it helped to establish Soyinka as a dramatist. A relatively lighthearted satiric comedy, *The Lion and the Jewel* nevertheless explores the real conflicts surrounding the role of men and that of women, modernization and conservatism, and the meeting of Western material culture and Yoruban tradition. Though characters like Lakunle and Baroka may seem at first to be fairly straightforward representations of opposing value systems, closer inspection broadens this view. For example, though Lakunle is an educator and purveyor of "civilizing" influences, his infatuation with symbols of "Englishness" often reaches the point of absurdity, and he is not taken seriously by the villagers. Similarly, Baroka clearly uses his position to uphold the traditional ways of his people, yet he has allowed his workers to form a labor union and has invested in a stamp machine. Soyinka's experimental combination of dialogue, song, and dance in this drama is both structurally and thematically important. The mimes, in particular, provide important background information, reveal communal values through performance, and interrupt the dialogue with powerful aural and visual experiences.

A note on the text: The play reprinted here is from *Collected Plays 2*. All notes are the editors' unless otherwise indicated.

LAKUNLE: Let me take it.

SIDI: No.

LAKUNLE: Let me. [*Seizes the pail. Some water spills on him.*]

SIDI [*delighted.*]:
    There. Wet for your pains.
    Have you no shame?

LAKUNLE: That is what the stewpot said to the fire.
    Have you no shame—at your age
    Licking my bottom? But she was tickled
    Just the same.

SIDI: The school teacher is full of stories
    This morning. And now, if the lesson
    Is over, may I have the pail?

LAKUNLE: No. I have told you not to carry loads
    On your head. But you are as stubborn
    As an illiterate goat. It is bad for the spine.
    And it shortens your neck, so that very soon
    You will have no neck at all. Do you wish to look
    Squashed like my pupils' drawings?

SIDI: Why should that worry me? Haven't you sworn
    That my looks do not affect your love?
    Yesterday, dragging your knees in the dust
    You said, Sidi, if you were crooked or fat,
    And your skin was scaly like a . . .

LAKUNLE: Stop!

SIDI: I only repeat what you said.

LAKUNLE: Yes, and I will stand by every word I spoke.
    But must you throw away your neck on that account?
    Sidi, it is so unwomanly. Only spiders
    Carry loads the way you do.

SIDI [*huffily, exposing the neck to advantage.*]:
    Well, it is my neck, not your spider.

LAKUNLE [*looks, and gets suddenly agitated.*]:
    And look at that! Look, look at that!
    [*Makes a general sweep in the direction of her breasts.*]
    Who was it talked of shame just now?
    How often must I tell you, Sidi, that
    A grown-up girl must cover up her . . .
    Her . . . shoulders? I can see quite . . . quite
    A good portion of—that! And so I imagine
    Can every man in the village. Idlers
    All of them, good-for-nothing shameless men
    Casting their lustful eyes where
    They have no business. . . .

SIDI: Are you at that again? Why, I've done the fold

So high and so tight, I can hardly breathe.
And all because you keep at me so much.
I have to leave my arms so I can use them . . .
Or don't you know that?
LAKUNLE: You could wear something.
Most modest women do. But you, no.
You must run about naked in the streets.
Does it not worry you . . . the bad names,
The lewd jokes, the tongue-licking noises
Which girls, uncovered like you,
Draw after them?
SIDI: This is too much. Is it you, Lakunle,
Telling me that I make myself common talk?
When the whole world knows of the madman
Of Ilujinle, who calls himself a teacher!
Is it Sidi who makes the men choke
In their cups, or you, with your big loud words
And no meaning? You and your ragged books
Dragging your feet to every threshold
And rushing them out again as curses
Greet you instead of welcome. Is it Sidi
They call a fool—even the children—
Or you with your fine airs and little sense!
LAKUNLE [*first indignant, then recovers composure.*]:
For that, what is a jewel to pigs?
If now I am misunderstood by you
And your race of savages, I rise above taunts
And remain unruffled.
SIDI [*furious, shakes both fists at him.*]:
O . . . oh, you make me want to pulp your brain.
LAKUNLE [*retreats a little, but puts her aside with a very lofty gesture.*]:
A natural feeling, arising out of envy;
For, as a woman, you have a smaller brain
Than mine.
SIDI [*madder still.*]:
Again! I'd like to know
Just what gives you these thoughts
Of manly conceit.
LAKUNLE [*very, very patronizing.*]:
No, no. I have fallen for that trick before.
You can no longer draw me into arguments
Which go above your head.
SIDI [*can't find the right words, chokes back.*]:
Give me the pail now. And if you ever dare
To stop me in the streets again . . .

LAKUNLE: Now, now, Sidi . . .

SIDI: Give it or I'll . . .

LAKUNLE [*holds on to her.*]:
> Please, don't be angry with me.
> I didn't mean you in particular.
> And anyway, it isn't what I say.
> The scientists have proved it. It's in my books.
> Women have a smaller brain than men
> That's why they are called the weaker sex.

SIDI [*throws him off.*]:
> The weaker sex, is it?
> Is it a weaker breed who pounds the yam
> Or bends all day to plant the millet
> With a child strapped to her back?

LAKUNLE: That is all part of what I say.
> But don't you worry. In a year or two
> You will have machines which will do
> Your pounding, which will grind your pepper
> Without it getting in your eyes.

SIDI: O-oh. You really mean to turn
> The whole world upside down.

LAKUNLE: The world? Oh, that. Well, maybe later.
> Charity, they say, begins at home.
> For now, it is this village I shall turn
> Inside out. Beginning with that crafty rogue,
> Your past master of self-indulgence—Baroka.

SIDI: Are you still on about the Bale?°   chief of a village
> What has he done to you?

LAKUNLE: He'll find out. Soon enough, I'll let him know.

SIDI: These thoughts of future wonders—do you buy them
> Or merely go mad and dream of them?

LAKUNLE: A prophet has honour except
> In his own home. Wise men have been called mad
> Before me and after, many more shall be
> So abused. But to answer you, the measure
> Is not entirely of my own coinage.
> What I boast is known in Lagos, that city
> Of magic, in Badagry where Saro[1] women bathe
> In gold, even in smaller towns less than
> Twelve miles from here. . . .

SIDI: Well go there. Go to these places where
> Women would understand you

---

[1]**Lagos . . . Saro:** Lagos and Badagry are major port cities in Nigeria. The Saro, descended from emancipated slaves from Sierra Leone, are a group of peoples influenced by European culture.

If you told them of your plans with which
You oppress me daily. Do you not know
What name they give you here?
Have you lost shame completely that jeers
Pass you over.

LAKUNLE: No. I have told you no. Shame belongs
Only to the ignorant.

SIDI: Well, I am going.
Shall I take the pail or not?

LAKUNLE: Not till you swear to marry me.
[*Takes her hand, instantly soulful.*]
Sidi, a man must prepare to fight alone.
But it helps if he has a woman
To stand by him, a woman who . . .
Can understand . . . like you.

SIDI: I do?

LAKUNLE: Sidi, my love will open your mind
Like the chaste leaf in the morning, when
The sun first touches it.

SIDI: If you start that I will run away.
I had enough of that nonsense yesterday.

LAKUNLE: Nonsense? Nonsense? Do you hear?
Does anybody listen? Can the stones
Bear to listen to this? Do you call it
Nonsense that I poured the waters of my soul
To wash your feet?

SIDI: You did what!

LAKUNLE: Wasted! Wasted! Sidi, my heart
Bursts into flowers with my love.
But you, you and the dead of this village
Trample it with feet of ignorance.

SIDI [*shakes her head in bafflement.*]:
If the snail finds splinters in his shell
He changes house. Why do you stay?

LAKUNLE: Faith. Because I have faith.
Oh Sidi, vow to me your own undying love
And I will scorn the jibes of these bush minds
Who know no better. Swear, Sidi,
Swear you will be my wife and I will
Stand against earth, heaven, and the nine
Hells. . . .

SIDI: Now there you go again.
One little thing
And you must chirrup like a cockatoo.
You talk and talk and deafen me

With words which always sound the same
And make no meaning.
I've told you, and I say it again
I shall marry you today, next week
Or any day you name.
But my bride-price must first be paid.
Aha, now you turn away.
But I tell you, Lakunle, I must have
The full bride-price. Will you make me
A laughingstock? Well, do as you please.
But Sidi will not make herself
A cheap bowl for the village spit.

LAKUNLE: On my head let fall their scorn.

SIDI: They will say I was no virgin
That I was forced to sell my shame
And marry you without a price.

LAKUNLE: A savage custom, barbaric, outdated,
Rejected, denounced, accursed,
Excommunicated, archaic, degrading,
Humiliating, unspeakable, redundant.
Retrogressive, remarkable, unpalatable.

SIDI: Is the bag empty? Why did you stop?

LAKUNLE: I own only the Shorter Companion
Dictionary, but I have ordered
The Longer One — you wait!

SIDI: Just pay the price.

LAKUNLE [*with a sudden shout.*]:
An ignoble custom, infamous, ignominious
Shaming our heritage before the world.
Sidi, I do not seek a wife
To fetch and carry,
To cook and scrub,
To bring forth children by the gross. . . .

SIDI: Heaven forgive you! Do you now scorn
Childbearing in a wife?

LAKUNLE: Of course I do not. I only mean . . .
Oh Sidi, I want to wed
Because I love,
I seek a life-companion . . .
[*Pulpit-declamatory.*]
"And the man shall take the woman
And the two shall be together
As one flesh."°   Genesis 2:24
Sidi, I seek a friend in need.
An equal partner in my race of life.

SIDI [*attentive no more. Deeply engrossed in counting the beads on her neck.*]:
    Then pay the price.
LAKUNLE: Ignorant girl, can you not understand?
    To pay the price would be
    To buy a heifer off the market stall.
    You'd be my chattel, my mere property.
    No, Sidi! [*Very tenderly.*]
    When we are wed, you shall not walk or sit
    Tethered, as it were, to my dirtied heels.
    Together we shall sit at table
    —Not on the floor—and eat,
    Not with fingers, but with knives
    And forks, and breakable plates
    Like civilized beings.
    I will not have you wait on me
    Till I have dined my fill.
    No wife of mine, no lawful wedded wife
    Shall eat the leavings off my plate—
    That is for the children.
    I want to walk beside you in the street,
    Side by side and arm in arm
    Just like the Lagos couples I have seen
    High-heeled shoes for the lady, red paint
    On her lips. And her hair is stretched
    Like a magazine photo. I will teach you
    The waltz and we'll both learn the foxtrot
    And we'll spend the weekend in night clubs at Ibadan.[2]
    Oh I must show you the grandeur of towns
    We'll live there if you like or merely pay visits.
    So choose. Be a modern wife, look me in the eye
    And give me a little kiss—like this.
    [*Kisses her.*]
SIDI [*backs away.*]:
    No, don't! I tell you I dislike
    This strange unhealthy mouthing you perform.
    Every time, your action deceives me
    Making me think that you merely wish
    To whisper something in my ear.
    Then comes this licking of my lips with yours.
    It's so unclean. And then,
    The sound you make— "Pyout!"
    Are you being rude to me?

---

[2] Ibadan: One of the largest cities in Nigeria, located in the southwestern part of the country.

LAKUNLE [*wearily.*]: It's never any use.
    Bush girl you are, bush girl you'll always be;
    Uncivilized and primitive—bush girl!
    I kissed you as all educated men—
    And Christians—kiss their wives.
    It is the way of civilized romance.
SIDI [*lightly.*] A way you mean, to avoid
    Payment of lawful bride-price
    A cheating way, mean and miserly.
LAKUNLE [*violently.*]: It is not.
    [*Sidi bursts out laughing. Lakunle changes his tone to a soulful one, both eyes dreamily shut.*]
    Romance is the sweetening of the soul
    With fragrance offered by the stricken heart.
SIDI [*looks at him in wonder for a while.*]:
    Away with you. The village says you're mad,
    And I begin to understand.
    I wonder that they let you run the school.
    You and your talk. You'll ruin your pupils too
    And then they'll utter madness just like you.
    [*Noise offstage.*]
    There are people coming
    Give me the bucket or they'll jeer.
    [*Enter a crowd of youths and drummers, the girls being in various stages of excitement.*]
FIRST GIRL: Sidi, he has returned. He came back just as he said he would.
SIDI: Who has?
FIRST GIRL: The stranger. The man from the outside world.
    The clown who fell in the river for you.
    [*They all burst out laughing.*]
SIDI: The one who rode on the devil's own horse?
SECOND GIRL: Yes, the same. The stranger with the one-eyed box.
    [*She demonstrates the action of a camera amidst admiring titters.*]
THIRD GIRL: And he brought his new horse right into the village square this time.
    This one has only two feet. You should have seen him. B-r-r-r-r.
    [*Runs round the platform driving an imaginary motorbike.*]
SIDI: And has he brought . . . ?
FIRST GIRL: The images? He brought them all. There was hardly any part of the village which does not show in the book.
    [*Clicks the imaginary shutter.*]
SIDI: The book? Did you see the book?
    Had he the precious book
    That would bestow upon me
    Beauty beyond the dreams of a goddess?
    For so he said.

> The book which would announce
> This beauty to the world—
> Have you seen it?

THIRD GIRL: Yes, yes, he did. But the Bale is still feasting his eyes on the images. Oh, Sidi, he was right. You *are* beautiful. On the cover of the book is an image of you from here [*touches the top of her head.*] to here [*her stomach.*]. And in the middle leaves, from the beginning of one leaf right across to the end of another, is one of you from head to toe. Do you remember it? It was the one for which he made you stretch your arms towards the sun. [*Rapturously.*] Oh, Sidi, you looked as if, at that moment, the sun himself had been your lover. [*They all gasp with pretended shock at this blasphemy and one slaps her playfully on the buttocks.*]

FIRST GIRL: The Bale is jealous, but he pretends to be proud of you. And when this man tells him how famous you are in the capital, he pretends to be pleased, saying how much honour and fame you have brought to the village.

SIDI [*with amazement.*]: Is not Baroka's image in the book at all?

SECOND GIRL [*contemptuous.*]: Oh yes, it is. But it would have been much better for the Bale if the stranger had omitted him altogether. His image is in a little corner somewhere in the book, and even that corner he shares with one of the village latrines.

SIDI: Is that the truth? Swear! Ask Ogun[3] to
> Strike you dead.

GIRL: Ogun strike me dead if I lie.

SIDI: If that is true, then I am more esteemed
> Than Bale Baroka,
> The Lion of Ilujinle.
> This means that I am greater than
> The Fox of the Undergrowth,
> The living god among men . . .

LAKUNLE [*peevishly.*]: And devil among women.

SIDI: Be silent, you.
> You are merely filled with spite.

LAKUNLE: I know him what he is. This is
> Divine justice that a mere woman
> Should outstrip him in the end.

SIDI: Be quiet;
> Or I swear I'll never speak to you again.
> [*Affects sudden coyness.*]
> In fact, I am not so sure I'll want to wed you now.

LAKUNLE: Sidi!

SIDI: Well, why should I?
> Known as I am to the whole wide world,

---

[3] **Ogun:** As the patron deity of hunters and soldiers, Ogun embodies the forces of both creation and destruction, the tension between which is a theme repeatedly explored in Soyinka's writing.

  I would demean my worth to wed
  A mere village school teacher.
LAKUNLE [*in agony.*]: Sidi!
SIDI: And one who is too mean
  To pay the bride-price like a man.
LAKUNLE: Oh, Sidi, don't!
SIDI [*plunging into an enjoyment of Lakunle's misery.*]:
  Well, don't you know?
  Sidi is more important even than the Bale.
  More famous than that panther of the trees.
  He is beneath me now—
  Your fearless rake, the scourge of womanhood!
  But now,
  He shares the corner of the leaf
  With the lowest of the low—
  With the dug-out village latrine!
  While I—How many leaves did my own image take?
FIRST GIRL: Two in the middle and . . .
SIDI: No, no. Let the school teacher count!
  How many were there, teacher-man?
LAKUNLE: Three leaves.
SIDI [*threateningly.*]: One leaf for every heart that I shall break.
  Beware!
  [*Leaps suddenly into the air.*]
  Hurray! I'm beautiful!
  Hurray for the wandering stranger!
CROWD: Hurray for the Lagos man!
SIDI [*wildly excited.*]: I know. Let us dance the dance of the lost
  Traveller.[4]
SHOUTS: Yes, let's.
SIDI: Who will dance the devil-horse?
  You, you, you, and you.
  [*The four girls fall out.*]
  A python. Who will dance the snake?
  Ha ha! Your eyes are shifty and your ways are sly.
  [*The selected youth is pushed out amidst jeers.*]
  The stranger. We've got to have the being
  From the mad outer world. . . . You there,
  No, you have never felt the surge
  Of burning liquor in your milky veins.
  Who can we pick that knows the walk of drunks?

---

[4] **dance . . . Traveller:** In Yoruban tradition, events are often told and interpreted through rhythmic dance and pantomime.

You? . . . No, the thought itself
Would knock you out as sure as wine. . . . Ah!
[*Turns round slowly to where Lakunle is standing with a kindly, fatherly smile for the children at play.*]
Come on bookworm, you'll play his part.

LAKUNLE: No, no. I've never been drunk in all my life.

SIDI: We know. But your father drank so much,
He must have drunk your share, and that
Of his great-grandsons.

LAKUNLE [*tries to escape.*]: I won't take part.

SIDI: You must.

LAKUNLE: I cannot stay. It's nearly time to take
Primary four in Geography.

SIDI [*goes over to the window and throws it open.*]:
Did you think your pupils would remain in school
Now that the stranger has returned?
The village is on holiday, you fool.

LAKUNLE [*as they drag him towards the platform.*]:
No, no. I won't. This foolery bores me.
It is a game of idiots. I have work of more importance.

SIDI [*bending down over Lakunle who has been seated forcibly on the platform.*]:
You are dressed like him
You look like him
You speak his tongue
You think like him
You're just as clumsy
In your Lagos ways—
You'll do for him!

[*This chant is taken up by all and they begin to dance round Lakunle, speaking the words in a fast rhythm. The drummers join in after the first time, keeping up a steady beat as the others whirl round their victim. They go faster and faster and chant faster and faster with each round. By the sixth or seventh, Lakunle has obviously had enough.*]

LAKUNLE [*raising his voice above the din.*]: All right! I'll do it.
Come now, let's get it over with.

[*A terrific shout and a clap of drums. Lakunle enters into the spirit of the dance with enthusiasm. He takes over from Sidi, stations his cast all over the stage as the jungle, leaves the right topstage clear for the four girls who are to dance the motorcar. A mime follows of the visitor's entry into Ilujinle, and his short stay among the villagers. The four girls crouch on the floor, as four wheels of a car. Lakunle directs their spacing, then takes his place in the middle, and sits on air. He alone does not dance. He does realistic miming. Soft throbbing drums, gradually swelling in volume, and the four "wheels" begin to rotate the upper halves of their bodies in perpendicular circles. Lakunle clowning the driving motions, obviously enjoying this fully. The drums gain tempo, faster, faster, faster. A sudden crash of drums and the girls quiver and dance the stall. Another effort at a rhythm fails, and the "stalling wheels" give a corresponding*] *shudder, finally, and let their faces fall on to their laps. Lakunle tampers with a number of controls, climbs out of the car and looks underneath it. His lips indicate that he is swearing violently.*

Examines the wheels, pressing them to test the pressure, betrays the devil in him by seizing his chance to pinch the girls' bottoms. One yells and bites him on the ankle. He climbs hurriedly back into the car, makes a final attempt to restart it, gives it up and decides to abandon it. Picks up his camera and his helmet, pockets a flask of whisky from which he takes a swig, before beginning the trek. The drums resume beating, a different, darker tone and rhythm, varying with the journey. Full use of "gangan" and "iya ilu."[5] The "trees" perform a subdued and unobtrusive dance on the same spot. Details as a snake slithering out of the branches and poising over Lakunle's head when he leans against a tree for a rest. He flees, restoring his nerves shortly after by a swig. A monkey drops suddenly in his path and gibbers at him before scampering off. A roar comes from somewhere, etc. His nerves go rapidly and he recuperates himself by copious draughts. He is soon tipsy, battles violently with the undergrowth and curses silently as he swats the flies off his tortured body.

Suddenly, from somewhere in the bush comes the sound of a girl singing. The Traveller shakes his head but the sound persists. Convinced he is suffering from sunstroke, he drinks again. His last drop, so he tosses the bottle in the direction of the sound, only to be rewarded by a splash, a scream, and a torrent of abuse, and finally, silence again. He tip-toes, clears away the obstructing growth, blinks hard, and rubs his eyes. Whatever he has seen still remains. He whistles softly, unhitches his camera, and begins to jockey himself into a good position for a take. Backwards and forwards, and his eyes are so closely glued to the lens that he puts forward a careless foot and disappears completely. There is a loud splash and the invisible singer alters her next tone to a sustained scream. Quickened rhythm and shortly afterwards, amidst sounds of splashes, Sidi appears on the stage, with a piece of cloth only partially covering her.

Lakunle follows a little later, more slowly, trying to wring out the water from his clothes. He has lost all his appendages except the camera. Sidi has run right across the stage, and returns a short while later, accompanied by the villagers. The same cast has disappeared and re-forms behind Sidi as the villagers. They are in an ugly mood, and in spite of his protests, haul him off to the town centre, in front of the "odan" tree.

Everything comes to a sudden stop as Baroka the Bale, wiry, goateed, tougher than his sixty-two years, himself emerges at this point from behind the tree. All go down, prostrate or kneeling with the greetings of "Kabiyesi," "Baba,"[6] etc. All except Lakunle who begins to sneak off.]

BAROKA: Akowe. Teacher wa. Misita Lakunle.[7]

[*As the others take up the cry "Misita Lakunle" he is forced to stop. He returns and bows deeply from the waist.*]

LAKUNLE: A good morning to you sir.

BAROKA: Guru morin guru morin, ngh-hn! That is
    All we get from "alakowe." You call at his house

---

[5] "gangan" . . . "iya ilu": Types of drums.

[6] "Kabiyesi," "Baba": Traditional greetings for a ruler, acknowledging his social position and his age, respectively.

[7] Akowe. . . . Lakunle: *Akowe* means "person who can write." Baroka offers Lakunle a traditional greeting and is disappointed to get a European one in return.

> Hoping he sends for beer, but all you get is
> Guru morin. Will guru morin wet my throat?
> Well, well our man of knowledge, I hope you have no
> Query for an old man today.

LAKUNLE: No complaints.

BAROKA: And we are not feuding in something
> I have forgotten.

LAKUNLE: Feuding sir? I see no cause at all.

BAROKA: Well, the play was much alive until I came.
> And now everything stops, and you were leaving
> Us. After all, I knew the story and I came in
> Right on cue. It makes me feel as if I was
> Chief Baseje.°   a person who spoils a celebration

LAKUNLE: One hardly thinks the Bale would have the time
> For such childish nonsense.

BAROKA: A-ah Mister Lakunle. Without these things you call
> Nonsense, a Bale's life would be pretty dull.
> Well, now that you say I am welcome, shall we
> Resume your play?
> [*Turns suddenly to his attendants.*]
> Seize him!

LAKUNLE [*momentarily baffled*]: What for? What have I done?

BAROKA: You tried to steal our village maidenhead
> Have you forgotten? If he has, serve him a slap
> To wake his brain.

[*An uplifted arm being proffered, Lakunle quickly recollects and nods his head vigorously. So the play is back in performance. The villagers gather round threatening, clamouring for his blood. Lakunle tries bluff, indignation, appeasement in turn. At a sudden signal from the Bale, they throw him down prostrate on his face. Only then does the Chief begin to show him sympathy, appear to understand the stranger's plight, and pacify the villagers on his behalf. He orders dry clothes for him, seats him on his right, and orders a feast in his honour. The stranger springs up every second to take photographs of the party, but most of the time his attention is fixed on Sidi dancing with abandon. Eventually he whispers to the Chief, who nods in consent, and Sidi is sent for. The stranger arranges Sidi in all sorts of magazine postures and takes innumerable photographs of her. Drinks are pressed upon him; he refuses at first, eventually tries the local brew with scepticism, appears to relish it, and drinks profusely. Before long, however, he leaves the party to be sick. They clap him on the back as he goes out, and two drummers who insist on dancing round him nearly cause the calamity to happen on the spot. However, he rushes out with his hand held to his mouth. Lakunle's exit seems to signify the end of the mime. He returns almost at once and the others discard their roles.*]

SIDI [*delightedly.*]: What did I say? You played him to the bone,
> A court jester would have been the life for you,
> Instead of school.
> [*Points contemptuously to the school.*]

BAROKA: And where would the village be, robbed of

Such wisdom as Mister Lakunle dispenses
Daily? Who would tell us where we go wrong?
Eh, Mister Lakunle?
SIDI [*hardly listening, still in the full grip of her excitement.*]:
Who comes with me to find the man?
But Lakunle, you'll have to come and find sense
In his clipping tongue. You see book-man
We cannot really do
Without your head.

[*Lakunle begins to protest, but they crowd him and try to bear him down. Suddenly he breaks free and takes to his heels with all the women in full pursuit. Baroka is left sitting by himself— his wrestler, who accompanied him on his entry, stands a respectful distance away—staring at the flock of women in flight. From the folds of his "agbada"*[8] *he brings out his copy of the magazine and admires the heroine of the publication. Nods slowly to himself.*]

BAROKA: Yes, yes . . . it is five full months since last
I took a wife . . . five full months . . .

NOON

A road by the market. Enter Sidi, happily engrossed in the pictures of herself in the magazine. Lakunle follows one or two paces behind carrying a bundle of firewood which Sidi has set out to obtain. They are met in the centre by Sadiku, who has entered from the opposite side. Sadiku is an old woman, with a shawl over her head.

SADIKU: Fortune is with me. I was going to your house to see you.
SIDI [*startled out of her occupation.*]: What! Oh, it is you, Sadiku.
SADIKU: The Lion sent me. He wishes you well.
SIDI: Thank him for me.
      [*Then excitedly.*]
Have you seen these?
Have you seen these images of me
Wrought by the man from the capital city?
Have you felt the gloss? [*Caresses the page.*]
Smoother by far than the parrot's breast.
SADIKU: I have. I saw them as soon as the city man came. . . . Sidi, I bring a message
      from my lord. [*Jerks her head at Lakunle.*] Shall we draw aside a little?
SIDI: Him? Pay no more heed to that
Than you would a eunuch.
SADIKU: Then, in as few words as it takes to tell, Baroka wants you for a wife.
LAKUNLE [*bounds forward, dropping the wood.*]:
What! The greedy dog!
Insatiate camel of a foolish, doting race;
Is he at his tricks again?

---

[8] "agbada": Robe.

SIDI: Be quiet, 'Kunle. You get so tiresome.
   The message is for me, not you.
LAKUNLE [*down on his knees at once. Covers Sidi's hands with kisses.*]:
   My Ruth, my Rachel, Esther, Bathsheba[9]
   Thou sum of fabled perfections
   From Genesis to the Revelations
   Listen not to the voice of this infidel. . . .
SIDI [*snatches her hand away.*]:
   Now that's your other game;
   Giving me funny names you pick up
   In your wretched books.
   My name is Sidi. And now, let me be.
   My name is Sidi, and I am beautiful.
   The stranger took my beauty
   And placed it in my hands.
   Here, here it is. I need no funny names
   To tell me of my fame.
   Loveliness beyond the jewels of a throne—
   That is what he said.
SADIKU [*gleefully.*]: Well, will you be Baroka's own jewel? Will you be his sweetest
   princess, soothing him on weary nights? What answer shall I give my lord?
SIDI [*wags her finger playfully at the woman.*]:
   Ha ha. Sadiku of the honey tongue.
   Sadiku, head of the Lion's wives.
   You'll make no prey of Sidi with your wooing tongue
   Not this Sidi whose fame has spread to Lagos
   And beyond the seas.
   [*Lakunle beams with satisfaction and rises.*]
SADIKU: Sidi, have you considered what a life of bliss awaits you? Baroka swears to
   take no other wife after you. Do you know what it is to be the Bale's last wife? I'll
   tell you. When he dies—and that should not be long; even the Lion has to die
   sometime—well, when he does, it means that you will have the honour of being
   the senior wife of the new Bale. And just think, until Baroka dies, you shall be his
   favourite. No living in the outhouses for you, my girl. Your place will always be
   in the palace; first as the latest bride, and afterwards, as the head of the new
   harem. . . . It is a rich life, Sidi. I know. I have been in that position for forty-one
   years.
SIDI: You waste your breath.
   Why did Baroka not request my hand
   Before the stranger
   Brought his book of images?
   Why did the Lion not bestow his gift

---

[9] **Ruth . . . Bathsheba:** Women who figure prominently in Hebrew Scriptures.

Before my face was lauded to the world?
Can you not see? Because he sees my worth
Increased and multiplied above his own;
Because he can already hear
The ballad-makers and their songs
In praise of Sidi, the incomparable,
While the Lion is forgotten.
He seeks to have me as his property
Where I must fade beneath his jealous hold.
Ah, Sadiku,
The school-man here has taught me certain things
And my images have taught me all the rest.
Baroka merely seeks to raise his manhood
Above my beauty.
He seeks new fame
As the one man who has possessed
The jewel of Ilujinle!

SADIKU [*shocked, bewildered, incapable of making any sense of Sidi's words.*]: But Sidi, are you well? Such nonsense never passed your lips before. Did you not sound strange, even in your own hearing? [*Rushes suddenly at Lakunle.*] Is this your doing, you popinjay? Have you driven the poor girl mad at last? Such rubbish . . . I will beat your head for this!

LAKUNLE [*retreating in panic.*]: Keep away from me, old hag.

SIDI: Sadiku, let him be.
Tell your lord that I can read his mind,
That I will none of him.
Look—judge for yourself.
[*Opens the magazine and points out the pictures.*]
He's old. I never knew till now,
He was that old . . .
[*During the rest of her speech, Sidi runs her hand over the surface of the relevant part of the photographs, tracing the contours with her fingers.*]
         . . . To think I took
No notice of my velvet skin.
How smooth it is!
And no man ever thought
To praise the fulness of my breasts. . . .

LAKUNLE [*laden with guilt and full of apology.*]:
Well, Sidi, I did think . . .
But somehow it was not the proper thing.

SIDI [*ignores the interruption.*]:
See I hold them to the warm caress
[*Unconsciously pushes out her chest.*]
Of a desire-filled sun.
[*Smiles mischievously.*]

There's a deceitful message in my eyes
Beckoning insatiate men to certain doom.
And teeth that flash the sign of happiness,
Strong and evenly, beaming full of life.
Be just, Sadiku,
Compare my image and your lord's—
An age of difference!
See how the water glistens on my face
Like the dew-moistened leaves on a Harmattan[10] morning
But he—his face is like a leather piece
Torn rudely from the saddle of his horse,
[*Sadiku gasps.*]
Sprinkled with the musty ashes
From a pipe that is long over-smoked.
And this goat-like tuft
Which I once thought was manly;
It is like scattered twists of grass—
Not even green—
But charred and lifeless, as after a forest fire!
Sadiku, I am young and brimming; he is spent.
I am the twinkle of a jewel
But he is the hind quarters of a lion!

SADIKU [*recovering at last from helpless amazement.*]: May Sango[11] restore your wits. For most surely some angry god has taken possession of you. [*Turns around and walks away. Stops again as she remembers something else.*] Your ranting put this clean out of my head. My lord says that if you would not be his wife, would you at least come to supper at his house tonight. There is a small feast in your honour. He wishes to tell you how happy he is that the great capital city has done so much honour to a daughter of Ilujinle. You have brought great fame to your people.

SIDI: Ho ho! Do you think that I was only born
Yesterday?
The tales of Baroka's little suppers,
I know all.
Tell your lord that Sidi does not sup with
Married men.

SADIKU: They are lies, lies. You must not believe everything you hear. Sidi, would I deceive you? I swear to you . . .

SIDI: Can you deny that
Every woman who has supped with him one night,
Becomes his wife or concubine the next?

---

[10]**Harmattan:** A hot, dry wind that blows in the Sahara desert.   [11]**Sango:** West African god of storms, associated with thunder and lightning.

LAKUNLE: Is it for nothing he is called the Fox?

SADIKU [*advancing on him.*]: You keep out of this, or so Sango be my witness . . .

LAKUNLE [*retreats just a little, but continues to talk.*]:
>His wiliness is known even in the larger towns.
>Did you never hear
>Of how he foiled the Public Works attempt
>To build the railway through Ilujinle.

SADIKU: Nobody knows the truth of that. It is all hearsay.

SIDI: I love hearsays. Lakunle, tell me all.

LAKUNLE: Did you not know it? Well sit down and listen.
>My father told me, before he died. And few men
>Know of this trick—oh he's a die-hard rogue
>Sworn against our progress . . . yes . . . it was . . . somewhere here
>The track should have been laid just along
>The outskirts. Well, the workers came, in fact
>It was prisoners who were brought to do
>The harder part . . . to break the jungle's back . . .

[*Enter the prisoners, guarded by two warders. A white surveyor examines his map (khaki helmet, spats,*[12] *etc.). The foreman runs up with his camp stool, table, etc., erects the umbrella over him and unpacks the usual box of bush comforts—soda siphon, whisky bottle, and geometric sandwiches. His map consulted, he directs the sweat team to where to work. They begin felling, machete swinging, log dragging, all to the rhythm of the work gang's metal percussion (rod on gong or rude triangle, etc.). The two performers are also the song leaders and the others fill the chorus. "N'ijo itoro," "Amuda el 'ebe l'aiya," "Gbe je on'ipa," etc.*][13]

LAKUNLE: They marked the route with stakes, ate
>Through the jungle and began the tracks. Trade,
>Progress, adventure, success, civilization,
>Fame, international conspicuousity . . . it was
>All within the grasp of Ilujinle. . . .

[*The wrestler enters, stands horrified at the sight and flees. Returns later with the Bale himself who soon assesses the situation.*

>*They disappear. The work continues, the surveyor occupies himself with the fly-whisk and whisky. Shortly after, a bull-roarer*[14] *is heard. The prisoners falter a little, pick up again. The bull-roarer continues on its way, nearer and farther, moving in circles, so that it appears to come from all round them. The foreman is the first to break and then the rest is chaos. Sole survivor of the rout is the surveyor who is too surprised to move.*

>*Baroka enters a few minutes later accompanied by some attendants and preceded by a young girl bearing a calabash bowl.*[15] *The surveyor, angry and threatening, is prevailed upon to*

---

[12] **spats:** Short cloth or leather ankle coverings worn over the instep and fastened under the foot with a strap. [13] **"N'ijo itoro . . . on'ipa' ":** "In the dance of itoro" (itoro is a neighborhood); "Amuda is a big man"; "Keep the strong one cool." [14] **bull-roarer:** A carved piece of wood or stone that makes a roaring sound when whirled at the end of a long string. [15] **calabash bowl:** Bowl made by hollowing out the hardened shell of the large round fruit of the calabash tree.

open his gift. From it he reveals a wad of pound notes and kola nuts.[16] *Mutual understanding is established. The surveyor frowns heavily, rubs his chin, and consults his map. Re-examines the contents of the bowl, shakes his head. Baroka adds more money, and a coop of hens. A goat follows, and more money. This time "truth" dawns on him at last, he has made a mistake. The track really should go the other way. What an unfortunate error, discovered just in time! No, no, no possibility of a mistake this time, the track should be much further away. In fact (scooping up the soil) the earth is most unsuitable, couldn't possibly support the weight of a railway engine. A gourd of palm wine is brought to seal the agreement and a kola nut is broken. Baroka's men help the surveyor pack and they leave with their arms round each other followed by the surveyor's booty.*]

LAKUNLE [*as the last of the procession disappears, shakes his fist at them, stamping on the ground.*]:

> Voluptuous beast! He loves this life too well
> To bear to part from it. And motor roads
> And railways would do just that, forcing
> Civilization at his door. He foresaw it
> And he barred the gates, securing fast
> His dogs and horses, his wives and all his
> Concubines . . . ah, yes . . . all those concubines.
> Baroka has such a selective eye, none suits him
> But the best. . . .
> [*His eyes truly light up. Sidi and Sadiku snigger, tip-toe offstage.*]
>   . . . Yes, one must grant him that.
> Ah, I sometimes wish I led his kind of life.
> Such luscious bosoms make his nightly pillow.
> I am sure he keeps a timetable just as
> I do at school. Only way to ensure fair play.
> He must be healthy to keep going as he does.
> I don't know what the women see in him. His eyes
> Are small and always red with wine. He must
> Possess some secret. . . . No! I do not envy him!
> Just the one woman for me. Alone I stand
> For progress, with Sidi my chosen soul-mate, the one
> Woman of my life. . . . Sidi! Sidi where are you?
> [*Rushes out after them, returns to fetch the discarded firewood and runs out again.*]

[*Baroka in bed, naked except for baggy trousers, calf-length. It is a rich bedroom covered in animal skins and rugs. Weapons round the wall. Also a strange machine, a most peculiar contraption with a long lever. Kneeling beside the bed is Baroka's current Favourite, engaged in plucking the hairs from his armpit. She does this by first massaging the spot around the selected hair very gently with her forefinger. Then, with hardly a break, she pulls out the hair between her finger and the thumb with a sudden sharp movement. Baroka twitches slightly with each pull. Then an aspirated "A-ah," and a look of complete beatitude spreads all over his face.*]

---

[16] **kola nuts:** Nut of the kola tree containing caffeine and traditionally given to guests as a sign of hospitality.

FAVOURITE: Do I improve my lord?

BAROKA: You are still somewhat over-gentle with the pull
  As if you feared to hurt the panther of the trees.
  Be sharp and sweet
  Like the swift sting of a vicious wasp
  For there the pleasure lies — the cooling aftermath.

FAVOURITE: I'll learn, my lord.

BAROKA: You have not time, my dear.
  Tonight I hope to take another wife.
  And the honour of this task, you know,
  Belongs by right to my latest choice.
  But — A-ah — Now that was sharp.
  It had in it the scorpion's sudden sting
  Without its poison.
  It was an angry pull; you tried to hurt
  For I had made you wrathful with my boast.
  But now your anger flows in my bloodstream.
  How sweet it is! A-ah! That was sweeter still.
  I think perhaps that I shall let you stay,
  The sole out-puller of my sweat-bathed hairs.
  Ach!
  [*Sits up suddenly and rubs the sore point angrily.*]
      Now that had far more pain than pleasure
  Vengeful creature, you did not caress
  The area of extraction long enough!
  [*Enter Sadiku. She goes down on her knees at once and bows her head into her lap.*]
  Aha! Here comes Sadiku.
  Do you bring some balm,
  To soothe the smart of my misused armpit?
  Away, you enemy!
  [*Exit the Favourite.*]

SADIKU: My lord . . .

BAROKA: You have my leave to speak.
  What did she say?

SADIKU: She will not my lord. I did my best, but she will have none of you.

BAROKA: It follows the pattern — a firm refusal
  At the start. Why will she not?

SADIKU: That is the strange part of it. She says you're much too old. If you ask me, I think that she is really off her head. All this excitement of the books has been too much for her.

BAROKA [*springs to his feet.*]:
  She says . . . That I am old
  That I am much too old? Did a slight
  Unripened girl say this of me?

SADIKU: My lord, I heard the incredible words with my ears, and I thought the world
    was mad.
BAROKA: But is it possible, Sadiku? Is this right?
    Did I not, at the festival of Rain,
    Defeat the men in the log-tossing match?
    Do I not still with the most fearless ones,
    Hunt the leopard and the boa at night
    And save the farmers' goats from further harm?
    And does she say I'm old?
    Did I not, to announce the Harmattan,
    Climb to the top of the silk-cotton tree,
    Break the first pod, and scatter tasselled seeds
    To the four winds — and this but yesterday?
    Do any of my wives report
    A failing in my manliness?
    The strongest of them all
    Still wearies long before the Lion does!
    And so would she, had I the briefest chance
    To teach this unfledged birdling
    That lacks the wisdom to embrace
    The rich mustiness of age . . . if I could once . . .
    Come hither, soothe me, Sadiku
    For I am wroth at heart.
    [*Lies back on the bed, staring up as before. Sadiku takes her place at the foot of the
    bed and begins to tickle the soles of his feet. Baroka turns to the left suddenly,
    reaches down the side, and comes up with a copy of the magazine. Opens it and
    begins to study the pictures. He heaves a long sigh.*]
    That is good, Sadiku, very good.
    [*He begins to compare some pictures in the book, obviously his own and Sidi's.
    Flings the book away suddenly and stares at the ceiling for a second or two. Then,
    unsmiling.*]
    Perhaps it is as well, Sadiku.
SADIKU: My lord, what did you say?
BAROKA: Yes, faithful one, I say it is as well.
    The scorn, the laughter, and the jeers
    Would have been bitter
    Had she consented and my purpose failed,
    I would have sunk with shame.
SADIKU: My lord, I do not understand.
BAROKA: The time has come when I can fool myself
    No more. I am no man, Sadiku. My manhood
    Ended near a week ago.
SADIKU: The gods forbid.
BAROKA: I wanted Sidi because I still hoped —
    A foolish thought I know, but still — I hoped

That, with a virgin young and hot within,
My failing strength would rise and save my pride.
[*Sadiku begins to moan.*]
A waste of hope. I knew it even then.
But it's a human failing never to accept
The worst; and so I pandered to my vanity.
When manhood must, it ends.
The well of living, tapped beyond its depth,
Dries up, and mocks the wastrel in the end.
I am withered and unsapped, the joy
Of ballad-mongers, the aged butt
Of youth's ribaldry.

SADIKU [*tearfully.*]: The gods must have mercy yet.

BAROKA [*as if suddenly aware of her presence, starts up.*]:
I have told this to no one but you,
Who are my eldest, my most faithful wife.
But if you dare parade my shame before the world . . .
[*Sadiku shakes her head in protest and begins to stroke the soles of his feet with renewed tenderness. Baroka sighs and falls back slowly.*]
How irritable I have grown of late
Such doubts to harbour of your loyalty . . .
But this disaster is too much for one
Checked thus as I upon the prime of youth.
That rains that blessed me from my birth
Number a meagre sixty-two;
While my grandfather, that man of teak,
Fathered two sons, late on sixty-five.
But Okiki, my father beat them all
Producing female twins at sixty-seven.
Why then must I, descendant of these lions
Forswear my wives at a youthful sixty-two
My veins of life run dry, my manhood gone!
[*His voice goes drowsy; Sadiku sighs and moans and caresses his feet. His face lights up suddenly with rapture.*]
Sango bear witness! These weary feet
Have felt the loving hands of much design
In women.
My soles have felt the scratch of harsh,
Gravelled hands.
They have borne the heaviness of clumsy,
Gorilla paws.
And I have known the tease of tiny,
Dainty hands,
Toylike hands that tantalized
My eager senses,

Promised of thrills to come
Remaining
Unfulfilled because the fingers
Were too frail,
The touch too light and faint to pierce
The incredible thickness of my soles.
But thou Sadiku, thy plain unadorned hands
Encase a sweet sensuality which age
Will not destroy. A-ah,
Oyayi! Beyond a doubt Sadiku,
Thou art the queen of them all.
[*Falls asleep.*]

NIGHT

The village centre. Sidi stands by the schoolroom window, admiring her photos as before. Enter Sadiku with a longish bundle. She is very furtive. Unveils the object which turns out to be a carved figure of the Bale, naked and in full detail. She takes a good look at it, bursts suddenly into derisive laughter, sets the figure in front of the tree. Sidi stares in utter amazement.

SADIKU: So we did for you too did we? We did for you in the end. Oh high and mighty lion, have we really scotched[17] you? A—ya-ya-ya . . . we women undid you in the end. I was there when it happened to your father, the great Okiki. I did for him, I, the youngest and freshest of the wives. I killed him with my strength. I called him and he came at me, but no, for him, this was not like other times. I, Sadiku, was I not flame itself and he the flax on old women's spindles? I ate him up! Race of mighty lions, we always consume you, at our pleasure we spin you, at our whim we make you dance; like the foolish top you think the world revolves around you . . . fools! fools! . . . it is you who run giddy while we stand still and watch, and draw your frail thread from you, slowly, till nothing is left but a runty old stick. I scotched Okiki, Sadiku's unopened treasure-house demanded sacrifice, and Okiki came with his rusted key. Like a snake he came at me, like a rag he went back; a limp rag, smeared in shame. . . . [*Her ghoulish laugh repossesses her.*]
Ah, take warning my masters, we'll scotch you in the end. . . .
[*With a yell she leaps up, begins to dance round the tree, chanting.*]
Take warning, my masters
We'll scotch you in the end.
[*Sidi shuts the window gently, comes out; Sadiku, as she comes round again, gasps and is checked in mid-song.*]
SADIKU: Oh it is you my daughter. You should have chosen a better time to scare me to death. The hour of victory is no time for any woman to die.

---

[17] **scotched:** To injure something to the point that it is harmless.

SIDI: Why? What battle have you won?

SADIKU: Not me alone girl. You too. Every woman. Oh my daughter, that I have lived to see this day . . . To see him fizzle with the drabbest puff of a mis-primed "sakabula."[18]

[*Resumes her dance.*]

Take warning, my masters
We'll scotch you in the end.

SIDI: Wait Sadiku. I cannot understand.

SADIKU: You will my girl. You will.

Take warning my masters . . .

SIDI: Sadiku, are you well?

SADIKU: Ask no questions my girl. Just join my victory dance. Oh Sango my lord, who of us possessed your lightning and ran like fire through that lion's tail . . .

SIDI [*holds her firmly as she is about to go off again.*]:

Stop your loose ranting. You will not
Move from here until you make some sense.

SADIKU: Oh you are troublesome. Do you promise to tell no one?

SIDI: I swear it. Now tell me quickly.

[*As Sadiku whispers, her eyes widen.*]

O-ho-o-o-o-!
But Sadiku, if he knew the truth, why
Did he ask me to . . .

[*Again Sadiku whispers.*]

Ha ha! Some hope indeed. Oh Sadiku
I suddenly am glad to be a woman.

[*Leaps in the air.*]

We won. We won! Hurray for womankind!

[*Falls in behind Sadiku.*]

Take warning, my masters
We'll scotch you in the end. [*Lakunle enters unobserved.*]

LAKUNLE: The full moon is not yet, but
The women cannot wait.
They must go mad without it.

[*The dancing stops. Sadiku frowns.*]

SADIKU: The scarecrow is here. Begone fop! This is the world of women. At this moment our star sits in the centre of the sky. We are supreme. What is more, we are about to perform a ritual. If you remain, we will chop you up, we will make you the sacrifice.

LAKUNLE: What is the hag gibbering?

SADIKU [*advances menacingly.*]: You less than man, you less than the littlest woman, I say begone!

---

[18] "sakabula": A type of gun that is not particularly effective.

LAKUNLE [*nettled.*]: I will have you know that I am a man
  As you will find out if you dare
  To lay a hand on me.
SADIKU [*throws back her head in laughter.*]: You a man? Is Baroka not more of a man
  than you? And if he is no longer a man, then what are you? [*Lakunle, under-
  standing the meaning, stands rooted, shocked.*] Come on, dear girl, let him look
  on if he will. After all, only *men* are barred from watching this ceremony.
  Take warning, my masters
  We'll . . .
SIDI: Stop. Sadiku stop. Oh such an idea
  Is running in my head. Let me to the palace for
  This supper he promised me. Sadiku, what a way
  To mock the devil. I shall ask forgiveness
  For my hasty words. . . . No need to change
  My answers and consent to be his bride—he might
  Suspect you've told me. But I shall ask a month
  To think on it.
SADIKU [*somewhat doubtful.*]: Baroka is no child you know, he will know I have
  betrayed him.
SIDI: No, he will not. Oh Sadiku let me go.
  I long to see him thwarted, to watch his longing
  His twitching hands which this time cannot
  Rush to loosen his trouser cords.
SADIKU: You will have to match the fox's cunning. Use your bashful looks and be
  truly repentant. Goad him my child, torment him until he weeps for shame.
SIDI: Leave it to me. He will never suspect you of deceit.
SADIKU [*with another of her energetic leaps.*]: Yo-rooo o! Yo-rororo o!
  Shall I come with you?
SIDI: Will that be wise? You forget
  We have not seen each other.
SADIKU: Away then. Away woman. I shall bide here.
  Haste back and tell Sadiku how the no-man is.
  Away, my lovely child.
LAKUNLE [*he has listened with increasing horror.*]:
  No, Sidi, don't. If you care
  One little bit for what I feel,
  Do not go to torment the man.
  Suppose he knows that you have come to jeer—
  And he will know, if he is not a fool—
  He is a savage thing, degenerate
  He would beat a helpless woman if he could. . . .
SIDI [*running off gleefully.*]: Ta-raa school teacher. Wait here for me.
LAKUNLE [*stamps his foot helplessly.*]:
  Foolish girl! . . . And this is all your work.
  Could you not keep a secret?

Must every word leak out of you
As surely as the final drops
Of mother's milk
Oozed from your flattened breast
Generations ago?

SADIKU: Watch your wagging tongue, unformed creature!

LAKUNLE: If any harm befalls her . . .

SADIKU: Woman though she is, she can take better care of herself than you can of her. Fancy a thing like you actually wanting a girl like that, all to your little self. [*Walks round him and looks him up and down.*] Ah! Oba Ala[19] is an accommodating god. What a poor figure you cut!

LAKUNLE: I wouldn't demean myself to bandy words
With a woman of the bush.

SADIKU: At this moment, your betrothed is supping with the Lion.

LAKUNLE [*pleased at the use of the word "betrothed."*]:
Well, we are not really betrothed as yet,
I mean, she is not promised yet.
But it will come in time, I'm sure.

SADIKU [*bursts into her cackling laughter.*]: The bride-price, is that paid?

LAKUNLE: Mind your own business.

SADIKU: Why don't you do what other men have done. Take a farm for a season. One harvest will be enough to pay the price, even for a girl like Sidi. Or will the smell of the wet soil be too much for your delicate nostrils?

LAKUNLE: I said mind your own business.

SADIKU: A — a — ah. It is true what they say then. You are going to convert the whole village so that no one will ever pay the bride-price again. Ah, you're a clever man. I must admit that it is a good way for getting out of it, but don't you think you'd use more time and energy that way than you would if . . .

LAKUNLE [*with conviction.*]: Within a year or two, I swear,
This town shall see a transformation
Bride-price will be a thing forgotten
And wives shall take their place by men.
A motor road will pass this spot
And bring the city ways to us.
We'll buy saucepans for all the women
Clay pots are crude and unhygienic
No man shall take more wives than one
That's why they're impotent too soon.
The ruler shall ride cars, not horses
Or a bicycle at the very least.
We'll burn the forest, cut the trees
Then plant a modern park for lovers

---

[19] **Oba Ala:** Obatala, the god who shaped human beings.

We'll print newspapers every day
With pictures of seductive girls.
The world will judge our progress by
The girls that win beauty contests.
While Lagos builds new factories daily
We only play "ayo"° and gossip.   a board game
Where is our school of ballroom dancing?
Who here can throw a cocktail party?
We must be modern with the rest
Or live forgotten by the world
We must reject the palm wine habit
And take to tea, with milk and sugar.
[*Turns on Sadiku who has been staring at him in terror. She retreats, and he continues to talk down at her as they go round, then down and offstage, Lakunle's hectoring voice trailing away in the distance.*]
This is my plan, you withered face
And I shall start by teaching you.
From now you shall attend my school
And take your place with twelve-year olds.
For though you're nearly seventy,
Your mind is simple and unformed.
Have you no shame that at your age,
You neither read nor write nor think?
You spend your days as senior wife,
Collecting brides for Baroka.
And now because you've sucked him dry,
You send my Sidi to his shame. . . .

[*The scene changes to Baroka's bedroom. On the left in a one-knee-on-floor posture, two men are engaged in a kind of wrestling, their arms clasped round each other's waist, testing the right moment to heave. One is Baroka, the other a short squat figure of apparent muscular power. The contest is still in the balanced stage. In some distant part of the house, Sidi's voice is heard lifted in the familiar general greeting, addressed to no one in particular.*]
SIDI: A good day to the head and people
    Of this house.
    [*Baroka lifts his head, frowns as if he is trying to place the voice.*]
    A good day to the head and people
    Of this house.

[*Baroka now decides to ignore it and to concentrate on the contest. Sidi's voice draws progressively nearer. She enters nearly backwards, as she is still busy admiring the room through which she has just passed. Gasps on turning round to see the two men.*]
BAROKA [*without looking up.*]: Is Sadiku not at home then?
SIDI [*absent-mindedly.*]: Hm?
BAROKA: I asked, is Sadiku not at home?

SIDI [*recollecting herself, she curtseys quickly.*]: I saw no one, Baroka.
BAROKA: No one? Do you mean there was no one
    To bar unwanted strangers from my privacy?
SIDI [*retreating.*]: The house . . . seemed . . . empty.
BAROKA: Ah, I forget. This is the price I pay
    Once every week, for being progressive.
    Prompted by the school teacher, my servants
    Were prevailed upon to form something they call
    The Palace Workers' Union. And in keeping
    With the habits—I am told—of modern towns,
    This is their day off.
SIDI [*seeing that Baroka seems to be in a better mood, she becomes somewhat bolder. Moves forward—saucily.*]:
    Is this also a day off
    For Baroka's wives?
BAROKA [*looks up sharply, relaxes, and speaks with a casual voice.*]:
    No, the madness has not gripped them—yet.
    Did you not meet with one of them?
SIDI: No, Baroka. There was no one about.
BAROKA: Not even Ailatu, my favourite?
    Was she not at her usual place,
    Beside my door?
SIDI [*absently. She is deeply engrossed in watching the contest.*]:
    Her stool is there. And I saw
    The slippers she was embroidering.
BAROKA: Hm. Hm. I think I know
    Where she'll be found. In a dark corner
    Sulking like a slighted cockroach.
    By the way, look and tell me
    If she left her shawl behind.
    [*So as not to miss any part of the tussle, she moves backwards, darts a quick look round the door and back again.*]
SIDI: There is a black shawl on the stool.
BAROKA [*a regretful sigh.*]:
    Then she'll be back tonight. I had hoped
    My words were harsh enough
    To free me from her spite for a week or more.
SIDI: Did Ailatu offend her husband?
BAROKA: Offend? My armpit still weeps blood
    For the gross abuse I suffered from one
    I called my favourite.
SIDI [*in a disappointed voice.*]:
    Oh. Is that all?
BAROKA: Is that not enough? Why child?
    What more could the woman do?

SIDI: Nothing. Nothing, Baroka. I thought perhaps—
    Well—young wives are known to be—
    Forward—sometimes—to their husbands.
BAROKA: In an ill-kept household perhaps. But not
    Under Baroka's roof. And yet,
    Such are the sudden spites of women
    That even I cannot foresee them all.
    And child—if I lose this little match
    Remember that my armpit
    Burns and itches turn by turn.
    [*Sidi continues watching for some time, then clasps her hand over her mouth as she*
    remembers what she should have done to begin with. Doubtful how to proceed, she
    hesitates for some moments, then comes to a decision and kneels.]
SIDI: I have come, Bale, as a repentant child.
BAROKA: What?
SIDI [*very hesitantly, eyes to the floor, but she darts a quick look up when*
she thinks the Bale isn't looking.]
    The answer which I sent to the Bale
    Was given in a thoughtless moment. . . .
BAROKA: Answer, child? To what?
SIDI: A message brought by . . .
BAROKA [*groans and strains in a muscular effort.*]:
    Will you say that again? It is true that for supper
    I did require your company. But up till now
    Sadiku has brought no reply.
SIDI [*amazed.*]: But the other matter! Did not the Bale
    Send . . . did Baroka not send . . . ?
BAROKA [*with sinister encouragement.*]:
    What did Baroka not, my child?
SIDI [*cowed, but angry, rises.*]:
    It is nothing, Bale. I only hope
    That I am here at the Bale's invitation.
BAROKA [*as if trying to understand, he frowns as he looks at her.*]:
    A-ah, at last I understand. You think
    I took offence because you entered
    Unannounced?
SIDI: I remember that the Bale called me
    An unwanted stranger.
BAROKA: That could be expected. Is a man's bedroom
    To be made naked to any flea
    That chances to wander through?
    [*Sidi turns away, very hurt.*]
    Come, come, my child. You are too quick
    To feel aggrieved. Of course you are
    More than welcome. But I expected Ailatu

To tell me you were here.

[*Sidi curtseys briefly with her back to Baroka. After a while, she turns round. The mischief returns to her face. Baroka's attitude of denial has been a setback but she is now ready to pursue her mission.*]

SIDI: I hope the Bale will not think me
Forward. But, like everyone, I had thought
The Favourite was a gentle woman.

BAROKA: And so had I.

SIDI [*slyly.*]: One would hardly think that *she*
Would give offence without a cause
Was the Favourite . . . in some way . . .
Dissatisfied . . . with her lord and husband?

[*With a mock curtsey, quickly executed as Baroka begins to look up.*]

BAROKA [*slowly turns towards her.*]:
Now that
Is a question which I never thought to hear
Except from a school teacher. Do you think
The Lion has such leisure that he asks
The whys and wherefores of a woman's
Squint?

[*Sidi steps back and curtseys. As before, and throughout this scene, she is easily cowed by Baroka's change of mood, all the more easily as she is, in any case, frightened by her own boldness.*]

SIDI: I mean no disrespect . . .

BAROKA [*gently.*]: I know. [*Breaks off.*] Christians on my
Fathers' shrines, child!
Do you think I took offence? A — aw
Come in and seat yourself. Since you broke in
Unawares, and appear resolved to stay,
Try, if you can, not to make me feel
A humourless old ram. I allow no one
To watch my daily exercise, but as we say,
The woman gets lost in the woods one day
And every wood deity dies the next.

[*Sidi curtseys, watches, and moves forward warily, as if expecting the two men to spring apart too suddenly.*]

SIDI: I think he will win.

BAROKA: Is that a wish, my daughter?

SIDI: No, but— [*Hesitates, but boldness wins.*]
If the tortoise cannot tumble
It does not mean that he can stand.

[*Baroka looks at her, seemingly puzzled. Sidi turns away, humming.*]

BAROKA: When the child is full of riddles, the mother
Has one water-pot the less.

[*Sidi tip-toes to Baroka's back and pulls asses' ears at him.*]

SIDI: I think he will win.

BAROKA: He knows he must. Would it profit me
    To pit my strength against a weakling?
    Only yesterday, this son of—I suspect—
    A python for a mother, and fathered beyond doubt
    By a blubber-bottomed baboon,
    [*The complimented man grins.*]
    Only yesterday, he nearly
    Ploughed my tongue with my front teeth
    In a friendly wrestling bout.

WRESTLER [*encouraged, makes an effort.*]: Ugh. Ugh.

SIDI [*bent almost over them. Genuinely worried.*]:
    Oh! Does it hurt?

BAROKA: Not yet . . . but, as I was saying
    I change my wrestlers when I have learnt
    To throw them. I also change my wives
    When I have learnt to tire them.

SIDI: And is this another . . . changing time
    For the Bale?

BAROKA: Who knows? Until the finger nails
    Have scraped the dust, no one can tell
    Which insect released his bowels.
    [*Sidi grimaces in disgust and walks away. Returns as she thinks up a new idea.*]

SIDI: A woman spoke to me this afternoon.

BAROKA: Indeed. And does Sidi find this unusual—
    That a woman speak with her in the afternoon?

SIDI [*stamping.*]: No. She had the message of a go-between.

BAROKA: Did she? Then I rejoice with you.
    [*Sidi stands biting her lips. Baroka looks at her, this time with deliberate appreciation.*]
    And now I think of it, why not?
    There must be many men who
    Build their loft to fit your height.

SIDI [*unmoving, pointedly.*]: Her message came from one
    With many lofts.

BAROKA: Ah! Such is the greed of men.

SIDI: If Baroka were my father
    [*Aside.*] —which many would take him to be—
    [*Makes a rude sign.*]
    Would he pay my dowry to this man
    And give his blessings?

BAROKA: Well, I must know his character.
    For instance, is the man rich?

SIDI: Rumour has it so.

BAROKA: Is he repulsive?

SIDI: He is old. [*Baroka winces.*]

BAROKA: Is he mean and miserly?

SIDI: To strangers—no. There are tales
  Of his open-handedness, which are never
  Quite without a motive. But his wives report
  —To take one little story—
  How he grew the taste for ground corn
  And pepper—because he would not pay
  The price of snuff!
  [*With a sudden burst of angry energy, Baroka lifts his opponent and throws him
  over his shoulder.*]

BAROKA: A lie! The price of snuff
  Had nothing to do with it.

SIDI [*too excited to listen.*]: You won!

BAROKA: By the years on my beard, I swear
  They slander me!

SIDI [*excitedly.*]: You won. You won!
  [*She breaks into a kind of shoulder dance and sings.*]
  Yokolu Yokolu. Ko ha tan bi
  Iyawo gb'oko san'le.
  Oko yo 'ke . . .²⁰
  [*She repeats this throughout Baroka's protests. Baroka is pacing angrily up and
  down. The defeated man, nursing a hip, goes to the corner of the room and lifts out
  a low "ako" bench. He sits on the floor, and soon, Baroka joins him; using only their
  arms now, they place their elbows on the bench and grip hands. Baroka takes his off
  again, replaces it, takes it off again, and so on during the rest of his outburst.*]

BAROKA: This means nothing to me of course. Nothing!
  But I know the ways of women, and I know
  Their ruinous tongues.
  Suppose that, as a child—only suppose—
  Suppose then, that as a child, I—
  And remember, I only use myself
  To illustrate the plight of many men. . . .
  So, once again, suppose that as a child
  I grew to love "tanfiri"²¹—with a good dose of pepper
  And growing old, I found that—
  Sooner than die away, my passion only
  Bred itself upon each mouthful of
  Ground corn and pepper I consumed.
  Now, think child, would it be seemly
  At my age, and the father of children,

---

²⁰Yokolu . . . yo 'ke: A song; often used to insult someone after he or she suffers a great defeat.

²¹"tanfiri": A type of food; possibly an aphrodisiac.

To be discovered, in public
Thrusting fistfuls of corn dust and pepper
In my mouth? Is it not wise to indulge
In the little masquerade of a dignified
Snuff box?—But remember, I only make
A pleading for this prey of women's
Malice. I feel his own injustice,
Being myself, a daily fellow-sufferer!
[*Baroka seems to realize for the first time that Sidi has paid no attention to his explanation. She is, in fact, still humming and shaking her shoulders. He stares questioningly at her. Sidi stops, somewhat confused and embarrassed, points sheepishly to the wrestler.*]

SIDI: I think this time he will win.
[*Baroka's grumbling subsides slowly. He is now attentive to the present bout.*]

BAROKA: Now let us once again take up
The questioning. [*Almost timidly.*] Is this man
Good and kindly.

SIDI: They say he uses well
His dogs and horses.

BAROKA [*desperately.*]:
Well is he fierce then? Reckless!
Does the bush cow run to hole
When he hears his beaters' Hei-ei-wo-rah!

SIDI: There are heads and skins of leopards
Hung around his council room.
But the market is also
Full of them.

BAROKA: Is he not wise? Is he not sagely?
Do the young and old not seek
His counsel?

SIDI: The fox is said to be wise
So cunning that he stalks and dines on
New-hatched chickens.

BAROKA [*more and more desperate.*]:
Does he not beget strength on wombs?
Are his children not tall and stout-limbed?

SIDI: Once upon a time.

BAROKA: Once upon a time?
What do you mean, girl?

SIDI: Just once upon a time.
Perhaps his children have of late
Been plagued with shyness and refuse
To come into the world. Or else
He is so tired with the day's affairs
That at night, he turns his buttocks

To his wives. But there have been
No new reeds cut by his servants,
No new cots woven.
And his household gods are starved
For want of child-naming festivities
Since the last two rains went by.

BAROKA: Perhaps he is a frugal man.
Mindful of years to come,
Planning for a final burst of life, he
Husbands his strength.

SIDI [*giggling. She is actually stopped, half-way, by giggling at the cleverness of her remark.*]:
To husband his wives surely ought to be
A man's first duties — at all times.

BAROKA: My beard tells me you've been a pupil,
A most diligent pupil of Sadiku.
Among all shameless women,
The sharpest tongues grow from that one
Peeling bark — Sadiku, my faithful lizard!
[*Growing steadily warmer during the speech, he again slaps down his opponent's arm as he shouts "Sadiku."*]

SIDI [*backing away, aware that she has perhaps gone too far and betrayed knowledge of the "secret."*]:
I have learnt nothing of anyone.

BAROKA: No more. No more.
Already I have lost a wrestler
On your account. This town-bred daring
Of little girls, awakes in me
A seven-horned devil of strength.
Let one woman speak a careless word
And I can pin a wriggling — Bah!
[*Lets go the man's arm. He has risen during the last speech but held on to the man's arm, who is forced to rise with him.*]
The tappers[22] should have called by now.
See if we have a fresh gourd by the door.
[*The wrestler goes out. Baroka goes to sit on the bed, Sidi eyeing him, doubtfully.*]
What an ill-tempered man I daily grow
Towards. Soon my voice will be
The sand between two grinding stones.
But I have my scattered kindliness
Though few occasions serve to herald it.
And Sidi, my daughter, you do not know

---

[22] **The tappers:** A reference to the drawing of palm wine by tapping.

     The thoughts which prompted me
     To ask the pleasure that I be your host
     This evening. I would not tell Sadiku,
     Meaning to give delight
     With the surprise of it. Now, tell me, child
     Can you guess a little at this thing?

SIDI: Sadiku told me nothing.

BAROKA: You are hasty with denial. For how indeed
     Could Sadiku, since I told her
     Nothing of my mind? But, my daughter,
     Did she not, perhaps . . . invent some tale?
     For I know Sadiku loves to be
     All-knowing.

SIDI: She said no more, except the Bale
     Begged my presence.

BAROKA [*rises quickly to the bait.*]:
     Begged? Bale Baroka begged?
     [*Wrestler enters with gourd and calabash cups. Baroka relapses.*]
     Ah! I see you love to bait your elders.
     One way the world remains the same,
     The child still thinks she is wiser than
     The cotton head of age.
     Do you think Baroka deaf or blind
     To little signs? But let that pass.
     Only, lest you fall victim to the schemes
     Of busy women, I will tell you this —
     I know Sadiku plays the matchmaker
     Without the prompting. If I look
     On any maid, or call her name
     Even in the course of harmless, neighbourly
     Well-wishing — How fares your daughter?
     — Is your sister now recovered from her
     Whooping cough? — How fast your ward
     Approaches womanhood! Have the village lads
     Begun to gather at your door? —
     Or any word at all which shows I am
     The thoughtful guardian of the village health,
     If it concerns a woman, Sadiku straightway
     Flings herself into the role of go-between
     And before I even don a cap, I find
     Yet another stranger in my bed!

SIDI: It seems a Bale's life
     Is full of great unhappiness.

BAROKA: I do not complain. No, my child

I accept the sweet and sour with
A ruler's grace. I lose my patience
Only when I meet with
The new immodesty with women.
Now, my Sidi, you have not caught
This new and strange disease, I hope.

SIDI [*curtseying.*]: The threading of my smock—
Does Baroka not know the marking
Of the village loom?

BAROKA: But will Sidi, the pride of mothers,
Will she always wear it?

SIDI: Will Sidi, the proud daughter of Baroka,
Will she step out naked?
[*A pause. Baroka surveys Sidi in an almost fatherly manner and she bashfully drops her eyes.*]

BAROKA: To think that once I thought,
Sidi is the eye's delight, but
She is vain, and her head
Is feather-light, and always giddy
With a trivial thought. And now
I find her deep and wise beyond her years.
[*Reaches under his pillow, brings out the now familiar magazine, and also an addressed envelope. Retains the former and gives her the envelope.*]
Do you know what this means?
The trim red piece of paper
In the corner?

SIDI: I know it. A stamp. Lakunle receives
Letters from Lagos marked with it.

BAROKA [*obviously disappointed*]:
Hm. Lakunle. But more about him
Later. Do you know what it means—
This little frippery?

SIDI [*very proudly.*]:
Yes. I know that too. Is it not a tax on
The habit of talking with paper?

BAROKA: Oh. Oh. I see you dip your hand
Into the pockets of the school teacher
And retrieve it bulging with knowledge.
[*Goes to the strange machine, and pulls the lever up and down.*]
Now this, not even the school teacher can tell
What magic this performs. Come nearer,
It will not bite.

SIDI: I have never seen the like.

BAROKA: The work dear child, of the palace blacksmiths

Built in full secrecy. All is not well with it—
But I will find the cause and then Ilujinle
Will boast its own tax on paper, made with
Stamps[23] like this. For long I dreamt it
And here it stands, child of my thoughts.

SIDI [*wonder-struck.*]: You mean . . . this will work some day?

BAROKA: Ogun has said the word. And now my girl
What think you of that image on the stamp
This spiderwork of iron, wood, and mortar?

SIDI: Is it not a bridge?

BAROKA: It is a bridge. The longest—so they say
In the whole country. When not a bridge,
You'll find a print of groundnuts
Stacked like pyramids,
Or palm trees, or cocoa trees, and farmers
Hacking pods, and workmen
Felling trees and tying skinned logs
Into rafts. A thousand thousand letters
By road, by rail, by air,
From one end of the world to another,
And not one human head among them.
Not one head of beauty on the stamp!

SIDI: But I once saw Lakunle's letter
With a head of bronze.

BAROKA: A figurehead, my child, a lifeless work
Of craft, with holes for eyes, and coldness
For the warmth of life and love
In youthful cheeks like yours,
My daughter . . .
[*Pauses to watch the effect on Sidi.*]
⠀⠀⠀⠀⠀⠀⠀. . . Can you see it, Sidi?
Tens of thousands of these dainty prints
And each one with this legend of Sidi.
[*Flourishes the magazine, open in the middle.*]
The village goddess, reaching out
Towards the sun, her lover.
Can you see it, my daughter!
[*Sidi drowns herself totally in the contemplation, takes the magazine but does not even look at it. Sits on the bed.*]

---

[23] **Stamps:** It was not uncommon for small African nations to make part of their national income by selling decorative stamps to collectors.

BAROKA [*very gently.*]:
  I hope you will not think it too great
  A burden, to carry the country's mail
  All on your comeliness.
  [*Walks away, an almost business-like tone.*]
                    Our beginnings will
  Of course be modest. We shall begin
  By cutting stamps for our own village alone.
  As the schoolmaster himself would say—
  Charity begins at home.
  [*Pause. Faces Sidi from nearly the distance of the room.*]
                    For a long time now,
  The town-dwellers have made up tales
  Of the backwardness of Ilujinle
  Until it hurts Baroka, who holds
  The welfare of his people deep at heart.
  Now, if we do this thing, it will prove more
  Than any single town has done!
  [*The wrestler, who has been listening open-mouthed, drops his cup in admiration. Baroka, annoyed, realizing only now in fact that he is still in the room, waves him impatiently out.*]
  I do not hate progress, only its nature
  Which makes all roofs and faces look the same,
  And the wish of one old man is
  That here and there,
  [*Goes progressively towards Sidi, until he bends over her, then sits beside her on the bed.*]
  Among the bridges and the murderous roads,
  Below the humming birds which
  Smoke the face of Sango, dispenser of
  The snake-tongue lightning; between this moment
  And the reckless broom that will be wielded
  In these years to come, we must leave
  Virgin plots of lives, rich decay
  And the tang of vapour rising from
  Forgotten heaps of compost, lying
  Undisturbed . . . But the skin of progress
  Masks, unknown, the spotted wolf of sameness . . .
  Does sameness not revolt your being,
  My daughter?
  [*Sidi is capable only of a bewildered nod, slowly.*]
BAROKA [*sighs, hands folded piously on his lap.*]:
  I find my soul is sensitive, like yours.
  Indeed, although there is one—no more think I—

One generation between yours and mine,
Our thoughts fly crisply through the air
And meet, purified, as one.
And our first union
Is the making of this stamp.
The one redeeming grace on any paper tax
Shall be your face. And mine,
The soul behind it all, worshipful
Of Nature for her gift of youth
And beauty to our earth. Does this
Please you, my daughter?

SIDI: I can no longer see the meaning, Baroka.
Now that you speak
Almost like the school teacher, except
Your words fly on a different path,
I find . . .

BAROKA: It is a bad thing, then, to sound
Like your school teacher?

SIDI: No, Bale, but words are like beetles
Boring at my ears, and my head
Becomes a jumping bean. Perhaps after all,
As the school teacher tells me often,
[*Very miserably.*]
I have a simple mind.

BAROKA [*pats her kindly on the head*]:
No, Sidi, not simple, only straight and truthful
Like a freshwater reed. But I do find
Your school teacher and I are much alike.
The proof of wisdom is the wish to learn
Even from children. And the haste of youth
Must learn its temper from the gloss
Of ancient leather, from a strength
Knit close along the grain. The school teacher
And I, must learn one from the other.
Is this not right?
[*A tearful nod.*]

BAROKA: The old must flow into the new, Sidi,
Not blind itself or stand foolishly
Apart. A girl like you must inherit
Miracles which age alone reveals.
Is this not so?

SIDI: Everything you say, Bale,
Seems wise to me.

BAROKA: Yesterday's wine alone is strong and blooded, child,

And though the Christians' holy book denies
The truth of this, old wine thrives best
Within a new bottle.[24] The coarseness
Is mellowed down, and the rugged wine
Acquires a full and rounded body. . . .
Is this not so — my child?
[*Quite overcome, Sidi nods.*]

BAROKA: Those who know little of Baroka think
His life one pleasure-living course.
But the monkey sweats, my child,
The monkey sweats,
It is only the hair upon his back
Which still deceives the world. . . .

[*Sidi's head falls slowly on the Bale's shoulder. The Bale remains in his final body-weighed-down-by-burdens-of-State attitude.*

Even before the scene is completely shut off a crowd of dancers burst in at the front and dance off at the opposite side without slackening pace. In their brief appearance it should be apparent that they comprise a group of female dancers pursuing a masked male. Drumming and shouts continue quite audibly and shortly afterwards. They enter and recross the stage in the same manner.

The shouts fade away and they next appear at the market clearing. It is now full evening. Lakunle and Sadiku are still waiting for Sidi's return. The traders are beginning to assemble one by one, ready for the evening market. Hawkers pass through with oil-lamps beside their ware. Food sellers enter with cooking-pots and foodstuffs, set up their "adogan" or stone hearth and build a fire.

All this while, Lakunle is pacing wretchedly, Sadiku looks on placidly.]

LAKUNLE [*he is pacing furiously.*]:
He's killed her.
I warned you. You know him,
And I warned you.
[*Goes up all the approaches to look.*]
She's been gone half the day. It will soon
Be daylight. And still no news.
Women have disappeared before.
No trace. Vanished. Now we know how.
[*Checks, turns round.*]
And why!
Mock an old man, will you? So?
You can laugh? Ha ha! You wait.

---

[24] **old wine . . . new bottle:** According to the parable in Mark 2:22, new wine should not be put into old "bottles," wineskins that have already been stretched out and may burst when the new wine begins to ferment.

I'll come and see you
Whipped like a dog. Baroka's head wife
Driven out of the house for plotting
With a girl.
[*Each approaching footstep brings Lakunle to attention, but it is only a hawker or a passer-by. The wrestler passes. Sadiku greets him familiarly. Then, after he has passed, some significance of this breaks on Sadiku and she begins to look a little puzzled.*]

LAKUNLE: I know he has dungeons. Secret holes
Where a helpless girl will lie
And rot forever. But not for nothing
Was I born a man. I'll find my way
To rescue her. She little deserves it, but
I shall risk my life for her.
[*The mummers*[25] *can now be heard again, distantly. Sadiku and Lakunle become attentive as the noise approaches, Lakunle increasingly uneasy. A little, but not too much notice is paid by the market people.*]
What is that?

SADIKU: If my guess is right, it will be mummers.
[*Adds slyly.*]
Somebody must have told them the news.

LAKUNLE: What news?
[*Sadiku chuckles darkly and comprehension breaks on the school teacher.*]
Baroka! You dared . . . ?
Woman, is there no mercy in your veins?
He gave you children, and he stood
Faithfully by you and them.
He risked his life that you may boast
A warrior-hunter for your lord . . . But you—
You sell him to the rhyming rabble
Gloating in your disloyalty . . .

SADIKU [*calmly dips her hand in his pocket.*]:
Have you any money?

LAKUNLE [*snatching out her hand.*]:
Why? What? . . . Keep away, witch! Have you
Turned pickpocket in your dotage?

SADIKU: Don't be a miser. Will you let them go without giving you a special performance?

LAKUNLE: If you think I care for their obscenity . . .

SADIKU [*wheedling.*]: Come on, school teacher. They'll expect it of you . . . The man of learning . . . the young sprig of foreign wisdom . . . You must not demean yourself in their eyes . . . you must give them money to perform for your lordship. . . .

---

[25] **mummers:** Dancers of pantomime stories.

[*Re-enter the mummers, dancing straight through (more centrally this time) as before. Male dancer enters first, pursued by a number of young women and other choral idlers. The man dances in tortured movements. He and about half of his pursuers have already danced offstage on the opposite side when Sadiku dips her hand briskly in Lakunle's pocket, this time with greater success. Before Lakunle can stop her, she has darted to the drummers and pressed a coin apiece on their foreheads, waving them to possession of the floor. Tilting their heads backwards, they drum her praises. Sadiku denies the credit, points to Lakunle as the generous benefactor. They transfer their attention to him where he stands biting his lips at the trick. The other dancers have now been brought back and the drummers resume the beat of the interrupted dance. The treasurer removes the coins from their foreheads and places them in a pouch. Now begins the dance of virility which is of course none other than the Baroka story. Very athletic movements. Even in his prime, "Baroka" is made a comic figure, held in a kind of tolerant respect by his women. At his decline and final downfall, they are most unsparing in their taunts and tantalizing motions. Sadiku has never stopped bouncing on her toes through the dance, now she is done the honour of being invited to join at the kill. A dumb show of bashful refusals, then she joins them, reveals surprising agility for her age, to the wild enthusiasm of the rest who surround and spur her on. With "Baroka" finally scotched, the crowd dances away to their incoming movement, leaving Sadiku to dance on oblivious of their departure. The drumming becomes more distant and she unwraps her eyelids. Sighs, looks around her, and walks content-edly towards Lakunle. As usual he has enjoyed the spectacle in spite of himself, showing especial relish where "Baroka" gets the worst of it from his women. Sadiku looks at him for a moment while he tries to replace his obvious enjoyment with disdain. She shouts "Boo" at him, and breaks into a dance movement, shakes a sudden leg at Lakunle.*]

SADIKU: Sadiku of the duiker's[26] feet . . . that's what the men used to call me. I could twist and untwist my waist with the smoothness of a water snake . . .

LAKUNLE: No doubt. And you are still just as slippery.
   I hope Baroka kills you for this.
   When he finds out what your wagging tongue
   Has done to him, I hope he beats you
   Till you choke on your own breath. . . .

   [*Sidi bursts in, she has been running all the way. She throws herself on the ground against the tree and sobs violently, beating herself on the ground.*]

SADIKU [*on her knees beside her.*]: Why, child. What is the matter?

SIDI [*pushes her off.*]:
   Get away from me. Do not touch me.

LAKUNLE [*with a triumphant smile, he pulls Sadiku away and takes her place.*]:
   Oh, Sidi, let me kiss your tears. . . .

SIDI [*pushes him so hard that he sits down abruptly.*]:
   Don't touch me.

LAKUNLE [*dusting himself.*]:
   He must have beaten her.
   Did I not warn you both?

---

[26] **duiker:** A small antelope able to leap high in the air.

Baroka is a creature of the wilds,
Untutored, mannerless, devoid of grace.
[*Sidi only cries all the more, beats on the ground with clenched fists, and stubs her toes in the ground.*]
Chief though he is,
I shall kill him for this . . .
No. Better still, I shall demand
Redress from the central courts.
I shall make him spend
The remainder of his wretched life
In prison—with hard labour.
I'll teach him
To beat defenceless women. . . .

SIDI [*lifting her head.*]:
Fool! You little fools! It was a lie.
The frog. The cunning frog!
He lied to you, Sadiku.

SADIKU: Sango forbid!

SIDI: He told me . . . afterwards, crowing.
It was a trick.
He knew Sadiku would not keep it to herself,
That I, or maybe other maids would hear of it
And go to mock his plight.
And how he laughed!
How his frog-face croaked and croaked
And called me little fool!
Oh how I hate him! How I loathe
And long to kill the man!

LAKUNLE [*retreating.*]: But Sidi, did he . . . ? I mean . . .
Did you escape?
[*Louder sobs from Sidi.*]
Speak, Sidi, this is agony.
Tell me the worst; I'll take it like a man.
Is it the fright which affects you so,
Or did he . . . ? Sidi, I cannot bear the thought.
The words refuse to form.
Do not unman me, Sidi. Speak
Before I burst in tears.

SADIKU [*raises Sidi's chin in her hand.*]:
Sidi, are you a maid or not?
[*Sidi shakes her head violently and bursts afresh in tears.*]

LAKUNLE: The Lord forbid!

SADIKU: Too late for prayers. Cheer up. It happens to the best of us.

LAKUNLE: Oh heavens, strike me dead!
Earth, open up and swallow Lakunle.

For he no longer has the wish to live.
Let the lightning fall and shrivel me
To dust and ashes. . . .
[*Recoils.*]
No, that wish is cowardly. This trial is my own.
Let Sango and his lightning keep out of this. It
Is my cross, and let it not be spoken that
In the hour of need, Lakunle stood
Upon the scales and was proved wanting.
My love is selfless—the love of spirit
Not of flesh.
[*Stands over Sidi.*]
Dear Sidi, we shall forget the past.
This great misfortune touches not
The treasury of my love.
But you will agree, it is only fair
That we forget the bride-price totally
Since you no longer can be called a maid.
Here is my hand, if on these terms
You'll be my cherished wife.
We'll take an oath, between us three
That this shall stay
A secret to our dying days . . .
[*Takes a look at Sadiku and adds quickly.*]
Oh no, a secret even after we're dead and gone.
And if Baroka dares to boast of it,
I'll swear he is a liar—and swear by Sango too!
[*Sidi raises herself slowly, staring at Lakunle with unbelieving eyes. She is unsmiling, her face a puzzle.*]

SIDI: You would? You would marry me?
LAKUNLE [*puffs out his chest.*]: Yes.
[*Without a change of expression, Sidi dashes suddenly off the stage.*]
SADIKU: What on earth has got into her?
LAKUNLE: I wish I knew
She took off suddenly
Like a hunted buck.
[*Looks offstage.*]
I think—yes, she is,
She is going home.
Sadiku, will you go?
Find out if you can
What she plans to do.
[*Sadiku nods and goes. Lakunle walks up and down.*]
And now I know I am the biggest fool
That ever walked this earth.

There are women to be found
In every town or village in these parts,
And every one a virgin.
But I obey my books.
[*Distant music. Light drums, flutes, box-guitars, "sekere."*[27]]
"Man takes the fallen woman by the hand"
And ever after they live happily.
Moreover, I will admit,
It solves the problem of her bride-price too.
A man must live or fall by his true
Principles. That, I had sworn,
Never to pay.
[*Enter Sadiku.*]

SADIKU: She is packing her things. She is gathering her clothes and trinkets together, and oiling herself as a bride does before her wedding.

LAKUNLE: Heaven help us! I am not impatient.
Surely she can wait a day or two at least.
There is the asking to be done,
And then I have to hire a praise-singer,
And such a number of ceremonies
Must firstly be performed.

SADIKU: Just what I said but she only laughed at me and called me a . . . a . . . what was it now . . . a bra . . . braba . . . brabararian. It serves you right. It all comes of your teaching. I said what about the asking and the other ceremonies. And she looked at me and said, leave all that nonsense to savages and brabararians.

LAKUNLE: But I must prepare myself
I cannot be
A single man one day and a married one the next.
It must come gradually.
I will not wed in haste.
A man must have time to prepare,
To learn to like the thought.
I must think of my pupils too:
Would they be pleased if I were married
Not asking their consent . . . ?
[*The singing group is now audible even to him.*]
What is that? The musicians?
Could they have learnt so soon?

SADIKU: The news of a festivity travels fast. You ought to know that.

LAKUNLE: The goddess of malicious gossip
Herself must have a hand in my undoing.

---

[27] "**sekere**": Percussion instrument made by lacing strings of shells around a calabash.

The very spirits of the partial air
Have all conspired to blow me, willy-nilly
Down the slippery slope of grim matrimony.
What evil have I done . . . ? Ah, here they come!
[*Enter crowd and musicians.*]
Go back. You are not needed yet. Nor ever.
Hence parasites, you've made a big mistake.
There is no one getting wedded; get you home.
[*Sidi now enters. In one hand she holds a bundle, done up in a richly embroidered
cloth: in the other the magazine. She is radiant, jewelled, lightly clothed, and wears
light leather-thong sandals. They all go suddenly silent except for the long-drawn
O-Ohs of admiration. She goes up to Lakunle and hands him the book.*]

SIDI: A present from Sidi.
I tried to tear it up
But my fingers were too frail.
[*To the crowd.*]
Let us go.
[*To Lakunle.*]
You may come too if you wish,
You are invited.

LAKUNLE [*lost in the miracle of transformation.*]:
Well I should hope so indeed
Since I am to marry you.

SIDI [*turns round in surprise.*]:
Marry who . . . ? You thought . . .
Did you really think that you, and I . . .
Why, did you think that after him,
I could endure the touch of another man?
I who have felt the strength,
The perpetual youthful zest
Of the panther of the trees?
And would I choose a watered-down,
A beardless version of unripened man?

LAKUNLE [*bars her way.*]:
I shall not let you.
I shall protect you from yourself.

SIDI [*gives him a shove that sits him down again, hard against the tree base.*]:
Out of my way, book-nourished shrimp.
Do you see what strength he has given me?
That was not bad. For a man of sixty,
It was the secret of God's own draught
A deed for drums and ballads.
But you, at sixty, you'll be ten years dead!
In fact, you'll not survive your honeymoon. . . .

Come to my wedding if you will. If not . . .
[*She shrugs her shoulders. Kneels down at Sadiku's feet.*]
Mother of brides, your blessing . . .

SADIKU [*lays her hand on Sidi's head.*]: I invoke the fertile gods. They will stay with you. May the time come soon when you shall be as round-bellied as a full moon in a low sky.

SIDI [*hands her the bundle.*]:
Now bless my worldly goods.
[*Turns to the musicians.*]
Come, sing to me of seeds
Of children, sired of the lion stock.
[*The musicians resume their tune. Sidi sings and dances.*]
Mo te'ni. Mo te'ni.
Mo te'ni. Mo te'ni.
Sun mo mi, we mo mi
Sun mo mi, fa mo mi
Yarabi lo m'eyi t'o le d'omo . . .
[*Festive air, fully pervasive. Oil lamps from the market multiply as traders desert their stalls to join them. A young girl flaunts her dancing buttocks at Lakunle and he rises to the bait. Sadiku gets in his way as he gives chase. Tries to make him dance with her. Lakunle last seen, having freed himself of Sadiku, clearing a space in the crowd for the young girl.*
The crowd repeat the song after Sidi.]
Tolani Tolani
T'emi ni T'emi ni
Sun mo mi, we mo mi
Sun mo mi, fa mo mi
Yarabi lo m'eyi t'o le d'omo.[28]

THE END

---

[28]Mo te'ni . . . d'omo:
My net is spread. My net is spread.
Come close to me, wrap yourself around me.
Only God knows which moment makes the child . . .

Tolani Tolani
She belongs to me, belongs to me.
Come close to me, wrap yourself around me.
Only God knows which moment makes the child.
[From *Collected Plays 2.*]

～ ANITA DESAI
B. INDIA, 1937

There is a strong tradition in India of women as storytellers, as transmitters of tales of the gods, animal fables, and family and village histories. It is not surprising, therefore, that when the Western literary genre of the short story was introduced into India in the nineteenth century, women soon followed the early example of the Bengali writer Rabindranath Tagore[1] and began writing short fiction themselves. By the late 1920s, there were already several journals in India dedicated exclusively to the publication of women's writing. Contemporary India boasts a large number of women writers, some of whom, like **Amrita Pritam**, Kamala Das, **Bharati Mukherjee**,[2] and Anita Desai, have attracted international admiration for their work. Like their male colleagues, they are often drawn to postcolonial themes: the movement of rural populations into cities, the violent displacement of tribal peoples and families in the 1947 partition of India into India and Pakistan, the conflict between European and Indian ways and the anxiety of choosing among them, and the rapid changes in social conditions as contemporary India moves further and further away from Gandhi's spiritual and social vision[3] toward a multi-corporate capitalist state. In addition, Indian women writers are especially concerned with what happens to women in the midst of these circumstances, with the specific oppressions Indian women continue to endure, with Indian women's anger and survival strategies, with women's strengths and the bonds among women. Desai's fiction in particular often centers on women from urban and somewhat Westernized middle-class Indian families who are troubled by conflicts between the cultures, the generations, and the sexes.

UM-rih-tuh PREE-tum;
BAH-ruh-tee
MUCK-ur-jee

A Multicultural Background. **Anita Desai** was born on June 24, 1937, in Mussoorie, India, to Toni Nime Mazumdar, a German woman, and D. N. Mazumdar, a successful Bengali businessman. She grew up in a comfortable multilingual and multicultural household in Old Delhi with her brothers and sisters, the sort of child her mother gently teased for

uh-NEE-tuh deh-SIGH

---

[1] **Rabindranath Tagore** (1861–1941): The leading writer of the Bengali Renaissance, Tagore inspired many younger writers to write poetry and fiction in the Bengali language. See Book 5.

[2] **Pritam . . . Mukherjee:** Amrita Pritam (b. 1919), first prominent Punjabi woman poet and fiction writer, author of twenty-eight novels, eighteen collections of poetry, and numerous other works. Kamala Das (b. 1934, now Kamala Surayya, after converting to Islam), poet, fiction writer, and columnist best known for her Krishna poems, her frank autobiography, *My Story*, and her many collections of poems, including *Only the Soul Knows How to Sing* (1996). Bharati Mukherjee (b. 1940), novelist best known for *The Tiger's Daughter* (1971) and *Jasmine* (1989). See page 1316.

[3] **Gandhi's . . . vision:** As leader of the Indian independence movement, Mohandas Gandhi advocated nonviolent resistance to colonial rule and a return to a simple economy based on hand crafts, home industries, and local self-sufficiency.

www For links to more information about Anita Desai and a quiz on "The Farewell Party," and for information about the culture and context of India in the twentieth century, see *World Literature Online* at bedfordstmartins .com/worldlit.

being a *lese Ratte,* or "reading rat," the German term for a bookworm. Although she spoke German and Hindi at home, Desai learned English at school. "It was the first language that I learned to read and write," the author has commented, "so it became my literary language. Languages tend to proliferate around one in India, and one tends to use whatever is at hand. It makes one realize each language has its own distinct genius." Her true awakening as a reader and writer came when she was nine and chose idly from her parents' bookshelves a copy of Emily Brontë's *Wuthering Heights.* As she read on, she recalls, "my own world of an Old Delhi bungalow, its verandas and plastered walls and ceiling fans, its gardens of papaya and guava trees full of shrieking parakeets, the gritty dust that settled on the pages of a book before one could turn them, all receded. What became real, dazzlingly real, through the power of Emily Brontë's pen was the Yorkshire moors, the storm-driven heath."

Desai earned her B.A. from Delhi University in 1957, having come to admire the work of Chekhov, Dostoevsky, D. H. Lawrence, and E. M. Forster,[4] and began to publish her own short fiction. She married Ashvin Desai, a corporate executive, in the year after her graduation. The Desais, now the parents of four children, have lived in New Delhi, Calcutta, Bombay, and other Indian cities. Anita Desai has taught at several colleges and universities in England and the United States. She currently divides her time between India and America, teaching one semester each year at the Massachusetts Institute of Technology.

Desai's Literary Career.   In her early novels, Desai told the stories of women living in a variety of social situations in India. Her first novel, *Cry, The Peacock,* appeared in 1963; its main character is an Indian woman whose traditional upbringing has made it nearly impossible for her to voice or act on her personal desires. *Voices of the City* (1965) describes the lives of three sisters in Calcutta and their differing responses to the city, while *Fire on the Mountain* (1977) examines the oppressed lives of three women in a rural hill village and the generational conflicts in Indian families. Although Desai has asserted that her novels "are no reflection of Indian society, politics, or character" but rather her "private attempt to seize upon the new material of life," they do provide a personal perspective on India, its contemporary history and situation. In *The Clear Light of Day,* for example, two sisters view the partition of India, in 1947, from differing points of view. *Baumgartner's Bombay* (1988) draws from both sides of Desai's heritage, as it tells the story of a gentle German Jew who flees the Holocaust to make his home in India, only to meet his end in the contemporary Bombay underworld of drug dealing and violence. *Journey to Ithaca* (1995) looks at India from both Indian and European per-

---

[4] **Chekhov . . . Forster:** Realist writers of the late nineteenth and early twentieth century. Anton Chekhov (1860–1904) was a Russian short-story writer and playwright. Fyodor Dostoevsky (1821–1881) was a Russian novelist and author of *The Brothers Karamazov* (1879–80) and other works of psychological fiction. D. H. Lawrence (1885–1930), the English novelist, poet, and travel writer, was best known for *Sons and Lovers* (1913). E. M. Forster (1879–1970) was an English novelist whose *A Passage to India* (1924) is a classic on late British colonialism in India.

spectives as it tells the stories of three Europeans who come to India seeking spiritual enlightenment. In addition to her novels, Desai has written several children's books and a collection of short stories, *Games at Twilight* (1978), which includes "The Farewell Party."

■ CONNECTIONS

Rassundari Devi, *Amar Jiban* (Book 5); Rabindranath Tagore, "Broken Ties" (Book 5); Rokeya Hossain, "Sultana's Dream," p. 323; Bharati Mukherjee, "A Wife's Story," p. 1316. Desai's take on Bina's place as a woman in middle-class Indian culture adds another dimension to the accounts of the lives of Indian women in Devi's *My Life (Amar Jiban)*, Tagore's "Broken Ties," Hossain's "Sultana's Dream," and Mukherjee's "A Wife's Story." Do these works, spanning the last century or so, indicate significant changes in the situation of women in India? What continuities do you see between the lives of the women in the earlier works and those in works written more recently?

James Joyce, "The Dead," p. 372. Both "The Farewell Party" and Joyce's "The Dead" use a party to bring out the differences between their protagonists and the cultures in which they live. How are Bina and her husband alienated from the town they are leaving? Is their alienation similar to Gabriel's in "The Dead"? Consider the use of music in the two stories. Do the Irish folk songs in Joyce's story have a similar significance to the Tagore song in "The Farewell Party"?

Petronius, *The Satyricon* (Book 1); Leo Tolstoy, *The Death of Ivan Ilych* (Book 5). Desai's treatment of the corporate culture of a provincial Indian town mildly satirizes middle-class mores and values. What specifically does Desai satirize? Is the overall effect of her story, like that of Petronius's account of Trimalchio's feast, satiric? Think about the point of view from which the story is told. With which character in the story is the narrator most closely allied? Compare the point of view with that in Tolstoy's *The Death of Ivan Ilych*. Both Ivan and Bina learn through suffering. Is the tone at the end of the two stories similar? With whom do you sympathize more, Ivan or Bina?

■ FURTHER RESEARCH

Criticism
Bande, U. *The Novels of Anita Desai.* 1988.
Belliopa, Meena. *The Fiction of Anita Desai.* 1971.
Dash, Sandhyarani. *Novels of Anita Desai.* 1997.
Prasad, V. V. N. Rajendra. *Anita Desai.* 1997.
Solanki, M. *Anita Desai's Fiction.* 1993.

■ PRONUNCIATION

Anita Desai: un-NEE-tuh deh-SIGH
Bharati Mukherjee: BAH-ruh-tee MUCK-ur-jee
Amrita Pritam: UM-rih-tuh PREE-tum
Shantiniketan: shun-tee-nee-KAY-tun

[English] was the first language that I learned to read and write, so it became my literary language. Languages tend to proliferate around one in India, and one tends to use whatever is at hand. It makes one realize each language has its own distinct genius.

– Anita Desai

Desai has been compared to Jane Austen, and, indeed, she is a deceptively gracious storyteller, writing like an embroiderer concealing a sword as she creates family microcosms that embody all the delusions and cruelties of society-at-large.

– Donna Seaman, 1999

∽ The Farewell Party

Before the party she had made a list, faintheartedly, and marked off the items as they were dealt with, inexorably—cigarettes, soft drinks, ice, *kebabs,* and so on. But she had forgotten to provide lights. The party was to be held on the lawn: On these dry summer nights one could plan a lawn party weeks in advance and be certain of fine weather, and she had thought happily of how the roses would be in bloom and of the stars and perhaps even fireflies, so decorative and discreet, all gracefully underlining her unsuspected talent as a hostess. But she had not realised that there would be no moon and therefore it would be very dark on the lawn. All the lights on the verandah, in the portico, and indoors were on, like so many lanterns, richly copper and glowing with extraordinary beauty as though aware that the house would soon be empty and these were the last few days of illumination and family life, but they did very little to light the lawn which was vast, a still lake of inky grass.

Wandering about with a glass in one hand and a plate of cheese biscuits in another, she gave a start now and then to see an acquaintance emerge from the darkness, which had the gloss, the sheen, the coolness but not the weight of water, and present her with a face, vague and without outlines but eventually recognisable. "Oh," she cried several times that evening, "I didn't know you had arrived. I've been looking for you," she would add with unaccustomed intimacy (was it because of the gin and lime, her second, or because such warmth could safely be held to lead to

---

"The Farewell Party." From Desai's 1978 collection *Games at Twilight,* this story displays the author's sure touch with imagery and dialogue. As James Joyce does in "The Dead," Desai here follows her characters through the unfolding of an evening gathering, where seemingly banal conversation becomes fascinating as it reveals more and more about the story's main characters and the Euro-Indian corporate world they inhabit, a world neither wholly European nor Indian. Forced to be competitive and mobile, these executives find themselves and their families cut off from the intimacy that once characterized Indian life. Only at a farewell party, when there is no danger of seeing the departing couple again and all exchanges are made easier by alcohol can these people express affection for one another. The adults' more thoroughly Westernized teenaged children twist to Beatles records and giggle and shriek while they swig Coca-Cola, but the uneasy parents have nearly forgotten how to enjoy themselves.

As the night deepens, more is learned about the host couple, the Ramans, who have been further isolated by their own natural shyness and by the needs of Nono, their severely handicapped eldest child. Finally, when most of the guests have gone, the doctors from the local hospital come forward. They have been hanging back in the shadows, shy before the corporate executives, but of all the partygoers they alone have truly shared a part of the Ramans' lives in their joint concern for Nono, even though they have never socialized with his parents before. Free now to bring Nono out to the party, Bina sits with her son among people who care about him and relaxes at last. One of the doctors' wives sings into the darkness an old Rabindranath Tagore song in Bengali about a woman compelled to sail away and leave her family behind. Even as the song creates a bond for this small circle of newly intimate people soon to be separated, its simple lyrics and the regional language in which it is sung evoke all the poignancy of lost relationships and connectedness.

All notes are the editors'.

nothing now that they were leaving town?). The guest, also having had several drinks between beds of flowering balsam and torenias before launching out onto the lawn, responded with an equal vivacity. Sometimes she had her arm squeezed or a hand slid down the bareness of her back—which was athletic: she had once played tennis, rather well—and once someone said, "I've been hiding in this corner, watching you," while another went so far as to say, "Is it true you are leaving us, Bina? How can you be so cruel?" And if it were a woman guest, the words were that much more effusive. It was all heady, astonishing.

It was astonishing because Bina was a frigid and friendless woman. She was thirty-five. For fifteen years she had been bringing up her children and, in particular, nursing the eldest who was severely spastic. This had involved her deeply in the workings of the local hospital and with its many departments and doctors, but her care for this child was so intense and so desperate that her relationship with them was purely professional. Outside this circle of family and hospital—ringed, as it were, with barbed wire and lit with one single floodlight—Bina had no life. The town had scarcely come to know her for its life turned in the more jovial circles of mah-jong, bridge, coffee parties, club evenings, and, occasionally, a charity show in aid of the Red Cross. For these Bina had a kind of sad contempt and certainly no time. A tall, pale woman, heavy-boned and sallow, she had a certain presence, a certain dignity, and people, having heard of the spastic child, liked and admired her, but she had not thought she had friends. Yet tonight they were coming forth from the darkness in waves that quite overwhelmed.

Now here was Mrs. Ray, the Commissioner's wife, chirping inside a nest of rustling embroidered organza. "Why are you leaving us so soon, Mrs. Raman? You've only been here—two years, is it?"

"Five," exclaimed Bina, widening her eyes, herself surprised at such a length of time. Although time dragged heavily in their household, agonisingly slow, and the five years had been so hard that sometimes, at night, she did not know how she had crawled through the day and if she would crawl through another, her back almost literally broken by the weight of the totally dependent child and of the three smaller ones who seemed perpetually to clamour for their share of attention, which they felt they never got. Yet now these five years had telescoped. They were over. The Raman family was moving and their time here was spent. There had been the hospital, the girls' school, the boys' school, picnics, monsoons, birthday parties, and measles. Crushed together into a handful. She gazed down at her hands, tightened around glass and plate. "Time has flown," she murmured incredulously.

"Oh, I wish you were staying, Mrs. Raman," cried the Commissioner's wife and, as she squeezed Bina's arm, her fragrant talcum powder seemed to lift off her chalky shoulders and some of it settled on Bina who sneezed. "It's been so nice to have a family like yours here. It's a small town, so little to do, at least one must have good friends . . ."

Bina blinked at such words of affection from a woman she had met twice, perhaps thrice before. Bina and her husband did not go in for society. The shock of their first child's birth had made them both fanatic parents. But she knew that not everyone considered this vital factor in their lives, and spoke of "social duties" in a somehow reproving tone. The Commissioner's wife had been annoyed, she always felt, by her refusal to help out at the Red Cross fair. The hurt silence with which her refusal had been accepted had implied the importance of these "social duties" of which Bina remained so stubbornly unaware.

However, this one evening, this last party, was certainly given over to their recognition and celebration. "Oh, everyone, everyone is here," rejoiced the Commissioner's wife, her eyes snapping from face to face in that crowded aquarium, and, at a higher pitch, cried "Renu, why weren't you at the mah-jong party this morning?" and moved off into another powdery organza embrace that rose to meet her from the night like a moth and then was submerged again in the shadows of the lawn. Bina gave one of those smiles that easily frightened people found mocking, a shade too superior, somewhat scornful. Looking down into her glass of gin and lime, she moved on and in a minute found herself brought up short against the quite regal although overweight figure, in raw silk and homespun and the somewhat saturnine air of underpaid culture, of Bose, an employee of the local museum whom she had met once or twice at the art competitions and exhibitions to which she was fond of hauling her children, whether reluctant or enthusiastic, because "it made a change," she said.

"Mrs. Raman," he said in the fruity tones of the culture-bent Bengali, "how we'll miss you at the next children's art competitions. You used to be my chief inspiration—"

"Inspiration?" she laughed, incredulously, spilling some of her drink and proffering the plate of cheese biscuits from which he helped himself, half-bowing as though it were gold she offered, gems.

"Yes, yes, inspiration," he went on, even more fruitily now that his mouth was full. "Think of me—alone, the hapless organiser—surrounded by mammas, by primary school teachers, by three, four, five hundred children. And the judges—they are always the most trouble, those judges. And then I look at you—so cool, controlling your children, handling them so wonderfully and with such superb results—my inspiration!"

She was flustered by this unaccustomed vision of herself and half-turned her face away from Bose the better to contemplate it, but could find no reflection of it in the ghostly white bush of the Queen of the Night, and listened to him murmur on about her unkindness in deserting him in this cultural backwater to that darkest of dooms—guardian of a provincial museum—where he saw no one but school teachers herding children through his halls or, worse, Government officials who periodically and inexplicably stirred to create trouble for him and made their official presences felt amongst the copies of the Ajanta frescoes (in which even the mouldy and peeled-off portions were carefully reproduced) and the cupboards of Indus Valley seals. Murmuring commiseration, she left him to a gloomy young professor of history who was languishing at another of the institutions of provincial backwaters that they so deplored and whose wife was always having a baby, and slipped away, still feeling an unease at Bose's unexpected vision of her which did not tally with the cruder reality, into the less equivocal company provided by a ring of twittering "company wives."

These women she had always encountered in just such a ring as they formed now, the kind that garden babblers form under a hedge where they sit gabbling and whirring with social bitchiness, and she had always stood outside it, smiling stiffly, not wanting to join and refusing their effusively nodded invitation. They were the wives of men who represented various mercantile companies in the town—Imperial Tobacco, Brooke Bond, Esso, and so on—and although they might seem exactly alike to one who did not belong to this circle, inside it were subtle gradations of importance according to the particular company for which each one's husband worked and of these only they themselves were initiates. Bina was, however unwillingly, an initiate. Her husband worked for one of these companies but she had always stiffly refused to recognise these gradations, or consider them. They noted the rather set sulkiness of her silence when amongst them and privately labelled her queer, proud, boring, and difficult. Also, they felt she belonged to their circle whether she liked it or not.

Now she entered this circle with diffidence, wishing she had stayed with the more congenial Bose (why hadn't she? What was it in her that made her retreat from anything like a friendly approach?) and was taken aback to find their circle parting to admit her and hear their cries of welcome and affection that did not, however, lose the stridency and harshness of garden babblers' voices.

"Bina, how do you like the idea of going back to Bombay?"

"Have you started packing, Bina? Poor you. Oh, are you having packers over from Delhi? Oh well, then it's not so bad."

Never had they been so vociferous in her company, so easy, so warm. They were women to whom the most awful thing that had ever happened was the screw of a golden earring disappearing down the bathroom sink or a mother-in-law's visit or an ayah[1] deserting just before the arrival of guests: what could they know of Bina's life, Bina's ordeal? She cast her glance at the drinks they held—but they were mostly of orange squash. Only the Esso wife, who participated in amateur dramatics and ran a boutique and was rather taller and bolder than the rest, held a whisky and soda. So much affection generated by just orange squash? Impossible. Rather tentatively, she offered them the remains of the cheese biscuits, found herself chirping replies, deploring the nuisance of having packing crates all over the house, talking of the flat they would move into in Bombay, and then, sweating unobtrusively with the strain, saw another recognisable fish swim towards her from the edge of the liquescent lawn, and swung away in relief, saying, "Mrs. D'Souza! How late you are, but I'm so glad—" for she really was.

Mrs. D'Souza was her daughter's teacher at the convent school and had clearly never been to a cocktail party before so that all Bina's compassion was aroused by those school-scuffed shoes and her tea-party best—quite apart from the simple truth that she found in her an honest individuality that all those beautifully dressed and poised babblers lacked, being stamped all over by the plain rubber stamps of their husbands' companies—and she hurried off to find Mrs. D'Souza something

---

[1] ayah: A nanny or maidservant.

suitable to drink. "Sherry? Why yes, I think I'll be able to find you some," she said, a bit flabbergasted at such an unexpected fancy of the pepper-haired school teacher, "and I'll see if Tara's around—she'll want to see you," she added, vaguely and fraudulently, wondering why she had asked Mrs. D'Souza to a cocktail party, only to see, as she skirted the rose bed, the admirable Bose appear at her side and envelop her in this strange intimacy that marked the whole evening, and went off, light-hearted, towards the table where her husband was trying, with the help of some hired waiters in soggy white uniforms with the name of the restaurant from which they were hired embroidered in red across their pockets, to cope with the flood of drinks this party atmosphere had called for and released.

Harassed, perspiring, his feet burning, Raman was nevertheless pleased to be so obviously employed and be saved the strain of having to converse with his motley assembly of guests: he had no more gift for society than his wife had. Ice cubes were melting on the tablecloth in sopping puddles and he had trouble in keeping track of his bottles: They were, besides the newly bought dozens of beer bottles and Black Knight whisky, the remains of their five years in this town that he now wished to bring to their end—bottles brought by friends from trips abroad, bottles bought cheap through "contacts" in the army or air force, some gems, extravaganzas bought for anniversaries such as a nearly full bottle of Vat 69, a bottle with a bit of *crème de menthe* growing sticky at the bottom, some brown sherry with a great deal of rusty sediment, a red Golconda wine from Hyderabad, and a bottle of Remy Martin that he was keeping guiltily to himself, pouring small quantities into a whisky glass at his elbow and gulping it down in between mixing some very weird cocktails for his guests. There was no one at the party he liked well enough to share it with. Oh, one of the doctors perhaps, but where were they? Submerged in grass, in dark, in night and chatter, clatter of ice in glass, teeth on biscuit, teeth on teeth. Enamel and gold. Crumbs and dregs. All awash, all soaked in night. Watery sound of speech, liquid sound of drink. Water and ice and night. It occurred to him that everyone had forgotten him, the host, that it was a mistake to have stationed himself amongst the waiters, that he ought to move out, mingle with the guests. But he felt himself drowned, helplessly and quite delightfully, in Remy Martin, in grass, in a border of purple torenias.

Then he was discovered by his son who galloped through the ranks of guests and waiters to fling himself at his father and ask if he could play the new Beatles record, his friends had asked to hear it.

Raman considered, taking the opportunity to pour out and gulp down some more of the precious Remy Martin. "All right," he said, after a judicious minute or two, "but keep it low, everyone won't want to hear it," not adding that he himself didn't, for his taste in music ran to slow and melancholy, folk at its most frivolous. Still, he glanced into the lighted room where his children and the children of neighbours and guests had collected, making themselves tipsy on Fanta and Coca-Cola, the girls giggling in a multicoloured huddle and the boys swaggering around the record-player with a kind of lounging strut, holding bottles in their hands with a sophisticated ease, exactly like experienced cocktail party guests, so that he smiled and wished he had a ticket, a passport that would make it possible to break into that party within a party. It was chillingly obvious to him that he hadn't one. He also saw that a good deal of their riotousness was due to the fact that they were raiding the snack trays that the waiters carried through the room to the lawn, and that they were seeing to it that the trays emerged half-empty. He knew he ought to go in and see about it but he hadn't the heart, or the nerve. He couldn't join that party but he wouldn't wreck it either so he only caught hold of one of the waiters and suggested that the snack trays be carried out from the kitchen straight onto the lawn, not by way of the drawing-room, and led him towards a group that seemed to be without snacks and saw too late that it was a group of the company executives that he loathed most. He half-groaned, then hiccuped at his mistake, but it was too late to alter course now. He told himself that he ought to see to it that the snacks were offered around without snag or error.

Poor Raman was placed in one of the lower ranks of the companies' hierarchy. That is, he did not belong to a British concern, or even to an American-collaboration one, but merely to an Indian one. Oh, a long-established, prosperous, and solid one but, still, only Indian. Those cigarettes that he passed around were made by his own company. Somehow it struck a note of bad taste amongst these fastidious men who played golf, danced at the club on Independence Eve and New Year's Eve, invited at least one foreign couple to every party, and called their decorative wives "darling" when in public. Poor Raman never had belonged. It was so obvious to everyone, even to himself, as he passed around those awful cigarettes that sold so well in the market. It had been obvious since their first disastrous dinner party for this very ring of jocular gentlemen, five years ago. Nono had cried right through the party, Bina had spent the evening racing upstairs to see to the babies' baths and bedtime and then crawling reluctantly down, the hired cook had got drunk and stolen two of the chickens so that there was not enough on the table, no one had relaxed for a minute or enjoyed a second—it had been too sad and harrowing even to make a good story or a funny anecdote. They had all let it sink by mutual consent and the invitations to play a round of golf on Saturday afternoon or a rubber of bridge on Sunday morning had been issued and refused with conspiratorial smoothness. Then there was that distressing hobby of Raman's: his impossibly long walks on which he picked up bits of wood and took them home to sandpaper and chisel and then call wood sculpture. What could one do with a chap who did that? He himself wasn't sure if he pursued such odd tastes because he was a social pariah or if he was one on account of this oddity. Not to speak of the spastic child. Now that didn't even bear thinking of, and so it was no wonder that Raman swayed towards them so hesitantly, as though he were wading through water instead of over clipped grass, and handed his cigarettes around with such an apologetic air.

But, after all, hesitation and apology proved unnecessary. One of them—was he Polson's Coffee or Brooke Bond Tea?—clasped Raman about the shoulders as proper men do on meeting, and hearty voices rose together, congratulating him on his promotion (it wasn't one, merely a transfer, and they knew it), envying him his move to the metropolis. They talked as if they had known each other for years, shared all kinds of public schoolboy fun. One—was he Voltas or Ciba?—talked of golf matches at the Willingdon as though he had often played there with Raman, another spoke of *kebabs* eaten on the roadside after a party as though Raman had been one of the gang. Amazed and grateful as a schoolboy admitted to a closed society, Raman nodded and put in a few cautious words, put away his cigarettes, called a waiter to refill their glasses, and broke away before the clock struck twelve and the golden carriage turned into a pumpkin, he himself into a mouse. He hated mice.

Walking backwards, he walked straight into the soft barrier of Miss Dutta's ample back wrapped and bound in rich Madras silk.

"Sorry, sorry, Miss Dutta, I'm clumsy as a bear," he apologised, but here, too, there was no call for apology for Miss Dutta was obviously delighted at having been bumped into.

"My dear Mr. Raman, what can you expect if you invite the whole town to your party?" she asked in that piercing voice that invariably made her companions drop theirs self-consciously. "You and Bina have been so popular—what are we going to do without you?"

He stood pressing his glass with white-tipped fingers and tried to think what he or Bina had provided her with that she could possibly miss. In any case, Miss Dutta could always manage, and did manage, everything single-handedly. She was the town busybody, secretary and chairman of more committees than he could count: They ranged from the Film Society to the Blood Bank, from the Red Cross to the Friends of the Museum, for Miss Dutta was nothing if not versatile. "We hardly ever saw you at our film shows of course," her voice rang out, making him glance furtively over his shoulder to see if anyone were listening, "but it was so nice *knowing* you were in town and that I could count on you. So few people here *care,* you know," she went on, and affectionately bumped her comfortable middle-aged body into his as someone squeezed by, making him remember that he had once heard her called a man-eater, and wonder which man she had eaten and even consider, for a moment, if there were not, after all, some charm in those powdered creases of her creamy arms, equalling if not surpassing that of his worn and harassed wife's bony angles. Why did suffering make for angularity? he even asked himself with uncharacteristic unkindness. But when Miss Dutta laid an arm on top of his glass-holding one and raised herself on her toes to bray something into his ear, he loyally decided that he was too accustomed to sharp angles to change them for such unashamed luxuriance, and, contriving to remove her arm by grasping her elbow—how one's fingers sank into the stuff!—he steered her towards his wife who was standing at the table and inefficiently pouring herself another gin and lime.

"This is my third," she confessed hurriedly, "and I can't tell you how gay it makes me feel. I giggle at everything everyone says."

"Good," he pronounced, feeling inside a warm expansion of relief at seeing her lose, for the moment, her tension and anxiety. "Let's hear you giggle," he said, sloshing some more gin into her glass.

"Look at those children," she exclaimed, and they stood in a bed of balsam, irredeemably crushed, and looked into the lighted drawing room where their daughter was at the moment the cynosure of all juvenile eyes, having thrown herself with abandon into a dance of monkey-like movements. "What is it, Miss Dutta?" the awed mother enquired. "You're more up in the latest fashions than I am—is it the twist, the rock, or the jungle?" and all three watched, enthralled, till Tara began to totter and, losing her simian grace, collapsed against some wildly shrieking girlfriends.

A bit embarrassed by their daughter's reckless abandon, the parents discussed with Miss Dutta, whose finger by her own admission was placed squarely on the pulse of youth, the latest trends in juvenile culture on which Miss Dutta gave a neat sociological discourse (all the neater for having been given earlier that day at the convocation of the Home Science College) and Raman wondered uneasily at this opening of floodgates in his own family—his wife grown giggly with gin, his daughter performing wildly to a Chubby Checker record—how had it all come about? Was it the darkness all about them, dense as the heavy curtains about a stage, that made them act, for an hour or so, on the tiny lighted stage of brief intimacy with such a lack of inhibition? Was it the drink, so freely sloshing from end to end of the house and lawn on account of his determination to clear out his "cellar" (actually one-half of the sideboard and the top shelf of the wardrobe in his dressing-room) and his muddling and mixing them, making up untried and experimental cocktails and lavishly pouring out the whisky without a measure? But these were solid and everyday explanations and there was about this party something out of the ordinary and everyday—at least to the Ramans, normally so austere and unpopular. He knew the real reason too—it was all because the party had been labelled a "farewell party," everyone knew it was the last one, that the Ramans were leaving and they would not meet up again. There was about it exactly that kind of sentimental euphoria that is generated at a shipboard party, the one given on the last night before the end of the voyage. Everyone draws together with an intimacy, a lack of inhibition not displayed or guessed at before, knowing this is the last time, tomorrow they will be dispersed, it will be over. They will not meet, be reminded of it or be required to repeat it.

As if to underline this new and Cinderella's ball–like atmosphere of friendliness and gaiety, three pairs of neighbours now swept in (and three kochias lay down and died under their feet, to the gardener's rage and sorrow): the couple who lived to the Ramans' left, the couple who lived to their right, and the couple from across the road, all crying, "So sorry to be late, but you know what a long way we had to come," making everyone laugh identically at the identical joke. Despite the disparity in their looks and ages—one couple was very young, another middle-aged, the third grandparents—they were, in a sense, as alike as the company executives and their wives, for they too bore a label if a less alarming one: neighbours, it said. Because they were neighbours, and although they had never been more than nodded to over the hedge, waved to in passing cars or spoken to about anything other than their children, dogs, flowers, and gardens, their talk had a vivid immediacy that went straight to the heart.

"Diamond's going to miss you so—he'll be heartbroken," moaned the grandparents who lived alone in their spotless house with a black labrador who had made a habit of visiting the Ramans whenever he wanted young company, a romp on the lawn, or an illicit biscuit.

"I don't know what my son will do without Diamond," reciprocated Bina with her new and sympathetic warmth. "He'll force me to get a dog of his own, I know, and how will I ever keep one in a flat in Bombay?"

"When are you going to throw out those rascals?" a father demanded of Raman, pointing at the juvenile revellers indoors. "My boy has an exam tomorrow, you know, but he said he couldn't be bothered about it—he had to go to the Ramans' farewell party."

One mother confided to Bina, winning her heart forever, "Now that you are leaving, I can talk to you about it at last: did you know my Vinod is sweet on your Tara? Last night when I was putting him to bed, he said, 'Mama, when I grow up I will marry Tara. I will sit on a white horse and wear a turban and carry a sword in my belt and I will go and marry Tara.' What shall we do about that, eh? Only a ten year difference in age, isn't there—or twelve?" and both women rocked with laughter.

The party had reached its crest, like a festive ship, loud and illuminated for that last party before the journey's end, perched on the dizzy top of the dark wave. It could do nothing now but descend and dissolve. As if by simultaneous and unanimous consent, the guests began to leave (in the wake of the Commissioner and his wife who left first, like royalty) streaming towards the drive where cars stood bumper to bumper—more than had visited the Ramans' house in the previous five years put together. The light in the portico fell on Bina's pride and joy, a Chinese orange tree, lighting its miniature globes of fruit like golden lanterns. There was a babble, an uproar of leave-taking (the smaller children, already in pyjamas, watched open-mouthed from a dark window upstairs). Esso and Caltex left together, arms about each other and smoking cigars, like figures in a comic act. Miss Dutta held firmly to Bose's arm as they dipped, bowed, swayed, and tripped on their way out. Bina was clasped, kissed—earrings grazed her cheek, talcum powder tickled her nose. Raman had his back slapped till he thrummed and vibrated like a beaten gong.

It seemed as if Bina and Raman were to be left alone at last, left to pack up and leave—now the good-byes had been said, there was nothing else they could possibly do—but no, out popped the good doctors from the hospital who had held themselves back in the darkest corners and made themselves inconspicuous throughout the party, and now, in the manner in which they clasped the host by the shoulders and the hostess by her hands, and said "Ah, *now* we have a chance to be with you at last, now we can begin *our* party," revealed that although this was the first time they had come to the Ramans' house on any but professional visits, they were not merely friends—they were almost a part of that self-defensive family, the closest to them in sympathy. Raman and Bina felt a warm, moist expansion of tenderness inside themselves, the tenderness they had till today restricted to the limits of their family, no farther, as though they feared it had not an unlimited capacity. Now its close horizons stepped backwards, with some surprise.

And it was as the doctors said—the party now truly began. Cane chairs were dragged out of the verandah onto the lawn, placed in a ring next to the flowering Queen of the Night which shook out flounces and frills of white scent with every rustle of night breeze. Bina could give in now to her two most urgent needs and dash indoors to smear her mosquito-bitten arms and feet with Citronella and fetch Nono to sit on her lap, to let Nono have a share, too, in the party. The good doctors and their wives leant forward and gave Nono the attention that made the parents' throats tighten with gratitude. Raman insisted on their each having a glass of Remy

Martin—they must finish it tonight, he said, and would not let the waiters clear away the ice or glasses yet. So they sat on the verandah steps, smoking and yawning.

Now it turned out that Dr. Bannerji's wife, the lady in the Dacca sari and the steel-rimmed spectacles, had studied in Shantiniketan,[2] and she sang, at her husband's and his colleagues' urging, Tagore's sweetest, saddest songs. When she sang, in heartbroken tones that seemed to come from some distance away, from the damp corners of the darkness where the fireflies flitted,

> Father, the boat is carrying me away,
> Father, it is carrying me away from home,

the eyes of her listeners, sitting tensely in that grassy, inky dark, glazed with tears that were compounded equally of drink, relief, and regret.

---

[2] **Shantiniketan:** School founded in 1901 by the Bengali Renaissance poet Rabindranath Tagore to teach students in a natural setting. Later, the school became a university devoted to bringing East and West together.

❧ BESSIE HEAD
B. SOUTH AFRICA, 1937–1986

The short and unhappy life of Bessie Head, the black South African novelist and short-story writer, reflects the troubled times in which she lived. Because her own identity was clouded by a painful family history and complicated by the twin oppressions of South African apartheid and sexism, she found in her own story a way to understand the troubled history of her country. "We black Africans," she wrote, "did not know who or what we were, apart from objects of abuse and exploitation." Her search for her own identity in her writing embodies a search for the identity of black Africa. Just as she was cut off from a knowledge of her own origins, the Africa Bessie Head describes has been separated from its past and is caught between conflicting cultural forces.

A Troubled Personal History.   Bessie Head was born in 1937 in a Pietermaritzburg psychiatric hospital where her mother, Bessie Amelia Emery, was a patient. From a family of wealthy Scottish immigrants, Bessie Emery had fallen prey to mental illness after her eldest son, at age four, was run over and killed. Her marriage gradually disintegrated, and after her divorce in 1928 she was in and out of mental hospitals. She was forty-two when her illegitimate daughter was born, the child of a secret relationship with a black household servant. Although Bessie's mother never disclosed her father's identity to her, by naming the child with her own name she provided the key by which Bessie Head's parentage would be deciphered fifty-three years later. As a baby Head was classified as "white"

www   For links to more information about Bessie Head and quizzes on "The Deep River" and "Snapshots of a Wedding," and for information about the culture and context of Africa in the twentieth century, see *World Literature Online* at bedfordstmartins.com/worldlit.

on her birth certificate and adopted by a white family, but when her features began to show some African characteristics, she was placed with a new "colored" family. Under APARTHEID, the South African system of racial segregation, "white," "colored," and "black" were strictly defined racial categories. In 1937 sexual intercourse across racial lines was a punishable offense. The identity of Bessie Head's black father, a servant in her mother's household, was uncovered only after Head's death many years later.

When Bessie was twelve, her adoptive parents suffered financial reverses and placed her in a home for "colored" girls where she was sent to a mission school. There she trained to be a teacher, earning her teaching certificate in 1955. But she did not like teaching, and after biting the principal's hand and accusing him of sexually molesting her, she turned to journalism. In 1960 she married fellow journalist Harold Head, but the marriage soon soured, ending in 1964. Then, leaving behind a troubled personal history and escaping from the oppression of apartheid in South Africa, Head took her infant son and moved to Botswana. Although she hoped to begin a new life there, she took her anger and unhappiness with her. She struggled to make a living, always on the edge of poverty, and felt like an outsider who was not welcomed in the recently independent Botswana.

Bessie Head and Black South Africa. In "The Collector of Treasures," a short story about a woman in circumstances similar to her own, Head traces African history through three periods: "In the old days, before the colonial invasion of Africa, he [the African] was a man who lived by tradition and taboos outlined for all the people by the forefathers of the tribe. He had little individual freedom to assess whether these traditions were compassionate or not—they demanded that he comply and obey the rules, without thought." Traditional African culture, Head goes on to point out, "relegated men to a superior position . . . while women were regarded, in a congenital sense, as being an inferior form of human life." The next period, the colonial era, "broke the hold of the ancestors." The black man was sent to work in the mines and separated from his family; he became "'the boy' of the white man and a machine tool of the South African mines." Finally, African independence brought "one more affliction." It offered jobs and opportunities for a "family life of a new order, above the childlike discipline of custom, the degradation of colonialism. Men and women, in order to survive, had to turn inwards to their own resources." But tribalism and colonialism had drained them of those inner resources, and the African, "in an effort to flee his own inner emptiness, . . . spun away from himself in a dizzy kind of death dance of wild destruction and dissipation."

Bessie Head's own life can be seen as representative of the black South African's experience in the emerging postcolonial era. In her own struggle to transcend apartheid and live independently, Head found herself alienated, tormented, and subject to spells of mental illness that required hospitalization.

Bessie Head never returned to South Africa from her exile in Botswana. When she died from a lung infection at age forty-nine in 1986, she was working on her autobiography, a story she did not finish. Much of her troubled and suppressed personal history came to light only after her death.

Novels and Head's Personal Story.   Head's first novel, *When Rain Clouds Gather* (1968), turned her personal situation into a parable about the new Africa. The hero, Makhaya, a Zulu from South Africa, escapes apartheid by fleeing to Botswana. Though he becomes part of an agricultural cooperative developing new methods of agriculture and social organization, the traditional ways of doing things frustrate his idealistic program for the future and drive Makhaya to suicide. *A Question of Power* (1973) is even more autobiographical. It tells the story of a colored South African woman, Elizabeth, who has settled in a rural Botswanan village and is tormented there by loneliness and alienation. In her relationships with men she is unable to separate her imaginings from reality, and, eventually, she is driven to insanity and spends time in a mental hospital. In the end she leaves the hospital and returns to the village and to her son.

Short Stories.   Drawing on the experience of exile, Bessie Head's short stories deal with the same themes as her novels: identity, tradition, exile, colonialism, and the influence of the West in Africa. "The Deep River: A Story of Ancient Tribal Migration" (1977) records the fragmentary history of the **Botalaote** tribe. A story of exile and migration, it is representative of the dislocation and loss of identity suffered by many African peoples. "Snapshots of a Wedding" (1977) treats similar issues in its account of a contemporary wedding ceremony that awkwardly combines traditional ritual and contemporary ways.

■ CONNECTIONS

In the World: **Imagining Africa, p. 853.** Léopold Sédar Senghor's "Prayer to the Masks" and Countee Cullen's "Heritage" are works that treat the subject of African roots. Both Senghor and Cullen celebrate Africa and could be said to romanticize their heritage. Why is Bessie Head unable to do the same?

T. S. Eliot, *The Waste Land,* **p. 486.** Bessie Head views the Botalaote as a tribe that has largely lost touch with its traditions, much as T. S. Eliot implicitly compares Western culture after World War I to a wasteland. How do Head and Eliot each indicate this loss of connection with the past? Are the differences between their approaches indicative of the disparity between oral and writing cultures? What indications of similar cultural losses are there in "Snapshots of a Wedding"?

Sunjata **(Book 3).** Compare "The Deep River" with *Sunjata,* a traditional African founding epic. How do they differ as founding stories? What elements in the traditional epic are lacking in "The Deep River"? How do the characterizations of the founders differ? Is Sebembele a heroic figure? Had Bessie Head been a *griot,* could she have recited the story of the founding of the Botalaote tribe?

[Head's stories are] rooted folkloristic tales woven from the fabric of village life and intended to entertain and enlighten, not to engage the modern close critic.

– MICHAEL THORPE, critic, 1977

boh-tah-LOW-teh

Head puts a woman's as well as a black case in tales that both reach back into tribal legend and cut deep into modern Africa.

– VALERIE CUNNINGHAM, critic, 1977

■ **FURTHER RESEARCH**

Biography
Eilersen, Gillian Stead. *Bessie Head, Thunder behind Her Ears: Her Life and Writing.*
    1995.

Criticism
Abrahams, Cecil, ed. *The Tragic Life: Bessie Head and Literature in Southern Africa.* 1991.
Barnett, Ursula A. *A Vision of Order: A Study of Black South African Literature in English*
    (1914–1980). 1984.
Hurna, Ibrahim. *Bessie Head: Subversive Identities in Exile.* 1996.
Ravenscroft, A. "The Novels of Bessie Head," in *Aspects of South African Literature.*
    Christopher Heywood, ed. 1976.

■ **PRONUNCIATION**

Bakaa: bah-KAH
Bamangwato: bah-mahng-WAH-toh
Baphaleng: bah-PEH-leng
Batswapong: bah-TSWAH-pong
Botalaote: boh-tah-LOW-teh
Kegoletile: keh-goh-leh-TEE-leh
Makobi: mah-KOH-bee
Mathata: mah-TAH-tah
MmaKhudu: mah-KOO-doo
Monemapee: moh-neh-mah-PAY-eh
Neo: NAY-oh
Ntema: en-TAY-mah
Rankwana: rahng-KWAH-nah
Sebembele: seh-bem-BEH-leh
Talaote: tah-lah-OH-teh

ᴖ The Deep River:
A Story of Ancient Tribal Migration

Long ago, when the land was only cattle tracks and footpaths, the people lived together like a deep river. In this deep river which was unruffled by conflict or a movement forward, the people lived without faces, except for their chief, whose face was the face of all the people; that is, if their chief's name was Monemapee, then they

---

"The Deep River." Included in Bessie Head's first collection of short stories, *"The Collector of Treasures" and Other Botswana Village Tales* (1977), this story is a founding myth, like *The Aeneid* or the landing of the Pilgrims at Plymouth Rock, that traces the origins of a particular culture. It is, however, a troubled story, for it traces a culture's loss of identity and shows its alienation. The conflict between tribal traditions and Sebembele's individual desires cuts Sebembele off from his origins and forces him and his followers into exile. Over time the members of the exiled group and their descendants lose their identity, ironically naming themselves *Talaote,* meaning "all

were all the people of Monemapee. The Talaote tribe have forgotten their origins and their original language during their journey southwards—they have merged and remerged again with many other tribes—and the name, Talaote, is all they have retained in memory of their history. Before a conflict ruffled their deep river, they were all the people of Monemapee, whose kingdom was somewhere in the central part of Africa.

They remembered that Monemapee ruled the tribe for many years as the hairs on his head were already saying white! by the time he died. On either side of the deep river there might be hostile tribes or great dangers, so all the people lived in one great town. The lands where they ploughed their crops were always near the town. That was done by all the tribes for their own protection, and their day-to-day lives granted them no individual faces either for they ploughed their crops, reared their children, and held their festivities according to the laws of the land.

Although the people were given their own ploughing lands, they had no authority to plough them without the chief's order. When the people left home to go to plough, the chief sent out the proclamation for the beginning of the ploughing season. When harvest time came, the chief perceived that the corn was ripe. He gathered the people together and said:

"Reap now, and come home."

When the people brought home their crops, the chief called the thanksgiving for the harvest. Then the women of the whole town carried their corn in flat baskets, to the chief's place. Some of that corn was accepted on its arrival, but the rest was returned so that the women might soak it in their own yards. After a few days, the chief sent his special messenger to proclaim that the harvest thanksgiving corn was to be pounded. The special messenger went around the whole town and in each place where there was a little hill or mound, he climbed it and shouted:

"Listen, the corn is to be pounded!"

So the people took their sprouting corn and pounded it. After some days the special messenger came back and called out:

"The corn is to be fermented now!"

A few days passed and then he called out:

"The corn is to be cooked now!"

---

right, you can go"; they are marked as being in exile. Bessie Head, who was adopted and not informed of her parentage, uses this founding myth to generalize her situation to that of the African dispossessed.

In a note appended to this story, Head commented: "The story is an entirely romanticized and fictionalized version of the history of the Botalaote tribe. Some historical data was given to me by the old men of the tribe, but it was unreliable as their memories had tended to fail them. A reconstruction was made therefore in my own imagination; I am also partly indebted to the London Missionary Society's *'Livingstone Tswana Readers,' Padiso III,* [a] school textbook, for those graphic paragraphs on the harvest thanksgiving ceremony which appear in the story."

So throughout the whole town the beer was boiled and when it had been strained, the special messenger called out for the last time:

"The beer is to be brought now!"

On the day on which thanksgiving was to be held, the women all followed one another in single file to the chief's place. Large vessels had been prepared at the chief's place, so that when the women came they poured the beer into them. Then there was a gathering of all the people to celebrate thanksgiving for the harvest time. All the people lived this way, like one face, under their chief. They accepted this regimental levelling down of their individual souls, but on the day of dispute or when strife and conflict and greed blew stormy winds over their deep river, the people awoke and showed their individual faces.

Now, during his lifetime Monemapee had had three wives. Of these marriages he had four sons: Sebembele by the senior wife; Ntema and Mosemme by the second junior wife; and Kgagodi by the third junior wife. There was a fifth son, Makobi, a small baby who was still suckling at his mother's breast by the time the old chief, Monemapee, died. This mother was the third junior wife, Rankwana. It was about the fifth son, Makobi, that the dispute arose. There was a secret there. Monemapee had married the third junior wife, Rankwana, late in his years. She was young and beautiful and Sebembele, the senior son, fell in love with her—but in secret. On the death of Monemapee, Sebembele, as senior son, was installed chief of the tribe and immediately made a blunder. He claimed Rankwana as his wife and exposed the secret that the fifth son, Makobi, was his own child and not that of his father.

This news was received with alarm by the people as the first ripples of trouble stirred over the even surface of the river of their lives. If both the young man and the old man were visiting the same hut, they reasoned, perhaps the old man had not died a normal death. They questioned the councillors who knew all secrets.

"Monemapee died just walking on his own feet," they said reassuringly.

That matter settled, the next challenge came from the two junior brothers, Ntema and Mosemme. If Sebembele were claiming the child, Makobi, as his son, they said, it meant that the young child displaced them in seniority. That they could not allow. The subtle pressure exerted on Sebembele by his junior brothers and the councillors was that he should renounce Rankwana and the child and all would be well. A chief lacked nothing and there were many other women more suitable as wives. Then Sebembele made the second blunder. In a world where women were of no account, he said truthfully:

"The love between Rankwana and I is great."

This was received with cold disapproval by the councillors.

"If we were you," they said, "we would look for a wife somewhere else. A ruler must not be carried away by his emotions. This matter is going to cause disputes among the people."

They noted that on being given this advice, Sebembele became very quiet, and they left him to his own thoughts, thinking that sooner or later he would come to a decision that agreed with theirs.

In the meanwhile the people quietly split into two camps. The one camp said:

"If he loves her, let him keep her. We all know Rankwana. She is a lovely person, deserving to be the wife of a chief."

The other camp said:

"He must be mad. A man who is influenced by a woman is no ruler. He is like one who listens to the advice of a child. This story is really bad."

There was at first no direct challenge to the chieftaincy which Sebembele occupied. But the nature of the surprising dispute, that of his love for a woman and a child, caused it to drag on longer than time would allow. Many evils began to rear their heads like impatient hissing snakes, while Sebembele argued with his own heart or engaged in tender dialogues with his love, Rankwana.

"I don't know what I can do," Sebembele said, torn between the demands of his position and the strain of a love affair which had been conducted in deep secrecy for many, many months. The very secrecy of the affair seemed to make it shout all the louder for public recognition. At one moment his heart would urge him to renounce the woman and child, but each time he saw Rankwana it abruptly said the opposite. He could come to no decision.

It seemed little enough that he wanted for himself—the companionship of a beautiful woman to whom life had given many other attractive gifts; she was gentle and kind and loving. As soon as Sebembele communicated to her the advice of the councillors, she bowed her head and cried a little.

"If that is what they say, my love," she said in despair, "I have no hope left for myself and the child. It were better if we were both dead."

"Another husband could be chosen for you," he suggested.

"You doubt my love for you, Sebembele," she said. "I would kill myself if I lose you. If you leave me, I would kill myself."

Her words had meaning for him because he was trapped in the same kind of anguish. It was a terrible pain which seemed to paralyse his movements and thoughts. It filled his mind so completely that he could think of nothing else, day and night. It was like a sickness, this paralysis, and like all ailments it could not be concealed from sight; Sebembele carried it all around with him.

"Our hearts are saying many things about this man," the councillors said among themselves. They were saying that he was unmanly; that he was unfit to be a ruler; that things were slipping from his hands. Those still sympathetic approached him and said:

"Why are you worrying yourself like this over a woman, Sebembele? There are no limits to the amount of wives a chief may have, but you cannot have that woman and that child."

And he only replied with a distracted mind: "I don't know what I can do."

But things had been set in motion. All the people were astir over events; if a man couldn't make up his mind, other men could make it up for him.

Everything was arranged in secret and on an appointed day Rankwana and the child were forcibly removed back to her father's home. Ever since the controversy had started, her father had been harassed day and night by the councillors as an influence that could help to end it. He had been reduced to a state of agitated muttering to himself by the time she was brought before him. The plan was to set her up with a husband immediately and settle the matter. She was not yet formally married to Sebembele.

"You have put me in great difficulties, my child," her father said, looking away from her distressed face. "Women never know their own minds and once this has passed away and you have many children you will wonder what all the fuss was about."

"Other women may not know their minds . . ." she began, but he stopped her with a raised hand, indicating the husband who had been chosen for her. In all the faces surrounding her there was no sympathy or help, and she quietly allowed herself to be led away to her new home.

When Sebembele arrived in his own yard after a morning of attending to the affairs of the land, he found his brothers, Ntema and Mosemme there.

"Why have you come to visit me?" he asked with foreboding. "You never come to visit me. It would seem that we are bitter enemies rather than brothers."

"You have shaken the whole town with your madness over a woman," they replied mockingly. "She is no longer here so you don't have to say any longer 'I-don't-know-what-I-can-do.' But we still request that you renounce the child, Makobi, in a gathering before all the people, in order that our position is clear. You must say: 'That child Makobi is the younger brother of my brothers, Ntema and Mosemme, and not the son of Sebembele who rules.'"

Sebembele looked at them for a long moment. It was not hatred he felt but peace at last. His brothers were forcing him to leave the tribe.

"Tell the people that they should all gather together," he said. "But what I say to them is my own affair."

The next morning the people of the whole town saw an amazing sight which stirred their hearts. They saw their ruler walk slowly and unaccompanied through the town. They saw him pause at the yard of Rankwana's father. They saw Sebembele and Rankwana's father walk to the home of her new husband where she had been secreted. They saw Rankwana and Sebembele walk together through the town. Sebembele held the child Makobi in his arms. They saw that they had a ruler who talked with deeds rather than words. They saw that the time had come for them to offer up their individual faces to the face of this ruler. But the people were still in two camps. There was a whole section of the people who did not like this face; it was too out-of-the-way and shocking; it made them very uneasy. Theirs was not a tender, compassionate, and romantic world. And yet in a way it was. The arguments in the other camp which supported Sebembele had flown thick and fast all this time, and they said:

"Ntema and Mosemme are at the bottom of all this trouble. What are they after for they have set a difficult problem before us all? We don't trust them. But why not? They have not yet had time to take anything from us. Perhaps we ought to wait until they do something really bad; at present they are only filled with indignation at the behaviour of Sebembele. But no, we don't trust them. We don't like them. It is Sebembele we love, even though he has shown himself to be a man with a weakness . . ."

That morning, Sebembele completely won over his camp with his extravagant, romantic gesture, but he lost everything else and the rulership of the kingdom of Monemapee.

When all the people had gathered at the meeting place of the town, there were not many arguments left. One by one the councillors stood up and condemned the behaviour of Sebembele. So the two brothers, Ntema and Mosemme won the day. Still working together as one voice, they stood up and asked if their senior brother had any words to say before he left with his people.

"Makobi is my child," he said.

"Talaote," they replied, meaning in the language then spoken by the tribe — "all right, you can go."

And the name Talaote was all they were to retain of their identity as the people of the kingdom of Monemapee. That day, Sebembele and his people packed their belongings on the backs of their cattle and slowly began the journey southwards. They were to leave many ruins behind them and it is said that they lived, on the journey southwards, with many other tribes like the Baphaleng, Bakaa, and Batswapong until they finally settled in the land of the Bamangwato. To this day there is a separate Botalaote ward in the capital village of the Bamangwato, and the people refer to themselves still as the people of Talaote. The old men there keep on giving confused and contradictory accounts of their origins, but they say they lost their place of birth over a woman. They shake their heads and say that women have always caused a lot of trouble in the world. They say that the child of their chief was named, Talaote, to commemorate their expulsion from the kingdom of Monemapee.

∾ Snapshots of a Wedding

Wedding days always started at the haunting magical hour of early dawn when there was only a pale crack of light on the horizon. For those who were awake, it took the earth hours to adjust to daylight. The cool and damp of the night slowly arose in shimmering waves like water and even the forms of the people who bestirred themselves at this unearthly hour were distorted in the haze; they appeared to be dancers in slow motion, with fluid, watery forms. In the dim light, four men, the relatives of

---

"Snapshots of a Wedding." This story, also included in Bessie Head's first collection, *"The Collector of Treasures" and Other Botswana Village Tales* (1977), explores the simultaneous loss and persistence of tradition in a wedding ceremony. Even though Neo's wedding is to be a "modern" one, many elements of the traditional ceremony are invoked by her aunts and by other members of the village who are clearly uneasy about the deviations from tradition and about Neo's position as a "liberated" woman. In the story Neo is seen responding to her aunt's scolding, compromising with tradition, and finally succumbing to joyful laughter during the ceremony. But in her aunt's final assertion, "Be a good wife," the conflicting implications of that admonition, warning, and wish resonate.

All notes are the editors'.

the bridegroom, Kegoletile, slowly herded an ox before them towards the yard of MmaKhudu, where the bride, Neo, lived. People were already astir in MmaKhudu's yard, yet for a while they all came and peered closely at the distorted fluid forms that approached, to ascertain if it were indeed the relatives of the bridegroom. Then the ox, who was a rather stupid fellow and unaware of his sudden and impending end as meat for the wedding feast, bellowed casually his early morning yawn. At this, the beautiful ululating of the women rose and swelled over the air like water bubbling rapidly and melodiously over the stones of a clear, sparkling stream. In between ululating all the while, the women began to weave about the yard in the wedding dance; now and then they bent over and shook their buttocks in the air. As they handed over the ox, one of the bridegroom's relatives joked:

"This is going to be a modern wedding." He meant that a lot of the traditional courtesies had been left out of the planning for the wedding day; no one had been awake all night preparing diphiri or the traditional wedding breakfast of pounded meat and samp;[1] the bridegroom said he had no church and did not care about such things; the bride was six months pregnant and showing it, so there was just going to be a quick marriage ceremony at the police camp.

"Oh, we all have our own ways," one of the bride's relatives joked back. "If the times are changing, we keep up with them." And she weaved away ululating joyously.

Whenever there was a wedding the talk and gossip that preceded it were appalling, except that this time the relatives of the bride, Neo, kept their talk a strict secret among themselves. They were anxious to be rid of her; she was an impossible girl with haughty, arrogant ways. Of all her family and relatives, she was the only one who had completed her "O" levels[2] and she never failed to rub in this fact. She walked around with her nose in the air; illiterate relatives were beneath her greeting — it was done in a clever way, she just turned her head to one side and smiled to herself or when she greeted it was like an insult; she stretched her hand out, palm outspread, swung it down laughing with a gesture that plainly said: "Oh, that's you!" Only her mother seemed bemused by her education. At her own home Neo was waited on hand and foot. Outside her home nasty remarks were passed. People bitterly disliked conceit and pride.

"That girl has no manners!" the relatives would remark. "What's the good of education if it goes to someone's head so badly they have no respect for the people? Oh, she is not a person."

Then they would nod their heads in that fatal way, with predictions that one day life would bring her down. Actually, life had treated Neo rather nicely. Two months after completing her "O" levels she became pregnant by Kegoletile with their first child. It soon became known that another girl, Mathata, was also pregnant by Kegoletile. The difference between the two girls was that Mathata was completely uneducated; the only work she would ever do was that of a housemaid, while Neo had endless opportunities before her — typist, bookkeeper, or secretary. So Neo merely

---

[1] **samp:** Cornmeal.

[2] **"O" levels:** Examinations taken to qualify for an ordinary-level secondary-school diploma.

smiled; Mathata was no rival. It was as though the decision had been worked out by circumstance because when the families converged on Kegoletile at the birth of the children—he was rich in cattle and they wanted to see what they could get—he of course immediately proposed marriage to Neo; and for Mathata, he agreed to a court order to pay a maintenance of R10.00 a month until the child was twenty years old. Mathata merely smiled too. Girls like her offered no resistance to the approaches of men; when they lost them, they just let things ride.

"He is of course just running after the education and not the manners," Neo's relatives commented, to show they were not fooled by human nature. "He thinks that since she is as educated as he is they will both get good jobs and be rich in no time . . ."

Educated as he was, Kegoletile seemed to go through a secret conflict during that year he prepared a yard for his future married life with Neo. He spent most of his free time in the yard of Mathata. His behaviour there wasn't too alarming but he showered Mathata with gifts of all kinds—food, fancy dresses, shoes, and underwear. Each time he came, he brought a gift and each time Mathata would burst out laughing and comment: "Ow, Kegoletile, how can I wear all these dresses? It's just a waste of money! Besides, I manage quite well with the R10.00 you give every month for the child . . ."

She was a very pretty girl with black eyes like stars; she was always smiling and happy; immediately and always her own natural self. He knew what he was marrying—something quite the opposite, a new kind of girl with false postures and acquired, grand-madame ways. And yet, it didn't pay a man these days to look too closely into his heart. They all wanted as wives, women who were big money-earners and were so ruthless about it! And yet it was as though the society itself stamped each of its individuals with its own particular brand of wealth and Kegoletile had not yet escaped it; he had about him an engaging humility and eagerness to help and please that made him loved and respected by all who knew him. During those times he sat in Mathata's yard, he communicated nothing of the conflict he felt but he would sit on a chair with his arms spread out across its back, turn his head sideways and stare at what seemed to be an empty space beside him. Then he would smile, stand up, and walk away. Nothing dramatic. During the year he prepared the huts in his new yard, he frequently slept at the home of Neo.

Relatives on both sides watched this division of interest between the two yards and one day when Neo walked patronizingly into the yard of an aunt, the aunt decided to frighten her a little.

"Well aunt," she said, with the familiar careless disrespect which went with her so-called, educated, status. "Will you make me some tea? And how's things?"

The aunt spoke very quietly.

"You may not know it, my girl, but you are hated by everyone around here. The debate we have going is whether a nice young man like Kegoletile should marry bad-mannered rubbish like you. He would be far better off if he married a girl like Mathata, who though uneducated, still treats people with respect."

The shock the silly girl received made her stare for a terrified moment at her aunt. Then she stood up and ran out of the house. It wiped the superior smile off her face and brought her down a little. She developed an anxiety to greet people and also an anxiety about securing Kegoletile as a husband—that was why she became pregnant six months before the marriage could take place. In spite of this, her own relatives still disliked her and right up to the day of the wedding they were still debating whether Neo was a suitable wife for any man. No one would have guessed it though with all the dancing, ululating, and happiness expressed in the yard and streams of guests gaily ululated themselves along the pathways with wedding gifts precariously balanced on their heads. Neo's maternal aunts, all sedately decked up in shawls, sat in a select group by themselves in a corner of the yard. They sat on the bare ground with their legs stretched out before them but they were served like queens the whole day long. Trays of tea, dry white bread, plates of meat, rice, and salad were constantly placed before them. Their important task was to formally hand over the bride to Kegoletile's maternal aunts when they approached the yard at sunset. So they sat the whole day with still, expressionless faces, waiting to fulfill this ancient rite.

Equally still and expressionless were the faces of the long column of women, Kegoletile's maternal aunts, who appeared outside the yard just as the sun sank low. They walked slowly into the yard indifferent to the ululating that greeted them and seated themselves in a group opposite Neo's maternal aunts. The yard became very silent while each group made its report. Kegoletile had provided all the food for the wedding feast and a maternal aunt from his side first asked:

"Is there any complaint? Has all gone well?"

"We have no complaint," the opposite party replied.

"We have come to ask for water," Kegoletile's side said, meaning that from times past the bride was supposed to carry water at her in-law's home.

"It is agreed to," the opposite party replied.

Neo's maternal aunts then turned to the bridegroom and counselled him: "Son, you must plough and supply us with corn each year."

Then Kegoletile's maternal aunts turned to the bride and counselled her: "Daughter, you must carry water for your husband. Beware, that at all times, he is the owner of the house and must be obeyed. Do not mind if he stops now and then and talks to other ladies. Let him feel free to come and go as he likes . . ."

The formalities over, it was now time for Kegoletile's maternal aunts to get up, ululate and weave and dance about the yard. Then, still dancing and ululating, accompanied by the bride and groom they slowly wound their way to the yard of Kegoletile where another feast had been prepared. As they approached his yard, an old woman suddenly dashed out and chopped at the ground with a hoe. It was all only a formality. Neo would never be the kind of wife who went to the lands to plough. She already had a well-paid job in an office as a secretary. Following on this another old woman took the bride by the hand and led her to a smeared and decorated courtyard wherein had been placed a traditional animal skin Tswana[3] mat. She was made to sit on the mat and a shawl and kerchief were placed before her. The shawl was ceremonially wrapped around her shoulders; the kerchief tied around her head—the symbols that she was now a married woman.

---

[3] Tswana: Botswanan.

Guests quietly moved forward to greet the bride. Then two girls started to ululate and dance in front of the bride. As they both turned and bent over to shake their buttocks in the air, they bumped into each other and toppled over. The wedding guests roared with laughter. Neo, who had all this time been stiff, immobile, and rigid, bent forward and her shoulders shook with laughter.

The hoe, the mat, the shawl, the kerchief, the beautiful flute-like ululating of the women seemed in itself a blessing on the marriage but all the guests were deeply moved when out of the crowd, a woman of majestic, regal bearing slowly approached the bride. It was the aunt who had scolded Neo for her bad manners and modern ways. She dropped to her knees before the bride, clenched her fists together and pounded the ground hard with each clenched fist on either side of the bride's legs. As she pounded her fists she said loudly:

"Be a good wife! Be a good wife!"

꩜ GAO XINGJIAN
B. CHINA, 1940

Although Gao Xingjian is usually characterized as a political dissident in exile from his native China, he challenges descriptions of himself and other writers that are couched in political terms. Literature can only be destroyed, he asserted when accepting the Nobel Prize in literature in 2000, if it becomes "the tool of politics." Gao Xingjian has championed instead a literature of the individual. "A writer does not speak as the spokesperson of the people or as the embodiment of righteousness. His voice is inevitably weak but it is precisely this voice of the individual that is more authentic." In plays, novels, and works of nonfiction, Gao Xingjian has experimented with ways to express such a voice. His plays, which bring the theatrical traditions of China together with those of the West, especially the THEATER OF THE ABSURD, are an exploration of the situation of modern man outside the limitations imposed by political or national identities.

Coming of Age in Mao's China.   Born in 1940 in Ganzhow in Jiangxi province in eastern China, **Gao Xingjian** grew up under the shadow of the Japanese invasion of China. His banker father and actress mother provided a comfortable home, a well-stocked library, and inspiration for their son's literary ambitions. His mother insisted that he keep a diary, prompting the habit of writing in her son who produced his first story at age ten, at just the time when the Communist regime under Mao Zedong came to power. A good student in high school, Gao Xingjian was directed to enter the Foreign Languages Institute in Beijing, from which he graduated in 1962 with a degree in French literature. His first job was

www   For links to more information about Gao Xingjian and a quiz on *Dialogue and Rebuttal,* and for information about the culture and context of China in the twentieth century, see *World Literature Online* at bedfordstmartins .com/worldlit.

gow shing-JEN

François Guillot, *Gao Xingjian*, 2000
The Nobel Prize–winning author and playwright standing before one of his paintings in his house in suburban Paris. (© AFP / CORBIS)

as a translator and editor on the French edition of the magazine *China Reconstructs.*

The Cultural Revolution.   Gao Xingjian was active in the Communist Party and a leader of a Red Guard brigade in the mid sixties, but like many other urban intellectuals, he was banished to a reeducation camp in the countryside during the Cultural Revolution to do farm work with the peasants. This "reeducation" spanned a period of ten years during which he was cut off from urban intellectual life, from his lifelong engagement with French culture, and from reading and discussing literature. Despite a prohibition, he did continue to write, hiding his work from the authorities by wrapping it in plastic and burying it in the earthen floor of his hut. When his deception was about to be discovered, in a final desperate act of self-protection he burned many manuscripts — short stories, essays, poems, and ten plays.

In the Literary Avant-Garde.   When the Cultural Revolution gave way to more moderate forces in the Chinese government, Gao Xingjian was released from the labor camp and sent to southwestern China to work as a schoolteacher for six years before being assigned in 1981 to the Beijing People's Art Theater, the foremost theatrical company in China. In 1980 he published his first work, the novella *Stars on a Cold Night.* The series of publications that followed during the 1980s brought him recognition as the leader of the literary AVANT-GARDE in China. He produced stories, critical essays, and, especially, plays as well as translations of modernist European playwrights like Samuel Beckett (1906–1989; p. 770) and Eugène Ionesco (1912–1994) and of the poet Jacques Prévert (1900–1977). *A Preliminary Discussion of the Art of Modern Fiction,* despite being a book of criticism written in an academic manner, provoked much discussion and went through three editions in three years (1980, 1981, and 1982), before it was banned for challenging the doctrines of SOCIALIST REALISM[1] of Mao Zedong. Gao Xingjian's plays were also suppressed. *Bus Stop* (1983) was cheered by those lucky enough to see it before authorities halted its performances, calling it the "most pernicious play since the establishment of the People's Republic of China." Reminiscent in some ways of Samuel Beckett's *Waiting for Godot* (1951), *Bus Stop* involves a group of people waiting for a bus that never comes and employs language reminiscent of the spare and ambiguous dialogue of European absurdist drama. As Gao Xingjian's profile rose in literary circles, he became increasingly suspect to the authorities. In 1983 a new production of his play *Absolute Signal* was closed. Barred from publishing anything else for a year and about to be sent again to a "reeducation camp," Gao Xingjian went into self-imposed exile, taking a six-month trek in the hinterlands of China, following the Yangtze River from its source to the coast. This wilderness

---

[1] **socialist realism:** A standard for art and literature developed in the Soviet Union in the 1930s that demanded that art depict the life of the people realistically and celebrate the ideals of the Bolshevik revolution. Mao Zedong enforced similar standards in China after the People's Republic was established in 1949.

experience inspired his autobiographical novel *Soul Mountain* (1989), a meditation on the meaning of life that was also shaped by the author's confrontation with death when he was misdiagnosed with terminal cancer.

Exile in the West.   When Gao Xingjian, also an accomplished Chinese brush painter, had a chance to tour Europe with his paintings in 1987, he decided to leave China and not return. Taking the manuscript of *Soul Mountain* with him, he applied for permanent residence in France in 1988 and a decade later became a French citizen. In 2000 he was the first Chinese writer to receive the Nobel Prize, "for an oeuvre of universal validity, bitter insights, and linguistic ingenuity," cited the Nobel Committee, "which has opened new paths for the Chinese novel and drama." The Chinese authorities have considered the prize a political rather than a literary award, and Gao Xingjian's plays are still not performed in his native country.

Although Gao Xingjian admires the works of Lu Xun (1881–1936; p. 331), the Chinese writer from the beginning of the twentieth century who was celebrated by Mao Zedong as the spiritual father to the revolution, he rejects Lu Xun's politicization of literature. "Literature is not concerned with politics," Gao Xingjian has asserted, "but is purely a matter of the individual." His acceptance speech for the Nobel Prize elaborates this point of view, arguing that literature can be true to its mission only if it avoids politicization: "In order that literature safeguard the reason for its own existence and not become the tool of politics it must return to the voice of the individual, for literature is primarily derived from the feelings of the individual and is the result of feelings."

Gao Xingjian did touch on politics in *Exile* (1989), a play written in the aftermath of the struggle in Tiananmen Square. The play centers on three characters who are running from the soldiers who attacked the student protesters in the square. The play was, of course, condemned by the Chinese government, but it was also criticized in the West for not presenting its characters as heroic figures but rather as people susceptible to doubt. The American theater company that originally commissioned it turned down the finished play.

Cold Literature.   Since *Exile,* Gao Xingjian has become increasingly committed to what he calls "cold literature," writing stripped of didactic, political, or social agendas. Proclaiming himself a "nothingist," he refuses to advocate any "ism," a position he develops in the essay "Without isms" (1996) and in the autobiographical novel *One Man's Bible* (2000). The writer must be free—free of outside limitations, free of conventional expectations, free to validate in his writing the deepest impulses of his being. Gao Xingjian left China to escape political agendas and censorship; but in the West he finds the pressures of the capitalistic marketplace also threatening to his freedom as a writer. To stay in touch with the sources of his creativity, the writer, regardless of whether he is in the East or the West, must retreat into himself.

"Talking to oneself," Gao Xingjian remarked in his Nobel speech, "is the starting point of literature." His years writing secretly during the

[Gao Xingjian] rejects Nietzsche and the individualism of the West, which he considers destructive. His attitude is not unlike that of the traditional Taoist or Zen Buddhist who, bent on seclusion or exile from society to cultivate his inner virtues and strengths, still casts an indifferent eye to observe the world of humans in his somewhat aloof and detached position.

– GILBERT C. F. FONG, translator and critic, 1999

[Gao Xingjian] forces
his way into the self
and compels it to
reluctantly admit its
own inadequacies, its
fragmentation, its
impotence to act,
and its inability to
eradicate the evil in
and around it.
– GILBERT C. F. FONG,
translator and critic,
1999

Cultural Revolution, on his wilderness trek meditated on in *Soul Mountain,* and during his years of exile both within China and in the West have given Gao Xingjian many opportunities for such communication with himself. His unusual personal history also explains the evolution in his work from public themes to a much more private subject matter. The self has been the subject of Gao Xingjian's plays and novels for the last decade and a half.

Gao Xingjian's Plays. Elemental figures from a realm beneath the social world where names are used to make public distinctions, the characters in Gao Xingjian's plays appear on a bare stage with few props and usually have generic names — Man or Woman, Girl or Monk, He or She. Writing about the novel *Soul Mountain,* in which the characters are similarly named, Mabel Lee describes this method of characterization:

> The characters of the novel are the pronouns "I," "you," "she," and "he." Plural forms of pronouns are not employed, as for Gao Xingjian having another person representing the thinking and emotions of the individual self is anathema. The narrator "I" experiences loneliness on his journey and creates a "you" to have someone to talk with. "You," being a reflection of the "I," also experiences loneliness and in turn creates "she."

In the plays, Gao Xingjian's elemental characters shift in their speech from using the pronoun "I" to "you" and "s/he" to indicate dimensions in their self-awareness, for they are characters engrossed in observing themselves. The subject of the plays thus becomes the processes of consciousness of the self. The various territories of the self are sometimes dramatically represented as body parts; heads, for example, become props for the characters to observe. An individual character's dialogue with himself or parts of himself is more telling of loneliness in these dramas than are the conversations that take place between characters, which are often just trivial chatter, talk that leads nowhere except to the recognition of the radical isolation in which individuals live.

There is much in Gao Xingjian's plays to remind the viewer of the works of Pirandello (p. 201), Beckett, Ionesco, and other European dramatists of the absurd:[2] the bare stage, minimal use of props, banal and repetitive dialogue, generic characters, and a lack of action. But Gao Xingjian insists that his work is different from that of the European modernists. Translator Gilbert C. F. Fong describes it as "a new kind of modernism . . . that . . . constitutes an affirmation of the self, not its negation, as in Western modernism, and a rediscovery of humanism which has been lost among the insistence on the denial of rationality and the equation of absurdity with existence." Gao Xingjian asserts that the aim of his

---

[2] **dramatists of the absurd:** Writers associated with a school of modernist, non-Realist drama especially influential from the 1950s to the 1970s. Italian playwright Eugène Ionesco (1912–1994; *The Bald Soprano,* 1950) described its subject matter as "man . . . lost in the world, [so] all his actions become senseless, absurd, useless." Ionesco, Irish/French dramatist Samuel Beckett (1906–1989; *Waiting for Godot,* 1952), and English playwright Harold Pinter (b. 1930; *The Homecoming,* 1964) are among the most important absurdists.

work is to liberate the spirit by bringing his audience to a state of contemplation in which they become aware of the wordless emotions that lie beneath the banalities of language.

Dialogue and Rebuttal.   Characteristic of the plays written after *Exile,* the drama *Dialogue and Rebuttal* confronts the audience with three generic characters: Man, Girl, and Monk; but Monk rarely speaks. The play opens after a brief sexual encounter between Man and Girl; their conversations are a series of games, strategies of sexual flirtation and avoidance, dominance and evasion. As they skip from one topic to another — from gender relationships to the weather, drugs, dreams, love, games, philosophy, and feminism — they avoid real contact and self-revelation. A monk punctuates their interactions with a series of stunts — handstands, balancing sticks on end, balancing eggs on the end of sticks — many of which end in failure or frustration. These voiceless interludes of pantomime echo the dynamics of the dialogue between the two principals, which fails to communicate and moves toward and away from moments of enlightenment. Man and Girl approach such revelations when they observe themselves rather than the other, for self-understanding comes only in moments when one is really talking to oneself. The negative logic of the language games between Man and Girl ends in their simultaneous murders at the end of the first act.

In the ritualistic second act, the dialogue of the dead becomes a kind of chant, ultimately bringing Man and Girl together to contemplate "the crack," the gap, perhaps, between them, between language and understanding, between the spoken word and the voiceless rituals of the monk. In his notes on producing the play, Gao Xingjian says that the dialogue and rebuttal form was "inspired by the *gonzan* style of question and answer in Chinese **BUDDHISM.**" If the dialogue between Man and Girl articulates the question, then the wordless pantomime of Monk may be the answer. In the interplay between dialogue and rebuttal the audience may be brought to contemplate meaning beyond or beneath that of the spoken word.

> Gao is an exile writer who now writes in two languages: He represents that underrated yet increasingly frequent writer and artist who is "in-between," that is, in between the still reigning paradigm of national literatures and cultures.
>
> – MABEL LEE, critic and translator, 2000

■ CONNECTIONS

Samuel Beckett, *Krapp's Last Tape*, p. 774; Luigi Pirandello, *Six Characters in Search of an Author*, p. 205. Gao Xingjian learned some of his dramatic techniques by translating European absurdist playwrights like Samuel Beckett. What techniques used by Beckett in *Krapp's Last Tape* can be found in *Dialogue and Rebuttal*? What if any elements of influence from Pirandello are there in *Dialogue*? Gao Xingjian claims to have a more positive message than that of the European absurdists. How might *Dialogue and Rebuttal* be seen as conveying a positive message?

Laozi (Lao Tzu), *Dao De Jing* (Book 1); Zhuangzi (Chuang Tzu), *Writings* (Book 1). Gao Xingjian considers the contemplative dimension in his plays, represented in *Dialogue and Rebuttal* by Monk, as significantly related to Asian Zen Buddhism. The Dao De Jing (Tao Te Ching) and the writings of Zhuangzi are representative works of Asian contemplative literature. How might they help to explain the role of Monk in Gao Xingjian's play? How might Zhuangzi describe one of Monk's successful "stunts"?

Dante, *The Inferno* (Book 2). The second act of *Dialogue and Rebuttal* takes place after the deaths of the two central characters at the end of Act One. Compare the "afterlife" presented by Gao Xingjian with that in *The Inferno*. Are his characters being punished for their life on earth? Is the afterlife simply a continuation of their earlier lives? What do you make of the ritualistic elements — chanting, repetition, etc. — in the second act?

■ **FURTHER RESEARCH**

Other Works of Gao Xingjian in English Translation
The Bus Stop: A Lyrical Comedy on Life in One Act. Gilbert C. F. Fong, ed., *Theatre and Society: An Anthology of Contemporary Chinese Drama.* 1998.
The Other Shore: Plays by Gao Xingjian. Gilbert C. F. Fong, trans. and ed. 1999.
Soul Mountain. Mabel Lee, trans. 1999.

Criticism
Fong, Gilbert C. F. Introduction to *The Other Shore.* 1999.
Zhao, Henry Y. H. *Towards a Modern Zen Theatre: Gao Xingjian and the Chinese Theatre Experimentalism.* 2000.

■ **PRONUNCIATION**
Gao Xingjian: gow shing-JEN

Dialogue and Rebuttal

(A Play in Two Parts)

Translated by Gilbert C. F. Fong

Time and location uncertain.
An empty stage, some clothing, several objects.

CHARACTERS:

A YOUNG GIRL
A MIDDLE-AGED MAN
A MONK
TWO HEADS: ONE MALE, ONE FEMALE

Dialogue and Rebuttal. Written in 1992, this play was first produced in the same year at the Theater des Augenblicks in Vienna and directed by its author, Gao Xingjian. He also directed a 1995 production of the play in Paris at the Théâtre Molière. The English translation, by Gilbert C. F. Fong, was included in *The Other Shore: Plays by Gao Xingjian,* published in 1999.

Gao Xingjian's notes for producing the play, which appear at the end of the text, suggest several ways of reading the play. In the notes the actors are instructed to work more to distinguish the several different voices in which each character speaks than to draw sharp distinctions between the characters, for the subject of the play is not the interactions between the characters but rather different dimensions within the self. The monk, who provides wordless commentary on the action,

FIRST HALF

(The stage is white [if possible], on which one sees a young girl and a middle-aged man. A black overcoat and a travelling tote bag have been thrown to one side; on the other side towards the back, there lies a bathrobe, which has been tossed down in a heap. At front stage on the right, a wooden fish[1] has been placed on the floor.)

GIRL: Finished?

MAN: Finished.

GIRL: How was it?

MAN: Quite good. *(Pause.)* How about you?

GIRL: Not bad. *(Pause.)* Quite good, I should say.

(Man tries to say something but stops.)

GIRL: So . . .

MAN: What?

GIRL: Nothing much.

MAN: Nothing much what?

(Girl smiles slightly.)

MAN: What are you smiling at?

GIRL: Nothing.

MAN: Why are you still smiling?

GIRL: I'm not smiling.

(Helpless, Man stares at her.
Girl avoids his stare and looks away.)

MAN: Is it over?

GIRL: Isn't it better this way?

MAN: Are you always like this?

GIRL: What?

MAN: With men . . .

GIRL: Of course, you're not the first one.

(Man is taken aback, then laughs out loud.)

GIRL: You're all the same.

MAN: *(Happily.)* Do you mean we—

GIRL: I mean you, you men!

MAN: *(Corrects her.)* Men and women!

---

may offer the most clues to Gao Xingjian's theme, for his pantomime echoes and ironically comments on the interactions between the two central players. He also connects the drama to Gao Xingjian's Chinese roots, for he articulates the unspoken wisdom of Zen Buddhism through his mimes. Appropriately, he closes the play.

All notes are the editors' unless otherwise indicated.

---

[1] **wooden fish:** A percussion instrument made of a hollow wooden block, used by Buddhist priests to make rhythm while chanting scriptures. [Author's note.]

(Both laugh. Girl stops laughing abruptly. Man also stops.)
MAN: What's wrong?
GIRL: Nothing.
MAN: I'm sorry.
GIRL: *(Coldly.)* There's nothing to be sorry about.

(Man walks away and puts on bathrobe.)
GIRL: If we had known . . .
MAN: Speak for yourself.
GIRL: Hypocrite!
MAN: But I love you—

(Immediately Girl starts to laugh out loud. Man also laughs heartily. Monk enters slowly from the right side of the stage. He is bald, wearing a kasaya, *a Buddhist robe, and a pair of straw sandals. With his eyes lowered and his palms clasped, he is chanting "Amitabha Buddha!"[2] Man and Girl stop laughing.*
Monk walks to a corner at right stage, turns around until his back is facing the audience, sits down with his legs crossed and starts to beat the wooden fish.
Man and Girl restrain themselves. They both look down, listening carefully to the continuous beating of the wooden fish.)
GIRL: *(Softly.)* She doesn't understand why, why she followed such a man, but she followed him anyway, following him to . . .
MAN: *(Softly.)* She understands everything, she knew it very well, it's all very simple and clear, both had the need . . .
GIRL: *(Softly.)* No, she only wanted to know if it could happen . . . She knew it was possible but not entirely unavoidable . . .
MAN: *(Softly.)* Things are bound to happen anytime, anywhere in the world, when something happens, you'll just have to go along with it and have some fun.
GIRL: *(Softly.)* He may look eager and willing, but she knows very well that he's faking it, if she'd only arched her back and held him off, the whole thing wouldn't have happened.
MAN: *(Softly.)* One minute early or one minute late, it's all the same. Why put on an act? You and I are no different, that's the way it is.
GIRL: *(Softly.)* Of course she'd been expecting it, she knew right from the beginning how it would end, but she never thought it would be so sudden, so hasty, and the end would come so fast.

(Monk beats the wooden fish twice.)
GIRL: Forget it! There's nothing worth celebrating.
MAN: I didn't say anything.
GIRL: Better keep it that way.

(Man droops his head.

---

[2] **Amitabha Buddha:** "The Buddha of Infinite Light." The believer who repeats this Buddha's name in meditation will be reborn in Paradise.

Monk starts to beat lightly on the wooden fish, chanting softly and continually: "Amitabha Buddha.")
GIRL: How come you're not saying anything?
MAN: What's there to say?
GIRL: Anything you want.
MAN: You talk, I'll listen.
GIRL: Tell me about yourself.
MAN: I'm a man.
GIRL: You don't have to tell me that.
MAN: What shall I tell you then?
GIRL: Don't you know how to talk with people?
MAN: I'm afraid you won't like it.
GIRL: The problem is you've got to have something to talk about.
MAN: Except love—
GIRL: Don't talk to me about love!
MAN: Tell me, what else is there to talk about with a woman?

(Girl stands up to get her overcoat.)
MAN: Where are you going?
GIRL: It's none of your business.
MAN: I can ask, can't I?
GIRL: But you really don't want to know.
MAN: Why not? I do want to know.
GIRL: You only want a woman's body, you don't understand women, not even a tiny bit.
MAN: I don't understand myself either.
GIRL: Well said. You're such a pig!
MAN: And you?
GIRL: You think I'm that low-down?
MAN: That's not what I meant.
GIRL: Your attitude, it's disgusting!
MAN: To tell you the truth, I also disgust myself.
GIRL: What a wonderful confession! *(Turns and puts on her overcoat.)*
MAN: *(Snatches away her overcoat.)* Don't go!
GIRL: What more do you want?
MAN: Don't go! You've got to listen to me.
GIRL: You don't have the right to stop me. *(Struggles free.)* I've got to agree first!
MAN: *(Apprehensive.)* Now that you're here, well, of course I invited you, and I'm very glad—
GIRL: You—you're an out-and-out bastard!

(Man laughs.)
GIRL: What are you laughing at?
MAN: Myself, I'm laughing at myself. What is it to you?
GIRL: Fine then, let me go.
MAN: *(Blocking her.)* I love you, really I do!
GIRL: Stop acting. *(Pushes him away.)*

(Monk picks up wooden fish and beats on it while chanting "Amitabha Buddha." He exits left stage as Girl watches.)

MAN: I don't understand, it's really hard to figure you out. Tell me, what are you going to do? What is it that you want?

GIRL: *(Nonchalantly.)* Don't ask me, I don't know. I only, only wanted to know . . .

MAN: You already know everything there is to know.

GIRL: What do I know?

MAN: That I'm a man. Other men, aren't they the same?

GIRL: Don't talk to me about men!

MAN: Then what shall we talk about?

GIRL: Something interesting, cheerful, something which makes people happy. How stupid can you get?

MAN: Really?

GIRL: You only think you're smart.

MAN: And you're a smart Girl.

GIRL: Not necessarily. Otherwise I wouldn't have come here with you.

MAN: In fact I prefer stupid women.

GIRL: Because they're submissive, gullible, and easy to manipulate, is that it?

MAN: No, I'm only talking about myself, that way I can be more relaxed.

(Monotonous beating on the wooden fish. Monk has not yet entered.)

MAN: You want to drink something?

GIRL: No, I guess I'd better be going.

MAN: It's raining outside.

GIRL: *(Listening.)* I don't think so.

MAN: If I say it's raining, it's got to be raining.

GIRL: Who do you think you are, God?

MAN: I can hear it raining. I know all the sounds in and outside this place, the wind, the rain, the water heater, and the leaking toilet, every single one of them. I've owned this place for years.

GIRL: Leave me out of your ownership, I belong to me, and me only.

MAN: Is that very important?

GIRL: I don't know, maybe. Anyway, I still haven't found the right person to belong to.

MAN: Obviously I'm not that person.

GIRL: At last you've said something intelligent.

MAN: Thanks for the compliment.

GIRL: Intelligent men are a rare breed nowadays.

MAN: Most women are also stupid dingbats. Of course you're an exception.

GIRL: Do you really think so?

MAN: I never lie, don't you believe me?

GIRL: Do you say the same thing to every woman you're with?

MAN: You know why I said it to you? It's only because you like to hear people say that about you.

GIRL: You're — really — very bad.

(Man laughs, and Girl laughs with him.)

MAN: Are you sure you don't want anything to drink?

GIRL: Only if you promise not to mix anything in it. Nothing's worse than that.

MAN: That's to say you must have done it yourself. I'm sure you must've had tons of strange things happening to you before.

GIRL: I mean when somebody puts something in your drink and you don't realize it even after you've drunk the darn thing.

MAN: You mean just now, at the bar? If anybody put anything in it, it was definitely not me.

GIRL: I meant it happened once, in India.

MAN: But this certainly isn't India.

GIRL: I'm saying I went on a trip to India once.

MAN: With your friend, one of your many boyfriends, if I'm not mistaken?

GIRL: You might as well save that little bit of intelligence you have for something else. Of course I wasn't alone. Travelling alone can bore you to tears.

MAN: But if I were going on a trip, I'd never coax my female companion into doing drugs.

GIRL: It doesn't take any coaxing, does it? We're not kids any more.

MAN: Of course taking drugs is only human. Tell me, what do you use as a regular?

GIRL: I'm telling you I don't have the habit!

MAN: But how come you said when you were in India—

GIRL: I was in this small village close to the Tibetan border. The sky was real blue, I've never seen such a blue sky before. The clouds were real close, and as I watched them dissipating strand by strand in mid-air, I got dizzy, I couldn't climb up any more. My head was aching, my ears were ringing, as if some guy was ringing a bell like crazy next to my ears . . . He wanted to take some shots of the glaciers, you know, my friend was into photography, so I took the car and went back alone to a town where there was a small inn. There was this Indian man standing by the door and he asked me if I wanted any marijuana. He spoke some English, and he led me to his house to get some.

MAN: And you went with him just like that?

GIRL: Yes, I did, so what?

MAN: So what? It's the same as your coming here with me, isn't it?

GIRL: You sell marijuana too?

MAN: If you really want some.

GIRL: You don't know how to listen, do you?

MAN: Go on!

GIRL: I don't want to tell you any more.

(Monk enters, one hand holding an alms bowl, the other carrying a small bell. As he chants "Amitabha Buddha" in a low voice, he sprinkles some water into the bowl with his middle finger and rings the bell softly.)

MAN: Did he force you to take any drugs?

GIRL: No.

MAN: Did he make love to you?

GIRL: He was very gentle and very polite.

(Man wants to say something but stops.)

GIRL: There were these two women in his house, the younger one must have been his daughter, and they both bowed to me. He asked me to sit down and told the women to bring some wine, it was kind of sweet. The women stood on the side waiting on us, they only watched and smiled at me. I drank two cups in one go, and then they brought in some dried fruit and some sticky rice cakes.

(Girl listens attentively to the ringing of the bell.)

MAN: Go on, go on.

GIRL: I didn't know why but somehow I felt sleepy. I think for a whole week I was just lying down, not wanting to move.

MAN: Did you go back to the inn?

GIRL: No, I was in his room, on his bed—

MAN: Naked?

GIRL: Is that important?

MAN: When you're telling a story, you've got to give details.

GIRL: Anyway, my body didn't seem to belong to me, my hands and feet were too heavy to move, and my mind was totally blank . . . But I was still conscious . . .

MAN: Weren't you scared?

GIRL: The two women would come in every now and then, whenever he was not there they would come to give me something to eat or drink. I wanted to speak and scream, but they didn't say anything except to touch and stroke me all the time. Then without knowing it I fell asleep again until he came back and woke me up . . .

MAN: Did he rape you?

GIRL: No, I think . . . I don't know . . . Maybe I accepted it, I also, enjoyed . . . Maybe I wanted it too, there was no way out. Do you find this exciting?

MAN: Not really, I mean, he ruined you.

GIRL: Didn't you?

MAN: It's not the same, under the circumstances, he could have abused you until you died and no one would know anything about it.

GIRL: He was very gentle from beginning to end, he didn't force me at all, I gave him all he wanted without holding anything back . . . You know, I gave him everything I had until I became a total void . . . Except that after one week, I realized later that it'd been a whole week, it was either daytime or at night when I found myself completely paralysed, I didn't even want to move a finger, the room had only one oil lamp and it smelled real bad.

MAN: Maybe it was burning tallow, or animal fat, a kind of beef oil.

GIRL: Have you been there as well?

MAN: I read about it in some travel book on Tibet. Didn't you say the place was right next to Tibet?

GIRL: Uh-huh . . .

(The bell stops ringing.)

MAN: Go on, why have you stopped talking?

GIRL: What else should I talk about?

MAN: Talk about the smell.

GIRL: As I was saying, that was when I woke up for the first time, afterwards I didn't smell it any more, I only felt I was warm all over, I thought, I must have had that smell on me as well. Afterwards I washed again and again but I just couldn't get rid of . . .

MAN: That greasy muttony smell?

GIRL: No, the smell of his body.

MAN: Stop it! I've had enough.

(Monk has finished sprinkling and bends down as if to splash water onto the ground. He exits, holding up his sleeves with his hands.)

GIRL: *(Collects her thoughts and turns to look at him.)* Why?

MAN: There's no why.

GIRL: You don't like what I said?

MAN: I'm listening.

GIRL: What do you want to listen to?

MAN: It's up to you, whatever you want to say.

GIRL: You want me to say that I'm horny all the time?

MAN: You said it, not me.

GIRL: Don't you want every woman to be horny?

MAN: Women, they're actually like that.

GIRL: That's only in a man's imagination.

MAN: Believe me, men are no different.

GIRL: Then what's there to be curious about?

MAN: It's just the sex that's different.

GIRL: How about between one woman and another, are they the same to you?

MAN: Can't you change the subject?

GIRL: Shall we talk about the smell then?

MAN: To hell with the smell!

GIRL: You're really no fun!

MAN: What? Fine, fine, let's talk about the smell then.

GIRL: I don't want to talk about it any more.

(Monk enters tumbling in the air. He has taken off his kasaya *and is dressed in a casual jacket and pants. He holds his breath and stands motionlessly kungfu style.)*

MAN: *(Looks towards Monk and speaks softly.)* You can never understand what really goes on in a woman's mind. *(Loudly.)* An interesting story, very interesting. *(Turns to look at Girl.)* How come he didn't kill you?

GIRL: Why?

MAN: There's no why.

GIRL: All you men want to do is to possess, possess, and possess until everything's all busted and gone! *(Sighs.)* Men are so selfish, they only think of themselves.

MAN: Men this, men that, why do you have to keep babbling on about men?

GIRL: Aren't you one of them?

MAN: If anything, I'm still a person, a real, tangible, living human being.

GIRL: But you haven't been treating me like one. Let me tell you, I'm not just some plaything for venting your sexual desires. And one woman is different from another—

MAN: When we first started, we were talking in general terms, now it's different—

GIRL: How different?

MAN: Now it's you and me, and not men and women in the general sense. We're face to face with each other, we can see each other, and we've had some contact, I don't just mean physical contact, we're bound to have some feelings, some understanding of each other, because we're two living human beings.

GIRL: Wait a minute. You mean when you made love to me just now, you were treating me like your so-called women in the general sense, in other words, just a plaything.

MAN: Don't talk like that, because you and I were in the same boat, weren't we? We were like two people possessed—

GIRL: Let me finish. You didn't even ask me my name, as soon as we entered the door, you . . .

MAN: Don't forget, you didn't exactly refuse me.

GIRL: That's true, but . . .

MAN: I see, my sincerest apologies.

(Monk successfully completes a handstand. Then he tries to take away one hand to attempt a one-hand handstand, but at once he loses his balance and hurriedly lands his feet on the ground.)

MAN: *(Softly.)* What's wrong?

GIRL: *(At a loss.)* Nothing.

(Silence. Monk again attempts a one-hand handstand.)

MAN: *(Takes a look at her tote bag.)* Tell me, what happened afterwards? How about that friend of yours?

GIRL: We split up a long time ago.

MAN: So now you're on your own and you're wandering all over the globe?

GIRL: I've been looking for a companion, but none lasted.

MAN: Yes, nowadays it's the in thing to do, like fashion, which tends to change from one year to another, or from one season to the next.

GIRL: *(Looks around.)* You don't look like you're living alone, eh?

MAN: Of course I've had, how should I put it, a wife? What's the matter? You don't like that word?

GIRL: I can't stand being tied down.

MAN: Well, I guess we're no different from each other there.

(Both laugh heartily. Monk, who is doing a handstand, again takes away one hand and fails once more. He hurriedly lands his feet on the ground.)

MAN: *(Very carefully.)* May I ask your name?

GIRL: Is that important? Try to remember it well and make sure that you don't get it wrong.

MAN: Why? Somebody did?

GIRL: I hope you're not as bad.

(Both laugh somewhat bitterly.
Monk kneads his hands and attempts a handstand for the third time.)

GIRL: Maria or Anna, which one do you prefer?

MAN: The question is which one is your real name?

GIRL: If I told you it's Maria, then would I surely be Maria?

MAN: That's a real problem. But if I called you Anna, you'd still be you and not some-one called Anna, therefore, you really shouldn't worry too much about it.

GIRL: *(Dryly.)* I don't want to be a stand-in for somebody else!

MAN: Of course. A name is just a code, what's important is not the sign itself but the actual person behind that sign. You can call me whatever you like, even if it's some name you're familiar with, or some name that accidentally slips from your tongue, anything, I don't think I'd mind.

GIRL: I don't want to waste any more time on this subject. I don't want to know your name either, it's useless to me. And don't bother making up a fake name and then forget about it in short order. When it's over, it's over.

MAN: But we've just begun, how could it be over so soon? Now that you've agreed that a name isn't important and that it's a real burden, let's get to the important part: between you and me . . .

GIRL: Between a man and a woman? How interesting!

MAN: The whole thing would become more pure, and the relationship more sincere and more real, don't you think?

(Monk completes a handstand and takes away one hand, but he fails again just when it looks as if he is going to succeed. He exits dejected.)

GIRL: You really can't get it.

MAN: *(Quite interested.)* Get what?

GIRL: Impossible, it's impossible. I mean, a woman's heart.

MAN: If I guessed right, you're talking about love, aren't you? That of course is a very delicate subject.

GIRL: I'm talking about emotion, which you can't possibly understand.

MAN: Try me, you never know.

GIRL: How?

MAN: Between you and me—

GIRL: We've tried that before.

MAN: Try again. If it doesn't work, we'll just try again.

GIRL: *(On guard.)* No, you can never have it, you can never have anything!

MAN: Just now I was too rushed, really.

GIRL: *(Smiles coldly.)* You're always in a rush.

MAN: *(Somewhat repentant.)* Can I make it up to you in any way?

GIRL: Don't think that because you've had a lot of women . . . You don't know women, you'll never be loved, it's in your destiny.

(Girl turns around. Monk enters carrying a wooden stick. He looks around for something.)

MAN: *(Sarcastically.)* What's love? Try to explain it to me.

GIRL: It can't be explained.

MAN: There's no harm in trying.

GIRL: There are things you can explain, and there are things you can't. Don't you know that?

MAN: Of course I do, but I still want to know about love.

GIRL: What a fool!

MAN: Then go find yourself someone who isn't.

GIRL: Aren't we discussing something? And the topic is love?

MAN: We just made love, do we have to discuss it too?

GIRL: Isn't it true that you like to discuss all kinds of things?

MAN: Well, go find someone that you can discuss with and discuss them all you want!

GIRL: Why are you so hotheaded?

(Monk finally finds a spot and tries very carefully to stand the stick up on the floor. But once he removes his hand, the stick falls and he at once grabs it and holds on to it. He turns to find another spot.
Man looks at Monk and can't help feeling a bit depressed.)

GIRL: Answer me, are you or are you not a philosopher?

MAN: Philosophy can go to hell.

GIRL: You're such an overgrown kid. *(Embraces his head.)* Be careful, I'm beginning to like you.

MAN: Isn't that nice?

GIRL: It's very dangerous.

MAN: *(Gets away from her.)* Why?

GIRL: Dangerous for you and for me.

MAN: As far as I'm concerned, if you want to stay then stay, you won't be in my way. I've got everything here, a bathroom, a kitchen, a bedroom, and a bed, of course, there's only one bed, but there's everything that a woman needs.

GIRL: Do you have shampoo, make-up, and a nightgown too?

MAN: Yes, if you need them, except underwear, you know, everyone is a different size. Make yourself at home, as a matter of fact, I won't mind if you treat this place like your own home—

GIRL: As long as none of your girlfriends is coming?

MAN: At least none is coming right now. You can stay as long as you like, it's free. When you want to eat something, just go to the fridge and help yourself, and don't bother to pay me.

GIRL: I can't stay with a man all the time.

MAN: There's no need to. Anyway, if you want to go, it'll be very simple.

GIRL: And very cheap.

MAN: I'm doing this out of good will, you can stay if you don't have anywhere else to go, that is, if you really want to stay.

GIRL: Thanks, I don't live off men, so you don't have to worry about that.

MAN: I'm not worrying. I can even give you a key, just leave it behind when you go.

GIRL: Do you entertain women like this all the time?

MAN: Not all the time, only sometimes, it's the same with any other single man, there's nothing unusual about it.

GIRL: What's unusual is—Is there anything that's unusual about you?

MAN: Well, I do have a strange habit. I can't stand people shaving their armpits in front of me. Don't get me wrong, I'm not against hair or anything. We're born with it, and it's natural and it can be very exciting. And of course, I have no objection to a woman dressing herself up.

GIRL: For me, I can't stand anyone snoring beside me.

MAN: Fortunately I'm not that old yet, well, at least I haven't noticed it, and no women have left me because of it.

GIRL: Why did they leave you then?

MAN: It's very simple, either I couldn't stand them or they couldn't stand me.

GIRL: May I ask why couldn't they stand you?

MAN: I like eating raw garlic.

GIRL: It shouldn't be much of a problem, as long as you brush your teeth afterwards.

MAN: Another thing is probably that I don't have patience, and I just can't stand neurotic behaviour.

GIRL: Well, there's no woman who isn't neurotic.

MAN: And you too?

GIRL: It depends on the person and the time. *(Silence.)* What else shall we talk about?

MAN: *(Scrutinizing her.)* Are you still at school? I'm just asking. What I mean is, you're so young.

GIRL: You want to see my diploma or something? Are you planning to hire me?

MAN: Come to think of it, I might. But how shall I put it, I can't afford to pay you.

GIRL: I don't want to be a maid to wait on people, I don't do cleaning, and I hate washing dishes.

MAN: I don't entertain at home much, unless it's some young girl like you. What I mean to say is, sometimes I do need to use the desk at night. If you're still at school and you've got homework to do, there could be a slight problem.

GIRL: Do you write? Are you a writer?

MAN: *(Hurriedly.)* No, we're living in an age of women writers, every woman likes to write something. All men's books have already been written. And when men write about women it's just not as realistic as women writing about themselves.

GIRL: Do you read only books written by women?

MAN: Not necessarily. I've read some. As for women writing about men . . . How shall I put it? . . .

GIRL: Too exciting? Or too neurotic?

MAN: Too sissyish. I don't mean to criticize, let's leave criticism to the critics, it's their job. What I mean is, women don't understand men, just as men don't understand women.

GIRL: If I were to write about men —

MAN: They'd all be bastards?

GIRL: Not necessarily.

MAN: Even worse than bastards?

GIRL: They don't even qualify, they'd just be cowards.

MAN: *(Hesitantly.)* Actually, it'd be quite interesting if you were to write like that. Have you written anything yet?

GIRL: I want to write, but I know I'll never be a writer.

MAN: Whoever writes is a writer, you don't need a diploma to be one. It's as simple as that.

GIRL: But who's going to support me? I've got to pay my rent first, you know.

MAN: Of course, you can't live on writing. Nowadays writing has become a luxury and an extravagant habit.

GIRL: You seem to like literature, don't you? Do you prefer poetry or fiction?

MAN: Why just poetry or fiction? Only women read those nowadays. Oh, I beg your pardon, what I mean is—

GIRL: Why apologize? *(Teasing him.)* I'm no poet and I can't write fiction, I'm not any of those, I'm just a woman.

MAN: Thank God for that. These days men are always busy earning money and making deals. On weekends? Well, they either have business engagements or they can't wait to go away with their girlfriends. Only women can afford to have the leisure and the time to read.

GIRL: Not all women read, they're also busy living. We only live once, don't you think?

MAN: I know. Nowadays, anyone who writes a book has to read it himself.

GIRL: You don't look like a businessman. Tell me, do you write books just for yourself to read?

MAN: I don't have the luxury. Once in a while, I'll take a look at the books other people have written.

GIRL: May I ask what kind of books do you read?

MAN: Books on politics.

GIRL: Wow! Are you a politician? Are you involved in politics in any way?

MAN: Thank God no, I think it's better to leave the politicians alone.

GIRL: Then why do you still read about politics then?

MAN: I only read political memoirs.

GIRL: Then you must be studying history, right?

MAN: Not exactly studying. I only want to see how the politicians can lie with a straight face, cheat on one another, swindle, and play with public opinion as if it were a card game. And you know, they'll only let out a little bit of truth in their memoirs after they've been kicked out. And like you said, we only live once, right? So don't let them take you for a ride.

GIRL: Please don't talk to me about politics. All men like politics, 'cause they want to show people they have the talent and the intelligence to run the ship of the state.

MAN: Relax, it's more interesting to talk about women when you're with a woman.

GIRL: You've got to know how, otherwise you'll just make a real pest of yourself.

MAN: Of course, flirting is an art, or the art of living even. It's a lot more interesting than playing cards. Cards are dead and people are living creatures, and they're all different from one another, don't you think?

GIRL: Are you done yet?

MAN: Yes.

(Monk finally manages to stand the stick up. Man and Girl both look at him.)

GIRL: What else shall we talk about?

MAN: We'll keep on talking about women of course.

GIRL: Generally, or shall we pick a specific one?

MAN: Why don't you talk about yourself? I want to get to know you, but please don't mention that India thing again.

GIRL: You wouldn't believe me if I did.

MAN: Have you been feeding me lies?

GIRL: Haven't you lied before? Haven't you ever cheated on your wife? Don't lie to me!

MAN: Of course I did, I never said I was a saint.

GIRL: Exactly. You know why women cheat? It's only because they've learned the tricks from men first.

MAN: You mean people cheat on you all the time?

GIRL: Cheating is a form of self-defence.

MAN: Does that include cheating on oneself?

GIRL: Everyone cheats, otherwise it'd be impossible to live.

MAN: You seem to be living quite painfully, don't you?

GIRL: Everyone's in pain. You don't look like you're too happy yourself.

MAN: Can't you change the way you talk?

GIRL: How? How should I change it? C'mon, tell me.

MAN: You're always so defensive, it's so hard to talk to you.

GIRL: The same here. It's really tiring talking to you.

MAN: You're like that too. Now I've got a headache.

GIRL: (*Somewhat sympathetic.*) Come on, let's change to a lighter subject, something that'll cheer us up.

(*Having completed his previous stunt, Monk rubs his hands and starts to become enthusiastic again. He takes out an egg from inside his robe and tries to stand the egg on the tip of the stick.*)

MAN: What else shall we talk about? Something in praise of women or what? But everything that has to be said has been said already, there's really nothing new left to say any more. Perhaps I should say that you're young and beautiful? That you're charming and attractive? Or that you're sexy? By the way, these are not empty words, and they're not meant to flatter you or to make you feel good, they're all true.

GIRL: My dear, you seem to be more lovely when you're not using your brain. For once can't you just honestly talk about yourself? Tell me, how do you spend your time?

MAN: You mean right now?

GIRL: Yes, at this very moment —

MAN: Make love, if someone's willing.

GIRL: What if there's nobody around? Then what would you do?

MAN: I dream, when I'm doing nothing I always dream. Dreams are more real than reality itself, they're closer to the self. Don't you think so? (*Lights a candle.*)

GIRL: Me too, I dream almost every day. Tell me about your dreams.

MAN: One day, I dreamt that I was sinking into the ground, my whole body was trapped deep inside, there were two extremely high walls on either side of me, or should I say huge crags, no matter how hard I tried I just couldn't climb over them and get out . . . What are you laughing at?

GIRL: You made it all up, you're only thinking about women.

MAN: You can't really tell what happens in your dream, can you? If you're dreaming things happen in no particular order and you're confused, when you wake up and try to talk about it, you'd simply lay it on and fabricate, or you'd deceive yourself, and later when you tell your dream to somebody, you'd add on your own fantasies for self-gratification. In a dream, you're only living in your feelings at the time, that's all. *(Looks at Monk.)* There's no plot, just narration.

(The egg falls from the tip of the stick onto the ground. Monk takes another egg from inside his robe and tries patiently to stand it on the tip of the stick again.
Girl smiles surreptitiously.)

MAN: It's just wishful thinking trying to tell a dream.

GIRL: You're an idiot.

MAN: That's right. You're you only when you're dreaming.

GIRL: *(Steps back to inspect him.)* Are you saying that at this very moment you aren't real?

MAN: Who cares if I'm real or not? You're only concerned with how you feel, right? Only feelings can be real.

GIRL: Now you're beginning to scare me.

MAN: You weren't scared when that Indian guy raped you, and you're telling me that you're scared now? *(Walking closer to her.)*

GIRL: Don't even try, I'm going.

MAN: You're not going anywhere.

GIRL: Don't try to intimidate me.

MAN: Just playing. You get scared easily when we play for real.

GIRL: Because it's not fun.

MAN: Well then, why don't you tell me how we should play?

GIRL: It's got to be more relaxing, more cheerful. But you just keep annoying people.

MAN: All right. Whatever you say, I'm game. Tell me, how do you want to play?
     (Puts down the candlestick.)

(Again the egg falls and rolls on the ground. Monk takes out a third egg from inside his robe. He rubs it in his palms and then places it on the tip of the stick.)

GIRL: Fine. Take off your clothes for me, take them all off! That's what you want, right?

(Monk turns his head as if to take a glance at them.)

GIRL: I can't stand your bathrobe, don't you think it's ugly? It makes me sick!

(Monk turns back his head to continue with his task.
Man takes off his bathrobe and throws it on the ground.)

MAN: Okay, now it's your turn.

GIRL: Can't you put it more gently?

MAN: How?

GIRL: Do I have to teach you that too?

MAN: When you're stark naked you're more natural, and more beautiful.

GIRL: *(Sighs.)* Your trouble is you're lonely, so lonely that you're dying for someone to give you a little tender loving care.

(When Monk takes his hand away, the egg falls rolling onto the ground as before.
Girl takes off her blouse. Monk keeps looking at the egg, not knowing what to do.)

MAN: *(At once getting excited.)* You're a real knockout!

GIRL: You only found out just now? It sure took you long enough. You really don't
know how to appreciate what you've got, or how to cherish it.

MAN: It's still not too late. Come over here . . . No, go stand over there!

GIRL: Where?

MAN: On the opposite side. Look at me, and put your hands down.

(Girl drops her hands and laughs, facing him.
Monk sighs and again takes out an egg from inside his robe.)

MAN: Spread your arms like a bird in flight. You're a bird, a living and breathing big
bird. Spread your arms for me!

GIRL: What if I don't?

(Monk is persisting, still trying to place the egg on the tip of the stick.)

MAN: When I say spread, spread. Don't you like birds?

GIRL: You're a bird, not me.

MAN: Spread your arms!

GIRL: No.

(Man and Girl are locked in a stalemate.
Frustrated, Monk cracks the egg on the tip of the stick, and the egg shell finally stands on the stick.)

GIRL: *(Begging.)* Say something nice to me.

MAN: I want you . . . Close your eyes.

(Girl reluctantly spreads her arms and closes her eyes.
Monk rubs his hands and exits satisfied.)

MAN: *(Man quietly circles to the back of Girl.)* On your knees now. *(Takes a knife from
inside his bathrobe.)*

GIRL: No, you're disgusting. *(Reluctant, half kneeling and half sitting down.)*

MAN: Put your hands on the floor. We're playing a game, are we not? *(He hides the
knife behind him and pulls her hands down on the floor and holds them there with
his other hand.)*

GIRL: *(Frees herself from his hand.)* No, I'm not a dog! You're really sick. *(Gets up.)*

MAN: Are we playing or not? You wanted it, and you started it first—

GIRL: That's enough. Can't you just use your imagination?

MAN: *(Coaxing her.)* All right, then you'll be a fish, now try to imagine you're a fish, a
bouncy and jumping mermaid fish dragged out of the water and landed on dry
land, okay?

GIRL: To hell with you. I'm not your plaything, go play with yourself.

MAN: But you started it first. After you've got people interested, you turn around and
say you don't want to play any more. It just isn't fair.

GIRL: You make me sick! You understand?

MAN: Has it ever crossed your mind that you make people sick also? Everybody's sick
of everybody! Everyone is sickening!

GIRL: You're just a log! A rotten log, rotten to the core!

(Man and Girl face each other in silence. Suddenly Girl laughs out loud. Man is dejected. He quietly puts the knife back inside his bathrobe.)

GIRL: Dance for me!

MAN: *(Confounded.)* What?

GIRL: Are you playing or not?

MAN: Forget it, let's knock it off. I'm not interested any more.

GIRL: But now I am. You forced me to play when I wasn't interested, didn't you? *(Pleading with him.)* Please, dance for me, just one dance, okay?

MAN: I don't know how to.

GIRL: Then what do you know? Or do you only know how to think?

MAN: Don't talk to me about thinking or not thinking.

GIRL: Then go and stand over there, you do know how, don't you? Please, please do me a favour, go and stand over there.

MAN: Where?

GIRL: There, stand there like Michelangelo's David,[3] but act like you're thinking.

MAN: *(Goes to the other side reluctantly.)* You act like one of those woman executives. Do you enjoy ordering men around?

GIRL: It'd be nice if I could. Listen, David represents man at his best, I'm making it easy for you.

MAN: You're an unqualified witch!

GIRL: That's it! Raise your hands for me, just like a Michelangelo.

MAN: Michelangelo was gay.

(Girl laughs heartily. Man reluctantly raises his hands and laughs.)

GIRL: I like being gay. Nobody asked you to become impotent!

MAN: Gosh, what a she-devil!

GIRL: I'm going to hurt you, hurt you real bad! Run, I say run!

(Continuous beating of the cymbal. Monk still has not entered.)

MAN: How?

GIRL: Run in a circle around me!

MAN: Do you want everyone to run around you?

GIRL: Aren't you the same? You won't be happy until you turn every woman into your slave. *(Very excited.)* Raise your hand now like you're throwing a javelin.

MAN: *(Screaming.)* I'm not a model!

GIRL: Why is it that only women can be models? Now try it and see what it's like! Didn't you say this is the age of women? Who told you to lose your sense of imagination? Run! I say run!

MAN: *(Running and shouting.)* If a woman became God, the world would turn into a pandemonium, much more horrible than it is now. I don't know, maybe it'd be better, but it'd more likely be much worse, like some chick's tantrum!

GIRL: So what if for once we were God Almighty? *(Blocks his way.)* Blindfold yourself!

---

[3] **Michelangelo's David:** A marble statue of the nude David by Italian sculptor and painter Michelangelo Buonarroti (1475–1564). Produced between 1501 and 1504, the figure, more than thirteen feet tall, now stands in a museum in Florence, Italy.

MAN: Stop fooling around, I beg you. Okay?

GIRL: Oh, so you can fool around but I can't, is that what you're saying? If we're going to fool around, let's fool around together, you and I, until we both can't take it any more!

(Girl takes the chance to strip Man of his clothes. He kisses her, taking advantage of the situation. She wraps the clothes around his head, covering his eyes.
Monk enters beating a gong.
Girl hurriedly takes out a pair of pantyhose from her handbag, ties it around Man's clothes and pushes him away.)

GIRL: Over here.

MAN: I'm going to get you! You little devil you!

(Man chases after Girl. Both of them run in circles.)

MAN: You pigfeet — you dirty little rat — where are you?

GIRL: Here I am . . . *(Quietly picks up the overcoat.)*

MAN: You won't get away this time! *(Jumps on Girl.)*

(Just as he is about to catch her, she sticks out a leg and he trips and misses her.
Monk is stunned and exits.)

MAN: *(Yanks off her pantyhose and throws it on the ground.)* What the hell are you doing?

GIRL: *(Giggling.)* Isn't this what you want? Isn't it?

MAN: *(Irritated.)* You must be out of your mind. Are you crazy or something?

GIRL: You're crazy, you're sick, not me! All you want is sex, sex, sex and getting yourself turned on. It's your sexual fantasy, not mine.

MAN: *(Grabs her at once.)* Now let's see if you can go on bullshitting!

GIRL: *(Pushes him away.)* Get away from me! You want fantasies, right? Go fantasize yourself! *(Picks up the handbag.)*

MAN: *(Knocks her to the ground.)* Don't even think of running away! You'll never make it! *(Fishes out the knife from inside his bathrobe.)* I'll kill you first!

GIRL: *(Startled. She moves back and tries to block him with her handbag.)* What? Are you crazy or something? Stay away from me!

MAN: *(Forces his way towards her and grabs her handbag.)* Slut! Whore! You want to run? Go ahead and try! — *(Kisses her by force.)*

GIRL: *(Seizes a pencil case, wallet, underwear, notebook, book, make-up, a set of keys, and other unimaginable sundry items from her handbag and throws them at Man one after another.)* No, don't! Don't — !

MAN: Stop — it! *(Grabs her.)* I'm going to make a whore out of you yet!

GIRL: I'm no —

MAN: I don't care if you aren't, you still have to pretend once —

GIRL: No! Get away from me! Let — me — go — ! Let me go! Let go! I — don't — *(Becomes hysterical and strikes him again and again.)*

MAN: *(Letting go of her, stunned.)* I was just fooling around. Didn't you start it first? You started the whole thing, didn't you?

(Man puts down the knife and walks away perplexed.)

Monk enters, beating the wooden fish in his hand. He chants loudly:

"A . . . mi . . . tabha! Great mercy, great pity, Amitabha! Sympathy . . . goodness! Virtuous men, virtuous women, purify your hearts! And in your highest voices, recite the Five Wisdoms Sutra![4] Since the time of the ancients, such a doctrine, this doctrine of thoughtlessness, has been upheld in sudden enlightenment, and in gradual enlightenment. The body is without form, the essence without entity."

Girl covers her face with her hands and crouches down slowly. She starts to sob.
When Man hears her sobbing, he shakes his head and frowns, finally turns around and returns to her side. He stretches out his hand and bends down to stroke her head and neck.)
GIRL: Don't touch me, I have no feelings . . . *(Starts to wail loudly.)* No feelings! No feelings! No feelings . . .

(Man jumps on Girl. She falls onto the ground and wails and cries continuously.
Monk walks slowly to front stage and sits down, his legs crossed. He beats the wooden fish and chants the sutra:

"Monks of the Buddha, nuns of the Buddha, and man disciples, woman disciples, and the wise men in all directions, they all subscribe to the Law. The Law is neither long nor short, one moment is ten thousand years. No being is not being, all directions are before your eyes. The extremely big is the same as small, all boundaries forgotten; the extremely small is the same as big, all limits disappeared. Presence is absence, absence is presence. Anything that is not so, it is not worth keeping. One is all, all is one. If this could be so, how could any worry remain unresolved?")

MAN: This world, it's all gone crazy,
GIRL: *(Mumbling.)* Just because of loneliness,
MAN: *(Whispering.)* Just because of boredom,
GIRL: Just because of thirst and hunger,
MAN: Just because of desires,
GIRL: It's unbearable,
MAN: Just because it's unbearable,
GIRL: Just because it's unbearable to be a woman,
MAN: Just because to be a man is unbearable,
GIRL: Just because not only being a woman but also being human,
MAN: A living human being, a body of flesh and blood,
GIRL: It's only to have feelings,
MAN: It's only to resist death,
GIRL: Just because of the fear of death,
MAN: Just because the yearning for life,
GIRL: It's only to experience the fear of death,

---

[4] **Five Wisdoms Sutra:** A Buddhist text describing the five wisdoms: Wisdom of the Embodied Nature of the Dharma Realm; Wisdom of the Great Round Mirror; Wisdom in regard to all things equally and universally; Wisdom of profound insight, or discrimination, for exposition and doubt—destruction—derived from the mind consciousness; Wisdom of perfecting the double work of self-welfare and the welfare of others.

MAN: It's only to prove the existence of the self,
GIRL: It's only for the reason of just because —
MAN: Just because of the reason of it's only for —
GIRL: It's only because just because . . .
MAN: No therefore there is no purpose.

(Monk starts to turn the beads of his Buddhist rosary, reciting the sutra in silence. The sound of the wooden fish becomes increasingly lighter, and Monk closes his eyes in meditation. Sound of wooden fish fades completely.)

GIRL: A sound, sharp and piercing . . .
MAN: A greenish grey sun, gyrating in the dark . . .
GIRL: Dead at knife-point, dead in space . . .
MAN: Motorcars howling ferociously —
GIRL: And the fingers are very cruel!
MAN: Zooming past, zooming, zooming and gone . . .
GIRL: Void and empty, all over the body . . .
MAN: A swollen leather bag . . .
GIRL: Flowing from the inside of the body to the outside . . .
MAN: Window panes shaking furiously forever . . .
GIRL: Up and down and all over, no more existence, no more weight, all shapes have vanished —
MAN: Only hear something breathing —
GIRL: Water's dripping, where is it?
MAN: *(Listening.)* No sound.
GIRL: Still dripping, and still dripping . . .
MAN: Any more troubles?
GIRL: Not turned off properly . . . How come it can't be turned off completely?
MAN: Turn off what completely?
GIRL: The tap, the tap in the bathroom.
MAN: Let it drip.
GIRL: Go turn it off, I beg you.
MAN: *(Sits up and observes her.)* The doors, the windows, and all the taps have been shut off properly!
GIRL: But I'm still uneasy . . .
MAN: You're hypersensitive.
GIRL: I'm always frightened, always afraid . . .
MAN: What's there to be afraid of?
GIRL: Afraid of death, afraid of dark houses, I've been afraid of staying in a room by myself since I was young, even when I was sleeping, I had got to turn on the light. First I was afraid of growing up, then I was afraid of men, and afraid of becoming a woman, a real woman, of course I'm not afraid of that any more, but I'm still afraid, afraid that someone might just suddenly kill me, just like that, with no particular reason . . .
MAN: *(Becoming alert.)* What are you talking about? Who wants to kill you?
GIRL: I don't know, but I'm afraid, there's always a certain fear, always afraid that . . . When I was eighteen I was afraid of being twenty, when I was twenty I was afraid

of being over twenty, and after twenty I felt that death was getting closer day by day.

MAN: *(Relieved.)* According to what you said, it's the same with everybody. But you're still young.

GIRL: When I'm alone at night I'm always jumpy. I'm afraid of weekends, afraid of spending the days by myself. I'm afraid of mornings, afraid that someday crinkles might appear at the corner of my eyes, I'm afraid, afraid that someday I'll suddenly grow old.

MAN: Tell me, how old are you really?

GIRL: I'm close to twenty six, I'm not young any more.

MAN: What is twenty six? I was still a kid when I was twenty six. I didn't even know how to fart properly, let alone knowing women.

GIRL: But that's you, to a woman, once she reaches thirty it spells death, and that's the truth!

MAN: According to you, I should have been dead a long time ago, shouldn't I?

GIRL: For a man, life begins at thirty, but for a woman, the best time of her life is over and done with already.

MAN: There's no need to worry. You're still in your prime, still fresh as a daisy —

GIRL: Really? Am I still fresh?

MAN: When did you first do it? Your first time?

GIRL: Let me think, sixteen, no, at that time I was . . . only fourteen.

MAN: Did you do it with a classmate? Or with a dirty old man?

GIRL: No, my teacher, a physical education teacher.

MAN: The bastard!

GIRL: He told me that I had a good figure, that I had long legs and I was agile, so he would give me special lessons. He invited me to his place and gave me some candies, I was very fond of candies then. He told me to take off my clothes. You see, there wasn't anybody else at his place. Then he told me to demonstrate some movements for him to look at and he would correct me. First he held my waist to help me press my legs down, then . . . he . . . raped me.

MAN: *(Letting go of her.)* You only thought he did?

GIRL: At the time I felt . . . I also wanted to know something about my body . . .

MAN: And since then you've been going all out to use yourself up, to consume it all. *(Sits up.)*

GIRL: Aren't you also using yourself up? And you think that's love, don't you? Go pull a fast one on some wide-eyed teenybopper!

MAN: You're always flirting, has it ever occurred to you that you've got some kind of psychological problem?

GIRL: Problem? Everyone has a problem, including you, me, everyone. Have you seen how men stare at women? The look in your eyes, the way you whisper, the way you behave, and the way you leer at women's clothing, aren't they all meant to encourage women, so that they'll make themselves sexy for men? The bras, panties, necklaces, jewellery, and perfume, by the way, men also use perfume, only the brand names are different, aren't they all designed by men and for men's excitement? Women themselves don't need these things at all. Movies, television, fashion, advertisements, pop songs, bars and nightclubs, is there anything that's not meant to turn people on? You men all want to turn women into playthings, and you, you're not much better.

MAN: I knew it, I knew it. You're a feminist!

GIRL: You don't know anything. I'm no believer in feminism or any other ism. I'm a living human being, I only want to live life to the fullest as a woman.

MAN: Wonderful! So why are you still complaining?

GIRL: I'm not complaining, I'm only saying that I'm afraid, afraid that all these will disappear . . .

MAN: That's why you're trying desperately to seize every moment?

GIRL: Aren't you doing the same thing? Whenever you see an opportunity, you never let it go.

MAN: *(Stands up.)* Everybody is sick, the whole world is sick.

(Girl tenderly caresses Man's leg, her face leaning close to him.
Monk lifts his head and beats softly on the wooden fish.)

MAN: *(Looks at Monk and talks to himself.)* We'll all be used up before we die.

(Monk holds up the wooden fish and beats on it. The sounds become louder. Monk exits.)

GIRL: Don't leave me.

MAN: *(Stroking her head.)* I'm right by your side, am I not?

GIRL: I don't have anybody to rely on, you wouldn't understand even if I told you.

MAN: You and I are in the same boat, the world is a desert.

GIRL: I'm afraid that tomorrow . . .

MAN: Tomorrow, tomorrow, it's still early . . .

GIRL: No one's coming?

MAN: Tomorrow, no one.

GIRL: Do I have your word for it?

MAN: You're a silly girl.

GIRL: A silly woman.

MAN: And a silly child.

GIRL: Do you deserve to have a child?

(Man is silent. He just holds her head and looks at it closely.)

GIRL: You must be thinking of something. Don't look at me like that! *(Pushes him away.)*

MAN: What's wrong with that?

GIRL: You know exactly what's wrong.

MAN: *(Letting her go.)* I don't understand you, I just don't understand what goes on in your mind.

GIRL: Is that important?

MAN: *(Somewhat troubled.)* I can't decide whether or not I should love you.

GIRL: It's the same here.

MAN: You mean you love me?

GIRL: Don't take it too seriously. *(Sincerely.)* At least, I like you.

MAN: You've set my mind at ease. I like you too, really.

GIRL: Since when?

MAN: In the pub, when I caught sight of you right away. Remember that corner with the light hanging on the wall? You were sitting there, your face towards the entrance.

GIRL: *(Smiling.)* And you came over to me just like that, without even asking, right?

MAN: The light was shining on your neck . . . in the shadow, I couldn't quite see your eyes.

GIRL: It's not nice to look at other people's eyes.

MAN: Tell me, what should I look at then?

GIRL: Anyway, you shouldn't look without asking, it's very rude.

MAN: I was only looking at a shadow, that soft shadow in between your breasts. And then the old black guy on the stage was singing some jazz song, it was so melancholy. When I sat down in the chair opposite you, you didn't say anything, did you?

GIRL: For a girl you didn't know, you really shouldn't have looked at her that way.

MAN: But you didn't exactly refuse me at the time. You didn't have a date, you were only waiting, waiting for that someone, until he sat down opposite you, weren't you?

GIRL: Remember, you just said something very pleasing to the ear.

MAN: Good, then I'll keep my mouth shut.

GIRL: You know, . . . today is my birthday.

MAN: Why didn't you tell me earlier? Let's celebrate!

GIRL: We did already. *(Silence. Then softly.)* Just now.

MAN: That was your birthday celebration?

GIRL: Yes, my twenty-sixth birthday. I was born at midnight, what time is it?

MAN: I know now, you just wanted to prove that you're still young, still attractive to men.

GIRL: There's no need to prove anything. All women at my age are still attractive. I just wanted . . .

MAN: What?

GIRL: To wait for a miracle.

(Girl does not say anything. Man walks away.)

MAN: I didn't know. At first I thought . . .

GIRL: I'm exactly what you thought I was, don't you see? *(Pulls up her dress.)*

MAN: *(Begging.)* Fine, fine. Stop flirting, please . . .

GIRL: Who's flirting? Tell me, how much were you prepared to pay me?

MAN: Really, you devil you!

GIRL: No, not a devil, but a cock-teasing goddess! Your idol, your whore. *(Opens her arms to him.)*

MAN: Don't abuse yourself.

GIRL: You did already. Stop acting like you're a gentleman.

MAN: All right then. You want a cheque or something? A ring? Or a necklace?

GIRL: Things that've been thrown away by other women, right?

MAN: Then how much? Give it to me straight, don't give me the run-around!

GIRL: I want you to make up for my birthday, I want you to spend the night with me before I turn into a totally incurable slut. You think I'm still sexy, don't you?

MAN: Wait, wait, calm down. Listen, you're still young, you can start all over again, there's no need to destroy yourself like that.

GIRL: *(Laughs loudly.)* You're more honest when you're not preaching. Hypocrite, an out-and-out hypocrite!

MAN: What is it that you really want? Tell me!

GIRL: *(Looking at the knife on the floor.)* I want your head.

MAN: That'd be kind of hard. Have you had too much to drink? Are you on drugs or something?

GIRL: This isn't India.

MAN: Will you stop making up stories? You just can't quit playing your game, can you?

GIRL: Isn't making love like playing a game? Either you're playing with me or I'm playing with you. What are you going to say to that?

MAN: I really should have killed you!

GIRL: I know. You're only wishing, you wouldn't dare. I've already seen through you ever since I first caught sight of you. You know, the look in your eyes actually gave you away. I'm telling you, you're a piece of crap.

MAN: *(Becoming very angry.)* Why did you come here then? You stinking whore!

GIRL: *(Calmly.)* I just wanted to prove something.

MAN: That you also put yourself up for sale?

GIRL: All women do, there's no need to prove that.

MAN: *(Puzzled.)* Then what were you trying to prove?

GIRL: *(Pauses. Laughs.)* . . . Do you want to play one last game with me?

MAN: What more is there to play?

GIRL: Play with death, a game of death.

MAN: That's not a bad idea. How do we play?

GIRL: Let's borrow your head for the time being.

MAN: Do you really want my head?

GIRL: *(Giggles.)* I said borrow.

MAN: *(Thinks for a moment. Goes over to her and lowers his head.)* All right, take it.

(Girl circles to Man's back. Suddenly she seizes the knife and raises it up high. Immediately the lights on the stage darken. Two loud and clear drum beats. Man falls down.

Monk enters, bareback and with a piece of red cloth tied around his waist. He is holding an axe in one hand and a wooden stick in the other, his head lowered.

Girl picks up the black overcoat and quietly covers Man's body with it. Monk bends down to look for a spot. He finally finds it at the other corner of the stage. He supports the wooden stick with one hand and softly bangs on it with the axe.

Man walks to the back of Girl. He is wrapped in the black overcoat with its collar pulled up. His face is cold and grey.)

GIRL: *(Without turning her head.)* You . . . you're not dead yet?

MAN: *(In a low voice.)* An eye for an eye? It's only fair. *(Raises the knife.)*

(Monk succeeds in making the wooden stick stand up. He raises the axe with both hands and hammers it down. The stick is nailed onto the floor. Monk is stupefied.

In the dark, both Man and Girl fall down quietly at the same time.

Monk picks up an egg from the floor and exits.)

SECOND HALF

(The stage has been cleaned and tidied up. It is empty except for two heads under the beaming light, one male and the other female.
Man and Girl are lying down and resting in the dark.
Sound of a tinkling bell.)

GIRL: The place is so quiet . . . as if it would break once you touched it . . .

MAN: What?

GIRL: Listen, how can it be so quiet, like there's absolutely nothing here, nothing has happened . . .

MAN: What's happening?

GIRL: Hush! Don't say a word—

(Girl gets to her feet and listens. The ringing disappears.)

GIRL: Someone's coming!

MAN: No one would come at this hour.

GIRL: Listen! Listen carefully—

MAN: *(Lifts his head.)* You're too sensitive. *(Lies down again.)*

(Crystal clear sound of bell ringing as if it's unreal.)

GIRL: Someone's at the door!

MAN: It's impossible.

GIRL: There's a knock on the door, I heard it. Someone's right there at the door.

MAN: Yeah, you heard it, so? Nobody can possibly come in here.

GIRL: Didn't you give someone the key?

MAN: That was a long time ago . . .

GIRL: How long ago?

MAN: I can't remember. It must have been years ago.

GIRL: Why didn't you ask for the key back?

MAN: I didn't bother. Anyway, it was ancient history, why mention it now?

GIRL: But if that someone suddenly remembered?

MAN: Who are you talking about? Who remembered?

GIRL: The one you gave the key to.

MAN: Remembered what?

GIRL: Remembered you. That person can come here any time, right?

MAN: Apart from you, is there anyone else who'd be thinking of me right now?

GIRL: You're so screwy.

MAN: *(Sits up and looks at her.)* Don't worry, no one's going to come any more. There's only you and me. Besides, we're dead already. Who'd think of visiting the dead? Don't be daft.

GIRL: Listen, listen, it's right above us. *(Looks up.)*

MAN: *(Listening.)* I don't hear anything. Besides, the place is so big, even if there were dead bodies rotting in here our neighbours wouldn't know anything about it, and they won't come knocking at the door unless the corridor smells.

GIRL: But we're both dead already, aren't we?

(Man and Girl lower their heads, silently gathering their thoughts.)

MAN: It looks like it. *(Looking at the two heads.)* Only you and me, nobody else knows. Besides, you can't tell, I can't tell, and it's impossible, absolutely impossible for anybody to tell the outside world!

GIRL: Are we going to be locked up here forever?

MAN: It wouldn't be too bad if this were a desert island, isolated from the rest of the world and without any sign of human habitation. But there's no blue sky to look at, and no beautiful sea to behold. If only we could hear the sound of surging waves from the sea . . .

GIRL: And you can't tell if it's day or night.

MAN: There's no sound, there's no movement, we're left in oblivion and stuck in a forgotten corner, no, an enclosed black box. It's not a coffin, it's not anything. We don't even know the time, is there time any more? Ah, time is no more than a notion, if you think there's time, then there's time. And death, it isn't such a horrible thing, is it?

GIRL: What's so scary is that you can't die quickly, this fear . . .

MAN: Nonsense! What's there to be scared of any more? You and I are already dead.

GIRL: I don't know, am I . . . ?

MAN: Are you what? Now you want to change your mind?

GIRL: I don't know, I don't know anything, is death better than living? I really can't say, everything is so confusing, so elusive . . . Please, please don't ask me any more questions.

MAN: *(Delightedly, like a child.)* You and I can't go back any more! Whether you like it or not, ha ha, we are stuck together forever like a man and his shadow. You and I, we're each other's shadow.

GIRL: Why are you still gloating now that you've turned into a shadow, a slave at the feet of a woman? I don't get you.

MAN: It doesn't matter, you and I are in the same boat, nobody can leave anybody. It makes no difference if you're my shadow or if I'm your shadow.

GIRL: You said it, not me.

MAN: So? The bottom line is . . . I love you.

GIRL: Me too.

MAN: We can't afford not to, we're inseparable now! Inseparable forever . . .

GIRL: *(Moved.)* Stay by me, like a good kid. *(Wants to kiss him.)*

MAN: *(Moves away.)* I'm tired. I don't have the urge.

GIRL: It's better this way. Stay by me, as long as I can hear your voice.

MAN: What more shall we talk about?

GIRL: You decide, anything's fine with me. Just say something, for instance, something you're thinking of.

MAN: I . . . can't think.

GIRL: How about your sarcasm, your mockery, and your ridicule? You enjoy doing these things, don't you?

MAN: I've said everything I can say . . . I really can't think of anything else . . . what else can I say?

GIRL: Maybe you could fantasize. Let's talk about your fantasies about women.

MAN: I've become impotent.

GIRL: *(Startled.)* That's no fun, what has become of that little bit of intelligence you had?

MAN: I'm really very drowsy . . .

GIRL: Don't close your eyes. Look at me and say something!

MAN: Leave me alone, I'm totally exhausted . . .

GIRL: How miserable . . . How can you be so boring . . .

MAN: Who? Who's boring?

GIRL: I mean it's really boring when a person dies. *(Looks at Girl's head.)*

(Girl crawls in front of the head and stares at it.)

MAN: What are you doing?

GIRL: Nothing.

MAN: *(Sits up.)* Just like a nightmare. *(Also looks at Man's head.)* This is . . . is this my head? Do you believe in resurrection?

GIRL: What?

MAN: Transmigration.

GIRL: What did you say?

MAN: Nothing.

(The two sit quietly back to back.)

GIRL: *(Persistently.)* She asks, what did you say?

MAN: *(Wearily.)* You say, you didn't say anything.

GIRL: She says she clearly heard you say something.

MAN: *(Without looking at her.)* You ask what did she hear you say?

GIRL: She says would she ask you if she knew?

MAN: You say that means you didn't say anything.

GIRL: Then she says, Oh. *(Turns to face the audience:)*

(Girl sits up straight, then she covers her face with her hands, her head lowered.
Man looks at woman's head.)

MAN: Then you see a contemptuous face. You say even if you wanted to say something, you wouldn't be saying it to her, and you say even if you actually said something, it wouldn't have anything to do with her, you're only talking about yourself. And the you that you're referring to only means you, which is no more than your self, you mean you, that self of yourself, keep on troubling you.

GIRL: She says she's afraid of silence, she can't stand people not talking when they're face to face with each other, she finds that suffocating. She's much more afraid of silence than of death, death is more bearable than not talking to each other like this.

MAN: You say you, you're only talking to yourself.

GIRL: She says she, she's only left with her memories.

MAN: You say you, the only way you can get a little bit of comfort is by talking to yourself.

GIRL: She says she, the only way she can invoke a little bit of fantasy is through her memories.

MAN: You say you, you can feel somewhat relaxed only when you're talking to yourself.

GIRL: She says she, she can see herself clearly only when she's fantasizing.

MAN: You say it's not that you don't want to get away from your self, but you're always talking to yourself, in that way the self will never go away and it'll never stop haunting you.

GIRL: She says only when she indulges herself in fantasies can she empty herself of her worries, be carefree and recall her past feelings. Even though they may have been scary feelings, they still manage to touch her heart.

(Man stands up slowly and walks in front of man's head.)

MAN: You have to get rid of the baggage in your mind completely, let bygones be bygones, get away from it all, and get it off your back forever.

GIRL: She's falling asleep . . . It's best to sleep deeply and never wake up, but she just can't sleep well, she's suffering from anxieties all the time . . .

MAN: *(Circles around the head and inspects it.)* You've got to find a way to get out of here!

GIRL: Dreams, one after another, intermittent and disjointed, there's no beginning, there's no end . . .

MAN: *(Lifts his head.)* It doesn't matter where you're going, when you've got to go, you've got to go!

GIRL: Her head is swooning and she's unsteady on her feet, she has no idea where she is . . .

MAN: You're groping around, you're trying hard to find a way out, you're afraid that you might bump into something . . .

GIRL: A wall, it is collapsing in silence, right in front of her eyes . . .

MAN: Finally you manage to find a door, it must be a door, it is tightly shut . . .

GIRL: That high wall, the one which has been standing erect in front of her, suddenly collapses just like that, without a sound, nobody has touched it . . .

MAN: You must open the door, even if it's only a little crack, as long as you can . . . squeeze through it sideways . . .

GIRL: She actually sees a patch of sky, misty and grey . . . just like fog . . .

MAN: You carefully walk into a dark and shady long corridor . . . it's curved and bent . . . there's no end . . .

GIRL: A big patch of misty grey sky, it's dark and light at the same time, like it's neither morning nor evening . . .

MAN: *(Lowers his head.)* Strange, where did this top hat come from? You don't know, should you or shouldn't you pick it up?

GIRL: Then she clearly hears a squeaking sound.

MAN: But you're afraid it might be a trap—*(Lifts his head.)*

GIRL: She knows that a knife is cutting—

MAN: You lift it up—*(Bends down to pick up the top hat.)*

GIRL: Cutting open a naked body—

MAN: Oh, a nest of ants! *(Immediately retreats.)*

GIRL: She sees it now, there's a crowd surrounding a woman, they're cutting open her stomach to dig out her internal organs.

MAN: *(Inspecting the top hat in his hand.)* It looks like your own hat, you haven't worn it for a long time, how could you have forgotten about it?

GIRL: They're butchering her, they're dissecting and discussing at the same time. There's also a woman mixed in among them, can't tell how old she is.

MAN: *(Puts on the hat.)* It actually fits. Only your own hat would fit this well.

GIRL: She lifts her head and looks around. A pair of hollow eye sockets! She takes to her feet at once!

MAN: *(Pulls down the brim of the hat.)* You can't go without a hat, a man without a hat is like a man without clothes.

GIRL: *(She bends down until her head touches the ground.)* Something's flowing down her thigh, she knows it may be blood, she feels awfully embarrassed.

MAN: *(Somewhat comforted, he raises his voice slightly.)* You walk down the pitch-dark corridor, at the same time you're groping for a way, you know what you should avoid, as if you've passed through the same corridor once, twice, and even three times before.

GIRL: She's actually not afraid of bleeding, just that she's afraid of the sight of blood. Once when she was a small girl she went fishing with the grownups, she saw them toss a big fish onto the shore, they'd just caught that fish, it was all shiny and glittering, and then they started to cut it open right there on a piece of rock, their fingers became sticky with blood, and the fish was still struggling and jerking up and down. She felt rather sorry for that fish, it hadn't died and yet it couldn't live any longer.

MAN: *(Wobbles backward rather purposely.)* You know it very well, there is no end, but still you have to keep on going, turning wherever there's a turn. There's no end, you can't stop because you have to go on, even though you know nothing will ever come of it.

GIRL: She really wants to cry, but she can't, she has no more tears. She knows her heart is hardened and dried, a barren stretch of desolation, just like those naked hills behind the old house she lived in when she was a child. She only went there once, she was alone, after that she didn't dare to go any more, the naked branches in the bushes were shaking, shaking with the wailing wind among those hills.

MAN: *(Finally he cannot stand steadily.)* You don't know where you should go, should you stop, or perhaps should you turn and go back?

GIRL: *(Gets up, at a loss.)* She doesn't know how it happened, but somehow she's in this railway station, it's all deserted and empty, there're no signs on the platform. She wants to know where the next train is going, but she can't find anyone to ask. She feels a bit scared, from here to there in this mammoth platform, she can only hear the hollow tapping of her own footsteps.

(Man walks behind her, staring at her back.
She walks away at once and then suddenly stops.
He takes two steps forward and follows her.)

GIRL: *(Closes her eyes and holds her breath.)* She knows there's someone behind her, she can feel that he's staring at her, her back is cold, she is waiting for that someone to raise the knife, she has no strength to lift her feet— *(Panting.)*

(Man extends his hands towards her, and she runs away as if she is possessed.
Man drops his hands.)

GIRL: *(Running and panting for breath.)* She says she's terrified, but then she's not really terrified, she knows she's only terrified of her memories of terror.

(Man droops his head.)

GIRL: Nobody can save her except herself, but she feels too weak even to think of saving herself. *(Dejected.)*

(Man stares at his feet.
Girl looks at him at a distance.)

GIRL: At last she sees someone in front of her, a man she's long been waiting for, a man who can perhaps save her! She really wants to see his face clearly, but it's just a blur, she can't quite make it out no matter how hard she tries. *(Walks around him and looks at him closely.)* My God, it's only a shadow!

(Disappointed, she retreats step by step, head down.)

MAN: *(Slowly lifts his head and marches forward.)* Shit. *(Crouches down to tie the shoelace on his right shoe, gets up, and starts to put forward his right foot.)* Shit! *(Crouches down to tie the shoelace on his left shoe, gets up, and starts to put forward his left foot.)* Shit! *(Crouches down to tie right shoelace again, gets up, and puts forward his right foot.)* Fucking shi— *(Turns to look at left foot, takes back right foot, crouches down to tie left shoelace again, gets up, and starts to lift right foot.)* Mother fucking shit! *(Lifts his right foot in the air to tie shoelace. Then with his right foot touching the ground, he raises the tip of his left foot.)* Mother fucking sh— *(Frustrated, he takes off both shoes, throws them away and sits on the ground trying to figure out what to do next.)*

GIRL: *(Looks at herself all over.)* She has no idea, is she also a shadow herself? *(Looks at the shadow under her feet and turns around again and again on the same spot.)* Is the shadow herself? *(Becoming dizzy.)* Or is she no more than the shadow of this shadow? *(Closes her eyes.)* Who is the real she?

(Monk enters dancing. He is holding a horsetail whisk to dust himself. He picks up an imaginary leaf from his shoulder and blows on it, making a whistling sound. Then he closes his eyes and chants: "Good men and women, good knowledge, purify your nature, purify your heart, Amitabha Buddha!" Monk exits.
Afterwards Man and Girl's behaviour becomes increasingly abnormal and strange.)

MAN: *(Talking to himself.)* Behind that door, perhaps there is nothing.

GIRL: *(Asking herself.)* No memories?

MAN: *(Ruminating.)* That door, behind that door, perhaps there is really nothing, do you believe that?

GIRL: No fantasies?

MAN: That's right, there's nothing behind that door, you thought there was something, but there's nothing.

GIRL: And no dreams either?

MAN: *(To audience.)* That door, behind that door, there's nothing.

GIRL: She can't remember anything.

MAN: *(To himself.)* There's absolutely nothing behind that door. *(Giggles.)*

GIRL: *(To audience.)* What happened?

MAN: *(Softly, his back facing Girl.)* That door, behind that door, there is nothing.

GIRL: *(Softly.)* And no memories.

MAN: Absolutely, absolutely.

GIRL: And no fantasies.

MAN: Absolutely, absolutely. *(Nods his head.)*

GIRL: And no dreams either.

MAN: Absolutely, absolutely! *(Becoming contemptuous, his head to one side.)*

GIRL: *(More softly.)* Can't say.

MAN: *(Very softly.)* Why?

GIRL: *(With certainty.)* Can't say.

MAN: Why can't you say it?

GIRL: *(Almost whispering.)* Can't say!

(Man is speechless.
Monk enters. Sound of running water.
Monk hastens forward, kneels on one knee, bends down and clasps his hands as if to cup the water. He dips his little finger in the water to wash his ears. After cleaning both ears, he rises and listens respectfully. His mouth opens slowly and reveals a Buddha-like smile. He exits quietly.)

GIRL: She can't believe that she actually said it, she said something that can't be said, but she said it, clearly this can't be said but why did she have to say it? It ought not to be said it can't be said but she said it regardless, it's her misfortune, it's her disaster, it's her sin.

MAN: *(Gets up, looks around and speaks loudly.)* And no door! *(Facing audience.)* The door? Where's the door? The door? The door? The door . . . *(Lowers his head.)* If you think you see it then you see it, if you think there's something then there's something, but what if you think there isn't? The door? Of course it's not there. *(Laughs to himself.)* That door of yours — no doubt it's something out of nothing, you're just being nosy, you just want to find a way out. What if you can't find a way out? Isn't that just as good? *(Laughs loudly.)*

GIRL: *(On her knees, murmuring.)* Her sin, well, if she feels guilty then she's guilty. She's afraid of this and afraid of that, afraid of this, afraid of that, afraid, afraid, afraid, but she's not afraid of her, not afraid of herself. But what happens if she's also afraid of herself? Then wouldn't she be not afraid?

MAN: A way out, a way out, since there's no way out, why go and look for it? You only want to prove you're not trapped, or look at it another way, you're looking just to prove that you're trapped? What if you were to stop looking? Then you're not trapped, and you aren't not trapped? Either you're trapped or you're not trapped, either you're not trapped or you aren't not trapped, isn't it all your own doing?

GIRL: If she feels she's not guilty, what's there to be afraid of? She's afraid because she feels she's guilty, she feels guilty because she's afraid. And if she's not afraid then she no longer — *(Pauses.)* That's even more horrifying than Silent Extinction . . .

MAN: If you weren't you, there wouldn't be the need to prove anything, would it? But if you weren't you, then who are you?

GIRL: A silkworm, which gets enmeshed in its own cocoon.

MAN: Do you care who you are? Why can't you put down this you of yours?

GIRL: Left with only the remnants of a broken wish?

MAN: You keep on babbling only to show that you are you, that you're not like other people.

GIRL: A wisp of silk at large.

MAN: You are you because you're still talking, that's all there is to it.

GIRL: Wind.

MAN: Actually you don't know what you're talking about, you talk only because you want to. *(Shakes his head.)*

GIRL: Hollow.

MAN: You can't understand the meaning of your own words, you're just the slave of language, but you can't stop yourself from talking endlessly — *(Shakes his head.)*

GIRL: Tin soldier.

MAN: You can't free yourself from language's entanglement, just like a spider — *(Shakes his head.)* No, you're not a spider, but you're still a spider. *(Shakes his head.)*

GIRL: Candle.

MAN: You're not free to move, being trapped in the web of language of your own making — *(Shakes his head.)*

GIRL: Sa, send, da, la, wood —

MAN: Drunk city, mourning, stone statue — *(Listening to himself attentively.)* Why mourn a stone statue? Is the whole city drunk, or is everyone drunk all over the city? Or is someone or something mourning the idol with drunkenness? Stones are heartless, do humans have a heart? Is the city drunk? Does the stone know?

GIRL: Trap, jump, show, mouth, cut —

MAN: Hut — sin — grief — chime — bell. *(Tilting his head to think.)* Who's actually grieving for who? Is this the hut owner's death or the instruments' pain? Do the instruments know their suffering? If they don't, how can they mourn? Where is the mourner? How does one know? This one, that one, what are they mourning? What is there to mourn? It's all utter nonsense!

(Monk enters sweeping the floor. He is holding a big broom, his back to the audience. He stops when he comes to front stage and sees the two heads.

The lights on stage gradually darken, except for the light shining on the heads, which becomes brighter. Monk turns to observe Man and Girl.

Man and Girl's movements become very slow.)

GIRL: *(Murmuring.)* Win — ter . . .

MAN: *(Observing her.)* Aha!

GIRL: Makes . . .

MAN: What?

GIRL: Tea — pot . . .

MAN: *(Sarcastically.)* Winter makes teapot?

GIRL: Teapot . . .

MAN: Teapot what?

GIRL: Makes . . .

MAN: Makes what?

GIRL: Winter . . .

MAN: Teapot makes winter?

GIRL: Makes . . .

MAN: And then—?

GIRL: Teapot . . .

MAN: And then makes teapot?

GIRL: It is . . .

MAN: It is what? Speak!

GIRL: It is not . . .

MAN: It is it is not?

GIRL: Is . . .

MAN: Is it is it not—is it winter makes teapot or teapot makes winter? (*Getting angry.*) Or is it it is not winter makes teapot or teapot makes winter? Or it is it is not is it not winter makes teapot or is it it is teapot makes winter? Or is it winter makes teapot makes winter? Or it is it is not is it winter makes teapot and then makes winter? Speak, speak, speak, go on!

(*Monk ignores them, sweeping more earnestly.*
Man and Girl move and speak faster with the quickening rhythm of the broom. Their bodies become more contorted, like two strange crawling reptiles.)

GIRL: Crack . . .

MAN: What crack?

GIRL: A crack . . .

MAN: What kind of a crack?

GIRL: A crack line . . .

MAN: What crack line?

GIRL: A crack . . .

MAN: What's this crack like?

GIRL: A crack . . .

MAN: Why a crack?

GIRL: A crack . . .

MAN: Where's this crack?

GIRL: A crack . . .

MAN: Why is it called a crack?

GIRL: A crack . . .

MAN: A crack and a crack!

GIRL: A crack . . .

MAN: Why is there just a crack?

GIRL: A crack . . .

MAN: A crack is a crack!

GIRL: A crack . . .

MAN: Okay, fine, a crack, so? What about it?

GIRL: A crack . . .

MAN: To hell with the crack!

GIRL: A crack . . .

MAN: Only one crack?
GIRL: A crack . . .
MAN: Another crack?
GIRL: A crack . . .
MAN: *(Exploding.)* A cr — a — ck — ?
GIRL: A crack . . .
MAN: *(Laughs bitterly.)* A crack.
GIRL: A crack . . .
MAN: *(Talking to himself.)* A crack . . .
GIRL: A crack . . .
MAN: *(Murmuring.)* A crack . . .
MAN & GIRL: *(Almost simultaneously.)* A crack —

(Monk coughs and throws the broom on the ground at the same time. He halts.
Man and Girl are stunned by the noise, staring at Monk. Monk turns to face the audience. He
inhales deeply and slowly and then exhales as slowly. All lights go out.
Monk turns to open a curtain, revealing a greyish blue sky. Monk stands motionless and looks
outside the door, his back to the audience. Gradually the wind starts to blow.)

THE END

∾ SALMAN RUSHDIE
B. INDIA, 1947

After Ayatollah Khomeini of Iran urged zealous Muslims to assassinate him, Salman Rushdie, a Muslim born in India who has since become a British citizen, became a story on the evening news. His crime, according to the ayatollah, was demonizing the Prophet Muhammad in his novel *The Satanic Verses* (1989). For Rushdie, the conflict with Islamic fundamentalism was probably inevitable, for his varied cultural heritage and multicultural identity made of him what he calls a "translated man." A product of Indian and Islamic roots, a British education, and total self-immersion in Western popular culture, Rushdie is seen by Muslim fundamentalists as someone who has been corrupted by the secular materialism of the West. From another perspective, Rushdie can be seen as a successor to Indian writers who sought to integrate East and West such as Ram Mohun Roy (1772–1833), Syed Ahmed Khan (1817–1898), and Rabindranath Tagore (1861–1941). From still another viewpoint, Rushdie becomes an avatar of POSTMODERNISM, a citizen of many cultures who speaks for an emerging global consciousness. "The Courter," which follows, is an autobiographical story that explores some of the gains and losses of such a cultural translation.

Phil Wilkinson,
Salman Rushdie, 1998
Since the Iranian
threat on his life was
lifted in 1999, Rushdie
has lived in full view
of the public. (© Star
Images / Topham /
The Image Works)

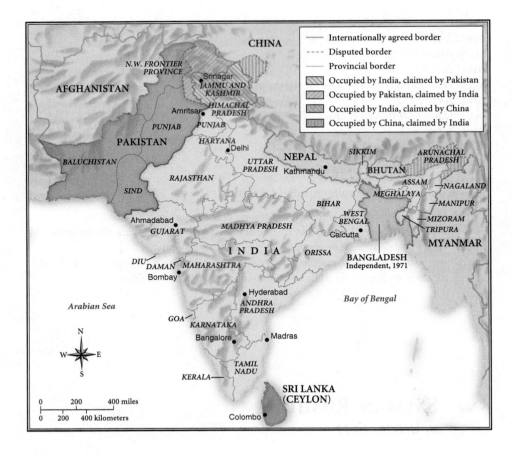

The Partition of India, 1947
*Led by Mohandas Gandhi, the Mahatma, the Indian independence movement realized
its goal in 1947, winning independence from the United Kingdom. The mainly Muslim
western provinces and Bengal became Pakistan, the rest remained India. Bengal was
known as East Pakistan until a civil war in 1971 between West and East Pakistan
resulted in the latter's independence and new name, Bangladesh. Ownership of the territory of Kashmir, which lies north of India and northeast of Pakistan, is still disputed.*

Almost One of "Midnight's Children."   Born in Bombay in 1947, the
year that India gained its independence from Britain, **Salman Rushdie**,
though not one of "Midnight's Children"—children born in the first
hour of Indian independence—was a postcolonial child. His father, a
Cambridge-educated Muslim businessman who would move his family
to Pakistan when his son was seventeen, kept the family in the cosmopolitan and predominantly Hindu Bombay during the years of Salman's
childhood. There the boy received a British education, read the Hindu

SAL-mun RUSH-dee

classics, and watched the films produced by Bollywood, India's prolific film industry. At fourteen, Salman was sent to Rugby, a famous English public school near London where he was considered an outsider, treated as an inferior, and excluded from many social activities. After three years in England, Rushdie rejoined his family, who had moved to Pakistan while he was away, but he was equally uncomfortable in Pakistan, where his English accent marked him as different. At his father's urging to accept a scholarship to attend Cambridge University, Rushdie reluctantly returned to England in 1965, a choice he has characterized as "one of the most disorienting moments of my life."

But Cambridge proved to be friendlier than Rugby, and Rushdie thrived there as a student. After completing a degree in history in 1968, he returned to Pakistan and worked for a television station in Karachi. His stay didn't last long. Displaced from the intellectual and cosmopolitan life he had known in England and frustrated by the censorship of media in Pakistan, he returned to London in 1970 to work as an actor and advertising copywriter while setting out on a writing career. His first work, *Grimus: A Novel* (1975), a science-fiction version of the classical Sufi poem, *Conference of the Birds,* received mixed reviews and generated little interest. His breakthrough as an author came with his second novel, *Midnight's Children* (1981), the story of his childhood and youth in Bombay between 1947 and 1977 and the lives of his parents and grandparents in the three decades before his birth. The novel doubles as a national ALLEGORY,[1] telling the story of the emergence of India as an independent country. With complex plotting and extravagant invention, Rushdie brings nearly every major event in the sixty years of Indian history that the novel spans into the lives of his two central characters. The novel received the most prestigious British literary award, the Booker Prize, in 1981.

Confronting Islam.   In *Shame* (1983), Rushdie wrote a similarly extravagant but less successful tale of the modern history of Pakistan. Its fictional versions of the vagaries and brutalities in Pakistani politics offended some Muslim readers, but Rushdie escaped direct censure and censorship by not identifying the setting as Pakistan. He was less cautious in his next novel. *The Satanic Verses* (1988) takes Islamic history as its subject matter, working legends about Muhammad into a contemporary story of movie actors and popular culture. Rushdie's license with Muhammad and the Qur'an (Koran) so offended many orthodox Muslims that Iran's ayatollah Khomeini issued a *fatwa,* a decree calling on "all zealous Muslims to execute [those responsible for the novel] quickly, wherever they may find them, so that no one will dare to insult the Islamic sanctions. Whoever is killed on this path will be regarded as a martyr, God willing." Rushdie went into hiding; the Norwegian publisher of *The Satanic Verses* was shot and wounded; an Italian translator stabbed;

www For links to more information about Salman Rushdie and a quiz on "The Courter," and for information about the culture and context of India in the twentieth century, see *World Literature Online* at bedfordstmartins .com/worldlit.

Having been borne across the ocean, we are translated men. It is normally supposed that something always gets lost in translation; I cling, obstinately, to the notion that something can also be gained.

– SALMAN RUSHDIE,
"Imaginary
Homelands," 1991

---

[1] **national allegory:** A story in which the characters represent forces or figures in the history of a nation, often a nation in the process of asserting its independence or establishing its national identity.

"We Are Ready to Kill Rushdy," 1989

At a pro-Iranian rally, a girl in Beirut, Lebanon, calls for the death of Salman Rushdie. Behind her is a portrait of Ayatollah Khomeini, who declared a fatwa, *or death sentence, on Rushdie after he allegedly blasphemed Islam in his novel* The Satanic Verses. *(© Reuters / CORBIS)*

If somebody's trying to shut you up, sing louder and louder and if possible, better. My experience just made me all the more determined to write the very best books I could find it in myself to write.

– SALMAN RUSHDIE

a Japanese translator killed. In Islamic countries several deaths reportedly occurred as a result of the decree. While Western writers defended Rushdie's novel and his right to speak, many moderate Muslims in the West considered the novel an "unprecedented assault on Islam" and, like the president of the Massachusetts Institute of Technology (M.I.T.) Islamic Society, considered "the reaction of the vast majority of Muslims . . . remarkably mild." Even Naguib Mahfouz (p. 797), the Egyptian novelist whose *Children of the Alley* (1959) had been attacked by Islamic fundamentalists and banned in nearly every Islamic country, criticized Rushdie—and Khomeini: "I believe that the wrong done by Khomeini towards Islam and the Muslims," he wrote, "is no less than that done by the author himself."

Rushdie's Response.   Forced into seclusion, Rushdie wrote a "children's book," *Haroun and the Sea of Stories* (1990), that made the tradition of the *Arabian Nights* into an allegory of the author's predicament.

Haroun, son of the storyteller Rashid Khalifa, sets out on a journey to restore his father's voice and to cleanse the sea of stories that has been poisoned by the tyrant Khattam-Shud, who claims that "stories make trouble." Haroun asserts that "stories are fun," but Khattam-Shud counters, "The world, however, is not for fun. . . . The world is for Controlling." Even in seclusion Rushdie was not to be silenced; his children's book was a tribute to the imagination, which tyranny would suppress. Rushdie once said, "If somebody's trying to shut you up, sing louder and louder and if possible, better. My experience just made me all the more determined to write the very best books I could find it in myself to write."

Rushdie's novels and stories are filled with extravagant inventions, bizarre plot twists, and a melange of allusions to songs, movies, and other elements of popular culture. Rushdie has been compared to Swift and Sterne[2] as a satirist, to Kafka and Günter Grass[3] as an allegorist, and to Gabriel García Márquez and the MAGICAL REALISTS as an inventor of bizarre and surreal worlds. Since the *fatwa* was lifted in 1999, Rushdie has come out of hiding and moved from London to New York City. He has recently published *The Ground beneath Her Feet* (1999), a rock-and-roll retelling of the myth of Orpheus and Eurydice, and *Fury* (2001), about a doll-obsessed professor who moves from London to New York.

"The Courter."   The volume of short stories in which "The Courter" originally appeared, *East, West* (1994), illustrates in its organization Rushdie's hybrid self. Of the nine stories in the collection, three are about the East, three are about the West, and three concern the meeting of East and West. "The Courter" comes from the book's final section. Set in an apartment building in London inhabited by a colony of displaced Indians, the story contrasts the connection of the Indian maid Certainly-Mary to her homeland with that of the narrator, an adolescent schoolboy at the time of the action, to his. The difficulties of adjusting to a foreign culture are comically exaggerated in Certainly-Mary, whose relationship with Mixed-Up is emblematic of her life in a strange land, where she mispronounces the language, gets her sari entangled in an escalator, and suffers from a heart condition. Her difficulties are similar to those that nearly all Indians of the older generation experience in their adopted countries. The narrator's father gets slapped for confusing the words *teats* and *nipples,* and the various maharajas become entangled with British hoodlums. The narrator and his sisters, on the other hand, are much more savvy about British ways. Their knowledge of British popular music, movies, and sports has already "translated" and assimilated them

> No one writes more convincingly of the tug between old and new, home and the culture of the unknown.
>
> – PAUL GRAY, 1995, on Salman Rushdie

> If Rushdie's persecutors have made the experience of rootless nomadism all too literal for him, he's still teaching the rest of us why we can't go home again.
>
> – HENRY LOUIS GATES JR., writer and critic, 1995

---

[2] **Swift and Sterne:** Jonathan Swift (1667–1745; see Book 4) used fantasy and bizarre inventions in *Gulliver's Travels* and other works to satirize British institutions. Laurence Sterne (1713–1768) in *Tristram Shandy* employed a digressive and allusive, stream-of-consciousness style of writing for comic and satiric purposes. Rushdie has acknowledged his indebtedness to Sterne as well as to James Joyce (1882–1941; see p. 366), the Irish stream-of-consciousness writer who reveled in wordplay and allusions.

[3] **Günter Grass** (b. 1927): German novelist who authored *The Tin Drum* (1959), an allegory of German history in the twentieth century much like Rushdie's treatment of Indian and Pakistani history.

into British life. The narrator moves back and forth between Eastern and Western traditions, punning, playing on song titles, movie scenes, and Indian mythology as if there were no separation between East and West in his language or consciousness. The contrasting choices at the end of the story — Certainly-Mary's decision to return to Bombay where she recovers from her heart condition, and the narrator's to stay in England and seek British citizenship — carry out the logic of the generational differences explored in the story. For neither the maid nor the school-boy, however, is the decision unequivocal: Certainly-Mary must leave behind her London lover, and the schoolboy, as he narrates this tale many years later, still feels caught between two cultures and pulled in opposite directions.

■ **CONNECTIONS**

In the World, **Crossing Cultures, p. 1278.** Writers of Indian ancestry serve as examples of the globalization of literature in *In the World: Crossing Cultures,* which presents writers who have left their homeland or emerged from the Indian diaspora to adopt a new cultural identity. The section includes Salman Rushdie's essay "Imaginary Homelands," in which he describes himself as a "translated man." Which other writers in this section might be called "translated people"?

Mori Ogai, "The Dancing Girl" (Book 5). "The Dancing Girl" is about a young man torn between two cultures, whose decision to return to Japan differs from that of Rushdie's narrator, who decides to remain in the West. Do you think this dissimilarity is indicative of a difference between the nineteenth and twentieth centuries or between the Indians and the Japanese?

Virgil, *The Aeneid* **(Book 1); Jonathan Swift,** *Gulliver's Travels* **(Book 4); Voltaire,** *Candide* **(Book 4).** Travelers can acquire a perspective on their own culture and experiment with different ways of living. Some discover a new appreciation for the culture they left behind; others learn that they cannot "go home again." Does Rushdie's narrator fit in either of these two categories? What does he appreciate about India? What has he taken from the West? Consider Virgil's Aeneas, Swift's Gulliver, and Voltaire's Candide in this context. How do these characters feel about their homelands? Can they go home again? Are any torn, like Rushdie's narrator, between two cultures?

■ **FURTHER RESEARCH**

Booker, M. Keith, ed. *Critical Essays on Salman Rushdie.* 1999.
Cundy, Catherine. *Salman Rushdie.* 1996.
Goonetilleke, D. C. R. A. *Salman Rushdie.* 1998.
Israel, Nico. *Outlandish, Writing between Exile and Diaspora.* 2000.

■ **PRONUNCIATION**

Chhoti: CHOH-tee
Dasashwamedh-ghat: duh-suh-shwah-MADE GAHT
Salman Rushdie: SAL-mun RUSH-dee
Varanasi: vuh-RAH-nuh-see
Zbigniew: ZBIG-nyef

❧ The Courter

1

Certainly-Mary was the smallest woman Mixed-Up the hall porter had come across, dwarfs excepted, a tiny sixty-year-old Indian lady with her greying hair tied behind her head in a neat bun, hitching up her red-hemmed white sari in the front and negotiating the apartment block's front steps as if they were Alps. "No," he said aloud, furrowing his brow. What would be the right peaks. Ah, good, that was the name. "Ghats,"[1] he said proudly. Word from a schoolboy atlas long ago, when India felt as far away as Paradise. (Nowadays Paradise seemed even further away but India, and Hell, had come a good bit closer.) "Western Ghats, Eastern Ghats, and now Kensington Ghats," he said, giggling. "Mountains."

She stopped in front of him in the oak-panelled lobby. "But ghats in India are also stairs," she said. "Yes yes certainly. For instance in Hindu holy city of Varanasi, where the Brahmins sit taking the filgrims' money is called Dasashwamedh-ghat. Broad-broad staircase down to River Ganga.[2] O, most certainly! Also Manikarnika-ghat.[3] They buy fire from a house with a tiger leaping from the roof—yes certainly, a statue tiger, coloured by Technicolor, what are you thinking?—and they bring it in a

---

"The Courter." First collected in the volume *East, West* (1994), this short story is, suitably, about crossing cultures. All of the major figures in the story—the narrator and his Indian family, the porter from Eastern Europe, and the Indian ayah, Certainly-Mary—have been separated from their homelands and their pasts. Rushdie contrasts the narrator's story with that of Certainly-Mary as a way of dramatizing being caught between two cultures. The narrator, a teenager attending an English public school at the time of the action, is determined to break with his family and take on an English identity, even though he recognizes the ways in which he is different from his English schoolmates. Mary, even though she and her "courter" have turned chess from a game of war into a game of love, decides to return to Bombay, a move that cures her heart trouble. She is "still going strong" at the age of ninety-one because she recovered her homeland. The narrator, however, comparing himself to the wild horses in the film *The Misfits*, is pulled in two directions:

> But I, too, have ropes around my neck, I have them to this day, pulling me this way and that, East and West, the nooses tightening, commanding, *choose, choose.*
>
> I buck, I snort, I whinny, I rear, I kick. Ropes, I do not choose between you. Lassoes, lariats, I choose neither of you, and both. Do you hear? I refuse to choose.

All notes are the editors'.

---

[1] **"Ghats":** Hindi word for a mountain range and also for a flight of steps leading down to a river. Two particular ranges in India are the Eastern Ghats, along the Bay of Bengal, and the Western Ghats, along the Arabian Sea.

[2] **Varanasi . . . Ganga:** Varanasi, formerly Benares, a sacred city on the River Ganga (Ganges)—the sacred Hindu river running through the heart of Bengal—where Hindu pilgrims come to bathe in the river and to cremate their dead. The Dasashwamedh-ghat is a series of steps leading down to the river, the most popular ghat for pilgrims who come to bathe.

[3] **Manikarnika-ghat:** The "burning ghat" is a set of stairs where bodies are brought to be cremated.

box to set fire to their loved ones' bodies. Funeral fires are of sandal. Photographs not allowed; no, certainly not."

He began thinking of her as Certainly-Mary because she never said plain yes or no; always this O-yes-certainly or no-certainly-not. In the confused circumstances that had prevailed ever since his brain, his one sure thing, had let him down, he could hardly be certain of anything any more; so he was stunned by her sureness, first into nostalgia, then envy, then attraction. And attraction was a thing so long forgotten that when the churning started he thought for a long time it must be the Chinese dumplings he had brought home from the High Street carry-out.

English was hard for Certainly-Mary, and this was a part of what drew damaged old Mixed-Up towards her. The letter p was a particular problem, often turning into an f or a c; when she proceeded through the lobby with a wheeled wicker shopping basket, she would say, "Going shocking," and when, on her return, he offered to help lift the basket up the front ghats, she would answer, "Yes, fleas." As the elevator lifted her away, she called through the grille: "Oé, courter! Thank you, courter. O, yes, certainly." (In Hindi and Konkani,[4] however, her p's knew their place.)

So: thanks to her unexpected, somehow stomach-churning magic, he was no longer porter, but courter. "Courter," he repeated to the mirror when she had gone. His breath made a little dwindling picture of the word on the glass. "Courter courter caught." Okay. People called him many things, he did not mind. But this name, this courter, this he would try to be.

2

For years now I've been meaning to write down the story of Certainly-Mary, our ayah,[5] the woman who did as much as my mother to raise my sisters and me, and her great adventure with her "courter" in London, where we all lived for a time in the early sixties in a block called Waverley House; but what with one thing and another I never got round to it.

Then recently I heard from Certainly-Mary after a longish silence. She wrote to say that she was ninety-one, had had a serious operation, and would I kindly send her some money, because she was embarrassed that her niece, with whom she was now living in the Kurla district of Bombay, was so badly out of pocket.

I sent the money, and soon afterwards received a pleasant letter from the niece, Stella, written in the same hand as the letter from "Aya" — as we had always called Mary, palindromically dropping the "h." Aya had been so touched, the niece wrote, that I remembered her after all these years. "I have been hearing the stories about you folks all my life," the letter went on, "and I think of you a little bit as family. Maybe you recall my mother, Mary's sister. She unfortunately passed on. Now it is I who write Mary's letters for her. We all wish you the best."

---

[4] Konkani: The language of an ethnic group living mainly along the west coast of India.

[5] ayah: Maid or nursemaid.

This message from an intimate stranger reached out to me in my enforced exile from the beloved country of my birth and moved me, stirring things that had been buried very deep. Of course it also made me feel guilty about having done so little for Mary over the years. For whatever reason, it has become more important than ever to set down the story I've been carrying around unwritten for so long, the story of Aya and the gentle man whom she renamed—with unintentional but prophetic overtones of romance—"the courter." I see now that it is not just their story, but ours, mine, as well.

3

His real name was Mecir: You were supposed to say Mishirsh because it had invisible accents on it in some Iron Curtain language in which the accents had to be invisible, my sister Durré said solemnly, in case somebody spied on them or rubbed them out or something. His first name also began with an m but it was so full of what we called Communist consonants, all those z's and c's and w's walled up together without vowels to give them breathing space, that I never even tried to learn it.

At first we thought of nicknaming him after a mischievous little comic-book character, Mr. Mxyztplk from the Fifth Dimension, who looked a bit like Elmer Fudd and used to make Superman's life hell until ole Supe could trick him into saying his name backwards, Klptzyxm, whereupon he disappeared back into the Fifth Dimension; but because we weren't too sure how to say Mxyztplk (not to mention Klptzyxm) we dropped that idea. "We'll just call you Mixed-Up," I told him in the end, to simplify life. "Mishter Mikshed-Up Mishirsh." I was fifteen then and bursting with unemployed cock and it meant I could say things like that right into people's faces, even people less accommodating than Mr. Mecir with his stroke.

What I remember most vividly are his pink rubber washing-up gloves, which he seemed never to remove, at least not until he came calling for Certainly-Mary . . . At any rate, when I insulted him, with my sisters Durré and Muneeza cackling in the lift, Mecir just grinned an empty good-natured grin, nodded, "You call me what you like, okay," and went back to buffing and polishing the brasswork. There was no point teasing him if he was going to be like that, so I got into the lift and all the way to the fourth floor we sang *I Can't Stop Loving You* at the top of our best Ray Charles voices, which were pretty awful. But we were wearing our dark glasses, so it didn't matter.

4

It was the summer of 1962, and school was out. My baby sister Scheherazade was just one year old. Durré was a beehived fourteen; Muneeza was ten, and already quite a handful. The three of us—or rather Durré and me, with Muneeza trying desperately and unsuccessfully to be included in our gang—would stand over Scheherazade's cot and sing to her. "No nursery rhymes," Durré had decreed, and so there were none, for though she was a year my junior she was a natural leader. The infant Scheherazade's lullabies were our cover versions of recent hits by Chubby Checker, Neil Sedaka, Elvis, and Pat Boone.

"Why don't you come home, Speedy Gonzales?" we bellowed in sweet disharmony: But most of all, and with actions, we would jump down, turn around, and pick a bale of cotton. We would have jumped down, turned around, and picked those bales all day except that the Maharaja of B—— in the flat below complained, and Aya Mary came in to plead with us to be quiet.

"Look, see, it's Jumble-Aya who's fallen for Mixed-Up," Durré shouted, and Mary blushed a truly immense blush. So naturally we segued right into a quick me-oh-my-oh; son of a gun, we had big fun. But then the baby began to yell, my father came in with his head down bull-fashion and steaming from both ears, and we needed all the good-luck charms we could find.

I had been at boarding school in England for a year or so when Abba took the decision to bring the family over. Like all his decisions, it was neither explained to nor discussed with anyone, not even my mother. When they first arrived he rented two adjacent flats in a seedy Bayswater mansion block called Graham Court, which lurked furtively in a nothing street that crawled along the side of the ABC Queensway cinema towards the Porchester Baths. He commandeered one of these flats for himself and put my mother, three sisters, and Aya in the other; also, on school holidays, me. England, where liquor was freely available, did little for my father's *bonhomie,* so in a way it was a relief to have a flat to ourselves.

Most nights he emptied a bottle of Johnnie Walker Red Label and a soda-siphon. My mother did not dare to go across to "his place" in the evenings. She said: "He makes faces at me."

Aya Mary took Abba his dinner and answered all his calls (if he wanted anything, he would phone us up and ask for it). I am not sure why Mary was spared his drunken rages. She said it was because she was nine years his senior, so she could tell him to show due respect.

After a few months, however, my father leased a three-bedroom fourth-floor apartment with a fancy address. This was Waverley House in Kensington Court, W8. Among its other residents were not one but two Indian Maharajas, the sporting Prince P—— as well as the old B—— who has already been mentioned. Now we were jammed in together, my parents and Baby Scare-zade (as her siblings had affectionately begun to call her) in the master bedroom, the three of us in a much smaller room, and Mary, I regret to admit, on a straw mat laid on the fitted carpet in the hall. The third bedroom became my father's office, where he made phone calls and kept his *Encyclopaedia Britannica,* his *Reader's Digests,* and (under lock and key) the television cabinet. We entered it at our peril. It was the Minotaur's[6] lair.

---

[6] **Minotaur:** In Greek mythology, the threatening creature, half bull and half man, at the center of the labyrinth in Crete who is slain by Theseus.

One morning he was persuaded to drop in at the corner pharmacy and pick up some supplies for the baby. When he returned there was a hurt, schoolboyish look on his face that I had never seen before, and he was pressing his hand against his cheek.

"She hit me," he said plaintively.

"Hai! Allah-tobah![7] Darling!" cried my mother, fussing. "Who hit you? Are you injured? Show me, let me see."

"I did nothing," he said, standing there in the hall with the pharmacy bag in his other hand and a face as pink as Mecir's rubber gloves. "I just went in with your list. The girl seemed very helpful. I asked for baby compound, Johnson's powder, teething jelly, and she brought them out. Then I asked did she have any nipples, and she slapped my face."

My mother was appalled. "Just for that?" And Certainly-Mary backed her up. "What is this nonsense?" she wanted to know. "I have been in that chemist's shock, and they have flenty nickels, different sizes, all on view."

Durré and Muneeza could not contain themselves. They were rolling round on the floor, laughing and kicking their legs in the air.

"You both shut your face at once," my mother ordered. "A madwoman has hit your father. Where is the comedy?"

"I don't believe it," Durré gasped. "You just went up to that girl and said," and here she fell apart again, stamping her feet and holding her stomach, "'*have you got any nipples?*'"

My father grew thunderous, empurpled. Durré controlled herself. "But Abba," she said, at length, "here they call them teats."

Now my mother's and Mary's hands flew to their mouths, and even my father looked shocked. "But how shameless!" my mother said. "The same word as for what's on your bosoms?" She coloured, and stuck out her tongue for shame.

"These English," sighed Certainly-Mary. "But aren't they the limit? Certainly-yes; they are."

I remember this story with delight, because it was the only time I ever saw my father so discomfited, and the incident became legendary and the girl in the pharmacy was installed as the object of our great veneration. (Durré and I went in there just to take a look at her—she was a plain, short girl of about seventeen, with large, unavoidable breasts—but she caught us whispering and glared so fiercely that we fled.) And also because in the general hilarity I was able to conceal the shaming truth that I, who had been in England for so long, would have made the same mistake as Abba did.

It wasn't just Certainly-Mary and my parents who had trouble with the English language. My schoolfellows tittered when in my Bombay way I said "brought-up" for upbringing (as in "where was your brought-up?") and "thrice" for three times and

---

[7] **Allah-tobah!:** Oh my God!

"quarter-plate" for side-plate and "macaroni" for pasta in general. As for learning the difference between nipples and teats, I really hadn't had any opportunities to increase my word power in that area at all.

5

So I was a little jealous of Certainly-Mary when Mixed-Up came to call. He rang our bell, his body quivering with deference in an old suit grown too loose, the trousers tightly gathered by a belt; he had taken off his rubber gloves and there were roses in his hand. My father opened the door and gave him a withering look. Being a snob, Abba was not pleased that the flat lacked a separate service entrance, so that even a porter had to be treated as a member of the same universe as himself.

"Mary," Mixed-Up managed, licking his lips and pushing back his floppy white hair. "I, to see Miss Mary, come, am."

"Wait on," Abba said, and shut the door in his face.

Certainly-Mary spent all her afternoons off with old Mixed-Up from then on, even though that first date was not a complete success. He took her "up West" to show her the visitors' London she had never seen, but at the top of an up escalator at Piccadilly Circus, while Mecir was painfully enunciating the words on the posters she couldn't read—*Unzip a banana*, and *Idris when I's dri*—she got her sari stuck in the jaws of the machine, and as the escalator pulled at the garment it began to unwind. She was forced to spin round and round like a top, and screamed at the top of her voice, "O BAAP! BAAPU-RÉ! BAAP-RÉ-BAAP-RÉ-BAAP!"[8] It was Mixed-Up who saved her by pushing the emergency stop button before the sari was completely unwound and she was exposed in her petticoat for all the world to see.

"O, courter!" she wept on his shoulder. "O, no more escaleater, courter, nevermore, surely not!"

My own amorous longings were aimed at Durré's best friend, a Polish girl called Rozalia, who had a holiday job at Faiman's shoe shop on Oxford Street. I pursued her pathetically throughout the holidays and, on and off, for the next two years. She would let me have lunch with her sometimes and buy her a Coke and a sandwich, and once she came with me to stand on the terraces at White Hart Lane[9] to watch Jimmy Greaves's first game for the Spurs. "Come on you whoi-oites," we both shouted dutifully. "Come on you *Lily-whoites*." After that she even invited me into the back room at Faiman's, where she kissed me twice and let me touch her breast, but that was as far as I got.

And then there was my sort-of-cousin Chandni, whose mother's sister had married my mother's brother, though they had since split up. Chandni was eighteen

---

[8] **"O BAAP! . . . BAAP!":** An expression of embarrassment; "Oh God!"

[9] **White Hart Lane:** The home stadium in London of the professional soccer team the Tottenham Hot Spurs. Jimmy Greaves was one of the Spurs' star players.

months older than me, and so sexy it made you sick. She was training to be an Indian classical dancer, Odissi as well as Natyam,[10] but in the meantime she dressed in tight black jeans and a clinging black polo-neck jumper and took me, now and then, to hang out at Bunjie's, where she knew most of the folk-music crowd that frequented the place, and where she answered to the name of Moonlight, which is what *chandni* means. I chain-smoked with the folkies and then went to the toilet to throw up.

Chandni was the stuff of obsessions. She was a teenage dream, the Moon River come to Earth like the Goddess Ganga,[11] dolled up in slinky black. But for her I was just the young greenhorn cousin to whom she was being nice because he hadn't learned his way around.

She-E-rry, won't you come out tonight? yodelled the Four Seasons. I knew exactly how they felt. *Come, come, come out toni-yi-yight.* And while you're at it, love me do.

6

They went for walks in Kensington Gardens. "Pan," Mixed-Up said, pointing at a statue. "Los' boy. Nev' grew up."[12] They went to Barkers and Pontings and Derry & Toms[13] and picked out furniture and curtains for imaginary homes. They cruised supermarkets and chose little delicacies to eat. In Mecir's cramped lounge they sipped what he called "chimpanzee tea"[14] and toasted crumpets in front of an electric bar fire.

Thanks to Mixed-Up, Mary was at last able to watch television. She liked children's programmes best, especially *The Flintstones.* Once, giggling at her daring, Mary confided to Mixed-Up that Fred and Wilma reminded her of her Sahib and Begum Sahiba upstairs; at which the courter, matching her audaciousness, pointed first at Certainly-Mary and then at himself, grinned a wide gappy smile and said, "Rubble."

Later, on the news, a vulpine Englishman with a thin moustache and mad eyes declaimed a warning about immigrants, and Certainly-Mary flapped her hand at the set: "Khali-pili bom marta," she objected, and then, for her host's benefit translated: "For nothing he is shouting shouting. Bad life! Switch it off."

They were often interrupted by the Maharajas of and B——— and P———, who came downstairs to escape their wives and ring other women from the call-box in the porter's room.

---

[10] **Odissi . . . Natyam:** Odissi is the traditional dance of Orissa, a state on the east coast of India. Natyam is one of the oldest dance forms in southern India.

[11] **Goddess Ganga:** The Hindu goddess of the sacred Ganga River.

[12] **"Pan . . . grew up":** A statue of Peter Pan in Kensington Gardens celebrates James Barrie's tale of the lost boy who never grew up, *Peter Pan.*

[13] **Barkers . . . Toms:** Fashionable London stores.

[14] **"chimpanzee tea":** The television advertisements for a popular brand of English tea featured chimpanzees dressed as humans.

"Oh, baby, forget that guy," said sporty Prince P——, who seemed to spend all his days in tennis whites, and whose plump gold Rolex was almost lost in the thick hair on his arm. "I'll show you a better time than him, baby; step into my world."

The Maharaja of B—— was older, uglier, more matter-of-fact. "Yes, bring all appliances. Room is booked in name of Mr. Douglas Home. Six forty-five to seven fifteen. You have printed rate card? Please. Also a two-foot ruler, must be wooden. Frilly apron, plus."

This is what has lasted in my memory of Waverley House, this seething mass of bad marriages, booze, philanderers, and unfulfilled young lusts; of the Maharaja of P—— roaring away towards London's casinoland every night, in a red sports car with fitted blondes, and of the Maharaja of B—— skulking off to Kensington High Street wearing dark glasses in the dark, and a coat with the collar turned up even though it was high summer; and at the heart of our little universe were Certainly-Mary and her courter, drinking chimpanzee tea and singing along with the national anthem of Bedrock.

But they were not really like Barney and Betty Rubble at all. They were formal, polite. They were . . . courtly. He courted her, and, like a coy, ringleted ingénue with a fan, she inclined her head, and entertained his suit.

7

I spent one half-term weekend in 1963 at the home in Beccles, Suffolk of Field Marshal Sir Charles Lutwidge-Dodgson, an old India hand and a family friend who was supporting my application for British citizenship. "The Dodo,"[15] as he was known, invited me down by myself, saying he wanted to get to know me better.

He was a huge man whose skin had started hanging too loosely on his face, a giant living in a tiny thatched cottage and forever bumping his head. No wonder he was irascible at times; he was in Hell, a Gulliver trapped in that rose-garden Lilliput[16] of croquet hoops, church bells, sepia photographs, and old battle-trumpets.

The weekend was fitful and awkward until the Dodo asked if I played chess. Slightly awestruck at the prospect of playing a Field Marshal, I nodded; and ninety minutes later, to my amazement, won the game.

I went into the kitchen, strutting somewhat, planning to boast a little to the old soldier's long-time housekeeper, Mrs. Liddell. But as soon as I entered she said: "Don't tell me. You never went and won?"

"Yes," I said, affecting nonchalance. "As a matter of fact, yes, I did."

---

[15] **Dodgson . . . "The Dodo":** Charles Lutwidge Dodgson was the given name of Lewis Carroll (1832–1898), author of *Alice in Wonderland,* a novel he based on a story he told to Alice Liddell and her sisters. The Dodo, a character in the story, is said to be Carroll's projection of himself. The author could not pronounce his given name without stuttering.

[16] **Gulliver . . . Lilliput:** On the first of his voyages in Jonathan Swift's *Gulliver's Travels* (1726), Gulliver visits Lilliput, a land whose inhabitants are tiny human beings.

"Gawd," said Mrs. Liddell. "Now there'll be hell to pay. You go back in there and ask him for another game, and this time make sure you lose."

I did as I was told, but was never invited to Beccles again.

Still, the defeat of the Dodo gave me new confidence at the chessboard, so when I returned to Waverley House after finishing my O levels,[17] and was at once invited to play a game by Mixed-Up (Mary had told him about my victory in the Battle of Beccles with great pride and some hyperbole), I said: "Sure, I don't mind." How long could it take to thrash the old duffer, after all?

There followed a massacre royal. Mixed-Up did not just beat me; he had me for breakfast, over easy. I couldn't believe it—the canny opening, the fluency of his combination play, the force of his attacks, my own impossibly cramped, strangled positions—and asked for a second game. This time he tucked into me even more heartily. I sat broken in my chair at the end, close to tears. *Big girls don't cry,* I reminded myself, but the song went on playing in my head: *That's just an alibi.*

"Who are you?" I demanded, humiliation weighing down every syllable. "The devil in disguise?"

Mixed-Up gave his big, silly grin. "Grand Master," he said. "Long time. Before head."

"You're a Grand Master," I repeated, still in a daze. Then in a moment of horror I remembered that I had seen the name Mecir in books of classic games. "Nimzo-Indian," I said aloud. He beamed and nodded furiously.

"That Mecir?" I asked wonderingly.

"That," he said. There was saliva dribbling out of a corner of his sloppy old mouth. This ruined old man was in the books. He was in the books. And even with his mind turned to rubble he could still wipe the floor with me.

"Now play lady," he grinned. I didn't get it. "Mary lady," he said. "Yes yes certainly."

She was pouring tea, waiting for my answer. "Aya, you can't play," I said, bewildered.

"Learning, baba," she said. "What is it, na? Only a game."

And then she, too, beat me senseless, and with the black pieces, at that. It was not the greatest day of my life.

8

From *100 Most Instructive Chess Games* by Robert Reshevsky, 1961:

> *M. Mecir—M. Najdorf*
> *Dallas 1950, Nimzo-Indian Defense*
> The attack of a tactician can be troublesome to meet—that of a strategist even more so. Whereas the tactician's threats may be unmistakable, the strategist confuses the issue by keeping things in abeyance. He threatens to threaten!

---

[17] **O levels:** Exams given at the end of an "ordinary-level" secondary education to establish eligibility for a diploma.

Take this game for instance: Mecir posts a Knight at Q6 to get a grip on the center. Then he establishes a passed Pawn on one wing to occupy his opponent on the Queen side. Finally he stirs up the position on the King-side. What does the poor bewildered opponent do? How can he defend everything at once? Where will the blow fall?

Watch Mecir keep Najdorf on the run, as he shifts the attack from side to side!

Chess had become their private language. Old Mixed-Up, lost as he was for words, retained, on the chessboard, much of the articulacy and subtlety which had vanished from his speech. As Certainly-Mary gained in skill—and she had learned with astonishing speed, I thought bitterly, for someone who couldn't read or write or pronounce the letter p—she was better able to understand, and respond to, the wit of the reduced maestro with whom she had so unexpectedly forged a bond.

He taught her with great patience, showing-not-telling, repeating openings and combinations and endgame techniques over and over until she began to see the meaning in the patterns. When they played, he handicapped himself, he told her her best moves and demonstrated their consequences, drawing her, step by step, into the infinite possibilities of the game.

Such was their courtship. "It is like an adventure, baba," Mary once tried to explain to me. "It is like going with him to his country, you know? What a place, baap-ré! Beautiful and dangerous and funny and full of fuzzles. For me it is a big-big discovery. What to tell you? I go for the game. It is a wonder."

I understood, then, how far things had gone between them. Certainly-Mary had never married, and had made it clear to old Mixed-Up that it was too late to start any of that monkey business at her age. The courter was a widower, and had grown-up children somewhere, lost long ago behind the ever-higher walls of Eastern Europe. But in the game of chess they had found a form of flirtation, an endless renewal that precluded the possibility of boredom, a courtly wonderland of the aging heart.

What would the Dodo have made of it all? No doubt it would have scandalised him to see chess, chess of all games, the great formalisation of war, transformed into an art of love.

As for me: My defeats by Certainly-Mary and her courter ushered in further humiliations. Durré and Muneeza went down with the mumps, and so, finally, in spite of my mother's efforts to segregate us, did I. I lay terrified in bed while the doctor warned me not to stand up and move around if I could possibly help it. "If you do," he said, "your parents won't need to punish you. You will have punished yourself quite enough."

I spent the following few weeks tormented day and night by visions of grotesquely swollen testicles and a subsequent life of limp impotence—finished before I'd even started, it wasn't fair!—which were made much worse by my sisters' quick recovery and incessant gibes. But in the end I was lucky; the illness didn't spread to the deep South. "Think how happy your hundred and one girlfriends will be, bhai,"[18] sneered

---

[18] **bhai**: Brother.

Durré, who knew all about my continued failures in the Rozalia and Chandni departments.

On the radio, people were always singing about the joys of being sixteen years old. I wondered where they were, all those boys and girls of my age having the time of their lives. Were they driving around America in Studebaker convertibles? They certainly weren't in my neighbourhood. London, W8 was Sam Cooke country that summer. *Another Saturday night* . . . There might be a mop-top love-song stuck at number one, but I was down with lonely Sam in the lower depths of the charts, how-I-wishing I had someone, etc., and generally feeling in a pretty goddamn dreadful way.

9

"Baba, come quick."

It was late at night when Aya Mary shook me awake. After many urgent hisses, she managed to drag me out of sleep and pull me, pajama'ed and yawning, down the hall. On the landing outside our flat was Mixed-Up the courter, huddled up against a wall, weeping. He had a black eye and there was dried blood on his mouth.

"What happened?" I asked Mary, shocked.

"Men," wailed Mixed-Up. "Threaten. Beat."

He had been in his lounge earlier that evening when the sporting Maharaja of P—— burst in to say, "If anybody comes looking for me, okay, any tough-guy type guys, okay, I am out, okay? Oh you tea. Don't let them go upstairs, okay? Big tip, okay?"

A short time later, the old Maharaja of B—— also arrived in Mecir's lounge, looking distressed.

"Suno, listen on," said the Maharaja of B——. "You don't know where I am, samajh liya?[19] Understood? Some low persons may inquire. You don't know. I am abroad, achha?[20] On extended travels abroad. Do your job, porter. Handsome recompense."

Late at night two tough-guy types did indeed turn up. It seemed the hairy Prince P—— had gambling debts. "Out," Mixed-Up grinned in his sweetest way. The tough-guy types nodded, slowly. They had long hair and thick lips like Mick Jagger's. "He's a busy gent. We should of made an appointment," said the first type to the second. "Didn't I tell you we should of called?"

"You did," agreed the second type. "Got to do these things right, you said, he's royalty. And you was right, my son, I put my hand up, I was dead wrong. I put my hand up to that."

"Let's leave our card," said the first type. "Then he'll know to expect us."

"Ideal," said the second type, and smashed his fist into old Mixed-Up's mouth. "You tell him," the second type said, and struck the old man in the eye. "When he's in. You mention it."

He had locked the front door after that; but much later, well after midnight, there was a hammering. Mixed-Up called out, "Who?"

---

[19] **samajh liya?:** Do you understand?   [20] **achha?:** Yeah?

"We are close friends of the Maharaja of B——" said a voice. "No, I tell a lie. Acquaintances."

"He calls upon a lady of our acquaintance," said a second voice. "To be precise."

"It is in that connection that we crave audience," said the first voice.

"Gone," said Mecir. "Jet plane. Gone."

There was a silence. Then the second voice said, "Can't be in the jet set if you never jump on a jet, eh? Biarritz, Monte, all of that."

"Be sure and let His Highness know," said the first voice, "that we eagerly await his return."

"With regard to our mutual friend," said the second voice. "Eagerly."

What does the poor bewildered opponent do? The words from the chess book popped unbidden into my head. *How can he defend everything at once? Where will the blow fall? Watch Mecir keep Najdorf on the run, as he shifts the attack from side to side!*

Mixed-Up returned to his lounge and on this occasion, even though there had been no use of force, he began to weep. After a time he took the elevator up to the fourth floor and whispered through our letter-box to Certainly-Mary sleeping on her mat.

"I didn't want to wake Sahib," Mary said. "You know his trouble, na? And Begum Sahiba is so tired at end of the day. So now you tell, baba, what to do?"

What did she expect me to come up with? I was sixteen years old. "Mixed-Up must call the police," I unoriginally offered.

"No, no, baba," said Certainly-Mary emphatically. "If the courter makes a scandal for Maharaja-log, then in the end it is the courter only who will be out on his ear."

I had no other ideas. I stood before them feeling like a fool, while they both turned upon me their frightened, supplicant eyes.

"Go to sleep," I said. "We'll think about it in the morning." *The first pair of thugs were tacticians,* I was thinking. *They were troublesome to meet. But the second pair were scarier; they were strategists. They threatened to threaten.*

Nothing happened in the morning, and the sky was clear. It was almost impossible to believe in fists, and menacing voices at the door. During the course of the day both Maharajas visited the porter's lounge and stuck five-pound notes in Mixed-Up's waistcoat pocket. "Held the fort, good man," said Prince P——, and the Maharaja of B—— echoed those sentiments: "Spot on. All handled now, achha? Problem over."

The three of us—Aya Mary, her courter, and me—held a council of war that afternoon and decided that no further action was necessary. The hall porter was the front line in any such situation, I argued, and the front line had held. And now the risks were past. Assurances had been given. End of story.

"End of story," repeated Certainly-Mary doubtfully, but then, seeking to reassure Mecir, she brightened. "Correct," she said. "Most certainly! All-done, finis." She slapped her hands against each other for emphasis. She asked Mixed-Up if he wanted a game of chess; but for once the courter didn't want to play.

10

After that I was distracted, for a time, from the story of Mixed-Up and Certainly-Mary by violence nearer home.

My middle sister Muneeza, now eleven, was entering her delinquent phase a little early. She was the true inheritor of my father's black rage, and when she lost control it was terrible to behold. That summer she seemed to pick fights with my father on purpose; seemed prepared, at her young age, to test her strength against his. (I intervened in her rows with Abba only once, in the kitchen. She grabbed the kitchen scissors and flung them at me. They cut me on the thigh. After that I kept my distance.)

As I witnessed their wars I felt myself coming unstuck from the idea of family itself. I looked at my screaming sister and thought how brilliantly self-destructive she was, how triumphantly she was ruining her relations with the people she needed most.

And I looked at my choleric, face-pulling father and thought about British citizenship. My existing Indian passport permitted me to travel only to a very few countries, which were carefully listed on the second right-hand page. But I might soon have a British passport and then, by hook or by crook, I would get away from him. I would not have this face-pulling in my life.

At sixteen, you still think you can escape from your father. You aren't listening to his voice speaking through your mouth, you don't see how your gestures already mirror his; you don't see him in the way you hold your body, in the way you sign your name. You don't hear his whisper in your blood.

On the day I have to tell you about, my two-year-old sister Chhoti Scheherazade, Little Scare-zade, started crying as she often did during one of our family rows. Amma and Aya Mary loaded her into her push-chair and made a rapid getaway. They pushed her to Kensington Square and then sat on the grass, turned Scheherazade loose and made philosophical remarks while she tired herself out. Finally, she fell asleep, and they made their way home in the fading light of the evening. Outside Waverley House they were approached by two well-turned-out young men with Beatle haircuts and the buttoned-up, collarless jackets made popular by the band. The first of these young men asked my mother, very politely, if she might be the Maharani of B——.

"No," my mother answered, flattered.

"Oh, but you are, madam," said the second Beatle, equally politely. "For you are heading for Waverley House and that is the Maharaja's place of residence."

"No, no," my mother said, still blushing with pleasure. "We are a different Indian family."

"Quite so," the first Beatle nodded understandingly, and then, to my mother's great surprise, placed a finger alongside his nose, and winked. "Incognito, eh. Mum's the word."

"Now excuse us," my mother said, losing patience. "We are not the ladies you seek."

The second Beatle tapped a foot lightly against a wheel of the push-chair. "Your husband seeks ladies, madam, were you aware of that fact? Yes, he does. Most assiduously, may I add."

"Too assiduously," said the first Beatle, his face darkening.

"I tell you I am not the Maharani Begum," my mother said, growing suddenly alarmed. "Her business is not my business. Kindly let me pass."

The second Beatle stepped closer to her. She could feel his breath, which was minty. "One of the ladies he sought out was our ward, as you might say," he explained. "That would be the term. Under our protection, you follow. Us, therefore, being responsible for her welfare."

"Your husband," said the first Beatle, showing his teeth in a frightening way, and raising his voice one notch, "damaged the goods. Do you hear me, Queenie? He damaged the fucking goods."

"Mistaken identity, fleas," said Certainly-Mary. "Many Indian residents in Waverley House. We are decent ladies; *fleas.*"

The second Beatle had taken out something from an inside pocket. A blade caught the light. "Fucking wogs," he said. "You fucking come over here, you don't fucking know how to fucking behave. Why don't you fucking fuck off to fucking Wogistan? Fuck your fucking wog arses. Now then," he added in a quiet voice, holding up the knife, "unbutton your blouses."

Just then a loud noise emanated from the doorway of Waverley House. The two women and the two men turned to look, and out came Mixed-Up, yelling at the top of his voice and windmilling his arms like a mad old loon.

"Hullo," said the Beatle with the knife, looking amused. "Who's this, then? Oh oh fucking seven?"

Mixed-Up was trying to speak, he was in a mighty agony of effort, but all that was coming out of his mouth was raw, unshaped noise. Scheherazade woke up and joined in. The two Beatles looked displeased. But then something happened inside old Mixed-Up; something popped, and in a great rush he gabbled, "Sirs sirs no sirs these not B—— women sirs B—— women upstairs on floor three sirs Maharaja of B—— also sirs God's truth mother's grave swear."

It was the longest sentence he had spoken since the stroke that had broken his tongue long ago.

And what with his torrent and Scheherazade's squalls there were suddenly heads poking out from doorways, attention was being paid, and the two Beatles nodded gravely. "Honest mistake," the first of them said apologetically to my mother, and actually bowed from the waist. "Could happen to anyone," the knife-man added, ruefully. They turned and began to walk quickly away. As they passed Mecir, however, they paused. "I know you, though," said the knife-man. "'*Jet plane. Gone.*'" He made a short movement of the arm, and then Mixed-Up the courter was lying on the pavement with blood leaking from a wound in his stomach. "All okay now," he gasped, and passed out.

11

He was on the road to recovery by Christmas; my mother's letter to the landlords, in which she called him a "knight in shining armour," ensured that he was well looked after, and his job was kept open for him. He continued to live in his little ground-floor cubbyhole, while the hall porter's duties were carried out by shift-duty staff. "Nothing but the best for our very own hero," the landlords assured my mother in their reply.

The two Maharajas and their retinues had moved out before I came home for the Christmas holidays, so we had no further visits from the Beatles or the Rolling Stones. Certainly-Mary spent as much time as she could with Mecir; but it was the look of my old Aya that worried me more than poor Mixed-Up. She looked older, and powdery, as if she might crumble away at any moment into dust.

"We didn't want to worry you at school," my mother said. "She has been having heart trouble. Palpitations. Not all the time, but."

Mary's health problems had sobered up the whole family. Muneeza's tantrums had stopped, and even my father was making an effort. They had put up a Christmas tree in the sitting-room and decorated it with all sorts of baubles. It was so odd to see a Christmas tree at our place that I realised things must be fairly serious.

On Christmas Eve my mother suggested that Mary might like it if we all sang some carols. Amma had made song-sheets, six copies, by hand. When we did *O come, all ye faithful* I showed off by singing from memory in Latin. Everybody behaved perfectly. When Muneeza suggested that we should try *Swinging on a Star* or *I Wanna Hold Your Hand* instead of this boring stuff, she wasn't really being serious. So this is family life, I thought. This is it.

But we were only playacting.

A few weeks earlier, at school, I'd come across an American boy, the star of the school's Rugby football team, crying in the Chapel cloisters. I asked him what the matter was and he told me that President Kennedy had been assassinated. "I don't believe you," I said, but I could see that it was true. The football star sobbed and sobbed. I took his hand.

"When the President dies, the nation is orphaned," he eventually said, broken-heartedly parroting a piece of cracker-barrel wisdom he'd probably heard on Voice of America.

"I know how you feel," I lied. "My father just died, too."

Mary's heart trouble turned out to be a mystery; unpredictably, it came and went. She was subjected to all sorts of tests during the next six months, but each time the doctors ended up by shaking their heads: They couldn't find anything wrong with her. Physically, she was right as rain; except that there were these periods when her heart kicked and bucked in her chest like the wild horses in *The Misfits*,[21] the ones whose roping and tying made Marilyn Monroe so mad.

Mecir went back to work in the spring, but his experience had knocked the stuffing out of him. He was slower to smile, duller of eye, more inward. Mary, too, had turned in upon herself. They still met for tea, crumpets, and *The Flintstones,* but something was no longer quite right.

At the beginning of the summer Mary made an announcement.

"I know what is wrong with me," she told my parents, out of the blue. "I need to go home."

"But, Aya," my mother argued, "homesickness is not a real disease."

"God knows for what-all we came over to this country," Mary said. "But I can no longer stay. No. Certainly not." Her determination was absolute.

So it was England that was breaking her heart, breaking it by not being India. London was killing her, by not being Bombay. And Mixed-Up? I wondered. Was the courter killing her, too, because he was no longer himself? Or was it that her heart, roped by two different loves, was being pulled both East and West, whinnying and rearing, like those movie horses being yanked this way by Clark Gable and that way by Montgomery Clift, and she knew that to live she would have to choose?

"I must go," said Certainly-Mary. "Yes, certainly. *Bas.* Enough."

That summer, the summer of '64, I turned seventeen. Chandni went back to India. Durré's Polish friend Rozalia informed me over a sandwich in Oxford Street that she was getting engaged to a "real man," so I could forget about seeing her again, because this Zbigniew was the jealous type. Roy Orbison sang *It's Over* in my ears as I walked away to the Tube, but the truth was that nothing had really begun.

Certainly-Mary left us in mid-July. My father bought her a one-way ticket to Bombay, and that last morning was heavy with the pain of ending. When we took her bags down to the car, Mecir the hall porter was nowhere to be seen. Mary did not knock on the door of his lounge, but walked straight out through the freshly polished oak-panelled lobby, whose mirrors and brasses were sparkling brightly; she climbed into the back seat of our Ford Zodiac and sat there stiffly with her carry-on grip on her lap, staring straight ahead. I had known and loved her all my life. *Never mind your damned courter,* I wanted to shout at her, *what about me?*

As it happened, she was right about the homesickness. After her return to Bombay, she never had a day's heart trouble again; and, as the letter from her niece Stella confirmed, at ninety-one she was still going strong.

Soon after she left, my father told us he had decided to "shift location" to Pakistan. As usual, there were no discussions, no explanations, just the simple fiat. He gave up the lease on the flat in Waverley House at the end of the summer holidays, and they all went off to Karachi, while I went back to school.

---

[21] *The Misfits:* A western film (1960) written by Arthur Miller and starring Marilyn Monroe, Clark Gable, and Montgomery Clift about a roundup of wild horses.

I became a British citizen that year. I was one of the lucky ones, I guess, because in spite of that chess game I had the Dodo on my side. And the passport did, in many ways, set me free. It allowed me to come and go, to make choices that were not the ones my father would have wished. But I, too, have ropes around my neck, I have them to this day, pulling me this way and that, East and West, the nooses tightening, commanding, *choose, choose.*

I buck, I snort, I whinny, I rear, I kick. Ropes, I do not choose between you. Lassoes, lariats, I choose neither of you, and both. Do you hear? I refuse to choose.

A year or so after we moved out I was in the area and dropped in at Waverley House to see how the old courter was doing. Maybe, I thought, we could have a game of chess, and he could beat me to a pulp. The lobby was empty, so I knocked on the door of his little lounge. A stranger answered.

"Where's Mixed-Up?" I cried, taken by surprise. I apologised at once, embarrassed. "Mr. Mecir, I meant, the porter."

"I'm the porter, sir," the man said. "I don't know anything about any mix-up."

Crossing Cultures:
The Example of India

> Those of us who do use English do so in spite of our ambiguity towards it, or perhaps because of that, perhaps because we can find in that linguistic struggle a reflection of other struggles taking place in the real world, struggles between the cultures within ourselves and the influences at work upon our societies. To conquer English may be to complete the process of making ourselves free.
>
> – SALMAN RUSHDIE

Beginning with Joseph Conrad—born a Pole but writing in English as a naturalized citizen of England—modern writers have increasingly become citizens of more than one nation and inheritors of multiple cultural traditions. Salman Rushdie, a representative of such cultural hybridity, was born in India, educated in Britain where he became a citizen, and now lives in New York. He describes himself as an English writer, even though many of his works are about India, Pakistan, and the Islamic world. He uses an idiom and techniques found in much POSTMODERN literature and is often linked with the MAGICAL REALISTS of Latin America and with the European and American postmodernists whose work is steeped in the artifacts of popular culture. Like Rushdie, contemporary writers increasingly are part of an emerging global culture in which a particular national origin has less and less significance.

CULTURAL HYBRIDITY

If colonialism began the cross-cultural dialogue, however unequally, POSTCOLONIAL INDUSTRIALIZATION has extended it. We are all aware of the international ubiquity of blue jeans, Coca Cola, and McDonald's. Western literary forms—the drama of the ABSURD, for example, and the REALIST novel—have had similar currency in many cultures that formerly had only traditional or oral literatures. Critics object that such globalization is just the latest form of Western cultural imperialism, robbing indigenous cultures of their distinctive character and traditions. Such objections are similar to those raised by the ROMANTIC poets against industrialization and urbanization at the beginning of the nineteenth century; industrialization inevitably brings change

Bojan Brecelj,
Sikh Taxi Drivers,
New York, 1995
Sikh taxi drivers in
New York City
notably demonstrate
the mixing of cultures
in the twenty-first
century. (© Bojan
Brecelj / © Rune
Hellestad / CORBIS)

and may irreversibly alter a society. Yet the emerging global culture also involves exchange: Afro-pop music, Japanese animé, and Indian meditative practices are as much a part of it as are Coca Cola and blue jeans.

The fluidity of modern life and the ease with which one can move about the world have also contributed to the emergence of cross-cultural literature. Many modern writers—Graham Greene, D. H. Lawrence,[1] and V. S. Naipaul, for example—have been lifelong travelers who have traced their journeys in their novels. Others have gone to study or teach at foreign universities: Chinua Achebe at Boston University, for example, Anita Desai at M.I.T., and Raja Rao at the University of Texas. Still others have been driven into exile for political reasons or have chosen to migrate to such centers of literary culture as Paris or New York City. One has only to survey the selections available in any large bookstore to get some sense of how international literature has become in the last half century.

> In Trinidad I grew up in the last days of that kind of [colonial] racialism. And that, perhaps, has given me a greater appreciation of the immense changes that have taken place since the end of the war, the extraordinary attempt to accommodate the rest of the world, and all the currents of that world's thought.
> – V. S. NAIPAUL

---

[1]**Greene . . . Lawrence:** Among the many novels by English novelist Graham Greene (1904–1991) are works set in Mexico (*The Power and the Glory*, 1940), Vietnam (*The Quiet American*, 1955), Cuba (*Our Man in Havana*, 1958), Spain (*Monsignor Quixote*, 1982), and several other countries; D. H. Lawrence (1885–1930) wrote about Italy (*Sea and Sardinia*, 1921), Australia (*Kangaroo*, 1923), and Mexico (*The Plumed Serpent*, 1926) as well as his native England.

We are all instinctively bilingual, many of us writing in our own language and in English. We cannot write like the English. . . . Our method of expression therefore has to be a dialect which will some day prove to be as distinctive and colorful as the Irish or the American.

– RAJA RAO

THE EXAMPLE OF INDIA

India is an excellent case study in such cross-fertilization. A great number of Indian writers' works are available in the West. With a population of more than one billion, India has the second largest population in the world, behind the People's Republic of China. India has a more open society than China; it is the world's largest democracy, and its multiculturalism, traditions of tolerance, and history of absorbing foreign influences have given it an especially international literary culture. A British colony until 1947, India uses English as one of its major languages, and many Indian writers choose to work in English because it transcends the barrier of the various local languages of India and is known to more of the reading public. Finally, the Indian DIASPORA, those Indians dispersed and living outside of India, is the largest displaced group in the world. At the beginning of the twenty-first century, more than twenty million Indians live in countries other than India. The largest single group, nearly three million, lives in Britain. Close to half a million Indians live in the United States.

THREE TRAVELERS

In spite of strictures in the ancient Hindu shastras, or canonical writings, against traveling overseas, Indians have long traveled throughout Southeast Asia and in the regions surrounding the Indian Ocean. Then with the consolidation of British colonial power after the SEPOY MUTINY[2] in 1857–58, Indians assumed increasingly important roles in administering the British colonies throughout south Asia and Africa. By the time Mohandas Gandhi (p. 1284) arrived in South Africa as a young lawyer in the late nineteenth century, there were substantial numbers of Indian business and professional people already there. A young man of extraordinary intellect, tolerance, and curiosity, Gandhi combined his Hindu background with a British legal education and a commitment to the ethics of Christianity and Islam and the ideals of Hinduism. In South Africa he confronted a system of racial prejudice that violated the principles of British law and the ethics of the world's major religions. The excerpt from Gandhi's *Autobiography* that follows

p. 1285

---

[2] Sepoy Mutiny: A rebellion against the British in 1857–58 by native Indian soldiers, or Sepoys, in the Bengali army. It is sometimes seen as the first stirring of Indian nationalism.

describes his initial encounter with South African racism. In his reaction to mistreatment, those aspects of his character and background that lead him to conceive of a nonviolent resistance movement and begin the lifelong mission that would make him one of the great men of the twentieth century are already in evidence. In India, he combines his knowledge of the law with a spiritual mission and an economic strategy of boycotts and strikes to form a mass movement for Indian independence from Britain. In fact, by the time he leaves South Africa to return to India in 1914, he has given up the law; forced the South African government to recognize the rights of Indian citizens; adopted the Hindu asceticism that he would practice for the rest of his life and that has since guided the spiritual communities, or ashrams, that he founded; and formulated his philosophy of nonviolent resistance, *satyagraha,* which he would eventually use to lead India to independence in 1947.

Gandhi was the greatest in a long line of Indian spiritual leaders who had sought to synthesize a reformed Hinduism with the ethics of Christianity. Ram Mohun Roy (c. 1772–1833), Keshub Chunder Sen (1838–1884), and Swami Vivekananda (1863–1902) led such movements in the nineteenth century. Gandhi, embodying their spiritual ideals, applied them to the political end of achieving Indian independence. He inspired religious leaders and anticolonialism movements throughout the world, most notably, perhaps, Martin Luther King Jr. and the nonviolent civil rights movement in the United States. In 1959, just after the successful Montgomery bus boycott that inaugurated his protest movement, King made a pilgrimage to India, which he describes in **"My Trip to the Land of Gandhi,"** to meet the assassinated leader's followers and to observe the results of his campaigns. In India King found support for his belief in nonviolence, and linking his movement with the worldwide movement against colonialism, he urged others — especially those colonial peoples who thought that they could liberate themselves only through violence — to follow the example of Gandhi.

Octavio Paz (p. 1292) did not go to India as a religious pilgrim, but his account of his involvement with India over a span of nearly forty years could be taken as indicative of the "familiarization" of India in the Western imagination over the last half-century. On his first visit in 1951 the Mexican viewed India at least in part through the eyes of Western **"Orientalism"** — seeing before him an exotic,

Massacres along the railroad tracks, the same in India as in Mexico . . . From the beginning, everything that I saw inadvertently evoked forgotten images of Mexico. The strangeness of India brought to mind that other strangeness: my own country.

– Octavio Paz

suh-tyuh-GRAH-huh

p. 1290

English has been with
us for over a century
and a half. I am par-
ticularly fond of the
language. I was never
aware that I was
using a different, a
foreign language
when I wrote in
English, because it
came very easily.

– R. K. NARAYAN

strange, and romantic land. By the time he served as Mexican ambassador to India in the 1960s, he had a circle of Indian friends and an appreciation for Indian culture that allowed him to consult and accept the counsel of a spiritual director, Mother Ananda Mai. Finally, on a visit in 1985, Paz collaborated with two Indian poets in writing a poem, symbolically bridging the distance between East and West. The stages in Paz's relationship with India reflect the changes in the West's perception of that country in the last half-century or so, from the Eastern exoticism seen in such films as *The Jungle Book* (1942) to the engagement with Indian gurus like the Maharishi Mahesh Yogi[3] in the 1960s to the assimilation of Indian doctors, computer specialists, and other Indian immigrants into American society since the 1980s.

WRITING INDIA

p. 1301

Raja Rao, in the foreword to his novel **Kanthapura** (1938), succinctly identifies two of the central issues facing Indian writers, both within India and in the diaspora: first, whether to write in English and second, whether English, if one chooses to use it, can accurately capture Indian life. For many authors, European languages are the languages of the colonial oppressors. Some, like Kenyan writer **Ngugi Wa Thiong'o** (p. 149), who began his literary career writing in English, have returned to their native tongues as a way of renounc-ing the colonial legacy. The majority of Indian writers have, however, chosen to use English. Its nearly two centuries of use in India estab-lished it as a shared second language for speakers of Hindi, Urdu, Tamil, and the many other regional languages and dialects of India. To write in English enables an Indian writer to reach a broad multi-cultural audience within India as well as the large English-speaking audience throughout the world. Although English may, as Rao sug-gests, present some difficulties in representing Indian culture, its virtues outweigh its disadvantages. R. K. Narayan speaks for many Indian writers when he says: "English has been with us for over a century and a half. I am particularly fond of the language. I was never aware that I was using a different, a foreign language when I wrote in English, because it came very easily."

en-GOO-gee wah
thee-ONG-oh

---

[3] **Maharishi Mahesh Yogi:** Leader of the Transcendental Meditation movement; his numerous Western follow-ers included the Beatles for a while.

The difficult thing, as Narayan shares in **"A Passage to America,"** is trying to maintain a deep involvement with Indian culture while living outside of India. He remained in the same region of southern India where he grew up and nearly all of his novels take place in the fictional city of Malgudi, a town deeply rooted in Indian history and culture. On one of his rare trips outside southern India, Narayan traveled to America in 1956, a journey that led to the travel narrative *My Dateless Diary* (1964) and the essay "A Passage to America" (1985). In the diaspora, at least in America, as Narayan saw it, life lacks "variety and richness," and the imported priests and ceremonies are "only imitating Indian existence." Indians who have been "translated" (to use Rushdie's term) into Americans have, in Narayan's view, lost much of the depth and spiritual dimension of their culture.

p. 1302

Indian-born but now a citizen of Britain and a resident of the United States, Salman Rushdie takes an opposite view in **"Imaginary Homelands."** He suggests that even a writer as rooted in India as Narayan was has only a "broken mirror" with which to view his society. The fragmentation in all human experience may just be more evident to exiles, expatriates, and émigrés like Rushdie than to a writer like Narayan who can entertain the illusion that he sees it whole. Rushdie sees translation—living in more than one culture—as a gain. It gives the individual the freedom to choose his heritage and connects him with historical migrants, such as Jews, Huguenots, and the Irish, whose lives were enriched by "cultural transplantation." V. S. Naipaul, born in Trinidad in the West Indies, a descendant of grandparents who migrated there in the nineteenth century as indentured servants, also celebrates the migrant in **"Our Universal Civilization."** The gain, as he sees it, is in becoming part of a global culture centered in the values of the West—"the idea of the individual, responsibility, choice, the life of the intellect, the idea of vocation and perfectibility and achievement"—values that grant to the individual the pursuit of happiness.

p. 1308

p. 1313

A MIGRANT'S STORY

Bharati Mukherjee was born in Calcutta, educated in Britain, India, and the United States, has lived in Canada, and is now a U.S. citizen and a professor at the University of California at Berkeley. She often writes about Indian women who have left India and are part of the

BAH-ruh-tee
MUCK-ur-jee

p. 1316

diaspora. In **"A Wife's Story,"** she tells of a woman who is visited by her Indian husband who has remained in India while she attends graduate school in New York City. She resists his plea that she return

p. 1261

with him to India, for she, like the narrator in **"The Courter,"** has found a new and fulfilling life away from her native land. The situation has similarities to that in "The Courter," but the rewards and difficulties of translation are different for a married woman than they are for the schoolboy at the center of Rushdie's story.

■ CONNECTIONS

R. K. Narayan, "A Horse and Two Goats," p. 785; Rokeya Hossain, "Sultana's Dream," p. 323; Rabindranath Tagore, *Broken Ties* (Book 5); Anita Desai, "The Farewell Party," p. 1196; Salman Rushdie, "The Courter," p. 1261. Although Rushdie's "The Courter" and Mukherjee's "A Wife's Story" are the only works in this anthology by writers in the Indian diaspora that directly address the issue of crossing cultures, how do other works by Indian writers — Tagore, Hossain, Narayan, and Desai, for example — raise questions relating to cultural pluralism?

In the World: Colonialism, p. 97; *In the World:* Imagining Africa, p. 853. Several selections by writers in the African diaspora in these two *In the World* sections deal with cultural "translation." How, if at all, do views of the native land and of living globally differ between African and Indian writers?

■ PRONUNCIATION

Bharati Mukherjee: BAH-ruh-tee MUCK-ur-jee
Ngugi wa Thiong'o: en-GOO-gee wah thee-ONG-oh
satyagraha: suh-tyuh-GRAH-huh

❧ MOHANDAS K. GANDHI
B. INDIA, 1869–1948

Political leader of the Indian independence movement and its first martyr, spiritual leader of modern India, and philosopher of nonviolence, Mohandas Gandhi has influenced independence leaders around the globe, including Nelson Mandela and Dr. Martin Luther King Jr. Schooled in law in India and London, Gandhi began legal practice in South Africa in 1893 but soon gave up the law to organize a campaign to secure better treatment of Indians in that country, where he stayed for nearly twenty years, until 1914. In this selection from his *Autobiography* Gandhi describes his introduction to South Africa on a train journey from Durban to Pretoria. Although he had not yet formulated his philos-

Gandhi in London, 1931
Gandhi leaving the Round Table Conference on Indian constitutional reform in London. (Hulton / Archive)

ophy of *satyagraha*—nonviolent direct action as a way of forcing social change—Gandhi refused to be demeaned or intimidated by his treatment on the train. That refusal illustrates the attitude and state of mind that would later enable him to mount successful campaigns to secure civil rights for Indians in South Africa and to win independence for India from the British. Returning to India in 1914, he applied the lessons he had learned in South Africa to the cause of Indian independence. His goal was achieved in 1947 when Britain withdrew; Britain required that the country be partitioned into India and Pakistan first. A few months later, on January 30, 1948, Gandhi was assassinated by a Hindu who blamed him for the partition.

❧ Autobiography

ON THE WAY TO PRETORIA

On the seventh or eighth day after my arrival, I left Durban. A first-class seat was booked for me. It was usual there to pay five shillings extra, if one needed a bedding. Abdulla Sheth[1] insisted that I should book one bedding but, out of obstinacy and pride and with a view to saving five shillings, I declined. Abdulla Sheth warned me.

---

[1] **Abdulla Sheth:** An affluent Indian businessman in South Africa who served as Gandhi's host when he first arrived in the country. [Editors' note.]

"Look, now," said he, "this is a different country from India. Thank God, we have enough and to spare. Please do not stint yourself in anything that you may need."

I thanked him and asked him not to be anxious.

The train reached Maritzburg, the capital of Natal, at about 9 P.M. Beddings used to be provided at this station. A railway servant came and asked me if I wanted one. "No," said I. "I have one with me." He went away. But a passenger came next, and looked me up and down. He saw that I was a "colored" man. This disturbed him. Out he went and came in again with one or two officials. They all kept quiet, when another official came to me and said, "Come along, you must go to the van compartment."

"But I have a first-class ticket," said I.

"That doesn't matter," rejoined the other. "I tell you, you must go to the van compartment."

"I tell you, I was permitted to travel in this compartment at Durban, and I insist on going on in it."

"No, you won't," said the official. "You must leave this compartment, or else I shall have to call a police constable to push you out."

"Yes, you may. I refuse to get out voluntarily."

The constable came. He took me by the hand and pushed me out. My luggage was also taken out. I refused to go to the other compartment and the train steamed away. I went and sat in the waiting room, keeping my hand-bag with me, and leaving the other luggage where it was. The railway authorities had taken charge of it.

It was winter, and winter in the higher regions of South Africa is severely cold. Maritzburg being at a high altitude, the cold was extremely bitter. My overcoat was in my luggage, but I did not dare to ask for it lest I should be insulted again, so I sat and shivered. There was no light in the room. A passenger came in at about midnight and possibly wanted to talk to me. But I was in no mood to talk.

I began to think of my duty. Should I fight for my rights or go back to India, or should I go on to Pretoria without minding the insults, and return to India after finishing the case? It would be cowardice to run back to India without fulfilling my obligation. The hardship to which I was subjected was superficial — only a symptom of the deep disease of color prejudice. I should try, if possible, to root out the disease and suffer hardships in the process. Redress for wrongs I should seek only to the extent that would be necessary for the removal of the color prejudice.

So I decided to take the next available train to Pretoria.

The following morning I sent a long telegram to the General Manager of the Railway and also informed Abdulla Sheth, who immediately met the General Manager. The Manager justified the conduct of the railway authorities, but informed him that he had already instructed the Station Master to see that I reached my destination safely. Abdulla Sheth wired to the Indian merchants in Maritzburg and to friends in other places to meet me and look after me. The merchants came to see me at the station and tried to comfort me by narrating their own hardships and explaining that what had happened to me was nothing unusual. They also said that Indians traveling first or second class had to expect trouble from railway officials and white passengers. The day was thus spent in listening to these tales of woe. The evening train arrived. There was a reserved berth for me. I now purchased at Maritzburg the bedding ticket I had refused to book at Durban.

The train reached Charlestown in the morning. There was no railway, in those days, between Charlestown and Johannesburg, but only a stagecoach, which halted at Standerton for the night en route. I possessed a ticket for the coach, which was not cancelled by the break of the journey at Maritzburg for a day; besides, Abdulla Sheth had sent a wire to the coach agent at Charlestown.

But the agent only needed a pretext for putting me off, and so, when he discovered me to be a stranger, he said, "Your ticket is cancelled." I gave him the proper reply. The reason at the back of his mind was not want of accommodation, but quite another. Passengers had to be accommodated inside the coach, but as I was regarded as a "coolie" and looked a stranger, it would be proper, thought the "leader," as the white man in charge of the coach was called, not to seat me with the white passengers. There were seats on either side of the coachbox. The leader sat on one of these as a rule. Today he sat inside and gave me his seat. I knew it was sheer injustice and an insult, but I thought it better to pocket it. I could not have forced myself inside, and if I had raised a protest, the coach would have gone off without me. This would have meant the loss of another day, and Heaven only knows what would have happened the next day. So, much as I fretted within myself, I prudently sat next the coachman.

At about three o'clock the coach reached Pardekoph. Now the leader desired to sit where I was seated, as he wanted to smoke and possibly to have some fresh air. So he took a piece of dirty sackcloth from the driver, spread it on the footboard and, addressing me said, "Sami, you sit on this, I want to sit near the driver." The insult was more than I could bear. In fear and trembling I said to him, "It was you who seated me here, though I should have been accommodated inside. I put up with the insult. Now that you want to sit outside and smoke, you would have me sit at your feet. I will not do so, but I am prepared to sit inside."

As I was struggling through these sentences, the man came down upon me and began heavily to box my ears. He seized me by the arm and tried to drag me down. I clung to the brass rails of the coachbox and was determined to keep my hold even at the risk of breaking my wristbones. The passengers were witnessing the scene — the man swearing at me, dragging and belaboring me, and I remaining still. He was strong and I was weak. Some of the passengers were moved to pity and exclaimed: "Man, let him alone. Don't beat him. He is not to blame. He is right. If he can't stay there, let him come and sit with us." "No fear," cried the man, but he seemed somewhat crestfallen and stopped beating me. He let go my arm, swore at me a little more, and asking the Hottentot servant who was sitting on the other side of the coachbox to sit on the footboard, took the seat so vacated.

The passengers took their seats and, the whistle given, the coach rattled away. My heart was beating fast within my breast, and I was wondering whether I should ever reach my destination alive. The man cast an angry look at me now and then and, pointing his finger at me, growled: "Take care, let me once get to Standerton and I shall show you what I do." I sat speechless and prayed to God to help me.

After dark we reached Standerton and I heaved a sigh of relief on seeing some Indian faces. As soon as I got down, these friends said: "We are here to receive you and take you to Isa Sheth's shop. We have had a telegram from Dada Abdulla." I was very glad, and we went to Sheth Isa Haji Sumar's shop. The Sheth and his clerks gathered around me. I told them all that I had gone through. They were very sorry to hear it and comforted me by relating to me their own bitter experiences.

I wanted to inform the agent of the Coach Company of the whole affair. So I wrote him a letter, narrating everything that had happened, and drawing his attention to the threat his man had held out. I also asked for an assurance that he would accommodate me with the other passengers inside the coach when we started the next morning. To which the agent replied to this effect: "From Standerton we have a bigger coach with different men in charge. The man complained of will not be there tomorrow, and you will have a seat with the other passengers." This somewhat relieved me. I had, of course, no intention of proceeding against the man who had assaulted me, and so the chapter of the assault closed there.

In the morning Isa Sheth's man took me to the coach. I got a good seat and reached Johannesburg quite safely that night.

Standerton is a small village and Johannesburg a big city. Abdulla Sheth had wired to Johannesburg also, and given me the name and address of Muhammad Kasam Kamruddin's firm there. Their man had come to receive me at the stage, but neither did I see him nor did he recognize me. So I decided to go to a hotel. I knew the names of several. Taking a cab I asked to be driven to the Grand National Hotel. I saw the Manager and asked for a room. He eyed me for a moment, and politely saying, "I am very sorry, we are full up," bade me good-bye. So I asked the cabman to drive to Muhammad Kasam Kamruddin's shop. Here I found Abdul Gani Sheth expecting me, and he gave me a cordial greeting. He had a hearty laugh over the story of my experience at the hotel. "How ever did you expect to be admitted to a hotel?" he said.

"Why not?" I asked.

"You will come to know after you have stayed here a few days," said he. "Only we can live in a land like this, because, for making money, we do not mind pocketing insults, and here we are." With this he narrated to me the story of the hardships of Indians in South Africa.

◎ Martin Luther King Jr.
b. United States, 1929–1968

Dr. Martin Luther King Jr. was raised in a middle-class home in Atlanta, the son of a prominent Baptist clergyman. After earning a Ph.D. in theology from Boston University in 1955, King became a pastor in Montgomery, Alabama, where one of his parishioners, Rosa Parks, defied segregation laws by sitting in the white section of a city bus. Following her arrest King led a bus boycott that came to a successful conclusion more than a year later and inaugurated the civil rights movement. King saw the struggle of American blacks for equal rights as part of the worldwide fight against colonial oppression, and he modeled his campaign on the nonviolent independence movement led by Mohandas Gandhi in India. Through the Southern Christian Leadership Conference, a group he founded in 1957, King promoted the Gandhian principle of *satyagraha*, or nonviolent resistance. His speeches, particularly the inspired "I Have a Dream" speech delivered on the steps of the Lincoln Memorial during the March on Washington in 1963 and the extraordinary "I See the Promised Land" speech delivered the evening before his assassination in 1968, are classics of American oratory and pivotal documents of American history.

In the essay "My Trip to the Land of Gandhi," from which the selection here is taken, King describes a pilgrimage that he and his wife, Coretta, made to India in 1959 to pay homage to Gandhi and to observe India in the aftermath of independence.

> By all standards of measurement, [Gandhi] is one of the half-dozen greatest men in world history.
>
> — Martin Luther King Jr.

Equal Rights Now, 1963

Martin Luther King Jr. leads some two-hundred thousand protesters in Washington, D.C., in a march for equal rights. King's nonviolent philosophy had been profoundly influenced by that of Gandhi. (Hulton / Archive)

FROM

↜ My Trip to the Land of Gandhi

At the outset, let me say that we had a grand reception in India. The people showered upon us the most generous hospitality imaginable. We were graciously received by the prime minister, the president, and the vice president of the nation: members of Parliament, governors and chief ministers of various Indian states; writers, professors, social reformers, and at least one saint. Since our pictures were in the newspapers very often it was not unusual for us to be recognized by crowds in public places and on public conveyances. Occasionally I would take a morning walk in the large cities, and out of the most unexpected places someone would emerge and ask: "Are you Martin Luther King?"

Virtually every door was open to us. We had hundreds of invitations that the limited time did not allow us to accept. We were looked upon as brothers with the color of our skins as something of an asset. But the strongest bond of fraternity was the common cause of minority and colonial peoples in America, Africa, and Asia struggling to throw off racialism and imperialism.

We had the opportunity to share our views with thousands of Indian people through endless conversations and numerous discussion sessions. I spoke before university groups and public meetings all over India. Because of the keen interest that the Indian people have in the race problem these meetings were usually packed. Occasionally interpreters were used, but on the whole I spoke to audiences that understood English.

The Indian people love to listen to the Negro spirituals. Therefore, Coretta ended up singing as much as I lectured. We discovered that autograph seekers are not confined to America. After appearances in public meetings and while visiting villages we were often besieged for autographs. Even while riding planes, more than once pilots came into the cabin from the cockpit requesting our signatures.

We got a good press throughout our stay. Thanks to the Indian papers, the Montgomery bus boycott was already well known in that country. Indian publications perhaps gave a better continuity of our 381-day bus strike than did most of our papers in the United States. Occasionally I meet some American fellow citizen who even now asks me how the bus boycott is going, apparently never having read that our great day of bus integration, December 21, 1956, closed that chapter of our history.

We held press conferences in all of the larger cities—Delhi, Calcutta, Madras, and Bombay—and talked with newspapermen almost everywhere we went. They asked sharp questions and at times appeared to be hostile but that was just their way of bringing out the story that they were after. As reporters, they were scrupulously fair with us and in their editorials showed an amazing grasp of what was going on in America and other parts of the world.

The trip had a great impact upon me personally. It was wonderful to be in Gandhi's land, to talk with his son, his grandsons, his cousins, and other relatives; to share the reminiscences of his close comrades, to visit his ashrama,[1] to see the countless memorials for him, and finally to lay a wreath on his entombed ashes at Rajghat. I left India more convinced than ever before that nonviolent resistance is the most potent weapon available to oppressed people in their struggle for freedom. It was a marvelous thing to see the amazing results of a nonviolent campaign. The aftermath of hatred and bitterness that usually follows a violent campaign was found nowhere in India. Today a mutual friendship based on complete equality exists between the Indian and British people within the commonwealth. The way of acquiescence leads to moral and spiritual suicide. The way of violence leads to bitterness in the survivors and brutality in the destroyers. But, the way of nonviolence leads to redemption and the creation of the beloved community.

The spirit of Gandhi is very much alive in India today. Some of his disciples have misgivings about this when they remember the drama of the fight for national independence and when they look around and find nobody today who comes near the stature of the Mahatma. But any objective observer must report that Gandhi is not only the greatest figure in India's history but that his influence is felt in almost every aspect of life and public policy today.

India can never forget Gandhi. For example, the Gandhi Memorial Trust (also known as the Gandhi Smarak Nidhi) collected some $130 million soon after the death of "the father of the nation." This was perhaps the largest, spontaneous, mass monetary contribution to the memory of a single individual in the history of the world. This fund, along with support from the Government and other institutions, is resulting in the spread and development of Gandhian philosophy, the implementing of his constructive program, the erection of libraries, and the publication of works by and about the life and times of Gandhi. Posterity could not escape him even if it tried. By all standards of measurement, he is one of the half-dozen greatest men in world history.

I was delighted that the Gandhians accepted us with open arms. They praised our experiment with the nonviolent resistance technique at Montgomery. They seem to look upon it as an outstanding example of the possibilities of its use in Western civilization. To them as to me it also suggests that nonviolent resistance *when planned and positive in action* can work effectively even under totalitarian regimes.

We argued this point at some length with the groups of African students who are today studying in India. They felt that nonviolent resistance could only work in a situation where the resisters had a potential ally in the conscience of the opponent. We soon discovered that they, like many others, tended to confuse passive resistance with nonresistance. This is completely wrong. True nonviolent resistance is not unrealistic submission to evil power. It is rather a courageous confrontation of evil by the power of love, in the faith that it is better to be the recipient of violence than the inflictor of it, since the latter only multiplies the existence of violence and bitterness in the universe, while the former may develop a sense of shame in the opponent, and thereby bring about a transformation and change of heart.

---

[1]**ashrama:** A spiritual community. [Editors' note.]

Nonviolent resistance does call for love, but it is not a sentimental love. It is a very stern love that would organize itself into collective action to right a wrong by taking on itself suffering. While I understand the reasons why oppressed people often turn to violence in their struggle for freedom, it is my firm belief that the crusade for independence and human dignity that is now reaching a climax in Africa will have a more positive effect on the world, if it is waged along the lines that were first demonstrated in that continent by Gandhi himself.

∾ OCTAVIO PAZ
B. MEXICO, 1914–1998

Octavio Paz, c. 1958
*The Mexican Nobel
Prize–winner.
(Bernard Diederich /
Timepix)*

The most important Mexican poet of the twentieth century and the winner of the Nobel Prize in literature in 1990, Octavio Paz came from a prominent family of writers, intellectuals, and journalists. Besides poetry, Paz wrote many volumes of essays, including *The Labyrinth of Solitude* (1950), a study of Mexican identity. As a member of the Mexican diplomatic service, Paz served in France and then as the Mexican ambassador to India between 1962 and 1968. *In Light of India* (1996), from which the following selection is taken, tells of his long association with that Asian nation, beginning in 1951 when he first went to India as a traveler and ending with a return in 1985 as an invited lecturer. If Paz begins as an observer of an exotic "oriental" culture in 1951, by the time of his 1985 visit he has become a participant in Indian culture, even collaborating with Indian poets.

All notes are the editors'.

∾ Three Visits to India[1]

Translated by Eliot Weinberger

I

We arrived in Bombay on an early morning in November 1951. I remember the intensity of the light despite the early hour, and my impatience at the sluggishness with which the boat crossed the quiet bay. An enormous mass of liquid mercury, barely undulating; vague hills in the distance; flocks of birds; a pale sky and scraps of pink clouds. As the boat moved forward, the excitement of the passengers grew. Little by little the white-and-blue architecture of the city sprouted up, a stream of

---

[1]Editors' title.

smoke from a chimney, the ocher and green stains of a distant garden. An arch of stone appeared, planted on a dock and crowned with four little towers in the shape of pine trees. Someone leaning on the railing beside me exclaimed, "The Gateway of India!" He was an Englishman, a geologist bound for Calcutta. We had met two days before, and I had discovered that he was W. H. Auden's[2] brother. He explained that the arch was a monument erected to commemorate the visit of King George V[3] and his wife, Queen Mary, in 1911. It seemed to me a fantasy version of the Roman arches; later I learned it was inspired by an architectural style that had flourished in Gujarat, an Indian state, in the sixteenth century. Behind the monument, floating in the warm air, was the silhouette of the Taj Mahal Hotel, an enormous cake, a delirium of the fin-de-siècle Orient fallen like a gigantic bubble, not of soap but of stone, on Bombay's lap. I rubbed my eyes: Was the hotel getting closer or farther away? Seeing my surprise, Auden explained to me that the hotel's strange appearance was due to a mistake: The builders could not read the plans that the architect had sent from Paris, and they built it backward, its front facing the city, its back turned to the sea. The mistake seemed to me a deliberate one that revealed an unconscious negation of Europe and the desire to confine the building forever in India. A symbolic gesture, much like that of Cortés[4] burning the boats so that his men could not leave. How often have we experienced similar temptations?

Once on land, surrounded by crowds shouting at us in English and various native languages, we walked fifty meters along the filthy dock and entered the ramshackle customs building, an enormous shed. The heat was unbearable and the chaos indescribable. I found, not easily, my few pieces of luggage, and subjected myself to a tedious interrogation by a customs official. Free at last, I left the building and found myself on the street, in the middle of an uproar of porters, guides, and drivers. I managed to find a taxi, and it took me on a crazed drive to my hotel, the Taj Mahal.

If this book were a memoir and not an essay, I would devote pages to that hotel. It is real and chimerical, ostentatious and comfortable, vulgar and sublime. It is the English dream of India at the beginning of the century, an India populated by dark men with pointed mustaches and scimitars at their waists, by women with amber-colored skin, hair and eyebrows as black as crows' wings, and the huge eyes of lionesses in heat. Its elaborately ornamented archways, its unexpected nooks, its patios, terraces, and gardens are both enchanting and dizzying. It is a literary architecture, a serialized novel. Its passageways are the corridors of a lavish, sinister, and endless dream. A setting for a sentimental tale or a chronicle of depravity. But that Taj Mahal no longer exists: It has been modernized and degraded, as though it were a motel for tourists from the Midwest. . . . A bellboy in a turban and an immaculate

---

[2] W. H. Auden (1907–1973): English-born American poet and playwright, author of *On the Frontier* (1938), *The Age of Anxiety* (1947), and other volumes of poetry. He left Britain in 1939 and spent the rest of his life in the United States.

[3] King George V: King of England from 1910 to 1936; he took an active interest in England's colonies.

[4] Cortés: Hernán Cortés (1485–1547), Spanish conqueror of Mexico. When he arrived on the coast of Mexico in 1519, he burned his ships so that neither he nor his men could turn around and return to Spain.

white jacket took me to my room. It was tiny but agreeable. I put my things in the closet, bathed quickly, and put on a white shirt. I ran down the stairs and plunged into the streets. There, awaiting me, was an unimagined reality:

> waves of heat; huge grey and red buildings, a Victorian London growing among palm trees and banyans like a recurrent nightmare, leprous walls, wide and beautiful avenues, huge unfamiliar trees, stinking alleyways,
>
> torrents of cars, people coming and going, skeletal cows with no owners, beggars, creaking carts drawn by enervated oxen, rivers of bicycles,
>
> a survivor of the British Raj, in a meticulous and threadbare white suit, with a black umbrella,
>
> another beggar, four half-naked would-be saints daubed with paint, red betel stains on the sidewalk,
>
> horn battles between a taxi and a dusty bus, more bicycles, more cows, another half-naked saint,
>
> turning the corner, the apparition of a girl like a half-opened flower,
>
> gusts of stench, decomposing matter, whiffs of pure and fresh perfumes,
>
> stalls selling coconuts and slices of pineapple, ragged vagrants with no job and no luck, a gang of adolescents like an escaping herd of deer,
>
> women in red, blue, yellow, deliriously colored saris, some solar, some nocturnal, dark-haired women with bracelets on their ankles and sandals made not for the burning asphalt but for fields,
>
> public gardens overwhelmed by the heat, monkeys in the cornices of the buildings, shit and jasmine, homeless boys,
>
> a banyan, image of the rain as the cactus is the emblem of aridity, and, leaning against a wall, a stone daubed with red paint, at its feet a few faded flowers: the silhouette of the monkey god,
>
> the laughter of a young girl, slender as a lily stalk, a leper sitting under the statue of an eminent Parsi,
>
> in the doorway of a shack, watching everyone with indifference, an old man with a noble face,
>
> a magnificent eucalyptus in the desolation of a garbage dump, an enormous billboard in an empty lot with a picture of a movie star: full moon over the sultan's terrace,
>
> more decrepit walls, whitewashed walls covered with political slogans written in red and black letters I couldn't read,
>
> the gold and black grillwork of a luxurious villa with a contemptuous inscription: EASY MONEY; more grilles even more luxurious, which allowed a glimpse of an exuberant garden; on the door, an inscription in gold on the black marble,
>
> in the violently blue sky, in zigzags or in circles, the flights of seagulls or vultures, crows, crows, crows . . .

As night fell, I returned to my hotel, exhausted. I had dinner in my room, but my curiosity was greater than my fatigue: After another bath, I went out again into the city. I found many white bundles lying on the sidewalks: men and women who had no home. I took a taxi and drove through deserted districts and lively neighborhoods, streets animated by the twin fevers of vice and money. I saw monsters and was blinded by flashes of beauty. I strolled through infamous alleyways and stared at the bordellos and little shops: painted prostitutes and transvestites with glass beads and loud skirts. I wandered toward Malabar Hill and its serene gardens. I walked down a quiet street to its end and found a dizzying vision: There, below, the black sea beat against the rocks of the coast and covered them with a rippling shawl of foam. I took another taxi back to my hotel, but I did not go in. The night lured me on, and I decided to take another walk along the great avenue that ran beside the docks. It was a zone of calm. In the sky the stars burned silently. I sat at the foot of a huge tree, a statue of the night, and tried to make an inventory of all I had seen, heard, smelled, and felt: dizziness, horror, stupor, astonishment, joy, enthusiasm, nausea, inescapable attraction. What had attracted me? It was difficult to say: *Human kind cannot bear much reality.* Yes, the excess of reality had become an unreality, but that unreality had turned suddenly into a balcony from which I peered into — what? Into that which is beyond and still has no name . . .

In retrospect, my immediate fascination doesn't strike me as strange: In those days I was a young barbarian poet. Youth, poetry, and barbarism are not opposed to one another: In the gaze of a barbarian there is innocence; in that of a young man, an appetite for life; and in a poet's gaze, astonishment. The next day I called Santha and Faubian. They invited me for a drink at their house. They were living with Santha's parents in an elegant mansion that, like the others in Bombay, was surrounded by a garden. We sat on the terrace, around a table with refreshments. Soon after, her father joined us, a courtly man who had been the first Indian ambassador to Washington and had recently left his post. On hearing my nationality, he burst out laughing and asked: "And is Mexico one of the stars or one of the stripes?" I turned red and was about to answer rudely, when Santha intervened with a smile: "Forgive us, Octavio. The Europeans know nothing of geography, and we know nothing of history." Her father apologized. "It was only a joke. . . . We too, not so long ago, were also a colony." I thought of my compatriots: They say similar nonsense when talking about India. Santha and Faubian asked me if I had visited any of the famous sites. They told me to go to the museum and, above all, to visit the island of Elephanta.

The next day I went back to the dock and bought a ticket for the small boat that runs between Bombay and Elephanta. With me were various foreign tourists and a few Indians. The sea was calm; we crossed the bay under a cloudless sky and arrived at the small island in less than an hour. Tall white cliffs, and a rich and startling vegetation. We walked up a gray and red path that led to the mouth of an enormous cave, and I entered a world made of shadows and sudden brightness. The play of the light, the vastness of the space and its irregular form, the figures carved on the walls: All of it gave the place a sacred character, sacred in the deepest meaning of the word. In the shadows were the powerful reliefs and statues, many of them mutilated by the fanaticism of the Portuguese and the Muslims, but all of them majestic, solid, made of a solar material. Corporeal beauty, turned into living stone. Divinities of the earth, sexual incarnations of the most abstract thought, gods that were simultaneously intellectual and carnal, terrible and peaceful. Shiva smiles from a beyond where time is a small drifting cloud, and that cloud soon turns into a stream of water, and the stream into a slender maiden who is spring itself: the goddess Pārvatī. The divine couple are the image of a happiness that our mortal condition grants us only for a moment before it vanishes. That palpable, tangible, eternal world is not for us. A vision of a happiness that is both terrestrial and unreachable. This was my initiation into the art of India.

Delhi

A week later I took the train for Delhi. I didn't take a camera with me, but I took a trusty guide: *Murray's Handbook of India, Pakistan, Burma, and Ceylon,* in the 1949 edition, purchased the day before in the bookstall of the Taj Mahal. On the first page were three lines by Milton:

> India and the Golden Chersonese
> And utmost Indian Isle Taprobane,
> Dusk faces with white silken turbans wreathed.

That interminable journey, with its stations full of people and the vendors of trinkets and sweets, made me think not of the visions of an English poet of the seventeenth century, but of some lines from a Mexican in the twentieth, Ramón López Velarde:

> My country: your house is still
> so vast that the train going by
> seems like a Christmas box from a toyshop.

It was impossible not to recall another long train ride, as desolate and with the same monotony which is one of the attributes of immensity, that I took as a child with my mother from Mexico City to San Antonio, Texas. It was near the end of the Mexican Revolution, and we had a military escort on board to protect us from the insurgents who were attacking the trains. My mother was suspicious of the officials: We were going to join my father, a political exile in the United States and the enemy of these military men. She was haunted by the hanged men she had seen on trips from Mexico City to Puebla, swaying from the telegraph poles along the way, their tongues dangling. Whenever we reached a station where the rebels had recently been fighting the federal troops, she would cover my face with one hand and with the other quickly lower the blinds on the window. I would be sleeping, and her gesture would make me open my eyes: Once I saw an elongated shadow hanging from a pole. It was a brief glimpse, and before I could realize what it was, it vanished. I was six years old then. Remembering that incident as I watched the interminable plains of India, I thought of the massacres of Hindus and Muslims in 1947. Massacres along the railroad tracks, the same in India as in Mexico . . . From the beginning, everything that I saw inadvertently evoked forgotten images of Mexico. The strangeness of India brought to mind that other strangeness: my own country. The lines of Milton with their exoticism blended into my own familiar exoticism of being Mexican. I had just written *The Labyrinth of Solitude,* an attempt to answer the question that Mexico asked me; now India was asking another question, one that was far more vast and enigmatic. . . .

. . . My education in India lasted for years and was not confined to books. Although it is far from complete and will remain forever rudimentary, it has marked me deeply. It has been a sentimental, artistic, and spiritual education. Its influence can be seen in my poems, my prose writings, and in my life itself.

II

During those years [1962–1968, when Paz was Mexico's ambassador to India] I made various friends. One of them was the novelist and essayist Raja Rao, whom I had met in Paris at the home of the poet Yves Bonnefoy shortly before my second stay in India. That night we discovered that both of us, for different reasons, were interested in the Cathar heresy:[5] he for its philosophical and religious spirit, I for its somewhat tenuous and circumstantial relation with courtly love. We became friends, and on each of his trips to Delhi—he was a professor at an American university—he never failed to visit me. Later we saw each other in different places. The last time was in Austin, Texas, at a festival of poetry. Czeslaw Milosz[6] was also there, another profoundly religious man with a philosophical temperament. Rao and Milosz immediately became friends and launched into long and passionate dialogues. Hearing them, I remembered this fable: After the final battle foretold by the holy books, among the corpses and the rubble, two men appear, the only survivors. One is a Hindu, a follower of Vedānta; the other a Christian, a Thomist.[7] No sooner do they discover each other than they begin to debate. The Christian says: The world is an accident; it was born from the divine *fiat lux;*[8] it was created, and like everything that has a beginning, it will have an end; salvation is beyond time. The Hindu answers: The world had no beginning and will have no end; it is necessary and self-sufficient; change doesn't change it; it is, has been, and will always be identical to itself. And the dialogue continues, the debate never ends. . . .

Late in 1963, I received a telegram from Brussels informing me that I had been awarded the Knokke le Zoute International Prize for Poetry. At that time it was a prestigious award that had been given to Saint-John Perse, Ungaretti, and

---

[5] **Cathar heresy:** Dualistic philosophy of the eleventh and twelfth centuries that divided the universe into a realm of the spiritual ruled by God and a realm of matter ruled by an evil god, Satan.

[6] **Czeslaw Milosz** (b. 1911): Polish poet, winner of the Nobel Prize in literature in 1980.

[7] **Thomist:** A follower of Saint Thomas Aquinas (1225–1274), Dominican monk and founder of Scholasticism.

[8] *fiat lux:* Latin for "Let there be light."

Jorge Guillén.[9] Not a well-known prize, but among those who knew it — people who truly interested me — it was, more than a distinction, a kind of confirmation. The news disturbed me. Since my adolescence I had written poems and had published various books, but for me poetry had always been a secret religion, celebrated outside the public eye. I had never received a prize for it, and had never wanted one. Prizes were public, poems private. If I accepted the prize, wouldn't I be revealing the secret and betraying myself? I was in this dilemma when I happened to see Raja Rao. I told him my problem. He replied: "I cannot give you advice, but I know someone who can. I'll take you to that person tomorrow, if you like." I accepted, without asking anything further. The next day, early in the afternoon, he came by and took me to a modest house on the outskirts of Delhi. It was an *ashram,* a place for retreat and meditation. The spiritual director was a woman who was well known in certain circles, Mother Ananda Mai.

The ashram was simple, sober rather than severe, and seemed more like a college than a convent. We crossed a small patio with two withered lawns and two small trees. There was an open door, and we entered a small room. There we found about a dozen people sitting on chairs in a semicircle around a woman who was seated on the floor. She was around fifty, dark-skinned, with loose black hair, deep and liquid eyes, thick, well-defined lips, wide nostrils as though made for deep breathing, her body full and powerful, her hands eloquent. She was dressed in a dark-blue cotton sari. Receiving us with a smile — she had known Raja Rao for a long time — she gestured to us to take a seat. The conversation, interrupted by our arrival, continued. She spoke in Hindi, but would answer a foreigner in English. As she spoke, she played with some oranges in a basket next to her. She soon looked at me, smiled, and threw an orange at me, which I caught and held on to. I realized that this was a game, and that the game contained some sort of symbolism. Perhaps she wanted to say that what we call "life" is a game and nothing more. Ananda began to speak in English and said:

> I am frequently asked who I am. And I answer you: I am a puppet, the puppet of each one of you. I am what you want me to be. In reality, I am nobody. A woman like any other. But the puppet whom you call Ananda the Mother is your fabrication. I am your toy . . . Ask me whatever you like, but first I must say that the answer will not be mine, but rather your own. It is like a game in which each person answers himself.

There were various questions — in the group were four or five Europeans and Americans, men and women — and then it was my turn. Before I could speak, Ananda interrupted me: "Raja Rao has already told me about your little problem." "And what do you think?" I said. She began to laugh:

> What vanity! Be humble and accept this prize. But accept it knowing that it is worth little or nothing, like all prizes. To not accept it is to overvalue it, to give it an impor-

---

[9] **Saint-John Perse . . . Guillén:** Saint-John Perse (1887–1975), French poet and diplomat, winner of the Nobel Prize in 1960; Giuseppe Ungaretti (1888–1970), Italian symbolist poet; Jorge Guillén (1893–1984), Spanish poet, exiled from Spain during the Spanish civil war.

tance that it does not have. It would be a presumptuous gesture. A false purity, a mask of pride . . . True disinterest is accepting it with a smile, as you received the orange I threw you. The prize will neither make you nor your poems better. But don't offend those who awarded it to you. You wrote those poems not in the spirit of gain. Do the same now. What matters is not prizes but the way they are received. Disinterest is the only thing that matters. . . .

An old German woman wanted to ask something more, but Ananda said, "We have ended for today. . . ." I was hoping that, as in other congregations, the session would end with the singing of some hymn. But without ceremony, two assistants invited us to leave. Some people remained on the patio, no doubt hoping for a private interview. Raja Rao took me by the arm and, when we reached our car, asked, "Are you happy?" "Yes, I am," I replied, "not because of the prize, but for what I heard." Rao said, "I don't know if you realized that everything Ananda said is in the *Gītā*."[10] I hadn't known. A few years later, I understood: To give and to receive are identical acts if they are realized with disinterest. . . .

III

The new prime minister, Rajiv Gandhi, renewed the invitation [to give the annual lecture honoring Jawaharlal Nehru]. I gave the lecture in 1985, never imagining that a few years later he too would be assassinated. One night on that visit, our last to India, the writer Sham Lal gathered a group of friends in his house. He had read *Renga*, a poem that had been written in Paris in 1969 by four poets (Charles Tomlinson, Jacques Roubaud, Edoardo Sanguinetti,[11] and myself). It occurred to him that the experiment could be repeated with Hindi poets. We agreed, and sheets of paper were passed out to three of us: Agyeya (S. Vatsyanan), the patriarch of Hindi poetry; Shirkant Verma, a young poet; and myself. Our poem was composed according to the tradition of Hindi and Urdu poetry: a six-line stanza followed by a concluding couplet. The first line was written by me in Spanish; the second and third by Agyeya in Hindi; the fourth and fifth by Verma, also in Hindi; the sixth, again by me, in Spanish. The last two lines, the coda, were written three times, once by each of us, so that the poem would have three different endings. I present it here in memory of Shirkant Verma, who died in his youth:

POEM OF FRIENDSHIP

O. P. Friendship is a river and a ring.
A.   The river flows through the ring.
      The ring is an island in the river.
S. V. The river says: before there was no river,
       after there is only a river.

---

[10] the *Gītā*: The Bhagavad Gita; part of the *Mahabarata,* this poem is considered the major devotional book of Hinduism.

[11] Tomlinson . . . Sanguinetti: Charles Tomlinson (b. 1927), British poet, professor emeritus from Bristol University; Jacques Roubaud (b. 1932), French experimental poet and mathematician, professor at the University of Paris; Edoardo Sanguinetti (b. 1930), Italian avant-garde poet.

Before and after: that which erases friendship.

O. P. Erases it? The river flows, forming the ring.

A. Friendship erases time and thus it frees us.
It is a river that, flowing, invents its rings.

S. V. In the sands of the river our tracks are erased.
In the sands we seek the river: where has it gone?

O. P. We live between oblivion and memory:
this moment
is an island weathered by incessant time.

✎ RAJA RAO
B. INDIA, 1909

Novelist Raja Rao, a Brahman from south India educated in Muslim schools, took part in the Indian independence movement and spent several years in a Gandhian ashram. (Brahmans are Hindus of the highest social caste.) He has also spent long periods of his life in Europe and America, studying in France for most of the 1930s and teaching at the University of Texas from 1965 to 1983. His novel *The Serpent and the Rope* (1960) is the story of a search for spiritual truth in Europe and India. *Kanthapura* (1938), the novel whose foreword is reprinted here, describes Gandhi's nonviolent resistance to the British Raj in the context of a small Indian village. Rao briefly addresses two of the central issues facing Indian and other postcolonial writers: the use of the language of the colonial masters and its adequacy to convey the language and culture of an Indian village.

All notes are the editors'.

∽　Foreword to *Kanthapura*

There is no village in India, however mean, that has not a rich *sthala-purana*, or legendary history, of its own. Some god or godlike hero has passed by the village—Rama[1] might have rested under this pipal-tree, Sita[2] might have dried her clothes, after her bath, on this yellow stone, or the Mahatma[3] himself, on one of his many pilgrimages through the country, might have slept in this hut, the low one, by the village gate. In this way the past mingles with the present, and the gods mingle with men to make the repertory of your grandmother always bright. One such story from the contemporary annals of a village I have tried to tell.

The telling has not been easy. One has to convey in a language that is not one's own the spirit that is one's own. One has to convey the various shades and omissions of a certain thought-movement that looks maltreated in an alien language. I use the word "alien," yet English is not really an alien language to us. It is the language of our intellectual make-up—like Sanskrit or Persian was before—but not of our emotional make-up. We are all instinctively bilingual, many of us writing in our own language and in English. We cannot write like the English. We should not. We cannot write only as Indians. We have grown to look at the large world as part of us. Our method of expression therefore has to be a dialect which will some day prove to be as distinctive and colorful as the Irish or the American. Time alone will justify it.

After language the next problem is that of style. The tempo of Indian life must be infused into our English expression, even as the tempo of American or Irish life has gone into the making of theirs. We, in India, think quickly, we talk quickly, and when we move we move quickly. There must be something in the sun of India that makes us rush and tumble and run on. And our paths are paths interminable. The *Mahabharata* has 214,778 verses and the *Ramayana* 48,000. The *Puranas* are endless and innumerable.[4] We have neither punctuation nor the treacherous "ats" and "ons" to bother us—we tell one interminable tale. Episode follows episode, and when our thoughts stop our breath stops, and we move on to another thought. This was and still is the ordinary style of our storytelling. I have tried to follow it myself in this story.

It may have been told of an evening, when as the dusk falls, and through the sudden quiet, lights leap up in house after house, and stretching her bedding on the veranda, a grandmother might have told you, newcomer, the sad tale of her village.

---

[1] Rama: An incarnation of Vishnu, one of the three central Hindu gods.

[2] Sita: Or Shiva, one of the gods in the central triad of Hinduism along with Brahma and Vishnu.

[3] the Mahatma: Hindu title of respect for a man of spirituality and high-mindedness; *the* Mahatma is Mohandas Gandhi; the appellation was first bestowed on him by Rabindranath Tagore.

[4] *Mahabharata . . .* innumerable: *Mahabharata* and *Ramayana* are the two great ancient Indian epics (see Book 1). *Puranas* are ancient poetic texts written between the fourth century B.C.E. and 1000 C.E. on metaphysical, mythical, and historical subjects for a popular audience.

R. K. NARAYAN
B. INDIA, 1906–2001

> Unlike many Indian writers who left India for long periods to teach in foreign universities or who resettled in foreign countries, Narayan remained rooted in his homeland. He took only a few relatively brief trips outside of India, preferring to remain in Mysore, the town in southern India that he immortalized as Malgudi, the fictional setting of most of his novels. Narayan's commitment to India and its way of life and his refusal to adopt non-Indian ways give him a different perspective from that of Salman Rushdie and other Indian writers of the new globalism on what it means to be an Indian translated into another culture.
>
> All notes are the editors'.

A Passage to America

The silent movies of the twenties were the main source of our knowledge of America when I was growing up in Madras. We had a theater called the Roxy in our neighborhood. For an outlay of two annas (about two cents) one could sit with a lot of others on a long teakwood bench, facing the screen. When the hall darkened, there appeared before us our idols and heroes — those hard-hitting, valorous men, such as Eddie Polo and Elmo Lincoln, who smashed up the evil-minded gang no matter how many came on at a time, retrieved the treasure plan, and rescued the heroine, who was on the verge of losing either her life or her chastity. The entire saga as a serial would be covered in twenty-four installments at a rate of six a week, with new episodes presented every Saturday. When Eddie Polo went out of vogue, we were shown wild men of the Wild West, cowboys in broad-brimmed hats and cartridge-studded belts, walking arsenals who lived on horseback, forever chasing, lassoing, and shooting. We watched this daredeviltry enthralled, but now and then we questioned, When and where do Americans sit down to eat or sleep? Do they never have walls and doors and roofs under which to live? In essence the question amounted to, After Columbus, what?

In the thirties, as Hollywood progressed, we were presented with more plausible types on the screen. Greta Garbo and Bette Davis — and who else? Ramon Novarro, John Gilbert, and other pensive, poignant, or turbulent romantics acting against the more versatile backdrops of Arabian deserts, European mansions, and glamorous drawing rooms.

Our knowledge of America was still undergoing an evolutionary process. It took time, but ultimately one was bound to hear of Lincoln, Emerson, Mark Twain, and Thoreau. The British connection had been firmly established. The British way of life and culture were the only other ones we Indians knew. All our books, periodicals, and educational material were British. These said very little about America, except for Dickens or Chesterton, who had traveled and lectured in America and had written of American scenes and character—after accepting a great deal of hospitality, and dollars of course. This seemed to us a peculiar trait of Americans—why should they invest so heavily in foreign authors, we Indians wondered, only to be presented as oddities at the end?

After World War II, the Indian media focused attention on American affairs and personalities and we became familiar with such esoteric terms as the Point-Four Plan, Public Law 480, and grants and fellowships, which in practical terms meant technical training and cultural exchanges. In the postwar period, more and more Americans were to be seen in India while more and more Indians went to America. Americans came to India as consultants, technicians, and engineers and to participate in the vast projects of our Five Year Plan. We noticed that Coca-Cola and Virginia tobacco and chewing gum were soon making their appearance in shop windows, and American best-sellers were to be found in the bookstores. For their part, Americans displayed on their mantelpieces Indian bric-a-brac of ivory, sandalwood, and bronze. Academicians from America came to India to study its culture and social organizations, as did political scientists (who were suspected of having CIA connections), and returned home to establish departments of South Asian studies in such universities as Chicago, Columbia, and the University of California at Berkeley. (Some American scholars of Sanskrit, Hindi, or Tamil are unquestioned authorities, and a match for the orthodox pundits in India.)

Americans working in India adapted themselves to Indian style with ease—visited Indian homes, sat down to eat with their fingers, savored Indian curry, wore *kurta* and pajamas, enjoyed Indian music. Some even mastered Indian music well enough to be able to give public concerts at a professional level before Indian audiences. Such colleges as Wesleyan and Colgate started regular programs in Indian music. Given this American cultural impact, young Indians began applying for admission to American institutions for higher studies or training.

My first chance to visit America came when I was offered a Rockefeller grant, which enabled me to see a great deal of the country—perhaps more than any American could—by train from New York to the Midwest and the West Coast, down south to Santa Fe, then through Texas to Nashville and Washington and back to New York, where I spent a couple of months. The more cities I saw, the more I was convinced that all America was contained in New York. For more than two decades I have been visiting New York off and on and never tire of it. I could not send down roots anywhere in America outside of New York.

An exception might be Berkeley, where I stayed, in a hotel room, long enough to write a novel. From my window I could watch young men and women hurrying along to their classes or hanging around the café or bookstore across the street. I divided my time between writing and window-shopping along Telegraph Avenue or strolling along the mountain paths. When the time came for me to leave Berkeley, I felt depressed. I could not imagine how I was to survive without all those enchantments I had gotten used to: the day's routine in my hotel on the fringe of the campus, the familiar shops, the Campanile, which I could see from my hotel window if the Bay smog was not too dense and by whose chime I regulated my daily activities (I had sworn to live through the American trip without a watch), the walk along picturesque highways and byways with such sonorous names as Sonoma, Pomona, and Venice. Even the voice of the ice-cream vendor who parked his cart at Sather Gate and sounded his bell, crying out, "Crunchymunchies, them's good for you," was part of the charm.

On the whole, my memories of America are happy ones. I enjoy them in retrospect. If I were to mention a single outstanding experience, it would be my visit to the Grand Canyon. To call it a visit is not right; a better word is "pilgrimage." I understood why certain areas of the canyon's outcrops have been named after the temples of Brahma, Shiva, and Zoroaster. I spent a day at the canyon. At dawn or a little before, I left my room at El Tovaro before other guests woke up, then took myself to a seat on the brink of the canyon. It was still dark under a starry sky. At that hour the whole scene acquired a different dimension and a strange, indescribable quality. Far below, the Colorado River wound its course, muffled and softened. The wind roared in the valley; as the stars gradually vanished a faint light appeared on the horizon. At first there was absolute, enveloping darkness. But as I kept looking on, contours gently emerged, little by little, as if at the beginning of creation itself. The Grand Canyon seemed to me not a geological object, but some cosmic creature spanning the horizons. I felt a thrill more mystic than physical, and that sensation has unfadingly remained with me all through the years. At any moment I can relive that ecstasy. For me the word *immortal* has a meaning now.

The variety of college campuses is an impressive feature of American life. One can lead a life of complete satisfaction at any campus, whether Berkeley or Michigan State or the tiny University of the South in Sewanee, Tennessee. Any university campus is a self-contained world, with its avenues and lawns, libraries, student union, tuck-shops, campus stores, and restaurants. I spent a term or two as Lecturer or Distinguished Visiting Professor or Very Distinguished Visiting Professor in various universities. Whatever my designation, it provided me with an opportunity to enjoy the facilities of a campus in comfortable surroundings, among agreeable and intelligent people. The duties I was expected to perform were light — give a couple of lectures and be accessible to students or faculty members when they desired to meet me. I have found campus life enjoyable when the lakes froze in Wisconsin or the snows piled up ten feet high in Michigan; in the ever-moderate climate of Berkeley or springtime at Columbia.

If I were asked where I would rather not live, I would say, "No American suburban life for me, please." It is boring. The sameness of houses, gardens, lawns, and dogs and two automobiles parked at every door, with not a soul or shop in sight except in a one-block stretch containing a post office, firehouse, and bank, similar to a hundred other places in the country. Interesting at first, but monotonous in the long run. I have lived for weeks at a stretch in Briarcliff Manor, an hour's run from Grand Central Station. I could survive it because of the lovely home of my hosts and their family, but outside their home the only relief was when I could escape to Manhattan. The surroundings of Briarcliff were perfect and charming, but life there was like existing amid painted cardboard scenes. I never felt this kind of desolation in

New York at any time, although I have stayed there for months at a time, usually at the Chelsea Hotel.

New York takes you out of yourself. A walk along Fifth Avenue or Madison or even 14th Street, with its dazzling variety of merchandise displayed on the pavement, can be a completely satisfying experience. You can visit a new ethnic quarter every day—German, Italian, Spanish, even Arab and Chinese—or choose an entertainment or concert or show from the newspaper, from page after page of listings. If you prefer to stay awake all night and jostle with a crowd, you can always go to Washington Square or Times Square, especially on a weekend.

At the American consulate the visa section is kept busy nowadays as more and more young men from India seek the green card or profess to enter on a limited visa, then try to extend their stay once they get in. The official has a difficult task filtering out the "permanent" in order to let in only the "transient." The average American is liberal-minded and isn't bothered that more and more Indian engineers and doctors are snapping up the opportunities available in the United States, possibly to the disadvantage of an American. I discussed the subject with Professor Ainslie T. Embree, chairman of Columbia University's history department, who has had a long association with Indian affairs and culture. His reply was noteworthy: "Why not Indians as well? In the course of time they will be Americans. The American citizen of today was once an expatriate, a foreigner who had come out of a European or African country. Why not Indians too? We certainly love to have Indians in the country."

The young man who goes to the States for higher training or studies declares when leaving home, "I will come back as soon as I complete my course, maybe two years or more, but I'll surely come and work for our country—of course, also to help the family." Excellent intentions, but it will not work out that way. Later, when he returns home full of dreams, plans, and projects, he finds only hurdles wherever he tries to get a job or to start an enterprise of his own. Form-filling, bureaucracy, caste, and other restrictions and a generally feudal style of functioning waste a lot of time for the young aspirant. He frets and fumes as he spends his days running about presenting or collecting papers at various places, achieving nothing. He is not used to this sort of treatment in America, where, he claims, he can walk into the office of the top man anywhere, address him by his first name, and explain his purpose. When he attempts to visit a man of similar rank in India to discuss his plans, he finds he has no access to him, but is forced to meet only subordinates in a hierarchical system. Some years ago a biochemist returning from America with a lot of experience and bursting with proposals pushed open the door of a big executive's office, stepped in innocently, and was curtly told off: "You should not come to me directly. Send your papers through proper channels." Thereafter the young Indian biochemist left India once and for all, having kept his retreat open with the help of a sympathetic professor at the American end.

In this respect American democratic habits have rather spoiled our young men. They have no patience with our Indian tempo, whereas the non-Americanized Indian accepts the hurdles as inevitable karma. An Indian who returns from America expects special treatment, forgetting the fact that the chancellors of Indian universities will see only other chancellors, and top executives will see only other top executives, and no one of lesser position under any circumstances.

Another reason for a young man's final retreat from India could be a lack of jobs for one with his particular training and qualifications. A young engineer qualified in robotics spent hours explaining the value of his specialty to prospective sponsors, until eventually he realized that there could be no place for robots in an over-crowded country.

The Indian in America is a rather lonely being, having lost his roots in one place and not grown them in the other. Few Indians in America make any attempt to integrate into American culture or social life. Few visit an American home or a theater or an opera, or try to understand the American psyche. An Indian's contact with Americans is confined to work situations and official luncheons. He may mutter a "Hi" across the hedge to an American neighbor while mowing the lawn.

After he has equipped his new home with the latest dishwasher and video and his garage with two cars, once he has acquired all that the others have, he sits back with his family and counts his blessings. Outwardly happy, he is secretly gnawed at by some vague discontent and aware of some inner turbulence or vacuum he cannot define. All the comfort is physically satisfying, he has immense "job satisfaction"— and that is about all. On weekends he drives his family fifty miles or more to visit another Indian family so they can eat an Indian dinner and discuss Indian politics or tax problems (for doctors, who are in the highest income bracket, this is a constant topic of conversation).

There is monotony in this pattern of life, so mechanical and standardized. India may have lost an intellectual or an expert, but it must not be forgotten that he has lost India too—and that is a more serious loss in the final reckoning. The quality of life in India is different. Despite all the deficiencies, irritations, lack of material comforts and amenities, and general confusions, Indian life builds inner strength. It is the subtle, inexplicable influences—religion, family ties, and human relationships in general (let us call them psychological "inputs," to use a modern term)—that cumulatively sustain and lend variety and richness to existence. Building imposing Indian temples in America, installing our gods therein and importing Indian priests to perform the *pooja*[1] ritual and preside at festivals is only imitating Indian existence and can have only a limited value. Social and religious assemblies at the temples in America might mitigate boredom, but only temporarily. I have lived as a guest in many Indian homes in America and have noticed the ennui that descends on a family when they are stuck at home.

Indian children growing up in America present a special problem. Without the gentleness and courtesy and respect for parents that—unlike the American upbringing, whereby a child is left alone to discover for himself the right code of conduct—is the basic training for a child in India, Indian children have to develop themselves on a shallow foundation without a cultural basis either Indian or American. They are ignorant of Indian life; aware of this, the Indian parent tries to cram

---

[1] *pooja:* Or *puja;* a form of Hindu meditation.

into his children's little heads every possible bit of cultural information he can during a rushed trip to the mother country.

Ultimately, America and India are profoundly different in attitude and philosophy, though it would be wonderful if they could complement each other's values. Indian philosophy stresses austerity and unencumbered, uncomplicated day-to-day living. America's emphasis, on the other hand, is on material acquisition and the limitless pursuit of prosperity. From childhood an Indian is brought up on the notion that austerity and a contented life are good; a certain otherworldliness is inculcated through a grandmother's tales, the discourses at the temple hall, and moral books. The American temperament, on the contrary, is pragmatic. The American has a robust indifference to eternity. "Attend church on Sunday and listen to the sermon, but don't bother about the future," he seems to say. Also, he seems to echo Omar Khayyam's[2] philosophy: "Dead yesterday and unborn tomorrow, why fret about them if today be sweet?" He works hard and earnestly, acquires wealth and enjoys life. He has no time to worry about the afterlife, only taking care to draw up a proper will and trusting the funeral home to take care of the rest. The Indian in America who is not able to live wholeheartedly on this basis finds himself in a halfway house; he is unable to overcome his conflicts while physically flourishing on American soil. One may hope that the next generation of American-grown Indians will do better by accepting the American climate spontaneously or, alternatively, returning to India to live a different life.

---

[2] **Omar Khayyam:** Eleventh-century Persian poet and mathematician known for the poem *The Rubaiyat*, which expresses a hedonistic fatalism: "Eat, drink, and be merry, for tomorrow you may die."

❧ SALMAN RUSHDIE
B. INDIA, 1947

For postcolonial critics, Salman Rushdie is the model of both postcolonialism and hybridity—belonging to more than one culture. Born in the year of Indian independence in Bombay, Rushdie was educated in England, worked for a time in Pakistan where his family had relocated, then returned to England where he became a citizen. He now lives in New York but describes himself as an English writer—not an Indian writer, a Pakistani writer, or a Commonwealth writer. He discusses this self-identification in his essay "'Commonwealth Literature' Does Not Exist."

In "Imaginary Homelands," Rushdie explores his hybridity and his lack of a single homeland. Describing himself as a "translated man," he sees his situation as similar to that of many modern writers and one in which he has gained rather than lost.

All notes are the editors' unless otherwise indicated.

FROM

❧ Imaginary Homelands

An old photograph in a cheap frame hangs on a wall of the room where I work. It's a picture dating from 1946 of a house into which, at the time of its taking, I had not yet been born. The house is rather peculiar—a three-storeyed gabled affair with tiled roofs and round towers in two corners, each wearing a pointy tiled hat. "The past is a foreign country," goes the famous opening sentence of L. P. Hartley's novel *The Go-Between,* "they do things differently there." But the photograph tells me to invert this idea; it reminds me that it's my present that is foreign, and that the past is home, albeit a lost home in a lost city in the mists of lost time.

A few years ago I revisited Bombay, which is my lost city, after an absence of something like half my life. Shortly after arriving, acting on an impulse, I opened the telephone directory and looked for my father's name. And, amazingly, there it was; his name, our old address, the unchanged telephone number, as if we had never gone away to the unmentionable country[1] across the border. It was an eerie discovery. I felt as if I were being claimed, or informed that the facts of my faraway life were illusions, and that this continuity was the reality. Then I went to visit the house in the photograph and stood outside it, neither daring nor wishing to announce myself to its new owners. (I didn't want to see how they'd ruined the interior.) I was overwhelmed. The photograph had naturally been taken in black and white; and my memory, feeding on such images as this, had begun to see my childhood in the same way, monochromatically. The colours of my history had seeped out of my mind's eye; now my other two eyes were assaulted by colours, by the vividness of the red tiles, the yellow-edged green of cactus-leaves, the brilliance of bougainvillaea creeper. It is probably not too romantic to say that that was when my novel *Midnight's Children* was really born; when I realized how much I wanted to restore the past to myself, not in the faded greys of old family-album snapshots, but whole, in CinemaScope and glorious Technicolor.

Bombay is a city built by foreigners upon reclaimed land; I, who had been away so long that I almost qualified for the title, was gripped by the conviction that I, too, had a city and a history to reclaim.

It may be that writers in my position, exiles or emigrants or expatriates, are haunted by some sense of loss, some urge to reclaim, to look back, even at the risk of being mutated into pillars of salt.[2] But if we do look back, we must also do so in the knowledge—which gives rise to profound uncertainties—that our physical alienation from India almost inevitably means that we will not be capable of reclaiming precisely the thing that was lost; that we will, in short, create fictions, not actual cities or villages, but invisible ones, imaginary homelands, Indias of the mind.

Writing my book in North London, looking out through my window onto a city scene totally unlike the ones I was imagining onto paper, I was constantly plagued by

---

[1] **the unmentionable country:** Pakistan, created as an independent nation at the time of Indian independence by a partition of India in 1947. Rushdie's parents resettled there from Bombay in 1964.

[2] **pillars of salt:** As Lot and his wife are escaping the destruction of Sodom and Gomorrah, Lot's wife disobeys the Lord by looking back and is turned into a pillar of salt. See Genesis 19:26.

this problem, until I felt obliged to face it in the text, to make clear that (in spite of my original and I suppose somewhat Proustian ambition[3] to unlock the gates of lost time so that the past reappeared as it actually had been, unaffected by the distortions of memory) what I was actually doing was a novel of memory and about memory, so that my India was just that: "my" India, a version and no more than one version of all the hundreds of millions of possible versions. I tried to make it as imaginatively true as I could, but imaginative truth is simultaneously honourable and suspect, and I knew that my India may only have been one to which I (who am no longer what I was, and who by quitting Bombay never became what perhaps I was meant to be) was, let us say, willing to admit I belonged.

This is why I made my narrator, Saleem, suspect in his narration; his mistakes are the mistakes of a fallible memory compounded by quirks of character and of circumstance, and his vision is fragmentary. It may be that when the Indian writer who writes from outside India tries to reflect that world, he is obliged to deal in broken mirrors, some of whose fragments have been irretrievably lost.

But there is a paradox here. The broken mirror may actually be as valuable as the one which is supposedly unflawed. Let me again try and explain this from my own experience. Before beginning *Midnight's Children,* I spent many months trying simply to recall as much of the Bombay of the 1950s and 1960s as I could; and not only Bombay—Kashmir, too, and Delhi and Aligarh, which, in my book, I've moved to Agra to heighten a certain joke about the Taj Mahal. I was genuinely amazed by how much came back to me. I found myself remembering what clothes people had worn on certain days, and school scenes, and whole passages of Bombay dialogue verbatim, or so it seemed; I even remembered advertisements, film-posters, the neon Jeep sign on Marine Drive, toothpaste ads for Binaca and for Kolynos, and a footbridge over the local railway line which bore, on one side, the legend "Esso puts a tiger in your tank" and, on the other, the curiously contradictory admonition: "Drive like Hell and you will get there." Old songs came back to me from nowhere: a street entertainer's version of "Good Night, Ladies," and, from the film *Mr 420* (a very appropriate source for my narrator to have used), the hit number "Mera Joota Hai Japani,"[4] which could almost be Saleem's theme song.

---

[3] **Proustian ambition:** French novelist Marcel Proust (1871–1922) undertook a lifelong exercise in exploring the distortions of time and the powers of memory in a series of semiautobiographical novels under the general title of *À la recherche du temps perdu* (1913–1927), translated into English as *Remembrance of Things Past.*

[4] *Mera joota hai Japani*
Yé patloon Inglistani
Sar pé lal topi Rusi—
Phir bhi dil hai Hindustani
—which translates roughly as:
O, my shoes are Japanese
These trousers English, if you please
On my head, red Russian hat—
My heart's Indian for all that.
[This is also the song sung by Gibreel Farishta as he tumbles from the heavens at the beginning of *The Satanic Verses.*] [Author's note.]

I knew that I had tapped a rich seam; but the point I want to make is that of course I'm not gifted with total recall, and it was precisely the partial nature of these memories, their fragmentation, that made them so evocative for me. The shards of memory acquired greater status, greater resonance, because they were *remains;* fragmentation made trivial things seem like symbols, and the mundane acquired numinous qualities. There is an obvious parallel here with archaeology. The broken pots of antiquity, from which the past can sometimes, but always provisionally, be reconstructed, are exciting to discover, even if they are pieces of the most quotidian objects.

It may be argued that the past is a country from which we have all emigrated, that its loss is part of our common humanity. Which seems to me self-evidently true; but I suggest that the writer who is out-of-country and even out-of-language may experience this loss in an intensified form. It is made more concrete for him by the physical fact of discontinuity, of his present being in a different place from his past, of his being "elsewhere." This may enable him to speak properly and concretely on a subject of universal significance and appeal.

But let me go further. The broken glass is not merely a mirror of nostalgia. It is also, I believe, a useful tool with which to work in the present.

John Fowles[5] begins *Daniel Martin* with the words: "Whole sight: or all the rest is desolation." But human beings do not perceive things whole; we are not gods but wounded creatures, cracked lenses, capable only of fractured perceptions. Partial beings, in all the senses of that phrase. Meaning is a shaky edifice we build out of scraps, dogmas, childhood injuries, newspaper articles, chance remarks, old films, small victories, people hated, people loved; perhaps it is because our sense of what is the case is constructed from such inadequate materials that we defend it so fiercely, even to the death. The Fowles position seems to me a way of succumbing to the guru-illusion. Writers are no longer sages, dispensing the wisdom of the centuries. And those of us who have been forced by cultural displacement to accept the provisional nature of all truths, all certainties, have perhaps had modernism forced upon us. We can't lay claim to Olympus, and are thus released to describe our worlds in the way in which all of us, whether writers or not, perceive it from day to day. . . .

England's Indian writers are by no means all the same type of animal. Some of us, for instance, are Pakistani. Others Bangladeshi. Others West, or East, or even South African. And V. S. Naipaul, by now, is something else entirely. This word "Indian" is getting to be a pretty scattered concept. Indian writers in England include political exiles, first-generation migrants, affluent expatriates whose residence here is frequently temporary, naturalized Britons, and people born here who may never have laid eyes on the subcontinent. Clearly, nothing that I say can apply across all these categories. But one of the interesting things about this diverse community is that, as far as Indo-British fiction is concerned, its existence changes the ball game, because that fiction is in future going to come as much from addresses in London, Birmingham, and Yorkshire as from Delhi or Bombay.

---

[5]John Fowles (b. 1926): English novelist, influenced by the French existentialists; author of *The Collector* (1963), *The Magus* (1965), *The French Lieutenant's Woman* (1969), and other works.

One of the changes has to do with attitudes towards the use of English. Many have referred to the argument about the appropriateness of this language to Indian themes. And I hope all of us share the view that we can't simply use the language in the way the British did; that it needs remaking for our own purposes. Those of us who do use English do so in spite of our ambiguity towards it, or perhaps because of that, perhaps because we can find in that linguistic struggle a reflection of other struggles taking place in the real world, struggles between the cultures within ourselves and the influences at work upon our societies. To conquer English may be to complete the process of making ourselves free.

But the British Indian writer simply does not have the option of rejecting English, anyway. His children, her children, will grow up speaking it, probably as a first language; and in the forging of a British Indian identity the English language is of central importance. It must, in spite of everything, be embraced. (The word "translation" comes, etymologically, from the Latin for "bearing across." Having been borne across the world, we are translated men. It is normally supposed that something always gets lost in translation; I cling, obstinately, to the notion that something can also be gained.)

To be an Indian writer in this society is to face, every day, problems of definition. What does it mean to be "Indian" outside India? How can culture be preserved without becoming ossified? How should we discuss the need for change within ourselves and our community without seeming to play into the hands of our racial enemies? What are the consequences, both spiritual and practical, of refusing to make any concessions to Western ideas and practices? What are the consequences of embracing those ideas and practices and turning away from the ones that came here with us? These questions are all a single, existential question: How are we to live in the world?

I do not propose to offer, prescriptively, any answers to these questions; only to state that these are some of the issues with which each of us will have to come to terms. . . .

Let me suggest that Indian writers in England have access to a second tradition, quite apart from their own racial history. It is the culture and political history of the phenomenon of migration, displacement, life in a minority group. We can quite legitimately claim as our ancestors the Huguenots, the Irish, the Jews;[6] the past to which we belong is an English past, the history of immigrant Britain. Swift, Conrad, Marx[7] are as much our literary forebears as Tagore or Ram Mohun Roy.[8] America, a

---

[6] **Huguenots . . . Jews:** Religious and ethnic minorities forced by persecution to emigrate; the Huguenots were French Protestants who left France in the seventeenth century; the Irish fled from English colonial persecution in the nineteenth and early twentieth centuries; Jews were persecuted in many European countries, especially in Germany and eastern Europe.

[7] **Swift . . . Marx:** Jonathan Swift (1667–1745; see Book 4), author of *Gulliver's Travels* (1726), emigrated from Ireland to England; Joseph Conrad (1857–1924; see p. 30), author of *Heart of Darkness* (1902), emigrated from Poland and eventually became a British citizen; Karl Marx (1818–1883; see Book 5), author of *The Communist Manifesto* (1848), emigrated from Germany to England.

[8] **Tagore . . . Roy:** Indian novelist, poet, and playwright Rabindranath Tagore (1861–1941; see Book 5), author of *Broken Ties* (1916), made several trips to Britain where he was recognized as an important Indian writer, especially by W. B. Yeats; Ram Mohun Roy (1772–1833), Indian writer and reformer, was one of the first Indian intellectuals to travel to England; he died there in Bristol in 1833.

nation of immigrants, has created great literature out of the phenomenon of cultural transplantation, out of examining the ways in which people cope with a new world; it may be that by discovering what we have in common with those who preceded us into this country, we can begin to do the same.

I stress this is only one of many possible strategies. But we are inescapably international writers at a time when the novel has never been a more international form (a writer like Borges speaks of the influence of Robert Louis Stevenson[9] on his work; Heinrich Böll[10] acknowledges the influence of Irish literature; cross-pollination is everywhere); and it is perhaps one of the more pleasant freedoms of the literary migrant to be able to choose his parents. My own — selected half consciously, half not — include Gogol, Cervantes, Kafka, Melville, Machado de Assis;[11] a polyglot family tree, against which I measure myself, and to which I would be honoured to belong.

There's a beautiful image in Saul Bellow's latest novel, *The Dean's December*. The central character, the Dean, Corde, hears a dog barking wildly somewhere. He imagines that the barking is the dog's protest against the limit of dog experience. "For God's sake," the dog is saying, "open the universe a little more!" And because Bellow is, of course, not really talking about dogs, or not only about dogs, I have the feeling that the dog's rage, and its desire, is also mine, ours, everyone's. "For God's sake, open the universe a little more!"

---

[9] **Borges . . . Stevenson:** Argentine poet, critic, and fiction writer Jorge Luis Borges (1899–1986; see p. 648), author of "The Garden of Forking Paths"; Scottish novelist Robert Louis Stevenson (1850–1894), author of *Treasure Island* (1883), wrote many books based on his travels in Europe and the South Pacific.

[10] **Heinrich Böll** (1917–1985): German novelist, winner of the Nobel Prize in 1972; author of *And Where Were You Adam?* (1951), *Billiards at Half-Past Nine* (1959), and other works.

[11] **Gogol . . . Machado de Assis:** Russian Realist novelist Nikolai Gogol (1809–1852), author of *Dead Souls* (1842) and *The Inspector General* (1836); Spanish novelist Miguel de Cervantes Saavedra (1547–1616; see Book 3), known for *Don Quixote de la Mancha* (1605–1615); Austrian-Czech novelist Franz Kafka (1883–1924; see p. 423), author of *The Metamorphosis;* American novelist Herman Melville (1819–1891; see Book 5), author of "Bartleby, the Scrivener" and *Moby Dick* (1851); Brazilian novelist Joaquim Maria Machado de Assis (1839–1908; see Book 5), author of "Adam and Eve" and *Epitaph for a Small Winner* (1891).

❧ V. S. NAIPAUL

B. TRINIDAD, 1932

Although descended from Hindu parents from northern India, V. S. Naipaul was born in Trinidad, educated at Oxford, and became a British citizen after, as he describes it, migrating "from the periphery to the center." His many novels and travel books reflect the diversity of his experience and his role as a kind of rootless wanderer. Equally critical of the colonizers and the colonized in his many books about Third-World cultures, Naipaul has been harshly criticized himself, particularly for his unblinking and often scathing accounts of the West Indies, India, and Islamic societies. Naipaul has written three books about India: The first, *An Area of Darkness* (1964), records his first trip to his ancestral homeland. He reevaluated his somewhat denigrating first impression in two later books: *India: A Wounded Civilization* (1977) and *India: A Million Mutinies Now* (1991).

Naipaul has consistently challenged tribalism, chauvinism, and the "politically correct" refusal to criticize Third-World cultures. In "Our Universal Civilization," he speaks of individualism and the pursuit of happiness, Western values that characterize the emerging global culture.

All notes are the editors'.

V. S. Naipaul, 1968
Trinidad-born novel-ist V. S. Naipaul is of Indian heritage, and many of his novels portray the immigrant Indian population in the West Indies.
(© Hulton-Deutsch Collection / CORBIS)

❧ Our Universal Civilization

I never formulated the idea of the universal civilization until eleven years ago, when I traveled for many months in a number of non-Arab Muslim countries — Iran, Indonesia, Malaysia, and Pakistan — to try to understand what had driven them to their rage. That Muslim rage was just beginning to be apparent.

I thought I would be traveling among people who would be like the people of my own community, the Trinidad Indian community. A large portion of Indians were Muslims; we both had a similar nineteenth-century imperial or colonial history. But it wasn't like that.

Despite the history we had in common, I had traveled a different way. Starting with the Hindu background of the instinctive, ritualized life; growing up in the unpromising conditions of colonial Trinidad; I had gone through many stages of knowledge and self-knowledge. I had been granted the ideas of inquiry and the tools of scholarship. I could carry four or five or six different cultural ideas in my head. Now, traveling among non-Arab Muslims, I found myself among a colonized people who had been stripped by their faith of all that expanding cultural and historical knowledge of the world that I had been growing into on the other side of the world.

Before I began my journey—while the Shah[1] still ruled—there had appeared in the United States a small novel, *Foreigner,* by Nahid Rachlin, a young Iranian woman, that in its subdued, unpolitical way foreshadowed the hysteria that was to come. The central figure is a young Iranian woman who does research work in Boston as a biologist. She is married to an American, and she might seem well adapted.

But when she goes back on a holiday to Teheran, she begins to feel lost. She reflects on her time in the United States. It is not a time of clarity; she sees it now to be a time of emptiness. She has never been in control. We can see that she was not prepared for the movement out of the shut-in Iranian world—where the faith was the complete way, filled everything, left no spare corner of the mind or will or soul—to the other world where it was necessary to be an individual and responsible; where people developed vocations and were stirred by ambition and achievement, and believed in perfectibility.

In her distress, she falls ill. She goes to a hospital. The doctor understands her unhappiness. He tells the young woman that her pain comes from an old ulcer. "What you have," he says in his melancholy, seductive way, "is a Western disease." And the research biologist arrives at a decision. She will give up that Boston-imposed life of the intellect and meaningless work; she will stay in Iran and put on the veil.

Immensely satisfying, that renunciation. But it is intellectually flawed: It assumes that there will continue to be people striving out there, in the stressed world, making drugs and medical equipment, to keep the Iranian doctor's hospital going.

Again and again, on my Islamic journey in 1979, I found a similar unconscious contradiction in people's attitudes. I remember especially a newspaper editor in Teheran. His paper had been at the heart of the revolution. In the middle of 1979 it was busy, in a state of glory. Seven months later, when I went back to Teheran, it had lost its heart; the once busy main room was empty; all but two of the staff had disappeared. The American Embassy had been seized; a financial crisis had followed; many foreign firms had closed down; advertising had dried up; the newspaper editor could hardly see his way ahead; every issue of the paper lost money; the editor, it might be said, had become as much a hostage as the diplomats.

He also, as I now learned, had two sons of university age. One was studying in the United States; the other had applied for a visa, but then the hostage crisis had occurred. This was news to me—that the United States should have been so important to the sons of one of the spokesmen of the Islamic revolution. I told the editor I was surprised. He said, speaking especially of the son waiting for the visa, "It's his future."

Emotional satisfaction on one hand; thought for the future on the other. The editor was as divided as nearly everyone else.

One of Joseph Conrad's earliest stories[2] of the East Indies, from the 1890s, was about a local raja or chieftain, a murderous man, a Muslim (though it is never

---

[1] **the Shah:** The Shah of Iran, Muhammad Reza Pahlevi (1919–1980), who was deposed by the Islamic Revolution in 1979.

[2] **One of . . . stories:** "Karain: A Memory," collected in *Tales of Unrest* (1898).

explicitly said), who, in a crisis, having lost his magical counselor, swims out one night to one of the English merchant ships in the harbor to ask the sailors, representatives of the immense power that had come from the other end of the world, for an amulet, a magical charm. The sailors are at a loss; but then someone among them gives the raja a British coin, a sixpence commemorating Queen Victoria's Jubilee; and the raja is well pleased. Conrad didn't treat the story as a joke; he loaded it with philosophical implications for both sides, and I feel now that he saw truly.

In the one hundred years since that story, the wealth of the world has grown, power has grown, education has spread; the disturbance, the "philosophical shriek" of men at the margin (to use Conrad's words), has been amplified. The division in the revolutionary editor's spirit, and the renunciation of the fictional biologist, both contain a tribute—unacknowledged, but all the more profound—to the universal civilization. Simple charms alone cannot be acquired from it; other, difficult things come with it as well: ambition, endeavor, individuality.

The universal civilization has been a long time in the making. It wasn't always universal; it wasn't always as attractive as it is today. The expansion of Europe gave it for at least three centuries a racial taint, which still causes pain.

In Trinidad I grew up in the last days of that kind of racialism. And that, perhaps, has given me a greater appreciation of the immense changes that have taken place since the end of the war, the extraordinary attempt to accommodate the rest of the world, and all the currents of that world's thought.

Because my movement within this civilization has been from Trinidad to England, from the periphery to the center, I may have felt certain of its guiding principles more freshly than people to whom these things were everyday. One such realization—I suppose I have sensed it most of my life, but I have understood it philosophically only during the preparation of this talk—has been the beauty of the idea of the pursuit of happiness. Familiar words, easy to take for granted; easy to misconstrue.

This idea of the pursuit of happiness is at the heart of the attractiveness of the civilization to so many outside it or on its periphery. I find it marvelous to contemplate to what an extent, after two centuries, and after the terrible history of the earlier part of this century, the idea has come to a kind of fruition. It is an elastic idea; it fits all men. It implies a certain kind of society, a certain kind of awakened spirit. I don't imagine my father's Hindu parents would have been able to understand the idea. So much is contained in it: the idea of the individual, responsibility, choice, the life of the intellect, the idea of vocation and perfectibility and achievement. It is an immense human idea. It cannot be reduced to a fixed system. It cannot generate fanaticism. But it is known to exist, and because of that, other more rigid systems in the end blow away.

BHARATI MUKHERJEE
B. INDIA, 1940

Others who write
stories of migration
often talk of arrival
at a new place as a
loss, the loss of com-
munal memory and
the erosion of an
original culture. I
want to talk of arrival
as gain.

– BHARATI MUKHERJEE

Now a distinguished professor of English at the University of California, Berkeley, Bharati Mukherjee traveled to California from Calcutta via England, Iowa, and Canada. The second of three daughters in an upper-middle-class Brahman family, Mukherjee spent some of her primary-school years in England and then returned to India where she completed a master's degree in English and ancient Indian culture before leaving to continue studying in the United States. Marrying a Canadian while earning degrees in English and creative writing at the University of Iowa, Mukherjee spent fourteen years in Canada, a country she considers hostile to immigrants and cultural assimilation. She returned with her family to the United States in 1980 and has since become an American citizen. She cherishes the United States' "melting pot," and says that "America has transformed me." She also admits, however, that "the transition from foreign student to U.S. citizen, from detached onlooker to committed immigrant, has not been easy."

In her work, Mukherjee writes about such transitions and about the difficulties of crossing cultural borders. Her first novel, *The Tiger's Daughter* (1971), and a nonfiction work coauthored with her husband, Clark Blaise, *Days and Nights in Calcutta* (1986), both describe returning to India from America and explore being caught between two worlds. "A Wife's Story," from the collection *The Middleman and Other Stories* (1988), describes a similar dilemma from the point of view of a woman who has come to the United States to do graduate work.

All notes are the editors'.

A Wife's Story

Imre says forget it, but I'm going to write David Mamet.[1] So Patels are hard to sell real estate to. You buy them a beer, whisper Glengarry Glen Ross, and they smell swamp instead of sun and surf. They work hard, eat cheap, live ten to a room, stash their savings under futons in Queens, and before you know it they own half of Hoboken. You say, where's the sweet gullibility that made this nation great?

Polish jokes, Patel jokes: That's not why I want to write Mamet.

Seen their women?

Everybody laughs. Imre laughs. The dozing fat man with the Barnes & Noble sack between his legs, the woman next to him, the usher, everybody. The theater isn't

---

[1] Mamet: In *Glengarry Glen Ross* (1984), a satiric look at the real estate business by Chicago playwright David Mamet (b. 1947), the real estate salesmen call potential Indian clients "Patels" — a surname as common in India as "Smith" in the United States — to denigrate them.

so dark that they can't see me. In my red silk sari I'm conspicuous. Plump, gold paisleys sparkle on my chest.

The actor is just warming up. *Seen their women?* He plays a salesman, he's had a bad day and now he's in a Chinese restaurant trying to loosen up. His face is pink. His wool-blend slacks are creased at the crotch. We bought our tickets at half-price, we're sitting in the front row, but at the edge, and we see things we shouldn't be seeing. At least I do, or think I do. Spittle, actors goosing each other, little winks, streaks of makeup.

Maybe they're improvising dialogue too. Maybe Mamet's provided them with insult kits, Thursdays for Chinese, Wednesdays for Hispanics, today for Indians. Maybe they get together before curtain time, see an Indian woman settling in the front row off to the side, and say to each other: "Hey, forget Friday. Let's get *her* today. See if she cries. See if she walks out." Maybe, like the salesmen they play, they have a little bet on.

Maybe I shouldn't feel betrayed.

Their women, he goes again. *They look like they've just been fucked by a dead cat.*

The fat man hoots so hard he nudges my elbow off our shared armrest.

"Imre. I'm going home." But Imre's hunched so far forward he doesn't hear. English isn't his best language. A refugee from Budapest, he has to listen hard. "I didn't pay eighteen dollars to be insulted."

I don't hate Mamet. It's the tyranny of the American dream that scares me. First, you don't exist. Then you're invisible. Then you're funny. Then you're disgusting. Insult, my American friends will tell me, is a kind of acceptance. No instant dignity here. A play like this, back home, would cause riots. Communal, racist, and antisocial. The actors wouldn't make it off stage. This play, and all these awful feelings, would be safely locked up.

I long, at times, for clear-cut answers. Offer me instant dignity, today, and I'll take it.

"What?" Imre moves toward me without taking his eyes off the actor. "Come again?"

Tears come. I want to stand, scream, make an awful scene. I long for ugly, nasty rage.

The actor is ranting, flinging spittle. *Give me a chance. I'm not finished, I can get back on the board. I tell that asshole, give me a real lead. And what does that asshole give me? Patels. Nothing but Patels.*

This time Imre works an arm around my shoulders. "Panna, what is Patel? Why are you taking it all so personally?"

I shrink from his touch, but I don't walk out. Expensive girls' schools in Lausanne and Bombay have trained me to behave well. My manners are exquisite, my feelings are delicate, my gestures refined, my moods undetectable. They have seen me through riots, uprootings, separation, my son's death.

"I'm not taking it personally."

The fat man looks at us. The woman looks too, and shushes.

I stare back at the two of them. Then I stare, mean and cool, at the man's elbow. Under the bright blue polyester Hawaiian shirt sleeve, the elbow looks soft and runny. "Excuse me," I say. My voice has the effortless meanness of well-bred displaced Third World women, though my rhetoric has been learned elsewhere. "You're exploiting my space."

Startled, the man snatches his arm away from me. He cradles it against his breast. By the time he's ready with comebacks, I've turned my back on him. I've probably ruined the first act for him. I know I've ruined it for Imre.

It's not my fault; it's the *situation*. Old colonies wear down. Patels—the new pioneers—have to be suspicious. Idi Amin's[2] lesson is permanent. AT&T wires move good advice from continent to continent. Keep all assets liquid. Get into 7-11s, get out of condos and motels.[3] I know how both sides feel, that's the trouble. The Patel sniffing out scams, the sad salesmen on the stage: Postcolonialism has made me their referee. It's hate I long for; simple, brutish, partisan hate.

After the show Imre and I make our way toward Broadway. Sometimes he holds my hand; it doesn't mean anything more than that crazies and drunks are crouched in doorways. Imre's been here over two years, but he's stayed very old-world, very courtly, openly protective of women. I met him in a seminar on special ed. last semester. His wife is a nurse somewhere in the Hungarian countryside. There are two sons, and miles of petitions for their emigration. My husband manages a mill two hundred miles north of Bombay. There are no children.

"You make things tough on yourself," Imre says. He assumed Patel was a Jewish name or maybe Hispanic; everything makes equal sense to him. He found the play tasteless, he worried about the effect of vulgar language on my sensitive ears. "You have to let go a bit." And as though to show me how to let go, he breaks away from me, bounds ahead with his head ducked tight, then dances on amazingly jerky legs. He's a Magyar, he often tells me, and deep down, he's an Asian too. I catch glimpses of it, knife-blade Attila cheekbones, despite the blondish hair. In his faded jeans and leather jacket, he's a rock video star. I watch MTV for hours in the apartment when Charity's working the evening shift at Macy's. I listen to WPLJ on Charity's earphones. Why should I be ashamed? Television in India is so uplifting.

Imre stops as suddenly as he'd started. People walk around us. The summer sidewalk is full of theatergoers in seersucker suits; Imre's year-round jacket is out of place. European. Cops in twos and threes huddle, lightly tap their thighs with night sticks and smile at me with benevolence. I want to wink at them, get us all in trouble, tell them the crazy dancing man is from the Warsaw Pact. I'm too shy to break into dance on Broadway. So I hug Imre instead.

The hug takes him by surprise. He wants me to let go, but he doesn't really expect me to let go. He staggers, though I weigh no more than 104 pounds, and with him, I pitch forward slightly. Then he catches me, and we walk arm in arm to the bus stop. My husband would never dance or hug a woman on Broadway. Nor would my

---

[2] **Idi Amin** (b. 1925): Military dictator who ruled Uganda from 1971 to 1979. During his regime he expelled the Indian population of the country and killed an estimated two hundred thousand people before being deposed. He escaped into exile in Saudi Arabia.

[3] **condos and motels:** Businesses that many Indian immigrants bought into.

brothers. They aren't stuffy people, but they went to Anglican boarding schools and they have a well-developed sense of what's silly.

"Imre." I squeeze his big, rough hand. "I'm sorry I ruined the evening for you."

"You did nothing of the kind." He sounds tired. "Let's not wait for the bus. Let's splurge and take a cab instead."

Imre always has unexpected funds. The Network, he calls it, Class of '56.

In the back of the cab, without even trying, I feel light, almost free. Memories of Indian destitutes mix with the hordes of New York street people, and they float free, like astronauts, inside my head. I've made it. I'm making something of my life. I've left home, my husband, to get a Ph.D. in special ed. I have a multiple-entry visa and a small scholarship for two years. After that, we'll see. My mother was beaten by her mother-in-law, my grandmother, when she'd registered for French lessons at the Alliance Française. My grandmother, the eldest daughter of a rich zamindar,[4] was illiterate.

Imre and the cabdriver talk away in Russian. I keep my eyes closed. That way I can feel the floaters better. I'll write Mamet tonight. I feel strong, reckless. Maybe I'll write Steven Spielberg[5] too; tell him that Indians don't eat monkey brains.

We've made it. Patels must have made it. Mamet, Spielberg: They're not condescending to us. Maybe they're a little bit afraid.

Charity Chin, my roommate, is sitting on the floor drinking Chablis out of a plastic wineglass. She is five foot six, three inches taller than me, but weighs a kilo and a half less than I do. She is a "hands" model. Orientals are supposed to have a monopoly in the hands-modelling business, she says. She had her eyes fixed eight or nine months ago and out of gratitude sleeps with her plastic surgeon every third Wednesday.

"Oh, good," Charity says. "I'm glad you're back early. I need to talk."

She's been writing checks. MCI, Con Ed, Bonwit Teller. Envelopes, already stamped and sealed, form a pyramid between her shapely, knee-socked legs. The checkbook's cover is brown plastic, grained to look like cowhide. Each time Charity flips back the cover, white geese fly over sky-colored checks. She makes good money, but she's extravagant. The difference adds up to this shared, rent-controlled Chelsea one-bedroom.

"All right. Talk."

When I first moved in, she was seeing an analyst. Now she sees a nutritionist.

"Eric called. From Oregon."

"What did he want?"

"He wants me to pay half the rent on his loft for last spring. He asked me to move back, remember? He *begged* me."

Eric is Charity's estranged husband.

---

[4] zamindar: Landowner.

[5] **Spielberg:** In Steven Spielberg's film *Indiana Jones and the Temple of Doom* (1984), Indians prepare a feast at which monkey brains are served.

"What does your nutritionist say?" Eric now wears a red jumpsuit and tills the soil in Rajneeshpuram.[6]

"You think Phil's a creep too, don't you? What else can he be when creeps are all I attract?"

Phil is a flutist with thinning hair. He's very touchy on the subject of *flautists* versus *flutists*. He's touchy on every subject, from music to books to foods to clothes. He teaches at a small college upstate, and Charity bought a used blue Datsun ("Nissan," Phil insists) last month so she could spend weekends with him. She returns every Sunday night, exhausted and exasperated. Phil and I don't have much to say to each other—he's the only musician I know; the men in my family are lawyers, engineers, or in business—but I like him. Around me, he loosens up. When he visits, he bakes us loaves of pumpernickel bread. He waxes our kitchen floor. Like many men in this country, he seems to me a displaced child, or even a woman, looking for something that passed him by, or for something that he can never have. If he thinks I'm not looking, he sneaks his hands under Charity's sweater, but there isn't too much there. Here, she's a model with high ambitions. In India, she'd be a flat-chested old maid.

I'm shy in front of the lovers. A darkness comes over me when I see them horsing around.

"It isn't the money," Charity says. Oh? I think. "He says he still loves me. Then he turns around and asks me for five hundred."

What's so strange about that, I want to ask. She still loves Eric, and Eric, red jumpsuit and all, is smart enough to know it. Love is a commodity, hoarded like any other. Mamet knows. But I say, "I'm not the person to ask about love." Charity knows that mine was a traditional Hindu marriage. My parents, with the help of a marriage broker, who was my mother's cousin, picked out a groom. All I had to do was get to know his taste in food.

It'll be a long evening, I'm afraid. Charity likes to confess. I unpleat my silk sari—it no longer looks too showy—wrap it in muslin cloth and put it away in a dresser drawer. Saris are hard to have laundered in Manhattan, though there's a good man in Jackson Heights. My next step will be to brew us a pot of chrysanthemum tea. It's a very special tea from the mainland. Charity's uncle gave it to us. I like him. He's a humpbacked, awkward, terrified man. He runs a gift store on Mott Street, and though he doesn't speak much English, he seems to have done well. Once upon a time he worked for the railways in Chengdu, Szechwan Province, and during the Wuchang Uprising,[7] he was shot at. When I'm down, when I'm lonely for my husband, when I think of our son, or when I need to be held, I think of Charity's uncle. If I hadn't left home, I'd never have heard of the Wuchang Uprising. I've broadened my horizons.

Very late that night my husband calls me from Ahmadabad, a town of textile mills north of Bombay. My husband is a vice president at Lakshmi Cotton Mills.

---

[6] **Rajneeshpuram:** An ashram in Oregon founded in the 1980s by the controversial Indian guru, Bhagwan Shree Rajneesh.

[7] **Wuchang Uprising:** A crucial event in the Chinese Revolution in October 1911 that led in December to the founding of the Republic of China under the leadership of Sun Yat-sen.

Lakshmi is the goddess of wealth, but LCM (Priv.), Ltd., is doing poorly. Lockouts, strikes, rock-throwings. My husband lives on digitalis, which he calls the food for our *yuga*[8] of discontent.

"We had a bad mishap at the mill today." Then he says nothing for seconds.

The operator comes on. "Do you have the right party, sir? We're trying to reach Mrs. Butt."

"Bhatt," I insist. "*B* for Bombay, *H* for Haryana, *A* for Ahmadabad, double *T* for Tamil Nadu." It's a litany. "This is she."

"One of our lorries was firebombed today. Resulting in three deaths. The driver, old Karamchand, and his two children."

I know how my husband's eyes look this minute, how the eye rims sag and the yellow corneas shine and bulge with pain. He is not an emotional man — the Ahmadabad Institute of Management has trained him to cut losses, to look on the bright side of economic catastrophes — but tonight he's feeling low. I try to remember a driver named Karamchand, but can't. That part of my life is over, the way *trucks* have replaced *lorries* in my vocabulary, the way Charity Chin and her lurid love life have replaced inherited notions of marital duty. Tomorrow he'll come out of it. Soon he'll be eating again. He'll sleep like a baby. He's been trained to believe in turnovers. Every morning he rubs his scalp with cantharidine oil so his hair will grow back again.

"It could be your car next." Affection, love. Who can tell the difference in a traditional marriage in which a wife still doesn't call her husband by his first name?

"No. They know I'm a flunky, just like them. Well paid, maybe. No need for undue anxiety, please."

Then his voice breaks. He says he needs me, he misses me, he wants me to come to him damp from my evening shower, smelling of sandalwood soap, my braid decorated with jasmines.

"I need you too."

"Not to worry, please," he says. "I am coming in a fortnight's time. I have already made arrangements."

Outside my window, fire trucks whine, up Eighth Avenue. I wonder if he can hear them, what he thinks of a life like mine, led amid disorder.

"I am thinking it'll be like a honeymoon. More or less."

When I was in college, waiting to be married, I imagined honeymoons were only for the more fashionable girls, the girls who came from slightly racy families, smoked Sobranies[9] in the dorm lavatories and put up posters of Kabir Bedi,[10] who was supposed to have made it as a big star in the West. My husband wants us to go to Niagara. I'm not to worry about foreign exchange. He's arranged for extra dollars through the Gujarati Network,[11] with a cousin in San Jose. And he's bought four hundred more on the black market. "Tell me you need me. Panna, please tell me again."

I change out of the cotton pants and shirt I've been wearing all day and put on a sari to meet my husband at JFK. I don't forget the jewelry; the marriage necklace of

---

[8] *yuga:* Age.   [9] **Sobranies:** A brand of Balkan cigarettes.   [10] **Kabir Bedi:** A popular Indian film star.
[11] **Gujarati Network:** Network of the Gujarati people, an ethnic group from west central India.

mangalsutra,[12] gold drop earrings, heavy gold bangles. I don't wear them every day. In this borough of vice and greed, who knows when, or whom, desire will overwhelm.

My husband spots me in the crowd and waves. He has lost weight, and changed his glasses. The arm, uplifted in a cheery wave, is bony, frail, almost opalescent.

In the Carey Coach, we hold hands. He strokes my fingers one by one. "How come you aren't wearing my mother's ring?"

"Because muggers know about Indian women," I say. They know with us it's 24-karat. His mother's ring is showy, in ghastly taste anywhere but India: a blood-red Burma ruby set in a gold frame of floral sprays. My mother-in-law got her guru to bless the ring before I left for the States.

He looks disconcerted. He's used to a different role. He's the knowing, suspicious one in the family. He seems to be sulking, and finally he comes out with it. "You've said nothing about my new glasses." I compliment him on the glasses, how chic and Western-executive they make him look. But I can't help the other things, necessities until he learns the ropes. I handle the money, buy the tickets. I don't know if this makes me unhappy.

Charity drives her Nissan upstate, so for two weeks we are to have the apartment to ourselves. This is more privacy than we ever had in India. No parents, no servants, to keep us modest. We play at housekeeping. Imre has lent us a hibachi, and I grill saffron chicken breasts. My husband marvels at the size of the Perdue hens. "They're big like peacocks, no? These Americans, they're really something!" He tries out pizzas, burgers, McNuggets. He chews. He explores. He judges. He loves it all, fears nothing, feels at home in the summer odors, the clutter of Manhattan streets. Since he thinks that the American palate is bland, he carries a bottle of red peppers in his pocket. I wheel a shopping cart down the aisles of the neighborhood Grand Union, and he follows, swiftly, greedily. He picks up hair rinses and high-protein diet powders. There's so much I already take for granted.

One night, Imre stops by. He wants us to go with him to a movie. In his work shirt and red leather tie, he looks arty or strung out. It's only been a week, but I feel as though I am really seeing him for the first time. The yellow hair worn very short at the sides, the wide, narrow lips. He's a good-looking man, but self-conscious, almost arrogant. He's picked the movie we should see. He always tells me what to see, what to read. He buys the *Voice*. He's a natural avant-gardist. For tonight he's chosen *Numéro Deux*.[13]

"Is it a musical?" my husband asks. The Radio City Music Hall is on his list of sights to see. He's read up on the history of the Rockettes.[14] He doesn't catch Imre's sympathetic wink.

Guilt, shame, loyalty. I long to be ungracious, not ingratiate myself with both men.

---

[12] *mangalsutra:* A gold necklace signifying a married woman.

[13] *Numéro Deux* (1975): A film by French New Wave director, Jean-Luc Godard (b. 1930).

[14] **Rockettes:** High-kicking chorus girls who dance at Radio City Music Hall.

That night my husband calculates in rupees the money we've wasted on Godard. "That refugee fellow, Nagy, must have a screw loose in his head. I paid very steep price for dollars on the black market."

Some afternoons we go shopping. Back home we hated shopping, but now it is a lovers' project. My husband's shopping list startles me. I feel I am just getting to know him. Maybe, like Imre, freed from the dignities of old-world culture, he too could get drunk and squirt Cheez Whiz on a guest. I watch him dart into stores in his gleaming leather shoes. Jockey shorts on sale in outdoor bins on Broadway entrance him. White tube socks with different bands of color delight him. He looks for micro-cassettes, for anything small and electronic and smuggleable. He needs a garment bag. He calls it a "wardrobe," and I have to translate.

"All of New York is having sales, no?"

My heart speeds watching him this happy. It's the third week in August, almost the end of summer, and the city smells ripe, it cannot bear more heat, more money, more energy.

"This is so smashing! The prices are so excellent!" Recklessly, my prudent husband signs away traveller's checks. How he intends to smuggle it all back I don't dare ask. With a microwave, he calculates, we could get rid of our cook.

This has to be love, I think. Charity, Eric, Phil: They may be experts on sex. My husband doesn't chase me around the sofa, but he pushes me down on Charity's battered cushions, and the man who has never entered the kitchen of our Ahmadabad house now comes toward me with a dish tub of steamy water to massage away the pavement heat.

Ten days into his vacation my husband checks out brochures for sightseeing tours. Shortline, Grayline, Crossroads: His new vinyl briefcase is full of schedules and pamphlets. While I make pancakes out of a mix, he comparison-shops. Tour number one costs $10.95 and will give us the World Trade Center, Chinatown, and the United Nations. Tour number three would take us both uptown *and* downtown for $14.95, but my husband is absolutely sure he doesn't want to see Harlem. We settle for tour number four: Downtown and the Dame. It's offered by a new tour company with a small, dirty office at Eighth and Forty-eighth.

The sidewalk outside the office is colorful with tourists. My husband sends me in to buy the tickets because he has come to feel Americans don't understand his accent.

The dark man, Lebanese probably, behind the counter comes on too friendly. "Come on, doll, make my day!" He won't say which tour is his. "Number four? Honey, no! Look, you've wrecked me! Say you'll change your mind." He takes two twenties and gives back change. He holds the tickets, forcing me to pull. He leans closer. "I'm off after lunch."

My husband must have been watching me from the sidewalk. "What was the chap saying?" he demands. "I told you not to wear pants. He thinks you are Puerto Rican. He thinks he can treat you with disrespect."

The bus is crowded and we have to sit across the aisle from each other. The tour guide begins his patter on Forty-sixth. He looks like an actor, his hair bleached and blow-dried. Up close he must look middle-aged, but from where I sit his skin is smooth and his cheeks faintly red.

"Welcome to the Big Apple, folks." The guide uses a microphone. "Big Apple. That's what we native Manhattan degenerates call our city. Today we have guests from fifteen foreign countries and six states from this U.S. of A. That makes the Tourist Bureau real happy. And let me assure you that while we may be the richest city in the richest country in the world, it's okay to tip your charming and talented attendant." He laughs. Then he swings his hip out into the aisle and sings a song.

"And it's mighty fancy on old Delancey Street, you know. . . ."

My husband looks irritable. The guide is, as expected, a good singer. "The bloody man should be giving us histories of buildings we are passing, no?" I pat his hand, the mood passes. He cranes his neck. Our window seats have both gone to Japanese. It's the tour of his life. Next to this, the quick business trips to Manchester and Glasgow pale.

"And tell me what street compares to Mott Street, in July. . . ."

The guide wants applause. He manages a derisive laugh from the Americans up front. He's working the aisles now. "I coulda been somebody, right? I coulda been a star!" Two or three of us smile, those of us who recognize the parody. He catches my smile. The sun is on his harsh, bleached hair. "Right, your highness? Look, we gotta maharani with us! Couldn't I have been a star?"

"Right!" I say, my voice coming out a squeal. I've been trained to adapt; what else can I say?

We drive through traffic past landmark office buildings and churches. The guide flips his hands. "Art deco," he keeps saying. I hear him confide to one of the Americans: "Beats me. I went to a cheap guide's school." My husband wants to know more about this Art Deco, but the guide sings another song.

"We made a foolish choice," my husband grumbles. "We are sitting in the bus only. We're not going into famous buildings." He scrutinizes the pamphlets in his jacket pocket. I think, at least it's air-conditioned in here. I could sit here in the cool shadows of the city forever.

Only five of us appear to have opted for the "Downtown and the Dame" tour. The others will ride back uptown past the United Nations after we've been dropped off at the pier for the ferry to the Statue of Liberty.

An elderly European pulls a camera out of his wife's designer tote bag. He takes pictures of the boats in the harbor, the Japanese in kimonos eating popcorn, scavenging pigeons, me. Then, pushing his wife ahead of him, he climbs back on the bus and waves to us. For a second I feel terribly lost. I wish we were on the bus going back to the apartment. I know I'll not be able to describe any of this to Charity, or to Imre. I'm too proud to admit I went on a guided tour.

The view of the city from the Circle Line ferry is seductive, unreal. The skyline wavers out of reach, but never quite vanishes. The summer sun pushes through fluffy clouds and dapples the glass of office towers. My husband looks thrilled, even more than he had on the shopping trips down Broadway. Tourists and dreamers, we have spent our life's savings to see this skyline, this statue.

"Quick, take a picture of me!" my husband yells as he moves toward a gap of railings. A Japanese matron has given up her position in order to change film. "Before the Twin Towers disappear!"

I focus, I wait for a large Oriental family to walk out of my range. My husband holds his pose tight against the railing. He wants to look relaxed, an international businessman at home in all the financial markets.

A bearded man slides across the bench toward me. "Like this," he says and helps me get my husband in focus. "You want me to take the photo for you?" His name, he says, is Goran. He is Goran from Yugoslavia, as though that were enough for tracking him down. Imre from Hungary. Panna from India. He pulls the old Leica out of my hand, signaling the Orientals to beat it, and clicks away. "I'm a photographer," he says. He could have been a camera thief. That's what my husband would have assumed. Somehow, I trusted. "Get you a beer?" he asks.

"I don't. Drink, I mean. Thank you very much." I say those last words very loud, for everyone's benefit. The odd bottles of Soave with Imre don't count.

"Too bad." Goran gives back the camera.

"Take one more!" my husband shouts from the railing. "Just to be sure!"

The island itself disappoints. The Lady has brutal scaffolding holding her in. The museum is closed. The snack bar is dirty and expensive. My husband reads out the prices to me. He orders two french fries and two Cokes. We sit at picnic tables and wait for the ferry to take us back.

"What was that hippie chap saying?"

As if I could say. A day-care center has brought its kids, at least forty of them, to the island for the day. The kids, all wearing name tags, run around us. I can't help noticing how many are Indian. Even a Patel, probably a Bhatt if I looked hard enough. They toss hamburger bits at pigeons. They kick styrofoam cups. The pigeons are slow, greedy, persistent. I have to shoo one off the table top. I don't think my husband thinks about our son.

"What hippie?"

"The one on the boat. With the beard and the hair."

My husband doesn't look at me. He shakes out his paper napkin and tries to protect his french fries from pigeon feathers.

"Oh, him. He said he was from Dubrovnik." It isn't true, but I don't want trouble.

"What did he say about Dubrovnik?"

I know enough about Dubrovnik to get by. Imre's told me about it. And about Mostar and Zagreb. In Mostar white Muslims sing the call to prayer. I would like to see that before I die: white Muslims. Whole peoples have moved before me; they've adapted. The night Imre told me about Mostar was also the night I saw my first snow in Manhattan. We'd walked down to Chelsea from Columbia. We'd walked and talked and I hadn't felt tired at all.

"You're too innocent," my husband says. He reaches for my hand. "Panna," he cries with pain in his voice, and I am brought back from perfect, floating memories of snow, "I've come to take you back. I have seen how men watch you."

"What?"

"Come back, now. I have tickets. We have all the things we will ever need. I can't live without you."

A little girl with wiry braids kicks a bottle cap at his shoes. The pigeons wheel and scuttle around us. My husband covers his fries with spread-out fingers. "No kicking," he tells the girl. Her name, Beulah, is printed in green ink on a heart-shaped name tag. He forces a smile, and Beulah smiles back. Then she starts to flap her arms. She flaps, she hops. The pigeons go crazy for fries and scraps.

"Special ed. course is two years," I remind him. "I can't go back."

My husband picks up our trays and throws them into the garbage before I can stop him. He's carried disposability a little too far. "We've been taken," he says, moving toward the dock, though the ferry will not arrive for another twenty minutes. "The ferry costs only two dollars round-trip per person. We should have chosen tour number one for $10.95 instead of tour number four for $14.95."

With my Lebanese friend, I think. "But this way we don't have to worry about cabs. The bus will pick us up at the pier and take us back to midtown. Then we can walk home."

"New York is full of cheats and whatnot. Just like Bombay." He is not accusing me of infidelity. I feel dread all the same.

That night, after we've gone to bed, the phone rings. My husband listens, then hands the phone to me. "What is this woman saying?" He turns on the pink Macy's lamp by the bed. "I am not understanding these Negro people's accents."

The operator repeats the message. It's a cable from one of the directors of Lakshmi Cotton Mills. "Massive violent labor confrontation anticipated. Stop. Return posthaste. Stop. Cable flight details. Signed Kantilal Shah."

"It's not your factory," I say. "You're supposed to be on vacation."

"So, you are worrying about me? Yes? You reject my heartfelt wishes but you worry about me?" He pulls me close, slips the straps of my nightdress off my shoulder. "Wait a minute."

I wait, unclothed, for my husband to come back to me. The water is running in the bathroom. In the ten days he has been here he has learned American rites: deodorants, fragrances. Tomorrow morning he'll call Air India; tomorrow evening he'll be on his way back to Bombay. Tonight I should make up to him for my years away, the gutted trucks, the degree I'll never use in India. I want to pretend with him that nothing has changed.

In the mirror that hangs on the bathroom door, I watch my naked body turn, the breasts, the thighs glow. The body's beauty amazes. I stand here shameless, in ways he has never seen me. I am free, afloat, watching somebody else.

❧ LESLIE MARMON SILKO
B. UNITED STATES, 1948

More than any other Native American writer, Leslie Marmon Silko has introduced a large popular audience to the culture into which she was born. Through her poetry, essays, and, especially, her fiction, Silko has conveyed the importance of storytelling, including the way the drama of contemporary life both fulfills and transforms the myths and stories of the past. Like Nigerian novelist Chinua Achebe (b. 1930; see p. 1017), Silko recontextualizes the wisdom of oral tradition in poems and in the adages in her stories, teasing out new significances while contrasting and adapting old ways with the new. Also like Achebe, Silko explores the psychological, cultural, and social consequences of the contact between native populations and colonizers. Through the masterful tale of the power of myth to affirm identity in *Ceremony* (1977), the richly diverse short stories in *Storyteller* (1981), the disturbing apocalyptic vision of a Mesoamerican race war in *Almanac of the Dead* (1991), and the vivid and instructive historical contrast of Native and European relationships to the environment in *Gardens in the Dunes* (1999), Silko has changed the shape of contemporary fiction, contributing to an American vision of the POSTCOLONIAL world at the end of the twentieth century.

Beginnings at Laguna Pueblo.   A mixedblood Indian (of Laguna, Hispanic, and Anglo-American ancestry), Leslie Marmon Silko was born in 1948 and grew up in the pueblo of Laguna in western New Mexico.

www   For links to more information about Leslie Marmon Silko and a quiz on "Lullaby," and for information about the culture and context of America in the twentieth century, see *World Literature Online* at bedfordstmartins .com/worldlit.

Laguna Reservation, 1943
Born just a few years after this photo was taken, Leslie Marmon Silko grew up in the pueblo of Laguna in western New Mexico; its landscape and diverse culture has been a major influence on her life and work. (Library of Congress LC-USW361-713)

Laguna, named after the now dry lake at the site, sits on a shoulder rising above the San José River; it is surrounded by lava flows, grassy plains, desert, sandstone hills, and, to the northeast, the sacred *Tsé Pi Na* (Woman Veiled in Clouds), an ancient volcanic mountain renamed Mount Taylor by Anglo-Americans. Old Laguna and its surroundings were extremely important to the early development of Silko's imagination. As she says, "I grew up at Laguna Pueblo. I am of mixed-breed ancestry, but what I know is Laguna. This place I am from is everything I am as a writer and human being."

Founded in 1699 by refugees from the nearby pueblos of Cochiti and Santo Domingo, Laguna has always been a place of ethnic diversity, bringing into its extended community Acoma, Zuni, Hopi, and Navajo peoples as well as Mexican Americans, Spanish, Anglos, and even Lebanese. Among the important newcomers arriving in the late nineteenth century was Ohio surveyor Robert Marmon, Silko's great-grandfather; like his brother Walter, the first Marmon to settle in Laguna, Robert married a Laguna woman. He also eventually served as governor of the pueblo. Robert Marmon's son, Lee Marmon, a highly recognized photographer who learned his trade in the army in World War II, operated a trading post in the village of Old Laguna. Among the major influences on her young life, Silko credits her grandmother, "A'mooh" (Marie Anaya Marmon), and her "Aunt Susie" (her great-aunt Susan Reyes Marmon). From these women and others in the village, Silko learned the art of narrative, which she later celebrated and exemplified in *Storyteller* (1981), a collection of oral and literary stories, occasional tales, poems, and photographs. About the mixed heritage that gave rise to her distinctive voice, Silko says, "We are . . . Laguna, Mexican, White—but the way we live is like Marmons, and if you are from Laguna Pueblo, you will understand what I mean. All those languages, all those ways of living are combined, and we live somewhere on the fringes of all three." Laguna and its surroundings—the buildings, waterways, highways, and physical environs—figure prominently in Silko's stories and in the novel *Ceremony*.

Albuquerque and Beyond. Silko attended Laguna Day School, where she was forbidden to speak Keres, the Laguna language, until the fifth grade; she then began commuting to a private day school in Albuquerque. She also benefited educationally from her home environment: Both her great-grandmother and great-aunt were graduates of Carlisle Indian School in Pennsylvania, and her aunt Susan, after attending Dickinson College, taught school at Laguna and served as Keresan cultural historian. Silko enrolled in the University of New Mexico in 1964. Four years later she went on to enroll in its American Indian Law Program. During this time she taught courses at the university and published *Tony's Story*, a work anticipating her first novel, *Ceremony* (1977). In 1971 she received a National Endowment for the Arts Discovery Grant, allowing her to focus on her writing; "Yellow Woman" and several other stories, including the title story, appeared in Kenneth Rosen's collection entitled *The Man to Send Rain Clouds* (1974). A collection of her poetry, *Laguna Woman: Poems by Leslie Silko*, also appeared in 1974.

Silko, her husband, and her two young children — Cazimir Silko and Robert William Chapman — moved in 1976 to Ketchikan, Alaska, where she completed work on *Ceremony,* her highly acclaimed masterpiece. Two years later she returned to the Southwest where she taught at the University of New Mexico, Navajo Community College, and the University of Arizona. *Storyteller,* a mixed-genre collection of poems, short stories, and photographs, was published in 1981. During the 1980s, while writing *Almanac of the Dead,* Silko was supported by a grant from the MacArthur Foundation; since then she has dedicated her time to writing. For many years she has lived on a ranch a few miles northwest of Tucson, Arizona.

The Storyteller.   Silko's reputation as a mixedblood writer has served as an inspiration to other writers. She is also highly regarded by the many major artists of what some are beginning to call the Native American Renaissance, including N. Scott Momaday (Kiowa), winner of the Pulitzer Prize for *House Made of Dawn;* Joy Harjo (Muskogee Creek), poet and musician (p. 1363); Simon Ortiz (Acoma Pueblo), novelist; and Louis Owens[1] (Choctaw-Cherokee-Irish), novelist and critic. Particularly in works such as *The Almanac of the Dead* and *The Gardens in the Dunes,* which broaden Silko's scope to include all of North America, Mexico, Brazil, and Europe, her stories attempt to weave together disparate times and traditions into a coherent, if often troubling and troubled, story. Her goal is nothing less than a comprehensive vision that might enable readers to rethink their relation to others, the land, history, and themselves in such a way as to promote balance and understanding in a world otherwise likely to unravel at its rough-hewn seams. Stories, as she says, are not just for entertainment — and, one might add, not only for instruction. In Pueblo tradition, stories play a significant, even ritualistic role in bringing the world into being and in maintaining its precious balance. Such stories must be flexible, engaging in a give-and-take with current events, but must also always aim to integrate the new ways with the old. As Silko has commented, "When I say 'storytelling,' I don't just mean sitting down and telling a once-upon-a-time kind of story. I mean a whole way of seeing yourself, the people around you, your life, the place of your life in the bigger context, not just in terms of nature and location, but in terms of what has gone on before, what's happened to other people."

The Novels.   *Ceremony* (1977), still Silko's most popular work, not only aims to achieve such a balance and reorientation but has as its theme that

Like James Welch's *Winter in the Blood* and, more fully, *Fool's Crow,* Laguna author Leslie Marmon Silko's novel *Ceremony* is a remembering, a putting together of past, present, and future into a coherent fabric of timeless identity.
     – LOUIS OWENS, novelist and critic, 1992

---

[1]*Momaday . . . Owens:* Four important Native American writers. N. Scott Momaday (b. 1934) wrote the Pulitzer Prize–winning novel *House Made of Dawn* in 1969. His autobiographical work *The Way to Rainy Mountain,* was published the same year. Joy Harjo (b. 1951; see p. 1363) is an accomplished poet and musician: Her works include *She Had Some Horses* (1983) and *In Mad Love and War* (1990). Simon Ortiz (b. 1941) is equally talented as a poet and short-story writer: His works are collected in *Woven Stone* (1990) and *Men on the Moon* (1999). Louis Owens (1948–2002) is the author of several novels, including *The Sharpest Sight* (1992), *Nightland* (1996), and *Dark River* (1999), as well as works of criticism, including *Other Destinies: Understanding the American Indian Novel* (1992) and *Mixedblood Messages: Literature, Film, Family, Place* (1998).

very process in the story of Tayo's quest for psychic wholeness. Ostensibly about the Bataan Death March[2] in World War II, *Ceremony* was published after the conclusion of the Vietnam War. In the novel, Tayo, a mixedblood Indian from Laguna who bears terrible memories of the Vietnam War, returns to his village in a state of spiritual sickness. He is sent to a Navajo medicine man for a cure, in the course of which it is discovered that his illness holds the key to the possible destruction of the world. The historical setting of the making of the atomic bomb is inextricably related to Laguna, since Jackpile Mine, the source of the uranium used to make the bomb, is located only a few miles away. Through a series of ritual encounters that draw Tayo into a web of stories involving his immediate family, a Mexican dancer, a Navajo medicine man, and avatars from the spirit world and from nature, Tayo restores a balance within himself and in his community that brings about the temporary redemption of mankind from the threat of mass destruction.

Silko's second novel, *Almanac of the Dead* (1991), is even more fraught with destruction than *Ceremony*. This time the source of prophecy is the Aztec calendar, which predicts the rise of the indigenous tribes of the South and their reconquest of North America. In a world turned upside down, criminals and prophets conspire in the overthrow of the dominant social order. The harshness of the imagery, the connections with an underground drug culture, and the often gratuitous violence of this novel have proved offensive to some, but the MILLENARIAN feel of the text is chilling and its political thrust has put Silko in the company of postcolonial resistance writers. *Gardens in the Dunes* (1999), Silko's most recent novel—a sensuous evocation of the colors, smells, shapes, and textures of gardens—might be considered an ecological novel because it emphasizes the interrelations among human beings, animals, and plants, but it also examines the relations between Europeans and Native Americans, demonstrating the way that sociopolitical relations in many ways reflect and inform our relation to the land and to nature.

Focusing on the plight of the Sand Lizard People, a tribe threatened by European settlement, the novel recounts the experiences of Indigo, a member of the tribe who travels the world with Hattie, a wealthy American who represents something of the "new woman" of the late nineteenth century—independent, intelligent, even rebellious to some degree. Hattie takes Indigo under her care, hoping to cultivate her Indian protégée, rather in the way her botanist husband cultivates exotic plants, into a fully assimilated Euro-American. Although drawn to the luxuries and

---

[2] **Bataan Death March:** The deadly march of some 10,000 American and four to five times as many Filipino soldiers captured by the Japanese on the Bataan Peninsula of Luzon, the main island of the Philippines; the captives, many of whom were suffering from exhaustion, malaria, and other ailments, were forced to march 55 miles from Marivales to San Fernando, packed into railroad cars, taken to Capas, and made to march another 8 miles to the prison camp. Stragglers were beaten or killed; up to 650 Americans and 10,000 Filipinos died before reaching the camp, where many more died. Among the soldiers were many New Mexicans, including Hispanic, Navajo, and Pueblo men.

wealth that she witnesses in her travels, Indigo nonetheless never relinquishes her sense of place or her native beliefs and traditions, particularly her faith that her people eventually will be restored.

The Short Stories.   The collection *Storyteller* (1981), which included "Lullaby," is unique in recent literature. Silko arranged the modern tales in this volume in a sequence whose transitions are marked by prose and poetry. Some of the transitional pieces are traditional tales; some are evocations of ancient or modern Pueblo Indian life, especially at Laguna Pueblo; some are pure local gossip. Also included are photographs taken by Silko and family members. There is a hint of thematic development in the stories that critics have tried to account for. The collection's first two stories, "Storyteller" and "Lullaby," are often understood as tales of survival. "Storyteller" is a dark tale of a young girl's semicaptivity with an old man of her tribe, her cunning murder of the man who killed her parents, and her refusal to compromise the truth when she is brought before the local courts. "Lullaby" is the story of a Navajo woman who has experienced several tragedies in her life and who gathers her waning strength to sing a traditional song of support and sustenance as her husband lies freezing to death in the snow.

Other stories in the collection include "Yellow Woman," a modern version of an ancient Pueblo abduction story; "Tony's Story," Silko's account of the killing of a state policeman on the reservation; "The Man to Send Rain Clouds," on the death of an old sheepherder and the way that his relatives arrange his burial; and "A Geronimo Story," in which Pueblo scouts sabotage the U.S. cavalry's attempt to capture the famed Apache warrior. Critics have said that these stories turn inward to consider the mysteries and local knowledge of Laguna Pueblo culture, working their way through myth, legend, and what the author calls "accidents of history." The stories also criticize Anglo-American cultural beliefs and practices while upholding a Pueblo cultural viewpoint. For all these reasons as well as the range and depth of its feeling, *Storyteller* has maintained a presence in the public eye.

"Lullaby" is in many respects one of Silko's simplest stories, recounting the story of **Ayah**, a Navajo woman, and her husband, **Chato**, whom she protects as he lies dying on a freezing winter night. The heart of "Lullaby" surfaces in Ayah's memories, which reverberate throughout the tale. In a dreamlike reverie Ayah recalls how she has lost all three of her children: her oldest son, Jimmie, to war, and her two younger children to the state when she unwittingly signed a paper releasing them into its custody. Blaming her husband for her loss because he tried to adapt to the white culture that was dismantling his own and because he was the one who taught her how to sign her name, she nonetheless shelters and comforts him with her son's army blanket and a lullaby that her mother once sang to her. Through her memories—of combing wool for her grandmother, of Jimmie's birth, the loss of Danny and Ella and their growing alienation from their mother and their home—Ayah relives formative moments of her past, recalls her anger with Chato and the white doctors who took her children, and revisits the pain of her separation from them. Through

AH-yah; CHAH-toh

these memories Ayah weaves a story of survival and continuity; from that story and from the healing song of the wind and snow she gains a sense of peace. Nonetheless, although "Lullaby" ends with an expression of enduring presence and the promise of restoration in the natural cycles of life, the contexts of betrayal, cultural dissolution, family separation, poverty, and death undermine a fully positive conclusion.

■ CONNECTIONS

Chinua Achebe, *Things Fall Apart*, p. 1023. Silko's "Lullaby" is a story about tragic losses that in part result from colonial contact and racial prejudice. Achebe's *Things Fall Apart* tells of tragic losses stemming from similar causes, in this case when Europeans bring their laws and administrative mechanisms to the Ibo and disrupt the native ways of life. How is the Euro-African contact in Achebe's novel similar to the contact between whites and Native Americans in Silko's story? Are there any similarities between Okonkwo and Ayah? Are both characters tragic heroes?

Anna Akhmatova, *Requiem*, p. 560. As the title in part implies, "Lullaby" is a kind of requiem sung to commemorate the loss of a loved one, a culture, and a way of life as well as a song of healing and possible renewal. The surviving women in Akhmatova's poem and in Silko's story go through the stages of denial, anger, despair, and acceptance or reconciliation that psychologists have identified in the grieving process. What other similarities are there between *Requiem* and "Lullaby"? In what way, for example, is Silko's story an elegy?

■ FURTHER RESEARCH

Allen, Paula Gunn. "The Feminine Landscape of Leslie Marmon Silko's *Ceremony.*" In Paula Gunn Allen, *Studies in American Indian Literature: Critical Essays and Course Designs.* 1983.

Barnett, Louise K., and James Thorson. *Leslie Marmon Silko: A Collection of Critical Essays.* 1999.

Owens, Louis. "The Very Essence of Our Lives: Leslie Silko's Webs of Identity." In Louis Owens, *Other Destinies: Understanding the American Indian Novel.* 1992.

Ruppert, James. "Story Telling: The Fiction of Leslie Silko." *Journal of Ethnic Studies* 9.1 (1981): 53–58.

Silko, Leslie. *Yellow Woman and a Beauty of the Spirit.* 1996.

Smith, Patricia Clark, with Paula Gunn Allen. "Earthy Relations, Carnal Knowledge: Southwestern American Indian Women Writers and Landscape." In Vera Norwood, ed., *The Desert Is No Lady: Southwestern Landscapes in Women's Writing and Art.* 1987.

■ PRONUNCIATION

Ayah: AH-yah
Cañoncito: kah-nyon-SEE-toh
Cebolleta: seh-boh-YEH-tah
Chato: CHAH-toh
Cholla: CHOH-yah
Yeibechei: YAY-buh-chigh

⌇ Lullaby

The sun had gone down but the snow in the wind gave off its own light. It came in thick tufts like new wool—washed before the weaver spins it. Ayah reached out for it like her own babies had, and she smiled when she remembered how she had laughed at them. She was an old woman now, and her life had become memories. She sat down with her back against the wide cottonwood tree, feeling the rough bark on her back bones; she faced east and listened to the wind and snow sing a high-pitched Yeibechei song.[1] Out of the wind she felt warmer, and she could watch the wide fluffy snow fill in her tracks, steadily, until the direction she had come from was gone. By the light of the snow she could see the dark outline of the big arroyo[2] a few feet away. She was sitting on the edge of Cebolleta Creek,[3] where in the springtime the thin cows would graze on grass already chewed flat to the ground. In the wide deep creek bed where only a trickle of water flowed in the summer, the skinny cows would wander, looking for new grass along winding paths splashed with manure.

Ayah pulled the old Army blanket over her head like a shawl. Jimmie's blanket—the one he had sent to her. That was a long time ago and the green wool was faded, and it was unraveling on the edges. She did not want to think about Jimmie. So she

"Lullaby." This story from the 1981 collection *Storyteller* first appeared separately in *The Chicago Review* in 1974. "Lullaby" may be viewed either as a nearly stereotypic account of the dissolution of an Indian family or as a reflection on the importance of memory and tradition in establishing a sense of continuity. That tradition, however, is strikingly and perhaps ironically altered in the context of the subordination and oppression that surrounds the Native Americans in what once was their homeland. Ayah's memories and the healing presence of nature bring to life the traditions that are her legacy. Yet that sense of tradition, symbolized in part by the faded green blanket and the dilapidated hogan, and that sense of nature, most poignantly figured in the healing song of wind and snow, yield little hope for any real recovery from the tragic loss of Ayah's children and the approaching death of her husband, Chato. The strength we do find from the story comes from Ayah herself, who at one point is compared to Spider Woman, the creator whose web of stories brings the world into being. Ayah, a weaver, adapts her grandmother's lullaby to the desperate conditions of her life, clinging to the power of the words even as her world spins apart. Ayah's power and striving are most starkly communicated in a poem near the end of *Storyteller:* "No matter what is said to you by anyone / you must take care of those most dear to you."

All notes are the editors'.

[1] **Yeibechei song:** (also Yeibechai) A healing song; Yeibechei, named after the grandfather of the gods, is the last and most significant night of the Night Chant or Nightway ceremony, which is held at harvest time to restore balance and health for the community, symbolized by a person who has been sick in whose name the ceremony is held.

[2] **arroyo:** The Spanish word for "ditch"; arroyos, which can be dangerous, are special places, sites of encounter with avatars from the spirit world and nature.

[3] **Cebolleta Creek:** The story takes place in and outside of Seboyeta (an alternate and now preferred spelling), a small town near the pueblo of Laguna; in the nineteenth century, Seboyeta was the site of conflict between the Navajos, Pueblos, and Spanish settlers.

thought about the weaving and the way her mother had done it. On the tall wooden loom set into the sand under a tamarack tree for shade. She could see it clearly. She had been only a little girl when her grandma gave her the wooden combs to pull the twigs and burrs from the raw, freshly washed wool. And while she combed the wool, her grandma sat beside her, spinning a silvery strand of yarn around the smooth cedar spindle. Her mother worked at the loom with yarns dyed bright yellow and red and gold. She watched them dye the yarn in boiling black pots full of beeweed petals, juniper berries, and sage. The blankets her mother made were soft and woven so tight that rain rolled off them like birds' feathers. Ayah remembered sleeping warm on cold windy nights, wrapped in her mother's blankets on the hogan's[4] sandy floor.

The snow drifted now, with the northwest wind hurling it in gusts. It drifted up around her black overshoes—old ones with little metal buckles. She smiled at the snow which was trying to cover her little by little. She could remember when they had no black rubber overshoes; only the high buckskin leggings that they wrapped over their elkhide moccasins. If the snow was dry or frozen, a person could walk all day and not get wet; and in the evenings the beams of the ceiling would hang with lengths of pale buckskin leggings, drying out slowly.

She felt peaceful remembering. She didn't feel cold anymore. Jimmie's blanket seemed warmer than it had ever been. And she could remember the morning he was born. She could remember whispering to her mother, who was sleeping on the other side of the hogan, to tell her it was time now. She did not want to wake the others. The second time she called to her, her mother stood up and pulled on her shoes; she knew. They walked to the old stone hogan together, Ayah walking a step behind her mother. She waited alone, learning the rhythms of the pains while her mother went to call the old woman to help them. The morning was already warm even before dawn and Ayah smelled the bee flowers blooming and the young willow growing at the springs. She could remember that so clearly, but his birth merged into the births of the other children and to her it became all the same birth. They named him for the summer morning and in English they called him Jimmie.

It wasn't like Jimmie died. He just never came back, and one day a dark blue sedan with white writing on its doors pulled up in front of the boxcar shack where the rancher let the Indians live. A man in a khaki uniform trimmed in gold gave them a yellow piece of paper and told them that Jimmie was dead. He said the Army would try to get the body back and then it would be shipped to them; but it wasn't likely because the helicopter had burned after it crashed. All of this was told to Chato because he could understand English. She stood inside the doorway holding the baby while Chato listened. Chato spoke English like a white man and he spoke Spanish too. He was taller than the white man and he stood straighter too. Chato didn't explain why; he just told the military man they could keep the body if they found it. The white man looked bewildered; he nodded his head and he left. Then Chato looked at her and shook his head, and then he told her, "Jimmie isn't coming home anymore," and when he spoke, he used the words to speak of the dead. She didn't cry

---

[4] hogan: A rounded building made of adobe and timber, the traditional dwelling of the Navajo.

then, but she hurt inside with anger. And she mourned him as the years passed, when a horse fell with Chato and broke his leg, and the white rancher told them he wouldn't pay Chato until he could work again. She mourned Jimmie because he would have worked for his father then; he would have saddled the big bay horse and ridden the fence lines each day, with wire cutters and heavy gloves, fixing the breaks in the barbed wire and putting the stray cattle back inside again.

She mourned him after the white doctors came to take Danny and Ella away. She was at the shack alone that day they came. It was back in the days before they hired Navajo women to go with them as interpreters. She recognized one of the doctors. She had seen him at the children's clinic at Cañoncito about a month ago. They were wearing khaki uniforms and they waved papers at her and a black ball-point pen, trying to make her understand their English words. She was frightened by the way they looked at the children, like the lizard watches the fly. Danny was swinging on the tire swing on the elm tree behind the rancher's house, and Ella was toddling around the front door, dragging the broomstick horse Chato made for her. Ayah could see they wanted her to sign the papers, and Chato had taught her to sign her name. It was something she was proud of. She only wanted them to go, and to take their eyes away from her children.

She took the pen from the man without looking at his face and she signed the papers in three different places he pointed to. She stared at the ground by their feet and waited for them to leave. But they stood there and began to point and gesture at the children. Danny stopped swinging. Ayah could see his fear. She moved suddenly and grabbed Ella into her arms; the child squirmed, trying to get back to her toys. Ayah ran with the baby toward Danny; she screamed for him to run and then she grabbed him around his chest and carried him too. She ran south into the foothills of juniper trees and black lava rock. Behind her she heard the doctors running, but they had been taken by surprise, and as the hills became steeper and the cholla cactus were thicker, they stopped. When she reached the top of the hill, she stopped to listen in case they were circling around her. But in a few minutes she heard a car engine start and they drove away. The children had been too surprised to cry while she ran with them. Danny was shaking and Ella's little fingers were gripping Ayah's blouse.

She stayed up in the hills for the rest of the day, sitting on a black lava boulder in the sunshine where she could see for miles all around her. The sky was light blue and cloudless, and it was warm for late April. The sun warmth relaxed her and took the fear and anger away. She lay back on the rock and watched the sky. It seemed to her that she could walk into the sky, stepping through clouds endlessly. Danny played with little pebbles and stones, pretending they were birds' eggs and then little rabbits. Ella sat at her feet and dropped fistfuls of dirt into the breeze, watching the dust and particles of sand intently. Ayah watched a hawk soar high above them, dark wings gliding; hunting or only watching, she did not know. The hawk was patient and he circled all afternoon before he disappeared around the high volcanic peak the Mexicans called Guadalupe.

Late in the afternoon, Ayah looked down at the gray boxcar shack with the paint all peeled from the wood; the stove pipe on the roof was rusted and crooked. The fire she had built that morning in the oil drum stove had burned out. Ella was asleep in her lap now and Danny sat close to her, complaining that he was hungry; he asked when they would go to the house. "We will stay up here until your father comes," she told him, "because those white men were chasing us." The boy remembered then and he nodded at her silently.

If Jimmie had been there he could have read those papers and explained to her what they said. Ayah would have known then, never to sign them. The doctors came back the next day and they brought a BIA policeman with them. They told Chato they had her signature and that was all they needed. Except for the kids. She listened to Chato sullenly; she hated him when he told her it was the old woman who died in the winter, spitting blood; it was her old grandma who had given the children this disease. "They don't spit blood," she said coldly. "The whites lie." She held Ella and Danny close to her, ready to run to the hills again. "I want a medicine man first," she said to Chato, not looking at him. He shook his head. "It's too late now. The police-man is with them. You signed the paper." His voice was gentle.

It was worse than if they had died: to lose the children and to know that some-where, in a place called Colorado, in a place full of sick and dying strangers, her chil-dren were without her. There had been babies that died soon after they were born, and one that died before he could walk. She had carried them herself, up to the boul-ders and great pieces of the cliff that long ago crashed down from Long Mesa; she laid them in the crevices of sandstone and buried them in fine brown sand with round quartz pebbles that washed down the hills in the rain. She had endured it because they had been with her. But she could not bear this pain. She did not sleep for a long time after they took her children. She stayed on the hill where they had fled the first time, and she slept rolled up in the blanket Jimmie had sent her. She car-ried the pain in her belly and it was fed by everything she saw: the blue sky of their last day together and the dust and pebbles they played with; the swing in the elm tree and broomstick horse choked life from her. The pain filled her stomach and there was no room for food or for her lungs to fill with air. The air and the food would have been theirs.

She hated Chato, not because he let the policeman and doctors put the scream-ing children in the government car, but because he had taught her to sign her name. Because it was like the old ones always told her about learning their language or any of their ways: It endangered you. She slept alone on the hill until the middle of November when the first snows came. Then she made a bed for herself where the children had slept. She did not lie down beside Chato again until many years later, when he was sick and shivering and only her body could keep him warm. The illness came after the white rancher told Chato he was too old to work for him anymore, and Chato and his old woman should be out of the shack by the next afternoon because the rancher had hired new people to work there. That had satisfied her. To see how the white man repaid Chato's years of loyalty and work. All of Chato's fine-sounding English talk didn't change things.

It snowed steadily and the luminous light from the snow gradually diminished into the darkness. Somewhere in Cebolleta a dog barked and other village dogs joined with it. Ayah looked in the direction she had come, from the bar where Chato was buying the wine. Sometimes he told her to go on ahead and wait; and then he never came. And when she finally went back looking for him, she would find him passed out at the bottom of the wooden steps to Azzie's Bar. All the wine would be gone and most of the money too, from the pale blue check that came to them once a month in a government envelope. It was then that she would look at his face and his hands, scarred by ropes and the barbed wire of all those years, and she would think, this man is a stranger; for forty years she had smiled at him and cooked his food, but he remained a stranger. She stood up again, with the snow almost to her knees, and she walked back to find Chato.

It was hard to walk in the deep snow and she felt the air burn in her lungs. She stopped a short distance from the bar to rest and readjust the blanket. But this time he wasn't waiting for her on the bottom step with his old Stetson hat pulled down and his shoulders hunched up in his long wool overcoat.

She was careful not to slip on the wooden steps. When she pushed the door open, warm air and cigarette smoke hit her face. She looked around slowly and deliberately, in every corner, in every dark place that the old man might find to sleep. The bar owner didn't like Indians in there, especially Navajos, but he let Chato come in because he could talk Spanish like he was one of them. The men at the bar stared at her, and the bartender saw that she left the door open wide. Snowflakes were flying inside like moths and melting into a puddle on the oiled wood floor. He motioned to her to close the door, but she did not see him. She held herself straight and walked across the room slowly, searching the room with every step. The snow in her hair melted and she could feel it on her forehead. At the far corner of the room, she saw red flames at the mica window of the old stove door; she looked behind the stove just to make sure. The bar got quiet except for the Spanish polka music playing on the jukebox. She stood by the stove and shook the snow from her blanket and held it near the stove to dry. The wet wool smell reminded her of new-born goats in early March, brought inside to warm near the fire. She felt calm.

In past years they would have told her to get out. But her hair was white now and her face was wrinkled. They looked at her like she was a spider crawling slowly across the room. They were afraid; she could feel the fear. She looked at their faces steadily. They reminded her of the first time the white people brought her children back to her that winter. Danny had been shy and hid behind the thin white woman who brought them. And the baby had not known her until Ayah took her into her arms, and then Ella had nuzzled close to her as she had when she was nursing. The blonde woman was nervous and kept looking at a dainty gold watch on her wrist. She sat on the bench near the small window and watched the dark snow clouds gather around the mountains; she was worrying about the unpaved road. She was frightened by what she saw inside too: the strips of venison drying on a rope across the ceiling and the children jabbering excitedly in a language she did not know. So they stayed for only a few hours. Ayah watched the government car disappear down the road and she knew they were already being weaned from these lava hills and from this sky. The last time they came was in early June, and Ella stared at her the way the men in the bar were now staring. Ayah did not try to pick her up; she smiled at her instead and spoke cheerfully to Danny. When he tried to answer her, he could not seem to remember and he spoke English words with the Navajo. But he gave her a scrap of paper that he had found somewhere and carried in his pocket; it was folded in half, and he shyly looked up at her and said it was a bird. She asked Chato if they were home for good this time. He spoke to the white woman and she shook her head. "How much longer?" he asked, and she said she didn't know; but Chato saw how she stared at the boxcar shack. Ayah turned away then. She did not say good-bye.

She felt satisfied that the men in the bar feared her. Maybe it was her face and the way she held her mouth with teeth clenched tight, like there was nothing anyone could do to her now. She walked north down the road, searching for the old man. She did this because she had the blanket, and there would be no place for him except with her and the blanket in the old adobe barn near the arroyo. They always slept there when they came to Cebolleta. If the money and the wine were gone, she would be relieved because then they could go home again; back to the old hogan with a dirt roof and rock walls where she herself had been born. And the next day the old man could go back to the few sheep they still had, to follow along behind them, guiding them, into dry sandy arroyos where sparse grass grew. She knew he did not like walking behind old ewes when for so many years he rode big quarter horses and worked with cattle. But she wasn't sorry for him; he should have known all along what would happen.

There had not been enough rain for their garden in five years; and that was when Chato finally hitched a ride into the town and brought back brown boxes of rice and sugar and big tin cans of welfare peaches. After that, at the first of the month they went to Cebolleta to ask the postmaster for the check; and then Chato would go to the bar and cash it. They did this as they planted the garden every May, not because anything would survive the summer dust, but because it was time to do this. The journey passed the days that smelled silent and dry like the caves above the canyon with yellow painted buffaloes on their walls.

He was walking along the pavement when she found him. He did not stop or turn around when he heard her behind him. She walked beside him and she noticed how slowly he moved now. He smelled strong of woodsmoke and urine. Lately he had been forgetting. Sometimes he called her by his sister's name and she had been gone for a long time. Once she had found him wandering on the road to the white man's ranch, and she asked him why he was going that way; he laughed at her and said, "You know they can't run that ranch without me," and he walked on determined, limping on the leg that had been crushed many years before. Now he looked at her curiously, as if for the first time, but he kept shuffling along, moving slowly along the side of the highway. His gray hair had grown long and spread out on the shoulders of the long overcoat. He wore the old felt hat pulled down over his ears. His boots were worn out at the toes and he had stuffed pieces of an old red shirt in the holes. The rags made his feet look like little animals up to their ears in snow. She laughed at his feet; the snow muffled the sound of her laugh. He stopped and looked at her again. The wind had quit blowing and the snow was falling straight down; the southeast sky was beginning to clear and Ayah could see a star.

"Let's rest awhile," she said to him. They walked away from the road and up the slope to the giant boulders that had tumbled down from the red sandrock mesa throughout the centuries of rainstorms and earth tremors. In a place where the boulders shut out the wind, they sat down with their backs against the rock. She offered half of the blanket to him and they sat wrapped together.

The storm passed swiftly. The clouds moved east. They were massive and full, crowding together across the sky. She watched them with the feeling of horses— steely blue-gray horses startled across the sky. The powerful haunches pushed into the distances and the tail hairs streamed white mist behind them. The sky cleared. Ayah saw that there was nothing between her and the stars. The light was crystalline. There was no shimmer, no distortion through earth haze. She breathed the clarity of the night sky; she smelled the purity of the half moon and the stars. He was lying on his side with his knees pulled up near his belly for warmth. His eyes were closed now, and in the light from the stars and the moon, he looked young again.

She could see it descend out of the night sky: an icy stillness from the edge of the thin moon. She recognized the freezing. It came gradually, sinking snowflake by snowflake until the crust was heavy and deep. It had the strength of the stars in Orion, and its journey was endless. Ayah knew that with the wine he would sleep. He would not feel it. She tucked the blanket around him, remembering how it was when Ella had been with her; and she felt the rush so big inside her heart for the babies. And she sang the only song she knew to sing for babies. She could not remember if she had ever sung it to her children, but she knew that her grandmother had sung it and her mother had sung it:

> The earth is your mother,
>   she holds you.
> The sky is your father,
>   he protects you.
> Sleep,
> sleep.
> Rainbow is your sister,
>   she loves you.
> The winds are your brothers,
>   they sing to you.
> Sleep,
> sleep.
> We are together always
> We are together always
> There never was a time
> when this
> was not so.

American Borderlands: Voices from the United States's Many Cultures

My family took me to my first pow-wow. I kept asking my grandmother, "Where are the Indians? Where are the Indians? Are they going to have bows and arrows?" I was very curious and excited about the prospect of seeing real live Indians even though I myself was one.

– Barbara Cameron, writer, 1981

The global culture that emerged during the twentieth century gave blue jeans, Coca-Cola, and the Beatles international currency and simultaneously nurtured a growing awareness of humanity's shared dreams and difficulties. Paradoxically it also aroused an appreciation of difference, of the things that make a particular culture distinctive. The writers of the IRISH RENAISSANCE, for example, celebrated Irishness and at the same time contributed to a global interest in ethnicity, influencing, among others, the writers of the HARLEM RENAISSANCE and their search for African roots. The discovery, recovery, or creation of one's ethnic heritage has become an endeavor undertaken by writers worldwide as they seek to establish a cultural identity for themselves and their people—often in works that reach far beyond their native culture to be read by a worldwide audience. This anthology concludes with several works by younger American writers engaged in the seemingly contradictory project of writing for the world by writing of their own identity.

MELTING POT, LAYER CAKE, OR McDONALDIZATION?

The rise of multicultural literature over the past twenty to thirty years has sparked a debate over the appropriate metaphor to describe American society. Is the United States really a "melting pot," a country in which the disparate elements are blended into a common culture? Or is it more like a layer cake, stratified by differences in race, ethnicity, class, and gender? And with the increasing globalization of the world economy and the proliferation of multinational corporations many of which are owned by Americans, some have suggested that neither the melting pot nor the cake

Teri Greeves, *We Gave Two Horses for Our Son*. 1999
American art, literature, and culture in the twentieth and twenty-first centuries is largely about cultures colliding. Greeves, a Kiowa beadworker, blends traditional Native American beadwork with images of popular culture, such as sneakers and umbrellas. She says of her work: "Indian beadwork comes from a long tradition. Techniques and ideas come from before me. My grandmother, a beadworker, is present in everything I do. We are Native peoples of the year 2000." (Fine Art Collection, Heard Museum. Phoenix, Arizona)

adequately describes contemporary American culture, which has been McDonaldized. The creation of commercial interests and the media, the United States as Big Mac, they suggest, has replaced the richness of the mixture with empty calories and the different layers in the cake with a homogenized and superficial version of America.

In response to these alternatives, artists and writers within the United States from various ethnic backgrounds have grown more active and visible during the last several decades, expressing their views on the cultural choices of assimilating into the American mainstream, remaining loyal to family or cultural traditions, or exploring new avenues of self-realization. Some are overtly political, challenging years of prejudice and repression or celebrating their ability to overcome previously impervious cultural, linguistic, racial, or sexual barriers. Others look to move beyond the pain of the past into a present in which they can claim a more empowered role in society by articulating their distinctive view of America.

> The exile knows that in a secular and contingent world, homes are always provisional. Borders and barriers, which enclose us within the safety of familiar territory, can also become prisons, and are often defended beyond reason or necessity. Exiles cross borders, break barriers of thought and experience.
> – EDWARD SAID, critic, 1984

I always tell people that the five primary influences in my life are my father, for his nontraditional Indian stories, my grandmother for her traditional Indian stories, Stephen King, John Steinbeck, and *The Brady Bunch*. That's who I am. I think a lot of Indian artists like to pretend that they're not influenced by pop culture or Western culture, but I am, and I'm happy to admit it. . . . It's a cultural currency.

– SHERMAN ALEXIE

p. 1350

p. 1346

RE-VISIONING HISTORY

Many ethnic writers in the United States have had difficulty acquiring a voice that can be heard by the mainstream culture. Members of the dominant Euro-American culture often express fear or distrust of the "others" among them. Native Americans, of course, are the original Americans, yet their ongoing encounter with invading Europeans over the past several hundred years has by and large been one of great suffering. And despite the fact that the Spaniards were the first Europeans to explore the New World, it is only in recent years that Hispanic Americans have begun to achieve economic security and political representation in this country. Asian Americans have had a long, complex, and varied history on this continent, as have people from other parts of the world, such as the Caribbean, Africa, and the Middle East.

For many years American history and literature textbooks did not include the perspectives of the conquered or the subordinated. The multiethnic American literature of the last few decades attempts to correct that oversight by cataloging the cruelties of the past and recovering the history and culture of neglected ancestors. The work of Sherman Alexie (b. 1966), Martín Espada (b. 1957), Joy Harjo (b. 1951), and Jimmy Santiago Baca (b. 1952) recounts the historical past and the losses of the indigenous peoples of the Americas as well as their determination to survive and to pass on that determination to others. Alexie, for example, has said that his main goal is to get his books read by twelve-year-old reservation kids who, like him, grew up with heroes created by the white media or with no heroes at all. To reach these readers Alexie writes accessible literature, such as **"Class,"** for a pop-culture audience. Espada, like many Latino writers, exposes a Puerto Rican history entangled in Euro-American imperialism. His poem **"Bully"** weaves together images of Theodore Roosevelt, the Spanish colonization, the Taíno Indians who were the island's original inhabitants, the children of today, and U.S. Marines to challenge the imperial view of his native land. In poems that use repetition to create the tone of ceremony, Joy Harjo, a Creek Indian, seeks to recover a remembrance of her native traditions and to exorcise the pain and fear that her people have suffered. Baca, who writes "to give voice to the voiceless," looks at America from the perspective of the barrios of the Southwest.

Joseph Rodríguez, *Puerto Rican Flag, 1986* *In Spanish Harlem in New York City, a heavily Puerto Rican area, a girl stands in front of boarded-up storefronts with peeling paint that attest to the area's poverty. The bright flag of Puerto Rico stands in ironic contrast to its surroundings. (Smithsonian American Art Museum, Washington, D.C. / Art Resource, NY)*

THE MEANING OF ASSIMILATION

Some American writers, particularly those who are "hybrids," mixed-blood children of more than one heritage, or those who are part of an assimilated younger generation caught between their parents' past and a new cultural present, grapple with the complexities of their cultural situation. The narrator of the short story **"Never Marry a Mexican"** by Sandra Cisneros (b. 1954) is caught in the borderlands of love between Mexico and a new Mexican American culture in which white men and women say, "never marry a Mexican." The narrator in Sherman Alexie's "Class," Edgar Eagle Runner, is a Spokane Indian who has become a corporate attorney and has married into the mainstream. The Chinese grandmother in **"Who's Irish?"** by Gish Jen (b. 1956) struggles to understand her granddaughter, who doesn't act like any Chinese girl she's ever seen. Her traditional ideas about discipline and appropriate behavior conflict with the Western attitudes of her daughter.

p. 1370

p. 1389

Another aspect of assimilation that creates difficulties is language. The situation of Native Americans and of many Hispanics in the United States is similar to that of formerly colonized people in other parts of the world, for they joined the United States by force rather than choice. **POSTCOLONIAL** writers take contradictory positions on language. Some resent and reject the language of their former colonizers as a tool of oppression; others embrace it as one of their native tongues or as a mark of their global identity. Bilingual American writers are also often conflicted about English, affirming it as the tongue of their national life, but worrying that their native culture will be lost with their original language. In her poem p. 1388 **"Arabic,"** Naomi Shihab Nye (b. 1952), for example, questions whether she must speak her father's language in order to understand pain. In p. 1348 **"Revolutionary Spanish Lesson,"** Martín Espada expresses his rage toward "average" Americans who are unable to correctly pronounce the names of their fellow citizens.

One's cultural heritage sometimes can be remembered only with pain. Haitian American writer Edwidge Danticat (b. 1969) affirms the freedom and security in the United States by revealing their absence in Haiti in her story p. 1398 **"Children of the Sea."** Alternating diary entries by two Haitian young people, a radical activist who has escaped Haiti on a boat headed for Florida and his girlfriend left behind in Haiti, Danticat dramatizes the horrors that prompt them and other Haitians to risk their lives to reach the United States. Like many other refugees who have come to America to escape persecution in their native lands, the Haitians who reach the United States are scarred by the traumas of their past and their passage.

**Flea Market,
New York City**

On any given day, the streets of New York City display the city's multiculturalism. Omnipresent flea markets feature goods ranging from strange pieces of art to antiques to limitless household items, all of which reflect the diversity of the metropolis. (Travelsite / Neil Setchfield)

The writers whose work appears in the following pages are contributing to a conversation about what it means to be American in a globalizing world. Like their counterparts in postcolonial India, Africa, and Latin America, these writers seek an identity that comprehends both their ethnic heritage and their present situation. For them the past is a work-in-progress, something to be rediscovered or recovered, and the present points toward a future reshaped by new visions, new paradigms for being.

■ CONNECTIONS

In the World: **Crossing Cultures, p. 1278.** Many postcolonial writers are ambivalent about using the language of their former colonizers, while others embrace that language as a suitable medium to reach a wide audience and exercise their talent. How do Rao's, Narayan's, and Rushdie's views on writing in English compare with the stance taken by the American multicultural writers in this American Borderlands section?

Euripides, *Medea* (Book 1); Aphra Behn, *Oroonoko* (Book 4); Jonathan Swift, *Gulliver's Travels* (Book 4); Mary Rowlandson, *Narrative of the Captivity and Restoration of Mrs. Mary Rowlandson* (Book 4). Outsiders are often viewed as barbarians whose customs are uncivilized. From Euripides' *Medea* to the eighteenth-century travel narrative to today's works of multicultural literature, encounters with new places and people have been framed as a pairing of the civilized and the uncivilized — or of the "cooked" and the "raw," to quote social anthropologist Claude Lévi-Strauss (b. 1908). How does this dichotomy play out in the works of American multicultural writers? How does their use of this opposition compare with its use by Euripides, Behn, Swift, and Rowlandson?

In the World: **Europe Meets America (Book 3).** The Spanish conquest of the Americas continues to reverberate through the works of many writers in the United States, particularly those of the Southwest. Compare the writings in *In the World: Europe Meets America* with the works of Espada, Alexie, Harjo, Cisneros, and Baca. Can their work be seen as an answer to Columbus, Ponce de León, and Cortés? How do Native Americans view early Spanish conquerors? How does the history of conquest and exploitation in the Americas figure in the works of these contemporary writers?

ᘒ MARTÍN ESPADA
B. UNITED STATES, 1957

Martín Espada moved frequently when he was young, often to neighborhoods hostile to Latinos and far removed from his original *barrio* home in Brooklyn, New York, where he was born in 1957. Espada says that he began writing as an adolescent because "nothing fit me," but he also proposes that the experience of being an outcast is the determinant in all Puerto Rican immigrant life. This perpetual malaise is brought on not only by each immigrant's sense of exile from home but also by the fact that the island's political identity remains in limbo. Puerto Rico is a U.S. commonwealth and its citizens are U.S. citizens, but they cannot vote in federal elections unless they move to the United States. While they reside on the island, they do not pay federal taxes, but they can be conscripted into military service. Thus the anxiety about identity that many Puerto Ricans feel is both personal and communal, an ambivalence reflected in the results of a 1998 referendum on whether the island should be independent, made a state of the United States, or remain in protectorate status: A winning plurality voted for "none of the above."

Espada's work reflects not only the contemporary Puerto Rican immigrant experience but also his culture's earliest history. His latest collection of poetry, *A Mayan Astronomer in Hell's Kitchen: Poems* (2000), was preceded by *Imagine the Angels of Bread* (1996), an American Book Award recipient; *City of Coughing and Dead Radiators* (1993); *Rebellion Is the Circle of a Lover's Hands* (1990); and *Trumpets from the Islands of Their Eviction* (1987). A prose collection, *Zapata's Disciple: Essays*, was published in 1998. Espada's honors include the PEN/Voelker Award for Poetry, the Paterson Poetry Prize, and fellowships from the National Endowment for the Arts. Espada lives with his wife and son in Amherst, Massachusetts, where he is an associate professor of English at the University of Massachusetts, Amherst.

All notes are the editors'.

❧ Bully

In the school auditorium,
the Theodore Roosevelt[1] statue
is nostalgic
for the Spanish-American war,[2]
each fist lonely for a saber
or the reins of anguish-eyed horses,

---

[1] Theodore Roosevelt (1858–1919): Twenty-sixth president of the United States (1901–09); Roosevelt's Rough Riders, a volunteer cavalry unit, fought in Cuba at the beginning of the Spanish-American War. Roosevelt's policies toward Latin America may be categorized by his own motto: "Walk softly and carry a big stick."

[2] Spanish-American War (1898): In the waning years of the nineteenth century, the United States went to war to expell Spain from Cuba. The war, in which Theodore Roosevelt led the famous charge on San Juan Hill, was over in a few months. The Treaty of Paris, which concluded the war, acknowledged Cuban independence, ceded Puerto Rico and the island of Guam to the United States, liquidated Spanish possessions in the West Indies, and sold the Philippines to the United States for $20 million.

or a podium to clatter with speeches
glorying in the malaria of conquest.

But now the Roosevelt school
10   is pronounced Hernández.
Puerto Rico has invaded Roosevelt[3]
with its army of Spanish-singing children
in the hallways,
brown children devouring
the stockpiles of the cafeteria,
children painting Taíno ancestors[4]
that leap naked across murals.

Roosevelt is surrounded
by all the faces
20   he ever shoved in eugenic spite
and cursed as mongrels, skin of one race,
hair and cheekbones of another.

Once Marines tramped
from the newsreel of his imagination;
now children plot to spray graffiti
in parrot-brilliant colors
across the Victorian mustache
and monocle.

---

[3] **Puerto Rico . . . Roosevelt:** In the 1950s a mass immigration of Puerto Ricans to the U.S. mainland began, encouraged by the U.S. government and resulting from many factors, including a poor economy, collapsing agriculture, and an increase in population on the island.

[4] **Taíno ancestors:** A Spanish colony since 1508, by 1520 Puerto Rico had become strategically important as the "key to the Indies." According to some historians, there were 426 Spaniards and 2,264 black slaves on the island in 1531 but only 473 Taíno Indians out of what had been tens of thousands; those who remained had been enslaved by the *encomienda* system, under which the Spanish king granted to his agent the right to enslave all the Indians within a territory. Others believe that many Taínos escaped to the mountainous regions or inter-married with the newcomers. Recent preliminary research demonstrates that Taíno DNA is found at a much higher rate than was previously thought to be the case among current residents of Puerto Rico.

✍ From an Island You Cannot Name

Thirty years ago,
your linen-gowned father stood
in the dayroom of the VA hospital,
grabbing at the plastic

identification bracelet
marked Negro,
shouting "I'm not!
Take it off!
I'm Other!"

10   The army photograph
pinned to your mirror
says he was,
black, Negro,
dark as West Indian rum.

And this morning,
daughter of a man
from an island you cannot name,
you gasp tears
trying to explain
20   that you're Other,
that you're not.

❧ Revolutionary Spanish Lesson

Whenever my name
is mispronounced,
I want to buy a toy pistol,
put on dark sunglasses,
push my beret to an angle,
comb my beard to a point,
hijack a busload
of Republican tourists
from Wisconsin,
10   force them to chant
anti-American slogans
in Spanish,
and wait
for the bilingual SWAT team
to helicopter overhead,
begging me
to be reasonable

⚱ SHERMAN ALEXIE
B. UNITED STATES, 1966

Sherman Alexie's college writing professor once said that as a student
Alexie showed an extraordinary amount of dedication to his work as
a writer. That dedication has paid off in a career that has been on fire
for more than a decade. Alexie has published seven books of poetry,
including *I Would Steal Horses* and *The Business of Fancydancing* (both
published in 1991); two collections of short stories, *The Lone Ranger
and Tonto Fistfight in Heaven* (1993) and *The Toughest Indian in the
World* (1998), which included "Class"; and two novels, *Reservation Blues*
(1995) and *Indian Killer* (1996), a *New York Times* Notable Book. In 1998
he produced the film *Smoke Signals,* based on *The Lone Ranger and
Tonto,* which was the first-ever film distributed in the United States
produced, directed, and written by a Native American. Alexie's honors

**Still from *Smoke
Signals,* 1998**

Smoke Signals, *a film
based on the short
stories of Sherman
Alexie, documents the
journey of two young
Native Americans
coping with the loss of
their parents and
forming a bond with
each other. (The
Kobal Collection /
Miramax / Duchin,
Courtnay)*

include awards from PEN and the National Endowment for the Arts; in 1998 and 1999 he was named by *Granta* and *The New Yorker* as one of the best American fiction writers under forty. Born on the Spokane Reservation to a Coeur d'Alene father and a Spokane mother, Alexie currently lives in Seattle.

All notes are the editors'.

∾ Class

She wanted to know if I was Catholic.

I was completely unprepared to respond with any degree of clarity to such a dangerous question. After all, we had been talking about the shrimp appetizers (which were covered with an ambitious pesto sauce) and where they fit, in terms of quality, in our very different histories of shrimp appetizers in particular and seafood appetizers in general. I'd just been describing to her how cayenne and lobster seemed to be mortal enemies, one of the more secular and inane culinary observations I'd ever made, when she'd focused her blue eyes on me, really looked at me for the first time in the one minute and thirty-five seconds we'd known each other, and asked me if I was Catholic.

How do you answer a question like that, especially when you've just met the woman at one of those house parties where you'd expected to know everybody in attendance but had gradually come to realize that you knew only the host couple, and then only well enough to ask about the welfare of the two kids (a boy and a girl or two boys) you thought they parented? As far as I could tell, there were no priests, ministers, or pastors milling about, so I had no easy visual aids in guessing at the dominant denomination in the room. If there'd been a Jesuit priest, Hasidic rabbi, or Tibetan monk drinking a pale ale over by the saltwater aquarium, I might have known the best response, the clever, scintillating answer that would have compelled her to take me home with her for a long night of safe and casual sex.

"Well," she asked again, with a musical lilt in her voice. "Are you Catholic?"

Her left eye was a significantly darker blue than the right.

"Your eyes," I said, trying to change the subject. "They're different."

"I'm blind in this one," she said, pointing to the left eye.

"Oh, I'm sorry," I said, mortified by my lack of decorum.

"Why? It was my big brother who stabbed me with the pencil. He didn't mean it, though."

She told the story as if she'd only skinned a knee or received a slight concussion, as if the injury had been temporary.

"He was aiming for my little sister's eye," she added. "But she ducked. She was always more athletic than me."

"Where's your sister now?"

"She's dead. Car wreck. Bang, bang, bang."

So much pain for such a white woman. I wondered how often a man can say the wrong thing during the course of a particular conversation.

"What about your brother?" I asked, praying that he had not been driving the car that killed her sister.

"He's right over there," she said and pointed at a handsome man, taller than everybody else in the room, who was sitting on the carpeted stairs with a woman whose red hair I'd been admiring all evening. Though engaged in what appeared to be a passionate conversation, the brother sensed his sister's attention and looked up. Both of his eyes were the same shade of blue as her good eye.

"He's the one who did it," she said and tapped her blind eye.

In response, the brother smiled and tapped his left eye. He could see perfectly.

"You cruel bastard," she mouthed at him, though she made it sound like an affectionate nickname, like a tender legacy from childhood.

"You cruel bastard," she repeated. Her brother could obviously read her lips because he laughed again, loud enough for me to hear him over the din of the party, and hugged the redhead in a tender but formal way that indicated they'd made love only three or four times in their young relationship.

"Your brother," I said, trying to compliment her by complimenting the family genetics. "He's good-looking."

"He's okay," she said.

"He's got your eyes."

"Only one of them, remember," she said and moved one step closer to me. "Now, quit trying to change the subject. Tell me. Are you Catholic or are you not Catholic?"

"Baptized," I said. "But not confirmed."

"That's very ambiguous."

"I read somewhere that many women think ambiguity is sexy."

"Not me. I like men who are very specific."

"You don't like mystery?"

"I always know who did it," she said and moved so close that I could smell the red wine and dinner mints on her breath.

I took a step back.

"Don't be afraid," she said. "I'm not drunk. And I just chewed on a few Altoids because I thought I might be kissing somebody very soon."

She could read minds. She was also drunk enough that her brother had already pocketed the keys to her Lexus.

"Who is this somebody you're going to be kissing?" I asked. "And why just somebody? That sounds very ambiguous to me."

"And very sexy," she said and touched my hand. Blond, maybe thirty-five, and taller than me, she was the tenth most attractive white woman in the room. I always approached the tenth most attractive white woman at any gathering. I didn't have enough looks, charm, intelligence, or money to approach anybody more attractive than that, and I didn't have enough character to approach the less attractive. Crassly speaking, I'd always made sure to play ball only with my equals.

"You're Indian," she said, stretching the word into three syllables and nearly a fourth.

"Do you like that?"

"I like your hair," she said, touching the black braids that hung down past my chest. I'd been growing the braids since I'd graduated from law school. My hair impressed jurors but irritated judges. Perfect.

"I like your hair, too," I said and brushed a pale strand away from her forehead. I counted three blemishes and one mole on her face. I wanted to kiss the tips of her fingers. Woman expected kisses on the parts of their bodies hidden by clothes, the private places, but were often surprised when I paid more attention to their public features: hands, hairline, the soft skin around their eyes.

"You're beautiful," I said.

"No, I'm not," she said. "I'm just pretty. But pretty is good enough."

I still didn't know her name, but I could have guessed at it. Her generation of white women usually carried two-syllable names, like Becky, Erin, and Wendy, or monosyllabic nicknames that lacked any adornment. Peg, Deb, or Sam. Efficient names, quick-in-the-shower names, just-brush-it-and-go names. Her mother and her mother's friends would be known by more ornate monikers, and if she had daughters, they would be named after their grandmothers. The country was filling up with little white girls named Rebecca, Elizabeth, and Willamena.

"Sara," I guessed. "Your name is Sara."

"With or without an *h*?" she asked.

"Without," I said, pleased with my psychic ability.

"Actually, it's neither. My name is Susan. Susan McDermott. Without the *h*."

"I'm Edgar Eagle Runner," I said, though my driver's license still read Edgar Joseph.

"Eagle Runner," she repeated, feeling the shape of my name fill her mouth, then roll past her tongue, teeth, and lips.

"Susan," I said.

"Eagle Runner," she whispered. "What kind of Indian are you?"

"Spokane."

"Never heard of it."

"We're a small tribe. Salmon people."

"The salmon are disappearing," she said.

"Yes," I said. "Yes, they are."

Susan McDermott and I were married in a small ceremony seven months later in St. Therese Catholic Church in Madrona, a gentrified neighborhood ten minutes from downtown Seattle. She'd been baptized at St. Therese as a toddler by a Jesuit who many years later went hiking on Mount Rainier and vanished. Father David or Joseph or Father Something Biblical. She didn't remember anything about him, neither the color of his hair nor the exact shape of his theology, but she thought that his disappearance was a metaphor for her love life.

"One day, many years ago," she said, "my heart walked into the snow and vanished. But then you found it and gave it heat."

"Is that a simile or a metaphor?" I asked.

"It might be an analogy," she said.

Our vows were witnessed by three dozen of Susan's best friends, along with most of her coworkers at the architecture firm, but Susan's handsome brother and parents stayed away as a protest against my pigmentation.

"I can understand fucking him," her brother had said upon hearing the news of our engagement. "But why do you want to share a checking account?"

He was so practical.

Half of the partners and all of my fellow associates from the law firm showed up to watch me tie the knot.

Velma, my dark-skinned mother, was overjoyed by my choice of mate. She'd always wanted me to marry a white woman and beget half-breed children who would marry white people who would beget quarter-bloods, and so on and so on, until simple mathematics killed the Indian in us.

When asked, my mother told white people she was Spanish, not Mexican, not Hispanic, not Chicana, and certainly not Spokane Indian with a little bit of Aztec thrown in for spice, even though she was all of these things.

As for me, I'd told any number of white women that I was part Aztec and I'd told a few that I was completely Aztec. That gave me some mystery, some ethnic weight, a history of glorious color and mass executions. Strangely enough, there were aphrodisiacal benefits to claiming to be descended from ritual cannibals. In any event, pretending to be an Aztec warrior was a lot more impressive than revealing I was just some bright kid who'd fought his way off the Spokane Indian Reservation in Washington State and was now a corporate lawyer in Seattle who pretended to have a lot more money than he did.

I'd emptied my meager savings account to pay for the wedding and reception, refusing to allow Susan to help, though she made twice what I did. I was living paycheck to paycheck, a bizarre circumstance for a man whose monthly wage exceeded his mother's yearly income as a social worker in the small city of Spokane, Washington.

My mother was an Indian woman who taught drunk white people not to drink, stoned whites not to smoke, and abusive whites not to throw the punch. A simple and honorable job. She was very good at it and I loved her. She wore a black dress to the wedding, nearly funeral wear, but brightened it with a salmon-colored scarf and matching shoes.

I counted seventeen white women at the wedding. On an average day, Susan would have been the fourth or fifth most attractive. On this, her wedding day, dressed in an ivory gown with plunging neckline, she was easily the most beautiful white woman in the chapel; she was more serene, sexy, and spiritual than the wooden Mary hanging on the west wall or the stained-glassed Mary filling up one of the windows.

Susan's niece, an eighteen-year-old, served as her maid of honor. She modeled teen wear for Nordstrom's. I tried not to stare at her. My best man was one of the partners in the law firm where I worked.

"Hey, Runner," he had said just before the ceremony began. "I love you, man."

I'd hugged him, feeling guilty. My friendship with him was strictly professional.

During the ceremony, he cried. I couldn't believe it. I'm not one of those men who believe tears are a sign of weakness. On the contrary, I believe it's entirely appropriate, even attractive, for a man to cry under certain circumstances, but my wedding was not tearworthy. In fact, there was a decided lack of emotion during the ceremony, mostly due to the absence of Susan's immediate family.

My mother was the only member of my family sitting in the pews, but that didn't bother or surprise me. She was the only one I had invited.

The ceremony itself was short and simple, because Susan believed brevity was always more elegant, and more sexy, than excess. I agreed with her.

"I will," she said.

"I will," I said.

We did.

During the first two years of our marriage, we attended thirty-seven cocktail parties, eighteen weddings, one divorce, seven Christmas parties, two New Year's Eve parties, three New Year's Day parties, nine birthday parties—only one of them for a child under the age of eighteen—six opera performances, nine literary readings, twelve museum openings, one museum closing, three ballets, including a revival of *Swan Lake* in New York City, one spouse-swapping party we left before we took off our coats, and thirty-two films, including most of those nominated for Oscars and two or three that had screened at the Sundance Film Festival.

I attended business lunches Monday through Friday, and occasionally on Saturdays, while Susan kept her Friday lunches free so she could carry on an affair with an architect named Harry. She'd begun the affair a few days after our first anniversary and it had gone on for seven months before she'd voluntarily quit him, never having known that I'd known about the tryst, that I'd discovered his love letters hidden in a shoe box at the bottom of her walk-in closet.

I hadn't been snooping on her when I'd found the letters and I didn't bother to read any of them past the salutation that began each. "My love, my love, my love," they'd read, three times, always three times, like a chant, like a prayer. Brokenhearted, betrayed, I'd kept the letters sacred by carefully placing them back, intact and unread, in the shoe box and sliding the box back into its hiding place.

I suppose I could have exacted revenge on her by sleeping with one or more of her friends or coworkers. I'd received any number of subtle offers to do such a thing, but I didn't want to embarrass her. Personal pain should never be made public. Instead, in quiet retaliation, I patronized prostitutes whenever I traveled out of town. Miami, Los Angeles, Boston, Chicago, Minneapolis, Houston.

In San Francisco for a deposition hearing, I called the first service listed in the Yellow Pages.

"A-1 Escorts," said the woman. A husky voice, somehow menacing. I'm sure her children hated the sound of it, even as I found myself aroused by its timbre.

"A-1 Escorts," she said again when I did not speak.

"Oh," I said. "Hi. Hello. Uh, I'm looking for some company this evening."

"Where you at?"

"The Prescott."

"Nice place."

"Yeah, they have whirlpool bathtubs."

"Water sports will cost you extra."

"Oh, no, no, no. I'm, uh, rather traditional."

"Okay, Mr. Traditional, what are you looking for?"

I'd slept with seventeen prostitutes, all of them blond and blue-eyed. Twelve of them had been busty while the other five had been small-breasted. Eight of them had claimed to be college students; one of them even had a chemistry textbook in her backpack.

"Do you employ any Indian women?" I asked.

"Indian? Like with the dot in the forehead?"

"No, no, that's East Indian. From India. I'm looking for American Indian. You know, like Tonto."[1]

"We don't have any boys."

"Oh, no, I mean, I want an Indian woman."

There was a long silence on the other end. Was she looking through some kind of catalog? Searching her inventory for the perfect woman for me? Was she calling other escort companies, looking for a referral? I wanted to hang up the phone. I'd never had intercourse with an Indian woman.

"Yeah, we got somebody. She's a pro."

"What do you mean by pro?"

"She used to work pornos."

"Pornos?"

"Dirty movies? X-rated? You got them right there on the pay-per-view in your room, buddy."

"What's her name?"

"She calls herself Tawny Feather."

"You're kidding."

"I never kid."

I wondered what kind of Indian woman would call herself Tawny Feather. Sexually speaking, Indian women and men are simultaneously promiscuous and modest. That's a contradiction, but it also happens to be the truth. I just couldn't imagine an Indian woman who would star in pornographic movies.

"Well, you want a date or not?" asked the husky-voiced woman.

"How much?"

"How much you got?"

"How much you want?"

"Two hundred."

"Sold," I said.

"What room?"

"1216."

---

[1] **Tonto:** Stereotypical subordinate and faithful Native American companion to the Lone Ranger in the radio and television series of the same name in the 1940s and 1950s.

"Who should she ask for?"

"Geronimo."

"Ha, ha," she said and hung up the phone.

Less than an hour later, there was a knock on the door. I peered through the peephole and saw her.

Tawny Feather.

She wore a conservative tan suit and a string of fake pearls. Dream-catcher earrings, turquoise rings, a stainless-steel eagle pinned to her lapel. Good camouflage. Professional but eccentric. She looked like a woman on her way to or from a meeting. She looked like a woman with an Individualized Retirement Account.

She was also a white woman wearing a black wig over her short blond hair.

"You're not Indian," I said when I opened the door.

She looked me up and down.

"No, I'm not," she said. "But you are."

"Mostly."

"Well," she said as she stepped into the room and kissed my neck. "Then you can mostly pretend I'm Indian."

She stayed all night, which cost me another five hundred dollars, and ordered eggs and toast for breakfast, which cost me another twenty.

"You're the last one," I said as she prepared to leave.

"The last what?"

"My last prostitute."

"The last one today?" she asked. "Or the last one this month? What kind of time period are we talking about here?"

She swore she was an English major.

"The last one forever," I said.

She smiled, convinced that I was lying and/or fooling myself, having heard these same words from any number of customers. She knew that she and her coworkers were drugs for men like me.

"Sure I am," she said.

"No, really," I said. "I promise."

She laughed.

"Son," she said, though she was ten years younger than me. "You don't have to make me any damn promises."

She took off her black wig and handed it to me.

"You keep it," she said and gave me a free good-bye kiss.

Exactly three years after our wedding, Susan gave birth to our first child, a boy. He weighed eight pounds, seven ounces, and was twenty-two inches long. A big baby. His hair was black and his eyes were a strange gray. He died ten minutes after leaving Susan's body.

After our child died, Susan and I quit having sex. Or rather, she stopped wanting to have sex. I just want to tell the whole story. For months I pressured, coerced, seduced, and emotionally blackmailed her into sleeping with me. At first, I assumed she'd been engaged in another affair with another architect named Harry, but my private detective found only evidence of her grief, crying jags in public rest rooms, aimless wandering in the children's departments of Nordstrom's and the Bon Marche, and visits to a therapist I'd never heard about.

She wasn't touching anybody else but me. Our lives moved on.

After a year of reluctant sex, I believed her orgasms were mostly due to my refusal to quit touching her until she did come, the arduous culmination of my physical endeavors rather than the result of any emotional investment she might have had in fulfillment. And then, one night, while I was still inside her, moving my hips in rhythm with hers, I looked into her eyes, her blue eyes, and saw that her good eye held no more light in it than her dead eye. She wasn't literally blind, of course. She'd just stopped seeing me. I was startled by the sudden epiphany that she'd been faking her orgasms all along, certainly since our child had died, and probably since the first time we'd made love.

"What?" she asked, a huge question to ask and answer at any time in our lives. Her hands never left their usual place at the small of my back.

"I'm sorry," I told her, and I was sorry, and left her naked and alone in bed while I quickly dressed and went out for a drink.

I don't drink alcohol, never have, mostly because I don't want to maintain and confirm any of my ethnic stereotypes, let alone the most prevalent one, but also because my long-lost father, a half-breed, is still missing somewhere in the bottom of a tequila bottle. I had always wondered if he was a drunk because he was Indian or because he was white or because he was both.

Personally, I like bottled water, with gas, as the Europeans like to say. If I drink enough of that bubbly water in the right environment, I can get drunk. After a long night of Perrier or Pellegrino, I can still wake up with a vicious hangover. Obviously, I place entirely too much faith in the power of metaphor.

When I went out carousing with my fellow lawyers, I ended up in fancy hotel lounges, private clubs, and golf course cigar rooms, the places where the alcoholics adhere to a rigid dress code, but after leaving my marriage bed I wanted to drink in a place free from lawyers and their dress codes, from emotional obligations and beautiful white women, even the kind of white woman who might be the tenth most attractive in any room in the world.

I chose Chuck's, a dive near the corner of Virginia and First.

I'd driven by the place any number of times, had seen the Indians who loitered outside. I assumed it was an Indian bar, one of those establishments where the clientele, through chance and design, is mostly indigenous. I'd heard about these kinds of places. They are supposed to exist in every city.

"What can I get you?" asked the bartender when I sat on the stool closest to the door. She was an Indian woman with scars on her face and knuckles. A fighter. She was a woman who had once been pretty but had grown up in a place where pretty was punished. Now, twenty pounds overweight, on her way to forty pounds more, she was most likely saving money for a complete move to a city yet to be determined.

"Hey, handsome," she asked again as I stared blankly at her oft-broken nose. I decided that her face resembled most of the furniture in the bar: dark, stained by unknown insults, and in a continual state of repair. "What the fuck would you like to drink?"

"Water," I said, surprised that the word "fuck" could sound so friendly.

"Water?"

"Yeah, water."

She filled a glass from the tap behind her and plunked it down in front of me.

"A dollar," she said.

"For tap water?"

"For space rental."

I handed her a five-dollar bill.

"Keep the change," I said and took a big drink.

"Cool. Next time, you get a clean glass," she said and waited for my reaction.

I swallowed hard, kept my dinner down, and smiled.

"I don't need to know what's coming next," I said. "I like mysteries."

"What kind of mysteries?"

"Hard-boiled. The kind where the dog gets run over, the hero gets punched in the head, and the bad guy gets eaten by sharks."

"Not me," she said. "I got too much blood in my life already. I like romances."

I wondered if she wanted to sleep with me.

"You want something else," she said, "just shout it out. I'll hear you."

She moved to the other end of the bar where an old Indian man sipped at a cup of coffee. They talked and laughed. Surprisingly jealous of their camaraderie, I turned away and looked around the bar. It was a small place, maybe fifty feet long by twenty feet wide, with one pinball machine, one pool table, and two bathrooms. I supposed the place would be packed on a weekend.

As it was, on a cold Thursday, there were only five Indians in the bar, other than the bartender, her old friend, and me.

Two obese Indian women shared a table in the back, an Indian couple danced in front of a broken jukebox, and one large and muscular Indian guy played pool by himself. In his white T-shirt, blue-jean jacket, tight jeans, and cowboy boots, he looked like Chief Broom[2] from *One Flew Over the Cuckoo's Nest.* I decided he could have killed me with a flick of one finger.

He looked up from his pool cue when he felt my eyes on him.

"What the fuck are you looking at?" he asked. His eyes were darker than the eight ball. I had no idea that "fuck" could be such a dangerous word.

"Nothing," I said.

Still holding his cue stick, he walked a few paces closer to me. I was afraid, very afraid.

---

[2] **Chief Broom:** Chief Broom, or Bromden, is the tall, "mute" Native American chief who narrates the story in Ken Kesey's novel *One Flew Over the Cuckoo's Nest.* He was relegated to a minor and silent role in the 1975 film of the same name directed by Milos Forman. The flamboyant, wise-guy antihero McMurphy, played by Jack Nicholson, rebels against the establishment and the institutional authority of the mental hospital. By the end of the movie he has been lobotomized, and Chief Broom, knowing his friend has lost his spirit, suffocates him in a mercy killing and then escapes.

"Nothing?" he asked. "Do I look like nothing to you?"

"No, no, that's not what I meant. I mean, I was just watching you play pool. That's all."

He stared at me, studied me like an owl might study a field mouse.

"You just keep your eyes to yourself," he said and turned back to his game.

I thought I was safe. I looked down to the bartender, who was shaking her head at me.

"Because I just, I just want to know," sputtered the big Indian. "I just want to know who the hell you think you are."

Furious, he shouted, a primal sort of noise, as he threw the cue stick against the wall. He rushed at me and lifted me by the collar.

"Who are you?" he shouted. "Who the fuck are you?"

"I'm nobody," I said, wet with fear. "Nobody. Nobody."

"Put him down, Junior," said the bartender.

Junior and I both turned to look at her. She held a pistol down by her hip, not as a threat, but more like a promise. Junior studied the bartender's face, estimated the level of her commitment, and dropped me back onto the stool.

He took a few steps back, pointed at me.

"I'm sick of little shits like you," he said. "Fucking urban Indians in your fancy fucking clothes. Fuck you. Fuck you."

I looked down and saw my denim jacket and polo shirt, the khakis and brown leather loafers. I looked like a Gap ad.

"I ever see you again," Junior said. "I'm going to dislocate your hips."

I flinched. Junior obviously had some working knowledge of human anatomy and the most effective means of creating pain therein. He saw my fear, examined its corners and edges, and decided it was large enough.

"Jesus," he said. "I don't know why I'm even talking to you. What are you going to do? You fucking wimp. You're not worth my time. Why don't you get the fuck out of here? Why don't you just get in your BMW, that's what you drive, enit? Why don't you get in your fucking BMW and get out of here before I change my mind, before I pop out one of your eyes with a fucking spoon, all right?"

I didn't drive a BMW; I drove a Saab.

"Yeah, fuck you," Junior said, thoroughly enjoying himself now. "Just drive back to your fucking mansion on Mercer Island or Edmonds or whatever white fucking neighborhood you live in. Drive back to your white wife. She's white, enit? Yeah, blond and blue-eyed, I bet. White, white. I bet her pussy hair is blond, too. Isn't it? Isn't it?"

I wanted to hate him.

"Go back to your mansion and read some fucking Teletubbies to your white fucking kids."

"What?" I asked.

"I said, go home to your white fucking kids."

"Fuck you," I said and completely surprised Junior. Good thing. He hesitated for a brief moment before he rushed at me again. His hesitation gave the bartender enough time to vault the bar and step in between Junior and me. I couldn't believe how fast she was.

She pressed the pistol tightly against Junior's forehead.

"Let it go, Junior," said the bartender.

"Why are you protecting him?" Junior asked.

"I don't give a shit about him," she said. "But I do care about you. You get into trouble again and you're going to jail forever. You know that."

Junior smiled.

"Sissy," he said to the bartender. "In another world, you and I are Romeo and Juliet."

"But we live in this world, Junior."

"Okay," said Sissy. "This is what's going to happen, Junior. You're going to walk over behind the bar, get yourself another Diet Pepsi, and mellow out. And Mr. Tap Water here is going to walk out the front door and never return. How does that sound to the both of you?"

"Make it two Pepsis," said Junior.

"Deal," said Sissy. "How about you, Polo?"

"Fuck him," I said.

Junior didn't move anything except his mouth.

"Sissy," he said. "How can you expect me to remain calm, how can you expect me to stay reasonable, when this guy so obviously wants to die?"

"I'll fight you," I said.

"What?" asked Sissy and Junior, both amazed.

"I'll fight you," I said again.

"All right, that's what I want to hear," said Junior. "Maybe you do have some balls. There's an alley out back."

"You don't want to do this," Sissy said to me.

"I'll meet you out there, Junior," I said.

Junior laughed and shook his head.

"Listen up, Tommy Hilfiger," he said. "I'm not stupid. I go out the back door and you're going to run out the front door. You don't have to make things so complicated. You want to leave, I'll let you leave. Just do it now, man."

"He's giving you a chance," Sissy said to me. "You better take it."

"No," I said. "I want to fight. I'll meet you out there. I promise."

Junior studied my eyes.

"You don't lie, do you?"

"I lie all the time," I said. "Most of the time. But I'm not lying now. I want to fight."

"All right, then, bring your best," he said and walked out the back door.

"Are you out of your mind?" Sissy asked. "Have you ever been in a fight?"

"I boxed a little in college."

"You boxed a little in college? You boxed a little in college? I can't believe this. Do you have any idea who Junior is?"

"No, why should I?"

"He's a pro."

"What? You mean, like a professional boxer?"

"No, man. A professional street fighter. No judges, no ring, no rules. The loser is the guy who don't get up."

"Isn't that illegal?"

"Illegal? Illegal? What, you think you're a lawyer now?"

"Actually, I am a lawyer."

Sissy laughed until tears ran down her face.

"Sweetheart," she said after she'd finally calmed down. "You need to leave. Please. Junior's got a wicked temper but he'll calm down soon enough. Hell, you come in a week from now and he'll probably buy you some water."

"Really?"

"No, not at all. I'm lying. You come in a week from now and Junior will break your thumbs."

She laughed again, laughed until she had to lean against the bar for support.

"Stop it," I said.

She kept laughing.

"Stop it," I shouted.

She kept laughing.

"Sweetheart," she said, trying to catch her breath. "I could kick your ass."

I shrugged off my denim jacket and marched for the back door. Sissy tried to stop me, but I pulled away from her and stepped into the alley.

Junior was surprised to see me. I felt a strange sense of pride. Without another word, I rushed at Junior, swinging at him with a wide right hook, with dreams of connecting with his jaw and knocking him out with one punch.

Deep in the heart of the heart of every Indian man's heart, he believes he is Crazy Horse.[3]

My half-closed right hand whizzed over Junior's head as he expertly ducked under my wild punch and then rose, surely and accurately, with a left uppercut that carried with it the moon and half of every star in the universe.

I woke up with my head in Sissy's lap. She was washing my face with a cold towel.

"Where are we?" I asked.

"In the storeroom," she said.

"Where is he?"

"Gone."

My face hurt.

"Am I missing any teeth?"

---

[3] **Crazy Horse** (1849–1877): Celebrated for his ferocity in battle, Crazy Horse, *Tashunca-uitco*, was recognized among his own people as a visionary leader committed to preserving the traditions and values of the Lakota way of life. He fought to prevent American encroachment on Lakota lands following the Fort Laramie Treaty of 1868, helping to attack a surveying party sent into the Black Hills by General George Armstrong Custer in 1873. When the War Department ordered all Lakota bands onto their reservations in 1876, Crazy Horse led the resistance with others. Following the Lakota victory at the Little Big Horn, Crazy Horse stayed on to battle General Nelson Miles as the latter pursued the Lakota and their allies relentlessly throughout the winter of 1876–77. Constant military harassment and the decline of the buffalo population eventually forced Crazy Horse to surrender on May 6, 1877; except for Gall and Sitting Bull, he was the last important chief to yield. He died resisting arrest in September 1877 when he left the reservation without authorization to take his sick wife to her parents.

"No," said Sissy. "But your nose is broken."

"Are you sure?"

"Trust me."

I looked up at her. I decided she was still pretty and pretty was good enough. I grabbed her breast.

"Shit," she said and shoved me away.

I sprawled on the floor while she scrambled to her feet.

"What's wrong with you?" she asked. "What is wrong with you?"

"What do you mean? What?"

"Did you think, did you somehow get it into your crazy head that I was going to fuck you back here? On the goddamn floor in the goddamn dirt?"

I didn't know what to say.

"Jesus Christ, you really thought I was going to fuck you, didn't you?"

"Well, I mean, I just . . ."

"You just thought because I'm an ugly woman that I'd be easy."

"You're not ugly," I said.

"Do you think I'm impressed by this fighting bullshit? Do you think it makes you some kind of warrior or something?"

She could read minds.

"You did, didn't you? All of you Indian guys think you're Crazy Horse."

I struggled to my feet and walked over to the sink. I looked in the mirror and saw a bloody mess. I also noticed that one of my braids was missing.

"Junior cut it off," said Sissy. "And took it with him. You're lucky he liked you. Otherwise, he would have taken a toe. He's done that before."

I couldn't imagine what that would have meant to my life.

"Look at you," she said. "Do you think that's attractive? Is that who you want to be?"

I carefully washed my face. My nose was most certainly broken.

"I just want to know, man. What are you doing here? Why'd you come here?"

My left eye was swelling shut. I wouldn't be able to see out of it in the morning.

"I wanted to be with my people," I said.

"Your people?" asked Sissy. "Your people? We're not your people."

"We're Indians."

"Yeah, we're Indians. You, me, Junior. But we live in this world and you live in your world."

"I don't like my world."

"You pathetic bastard," she said, her eyes swelling with tears that had nothing to do with laughter. "You sorry, sorry piece of shit. Do you know how much I want to live in your world? Do you know how much Junior wants to live in your world?"

Of course I knew. For most of my life, I'd dreamed about the world where I currently resided.

"Junior and me," she said. "We have to worry about having enough to eat. What do you have to worry about? That you're lonely? That you have a mortgage? That your wife doesn't love you? Fuck you, fuck you. *I have to worry about having enough to eat.*"

She stormed out of the room, leaving me alone.

I stood there in the dark for a long time. When I walked out, the bar was nearly empty. Another bartender was cleaning glasses. He didn't look at me. Sissy was gone. The front door was wide open. I stepped into the street and saw her sitting at the bus stop.

"I'm sorry," I said.

"Whatever."

"Can I give you a ride somewhere?"

"Do you really want to do that?" she asked.

"No," I said.

"Finally, you're being honest."

I stared at her. I wanted to say the exact right thing.

"Go home," she said. "Just go home."

I walked away, stopped halfway down the block.

"Do you have any kids?" I shouted back at her.

"Three," she said.

Without changing my clothes, I crawled back into bed with Susan. Her skin was warm to the touch. The house ticked, ticked, ticked. In the morning, my pillow would be soaked with my blood.

"Where did you go?" Susan asked me.

"I was gone," I said. "But now I'm back."

❧ JOY HARJO
B. UNITED STATES, 1951

Born in Tulsa, Oklahoma, and an enrolled member of the Muskogee tribe, Joy Harjo went to New Mexico at sixteen to attend the Institute of American Indian Arts where she studied painting and theater. Switching her focus to poetry, she received a B.A. in creative writing from the University of New Mexico in 1976 and an M.F.A. from the University of Iowa in 1978. Her most recent book of poetry, *How We Became Human: New and Selected Poems: 1975–2001* (2002), was preceded by seven others: *The Last Song* (1975), *What Moon Drove Me to This* (1979), *She Had Some Horses* (1983), *Secrets from the Center of the World* (1989), *In Mad Love and War* (1990), *The Woman Who Fell from the Sky* (1994), and *A Map to the Next World: Poems and Tales* (2000). Harjo founded the musical band Poetic Justice, which combined elements of tribal musics, jazz, and rock with poetry and allowed Harjo to sing and play her compositions. Harjo's poems are imbued with an awareness and understanding of the strength of memory, and themes of continuance and survival underlie much of her work. She has received many honors for her work, including the American Book Award from the Before Columbus Foundation, the Poetry Society of America's William Carlos Williams Award, and the American Indian Distinguished Achievement Award, as well as a National Endowment for the Arts Fellowship.

❧ Remember

Remember the sky you were born under,
know each of the star's stories.
Remember the moon, know who she is.
Remember the sun's birth at dawn, that is the
strongest point of time. Remember sundown
and the giving away to night.
Remember your birth, how your mother struggled
to give you form and breath. You are evidence of
her life, and her mother's, and hers.
Remember your father. He is your life, also.
Remember the earth whose skin you are:
red earth, black earth, yellow earth, white earth
brown earth, we are earth.
Remember the plants, trees, animal life who all have their
tribes, their families, their histories, too. Talk to them,
listen to them. They are alive poems.
Remember the wind. Remember her voice. She knows the
origin of this universe.
Remember you are all people and all people
are you.
Remember you are this universe and this
universe is you.
Remember all is in motion, is growing, is you.
Remember language comes from this.
Remember the dance language is, that life is.
Remember.

❧ New Orleans

This is the south. I look for evidence
of other Creeks, for remnants of voices,
or for tobacco brown bones to come wandering
down Conti Street, Royal, or Decatur.
Near the French Market I see a blue horse

caught frozen in stone in the middle of
a square. Brought in by the Spanish on
an endless ocean voyage he became mad
and crazy. They caught him in blue

10   rock, said
          don't talk.

I know it wasn't just a horse
              that went crazy.

Nearby is a shop with ivory and knives.
There are red rocks. The man behind the
counter has no idea that he is inside
magic stones. He should find out before
they destroy him. These things
have memory,

20   you know.

I have a memory.
              It swims deep in blood,
a delta in the skin. It swims out of Oklahoma,
deep the Mississippi River. It carries my
feet to these places: the French Quarter,
stale rooms, the sun behind thick and moist
clouds, and I hear boats hauling themselves up
and down the river.

My spirit comes here to drink.

30   My spirit comes here to drink.
Blood is the undercurrent.

There are voices buried in the Mississippi mud.
There are ancestors and future children
buried beneath the currents stirred up by
pleasure boats going up and down.
There are stories here made of memory.

I remember DeSoto.[1] He is buried somewhere in
this river, his bones sunk like the golden

---

[1] **DeSoto:** Hernando De Soto (1500–1542), Spanish explorer who led an expedition from Florida to the Mississippi delta; he was probably the first European to see the Mississippi River. When he died there, his men buried
his body in the river so that the Indians, whom he had bullied and mistreated, would not know of his death.
[Editors' note.]

40 treasure he traveled half the earth to find,
came looking for gold cities, for shining streets
of beaten gold to dance on with silk ladies.

He should have stayed home.

                    (Creeks knew of him for miles
                    before he came into town.
                    Dreamed of silver blades
                    and crosses.)

And knew he was one of the ones who yearned
for something his heart wasn't big enough
to handle.
50   (And DeSoto thought it was gold.)

The Creeks lived in earth towns,
                    not gold,
          spun children, not gold.
That's not what DeSoto thought he wanted to see.
The Creeks knew it, and drowned him in
          the Mississippi River
                    so he wouldn't have to drown himself.

Maybe his body is what I am looking for
as evidence. To know in another way
60 that my memory is alive.
But he must have got away, somehow,
because I have seen New Orleans,
the lace and silk buildings,
trolley cars on beaten silver paths,
graves that rise up out of soft earth in the rain,
shops that sell black mammy dolls
holding white babies.

And I know I have seen DeSoto,
                    having a drink on Bourbon Street,
70   mad and crazy
                    dancing with a woman as gold
                    as the river bottom.

She Had Some Horses

She had some horses.

She had horses who were bodies of sand.
She had horses who were maps drawn of blood.
She had horses who were skins of ocean water.
She had horses who were the blue air of sky.
She had horses who were fur and teeth.
She had horses who were clay and would break.
She had horses who were splintered red cliff.

She had some horses.

10   She had horses with eyes of trains.
She had horses with full, brown thighs.
She had horses who laughed too much.
She had horses who threw rocks at glass houses.
She had horses who liked razor blades.

She had some horses.

She had horses who danced in their mothers' arms.
She had horses who thought they were the sun and their
    bodies shone and burned like stars.
She had horses who waltzed nightly on the moon.
20   She had horses who were much too shy, and kept quiet
    in stalls of their own making.

She had some horses.

She had horses who liked Creek Stomp Dance songs.
She had horses who cried in their beer.
She had horses who spit at male queens who made
    them afraid of themselves.
She had horses who said they weren't afraid.
She had horses who lied.
She had horses who told the truth, who were stripped
30   bare of their tongues.

She had some horses.

She had horses who called themselves, *horse.*
She had horses who called themselves, *spirit,* and kept

their voices secret and to themselves.
She had horses who had no names.
She had horses who had books of names.

She had some horses.

She had horses who whispered in the dark, who were afraid to speak.
She had horses who screamed out of fear of the silence, who
40   carried knives to protect themselves from ghosts.
She had horses who waited for destruction.
She had horses who waited for resurrection.

She had some horses.

She had horses who got down on their knees for any saviour.
She had horses who thought their high price had saved them.
She had horses who tried to save her, who climbed in her
bed at night and prayed as they raped her.

She had some horses.

She had some horses she loved.
50   She had some horses she hated.

These were the same horses.

෴ I Give You Back

I release you, my beautiful and terrible
fear. I release you. You were my beloved
and hated twin, but now, I don't know you
as myself. I release you with all the
pain I would know at the death of
my children.

You are not my blood anymore.

I give you back to the soldiers
who burned down my home, beheaded my children,
10   raped and sodomized my brothers and sisters.

I give you back to those who stole the
food from our plates when we were starving.

I release you, fear, because you hold
these scenes in front of me and I was born
with eyes that can never close.

I release you
I release you
I release you
I release you

20   I am not afraid to be angry.
I am not afraid to rejoice.
I am not afraid to be black.
I am not afraid to be white.
I am not afraid to be hungry.
I am not afraid to be full.
I am not afraid to be hated.
I am not afraid to be loved.

to be loved, to be loved, fear.

Oh, you have choked me, but I gave you the leash.
30   You have gutted me but I gave you the knife.
You have devoured me, but I laid myself across the fire.

I take myself back, fear.
You are not my shadow any longer.
I won't hold you in my hands.
You can't live in my eyes, my ears, my voice
my belly, or in my heart my heart
my heart my heart

But come here, fear
I am alive and you are so afraid
40   of dying.

SANDRA CISNEROS
B. UNITED STATES, 1954

Throughout Sandra Cisneros's childhood, her Mexican American mother, her Mexican father, her six brothers, and she moved often between Mexico City and Chicago, never allowing her much time to get settled in either place. As a child she couldn't understand why her life didn't seem like the one projected onto her television screen. Her loneliness from not having sisters or friends drove her to bury herself in books. In high school she wrote poetry, but she didn't start writing seriously until her first creative writing class in college in 1974. After that it took a while to find her own voice: "I rejected what was at hand and emulated the voices of the poets I admired in books: big male voices like James Wright and Richard Hugo and Theodore Roethke, all wrong for me." Cisneros realized that she needed to write what she knew and adopted a writing style that was deliberately opposite to that of her classmates. After receiving her M.F.A. from the University of Iowa, she returned to Chicago to work in the Chicano barrio teaching high-school dropouts, a job that helped her develop the voice of a working-class Latina with an independent sexuality. Her work explores issues that are important to her: feminism, love, oppression, and religion. Her first novel, *The House on Mango Street* (1983), was awarded the Before Columbus American Book Award in 1985. Her other works include *Loose Woman: Poems* (1994); *Woman Hollering Creek and Other Stories* (1991), from which "Never Marry a Mexican" is taken; and another collection of poems, *My Wicked Wicked Ways* (1987). Cisneros has received the prestigious MacArthur Foundation Fellowship (1995) as well as many other national recognitions.

All notes are the editors'.

Never Marry a Mexican

Never marry a Mexican, my ma said once and always. She said this because of my father. She said this though she was Mexican too. But she was born here in the U.S., and he was born there, and it's *not* the same, you know.

I'll *never* marry. Not any man. I've known men too intimately. I've witnessed their infidelities, and I've helped them to it. Unzipped and unhooked and agreed to clandestine maneuvers. I've been accomplice, committed premeditated crimes. I'm guilty of having caused deliberate pain to other women. I'm vindictive and cruel, and I'm capable of anything.

I admit, there was a time when all I wanted was to belong to a man. To wear that gold band on my left hand and be worn on his arm like an expensive jewel brilliant in the light of day. Not the sneaking around I did in different bars that all looked the same, red carpets with a black grillwork design, flocked wallpaper, wooden wagon-wheel light fixtures with hurricane lampshades a sick amber color like the drinking glasses you get for free at gas stations.

Dark bars, dark restaurants then. And if not—my apartment, with his tooth-brush firmly planted in the toothbrush holder like a flag on the North Pole. The bed so big because he never stayed the whole night. Of course not.

Borrowed. That's how I've had my men. Just the cream skimmed off the top. Just the sweetest part of the fruit, without the bitter skin that daily living with a spouse can rend. They've come to me when they wanted the sweet meat then.

So, no. I've never married and never will. Not because I couldn't, but because I'm too romantic for marriage. Marriage has failed me, you could say. Not a man exists who hasn't disappointed me, whom I could trust to love the way I've loved. It's because I believe too much in marriage that I don't. Better to not marry than live a lie.

Mexican men, forget it. For a long time the men clearing off the tables or chop-ping meat behind the butcher counter or driving the bus I rode to school every day, those weren't men. Not men I considered as potential lovers. Mexican, Puerto Rican, Cuban, Chilean, Colombian, Panamanian, Salvadorean, Bolivian, Honduran, Argentine, Dominican, Venezuelan, Guatemalan, Ecuadorean, Nicaraguan, Peruvian, Costa Rican, Paraguayan, Uruguayan, I don't care. I never saw them. My mother did this to me.

I guess she did it to spare me and Ximena the pain she went through. Having married a Mexican man at seventeen. Having had to put up with all the grief a Mex-ican family can put on a girl because she was from *el otro lado,* the other side, and my father had married down by marrying her. If he had married a white woman from *el otro lado,* that would've been different. That would've been marrying up, even if the white girl was poor. But what could be more ridiculous than a Mexican girl who couldn't even speak Spanish, who didn't know enough to set a separate plate for each course at dinner, nor how to fold cloth napkins, nor how to set the silverware.

In my ma's house the plates were always stacked in the center of the table, the knives and forks and spoons standing in a jar, help yourself. All the dishes chipped or cracked and nothing matched. And no tablecloth, ever. And newspapers set on the table whenever my grandpa sliced watermelons, and how embarrassed she would be when her boyfriend, my father, would come over and there were newspapers all over the kitchen floor and table. And my grandpa, big hardworking Mexican man, saying Come, come and eat, and slicing a big wedge of those dark green watermelons, a big slice, he wasn't stingy with food. Never, even during the Depression. Come, come and eat, to whoever came knocking on the back door. Hobos sitting at the dinner table and the children staring and staring. Because my grandfather always made sure they never went without. Flour and rice, by the barrel and by the sack. Potatoes. Big bags of pinto beans. And watermelons, bought three or four at a time, rolled under his bed and brought out when you least expected. My grandpa had survived three wars, one Mexican, two American, and he knew what living without meant. He knew.

My father, on the other hand, did not. True, when he first came to this country he had worked shelling clams, washing dishes, planting hedges, sat on the back of the bus in Little Rock and had the bus driver shout, You — sit up here, and my father had shrugged sheepishly and said, No speak English.

But he was no economic refugee, no immigrant fleeing a war. My father ran away from home because he was afraid of facing his father after his first-year grades at the university proved he'd spent more time fooling around than studying. He left behind a house in Mexico City that was neither poor nor rich, but thought itself better than both. A boy who would get off a bus when he saw a girl he knew board if he didn't have the money to pay her fare. That was the world my father left behind.

I imagine my father in his *fanfarrón* clothes, because that's what he was, a *fanfarrón*. That's what my mother thought the moment she turned around to the voice that was asking her to dance. A big show-off, she'd say years later. Nothing but a big show-off. But she never said why she married him. My father in his shark-blue suits with the starched handkerchief in the breast pocket, his felt fedora, his tweed topcoat with the big shoulders, and heavy British wing tips with the pin-hole design on the heel and toe. Clothes that cost a lot. Expensive. That's what my father's things said. *Calidad.* Quality.

My father must've found the U.S. Mexicans very strange, so foreign from what he knew at home in Mexico City where the servant served watermelon on a plate with silverware and a cloth napkin, or mangos with their own special prongs. Not like this, eating with your legs wide open in the yard, or in the kitchen hunkered over newspapers. *Come, come and eat.* No, never like this.

How I make my living depends. Sometimes I work as a translator. Sometimes I get paid by the word and sometimes by the hour, depending on the job. I do this in the day, and at night I paint. I'd do anything in the day just so I can keep on painting.

I work as a substitute teacher, too, for the San Antonio Independent School District. And that's worse than translating those travel brochures with their tiny print, believe me. I can't stand kids. Not any age. But it pays the rent.

Any way you look at it, what I do to make a living is a form of prostitution. People say, "A painter? How nice," and want to invite me to their parties, have me decorate the lawn like an exotic orchid for hire. But do they buy art?

I'm amphibious. I'm a person who doesn't belong to any class. The rich like to have me around because they envy my creativity; they know they can't buy *that.* The poor don't mind if I live in their neighborhood because they know I'm poor like they are, even if my education and the way I dress keeps us worlds apart. I don't belong to any class. Not to the poor, whose neighborhood I share. Not to the rich, who come to my exhibitions and buy my work. Not to the middle class from which my sister Ximena and I fled.

When I was young, when I first left home and rented that apartment with my sister and her kids right after her husband left, I thought it would be glamorous to be an artist. I wanted to be like Frida or Tina.[1] I was ready to suffer with my camera and

---

[1]**Frida or Tina:** Frida Kahlo (1907–1954), Mexican painter famous for her self-portraits. Tina Modotti (1896–1942), Italian-born photographer who lived and worked in Hollywood and Mexico. Both artists are known for their bohemian lifestyles and association with Communist revolutionaries.

my paint brushes in that awful apartment we rented for $150 each because it had high ceilings and those wonderful glass skylights that convinced us we had to have it. Never mind there was no sink in the bathroom, and a tub that looked like a sarcophagus, and floorboards that didn't meet, and a hallway to scare away the dead. But fourteen-foot ceilings was enough for us to write a check for the deposit right then and there. We thought it all romantic. You know the place, the one on Zarzamora on top of the barber shop with the Casasola prints of the Mexican Revolution.[2] Neon BIRRIA TEPATITLÁN sign round the corner, two goats knocking their heads together, and all those Mexican bakeries, Las Brisas for *huevos rancheros* and *carnitas* and *barbacoa* on Sundays, and fresh fruit milk shakes, and mango *paletas*,[3] and more signs in Spanish than in English. We thought it was great, great. The barrio looked cute in the daytime, like Sesame Street. Kids hopscotching on the sidewalk, blessed little boogers. And hardware stores that still sold ostrich-feather dusters, and whole families marching out of Our Lady of Guadalupe Church on Sundays, girls in their swirly-whirly dresses and patent-leather shoes, boys in their dress Stacys and shiny shirts.

But nights, that was nothing like what we knew up on the north side. Pistols going off like the wild, wild West, and me and Ximena and the kids huddled in one bed with the lights off listening to it all, saying, Go to sleep, babies, it's just firecrackers. But we knew better. Ximena would say, Clemencia, maybe we should go home. And I'd say, Shit! Because she knew as well as I did there was no home to go home to. Not with our mother. Not with that man she married. After Daddy died, it was like we didn't matter. Like Ma was so busy feeling sorry for herself, I don't know. I'm not like Ximena. I still haven't worked it out after all this time, even though our mother's dead now. My half brothers living in that house that should've been ours, me and Ximena's. But that's—how do you say it?—water under the damn? I can't ever get the sayings right even though I was born in this country. We didn't say shit like that in our house.

Once Daddy was gone, it was like my ma didn't exist, like if she died, too. I used to have a little finch, twisted one of its tiny red legs between the bars of the cage once, who knows how. The leg just dried up and fell off. My bird lived a long time without it, just a little red stump of a leg. He was fine, really. My mother's memory is like that, like if something already dead dried up and fell off, and I stopped missing where she used to be. Like if I never had a mother. And I'm not ashamed to say it either. When she married that white man, and he and his boys moved into my father's house, it was as if she stopped being my mother. Like I never even had one.

Ma always sick and too busy worrying about her own life, she would've sold us to the Devil if she could. "Because I married so young, *mi'ja*,"[4] she'd say. "Because

---

[2] **Casasola . . . Revolution:** The Casasola brothers, Agustín Victor (1874–1938) and Miguel, began Mexico's first photo agency during revolution-era Mexico, around 1912. Agustín Victor is considered the photographer of the Mexican Revolution.

[3] *huevos rancheros . . . paletas:* Traditional Mexican egg-and-chile dish; Mexican dish of braised pork; barbeque; mango popsicle.

[4] *mi'ja:* Abbreviation of the Spanish *mi hija*, a term of endearment meaning "my daughter."

your father, he was so much older than me, and I never had a chance to be young. Honey, try to understand . . ." Then I'd stop listening.

That man she met at work, Owen Lambert, the foreman at the photo-finishing plant, who she was seeing even while my father was sick. Even then. That's what I can't forgive.

When my father was coughing up blood and phlegm in the hospital, half his face frozen, and his tongue so fat he couldn't talk, he looked so small with all those tubes and plastic sacks dangling around him. But what I remember most is the smell, like death was already sitting on his chest. And I remember the doctor scraping the phlegm out of my father's mouth with a white washcloth, and my daddy gagging and I wanted to yell, Stop, you stop that, he's my daddy. Goddamn you. Make him live. Daddy, don't. Not yet, not yet, not yet. And how I couldn't hold myself up, I couldn't hold myself up. Like if they'd beaten me, or pulled my insides out through my nostrils, like if they'd stuffed me with cinnamon and cloves, and I just stood there dry-eyed next to Ximena and my mother, Ximena between us because I wouldn't let her stand next to me. Everyone repeating over and over the Ave Marías and Padre Nuestros.[5] The priest sprinkling holy water, *mundo sin fin, amén.*[6]

Drew, remember when you used to call me your Malinalli?[7] It was a joke, a private game between us, because you looked like a Cortez with that beard of yours. My skin dark against yours. Beautiful, you said. You said I was beautiful, and when you said it, Drew, I was.

My Malinalli, Malinche,[8] my courtesan, you said, and yanked my head back by the braid. Calling me that name in between little gulps of breath and the raw kisses you gave, laughing from that black beard of yours.

Before daybreak, you'd be gone, same as always, before I even knew it. And it was as if I'd imagined you, only the teeth marks on my belly and nipples proving me wrong.

Your skin pale, but your hair blacker than a pirate's. Malinalli, you called me,

---

[5] **Ave . . . Nuestros:** Spanish for Hail Marys and Our Fathers.

[6] *mundo . . . amén:* Spanish for "World without end, amen."

[7] **Malinalli:** Another name for La Malinche (see footnote 8); native peoples called the young woman both Malintzin, "princess of suffering," and Malinalli, which refers to the twisted grass used as penance, which was passed through a hole in the tongue and knotted according to the number of sins being acknowledged. From the native point of view, Malintzin or Malinalli was a bringer of misfortune, a betrayer of her people.

[8] **Malinche:** La Malinche, or Doña Marina, is said to be the first woman to give birth to a *mestizo* Mexican. The daughter of a noble Aztec family at the time of the Spanish conquest of Mexico, she was sold into slavery by her people. Offered to Hernán Cortés (1485–1547), conqueror of Mexico, as a slave, she served as the interpreter at the first meetings between him and the representatives of Moctezuma. Some saw her as a prostitute who betrayed her people, others as an intelligent, religious, and loyal woman. The term "Malinchista" is often used today to describe a woman who acts out against the preestablished rules and norms of her community or her man. In the past twenty years many Chicana feminist theorists have rewritten the Malinche myth in order to understand Malintzin, as she is also known, in a more realistic context.

Your skin pale, but your hair blacker than a pirate's. Malinalli, you called me, remember? *Mi doradita.*[9] I liked when you spoke to me in my language. I could love myself and think myself worth loving.

Your son. Does he know how much I had to do with his birth? I was the one who convinced you to let him be born. Did you tell him, while his mother lay on her back laboring his birth, I lay in his mother's bed making love to you.

You're nothing without me. I created you from spit and red dust. And I can snuff you between my finger and thumb if I want to. Blow you to kingdom come. You're just a smudge of paint I chose to birth on canvas. And when I made you over, you were no longer a part of her, you were all mine. The landscape of your body taut as a drum. The heart beneath that hide thrumming and thrumming. Not an inch did I give back.

I paint and repaint you the way I see fit, even now. After all these years. Did you know that? Little fool. You think I went hobbling along with my life, whimpering and whining like some twangy country-and-western when you went back to her. But I've been waiting. Making the world look at you from my eyes. And if that's not power, what is?

Nights I light all the candles in the house, the ones to La Virgen de Guadalupe, the ones to El Niño Fidencio, Don Pedrito Jaramillo, Santo Niño de Atocha, Nuestra Señora de San Juan de los Lagos, and especially, Santa Lucía,[10] with her beautiful eyes on a plate.

Your eyes are beautiful, you said. You said they were the darkest eyes you'd ever seen and kissed each one as if they were capable of miracles. And after you left, I wanted to scoop them out with a spoon, place them on a plate under these blue blue skies, food for the blackbirds.

The boy, your son. The one with the face of that redheaded woman who is your wife. The boy red-freckled like fish food floating on the skin of water. That boy.

I've been waiting patient as a spider all these years, since I was nineteen and he was just an idea hovering in his mother's head, and I'm the one that gave him permission and made it happen, see.

Because your father wanted to leave your mother and live with me. Your mother whining for a child, at least *that.* And he kept saying, Later, we'll see, later. But all along it was me he wanted to be with, it was me, he said.

I want to tell you this evenings when you come to see me. When you're full of talk about what kind of clothes you're going to buy, and what you used to be like when you started high school and what you're like now that you're almost finished. And how everyone knows you as a rocker, and your band, and your new red guitar that you just got because your mother gave you a choice, a guitar or a car, but you don't need a car, do you, because I drive you everywhere. You could be my son if you weren't so light-skinned.

---

[9] *Mi doradita:* Spanish for "my little golden one."

[10] La Virgen . . . Lucía: Catholic and folk saints, many particular to Mexican culture and all popular along the Texas-Mexico border.

This happened. A long time ago. Before you were born. When you were a moth inside your mother's heart, I was your father's student, yes, just like you're mine now. And your father painted and painted me, because he said, I was his *doradita*, all golden and sun-baked, and that's the kind of woman he likes best, the ones brown as river sand, yes. And he took me under his wing and in his bed, this man, this teacher, your father. I was honored that he'd done me the favor. I was that young.

All I know is I was sleeping with your father the night you were born. In the same bed where you were conceived. I was sleeping with your father and didn't give a damn about that woman, your mother. If she was a brown woman like me, I might've had a harder time living with myself, but since she's not, I don't care. I was there first, always. I've always been there, in the mirror, under his skin, in the blood, before you were born. And he's been here in my heart before I even knew him. Understand? He's always been here. Always. Dissolving like a hibiscus flower, exploding like a rope into dust. I don't care what's right anymore. I don't care about his wife. She's not *my* sister.

And it's not the last time I've slept with a man the night his wife is birthing a baby. Why do I do that, I wonder? Sleep with a man when his wife is giving life, being suckled by a thing with its eyes still shut. Why do that? It's always given me a bit of crazy joy to be able to kill those women like that, without their knowing it. To know I've had their husbands when they were anchored in blue hospital rooms, their guts yanked inside out, the baby sucking their breasts while their husband sucked mine. All this while their ass stitches were still hurting.

Once, drunk on margaritas, I telephoned your father at four in the morning, woke the bitch up. Hello, she chirped. I want to talk to Drew. Just a moment, she said in her most polite drawing-room English. Just a moment. I laughed about that for weeks. What a stupid ass to pass the phone over to the lug asleep beside her. Excuse me, honey, it's for you. When Drew mumbled hello I was laughing so hard I could hardly talk. Drew? That dumb bitch of a wife of yours, I said, and that's all I could manage. That stupid stupid stupid. No Mexican woman would react like that. Excuse me, honey. It cracked me up.

He's got the same kind of skin, the boy. All the blue veins pale and clear just like his mama. Skin like roses in December. Pretty boy. Little clone. Little cells split into you and you and you. Tell me, baby, which part of you is your mother. I try to imagine her lips, her jaw, her long long legs that wrapped themselves around this father who took me to his bed.

This happened. I'm asleep. Or pretend to be. You're watching me, Drew. I feel your weight when you sit on the corner of the bed, dressed and ready to go, but now you're just watching me sleep. Nothing. Not a word. Not a kiss. Just sitting. You're taking me in, under inspection. What do you think already?

I haven't stopped dreaming you. Did you know that? Do you think it's strange? I never tell, though. I keep it to myself like I do all the thoughts I think of you.

After all these years.

I don't want you looking at me. I don't want you taking me in while I'm asleep. I'll open my eyes and frighten you away.

There. What did I tell you? *Drew? What is it?* Nothing. I'd knew you'd say that.

Let's not talk. We're no good at it. With you I'm useless with words. As if somehow I had to learn to speak all over again, as if the words I needed haven't been invented yet. We're cowards. Come back to bed. At least there I feel I have you for a little. For a moment. For a catch of the breath. You let go. You ache and tug. You rip my skin.

You're almost not a man without your clothes. How do I explain it? You're so much a child in my bed. Nothing but a big boy who needs to be held. I won't let anyone hurt you. My pirate. My slender boy of a man.

After all these years.

I didn't imagine it, did I? A Ganges,[11] an eye of the storm. For a little. When we forgot ourselves, you tugged me, I leapt inside you and split you like an apple. Opened for the other to look and not give back. Something wrenched itself loose. Your body doesn't lie. It's not silent like you.

You're nude as a pearl. You've lost your train of smoke. You're tender as rain. If I'd put you in my mouth you'd dissolve like snow.

You were ashamed to be so naked. Pulled back. But I saw you for what you are, when you opened yourself for me. When you were careless and let yourself through. I caught that catch of the breath. I'm not crazy.

When you slept, you tugged me toward you. You sought me in the dark. I didn't sleep. Every cell, every follicle, every nerve, alert. Watching you sigh and roll and turn and hug me closer to you. I didn't sleep. I was taking *you* in that time.

Your mother? Only once. Years after your father and I stopped seeing each other. At an art exhibition. A show on the photographs of Eugène Atget.[12] Those images, I could look at them for hours. I'd taken a group of students with me.

It was your father I saw first. And in that instant I felt as if everyone in the room, all the sepia-toned photographs, my students, the men in business suits, the high-heeled women, the security guards, everyone, could see me for what I was. I had to scurry out, lead my kids to another gallery, but some things destiny has cut out for you.

He caught up with us in the coat-check area, arm in arm with a redheaded Barbie doll in a fur coat. One of those scary Dallas types, hair yanked into a ponytail, big shiny face like the women behind the cosmetic counters at Neiman's.[13] That's what I remember. She must've been with him all along, only I swear I never saw her until that second.

---

[11] **Ganges:** A major river of the Indian subcontinent and an integral part of both the myth and reality of Indian and Bangladeshi cultures.

[12] **Eugène Atget** (1856–1927): The renowned French photographer Atget recorded Paris for thirty years, evoking a dream city replete with contradictions; his most famous images are evocative black-and-whites of the city's gardens, sculptures, and architecture.

[13] **Neiman's:** Neiman Marcus, an upscale department store chain.

You could tell from a slight hesitancy, only slight because he's too suave to hesitate, that he was nervous. Then he's walking toward me, and I didn't know what to do, just stood there dazed like those animals crossing the road at night when the headlights stun them.

And I don't know why, but all of a sudden I looked at my shoes and felt ashamed at how old they looked. And he comes up to me, my love, your father, in that way of his with that grin that makes me want to beat him, makes me want to make love to him, and he says in the most sincere voice you ever heard, "Ah, Clemencia! *This* is Megan." No introduction could've been meaner. *This* is Megan. Just like that.

I grinned like an idiot and held out my paw — "Hello, Megan" — and smiled too much the way you do when you can't stand someone. Then I got the hell out of there, chattering like a monkey all the ride back with my kids. When I got home I had to lie down with a cold washcloth on my forehead and the TV on. All I could hear throbbing under the washcloth in that deep part behind my eyes: *This* is Megan.

And that's how I fell asleep, with the TV on and every light in the house burning. When I woke up it was something like three in the morning. I shut the lights and TV and went to get some aspirin, and the cats, who'd been asleep with me on the couch, got up too and followed me into the bathroom as if they knew what's what. And then they followed me into bed, where they aren't allowed, but this time I just let them, fleas and all.

This happened, too. I swear I'm not making this up. It's all true. It was the last time I was going to be with your father. We had agreed. All for the best. Surely I could see that, couldn't I? My own good. A good sport. A young girl like me. Hadn't I understood . . . responsibilities. Besides, he could *never* marry *me*. You didn't think . . . ? *Never marry a Mexican. Never marry a Mexican* . . . No, of course not. I see. I see.

We had the house to ourselves for a few days, who knows how. You and your mother had gone somewhere. Was it Christmas? I don't remember.

I remember the leaded-glass lamp with the milk glass above the dining-room table. I made a mental inventory of everything. The Egyptian lotus design on the hinges of the doors. The narrow, dark hall where your father and I had made love once. The four-clawed tub where he had washed my hair and rinsed it with a tin bowl. This window. That counter. The bedroom with its light in the morning, incredibly soft, like the light from a polished dime.

The house was immaculate, as always, not a stray hair anywhere, not a flake of dandruff or a crumpled towel. Even the roses on the dining-room table held their breath. A kind of airless cleanliness that always made me want to sneeze.

Why was I so curious about this woman he lived with? Every time I went to the bathroom, I found myself opening the medicine cabinet, looking at all the things that were hers. Her Estée Lauder lipsticks. Corals and pinks, of course. Her nail polishes — mauve was as brave as she could wear. Her cotton balls and blond hairpins. A pair of bone-colored sheepskin slippers, as clean as the day she'd bought them. On the door hook — a white robe with a MADE IN ITALY label, and a silky nightshirt with pearl buttons. I touched the fabrics. *Calidad.* Quality.

I don't know how to explain what I did next. While your father was busy in the kitchen, I went over to where I'd left my backpack, and took out a bag of gummy bears I'd bought. And while he was banging pots, I went around the house and left a trail of them in places I was sure *she* would find them. One in her lucite makeup organizer. One stuffed inside each bottle of nail polish. I untwisted the expensive lipsticks to their full length and smushed a bear on the top before recapping them. I even put a gummy bear in her diaphragm case in the very center of that luminescent rubber moon.

Why bother? Drew could take the blame. Or he could say it was the cleaning woman's Mexican voodoo. I knew that, too. It didn't matter. I got a strange satisfaction wandering about the house leaving them in places only she would look.

And just as Drew was shouting, "Dinner!" I saw it on the desk. One of those wooden babushka dolls Drew had brought her from his trip to Russia. I know. He'd bought one just like it for me.

I just did what I did, uncapped the doll inside a doll inside a doll, until I got to the very center, the tiniest baby inside all the others, and this I replaced with a gummy bear. And then I put the dolls back, just like I'd found them, one inside the other, inside the other. Except for the baby, which I put inside my pocket. All through dinner I kept reaching in the pocket of my jean jacket. When I touched it, it made me feel good.

On the way home, on the bridge over the *arroyo*[14] on Guadalupe Street, I stopped the car, switched on the emergency blinkers, got out, and dropped the wooden toy into that muddy creek where winos piss and rats swim. The Barbie doll's toy stewing there in that muck. It gave me a feeling like nothing before and since.

Then I drove home and slept like the dead.

These mornings, I fix coffee for me, milk for the boy. I think of that woman, and I can't see a trace of my lover in this boy, as if she conceived him by immaculate conception.

I sleep with this boy, their son. To make the boy love me the way I love his father. To make him want me, hunger, twist in his sleep, as if he'd swallowed glass. I put him in my mouth. Here, little piece of my *corazón*.[15] Boy with hard thighs and just a bit of down and a small hard downy ass like his father's, and that back like a valentine. Come here, *mi cariñito*.[16] Come to *mamita*.[17] Here's a bit of toast.

I can tell from the way he looks at me, I have him in my power. Come, sparrow. I have the patience of eternity. Come to *mamita*. My stupid little bird. I don't move. I don't startle him. I let him nibble. All, all for you. Rub his belly. Stroke him. Before I snap my teeth.

What is it inside me that makes me so crazy at 2 A.M.? I can't blame it on alcohol in my blood when there isn't any. It's something worse. Something that poisons the

---

[14] *arroyo:* Spanish for "canyon" or "gully."   [15] *corazón:* Spanish for "heart."   [16] *mi cariñito:* Spanish for "My little beloved one."   [17] *mamita:* Spanish for "little mama"; diminutive form of *mother.*

blood and tips me when the night swells and I feel as if the whole sky were leaning against my brain.

And if I killed someone on a night like this? And if it was *me* I killed instead, I'd be guilty of getting in the line of crossfire, innocent bystander, isn't it a shame. I'd be walking with my head full of images and my back to the guilty. Suicide? I couldn't say. I didn't see it.

Except it's not me who I want to kill. When the gravity of the planets is just right, it all tilts and upsets the visible balance. And that's when it wants to out from my eyes. That's when I get on the telephone, dangerous as a terrorist. There's nothing to do but let it come.

So. What do you think? Are you convinced now I'm as crazy as a tulip or a taxi? As vagrant as a cloud?

Sometimes the sky is so big and I feel so little at night. That's the problem with being cloud. The sky is so terribly big. Why is it worse at night, when I have such an urge to communicate and no language with which to form the words? Only colors. Pictures. And you know what I have to say isn't always pleasant.

Oh, love, there. I've gone and done it. What good is it? Good or bad, I've done what I had to do and needed to. And you've answered the phone, and startled me away like a bird. And now you're probably swearing under your breath and going back to sleep, with that wife beside you, warm, radiating her own heat, alive under the flannel and down and smelling a bit like milk and hand cream, and that smell familiar and dear to you, oh.

Human beings pass me on the street, and I want to reach out and strum them as if they were guitars. Sometimes all humanity strikes me as lovely. I just want to reach out and stroke someone, and say There, there, it's all right, honey. There, there, there.

ᔕ Jimmy Santiago Baca
b. United States, 1952

A winner of the Pushcart Prize, the Before Columbus Foundation American Book Award, and a National Endowment of the Arts Literary Fellowship, Jimmy Santiago Baca has been called an heir to Pablo Neruda and one of the best poets in America today. Abandoned by both his parents, he and his brother were sent to an orphanage in Albuquerque, New Mexico. By thirteen he had been incarcerated for the first time, and at age twenty-one he was illiterate and jailed in a maximum-security facility for selling drugs. He emerged from prison five years later with a passion for reading and writing poetry. Baca received his B.A. from the University of New Mexico in 1984. He is the author of a memoir, *A Place to Stand* (1991), and numerous books of poetry, including *Martín and Meditations on the South Valley* (1987), *Black Mesa Poems* (1989), *Immigrants in Our*

Own Land (1991), *Healing Earthquakes* (2001), *C-Train* (2002), and *13 Mexicans* (2002). He has also written an essay collection, *Working in the Dark: Reflections on a Poet in the Barrio* (1992) and has worked with films, scripts, and productions. Baca's vision of himself as a "poet of the people" manifests in his involvement with writing workshops for children and adults at countless elementary, junior high and high schools, colleges, universities, reservations, barrio community centers, white ghettos, housing projects, and correctional facilities and prisons from coast to coast. He says in *A Place to Stand,* "I am a witness, not a victim. . . . My role as a witness is to give voice to the voiceless, hope to the hopeless, of which I am one."

All notes are the editors'.

∾ What We Don't Tell the Children

Feathers in the yard this morning.
My cat?
Or the two black strays,
ominously staring with orange eyes
from corrugated, rusted sheep-shed roof?
I hear them at night
yeowling—

shush of branches, squeals and shrieks,
then silence.

10   Tufts of rabbit fur
in backfield weeds, shred of meat
still warm on bones,
blood drops in warm earth.

Artist couple rented around the
corner last month. Were ecstatic
about this *primitive place.*
She came over one morning,
arm bandaged, boyfriend
stern-faced, sucking air through teeth,
20   she said, "My cat went belly up,
no animal is supposed to attack another
belly up. Those blacks are vicious.
Ought to be put to sleep."
Her Siamese crossed Blacks' territory,
she came upon them, kicked one Black,
and it scratched her arm in defense.

They moved out month after they moved in,
truck loaded with paintbrushes, canvasses,
cameras, to find another *primitive place*
30   near Santa Fe,[1] quaint artistic place,
tranquil as a pond in autumn evening
where golden-tipped wheat leans,
place with no problems, no animal
attacks another, where gentle folk
are as groomed as heirloom porcelain,
where there is no pollution, no drugs,
no world gone belly-up
the rest of us are trying to heal.

After they left, Antonio and I
40   sat on the patio, talking how he
and Blacks played hide-n-seek,
how he crouched in cool cracks
reaching his arm under boards

---

[1] **Santa Fe:** Capital of New Mexico and the oldest capital in the United States, founded by the Spanish conquistadors in 1610. Today it is known as an artists' mecca, attracting tourists from around the globe.

by the fence, they squirmed under,
pawing at him playfully, their claws
tucked in their furry mitten-paws
safely.
"Where's the other Black Papi²?"

"I don't know, *mejito,*³" I said.

---

² **Papi:** Spanish for "father"; diminutive form.
³ *mejito:* Abbreviation of the Spanish *mi hijito,* meaning "my little son."

❧ Family Ties

Mountain barbecue.
They arrive, young cousins singly,
older aunts and uncle in twos and threes,
like trees. I play with a new generation
of children, my hands in streambed silt
of their lives, a scuba diver's hands, dusting
surface sand for buried treasure.
Freshly shaved and powdered faces
of uncles and aunts surround taco
and tamale tables. Mounted elk head on wall,   10
brass rearing horse cowboy clock
on fireplace mantle. Sons and daughters
converse round beer and whiskey table.
Tempers ignite on land grant issues.¹
Children scurry round my legs.
Old bow-legged men toss horseshoes on lawn,
other farmhands from Mexico sit on a bench,
broken lives repaired for this occasion.
I feel no love or family tie here. I rise
to go hiking, to find abandoned rock cabins   20
in the mountains. We come to a grass clearing,
my wife rolls her jeans up past ankles,
wades ice cold stream, and I barefooted,
carry a son in each arm and follow.

---

¹ **land grant issues:** When New Mexico belonged to Spain and later to Mexico, land was distributed to citizens through a system of land grants, the three main types of which were Pueblo grants, given to the Indian pueblos; private grants; and community grants.

We cannot afford a place like this.
At the party again, I eat bean and chile
burrito, and after my third glass of rum,
we climb in the car and my wife drives
us home. My sons sleep in the back,
30   dream of the open clearing,
they are chasing each other with cattails
in the sunlit pasture, giggling,
as I stare out the window
at no trespassing signs white flashing past.

∾ Work We Hate and Dreams We Love

Every morning
Meiyo[1] revs his truck up
and lets it idle. Inside the small adobe house,
he sips coffee
while his Isleta[2] girlfriend
Cristi
brownbags his lunch.
Life is filled with work
Meiyo hates,
10   and while he saws, 2 × 4's,
trims lengths of 2 × 10's on table saw,
inside his veins another world
in full color etches
a blue sky on his bones,
a man following a bison herd,
and suddenly his hammer becomes a spear
he tosses to the ground
uttering a sound we do not understand.

[1] Meiyo: The name of Baca's brother.
[2] Isleta: Located just south of Albuquerque; one of the Indian pueblos whose ancestors have been traced to 700 B.C.E.

ℰ Meditations on the South Valley

XVI

Jefe,
todavía no saben[1] . . .

Under color of race
on your death certificate,
they have you down
as White.

You fought against that
label
all your short life, jefe,
and now they have you down
as White.

They had you down
when you lived, down
because you were too brown.

Dead on arrival
when you tried to be White.
You were brown as empty whiskey bottles,
and your accent was brown adobe dirt
you shattered bottles against.

Dead now,
you are White.
Under specify suicide or homicide,
I scribbled out accident and wrote in
Suicide—
scribbled out White and wrote in
Chicano. Erased caused by aspiration of meat
and wrote in
trying to be White.

---

[1] Jefe, . . . saben: Spanish for "Boss, they still don't know."

❧ Naomi Shihab Nye

b. *United States, 1952*

Born to a Palestinian father and an American mother, Naomi Shihab Nye grew up in St. Louis, Missouri; Jerusalem; and San Antonio, Texas. She received her B.A. from Trinity University in San Antonio, where she still resides with her family. She is the author of six books of poems, including *Fuel* (1998), *Red Suitcase* (1994), and *Hugging the Jukebox* (1982), and has also written books for children. She has twice traveled to the Middle East and Asia for the United States Information Agency, promoting international goodwill through the arts, and has worked as a visiting writer in schools for twenty-one years. Nye has received many awards, including the Pushcart Prize and the Texas Institute of Letters award. In her writing she draws on the voices of the Mexican Americans who live near her as well as on the perspectives of Arab Americans like herself and the ideas and practices of the different subcultures in America.

❧ Blood

"A true Arab knows how to catch a fly in his hands,"
my father would say. And he'd prove it,
cupping the buzzer instantly
while the host with the swatter stared.

In the spring our palms peeled like snakes.
True Arabs believed watermelon could heal fifty ways.
I changed these to fit the occasion.

Years before, a girl knocked,
wanted to see the Arab.
I said we didn't have one.
After that, my father told me who he was,
"Shihab" — "shooting star" —
a good name, borrowed from the sky.
Once I said, "When we die, we give it back?"
He said that's what a true Arab would say.

Today the headlines clot in my blood.
A little Palestinian dangles a truck on the front page.
Homeless fig, this tragedy with a terrible root

10

is too big for us. What flag can we wave?
20   I wave the flag of stone and seed,
    table mat stitched in blue.

I call my father, we talk around the news.
It is too much for him,
neither of his two languages can reach it.
I drive into the country to find sheep, cows,
to plead with the air:
Who calls anyone *civilized*?
Where can the crying heart graze?
What does a true Arab do now?

❧ My Father and the Figtree

For other fruits my father was indifferent.
He'd point at the cherry trees and say,
"See those? I wish they were figs."
In the evenings he sat by my bed
weaving folktales like vivid little scarves.
They always involved a figtree.
Even when it didn't fit, he'd stick it in.
Once Joha was walking down the road
and he saw a figtree.
10   Or, he tied his camel to a figtree
and went to sleep.
Or, later when they caught and arrested him,
his pockets were full of figs.

At age six I ate a dried fig and shrugged.
"That's not what I'm talking about!" he said.
"I'm talking about a fig straight from the earth—
gift of Allah!—on a branch so heavy it touches the ground.
I'm talking about picking the largest fattest sweetest fig
in the world and putting it in my mouth."
20   (Here he'd stop and close his eyes.)

Years passed, we lived in many houses, none had figtrees.
We had lima beans, zucchini, parsley, beets.
"Plant one!" my mother said, but my father never did.
He tended garden half-heartedly, forgot to water,

let the okra get too big.
"What a dreamer he is. Look how many things he starts
and doesn't finish."

The last time he moved, I had a phone call,
my father, in Arabic, chanting a song I'd never heard.
30   "What's that?"
"Wait till you see!"

He took me out to the new yard.
There, in the middle of Dallas, Texas,
a tree with the largest, fattest, sweetest figs in the world.
"It's a figtree song!" he said,
plucking his fruits like ripe tokens,
emblems, assurance
of a world that was always his own.

⌣ Arabic

(Jordan, 1992)

The man with laughing eyes stopped smiling
to say, "Until you speak Arabic —
— you will not understand pain."

Something to do with the back of the head,
an Arab carries sorrow in the back of the head
that only language cracks, the thrum of stones

weeping, grating hinge on an old metal gate.
"Once you know," he whispered, "you can enter the room
whenever you need to. Music you heard from a distance,

10   the slapped drum of a stranger's wedding,
wells up inside your skin, inside rain, a thousand
pulsing tongues. You are changed."

Outside, the snow had finally stopped.
In a land where snow rarely falls,
we had felt our days grow white and still.

I thought pain had no tongue. Or every tongue
at once, supreme translator, sieve. I admit my
shame. To live on the brink of Arabic, tugging

20 its rich threads without understanding
how to weave the rug . . . I have no gift.
The sound, but not the sense.

I kept looking over his shoulder for someone else
to talk to, recalling my dying friend who only scrawled
I can't write. What good would any grammar have been

to her then? I touched his arm, held it hard,
which sometimes you don't do in the Middle East, and said,
I'll work on it, feeling sad

for his good strict heart, but later in the slick street
hailed a taxi by shouting *Pain!* and it stopped
30 in every language and opened its doors.

✎ GISH JEN
B. UNITED STATES, 1956

The daughter of Chinese immigrants, Gish Jen grew up in Yonkers and Scarsdale, New York, and was educated at Harvard, Stanford, and the Iowa Writers' Workshop. Her first novel, *Typical American* (1991), described how Chinese immigrants in the United States are transformed by their efforts to pursue the American dream. Of herself she says, "My parents were born into a culture that puts society first [but] I was born into a culture that puts the individual first. This forced me to carve out a balance for myself." Jen's work has appeared in *The New Yorker, The New Republic,* and the *New York Times* as well as in a variety of anthologies, including *The Best American Short Stories of the Century.* Her two novels, *Typical American* and *Mona in the Promised Land* (1996), were both *New York Times* Notable Books. Her collection of short stories, *Who's Irish?,* from which this selection is taken, was published in 1999.

✎ Who's Irish?

In China, people say mixed children are supposed to be smart, and definitely my granddaughter Sophie is smart. But Sophie is wild, Sophie is not like my daughter Natalie, or like me. I am work hard my whole life, and fierce besides. My husband always used to say he is afraid of me, and in our restaurant, busboys and cooks all

Dean Wong,
*Grandmother Carries
Baby to Market
Chinese-Style,* 1993
*The Chinese woman
in this photograph
carries her grandchild
through the streets
of San Francisco's
Chinatown. (© Dean
Wong/CORBIS)*

afraid of me too. Even the gang members come for protection money, they try to talk to my husband. When I am there, they stay away. If they come by mistake, they pretend they are come to eat. They hide behind the menu, they order a lot of food. They talk about their mothers. Oh, my mother have some arthritis, need to take herbal medicine, they say. Oh, my mother getting old, her hair all white now.

I say, Your mother's hair used to be white, but since she dye it, it become black again. Why don't you go home once in a while and take a look? I tell them, Confucius say a filial son knows what color his mother's hair is.

My daughter is fierce too, she is vice president in the bank now. Her new house is big enough for everybody to have their own room, including me. But Sophie take after Natalie's husband's family, their name is Shea. Irish. I always thought Irish people are like Chinese people, work so hard on the railroad, but now I know why the Chinese beat the Irish. Of course, not all Irish are like the Shea family, of course not. My daughter tell me I should not say Irish this, Irish that.

How do you like it when people say the Chinese this, the Chinese that, she say.

You know, the British call the Irish heathen, just like they call the Chinese, she say.

You think the Opium War[1] was bad, how would you like to live right next door to the British, she say.

And that is that. My daughter have a funny habit when she win an argument, she take a sip of something and look away, so the other person is not embarrassed. So I am not embarrassed. I do not call anybody anything either. I just happen to mention

---

[1] **Opium War:** The first war between China and Britain, 1839–42, fought over trade imbalances. [Editors' note.]

about the Shea family, an interesting fact: four brothers in the family, and not one of them work. The mother, Bess, have a job before she got sick, she was executive secretary in a big company. She is handle everything for a big shot, you would be surprised how complicated her job is, not just type this, type that. Now she is a nice woman with a clean house. But her boys, every one of them is on welfare, or so-called severance pay, or so-called disability pay. Something. They say they cannot find work, this is not the economy of the fifties, but I say, Even the black people doing better these days, some of them live so fancy, you'd be surprised. Why the Shea family have so much trouble? They are white people, they speak English. When I come to this country, I have no money and do not speak English. But my husband and I own our restaurant before he die. Free and clear, no mortgage. Of course, I understand I am just lucky, come from a country where the food is popular all over the world. I understand it is not the Shea family's fault they come from a country where everything is boiled. Still, I say.

She's right, we should broaden our horizons, say one brother, Jim, at Thanksgiving. Forget about the car business. Think about egg rolls.

Pad thai, say another brother, Mike. I'm going to make my fortune in pad thai. It's going to be the new pizza.

I say, You people too picky about what you sell. Selling egg rolls not good enough for you, but at least my husband and I can say, We made it. What can you say? Tell me. What can you say?

Everybody chew their tough turkey.

I especially cannot understand my daughter's husband John, who has no job but cannot take care of Sophie either. Because he is a man, he say, and that's the end of the sentence.

Plain boiled food, plain boiled thinking. Even his name is plain boiled: John. Maybe because I grew up with black bean sauce and hoisin sauce and garlic sauce, I always feel something is missing when my son-in-law talk.

But, okay: so my son-in-law can be man, I am baby-sitter. Six hours a day, same as the old sitter, crazy Amy, who quit. This is not so easy, now that I am sixty-eight, Chinese age almost seventy. Still, I try. In China, daughter take care of mother. Here it is the other way around. Mother help daughter, mother ask, Anything else I can do? Otherwise daughter complain mother is not supportive. I tell daughter, We do not have this word in Chinese, *supportive.* But my daughter too busy to listen, she has to go to meeting, she has to write memo while her husband go to the gym to be a man. My daughter say otherwise he will be depressed. Seems like all his life he has this trouble, depression.

No one wants to hire someone who is depressed, she say. It is important for him to keep his spirits up.

Beautiful wife, beautiful daughter, beautiful house, oven can clean itself automatically. No money left over, because only one income, but lucky enough, got the baby-sitter for free. If John lived in China, he would be very happy. But he is not happy. Even at the gym things go wrong. One day, he pull a muscle. Another day, weight room too crowded. Always something.

Until finally, hooray, he has a job. Then he feel pressure.

I need to concentrate, he say. I need to focus.

He is going to work for insurance company. Salesman job. A paycheck, he say, and at least he will wear clothes instead of gym shorts. My daughter buy him some special candy bars from the health-food store. They say THINK! on them, and are supposed to help John think.

John is a good-looking boy, you have to say that, especially now that he shave so you can see his face.

I am an old man in a young man's game, say John.

I will need a new suit, say John.

This time I am not going to shoot myself in the foot, say John.

Good, I say.

She means to be supportive, my daughter say. Don't start the send her back to China thing, because we can't.

Sophie is three years old American age, but already I see her nice Chinese side swallowed up by her wild Shea side. She looks like mostly Chinese. Beautiful black hair, beautiful black eyes. Nose perfect size, not so flat looks like something fell down, not so large looks like some big deal got stuck in wrong face. Everything just right, only her skin is a brown surprise to John's family. So brown, they say. Even John say it. She never goes in the sun, still she is that color, he say. Brown. They say, Nothing the matter with brown. They are just surprised. So brown. Nattie is not that brown, they say. They say, It seems like Sophie should be a color in between Nattie and John. Seems funny, a girl named Sophie Shea be brown. But she is brown, maybe her name should be Sophie Brown. She never go in the sun, still she is that color, they say. Nothing the matter with brown. They are just surprised.

The Shea family talk is like this sometimes, going around and around like a Christmas-tree train.

Maybe John is not her father, I say one day, to stop the train. And sure enough, train wreck. None of the brothers ever say the word *brown* to me again.

Instead, John's mother, Bess, say, I hope you are not offended.

She say, I did my best on those boys. But raising four boys with no father is no picnic.

You have a beautiful family, I say.

I'm getting old, she say.

You deserve a rest, I say. Too many boys make you old.

I never had a daughter, she say. You have a daughter.

I have a daughter, I say. Chinese people don't think a daughter is so great, but you're right. I have a daughter.

I was never against the marriage, you know, she say. I never thought John was marrying down. I always thought Nattie was just as good as white.

I was never against the marriage either, I say. I just wonder if they look at the whole problem.

Of course you pointed out the problem, you are a mother, she say. And now we both have a granddaughter. A little brown granddaughter, she is so precious to me.

I laugh. A little brown granddaughter, I say. To tell you the truth, I don't know how she came out so brown.

We laugh some more. These days Bess need a walker to walk. She take so many pills, she need two glasses of water to get them all down. Her favorite TV show is about bloopers, and she love her bird feeder. All day long, she can watch that bird feeder, like a cat.

I can't wait for her to grow up, Bess say. I could use some female company.

Too many boys, I say.

Boys are fine, she say. But they do surround you after a while.

You should take a break, come live with us, I say. Lots of girls at our house.

Be careful what you offer, say Bess with a wink. Where I come from, people mean for you to move in when they say a thing like that.

Nothing the matter with Sophie's outside, that's the truth. It is inside that she is like not any Chinese girl I ever see. We go to the park, and this is what she does. She stand up in the stroller. She take off all her clothes and throw them in the fountain.

Sophie! I say. Stop!

But she just laugh like a crazy person. Before I take over as baby-sitter, Sophie has that crazy-person sitter, Amy the guitar player. My daughter thought this Amy very creative — another word we do not talk about in China. In China, we talk about whether we have difficulty or no difficulty. We talk about whether life is bitter or not bitter. In America, all day long, people talk about creative. Never mind that I cannot even look at this Amy, with her shirt so short that her belly button showing. This Amy think Sophie should love her body. So when Sophie take off her diaper, Amy laugh. When Sophie run around naked, Amy say she wouldn't want to wear a diaper either. When Sophie go *shu-shu,* in her lap, Amy laugh and say there are no germs in pee. When Sophie take off her shoes, Amy say bare feet is best, even the pediatrician say so. That is why Sophie now walk around with no shoes like a beggar child. Also why Sophie love to take off her clothes.

Turn around! say the boys in the park. Let's see that ass!

Of course, Sophie does not understand, Sophie clap her hands, I am the only one to say, No! This is not a game.

It has nothing to do with John's family, my daughter say, Amy was too permissive, that's all.

But I think if Sophie was not wild inside, she would not take off her shoes and clothes to begin with.

You never take off your clothes when you were little, I say. All my Chinese friends had babies, I never saw one of them act wild like that.

Look, my daughter say. I have a big presentation tomorrow.

John and my daughter agree Sophie is a problem, but they don't know what to do.

You spank her, she'll stop, I say another day.

But they say, Oh no.

In America, parents not supposed to spank the child.

It gives them low self-esteem, my daughter say. And that leads to problems later, as I happen to know.

My daughter never have big presentation the next day when the subject of spanking come up.

I don't want you to touch Sophie, she say. No spanking, period.

Don't tell me what to do, I say.

I'm not telling you what to do, say my daughter. I'm telling you how I feel.

I am not your servant, I say. Don't you dare talk to me like that.

My daughter have another funny habit when she lose an argument. She spread out all her fingers and look at them, as if she like to make sure they are still there.

My daughter is fierce like me, but she and John think it is better to explain to Sophie that clothes are a good idea. This is not so hard in the cold weather. In the warm weather, it is very hard.

Use your words, my daughter say. That's what we tell Sophie. How about if you set a good example.

As if good example mean anything to Sophie. I am so fierce, the gang members who used to come to the restaurant all afraid of me, but Sophie is not afraid.

I say, Sophie, if you take off your clothes, no snack.

I say, Sophie, if you take off your clothes, no lunch.

I say, Sophie, if you take off your clothes, no park.

Pretty soon we are stay home all day, and by the end of six hours she still did not have one thing to eat. You never saw a child stubborn like that.

I'm hungry! she cry when my daughter come home.

What's the matter, doesn't your grandmother feed you? My daughter laugh.

No! Sophie say. She doesn't feed me anything!

My daughter laugh again. Here you go, she say.

She say to John, Sophie must be growing.

Growing like a weed, I say.

Still Sophie take off her clothes, until one day I spank her. Not too hard, but she cry and cry, and when I tell her if she doesn't put her clothes back on I'll spank her again, she put her clothes back on. Then I tell her she is good girl, and give her some food to eat. The next day we go to the park and, like a nice Chinese girl, she does not take off her clothes.

She stop taking off her clothes, I report. Finally!

How did you do it? my daughter ask.

After twenty-eight years experience with you, I guess I learn something, I say.

It must have been a phase, John say, and his voice is suddenly like an expert.

His voice is like an expert about everything these days, now that he carry a leather briefcase, and wear shiny shoes, and can go shopping for a new car. On the company, he say. The company will pay for it, but he will be able to drive it whenever he want.

A free car, he say. How do you like that.

It's good to see you in the saddle again, my daughter say. Some of your family patterns are scary.

At least I don't drink, he say. He say, And I'm not the only one with scary family patterns.

That's for sure, say my daughter.

Everyone is happy. Even I am happy, because there is more trouble with Sophie, but now I think I can help her Chinese side fight against her wild side. I teach her to eat food with fork or spoon or chopsticks, she cannot just grab into the middle of a bowl of noodles. I teach her not to play with garbage cans. Sometimes I spank her, but not too often, and not too hard.

Still, there are problems. Sophie like to climb everything. If there is a railing, she is never next to it. Always she is on top of it. Also, Sophie like to hit the mommies of her friends. She learn this from her playground best friend, Sinbad, who is four. Sinbad wear army clothes every day and like to ambush his mommy. He is the one who dug a big hole under the play structure, a foxhole he call it, all by himself. Very hardworking. Now he wait in the foxhole with a shovel full of wet sand. When his mommy come, he throw it right at her.

Oh, it's all right, his mommy say. You can't get rid of war games, it's part of their imaginative play. All the boys go through it.

Also, he like to kick his mommy, and one day he tell Sophie to kick his mommy too.

I wish this story is not true.

Kick her, kick her! Sinbad say.

Sophie kick her. A little kick, as if she just so happened was swinging her little leg and didn't realize that big mommy leg was in the way. Still I spank Sophie and make Sophie say sorry, and what does the mommy say?

Really, it's all right, she say. It didn't hurt.

After that, Sophie learn she can attack mommies in the playground, and some will say, Stop, but others will say, Oh, she didn't mean it, especially if they realize Sophie will be punished.

This is how, one day, bigger trouble come. The bigger trouble start when Sophie hide in the foxhole with that shovel full of sand. She wait, and when I come look for her, she throw it at me. All over my nice clean clothes.

Did you ever see a Chinese girl act this way?

Sophie! I say. Come out of there, say you're sorry.

But she does not come out. Instead, she laugh. Naaah, naah-na, naaa-naaa, she say.

I am not exaggerate: millions of children in China, not one act like this.

Sophie! I say. Now! Come out now!

But she know she is in big trouble. She know if she come out, what will happen next. So she does not come out. I am sixty-eight, Chinese age almost seventy, how can I crawl under there to catch her? Impossible. So I yell, yell, yell, and what happen? Nothing. A Chinese mother would help, but American mothers, they look at you, they shake their head, they go home. And, of course, a Chinese child would give up, but not Sophie.

I hate you! she yell. I hate you, Meanie!

Meanie is my new name these days.

Long time this goes on, long long time. The foxhole is deep, you cannot see too much, you don't know where is the bottom. You cannot hear too much either. If she does not yell, you cannot even know she is still there or not. After a while, getting cold out, getting dark out. No one left in the playground, only us.

Sophie, I say. How did you become stubborn like this? I am go home without you now.

I try to use a stick, chase her out of there, and once or twice I hit her, but still she does not come out. So finally I leave. I go outside the gate.

Bye-bye! I say. I'm go home now.

But still she does not come out and does not come out. Now it is dinnertime, the sky is black. I think I should maybe go get help, but how can I leave a little girl by herself in the playground? A bad man could come. A rat could come. I go back in to see what is happen to Sophie. What if she have a shovel and is making a tunnel to escape?

Sophie! I say.

No answer.

Sophie!

I don't know if she is alive. I don't know if she is fall asleep down there. If she is crying, I cannot hear her.

So I take the stick and poke.

Sophie! I say. I promise I no hit you. If you come out, I give you a lollipop.

No answer. By now I worried. What to do, what to do, what to do? I poke some more, even harder, so that I am poking and poking when my daughter and John suddenly appear.

What are you doing? What is going on? say my daughter.

Put down that stick! say my daughter.

You are crazy! say my daughter.

John wiggle under the structure, into the foxhole, to rescue Sophie.

She fell asleep, say John the expert. She's okay. That is one big hole.

Now Sophie is crying and crying.

Sophia, my daughter say, hugging her. Are you okay, peanut? Are you okay?

She's just scared, say John.

Are you okay? I say too. I don't know what happen, I say.

She's okay, say John. He is not like my daughter, full of questions. He is full of answers until we get home and can see by the lamplight.

Will you look at her? he yell then. What the hell happened?

Bruises all over her brown skin, and a swollen-up eye.

You are crazy! say my daughter. Look at what you did! You are crazy!

I try very hard, I say.

How could you use a stick? I told you to use your words!

She is hard to handle, I say.

She's three years old! You cannot use a stick! say my daughter.

She is not like any Chinese girl I ever saw, I say.

I brush some sand off my clothes. Sophie's clothes are dirty too, but at least she has her clothes on.

Has she done this before? ask my daughter. Has she hit you before?

She hits me all the time, Sophie say, eating ice cream.

Your family, say John.

Believe me, say my daughter.

A daughter I have, a beautiful daughter, I took care of her when she could not hold her head up. I took care of her before she could argue with me, when she was a little girl with two pigtails, one of them always crooked. I took care of her when we have to escape from China, I took care of her when suddenly we live in a country with cars everywhere, if you are not careful your little girl get run over. When my husband die, I promise him I will keep the family together, even though it was just two of us, hardly a family at all.

But now my daughter take me around to look at apartments. After all, I can cook, I can clean, there's no reason I cannot live by myself, all I need is a telephone. Of course, she is sorry. Sometimes she cry, I am the one to say everything will be okay. She say she have no choice, she doesn't want to end up divorced. I say divorce is terrible, I don't know who invented this terrible idea. Instead of live with a telephone, though, surprise, I come to live with Bess. Imagine that. Bess make an offer and, sure enough, where she come from, people mean for you to move in when they say things like that. A crazy idea, go to live with someone else's family, but she like to have some female company, not like my daughter, who does not believe in company. These days when my daughter visit, she does not bring Sophie. Bess say we should give Nattie time, we will see Sophie again soon. But seems like my daughter have more presentation than ever before, every time she come she have to leave.

I have a family to support, she say, and her voice is heavy, as if soaking wet. I have a young daughter and a depressed husband and no one to turn to.

When she say no one to turn to, she mean me.

These days my beautiful daughter is so tired she can just sit there in a chair and fall asleep. John lost his job again, already, but still they rather hire a baby-sitter than ask me to help, even they can't afford it. Of course, the new baby-sitter is much younger, can run around. I don't know if Sophie these days is wild or not wild. She call me Meanie, but she like to kiss me too, sometimes. I remember that every time I see a child on TV. Sophie like to grab my hair, a fistful in each hand, and then kiss me smack on the nose. I never see any other child kiss that way.

The satellite TV has so many channels, more channels than I can count, including a Chinese channel from the Mainland and a Chinese channel from Taiwan, but most of the time I watch bloopers with Bess. Also, I watch the bird feeder—so many, many kinds of birds come. The Shea sons hang around all the time, asking when will I go home, but Bess tell them, Get lost.

She's a permanent resident, say Bess. She isn't going anywhere.

Then she wink at me, and switch the channel with the remote control.

Of course, I shouldn't say Irish this, Irish that, especially now I am become honorary Irish myself, according to Bess. Me! Who's Irish? I say, and she laugh. All the same, if I could mention one thing about some of the Irish, not all of them of course, I like to mention this: Their talk just stick. I don't know how Bess Shea learn to use her words, but sometimes I hear what she say a long time later. *Permanent resident. Not going anywhere.* Over and over I hear it, the voice of Bess.

❧ EDWIDGE DANTICAT
B. HAITI, 1969

> Edwidge Danticat emigrated from Haiti to the United States in 1981, studying French at Barnard College and receiving an M.F.A. from Brown University in 1993. At the age of twenty-six, in 1995, she became a finalist for the National Book Award for *Krik? Krak!* and received the Pushcart Short Story Prize. When she was a child, her parents immigrated to New York without her; until she joined them at the age of twelve, Danticat was raised by an aunt. As a result her childhood was deeply influenced by Haitian oral storytelling. Her first novel, *Breath, Eyes, Memory* (1994), speaks of four generations of Haitian women who must overcome their poverty and powerlessness. Her latest novel, *The Farming of Bones* (1998), highlights the connection between language and personal and social meaning. The characters in the novel actively create histories through the stories they tell about the 1937 massacre, when some ten to fifteen thousand Haitians were killed by Dominican troops in a border struggle between Haiti and its neighbor, the Dominican Republic. The book's title plays on the multiple meanings of language, referring to both the massacre and the gathering of cane, and so invokes the events of 1937 as well as the economic history that created them. *Krik? Krak!* (1995), from which the selection here is taken, is a collection of short stories about Haiti and Haitian Americans. The title originates from the Haitian tradition of a storyteller calling out "Krik?" and willing listeners gathering around and answering "Krak!"
>
> All notes are the editors'.

❧ Children of the Sea

They say behind the mountains are more mountains. Now I know it's true. I also know there are timeless waters, endless seas, and lots of people in this world whose names don't matter to anyone but themselves. I look up at the sky and I see you there. I see you crying like a crushed snail, the way you cried when I helped you pull out your first loose tooth. Yes, I did love you then. Somehow when I looked at you, I thought of fiery red ants. I wanted you to dig your fingernails into my skin and drain out all my blood.

I don't know how long we'll be at sea. There are thirty-six other deserting souls on this little boat with me. White sheets with bright red spots float as our sail.

When I got on board I thought I could still smell the semen and the innocence lost to those sheets. I look up there and I think of you and all those times you resisted. Sometimes I felt like you wanted to, but I knew you wanted me to respect you. You thought I was testing your will, but all I wanted was to be near you. Maybe it's like you've always said. I imagine too much. I am afraid I am going to start having nightmares once we get deep at sea. I really hate having the sun in my face all day long. If you see me again, I'll be so dark.

Your father will probably marry you off now, since I am gone. Whatever you do, please don't marry a soldier. They're almost not human.

haiti est comme tu l'as laissé. yes, just the way you left it. bullets day and night. same hole. same everything. i'm tired of the whole mess. i get so cross and irritable. i pass the time by chasing roaches around the house. i pound my heel on their heads. they make me so mad. everything makes me mad. i am cramped inside all day. they've closed the schools since the army took over. no one is mentioning the old president's[1] name. papa burnt all his campaign posters and old buttons. manman buried her buttons in a hole behind the house. she thinks he might come back. she says she will unearth them when he does. no one comes out of their house. not a single person. papa wants me to throw out those tapes of your radio shows. i destroyed some music tapes, but i still have your voice. i thank god you got out when you did. all the other youth federation members have disappeared. no one has heard from them. i think they might all be in prison. maybe they're all dead. papa worries a little about you. he doesn't hate you as much as you think. the other day i heard him asking manman, do you think the boy is dead? manman said she didn't know. i think he regrets being so mean to you. i don't sketch my butterflies anymore because i don't even like seeing the sun. besides, manman says that butterflies can bring news. the bright ones bring happy news and the black ones warn us of deaths. we have our whole lives ahead of us. you used to say that, remember? but then again things were so very different then.

There is a pregnant girl on board. She looks like she might be our age. Nineteen or twenty. Her face is covered with scars that look like razor marks. She is short and speaks in a singsong that reminds me of the villagers in the north. Most of the other people on the boat are much older than I am. I have heard that a lot of these boats have young children on board. I am glad this one does not. I think it would break my heart watching some little boy or girl every single day on this sea, looking into their

---

[1] **the old president:** Jean-Bertrand Aristide (b. 1953), democratically elected president of Haiti in 1990, held office for seven months in 1991 and again from 1994 to 1996.

empty faces to remind me of the hopelessness of the future in our country. It's hard enough with the adults. It's hard enough with me.

I used to read a lot about America before I had to study so much for the university exams. I am trying to think, to see if I read anything more about Miami. It is sunny. It doesn't snow there like it does in other parts of America. I can't tell exactly how far we are from there. We might be barely out of our own shores. There are no borderlines on the sea. The whole thing looks like one. I cannot even tell if we are about to drop off the face of the earth. Maybe the world is flat and we are going to find out, like the navigators of old. As you know, I am not very religious. Still I pray every night that we won't hit a storm. When I do manage to sleep, I dream that we are caught in one hurricane after another. I dream that the winds come of the sky and claim us for the sea. We go under and no one hears from us again.

I am more comfortable now with the idea of dying. Not that I have completely accepted it, but I know that it might happen. Don't be mistaken. I really do not want to be a martyr. I know I am no good to anybody dead, but if that is what's coming, I know I cannot just scream at it and tell it to go away.

I hope another group of young people can do the radio show. For a long time that radio show was my whole life. It was nice to have radio like that for a while, where we could talk about what we wanted from government, what we wanted for the future of our country.

There are a lot of Protestants on this boat. A lot of them see themselves as Job or the Children of Israel. I think some of them are hoping something will plunge down from the sky and part the sea for us. They say the Lord gives and the Lord takes away. I have never been given very much. What was there to take away?

if only I could kill. if i knew some good *wanga* magic,[2] i would wipe them off the face of the earth. a group of students got shot in front of fort dimanche prison today. they were demonstrating for the bodies of the radio six. that is what they are calling you all. the radio six. you have a name. you have a reputation. a lot of people think you are dead like the others. they want the bodies turned over to the families. this afternoon, the army finally did give some bodies back. they told the families to go collect them at the rooms for indigents at the morgue. our neighbor madan roger came home with her son's head and not much else. honest to god, it was just his head. at the morgue, they say a car ran over him and took the head off his body. when madan roger went to the morgue, they gave her the head. by the time we saw her, she had been carrying the head all over port-au-prince.[3] just to show what's

---

[2] *wanga* magic: *Wanga,* or magic charms in the *vodou* religion of Haiti, are fetishes that concentrate spiritual power in order to protect oneself from or to attack one's enemies, but not to the extent of death. This religion is a syncretization, or intermixing, of African Benin and Christian faiths whose intricate and complex set of practices do not much resemble those of Western religions. At its foundation is a belief in spirits, or *lwa,* that mediate between the human and the natural and supernatural worlds. Together, the *lwa* form a pantheon much like a family or ensemble, each *lwa* having a particular realm over which it rules. They are not gods, but mediators between a monotheistic god and humans; each *lwa* has been associated with a Catholic saint.

[3] port-au-prince: Port-au-Prince, the capital of Haiti and its largest city.

been done to her son. the macoutes[4] by the house were laughing at her. they asked her if that was her dinner. it took ten people to hold her back from jumping on them. they would have killed her, the dogs. i will never go outside again. not even in the yard to breathe the air. they are always watching you, like vultures. at night i can't sleep. i count the bullets in the dark. i keep wondering if it is true. did you really get out? i wish there was some way i could be sure that you really went away. yes, i will. i will keep writing like we promised to do. i hate it, but i will keep writing. you keep writing too, okay? and when we see each other again, it will seem like we lost no time.

Today was our first real day at sea. Everyone was vomiting with each small rocking of the boat. The faces around me are showing their first charcoal layer of sunburn. "Now we will never be mistaken for Cubans,"[5] one man said. Even though some of the Cubans are black too. The man said he was once on a boat with a group of Cubans. His boat had stopped to pick up the Cubans on an island off the Bahamas. When the Coast Guard came for them, they took the Cubans to Miami and sent him back to Haiti. Now he was back on the boat with some papers and documents to show that the police in Haiti were after him. He had a broken leg too, in case there was any doubt.

One old lady fainted from sunstroke. I helped revive her by rubbing some of the salt water on her lips. During the day it can be so hot. At night, it is so cold. Since there are no mirrors, we look at each others faces to see just how frail and sick we are starting to look.

Some of the women sing and tell stories to each other to appease the vomiting. Still, I watch the sea. At night, the sky and the sea are one. The stars look so huge and so close. They make for very bright reflections in the sea. At times I feel like I can just reach out and pull a star down from the sky as though it is a breadfruit or a calabash or something that could be of use to us on this journey.

When we sing, *Beloved Haiti, there is no place like you. I had to leave you before I could understand you,* some of the women start crying. At times, I just want to stop in the middle of the song and cry myself. To hide my tears, I pretend like I am getting another attack of nausea, from the sea smell. I no longer join in the singing.

You probably do not know much about this, because you have always been so closely watched by your father in that well-guarded house with your genteel mother. No, I am not making fun of you for this. If anything, I am jealous. If I was a girl, maybe I would have been at home and not out politicking and getting myself into something like this. Once you have been at sea for a couple of days, it smells like every fish you have ever eaten, every crab you have ever caught, every jellyfish that

---

[4] **the macoutes:** The *tonton macoutes,* the infamously brutal paramilitary troops who pursued and executed the opponents of "Papa Doc" Duvalier (1907–1971), the president of Haiti. Duvalier was elected president in 1957, and in 1964 he declared himself president for life. His rule of Haiti was a cruel dictatorship. The *tonton macoutes* are still a potent military force in the country.

[5] **". . . mistaken for Cubans":** Many Cuban people leave their home for the United States in the same manner as the Haitian boat people described in this story.

has ever bitten your leg. I am so tired of the smell. I am also tired of the way the people on this boat are starting to stink. The pregnant girl, Célianne, I don't know how she takes it. She stares into space all the time and rubs her stomach.

I have never seen her eat. Sometimes the other women offer her a piece of bread and she takes it, but she has no food of her own. I cannot help feeling like she will have this child as soon as she gets hungry enough.

She woke up screaming the other night. I thought she had a stomach ache. Some water started coming into the boat in the spot where she was sleeping. There is a crack at the bottom of the boat that looks as though, if it gets any bigger, it will split the boat in two. The captain cleared us aside and used some tar to clog up the hole. Everyone started asking him if it was okay, if they were going to be okay. He said he hoped the Coast Guard would find us soon.

You can't really go to sleep after that. So we all stared at the tar by the moonlight. We did this until dawn. I cannot help but wonder how long this tar will hold out.

papa found your tapes. he started yelling at me, asking if I was crazy keeping them. he is just waiting for the gasoline ban to be lifted so we can get out of the city. he is always pestering me these days because he cannot go out driving his van. all the american factories are closed.[6] he kept yelling at me about the tapes. he called me selfish, and he asked if i hadn't seen or heard what was happening to man-crazy whores like me. i shouted that i wasn't a whore. he had no business calling me that. he pushed me against the wall for disrespecting him. he spat in my face. i wish those macoutes would kill him. i wish he would catch a bullet so we could see how scared he really is. he said to me, i didn't send your stupid trouble maker away. i started yelling at him. yes, you did. yes, you did. yes, you did, you pig peasant. i don't know why i said that. he slapped me and kept slapping me really hard until manman came and grabbed me away from him. i wish one of those bullets would hit me.

The tar is holding up so far. Two days and no more leaks. Yes, I am finally an African. I am even darker than your father. I wanted to buy a straw hat from one of the ladies, but she would not sell it to me for the last two gourdes[7] I have left in change. Do you think your money is worth anything to me here? she asked me. Sometimes, I forget where I am. If I keep daydreaming like I have been doing, I will walk off the boat to go for a stroll.

The other night I dreamt that I died and went to heaven. This heaven was nothing like I expected. It was at the bottom of the sea. There were starfishes and mermaids all around me. The mermaids were dancing and singing in Latin like the priests do at the cathedral during Mass. You were there with me too, at the bottom of the sea. You were with your family, off to the side. Your father was acting like he was better than everyone else and he was standing in front of a sea cave blocking

---

[6] **all . . . closed:** Many North American companies, attracted to Haiti because of the low labor costs, pulled out during the political uncertainties of the 1990s.

[7] **gourdes:** Official currency of Haiti.

you from my view. I tried to talk to you, but every time I opened my mouth, water bubbles came out. No sounds.

they have this thing now that they do. if they come into a house and there is a son and mother there, they hold a gun to their heads. they make the son sleep with his mother. if it is a daughter and father, they do the same thing. some nights papa sleeps at his brother's, uncle pressoir's house. uncle pressoir sleeps at our house, just in case they come. that way papa will never be forced to lie down in bed with me. instead, uncle pressoir would be forced to, but that would not be so bad. we know a girl who had a child by her father that way. that is what papa does not want to happen, even if he is killed. there is still no gasoline to buy. otherwise we would be in ville rose already. papa has a friend who is going to get him some gasoline from a soldier. as soon as we get the gasoline, we are going to drive quick and fast until we find civilization. that's how papa puts it, civilization. he says things are not as bad in the provinces. i am still not talking to him. i don't think i ever will. manman says it is not his fault. he is trying to protect us. he cannot protect us. only god can protect us. the soldiers can come and do with us what they want. that makes papa feel weak, she says. he gets angry when he feels weak. why should he be angry with me? i am not one of the pigs with the machine guns. she asked me what really happened to you. she said she saw your parents before they left for the provinces. they did not want to tell her anything. i told her you took a boat after they raided the radio station. you escaped and took a boat to heaven knows where. she said, he was going to make a good man, that boy. sharp, like a needle point, that boy, he took the university exams a year before everyone else in this area. manman has respect for people with ambitions. she said papa did not want you for me because it did not seem as though you were going to do any better for me than he and manman could. he wants me to find a man who will do me some good. someone who will make sure that i have more than i have now. it is not enough for a girl to be just pretty anymore. we are not that well connected in society. the kind of man that papa wants for me would never have anything to do with me. all anyone can hope for is just a tiny bit of love, manman says, like a drop in a cup if you can get it, or a waterfall, a flood, if you can get that too. we do not have all that many high-up connections, she says, but you are an educated girl. what she counts for educated is not much to anyone but us anyway. they should be announcing the university exams on the radio next week. then i will know if you passed. i will listen for your name.

We spent most of yesterday telling stories. Someone says, Krik? You answer, Krak! And they say, I have many stories I could tell you, and then they go on and tell these stories to you, but mostly to themselves. Sometimes it feels like we have been at sea longer than the many years that I have been on this earth. The sun comes up and goes down. That is how you know it has been a whole day. I feel like we are sailing for Africa. Maybe we will go to Guinin,[8] to live with the spirits, to be with everyone who

---

[8] **Guinin:** Guinea, in Africa, where the *vodou* faithful believe the *lwa*, or spirits, originated. It is a region considered irretrievably lost and purely mythical.

has come and has died before us. They would probably turn us away from there too. Someone has a transistor and sometimes we listen to radio from the Bahamas. They treat Haitians like dogs in the Bahamas, a woman says. To them, we are not human. Even though their music sounds like ours. Their people look like ours. Even though we had the same African fathers who probably crossed these same seas together.

Do you want to know how people go to the bathroom on the boat? Probably the same way they did on those slaves ships years ago. They set aside a little corner for that. When I have to pee, I just pull it, lean over the rail, and do it very quickly. When I have to do the other thing, I rip a piece of something, squat down and do it, and throw the waste in the sea. I am always embarrassed by the smell. It is so demeaning having to squat in front of so many people. People turn away, but not always. At times I wonder if there is really land on the other side of the sea. Maybe the sea is endless. Like my love for you.

last night they came to madan roger's house. papa hurried inside as soon as madan roger's screaming started. the soldiers were looking for her son. madan roger was screaming, you killed him already. we buried his head. you can't kill him twice. they were shouting at her, do you belong to the youth federation with those vagabonds who were on the radio? she was yelling, do i look like a youth to you? can you identify your son's other associates? they asked her. papa had us tiptoe from the house into the latrine out back. we could hear it all from there. i thought i was going to choke on the smell of rotting poupou. they kept shouting at madan roger, did your son belong to the youth federation? wasn't he on the radio talking about the police? did he say, down with tonton macoutes? did he say, down with the army? he said that the military had to go; didn't he write slogans? he had meetings, didn't he? he demonstrated on the streets. you should have advised him better. she cursed on their mothers' graves. she just came out and shouted it, i hope your mothers will never rest in their cursed graves! she was just shouting it out, you killed him once already! you want to kill me too? go ahead. i don't care anymore. i'm dead already. you have already done the worst to me that you can do. you have killed my soul. they kept at it, asking her questions at the top of their voices: was your son a traitor? tell me all the names of his friends who were traitors just like him. madan roger finally shouts, yes, he was one! he belonged to that group. he was on the radio. he was on the streets at these demonstrations. he hated you like i hate you criminals. you killed him. they start to pound at her. you can hear it. you can hear the guns coming down on her head. it sounds like they are cracking all the bones in her body. manman whispers to papa, you can't just let them kill her. go and give them some money like you gave them for your daughter. papa says, the only money i have left is to get us out of here tomorrow. manman whispers, we cannot just stay here and let them kill her. manman starts moving like she is going out the door. papa grabs her neck and pins her to the latrine wall. tomorrow we are going to ville rose, he says. you will not spoil that for the family. you will not put us in that situation. you will not get us killed. going out there will be like trying to raise the dead. she is not dead yet, manman says, maybe we can help her. i will make you stay if i have to, he says to her. my mother buries her face in the latrine wall. she starts to cry. you can hear madan roger screaming. they are beating her, pounding on her until you don't hear anything else. manman tells papa, you cannot let them kill somebody just because you are afraid. papa says, oh yes, you *can* let them kill somebody because you are afraid. they are the law. it is their right. we are just being good citizens, following the law of the land. it has happened before all over this country and tonight it will happen again and there is nothing we can do.

Célianne spent the night groaning. She looks like she has been ready for a while, but maybe the child is being stubborn. She just screamed that she is bleeding. There is an older woman here who looks like she has had a lot of children herself. She says Célianne is not bleeding at all. Her water sack has broken.

The only babies I have ever seen right after birth are baby mice. Their skin looks veil thin. You can see all the blood vessels and all their organs. I have always wanted to poke them to see if my finger would go all the way through the skin.

I have moved to the other side of the boat so I will not have to look *inside* Célianne. People are just watching. The captain asks the midwife to keep Célianne steady so she will not rock any more holes into the boat. Now we have three cracks covered with tar. I am scared to think of what would happen if we had to choose among ourselves who would stay on the boat and who should die. Given the choice to make a decision like that, we would all act like vultures, including me.

The sun will set soon. Someone says that this child will be just another pair of hungry lips. At least it will have its mother's breasts, says an old man. Everyone will eat their last scraps of food today.

there is a rumor that the old president is coming back. there is a whole bunch of people going to the airport to meet him. papa says we are not going to stay in port-au-prince to find out if this is true or if it is a lie. they are selling gasoline at the market again. the carnival groups[9] have taken to the streets. we are heading the other way, to ville rose. maybe there i will be able to sleep at night. it is not going to turn out well with the old president coming back, manman now says. people are just too hopeful, and sometimes hope is the biggest weapon of all to use against us. people will believe anything. they will claim to see the christ return and march on the cross backwards if there is enough hope. manman told papa that you took the boat. papa told me before we left this morning that he thought himself a bad father for everything that happened. he says a father should be able to speak to his children like a civilized man. all the craziness here has made him feel like he cannot do that anymore. all he wants to do is live. he and manman have not said a word to one another since we left the latrine. i know that papa does not hate us, not in the way that i hate those soldiers, those macoutes, and all those people here who shoot guns. on our way to ville rose, we saw dogs licking two dead faces. one of them was a little boy who was lying on the side of the road with the sun in his dead open eyes. we saw a soldier

---

[9] **carnival groups:** Traditionally, groups of people form to sing and dance in procession throughout the Haitian countryside, starting at Mardi Gras and continuing each weekend during Lent.

shoving a woman out of a hut, calling her a witch. he was shaving the woman's head, but of course we never stopped. papa didn't want to go in madan roger's house and check on her before we left. he thought the soldiers might still be there. papa was driving the van real fast. i thought he was going to kill us. we stopped at an open market on the way. manman got some black cloth for herself and for me. she cut the cloth in two pieces and we wrapped them around our heads to mourn madan roger. when i am used to ville rose, maybe i will sketch you some butterflies, depending on the news that they bring me.

Célianne had a girl baby. The woman acting as a midwife is holding the baby to the moon and whispering prayers. . . . *God, this child You bring into the world, please guide her as You please through all her days on this earth.* The baby has not cried.

We had to throw our extra things in the sea because the water is beginning to creep in slowly. The boat needs to be lighter. My two gourdes in change had to be thrown overboard as an offering to Agwé,[10] the spirit of the water. I heard the captain whisper to someone yesterday that they might have to *do something* with some of the people who never recovered from seasickness. I am afraid that soon they may ask me to throw out this notebook. We might all have to strip down to the way we were born, to keep ourselves from drowning.

Célianne's child is a beautiful child. They are calling her Swiss, because the word *Swiss* was written on the small knife they used to cut her umbilical cord. If she was my daughter, I would call her soleil, sun, moon, or star, after the elements. She still hasn't cried. There is gossip circulating about how Célianne became pregnant. Some people are saying that she had an affair with a married man and her parents threw her out. Gossip spreads here like everywhere else.

Do you remember our silly dreams? Passing the university exams and then studying hard to go until the end, the farthest of all that we can go in school. I know your father might never approve of me. I was going to try to win him over. He would have to cut out my heart to keep me from loving you. I hope you are writing like you promised. Jésus, Marie, Joseph! Everyone smells so bad. They get into arguments and they say to one another, "It is only my misfortune that would lump me together with an indigent like you." Think of it. They are fighting about being superior when we all might drown like straw.

There is an old toothless man leaning over to see what I am writing. He is sucking on the end of an old wooden pipe that has not seen any fire for a very long time now. He looks like a painting. Seeing things simply, you could fill a museum with the sights you have here. I still feel like such a coward for running away. Have you heard anything about my parents? Last time I saw them on the beach, my mother had a *kriz*.[11]

---

[10] Agwé: One of the *lwa*, he is captain and protector of ships on the sea and ruler of fishing. His consort, Lasiren, is a *lwa* in the form of a mermaid. She brings luck and money from the ocean's depths, where she makes her own unearthly music.

[11] *kriz*: Probably "crisis" — meaning "fit" — in *kreyol*, the Haitian language.

She just fainted on the sand. I saw her coming to as we started sailing away. But of course I don't know if she is doing all right.

The water is really piling into the boat. We take turns pouring bowls of it out. I don't know what is keeping the boat from splitting in two. Swiss isn't crying. They keep slapping her behind, but she is not crying.

of course the old president didn't come. they arrested a lot of people at the airport, shot a whole bunch of them down. i heard it on the radio. while we were eating tonight, i told papa that i love you. i don't know if it will make a difference. i just want him to know that i have loved somebody in my life. in case something happens to one of us, i think he should know this about me, that i have loved someone besides only my mother and father in my life. i know you would understand. you are the one for large noble gestures. i just wanted him to know that i was capable of loving somebody. he looked me straight in the eye and said nothing to me. i love you until my hair shivers at the thought of anything happening to you. papa just turned his face away like he was rejecting my very birth. i am writing you from under the banyan tree in the yard in our new house. there are only two rooms and a tin roof that makes music when it rains, especially when there is hail, which falls like angry tears from heaven. there is a stream down the hill from the house, a stream that is too shallow for me to drown myself. manman and i spend a lot of time talking under the banyan tree. she told me today that sometimes you have to choose between your father and the man you love. her whole family did not want her to marry papa because he was a gardener from ville rose and her family was from the city and some of them had even gone to university. she whispered everything under the banyan tree in the yard so as not to hurt his feelings. i saw him looking at us hard from the house. i heard him clearing his throat like he heard us anyway, like we hurt him very deeply somehow just by being together.

Célianne is lying with her head against the side of the boat. The baby still will not cry. They both look very peaceful in all this chaos. Célianne is holding her baby tight against her chest. She just cannot seem to let herself throw it in the ocean. I asked her about the baby's father. She keeps repeating the story now with her eyes closed, her lips barely moving.

She was home one night with her mother and brother Lionel when some ten or twelve soldiers burst into the house. The soldiers held a gun to Lionel's head and ordered him to lie down and become intimate with his mother. Lionel refused. Their mother told him to go ahead and obey the soldiers because she was afraid that they would kill Lionel on the spot if he put up more of a fight. Lionel did as his mother told him, crying as the soldiers laughed at him, pressing the gun barrels farther and farther into his neck.

Afterwards, the soldiers tied up Lionel and their mother, then they each took turns raping Célianne. When they were done, they arrested Lionel, accusing him of moral crimes. After that night, Célianne never heard from Lionel again.

The same night, Célianne cut her face with a razor so that no one would know who she was. Then as facial scars were healing, she started throwing up and getting rashes. Next thing she knew, she was getting big. She found out about the boat and got on. She is fifteen.

manman told me the whole story today under the banyan tree. the bastards were coming to get me. they were going to arrest me. they were going to peg me as a member of the youth federation and then take me away. papa heard about it. he went to the post and paid them money, all the money he had. our house in port-au-prince and all the land his father had left him, he gave it all away to save my life. this is why he was so mad. tonight manman told me this under the banyan tree. i have no words to thank him for this. i don't know how. you must love him for this, manman says, you must. it is something you can never forget, the sacrifice he has made. i cannot bring myself to say thank you. now he is more than my father. he is a man who gave everything he had to save my life. on the radio tonight, they read the list of names of people who passed the university exams. you passed.

We got some relief from the seawater coming in. The captain used the last of his tar, and most of the water is staying out for a while. Many people have volunteered to throw Célianne's baby overboard for her. She will not let them. They are waiting for her to go to sleep so they can do it, but she will not sleep. I never knew before that dead children looked purple. The lips are the most purple because the baby is so dark. Purple like the sea after the sun has set.

Célianne is slowly drifting off to sleep. She is very tired from the labor. I do not want to touch the child. If anybody is going to throw it in the ocean, I think it should be her. I keep thinking, they have thrown every piece of flesh that followed the child out of her body into the water. They are going to throw the dead baby in the water. Won't these things attract sharks?

Célianne's fingernails are buried deep in the child's naked back. The old man with the pipe just asked, "Kompè, what are you writing?" I told him, "My will."

i am getting used to ville rose. there are butterflies here, tons of butterflies. so far none has landed on my hand, which means they have no news for me. i cannot always bathe in the stream near the house because the water is freezing cold. the only time it feels just right is at noon, and then there are a dozen eyes who might see me bathing. i solved that by getting a bucket of water in the morning and leaving it in the sun and then bathing myself once it is night under the banyan tree. the banyan now is my most trusted friend. they say banyans can last hundreds of years. even the branches that lean down from them become like trees themselves. a banyan could become a forest, manman says, if it were given a chance. from the spot where i stand under the banyan, i see the mountains, and behind those are more mountains still. so many mountains that are bare like rocks. i feel like all those mountains are pushing me farther and farther away from you.

She threw it overboard. I watched her face knot up like a thread, and then she let go. It fell in a splash, floated for a while, and then sank. And quickly after that she jumped in too. And just as the baby's head sank, so did hers. They went together like two bottles beneath a waterfall. The shock lasts only so long. There was no time to even try and save her. There was no question of it. The sea in that spot is like the sharks that live there. It has no mercy.

They say I have to throw my notebook out. The old man has to throw out his hat and his pipe. The water is rising again and they are scooping it out. I asked for a few seconds to write this last page and then promised that I would let it go. I know you will probably never see this, but it was nice imagining that I had you here to talk to.

I hope my parents are alive. I asked the old man to tell them what happened to me, if he makes it anywhere. He asked me to write his name in "my book." I asked him for his full name. It is Justin Moïse André Nozius Joseph Frank Osnac Maximilien. He says it all with such an air that you would think him a king. The old man says, "I know a Coast Guard ship is coming. It came to me in my dream." He points to a spot far into the distance. I look where he is pointing. I see nothing. From here, ships must be like a mirage in the desert.

I must throw my book out now. It goes down to them, Célianne and her daughter and all those children of the sea who might soon be claiming me.

I go to them now as though it was always meant to be, as though the very day that my mother birthed me, she had chosen me to live life eternal, among the children of the deep blue sea, those who have escaped the chains of slavery to form a world beneath the heavens and the blood-drenched earth where you live.

Perhaps I was chosen from the beginning of time to live there with Agwé at the bottom of the sea. Maybe this is why I dreamed of the starfish and the mermaids having the Catholic Mass under the sea. Maybe this was my invitation to go. In any case, I know that my memory of you will live even there as I too become a child of the sea.

today i said thank you. i said thank you, papa, because you saved my life. he groaned and just touched my shoulder, moving his hand quickly away like a butterfly. and then there it was, the black butterfly floating around us. i began to run and run so it wouldn't land on me, but it had already carried its news. i know what must have happened. tonight i listened to manman's transistor under the banyan tree. all i hear from the radio is more killing in port-au-prince. the pigs are refusing to let up. i don't know what's going to happen, but i cannot see staying here forever. i am writing to you from the bottom of the banyan tree. manman says that banyan trees are holy and sometimes if we call the gods from beneath them, they will hear our voices clearer. now there are always butterflies around me, black ones that i refuse to let find my hand. i throw big rocks at them, but they are always too fast. last night on the radio, i heard that another boat sank off the coast of the bahamas. i can't think about you being in there in the waves. my hair shivers. from here, i cannot even see the sea. behind these mountains are more mountains and more black butterflies still and a sea that is endless like my love for you.

GLOSSARY OF LITERARY AND CRITICAL TERMS

Absurd Literary movement that evolved in France in the 1950s. The Absurdists saw the universe as irrational and meaningless. They rejected conventional PLOT and DIALOGUE in their work, emphasizing the incoherence of the world.

Accent The emphasis, or stress, given to a syllable or word in pronunciation. Accents can be used to emphasize a particular word in a sentence: *Is* she con*tent* with the *con*tents of the *yel*low *pack*age?

Acmeists A group of twentieth-century Russian poets, most notably Anna Akhmatova (1889–1966), who rejected Symbolism in favor of linguistic clarity.

Acropolis The most fortified part of a Greek city, located on a hill; the most famous acropolis is in Athens and is the site of the Parthenon.

Act A major division in the action of a play. In many full-length plays, acts are further divided into SCENES, which often mark a point in the action when the location changes or when a new character arrives.

Age of Pericles The golden age of Athens in the fifth century B.C.E. when Pericles (c. 495–429 B.C.E.) was the head of the Athenian government. During this period, Athenian democ-racy reached its height; the Parthenon was constructed and drama and music flourished.

Agnosticism The belief that the existence of God or anything beyond material phenom-ena can be neither proved nor disproved. The French ENLIGHTENMENT philosopher Fran-çois Voltaire (1694–1778) is considered by many to be the father of agnosticism. The term *agnostic,* however, was first used by the English biologist Thomas Huxley (1825–1895) in 1869.

Ahasuarus, the Wandering Jew A legendary figure during ancient times who was said to have mocked Jesus en route to the crucifixion and was therefore doomed to wander the earth in penance until Judgment Day.

Allegory A narrative in which the characters, settings, and episodes stand for something else. Traditionally, most allegories come in the form of stories that correlate to spiritual concepts; examples of these can be found in Dante's *Divine Comedy* (1321). Some later allegories allude to political, historical, and sociological ideas.

Alliteration The repetition of the same conso-nant sound or sounds in a sequence of words, usually at the beginning of a word or stressed syllable: "*d*escending *d*ew *d*rops"; "*l*uscious *l*emons." The repetition is based on the sounds of the letters, not the spelling of the words; for example, "*keen*" and "*car*" alliterate, but "*car*" and "*cite*" do not, even though both begin with *c.* Used sparingly, alliteration can intensify ideas by emphasizing key words.

Allusion A brief reference to a person, place, thing, event, or idea in history or literature. These references can be to a scene from one of Shakespeare's plays, a historic figure, a war, a great love story, a biblical authority, or anything else that might enrich an author's work. Allusions imply that the writer and the reader share similar knowledge and function as a kind of shorthand.

Ambiguity Allows for two or more simultaneous interpretations of a word, phrase, action, or situation, all of whose meanings are supported by the work. Deliberate ambiguity can contribute to the effectiveness and richness of a piece of writing; unintentional ambiguity obscures meaning and may confuse readers.

Anagram A word or phrase made up of the same letters as another word or phrase; *heart* is an anagram of *earth.* Often considered merely an exercise of one's ingenuity, anagrams are sometimes used by writers to conceal proper names, veil messages, or suggest important connections between words, such as between *hated* and *death.*

Antagonist The character, force, or collection of forces in fiction or drama that opposes the PROTAGONIST and gives rise to the conflict in the story; an opponent of the protagonist, such as Caliban in Shakespeare's play *The Tempest.*

Antihero A PROTAGONIST who has the opposite of most of the traditional attributes of a hero. He or she may be bewildered, ineffectual, deluded, or merely pathetic. Often what antiheroes learn, if they learn anything at all, is that they are isolated in an existence devoid of God or any absolute value.

Apartheid The South African system of official racial segregation, which was established in 1948 and lasted until the early 1990s. The term *apartheid* means "state of being separate." Apartheid divided people into racial categories—colored, or Indian, as well as black and white—and severely limited the movements and activities of the colored and black groups, giving particular privilege to people of European heritage. After intense international pressure, the resistance movement leader, Nelson Mandela (b. 1918), was released from prison in 1990. One year later he became the country's first black president.

Apostrophe A statement or address made either to an implied interlocutor, sometimes a nonhuman figure or PERSONIFICATION. Apostrophes often provide a speaker with the opportunity to reveal his or her internal thoughts.

Archetype A universal symbol that evokes deep and sometimes unconscious responses in a reader. In literature, characters, images, and themes that symbolize universal meanings and basic human experiences are considered archetypes. Common literary archetypes include quests, initiations, scapegoats, descents to the underworld, and ascents to heaven.

Aryans A people who settled in Iran (Persia) and northern India in prehistoric times. Their language was also called Aryan, and it gave rise to the Indo-European languages of South Asia. Linguists now use the term *Aryan* to refer to Indo-Aryan languages. In the nineteenth and twentieth century the term was appropriated (most infamously by Adolf Hitler and the Nazi government) to define a "pure" race of people responsible for the progress of the modern world and superior to non-Aryans.

Aside In drama, a speech directed to the audience that supposedly is not audible to the other characters onstage.

Associationism A British eighteenth- and nineteenth-century school of philosophy that derived its ideas from, among others, philosophers John Locke (1632–1704) and David Hume (1711–1776). Associationists believed that one's view of reality is formed from bits and pieces of sensations that join together through patterns of association.

Assonance The repetition of vowel sounds in nearby words, as in "as*ee*p under a tr*ee*" or "*each* *e*vening." When the words also share similar endings, as in "as*ee*p in the d*ee*p," rhyme occurs. Assonance is an effective means of emphasizing important words.

Atheism The belief that God does not exist and that the Earth evolved naturally.

Avant-garde Writers, artists, filmmakers, and musicians whose work is innovative, experimental, or unconventional.

Bataan Death March The forced march of 10,000 American and 65,000 Filipino soldiers who were captured in 1942 by the Japanese on the Bataan Peninsula of the Philippines during World War II; the prisoners of war, many of whom were suffering from exhaustion, malaria, and other ailments, were compelled to march 55 miles from Marivales to San Fernando. They were then packed into railroad cars and taken to Capas, where they were made to march another 8 miles to a prison camp. Up to 650 Americans and some 10,000 Filipinos died before reaching the camp, where still many others died.

Ballad An uncomplicated verse originally meant to be sung; it generally tells a dramatic tale or simple story. Ballads are associated with the oral traditions or folklore of common people. The folk ballad stanza usually consists of four lines of alternating tetrameter (four accented syllables) and trimeter (three accented syllables) following a rhyme scheme of *abab* or *abcb.*

Ballad stanza A four-line stanza, known as a QUATRAIN, consisting of alternating eight- and six-syllable lines. Usually, only the second and fourth lines rhyme (an *abcb* pattern). Samuel Taylor Coleridge adapted the ballad stanza in *The Rime of the Ancient Mariner* (1798).

Battle of Dresden A battle in 1813 outside the capital of Saxony, where Napoleon defeated an allied army of 400,000 men. It was Napoleon's last great victory before his final defeat one year later.

Battle of Plassey Plassey was the village in West Bengal, India, where the British defeated the Bengal army in 1757, which led to Britain's domination of northeast India.

Bengali Traditional language of Bengal in eastern India, now the national language of Bangladesh and the official language of the West Bengal region of India; also, someone who comes from Bangladesh or West Bengal.

Bengali literary renaissance A movement in the second half of the nineteenth century to develop literature in the Bengali language that would describe the everyday life of contemporary Bengal. Rabindranath Tagore, Madhusudan Dutta, and Bankim Chandra Chatterjee were important writers of the movement.

Bhagavad Gita An ancient text of Hindu wisdom from the first century B.C.E. or first century C.E. inserted into the epic poem *The Mahabharata.*

Bible-based calendar Calendar based on Scripture that dates the creation of the earth at 4004 B.C.E. Archbishop James Ussher constructed it in the mid seventeenth century.

Bildungsroman A novel that traces the PROTAGONIST's development, generally from birth or childhood into maturity. An early prototype is Goethe's *Wilhelm Meister's Apprenticeship* (1795–96). The form has flourished in the ensuing two centuries and includes such modern masterpieces as James Joyce's *Portrait of the Artist as a Young Man* (1916).

Bill of Rights A document that spells out the rights of a citizen in either England or the United States of America. The American Bill of Rights, the first ten amendments to the Constitution, was ratified in 1791 and guarantees freedom of religion, press, assembly, and petition; the right to bear arms; protection under the law; and the right to a speedy trial. See also ENGLISH BILL OF RIGHTS.

Biographical criticism An approach to literature that maintains that knowledge of an author's life experiences can aid in the understanding of his or her work. Although biographical information can sometimes complicate one's interpretation of a work and some FORMALIST CRITICS, such as the NEW

CRITICS, disparage the use of an author's biography as a tool for textual interpretation, learning about the life of an author can often enrich a reader's appreciation for that author's work.

Blank verse Unrhymed IAMBIC PENTAMETER. Blank verse is the form closest to the natural rhythms of English speech and is therefore the most common pattern found in traditional English narrative and dramatic poetry, from Shakespeare to the writers of the early twentieth century.

Bolshevik Revolution The revolution in Russia in 1917 in which the government of the hereditary tsar was overthrown and replaced by a Communist regime under the leadership of Vladimir Lenin. After the Bolshevik Revolution, the Russian empire became the Union of Soviet Socialist Republics, or USSR.

Bourgeoisie Prosperous urban middle class that emerged in the wake of the INDUSTRIAL REVOLUTION and gained wealth and power in the nineteenth century. In MARXIST theory, the bourgeoisie is identified as the owners and operators of industry, as opposed to the PROLETARIAT, who live by the sale of their labor.

Brahman In the UPANISHADS—sacred Hindu texts—Brahman is the ultimate reality that transcends all names and descriptions and is the single unifying essence of the universe. A brahman, or brahmin, is also a Hindu priest and thus of the highest caste in the traditional Hindu caste system.

Brahmanism A religion that recognizes the creator, Brahma, and the priestly class of brahmans who administer Hindu rituals.

Buddhism A religion founded in India in the sixth century B.C.E. by Siddhartha Gautama, the Buddha. While Buddhism has taken different forms in the many areas of the world to which it has spread, its central tenet is that life is suffering caused by desire. In order to obtain salvation, or nirvana, one must transcend desire through following an eightfold path that includes the practice of right action and right mindfulness.

Bunraku New name for JORURI, traditional Japanese puppet theater.

Bushido The code of honor and conduct of the Japanese SAMURAI class. *Bushido* emphasizes self-discipline and bravery.

Byronic hero A character based on the heroes in the poems of Lord Byron (1788–1824), such as Childe Harold, Manfred, and Cain. The Byronic hero is an outsider, even an outlaw—proud, defiant, and moody—who seems burdened by an undefined sense of guilt or misery.

Cacophony In literature, language that is discordant and difficult to pronounce, such as the line "never my numb plunker fumbles" from John Updike's "Player Piano." Cacophony (from the Greek for "bad sound") may be unintentional, or it may be used for deliberate dramatic effect; also refers to the combination of loud, jarring sounds.

Caesura A pause within a line of poetry that contributes to the line's RHYTHM. A caesura can occur anywhere within a line and need not be indicated by punctuation. In SCANSION, caesuras are indicated by a double vertical line.

Canon The works generally considered by scholars, critics, and teachers to be the most important to read and study and that collectively constitute the masterpieces of literature. Since the 1960s, the traditional English and American literary canons, consisting mostly of works by white male writers, have been expanding to include many female writers and writers of varying ethnic backgrounds.

Captivity narratives Autobiographical accounts detailing American colonists' experiences as prisoners of Native Americans; extremely popular from the late seventeenth century through the nineteenth century. Often written to illustrate spiritual or moral growth through trials, these narratives typically describe a dramatic capture and lengthy travels and ordeals, culminating in escape or release. Much was made of the divide between "savage" and "civilized" society, of fear of assimilation into an alien culture, and of the promise of salvation for the chosen few.

Carpe diem Latin phrase meaning "seize the day." This is a common literary theme, especially in lyric poetry, conveying that life is short, time is fleeting, and one should make the most of present pleasures. Andrew Marvell's poem "To His Coy Mistress" is a good example.

Catharsis Meaning "purgation," or the release of the emotions of pity and fear by the audience at the end of a tragedy. In *Poetics,* Aristotle discusses the importance of catharsis. The audience faces the misfortunes of the PROTAGONIST, which elicit pity and compassion. Simultaneously, the audience confronts the protagonist's failure, thus receiving a frightening reminder of human limitations and frailties.

Character, characterization A character is a person presented in a dramatic or narrative work; characterization is the process by which a writer makes a character seem real to the reader.

Chivalric romances Idealized stories from the medieval period that espoused the values of a sophisticated courtly society. These tales centered around the lives of knights who were faithful to God, king, and country and willing to sacrifice themselves for these causes and for the love and protection of women. Chivalric romances were highly moral and fanciful, often pitting knights against dark or supernatural forces.

Chorus In Greek tragedies, a group of people who serve mainly as commentators on the play's characters and events, adding to the audience's understanding of a play by expressing traditional moral, religious, and social attitudes. The role of the chorus is occasionally used by modern playwrights.

Cliché An idea or expression that has become tired and trite from overuse. Clichés often anesthetize readers and are usually signs of weak writing.

Closet drama A play that is to be read rather than performed onstage. In closet dramas, literary art outweighs all other considerations.

Colloquial Informal diction that reflects casual, conversational language and often includes slang expressions.

Comedy A work intended to interest, involve, and amuse readers or an audience, in which no terrible disaster occurs and which ends happily for the main characters.

Comic epic One of the earliest English novelists, Henry Fielding (1707–1754) characterized the kind of literature he was creating in his novel *Joseph Andrews* (1742) as "a comic epic in prose," thus distinguishing it from serious or tragic epic poems that treated noble characters and elevated subjects. His novel was about common people and everyday events.

Comic relief A humorous scene or incident that alleviates tension in an otherwise serious work. Often these moments enhance the thematic significance of a story in addition to providing humor.

Communist A supporter of the political system in which all property and wealth is owned collectively by and shared equally among all members of society. Communism derived largely from the theories of Karl Marx and Friedrich Engels, as presented in *The Communist Manifesto* (1848).

Conflict In a literary work, the struggle within the PLOT between opposing forces. The PROTAGONIST is engaged in a conflict with the ANTAGONIST.

Confucianism A religion/philosophy that has influenced Chinese and East Asian spirituality and culture for over two thousand years. Based on the writings of Confucius (Kongfuzi; 551–479 B.C.E.), Confucianism asserts that humans can improve and even perfect themselves through education and moral reform. In its various manifestations, Confucianism has affected the social and political evolution of China and East Asia while providing a spiritual and moral template.

Connotation Implications going beyond the literal meaning of a word that derive from how the word has been commonly used and from ideas or things associated with it. For example, the word *eagle* in the United States connotes ideas of liberty and freedom that have little to do with the term's literal meaning.

Consonance A common type of near-rhyme or half rhyme that consists of identical consonant sounds preceded by different vowel sounds: *home, same; worth, breath.*

Continental Congress Assembly of delegates representing the thirteen British colonies in North America. The First Continental Congress convened in 1774 and drafted a petition to King George III; the Second Continental Congress met in 1775, organized an army under the leadership of George Washington, and adopted the Declaration of Independence on July 4, 1776.

Convention A characteristic of a literary GENRE that is understood and accepted by readers and audiences because it has become familiar. For example, the division of a play into acts and scenes is a dramatic convention, as are SOLILOQUIES and ASIDES.

Cosmogony A theory that explains the origins of the universe.

Council of Areopagus Council in Athens—named after the place where it held its meetings—that was the political forum prior to the establishment of the COUNCIL OF FOUR HUNDRED. Areopagus later remained active as a criminal court.

Council of Four Hundred A council established by Solon in Athens in 594 B.C.E. as a rival to the COUNCIL OF AREOPAGUS, which, according to Solon, had become too corrupt. Solon granted each of Athens's social classes equal representation in the senate. Each class was represented by one hundred men.

Couplet A two-line, rhymed stanza. Pope is the master of the HEROIC COUPLET, a two-line, rhymed, iambic-pentameter stanza that completes its thought within the closed two-line form.

Creole The culture and language of some of the Spanish and French settlers of South and North America. Many Creoles speak a mixed form of French, Spanish, and English.

Crimean War (1853–1856) A war fought on the Crimean peninsula in the Black Sea between the Russians and the allied forces of the British, the French, and the Ottoman Turks. The war arose from religious conflicts in the Middle East. When Austria threatened to enter the war, Russia agreed to peace terms resulting in the Treaty of Paris (1856), but the shift in power had long-lasting effects, notably the unification of Germany and Italy.

Crisis The moment in a work of drama or fiction where the elements of the conflict reach the point of maximum tension. The crisis is part of the work's structure but is not necessarily the emotional crescendo, or climax.

Critical realism Politically driven, early-twentieth-century school of Chinese literature pioneered by Lu Xun (1881–1936); examines societal tendencies through the actions of realistic characters.

Cubism An early-twentieth-century movement centered in France, primarily in painting and collage, that attempted to show objects from several perspectives at once; proponents included the artists Pablo Picasso (1881–1973) and Georges Braque (1882–1963).

Cultural criticism An approach to literature that focuses on the historical as well as the social, political, and economic contexts of a work. Popular culture—mass-produced and mass-consumed cultural artifacts ranging from advertising to popular fiction to television to rock music—is seen on equal footing with "high culture." Cultural critics use widely eclectic strategies, such as NEW HISTORICISM, psychology, gender studies, and DECONSTRUCTION, to analyze not only literary texts but everything from radio talk shows to comic strips, calendar art, commercials, travel guides, and baseball cards.

Dadaism An early-twentieth-century AVANT-GARDE movement inaugurated by French poets Tristan Tzara (1896–1963) and Hans Arp (1887–1966) and German poet Hugo Ball (1886–1927), all living in Zurich during World War I. Stressing irrationality and the absurdity of life in an era of mechanized mass-destruction, dadaism is often seen as nihilistic; in its emphasis on free association and instinctive composition, it can be viewed as a precursor to surrealism. The French painter Marcel Duchamp (1887–1968) may be dadaism's most renowned practitioner.

Daoism (Taoism) A religion / philosophy based on the *Dao De Jing* of Laozi (Lao-tzu) that emphasizes individual freedom, spontaneity, mystical experience, and self-transformation, and is the antithesis of CONFUCIANISM. In pursuit of the *dao,* or the Way—the eternal creative reality that is the essence of all things—practitioners embrace simplicity and reject learned wisdom. The Daoist tradition has flourished in China and East Asia for two thousand years.

Decembrist Revolt After the death of Tsar Alexander I (r. 1801–25), a group of liberal officers, many of whom had served in the Napoleonic Wars, attempted in December 1825 to depose his heir, Nicholas I (r. 1825–55), in the hope of bringing to power a ruler who would guarantee them a constitutional monarchy. The officers were crushed by Nicholas, who punished them severely to discourage other reform-minded Russians.

Deconstructionism An approach to literature that suggests that literary works do not yield single fixed meanings because language can never say exactly what one intends it to mean. Deconstructionism seeks to destabilize meaning by examining the gaps in and ambiguities of a text's language. Deconstructionists pay close attention to language in order to discover and describe how a variety of close readings can be generated.

Deism An unorthodox religious philosophy prominent in the seventeenth and eighteenth centuries in northern Europe and America. Deists believe that religious knowledge can be arrived at through reason rather than through revelation or formal religious instruction. Deism constructs God as a rational architect of an orderly world; the deist God creates the world and sets it in motion but does not become directly involved in human affairs.

Denouement French term meaning "unraveling" or "unknotting" used to describe the resolution of a PLOT following the climax.

Dialect A type of informal DICTION. Dialects are spoken by definable groups of people from a particular geographic region, economic group, or social class. Writers use dialect to express and contrast the education, class, and social and regional backgrounds of their characters.

Dialogue Verbal exchange between CHARACTERS. Dialogue reveals firsthand characters' thoughts, responses, and emotional states, and thus makes the characters real to readers or the audience.

Diaspora The wide dispersion of a people or a culture that was formerly located in one place. Two historical diasporas of note are the diaspora of the Jews from Palestine following the Roman destruction of the Second Temple in 70 C.E. and the African diaspora caused by the slave trade. Both the Jews and the Africans were dispersed across many continents.

Diction A writer's choice of words, phrases, sentence structure, and figurative language, which combine to help create meaning.

Didactic poetry Poetry designed to teach an ethical, moral, or religious lesson.

Dionysus The god of wine in Greek mythology, whose cult originated in Thrace and Phrygia—north and east of the Greek peninsula. Dionysus was often blamed for people's irrational behavior and for chaotic situations. However, many Greeks also believed that Dionysus taught them good farming skills, especially those related to wine production. Greek tragedy evolved from a ceremony that honored Dionysus, and the theater in Athens was dedicated to him.

Doggerel A derogatory term for poetry whose subject is trite and whose rhythm and sounds are monotonously heavy-handed.

Drama Derived from the Greek word *dram,* meaning "to do" or "to perform," the term *drama* may refer to a single play, a group of plays, or to plays in general. Drama is designed to be performed in a theater: Actors take on the roles of its characters, perform indicated actions, and deliver the script's DIALOGUE.

Dramatic monologue A type of lyric or narrative poem in which a speaker addresses an imagined and distinct but silent audience in such a way as to reveal a dramatic situation and, often unintentionally, some aspect of the speaker's temperament or personality.

Dualistic tradition Religious and philosophical doctrine dating from ancient times in which the antagonistic forces of good and evil determine the course of events.

Early Modern era Period extending from about 1500 to 1800, marked by the advent of colonialism and capitalism.

Edenic New World Early European immigrants to the New World often described it as a new Eden, a Garden of Paradise.

Edo The ancient name for Tokyo. During the TOKUGAWA period (1600–1868), Edo became the imperial capital of Japan.

Eight-legged essay The *ba-gu wen*, an essay of eight parts written on a Confucian theme and developed during the MING DYNASTY in China (1368–1644) as a requirement for the civil service examinations.

Electra complex The female version of the Oedipus complex as theorized by Sigmund Freud to describe a daughter's unconscious rivalry with her mother for her father's attention. The name comes from the Greek legend of Electra, who avenged the death of her father by plotting the death of her mother.

Elegiac couplets The conventional strophic form of Latin elegiac love poetry, consisting of one dactylic hexameter line followed by one dactylic pentameter line. A dactylic hexameter line is composed of six feet, each foot comprising one long, or accented, and two short, or unaccented, syllables; the sixth foot may be shortened by one or two syllables; the pentameter line consists of five such feet. The elegiac couplet is also known as a "distich."

Elegy A mournful, contemplative lyric poem often ending in consolation, written to commemorate someone who has died. *Elegy* may also refer to a serious, meditative poem that expresses the speaker's melancholy thoughts.

Elysian land In Greek mythology, some fortunate mortals spend their afterlife in the bliss of the Elysian Fields, or Islands of the Blest, rather than in Hades, the underworld.

End-stopped line A line in a poem after which a pause occurs. End-stopped lines reflect normal speech patterns and are often marked by punctuation.

English Bill of Rights Formally known as "An Act declaring the Rights and Liberties of the Subject, and settling the Succession of the Crown," the English Bill of Rights was passed in December 1689. It conferred the crown upon William and Mary, who succeeded the ousted James II; it stated that no Catholic would ever be king or queen of England, extended civil rights and liberties to the people of England, and confirmed Parliament's power in a constitutional government. See also BILL OF RIGHTS.

Enjambment In poetry, a line continuing without a pause into the next line for its meaning; also called a run-on line.

Enlightenment Refers to a period of time in Europe from the late seventeenth through the eighteenth century, also called the Age of Reason, in which reason, human progress, and order were venerated. The Enlightenment intensified the process of secularization that had begun during the Renaissance and favored the use of empirical science to resolve social problems. Enlightenment philosophers questioned the existing forms of education and politics and fought tyranny and social injustice. Enlightenment ideas led to the American and French Revolutions in the late 1700s. Leading philosophers also questioned the Bible and gave rise to a new movement of freethinkers—people who rejected the church's dogma and encouraged rational inquiry and speculation.

Ennui French for boredom or lack of interest; the term is associated with a widespread discontent with the pleasures of the modern world.

Eos The Greek goddess of the dawn who loved the young men Cleitus, Cephalus, and Orion, the hunter.

Epic A long narrative poem told in a formal, elevated style that focuses on a serious subject and chronicles heroic deeds and events important to a culture or nation.

Epigram A brief, pointed, and witty poem that usually makes a satiric or humorous point. Epigrams are most often written in couplets but can be written in any form.

Epiphany In fiction, when a character suddenly experiences a deep realization about himself or herself; a truth which is grasped in an ordinary rather than a melodramatic moment.

Eros The Greek god of love, associated with both passion and fertility. Freud used the term *Eros* in modern times to signify the human life-drive (desire) at war with THANATOS, the death-drive.

Euphony From the Greek for "good sound"; refers to language that is smooth and musically pleasant to the ear.

Existentialism A school of modern philosophy associated with Jean-Paul Sartre (1905–1980) and Albert Camus (1913–1960) that dominated European thought in the years following World War II. Existentialists are interested in the nature of consciousness and emphasize the role of individual will in shaping existence. Existentialism holds that discrete, willful acts of choice create the only meaning that exists in an otherwise meaningless universe.

Exposition A narrative device often used at the beginning of a work that provides necessary background information about characters and their circumstances. Exposition explains such matters as what has gone on before, the relationships between characters, theme, and conflict.

Expressionism An artistic and literary movement that originated in Germany in the early twentieth century. Expressionism departs from the conventions of realism to focus on the inner impressions or moods of a character or of the artist. Influenced by the increased mechanization of the modern world and by MARXISM, expressionism often reveals the alienation of the individual.

Fabliau Although the *fabliau* originated in France as a comic or satiric tale in verse, by the time of Giovanni Boccaccio (1313–1375) and Geoffrey Chaucer (1340–1400) the term also stood for bawdy and ribald prose tales like "The Miller's Tale" in Chaucer's *Canterbury Tales* or Boccaccio's "Rustico and Alibech."

Farce A form of humor based on exaggerated, improbable incongruities. Farce involves rapid shifts in action and emotion as well as slapstick comedy and extravagant dialogue.

Fascism An ideology that combines dictatorial government, militarism, control of the personal freedom of a people, extreme nationalism, and government control of business. Fascism peaked between the 1920s and '40s, when Adolf Hitler, Benito Mussolini, and Francisco Franco gained power in Germany, Italy, and Spain respectively.

Feminism A school of thought that examines the oppression, subjugation, or inequality of women. Feminism has flourished since the middle of the twentieth century and has taken different forms, focusing variously on language, the meaning of power, and the institutions that perpetuate sexism.

Feminist criticism An approach to literature that seeks to correct or supplement a predominantly male-dominated critical perspective with a feminist consciousness. Feminist criticism places literature in a social context and uses a broad range of disciplines, including history, sociology, psychology, and linguistics, to provide interpretations that are sensitive to feminist issues.

Fenian Society A secret organization of Irish nationalists founded in 1858 promoting Irish independence from England by means of violent revolution. The organization was named after the Fenians, professional soldiers who served Irish kings in third-century Ireland. With support from cells among Irish emigrants in America, South Africa, and Australia, the Fenian Society, led by James Stephens, launched a rebellion in 1867 that, although it failed, helped to galvanize political opposition to English rule and call attention to the problems in Ireland.

Feudal aristocracy A system of government that existed in Europe in the Middle Ages. The feudal system refers to a mode of agricultural production in which peasants worked for landowners, or lords, in return for debt forgiveness, food, and governmental responsibilities such as military protection. The lords or landowners constitute the upper class, or aristocracy, but at the top of the hierarchy was the monarch who controlled the government and the granting of fiefs, or tracts of land.

Figures of speech Ways of using language that deviate from the literal, denotative meanings of words in order to suggest additional meanings or effects. Figures of speech say one thing in terms of something else, such as when an eager funeral director is described as a vulture.

Fin de siècle French for "end of the century"; generally refers to the final years of the nineteenth century, a time characterized by decadence and ENNUI. Artists of this era romanticized drug addiction and prostitution; open sexuality, including homosexuality, also marked the period. In Paris and Vienna, the Art Nouveau movement in the fine arts flourished and was informed by the blossoming of radical ideas in the wake of the Paris Commune of 1871. Notable fin-de-siècle figures include artists such as Aubrey Beardsley and writers such as Oscar Wilde.

Fixed form A poem characterized by a fixed pattern of lines, syllables, or meter. A SONNET is a fixed form of poetry because it must have fourteen lines.

Flashback A literary or dramatic device that allows a past occurrence to be inserted into the chronological order of a narrative.

Floating World (*ukiyo-e*) A Japanese artistic movement that flourished in the seventeenth, eighteenth, and nineteenth centuries in Tokyo. Ukiyo-e depicts the floating or sorrowful world; its most frequent media are woodblock prints, books, and drawings. Originally considered a popular rather than a high art, ukiyo-e treated literary, classic, and historical themes within a contemporary context, and it was particularly appealing to the emerging merchant classes.

Flying Dutchman The legend of a ghostly ship doomed to sail for eternity. If a vision of it appears to sailors, it signals imminent disaster. Most versions of the story have the captain of the ship playing dice or gambling with the Devil.

Foil A character in a literary work or drama whose behavior or values contrast with those of another character, typically the PROTAGONIST.

Foot A poetic foot is a poem's unit of measurement and decides the rhythm. In English, the iambic, or ascending, foot is the most common.

Foreshadowing Providing hints of what is to happen next in order to build suspense.

Formalist A type of criticism dominant in the early twentieth century that emphasizes the form of an artwork. Two of its prominent schools are Russian formalism, which favors the form of an artwork over its content and argues for the necessity of literature to defamiliarize the ordinary objects of the world, and American NEW CRITICISM, which treats a work of art as an object and seeks to understand it through close, careful analysis.

Formula literature Literature that fulfills a reader's expectations. In detective novels, for instance, the plot may vary among different works, but in the end the detective solves the case in all of them. Science fiction, romance, and Westerns are other examples of formula literature.

Found poem An ordinary collection of words that can be understood differently when arranged or labeled as a poem. A found poem could be something as banal as a "to do" list or personal advertisement, but the poet who "finds" it argues that it has special, unintentional value when presented as a poem.

Founding myth A story that explains how a particular nation or culture came to be, such as Virgil's *Aeneid,* which describes the founding of Rome. Many epic poems, sometimes called national epics, are founding myths.

Four classes In Hindu tradition, humans are created as one of four classes, or *varna:* in descending order, the BRAHMANS (priests), the *Kohatriya* (warriors), the *Vaishya* (merchants and farmers), and the *Shudra* (laborers and servants).

Framed narration Also called *framed tale.* A story within a story. In Chaucer's *Canterbury Tales,* each pilgrim's story is framed by the story of the pilgrimage itself. This device, used by writers from ancient times to the present, enjoyed particular popularity during the thirteenth, fourteenth, and fifteenth centuries and was most fully developed in *The Arabian Nights,* a work in which the framing is multilayered.

Free association A Freudian exercise wherein a patient relates to an analyst anything that comes to his or her mind, no matter how illogical or apparently trivial, without any attempt to censor, shape, or otherwise organize the material. In literature, the term refers to a free flow of the mind's thoughts; it is an important element of stream-of-consciousness writing.

Free verse Highly irregular poetry; typically, free verse does not rhyme.

French Revolution The first of four major revolutions in France in the late eighteenth and nineteenth centuries; it began with the storming of the Bastille in 1789 and ended in the coup of the Eighteenth Brumaire, on November 9–10, 1799, when Napoleon overthrew the revolutionary government. The original goal of the revolution had been to establish a constitutional monarchy that would transfer power from the nobility, headed by King Louis XVI, and the clergy to the middle classes. That aim was abandoned, however, when the king and queen were beheaded in 1793 and a republic was created.

French Symbolists Symbolism was an AVANT-GARDE movement in France in the late nineteenth century that arose from revolutionary experiments with language, verse form, and the use of symbols in the poetry of Stéphane Mallarmé (1842–1898) and Paul Verlaine (1844–1896); according to the Symbolists, poetic language should not delineate ideas but rather evoke feeling and moods, insinuate impressions and connections. French Symbolism, which often is extended to include the poetry of Charles Baudelaire (1821–1867) and Arthur Rimbaud (1854–1891), who anticipated some of its principles, exerted a profound influence on modernist poetry in Russia as well as throughout Europe and the United States.

Freudian criticism A method of literary criticism associated with Freud's theories of psychoanalysis. Early Freudian critics sought to illustrate how literature is shaped by the unconscious desires of the author, but the term has developed and become more broadly defined to encompass many schools of thought that link psychoanalysis to the interpretation of literature.

Gay and lesbian criticism School of literary criticism that focuses on the representation of homosexuality in literature; also interested in how homosexuals read literature and to what extent sexuality and gender is culturally constructed.

Gender criticism Literary school that analyzes how an author's or a reader's sex affects the writing and reading experiences.

Genre A category of artistic works or literary compositions that have a distinctive style or content. Poetry, fiction, and drama are genres. Different genres have dominated at various times and places: In eighteenth-century Europe, the dramatic comedy was the preferred form of theater; in the nineteenth century, the novel was the dominant genre.

Genroku period (1688–1703) A Japanese cultural period during the EDO era when a growing number of affluent *chonin,* or townsmen, sought diversion in the FLOATING WORLD, or *ukiyo-e* — city districts where courtesans, along with theater, dance, song, and the arts, flourished.

German Romanticism A German form of nineteenth-century Romanticism. In addition to German Romantic poets like Friedrich Holderlin (1770–1843), Novalis (1772–1801), and Heinrich Heine (1797–1856), Germany produced the Romantic theorists Friedrich Schlegel (1772–1829), F. W. J. Schelling (1775–1854), and August Wilhelm Schlegel (1767–1845), who believed that the Christian myth needed to be replaced with a modern one.

Ghazal A form of lyric poetry composed of three to seven couplets, called *sh'ir,* that follow the strict rhyme scheme of *aa ba ca da,* and so on, known as the *qafiyah.* Strict adherence to the form requires the use of the *radif,* a word that is repeated in a pattern dictated by the first couplet, throughout the poem. Literally meaning "dialogue with the beloved," the *ghazal,* as practiced in Arabia, Persia, Turkey, and India beginning around 1200, became the predominant form for love poetry.

Giri Japanese term for social duty and responsibility.

Glorious Revolution of 1688 The forced abdication of the Catholic king James II of England, whose attempts to exercise royal authority over Parliament galvanized the largely Protestant English nation against him. Although largely a bloodless revolution, some fighting between Catholics and Protestants took place in Ireland and Scotland.

Gnostics Members of an ancient sect in the Middle East who believed that hidden knowledge held the key to the universe. Throughout history there have been Gnostics who have formed secret societies with secret scriptures and who have believed they understood the workings of the cosmos.

Gokan A book combining pictures and text; often adapted from classic Chinese or Japanese stories.

Gothic A style of literature (especially novels) in the late eighteenth and early nineteenth centuries that reacted against the mannered decorum of earlier literature. Gothic novels explore the darker side of human experience; they are often set in the past and in foreign countries, and they employ elements of horror, mystery, and the supernatural.

Gothic novel A subgenre of the novel whose works concentrate on mystery, magic, and horror. Especially popular during the late eighteenth and early nineteenth centuries, gothic novels are often set in castles or mansions whose dungeons or secret rooms contribute to the atmosphere of mystery.

Greater Dionysia In ancient Greece, dramas were performed at festivals that honored the god Dionysus: the Lenaea during January and February and the Greater Dionysia in March and April. The best tragedies and comedies were awarded prizes by an Athenian jury.

Hadith Islamic source of religious law and moral guidance. According to tradition, the Hadith were passed down orally to the prophet Muhammad, and today they are critical to the study of the early development of Islam.

Haikai A form of Japanese linked verse that flourished from the sixteenth through the nineteenth centuries, *haikai* is a sequence of alternating stanzas usually composed by two or more writers. The sequence opens with a *hokku,* a three-line stanza of seventeen syllables that alternate 5, 7, 5; the hokku is followed by alternating three- and two-line stanzas of seventeen and fourteen syllables, respectively. Bashō, the greatest of the haikai masters, preferred a sequence of thirty-six stanzas. Haikai is distinguished from RENGA, an earlier form of Japanese linked verse, primarily by diction and tone; whereas renga, with its origins in court poetry, uses elevated diction and reflects a cultivated seriousness, haikai introduces more colloquial diction, is more lighthearted, and treats common aspects of human experience. The hokku eventually became a separate form, now known as HAIKU.

Haiku Unrhymed Japanese poetic form that consists of seventeen syllables arranged in three lines. Although its origins can be traced to the seventeenth century, it is the most popular poetic form in Japan today. See HAIKAI.

Hamartia Error or flaw. In ancient Greek tragedies, the hero falls through his own *hamartia.*

Hellene Greek.

Heroic couplet A rhymed, iambic-pentameter stanza of two lines that completes its thought within the two-line form. Alexander Pope

(1688–1744), the most accomplished practitioner of the form in English, included this couplet in his *Essay on Criticism:* "True wit is nature to advantage dressed, / What oft was thought, but ne'er so well expressed."

Hexameter couplets The conventional strophic form of Greek and Latin epic poetry consisting of two dactylic hexameter lines; each line is composed of six feet and each foot comprises one long (accented) and two short (unaccented) syllables. The final foot is known as a catalectic foot, for it is generally shortened by one or two syllables.

Hieros gamos Literally, "sacred marriage"; a fertility ritual in which the god-king or priest-king is united with the goddess or priestess-queen in order to provide a model for the kingdom and establish the king's right to rule.

Hinduism The major religion of India, based upon the ancient doctrines found in the Sanskrit texts known as the Vedas and the Upanishads, dating from 1000 B.C.E.

Historical criticism An approach to literature that uses history as a means of understanding a literary work. Such criticism moves beyond both the facts of an author's life and the text itself to examine the social and intellectual contexts in which the author composed the work.

Homeric Hymns At one time attributed to Homer, the *Homeric Hymns* (seventh–sixth centuries B.C.E.) are now believed to have been created by poets from a Homeric school or simply in the style of Homer. Five of the longer hymns contain important stories about gods such as Demeter, Dionysus, Apollo, Aphrodite, and Hermes.

Hubris Exaggerated pride or arrogance; in Greek tragedies, hubris always causes fatal errors.

Huguenots French Protestant members of the Reformed Church established in France by John Calvin in about 1555. Due to religious persecution, many fled to other countries in the sixteenth and seventeenth centuries.

Hyperbole An exaggerated figure of speech; for example, "I nearly died laughing."

Iambic pentameter A poetic line made up of five feet, or iambs, or a ten-syllable line.

Ibsenism After the plays of Norwegian dramatist Henrik Ibsen (1828–1906): a concern in drama with social problems treated realistically rather than romantically.

Idealism Philosophical Idealism in its various forms holds that objects of perception are in reality mental constructs and not the material objects themselves.

Image The two types of images are literal and figurative. Literal images are very detailed, almost photographic; figurative images are more abstract and often use symbols, such as this image of the night in T. S. Eliot's "The Love Song of J. Alfred Prufrock" (1917):

> Let us go then, you and I,
> When the evening is spread out
>   against the sky
> Like a patient etherized upon a table

Industrial Revolution Advancements in mechanization beginning in the mid eighteenth century that transformed manufacturing, transportation, and agriculture over the next century and a half. Most historians regard the Industrial Revolution as the phenomenon that has had the largest impact on the present, changing the Western world from a rural to an urban society and moving the workplace from the fields to the factories. Because of it, the economy changed rapidly, and the production of goods increased exponentially, raising the West's standard of living. The new working class, however, lived in horrible conditions in the cities.

Industrialization The process of building factories and mass producing goods; typically, also part of urbanization.

Inquisition A medieval institution set up by the Roman Catholic pope to judge and convict anyone who might constitute a threat to papal power. The threats took various forms, including heresy, witchcraft, alchemy, and sorcery. The Inquisition held a great amount of power in medieval Europe, especially in southern European countries. The most powerful was the Spanish Inquisition, authorized in 1478, which executed thousands of victims, among them Jews, Muslims, and heretics, through public burning.

Irish Literary Renaissance A movement of the late nineteenth century of Irish writers, including William Butler Yeats (1865–1939), Lady Gregory (1852–1932), and J. M. Synge (1871–1909), who aimed to revitalize Irish literature and to renew interest in and reevaluate Irish myth, legend, folklore, history, and literature. The literary renaissance was part of a broader cultural effervescence in Ireland in the late 1890s that included the founding of the Gaelic League, which promoted the use of the Irish language, and the startup of the Gaelic Athletic Association, which restored Irish sports.

Irony A device used in writing and speech to deliberately express ideas so they can be understood in two ways. In drama, irony occurs when a character does not know something that the other characters or the audience knows.

Jainism A religion founded in India in the sixth century B.C.E. by Vardhaman, who is known as Mahavira, or the "great hero." Formed in direct opposition to the rigid ritualism and hierarchical structure of traditional Hinduism, Jainism espoused asceticism, renunciation of the world, nonviolence, and the sanctity of all living beings.

Jewish mysticism Like all forms of mysticism, Jewish mysticism focuses on learning and practices that lead to unity with the creator; its teachings are referred to as the Cabala, or Kabala.

Joruri The form of puppet theater that developed in Japan in the seventeenth and eighteenth centuries in which expert puppeteers manipulate lifelike dolls while a master chanter, accompanied by the SAMISEN, sings and chants the story, speaks for the characters, and describes the scenes. The term derives from *ningyo,* meaning puppet or doll, and *joruri,* which alludes to the often-told story of Lady Joruri, the main character of a popular story dating back to the fifteenth century who was the subject of the first puppet play. Today joruri is known as *BUNRAKU,*

after the great puppeteer Bunraku-ken Uemura (d. 1810), and Bunraku-ken Uemura II (1813–1873), who established a puppet theater in Osaka in 1842 after interest in joruri declined.

Judgment of Paris In Greek legend, Paris (Alexandros) was selected by the god Zeus to judge which of three goddesses was the most beautiful. He chose Aphrodite, who bribed him by agreeing to help him seduce Helen, the most beautiful woman alive. His stealing of Helen and refusal to return her was the cause of the Trojan War.

Julian calendar Calendar used in the Western world from the time of Julius Caesar, c. 46 B.C.E., until 1582, when it was generally replaced by the Gregorian calendar, which is still in wide use today.

Kabuki A popular form of Japanese theater primarily about and aimed at the middle classes and that uses only male actors; Kabuki developed in the sixteenth and seventeenth centuries, parallel to *JORURI,* or puppet theater, which often shares the same plots and stories and even the same plays.

Kibyoshi Literally, "yellow back"; a simple illustrated book usually concerned with life in the licensed quarters.

Laissez-faire A French phrase meaning "let them do"; a doctrine in classical economics that asserts the economy should operate on its own, without interference from the government.

Leatherstocking Tales Novels by James Fenimore Cooper (1789–1851), including *The Pioneers* (1823), *The Last of the Mohicans* (1826), *The Prairie* (1827), *The Pathfinder* (1840), and *The Deerslayer* (1841). All featured a PROTAGONIST nicknamed "Leatherstocking."

Leitmotifs Themes, brief passages, or single words repeated within a work.

Leviathan A dragon or sea monster mentioned in the Hebrew Scriptures, suggesting an ancient combat myth. See Isaiah 51:9–10, Isaiah 27:1, Psalm 74:12–14, Psalm 89:10, and Job 26:12–13. See also RAHAB.

Liberalism An ideology that rejects authoritarian government and defends freedom of speech, association, and religion as well as the right to own property. Liberalism evolved during the ENLIGHTENMENT and became the dominant political idea of the nineteenth century. Both the American and French Revolutions were based on liberal thought.

Limerick A humorous, sometimes nonsensical poem of five lines, with a strict scheme of meter and rhyme.

Line A sequence of words. In poetry, lines are typically measured by the number of feet they contain.

Literary epic A literary epic—as distinguished from folk epics such as the *Mahabharata* or *The Iliad*—that are made up of somewhat loosely linked episodes and closely follow oral conventions—is written with self-conscious artistry, has a tightly knit organic unity, and is stylistically rooted in a written, literate culture. In actuality, great epics often blur the distinction between the oral or folk epic and the literary epic.

Local-color tales Stories that seek to portray the people and way of life of a particular region by describing the speech, dress, and customs of its inhabitants.

Lyric A brief poem that reflects the imagination and emotion of the speaker. With its etymology in the word *lyre*, a lyric poem was originally meant to be sung to the accompaniment of a lyre, a medieval stringed instrument that is associated with poetic inspiration. Although modern lyric poetry is not necessarily meant to be sung, it does retain its melodic quality. Lyric poetry is highly subjective and informed by the speaker's imagination; it has flourished throughout literary history.

Magical realism A movement in fiction in which REALIST technique is used to narrate stories that combine mundane and miraculous events, everyday realities and the supernatural. The term is most often used to describe the work of Colombian novelist Gabriel García Márquez (b. 1928), Mexican author Carlos Fuentes (b. 1928), Peruvian novelist Mario Vargas Llosa (b. 1936), and Argentine author Julio Cortázar (1914–1984).

Manchu Also known as the Jurchen, a people who lived northeast of the Great Wall of China, in the area now known as Manchuria; when civil disturbances weakened the authority of the Ming emperor, the Manchu, with the assistance of some from inside China, took control of Beijing and founded a new empire. Their dynasty, known as the QING or Manchu dynasty, lasted from 1644 to 1911.

Manifest Destiny Term coined in 1845 for the American belief that the United States was not only destined but obligated to expand its territory westward to the Pacific Ocean.

Marxism A school of thought based on the writings of German Socialist thinker Karl Marx. Among its main tenets are the ideas that class struggle is the central element of Western culture, that a capitalist class thrives by exploiting the labor of a working class, and that workers must struggle to overcome their capitalist exploiters through revolution and thereafter establish a socialist society in which private property does not exist and all people have collective control of the means of production and distribution.

Marxist criticism Literary criticism that evolved from Karl Marx's political and economic theories. Marxist critics believe that texts must be understood in terms of the social class and the economic and political positions of their characters and plot.

Masque Developed in the Renaissance, masques are highly stylized and structured performances with an often mythological or allegorical plot, combining drama, music, song, and dance in an elaborate display.

Materialism A worldview that explains the nature of reality in terms of physical matter and material conditions rather than by way of ideas, emotions, or the supernatural.

Mathnavi Persian poetic form used for romantic, epic, didactic, and other types of poems whose subjects demand a lengthy treatment; its verse structure is similar to that of the Western heroic couplet, but with two rhyming halves in a single line.

Meiji Restoration After years of feudal reign in Japan, the emperor was restored to his position in 1868. He adopted *Meiji,* meaning "enlightened rule," as the name of his era. In this period, massive INDUSTRIALIZATION took place in Japan, which became a significant competitor for world power. The military was also strengthened to combat European and American imperialism.

Melodrama A dramatic genre characterized by suspense, romance, and sensation. Melodramas typically have a happy ending.

Mestizos Peoples in the Americas of mixed ethnic or cultural heritage, usually a combination of Spanish and Native American.

Metaphor A comparison of two things that does not use the words *like* or *as.* For example, "love is a rose."

Meter The rhythm of a poem based on the number of syllables in each line and which syllables are accented. See also FOOT.

Michiyuki A conventional form in Japanese drama (and also in fiction) wherein a character's thoughts and feelings are evoked through the places he or she visits on a journey; often, by means of symbolism and allusion, the journey suggests a spiritual transformation.

Middle Passage The transatlantic journey from West Africa to the Caribbean or the Americas of slave ships transporting their human cargo during the time of the slave trade (sixteenth–nineteenth centuries).

Millenarianism A utopian belief that the end of time is imminent, after which there will be a thousand-year era of perfect peace on earth.

Ming dynasty (1368–1644) Founded by Zhu Yuan-zhang, who restored native Chinese rule from the Mongols who had ruled China during the previous Yuan dynasty (1271–1368) established by Kubla Khan. The Ming dynasty saw a flourishing of Chinese culture, the restoration of Confucianism, and the rise of the arts, including porcelain, architecture, drama, and the novel.

Mock epic A form that parodies the EPIC by treating a trivial subject in the elevated style of the epic, employing such conventions as an invocation to the muse, an extended simile, and a heroic epithet that burlesques its subject.

Modernism In its broadest sense, this term refers to European writing and art from approximately 1914, the beginning of World War I, to about 1945, the end of World War II. Although many writers of this time continued to work with the forms of fiction and poetry that had been in place since the nineteenth century, others such as James Joyce (1882–1941), Virginia Woolf (1882–1941), William Faulkner (1897–1962), Rainer Maria Rilke (1875–1926), and Thomas Mann (1875–1955) broke with the past, introducing experimentation and innovation in structure, style, and language. *Modernism* can also refer to a spirit of innovation and experimentation, or the break with nineteenth-century aesthetic and literary thinking and forms, or the exploration of psychological states of mind, alienation, and social rupture that characterized the era between the two world wars.

Monologue A speech of significant length delivered by one person; in drama, a CHARACTER talks to himself or reveals personal secrets without addressing another character.

Mystery religions Mystery cults were very popular in ancient Greece and Rome for at least one thousand years, beginning around 1000 B.C.E. The details of each cult were kept a secret, but all cults shared a rigorous rite of initiation, a concern about death, and a hope for immortality centered on a deity who had personal knowledge of the afterlife. The most popular Greek versions were the Orphic and Eleusinian mysteries. The mysteries of Isis and Mithra were favored in the Roman world.

Mythological criticism A type of literary criticism that focuses on the archetypal stories common to all cultures. Initiated by Carl Jung in the early twentieth century, mythological criticism seeks to reveal how the structures lodged deep in the human consciousness take the form of archetypal stories and are the basis for literature. Jung identified four principal ARCHETYPES that together constitute the Self: Shadow (rejected evil), Anima (feminine side of male self), Animus (masculine side of female self), and Spirit (wise old man or woman).

Narrative poem A poem with only one basic rule: It must tell a story. Ballads, epics, and romances are typically narrative poems.

Narrator The voice that in fiction describes the PLOT or action of a story. The narrator can speak in the first or the third person and, depending on the effect the author wishes to create, can be very visible or almost invisible (an explicit or an implicit narrator); he or she can be involved in the plot or be more distant. See also POINT OF VIEW and SPEAKER.

Naturalism A late-nineteenth-century literary school that sought to apply scientific objectivity to the novel. Led by Émile Zola (1840–1902) and influenced by Darwinism, Naturalists created characters who were ordinary people, whose lives were shaped by the forces of heredity and the environment.

Nawab The title given to a local Muslim ruler in India during the Mughal empire (1526–1857).

Négritude A literary movement founded in the early 1930s by three Black Francophone writers in Paris: Léopold Sédar Senghor (1906–2001), Aimé Césaire (b. 1913), and Léon Damas (1912–1978). In their work, these Négritude writers protested French colonial rule and the European assumption of superiority. They wanted their writings, which honored the traditions and special qualities of the African and Caribbean peoples, to inspire independence movements in the colonies.

Neoclassicism A style of art and architecture that was characterized by the simple, symmetrical forms of classical Greek and Roman art. It originated as a reaction to the Rococo and Baroque styles and was the result of a revival of classical thought in Europe and America. Neoclassical writing characterized the Augustan Age, a period comprising roughly the first half of the eighteenth century. Its name suggests an analogy to the reign of Emperor Augustus in the Roman Empire (63 B.C.E.–14 C.E.), when many of the great Latin poets, especially Virgil, were writing.

Neo-Confucianism Refers generally to the philosophical tradition in China and Japan based on the thought of Confucius (551–479 B.C.E.) and his commentators, particularly Mencius (c. 371–c. 288 B.C.E.) and Zhu Xi (1130–1200). Neo-Confucianism, which arose during the Sung dynasty (960–1279), asserts that the understanding of things must be based on an understanding of their underlying principles; in moral and political philosophy, it emphasizes the study of history, loyalty to family and nation, and order.

Neo-Sensualism Also known as the New Sensibilities or New Perceptionist school, this approach was founded by Kawabata Yasunari and other AVANT-GARDE writers, including Riichi Yokomitsu (1898–1947), and headquartered at the University of Tokyo in the 1920s. In 1924 these writers founded a magazine called *The Literary Age*. Influenced by European writers as well as by Japanese poetic traditions and *Nō* drama, neo-Sensualists sought to break with the confessional style of REALIST and NATURALIST writers and aimed for a more purely aesthetic, nonlinear style of fiction writing.

Neo-Shintoism *Shinto* is a term given to indigenous Japanese beliefs as distinguished from Buddhism, which was introduced to Japan in the sixth century C.E. In the seventeenth century, Shinto and Confucianist ideals came into contact with one another and produced an ideology that emphasized political philosophy and valued the virtues of wisdom, benevolence, and courage.

New Criticism A type of formalist literary criticism that completely disregards historical and biographical information to focus on the actual text. The New Critics perform a close reading of a work and give special attention to technical devices such as symbols and images and, in poetry, rhythm.

New Historicism A literary school developed as a reaction to NEW CRITICISM in the 1980s; presently, it is one of the leading schools of literary criticism. Like the nineteenth-century historicists, the New Historicists argue that historical and other external contexts must be part of textual analysis.

Nigerian-Biafran War Nigerian civil war that started when the Igbo people declared the eastern region of Nigeria an independent state named the Republic of Biafra. Recognized by only three countries, Biafra was almost immediately attacked by Nigerian troops. After a bloody fight resulting in close to three million casualties, the Biafran government surrendered in January 1970.

Ninjo Japanese term that denotes human feelings or passion, drives that often come into conflict with *GIRI*, or social duty and responsibility.

Nō The highly elaborate and ritualistic classical theater of Japan, known for its minimalist approach to plot, scenery, and stage effects and the stately performance and Zen-like mastery of its actors; *nō* means "talent" or "accomplishment." The great master and theorist of *Nō* drama is Zeami Motokiyo (1363–1443), who wrote several of the most famous *Nō* plays, including *Atsumori* and *The Lady Aoi.*

Novel An extended work of fictional prose narrative. The novel is a modern outgrowth of earlier genres such as the romance. There is considerable debate as to the origins of the novel; some critics trace it to Cervantes's *Don Quixote* in 1605. In England, the novel came into being in the beginning of the eighteenth century and has since developed far beyond its original realistic and moralistic aims, making it one of the most flexible of literary genres.

Octave A STANZA of eight lines in poetry.

Ode An elevated form of LYRIC generally written on a single theme, using varied metric and rhyme patterns. With the ode, poets working within classical schemes can introduce considerable innovation. There are three major types of odes in English: the Pindaric, or Regular; the Horatian; and the Irregular. The Pindaric ode is structured by three-strophe divisions, modulating between the strophe, antistrophe, and epode, which vary in tone. The Horatian ode uses only one STANZA type with variation introduced within each stanza. The Irregular ode, sometimes called the English ode, allows wide variety among stanza forms, rhyme schemes, and metrical patterns.

Oedipus complex A term from Freudian psychoanalysis that refers to the unconscious male desire to kill one's own father and to sleep with one's own mother. The term derives from the Greek myth of Oedipus, who unknowingly murdered his father and married his mother; his self-inflicted punishment was to blind himself. FREUDIAN CRITICS do not take the complex or the story literally, but frequently use it to examine in literature the guilt associated with sexual desire and competition with or hostility toward one's father.

Onomatopoeia A word that sounds like the thing it refers to: for example, the *buzz* of bees.

Open form Also known as FREE VERSE. A type of poetry that does not follow established conventions of METER, RHYME, and STANZA.

Organic form The concept that the structure of a literary work develops according to an internal logic. The literary work grows and becomes an organic whole that follows the principles of nature, not mechanics. The created work of art is akin to a growing plant that relies on all of its parts working together.

Orientalism The academic study and knowledge of the Middle East and Asia that developed during the imperialism of the nineteenth century. Orientalism is a Western approach to understanding the cultures, languages, and religions of the East. Especially in the early studies, the Orient was seen as exotic and romantic, but its inhabitants were regarded as uncivilized and inferior. Although by now these views have been challenged and changed, they are arguably still prevalent.

Oxymoron A rhetorical figure of speech in which contradictory terms are combined, such as "jumbo shrimp" and "deafening silence."

Parable A short narrative designed to teach a lesson about life in which the moral isn't directly stated; a form popular during biblical times.

Paradox An argument or opinion that is contradictory but true. For instance, "You have to be cruel to be kind."

Paraphrase To rewrite or say the same thing using different words.

Parian White marble from the Greek island of Paros.

Parody A humorous imitation of another, usually serious, work. Parody can be a form of literary criticism that exposes defects in a work, or it can function as an acknowledgement of a work's cultural and literary importance.

Patois A regional dialect of a language.

Peloponnesian War (431–404 B.C.E.) War between the Athenian and Spartan alliance systems that encompassed most of the Greek world. The war set new standards for warfare—Athens used the navy to support the land offensive, for instance—but the new tactics also prolonged the fight; instead of there being one decisive battle, the war dragged on for three decades. Eventually, Athens was defeated, and Sparta took over the defeated power's overseas empire.

Persian Wars A series of wars between a coalition of Greek city-states and the Persian empire fought between 500 and 449 B.C.E.; the Greek victory set the stage for the flourishing of Greek culture.

Persona Literally, a persona is a mask. In literature, a persona is a speaker created by a writer to tell a story or to speak in a poem. A persona is not a character in a story or narrative, nor does a persona necessarily directly reflect the author's personal voice. A persona is a separate self, created by and distinct from the author, through which he or she speaks.

Personification A figure of speech in which abstractions or inanimate objects are given human qualities or form.

Picaresque Term used to describe a novel that is loosely structured around a succession of episodes that focus on a rather thinly drawn *picaro,* or hero. The hero's adventures generally provide a sweeping and detailed view of a society and its customs, which are often satirized by the writer. Examples include Cervantes's *Don Quixote* and Voltaire's *Candide.*

Picture poem A poem whose lines form the image of the object it describes.

Plot The pattern of events or the story told in a narrative or drama.

Point of view The perspective from which the author, SPEAKER, or NARRATOR presents a story. A point of view might be localized within a CHARACTER, in which case the story is told from a first-person point of view. There is a range of possibilities between first-person point of view and omniscience, wherein the story is told from a perspective unlimited by time, place, or character.

Polis Greek term meaning "city"; designates the Greek city-states, such as Athens and Sparta, that arose in the sixth century B.C.E.

Postcolonial criticism Literary analysis of works produced in countries such as India, Africa, and the Caribbean that were once under the control of a colonial power. In some cases the term refers to the analysis of works about the colony written by authors who have been heavily influenced by the colonizing culture.

Postcolonialism The social, political, cultural, and economic practices that arose in response and resistance to colonialism and imperialism. This term also refers to the historical period following the colonial era, corresponding roughly to the second half of the twentieth century.

Postmodernism A literary and artistic movement that flourished in the late twentieth century as both a departure from and a development of MODERNISM. Postmodernism is frequently characterized by self-consciousness and self-reflexiveness: Postmodern literature is aware of the way it operates in a long literary tradition and responds to this awareness by revealing or referring to itself. Postmodern literature differs from modern literature in its emphasis on surface rather than depth, humor rather than psychological anguish, and space rather than time.

Pragmatism A philosophical approach that explains meaning and truth in terms of the application of ideas and beliefs to practical action.

Pre-Raphaelites A group of artists and writers, including John Everett Millais (1829–1896),

Dante Gabriel Rossetti (1828–1882), and William Holman Hunt (1827–1910), who rebelled against convention in poetry and painting by means of a strict adherence to details of nature; they aimed to capture what they perceived to be the truth, simplicity, and clarity of medieval painting—its pure colors, spiritual or mystical ambience, and sensuousness.

Problem play A drama in which the conflict arises from contemporary social problems. Bernard Shaw's *Mrs. Warren's Profession* (1893) and Shakespeare's *All's Well That Ends Well* (1602–04) are problem plays.

Proletariat The modern industrial working class, which, as defined by Karl Marx, lives solely by the sale of its labor. See also Bourgeoisie.

Prologue Text that typically is placed prior to an introduction or that replaces a traditional introduction; often discusses events of importance for the general understanding of the narrative.

Prose poem A poem printed as prose without attention to line breaks. The prose poem argues for the flexibility of poetry by eschewing strict attention to meter and even rhythm, yet the language of a prose poem is frequently figurative and characterized by other poetic conventions such as alliteration or internal rhyme.

Protagonist A leading figure or the main character in a drama or other literary work.

Protestant work ethic German sociologist Max Weber (1864–1920) first linked Protestantism to the habits of diligence and hard work that contributed to the rise of capitalism. The Puritans, whose form of Protestantism influenced early American life, interpreted prosperity resulting from work as a sign of God's favor.

Psychological criticism An approach to literature that draws on psychoanalytic theories, especially those of Sigmund Freud (1856–1939) and Jacques Lacan (1901–1981), to understand more fully the text, the writer, and the reader.

Pun A play on words that relies on a word's having more than one meaning or sounding like another word.

Purdah Practice adopted by some Muslims and Hindus that obscures women from public sight by mandating that they wear concealing clothing, especially veils. The custom originated in the seventh century c.e. and is still common in Islamic countries, though it has largely disappeared in Hinduism.

Qing dynasty (1644–1911) Also known as the Manchu dynasty, named after the Manchu, a people from the north of China who took over China in 1644 with the help of rebel Chinese; the last dynasty in Chinese history, the Qing saw an increase in the influence of foreign interests and trade.

Quatrain A stanza of four lines in a poem.

Qur'an Or Koran; the sacred scriptures of Islam.

Rahab A term appearing several times in the Hebrew Scriptures; literally means "stormer," an allusion to the ancient monster of chaos in earlier Semitic creation myths. See also Leviathan.

Rastafarianism An African-influenced religion that originated in the Caribbean in the twentieth century; venerates the former emperor of Ethiopia, Haile Selassie, forbids the cutting of hair, and embraces black culture and identity.

Rationalist Utilitarianism Revolutionary way of thinking established by, among others, Leon Trotsky (1879–1940). The Rationalist Utilitarians adopted the ethical theory proposed by John Stuart Mill (1806–1873) that all political actions should be directed toward achieving the greatest good for the greatest number of people. Mill, however, believed that decisions based on direct observation should determine action, while the Rationalist Utilitarians held that logical reasoning should play that role.

Reader-response criticism A critical approach to literature in which the primary focus falls on the reader, or the process of reading, not on the author. Reader-response critics believe that a literary work does not possess a fixed idea or meaning; meaning is a function of the perspective of the reader.

Realism Most broadly defined, realism is the attempt to represent the world accurately in literature. As a literary movement, Realism flourished in Russia, France, England, and America in the latter half of the nineteenth century. It emphasized not only accurate representation but the "truth," usually expressed as the consequence of a moral choice. Realist writers deemphasized the shaping power of the imagination and concerned themselves with the experiences of ordinary, middle-class subjects and the dilemmas they faced.

Recognition Based on the Greek concept of tragedy, recognition, or *anagnorisis,* is the point in a story when the PROTAGONIST discovers the truth about his or her situation. Usually this results in a drastic change in the course of the plot.

Reformation Also known as the Protestant Reformation, this sixteenth-century challenge to the authority of the Catholic Church caused a permanent rift in the Christian world, with those loyal to the pope remaining Catholic and those rejecting papal authority forming new Protestant faiths such as the Anglican, Lutheran, Calvinist, Anabaptist, and Presbyterian. The Reformation originated — and was most successful — in Northern Europe, especially Germany; its notable leaders include Martin Luther and John Calvin.

Renaissance man A term used to describe someone accomplished in many disciplines, especially in both science and the arts, like Leonardo da Vinci and other figures from the European Renaissance who were talented in many fields.

Renaissance sonneteers Poets of the European Renaissance who wrote fourteen-line love poems, often addressed to lovers who resisted or ignored their entreaties. Two types of Renaissance sonnets are commonly identified, the Italian and the English. These are alternatively known as the Petrarchan, after the Italian poet Petrarch who originated the form, and the Shakespearean, after the form's preeminent English practitioner. The major difference between the two types is that the Italian usually has five rhymes and the English seven.

Renga A form of traditional Japanese court poetry that uses elevated diction and links a number of haiku-like poems. Usually written by two or more poets who alternate verses, the traditional *renga* is a succession of three- and two-line compositions that evokes a particular season in each verse.

Resolution The point in the plot of a narrative work or drama that occurs after the climax and generally establishes a new understanding; also known as *falling action.*

Reversal The point in the plot of a story or drama when the fortunes of the PROTAGONIST change unexpectedly; also known as the *peripiteia.*

Revolution of 1830 In July 1830, the opponents of King Charles X (r. 1818–24) took to the streets of Paris to protest his corruption and the undermining of liberal reforms. Charles abdicated the throne, and bankers and industrialists brought in King Louis-Philippe (r. 1830–48), who promised to uphold the reforms Charles had tried to dissolve.

Revolution of 1848 Often called the February Revolution, when French king Louis-Philippe (r. 1830–48) was overthrown and the Second Republic was established. This revolution inspired uprisings in many European countries.

Rhyme The repetition of identical or similar-sounding words or syllables, usually accented, in lines of poetry. Rhymes may be at the end of lines or internal to the lines.

Rhythm The pattern of stressed and unstressed syllables in prose and especially in poetry that can lend emphasis, reinforce a sound association, or suggest regularity or recurrence. The rhythm of a literary work can affect the emotional response of the reader or listener.

Romantic hero The PROTAGONIST of a romance, novel, or poem who is shaped by experiences that frequently take the form of combat, love, or adventure. The romantic hero is judged by his actions more than his thoughts, and he is often on a journey that will affect his moral development.

Romanticism A literary and artistic movement that swept through Europe in the early nineteenth century; its defiance of neoclassical principles and rationalism roughly parallels the political upheaval of the French Revolution, with which it is often associated. Romanticism in its simplest form exalts nature, the innocence of children and rustics, private emotion and experience, and the pursuit of political freedom and spiritual transcendence.

Rosetta stone A slab of basalt inscribed with texts in hieroglyphic, demotic, and Greek. Found by Napoleon's troops in Northern Egypt in 1799, it enabled Egyptologist J.-F. Champollion (1790–1832) to decipher Egyptian hieroglyphics for the first time (1821).

Russo-Japanese War (1904–1905) Russia's aggressive Far-Eastern policy following the SINO-JAPANESE WAR (1894–95) and the Russian construction of a railway across Manchuria resulted in increasing animosity between the two nations. Russia twice violated the treaty with China and lost the year-long war with Japan, destabilizing Russian power in the region.

Salamis Site of an important naval battle where the Greek fleet defeated the Persians in 480 B.C.E.

Samian War The Samian War (441–439 B.C.E.) was fought to bring the island of Samos — which had broken off from the league of Greek states led by Athens — back into the alliance and into compliance with Athenian hegemony.

Samisen A three-stringed instrument with a long fretless neck and a nearly square sound box introduced in Japan in the late sixteenth century; the samisen became the preferred instrument for accompanying the narration of JORURI.

Samsara A HINDU term for the cycle of birth, life, death, and rebirth; many Hindu practices aimed at obtaining release, *moksa,* from the otherwise endless repetition of life and death.

Samurai Japanese feudal aristocrat and member of the hereditary warrior class. Denied recognition in the MEIJI RESTORATION (1867).

Sanskrit The classical language of ancient India, in which many of the major HINDU religious and literary texts were written.

Satire A literary or dramatic genre whose works, such as Jonathan Swift's (1667–1745) *Gulliver's Travels,* attack and ridicule human behavior.

Scansion A system of poetic analysis that involves dividing lines into feet and examining patterns of stressed and unstressed syllables. Scansion is a mechanical way of breaking down verse in order to understand the regularities and irregularities of its METER.

Scene In drama, a subdivision of an ACT.

Script The written version or text of a play or movie that is used by the actors.

Sentimentality Extravagant emotion; T. S. Eliot defined this as "emotion in excess of the facts."

Sepoy The name given to Indians serving in the British army.

Sepoy Mutiny A rebellion in southern India in 1857 started by local Sepoys in reaction to regulations that violated their religion. The rebellion ended in 1858 after the British army intervened.

Sestet A STANZA of six lines; the last stanza of a Petrarchan SONNET is a sestet.

Setting The time, place, and social environment that frame the characters in a story.

Shinju play A play culminating in suicide; one of three major types of JORURI plays. The others are the *jidaimono,* or history play, and the *sewamono,* a play about contemporary domestic life. Some critics see the *shinju* play as a type of *sewamono.*

Shogun A military ruler of feudal Japan between 1192 and 1867. The shogunate was an inherited position in the military that operated under the nominal control of the emperor.

Simile A figure of speech, introduced by *like* or *as,* in which two things are compared as equals.

Sino-Japanese War (1894–1895) A conflict between Japan and China that revealed the weakness of the declining Chinese empire and the emerging strength of Japan. The war, which developed from a conflict over the control of Korea, culminated in Japan's victory: China recognized the independence of Korea, ceded Taiwan, and lifted trade restrictions with Japan.

Slave narrative Autobiographical narrative by a former slave describing his or her life and mistreatment under slavery, attempts to escape, and ultimate liberation. The narratives, which employed many devices from popular fiction, were accompanied by testimonials to their authenticity.

Slavophile Literally, someone who admires Slavs, a people of Eastern Europe. In nineteenth-century Russia, the term referred to someone who believed in the national traditions of Russia, who felt that Russia had the true religion, and who believed he or she was destined to export Russian teachings and establish the kingdom of God on earth.

Social Realism A type of realism that concentrates on the unpleasant realities of the modern world and attempts to expose injustice and to encourage political reaction.

Socialist Realism A standard for art and literature developed in the Soviet Union in the 1930s; it demanded that art depict the life of the people realistically and celebrate the ideals of the revolution. Mao Zedong (1893–1976) enforced similar standards in China after the People's Republic was established in 1949.

Sociological criticism School of literary criticism that seeks to place a work of art in its social context and define the relationship between the two. Like Marxist critics, sociological critics are oriented toward social class, political ideology, gender roles, and economic conditions in their analyses.

Soliloquy A literary or dramatic discourse in which a character speaks without addressing a listener.

Sonnet A fourteen-line LYRIC poem. The first basic sonnet form is the Italian or Petrarchan sonnet, which is divided into an eight-line octet and a six-line SESTET, each with a specific but varied rhyme pattern. The English or Shakespearean sonnet is divided into three four-line QUATRAINS followed by a two-line COUPLET; the quatrains are rhymed *abab cdcd efef* and the couplet is also end rhymed, *gg*.

Sophists Literally, wise men. Greek teachers who provided instruction in logic and rhetoric to pupils who could afford their expensive fees. Rhetoric was a new discipline whose study was observed to provide an advantage in politics and in the courts. Soon *Sophist* came to mean one who used methods of argumentation that undermined traditional beliefs and manipulated reality. When Socrates (c. 470–399 B.C.E.) challenged the authority of the Sophists, he was brought to trial and executed.

Spanish civil war (1936–39) War between the Falange Fascist Party led by General Francisco Franco and liberal republican loyalist forces; often seen as the staging ground for World War II. The war ended with republican defeat and the establishment of a right-wing dictatorship.

Speaker The person or PERSONA who speaks in a poem—often a created identity who cannot be equated with the poet.

Spiritual autobiography An autobiography that gives special importance to self-examination, interpretation of Scripture, and belief in predestination. St. Augustine's *Confessions* (c. 400), detailing a life of sin, conversion, and spiritual rebirth, is generally regarded as the archetypal spiritual autobiography.

St. Augustine (354–430) Influential Catholic theologian from North Africa whose *Confessions* (c. 400) tells the story of his conversion to Christianity.

St. Francis (c. 1181–1226) Founder of the Franciscan religious order; known for his kindness.

Stage directions Written directions explaining how actors are to move onstage. See also SCRIPT.

Stanza A poetic verse of two or more lines, sometimes characterized by a common pattern of RHYME and METER.

Stock responses Predictable responses to language and symbols. See also CLICHÉ.

Stream of consciousness A term first used by the American philosopher and psychologist William James (1842–1910) to denote the often disjointed and even incoherent flow of ideas, sensations, thoughts, and images running through the conscious mind at any given moment. In literature, "stream of consciousness" generally refers to novels or short stories that attempt to achieve psychological realism by depicting the raw, unedited contents of a character's mind. Such depictions may involve "interior monologues" wherein an author presents a character's thoughts either with (indirect) or without (direct) any commentary, ordering, or editing. This device, associated with high modernism, reached its height in the work of James Joyce.

Stress A syllable receiving emphasis in accordance with a metrical pattern.

Sturm und Drang Literally, "storm and stress." Refers to a period of intense literary activity in the late eighteenth century associated with Idealism and the revolt against stale convention. The movement was named after a play about the American Revolution, and its leading participants included Goethe (1749–1832) and Schiller (1759–1805).

Style The distinctive manner in which an author writes and thus makes his or her work unique. A style provides a kind of literary signature for the writer.

Subplot A PLOT subordinate to the main plot of a literary work or drama.

Superman Also called "overman," or *Übermensch* in German. A term introduced by the German philosopher Friedrich Nietzsche (1844–1900) to denote a superior man who would exercise creative power and live at a level of experience beyond the standards of good and evil and thus represent the goal of human evolution.

Surrealism An aesthetic movement centered in twentieth-century France that extolled the direct and free expression of the unconscious as understood by Freudian psychology; proponents of surrealism include the writer André Breton (1896–1966), who wrote *Manifesto of Surrealism* in 1924; the filmmaker Jean Cocteau (1889–1963); and the painters Salvador Dalí (1904–1989) from France and Joan Miró (1893–1983) from Spain. A combination of precise, realistic detail and dreamlike fantasy characterizes surrealism.

Suspense The anxious emotion of the audience or reader anticipating the outcome of a story or drama, typically having to do with the fate of the PROTAGONIST or another character with whom a sympathetic attachment has been formed.

Symbol A representative of something by association. Though a symbol is often confused with a metaphor, a metaphor compares two dissimilar things while a symbol associates two things. For example, the *word* "tree" is a symbol for an *actual* tree. Some symbols have values that are accepted by most people. A flag, for instance, is for many a symbol of national pride, just as a cross is widely seen as a symbol of Christianity. Knowledge of a symbol's cultural context is sometimes necessary to understand its meaning; an apple pie is an American symbol of innocence that a Japanese person, for example, would not necessarily recognize.

Symbolism As the French writer Paul Valéry (1871–1945) notes in *The Existence of Symbolism* (1939), Symbolism "was not a school. On the contrary, it included many schools of the most divergent types." Symbolism generally refers to a movement among poets in France anticipated in the work of Charles Baudelaire (1821–1867) and Arthur Rimbaud (1854–1891) but practiced as a self-conscious movement by Stéphane Mallarmé (1842–1898), Paul Verlaine (1844–1896), and Jules Laforgue (1860–1887). Symbolists sought to convey the fluidity and evocative harmony of music in their work, and to capture tones, fragrances, sensations, and intuitions rather than concrete images or rational ideas.

Syncretism The attempt to combine differing beliefs, such as philosophy and religion, or two religious systems, such as Christianity and a native African tradition.

Syntax The way parts of speech are arranged in a sentence.

Tantrism A minor HINDU tradition written down in scriptures called Tantras. Tantrism holds the supreme deity to be feminine and teaches that spiritual liberation can be won through erotic practices.

Terza rima A verse form composed of iambic three-line STANZAS. The triplets have ten- or eleven-syllable lines. Terza rima is used to perhaps its most brilliant end in Dante's (1265–1321) *Divine Comedy.*

Tetragrammaton The four consonants of the Hebrew alphabet YHWH used to approximate God's secret name; this name and its utterances are believed to contain special powers.

Thanatos "Death" in Greek. According to Sigmund Freud, our two primary drives are EROS (love) and Thanatos (death).

Theater of the absurd A school of modernist, non-realistic drama especially influential from the 1950s to the '70s. Italian playwright Eugene Ionesco described its subject matter as "man . . . lost in the world, [so] all his actions become senseless, absurd, useless."

Theme A topic of discussion or a point of view embodied in a work of art.

Theosophical Society Founded in 1875 in London by Helena Petrovna Blavatsky in order to promote the reconciliation of Eastern religious doctrines with Western mysticism. Blavatsky, who wrote *Isis Unveiled* (1877) and faced charges of charlatanism, believed in the spiritual nature of things, the reincarnation of the soul, and the power of grasping one's spiritual essence, particularly by means of mystical experience.

Thesis The presentation of a purpose or hypothetical proposition, or a dissertation with an original point based on research.

Tokugawa era (1600–1868) Period of Japanese history named after Tokugawa Ieyasu (1542–1616), who was named shogun in 1603; also known as the EDO era because Tokugawa made Edo (now Tokyo) the capital. The early Tokugawa was a period of international isolation, political stability, nation building, and prosperity for the middle classes; it was also a time of great literary and cultural growth, particularly in the popular cultural forms such as KABUKI and *JORURI* (puppet) theater, the popular novel, and colored woodblock art, all aimed at the flourishing middle classes.

The Tokugawa era ended in 1867 when a group of disaffected SAMURAI restored imperial rule under the teenage emperor Meiji (r. 1867–1912) in the MEIJI RESTORATION and opened Japan's doors to Western trade and cultural exchange.

Tone A manner of expression in writing that indicates a certain attitude toward the subject or the implied audience.

Totalitarianism A system of centralized government in which a single unopposed party exerts total and repressive control over a country's political, social, economic, and cultural life.

Tragedy A dramatic or literary form originating in Greece that deals with serious human actions and issues. The actions must create feelings of fear and compassion in the spectator that are later released (CATHARSIS). Typically, the main character is of a high stature or rank, so his or her fall is substantial. Even though tragedies are sad, they seem both just and believable. The tragedy raises serious moral and philosophical questions about the meaning of life and fate.

Tragicomedy A drama that combines tragedy and comedy and in which moral values are particularly questioned or ridiculed.

Transcendentalism A philosophy derived from ROMANTICISM that flourished in the United States in the early nineteenth century. American writers Ralph Waldo Emerson and Henry David Thoreau championed and articulated the philosophy, which contends that the individual mind has the capability to transcend the human institutions that seek to fetter it. The transcendentalists believed that the most valuable pursuit was to experience, reflect upon, and study nature and its relation to the individual.

Travel narratives A form of narrative that recounts the incidents that occur and the people and things that the narrator meets and sees while visiting a place with which she or he is typically unfamiliar. Prose and poetic accounts about exploration and adventure in unfamiliar lands and places as well as in more or less familiar locations are considered travel narratives. Such narratives typically are told episodically and chronologically, engage in elaborate strategies to validate their authenticity, and raise important and complex questions about the representation of the "other" — that is, the ability of the traveler to depict accurately the people, places, and cultures he or she is describing.

Triplet In poetry, a group of three lines of verse.

Ukiyo-e A school of Japanese woodblock printing arising in the EDO period that captured images of everyday life in the FLOATING WORLD (*ukiyo*). The greatest *ukiyo-e* artists include Moronobu (c. 1618–c. 1694), Harunobu (1725–1770), and Hiroshige (1797–1858).

Ukiyo-zoshi "Stories of the FLOATING WORLD" or "tales of the floating world"; a Japanese style of fiction associated with the hundred-year period from about 1683 to 1783 that took as its subject matter the everyday lives of *chonin,* or townspeople, and was written in colloquial language. Ihara Saikaku is said to be the originator of *ukiyo-zoshi;* many authors in this tradition not only imitated his style but plagiarized his works.

Ultraists A group of Spanish writers who influenced Jorge Luis Borges. The Ultraists rejected middle-class materialism and sought refuge in the artifice of poetry and in exotic images and metaphors.

Understatement A figure of speech that says less than what is intended.

Upanishads A body of sacred texts dating from the ninth century B.C.E. that provide a mystical development of and commentary on earlier Vedic texts.

Urdu An Indo-European language closely related to Hindi. Urdu is the official language of Pakistan and is also spoken in India and Bangladesh.

Utilitarianism An ethical tradition dating from the late eighteenth century that assumes an action is right if it promotes happiness of both the agent and those affected by the act. Judgments of right and wrong depend upon

the consequence of an action rather than strictly on motives.

Vedas The earliest Indian sacred texts, written in SANSKRIT, dating from sometime between 1000 and 500 B.C.E.; they contain hymns and ritual lore considered to be revelation, or *sruti.*

Verisimo Italian school of literary Realism influenced by Gustave Flaubert and Émile Zola.

Vernacular fiction Fiction that attempts to capture accurately the typical speech, mannerisms, or dialect of region. *The Satyricon* of the Roman author Petronius is often considered the first work of vernacular fiction.

Verse Poetic writing arranged according to a metrical pattern and composed of a varied number of lines.

Victorian In English history, *Victorian* refers to the age of Queen Victoria (1837–1901) and the values of respectability, social conservatism, and sexual repression characteristic of that time.

Villanelle Originally a complicated French verse form that appeared in English in the 1800s. The villanelle is a nineteen-line poem of five tercets (three-line STANZAS) and a final two-rhyme QUATRAIN. The first and third line of the first tercet repeat alternately, closing the succeeding stanzas.

Wampanoag One of several Algonquin peoples residing in New England in the seventeenth century. Their territory extended from Narragansett Bay to Cape Cod.

Well-made play The plays of Augustin Eugène Scribe (1791–1861) and those of his followers, whose popular comedies were especially in vogue during the second half of the nineteenth century, established the rules for the "well-made play." The well-made play was carefully constructed around a single situation that built scene by scene to a climactic revelation. The situation usually involved a misunderstanding, a secret, or a suppressed document that, when discovered, prompted a REVERSAL and a DENOUEMENT. The dialogue was colloquial and realistic, and the subject matter commonplace and trivial. The well-made play was intended to amuse, not instruct.

Weltliteratur Term coined by Goethe for works of literature that transcend local and national concerns to treat universal human themes.

Yin and yang A pair of opposites derived from a dualistic system of ancient Chinese philosophy; symbolically representing the sun and the moon, *yang* is positive, active, and strong, while *yin* is negative, passive, and weak. All things in the universe are formed from the dynamic interaction of these forces.

Yomihon A serious, often didactic "reading book," as opposed to a picture book. This GENRE, popular in the early nineteenth century, often presented historical romances influenced by classic Chinese fiction.

Zen A prominent school of Buddhism that seeks to reveal the essence of the enlightened mind. Zen teaches that everyone has the potential to attain enlightenment but that most are unaware of this potential because they are ignorant. The way to attain enlightenment is through transcending the boundaries of common thought, and the method of study is most frequently the intense, personal instruction of a student by a Zen master.

Acknowledgments (continued from p. iv)

Chinua Achebe, "An Image of Africa: Racism in Conrad's *Heart of Darkness*" from *The Massachusetts Review* 18, no. 4 (Winter 1977), pp. 782–94. Copyright © 1978 by The Massachusetts Review, Inc. Reprinted with permission. *Things Fall Apart.* Copyright © 1958 by Chinua Achebe. First published by William Heinemann, Ltd., 1958. Reprinted with the permission of Reed Consumer Books, London.

Anna Akhmatova, "Voronezh," "To the Memory of M. B.," and "Requiem" from *The Complete Poems of Anna Akhmatova,* Second Edition, translated by Judith Hemschemeyer, edited by Roberta Reeder. Copyright © 1989, 1992 by Judith Hemschemeyer. Reprinted with the permission of Zephyr Press.

Sherman Alexie, "Class" from *The Toughest Indian in the World.* Copyright © 2001 by Sherman Alexie. Reprinted with the permission of Grove / Atlantic, Inc.

Yehuda Amichai, "Sort of an Apocalypse," translated by Chana Bloch and Stephen Mitchell, from *Selected Poetry of Yehuda Amichai,* edited by Chana Bloch and Stephen Mitchell (New York: HarperCollins, 1986). Copyright © 1986, 1996 by Chana Bloch and Stephen Mitchell. Reprinted with the permission of the University of California Press. "God Has Pity on Kindergarten Children," translated by Assia Guttmann, from *Poems.* Copyright © 1968 by Assia Guttmann. Reprinted with the permission of HarperCollins Publishers, Inc.

Jimmy Santiago Baca, "What We Don't Tell the Children," "Family Ties," and "Work We Hate and Dreams We Love" from *Black Mesa Poems.* Copyright © 1986, 1987, 1988, 1989 by Jimmy Santiago Baca. "Meditations on the South Valley, XVI" from *Martin & Meditations on the South Valley.* Copyright © 1986, 1987 by Jimmy Santiago Baca. All reprinted with the permission of New Directions Publishing Corporation.

James Baldwin, "Sonny's Blues" from *Going to Meet the Man* (New York: Doubleday, 1957). Copyright © 1957 and renewed 1985 by James Baldwin. Excerpt from "Princes and Powers" from *Nobody Knows My Name* (New York: The Dial Press, 1961). Copyright © 1961 by James Baldwin. Both reprinted with the permission of the James Baldwin Estate.

Samuel Beckett, *Krapp's Last Tape.* Copyright © 1958 by Samuel Beckett. Reprinted with the permission of Grove / Atlantic, Inc.

Bei Dao, "The Answer," "Declaration," and "An End or a Beginning," translated by Bonnie S. McDougall, from *The August Sleepwalker.* Copyright © 1988 by Bei Dao. Translation copyright © 1988, 1990 by Bonnie S. McDougall. Reprinted with the permission of New Directions Publishing Corporation.

Black Elk, "The Gift of the Sacred Pipe" from *The Sacred Pipe: Black Elk's Account of the Seven Rites of the Oglala Sioux,* recorded and edited by Joseph Epes Brown. Copyright 1953. Reprinted with the permission of the University of Oklahoma Press. Excerpt from *Black Elk Speaks: Being the Life Story of a Holy Man of the Oglala Sioux,* recorded and edited by John Neihardt. Copyright 1932, © 1959, 1972 by John G. Neihardt. Copyright © 1961 by the John G. Neihardt Trust. Reprinted with the permission of University of Nebraska Press. Excerpt from *The Sixth Grandfather: Black Elk's Teachings Given to John G. Neihardt,* edited by Raymond J. DeMallie. Copyright © 1984 by the University of Nebraska Press. Reprinted with the permission of the University of Nebraska Press.

Jorge Luis Borges, "The Garden of Forking Paths" from *Labyrinths: Selected Stories and Other Writings,* translated by Donald A. Yates. Copyright © 1963, 1963 by New Directions Publishing Corporation. Reprinted with the permission of the publisher.

Bertolt Brecht, "When Evil-Doing Comes like Falling Rain" from *Bertolt Brecht: Poems 1913–1916,* translated by John Willett. Copyright © 1976, 1979 by Methuen, Ltd. Reprinted with the permission of Methuen Publishing, Ltd.

Gwendolyn Brooks, "To the Diaspora" from *Blacks.* Copyright © 1987 by Gwendolyn Brooks Blakely. "To the Diaspora" reprinted with the permission of the Estate of Gwendolyn Brooks.

Albert Camus, "The Myth of Sisyphus" from *The Myth of Sisyphus and Other Essays,* translated by Justin O'Brien. Copyright © 1955 by Alfred A. Knopf, Inc. "The Guest" from *Exile and the Kingdom,* translated by Justin O'Brien. Copyright © 1957, 1958 by Alfred A. Knopf, Inc. Both reprinted with the permission of Alfred A. Knopf, a division of Random House, Inc.

Paul Celan, "Death Fugue," translated by John Felstiner, from *Selected Poems and Prose of Paul Celan.* Copyright © 2001 by John Felstiner. Reprinted with the permission of W. W. Norton & Company, Inc.

Aimé Césaire, excerpt from *A Tempest,* translated by Richard Miller. Copyright © 1986 by Richard Miller. Reprinted with the permission of Theatre Communications Group. Excerpt from *Notebook of a Return to the Native Land* from *Aimé Césaire: The Collected Poetry,* translated by Clayton Eshleman and Annette Smith. Copyright © 1983 by The Regents of the University of California. Reprinted with the permission of the University of California Press.

Chinweizu, excerpt from "Calibans vs. Ariels" from *Decolonizing the African Mind* (Lagos, Nigeria: Pero Press, 1987). Copyright © 1987 by Chinweizu. Reprinted by permission.

Chinweizu, Onwuchekwa Jemie, and Ihechukwu Madubuike, excerpt from "The African Writer and the

African Past" from *Toward the Decolonization of African Literature* (Enugu, Nigeria: Fourth Dimension, 1980). Copyright © 1980, 1993 by Chinweizu, Onwuchekwa Jemie, and Ihechukwu Madubuike. Reprinted by permission.

Sandra Cisneros, "Never Marry a Mexican" from *Woman Hollering Creek and Other Stories* (New York: Random House, 1991). Copyright © 1991 by Sandra Cisneros. Reprinted with the permission of Susan Bergholz Literary Services, New York. All rights reserved.

Countee Cullen, "Heritage" and "Yet Do I Marvel" from *Color.* Copyright 1925 by Harper & Brothers, renewed © 1969 by Ida M. Cullen. Reprinted with the permission of Thompson and Thompson, as agents for the Estate of Countee Cullen.

Edwidge Danticat, "Children of the Sea" from *Krik? Krak!* Copyright © 1995 by Edwidge Danticat. Reprinted with the permission of Soho Press.

Mahmoud Darwish, "Identity Card" and "Victim Number 18," translated by Denys Johnson-Davies, from *The Music of Human Flesh* (Washington, D.C.: Three Continents Press, 1980). Copyright © 1980 by Denys Johnson-Davies. Reprinted with the permission of the translator.

Anita Desai, "The Farewell Party" from *Games at Twilight and Other Stories.* Copyright © 1978 by Anita Desai. Reprinted with the permission of HarperCollins Publishers, Inc.

W. E. B. Du Bois, excerpt from "Of Our Spiritual Strivings" and "The Sorrow Songs" from *The Souls of Black Folk: Essays and Sketches* (New York: A. C. McClurg, 1903). Reprinted with the permission of David Graham Du Bois.

T. S. Eliot, "The Waste Land" and "The Love Song of J. Alfred Prufrock" from *Collected Poems, 1909–1962.* Copyright 1936 by Harcourt Brace & Company, renewed © 1964 by T. S. Eliot. Reprinted with the permission of Faber and Faber Limited.

Martín Espada, "From an Island You Cannot Name" from *Trumpets: From the Islands of the Eviction* (Tempe: Bilingual Review/Press, 1987). Copyright © 1987 by Martín Espada. Reprinted with the permission of Bilingual Press/Editorial Bilingüe. "Bully" and "Revolutionary Spanish Lesson" from *Rebellion Is the Circle of a Lover's Hands.* Copyright © 1990 by Martín Espada. Reprinted with the permission of Curbstone Press. Distributed by Consortium.

Frantz Fanon, excerpt from *The Wretched of the Earth,* translated by Constance Farrington. Copyright © 1963 by Presence Africaine. "By Way of Conclusion" from *Black Skin, White Masks,* translated by Charles Lam Markmann. Copyright © 1967 by Charles Lam Markmann. Both reprinted with the permission of Grove/Atlantic, Inc.

Carlos Fuentes, "The Prisoner of Las Lomas" from *Constancia and Other Stories for Virgins,* translated by Thomas Christensen. English translation copyright © 1990 by Farrar, Straus & Giroux, Inc. Reprinted with the permission of the publisher.

Gao Xingjian, "Dialogue and Rebuttal" from *The Other Shore,* translated by Gilbert C. Fong. Copyright © 1999. Reprinted with the permission of The Chinese University Press.

Federico García Lorca, "The Faithless Wife," "Ode to Walt Whitman," and "Lament for Ignacio Sanchez Mejías," translated by Stephen Spender and J. L. Gill, from *The Selected Poems of Federico García Lorca,* edited by Francisco García Lorca and Donald M. Allen. Copyright © 1955 by New Directions Publishing Corporation. Reprinted with the permission of the publisher.

Gabriel García Márquez, "A Very Old Man With Enormous Wings," translated by Gregory Rabassa, from *Leaf Storm and Other Stories.* Copyright © 1971 by Gabriel García Márquez. Reprinted with the permission of HarperCollins Publishers, Inc.

Nadine Gordimer, "As Others See Us" from *Living in Hope and History.* Copyright © 1999 by Nadine Gordimer. Reprinted with the permission of Farrar, Straus & Giroux, LLC and Russell & Volkening as agents for the author.

Tawfiq al-Hakim, "The Fate of a Cockroach" from *The Fate of a Cockroach and Other Plays,* translated by Denys Johnson-Davies (London: Heinemann, 1966). Copyright © 1966 by Denys Johnson-Davies. Reprinted with the permission of the translator.

Joy Harjo, "She Had Some Horses," "Remember," "New Orleans," and "I Give You Back" from *She Had Some Horses.* Copyright © 1983 by Thunder's Mouth Press. Reprinted with the permission of the publishers.

Bessie Head, "The Deep River: A Story of Ancient Tribal Migration" and "Snapshots of a Wedding" from *The Collector of Treasures and Other Botswana Village Tales* (London: Wm. Heinemann, 1977). Copyright © 1977 by the Estate of Bessie Head. Reprinted with the permission of John Johnson, Authors' Agent, Ltd.

Langston Hughes, "The Negro Speaks of Rivers," "The Weary Blues," and "Jazzonia" from *The Collected Poems of Langston Hughes,* edited by Arnold Rampersad and David Roessel. Copyright 1994 by The Estate of Langston Hughes. Reprinted with the permission of Alfred A. Knopf, a division of Random House, Inc.

Gish Jen, "Who's Irish?" from *Who's Irish?* Copyright © 1999 by Gish Jen. Reprinted with the permission of Alfred A. Knopf, a division of Random House, Inc.

Franz Kafka, "The Metamorphosis," translated by Willa and Edwin Muir, from *Franz Kafka: The Complete Stories,* edited by Nahum N. Glatzer. Copyright 1946, 1947, 1948, 1949, 1954, © 1958, 1971 by Schocken Books,

Inc. Reprinted with the permission of Schocken Books, published by Pantheon Books, a division of Random House, Inc.

Kawabata Yasunari, "The Moon on the Water," translated by George Saitō, from *Modern Japanese Stories: An Anthology,* edited by Ivan Morris. Copyright © 1962 by Charles E. Tuttle Co., Inc. Reprinted with the permission of Charles E. Tuttle Co., Inc. of Boston, Massachusetts and Tokyo, Japan. "Snow," translated by Lane Dunlop and J. Martin Holman, from *Palm-of-the-Hand Stories* (San Francisco: North Point Press, 1988). Copyright © 1988 by Lane Dunlop. Reprinted with the permission of the translator.

Martin Luther King Jr., excerpt from "My Trip to the Land of Gandhi" from *A Testament of Hope: The Essential Writings and Speeches of Martin Luther King Jr.,* edited by James W. Washington (New York: Harper & Row, Publishers, 1986). Copyright © 1966 by Martin Luther King Jr. Copyright renewed 1994 by The Heirs to the Estate of Martin Luther King Jr. Reprinted with the permission of The Heirs to the Estate of Martin Luther King Jr., c/o Writers House, Inc. as agents for the proprietor.

Milan Kundera, "The Hitchhiking Game" from *Laughable Loves,* translated by Suzanne Rappaport. Copyright © 1974 by Alfred A. Knopf, Inc. Reprinted with the permission of the publishers.

Lu Xun, "The True Story of Ah Q," translated by Yang Xianyi and Gladys Yang from *The Complete Stories of Lu Hsun.* Copyright © 1981 by Foreign Languages Press, Beijing, China. Reprinted with the permission of the publisher.

Naguib Mahfouz, "Zaabalawi" from *Modern Arabic Short Stories,* translated by Denys Johnson-Davies (London: Oxford University Press, 1967). Reprinted with the permission of the translator.

Thomas Mann, "Death in Venice" from *Death in Venice and Other Stories,* translated by David Luke, published by Secker & Warburg. Copyright © 1988 by David Luke. Reprinted with the permission of Bantam Books, a division of Random House, Inc. and The Random House Group Limited.

Felix Mnthali, "The Stranglehold of English Lit." from *Echoes from Ibadan* (privately printed, 1961). Copyright © 1961 by Felix Mnthali. Reprinted with the permission of the author.

Toni Morrison, excerpt from Chapter 14 from *Song of Solomon* (New York: Alfred A. Knopf, 1977). Copyright © 1977 by Toni Morrison. Reprinted with the permission of International Creative Management, Inc.

Bharati Mukherjee, "A Wife's Story" from *The Middleman and Other Stories.* Copyright © 1988 by Bharati Mukherjee. Reprinted with the permission of Grove / Atlantic, Inc. and Penguin Books Canada Limited.

V. S. Naipaul, "Our Universal Civilization" from *The New York Times* (November 5, 1990). Copyright © 1990 by The New York Times Company. Reprinted by permission.

R. K. Narayan, "A Horse and Two Goats" from *Under the Banyan Tree.* Copyright © 1985 by R. K. Narayan. Reprinted with the permission of Viking Penguin, a division of Penguin Putnam Inc. "A Passage to America" from *Town and Country* (May 1985). Copyright © 1985 by R. K. Narayan. Reprinted with the permission of The Wallace Literary Agency.

Pablo Neruda, "The United Fruit Co.," "Hymn and Return," and "Ode to Salt" from *Neruda and Vallejo: Selected Poems* (Boston: Beacon Press, 1962), translated by Robert Bly, James Wright, and John Knoeptle. Reprinted with the permission of Robert Bly. "Ode with a Lament," "Alberto Rojas Jimenez Comes Flying," "Ode of the Sun to the People's Army," and "Sexual Water" from *Twelve Spanish Poets: An Anthology* (Boston: Beacon Press, 1972), translated by H. R. Hays. Reprinted with the permission of The Estate of H. R. Hays. Section VI from "The Heights of Macchu Picchu," translated by Jack Schmitt, from *Canto General.* Copyright © 1991. Reprinted with the permission of the University of California Press. "Poet's Obligation," translated by Alastair Reid, from *Neruda: Selected Poems.* Copyright © 1970 by Alastair Reid. Reprinted with the permission of the translator.

Ngugi Wa Thiong'o, excerpt from "Creating Space for a Hundred Flowers to Bloom: The Wealth of a Common Global Culture" from *Moving the Centre.* Copyright © 1993 by Ngugi Wa Thiong'o. Reprinted with the permission of Heinemann, a division of Reed Elsevier, Inc., Portsmouth, NH.

Naomi Shihab Nye, "Blood" and "My Father and the Figtree" from *19 Varieties of Gazelle: Poems of the Middle East* (New York: Greenwillow Books, 2002). Copyright © 2002 by Naomi Shihab Nye. Reprinted with the permission of Far Corner Books, Portland, Oregon. "Arabic" from *Red Suitcase.* Copyright © 1994 by Naomi Shihab Nye. Reprinted with the permission of BOA Editions, Ltd.

Tim O'Brien, "The Man I Killed" from *The Things They Carried.* Copyright © 1989 by Tim O'Brien. Reprinted with the permission of Houghton Mifflin Company. All rights reserved.

Oe Kenzaburo, excerpt from "The Moralists of Hiroshima, September 1964" from *Hiroshima Notes,* translated by David L. Swain & Toshi Yonezawa. Reprinted with the permission of Marion Boyers Publishers, London and New York.

Octavio Paz, excerpts from "Three Visits to India" from *The Light of India,* translated by Eliot Weinberger. Copyright © 1995 by Octavio Paz. English translation

Fadwa Tuqan, "Enough for Me," translated by Olive Kenny, from *Anthology of Modern Palestinian Literature,* edited and introduced by Salma Khadra Jayyusi (New York: Columbia University Press, 1992). Reprinted with the permission of the author. "Song of Becoming," translated by Naomi Shihab Nye, from *Anthology of Modern Palestinian Literature,* edited and introduced by Salma Khadra Jayyusi (New York: Columbia University Press, 1992). Reprinted with the permission of the translator.

Andrei Voznesensky, "I Am Goya," translated by Stanley Kunitz, from *Antiworlds and the Fifth Ace,* edited by Patricia Blake and Max Hayward. Copyright © 1966, 1967 by Basic Books, Inc., © 1963 by Encounter, Ltd. Copyright renewed. Reprinted with the permission of Basic Books, a member of Perseus Books, L.L.C.

Derek Walcott, "A Latin Primer," "White Magic," and "The Light of the World" from *The Arkansas Testament.* Copyright © 1987 by Derek Walcott. "For Pablo Neruda" from *Sea Grapes.* Copyright © 1976 by Derek Walcott. All reprinted with the permission of Farrar, Straus & Giroux, LLC.

Virginia Woolf, "Shakespeare's Sister" from *A Room of One's Own.* Copyright 1929 by Harcourt Brace & World, Inc., renewed © 1957 by Leonard Woolf. Reprinted with the permission of Harcourt, Inc. "Three Pictures" from *The Death of the Moth and Other Essays.* Copyright 1942 by Harcourt, Inc., renewed © 1970 by Marjorie T. Parsons, Executrix. Reprinted with the permission of Harcourt, Inc. "The Fascination of the Pool" from *The Complete Shorter Fiction of Virginia Woolf,* edited by Susan Dick. Copyright © 1985 by Quentin Bell and Angelica Garnett. Reprinted with the permission of Harcourt, Inc. and The Random House Group.

William Butler Yeats, "Sailing to Byzantium," "Leda and the Swan," "Among School Children," "Easter 1916," and "The Second Coming" from *The Poems of W. B. Yeats: A New Edition,* edited by Richard J. Finneran. Copyright 1940 by Georgie Yeats, renewed © 1968 by Bertha Georgie Yeats, Michael Butler Yeats, and Anne Yeats. Reprinted with the permission of Scribner, a division of the Simon & Schuster Adult Publishing Group.

Image Credits

Page 1: Travelsite / Neil Setchfield
Page 30: Hulton / Archive
Page 32: The Kobal Collection / Zoetrope / USA)
Page 98: The Art Archive / Imperial War Museum
Page 105: Hulton / Archive
Page 119: The Art Archive / Bibliotheque Municipale Dijon / Dagli Orti

Page 126: Courtesy of Anti-Slavery International, London
Page 136: The Art Archive / Dagli Orti
Page 142: The Art Archive / Private Collection Paris / Dagli Orti
Page 159: National Anthropological Archives
Page 160: National Anthropological Archives
Page 181: Hulton / Archive
Page 184: Hulton / Archive
Page 185: The Art Archive / Dagli Orti
Page 201: Courtesy of the Biblioteca e Raccolta Teatrale del Burcardo, S.I.A.E.
Page 261: Hulton / Archive
Page 332: © Bettmann / CORBIS
Page 366: Hulton / Archive
Page 368: Hulton / Archive
Page 402: Hulton / Archive
Page 423: Hulton / Archive
Page 425: The Art Archive / Museum der Stadt Wien / Dagli Orti(A)
Page 473: Hulton / Archive
Page 503: Mandeville Special Collections, UC San Diego
Page 505: Library of Congress, LC-USZ62 112445
Page 506: © Hulton-Deutsch Collection / CORBIS
Page 507: Courtesy of the Auschwitz-Birkenau State Museum
Page 508: © Bettmann / CORBIS
Page 509: © Bettmann / CORBIS
Page 510: © Bettmann / CORBIS
Page 553: Scala / Art Resource, NY
Page 648: Charles H. Phillips / TimePix
Page 659: © Bettmann / CORBIS
Page 693: © Pierre George / Corbis-Sygma
Page 747: Alberto Giacometti. *Diego,* 1953. Oil on canvas. 100.5 x 80.5 (39½ x 31¼ inches). Solomon R. Guggenheim Museum, New York. 55.1431. © 2003 Artists Rights Society (ARS), New York / ADAGP, Paris. Photograph by Robert E. Mates. © The Solomon R. Guggenheim Foundation, New York.
Page 749: Victoria & Albert Museum, London / Art Resource, NY. © 2003 Artists Rights Society (ARS), New York / ADAGP, Paris
Page 756: Visual Arts Library / Art Resource, NY. © 2003 Artists Rights Society (ARS), New York / ADAGP, Paris
Page 765: © Michael Schwarz / The Image Works
Page 770: © Topham / The Image Works
Page 781: © DPA / The Image Works
Page 783: © Bettmann / CORBIS
Page 797: © Topham / The Image Works
Page 799: Library of Congress, LC USZ62 099022
Page 812: Hulton / Archive
Page 826: Steve Shapiro / Stockphoto.com
Page 854: In the Collection of The Corcoran Gallery of Art, Museum Purchase and partial gift from Thurlow Evans Tibbs Jr., The Evans Tibbs Collection

Page 860: Photographs and Prints Division, Schomburg Center for Research in Black Culture, The New York Public Library, Astor, Lenox and Tilden Foundations

Page 875: Photographs and Prints Division, Schomburg Center for Research in Black Culture, The New York Public Library, Astor, Lenox and Tilden Foundations

Page 877: Smithsonian American Art Museum, Washington, DC / Art Resource, NY

Page 899: Manuscripts, Archives & Rare Books Division, Schomburg Center for Research in Black Culture, The New York Public Library, Astor, Lenox and Tilden Foundations

Page 924: Ben Martin / TimePix

Page 933: © Bob Daemmrich / The Image Works

Page 935: The Art Archive

Page 969: The Art Archive

Page 991: © Bettmann / CORBIS

Page 1018: Hulton / Archive

Page 1113: © Rune Hellestad / CORBIS

Page 1141: © Reuters NewMedia Inc. / CORBIS

Page 1218: © AFP / CORBIS

Page 1255: © Star Images / Topham / The Image Works

Page 1258: © Reuters / CORBIS

Page 1279: © Bojan Brecelj / ©Rune Hellestad / CORBIS

Page 1285: Hulton / Archive

Page 1289: Hulton / Archive

Page 1292: Bernard Diederich / Timepix

Page 1313: © Hulton-Deutsch Collection / CORBIS

Page 1327: Library of Congress, LC-USW361-713

Page 1341: Fine Art Collection, Heard Museum. Phoenix, Arizona

Page 1343: Smithsonian American Art Museum, Washington, DC / Art Resource, NY

Page 1344: Travelsite / Neil Setchfield

Page 1349: The Kobal Collection / Miramax / Duchin, Courtnay

Page 1381: Smithsonian American Art Museum, Washington, DC / Art Resource, NY

Page 1390: © Dean Wong / CORBIS

INDEX